BUSINESS AND COMPANY LEGISLATION

BUSINESS AND COMPANY LEGISLATION

Jason Ellis

CLP

Published by
College of Law Publishing,
Braboeuf Manor, Portsmouth Road, St Catherines, Guildford GU3 1HA

British Library Cataloguing-in-Publication Data
A catalogue record for this book is available from the British Library.

ISBN 978 1 909176 66 9

Typeset by Style Photosetting Ltd, Mayfield, East Sussex
Printed in Great Britain by Polestar Wheatons, Exeter

Contents

Note: The text of the legislation incorporates amendments and repeals to 6 April 2013. Amendments deriving from the Companies Act 2006 (Amendment of Part 18) Regulations 2013 (SI 2013/999), which came into force on 30 April 2013, are also incorporated. Repeals and provisions omitted because they are amending only are indicated by an ellipsis and prospective repeals and legislation not yet brought into force are printed in italics.

Financial Services and Securities Regulation

Companies Act 2006

Arrangement of sections

Companies Act 2006

2006 c. 46

An Act to reform company law and restate the greater part of the enactments relating to companies; to make other provision relating to companies and other forms of business organisation; to make provision about directors' disqualification, business names, auditors and actuaries; to amend Part 9 of the Enterprise Act 2002; and for connected purposes. [8th November 2006]

PART 1
GENERAL INTRODUCTORY PROVISIONS

Companies and Companies Acts

1 Companies

(1) In the Companies Acts, unless the context otherwise requires—
"company" means a company formed and registered under this Act, that is—
(a) a company so formed and registered after the commencement of this Part, or
(b) a company that immediately before the commencement of this Part—
(i) was formed and registered under the Companies Act 1985 or the Companies (Northern Ireland) Order 1986, or
(ii) was an existing company for the purposes of that Act or that Order,
(which is to be treated on commencement as if formed and registered under this Act).

(2) Certain provisions of the Companies Acts apply to—
(a) companies registered, but not formed, under this Act (see Chapter 1 of Part 33), and
(b) bodies incorporated in the United Kingdom but not registered under this Act (see Chapter 2 of that Part).

(3) For provisions applying to companies incorporated outside the United Kingdom, see Part 34 (overseas companies).

2 The Companies Acts

(1) In this Act "the Companies Acts" means—
(a) the company law provisions of this Act,
(b) Part 2 of the Companies (Audit, Investigations and Community Enterprise) Act 2004 (community interest companies), and
(c) the provisions of the Companies Act 1985 and the Companies Consolidation (Consequential Provisions) Act 1985 that remain in force.

(2) The company law provisions of this Act are—
(a) the provisions of Parts 1 to 39 of this Act, and
(b) the provisions of Parts 45 to 47 of this Act so far as they apply for the purposes of those Parts.

Types of company

3 Limited and unlimited companies

(1) A company is a "limited company" if the liability of its members is limited by its constitution. It may be limited by shares or limited by guarantee.

(2) If their liability is limited to the amount, if any, unpaid on the shares held by them, the company is "limited by shares".

(3) If their liability is limited to such amount as the members undertake to contribute to the assets of the company in the event of its being wound up, the company is "limited by guarantee".

(4) If there is no limit on the liability of its members, the company is an "unlimited company".

4 Private and public companies

(1) A "private company" is any company that is not a public company.

(2) A "public company" is a company limited by shares or limited by guarantee and having a share capital—

(a) whose certificate of incorporation states that it is a public company, and

(b) in relation to which the requirements of this Act, or the former Companies Acts, as to registration or re-registration as a public company have been complied with on or after the relevant date.

(3) For the purposes of subsection (2)(b) the relevant date is—

(a) in relation to registration or re-registration in Great Britain, 22nd December 1980;

(b) in relation to registration or re-registration in Northern Ireland, 1st July 1983.

(4) For the two major differences between private and public companies, see Part 20.

5 Companies limited by guarantee and having share capital

(1) A company cannot be formed as, or become, a company limited by guarantee with a share capital.

(2) Provision to this effect has been in force—

(a) in Great Britain since 22nd December 1980, and

(b) in Northern Ireland since 1st July 1983.

(3) Any provision in the constitution of a company limited by guarantee that purports to divide the company's undertaking into shares or interests is a provision for a share capital.

This applies whether or not the nominal value or number of the shares or interests is specified by the provision.

6 Community interest companies

(1) In accordance with Part 2 of the Companies (Audit, Investigations and Community Enterprise) Act 2004—

(a) a company limited by shares or a company limited by guarantee and not having a share capital may be formed as or become a community interest company, and

(b) a company limited by guarantee and having a share capital may become a community interest company.

(2) The other provisions of the Companies Acts have effect subject to that Part.

PART 2
COMPANY FORMATION

General

7 Method of forming company

(1) A company is formed under this Act by one or more persons—

(a) subscribing their names to a memorandum of association (see section 8), and

(b) complying with the requirements of this Act as to registration (see sections 9 to 13).

(2) A company may not be so formed for an unlawful purpose.

8 Memorandum of association

(1) A memorandum of association is a memorandum stating that the subscribers—

(a) wish to form a company under this Act, and

(b) agree to become members of the company and, in the case of a company that is to have a share capital, to take at least one share each.

(2) The memorandum must be in the prescribed form and must be authenticated by each subscriber.

Requirements for registration

9 Registration documents

(1) The memorandum of association must be delivered to the registrar together with an application for registration of the company, the documents required by this section and a statement of compliance.

(2) The application for registration must state—

(a) the company's proposed name,

(b) whether the company's registered office is to be situated in England and Wales (or in Wales), in Scotland or in Northern Ireland,

(c) whether the liability of the members of the company is to be limited, and if so whether it is to be limited by shares or by guarantee, and

(d) whether the company is to be a private or a public company.

(3) If the application is delivered by a person as agent for the subscribers to the memorandum of association, it must state his name and address.

(4) The application must contain—

(a) in the case of a company that is to have a share capital, a statement of capital and initial shareholdings (see section 10);

(b) in the case of a company that is to be limited by guarantee, a statement of guarantee (see section 11);

(c) a statement of the company's proposed officers (see section 12).

(5) The application must also contain—

(a) a statement of the intended address of the company's registered office; and

(b) a copy of any proposed articles of association (to the extent that these are not supplied by the default application of model articles: see section 20).

(6) The application must be delivered—

(a) to the registrar of companies for England and Wales, if the registered office of the company is to be situated in England and Wales (or in Wales);

(b) to the registrar of companies for Scotland, if the registered office of the company is to be situated in Scotland;

(c) to the registrar of companies for Northern Ireland, if the registered office of the company is to be situated in Northern Ireland.

10 Statement of capital and initial shareholdings

(1) The statement of capital and initial shareholdings required to be delivered in the case of a company that is to have a share capital must comply with this section.

(2) It must state—

(a) the total number of shares of the company to be taken on formation by the subscribers to the memorandum of association,

(b) the aggregate nominal value of those shares,

(c) for each class of shares—

(i) prescribed particulars of the rights attached to the shares,

(ii) the total number of shares of that class, and

(iii) the aggregate nominal value of shares of that class, and

(d) the amount to be paid up and the amount (if any) to be unpaid on each share (whether on account of the nominal value of the share or by way of premium).

(3) It must contain such information as may be prescribed for the purpose of identifying the subscribers to the memorandum of association.

(4) It must state, with respect to each subscriber to the memorandum—

(a) the number, nominal value (of each share) and class of shares to be taken by him on formation, and

(b) the amount to be paid up and the amount (if any) to be unpaid on each share (whether on account of the nominal value of the share or by way of premium).

(5) Where a subscriber to the memorandum is to take shares of more than one class, the information required under subsection (4) (a) is required for each class.

11 Statement of guarantee

(1) The statement of guarantee required to be delivered in the case of a company that is to be limited by guarantee must comply with this section.

(2) It must contain such information as may be prescribed for the purpose of identifying the subscribers to the memorandum of association.

(3) It must state that each member undertakes that, if the company is wound up while he is a member, or within one year after he ceases to be a member, he will contribute to the assets of the company such amount as may be required for—
   (a) payment of the debts and liabilities of the company contracted before he ceases to be a member,
   (b) payment of the costs, charges and expenses of winding up, and
   (c) adjustment of the rights of the contributories among themselves, not exceeding a specified amount.

12 Statement of proposed officers

(1) The statement of the company's proposed officers required to be delivered to the registrar must contain the required particulars of—
   (a) the person who is, or persons who are, to be the first director or directors of the company;
   (b) in the case of a company that is to be a private company, any person who is (or any persons who are) to be the first secretary (or joint secretaries) of the company;
   (c) in the case of a company that is to be a public company, the person who is (or the persons who are) to be the first secretary (or joint secretaries) of the company.

(2) The required particulars are the particulars that will be required to be stated—
   (a) in the case of a director, in the company's register of directors and register of directors' residential addresses (see sections 162 to 166);
   (b) in the case of a secretary, in the company's register of secretaries (see sections 277 to 279).

(3) The statement must also contain a consent by each of the persons named as a director, as secretary or as one of joint secretaries, to act in the relevant capacity.
If all the partners in a firm are to be joint secretaries, consent may be given by one partner on behalf of all of them.

13 Statement of compliance

(1) The statement of compliance required to be delivered to the registrar is a statement that the requirements of this Act as to registration have been complied with.

(2) The registrar may accept the statement of compliance as sufficient evidence of compliance.

Registration and its effect

14 Registration

If the registrar is satisfied that the requirements of this Act as to registration are complied with, he shall register the documents delivered to him.

15 Issue of certificate of incorporation

(1) On the registration of a company, the registrar of companies shall give a certificate that the company is incorporated.

(2) The certificate must state—
   (a) the name and registered number of the company,
   (b) the date of its incorporation,
   (c) whether it is a limited or unlimited company, and if it is limited whether it is limited by shares or limited by guarantee,
   (d) whether it is a private or a public company, and

(e) whether the company's registered office is situated in England and Wales (or in Wales), in Scotland or in Northern Ireland.

(3) The certificate must be signed by the registrar or authenticated by the registrar's official seal.

(4) The certificate is conclusive evidence that the requirements of this Act as to registration have been complied with and that the company is duly registered under this Act.

16 Effect of registration

(1) The registration of a company has the following effects as from the date of incorporation.

(2) The subscribers to the memorandum, together with such other persons as may from time to time become members of the company, are a body corporate by the name stated in the certificate of incorporation.

(3) That body corporate is capable of exercising all the functions of an incorporated company.

(4) The status and registered office of the company are as stated in, or in connection with, the application for registration.

(5) In the case of a company having a share capital, the subscribers to the memorandum become holders of the shares specified in the statement of capital and initial shareholdings.

(6) The persons named in the statement of proposed officers—

(a) as director, or

(b) as secretary or joint secretary of the company,

are deemed to have been appointed to that office.

PART 3
A COMPANY'S CONSTITUTION

CHAPTER 1
INTRODUCTORY

17 A company's constitution

Unless the context otherwise requires, references in the Companies Acts to a company's constitution include—

(a) the company's articles, and

(b) any resolutions and agreements to which Chapter 3 applies (see section 29).

CHAPTER 2
ARTICLES OF ASSOCIATION

General

18 Articles of association

(1) A company must have articles of association prescribing regulations for the company.

(2) Unless it is a company to which model articles apply by virtue of section 20 (default application of model articles in case of limited company), it must register articles of association.

(3) Articles of association registered by a company must—

(a) be contained in a single document, and

(b) be divided into paragraphs numbered consecutively.

(4) References in the Companies Acts to a company's "articles" are to its articles of association.

19 Power of Secretary of State to prescribe model articles

(1) The Secretary of State may by regulations prescribe model articles of association for companies.

(2) Different model articles may be prescribed for different descriptions of company.

(3) A company may adopt all or any of the provisions of model articles.

(4) Any amendment of model articles by regulations under this section does not affect a company registered before the amendment takes effect. "Amendment" here includes addition, alteration or repeal.

(5) Regulations under this section are subject to negative resolution procedure.

20 Default application of model articles

(1) On the formation of a limited company—

(a) if articles are not registered, or

(b) if articles are registered, in so far as they do not exclude or modify the relevant model articles,

the relevant model articles (so far as applicable) form part of the company's articles in the same manner and to the same extent as if articles in the form of those articles had been duly registered.

(2) The "relevant model articles" means the model articles prescribed for a company of that description as in force at the date on which the company is registered.

Alteration of articles

21 Amendment of articles

(1) A company may amend its articles by special resolution.

(2) In the case of a company that is a charity, this is subject to—

(a) in England and Wales, sections 197 and 198 of the Charities Act 2011;

(b) in Northern Ireland, Article 9 of the Charities (Northern Ireland) Order 1987.

(3) In the case of a company that is registered in the Scottish Charity Register, this is subject to—

(a) section 112 of the Companies Act 1989, and

(b) section 16 of the Charities and Trustee Investment (Scotland) Act 2005.

22 Entrenched provisions of the articles

(1) A company's articles may contain provision ("provision for entrenchment") to the effect that specified provisions of the articles may be amended or repealed only if conditions are met, or procedures are complied with, that are more restrictive than those applicable in the case of a special resolution.

(2) Provision for entrenchment may only be made—

(a) in the company's articles on formation, or

(b) by an amendment of the company's articles agreed to by all the members of the company.

(3) Provision for entrenchment does not prevent amendment of the company's articles—

(a) by agreement of all the members of the company, or

(b) by order of a court or other authority having power to alter the company's articles.

(4) Nothing in this section affects any power of a court or other authority to alter a company's articles.

23 Notice to registrar of existence of restriction on amendment of articles

(1) Where a company's articles—

(a) on formation contain provision for entrenchment,

(b) are amended so as to include such provision, or

(c) are altered by order of a court or other authority so as to restrict or exclude the power of the company to amend its articles,

the company must give notice of that fact to the registrar.

(2) Where a company's articles—

(a) are amended so as to remove provision for entrenchment, or

(b) are altered by order of a court or other authority—

(i) so as to remove such provision, or

(ii) so as to remove any other restriction on, or any exclusion of, the power of the company to amend its articles,

the company must give notice of that fact to the registrar.

24 Statement of compliance where amendment of articles restricted

(1) This section applies where a company's articles are subject—

(a) to provision for entrenchment, or

(b) to an order of a court or other authority restricting or excluding the company's power to amend the articles.

(2) If the company—

(a) amends its articles, and

(b) is required to send to the registrar a document making or evidencing the amendment,

the company must deliver with that document a statement of compliance.

(3) The statement of compliance required is a statement certifying that the amendment has been made in accordance with the company's articles and, where relevant, any applicable order of a court or other authority.

(4) The registrar may rely on the statement of compliance as sufficient evidence of the matters stated in it.

25 Effect of alteration of articles on company's members

(1) A member of a company is not bound by an alteration to its articles after the date on which he became a member, if and so far as the alteration—

(a) requires him to take or subscribe for more shares than the number held by him at the date on which the alteration is made, or

(b) in any way increases his liability as at that date to contribute to the company's share capital or otherwise to pay money to the company.

(2) Subsection (1) does not apply in a case where the member agrees in writing, either before or after the alteration is made, to be bound by the alteration.

26 Registrar to be sent copy of amended articles

(1) Where a company amends its articles it must send to the registrar a copy of the articles as amended not later than 15 days after the amendment takes effect.

(2) This section does not require a company to set out in its articles any provisions of model articles that—

(a) are applied by the articles, or

(b) apply by virtue of section 20 (default application of model articles).

(3) If a company fails to comply with this section an offence is committed by—

(a) the company, and

(b) every officer of the company who is in default.

(4) A person guilty of an offence under this section is liable on summary conviction to a fine not exceeding level 3 on the standard scale and, for continued contravention, a daily default fine not exceeding one-tenth of level 3 on the standard scale.

27 Registrar's notice to comply in case of failure with respect to amended articles

(1) If it appears to the registrar that a company has failed to comply with any enactment requiring it—

(a) to send to the registrar a document making or evidencing an alteration in the company's articles, or

(b) to send to the registrar a copy of the company's articles as amended, the registrar may give notice to the company requiring it to comply.

(2) The notice must—

(a) state the date on which it is issued, and

(b) require the company to comply within 28 days from that date.

(3) If the company complies with the notice within the specified time, no criminal proceedings may be brought in respect of the failure to comply with the enactment mentioned in subsection (1).

(4) If the company does not comply with the notice within the specified time, it is liable to a civil penalty of £200.

This is in addition to any liability to criminal proceedings in respect of the failure mentioned in subsection (1).

(5) The penalty may be recovered by the registrar and is to be paid into the Consolidated Fund.

Supplementary

28 Existing companies: provisions of memorandum treated as provisions of articles

(1) Provisions that immediately before the commencement of this Part were contained in a company's memorandum but are not provisions of the kind mentioned in section 8 (provisions of new-style memorandum) are to be treated after the commencement of this Part as provisions of the company's articles.

(2) This applies not only to substantive provisions but also to provision for entrenchment (as defined in section 22).

(3) The provisions of this Part about provision for entrenchment apply to such provision as they apply to provision made on the company's formation, except that the duty under section 23(1)(a) to give notice to the registrar does not apply.

CHAPTER 3
RESOLUTIONS AND AGREEMENTS AFFECTING A COMPANY'S CONSTITUTION

29 Resolutions and agreements affecting a company's constitution

(1) This Chapter applies to—

(a) any special resolution;

(b) any resolution or agreement agreed to by all the members of a company that, if not so agreed to, would not have been effective for its purpose unless passed as a special resolution;

(c) any resolution or agreement agreed to by all the members of a class of shareholders that, if not so agreed to, would not have been effective for its purpose unless passed by some particular majority or otherwise in some particular manner;

(d) any resolution or agreement that effectively binds all members of a class of shareholders though not agreed to by all those members;

(e) any other resolution or agreement to which this Chapter applies by virtue of any enactment.

(2) References in subsection (1) to a member of a company, or of a class of members of a company, do not include the company itself where it is such a member by virtue only of its holding shares as treasury shares.

30 Copies of resolutions or agreements to be forwarded to registrar

(1) A copy of every resolution or agreement to which this Chapter applies, or (in the case of a resolution or agreement that is not in writing) a written memorandum setting out its terms, must be forwarded to the registrar within 15 days after it is passed or made.

(2) If a company fails to comply with this section, an offence is committed by—

(a) the company, and

(b) every officer of it who is in default.

(3) A person guilty of an offence under this section is liable on summary conviction to a fine not exceeding level 3 on the standard scale and, for continued contravention, a daily default fine not exceeding one-tenth of level 3 on the standard scale.

(4) For the purposes of this section, a liquidator of the company is treated as an officer of it.

CHAPTER 4
MISCELLANEOUS AND SUPPLEMENTARY PROVISIONS

Statement of company's objects

31 Statement of company's objects

(1) Unless a company's articles specifically restrict the objects of the company, its objects are unrestricted.

(2) Where a company amends its articles so as to add, remove or alter a statement of the company's objects—

(a) it must give notice to the registrar,

(b) on receipt of the notice, the registrar shall register it, and

(c) the amendment is not effective until entry of that notice on the register.

(3) Any such amendment does not affect any rights or obligations of the company or render defective any legal proceedings by or against it.

(4) In the case of a company that is a charity, the provisions of this section have effect subject to—

(a) in England and Wales, sections 197 and 198 of the Charities Act 2011;

(b) in Northern Ireland, Article 9 of the Charities (Northern Ireland) Order 1987.

(5) In the case of a company that is entered in the Scottish Charity Register, the provisions of this section have effect subject to the provisions of the Charities and Trustee Investment (Scotland) Act 2005.

Other provisions with respect to a company's constitution

32 Constitutional documents to be provided to members

(1) A company must, on request by any member, send to him the following documents—

(a) an up-to-date copy of the company's articles;

(b) a copy of any resolution or agreement relating to the company to which Chapter 3 applies (resolutions and agreements affecting a company's constitution) and that is for the time being in force;

(c) a copy of any document required to be sent to the registrar under—

(i) section 34(2) (notice where company's constitution altered by enactment), or

(ii) section 35(2)(a) (notice where order of court or other authority alters company's constitution);

(d) a copy of any court order under section 899 (order sanctioning compromise or arrangement) or section 900 (order facilitating reconstruction or amalgamation);

(e) a copy of any court order under section 996 (protection of members against unfair prejudice: powers of the court) that alters the company's constitution;

(f) a copy of the company's current certificate of incorporation, and of any past certificates of incorporation;

(g) in the case of a company with a share capital, a current statement of capital;

(h) in the case of a company limited by guarantee, a copy of the statement of guarantee.

(2) The statement of capital required by subsection (1)(g) is a statement of—

(a) the total number of shares of the company,

(b) the aggregate nominal value of those shares,

(c) for each class of shares—

(i) prescribed particulars of the rights attached to the shares,

(ii) the total number of shares of that class, and

(iii) the aggregate nominal value of shares of that class, and

(d) the amount paid up and the amount (if any) unpaid on each share (whether on account of the nominal value of the share or by way of premium).

(3) If a company makes default in complying with this section, an offence is committed by every officer of the company who is in default.

(4) A person guilty of an offence under this section is liable on summary conviction to a fine not exceeding level 3 on the standard scale.

33 Effect of company's constitution

(1) The provisions of a company's constitution bind the company and its members to the same extent as if there were covenants on the part of the company and of each member to observe those provisions.

(2) Money payable by a member to the company under its constitution is a debt due from him to the company.

In England and Wales and Northern Ireland it is of the nature of an ordinary contract debt.

34 Notice to registrar where company's constitution altered by enactment

(1) This section applies where a company's constitution is altered by an enactment, other than an enactment amending the general law.

(2) The company must give notice of the alteration to the registrar, specifying the enactment, not later than 15 days after the enactment comes into force. In the case of a special enactment the notice must be accompanied by a copy of the enactment.

(3) If the enactment amends—

(a) the company's articles, or

(b) a resolution or agreement to which Chapter 3 applies (resolutions and agreements affecting a company's constitution),

the notice must be accompanied by a copy of the company's articles, or the resolution or agreement in question, as amended.

(4) A "special enactment" means an enactment that is not a public general enactment, and includes—

(a) an Act for confirming a provisional order,

(b) any provision of a public general Act in relation to the passing of which any of the standing orders of the House of Lords or the House of Commons relating to Private Business applied, or

(c) any enactment to the extent that it is incorporated in or applied for the purposes of a special enactment.

(5) If a company fails to comply with this section an offence is committed by—

(a) the company, and

(b) every officer of the company who is in default.

(6) A person guilty of an offence under this section is liable on summary conviction to a fine not exceeding level 3 on the standard scale and, for continued contravention, a daily default fine not exceeding one-tenth of level 3 on the standard scale.

35 Notice to registrar where company's constitution altered by order

(1) Where a company's constitution is altered by an order of a court or other authority, the company must give notice to the registrar of the alteration not later than 15 days after the alteration takes effect.

(2) The notice must be accompanied by—

(a) a copy of the order, and

(b) if the order amends—

(i) the company's articles, or

(ii) a resolution or agreement to which Chapter 3 applies (resolutions and agreements affecting the company's constitution),

a copy of the company's articles, or the resolution or agreement in question, as amended.

(3) If a company fails to comply with this section an offence is committed by—

(a) the company, and

(b) every officer of the company who is in default.

(4) A person guilty of an offence under this section is liable on summary conviction to a fine not exceeding level 3 on the standard scale and, for continued contravention, a daily default fine not exceeding one-tenth of level 3 on the standard scale.

(5) This section does not apply where provision is made by another enactment for the delivery to the registrar of a copy of the order in question.

36 Documents to be incorporated in or accompany copies of articles issued by company

(1) Every copy of a company's articles issued by the company must be accompanied by—

(a) a copy of any resolution or agreement relating to the company to which Chapter 3 applies (resolutions and agreements affecting a company's constitution),

(b) where the company has been required to give notice to the registrar under section 34(2) (notice where company's constitution altered by enactment), a statement that the enactment in question alters the effect of the company's constitution,

(c) where the company's constitution is altered by a special enactment (see section 34(4)), a copy of the enactment, and

(d) a copy of any order required to be sent to the registrar under section 35(2)(a) (order of court or other authority altering company's constitution).

(2) This does not require the articles to be accompanied by a copy of a document or by a statement if—

(a) the effect of the resolution, agreement, enactment or order (as the case may be) on the company's constitution has been incorporated into the articles by amendment, or

(b) the resolution, agreement, enactment or order (as the case may be) is not for the time being in force.

(3) If the company fails to comply with this section, an offence is committed by every officer of the company who is in default.

(4) A person guilty of an offence under this section is liable on summary conviction to a fine not exceeding level 3 on the standard scale for each occasion on which copies are issued, or, as the case may be, requested.

(5) For the purposes of this section, a liquidator of the company is treated as an officer of it.

Supplementary provisions

37 Right to participate in profits otherwise than as member void

In the case of a company limited by guarantee and not having a share capital any provision in the company's articles, or in any resolution of the company, purporting to give a person a right to participate in the divisible profits of the company otherwise than as a member is void.

38 Application to single member companies of enactments and rules of law

Any enactment or rule of law applicable to companies formed by two or more persons or having two or more members applies with any necessary modification in relation to a company formed by one person or having only one person as a member.

PART 4
A COMPANY'S CAPACITY AND RELATED MATTERS

Capacity of company and power of directors to bind it

39 A company's capacity

(1) The validity of an act done by a company shall not be called into question on the ground of lack of capacity by reason of anything in the company's constitution.

(2) This section has effect subject to section 42 (companies that are charities).

40 Power of directors to bind the company

(1) In favour of a person dealing with a company in good faith, the power of the directors to bind the company, or authorise others to do so, is deemed to be free of any limitation under the company's constitution.

(2) For this purpose—

(a) a person "deals with" a company if he is a party to any transaction or other act to which the company is a party,

(b) a person dealing with a company—

(i) is not bound to enquire as to any limitation on the powers of the directors to bind the company or authorise others to do so,

(ii) is presumed to have acted in good faith unless the contrary is proved, and

(iii) is not to be regarded as acting in bad faith by reason only of his knowing that an act is beyond the powers of the directors under the company's constitution.

(3) The references above to limitations on the directors' powers under the company's constitution include limitations deriving—

(a) from a resolution of the company or of any class of shareholders, or

(b) from any agreement between the members of the company or of any class of shareholders.

(4) This section does not affect any right of a member of the company to bring proceedings to restrain the doing of an action that is beyond the powers of the directors.

But no such proceedings lie in respect of an act to be done in fulfilment of a legal obligation arising from a previous act of the company.

(5) This section does not affect any liability incurred by the directors, or any other person, by reason of the directors' exceeding their powers.

(6) This section has effect subject to—

section 41 (transactions with directors or their associates), and

section 42 (companies that are charities).

41 Constitutional limitations: transactions involving directors or their associates

(1) This section applies to a transaction if or to the extent that its validity depends on section 40 (power of directors deemed to be free of limitations under company's constitution in favour of person dealing with company in good faith).

Nothing in this section shall be read as excluding the operation of any other enactment or rule of law by virtue of which the transaction may be called in question or any liability to the company may arise.

(2) Where—

(a) a company enters into such a transaction, and

(b) the parties to the transaction include—

(i) a director of the company or of its holding company, or

(ii) a person connected with any such director,

the transaction is voidable at the instance of the company.

(3) Whether or not it is avoided, any such party to the transaction as is mentioned in subsection (2)(b)(i) or (ii), and any director of the company who authorised the transaction, is liable—

(a) to account to the company for any gain he has made directly or indirectly by the transaction, and

(b) to indemnify the company for any loss or damage resulting from the transaction.

(4) The transaction ceases to be voidable if—

(a) restitution of any money or other asset which was the subject matter of the transaction is no longer possible, or

(b) the company is indemnified for any loss or damage resulting from the transaction, or

(c) rights acquired bona fide for value and without actual notice of the directors' exceeding their powers by a person who is not party to the transaction would be affected by the avoidance, or

(d) the transaction is affirmed by the company.

(5) A person other than a director of the company is not liable under subsection (3) if he shows that at the time the transaction was entered into he did not know that the directors were exceeding their powers.

(6) Nothing in the preceding provisions of this section affects the rights of any party to the transaction not within subsection (2)(b)(i) or (ii).

But the court may, on the application of the company or any such party, make an order affirming, severing or setting aside the transaction on such terms as appear to the court to be just.

(7) In this section—

(a) "transaction" includes any act; and

(b) the reference to a person connected with a director has the same meaning as in Part 10 (company directors).

42 Constitutional limitations: companies that are charities

(1) Sections 39 and 40 (company's capacity and power of directors to bind company) do not apply to the acts of a company that is a charity except in favour of a person who—

(a) does not know at the time the act is done that the company is a charity, or

(b) gives full consideration in money or money's worth in relation to the act in question and does not know (as the case may be)—

(i) that the act is not permitted by the company's constitution, or

(ii)) that the act is beyond the powers of the directors.

(2) Where a company that is a charity purports to transfer or grant an interest in property, the fact that (as the case may be)—

(a) the act was not permitted by the company's constitution, or

(b) the directors in connection with the act exceeded any limitation on their powers under the company's constitution,

does not affect the title of a person who subsequently acquires the property or any interest in it for full consideration without actual notice of any such circumstances affecting the validity of the company's act.

(3) In any proceedings arising out of subsection (1) or (2) the burden of proving—

(a) that a person knew that the company was a charity, or

(b) that a person knew that an act was not permitted by the company's constitution or was beyond the powers of the directors,

lies on the person asserting that fact.

(4) In the case of a company that is a charity the affirmation of a transaction to which section 41 applies (transactions with directors or their associates) is ineffective without the prior written consent of—

(a) in England and Wales, the Charity Commission;

(b) in Northern Ireland, the Department for Social Development.

(5) This section does not extend to Scotland (but see section 112 of the Companies Act 1989).

Formalities of doing business under the law of England and Wales or Northern Ireland

43 Company contracts

(1) Under the law of England and Wales or Northern Ireland a contract may be made—

(a) by a company, by writing under its common seal, or

(b) on behalf of a company, by a person acting under its authority, express or implied.

(2) Any formalities required by law in the case of a contract made by an individual also apply, unless a contrary intention appears, to a contract made by or on behalf of a company.

44 Execution of documents

(1) Under the law of England and Wales or Northern Ireland a document is executed by a company—

(a) by the affixing of its common seal, or

(b) by signature in accordance with the following provisions.

(2) A document is validly executed by a company if it is signed on behalf of the company—

(a) by two authorised signatories, or

(b) by a director of the company in the presence of a witness who attests the signature.

(3) The following are "authorised signatories" for the purposes of subsection (2)—

(a) every director of the company, and

(b) in the case of a private company with a secretary or a public company, the secretary (or any joint secretary) of the company.

(4) A document signed in accordance with subsection (2) and expressed, in whatever words, to be executed by the company has the same effect as if executed under the common seal of the company.

(5) In favour of a purchaser a document is deemed to have been duly executed by a company if it purports to be signed in accordance with subsection (2).

A "purchaser" means a purchaser in good faith for valuable consideration and includes a lessee, mortgagee or other person who for valuable consideration acquires an interest in property.

(6) Where a document is to be signed by a person on behalf of more than one company, it is not duly signed by that person for the purposes of this section unless he signs it separately in each capacity.

(7) References in this section to a document being (or purporting to be) signed by a director or secretary are to be read, in a case where that office is held by a firm, as references to its being (or purporting to be) signed by an individual authorised by the firm to sign on its behalf.

(8) This section applies to a document that is (or purports to be) executed by a company in the name of or on behalf of another person whether or not that person is also a company.

45 Common seal

(1) A company may have a common seal, but need not have one.

(2) A company which has a common seal shall have its name engraved in legible characters on the seal.

(3) If a company fails to comply with subsection (2) an offence is committed by—
 (a) the company, and
 (b) every officer of the company who is in default.

(4) An officer of a company, or a person acting on behalf of a company, commits an offence if he uses, or authorises the use of, a seal purporting to be a seal of the company on which its name is not engraved as required by subsection (2).

(5) A person guilty of an offence under this section is liable on summary conviction to a fine not exceeding level 3 on the standard scale.

(6) This section does not form part of the law of Scotland.

46 Execution of deeds

(1) A document is validly executed by a company as a deed for the purposes of section 1(2)(b) of the Law of Property (Miscellaneous Provisions) Act 1989 and for the purposes of the law of Northern Ireland if, and only if—
 (a) it is duly executed by the company, and
 (b) it is delivered as a deed.

(2) For the purposes of subsection (1)(b) a document is presumed to be delivered upon its being executed, unless a contrary intention is proved.

47 Execution of deeds or other documents by attorney

(1) Under the law of England and Wales or Northern Ireland a company may, by instrument executed as a deed, empower a person, either generally or in respect of specified matters, as its attorney to execute deeds or other documents on its behalf.

(2) A deed or other document so executed, whether in the United Kingdom or elsewhere, has effect as if executed by the company.

Formalities of doing business under the law of Scotland

48 Execution of documents by companies

(1) The following provisions form part of the law of Scotland only.

(2) Notwithstanding the provisions of any enactment, a company need not have a company seal.

(3) For the purposes of any enactment—
 (a) providing for a document to be executed by a company by affixing its common seal, or
 (b) referring (in whatever terms) to a document so executed,

a document signed or subscribed by or on behalf of the company in accordance with the provisions of the Requirements of Writing (Scotland) Act 1995 has effect as if so executed.

Note. The words "(or, in the case of an electronic document, authenticated)" are inserted after "a document signed or subscribed" in subsection (3), in relation to Scotland, by the Land Registration etc. (Scotland) Act 2012, s. 119, Sch. 5, para. 50(1), (2), as from a day to be appointed.

Other matters

49 Official seal for use abroad

(1) A company that has a common seal may have an official seal for use outside the United Kingdom.

(2) The official seal must be a facsimile of the company's common seal, with the addition on its face of the place or places where it is to be used.

(3) The official seal when duly affixed to a document has the same effect as the company's common seal.

This subsection does not extend to Scotland.

(4) A company having an official seal for use outside the United Kingdom may—

(a) by writing under its common seal, or

(b) as respects Scotland, by writing subscribed in accordance with the Requirements of Writing (Scotland) Act 1995,

authorise any person appointed for the purpose to affix the official seal to any deed or other document to which the company is party.

(5) As between the company and a person dealing with such an agent, the agent's authority continues—

(a) during the period mentioned in the instrument conferring the authority, or

(b) if no period is mentioned, until notice of the revocation or termination of the agent's authority has been given to the person dealing with him.

(6) The person affixing the official seal must certify in writing on the deed or other document to which the seal is affixed the date on which, and place at which, it is affixed.

Note. The words "or authenticated" are inserted after "by writing subscribed" in subsection (4)(b), in relation to Scotland, by the Land Registration etc. (Scotland) Act 2012, s. 119, Sch. 5, para. 50(1), (3), as from a day to be appointed.

50 Official seal for share certificates etc

(1) A company that has a common seal may have an official seal for use—

(a) for sealing securities issued by the company, or

(b) for sealing documents creating or evidencing securities so issued.

(2) The official seal—

(a) must be a facsimile of the company's common seal, with the addition on its face of the word "Securities", and

(b) when duly affixed to the document has the same effect as the company's common seal.

51 Pre-incorporation contracts, deeds and obligations

(1) A contract that purports to be made by or on behalf of a company at a time when the company has not been formed has effect, subject to any agreement to the contrary, as one made with the person purporting to act for the company or as agent for it, and he is personally liable on the contract accordingly.

(2) Subsection (1) applies—

(a) to the making of a deed under the law of England and Wales or Northern Ireland, and

(b) to the undertaking of an obligation under the law of Scotland,

as it applies to the making of a contract.

52 Bills of exchange and promissory notes

A bill of exchange or promissory note is deemed to have been made, accepted or endorsed on behalf of a company if made, accepted or endorsed in the name of, or by or on behalf or on account of, the company by a person acting under its authority.

PART 5
A COMPANY'S NAME

CHAPTER 1
GENERAL REQUIREMENTS

Prohibited names

53 Prohibited names

A company must not be registered under this Act by a name if, in the opinion of the Secretary of State—

(a) its use by the company would constitute an offence, or
(b) it is offensive.

Sensitive words and expressions

54 Names suggesting connection with government or public authority

(1) The approval of the Secretary of State is required for a company to be registered under this Act by a name that would be likely to give the impression that the company is connected with—
(a) Her Majesty's Government, any part of the Scottish administration, the Welsh Assembly Government or Her Majesty's Government in Northern Ireland,
(b) a local authority, or
(c) any public authority specified for the purposes of this section by regulations made by the Secretary of State.

(2) For the purposes of this section—
"local authority" means—
(a) a local authority within the meaning of the Local Government Act 1972, the Common Council of the City of London or the Council of the Isles of Scilly,
(b) a council constituted under section 2 of the Local Government etc. (Scotland) Act 1994, or
(c) a district council in Northern Ireland;
"public authority" includes any person or body having functions of a public nature.

(3) Regulations under this section are subject to affirmative resolution procedure.

55 Other sensitive words or expressions

(1) The approval of the Secretary of State is required for a company to be registered under this Act by a name that includes a word or expression for the time being specified in regulations made by the Secretary of State under this section.

(2) Regulations under this section are subject to approval after being made.

56 Duty to seek comments of government department or other specified body

(1) The Secretary of State may by regulations under—
(a) section 54 (name suggesting connection with government or public authority), or
(b) section 55 (other sensitive words or expressions),
require that, in connection with an application for the approval of the Secretary of State under that section, the applicant must seek the view of a specified Government department or other body.

(2) Where such a requirement applies, the applicant must request the specified department or other body (in writing) to indicate whether (and if so why) it has any objections to the proposed name.

(3) Where a request under this section is made in connection with an application for the registration of a company under this Act, the application must—
(a) include a statement that a request under this section has been made, and
(b) be accompanied by a copy of any response received.

(4) Where a request under this section is made in connection with a change in a company's name, the notice of the change sent to the registrar must be accompanied by—
(a) a statement by a director or secretary of the company that a request under this section has been made, and
(b) a copy of any response received.

(5) In this section "specified" means specified in the regulations.

Permitted characters etc

57 Permitted characters etc

(1) The Secretary of State may make provision by regulations—
(a) as to the letters or other characters, signs or symbols (including accents and other diacritical marks) and punctuation that may be used in the name of a company registered under this Act; and

(b) specifying a standard style or format for the name of a company for the purposes of registration.

(2) The regulations may prohibit the use of specified characters, signs or symbols when appearing in a specified position (in particular, at the beginning of a name).

(3) A company may not be registered under this Act by a name that consists of or includes anything that is not permitted in accordance with regulations under this section.

(4) Regulations under this section are subject to negative resolution procedure.

(5) In this section "specified" means specified in the regulations.

CHAPTER 2
INDICATIONS OF COMPANY TYPE OR LEGAL FORM

Required indications for limited companies

58 Public limited companies

(1) The name of a limited company that is a public company must end with "public limited company" or "p.l.c.".

(2) In the case of a Welsh company, its name may instead end with "cwmni cyfyngedig cyhoeddus" or "c.c.c.".

(3) This section does not apply to community interest companies (but see section 33(3) and (4) of the Companies (Audit, Investigations and Community Enterprise) Act 2004).

59 Private limited companies

(1) The name of a limited company that is a private company must end with "limited" or "ltd.".

(2) In the case of a Welsh company, its name may instead end with "cyfyngedig" or "cyf.".

(3) Certain companies are exempt from this requirement (see section 60).

(4) This section does not apply to community interest companies (but see section 33(1) and (2) of the Companies (Audit, Investigations and Community Enterprise) Act 2004).

60 Exemption from requirement as to use of "limited"

(1) A private company is exempt from section 59 (requirement to have name ending with "limited" or permitted alternative) if—

(a) it is a charity,

(b) it is exempted from the requirement of that section by regulations made by the Secretary of State, or

(c) it meets the conditions specified in—

section 61 (continuation of existing exemption: companies limited by shares), or

section 62 (continuation of existing exemption: companies limited by guarantee).

(2) The registrar may refuse to register a private limited company by a name that does not include the word "limited" (or a permitted alternative) unless a statement has been delivered to him that the company meets the conditions for exemption.

(3) The registrar may accept the statement as sufficient evidence of the matters stated in it.

(4) Regulations under this section are subject to negative resolution procedure.

61 Continuation of existing exemption: companies limited by shares

(1) This section applies to a private company limited by shares—

(a) that on 25th February 1982—

(i) was registered in Great Britain, and

(ii) had a name that, by virtue of a licence under section 19 of the Companies Act 1948 (or corresponding earlier legislation), did not include the word "limited" or any of the permitted alternatives, or

(b) that on 30th June 1983—

(i) was registered in Northern Ireland, and

(ii) had a name that, by virtue of a licence under section 19 of the Companies Act (Northern Ireland) 1960 (or corresponding earlier legislation), did not include the word "limited" or any of the permitted alternatives.

(2) A company to which this section applies is exempt from section 59 (requirement to have name ending with "limited" or permitted alternative) so long as—

(a) it continues to meet the following two conditions, and

(b) it does not change its name.

(3) The first condition is that the objects of the company are the promotion of commerce, art, science, education, religion, charity or any profession, and anything incidental or conducive to any of those objects.

(4) The second condition is that the company's articles—

(a) require its income to be applied in promoting its objects,

(b) prohibit the payment of dividends, or any return of capital, to its members, and

(c) require all the assets that would otherwise be available to its members generally to be transferred on its winding up either—

(i) to another body with objects similar to its own, or

(ii) to another body the objects of which are the promotion of charity and anything incidental or conducive thereto,

(whether or not the body is a member of the company).

62 Continuation of existing exemption: companies limited by guarantee

(1) A private company limited by guarantee that immediately before the commencement of this Part—

(a) was exempt by virtue of section 30 of the Companies Act 1985 or Article 40 of the Companies (Northern Ireland) Order 1986 from the requirement to have a name including the word "limited" or a permitted alternative, and

(b) had a name that did not include the word "limited" or any of the permitted alternatives,

is exempt from section 59 (requirement to have name ending with "limited" or permitted alternative) so long as it continues to meet the following two conditions and does not change its name.

(2) The first condition is that the objects of the company are the promotion of commerce, art, science, education, religion, charity or any profession, and anything incidental or conducive to any of those objects.

(3) The second condition is that the company's articles—

(a) require its income to be applied in promoting its objects,

(b) prohibit the payment of dividends to its members, and

(c) require all the assets that would otherwise be available to its members generally to be transferred on its winding up either—

(i) to another body with objects similar to its own, or

(ii) to another body the objects of which are the promotion of charity and anything incidental or conducive thereto,

(whether or not the body is a member of the company).

63 Exempt company: restriction on amendment of articles

(1) A private company—

(a) that is exempt under section 61 or 62 from the requirement to use "limited" (or a permitted alternative) as part of its name, and

(b) whose name does not include "limited" or any of the permitted alternatives,

must not amend its articles so that it ceases to comply with the conditions for exemption under that section.

(2) If subsection (1) above is contravened an offence is committed by—

(a) the company, and

(b) every officer of the company who is in default.

For this purpose a shadow director is treated as an officer of the company.

(3) A person guilty of an offence under this section is liable on summary conviction to a fine not exceeding level 5 on the standard scale and, for continued contravention, a daily default fine not exceeding one-tenth of level 5 on the standard scale.

(4) Where immediately before the commencement of this section—

(a) a company was exempt by virtue of section 30 of the Companies Act 1985 or Article 40 of the Companies (Northern Ireland) Order 1986 from the requirement to have a name including the word "limited" (or a permitted alternative), and

(b) the company's memorandum or articles contained provision preventing an alteration of them without the approval of—

(i) the Board of Trade or a Northern Ireland department (or any other department or Minister), or

(ii) the Charity Commission,

that provision, and any condition of any such licence as is mentioned in section 61(1) (a) (ii) or (b) (ii) requiring such provision, shall cease to have effect. This does not apply if, or to the extent that, the provision is required by or under any other enactment.

(5) It is hereby declared that any such provision as is mentioned in subsection (4) (b) formerly contained in a company's memorandum was at all material times capable, with the appropriate approval, of being altered or removed under section 17 of the Companies Act 1985 or Article 28 of the Companies (Northern Ireland) Order 1986 (or corresponding earlier enactments).

64 Power to direct change of name in case of company ceasing to be entitled to exemption

(1) If it appears to the Secretary of State that a company whose name does not include "limited" or any of the permitted alternatives—

(a) has ceased to be entitled to exemption under section 60(1)(a) or (b), or

(b) in the case of a company within section 61 or 62 (which impose conditions as to the objects and articles of the company)—

(i) has carried on any business other than the promotion of any of the objects mentioned in subsection (3) of section 61 or, as the case may be, subsection (2) of section 62, or

(ii) has acted inconsistently with the provision required by subsection (4)(a) or (b) of section 61 or, as the case may be, subsection (3)(a) or (b) of section 62,

the Secretary of State may direct the company to change its name so that it ends with "limited" or one of the permitted alternatives.

(2) The direction must be in writing and must specify the period within which the company is to change its name.

(3) A change of name in order to comply with a direction under this section may be made by resolution of the directors.

This is without prejudice to any other method of changing the company's name.

(4) Where a resolution of the directors is passed in accordance with subsection (3), the company must give notice to the registrar of the change.

Sections 80 and 81 apply as regards the registration and effect of the change.

(5) If the company fails to comply with a direction under this section an offence is committed by—

(a) the company, and

(b) every officer of the company who is in default.

(6) A person guilty of an offence under this section is liable on summary conviction to a fine not exceeding level 5 on the standard scale and, for continued contravention, a daily default fine not exceeding one-tenth of level 5 on the standard scale.

(7) A company that has been directed to change its name under this section may not, without the approval of the Secretary of State, subsequently change its name so that it does not include "limited" or one of the permitted alternatives.

This does not apply to a change of name on re-registration or on conversion to a community interest company.

Inappropriate use of indications of company type or legal form

65 Inappropriate use of indications of company type or legal form

(1) The Secretary of State may make provision by regulations prohibiting the use in a company name of specified words, expressions or other indications—
(a) that are associated with a particular type of company or form of organisation, or
(b) that are similar to words, expressions or other indications associated with a particular type of company or form of organisation.

(2) The regulations may prohibit the use of words, expressions or other indications—
(a) in a specified part, or otherwise than in a specified part, of a company's name;
(b) in conjunction with, or otherwise than in conjunction with, such other words, expressions or indications as may be specified.

(3) A company must not be registered under this Act by a name that consists of or includes anything prohibited by regulations under this section.

(4) In this section "specified" means specified in the regulations.

(5) Regulations under this section are subject to negative resolution procedure.

CHAPTER 3
SIMILARITY TO OTHER NAMES

Similarity to other name on registrar's index

66 Name not to be the same as another in the index

(1) A company must not be registered under this Act by a name that is the same as another name appearing in the registrar's index of company names.

(2) The Secretary of State may make provision by regulations supplementing this section.

(3) The regulations may make provision—
(a) as to matters that are to be disregarded, and
(b) as to words, expressions, signs or symbols that are, or are not, to be regarded as the same,
for the purposes of this section.

(4) The regulations may provide—
(a) that registration by a name that would otherwise be prohibited under this section is permitted—
(i) in specified circumstances, or
(ii) with specified consent, and
(b) that if those circumstances obtain or that consent is given at the time a company is registered by a name, a subsequent change of circumstances or withdrawal of consent does not affect the registration.

(5) Regulations under this section are subject to negative resolution procedure.

(6) In this section "specified" means specified in the regulations.

67 Power to direct change of name in case of similarity to existing name

(1) The Secretary of State may direct a company to change its name if it has been registered in a name that is the same as or, in the opinion of the Secretary of State, too like—
(a) a name appearing at the time of the registration in the registrar's index of company names, or
(b) a name that should have appeared in that index at that time.

(2) The Secretary of State may make provision by regulations supplementing this section.

(3) The regulations may make provision—
(a) as to matters that are to be disregarded, and
(b) as to words, expressions, signs or symbols that are, or are not, to be regarded as the same,
for the purposes of this section.

(4) The regulations may provide—
(a) that no direction is to be given under this section in respect of a name—

(i) in specified circumstances, or
(ii) if specified consent is given, and
(b) that a subsequent change of circumstances or withdrawal of consent does not give rise to grounds for a direction under this section.

(5) Regulations under this section are subject to negative resolution procedure.

(6) In this section "specified" means specified in the regulations.

68 Direction to change name: supplementary provisions

(1) The following provisions have effect in relation to a direction under section 67 (power to direct change of name in case of similarity to existing name).

(2) Any such direction—
(a) must be given within twelve months of the company's registration by the name in question, and
(b) must specify the period within which the company is to change its name.

(3) The Secretary of State may by a further direction extend that period.
Any such direction must be given before the end of the period for the time being specified.

(4) A direction under section 67 or this section must be in writing.

(5) If a company fails to comply with the direction, an offence is committed by—
(a) the company, and
(b) every officer of the company who is in default.
For this purpose a shadow director is treated as an officer of the company.

(6) A person guilty of an offence under this section is liable on summary conviction to a fine not exceeding level 3 on the standard scale and, for continued contravention, a daily default fine not exceeding one-tenth of level 3 on the standard scale.

Similarity to other name in which person has goodwill

69 Objection to company's registered name

(1) A person ("the applicant") may object to a company's registered name on the ground—
(a) that it is the same as a name associated with the applicant in which he has goodwill, or
(b) that it is sufficiently similar to such a name that its use in the United Kingdom would be likely to mislead by suggesting a connection between the company and the applicant.

(2) The objection must be made by application to a company names adjudicator (see section 70).

(3) The company concerned shall be the primary respondent to the application. Any of its members or directors may be joined as respondents.

(4) If the ground specified in subsection (1) (a) or (b) is established, it is for the respondents to show—
(a) that the name was registered before the commencement of the activities on which the applicant relies to show goodwill; or
(b) that the company—
(i) is operating under the name, or
(ii) is proposing to do so and has incurred substantial start-up costs in preparation, or
(iii) was formerly operating under the name and is now dormant; or
(c) that the name was registered in the ordinary course of a company formation business and the company is available for sale to the applicant on the standard terms of that business; or
(d) that the name was adopted in good faith; or
(e) that the interests of the applicant are not adversely affected to any significant extent.
If none of those is shown, the objection shall be upheld.

(5) If the facts mentioned in subsection (4)(a), (b) or (c) are established, the objection shall nevertheless be upheld if the applicant shows that the main purpose of the respondents (or any of them) in registering the name was to obtain money (or other consideration) from the applicant or prevent him from registering the name.

(6) If the objection is not upheld under subsection (4) or (5), it shall be dismissed.

(7) In this section "goodwill" includes reputation of any description.

70 Company names adjudicators

(1) The Secretary of State shall appoint persons to be company names adjudicators.

(2) The persons appointed must have such legal or other experience as, in the Secretary of State's opinion, makes them suitable for appointment.

(3) An adjudicator—

(a) holds office in accordance with the terms of his appointment,

(b) is eligible for re-appointment when his term of office ends,

(c) may resign at any time by notice in writing given to the Secretary of State, and

(d) may be dismissed by the Secretary of State on the ground of incapacity or misconduct.

(4) One of the adjudicators shall be appointed Chief Adjudicator.
He shall perform such functions as the Secretary of State may assign to him.

(5) The other adjudicators shall undertake such duties as the Chief Adjudicator may determine.

(6) The Secretary of State may—

(a) appoint staff for the adjudicators;

(b) pay remuneration and expenses to the adjudicators and their staff;

(c) defray other costs arising in relation to the performance by the adjudicators of their functions;

(d) compensate persons for ceasing to be adjudicators.

71 Procedural rules

(1) The Secretary of State may make rules about proceedings before a company names adjudicator.

(2) The rules may, in particular, make provision—

(a) as to how an application is to be made and the form and content of an application or other documents;

(b) for fees to be charged;

(c) about the service of documents and the consequences of failure to serve them;

(d) as to the form and manner in which evidence is to be given;

(e) for circumstances in which hearings are required and those in which they are not;

(f) for cases to be heard by more than one adjudicator;

(g) setting time limits for anything required to be done in connection with the proceedings (and allowing for such limits to be extended, even if they have expired);

(h) enabling the adjudicator to strike out an application, or any defence, in whole or in part—

(i) on the ground that it is vexatious, has no reasonable prospect of success or is otherwise misconceived, or

(ii) for failure to comply with the requirements of the rules;

(i) conferring power to order security for costs (in Scotland, caution for expenses);

(j) as to how far proceedings are to be held in public;

(k) requiring one party to bear the costs (in Scotland, expenses) of another and as to the taxing (or settling) the amount of such costs (or expenses).

(3) The rules may confer on the Chief Adjudicator power to determine any matter that could be the subject of provision in the rules.

(4) Rules under this section shall be made by statutory instrument which shall be subject to annulment in pursuance of a resolution of either House of Parliament.

72 Decision of adjudicator to be made available to public

(1) A company names adjudicator must, within 90 days of determining an application under section 69, make his decision and his reasons for it available to the public.

(2) He may do so by means of a website or by such other means as appear to him to be appropriate.

73 Order requiring name to be changed

(1) If an application under section 69 is upheld, the adjudicator shall make an order—

(a) requiring the respondent company to change its name to one that is not an offending name, and

(b) requiring all the respondents—

(i) to take all such steps as are within their power to make, or facilitate the making, of that change, and

(ii) not to cause or permit any steps to be taken calculated to result in another company being registered with a name that is an offending name.

(2) An "offending name" means a name that, by reason of its similarity to the name associated with the applicant in which he claims goodwill, would be likely—

(a) to be the subject of a direction under section 67 (power of Secretary of State to direct change of name), or

(b) to give rise to a further application under section 69.

(3) The order must specify a date by which the respondent company's name is to be changed and may be enforced—

(a) in England and Wales or Northern Ireland, in the same way as an order of the High Court;

(b) in Scotland, in the same way as a decree of the Court of Session.

(4) If the respondent company's name is not changed in accordance with the order by the specified date, the adjudicator may determine a new name for the company.

(5) If the adjudicator determines a new name for the respondent company he must give notice of his determination—

(a) to the applicant,

(b) to the respondents, and

(c) to the registrar.

(6) For the purposes of this section a company's name is changed when the change takes effect in accordance with section 81(1) (on the issue of the new certification of incorporation).

74 Appeal from adjudicator's decision

(1) An appeal lies to the court from any decision of a company names adjudicator to uphold or dismiss an application under section 69.

(2) Notice of appeal against a decision upholding an application must be given before the date specified in the adjudicator's order by which the respondent company's name is to be changed.

(3) If notice of appeal is given against a decision upholding an application, the effect of the adjudicator's order is suspended.

(4) If on appeal the court—

(a) affirms the decision of the adjudicator to uphold the application, or

(b) reverses the decision of the adjudicator to dismiss the application,

the court may (as the case may require) specify the date by which the adjudicator's order is to be complied with, remit the matter to the adjudicator or make any order or determination that the adjudicator might have made.

(5) If the court determines a new name for the company it must give notice of the determination—

(a) to the parties to the appeal, and

(b) to the registrar.

CHAPTER 4
OTHER POWERS OF THE SECRETARY OF STATE

75 Provision of misleading information etc

(1) If it appears to the Secretary of State—

(a) that misleading information has been given for the purposes of a company's registration by a particular name, or

(b) that an undertaking or assurance has been given for that purpose and has not been fulfilled,

the Secretary of State may direct the company to change its name.

(2) Any such direction—

(a) must be given within five years of the company's registration by that name, and

(b) must specify the period within which the company is to change its name.

(3) The Secretary of State may by a further direction extend the period within which the company is to change its name.
Any such direction must be given before the end of the period for the time being specified.

(4) A direction under this section must be in writing.

(5) If a company fails to comply with a direction under this section, an offence is committed by—
(a) the company, and
(b) every officer of the company who is in default.
For this purpose a shadow director is treated as an officer of the company.

(6) A person guilty of an offence under this section is liable on summary conviction to a fine not exceeding level 3 on the standard scale and, for continued contravention, a daily default fine not exceeding one-tenth of level 3 on the standard scale.

76 Misleading indication of activities

(1) If in the opinion of the Secretary of State the name by which a company is registered gives so misleading an indication of the nature of its activities as to be likely to cause harm to the public, the Secretary of State may direct the company to change its name.

(2) The direction must be in writing.

(3) The direction must be complied with within a period of six weeks from the date of the direction or such longer period as the Secretary of State may think fit to allow.
This does not apply if an application is duly made to the court under the following provisions.

(4) The company may apply to the court to set the direction aside.
The application must be made within the period of three weeks from the date of the direction.

(5) The court may set the direction aside or confirm it.
If the direction is confirmed, the court shall specify the period within which the direction is to be complied with.

(6) If a company fails to comply with a direction under this section, an offence is committed by—
(a) the company, and
(b) every officer of the company who is in default.
For this purpose a shadow director is treated as an officer of the company.

(7) A person guilty of an offence under this section is liable on summary conviction to a fine not exceeding level 3 on the standard scale and, for continued contravention, a daily default fine not exceeding one-tenth of level 3 on the standard scale.

CHAPTER 5
CHANGE OF NAME

77 Change of name

(1) A company may change its name—
(a) by special resolution (see section 78), or
(b) by other means provided for by the company's articles (see section 79).

(2) The name of a company may also be changed—
(a) by resolution of the directors acting under section 64 (change of name to comply with direction of Secretary of State under that section);
(b) on the determination of a new name by a company names adjudicator under section 73 (powers of adjudicator on upholding objection to company name);
(c) on the determination of a new name by the court under section 74 (appeal against decision of company names adjudicator);
(d) under section 1033 (company's name on restoration to the register).

78 Change of name by special resolution

(1) Where a change of name has been agreed to by a company by special resolution, the company must give notice to the registrar.
This is in addition to the obligation to forward a copy of the resolution to the registrar.

(2) Where a change of name by special resolution is conditional on the occurrence of an event, the notice given to the registrar of the change must—

(a) specify that the change is conditional, and

(b) state whether the event has occurred.

(3) If the notice states that the event has not occurred—

(a) the registrar is not required to act under section 80 (registration and issue of new certificate of incorporation) until further notice,

(b) when the event occurs, the company must give notice to the registrar stating that it has occurred, and

(c) the registrar may rely on the statement as sufficient evidence of the matters stated in it.

79 Change of name by means provided for in company's articles

(1) Where a change of a company's name has been made by other means provided for by its articles—

(a) the company must give notice to the registrar, and

(b) the notice must be accompanied by a statement that the change of name has been made by means provided for by the company's articles.

(2) The registrar may rely on the statement as sufficient evidence of the matters stated in it.

80 Change of name: registration and issue of new certificate of incorporation

(1) This section applies where the registrar receives notice of a change of a company's name.

(2) If the registrar is satisfied—

(a) that the new name complies with the requirements of this Part, and

(b) that the requirements of the Companies Acts, and any relevant requirements of the company's articles, with respect to a change of name are complied with,

the registrar must enter the new name on the register in place of the former name.

(3) On the registration of the new name, the registrar must issue a certificate of incorporation altered to meet the circumstances of the case.

81 Change of name: effect

(1) A change of a company's name has effect from the date on which the new certificate of incorporation is issued.

(2) The change does not affect any rights or obligations of the company or render defective any legal proceedings by or against it.

(3) Any legal proceedings that might have been continued or commenced against it by its former name may be continued or commenced against it by its new name.

CHAPTER 6
TRADING DISCLOSURES

82 Requirement to disclose company name etc

(1) The Secretary of State may by regulations make provision requiring companies—

(a) to display specified information in specified locations,

(b) to state specified information in specified descriptions of document or communication, and

(c) to provide specified information on request to those they deal with in the course of their business.

(2) The regulations—

(a) must in every case require disclosure of the name of the company, and

(b) may make provision as to the manner in which any specified information is to be displayed, stated or provided.

(3) The regulations may provide that, for the purposes of any requirement to disclose a company's name, any variation between a word or words required to be part of the name and a permitted abbreviation of that word or those words (or vice versa) shall be disregarded.

(4) In this section "specified" means specified in the regulations.

(5) Regulations under this section are subject to affirmative resolution procedure.

83 Civil consequences of failure to make required disclosure

(1) This section applies to any legal proceedings brought by a company to which section 82 applies (requirement to disclose company name etc) to enforce a right arising out of a contract made in the course of a business in respect of which the company was, at the time the contract was made, in breach of regulations under that section.

(2) The proceedings shall be dismissed if the defendant (in Scotland, the defender) to the proceedings shows—

(a) that he has a claim against the claimant (pursuer) arising out of the contract that he has been unable to pursue by reason of the latter's breach of the regulations, or

(b) that he has suffered some financial loss in connection with the contract by reason of the claimant's (pursuer's) breach of the regulations,

unless the court before which the proceedings are brought is satisfied that it is just and equitable to permit the proceedings to continue.

(3) This section does not affect the right of any person to enforce such rights as he may have against another person in any proceedings brought by that person.

84 Criminal consequences of failure to make required disclosures

(1) Regulations under section 82 may provide—

(a) that where a company fails, without reasonable excuse, to comply with any specified requirement of regulations under that section an offence is committed by—

(i) the company, and

(ii) every officer of the company who is in default;

(b) that a person guilty of such an offence is liable on summary conviction to a fine not exceeding level 3 on the standard scale and, for continued contravention, a daily default fine not exceeding one-tenth of level 3 on the standard scale.

(2) The regulations may provide that, for the purposes of any provision made under subsection (1), a shadow director of the company is to be treated as an officer of the company.

(3) In subsection (1)(a) "specified" means specified in the regulations.

85 Minor variations in form of name to be left out of account

(1) For the purposes of this Chapter, in considering a company's name no account is to be taken of—

(a)whether upper or lower case characters (or a combination of the two) are used,

(b) whether diacritical marks or punctuation are present or absent,

(c) whether the name is in the same format or style as is specified under section 57(1)(b) for the purposes of registration,

provided there is no real likelihood of names differing only in those respects being taken to be different names.

(2) This does not affect the operation of regulations under section 57(1)(a) permitting only specified characters, diacritical marks or punctuation.

PART 6
A COMPANY'S REGISTERED OFFICE

General

86 A company's registered office

A company must at all times have a registered office to which all communications and notices may be addressed.

87 Change of address of registered office

(1) A company may change the address of its registered office by giving notice to the registrar.

(2) The change takes effect upon the notice being registered by the registrar, but until the end of the period of 14 days beginning with the date on which it is registered a person may validly serve any document on the company at the address previously registered.

(3) For the purposes of any duty of a company—

(a) to keep available for inspection at its registered office any register, index or other document, or

(b) to mention the address of its registered office in any document,

a company that has given notice to the registrar of a change in the address of its registered office may act on the change as from such date, not more than 14 days after the notice is given, as it may determine.

(4) Where a company unavoidably ceases to perform at its registered office any such duty as is mentioned in subsection (3)(a) in circumstances in which it was not practicable to give prior notice to the registrar of a change in the address of its registered office, but—

(a) resumes performance of that duty at other premises as soon as practicable, and

(b) gives notice accordingly to the registrar of a change in the situation of its registered office within 14 days of doing so,

it is not to be treated as having failed to comply with that duty.

Welsh companies

88 Welsh companies

(1) In the Companies Acts a "Welsh company" means a company as to which it is stated in the register that its registered office is to be situated in Wales.

(2) A company—

(a) whose registered office is in Wales, and

(b) as to which it is stated in the register that its registered office is to be situated in England and Wales,

may by special resolution require the register to be amended so that it states that the company's registered office is to be situated in Wales.

(3) A company—

(a) whose registered office is in Wales, and

(b) as to which it is stated in the register that its registered office is to be situated in Wales,

may by special resolution require the register to be amended so that it states that the company's registered office is to be situated in England and Wales.

(4) Where a company passes a resolution under this section it must give notice to the registrar, who shall—

(a) amend the register accordingly, and

(b) issue a new certificate of incorporation altered to meet the circumstances of the case.

PART 7
RE-REGISTRATION AS A MEANS OF ALTERING A COMPANY'S STATUS

Introductory

89 Alteration of status by re-registration

A company may by re-registration under this Part alter its status—

(a) from a private company to a public company (see sections 90 to 96);

(b) from a public company to a private company (see sections 97 to 101);

(c) from a private limited company to an unlimited company (see sections 102 to 104);

(d) from an unlimited private company to a limited company (see sections 105 to 108);

(e) from a public company to an unlimited private company (see sections 109 to 111).

Private company becoming public

90 Re-registration of private company as public

(1) A private company (whether limited or unlimited) may be re-registered as a public company limited by shares if—

(a) a special resolution that it should be so re-registered is passed,

(b) the conditions specified below are met, and

(c) an application for re-registration is delivered to the registrar in accordance with section 94, together with—

(i) the other documents required by that section, and

(ii) a statement of compliance.

(2) The conditions are—

(a) that the company has a share capital;

(b) that the requirements of section 91 are met as regards its share capital;

(c) that the requirements of section 92 are met as regards its net assets;

(d) if section 93 applies (recent allotment of shares for non-cash consideration), that the requirements of that section are met; and

(e) that the company has not previously been re-registered as unlimited.

(3) The company must make such changes—

(a) in its name, and

(b) in its articles,

as are necessary in connection with its becoming a public company.

(4) If the company is unlimited it must also make such changes in its articles as are necessary in connection with its becoming a company limited by shares.

91 Requirements as to share capital

(1) The following requirements must be met at the time the special resolution is passed that the company should be re-registered as a public company—

(a) the nominal value of the company's allotted share capital must be not less than the authorised minimum;

(b) each of the company's allotted shares must be paid up at least as to one-quarter of the nominal value of that share and the whole of any premium on it;

(c) if any shares in the company or any premium on them have been fully or partly paid up by an undertaking given by any person that he or another should do work or perform services (whether for the company or any other person), the undertaking must have been performed or otherwise discharged;

(d) if shares have been allotted as fully or partly paid up as to their nominal value or any premium on them otherwise than in cash, and the consideration for the allotment consists of or includes an undertaking to the company (other than one to which paragraph (c) applies), then either—

(i) the undertaking must have been performed or otherwise discharged, or

(ii) there must be a contract between the company and some person pursuant to which the undertaking is to be performed within five years from the time the special resolution is passed.

(2) For the purpose of determining whether the requirements in subsection (1)(b), (c)and (d) are met, the following may be disregarded—

(a) shares allotted—

(i) before 22nd June 1982 in the case of a company then registered in Great Britain, or

(ii) before 31st December 1984 in the case of a company then registered in Northern Ireland;

(b) shares allotted in pursuance of an employees' share scheme by reason of which the company would, but for this subsection, be precluded under subsection (1)(b) (but not otherwise) from being re-registered as a public company.

(3) No more than one-tenth of the nominal value of the company's allotted share capital is to be disregarded under subsection (2)(a).

For this purpose the allotted share capital is treated as not including shares disregarded under subsection (2)(b).

(4) Shares disregarded under subsection (2) are treated as not forming part of the allotted share capital for the purposes of subsection (1)(a).

(5) A company must not be re-registered as a public company if it appears to the registrar that—

(a) the company has resolved to reduce its share capital,

(b) the reduction—

(i) is made under section 626 (reduction in connection with redenomination of share capital),

(iii) is supported by a solvency statement in accordance with section 643, or

(iii) has been confirmed by an order of the court under section 648, and

(c) the effect of the reduction is, or will be, that the nominal value of the company's allotted share capital is below the authorised minimum.

92 Requirements as to net assets

(1) A company applying to re-register as a public company must obtain—

(a) a balance sheet prepared as at a date not more than seven months before the date on which the application is delivered to the registrar,

(b) an unqualified report by the company's auditor on that balance sheet, and

(c) a written statement by the company's auditor that in his opinion at the balance sheet date the amount of the company's net assets was not less than the aggregate of its called-up share capital and undistributable reserves.

(2) Between the balance sheet date and the date on which the application for re-registration is delivered to the registrar, there must be no change in the company's financial position that results in the amount of its net assets becoming less than the aggregate of its called-up share capital and undistributable reserves.

(3) In subsection (1)(b) an "unqualified report" means—

(a) if the balance sheet was prepared for a financial year of the company, a report stating without material qualification the auditor's opinion that the balance sheet has been properly prepared in accordance with the requirements of this Act;

(b) if the balance sheet was not prepared for a financial year of the company, a report stating without material qualification the auditor's opinion that the balance sheet has been properly prepared in accordance with the provisions of this Act which would have applied if it had been prepared for a financial year of the company.

(4) For the purposes of an auditor's report on a balance sheet that was not prepared for a financial year of the company, the provisions of this Act apply with such modifications as are necessary by reason of that fact.

(5) For the purposes of subsection (3) a qualification is material unless the auditor states in his report that the matter giving rise to the qualification is not material for the purpose of determining (by reference to the company's balance sheet) whether at the balance sheet date the amount of the company's net assets was not less than the aggregate of its called-up share capital and undistributable reserves.

(6) In this Part "net assets" and "undistributable reserves" have the same meaning as in section 831 (net asset restriction on distributions by public companies).

93 Recent allotment of shares for non-cash consideration

(1) This section applies where—

(a) shares are allotted by the company in the period between the date as at which the balance sheet required by section 92 is prepared and the passing of the resolution that the company should re-register as a public company, and

(b) the shares are allotted as fully or partly paid up as to their nominal value or any premium on them otherwise than in cash.

(2) The registrar shall not entertain an application by the company for re-registration as a public company unless—

(a) the requirements of section 593(1)(a) and (b) have been complied with (independent valuation of non-cash consideration; valuer's report to company not more than six months before allotment), or

(b) the allotment is in connection with—

(i) a share exchange (see subsections (3) to (5) below), or

(ii) a proposed merger with another company (see subsection (6) below).

(3) An allotment is in connection with a share exchange if—

(a) the shares are allotted in connection with an arrangement under which the whole or part of the consideration for the shares allotted is provided by—

(i) the transfer to the company allotting the shares of shares (or shares of a particular class) in another company, or

(ii) the cancellation of shares (or shares of a particular class) in another company; and

(b) the allotment is open to all the holders of the shares of the other company in question (or, where the arrangement applies only to shares of a particular class, to all the holders of the company's shares of that class) to take part in the arrangement in connection with which the shares are allotted.

(4) In determining whether a person is a holder of shares for the purposes of subsection (3), there shall be disregarded—

(a) shares held by, or by a nominee of, the company allotting the shares;

(b) shares held by, or by a nominee of—

(i) the holding company of the company allotting the shares,

(ii) a subsidiary of the company allotting the shares, or

(iii) a subsidiary of the holding company of the company allotting the shares.

(5) It is immaterial, for the purposes of deciding whether an allotment is in connection with a share exchange, whether or not the arrangement in connection with which the shares are allotted involves the issue to the company allotting the shares of shares (or shares of a particular class) in the other company.

(6) There is a proposed merger with another company if one of the companies concerned proposes to acquire all the assets and liabilities of the other in exchange for the issue of its shares or other securities to shareholders of the other (whether or not accompanied by a cash payment). "Another company" includes any body corporate.

(7) For the purposes of this section—

(a) the consideration for an allotment does not include any amount standing to the credit of any of the company's reserve accounts, or of its profit and loss account, that has been applied in paying up (to any extent) any of the shares allotted or any premium on those shares; and

(b) "arrangement" means any agreement, scheme or arrangement, (including an arrangement sanctioned in accordance with—

(i) Part 26 of this Act (arrangements and reconstructions), or

(ii) section 110 of the Insolvency Act 1986 or Article 96 of the Insolvency (Northern Ireland) Order 1989 (liquidator in winding up accepting shares as consideration for sale of company's property)).

94 Application and accompanying documents

(1) An application for re-registration as a public company must contain—

(a) a statement of the company's proposed name on re-registration; and

(b) in the case of a company without a secretary, a statement of the company's proposed secretary (see section 95).

(2) The application must be accompanied by—

(a) a copy of the special resolution that the company should re-register as a public company (unless a copy has already been forwarded to the registrar under Chapter 3 of Part 3);
(b) a copy of the company's articles as proposed to be amended;
(c) a copy of the balance sheet and other documents referred to in section 92(1); and
(d) if section 93 applies (recent allotment of shares for non-cash consideration), a copy of the valuation report (if any) under subsection (2) (a) of that section.

(3) The statement of compliance required to be delivered together with the application is a statement that the requirements of this Part as to re-registration as a public company have been complied with.

(4) The registrar may accept the statement of compliance as sufficient evidence that the company is entitled to be re-registered as a public company.

95 Statement of proposed secretary

(1) The statement of the company's proposed secretary must contain the required particulars of the person who is or the persons who are to be the secretary or joint secretaries of the company.

(2) The required particulars are the particulars that will be required to be stated in the company's register of secretaries (see sections 277 to 279).

(3) The statement must also contain a consent by the person named as secretary, or each of the persons named as joint secretaries, to act in the relevant capacity. If all the partners in a firm are to be joint secretaries, consent may be given by one partner on behalf of all of them.

96 Issue of certificate of incorporation on re-registration

(1) If on an application for re-registration as a public company the registrar is satisfied that the company is entitled to be so re-registered, the company shall be re-registered accordingly.

(2) The registrar must issue a certificate of incorporation altered to meet the circumstances of the case.

(3) The certificate must state that it is issued on re-registration and the date on which it is issued.

(4) On the issue of the certificate—
(a) the company by virtue of the issue of the certificate becomes a public company,
(b) the changes in the company's name and articles take effect, and
(c) where the application contained a statement under section 95 (statement of proposed secretary), the person or persons named in the statement as secretary or joint secretary of the company are deemed to have been appointed to that office.

(5) The certificate is conclusive evidence that the requirements of this Act as to re-registration have been complied with.

Public company becoming private

97 Re-registration of public company as private limited company

(1) A public company may be re-registered as a private limited company if—
(a) a special resolution that it should be so re-registered is passed,
(b) the conditions specified below are met, and
(c) an application for re-registration is delivered to the registrar in accordance with section 100, together with—
(i) the other documents required by that section, and
(ii) a statement of compliance.

(2) The conditions are that—
(a) where no application under section 98 for cancellation of the resolution has been made—
(i) having regard to the number of members who consented to or voted in favour of the resolution, no such application may be made, or
(ii) the period within which such an application could be made has expired, or
(b) where such an application has been made—
(i) the application has been withdrawn, or

(ii) an order has been made confirming the resolution and a copy of that order has been delivered to the registrar.

(3) The company must make such changes—
(a) in its name, and
(b) in its articles,
as are necessary in connection with its becoming a private company limited by shares or, as the case may be, by guarantee.

98 Application to court to cancel resolution

(1) Where a special resolution by a public company to be re-registered as a private limited company has been passed, an application to the court for the cancellation of the resolution may be made—
(a) by the holders of not less in the aggregate than 5% in nominal value of the company's issued share capital or any class of the company's issued share capital (disregarding any shares held by the company as treasury shares);
(b) if the company is not limited by shares, by not less than 5% of its members; or
(c) by not less than 50 of the company's members;
but not by a person who has consented to or voted in favour of the resolution.

(2) The application must be made within 28 days after the passing of the resolution and may be made on behalf of the persons entitled to make it by such one or more of their number as they may appoint for the purpose.

(3) On the hearing of the application the court shall make an order either cancelling or confirming the resolution.

(4) The court may—
(a) make that order on such terms and conditions as it thinks fit,
(b) if it thinks fit adjourn the proceedings in order that an arrangement may be made to the satisfaction of the court for the purchase of the interests of dissentient members, and
(c) give such directions, and make such orders, as it thinks expedient for facilitating or carrying into effect any such arrangement.

(5) The court's order may, if the court thinks fit—
(a) provide for the purchase by the company of the shares of any of its members and for the reduction accordingly of the company's capital; and
(b) make such alteration in the company's articles as may be required in consequence of that provision.

(6) The court's order may, if the court thinks fit, require the company not to make any, or any specified, amendments to its articles without the leave of the court.

99 Notice to registrar of court application or order

(1) On making an application under section 98 (application to court to cancel resolution) the applicants, or the person making the application on their behalf, must immediately give notice to the registrar.
This is without prejudice to any provision of rules of court as to service of notice of the application.

(2) On being served with notice of any such application, the company must immediately give notice to the registrar.

(3) Within 15 days of the making of the court's order on the application, or such longer period as the court may at any time direct, the company must deliver to the registrar a copy of the order.

(4) If a company fails to comply with subsection (2) or (3) an offence is committed by—
(a) the company, and
(b) every officer of the company who is in default.

(5) A person guilty of an offence under this section is liable on summary conviction to a fine not exceeding level 3 on the standard scale and, for continued contravention, a daily default fine not exceeding one-tenth of level 3 on the standard scale.

100 Application and accompanying documents

(1) An application for re-registration as a private limited company must contain a statement of the company's proposed name on re-registration.

(2) The application must be accompanied by—

(a) a copy of the resolution that the company should re-register as a private limited company (unless a copy has already been forwarded to the registrar under Chapter 3 of Part 3); and

(b) a copy of the company's articles as proposed to be amended.

(3) The statement of compliance required to be delivered together with the application is a statement that the requirements of this Part as to re-registration as a private limited company have been complied with.

(4) The registrar may accept the statement of compliance as sufficient evidence that the company is entitled to be re-registered as a private limited company.

101 Issue of certificate of incorporation on re-registration

(1) If on an application for re-registration as a private limited company the registrar is satisfied that the company is entitled to be so re-registered, the company shall be re-registered accordingly.

(2) The registrar must issue a certificate of incorporation altered to meet the circumstances of the case.

(3) The certificate must state that it is issued on re-registration and the date on which it is issued.

(4) On the issue of the certificate—

(a) the company by virtue of the issue of the certificate becomes a private limited company, and

(b) the changes in the company's name and articles take effect.

(5) The certificate is conclusive evidence that the requirements of this Act as to re-registration have been complied with.

Private limited company becoming unlimited

102 Re-registration of private limited company as unlimited

(1) A private limited company may be re-registered as an unlimited company if—

(a) all the members of the company have assented to its being so re-registered,

(b) the condition specified below is met, and

(c) an application for re-registration is delivered to the registrar in accordance with section 103, together with—

(i) the other documents required by that section, and

(ii) a statement of compliance.

(2) The condition is that the company has not previously been re-registered as limited.

(3) The company must make such changes in its name and its articles—

(a) as are necessary in connection with its becoming an unlimited company; and

(b) if it is to have a share capital, as are necessary in connection with its becoming an unlimited company having a share capital.

(4) For the purposes of this section—

(a) a trustee in bankruptcy of a member of the company is entitled, to the exclusion of the member, to assent to the company's becoming unlimited; and

(b) the personal representative of a deceased member of the company may assent on behalf of the deceased.

(5) In subsection (4)(a), "a trustee in bankruptcy of a member of the company" includes—

(a) a permanent trustee or an interim trustee (within the meaning of the Bankruptcy (Scotland) Act 1985 on the sequestrated estate of a member of the company;

(b) a trustee under a protected trustee deed (within the meaning of the Bankruptcy (Scotland) Act 1985) granted by a member of the company.

103 Application and accompanying documents

(1) An application for re-registration as an unlimited company must contain a statement of the company's proposed name on re-registration.

(2) The application must be accompanied by—
(a) the prescribed form of assent to the company's being registered as an unlimited company, authenticated by or on behalf of all the members of the company;
(b) a copy of the company's articles as proposed to be amended.

(3) The statement of compliance required to be delivered together with the application is a statement that the requirements of this Part as to re-registration as an unlimited company have been complied with.

(4) The statement must contain a statement by the directors of the company—
(a) that the persons by whom or on whose behalf the form of assent is authenticated constitute the whole membership of the company, and
(b) if any of the members have not authenticated that form themselves, that the directors have taken all reasonable steps to satisfy themselves that each person who authenticated it on behalf of a member was lawfully empowered to do so.

(5) The registrar may accept the statement of compliance as sufficient evidence that the company is entitled to be re-registered as an unlimited company.

104 Issue of certificate of incorporation on re-registration

(1) If on an application for re-registration of a private limited company as an unlimited company the registrar is satisfied that the company is entitled to be so re-registered, the company shall be re-registered accordingly.

(2) The registrar must issue a certificate of incorporation altered to meet the circumstances of the case.

(3) The certificate must state that it is issued on re-registration and the date on which it is issued.

(4) On the issue of the certificate—
(a) the company by virtue of the issue of the certificate becomes an unlimited company, and
(b) the changes in the company's name and articles take effect.

(5) The certificate is conclusive evidence that the requirements of this Act as to re-registration have been complied with.

Unlimited private company becoming limited

105 Re-registration of unlimited company as limited

(1) An unlimited company may be re-registered as a private limited company if—
(a) a special resolution that it should be so re-registered is passed,
(b) the condition specified below is met, and
(c) an application for re-registration is delivered to the registrar in accordance with section 106, together with—
(i) the other documents required by that section, and
(ii) a statement of compliance.

(2) The condition is that the company has not previously been re-registered as unlimited.

(3) The special resolution must state whether the company is to be limited by shares or by guarantee.

(4) The company must make such changes—
(a) in its name, and
(b) in its articles,
as are necessary in connection with its becoming a company limited by shares or, as the case may be, by guarantee.

106 Application and accompanying documents

(1) An application for re-registration as a limited company must contain a statement of the company's proposed name on re-registration.

(2) The application must be accompanied by—
(a) a copy of the resolution that the company should re-register as a private limited company (unless a copy has already been forwarded to the registrar under Chapter 3 of Part 3);
(b) if the company is to be limited by guarantee, a statement of guarantee;

(c) a copy of the company's articles as proposed to be amended.

(3) The statement of guarantee required to be delivered in the case of a company that is to be limited by guarantee must state that each member undertakes that, if the company is wound up while he is a member, or within one year after he ceases to be a member, he will contribute to the assets of the company such amount as may be required for—

(a) payment of the debts and liabilities of the company contracted before he ceases to be a member,

(b) payment of the costs, charges and expenses of winding up, and

(c) adjustment of the rights of the contributories among themselves,

not exceeding a specified amount.

(4) The statement of compliance required to be delivered together with the application is a statement that the requirements of this Part as to re-registration as a limited company have been complied with.

(5) The registrar may accept the statement of compliance as sufficient evidence that the company is entitled to be re-registered as a limited company.

107 Issue of certificate of incorporation on re-registration

(1) If on an application for re-registration of an unlimited company as a limited company the registrar is satisfied that the company is entitled to be so re-registered, the company shall be re-registered accordingly.

(2) The registrar must issue a certificate of incorporation altered to meet the circumstances of the case.

(3) The certificate must state that it is issued on re-registration and the date on which it is so issued.

(4) On the issue of the certificate—

(a) the company by virtue of the issue of the certificate becomes a limited company, and

(b) the changes in the company's name and articles take effect.

(5) The certificate is conclusive evidence that the requirements of this Act as to re-registration have been complied with.

108 Statement of capital required where company already has share capital

(1) A company which on re-registration under section 107 already has allotted share capital must within 15 days after the re-registration deliver a statement of capital to the registrar.

(2) This does not apply if the information which would be included in the statement has already been sent to the registrar in—

(a) a statement of capital and initial shareholdings (see section 10), or

(b) a statement of capital contained in an annual return (see section 856(2)).

(3) The statement of capital must state with respect to the company's share capital on re-registration—

(a) the total number of shares of the company,

(b) the aggregate nominal value of those shares,

(c) for each class of shares—

(i) prescribed particulars of the rights attached to the shares,

(ii) the total number of shares of that class, and

(iii) the aggregate nominal value of shares of that class, and

(d) the amount paid up and the amount (if any) unpaid on each share (whether on account of the nominal value of the share or by way of premium).

(4) If default is made in complying with this section, an offence is committed by—

(a) the company, and

(b) every officer of the company who is in default.

(5) A person guilty of an offence under this section is liable on summary conviction to a fine not exceeding level 3 on the standard scale and, for continued contravention, a daily default fine not exceeding one-tenth of level 3 on the standard scale.

Public company becoming private and unlimited

109 Re-registration of public company as private and unlimited

(1) A public company limited by shares may be re-registered as an unlimited private company with a share capital if—

(a) all the members of the company have assented to its being so re-registered,

(b) the condition specified below is met, and

(c) an application for re-registration is delivered to the registrar in accordance with section 110, together with—

(i) the other documents required by that section, and

(ii) a statement of compliance.

(2) The condition is that the company has not previously been re-registered—

(a) as limited, or

(b) as unlimited.

(3) The company must make such changes—

(a) in its name, and

(b) in its articles,

as are necessary in connection with its becoming an unlimited private company.

(4) For the purposes of this section—

(a) a trustee in bankruptcy of a member of the company is entitled, to the exclusion of the member, to assent to the company's re-registration; and

(b) the personal representative of a deceased member of the company may assent on behalf of the deceased.

(5) In subsection (4)(a), "a trustee in bankruptcy of a member of the company" includes—

(a) a permanent trustee or an interim trustee (within the meaning of the Bankruptcy (Scotland) Act 1985 on the sequestrated estate of a member of the company;

(b) a trustee under a protected trustee deed (within the meaning of the Bankruptcy (Scotland) Act 1985) granted by a member of the company.

110 Application and accompanying documents

(1) An application for re-registration of a public company as an unlimited private company must contain a statement of the company's proposed name on re-registration.

(2) The application must be accompanied by—

(a) the prescribed form of assent to the company's being registered as an unlimited company, authenticated by or on behalf of all the members of the company, and

(b) a copy of the company's articles as proposed to be amended.

(3) The statement of compliance required to be delivered together with the application is a statement that the requirements of this Part as to re-registration as an unlimited private company have been complied with.

(4) The statement must contain a statement by the directors of the company—

(a) that the persons by whom or on whose behalf the form of assent is authenticated constitute the whole membership of the company, and

(b) if any of the members have not authenticated that form themselves, that the directors have taken all reasonable steps to satisfy themselves that each person who authenticated it on behalf of a member was lawfully empowered to do so.

(5) The registrar may accept the statement of compliance as sufficient evidence that the company is entitled to be re-registered as an unlimited private company.

111 Issue of certificate of incorporation on re-registration

(1) If on an application for re-registration of a public company as an unlimited private company the registrar is satisfied that the company is entitled to be so re-registered, the company shall be re-registered accordingly.

(2) The registrar must issue a certificate of incorporation altered to meet the circumstances of the case.

(3) The certificate must state that it is issued on re-registration and the date on which it is so issued.

(4) On the issue of the certificate—

(a) the company by virtue of the issue of the certificate becomes an unlimited private company, and

(b) the changes in the company's name and articles take effect.

(5) The certificate is conclusive evidence that the requirements of this Act as to re-registration have been complied with.

PART 8
A COMPANY'S MEMBERS

CHAPTER 1
THE MEMBERS OF A COMPANY

112 The members of a company

(1) The subscribers of a company's memorandum are deemed to have agreed to become members of the company, and on its registration become members and must be entered as such in its register of members.

(2) Every other person who agrees to become a member of a company, and whose name is entered in its register of members, is a member of the company.

CHAPTER 2
REGISTER OF MEMBERS

General

113 Register of members

(1) Every company must keep a register of its members.

(2) There must be entered in the register—

(a) the names and addresses of the members,

(b) the date on which each person was registered as a member, and

(c) the date at which any person ceased to be a member.

(3) In the case of a company having a share capital, there must be entered in the register, with the names and addresses of the members, a statement of—

(a) the shares held by each member, distinguishing each share—

(i) by its number (so long as the share has a number), and

(ii) where the company has more than one class of issued shares, by its class, and

(b) the amount paid or agreed to be considered as paid on the shares of each member.

(4) If the company has converted any of its shares into stock, and given notice of the conversion to the registrar, the register of members must show the amount and class of stock held by each member instead of the amount of shares and the particulars relating to shares specified above.

(5) In the case of joint holders of shares or stock in a company, the company's register of members must state the names of each joint holder.

In other respects joint holders are regarded for the purposes of this Chapter as a single member (so that the register must show a single address).

(6) In the case of a company that does not have a share capital but has more than one class of members, there must be entered in the register, with the names and addresses of the members, a statement of the class to which each member belongs.

(7) If a company makes default in complying with this section an offence is committed by—

(a) the company, and

(b) every officer of the company who is in default.

(8) A person guilty of an offence under this section is liable on summary conviction to a fine not exceeding level 3 on the standard scale and, for continued contravention, a daily default fine not exceeding one-tenth of level 3 on the standard scale.

114 Register to be kept available for inspection

(1) A company's register of members must be kept available for inspection—

(a) at its registered office, or

(b) at a place specified in regulations under section 1136.

(2) A company must give notice to the registrar of the place where its register of members is kept available for inspection and of any change in that place.

(3) No such notice is required if the register has, at all times since it came into existence (or, in the case of a register in existence on the relevant date, at all times since then) been kept available for inspection at the company's registered office.

(4) The relevant date for the purposes of subsection (3) is—

(a) 1st July 1948 in the case of a company registered in Great Britain, and

(b) 1st April 1961 in the case of a company registered in Northern Ireland.

(5) If a company makes default for 14 days in complying with subsection (2), an offence is committed by—

(a) the company, and

(b) every officer of the company who is in default.

(6) A person guilty of an offence under this section is liable on summary conviction to a fine not exceeding level 3 on the standard scale and, for continued contravention, a daily default fine not exceeding one-tenth of level 3 on the standard scale.

115 Index of members

(1) Every company having more than 50 members must keep an index of the names of the members of the company, unless the register of members is in such a form as to constitute in itself an index.

(2) The company must make any necessary alteration in the index within 14 days after the date on which any alteration is made in the register of members.

(3) The index must contain, in respect of each member, a sufficient indication to enable the account of that member in the register to be readily found.

(4) The index must be at all times kept available for inspection at the same place as the register of members.

(5) If default is made in complying with this section, an offence is committed by—

(a) the company, and

(b) every officer of the company who is in default.

(6) A person guilty of an offence under this section is liable on summary conviction to a fine not exceeding level 3 on the standard scale and, for continued contravention, a daily default fine not exceeding one-tenth of level 3 on the standard scale.

116 Rights to inspect and require copies

(1) The register and the index of members' names must be open to the inspection—

(a) of any member of the company without charge, and

(b) of any other person on payment of such fee as may be prescribed.

(2) Any person may require a copy of a company's register of members, or of any part of it, on payment of such fee as may be prescribed.

(3) A person seeking to exercise either of the rights conferred by this section must make a request to the company to that effect.

(4) The request must contain the following information—

(a) in the case of an individual, his name and address;

(b) in the case of an organisation, the name and address of an individual responsible for making the request on behalf of the organisation;

(c) the purpose for which the information is to be used; and

(d) whether the information will be disclosed to any other person, and if so—

(i) where that person is an individual, his name and address,

(ii) where that person is an organisation, the name and address of an individual responsible for receiving the information on its behalf, and

(iii) the purpose for which the information is to be used by that person.

117 Register of members: response to request for inspection or copy

(1) Where a company receives a request under section 116 (register of members: right to inspect and require copy), it must within five working days either—

(a) comply with the request, or

(b) apply to the court.

(2) If it applies to the court it must notify the person making the request.

(3) If on an application under this section the court is satisfied that the inspection or copy is not sought for a proper purpose—

(a) it shall direct the company not to comply with the request, and

(b) it may further order that the company's costs (in Scotland, expenses) on the application be paid in whole or in part by the person who made the request, even if he is not a party to the application.

(4) If the court makes such a direction and it appears to the court that the company is or may be subject to other requests made for a similar purpose (whether made by the same person or different persons), it may direct that the company is not to comply with any such request.

The order must contain such provision as appears to the court appropriate to identify the requests to which it applies.

(5) If on an application under this section the court does not direct the company not to comply with the request, the company must comply with the request immediately upon the court giving its decision or, as the case may be, the proceedings being discontinued.

118 Register of members: refusal of inspection or default in providing copy

(1) If an inspection required under section 116 (register of members: right to inspect and require copy) is refused or default is made in providing a copy required under that section, otherwise than in accordance with an order of the court, an offence is committed by—

(a) the company, and

(b) every officer of the company who is in default.

(2) A person guilty of an offence under this section is liable on summary conviction to a fine not exceeding level 3 on the standard scale and, for continued contravention, a daily default fine not exceeding one-tenth of level 3 on the standard scale.

(3) In the case of any such refusal or default the court may by order compel an immediate inspection or, as the case may be, direct that the copy required be sent to the person requesting it.

119 Register of members: offences in connection with request for or disclosure of information

(1) It is an offence for a person knowingly or recklessly to make in a request under section 116 (register of members: right to inspect or require copy) a statement that is misleading, false or deceptive in a material particular.

(2) It is an offence for a person in possession of information obtained by exercise of either of the rights conferred by that section—

(a) to do anything that results in the information being disclosed to another person, or

(b) to fail to do anything with the result that the information is disclosed to another person,

knowing, or having reason to suspect, that person may use the information for a purpose that is not a proper purpose.

(3) A person guilty of an offence under this section is liable—

(a) on conviction on indictment, to imprisonment for a term not exceeding two years or a fine (or both);

(b) on summary conviction—

(i) in England and Wales, to imprisonment for a term not exceeding twelve months or to a fine not exceeding the statutory maximum (or both);

(ii) in Scotland or Northern Ireland, to imprisonment for a term not exceeding six months, or to a fine not exceeding the statutory maximum (or both).

120 Information as to state of register and index

(1) When a person inspects the register, or the company provides him with a copy of the register or any part of it, the company must inform him of the most recent date (if any) on which alterations were made to the register and there were no further alterations to be made.

(2) When a person inspects the index of members' names, the company must inform him whether there is any alteration to the register that is not reflected in the index.

(3) If a company fails to provide the information required under subsection (1) or (2), an offence is committed by—
 (a) the company, and
 (b) every officer of the company who is in default.

(4) A person guilty of an offence under this section is liable on summary conviction to a fine not exceeding level 3 on the standard scale.

121 Removal of entries relating to former members

An entry relating to a former member of the company may be removed from the register after the expiration of ten years from the date on which he ceased to be a member.

Special cases

122 Share warrants

(1) On the issue of a share warrant the company must—
 (a) enter in the register of members—
  (i) the fact of the issue of the warrant,
  (ii) a statement of the shares included in the warrant, distinguishing each share by its number so long as the share has a number, and
  (iii) the date of the issue of the warrant,
 and
 (b) amend the register, if necessary, so that no person is named on the register as the holder of the shares specified in the warrant.

(2) Until the warrant is surrendered, the particulars specified in subsection (1)(a) are deemed to be those required by this Act to be entered in the register of members.

(3) The bearer of a share warrant may, if the articles of the company so provide, be deemed a member of the company within the meaning of this Act, either to the full extent or for any purposes defined in the articles.

(4) Subject to the company's articles, the bearer of a share warrant is entitled, on surrendering it for cancellation, to have his name entered as a member in the register of members.

(5) The company is responsible for any loss incurred by any person by reason of the company entering in the register the name of a bearer of a share warrant in respect of the shares specified in it without the warrant being surrendered and cancelled.

(6) On the surrender of a share warrant, the date of the surrender must be entered in the register.

123 Single member companies

(1) If a limited company is formed under this Act with only one member there shall be entered in the company's register of members, with the name and address of the sole member, a statement that the company has only one member.

(2) If the number of members of a limited company falls to one, or if an unlimited company with only one member becomes a limited company on re-registration, there shall upon the occurrence of that event be entered in the company's register of members, with the name and address of the sole member—
 (a) a statement that the company has only one member, and
 (b) the date on which the company became a company having only one member.

(3) If the membership of a limited company increases from one to two or more members, there shall upon the occurrence of that event be entered in the company's register of members, with the name and address of the person who was formerly the sole member—

(a) a statement that the company has ceased to have only one member, and
(b) the date on which that event occurred.

(4) If a company makes default in complying with this section, an offence is committed by—
(a) the company, and
(b) every officer of the company who is in default.

(5) A person guilty of an offence under this section is liable on summary conviction to a fine not exceeding level 3 on the standard scale and, for continued contravention, a daily default fine not exceeding one-tenth of level 3 on the standard scale.

124 Company holding its own shares as treasury shares

(1) Where a company purchases its own shares in circumstances in which section 724 (treasury shares) applies—
(a) the requirements of section 113 (register of members) need not be complied with if the company cancels all of the shares forthwith after the purchase, and
(b) if the company does not cancel all of the shares forthwith after the purchase, any share that is so cancelled shall be disregarded for the purposes of that section.

(2) Subject to subsection (1), where a company holds shares as treasury shares the company must be entered in the register as the member holding those shares.

Supplementary

125 Power of court to rectify register

(1) If—
(a) the name of any person is, without sufficient cause, entered in or omitted from a company's register of members, or
(b) default is made or unnecessary delay takes place in entering on the register the fact of any person having ceased to be a member,

the person aggrieved, or any member of the company, or the company, may apply to the court for rectification of the register.

(2) The court may either refuse the application or may order rectification of the register and payment by the company of any damages sustained by any party aggrieved.

(3) On such an application the court may decide any question relating to the title of a person who is a party to the application to have his name entered in or omitted from the register, whether the question arises between members or alleged members, or between members or alleged members on the one hand and the company on the other hand, and generally may decide any question necessary or expedient to be decided for rectification of the register.

(4) In the case of a company required by this Act to send a list of its members to the registrar of companies, the court, when making an order for rectification of the register, shall by its order direct notice of the rectification to be given to the registrar.

126 Trusts not to be entered on register

No notice of any trust, expressed, implied or constructive, shall be entered on the register of members of a company registered in England and Wales or Northern Ireland, or be receivable by the registrar.

127 Register to be evidence

The register of members is prima facie evidence of any matters which are by this Act directed or authorised to be inserted in it.

128 Time limit for claims arising from entry in register

(1) Liability incurred by a company—
(a) from the making or deletion of an entry in the register of members, or
(b) from a failure to make or delete any such entry,

is not enforceable more than ten years after the date on which the entry was made or deleted or, as the case may be, the failure first occurred.

(2) This is without prejudice to any lesser period of limitation (and, in Scotland, to any rule that the obligation giving rise to the liability prescribes before the expiry of that period).

CHAPTER 3
OVERSEAS BRANCH REGISTERS

129 Overseas branch registers

(1) A company having a share capital may, if it transacts business in a country or territory to which this Chapter applies, cause to be kept there a branch register of members resident there (an "overseas branch register").

(2) This Chapter applies to—

(a) any part of Her Majesty's dominions outside the United Kingdom, the Channel Islands and the Isle of Man, and

(b) the countries or territories listed below.

Bangladesh	Malaysia
Cyprus	Malta
Dominica	Nigeria
The Gambia	Pakistan
Ghana	Seychelles
Guyana	Sierra Leone
The Hong Kong Special Administrative Region of the People's Republic of China	Singapore
India	South Africa
Ireland	Sri Lanka
Kenya	Swaziland
Kiribati	Trinidad and Tobago
Lesotho	Uganda
Malawi	Zimbabwe

(3) The Secretary of State may make provision by regulations as to the circumstances in which a company is to be regarded as keeping a register in a particular country or territory.

(4) Regulations under this section are subject to negative resolution procedure.

(5) References—

(a) in any Act or instrument (including, in particular, a company's articles) to a dominion register, or

(b) in articles registered before 1st November 1929 to a colonial register,

are to be read (unless the context otherwise requires) as a reference to an overseas branch register kept under this section.

130 Notice of opening of overseas branch register

(1) A company that begins to keep an overseas branch register must give notice to the registrar within 14 days of doing so, stating the country or territory in which the register is kept.

(2) If default is made in complying with subsection (1), an offence is committed by—

(a) the company, and

(b) every officer of the company who is in default.

(3) A person guilty of an offence under subsection (2) is liable on summary conviction to a fine not exceeding level 3 on the standard scale and, for continued contravention, a daily default fine not exceeding one-tenth of level 3 on the standard scale.

131 Keeping of overseas branch register

(1) An overseas branch register is regarded as part of the company's register of members ("the main register").

(2) The Secretary of State may make provision by regulations modifying any provision of Chapter 2 (register of members) as it applies in relation to an overseas branch register.

(3) Regulations under this section are subject to negative resolution procedure.

(4) Subject to the provisions of this Act, a company may by its articles make such provision as it thinks fit as to the keeping of overseas branch registers.

132 Register or duplicate to be kept available for inspection in UK

(1) A company that keeps an overseas branch register must keep available for inspection—
(a) the register, or
(b) a duplicate of the register duly entered up from time to time,
at the place in the United Kingdom where the company's main register is kept available for inspection.

(2) Any such duplicate is treated for all purposes of this Act as part of the main register.

(3) If default is made in complying with subsection (1), an offence is committed by—
(a) the company, and
(b) every officer of the company who is in default.

(4) A person guilty of an offence under subsection (3) is liable on summary conviction to a fine not exceeding level 3 on the standard scale and, for continued contravention, a daily default fine not exceeding one-tenth of level 3 on the standard scale.

133 Transactions in shares registered in overseas branch register

(1) Shares registered in an overseas branch register must be distinguished from those registered in the main register.

(2) No transaction with respect to shares registered in an overseas branch register may be registered in any other register.

(3) An instrument of transfer of a share registered in an overseas branch register—
(a) is regarded as a transfer of property situated outside the United Kingdom, and
(b) unless executed in a part of the United Kingdom, is exempt from stamp duty.

134 Jurisdiction of local courts

(1) A competent court in a country or territory where an overseas branch register is kept may exercise the same jurisdiction as is exercisable by a court in the United Kingdom—
(a) to rectify the register (see section 125), or
(b) in relation to a request for inspection or a copy of the register (see section 117).

(2) The offences—
(a) of refusing inspection or failing to provide a copy of the register (see section 118), and
(b) of making a false, misleading or deceptive statement in a request for inspection or a copy (see section 119),
may be prosecuted summarily before any tribunal having summary criminal jurisdiction in the country or territory where the register is kept.

(3) This section extends only to those countries and territories to which paragraph 3 of Schedule 14 to the Companies Act 1985 (which made similar provision) extended immediately before the coming into force of this Chapter.

135 Discontinuance of overseas branch register

(1) A company may discontinue an overseas branch register.

(2) If it does so all the entries in that register must be transferred—
(a) to some other overseas branch register kept in the same country or territory, or
(b) to the main register.

(3) The company must give notice to the registrar within 14 days of the discontinuance.

(4) If default is made in complying with subsection (3), an offence is committed by—
(a) the company, and
(b) every officer of the company who is in default.

(5) A person guilty of an offence under subsection (4) is liable on summary conviction to a fine not exceeding level 3 on the standard scale and, for continued contravention, a daily default fine not exceeding one-tenth of level 3 on the standard scale.

CHAPTER 4
PROHIBITION ON SUBSIDIARY BEING MEMBER OF ITS HOLDING COMPANY

General prohibition

136 Prohibition on subsidiary being a member of its holding company

(1) Except as provided by this Chapter—
(a) a body corporate cannot be a member of a company that is its holding company, and
(b) any allotment or transfer of shares in a company to its subsidiary is void.

(2) The exceptions are provided for in—
section 138 (subsidiary acting as personal representative or trustee), and
section 141 (subsidiary acting as authorised dealer in securities).

137 Shares acquired before prohibition became applicable

(1) Where a body corporate became a holder of shares in a company—
(a) before the relevant date, or
(b) on or after that date and before the commencement of this Chapter in circumstances in which the prohibition in section 23(1) of the Companies Act 1985 or Article 33(1) of the Companies (Northern Ireland) Order 1986 (or any corresponding earlier enactment), as it then had effect, did not apply, or
(c) on or after the commencement of this Chapter in circumstances in which the prohibition in section 136 did not apply,
it may continue to be a member of the company.

(2) The relevant date for the purposes of subsection (1)(a) is—
(a) 1st July 1948 in the case of a company registered in Great Britain, and
(b) 1st April 1961 in the case of a company registered in Northern Ireland.

(3) So long as it is permitted to continue as a member of a company by virtue of this section, an allotment to it of fully paid shares in the company may be validly made by way of capitalisation of reserves of the company.

(4) But, so long as the prohibition in section 136 would (apart from this section) apply, it has no right to vote in respect of the shares mentioned in subsection (1) above, or any shares allotted as mentioned in subsection (3) above, on a written resolution or at meetings of the company or of any class of its members.

Subsidiary acting as personal representative or trustee

138 Subsidiary acting as personal representative or trustee

(1) The prohibition in section 136 (prohibition on subsidiary being a member of its holding company) does not apply where the subsidiary is concerned only—
(a) as personal representative, or
(b) as trustee,
unless, in the latter case, the holding company or a subsidiary of it is beneficially interested under the trust.

(2) For the purpose of ascertaining whether the holding company or a subsidiary is so interested, there shall be disregarded—
(a) any interest held only by way of security for the purposes of a transaction entered into by the holding company or subsidiary in the ordinary course of a business that includes the lending of money;
(b) any interest within—
section 139 (interests to be disregarded: residual interest under pension scheme or employees' share scheme), or
section 140 (interests to be disregarded: employer's rights of recovery under pension scheme or employees' share scheme);

(c) any rights that the company or subsidiary has in its capacity as trustee, including in particular—
(i) any right to recover its expenses or be remunerated out of the trust property, and
(ii) any right to be indemnified out of the trust property for any liability incurred by reason of any act or omission in the performance of its duties as trustee.

139 Interests to be disregarded: residual interest under pension scheme or employees' share scheme

(1) Where shares in a company are held on trust for the purposes of a pension scheme or employees' share scheme, there shall be disregarded for the purposes of section 138 any residual interest that has not vested in possession.

(2) A "residual interest" means a right of the company or subsidiary ("the residual beneficiary") to receive any of the trust property in the event of—
(a) all the liabilities arising under the scheme having been satisfied or provided for, or
(b) the residual beneficiary ceasing to participate in the scheme, or
(c) the trust property at any time exceeding what is necessary for satisfying the liabilities arising or expected to arise under the scheme.

(3) In subsection (2)—
(a) the reference to a right includes a right dependent on the exercise of a discretion vested by the scheme in the trustee or another person, and
(b) the reference to liabilities arising under a scheme includes liabilities that have resulted, or may result, from the exercise of any such discretion.

(4) For the purposes of this section a residual interest vests in possession—
(a) in a case within subsection (2)(a), on the occurrence of the event mentioned there (whether or not the amount of the property receivable pursuant to the right is ascertained);
(b) in a case within subsection (2)(b) or (c), when the residual beneficiary becomes entitled to require the trustee to transfer to him any of the property receivable pursuant to the right.

(5) In this section "pension scheme" means a scheme for the provision of benefits consisting of or including relevant benefits for or in respect of employees or former employees.

(6) In subsection (5)—
(a) "relevant benefits" means any pension, lump sum, gratuity or other like benefit given or to be given on retirement or on death or in anticipation of retirement or, in connection with past service, after retirement or death; and
(b) "employee" shall be read as if a director of a company were employed by it.

140 Interests to be disregarded: employer's rights of recovery under pension scheme or employees' share scheme

(1) Where shares in a company are held on trust for the purposes of a pension scheme or employees' share scheme, there shall be disregarded for the purposes of section 138 any charge or lien on, or set-off against, any benefit or other right or interest under the scheme for the purpose of enabling the employer or former employer of a member of the scheme to obtain the discharge of a monetary obligation due to him from the member.

(2) In the case of a trust for the purposes of a pension scheme there shall also be disregarded any right to receive from the trustee of the scheme, or as trustee of the scheme to retain, an amount that can be recovered or retained, under section 61 of the Pension Schemes Act 1993 or section 57 of the Pension Schemes (Northern Ireland) Act 1993 (deduction of contributions equivalent premium from refund of scheme contributions) or otherwise, as reimbursement or partial reimbursement for any contributions equivalent premium paid in connection with the scheme under Part 3 of that Act.

(3) In this section "pension scheme" means a scheme for the provision of benefits consisting of or including relevant benefits for or in respect of employees or former employees.

"Relevant benefits" here means any pension, lump sum, gratuity or other like benefit given or to be given on retirement or on death or in anticipation of retirement or, in connection with past service, after retirement or death.

(4) In this section "employer" and "employee" shall be read as if a director of a company were employed by it.

Subsidiary acting as dealer in securities

141 Subsidiary acting as authorised dealer in securities

(1) The prohibition in section 136 (prohibition on subsidiary being a member of its holding company) does not apply where the shares are held by the subsidiary in the ordinary course of its business as an intermediary.

(2) For this purpose a person is an intermediary if he—

(a) carries on a bona fide business of dealing in securities,

(b) is a member of or has access to a regulated market, and

(c) does not carry on an excluded business.

(3) The following are excluded businesses—

(a) a business that consists wholly or mainly in the making or managing of investments;

(b) a business that consists wholly or mainly in, or is carried on wholly or mainly for the purposes of, providing services to persons who are connected with the person carrying on the business;

(c) a business that consists in insurance business;

(d) a business that consists in managing or acting as trustee in relation to a pension scheme, or that is carried on by the manager or trustee of such a scheme in connection with or for the purposes of the scheme;

(e) a business that consists in operating or acting as trustee in relation to a collective investment scheme, or that is carried on by the operator or trustee of such a scheme in connection with and for the purposes of the scheme.

(4) For the purposes of this section—

(a) the question whether a person is connected with another shall be determined in accordance with section 1122 of the Corporation Tax Act 2010;

(b) ""collective investment scheme" has the meaning given in section 235 of the Financial Services and Markets Act 2000;

(c) "insurance business" means business that consists in the effecting or carrying out of contracts of insurance;

(d) "securities" includes—

(i) options,

(ii) futures, and

(iii) contracts for differences,

and rights or interests in those investments;

(e) "trustee" and "the operator" in relation to a collective investment scheme shall be construed in accordance with section 237(2) of the Financial Services and Markets Act 2000.

(5) Expressions used in this section that are also used in the provisions regulating activities under the Financial Services and Markets Act 2000 have the same meaning here as they do in those provisions.

See section 22 of that Act, orders made under that section and Schedule 2 to that Act.

142 Protection of third parties in other cases where subsidiary acting as dealer in securities

(1) This section applies where—

(a) a subsidiary that is a dealer in securities has purportedly acquired shares in its holding company in contravention of the prohibition in section 136, and

(b) a person acting in good faith has agreed, for value and without notice of the contravention, to acquire shares in the holding company—

(i) from the subsidiary, or

(ii) from someone who has purportedly acquired the shares after their disposal by the subsidiary.

(2) A transfer to that person of the shares mentioned in subsection (1)(a) has the same effect as it would have had if their original acquisition by the subsidiary had not been in contravention of the prohibition.

Supplementary

143 Application of provisions to companies not limited by shares

In relation to a company other than a company limited by shares, the references in this Chapter to shares shall be read as references to the interest of its members as such, whatever the form of that interest.

144 Application of provisions to nominees

The provisions of this Chapter apply to a nominee acting on behalf of a subsidiary as to the subsidiary itself.

PART 9
EXERCISE OF MEMBERS' RIGHTS

Effect of provisions in company's articles

145 Effect of provisions of articles as to enjoyment or exercise of members' rights

(1) This section applies where provision is made by a company's articles enabling a member to nominate another person or persons as entitled to enjoy or exercise all or any specified rights of the member in relation to the company.

(2) So far as is necessary to give effect to that provision, anything required or authorised by any provision of the Companies Acts to be done by or in relation to the member shall instead be done, or (as the case may be) may instead be done, by or in relation to the nominated person (or each of them) as if he were a member of the company.

(3) This applies, in particular, to the rights conferred by—

(a) sections 291 and 293 (right to be sent proposed written resolution);
(b) section 292 (right to require circulation of written resolution);
(c) section 303 (right to require directors to call general meeting);
(d) section 310 (right to notice of general meetings);
(e) section 314 (right to require circulation of a statement);
(ea) section 319A (right to ask question at meeting of traded company);
(f) section 324 (right to appoint proxy to act at meeting);
(g) section 338 (right to require circulation of resolution for AGM of public company); and
(ga) section 338A (traded companies: members' power to include matters in business dealt with at AGM);
(h) section 423 (right to be sent a copy of annual accounts and reports).

(4) This section and any such provision as is mentioned in subsection (1)—

(a) do not confer rights enforceable against the company by anyone other than the member, and
(b) do not affect the requirements for an effective transfer or other disposition of the whole or part of a member's interest in the company.

Information rights

146 Traded companies: nomination of persons to enjoy information rights

(1) This section applies to a company whose shares are admitted to trading on a regulated market.

(2) A member of such a company who holds shares on behalf of another person may nominate that person to enjoy information rights.

(3) "Information rights" means—

(a) the right to receive a copy of all communications that the company sends to its members generally or to any class of its members that includes the person making the nomination, and

(b) the rights conferred by—
(i) section 431 or 432 (right to require copies of accounts and reports), and
(ii) section 1145 (right to require hard copy version of document or information provided in another form).

(4) The reference in subsection (3) (a) to communications that a company sends to its members generally includes the company's annual accounts and reports. For the application of section 426 (option to provide summary financial statement) in relation to a person nominated to enjoy information rights, see subsection (5) of that section.

(5) A company need not act on a nomination purporting to relate to certain information rights only.

147 Information rights: form in which copies to be provided

(1) This section applies as regards the form in which copies are to be provided to a person nominated under section 146 (nomination of person to enjoy information rights).

(2) If the person to be nominated wishes to receive hard copy communications, he must—
(a) request the person making the nomination to notify the company of that fact, and
(b) provide an address to which such copies may be sent.
This must be done before the nomination is made.

(3) If having received such a request the person making the nomination—
(a) notifies the company that the nominated person wishes to receive hard copy communications, and
(b) provides the company with that address,
the right of the nominated person is to receive hard copy communications accordingly.

(4) This is subject to the provisions of Parts 3 and 4 of Schedule 5 (communications by company) under which the company may take steps to enable it to communicate in electronic form or by means of a website.

(5) If no such notification is given (or no address is provided), the nominated person is taken to have agreed that documents or information may be sent or supplied to him by the company by means of a website.

(6) That agreement—
(a) may be revoked by the nominated person, and
(b) does not affect his right under section 1145 to require a hard copy version of a document or information provided in any other form.

148 Termination or suspension of nomination

(1) The following provisions have effect in relation to a nomination under section 146 (nomination of person to enjoy information rights).

(2) The nomination may be terminated at the request of the member or of the nominated person.

(3) The nomination ceases to have effect on the occurrence in relation to the member or the nominated person of any of the following—
(a) in the case of an individual, death or bankruptcy;
(b) in the case of a body corporate, dissolution or the making of an order for the winding up of the body otherwise than for the purposes of reconstruction.

(4) In subsection (3)—
(a) the reference to bankruptcy includes—
(i) the sequestration of a person's estate, and
(ii) a person's estate being the subject of a protected trust deed (within the meaning of the Bankruptcy (Scotland) Act 1985); and
(b) the reference to the making of an order for winding up is to—
(i) the making of such an order under the Insolvency Act 1986 or the Insolvency (Northern Ireland) Order 1989, or
(ii) any corresponding proceeding under the law of a country or territory outside the United Kingdom.

(5) The effect of any nominations made by a member is suspended at any time when there are more nominated persons than the member has shares in the company.

(6) Where—

(a) the member holds different classes of shares with different information rights, and

(b) there are more nominated persons than he has shares conferring a particular right,

the effect of any nominations made by him is suspended to the extent that they confer that right.

(7) Where the company—

(a) enquires of a nominated person whether he wishes to retain information rights, and

(b) does not receive a response within the period of 28 days beginning with the date on which the company's enquiry was sent,

the nomination ceases to have effect at the end of that period.

Such an enquiry is not to be made of a person more than once in any twelve-month period.

(8) The termination or suspension of a nomination means that the company is not required to act on it.

It does not prevent the company from continuing to do so, to such extent or for such period as it thinks fit.

149 Information as to possible rights in relation to voting

(1) This section applies where a company sends a copy of a notice of a meeting to a person nominated under section 146 (nomination of person to enjoy information rights)

(2) The copy of the notice must be accompanied by a statement that—

(a) he may have a right under an agreement between him and the member by whom he was nominated to be appointed, or to have someone else appointed, as a proxy for the meeting, and

(b) if he has no such right or does not wish to exercise it, he may have a right under such an agreement to give instructions to the member as to the exercise of voting rights.

(3) Section 325 (notice of meeting to contain statement of member's rights in relation to appointment of proxy) does not apply to the copy, and the company must either—

(a) omit the notice required by that section, or

(b) include it but state that it does not apply to the nominated person.

150 Information rights: status of rights

(1) This section has effect as regards the rights conferred by a nomination under section 146 (nomination of person to enjoy information rights).

(2) Enjoyment by the nominated person of the rights conferred by the nomination is enforceable against the company by the member as if they were rights conferred by the company's articles.

(3) Any enactment, and any provision of the company's articles, having effect in relation to communications with members has a corresponding effect (subject to any necessary adaptations) in relation to communications with the nominated person.

(4) In particular—

(a) where under any enactment, or any provision of the company's articles, the members of a company entitled to receive a document or information are determined as at a date or time before it is sent or supplied, the company need not send or supply it to a nominated person—

(i) whose nomination was received by the company after that date or time, or

(ii) if that date or time falls in a period of suspension of his nomination; and

(b) where under any enactment, or any provision of the company's articles, the right of a member to receive a document or information depends on the company having a current address for him, the same applies to any person nominated by him.

(5) The rights conferred by the nomination—

(a) are in addition to the rights of the member himself, and

(b) do not affect any rights exercisable by virtue of any such provision as is mentioned in section 145 (provisions of company's articles as to enjoyment or exercise of members' rights).

(6) A failure to give effect to the rights conferred by the nomination does not affect the validity of anything done by or on behalf of the company.

(7) References in this section to the rights conferred by the nomination are to—

(a) the rights referred to in section 146(3) (information rights), and

(b) where applicable, the rights conferred by section 147(3) (right to hard copy communications) and section 149 (information as to possible voting rights).

151 Information rights: power to amend

(1) The Secretary of State may by regulations amend the provisions of sections 146 to 150 (information rights) so as to—

(a) extend or restrict the classes of companies to which section 146 applies,

(b) make other provision as to the circumstances in which a nomination may be made under that section, or

(c) extend or restrict the rights conferred by such a nomination.

(2) The regulations may make such consequential modifications of any other provisions of this Part, or of any other enactment, as appear to the Secretary of State to be necessary.

(3) Regulations under this section are subject to affirmative resolution procedure.

Exercise of rights where shares held on behalf of others

152 Exercise of rights where shares held on behalf of others: exercise in different ways

(1) Where a member holds shares in a company on behalf of more than one person—

(a) rights attached to the shares, and

(b) rights under any enactment exercisable by virtue of holding the shares,

need not all be exercised, and if exercised, need not all be exercised in the same way.

(2) A member who exercises such rights but does not exercise all his rights, must inform the company to what extent he is exercising the rights.

(3) A member who exercises such rights in different ways must inform the company of the ways in which he is exercising them and to what extent they are exercised in each way.

(4) If a member exercises such rights without informing the company—

(a) that he is not exercising all his rights, or

(b) that he is exercising his rights in different ways,

the company is entitled to assume that he is exercising all his rights and is exercising them in the same way.

153 Exercise of rights where shares held on behalf of others: members' requests

(1) This section applies for the purposes of—

(a) section 314 (power to require circulation of statement),

(b) section 338 (public companies: power to require circulation of resolution for AGM),

(ba) section 338A (traded companies: members' power to include matters in business dealt with at AGM),

(c) section 342 (power to require independent report on poll), and

(d) section 527 (power to require website publication of audit concerns).

(2) A company is required to act under any of those sections if it receives a request in relation to which the following conditions are met—

(a) it is made by at least 100 persons;

(b) it is authenticated by all the persons making it;

(c) in the case of any of those persons who is not a member of the company, it is accompanied by a statement—

(i) of the full name and address of a person ("the member") who is a member of the company and holds shares on behalf of that person,

(ii) that the member is holding those shares on behalf of that person in the course of a business,

(iii) of the number of shares in the company that the member holds on behalf of that person,
(iv) of the total amount paid up on those shares,
(v) that those shares are not held on behalf of anyone else or, if they are, that the other person or persons are not among the other persons making the request,
(vi) that some or all of those shares confer voting rights that are relevant for the purposes of making a request under the section in question, and
(vii) that the person has the right to instruct the member how to exercise those rights;

(d) in the case of any of those persons who is a member of the company, it is accompanied by a statement—
(i) that he holds shares otherwise than on behalf of another person, or
(ii) that he holds shares on behalf of one or more other persons but those persons are not among the other persons making the request;

(e) it is accompanied by such evidence as the company may reasonably require of the matters mentioned in paragraph (c) and (d);

(f) the total amount of the sums paid up on—
(i) shares held as mentioned in paragraph (c), and
(ii) shares held as mentioned in paragraph (d),
divided by the number of persons making the request, is not less than £100;

(g) the request complies with any other requirements of the section in question as to contents, timing and otherwise.

PART 10
A COMPANY'S DIRECTORS

CHAPTER 1
APPOINTMENT AND REMOVAL OF DIRECTORS

Requirement to have directors

154 Companies required to have directors

(1) A private company must have at least one director.
(2) A public company must have at least two directors.

155 Companies required to have at least one director who is a natural person

(1) A company must have at least one director who is a natural person.
(2) This requirement is met if the office of director is held by a natural person as a corporation sole or otherwise by virtue of an office.

156 Direction requiring company to make appointment

(1) If it appears to the Secretary of State that a company is in breach of—
section 154 (requirements as to number of directors), or
section 155 (requirement to have at least one director who is a natural person),
the Secretary of State may give the company a direction under this section.

(2) The direction must specify—
(a) the statutory requirement the company appears to be in breach of,
(b) what the company must do in order to comply with the direction, and
(c) the period within which it must do so.
That period must be not less than one month or more than three months after the date on which the direction is given.

(3) The direction must also inform the company of the consequences of failing to comply.

(4) Where the company is in breach of section 154 or 155 it must comply with the direction by—
(a) making the necessary appointment or appointments, and
(b) giving notice of them under section 167,
before the end of the period specified in the direction.

(5) If the company has already made the necessary appointment or appointments (or so far as it has done so), it must comply with the direction by giving notice of them under section 167 before the end of the period specified in the direction.

(6) If a company fails to comply with a direction under this section, an offence is committed by—

(a) the company, and

(b) every officer of the company who is in default.

For this purpose a shadow director is treated as an officer of the company.

(7) A person guilty of an offence under this section is liable on summary conviction to a fine not exceeding level 5 on the standard scale and, for continued contravention, a daily default fine not exceeding one-tenth of level 5 on the standard scale.

Appointment

157 Minimum age for appointment as director

(1) A person may not be appointed a director of a company unless he has attained the age of 16 years.

(2) This does not affect the validity of an appointment that is not to take effect until the person appointed attains that age.

(3) Where the office of director of a company is held by a corporation sole, or otherwise by virtue of another office, the appointment to that other office of a person who has not attained the age of 16 years is not effective also to make him a director of the company until he attains the age of 16 years.

(4) An appointment made in contravention of this section is void.

(5) Nothing in this section affects any liability of a person under any provision of the Companies Acts if he—

(a) purports to act as director, or

(b) acts as a shadow director,

although he could not, by virtue of this section, be validly appointed as a director.

(6) This section has effect subject to section 158 (power to provide for exceptions from minimum age requirement).

158 Power to provide for exceptions from minimum age requirement

(1) The Secretary of State may make provision by regulations for cases in which a person who has not attained the age of 16 years may be appointed a director of a company.

(2) The regulations must specify the circumstances in which, and any conditions subject to which, the appointment may be made.

(3) If the specified circumstances cease to obtain, or any specified conditions cease to be met, a person who was appointed by virtue of the regulations and who has not since attained the age of 16 years ceases to hold office.

(4) The regulations may make different provision for different parts of the United Kingdom.
This is without prejudice to the general power to make different provision for different cases.

(5) Regulations under this section are subject to negative resolution procedure.

159 Existing under-age directors

(1) This section applies where—

(a) a person appointed a director of a company before section 157 (minimum age for appointment as director) comes into force has not attained the age of 16 when that section comes into force, or

(b) the office of director of a company is held by a corporation sole, or otherwise by virtue of another office, and the person appointed to that other office has not attained the age of 16 years when that section comes into force,

and the case is not one excepted from that section by regulations under section 158.

(2) That person ceases to be a director on section 157 coming into force.

(3) The company must make the necessary consequential alteration in its register of directors but need not give notice to the registrar of the change.

(4) If it appears to the registrar (from other information) that a person has ceased by virtue of this section to be a director of a company, the registrar shall note that fact on the register.

160 Appointment of directors of public company to be voted on individually

(1) At a general meeting of a public company a motion for the appointment of two or more persons as directors of the company by a single resolution must not be made unless a resolution that it should be so made has first been agreed to by the meeting without any vote being given against it.

(2) A resolution moved in contravention of this section is void, whether or not its being so moved was objected to at the time.

But where a resolution so moved is passed, no provision for the automatic reappointment of retiring directors in default of another appointment applies.

(3) For the purposes of this section a motion for approving a person's appointment, or for nominating a person for appointment, is treated as a motion for his appointment.

(4) Nothing in this section applies to a resolution amending the company's articles.

161 Validity of acts of directors

(1) The acts of a person acting as a director are valid notwithstanding that it is afterwards discovered—

(a) that there was a defect in his appointment;
(b) that he was disqualified from holding office;
(c) that he had ceased to hold office;
(d) that he was not entitled to vote on the matter in question.

(2) This applies even if the resolution for his appointment is void under section 160 (appointment of directors of public company to be voted on individually).

Register of directors, etc

162 Register of directors

(1) Every company must keep a register of its directors.

(2) The register must contain the required particulars (see sections 163, 164 and 166) of each person who is a director of the company.

(3) The register must be kept available for inspection—

(a) at the company's registered office, or
(b) at a place specified in regulations under section 1136.

(4) The company must give notice to the registrar—

(a) of the place at which the register is kept available for inspection, and
(b) of any change in that place,

unless it has at all times been kept at the company's registered office.

(5) The register must be open to the inspection—

(a) of any member of the company without charge, and
(b) of any other person on payment of such fee as may be prescribed.

(6) If default is made in complying with subsection (1), (2) or (3) or if default is made for 14 days in complying with subsection (4), or if an inspection required under subsection (5) is refused, an offence is committed by—

(a) the company, and
(b) every officer of the company who is in default.

For this purpose a shadow director is treated as an officer of the company.

(7) A person guilty of an offence under this section is liable on summary conviction to a fine not exceeding level 5 on the standard scale and, for continued contravention, a daily default fine not exceeding one-tenth of level 5 on the standard scale.

(8) In the case of a refusal of inspection of the register, the court may by order compel an immediate inspection of it.

163 Particulars of directors to be registered: individuals

(1) A company's register of directors must contain the following particulars in the case of an individual—
(a) name and any former name;
(b) a service address;
(c) the country or state (or part of the United Kingdom) in which he is usually resident;
(d) nationality;
(e) business occupation (if any);
(f) date of birth.

(2) For the purposes of this section "name" means a person's Christian name (or other forename) and surname, except that in the case of—
(a) a peer, or
(b) an individual usually known by a title,
the title may be stated instead of his Christian name (or other forename) and surname or in addition to either or both of them.

(3) For the purposes of this section a "former name" means a name by which the individual was formerly known for business purposes.
Where a person is or was formerly known by more than one such name, each of them must be stated.

(4) It is not necessary for the register to contain particulars of a former name in the following cases—
(a) in the case of a peer or an individual normally known by a British title, where the name is one by which the person was known previous to the adoption of or succession to the title;
(b) in the case of any person, where the former name—
(i) was changed or disused before the person attained the age of 16 years, or
(ii) has been changed or disused for 20 years or more.

(5) A person's service address may be stated to be "The company's registered office".

164 Particulars of directors to be registered: corporate directors and firms

A company's register of directors must contain the following particulars in the case of a body corporate, or a firm that is a legal person under the law by which it is governed—
(a) corporate or firm name;
(b) registered or principal office;
(c) in the case of an EEA company to which the First Company Law Directive (68/151/EEC) applies, particulars of—
(i) the register in which the company file mentioned in Article 3 of that Directive is kept (including details of the relevant state), and
(ii) the registration number in that register;
(d) in any other case, particulars of—
(i) the legal form of the company or firm and the law by which it is governed, and
(ii) if applicable, the register in which it is entered (including details of the state) and its registration number in that register.

165 Register of directors' residential addresses

(1) Every company must keep a register of directors' residential addresses.

(2) The register must state the usual residential address of each of the company's directors.

(3) If a director's usual residential address is the same as his service address (as stated in the company's register of directors), the register of directors' residential addresses need only contain an entry to that effect.
This does not apply if his service address is stated to be "The company's registered office".

(4) If default is made in complying with this section, an offence is committed by—
(a) the company, and
(b) every officer of the company who is in default.
For this purpose a shadow director is treated as an officer of the company.

(5) A person guilty of an offence under this section is liable on summary conviction to a fine not exceeding level 5 on the standard scale and, for continued contravention, a daily default fine not exceeding one-tenth of level 5 on the standard scale.

(6) This section applies only to directors who are individuals, not where the director is a body corporate or a firm that is a legal person under the law by which it is governed.

166 Particulars of directors to be registered: power to make regulations

(1) The Secretary of State may make provision by regulations amending—
section 163 (particulars of directors to be registered: individuals),
section 164 (particulars of directors to be registered: corporate directors and firms), or
section 165 (register of directors' residential addresses),
so as to add to or remove items from the particulars required to be contained in a company's register of directors or register of directors' residential addresses.

(2) Regulations under this section are subject to affirmative resolution procedure.

167 Duty to notify registrar of changes

(1) A company must, within the period of 14 days from—
(a) a person becoming or ceasing to be a director, or
(b) the occurrence of any change in the particulars contained in its register of directors or its register of directors' residential addresses,
give notice to the registrar of the change and of the date on which it occurred.

(2) Notice of a person having become a director of the company must—
(a) contain a statement of the particulars of the new director that are required to be included in the company's register of directors and its register of directors' residential addresses, and
(b) be accompanied by a consent, by that person, to act in that capacity.

(3) Where—
(a) a company gives notice of a change of a director's service address as stated in the company's register of directors, and
(b) the notice is not accompanied by notice of any resulting change in the particulars contained in the company's register of directors' residential addresses,
the notice must be accompanied by a statement that no such change is required.

(4) If default is made in complying with this section, an offence is committed by—
(a) the company, and
(b) every officer of the company who is in default.
For this purpose a shadow director is treated as an officer of the company.

(5) A person guilty of an offence under this section is liable on summary conviction to a fine not exceeding level 5 on the standard scale and, for continued contravention, a daily default fine not exceeding one-tenth of level 5 on the standard scale.

Removal

168 Resolution to remove director

(1) A company may by ordinary resolution at a meeting remove a director before the expiration of his period of office, notwithstanding anything in any agreement between it and him.

(2) Special notice is required of a resolution to remove a director under this section or to appoint somebody instead of a director so removed at the meeting at which he is removed.

(3) A vacancy created by the removal of a director under this section, if not filled at the meeting at which he is removed, may be filled as a casual vacancy.

(4) A person appointed director in place of a person removed under this section is treated, for the purpose of determining the time at which he or any other director is to retire, as if he had become director on the day on which the person in whose place he is appointed was last appointed a director.

(5) This section is not to be taken—

(a) as depriving a person removed under it of compensation or damages payable to him in respect of the termination of his appointment as director or of any appointment terminating with that as director, or

(b) as derogating from any power to remove a director that may exist apart from this section.

169 Director's right to protest against removal

(1) On receipt of notice of an intended resolution to remove a director under section 168, the company must forthwith send a copy of the notice to the director concerned.

(2) The director (whether or not a member of the company) is entitled to be heard on the resolution at the meeting.

(3) Where notice is given of an intended resolution to remove a director under that section, and the director concerned makes with respect to it representations in writing to the company (not exceeding a reasonable length) and requests their notification to members of the company, the company shall, unless the representations are received by it too late for it to do so—

(a) in any notice of the resolution given to members of the company state the fact of the representations having been made; and

(b) send a copy of the representations to every member of the company to whom notice of the meeting is sent (whether before or after receipt of the representations by the company).

(4) If a copy of the representations is not sent as required by subsection (3) because received too late or because of the company's default, the director may (without prejudice to his right to be heard orally) require that the representations shall be read out at the meeting.

(5) Copies of the representations need not be sent out and the representations need not be read out at the meeting if, on the application either of the company or of any other person who claims to be aggrieved, the court is satisfied that the rights conferred by this section are being abused.

(6) The court may order the company's costs (in Scotland, expenses) on an application under subsection (5) to be paid in whole or in part by the director, notwithstanding that he is not a party to the application.

CHAPTER 2
GENERAL DUTIES OF DIRECTORS

Introductory

170 Scope and nature of general duties

(1) The general duties specified in sections 171 to 177 are owed by a director of a company to the company.

(2) A person who ceases to be a director continues to be subject—

(a) to the duty in section 175 (duty to avoid conflicts of interest) as regards the exploitation of any property, information or opportunity of which he became aware at a time when he was a director, and

(b) to the duty in section 176 (duty not to accept benefits from third parties) as regards things done or omitted by him before he ceased to be a director.

To that extent those duties apply to a former director as to a director, subject to any necessary adaptations.

(3) The general duties are based on certain common law rules and equitable principles as they apply in relation to directors and have effect in place of those rules and principles as regards the duties owed to a company by a director.

(4) The general duties shall be interpreted and applied in the same way as common law rules or equitable principles, and regard shall be had to the corresponding common law rules and equitable principles in interpreting and applying the general duties.

(5) The general duties apply to shadow directors where, and to the extent that, the corresponding common law rules or equitable principles so apply.

The general duties

171 Duty to act within powers

A director of a company must—

(a) act in accordance with the company's constitution, and

(b) only exercise powers for the purposes for which they are conferred.

172 Duty to promote the success of the company

(1) A director of a company must act in the way he considers, in good faith, would be most likely to promote the success of the company for the benefit of its members as a whole, and in doing so have regard (amongst other matters) to—

(a) the likely consequences of any decision in the long term,

(b) the interests of the company's employees,

(c) the need to foster the company's business relationships with suppliers, customers and others,

(d) the impact of the company's operations on the community and the environment,

(e) the desirability of the company maintaining a reputation for high standards of business conduct, and

(f) the need to act fairly as between members of the company.

(2) Where or to the extent that the purposes of the company consist of or include purposes other than the benefit of its members, subsection (1) has effect as if the reference to promoting the success of the company for the benefit of its members were to achieving those purposes.

(3) The duty imposed by this section has effect subject to any enactment or rule of law requiring directors, in certain circumstances, to consider or act in the interests of creditors of the company.

173 Duty to exercise independent judgment

(1) A director of a company must exercise independent judgment.

(2) This duty is not infringed by his acting—

(a) in accordance with an agreement duly entered into by the company that restricts the future exercise of discretion by its directors, or

(b) in a way authorised by the company's constitution.

174 Duty to exercise reasonable care, skill and diligence

(1) A director of a company must exercise reasonable care, skill and diligence.

(2) This means the care, skill and diligence that would be exercised by a reasonably diligent person with—

(a) the general knowledge, skill and experience that may reasonably be expected of a person carrying out the functions carried out by the director in relation to the company, and

(b) the general knowledge, skill and experience that the director has.

175 Duty to avoid conflicts of interest

(1) A director of a company must avoid a situation in which he has, or can have, a direct or indirect interest that conflicts, or possibly may conflict, with the interests of the company.

(2) This applies in particular to the exploitation of any property, information or opportunity (and it is immaterial whether the company could take advantage of the property, information or opportunity).

(3) This duty does not apply to a conflict of interest arising in relation to a transaction or arrangement with the company.

(4) This duty is not infringed—

(a) if the situation cannot reasonably be regarded as likely to give rise to a conflict of interest; or

(b) if the matter has been authorised by the directors.

(5) Authorisation may be given by the directors—

Nothing in Model Arts to prevent such auth.

(a) where the company is a private company and nothing in the company's constitution invalidates such authorisation, by the matter being proposed to and authorised by the directors; or

(b) where the company is a public company and its constitution includes provision enabling the directors to authorise the matter, by the matter being proposed to and authorised by them in accordance with the constitution.

(6) The authorisation is effective only if—

(a) any requirement as to the quorum at the meeting at which the matter is considered is met without counting the director in question or any other interested director, and

(b) the matter was agreed to without their voting or would have been agreed to if their votes had not been counted.

(7) Any reference in this section to a conflict of interest includes a conflict of interest and duty and a conflict of duties.

176 Duty not to accept benefits from third parties

(1) A director of a company must not accept a benefit from a third party conferred by reason of—

(a) his being a director, or

(b) his doing (or not doing) anything as director.

(2) A "third party" means a person other than the company, an associated body corporate or a person acting on behalf of the company or an associated body corporate.

(3) Benefits received by a director from a person by whom his services (as a director or otherwise) are provided to the company are not regarded as conferred by a third party.

(4) This duty is not infringed if the acceptance of the benefit cannot reasonably be regarded as likely to give rise to a conflict of interest.

(5) Any reference in this section to a conflict of interest includes a conflict of interest and duty and a conflict of duties.

177 Duty to declare interest in proposed transaction or arrangement

(1) If a director of a company is in any way, directly or indirectly, interested in a proposed transaction or arrangement with the company, he must declare the nature and extent of that interest to the other directors.

(2) The declaration may (but need not) be made—

(a) at a meeting of the directors, or

(b) by notice to the directors in accordance with—

(i) section 184 (notice in writing), or

(ii) section 185 (general notice).

(3) If a declaration of interest under this section proves to be, or becomes, inaccurate or incomplete, a further declaration must be made.

(4) Any declaration required by this section must be made before the company enters into the transaction or arrangement.

(5) This section does not require a declaration of an interest of which the director is not aware or where the director is not aware of the transaction or arrangement in question.

For this purpose a director is treated as being aware of matters of which he ought reasonably to be aware.

(6) A director need not declare an interest—

(a) if it cannot reasonably be regarded as likely to give rise to a conflict of interest;

(b) if, or to the extent that, the other directors are already aware of it (and for this purpose the other directors are treated as aware of anything of which they ought reasonably to be aware); or

(c) if, or to the extent that, it concerns terms of his service contract that have been or are to be considered—

(i) by a meeting of the directors, or

(ii) by a committee of the directors appointed for the purpose under the company's constitution.

Supplementary provisions

178 Civil consequences of breach of general duties

(1) The consequences of breach (or threatened breach) of sections 171 to 177 are the same as would apply if the corresponding common law rule or equitable principle applied.

(2) The duties in those sections (with the exception of section 174 (duty to exercise reasonable care, skill and diligence)) are, accordingly, enforceable in the same way as any other fiduciary duty owed to a company by its directors.

179 Cases within more than one of the general duties

Except as otherwise provided, more than one of the general duties may apply in any given case.

180 Consent, approval or authorisation by members

(1) In a case where—

(a) section 175 (duty to avoid conflicts of interest) is complied with by authorisation by the directors, or

(b) section 177 (duty to declare interest in proposed transaction or arrangement) is complied with,

the transaction or arrangement is not liable to be set aside by virtue of any common law rule or equitable principle requiring the consent or approval of the members of the company.

This is without prejudice to any enactment, or provision of the company's constitution, requiring such consent or approval.

(2) The application of the general duties is not affected by the fact that the case also falls within Chapter 4 (transactions requiring approval of members), except that where that Chapter applies and—

(a) approval is given under that Chapter, or

(b) the matter is one as to which it is provided that approval is not needed,

it is not necessary also to comply with section 175 (duty to avoid conflicts of interest) or section 176 (duty not to accept benefits from third parties).

(3) Compliance with the general duties does not remove the need for approval under any applicable provision of Chapter 4 (transactions requiring approval of members).

(4) The general duties—

(a) have effect subject to any rule of law enabling the company to give authority, specifically or generally, for anything to be done (or omitted) by the directors, or any of them, that would otherwise be a breach of duty, and

(b) where the company's articles contain provisions for dealing with conflicts of interest, are not infringed by anything done (or omitted) by the directors, or any of them, in accordance with those provisions.

(5) Otherwise, the general duties have effect (except as otherwise provided or the context otherwise requires) notwithstanding any enactment or rule of law.

181 Modification of provisions in relation to charitable companies

(1) In their application to a company that is a charity, the provisions of this Chapter have effect subject to this section.

(2) Section 175 (duty to avoid conflicts of interest) has effect as if—

(a) for subsection (3) (which disapplies the duty to avoid conflicts of interest in the case of a transaction or arrangement with the company) there were substituted—

"(3) This duty does not apply to a conflict of interest arising in relation to a transaction or arrangement with the company if or to the extent that the company's articles allow that duty to be so disapplied, which they may do only in relation to descriptions of transaction or arrangement specified in the company's articles.";

(b) for subsection (5) (which specifies how directors of a company may give authority under that section for a transaction or arrangement) there were substituted—

"(5) Authorisation may be given by the directors where the company's constitution includes provision enabling them to authorise the matter, by the matter being proposed to and authorised by them in accordance with the constitution.".

(3) Section 180(2)(b) (which disapplies certain duties under this Chapter in relation to cases excepted from requirement to obtain approval by members under Chapter 4) applies only if or to the extent that the company's articles allow those duties to be so disapplied, which they may do only in relation to descriptions of transaction or arrangement specified in the company's articles.

(4) . . .

(5) This section does not extend to Scotland.

CHAPTER 3
DECLARATION OF INTEREST IN EXISTING TRANSACTION OR ARRANGEMENT

182 Declaration of interest in existing transaction or arrangement

(1) Where a director of a company is in any way, directly or indirectly, interested in a transaction or arrangement that has been entered into by the company, he must declare the nature and extent of the interest to the other directors in accordance with this section.

This section does not apply if or to the extent that the interest has been declared under section 177 (duty to declare interest in proposed transaction or arrangement).

(2) The declaration must be made—

(a) at a meeting of the directors, or

(b) by notice in writing (see section 184), or

(c) by general notice (see section 185).

(3) If a declaration of interest under this section proves to be, or becomes, inaccurate or incomplete, a further declaration must be made.

(4) Any declaration required by this section must be made as soon as is reasonably practicable.

Failure to comply with this requirement does not affect the underlying duty to make the declaration.

(5) This section does not require a declaration of an interest of which the director is not aware or where the director is not aware of the transaction or arrangement in question.

For this purpose a director is treated as being aware of matters of which he ought reasonably to be aware.

(6) A director need not declare an interest under this section—

(a) if it cannot reasonably be regarded as likely to give rise to a conflict of interest;

(b) if, or to the extent that, the other directors are already aware of it (and for this purpose the other directors are treated as aware of anything of which they ought reasonably to be aware); or

(c) if, or to the extent that, it concerns terms of his service contract that have been or are to be considered–

(i) by a meeting of the directors, or

(ii) by a committee of the directors appointed for the purpose under the company's constitution.

183 Offence of failure to declare interest

(1) A director who fails to comply with the requirements of section 182 (declaration of interest in existing transaction or arrangement) commits an offence.

(2) A person guilty of an offence under this section is liable—

(a) on conviction on indictment, to a fine;

(b) on summary conviction, to a fine not exceeding the statutory maximum.

184 Declaration made by notice in writing

(1) This section applies to a declaration of interest made by notice in writing.

(2) The director must send the notice to the other directors.

(3) The notice may be sent in hard copy form or, if the recipient has agreed to receive it in electronic form, in an agreed electronic form.

(4) The notice may be sent—

(a) by hand or by post, or

(b) if the recipient has agreed to receive it by electronic means, by agreed electronic means.

(5) Where a director declares an interest by notice in writing in accordance with this section—

(a) the making of the declaration is deemed to form part of the proceedings at the next meeting of the directors after the notice is given, and

(b) the provisions of section 248 (minutes of meetings of directors) apply as if the declaration had been made at that meeting.

185 General notice treated as sufficient declaration

(1) General notice in accordance with this section is a sufficient declaration of interest in relation to the matters to which it relates.

(2) General notice is notice given to the directors of a company to the effect that the director—

(a) has an interest (as member, officer, employee or otherwise) in a specified body corporate or firm and is to be regarded as interested in any transaction or arrangement that may, after the date of the notice, be made with that body corporate or firm, or

(b) is connected with a specified person (other than a body corporate or firm) and is to be regarded as interested in any transaction or arrangement that may, after the date of the notice, be made with that person.

(3) The notice must state the nature and extent of the director's interest in the body corporate or firm or, as the case may be, the nature of his connection with the person.

(4) General notice is not effective unless—

(a) it is given at a meeting of the directors, or

(b) the director takes reasonable steps to secure that it is brought up and read at the next meeting of the directors after it is given.

186 Declaration of interest in case of company with sole director

(1) Where a declaration of interest under section 182 (duty to declare interest in existing transaction or arrangement) is required of a sole director of a company that is required to have more than one director—

(a) the declaration must be recorded in writing,

(b) the making of the declaration is deemed to form part of the proceedings at the next meeting of the directors after the notice is given, and

(c) the provisions of section 248 (minutes of meetings of directors) apply as if the declaration had been made at that meeting.

(2) Nothing in this section affects the operation of section 231 (contract with sole member who is also a director: terms to be set out in writing or recorded in minutes).

187 Declaration of interest in existing transaction by shadow director

(1) The provisions of this Chapter relating to the duty under section 182 (duty to declare interest in existing transaction or arrangement) apply to a shadow director as to a director, but with the following adaptations.

(2) Subsection (2)(a) of that section (declaration at meeting of directors) does not apply.

(3) In section 185 (general notice treated as sufficient declaration), subsection (4) (notice to be given at or brought up and read at meeting of directors) does not apply.

(4) General notice by a shadow director is not effective unless given by notice in writing in accordance with section 184.

CHAPTER 4
TRANSACTIONS WITH DIRECTORS REQUIRING APPROVAL OF MEMBERS

Service contracts

188 Directors' long-term service contracts: requirement of members' approval

(1) This section applies to provision under which the guaranteed term of a director's employment—
(a) with the company of which he is a director, or
(b) where he is the director of a holding company, within the group consisting of that company and its subsidiaries,
is, or may be, longer than two years.

(2) A company may not agree to such provision unless it has been approved—
(a) by resolution of the members of the company, and
(b) in the case of a director of a holding company, by resolution of the members of that company.

(3) The guaranteed term of a director's employment is—
(a) the period (if any) during which the director's employment—
(i) is to continue, or may be continued otherwise than at the instance of the company (whether under the original agreement or under a new agreement entered into in pursuance of it), and
(ii) cannot be terminated by the company by notice, or can be so terminated only in specified circumstances, or
(b) in the case of employment terminable by the company by notice, the period of notice required to be given,
or, in the case of employment having a period within paragraph (a) and a period within paragraph (b), the aggregate of those periods.

(4) If more than six months before the end of the guaranteed term of a director's employment the company enters into a further service contract (otherwise than in pursuance of a right conferred, by or under the original contract, on the other party to it), this section applies as if there were added to the guaranteed term of the new contract the unexpired period of the guaranteed term of the original contract.

(5) A resolution approving provision to which this section applies must not be passed unless a memorandum setting out the proposed contract incorporating the provision is made available to members—
(a) in the case of a written resolution, by being sent or submitted to every eligible member at or before the time at which the proposed resolution is sent or submitted to him;
(b) in the case of a resolution at a meeting, by being made available for inspection by members of the company both—
(i) at the company's registered office for not less than 15 days ending with the date of the meeting, and
(ii) at the meeting itself.

(6) No approval is required under this section on the part of the members of a body corporate that—
(a) is not a UK-registered company, or
(b) is a wholly-owned subsidiary of another body corporate.

(7) In this section "employment" means any employment under a director's service contract.

189 Directors' long-term service contracts: civil consequences of contravention

If a company agrees to provision in contravention of section 188 (directors' long-term service contracts: requirement of members' approval)—
(a) the provision is void, to the extent of the contravention, and
(b) the contract is deemed to contain a term entitling the company to terminate it at any time by the giving of reasonable notice.

Substantial property transactions

190 Substantial property transactions: requirement of members' approval

(1) A company may not enter into an arrangement under which—

(a) a director of the company or of its holding company, or a person connected with such a director, acquires or is to acquire from the company (directly or indirectly) a substantial non-cash asset, or

(b) the company acquires or is to acquire a substantial non-cash asset (directly or indirectly) from such a director or a person so connected,

unless the arrangement has been approved by a resolution of the members of the company or is conditional on such approval being obtained.

For the meaning of "substantial non-cash asset" see section 191.

(2) If the director or connected person is a director of the company's holding company or a person connected with such a director, the arrangement must also have been approved by a resolution of the members of the holding company or be conditional on such approval being obtained.

(3) A company shall not be subject to any liability by reason of a failure to obtain approval required by this section.

(4) No approval is required under this section on the part of the members of a body corporate that—

(a) is not a UK-registered company, or

(b) is a wholly-owned subsidiary of another body corporate.

(5) For the purposes of this section—

(a) an arrangement involving more than one non-cash asset, or

(b) an arrangement that is one of a series involving non-cash assets,

shall be treated as if they involved a non-cash asset of a value equal to the aggregate value of all the non-cash assets involved in the arrangement or, as the case may be, the series.

(6) This section does not apply to a transaction so far as it relates—

(a) to anything to which a director of a company is entitled under his service contract, or

(b) to payment for loss of office as defined in section 215 (payments requiring members' approval).

191 Meaning of "substantial"

(1) This section explains what is meant in section 190 (requirement of approval for substantial property transactions) by a "substantial" non-cash asset.

(2) An asset is a substantial asset in relation to a company if its value—

(a) exceeds 10% of the company's asset value and is more than £5,000, or

(b) exceeds £100,000.

(3) For this purpose a company's "asset value" at any time is—

(a) the value of the company's net assets determined by reference to its most recent statutory accounts, or

(b) if no statutory accounts have been prepared, the amount of the company's called-up share capital.

(4) A company's "statutory accounts" means its annual accounts prepared in accordance with Part 15, and its "most recent" statutory accounts means those in relation to which the time for sending them out to members (see section 424) is most recent.

(5) Whether an asset is a substantial asset shall be determined as at the time the arrangement is entered into.

192 Exception for transactions with members or other group companies

Approval is not required under section 190 (requirement of members' approval for substantial property transactions)—

(a) for a transaction between a company and a person in his character as a member of that company, or

(b) for a transaction between—

(i) a holding company and its wholly-owned subsidiary, or

(ii) two wholly-owned subsidiaries of the same holding company.

193 Exception in case of company in winding up or administration

(1) This section applies to a company—
(a) that is being wound up (unless the winding up is a members' voluntary winding up), or
(b) that is in administration within the meaning of Schedule B1 to the Insolvency Act 1986 or the Insolvency (Northern Ireland) Order 1989.

(2) Approval is not required under section 190 (requirement of members' approval for substantial property transactions)—
(a) on the part of the members of a company to which this section applies, or
(b) for an arrangement entered into by a company to which this section applies.

194 Exception for transactions on recognised investment exchange

(1) Approval is not required under section 190 (requirement of members' approval for substantial property transactions) for a transaction on a recognised investment exchange effected by a director, or a person connected with him, through the agency of a person who in relation to the transaction acts as an independent broker.

(2) For this purpose—
(a) "independent broker" means a person who, independently of the director or any person connected with him, selects the person with whom the transaction is to be effected; and
(b) "recognised investment exchange" has the same meaning as in Part 18 of the Financial Services and Markets Act 2000.

195 Property transactions: civil consequences of contravention

(1) This section applies where a company enters into an arrangement in contravention of section 190 (requirement of members' approval for substantial property transactions).

(2) The arrangement, and any transaction entered into in pursuance of the arrangement (whether by the company or any other person), is voidable at the instance of the company, unless—
(a) restitution of any money or other asset that was the subject matter of the arrangement or transaction is no longer possible,
(b) the company has been indemnified in pursuance of this section by any other persons for the loss or damage suffered by it, or
(c) rights acquired in good faith, for value and without actual notice of the contravention by a person who is not a party to the arrangement or transaction would be affected by the avoidance.

(3) Whether or not the arrangement or any such transaction has been avoided, each of the persons specified in subsection (4) is liable—
(a) to account to the company for any gain that he has made directly or indirectly by the arrangement or transaction, and
(b) (jointly and severally with any other person so liable under this section) to indemnify the company for any loss or damage resulting from the arrangement or transaction.

(4) The persons so liable are—
(a) any director of the company or of its holding company with whom the company entered into the arrangement in contravention of section 190,
(b) any person with whom the company entered into the arrangement in contravention of that section who is connected with a director of the company or of its holding company,
(c) the director of the company or of its holding company with whom any such person is connected, and
(d) any other director of the company who authorised the arrangement or any transaction entered into in pursuance of such an arrangement.

(5) Subsections (3) and (4) are subject to the following two subsections.

(6) In the case of an arrangement entered into by a company in contravention of section 190 with a person connected with a director of the company or of its holding company, that director is not

liable by virtue of subsection (4) (c) if he shows that he took all reasonable steps to secure the company's compliance with that section.

(7) In any case—

(a) a person so connected is not liable by virtue of subsection (4)(b), and

(b) a director is not liable by virtue of subsection (4) (d),

if he shows that, at the time the arrangement was entered into, he did not know the relevant circumstances constituting the contravention.

(8) Nothing in this section shall be read as excluding the operation of any other enactment or rule of law by virtue of which the arrangement or transaction may be called in question or any liability to the company may arise.

196 Property transactions: effect of subsequent affirmation

Where a transaction or arrangement is entered into by a company in contravention of section 190 (requirement of members' approval) but, within a reasonable period, it is affirmed—

(a) in the case of a contravention of subsection (1) of that section, by resolution of the members of the company, and

(b) in the case of a contravention of subsection (2) of that section, by resolution of the members of the holding company,

the transaction or arrangement may no longer be avoided under section 195.

Loans, quasi-loans and credit transactions

197 Loans to directors: requirement of members' approval

(1) A company may not—

(a) make a loan to a director of the company or of its holding company, or

(b) give a guarantee or provide security in connection with a loan made by any person to such a director,

unless the transaction has been approved by a resolution of the members of the company.

(2) If the director is a director of the company's holding company, the transaction must also have been approved by a resolution of the members of the holding company.

(3) A resolution approving a transaction to which this section applies must not be passed unless a memorandum setting out the matters mentioned in subsection (4) is made available to members—

(a) in the case of a written resolution, by being sent or submitted to every eligible member at or before the time at which the proposed resolution is sent or submitted to him;

(b) in the case of a resolution at a meeting, by being made available for inspection by members of the company both—

(i) at the company's registered office for not less than 15 days ending with the date of the meeting, and

(ii) at the meeting itself.

(4) The matters to be disclosed are—

(a) the nature of the transaction,

(b) the amount of the loan and the purpose for which it is required, and

(c) the extent of the company's liability under any transaction connected with the loan.

(5) No approval is required under this section on the part of the members of a body corporate that—

(a) is not a UK-registered company, or

(b) is a wholly-owned subsidiary of another body corporate.

198 Quasi-loans to directors: requirement of members' approval

(1) This section applies to a company if it is—

(a) a public company, or

(b) a company associated with a public company.

(2) A company to which this section applies may not—

(a) make a quasi-loan to a director of the company or of its holding company, or

(b) give a guarantee or provide security in connection with a quasi-loan made by any person to such a director,

unless the transaction has been approved by a resolution of the members of the company.

(3) If the director is a director of the company's holding company, the transaction must also have been approved by a resolution of the members of the holding company.

(4) A resolution approving a transaction to which this section applies must not be passed unless a memorandum setting out the matters mentioned in subsection (5) is made available to members—

(a) in the case of a written resolution, by being sent or submitted to every eligible member at or before the time at which the proposed resolution is sent or submitted to him;

(b) in the case of a resolution at a meeting, by being made available for inspection by members of the company both—

(i) at the company's registered office for not less than 15 days ending with the date of the meeting, and

(ii) at the meeting itself.

(5) The matters to be disclosed are—

(a) the nature of the transaction,

(b) the amount of the quasi-loan and the purpose for which it is required, and

(c) the extent of the company's liability under any transaction connected with the quasi-loan.

(6) No approval is required under this section on the part of the members of a body corporate that—

(a) is not a UK-registered company, or

(b) is a wholly-owned subsidiary of another body corporate.

199 Meaning of "quasi-loan" and related expressions

(1) A "quasi-loan" is a transaction under which one party ("the creditor") agrees to pay, or pays otherwise than in pursuance of an agreement, a sum for another ("the borrower") or agrees to reimburse, or reimburses otherwise than in pursuance of an agreement, expenditure incurred by another party for another ("the borrower")—

(a) on terms that the borrower (or a person on his behalf) will reimburse the creditor; or

(b) in circumstances giving rise to a liability on the borrower to reimburse the creditor.

(2) Any reference to the person to whom a quasi-loan is made is a reference to the borrower.

(3) The liabilities of the borrower under a quasi-loan include the liabilities of any person who has agreed to reimburse the creditor on behalf of the borrower.

200 Loans or quasi-loans to persons connected with directors: requirement of members' approval

(1) This section applies to a company if it is—

(a) a public company, or

(b) a company associated with a public company.

(2) A company to which this section applies may not—

(a) make a loan or quasi-loan to a person connected with a director of the company or of its holding company, or

(b) give a guarantee or provide security in connection with a loan or quasi-loan made by any person to a person connected with such a director,

unless the transaction has been approved by a resolution of the members of the company.

(3) If the connected person is a person connected with a director of the company's holding company, the transaction must also have been approved by a resolution of the members of the holding company.

(4) A resolution approving a transaction to which this section applies must not be passed unless a memorandum setting out the matters mentioned in subsection (5) is made available to members—

(a) in the case of a written resolution, by being sent or submitted to every eligible member at or before the time at which the proposed resolution is sent or submitted to him;

(b) in the case of a resolution at a meeting, by being made available for inspection by members of the company both—

(i) at the company's registered office for not less than 15 days ending with the date of the meeting, and

(ii) at the meeting itself.

(5) The matters to be disclosed are—

(a) the nature of the transaction,

(b) the amount of the loan or quasi-loan and the purpose for which it is required, and

(c) the extent of the company's liability under any transaction connected with the loan or quasi-loan.

(6) No approval is required under this section on the part of the members of a body corporate that—

(a) is not a UK-registered company, or

(b) is a wholly-owned subsidiary of another body corporate.

201 Credit transactions: requirement of members' approval

(1) This section applies to a company if it is—

(a) a public company, or

(b) a company associated with a public company.

(2) A company to which this section applies may not—

(a) enter into a credit transaction as creditor for the benefit of a director of the company or of its holding company, or a person connected with such a director, or

(b) give a guarantee or provide security in connection with a credit transaction entered into by any person for the benefit of such a director, or a person connected with such a director,

unless the transaction (that is, the credit transaction, the giving of the guarantee or the provision of security, as the case may be) has been approved by a resolution of the members of the company.

(3) If the director or connected person is a director of its holding company or a person connected with such a director, the transaction must also have been approved by a resolution of the members of the holding company.

(4) A resolution approving a transaction to which this section applies must not be passed unless a memorandum setting out the matters mentioned in subsection (5) is made available to members—

(a) in the case of a written resolution, by being sent or submitted to every eligible member at or before the time at which the proposed resolution is sent or submitted to him;

(b) in the case of a resolution at a meeting, by being made available for inspection by members of the company both—

(i) at the company's registered office for not less than 15 days ending with the date of the meeting, and

(ii) at the meeting itself.

(5) The matters to be disclosed are—

(a) the nature of the transaction,

(b) the value of the credit transaction and the purpose for which the land, goods or services sold or otherwise disposed of, leased, hired or supplied under the credit transaction are required, and

(c) the extent of the company's liability under any transaction connected with the credit transaction.

(6) No approval is required under this section on the part of the members of a body corporate that—

(a) is not a UK-registered company, or

(b) is a wholly-owned subsidiary of another body corporate.

202 Meaning of "credit transaction"

(1) A "credit transaction" is a transaction under which one party ("the creditor")—

(a) supplies any goods or sells any land under a hire-purchase agreement or a conditional sale agreement,

(b) leases or hires any land or goods in return for periodical payments, or

(c) otherwise disposes of land or supplies goods or services on the understanding that payment (whether in a lump sum or instalments or by way of periodical payments or otherwise) is to be deferred.

(2) Any reference to the person for whose benefit a credit transaction is entered into is to the person to whom goods, land or services are supplied, sold, leased, hired or otherwise disposed of under the transaction.

(3) In this section—

"conditional sale agreement" has the same meaning as in the Consumer Credit Act 1974; and

"services" means anything other than goods or land.

203 Related arrangements: requirement of members' approval

(1) A company may not—

(a) take part in an arrangement under which—

(i) another person enters into a transaction that, if it had been entered into by the company, would have required approval under section 197, 198, 200 or 201, and

(ii) that person, in pursuance of the arrangement, obtains a benefit from the company or a body corporate associated with it, or

(b) arrange for the assignment to it, or assumption by it, of any rights, obligations or liabilities under a transaction that, if it had been entered into by the company, would have required such approval,

unless the arrangement in question has been approved by a resolution of the members of the company.

(2) If the director or connected person for whom the transaction is entered into is a director of its holding company or a person connected with such a director, the arrangement must also have been approved by a resolution of the members of the holding company.

(3) A resolution approving an arrangement to which this section applies must not be passed unless a memorandum setting out the matters mentioned in subsection (4) is made available to members—

(a) in the case of a written resolution, by being sent or submitted to every eligible member at or before the time at which the proposed resolution is sent or submitted to him;

(b) in the case of a resolution at a meeting, by being made available for inspection by members of the company both—

(i) at the company's registered office for not less than 15 days ending with the date of the meeting, and

(ii) at the meeting itself.

(4) The matters to be disclosed are—

(a) the matters that would have to be disclosed if the company were seeking approval of the transaction to which the arrangement relates,

(b) the nature of the arrangement, and

(c) the extent of the company's liability under the arrangement or any transaction connected with it.

(5) No approval is required under this section on the part of the members of a body corporate that—

(a) is not a UK-registered company, or

(b) is a wholly-owned subsidiary of another body corporate.

(6) In determining for the purposes of this section whether a transaction is one that would have required approval under section 197, 198, 200 or 201 if it had been entered into by the company, the transaction shall be treated as having been entered into on the date of the arrangement.

204 Exception for expenditure on company business

(1) Approval is not required under section 197, 198, 200 or 201 (requirement of members' approval for loans etc) for anything done by a company—

(a) to provide a director of the company or of its holding company, or a person connected with any such director, with funds to meet expenditure incurred or to be incurred by him—

(i) for the purposes of the company, or

(ii) for the purpose of enabling him properly to perform his duties as an officer of the company, or

(b) to enable any such person to avoid incurring such expenditure.

(2) This section does not authorise a company to enter into a transaction if the aggregate of—

(a) the value of the transaction in question, and

(b) the value of any other relevant transactions or arrangements, exceeds £50,000.

205 Exception for expenditure on defending proceedings etc

(1) Approval is not required under section 197, 198, 200 or 201 (requirement of members' approval for loans etc) for anything done by a company—

(a) to provide a director of the company or of its holding company with funds to meet expenditure incurred or to be incurred by him—

(i) in defending any criminal or civil proceedings in connection with any alleged negligence, default, breach of duty or breach of trust by him in relation to the company or an associated company, or

(ii) in connection with an application for relief (see subsection (5)), or

(b) to enable any such director to avoid incurring such expenditure, if it is done on the following terms.

(2) The terms are—

(a) that the loan is to be repaid, or (as the case may be) any liability of the company incurred under any transaction connected with the thing done is to be discharged, in the event of—

(i) the director being convicted in the proceedings,

(ii) judgment being given against him in the proceedings, or

(iii) the court refusing to grant him relief on the application; and

(b) that it is to be so repaid or discharged not later than—

(i) the date when the conviction becomes final,

(ii) the date when the judgment becomes final, or

(iii) the date when the refusal of relief becomes final.

(3) For this purpose a conviction, judgment or refusal of relief becomes final—

(a) if not appealed against, at the end of the period for bringing an appeal;

(b) if appealed against, when the appeal (or any further appeal) is disposed of.

(4) An appeal is disposed of—

(a) if it is determined and the period for bringing any further appeal has ended, or

(b) if it is abandoned or otherwise ceases to have effect.

(5) The reference in subsection (1)(a)(ii) to an application for relief is to an application for relief under—

section 661(3) or (4) (power of court to grant relief in case of acquisition of shares by innocent nominee), or

section 1157 (general power of court to grant relief in case of honest and reasonable conduct).

206 Exception for expenditure in connection with regulatory action or investigation

Approval is not required under section 197, 198, 200 or 201 (requirement of members' approval for loans etc) for anything done by a company—

(a) to provide a director of the company or of its holding company with funds to meet expenditure incurred or to be incurred by him in defending himself—

(i) in an investigation by a regulatory authority, or

(ii) against action proposed to be taken by a regulatory authority,

in connection with any alleged negligence, default, breach of duty or breach of trust by him in relation to the company or an associated company, or

(b) to enable any such director to avoid incurring such expenditure.

207 Exceptions for minor and business transactions

(1) Approval is not required under section 197, 198 or 200 for a company to make a loan or quasi-loan, or to give a guarantee or provide security in connection with a loan or quasi-loan, if the aggregate of—

(a) the value of the transaction, and

(b) the value of any other relevant transactions or arrangements, does not exceed £10,000.

(2) Approval is not required under section 201 for a company to enter into a credit transaction, or to give a guarantee or provide security in connection with a credit transaction, if the aggregate of—

(a) the value of the transaction (that is, of the credit transaction, guarantee or security), and

(b) the value of any other relevant transactions or arrangements,

does not exceed £15,000.

(3) Approval is not required under section 201 for a company to enter into a credit transaction, or to give a guarantee or provide security in connection with a credit transaction, if—

(a) the transaction is entered into by the company in the ordinary course of the company's business, and

(b) the value of the transaction is not greater, and the terms on which it is entered into are not more favourable, than it is reasonable to expect the company would have offered to, or in respect of, a person of the same financial standing but unconnected with the company.

208 Exceptions for intra-group transactions

(1) Approval is not required under section 197, 198 or 200 for—

(a) the making of a loan or quasi-loan to an associated body corporate, or

(b) the giving of a guarantee or provision of security in connection with a loan or quasi-loan made to an associated body corporate.

(2) Approval is not required under section 201—

(a) to enter into a credit transaction as creditor for the benefit of an associated body corporate, or

(b) to give a guarantee or provide security in connection with a credit transaction entered into by any person for the benefit of an associated body corporate.

209 Exceptions for money-lending companies

(1) Approval is not required under section 197, 198 or 200 for the making of a loan or quasi-loan, or the giving of a guarantee or provision of security in connection with a loan or quasi-loan, by a money-lending company if—

(a) the transaction (that is, the loan, quasi-loan, guarantee or security) is entered into by the company in the ordinary course of the company's business, and

(b) the value of the transaction is not greater, and its terms are not more favourable, than it is reasonable to expect the company would have offered to a person of the same financial standing but unconnected with the company.

(2) A "money-lending company" means a company whose ordinary business includes the making of loans or quasi-loans, or the giving of guarantees or provision of security in connection with loans or quasi-loans.

(3) The condition specified in subsection (1)(b) does not of itself prevent a company from making a home loan—

(a) to a director of the company or of its holding company, or

(b) to an employee of the company,

if loans of that description are ordinarily made by the company to its employees and the terms of the loan in question are no more favourable than those on which such loans are ordinarily made.

(4) For the purposes of subsection (3) a "home loan" means a loan—

(a) for the purpose of facilitating the purchase, for use as the only or main residence of the person to whom the loan is made, of the whole or part of any dwelling-house together with any land to be occupied and enjoyed with it,

(b) for the purpose of improving a dwelling-house or part of a dwelling-house so used or any land occupied and enjoyed with it, or

(c) in substitution for any loan made by any person and falling within paragraph (a) or (b).

210 Other relevant transactions or arrangements

(1) This section has effect for determining what are "other relevant transactions or arrangements" for the purposes of any exception to section 197, 198, 200 or 201. In the following provisions "the relevant exception" means the exception for the purposes of which that falls to be determined.

(2) Other relevant transactions or arrangements are those previously entered into, or entered into at the same time as the transaction or arrangement in question in relation to which the following conditions are met.

(3) Where the transaction or arrangement in question is entered into—

(a) for a director of the company entering into it, or

(b) for a person connected with such a director,

the conditions are that the transaction or arrangement was (or is) entered into for that director, or a person connected with him, by virtue of the relevant exception by that company or by any of its subsidiaries.

(4) Where the transaction or arrangement in question is entered into—

(a) for a director of the holding company of the company entering into it, or

(b) for a person connected with such a director,

the conditions are that the transaction or arrangement was (or is) entered into for that director, or a person connected with him, by virtue of the relevant exception by the holding company or by any of its subsidiaries.

(5) A transaction or arrangement entered into by a company that at the time it was entered into—

(a) was a subsidiary of the company entering into the transaction or arrangement in question, or

(b) was a subsidiary of that company's holding company,

is not a relevant transaction or arrangement if, at the time the question arises whether the transaction or arrangement in question falls within a relevant exception, it is no longer such a subsidiary.

211 The value of transactions and arrangements

(1) For the purposes of sections 197 to 214 (loans etc)—

(a) the value of a transaction or arrangement is determined as follows, and

(b) the value of any other relevant transaction or arrangement is taken to be the value so determined reduced by any amount by which the liabilities of the person for whom the transaction or arrangement was made have been reduced.

(2) The value of a loan is the amount of its principal.

(3) The value of a quasi-loan is the amount, or maximum amount, that the person to whom the quasi-loan is made is liable to reimburse the creditor.

(4) The value of a credit transaction is the price that it is reasonable to expect could be obtained for the goods, services or land to which the transaction relates if they had been supplied (at the time the transaction is entered into) in the ordinary course of business and on the same terms (apart from price) as they have been supplied, or are to be supplied, under the transaction in question.

(5) The value of a guarantee or security is the amount guaranteed or secured.

(6) The value of an arrangement to which section 203 (related arrangements) applies is the value of the transaction to which the arrangement relates.

(7) If the value of a transaction or arrangement is not capable of being expressed as a specific sum of money—

(a) whether because the amount of any liability arising under the transaction or arrangement is unascertainable, or for any other reason, and

(b) whether or not any liability under the transaction or arrangement has been reduced,

its value is deemed to exceed £50,000.

212 The person for whom a transaction or arrangement is entered into

For the purposes of sections 197 to 214 (loans etc) the person for whom a transaction or arrangement is entered into is—

(a) in the case of a loan or quasi-loan, the person to whom it is made;

(b) in the case of a credit transaction, the person to whom goods, land or services are supplied, sold, hired, leased or otherwise disposed of under the transaction;

(c) in the case of a guarantee or security, the person for whom the transaction is made in connection with which the guarantee or security is entered into;

(d) in the case of an arrangement within section 203 (related arrangements), the person for whom the transaction is made to which the arrangement relates.

213 Loans etc: civil consequences of contravention

(1) This section applies where a company enters into a transaction or arrangement in contravention of section 197, 198, 200, 201 or 203 (requirement of members' approval for loans etc).

(2) The transaction or arrangement is voidable at the instance of the company, unless—

(a) restitution of any money or other asset that was the subject matter of the transaction or arrangement is no longer possible,

(b) the company has been indemnified for any loss or damage resulting from the transaction or arrangement, or

(c) rights acquired in good faith, for value and without actual notice of the contravention by a person who is not a party to the transaction or arrangement would be affected by the avoidance.

(3) Whether or not the transaction or arrangement has been avoided, each of the persons specified in subsection (4) is liable—

(a) to account to the company for any gain that he has made directly or indirectly by the transaction or arrangement, and

(b) (jointly and severally with any other person so liable under this section) to indemnify the company for any loss or damage resulting from the transaction or arrangement.

(4) The persons so liable are—

(a) any director of the company or of its holding company with whom the company entered into the transaction or arrangement in contravention of section 197, 198, 201 or 203,

(b) any person with whom the company entered into the transaction or arrangement in contravention of any of those sections who is connected with a director of the company or of its holding company,

(c) the director of the company or of its holding company with whom any such person is connected, and

(d) any other director of the company who authorised the transaction or arrangement.

(5) Subsections (3) and (4) are subject to the following two subsections.

(6) In the case of a transaction or arrangement entered into by a company in contravention of section 200, 201 or 203 with a person connected with a director of the company or of its holding company, that director is not liable by virtue of subsection (4)(c) if he shows that he took all reasonable steps to secure the company's compliance with the section concerned.

(7) In any case—

(a) a person so connected is not liable by virtue of subsection (4)(b), and

(b) a director is not liable by virtue of subsection (4) (d),

if he shows that, at the time the transaction or arrangement was entered into, he did not know the relevant circumstances constituting the contravention.

(8) Nothing in this section shall be read as excluding the operation of any other enactment or rule of law by virtue of which the transaction or arrangement may be called in question or any liability to the company may arise.

214 Loans etc: effect of subsequent affirmation

(1) Where a transaction or arrangement is entered into by a company in contravention of section 197, 198, 200, 201 or 203 (requirement of members' approval for loans etc) but, within a reasonable period, it is affirmed—

(a) in the case of a contravention of the requirement for a resolution of the members of the company, by a resolution of the members of the company, and

(b) in the case of a contravention of the requirement for a resolution of the members of the company's holding company, by a resolution of the members of the holding company,

the transaction or arrangement may no longer be avoided under section 213.

Payments for loss of office

215 Payments for loss of office

(1) In this Chapter a "payment for loss of office" means a payment made to a director or past director of a company—

(a) by way of compensation for loss of office as director of the company,

(b) by way of compensation for loss, while director of the company or in connection with his ceasing to be a director of it, of—

(i) any other office or employment in connection with the management of the affairs of the company, or

(ii) any office (as director or otherwise) or employment in connection with the management of the affairs of any subsidiary undertaking of the company,

(c) as consideration for or in connection with his retirement from his office as director of the company, or

(d) as consideration for or in connection with his retirement, while director of the company or in connection with his ceasing to be a director of it, from—

(i) any other office or employment in connection with the management of the affairs of the company, or

(ii) any office (as director or otherwise) or employment in connection with the management of the affairs of any subsidiary undertaking of the company.

(2) The references to compensation and consideration include benefits otherwise than in cash and references in this Chapter to payment have a corresponding meaning.

(3) For the purposes of sections 217 to 221 (payments requiring members' approval)—

(a) payment to a person connected with a director, or

(b) payment to any person at the direction of, or for the benefit of, a director or a person connected with him,

is treated as payment to the director.

(4) References in those sections to payment by a person include payment by another person at the direction of, or on behalf of, the person referred to.

216 Amounts taken to be payments for loss of office

(1) This section applies where in connection with any such transfer as is mentioned in section 218 or 219 (payment in connection with transfer of undertaking, property or shares) a director of the company—

(a) is to cease to hold office, or

(b) is to cease to be the holder of—

(i) any other office or employment in connection with the management of the affairs of the company, or

(ii) any office (as director or otherwise) or employment in connection with the management of the affairs of any subsidiary undertaking of the company.

(2) If in connection with any such transfer—

(a) the price to be paid to the director for any shares in the company held by him is in excess of the price which could at the time have been obtained by other holders of like shares, or

(b) any valuable consideration is given to the director by a person other than the company,

the excess or, as the case may be, the money value of the consideration is taken for the purposes of those sections to have been a payment for loss of office.

217 Payment by company: requirement of members' approval

(1) A company may not make a payment for loss of office to a director of the company unless the payment has been approved by a resolution of the members of the company.

(2) A company may not make a payment for loss of office to a director of its holding company unless the payment has been approved by a resolution of the members of each of those companies.

(3) A resolution approving a payment to which this section applies must not be passed unless a memorandum setting out particulars of the proposed payment (including its amount) is made available to the members of the company whose approval is sought—

(a) in the case of a written resolution, by being sent or submitted to every eligible member at or before the time at which the proposed resolution is sent or submitted to him;

(b) in the case of a resolution at a meeting, by being made available for inspection by the members both—

(i) at the company's registered office for not less than 15 days ending with the date of the meeting, and

(ii) at the meeting itself.

(4) No approval is required under this section on the part of the members of a body corporate that—

(a) is not a UK-registered company, or

(b) is a wholly-owned subsidiary of another body corporate.

218 Payment in connection with transfer of undertaking etc: requirement of members' approval

(1) No payment for loss of office may be made by any person to a director of a company in connection with the transfer of the whole or any part of the undertaking or property of the company unless the payment has been approved by a resolution of the members of the company.

(2) No payment for loss of office may be made by any person to a director of a company in connection with the transfer of the whole or any part of the undertaking or property of a subsidiary of the company unless the payment has been approved by a resolution of the members of each of the companies.

(3) A resolution approving a payment to which this section applies must not be passed unless a memorandum setting out particulars of the proposed payment (including its amount) is made available to the members of the company whose approval is sought—

(a) in the case of a written resolution, by being sent or submitted to every eligible member at or before the time at which the proposed resolution is sent or submitted to him;

(b) in the case of a resolution at a meeting, by being made available for inspection by the members both—

(i) at the company's registered office for not less than 15 days ending with the date of the meeting, and

(ii) at the meeting itself.

(4) No approval is required under this section on the part of the members of a body corporate that—

(a) is not a UK-registered company, or

(b) is a wholly-owned subsidiary of another body corporate.

(5) A payment made in pursuance of an arrangement—

(a) entered into as part of the agreement for the transfer in question, or within one year before or two years after that agreement, and

(b) to which the company whose undertaking or property is transferred, or any person to whom the transfer is made, is privy,

is presumed, except in so far as the contrary is shown, to be a payment to which this section applies.

219 Payment in connection with share transfer: requirement of members' approval

(1) No payment for loss of office may be made by any person to a director of a company in connection with a transfer of shares in the company, or in a subsidiary of the company, resulting from a takeover bid unless the payment has been approved by a resolution of the relevant shareholders.

(2) The relevant shareholders are the holders of the shares to which the bid relates and any holders of shares of the same class as any of those shares.

(3) A resolution approving a payment to which this section applies must not be passed unless a memorandum setting out particulars of the proposed payment (including its amount) is made available to the members of the company whose approval is sought—

(a) in the case of a written resolution, by being sent or submitted to every eligible member at or before the time at which the proposed resolution is sent or submitted to him;

(b) in the case of a resolution at a meeting, by being made available for inspection by the members both—

(i) at the company's registered office for not less than 15 days ending with the date of the meeting, and

(ii) at the meeting itself.

(4) Neither the person making the offer, nor any associate of his (as defined in section 988), is entitled to vote on the resolution, but—

(a) where the resolution is proposed as a written resolution, they are entitled (if they would otherwise be so entitled) to be sent a copy of it, and

(b) at any meeting to consider the resolution they are entitled (if they would otherwise be so entitled) to be given notice of the meeting, to attend and speak and if present (in person or by proxy) to count towards the quorum.

(5) If at a meeting to consider the resolution a quorum is not present, and after the meeting has been adjourned to a later date a quorum is again not present, the payment is (for the purposes of this section) deemed to have been approved.

(6) No approval is required under this section on the part of shareholders in a body corporate that—

(a) is not a UK-registered company, or

(b) is a wholly-owned subsidiary of another body corporate.

(7) A payment made in pursuance of an arrangement—

(a) entered into as part of the agreement for the transfer in question, or within one year before or two years after that agreement, and

(b) to which the company whose shares are the subject of the bid, or any person to whom the transfer is made, is privy,

is presumed, except in so far as the contrary is shown, to be a payment to which this section applies.

220 Exception for payments in discharge of legal obligations etc

(1) Approval is not required under section 217, 218 or 219 (payments requiring members' approval) for a payment made in good faith—

(a) in discharge of an existing legal obligation (as defined below),

(b) by way of damages for breach of such an obligation,

(c) by way of settlement or compromise of any claim arising in connection with the termination of a person's office or employment, or

(d) by way of pension in respect of past services.

(2) In relation to a payment within section 217 (payment by company) an existing legal obligation means an obligation of the company, or any body corporate associated with it, that was not entered into in connection with, or in consequence of, the event giving rise to the payment for loss of office.

(3) In relation to a payment within section 218 or 219 (payment in connection with transfer of undertaking, property or shares) an existing legal obligation means an obligation of the person

making the payment that was not entered into for the purposes of, in connection with or in consequence of, the transfer in question.

(4) In the case of a payment within both section 217 and section 218, or within both section 217 and section 219, subsection (2) above applies and not subsection (3).

(5) A payment part of which falls within subsection (1) above and part of which does not is treated as if the parts were separate payments.

221 Exception for small payments

(1) Approval is not required under section 217, 218 or 219 (payments requiring members' approval) if—

(a) the payment in question is made by the company or any of its subsidiaries, and

(b) the amount or value of the payment, together with the amount or value of any other relevant payments, does not exceed £200.

(2) For this purpose "other relevant payments" are payments for loss of office in relation to which the following conditions are met.

(3) Where the payment in question is one to which section 217 (payment by company) applies, the conditions are that the other payment was or is paid—

(a) by the company making the payment in question or any of its subsidiaries,

(b) to the director to whom that payment is made, and

(c) in connection with the same event.

(4) Where the payment in question is one to which section 218 or 219 applies (payment in connection with transfer of undertaking, property or shares), the conditions are that the other payment was (or is) paid in connection with the same transfer—

(a) to the director to whom the payment in question was made, and

(b) by the company making the payment or any of its subsidiaries.

222 Payments made without approval: civil consequences

(1) If a payment is made in contravention of section 217 (payment by company)—

(a) it is held by the recipient on trust for the company making the payment, and

(b) any director who authorised the payment is jointly and severally liable to indemnify the company that made the payment for any loss resulting from it.

(2) If a payment is made in contravention of section 218 (payment in connection with transfer of undertaking etc), it is held by the recipient on trust for the company whose undertaking or property is or is proposed to be transferred.

(3) If a payment is made in contravention of section 219 (payment in connection with share transfer)—

(a) it is held by the recipient on trust for persons who have sold their shares as a result of the offer made, and

(b) the expenses incurred by the recipient in distributing that sum amongst those persons shall be borne by him and not retained out of that sum.

(4) If a payment is in contravention of section 217 and section 218, subsection (2) of this section applies rather than subsection (1).

(5) If a payment is in contravention of section 217 and section 219, subsection (3) of this section applies rather than subsection (1), unless the court directs otherwise.

Supplementary

223 Transactions requiring members' approval: application of provisions to shadow directors

(1) For the purposes of—

(a) sections 188 and 189 (directors' service contracts),

(b) sections 190 to 196 (property transactions),

(c) sections 197 to 214 (loans etc), and

(d) sections 215 to 222 (payments for loss of office),

a shadow director is treated as a director.

(2) Any reference in those provisions to loss of office as a director does not apply in relation to loss of a person's status as a shadow director.

224 Approval by written resolution: accidental failure to send memorandum

(1) Where—

(a) approval under this Chapter is sought by written resolution, and

(b) a memorandum is required under this Chapter to be sent or submitted to every eligible member before the resolution is passed,

any accidental failure to send or submit the memorandum to one or more members shall be disregarded for the purpose of determining whether the requirement has been met.

(2) Subsection (1) has effect subject to any provision of the company's articles.

225 Cases where approval is required under more than one provision

(1) Approval may be required under more than one provision of this Chapter.

(2) If so, the requirements of each applicable provision must be met.

(3) This does not require a separate resolution for the purposes of each provision.

226 . . .

CHAPTER 5
DIRECTORS' SERVICE CONTRACTS

227 Directors' service contracts

(1) For the purposes of this Part a director's "service contract", in relation to a company, means a contract under which—

(a) a director of the company undertakes personally to perform services (as director or otherwise) for the company, or for a subsidiary of the company, or

(b) services (as director or otherwise) that a director of the company undertakes personally to perform are made available by a third party to the company, or to a subsidiary of the company.

(2) The provisions of this Part relating to directors' service contracts apply to the terms of a person's appointment as a director of a company.

They are not restricted to contracts for the performance of services outside the scope of the ordinary duties of a director.

228 Copy of contract or memorandum of terms to be available for inspection

(1) A company must keep available for inspection—

(a) a copy of every director's service contract with the company or with a subsidiary of the company, or

(b) if the contract is not in writing, a written memorandum setting out the terms of the contract.

(2) All the copies and memoranda must be kept available for inspection at—

(a) the company's registered office, or

(b) a place specified in regulations under section 1136.

(3) The copies and memoranda must be retained by the company for at least one year from the date of termination or expiry of the contract and must be kept available for inspection during that time.

(4) The company must give notice to the registrar—

(a) of the place at which the copies and memoranda are kept available for inspection, and

(b) of any change in that place,

unless they have at all times been kept at the company's registered office.

(5) If default is made in complying with subsection (1), (2) or (3), or default is made for 14 days in complying with subsection (4), an offence is committed by every officer of the company who is in default.

(6) A person guilty of an offence under this section is liable on summary conviction to a fine not exceeding level 3 on the standard scale and, for continued contravention, a daily default fine not exceeding one-tenth of level 3 on the standard scale.

(7) The provisions of this section apply to a variation of a director's service contract as they apply to the original contract.

229 Right of member to inspect and request copy

(1) Every copy or memorandum required to be kept under section 228 must be open to inspection by any member of the company without charge.

(2) Any member of the company is entitled, on request and on payment of such fee as may be prescribed, to be provided with a copy of any such copy or memorandum.
The copy must be provided within seven days after the request is received by the company.

(3) If an inspection required under subsection (1) is refused, or default is made in complying with subsection (2), an offence is committed by every officer of the company who is in default.

(4) A person guilty of an offence under this section is liable on summary conviction to a fine not exceeding level 3 on the standard scale and, for continued contravention, a daily default fine not exceeding one-tenth of level 3 on the standard scale.

(5) In the case of any such refusal or default the court may by order compel an immediate inspection or, as the case may be, direct that the copy required be sent to the person requiring it.

230 Directors' service contracts: application of provisions to shadow directors

A shadow director is treated as a director for the purposes of the provisions of this Chapter.

CHAPTER 6
CONTRACTS WITH SOLE MEMBERS WHO ARE DIRECTORS

231 Contract with sole member who is also a director

(1) This section applies where—
   (a) a limited company having only one member enters into a contract with the sole member,
   (b) the sole member is also a director of the company, and
   (c) the contract is not entered into in the ordinary course of the company's business.

(2) The company must, unless the contract is in writing, ensure that the terms of the contract are either—
   (a) set out in a written memorandum, or
   (b) recorded in the minutes of the first meeting of the directors of the company following the making of the contract.

(3) If a company fails to comply with this section an offence is committed by every officer of the company who is in default.

(4) A person guilty of an offence under this section is liable on summary conviction to a fine not exceeding level 5 on the standard scale.

(5) For the purposes of this section a shadow director is treated as a director.

(6) Failure to comply with this section in relation to a contract does not affect the validity of the contract.

(7) Nothing in this section shall be read as excluding the operation of any other enactment or rule of law applying to contracts between a company and a director of the company.

CHAPTER 7
DIRECTORS' LIABILITIES

Provision protecting directors from liability

232 Provisions protecting directors from liability

(1) Any provision that purports to exempt a director of a company (to any extent) from any liability that would otherwise attach to him in connection with any negligence, default, breach of duty or breach of trust in relation to the company is void.

(2) Any provision by which a company directly or indirectly provides an indemnity (to any extent) for a director of the company, or of an associated company, against any liability attaching to him in connection with any negligence, default, breach of duty or breach of trust in relation to the company of which he is a director is void, except as permitted by—

(a) section 233 (provision of insurance),

(b) section 234 (qualifying third party indemnity provision), or

(c) section 235 (qualifying pension scheme indemnity provision).

(3) This section applies to any provision, whether contained in a company's articles or in any contract with the company or otherwise.

(4) Nothing in this section prevents a company's articles from making such provision as has previously been lawful for dealing with conflicts of interest.

233 Provision of insurance

Section 232(2) (voidness of provisions for indemnifying directors) does not prevent a company from purchasing and maintaining for a director of the company, or of an associated company, insurance against any such liability as is mentioned in that subsection.

234 Qualifying third party indemnity provision

(1) Section 232(2) (voidness of provisions for indemnifying directors) does not apply to qualifying third party indemnity provision.

(2) Third party indemnity provision means provision for indemnity against liability incurred by the director to a person other than the company or an associated company.

Such provision is qualifying third party indemnity provision if the following requirements are met.

(3) The provision must not provide any indemnity against—

(a) any liability of the director to pay—

(i) a fine imposed in criminal proceedings, or

(ii) a sum payable to a regulatory authority by way of a penalty in respect of non-compliance with any requirement of a regulatory nature (however arising); or

(b) any liability incurred by the director—

(i) in defending criminal proceedings in which he is convicted, or

(ii) in defending civil proceedings brought by the company, or an associated company, in which judgment is given against him, or

(iii) in connection with an application for relief (see subsection (6)) in which the court refuses to grant him relief.

(4) The references in subsection (3)(b) to a conviction, judgment or refusal of relief are to the final decision in the proceedings.

(5) For this purpose—

(a) a conviction, judgment or refusal of relief becomes final—

(i) if not appealed against, at the end of the period for bringing an appeal, or

(ii) if appealed against, at the time when the appeal (or any further appeal) is disposed of; and

(b) an appeal is disposed of—

(i) if it is determined and the period for bringing any further appeal has ended, or

(ii) if it is abandoned or otherwise ceases to have effect.

(6) The reference in subsection (3) (b) (iii) to an application for relief is to an application for relief under—

section 661(3) or (4) (power of court to grant relief in case of acquisition of shares by innocent nominee), or

section 1157 (general power of court to grant relief in case of honest and reasonable conduct).

235 Qualifying pension scheme indemnity provision

(1) Section 232(2) (voidness of provisions for indemnifying directors) does not apply to qualifying pension scheme indemnity provision.

(2) Pension scheme indemnity provision means provision indemnifying a director of a company that is a trustee of an occupational pension scheme against liability incurred in connection with the company's activities as trustee of the scheme.

Such provision is qualifying pension scheme indemnity provision if the following requirements are met.

(3) The provision must not provide any indemnity against—

(a) any liability of the director to pay—

(i) a fine imposed in criminal proceedings, or

(ii) a sum payable to a regulatory authority by way of a penalty in respect of non-compliance with any requirement of a regulatory nature (however arising); or

(b) any liability incurred by the director in defending criminal proceedings in which he is convicted.

(4) The reference in subsection (3) (b) to a conviction is to the final decision in the proceedings.

(5) For this purpose—

(a) a conviction becomes final—

(i) if not appealed against, at the end of the period for bringing an appeal, or

(ii) if appealed against, at the time when the appeal (or any further appeal) is disposed of; and

(b) an appeal is disposed of—

(i) if it is determined and the period for bringing any further appeal has ended, or

(ii) if it is abandoned or otherwise ceases to have effect.

(6) In this section "occupational pension scheme" means an occupational pension scheme as defined in section 150(5) of the Finance Act 2004 that is established under a trust.

236 Qualifying indemnity provision to be disclosed in directors' report

(1) This section requires disclosure in the directors' report of—

(a) qualifying third party indemnity provision, and

(b) qualifying pension scheme indemnity provision.

Such provision is referred to in this section as "qualifying indemnity provision".

(2) If when a directors' report is approved any qualifying indemnity provision (whether made by the company or otherwise) is in force for the benefit of one or more directors of the company, the report must state that such provision is in force.

(3) If at any time during the financial year to which a directors' report relates any such provision was in force for the benefit of one or more persons who were then directors of the company, the report must state that such provision was in force.

(4) If when a directors' report is approved qualifying indemnity provision made by the company is in force for the benefit of one or more directors of an associated company, the report must state that such provision is in force.

(5) If at any time during the financial year to which a directors' report relates any such provision was in force for the benefit of one or more persons who were then directors of an associated company, the report must state that such provision was in force.

237 Copy of qualifying indemnity provision to be available for inspection

(1) This section has effect where qualifying indemnity provision is made for a director of a company, and applies—

(a) to the company of which he is a director (whether the provision is made by that company or an associated company), and

(b) where the provision is made by an associated company, to that company.

(2) That company or, as the case may be, each of them must keep available for inspection—

(a) a copy of the qualifying indemnity provision, or

(b) if the provision is not in writing, a written memorandum setting out its terms.

(3) The copy or memorandum must be kept available for inspection at—

(a) the company's registered office, or

(b) a place specified in regulations under section 1136.

(4) The copy or memorandum must be retained by the company for at least one year from the date of termination or expiry of the provision and must be kept available for inspection during that time.

(5) The company must give notice to the registrar—

(a) of the place at which the copy or memorandum is kept available for inspection, and

(b) of any change in that place,

unless it has at all times been kept at the company's registered office.

(6) If default is made in complying with subsection (2), (3) or (4), or default is made for 14 days in complying with subsection (5), an offence is committed by every officer of the company who is in default.

(7) A person guilty of an offence under this section is liable on summary conviction to a fine not exceeding level 3 on the standard scale and, for continued contravention, a daily default fine not exceeding one-tenth of level 3 on the standard scale.

(8) The provisions of this section apply to a variation of a qualifying indemnity provision as they apply to the original provision.

(9) In this section "qualifying indemnity provision" means—

(a) qualifying third party indemnity provision, and

(b) qualifying pension scheme indemnity provision.

238 Right of member to inspect and request copy

(1) Every copy or memorandum required to be kept by a company under section 237 must be open to inspection by any member of the company without charge.

(2) Any member of the company is entitled, on request and on payment of such fee as may be prescribed, to be provided with a copy of any such copy or memorandum.

The copy must be provided within seven days after the request is received by the company.

(3) If an inspection required under subsection (1) is refused, or default is made in complying with subsection (2), an offence is committed by every officer of the company who is in default.

(4) A person guilty of an offence under this section is liable on summary conviction to a fine not exceeding level 3 on the standard scale and, for continued contravention, a daily default fine not exceeding one-tenth of level 3 on the standard scale.

(5) In the case of any such refusal or default the court may by order compel an immediate inspection or, as the case may be, direct that the copy required be sent to the person requiring it.

Ratification of acts giving rise to liability

239 Ratification of acts of directors

(1) This section applies to the ratification by a company of conduct by a director amounting to negligence, default, breach of duty or breach of trust in relation to the company.

(2) The decision of the company to ratify such conduct must be made by resolution of the members of the company.

(3) Where the resolution is proposed as a written resolution neither the director (if a member of the company) nor any member connected with him is an eligible member.

(4) Where the resolution is proposed at a meeting, it is passed only if the necessary majority is obtained disregarding votes in favour of the resolution by the director (if a member of the company) and any member connected with him.

This does not prevent the director or any such member from attending, being counted towards the quorum and taking part in the proceedings at any meeting at which the decision is considered.

(5) For the purposes of this section—

(a) "conduct" includes acts and omissions;

(b) "director" includes a former director;

(c) a shadow director is treated as a director; and

(d) in section 252 (meaning of "connected person"), subsection (3) does not apply (exclusion of person who is himself a director).

(6) Nothing in this section affects—

(a) the validity of a decision taken by unanimous consent of the members of the company, or
(b) any power of the directors to agree not to sue, or to settle or release a claim made by them on behalf of the company.

(7) This section does not affect any other enactment or rule of law imposing additional requirements for valid ratification or any rule of law as to acts that are incapable of being ratified by the company.

CHAPTER 8
DIRECTORS' RESIDENTIAL ADDRESSES: PROTECTION FROM DISCLOSURE

240 Protected information

(1) This Chapter makes provision for protecting, in the case of a company director who is an individual—
(a) information as to his usual residential address;
(b) the information that his service address is his usual residential address.

(2) That information is referred to in this Chapter as "protected information".

(3) Information does not cease to be protected information on the individual ceasing to be a director of the company.
References in this Chapter to a director include, to that extent, a former director.

241 Protected information: restriction on use or disclosure by company

(1) A company must not use or disclose protected information about any of its directors, except—
(a) for communicating with the director concerned,
(b) in order to comply with any requirement of the Companies Acts as to particulars to be sent to the registrar, or
(c) in accordance with section 244 (disclosure under court order).

(2) Subsection (1) does not prohibit any use or disclosure of protected information with the consent of the director concerned.

242 Protected information: restriction on use or disclosure by registrar

(1) The registrar must omit protected information from the material on the register that is available for inspection where—
(a) it is contained in a document delivered to him in which such information is required to be stated, and
(b) in the case of a document having more than one part, it is contained in a part of the document in which such information is required to be stated.

(2) The registrar is not obliged—
(a) to check other documents or (as the case may be) other parts of the document to ensure the absence of protected information, or
(b) to omit from the material that is available for public inspection anything registered before this Chapter comes into force.

(3) The registrar must not use or disclose protected information except—
(a) as permitted by section 243 (permitted use or disclosure by registrar), or
(b) in accordance with section 244 (disclosure under court order).

243 Permitted use or disclosure by the registrar

(1) The registrar may use protected information for communicating with the director in question.

(2) The registrar may disclose protected information—
(a) to a public authority specified for the purposes of this section by regulations made by the Secretary of State, or
(b) to a credit reference agency.

(3) The Secretary of State may make provision by regulations—
(a) specifying conditions for the disclosure of protected information in accordance with this section, and

(b) providing for the charging of fees.

(4) The Secretary of State may make provision by regulations requiring the registrar, on application, to refrain from disclosing protected information relating to a director to a credit reference agency.

(5) Regulations under subsection (4) may make provision as to—

(a) who may make an application,

(b) the grounds on which an application may be made,

(c) the information to be included in and documents to accompany an application, and

(d) how an application is to be determined.

(6) Provision under subsection (5) (d) may in particular—

(a) confer a discretion on the registrar;

(b) provide for a question to be referred to a person other than the registrar for the purposes of determining the application.

(7) In this section—

"credit reference agency" means a person carrying on a business comprising the furnishing of information relevant to the financial standing of individuals, being information collected by the agency for that purpose; and

"public authority" includes any person or body having functions of a public nature.

(8) Regulations under this section are subject to negative resolution procedure.

244 Disclosure under court order

(1) The court may make an order for the disclosure of protected information by the company or by the registrar if—

(a) there is evidence that service of documents at a service address other than the director's usual residential address is not effective to bring them to the notice of the director, or

(b) it is necessary or expedient for the information to be provided in connection with the enforcement of an order or decree of the court,

and the court is otherwise satisfied that it is appropriate to make the order.

(2) An order for disclosure by the registrar is to be made only if the company—

(a) does not have the director's usual residential address, or

(b) has been dissolved.

(3) The order may be made on the application of a liquidator, creditor or member of the company, or any other person appearing to the court to have a sufficient interest.

(4) The order must specify the persons to whom, and purposes for which, disclosure is authorised.

245 Circumstances in which registrar may put address on the public record

(1) The registrar may put a director's usual residential address on the public record if—

(a) communications sent by the registrar to the director and requiring a response within a specified period remain unanswered, or

(b) there is evidence that service of documents at a service address provided in place of the director's usual residential address is not effective to bring them to the notice of the director.

(2) The registrar must give notice of the proposal—

(a) to the director, and

(b) to every company of which the registrar has been notified that the individual is a director.

(3) The notice must—

(a) state the grounds on which it is proposed to put the director's usual residential address on the public record, and

(b) specify a period within which representations may be made before that is done.

(4) It must be sent to the director at his usual residential address, unless it appears to the registrar that service at that address may be ineffective to bring it to the individual's notice, in which case it may be sent to any service address provided in place of that address.

(5) The registrar must take account of any representations received within the specified period.

(6) What is meant by putting the address on the public record is explained in section 246.

246 Putting the address on the public record

(1) The registrar, on deciding in accordance with section 245 that a director's usual residential address is to be put on the public record, shall proceed as if notice of a change of registered particulars had been given—
(a) stating that address as the director's service address, and
(b) stating that the director's usual residential address is the same as his service address.

(2) The registrar must give notice of having done so—
(a) to the director, and
(b) to the company.

(3) On receipt of the notice the company must—
(a) enter the director's usual residential address in its register of directors as his service address, and
(b) state in its register of directors' residential addresses that his usual residential address is the same as his service address.

(4) If the company has been notified by the director in question of a more recent address as his usual residential address, it must—
(a) enter that address in its register of directors as the director's service address, and
(b) give notice to the registrar as on a change of registered particulars.

(5) If a company fails to comply with subsection (3) or (4), an offence is committed by—
(a) the company, and
(b) every officer of the company who is in default.

(6) A person guilty of an offence under subsection (5) is liable on summary conviction to a fine not exceeding level 5 on the standard scale and, for continued contravention, a daily default fine not exceeding one-tenth of level 5 on the standard scale.

(7) A director whose usual residential address has been put on the public record by the registrar under this section may not register a service address other than his usual residential address for a period of five years from the date of the registrar's decision.

CHAPTER 9
SUPPLEMENTARY PROVISIONS

Provision for employees on cessation or transfer of business

247 Power to make provision for employees on cessation or transfer of business

(1) The powers of the directors of a company include (if they would not otherwise do so) power to make provision for the benefit of persons employed or formerly employed by the company, or any of its subsidiaries, in connection with the cessation or the transfer to any person of the whole or part of the undertaking of the company or that subsidiary.

(2) This power is exercisable notwithstanding the general duty imposed by section 172 (duty to promote the success of the company).

(3) In the case of a company that is a charity it is exercisable notwithstanding any restrictions on the directors' powers (or the company's capacity) flowing from the objects of the company.

(4) The power may only be exercised if sanctioned—
(a) by a resolution of the company, or
(b) by a resolution of the directors,
in accordance with the following provisions.

(5) A resolution of the directors—
(a) must be authorised by the company's articles, and
(b) is not sufficient sanction for payments to or for the benefit of directors, former directors or shadow directors.

(6) Any other requirements of the company's articles as to the exercise of the power conferred by this section must be complied with.

(7) Any payment under this section must be made—

(a) before the commencement of any winding up of the company, and
(b) out of profits of the company that are available for dividend.

Records of meetings of directors

248 Minutes of directors' meetings

(1) Every company must cause minutes of all proceedings at meetings of its directors to be recorded.
(2) The records must be kept for at least ten years from the date of the meeting.
(3) If a company fails to comply with this section, an offence is committed by every officer of the company who is in default.
(4) A person guilty of an offence under this section is liable on summary conviction to a fine not exceeding level 3 on the standard scale and, for continued contravention, a daily default fine not exceeding one-tenth of level 3 on the standard scale.

249 Minutes as evidence

(1) Minutes recorded in accordance with section 248, if purporting to be authenticated by the chairman of the meeting or by the chairman of the next directors' meeting, are evidence (in Scotland, sufficient evidence) of the proceedings at the meeting.
(2) Where minutes have been made in accordance with that section of the proceedings of a meeting of directors, then, until the contrary is proved—
(a) the meeting is deemed duly held and convened,
(b) all proceedings at the meeting are deemed to have duly taken place, and
(c) all appointments at the meeting are deemed valid.

Meaning of 'director' and 'shadow director'

250 "Director"

In the Companies Acts "director" includes any person occupying the position of director, by whatever name called.

251 "Shadow director"

(1) In the Companies Acts "shadow director", in relation to a company, means a person in accordance with whose directions or instructions the directors of the company are accustomed to act.
(2) A person is not to be regarded as a shadow director by reason only that the directors act on advice given by him in a professional capacity.
(3) A body corporate is not to be regarded as a shadow director of any of its subsidiary companies for the purposes of—
Chapter 2 (general duties of directors),
Chapter 4 (transactions requiring members' approval), or
Chapter 6 (contract with sole member who is also a director),
by reason only that the directors of the subsidiary are accustomed to act in accordance with its directions or instructions.

Other definitions

252 Persons connected with a director

(1) This section defines what is meant by references in this Part to a person being "connected" with a director of a company (or a director being "connected" with a person).
(2) The following persons (and only those persons) are connected with a director of a company—
(a) members of the director's family (see section 253);
(b) a body corporate with which the director is connected (as defined in section 254);
(c) a person acting in his capacity as trustee of a trust—
(i) the beneficiaries of which include the director or a person who by virtue of paragraph (a) or (b) is connected with him, or

(ii) the terms of which confer a power on the trustees that may be exercised for the benefit of the director or any such person,

other than a trust for the purposes of an employees' share scheme or a pension scheme;

(d) a person acting in his capacity as partner—

(i) of the director, or

(ii) of a person who, by virtue of paragraph (a), (b) or (c), is connected with that director;

(e) a firm that is a legal person under the law by which it is governed and in which—

(i) the director is a partner,

(ii) a partner is a person who, by virtue of paragraph (a), (b) or (c) is connected with the director, or

(iii) a partner is a firm in which the director is a partner or in which there is a partner who, by virtue of paragraph (a), (b) or (c), is connected with the director.

(3) References in this Part to a person connected with a director of a company do not include a person who is himself a director of the company.

253 Members of a director's family

(1) This section defines what is meant by references in this Part to members of a director's family.

(2) For the purposes of this Part the members of a director's family are—

(a) the director's spouse or civil partner;

(b) any other person (whether of a different sex or the same sex) with whom the director lives as partner in an enduring family relationship;

(c) the director's children or step-children;

(d) any children or step-children of a person within paragraph (b) (and who are not children or step-children of the director) who live with the director and have not attained the age of 18;

(e) the director's parents.

(3) Subsection (2)(b) does not apply if the other person is the director's grandparent or grandchild, sister, brother, aunt or uncle, or nephew or niece.

254 Director "connected with" a body corporate

(1) This section defines what is meant by references in this Part to a director being "connected with" a body corporate.

(2) A director is connected with a body corporate if, but only if, he and the persons connected with him together—

(a) are interested in shares comprised in the equity share capital of that body corporate of a nominal value equal to at least 20% of that share capital, or

(b) are entitled to exercise or control the exercise of more than 20% of the voting power at any general meeting of that body.

(3) The rules set out in Schedule 1 (references to interest in shares or debentures) apply for the purposes of this section.

(4) References in this section to voting power the exercise of which is controlled by a director include voting power whose exercise is controlled by a body corporate controlled by him.

(5) Shares in a company held as treasury shares, and any voting rights attached to such shares, are disregarded for the purposes of this section.

(6) For the avoidance of circularity in the application of section 252 (meaning of "connected person")—

(a) a body corporate with which a director is connected is not treated for the purposes of this section as connected with him unless it is also connected with him by virtue of subsection (2)(c) or (d) of that section (connection as trustee or partner); and

(b) a trustee of a trust the beneficiaries of which include (or may include) a body corporate with which a director is connected is not treated for the purposes of this section as connected with a director by reason only of that fact.

255 Director "controlling" a body corporate

(1) This section defines what is meant by references in this Part to a director "controlling" a body corporate.

(2) A director of a company is taken to control a body corporate if, but only if—

(a) he or any person connected with him—

(i) is interested in any part of the equity share capital of that body, or

(ii) is entitled to exercise or control the exercise of any part of the voting power at any general meeting of that body, and

(b) he, the persons connected with him and the other directors of that company, together—

(i) are interested in more than 50% of that share capital, or

(ii) are entitled to exercise or control the exercise of more than 50% of that voting power.

(3) The rules set out in Schedule 1 (references to interest in shares or debentures) apply for the purposes of this section.

(4) References in this section to voting power the exercise of which is controlled by a director include voting power whose exercise is controlled by a body corporate controlled by him.

(5) Shares in a company held as treasury shares, and any voting rights attached to such shares, are disregarded for the purposes of this section.

(6) For the avoidance of circularity in the application of section 252 (meaning of "connected person")—

(a) a body corporate with which a director is connected is not treated for the purposes of this section as connected with him unless it is also connected with him by virtue of subsection (2)(c) or (d) of that section (connection as trustee or partner); and

(b) a trustee of a trust the beneficiaries of which include (or may include) a body corporate with which a director is connected is not treated for the purposes of this section as connected with a director by reason only of that fact.

256 Associated bodies corporate

For the purposes of this Part—

(a) bodies corporate are associated if one is a subsidiary of the other or both are subsidiaries of the same body corporate, and

(b) companies are associated if one is a subsidiary of the other or both are subsidiaries of the same body corporate.

257 References to company's constitution

(1) References in this Part to a company's constitution include—

(a) any resolution or other decision come to in accordance with the constitution, and

(b) any decision by the members of the company, or a class of members, that is treated by virtue of any enactment or rule of law as equivalent to a decision by the company.

(2) This is in addition to the matters mentioned in section 17 (general provision as to matters contained in company's constitution).

General

258 Power to increase financial limits

(1) The Secretary of State may by order substitute for any sum of money specified in this Part a larger sum specified in the order.

(2) An order under this section is subject to negative resolution procedure.

(3) An order does not have effect in relation to anything done or not done before it comes into force. Accordingly, proceedings in respect of any liability incurred before that time may be continued or instituted as if the order had not been made.

259 Transactions under foreign law

For the purposes of this Part it is immaterial whether the law that (apart from this Act) governs an arrangement or transaction is the law of the United Kingdom, or a part of it, or not.

PART 11
DERIVATIVE CLAIMS AND PROCEEDINGS BY MEMBERS

CHAPTER 1
DERIVATIVE CLAIMS IN ENGLAND AND WALES OR NORTHERN IRELAND

260 Derivative claims

(1) This Chapter applies to proceedings in England and Wales or Northern Ireland by a member of a company—
- (a) in respect of a cause of action vested in the company, and
- (b) seeking relief on behalf of the company.

This is referred to in this Chapter as a "derivative claim".

(2) A derivative claim may only be brought—
- (a) under this Chapter, or
- (b) in pursuance of an order of the court in proceedings under section 994 (proceedings for protection of members against unfair prejudice).

(3) A derivative claim under this Chapter may be brought only in respect of a cause of action arising from an actual or proposed act or omission involving negligence, default, breach of duty or breach of trust by a director of the company.

The cause of action may be against the director or another person (or both).

(4) It is immaterial whether the cause of action arose before or after the person seeking to bring or continue the derivative claim became a member of the company.

(5) For the purposes of this Chapter—
- (a) "director" includes a former director;
- (b) a shadow director is treated as a director; and
- (c) references to a member of a company include a person who is not a member but to whom shares in the company have been transferred or transmitted by operation of law.

261 Application for permission to continue derivative claim

(1) A member of a company who brings a derivative claim under this Chapter must apply to the court for permission (in Northern Ireland, leave) to continue it.

(2) If it appears to the court that the application and the evidence filed by the applicant in support of it do not disclose a prima facie case for giving permission (or leave), the court—
- (a) must dismiss the application, and
- (b) may make any consequential order it considers appropriate.

(3) If the application is not dismissed under subsection (2), the court—
- (a) may give directions as to the evidence to be provided by the company, and
- (b) may adjourn the proceedings to enable the evidence to be obtained.

(4) On hearing the application, the court may—
- (a) give permission (or leave) to continue the claim on such terms as it thinks fit,
- (b) refuse permission (or leave) and dismiss the claim, or
- (c) adjourn the proceedings on the application and give such directions as it thinks fit.

262 Application for permission to continue claim as a derivative claim

(1) This section applies where—
- (a) a company has brought a claim, and
- (b) the cause of action on which the claim is based could be pursued as a derivative claim under this Chapter.

(2) A member of the company may apply to the court for permission (in Northern Ireland, leave) to continue the claim as a derivative claim on the ground that—
- (a) the manner in which the company commenced or continued the claim amounts to an abuse of the process of the court,
- (b) the company has failed to prosecute the claim diligently, and
- (c) it is appropriate for the member to continue the claim as a derivative claim.

(3) If it appears to the court that the application and the evidence filed by the applicant in support of it do not disclose a prima facie case for giving permission (or leave), the court—
(a) must dismiss the application, and
(b) may make any consequential order it considers appropriate.

(4) If the application is not dismissed under subsection (3), the court—
(a) may give directions as to the evidence to be provided by the company, and
(b) may adjourn the proceedings to enable the evidence to be obtained.

(5) On hearing the application, the court may—
(a) give permission (or leave) to continue the claim as a derivative claim on such terms as it thinks fit,
(b) refuse permission (or leave) and dismiss the application, or
(c) adjourn the proceedings on the application and give such directions as it thinks fit.

263 Whether permission to be given

(1) The following provisions have effect where a member of a company applies for permission (in Northern Ireland, leave) under section 261 or 262.

(2) Permission (or leave) must be refused if the court is satisfied—
(a) that a person acting in accordance with section 172 (duty to promote the success of the company) would not seek to continue the claim, or
(b) where the cause of action arises from an act or omission that is yet to occur, that the act or omission has been authorised by the company, or
(c) where the cause of action arises from an act or omission that has already occurred, that the act or omission—
(i) was authorised by the company before it occurred, or
(ii) has been ratified by the company since it occurred.

(3) In considering whether to give permission (or leave) the court must take into account, in particular—
(a) whether the member is acting in good faith in seeking to continue the claim;
(b) the importance that a person acting in accordance with section 172 (duty to promote the success of the company) would attach to continuing it;
(c) where the cause of action results from an act or omission that is yet to occur, whether the act or omission could be, and in the circumstances would be likely to be—
(i) authorised by the company before it occurs, or
(ii) ratified by the company after it occurs;
(d) where the cause of action arises from an act or omission that has already occurred, whether the act or omission could be, and in the circumstances would be likely to be, ratified by the company;
(e) whether the company has decided not to pursue the claim;
(f) whether the act or omission in respect of which the claim is brought gives rise to a cause of action that the member could pursue in his own right rather than on behalf of the company.

(4) In considering whether to give permission (or leave) the court shall have particular regard to any evidence before it as to the views of members of the company who have no personal interest, direct or indirect, in the matter.

(5) The Secretary of State may by regulations—
(a) amend subsection (2) so as to alter or add to the circumstances in which permission (or leave) is to be refused;
(b) amend subsection (3) so as to alter or add to the matters that the court is required to take into account in considering whether to give permission (or leave).

(6) Before making any such regulations the Secretary of State shall consult such persons as he considers appropriate.

(7) Regulations under this section are subject to affirmative resolution procedure.

264 Application for permission to continue derivative claim brought by another member

(1) This section applies where a member of a company ("the claimant")—
(a) has brought a derivative claim,
(b) has continued as a derivative claim a claim brought by the company, or
(c) has continued a derivative claim under this section.

(2) Another member of the company ("the applicant") may apply to the court for permission (in Northern Ireland, leave) to continue the claim on the ground that—
(a) the manner in which the proceedings have been commenced or continued by the claimant amounts to an abuse of the process of the court,
(b) the claimant has failed to prosecute the claim diligently, and
(c) it is appropriate for the applicant to continue the claim as a derivative claim.

(3) If it appears to the court that the application and the evidence filed by the applicant in support of it do not disclose a prima facie case for giving permission (or leave), the court—
(a) must dismiss the application, and
(b) may make any consequential order it considers appropriate.

(4) If the application is not dismissed under subsection (3), the court—
(a) may give directions as to the evidence to be provided by the company, and
(b) may adjourn the proceedings to enable the evidence to be obtained.

(5) On hearing the application, the court may—
(a) give permission (or leave) to continue the claim on such terms as it thinks fit,
(b) refuse permission (or leave) and dismiss the application, or
(c) adjourn the proceedings on the application and give such directions as it thinks fit.

CHAPTER 2
DERIVATIVE PROCEEDINGS IN SCOTLAND

265 Derivative proceedings

(1) In Scotland, a member of a company may raise proceedings in respect of an act or omission specified in subsection (3) in order to protect the interests of the company and obtain a remedy on its behalf.

(2) A member of a company may raise such proceedings only under subsection (1).

(3) The act or omission referred to in subsection (1) is any actual or proposed act or omission involving negligence, default, breach of duty or breach of trust by a director of the company.

(4) Proceedings may be raised under subsection (1) against (either or both)—
(a) the director referred to in subsection (3), or
(b) another person.

(5) It is immaterial whether the act or omission in respect of which the proceedings are to be raised or, in the case of continuing proceedings under section 267 or 269, are raised, arose before or after the person seeking to raise or continue them became a member of the company.

(6) This section does not affect—
(a) any right of a member of a company to raise proceedings in respect of an act or omission specified in subsection (3) in order to protect his own interests and obtain a remedy on his own behalf, or
(b) the court's power to make an order under section 996(2) (c) or anything done under such an order.

(7) In this Chapter—
(a) proceedings raised under subsection (1) are referred to as "derivative proceedings",
(b) the act or omission in respect of which they are raised is referred to as the "cause of action",
(c) "director" includes a former director,
(d) references to a director include a shadow director, and
(e) references to a member of a company include a person who is not a member but to whom shares in the company have been transferred or transmitted by operation of law.

266 Requirement for leave and notice

(1) Derivative proceedings may be raised by a member of a company only with the leave of the court.

(2) An application for leave must—

(a) specify the cause of action, and

(b) summarise the facts on which the derivative proceedings are to be based.

(3) If it appears to the court that the application and the evidence produced by the applicant in support of it do not disclose a prima facie case for granting it, the court—

(a) must refuse the application, and

(b) may make any consequential order it considers appropriate.

(4) If the application is not refused under subsection (3)—

(a) the applicant must serve the application on the company,

(b) the court—

(i) may make an order requiring evidence to be produced by the company, and

(ii) may adjourn the proceedings on the application to enable the evidence to be obtained, and

(c) the company is entitled to take part in the further proceedings on the application.

(5) On hearing the application, the court may—

(a) grant the application on such terms as it thinks fit,

(b) refuse the application, or

(c) adjourn the proceedings on the application and make such order as to further procedure as it thinks fit.

267 Application to continue proceedings as derivative proceedings

(1) This section applies where—

(a) a company has raised proceedings, and

(b) the proceedings are in respect of an act or omission which could be the basis for derivative proceedings.

(2) A member of the company may apply to the court to be substituted for the company in the proceedings, and for the proceedings to continue in consequence as derivative proceedings, on the ground that—

(a) the manner in which the company commenced or continued the proceedings amounts to an abuse of the process of the court,

(b) the company has failed to prosecute the proceedings diligently, and

(c) it is appropriate for the member to be substituted for the company in the proceedings.

(3) If it appears to the court that the application and the evidence produced by the applicant in support of it do not disclose a prima facie case for granting it, the court—

(a) must refuse the application, and

(b) may make any consequential order it considers appropriate.

(4) If the application is not refused under subsection (3)—

(a) the applicant must serve the application on the company,

(b) the court—

(i) may make an order requiring evidence to be produced by the company, and

(ii) may adjourn the proceedings on the application to enable the evidence to be obtained, and

(c) the company is entitled to take part in the further proceedings on the application.

(5) On hearing the application, the court may—

(a) grant the application on such terms as it thinks fit,

(b) refuse the application, or

(c) adjourn the proceedings on the application and make such order as to further procedure as it thinks fit.

268 Granting of leave

(1) The court must refuse leave to raise derivative proceedings or an application under section 267 if satisfied—

(a) that a person acting in accordance with section 172 (duty to promote the success of the company) would not seek to raise or continue the proceedings (as the case may be), or

(b) where the cause of action is an act or omission that is yet to occur, that the act or omission has been authorised by the company, or

(c) where the cause of action is an act or omission that has already occurred, that the act or omission—

(i) was authorised by the company before it occurred, or

(ii) has been ratified by the company since it occurred.

(2) In considering whether to grant leave to raise derivative proceedings or an application under section 267, the court must take into account, in particular—

(a) whether the member is acting in good faith in seeking to raise or continue the proceedings (as the case may be),

(b) the importance that a person acting in accordance with section 172 (duty to promote the success of the company) would attach to raising or continuing them (as the case may be),

(c) where the cause of action is an act or omission that is yet to occur, whether the act or omission could be, and in the circumstances would be likely to be—

(i) authorised by the company before it occurs, or

(ii) ratified by the company after it occurs,

(d) where the cause of action is an act or omission that has already occurred, whether the act or omission could be, and in the circumstances would be likely to be, ratified by the company,

(e) whether the company has decided not to raise proceedings in respect of the same cause of action or to persist in the proceedings (as the case may be),

(f) whether the cause of action is one which the member could pursue in his own right rather than on behalf of the company.

(3) In considering whether to grant leave to raise derivative proceedings or an application under section 267, the court shall have particular regard to any evidence before it as to the views of members of the company who have no personal interest, direct or indirect, in the matter.

(4) The Secretary of State may by regulations—

(a) amend subsection (1) so as to alter or add to the circumstances in which leave or an application is to be refused,

(b) amend subsection (2) so as to alter or add to the matters that the court is required to take into account in considering whether to grant leave or an application.

(5) Before making any such regulations the Secretary of State shall consult such persons as he considers appropriate.

(6) Regulations under this section are subject to affirmative resolution procedure.

269 Application by member to be substituted for member pursuing derivative proceedings

(1) This section applies where a member of a company ("the claimant")—

(a) has raised derivative proceedings,

(b) has continued as derivative proceedings raised by the company, or

(c) has continued derivative proceedings under this section.

(2) Another member of the company ("the applicant") may apply to the court to be substituted for the claimant in the action on the ground that—

(a) the manner in which the proceedings have been commenced or continued by the claimant amounts to an abuse of the process of the court,

(b) the claimant has failed to prosecute the proceedings diligently, and

(c) it is appropriate for the applicant to be substituted for the claimant in the proceedings.

(3) If it appears to the court that the application and the evidence produced by the applicant in support of it do not disclose a prima facie case for granting it, the court—

(a) must refuse the application, and

(b) may make any consequential order it considers appropriate.

(4) If the application is not refused under subsection (3)—

(a) the applicant must serve the application on the company,

(b) the court—

(i) may make an order requiring evidence to be produced by the company, and

(ii) may adjourn the proceedings on the application to enable the evidence to be obtained, and

(c) the company is entitled to take part in the further proceedings on the application.

(5) On hearing the application, the court may—

(a) grant the application on such terms as it thinks fit,

(b) refuse the application, or

(c) adjourn the proceedings on the application and make such order as to further procedure as it thinks fit.

PART 12
COMPANY SECRETARIES

Private companies

270 Private company not required to have secretary

(1) A private company is not required to have a secretary.

(2) References in the Companies Acts to a private company "without a secretary" are to a private company that for the time being is taking advantage of the exemption in subsection (1); and references to a private company "with a secretary" shall be construed accordingly.

(3) In the case of a private company without a secretary—

(a) anything authorised or required to be given or sent to, or served on, the company by being sent to its secretary—

(i) may be given or sent to, or served on, the company itself, and

(ii) if addressed to the secretary shall be treated as addressed to the company; and

(b) anything else required or authorised to be done by or to the secretary of the company may be done by or to—

(i) a director, or

(ii) a person authorised generally or specifically in that behalf by the directors.

Public companies

271 Public company required to have secretary

A public company must have a secretary.

272 Direction requiring public company to appoint secretary

(1) If it appears to the Secretary of State that a public company is in breach of section 271 (requirement to have secretary), the Secretary of State may give the company a direction under this section.

(2) The direction must state that the company appears to be in breach of that section and specify—

(a) what the company must do in order to comply with the direction, and

(b) the period within which it must do so.

That period must be not less than one month or more than three months after the date on which the direction is given.

(3) The direction must also inform the company of the consequences of failing to comply.

(4) Where the company is in breach of section 271 it must comply with the direction by—

(a) making the necessary appointment, and

(b) giving notice of it under section 276,

before the end of the period specified in the direction.

(5) If the company has already made the necessary appointment, it must comply with the direction by giving notice of it under section 276 before the end of the period specified in the direction.

(6) If a company fails to comply with a direction under this section, an offence is committed by—
(a) the company, and
(b) every officer of the company who is in default.
For this purpose a shadow director is treated as an officer of the company.

(7) A person guilty of an offence under this section is liable on summary conviction to a fine not exceeding level 5 on the standard scale and, for continued contravention, a daily default fine not exceeding one-tenth of level 5 on the standard scale.

273 Qualifications of secretaries of public companies

(1) It is the duty of the directors of a public company to take all reasonable steps to secure that the secretary (or each joint secretary) of the company—
(a) is a person who appears to them to have the requisite knowledge and experience to discharge the functions of secretary of the company, and
(b) has one or more of the following qualifications.

(2) The qualifications are—
(a) that he has held the office of secretary of a public company for at least three of the five years immediately preceding his appointment as secretary;
(b) that he is a member of any of the bodies specified in subsection (3);
(c) that he is a barrister, advocate or solicitor called or admitted in any part of the United Kingdom;
(d) that he is a person who, by virtue of his holding or having held any other position or his being a member of any other body, appears to the directors to be capable of discharging the functions of secretary of the company.

(3) The bodies referred to in subsection (2)(b) are—
(a) the Institute of Chartered Accountants in England and Wales;
(b) the Institute of Chartered Accountants of Scotland;
(c) the Association of Chartered Certified Accountants;
(d) the Institute of Chartered Accountants in Ireland;
(e) the Institute of Chartered Secretaries and Administrators;
(f) the Chartered Institute of Management Accountants;
(g) the Chartered Institute of Public Finance and Accountancy.

Provisions applying to private companies with a secretary and to public companies

274 Discharge of functions where office vacant or secretary unable to act

Where in the case of any company the office of secretary is vacant, or there is for any other reason no secretary capable of acting, anything required or authorised to be done by or to the secretary may be done—
(a) by or to an assistant or deputy secretary (if any), or
(b) if there is no assistant or deputy secretary or none capable of acting, by or to any person authorised generally or specifically in that behalf by the directors.

275 Duty to keep register of secretaries

(1) A company must keep a register of its secretaries.

(2) The register must contain the required particulars (see sections 277 to 279) of the person who is, or persons who are, the secretary or joint secretaries of the company.

(3) The register must be kept available for inspection—
(a) at the company's registered office, or
(b) at a place specified in regulations under section 1136.

(4) The company must give notice to the registrar—
(a) of the place at which the register is kept available for inspection, and
(b) of any change in that place,
unless it has at all times been kept at the company's registered office.

(5) The register must be open to the inspection—

(a) of any member of the company without charge, and

(b) of any other person on payment of such fee as may be prescribed.

(6) If default is made in complying with subsection (1), (2) or (3), or if default is made for 14 days in complying with subsection (4), or if an inspection required under subsection (5) is refused, an offence is committed by—

(a) the company, and

(b) every officer of the company who is in default.

For this purpose a shadow director is treated as an officer of the company.

(7) A person guilty of an offence under this section is liable on summary conviction to a fine not exceeding level 5 on the standard scale and, for continued contravention, a daily default fine not exceeding one-tenth of level 5 on the standard scale.

(8) In the case of a refusal of inspection of the register, the court may by order compel an immediate inspection of it.

276 Duty to notify registrar of changes

(1) A company must, within the period of 14 days from—

(a) a person becoming or ceasing to be its secretary or one of its joint secretaries, or

(b) the occurrence of any change in the particulars contained in its register of secretaries,

give notice to the registrar of the change and of the date on which it occurred.

(2) Notice of a person having become secretary, or one of joint secretaries, of the company must be accompanied by a consent by that person to act in the relevant capacity.

(3) If default is made in complying with this section, an offence is committed by every officer of the company who is in default.

For this purpose a shadow director is treated as an officer of the company.

(4) A person guilty of an offence under this section is liable on summary conviction to a fine not exceeding level 5 on the standard scale and, for continued contravention, a daily default fine not exceeding one-tenth of level 5 on the standard scale.

277 Particulars of secretaries to be registered: individuals

(1) A company's register of secretaries must contain the following particulars in the case of an individual—

(a) name and any former name;

(b) address.

(2) For the purposes of this section "name" means a person's Christian name (or other forename) and surname, except that in the case of—

(a) a peer, or

(b) an individual usually known by a title,

the title may be stated instead of his Christian name (or other forename) and surname or in addition to either or both of them.

(3) For the purposes of this section a "former name" means a name by which the individual was formerly known for business purposes.

Where a person is or was formerly known by more than one such name, each of them must be stated.

(4) It is not necessary for the register to contain particulars of a former name in the following cases—

(a) in the case of a peer or an individual normally known by a British title, where the name is one by which the person was known previous to the adoption of or succession to the title;

(b) in the case of any person, where the former name—

(i) was changed or disused before the person attained the age of 16 years, or

(ii) has been changed or disused for 20 years or more.

(5) The address required to be stated in the register is a service address. This may be stated to be "The company's registered office".

278 Particulars of secretaries to be registered: corporate secretaries and firms

(1) A company's register of secretaries must contain the following particulars in the case of a body corporate, or a firm that is a legal person under the law by which it is governed—
(a) corporate or firm name;
(b) registered or principal office;
(c) in the case of an EEA company to which the First Company Law Directive (68/151/EEC) applies, particulars of—
(i) the register in which the company file mentioned in Article 3 of that Directive is kept (including details of the relevant state), and
(ii) the registration number in that register;
(d) in any other case, particulars of—
(i) the legal form of the company or firm and the law by which it is governed, and
(ii) if applicable, the register in which it is entered (including details of the state) and its registration number in that register.

(2) If all the partners in a firm are joint secretaries it is sufficient to state the particulars that would be required if the firm were a legal person and the firm had been appointed secretary.

279 Particulars of secretaries to be registered: power to make regulations

(1) The Secretary of State may make provision by regulations amending—
section 277 (particulars of secretaries to be registered: individuals), or
section 278 (particulars of secretaries to be registered: corporate secretaries and firms),
so as to add to or remove items from the particulars required to be contained in a company's register of secretaries.

(2) Regulations under this section are subject to affirmative resolution procedure.

280 Acts done by person in dual capacity

A provision requiring or authorising a thing to be done by or to a director and the secretary of a company is not satisfied by its being done by or to the same person acting both as director and as, or in place of, the secretary.

PART 13
RESOLUTIONS AND MEETINGS

CHAPTER 1
GENERAL PROVISIONS ABOUT RESOLUTIONS

281 Resolutions

(1) A resolution of the members (or of a class of members) of a private company must be passed—
(a) as a written resolution in accordance with Chapter 2, or
(b) at a meeting of the members (to which the provisions of Chapter 3 apply).

(2) A resolution of the members (or of a class of members) of a public company must be passed at a meeting of the members (to which the provisions of Chapter 3 and, where relevant, Chapter 4 apply).

(3) Where a provision of the Companies Acts—
(a) requires a resolution of a company, or of the members (or a class of members) of a company, and
(b) does not specify what kind of resolution is required,
what is required is an ordinary resolution unless the company's articles require a higher majority (or unanimity).

(4) Nothing in this Part affects any enactment or rule of law as to—
(a) things done otherwise than by passing a resolution,
(b) circumstances in which a resolution is or is not treated as having been passed, or
(c) cases in which a person is precluded from alleging that a resolution has not been duly passed.

282 Ordinary resolutions

(1) An ordinary resolution of the members (or of a class of members) of a company means a resolution that is passed by a simple majority.

(2) A written resolution is passed by a simple majority if it is passed by members representing a simple majority of the total voting rights of eligible members (see Chapter 2).

(3) A resolution passed at a meeting on a show of hands is passed by a simple majority if it is passed by a simple majority of the votes cast by those entitled to vote

(4) A resolution passed on a poll taken at a meeting is passed by a simple majority if it is passed by members representing a simple majority of the total voting rights of members who (being entitled to do so) vote in person, by proxy or in advance (see section 322A) on the resolution.

(5) Anything that may be done by ordinary resolution may also be done by special resolution.

283 Special resolutions

(1) A special resolution of the members (or of a class of members) of a company means a resolution passed by a majority of not less than 75%.

(2) A written resolution is passed by a majority of not less than 75% if it is passed by members representing not less than 75% of the total voting rights of eligible members (see Chapter 2).

(3) Where a resolution of a private company is passed as a written resolution—
   (a) the resolution is not a special resolution unless it stated that it was proposed as a special resolution, and
   (b) if the resolution so stated, it may only be passed as a special resolution.

(4) A resolution passed at a meeting on a show of hands is passed by a majority of not less than 75% if it is passed by not less than 75% of the votes cast by those entitled to vote.

(5) A resolution passed on a poll taken at a meeting is passed by a majority of not less than 75% if it is passed by members representing not less than 75% of the total voting rights of the members who (being entitled to do so) vote in person, by proxy or in advance (see section 322A) on the resolution.

(6) Where a resolution is passed at a meeting—
   (a) the resolution is not a special resolution unless the notice of the meeting included the text of the resolution and specified the intention to propose the resolution as a special resolution, and
   (b) if the notice of the meeting so specified, the resolution may only be passed as a special resolution.

284 Votes: general rules

(1) On a vote on a written resolution—
   (a) in the case of a company having a share capital, every member has one vote in respect of each share or each £10 of stock held by him, and
   (b) in any other case, every member has one vote.

(2) On a vote on a resolution on a show of hands at a meeting, each member present in person has one vote.

(3) On a vote on a resolution on a poll taken at a meeting—
   (a) in the case of a company having a share capital, every member has one vote in respect of each share or each £10 of stock held by him, and
   (b) in any other case, every member has one vote.

(4) The provisions of this section have effect subject to any provision of the company's articles.

(5) Nothing in this section is to be read as restricting the effect of—
section 152 (exercise of rights by nominees),
section 285 (voting by proxy),
section 322 (exercise of voting rights on poll),
section 322A (voting on a poll: votes cast in advance), or
section 323 (representation of corporations at meetings).

285 Voting by proxy

(1) On a vote on a resolution on a show of hands at a meeting, every proxy present who has been duly appointed by one or more members entitled to vote on the resolution has one vote.

This is subject to subsection (2).

(2) On a vote on a resolution on a show of hands at a meeting, a proxy has one vote for and one vote against the resolution if—

(a) the proxy has been duly appointed by more than one member entitled to vote on the resolution, and

(b) the proxy has been instructed by one or more of those members to vote for the resolution and by one or more other of those members to vote against it.

(3) On a poll taken at a meeting of a company all or any of the voting rights of a member may be exercised by one or more duly appointed proxies.

(4) Where a member appoints more than one proxy, subsection (3) does not authorise the exercise by the proxies taken together of more extensive voting rights than could be exercised by the member in person.

(5) Subsections (1) and (2) have effect subject to any provision of the company's articles.

285A Voting rights on poll or written resolution

In relation to a resolution required or authorised by an enactment, if a private company's articles provide that a member has a different number of votes in relation to a resolution when it is passed as a written resolution and when it is passed on a poll taken at a meeting—

(a) the provision about how many votes a member has in relation to the resolution passed on a poll is void, and

(b) a member has the same number of votes in relation to the resolution when it is passed on a poll as the member has when it is passed as a written resolution.

286 Votes of joint holders of shares

(1) In the case of joint holders of shares of a company, only the vote of the senior holder who votes (and any proxies duly authorised by him) may be counted by the company.

(2) For the purposes of this section, the senior holder of a share is determined by the order in which the names of the joint holders appear in the register of members.

(3) Subsections (1) and (2) have effect subject to any provision of the company's articles.

287 Saving for provisions of articles as to determination of entitlement to vote

Nothing in this Chapter affects—

(a) any provision of a company's articles—

(i) requiring an objection to a person's entitlement to vote on a resolution to be made in accordance with the articles, and

(ii) for the determination of any such objection to be final and conclusive, or

(b) the grounds on which such a determination may be questioned in legal proceedings.

CHAPTER 2
WRITTEN RESOLUTIONS

General provisions about written resolutions

288 Written resolutions of private companies

(1) In the Companies Acts a "written resolution" means a resolution of a private company proposed and passed in accordance with this Chapter.

(2) The following may not be passed as a written resolution—

(a) a resolution under section 168 removing a director before the expiration of his period of office;

(b) a resolution under section 510 removing an auditor before the expiration of his term of office.

(3) A resolution may be proposed as a written resolution—
(a) by the directors of a private company (see section 291), or
(b) by the members of a private company (see sections 292 to 295).

(4) References in enactments passed or made before this Chapter comes into force to—
(a) a resolution of a company in general meeting, or
(b) a resolution of a meeting of a class of members of the company,
have effect as if they included references to a written resolution of the members, or of a class of members, of a private company (as appropriate).

(5) A written resolution of a private company has effect as if passed (as the case may be)—
(a) by the company in general meeting, or
(b) by a meeting of a class of members of the company,
and references in enactments passed or made before this section comes into force to a meeting at which a resolution is passed or to members voting in favour of a resolution shall be construed accordingly.

289 Eligible members

(1) In relation to a resolution proposed as a written resolution of a private company, the eligible members are the members who would have been entitled to vote on the resolution on the circulation date of the resolution (see section 290).

(2) If the persons entitled to vote on a written resolution change during the course of the day that is the circulation date of the resolution, the eligible members are the persons entitled to vote on the resolution at the time that the first copy of the resolution is sent or submitted to a member for his agreement.

Circulation of written resolutions

290 Circulation date

References in this Part to the circulation date of a written resolution are to the date on which copies of it are sent or submitted to members in accordance with this Chapter (or if copies are sent or submitted to members on different days, to the first of those days).

291 Circulation of written resolutions proposed by directors

(1) This section applies to a resolution proposed as a written resolution by the directors of the company.

(2) The company must send or submit a copy of the resolution to every eligible member.

(3) The company must do so—
(a) by sending copies at the same time (so far as reasonably practicable) to all eligible members in hard copy form, in electronic form or by means of a website, or
(b) if it is possible to do so without undue delay, by submitting the same copy to each eligible member in turn (or different copies to each of a number of eligible members in turn),
or by sending copies to some members in accordance with paragraph (a) and submitting a copy or copies to other members in accordance with paragraph (b).

(4) The copy of the resolution must be accompanied by a statement informing the member—
(a) how to signify agreement to the resolution (see section 296), and
(b) as to the date by which the resolution must be passed if it is not to lapse (see section 297).

(5) In the event of default in complying with this section, an offence is committed by every officer of the company who is in default.

(6) A person guilty of an offence under this section is liable—
(a) on conviction on indictment, to a fine;
(b) on summary conviction, to a fine not exceeding the statutory maximum.

(7) The validity of the resolution, if passed, is not affected by a failure to comply with this section.

292 Members' power to require circulation of written resolution

(1) The members of a private company may require the company to circulate a resolution that may properly be moved and is proposed to be moved as a written resolution.

(2) Any resolution may properly be moved as a written resolution unless—

(a) it would, if passed, be ineffective (whether by reason of inconsistency with any enactment or the company's constitution or otherwise),

(b) it is defamatory of any person, or

(c) it is frivolous or vexatious.

(3) Where the members require a company to circulate a resolution they may require the company to circulate with it a statement of not more than 1,000 words on the subject matter of the resolution.

(4) A company is required to circulate the resolution and any accompanying statement once it has received requests that it do so from members representing not less than the requisite percentage of the total voting rights of all members entitled to vote on the resolution.

(5) The "requisite percentage" is 5% or such lower percentage as is specified for this purpose in the company's articles.

(6) A request—

(a) may be in hard copy form or in electronic form,

(b) must identify the resolution and any accompanying statement, and

(c) must be authenticated by the person or persons making it.

293 Circulation of written resolution proposed by members

(1) A company that is required under section 292 to circulate a resolution must send or submit to every eligible member—

(a) a copy of the resolution, and

(b) a copy of any accompanying statement.

This is subject to section 294(2) (deposit or tender of sum in respect of expenses of circulation) and section 295 (application not to circulate members' statement).

(2) The company must do so—

(a) by sending copies at the same time (so far as reasonably practicable) to all eligible members in hard copy form, in electronic form or by means of a website, or

(b) if it is possible to do so without undue delay, by submitting the same copy to each eligible member in turn (or different copies to each of a number of eligible members in turn),

or by sending copies to some members in accordance with paragraph (a) and submitting a copy or copies to other members in accordance with paragraph (b).

(3) The company must send or submit the copies (or, if copies are sent or submitted to members on different days, the first of those copies) not more than 21 days after it becomes subject to the requirement under section 292 to circulate the resolution.

(4) The copy of the resolution must be accompanied by guidance as to—

(a) how to signify agreement to the resolution (see section 296), and

(b) the date by which the resolution must be passed if it is not to lapse (see section 297).

(5) In the event of default in complying with this section, an offence is committed by every officer of the company who is in default.

(6) A person guilty of an offence under this section is liable—

(a) on conviction on indictment, to a fine;

(b) on summary conviction, to a fine not exceeding the statutory maximum.

(7) The validity of the resolution, if passed, is not affected by a failure to comply with this section.

294 Expenses of circulation

(1) The expenses of the company in complying with section 293 must be paid by the members who requested the circulation of the resolution unless the company resolves otherwise.

(2) Unless the company has previously so resolved, it is not bound to comply with that section unless there is deposited with or tendered to it a sum reasonably sufficient to meet its expenses in doing so.

295 Application not to circulate members' statement

(1) A company is not required to circulate a members' statement under section 293 if, on an application by the company or another person who claims to be aggrieved, the court is satisfied that the rights conferred by section 292 and that section are being abused.

(2) The court may order the members who requested the circulation of the statement to pay the whole or part of the company's costs (in Scotland, expenses) on such an application, even if they are not parties to the application.

Agreeing to written resolutions

296 Procedure for signifying agreement to written resolution

(1) A member signifies his agreement to a proposed written resolution when the company receives from him (or from someone acting on his behalf) an authenticated document—

(a) identifying the resolution to which it relates, and

(b) indicating his agreement to the resolution.

(2) The document must be sent to the company in hard copy form or in electronic form.

(3) A member's agreement to a written resolution, once signified, may not be revoked.

(4) A written resolution is passed when the required majority of eligible members have signified their agreement to it.

297 Period for agreeing to written resolution

(1) A proposed written resolution lapses if it is not passed before the end of—

(a) the period specified for this purpose in the company's articles, or

(b) if none is specified, the period of 28 days beginning with the circulation date.

(2) The agreement of a member to a written resolution is ineffective if signified after the expiry of that period.

Supplementary

298 Sending documents relating to written resolutions by electronic means

(1) Where a company has given an electronic address in any document containing or accompanying a proposed written resolution, it is deemed to have agreed that any document or information relating to that resolution may be sent by electronic means to that address (subject to any conditions or limitations specified in the document).

(2) In this section "electronic address" means any address or number used for the purposes of sending or receiving documents or information by electronic means.

299 Publication of written resolution on website

(1) This section applies where a company sends—

(a) a written resolution, or

(b) a statement relating to a written resolution,

to a person by means of a website.

(2) The resolution or statement is not validly sent for the purposes of this Chapter unless the resolution is available on the website throughout the period beginning with the circulation date and ending on the date on which the resolution lapses under section 297.

300 Relationship between this Chapter and provisions of company's articles

A provision of the articles of a private company is void in so far as it would have the effect that a resolution that is required by or otherwise provided for in an enactment could not be proposed and passed as a written resolution.

CHAPTER 3
RESOLUTIONS AT MEETINGS

General provisions about resolutions at meetings

301 Resolutions at general meetings

A resolution of the members of a company is validly passed at a general meeting if—

(a) notice of the meeting and of the resolution is given, and

(b) the meeting is held and conducted,

in accordance with the provisions of this Chapter (and, where relevant, Chapter 4) and the company's articles.

Calling meetings

302 Directors' power to call general meetings

The directors of a company may call a general meeting of the company.

303 Members' power to require directors to call general meeting

(1) The members of a company may require the directors to call a general meeting of the company.

(2) The directors are required to call a general meeting once the company has received requests to do so from—

(a) members representing at least 5% of such of the paid-up capital of the company as carries the right of voting at general meetings of the company (excluding any paid-up capital held as treasury shares); or

(b) in the case of a company not having a share capital, members who represent at least 5% of the total voting rights of all the members having a right to vote at general meetings.

(3) . . .

(4) A request—

(a) must state the general nature of the business to be dealt with at the meeting, and

(b) may include the text of a resolution that may properly be moved and is intended to be moved at the meeting.

(5) A resolution may properly be moved at a meeting unless—

(a) it would, if passed, be ineffective (whether by reason of inconsistency with any enactment or the company's constitution or otherwise),

(b) it is defamatory of any person, or

(c) it is frivolous or vexatious.

(6) A request—

(a) may be in hard copy form or in electronic form, and

(b) must be authenticated by the person or persons making it.

304 Directors' duty to call meetings required by members

(1) Directors required under section 303 to call a general meeting of the company must call a meeting—

(a) within 21 days from the date on which they become subject to the requirement, and

(b) to be held on a date not more than 28 days after the date of the notice convening the meeting.

(2) If the requests received by the company identify a resolution intended to be moved at the meeting, the notice of the meeting must include notice of the resolution.

(3) The business that may be dealt with at the meeting includes a resolution of which notice is given in accordance with this section.

(4) If the resolution is to be proposed as a special resolution, the directors are treated as not having duly called the meeting if they do not give the required notice of the resolution in accordance with section 283.

305 Power of members to call meeting at company's expense

(1) If the directors—

(a) are required under section 303 to call a meeting, and

(b) do not do so in accordance with section 304,

the members who requested the meeting, or any of them representing more than one half of the total voting rights of all of them, may themselves call a general meeting.

(2) Where the requests received by the company included the text of a resolution intended to be moved at the meeting, the notice of the meeting must include notice of the resolution.

(3) The meeting must be called for a date not more than three months after the date on which the directors become subject to the requirement to call a meeting.

(4) The meeting must be called in the same manner, as nearly as possible, as that in which meetings are required to be called by directors of the company.

(5) The business which may be dealt with at the meeting includes a resolution of which notice is given in accordance with this section.

(6) Any reasonable expenses incurred by the members requesting the meeting by reason of the failure of the directors duly to call a meeting must be reimbursed by the company.

(7) Any sum so reimbursed shall be retained by the company out of any sums due or to become due from the company by way of fees or other remuneration in respect of the services of such of the directors as were in default.

306 Power of court to order meeting

(1) This section applies if for any reason it is impracticable—

(a) to call a meeting of a company in any manner in which meetings of that company may be called, or

(b) to conduct the meeting in the manner prescribed by the company's articles or this Act.

(2) The court may, either of its own motion or on the application—

(a) of a director of the company, or

(b) of a member of the company who would be entitled to vote at the meeting,

order a meeting to be called, held and conducted in any manner the court thinks fit.

(3) Where such an order is made, the court may give such ancillary or consequential directions as it thinks expedient.

(4) Such directions may include a direction that one member of the company present at the meeting be deemed to constitute a quorum.

(5) A meeting called, held and conducted in accordance with an order under this section is deemed for all purposes to be a meeting of the company duly called, held and conducted.

Notice of meetings

307 Notice required of general meeting

(A1) This section applies to—

(a) a general meeting of a company that is not a traded company; and

(b) a general meeting of a traded company that is an opted-in company (as defined by section 971(1)), where—

(i) the meeting is held to decide whether to take any action that might result in the frustration of a takeover bid for the company; or

(ii) the meeting is held by virtue of section 969 (power of offeror to require general meeting to be held).

(A2) For corresponding provision in relation to general meetings of traded companies (other than meetings within subsection (A1)(b)), see section 307A.

(1) A general meeting of a private company (other than an adjourned meeting) must be called by notice of at least 14 days.

(2) A general meeting of a public company (other than an adjourned meeting) must be called by notice of—

(a) in the case of an annual general meeting, at least 21 days, and
(b) in any other case, at least 14 days.

(3) The company's articles may require a longer period of notice than that specified in subsection (1) or (2).

(4) A general meeting may be called by shorter notice than that otherwise required if shorter notice is agreed by the members.

(5) The shorter notice must be agreed to by a majority in number of the members having a right to attend and vote at the meeting, being a majority who—
(a) together hold not less than the requisite percentage in nominal value of the shares giving a right to attend and vote at the meeting (excluding any shares in the company held as treasury shares), or
(b) in the case of a company not having a share capital, together represent not less than the requisite percentage of the total voting rights at that meeting of all the members.

(6) The requisite percentage is—
(a) in the case of a private company, 90% or such higher percentage (not exceeding 95%) as may be specified in the company's articles;
(b) in the case of a public company, 95%.

(7) Subsections (5) and (6) do not apply to an annual general meeting of a public company (see instead section 337(2)).

307A Notice required of general meeting: certain meetings of traded companies

(1) A general meeting of a traded company must be called by notice of—
(a) in a case where conditions A to C (set out below) are met, at least 14 days;
(b) in any other case, at least 21 days.

(2) Condition A is that the general meeting is not an annual general meeting.

(3) Condition B is that the company offers the facility for members to vote by electronic means accessible to all members who hold shares that carry rights to vote at general meetings.
This condition is met if there is a facility, offered by the company and accessible to all such members, to appoint a proxy by means of a website.

(4) Condition C is that a special resolution reducing the period of notice to not less than 14 days has been passed—
(a) at the immediately preceding annual general meeting, or
(b) at a general meeting held since that annual general meeting.

(5) In the case of a company which has not yet held an annual general meeting, condition C is that a special resolution reducing the period of notice to not less than 14 days has been passed at a general meeting.

(6) The company's articles may require a longer period of notice than that specified in subsection (1).

(7) Where a general meeting is adjourned, the adjourned meeting may be called by shorter notice than required by subsection (1).
But in the case of an adjournment for lack of a quorum this subsection applies only if—
(a) no business is to be dealt with at the adjourned meeting the general nature of which was not stated in the notice of the original meeting, and
(b) the adjourned meeting is to be held at least 10 days after the original meeting.

(8) Nothing in this section applies in relation to a general meeting of a kind mentioned in section 307(A1)(b) (certain meetings regarding takeover of opted-in company).

308 Manner in which notice to be given

Notice of a general meeting of a company must be given—
(a) in hard copy form,
(b) in electronic form, or
(c) by means of a website (see section 309),
or partly by one such means and partly by another.

309 Publication of notice of meeting on website

(1) Notice of a meeting is not validly given by a company by means of a website unless it is given in accordance with this section.

(2) When the company notifies a member of the presence of the notice on the website the notification must—

(a) state that it concerns a notice of a company meeting,

(b) specify the place, date and time of the meeting, and

(c) in the case of a public company, state whether the meeting will be an annual general meeting.

(3) The notice must be available on the website throughout the period beginning with the date of that notification and ending with the conclusion of the meeting.

310 Persons entitled to receive notice of meetings

(1) Notice of a general meeting of a company must be sent to—

(a) every member of the company, and

(b) every director.

(2) In subsection (1), the reference to members includes any person who is entitled to a share in consequence of the death or bankruptcy of a member, if the company has been notified of their entitlement.

(3) In subsection (2), the reference to the bankruptcy of a member includes—

(a) the sequestration of the estate of a member;

(b) a member's estate being the subject of a protected trust deed (within the meaning of the Bankruptcy (Scotland) Act 1985).

(4) This section has effect subject to—

(a) any enactment, and

(b) any provision of the company's articles.

311 Contents of notices of meetings

(1) Notice of a general meeting of a company must state—

(a) the time and date of the meeting, and

(b) the place of the meeting.

(2) Notice of a general meeting of a company must state the general nature of the business to be dealt with at the meeting.

In relation to a company other than a traded company, this subsection has effect subject to any provision of the company's articles.

(3) Notice of a general meeting of a traded company must also include—

(a) a statement giving the address of the website on which the information required by section 311A (traded companies: publication of information in advance of general meeting) is published;

(b) a statement—

(i) that the right to vote at the meeting is determined by reference to the register of members, and

(ii) of the time when that right will be determined in accordance with section 360B(2) (traded companies: share dealings before general meetings);

(c) a statement of the procedures with which members must comply in order to be able to attend and vote at the meeting (including the date by which they must comply);

(d) a statement giving details of any forms to be used for the appointment of a proxy;

(e) where the company offers the facility for members to vote in advance (see section 322A) or by electronic means (see section 360A), a statement of the procedure for doing so (including the date by which it must be done, and details of any forms to be used); and

(f) a statement of the right of members to ask questions in accordance with section 319A (traded companies: questions at meetings).

311A Traded companies: publication of information in advance of general meeting

(1) A traded company must ensure that the following information relating to a general meeting of the company is made available on a website—
(a) the matters set out in the notice of the meeting;
(b) the total numbers of—
(i) shares in the company, and
(ii) shares of each class,
in respect of which members are entitled to exercise voting rights at the meeting;
(c) the totals of the voting rights that members are entitled to exercise at the meeting in respect of the shares of each class;
(d) members' statements, members' resolutions and members' matters of business received by the company after the first date on which notice of the meeting is given.

(2) The information must be made available on a website that—
(a) is maintained by or on behalf of the company, and
(b) identifies the company.

(3) Access to the information on the website, and the ability to obtain a hard copy of the information from the website, must not be conditional on payment of a fee or otherwise restricted.

(4) The information—
(a) must be made available—
(i) in the case of information required by subsection (1)(a) to (c), on or before the first date on which notice of the meeting is given, and
(ii) in the case of information required by subsection (1)(d), as soon as reasonably practicable, and
(b) must be kept available throughout the period of two years beginning with the date on which it is first made available on a website in accordance with this section.

(5) A failure to make information available throughout the period specified in subsection (4)(b) is disregarded if—
(a) the information is made available on the website for part of that period, and
(b) the failure is wholly attributable to circumstances that it would not be reasonable to have expected the company to prevent or avoid.

(6) The amounts mentioned in subsection (1)(b) and (c) must be ascertained at the latest practicable time before the first date on which notice of the meeting is given.

(7) Failure to comply with this section does not affect the validity of the meeting or of anything done at the meeting.

(8) If this section is not complied with as respects any meeting, an offence is committed by every officer of the company who is in default.

(9) A person guilty of an offence under this section is liable on summary conviction to a fine not exceeding level 3 on the standard scale.

312 Resolution requiring special notice

(1) Where by any provision of the Companies Acts special notice is required of a resolution, the resolution is not effective unless notice of the intention to move it has been given to the company at least 28 days before the meeting at which it is moved.

(2) The company must, where practicable, give its members notice of any such resolution in the same manner and at the same time as it gives notice of the meeting.

(3) Where that is not practicable, the company must give its members notice at least 14 days before the meeting—
(a) by advertisement in a newspaper having an appropriate circulation, or
(b) in any other manner allowed by the company's articles.

(4) If, after notice of the intention to move such a resolution has been given to the company, a meeting is called for a date 28 days or less after the notice has been given, the notice is deemed to have been properly given, though not given within the time required.

313 Accidental failure to give notice of resolution or meeting

(1) Where a company gives notice of—

(a) a general meeting, or

(b) a resolution intended to be moved at a general meeting,

any accidental failure to give notice to one or more persons shall be disregarded for the purpose of determining whether notice of the meeting or resolution (as the case may be) is duly given.

(2) Except in relation to notice given under—

(a) section 304 (notice of meetings required by members),

(b) section 305 (notice of meetings called by members), or

(c) section 339 (notice of resolutions at AGMs proposed by members),

subsection (1) has effect subject to any provision of the company's articles.

Members' statements

314 Members' power to require circulation of statements

(1) The members of a company may require the company to circulate, to members of the company entitled to receive notice of a general meeting, a statement of not more than 1,000 words with respect to—

(a) a matter referred to in a proposed resolution to be dealt with at that meeting, or

(b) other business to be dealt with at that meeting.

(2) A company is required to circulate a statement once it has received requests to do so from—

(a) members representing at least 5% of the total voting rights of all the members who have a relevant right to vote (excluding any voting rights attached to any shares in the company held as treasury shares), or

(b) at least 100 members who have a relevant right to vote and hold shares in the company on which there has been paid up an average sum, per member, of at least £100.

See also section 153 (exercise of rights where shares held on behalf of others).

(3) In subsection (2), a "relevant right to vote" means—

(a) in relation to a statement with respect to a matter referred to in a proposed resolution, a right to vote on that resolution at the meeting to which the requests relate, and

(b) in relation to any other statement, a right to vote at the meeting to which the requests relate.

(4) A request—

(a) may be in hard copy form or in electronic form,

(b) must identify the statement to be circulated,

(c) must be authenticated by the person or persons making it, and

(d) must be received by the company at least one week before the meeting to which it relates.

315 Company's duty to circulate members' statement

(1) A company that is required under section 314, to circulate a statement must send a copy of it to each member of the company entitled to receive notice of the meeting—

(a) in the same manner as the notice of the meeting, and

(b) at the same time as, or as soon as reasonably practicable after, it gives notice of the meeting.

(2) Subsection (1) has effect subject to section 316(2) (deposit or tender of sum in respect of expenses of circulation) and section 317 (application not to circulate members' statement).

(3) In the event of default in complying with this section, an offence is committed by every officer of the company who is in default.

(4) A person guilty of an offence under this section is liable—

(a) on conviction on indictment, to a fine;

(b) on summary conviction, to a fine not exceeding the statutory maximum.

316 Expenses of circulating members' statement

(1) The expenses of the company in complying with section 315 need not be paid by the members who requested the circulation of the statement if—

(a) the meeting to which the requests relate is an annual general meeting of a public company, and
(b) requests sufficient to require the company to circulate the statement are received before the end of the financial year preceding the meeting.

(2) Otherwise—
(a) the expenses of the company in complying with that section must be paid by the members who requested the circulation of the statement unless the company resolves otherwise, and
(b) unless the company has previously so resolved, it is not bound to comply with that section unless there is deposited with or tendered to it, not later than one week before the meeting, a sum reasonably sufficient to meet its expenses in doing so.

317 Application not to circulate members' statement

(1) A company is not required to circulate a members' statement under section 315 if, on an application by the company or another person who claims to be aggrieved, the court is satisfied that the rights conferred by section 314 and that section are being abused.

(2) The court may order the members who requested the circulation of the statement to pay the whole or part of the company's costs (in Scotland, expenses) on such an application, even if they are not parties to the application.

Procedure at meetings

318 Quorum at meetings

(1) In the case of a company limited by shares or guarantee and having only one member, one qualifying person present at a meeting is a quorum.

(2) In any other case, subject to the provisions of the company's articles, two qualifying persons present at a meeting are a quorum, unless—
(a) each is a qualifying person only because he is authorised under section 323 to act as the representative of a corporation in relation to the meeting, and they are representatives of the same corporation; or
(b) each is a qualifying person only because he is appointed as proxy of a member in relation to the meeting, and they are proxies of the same member.

(3) For the purposes of this section a "qualifying person" means—
(a) an individual who is a member of the company,
(b) a person authorised under section 323 (representation of corporations at meetings) to act as the representative of a corporation in relation to the meeting, or
(c) a person appointed as proxy of a member in relation to the meeting.

319 Chairman of meeting

(1) A member may be elected to be the chairman of a general meeting by a resolution of the company passed at the meeting.

(2) Subsection (1) is subject to any provision of the company's articles that states who may or may not be chairman.

319A Traded companies: questions at meetings

(1) At a general meeting of a traded company, the company must cause to be answered any question relating to the business being dealt with at the meeting put by a member attending the meeting.

(2) No such answer need be given—
(a) if to do so would—
(i) interfere unduly with the preparation for the meeting, or
(ii) involve the disclosure of confidential information;
(b) if the answer has already been given on a website in the form of an answer to a question; or
(c) if it is undesirable in the interests of the company or the good order of the meeting that the question be answered.

320 Declaration by chairman on a show of hands

(1) On a vote on a resolution at a meeting on a show of hands, a declaration by the chairman that the resolution—

(a) has or has not been passed, or

(b) passed with a particular majority,

is conclusive evidence of that fact without proof of the number or proportion of the votes recorded in favour of or against the resolution.

(2) An entry in respect of such a declaration in minutes of the meeting recorded in accordance with section 355 is also conclusive evidence of that fact without such proof.

(3) This section does not have effect if a poll is demanded in respect of the resolution (and the demand is not subsequently withdrawn).

321 Right to demand a poll

(1) A provision of a company's articles is void in so far as it would have the effect of excluding the right to demand a poll at a general meeting on any question other than—

(a) the election of the chairman of the meeting, or

(b) the adjournment of the meeting.

(2) A provision of a company's articles is void in so far as it would have the effect of making ineffective a demand for a poll on any such question which is made—

(a) by not less than 5 members having the right to vote on the resolution; or

(b) by a member or members representing not less than 10% of the total voting rights of all the members having the right to vote on the resolution (excluding any voting rights attached to any shares in the company held as treasury shares); or

(c) by a member or members holding shares in the company conferring a right to vote on the resolution, being shares on which an aggregate sum has been paid up equal to not less than 10% of the total sum paid up on all the shares conferring that right (excluding shares in the company conferring a right to vote on the resolution which are held as treasury shares).

322 Voting on a poll

On a poll taken at a general meeting of a company, a member entitled to more than one vote need not, if he votes, use all his votes or cast all the votes he uses in the same way.

322A Voting on a poll: votes cast in advance

(1) A company's articles may contain provision to the effect that on a vote on a resolution on a poll taken at a meeting, the votes may include votes cast in advance.

(2) In the case of a traded company any such provision in relation to voting at a general meeting may be made subject only to such requirements and restrictions as are—

(a) necessary to ensure the identification of the person voting, and

(b) proportionate to the achievement of that objective.

Nothing in this subsection affects any power of a company to require reasonable evidence of the entitlement of any person who is not a member to vote.

(3) Any provision of a company's articles is void in so far as it would have the effect of requiring any document casting a vote in advance to be received by the company or another person earlier than the following time—

(a) in the case of a poll taken more than 48 hours after it was demanded, 24 hours before the time appointed for the taking of the poll;

(b) in the case of any other poll, 48 hours before the time for holding the meeting or adjourned meeting.

(4) In calculating the periods mentioned in subsection (3), no account is to be taken of any part of a day that is not a working day.

323 Representation of corporations at meetings

(1) If a corporation (whether or not a company within the meaning of this Act) is a member of a company, it may by resolution of its directors or other governing body authorise a person or persons to act as its representative or representatives at any meeting of the company.

(2) A person authorised by a corporation is entitled to exercise (on behalf of the corporation) the same powers as the corporation could exercise if it were an individual member of the company. Where a corporation authorises more than one person, this subsection is subject to subsections (3) and (4).

(3) On a vote on a resolution on a show of hands at a meeting of the company, each authorised person has the same voting rights as the corporation would be entitled to.

(4) Where subsection (3) does not apply and more than one authorised person purport to exercise a power under subsection (2) in respect of the same shares—

(a) if they purport to exercise the power in the same way as each other, the power is treated as exercised in that way;

(b) if they do not purport to exercise the power in the same way as each other, the power is treated as not exercised.

Proxies

324 Rights to appoint proxies

(1) A member of a company is entitled to appoint another person as his proxy to exercise all or any of his rights to attend and to speak and vote at a meeting of the company.

(2) In the case of a company having a share capital, a member may appoint more than one proxy in relation to a meeting, provided that each proxy is appointed to exercise the rights attached to a different share or shares held by him, or (as the case may be) to a different £10, or multiple of £10, of stock held by him.

324A Obligation of proxy to vote in accordance with instructions

A proxy must vote in accordance with any instructions given by the member by whom the proxy is appointed.

325 Notice of meeting to contain statement of rights

(1) In every notice calling a meeting of a company there must appear, with reasonable prominence, a statement informing the member of—

(a) his rights under section 324, and

(b) any more extensive rights conferred by the company's articles to appoint more than one proxy.

(2) Failure to comply with this section does not affect the validity of the meeting or of anything done at the meeting.

(3) If this section is not complied with as respects any meeting, an offence is committed by every officer of the company who is in default.

(4) A person guilty of an offence under this section is liable on summary conviction to a fine not exceeding level 3 on the standard scale.

326 Company-sponsored invitations to appoint proxies

(1) If for the purposes of a meeting there are issued at the company's expense invitations to members to appoint as proxy a specified person or a number of specified persons, the invitations must be issued to all members entitled to vote at the meeting.

(2) Subsection (1) is not contravened if—

(a) there is issued to a member at his request a form of appointment naming the proxy or a list of persons willing to act as proxy, and

(b) the form or list is available on request to all members entitled to vote at the meeting.

(3) If subsection (1) is contravened as respects a meeting, an offence is committed by every officer of the company who is in default.

(4) A person guilty of an offence under this section is liable on summary conviction to a fine not exceeding level 3 on the standard scale.

327 Notice required of appointment of proxy etc

(A1) In the case of a traded company—
(a) the appointment of a person as proxy for a member must be notified to the company in writing;
(b) where such an appointment is made, the company may require reasonable evidence of—
(i) the identity of the member and of the proxy,
(ii) the member's instructions (if any) as to how the proxy is to vote, and
(iii) where the proxy is appointed by a person acting on behalf of the member, authority of that person to make the appointment;
but may not require to be provided with anything else relating to the appointment.

(1) The following provisions apply in the case of traded companies and other companies as regards—
(a) the appointment of a proxy, and
(b) any document necessary to show the validity of, or otherwise relating to, the appointment of a proxy.

(2) Any provision of the company's articles is void in so far as it would have the effect of requiring any such appointment or document to be received by the company or another person earlier than the following time—
(a) in the case of a meeting or adjourned meeting, 48 hours before the time for holding the meeting or adjourned meeting;
(b) in the case of a poll taken more than 48 hours after it was demanded, 24 hours before the time appointed for the taking of the poll;
(c) in the case of a poll taken not more than 48 hours after it was demanded, the time at which it was demanded.

(3) In calculating the periods mentioned in subsection (2) no account shall be taken of any part of a day that is not a working day.

328 Chairing meetings

(1) A proxy may be elected to be the chairman of a general meeting by a resolution of the company passed at the meeting.

(2) Subsection (1) is subject to any provision of the company's articles that states who may or who may not be chairman.

329 Right of proxy to demand a poll

(1) The appointment of a proxy to vote on a matter at a meeting of a company authorises the proxy to demand, or join in demanding, a poll on that matter.

(2) In applying the provisions of section 321(2) (requirements for effective demand), a demand by a proxy counts—
(a) for the purposes of paragraph (a), as a demand by the member;
(b) for the purposes of paragraph (b), as a demand by a member representing the voting rights that the proxy is authorised to exercise;
(c) for the purposes of paragraph (c), as a demand by a member holding the shares to which those rights are attached.

330 Notice required of termination of proxy's authority

(A1) In the case of a traded company the termination of the authority of a person to act as proxy must be notified to the company in writing.

(1) The following provisions apply in the case of traded companies and other companies as regards notice that the authority of a person to act as proxy is terminated ("notice of termination").

(2) The termination of the authority of a person to act as proxy does not affect—
(a) whether he counts in deciding whether there is a quorum at a meeting,
(b) the validity of anything he does as chairman of a meeting, or

(c) the validity of a poll demanded by him at a meeting,

unless the company receives notice of the termination before the commencement of the meeting.

(3) The termination of the authority of a person to act as proxy does not affect the validity of a vote given by that person unless the company receives notice of the termination—

(a) before the commencement of the meeting or adjourned meeting at which the vote is given, or

(b) in the case of a poll taken more than 48 hours after it is demanded, before the time appointed for taking the poll.

(4) If the company's articles require or permit members to give notice of termination to a person other than the company, the references above to the company receiving notice have effect as if they were or (as the case may be) included a reference to that person.

(5) Subsections (2) and (3) have effect subject to any provision of the company's articles which has the effect of requiring notice of termination to be received by the company or another person at a time earlier than that specified in those subsections.

This is subject to subsection (6).

(6) Any provision of the company's articles is void in so far as it would have the effect of requiring notice of termination to be received by the company or another person earlier than the following time—

(a) in the case of a meeting or adjourned meeting, 48 hours before the time for holding the meeting or adjourned meeting;

(b) in the case of a poll taken more than 48 hours after it was demanded, 24 hours before the time appointed for the taking of the poll;

(c) in the case of a poll taken not more than 48 hours after it was demanded, the time at which it was demanded.

(7) In calculating the periods mentioned in subsections (3)(b) and (6) no account shall be taken of any part of a day that is not a working day.

331 Saving for more extensive rights conferred by articles

Nothing in sections 324 to 330 (proxies) prevents a company's articles from conferring more extensive rights on members or proxies than are conferred by those sections.

Adjourned meetings

332 Resolution passed at adjourned meeting

Where a resolution is passed at an adjourned meeting of a company, the resolution is for all purposes to be treated as having been passed on the date on which it was in fact passed, and is not to be deemed passed on any earlier date.

Electronic communications

333 Sending documents relating to meetings etc in electronic form

(1) Where a company has given an electronic address in a notice calling a meeting, it is deemed to have agreed that any document or information relating to proceedings at the meeting may be sent by electronic means to that address (subject to any conditions or limitations specified in the notice).

(2) Where a company has given an electronic address—

(a) in an instrument of proxy sent out by the company in relation to the meeting, or

(b) in an invitation to appoint a proxy issued by the company in relation to the meeting,

it is deemed to have agreed that any document or information relating to proxies for that meeting may be sent by electronic means to that address (subject to any conditions or limitations specified in the notice).

(3) In subsection (2), documents relating to proxies include—

(a) the appointment of a proxy in relation to a meeting,

(b) any document necessary to show the validity of, or otherwise relating to, the appointment of a proxy, and

(c) notice of the termination of the authority of a proxy.

(4) In this section "electronic address" means any address or number used for the purposes of sending or receiving documents or information by electronic means.

333A Traded company: duty to provide electronic address for receipt of proxies etc

(1) A traded company must provide an electronic address for the receipt of any document or information relating to proxies for a general meeting.

(2) The company must provide the address either—

(a) by giving it when sending out an instrument of proxy for the purposes of the meeting or issuing an invitation to appoint a proxy for those purposes; or

(b) by ensuring that it is made available, throughout the period beginning with the first date on which notice of the meeting is given and ending with the conclusion of the meeting, on the website on which the information required by section 311A(1) is made available.

(3) The company is deemed to have agreed that any document or information relating to proxies for the meeting may be sent by electronic means to the address provided (subject to any limitations specified by the company when providing the address).

(4) In this section—

(a) documents relating to proxies include—

(i) the appointment of a proxy for a meeting,

(ii) any document necessary to show the validity of, or otherwise relating to, the appointment of a proxy, and

(iii) notice of the termination of the authority of a proxy;

(b) "electronic address" has the meaning given by section 333(4).

Application to class meetings

334 Application to class meetings

(1) The provisions of this Chapter apply (with necessary modifications) in relation to a meeting of holders of a class of shares as they apply in relation to a general meeting.
This is subject to subsections (2) to (3).

(2) The following provisions of this Chapter do not apply in relation to a meeting of holders of a class of shares—

(a) sections 303 to 305 (members' power to require directors to call general meeting), . . .

(b) section 306 (power of court to order meeting), and

(c) sections 311(3), 311A, 319A, 327(A1), 330(A1) and 333A (additional requirements relating to traded companies).

(2A) Section 307(1) to (6) apply in relation to a meeting of holders of a class of shares in a traded company as they apply in relation to a meeting of holders of a class of shares in a company other than a traded company (and, accordingly, section 307A does not apply in relation to such a meeting).

(3) The following provisions (in addition to those mentioned in subsection (2)) do not apply in relation to a meeting in connection with the variation of rights attached to a class of shares (a "variation of class rights meeting")—

(a) section 318 (quorum), and

(b) section 321 (right to demand a poll).

(4) The quorum for a variation of class rights meeting is—

(a) for a meeting other than an adjourned meeting, two persons present holding at least one-third in nominal value of the issued shares of the class in question (excluding any shares of that class held as treasury shares);

(b) for an adjourned meeting, one person present holding shares of the class in question.

(5) For the purposes of subsection (4), where a person is present by proxy or proxies, he is treated as holding only the shares in respect of which those proxies are authorised to exercise voting rights.

(6) At a variation of class rights meeting, any holder of shares of the class in question present may demand a poll.

(7) For the purposes of this section—

(a) any amendment of a provision contained in a company's articles for the variation of the rights attached to a class of shares, or the insertion of any such provision into the articles, is itself to be treated as a variation of those rights, and

(b) references to the variation of rights attached to a class of shares include references to their abrogation.

335 Application to class meetings: companies without a share capital

(1) The provisions of this Chapter apply (with necessary modifications) in relation to a meeting of a class of members of a company without a share capital as they apply in relation to a general meeting.

This is subject to subsections (2) and (3).

(2) The following provisions of this Chapter do not apply in relation to a meeting of a class of members—

(a) sections 303 to 305 (members' power to require directors to call general meeting), and

(b) section 306 (power of court to order meeting).

(3) The following provisions (in addition to those mentioned in subsection (2)) do not apply in relation to a meeting in connection with the variation of the rights of a class of members (a "variation of class rights meeting")—

(a) section 318 (quorum), and

(b) section 321 (right to demand a poll).

(4) The quorum for a variation of class rights meeting is—

(a) for a meeting other than an adjourned meeting, two members of the class present (in person or by proxy) who together represent at least one-third of the voting rights of the class;

(b) for an adjourned meeting, one member of the class present (in person or by proxy).

(5) At a variation of class rights meeting, any member present (in person or by proxy) may demand a poll.

(6) For the purposes of this section—

(a) any amendment of a provision contained in a company's articles for the variation of the rights of a class of members, or the insertion of any such provision into the articles, is itself to be treated as a variation of those rights, and

(b) references to the variation of rights of a class of members include references to their abrogation.

CHAPTER 4
PUBLIC COMPANIES AND TRADED COMPANIES: ADDITIONAL REQUIREMENTS FOR AGMS

336 Public companies and traded companies: annual general meeting

(1) Every public company must hold a general meeting as its annual general meeting in each period of 6 months beginning with the day following its accounting reference date (in addition to any other meetings held during that period).

(1A) Every private company that is a traded company must hold a general meeting as its annual general meeting in each period of 9 months beginning with the day following its accounting reference date (in addition to any other meetings held during that period).

(2) A company that fails to comply with subsection (1) or (1A) as a result of giving notice under section 392 (alteration of accounting reference date)—

(a) specifying a new accounting reference date, and

(b) stating that the current accounting reference period or the previous accounting reference period is to be shortened, shall be treated as if it had complied with subsection (1) or (1A) if it holds a general meeting as its annual general meeting within 3 months of giving that notice.

(3) If a company fails to comply with subsection (1) or (1A), an offence is committed by every officer of the company who is in default.

(4) A person guilty of an offence under this section is liable—

(a) on conviction on indictment, to a fine;

(b) on summary conviction, to a fine not exceeding the statutory maximum.

337 Public companies and traded companies: notice of AGM

(1) A notice calling an annual general meeting of a public company or a private company that is a traded company must state that the meeting is an annual general meeting.

(2) An annual general meeting of a public company that is not a traded company may be called by shorter notice than that required by section 307(2) or by the company's articles (as the case may be), if all the members entitled to attend and vote at the meeting agree to the shorter notice.

(3) Where a notice calling an annual general meeting of a traded company is given more than 6 weeks before the meeting, the notice must include—

(a) if the company is a public company, a statement of the right under section 338 to require the company to give notice of a resolution to be moved at the meeting, and

(b) whether or not the company is a public company, a statement of the right under section 338A to require the company to include a matter in the business to be dealt with at the meeting.

338 Public companies: members' power to require circulation of resolutions for AGMs

(1) The members of a public company may require the company to give, to members of the company entitled to receive notice of the next annual general meeting, notice of a resolution which may properly be moved and is intended to be moved at that meeting.

(2) A resolution may properly be moved at an annual general meeting unless—

(a) it would, if passed, be ineffective (whether by reason of inconsistency with any enactment or the company's constitution or otherwise),

(b) it is defamatory of any person, or

(c) it is frivolous or vexatious.

(3) A company is required to give notice of a resolution once it has received requests that it do so from—

(a) members representing at least 5% of the total voting rights of all the members who have a right to vote on the resolution at the annual general meeting to which the requests relate (excluding any voting rights attached to any shares in the company held as treasury shares), or

(b) at least 100 members who have a right to vote on the resolution at the annual general meeting to which the requests relate and hold shares in the company on which there has been paid up an average sum, per member, of at least £100.

See also section 153 (exercise of rights where shares held on behalf of others).

(4) A request—

(a) may be in hard copy form or in electronic form,

(b) must identify the resolution of which notice is to be given,

(c) must be authenticated by the person or persons making it, and

(d) must be received by the company not later than—

(i) 6 weeks before the annual general meeting to which the requests relate, or

(ii) if later, the time at which notice is given of that meeting.

338A Traded companies: members' power to include other matters in business dealt with at AGM

(1) The members of a traded company may request the company to include in the business to be dealt with at an annual general meeting any matter (other than a proposed resolution) which may properly be included in the business.

(2) A matter may properly be included in the business at an annual general meeting unless—
- (a) it is defamatory of any person, or
- (b) it is frivolous or vexatious.

(3) A company is required to include such a matter once it has received requests that it do so from—
- (a) members representing at least 5% of the total voting rights of all the members who have a right to vote at the meeting, or
- (b) at least 100 members who have a right to vote at the meeting and hold shares in the company on which there has been paid up an average sum, per member, of at least £100.

See also section 153 (exercise of rights where shares held on behalf of others).

(4) A request—
- (a) may be in hard copy form or in electronic form,
- (b) must identify the matter to be included in the business,
- (c) must be accompanied by a statement setting out the grounds for the request, and
- (d) must be authenticated by the person or persons making it.

(5) A request must be received by the company not later than—
- (a) 6 weeks before the meeting, or
- (b) if later, the time at which notice is given of the meeting.

339 Public companies: company's duty to circulate members' resolutions for AGMs

(1) A company that is required under section 338 to give notice of a resolution must send a copy of it to each member of the company entitled to receive notice of the annual general meeting—
- (a) in the same manner as notice of the meeting, and
- (b) at the same time as, or as soon as reasonably practicable after, it gives notice of the meeting.

(2) Subsection (1) has effect subject to section 340(2) (deposit or tender of sum in respect of expenses of circulation).

(3) The business which may be dealt with at an annual general meeting includes a resolution of which notice is given in accordance with this section.

(4) In the event of default in complying with this section, an offence is committed by every officer of the company who is in default.

(5) A person guilty of an offence under this section is liable—
- (a) on conviction on indictment, to a fine;
- (b) on summary conviction, to a fine not exceeding the statutory maximum.

340 Public companies: expenses of circulating members' resolutions for AGM

(1) The expenses of the company in complying with section 339 need not be paid by the members who requested the circulation of the resolution if requests sufficient to require the company to circulate it are received before the end of the financial year preceding the meeting.

(2) Otherwise—
- (a) the expenses of the company in complying with that section must be paid by the members who requested the circulation of the resolution unless the company resolves otherwise, and
- (b) unless the company has previously so resolved, it is not bound to comply with that section unless there is deposited with or tendered to it, not later than—
  - (i) six weeks before the annual general meeting to which the requests relate, or
  - (ii) if later, the time at which notice is given of that meeting,

  a sum reasonably sufficient to meet its expenses in complying with that section.

340A Traded companies: duty to circulate members' matters for AGM

(1) A company that is required under section 338A to include any matter in the business to be dealt with at an annual general meeting must—
- (a) give notice of it to each member of the company entitled to receive notice of the annual general meeting—
  - (i) in the same manner as notice of the meeting, and
  - (ii) at the same time as, or as soon as reasonably practicable after, it gives notice of the meeting, and

(b) publish it on the same website as that on which the company published the information required by section 311A.

(2) Subsection (1) has effect subject to section 340B(2) (deposit or tender of sum in respect of expenses of circulation).

(3) In the event of default in complying with this section, an offence is committed by every officer of the company who is in default.

(4) A person guilty of an offence under this section is liable—

(a) on conviction on indictment, to a fine;

(b) on summary conviction, to a fine not exceeding the statutory maximum.

340B Traded companies: expenses of circulating members' matters to be dealt with at AGM

(1) The expenses of the company in complying with section 340A need not be paid by the members who requested the inclusion of the matter in the business to be dealt with at the annual general meeting if requests sufficient to require the company to include the matter are received before the end of the financial year preceding the meeting.

(2) Otherwise—

(a) the expenses of the company in complying with that section must be paid by the members who requested the inclusion of the matter unless the company resolves otherwise, and

(b) unless the company has previously so resolved, it is not bound to comply with that section unless there is deposited with or tendered to it, not later than—

(i) six weeks before the annual general meeting to which the requests relate, or

(ii) if later, the time at which notice is given of that meeting,

a sum reasonably sufficient to meet its expenses in complying with that section.

CHAPTER 5
ADDITIONAL REQUIREMENTS FOR QUOTED COMPANIES AND TRADED COMPANIES

Website publication of poll results

341 Results of poll to be made available on website

(1) Where a poll is taken at a general meeting of a quoted company that is not a traded company, the company must ensure that the following information is made available on a website—

(a) the date of the meeting,

(b) the text of the resolution or, as the case may be, a description of the subject matter of the poll,

(c) the number of votes cast in favour, and

(d) the number of votes cast against.

(1A) Where a poll is taken at a general meeting of a traded company, the company must ensure that the following information is made available on a website—

(a) the date of the meeting,

(b) the text of the resolution or, as the case may be, a description of the subject matter of the poll,

(c) the number of votes validly cast,

(d) the proportion of the company's issued share capital (determined at the time at which the right to vote is determined under section 360B(2)) represented by those votes,

(e) the number of votes cast in favour,

(f) the number of votes cast against, and

(g) the number of abstentions (if counted).

(1B) A traded company must comply with subsection (1A) by—

(a) the end of 16 days beginning with the day of the meeting, or

(b) if later, the end of the first working day after the day on which the result of the poll is declared.

(2) The provisions of section 353 (requirements as to website availability) apply.

(3) In the event of default in complying with this section (or with the requirements of section 353 as it applies for the purposes of this section), an offence is committed by every officer of the company who is in default.

(4) A person guilty of an offence under subsection (3) is liable on summary conviction to a fine not exceeding level 3 on the standard scale.

(5) Failure to comply with this section (or the requirements of section 353) does not affect the validity of—

(a) the poll, or

(b) the resolution or other business (if passed or agreed to) to which the poll relates.

(6) This section only applies to polls taken after this section comes into force.

Independent report on poll

342 Members' power to require independent report on poll

(1) The members of a quoted company may require the directors to obtain an independent report on any poll taken, or to be taken, at a general meeting of the company.

(2) The directors are required to obtain an independent report if they receive requests to do so from—

(a) members representing not less than 5% of the total voting rights of all the members who have a right to vote on the matter to which the poll relates (excluding any voting rights attached to any shares in the company held as treasury shares), or

(b) not less than 100 members who have a right to vote on the matter to which the poll relates and hold shares in the company on which there has been paid up an average sum, per member, of not less than £100.

See also section 153 (exercise of rights where shares held on behalf of others).

(3) Where the requests relate to more than one poll, subsection (2) must be satisfied in relation to each of them.

(4) A request—

(a) may be in hard copy form or in electronic form,

(b) must identify the poll or polls to which it relates,

(c) must be authenticated by the person or persons making it, and

(d) must be received by the company not later than one week after the date on which the poll is taken.

343 Appointment of independent assessor

(1) Directors who are required under section 342 to obtain an independent report on a poll or polls must appoint a person they consider to be appropriate (an "independent assessor") to prepare a report for the company on it or them.

(2) The appointment must be made within one week after the company being required to obtain the report.

(3) The directors must not appoint a person who—

(a) does not meet the independence requirement in section 344, or

(b) has another role in relation to any poll on which he is to report (including, in particular, a role in connection with collecting or counting votes or with the appointment of proxies).

(4) In the event of default in complying with this section, an offence is committed by every officer of the company who is in default.

(5) A person guilty of an offence under this section is liable on summary conviction to a fine not exceeding level 5 on the standard scale.

(6) If at the meeting no poll on which a report is required is taken—

(a) the directors are not required to obtain a report from the independent assessor, and

(b) his appointment ceases (but without prejudice to any right to be paid for work done before the appointment ceased).

344 Independence requirement

(1) A person may not be appointed as an independent assessor—

(a) if he is—
(i) an officer or employee of the company, or
(ii) a partner or employee of such a person, or a partnership of which such a person is a partner;
(b) if he is—
(i) an officer or employee of an associated undertaking of the company, or
(ii) a partner or employee of such a person, or a partnership of which such a person is a partner;
(c) if there exists between—
(i) the person or an associate of his, and
(ii) the company or an associated undertaking of the company, a connection of any such description as may be specified by regulations made by the Secretary of State.

(2) An auditor of the company is not regarded as an officer or employee of the company for this purpose.

(3) In this section—
"associated undertaking" means—
(a) a parent undertaking or subsidiary undertaking of the company, or
(b) a subsidiary undertaking of a parent undertaking of the company; and
"associate" has the meaning given by section 345.

(4) Regulations under this section are subject to negative resolution procedure.

345 Meaning of "associate"

(1) This section defines "associate" for the purposes of section 344 (independence requirement).

(2) In relation to an individual, "associate" means—
(a) that individual's spouse or civil partner or minor child or step-child,
(b) any body corporate of which that individual is a director, and
(c) any employee or partner of that individual.

(3) In relation to a body corporate, "associate" means—
(a) any body corporate of which that body is a director,
(b) any body corporate in the same group as that body, and
(c) any employee or partner of that body or of any body corporate in the same group.

(4) In relation to a partnership that is a legal person under the law by which it is governed, "associate" means—
(a) any body corporate of which that partnership is a director,
(b) any employee of or partner in that partnership, and
(c) any person who is an associate of a partner in that partnership.

(5) In relation to a partnership that is not a legal person under the law by which it is governed, "associate" means any person who is an associate of any of the partners.

(6) In this section, in relation to a limited liability partnership, for "director" read "member".

346 Effect of appointment of a partnership

(1) This section applies where a partnership that is not a legal person under the law by which it is governed is appointed as an independent assessor.

(2) Unless a contrary intention appears, the appointment is of the partnership as such and not of the partners.

(3) Where the partnership ceases, the appointment is to be treated as extending to—
(a) any partnership that succeeds to the practice of that partnership, or
(b) any other person who succeeds to that practice having previously carried it on in partnership.

(4) For the purposes of subsection (3)—
(a) a partnership is regarded as succeeding to the practice of another partnership only if the members of the successor partnership are substantially the same as those of the former partnership, and

(b) a partnership or other person is regarded as succeeding to the practice of a partnership only if it or he succeeds to the whole or substantially the whole of the business of the former partnership.

(5) Where the partnership ceases and the appointment is not treated under subsection (3) as extending to any partnership or other person, the appointment may with the consent of the company be treated as extending to a partnership, or other person, who succeeds to—

(a) the business of the former partnership, or

(b) such part of it as is agreed by the company is to be treated as comprising the appointment.

347 The independent assessor's report

(1) The report of the independent assessor must state his opinion whether—

(a) the procedures adopted in connection with the poll or polls were adequate;

(b) the votes cast (including proxy votes) were fairly and accurately recorded and counted;

(c) the validity of members' appointments of proxies was fairly assessed;

(d) the notice of the meeting complied with section 325 (notice of meeting to contain statement of rights to appoint proxy);

(e) section 326 (company-sponsored invitations to appoint proxies) was complied with in relation to the meeting.

(2) The report must give his reasons for the opinions stated.

(3) If he is unable to form an opinion on any of those matters, the report must record that fact and state the reasons for it.

(4) The report must state the name of the independent assessor.

348 Rights of independent assessor: right to attend meeting etc

(1) Where an independent assessor has been appointed to report on a poll, he is entitled to attend—

(a) the meeting at which the poll may be taken, and

(b) any subsequent proceedings in connection with the poll.

(2) He is also entitled to be provided by the company with a copy of—

(a) the notice of the meeting, and

(b) any other communication provided by the company in connection with the meeting to persons who have a right to vote on the matter to which the poll relates.

(3) The rights conferred by this section are only to be exercised to the extent that the independent assessor considers necessary for the preparation of his report.

(4) If the independent assessor is a firm, the right under subsection (1) to attend the meeting and any subsequent proceedings in connection with the poll is exercisable by an individual authorised by the firm in writing to act as its representative for that purpose.

349 Rights of independent assessor: right to information

(1) The independent assessor is entitled to access to the company's records relating to—

(a) any poll on which he is to report;

(b) the meeting at which the poll or polls may be, or were, taken.

(2) The independent assessor may require anyone who at any material time was—

(a) a director or secretary of the company,

(b) an employee of the company,

(c) a person holding or accountable for any of the company's records,

(d) a member of the company, or

(e) an agent of the company,

to provide him with information or explanations for the purpose of preparing his report.

(3) For this purpose "agent" includes the company's bankers, solicitors and auditor.

(4) A statement made by a person in response to a requirement under this section may not be used in evidence against him in criminal proceedings except proceedings for an offence under section 350 (offences relating to provision of information).

(5) A person is not required by this section to disclose information in respect of which a claim to legal professional privilege (in Scotland, to confidentiality of communications) could be maintained in legal proceedings.

350 Offences relating to provision of information

(1) A person who fails to comply with a requirement under section 349 without delay commits an offence unless it was not reasonably practicable for him to provide the required information or explanation.

(2) A person guilty of an offence under subsection (1) is liable on summary conviction to a fine not exceeding level 3 on the standard scale.

(3) A person commits an offence who knowingly or recklessly makes to an independent assessor a statement (oral or written) that—

(a) conveys or purports to convey any information or explanations which the independent assessor requires, or is entitled to require, under section 349, and

(b) is misleading, false or deceptive in a material particular.

(4) A person guilty of an offence under subsection (3) is liable—

(a) on conviction on indictment, to imprisonment for a term not exceeding two years or a fine (or both);

(b) on summary conviction—

(i) in England and Wales, to imprisonment for a term not exceeding twelve months or to a fine not exceeding the statutory maximum (or both);

(ii) in Scotland or Northern Ireland, to imprisonment for a term not exceeding six months, or to a fine not exceeding the statutory maximum (or both).

(5) Nothing in this section affects any right of an independent assessor to apply for an injunction (in Scotland, an interdict or an order for specific performance) to enforce any of his rights under section 348 or 349.

351 Information to be made available on website

(1) Where an independent assessor has been appointed to report on a poll, the company must ensure that the following information is made available on a website—

(a) the fact of his appointment,

(b) his identity,

(c) the text of the resolution or, as the case may be, a description of the subject matter of the poll to which his appointment relates, and

(d) a copy of a report by him which complies with section 347.

(2) The provisions of section 353 (requirements as to website availability) apply.

(3) In the event of default in complying with this section (or with the requirements of section 353 as it applies for the purposes of this section), an offence is committed by every officer of the company who is in default.

(4) A person guilty of an offence under subsection (3) is liable on summary conviction to a fine not exceeding level 3 on the standard scale.

(5) Failure to comply with this section (or the requirements of section 353) does not affect the validity of—

(a) the poll, or

(b) the resolution or other business (if passed or agreed to) to which the poll relates.

Supplementary

352 Application of provisions to class meetings

(1) The provisions of section 341 (results of poll to be made available on website) apply (with any necessary modifications) in relation to a meeting of holders of a class of shares of a quoted company or traded company in connection with the variation of the rights attached to such shares as they apply in relation to a general meeting of the company.

(1A) The provisions of section 342 to 351 (independent report on poll) apply (with any necessary modifications) in relation to a meeting of holders of a class of shares of a quoted company in connection with the variation of the rights attached to such shares as they apply in relation to a general meeting of the company.

(2) For the purposes of this section—

(a) any amendment of a provision contained in a company's articles for the variation of the rights attached to a class of shares, or the insertion of any such provision into the articles, is itself to be treated as a variation of those rights, and

(b) references to the variation of rights attached to a class of shares include references to their abrogation.

353 Requirements as to website availability

(1) The following provisions apply for the purposes of—

section 341 (results of poll to be made available on website), and

section 351 (report of independent observer to be made available on website).

(2) The information must be made available on a website that—

(a) is maintained by or on behalf of the company, and

(b) identifies the company in question.

(3) Access to the information on the website, and the ability to obtain a hard copy of the information from the website, must not be conditional on the payment of a fee or otherwise restricted.

(4) The information—

(a) must be made available as soon as reasonably practicable, and

(b) must be kept available throughout the period of two years beginning with the date on which it is first made available on a website in accordance with this section.

(5) A failure to make information available on a website throughout the period specified in subsection (4)(b) is disregarded if—

(a) the information is made available on the website for part of that period, and

(b) the failure is wholly attributable to circumstances that it would not be reasonable to have expected the company to prevent or avoid.

354 Power to limit or extend the types of company to which provisions of this Chapter apply

(1) The Secretary of State may by regulations—

(a) limit the types of company to which some or all of the provisions of this Chapter apply, or

(b) extend some or all of the provisions of this Chapter to additional types of company.

(2) Regulations under this section extending the application of any provision of this Chapter are subject to affirmative resolution procedure.

(3) Any other regulations under this section are subject to negative resolution procedure.

(4) Regulations under this section may—

(a) amend the provisions of this Chapter (apart from this section);

(b) repeal and re-enact provisions of this Chapter with modifications of form or arrangement, whether or not they are modified in substance;

(c) contain such consequential, incidental and supplementary provisions (including provisions amending, repealing or revoking enactments) as the Secretary of State thinks fit.

CHAPTER 6
RECORDS OF RESOLUTIONS AND MEETINGS

355 Records of resolutions and meetings etc

(1) Every company must keep records comprising—

(a) copies of all resolutions of members passed otherwise than at general meetings,

(b) minutes of all proceedings of general meetings, and

(c) details provided to the company in accordance with section 357 (decisions of sole member).

(2) The records must be kept for at least ten years from the date of the resolution, meeting or decision (as appropriate).

(3) If a company fails to comply with this section, an offence is committed by every officer of the company who is in default.

(4) A person guilty of an offence under this section is liable on summary conviction to a fine not exceeding level 3 on the standard scale and, for continued contravention, a daily default fine not exceeding one-tenth of level 3 on the standard scale.

356 Records as evidence of resolutions etc

(1) This section applies to the records kept in accordance with section 355.

(2) The record of a resolution passed otherwise than at a general meeting, if purporting to be signed by a director of the company or by the company secretary, is evidence (in Scotland, sufficient evidence) of the passing of the resolution.

(3) Where there is a record of a written resolution of a private company, the requirements of this Act with respect to the passing of the resolution are deemed to be complied with unless the contrary is proved.

(4) The minutes of proceedings of a general meeting, if purporting to be signed by the chairman of that meeting or by the chairman of the next general meeting, are evidence (in Scotland, sufficient evidence) of the proceedings at the meeting.

(5) Where there is a record of proceedings of a general meeting of a company, then, until the contrary is proved—

(a) the meeting is deemed duly held and convened,

(b) all proceedings at the meeting are deemed to have duly taken place, and

(c) all appointments at the meeting are deemed valid.

357 Records of decisions by sole member

(1) This section applies to a company limited by shares or by guarantee that has only one member.

(2) Where the member takes any decision that—

(a) may be taken by the company in general meeting, and

(b) has effect as if agreed by the company in general meeting, he must (unless that decision is taken by way of a written resolution) provide the company with details of that decision.

(3) If a person fails to comply with this section he commits an offence.

(4) A person guilty of an offence under this section is liable on summary conviction to a fine not exceeding level 2 on the standard scale.

(5) Failure to comply with this section does not affect the validity of any decision referred to in subsection (2).

358 Inspection of records of resolutions and meetings

(1) The records referred to in section 355 (records of resolutions etc) relating to the previous ten years must be kept available for inspection—

(a) at the company's registered office, or

(b) at a place specified in regulations under section 1136.

(2) The company must give notice to the registrar—

(a) of the place at which the records are kept available for inspection, and

(b) of any change in that place,

unless they have at all times been kept at the company's registered office.

(3) The records must be open to the inspection of any member of the company without charge.

(4) Any member may require a copy of any of the records on payment of such fee as may be prescribed.

(5) If default is made for 14 days in complying with subsection (2) or an inspection required under subsection (3) is refused, or a copy requested under subsection (4) is not sent, an offence is committed by every officer of the company who is in default.

(6) A person guilty of an offence under this section is liable on summary conviction to a fine not exceeding level 3 on the standard scale and, for continued contravention, a daily default fine not exceeding one-tenth of level 3 on the standard scale.

(7) In a case in which an inspection required under subsection (3) is refused or a copy requested under subsection (4) is not sent, the court may by order compel an immediate inspection of the records or direct that the copies required be sent to the persons who requested them.

359 Records of resolutions and meetings of class of members

The provisions of this Chapter apply (with necessary modifications) in relation to resolutions and meetings of—

(a) holders of a class of shares, and

(b) in the case of a company without a share capital, a class of members, as they apply in relation to resolutions of members generally and to general meetings.

CHAPTER 7
SUPPLEMENTARY PROVISIONS

360 Computation of periods of notice etc: clear day rule

(1) This section applies for the purposes of the following provisions of this Part—
section 307(1) and (2) (notice required of general meeting),
section 307A(1), (4), (5) and (7)(b) (notice required of general meeting of traded company),
section 312(1) and (3) (resolution requiring special notice),
section 314(4)(d) (request to circulate members' statement),
section 316(2)(b) (expenses of circulating statement to be deposited or tendered before meeting),
section 337(3) (contents of notice of AGM of traded company),
section 338(4)(d)(i) (request to circulate member's resolution at AGM of public company), . . .
section 338A(5) (request to include matter in the business to be dealt with at AGM of traded company),
section 340(2)(b)(i) (expenses of circulating statement to be deposited or tendered before meeting), and
section 340B(2)(b) (traded companies: duty to circulate members' matters for AGM).

(2) Any reference in those provisions to a period of notice, or to a period before a meeting by which a request must be received or sum deposited or tendered, is to a period of the specified length excluding—

(a) the day of the meeting, and

(b) the day on which the notice is given, the request received or the sum deposited or tendered.

360A Electronic meetings and voting

(1) Nothing in this Part is to be taken to preclude the holding and conducting of a meeting in such a way that persons who are not present together at the same place may by electronic means attend and speak and vote at it.

(2) In the case of a traded company the use of electronic means for the purpose of enabling members to participate in a general meeting may be made subject only to such requirements and restrictions as are—

(a) necessary to ensure the identification of those taking part and the security of the electronic communication, and

(b) proportionate to the achievement of those objectives.

(3) Nothing in subsection (2) affects any power of a company to require reasonable evidence of the entitlement of any person who is not a member to participate in the meeting.

360B Traded companies: requirements for participating in and voting at general meetings

(1) Any provision of a traded company's articles is void in so far as it would have the effect of—

(a) imposing a restriction on a right of a member to participate in and vote at a general meeting of the company unless the member's shares have (after having been acquired by the member and before the meeting) been deposited with, or transferred to, or registered in the name of another person, or

(b) imposing a restriction on the right of a member to transfer shares in the company during the period of 48 hours before the time for the holding of a general meeting of the company if that right would not otherwise be subject to that restriction.

(2) A traded company must determine the right to vote at a general meeting of the company by reference to the register of members as at a time (determined by the company) that is not more than 48 hours before the time for the holding of the meeting.

(3) In calculating the period mentioned in subsection (1)(b) or (2), no account is to be taken of any part of a day that is not a working day.

(4) Nothing in this section affects—

(a) the operation of—

(i) Part 22 of this Act (information about interests in a company's shares),

(ii) Part 15 of the Companies Act 1985 (orders imposing restrictions on shares), or

(iii) any provision in a company's articles relating to the application of any provision of either of those Parts; or

(b) the validity of articles prescribed, or to the same effect as articles prescribed, under section 19 of this Act (power of Secretary of State to prescribe model articles).

360C Meaning of "traded company"

In this Part, "traded company" means a company any shares of which—

(a) carry rights to vote at general meetings, and

(b) are admitted to trading on a regulated market in an EEA State by or with the consent of the company.

361 Meaning of "quoted company"

In this Part "quoted company" has the same meaning as in Part 15 of this Act.

PART 14
CONTROL OF POLITICAL DONATIONS AND EXPENDITURE

Introductory

362 Introductory

This Part has effect for controlling—

(a) political donations made by companies to political parties, to other political organisations and to independent election candidates, and

(b) political expenditure incurred by companies.

Donations and expenditure to which this Part applies

363 Political parties, organisations etc to which this Part applies

(1) This Part applies to a political party if—

(a) it is registered under Part 2 of the Political Parties, Elections and Referendums Act 2000, or

(b) it carries on, or proposes to carry on, activities for the purposes of or in connection with the participation of the party in any election or elections to public office held in a member State other than the United Kingdom.

(2) This Part applies to an organisation (a "political organisation") if it carries on, or proposes to carry on, activities that are capable of being reasonably regarded as intended—

(a) to affect public support for a political party to which, or an independent election candidate to whom, this Part applies, or

(b) to influence voters in relation to any national or regional referendum held under the law of the United Kingdom or another member State.

(3) This Part applies to an independent election candidate at any election to public office held in the United Kingdom or another member State.

(4) Any reference in the following provisions of this Part to a political party, political organisation or independent election candidate, or to political expenditure, is to a party, organisation, independent candidate or expenditure to which this Part applies.

364 Meaning of "political donation"

(1) The following provisions have effect for the purposes of this Part as regards the meaning of "political donation".

(2) In relation to a political party or other political organisation—

(a) "political donation" means anything that in accordance with sections 50 to 52 of the Political Parties, Elections and Referendums Act 2000—

(i) constitutes a donation for the purposes of Chapter 1 of Part 4 of that Act (control of donations to registered parties), or

(ii) would constitute such a donation reading references in those sections to a registered party as references to any political party or other political organisation,

and

(b) section 53 of that Act applies, in the same way, for the purpose of determining the value of a donation.

(3) In relation to an independent election candidate—

(a) "political donation" means anything that, in accordance with sections 50 to 52 of that Act, would constitute a donation for the purposes of Chapter 1 of Part 4 of that Act (control of donations to registered parties) reading references in those sections to a registered party as references to the independent election candidate,

and

(b) section 53 of that Act applies, in the same way, for the purpose of determining the value of a donation.

(4) For the purposes of this section, sections 50 and 53 of the Political Parties, Elections and Referendums Act 2000 (definition of "donation" and value of donations) shall be treated as if the amendments to those sections made by the Electoral Administration Act 2006 (which remove from the definition of "donation" loans made otherwise than on commercial terms) had not been made.

365 Meaning of "political expenditure"

(1) In this Part "political expenditure", in relation to a company, means expenditure incurred by the company on—

(a) the preparation, publication or dissemination of advertising or other promotional or publicity material—

(i) of whatever nature, and

(ii) however published or otherwise disseminated,

that, at the time of publication or dissemination, is capable of being reasonably regarded as intended to affect public support for a political party or other political organisation, or an independent election candidate, or

(b) activities on the part of the company that are capable of being reasonably regarded as intended—

(i) to affect public support for a political party or other political organisation, or an independent election candidate, or

(ii) to influence voters in relation to any national or regional referendum held under the law of a member State.

(2) For the purposes of this Part a political donation does not count as political expenditure.

Authorisation required for donations or expenditure

366 Authorisation required for donations or expenditure

(1) A company must not—

(a) make a political donation to a political party or other political organisation, or to an independent election candidate, or

(b) incur any political expenditure,

unless the donation or expenditure is authorised in accordance with the following provisions.

(2) The donation or expenditure must be authorised—

(a) in the case of a company that is not a subsidiary of another company, by a resolution of the members of the company;

(b) in the case of a company that is a subsidiary of another company by—

(i) a resolution of the members of the company, and

(ii) a resolution of the members of any relevant holding company.

(3) No resolution is required on the part of a company that is a wholly-owned subsidiary of a UK-registered company.

(4) For the purposes of subsection (2)(b)(ii) a "relevant holding company" means a company that, at the time the donation was made or the expenditure was incurred—

(a) was a holding company of the company by which the donation was made or the expenditure was incurred,

(b) was a UK-registered company, and

(c) was not a subsidiary of another UK-registered company.

(5) The resolution or resolutions required by this section—

(a) must comply with section 367 (form of authorising resolution), and

(b) must be passed before the donation is made or the expenditure incurred.

(6) Nothing in this section enables a company to be authorised to do anything that it could not lawfully do apart from this section.

367 Form of authorising resolution

(1) A resolution conferring authorisation for the purposes of this Part may relate to—

(a) the company passing the resolution,

(b) one or more subsidiaries of that company, or

(c) the company passing the resolution and one or more subsidiaries of that company.

(2) A resolution may be expressed to relate to all companies that are subsidiaries of the company passing the resolution—

(a) at the time the resolution is passed, or

(b) at any time during the period for which the resolution has effect, without identifying them individually.

(3) The resolution may authorise donations or expenditure under one or more of the following heads—

(a) donations to political parties or independent election candidates;

(b) donations to political organisations other than political parties;

(c) political expenditure.

(4) The resolution must specify a head or heads—

(a) in the case of a resolution under subsection (2), for all of the companies to which it relates taken together;

(b) in the case of any other resolution, for each company to which it relates.

(5) The resolution must be expressed in general terms conforming with subsection (3) and must not purport to authorise particular donations or expenditure.

(6) For each of the specified heads the resolution must authorise donations or, as the case may be, expenditure up to a specified amount in the period for which the resolution has effect (see section 368).

(7) The resolution must specify such amounts—

(a) in the case of a resolution under subsection (2), for all of the companies to which it relates taken together;

(b) in the case of any other resolution, for each company to which it relates.

368 Period for which resolution has effect

(1) A resolution conferring authorisation for the purposes of this Part has effect for a period of four years beginning with the date on which it is passed unless the directors determine, or the articles require, that it is to have effect for a shorter period beginning with that date.

(2) The power of the directors to make a determination under this section is subject to any provision of the articles that operates to prevent them from doing so.

Remedies in case of unauthorised donations or expenditure

369 Liability of directors in case of unauthorised donation or expenditure

(1) This section applies where a company has made a political donation or incurred political expenditure without the authorisation required by this Part.

(2) The directors in default are jointly and severally liable—

(a) to make good to the company the amount of the unauthorised donation or expenditure, with interest, and

(b) to compensate the company for any loss or damage sustained by it as a result of the unauthorised donation or expenditure having been made.

(3) The directors in default are—

(a) those who, at the time the unauthorised donation was made or the unauthorised expenditure was incurred, were directors of the company by which the donation was made or the expenditure was incurred, and

(b) where—

(i) that company was a subsidiary of a relevant holding company, and

(ii) the directors of the relevant holding company failed to take all reasonable steps to prevent the donation being made or the expenditure being incurred,

the directors of the relevant holding company.

(4) For the purposes of subsection (3)(b) a "relevant holding company" means a company that, at the time the donation was made or the expenditure was incurred—

(a) was a holding company of the company by which the donation was made or the expenditure was incurred,

(b) was a UK-registered company, and

(c) was not a subsidiary of another UK-registered company.

(5) The interest referred to in subsection (2)(a) is interest on the amount of the unauthorised donation or expenditure, so far as not made good to the company—

(a) in respect of the period beginning with the date when the donation was made or the expenditure was incurred, and

(b) at such rate as the Secretary of State may prescribe by regulations.

Section 379(2) (construction of references to date when donation made or expenditure incurred) does not apply for the purposes of this subsection.

(6) Where only part of a donation or expenditure was unauthorised, this section applies only to so much of it as was unauthorised.

370 Enforcement of directors' liabilities by shareholder action

(1) Any liability of a director under section 369 is enforceable—

(a) in the case of a liability of a director of a company to that company, by proceedings brought under this section in the name of the company by an authorised group of its members;

(b) in the case of a liability of a director of a holding company to a subsidiary, by proceedings brought under this section in the name of the subsidiary by—

(i) an authorised group of members of the subsidiary, or

(ii) an authorised group of members of the holding company.

(2) This is in addition to the right of the company to which the liability is owed to bring proceedings itself to enforce the liability.

(3) An "authorised group" of members of a company means—

(a) the holders of not less than 5% in nominal value of the company's issued share capital,
(b) if the company is not limited by shares, not less than 5 % of its members, or
(c) not less than 50 of the company's members.

(4) The right to bring proceedings under this section is subject to the provisions of section 371.

(5) Nothing in this section affects any right of a member of a company to bring or continue proceedings under Part 11 (derivative claims or proceedings).

371 Enforcement of directors' liabilities by shareholder action: supplementary

(1) A group of members may not bring proceedings under section 370 in the name of a company unless—
(a) the group has given written notice to the company stating—
(i) the cause of action and a summary of the facts on which the proceedings are to be based,
(ii) the names and addresses of the members comprising the group, and
(iii) the grounds on which it is alleged that those members constitute an authorised group; and
(b) not less than 28 days have elapsed between the date of the giving of the notice to the company and the bringing of the proceedings.

(2) Where such a notice is given to a company, any director of the company may apply to the court within the period of 28 days beginning with the date of the giving of the notice for an order directing that the proposed proceedings shall not be brought, on one or more of the following grounds—
(a) that the unauthorised amount has been made good to the company;
(b) that proceedings to enforce the liability have been brought, and are being pursued with due diligence, by the company;
(c) that the members proposing to bring proceedings under this section do not constitute an authorised group.

(3) Where an application is made on the ground mentioned in subsection (2)(b), the court may as an alternative to directing that the proposed proceedings under section 370 are not to be brought, direct—
(a) that such proceedings may be brought on such terms and conditions as the court thinks fit, and
(b) that the proceedings brought by the company—
(i) shall be discontinued, or
(ii) may be continued on such terms and conditions as the court thinks fit.

(4) The members by whom proceedings are brought under section 370 owe to the company in whose name they are brought the same duties in relation to the proceedings as would be owed by the company's directors if the proceedings were being brought by the company.
But proceedings to enforce any such duty may be brought by the company only with the permission of the court.

(5) Proceedings brought under section 370 may not be discontinued or settled by the group except with the permission of the court, which may be given on such terms as the court thinks fit.

372 Costs of shareholder action

(1) This section applies in relation to proceedings brought under section 370 in the name of a company ("the company") by an authorised group ("the group").

(2) The group may apply to the court for an order directing the company to indemnify the group in respect of costs incurred or to be incurred by the group in connection with the proceedings.
The court may make such an order on such terms as it thinks fit.

(3) The group is not entitled to be paid any such costs out of the assets of the company except by virtue of such an order.

(4) If no such order has been made with respect to the proceedings, then—

(a) if the company is awarded costs in connection with the proceedings, or it is agreed that costs incurred by the company in connection with the proceedings should be paid by any defendant, the costs shall be paid to the group; and
(b) if any defendant is awarded costs in connection with the proceedings, or it is agreed that any defendant should be paid costs incurred by him in connection with the proceedings, the costs shall be paid by the group.

(5) In the application of this section to Scotland for "costs" read "expenses" and for "defendant" read "defender".

373 Information for purposes of shareholder action

(1) Where proceedings have been brought under section 370 in the name of a company by an authorised group, the group is entitled to require the company to provide it with all information relating to the subject matter of the proceedings that is in the company's possession or under its control or which is reasonably obtainable by it.

(2) If the company, having been required by the group to do so, refuses to provide the group with all or any of that information, the court may, on an application made by the group, make an order directing—
(a) the company, and
(b) any of its officers or employees specified in the application, to provide the group with the information in question in such form and by such means as the court may direct.

Exemptions

374 Trade unions

(1) A donation to a trade union, other than a contribution to the union's political fund, is not a political donation for the purposes of this Part.

(2) A trade union is not a political organisation for the purposes of section 365 (meaning of "political expenditure").

(3) In this section—
"trade union" has the meaning given by section 1 of Trade Union and Labour Relations (Consolidation) Act 1992 or Article 3 of the Industrial Relations (Northern Ireland) Order 1992;
"political fund" means the fund from which payments by a trade union in the furtherance of political objects are required to be made by virtue of section 82(1)(a) of that Act or Article 57(2)(a) of that Order.

375 Subscription for membership of trade association

(1) A subscription paid to a trade association for membership of the association is not a political donation for the purposes of this Part.

(2) For this purpose—
"trade association" means an organisation formed for the purpose of furthering the trade interests of its members, or of persons represented by its members, and
subscription" does not include a payment to the association to the extent that it is made for the purpose of financing any particular activity of the association.

376 All-party parliamentary groups

(1) An all-party parliamentary group is not a political organisation for the purposes of this Part.

(2) An "all-party parliamentary group" means an all-party group composed of members of one or both of the Houses of Parliament (or of such members and other persons).

377 Political expenditure exempted by order

(1) Authorisation under this Part is not needed for political expenditure that is exempt by virtue of an order of the Secretary of State under this section.

(2) An order may confer an exemption in relation to—
(a) companies of any description or category specified in the order, or

(b) expenditure of any description or category so specified (whether framed by reference to goods, services or other matters in respect of which such expenditure is incurred or otherwise),

or both.

(3) If or to the extent that expenditure is exempt from the requirement of authorisation under this Part by virtue of an order under this section, it shall be disregarded in determining what donations are authorised by any resolution of the company passed for the purposes of this Part.

(4) An order under this section is subject to affirmative resolution procedure.

378 Donations not amounting to more than £5,000 in any twelve month period

(1) Authorisation under this Part is not needed for a donation except to the extent that the total amount of—

(a) that donation, and

(b) other relevant donations made in the period of 12 months ending with the date on which that donation is made,

exceeds £5,000.

(2) In this section—

"donation" means a donation to a political party or other political organisation or to an independent election candidate; and

"other relevant donations" means—

(a) in relation to a donation made by a company that is not a subsidiary, any other donations made by that company or by any of its subsidiaries;

(b) in relation to a donation made by a company that is a subsidiary, any other donations made by that company, by any holding company of that company or by any other subsidiary of any such holding company.

(3) If or to the extent that a donation is exempt by virtue of this section from the requirement of authorisation under this Part, it shall be disregarded in determining what donations are authorised by any resolution passed for the purposes of this Part.

Supplementary provisions

379 Minor definitions

(1) In this Part—

"director" includes shadow director; and

"organisation" includes any body corporate or unincorporated association and any combination of persons.

(2) Except as otherwise provided, any reference in this Part to the time at which a donation is made or expenditure is incurred is, in a case where the donation is made or expenditure incurred in pursuance of a contract, any earlier time at which that contract is entered into by the company.

PART 15
ACCOUNTS AND REPORTS

CHAPTER 1
INTRODUCTION

General

380 Scheme of this Part

(1) The requirements of this Part as to accounts and reports apply in relation to each financial year of a company.

(2) In certain respects different provisions apply to different kinds of company.

(3) The main distinctions for this purpose are—

(a) between companies subject to the small companies regime (see section 381) and companies that are not subject to that regime; and

(b) between quoted companies (see section 385) and companies that are not quoted.

(4) In this Part, where provisions do not apply to all kinds of company—

(a) provisions applying to companies subject to the small companies regime appear before the provisions applying to other companies,

(b) provisions applying to private companies appear before the provisions applying to public companies, and

(c) provisions applying to quoted companies appear after the provisions applying to other companies.

Companies subject to the small companies regime

381 Companies subject to the small companies regime

The small companies regime ... applies to a company for a financial year in relation to which the company—

(a) qualifies as small (see sections 382 and 383), and

(b) is not excluded from the regime (see section 384).

382 Companies qualifying as small: general

(1) A company qualifies as small in relation to its first financial year if the qualifying conditions are met in that year.

(2) A company qualifies as small in relation to a subsequent financial year—

(a) if the qualifying conditions are met in that year and the preceding financial year;

(b) if the qualifying conditions are met in that year and the company qualified as small in relation to the preceding financial year;

(c) if the qualifying conditions were met in the preceding financial year and the company qualified as small in relation to that year.

(3) The qualifying conditions are met by a company in a year in which it satisfies two or more of the following requirements—

1.	Turnover	Not more than £6.5 million
2.	Balance sheet total	Not more than £3.26 million
3.	Number of employees	Not more than 50

(4) For a period that is a company's financial year but not in fact a year the maximum figures for turnover must be proportionately adjusted.

(5) The balance sheet total means the aggregate of the amounts shown as assets in the company's balance sheet.

(6) The number of employees means the average number of persons employed by the company in the year, determined as follows—

(a) find for each month in the financial year the number of persons employed under contracts of service by the company in that month (whether throughout the month or not),

(b) add together the monthly totals, and

(c) divide by the number of months in the financial year.

(7) This section is subject to section 383 (companies qualifying as small: parent companies).

383 Companies qualifying as small: parent companies

(1) A parent company qualifies as a small company in relation to a financial year only if the group headed by it qualifies as a small group.

(2) A group qualifies as small in relation to the parent company's first financial year if the qualifying conditions are met in that year.

(3) A group qualifies as small in relation to a subsequent financial year of the parent company—

(a) if the qualifying conditions are met in that year and the preceding financial year;

(b) if the qualifying conditions are met in that year and the group qualified as small in relation to the preceding financial year;

(c) if the qualifying conditions were met in the preceding financial year and the group qualified as small in relation to that year.

(4) The qualifying conditions are met by a group in a year in which it satisfies two or more of the following requirements—

1.	Aggregate turnover	Not more than £6.5 million net (or £7.8 million gross)
2.	Aggregate balance sheet total	Not more than £3.26 million net (or £3.9 million gross)
3.	Aggregate number of employees	Not more than 50

(5) The aggregate figures are ascertained by aggregating the relevant figures determined in accordance with section 382 for each member of the group.

(6) In relation to the aggregate figures for turnover and balance sheet total—
"net" means after any set-offs and other adjustments made to eliminate group transactions—
(a) in the case of Companies Act accounts, in accordance with regulations under section 404,
(b) in the case of IAS accounts, in accordance with international accounting standards; and
"gross" means without those set-offs and other adjustments.
A company may satisfy any relevant requirement on the basis of either the net or the gross figure.

(7) The figures for each subsidiary undertaking shall be those included in its individual accounts for the relevant financial year, that is—
(a) if its financial year ends with that of the parent company, that financial year, and
(b) if not, its financial year ending last before the end of the financial year of the parent company.
If those figures cannot be obtained without disproportionate expense or undue delay, the latest available figures shall be taken.

384 Companies excluded from the small companies regime

(1) The small companies regime does not apply to a company that is, or was at any time within the financial year to which the accounts relate—
(a) a public company,
(b) a company that—
(i) is an authorised insurance company, a banking company, an e-money issuer, a MiFID investment firm or a UCITS management company, or
(ii) carries on insurance market activity, or
(c) a member of an ineligible group.

(2) A group is ineligible if any of its members is—
(a) a public company,
(b) a body corporate (other than a company) whose shares are admitted to trading on a regulated market in an EEA State,
(c) a person (other than a small company) who has permission under Part 4A of the Financial Services and Markets Act 2000 to carry on a regulated activity,
(d) a small company that is an authorised insurance company, a banking company, an e-money issuer, a MiFID investment firm or a UCITS management company, or
(e) a person who carries on insurance market activity.

(3) A company is a small company for the purposes of subsection (2) if it qualified as small in relation to its last financial year ending on or before the end of the financial year to which the accounts relate.

Quoted and unquoted companies

385 Quoted and unquoted companies

(1) For the purposes of this Part a company is a quoted company in relation to a financial year if it is a quoted company immediately before the end of the accounting reference period by reference to which that financial year was determined.

(2) A "quoted company" means a company whose equity share capital—
(a) has been included in the official list in accordance with the provisions of Part 6 of the Financial Services and Markets Act 2000, or
(b) is officially listed in an EEA State, or

(c) is admitted to dealing on either the New York Stock Exchange or the exchange known as Nasdaq.

In paragraph (a) "the official list" has the meaning given by section 103(1) of the Financial Services and Markets Act 2000.

(3) An "unquoted company" means a company that is not a quoted company.

(4) The Secretary of State may by regulations amend or replace the provisions of subsections (1) to (2) so as to limit or extend the application of some or all of the provisions of this Part that are expressed to apply to quoted companies.

(5) Regulations under this section extending the application of any such provision of this Part are subject to affirmative resolution procedure.

(6) Any other regulations under this section are subject to negative resolution procedure.

CHAPTER 2
ACCOUNTING RECORDS

386 Duty to keep accounting records

(1) Every company must keep adequate accounting records.

(2) Adequate accounting records means records that are sufficient—

(a) to show and explain the company's transactions,

(b) to disclose with reasonable accuracy, at any time, the financial position of the company at that time, and

(c) to enable the directors to ensure that any accounts required to be prepared comply with the requirements of this Act (and, where applicable, of Article 4 of the IAS Regulation).

(3) Accounting records must, in particular, contain—

(a) entries from day to day of all sums of money received and expended by the company and the matters in respect of which the receipt and expenditure takes place, and

(b) a record of the assets and liabilities of the company.

(4) If the company's business involves dealing in goods, the accounting records must contain—

(a) statements of stock held by the company at the end of each financial year of the company,

(b) all statements of stocktakings from which any statement of stock as is mentioned in paragraph (a) has been or is to be prepared, and

(c) except in the case of goods sold by way of ordinary retail trade, statements of all goods sold and purchased, showing the goods and the buyers and sellers in sufficient detail to enable all these to be identified.

(5) A parent company that has a subsidiary undertaking in relation to which the above requirements do not apply must take reasonable steps to secure that the undertaking keeps such accounting records as to enable the directors of the parent company to ensure that any accounts required to be prepared under this Part comply with the requirements of this Act (and, where applicable, of Article 4 of the IAS Regulation).

387 Duty to keep accounting records: offence

(1) If a company fails to comply with any provision of section 386 (duty to keep accounting records), an offence is committed by every officer of the company who is in default.

(2) It is a defence for a person charged with such an offence to show that he acted honestly and that in the circumstances in which the company's business was carried on the default was excusable.

(3) A person guilty of an offence under this section is liable—

(a) on conviction on indictment, to imprisonment for a term not exceeding two years or a fine (or both);

(b) on summary conviction—

(i) in England and Wales, to imprisonment for a term not exceeding twelve months or to a fine not exceeding the statutory maximum (or both);

(ii) in Scotland or Northern Ireland, to imprisonment for a term not exceeding six months, or to a fine not exceeding the statutory maximum (or both).

388 Where and for how long records to be kept

(1) A company's accounting records—

(a) must be kept at its registered office or such other place as the directors think fit, and

(b) must at all times be open to inspection by the company's officers.

(2) If accounting records are kept at a place outside the United Kingdom, accounts and returns with respect to the business dealt with in the accounting records so kept must be sent to, and kept at, a place in the United Kingdom, and must at all times be open to such inspection.

(3) The accounts and returns to be sent to the United Kingdom must be such as to—

(a) disclose with reasonable accuracy the financial position of the business in question at intervals of not more than six months, and

(b) enable the directors to ensure that the accounts required to be prepared under this Part comply with the requirements of this Act (and, where applicable, of Article 4 of the IAS Regulation).

(4) Accounting records that a company is required by section 386 to keep must be preserved by it—

(a) in the case of a private company, for three years from the date on which they are made;

(b) in the case of a public company, for six years from the date on which they are made.

(5) Subsection (4) is subject to any provision contained in rules made under section 411 of the Insolvency Act 1986 (company insolvency rules) or Article 359 of the Insolvency (Northern Ireland) Order 1989.

389 Where and for how long records to be kept: offences

(1) If a company fails to comply with any provision of subsections (1) to (3) of section 388 (requirements as to keeping of accounting records), an offence is committed by every officer of the company who is in default.

(2) It is a defence for a person charged with such an offence to show that he acted honestly and that in the circumstances in which the company's business was carried on the default was excusable.

(3) An officer of a company commits an offence if he—

(a) fails to take all reasonable steps for securing compliance by the company with subsection (4) of that section (period for which records to be preserved), or

(b) intentionally causes any default by the company under that subsection.

(4) A person guilty of an offence under this section is liable—

(a) on conviction on indictment, to imprisonment for a term not exceeding two years or a fine (or both);

(b) on summary conviction—

(i) in England and Wales, to imprisonment for a term not exceeding twelve months or to a fine not exceeding the statutory maximum (or both);

(ii) in Scotland or Northern Ireland, to imprisonment for a term not exceeding six months, or to a fine not exceeding the statutory maximum (or both).

CHAPTER 3
A COMPANY'S FINANCIAL YEAR

390 A company's financial year

(1) A company's financial year is determined as follows.

(2) Its first financial year—

(a) begins with the first day of its first accounting reference period, and

(b) ends with the last day of that period or such other date, not more than seven days before or after the end of that period, as the directors may determine.

(3) Subsequent financial years—

(a) begin with the day immediately following the end of the company's previous financial year, and

(b) end with the last day of its next accounting reference period or such other date, not more than seven days before or after the end of that period, as the directors may determine.

(4) In relation to an undertaking that is not a company, references in this Act to its financial year are to any period in respect of which a profit and loss account of the undertaking is required to be made up (by its constitution or by the law under which it is established), whether that period is a year or not.

(5) The directors of a parent company must secure that, except where in their opinion there are good reasons against it, the financial year of each of its subsidiary undertakings coincides with the company's own financial year.

391 Accounting reference periods and accounting reference date

(1) A company's accounting reference periods are determined according to its accounting reference date in each calendar year.

(2) The accounting reference date of a company incorporated in Great Britain before 1st April 1996 is—

(a) the date specified by notice to the registrar in accordance with section 224(2) of the Companies Act 1985 (notice specifying accounting reference date given within nine months of incorporation), or

(b) failing such notice—

(i) in the case of a company incorporated before 1st April 1990, 31st March, and

(ii) in the case of a company incorporated on or after 1st April 1990, the last day of the month in which the anniversary of its incorporation falls.

(3) The accounting reference date of a company incorporated in Northern Ireland before 22nd August 1997 is—

(a) the date specified by notice to the registrar in accordance with article 232(2) of the Companies (Northern Ireland) Order 1986 (notice specifying accounting reference date given within nine months of incorporation), or

(b) failing such notice—

(i) in the case of a company incorporated before the coming into operation of Article 5 of the Companies (Northern Ireland) Order 1990, 31st March, and

(ii) in the case of a company incorporated after the coming into operation of that Article, the last day of the month in which the anniversary of its incorporation falls.

(4) The accounting reference date of a company incorporated—

(a) in Great Britain on or after 1st April 1996 and before the commencement of this Act,

(b) in Northern Ireland on or after 22nd August 1997 and before the commencement of this Act, or

(c) after the commencement of this Act,

is the last day of the month in which the anniversary of its incorporation falls.

(5) A company's first accounting reference period is the period of more than six months, but not more than 18 months, beginning with the date of its incorporation and ending with its accounting reference date.

(6) Its subsequent accounting reference periods are successive periods of twelve months beginning immediately after the end of the previous accounting reference period and ending with its accounting reference date.

(7) This section has effect subject to the provisions of section 392 (alteration of accounting reference date).

392 Alteration of accounting reference date

(1) A company may by notice given to the registrar specify a new accounting reference date having effect in relation to—

(a) the company's current accounting reference period and subsequent periods, or

(b) the company's previous accounting reference period and subsequent periods.

A company's "previous accounting reference period" means the one immediately preceding its current accounting reference period.

(2) The notice must state whether the current or previous accounting reference period—

(a) is to be shortened, so as to come to an end on the first occasion on which the new accounting reference date falls or fell after the beginning of the period, or

(b) is to be extended, so as to come to an end on the second occasion on which that date falls or fell after the beginning of the period.

(3) A notice extending a company's current or previous accounting reference period is not effective if given less than five years after the end of an earlier accounting reference period of the company that was extended under this section.

This does not apply—

(a) to a notice given by a company that is a subsidiary undertaking or parent undertaking of another EEA undertaking if the new accounting reference date coincides with that of the other EEA undertaking or, where that undertaking is not a company, with the last day of its financial year, or

(b) where the company is in administration under Part 2 of the Insolvency Act 1986 or Part 3 of the Insolvency (Northern Ireland) Order 1989, or

(c) where the Secretary of State directs that it should not apply, which he may do with respect to a notice that has been given or that may be given.

(4) A notice under this section may not be given in respect of a previous accounting reference period if the period for filing accounts and reports for the financial year determined by reference to that accounting reference period has already expired.

(5) An accounting reference period may not be extended so as to exceed 18 months and a notice under this section is ineffective if the current or previous accounting reference period as extended in accordance with the notice would exceed that limit.

This does not apply where the company is in administration under Part 2 of the Insolvency Act 1986 or Part 3 of the Insolvency (Northern Ireland) Order 1989.

(6) In this section "EEA undertaking" means an undertaking established under the law of any part of the United Kingdom or the law of any other EEA State.

CHAPTER 4
ANNUAL ACCOUNTS

General

393 Accounts to give true and fair view

(1) The directors of a company must not approve accounts for the purposes of this Chapter unless they are satisfied that they give a true and fair view of the assets, liabilities, financial position and profit or loss—

(a) in the case of the company's individual accounts, of the company;

(b) in the case of the company's group accounts, of the undertakings included in the consolidation as a whole, so far as concerns members of the company.

(2) The auditor of a company in carrying out his functions under this Act in relation to the company's annual accounts must have regard to the directors' duty under subsection (1).

Individual accounts

394 Duty to prepare individual accounts

The directors of every company must prepare accounts for the company for each of its financial years unless the company is exempt from that requirement under section 394A.

Those accounts are referred to as the company's "individual accounts".

394A Individual accounts: exemption for dormant subsidiaries

(1) A company is exempt from the requirement to prepare individual accounts for a financial year if—

(a) it is itself a subsidiary undertaking,

(b) it has been dormant throughout the whole of that year, and

(c) its parent undertaking is established under the law of an EEA State.

(2) Exemption is conditional upon compliance with all of the following conditions—
(a) all members of the company must agree to the exemption in respect of the financial year in question,
(b) the parent undertaking must give a guarantee under section 394C in respect of that year,
(c) the company must be included in the consolidated accounts drawn up for that year or to an earlier date in that year by the parent undertaking in accordance with—
(i) the provisions of the Seventh Directive (83/349/EEC), or
(ii) international accounting standards,
(d) the parent undertaking must disclose in the notes to the consolidated accounts that the company is exempt from the requirement to prepare individual accounts by virtue of this section, and
(e) the directors of the company must deliver to the registrar within the period for filing the company's accounts and reports for that year—
(i) a written notice of the agreement referred to in subsection (2)(a),
(ii) the statement referred to in section 394C(1),
(iii) a copy of the consolidated accounts referred to in subsection (2)(c),
(iv) a copy of the auditor's report on those accounts, and
(v) a copy of the consolidated annual report drawn up by the parent undertaking.

394B Companies excluded from the dormant subsidiaries exemption

A company is not entitled to the exemption conferred by section 394A (dormant subsidiaries) if it was at any time within the financial year in question—
(a) a quoted company as defined in section 385(2) of this Act,
(b) a company that—
(i) is an authorised insurance company, a banking company, an e-money issuer, a MiFID investment firm or a UCITS management company, or
(ii) carries on insurance market activity, or
(c) a special register body as defined in section 117(1) of the Trade Union and Labour Relations (Consolidation) Act 1992 (c 52) or an employers' association as defined in section 122 of that Act or Article 4 of the Industrial Relations (Northern Ireland) Order 1992 (SI 1992/807) (NI 5).

394C Dormant subsidiaries exemption: parent undertaking declaration of guarantee

(1) A guarantee is given by a parent undertaking under this section when the directors of the subsidiary company deliver to the registrar a statement by the parent undertaking that it guarantees the subsidiary company under this section.
(2) The statement under subsection (1) must be authenticated by the parent undertaking and must specify—
(a) the name of the parent undertaking,
(b) if the parent undertaking is incorporated in the United Kingdom, its registered number (if any),
(c) if the parent undertaking is incorporated outside the United Kingdom and registered in the country in which it is incorporated, the identity of the register on which it is registered and the number with which it is so registered,
(d) the name and registered number of the subsidiary company in respect of which the guarantee is being given,
(e) the date of the statement, and
(f) the financial year to which the guarantee relates.
(3) A guarantee given under this section has the effect that—
(a) the parent undertaking guarantees all outstanding liabilities to which the subsidiary company is subject at the end of the financial year to which the guarantee relates, until they are satisfied in full, and

(b) the guarantee is enforceable against the parent undertaking by any person to whom the subsidiary company is liable in respect of those liabilities.

395 Individual accounts: applicable accounting framework

(1) A company's individual accounts may be prepared—

(a) in accordance with section 396 ("Companies Act individual accounts"), or

(b) in accordance with international accounting standards ("IAS individual accounts").

This is subject to the following provisions of this section and to section 407 (consistency of financial reporting within group).

(2) The individual accounts of a company that is a charity must be Companies Act individual accounts.

(3) After the first financial year in which the directors of a company prepare IAS individual accounts ("the first IAS year"), all subsequent individual accounts of the company must be prepared in accordance with international accounting standards unless there is a relevant change of circumstance.

This is subject to subsection (4A).

(4) There is a relevant change of circumstance if, at any time during or after the first IAS year—

(a) the company becomes a subsidiary undertaking of another undertaking that does not prepare IAS individual accounts,

(aa) the company ceases to be a subsidiary undertaking,

(b) the company ceases to be a company with securities admitted to trading on a regulated market in an EEA State, or

(c) a parent undertaking of the company ceases to be an undertaking with securities admitted to trading on a regulated market in an EEA State.

(4A) After a financial year in which the directors of a company prepare IAS individual accounts for the company, the directors may change to preparing Companies Act individual accounts for a reason other than a relevant change of circumstance provided they have not changed to Companies Act individual accounts in the period of five years preceding the first day of that financial year.

(4B) In calculating the five year period for the purpose of subsection (4A), no account should be taken of a change due to a relevant change of circumstance.

(5) If, having changed to preparing Companies Act individual accounts ..., the directors again prepare IAS individual accounts for the company, subsections (3) and (4) apply again as if the first financial year for which such accounts are again prepared were the first IAS year.

396 Companies Act individual accounts

(1) Companies Act individual accounts must comprise—

(a) a balance sheet as at the last day of the financial year, and

(b) a profit and loss account.

(2) The accounts must—

(a) in the case of the balance sheet, give a true and fair view of the state of affairs of the company as at the end of the financial year, and

(b) in the case of the profit and loss account, give a true and fair view of the profit or loss of the company for the financial year.

(3) The accounts must comply with provision made by the Secretary of State by regulations as to—

(a) the form and content of the balance sheet and profit and loss account, and

(b) additional information to be provided by way of notes to the accounts.

(4) If compliance with the regulations, and any other provision made by or under this Act as to the matters to be included in a company's individual accounts or in notes to those accounts, would not be sufficient to give a true and fair view, the necessary additional information must be given in the accounts or in a note to them.

(5) If in special circumstances compliance with any of those provisions is inconsistent with the requirement to give a true and fair view, the directors must depart from that provision to the extent necessary to give a true and fair view.

Particulars of any such departure, the reasons for it and its effect must be given in a note to the accounts.

397 IAS individual accounts

Where the directors of a company prepare IAS individual accounts, they must state in the notes to the accounts that the accounts have been prepared in accordance with international accounting standards.

Group accounts: small companies

398 Option to prepare group accounts

If at the end of a financial year a company subject to the small companies regime is a parent company the directors, as well as preparing individual accounts for the year, may prepare group accounts for the year.

Group accounts: other companies

399 Duty to prepare group accounts

(1) This section applies to companies that are not subject to the small companies regime.

(2) If at the end of a financial year the company is a parent company the directors, as well as preparing individual accounts for the year, must prepare group accounts for the year unless the company is exempt from that requirement.

(3) There are exemptions under-
section 400 (company included in EEA accounts of larger group),
section 401 (company included in non-EEA accounts of larger group), and section 402 (company none of whose subsidiary undertakings need be included in the consolidation).

(4) A company to which this section applies but which is exempt from the requirement to prepare group accounts, may do so.

400 Exemption for company included in EEA group accounts of larger group

(1) A company is exempt from the requirement to prepare group accounts if it is itself a subsidiary undertaking and its immediate parent undertaking is established under the law of an EEA State, in the following cases—

(a) where the company is a wholly-owned subsidiary of that parent undertaking;

(b) where that parent undertaking holds more than 50% of the allotted shares in the company and notice requesting the preparation of group accounts has not been served on the company by shareholders holding in aggregate—

(i) more than half of the remaining allotted shares in the company, or

(ii) 5% of the total allotted shares in the company.

Such notice must be served not later than six months after the end of the financial year before that to which it relates.

(2) Exemption is conditional upon compliance with all of the following conditions—

(a) the company must be included in consolidated accounts for a larger group drawn up to the same date, or to an earlier date in the same financial year, by a parent undertaking established under the law of an EEA State;

(b) those accounts must be drawn up and audited, and that parent undertaking's annual report must be drawn up, according to that law—

(i) in accordance with the provisions of the Seventh Directive (83/349/EEC) (as modified, where relevant, by the provisions of the Bank Accounts Directive (86/635/EEC) or the Insurance Accounts Directive (91/674/ EEC)), or

(ii) in accordance with international accounting standards;

(c) the company must disclose in its individual accounts that it is exempt from the obligation to prepare and deliver group accounts;

(d) the company must state in its individual accounts the name of the parent undertaking that draws up the group accounts referred to above and—

(i) if it is incorporated outside the United Kingdom, the country in which it is incorporated, or

(ii) if it is unincorporated, the address of its principal place of business;

(e) the company must deliver to the registrar, within the period for filing its accounts and reports for the financial year in question, copies of—

(i) those group accounts, and

(ii) the parent undertaking's annual report,

together with the auditor's report on them;

(f) any requirement of Part 35 of this Act as to the delivery to the registrar of a certified translation into English must be met in relation to any document comprised in the accounts and reports delivered in accordance with paragraph (e).

(3) For the purposes of subsection (1)(b) shares held by a wholly-owned subsidiary of the parent undertaking, or held on behalf of the parent undertaking or a wholly-owned subsidiary, shall be attributed to the parent undertaking.

(4) The exemption does not apply to a company any of whose securities are admitted to trading on a regulated market in an EEA State.

(5) Shares held by directors of a company for the purpose of complying with any share qualification requirement shall be disregarded in determining for the purposes of this section whether the company is a wholly-owned subsidiary.

(6) In subsection (4) "securities" includes—

(a) shares and stock,

(b) debentures, including debenture stock, loan stock, bonds, certificates of deposit and other instruments creating or acknowledging indebtedness,

(c) warrants or other instruments entitling the holder to subscribe for securities falling within paragraph (a) or (b), and

(d) certificates or other instruments that confer—

(i) property rights in respect of a security falling within paragraph (a), (b) or (c),

(ii) any right to acquire, dispose of, underwrite or convert a security, being a right to which the holder would be entitled if he held any such security to which the certificate or other instrument relates, or

(iii) a contractual right (other than an option) to acquire any such security otherwise than by subscription.

401 Exemption for company included in non-EEA group accounts of larger group

(1) A company is exempt from the requirement to prepare group accounts if it is itself a subsidiary undertaking and its parent undertaking is not established under the law of an EEA State, in the following cases—

(a) where the company is a wholly-owned subsidiary of that parent undertaking;

(b) where that parent undertaking holds more than 50% of the allotted shares in the company and notice requesting the preparation of group accounts has not been served on the company by shareholders holding in aggregate—

(i) more than half of the remaining allotted shares in the company, or

(ii) 5% of the total allotted shares in the company.

Such notice must be served not later than six months after the end of the financial year before that to which it relates.

(2) Exemption is conditional upon compliance with all of the following conditions—

(a) the company and all of its subsidiary undertakings must be included in consolidated accounts for a larger group drawn up to the same date, or to an earlier date in the same financial year, by a parent undertaking;

(b) those accounts and, where appropriate, the group's annual report, must be drawn up—

(i) in accordance with the provisions of the Seventh Directive (83/349/EEC) (as modified, where relevant, by the provisions of the Bank Accounts Directive (86/635/EEC) or the Insurance Accounts Directive (91/674/ EEC)), or

(ii) in a manner equivalent to consolidated accounts and consolidated annual reports so drawn up;

(c) the group accounts must be audited by one or more persons authorised to audit accounts under the law under which the parent undertaking which draws them up is established;

(d) the company must disclose in its individual accounts that it is exempt from the obligation to prepare and deliver group accounts;

(e) the company must state in its individual accounts the name of the parent undertaking which draws up the group accounts referred to above and—

(i) if it is incorporated outside the United Kingdom, the country in which it is incorporated, or

(ii) if it is unincorporated, the address of its principal place of business;

(f) the company must deliver to the registrar, within the period for filing its accounts and reports for the financial year in question, copies of—

(i) the group accounts, and

(ii) where appropriate, the consolidated annual report,

together with the auditor's report on them;

(g) any requirement of Part 35 of this Act as to the delivery to the registrar of a certified translation into English must be met in relation to any document comprised in the accounts and reports delivered in accordance with paragraph (f).

(3) For the purposes of subsection (1)(b), shares held by a wholly-owned subsidiary of the parent undertaking, or held on behalf of the parent undertaking or a wholly-owned subsidiary, are attributed to the parent undertaking.

(4) The exemption does not apply to a company any of whose securities are admitted to trading on a regulated market in an EEA State.

(5) Shares held by directors of a company for the purpose of complying with any share qualification requirement shall be disregarded in determining for the purposes of this section whether the company is a wholly-owned subsidiary.

(6) In subsection (4) "securities" includes—

(a) shares and stock,

(b) debentures, including debenture stock, loan stock, bonds, certificates of deposit and other instruments creating or acknowledging indebtedness,

(c) warrants or other instruments entitling the holder to subscribe for securities falling within paragraph (a) or (b), and

(d) certificates or other instruments that confer—

(i) property rights in respect of a security falling within paragraph (a), (b) or (c),

(ii) any right to acquire, dispose of, underwrite or convert a security, being a right to which the holder would be entitled if he held any such security to which the certificate or other instrument relates, or

(iii) a contractual right (other than an option) to acquire any such security otherwise than by subscription.

402 Exemption if no subsidiary undertakings need be included in the consolidation

A parent company is exempt from the requirement to prepare group accounts if under section 405 all of its subsidiary undertakings could be excluded from consolidation in Companies Act group accounts.

Group accounts: general

403 Group accounts: applicable accounting framework

(1) The group accounts of certain parent companies are required by Article 4 of the IAS Regulation to be prepared in accordance with international accounting standards ("IAS group accounts").

(2) The group accounts of other companies may be prepared—

(a) in accordance with section 404 ("Companies Act group accounts"), or

(b) in accordance with international accounting standards ("IAS group accounts").

This is subject to the following provisions of this section.

(3) The group accounts of a parent company that is a charity must be Companies Act group accounts.

(4) After the first financial year in which the directors of a parent company prepare IAS group accounts ("the first IAS year"), all subsequent group accounts of the company must be prepared in accordance with international accounting standards unless there is a relevant change of circumstance.

This is subject to subsection (5A).

(5) There is a relevant change of circumstance if, at any time during or after the first IAS year—

(a) the company becomes a subsidiary undertaking of another undertaking that does not prepare IAS group accounts,

(b) the company ceases to be a company with securities admitted to trading on a regulated market in an EEA State, or

(c) a parent undertaking of the company ceases to be an undertaking with securities admitted to trading on a regulated market in an EEA State.

(5A) After a financial year in which the directors of a parent company prepare IAS group accounts for the company, the directors may change to preparing Companies Act group accounts for a reason other than a relevant change of circumstance provided they have not changed to Companies Act group accounts in the period of five years preceding the first day of that financial year.

(5B) In calculating the five year period for the purpose of subsection (5A), no account should be taken of a change due to a relevant change of circumstance.

(6) If, having changed to preparing Companies Act group accounts ..., the directors again prepare IAS group accounts for the company, subsections (4) and (5) apply again as if the first financial year for which such accounts are again prepared were the first IAS year.

404 Companies Act group accounts

(1) Companies Act group accounts must comprise—

(a) a consolidated balance sheet dealing with the state of affairs of the parent company and its subsidiary undertakings, and

(b) a consolidated profit and loss account dealing with the profit or loss of the parent company and its subsidiary undertakings.

(2) The accounts must give a true and fair view of the state of affairs as at the end of the financial year, and the profit or loss for the financial year, of the undertakings included in the consolidation as a whole, so far as concerns members of the company.

(3) The accounts must comply with provision made by the Secretary of State by regulations as to—

(a) the form and content of the consolidated balance sheet and consolidated profit and loss account, and

(b) additional information to be provided by way of notes to the accounts.

(4) If compliance with the regulations, and any other provision made by or under this Act as to the matters to be included in a company's group accounts or in notes to those accounts, would not be sufficient to give a true and fair view, the necessary additional information must be given in the accounts or in a note to them.

(5) If in special circumstances compliance with any of those provisions is inconsistent with the requirement to give a true and fair view, the directors must depart from that provision to the extent necessary to give a true and fair view.

Particulars of any such departure, the reasons for it and its effect must be given in a note to the accounts.

405 Companies Act group accounts: subsidiary undertakings included in the consolidation

(1) Where a parent company prepares Companies Act group accounts, all the subsidiary undertakings of the company must be included in the consolidation, subject to the following exceptions.

(2) A subsidiary undertaking may be excluded from consolidation if its inclusion is not material for the purpose of giving a true and fair view (but two or more undertakings may be excluded only if they are not material taken together).

(3) A subsidiary undertaking may be excluded from consolidation where—
(a) severe long-term restrictions substantially hinder the exercise of the rights of the parent company over the assets or management of that undertaking, or
(b) the information necessary for the preparation of group accounts cannot be obtained without disproportionate expense or undue delay, or
(c) the interest of the parent company is held exclusively with a view to subsequent resale.

(4) The reference in subsection (3)(a) to the rights of the parent company and the reference in subsection (3)(c) to the interest of the parent company are, respectively, to rights and interests held by or attributed to the company for the purposes of the definition of "parent undertaking" (see section 1162) in the absence of which it would not be the parent company.

406 IAS group accounts

Where the directors of a company prepare IAS group accounts, they must state in the notes to those accounts that the accounts have been prepared in accordance with international accounting standards.

407 Consistency of financial reporting within group

(1) The directors of a parent company must secure that the individual accounts of—
(a) the parent company, and
(b) each of its subsidiary undertakings,
are all prepared using the same financial reporting framework, except to the extent that in their opinion there are good reasons for not doing so.

(2) Subsection (1) does not apply if the directors do not prepare group accounts for the parent company.

(3) Subsection (1) only applies to accounts of subsidiary undertakings that are required to be prepared under this Part.

(4) Subsection (1) does not require accounts of undertakings that are charities to be prepared using the same financial reporting framework as accounts of undertakings which are not charities.

(5) Subsection (1)(a) does not apply where the directors of a parent company prepare IAS group accounts and IAS individual accounts.

408 Individual profit and loss account where group accounts prepared

(1) This section applies where—
(a) a company prepares group accounts in accordance with this Act, and
(b) the notes to the company's individual balance sheet show the company's profit or loss for the financial year determined in accordance with this Act.

(2) The company's individual profit and loss account need not contain the information specified in section 411 (information about employee numbers and costs).

(3) The company's individual profit and loss account must be approved in accordance with section 414(1) (approval by directors) but may be omitted from the company's annual accounts for the purposes of the other provisions of the Companies Acts.

(4) The exemption conferred by this section is conditional upon its being disclosed in the company's annual accounts that the exemption applies.

Information to be given in notes to the accounts

409 Information about related undertakings

(1) The Secretary of State may make provision by regulations requiring information about related undertakings to be given in notes to a company's annual accounts.

(2) The regulations—
(a) may make different provision according to whether or not the company prepares group accounts, and
(b) may specify the descriptions of undertaking in relation to which they apply, and make different provision in relation to different descriptions of related undertaking.

(3) The regulations may provide that information need not be disclosed with respect to an undertaking that—

(a) is established under the law of a country outside the United Kingdom, or

(b) carries on business outside the United Kingdom,

if the following conditions are met.

(4) The conditions are—

(a) that in the opinion of the directors of the company the disclosure would be seriously prejudicial to the business of—

(i) that undertaking,

(ii) the company,

(iii) any of the company's subsidiary undertakings, or

(iv) any other undertaking which is included in the consolidation;

(b) that the Secretary of State agrees that the information need not be disclosed.

(5) Where advantage is taken of any such exemption, that fact must be stated in a note to the company's annual accounts.

410 Information about related undertakings: alternative compliance

(1) This section applies where the directors of a company are of the opinion that the number of undertakings in respect of which the company is required to disclose information under any provision of regulations under section 409 (related undertakings) is such that compliance with that provision would result in information of excessive length being given in notes to the company's annual accounts.

(2) The information need only be given in respect of—

(a) the undertakings whose results or financial position, in the opinion of the directors, principally affected the figures shown in the company's annual accounts, and

(b) where the company prepares group accounts, undertakings excluded from consolidation under section 405(3) (undertakings excluded on grounds other than materiality).

(3) If advantage is taken of subsection (2)—

(a) there must be included in the notes to the company's annual accounts a statement that the information is given only with respect to such undertakings as are mentioned in that subsection, and

(b) the full information (both that which is disclosed in the notes to the accounts and that which is not) must be annexed to the company's next annual return.

For this purpose the "next annual return" means that next delivered to the registrar after the accounts in question have been approved under section 414.

(4) If a company fails to comply with subsection (3) (b), an offence is committed by—

(a) the company, and

(b) every officer of the company who is in default.

(5) A person guilty of an offence under subsection (4) is liable on summary conviction to a fine not exceeding level 3 on the standard scale and, for continued contravention, a daily default fine not exceeding one-tenth of level 3 on the standard scale.

410A Information about off-balance sheet arrangements

(1) In the case of a company that is not subject to the small companies regime, if in any financial year—

(a) the company is or has been party to arrangements that are not reflected in its balance sheet, and

(b) at the balance sheet date the risks or benefits arising from those arrangements are material,

the information required by this section must be given in notes to the company's annual accounts.

(2) The information required is—

(a) the nature and business purpose of the arrangements, and

(b) the financial impact of the arrangements on the company.

(3) The information need only be given to the extent necessary for enabling the financial position of the company to be assessed.

(4) If the company qualifies as medium-sized in relation to the financial year (see sections 465 to 467) it need not comply with subsection (2)(b).

(5) This section applies in relation to group accounts as if the undertakings included in the consolidation were a single company.

411 Information about employee numbers and costs

(1) In the case of a company not subject to the small companies regime, the following information with respect to the employees of the company must be given in notes to the company's annual accounts—

(a) the average number of persons employed by the company in the financial year, and

(b) the average number of persons so employed within each category of persons employed by the company.

(2) The categories by reference to which the number required to be disclosed by subsection (1)(b) is to be determined must be such as the directors may select having regard to the manner in which the company's activities are organised.

(3) The average number required by subsection (1)(a) or (b) is determined by dividing the relevant annual number by the number of months in the financial year.

(4) The relevant annual number is determined by ascertaining for each month in the financial year—

(a) for the purposes of subsection (1) (a), the number of persons employed under contracts of service by the company in that month (whether throughout the month or not);

(b) for the purposes of subsection (1)(b), the number of persons in the category in question of persons so employed;

and adding together all the monthly numbers.

(5) In respect of all persons employed by the company during the financial year who are taken into account in determining the relevant annual number for the purposes of subsection (1)(a) there must also be stated the aggregate amounts respectively of—

(a) wages and salaries paid or payable in respect of that year to those persons;

(b) social security costs incurred by the company on their behalf; and

(c) other pension costs so incurred.

This does not apply in so far as those amounts, or any of them, are stated elsewhere in the company's accounts.

(6) In subsection (5)—

"pension costs" includes any costs incurred by the company in respect of—

(a) any pension scheme established for the purpose of providing pensions for persons currently or formerly employed by the company,

(b) any sums set aside for the future payment of pensions directly by the company to current or former employees, and

(c) any pensions paid directly to such persons without having first been set aside;

"social security costs" means any contributions by the company to any state social security or pension scheme, fund or arrangement.

(7) This section applies in relation to group accounts as if the undertakings included in the consolidation were a single company.

412 Information about directors' benefits: remuneration

(1) The Secretary of State may make provision by regulations requiring information to be given in notes to a company's annual accounts about directors' remuneration.

(2) The matters about which information may be required include—

(a) gains made by directors on the exercise of share options;

(b) benefits received or receivable by directors under long-term incentive schemes;

(c) payments for loss of office (as defined in section 215);

(d) benefits receivable, and contributions for the purpose of providing benefits, in respect of past services of a person as director or in any other capacity while director;

(e) consideration paid to or receivable by third parties for making available the services of a person as director or in any other capacity while director.

(3) Without prejudice to the generality of subsection (1), regulations under this section may make any such provision as was made immediately before the commencement of this Part by Part 1 of Schedule 6 to the Companies Act 1985.

(4) For the purposes of this section, and regulations made under it, amounts paid to or receivable by—

(a) a person connected with a director, or

(b) a body corporate controlled by a director,

are treated as paid to or receivable by the director.

The expressions "connected with" and "controlled by" in this subsection have the same meaning as in Part 10 (company directors).

(5) It is the duty of—

(a) any director of a company, and

(b) any person who is or has at any time in the preceding five years been a director of the company,

to give notice to the company of such matters relating to himself as may be necessary for the purposes of regulations under this section.

(6) A person who makes default in complying with subsection (5) commits an offence and is liable on summary conviction to a fine not exceeding level 3 on the standard scale.

413 Information about directors' benefits: advances, credit and guarantees

(1) In the case of a company that does not prepare group accounts, details of—

(a) advances and credits granted by the company to its directors, and

(b) guarantees of any kind entered into by the company on behalf of its directors,

must be shown in the notes to its individual accounts.

(2) In the case of a parent company that prepares group accounts, details of—

(a) advances and credits granted to the directors of the parent company, by that company or by any of its subsidiary undertakings, and

(b) guarantees of any kind entered into on behalf of the directors of the parent company, by that company or by any of its subsidiary undertakings,

must be shown in the notes to the group accounts.

(3) The details required of an advance or credit are—

(a) its amount,

(b) an indication of the interest rate,

(c) its main conditions, and

(d) any amounts repaid.

(4) The details required of a guarantee are—

(a) its main terms,

(b) the amount of the maximum liability that may be incurred by the company (or its subsidiary), and

(c) any amount paid and any liability incurred by the company (or its subsidiary) for the purpose of fulfilling the guarantee (including any loss incurred by reason of enforcement of the guarantee).

(5) There must also be stated in the notes to the accounts the totals—

(a) of amounts stated under subsection (3) (a),

(b) of amounts stated under subsection (3) (d),

(c) of amounts stated under subsection (4)(b), and

(d) of amounts stated under subsection (4)(c).

(6) References in this section to the directors of a company are to the persons who were a director at any time in the financial year to which the accounts relate.

(7) The requirements of this section apply in relation to every advance, credit or guarantee subsisting at any time in the financial year to which the accounts relate—
(a) whenever it was entered into,
(b) whether or not the person concerned was a director of the company in question at the time it was entered into, and
(c) in the case of an advance, credit or guarantee involving a subsidiary undertaking of that company, whether or not that undertaking was such a subsidiary undertaking at the time it was entered into.

(8) Banking companies and the holding companies of credit institutions need only state the details required by subsection (5)(a) and (c).

Approval and signing of accounts

414 Approval and signing of accounts

(1) A company's annual accounts must be approved by the board of directors and signed on behalf of the board by a director of the company.

(2) The signature must be on the company's balance sheet.

(3) If the accounts are prepared in accordance with the provisions applicable to companies subject to the small companies regime, the balance sheet must contain a statement to that effect in a prominent position above the signature.

(4) If annual accounts are approved that do not comply with the requirements of this Act (and, where applicable, of Article 4 of the IAS Regulation), every director of the company who—
(a) knew that they did not comply, or was reckless as to whether they complied, and
(b) failed to take reasonable steps to secure compliance with those requirements or, as the case may be, to prevent the accounts from being approved,
commits an offence.

(5) A person guilty of an offence under this section is liable—
(a) on conviction on indictment, to a fine;
(b) on summary conviction, to a fine not exceeding the statutory maximum.

CHAPTER 5
DIRECTORS' REPORT

Directors' report

415 Duty to prepare directors' report

(1) The directors of a company must prepare a directors' report for each financial year of the company.

(2) For a financial year in which—
(a) the company is a parent company, and
(b) the directors of the company prepare group accounts,
the directors' report must be a consolidated report (a "group directors' report") relating to the undertakings included in the consolidation.

(3) A group directors' report may, where appropriate, give greater emphasis to the matters that are significant to the undertakings included in the consolidation, taken as a whole.

(4) In the case of failure to comply with the requirement to prepare a directors' report, an offence is committed by every person who—
(a) was a director of the company immediately before the end of the period for filing accounts and reports for the financial year in question, and
(b) failed to take all reasonable steps for securing compliance with that requirement.

(5) A person guilty of an offence under this section is liable—
(a) on conviction on indictment, to a fine;
(b) on summary conviction, to a fine not exceeding the statutory maximum.

415A Directors' report: small companies exemption

(1) A company is entitled to small companies exemption in relation to the directors' report for a financial year if—

(a) it is entitled to prepare accounts for the year in accordance with the small companies regime, or

(b) it would be so entitled but for being or having been a member of an ineligible group.

(2) The exemption is relevant to—

section 416(3) (contents of report: statement of amount recommended by way of dividend),
section 417 (contents of report: business review), and
sections 444 to 446 (filing obligations of different descriptions of company).

416 Contents of directors' report: general

(1) The directors' report for a financial year must state—

(a) the names of the persons who, at any time during the financial year, were directors of the company, and

(b) the principal activities of the company in the course of the year.

(2) In relation to a group directors' report subsection (1)(b) has effect as if the reference to the company was to the undertakings included in the consolidation.

(3) Except in the case of a company entitled to the small companies exemption, the report must state the amount (if any) that the directors recommend should be paid by way of dividend.

(4) The Secretary of State may make provision by regulations as to other matters that must be disclosed in a directors' report.

Without prejudice to the generality of this power, the regulations may make any such provision as was formerly made by Schedule 7 to the Companies Act 1985.

417 Contents of directors' report: business review

(1) Unless the company is entitled to the small companies exemption, the directors' report must contain a business review.

(2) The purpose of the business review is to inform members of the company and help them assess how the directors have performed their duty under section 172 (duty to promote the success of the company).

(3) The business review must contain—

(a) a fair review of the company's business, and

(b) a description of the principal risks and uncertainties facing the company.

(4) The review required is a balanced and comprehensive analysis of—

(a) the development and performance of the company's business during the financial year, and

(b) the position of the company's business at the end of that year, consistent with the size and complexity of the business.

(5) In the case of a quoted company the business review must, to the extent necessary for an understanding of the development, performance or position of the company's business, include—

(a) the main trends and factors likely to affect the future development, performance and position of the company's business; and

(b) information about—

(i) environmental matters (including the impact of the company's business on the environment),

(ii) the company's employees, and

(iii) social and community issues,

including information about any policies of the company in relation to those matters and the effectiveness of those policies; and

(c) subject to subsection (11), information about persons with whom the company has contractual or other arrangements which are essential to the business of the company.

If the review does not contain information of each kind mentioned in paragraphs (b)(i), (ii) and (iii) and (c), it must state which of those kinds of information it does not contain.

(6) The review must, to the extent necessary for an understanding of the development, performance or position of the company's business, include—
(a) analysis using financial key performance indicators, and
(b) where appropriate, analysis using other key performance indicators, including information relating to environmental matters and employee matters.
"Key performance indicators" means factors by reference to which the development, performance or position of the company's business can be measured effectively.
(7) Where a company qualifies as medium-sized in relation to a financial year (see sections 465 to 467), the directors' report for the year need not comply with the requirements of subsection (6) so far as they relate to non-financial information.
(8) The review must, where appropriate, include references to, and additional explanations of, amounts included in the company's annual accounts.
(9) In relation to a group directors' report this section has effect as if the references to the company were references to the undertakings included in the consolidation.
(10) Nothing in this section requires the disclosure of information about impending developments or matters in the course of negotiation if the disclosure would, in the opinion of the directors, be seriously prejudicial to the interests of the company.
(11) Nothing in subsection (5)(c) requires the disclosure of information about a person if the disclosure would, in the opinion of the directors, be seriously prejudicial to that person and contrary to the public interest.

418 Contents of directors' report: statement as to disclosure to auditors

(1) This section applies to a company unless—
(a) it is exempt for the financial year in question from the requirements of Part 16 as to audit of accounts, and
(b) the directors take advantage of that exemption.
(2) The directors' report must contain a statement to the effect that, in the case of each of the persons who are directors at the time the report is approved—
(a) so far as the director is aware, there is no relevant audit information of which the company's auditor is unaware, and
(b) he has taken all the steps that he ought to have taken as a director in order to make himself aware of any relevant audit information and to establish that the company's auditor is aware of that information.
(3) "Relevant audit information" means information needed by the company's auditor in connection with preparing his report.
(4) A director is regarded as having taken all the steps that he ought to have taken as a director in order to do the things mentioned in subsection (2) (b) if he has—
(a) made such enquiries of his fellow directors and of the company's auditors for that purpose, and
(b) taken such other steps (if any) for that purpose,
as are required by his duty as a director of the company to exercise reasonable care, skill and diligence.
(5) Where a directors' report containing the statement required by this section is approved but the statement is false, every director of the company who—
(a) knew that the statement was false, or was reckless as to whether it was false, and
(b) failed to take reasonable steps to prevent the report from being approved,
commits an offence.
(6) A person guilty of an offence under subsection (5) is liable—
(a) on conviction on indictment, to imprisonment for a term not exceeding two years or a fine (or both);
(b) on summary conviction—
(i) in England and Wales, to imprisonment for a term not exceeding twelve months or to a fine not exceeding the statutory maximum (or both);

(ii) in Scotland or Northern Ireland, to imprisonment for a term not exceeding six months, or to a fine not exceeding the statutory maximum (or both).

419 Approval and signing of directors' report

(1) The directors' report must be approved by the board of directors and signed on behalf of the board by a director or the secretary of the company.

(2) If in preparing the report advantage is taken of the small companies exemption, it must contain a statement to that effect in a prominent position above the signature.

(3) If a directors' report is approved that does not comply with the requirements of this Act, every director of the company who—

(a) knew that it did not comply, or was reckless as to whether it complied, and

(b) failed to take reasonable steps to secure compliance with those requirements or, as the case may be, to prevent the report from being approved,

commits an offence.

(4) A person guilty of an offence under this section is liable—

(a) on conviction on indictment, to a fine;

(b) on summary conviction, to a fine not exceeding the statutory maximum.

419A Approval and signing of separate corporate governance statement

Any separate corporate governance statement must be approved by the board of directors and signed on behalf of the board by a director or the secretary of the company.

CHAPTER 6
QUOTED COMPANIES: DIRECTORS' REMUNERATION REPORT

420 Duty to prepare directors' remuneration report

(1) The directors of a quoted company must prepare a directors' remuneration report for each financial year of the company.

(2) In the case of failure to comply with the requirement to prepare a directors' remuneration report, every person who—

(a) was a director of the company immediately before the end of the period for filing accounts and reports for the financial year in question, and

(b) failed to take all reasonable steps for securing compliance with that requirement,

commits an offence.

(3) A person guilty of an offence under this section is liable—

(a) on conviction on indictment, to a fine;

(b) on summary conviction, to a fine not exceeding the statutory maximum.

421 Contents of directors' remuneration report

(1) The Secretary of State may make provision by regulations as to—

(a) the information that must be contained in a directors' remuneration report,

(b) how information is to be set out in the report, and

(c) what is to be the auditable part of the report.

(2) Without prejudice to the generality of this power, the regulations may make any such provision as was made, immediately before the commencement of this Part, by Schedule 7A to the Companies Act 1985.

(3) It is the duty of—

(a) any director of a company, and

(b) any person who is or has at any time in the preceding five years been a director of the company,

to give notice to the company of such matters relating to himself as may be necessary for the purposes of regulations under this section.

(4) A person who makes default in complying with subsection (3) commits an offence and is liable on summary conviction to a fine not exceeding level 3 on the standard scale.

422 Approval and signing of directors' remuneration report

(1) The directors' remuneration report must be approved by the board of directors and signed on behalf of the board by a director or the secretary of the company.

(2) If a directors' remuneration report is approved that does not comply with the requirements of this Act, every director of the company who—

(a) knew that it did not comply, or was reckless as to whether it complied, and

(b) failed to take reasonable steps to secure compliance with those requirements or, as the case may be, to prevent the report from being approved,

commits an offence.

(3) A person guilty of an offence under this section is liable—

(a) on conviction on indictment, to a fine;

(b) on summary conviction, to a fine not exceeding the statutory maximum.

CHAPTER 7
PUBLICATION OF ACCOUNTS AND REPORTS

Duty to circulate copies of accounts and reports

423 Duty to circulate copies of annual accounts and reports

(1) Every company must send a copy of its annual accounts and reports for each financial year to—

(a) every member of the company,

(b) every holder of the company's debentures, and

(c) every person who is entitled to receive notice of general meetings.

(2) Copies need not be sent to a person for whom the company does not have a current address.

(3) A company has a "current address" for a person if—

(a) an address has been notified to the company by the person as one at which documents may be sent to him, and

(b) the company has no reason to believe that documents sent to him at that address will not reach him.

(4) In the case of a company not having a share capital, copies need not be sent to anyone who is not entitled to receive notices of general meetings of the company.

(5) Where copies are sent out over a period of days, references in the Companies Acts to the day on which copies are sent out shall be read as references to the last day of that period.

(6) This section has effect subject to section 426 (option to provide summary financial statement).

424 Time allowed for sending out copies of accounts and reports

(1) The time allowed for sending out copies of the company's annual accounts and reports is as follows.

(2) A private company must comply with section 423 not later than—

(a) the end of the period for filing accounts and reports, or

(b) if earlier, the date on which it actually delivers its accounts and reports to the registrar.

(3) A public company must comply with section 423 at least 21 days before the date of the relevant accounts meeting.

(4) If in the case of a public company copies are sent out later than is required by subsection (3), they shall, despite that, be deemed to have been duly sent if it is so agreed by all the members entitled to attend and vote at the relevant accounts meeting.

(5) Whether the time allowed is that for a private company or a public company is determined by reference to the company's status immediately before the end of the accounting reference period by reference to which the financial year for the accounts in question was determined.

(6) In this section the "relevant accounts meeting" means the accounts meeting of the company at which the accounts and reports in question are to be laid.

425 Default in sending out copies of accounts and reports: offences

(1) If default is made in complying with section 423 or 424, an offence is committed by—

(a) the company, and

(b) every officer of the company who is in default.

(2) A person guilty of an offence under this section is liable—

(a) on conviction on indictment, to a fine;

(b) on summary conviction, to a fine not exceeding the statutory maximum.

Option to provide summary financial statement

426 Option to provide summary financial statement

(1) A company may—

(a) in such cases as may be specified by regulations made by the Secretary of State, and

(b) provided any conditions so specified are complied with,

provide a summary financial statement instead of copies of the accounts and reports required to be sent out in accordance with section 423.

(2) Copies of those accounts and reports must, however, be sent to any person entitled to be sent them in accordance with that section and who wishes to receive them.

(3) The Secretary of State may make provision by regulations as to the manner in which it is to be ascertained, whether before or after a person becomes entitled to be sent a copy of those accounts and reports, whether he wishes to receive them.

(4) A summary financial statement must comply with the requirements of—

section 427 (form and contents of summary financial statement: unquoted companies), or

section 428 (form and contents of summary financial statement: quoted companies).

(5) This section applies to copies of accounts and reports required to be sent out by virtue of section 146 to a person nominated to enjoy information rights as it applies to copies of accounts and reports required to be sent out in accordance with section 423 to a member of the company.

(6) Regulations under this section are subject to negative resolution procedure.

427 Form and contents of summary financial statement: unquoted companies

(1) A summary financial statement by a company that is not a quoted company must—

(a) be derived from the company's annual accounts, and

(b) be prepared in accordance with this section and regulations made under it.

(2) The summary financial statement must be in such form, and contain such information, as the Secretary of State may specify by regulations. The regulations may require the statement to include information derived from the directors' report.

(3) Nothing in this section or regulations made under it prevents a company from including in a summary financial statement additional information derived from the company's annual accounts or the directors' report.

(4) The summary financial statement must—

(a) state that it is only a summary of information derived from the company's annual accounts;

(b) state whether it contains additional information derived from the directors' report and, if so, that it does not contain the full text of that report;

(c) state how a person entitled to them can obtain a full copy of the company's annual accounts and the directors' report;

(d) contain a statement by the company's auditor of his opinion as to whether the summary financial statement—

(i) is consistent with the company's annual accounts and, where information derived from the directors' report is included in the statement, with that report, and

(ii) complies with the requirements of this section and regulations made under it;

(e) state whether the auditor's report on the annual accounts was unqualified or qualified and, if it was qualified, set out the report in full together with any further material needed to understand the qualification;

(f) state whether, in that report, the auditor's statement under section 496 (whether directors' report consistent with accounts) was qualified or unqualified and, if it was qualified, set out the qualified statement in full together with any further material needed to understand the qualification;

(g) state whether that auditor's report contained a statement under—

(i) section 498(2)(a) or (b) (accounting records or returns inadequate or accounts not agreeing with records and returns), or

(ii) section 498(3) (failure to obtain necessary information and explanations),

and if so, set out the statement in full.

(5) Regulations under this section may provide that any specified material may, instead of being included in the summary financial statement, be sent separately at the same time as the statement.

(6) Regulations under this section are subject to negative resolution procedure.

428 Form and contents of summary financial statement: quoted companies

(1) A summary financial statement by a quoted company must—

(a) be derived from the company's annual accounts and the directors' remuneration report, and

(b) be prepared in accordance with this section and regulations made under it.

(2) The summary financial statement must be in such form, and contain such information, as the Secretary of State may specify by regulations.

The regulations may require the statement to include information derived from the directors' report.

(3) Nothing in this section or regulations made under it prevents a company from including in a summary financial statement additional information derived from the company's annual accounts, the directors' remuneration report or the directors' report.

(4) The summary financial statement must—

(a) state that it is only a summary of information derived from the company's annual accounts and the directors' remuneration report;

(b) state whether it contains additional information derived from the directors' report and, if so, that it does not contain the full text of that report;

(c) state how a person entitled to them can obtain a full copy of the company's annual accounts, the directors' remuneration report or the directors' report;

(d) contain a statement by the company's auditor of his opinion as to whether the summary financial statement—

(i) is consistent with the company's annual accounts and the directors' remuneration report and, where information derived from the directors' report is included in the statement, with that report, and

(ii) complies with the requirements of this section and regulations made under it;

(e) state whether the auditor's report on the annual accounts and the auditable part of the directors' remuneration report was unqualified or qualified and, if it was qualified, set out the report in full together with any further material needed to understand the qualification;

(f) state whether that auditor's report contained a statement under—

(i) section 498(2) (accounting records or returns inadequate or accounts or directors' remuneration report not agreeing with records and returns), or

(ii) section 498(3) (failure to obtain necessary information and explanations),

and if so, set out the statement in full;

(g) state whether, in that report, the auditor's statement under section 496 (whether directors' report consistent with accounts) was qualified or unqualified and, if it was qualified, set out the qualified statement in full together with any further material needed to understand the qualification.

(5) Regulations under this section may provide that any specified material may, instead of being included in the summary financial statement, be sent separately at the same time as the statement.

(6) Regulations under this section are subject to negative resolution procedure.

429 Summary financial statements: offences

(1) If default is made in complying with any provision of section 426, 427 or 428, or of regulations under any of those sections, an offence is committed by—

(a) the company, and

(b) every officer of the company who is in default.

(2) A person guilty of an offence under this section is liable on summary conviction to a fine not exceeding level 3 on the standard scale.

Quoted companies: requirements as to website publication

430 Quoted companies: annual accounts and reports to be made available on website

(1) A quoted company must ensure that its annual accounts and reports—

(a) are made available on a website, and

(b) remain so available until the annual accounts and reports for the company's next financial year are made available in accordance with this section.

(2) The annual accounts and reports must be made available on a website that—

(a) is maintained by or on behalf of the company, and

(b) identifies the company in question.

(3) Access to the annual accounts and reports on the website, and the ability to obtain a hard copy of the annual accounts and reports from the website, must not be—

(a) conditional on the payment of a fee, or

(b) otherwise restricted, except so far as necessary to comply with any enactment or regulatory requirement (in the United Kingdom or elsewhere).

(4) The annual accounts and reports—

(a) must be made available as soon as reasonably practicable, and

(b) must be kept available throughout the period specified in subsection (1)(b).

(5) A failure to make the annual accounts and reports available on a website throughout that period is disregarded if—

(a) the annual accounts and reports are made available on the website for part of that period, and

(b) the failure is wholly attributable to circumstances that it would not be reasonable to have expected the company to prevent or avoid.

(6) In the event of default in complying with this section, an offence is committed by every officer of the company who is in default.

(7) A person guilty of an offence under subsection (6) is liable on summary conviction to a fine not exceeding level 3 on the standard scale.

Right of member or debenture holder to demand copies of accounts and reports

431 Right of member or debenture holder to copies of accounts and reports: unquoted companies

(1) A member of, or holder of debentures of, an unquoted company is entitled to be provided, on demand and without charge, with a copy of—

(a) the company's last annual accounts,

(b) the last directors' report, and

(c) the auditor's report on those accounts (including the statement on that report).

(2) The entitlement under this section is to a single copy of those documents, but that is in addition to any copy to which a person may be entitled under section 423.

(3) If a demand made under this section is not complied with within seven days of receipt by the company, an offence is committed by—

(a) the company, and

(b) every officer of the company who is in default.

(4) A person guilty of an offence under this section is liable on summary conviction to a fine not exceeding level 3 on the standard scale and, for continued contravention, a daily default fine not exceeding one-tenth of level 3 on the standard scale.

432 Right of member or debenture holder to copies of accounts and reports: quoted companies

(1) A member of, or holder of debentures of, a quoted company is entitled to be provided, on demand and without charge, with a copy of—
(a) the company's last annual accounts,
(b) the last directors' remuneration report,
(c) the last directors' report, and
(d) the auditor's report on those accounts (including the report on the directors' remuneration report and on the directors' report).

(2) The entitlement under this section is to a single copy of those documents, but that is in addition to any copy to which a person may be entitled under section 423.

(3) If a demand made under this section is not complied with within seven days of receipt by the company, an offence is committed by—
(a) the company, and
(b) every officer of the company who is in default.

(4) A person guilty of an offence under this section is liable on summary conviction to a fine not exceeding level 3 on the standard scale and, for continued contravention, a daily default fine not exceeding one-tenth of level 3 on the standard scale.

Requirements in connection with publication of accounts and reports

433 Name of signatory to be stated in published copies of accounts and reports

(1) Every copy of a document to which this section applies that is published by or on behalf of the company must state the name of the person who signed it on behalf of the board.

(2) In the case of an unquoted company, this section applies to copies of—
(a) the company's balance sheet, and
(b) the directors' report.

(3) In the case of a quoted company, this section applies to copies of—
(a) the company's balance sheet,
(b) the directors' remuneration report, and
(c) the directors' report.

(4) If a copy is published without the required statement of the signatory's name, an offence is committed by—
(a) the company, and
(b) every officer of the company who is in default.

(5) A person guilty of an offence under this section is liable on summary conviction to a fine not exceeding level 3 on the standard scale.

434 Requirements in connection with publication of statutory accounts

(1) If a company publishes any of its statutory accounts, they must be accompanied by the auditor's report on those accounts (unless the company is exempt from audit and the directors have taken advantage of that exemption).

(2) A company that prepares statutory group accounts for a financial year must not publish its statutory individual accounts for that year without also publishing with them its statutory group accounts.

(3) A company's "statutory accounts" are its accounts for a financial year as required to be delivered to the registrar under section 441.

(4) If a company contravenes any provision of this section, an offence is committed by—
(a) the company, and
(b) every officer of the company who is in default.

(5) A person guilty of an offence under this section is liable on summary conviction to a fine not exceeding level 3 on the standard scale.

(6) This section does not apply in relation to the provision by a company of a summary financial statement (see section 426).

435 Requirements in connection with publication of non-statutory accounts

(1) If a company publishes non-statutory accounts, it must publish with them a statement indicating—

(a) that they are not the company's statutory accounts,

(b) whether statutory accounts dealing with any financial year with which the non-statutory accounts purport to deal have been delivered to the registrar, and

(c) whether an auditor's report has been made on the company's statutory accounts for any such financial year, and if so whether the report—

(i) was qualified or unqualified, or included a reference to any matters to which the auditor drew attention by way of emphasis without qualifying the report, or

(ii) contained a statement under section 498(2) (accounting records or returns inadequate or accounts or directors' remuneration report not agreeing with records and returns), or section 498(3) (failure to obtain necessary information and explanations).

(2) The company must not publish with non-statutory accounts the auditor's report on the company's statutory accounts.

(3) References in this section to the publication by a company of "non-statutory accounts" are to the publication of—

(a) any balance sheet or profit and loss account relating to, or purporting to deal with, a financial year of the company, or

(b) an account in any form purporting to be a balance sheet or profit and loss account for a group headed by the company relating to, or purporting to deal with, a financial year of the company,

otherwise than as part of the company's statutory accounts.

(4) In subsection (3)(b) "a group headed by the company" means a group consisting of the company and any other undertaking (regardless of whether it is a subsidiary undertaking of the company) other than a parent undertaking of the company.

(5) If a company contravenes any provision of this section, an offence is committed by—

(a) the company, and

(b) every officer of the company who is in default.

(6) A person guilty of an offence under this section is liable on summary conviction to a fine not exceeding level 3 on the standard scale.

(7) This section does not apply in relation to the provision by a company of a summary financial statement (see section 426).

436 Meaning of "publication" in relation to accounts and reports

(1) This section has effect for the purposes of—

section 433 (name of signatory to be stated in published copies of accounts and reports),
section 434 (requirements in connection with publication of statutory accounts), and
section 435 (requirements in connection with publication of non-statutory accounts).

(2) For the purposes of those sections a company is regarded as publishing a document if it publishes, issues or circulates it or otherwise makes it available for public inspection in a manner calculated to invite members of the public generally, or any class of members of the public, to read it.

CHAPTER 8
PUBLIC COMPANIES: LAYING OF ACCOUNTS AND REPORTS BEFORE GENERAL MEETING

437 Public companies: laying of accounts and reports before general meeting

(1) The directors of a public company must lay before the company in general meeting copies of its annual accounts and reports.

(2) This section must be complied with not later than the end of the period for filing the accounts and reports in question.

(3) In the Companies Acts "accounts meeting", in relation to a public company, means a general meeting of the company at which the company's annual accounts and reports are (or are to be) laid in accordance with this section.

438 Public companies: offence of failure to lay accounts and reports

(1) If the requirements of section 437 (public companies: laying of accounts and reports before general meeting) are not complied with before the end of the period allowed, every person who immediately before the end of that period was a director of the company commits an offence.

(2) It is a defence for a person charged with such an offence to prove that he took all reasonable steps for securing that those requirements would be complied with before the end of that period.

(3) It is not a defence to prove that the documents in question were not in fact prepared as required by this Part.

(4) A person guilty of an offence under this section is liable on summary conviction to a fine not exceeding level 5 on the standard scale and, for continued contravention, a daily default fine not exceeding one-tenth of level 5 on the standard scale.

CHAPTER 9
QUOTED COMPANIES: MEMBERS' APPROVAL OF DIRECTORS' REMUNERATION REPORT

439 Quoted companies: members' approval of directors' remuneration report

(1) A quoted company must, prior to the accounts meeting, give to the members of the company entitled to be sent notice of the meeting notice of the intention to move at the meeting, as an ordinary resolution, a resolution approving the directors' remuneration report for the financial year.

(2) The notice may be given in any manner permitted for the service on the member of notice of the meeting.

(3) The business that may be dealt with at the accounts meeting includes the resolution.
This is so notwithstanding any default in complying with subsection (1) or (2).

(4) The existing directors must ensure that the resolution is put to the vote of the meeting.

(5) No entitlement of a person to remuneration is made conditional on the resolution being passed by reason only of the provision made by this section.

(6) In this section—
"the accounts meeting" means the general meeting of the company before which the company's annual accounts for the financial year are to be laid; and
"existing director" means a person who is a director of the company immediately before that meeting.

440 Quoted companies: offences in connection with procedure for approval

(1) In the event of default in complying with section 439(1) (notice to be given of resolution for approval of directors' remuneration report), an offence is committed by every officer of the company who is in default.

(2) If the resolution is not put to the vote of the accounts meeting, an offence is committed by each existing director.

(3) It is a defence for a person charged with an offence under subsection (2) to prove that he took all reasonable steps for securing that the resolution was put to the vote of the meeting.

(4) A person guilty of an offence under this section is liable on summary conviction to a fine not exceeding level 3 on the standard scale.

(5) In this section—

"the accounts meeting" means the general meeting of the company before which the company's annual accounts for the financial year are to be laid; and

"existing director" means a person who is a director of the company immediately before that meeting.

CHAPTER 10
FILING OF ACCOUNTS AND REPORTS

Duty to file accounts and reports

441 Duty to file accounts and reports with the registrar

(1) The directors of a company must deliver to the registrar for each financial year the accounts and reports required by—

section 444 (filing obligations of companies subject to small companies regime),

section 444A (filing obligations of companies entitled to small companies exemption in relation to directors' report),

section 445 (filing obligations of medium-sized companies),

section 446 (filing obligations of unquoted companies), or

section 447 (filing obligations of quoted companies).

(2) This is subject to—

section 448 (unlimited companies exempt from filing obligations), and

section 448A (dormant subsidiaries exempt from filing obligations).

442 Period allowed for filing accounts

(1) This section specifies the period allowed for the directors of a company to comply with their obligation under section 441 to deliver accounts and reports for a financial year to the registrar. This is referred to in the Companies Acts as the "period for filing" those accounts and reports.

(2) The period is—

(a) for a private company, nine months after the end of the relevant accounting reference period, and

(b) for a public company, six months after the end of that period. This is subject to the following provisions of this section.

(3) If the relevant accounting reference period is the company's first and is a period of more than twelve months, the period is—

(a) nine months or six months, as the case may be, from the first anniversary of the incorporation of the company, or

(b) three months after the end of the accounting reference period,

whichever last expires.

(4) If the relevant accounting reference period is treated as shortened by virtue of a notice given by the company under section 392 (alteration of accounting reference date), the period is—

(a) that applicable in accordance with the above provisions, or

(b) three months from the date of the notice under that section, whichever last expires.

(5) If for any special reason the Secretary of State thinks fit he may, on an application made before the expiry of the period otherwise allowed, by notice in writing to a company extend that period by such further period as may be specified in the notice.

(6) Whether the period allowed is that for a private company or a public company is determined by reference to the company's status immediately before the end of the relevant accounting reference period.

(7) In this section "the relevant accounting reference period" means the accounting reference period by reference to which the financial year for the accounts in question was determined.

443 Calculation of period allowed

(1) This section applies for the purposes of calculating the period for filing a company's accounts and reports which is expressed as a specified number of months from a specified date or after the end of a specified previous period.

(2) Subject to the following provisions, the period ends with the date in the appropriate month corresponding to the specified date or the last day of the specified previous period.

(3) If the specified date, or the last day of the specified previous period, is the last day of a month, the period ends with the last day of the appropriate month (whether or not that is the corresponding date).

(4) If—

(a) the specified date, or the last day of the specified previous period, is not the last day of a month but is the 29th or 30th, and

(b) the appropriate month is February,

the period ends with the last day of February.

(5) "The appropriate month" means the month that is the specified number of months after the month in which the specified date, or the end of the specified previous period, falls.

Filing obligations of different descriptions of company

444 Filing obligations of companies subject to small companies regime

(1) The directors of a company subject to the small companies regime—

(a) must deliver to the registrar for each financial year a copy of a balance sheet drawn up as at the last day of that year, and

(b) may also deliver to the registrar—

(i) a copy of the company's profit and loss account for that year, and

(ii) a copy of the directors' report for that year.

(2) The directors must also deliver to the registrar a copy of the auditor's report on the accounts (and any directors' report) that it delivers.

This does not apply if the company is exempt from audit and the directors have taken advantage of that exemption.

(3) The copies of accounts and reports delivered to the registrar must be copies of the company's annual accounts and reports, except that where the company prepares Companies Act accounts—

(a) the directors may deliver to the registrar a copy of a balance sheet drawn up in accordance with regulations made by the Secretary of State, and

(b) there may be omitted from the copy profit and loss account delivered to the registrar such items as may be specified by the regulations.

These are referred to in this Part as "abbreviated accounts".

(4) If abbreviated accounts are delivered to the registrar the obligation to deliver a copy of the auditor's report on the accounts is to deliver a copy of the special auditor's report required by section 449.

(5) Where the directors of a company subject to the small companies regime deliver to the registrar IAS accounts, or Companies Act accounts that are not abbreviated accounts, and in accordance with this section—

(a) do not deliver to the registrar a copy of the company's profit and loss account, or

(b) do not deliver to the registrar a copy of the directors' report,

the copy of the balance sheet delivered to the registrar must contain in a prominent position a statement that the company's annual accounts and reports have been delivered in accordance with the provisions applicable to companies subject to the small companies regime.

(6) The copies of the balance sheet and any directors' report delivered to the registrar under this section must state the name of the person who signed it on behalf of the board.

(7) The copy of the auditor's report delivered to the registrar under this section must—

(a) state the name of the auditor and (where the auditor is a firm) the name of the person who signed it as senior statutory auditor, or

(b) if the conditions in section 506 (circumstances in which names may be omitted) are met, state that a resolution has been passed and notified to the Secretary of State in accordance with that section.

444A Filing obligations of companies entitled to small companies exemption in relation to directors' report

(1) The directors of a company that is entitled to small companies exemption in relation to the directors' report for a financial year—

(a) must deliver to the registrar a copy of the company's annual accounts for that year, and

(b) may also deliver to the registrar a copy of the directors' report.

(2) The directors must also deliver to the registrar a copy of the auditor's report on the accounts (and any directors' report) that it delivers.

This does not apply if the company is exempt from audit and the directors have taken advantage of that exception.

(3) The copies of the balance sheet and directors' report delivered to the registrar under this section must state the name of the person who signed it on behalf of the board.

(4) The copy of the auditor's report delivered to the registrar under this section must—

(a) state the name of the auditor and (where the auditor is a firm) the name of the person who signed it as senior statutory auditor, or

(b) if the conditions in section 506 (circumstances in which names may be omitted) are met, state that a resolution has been passed and notified to the Secretary of State in accordance with that section.

(5) This section does not apply to companies within section 444 (filing obligations of companies subject to the small companies regime).

445 Filing obligations of medium-sized companies

(1) The directors of a company that qualifies as a medium-sized company in relation to a financial year (see sections 465 to 467) must deliver to the registrar a copy of—

(a) the company's annual accounts, and

(b) the directors' report.

(2) They must also deliver to the registrar a copy of the auditor's report on those accounts (and on the directors' report).

This does not apply if the company is exempt from audit and the directors have taken advantage of that exemption.

(3) Where the company prepares Companies Act accounts, the directors may deliver to the registrar a copy of the company's annual accounts for the financial year—

(a) that includes a profit and loss account in which items are combined in accordance with regulations made by the Secretary of State, and

(b) that does not contain items whose omission is authorised by the regulations.

These are referred to in this Part as "abbreviated accounts".

(4) If abbreviated accounts are delivered to the registrar the obligation to deliver a copy of the auditor's report on the accounts is to deliver a copy of the special auditor's report required by section 449.

(5) The copies of the balance sheet and directors' report delivered to the registrar under this section must state the name of the person who signed it on behalf of the board.

(6) The copy of the auditor's report delivered to the registrar under this section must—

(a) state the name of the auditor and (where the auditor is a firm) the name of the person who signed it as senior statutory auditor, or

(b) if the conditions in section 506 (circumstances in which names may be omitted) are met, state that a resolution has been passed and notified to the Secretary of State in accordance with that section.

(7) This section does not apply to companies within—
(a) section 444 (filing obligations of companies subject to the small companies regime), or
(b) section 444A (filing obligations of companies entitled to small companies exemption in relation to directors' report).

446 Filing obligations of unquoted companies

(1) The directors of an unquoted company must deliver to the registrar for each financial year of the company a copy of—
(a) the company's annual accounts, . . .
(b) the directors' report, and
(c) any separate corporate governance statement.

(2) The directors must also deliver to the registrar a copy of the auditor's report on those accounts (and the directors' report and any separate corporate governance statement).

This does not apply if the company is exempt from audit and the directors have taken advantage of that exemption.

(3) The copies of the balance sheet and directors' report delivered to the registrar under this section must state the name of the person who signed it on behalf of the board.

(4) The copy of the auditor's report delivered to the registrar under this section must—
(a) state the name of the auditor and (where the auditor is a firm) the name of the person who signed it as senior statutory auditor, or
(b) if the conditions in section 506 (circumstances in which names may be omitted) are met, state that a resolution has been passed and notified to the Secretary of State in accordance with that section.

(5) This section does not apply to companies within—
(a) section 444 (filing obligations of companies subject to the small companies regime), ...
(aa) section 444A (filing obligations of companies entitled to small companies exemption in relation to directors' report), or
(b) section 445 (filing obligations of medium-sized companies).

447 Filing obligations of quoted companies

(1) The directors of a quoted company must deliver to the registrar for each financial year of the company a copy of—
(a) the company's annual accounts,
(b) the directors' remuneration report, . . .
(c) the directors' report, and
(d) any separate corporate governance statement.

(2) They must also deliver a copy of the auditor's report on those accounts (and on the directors' remuneration report , the directors' report and any separate corporate governance statement).

(3) The copies of the balance sheet, the directors' remuneration report and the directors' report delivered to the registrar under this section must state the name of the person who signed it on behalf of the board.

(4) The copy of the auditor's report delivered to the registrar under this section must—
(a) state the name of the auditor and (where the auditor is a firm) the name of the person who signed it as senior statutory auditor, or
(b) if the conditions in section 506 (circumstances in which names may be omitted) are met, state that a resolution has been passed and notified to the Secretary of State in accordance with that section.

448 Unlimited companies exempt from obligation to file accounts

(1) The directors of an unlimited company are not required to deliver accounts and reports to the registrar in respect of a financial year if the following conditions are met.

(2) The conditions are that at no time during the relevant accounting reference period—
(a) has the company been, to its knowledge, a subsidiary undertaking of an undertaking which was then limited, or

(b) have there been, to its knowledge, exercisable by or on behalf of two or more undertakings which were then limited, rights which if exercisable by one of them would have made the company a subsidiary undertaking of it, or

(c) has the company been a parent company of an undertaking which was then limited.

The references above to an undertaking being limited at a particular time are to an undertaking (under whatever law established) the liability of whose members is at that time limited.

(3) The exemption conferred by this section does not apply if—

(a) the company is a banking or insurance company or the parent company of a banking or insurance group, or

(b) each of the members of the company is—

(i) a limited company,

(ii) another unlimited company each of whose members is a limited company, or

(iii) a Scottish partnership each of whose members is a limited company.

The references in paragraph (b) to a limited company, another unlimited company or a Scottish partnership include a comparable undertaking incorporated in or formed under the law of a country or territory outside the United Kingdom.

(4) Where a company is exempt by virtue of this section from the obligation to deliver accounts—

(a) section 434(3) (requirements in connection with publication of statutory accounts: meaning of "statutory accounts") has effect with the substitution for the words "as required to be delivered to the registrar under section 441" of the words "as prepared in accordance with this Part and approved by the board of directors"; and

(b) section 435(1)(b) (requirements in connection with publication of non-statutory accounts: statement whether statutory accounts delivered) has effect with the substitution for the words from "whether statutory accounts" to "have been delivered to the registrar" of the words "that the company is exempt from the requirement to deliver statutory accounts".

(5) In this section the "relevant accounting reference period", in relation to a financial year, means the accounting reference period by reference to which that financial year was determined.

448A Dormant subsidiaries exempt from obligation to file accounts

(1) The directors of a company are not required to deliver a copy of the company's individual accounts to the registrar in respect of a financial year if—

(a) the company is a subsidiary undertaking,

(b) it has been dormant throughout the whole of that year, and

(c) its parent undertaking is established under the law of an EEA State.

(2) Exemption is conditional upon compliance with all of the following conditions—

(a) all members of the company must agree to the exemption in respect of the financial year in question,

(b) the parent undertaking must give a guarantee under section 448C in respect of that year,

(c) the company must be included in the consolidated accounts drawn up for that year or to an earlier date in that year by the parent undertaking in accordance with—

(i) the provisions of the Seventh Directive (83/349/EEC), or

(ii) international accounting standards,

(d) the parent undertaking must disclose in the notes to the consolidated accounts that the directors of the company are exempt from the requirement to deliver a copy of the company's individual accounts to the registrar by virtue of this section, and

(e) the directors of the company must deliver to the registrar within the period for filing the company's accounts and reports for that year—

(i) a written notice of the agreement referred to in subsection (2)(a),

(ii) the statement referred to in section 448C(1),

(iii) a copy of the consolidated accounts referred to in subsection (2)(c),

(iv) a copy of the auditor's report on those accounts, and

(v) a copy of the consolidated annual report drawn up by the parent undertaking.

448B Companies excluded from the dormant subsidiaries exemption

The directors of a company are not entitled to the exemption conferred by section 448A (dormant subsidiaries) if the company was at any time within the financial year in question—

(a) a quoted company as defined in section 385(2) of this Act,

(b) a company that—

(i) is an authorised insurance company, a banking company, an e-Money issuer, a MiFID investment firm or a UCITS management company, or

(ii) carries on insurance market activity, or

(c) a special register body as defined in section 117(1) of the Trade Union and Labour Relations (Consolidation) Act 1992 (c 52) or an employers' association as defined in section 122 of that Act or Article 4 of the Industrial Relations (Northern Ireland) Order 1992 (SI 1992/807) (NI 5).

448C Dormant subsidiaries filing exemption: parent undertaking declaration of guarantee

(1) A guarantee is given by a parent undertaking under this section when the directors of the subsidiary company deliver to the registrar a statement by the parent undertaking that it guarantees the subsidiary company under this section.

(2) The statement under subsection (1) must be authenticated by the parent undertaking and must specify—

(a) the name of the parent undertaking,

(b) if the parent undertaking is incorporated in the United Kingdom, its registered number (if any),

(c) if the parent undertaking is incorporated outside the United Kingdom and registered in the country in which it is incorporated, the identity of the register on which it is registered and the number with which it is so registered,

(d) the name and registered number of the subsidiary company in respect of which the guarantee is being given,

(e) the date of the statement, and

(f) the financial year to which the guarantee relates.

(3) A guarantee given under this section has the effect that—

(a) the parent undertaking guarantees all outstanding liabilities to which the subsidiary company is subject at the end of the financial year to which the guarantee relates, until they are satisfied in full, and

(b) the guarantee is enforceable against the parent undertaking by any person to whom the subsidiary company is liable in respect of those liabilities.

Requirements where abbreviated accounts delivered

449 Special auditor's report where abbreviated accounts delivered

(1) This section applies where—

(a) the directors of a company deliver abbreviated accounts to the registrar, and

(b) the company is not exempt from audit (or the directors have not taken advantage of any such exemption).

(2) The directors must also deliver to the registrar a copy of a special report of the company's auditor stating that in his opinion—

(a) the company is entitled to deliver abbreviated accounts in accordance with the section in question, and

(b) the abbreviated accounts to be delivered are properly prepared in accordance with regulations under that section.

(3) The auditor's report on the company's annual accounts need not be delivered, but—

(a) if that report was qualified, the special report must set out that report in full together with any further material necessary to understand the qualification, and

(b) if that report contained a statement under—

(i) section 498(2)(a) or (b) (accounts, records or returns inadequate or accounts not agreeing with records and returns), or

(ii) section 498(3) (failure to obtain necessary information and explanations),

the special report must set out that statement in full.

(4) The provisions of—

sections 503 to 506 (signature of auditor's report), and

sections 507 to 509 (offences in connection with auditor's report),

apply to a special report under this section as they apply to an auditor's report on the company's annual accounts prepared under Part 16.

(5) If abbreviated accounts are delivered to the registrar, the references in section 434 or 435 (requirements in connection with publication of accounts) to the auditor's report on the company's annual accounts shall be read as references to the special auditor's report required by this section.

450 Approval and signing of abbreviated accounts

(1) Abbreviated accounts must be approved by the board of directors and signed on behalf of the board by a director of the company.

(2) The signature must be on the balance sheet.

(3) The balance sheet must contain in a prominent position above the signature a statement to the effect that it is prepared in accordance with the special provisions of this Act relating (as the case may be) to companies subject to the small companies regime or to medium-sized companies.

(4) If abbreviated accounts are approved that do not comply with the requirements of regulations under the relevant section, every director of the company who—

(a) knew that they did not comply, or was reckless as to whether they complied, and

(b) failed to take reasonable steps to prevent them from being approved, commits an offence.

(5) A person guilty of an offence under subsection (4) is liable—

(a) on conviction on indictment, to a fine;

(b) on summary conviction, to a fine not exceeding the statutory maximum.

Failure to file accounts and reports

451 Default in filing accounts and reports: offences

(1) If the requirements of section 441 (duty to file accounts and reports) are not complied with in relation to a company's accounts and reports for a financial year before the end of the period for filing those accounts and reports, every person who immediately before the end of that period was a director of the company commits an offence.

(2) It is a defence for a person charged with such an offence to prove that he took all reasonable steps for securing that those requirements would be complied with before the end of that period.

(3) It is not a defence to prove that the documents in question were not in fact prepared as required by this Part.

(4) A person guilty of an offence under this section is liable on summary conviction to a fine not exceeding level 5 on the standard scale and, for continued contravention, a daily default fine not exceeding one-tenth of level 5 on the standard scale.

452 Default in filing accounts and reports: court order

(1) If—

(a) the requirements of section 441 (duty to file accounts and reports) are not complied with in relation to a company's accounts and reports for a financial year before the end of the period for filing those accounts and reports, and

(b) the directors of the company fail to make good the default within 14 days after the service of a notice on them requiring compliance,

the court may, on the application of any member or creditor of the company or of the registrar, make an order directing the directors (or any of them) to make good the default within such time as may be specified in the order.

(2) The court's order may provide that all costs (in Scotland, expenses) of and incidental to the application are to be borne by the directors.

453 Civil penalty for failure to file accounts and reports

(1) Where the requirements of section 441 are not complied with in relation to a company's accounts and reports for a financial year before the end of the period for filing those accounts and reports, the company is liable to a civil penalty.
This is in addition to any liability of the directors under section 451.

(2) The amount of the penalty shall be determined in accordance with regulations made by the Secretary of State by reference to—
(a) the length of the period between the end of the period for filing the accounts and reports in question and the day on which the requirements are complied with, and
(b) whether the company is a private or public company.

(3) The penalty may be recovered by the registrar and is to be paid into the Consolidated Fund.

(4) It is not a defence in proceedings under this section to prove that the documents in question were not in fact prepared as required by this Part.

(5) Regulations under this section having the effect of increasing the penalty payable in any case are subject to affirmative resolution procedure. Otherwise, the regulations are subject to negative resolution procedure.

CHAPTER 11
REVISION OF DEFECTIVE ACCOUNTS AND REPORTS

Voluntary revision

454 Voluntary revision of accounts etc

(1) If it appears to the directors of a company that—
(a) the company's annual accounts,
(b) the directors' remuneration report or the directors' report, or
(c) a summary financial statement of the company,
did not comply with the requirements of this Act (or, where applicable, of Article 4 of the IAS Regulation), they may prepare revised accounts or a revised report or statement.

(2) Where copies of the previous accounts or report have been sent out to members, delivered to the registrar or (in the case of a public company) laid before the company in general meeting, the revisions must be confined to—
(a) the correction of those respects in which the previous accounts or report did not comply with the requirements of this Act (or, where applicable, of Article 4 of the IAS Regulation), and
(b) the making of any necessary consequential alterations.

(3) The Secretary of State may make provision by regulations as to the application of the provisions of this Act in relation to—
(a) revised annual accounts,
(b) a revised directors' remuneration report or directors' report, or
(c) a revised summary financial statement.

(4) The regulations may, in particular—
(a) make different provision according to whether the previous accounts, report or statement are replaced or are supplemented by a document indicating the corrections to be made;
(b) make provision with respect to the functions of the company's auditor in relation to the revised accounts, report or statement;
(c) require the directors to take such steps as may be specified in the regulations where the previous accounts or report have been—
(i) sent out to members and others under section 423,
(ii) laid before the company in general meeting, or
(iii) delivered to the registrar,

or where a summary financial statement containing information derived from the previous accounts or report has been sent to members under section 426;

(d) apply the provisions of this Act (including those creating criminal offences) subject to such additions, exceptions and modifications as are specified in the regulations.

(5) Regulations under this section are subject to negative resolution procedure.

Secretary of State's notice

455 Secretary of State's notice in respect of accounts or reports

(1) This section applies where—

(a) copies of a company's annual accounts or directors' report have been sent out under section 423, or

(b) a copy of a company's annual accounts or directors' report has been delivered to the registrar or (in the case of a public company) laid before the company in general meeting,

and it appears to the Secretary of State that there is, or may be, a question whether the accounts or report comply with the requirements of this Act (or, where applicable, of Article 4 of the IAS Regulation).

(2) The Secretary of State may give notice to the directors of the company indicating the respects in which it appears that such a question arises or may arise.

(3) The notice must specify a period of not less than one month for the directors to give an explanation of the accounts or report or prepare revised accounts or a revised report.

(4) If at the end of the specified period, or such longer period as the Secretary of State may allow, it appears to the Secretary of State that the directors have not—

(a) given a satisfactory explanation of the accounts or report, or

(b) revised the accounts or report so as to comply with the requirements of this Act (or, where applicable, of Article 4 of the IAS Regulation),

the Secretary of State may apply to the court.

(5) The provisions of this section apply equally to revised annual accounts and revised directors' reports, in which case they have effect as if the references to revised accounts or reports were references to further revised accounts or reports.

Application to court

456 Application to court in respect of defective accounts or reports

(1) An application may be made to the court—

(a) by the Secretary of State, after having complied with section 455, or

(b) by a person authorised by the Secretary of State for the purposes of this section,

for a declaration (in Scotland, a declarator) that the annual accounts of a company do not comply, or a directors' report does not comply, with the requirements of this Act (or, where applicable, of Article 4 of the IAS Regulation) and for an order requiring the directors of the company to prepare revised accounts or a revised report.

(2) Notice of the application, together with a general statement of the matters at issue in the proceedings, shall be given by the applicant to the registrar for registration.

(3) If the court orders the preparation of revised accounts, it may give directions as to—

(a) the auditing of the accounts,

(b) the revision of any directors' remuneration report, directors' report or summary financial statement, and

(c) the taking of steps by the directors to bring the making of the order to the notice of persons likely to rely on the previous accounts, and such other matters as the court thinks fit.

(4) If the court orders the preparation of a revised directors' report it may give directions as to—

(a) the review of the report by the auditors,

(b) the revision of any summary financial statement,

(c) the taking of steps by the directors to bring the making of the order to the notice of persons likely to rely on the previous report, and

(d) such other matters as the court thinks fit.

(5) If the court finds that the accounts or report did not comply with the requirements of this Act (or, where applicable, of Article 4 of the IAS Regulation) it may order that all or part of—

(a) the costs (in Scotland, expenses) of and incidental to the application, and

(b) any reasonable expenses incurred by the company in connection with or in consequence of the preparation of revised accounts or a revised report,

are to be borne by such of the directors as were party to the approval of the defective accounts or report.

For this purpose every director of the company at the time of the approval of the accounts or report shall be taken to have been a party to the approval unless he shows that he took all reasonable steps to prevent that approval.

(6) Where the court makes an order under subsection (5) it shall have regard to whether the directors party to the approval of the defective accounts or report knew or ought to have known that the accounts or report did not comply with the requirements of this Act (or, where applicable, of Article 4 of the IAS Regulation), and it may exclude one or more directors from the order or order the payment of different amounts by different directors.

(7) On the conclusion of proceedings on an application under this section, the applicant must send to the registrar for registration a copy of the court order or, as the case may be, give notice to the registrar that the application has failed or been withdrawn.

(8) The provisions of this section apply equally to revised annual accounts and revised directors' reports, in which case they have effect as if the references to revised accounts or reports were references to further revised accounts or reports.

457 Other persons authorised to apply to the court

(1) The Secretary of State may by order (an "authorisation order") authorise for the purposes of section 456 any person appearing to him—

(a) to have an interest in, and to have satisfactory procedures directed to securing, compliance by companies with the requirements of this Act (or, where applicable, of Article 4 of the IAS Regulation) relating to accounts and directors' reports,

(b) to have satisfactory procedures for receiving and investigating complaints about companies' annual accounts and directors' reports, and

(c) otherwise to be a fit and proper person to be authorised.

(2) A person may be authorised generally or in respect of particular classes of case, and different persons may be authorised in respect of different classes of case.

(3) The Secretary of State may refuse to authorise a person if he considers that his authorisation is unnecessary having regard to the fact that there are one or more other persons who have been or are likely to be authorised.

(4) If the authorised person is an unincorporated association, proceedings brought in, or in connection with, the exercise of any function by the association as an authorised person may be brought by or against the association in the name of a body corporate whose constitution provides for the establishment of the association.

(5) An authorisation order may contain such requirements or other provisions relating to the exercise of functions by the authorised person as appear to the Secretary of State to be appropriate.

No such order is to be made unless it appears to the Secretary of State that the person would, if authorised, exercise his functions as an authorised person in accordance with the provisions proposed.

(6) Where authorisation is revoked, the revoking order may make such provision as the Secretary of State thinks fit with respect to pending proceedings.

(7) An order under this section is subject to negative resolution procedure.

458 Disclosure of information by tax authorities

(1) The Commissioners for Her Majesty's Revenue and Customs may disclose information to a person authorised under section 457 for the purpose of facilitating—

(a) the taking of steps by that person to discover whether there are grounds for an application to the court under section 456 (application in respect of defective accounts etc), or
(b) a decision by the authorised person whether to make such an application.

(2) This section applies despite any statutory or other restriction on the disclosure of information.
Provided that, in the case of personal data within the meaning of the Data Protection Act 1998, information is not to be disclosed in contravention of that Act.

(3) Information disclosed to an authorised person under this section—
(a) may not be used except in or in connection with—
(i) taking steps to discover whether there are grounds for an application to the court under section 456, or
(ii) deciding whether or not to make such an application,
or in, or in connection with, proceedings on such an application; and
(b) must not be further disclosed except—
(i) to the person to whom the information relates, or
(ii) in, or in connection with, proceedings on any such application to the court.

(4) A person who contravenes subsection (3) commits an offence unless—
(a) he did not know, and had no reason to suspect, that the information had been disclosed under this section, or
(b) he took all reasonable steps and exercised all due diligence to avoid the commission of the offence.

(5) A person guilty of an offence under subsection (4) is liable—
(a) on conviction on indictment, to imprisonment for a term not exceeding two years or a fine (or both);
(b) on summary conviction—
(i) in England and Wales, to imprisonment for a term not exceeding twelve months or to a fine not exceeding the statutory maximum (or both);
(ii) in Scotland or Northern Ireland, to imprisonment for a term not exceeding six months, or to a fine not exceeding the statutory maximum (or both).

(6) Where an offence under this section is committed by a body corporate, every officer of the body who is in default also commits the offence.
For this purpose—
(a) any person who purports to act as director, manager or secretary of the body is treated as an officer of the body, and
(b) if the body is a company, any shadow director is treated as an officer of the company.

Power of authorised person to require documents etc

459 Power of authorised person to require documents, information and explanations

(1) This section applies where it appears to a person who is authorised under section 457 that there is, or may be, a question whether a company's annual accounts or directors' report comply with the requirements of this Act (or, where applicable, of Article 4 of the IAS Regulation).

(2) The authorised person may require any of the persons mentioned in subsection (3) to produce any document, or to provide him with any information or explanations, that he may reasonably require for the purpose of—
(a) discovering whether there are grounds for an application to the court under section 456, or
(b) deciding whether to make such an application.

(3) Those persons are—
(a) the company;
(b) any officer, employee, or auditor of the company;
(c) any persons who fell within paragraph (b) at a time to which the document or information required by the authorised person relates.

(4) If a person fails to comply with such a requirement, the authorised person may apply to the court.

(5) If it appears to the court that the person has failed to comply with a requirement under subsection (2), it may order the person to take such steps as it directs for securing that the documents are produced or the information or explanations are provided.

(6) A statement made by a person in response to a requirement under subsection (2) or an order under subsection (5) may not be used in evidence against him in any criminal proceedings.

(7) Nothing in this section compels any person to disclose documents or information in respect of which a claim to legal professional privilege (in Scotland, to confidentiality of communications) could be maintained in legal proceedings.

(8) In this section "document" includes information recorded in any form.

460 Restrictions on disclosure of information obtained under compulsory powers

(1) This section applies to information (in whatever form) obtained in pursuance of a requirement or order under section 459 (power of authorised person to require documents etc) that relates to the private affairs of an individual or to any particular business.

(2) No such information may, during the lifetime of that individual or so long as that business continues to be carried on, be disclosed without the consent of that individual or the person for the time being carrying on that business.

(3) This does not apply—

(a) to disclosure permitted by section 461 (permitted disclosure of information obtained under compulsory powers), or

(b) to the disclosure of information that is or has been available to the public from another source.

(4) A person who discloses information in contravention of this section commits an offence, unless—

(a) he did not know, and had no reason to suspect, that the information had been disclosed under section 459, or

(b) he took all reasonable steps and exercised all due diligence to avoid the commission of the offence.

(5) A person guilty of an offence under this section is liable—

(a) on conviction on indictment, to imprisonment for a term not exceeding two years or a fine (or both);

(b) on summary conviction—

(i) in England and Wales or Scotland, to imprisonment for a term not exceeding twelve months or to a fine not exceeding the statutory maximum (or both);

(ii) in . . . Northern Ireland, to imprisonment for a term not exceeding six months, or to a fine not exceeding the statutory maximum (or both).

(6) Where an offence under this section is committed by a body corporate, every officer of the body who is in default also commits the offence.

For this purpose—

(a) any person who purports to act as director, manager or secretary of the body is treated as an officer of the body, and

(b) if the body is a company, any shadow director is treated as an officer of the company.

461 Permitted disclosure of information obtained under compulsory powers

(1) The prohibition in section 460 of the disclosure of information obtained in pursuance of a requirement or order under section 459 (power of authorised person to require documents etc) that relates to the private affairs of an individual or to any particular business has effect subject to the following exceptions.

(2) It does not apply to the disclosure of information for the purpose of facilitating the carrying out by the authorised person of his functions under section 456.

(3) It does not apply to disclosure to—

(a) the Secretary of State,

(b) the Department of Enterprise, Trade and Investment for Northern Ireland,

(c) the Treasury,

(d) the Bank of England,
(e) the Financial Conduct Authority,
(ea) the Prudential Regulation Authority, or
(f) the Commissioners for Her Majesty's Revenue and Customs.

(4) It does not apply to disclosure—
(a) for the purpose of assisting a body designated by an order under section 1252 (delegation of functions of the Secretary of State) to exercise its functions under Part 42;
(aa) for the purpose of facilitating the carrying out of inspections under paragraph 23 of Schedule 10 (arrangements for independent monitoring of audits of listed companies and other major bodies);
(b) with a view to the institution of, or otherwise for the purposes of, disciplinary proceedings relating to the performance by an accountant or auditor of his professional duties;
(c) for the purpose of enabling or assisting the Secretary of State or the Treasury to exercise any of their functions under any of the following—
(i) the Companies Acts,
(ii) Part 5 of the Criminal Justice Act 1993 (insider dealing),
(iii) the Insolvency Act 1986 or the Insolvency (Northern Ireland) Order 1989,
(iv) the Company Directors Disqualification Act 1986 or the Company Directors Disqualification (Northern Ireland) Order 2002,
(v) the Financial Services and Markets Act 2000;
(d) for the purpose of enabling or assisting the Department of Enterprise, Trade and Investment for Northern Ireland to exercise any powers conferred on it by the enactments relating to companies, directors' disqualification or insolvency;
(e) for the purpose of enabling or assisting the Bank of England to exercise its functions;
(f) for the purpose of enabling or assisting the Commissioners for Her Majesty's Revenue and Customs to exercise their functions;
(g) for the purpose of enabling or assisting the Financial Conduct Authority or the Prudential Regulation Authority to exercise its functions under any of the following—
(i) the legislation relating to friendly societies or to industrial and provident societies,
(ii) the Building Societies Act 1986,
(iii) Part 7 of the Companies Act 1989,
(iv) the Financial Services and Markets Act 2000; or
(h) in pursuance of any EU obligation.

(5) It does not apply to disclosure to a body exercising functions of a public nature under legislation in any country or territory outside the United Kingdom that appear to the authorised person to be similar to his functions under section 456 for the purpose of enabling or assisting that body to exercise those functions.

(6) In determining whether to disclose information to a body in accordance with subsection (5), the authorised person must have regard to the following considerations—
(a) whether the use which the body is likely to make of the information is sufficiently important to justify making the disclosure;
(b) whether the body has adequate arrangements to prevent the information from being used or further disclosed other than—
(i) for the purposes of carrying out the functions mentioned in that subsection, or
(ii) for other purposes substantially similar to those for which information disclosed to the authorised person could be used or further disclosed.

(7) Nothing in this section authorises the making of a disclosure in contravention of the Data Protection Act 1998.

462 Power to amend categories of permitted disclosure

(1) The Secretary of State may by order amend section 461(3), (4) and (5).

(2) An order under this section must not—

(a) amend subsection (3) of that section (UK public authorities) by specifying a person unless the person exercises functions of a public nature (whether or not he exercises any other function);
(b) amend subsection (4) of that section (purposes for which disclosure permitted) by adding or modifying a description of disclosure unless the purpose for which the disclosure is permitted is likely to facilitate the exercise of a function of a public nature;
(c) amend subsection (5) of that section (overseas regulatory authorities) so as to have the effect of permitting disclosures to be made to a body other than one that exercises functions of a public nature in a country or territory outside the United Kingdom.

(3) An order under this section is subject to negative resolution procedure.

CHAPTER 12
SUPPLEMENTARY PROVISIONS

Liability for false or misleading statements in reports

463 Liability for false or misleading statements in reports

(1) The reports to which this section applies are—
(a) the directors' report,
(b) the directors' remuneration report, and
(c) a summary financial statement so far as it is derived from either of those reports.

(2) A director of a company is liable to compensate the company for any loss suffered by it as a result of—
(a) any untrue or misleading statement in a report to which this section applies, or
(b) the omission from a report to which this section applies of anything required to be included in it.

(3) He is so liable only if—
(a) he knew the statement to be untrue or misleading or was reckless as to whether it was untrue or misleading, or
(b) he knew the omission to be dishonest concealment of a material fact.

(4) No person shall be subject to any liability to a person other than the company resulting from reliance, by that person or another, on information in a report to which this section applies.

(5) The reference in subsection (4) to a person being subject to a liability includes a reference to another person being entitled as against him to be granted any civil remedy or to rescind or repudiate an agreement.

(6) This section does not affect—
(a) liability for a civil penalty, or
(b) liability for a criminal offence.

Accounting and reporting standards

464 Accounting standards

(1) In this Part "accounting standards" means statements of standard accounting practice issued by such body or bodies as may be prescribed by regulations.

(2) References in this Part to accounting standards applicable to a company's annual accounts are to such standards as are, in accordance with their terms, relevant to the company's circumstances and to the accounts.

(3) Regulations under this section may contain such transitional and other supplementary and incidental provisions as appear to the Secretary of State to be appropriate.

Companies qualifying as medium-sized

465 Companies qualifying as medium-sized: general

(1) A company qualifies as medium-sized in relation to its first financial year if the qualifying conditions are met in that year.

(2) A company qualifies as medium-sized in relation to a subsequent financial year—
(a) if the qualifying conditions are met in that year and the preceding financial year;
(b) if the qualifying conditions are met in that year and the company qualified as medium-sized in relation to the preceding financial year;
(c) if the qualifying conditions were met in the preceding financial year and the company qualified as medium-sized in relation to that year.

(3) The qualifying conditions are met by a company in a year in which it satisfies two or more of the following requirements—

1.	Turnover	Not more than £25.9 million
2.	Balance sheet total	Not more than £12.9 million
3.	Number of employees	Not more than 250

(4) For a period that is a company's financial year but not in fact a year the maximum figures for turnover must be proportionately adjusted.

(5) The balance sheet total means the aggregate of the amounts shown as assets in the company's balance sheet.

(6) The number of employees means the average number of persons employed by the company in the year, determined as follows—
(a) find for each month in the financial year the number of persons employed under contracts of service by the company in that month (whether throughout the month or not),
(b) add together the monthly totals, and
(c) divide by the number of months in the financial year.

(7) This section is subject to section 466 (companies qualifying as medium-sized: parent companies).

466 Companies qualifying as medium-sized: parent companies

(1) A parent company qualifies as a medium-sized company in relation to a financial year only if the group headed by it qualifies as a medium-sized group.

(2) A group qualifies as medium-sized in relation to the parent company's first financial year if the qualifying conditions are met in that year.

(3) A group qualifies as medium-sized in relation to a subsequent financial year of the parent company—
(a) if the qualifying conditions are met in that year and the preceding financial year;
(b) if the qualifying conditions are met in that year and the group qualified as medium-sized in relation to the preceding financial year;
(c) if the qualifying conditions were met in the preceding financial year and the group qualified as medium-sized in relation to that year.

(4) The qualifying conditions are met by a group in a year in which it satisfies two or more of the following requirements—

1.	Aggregate turnover	Not more than £25.9 million net (or £31.1 million gross)
2.	Aggregate balance sheet total	Not more than £12.9 million net (or £15.5 million gross)
3.	Aggregate number of employees	Not more than 250

(5) The aggregate figures are ascertained by aggregating the relevant figures determined in accordance with section 465 for each member of the group.

(6) In relation to the aggregate figures for turnover and balance sheet total—
"net" means after any set-offs and other adjustments made to eliminate group transactions—
(a) in the case of Companies Act accounts, in accordance with regulations under section 404,
(b) in the case of IAS accounts, in accordance with international accounting standards; and
"gross" means without those set-offs and other adjustments.
A company may satisfy any relevant requirement on the basis of either the net or the gross figure.

(7) The figures for each subsidiary undertaking shall be those included in its individual accounts for the relevant financial year, that is—
(a) if its financial year ends with that of the parent company, that financial year, and
(b) if not, its financial year ending last before the end of the financial year of the parent company.

If those figures cannot be obtained without disproportionate expense or undue delay, the latest available figures shall be taken.

467 Companies excluded from being treated as medium-sized

(1) A company is not entitled to take advantage of any of the provisions of this Part relating to companies qualifying as medium-sized if it was at any time within the financial year in question—
- (a) a public company,
- (b) a company that—
  - (i) has permission under Part 4A of the Financial Services and Markets Act 2000 to carry on a regulated activity, or
  - (ii) carries on insurance market activity, or
- (c) a member of an ineligible group.

(2) A group is ineligible if any of its members is—
- (a) a public company,
- (b) a body corporate (other than a company) whose shares are admitted to trading on a regulated market,
- (c) a person (other than a small company) who has permission under Part 4A of the Financial Services and Markets Act 2000 to carry on a regulated activity,
- (d) a small company that is an authorised insurance company, a banking company, an e-money issuer, a MiFID investment firm or a UCITS management company, or
- (e) a person who carries on insurance market activity.

(3) A company is a small company for the purposes of subsection (2) if it qualified as small in relation to its last financial year ending on or before the end of the financial year in question.

(4) This section does not prevent a company from taking advantage of section 417(7) (business review: non-financial information) by reason only of its having been a member of an ineligible group at any time within the financial year in question.

General power to make further provision about accounts and reports

468 General power to make further provision about accounts and reports

(1) The Secretary of State may make provision by regulations about—
- (a) the accounts and reports that companies are required to prepare;
- (b) the categories of companies required to prepare accounts and reports of any description;
- (c) the form and content of the accounts and reports that companies are required to prepare;
- (d) the obligations of companies and others as regards—
  - (i) the approval of accounts and reports,
  - (ii) the sending of accounts and reports to members and others,
  - (iii) the laying of accounts and reports before the company in general meeting,
  - (iv) the delivery of copies of accounts and reports to the registrar, and
  - (v) the publication of accounts and reports.

(2) The regulations may amend this Part by adding, altering or repealing provisions.

(3) But they must not amend (other than consequentially)—
- (a) section 393 (accounts to give true and fair view), or
- (b) the provisions of Chapter 11 (revision of defective accounts and reports).

(4) The regulations may create criminal offences in cases corresponding to those in which an offence is created by an existing provision of this Part. The maximum penalty for any such offence may not be greater than is provided in relation to an offence under the existing provision.

(5) The regulations may provide for civil penalties in circumstances corresponding to those within section 453(1) (civil penalty for failure to file accounts and reports).
The provisions of section 453(2) to (5) apply in relation to any such penalty.

Other supplementary provisions

469 Preparation and filing of accounts in euros

(1) The amounts set out in the annual accounts of a company may also be shown in the same accounts translated into euros.

(2) When complying with section 441 (duty to file accounts and reports), the directors of a company may deliver to the registrar an additional copy of the company's annual accounts in which the amounts have been translated into euros.

(3) In both cases—

(a) the amounts must have been translated at the exchange rate prevailing on the date to which the balance sheet is made up, and

(b) that rate must be disclosed in the notes to the accounts.

(4) For the purposes of sections 434 and 435 (requirements in connection with published accounts) any additional copy of the company's annual accounts delivered to the registrar under subsection (2) above shall be treated as statutory accounts of the company.

In the case of such a copy, references in those sections to the auditor's report on the company's annual accounts shall be read as references to the auditor's report on the annual accounts of which it is a copy.

470 Power to apply provisions to banking partnerships

(1) The Secretary of State may by regulations apply to banking partnerships, subject to such exceptions, adaptations and modifications as he considers appropriate, the provisions of this Part (and of regulations made under this Part) applying to banking companies.

(2) A "banking partnership" means a partnership which has permission under Part 4A of the Financial Services and Markets Act 2000.

But a partnership is not a banking partnership if it has permission to accept deposits only for the purpose of carrying on another regulated activity in accordance with that permission.

(3) Expressions used in this section that are also used in the provisions regulating activities under the Financial Services and Markets Act 2000 have the same meaning here as they do in those provisions.

See section 22 of that Act, orders made under that section and Schedule 2 to that Act.

(4) Regulations under this section are subject to affirmative resolution procedure.

471 Meaning of "annual accounts" and related expressions

(1) In this Part a company's "annual accounts", in relation to a financial year, means—

(a) any individual accounts prepared by the company for that year (see section 394), and

(b) any group accounts prepared by the company for that year (see sections 398 and 399).

This is subject to section 408 (option to omit individual profit and loss account from annual accounts where information given in group accounts).

(2) In the case of an unquoted company, its "annual accounts and reports" for a financial year are—

(a) its annual accounts,

(b) the directors' report, and

(c) the auditor's report on those accounts and the directors' report (unless the company is exempt from audit).

(3) In the case of a quoted company, its "annual accounts and reports" for a financial year are—

(a) its annual accounts,

(b) the directors' remuneration report,

(c) the directors' report, and

(d) the auditor's report on those accounts, on the auditable part of the directors' remuneration report and on the directors' report.

472 Notes to the accounts

(1) Information required by this Part to be given in notes to a company's annual accounts may be contained in the accounts or in a separate document annexed to the accounts.

(2) References in this Part to a company's annual accounts, or to a balance sheet or profit and loss account, include notes to the accounts giving information which is required by any provision of this Act or international accounting standards, and required or allowed by any such provision to be given in a note to company accounts.

472A Meaning of "corporate governance statement" etc

(1) In this Part "corporate governance statement" means the statement required by rules 7.2.1 to 7.2.11 in the Disclosure Rules and Transparency Rules sourcebook issued by the Financial Services Authority.

(2) Those rules were inserted by Annex C of the Disclosure Rules and Transparency Rules Sourcebook (Corporate Governance Rules) Instrument 2008 made by the Authority on 26th June 2008 (FSA 2008/32).

(3) A "separate" corporate governance statement means one that is not included in the directors' report.

473 Parliamentary procedure for certain regulations under this Part

(1) This section applies to regulations under the following provisions of this Part—
section 396 (Companies Act individual accounts),
section 404 (Companies Act group accounts),
section 409 (information about related undertakings),
section 412 (information about directors' benefits: remuneration, pensions and compensation for loss of office),
section 416 (contents of directors' report: general),
section 421 (contents of directors' remuneration report),
section 444 (filing obligations of companies subject to small companies regime),
section 445 (filing obligations of medium-sized companies),
section 468 (general power to make further provision about accounts and reports).

(2) Any such regulations may make consequential amendments or repeals in other provisions of this Act, or in other enactments.

(3) Regulations that—
(a) restrict the classes of company which have the benefit of any exemption, exception or special provision,
(b) require additional matter to be included in a document of any class, or
(c) otherwise render the requirements of this Part more onerous, are subject to affirmative resolution procedure.

(4) Otherwise, the regulations are subject to negative resolution procedure.

474 Minor definitions

(1) In this Part—

"e-money issuer" means a person who has permission under Part 4A of the Financial Services and Markets Act 2000 to carry on the activity of issuing electronic money within the meaning of article 9B of the Financial Services and Markets Act 2000 (Regulated Activities) Order 2001;

"group" means a parent undertaking and its subsidiary undertakings; "IAS Regulation" means EC Regulation No. 1606/2002 of the European Parliament and of the Council of 19 July 2002 on the application of international accounting standards;

"included in the consolidation", in relation to group accounts, or "included in consolidated group accounts", means that the undertaking is included in the accounts by the method of full (and not proportional) consolidation, and references to an undertaking excluded from consolidation shall be construed accordingly;

"international accounting standards" means the international accounting standards, within the meaning of the IAS Regulation, adopted from time to time by the European Commission in accordance with that Regulation;

…

"MiFID investment firm" means an investment firm within the meaning of Article 4.1.1 of Directive 2004/39/EC of the European Parliament and of the Council of 21 April 2004 on markets in financial instruments, other than—

(a) a company to which that Directive does not apply by virtue of Article 2 of that Directive,

(b) a company which is an exempt investment firm within the meaning of regulation 4A(3) of the Financial Services and Markets Act 2000 (Markets in Financial Instruments) Regulations 2007, and

(c) any other company which fulfils all the requirements set out in regulation 4C(3) of those Regulations;

"profit and loss account", in relation to a company that prepares IAS accounts, includes an income statement or other equivalent financial statement required to be prepared by international accounting standards;

"regulated activity" has the meaning given in section 22 of the Financial Services and Markets Act 2000, except that it does not include activities of the kind specified in any of the following provisions of the Financial Services and Markets Act 2000 (Regulated Activities) Order 2001—

(a) article 25A (arranging regulated mortgage contracts),

(b) article 25B (arranging regulated home reversion plans),

(c) article 25C (arranging regulated home purchase plans),

(ca) article 25E (arranging regulated sale and rent back agreements),

(d) article 39A (assisting administration and performance of a contract of insurance),

(e) article 53A (advising on regulated mortgage contracts),

(f) article 53B (advising on regulated home reversion plans),

(g) article 53C (advising on regulated home purchase plans),

(ga) article 53D (advising on regulated sale and rent back agreements),

(h) article 21 (dealing as agent), article 25 (arranging deals in investments) or article 53 (advising on investments) where the activity concerns relevant investments that are not contractually based investments (within the meaning of article 3 of that Order), or

(i) article 64 (agreeing to carry on a regulated activity of the kind mentioned in paragraphs (a) to (h));

"turnover", in relation to a company, means the amounts derived from the provision of goods and services falling within the company's ordinary activities, after deduction of—

(a) trade discounts,

(b) value added tax, and

(c) any other taxes based on the amounts so derived;

"UCITS management company" has the meaning given by the Glossary forming part of the Handbook made by the Financial Services Authority under the Financial Services and Markets Act 2000.

(2) In the case of an undertaking not trading for profit, any reference in this Part to a profit and loss account is to an income and expenditure account. References to profit and loss and, in relation to group accounts, to a consolidated profit and loss account shall be construed accordingly.

PART 16
AUDIT

CHAPTER 1
REQUIREMENT FOR AUDITED ACCOUNTS

Requirement for audited accounts

475 Requirement for audited accounts

(1) A company's annual accounts for a financial year must be audited in accordance with this Part unless the company—

(a) is exempt from audit under—
section 477 (small companies),

section 479A (subsidiary companies), or
section 480 (dormant companies);
or

(b) is exempt from the requirements of this Part under section 482 (non-profit-making companies subject to public sector audit).

(2) A company is not entitled to any such exemption unless its balance sheet contains a statement by the directors to that effect.

(3) A company is not entitled to exemption under any of the provisions mentioned in subsection (1)(a) unless its balance sheet contains a statement by the directors to the effect that—

(a) the members have not required the company to obtain an audit of its accounts for the year in question in accordance with section 476, and

(b) the directors acknowledge their responsibilities for complying with the requirements of this Act with respect to accounting records and the preparation of accounts.

(4) The statement required by subsection (2) or (3) must appear on the balance sheet above the signature required by section 414.

476 Right of members to require audit

(1) The members of a company that would otherwise be entitled to exemption from audit under any of the provisions mentioned in section 475(1)(a) may by notice under this section require it to obtain an audit of its accounts for a financial year.

(2) The notice must be given by—

(a) members representing not less in total than 10% in nominal value of the company's issued share capital, or any class of it, or

(b) if the company does not have a share capital, not less than 10% in number of the members of the company.

(3) The notice may not be given before the financial year to which it relates and must be given not later than one month before the end of that year.

Exemption from audit: small companies

477 Small companies: conditions for exemption from audit

(1) A company that qualifies as a small company in relation to a financial year is exempt from the requirements of this Act relating to the audit of accounts for that year.

(2), (3) ...

(4) For the purposes of this section—

(a) whether a company qualifies as a small company shall be determined in accordance with section 382(1) to (6), ...

(b) ...

(5) This section has effect subject to—
section 475(2) and (3) (requirements as to statements to be contained in balance sheet),
section 476 (right of members to require audit),
section 478 (companies excluded from small companies exemption), and
section 479 (availability of small companies exemption in case of group company).

478 Companies excluded from small companies exemption

A company is not entitled to the exemption conferred by section 477 (small companies) if it was at any time within the financial year in question—

(a) a public company,

(b) a company that—

(i) is an authorised insurance company, a banking company, an e-money issuer, a MiFID investment firm or a UCITS management company, or

(ii) carries on insurance market activity, or

(c) a special register body as defined in section 117(1) of the Trade Union and Labour Relations (Consolidation) Act 1992 or an employers' association as defined in section 122 of that Act or Article 4 of the Industrial Relations (Northern Ireland) Order 1992.

479 Availability of small companies exemption in case of group company

(1) A company is not entitled to the exemption conferred by section 477 (small companies) in respect of a financial year during any part of which it was a group company unless—

(a) the group—

(i) qualifies as a small group in relation to that financial year, and

(ii) was not at any time in that year an ineligible group, or

(b) subsection (3) applies.

(2) ...

(3) A company is not excluded by subsection (1) if, throughout the whole of the period or periods during the financial year when it was a group company, it was both a subsidiary undertaking and dormant.

(4) In this section—

(a) "group company" means a company that is a parent company or a subsidiary undertaking, and

(b) "the group", in relation to a group company, means that company together with all its associated undertakings.

For this purpose undertakings are associated if one is a subsidiary undertaking of the other or both are subsidiary undertakings of a third undertaking.

(5) For the purposes of this section—

(a) whether a group qualifies as small shall be determined in accordance with section 383 (companies qualifying as small: parent companies);

(b) "ineligible group" has the meaning given by section 384(2) and (3);

(c)–(e) ...

(6) The provisions mentioned in subsection (5) apply for the purposes of this section as if all the bodies corporate in the group were companies.

Exemption from audit: qualifying subsidiaries

479A Subsidiary companies: conditions for exemption from audit

(1) A company is exempt from the requirements of this Act relating to the audit of individual accounts for a financial year if—

(a) it is itself a subsidiary undertaking, and

(b) its parent undertaking is established under the law of an EEA State.

(2) Exemption is conditional upon compliance with all of the following conditions—

(a) all members of the company must agree to the exemption in respect of the financial year in question,

(b) the parent undertaking must give a guarantee under section 479C in respect of that year,

(c) the company must be included in the consolidated accounts drawn up for that year or to an earlier date in that year by the parent undertaking in accordance with—

(i) the provisions of the Seventh Directive (83/349/EEC), or

(ii) international accounting standards,

(d) the parent undertaking must disclose in the notes to the consolidated accounts that the company is exempt from the requirements of this Act relating to the audit of individual accounts by virtue of this section, and

(e) the directors of the company must deliver to the registrar on or before the date that they file the accounts for that year—

(i) a written notice of the agreement referred to in subsection (2)(a),

(ii) the statement referred to in section 479C(1),

(iii) a copy of the consolidated accounts referred to in subsection (2)(c),

(iv) a copy of the auditor's report on those accounts, and

(v) a copy of the consolidated annual report drawn up by the parent undertaking.

(3) This section has effect subject to—

section 475(2) and (3) (requirements as to statements contained in balance sheet), and

section 476 (right of members to require audit).

479B Companies excluded from the subsidiary companies audit exemption

A company is not entitled to the exemption conferred by section 479A (subsidiary companies) if it was at any time within the financial year in question—

(a) a quoted company as defined in section 385(2) of this Act,

(b) a company that—

(i) is an authorised insurance company, a banking company, an e-money issuer, a MiFID investment firm or a UCITS management company, or

(ii) carries on insurance market activity, or

(c) a special register body as defined in section 117(1) of the Trade Union and Labour Relations (Consolidation) Act 1992 (c 52) or an employers' association as defined in section 122 of that Act or Article 4 of the Industrial Relations (Northern Ireland) Order 1992 (SI 1992/807) (NI 5).

479C Subsidiary companies audit exemption: parent undertaking declaration of guarantee

(1) A guarantee is given by a parent undertaking under this section when the directors of the subsidiary company deliver to the registrar a statement by the parent undertaking that it guarantees the subsidiary company under this section.

(2) The statement under subsection (1) must be authenticated by the parent undertaking and must specify—

(a) the name of the parent undertaking,

(b) if the parent undertaking is incorporated in the United Kingdom, its registered number (if any),

(c) if the parent undertaking is incorporated outside the United Kingdom and registered in the country in which it is incorporated, the identity of the register on which it is registered and the number with which it is so registered,

(d) the name and registered number of the subsidiary company in respect of which the guarantee is being given,

(e) the date of the statement, and

(f) the financial year to which the guarantee relates.

(3) A guarantee given under this section has the effect that—

(a) the parent undertaking guarantees all outstanding liabilities to which the subsidiary company is subject at the end of the financial year to which the guarantee relates, until they are satisfied in full, and

(b) the guarantee is enforceable against the parent undertaking by any person to whom the subsidiary company is liable in respect of those liabilities.

Exemption from audit: dormant companies

480 Dormant companies: conditions for exemption from audit

(1) A company is exempt from the requirements of this Act relating to the audit of accounts in respect of a financial year if—

(a) it has been dormant since its formation, or

(b) it has been dormant since the end of the previous financial year and the following conditions are met.

(2) The conditions are that the company—

(a) as regards its individual accounts for the financial year in question—

(i) is entitled to prepare accounts in accordance with the small companies regime (see sections 381 to 384), or

(ii) would be so entitled but for having been a public company or a member of an ineligible group, and

(b) is not required to prepare group accounts for that year.

(3) This section has effect subject to—

section 475(2) and (3) (requirements as to statements to be contained in balance sheet),
section 476 (right of members to require audit), and
section 481 (companies excluded from dormant companies exemption).

481 Companies excluded from dormant companies exemption

A company is not entitled to the exemption conferred by section 480 (dormant companies) if it was at any time within the financial year in question a company that—

(a) is an authorised insurance company, a banking company, an e-money issuer, a MiFID investment firm or a UCITS management company, or

(b) carries on insurance market activity.

Companies subject to public sector audit

482 Non-profit-making companies subject to public sector audit

(1) The requirements of this Part as to audit of accounts do not apply to a company for a financial year if it is non-profit-making and its accounts—

(a) are subject to audit by the Comptroller and Auditor General by virtue of an order under section 25(6) of the Government Resources and Accounts Act 2000;

(ab) are subject to audit by the Auditor General for Wales by virtue of—

(i) an order under section 144 of the Government of Wales Act 1998, or

(ii) paragraph 18 of Schedule 8 to the Government of Wales Act 2006;

(b) are accounts—

(i) in relation to which section 21 of the Public Finance and Accountability (Scotland) Act 2000 (asp 1) (audit of accounts: Auditor General for Scotland) applies, or

(ii) that are subject to audit by the Auditor General for Scotland by virtue of an order under section 483 (Scottish public sector companies: audit by Auditor General for Scotland); or

(c) are subject to audit by the Comptroller and Auditor General for Northern Ireland by virtue of an order under Article 5(3) of the Audit and Accountability (Northern Ireland) Order 2003.

(2) In the case of a company that is a parent company or a subsidiary undertaking, subsection (1) applies only if every group undertaking is non-profit-making.

(3) In this section "non-profit-making" has the same meaning as in Article 54 of the Treaty on the Functioning of the European Union.

(4) This section has effect subject to section 475(2) (balance sheet to contain statement that company entitled to exemption under this section).

483 Scottish public sector companies: audit by Auditor General for Scotland

(1) The Scottish Ministers may by order provide for the accounts of a company having its registered office in Scotland to be audited by the Auditor General for Scotland.

(2) An order under subsection (1) may be made in relation to a company only if it appears to the Scottish Ministers that the company—

(a) exercises in or as regards Scotland functions of a public nature none of which relate to reserved matters (within the meaning of the Scotland Act 1998), or

(b) is entirely or substantially funded from a body having accounts falling within paragraph (a) or (b) of subsection (3).

(3) Those accounts are—

(a) accounts in relation to which section 21 of the Public Finance and Accountability (Scotland) Act 2000 (asp 1) (audit of accounts: Auditor General for Scotland) applies,

(b) accounts which are subject to audit by the Auditor General for Scotland by virtue of an order under this section.

(4) An order under subsection (1) may make such supplementary or consequential provision (including provision amending an enactment) as the Scottish Ministers think expedient.

(5) An order under subsection (1) shall not be made unless a draft of the statutory instrument containing it has been laid before, and approved by resolution of, the Scottish Parliament.

General power of amendment by regulations

484 General power of amendment by regulations

(1) The Secretary of State may by regulations amend this Chapter or section 539 (minor definitions) so far as applying to this Chapter by adding, altering or repealing provisions.

(2) The regulations may make consequential amendments or repeals in other provisions of this Act, or in other enactments.

(3) Regulations under this section imposing new requirements, or rendering existing requirements more onerous, are subject to affirmative resolution procedure.

(4) Other regulations under this section are subject to negative resolution procedure.

CHAPTER 2
APPOINTMENT OF AUDITORS

Private companies

485 Appointment of auditors of private company: general

(1) An auditor or auditors of a private company must be appointed for each financial year of the company, unless the directors reasonably resolve otherwise on the ground that audited accounts are unlikely to be required.

(2) For each financial year for which an auditor or auditors is or are to be appointed (other than the company's first financial year), the appointment must be made before the end of the period of 28 days beginning with—

(a) the end of the time allowed for sending out copies of the company's annual accounts and reports for the previous financial year (see section 424), or

(b) if earlier, the day on which copies of the company's annual accounts and reports for the previous financial year are sent out under section 423.

This is the "period for appointing auditors".

(3) The directors may appoint an auditor or auditors of the company—

(a) at any time before the company's first period for appointing auditors,

(b) following a period during which the company (being exempt from audit) did not have any auditor, at any time before the company's next period for appointing auditors, or

(c) to fill a casual vacancy in the office of auditor.

(4) The members may appoint an auditor or auditors by ordinary resolution—

(a) during a period for appointing auditors,

(b) if the company should have appointed an auditor or auditors during a period for appointing auditors but failed to do so, or

(c) where the directors had power to appoint under subsection (3) but have failed to make an appointment.

(5) An auditor or auditors of a private company may only be appointed—

(a) in accordance with this section, or

(b) in accordance with section 486 (default power of Secretary of State). This is without prejudice to any deemed re-appointment under section 487.

486 Appointment of auditors of private company: default power of Secretary of State

(1) If a private company fails to appoint an auditor or auditors in accordance with section 485, the Secretary of State may appoint one or more persons to fill the vacancy.

(2) Where subsection (2) of that section applies and the company fails to make the necessary appointment before the end of the period for appointing auditors, the company must within one week of the end of that period give notice to the Secretary of State of his power having become exercisable.

(3) If a company fails to give the notice required by this section, an offence is committed by—

(a) the company, and

(b) every officer of the company who is in default.

(4) A person guilty of an offence under this section is liable on summary conviction to a fine not exceeding level 3 on the standard scale and, for continued contravention, a daily default fine not exceeding one-tenth of level 3 on the standard scale.

487 Term of office of auditors of private company

(1) An auditor or auditors of a private company hold office in accordance with the terms of their appointment, subject to the requirements that—

(a) they do not take office until any previous auditor or auditors cease to hold office, and

(b) they cease to hold office at the end of the next period for appointing auditors unless re-appointed.

(2) Where no auditor has been appointed by the end of the next period for appointing auditors, any auditor in office immediately before that time is deemed to be re-appointed at that time, unless—

(a) he was appointed by the directors, or

(b) the company's articles require actual re-appointment, or

(c) the deemed re-appointment is prevented by the members under section 488, or

(d) the members have resolved that he should not be re-appointed, or

(e) the directors have resolved that no auditor or auditors should be appointed for the financial year in question.

(3) This is without prejudice to the provisions of this Part as to removal and resignation of auditors.

(4) No account shall be taken of any loss of the opportunity of deemed re-appointment under this section in ascertaining the amount of any compensation or damages payable to an auditor on his ceasing to hold office for any reason..

488 Prevention by members of deemed re-appointment of auditor

(1) An auditor of a private company is not deemed to be re-appointed under section 487(2) if the company has received notices under this section from members representing at least the requisite percentage of the total voting rights of all members who would be entitled to vote on a resolution that the auditor should not be re-appointed.

(2) The "requisite percentage" is 5%, or such lower percentage as is specified for this purpose in the company's articles.

(3) A notice under this section—

(a) may be in hard copy or electronic form,

(b) must be authenticated by the person or persons giving it, and

(c) must be received by the company before the end of the accounting reference period immediately preceding the time when the deemed reappointment would have effect.

Public companies

489 Appointment of auditors of public company: general

(1) An auditor or auditors of a public company must be appointed for each financial year of the company, unless the directors reasonably resolve otherwise on the ground that audited accounts are unlikely to be required.

(2) For each financial year for which an auditor or auditors is or are to be appointed (other than the company's first financial year), the appointment must be made before the end of the accounts meeting of the company at which the company's annual accounts and reports for the previous financial year are laid.

(3) The directors may appoint an auditor or auditors of the company—

(a) at any time before the company's first accounts meeting;
(b) following a period during which the company (being exempt from audit) did not have any auditor, at any time before the company's next accounts meeting;
(c) to fill a casual vacancy in the office of auditor.

(4) The members may appoint an auditor or auditors by ordinary resolution—
(a) at an accounts meeting;
(b) if the company should have appointed an auditor or auditors at an accounts meeting but failed to do so;
(c) where the directors had power to appoint under subsection (3) but have failed to make an appointment.

(5) An auditor or auditors of a public company may only be appointed—
(a) in accordance with this section, or
(b) in accordance with section 490 (default power of Secretary of State).

490 Appointment of auditors of public company: default power of Secretary of State

(1) If a public company fails to appoint an auditor or auditors in accordance with section 489, the Secretary of State may appoint one or more persons to fill the vacancy.

(2) Where subsection (2) of that section applies and the company fails to make the necessary appointment before the end of the accounts meeting, the company must within one week of the end of that meeting give notice to the Secretary of State of his power having become exercisable.

(3) If a company fails to give the notice required by this section, an offence is committed by—
(a) the company, and
(b) every officer of the company who is in default.

(4) A person guilty of an offence under this section is liable on summary conviction to a fine not exceeding level 3 on the standard scale and, for continued contravention, a daily default fine not exceeding one-tenth of level 3 on the standard scale.

491 Term of office of auditors of public company

(1) The auditor or auditors of a public company hold office in accordance with the terms of their appointment, subject to the requirements that—
(a) they do not take office until the previous auditor or auditors have ceased to hold office, and
(b) they cease to hold office at the conclusion of the accounts meeting next following their appointment, unless re-appointed.

(2) This is without prejudice to the provisions of this Part as to removal and resignation of auditors.

General provisions

492 Fixing of auditor's remuneration

(1) The remuneration of an auditor appointed by the members of a company must be fixed by the members by ordinary resolution or in such manner as the members may by ordinary resolution determine.

(2) The remuneration of an auditor appointed by the directors of a company must be fixed by the directors.

(3) The remuneration of an auditor appointed by the Secretary of State must be fixed by the Secretary of State.

(4) For the purposes of this section "remuneration" includes sums paid in respect of expenses.

(5) This section applies in relation to benefits in kind as to payments of money.

493 Disclosure of terms of audit appointment

(1) The Secretary of State may make provision by regulations for securing the disclosure of the terms on which a company's auditor is appointed, remunerated or performs his duties.
Nothing in the following provisions of this section affects the generality of this power.

(2) The regulations may—
(a) require disclosure of—
(i) a copy of any terms that are in writing, and

(ii) a written memorandum setting out any terms that are not in writing;

(b) require disclosure to be at such times, in such places and by such means as are specified in the regulations;

(c) require the place and means of disclosure to be stated—

(i) in a note to the company's annual accounts (in the case of its individual accounts) or in such manner as is specified in the regulations (in the case of group accounts),

(ii) in the directors' report, or

(iii) in the auditor's report on the company's annual accounts.

(3) The provisions of this section apply to a variation of the terms mentioned in subsection (1) as they apply to the original terms.

(4) Regulations under this section are subject to affirmative resolution procedure.

494 Disclosure of services provided by auditor or associates and related remuneration

(1) The Secretary of State may make provision by regulations for securing the disclosure of—

(a) the nature of any services provided for a company by the company's auditor (whether in his capacity as auditor or otherwise) or by his associates;

(b) the amount of any remuneration received or receivable by a company's auditor, or his associates, in respect of any such services.

Nothing in the following provisions of this section affects the generality of this power.

(2) The regulations may provide—

(a) for disclosure of the nature of any services provided to be made by reference to any class or description of services specified in the regulations (or any combination of services, however described);

(b) for the disclosure of amounts of remuneration received or receivable in respect of services of any class or description specified in the regulations (or any combination of services, however described);

(c) for the disclosure of separate amounts so received or receivable by the company's auditor or any of his associates, or of aggregate amounts so received or receivable by all or any of those persons.

(3) The regulations may—

(a) provide that "remuneration" includes sums paid in respect of expenses;

(b) apply to benefits in kind as well as to payments of money, and require the disclosure of the nature of any such benefits and their estimated money value;

(c) apply to services provided for associates of a company as well as to those provided for a company;

(d) define "associate" in relation to an auditor and a company respectively.

(4) The regulations may provide that any disclosure required by the regulations is to be made—

(a) in a note to the company's annual accounts (in the case of its individual accounts) or in such manner as is specified in the regulations (in the case of group accounts),

(b) in the directors' report, or

(c) in the auditor's report on the company's annual accounts.

(5) If the regulations provide that any such disclosure is to be made as mentioned in subsection (4)(a) or (b), the regulations may require the auditor to supply the directors of the company with any information necessary to enable the disclosure to be made.

(6) Regulations under this section are subject to negative resolution procedure.

CHAPTER 3
FUNCTIONS OF AUDITOR

Auditor's report

495 Auditor's report on company's annual accounts

(1) A company's auditor must make a report to the company's members on all annual accounts of the company of which copies are, during his tenure of office—

(a) in the case of a private company, to be sent out to members under section 423;
(b) in the case of a public company, to be laid before the company in general meeting under section 437.

(2) The auditor's report must include—
(a) an introduction identifying the annual accounts that are the subject of the audit and the financial reporting framework that has been applied in their preparation, and
(b) a description of the scope of the audit identifying the auditing standards in accordance with which the audit was conducted.

(3) The report must state clearly whether, in the auditor's opinion, the annual accounts—
(a) give a true and fair view—
(i) in the case of an individual balance sheet, of the state of affairs of the company as at the end of the financial year,
(ii) in the case of an individual profit and loss account, of the profit or loss of the company for the financial year,
(iii) in the case of group accounts, of the state of affairs as at the end of the financial year and of the profit or loss for the financial year of the undertakings included in the consolidation as a whole, so far as concerns members of the company;
(b) have been properly prepared in accordance with the relevant financial reporting framework; and
(c) have been prepared in accordance with the requirements of this Act (and, where applicable, Article 4 of the IAS Regulation).

Expressions used in this subsection that are defined for the purposes of Part 15 (see section 474) have the same meaning as in that Part.

(4) The auditor's report—
(a) must be either unqualified or qualified, and
(b) must include a reference to any matters to which the auditor wishes to draw attention by way of emphasis without qualifying the report.

496 Auditor's report on directors' report

The auditor must state in his report on the company's annual accounts whether in his opinion the information given in the directors' report for the financial year for which the accounts are prepared is consistent with those accounts.

497 Auditor's report on auditable part of directors' remuneration report

(1) If the company is a quoted company, the auditor, in his report on the company's annual accounts for the financial year, must—
(a) report to the company's members on the auditable part of the directors' remuneration report, and
(b) state whether in his opinion that part of the directors' remuneration report has been properly prepared in accordance with this Act.

(2) For the purposes of this Part, "the auditable part" of a directors' remuneration report is the part identified as such by regulations under section 421.

497A Auditor's report on separate corporate governance statement

(1) Where the company prepares a separate corporate governance statement in respect of a financial year the auditor must state in his report on the company's annual accounts for that year whether in his opinion the information given in the statement in compliance with rules 7.2.5 and 7.2.6 in the Disclosure Rules and Transparency Rules sourcebook issued by the Financial Services Authority (information about internal control and risk management systems in relation to financial reporting processes and about share capital structures) is consistent with those accounts.

(2) The rules referred to above were inserted by Annex C of the Disclosure Rules and Transparency Rules Sourcebook (Corporate Governance Rules) Instrument 2008 made by the Authority on 26th June 2008 (FSA 2008/32).

Duties and rights of auditors

498 Duties of auditor

(1) A company's auditor, in preparing his report, must carry out such investigations as will enable him to form an opinion as to—

(a) whether adequate accounting records have been kept by the company and returns adequate for their audit have been received from branches not visited by him, and

(b) whether the company's individual accounts are in agreement with the accounting records and returns, and

(c) in the case of a quoted company, whether the auditable part of the company's directors' remuneration report is in agreement with the accounting records and returns.

(2) If the auditor is of the opinion—

(a) that adequate accounting records have not been kept, or that returns adequate for their audit have not been received from branches not visited by him, or

(b) that the company's individual accounts are not in agreement with the accounting records and returns, or

(c) in the case of a quoted company, that the auditable part of its directors' remuneration report is not in agreement with the accounting records and returns,

the auditor shall state that fact in his report.

(3) If the auditor fails to obtain all the information and explanations which, to the best of his knowledge and belief, are necessary for the purposes of his audit, he shall state that fact in his report.

(4) If—

(a) the requirements of regulations under section 412 (disclosure of directors' benefits: remuneration, pensions and compensation for loss of office) are not complied with in the annual accounts, or

(b) in the case of a quoted company, the requirements of regulations under section 421 as to information forming the auditable part of the directors' remuneration report are not complied with in that report,

the auditor must include in his report, so far as he is reasonably able to do so, a statement giving the required particulars.

(5) If the directors of the company—

(a) have prepared accounts in accordance with the small companies regime, or

(b) have taken advantage of small companies exemption in preparing the directors' report,

and in the auditor's opinion they were not entitled to do so, the auditor shall state that fact in his report.

498A Auditor's duties in relation to separate corporate governance statement

Where the company is required to prepare a corporate governance statement in respect of a financial year and no such statement is included in the directors' report—

(a) the company's auditor, in preparing his report on the company's annual accounts for that year, must ascertain whether a corporate governance statement has been prepared, and

(b) if it appears to the auditor that no such statement has been prepared, he must state that fact in his report.

499 Auditor's general right to information

(1) An auditor of a company—

(a) has a right of access at all times to the company's books, accounts and vouchers (in whatever form they are held), and

(b) may require any of the following persons to provide him with such information or explanations as he thinks necessary for the performance of his duties as auditor.

(2) Those persons are—

(a) any officer or employee of the company;

(b) any person holding or accountable for any of the company's books, accounts or vouchers;

(c) any subsidiary undertaking of the company which is a body corporate incorporated in the United Kingdom;

(d) any officer, employee or auditor of any such subsidiary undertaking or any person holding or accountable for any books, accounts or vouchers of any such subsidiary undertaking;

(e) any person who fell within any of paragraphs (a) to (d) at a time to which the information or explanations required by the auditor relates or relate.

(3) A statement made by a person in response to a requirement under this section may not be used in evidence against him in criminal proceedings except proceedings for an offence under section 501.

(4) Nothing in this section compels a person to disclose information in respect of which a claim to legal professional privilege (in Scotland, to confidentiality of communications) could be maintained in legal proceedings.

500 Auditor's right to information from overseas subsidiaries

(1) Where a parent company has a subsidiary undertaking that is not a body corporate incorporated in the United Kingdom, the auditor of the parent company may require it to obtain from any of the following persons such information or explanations as he may reasonably require for the purposes of his duties as auditor.

(2) Those persons are—

(a) the undertaking;

(b) any officer, employee or auditor of the undertaking;

(c) any person holding or accountable for any of the undertaking's books, accounts or vouchers;

(d) any person who fell within paragraph (b) or (c) at a time to which the information or explanations relates or relate.

(3) If so required, the parent company must take all such steps as are reasonably open to it to obtain the information or explanations from the person concerned.

(4) A statement made by a person in response to a requirement under this section may not be used in evidence against him in criminal proceedings except proceedings for an offence under section 501.

(5) Nothing in this section compels a person to disclose information in respect of which a claim to legal professional privilege (in Scotland, to confidentiality of communications) could be maintained in legal proceedings.

501 Auditor's rights to information: offences

(1) A person commits an offence who knowingly or recklessly makes to an auditor of a company a statement (oral or written) that—

(a) conveys or purports to convey any information or explanations which the auditor requires, or is entitled to require, under section 499, and

(b) is misleading, false or deceptive in a material particular.

(2) A person guilty of an offence under subsection (1) is liable—

(a) on conviction on indictment, to imprisonment for a term not exceeding two years or a fine (or both);

(b) on summary conviction—

(i) in England and Wales, to imprisonment for a term not exceeding twelve months or to a fine not exceeding the statutory maximum (or both);

(ii) in Scotland or Northern Ireland, to imprisonment for a term not exceeding six months or to a fine not exceeding the statutory maximum (or both).

(3) A person who fails to comply with a requirement under section 499 without delay commits an offence unless it was not reasonably practicable for him to provide the required information or explanations.

(4) If a parent company fails to comply with section 500, an offence is committed by—

(a) the company, and

(b) every officer of the company who is in default.

(5) A person guilty of an offence under subsection (3) or (4) is liable on summary conviction to a fine not exceeding level 3 on the standard scale.

(6) Nothing in this section affects any right of an auditor to apply for an injunction (in Scotland, an interdict or an order for specific performance) to enforce any of his rights under section 499 or 500.

502 Auditor's rights in relation to resolutions and meetings

(1) In relation to a written resolution proposed to be agreed to by a private company, the company's auditor is entitled to receive all such communications relating to the resolution as, by virtue of any provision of Chapter 2 of Part 13 of this Act, are required to be supplied to a member of the company.

(2) A company's auditor is entitled—

(a) to receive all notices of, and other communications relating to, any general meeting which a member of the company is entitled to receive,

(b) to attend any general meeting of the company, and

(c) to be heard at any general meeting which he attends on any part of the business of the meeting which concerns him as auditor.

(3) Where the auditor is a firm, the right to attend or be heard at a meeting is exercisable by an individual authorised by the firm in writing to act as its representative at the meeting.

Signature of auditor's report

503 Signature of auditor's report

(1) The auditor's report must state the name of the auditor and be signed and dated.

(2) Where the auditor is an individual, the report must be signed by him.

(3) Where the auditor is a firm, the report must be signed by the senior statutory auditor in his own name, for and on behalf of the auditor.

504 Senior statutory auditor

(1) The senior statutory auditor means the individual identified by the firm as senior statutory auditor in relation to the audit in accordance with—

(a) standards issued by the European Commission, or

(b) if there is no applicable standard so issued, any relevant guidance issued by—

(i) the Secretary of State, or

(ii) a body appointed by order of the Secretary of State.

(2) The person identified as senior statutory auditor must be eligible for appointment as auditor of the company in question (see Chapter 2 of Part 42 of this Act).

(3) The senior statutory auditor is not, by reason of being named or identified as senior statutory auditor or by reason of his having signed the auditor's report, subject to any civil liability to which he would not otherwise be subject.

(4) An order appointing a body for the purpose of subsection (1)(b)(ii) is subject to negative resolution procedure.

505 Names to be stated in published copies of auditor's report

(1) Every copy of the auditor's report that is published by or on behalf of the company must—

(a) state the name of the auditor and (where the auditor is a firm) the name of the person who signed it as senior statutory auditor, or

(b) if the conditions in section 506 (circumstances in which names may be omitted) are met, state that a resolution has been passed and notified to the Secretary of State in accordance with that section.

(2) For the purposes of this section a company is regarded as publishing the report if it publishes, issues or circulates it or otherwise makes it available for public inspection in a manner calculated to invite members of the public generally, or any class of members of the public, to read it.

(3) If a copy of the auditor's report is published without the statement required by this section, an offence is committed by—

(a) the company, and

(b) every officer of the company who is in default.

(4) A person guilty of an offence under this section is liable on summary conviction to a fine not exceeding level 3 on the standard scale.

506 Circumstances in which names may be omitted

(1) The auditor's name and, where the auditor is a firm, the name of the person who signed the report as senior statutory auditor, may be omitted from—

(a) published copies of the report, and

(b) the copy of the report delivered to the registrar under Chapter 10 of Part 15 (filing of accounts and reports),

if the following conditions are met.

(2) The conditions are that the company—

(a) considering on reasonable grounds that statement of the name would create or be likely to create a serious risk that the auditor or senior statutory auditor, or any other person, would be subject to violence or intimidation, has resolved that the name should not be stated, and

(b) has given notice of the resolution to the Secretary of State, stating—

(i) the name and registered number of the company,

(ii) the financial year of the company to which the report relates, and

(iii) the name of the auditor and (where the auditor is a firm) the name of the person who signed the report as senior statutory auditor.

Offences in connection with auditor's report

507 Offences in connection with auditor's report

(1) A person to whom this section applies commits an offence if he knowingly or recklessly causes a report under section 495 (auditor's report on company's annual accounts) to include any matter that is misleading, false or deceptive in a material particular.

(2) A person to whom this section applies commits an offence if he knowingly or recklessly causes such a report to omit a statement required by—

(a) section 498(2)(b) (statement that company's accounts do not agree with accounting records and returns),

(b) section 498(3) (statement that necessary information and explanations not obtained), or

(c) section 498(5) (statement that directors wrongly took advantage of exemption from obligation to prepare group accounts).

(3) This section applies to—

(a) where the auditor is an individual, that individual and any employee or agent of his who is eligible for appointment as auditor of the company;

(b) where the auditor is a firm, any director, member, employee or agent of the firm who is eligible for appointment as auditor of the company.

(4) A person guilty of an offence under this section is liable—

(a) on conviction on indictment, to a fine;

(b) on summary conviction, to a fine not exceeding the statutory maximum.

508 Guidance for regulatory and prosecuting authorities: England, Wales and Northern Ireland

(1) The Secretary of State may issue guidance for the purpose of helping relevant regulatory and prosecuting authorities to determine how they should carry out their functions in cases where behaviour occurs that—

(a) appears to involve the commission of an offence under section 507 (offences in connection with auditor's report), and

(b) has been, is being or may be investigated pursuant to arrangements—

(i) under paragraph 15 of Schedule 10 (investigation of complaints against auditors and supervisory bodies), or

(ii) of a kind mentioned in paragraph 24 of that Schedule (independent investigation for disciplinary purposes of public interest cases).

(2) The Secretary of State must obtain the consent of the Attorney General before issuing any such guidance.

(3) In this section "relevant regulatory and prosecuting authorities" means—

(a) supervisory bodies within the meaning of Part 42 of this Act,

(b) bodies to which the Secretary of State may make grants under section 16(1) of the Companies (Audit, Investigations and Community Enterprise) Act 2004 (bodies concerned with accounting standards etc),

(c) the Director of the Serious Fraud Office,

(d) the Director of Public Prosecutions or the Director of Public Prosecutions for Northern Ireland, and

(e) the Secretary of State.

(4) This section does not apply to Scotland.

509 Guidance for regulatory authorities: Scotland

(1) The Lord Advocate may issue guidance for the purpose of helping relevant regulatory authorities to determine how they should carry out their functions in cases where behaviour occurs that—

(a) appears to involve the commission of an offence under section 507 (offences in connection with auditor's report), and

(b) has been, is being or may be investigated pursuant to arrangements—

(i) under paragraph 15 of Schedule 10 (investigation of complaints against auditors and supervisory bodies), or

(ii) of a kind mentioned in paragraph 24 of that Schedule (independent investigation for disciplinary purposes of public interest cases).

(2) The Lord Advocate must consult the Secretary of State before issuing any such guidance.

(3) In this section "relevant regulatory authorities" means—

(a) supervisory bodies within the meaning of Part 42 of this Act,

(b) bodies to which the Secretary of State may make grants under section 16(1) of the Companies (Audit, Investigations and Community Enterprise) Act 2004 (bodies concerned with accounting standards etc), and

(c) the Secretary of State.

(4) This section applies only to Scotland.

CHAPTER 4
REMOVAL, RESIGNATION, ETC OF AUDITORS

Removal of auditor

510 Resolution removing auditor from office

(1) The members of a company may remove an auditor from office at any time.

(2) This power is exercisable only—

(a) by ordinary resolution at a meeting, and

(b) in accordance with section 511 (special notice of resolution to remove auditor).

(3) Nothing in this section is to be taken as depriving the person removed of compensation or damages payable to him in respect of the termination—

(a) of his appointment as auditor, or

(b) of any appointment terminating with that as auditor.

(4) An auditor may not be removed from office before the expiration of his term of office except by resolution under this section.

511 Special notice required for resolution removing auditor from office

(1) Special notice is required for a resolution at a general meeting of a company removing an auditor from office.

(2) On receipt of notice of such an intended resolution the company must immediately send a copy of it to the auditor proposed to be removed.

(3) The auditor proposed to be removed may make with respect to the intended resolution representations in writing to the company (not exceeding a reasonable length) and request their notification to members of the company.

(4) The company must (unless the representations are received by it too late for it to do so)—

(a) in any notice of the resolution given to members of the company, state the fact of the representations having been made, and

(b) send a copy of the representations to every member of the company to whom notice of the meeting is or has been sent.

(5) If a copy of any such representations is not sent out as required because received too late or because of the company's default, the auditor may (without prejudice to his right to be heard orally) require that the representations be read out at the meeting.

(6) Copies of the representations need not be sent out and the representations need not be read at the meeting if, on the application either of the company or of any other person claiming to be aggrieved, the court is satisfied that the auditor is using the provisions of this section to secure needless publicity for defamatory matter.

The court may order the company's costs (in Scotland, expenses) on the application to be paid in whole or in part by the auditor, notwithstanding that he is not a party to the application.

512 Notice to registrar of resolution removing auditor from office

(1) Where a resolution is passed under section 510 (resolution removing auditor from office), the company must give notice of that fact to the registrar within 14 days.

(2) If a company fails to give the notice required by this section, an offence is committed by—

(a) the company, and

(b) every officer of it who is in default.

(3) A person guilty of an offence under this section is liable on summary conviction to a fine not exceeding level 3 on the standard scale and, for continued contravention, a daily default fine not exceeding one-tenth of level 3 on the standard scale.

513 Rights of auditor who has been removed from office

(1) An auditor who has been removed by resolution under section 510 has, notwithstanding his removal, the rights conferred by section 502(2) in relation to any general meeting of the company—

(a) at which his term of office would otherwise have expired, or

(b) at which it is proposed to fill the vacancy caused by his removal.

(2) In such a case the references in that section to matters concerning the auditor as auditor shall be construed as references to matters concerning him as a former auditor.

Failure to re-appoint auditor

514 Failure to re-appoint auditor: special procedure required for written resolution

(1) This section applies where a resolution is proposed as a written resolution of a private company whose effect would be to appoint a person as auditor in place of a person (the "outgoing auditor") whose term of office has expired, or is to expire, at the end of the period for appointing auditors.

(2) The following provisions apply if—

(a) no period for appointing auditors has ended since the outgoing auditor ceased to hold office, or

(b) such a period has ended and an auditor or auditors should have been appointed but were not.

(3) The company must send a copy of the proposed resolution to the person proposed to be appointed and to the outgoing auditor.

(4) The outgoing auditor may, within 14 days after receiving the notice, make with respect to the proposed resolution representations in writing to the company (not exceeding a reasonable length) and request their circulation to members of the company.

(5) The company must circulate the representations together with the copy or copies of the resolution circulated in accordance with section 291 (resolution proposed by directors) or section 293 (resolution proposed by members).

(6) Where subsection (5) applies—

(a) the period allowed under section 293(3) for service of copies of the proposed resolution is 28 days instead of 21 days, and

(b) the provisions of section 293(5) and (6) (offences) apply in relation to a failure to comply with that subsection as in relation to a default in complying with that section.

(7) Copies of the representations need not be circulated if, on the application either of the company or of any other person claiming to be aggrieved, the court is satisfied that the auditor is using the provisions of this section to secure needless publicity for defamatory matter.

The court may order the company's costs (in Scotland, expenses) on the application to be paid in whole or in part by the auditor, notwithstanding that he is not a party to the application.

(8) If any requirement of this section is not complied with, the resolution is ineffective.

515 Failure to re-appoint auditor: special notice required for resolution at general meeting

(1) This section applies to a resolution at a general meeting of a company whose effect would be to appoint a person as auditor in place of a person (the "outgoing auditor") whose term of office has ended, or is to end—

(a) in the case of a private company, at the end of the period for appointing auditors;

(b) in the case of a public company, at the end of the next accounts meeting.

(2) Special notice is required of such a resolution if—

(a) in the case of a private company—

(i) no period for appointing auditors has ended since the outgoing auditor ceased to hold office, or

(ii) such a period has ended and an auditor or auditors should have been appointed but were not;

(b) in the case of a public company—

(i) there has been no accounts meeting of the company since the outgoing auditor ceased to hold office, or

(ii) there has been an accounts meeting at which an auditor or auditors should have been appointed but were not.

(3) On receipt of notice of such an intended resolution the company shall forthwith send a copy of it to the person proposed to be appointed and to the outgoing auditor.

(4) The outgoing auditor may make with respect to the intended resolution representations in writing to the company (not exceeding a reasonable length) and request their notification to members of the company.

(5) The company must (unless the representations are received by it too late for it to do so)—

(a) in any notice of the resolution given to members of the company, state the fact of the representations having been made, and

(b) send a copy of the representations to every member of the company to whom notice of the meeting is or has been sent.

(6) If a copy of any such representations is not sent out as required because received too late or because of the company's default, the outgoing auditor may (without prejudice to his right to be heard orally) require that the representations be read out at the meeting.

(7) Copies of the representations need not be sent out and the representations need not be read at the meeting if, on the application either of the company or of any other person claiming to be aggrieved, the court is satisfied that the auditor is using the provisions of this section to secure needless publicity for defamatory matter.

The court may order the company's costs (in Scotland, expenses) on the application to be paid in whole or in part by the outgoing auditor, notwithstanding that he is not a party to the application.

Resignation of auditor

516 Resignation of auditor

(1) An auditor of a company may resign his office by depositing a notice in writing to that effect at the company's registered office.

(2) The notice is not effective unless it is accompanied by the statement required by section 519.

(3) An effective notice of resignation operates to bring the auditor's term of office to an end as of the date on which the notice is deposited or on such later date as may be specified in it.

517 Notice to registrar of resignation of auditor

(1) Where an auditor resigns the company must within 14 days of the deposit of a notice of resignation send a copy of the notice to the registrar of companies.

(2) If default is made in complying with this section, an offence is committed by—

(a) the company, and

(b) every officer of the company who is in default.

(3) A person guilty of an offence under this section is liable—

(a) on conviction on indictment, to a fine;

(b) on summary conviction, to a fine not exceeding the statutory maximum and, for continued contravention, a daily default fine not exceeding one-tenth of the statutory maximum.

518 Rights of resigning auditor

(1) This section applies where an auditor's notice of resignation is accompanied by a statement of the circumstances connected with his resignation (see section 519).

(2) He may deposit with the notice a signed requisition calling on the directors of the company forthwith duly to convene a general meeting of the company for the purpose of receiving and considering such explanation of the circumstances connected with his resignation as he may wish to place before the meeting.

(3) He may request the company to circulate to its members—

(a) before the meeting convened on his requisition, or

(b) before any general meeting at which his term of office would otherwise have expired or at which it is proposed to fill the vacancy caused by his resignation,

a statement in writing (not exceeding a reasonable length) of the circumstances connected with his resignation.

(4) The company must (unless the statement is received too late for it to comply)—

(a) in any notice of the meeting given to members of the company, state the fact of the statement having been made, and

(b) send a copy of the statement to every member of the company to whom notice of the meeting is or has been sent.

(5) The directors must within 21 days from the date of the deposit of a requisition under this section proceed duly to convene a meeting for a day not more than 28 days after the date on which the notice convening the meeting is given.

(6) If default is made in complying with subsection (5), every director who failed to take all reasonable steps to secure that a meeting was convened commits an offence.

(7) A person guilty of an offence under this section is liable—

(a) on conviction on indictment, to a fine;

(b) on summary conviction to a fine not exceeding the statutory maximum.

(8) If a copy of the statement mentioned above is not sent out as required because received too late or because of the company's default, the auditor may (without prejudice to his right to be heard orally) require that the statement be read out at the meeting.

(9) Copies of a statement need not be sent out and the statement need not be read out at the meeting if, on the application either of the company or of any other person who claims to be aggrieved, the

court is satisfied that the auditor is using the provisions of this section to secure needless publicity for defamatory matter.

The court may order the company's costs (in Scotland, expenses) on such an application to be paid in whole or in part by the auditor, notwithstanding that he is not a party to the application.

(10) An auditor who has resigned has, notwithstanding his resignation, the rights conferred by section 502(2) in relation to any such general meeting of the company as is mentioned in subsection (3) (a) or (b) above.

In such a case the references in that section to matters concerning the auditor as auditor shall be construed as references to matters concerning him as a former auditor.

Statement by auditor on ceasing to hold office

519 Statement by auditor to be deposited with company

(1) Where an auditor of an unquoted company ceases for any reason to hold office, he must deposit at the company's registered office a statement of the circumstances connected with his ceasing to hold office, unless he considers that there are no circumstances in connection with his ceasing to hold office that need to be brought to the attention of members or creditors of the company.

(2) If he considers that there are no circumstances in connection with his ceasing to hold office that need to be brought to the attention of members or creditors of the company, he must deposit at the company's registered office a statement to that effect.

(3) Where an auditor of a quoted company ceases for any reason to hold office, he must deposit at the company's registered office a statement of the circumstances connected with his ceasing to hold office.

(4) The statement required by this section must be deposited—

(a) in the case of resignation, along with the notice of resignation;

(b) in the case of failure to seek re-appointment, not less than 14 days before the end of the time allowed for next appointing an auditor;

(c) in any other case, not later than the end of the period of 14 days beginning with the date on which he ceases to hold office.

(5) A person ceasing to hold office as auditor who fails to comply with this section commits an offence.

(6) In proceedings for such an offence it is a defence for the person charged to show that he took all reasonable steps and exercised all due diligence to avoid the commission of the offence.

(7) A person guilty of an offence under this section is liable—

(a) on conviction on indictment, to a fine;

(b) on summary conviction, to a fine not exceeding the statutory maximum.

(8) Where an offence under this section is committed by a body corporate, every officer of the body who is in default also commits the offence.

For this purpose—

(a) any person who purports to act as director, manager or secretary of the body is treated as an officer of the body, and

(b) if the body is a company, any shadow director is treated as an officer of the company.

520 Company's duties in relation to statement

(1) This section applies where the statement deposited under section 519 states the circumstances connected with the auditor's ceasing to hold office.

(2) The company must within 14 days of the deposit of the statement either—

(a) send a copy of it to every person who under section 423 is entitled to be sent copies of the accounts, or

(b) apply to the court.

(3) If it applies to the court, the company must notify the auditor of the application.

(4) If the court is satisfied that the auditor is using the provisions of section 519 to secure needless publicity for defamatory matter—

(a) it shall direct that copies of the statement need not be sent out, and

(b) it may further order the company's costs (in Scotland, expenses) on the application to be paid in whole or in part by the auditor, even if he is not a party to the application.

The company must within 14 days of the court's decision send to the persons mentioned in subsection (2)(a) a statement setting out the effect of the order.

(5) If no such direction is made the company must send copies of the statement to the persons mentioned in subsection (2) (a) within 14 days of the court's decision or, as the case may be, of the discontinuance of the proceedings.

(6) In the event of default in complying with this section an offence is committed by every officer of the company who is in default.

(7) In proceedings for such an offence it is a defence for the person charged to show that he took all reasonable steps and exercised all due diligence to avoid the commission of the offence.

(8) A person guilty of an offence under this section is liable—

(a) on conviction on indictment, to a fine;

(b) on summary conviction, to a fine not exceeding the statutory maximum.

521 Copy of statement to be sent to registrar

(1) Unless within 21 days beginning with the day on which he deposited the statement under section 519 the auditor receives notice of an application to the court under section 520, he must within a further seven days send a copy of the statement to the registrar.

(2) If an application to the court is made under section 520 and the auditor subsequently receives notice under subsection (5) of that section, he must within seven days of receiving the notice send a copy of the statement to the registrar.

(3) An auditor who fails to comply with subsection (1) or (2) commits an offence.

(4) In proceedings for such an offence it is a defence for the person charged to show that he took all reasonable steps and exercised all due diligence to avoid the commission of the offence.

(5) A person guilty of an offence under this section is liable—

(a) on conviction on indictment, to a fine;

(b) on summary conviction, to a fine not exceeding the statutory maximum.

(6) Where an offence under this section is committed by a body corporate, every officer of the body who is in default also commits the offence.

For this purpose—

(a) any person who purports to act as director, manager or secretary of the body is treated as an officer of the body, and

(b) if the body is a company, any shadow director is treated as an officer of the company.

522 Duty of auditor to notify appropriate audit authority

(1) Where—

(a) in the case of a major audit, an auditor ceases for any reason to hold office, or

(b) in the case of an audit that is not a major audit, an auditor ceases to hold office before the end of his term of office,

the auditor ceasing to hold office must notify the appropriate audit authority.

(2) The notice must—

(a) inform the appropriate audit authority that he has ceased to hold office, and

(b) be accompanied by a copy of the statement deposited by him at the company's registered office in accordance with section 519.

(3) If the statement so deposited is to the effect that he considers that there are no circumstances in connection with his ceasing to hold office that need to be brought to the attention of members or creditors of the company, the notice must also be accompanied by a statement of the reasons for his ceasing to hold office.

(4) The auditor must comply with this section—

(a) in the case of a major audit, at the same time as he deposits a statement at the company's registered office in accordance with section 519;

(b) in the case of an audit that is not a major audit, at such time (not being earlier than the time mentioned in paragraph (a)) as the appropriate audit authority may require.

(5) A person ceasing to hold office as auditor who fails to comply with this section commits an offence.

(6) If that person is a firm an offence is committed by—

(a) the firm, and

(b) every officer of the firm who is in default.

(7) In proceedings for an offence under this section it is a defence for the person charged to show that he took all reasonable steps and exercised all due diligence to avoid the commission of the offence.

(8) A person guilty of an offence under this section is liable—

(a) on conviction on indictment, to a fine;

(b) on summary conviction, to a fine not exceeding the statutory maximum.

523 Duty of company to notify appropriate audit authority

(1) Where an auditor ceases to hold office before the end of his term of office, the company must notify the appropriate audit authority.

(2) The notice must—

(a) inform the appropriate audit authority that the auditor has ceased to hold office, and

(b) be accompanied by—

(i) a statement by the company of the reasons for his ceasing to hold office, or

(ii) if the copy of the statement deposited by the auditor at the company's registered office in accordance with section 519 contains a statement of circumstances in connection with his ceasing to hold office that need to be brought to the attention of members or creditors of the company, a copy of that statement.

(3) The company must give notice under this section not later than 14 days after the date on which the auditor's statement is deposited at the company's registered office in accordance with section 519.

(4) If a company fails to comply with this section, an offence is committed by—

(a) the company, and

(b) every officer of the company who is in default.

(5) In proceedings for such an offence it is a defence for the person charged to show that he took all reasonable steps and exercised all due diligence to avoid the commission of the offence.

(6) A person guilty of an offence under this section is liable—

(a) on conviction on indictment, to a fine;

(b) on summary conviction, to a fine not exceeding the statutory maximum.

524 Information to be given to accounting authorities

(1) The appropriate audit authority on receiving notice under section 522 or 523 of an auditor's ceasing to hold office—

(a) must inform the accounting authorities, and

(b) may if it thinks fit forward to those authorities a copy of the statement or statements accompanying the notice.

(2) The accounting authorities are—

(a) the Secretary of State, and

(b) any person authorised by the Secretary of State for the purposes of section 456 (revision of defective accounts: persons authorised to apply to court).

(3) If either of the accounting authorities is also the appropriate audit authority it is only necessary to comply with this section as regards any other accounting authority.

(4) If the court has made an order under section 520(4) directing that copies of the statement need not be sent out by the company, sections 460 and 461 (restriction on further disclosure) apply in relation to the copies sent to the accounting authorities as they apply to information obtained under section 459 (power to require documents etc).

525 Meaning of "appropriate audit authority" and "major audit"

(1) In sections 522, 523 and 524 "appropriate audit authority" means—

(a) in the case of a major audit (other than one conducted by an Auditor General)—

(i) the Secretary of State, or

(ii) if the Secretary of State has delegated functions under section 1252 to a body whose functions include receiving the notice in question, that body;

(b) in the case of an audit (other than one conducted by an Auditor General) that is not a major audit, the relevant supervisory body;

(c) in the case of an audit conducted by an Auditor General, the Independent Supervisor.

"Supervisory body" and "Independent Supervisor" have the same meaning as in Part 42 (statutory auditors) (see sections 1217 and 1228).

(2) In sections 522 and this section "major audit" means a statutory audit conducted in respect of—

(a) a company any of whose securities have been admitted to the official list (within the meaning of Part 6 of the Financial Services and Markets Act 2000), or

(b) any other person in whose financial condition there is a major public interest.

(3) In determining whether an audit is a major audit within subsection (2)(b), regard shall be had to any guidance issued by any of the authorities mentioned in subsection (1).

Supplementary

526 Effect of casual vacancies

If an auditor ceases to hold office for any reason, any surviving or continuing auditor or auditors may continue to act.

CHAPTER 5
QUOTED COMPANIES: RIGHT OF MEMBERS TO RAISE AUDIT CONCERNS AT ACCOUNTS MEETING

527 Members' power to require website publication of audit concerns

(1) The members of a quoted company may require the company to publish on a website a statement setting out any matter relating to—

(a) the audit of the company's accounts (including the auditor's report and the conduct of the audit) that are to be laid before the next accounts meeting, or

(b) any circumstances connected with an auditor of the company ceasing to hold office since the previous accounts meeting,

that the members propose to raise at the next accounts meeting of the company.

(2) A company is required to do so once it has received requests to that effect from—

(a) members representing at least 5% of the total voting rights of all the members who have a relevant right to vote (excluding any voting rights attached to any shares in the company held as treasury shares), or

(b) at least 100 members who have a relevant right to vote and hold shares in the company on which there has been paid up an average sum, per member, of at least £100.

See also section 153 (exercise of rights where shares held on behalf of others).

(3) In subsection (2) a "relevant right to vote" means a right to vote at the accounts meeting.

(4) A request—

(a) may be sent to the company in hard copy or electronic form,

(b) must identify the statement to which it relates,

(c) must be authenticated by the person or persons making it, and

(d) must be received by the company at least one week before the meeting to which it relates.

(5) A quoted company is not required to place on a website a statement under this section if, on an application by the company or another person who claims to be aggrieved, the court is satisfied that the rights conferred by this section are being abused.

(6) The court may order the members requesting website publication to pay the whole or part of the company's costs (in Scotland, expenses) on such an application, even if they are not parties to the application.

528 Requirements as to website availability

(1) The following provisions apply for the purposes of section 527 (website publication of members' statement of audit concerns).

(2) The information must be made available on a website that—

(a) is maintained by or on behalf of the company, and

(b) identifies the company in question.

(3) Access to the information on the website, and the ability to obtain a hard copy of the information from the website, must not be conditional on the payment of a fee or otherwise restricted.

(4) The statement—

(a) must be made available within three working days of the company being required to publish it on a website, and

(b) must be kept available until after the meeting to which it relates.

(5) A failure to make information available on a website throughout the period specified in subsection (4)(b) is disregarded if—

(a) the information is made available on the website for part of that period, and

(b) the failure is wholly attributable to circumstances that it would not be reasonable to have expected the company to prevent or avoid.

529 Website publication: company's supplementary duties

(1) A quoted company must in the notice it gives of the accounts meeting draw attention to—

(a) the possibility of a statement being placed on a website in pursuance of members' requests under section 527, and

(b) the effect of the following provisions of this section.

(2) A company may not require the members requesting website publication to pay its expenses in complying with that section or section 528 (requirements in connection with website publication).

(3) Where a company is required to place a statement on a website under section 527 it must forward the statement to the company's auditor not later than the time when it makes the statement available on the website.

(4) The business which may be dealt with at the accounts meeting includes any statement that the company has been required under section 527 to publish on a website.

530 Website publication: offences

(1) In the event of default in complying with

(a) section 528 (requirements as to website publication), or

(b) section 529 (companies' supplementary duties in relation to request for website publication),

an offence is committed by every officer of the company who is in default.

(2) A person guilty of an offence under this section is liable—

(a) on conviction on indictment, to a fine;

(b) on summary conviction, to a fine not exceeding the statutory maximum.

531 Meaning of "quoted company"

(1) For the purposes of this Chapter a company is a quoted company if it is a quoted company in accordance with section 385 (quoted and unquoted companies for the purposes of Part 15) in relation to the financial year to which the accounts to be laid at the next accounts meeting relate.

(2) The provisions of subsections (4) to (6) of that section (power to amend definition by regulations) apply in relation to the provisions of this Chapter as in relation to the provisions of that Part.

CHAPTER 6
AUDITORS' LIABILITY

Voidness of provisions protecting auditors from liability

532 Voidness of provisions protecting auditors from liability

(1) This section applies to any provision—

(a) for exempting an auditor of a company (to any extent) from any liability that would otherwise attach to him in connection with any negligence, default, breach of duty or breach of trust in relation to the company occurring in the course of the audit of accounts, or

(b) by which a company directly or indirectly provides an indemnity (to any extent) for an auditor of the company, or of an associated company, against any liability attaching to him in connection with any negligence, default, breach of duty or breach of trust in relation to the company of which he is auditor occurring in the course of the audit of accounts.

(2) Any such provision is void, except as permitted by—

(a) section 533 (indemnity for costs of successfully defending proceedings), or

(b) sections 534 to 536 (liability limitation agreements).

(3) This section applies to any provision, whether contained in a company's articles or in any contract with the company or otherwise.

(4) For the purposes of this section companies are associated if one is a subsidiary of the other or both are subsidiaries of the same body corporate.

Indemnity for costs of defending proceedings

533 Indemnity for costs of successfully defending proceedings

Section 532 (general voidness of provisions protecting auditors from liability) does not prevent a company from indemnifying an auditor against any liability incurred by him—

(a) in defending proceedings (whether civil or criminal) in which judgment is given in his favour or he is acquitted, or

(b) in connection with an application under section 1157 (power of court to grant relief in case of honest and reasonable conduct) in which relief is granted to him by the court.

Liability limitation agreements

534 Liability limitation agreements

(1) A "liability limitation agreement" is an agreement that purports to limit the amount of a liability owed to a company by its auditor in respect of any negligence, default, breach of duty or breach of trust, occurring in the course of the audit of accounts, of which the auditor may be guilty in relation to the company.

(2) Section 532 (general voidness of provisions protecting auditors from liability) does not affect the validity of a liability limitation agreement that—

(a) complies with section 535 (terms of liability limitation agreement) and of any regulations under that section, and

(b) is authorised by the members of the company (see section 536).

(3) Such an agreement—

(a) is effective to the extent provided by section 537, and

(b) is not subject—

(i) in England and Wales or Northern Ireland, to section 2(2) or 3(2)(a) of the Unfair Contract Terms Act 1977;

(ii) in Scotland, to section 16(1)(b) or 17(1)(a) of that Act.

535 Terms of liability limitation agreement

(1) A liability limitation agreement—

(a) must not apply in respect of acts or omissions occurring in the course of the audit of accounts for more than one financial year, and

(b) must specify the financial year in relation to which it applies.

(2) The Secretary of State may by regulations—

(a) require liability limitation agreements to contain specified provisions or provisions of a specified description;

(b) prohibit liability limitation agreements from containing specified provisions or provisions of a specified description.

"Specified" here means specified in the regulations.

(3) Without prejudice to the generality of the power conferred by subsection (2), that power may be exercised with a view to preventing adverse effects on competition.

(4) Subject to the preceding provisions of this section, it is immaterial how a liability limitation agreement is framed.

In particular, the limit on the amount of the auditor's liability need not be a sum of money, or a formula, specified in the agreement.

(5) Regulations under this section are subject to negative resolution procedure.

536 Authorisation of agreement by members of the company

(1) A liability limitation agreement is authorised by the members of the company if it has been authorised under this section and that authorisation has not been withdrawn.

(2) A liability limitation agreement between a private company and its auditor may be authorised—

(a) by the company passing a resolution, before it enters into the agreement, waiving the need for approval,

(b) by the company passing a resolution, before it enters into the agreement, approving the agreement's principal terms, or

(c) by the company passing a resolution, after it enters into the agreement, approving the agreement.

(3) A liability limitation agreement between a public company and its auditor may be authorised—

(a) by the company passing a resolution in general meeting, before it enters into the agreement, approving the agreement's principal terms, or

(b) by the company passing a resolution in general meeting, after it enters into the agreement, approving the agreement.

(4) The "principal terms" of an agreement are terms specifying, or relevant to the determination of—

(a) the kind (or kinds) of acts or omissions covered,

(b) the financial year to which the agreement relates, or

(c) the limit to which the auditor's liability is subject.

(5) Authorisation under this section may be withdrawn by the company passing an ordinary resolution to that effect—

(a) at any time before the company enters into the agreement, or

(b) if the company has already entered into the agreement, before the beginning of the financial year to which the agreement relates. Paragraph (b) has effect notwithstanding anything in the agreement.

537 Effect of liability limitation agreement

(1) A liability limitation agreement is not effective to limit the auditor's liability to less than such amount as is fair and reasonable in all the circumstances of the case having regard (in particular) to—

(a) the auditor's responsibilities under this Part,

(b) the nature and purpose of the auditor's contractual obligations to the company, and

(c) the professional standards expected of him.

(2) A liability limitation agreement that purports to limit the auditor's liability to less than the amount mentioned in subsection (1) shall have effect as if it limited his liability to that amount.

(3) In determining what is fair and reasonable in all the circumstances of the case no account is to be taken of—

(a) matters arising after the loss or damage in question has been incurred, or

(b) matters (whenever arising) affecting the possibility of recovering compensation from other persons liable in respect of the same loss or damage.

538 Disclosure of agreement by company

(1) A company which has entered into a liability limitation agreement must make such disclosure in connection with the agreement as the Secretary of State may require by regulations.

(2) The regulations may provide, in particular, that any disclosure required by the regulations shall be made—

(a) in a note to the company's annual accounts (in the case of its individual accounts) or in such manner as is specified in the regulations (in the case of group accounts), or

(b) in the directors' report.

(3) Regulations under this section are subject to negative resolution procedure.

CHAPTER 7
SUPPLEMENTARY PROVISIONS

538A Meaning of "corporate governance statement" etc

(1) In this Part "corporate governance statement" means the statement required by rules 7.2.1 to 7.2.11 in the Disclosure Rules and Transparency Rules sourcebook issued by the Financial Services Authority.

(2) Those rules were inserted by Annex C of the Disclosure Rules and Transparency Rules Sourcebook (Corporate Governance Rules) Instrument 2008 made by the Authority on 26th June 2008 (FSA 2008/32).

(3) A "separate" corporate governance statement means one that is not included in the directors' report.

539 Minor definitions

In this Part—

"e-money issuer" means a person who has permission under Part 4A of the Financial Services and Markets Act 2000 to carry on the activity of issuing electronic money within the meaning of article 9B of the Financial Services and Markets Act 2000 (Regulated Activities) Order 2001;

…

"MiFID investment firm" means an investment firm within the meaning of Article 4.1.1 of Directive 2004/39/EC of the European Parliament and of the Council of 21 April 2004 on markets in financial instruments, other than—

(a) a company to which that Directive does not apply by virtue of Article 2 of that Directive,

(b) a company which is an exempt investment firm within the meaning of regulation 4A(3) of the Financial Services and Markets Act 2000 (Markets in Financial Instruments) Regulations 2007, and

(c) any other company which fulfils all the requirements set out in regulation 4C(3) of those Regulations;

"qualified", in relation to an auditor's report (or a statement contained in an auditor's report), means that the report or statement does not state the auditor's unqualified opinion that the accounts have been properly prepared in accordance with this Act or, in the case of an undertaking not required to prepare accounts in accordance with this Act, under any corresponding legislation under which it is required to prepare accounts;

"turnover", in relation to a company, means the amounts derived from the provision of goods and services falling within the company's ordinary activities, after deduction of—

(a) trade discounts,

(b) value added tax, and

(c) any other taxes based on the amounts so derived;

"UCITS management company" has the meaning given by the Glossary forming part of the Handbook made by the Financial Services Authority under the Financial Services and Markets Act 2000.

PART 17
A COMPANY'S SHARE CAPITAL
CHAPTER 1
SHARES AND SHARE CAPITAL OF A COMPANY
Shares

540 Shares

(1) In the Companies Acts "share", in relation to a company, means share in the company's share capital.

(2) A company's shares may no longer be converted into stock.

(3) Stock created before the commencement of this Part may be reconverted into shares in accordance with section 620.

(4) In the Companies Acts—

(a) references to shares include stock except where a distinction between share and stock is express or implied, and

(b) references to a number of shares include an amount of stock where the context admits of the reference to shares being read as including stock.

541 Nature of shares

The shares or other interest of a member in a company are personal property (or, in Scotland, moveable property) and are not in the nature of real estate (or heritage).

542 Nominal value of shares

(1) Shares in a limited company having a share capital must each have a fixed nominal value.

(2) An allotment of a share that does not have a fixed nominal value is void.

(3) Shares in a limited company having a share capital may be denominated in any currency, and different classes of shares may be denominated in different currencies.

But see section 765 (initial authorised minimum share capital requirement for public company to be met by reference to share capital denominated in sterling or euros).

(4) If a company purports to allot shares in contravention of this section, an offence is committed by every officer of the company who is in default.

(5) A person guilty of an offence under this section is liable—

(a) on conviction on indictment, to a fine;

(b) on summary conviction, to a fine not exceeding the statutory maximum.

543 Numbering of shares

(1) Each share in a company having a share capital must be distinguished by its appropriate number, except in the following circumstances.

(2) If at any time—

(a) all the issued shares in a company are fully paid up and rank *pari passu* for all purposes, or

(b) all the issued shares of a particular class in a company are fully paid up and rank *pari passu* for all purposes,

none of those shares need thereafter have a distinguishing number so long as it remains fully paid up and ranks *pari passu* for all purposes with all shares of the same class for the time being issued and fully paid up.

544 Transferability of shares

(1) The shares or other interest of any member in a company are transferable in accordance with the company's articles.

(2) This is subject to—

(a) the Stock Transfer Act 1963 or the Stock Transfer Act (Northern Ireland) 1963 (which enables securities of certain descriptions to be transferred by a simplified process), and

(b) regulations under Chapter 2 of Part 21 of this Act (which enable title to securities to be evidenced and transferred without a written instrument).

(3) See Part 21 of this Act generally as regards share transfers.

545 Companies having a share capital

References in the Companies Acts to a company having a share capital are to a company that has power under its constitution to issue shares.

546 Issued and allotted share capital

(1) References in the Companies Acts—

(a) to "issued share capital" are to shares of a company that have been issued;

(b) to "allotted share capital" are to shares of a company that have been allotted.

(2) References in the Companies Acts to issued or allotted shares, or to issued or allotted share capital, include shares taken on the formation of the company by the subscribers to the company's memorandum.

Share capital

547 Called-up share capital

In the Companies Acts—

"called-up share capital", in relation to a company, means so much of its share capital as equals the aggregate amount of the calls made on its shares (whether or not those calls have been paid), together with—

(a) any share capital paid up without being called, and

(b) any share capital to be paid on a specified future date under the articles, the terms of allotment of the relevant shares or any other arrangements for payment of those shares; and

"uncalled share capital" is to be construed accordingly.

548 Equity share capital

In the Companies Acts "equity share capital", in relation to a company, means its issued share capital excluding any part of that capital that, neither as respects dividends nor as respects capital, carries any right to participate beyond a specified amount in a distribution.

CHAPTER 2
ALLOTMENT OF SHARES: GENERAL PROVISIONS

Power of directors to allot shares

549 Exercise by directors of power to allot shares etc

(1) The directors of a company must not exercise any power of the company—

(a) to allot shares in the company, or

(b) to grant rights to subscribe for, or to convert any security into, shares in the company,

except in accordance with section 550 (private company with single class of shares) or section 551 (authorisation by company).

(2) Subsection (1) does not apply—

(a) to the allotment of shares in pursuance of an employees' share scheme, or

(b) to the grant of a right to subscribe for, or to convert any security into, shares so allotted.

(3) Subsection (1) does not apply to the allotment of shares pursuant to a right to subscribe for, or to convert any security into, shares in the company.

(4) A director who knowingly contravenes, or permits or authorises a contravention of, this section commits an offence.

(5) A person guilty of an offence under this section is liable—

(a) on conviction on indictment, to a fine;

(b) on summary conviction, to a fine not exceeding the statutory maximum.

(6) Nothing in this section affects the validity of an allotment or other transaction.

550 Power of directors to allot shares etc: private company with only one class of shares

Where a private company has only one class of shares, the directors may exercise any power of the company—

(a) to allot shares of that class, or

(b) to grant rights to subscribe for or to convert any security into such shares,

except to the extent that they are prohibited from doing so by the company's articles.

551 Power of directors to allot shares etc: authorisation by company

(1) The directors of a company may exercise a power of the company—

(a) to allot shares in the company, or

(b) to grant rights to subscribe for or to convert any security into shares in the company,

if they are authorised to do so by the company's articles or by resolution of the company.

(2) Authorisation may be given for a particular exercise of the power or for its exercise generally, and may be unconditional or subject to conditions.

(3) Authorisation must—

(a) state the maximum amount of shares that may be allotted under it, and

(b) specify the date on which it will expire, which must be not more than five years from—

(i) in the case of authorisation contained in the company's articles at the time of its original incorporation, the date of that incorporation;

(ii) in any other case, the date on which the resolution is passed by virtue of which the authorisation is given.

(4) Authorisation may—

(a) be renewed or further renewed by resolution of the company for a further period not exceeding five years, and

(b) be revoked or varied at any time by resolution of the company.

(5) A resolution renewing authorisation must—

(a) state (or restate) the maximum amount of shares that may be allotted under the authorisation or, as the case may be, the amount remaining to be allotted under it, and

(b) specify the date on which the renewed authorisation will expire.

(6) In relation to rights to subscribe for or to convert any security into shares in the company, references in this section to the maximum amount of shares that may be allotted under the authorisation are to the maximum amount of shares that may be allotted pursuant to the rights.

(7) The directors may allot shares, or grant rights to subscribe for or to convert any security into shares, after authorisation has expired if—

(a) the shares are allotted, or the rights are granted, in pursuance of an offer or agreement made by the company before the authorisation expired, and

(b) the authorisation allowed the company to make an offer or agreement which would or might require shares to be allotted, or rights to be granted, after the authorisation had expired.

(8) A resolution of a company to give, vary, revoke or renew authorisation under this section may be an ordinary resolution, even though it amends the company's articles.

(9) Chapter 3 of Part 3 (resolutions affecting a company's constitution) applies to a resolution under this section.

Prohibition of commissions, discounts and allowances

552 General prohibition of commissions, discounts and allowances

(1) Except as permitted by section 553 (permitted commission), a company must not apply any of its shares or capital money, either directly or indirectly, in payment of any commission, discount or allowance to any person in consideration of his—

(a) subscribing or agreeing to subscribe (whether absolutely or conditionally) for shares in the company, or

(b) procuring or agreeing to procure subscriptions (whether absolute or conditional) for shares in the company.

(2) It is immaterial how the shares or money are so applied, whether by being added to the purchase money of property acquired by the company or to the contract price of work to be executed for the company, or being paid out of the nominal purchase money or contract price, or otherwise.

(3) Nothing in this section affects the payment of such brokerage as has previously been lawful.

553 Permitted commission

(1) A company may, if the following conditions are satisfied, pay a commission to a person in consideration of his subscribing or agreeing to subscribe (whether absolutely or conditionally) for shares in the company, or procuring or agreeing to procure subscriptions (whether absolute or conditional) for shares in the company.

(2) The conditions are that—

(a) the payment of the commission is authorised by the company's articles; and

(b) the commission paid or agreed to be paid does not exceed—

(i) 10% of the price at which the shares are issued, or

(ii) the amount or rate authorised by the articles,

whichever is the less.

(3) A vendor to, or promoter of, or other person who receives payment in money or shares from, a company may apply any part of the money or shares so received in payment of any commission the payment of which directly by the company would be permitted by this section.

Registration of allotment

554 Registration of allotment

(1) A company must register an allotment of shares as soon as practicable and in any event within two months after the date of the allotment.

(2) This does not apply if the company has issued a share warrant in respect of the shares (see section 779).

(3) If a company fails to comply with this section, an offence is committed by—

(a) the company, and

(b) every officer of the company who is in default.

(4) A person guilty of an offence under this section is liable on summary conviction to a fine not exceeding level 3 on the standard scale and, for continued contravention, a daily default fine not exceeding one-tenth of level 3 on the standard scale.

(5) For the company's duties as to the issue of share certificates etc, see Part 21 (certification and transfer of securities).

Return of allotment

555 Return of allotment by limited company

(1) This section applies to a company limited by shares and to a company limited by guarantee and having a share capital.

(2) The company must, within one month of making an allotment of shares, deliver to the registrar for registration a return of the allotment.

(3) The return must—

(a) contain the prescribed information, and

(b) be accompanied by a statement of capital.

(4) The statement of capital must state with respect to the company's share capital at the date to which the return is made up—

(a) the total number of shares of the company,

(b) the aggregate nominal value of those shares,

(c) for each class of shares—

(i) prescribed particulars of the rights attached to the shares,

(ii) the total number of shares of that class, and

(iii) the aggregate nominal value of shares of that class, and

(d) the amount paid up and the amount (if any) unpaid on each share (whether on account of the nominal value of the share or by way of premium).

556 Return of allotment by unlimited company allotting new class of shares

(1) This section applies to an unlimited company that allots shares of a class with rights that are not in all respects uniform with shares previously allotted.

(2) The company must, within one month of making such an allotment, deliver to the registrar for registration a return of the allotment.

(3) The return must contain the prescribed particulars of the rights attached to the shares.

(4) For the purposes of this section shares are not to be treated as different from shares previously allotted by reason only that the former do not carry the same rights to dividends as the latter during the twelve months immediately following the former's allotment.

557 Offence of failure to make return

(1) If a company makes default in complying with—

section 555 (return of allotment of shares by limited company), or section 556 (return of allotment of new class of shares by unlimited company),

an offence is committed by every officer of the company who is in default.

(2) A person guilty of an offence under this section is liable—

(a) on conviction on indictment, to a fine;

(b) on summary conviction, to a fine not exceeding the statutory maximum and, for continued contravention, a daily default fine not exceeding one-tenth of the statutory maximum.

(3) In the case of default in delivering to the registrar within one month after the allotment the return required by section 555 or 556—

(a) any person liable for the default may apply to the court for relief, and

(b) the court, if satisfied—

(i) that the omission to deliver the document was accidental or due to inadvertence, or

(ii) that it is just and equitable to grant relief,

may make an order extending the time for delivery of the document for such period as the court thinks proper.

Supplementary provisions

558 When shares are allotted

For the purposes of the Companies Acts shares in a company are taken to be allotted when a person acquires the unconditional right to be included in the company's register of members in respect of the shares.

559 Provisions about allotment not applicable to shares taken on formation

The provisions of this Chapter have no application in relation to the taking of shares by the subscribers to the memorandum on the formation of the company.

CHAPTER 3
ALLOTMENT OF EQUITY SECURITIES: EXISTING SHAREHOLDERS' RIGHT OF PRE-EMPTION

Introductory

560 Meaning of "equity securities" and related expressions

(1) In this Chapter—

"equity securities" means—

(a) ordinary shares in the company, or

(b) rights to subscribe for, or to convert securities into, ordinary shares in the company;

"ordinary shares" means shares other than shares that as respects dividends and capital carry a right to participate only up to a specified amount in a distribution.

(2) References in this Chapter to the allotment of equity securities—
  (a) include the grant of a right to subscribe for, or to convert any securities into, ordinary shares in the company, and
  (b) do not include the allotment of shares pursuant to such a right.

(3) References in this Chapter to the allotment of equity securities include the sale of ordinary shares in the company that immediately before the sale were held by the company as treasury shares.

Existing shareholders' right of pre-emption

561 Existing shareholders' right of pre-emption

(1) A company must not allot equity securities to a person on any terms unless—
  (a) it has made an offer to each person who holds ordinary shares in the company to allot to him on the same or more favourable terms a proportion of those securities that is as nearly as practicable equal to the proportion in nominal value held by him of the ordinary share capital of the company, and
  (b) the period during which any such offer may be accepted has expired or the company has received notice of the acceptance or refusal of every offer so made.

(2) Securities that a company has offered to allot to a holder of ordinary shares may be allotted to him, or anyone in whose favour he has renounced his right to their allotment, without contravening subsection (1)(b).

(3) . . .

(4) Shares held by the company as treasury shares are disregarded for the purposes of this section, so that—
  (a) the company is not treated as a person who holds ordinary shares, and
  (b) the shares are not treated as forming part of the ordinary share capital of the company.

(5) This section is subject to—
  (a) sections 564 to 566 (exceptions to pre-emption right),
  (b) sections 567 and 568 (exclusion of rights of pre-emption),
  (c) sections 569 to 573 (disapplication of pre-emption rights), and
  (d) section 576 (saving for certain older pre-emption procedures).

562 Communication of pre-emption offers to shareholders

(1) This section has effect as to the manner in which offers required by section 561 are to be made to holders of a company's shares.

(2) The offer may be made in hard copy or electronic form.

(3) If the holder—
  (a) has no registered address in an EEA State and has not given to the company an address in an EEA State for the service of notices on him, or
  (b) is the holder of a share warrant,

the offer may be made by causing it, or a notice specifying where a copy of it can be obtained or inspected, to be published in the Gazette.

(4) The offer must state a period during which it may be accepted and the offer shall not be withdrawn before the end of that period.

(5) The period must be a period of at least 14 days beginning—
  (a) in the case of an offer made in hard copy form, with the date on which the offer is sent or supplied;
  (b) in the case of an offer made in electronic form, with the date on which the offer is sent;
  (c) in the case of an offer made by publication in the Gazette, with the date of publication.

(6) The Secretary of State may by regulations made by statutory instrument—
  (a) reduce the period specified in subsection (5) (but not to less than 14 days), or
  (b) increase that period.

(7) A statutory instrument containing regulations made under subsection (6) is subject to affirmative resolution procedure.

563 Liability of company and officers in case of contravention

(1) This section applies where there is a contravention of—
section 561 (existing shareholders' right of pre-emption), or
section 562 (communication of pre-emption offers to shareholders).

(2) The company and every officer of it who knowingly authorised or permitted the contravention are jointly and severally liable to compensate any person to whom an offer should have been made in accordance with those provisions for any loss, damage, costs or expenses which the person has sustained or incurred by reason of the contravention.

(3) No proceedings to recover any such loss, damage, costs or expenses shall be commenced after the expiration of two years—
(a) from the delivery to the registrar of companies of the return of allotment, or
(b) where equity securities other than shares are granted, from the date of the grant.

Exceptions to right of pre-emption

564 Exception to pre-emption right: bonus shares

Section 561(1) (existing shareholders' right of pre-emption) does not apply in relation to the allotment of bonus shares.

565 Exception to pre-emption right: issue for non-cash consideration

Section 561(1) (existing shareholders' right of pre-emption) does not apply to a particular allotment of equity securities if these are, or are to be, wholly or partly paid up otherwise than in cash.

566 Exceptions to pre-emption right: employees' share schemes

Section 561 (existing shareholders' right of pre-emption) does not apply to the allotment of equity securities that would, apart from any renunciation or assignment of the right to their allotment, be held under or allotted or transferred pursuant to an employees' share scheme.

Exclusion of right of pre-emption

567 Exclusion of requirements by private companies

(1) All or any of the requirements of—
(a) section 561 (existing shareholders' right of pre-emption), or
(b) section 562 (communication of pre-emption offers to shareholders)
may be excluded by provision contained in the articles of a private company.

(2) They may be excluded—
(a) generally in relation to the allotment by the company of equity securities, or
(b) in relation to allotments of a particular description.

(3) Any requirement or authorisation contained in the articles of a private company that is inconsistent with either of those sections is treated for the purposes of this section as a provision excluding that section.

(4) A provision to which section 568 applies (exclusion of pre-emption right: corresponding right conferred by articles) is not to be treated as inconsistent with section 561.

568 Exclusion of pre-emption right: articles conferring corresponding right

(1) The provisions of this section apply where, in a case in which section 561 (existing shareholders' right of pre-emption) would otherwise apply—
(a) a company's articles contain provision ("pre-emption provision") prohibiting the company from allotting ordinary shares of a particular class unless it has complied with the condition that it makes such an offer as is described in section 561(1) to each person who holds ordinary shares of that class, and
(b) in accordance with that provision—
(i) the company makes an offer to allot shares to such a holder, and

(ii) he or anyone in whose favour he has renounced his right to their allotment accepts the offer.

(2) In that case, section 561 does not apply to the allotment of those shares and the company may allot them accordingly.

(3) The provisions of section 562 (communication of pre-emption offers to shareholders) apply in relation to offers made in pursuance of the pre-emption provision of the company's articles.
This is subject to section 567 (exclusion of requirements by private companies).

(4) If there is a contravention of the pre-emption provision of the company's articles, the company, and every officer of it who knowingly authorised or permitted the contravention, are jointly and severally liable to compensate any person to whom an offer should have been made under the provision for any loss, damage, costs or expenses which the person has sustained or incurred by reason of the contravention.

(5) No proceedings to recover any such loss, damage, costs or expenses may be commenced after the expiration of two years—
(a) from the delivery to the registrar of companies of the return of allotment, or
(b) where equity securities other than shares are granted, from the date of the grant.

Disapplication of pre-emption rights

569 Disapplication of pre-emption rights: private company with only one class of shares

(1) The directors of a private company that has only one class of shares may be given power by the articles, or by a special resolution of the company, to allot equity securities of that class as if section 561 (existing shareholders' right of pre-emption)—
(a) did not apply to the allotment, or
(b) applied to the allotment with such modifications as the directors may determine.

(2) Where the directors make an allotment under this section, the provisions of this Chapter have effect accordingly.

570 Disapplication of pre-emption rights: directors acting under general authorisation

(1) Where the directors of a company are generally authorised for the purposes of section 551 (power of directors to allot shares etc: authorisation by company), they may be given power by the articles, or by a special resolution of the company, to allot equity securities pursuant to that authorisation as if section 561 (existing shareholders' right of pre-emption)—
(a) did not apply to the allotment, or
(b) applied to the allotment with such modifications as the directors may determine.

(2) Where the directors make an allotment under this section, the provisions of this Chapter have effect accordingly.

(3) The power conferred by this section ceases to have effect when the authorisation to which it relates—
(a) is revoked, or
(b) would (if not renewed) expire.
But if the authorisation is renewed the power may also be renewed, for a period not longer than that for which the authorisation is renewed, by a special resolution of the company.

(4) Notwithstanding that the power conferred by this section has expired, the directors may allot equity securities in pursuance of an offer or agreement previously made by the company if the power enabled the company to make an offer or agreement that would or might require equity securities to be allotted after it expired.

571 Disapplication of pre-emption rights by special resolution

(1) Where the directors of a company are authorised for the purposes of section 551 (power of directors to allot shares etc: authorisation by company), whether generally or otherwise, the company may by special resolution resolve that section 561 (existing shareholders' right of pre-emption)—

(a) does not apply to a specified allotment of equity securities to be made pursuant to that authorisation, or

(b) applies to such an allotment with such modifications as may be specified in the resolution.

(2) Where such a resolution is passed the provisions of this Chapter have effect accordingly.

(3) A special resolution under this section ceases to have effect when the authorisation to which it relates—

(a) is revoked, or

(b) would (if not renewed) expire.

But if the authorisation is renewed the resolution may also be renewed, for a period not longer than that for which the authorisation is renewed, by a special resolution of the company.

(4) Notwithstanding that any such resolution has expired, the directors may allot equity securities in pursuance of an offer or agreement previously made by the company if the resolution enabled the company to make an offer or agreement that would or might require equity securities to be allotted after it expired.

(5) A special resolution under this section, or a special resolution to renew such a resolution, must not be proposed unless—

(a) it is recommended by the directors, and

(b) the directors have complied with the following provisions.

(6) Before such a resolution is proposed, the directors must make a written statement setting out—

(a) their reasons for making the recommendation,

(b) the amount to be paid to the company in respect of the equity securities to be allotted, and

(c) the directors' justification of that amount.

(7) The directors' statement must—

(a) if the resolution is proposed as a written resolution, be sent or submitted to every eligible member at or before the time at which the proposed resolution is sent or submitted to him;

(b) if the resolution is proposed at a general meeting, be circulated to the members entitled to notice of the meeting with that notice.

572 Liability for false statement in directors' statement

(1) This section applies in relation to a directors' statement under section 571 (special resolution disapplying pre-emption rights) that is sent, submitted or circulated under subsection (7) of that section.

(2) A person who knowingly or recklessly authorises or permits the inclusion of any matter that is misleading, false or deceptive in a material particular in such a statement commits an offence.

(3) A person guilty of an offence under this section is liable—

(a) on conviction on indictment, to imprisonment for a term not exceeding two years or a fine (or both);

(b) on summary conviction—

(i) in England and Wales, to imprisonment for a term not exceeding twelve months or to a fine not exceeding the statutory maximum (or both);

(ii) in Scotland or Northern Ireland, to imprisonment for a term not exceeding six months, or to a fine not exceeding the statutory maximum (or both).

573 Disapplication of pre-emption rights: sale of treasury shares

(1) This section applies in relation to a sale of shares that is an allotment of equity securities by virtue of section 560(3) (sale of shares held by company as treasury shares).

(2) The directors of a company may be given power by the articles, or by a special resolution of the company, to allot equity securities as if section 561 (existing shareholders' right of pre-emption)—

(a) did not apply to the allotment, or

(b) applied to the allotment with such modifications as the directors may determine.

(3) The provisions of section 570(2) and (4) apply in that case as they apply to a case within subsection (1) of that section.

(4) The company may by special resolution resolve that section 561—

(a) shall not apply to a specified allotment of securities, or

(b) shall apply to the allotment with such modifications as may be specified in the resolution.

(5) The provisions of section 571(2) and (4) to (7) apply in that case as they apply to a case within subsection (1) of that section.

Supplementary

574 References to holder of shares in relation to offer

(1) In this Chapter, in relation to an offer to allot securities required by—

(a) section 561 (existing shareholders' right of pre-emption), or

(b) any provision to which section 568 applies (articles conferring corresponding right),

a reference (however expressed) to the holder of shares of any description is to whoever was the holder of shares of that description at the close of business on a date to be specified in the offer.

(2) The specified date must fall within the period of 28 days immediately before the date of the offer.

575 Saving for other restrictions on offer or allotment

(1) The provisions of this Chapter are without prejudice to any other enactment by virtue of which a company is prohibited (whether generally or in specified circumstances) from offering or allotting equity securities to any person.

(2) Where a company cannot by virtue of such an enactment offer or allot equity securities to a holder of ordinary shares of the company, those shares are disregarded for the purposes of section 561 (existing shareholders' right of pre-emption), so that—

(a) the person is not treated as a person who holds ordinary shares, and

(b) the shares are not treated as forming part of the ordinary share capital of the company.

576 Saving for certain older pre-emption requirements

(1) In the case of a public company the provisions of this Chapter do not apply to an allotment of equity securities that are subject to a pre-emption requirement in relation to which section 96(1) of the Companies Act 1985 or Article 106(1) of the Companies (Northern Ireland) Order 1986 applied immediately before the commencement of this Chapter.

(2) In the case of a private company a pre-emption requirement to which section 96(3) of the Companies Act 1985 or Article 106(3) of the Companies (Northern Ireland) Order 1986 applied immediately before the commencement of this Chapter shall have effect, so long as the company remains a private company, as if it were contained in the company's articles.

(3) A pre-emption requirement to which section 96(4) of the Companies Act 1985 or Article 106(4) of the Companies (Northern Ireland) Order 1986 applied immediately before the commencement of this section shall be treated for the purposes of this Chapter as if it were contained in the company's articles.

577 Provisions about pre-emption not applicable to shares taken on formation

The provisions of this Chapter have no application in relation to the taking of shares by the subscribers to the memorandum on the formation of the company.

CHAPTER 4

PUBLIC COMPANIES: ALLOTMENT WHERE ISSUE NOT FULLY SUBSCRIBED

578 Public companies: allotment where issue not fully subscribed

(1) No allotment shall be made of shares of a public company offered for subscription unless—

(a) the issue is subscribed for in full, or

(b) the offer is made on terms that the shares subscribed for may be allotted—

(i) in any event, or

(ii) if specified conditions are met (and those conditions are met).

(2) If shares are prohibited from being allotted by subsection (1) and 40 days have elapsed after the first making of the offer, all money received from applicants for shares must be repaid to them forthwith, without interest.

(3) If any of the money is not repaid within 48 days after the first making of the offer, the directors of the company are jointly and severally liable to repay it, with interest at the rate for the time being specified under section 17 of the Judgments Act 1838 from the expiration of the 48th day.

A director is not so liable if he proves that the default in the repayment of the money was not due to any misconduct or negligence on his part.

(4) This section applies in the case of shares offered as wholly or partly payable otherwise than in cash as it applies in the case of shares offered for subscription.

(5) In that case—

(a) the references in subsection (1) to subscription shall be construed accordingly;

(b) references in subsections (2) and (3) to the repayment of money received from applicants for shares include—

(i) the return of any other consideration so received (including, if the case so requires, the release of the applicant from any undertaking), or

(ii) if it is not reasonably practicable to return the consideration, the payment of money equal to its value at the time it was so received;

(c) references to interest apply accordingly.

(6) Any condition requiring or binding an applicant for shares to waive compliance with any requirement of this section is void.

579 Public companies: effect of irregular allotment where issue not fully subscribed

(1) An allotment made by a public company to an applicant in contravention of section 578 (public companies: allotment where issue not fully subscribed) is voidable at the instance of the applicant within one month after the date of the allotment, and not later.

(2) It is so voidable even if the company is in the course of being wound up.

(3) A director of a public company who knowingly contravenes, or permits or authorises the contravention of, any provision of section 578 with respect to allotment is liable to compensate the company and the allottee respectively for any loss, damages, costs or expenses that the company or allottee may have sustained or incurred by the contravention.

(4) Proceedings to recover any such loss, damages, costs or expenses may not be brought more than two years after the date of the allotment.

CHAPTER 5
PAYMENT FOR SHARES

General rules

580 Shares not to be allotted at a discount

(1) A company's shares must not be allotted at a discount.

(2) If shares are allotted in contravention of this section, the allottee is liable to pay the company an amount equal to the amount of the discount, with interest at the appropriate rate.

581 Provision for different amounts to be paid on shares

A company, if so authorised by its articles, may—

(a) make arrangements on the issue of shares for a difference between the shareholders in the amounts and times of payment of calls on their shares;

(b) accept from any member the whole or part of the amount remaining unpaid on any shares held by him, although no part of that amount has been called up;

(c) pay a dividend in proportion to the amount paid up on each share where a larger amount is paid up on some shares than on others.

582 General rule as to means of payment

(1) Shares allotted by a company, and any premium on them, may be paid up in money or money's worth (including goodwill and know-how).

(2) This section does not prevent a company—

(a) from allotting bonus shares to its members, or
(b) from paying up, with sums available for the purpose, any amounts for the time being unpaid on any of its shares (whether on account of the nominal value of the shares or by way of premium).

(3) This section has effect subject to the following provisions of this Chapter (additional rules for public companies).

583 Meaning of payment in cash

(1) The following provisions have effect for the purposes of the Companies Acts.

(2) A share in a company is deemed paid up (as to its nominal value or any premium on it) in cash, or allotted for cash, if the consideration received for the allotment or payment up is a cash consideration.

(3) A "cash consideration" means—
(a) cash received by the company,
(b) a cheque received by the company in good faith that the directors have no reason for suspecting will not be paid,
(c) a release of a liability of the company for a liquidated sum,
(d) an undertaking to pay cash to the company at a future date, or
(e) payment by any other means giving rise to a present or future entitlement (of the company or a person acting on the company's behalf) to a payment, or credit equivalent to payment, in cash.

(4) The Secretary of State may by order provide that particular means of payment specified in the order are to be regarded as falling within subsection (3)(e).

(5) In relation to the allotment or payment up of shares in a company—
(a) the payment of cash to a person other than the company, or
(b) an undertaking to pay cash to a person other than the company, counts as consideration other than cash.

This does not apply for the purposes of Chapter 3 (allotment of equity securities: existing shareholders' right of pre-emption).

(6) For the purpose of determining whether a share is or is to be allotted for cash, or paid up in cash, "cash" includes foreign currency.

(7) An order under this section is subject to negative resolution procedure.

Additional rules for public companies

584 Public companies: shares taken by subscribers of memorandum

Shares taken by a subscriber to the memorandum of a public company in pursuance of an undertaking of his in the memorandum, and any premium on the shares, must be paid up in cash.

585 Public companies: must not accept undertaking to do work or perform services

(1) A public company must not accept at any time, in payment up of its shares or any premium on them, an undertaking given by any person that he or another should do work or perform services for the company or any other person.

(2) If a public company accepts such an undertaking in payment up of its shares or any premium on them, the holder of the shares when they or the premium are treated as paid up (in whole or in part) by the undertaking is liable—
(a) to pay the company in respect of those shares an amount equal to their nominal value, together with the whole of any premium or, if the case so requires, such proportion of that amount as is treated as paid up by the undertaking; and
(b) to pay interest at the appropriate rate on the amount payable under paragraph (a).

(3) The reference in subsection (2) to the holder of shares includes a person who has an unconditional right—
(a) to be included in the company's register of members in respect of those shares, or
(b) to have an instrument of transfer of them executed in his favour.

586 Public companies: shares must be at least one-quarter paid up

(1) A public company must not allot a share except as paid up at least as to one-quarter of its nominal value and the whole of any premium on it.

(2) This does not apply to shares allotted in pursuance of an employees' share scheme.

(3) If a company allots a share in contravention of this section—

(a) the share is to be treated as if one-quarter of its nominal value, together with the whole of any premium on it, had been received, and

(b) the allottee is liable to pay the company the minimum amount which should have been received in respect of the share under subsection (1) (less the value of any consideration actually applied in payment up, to any extent, of the share and any premium on it), with interest at the appropriate rate.

(4) Subsection (3) does not apply to the allotment of bonus shares, unless the allottee knew or ought to have known the shares were allotted in contravention of this section.

587 Public companies: payment by long-term undertaking

(1) A public company must not allot shares as fully or partly paid up (as to their nominal value or any premium on them) otherwise than in cash if the consideration for the allotment is or includes an undertaking which is to be, or may be, performed more than five years after the date of the allotment.

(2) If a company allots shares in contravention of subsection (1), the allottee is liable to pay the company an amount equal to the aggregate of their nominal value and the whole of any premium (or, if the case so requires, so much of that aggregate as is treated as paid up by the undertaking), with interest at the appropriate rate.

(3) Where a contract for the allotment of shares does not contravene subsection (1), any variation of the contract that has the effect that the contract would have contravened the subsection, if the terms of the contract as varied had been its original terms, is void.

This applies also to the variation by a public company of the terms of a contract entered into before the company was re-registered as a public company.

(4) Where—

(a) a public company allots shares for a consideration which consists of or includes (in accordance with subsection (1)) an undertaking that is to be performed within five years of the allotment, and

(b) the undertaking is not performed within the period allowed by the contract for the allotment of the shares,

the allottee is liable to pay the company, at the end of the period so allowed, an amount equal to the aggregate of the nominal value of the shares and the whole of any premium (or, if the case so requires, so much of that aggregate as is treated as paid up by the undertaking), with interest at the appropriate rate.

(5) References in this section to a contract for the allotment of shares include an ancillary contract relating to payment in respect of them.

Supplementary provisions

588 Liability of subsequent holders of shares

(1) If a person becomes a holder of shares in respect of which—

(a) there has been a contravention of any provision of this Chapter, and

(b) by virtue of that contravention another is liable to pay any amount under the provision contravened,

that person is also liable to pay that amount (jointly and severally with any other person so liable), subject as follows.

(2) A person otherwise liable under subsection (1) is exempted from that liability if either—

(a) he is a purchaser for value and, at the time of the purchase, he did not have actual notice of the contravention concerned, or

(b) he derived title to the shares (directly or indirectly) from a person who became a holder of them after the contravention and was not liable under subsection (1).

(3) References in this section to a holder, in relation to shares in a company, include any person who has an unconditional right—

(a) to be included in the company's register of members in respect of those shares, or

(b) to have an instrument of transfer of the shares executed in his favour.

(4) This section applies in relation to a failure to carry out a term of a contract as mentioned in section 587(4) (public companies: payment by long-term undertaking) as it applies in relation to a contravention of a provision of this Chapter.

589 Power of court to grant relief

(1) This section applies in relation to liability under—
section 585(2) (liability of allottee in case of breach by public company of
prohibition on accepting undertaking to do work or perform services), section 587(2) or (4) (liability of allottee in case of breach by public
company of prohibition on payment by long-term undertaking), or section 588 (liability of subsequent holders of shares),
as it applies in relation to a contravention of those sections.

(2) A person who—

(a) is subject to any such liability to a company in relation to payment in respect of shares in the company, or

(b) is subject to any such liability to a company by virtue of an undertaking given to it in, or in connection with, payment for shares in the company,

may apply to the court to be exempted in whole or in part from the liability.

(3) In the case of a liability within subsection (2) (a), the court may exempt the applicant from the liability only if and to the extent that it appears to the court just and equitable to do so having regard to—

(a) whether the applicant has paid, or is liable to pay, any amount in respect of—

(i) any other liability arising in relation to those shares under any provision of this Chapter or Chapter 6, or

(ii) any liability arising by virtue of any undertaking given in or in connection with payment for those shares;

(b) whether any person other than the applicant has paid or is likely to pay, whether in pursuance of any order of the court or otherwise, any such amount;

(c) whether the applicant or any other person—

(i) has performed in whole or in part, or is likely so to perform any such undertaking, or

(ii) has done or is likely to do any other thing in payment or part payment for the shares.

(4) In the case of a liability within subsection (2) (b), the court may exempt the applicant from the liability only if and to the extent that it appears to the court just and equitable to do so having regard to—

(a) whether the applicant has paid or is liable to pay any amount in respect of liability arising in relation to the shares under any provision of this Chapter or Chapter 6;

(b) whether any person other than the applicant has paid or is likely to pay, whether in pursuance of any order of the court or otherwise, any such amount.

(5) In determining whether it should exempt the applicant in whole or in part from any liability, the court must have regard to the following overriding principles—

(a) a company that has allotted shares should receive money or money's worth at least equal in value to the aggregate of the nominal value of those shares and the whole of any premium or, if the case so requires, so much of that aggregate as is treated as paid up;

(b) subject to that, where a company would, if the court did not grant the exemption, have more than one remedy against a particular person, it should be for the company to decide which remedy it should remain entitled to pursue.

(6) If a person brings proceedings against another ("the contributor") for a contribution in respect of liability to a company arising under any provision of this Chapter or Chapter 6 and it appears to the court that the contributor is liable to make such a contribution, the court may, if and to the extent that it appears to it just and equitable to do so having regard to the respective culpability (in respect of the liability to the company) of the contributor and the person bringing the proceedings—

(a) exempt the contributor in whole or in part from his liability to make such a contribution, or

(b) order the contributor to make a larger contribution than, but for this subsection, he would be liable to make.

590 Penalty for contravention of this Chapter

(1) If a company contravenes any of the provisions of this Chapter, an offence is committed by—

(a) the company, and

(b) every officer of the company who is in default.

(2) A person guilty of an offence under this section is liable—

(a) on conviction on indictment, to a fine;

(b) on summary conviction, to a fine not exceeding the statutory maximum.

591 Enforceability of undertakings to do work etc

(1) An undertaking given by any person, in or in connection with payment for shares in a company, to do work or perform services or to do any other thing, if it is enforceable by the company apart from this Chapter, is so enforceable notwithstanding that there has been a contravention in relation to it of a provision of this Chapter or Chapter 6.

(2) This is without prejudice to section 589 (power of court to grant relief etc in respect of liabilities).

592 The appropriate rate of interest

(1) For the purposes of this Chapter the "appropriate rate" of interest is 5% per annum or such other rate as may be specified by order made by the Secretary of State.

(2) An order under this section is subject to negative resolution procedure.

CHAPTER 6

PUBLIC COMPANIES: INDEPENDENT VALUATION OF NON-CASH CONSIDERATION

Non-cash consideration for shares

593 Public company: valuation of non-cash consideration for shares

(1) A public company must not allot shares as fully or partly paid up (as to their nominal value or any premium on them) otherwise than in cash unless—

(a) the consideration for the allotment has been independently valued in accordance with the provisions of this Chapter,

(b) the valuer's report has been made to the company during the six months immediately preceding the allotment of the shares, and

(c) a copy of the report has been sent to the proposed allottee.

(2) For this purpose the application of an amount standing to the credit of—

(a) any of a company's reserve accounts, or

(b) its profit and loss account,

in paying up (to any extent) shares allotted to members of the company, or premiums on shares so allotted, does not count as consideration for the allotment.

Accordingly, subsection (1) does not apply in that case.

(3) If a company allots shares in contravention of subsection (1) and either—

(a) the allottee has not received the valuer's report required to be sent to him, or

(b) there has been some other contravention of the requirements of this section or section 596 that the allottee knew or ought to have known amounted to a contravention,

the allottee is liable to pay the company an amount equal to the aggregate of the nominal value of the shares and the whole of any premium (or, if the case so requires, so much of that aggregate as is treated as paid up by the consideration), with interest at the appropriate rate.

(4) This section has effect subject to—

section 594 (exception to valuation requirement: arrangement with another company), and

section 595 (exception to valuation requirement: merger or division).

594 Exception to valuation requirement: arrangement with another company

(1) Section 593 (valuation of non-cash consideration) does not apply to the allotment of shares by a company ("company A") in connection with an arrangement to which this section applies.

(2) This section applies to an arrangement for the allotment of shares in company A on terms that the whole or part of the consideration for the shares allotted is to be provided by—

(a) the transfer to that company, or

(b) the cancellation,

of all or some of the shares, or of all or some of the shares of a particular class, in another company ("company B").

(3) It is immaterial whether the arrangement provides for the issue to company A of shares, or shares of any particular class, in company B.

(4) This section applies to an arrangement only if under the arrangement it is open to all the holders of the shares in company B (or, where the arrangement applies only to shares of a particular class, to all the holders of shares of that class) to take part in the arrangement.

(5) In determining whether that is the case, the following shall be disregarded—

(a) shares held by or by a nominee of company A;

(b) shares held by or by a nominee of a company which is—

(i) the holding company, or a subsidiary, of company A, or

(ii) a subsidiary of such a holding company;

(c) shares held as treasury shares by company B.

(6) In this section—

(a) "arrangement" means any agreement, scheme or arrangement (including an arrangement sanctioned in accordance with—

(i) Part 26 (arrangements and reconstructions), or

(ii) section 110 of the Insolvency Act 1986 or Article 96 of the Insolvency (Northern Ireland) Order 1989 (liquidator in winding up accepting shares as consideration for sale of company property)), and

(b) "company", except in reference to company A, includes any body corporate.

595 Exception to valuation requirement: merger or division

(1) Section 593 (valuation of non-cash consideration) does not apply to the allotment of shares by a company as part of a scheme to which Part 27 (mergers and divisions of public companies) applies if—

(a) in the case of a scheme involving a merger, an expert's report is drawn up as required by section 909, or

(b) in the case of a scheme involving a division, an expert's report is drawn up as required by section 924.

(2), (3) . . .

596 Non-cash consideration for shares: requirements as to valuation and report

(1) The provisions of sections 1150 to 1153 (general provisions as to independent valuation and report) apply to the valuation and report required by section 593 (public company: valuation of non-cash consideration for shares).

(2) The valuer's report must state—

(a) the nominal value of the shares to be wholly or partly paid for by the consideration in question;
(b) the amount of any premium payable on the shares;
(c) the description of the consideration and, as respects so much of the consideration as he himself has valued, a description of that part of the consideration, the method used to value it and the date of the valuation;
(d) the extent to which the nominal value of the shares and any premium are to be treated as paid up—
(i) by the consideration;
(ii) in cash.

(3) The valuer's report must contain or be accompanied by a note by him—
(a) in the case of a valuation made by a person other than himself, that it appeared to himself reasonable to arrange for it to be so made or to accept a valuation so made,
(b) whoever made the valuation, that the method of valuation was reasonable in all the circumstances,
(c) that it appears to the valuer that there has been no material change in the value of the consideration in question since the valuation, and
(d) that, on the basis of the valuation, the value of the consideration, together with any cash by which the nominal value of the shares or any premium payable on them is to be paid up, is not less than so much of the aggregate of the nominal value and the whole of any such premium as is treated as paid up by the consideration and any such cash.

(4) Where the consideration to be valued is accepted partly in payment up of the nominal value of the shares and any premium and partly for some other consideration given by the company, section 593 and the preceding provisions of this section apply as if references to the consideration accepted by the company included the proportion of that consideration that is properly attributable to the payment up of that value and any premium.

(5) In such a case—
(a) the valuer must carry out, or arrange for, such other valuations as will enable him to determine that proportion, and
(b) his report must state what valuations have been made under this subsection and also the reason for, and method and date of, any such valuation and any other matters which may be relevant to that determination.

597 Copy of report to be delivered to registrar

(1) A company to which a report is made under section 593 as to the value of any consideration for which, or partly for which, it proposes to allot shares must deliver a copy of the report to the registrar for registration.

(2) The copy must be delivered at the same time that the company files the return of the allotment of those shares under section 555 (return of allotment by limited company).

(3) If default is made in complying with subsection (1) or (2), an offence is committed by every officer of the company who is in default.

(4) A person guilty of an offence under this section is liable—
(a) on conviction on indictment, to a fine;
(b) on summary conviction, to a fine not exceeding the statutory maximum and, for continued contravention, a daily default fine not exceeding one-tenth of the statutory maximum.

(5) In the case of default in delivering to the registrar any document as required by this section, any person liable for the default may apply to the court for relief.

(6) The court, if satisfied—
(a) that the omission to deliver the document was accidental or due to inadvertence, or
(b) that it is just and equitable to grant relief,

may make an order extending the time for delivery of the document for such period as the court thinks proper.

Transfer of non-cash asset in initial period

598 Public company: agreement for transfer of non-cash asset in initial period

(1) A public company formed as such must not enter into an agreement—

(a) with a person who is a subscriber to the company's memorandum,

(b) for the transfer by him to the company, or another, before the end of the company's initial period of one or more non-cash assets, and

(c) under which the consideration for the transfer to be given by the company is at the time of the agreement equal in value to one-tenth or more of the company's issued share capital,

unless the conditions referred to below have been complied with.

(2) The company's "initial period" means the period of two years beginning with the date of the company being issued with a certificate under section 761 (trading certificate).

(3) The conditions are those specified in—

section 599 (requirement of independent valuation), and

section 601 (requirement of approval by members).

(4) This section does not apply where—

(a) it is part of the company's ordinary business to acquire, or arrange for other persons to acquire, assets of a particular description, and

(b) the agreement is entered into by the company in the ordinary course of that business.

(5) This section does not apply to an agreement entered into by the company under the supervision of the court or of an officer authorised by the court for the purpose.

599 Agreement for transfer of non-cash asset: requirement of independent valuation

(1) The following conditions must have been complied with—

(a) the consideration to be received by the company, and any consideration other than cash to be given by the company, must have been independently valued in accordance with the provisions of this Chapter,

(b) the valuer's report must have been made to the company during the six months immediately preceding the date of the agreement, and

(c) a copy of the report must have been sent to the other party to the proposed agreement not later than the date on which copies have to be circulated to members under section 601(3).

(2) The reference in subsection (1)(a) to the consideration to be received by the company is to the asset to be transferred to it or, as the case may be, to the advantage to the company of the asset's transfer to another person.

(3) The reference in subsection (1)(c) to the other party to the proposed agreement is to the person referred to in section 598(1)(a).

If he has received a copy of the report under section 601 in his capacity as a member of the company, it is not necessary to send another copy under this section.

(4) This section does not affect any requirement to value any consideration for purposes of section 593 (valuation of non-cash consideration for shares).

600 Agreement for transfer of non-cash asset: requirements as to valuation and report

(1) The provisions of sections 1150 to 1153 (general provisions as to independent valuation and report) apply to the valuation and report required by section 599 (public company: transfer of non-cash asset).

(2) The valuer's report must state—

(a) the consideration to be received by the company, describing the asset in question (specifying the amount to be received in cash) and the consideration to be given by the company (specifying the amount to be given in cash), and

(b) the method and date of valuation.

(3) The valuer's report must contain or be accompanied by a note by him—

(a) in the case of a valuation made by a person other than himself, that it appeared to himself reasonable to arrange for it to be so made or to accept a valuation so made,

(b) whoever made the valuation, that the method of valuation was reasonable in all the circumstances,

(c) that it appears to the valuer that there has been no material change in the value of the consideration in question since the valuation, and

(d) that, on the basis of the valuation, the value of the consideration to be received by the company is not less than the value of the consideration to be given by it.

(4) Any reference in section 599 or this section to consideration given for the transfer of an asset includes consideration given partly for its transfer.

(5) In such a case—

(a) the value of any consideration partly so given is to be taken as the proportion of the consideration properly attributable to its transfer,

(b) the valuer must carry out or arrange for such valuations of anything else as will enable him to determine that proportion, and

(c) his report must state what valuations have been made for that purpose and also the reason for and method and date of any such valuation and any other matters which may be relevant to that determination.

601 Agreement for transfer of non-cash asset: requirement of approval by members

(1) The following conditions must have been complied with—

(a) the terms of the agreement must have been approved by an ordinary resolution of the company,

(b) copies of the valuer's report must have been circulated to the members entitled to notice of the meeting at which the resolution is proposed, not later than the date on which notice of the meeting is given, and

(c) a copy of the proposed resolution must have been sent to the other party to the proposed agreement.

(2) The reference in subsection (1)(c) to the other party to the proposed agreement is to the person referred to in section 598(1)(a).

(3) . . .

602 Copy of resolution to be delivered to registrar

(1) A company that has passed a resolution under section 601 with respect to the transfer of an asset must, within 15 days of doing so, deliver to the registrar a copy of the resolution together with the valuer's report required by that section.

(2) If a company fails to comply with subsection (1), an offence is committed by—

(a) the company, and

(b) every officer of the company who is in default.

(3) A person guilty of an offence under this section is liable on summary conviction to a fine not exceeding level 3 on the standard scale and, for continued contravention, to a daily default fine not exceeding one-tenth of level 3 on the standard scale.

603 Adaptation of provisions in relation to company re-registering as public

The provisions of sections 598 to 602 (public companies: transfer of non-cash assets) apply with the following adaptations in relation to a company re-registered as a public company—

(a) the reference in section 598(1)(a) to a person who is a subscriber to the company's memorandum shall be read as a reference to a person who is a member of the company on the date of re-registration;

(b) the reference in section 598(2) to the date of the company being issued with a certificate under section 761 (trading certificate) shall be read as a reference to the date of re-registration.

604 Agreement for transfer of non-cash asset: effect of contravention

(1) This section applies where a public company enters into an agreement in contravention of section 598 and either—

(a) the other party to the agreement has not received the valuer's report required to be sent to him, or

(b) there has been some other contravention of the requirements of this Chapter that the other party to the agreement knew or ought to have known amounted to a contravention.

(2) In those circumstances—

(a) the company is entitled to recover from that person any consideration given by it under the agreement, or an amount equal to the value of the consideration at the time of the agreement, and

(b) the agreement, so far as not carried out, is void.

(3) If the agreement is or includes an agreement for the allotment of shares in the company, then—

(a) whether or not the agreement also contravenes section 593 (valuation of non-cash consideration for shares), this section does not apply to it in so far as it is for the allotment of shares, and

(b) the allottee is liable to pay the company an amount equal to the aggregate of the nominal value of the shares and the whole of any premium (or, if the case so requires, so much of that aggregate as is treated as paid up by the consideration), with interest at the appropriate rate.

Supplementary provisions

605 Liability of subsequent holders of shares

(1) If a person becomes a holder of shares in respect of which—

(a) there has been a contravention of section 593 (public company: valuation of non-cash consideration for shares), and

(b) by virtue of that contravention another is liable to pay any amount under the provision contravened,

that person is also liable to pay that amount (jointly and severally with any other person so liable), unless he is exempted from liability under subsection (3) below.

(2) If a company enters into an agreement in contravention of section 598 (public company: agreement for transfer of non-cash asset in initial period) and—

(a) the agreement is or includes an agreement for the allotment of shares in the company,

(b) a person becomes a holder of shares allotted under the agreement, and

(c) by virtue of the agreement and allotment under it another person is liable to pay an amount under section 604,

the person who becomes the holder of the shares is also liable to pay that amount (jointly and severally with any other person so liable), unless he is exempted from liability under subsection (3) below.

This applies whether or not the agreement also contravenes section 593.

(3) A person otherwise liable under subsection (1) or (2) is exempted from that liability if either—

(a) he is a purchaser for value and, at the time of the purchase, he did not have actual notice of the contravention concerned, or

(b) he derived title to the shares (directly or indirectly) from a person who became a holder of them after the contravention and was not liable under subsection (1) or (2).

(4) References in this section to a holder, in relation to shares in a company, include any person who has an unconditional right—

(a) to be included in the company's register of members in respect of those shares, or

(b) to have an instrument of transfer of the shares executed in his favour.

606 Power of court to grant relief

(1) A person who—

(a) is liable to a company under any provision of this Chapter in relation to payment in respect of any shares in the company, or

(b) is liable to a company by virtue of an undertaking given to it in, or in connection with, payment for any shares in the company, may apply to the court to be exempted in whole or in part from the liability.

(2) In the case of a liability within subsection (1)(a), the court may exempt the applicant from the liability only if and to the extent that it appears to the court just and equitable to do so having regard to—

(a) whether the applicant has paid, or is liable to pay, any amount in respect of—

(i) any other liability arising in relation to those shares under any provision of this Chapter or Chapter 5, or

(ii) any liability arising by virtue of any undertaking given in or in connection with payment for those shares;

(b) whether any person other than the applicant has paid or is likely to pay, whether in pursuance of any order of the court or otherwise, any such amount;

(c) whether the applicant or any other person—

(i) has performed in whole or in part, or is likely so to perform any such undertaking, or

(ii) has done or is likely to do any other thing in payment or part payment for the shares.

(3) In the case of a liability within subsection (1) (b), the court may exempt the applicant from the liability only if and to the extent that it appears to the court just and equitable to do so having regard to—

(a) whether the applicant has paid or is liable to pay any amount in respect of liability arising in relation to the shares under any provision of this Chapter or Chapter 5;

(b) whether any person other than the applicant has paid or is likely to pay, whether in pursuance of any order of the court or otherwise, any such amount.

(4) In determining whether it should exempt the applicant in whole or in part from any liability, the court must have regard to the following overriding principles—

(a) that a company that has allotted shares should receive money or money's worth at least equal in value to the aggregate of the nominal value of those shares and the whole of any premium or, if the case so requires, so much of that aggregate as is treated as paid up;

(b) subject to this, that where such a company would, if the court did not grant the exemption, have more than one remedy against a particular person, it should be for the company to decide which remedy it should remain entitled to pursue.

(5) If a person brings proceedings against another ("the contributor") for a contribution in respect of liability to a company arising under any provision of this Chapter or Chapter 5 and it appears to the court that the contributor is liable to make such a contribution, the court may, if and to the extent that it appears to it, just and equitable to do so having regard to the respective culpability (in respect of the liability to the company) of the contributor and the person bringing the proceedings—

(a) exempt the contributor in whole or in part from his liability to make such a contribution, or

(b) order the contributor to make a larger contribution than, but for this subsection, he would be liable to make.

(6) Where a person is liable to a company under section 604(2) (agreement for transfer of non-cash asset: effect of contravention), the court may, on application, exempt him in whole or in part from that liability if and to the extent that it appears to the court to be just and equitable to do so having regard to any benefit accruing to the company by virtue of anything done by him towards the carrying out of the agreement mentioned in that subsection.

607 Penalty for contravention of this Chapter

(1) This section applies where a company contravenes—

section 593 (public company allotting shares for non-cash consideration), or

section 598 (public company entering into agreement for transfer of non-cash asset).

(2) An offence is committed by—

(a) the company, and

(b) every officer of the company who is in default.

(3) A person guilty of an offence under this section is liable—
(a) on conviction on indictment, to a fine;
(b) on summary conviction, to a fine not exceeding the statutory maximum.

608 Enforceability of undertakings to do work etc

(1) An undertaking given by any person, in or in connection with payment for shares in a company, to do work or perform services or to do any other thing, if it is enforceable by the company apart from this Chapter, is so enforceable notwithstanding that there has been a contravention in relation to it of a provision of this Chapter or Chapter 5.

(2) This is without prejudice to section 606 (power of court to grant relief etc in respect of liabilities).

609 The appropriate rate of interest

(1) For the purposes of this Chapter the "appropriate rate" of interest is 5% per annum or such other rate as may be specified by order made by the Secretary of State.

(2) An order under this section is subject to negative resolution procedure.

CHAPTER 7
SHARE PREMIUMS

The share premium account

610 Application of share premiums

(1) If a company issues shares at a premium, whether for cash or otherwise, a sum equal to the aggregate amount or value of the premiums on those shares must be transferred to an account called "the share premium account".

(2) Where, on issuing shares, a company has transferred a sum to the share premium account, it may use that sum to write off—
(a) the expenses of the issue of those shares;
(b) any commission paid on the issue of those shares.

(3) The company may use the share premium account to pay up new shares to be allotted to members as fully paid bonus shares.

(4) Subject to subsections (2) and (3), the provisions of the Companies Acts relating to the reduction of a company's share capital apply as if the share premium account were part of its paid up share capital.

(5) This section has effect subject to—
section 611 (group reconstruction relief);
section 612 (merger relief);
section 614 (power to make further provisions by regulations).

(6) In this Chapter "the issuing company" means the company issuing shares as mentioned in subsection (1) above.

Relief from requirements as to share premiums

611 Group reconstruction relief

(1) This section applies where the issuing company—
(a) is a wholly-owned subsidiary of another company ("the holding company"), and
(b) allots shares—
(i) to the holding company, or
(ii) to another wholly-owned subsidiary of the holding company,
in consideration for the transfer to the issuing company of non-cash assets of a company ("the transferor company") that is a member of the group of companies that comprises the holding company and all its wholly-owned subsidiaries.

(2) Where the shares in the issuing company allotted in consideration for the transfer are issued at a premium, the issuing company is not required by section 610 to transfer any amount in excess of the minimum premium value to the share premium account.

(3) The minimum premium value means the amount (if any) by which the base value of the consideration for the shares allotted exceeds the aggregate nominal value of the shares.

(4) The base value of the consideration for the shares allotted is the amount by which the base value of the assets transferred exceeds the base value of any liabilities of the transferor company assumed by the issuing company as part of the consideration for the assets transferred.

(5) For the purposes of this section—

(a) the base value of assets transferred is taken as—

(i) the cost of those assets to the transferor company, or

(ii) if less, the amount at which those assets are stated in the transferor company's accounting records immediately before the transfer;

(b) the base value of the liabilities assumed is taken as the amount at which they are stated in the transferor company's accounting records immediately before the transfer.

612 Merger relief

(1) This section applies where the issuing company has secured at least a 90% equity holding in another company in pursuance of an arrangement providing for the allotment of equity shares in the issuing company on terms that the consideration for the shares allotted is to be provided—

(a) by the issue or transfer to the issuing company of equity shares in the other company, or

(b) by the cancellation of any such shares not held by the issuing company.

(2) If the equity shares in the issuing company allotted in pursuance of the arrangement in consideration for the acquisition or cancellation of equity shares in the other company are issued at a premium, section 610 does not apply to the premiums on those shares.

(3) Where the arrangement also provides for the allotment of any shares in the issuing company on terms that the consideration for those shares is to be provided—

(a) by the issue or transfer to the issuing company of non-equity shares in the other company, or

(b) by the cancellation of any such shares in that company not held by the issuing company,

relief under subsection (2) extends to any shares in the issuing company allotted on those terms in pursuance of the arrangement.

(4) This section does not apply in a case falling within section 611 (group reconstruction relief).

613 Merger relief: meaning of 90% equity holding

(1) The following provisions have effect to determine for the purposes of section 612 (merger relief) whether a company ("company A") has secured at least a 90% equity holding in another company ("company B") in pursuance of such an arrangement as is mentioned in subsection (1) of that section.

(2) Company A has secured at least a 90% equity holding in company B if in consequence of an acquisition or cancellation of equity shares in company B (in pursuance of that arrangement) it holds equity shares in company B of an aggregate amount equal to 90% or more of the nominal value of that company's equity share capital.

(3) For this purpose—

(a) it is immaterial whether any of those shares were acquired in pursuance of the arrangement; and

(b) shares in company B held by the company as treasury shares are excluded in determining the nominal value of company B's share capital.

(4) Where the equity share capital of company B is divided into different classes of shares, company A is not regarded as having secured at least a 90% equity holding in company B unless the requirements of subsection (2) are met in relation to each of those classes of shares taken separately.

(5) For the purposes of this section shares held by—

(a) a company that is company A's holding company or subsidiary, or

(b) a subsidiary of company A's holding company, or

(c) its or their nominees,

are treated as held by company A.

614 Power to make further provision by regulations

(1) The Secretary of State may by regulations make such provision as he thinks appropriate—

(a) for relieving companies from the requirements of section 610 (application of share premiums) in relation to premiums other than cash premiums;

(b) for restricting or otherwise modifying any relief from those requirements provided by this Chapter.

(2) Regulations under this section are subject to affirmative resolution procedure.

615 Relief may be reflected in company's balance sheet

An amount corresponding to the amount representing the premiums, or part of the premiums, on shares issued by a company that by virtue of any relief under this Chapter is not included in the company's share premium account may also be disregarded in determining the amount at which any shares or other consideration provided for the shares issued is to be included in the company's balance sheet.

Supplementary provisions

616 Interpretation of this Chapter

(1) In this Chapter—

"arrangement" means any agreement, scheme or arrangement (including an arrangement sanctioned in accordance with—

(a) Part 26 (arrangements and reconstructions), or

(b) section 110 of the Insolvency Act 1986 or Article 96 of the Insolvency (Northern Ireland) Order 1989 (liquidator in winding up accepting shares as consideration for sale of company property));

"company", except in reference to the issuing company, includes any body corporate;

"equity shares" means shares comprised in a company's equity share capital, and "non-equity shares" means shares (of any class) that are not so comprised;

"the issuing company" has the meaning given by section 610(6).

(2) References in this Chapter (however expressed) to—

(a) the acquisition by a company of shares in another company, and

(b) the issue or allotment of shares to, or the transfer of shares to or by, a company,

include (respectively) the acquisition of shares by, and the issue or allotment or transfer of shares to or by, a nominee of that company.

The reference in section 611 to the transferor company shall be read accordingly.

(3) References in this Chapter to the transfer of shares in a company include the transfer of a right to be included in the company's register of members in respect of those shares.

CHAPTER 8
ALTERATION OF SHARE CAPITAL

How share capital may be altered

617 Alteration of share capital of limited company

(1) A limited company having a share capital may not alter its share capital except in the following ways.

(2) The company may—

(a) increase its share capital by allotting new shares in accordance with this Part, or

(b) reduce its share capital in accordance with Chapter 10.

(3) The company may—

(a) sub-divide or consolidate all or any of its share capital in accordance with section 618, or

(b) reconvert stock into shares in accordance with section 620.

(4) The company may redenominate all or any of its shares in accordance with section 622, and may reduce its share capital in accordance with section 626 in connection with such a redenomination.

(5) Nothing in this section affects—

(a) the power of a company to purchase its own shares, or to redeem shares, in accordance with Part 18;

(b) the power of a company to purchase its own shares in pursuance of an order of the court under—

(i) section 98 (application to court to cancel resolution for re-registration as a private company);

(ii) section 721(6) (powers of court on objection to redemption or purchase of shares out of capital),

(iii) section 759 (remedial order in case of breach of prohibition of public offers by private company), or

(iv) Part 30 (protection of members against unfair prejudice);

(c) the forfeiture of shares, or the acceptance of shares surrendered in lieu, in pursuance of the company's articles, for failure to pay any sum payable in respect of the shares;

(d) the cancellation of shares under section 662 (duty to cancel shares held by or for a public company);

(e) the power of a company—

(i) to enter into a compromise or arrangement in accordance with Part 26 (arrangements and reconstructions), or

(ii) to do anything required to comply with an order of the court on an application under that Part.

Subdivision or consolidation of shares

618 Sub-division or consolidation of shares

(1) A limited company having a share capital may—

(a) sub-divide its shares, or any of them, into shares of a smaller nominal amount than its existing shares, or

(b) consolidate and divide all or any of its share capital into shares of a larger nominal amount than its existing shares.

(2) In any sub-division, consolidation or division of shares under this section, the proportion between the amount paid and the amount (if any) unpaid on each resulting share must be the same as it was in the case of the share from which that share is derived.

(3) A company may exercise a power conferred by this section only if its members have passed a resolution authorising it to do so.

(4) A resolution under subsection (3) may authorise a company—

(a) to exercise more than one of the powers conferred by this section;

(b) to exercise a power on more than one occasion;

(c) to exercise a power at a specified time or in specified circumstances.

(5) The company's articles may exclude or restrict the exercise of any power conferred by this section.

619 Notice to registrar of sub-division or consolidation

(1) If a company exercises the power conferred by section 618 (sub-division or consolidation of shares) it must within one month after doing so give notice to the registrar, specifying the shares affected.

(2) The notice must be accompanied by a statement of capital.

(3) The statement of capital must state with respect to the company's share capital immediately following the exercise of the power—

(a) the total number of shares of the company,

(b) the aggregate nominal value of those shares,

(c) for each class of shares—

(i) prescribed particulars of the rights attached to the shares,

(ii) the total number of shares of that class, and

(iii) the aggregate nominal value of shares of that class, and

(d) the amount paid up and the amount (if any) unpaid on each share (whether on account of the nominal value of the share or by way of premium).

(4) If default is made in complying with this section, an offence is committed by—

(a) the company, and

(b) every officer of the company who is in default.

(5) A person guilty of an offence under this section is liable on summary conviction to a fine not exceeding level 3 on the standard scale and, for continued contravention, a daily default fine not exceeding one-tenth of level 3 on the standard scale.

Reconversion of stock into shares

620 Reconversion of stock into shares

(1) A limited company that has converted paid-up shares into stock (before the repeal by this Act of the power to do so) may reconvert that stock into paid-up shares of any nominal value.

(2) A company may exercise the power conferred by this section only if its members have passed an ordinary resolution authorising it to do so.

(3) A resolution under subsection (2) may authorise a company to exercise the power conferred by this section—

(a) on more than one occasion;

(b) at a specified time or in specified circumstances.

621 Notice to registrar of reconversion of stock into shares

(1) If a company exercises a power conferred by section 620 (reconversion of stock into shares) it must within one month after doing so give notice to the registrar, specifying the stock affected.

(2) The notice must be accompanied by a statement of capital.

(3) The statement of capital must state with respect to the company's share capital immediately following the exercise of the power—

(a) the total number of shares of the company,

(b) the aggregate nominal value of those shares,

(c) for each class of shares—

(i) prescribed particulars of the rights attached to the shares,

(ii) the total number of shares of that class, and

(iii) the aggregate nominal value of shares of that class, and

(d) the amount paid up and the amount (if any) unpaid on each share (whether on account of the nominal value of the share or by way of premium).

(4) If default is made in complying with this section, an offence is committed by—

(a) the company, and

(b) every officer of the company who is in default.

(5) A person guilty of an offence under this section is liable on summary conviction to a fine not exceeding level 3 on the standard scale and, for continued contravention, a daily default fine not exceeding one-tenth of level 3 on the standard scale.

Redenomination of share capital

622 Redenomination of share capital

(1) A limited company having a share capital may by resolution redenominate its share capital or any class of its share capital.

"Redenominate" means convert shares from having a fixed nominal value in one currency to having a fixed nominal value in another currency.

(2) The conversion must be made at an appropriate spot rate of exchange specified in the resolution.

(3) The rate must be either—

(a) a rate prevailing on a day specified in the resolution, or

(b) a rate determined by taking the average of rates prevailing on each consecutive day of a period specified in the resolution.

The day or period specified for the purposes of paragraph (a) or (b) must be within the period of 28 days ending on the day before the resolution is passed.

(4) A resolution under this section may specify conditions which must be met before the redenomination takes effect.

(5) Redenomination in accordance with a resolution under this section takes effect—

(a) on the day on which the resolution is passed, or

(b) on such later day as may be determined in accordance with the resolution.

(6) A resolution under this section lapses if the redenomination for which it provides has not taken effect at the end of the period of 28 days beginning on the date on which it is passed.

(7) A company's articles may prohibit or restrict the exercise of the power conferred by this section.

(8) Chapter 3 of Part 3 (resolutions affecting a company's constitution) applies to a resolution under this section.

623 Calculation of new nominal values

For each class of share the new nominal value of each share is calculated as follows:

Step One

Take the aggregate of the old nominal values of all the shares of that class.

Step Two

Translate that amount into the new currency at the rate of exchange specified in the resolution.

Step Three

Divide that amount by the number of shares in the class.

624 Effect of redenomination

(1) The redenomination of shares does not affect any rights or obligations of members under the company's constitution, or any restrictions affecting members under the company's constitution.

In particular, it does not affect entitlement to dividends (including entitlement to dividends in a particular currency), voting rights or any liability in respect of amounts unpaid on shares.

(2) For this purpose the company's constitution includes the terms on which any shares of the company are allotted or held.

(3) Subject to subsection (1), references to the old nominal value of the shares in any agreement or statement, or in any deed, instrument or document, shall (unless the context otherwise requires) be read after the resolution takes effect as references to the new nominal value of the shares.

625 Notice to registrar of redenomination

(1) If a limited company having a share capital redenominates any of its share capital, it must within one month after doing so give notice to the registrar, specifying the shares redenominated.

(2) The notice must—

(a) state the date on which the resolution was passed, and

(b) be accompanied by a statement of capital.

(3) The statement of capital must state with respect to the company's share capital as redenominated by the resolution—

(a) the total number of shares of the company,

(b) the aggregate nominal value of those shares,

(c) for each class of shares—

(i) prescribed particulars of the rights attached to the shares,

(ii) the total number of shares of that class, and

(iii) the aggregate nominal value of shares of that class, and

(d) the amount paid up and the amount (if any) unpaid on each share (whether on account of the nominal value of the share or by way of premium).

(4) If default is made in complying with this section, an offence is committed by—

(a) the company, and

(b) every officer of the company who is in default.

(5) A person guilty of an offence under this section is liable on summary conviction to a fine not exceeding level 3 on the standard scale and, for continued contravention, a daily default fine not exceeding one-tenth of level 3 on the standard scale.

626 Reduction of capital in connection with redenomination

(1) A limited company that passes a resolution redenominating some or all of its shares may, for the purpose of adjusting the nominal values of the redenominated shares to obtain values that are, in the opinion of the company, more suitable, reduce its share capital under this section.

(2) A reduction of capital under this section requires a special resolution of the company.

(3) Any such resolution must be passed within three months of the resolution effecting the redenomination.

(4) The amount by which a company's share capital is reduced under this section must not exceed 10% of the nominal value of the company's allotted share capital immediately after the reduction.

(5) A reduction of capital under this section does not extinguish or reduce any liability in respect of share capital not paid up.

(6) Nothing in Chapter 10 applies to a reduction of capital under this section.

627 Notice to registrar of reduction of capital in connection with redenomination

(1) A company that passes a resolution under section 626 (reduction of capital in connection with redenomination) must within 15 days after the resolution is passed give notice to the registrar stating—

(a) the date of the resolution, and

(b) the date of the resolution under section 622 in connection with which it was passed.

This is in addition to the copies of the resolutions themselves that are required to be delivered to the registrar under Chapter 3 of Part 3.

(2) The notice must be accompanied by a statement of capital.

(3) The statement of capital must state with respect to the company's share capital as reduced by the resolution—

(a) the total number of shares of the company,

(b) the aggregate nominal value of those shares,

(c) for each class of shares—

(i) prescribed particulars of the rights attached to the shares,

(ii) the total number of shares of that class, and

(iii) the aggregate nominal value of shares of that class, and

(d) the amount paid up and the amount (if any) unpaid on each share (whether on account of the nominal value of the share or by way of premium).

(4) The registrar must register the notice and the statement on receipt.

(5) The reduction of capital is not effective until those documents are registered.

(6) The company must also deliver to the registrar, within 15 days after the resolution is passed, a statement by the directors confirming that the reduction in share capital is in accordance with section 626(4) (reduction of capital not to exceed 10% of nominal value of allotted shares immediately after reduction).

(7) If default is made in complying with this section, an offence is committed by—

(a) the company, and

(b) every officer of the company who is in default.

(8) A person guilty of an offence under this section is liable—

(a) on conviction on indictment to a fine, and

(b) on summary conviction to a fine not exceeding the statutory maximum.

628 Redenomination reserve

(1) The amount by which a company's share capital is reduced under section 626 (reduction of capital in connection with redenomination) must be transferred to a reserve, called "the redenomination reserve".

(2) The redenomination reserve may be applied by the company in paying up shares to be allotted to members as fully paid bonus shares.

(3) Subject to that, the provisions of the Companies Acts relating to the reduction of a company's share capital apply as if the redenomination reserve were paid-up share capital of the company.

CHAPTER 9
CLASSES OF SHARE AND CLASS RIGHTS

Introductory

629 Classes of shares

(1) For the purposes of the Companies Acts shares are of one class if the rights attached to them are in all respects uniform.

(2) For this purpose the rights attached to shares are not regarded as different from those attached to other shares by reason only that they do not carry the same rights to dividends in the twelve months immediately following their allotment.

Variation of class rights

630 Variation of class rights: companies having a share capital

(1) This section is concerned with the variation of the rights attached to a class of shares in a company having a share capital.

(2) Rights attached to a class of a company's shares may only be varied—
  (a) in accordance with provision in the company's articles for the variation of those rights, or
  (b) where the company's articles contain no such provision, if the holders of shares of that class consent to the variation in accordance with this section.

(3) This is without prejudice to any other restrictions on the variation of the rights.

(4) The consent required for the purposes of this section on the part of the holders of a class of a company's shares is—
  (a) consent in writing from the holders of at least three-quarters in nominal value of the issued shares of that class (excluding any shares held as treasury shares), or
  (b) a special resolution passed at a separate general meeting of the holders of that class sanctioning the variation.

(5) Any amendment of a provision contained in a company's articles for the variation of the rights attached to a class of shares, or the insertion of any such provision into the articles, is itself to be treated as a variation of those rights.

(6) In this section, and (except where the context otherwise requires) in any provision in a company's articles for the variation of the rights attached to a class of shares, references to the variation of those rights include references to their abrogation.

631 Variation of class rights: companies without a share capital

(1) This section is concerned with the variation of the rights of a class of members of a company where the company does not have a share capital.

(2) Rights of a class of members may only be varied—
  (a) in accordance with provision in the company's articles for the variation of those rights, or
  (b) where the company's articles contain no such provision, if the members of that class consent to the variation in accordance with this section.

(3) This is without prejudice to any other restrictions on the variation of the rights.

(4) The consent required for the purposes of this section on the part of the members of a class is—
  (a) consent in writing from at least three-quarters of the members of the class, or
  (b) a special resolution passed at a separate general meeting of the members of that class sanctioning the variation.

(5) Any amendment of a provision contained in a company's articles for the variation of the rights of a class of members, or the insertion of any such provision into the articles, is itself to be treated as a variation of those rights.

(6) In this section, and (except where the context otherwise requires) in any provision in a company's articles for the variation of the rights of a class of members, references to the variation of those rights include references to their abrogation.

632 Variation of class rights: saving for court's powers under other provisions

Nothing in section 630 or 631 (variation of class rights) affects the power of the court under—
section 98 (application to cancel resolution for public company to be re-registered as private),
Part 26 (arrangements and reconstructions), or
Part 30 (protection of members against unfair prejudice).

633 Right to object to variation: companies having a share capital

(1) This section applies where the rights attached to any class of shares in a company are varied under section 630 (variation of class rights: companies having a share capital).

(1) The holders of not less in the aggregate than 15% of the issued shares of the class in question (being persons who did not consent to or vote in favour of the resolution for the variation) may apply to the court to have the variation cancelled.

For this purpose any of the company's share capital held as treasury shares is disregarded.

(3) If such an application is made, the variation has no effect unless and until it is confirmed by the court.

(4) Application to the court—

(a) must be made within 21 days after the date on which the consent was given or the resolution was passed (as the case may be), and

(b) may be made on behalf of the shareholders entitled to make the application by such one or more of their number as they may appoint in writing for the purpose.

(5) The court, after hearing the applicant and any other persons who apply to the court to be heard and appear to the court to be interested in the application, may, if satisfied having regard to all the circumstances of the case that the variation would unfairly prejudice the shareholders of the class represented by the applicant, disallow the variation, and shall if not so satisfied confirm it. The decision of the court on any such application is final.

(6) References in this section to the variation of the rights of holders of a class of shares include references to their abrogation.

634 Right to object to variation: companies without a share capital

(1) This section applies where the rights of any class of members of a company are varied under section 631 (variation of class rights: companies without a share capital).

(2) Members amounting to not less than 15% of the members of the class in question (being persons who did not consent to or vote in favour of the resolution for the variation) may apply to the court to have the variation cancelled.

(3) If such an application is made, the variation has no effect unless and until it is confirmed by the court.

(4) Application to the court must be made within 21 days after the date on which the consent was given or the resolution was passed (as the case may be) and may be made on behalf of the members entitled to make the application by such one or more of their number as they may appoint in writing for the purpose.

(5) The court, after hearing the applicant and any other persons who apply to the court to be heard and appear to the court to be interested in the application, may, if satisfied having regard to all the circumstances of the case that the variation would unfairly prejudice the members of the class represented by the applicant, disallow the variation, and shall if not so satisfied confirm it. The decision of the court on any such application is final.

(6) References in this section to the variation of the rights of a class of members include references to their abrogation.

635 Copy of court order to be forwarded to the registrar

(1) The company must within 15 days after the making of an order by the court on an application under section 633 or 634 (objection to variation of class rights) forward a copy of the order to the registrar.

(2) If default is made in complying with this section an offence is committed by—

(a) the company, and

(b) every officer of the company who is in default.

(3) A person guilty of an offence under this section is liable on summary conviction to a fine not exceeding level 3 on the standard scale and, for continued contravention, a daily default fine not exceeding one-tenth of level 3 on the standard scale.

Matters to be notified to the registrar

636 Notice of name or other designation of class of shares

(1) Where a company assigns a name or other designation, or a new name or other designation, to any class or description of its shares, it must within one month from doing so deliver to the registrar a notice giving particulars of the name or designation so assigned.

(2) If default is made in complying with this section, an offence is committed by—

(a) the company, and

(b) every officer of the company who is in default.

(3) A person guilty of an offence under this section is liable on summary conviction to a fine not exceeding level 3 on the standard scale and, for continued contravention, a daily default fine not exceeding one-tenth of level 3 on the standard scale.

637 Notice of particulars of variation of rights attached to shares

(1) Where the rights attached to any shares of a company are varied, the company must within one month from the date on which the variation is made deliver to the registrar a notice giving particulars of the variation.

(2) If default is made in complying with this section, an offence is committed by—

(a) the company, and

(b) every officer of the company who is in default.

(3) A person guilty of an offence under this section is liable on summary conviction to a fine not exceeding level 3 on the standard scale and, for continued contravention, a daily default fine not exceeding one-tenth of level 3 on the standard scale.

638 Notice of new class of members

(1) If a company not having a share capital creates a new class of members, the company must within one month from the date on which the new class is created deliver to the registrar a notice containing particulars of the rights attached to that class.

(2) If default is made in complying with this section, an offence is committed by—

(a) the company, and

(b) every officer of the company who is in default.

(3) A person guilty of an offence under this section is liable on summary conviction to a fine not exceeding level 3 on the standard scale and, for continued contravention, a daily default fine not exceeding one-tenth of level 3 on the standard scale.

639 Notice of name or other designation of class of members

(1) Where a company not having a share capital assigns a name or other designation, or a new name or other designation, to any class of its members, it must within one month from doing so deliver to the registrar a notice giving particulars of the name or designation so assigned.

(2) If default is made in complying with this section, an offence is committed by—

(a) the company, and

(b) every officer of the company who is in default.

(3) A person guilty of an offence under this section is liable on summary conviction to a fine not exceeding level 3 on the standard scale and, for continued contravention, a daily default fine not exceeding one-tenth of level 3 on the standard scale.

640 Notice of particulars of variation of class rights

(1) If the rights of any class of members of a company not having a share capital are varied, the company must within one month from the date on which the variation is made deliver to the registrar a notice containing particulars of the variation.

(2) If default is made in complying with this section, an offence is committed by—

(a) the company, and

(b) every officer of the company who is in default.

(3) A person guilty of an offence under this section is liable on summary conviction to a fine not exceeding level 3 on the standard scale and, for continued contravention, a daily default fine not exceeding one-tenth of level 3 on the standard scale.

CHAPTER 10
REDUCTION OF SHARE CAPITAL

Introductory

641 Circumstances in which a company may reduce its share capital

(1) A limited company having a share capital may reduce its share capital—

(a) in the case of a private company limited by shares, by special resolution supported by a solvency statement (see sections 642 to 644);

(b) in any case, by special resolution confirmed by the court (see sections 645 to 651).

(2) A company may not reduce its capital under subsection (1)(a) if as a result of the reduction there would no longer be any member of the company holding shares other than redeemable shares.

(3) Subject to that, a company may reduce its share capital under this section in any way.

(4) In particular, a company may—

(a) extinguish or reduce the liability on any of its shares in respect of share capital not paid up, or

(b) either with or without extinguishing or reducing liability on any of its shares—

(i) cancel any paid-up share capital that is lost or unrepresented by available assets, or

(ii) repay any paid-up share capital in excess of the company's wants.

(5) A special resolution under this section may not provide for a reduction of share capital to take effect later than the date on which the resolution has effect in accordance with this Chapter.

(6) This Chapter (apart from subsection (5) above) has effect subject to any provision of the company's articles restricting or prohibiting the reduction of the company's share capital.

Private companies: reduction of capital supported by solvency statement

642 Reduction of capital supported by solvency statement

(1) A resolution for reducing share capital of a private company limited by shares is supported by a solvency statement if—

(a) the directors of the company make a statement of the solvency of the company in accordance with section 643 (a "solvency statement") not more than 15 days before the date on which the resolution is passed, and

(b) the resolution and solvency statement are registered in accordance with section 644.

(2) Where the resolution is proposed as a written resolution, a copy of the solvency statement must be sent or submitted to every eligible member at or before the time at which the proposed resolution is sent or submitted to him.

(3) Where the resolution is proposed at a general meeting, a copy of the solvency statement must be made available for inspection by members of the company throughout that meeting.

(4) The validity of a resolution is not affected by a failure to comply with subsection (2) or (3).

643 Solvency statement

(1) A solvency statement is a statement that each of the directors—

(a) has formed the opinion, as regards the company's situation at the date of the statement, that there is no ground on which the company could then be found to be unable to pay (or otherwise discharge) its debts; and

(b) has also formed the opinion—

(i) if it is intended to commence the winding up of the company within twelve months of that date, that the company will be able to pay (or otherwise discharge) its debts in full within twelve months of the commencement of the winding up; or

(ii) in any other case, that the company will be able to pay (or otherwise discharge) its debts as they fall due during the year immediately following that date.

(2) In forming those opinions, the directors must take into account all of the company's liabilities (including any contingent or prospective liabilities).

(3) The solvency statement must be in the prescribed form and must state—

(a) the date on which it is made, and

(b) the name of each director of the company.

(4) If the directors make a solvency statement without having reasonable grounds for the opinions expressed in it, and the statement is delivered to the registrar, an offence is committed by every director who is in default.

(5) A person guilty of an offence under subsection (4) is liable—

(a) on conviction on indictment, to imprisonment for a term not exceeding two years or a fine (or both);

(b) on summary conviction—

(i) in England and Wales, to imprisonment for a term not exceeding twelve months or to a fine not exceeding the statutory maximum (or both);

(ii) in Scotland or Northern Ireland, to imprisonment for a term not exceeding six months, or to a fine not exceeding the statutory maximum (or both).

644 Registration of resolution and supporting documents

(1) Within 15 days after the resolution for reducing share capital is passed the company must deliver to the registrar—

(a) a copy of the solvency statement, and

(b) a statement of capital.

This is in addition to the copy of the resolution itself that is required to be delivered to the registrar under Chapter 3 of Part 3.

(2) The statement of capital must state with respect to the company's share capital as reduced by the resolution—

(a) the total number of shares of the company,

(b) the aggregate nominal value of those shares,

(c) for each class of shares—

(i) prescribed particulars of the rights attached to the shares,

(ii) the total number of shares of that class, and

(iii) the aggregate nominal value of shares of that class, and

(d) the amount paid up and the amount (if any) unpaid on each share (whether on account of the nominal value of the share or by way of premium).

(3) The registrar must register the documents delivered to him under subsection (1) on receipt.

(4) The resolution does not take effect until those documents are registered.

(5) The company must also deliver to the registrar, within 15 days after the resolution is passed, a statement by the directors confirming that the solvency statement was—

(a) made not more than 15 days before the date on which the resolution was passed, and

(b) provided to members in accordance with section 642(2) or (3).

(6) The validity of a resolution is not affected by—

(a) a failure to deliver the documents required to be delivered to the registrar under subsection (1) within the time specified in that subsection, or
(b) a failure to comply with subsection (5).

(7) If the company delivers to the registrar a solvency statement that was not provided to members in accordance with section 642(2) or (3), an offence is committed by every officer of the company who is in default.

(8) If default is made in complying with this section, an offence is committed by—
(a) the company, and
(b) every officer of the company who is in default.

(9) A person guilty of an offence under subsection (7) or (8) is liable—
(a) on conviction on indictment, to a fine;
(b) on summary conviction, to a fine not exceeding the statutory maximum.

Reduction of capital confirmed by the court

645 Application to court for order of confirmation

(1) Where a company has passed a resolution for reducing share capital, it may apply to the court for an order confirming the reduction.

(2) If the proposed reduction of capital involves either—
(a) diminution of liability in respect of unpaid share capital, or
(b) the payment to a shareholder of any paid-up share capital,
section 646 (creditors entitled to object to reduction) applies unless the court directs otherwise.

(3) The court may, if having regard to any special circumstances of the case it thinks proper to do so, direct that section 646 is not to apply as regards any class or classes of creditors.

(4) The court may direct that section 646 is to apply in any other case.

646 Creditors entitled to object to reduction

(1) Where this section applies (see section 645(2) and (4)), every creditor of the company who—
(a) at the date fixed by the court is entitled to any debt or claim that, if that date were the commencement of the winding up of the company would be admissible in proof against the company, and
(b) can show that there is a real likelihood that the reduction would result in the company being unable to discharge his debt or claim when it fell due,
is entitled to object to the reduction of capital.

(2) The court shall settle a list of creditors entitled to object.

(3) For that purpose the court—
(a) shall ascertain, as far as possible without requiring an application from any creditor, the names of those creditors and the nature and amount of their debts or claims, and
(b) may publish notices fixing a day or days within which creditors not entered on the list are to claim to be so entered or are to be excluded from the right of objecting to the reduction of capital.

(4) If a creditor entered on the list whose debt or claim is not discharged or has not determined does not consent to the reduction, the court may, if it thinks fit, dispense with the consent of that creditor on the company securing payment of his debt or claim.

(5) For this purpose the debt or claim must be secured by appropriating (as the court may direct) the following amount—
(a) if the company admits the full amount of the debt or claim or, though not admitting it, is willing to provide for it, the full amount of the debt or claim;
(b) if the company does not admit, and is not willing to provide for, the full amount of the debt or claim, or if the amount is contingent or not ascertained, an amount fixed by the court after the like enquiry and adjudication as if the company were being wound up by the court.

647 Offences in connection with list of creditors

(1) If an officer of the company—
(a) intentionally or recklessly—

(i) conceals the name of a creditor entitled to object to the reduction of capital, or

(ii) misrepresents the nature or amount of the debt or claim of a creditor, or

(b) is knowingly concerned in any such concealment or misrepresentation, he commits an offence.

(2) A person guilty of an offence under this section is liable—

(a) on conviction on indictment, to a fine;

(b) on summary conviction, to a fine not exceeding the statutory maximum.

648 Court order confirming reduction

(1) The court may make an order confirming the reduction of capital on such terms and conditions as it thinks fit.

(2) The court must not confirm the reduction unless it is satisfied, with respect to every creditor of the company who is entitled to object to the reduction of capital that either—

(a) his consent to the reduction has been obtained, or

(b) his debt or claim has been discharged, or has determined or has been secured.

(3) Where the court confirms the reduction, it may order the company to publish (as the court directs) the reasons for reduction of capital, or such other information in regard to it as the court thinks expedient with a view to giving proper information to the public, and (if the court thinks fit) the causes that led to the reduction.

(4) The court may, if for any special reason it thinks proper to do so, make an order directing that the company must, during such period (commencing on or at any time after the date of the order) as is specified in the order, add to its name as its last words the words "and reduced".

If such an order is made, those words are, until the end of the period specified in the order, deemed to be part of the company's name.

649 Registration of order and statement of capital

(1) The registrar, on production of an order of the court confirming the reduction of a company's share capital and the delivery of a copy of the order and of a statement of capital (approved by the court), shall register the order and statement.

This is subject to section 650 (public company reducing capital below authorised minimum).

(2) The statement of capital must state with respect to the company's share capital as altered by the order—

(a) the total number of shares of the company,

(b) the aggregate nominal value of those shares,

(c) for each class of shares—

(i) prescribed particulars of the rights attached to the shares,

(ii) the total number of shares of that class, and

(iii) the aggregate nominal value of shares of that class, and

(d) the amount paid up and the amount (if any) unpaid on each share (whether on account of the nominal value of the share or by way of premium).

(3) The resolution for reducing share capital, as confirmed by the court's order, takes effect—

(a) in the case of a reduction of share capital that forms part of a compromise or arrangement sanctioned by the court under Part 26 (arrangements and reconstructions)—

(i) on delivery of the order and statement of capital to the registrar, or

(ii) if the court so orders, on the registration of the order and statement of capital;

(b) in any other case, on the registration of the order and statement of capital.

(4) Notice of the registration of the order and statement of capital must be published in such manner as the court may direct.

(5) The registrar must certify the registration of the order and statement of capital.

(6) The certificate—

(a) must be signed by the registrar or authenticated by the registrar's official seal, and

(b) is conclusive evidence—

(i) that the requirements of this Act with respect to the reduction of share capital have been complied with, and

(ii) that the company's share capital is as stated in the statement of capital.

Public company reducing capital below authorised minimum

650 Public company reducing capital below authorised minimum

(1) This section applies where the court makes an order confirming a reduction of a public company's capital that has the effect of bringing the nominal value of its allotted share capital below the authorised minimum.

(2) The registrar must not register the order unless either—

(a) the court so directs, or

(b) the company is first re-registered as a private company.

(3) Section 651 provides an expedited procedure for re-registration in these circumstances.

651 Expedited procedure for re-registration as a private company

(1) The court may authorise the company to be re-registered as a private company without its having passed the special resolution required by section 97.

(2) If it does so, the court must specify in the order the changes to the company's name and articles to be made in connection with the re-registration.

(3) The company may then be re-registered as a private company if an application to that effect is delivered to the registrar together with—

(a) a copy of the court's order, and

(b) notice of the company's name, and a copy of the company's articles, as altered by the court's order.

(4) On receipt of such an application the registrar must issue a certificate of incorporation altered to meet the circumstances of the case.

(5) The certificate must state that it is issued on re-registration and the date on which it is issued.

(6) On the issue of the certificate—

(a) the company by virtue of the issue of the certificate becomes a private company, and

(b) the changes in the company's name and articles take effect.

(7) The certificate is conclusive evidence that the requirements of this Act as to re-registration have been complied with.

Effect of reduction of capital

652 Liability of members following reduction of capital

(1) Where a company's share capital is reduced a member of the company (past or present) is not liable in respect of any share to any call or contribution exceeding in amount the difference (if any) between—

(a) the nominal amount of the share as notified to the registrar in the statement of capital delivered under section 644 or 649, and

(b) the amount paid on the share or the reduced amount (if any) which is deemed to have been paid on it, as the case may be.

(2) This is subject to section 653 (liability to creditor in case of omission from list).

(3) Nothing in this section affects the rights of the contributories among themselves.

653 Liability to creditor in case of omission from list of creditors

(1) This section applies where, in the case of a reduction of capital confirmed by the court—

(a) a creditor entitled to object to the reduction of share capital is by reason of his ignorance—

(i) of the proceedings for reduction of share capital, or

(ii) of their nature and effect with respect to his debt or claim, not entered on the list of creditors, and

(b) after the reduction of capital the company is unable to pay the amount of his debt or claim.

(2) Every person who was a member of the company at the date on which the resolution for reducing capital took effect under section 649(3) is liable to contribute for the payment of the debt or claim an amount not exceeding that which he would have been liable to contribute if the company had commenced to be wound up on the day before that date.

(3) If the company is wound up, the court on the application of the creditor in question, and proof of ignorance as mentioned in subsection (1)(a), may if it thinks fit—

(a) settle accordingly a list of persons liable to contribute under this section, and

(b) make and enforce calls and orders on them as if they were ordinary contributories in a winding up.

(4) The reference in subsection (1) (b) to a company being unable to pay the amount of a debt or claim has the same meaning as in section 123 of the Insolvency Act 1986 or Article 103 of the Insolvency (Northern Ireland) Order 1989.

CHAPTER 11
MISCELLANEOUS AND SUPPLEMENTARY PROVISIONS

654 Treatment of reserve arising from reduction of capital

(1) A reserve arising from the reduction of a company's share capital is not distributable, subject to any provision made by order under this section.

(2) The Secretary of State may by order specify cases in which—

(a) the prohibition in subsection (1) does not apply, and

(b) the reserve is to be treated for the purposes of Part 23 (distributions) as a realised profit.

(3) An order under this section is subject to affirmative resolution procedure.

655 Shares no bar to damages against company

A person is not debarred from obtaining damages or other compensation from a company by reason only of his holding or having held shares in the company or any right to apply or subscribe for shares or to be included in the company's register of members in respect of shares.

656 Public companies: duty of directors to call meeting on serious loss of capital

(1) Where the net assets of a public company are half or less of its called-up share capital, the directors must call a general meeting of the company to consider whether any, and if so what, steps should be taken to deal with the situation.

(2) They must do so not later than 28 days from the earliest day on which that fact is known to a director of the company.

(3) The meeting must be convened for a date not later than 56 days from that day.

(4) If there is a failure to convene a meeting as required by this section, each of the directors of the company who—

(a) knowingly authorises or permits the failure, or

(b) after the period during which the meeting should have been convened, knowingly authorises or permits the failure to continue,

commits an offence.

(5) A person guilty of an offence under this section is liable—

(a) on conviction on indictment, to a fine;

(b) on summary conviction, to a fine not exceeding the statutory maximum.

(6) Nothing in this section authorises the consideration at a meeting convened in pursuance of subsection (1) of any matter that could not have been considered at that meeting apart from this section.

657 General power to make further provision by regulations

(1) The Secretary of State may by regulations modify the following provisions of this Part—

sections 552 and 553 (prohibited commissions, discounts and allowances),

Chapter 5 (payment for shares),

Chapter 6 (public companies: independent valuation of non-cash consideration),

Chapter 7 (share premiums),
sections 622 to 628 (redenomination of share capital),
Chapter 10 (reduction of capital), and
section 656 (public companies: duty of directors to call meeting on serious loss of capital).

(2) The regulations may—

(a) amend or repeal any of those provisions, or

(b) make such other provision as appears to the Secretary of State appropriate in place of any of those provisions.

(3) Regulations under this section may make consequential amendments or repeals in other provisions of this Act, or in other enactments.

(4) Regulations under this section are subject to affirmative resolution procedure.

PART 18
ACQUISITION BY LIMITED COMPANY OF ITS OWN SHARES

CHAPTER 1
GENERAL PROVISIONS

Introductory

658 General rule against limited company acquiring its own shares

(1) A limited company must not acquire its own shares, whether by purchase, subscription or otherwise, except in accordance with the provisions of this Part.

(2) If a company purports to act in contravention of this section—

(a) an offence is committed by—

(i) the company, and

(i) every officer of the company who is in default, and

(b) the purported acquisition is void.

(3) A person guilty of an offence under this section is liable—

(a) on conviction on indictment, to imprisonment for a term not exceeding two years or a fine (or both);

(b) on summary conviction—

(i) in England and Wales, to imprisonment for a term not exceeding twelve months or a fine not exceeding the statutory maximum (or both);

(ii) in Scotland or Northern Ireland, to imprisonment for a term not exceeding six months or a fine not exceeding the statutory maximum (or both).

659 Exceptions to general rule

(1) A limited company may acquire any of its own fully paid shares otherwise than for valuable consideration.

(2) Section 658 does not prohibit—

(a) the acquisition of shares in a reduction of capital duly made;

(b) the purchase of shares in pursuance of an order of the court under—

(i) section 98 (application to court to cancel resolution for re-registration as a private company),

(ii) section 721(6) (powers of court on objection to redemption or purchase of shares out of capital),

(iii) section 759 (remedial order in case of breach of prohibition of public offers by private company), or

(iv) Part 30 (protection of members against unfair prejudice);

(c) the forfeiture of shares, or the acceptance of shares surrendered in lieu, in pursuance of the company's articles, for failure to pay any sum payable in respect of the shares.

Shares held by company's nominee

660 Treatment of shares held by nominee

(1) This section applies where shares in a limited company—
  (a) are taken by a subscriber to the memorandum as nominee of the company,
  (b) are issued to a nominee of the company, or
  (c) are acquired by a nominee of the company, partly paid up, from a third person.

(2) For all purposes—
  (a) the shares are to be treated as held by the nominee on his own account, and
  (b) the company is to be regarded as having no beneficial interest in them.

(3) This section does not apply—
  (a) to shares acquired otherwise than by subscription by a nominee of a public company, where—
    (i) a person acquires shares in the company with financial assistance given to him, directly or indirectly, by the company for the purpose of or in connection with the acquisition, and
    (ii) the company has a beneficial interest in the shares;
  (b) to shares acquired by a nominee of the company when the company has no beneficial interest in the shares.

661 Liability of others where nominee fails to make payment in respect of shares

(1) This section applies where shares in a limited company—
  (a) are taken by a subscriber to the memorandum as nominee of the company,
  (b) are issued to a nominee of the company, or
  (c) are acquired by a nominee of the company, partly paid up, from a third person.

(2) If the nominee, having been called on to pay any amount for the purposes of paying up, or paying any premium on, the shares, fails to pay that amount within 21 days from being called on to do so, then—
  (a) in the case of shares that he agreed to take as subscriber to the memorandum, the other subscribers to the memorandum, and
  (b) in any other case, the directors of the company when the shares were issued to or acquired by him,

are jointly and severally liable with him to pay that amount.

(3) If in proceedings for the recovery of an amount under subsection (2) it appears to the court that the subscriber or director—
  (a) has acted honestly and reasonably, and
  (b) having regard to all the circumstances of the case, ought fairly to be relieved from liability,

the court may relieve him, either wholly or in part, from his liability on such terms as the court thinks fit.

(4) If a subscriber to a company's memorandum or a director of a company has reason to apprehend that a claim will or might be made for the recovery of any such amount from him—
  (a) he may apply to the court for relief, and
  (b) the court has the same power to relieve him as it would have had in proceedings for recovery of that amount.

(5) This section does not apply to shares acquired by a nominee of the company when the company has no beneficial interest in the shares.

Shares held by or for public company

662 Duty to cancel shares in public company held by or for the company

(1) This section applies in the case of a public company—
  (a) where shares in the company are forfeited, or surrendered to the company in lieu of forfeiture, in pursuance of the articles, for failure to pay any sum payable in respect of the shares;

(b) where shares in the company are surrendered to the company in pursuance of section 102C(1)(b) of the Building Societies Act 1986;

(c) where shares in the company are acquired by it (otherwise than in accordance with this Part or Part 30 (protection of members against unfair prejudice)) and the company has a beneficial interest in the shares;

(d) where a nominee of the company acquires shares in the company from a third party without financial assistance being given directly or indirectly by the company and the company has a beneficial interest in the shares; or

(e) where a person acquires shares in the company, with financial assistance given to him, directly or indirectly, by the company for the purpose of or in connection with the acquisition, and the company has a beneficial interest in the shares.

(2) Unless the shares or any interest of the company in them are previously disposed of, the company must—

(a) cancel the shares and diminish the amount of the company's share capital by the nominal value of the shares cancelled, and

(b) where the effect is that the nominal value of the company's allotted share capital is brought below the authorised minimum, apply for re-registration as a private company, stating the effect of the cancellation.

(3) It must do so no later than—

(a) in a case within subsection (1)(a) or (b), three years from the date of the forfeiture or surrender;

(b) in a case within subsection (1)(c) or (d), three years from the date of the acquisition;

(c) in a case within subsection (1)(e), one year from the date of the acquisition.

(4) The directors of the company may take any steps necessary to enable the company to comply with this section, and may do so without complying with the provisions of Chapter 10 of Part 17 (reduction of capital).

See also section 664 (re-registration as private company in consequence of cancellation).

(5) Neither the company nor, in a case within subsection (1)(d) or (e), the nominee or other shareholder may exercise any voting rights in respect of the shares.

(6) Any purported exercise of those rights is void.

663 Notice of cancellation of shares

(1) Where a company cancels shares in order to comply with section 662, it must within one month after the shares are cancelled give notice to the registrar, specifying the shares cancelled.

(2) The notice must be accompanied by a statement of capital.

(3) The statement of capital must state with respect to the company's share capital immediately following the cancellation—

(a) the total number of shares of the company,

(b) the aggregate nominal value of those shares,

(c) for each class of shares—

(i) prescribed particulars of the rights attached to the shares,

(ii) the total number of shares of that class, and

(iii) the aggregate nominal value of shares of that class, and

(d) the amount paid up and the amount (if any) unpaid on each share (whether on account of the nominal value of the share or by way of premium).

(4) If default is made in complying with this section, an offence is committed by—

(a) the company, and

(b) every officer of the company who is in default.

(5) A person guilty of an offence under this section is liable on summary conviction to a fine not exceeding level 3 on the standard scale and, for continued contravention, a daily default fine not exceeding one-tenth of level 3 on the standard scale.

664 Re-registration as private company in consequence of cancellation

(1) Where a company is obliged to re-register as a private company to comply with section 662, the directors may resolve that the company should be so re-registered.

Chapter 3 of Part 3 (resolutions affecting a company's constitution) applies to any such resolution.

(2) The resolution may make such changes—

(a) in the company's name, and

(b) in the company's articles,

as are necessary in connection with its becoming a private company.

(3) The application for re-registration must contain a statement of the company's proposed name on re-registration.

(4) The application must be accompanied by—

(a) a copy of the resolution (unless a copy has already been forwarded under Chapter 3 of Part 3),

(b) a copy of the company's articles as amended by the resolution, and

(c) a statement of compliance.

(5) The statement of compliance required is a statement that the requirements of this section as to re-registration as a private company have been complied with.

(6) The registrar may accept the statement of compliance as sufficient evidence that the company is entitled to be re-registered as a private company.

665 Issue of certificate of incorporation on re-registration

(1) If on an application under section 664 the registrar is satisfied that the company is entitled to be re-registered as a private company, the company shall be re-registered accordingly.

(2) The registrar must issue a certificate of incorporation altered to meet the circumstances of the case.

(3) The certificate must state that it is issued on re-registration and the date on which it is issued.

(4) On the issue of the certificate—

(a) the company by virtue of the issue of the certificate becomes a private company, and

(b) the changes in the company's name and articles take effect.

(5) The certificate is conclusive evidence that the requirements of this Act as to re-registration have been complied with.

666 Effect of failure to re-register

(1) If a public company that is required by section 662 to apply to be re-registered as a private company fails to do so before the end of the period specified in subsection (3) of that section, Chapter 1 of Part 20 (prohibition of public offers by private company) applies to it as if it were a private company.

(2) Subject to that, the company continues to be treated as a public company until it is so re-registered.

667 Offence in case of failure to cancel shares or re-register

(1) This section applies where a company, when required to do by section 662—

(a) fails to cancel any shares, or

(b) fails to make an application for re-registration as a private company, within the time specified in subsection (3) of that section.

(2) An offence is committed by—

(a) the company, and

(b) every officer of the company who is in default.

(3) A person guilty of an offence under this section is liable on summary conviction to a fine not exceeding level 3 on the standard scale and, for continued contravention, a daily default fine not exceeding one-tenth of level 3 on the standard scale.

668 Application of provisions to company re-registering as public company

(1) This section applies where, after shares in a private company—

(a) are forfeited in pursuance of the company's articles or are surrendered to the company in lieu of forfeiture,
(b) are acquired by the company (otherwise than by any of the methods permitted by this Part or Part 30 (protection of members against unfair prejudice)), the company having a beneficial interest in the shares,
(c) are acquired by a nominee of the company from a third party without financial assistance being given directly or indirectly by the company, the company having a beneficial interest in the shares, or
(d) are acquired by a person with financial assistance given to him, directly or indirectly, by the company for the purpose of or in connection with the acquisition, the company having a beneficial interest in the shares,

the company is re-registered as a public company.

(2) In that case the provisions of sections 662 to 667 apply to the company as if it had been a public company at the time of the forfeiture, surrender or acquisition, subject to the following modification.

(3) The modification is that the period specified in section 662(3)(a), (b) or (c) (period for complying with obligations under that section) runs from the date of the re-registration of the company as a public company.

669 Transfer to reserve on acquisition of shares by public company or nominee

(1) Where—
(a) a public company, or a nominee of a public company, acquires shares in the company, and
(b) those shares are shown in a balance sheet of the company as an asset, an amount equal to the value of the shares must be transferred out of profits available for dividend to a reserve fund and is not then available for distribution.

(2) Subsection (1) applies to an interest in shares as it applies to shares.
As it so applies the reference to the value of the shares shall be read as a reference to the value to the company of its interest in the shares.

Charges of public company on own shares

670 Public companies: general rule against lien or charge on own shares

(1) A lien or other charge of a public company on its own shares (whether taken expressly or otherwise) is void, except as permitted by this section.

(2) In the case of any description of company, a charge is permitted if the shares are not fully paid up and the charge is for an amount payable in respect of the shares.

(3) In the case of a company whose ordinary business—
(a) includes the lending of money, or
(b) consists of the provision of credit or the bailment (in Scotland, hiring) of goods under a hire-purchase agreement, or both,

a charge is permitted (whether the shares are fully paid or not) if it arises in connection with a transaction entered into by the company in the ordinary course of that business.

(4) In the case of a company that has been re-registered as a public company, a charge is permitted if it was in existence immediately before the application for re-registration.

Supplementary provisions

671 Interests to be disregarded in determining whether company has beneficial interest

In determining for the purposes of this Chapter whether a company has a beneficial interest in shares, there shall be disregarded any such interest as is mentioned in—
section 672 (residual interest under pension scheme or employees' share scheme),
section 673 (employer's charges and other rights of recovery), or section 674 (rights as personal representative or trustee).

672 Residual interest under pension scheme or employees' share scheme

(1) Where the shares are held on trust for the purposes of a pension scheme or employees' share scheme, there shall be disregarded any residual interest of the company that has not vested in possession.

(2) A "residual interest" means a right of the company to receive any of the trust property in the event of—

(a) all the liabilities arising under the scheme having been satisfied or provided for, or
(b) the company ceasing to participate in the scheme, or
(c) the trust property at any time exceeding what is necessary for satisfying the liabilities arising or expected to arise under the scheme.

(3) In subsection (2)—

(a) the reference to a right includes a right dependent on the exercise of a discretion vested by the scheme in the trustee or another person, and
(b) the reference to liabilities arising under a scheme includes liabilities that have resulted, or may result, from the exercise of any such discretion.

(4) For the purposes of this section a residual interest vests in possession—

(a) in a case within subsection (2)(a), on the occurrence of the event mentioned there (whether or not the amount of the property receivable pursuant to the right is ascertained);
(b) in a case within subsection (2)(b) or (c), when the company becomes entitled to require the trustee to transfer to it any of the property receivable pursuant to that right.

(5) Where by virtue of this section shares are exempt from section 660 or 661 (shares held by company's nominee) at the time they are taken, issued or acquired but the residual interest in question vests in possession before they are disposed of or fully paid up, those sections apply to the shares as if they had been taken, issued or acquired on the date on which that interest vests in possession.

(6) Where by virtue of this section shares are exempt from sections 662 to 668 (shares held by or for public company) at the time they are acquired but the residual interest in question vests in possession before they are disposed of, those sections apply to the shares as if they had been acquired on the date on which the interest vests in possession.

673 Employer's charges and other rights of recovery

(1) Where the shares are held on trust for the purposes of a pension scheme there shall be disregarded—

(a) any charge or lien on, or set-off against, any benefit or other right or interest under the scheme for the purpose of enabling the employer or former employer of a member of the scheme to obtain the discharge of a monetary obligation due to him from the member;
(b) any right to receive from the trustee of the scheme, or as trustee of the scheme to retain, an amount that can be recovered or retained—
   (i) under section 61 of the Pension Schemes Act 1993, or otherwise, as reimbursement or partial reimbursement for any contributions equivalent premium paid in connection with the scheme under Part 3 of that Act, or
   (ii) under section 57 of the Pension Schemes (Northern Ireland) Act 1993, or otherwise, as reimbursement or partial reimbursement for any contributions equivalent premium paid in connection with the scheme under Part 3 of that Act.

(2) Where the shares are held on trust for the purposes of an employees' share scheme, there shall be disregarded any charge or lien on, or set-off against, any benefit or other right or interest under the scheme for the purpose of enabling the employer or former employer of a member of the scheme to obtain the discharge of a monetary obligation due to him from the member.

674 Rights as personal representative or trustee

Where the company is a personal representative or trustee, there shall be disregarded any rights that the company has in that capacity including, in particular—

(a) any right to recover its expenses or be remunerated out of the estate or trust property, and

(b) any right to be indemnified out of that property for any liability incurred by reason of any act or omission of the company in the performance of its duties as personal representative or trustee.

675 Meaning of "pension scheme"

(1) In this Chapter "pension scheme" means a scheme for the provision of benefits consisting of or including relevant benefits for or in respect of employees or former employees.

(2) In subsection (1) "relevant benefits" means any pension, lump sum, gratuity or other like benefit given or to be given on retirement or on death or in anticipation of retirement or, in connection with past service, after retirement or death.

676 Application of provisions to directors

For the purposes of this Chapter references to "employer" and "employee", in the context of a pension scheme or employees' share scheme, shall be read as if a director of a company were employed by it.

CHAPTER 2
FINANCIAL ASSISTANCE FOR PURCHASE OF OWN SHARES

Introductory

677 Meaning of "financial assistance"

(1) In this Chapter "financial assistance" means—

(a) financial assistance given by way of gift,

(b) financial assistance given—

(i) by way of guarantee, security or indemnity (other than an indemnity in respect of the indemnifier's own neglect or default), or

(ii) by way of release or waiver,

(c) financial assistance given—

(i) by way of a loan or any other agreement under which any of the obligations of the person giving the assistance are to be fulfilled at a time when in accordance with the agreement any obligation of another party to the agreement remains unfulfilled, or

(ii) by way of the novation of, or the assignment (in Scotland, assignation) of rights arising under, a loan or such other agreement, or

(d) any other financial assistance given by a company where—

(i) the net assets of the company are reduced to a material extent by the giving of the assistance, or

(ii) the company has no net assets.

(2) "Net assets" here means the aggregate amount of the company's assets less the aggregate amount of its liabilities.

(3) For this purpose a company's liabilities include—

(a) where the company draws up Companies Act individual accounts, any provision of a kind specified for the purposes of this subsection by regulations under section 396, and

(b) where the company draws up IAS individual accounts, any provision made in those accounts.

Circumstances in which financial assistance prohibited

678 Assistance for acquisition of shares in public company

(1) Where a person is acquiring or proposing to acquire shares in a public company, it is not lawful for that company, or a company that is a subsidiary of that company, to give financial assistance directly or indirectly for the purpose of the acquisition before or at the same time as the acquisition takes place.

(2) Subsection (1) does not prohibit a company from giving financial assistance for the acquisition of shares in it or its holding company if—

(a) the company's principal purpose in giving the assistance is not to give it for the purpose of any such acquisition, or

(b) the giving of the assistance for that purpose is only an incidental part of some larger purpose of the company,

and the assistance is given in good faith in the interests of the company.

(3) Where—

(a) a person has acquired shares in a company, and

(b) a liability has been incurred (by that or another person) for the purpose of the acquisition,

it is not lawful for that company, or a company that is a subsidiary of that company, to give financial assistance directly or indirectly for the purpose of reducing or discharging the liability if, at the time the assistance is given, the company in which the shares were acquired is a public company.

(4) Subsection (3) does not prohibit a company from giving financial assistance if—

(a) the company's principal purpose in giving the assistance is not to reduce or discharge any liability incurred by a person for the purpose of the acquisition of shares in the company or its holding company, or

(b) the reduction or discharge of any such liability is only an incidental part of some larger purpose of the company,

and the assistance is given in good faith in the interests of the company.

(5) This section has effect subject to sections 681 and 682 (unconditional and conditional exceptions to prohibition).

679 Assistance by public company for acquisition of shares in its private holding company

(1) Where a person is acquiring or proposing to acquire shares in a private company, it is not lawful for a public company that is a subsidiary of that company to give financial assistance directly or indirectly for the purpose of the acquisition before or at the same time as the acquisition takes place.

(2) Subsection (1) does not prohibit a company from giving financial assistance for the acquisition of shares in its holding company if—

(a) the company's principal purpose in giving the assistance is not to give it for the purpose of any such acquisition, or

(b) the giving of the assistance for that purpose is only an incidental part of some larger purpose of the company,

and the assistance is given in good faith in the interests of the company.

(3) Where—

(a) a person has acquired shares in a private company, and

(b) a liability has been incurred (by that or another person) for the purpose of the acquisition,

it is not lawful for a public company that is a subsidiary of that company to give financial assistance directly or indirectly for the purpose of reducing or discharging the liability.

(4) Subsection (3) does not prohibit a company from giving financial assistance if—

(a) the company's principal purpose in giving the assistance is not to reduce or discharge any liability incurred by a person for the purpose of the acquisition of shares in its holding company, or

(b) the reduction or discharge of any such liability is only an incidental part of some larger purpose of the company,

and the assistance is given in good faith in the interests of the company.

(5) This section has effect subject to sections 681 and 682 (unconditional and conditional exceptions to prohibition).

680 Prohibited financial assistance an offence

(1) If a company contravenes section 678(1) or (3) or section 679(1) or (3) (prohibited financial assistance) an offence is committed by—

(a) the company, and

(b) every officer of the company who is in default.

(2) A person guilty of an offence under this section is liable—

(a) on conviction on indictment, to imprisonment for a term not exceeding two years or a fine (or both);

(b) on summary conviction—

(i) in England and Wales, to imprisonment for a term not exceeding twelve months or to a fine not exceeding the statutory maximum (or both);

(ii) in Scotland or Northern Ireland, to imprisonment for a term not exceeding six months, or to a fine not exceeding the statutory maximum (or both).

Exceptions from prohibition

681 Unconditional exceptions

(1) Neither section 678 nor section 679 prohibits a transaction to which this section applies.

(2) Those transactions are—

(a) a distribution of the company's assets by way of—

(i) dividend lawfully made, or

(ii) distribution in the course of a company's winding up;

(b) an allotment of bonus shares;

(c) a reduction of capital under Chapter 10 of Part 17;

(d) a redemption of shares under Chapter 3 or a purchase of shares under Chapter 4 of this Part;

(e) anything done in pursuance of an order of the court under Part 26 (order sanctioning compromise or arrangement with members or creditors);

(f) anything done under an arrangement made in pursuance of section 110 of the Insolvency Act 1986 or Article 96 of the Insolvency (Northern Ireland) Order 1989 (liquidator in winding up accepting shares as consideration for sale of company's property);

(g) anything done under an arrangement made between a company and its creditors that is binding on the creditors by virtue of Part 1 of the Insolvency Act 1986 or Part 2 of the Insolvency (Northern Ireland) Order 1989.

682 Conditional exceptions

(1) Neither section 678 nor section 679 prohibits a transaction to which this section applies—

(a) if the company giving the assistance is a private company, or

(b) if the company giving the assistance is a public company and—

(i) the company has net assets that are not reduced by the giving of the assistance, or

(ii) to the extent that those assets are so reduced, the assistance is provided out of distributable profits.

(2) The transactions to which this section applies are—

(a) where the lending of money is part of the ordinary business of the company, the lending of money in the ordinary course of the company's business;

(b) the provision by the company, in good faith in the interests of the company or its holding company, of financial assistance for the purposes of an employees' share scheme;

(c) the provision of financial assistance by the company for the purposes of or in connection with anything done by the company (or another company in the same group) for the purpose of enabling or facilitating transactions in shares in the first-mentioned company or its holding company between, and involving the acquisition of beneficial ownership of those shares by—

(i) bona fide employees or former employees of that company (or another company in the same group), or

(ii) spouses or civil partners, widows, widowers or surviving civil partners, or minor children or step-children of any such employees or former employees;

(d) the making by the company of loans to persons (other than directors) employed in good faith by the company with a view to enabling those persons to acquire fully paid shares in the company or its holding company to be held by them by way of beneficial ownership.

(3) The references in this section to "net assets" are to the amount by which the aggregate of the company's assets exceeds the aggregate of its liabilities.

(4) For this purpose—

(a) the amount of both assets and liabilities shall be taken to be as stated in the company's accounting records immediately before the financial assistance is given, and

(b) "liabilities" includes any amount retained as reasonably necessary for the purpose of providing for a liability the nature of which is clearly defined and that is either likely to be incurred or certain to be incurred but uncertain as to amount or as to the date on which it will arise.

(5) For the purposes of subsection (2) (c) a company is in the same group as another company if it is a holding company or subsidiary of that company or a subsidiary of a holding company of that company.

Supplementary

683 Definitions for this Chapter

(1) In this Chapter—

"distributable profits", in relation to the giving of any financial assistance—

(a) means those profits out of which the company could lawfully make a distribution equal in value to that assistance, and

(b) includes, in a case where the financial assistance consists of or includes, or is treated as arising in consequence of, the sale, transfer or other disposition of a non-cash asset, any profit that, if the company were to make a distribution of that character would be available for that purpose (see section 846); and

"distribution" has the same meaning as in Part 23 (distributions) (see section 829).

(2) In this Chapter—

(a) a reference to a person incurring a liability includes his changing his financial position by making an agreement or arrangement (whether enforceable or unenforceable, and whether made on his own account or with any other person) or by any other means, and

(b) a reference to a company giving financial assistance for the purposes of reducing or discharging a liability incurred by a person for the purpose of the acquisition of shares includes its giving such assistance for the purpose of wholly or partly restoring his financial position to what it was before the acquisition took place.

CHAPTER 3
REDEEMABLE SHARES

684 Power of limited company to issue redeemable shares

(1) A limited company having a share capital may issue shares that are to be redeemed or are liable to be redeemed at the option of the company or the shareholder ("redeemable shares"), subject to the following provisions.

(2) The articles of a private limited company may exclude or restrict the issue of redeemable shares.

(3) A public limited company may only issue redeemable shares if it is authorised to do so by its articles.

(4) No redeemable shares may be issued at a time when there are no issued shares of the company that are not redeemable.

685 Terms and manner of redemption

(1) The directors of a limited company may determine the terms, conditions and manner of redemption of shares if they are authorised to do so—

(a) by the company's articles, or

(b) by a resolution of the company.

(2) A resolution under subsection (1)(b) may be an ordinary resolution, even though it amends the company's articles.

(3) Where the directors are authorised under subsection (1) to determine the terms, conditions and manner of redemption of shares—
(a) they must do so before the shares are allotted, and
(b) any obligation of the company to state in a statement of capital the rights attached to the shares extends to the terms, conditions and manner of redemption.
(4) Where the directors are not so authorised, the terms, conditions and manner of redemption of any redeemable shares must be stated in the company's articles.

686 Payment for redeemable shares

(1) Redeemable shares in a limited company may not be redeemed unless they are fully paid.
(2) The terms of redemption of shares in a limited company may provide that the amount payable on redemption may, by agreement between the company and the holder of the shares, be paid on a date later than the redemption date.
(3) Unless redeemed in accordance with a provision authorised by subsection (2), the shares must be paid for on redemption.

687 Financing of redemption

(1) A private limited company may redeem redeemable shares out of capital in accordance with Chapter 5.
(2) Subject to that, redeemable shares in a limited company may only be redeemed out of—
(a) distributable profits of the company, or
(b) the proceeds of a fresh issue of shares made for the purposes of the redemption.
(3) Any premium payable on redemption of shares in a limited company must be paid out of distributable profits of the company, subject to the following provision.
(4) If the redeemable shares were issued at a premium, any premium payable on their redemption may be paid out of the proceeds of a fresh issue of shares made for the purposes of the redemption, up to an amount equal to—
(a) the aggregate of the premiums received by the company on the issue of the shares redeemed, or
(b) the current amount of the company's share premium account (including any sum transferred to that account in respect of premiums on the new shares),

whichever is the less.
(5) The amount of the company's share premium account is reduced by a sum corresponding (or by sums in the aggregate corresponding) to the amount of any payment made under subsection (4).
(6) This section is subject to section 735(4) (terms of redemption enforceable in a winding up).

688 Redeemed shares treated as cancelled

Where shares in a limited company are redeemed—
(a) the shares are treated as cancelled, and
(b) the amount of the company's issued share capital is diminished accordingly by the nominal value of the shares redeemed.

689 Notice to registrar of redemption

(1) If a limited company redeems any redeemable shares it must within one month after doing so give notice to the registrar, specifying the shares redeemed.
(2) The notice must be accompanied by a statement of capital.
(3) The statement of capital must state with respect to the company's share capital immediately following the redemption—
(a) the total number of shares of the company,
(b) the aggregate nominal value of those shares,
(c) for each class of shares—
(i) prescribed particulars of the rights attached to the shares,
(ii) the total number of shares of that class, and
(iii) the aggregate nominal value of shares of that class, and

(d) the amount paid up and the amount (if any) unpaid on each share (whether on account of the nominal value of the share or by way of premium).

(4) If default is made in complying with this section, an offence is committed by—

(a) the company, and

(b) every officer of the company who is in default.

(5) A person guilty of an offence under this section is liable on summary conviction to a fine not exceeding level 3 on the standard scale and, for continued contravention, a daily default fine not exceeding one-tenth of level 3 on the standard scale.

CHAPTER 4
PURCHASE OF OWN SHARES

General provisions

690 Power of limited company to purchase own shares

(1) A limited company having a share capital may purchase its own shares (including any redeemable shares), subject to—

(a) the following provisions of this Chapter, and

(b) any restriction or prohibition in the company's articles.

(2) A limited company may not purchase its own shares if as a result of the purchase there would no longer be any issued shares of the company other than redeemable shares or shares held as treasury shares.

691 Payment for purchase of own shares

(1) A limited company may not purchase its own shares unless they are fully paid.

(2) Where a limited company purchases its own shares, the shares must be paid for on purchase.

(3) But subsection (2) does not apply in a case where a private limited company is purchasing shares for the purposes of or pursuant to an employees' share scheme.

692 Financing of purchase of own shares

(1) A private limited company may purchase its own shares—

(a) out of capital in accordance with Chapter 5, and

(b) with cash (if authorised to do so by its articles) up to an amount in a financial year not exceeding the lower of—

(i) £15,000, or

(ii) the value of 5% of its share capital.

(1A) If the share capital of the company is not denominated in sterling, the value in sterling of the share capital shall be calculated for the purposes of subsection (1)(b)(ii) at an appropriate spot rate of exchange.

(1B) The rate must be a rate prevailing on a day specified in the resolution authorising the purchase of the shares.

(2) Subject to subsection (1)—

(a) a limited company may only purchase its own shares out of—

(i) distributable profits of the company, or

(ii) the proceeds of a fresh issue of shares made for the purpose of financing the purchase, and

(b) any premium payable on the purchase by a limited company of its own shares must be paid out of distributable profits of the company, subject to subsection (3).

(3) If the shares to be purchased were issued at a premium, any premium payable on their purchase by the company may be paid out of the proceeds of a fresh issue of shares made for the purpose of financing the purchase, up to an amount equal to—

(a) the aggregate of the premiums received by the company on the issue of the shares purchased, or

(b) the current amount of the company's share premium account (including any sum transferred to that account in respect of premiums on the new shares),

whichever is the less.

(4) The amount of the company's share premium account is reduced by a sum corresponding (or by sums in the aggregate corresponding) to the amount of any payment made under subsection (3).

(5) This section has effect subject to section 735(4) (terms of purchase enforceable in a winding up).

Authority for purchase of own shares

693 Authority for purchase of own shares

(1) A limited company may only purchase its own shares—

(a) by an off-market purchase, authorised in accordance with section 693A or in pursuance of a contract approved in advance in accordance with section 694;

(b) by a market purchase, authorised in accordance with section 701.

(2) A purchase is "off-market" if the shares either—

(a) are purchased otherwise than on a recognised investment exchange, or

(b) are purchased on a recognised investment exchange but are not subject to a marketing arrangement on the exchange.

(3) For this purpose a company's shares are subject to a marketing arrangement on a recognised investment exchange if—

(a) they are listed under Part 6 of the Financial Services and Markets Act 2000, or

(b) the company has been afforded facilities for dealings in the shares to take place on the exchange—

(i) without prior permission for individual transactions from the authority governing that investment exchange, and

(ii) without limit as to the time during which those facilities are to be available.

(4) A purchase is a "market purchase" if it is made on a recognised investment exchange and is not an off-market purchase by virtue of subsection (2)(b).

(5) In this section "recognised investment exchange" means a recognised investment exchange (within the meaning of Part 18 of the Financial Services and Markets Act 2000) other than an overseas exchange (within the meaning of that Part).

693A Authority for off-market purchase for the purposes of or pursuant to an employees' share scheme

(1) A company may make an off-market purchase of its own shares for the purposes of or pursuant to an employees' share scheme if the purchase has first been authorised by a resolution of the company under this section.

(2) That authority—

(a) may be general or limited to the purchase of shares of a particular class or description, and

(b) may be unconditional or subject to conditions.

(3) The authority must—

(a) specify the maximum number of shares authorised to be acquired, and

(b) determine both the maximum and minimum prices that may be paid for the shares.

(4) The authority may be varied, revoked or from time to time renewed by a resolution of the company.

(5) A resolution conferring, varying or renewing authority must specify a date on which it is to expire, which must not be later than five years after the date on which the resolution is passed.

(6) A company may make a purchase of its own shares after the expiry of the time limit specified if—

(a) the contract of purchase was concluded before the authority expired, and

(b) the terms of the authority permitted the company to make a contract of purchase that would or might be executed wholly or partly after its expiration.

(7) A resolution to confer or vary authority under this section may determine the maximum or minimum price for purchase by—

(a) specifying a particular sum, or

(b) providing a basis or formula for calculating the amount of the price (but without reference to any person's discretion or opinion).

(8) Chapter 3 of Part 3 (resolutions affecting a company's constitution) applies to a resolution under this section.

Authority for off-market purchase

694 Authority for off-market purchase

(1) Subject to section 693A, a company may only make an off-market purchase of its own shares in pursuance of a contract approved prior to the purchase in accordance with this section.

(2) Either—

(a) the terms of the contract must be authorised by a resolution of the company before the contract is entered into, or

(b) the contract must provide that no shares may be purchased in pursuance of the contract until its terms have been authorised by a resolution of the company.

(3) The contract may be a contract, entered into by the company and relating to shares in the company, that does not amount to a contract to purchase the shares but under which the company may (subject to any conditions) become entitled or obliged to purchase the shares.

(4) The authority conferred by a resolution under this section may be varied, revoked or from time to time renewed by a resolution of the company.

(5) In the case of a public company a resolution conferring, varying or renewing authority must specify a date on which the authority is to expire, which must not be later than five years after the date on which the resolution is passed.

(6) A resolution conferring, varying, revoking or renewing authority under this section is subject to—
section 695 (exercise of voting rights), and
section 696 (disclosure of details of contract).

695 Resolution authorising off-market purchase: exercise of voting rights

(1) This section applies to a resolution to confer, vary, revoke or renew authority for the purposes of section 694 (authority for off-market purchase of own shares).

(2) Where the resolution is proposed as a written resolution, a member who holds shares to which the resolution relates is not an eligible member.

(3) Where the resolution is proposed at a meeting of the company, it is not effective if—

(a) any member of the company holding shares to which the resolution relates exercises the voting rights carried by any of those shares in voting on the resolution, and

(b) the resolution would not have been passed if he had not done so.

(4) For this purpose—

(a) a member who holds shares to which the resolution relates is regarded as exercising the voting rights carried by those shares not only if he votes in respect of them on a poll on the question whether the resolution shall be passed, but also if he votes on the resolution otherwise than on a poll;

(b) any member of the company may demand a poll on that question;

(c) a vote and a demand for a poll by a person as proxy for a member are the same respectively as a vote and a demand by the member.

696 Resolution authorising off-market purchase: disclosure of details of contract

(1) This section applies in relation to a resolution to confer, vary, revoke or renew authority for the purposes of section 694 (authority for off-market purchase of own shares).

(2) A copy of the contract (if it is in writing) or a memorandum setting out its terms (if it is not) must be made available to members—

(a) in the case of a written resolution, by being sent or submitted to every eligible member at or before the time at which the proposed resolution is sent or submitted to him;

(b) in the case of a resolution at a meeting, by being made available for inspection by members of the company both—

(i) at the company's registered office for not less than 15 days ending with the date of the meeting, and

(ii) at the meeting itself.

(3) A memorandum of contract terms so made available must include the names of the members holding shares to which the contract relates.

(4) A copy of the contract so made available must have annexed to it a written memorandum specifying such of those names as do not appear in the contract itself.

(5) The resolution is not validly passed if the requirements of this section are not complied with

697 Variation of contract for off-market purchase

(1) A company may only agree to a variation of a contract authorised under section 694 (authority for off-market purchase) if the variation is approved in advance in accordance with this section.

(2) The terms of the variation must be authorised by a resolution of the company before it is agreed to.

(3) That authority may be varied, revoked or from time to time renewed by a resolution of the company.

(4) In the case of a public company a resolution conferring, varying or renewing authority must specify a date on which the authority is to expire, which must not be later than five years after the date on which the resolution is passed.

(5) A resolution conferring, varying, revoking or renewing authority under this section is subject to—
section 698 (exercise of voting rights), and
section 699 (disclosure of details of variation).

698 Resolution authorising variation: exercise of voting rights

(1) This section applies to a resolution to confer, vary, revoke or renew authority for the purposes of section 697 (variation of contract for off-market purchase of own shares).

(2) Where the resolution is proposed as a written resolution, a member who holds shares to which the resolution relates is not an eligible member.

(3) Where the resolution is proposed at a meeting of the company, it is not effective if—

(a) any member of the company holding shares to which the resolution relates exercises the voting rights carried by any of those shares in voting on the resolution, and

(b) the resolution would not have been passed if he had not done so.

(4) For this purpose—

(a) a member who holds shares to which the resolution relates is regarded as exercising the voting rights carried by those shares not only if he votes in respect of them on a poll on the question whether the resolution shall be passed, but also if he votes on the resolution otherwise than on a poll;

(b) any member of the company may demand a poll on that question;

(c) a vote and a demand for a poll by a person as proxy for a member are the same respectively as a vote and a demand by the member.

699 Resolution authorising variation: disclosure of details of variation

(1) This section applies in relation to a resolution under section 697 (variation of contract for off-market purchase of own shares).

(2) A copy of the proposed variation (if it is in writing) or a written memorandum giving details of the proposed variation (if it is not) must be made available to members—

(a) in the case of a written resolution, by being sent or submitted to every eligible member at or before the time at which the proposed resolution is sent or submitted to him;

(b) in the case of a resolution at a meeting, by being made available for inspection by members of the company both—

(i) at the company's registered office for not less than 15 days ending with the date of the meeting, and

(ii) at the meeting itself.

(3) There must also be made available as mentioned in subsection (2) a copy of the original contract or, as the case may be, a memorandum of its terms, together with any variations previously made.

(4) A memorandum of the proposed variation so made available must include the names of the members holding shares to which the variation relates.

(5) A copy of the proposed variation so made available must have annexed to it a written memorandum specifying such of those names as do not appear in the variation itself.

(6) The resolution is not validly passed if the requirements of this section are not complied with.

700 Release of company's rights under contract for off-market purchase

(1) An agreement by a company to release its rights under a contract approved under section 694 (authorisation of off-market purchase) is void unless the terms of the release agreement are approved in advance in accordance with this section.

(2) The terms of the proposed agreement must be authorised by a resolution of the company before the agreement is entered into.

(3) That authority may be varied, revoked or from time to time renewed by a resolution of the company.

(4) In the case of a public company a resolution conferring, varying or renewing authority must specify a date on which the authority is to expire, which must not be later than five years after the date on which the resolution is passed.

(5) The provisions of—

section 698 (exercise of voting rights), and

section 699 (disclosure of details of variation),

apply to a resolution authorising a proposed release agreement as they apply to a resolution authorising a proposed variation.

Authority for market purchase

701 Authority for market purchase

(1) A company may only make a market purchase of its own shares if the purchase has first been authorised by a resolution of the company.

(2) That authority—

(a) may be general or limited to the purchase of shares of a particular class or description, and

(b) may be unconditional or subject to conditions.

(3) The authority must—

(a) specify the maximum number of shares authorised to be acquired, and

(b) determine both the maximum and minimum prices that may be paid for the shares.

(4) The authority may be varied, revoked or from time to time renewed by a resolution of the company.

(5) A resolution conferring, varying or renewing authority must specify a date on which it is to expire, which must not be later than five years after the date on which the resolution is passed.

(6) A company may make a purchase of its own shares after the expiry of the time limit specified if—

(a) the contract of purchase was concluded before the authority expired, and

(b) the terms of the authority permitted the company to make a contract of purchase that would or might be executed wholly or partly after its expiration.

(7) A resolution to confer or vary authority under this section may determine either or both the maximum and minimum price for purchase by—

(a) specifying a particular sum, or

(b) providing a basis or formula for calculating the amount of the price (but without reference to any person's discretion or opinion).

(8) Chapter 3 of Part 3 (resolutions affecting a company's constitution) applies to a resolution under this section.

Supplementary provisions

702 Copy of contract or memorandum to be available for inspection

(1) This section applies where a company has entered into—

(a) a contract approved under section 694 (authorisation of contract for off-market purchase), or

(b) a contract for a purchase authorised under section 701 (authorisation of market purchase).

(2) The company must keep available for inspection—

(a) a copy of the contract, or

(b) if the contract is not in writing, a written memorandum setting out its terms.

(3) The copy or memorandum must be kept available for inspection from the conclusion of the contract until the end of the period of ten years beginning with—

(a) the date on which the purchase of all the shares in pursuance of the contract is completed, or

(b) the date on which the contract otherwise determines.

(4) The copy or memorandum must be kept available for inspection—

(a) at the company's registered office, or

(b) at a place specified in regulations under section 1136.

(5) The company must give notice to the registrar—

(a) of the place at which the copy or memorandum is kept available for inspection, and

(b) of any change in that place,

unless it has at all times been kept at the company's registered office.

(6) Every copy or memorandum required to be kept under this section must be kept open to inspection without charge—

(a) by any member of the company, and

(b) in the case of a public company, by any other person.

(7) The provisions of this section apply to a variation of a contract as they apply to the original contract.

703 Enforcement of right to inspect copy or memorandum

(1) If default is made in complying with section 702(2), (3) or (4) or default is made for 14 days in complying with section 702(5), or an inspection required under section 702(6) is refused, an offence is committed by—

(a) the company, and

(b) every officer of the company who is in default.

(2) A person guilty of an offence under this section is liable on summary conviction to a fine not exceeding level 3 on the standard scale and, for continued contravention, a daily default fine not exceeding one-tenth of level 3 on the standard scale.

(3) In the case of refusal of an inspection required under section 702(6) the court may by order compel an immediate inspection.

704 No assignment of company's right to purchase own shares

The rights of a company under a contract authorised under—

(za) section 693A (authority for off-market purchase for the purposes of or pursuant to an employees' share scheme),

(a) section 694 (authority for off-market purchase), or

(b) section 701 (authority for market purchase)

are not capable of being assigned.

705 Payments apart from purchase price to be made out of distributable profits

(1) A payment made by a company in consideration of—

(a) acquiring any right with respect to the purchase of its own shares in pursuance of a contingent purchase contract approved under section 694 (authorisation of off-market purchase),

(b) the variation of any contract approved under that section, or

(c) the release of any of the company's obligations with respect to the purchase of any of its own shares under a contract—
(i) approved under section 694, or
(ii) authorised under section 701 (authorisation of market purchase),
must be made out of the company's distributable profits.

(2) If this requirement is not met in relation to a contract, then—
(a) in a case within subsection (1)(a), no purchase by the company of its own shares in pursuance of that contract may be made under this Chapter;
(b) in a case within subsection (1)(b), no such purchase following the variation may be made under this Chapter;
(c) in a case within subsection (1)(c), the purported release is void.

706 Treatment of shares purchased

Where a limited company makes a purchase of its own shares in accordance with this Chapter, then—
(a) if section 724 (treasury shares) applies, the shares may be held and dealt with in accordance with Chapter 6;
(b) if that section does not apply—
(i) the shares are treated as cancelled, and
(ii) the amount of the company's issued share capital is diminished accordingly by the nominal value of the shares cancelled.

707 Return to registrar of purchase of own shares

(1) Where a company purchases shares under this Chapter, it must deliver a return to the registrar within the period of 28 days beginning with the date on which the shares are delivered to it.

(2) The return must distinguish—
(a) shares in relation to which section 724 (treasury shares) applies and shares in relation to which that section does not apply, and
(b) shares in relation to which that section applies—
(i) that are cancelled forthwith (under section 729 (cancellation of treasury shares)), and
(ii) that are not so cancelled.

(3) The return must state, with respect to shares of each class purchased—
(a) the number and nominal value of the shares, and
(b) the date on which they were delivered to the company.

(4) In the case of a public company the return must also state—
(a) the aggregate amount paid by the company for the shares, and
(b) the maximum and minimum prices paid in respect of shares of each class purchased.

(5) Particulars of shares delivered to the company on different dates and under different contracts may be included in a single return.
In such a case the amount required to be stated under subsection (4)(a) is the aggregate amount paid by the company for all the shares to which the return relates.

(6) If default is made in complying with this section an offence is committed by every officer of the company who is in default.

(7) A person guilty of an offence under this section is liable—
(a) on conviction on indictment, to a fine;
(b) on summary conviction to a fine not exceeding the statutory maximum and, for continued contravention, a daily default fine not exceeding one-tenth of the statutory maximum.

708 Notice to registrar of cancellation of shares

(1) If on the purchase by a company of any of its own shares in accordance with this Part—
(a) section 724 (treasury shares) does not apply (so that the shares are treated as cancelled), or
(b) that section applies but the shares are cancelled forthwith (under section 729 (cancellation of treasury shares)),

the company must give notice of cancellation to the registrar, within the period of 28 days beginning with the date on which the shares are delivered to it, specifying the shares cancelled.

(2) The notice must be accompanied by a statement of capital.

(3) The statement of capital must state with respect to the company's share capital immediately following the cancellation—

(a) the total number of shares of the company,

(b) the aggregate nominal value of those shares,

(c) for each class of shares—

(i) prescribed particulars of the rights attached to the shares,

(ii) the total number of shares of that class, and

(iii) the aggregate nominal value of shares of that class, and

(d) the amount paid up and the amount (if any) unpaid on each share (whether on account of the nominal value of the share or by way of premium).

(4) If default is made in complying with this section, an offence is committed by—

(a) the company, and

(b) every officer of the company who is in default.

(5) A person guilty of an offence under this section is liable on summary conviction to a fine not exceeding level 3 on the standard scale and, for continued contravention, a daily default fine not exceeding one-tenth of level 3 on the standard scale.

CHAPTER 5
REDEMPTION OR PURCHASE BY PRIVATE COMPANY OUT OF CAPITAL

Introductory

709 Power of private limited company to redeem or purchase own shares out of capital

(1) A private limited company may in accordance with this Chapter, but subject to any restriction or prohibition in the company's articles, make a payment in respect of the redemption or purchase of its own shares otherwise than out of distributable profits or the proceeds of a fresh issue of shares.

(2) References below in this Chapter to payment out of capital are to any payment so made, whether or not it would be regarded apart from this section as a payment out of capital.

The permissible capital payment

710 The permissible capital payment

(1) The payment that may, in accordance with this Chapter, be made by a company out of capital in respect of the redemption or purchase of its own shares is such amount as, after applying for that purpose—

(a) any available profits of the company, and

(b) the proceeds of any fresh issue of shares made for the purposes of the redemption or purchase,

is required to meet the price of redemption or purchase.

(2) That is referred to below in this Chapter as "the permissible capital payment" for the shares.

711 Available profits

(1) For the purposes of this Chapter the available profits of the company, in relation to the redemption or purchase of any shares, are the profits of the company that are available for distribution (within the meaning of Part 23).

(2) But the question whether a company has any profits so available, and the amount of any such profits, shall be determined in accordance with section 712 instead of in accordance with sections 836 to 842 in that Part.

712 Determination of available profits

(1) The available profits of the company are determined as follows.

(2) First, determine the profits of the company by reference to the following items as stated in the relevant accounts—
(a) profits, losses, assets and liabilities,
(b) provisions of the following kinds—
(i) where the relevant accounts are Companies Act accounts, provisions of a kind specified for the purposes of this subsection by regulations under section 396;
(ii) where the relevant accounts are IAS accounts, provisions of any kind;
(c) share capital and reserves (including undistributable reserves).

(3) Second, reduce the amount so determined by the amount of—
(a) any distribution lawfully made by the company, and
(b) any other relevant payment lawfully made by the company out of distributable profits,
after the date of the relevant accounts and before the end of the relevant period.

(4) For this purpose "other relevant payment lawfully made" includes—
(a) financial assistance lawfully given out of distributable profits in accordance with Chapter 2,
(b) payments lawfully made out of distributable profits in respect of the purchase by the company of any shares in the company, and
(c) payments of any description specified in section 705 (payments other than purchase price to be made out of distributable profits) lawfully made by the company.

(5) The resulting figure is the amount of available profits.

(6) For the purposes of this section "the relevant accounts" are any accounts that—
(a) are prepared as at a date within the relevant period, and
(b) are such as to enable a reasonable judgment to be made as to the amounts of the items mentioned in subsection (2).

(7) In this section "the relevant period" means the period of three months ending with the date on which the solvency statement is made in accordance with section 720A or the directors' statement is made in accordance with section 714.

Requirements for payment out of capital

713 Requirements for payment out of capital

(1) A payment out of capital by a private company for the redemption or purchase of its own shares is not lawful unless the requirements of the following sections are met—
section 714 (directors' statement and auditor's report);
section 716 (approval by special resolution);
section 719 (public notice of proposed payment);
section 720 (directors' statement and auditor's report to be available for inspection).

(2) This is subject to section 720A and to any order of the court under section 721 (power of court to extend period for compliance on application by persons objecting to payment).

714 Directors' statement and auditor's report

(1) The company's directors must make a statement in accordance with this section.

(2) The statement must specify the amount of the permissible capital payment for the shares in question.

(3) It must state that, having made full inquiry into the affairs and prospects of the company, the directors have formed the opinion—
(a) as regards its initial situation immediately following the date on which the payment out of capital is proposed to be made, that there will be no grounds on which the company could then be found unable to pay its debts, and
(b) as regards its prospects for the year immediately following that date, that having regard to—
(i) their intentions with respect to the management of the company's business during that year, and
(ii) the amount and character of the financial resources that will in their view be available to the company during that year,

the company will be able to continue to carry on business as a going concern (and will accordingly be able to pay its debts as they fall due) throughout that year.

(4) In forming their opinion for the purposes of subsection (3)(a), the directors must take into account all of the company's liabilities (including any contingent or prospective liabilities).

(5) The directors' statement must be in the prescribed form and must contain such information with respect to the nature of the company's business as may be prescribed.

(6) It must in addition have annexed to it a report addressed to the directors by the company's auditor stating that—

(a) he has inquired into the company's state of affairs,

(b) the amount specified in the statement as the permissible capital payment for the shares in question is in his view properly determined in accordance with sections 710 to 712, and

(c) he is not aware of anything to indicate that the opinion expressed by the directors in their statement as to any of the matters mentioned in subsection (3) above is unreasonable in all the circumstances.

715 Directors' statement: offence if no reasonable grounds for opinion

(1) If the directors make a statement under section 714 without having reasonable grounds for the opinion expressed in it, an offence is committed by every director who is in default.

(2) A person guilty of an offence under this section is liable—

(a) on conviction on indictment, to imprisonment for a term not exceeding two years or a fine (or both);

(b) on summary conviction—

(i) in England and Wales, to imprisonment for a term not exceeding twelve months or a fine not exceeding the statutory maximum (or both);

(ii) in Scotland or Northern Ireland, to imprisonment for a term not exceeding six months or a fine not exceeding the statutory maximum (or both).

716 Payment to be approved by special resolution

(1) The payment out of capital must be approved by a special resolution of the company.

(2) The resolution must be passed on, or within the week immediately following, the date on which the directors make the statement required by section 714.

(3) A resolution under this section is subject to—

section 717 (exercise of voting rights), and

section 718 (disclosure of directors' statement and auditors' report).

717 Resolution authorising payment: exercise of voting rights

(1) This section applies to a resolution under section 716 (authority for payment out of capital for redemption or purchase of own shares).

(2) Where the resolution is proposed as a written resolution, a member who holds shares to which the resolution relates is not an eligible member.

(3) Where the resolution is proposed at a meeting of the company, it is not effective if—

(a) any member of the company holding shares to which the resolution relates exercises the voting rights carried by any of those shares in voting on the resolution, and

(b) the resolution would not have been passed if he had not done so.

(4) For this purpose—

(a) a member who holds shares to which the resolution relates is regarded as exercising the voting rights carried by those shares not only if he votes in respect of them on a poll on the question whether the resolution shall be passed, but also if he votes on the resolution otherwise than on a poll;

(b) any member of the company may demand a poll on that question;

(c) a vote and a demand for a poll by a person as proxy for a member are the same respectively as a vote and a demand by the member.

718 Resolution authorising payment: disclosure of directors' statement and auditor's report

(1) This section applies to a resolution under section 716 (resolution authorising payment out of capital for redemption or purchase of own shares).

(2) A copy of the directors' statement and auditor's report under section 714 must be made available to members—

(a) in the case of a written resolution, by being sent or submitted to every eligible member at or before the time at which the proposed resolution is sent or submitted to him;

(b) in the case of a resolution at a meeting, by being made available for inspection by members of the company at the meeting.

(3) The resolution is ineffective if this requirement is not complied with.

719 Public notice of proposed payment

(1) Within the week immediately following the date of the resolution under section 716 the company must cause to be published in the Gazette a notice—

(a) stating that the company has approved a payment out of capital for the purpose of acquiring its own shares by redemption or purchase or both (as the case may be),

(b) specifying—

(i) the amount of the permissible capital payment for the shares in question, and

(ii) the date of the resolution,

(c) stating where the directors' statement and auditor's report required by section 714 are available for inspection, and

(d) stating that any creditor of the company may at any time within the five weeks immediately following the date of the resolution apply to the court under section 721 for an order preventing the payment.

(2) Within the week immediately following the date of the resolution the company must also either—

(a) cause a notice to the same effect as that required by subsection (1) to be published in an appropriate national newspaper, or

(b) give notice in writing to that effect to each of its creditors.

(3) "An appropriate national newspaper" means a newspaper circulating throughout the part of the United Kingdom in which the company is registered.

(4) Not later than the day on which the company—

(a) first publishes the notice required by subsection (1), or

(b) if earlier, first publishes or gives the notice required by subsection (2),

the company must deliver to the registrar a copy of the directors' statement and auditor's report required by section 714.

720 Directors' statement and auditor's report to be available for inspection

(1) The directors' statement and auditor's report must be kept available for inspection throughout the period—

(a) beginning with the day on which the company—

(i) first publishes the notice required by section 719(1), or

(ii) if earlier, first publishes or gives the notice required by section 719(2), and

(b) ending five weeks after the date of the resolution for payment out of capital.

(2) They must be kept available for inspection—

(a) at the company's registered office, or

(b) at a place specified in regulations under section 1136.

(3) The company must give notice to the registrar—

(a) of the place at which the statement and report are kept available for inspection, and

(b) of any change in that place,

unless they have at all times been kept at the company's registered office.

(4) They must be open to the inspection of any member or creditor of the company without charge.

(5) If default is made for 14 days in complying with subsection (3), or an inspection under subsection (4) is refused, an offence is committed by—

(a) the company, and
(b) every officer of the company who is in default.

(6) A person guilty of an offence under this section is liable on summary conviction to a fine not exceeding level 3 on the standard scale and, for continued contravention, a daily default fine not exceeding one-tenth of level 3 on the standard scale.

(7) In the case of a refusal of an inspection required by subsection (4), the court may by order compel an immediate inspection.

Requirements for payment out of capital: employees' share schemes

720A Reduced requirements for payment out of capital for purchase of own shares for the purposes of or pursuant to an employees' share scheme

(1) Section 713(1) does not apply to the purchase out of capital by a private company of its own shares for the purposes of or pursuant to an employees' share scheme when approved by special resolution supported by a solvency statement.

(2) For the purposes of this section a resolution is supported by a solvency statement if—
(a) the directors of the company make a solvency statement (see section 643) not more than 15 days before the date on which the resolution is passed, and
(b) the resolution and solvency statement are registered in accordance with section 720B.

(3) Where the resolution is proposed as a written resolution, a copy of the solvency statement must be sent or submitted to every eligible member at or before the time at which the proposed resolution is sent or submitted to the member.

(4) Where the resolution is proposed at a general meeting, a copy of the solvency statement must be made available for inspection by members of the company throughout that meeting.

(5) The validity of a resolution is not affected by a failure to comply with subsection (3) or (4).

(6) Section 717 (resolution authorising payment: exercise of voting rights) applies to a resolution under this section as it applies to a resolution under section 716.

720B Registration of resolution and supporting documents for purchase of own shares for the purposes of or pursuant to an employees' share scheme

(1) Within 15 days after the passing of the resolution for a payment out of capital by a private company for the purchase of its own shares for the purposes of or pursuant to an employees' share scheme the company must deliver to the registrar—
(a) a copy of the solvency statement,
(b) a copy of the resolution, and
(c) a statement of capital.

(2) The statement of capital must state with respect to the company's share capital as reduced by the resolution—
(a) the total number of shares of the company,
(b) the aggregate nominal value of those shares,
(c) for each class of shares—
  (i) prescribed particulars of the rights attached to the shares,
  (ii) the total number of shares of that class, and
  (iii) the aggregate nominal value of shares of that class, and
(d) the amount paid up and the amount (if any) unpaid on each share (whether on account of the nominal value of the share of by way of premium).

(3) The registrar must register the documents delivered to him under subsection (1) on receipt.

(4) The resolution does not take effect until those documents are registered.

(5) The company must also deliver to the registrar, within 15 days after the resolution is passed, a statement by the directors confirming that the solvency statement was—
(a) made not more than 15 days before the date on which the resolution was passed, and
(b) provided to members in accordance with section 720A(3) or (4).

(6) The validity of a resolution is not affected by—

(a) a failure to deliver the documents required to be delivered to the registrar under subsection (1) within the time specified in that subsection, or

(b) a failure to comply with subsection (5).

(7) If the company delivers to the registrar a solvency statement that was not provided to members in accordance with section 720A(3) or (4), an offence is committed by every officer of the company who is in default.

(8) If default is made in complying with this section, an offence is committed by—

(a) the company, and

(b) every officer of the company who is in default.

(9) A person guilty of an offence under subsection (7) or (8) is liable—

(a) on conviction on indictment, to a fine;

(b) on summary conviction, to a fine not exceeding the statutory maximum.

Objection to payment by members or creditors

721 Application to court to cancel resolution

(1) Where a private company passes a special resolution approving a payment out of capital for the redemption or purchase of any of its shares—

(a) any member of the company (other than one who consented to or voted in favour of the resolution), and

(b) any creditor of the company,

may apply to the court for the cancellation of the resolution.

(2) The application—

(a) must be made within five weeks after the passing of the resolution, and

(b) may be made on behalf of the persons entitled to make it by such one or more of their number as they may appoint in writing for the purpose.

(3) On an application under this section the court may if it thinks fit—

(a) adjourn the proceedings in order that an arrangement may be made to the satisfaction of the court—

(i) for the purchase of the interests of dissentient members, or

(ii) for the protection of dissentient creditors, and

(b) give such directions and make such orders as it thinks expedient for facilitating or carrying into effect any such arrangement.

(4) Subject to that, the court must make an order either cancelling or confirming the resolution, and may do so on such terms and conditions as it thinks fit.

(5) If the court confirms the resolution, it may by order alter or extend any date or period of time specified—

(a) in the resolution, or

(b) in any provision of this Chapter applying to the redemption or purchase to which the resolution relates.

(6) The court's order may, if the court thinks fit—

(a) provide for the purchase by the company of the shares of any of its members and for the reduction accordingly of the company's capital, and

(b) make any alteration in the company's articles that may be required in consequence of that provision.

(7) The court's order may, if the court thinks fit, require the company not to make any, or any specified, amendments of its articles without the leave of the court.

722 Notice to registrar of court application or order

(1) On making an application under section 721 (application to court to cancel resolution) the applicants, or the person making the application on their behalf, must immediately give notice to the registrar.

This is without prejudice to any provision of rules of court as to service of notice of the application.

(2) On being served with notice of any such application, the company must immediately give notice to the registrar.

(3) Within 15 days of the making of the court's order on the application, or such longer period as the court may at any time direct, the company must deliver to the registrar a copy of the order.

(4) If a company fails to comply with subsection (2) or (3) an offence is committed by—
(a) the company, and
(b) every officer of the company who is in default.

(5) A person guilty of an offence under this section is liable on summary conviction to a fine not exceeding level 3 on the standard scale and, for continued contravention, a daily default fine not exceeding one-tenth of level 3 on the standard scale.

Supplementary provisions

723 When payment out of capital to be made

(1) The payment out of capital, if made in accordance with a resolution under section 716 must be made—
(a) no earlier than five weeks after the date on which the resolution under section 716 is passed, and
(b) no more than seven weeks after that date.

(1A) The payment out of capital, if made in accordance with a resolution under section 720A must be made—
(a) no earlier than five weeks after the date on which the shares to which the capital payment relates are surrendered, and
(b) no more than seven weeks after that date.

(2) This is subject to any exercise of the court's powers under section 721(5) (power to alter or extend time where resolution confirmed after objection).

CHAPTER 6
TREASURY SHARES

724 Treasury shares

(1) This section applies where—
(a) a limited company makes a purchase of its own shares in accordance with Chapter 4, and
(b) the purchase is made—
(i) out of distributable profits, or
(ii) with cash under section 692(1)(b).

(2) ...

(3) Where this section applies the company may—
(a) hold the shares (or any of them), or
(b) deal with any of them, at any time, in accordance with section 727 or 729.

(4) Where shares are held by the company, the company must be entered in its register of members as the member holding the shares.

(5) In the Companies Acts references to a company holding shares as treasury shares are to the company holding shares that—
(a) were (or are treated as having been) purchased by it in circumstances in which this section applies, and
(b) have been held by the company continuously since they were so purchased (or treated as purchased).

725 . . .

726 Treasury shares: exercise of rights

(1) This section applies where shares are held by a company as treasury shares.

(2) The company must not exercise any right in respect of the treasury shares, and any purported exercise of such a right is void.

This applies, in particular, to any right to attend or vote at meetings.

(3) No dividend may be paid, and no other distribution (whether in cash or otherwise) of the company's assets (including any distribution of assets to members on a winding up) may be made to the company, in respect of the treasury shares.

(4) Nothing in this section prevents—

(a) an allotment of shares as fully paid bonus shares in respect of the treasury shares, or

(b) the payment of any amount payable on the redemption of the treasury shares (if they are redeemable shares).

(5) Shares allotted as fully paid bonus shares in respect of the treasury shares are treated as if purchased by the company, at the time they were allotted, in circumstances in which section 724(1) (treasury shares) applied.

727 Treasury shares: disposal

(1) Where shares are held as treasury shares, the company may at any time—

(a) sell the shares (or any of them) for a cash consideration, or

(b) transfer the shares (or any of them) for the purposes of or pursuant to an employees' share scheme.

(2) In subsection (1) (a) "cash consideration" means—

(a) cash received by the company, or

(b) a cheque received by the company in good faith that the directors have no reason for suspecting will not be paid, or

(c) a release of a liability of the company for a liquidated sum, or

(d) an undertaking to pay cash to the company on or before a date not more than 90 days after the date on which the company agrees to sell the shares, or

(e) payment by any other means giving rise to a present or future entitlement (of the company or a person acting on the company's behalf) to a payment, or credit equivalent to payment, in cash.

For this purpose "cash" includes foreign currency.

(3) The Secretary of State may by order provide that particular means of payment specified in the order are to be regarded as falling within subsection (2)(e).

(4) If the company receives a notice under section 979 (takeover offers: right of offeror to buy out minority shareholders) that a person desires to acquire shares held by the company as treasury shares, the company must not sell or transfer the shares to which the notice relates except to that person.

(5) An order under this section is subject to negative resolution procedure.

728 Treasury shares: notice of disposal

(1) Where shares held by a company as treasury shares—

(a) are sold, or

(b) are transferred for the purposes of an employees' share scheme,

the company must deliver a return to the registrar not later than 28 days after the shares are disposed of.

(2) The return must state with respect to shares of each class disposed of—

(a) the number and nominal value of the shares, and

(b) the date on which they were disposed of.

(3) Particulars of shares disposed of on different dates may be included in a single return.

(4) If default is made in complying with this section an offence is committed by every officer of the company who is in default.

(5) A person guilty of an offence under this section is liable—

(a) on conviction on indictment, to a fine;

(b) on summary conviction, to a fine not exceeding the statutory maximum and, for continued contravention, a daily default fine not exceeding one-tenth of the statutory maximum.

729 Treasury shares: cancellation

(1) Where shares are held as treasury shares, the company may at any time cancel the shares (or any of them).

(2), (3) ...

(4) If company cancels shares held as treasury shares, the amount of the company's share capital is reduced accordingly by the nominal amount of the shares cancelled.

(5) The directors may take any steps required to enable the company to cancel its shares under this section without complying with the provisions of Chapter 10 of Part 17 (reduction of share capital).

730 Treasury shares: notice of cancellation

(1) Where shares held by a company as treasury shares are cancelled, the company must deliver a return to the registrar not later than 28 days after the shares are cancelled.
This does not apply to shares that are cancelled forthwith on their acquisition by the company (see section 708).

(2) The return must state with respect to shares of each class cancelled—
(a) the number and nominal value of the shares, and
(b) the date on which they were cancelled.

(3) Particulars of shares cancelled on different dates may be included in a single return.

(4) The notice must be accompanied by a statement of capital.

(5) The statement of capital must state with respect to the company's share capital immediately following the cancellation—
(a) the total number of shares of the company,
(b) the aggregate nominal value of those shares,
(c) for each class of shares—
(i) prescribed particulars of the rights attached to the shares,
(ii) the total number of shares of that class, and
(iii) the aggregate nominal value of shares of that class, and
(d) the amount paid up and the amount (if any) unpaid on each share (whether on account of the nominal value of the share or by way of premium).

(6) If default is made in complying with this section, an offence is committed by—
(a) the company, and
(b) every officer of the company who is in default.

(7) A person guilty of an offence under this section is liable on summary conviction to a fine not exceeding level 3 on the standard scale and, for continued contravention, a daily default fine not exceeding one-tenth of level 3 on the standard scale.

731 Treasury shares: treatment of proceeds of sale

(1) Where shares held as treasury shares are sold, the proceeds of sale must be dealt with in accordance with this section.

(2) If the proceeds of sale are equal to or less than the purchase price paid by the company for the shares, the proceeds are treated for the purposes of Part 23 (distributions) as a realised profit of the company.

(3) If the proceeds of sale exceed the purchase price paid by the company—
(a) an amount equal to the purchase price paid is treated as a realised profit of the company for the purposes of that Part, and
(b) the excess must be transferred to the company's share premium account.

(4) For the purposes of this section—
(a) the purchase price paid by the company must be determined by the application of a weighted average price method, and
(b) if the shares were allotted to the company as fully paid bonus shares, the purchase price paid for them is treated as nil.

732 Treasury shares: offences

(1) If a company contravenes any of the provisions of this Chapter (except section 730 (notice of cancellation)), an offence is committed by—

(a) the company, and

(b) every officer of the company who is in default.

(2) A person guilty of an offence under this section is liable—

(a) on conviction on indictment, to a fine;

(b) on summary conviction to a fine not exceeding the statutory maximum.

CHAPTER 7
SUPPLEMENTARY PROVISIONS

733 The capital redemption reserve

(1) In the following circumstances a company must transfer amounts to a reserve, called the "capital redemption reserve".

(2) Where under this Part shares of a limited company are redeemed or purchased wholly out of the company's profits, the amount by which the company's issued share capital is diminished in accordance with—

(a) section 688(b) (on the cancellation of shares redeemed), or

(b) section 706(b)(ii) (on the cancellation of shares purchased), must be transferred to the capital redemption reserve.

(3) If—

(a) the shares are redeemed or purchased wholly or partly out of the proceeds of a fresh issue, and

(b) the aggregate amount of the proceeds is less than the aggregate nominal value of the shares redeemed or purchased,

the amount of the difference must be transferred to the capital redemption reserve.

This does not apply in the case of a private company if, in addition to the proceeds of the fresh issue, the company applies a payment out of capital under Chapter 5 in making the redemption or purchase.

(4) The amount by which a company's share capital is diminished in accordance with section 729(4) (on the cancellation of shares held as treasury shares) must be transferred to the capital redemption reserve.

(5) The company may use the capital redemption reserve to pay up new shares to be allotted to members as fully paid bonus shares.

(6) Subject to that, the provisions of the Companies Acts relating to the reduction of a company's share capital apply as if the capital redemption reserve were part of its paid up share capital.

734 Accounting consequences of payment out of capital

(1) This section applies where a payment out of capital is made in accordance with Chapter 5 (redemption or purchase of own shares by private company out of capital).

(2) If the permissible capital payment is less than the nominal amount of the shares redeemed or purchased, the amount of the difference must be transferred to the company's capital redemption reserve.

(3) If the permissible capital payment is greater than the nominal amount of the shares redeemed or purchased—

(a) the amount of any capital redemption reserve, share premium account or fully paid share capital of the company, and

(b) any amount representing unrealised profits of the company for the time being standing to the credit of any revaluation reserve maintained by the company,

may be reduced by a sum not exceeding (or by sums not in total exceeding) the amount by which the permissible capital payment exceeds the nominal amount of the shares.

(4) Where the proceeds of a fresh issue are applied by the company in making a redemption or purchase of its own shares in addition to a payment out of capital under this Chapter, the references in subsections (2) and (3) to the permissible capital payment are to be read as referring to the aggregate of that payment and those proceeds.

735 Effect of company's failure to redeem or purchase

(1) This section applies where a company—

(a) issues shares on terms that they are or are liable to be redeemed, or

(b) agrees to purchase any of its shares.

(2) The company is not liable in damages in respect of any failure on its part to redeem or purchase any of the shares.

This is without prejudice to any right of the holder of the shares other than his right to sue the company for damages in respect of its failure.

(3) The court shall not grant an order for specific performance of the terms of redemption or purchase if the company shows that it is unable to meet the costs of redeeming or purchasing the shares in question out of distributable profits.

(4) If the company is wound up and at the commencement of the winding up any of the shares have not been redeemed or purchased, the terms of redemption or purchase may be enforced against the company.

When shares are redeemed or purchased under this subsection, they are treated as cancelled.

(5) Subsection (4) does not apply if—

(a) the terms provided for the redemption or purchase to take place at a date later than that of the commencement of the winding up, or

(b) during the period—

(i) beginning with the date on which the redemption or purchase was to have taken place, and

(ii) ending with the commencement of the winding up,

the company could not at any time have lawfully made a distribution equal in value to the price at which the shares were to have been redeemed or purchased.

(6) There shall be paid in priority to any amount that the company is liable under subsection (4) to pay in respect of any shares—

(a) all other debts and liabilities of the company (other than any due to members in their character as such), and

(b) if other shares carry rights (whether as to capital or as to income) that are preferred to the rights as to capital attaching to the first-mentioned shares, any amount due in satisfaction of those preferred rights.

Subject to that, any such amount shall be paid in priority to any amounts due to members in satisfaction of their rights (whether as to capital or income) as members.

736 Meaning of "distributable profits"

In this Part (except in Chapter 2 (financial assistance): see section 683) "distributable profits", in relation to the making of any payment by a company, means profits out of which the company could lawfully make a distribution (within the meaning given by section 830) equal in value to the payment.

737 General power to make further provision by regulations

(1) The Secretary of State may by regulations modify the provisions of this Part.

(2) The regulations may—

(a) amend or repeal any of the provisions of this Part, or

(b) make such other provision as appears to the Secretary of State appropriate in place of any of the provisions of this Part.

(3) Regulations under this section may make consequential amendments or repeals in other provisions of this Act, or in other enactments.

(4) Regulations under this section are subject to affirmative resolution procedure.

PART 19
DEBENTURES

General provisions

738 Meaning of "debenture"

In the Companies Acts "debenture" includes debenture stock, bonds and any other securities of a company, whether or not constituting a charge on the assets of the company.

739 Perpetual debentures

(1) A condition contained in debentures, or in a deed for securing debentures, is not invalid by reason only that the debentures are made—
- (a) irredeemable, or
- (b) redeemable only—
  - (i) on the happening of a contingency (however remote), or
  - (ii) on the expiration of a period (however long),

any rule of equity to the contrary notwithstanding.

(2) Subsection (1) applies to debentures whenever issued and to deeds whenever executed.

740 Enforcement of contract to subscribe for debentures

A contract with a company to take up and pay for debentures of the company may be enforced by an order for specific performance.

741 Registration of allotment of debentures

(1) A company must register an allotment of debentures as soon as practicable and in any event within two months after the date of the allotment.

(2) If a company fails to comply with this section, an offence is committed by—
- (a) the company, and
- (b) every officer of the company who is in default.

(3) A person guilty of an offence under this section is liable on summary conviction to a fine not exceeding level 3 on the standard scale and, for continued contravention, a daily default fine not exceeding one-tenth of level 3 on the standard scale.

(4) For the duties of the company as to the issue of the debentures, or certificates of debenture stock, see Part 21 (certification and transfer of securities)

742 Debentures to bearer (Scotland)

Notwithstanding anything in the statute of the Scots Parliament of 1696, chapter 25, debentures to bearer issued in Scotland are valid and binding according to their terms.

Register of debenture holders

743 Register of debenture holders

(1) Any register of debenture holders of a company that is kept by the company must be kept available for inspection—
- (a) at the company's registered office, or
- (b) at a place specified in regulations under section 1136.

(2) A company must give notice to the registrar of the place where any such register is kept available for inspection and of any change in that place.

(3) No such notice is required if the register has, at all times since it came into existence, been kept available for inspection at the company's registered office.

(4) If a company makes default for 14 days in complying with subsection (2), an offence is committed by—
- (a) the company, and
- (b) every officer of the company who is in default.

(5) A person guilty of an offence under this section is liable on summary conviction to a fine not exceeding level 3 on the standard scale and, for continued contravention, a daily default fine not exceeding one-tenth of level 3 on the standard scale.

(6) References in this section to a register of debenture holders include a duplicate—
(a) of a register of debenture holders that is kept outside the United Kingdom, or
(b) of any part of such a register.

744 Register of debenture holders: right to inspect and require copy

(1) Every register of debenture holders of a company must, except when duly closed, be open to the inspection—
(a) of the registered holder of any such debentures, or any holder of shares in the company, without charge, and
(b) of any other person on payment of such fee as may be prescribed.

(2) Any person may require a copy of the register, or any part of it, on payment of such fee as may be prescribed.

(3) A person seeking to exercise either of the rights conferred by this section must make a request to the company to that effect.

(4) The request must contain the following information—
(a) in the case of an individual, his name and address;
(b) in the case of an organisation, the name and address of an individual responsible for making the request on behalf of the organisation;
(c) the purpose for which the information is to be used; and
(d) whether the information will be disclosed to any other person, and if so—
(i) where that person is an individual, his name and address,
(ii) where that person is an organisation, the name and address of an individual responsible for receiving the information on its behalf, and
(iii) the purpose for which the information is to be used by that person.

(5) For the purposes of this section a register is "duly closed" if it is closed in accordance with provision contained—
(a) in the articles or in the debentures,
(b) in the case of debenture stock in the stock certificates, or
(c) in the trust deed or other document securing the debentures or debenture stock.
The total period for which a register is closed in any year must not exceed 30 days.

(6) References in this section to a register of debenture holders include a duplicate—
(a) of a register of debenture holders that is kept outside the United Kingdom, or
(b) of any part of such a register.

745 Register of debenture holders: response to request for inspection or copy

(1) Where a company receives a request under section 744 (register of debenture holders: right to inspect and require copy), it must within five working days either—
(a) comply with the request, or
(b) apply to the court.

(2) If it applies to the court it must notify the person making the request.

(3) If on an application under this section the court is satisfied that the inspection or copy is not sought for a proper purpose—
(a) it shall direct the company not to comply with the request, and
(b) it may further order that the company's costs (in Scotland, expenses) on the application be paid in whole or in part by the person who made the request, even if he is not a party to the application.

(4) If the court makes such a direction and it appears to the court that the company is or may be subject to other requests made for a similar purpose (whether made by the same person or different persons), it may direct that the company is not to comply with any such request.

The order must contain such provision as appears to the court appropriate to identify the requests to which it applies.

(5) If on an application under this section the court does not direct the company not to comply with the request, the company must comply with the request immediately upon the court giving its decision or, as the case may be, the proceedings being discontinued.

746 Register of debenture holders: refusal of inspection or default in providing copy

(1) If an inspection required under section 744 (register of debenture holders: right to inspect and require copy) is refused or default is made in providing a copy required under that section, otherwise than in accordance with an order of the court, an offence is committed by—

(a) the company, and

(b) every officer of the company who is in default.

(2) A person guilty of an offence under this section is liable on summary conviction to a fine not exceeding level 3 on the standard scale and, for continued contravention, a daily default fine not exceeding one-tenth of level 3 on the standard scale.

(3) In the case of any such refusal or default the court may by order compel an immediate inspection or, as the case may be, direct that the copy required be sent to the person requesting it.

747 Register of debenture holders: offences in connection with request for or disclosure of information

(1) It is an offence for a person knowingly or recklessly to make in a request under section 744 (register of debenture holders: right to inspect and require copy) a statement that is misleading, false or deceptive in a material particular.

(2) It is an offence for a person in possession of information obtained by exercise of either of the rights conferred by that section—

(a) to do anything that results in the information being disclosed to another person, or

(b) to fail to do anything with the result that the information is disclosed to another person,

knowing, or having reason to suspect, that person may use the information for a purpose that is not a proper purpose.

(3) A person guilty of an offence under this section is liable—

(a) on conviction on indictment, to imprisonment for a term not exceeding two years or a fine (or both);

(b) on summary conviction—

(i) in England and Wales, to imprisonment for a term not exceeding twelve months or to a fine not exceeding the statutory maximum (or both);

(ii) in Scotland or Northern Ireland, to imprisonment for a term not exceeding six months, or to a fine not exceeding the statutory maximum (or both).

748 Time limit for claims arising from entry in register

(1) Liability incurred by a company—

(a) from the making or deletion of an entry in the register of debenture holders, or

(b) from a failure to make or delete any such entry,

is not enforceable more than ten years after the date on which the entry was made or deleted or, as the case may be, the failure first occurred.

(2) This is without prejudice to any lesser period of limitation (and, in Scotland, to any rule that the obligation giving rise to the liability prescribes before the expiry of that period).

Supplementary provisions

749 Right of debenture holder to copy of deed

(1) Any holder of debentures of a company is entitled, on request and on payment of such fee as may be prescribed, to be provided with a copy of any trust deed for securing the debentures.

(2) If default is made in complying with this section, an offence is committed by every officer of the company who is in default.

(3) A person guilty of an offence under this section is liable on summary conviction to a fine not exceeding level 3 on the standard scale and, for continued contravention, a daily default fine not exceeding one-tenth of level 3 on the standard scale.

(4) In the case of any such default the court may direct that the copy required be sent to the person requiring it.

750 Liability of trustees of debentures

(1) Any provision contained in—

(a) a trust deed for securing an issue of debentures, or

(b) any contract with the holders of debentures secured by a trust deed,

is void in so far as it would have the effect of exempting a trustee of the deed from, or indemnifying him against, liability for breach of trust where he fails to show the degree of care and diligence required of him as trustee, having regard to the provisions of the trust deed conferring on him any powers, authorities or discretions.

(2) Subsection (1) does not invalidate—

(a) a release otherwise validly given in respect of anything done or omitted to be done by a trustee before the giving of the release;

(b) any provision enabling such a release to be given—

(i) on being agreed to by a majority of not less than 75% in value of the debenture holders present and voting in person or, where proxies are permitted, by proxy at a meeting summoned for the purpose, and

(ii) either with respect to specific acts or omissions or on the trustee dying or ceasing to act.

(3) This section is subject to section 751 (saving for certain older provisions).

751 Liability of trustees of debentures: saving for certain older provisions

(1) Section 750 (liability of trustees of debentures) does not operate—

(a) to invalidate any provision in force on the relevant date so long as any person—

(i) then entitled to the benefit of the provision, or

(ii) afterwards given the benefit of the provision under subsection (3) below,

remains a trustee of the deed in question, or

(b) to deprive any person of any exemption or right to be indemnified in respect of anything done or omitted to be done by him while any such provision was in force.

(2) The relevant date for this purpose is—

(a) 1st July 1948 in a case where section 192 of the Companies Act 1985 applied immediately before the commencement of this section;

(b) 1st July 1961 in a case where Article 201 of the Companies (Northern Ireland) Order 1986 then applied.

(3) While any trustee of a trust deed remains entitled to the benefit of a provision saved by subsection (1) above the benefit of that provision may be given either—

(a) to all trustees of the deed, present and future, or

(b) to any named trustees or proposed trustees of it,

by a resolution passed by a majority of not less than 75% in value of the debenture holders present in person or, where proxies are permitted, by proxy at a meeting summoned for the purpose.

(4) A meeting for that purpose must be summoned in accordance with the provisions of the deed or, if the deed makes no provision for summoning meetings, in a manner approved by the court.

752 Power to re-issue redeemed debentures

(1) Where a company has redeemed debentures previously issued, then unless—

(a) provision to the contrary (express or implied) is contained in the company's articles or in any contract made by the company, or

(b) the company has, by passing a resolution to that effect or by some other act, manifested its intention that the debentures shall be cancelled, the company may re-issue the debentures, either by re-issuing the same debentures or by issuing new debentures in their place.

This subsection is deemed always to have had effect.

(2) On a re-issue of redeemed debentures the person entitled to the debentures has (and is deemed always to have had) the same priorities as if the debentures had never been redeemed.

(3) The re-issue of a debenture or the issue of another debenture in its place under this section is treated as the issue of a new debenture for the purposes of stamp duty.

It is not so treated for the purposes of any provision limiting the amount or number of debentures to be issued.

(4) A person lending money on the security of a debenture re-issued under this section which appears to be duly stamped may give the debenture in evidence in any proceedings for enforcing his security without payment of the stamp duty or any penalty in respect of it, unless he had notice (or, but for his negligence, might have discovered) that the debenture was not duly stamped. In that case the company is liable to pay the proper stamp duty and penalty.

753 Deposit of debentures to secure advances

Where a company has deposited any of its debentures to secure advances from time to time on current account or otherwise, the debentures are not treated as redeemed by reason only of the company's account having ceased to be in debit while the debentures remained so deposited.

754 Priorities where debentures secured by floating charge

(1) This section applies where debentures of a company registered in England and Wales or Northern Ireland are secured by a charge that, as created, was a floating charge.

(2) If possession is taken, by or on behalf of the holders of the debentures, of any property comprised in or subject to the charge, and the company is not at that time in the course of being wound up, the company's preferential debts shall be paid out of assets coming to the hands of the persons taking possession in priority to any claims for principal or interest in respect of the debentures.

(3) "Preferential debts" means the categories of debts listed in Schedule 6 to the Insolvency Act 1986 or Schedule 4 to the Insolvency (Northern Ireland) Order 1989.

For the purposes of those Schedules "the relevant date" is the date of possession being taken as mentioned in subsection (2).

(4) Payments under this section shall be recouped, as far as may be, out of the assets of the company available for payment of general creditors.

PART 20
PRIVATE AND PUBLIC COMPANIES

CHAPTER 1
PROHIBITION OF PUBLIC OFFERS BY PRIVATE COMPANIES

755 Prohibition of public offers by private company

(1) A private company limited by shares or limited by guarantee and having a share capital must not—

(a) offer to the public any securities of the company, or

(b) allot or agree to allot any securities of the company with a view to their being offered to the public.

(2) Unless the contrary is proved, an allotment or agreement to allot securities is presumed to be made with a view to their being offered to the public if an offer of the securities (or any of them) to the public is made—

(a) within six months after the allotment or agreement to allot, or

(b) before the receipt by the company of the whole of the consideration to be received by it in respect of the securities.

(3) A company does not contravene this section if—

(a) it acts in good faith in pursuance of arrangements under which it is to re-register as a public company before the securities are allotted, or

(b) as part of the terms of the offer it undertakes to re-register as a public company within a specified period, and that undertaking is complied with.

(4) The specified period for the purposes of subsection (3)(b) must be a period ending not later than six months after the day on which the offer is made (or, in the case of an offer made on different days, first made).

(5) In this Chapter "securities" means shares or debentures.

756 Meaning of "offer to the public"

(1) This section explains what is meant in this Chapter by an offer of securities to the public.

(2) An offer to the public includes an offer to any section of the public, however selected.

(3) An offer is not regarded as an offer to the public if it can properly be regarded, in all the circumstances, as—

(a) not being calculated to result, directly or indirectly, in securities of the company becoming available to persons other than those receiving the offer, or

(b) otherwise being a private concern of the person receiving it and the person making it.

(4) An offer is to be regarded (unless the contrary is proved) as being a private concern of the person receiving it and the person making it if—

(a) it is made to a person already connected with the company and, where it is made on terms allowing that person to renounce his rights, the rights may only be renounced in favour of another person already connected with the company; or

(b) it is an offer to subscribe for securities to be held under an employees' share scheme and, where it is made on terms allowing that person to renounce his rights, the rights may only be renounced in favour of—

(i) another person entitled to hold securities under the scheme, or

(ii) a person already connected with the company.

(5) For the purposes of this section "person already connected with the company" means—

(a) an existing member or employee of the company,

(b) a member of the family of a person who is or was a member or employee of the company,

(c) the widow or widower, or surviving civil partner, of a person who was a member or employee of the company,

(d) an existing debenture holder of the company, or

(e) a trustee (acting in his capacity as such) of a trust of which the principal beneficiary is a person within any of paragraphs (a) to (d).

(6) For the purposes of subsection (5)(b) the members of a person's family are the person's spouse or civil partner and children (including step-children) and their descendants.

757 Enforcement of prohibition: order restraining proposed contravention

(1) If it appears to the court—

(a) on an application under this section, or

(b) in proceedings under Part 30 (protection of members against unfair prejudice),

that a company is proposing to act in contravention of section 755 (prohibition of public offers by private companies), the court shall make an order under this section.

(2) An order under this section is an order restraining the company from contravening that section.

(3) An application for an order under this section may be made by—

(a) a member or creditor of the company, or

(b) the Secretary of State.

758 Enforcement of prohibition: orders available to the court after contravention

(1) This section applies if it appears to the court—

(a) on an application under this section, or

(b) in proceedings under Part 30 (protection of members against unfair prejudice), that a company has acted in contravention of section 755 (prohibition of public offers by private companies).

(2) The court must make an order requiring the company to re-register as a public company unless it appears to the court—

(a) that the company does not meet the requirements for re-registration as a public company, and

(b) that it is impractical or undesirable to require it to take steps to do so.

(3) If it does not make an order for re-registration, the court may make either or both of the following—

(a) a remedial order (see section 759), or

(b) an order for the compulsory winding up of the company.

(4) An application under this section may be made by—

(a) a member of the company who—

(i) was a member at the time the offer was made (or, if the offer was made over a period, at any time during that period), or

(ii) became a member as a result of the offer,

(b) a creditor of the company who was a creditor at the time the offer was made (or, if the offer was made over a period, at any time during that period), or

(c) the Secretary of State.

759 Enforcement of prohibition: remedial order

(1) A "remedial order" is an order for the purpose of putting a person affected by anything done in contravention of section 755 (prohibition of public offers by private company) in the position he would have been in if it had not been done.

(2) The following provisions are without prejudice to the generality of the power to make such an order.

(3) Where a private company has—

(a) allotted securities pursuant to an offer to the public, or

(b) allotted or agreed to allot securities with a view to their being offered to the public,

a remedial order may require any person knowingly concerned in the contravention of section 755 to offer to purchase any of those securities at such price and on such other terms as the court thinks fit.

(4) A remedial order may be made—

(a) against any person knowingly concerned in the contravention, whether or not an officer of the company;

(b) notwithstanding anything in the company's constitution (which includes, for this purpose, the terms on which any securities of the company are allotted or held);

(c) whether or not the holder of the securities subject to the order is the person to whom the company allotted or agreed to allot them.

(5) Where a remedial order is made against the company itself, the court may provide for the reduction of the company's capital accordingly.

760 Validity of allotment etc not affected

Nothing in this Chapter affects the validity of any allotment or sale of securities or of any agreement to allot or sell securities.

CHAPTER 2
MINIMUM SHARE CAPITAL REQUIREMENT FOR PUBLIC COMPANIES

761 Public company: requirement as to minimum share capital

(1) A company that is a public company (otherwise than by virtue of re-registration as a public company) must not do business or exercise any borrowing powers unless the registrar has issued it with a certificate under this section (a "trading certificate").

(2) The registrar shall issue a trading certificate if, on an application made in accordance with section 762, he is satisfied that the nominal value of the company's allotted share capital is not less than the authorised minimum.

(3) For this purpose a share allotted in pursuance of an employees' share scheme shall not be taken into account unless paid up as to—
(a) at least one-quarter of the nominal value of the share, and
(b) the whole of any premium on the share.

(4) A trading certificate has effect from the date on which it is issued and is conclusive evidence that the company is entitled to do business and exercise any borrowing powers.

762 Procedure for obtaining certificate

(1) An application for a certificate under section 761 must—
(a) state that the nominal value of the company's allotted share capital is not less than the authorised minimum,
(b) specify the amount, or estimated amount, of the company's preliminary expenses,
(c) specify any amount or benefit paid or given, or intended to be paid or given, to any promoter of the company, and the consideration for the payment or benefit, and
(d) be accompanied by a statement of compliance.

(2) The statement of compliance is a statement that the company meets the requirements for the issue of a certificate under section 761.

(3) The registrar may accept the statement of compliance as sufficient evidence of the matters stated in it.

763 The authorised minimum

(1) "The authorised minimum", in relation to the nominal value of a public company's allotted share capital is—
(a) £50,000, or
(b) the prescribed euro equivalent.

(2) The Secretary of State may by order prescribe the amount in euros that is for the time being to be treated as equivalent to the sterling amount of the authorised minimum.

(3) This power may be exercised from time to time as appears to the Secretary of State to be appropriate.

(4) The amount prescribed shall be determined by applying an appropriate spot rate of exchange to the sterling amount and rounding to the nearest 100 euros.

(5) An order under this section is subject to negative resolution procedure.

(6) This section has effect subject to any exercise of the power conferred by section 764 (power to alter authorised minimum).

764 Power to alter authorised minimum

(1) The Secretary of State may by order—
(a) alter the sterling amount of the authorised minimum, and
(b) make a corresponding alteration of the prescribed euro equivalent.

(2) The amount of the prescribed euro equivalent shall be determined by applying an appropriate spot rate of exchange to the sterling amount and rounding to the nearest 100 euros.

(3) An order under this section that increases the authorised minimum may—
(a) require a public company having an allotted share capital of which the nominal value is less than the amount specified in the order to—
(i) increase that value to not less than that amount, or
(ii) re-register as a private company;
(b) make provision in connection with any such requirement for any of the matters for which provision is made by this Act relating to—
(i) a company's registration, re-registration or change of name,
(ii) payment for shares comprised in a company's share capital, and
(iii) offers to the public of shares in or debentures of a company,

including provision as to the consequences (in criminal law or otherwise) of a failure to comply with any requirement of the order;

(c) provide for any provision of the order to come into force on different days for different purposes.

(4) An order under this section is subject to affirmative resolution procedure.

765 Authorised minimum: application of initial requirement

(1) The initial requirement for a public company to have allotted share capital of a nominal value not less than the authorised minimum, that is—

(a) the requirement in section 761(2) for the issue of a trading certificate, or

(b) the requirement in section 91(1) (a) for re-registration as a public company,

must be met either by reference to allotted share capital denominated in sterling or by reference to allotted share capital denominated in euros (but not partly in one and partly in the other).

(2) Whether the requirement is met is determined in the first case by reference to the sterling amount and in the second case by reference to the prescribed euro equivalent.

(3) No account is to be taken of any allotted share capital of the company denominated in a currency other than sterling or, as the case may be, euros.

(4) If the company could meet the requirement either by reference to share capital denominated in sterling or by reference to share capital denominated in euros, it must elect in its application for a trading certificate or, as the case may be, for re-registration as a public company which is to be the currency by reference to which the matter is determined.

766 Authorised minimum: application where shares denominated in different currencies etc

(1) The Secretary of State may make provision by regulations as to the application of the authorised minimum in relation to a public company that—

(a) has shares denominated—

(i) in more than one currency, or

(ii) in a currency other than sterling or euros,

(b) redenominates the whole or part of its allotted share capital, or

(c) allots new shares.

(2) The regulations may make provision as to the currencies, exchange rates and dates by reference to which it is to be determined whether the nominal value of the company's allotted share capital is less than the authorised minimum.

(3) The regulations may provide that where—

(a) a company has redenominated the whole or part of its allotted share capital, and

(b) the effect of the redenomination is that the nominal value of the company's allotted share capital is less than the authorised minimum,

the company must re-register as a private company.

(4) Regulations under subsection (3) may make provision corresponding to any provision made by sections 664 to 667 (re-registration as private company in consequence of cancellation of shares).

(5) Any regulations under this section have effect subject to section 765 (authorised minimum: application of initial requirement).

(6) Regulations under this section are subject to negative resolution procedure.

767 Consequences of doing business etc without a trading certificate

(1) If a company does business or exercises any borrowing powers in contravention of section 761, an offence is committed by—

(a) the company, and

(b) every officer of the company who is in default.

(2) A person guilty of an offence under subsection (1) is liable—

(a) on conviction on indictment, to a fine;

(b) on summary conviction, to a fine not exceeding the statutory maximum.

(3) A contravention of section 761 does not affect the validity of a transaction entered into by the company, but if a company—

(a) enters into a transaction in contravention of that section, and

(b) fails to comply with its obligations in connection with the transaction within 21 days from being called on to do so,

the directors of the company are jointly and severally liable to indemnify any other party to the transaction in respect of any loss or damage suffered by him by reason of the company's failure to comply with its obligations.

(4) The directors who are so liable are those who were directors at the time the company entered into the transaction.

PART 21
CERTIFICATION AND TRANSFER OF SECURITIES

CHAPTER 1
CERTIFICATION AND TRANSFER OF SECURITIES: GENERAL

Share certificates

768 Share certificate to be evidence of title

(1) In the case of a company registered in England and Wales or Northern Ireland, a certificate under the common seal of the company specifying any shares held by a member is prima facie evidence of his title to the shares.

(2) In the case of a company registered in Scotland—

(a) a certificate under the common seal of the company specifying any shares held by a member, or

(b) a certificate specifying any shares held by a member and subscribed by the company in accordance with the Requirements of Writing (Scotland) Act 1995,

is sufficient evidence, unless the contrary is shown, of his title to the shares.

Issue of certificates etc on allotment

769 Duty of company as to issue of certificates etc on allotment

(1) A company must, within two months after the allotment of any of its shares, debentures or debenture stock, complete and have ready for delivery—

(a) the certificates of the shares allotted,

(b) the debentures allotted, or

(c) the certificates of the debenture stock allotted.

(2) Subsection (1) does not apply—

(a) if the conditions of issue of the shares, debentures or debenture stock provide otherwise,

(b) in the case of allotment to a financial institution (see section 778), or

(c) in the case of an allotment of shares if, following the allotment, the company has issued a share warrant in respect of the shares (see section 779).

(3) If default is made in complying with subsection (1) an offence is committed by every officer of the company who is in default.

(4) A person guilty of an offence under subsection (3) is liable on summary conviction to a fine not exceeding level 3 on the standard scale and, for continued contravention, a daily default fine not exceeding one-tenth of level 3 on the standard scale.

Transfer of securities

770 Registration of transfer

(1) A company may not register a transfer of shares in or debentures of the company unless—

(a) a proper instrument of transfer has been delivered to it, or

(b) the transfer—

(i) is an exempt transfer within the Stock Transfer Act 1982, or

(ii) is in accordance with regulations under Chapter 2 of this Part.

(2) Subsection (1) does not affect any power of the company to register as shareholder or debenture holder a person to whom the right to any shares in or debentures of the company has been transmitted by operation of law.

771 Procedure on transfer being lodged

(1) When a transfer of shares in or debentures of a company has been lodged with the company, the company must either—

(a) register the transfer, or

(b) give the transferee notice of refusal to register the transfer, together with its reasons for the refusal,

as soon as practicable and in any event within two months after the date on which the transfer is lodged with it.

(2) If the company refuses to register the transfer, it must provide the transferee with such further information about the reasons for the refusal as the transferee may reasonably request.

This does not include copies of minutes of meetings of directors.

(3) If a company fails to comply with this section, an offence is committed by—

(a) the company, and

(b) every officer of the company who is in default.

(4) A person guilty of an offence under this section is liable on summary conviction to a fine not exceeding level 3 on the standard scale and, for continued contravention, a daily default fine not exceeding one-tenth of level 3 on the standard scale.

(5) This section does not apply—

(a) in relation to a transfer of shares if the company has issued a share warrant in respect of the shares (see section 779);

(b) in relation to the transmission of shares or debentures by operation of law.

772 Transfer of shares on application of transferor

On the application of the transferor of any share or interest in a company, the company shall enter in its register of members the name of the transferee in the same manner and subject to the same conditions as if the application for the entry were made by the transferee.

773 Execution of share transfer by personal representative

An instrument of transfer of the share or other interest of a deceased member of a company—

(a) may be made by his personal representative although the personal representative is not himself a member of the company, and

(b) is as effective as if the personal representative had been such a member at the time of the execution of the instrument.

774 Evidence of grant of probate etc

The production to a company of any document that is by law sufficient evidence of the grant of—

(a) probate of the will of a deceased person,

(b) letters of administration of the estate of a deceased person, or

(c) confirmation as executor of a deceased person,

shall be accepted by the company as sufficient evidence of the grant.

775 Certification of instrument of transfer

(1) The certification by a company of an instrument of transfer of any shares in, or debentures of, the company is to be taken as a representation by the company to any person acting on the faith of the certification that there have been produced to the company such documents as on their face show a prima facie title to the shares or debentures in the transferor named in the instrument.

(2) The certification is not to be taken as a representation that the transferor has any title to the shares or debentures.

(3) Where a person acts on the faith of a false certification by a company made negligently, the company is under the same liability to him as if the certification had been made fraudulently.

(4) For the purposes of this section—
(a) an instrument of transfer is certificated if it bears the words "certificate lodged" (or words to the like effect);
(b) the certification of an instrument of transfer is made by a company if—
(i) the person issuing the instrument is a person authorised to issue certificated instruments of transfer on the company's behalf, and
(ii) the certification is signed by a person authorised to certificate transfers on the company's behalf or by an officer or employee either of the company or of a body corporate so authorised;
(c) a certification is treated as signed by a person if—
(i) it purports to be authenticated by his signature or initials (whether handwritten or not), and
(ii) it is not shown that the signature or initials was or were placed there neither by himself nor by a person authorised to use the signature or initials for the purpose of certificating transfers on the company's behalf.

Issue of certificates etc on transfer

776 Duty of company as to issue of certificates etc on transfer

(1) A company must, within two months after the date on which a transfer of any of its shares, debentures or debenture stock is lodged with the company, complete and have ready for delivery—
(a) the certificates of the shares transferred,
(b) the debentures transferred, or
(c) the certificates of the debenture stock transferred.
(2) For this purpose a "transfer" means—
(a) a transfer duly stamped and otherwise valid, or
(b) an exempt transfer within the Stock Transfer Act 1982,
but does not include a transfer that the company is for any reason entitled to refuse to register and does not register.
(3) Subsection (1) does not apply—
(a) if the conditions of issue of the shares, debentures or debenture stock provide otherwise,
(b) in the case of a transfer to a financial institution (see section 778), or
(c) in the case of a transfer of shares if, following the transfer, the company has issued a share warrant in respect of the shares (see section 779).
(4) Subsection (1) has effect subject to section 777 (cases where the Stock Transfer Act 1982 applies).
(5) If default is made in complying with subsection (1) an offence is committed by every officer of the company who is in default.
(6) A person guilty of an offence under this section is liable on summary conviction to a fine not exceeding level 3 on the standard scale and, for continued contravention, a daily default fine not exceeding one-tenth of level 3 on the standard scale.

777 Issue of certificates etc: cases within the Stock Transfer Act 1982

(1) Section 776(1) (duty of company as to issue of certificates etc on transfer) does not apply in the case of a transfer to a person where, by virtue of regulations under section 3 of the Stock Transfer Act 1982, he is not entitled to a certificate or other document of or evidencing title in respect of the securities transferred.
(2) But if in such a case the transferee—
(a) subsequently becomes entitled to such a certificate or other document by virtue of any provision of those regulations, and
(b) gives notice in writing of that fact to the company,

section 776 (duty to company as to issue of certificates etc) has effect as if the reference in subsection (1) of that section to the date of the lodging of the transfer were a reference to the date of the notice.

Issue of certificates etc on allotment or transfer to financial institution

778 Issue of certificates etc: allotment or transfer to financial institution

(1) A company—

(a) of which shares or debentures are allotted to a financial institution,

(b) of which debenture stock is allotted to a financial institution, or

(c) with which a transfer for transferring shares, debentures or debenture stock to a financial institution is lodged,

is not required in consequence of that allotment or transfer to comply with section 769(1) or 776(1) (duty of company as to issue of certificates etc).

(2) A "financial institution" means—

(a) a recognised clearing house acting in relation to a recognised investment exchange, or

(b) a nominee of—

(i) a recognised clearing house acting in that way, or

(ii) a recognised investment exchange,

designated for the purposes of this section in the rules of the recognised investment exchange in question.

(3) Expressions used in subsection (2) have the same meaning as in Part 18 of the Financial Services and Markets Act 2000.

Share warrants

779 Issue and effect of share warrant to bearer

(1) A company limited by shares may, if so authorised by its articles, issue with respect to any fully paid shares a warrant (a "share warrant") stating that the bearer of the warrant is entitled to the shares specified in it.

(2) A share warrant issued under the company's common seal or (in the case of a company registered in Scotland) subscribed in accordance with the Requirements of Writing (Scotland) Act 1995 entitles the bearer to the shares specified in it and the shares may be transferred by delivery of the warrant.

(3) A company that issues a share warrant may, if so authorised by its articles, provide (by coupons or otherwise) for the payment of the future dividends on the shares included in the warrant.

780 Duty of company as to issue of certificates on surrender of share warrant

(1) A company must, within two months of the surrender of a share warrant for cancellation, complete and have ready for delivery the certificates of the shares specified in the warrant.

(2) Subsection (1) does not apply if the company's articles provide otherwise.

(3) If default is made in complying with subsection (1) an offence is committed by every officer of the company who is in default.

(4) A person guilty of an offence under subsection (3) is liable on summary conviction to a fine not exceeding level 3 on the standard scale and, for continued contravention, a daily default fine not exceeding one-tenth of level 3 on the standard scale.

781 Offences in connection with share warrants (Scotland)

(1) If in Scotland a person—

(a) with intent to defraud, forges or alters, or offers, utters, disposes of, or puts off, knowing the same to be forged or altered, any share warrant or coupon, or any document purporting to be a share warrant or coupon issued in pursuance of this Act, or

(b) by means of any such forged or altered share warrant, coupon or document—

(i) demands or endeavours to obtain or receive any share or interest in a company under this Act, or

(ii) demands or endeavours to receive any dividend or money payment in respect of any such share or interest,

knowing the warrant, coupon or document to be forged or altered,

he commits an offence.

(2) If in Scotland a person without lawful authority or excuse (of which proof lies on him)—

(a) engraves or makes on any plate, wood, stone, or other material, any share warrant or coupon purporting to be—

(i) a share warrant or coupon issued or made by any particular company in pursuance of this Act, or

(ii) a blank share warrant or coupon so issued or made, or

(iii) a part of such a share warrant or coupon, or

(b) uses any such plate, wood, stone, or other material, for the making or printing of any such share warrant or coupon, or of any such blank share warrant or coupon or of any part of such a share warrant or coupon, or

(c) knowingly has in his custody or possession any such plate, wood, stone, or other material,

he commits an offence.

(3) A person guilty of an offence under subsection (1) is liable on summary conviction to imprisonment for a term not exceeding six months or to a fine not exceeding level 5 on the standard scale (or both).

(4) A person guilty of an offence under subsection (2) is liable—

(a) on conviction on indictment, to imprisonment for a term not exceeding seven years or a fine (or both);

(b) on summary conviction, to imprisonment for a term not exceeding six months or a fine not exceeding the statutory maximum (or both).

Supplementary provisions

782 Issue of certificates etc: court order to make good default

(1) If a company on which a notice has been served requiring it to make good any default in complying with—

(a) section 769(1) (duty of company as to issue of certificates etc on allotment),

(b) section 776(1) (duty of company as to issue of certificates etc on transfer), or

(c) section 780(1) (duty of company as to issue of certificates etc on surrender of share warrant),

fails to make good the default within ten days after service of the notice, the person entitled to have the certificates or the debentures delivered to him may apply to the court.

(2) The court may on such an application make an order directing the company and any officer of it to make good the default within such time as may be specified in the order.

(3) The order may provide that all costs (in Scotland, expenses) of and incidental to the application are to be borne by the company or by an officer of it responsible for the default.

CHAPTER 2
EVIDENCING AND TRANSFER OF TITLE TO SECURITIES WITHOUT WRITTEN INSTRUMENT

Introductory

783 Scope of this Chapter

In this Chapter—

(a) "securities" means shares, debentures, debenture stock, loan stock, bonds, units of a collective investment scheme within the meaning of the Financial Services and Markets Act 2000 and other securities of any description;

(b) references to title to securities include any legal or equitable interest in securities;

(c) references to a transfer of title include a transfer by way of security;

(d) references to transfer without a written instrument include, in relation to bearer securities, transfer without delivery.

784 Power to make regulations

(1) The power to make regulations under this Chapter is exercisable by the Treasury and the Secretary of State, either jointly or concurrently.

(2) References in this Chapter to the authority having power to make regulations shall accordingly be read as references to both or either of them, as the case may require.

(3) Regulations under this Chapter are subject to affirmative resolution procedure.

Powers exercisable

785 Provision enabling procedures for evidencing and transferring title

(1) Provision may be made by regulations for enabling title to securities to be evidenced and transferred without a written instrument.

(2) The regulations may make provision—

(a) for procedures for recording and transferring title to securities, and

(b) for the regulation of those procedures and the persons responsible for or involved in their operation.

(3) The regulations must contain such safeguards as appear to the authority making the regulations appropriate for the protection of investors and for ensuring that competition is not restricted, distorted or prevented.

(4) The regulations may, for the purpose of enabling or facilitating the operation of the procedures provided for by the regulations, make provision with respect to the rights and obligations of persons in relation to securities dealt with under the procedures.

(5) The regulations may include provision for the purpose of giving effect to—

(a) the transmission of title to securities by operation of law;

(b) any restriction on the transfer of title to securities arising by virtue of the provisions of any enactment or instrument, court order or agreement;

(c) any power conferred by any such provision on a person to deal with securities on behalf of the person entitled.

(6) The regulations may make provision with respect to the persons responsible for the operation of the procedures provided for by the regulations—

(a) as to the consequences of their insolvency or incapacity, or

(b) as to the transfer from them to other persons of their functions in relation to those procedures.

(7) The regulations may confer functions on any person, including—

(a) the function of giving guidance or issuing a code of practice in relation to any provision made by the regulations, and

(b) the function of making rules for the purposes of any provision made by the regulations.

(8) The regulations may, in prescribed cases, confer immunity from liability in damages.

786 Provision enabling or requiring arrangements to be adopted

(1) Regulations under this Chapter may make provision—

(a) enabling the members of a company or of any designated class of companies to adopt, by ordinary resolution, arrangements under which title to securities is required to be evidenced or transferred (or both) without a written instrument; or

(b) requiring companies, or any designated class of companies, to adopt such arrangements.

(2) The regulations may make such provision—

(a) in respect of all securities issued by a company, or

(b) in respect of all securities of a specified description.

(3) The arrangements provided for by regulations making such provision as is mentioned in subsection (1)—

(a) must not be such that a person who but for the arrangements would be entitled to have his name entered in the company's register of members ceases to be so entitled, and

(b) must be such that a person who but for the arrangements would be entitled to exercise any rights in respect of the securities continues to be able effectively to control the exercise of those rights.

(4) The regulations may—

(a) prohibit the issue of any certificate by the company in respect of the issue or transfer of securities,

(b) require the provision by the company to holders of securities of statements (at specified intervals or on specified occasions) of the securities held in their name, and

(c) make provision as to the matters of which any such certificate or statement is, or is not, evidence.

(5) In this section—

(a) references to a designated class of companies are to a class designated in the regulations or by order under section 787; and

(b) "specified" means specified in the regulations.

787 Provision enabling or requiring arrangements to be adopted: order-making powers

(1) The authority having power to make regulations under this Chapter may by order—

(a) designate classes of companies for the purposes of section 786 (provision enabling or requiring arrangements to be adopted);

(b) provide that, in relation to securities of a specified description—

(i) in a designated class of companies, or

(ii) in a specified company or class of companies,

specified provisions of regulations made under this Chapter by virtue of that section either do not apply or apply subject to specified modifications.

(2) In subsection (1) "specified" means specified in the order.

(3) An order under this section is subject to negative resolution procedure.

Supplementary

788 Provision that may be included in regulations

Regulations under this Chapter may—

(a) modify or exclude any provision of any enactment or instrument, or any rule of law;

(b) apply, with such modifications as may be appropriate, the provisions of any enactment or instrument (including provisions creating criminal offences);

(c) require the payment of fees, or enable persons to require the payment of fees, of such amounts as may be specified in the regulations or determined in accordance with them;

(d) empower the authority making the regulations to delegate to any person willing and able to discharge them any functions of the authority under the regulations.

789 Duty to consult

Before making—

(a) regulations under this Chapter, or

(b) any order under section 787,

the authority having power to make regulations under this Chapter must carry out such consultation as appears to it to be appropriate.

790 Resolutions to be forwarded to registrar

Chapter 3 of Part 3 (resolutions affecting a company's constitution) applies to a resolution passed by virtue of regulations under this Chapter.

PART 22
INFORMATION ABOUT INTERESTS IN A COMPANY'S SHARES

Introductory

791 Companies to which this Part applies

This Part applies only to public companies.

792 Shares to which this Part applies

(1) References in this Part to a company's shares are to the company's issued shares of a class carrying rights to vote in all circumstances at general meetings of the company (including any shares held as treasury shares).

(2) The temporary suspension of voting rights in respect of any shares does not affect the application of this Part in relation to interests in those or any other shares.

Notice requiring information about interests in shares

793 Notice by company requiring information about interests in its shares

(1) A public company may give notice under this section to any person whom the company knows or has reasonable cause to believe—

(a) to be interested in the company's shares, or

(b) to have been so interested at any time during the three years immediately preceding the date on which the notice is issued.

(2) The notice may require the person—

(a) to confirm that fact or (as the case may be) to state whether or not it is the case, and

(b) if he holds, or has during that time held, any such interest, to give such further information as may be required in accordance with the following provisions of this section.

(3) The notice may require the person to whom it is addressed to give particulars of his own present or past interest in the company's shares (held by him at any time during the three year period mentioned in subsection (1)(b)).

(4) The notice may require the person to whom it is addressed, where—

(a) his interest is a present interest and another interest in the shares subsists, or

(b) another interest in the shares subsisted during that three year period at a time when his interest subsisted,

to give, so far as lies within his knowledge, such particulars with respect to that other interest as may be required by the notice.

(5) The particulars referred to in subsections (3) and (4) include—

(a) the identity of persons interested in the shares in question, and

(b) whether persons interested in the same shares are or were parties to—

(i) an agreement to which section 824 applies (certain share acquisition agreements), or

(ii) an agreement or arrangement relating to the exercise of any rights conferred by the holding of the shares.

(6) The notice may require the person to whom it is addressed, where his interest is a past interest, to give (so far as lies within his knowledge) particulars of the identity of the person who held that interest immediately upon his ceasing to hold it.

(7) The information required by the notice must be given within such reasonable time as may be specified in the notice.

794 Notice requiring information: order imposing restrictions on shares

(1) Where—

(a) a notice under section 793 (notice requiring information about interests in company's shares) is served by a company on a person who is or was interested in shares in the company, and

(b) that person fails to give the company the information required by the notice within the time specified in it,

the company may apply to the court for an order directing that the shares in question be subject to restrictions.

For the effect of such an order see section 797.

(2) If the court is satisfied that such an order may unfairly affect the rights of third parties in respect of the shares, the court may, for the purpose of protecting those rights and subject to such terms as

it thinks fit, direct that such acts by such persons or descriptions of persons and for such purposes as may be set out in the order shall not constitute a breach of the restrictions.

(3) On an application under this section the court may make an interim order. Any such order may be made unconditionally or on such terms as the court thinks fit.

(4) Sections 798 to 802 make further provision about orders under this section.

795 Notice requiring information: offences

(1) A person who—

(a) fails to comply with a notice under section 793 (notice requiring information about interests in company's shares), or

(b) in purported compliance with such a notice—

(i) makes a statement that he knows to be false in a material particular, or

(ii) recklessly makes a statement that is false in a material particular,

commits an offence.

(2) A person does not commit an offence under subsection (1)(a) if he proves that the requirement to give information was frivolous or vexatious.

(3) A person guilty of an offence under this section is liable—

(a) on conviction on indictment, to imprisonment for a term not exceeding two years or a fine (or both);

(b) on summary conviction—

(i) in England and Wales, to imprisonment for a term not exceeding twelve months or to a fine not exceeding the statutory maximum (or both);

(ii) in Scotland or Northern Ireland, to imprisonment for a term not exceeding six months, or to a fine not exceeding the statutory maximum (or both).

796 Notice requiring information: persons exempted from obligation to comply

(1) A person is not obliged to comply with a notice under section 793 (notice requiring information about interests in company's shares) if he is for the time being exempted by the Secretary of State from the operation of that section.

(2) The Secretary of State must not grant any such exemption unless—

(a) he has consulted the Governor of the Bank of England, and

(b) he (the Secretary of State) is satisfied that, having regard to any undertaking given by the person in question with respect to any interest held or to be held by him in any shares, there are special reasons why that person should not be subject to the obligations imposed by that section.

Orders imposing restrictions on shares

797 Consequences of order imposing restrictions

(1) The effect of an order under section 794 that shares are subject to restrictions is as follows—

(a) any transfer of the shares is void;

(b) no voting rights are exercisable in respect of the shares;

(c) no further shares may be issued in right of the shares or in pursuance of an offer made to their holder;

(d) except in a liquidation, no payment may be made of sums due from the company on the shares, whether in respect of capital or otherwise.

(2) Where shares are subject to the restriction in subsection (1) (a), an agreement to transfer the shares is void.

This does not apply to an agreement to transfer the shares on the making of an order under section 800 made by virtue of subsection (3)(b) (removal of restrictions in case of court-approved transfer).

(3) Where shares are subject to the restriction in subsection (1)(c) or (d), an agreement to transfer any right to be issued with other shares in right of those shares, or to receive any payment on them (otherwise than in a liquidation), is void.

This does not apply to an agreement to transfer any such right on the making of an order under section 800 made by virtue of subsection (3)(b) (removal of restrictions in case of court-approved transfer).

(4) The provisions of this section are subject—

(a) to any directions under section 794(2) or section 799(3) (directions for protection of third parties), and

(b) in the case of an interim order under section 794(3), to the terms of the order.

798 Penalty for attempted evasion of restrictions

(1) This section applies where shares are subject to restrictions by virtue of an order under section 794.

(2) A person commits an offence if he—

(a) exercises or purports to exercise any right—

(i) to dispose of shares that to his knowledge, are for the time being subject to restrictions, or

(ii) to dispose of any right to be issued with any such shares, or

(b) votes in respect of any such shares (whether as holder or proxy), or appoints a proxy to vote in respect of them, or

(c) being the holder of any such shares, fails to notify of their being subject to those restrictions a person whom he does not know to be aware of that fact but does know to be entitled (apart from the restrictions) to vote in respect of those shares whether as holder or as proxy, or

(d) being the holder of any such shares, or being entitled to a right to be issued with other shares in right of them, or to receive any payment on them (otherwise than in a liquidation), enters into an agreement which is void under section 797(2) or (3).

(3) If shares in a company are issued in contravention of the restrictions, an offence is committed by—

(a) the company, and

(b) every officer of the company who is in default.

(4) A person guilty of an offence under this section is liable—

(a) on conviction on indictment, to a fine;

(b) on summary conviction, to a fine not exceeding the statutory maximum.

(5) The provisions of this section are subject—

(a) to any directions under—

section 794(2) (directions for protection of third parties), or

section 799 or 800 (relaxation or removal of restrictions), and

(b) in the case of an interim order under section 794(3), to the terms of the order.

799 Relaxation of restrictions

(1) An application may be made to the court on the ground that an order directing that shares shall be subject to restrictions unfairly affects the rights of third parties in respect of the shares.

(2) An application for an order under this section may be made by the company or by any person aggrieved.

(3) If the court is satisfied that the application is well-founded, it may, for the purpose of protecting the rights of third parties in respect of the shares, and subject to such terms as it thinks fit, direct that such acts by such persons or descriptions of persons and for such purposes as may be set out in the order do not constitute a breach of the restrictions.

800 Removal of restrictions

(1) An application may be made to the court for an order directing that the shares shall cease to be subject to restrictions.

(2) An application for an order under this section may be made by the company or by any person aggrieved.

(3) The court must not make an order under this section unless—

(a) it is satisfied that the relevant facts about the shares have been disclosed to the company and no unfair advantage has accrued to any person as a result of the earlier failure to make that disclosure, or

(b) the shares are to be transferred for valuable consideration and the court approves the transfer.

(4) An order under this section made by virtue of subsection (3)(b) may continue, in whole or in part, the restrictions mentioned in section 797(1)(c) and (d) (restrictions on issue of further shares or making of payments) so far as they relate to a right acquired or offer made before the transfer.

(5) Where any restrictions continue in force under subsection (4)—

(a) an application may be made under this section for an order directing that the shares shall cease to be subject to those restrictions, and

(b) subsection (3) does not apply in relation to the making of such an order.

801 Order for sale of shares

(1) The court may order that the shares subject to restrictions be sold, subject to the court's approval as to the sale.

(2) An application for an order under subsection (1) may only be made by the company.

(3) Where the court has made an order under this section, it may make such further order relating to the sale or transfer of the shares as it thinks fit.

(4) An application for an order under subsection (3) may be made—

(a) by the company,

(b) by the person appointed by or in pursuance of the order to effect the sale, or

(c) by any person interested in the shares.

(5) On making an order under subsection (1) or (3) the court may order that the applicant's costs (in Scotland, expenses) be paid out of the proceeds of sale.

802 Application of proceeds of sale under court order

(1) Where shares are sold in pursuance of an order of the court under section 801, the proceeds of the sale, less the costs of the sale, must be paid into court for the benefit of the persons who are beneficially interested in the shares.

(2) A person who is beneficially interested in the shares may apply to the court for the whole or part of those proceeds to be paid to him.

(3) On such an application the court shall order the payment to the applicant of—

(a) the whole of the proceeds of sale together with any interest on them, or

(b) if another person had a beneficial interest in the shares at the time of their sale, such proportion of the proceeds and interest as the value of the applicant's interest in the shares bears to the total value of the shares.

This is subject to the following qualification.

(4) If the court has ordered under section 801(5) that the costs (in Scotland, expenses) of an applicant under that section are to be paid out of the proceeds of sale, the applicant is entitled to payment of his costs (or expenses) out of those proceeds before any person interested in the shares receives any part of those proceeds.

Power of members to require company to act

803 Power of members to require company to act

(1) The members of a company may require it to exercise its powers under section 793 (notice requiring information about interests in shares).

(2) A company is required to do so once it has received requests (to the same effect) from members of the company holding at least 10% of such of the paid-up capital of the company as carries a right to vote at general meetings of the company (excluding any voting rights attached to any shares in the company held as treasury shares).

(3) A request—

(a) may be in hard copy form or in electronic form,

(b) must—
  (i) state that the company is requested to exercise its powers under section 793,
  (ii) specify the manner in which the company is requested to act, and
  (iii) give reasonable grounds for requiring the company to exercise those powers in the manner specified, and

(c) must be authenticated by the person or persons making it.

804 Duty of company to comply with requirement

(1) A company that is required under section 803 to exercise its powers under section 793 (notice requiring information about interests in company's shares) must exercise those powers in the manner specified in the requests.

(2) If default is made in complying with subsection (1) an offence is committed by every officer of the company who is in default.

(3) A person guilty of an offence under this section is liable—
(a) on conviction on indictment, to a fine;
(b) on summary conviction, to a fine not exceeding the statutory maximum.

805 Report to members on outcome of investigation

(1) On the conclusion of an investigation carried out by a company in pursuance of a requirement under section 803 the company must cause a report of the information received in pursuance of the investigation to be prepared.

The report must be made available for inspection within a reasonable period (not more than 15 days) after the conclusion of the investigation.

(2) Where—
(a) a company undertakes an investigation in pursuance of a requirement under section 803, and
(b) the investigation is not concluded within three months after the date on which the company became subject to the requirement,

the company must cause to be prepared in respect of that period, and in respect of each succeeding period of three months ending before the conclusion of the investigation, an interim report of the information received during that period in pursuance of the investigation.

(3) Each such report must be made available for inspection within a reasonable period (not more than 15 days) after the end of the period to which it relates.

(4) The reports must be retained by the company for at least six years from the date on which they are first made available for inspection and must be kept available for inspection during that time—
(a) at the company's registered office, or
(b) at a place specified in regulations under section 1136.

(5) The company must give notice to the registrar—
(a) of the place at which the reports are kept available for inspection, and
(b) of any change in that place,

unless they have at all times been kept at the company's registered office.

(6) The company must within three days of making any report prepared under this section available for inspection, notify the members who made the requests under section 803 where the report is so available.

(7) For the purposes of this section an investigation carried out by a company in pursuance of a requirement under section 803 is concluded when—
(a) the company has made all such inquiries as are necessary or expedient for the purposes of the requirement, and
(b) in the case of each such inquiry—
  (i) a response has been received by the company, or
  (ii) the time allowed for a response has elapsed.

806 Report to members: offences

(1) If default is made for 14 days in complying with section 805(5) (notice to registrar of place at which reports made available for inspection) an offence is committed by—
(a) the company, and
(b) every officer of the company who is in default.

(2) A person guilty of an offence under subsection (1) is liable on summary conviction to a fine not exceeding level 3 on the standard scale and, for continued contravention, a daily default fine not exceeding one-tenth of level 3 on the standard scale.

(3) If default is made in complying with any other provision of section 805 (report to members on outcome of investigation), an offence is committed by every officer of the company who is in default.

(4) A person guilty of an offence under subsection (3) is liable—
(a) on conviction on indictment, to a fine;
(b) on summary conviction, to a fine not exceeding the statutory maximum.

807 Right to inspect and request copy of reports

(1) Any report prepared under section 805 must be open to inspection by any person without charge.

(2) Any person is entitled, on request and on payment of such fee as may be prescribed, to be provided with a copy of any such report or any part of it. The copy must be provided within ten days after the request is received by the company.

(3) If an inspection required under subsection (1) is refused, or default is made in complying with subsection (2), an offence is committed by—
(a) the company, and
(b) every officer of the company who is in default.

(4) A person guilty of an offence under this section is liable on summary conviction to a fine not exceeding level 3 on the standard scale and, for continued contravention, a daily default fine not exceeding one-tenth of level 3 on the standard scale.

(5) In the case of any such refusal or default the court may by order compel an immediate inspection or, as the case may be, direct that the copy required be sent to the person requiring it.

Register of interests disclosed

808 Register of interests disclosed

(1) The company must keep a register of information received by it in pursuance of a requirement imposed under section 793 (notice requiring information about interests in company's shares).

(2) A company which receives any such information must, within three days of the receipt, enter in the register—
(a) the fact that the requirement was imposed and the date on which it was imposed, and
(b) the information received in pursuance of the requirement.

(3) The information must be entered against the name of the present holder of the shares in question or, if there is no present holder or the present holder is not known, against the name of the person holding the interest.

(4) The register must be made up so that the entries against the names entered in it appear in chronological order.

(5) If default is made in complying with this section an offence is committed by—
(a) the company, and
(b) every officer of the company who is in default.

(6) A person guilty of an offence under this section is liable on summary conviction to a fine not exceeding level 3 on the standard scale and, for continued contravention, a daily default fine not exceeding one-tenth of level 3 on the standard scale.

(7) The company is not by virtue of anything done for the purposes of this section affected with notice of, or put upon inquiry as to, the rights of any person in relation to any shares.

809 Register to be kept available for inspection

(1) The register kept under section 808 (register of interests disclosed) must be kept available for inspection—

(a) at the company's registered office, or

(b) at a place specified in regulations under section 1136.

(2) A company must give notice to the registrar of companies of the place where the register is kept available for inspection and of any change in that place.

(3) No such notice is required if the register has at all times been kept available for inspection at the company's registered office.

(4) If default is made in complying with subsection (1), or a company makes default for 14 days in complying with subsection (2), an offence is committed by—

(a) the company, and

(b) every officer of the company who is in default.

(5) A person guilty of an offence under this section is liable on summary conviction to a fine not exceeding level 3 on the standard scale and, for continued contravention, a daily default fine not exceeding one-tenth of level 3 on the standard scale.

810 Associated index

(1) Unless the register kept under section 808 (register of interests disclosed) is kept in such a form as itself to constitute an index, the company must keep an index of the names entered in it.

(2) The company must make any necessary entry or alteration in the index within ten days after the date on which any entry or alteration is made in the register.

(3) The index must contain, in respect of each name, a sufficient indication to enable the information entered against it to be readily found.

(4) The index must be at all times kept available for inspection at the same place as the register.

(5) If default is made in complying with this section, an offence is committed by—

(a) the company, and

(b) every officer of the company who is in default.

(6) A person guilty of an offence under this section is liable on summary conviction to a fine not exceeding level 3 on the standard scale and, for continued contravention, a daily default fine not exceeding one-tenth of level 3 on the standard scale.

811 Rights to inspect and require copy of entries

(1) The register required to be kept under section 808 (register of interests disclosed), and any associated index, must be open to inspection by any person without charge.

(2) Any person is entitled, on request and on payment of such fee as may be prescribed, to be provided with a copy of any entry in the register.

(3) A person seeking to exercise either of the rights conferred by this section must make a request to the company to that effect.

(4) The request must contain the following information—

(a) in the case of an individual, his name and address;

(b) in the case of an organisation, the name and address of an individual responsible for making the request on behalf of the organisation;

(c) the purpose for which the information is to be used; and

(d) whether the information will be disclosed to any other person, and if so—

(i) where that person is an individual, his name and address,

(ii) where that person is an organisation, the name and address of an individual responsible for receiving the information on its behalf, and

(iii) the purpose for which the information is to be used by that person.

812 Court supervision of purpose for which rights may be exercised

(1) Where a company receives a request under section 811 (register of interests disclosed: right to inspect and require copy), it must—

(a) comply with the request if it is satisfied that it is made for a proper purpose, and
(b) refuse the request if it is not so satisfied.

(2) If the company refuses the request, it must inform the person making the request, stating the reason why it is not satisfied.

(3) A person whose request is refused may apply to the court.

(4) If an application is made to the court—
(a) the person who made the request must notify the company, and
(b) the company must use its best endeavours to notify any persons whose details would be disclosed if the company were required to comply with the request.

(5) If the court is not satisfied that the inspection or copy is sought for a proper purpose, it shall direct the company not to comply with the request.

(6) If the court makes such a direction and it appears to the court that the company is or may be subject to other requests made for a similar purpose (whether made by the same person or different persons), it may direct that the company is not to comply with any such request.
The order must contain such provision as appears to the court appropriate to identify the requests to which it applies.

(7) If the court does not direct the company not to comply with the request, the company must comply with the request immediately upon the court giving its decision or, as the case may be, the proceedings being discontinued.

813 Register of interests disclosed: refusal of inspection or default in providing copy

(1) If an inspection required under section 811 (register of interests disclosed: right to inspect and require copy) is refused or default is made in providing a copy required under that section, otherwise than in accordance with an order of the court, an offence is committed by—
(a) the company, and
(b) every officer of the company who is in default.

(2) A person guilty of an offence under this section is liable on summary conviction to a fine not exceeding level 3 on the standard scale and, for continued contravention, a daily default fine not exceeding one-tenth of level 3 on the standard scale.

(3) In the case of any such refusal or default the court may by order compel an immediate inspection or, as the case may be, direct that the copy required be sent to the person requesting it.

814 Register of interests disclosed: offences in connection with request for or disclosure of information

(1) It is an offence for a person knowingly or recklessly to make in a request under section 811 (register of interests disclosed: right to inspect or require copy) a statement that is misleading, false or deceptive in a material particular.

(2) It is an offence for a person in possession of information obtained by exercise of either of the rights conferred by that section—
(a) to do anything that results in the information being disclosed to another person, or
(b) to fail to do anything with the result that the information is disclosed to another person,
knowing, or having reason to suspect, that person may use the information for a purpose that is not a proper purpose.

(3) A person guilty of an offence under this section is liable—
(a) on conviction on indictment, to imprisonment for a term not exceeding two years or a fine (or both);
(b) on summary conviction—
(i) in England and Wales, to imprisonment for a term not exceeding twelve months or to a fine not exceeding the statutory maximum (or both);
(ii) in Scotland or Northern Ireland, to imprisonment for a term not exceeding six months, or to a fine not exceeding the statutory maximum (or both).

815 Entries not to be removed from register

(1) Entries in the register kept under section 808 (register of interests disclosed) must not be deleted except in accordance with—
section 816 (old entries), or
section 817 (incorrect entry relating to third party).

(2) If an entry is deleted in contravention of subsection (1), the company must restore it as soon as reasonably practicable.

(3) If default is made in complying with subsection (1) or (2), an offence is committed by—
(a) the company, and
(b) every officer of the company who is in default.

(4) A person guilty of an offence under this section is liable on summary conviction to a fine not exceeding level 3 on the standard scale and, for continued contravention of subsection (2), a daily default fine not exceeding one-tenth of level 3 on the standard scale.

816 Removal of entries from register: old entries

A company may remove an entry from the register kept under section 808 (register of interests disclosed) if more than six years have elapsed since the entry was made.

817 Removal of entries from register: incorrect entry relating to third party

(1) This section applies where in pursuance of an obligation imposed by a notice under section 793 (notice requiring information about interests in company's shares) a person gives to a company the name and address of another person as being interested in shares in the company.

(2) That other person may apply to the company for the removal of the entry from the register.

(3) If the company is satisfied that the information in pursuance of which the entry was made is incorrect, it shall remove the entry.

(4) If an application under subsection (3) is refused, the applicant may apply to the court for an order directing the company to remove the entry in question from the register.
The court may make such an order if it thinks fit.

818 Adjustment of entry relating to share acquisition agreement

(1) If a person who is identified in the register kept by a company under section 808 (register of interests disclosed) as being a party to an agreement to which section 824 applies (certain share acquisition agreements) ceases to be a party to the agreement, he may apply to the company for the inclusion of that information in the register.

(2) If the company is satisfied that he has ceased to be a party to the agreement, it shall record that information (if not already recorded) in every place where his name appears in the register as a party to the agreement.

(3) If an application under this section is refused (otherwise than on the ground that the information has already been recorded), the applicant may apply to the court for an order directing the company to include the information in question in the register.
The court may make such an order if it thinks fit.

819 Duty of company ceasing to be public company

(1) If a company ceases to be a public company, it must continue to keep any register kept under section 808 (register of interests disclosed), and any associated index, until the end of the period of six years after it ceased to be such a company.

(2) If default is made in complying with this section, an offence is committed by—
(a) the company, and
(b) every officer of the company who is in default.

(3) A person guilty of an offence under this section is liable on summary conviction to a fine not exceeding level 3 on the standard scale and, for continued contravention, a daily default fine not exceeding one-tenth of level 3 on the standard scale.

Meaning of interest in shares

820 Interest in shares: general

(1) This section applies to determine for the purposes of this Part whether a person has an interest in shares.

(2) In this Part—

(a) a reference to an interest in shares includes an interest of any kind whatsoever in the shares, and

(b) any restraints or restrictions to which the exercise of any right attached to the interest is or may be subject shall be disregarded.

(3) Where an interest in shares is comprised in property held on trust, every beneficiary of the trust is treated as having an interest in the shares.

(4) A person is treated as having an interest in shares if—

(a) he enters into a contract to acquire them, or

(b) not being the registered holder, he is entitled—

(i) to exercise any right conferred by the holding of the shares, or

(ii) to control the exercise of any such right.

(5) For the purposes of subsection (4) (b) a person is entitled to exercise or control the exercise of a right conferred by the holding of shares if he—

(a) has a right (whether subject to conditions or not) the exercise of which would make him so entitled, or

(b) is under an obligation (whether subject to conditions or not) the fulfilment of which would make him so entitled.

(6) A person is treated as having an interest in shares if—

(a) he has a right to call for delivery of the shares to himself or to his order, or

(b) he has a right to acquire an interest in shares or is under an obligation to take an interest in shares.

This applies whether the right or obligation is conditional or absolute.

(7) Persons having a joint interest are treated as each having that interest.

(8) It is immaterial that shares in which a person has an interest are unidentifiable.

821 Interest in shares: right to subscribe for shares

(1) Section 793 (notice by company requiring information about interests in its shares) applies in relation to a person who has, or previously had, or is or was entitled to acquire, a right to subscribe for shares in the company as it applies in relation to a person who is or was interested in shares in that company.

(2) References in that section to an interest in shares shall be read accordingly.

822 Interest in shares: family interests

(1) For the purposes of this Part a person is taken to be interested in shares in which—

(a) his spouse or civil partner, or

(b) any infant child or step-child of his,

is interested.

(2) In relation to Scotland "infant" means a person under the age of 18 years.

823 Interest in shares: corporate interests

(1) For the purposes of this Part a person is taken to be interested in shares if a body corporate is interested in them and—

(a) the body or its directors are accustomed to act in accordance with his directions or instructions, or

(b) he is entitled to exercise or control the exercise of one-third or more of the voting power at general meetings of the body.

(2) For the purposes of this section a person is treated as entitled to exercise or control the exercise of voting power if—

(a) another body corporate is entitled to exercise or control the exercise of that voting power, and

(b) he is entitled to exercise or control the exercise of one-third or more of the voting power at general meetings of that body corporate.

(3) For the purposes of this section a person is treated as entitled to exercise or control the exercise of voting power if—

(a) he has a right (whether or not subject to conditions) the exercise of which would make him so entitled, or

(b) he is under an obligation (whether or not subject to conditions) the fulfilment of which would make him so entitled.

824 Interest in shares: agreement to acquire interests in a particular company

(1) For the purposes of this Part an interest in shares may arise from an agreement between two or more persons that includes provision for the acquisition by any one or more of them of interests in shares of a particular public company (the "target company" for that agreement).

(2) This section applies to such an agreement if—

(a) the agreement includes provision imposing obligations or restrictions on any one or more of the parties to it with respect to their use, retention or disposal of their interests in the shares of the target company acquired in pursuance of the agreement (whether or not together with any other interests of theirs in the company's shares to which the agreement relates), and

(b) an interest in the target company's shares is in fact acquired by any of the parties in pursuance of the agreement.

(3) The reference in subsection (2) to the use of interests in shares in the target company is to the exercise of any rights or of any control or influence arising from those interests (including the right to enter into an agreement for the exercise, or for control of the exercise, of any of those rights by another person).

(4) Once an interest in shares in the target company has been acquired in pursuance of the agreement, this section continues to apply to the agreement so long as the agreement continues to include provisions of any description mentioned in subsection (2).

This applies irrespective of—

(a) whether or not any further acquisitions of interests in the company's shares take place in pursuance of the agreement;

(b) any change in the persons who are for the time being parties to it;

(c) any variation of the agreement.

References in this subsection to the agreement include any agreement having effect (whether directly or indirectly) in substitution for the original agreement.

(5) In this section—

(a) "agreement" includes any agreement or arrangement, and

(b) references to provisions of an agreement include—

(i) undertakings, expectations or understandings operative under an arrangement, and

(ii) any provision whether express or implied and whether absolute or not.

References elsewhere in this Part to an agreement to which this section applies have a corresponding meaning.

(6) This section does not apply—

(a) to an agreement that is not legally binding unless it involves mutuality in the undertakings, expectations or understandings of the parties to it; or

(b) to an agreement to underwrite or sub-underwrite an offer of shares in a company, provided the agreement is confined to that purpose and any matters incidental to it.

825 Extent of obligation in case of share acquisition agreement

(1) For the purposes of this Part each party to an agreement to which section 824 applies is treated as interested in all shares in the target company in which any other party to the agreement is

interested apart from the agreement (whether or not the interest of the other party was acquired, or includes any interest that was acquired, in pursuance of the agreement).

(2) For those purposes an interest of a party to such an agreement in shares in the target company is an interest apart from the agreement if he is interested in those shares otherwise than by virtue of the application of section 824 (and this section) in relation to the agreement.

(3) Accordingly, any such interest of the person (apart from the agreement) includes for those purposes any interest treated as his under section 822 or 823 (family or corporate interests) or by the application of section 824 (and this section) in relation to any other agreement with respect to shares in the target company to which he is a party.

(4) A notification with respect to his interest in shares in the target company made to the company under this Part by a person who is for the time being a party to an agreement to which section 824 applies must—

(a) state that the person making the notification is a party to such an agreement,

(b) include the names and (so far as known to him) the addresses of the other parties to the agreement, identifying them as such, and

(c) state whether or not any of the shares to which the notification relates are shares in which he is interested by virtue of section 824 (and this section) and, if so, the number of those shares.

Other supplementary provisions

826 Information protected from wider disclosure

(1) Information in respect of which a company is for the time being entitled to any exemption conferred by regulations under section 409(3) (information about related undertakings to be given in notes to accounts: exemption where disclosure harmful to company's business)—

(a) must not be included in a report under section 805 (report to members on outcome of investigation), and

(b) must not be made available under section 811 (right to inspect and request copy of entries).

(2) Where any such information is omitted from a report under section 805, that fact must be stated in the report.

827 Reckoning of periods for fulfilling obligations

Where the period allowed by any provision of this Part for fulfilling an obligation is expressed as a number of days, any day that is not a working day shall be disregarded in reckoning that period.

828 Power to make further provision by regulations

(1) The Secretary of State may by regulations amend—

(a) the definition of shares to which this Part applies (section 792),

(b) the provisions as to notice by a company requiring information about interests in its shares (section 793), and

(c) the provisions as to what is taken to be an interest in shares (sections 820 and 821).

(2) The regulations may amend, repeal or replace those provisions and make such other consequential amendments or repeals of provisions of this Part as appear to the Secretary of State to be appropriate.

(3) Regulations under this section are subject to affirmative resolution procedure.

PART 23
DISTRIBUTIONS

CHAPTER 1
RESTRICTIONS ON WHEN DISTRIBUTIONS MAY BE MADE

Introductory

829 Meaning of "distribution"

(1) In this Part "distribution" means every description of distribution of a company's assets to its members, whether in cash or otherwise, subject to the following exceptions.

(2) The following are not distributions for the purposes of this Part—
(a) an issue of shares as fully or partly paid bonus shares;
(b) the reduction of share capital—
(i) by extinguishing or reducing the liability of any of the members on any of the company's shares in respect of share capital not paid up, or
(ii) by repaying paid-up share capital;
(c) the redemption or purchase of any of the company's own shares out of capital (including the proceeds of any fresh issue of shares) or out of unrealised profits in accordance with Chapter 3, 4 or 5 of Part 18;
(d) a distribution of assets to members of the company on its winding up.

General rules

830 Distributions to be made only out of profits available for the purpose

(1) A company may only make a distribution out of profits available for the purpose.
(2) A company's profits available for distribution are its accumulated, realised profits, so far as not previously utilised by distribution or capitalisation, less its accumulated, realised losses, so far as not previously written off in a reduction or reorganisation of capital duly made.
(3) Subsection (2) has effect subject to sections 832 and 835 (investment companies etc: distributions out of accumulated revenue profits).

831 Net asset restriction on distributions by public companies

(1) A public company may only make a distribution—
(a) if the amount of its net assets is not less than the aggregate of its called-up share capital and undistributable reserves, and
(b) if, and to the extent that, the distribution does not reduce the amount of those assets to less than that aggregate.
(2) For this purpose a company's "net assets" means the aggregate of the company's assets less the aggregate of its liabilities.
(3) "Liabilities" here includes—
(a) where the relevant accounts are Companies Act accounts, provisions of a kind specified for the purposes of this subsection by regulations under section 396;
(b) where the relevant accounts are IAS accounts, provisions of any kind.
(4) A company's undistributable reserves are—
(a) its share premium account;
(b) its capital redemption reserve;
(c) the amount by which its accumulated, unrealised profits (so far as not previously utilised by capitalisation) exceed its accumulated, unrealised losses (so far as not previously written off in a reduction or reorganisation of capital duly made);
(d) any other reserve that the company is prohibited from distributing—
(i) by any enactment (other than one contained in this Part), or
(ii) by its articles.

The reference in paragraph (c) to capitalisation does not include a transfer of profits of the company to its capital redemption reserve.
(5) A public company must not include any uncalled share capital as an asset in any accounts relevant for purposes of this section.
(6) Subsection (1) has effect subject to sections 832 and 835 (investment companies etc: distributions out of accumulated revenue profits).

Distributions by investment companies

832 Distributions by investment companies out of accumulated revenue profits

(1) An investment company may make a distribution out of its accumulated, realised revenue profits if the following conditions are met.

(2) It may make such a distribution only if, and to the extent that, its accumulated, realised revenue profits, so far as not previously utilised by a distribution or capitalisation, exceed its accumulated revenue losses (whether realised or unrealised), so far as not previously written off in a reduction or reorganisation of capital duly made.

(3) It may make such a distribution only—
(a) if the amount of its assets is at least equal to one and a half times the aggregate of its liabilities to creditors, and
(b) if, and to the extent that, the distribution does not reduce that amount to less than one and a half times that aggregate.

(4) For this purpose a company's liabilities to creditors include—
(a) in the case of Companies Act accounts, provisions of a kind specified for the purposes of this subsection by regulations under section 396;
(b) in the case of IAS accounts, provisions for liabilities to creditors.

(5) The following conditions must also be met—
(a) the company's shares must be shares admitted to trading on a regulated market;
(b) during the relevant period it must not have—
(i) ...
(ii) applied any unrealised profits ... in paying up debentures or amounts unpaid on its issued shares;
(c) it must have given notice to the registrar under section 833(1) (notice of intention to carry on business as an investment company)—
(i) before the beginning of the relevant period, or
(ii) as soon as reasonably practicable after the date of its incorporation.

(6) For the purposes of this section—
(a) ...
(b) the "relevant period" is the period beginning with—
(i) the first day of the accounting reference period immediately preceding that in which the proposed distribution is to be made, or
(ii) where the distribution is to be made in the company's first accounting reference period, the first day of that period, and ending with the date of the distribution.

(7) The company must not include any uncalled share capital as an asset in any accounts relevant for purposes of this section.

833 Meaning of "investment company"

(1) In this Part an "investment company" means a public company that—
(a) has given notice (which has not been revoked) to the registrar of its intention to carry on business as an investment company, and
(b) since the date of that notice has complied with the following requirement.

(2) The requirement is—
(a) that the business of the company consists of investing its funds in shares, land or other assets, with the aim of spreading investment risk and giving members of the company the benefit of the results of the management of its funds;
(b)–(d) ...

(3) ...

(4) Notice to the registrar under this section may be revoked at any time by the company on giving notice to the registrar that it no longer wishes to be an investment company within the meaning of this section.

(5) On giving such a notice, the company ceases to be such a company.

834, 835 ...

CHAPTER 2
JUSTIFICATION OF DISTRIBUTION BY REFERENCE TO ACCOUNTS

Justification of distribution by reference to accounts

836 Justification of distribution by reference to relevant accounts

(1) Whether a distribution may be made by a company without contravening this Part is determined by reference to the following items as stated in the relevant accounts—

(a) profits, losses, assets and liabilities;

(b) provisions of the following kinds—

(i) where the relevant accounts are Companies Act accounts, provisions of a kind specified for the purposes of this subsection by regulations under section 396;

(ii) where the relevant accounts are IAS accounts, provisions of any kind;

(c) share capital and reserves (including undistributable reserves).

(2) The relevant accounts are the company's last annual accounts, except that—

(a) where the distribution would be found to contravene this Part by reference to the company's last annual accounts, it may be justified by reference to interim accounts, and

(b) where the distribution is proposed to be declared during the company's first accounting reference period, or before any accounts have been circulated in respect of that period, it may be justified by reference to initial accounts.

(3) The requirements of—

section 837 (as regards the company's last annual accounts), section 838 (as regards interim accounts), and

section 839 (as regards initial accounts),

must be complied with, as and where applicable.

(4) If any applicable requirement of those sections is not complied with, the accounts may not be relied on for the purposes of this Part and the distribution is accordingly treated as contravening this Part.

Requirements applicable in relation to relevant accounts

837 Requirements where last annual accounts used

(1) The company's last annual accounts means the company's individual accounts—

(a) that were last circulated to members in accordance with section 423 (duty to circulate copies of annual accounts and reports), or

(b) if in accordance with section 426 the company provided a summary financial statement instead, that formed the basis of that statement.

(2) The accounts must have been properly prepared in accordance with this Act, or have been so prepared subject only to matters that are not material for determining (by reference to the items mentioned in section 836(1)) whether the distribution would contravene this Part.

(3) Unless the company is exempt from audit and the directors take advantage of that exemption, the auditor must have made his report on the accounts.

(4) If that report was qualified—

(a) the auditor must have stated in writing (either at the time of his report or subsequently) whether in his opinion the matters in respect of which his report is qualified are material for determining whether a distribution would contravene this Part, and

(b) a copy of that statement must—

(i) in the case of a private company, have been circulated to members in accordance with section 423, or

(ii) in the case of a public company, have been laid before the company in general meeting.

(5) An auditor's statement is sufficient for the purposes of a distribution if it relates to distributions of a description that includes the distribution in question, even if at the time of the statement it had not been proposed.

838 Requirements where interim accounts used

(1) Interim accounts must be accounts that enable a reasonable judgment to be made as to the amounts of the items mentioned in section 836(1).

(2) Where interim accounts are prepared for a proposed distribution by a public company, the following requirements apply.

(3) The accounts must have been properly prepared, or have been so prepared subject to matters that are not material for determining (by reference to the items mentioned in section 836(1)) whether the distribution would contravene this Part.

(4) "Properly prepared" means prepared in accordance with sections 395 to 397 (requirements for company individual accounts), applying those requirements with such modifications as are necessary because the accounts are prepared otherwise than in respect of an accounting reference period.

(5) The balance sheet comprised in the accounts must have been signed in accordance with section 414.

(6) A copy of the accounts must have been delivered to the registrar. Any requirement of Part 35 of this Act as to the delivery of a certified translation into English of any document forming part of the accounts must also have been met.

839 Requirements where initial accounts used

(1) Initial accounts must be accounts that enable a reasonable judgment to be made as to the amounts of the items mentioned in section 836(1).

(2) Where initial accounts are prepared for a proposed distribution by a public company, the following requirements apply.

(3) The accounts must have been properly prepared, or have been so prepared subject to matters that are not material for determining (by reference to the items mentioned in section 836(1)) whether the distribution would contravene this Part.

(4) "Properly prepared" means prepared in accordance with sections 395 to 397 (requirements for company individual accounts), applying those requirements with such modifications as are necessary because the accounts are prepared otherwise than in respect of an accounting reference period.

(5) The company's auditor must have made a report stating whether, in his opinion, the accounts have been properly prepared.

(6) If that report was qualified—

(a) the auditor must have stated in writing (either at the time of his report or subsequently) whether in his opinion the matters in respect of which his report is qualified are material for determining whether a distribution would contravene this Part, and

(b) a copy of that statement must have been laid before the company in general meeting.

(7) A copy of the accounts, of the auditor's report and of any auditor's statement must have been delivered to the registrar.

Any requirement of Part 35 of this Act as to the delivery of a certified translation into English of any of those documents must also have been met.

Application of provisions to successive distributions etc

840 Successive distributions etc by reference to the same accounts

(1) In determining whether a proposed distribution may be made by a company in a case where—

(a) one or more previous distributions have been made in pursuance of a determination made by reference to the same relevant accounts, or

(b) relevant financial assistance has been given, or other relevant payments have been made, since those accounts were prepared,

the provisions of this Part apply as if the amount of the proposed distribution was increased by the amount of the previous distributions, financial assistance and other payments.

(2) The financial assistance and other payments that are relevant for this purpose are—

(a) financial assistance lawfully given by the company out of its distributable profits;
(b) financial assistance given by the company in contravention of section 678 or 679 (prohibited financial assistance) in a case where the giving of that assistance reduces the company's net assets or increases its net liabilities;
(c) payments made by the company in respect of the purchase by it of shares in the company, except a payment lawfully made otherwise than out of distributable profits;
(d) payments of any description specified in section 705 (payments apart from purchase price of shares to be made out of distributable profits).

(3) In this section "financial assistance" has the same meaning as in Chapter 2 of Part 18 (see section 677).

(4) For the purpose of applying subsection (2)(b) in relation to any financial assistance—
(a) "net assets" means the amount by which the aggregate amount of the company's assets exceeds the aggregate amount of its liabilities, and
(b) "net liabilities" means the amount by which the aggregate amount of the company's liabilities exceeds the aggregate amount of its assets,

taking the amount of the assets and liabilities to be as stated in the company's accounting records immediately before the financial assistance is given.

(5) For this purpose a company's liabilities include any amount retained as reasonably necessary for the purposes of providing for any liability—
(a) the nature of which is clearly defined, and
(b) which is either likely to be incurred or certain to be incurred but uncertain as to amount or as to the date on which it will arise.

CHAPTER 3
SUPPLEMENTARY PROVISIONS

Accounting matters

841 Realised losses and profits and revaluation of fixed assets

(1) The following provisions have effect for the purposes of this Part.

(2) The following are treated as realised losses—
(a) in the case of Companies Act accounts, provisions of a kind specified for the purposes of this paragraph by regulations under section 396 (except revaluation provisions);
(b) in the case of IAS accounts, provisions of any kind (except revaluation provisions).

(3) A "revaluation provision" means a provision in respect of a diminution in value of a fixed asset appearing on a revaluation of all the fixed assets of the company, or of all of its fixed assets other than goodwill.

(4) For the purpose of subsections (2) and (3) any consideration by the directors of the value at a particular time of a fixed asset is treated as a revaluation provided—
(a) the directors are satisfied that the aggregate value at that time of the fixed assets of the company that have not actually been revalued is not less than the aggregate amount at which they are then stated in the company's accounts, and
(b) it is stated in a note to the accounts—
  (i) that the directors have considered the value of some or all of the fixed assets of the company without actually revaluing them,
  (ii) that they are satisfied that the aggregate value of those assets at the time of their consideration was not less than the aggregate amount at which they were then stated in the company's accounts, and
  (iii) that accordingly, by virtue of this subsection, amounts are stated in the accounts on the basis that a revaluation of fixed assets of the company is treated as having taken place at that time.

(5) Where—
(a) on the revaluation of a fixed asset, an unrealised profit is shown to have been made, and

(b) on or after the revaluation, a sum is written off or retained for depreciation of that asset over a period,

an amount equal to the amount by which that sum exceeds the sum which would have been so written off or retained for the depreciation of that asset over that period, if that profit had not been made, is treated as a realised profit made over that period.

842 Determination of profit or loss in respect of asset where records incomplete

In determining for the purposes of this Part whether a company has made a profit or loss in respect of an asset where—

(a) there is no record of the original cost of the asset, or

(b) a record cannot be obtained without unreasonable expense or delay, its cost is taken to be the value ascribed to it in the earliest available record of its value made on or after its acquisition by the company.

843 Realised profits and losses of long-term insurance business

(1) The provisions of this section have effect for the purposes of this Part as it applies in relation to an authorised insurance company, other than an insurance special purpose vehicle, carrying on long-term business.

(2) An amount included in the relevant part of the company's balance sheet that—

(a) represents a surplus in the fund or funds maintained by it in respect of its long-term business, and

(b) has not been allocated to policy holders or, as the case may be, carried forward unappropriated in accordance with asset identification rules made under Part 9A of the Financial Services and Markets Act 2000,

is treated as a realised profit.

(3) For the purposes of subsection (2)—

(a) the relevant part of the balance sheet is that part of the balance sheet that represents accumulated profit or loss;

(b) a surplus in the fund or funds maintained by the company in respect of its long-term business means an excess of the assets representing that fund or those funds over the liabilities of the company attributable to its long-term business, as shown by an actuarial investigation.

(4) A deficit in the fund or funds maintained by the company in respect of its long-term business is treated as a realised loss.

For this purpose a deficit in any such fund or funds means an excess of the liabilities of the company attributable to its long-term business over the assets representing that fund or those funds, as shown by an actuarial investigation.

(5) Subject to subsections (2) and (4), any profit or loss arising in the company's long-term business is to be left out of account.

(6) For the purposes of this section an "actuarial investigation" means an investigation made into the financial condition of an authorised insurance company in respect of its long-term business—

(a) carried out once in every period of twelve months in accordance with rules made under Part 9A of the Financial Services and Markets Act 2000, or

(b) carried out in accordance with a requirement imposed under section 166 of that Act,

by an actuary appointed as actuary to the company.

(7) In this section "long-term business" means business that consists of effecting or carrying out contracts of long-term insurance.

This definition must be read with section 22 of the Financial Services and Markets Act 2000, any relevant order under that section and Schedule 2 to that Act.

(8) In this section "insurance special purpose vehicle" means a special purpose vehicle within the meaning of Article 2.1(p) of Directive 2005/68/EC of the European Parliament and of the Council of 16 November 2005 on reinsurance and amending Council Directives 73/239/EEC, 92/49/EEC as well as Directives 98/78/EC and 2002/83/EC.

844 Treatment of development costs

(1) Where development costs are shown or included as an asset in a company's accounts, any amount shown or included in respect of those costs is treated—

(a) for the purposes of section 830 (distributions to be made out of profits available for the purpose) as a realised loss, and

(b) for the purposes of section 832 (distributions by investment companies out of accumulated revenue profits) as a realised revenue loss. This is subject to the following exceptions.

(2) Subsection (1) does not apply to any part of that amount representing an unrealised profit made on revaluation of those costs.

(3) Subsection (1) does not apply if—

(a) there are special circumstances in the company's case justifying the directors in deciding that the amount there mentioned is not to be treated as required by subsection (1),

(b) it is stated—

(i) in the case of Companies Act accounts, in the note required by regulations under section 396 as to the reasons for showing development costs as an asset, or

(ii) in the case of IAS accounts, in any note to the accounts,

that the amount is not to be so treated, and

(c) the note explains the circumstances relied upon to justify the decision of the directors to that effect.

Distributions in kind

845 Distributions in kind: determination of amount

(1) This section applies for determining the amount of a distribution consisting of or including, or treated as arising in consequence of, the sale, transfer or other disposition by a company of a non-cash asset where—

(a) at the time of the distribution the company has profits available for distribution, and

(b) if the amount of the distribution were to be determined in accordance with this section, the company could make the distribution without contravening this Part.

(2) The amount of the distribution (or the relevant part of it) is taken to be—

(a) in a case where the amount or value of the consideration for the disposition is not less than the book value of the asset, zero;

(b) in any other case, the amount by which the book value of the asset exceeds the amount or value of any consideration for the disposition.

(3) For the purposes of subsection (1) (a) the company's profits available for distribution are treated as increased by the amount (if any) by which the amount or value of any consideration for the disposition exceeds the book value of the asset.

(4) In this section "book value", in relation to an asset, means—

(a) the amount at which the asset is stated in the relevant accounts, or

(b) where the asset is not stated in those accounts at any amount, zero.

(5) The provisions of Chapter 2 (justification of distribution by reference to accounts) have effect subject to this section.

846 Distributions in kind: treatment of unrealised profits

(1) This section applies where—

(a) a company makes a distribution consisting of or including, or treated as arising in consequence of, the sale, transfer or other disposition by the company of a non-cash asset, and

(b) any part of the amount at which that asset is stated in the relevant accounts represents an unrealised profit.

(2) That profit is treated as a realised profit—

(a) for the purpose of determining the lawfulness of the distribution in accordance with this Part (whether before or after the distribution takes place), and

(b) for the purpose of the application, in relation to anything done with a view to or in connection with the making of the distribution, of any provision of regulations under section 396 under which only realised profits are to be included in or transferred to the profit and loss account.

Consequences of unlawful distribution

847 Consequences of unlawful distribution

(1) This section applies where a distribution, or part of one, made by a company to one of its members is made in contravention of this Part.

(2) If at the time of the distribution the member knows or has reasonable grounds for believing that it is so made, he is liable—

(a) to repay it (or that part of it, as the case may be) to the company, or

(b) in the case of a distribution made otherwise than in cash, to pay the company a sum equal to the value of the distribution (or part) at that time.

(3) This is without prejudice to any obligation imposed apart from this section on a member of a company to repay a distribution unlawfully made to him.

(4) This section does not apply in relation to—

(a) financial assistance given by a company in contravention of section 678 or 679, or

(b) any payment made by a company in respect of the redemption or purchase by the company of shares in itself.

Other matters

848 Saving for certain older provisions in articles

(1) Where immediately before the relevant date a company was authorised by a provision of its articles to apply its unrealised profits in paying up in full or in part unissued shares to be allotted to members of the company as fully or partly paid bonus shares, that provision continues (subject to any alteration of the articles) as authority for those profits to be so applied after that date.

(2) For this purpose the relevant date is—

(a) for companies registered in Great Britain, 22nd December 1980;

(b) for companies registered in Northern Ireland, 1st July 1983.

849 Restriction on application of unrealised profits

A company must not apply an unrealised profit in paying up debentures or any amounts unpaid on its issued shares.

850 Treatment of certain older profits or losses

(1) Where the directors of a company are, after making all reasonable enquiries, unable to determine whether a particular profit made before the relevant date is realised or unrealised, they may treat the profit as realised.

(2) Where the directors of a company, after making all reasonable enquiries, are unable to determine whether a particular loss made before the relevant date is realised or unrealised, they may treat the loss as unrealised.

(3) For the purposes of this section the relevant date is—

(a) for companies registered in Great Britain, 22nd December 1980;

(b) for companies registered in Northern Ireland, 1st July 1983.

851 Application of rules of law restricting distributions

(1) Except as provided in this section, the provisions of this Part are without prejudice to any rule of law restricting the sums out of which, or the cases in which, a distribution may be made.

(2) For the purposes of any rule of law requiring distributions to be paid out of profits or restricting the return of capital to members—

(a) section 845 (distributions in kind: determination of amount) applies to determine the amount of any distribution or return of capital consisting of or including, or treated as arising in consequence of the sale, transfer or other disposition by a company of a non-cash asset; and

(b) section 846 (distributions in kind: treatment of unrealised profits) applies as it applies for the purposes of this Part.

(3) In this section references to distributions are to amounts regarded as distributions for the purposes of any such rule of law as is referred to in subsection (1).

852 Saving for other restrictions on distributions

The provisions of this Part are without prejudice to any enactment, or any provision of a company's articles, restricting the sums out of which, or the cases in which, a distribution may be made.

853 Minor definitions

(1) The following provisions apply for the purposes of this Part.

(2) References to profit or losses of any description—

(a) are to profits or losses of that description made at any time, and

(b) except where the context otherwise requires, are to profits or losses of a revenue or capital character.

(3) "Capitalisation", in relation to a company's profits, means any of the following operations (whenever carried out)—

(a) applying the profits in wholly or partly paying up unissued shares in the company to be allotted to members of the company as fully or partly paid bonus shares, or

(b) transferring the profits to capital redemption reserve.

(4) References to "realised profits" and "realised losses", in relation to a company's accounts, are to such profits or losses of the company as fall to be treated as realised in accordance with principles generally accepted at the time when the accounts are prepared, with respect to the determination for accounting purposes of realised profits or losses.

(5) Subsection (4) is without prejudice to—

(a) the construction of any other expression (where appropriate) by reference to accepted accounting principles or practice, or

(b) any specific provision for the treatment of profits or losses of any description as realised.

(6) "Fixed assets" means assets of a company which are intended for use on a continuing basis in the company's activities.

PART 24
A COMPANY'S ANNUAL RETURN

854 Duty to deliver annual returns

(1) Every company must deliver to the registrar successive annual returns each of which is made up to a date not later than the date that is from time to time the company's return date.

(2) The company's return date is—

(a) the anniversary of the company's incorporation, or

(b) if the company's last return delivered in accordance with this Part was made up to a different date, the anniversary of that date.

(3) Each return must—

(a) contain the information required by or under the following provisions of this Part, and

(b) be delivered to the registrar within 28 days after the date to which it is made up.

855 Contents of annual return: general

(1) Every annual return must state the date to which it is made up and contain the following information—

(a) the address of the company's registered office;

(b) the type of company it is and its principal business activities;

(c) the required particulars (see section 855A) of—

(i) the directors of the company, and

(ii) in the case of a private company with a secretary or a public company, the secretary or joint secretaries;

(d) if any company records are (in accordance with regulations under section 1136) kept at a place other than the company's registered office, the address of that place and the records that are kept there;

(f) . . .

(2) The information as to the company's type must be given by reference to the classification scheme prescribed for the purposes of this section.

(3) The information as to the company's principal business activities may be given by reference to one or more categories of any prescribed system of classifying business activities.

(4) In this Part—

"DTR5 issuer" means an issuer to which Chapter 5 of the Disclosure Rules and Transparency Rules sourcebook issued by the Financial Services Authority applies;

"relevant market" means any of the markets mentioned in article 4(1) of the Financial Services and Markets Act 2000 (Prescribed Markets and Qualifying Investments) Order 2001; and

"return period", in relation to an annual return, means the period beginning immediately after the date to which the last return was made up (or, in the case of the first return, with the incorporation of the company) and ending with the date to which the return is made up; . . .

855A Required particulars of directors and secretaries

(1) For the purposes of section 855(1)(c) the required particulars of a director are—

(a) where the director is an individual, the particulars required by section 163 to be entered in the register of directors (subject to subsection (2) below); and

(b) where the director is a body corporate or a firm that is a legal person under the law by which it is governed, the particulars required by section 164 to be entered in the register of directors.

(2) The former name of a director who is an individual is a required particular in relation to an annual return only if the director was known by the name for business purposes during the return period.

(3) For the purposes of section 855(1)(c)(ii) the required particulars of a secretary are—

(a) where a secretary is an individual, the particulars required by section 277 to be entered in the register of secretaries (subject to subsection (4) below); and

(b) where a secretary is a body corporate or a firm that is a legal person under the law by which it is governed, the particulars required by section 278(1) to be entered in the register of secretaries.

(4) The former name of a secretary who is an individual is a required particular in relation to an annual return only if the secretary was known by the name for business purposes during the return period.

(5) Where all the partners in a firm are joint secretaries, the required particulars are the particulars that would be required to be entered in the register of secretaries if the firm were a legal person and the firm had been appointed secretary.

856 Contents of annual return: information about shares and share capital

(1) The annual return of a company having a share capital must also contain the following information.

(1A) The return must contain a statement of capital.

(2) The statement of capital must state with respect to the company's share capital at the date to which the return is made up—

(a) the total number of shares of the company,

(b) the aggregate nominal value of those shares,

(c) for each class of shares—

(i) the voting rights attached to the shares,

(ii) the total number of shares of that class, and

(iii) the aggregate nominal value of shares of that class, and

(d) the amount paid up and the amount (if any) unpaid on each share (whether on account of the nominal value of the share or by way of premium).

(2A) The annual return must also state whether any of the company's shares were, at any time during the return period, shares admitted to trading on a relevant market or on any other market which is outside the United Kingdom.

(2B) If any of the company's shares were shares admitted to trading as mentioned in subsection (2A), the annual return must also state whether both of the following conditions were satisfied throughout the return period—

(a) there were shares of the company which were shares admitted to trading on a relevant market;

(b) the company was a DTR5 issuer.

(3)–(6) . . .

856A Contents of annual return: information about shareholders: non-traded companies

(1) This section applies to the annual return of a company none of whose shares were, at any time during the return period, shares admitted to trading on a relevant market or on any other market which is outside the United Kingdom.

(2) The return must also contain the name (as it appears in the company's register of members) of every person who was a member of the company at any time during the return period.

The return must conform to the following requirements for the purpose of enabling the entries relating to any given person to be easily found—

(a) the entries must be listed in alphabetical order by name; or

(b) the return must have annexed to it an index that is sufficient to enable the name of the person in question to be easily found.

(3) The return must also state—

(a) the number of shares of each class held at the end of the date to which the return is made up by each person who was a member of the company at that time,

(b) the number of shares of each class transferred during the return period by or to each person who was a member of the company at any time during that period, and

(c) the dates of registration of those transfers.

(4) If either of the two immediately preceding returns has given the full particulars required by subsections (2) and (3), the return need only give such particulars as relate—

(a) to persons who became, or ceased to be, members during the return period, and

(b) to shares transferred during that period.

856B Contents of annual return: information about shareholders: certain traded companies

(1) This section applies to the annual return of a company any of whose shares were, at any time during the return period, shares admitted to trading on a relevant market or on any other market which is outside the United Kingdom.

(2) But this section does not apply to the annual return of a company if throughout the return period—

(a) there were shares of the company which were shares admitted to trading on a relevant market, and

(b) the company was a DTR5 issuer.

(3) The annual return of a company to which this section applies must also state, in respect of each person who held at least 5% of the issued shares of any class of the company at the end of the date to which the return is made up—

(a) the person's name and address (as they appear in the company's register of members); and

(b) the number of shares of each class held by the person at that time.

(4) The return must conform to the following requirements for the purpose of enabling entries relating to any given person to be easily found—

(a) the entries must be listed in alphabetical order by name; or

(b) the return must have annexed to it an index that is sufficient to enable the name of the person in question to be easily found.

857 Contents of annual return: power to make further provision by regulations

(1) The Secretary of State may by regulations make further provision as to the information to be given in a company's annual return.

(2) The regulations may—

(a) amend or repeal the provisions of sections 855 and 856, and

(b) provide for exceptions from the requirements of those sections as they have effect from time to time.

(3) Regulations under this section are subject to negative resolution procedure.

858 Failure to deliver annual return

(1) If a company fails to deliver an annual return before the end of the period of 28 days after a return date, an offence is committed by—

(a) the company,

(b) subject to subsection (4)—

(i) every director of the company, and

(ii) in the case of a private company with a secretary or a public company, every secretary of the company, and

(c) every other officer of the company who is in default.

For this purpose a shadow director is treated as a director.

(2) A person guilty of an offence under subsection (1) is liable on summary conviction to a fine not exceeding level 5 on the standard scale and, for continued contravention, a daily default fine not exceeding one-tenth of level 5 on the standard scale.

(3) The contravention continues until such time as an annual return made up to that return date is delivered by the company to the registrar.

(4) It is a defence for a director or secretary charged with an offence under subsection (1)(b) to prove that he took all reasonable steps to avoid the commission or continuation of the offence.

(5) In the case of continued contravention, an offence is also committed by every officer of the company who did not commit an offence under subsection (1) in relation to the initial contravention but is in default in relation to the continued contravention.

A person guilty of an offence under this subsection is liable on summary conviction to a fine not exceeding one-tenth of level 5 on the standard scale for each day on which the contravention continues and he is in default.

859 . . .

PART 25
COMPANY CHARGES

CHAPTER A1
REGISTRATION OF COMPANY CHARGES

Company charges

859A Charges created by a company

(1) Subject to subsection (6), this section applies where a company creates a charge.

(2) The registrar must register the charge if, before the end of the period allowed for delivery, the company or any person interested in the charge delivers to the registrar for registration a section 859D statement of particulars.

(3) Where the charge is created or evidenced by an instrument, the registrar is required to register it only if a certified copy of the instrument is delivered to the registrar with the statement of particulars.

(4) "The period allowed for delivery" is 21 days beginning with the day after the date of creation of the charge (see section 859E), unless an order allowing an extended period is made under section 859F(3).

(5) Where an order is made under section 859F(3) a copy of the order must be delivered to the registrar with the statement of particulars.

(6) This section does not apply to—

(a) a charge in favour of a landlord on a cash deposit given as a security in connection with the lease of land;

(b) a charge created by a member of Lloyd's (within the meaning of the Lloyd's Act 1982) to secure its obligations in connection with its underwriting business at Lloyd's;

(c) a charge excluded from the application of this section by or under any other Act.

(7) In this Part—

"cash" includes foreign currency,

"charge" includes—

(a) a mortgage;

(b) a standard security, assignation in security, and any other right in security constituted under the law of Scotland, including any heritable security, but not including a pledge, and

"company" means a UK-registered company.

859B Charge in series of debentures

(1) This section applies where—

(a) a company creates a series of debentures containing a charge, or giving a charge by reference to another instrument, and

(b) debenture holders of that series are entitled to the benefit of the charge pari passu.

(2) The registrar must register the charge if, before the end of the period allowed for delivery, the company or any person interested in the charge delivers to the registrar for registration, a section 859D statement of particulars which also contains the following—

(a) either—

(i) the name of each of the trustees for the debenture holders, or

(ii) where there are more than four such persons, the names of any four persons listed in the charge instrument as trustees for the debenture holders, and a statement that there are other such persons;

(b) the dates of the resolutions authorising the issue of the series;

(c) the date of the covering instrument (if any) by which the series is created or defined.

(3) Where the charge is created or evidenced by an instrument, the registrar is required to register it only if a certified copy of the instrument is delivered to the registrar with the statement of particulars.

(4) Where the charge is not created or evidenced by an instrument, the registrar is required to register it only if a certified copy of one of the debentures in the series is delivered to the registrar with the statement of particulars.

(5) For the purposes of this section a statement of particulars is taken to be a section 859D statement of particulars even if it does not contain the names of the debenture holders.

(6) "The period allowed for delivery" is—

(a) if there is a deed containing the charge, 21 days beginning with the day after the date on which the deed is executed;

(b) if there is no deed containing the charge, 21 days beginning with the day after the date on which the first debenture of the series is executed.

(7) Where an order is made under section 859F(3) a copy of the order must be delivered to the registrar with the statement of particulars.

(8) In this section "deed" means—

(a) a deed governed by the law of England and Wales or Northern Ireland, or

(b) an instrument governed by a law other than the law of England and Wales or Northern Ireland which requires delivery under that law in order to take effect.

859C Charges existing on property or undertaking acquired

(1) This section applies where a company acquires property or undertaking which is subject to a charge of a kind which would, if it had been created by the company after the acquisition of the property or undertaking, have been capable of being registered under section 859A.

(2) The registrar must register the charge if the company or any person interested in the charge delivers to the registrar for registration a section 859D statement of particulars.

(3) Where the charge is created or evidenced by an instrument, the registrar is required to register it only if a certified copy of the instrument is delivered to the registrar with the statement of particulars.

859D Particulars to be delivered to registrar

(1) A statement of particulars relating to a charge created by a company is a "section 859D statement of particulars" if it contains the following particulars—

(a) the registered name and number of the company;

(b) the date of creation of the charge and (if the charge is one to which section 859C applies) the date of acquisition of the property or undertaking concerned;

(c) where the charge is created or evidenced by an instrument, the particulars listed in subsection (2);

(d) where the charge is not created or evidenced by an instrument, the particulars listed in subsection (3).

(2) The particulars referred to in subsection (1)(c) are—

(a) any of the following—

(i) the name of each of the persons in whose favour the charge has been created or of the security agents or trustees holding the charge for the benefit of one or more persons; or,

(ii) where there are more than four such persons, security agents or trustees, the names of any four such persons, security agents or trustees listed in the charge instrument, and a statement that there are other such persons, security agents or trustees;

(b) whether the instrument is expressed to contain a floating charge and, if so, whether it is expressed to cover all the property and undertaking of the company;

(c) whether any of the terms of the charge prohibit or restrict the company from creating further security that will rank equally with or ahead of the charge;

(d) whether (and if so, a short description of) any land, ship, aircraft or intellectual property that is registered or required to be registered in the United Kingdom, is subject to a charge (which is not a floating charge) or fixed security included in the instrument;

(e) whether the instrument includes a charge (which is not a floating charge) or fixed security over—

(i) any tangible or corporeal property, or

(ii) any intangible or incorporeal property,

not described in paragraph (d).

(3) The particulars referred to in subsection (1)(d) are—

(a) a statement that there is no instrument creating or evidencing the charge;

(b) the names of each of the persons in whose favour the charge has been created or the names of any security agents or trustees holding the charge for the benefit of one or more persons;

(c) the nature of the charge;

(d) a short description of the property or undertaking charged;

(e) the obligations secured by the charge.

(4) In this section "fixed security" has the meaning given in section 486(1) of the Companies Act 1985.

(5) In this section "intellectual property" includes—

(a) any patent, trade mark, registered design, copyright or design right;

(b) any licence under or in respect of any such right.

859E Date of creation of charge

(1) For the purposes of this Part, a charge of the type described in column 1 of the Table below is taken to be created on the date given in relation to it in column 2 of that Table.

1 Type of charge	*2 When charge created*
Standard security	The date of its recording in the Register of Sasines or its registration in the Land Register of Scotland
Charge other than a standard security, where created or evidenced by an instrument	Where the instrument is a deed that has been executed and has immediate effect on execution and delivery, the date of delivery
	Where the instrument is a deed that has been executed and held in escrow, the date of delivery into escrow
	Where the instrument is a deed that has been executed and held as undelivered, the date of delivery
	Where the instrument is not a deed and has immediate effect on execution, the date of execution
	Where the instrument is not a deed and does not have immediate effect on execution, the date on which the instrument takes effect
Charge other than a standard security, where not created or evidenced by an instrument	The date on which the charge comes into effect.

(2) Where a charge is created or evidenced by an instrument made between two or more parties, references in the Table in subsection (1) to execution are to execution by all the parties to the instrument whose execution is essential for the instrument to take effect as a charge.

(3) This section applies for the purposes of this Chapter even if further forms, notices, registrations or other actions or proceedings are necessary to make the charge valid or effectual for any other purposes.

(4) For the purposes of this Chapter, the registrar is entitled without further enquiry to accept a charge as created on the date given as the date of creation of the charge in a section 859D statement of particulars.

(5) In this section "deed" means—

(a) a deed governed by the law of England and Wales or Northern Ireland, or

(b) an instrument governed by a law other than the law of England and Wales or Northern Ireland which requires delivery under that law in order to take effect.

(6) References in this section to delivery, in relation to a deed, include delivery as a deed where required.

859F Extension of period allowed for delivery

(1) Subsection (3) applies if the court is satisfied that—

(a) neither the company nor any other person interested in the charge has delivered to the registrar the documents required under section 859A or (as the case may be) 859B before the end of the period allowed for delivery under the section concerned, and

(b) the requirement in subsection (2) is met.

(2) The requirement is—

(a) that the failure to deliver those documents—

(i) was accidental or due to inadvertence or to some other sufficient cause, or
(ii) is not of a nature to prejudice the position of creditors or shareholders of the company, or

(b) that on other grounds it is just and equitable to grant relief.

(3) The court may, on the application of the company or a person interested, and on such terms and conditions as seem to the court just and expedient, order that the period allowed for delivery be extended.

859G Personal information etc in certified copies

(1) The following are not required to be included in a certified copy of an instrument or debenture delivered to the registrar for the purposes of any provision of this Chapter—
(a) personal information relating to an individual (other than the name of an individual);
(b) the number or other identifier of a bank or securities account of a company or individual;
(c) a signature.

(2) The registrar is entitled without further enquiry, to accept the certified copy of an instrument whether or not any of the information in subsection (1) is contained within the instrument.

Consequence of non-delivery

859H Consequence of failure to deliver charges

(1) This section applies if—
(a) a company creates a charge to which section 859A or 859B applies, and
(b) the documents required by section 859A or (as the case may be) 859B are not delivered to the registrar by the company or another person interested in the charge before the end of the relevant period allowed for delivery.

(2) "The relevant period allowed for delivery" is—
(a) the period allowed for delivery under the section in question, or
(b) if an order under section 859F(3) has been made, the period allowed by the order.

(3) Where this section applies, the charge is void (so far as any security on the company's property or undertaking is conferred by it) against—
(a) a liquidator of the company,
(b) an administrator of the company, and
(c) a creditor of the company.

(4) Subsection (3) is without prejudice to any contract or obligation for repayment of the money secured by the charge; and when a charge becomes void under this section, the money secured by it immediately becomes payable.

The register

859I Entries on the register

(1) This section applies where a charge is registered in accordance with a provision of this Chapter.

(2) The registrar must—
(a) allocate to the charge a unique reference code and place a note in the register recording that reference code; and
(b) include in the register any documents delivered under section 859A(3) or (5), 859B(3), (4) or (7), or 859C(3).

(3) The registrar must give a certificate of the registration of the charge to the person who delivered to the registrar a section 859D statement of particulars relating to the charge.

(4) The certificate must state—
(a) the registered name and number of the company in respect of which the charge was registered; and
(b) the unique reference code allocated to the charge.

(5) The certificate must be signed by the registrar or authenticated by the registrar's official seal.

(6) In the case of registration under section 859A or 859B, the certificate is conclusive evidence that the documents required by the section concerned were delivered to the registrar before the end of the relevant period allowed for delivery.

(7) "The relevant period allowed for delivery" is—
(a) the period allowed for delivery under the section in question, or
(b) if an order under section 859F(3) has been made, the period allowed by the order.

859J Company holding property or undertaking as trustee

(1) Where a company is acting as trustee of property or undertaking which is the subject of a charge delivered for registration under this Chapter, the company or any person interested in the charge may deliver to the registrar a statement to that effect.

(2) A statement delivered after the delivery for registration of the charge must include—
(a) the registered name and number of the company; and
(b) the unique reference code allocated to the charge.

859K Registration of enforcement of security

(1) Subsection (2) applies where a person—
(a) obtains an order for the appointment of a receiver or manager of a company's property or undertaking, or
(b) appoints such a receiver or manager under powers contained in an instrument.

(2) The person must, within 7 days of the order or of the appointment under those powers—
(a) give notice to the registrar of that fact, and
(b) if the order was obtained, or the appointment made, by virtue of a registered charge held by the person give the registrar a notice containing—
(i) in the case of a charge created before 6th April 2013, the information specified in subsection (4);
(ii) in the case of a charge created on or after 6th April 2013, the unique reference code allocated to the charge.

(3) Where a person appointed receiver or manager of a company's property or undertaking under powers contained in an instrument ceases to act as such a receiver or manager, the person must, on so ceasing—
(a) give notice to the registrar of that fact, and
(b) give the registrar a notice containing—
(i) in the case of a charge created before 6th April 2013, the information specified in subsection (4), or
(ii) in the case of a charge created on or after 6th April 2013, the unique reference code allocated to the charge.

(4) The information referred to in subsections (2)(b)(i) and (3)(b)(i) is—
(a) the date of the creation of the charge;
(b) a description of the instrument (if any) creating or evidencing the charge;
(c) short particulars of the property or undertaking charged.

(5) The registrar must include in the register—
(a) a fact of which notice is given under subsection (2)(a), and
(b) a fact of which notice is given under subsection (3)(a).

(6) A person who makes default in complying with the requirements of subsections (2) or (3) of this section commits an offence.

(7) A person guilty of an offence under this section is liable on summary conviction to a fine not exceeding level 3 on the standard scale and, for continued contravention, a daily default fine not exceeding one-tenth of level 3 on the standard scale.

(8) This section applies only to a receiver or manager appointed—
(a) by a court in England and Wales or Northern Ireland, or
(b) under an instrument governed by the law of England and Wales or Northern Ireland.

(9) This section does not apply to a receiver appointed under Chapter 2 of Part 3 of the Insolvency Act 1986 (receivers (Scotland)).

859L Entries of satisfaction and release

(1) Subsection (5) applies if the statement set out in subsection (2) and the particulars set out in subsection (4) are delivered to the registrar with respect to a registered charge.

(2) The statement referred to in subsection (1) is a statement to the effect that—
(a) the debt for which the charge was given has been paid or satisfied in whole or in part, or
(b) all or part of the property or undertaking charged—
(i) has been released from the charge, or
(ii) has ceased to form part of the company's property or undertaking.

(3) Where a statement within subsection (2)(b) relates to part only of the property or undertaking charged, the statement must include a short description of that part.

(4) The particulars referred to in subsection (1) are—
(a) the name and address of the person delivering the statement and an indication of their interest in the charge;
(b) the registered name and number of the company that—
(i) created the charge (in a case within section 859A or 859B), or
(ii) acquired the property or undertaking subject to the charge (in a case within section 859C);
(c) in respect of a charge created before 6th April 2013—
(i) the date of creation of the charge;
(ii) a description of the instrument (if any) by which the charge is created or evidenced;
(iii) short particulars of the property or undertaking charged;
(d) in respect of a charge created on or after 6th April 2013, the unique reference code allocated to the charge.

(5) The registrar must include in the register—
(a) a statement of satisfaction in whole or in part, or
(b) a statement of the fact that all or part of the property or undertaking has been released from the charge or has ceased to form part of the company's property or undertaking (as the case may be).

859M Rectification of register

(1) Subsection (3) applies if the court is satisfied that—
(a) there has been an omission or mis-statement in any statement or notice delivered to the registrar in accordance with this Chapter, and
(b) the requirement in subsection (2) is met.

(2) The requirement is that the court is satisfied—
(a) that the omission or mis-statement—
(i) was accidental or due to inadvertence or to some other sufficient cause, or
(ii) is not of a nature to prejudice the position of creditors or shareholders of the company, or
(b) that on other grounds it is just and equitable to grant relief.

(3) The court may, on the application of the company or a person interested, and on such terms and conditions as seem to the court just and expedient, order that the omission or mis-statement be rectified.

(4) A copy of the court's order must be sent by the applicant to the registrar for registration.

859N Replacement of instrument or debenture

(1) Subsection (2) applies if the court is satisfied that—
(a) a copy of an instrument or debenture delivered to the registrar under this Chapter contains material which could have been omitted under section 859G;
(b) the wrong instrument or debenture was delivered to the registrar; or
(c) the copy was defective.

(2) The court may, on the application of the company or a person interested, and on such terms and conditions as seem to the court just and expedient, order that the copy of the instrument or debenture be removed from the register and replaced.

(3) A copy of the court's order must be sent by the applicant to the registrar for registration.

859O Notification of addition to or amendment of charge

(1) This section applies where, after the creation of a charge, the charge is amended by adding or amending a term that—

(a) prohibits or restricts the creation of any fixed security or any other charge having priority over, or ranking pari passu with, the charge; or

(b) varies, or otherwise regulates the order of, the ranking of the charge in relation to any fixed security or any other charge.

(2) Either the company that created the charge or the person taking the benefit of the charge (or another charge referred to in subsection (1)(b)) may deliver to the registrar for registration—

(a) a certified copy of the instrument effecting the amendment, variation or regulation, and

(b) a statement of the particulars set out in subsection (3).

(3) The particulars to be included in the statement are—

(a) the registered name and number of the company;

(b) in the case of a charge created before 6th April 2013—

(i) the date of creation of the charge;

(ii) a description of the instrument (if any) by which the charge was created or evidenced;

(iii) short particulars of the property or undertaking charged as set out when the charge was registered;

(c) in the case of a charge created on or after 6th April 2013, (where allocated) the unique reference code allocated to the charge.

(4) Subsections (1) to (3) do not affect the continued application of section 466 of the Companies Act 1985.

(5) In this section "fixed security" has the meaning given in section 486(1) of the Companies Act 1985.

Companies' records and registers

859P Companies to keep copies of instruments creating and amending charges

(1) A company must keep available for inspection a copy of every—

(a) instrument creating a charge capable of registration under this Chapter, and

(b) instrument effecting any variation or amendment of such a charge.

(2) In the case of a charge contained in a series of uniform debentures, a copy of one of the debentures of the series is sufficient for the purposes of subsection (1)(a).

(3) If the particulars referred to in section 859D(1) or the particulars of the property or undertaking charged are not contained in the instrument creating the charge, but are instead contained in other documents which are referred to in or otherwise incorporated into the instrument, then the company must also keep available for inspection a copy of those other documents.

(4) It is sufficient for the purposes of subsection (1)(a) if the company keeps a copy of the instrument in the form delivered to the registrar under section 859A(3), 859B(3) or (4) or 859C(3).

(5) Where a translation has been delivered to the registrar in accordance with section 1105, the company must keep available for inspection a copy of the translation.

859Q Instruments creating charges to be available for inspection

(1) This section applies to documents required to be kept available for inspection under section 859P (copies of instruments creating and amending charges).

(2) The documents must be kept available for inspection—

(a) at the company's registered office, or

(b) at a place specified in regulations under section 1136.

(3) The company must give notice to the registrar—
(a) of the place at which the documents are kept available for inspection, and
(b) of any change in that place,
unless they have at all times been kept at the company's registered office.

(4) The documents must be open to the inspection—
(a) of any creditor or member of the company, without charge, and
(b) of any other person, on payment of such fee as may be prescribed.

(5) If default is made for 14 days in complying with subsection (3) or an inspection required under subsection (4) is refused, an offence is committed by—
(a) the company, and
(b) every officer of the company who is in default.

(6) A person guilty of an offence under this section is liable on summary conviction to a fine not exceeding level 3 on the standard scale and, for continued contravention, a daily default fine not exceeding one-tenth of level 3 on the standard scale.

(7) If an inspection required under subsection (4) is refused the court may by order compel an immediate inspection.

(8) Where the company and a person wishing to carry out an inspection under subsection (4) agree, the inspection may be carried out by electronic means.

860–892 ...

CHAPTER 3
POWERS OF THE SECRETARY OF STATE

893 Power to make provision for effect of registration in special register

(1) In this section a "special register" means a register, other than the register, in which a charge to which Chapter A1 applies is required or authorised to be registered.

(2) The Secretary of State may by order make provision for facilitating the making of information-sharing arrangements between the person responsible for maintaining a special register ("the responsible person") and the registrar that meet the requirement in subsection (4).
"Information-sharing arrangements" are arrangements to share and make use of information held by the registrar or by the responsible person.

(3) If the Secretary of State is satisfied that appropriate information-sharing arrangements have been made, he may by order provide that—
(a) the registrar is authorised not to register a charge of a specified description under Chapter A1,
(b) a charge of a specified description that is registered in the special register within a specified period is to be treated as if it had been registered (and certified by the registrar as registered) in accordance with the requirements of Chapter A1, and
(c) the other provisions of Chapter A1 apply to a charge so treated with specified modifications.

(4) The information-sharing arrangements must ensure that persons inspecting the register—
(a) are made aware, in a manner appropriate to the inspection, of the existence of charges in the special register which are treated in accordance with provision so made, and
(b) are able to obtain information from the special register about any such charge.

(5) An order under this section may—
(a) modify any enactment or rule of law which would otherwise restrict or prevent the responsible person from entering into or giving effect to information-sharing arrangements,
(b) authorise the responsible person to require information to be provided to him for the purposes of the arrangements,
(c) make provision about—
(i) the charging by the responsible person of fees in connection with the arrangements and the destination of such fees (including provision modifying any enactment which would otherwise apply in relation to fees payable to the responsible person), and

(ii) the making of payments under the arrangements by the registrar to the responsible person,

(d) require the registrar to make copies of the arrangements available to the public (in hard copy or electronic form).

(6) In this section "specified" means specified in an order under this section.

(7) A description of charge may be specified, in particular, by reference to one or more of the following—

(a) the type of company by which it is created,

(b) the form of charge which it is,

(c) the description of assets over which it is granted,

(d) the length of the period between the date of its registration in the special register and the date of its creation.

(8) Provision may be made under this section relating to registers maintained under the law of a country or territory outside the United Kingdom.

(9) An order under this section is subject to negative resolution procedure.

894 General power to make amendments to this Part

(1) The Secretary of State may by regulations under this section—

(a) amend this Part by altering, adding or repealing provisions,

(b) make consequential amendments or repeals in this Act or any other enactment (whether passed or made before or after this Act).

(2) Regulations under this section are subject to affirmative resolution procedure.

PART 26
ARRANGEMENTS AND RECONSTRUCTIONS

Application of this Part

895 Application of this Part

(1) The provisions of this Part apply where a compromise or arrangement is proposed between a company and—

(a) its creditors, or any class of them, or

(b) its members, or any class of them.

(2) In this Part—

"arrangement" includes a reorganisation of the company's share capital by the consolidation of shares of different classes or by the division of shares into shares of different classes, or by both of those methods; and

"company"—

(a) in section 900 (powers of court to facilitate reconstruction or amalgamation) means a company within the meaning of this Act, and

(b) elsewhere in this Part means any company liable to be wound up under the Insolvency Act 1986 or the Insolvency (Northern Ireland) Order 1989.

(3) The provisions of this Part have effect subject to Part 27 (mergers and divisions of public companies) where that Part applies (see sections 902 and 903).

Meeting of creditors or members

896 Court order for holding of meeting

(1) The court may, on an application under this section, order a meeting of the creditors or class of creditors, or of the members of the company or class of members (as the case may be), to be summoned in such manner as the court directs.

(2) An application under this section may be made by—

(a) the company,

(b) any creditor or member of the company,

(c) if the company is being wound up, the liquidator, or

(d) if the company is in administration, the administrator.

(3) Section 323 (representation of corporations at meetings) applies to a meeting of creditors under this section as to a meeting of the company (references to a member of the company being read as references to a creditor).

897 Statement to be circulated or made available

(1) Where a meeting is summoned under section 896—

(a) every notice summoning the meeting that is sent to a creditor or member must be accompanied by a statement complying with this section, and

(b) every notice summoning the meeting that is given by advertisement must either—

(i) include such a statement, or

(ii) state where and how creditors or members entitled to attend the meeting may obtain copies of such a statement.

(2) The statement must—

(a) explain the effect of the compromise or arrangement, and

(b) in particular, state—

(i) any material interests of the directors of the company (whether as directors or as members or as creditors of the company or otherwise), and

(ii) the effect on those interests of the compromise or arrangement, in so far as it is different from the effect on the like interests of other persons.

(3) Where the compromise or arrangement affects the rights of debenture holders of the company, the statement must give the like explanation as respects the trustees of any deed for securing the issue of the debentures as it is required to give as respects the company's directors.

(4) Where a notice given by advertisement states that copies of an explanatory statement can be obtained by creditors or members entitled to attend the meeting, every such creditor or member is entitled, on making application in the manner indicated by the notice, to be provided by the company with a copy of the statement free of charge.

(5) If a company makes default in complying with any requirement of this section, an offence is committed by—

(a) the company, and

(b) every officer of the company who is in default.

This is subject to subsection (7) below.

(6) For this purpose the following are treated as officers of the company—

(a) a liquidator or administrator of the company, and

(b) a trustee of a deed for securing the issue of debentures of the company.

(7) A person is not guilty of an offence under this section if he shows that the default was due to the refusal of a director or trustee for debenture holders to supply the necessary particulars of his interests.

(8) A person guilty of an offence under this section is liable—

(a) on conviction on indictment, to a fine;

(b) on summary conviction, to a fine not exceeding the statutory maximum.

898 Duty of directors and trustees to provide information

(1) It is the duty of—

(a) any director of the company, and

(b) any trustee for its debenture holders,

to give notice to the company of such matters relating to himself as may be necessary for the purposes of section 897 (explanatory statement to be circulated or made available).

(2) Any person who makes default in complying with this section commits an offence.

(3) A person guilty of an offence under this section is liable on summary conviction to a fine not exceeding level 3 on the standard scale.

Court sanction for compromise or arrangement

899 Court sanction for compromise or arrangement

(1) If a majority in number representing 75% in value of the creditors or class of creditors or members or class of members (as the case may be), present and voting either in person or by proxy at the meeting summoned under section 896, agree a compromise or arrangement, the court may, on an application under this section, sanction the compromise or arrangement.

(2) An application under this section may be made by—
(a) the company,
(b) any creditor or member of the company,
(c) if the company is being wound up, the liquidator, or
(d) if the company is in administration, the administrator.

(3) A compromise or arrangement sanctioned by the court is binding on—
(a) all creditors or the class of creditors or on the members or class of members (as the case may be), and
(b) the company or, in the case of a company in the course of being wound up, the liquidator and contributories of the company.

(4) The court's order has no effect until a copy of it has been delivered to the registrar.

(5) Section 323 (representation of corporations at meetings) applies to a meeting of creditors under this section as to a meeting of the company (references to a member of the company being read as references to a creditor).

Reconstructions and amalgamations

900 Powers of court to facilitate reconstruction or amalgamation

(1) This section applies where application is made to the court under section 899 to sanction a compromise or arrangement and it is shown that—
(a) the compromise or arrangement is proposed for the purposes of, or in connection with, a scheme for the reconstruction of any company or companies, or the amalgamation of any two or more companies, and
(b) under the scheme the whole or any part of the undertaking or the property of any company concerned in the scheme ("a transferor company") is to be transferred to another company ("the transferee company").

(2) The court may, either by the order sanctioning the compromise or arrangement or by a subsequent order, make provision for all or any of the following matters—
(a) the transfer to the transferee company of the whole or any part of the undertaking and of the property or liabilities of any transferor company;
(b) the allotting or appropriation by the transferee company of any shares, debentures, policies or other like interests in that company which under the compromise or arrangement are to be allotted or appropriated by that company to or for any person;
(c) the continuation by or against the transferee company of any legal proceedings pending by or against any transferor company;
(d) the dissolution, without winding up, of any transferor company;
(e) the provision to be made for any persons who, within such time and in such manner as the court directs, dissent from the compromise or arrangement;
(f) such incidental, consequential and supplemental matters as are necessary to secure that the reconstruction or amalgamation is fully and effectively carried out.

(3) If an order under this section provides for the transfer of property or liabilities—
(a) the property is by virtue of the order transferred to, and vests in, the transferee company, and
(b) the liabilities are, by virtue of the order, transferred to and become liabilities of that company.

(4) The property (if the order so directs) vests freed from any charge that is by virtue of the compromise or arrangement to cease to have effect.

(5) In this section—

"property" includes property, rights and powers of every description; and

"liabilities" includes duties.

(6) Every company in relation to which an order is made under this section must cause a copy of the order to be delivered to the registrar within seven days after its making.

(7) If default is made in complying with subsection (6) an offence is committed by—

(a) the company, and

(b) every officer of the company who is in default.

(8) A person guilty of an offence under subsection (7) is liable on summary conviction to a fine not exceeding level 3 on the standard scale and, for continued contravention, a daily default fine not exceeding one-tenth of level 3 on the standard scale.

Obligations of company with respect to articles etc

901 Obligations of company with respect to articles etc

(1) This section applies—

(a) to any order under section 899 (order sanctioning compromise or arrangement), and

(b) to any order under section 900 (order facilitating reconstruction or amalgamation) that alters the company's constitution.

(2) If the order amends—

(a) the company's articles, or

(b) any resolution or agreement to which Chapter 3 of Part 3 applies (resolution or agreement affecting a company's constitution),

the copy of the order delivered to the registrar by the company under section 899(4) or section 900(6) must be accompanied by a copy of the company's articles, or the resolution or agreement in question, as amended.

(3) Every copy of the company's articles issued by the company after the order is made must be accompanied by a copy of the order, unless the effect of the order has been incorporated into the articles by amendment.

(4) In this section—

(a) references to the effect of the order include the effect of the compromise or arrangement to which the order relates; and

(b) in the case of a company not having articles, references to its articles shall be read as references to the instrument constituting the company or defining its constitution.

(5) If a company makes default in complying with this section an offence is committed by—

(a) the company, and

(b) every officer of the company who is in default.

(6) A person guilty of an offence under this section is liable on summary conviction to a fine not exceeding level 3 on the standard scale.

PART 27
MERGERS AND DIVISIONS OF PUBLIC COMPANIES

CHAPTER 1
INTRODUCTORY

902 Application of this Part

(1) This Part applies where—

(a) a compromise or arrangement is proposed between a public company and—

(i) its creditors or any class of them, or

(ii) its members or any class of them,

for the purposes of, or in connection with, a scheme for the reconstruction of any company or companies or the amalgamation of any two or more companies,

(b) the scheme involves—

(i) a merger (as defined in section 904), or

(ii) a division (as defined in section 919), and

(c) the consideration for the transfer (or each of the transfers) envisaged is to be shares in the transferee company (or one or more of the transferee companies) receivable by members of the transferor company (or transferor companies), with or without any cash payment to members.

(2) In this Part—

(a) a "new company" means a company formed for the purposes of, or in connection with, the scheme, and

(b) an "existing company" means a company other than one formed for the purposes of, or in connection with, the scheme.

(3) This Part does not apply where the company in respect of which the compromise or arrangement is proposed is being wound up.

903 Relationship of this Part to Part 26

(1) The court must not sanction the compromise or arrangement under Part 26 (arrangements and reconstructions) unless the relevant requirements of this Part have been complied with.

(2) The requirements applicable to a merger are specified in sections 905 to 914. Certain of those requirements, and certain general requirements of Part 26, are modified or excluded by the provisions of sections 915 to 918A.

(3) The requirements applicable to a division are specified in sections 920 to 930. Certain of those requirements, and certain general requirements of Part 26, are modified or excluded by the provisions of sections 931 to 934.

CHAPTER 2
MERGER

Introductory

904 Mergers and merging companies

(1) The scheme involves a merger where under the scheme—

(a) the undertaking, property and liabilities of one or more public companies, including the company in respect of which the compromise or arrangement is proposed, are to be transferred to another existing public company (a "merger by absorption"), or

(b) the undertaking, property and liabilities of two or more public companies, including the company in respect of which the compromise or arrangement is proposed, are to be transferred to a new company, whether or not a public company, (a "merger by formation of a new company").

(2) References in this Part to "the merging companies" are—

(a) in relation to a merger by absorption, to the transferor and transferee companies;

(b) in relation to a merger by formation of a new company, to the transferor companies.

Requirements applicable to merger

905 Draft terms of scheme (merger)

(1) A draft of the proposed terms of the scheme must be drawn up and adopted by the directors of the merging companies.

(2) The draft terms must give particulars of at least the following matters—

(a) in respect of each transferor company and the transferee company—

(i) its name,

(ii) the address of its registered office, and

(iii) whether it is a company limited by shares or a company limited by guarantee and having a share capital;

(b) the number of shares in the transferee company to be allotted to members of a transferor company for a given number of their shares (the "share exchange ratio") and the amount of any cash payment;
(c) the terms relating to the allotment of shares in the transferee company;
(d) the date from which the holding of shares in the transferee company will entitle the holders to participate in profits, and any special conditions affecting that entitlement;
(e) the date from which the transactions of a transferor company are to be treated for accounting purposes as being those of the transferee company;
(f) any rights or restrictions attaching to shares or other securities in the transferee company to be allotted under the scheme to the holders of shares or other securities in a transferor company to which any special rights or restrictions attach, or the measures proposed concerning them;
(g) any amount of benefit paid or given or intended to be paid or given—
(i) to any of the experts referred to in section 909 (expert's report), or
(ii) to any director of a merging company,
and the consideration for the payment of benefit.

(3) The requirements in subsection (2)(b), (c) and (d) are subject to section 915 (circumstances in which certain particulars not required).

906 Publication of draft terms by registrar (merger)

(1) The directors of each of the merging companies must deliver a copy of the draft terms to the registrar.
(2) The registrar must publish in the Gazette notice of receipt by him from that company of a copy of the draft terms.
(3) That notice must be published at least one month before the date of any meeting of that company summoned for the purpose of approving the scheme.
(4) The requirements in this section are subject to section 906A (publication of draft terms on company website).

906A Publication of draft terms on company website (merger)

(1) Section 906 does not apply in respect of a company if the conditions in subsections (2) to (6) are met.
(2) The first condition is that the draft terms are made available on a website which—
(a) is maintained by or on behalf of the company, and
(b) identifies the company.
(3) The second condition is that neither access to the draft terms on the website nor the supply of a hard copy of them from the website is conditional on payment of a fee or otherwise restricted.
(4) The third condition is that the directors of the company deliver to the registrar a notice giving details of the website.
(5) The fourth condition is that the registrar publishes the notice in the Gazette at least one month before the date of any meeting of the company summoned for the purpose of approving the scheme.
(6) The fifth condition is that the draft terms remain available on the website throughout the period beginning one month before, and ending on, the date of any such meeting.

907 Approval of members of merging companies

(1) The scheme must be approved by a majority in number, representing 75% in value, of each class of members of each of the merging companies, present and voting either in person or by proxy at a meeting.
(2) This requirement is subject to sections 916, 917 and 918 (circumstances in which meetings of members not required).

908 Directors' explanatory report (merger)

(1) The directors of each of the merging companies must draw up and adopt a report.

(2) The report must consist of—
(a) the statement required by section 897 (statement explaining effect of compromise or arrangement), and
(b) insofar as that statement does not deal with the following matters, a further statement—
(i) setting out the legal and economic grounds for the draft terms, and in particular for the share exchange ratio, and
(ii) specifying any special valuation difficulties.

(3) The requirement in this section is subject to section 915 (circumstances in which reports not required), section 915A (other circumstances in which reports and inspection not required) and section 918A (agreement to dispense with reports etc).

909 Expert's report (merger)

(1) An expert's report must be drawn up on behalf of each of the merging companies.

(2) The report required is a written report on the draft terms to the members of the company.

(3) The court may on the joint application of all the merging companies approve the appointment of a joint expert to draw up a single report on behalf of all those companies.
If no such appointment is made, there must be a separate expert's report to the members of each merging company drawn up by a separate expert appointed on behalf of that company.

(4) The expert must be a person who—
(a) is eligible for appointment as a statutory auditor (see section 1212), and
(b) meets the independence requirement in section 936.

(5) The expert's report must—
(a) indicate the method or methods used to arrive at the share exchange ratio;
(b) give an opinion as to whether the method or methods used are reasonable in all the circumstances of the case, indicate the values arrived at using each such method and (if there is more than one method) give an opinion on the relative importance attributed to such methods in arriving at the value decided on;
(c) describe any special valuation difficulties that have arisen;
(d) state whether in the expert's opinion the share exchange ratio is reasonable; and
(e) in the case of a valuation made by a person other than himself (see section 935), state that it appeared to him reasonable to arrange for it to be so made or to accept a valuation so made.

(6) The expert (or each of them) has—
(a) the right of access to all such documents of all the merging companies, and
(b) the right to require from the companies' officers all such information, as he thinks necessary for the purposes of making his report.

(7) The requirement in this section is subject to section 915 (circumstances in which reports not required), section 915A (other circumstances in which reports and inspection not required) and section 918A (agreement to dispense with expert's report).

910 Supplementary accounting statement (merger)

(1) This section applies if the last annual accounts of any of the merging companies relate to a financial year ending before—
(a) the date seven months before the first meeting of the company summoned for the purposes of approving the scheme, or
(b) if no meeting of the company is required (by virtue of any of sections 916 to 918), the date six months before the directors of the company adopt the draft terms of the scheme.

(1A) If the company has not made public a half-yearly financial report relating to a period ending on or after the date mentioned in subsection (1), the directors of the company must prepare a supplementary accounting statement.

(2) That statement must consist of—
(a) a balance sheet dealing with the state of affairs of the company as at a date not more than three months before the draft terms were adopted by the directors, and

(b) where the company would be required under section 399 to prepare group accounts if that date were the last day of a financial year, a consolidated balance sheet dealing with the state of affairs of the company and the undertakings that would be included in such a consolidation.

(3) The requirements of this Act (and where relevant Article 4 of the IAS Regulation) as to the balance sheet forming part of a company's annual accounts, and the matters to be included in notes to it, apply to the balance sheet required for an accounting statement under this section, with such modifications as are necessary by reason of its being prepared otherwise than as at the last day of a financial year.

(4) The provisions of section 414 as to the approval and signing of accounts apply to the balance sheet required for an accounting statement under this section.

(5) In this section "half-yearly financial report" means a report of that description required to be made public by rules under section 89A of the Financial Services and Markets Act 2000 (transparency rules).

(6) The requirement in this section is subject to section 915A (other circumstances in which reports and inspection not required) and section 918A (agreement to dispense with reports etc).

911 Inspection of documents (merger)

(1) The members of each of the merging companies must be able, during the period specified below—
   (a) to inspect at the registered office of that company copies of the documents listed below relating to that company and every other merging company, and
   (b) to obtain copies of those documents or any part of them on request free of charge.

(2) The period referred to above is the period—
   (a) beginning one month before, and
   (b) ending on the date of,

the first meeting of the members, or any class of members, of the company for the purposes of approving the scheme.

(3) The documents referred to above are—
   (a) the draft terms;
   (b) the directors' explanatory report;
   (c) the expert's report;
   (d) the company's annual accounts and reports for the last three financial years ending on or before the first meeting of the members, or any class of members, of the company summoned for the purposes of approving the scheme; . . .
   (e) any supplementary accounting statement required by section 910; and
   (f) if no statement is required by section 910 because the company has made public a recent half-yearly financial report (see subsection (1A) of that section), that report.

(3A) The requirement in subsection (1)(a) is subject to section 911A(1) (publication of documents on company website).

(4) The requirements of subsection (3)(b) and (c) are subject to section 915 (circumstances in which reports not required) and section 918A (agreement to dispense with reports etc).

(5) Section 1145 (right to hard copy) does not apply to a document sent or supplied in accordance with subsection (1)(b) to a member who has consented to information being sent or supplied by the company by electronic means and has not revoked that consent.

(6) Part 4 of Schedule 5 (communications by means of a website) does not apply for the purposes of subsection (1)(b) (but see section 911A(5)).

(7) The requirements in this section are subject to section 915A (other circumstances in which reports and inspection not required).

911A Publication of documents on company website (merger)

(1) Section 911(1)(a) does not apply to a document if the conditions in subsections (2) to (4) are met in relation to that document.

This is subject to subsection (6).

(2) The first condition is that the document is made available on a website which—

(a) is maintained by or on behalf of the company, and

(b) identifies the company.

(3) The second condition is that access to the document on the website is not conditional on payment of a fee or otherwise restricted.

(4) The third condition is that the document remains available on the website throughout the period beginning one month before, and ending on, the date of any meeting of the company summoned for the purpose of approving the scheme.

(5) A person is able to obtain a copy of a document as required by section 911(1)(b) if—

(a) the conditions in subsections (2) and (3) are met in relation to that document, and

(b) the person is able, throughout the period specified in subsection (4)—

(i) to retain a copy of the document as made available on the website, and

(ii) to produce a hard copy of it.

(6) Where members of a company are able to obtain copies of a document only as mentioned in subsection (5), section 911(1)(a) applies to that document even if the conditions in subsections (2) to (4) are met.

911B Report on material changes of assets of merging companies

(1) The directors of each of the merging companies must report—

(a) to every meeting of the members, or any class of members, of that company summoned for the purpose of agreeing to the scheme, and

(b) to the directors of every other merging company,

any material changes in the property and liabilities of that company between the date when the draft terms were adopted and the date of the meeting in question.

(2) The directors of each of the other merging companies must in turn—

(a) report those matters to every meeting of the members, or any class of members, of that company summoned for the purpose of agreeing to the scheme, or

(b) send a report of those matters to every member entitled to receive notice of such a meeting.

(3) The requirement in this section is subject to section 915A (other circumstances in which reports and inspection not required) and section 918A (agreement to dispense with reports etc).

912 Approval of articles of new transferee company (merger)

In the case of a merger by formation of a new company, the articles of the transferee company, or a draft of them, must be approved by ordinary resolution of . . . each of the transferor companies.

913 Protection of holders of securities to which special rights attached (merger)

(1) The scheme must provide that where any securities of a transferor company (other than shares) to which special rights are attached are held by a person otherwise than as a member or creditor of the company, that person is to receive rights in the transferee company of equivalent value.

(2) Subsection (1) does not apply if—

(a) the holder has agreed otherwise, or

(b) the holder is, or under the scheme is to be, entitled to have the securities purchased by the transferee company on terms that the court considers reasonable.

914 No allotment of shares to transferor company or transferee company (merger)

The scheme must not provide for any shares in the transferee company to be allotted to—

(a) a transferor company (or its nominee) in respect of shares in the transferor company held by the transferor company itself (or its nominee); or

(b) the transferee company (or its nominee) in respect of shares in a transferor company held by the transferee company (or its nominee).

Exceptions where shares of transferor company held by transferee company

915 Circumstances in which certain particulars and reports not required (merger)

(1) This section applies in the case of a merger by absorption where all of the relevant securities of the transferor company (or, if there is more than one transferor company, of each of them) are held by or on behalf of the transferee company.

(2) The draft terms of the scheme need not give the particulars mentioned in section 905(2)(b), (c) or (d) (particulars relating to allotment of shares to members of transferor company).

(3) Section 897 (explanatory statement to be circulated or made available) does not apply.

(4) The requirements of the following sections do not apply—
section 908 (directors' explanatory report),
section 909 (expert's report).

(5) The requirements of section 911 (inspection of documents) so far as relating to any document required to be drawn up under the provisions mentioned in subsection (4) above do not apply.

(6) In this section "relevant securities", in relation to a company, means shares or other securities carrying the right to vote at general meetings of the company.

915A Other circumstances in which reports and inspection not required (merger)

(1) This section applies in the case of a merger by absorption where 90% or more (but not all) of the relevant securities of the transferor company (or, if there is more than one transferor company, of each of them) are held by or on behalf of the transferee company.

(2) If the conditions in subsections (3) and (4) are met, the requirements of the following sections do not apply—
(a) section 908 (directors' explanatory report),
(b) section 909 (expert's report),
(c) section 910 (supplementary accounting statement),
(d) section 911 (inspection of documents), and
(e) section 911B (report on material changes of assets of merging company).

(3) The first condition is that the scheme provides that every other holder of relevant securities has the right to require the transferee company to acquire those securities.

(4) The second condition is that, if a holder of securities exercises that right, the consideration to be given for those securities is fair and reasonable.

(5) The powers of the court under section 900(2) (power to facilitate reconstruction or amalgamation) include the power to determine, or make provision for the determination of, the consideration to be given for securities acquired under this section.

(6) In this section—
"other holder" means a person who holds securities of the transferor company otherwise than on behalf of the transferee company (and does not include the transferee company itself);
"relevant securities", in relation to a company, means shares or other securities carrying the right to vote at general meetings of the company.

916 Circumstances in which meeting of members of transferee company not required (merger)

(1) This section applies in the case of a merger by absorption where 90% or more (but not all) of the relevant securities of the transferor company (or, if there is more than one transferor company, of each of them) are held by or on behalf of the transferee company.

(2) It is not necessary for the scheme to be approved at a meeting of the members, or any class of members, of the transferee company if the court is satisfied that the following conditions have been complied with.

(3) The first condition is that either subsection (3A) or subsection (3B) is satisfied.

(3A) This subsection is satisfied if publication of notice of receipt of the draft terms by the registrar took place in respect of the transferee company at least one month before the date of the first meeting of members, or any class of members, of the transferor company summoned for the purpose of agreeing to the scheme.

(3B) This subsection is satisfied if—

(a) the conditions in section 906A(2) to (4) are met in respect of the transferee company,
(b) the registrar published the notice mentioned in subsection (4) of that section in the Gazette at least one month before the date of the first meeting of members, or any class of members, of the transferor company summoned for the purpose of agreeing to the scheme, and
(c) the draft terms remained available on the website throughout the period beginning one month before, and ending on, that date.

(4) The second condition is that subsection (4A) or (4B) is satisfied for each of the documents listed in the applicable paragraphs of section 911(3)(a) to (f) relating to the transferee company and the transferor company (or, if there is more than one transferor company, each of them).

(4A) This subsection is satisfied for a document if the members of the transferee company were able during the period beginning one month before, and ending on, the date mentioned in subsection (3A) to inspect that document at the registered office of that company.

(4B) This subsection is satisfied for a document if—
(a) the document is made available on a website which is maintained by or on behalf of the transferee company and identifies the company,
(b) access to the document on the website is not conditional on the payment of a fee or otherwise restricted, and
(c) the document remains available on the website throughout the period beginning one month before, and ending on, the date mentioned in subsection (3A).

(4C) The third condition is that the members of the transferee company were able to obtain copies of the documents mentioned in subsection (4), or any part of those documents, on request and free of charge, throughout the period beginning one month before, and ending on, the date mentioned in subsection (3A).

(4D) For the purposes of subsection (4C)—
(a) section 911A(5) applies as it applies for the purposes of section 911(1)(b), and
(b) Part 4 of Schedule 5 (communications by means of a website) does not apply.

(5) The fourth condition is that—
(a) one or more members of the transferee company, who together held not less than 5% of the paid-up capital of the company which carried the right to vote at general meetings of the company (excluding any shares in the company held as treasury shares) would have been able, during that period, to require a meeting of each class of members to be called for the purpose of deciding whether or not to agree to the scheme, and
(b) no such requirement was made.

(6) In this section "relevant securities", in relation to a company, means shares or other securities carrying the right to vote at general meetings of the company.

917 Circumstances in which no meetings required (merger)

(1) This section applies in the case of a merger by absorption where all of the relevant securities of the transferor company (or, if there is more than one transferor company, of each of them) are held by or on behalf of the transferee company.

(2) It is not necessary for the scheme to be approved at a meeting of the members, or any class of members, of any of the merging companies if the court is satisfied that the following conditions have been complied with.

(3) The first condition is that either subsection (3A) or subsection (3B) is satisfied.

(3A) This subsection is satisfied if publication of notice of receipt of the draft terms by the registrar took place in respect of all the merging companies at least one month before the date of the court's order.

(3B) This subsection is satisfied if—
(a) the conditions in section 906A(2) to (4) are met in respect of each of the merging companies,
(b) in each case, the registrar published the notice mentioned in subsection (4) of that section in the Gazette at least one month before the date of the court's order, and

(c) the draft terms remained available on the website throughout the period beginning one month before, and ending on, that date.

(4) The second condition is that subsection (4A) or (4B) is satisfied for each of the documents listed in the applicable paragraphs of section 911(3)(a) to (f) relating to the transferee company and the transferor company (or, if there is more than one transferor company, each of them).

(4A) This subsection is satisfied for a document if the members of the transferee company were able during the period beginning one month before, and ending on, the date mentioned in subsection (3A) to inspect that document at the registered office of that company.

(4B) This subsection is satisfied for a document if—

(a) the document is made available on a website which is maintained by or on behalf of the transferee company and identifies the company,

(b) access to the document on the website is not conditional on the payment of a fee or otherwise restricted, and

(c) the document remains available on the website throughout the period beginning one month before, and ending on, the date mentioned in subsection (3A).

(4C) The third condition is that the members of the transferee company were able to obtain copies of the documents mentioned in subsection (4), or any part of those documents, on request and free of charge, throughout the period beginning one month before, and ending on, the date mentioned in subsection (3A).

(4D) For the purposes of subsection (4C)—

(a) section 911A(5) applies as it applies for the purposes of section 911(1)(b), and

(b) Part 4 of Schedule 5 (communications by means of a website) does not apply.

(5) The fourth condition is that—

(a) one or more members of the transferee company, who together held not less than 5% of the paid-up capital of the company which carried the right to vote at general meetings of the company (excluding any shares in the company held as treasury shares) would have been able, during that period, to require a meeting of each class of members to be called for the purpose of deciding whether or not to agree to the scheme, and

(b) no such requirement was made.

(6) In this section "relevant securities", in relation to a company, means shares or other securities carrying the right to vote at general meetings of the company.

Other exceptions

918 Other circumstances in which meeting of members of transferee company not required (merger)

(1) In the case of any merger by absorption, it is not necessary for the scheme to be approved by the members of the transferee company if the court is satisfied that the following conditions have been complied with.

(2) The first condition is that either subsection (2A) or subsection (2B) is satisfied.

(2A) This subsection is satisfied if publication of notice of receipt of the draft terms by the registrar took place in respect of the transferee company at least one month before the date of the first meeting of members, or any class of members, of the transferor company (or, if there is more than one transferor company, any of them) summoned for the purposes of agreeing to the scheme.

(2B) This subsection is satisfied if—

(a) the conditions in section 906A(2) to (4) are met in respect of the transferee company,

(b) the registrar published the notice mentioned in subsection (4) of that section in the Gazette at least one month before the date of the first meeting of members, or any class of members, of the transferor company (or, if there is more than one transferor company, any of them) summoned for the purposes of agreeing to the scheme, and

(c) the draft terms remained available on the website throughout the period beginning one month before, and ending on, that date.

(3) The second condition is that subsection (3A) or (3B) is satisfied for each of the documents listed in the applicable paragraphs of section 911(3) relating to the transferee company and the transferor company (or, if there is more than one transferor company, each of them).

(3A) This subsection is satisfied for a document if the members of the transferee company were able during the period beginning one month before, and ending on, the date of any such meeting as is mentioned in subsection (2A) to inspect that document at the registered office of that company.

(3B) This subsection is satisfied for a document if—

(a) the document is made available on a website which is maintained by or on behalf of the transferee company and identifies the company,

(b) access to the document on the website is not conditional on the payment of a fee or otherwise restricted, and

(c) the document remains available on the website throughout the period beginning one month before, and ending on, the date of any such meeting as is mentioned in subsection (2A).

(3C) The third condition is that the members of the transferee company were able to obtain copies of the documents mentioned in subsection (3), or any part of those documents, on request and free of charge, throughout the period beginning one month before, and ending on, the date of any such meeting as is mentioned in subsection (2A).

(3D) For the purposes of subsection (3C)—

(a) section 911A(5) applies as it applies for the purposes of section 911(1)(b), and

(b) Part 4 of Schedule 5 (communications by means of a website) does not apply.

(4) The fourth condition is that—

(a) one or more members of that company, who together held not less than 5 % of the paid-up capital of the company which carried the right to vote at general meetings of the company (excluding any shares in the company held as treasury shares) would have been able, during that period, to require a meeting of each class of members to be called for the purpose of deciding whether or not to agree to the scheme, and

(b) no such requirement was made.

918A Agreement to dispense with reports etc

(1) If all members holding shares in, and all persons holding other securities of, the merging companies, being shares or securities that carry a right to vote in general meetings of the company in question, so agree, the following requirements do not apply.

(1A) The requirements that may be dispensed with under this section are—

(a) the requirements of—

(i) section 908 (directors' explanatory report),

(ii) section 909 (expert's report),

(iii) section 910 (supplementary accounting statement), and

(iv) section 911B (report on material changes of assets of merging company); and

(b) the requirements of section 911 (inspection of documents) so far as relating to any document required to be drawn up under sections 908, 909 or 910.

(2) For the purposes of this section—

(a) the members, or holders of other securities, of a company, and

(b) whether shares or other securities carry a right to vote in general meetings of the company,

are determined as at the date of the application to the court under section 896.

CHAPTER 3
DIVISION

Introductory

919 Divisions and companies involved in a division

(1) The scheme involves a division where under the scheme the undertaking, property and liabilities of the company in respect of which the compromise or arrangement is proposed are to be divided among and transferred to two or more companies each of which is either—

(a) an existing public company, or
(b) a new company (whether or not a public company).

(2) References in this Part to the companies involved in the division are to the transferor company and any existing transferee companies.

Requirements to be complied with in case of division

920 Draft terms of scheme (division)

(1) A draft of the proposed terms of the scheme must be drawn up and adopted by the directors of each of the companies involved in the division.

(2) The draft terms must give particulars of at least the following matters—
(a) in respect of the transferor company and each transferee company—
(i) its name,
(ii) the address of its registered office, and
(iii) whether it is a company limited by shares or a company limited by guarantee and having a share capital;
(b) the number of shares in a transferee company to be allotted to members of the transferor company for a given number of their shares (the "share exchange ratio") and the amount of any cash payment;
(c) the terms relating to the allotment of shares in a transferee company;
(d) the date from which the holding of shares in a transferee company will entitle the holders to participate in profits, and any special conditions affecting that entitlement;
(e) the date from which the transactions of the transferor company are to be treated for accounting purposes as being those of a transferee company;
(f) any rights or restrictions attaching to shares or other securities in a transferee company to be allotted under the scheme to the holders of shares or other securities in the transferor company to which any special rights or restrictions attach, or the measures proposed concerning them;
(g) any amount of benefit paid or given or intended to be paid or given—
(i) to any of the experts referred to in section 924 (expert's report), or
(ii) to any director of a company involved in the division,
and the consideration for the payment of benefit.

(3) The draft terms must also—
(a) give particulars of the property and liabilities to be transferred (to the extent that these are known to the transferor company) and their allocation among the transferee companies;
(b) make provision for the allocation among and transfer to the transferee companies of any other property and liabilities that the transferor company has acquired or may subsequently acquire; and
(c) specify the allocation to members of the transferor company of shares in the transferee companies and the criteria upon which that allocation is based.

921 Publication of draft terms by registrar (division)

(1) The directors of each company involved in the division must deliver a copy of the draft terms to the registrar.

(2) The registrar must publish in the Gazette notice of receipt by him from that company of a copy of the draft terms.

(3) That notice must be published at least one month before the date of any meeting of that company summoned for the purposes of approving the scheme.

(4) The requirements in this section are subject to section 921A (publication of draft terms on company website) and section 934 (power of court to exclude certain requirements).

921A Publication of draft terms on company website (division)

(1) Section 921 does not apply in respect of a company if the conditions in subsections (2) to (6) are met.

(2) The first condition is that the draft terms are made available on a website which—
 (a) is maintained by or on behalf of the company, and
 (b) identifies the company.

(3) The second condition is that neither access to the draft terms on the website nor the supply of a hard copy of them from the website is conditional on payment of a fee or otherwise restricted.

(4) The third condition is that the directors of the company deliver to the registrar a notice giving details of the website.

(5) The fourth condition is that the registrar publishes the notice in the Gazette at least one month before the date of any meeting of the company summoned for the purpose of approving the scheme.

(6) The fifth condition is that the draft terms remain available on the website throughout the period beginning one month before, and ending on, the date of any such meeting.

922 Approval of members of companies involved in the division

(1) The compromise or arrangement must be approved by a majority in number, representing 75% in value, of each class of members of each of the companies involved in the division, present and voting either in person or by proxy at a meeting.

(2) This requirement is subject to sections 931 and 932 (circumstances in which meeting of members not required).

923 Directors' explanatory report (division)

(1) The directors of the transferor and each existing transferee company must draw up and adopt a report.

(2) The report must consist of—
 (a) the statement required by section 897 (statement explaining effect of compromise or arrangement), and
 (b) insofar as that statement does not deal with the following matters, a further statement—
  (i) setting out the legal and economic grounds for the draft terms, and in particular for the share exchange ratio and for the criteria on which the allocation to the members of the transferor company of shares in the transferee companies was based, and
  (ii) specifying any special valuation difficulties.

(3) The report must also state—
 (a) whether a report has been made to any transferee company under section 593 (valuation of non-cash consideration for shares), and
 (b) if so, whether that report has been delivered to the registrar of companies.

(4) The requirement in this section is subject to section 933 (agreement to dispense with reports etc) and section 933A (certain requirements excluded where shareholders given proportional rights).

924 Expert's report (division)

(1) An expert's report must be drawn up on behalf of each company involved in the division.

(2) The report required is a written report on the draft terms to the members of the company.

(3) The court may on the joint application of the companies involved in the division approve the appointment of a joint expert to draw up a single report on behalf of all those companies.
If no such appointment is made, there must be a separate expert's report to the members of each company involved in the division drawn up by a separate expert appointed on behalf of that company.

(4) The expert must be a person who—
 (a) is eligible for appointment as a statutory auditor (see section 1212), and
 (b) meets the independence requirement in section 936.

(5) The expert's report must—
 (a) indicate the method or methods used to arrive at the share exchange ratio;
 (b) give an opinion as to whether the method or methods used are reasonable in all the circumstances of the case, indicate the values arrived at using each such method and (if there is more than one method) give an opinion on the relative importance attributed to such methods in arriving at the value decided on;

(c) describe any special valuation difficulties that have arisen;
(d) state whether in the expert's opinion the share exchange ratio is reasonable; and
(e) in the case of a valuation made by a person other than himself (see section 935), state that it appeared to him reasonable to arrange for it to be so made or to accept a valuation so made.

(6) The expert (or each of them) has—
(a) the right of access to all such documents of the companies involved in the division, and
(b) the right to require from the companies' officers all such information, as he thinks necessary for the purposes of making his report.

(7) The requirement in this section is subject to section 933 (agreement to dispense with reports etc) and section 933A (certain requirements excluded where shareholders given proportional rights).

925 Supplementary accounting statement (division)

(1) This section applies if the last annual accounts of a company involved in the division relate to a financial year ending before—
(a) the date seven months before the first meeting of the company summoned for the purposes of approving the scheme, or
(b) if no meeting of the company is required (by virtue of section 931 or 932), the date six months before the directors of the company adopt the draft terms of the scheme.

(1A) If the company has not made public a half-yearly financial report relating to a period ending on or after the date mentioned in subsection (1), the directors of the company must prepare a supplementary accounting statement.

(2) That statement must consist of—
(a) a balance sheet dealing with the state of affairs of the company as at a date not more than three months before the draft terms were adopted by the directors, and
(b) where the company would be required under section 399 to prepare group accounts if that date were the last day of a financial year, a consolidated balance sheet dealing with the state of affairs of the company and the undertakings that would be included in such a consolidation.

(3) The requirements of this Act (and where relevant Article 4 of the IAS Regulation) as to the balance sheet forming part of a company's annual accounts, and the matters to be included in notes to it, apply to the balance sheet required for an accounting statement under this section, with such modifications as are necessary by reason of its being prepared otherwise than as at the last day of a financial year.

(4) The provisions of section 414 as to the approval and signing of accounts apply to the balance sheet required for an accounting statement under this section.

(4A) In this section "half-yearly financial report" means a report of that description required to be made public by rules under section 89A of the Financial Services and Markets Act 2000 (transparency rules).

(5) The requirement in this section is subject to section 933 (agreement to dispense with reports etc) and section 933A (certain requirements excluded where shareholders given proportional rights).

926 Inspection of documents (division)

(1) The members of each company involved in the division must be able, during the period specified below—
(a) to inspect at the registered office of that company copies of the documents listed below relating to that company and every other company involved in the division, and
(b) to obtain copies of those documents or any part of them on request free of charge.

(2) The period referred to above is the period—
(a) beginning one month before, and
(b) ending on the date of,
the first meeting of the members, or any class of members, of the company for the purposes of approving the scheme.

(3) The documents referred to above are—

(a) the draft terms;
(b) the directors' explanatory report;
(c) the expert's report;
(d) the company's annual accounts and reports for the last three financial years ending on or before the first meeting of the members, or any class of members, of the company summoned for the purposes of approving the scheme; . . .
(e) any supplementary accounting statement required by section 925; and
(f) if no statement is required by section 925 because the company has made public a recent half-yearly financial report (see subsection (1A) of that section), that report.

(3A) The requirement in subsection (1)(a) is subject to section 926A(1) (publication of documents on company website).

(4) The requirements in subsection (3)(b), (c) and (e) are subject to section 933 (agreement to dispense with reports etc), section 933A (certain requirements excluded where shareholders given proportional rights) and section 934 (power of court to exclude certain requirements).

(5) Section 1145 (right to hard copy) does not apply to a document sent or supplied in accordance with subsection (1)(b) to a member who has consented to information being sent or supplied by the company by electronic means and has not revoked that consent.

(6) Part 4 of Schedule 5 (communications by means of a website) does not apply for the purposes of subsection (1)(b) (but see section 926A(5)).

926A Publication of documents on company website (division)

(1) Section 926(1)(a) does not apply to a document if the conditions in subsections (2) to (4) are met in relation to that document.
This is subject to subsection (6).

(2) The first condition is that the document is made available on a website which—
(a) is maintained by or on behalf of the company, and
(b) identifies the company.

(3) The second condition is that access to the document on the website is not conditional on payment of a fee or otherwise restricted.

(4) The third condition is that the document remains available on the website throughout the period beginning one month before, and ending on, the date of any meeting of the company summoned for the purpose of approving the scheme.

(5) A person is able to obtain a copy of a document as required by section 926(1)(b) if—
(a) the conditions in subsections (2) and (3) are met in relation to that document, and
(b) the person is able, throughout the period specified in subsection (4)—
(i) to retain a copy of the document as made available on the website, and
(ii) to produce a hard copy of it.

(6) Where members of a company are able to obtain copies of a document only as mentioned in subsection (5), section 926(1)(a) applies to that document even if the conditions in subsections (2) to (4) are met.

927 Report on material changes of assets of transferor company (division)

(1) The directors of the transferor company must report—
(a) to every meeting of the members, or any class of members, of that company summoned for the purpose of agreeing to the scheme, and
(b) to the directors of each existing transferee company,
any material changes in the property and liabilities of the transferor company between the date when the draft terms were adopted and the date of the meeting in question.

(2) The directors of each existing transferee company must in turn—
(a) report those matters to every meeting of the members, or any class of members, of that company summoned for the purpose of agreeing to the scheme, or
(b) send a report of those matters to every member entitled to receive notice of such a meeting.

(3) The requirement in this section is subject to section 933 (agreement to dispense with reports etc) and section 933A (certain requirements excluded where shareholders given proportional rights).

928 Approval of articles of new transferee company (division)

The articles of every new transferee company, or a draft of them, must be approved by ordinary resolution of the transferor company.

929 Protection of holders of securities to which special rights attached (division)

(1) The scheme must provide that where any securities of the transferor company (other than shares) to which special rights are attached are held by a person otherwise than as a member or creditor of the company, that person is to receive rights in a transferee company of equivalent value.

(2) Subsection (1) does not apply if—

(a) the holder has agreed otherwise, or

(b) the holder is, or under the scheme is to be, entitled to have the securities purchased by a transferee company on terms that the court considers reasonable.

930 No allotment of shares to transferor company or to transferee company (division)

The scheme must not provide for any shares in a transferee company to be allotted to—

(a) the transferor company (or its nominee) in respect of shares in the transferor company held by the transferor company itself (or its nominee); or

(b) a transferee company (or its nominee) in respect of shares in the transferor company held by the transferee company (or its nominee).

Exceptions where shares of transferor company held by transferee company

931 Circumstances in which meeting of members of transferor company not required (division)

(1) This section applies in the case of a division where all of the shares or other securities of the transferor company carrying the right to vote at general meetings of the company are held by or on behalf of one or more existing transferee companies.

(2) It is not necessary for the scheme to be approved by a meeting of the members, or any class of members, of the transferor company if the court is satisfied that the following conditions have been complied with.

(3) The first condition is that either subsection (3A) or subsection (3B) is satisfied.

(3A) This subsection is satisfied if publication of notice of receipt of the draft terms by the registrar took place in respect of all the companies involved in the division at least one month before the date of the court's order.

(3B) This subsection is satisfied if—

(a) the conditions in section 921A(2) to (4) are met in respect of each of the companies involved in the division,

(b) in each case, the registrar published the notice mentioned in subsection (4) of that section in the Gazette at least one month before the date of the court's order, and

(c) the draft terms remained available on the website throughout the period beginning one month before, and ending on, that date.

(4) The second condition is that subsection (4A) or (4B) is satisfied for each of the documents listed in the applicable paragraphs of section 926(3) relating to every company involved in the division.

(4A) This subsection is satisfied for a document if the members of every company involved in the division were able during the period beginning one month before, and ending on, the date of the court's order to inspect that document at the registered office of their company.

(4B) This subsection is satisfied for a document if—

(a) the document is made available on a website which is maintained by or on behalf of the company to which it relates and identifies the company,

(b) access to the document on the website is not conditional on payment of a fee or otherwise restricted, and

(c) the document remains available on the website throughout the period beginning one month before, and ending on, the date of the court's order.

(4C) The third condition is that the members of every company involved in the division were able to obtain copies of the documents mentioned in subsection (4), or any part of those documents, on request and free of charge, throughout the period beginning one month before, and ending on, the date of the court's order.

(4D) For the purposes of subsection (4C)—

(a) section 926A(5) applies as it applies for the purposes of section 926(1)(b), and

(b) Part 4 of Schedule 5 (communications by means of a website) does not apply.

(5) . . .

(6) The fourth condition is that the directors of the transferor company have sent—

(a) to every member who would have been entitled to receive notice of a meeting to agree to the scheme (had any such meeting been called), and

(b) to the directors of every existing transferee company,

a report of any material change in the property and liabilities of the transferor company between the date when the terms were adopted by the directors and the date one month before the date of the court's order.

Other exceptions

932 Circumstances in which meeting of members of transferee company not required (division)

(1) In the case of a division, it is not necessary for the scheme to be approved by the members of a transferee company if the court is satisfied that the following conditions have been complied with in relation to that company.

(2) The first condition is that either subsection (2A) or subsection (2B) is satisfied.

(2A) This subsection is satisfied if publication of notice of receipt of the draft terms by the registrar took place in respect of the transferee company at least one month before the date of the first meeting of members of the transferor company summoned for the purposes of agreeing to the scheme.

(2B) This subsection is satisfied if—

(a) the conditions in section 921A(2) to (4) are met in respect of the transferee company,

(b) the registrar published the notice mentioned in subsection (4) of that section in the Gazette at least one month before the date of the first meeting of members of the transferor company summoned for the purposes of agreeing to the scheme, and

(c) the draft terms remained available on the website throughout the period beginning one month before, and ending on, that date.

(3) The second condition is that subsection (3A) or (3B) is satisfied for each of the documents listed in the applicable paragraphs of section 926(3) relating to the transferee company and every other company involved in the division.

(3A) This subsection is satisfied for a document if the members of the transferee company were able during the period beginning one month before, and ending on, the date mentioned in subsection (2A) to inspect that document at the registered office of that company.

(3B) This subsection is satisfied for a document if—

(a) the document is made available on a website which is maintained by or on behalf of the transferee company and identifies the company,

(b) access to the document on the website is not conditional on payment of a fee or otherwise restricted, and

(c) the document remains available on the website throughout the period beginning one month before, and ending on, the date mentioned in subsection (2A).

(3C) The third condition is that the members of the transferee company were able to obtain copies of the documents mentioned in subsection (3), or any part of those documents, on request and free of charge, throughout the period beginning one month before, and ending on, the date mentioned in subsection (2A).

(3D) For the purposes of subsection (3C)—

(a) section 926A(5) applies as it applies for the purposes of section 926(1)(b), and

(b) Part 4 of Schedule 5 (communications by means of a website) does not apply.

(4) The fourth condition is that—

(a) one or more members of that company, who together held not less than 5 % of the paid-up capital of the company which carried the right to vote at general meetings of the company (excluding any shares in the company held as treasury shares) would have been able, during that period, to require a meeting of each class of members to be called for the purpose of deciding whether or not to agree to the scheme, and

(b) no such requirement was made.

(5) The first, second and third conditions above are subject to section 934 (power of court to exclude certain requirements).

933 Agreement to dispense with reports etc (division)

(1) If all members holding shares in, and all persons holding other securities of, the companies involved in the division, being shares or securities that carry a right to vote in general meetings of the company in question, so agree, the following requirements do not apply.

(2) The requirements that may be dispensed with under this section are—

(a) the requirements of—

(i) section 923 (directors' explanatory report),

(ii) section 924 (expert's report),

(iii) section 925 (supplementary accounting statement), and

(iv) section 927 (report on material changes in assets of transferor company); and

(b) the requirements of section 926 (inspection of documents) so far as relating to any document required to be drawn up under the provisions mentioned in paragraph (a)(i), (ii) or (iii) above.

(3) For the purposes of this section—

(a) the members, or holders of other securities, of a company, and

(b) whether shares or other securities carry a right to vote in general meetings of the company,

are determined as at the date of the application to the court under section 896.

933A Certain requirements excluded where shareholders given proportional rights (division)

(1) This section applies in the case of a division where each of the transferee companies is a new company.

(2) If all the shares in each of the transferee companies are to be allotted to the members of the transferor company in proportion to their rights in the allotted share capital of the transferor company, the following requirements do not apply.

(3) The requirements which do not apply are—

(a) the requirements of—

(i) section 923 (directors' explanatory report),

(ii) section 924 (expert's report),

(iii) section 925 (supplementary accounting statement), and

(iv) section 927 (report on material changes in assets of transferor company); and

(b) the requirements of section 926 (inspection of documents) so far as relating to any document required to be drawn up under the provisions mentioned in paragraph (a)(i), (ii) or (iii) above.

934 Power of court to exclude certain requirements (division)

(1) In the case of a division, the court may by order direct that—

(a) in relation to any company involved in the division, the requirements of—

(i) section 921 (publication of draft terms), and

(ii) section 926 (inspection of documents),

do not apply, and

(b) in relation to an existing transferee company, section 932 (circumstances in which meeting of members of transferee company not required) has effect with the omission of the first, second and third conditions specified in that section,

if the court is satisfied that the following conditions will be fulfilled in relation to that company.

(2) The first condition is that the members of that company will have received, or will have been able to obtain free of charge, copies of the documents listed in section 926—

(a) in time to examine them before the date of the first meeting of the members, or any class of members, of that company summoned for the purposes of agreeing to the scheme, or

(b) in the case of an existing transferee company where in the circumstances described in section 932 no meeting is held, in time to require a meeting as mentioned in subsection (4) of that section.

(3) The second condition is that the creditors of that company will have received or will have been able to obtain free of charge copies of the draft terms in time to examine them—

(a) before the date of the first meeting of the members, or any class of members, of the company summoned for the purposes of agreeing to the scheme, or

(b) in the circumstances mentioned in subsection (2)(b) above, at the same time as the members of the company.

(4) The third condition is that no prejudice would be caused to the members or creditors of the transferor company or any transferee company by making the order in question.

CHAPTER 4
SUPPLEMENTARY PROVISIONS

Expert's report and related matters

935 Expert's report: valuation by another person

(1) Where it appears to an expert—

(a) that a valuation is reasonably necessary to enable him to draw up his report, and

(b) that it is reasonable for that valuation, or part of it, to be made by (or for him to accept a valuation made by) another person who—

(i) appears to him to have the requisite knowledge and experience to make the valuation or that part of it, and

(ii) meets the independence requirement in section 936,

he may arrange for or accept such a valuation, together with a report which will enable him to make his own report under section 909 or 924.

(2) Where any valuation is made by a person other than the expert himself, the latter's report must state that fact and must also—

(a) state the former's name and what knowledge and experience he has to carry out the valuation, and

(b) describe so much of the undertaking, property and liabilities as was valued by the other person, and the method used to value them, and specify the date of the valuation.

936 Experts and valuers: independence requirement

(1) A person meets the independence requirement for the purposes of section 909 or 924 (expert's report) or section 935 (valuation by another person) only if—

(a) he is not—

(i) an officer or employee of any of the companies concerned in the scheme, or

(ii) a partner or employee of such a person, or a partnership of which such a person is a partner;

(b) he is not—

(i) an officer or employee of an associated undertaking of any of the companies concerned in the scheme, or

(ii) a partner or employee of such a person, or a partnership of which such a person is a partner; and

(c) there does not exist between—
(i) the person or an associate of his, and
(ii) any of the companies concerned in the scheme or an associated undertaking of such a company,

a connection of any such description as may be specified by regulations made by the Secretary of State.

(2) An auditor of a company is not regarded as an officer or employee of the company for this purpose.

(3) For the purposes of this section—
(a) the "companies concerned in the scheme" means every transferor and existing transferee company;
(b) "associated undertaking", in relation to a company, means—
(i) a parent undertaking or subsidiary undertaking of the company, or
(ii) a subsidiary undertaking of a parent undertaking of the company; and
(c) "associate" has the meaning given by section 937.

(4) Regulations under this section are subject to negative resolution procedure.

937 Experts and valuers: meaning of "associate"

(1) This section defines "associate" for the purposes of section 936 (experts and valuers: independence requirement).

(2) In relation to an individual, "associate" means—
(a) that individual's spouse or civil partner or minor child or step-child,
(b) any body corporate of which that individual is a director, and
(c) any employee or partner of that individual.

(3) In relation to a body corporate, "associate" means—
(a) any body corporate of which that body is a director,
(b) any body corporate in the same group as that body, and
(c) any employee or partner of that body or of any body corporate in the same group.

(4) In relation to a partnership that is a legal person under the law by which it is governed, "associate" means—
(a) any body corporate of which that partnership is a director,
(b) any employee of or partner in that partnership, and
(c) any person who is an associate of a partner in that partnership.

(5) In relation to a partnership that is not a legal person under the law by which it is governed, "associate" means any person who is an associate of any of the partners.

(6) In this section, in relation to a limited liability partnership, for "director" read "member".

Powers of the court

938 Power of court to summon meeting of members or creditors of existing transferee company

(1) The court may order a meeting of—
(a) the members of an existing transferee company, or any class of them, or
(b) the creditors of an existing transferee company, or any class of them,

to be summoned in such manner as the court directs.

(2) An application for such an order may be made by—
(a) the company concerned,
(b) a member or creditor of the company, or
(c) if the company being wound up, the liquidator, or
(d) if the company is in administration, the administrator.

(3) Section 323 (representation of corporations at meetings) applies to a meeting of creditors under this section as to a meeting of the company (references to a member being read as references to a creditor).

939 Court to fix date for transfer of undertaking etc of transferor company

(1) Where the court sanctions the compromise or arrangement, it must—

(a) in the order sanctioning the compromise or arrangement, or

(b) in a subsequent order under section 900 (powers of court to facilitate reconstruction or amalgamation),

fix a date on which the transfer (or transfers) to the transferee company (or transferee companies) of the undertaking, property and liabilities of the transferor company is (or are) to take place.

(2) Any such order that provides for the dissolution of the transferor company must fix the same date for the dissolution.

(3) If it is necessary for the transferor company to take steps to ensure that the undertaking, property and liabilities are fully transferred, the court must fix a date, not later than six months after the date fixed under subsection (1), by which such steps must be taken.

(4) In that case, the court may postpone the dissolution of the transferor company until that date.

(5) The court may postpone or further postpone the date fixed under subsection (3) if it is satisfied that the steps mentioned cannot be completed by the date (or latest date) fixed under that subsection.

Liability of transferee companies

940 Liability of transferee companies for each other's defaults

(1) In the case of a division, each transferee company is jointly and severally liable for any liability transferred to any other transferee company under the scheme to the extent that the other company has made default in satisfying that liability.

This is subject to the following provisions.

(2) If a majority in number representing 75% in value of the creditors or any class of creditors of the transferor company, present and voting either in person or by proxy at a meeting summoned for the purposes of agreeing to the scheme, so agree, subsection (1) does not apply in relation to the liabilities owed to the creditors or that class of creditors.

(3) A transferee company is not liable under this section for an amount greater than the net value transferred to it under the scheme.

The "net value transferred" is the value at the time of the transfer of the property transferred to it under the scheme less the amount at that date of the liabilities so transferred.

Disruption of websites

940A Disregard of website failures beyond control of company

(1) A failure to make information or a document available on the website throughout a period specified in any of the provisions mentioned in subsection (2) is to be disregarded if—

(a) it is made available on the website for part of that period, and

(b) the failure to make it available throughout that period is wholly attributable to circumstances that it would not be reasonable to have expected the company to prevent or avoid.

(2) The provisions referred to above are—

(a) section 906A(6),

(b) section 911A(4),

(c) section 916(3B) and (4B),

(d) section 917(3B) and (4B),

(e) section 918(2B) and (3B),

(f) section 921A(6),

(g) section 926A(4),

(h) section 931(3B) and (4B), and

(i) section 932(2B) and (3B).

Interpretation

941 Meaning of "liabilities" and "property"

In this Part—

"liabilities" includes duties;

"property" includes property, rights and powers of every description.

PART 28
TAKEOVERS ETC

CHAPTER 1
THE TAKEOVER PANEL

The Panel and its rules

942 The Panel

(1) The body known as the Panel on Takeovers and Mergers ("the Panel") is to have the functions conferred on it by or under this Chapter.

(2) The Panel may do anything that it considers necessary or expedient for the purposes of, or in connection with, its functions.

(3) The Panel may make arrangements for any of its functions to be discharged by—

(a) a committee or sub-committee of the Panel, or

(b) an officer or member of staff of the Panel, or a person acting as such. This is subject to section 943(4) and (5).

943 Rules

(1) The Panel must make rules giving effect to Articles 3.1, 4.2, 5, 6.1 to 6.3, 7 to 9 and 13 of the Takeovers Directive.

(2) Rules made by the Panel may also make other provision—

(a) for or in connection with the regulation of—

(i) takeover bids,

(ii) merger transactions, and

(iii) transactions (not falling within sub-paragraph (i) or (ii)) that have or may have, directly or indirectly, an effect on the ownership or control of companies;

(b) for or in connection with the regulation of things done in consequence of, or otherwise in relation to, any such bid or transaction;

(c) about cases where—

(i) any such bid or transaction is, or has been, contemplated or apprehended, or

(ii) an announcement is made denying that any such bid or transaction is intended.

(3) The provision that may be made under subsection (2) includes, in particular, provision for a matter that is, or is similar to, a matter provided for by the Panel in the City Code on Takeovers and Mergers as it had effect immediately before the passing of this Act.

(4) In relation to rules made by virtue of section 957 (fees and charges), functions under this section may be discharged either by the Panel itself or by a committee of the Panel (but not otherwise).

(5) In relation to rules of any other description, the Panel must discharge its functions under this section by a committee of the Panel.

(6) Section 1 (meaning of "company") does not apply for the purposes of this section.

(7) In this section "takeover bid" includes a takeover bid within the meaning of the Takeovers Directive.

(8) In this Chapter "the Takeovers Directive" means Directive 2004/25/EC of the European Parliament and of the Council.

(9) A reference to rules in the following provisions of this Chapter is to rules under this section.

944 Further provisions about rules

(1) Rules may—

(a) make different provision for different purposes;

(b) make provision subject to exceptions or exemptions;

(c) contain incidental, supplemental, consequential or transitional provision;

(d) authorise the Panel to dispense with or modify the application of rules in particular cases and by reference to any circumstances.

Rules made by virtue of paragraph (d) must require the Panel to give reasons for acting as mentioned in that paragraph.

(2) Rules must be made by an instrument in writing.

(3) Immediately after an instrument containing rules is made, the text must be made available to the public, with or without payment, in whatever way the Panel thinks appropriate.

(4) A person is not to be taken to have contravened a rule if he shows that at the time of the alleged contravention the text of the rule had not been made available as required by subsection (3).

(5) The production of a printed copy of an instrument purporting to be made by the Panel on which is endorsed a certificate signed by an officer of the Panel authorised by it for that purpose and stating—

(a) that the instrument was made by the Panel,

(b) that the copy is a true copy of the instrument, and

(c) that on a specified date the text of the instrument was made available to the public as required by subsection (3),

is evidence (or in Scotland sufficient evidence) of the facts stated in the certificate.

(6) A certificate purporting to be signed as mentioned in subsection (5) is to be treated as having been properly signed unless the contrary is shown.

(7) A person who wishes in any legal proceedings to rely on an instrument by which rules are made may require the Panel to endorse a copy of the instrument with a certificate of the kind mentioned in subsection (5).

945 Rulings

(1) The Panel may give rulings on the interpretation, application or effect of rules.

(2) To the extent and in the circumstances specified in rules, and subject to any review or appeal, a ruling has binding effect.

946 Directions

Rules may contain provision conferring power on the Panel to give any direction that appears to the Panel to be necessary in order—

(a) to restrain a person from acting (or continuing to act) in breach of rules;

(b) to restrain a person from doing (or continuing to do) a particular thing, pending determination of whether that or any other conduct of his is or would be a breach of rules;

(c) otherwise to secure compliance with rules.

Information

947 Power to require documents and information

(1) The Panel may by notice in writing require a person—

(a) to produce any documents that are specified or described in the notice;

(b) to provide, in the form and manner specified in the notice, such information as may be specified or described in the notice.

(2) A requirement under subsection (1) must be complied with—

(a) at a place specified in the notice, and

(b) before the end of such reasonable period as may be so specified.

(3) This section applies only to documents and information reasonably required in connection with the exercise by the Panel of its functions.

(4) The Panel may require—

(a) any document produced to be authenticated, or

(b) any information provided (whether in a document or otherwise) to be verified,

in such manner as it may reasonably require.

(5) The Panel may authorise a person to exercise any of its powers under this section.

(6) A person exercising a power by virtue of subsection (5) must, if required to do so, produce evidence of his authority to exercise the power.

(7) The production of a document in pursuance of this section does not affect any lien that a person has on the document.

(8) The Panel may take copies of or extracts from a document produced in pursuance of this section.

(9) A reference in this section to the production of a document includes a reference to the production of—

(a) a hard copy of information recorded otherwise than in hard copy form, or

(b) information in a form from which a hard copy can be readily obtained.

(10) A person is not required by this section to disclose documents or information in respect of which a claim to legal professional privilege (in Scotland, to confidentiality of communications) could be maintained in legal proceedings.

948 Restrictions on disclosure

(1) This section applies to information (in whatever form)—

(a) relating to the private affairs of an individual, or

(b) relating to any particular business,

that is provided to the Panel in connection with the exercise of its functions.

(2) No such information may, during the lifetime of the individual or so long as the business continues to be carried on, be disclosed without the consent of that individual or (as the case may be) the person for the time being carrying on that business.

(3) Subsection (2) does not apply to any disclosure of information that—

(a) is made for the purpose of facilitating the carrying out by the Panel of any of its functions,

(b) is made to a person specified in Part 1 of Schedule 2,

(c) is of a description specified in Part 2 of that Schedule, or

(d) is made in accordance with Part 3 of that Schedule.

(4) The Secretary of State may amend Schedule 2 by order subject to negative resolution procedure.

(5) An order under subsection (4) must not—

(a) amend Part 1 of Schedule 2 by specifying a person unless the person exercises functions of a public nature (whether or not he exercises any other function);

(b) amend Part 2 of Schedule 2 by adding or modifying a description of disclosure unless the purpose for which the disclosure is permitted is likely to facilitate the exercise of a function of a public nature;

(c) amend Part 3 of Schedule 2 so as to have the effect of permitting disclosures to be made to a body other than one that exercises functions of a public nature in a country or territory outside the United Kingdom.

(6) Subsection (2) does not apply to—

(a) the disclosure by an authority within subsection (7) of information disclosed to it by the Panel in reliance on subsection (3);

(b) the disclosure of such information by anyone who has obtained it directly or indirectly from an authority within subsection (7).

(7) The authorities within this subsection are—

(a) the Financial Conduct Authority;

(aa) the Prudential Regulation Authority;

(ab) the Bank of England;

(b) an authority designated as a supervisory authority for the purposes of Article 4.1 of the Takeovers Directive;

(c) any other person or body that exercises functions of a public nature, under legislation in an EEA State other than the United Kingdom, that are similar to the Panel's functions or those of the Financial Conduct Authority or the Prudential Regulation Authority or similar to the regulatory functions of the Bank of England.

(8) This section does not prohibit the disclosure of information if the information is or has been available to the public from any other source.

(9) Nothing in this section authorises the making of a disclosure in contravention of the Data Protection Act 1998.

949 Offence of disclosure in contravention of section 948

(1) A person who discloses information in contravention of section 948 is guilty of an offence, unless—
  (a) he did not know, and had no reason to suspect, that the information had been provided as mentioned in section 948(1), or
  (b) he took all reasonable steps and exercised all due diligence to avoid the commission of the offence.

(2) A person guilty of an offence under this section is liable—
  (a) on conviction on indictment, to imprisonment for a term not exceeding two years or a fine (or both);
  (b) on summary conviction—
    (i) in England and Wales, to imprisonment for a term not exceeding twelve months or to a fine not exceeding the statutory maximum (or both);
    (ii) in Scotland or Northern Ireland, to imprisonment for a term not exceeding six months, or to a fine not exceeding the statutory maximum (or both).

(3) Where a company or other body corporate commits an offence under this section, an offence is also committed by every officer of the company or other body corporate who is in default.

Co-operation

950 Panel's duty of co-operation

(1) The Panel must take such steps as it considers appropriate to co-operate with—
  (a) the Financial Conduct Authority;
  (aa) the Prudential Regulation Authority;
  (ab) the Bank of England;
  (b) an authority designated as a supervisory authority for the purposes of Article 4.1 of the Takeovers Directive;
  (c) any other person or body that exercises functions of a public nature, under legislation in any country or territory outside the United Kingdom, that appear to the Panel to be similar to its own functions or those of the Financial Conduct Authority or the Prudential Regulation Authority or similar to the regulatory functions of the Bank of England.

(2) Co-operation may include the sharing of information that the Panel is not prevented from disclosing.

Hearings and appeals

951 Hearings and appeals

(1) Rules must provide for a decision of the Panel to be subject to review by a committee of the Panel (the "Hearings Committee") at the instance of such persons affected by the decision as are specified in the rules.

(2) Rules may also confer other functions on the Hearings Committee.

(3) Rules must provide for there to be a right of appeal against a decision of the Hearings Committee to an independent tribunal (the "Takeover Appeal Board") in such circumstances and subject to such conditions as are specified in the rules.

(4) Rules may contain—
  (a) provision as to matters of procedure in relation to proceedings before the Hearings Committee (including provision imposing time limits);
  (b) provision about evidence in such proceedings;
  (c) provision as to the powers of the Hearings Committee dealing with a matter referred to it;
  (d) provision about enforcement of decisions of the Hearings Committee and the Takeover Appeal Board.

(5) Rules must contain provision—

(a) requiring the Panel, when acting in relation to any proceedings before the Hearings Committee or the Takeover Appeal Board, to do so by an officer or member of staff of the Panel (or a person acting as such);

(b) preventing a person who is or has been a member of the committee mentioned in section 943(5) from being a member of the Hearings Committee or the Takeover Appeal Board;

(c) preventing a person who is a member of the committee mentioned in section 943(5), of the Hearings Committee or of the Takeover Appeal Board from acting as mentioned in paragraph (a).

Contravention of rules etc

952 Sanctions

(1) Rules may contain provision conferring power on the Panel to impose sanctions on a person who has—

(a) acted in breach of rules, or

(b) failed to comply with a direction given by virtue of section 946.

(2) Subsection (3) applies where rules made by virtue of subsection (1) confer power on the Panel to impose a sanction of a kind not provided for by the City Code on Takeovers and Mergers as it had effect immediately before the passing of this Act.

(3) The Panel must prepare a statement (a "policy statement") of its policy with respect to—

(a) the imposition of the sanction in question, and

(b) where the sanction is in the nature of a financial penalty, the amount of the penalty that may be imposed.

An element of the policy must be that, in making a decision about any such matter, the Panel has regard to the factors mentioned in subsection (4).

(4) The factors are—

(a) the seriousness of the breach or failure in question in relation to the nature of the rule or direction contravened;

(b) the extent to which the breach or failure was deliberate or reckless;

(c) whether the person on whom the sanction is to be imposed is an individual.

(5) The Panel may at any time revise a policy statement.

(6) The Panel must prepare a draft of any proposed policy statement (or revised policy statement) and consult such persons about the draft as the Panel considers appropriate.

(7) The Panel must publish, in whatever way it considers appropriate, any policy statement (or revised policy statement) that it prepares.

(8) In exercising, or deciding whether to exercise, its power to impose a sanction within subsection (2) in the case of any particular breach or failure, the Panel must have regard to any relevant policy statement published and in force at the time when the breach or failure occurred.

953 Failure to comply with rules about bid documentation

(1) This section applies where a takeover bid is made for a company that has securities carrying voting rights admitted to trading on a regulated market in the United Kingdom.

(2) Where an offer document published in respect of the bid does not comply with offer document rules, an offence is committed by—

(a) the person making the bid, and

(b) where the person making the bid is a body of persons, any director, officer or member of that body who caused the document to be published.

(3) A person commits an offence under subsection (2) only if—

(a) he knew that the offer document did not comply, or was reckless as to whether it complied, and

(b) he failed to take all reasonable steps to secure that it did comply.

(4) Where a response document published in respect of the bid does not comply with response document rules, an offence is committed by any director or other officer of the company referred to in subsection (1) who—

(a) knew that the response document did not comply, or was reckless as to whether it complied, and

(b) failed to take all reasonable steps to secure that it did comply.

(5) Where an offence is committed under subsection (2)(b) or (4) by a company or other body corporate ("the relevant body")—

(a) subsection (2)(b) has effect as if the reference to a director, officer or member of the person making the bid included a reference to a director, officer or member of the relevant body;

(b) subsection (4) has effect as if the reference to a director or other officer of the company referred to in subsection (1) included a reference to a director, officer or member of the relevant body.

(6) A person guilty of an offence under this section is liable—

(a) on conviction on indictment, to a fine;

(b) on summary conviction, to a fine not exceeding the statutory maximum.

(7) Nothing in this section affects any power of the Panel in relation to the enforcement of its rules.

(8) Section 1 (meaning of "company") does not apply for the purposes of this section.

(9) In this section—

"designated" means designated in rules;

"offer document" means a document required to be published by rules giving effect to Article 6.2 of the Takeovers Directive;

"offer document rules" means rules designated as rules that give effect to Article 6.3 of that Directive;

"response document" means a document required to be published by rules giving effect to Article 9.5 of that Directive;

"response document rules" means rules designated as rules that give effect to the first sentence of Article 9.5 of that Directive;

"securities" means shares or debentures;

"takeover bid" has the same meaning as in that Directive;

"voting rights" means rights to vote at general meetings of the company in question, including rights that arise only in certain circumstances.

954 Compensation

(1) Rules may confer power on the Panel to order a person to pay such compensation as it thinks just and reasonable if he is in breach of a rule the effect of which is to require the payment of money.

(2) Rules made by virtue of this section may include provision for the payment of interest (including compound interest).

955 Enforcement by the court

(1) If, on the application of the Panel, the court is satisfied—

(a) that there is a reasonable likelihood that a person will contravene a rule-based requirement, or

(b) that a person has contravened a rule-based requirement or a disclosure requirement,

the court may make any order it thinks fit to secure compliance with the requirement.

(2) In subsection (1) "the court" means the High Court or, in Scotland, the Court of Session.

(3) Except as provided by subsection (1), no person—

(a) has a right to seek an injunction, or

(b) in Scotland, has title or interest to seek an interdict or an order for specific performance,

to prevent a person from contravening (or continuing to contravene) a rule-based requirement or a disclosure requirement.

(4) In this section—

"contravene" includes fail to comply;

"disclosure requirement" means a requirement imposed under section 947;
"rule-based requirement" means a requirement imposed by or under rules.

956 No action for breach of statutory duty etc

(1) Contravention of a rule-based requirement or a disclosure requirement does not give rise to any right of action for breach of statutory duty.

(2) Contravention of a rule-based requirement does not make any transaction void or unenforceable or (subject to any provision made by rules) affect the validity of any other thing.

(3) In this section—

(a) "contravention" includes failure to comply;

(b) "disclosure requirement" and "rule-based requirement" have the same meaning as in section 955.

Funding

957 Fees and charges

(1) Rules may provide for fees or charges to be payable to the Panel for the purpose of meeting any part of its expenses.

(2) A reference in this section or section 958 to expenses of the Panel is to any expenses that have been or are to be incurred by the Panel in, or in connection with, the discharge of its functions, including in particular—

(a) payments in respect of the expenses of the Takeover Appeal Board;

(b) the cost of repaying the principal of, and of paying any interest on, any money borrowed by the Panel;

(c) the cost of maintaining adequate reserves.

958 Levy

(1) For the purpose of meeting any part of the expenses of the Panel, the Secretary of State may by regulations provide for a levy to be payable to the Panel—

(a) by specified persons or bodies, or persons or bodies of a specified description, or

(b) on transactions, of a specified description, in securities on specified markets.

In this subsection "specified" means specified in the regulations.

(2) The power to specify (or to specify descriptions of) persons or bodies must be exercised in such a way that the levy is payable only by persons or bodies that appear to the Secretary of State—

(a) to be capable of being directly affected by the exercise of any of the functions of the Panel, or

(b) otherwise to have a substantial interest in the exercise of any of those functions.

(3) Regulations under this section may in particular—

(a) specify the rate of the levy and the period in respect of which it is payable at that rate;

(b) make provision as to the times when, and the manner in which, payments are to be made in respect of the levy.

(4) In determining the rate of the levy payable in respect of a particular period, the Secretary of State—

(a) must take into account any other income received or expected by the Panel in respect of that period;

(b) may take into account estimated as well as actual expenses of the Panel in respect of that period.

(5) The Panel must—

(a) keep proper accounts in respect of any amounts of levy received by virtue of this section;

(b) prepare, in relation to each period in respect of which any such amounts are received, a statement of account relating to those amounts in such form and manner as is specified in the regulations.

Those accounts must be audited, and the statement certified, by persons appointed by the Secretary of State.

(6) Regulations under this section—
(a) are subject to affirmative resolution procedure if subsection (7) applies to them;
(b) otherwise, are subject to negative resolution procedure.

(7) This subsection applies to—
(a) the first regulations under this section;
(b) any other regulations under this section that would result in a change in the persons or bodies by whom, or the transactions on which, the levy is payable.

(8) If a draft of an instrument containing regulations under this section would, apart from this subsection, be treated for the purposes of the Standing Orders of either House of Parliament as a hybrid instrument, it is to proceed in that House as if it were not such an instrument.

959 Recovery of fees, charges or levy

An amount payable by any person or body by virtue of section 957 or 958 is a debt due from that person or body to the Panel, and is recoverable accordingly.

Miscellaneous and supplementary

960 Panel as party to proceedings

The Panel is capable (despite being an unincorporated body) of—
(a) bringing proceedings under this Chapter in its own name;
(b) bringing or defending any other proceedings in its own name.

961 Exemption from liability in damages

(1) Neither the Panel, nor any person within subsection (2), is to be liable in damages for anything done (or omitted to be done) in, or in connection with, the discharge or purported discharge of the Panel's functions.

(2) A person is within this subsection if—
(a) he is (or is acting as) a member, officer or member of staff of the Panel, or
(b) he is a person authorised under section 947(5).

(3) Subsection (1) does not apply—
(a) if the act or omission is shown to have been in bad faith, or
(b) so as to prevent an award of damages in respect of the act or omission on the ground that it was unlawful as a result of section 6(1) of the Human Rights Act 1998 (acts of public authorities incompatible with Convention rights).

962 Privilege against self-incrimination

(1) A statement made by a person in response to—
(a) a requirement under section 947(1), or
(b) an order made by the court under section 955 to secure compliance with such a requirement,

may not be used against him in criminal proceedings in which he is charged with an offence to which this subsection applies.

(2) Subsection (1) applies to any offence other than an offence under one of the following provisions (which concern false statements made otherwise than on oath)—
(a) section 5 of the Perjury Act 1911;
(b) section 44(2) of the Criminal Law (Consolidation) (Scotland) Act 1995;
(c) Article 10 of the Perjury (Northern Ireland) Order 1979.

963 Annual reports

(1) After the end of each financial year the Panel must publish a report.

(2) The report must—
(a) set out how the Panel's functions were discharged in the year in question;
(b) include the Panel's accounts for that year;
(c) mention any matters the Panel considers to be of relevance to the discharge of its functions.

964 Amendments to Financial Services and Markets Act 2000

(1) The Financial Services and Markets Act 2000 is amended as follows.

(2) Section 143 (power to make rules endorsing the City Code on Takeovers and Mergers etc) is repealed.

(3) ...

(4) In section 349 (exceptions from restrictions on disclosure of confidential information), after subsection (3) insert—

"(3A) Section 348 does not apply to—

(a) the disclosure by a recipient to which subsection (3B) applies of confidential information disclosed to it by the Authority in reliance on subsection (1);

(b) the disclosure of such information by a person obtaining it directly or indirectly from a recipient to which subsection (3B) applies.

(3B) This subsection applies to—

(a) the Panel on Takeovers and Mergers;

(b) an authority designated as a supervisory authority for the purposes of Article 4.1 of the Takeovers Directive;

(c) any other person or body that exercises public functions, under legislation in an EEA State other than the United Kingdom, that are similar to the Authority's functions or those of the Panel on Takeovers and Mergers.".

...

(6) In section 417(1) (definitions), insert at the appropriate place—

""Takeovers Directive" means Directive 2004/25/EC of the European Parliament and of the Council;".

965 Power to extend to Isle of Man and Channel Islands

Her Majesty may by Order in Council direct that any of the provisions of this Chapter extend, with such modifications as may be specified in the Order, to the Isle of Man or any of the Channel Islands.

CHAPTER 2
IMPEDIMENTS TO TAKEOVERS

Opting in and opting out

966 Opting in and opting out

(1) A company may by special resolution (an "opting-in resolution") opt in for the purposes of this Chapter if the following three conditions are met in relation to the company.

(2) The first condition is that the company has voting shares admitted to trading on a regulated market.

(3) The second condition is that—

(a) the company's articles of association—

(i) do not contain any such restrictions as are mentioned in Article 11 of the Takeovers Directive, or

(ii) if they do contain any such restrictions, provide for the restrictions not to apply at a time when, or in circumstances in which, they would be disapplied by that Article,

and

(b) those articles do not contain any other provision which would be incompatible with that Article.

(4) The third condition is that—

(a) no shares conferring special rights in the company are held by—

(i) a minister,

(ii) a nominee of, or any other person acting on behalf of, a minister, or

(iii) a company directly or indirectly controlled by a minister, and

(b) no such rights are exercisable by or on behalf of a minister under any enactment.

(5) A company may revoke an opting-in resolution by a further special resolution (an "opting-out resolution").

(6) For the purposes of subsection (3), a reference in Article 11 of the Takeovers Directive to Article 7.1 or 9 of that Directive is to be read as referring to rules under section 943(1) giving effect to the relevant Article.

(7) In subsection (4) "minister" means—

(a) the holder of an office in Her Majesty's Government in the United Kingdom;

(b) the Scottish Ministers;

(c) a Minister within the meaning given by section 7(3) of the Northern Ireland Act 1998;

(d) the Welsh Ministers;

and for the purposes of that subsection "minister" also includes the Treasury, the Board of Trade and, the Defence Council ...

(8) The Secretary of State may by order subject to negative resolution procedure provide that subsection (4) applies in relation to a specified person or body that exercises functions of a public nature as it applies in relation to a minister. "Specified" means specified in the order.

967 Further provision about opting-in and opting-out resolutions

(1) An opting-in resolution or an opting-out resolution must specify the date from which it is to have effect (the "effective date").

(2) The effective date of an opting-in resolution may not be earlier than the date on which the resolution is passed.

(3) The second and third conditions in section 966 must be met at the time when an opting-in resolution is passed, but the first one does not need to be met until the effective date.

(4) An opting-in resolution passed before the time when voting shares of the company are admitted to trading on a regulated market complies with the requirement in subsection (1) if, instead of specifying a particular date, it provides for the resolution to have effect from that time.

(5) An opting-in resolution passed before the commencement of this section complies with the requirement in subsection (1) if, instead of specifying a particular date, it provides for the resolution to have effect from that commencement.

(6) The effective date of an opting-out resolution may not be earlier than the first anniversary of the date on which a copy of the opting-in resolution was forwarded to the registrar.

(7) Where a company has passed an opting-in resolution, any alteration of its articles of association that would prevent the second condition in section 966 from being met is of no effect until the effective date of an opting-out resolution passed by the company.

Consequences of opting in

968 Effect on contractual restrictions

(1) The following provisions have effect where a takeover bid is made for an opted-in company.

(2) An agreement to which this section applies is invalid in so far as it places any restriction—

(a) on the transfer to the offeror, or at his direction to another person, of shares in the company during the offer period;

(b) on the transfer to any person of shares in the company at a time during the offer period when the offeror holds shares amounting to not less than 75% in value of all the voting shares in the company;

(c) on rights to vote at a general meeting of the company that decides whether to take any action which might result in the frustration of the bid;

(d) on rights to vote at a general meeting of the company that—

(i) is the first such meeting to be held after the end of the offer period, and

(ii) is held at a time when the offeror holds shares amounting to not less than 75% in value of all the voting shares in the company.

(3) This section applies to an agreement—

(a) entered into between a person holding shares in the company and another such person on or after 21st April 2004, or

(b) entered into at any time between such a person and the company, and it applies to such an agreement even if the law applicable to the agreement (apart from this section) is not the law of a part of the United Kingdom.

(4) The reference in subsection (2)(c) to rights to vote at a general meeting of the company that decides whether to take any action which might result in the frustration of the bid includes a reference to rights to vote on a written resolution concerned with that question.

(5) For the purposes of subsection (2)(c), action which might result in the frustration of a bid is any action of that kind specified in rules under section 943(1) giving effect to Article 9 of the Takeovers Directive.

(6) If a person suffers loss as a result of any act or omission that would (but for this section) be a breach of an agreement to which this section applies, he is entitled to compensation, of such amount as the court considers just and equitable, from any person who would (but for this section) be liable to him for committing or inducing the breach.

(7) In subsection (6) "the court" means the High Court or, in Scotland, the Court of Session.

(8) A reference in this section to voting shares in the company does not include—

(a) debentures, or

(b) shares that, under the company's articles of association, do not normally carry rights to vote at its general meetings (for example, shares carrying rights to vote that, under those articles, arise only where specified pecuniary advantages are not provided).

969 Power of offeror to require general meeting to be called

(1) Where a takeover bid is made for an opted-in company, the offeror may by making a request to the directors of the company require them to call a general meeting of the company if, at the date at which the request is made, he holds shares amounting to not less than 75% in value of all the voting shares in the company.

(2) The reference in subsection (1) to voting shares in the company does not include—

(a) debentures, or

(b) shares that, under the company's articles of association, do not normally carry rights to vote at its general meetings (for example, shares carrying rights to vote that, under those articles, arise only where specified pecuniary advantages are not provided).

(3) Sections 303 to 305 (members' power to require general meetings to be called) apply as they would do if subsection (1) above were substituted for subsections (1) to (3) of section 303, and with any other necessary modifications.

Supplementary

970 Communication of decisions

(1) A company that has passed an opting-in resolution or an opting-out resolution must notify—

(a) the Panel, and

(b) where the company—

(i) has voting shares admitted to trading on a regulated market in an EEA State other than the United Kingdom, or

(ii) has requested such admission,

the authority designated by that state as the supervisory authority for the purposes of Article 4.1 of the Takeovers Directive.

(2) Notification must be given within 15 days after the resolution is passed and, if any admission or request such as is mentioned in subsection (1)(b) occurs at a later time, within 15 days after that time.

(3) If a company fails to comply with this section, an offence is committed by—

(a) the company, and

(b) every officer of it who is in default.

(4) A person guilty of an offence under this section is liable on summary conviction to a fine not exceeding level 3 on the standard scale and, for continued contravention, a daily default fine not exceeding one-tenth of level 3 on the standard scale.

971 Interpretation of this Chapter

(1) In this Chapter—

"offeror" and "takeover bid" have the same meaning as in the Takeovers Directive;

"offer period", in relation to a takeover bid, means the time allowed for acceptance of the bid by—

(a) rules under section 943(1) giving effect to Article 7.1 of the Takeovers Directive, or

(b) where the rules giving effect to that Article which apply to the bid are those of an EEA State other than the United Kingdom, those rules;

"opted-in company" means a company in relation to which—

(a) an opting-in resolution has effect, and

(b) the conditions in section 966(2) and (4) continue to be met;

"opting-in resolution" has the meaning given by section 966(1);

"opting-out resolution" has the meaning given by section 966(5);

"the Takeovers Directive" means Directive 2004/25/EC of the European Parliament and of the Council;

"voting rights" means rights to vote at general meetings of the company in question, including rights that arise only in certain circumstances;

"voting shares" means shares carrying voting rights.

(2) For the purposes of this Chapter—

(a) securities of a company are treated as shares in the company if they are convertible into or entitle the holder to subscribe for such shares;

(b) debentures issued by a company are treated as shares in the company if they carry voting rights.

972 Transitory provision

(1) Where a takeover bid is made for an opted-in company, section 368 of the Companies Act 1985 (extraordinary general meeting on members' requisition) and section 378 of that Act (extraordinary and special resolutions) have effect as follows until their repeal by this Act.

(2) Section 368 has effect as if a members' requisition included a requisition of a person who—

(a) is the offeror in relation to the takeover bid, and

(b) holds at the date of the deposit of the requisition shares amounting to not less than 75% in value of all the voting shares in the company.

(3) In relation to a general meeting of the company that—

(a) is the first such meeting to be held after the end of the offer period, and

(b) is held at a time when the offeror holds shares amounting to not less than 75% in value of all the voting shares in the company,

section 378(2) (meaning of "special resolution") has effect as if "14 days' notice" were substituted for "21 days' notice".

(4) A reference in this section to voting shares in the company does not include—

(a) debentures, or

(b) shares that, under the company's articles of association, do not normally carry rights to vote at its general meetings (for example, shares carrying rights to vote that, under those articles, arise only where specified pecuniary advantages are not provided).

973 Power to extend to Isle of Man and Channel Islands

Her Majesty may by Order in Council direct that any of the provisions of this Chapter extend, with such modifications as may be specified in the Order, to the Isle of Man or any of the Channel Islands.

CHAPTER 3
"SQUEEZE-OUT" AND "SELL-OUT"

Takeover offers

974 Meaning of "takeover offer"

(1) For the purposes of this Chapter an offer to acquire shares in a company is a "takeover offer" if the following two conditions are satisfied in relation to the offer.

(2) The first condition is that it is an offer to acquire—

(a) all the shares in a company, or

(b) where there is more than one class of shares in a company, all the shares of one or more classes,

other than shares that at the date of the offer are already held by the offeror.

Section 975 contains provision supplementing this subsection.

(3) The second condition is that the terms of the offer are the same—

(a) in relation to all the shares to which the offer relates, or

(b) where the shares to which the offer relates include shares of different classes, in relation to all the shares of each class.

Section 976 contains provision treating this condition as satisfied in certain circumstances.

(4) In subsections (1) to (3) "shares" means shares, other than relevant treasury shares, that have been allotted on the date of the offer (but see subsection (5)).

(5) A takeover offer may include among the shares to which it relates—

(a) all or any shares that are allotted after the date of the offer but before a specified date;

(b) all or any relevant treasury shares that cease to be held as treasury shares before a specified date;

(c) all or any other relevant treasury shares.

(6) In this section—

"relevant treasury shares" means shares that—

(a) are held by the company as treasury shares on the date of the offer, or

(b) become shares held by the company as treasury shares after that date but before a specified date;

"specified date" means a date specified in or determined in accordance with the terms of the offer.

(7) Where the terms of an offer make provision for their revision and for acceptances on the previous terms to be treated as acceptances on the revised terms, then, if the terms of the offer are revised in accordance with that provision—

(a) the revision is not to be regarded for the purposes of this Chapter as the making of a fresh offer, and

(b) references in this Chapter to the date of the offer are accordingly to be read as references to the date of the original offer.

975 Shares already held by the offeror etc

(1) The reference in section 974(2) to shares already held by the offeror includes a reference to shares that he has contracted to acquire, whether unconditionally or subject to conditions being met.

This is subject to subsection (2).

(2) The reference in section 974(2) to shares already held by the offeror does not include a reference to shares that are the subject of a contract—

(a) intended to secure that the holder of the shares will accept the offer when it is made, and

(b) entered into—

(i) by deed and for no consideration,

(ii) for consideration of negligible value, or

(iii) for consideration consisting of a promise by the offeror to make the offer.

(3) In relation to Scotland, this section applies as if the words "by deed and" in subsection (2) (b) (i) were omitted.

(4) The condition in section 974(2) is treated as satisfied where—

(a) the offer does not extend to shares that associates of the offeror hold or have contracted to acquire (whether unconditionally or subject to conditions being met), and
(b) the condition would be satisfied if the offer did extend to those shares.
(For further provision about such shares, see section 977(2)).

976 Cases where offer treated as being on same terms

(1) The condition in section 974(3) (terms of offer to be the same for all shares or all shares of particular classes) is treated as satisfied where subsection (2) or (3) below applies.

(2) This subsection applies where—
(a) shares carry an entitlement to a particular dividend which other shares of the same class, by reason of being allotted later, do not carry,
(b) there is a difference in the value of consideration offered for the shares allotted earlier as against that offered for those allotted later,
(c) that difference merely reflects the difference in entitlement to the dividend, and
(d) the condition in section 974(3) would be satisfied but for that difference.

(3) This subsection applies where—
(a) the law of a country or territory outside the United Kingdom—
(i) precludes an offer of consideration in the form, or any of the forms, specified in the terms of the offer ("the specified form"), or
(ii) precludes it except after compliance by the offeror with conditions with which he is unable to comply or which he regards as unduly onerous,
(b) the persons to whom an offer of consideration in the specified form is precluded are able to receive consideration in another form that is of substantially equivalent value, and
(c) the condition in section 974(3) would be satisfied but for the fact that an offer of consideration in the specified form to those persons is precluded.

977 Shares to which an offer relates

(1) Where a takeover offer is made and, during the period beginning with the date of the offer and ending when the offer can no longer be accepted, the offeror—
(a) acquires or unconditionally contracts to acquire any of the shares to which the offer relates, but
(b) does not do so by virtue of acceptances of the offer,
those shares are treated for the purposes of this Chapter as excluded from those to which the offer relates.

(2) For the purposes of this Chapter shares that an associate of the offeror holds or has contracted to acquire, whether at the date of the offer or subsequently, are not treated as shares to which the offer relates, even if the offer extends to such shares.
In this subsection "contracted" means contracted unconditionally or subject to conditions being met.

(3) This section is subject to section 979(8) and (9).

978 Effect of impossibility etc of communicating or accepting offer

(1) Where there are holders of shares in a company to whom an offer to acquire shares in the company is not communicated, that does not prevent the offer from being a takeover offer for the purposes of this Chapter if—
(a) those shareholders have no registered address in the United Kingdom,
(b) the offer was not communicated to those shareholders in order not to contravene the law of a country or territory outside the United Kingdom, and
(c) either—
(i) the offer is published in the Gazette, or
(ii) the offer can be inspected, or a copy of it obtained, at a place in an EEA State or on a website, and a notice is published in the Gazette specifying the address of that place or website.

(2) Where an offer is made to acquire shares in a company and there are persons for whom, by reason of the law of a country or territory outside the United Kingdom, it is impossible to accept the offer, or more difficult to do so, that does not prevent the offer from being a takeover offer for the purposes of this Chapter.

(3) It is not to be inferred—

(a) that an offer which is not communicated to every holder of shares in the company cannot be a takeover offer for the purposes of this Chapter unless the requirements of paragraphs (a) to (c) of subsection (1) are met, or

(b) that an offer which is impossible, or more difficult, for certain persons to accept cannot be a takeover offer for those purposes unless the reason for the impossibility or difficulty is the one mentioned in subsection (2).

"Squeeze-out"

979 Right of offeror to buy out minority shareholder

(1) Subsection (2) applies in a case where a takeover offer does not relate to shares of different classes.

(2) If the offeror has, by virtue of acceptances of the offer, acquired or unconditionally contracted to acquire—

(a) not less than 90% in value of the shares to which the offer relates, and

(b) in a case where the shares to which the offer relates are voting shares, not less than 90% of the voting rights carried by those shares,

he may give notice to the holder of any shares to which the offer relates which the offeror has not acquired or unconditionally contracted to acquire that he desires to acquire those shares.

(3) Subsection (4) applies in a case where a takeover offer relates to shares of different classes.

(4) If the offeror has, by virtue of acceptances of the offer, acquired or unconditionally contracted to acquire—

(a) not less than 90% in value of the shares of any class to which the offer relates, and

(b) in a case where the shares of that class are voting shares, not less than 90% of the voting rights carried by those shares,

he may give notice to the holder of any shares of that class to which the offer relates which the offeror has not acquired or unconditionally contracted to acquire that he desires to acquire those shares.

(5) In the case of a takeover offer which includes among the shares to which it relates—

(a) shares that are allotted after the date of the offer, or

(b) relevant treasury shares (within the meaning of section 974) that cease to be held as treasury shares after the date of the offer,

the offeror's entitlement to give a notice under subsection (2) or (4) on any particular date shall be determined as if the shares to which the offer relates did not include any allotted, or ceasing to be held as treasury shares, on or after that date.

(6) Subsection (7) applies where—

(a) the requirements for the giving of a notice under subsection (2) or (4) are satisfied, and

(b) there are shares in the company which the offeror, or an associate of his, has contracted to acquire subject to conditions being met, and in relation to which the contract has not become unconditional.

(7) The offeror's entitlement to give a notice under subsection (2) or (4) shall be determined as if—

(a) the shares to which the offer relates included shares falling within paragraph (b) of subsection (6), and

(b) in relation to shares falling within that paragraph, the words "by virtue of acceptances of the offer" in subsection (2) or (4) were omitted.

(8) Where—

(a) a takeover offer is made,

(b) during the period beginning with the date of the offer and ending when the offer can no longer be accepted, the offeror—
   (i) acquires or unconditionally contracts to acquire any of the shares to which the offer relates, but
   (ii) does not do so by virtue of acceptances of the offer, and

(c) subsection (10) applies,

then for the purposes of this section those shares are not excluded by section 977(1) from those to which the offer relates, and the offeror is treated as having acquired or contracted to acquire them by virtue of acceptances of the offer.

(9) Where—

(a) a takeover offer is made,

(b) during the period beginning with the date of the offer and ending when the offer can no longer be accepted, an associate of the offeror acquires or unconditionally contracts to acquire any of the shares to which the offer relates, and

(c) subsection (10) applies,

then for the purposes of this section those shares are not excluded by section 977(2) from those to which the offer relates.

(10) This subsection applies if—

(a) at the time the shares are acquired or contracted to be acquired as mentioned in subsection (8) or (9) (as the case may be), the value of the consideration for which they are acquired or contracted to be acquired ("the acquisition consideration") does not exceed the value of the consideration specified in the terms of the offer, or

(b) those terms are subsequently revised so that when the revision is announced the value of the acquisition consideration, at the time mentioned in paragraph (a), no longer exceeds the value of the consideration specified in those terms.

980 Further provision about notices given under section 979

(1) A notice under section 979 must be given in the prescribed manner.

(2) No notice may be given under section 979(2) or (4) after the end of—

(a) the period of three months beginning with the day after the last day on which the offer can be accepted, or

(b) the period of six months beginning with the date of the offer, where that period ends earlier and the offer is one to which subsection (3) below applies.

(3) This subsection applies to an offer if the time allowed for acceptance of the offer is not governed by rules under section 943(1) that give effect to Article 7 of the Takeovers Directive.

In this subsection "the Takeovers Directive" has the same meaning as in section 943.

(4) At the time when the offeror first gives a notice under section 979 in relation to an offer, he must send to the company—

(a) a copy of the notice, and

(b) a statutory declaration by him in the prescribed form, stating that the conditions for the giving of the notice are satisfied.

(5) Where the offeror is a company (whether or not a company within the meaning of this Act) the statutory declaration must be signed by a director.

(6) A person commits an offence if—

(a) he fails to send a copy of a notice or a statutory declaration as required by subsection (4), or

(b) he makes such a declaration for the purposes of that subsection knowing it to be false or without having reasonable grounds for believing it to be true.

(7) It is a defence for a person charged with an offence for failing to send a copy of a notice as required by subsection (4) to prove that he took reasonable steps for securing compliance with that subsection.

(8) A person guilty of an offence under this section is liable—

(a) on conviction on indictment, to imprisonment for a term not exceeding two years or a fine (or both);

(b) on summary conviction—
  (i) in England and Wales, to imprisonment for a term not exceeding twelve months or to a fine not exceeding the statutory maximum (or both) and, for continued contravention, a daily default fine not exceeding one-fiftieth of the statutory maximum;
  (ii) in Scotland or Northern Ireland, to imprisonment for a term not exceeding six months, or to a fine not exceeding the statutory maximum (or both) and, for continued contravention, a daily default fine not exceeding one-fiftieth of the statutory maximum.

981 Effect of notice under section 979

(1) Subject to section 986 (applications to the court), this section applies where the offeror gives a shareholder a notice under section 979.

(2) The offeror is entitled and bound to acquire the shares to which the notice relates on the terms of the offer.

(3) Where the terms of an offer are such as to give the shareholder a choice of consideration, the notice must give particulars of the choice and state—
(a) that the shareholder may, within six weeks from the date of the notice, indicate his choice by a written communication sent to the offeror at an address specified in the notice, and
(b) which consideration specified in the offer will apply if he does not indicate a choice.
The reference in subsection (2) to the terms of the offer is to be read accordingly.

(4) Subsection (3) applies whether or not any time-limit or other conditions applicable to the choice under the terms of the offer can still be complied with.

(5) If the consideration offered to or (as the case may be) chosen by the shareholder—
(a) is not cash and the offeror is no longer able to provide it, or
(b) was to have been provided by a third party who is no longer bound or able to provide it,
the consideration is to be taken to consist of an amount of cash, payable by the offeror, which at the date of the notice is equivalent to the consideration offered or (as the case may be) chosen.

(6) At the end of six weeks from the date of the notice the offeror must immediately—
(a) send a copy of the notice to the company, and
(b) pay or transfer to the company the consideration for the shares to which the notice relates.
Where the consideration consists of shares or securities to be allotted by the offeror, the reference in paragraph (b) to the transfer of the consideration is to be read as a reference to the allotment of the shares or securities to the company.

(7) If the shares to which the notice relates are registered, the copy of the notice sent to the company under subsection (6)(a) must be accompanied by an instrument of transfer executed on behalf of the holder of the shares by a person appointed by the offeror.
On receipt of that instrument the company must register the offeror as the holder of those shares.

(8) If the shares to which the notice relates are transferable by the delivery of warrants or other instruments, the copy of the notice sent to the company under subsection (6)(a) must be accompanied by a statement to that effect. On receipt of that statement the company must issue the offeror with warrants or other instruments in respect of the shares, and those already in issue in respect of the shares become void.

(9) The company must hold any money or other consideration received by it under subsection (6)(b) on trust for the person who, before the offeror acquired them, was entitled to the shares in respect of which the money or other consideration was received.
Section 982 contains further provision about how the company should deal with such money or other consideration.

982 Further provision about consideration held on trust under section 981(9)

(1) This section applies where an offeror pays or transfers consideration to the company under section 981(6).

(2) The company must pay into a separate bank account that complies with subsection (3)—

(a) any money it receives under paragraph (b) of section 981(6), and
(b) any dividend or other sum accruing from any other consideration it receives under that paragraph.

(3) A bank account complies with this subsection if the balance on the account—
(a) bears interest at an appropriate rate, and
(b) can be withdrawn by such notice (if any) as is appropriate.

(4) If—
(a) the person entitled to the consideration held on trust by virtue of section 981(9) cannot be found, and
(b) subsection (5) applies,
the consideration (together with any interest, dividend or other benefit that has accrued from it) must be paid into court.

(5) This subsection applies where—
(a) reasonable enquiries have been made at reasonable intervals to find the person, and
(b) twelve years have elapsed since the consideration was received, or the company is wound up.

(6) In relation to a company registered in Scotland, subsections (7) and (8) apply instead of subsection (4).

(7) If the person entitled to the consideration held on trust by virtue of section 981(9) cannot be found and subsection (5) applies—
(a) the trust terminates,
(b) the company or (if the company is wound up) the liquidator must sell any consideration other than cash and any benefit other than cash that has accrued from the consideration, and
(c) a sum representing—
(i) the consideration so far as it is cash,
(ii) the proceeds of any sale under paragraph (b), and
(iii) any interest, dividend or other benefit that has accrued from the consideration,
must be deposited in the name of the Accountant of Court in a separate bank account complying with subsection (3) and the receipt for the deposit must be transmitted to the Accountant of Court.

(8) Section 58 of the Bankruptcy (Scotland) Act 1985 (so far as consistent with this Act) applies (with any necessary modifications) to sums deposited under subsection (7) as it applies to sums deposited under section 57(1)(a) of that Act.

(9) The expenses of any such enquiries as are mentioned in subsection (5) may be paid out of the money or other property held on trust for the person to whom the enquiry relates.

"Sell-out"

983 Right of minority shareholder to be bought out by offeror

(1) Subsections (2) and (3) apply in a case where a takeover offer relates to all the shares in a company.
For this purpose a takeover offer relates to all the shares in a company if it is an offer to acquire all the shares in the company within the meaning of section 974.

(2) The holder of any voting shares to which the offer relates who has not accepted the offer may require the offeror to acquire those shares if, at any time before the end of the period within which the offer can be accepted—
(a) the offeror has by virtue of acceptances of the offer acquired or unconditionally contracted to acquire some (but not all) of the shares to which the offer relates, and
(b) those shares, with or without any other shares in the company which he has acquired or contracted to acquire (whether unconditionally or subject to conditions being met)—
(i) amount to not less than 90% in value of all the voting shares in the company (or would do so but for section 990(1)), and

(ii) carry not less than 90% of the voting rights in the company (or would do so but for section 990(1)).

(3) The holder of any non-voting shares to which the offer relates who has not accepted the offer may require the offeror to acquire those shares if, at any time before the end of the period within which the offer can be accepted—

(a) the offeror has by virtue of acceptances of the offer acquired or unconditionally contracted to acquire some (but not all) of the shares to which the offer relates, and

(b) those shares, with or without any other shares in the company which he has acquired or contracted to acquire (whether unconditionally or subject to conditions being met), amount to not less than 90% in value of all the shares in the company (or would do so but for section 990(1)).

(4) If a takeover offer relates to shares of one or more classes and at any time before the end of the period within which the offer can be accepted—

(a) the offeror has by virtue of acceptances of the offer acquired or unconditionally contracted to acquire some (but not all) of the shares of any class to which the offer relates, and

(b) those shares, with or without any other shares of that class which he has acquired or contracted to acquire (whether unconditionally or subject to conditions being met)—

(i) amount to not less than 90% in value of all the shares of that class, and

(ii) in a case where the shares of that class are voting shares, carry not less than 90% of the voting rights carried by the shares of that class,

the holder of any shares of that class to which the offer relates who has not accepted the offer may require the offeror to acquire those shares.

(5) For the purposes of subsections (2) to (4), in calculating 90% of the value of any shares, shares held by the company as treasury shares are to be treated as having been acquired by the offeror.

(6) Subsection (7) applies where—

(a) a shareholder exercises rights conferred on him by subsection (2), (3) or (4),

(b) at the time when he does so, there are shares in the company which the offeror has contracted to acquire subject to conditions being met, and in relation to which the contract has not become unconditional, and

(c) the requirement imposed by subsection (2)(b), (3)(b) or (4)(b) (as the case may be) would not be satisfied if those shares were not taken into account.

(7) The shareholder is treated for the purposes of section 985 as not having exercised his rights under this section unless the requirement imposed by paragraph (b) of subsection (2), (3) or (4) (as the case may be) would be satisfied if—

(a) the reference in that paragraph to other shares in the company which the offeror has contracted to acquire unconditionally or subject to conditions being met were a reference to such shares which he has unconditionally contracted to acquire, and

(b) the reference in that subsection to the period within which the offer can be accepted were a reference to the period referred to in section 984(2).

(8) A reference in subsection (2) (b), (3) (b), (4) (b), (6) or (7) to shares which the offeror has acquired or contracted to acquire includes a reference to shares which an associate of his has acquired or contracted to acquire.

984 Further provision about rights conferred by section 983

(1) Rights conferred on a shareholder by subsection (2), (3) or (4) of section 983 are exercisable by a written communication addressed to the offeror.

(2) Rights conferred on a shareholder by subsection (2), (3) or (4) of that section are not exercisable after the end of the period of three months from—

(a) the end of the period within which the offer can be accepted, or

(b) if later, the date of the notice that must be given under subsection (3) below.

(3) Within one month of the time specified in subsection (2), (3) or (4) (as the case may be) of that section, the offeror must give any shareholder who has not accepted the offer notice in the prescribed manner of—

(a) the rights that are exercisable by the shareholder under that subsection, and
(b) the period within which the rights are exercisable.

If the notice is given before the end of the period within which the offer can be accepted, it must state that the offer is still open for acceptance.

(4) Subsection (3) does not apply if the offeror has given the shareholder a notice in respect of the shares in question under section 979.

(5) An offeror who fails to comply with subsection (3) commits an offence.

If the offeror is a company, every officer of that company who is in default or to whose neglect the failure is attributable also commits an offence.

(6) If an offeror other than a company is charged with an offence for failing to comply with subsection (3), it is a defence for him to prove that he took all reasonable steps for securing compliance with that subsection.

(7) A person guilty of an offence under this section is liable—
(a) on conviction on indictment, to a fine;
(b) on summary conviction, to a fine not exceeding the statutory maximum and, for continued contravention, a daily default fine not exceeding one-fiftieth of the statutory maximum.

985 Effect of requirement under section 983

(1) Subject to section 986, this section applies where a shareholder exercises his rights under section 983 in respect of any shares held by him.

(2) The offeror is entitled and bound to acquire those shares on the terms of the offer or on such other terms as may be agreed.

(3) Where the terms of an offer are such as to give the shareholder a choice of consideration—
(a) the shareholder may indicate his choice when requiring the offeror to acquire the shares, and
(b) the notice given to the shareholder under section 984(3)—
(i) must give particulars of the choice and of the rights conferred by this subsection, and
(ii) may state which consideration specified in the offer will apply if he does not indicate a choice.

The reference in subsection (2) to the terms of the offer is to be read accordingly.

(4) Subsection (3) applies whether or not any time-limit or other conditions applicable to the choice under the terms of the offer can still be complied with.

(5) If the consideration offered to or (as the case may be) chosen by the shareholder—
(a) is not cash and the offeror is no longer able to provide it, or
(b) was to have been provided by a third party who is no longer bound or able to provide it,

the consideration is to be taken to consist of an amount of cash, payable by the offeror, which at the date when the shareholder requires the offeror to acquire the shares is equivalent to the consideration offered or (as the case may be) chosen.

Supplementary

986 Applications to the court

(1) Where a notice is given under section 979 to a shareholder the court may, on an application made by him, order—
(a) that the offeror is not entitled and bound to acquire the shares to which the notice relates, or
(b) that the terms on which the offeror is entitled and bound to acquire the shares shall be such as the court thinks fit.

(2) An application under subsection (1) must be made within six weeks from the date on which the notice referred to in that subsection was given.

If an application to the court under subsection (1) is pending at the end of that period, section 981(6) does not have effect until the application has been disposed of.

(3) Where a shareholder exercises his rights under section 983 in respect of any shares held by him, the court may, on an application made by him or the offeror, order that the terms on which the offeror is entitled and bound to acquire the shares shall be such as the court thinks fit.

(4) On an application under subsection (1) or (3)—
(a) the court may not require consideration of a higher value than that specified in the terms of the offer ("the offer value") to be given for the shares to which the application relates unless the holder of the shares shows that the offer value would be unfair;
(b) the court may not require consideration of a lower value than the offer value to be given for the shares.

(5) No order for costs or expenses may be made against a shareholder making an application under subsection (1) or (3) unless the court considers that—
(a) the application was unnecessary, improper or vexatious,
(b) there has been unreasonable delay in making the application, or
(c) there has been unreasonable conduct on the shareholder's part in conducting the proceedings on the application.

(6) A shareholder who has made an application under subsection (1) or (3) must give notice of the application to the offeror.

(7) An offeror who is given notice of an application under subsection (1) or (3) must give a copy of the notice to—
(a) any person (other than the applicant) to whom a notice has been given under section 979;
(b) any person who has exercised his rights under section 983.

(8) An offeror who makes an application under subsection (3) must give notice of the application to—
(a) any person to whom a notice has been given under section 979;
(b) any person who has exercised his rights under section 983.

(9) Where a takeover offer has not been accepted to the extent necessary for entitling the offeror to give notices under subsection (2) or (4) of section 979 the court may, on an application made by him, make an order authorising him to give notices under that subsection if it is satisfied that—
(a) the offeror has after reasonable enquiry been unable to trace one or more of the persons holding shares to which the offer relates,
(b) the requirements of that subsection would have been met if the person, or all the persons, mentioned in paragraph (a) above had accepted the offer, and
(c) the consideration offered is fair and reasonable.

This is subject to subsection (10).

(10) The court may not make an order under subsection (9) unless it considers that it is just and equitable to do so having regard, in particular, to the number of shareholders who have been traced but who have not accepted the offer.

987 Joint offers

(1) In the case of a takeover offer made by two or more persons jointly, this Chapter has effect as follows.

(2) The conditions for the exercise of the rights conferred by section 979 are satisfied—
(a) in the case of acquisitions by virtue of acceptances of the offer, by the joint offerors acquiring or unconditionally contracting to acquire the necessary shares jointly;
(b) in other cases, by the joint offerors acquiring or unconditionally contracting to acquire the necessary shares either jointly or separately.

(3) The conditions for the exercise of the rights conferred by section 983 are satisfied—
(a) in the case of acquisitions by virtue of acceptances of the offer, by the joint offerors acquiring or unconditionally contracting to acquire the necessary shares jointly;
(b) in other cases, by the joint offerors acquiring or contracting (whether unconditionally or subject to conditions being met) to acquire the necessary shares either jointly or separately.

(4) Subject to the following provisions, the rights and obligations of the offeror under sections 979 to 985 are respectively joint rights and joint and several obligations of the joint offerors.

(5) A provision of sections 979 to 986 that requires or authorises a notice or other document to be given or sent by or to the joint offerors is complied with if the notice or document is given or sent by or to any of them (but see subsection (6)).

(6) The statutory declaration required by section 980(4) must be made by all of the joint offerors and, where one or more of them is a company, signed by a director of that company.

(7) In sections 974 to 977, 979(9), 981(6), 983(8) and 988 references to the offeror are to be read as references to the joint offerors or any of them.

(8) In section 981(7) and (8) references to the offeror are to be read as references to the joint offerors or such of them as they may determine.

(9) In sections 981(5)(a) and 985(5)(a) references to the offeror being no longer able to provide the relevant consideration are to be read as references to none of the joint offerors being able to do so.

(10) In section 986 references to the offeror are to be read as references to the joint offerors, except that—

(a) an application under subsection (3) or (9) may be made by any of them, and

(b) the reference in subsection (9)(a) to the offeror having been unable to trace one or more of the persons holding shares is to be read as a reference to none of the offerors having been able to do so.

Interpretation

988 Associates

(1) In this Chapter "associate", in relation to an offeror, means—

(a) a nominee of the offeror,

(b) a holding company, subsidiary or fellow subsidiary of the offeror or a nominee of such a holding company, subsidiary or fellow subsidiary,

(c) a body corporate in which the offeror is substantially interested,

(d) a person who is, or is a nominee of, a party to a share acquisition agreement with the offeror, or

(e) (where the offeror is an individual) his spouse or civil partner and any minor child or step-child of his.

(2) For the purposes of subsection (1)(b) a company is a fellow subsidiary of another body corporate if both are subsidiaries of the same body corporate but neither is a subsidiary of the other.

(3) For the purposes of subsection (1)(c) an offeror has a substantial interest in a body corporate if—

(a) the body or its directors are accustomed to act in accordance with his directions or instructions, or

(b) he is entitled to exercise or control the exercise of one-third or more of the voting power at general meetings of the body.

Subsections (2) and (3) of section 823 (which contain provision about when a person is treated as entitled to exercise or control the exercise of voting power) apply for the purposes of this subsection as they apply for the purposes of that section.

(4) For the purposes of subsection (1) (d) an agreement is a share acquisition agreement if—

(a) it is an agreement for the acquisition of, or of an interest in, shares to which the offer relates,

(b) it includes provisions imposing obligations or restrictions on any one or more of the parties to it with respect to their use, retention or disposal of such shares, or their interests in such shares, acquired in pursuance of the agreement (whether or not together with any other shares to which the offer relates or any other interests of theirs in such shares), and

(c) it is not an excluded agreement (see subsection (5)).

(5) An agreement is an "excluded agreement"—

(a) if it is not legally binding, unless it involves mutuality in the undertakings, expectations or understandings of the parties to it, or

(b) if it is an agreement to underwrite or sub-underwrite an offer of shares in a company, provided the agreement is confined to that purpose and any matters incidental to it.

(6) The reference in subsection (4)(b) to the use of interests in shares is to the exercise of any rights or of any control or influence arising from those interests (including the right to enter into an agreement for the exercise, or for control of the exercise, of any of those rights by another person).

(7) In this section—
(a) "agreement" includes any agreement or arrangement;
(b) references to provisions of an agreement include—
(i) undertakings, expectations or understandings operative under an arrangement, and
(ii) any provision whether express or implied and whether absolute or not.

989 Convertible securities

(1) For the purposes of this Chapter securities of a company are treated as shares in the company if they are convertible into or entitle the holder to subscribe for such shares.
References to the holder of shares or a shareholder are to be read accordingly.

(2) Subsection (1) is not to be read as requiring any securities to be treated—
(a) as shares of the same class as those into which they are convertible or for which the holder is entitled to subscribe, or
(b) as shares of the same class as other securities by reason only that the shares into which they are convertible or for which the holder is entitled to subscribe are of the same class.

990 Debentures carrying voting rights

(1) For the purposes of this Chapter debentures issued by a company to which subsection (2) applies are treated as shares in the company if they carry voting rights.

(2) This subsection applies to a company that has voting shares, or debentures carrying voting rights, which are admitted to trading on a regulated market.

(3) In this Chapter, in relation to debentures treated as shares by virtue of subsection (1)—
(a) references to the holder of shares or a shareholder are to be read accordingly;
(b) references to shares being allotted are to be read as references to debentures being issued.

991 Interpretation

(1) In this Chapter—
"the company" means the company whose shares are the subject of a takeover offer;
"date of the offer" means—
(a) where the offer is published, the date of publication;
(b) where the offer is not published, or where any notices of the offer are given before the date of publication, the date when notices of the offer (or the first such notices) are given;
and references to the date of the offer are to be read in accordance with section 974(7) (revision of offer terms) where that applies;
"non-voting shares" means shares that are not voting shares;
"offeror" means (subject to section 987) the person making a takeover offer;
"voting rights" means rights to vote at general meetings of the company, including rights that arise only in certain circumstances;
"voting shares" means shares carrying voting rights.

(2) For the purposes of this Chapter a person contracts unconditionally to acquire shares if his entitlement under the contract to acquire them is not (or is no longer) subject to conditions or if all conditions to which it was subject have been met.
A reference to a contract becoming unconditional is to be read accordingly.

CHAPTER 4
AMENDMENTS TO PART 7 OF THE COMPANIES ACT 1985

992 Matters to be dealt with in directors' report

(1) Part 7 of the Companies Act 1985 (accounts and audit) is amended as follows.

(2) In Schedule 7 (matters to be dealt with in directors' report), after Part 6 insert—

"PART 7

DISCLOSURE REQUIRED BY CERTAIN PUBLICLY-TRADED COMPANIES

13 (1) This Part of this Schedule applies to the directors' report for a financial year if the company had securities carrying voting rights admitted to trading on a regulated market at the end of that year.

(2) The report shall contain detailed information, by reference to the end of that year, on the following matters—

(a) the structure of the company's capital, including in particular—

(i) the rights and obligations attaching to the shares or, as the case may be, to each class of shares in the company, and

(ii) where there are two or more such classes, the percentage of the total share capital represented by each class;

(b) any restrictions on the transfer of securities in the company, including in particular—

(i) limitations on the holding of securities, and

(ii) requirements to obtain the approval of the company, or of other holders of securities in the company, for a transfer of securities;

(c) in the case of each person with a significant direct or indirect holding of securities in the company, such details as are known to the company of—

(i) the identity of the person,

(ii) the size of the holding, and

(iii) the nature of the holding;

(d) in the case of each person who holds securities carrying special rights with regard to control of the company—

(i) the identity of the person, and

(ii) the nature of the rights;

(e) where—

(i) the company has an employees' share scheme, and

(ii) shares to which the scheme relates have rights with regard to control of the company that are not exercisable directly by the employees,

how those rights are exercisable;

(f) any restrictions on voting rights, including in particular—

(i) limitations on voting rights of holders of a given percentage or number of votes,

(ii) deadlines for exercising voting rights, and

(iii) arrangements by which, with the company's co-operation, financial rights carried by securities are held by a person other than the holder of the securities;

(g) any agreements between holders of securities that are known to the company and may result in restrictions on the transfer of securities or on voting rights;

(h) any rules that the company has about—

(i) appointment and replacement of directors, or

(ii) amendment of the company's articles of association;

(i) the powers of the company's directors, including in particular any powers in relation to the issuing or buying back by the company of its shares;

(j) any significant agreements to which the company is a party that take effect, alter or terminate upon a change of control of the company following a takeover bid, and the effects of any such agreements;

(k) any agreements between the company and its directors or employees providing for compensation for loss of office or employment (whether through resignation, purported redundancy or otherwise) that occurs because of a takeover bid.

(3) For the purposes of sub-paragraph (2)(a) a company's capital includes any securities in the company that are not admitted to trading on a regulated market.

(4) For the purposes of sub-paragraph (2)(c) a person has an indirect holding of securities if—

(a) they are held on his behalf, or

(b) he is able to secure that rights carried by the securities are exercised in accordance with his wishes.

(5) Sub-paragraph (2)(j) does not apply to an agreement if—

(a) disclosure of the agreement would be seriously prejudicial to the company, and

(b) the company is not under any other obligation to disclose it.

(6) In this paragraph—

"securities" means shares or debentures;

"takeover bid" has the same meaning as in the Takeovers Directive;

"the Takeovers Directive" means Directive 2004/25/EC of the European Parliament and of the Council;

"voting rights" means rights to vote at general meetings of the company in question, including rights that arise only in certain circumstances.".

(3) In section 234ZZA (requirements of directors' reports), at the end of subsection (4)(contents of Schedule 7) insert—

"Part 7 specifies information to be disclosed by certain publicly-traded companies.".

(4) After that subsection insert—

"(5) A directors' report shall also contain any necessary explanatory material with regard to information that is required to be included in the report by Part 7 of Schedule 7.".

(5) In section 251 (summary financial statements), after subsection (2ZA) insert—

"(2ZB) A company that sends to an entitled person a summary financial statement instead of a copy of its directors' report shall—

(a) include in the statement the explanatory material required to be included in the directors' report by section 234ZZA(5), or

(b) send that material to the entitled person at the same time as it sends the statement.

For the purposes of paragraph (b), subsections (2A) to (2E) apply in relation to the material referred to in that paragraph as they apply in relation to a summary financial statement.".

(6) The amendments made by this section apply in relation to directors' reports for financial years beginning on or after 20th May 2006.

PART 29
FRAUDULENT TRADING

993 Offence of fraudulent trading

(1) If any business of a company is carried on with intent to defraud creditors of the company or creditors of any other person, or for any fraudulent purpose, every person who is knowingly a party to the carrying on of the business in that manner commits an offence.

(2) This applies whether or not the company has been, or is in the course of being, wound up.

(3) A person guilty of an offence under this section is liable—

(a) on conviction on indictment, to imprisonment for a term not exceeding ten years or a fine (or both);

(b) on summary conviction—

(i) in England and Wales, to imprisonment for a term not exceeding twelve months or a fine not exceeding the statutory maximum (or both);

(ii) in Scotland or Northern Ireland, to imprisonment for a term not exceeding six months or a fine not exceeding the statutory maximum (or both).

PART 30
PROTECTION OF MEMBERS AGAINST UNFAIR PREJUDICE

Main provisions

994 Petition by company member

(1) A member of a company may apply to the court by petition for an order under this Part on the ground—

(a) that the company's affairs are being or have been conducted in a manner that is unfairly prejudicial to the interests of members generally or of some part of its members (including at least himself), or

(b) that an actual or proposed act or omission of the company (including an act or omission on its behalf) is or would be so prejudicial.

(1A) For the purposes of subsection (1)(a), a removal of the company's auditor from office—

(a) on grounds of divergence of opinions on accounting treatments or audit procedures, or

(b) on any other improper grounds,

shall be treated as being unfairly prejudicial to the interests of some part of the company's members.

(2) The provisions of this Part apply to a person who is not a member of a company but to whom shares in the company have been transferred or transmitted by operation of law as they apply to a member of a company.

(3) In this section, and so far as applicable for the purposes of this section in the other provisions of this Part, "company" means—

(a) a company within the meaning of this Act, or

(b) a company that is not such a company but is a statutory water company within the meaning of the Statutory Water Companies Act 1991.

995 Petition by Secretary of State

(1) This section applies to a company in respect of which—

(a) the Secretary of State has received a report under section 437 of the Companies Act 1985 (inspector's report);

(b) the Secretary of State has exercised his powers under section 447 or 448 of that Act (powers to require documents and information or to enter and search premises);

(c) the Secretary of State, the Financial Conduct Authority, the Prudential Regulation Authority or the Bank of England has exercised his or its powers under Part 11 of the Financial Services and Markets Act 2000 (information gathering and investigations); or

(d) the Secretary of State has received a report from an investigator appointed by him, the Financial Conduct Authority, the Prudential Regulation Authority or the Bank of England under that Part.

(2) If it appears to the Secretary of State that in the case of such a company—

(a) the company's affairs are being or have been conducted in a manner that is unfairly prejudicial to the interests of members generally or of some part of its members, or

(b) an actual or proposed act or omission of the company (including an act or omission on its behalf) is or would be so prejudicial,

he may apply to the court by petition for an order under this Part.

(3) The Secretary of State may do this in addition to, or instead of, presenting a petition for the winding up of the company.

(4) In this section, and so far as applicable for the purposes of this section in the other provisions of this Part, "company" means any body corporate that is liable to be wound up under the Insolvency Act 1986 or the Insolvency (Northern Ireland) Order 1989.

996 Powers of the court under this Part

(1) If the court is satisfied that a petition under this Part is well founded, it may make such order as it thinks fit for giving relief in respect of the matters complained of.

(2) Without prejudice to the generality of subsection (1), the court's order may—
(a) regulate the conduct of the company's affairs in the future;
(b) require the company—
(i) to refrain from doing or continuing an act complained of, or
(ii) to do an act that the petitioner has complained it has omitted to do;
(c) authorise civil proceedings to be brought in the name and on behalf of the company by such person or persons and on such terms as the court may direct;
(d) require the company not to make any, or any specified, alterations in its articles without the leave of the court;
(e) provide for the purchase of the shares of any members of the company by other members or by the company itself and, in the case of a purchase by the company itself, the reduction of the company's capital accordingly.

Supplementary provisions

997 Application of general rule-making powers

The power to make rules under section 411 of the Insolvency Act 1986 or Article 359 of the Insolvency (Northern Ireland) Order 1989, so far as relating to a winding-up petition, applies for the purposes of a petition under this Part.

998 Copy of order affecting company's constitution to be delivered to registrar

(1) Where an order of the court under this Part—
(a) alters the company's constitution, or
(b) gives leave for the company to make any, or any specified, alterations to its constitution,
the company must deliver a copy of the order to the registrar.
(2) It must do so within 14 days from the making of the order or such longer period as the court may allow.
(3) If a company makes default in complying with this section, an offence is committed by—
(a) the company, and
(b) every officer of the company who is in default.
(4) A person guilty of an offence under this section is liable on summary conviction to a fine not exceeding level 3 on the standard scale and, for continued contravention, a daily default fine not exceeding one-tenth of level 3 on the standard scale.

999 Supplementary provisions where company's constitution altered

(1) This section applies where an order under this Part alters a company's constitution.
(2) If the order amends—
(a) a company's articles, or
(b) any resolution or agreement to which Chapter 3 of Part 3 applies (resolution or agreement affecting a company's constitution),
the copy of the order delivered to the registrar by the company under section 998 must be accompanied by a copy of the company's articles, or the resolution or agreement in question, as amended.
(3) Every copy of a company's articles issued by the company after the order is made must be accompanied by a copy of the order, unless the effect of the order has been incorporated into the articles by amendment.
(4) If a company makes default in complying with this section an offence is committed by—
(a) the company, and
(b) every officer of the company who is in default.
(5) A person guilty of an offence under this section is liable on summary conviction to a fine not exceeding level 3 on the standard scale.

PART 31
DISSOLUTION AND RESTORATION TO THE REGISTER

CHAPTER 1
STRIKING OFF

Registrar's power to strike off defunct company

1000 Power to strike off company not carrying on business or in operation

(1) If the registrar has reasonable cause to believe that a company is not carrying on business or in operation, the registrar may send to the company by post a letter inquiring whether the company is carrying on business or in operation.

(2) If the registrar does not within one month of sending the letter receive any answer to it, the registrar must within 14 days after the expiration of that month send to the company by post a registered letter referring to the first letter, and stating—

(a) that no answer to it has been received, and

(b) that if an answer is not received to the second letter within one month from its date, a notice will be published in the Gazette with a view to striking the company's name off the register.

(3) If the registrar—

(a) receives an answer to the effect that the company is not carrying on business or in operation, or

(b) does not within one month after sending the second letter receive any answer,

the registrar may publish in the Gazette, and send to the company by post, a notice that at the expiration of three months from the date of the notice the name of the company mentioned in it will, unless cause is shown to the contrary, be struck off the register and the company will be dissolved.

(4) At the expiration of the time mentioned in the notice the registrar may, unless cause to the contrary is previously shown by the company, strike its name off the register.

(5) The registrar must publish notice in the Gazette of the company's name having been struck off the register.

(6) On the publication of the notice in the Gazette the company is dissolved.

(7) However—

(a) the liability (if any) of every director, managing officer and member of the company continues and may be enforced as if the company had not been dissolved, and

(b) nothing in this section affects the power of the court to wind up a company the name of which has been struck off the register.

1001 Duty to act in case of company being wound up

(1) If, in a case where a company is being wound up—

(a) the registrar has reasonable cause to believe—

(i) that no liquidator is acting, or

(ii) that the affairs of the company are fully wound up, and

(b) the returns required to be made by the liquidator have not been made for a period of six consecutive months,

the registrar must publish in the Gazette and send to the company or the liquidator (if any) a notice that at the expiration of three months from the date of the notice the name of the company mentioned in it will, unless cause is shown to the contrary, be struck off the register and the company will be dissolved.

(2) At the expiration of the time mentioned in the notice the registrar may, unless cause to the contrary is previously shown by the company, strike its name off the register.

(3) The registrar must publish notice in the Gazette of the company's name having been struck off the register.

(4) On the publication of the notice in the Gazette the company is dissolved.

(5) However—

(a) the liability (if any) of every director, managing officer and member of the company continues and may be enforced as if the company had not been dissolved, and
(b) nothing in this section affects the power of the court to wind up a company the name of which has been struck off the register.

1002 Supplementary provisions as to service of letter or notice

(1) A letter or notice to be sent under section 1000 or 1001 to a company may be addressed to the company at its registered office or, if no office has been registered, to the care of some officer of the company.
(2) If there is no officer of the company whose name and address are known to the registrar, the letter or notice may be sent to each of the persons who subscribed the memorandum (if their addresses are known to the registrar).
(3) A notice to be sent to a liquidator under section 1001 may be addressed to him at his last known place of business.

Voluntary striking off

1003 Striking off on application by company

(1) On application by a company, the registrar of companies may strike the company's name off the register.
(2) The application—
(a) must be made on the company's behalf by its directors or by a majority of them, and
(b) must contain the prescribed information.
(3) The registrar may not strike a company off under this section until after the expiration of three months from the publication by the registrar in the Gazette of a notice—
(a) stating that the registrar may exercise the power under this section in relation to the company, and
(b) inviting any person to show cause why that should not be done.
(4) The registrar must publish notice in the Gazette of the company's name having been struck off.
(5) On the publication of the notice in the Gazette the company is dissolved.
(6) However—
(a) the liability (if any) of every director, managing officer and member of the company continues and may be enforced as if the company had not been dissolved, and
(b) nothing in this section affects the power of the court to wind up a company the name of which has been struck off the register.

1004 Circumstances in which application not to be made: activities of company

(1) An application under section 1003 (application for voluntary striking off) on behalf of a company must not be made if, at any time in the previous three months, the company has—
(a) changed its name,
(b) traded or otherwise carried on business,
(c) made a disposal for value of property or rights that, immediately before ceasing to trade or otherwise carry on business, it held for the purpose of disposal for gain in the normal course of trading or otherwise carrying on business, or
(d) engaged in any other activity, except one which is—
(i) necessary or expedient for the purpose of making an application under that section, or deciding whether to do so,
(ii) necessary or expedient for the purpose of concluding the affairs of the company,
(iii) necessary or expedient for the purpose of complying with any statutory requirement, or
(iv) specified by the Secretary of State by order for the purposes of this sub-paragraph.
(2) For the purposes of this section, a company is not to be treated as trading or otherwise carrying on business by virtue only of the fact that it makes a payment in respect of a liability incurred in the course of trading or otherwise carrying on business.

(3) The Secretary of State may by order amend subsection (1) for the purpose of altering the period in relation to which the doing of the things mentioned in paragraphs (a) to (d) of that subsection is relevant.

(4) An order under this section is subject to negative resolution procedure.

(5) It is an offence for a person to make an application in contravention of this section.

(6) In proceedings for such an offence it is a defence for the accused to prove that he did not know, and could not reasonably have known, of the existence of the facts that led to the contravention.

(7) A person guilty of an offence under this section is liable—

(a) on conviction on indictment, to a fine;

(b) on summary conviction, to a fine not exceeding the statutory maximum.

1005 Circumstances in which application not to be made: other proceedings not concluded

(1) An application under section 1003 (application for voluntary striking off) on behalf of a company must not be made at a time when—

(a) an application to the court under Part 26 has been made on behalf of the company for the sanctioning of a compromise or arrangement and the matter has not been finally concluded;

(b) a voluntary arrangement in relation to the company has been proposed under Part 1 of the Insolvency Act 1986 or Part 2 of the Insolvency (Northern Ireland) Order 1989 and the matter has not been finally concluded;

(c) the company is in administration under Part 2 of that Act or Part 3 of that Order;

(d) paragraph 44 of Schedule B1 to that Act or paragraph 45 of Schedule B1 to that Order applies (interim moratorium on proceedings where application to the court for an administration order has been made or notice of intention to appoint administrator has been filed);

(e) the company is being wound up under Part 4 of that Act or Part 5 of that Order, whether voluntarily or by the court, or a petition under that Part for winding up of the company by the court has been presented and not finally dealt with or withdrawn;

(f) there is a receiver or manager of the company's property;

(g) the company's estate is being administered by a judicial factor.

(2) For the purposes of subsection (1)(a), the matter is finally concluded if—

(a) the application has been withdrawn,

(b) the application has been finally dealt with without a compromise or arrangement being sanctioned by the court, or

(c) a compromise or arrangement has been sanctioned by the court and has, together with anything required to be done under any provision made in relation to the matter by order of the court, been fully carried out.

(3) For the purposes of subsection (1)(b), the matter is finally concluded if—

(a) no meetings are to be summoned under section 3 of the Insolvency Act 1986 or Article 16 of the Insolvency (Northern Ireland) Order 1989,

(b) meetings summoned under that section or Article fail to approve the arrangement with no, or the same, modifications,

(c) an arrangement approved by meetings summoned under that section, or in consequence of a direction under section 6(4)(b) of that Act or Article 19(4)(b) of that Order, has been fully implemented, or

(d) the court makes an order under section 6(5) of that Act or Article 19(5) of that Order revoking approval given at previous meetings and, if the court gives any directions under section 6(6) of that Act or Article 19(6) of that Order, the company has done whatever it is required to do under those directions.

(4) It is an offence for a person to make an application in contravention of this section.

(5) In proceedings for such an offence it is a defence for the accused to prove that he did not know, and could not reasonably have known, of the existence of the facts that led to the contravention.

(6) A person guilty of an offence under this section is liable—

(a) on conviction on indictment, to a fine;

(b) on summary conviction, to a fine not exceeding the statutory maximum.

1006 Copy of application to be given to members, employees, etc

(1) A person who makes an application under section 1003 (application for voluntary striking off) on behalf of a company must secure that, within seven days from the day on which the application is made, a copy of it is given to every person who at any time on that day is—

(a) a member of the company,
(b) an employee of the company,
(c) a creditor of the company,
(d) a director of the company,
(e) a manager or trustee of any pension fund established for the benefit of employees of the company, or
(f) a person of a description specified for the purposes of this paragraph by regulations made by the Secretary of State.

Regulations under paragraph (f) are subject to negative resolution procedure.

(2) Subsection (1) does not require a copy of the application to be given to a director who is a party to the application.

(3) The duty imposed by this section ceases to apply if the application is withdrawn before the end of the period for giving the copy application.

(4) A person who fails to perform the duty imposed on him by this section commits an offence. If he does so with the intention of concealing the making of the application from the person concerned, he commits an aggravated offence.

(5) In proceedings for an offence under this section it is a defence for the accused to prove that he took all reasonable steps to perform the duty.

(6) A person guilty of an offence under this section (other than an aggravated offence) is liable—

(a) on conviction on indictment, to a fine;
(b) on summary conviction, to a fine not exceeding the statutory maximum.

(7) A person guilty of an aggravated offence under this section is liable—

(a) on conviction on indictment, to imprisonment for a term not exceeding seven years or a fine (or both);
(b) on summary conviction—
    (i) in England and Wales, to imprisonment for a term not exceeding twelve months or to a fine not exceeding the statutory maximum (or both);
    (ii) in Scotland or Northern Ireland, to imprisonment for a term not exceeding six months, or to a fine not exceeding the statutory maximum (or both).

1007 Copy of application to be given to new members, employees, etc

(1) This section applies in relation to any time after the day on which a company makes an application under section 1003 (application for voluntary striking off) and before the day on which the application is finally dealt with or withdrawn.

(2) A person who is a director of the company at the end of a day on which a person (other than himself) becomes—

(a) a member of the company,
(b) an employee of the company,
(c) a creditor of the company,
(d) a director of the company,
(e) a manager or trustee of any pension fund established for the benefit of employees of the company, or
(f) a person of a description specified for the purposes of this paragraph by regulations made by the Secretary of State,

must secure that a copy of the application is given to that person within seven days from that day.

Regulations under paragraph (f) are subject to negative resolution procedure.

(3) The duty imposed by this section ceases to apply if the application is finally dealt with or withdrawn before the end of the period for giving the copy application.

(4) A person who fails to perform the duty imposed on him by this section commits an offence.

If he does so with the intention of concealing the making of the application from the person concerned, he commits an aggravated offence.

(5) In proceedings for an offence under this section it is a defence for the accused to prove—

(a) that at the time of the failure he was not aware of the fact that the company had made an application under section 1003, or

(b) that he took all reasonable steps to perform the duty.

(6) A person guilty of an offence under this section (other than an aggravated offence) is liable—

(a) on conviction on indictment, to a fine;

(b) on summary conviction, to a fine not exceeding the statutory maximum.

(7) A person guilty of an aggravated offence under this section is liable—

(a) on conviction on indictment, to imprisonment for a term not exceeding seven years or a fine (or both);

(b) on summary conviction—

(i) in England and Wales, to imprisonment for a term not exceeding twelve months or to a fine not exceeding the statutory maximum (or both);

(ii) in Scotland or Northern Ireland, to imprisonment for a term not exceeding six months, or to a fine not exceeding the statutory maximum (or both).

1008 Copy of application: provisions as to service of documents

(1) The following provisions have effect for the purposes of—

section 1006 (copy of application to be given to members, employees, etc), and

section 1007 (copy of application to be given to new members, employees, etc).

(2) A document is treated as given to a person if it is—

(a) delivered to him, or

(b) left at his proper address, or

(c) sent by post to him at that address.

(3) For the purposes of subsection (2) and section 7 of the Interpretation Act 1978 (service of documents by post) as it applies in relation to that subsection, the proper address of a person is—

(a) in the case of a firm incorporated or formed in the United Kingdom, its registered or principal office;

(b) in the case of a firm incorporated or formed outside the United Kingdom—

(i) if it has a place of business in the United Kingdom, its principal office in the United Kingdom, or

(ii) if it does not have a place of business in the United Kingdom, its registered or principal office;

(c) in the case of an individual, his last known address.

(4) In the case of a creditor of the company a document is treated as given to him if it is left or sent by post to him—

(a) at the place of business of his with which the company has had dealings by virtue of which he is a creditor of the company, or

(b) if there is more than one such place of business, at each of them.

1009 Circumstances in which application to be withdrawn

(1) This section applies where, at any time on or after the day on which a company makes an application under section 1003 (application for voluntary striking off) and before the day on which the application is finally dealt with or withdrawn—

(a) the company—

(i) changes its name,

(ii) trades or otherwise carries on business,

(iii) makes a disposal for value of any property or rights other than those which it was necessary or expedient for it to hold for the purpose of making, or proceeding with, an application under that section, or

(iv) engages in any activity, except one to which subsection (4) applies;

(b) an application is made to the court under Part 26 on behalf of the company for the sanctioning of a compromise or arrangement;

(c) a voluntary arrangement in relation to the company is proposed under Part 1 of the Insolvency Act 1986 or Part 2 of the Insolvency (Northern Ireland) Order 1989;

(d) an application to the court for administration order in respect of the company is made under paragraph 12 of Schedule B1 to that Act or paragraph 13 of Schedule B1 to that Order;

(e) an administrator is appointed in respect of the company under paragraph 14 or 22 of Schedule B1 to that Act or paragraph 15 or 23 of Schedule B1 to that Order, or a copy of notice of intention to appoint an administrator of the company under any of those provisions is filed with the court;

(f) there arise any of the circumstances in which, under section 84(1) of that Act or Article 70 of that Order, the company may be voluntarily wound up;

(g) a petition is presented for the winding up of the company by the court under Part 4 of that Act or Part 5 of that Order;

(h) a receiver or manager of the company's property is appointed; or

(i) a judicial factor is appointed to administer the company's estate.

(2) A person who, at the end of a day on which any of the events mentioned in subsection (1) occurs, is a director of the company must secure that the company's application is withdrawn forthwith.

(3) For the purposes of subsection (1)(a), a company is not treated as trading or otherwise carrying on business by virtue only of the fact that it makes a payment in respect of a liability incurred in the course of trading or otherwise carrying on business.

(4) The excepted activities referred to in subsection (1)(a)(iv) are—

(a) any activity necessary or expedient for the purposes of—

(i) making, or proceeding with, an application under section 1003 (application for voluntary striking off),

(ii) concluding affairs of the company that are outstanding because of what has been necessary or expedient for the purpose of making, or proceeding with, such an application, or

(iii) complying with any statutory requirement;

(b) any activity specified by the Secretary of State by order for the purposes of this subsection.

An order under paragraph (b) is subject to negative resolution procedure.

(5) A person who fails to perform the duty imposed on him by this section commits an offence.

(6) In proceedings for an offence under this section it is a defence for the accused to prove—

(a) that at the time of the failure he was not aware of the fact that the company had made an application under section 1003, or

(b) that he took all reasonable steps to perform the duty.

(7) A person guilty of an offence under this section is liable—

(a) on conviction on indictment, to a fine;

(b) on summary conviction, to a fine not exceeding the statutory maximum.

1010 Withdrawal of application

An application under section 1003 is withdrawn by notice to the registrar.

1011 Meaning of "creditor"

In this Chapter "creditor" includes a contingent or prospective creditor.

CHAPTER 2
PROPERTY OF DISSOLVED COMPANY

Property vesting as bona vacantia

1012 Property of dissolved company to be bona vacantia

(1) When a company is dissolved, all property and rights whatsoever vested in or held on trust for the company immediately before its dissolution (including leasehold property, but not including property held by the company on trust for another person) are deemed to be *bona vacantia* and—

(a) accordingly belong to the Crown, or to the Duchy of Lancaster or to the Duke of Cornwall for the time being (as the case may be), and

(b) vest and may be dealt with in the same manner as other *bona vacantia* accruing to the Crown, to the Duchy of Lancaster or to the Duke of Cornwall.

(2) Subsection (1) has effect subject to the possible restoration of the company to the register under Chapter 3 (see section 1034).

1013 Crown disclaimer of property vesting as bona vacantia

(1) Where property vests in the Crown under section 1012, the Crown's title to it under that section may be disclaimed by a notice signed by the Crown representative, that is to say the Treasury Solicitor, or, in relation to property in Scotland, the Queen's and Lord Treasurer's Remembrancer.

(2) The right to execute a notice of disclaimer under this section may be waived by or on behalf of the Crown either expressly or by taking possession.

(3) A notice of disclaimer must be executed within three years after—

(a) the date on which the fact that the property may have vested in the Crown under section 1012 first comes to the notice of the Crown representative, or

(b) if ownership of the property is not established at that date, the end of the period reasonably necessary for the Crown representative to establish the ownership of the property.

(4) If an application in writing is made to the Crown representative by a person interested in the property requiring him to decide whether he will or will not disclaim, any notice of disclaimer must be executed within twelve months after the making of the application or such further period as may be allowed by the court.

(5) A notice of disclaimer under this section is of no effect if it is shown to have been executed after the end of the period specified by subsection (3) or (4).

(6) A notice of disclaimer under this section must be delivered to the registrar and retained and registered by him.

(7) Copies of it must be published in the Gazette and sent to any persons who have given the Crown representative notice that they claim to be interested in the property.

(8) This section applies to property vested in the Duchy of Lancaster or the Duke of Cornwall under section 1012 as if for references to the Crown and the Crown representative there were respectively substituted references to the Duchy of Lancaster and to the Solicitor to that Duchy, or to the Duke of Cornwall and to the Solicitor to the Duchy of Cornwall, as the case may be.

1014 Effect of Crown disclaimer

(1) Where notice of disclaimer is executed under section 1013 as respects any property, that property is deemed not to have vested in the Crown under section 1012.

(2) The following sections contain provisions as to the effect of the Crown disclaimer—
sections 1015 to 1019 apply in relation to property in England and Wales or Northern Ireland;
sections 1020 to 1022 apply in relation to property in Scotland.

Effect of Crown disclaimer: England and Wales and Northern Ireland

1015 General effect of disclaimer

(1) The Crown's disclaimer operates so as to terminate, as from the date of the disclaimer, the rights, interests and liabilities of the company in or in respect of the property disclaimed.

(2) It does not, except so far as is necessary for the purpose of releasing the company from any liability, affect the rights or liabilities of any other person.

1016 Disclaimer of leaseholds

(1) The disclaimer of any property of a leasehold character does not take effect unless a copy of the disclaimer has been served (so far as the Crown representative is aware of their addresses) on every person claiming under the company as underlessee or mortgagee, and either—

(a) no application under section 1017 (power of court to make vesting order) is made with respect to that property before the end of the period of 14 days beginning with the day on which the last notice under this paragraph was served, or

(b) where such an application has been made, the court directs that the disclaimer shall take effect.

(2) Where the court gives a direction under subsection (1)(b) it may also, instead of or in addition to any order it makes under section 1017, make such order as it thinks fit with respect to fixtures, tenant's improvements and other matters arising out of the lease.

(3) In this section the "Crown representative" means—

(a) in relation to property vested in the Duchy of Lancaster, the Solicitor to that Duchy;

(b) in relation to property vested in the Duke of Cornwall, the Solicitor to the Duchy of Cornwall;

(c) in relation to property in Scotland, the Queen's and Lord Treasurer's Remembrancer;

(d) in relation to other property, the Treasury Solicitor.

1017 Power of court to make vesting order

(1) The court may on application by a person who—

(a) claims an interest in the disclaimed property, or

(b) is under a liability in respect of the disclaimed property that is not discharged by the disclaimer,

make an order under this section in respect of the property.

(2) An order under this section is an order for the vesting of the disclaimed property in, or its delivery to—

(a) a person entitled to it (or a trustee for such a person), or

(b) a person subject to such a liability as is mentioned in subsection (1)(b) (or a trustee for such a person).

(3) An order under subsection (2)(b) may only be made where it appears to the court that it would be just to do so for the purpose of compensating the person subject to the liability in respect of the disclaimer.

(4) An order under this section may be made on such terms as the court thinks fit.

(5) On a vesting order being made under this section, the property comprised in it vests in the person named in that behalf in the order without conveyance, assignment or transfer.

1018 Protection of persons holding under a lease

(1) The court must not make an order under section 1017 vesting property of a leasehold nature in a person claiming under the company as underlessee or mortgagee except on terms making that person—

(a) subject to the same liabilities and obligations as those to which the company was subject under the lease, or

(b) if the court thinks fit, subject to the same liabilities and obligations as if the lease had been assigned to him.

(2) Where the order relates to only part of the property comprised in the lease, subsection (1) applies as if the lease had comprised only the property comprised in the vesting order.

(3) A person claiming under the company as underlessee or mortgagee who declines to accept a vesting order on such terms is excluded from all interest in the property.

(4) If there is no person claiming under the company who is willing to accept an order on such terms, the court has power to vest the company's estate and interest in the property in any person who is

liable (whether personally or in a representative character, and whether alone or jointly with the company) to perform the lessee's covenants in the lease.

(5) The court may vest that estate and interest in such a person freed and discharged from all estates, incumbrances and interests created by the company.

1019 Land subject to rentcharge

Where in consequence of the disclaimer land that is subject to a rentcharge vests in any person, neither he nor his successors in title are subject to any personal liability in respect of sums becoming due under the rentcharge, except sums becoming due after he, or some person claiming under or through him, has taken possession or control of the land or has entered into occupation of it.

Effect of Crown disclaimer: Scotland

1020 General effect of disclaimer

(1) The Crown's disclaimer operates to determine, as from the date of the disclaimer, the rights, interests and liabilities of the company, and the property of the company, in or in respect of the property disclaimed.

(2) It does not (except so far as is necessary for the purpose of releasing the company and its property from liability) affect the rights or liabilities of any other person.

1021 Power of court to make vesting order

(1) The court may—

(a) on application by a person who either claims an interest in disclaimed property or is under a liability not discharged by this Act in respect of disclaimed property, and

(b) on hearing such persons as it thinks fit,

make an order for the vesting of the property in or its delivery to any persons entitled to it, or to whom it may seem just that the property should be delivered by way of compensation for such liability, or a trustee for him.

(2) The order may be made on such terms as the court thinks fit.

(3) On a vesting order being made under this section, the property comprised in it vests accordingly in the person named in that behalf in the order, without conveyance or assignation for that purpose.

1022 Protection of persons holding under a lease

(1) Where the property disclaimed is held under a lease the court must not make a vesting order in favour of a person claiming under the company, whether—

(a) as sub-lessee, or

(b) as creditor in a duly registered or (as the case may be) recorded heritable security over a lease,

except on the following terms.

(2) The person must by the order be made subject—

(a) to the same liabilities and obligations as those to which the company was subject under the lease in respect of the property, or

(b) if the court thinks fit, only to the same liabilities and obligations as if the lease had been assigned to him.

In either event (if the case so requires) the liabilities and obligations must be as if the lease had comprised only the property comprised in the vesting order.

(3) A sub-lessee or creditor declining to accept a vesting order on such terms is excluded from all interest in and security over the property.

(4) If there is no person claiming under the company who is willing to accept an order on such terms, the court has power to vest the company's estate and interest in the property in any person liable (either personally or in a representative character, and either alone or jointly with the company) to perform the lessee's obligations under the lease.

(5) The court may vest that estate and interest in such a person freed and discharged from all interests, rights and obligations created by the company in the lease or in relation to the lease.

(6) For the purposes of this section a heritable security—

(a) is duly recorded if it is recorded in the Register of Sasines, and

(b) is duly registered if registered in accordance with the *Land Registration (Scotland) Act 1979*.

Note. The words "Land Registration etc. (Scotland) Act 2012 (asp 5)" are substituted for the words "Land Registration (Scotland) Act 1979" in subsection (6)(b), in relation to Scotland, by the Land Registration etc. (Scotland) Act 2012, s. 119, Sch. 5, para. 50(1), (4), as from a day to be appointed.

Supplementary provisions

1023 Liability for rentcharge on company's land after dissolution

(1) This section applies where on the dissolution of a company land in England and Wales or Northern Ireland that is subject to a rentcharge vests by operation of law in the Crown or any other person ("the proprietor").

(2) Neither the proprietor nor his successors in title are subject to any personal liability in respect of sums becoming due under the rentcharge, except sums becoming due after the proprietor, or some person claiming under or through him, has taken possession or control of the land or has entered into occupation of it.

(3) In this section "company" includes any body corporate.

CHAPTER 3
RESTORATION TO THE REGISTER

Administrative restoration to the register

1024 Application for administrative restoration to the register

(1) An application may be made to the registrar to restore to the register a company that has been struck off the register under section 1000 or 1001 (power of registrar to strike off defunct company).

(2) An application under this section may be made whether or not the company has in consequence been dissolved.

(3) An application under this section may only be made by a former director or former member of the company.

(4) An application under this section may not be made after the end of the period of six years from the date of the dissolution of the company.

For this purpose an application is made when it is received by the registrar.

1025 Requirements for administrative restoration

(1) On an application under section 1024 the registrar shall restore the company to the register if, and only if, the following conditions are met.

(2) The first condition is that the company was carrying on business or in operation at the time of its striking off.

(3) The second condition is that, if any property or right previously vested in or held on trust for the company has vested as *bona vacantia,* the Crown representative has signified to the registrar in writing consent to the company's restoration to the register.

(4) It is the applicant's responsibility to obtain that consent and to pay any costs (in Scotland, expenses) of the Crown representative—

(a) in dealing with the property during the period of dissolution, or

(b) in connection with the proceedings on the application,

that may be demanded as a condition of giving consent.

(5) The third condition is that the applicant has—

(a) delivered to the registrar such documents relating to the company as are necessary to bring up to date the records kept by the registrar, and

(b) paid any penalties under section 453 or corresponding earlier provisions (civil penalty for failure to deliver accounts) that were outstanding at the date of dissolution or striking off.

(6) In this section the "Crown representative" means—

(a) in relation to property vested in the Duchy of Lancaster, the Solicitor to that Duchy;

(b) in relation to property vested in the Duke of Cornwall, the Solicitor to the Duchy of Cornwall;

(c) in relation to property in Scotland, the Queen's and Lord Treasurer's Remembrancer;

(d) in relation to other property, the Treasury Solicitor.

1026 Application to be accompanied by statement of compliance

(1) An application under section 1024 (application for administrative restoration to the register) must be accompanied by a statement of compliance.

(2) The statement of compliance required is a statement—

(a) that the person making the application has standing to apply (see subsection (3) of that section), and

(b) that the requirements for administrative restoration (see section 1025) are met.

(3) The registrar may accept the statement of compliance as sufficient evidence of those matters.

1027 Registrar's decision on application for administrative restoration

(1) The registrar must give notice to the applicant of the decision on an application under section 1024 (application for administrative restoration to the register).

(2) If the decision is that the company should be restored to the register, the restoration takes effect as from the date that notice is sent.

(3) In the case of such a decision, the registrar must—

(a) enter on the register a note of the date as from which the company's restoration to the register takes effect, and

(b) cause notice of the restoration to be published in the Gazette.

(4) The notice under subsection (3) (b) must state—

(a) the name of the company or, if the company is restored to the register under a different name (see section 1033), that name and its former name,

(b) the company's registered number, and

(c) the date as from which the restoration of the company to the register takes effect.

1028 Effect of administrative restoration

(1) The general effect of administrative restoration to the register is that the company is deemed to have continued in existence as if it had not been dissolved or struck off the register.

(2) The company is not liable to a penalty under section 453 or any corresponding earlier provision (civil penalty for failure to deliver accounts) for a financial year in relation to which the period for filing accounts and reports ended—

(a) after the date of dissolution or striking off, and

(b) before the restoration of the company to the register.

(3) The court may give such directions and make such provision as seems just for placing the company and all other persons in the same position (as nearly as may be) as if the company had not been dissolved or struck off the register.

(4) An application to the court for such directions or provision may be made any time within three years after the date of restoration of the company to the register.

Restoration to the register by the court

1029 Application to court for restoration to the register

(1) An application may be made to the court to restore to the register a company—

(a) that has been dissolved under Chapter 9 of Part 4 of the Insolvency Act 1986 or Chapter 9 of Part 5 of the Insolvency (Northern Ireland) Order 1989 (dissolution of company after winding up),

(b) that is deemed to have been dissolved under paragraph 84(6) of Schedule B1 to that Act or paragraph 85(6) of Schedule B1 to that Order (dissolution of company following administration), or

(c) that has been struck off the register—

(i) under section 1000 or 1001 (power of registrar to strike off defunct company), or

(ii) under section 1003 (voluntary striking off),

whether or not the company has in consequence been dissolved.

(2) An application under this section may be made by—

(a) the Secretary of State,

(b) any former director of the company,

(c) any person having an interest in land in which the company had a superior or derivative interest,

(d) any person having an interest in land or other property—

(i) that was subject to rights vested in the company, or

(ii) that was benefited by obligations owed by the company,

(e) any person who but for the company's dissolution would have been in a contractual relationship with it,

(f) any person with a potential legal claim against the company,

(g) any manager or trustee of a pension fund established for the benefit of employees of the company,

(h) any former member of the company (or the personal representatives of such a person),

(i) any person who was a creditor of the company at the time of its striking off or dissolution,

(j) any former liquidator of the company,

(k) where the company was struck off the register under section 1003 (voluntary striking off), any person of a description specified by regulations under section 1006(1)(f) or 1007(2)(f) (persons entitled to notice of application for voluntary striking off),

or by any other person appearing to the court to have an interest in the matter.

1030 When application to the court may be made

(1) An application to the court for restoration of a company to the register may be made at any time for the purpose of bringing proceedings against the company for damages for personal injury.

(2) No order shall be made on such an application if it appears to the court that the proceedings would fail by virtue of any enactment as to the time within which proceedings must be brought.

(3) In making that decision the court must have regard to its power under section 1032(3) (power to give consequential directions etc) to direct that the period between the dissolution (or striking off) of the company and the making of the order is not to count for the purposes of any such enactment.

(4) In any other case an application to the court for restoration of a company to the register may not be made after the end of the period of six years from the date of the dissolution of the company, subject as follows.

(5) In a case where—

(a) the company has been struck off the register under section 1000 or 1001 (power of registrar to strike off defunct company),

(b) an application to the registrar has been made under section 1024 (application for administrative restoration to the register) within the time allowed for making such an application, and

(c) the registrar has refused the application,

an application to the court under this section may be made within 28 days of notice of the registrar's decision being issued by the registrar, even if the period of six years mentioned in subsection (4) above has expired.

(6) For the purposes of this section—

(a) "personal injury" includes any disease and any impairment of a person's physical or mental condition; and

(b) references to damages for personal injury include—

(i) any sum claimed by virtue of section 1(2) (c) of the Law Reform (Miscellaneous Provisions) Act 1934 or section 14(2)(c) of the Law Reform (Miscellaneous Provisions) Act (Northern Ireland) 1937 (funeral expenses)), and

(ii) damages under the Fatal Accidents Act 1976, the Damages (Scotland) Act 2011 (asp 7) or the Fatal Accidents (Northern Ireland) Order 1977.

1031 Decision on application for restoration by the court

(1) On an application under section 1029 the court may order the restoration of the company to the register—

(a) if the company was struck off the register under section 1000 or 1001 (power of registrar to strike off defunct companies) and the company was, at the time of the striking off, carrying on business or in operation;

(b) if the company was struck off the register under section 1003 (voluntary striking off) and any of the requirements of sections 1004 to 1009 was not complied with;

(c) if in any other case the court considers it just to do so.

(2) If the court orders restoration of the company to the register, the restoration takes effect on a copy of the court's order being delivered to the registrar.

(3) The registrar must cause to be published in the Gazette notice of the restoration of the company to the register.

(4) The notice must state—

(a) the name of the company or, if the company is restored to the register under a different name (see section 1033), that name and its former name,

(b) the company's registered number, and

(c) the date on which the restoration took effect.

1032 Effect of court order for restoration to the register

(1) The general effect of an order by the court for restoration to the register is that the company is deemed to have continued in existence as if it had not been dissolved or struck off the register.

(2) The company is not liable to a penalty under section 453 or any corresponding earlier provision (civil penalty for failure to deliver accounts) for a financial year in relation to which the period for filing accounts and reports ended—

(a) after the date of dissolution or striking off, and

(b) before the restoration of the company to the register.

(3) The court may give such directions and make such provision as seems just for placing the company and all other persons in the same position (as nearly as may be) as if the company had not been dissolved or struck off the register.

(4) The court may also give directions as to—

(a) the delivery to the registrar of such documents relating to the company as are necessary to bring up to date the records kept by the registrar,

(b) the payment of the costs (in Scotland, expenses) of the registrar in connection with the proceedings for the restoration of the company to the register,

(c) where any property or right previously vested in or held on trust for the company has vested as *bona vacantia,* the payment of the costs (in Scotland, expenses) of the Crown representative—

(i) in dealing with the property during the period of dissolution, or

(ii) in connection with the proceedings on the application.

(5) In this section the "Crown representative" means—

(a) in relation to property vested in the Duchy of Lancaster, the Solicitor to that Duchy;

(b) in relation to property vested in the Duke of Cornwall, the Solicitor to the Duchy of Cornwall;

(c) in relation to property in Scotland, the Queen's and Lord Treasurer's Remembrancer;

(d) in relation to other property, the Treasury Solicitor.

Supplementary provisions

1033 Company's name on restoration

(1) A company is restored to the register with the name it had before it was dissolved or struck off the register, subject to the following provisions.

(2) If at the date of restoration the company could not be registered under its former name without contravening section 66 (name not to be the same as another in the registrar's index of company names), it must be restored to the register—

(a) under another name specified—

(i) in the case of administrative restoration, in the application to the registrar, or

(ii) in the case of restoration under a court order, in the court's order, or

(b) as if its registered number was also its name.

References to a company's being registered in a name, and to registration in that context, shall be read as including the company's being restored to the register.

(3) If a company is restored to the register under a name specified in the application to the registrar, the provisions of—

section 80 (change of name: registration and issue of new certificate of incorporation), and

section 81 (change of name: effect),

apply as if the application to the registrar were notice of a change of name.

(4) If a company is restored to the register under a name specified in the court's order, the provisions of—

section 80 (change of name: registration and issue of new certificate of incorporation), and

section 81 (change of name: effect),

apply as if the copy of the court order delivered to the registrar were notice of a change a name.

(5) If the company is restored to the register as if its registered number was also its name—

(a) the company must change its name within 14 days after the date of the restoration,

(b) the change may be made by resolution of the directors (without prejudice to any other method of changing the company's name),

(c) the company must give notice to the registrar of the change, and

(d) sections 80 and 81 apply as regards the registration and effect of the change.

(6) If the company fails to comply with subsection (5) (a) or (c) an offence is committed by—

(a) the company, and

(b) every officer of the company who is in default.

(7) A person guilty of an offence under subsection (6) is liable on summary conviction to a fine not exceeding level 5 on the standard scale and, for continued contravention, a daily default fine not exceeding one-tenth of level 5 on the standard scale.

1034 Effect of restoration to the register where property has vested as bona vacantia

(1) The person in whom any property or right is vested by section 1012 (property of dissolved company to be *bona vacantia)* may dispose of, or of an interest in, that property or right despite the fact that the company may be restored to the register under this Chapter.

(2) If the company is restored to the register—

(a) the restoration does not affect the disposition (but without prejudice to its effect in relation to any other property or right previously vested in or held on trust for the company), and

(b) the Crown or, as the case may be, the Duke of Cornwall shall pay to the company an amount equal to—

(i) the amount of any consideration received for the property or right or, as the case may be, the interest in it, or

(ii) the value of any such consideration at the time of the disposition,

or, if no consideration was received an amount equal to the value of the property, right or interest disposed of, as at the date of the disposition.

(3) There may be deducted from the amount payable under subsection (2)(b) the reasonable costs of the Crown representative in connection with the disposition (to the extent that they have not been paid as a condition of administrative restoration or pursuant to a court order for restoration).

(4) Where a liability accrues under subsection (2) in respect of any property or right which before the restoration of the company to the register had accrued as *bona vacantia* to the Duchy of Lancaster, the Attorney General of that Duchy shall represent Her Majesty in any proceedings arising in connection with that liability.

(5) Where a liability accrues under subsection (2) in respect of any property or right which before the restoration of the company to the register had accrued as *bona vacantia* to the Duchy of Cornwall, such persons as the Duke of Cornwall (or other possessor for the time being of the Duchy) may appoint shall represent the Duke (or other possessor) in any proceedings arising out of that liability.

(6) In this section the "Crown representative" means—

(a) in relation to property vested in the Duchy of Lancaster, the Solicitor to that Duchy;

(b) in relation to property vested in the Duke of Cornwall, the Solicitor to the Duchy of Cornwall;

(c) in relation to property in Scotland, the Queen's and Lord Treasurer's Remembrancer;

(d) in relation to other property, the Treasury Solicitor.

PART 32
COMPANY INVESTIGATIONS: AMENDMENTS

1035 Powers of Secretary of State to give directions to inspectors

(1) In Part 14 of the Companies Act 1985 (investigation of companies and their affairs), after section 446 insert—

"Powers of Secretary of State to give directions to inspectors

446A General powers to give directions

(1) In exercising his functions an inspector shall comply with any direction given to him by the Secretary of State under this section.

(2) The Secretary of State may give an inspector appointed under section 431, 432(2) or 442(1) a direction—

(a) as to the subject matter of his investigation (whether by reference to a specified area of a company's operation, a specified transaction, a period of time or otherwise), or

(b) which requires the inspector to take or not to take a specified step in his investigation.

(3) The Secretary of State may give an inspector appointed under any provision of this Part a direction requiring him to secure that a specified report under section 437—

(a) includes the inspector's views on a specified matter,

(b) does not include any reference to a specified matter,

(c) is made in a specified form or manner, or

(d) is made by a specified date.

(4) A direction under this section—

(a) may be given on an inspector's appointment,

(b) may vary or revoke a direction previously given, and

(c) may be given at the request of an inspector.

(5) In this section—

(a) a reference to an inspector's investigation includes any investigation he undertakes, or could undertake, under section 433(1) (power to investigate affairs of holding company or subsidiary);

(b) "specified" means specified in a direction under this section.

446B Direction to terminate investigation

(1) The Secretary of State may direct an inspector to take no further steps in his investigation.

(2) The Secretary of State may give a direction under this section to an inspector appointed under section 432(1) or 442(3) only on the grounds that it appears to him that—

(a) matters have come to light in the course of the inspector's investigation which suggest that a criminal offence has been committed, and

(b) those matters have been referred to the appropriate prosecuting authority.

(3) Where the Secretary of State gives a direction under this section, any direction already given to the inspector under section 437(1) to produce an interim report, and any direction given to him under section 446A(3) in relation to such a report, shall cease to have effect.

(4) Where the Secretary of State gives a direction under this section, the inspector shall not make a final report to the Secretary of State unless—

(a) the direction was made on the grounds mentioned in subsection (2) and the Secretary of State directs the inspector to make a final report to him, or

(b) the inspector was appointed under section 432(1) (appointment in pursuance of order of the court).

(5) An inspector shall comply with any direction given to him under this section.

(6) In this section, a reference to an inspector's investigation includes any investigation he undertakes, or could undertake, under section 433(1) (power to investigate affairs of holding company or subsidiary).".

(2) In section 431 of that Act (inspectors' powers during investigation) in subsection (1) for "report on them in such manner as he may direct" substitute "report the result of their investigations to him".

(3) In section 432 of that Act (other company investigations) in subsection (1) for "report on them in such manner as he directs" substitute "report the result of their investigations to him".

(4) In section 437 of that Act (inspectors' reports)—

(a) in subsection (1) omit the second sentence, and

(b) subsections (1B) and (1C) shall cease to have effect.

(5) In section 442 of that Act (power to investigate company ownership), omit subsection (2).

1036 Resignation, removal and replacement of inspectors

After section 446B of the Companies Act 1985 (inserted by section 1035 above) insert—

"Resignation, removal and replacement of inspectors

446C Resignation and revocation of appointment

(1) An inspector may resign by notice in writing to the Secretary of State.

(2) The Secretary of State may revoke the appointment of an inspector by notice in writing to the inspector.

446D Appointment of replacement inspectors

(1) Where—

(a) an inspector resigns,

(b) an inspector's appointment is revoked, or

(c) an inspector dies,

the Secretary of State may appoint one or more competent inspectors to continue the investigation.

(2) An appointment under subsection (1) shall be treated for the purposes of this Part (apart from this section) as an appointment under the provision of this Part under which the former inspector was appointed.

(3) The Secretary of State must exercise his power under subsection (1) so as to secure that at least one inspector continues the investigation.

(4) Subsection (3) does not apply if—

(a) the Secretary of State could give any replacement inspector a direction under section 446B (termination of investigation), and

(b) such a direction would (under subsection (4) of that section) result in a final report not being made.

(5) In this section, references to an investigation include any investigation the former inspector conducted under section 433(1) (power to investigate affairs of holding company or subsidiary).".

1037 Power to obtain information from former inspectors etc

(1) After section 446D of the Companies Act 1985 (inserted by section 1036 above) insert—

"Power to obtain information from former inspectors etc

446E Obtaining information from former inspectors etc

(1) This section applies to a person who was appointed as an inspector under this Part—

(a) who has resigned, or

(b) whose appointment has been revoked.

(2) This section also applies to an inspector to whom the Secretary of State has given a direction under section 446B (termination of investigation).

(3) The Secretary of State may direct a person to whom this section applies to produce documents obtained or generated by that person during the course of his investigation to—

(a) the Secretary of State, or

(b) an inspector appointed under this Part.

(4) The power under subsection (3) to require production of a document includes power, in the case of a document not in hard copy form, to require the production of a copy of the document—

(a) in hard copy form, or

(b) in a form from which a hard copy can be readily obtained.

(5) The Secretary of State may take copies of or extracts from a document produced in pursuance of this section.

(6) The Secretary of State may direct a person to whom this section applies to inform him of any matters that came to that person's knowledge as a result of his investigation.

(7) A person shall comply with any direction given to him under this section.

(8) In this section—

(a) references to the investigation of a former inspector or inspector include any investigation he conducted under section 433(1) (power to investigate affairs of holding company or subsidiary), and

(b) "document" includes information recorded in any form.".

(2) In section 451A of that Act (disclosure of information by Secretary of State or inspector), in subsection (1) (a) for "446" substitute "446E".

(3) In section 452(1) of that Act (privileged information) for "446" substitute "446E".

1038 Power to require production of documents

(1) In section 434 of the Companies Act 1985 (production of documents and evidence to inspectors), for subsection (6) substitute—

"(6) In this section "document" includes information recorded in any form.

(7) The power under this section to require production of a document includes power, in the case of a document not in hard copy form, to require the production of a copy of the document—

(a) in hard copy form, or

(b) in a form from which a hard copy can be readily obtained.

(8) An inspector may take copies of or extracts from a document produced in pursuance of this section.".

(2) In section 447 of the Companies Act 1985 (power of Secretary of State to require documents and information), for subsection (9) substitute—

(9) The power under this section to require production of a document includes power, in the case of a document not in hard copy form, to require the production of a copy of the document—

(a) in hard copy form, or

(b) in a form from which a hard copy can be readily obtained.".

1039 Disqualification orders: consequential amendments

In section 8(1A)(b)(i) of the Company Directors Disqualification Act 1986 (disqualification after investigation of company: meaning of "investigative material")—

(a) after "section" insert "437, 446E,", and

(b) after "448" insert ", 451A".

PART 33
UK COMPANIES NOT FORMED UNDER COMPANIES LEGISLATION

CHAPTER 1
COMPANIES NOT FORMED UNDER COMPANIES LEGISLATION BUT AUTHORISED TO REGISTER

1040 Companies authorised to register under this Act

(1) This section applies to—

(a) any company that was in existence on 2nd November 1862 (including any company registered under the Joint Stock Companies Acts), and

(b) any company formed after that date (whether before or after the commencement of this Act)—

(i) in pursuance of an Act of Parliament other than this Act or any of the former Companies Acts,

(ii) in pursuance of letters patent, or

(iii) that is otherwise duly constituted according to law.

(2) Any such company may on making application register under this Act.

(3) Subject to the following provisions, it may register as an unlimited company, as a company limited by shares or as a company limited by guarantee.

(4) A company having the liability of its members limited by Act of Parliament or letters patent—

(a) may not register under this section unless it is a joint stock company, and

(b) may not register under this section as an unlimited company or a company limited by guarantee.

(5) A company that is not a joint stock company may not register under this section as a company limited by shares.

(6) The registration of a company under this section is not invalid by reason that it has taken place with a view to the company's being wound up.

1041 Definition of "joint stock company"

(1) For the purposes of section 1040 (companies authorised to register under this Act) "joint stock company" means a company—

(a) having a permanent paid-up or nominal share capital of fixed amount divided into shares, also of fixed amount, or held and transferable as stock, or divided and held partly in one way and partly in the other, and

(b) formed on the principle of having for its members the holders of those shares or that stock, and no other persons.

(2) Such a company when registered with limited liability under this Act is deemed a company limited by shares.

1042 Power to make provision by regulations

(1) The Secretary of State may make provision by regulations—

(a) for and in connection with registration under section 1040 (companies authorised to register under this Act), and

(b) as to the application to companies so registered of the provisions of the Companies Acts.

(2) Without prejudice to the generality of that power, regulations under this section may make provision corresponding to any provision formerly made by Chapter 2 of Part 22 of the Companies Act 1985.

(3) Regulations under this section are subject to negative resolution procedure.

CHAPTER 2
UNREGISTERED COMPANIES

1043 Unregistered companies

(1) This section applies to bodies corporate incorporated in and having a principal place of business in the United Kingdom, other than—

(a) bodies incorporated by, or registered under, a public general Act of Parliament;

(b) bodies not formed for the purpose of carrying on a business that has for its object the acquisition of gain by the body or its individual members;

(c) bodies for the time being exempted from this section by direction of the Secretary of State;

(d) open-ended investment companies.

(2) The Secretary of State may make provision by regulations applying specified provisions of the Companies Acts to all, or any specified description of, the bodies to which this section applies.

(3) The regulations may provide that the specified provisions of the Companies Acts apply subject to any specified limitations and to such adaptations and modifications (if any) as may be specified.

(4) This section does not—

(a) repeal or revoke in whole or in part any enactment, royal charter or other instrument constituting or regulating any body in relation to which provisions of the Companies Acts are applied by regulations under this section, or

(b) restrict the power of Her Majesty to grant a charter in lieu or supplementary to any such charter.

But in relation to any such body the operation of any such enactment, charter or instrument is suspended in so far as it is inconsistent with any of those provisions as they apply for the time being to that body.

(5) In this section "specified" means specified in the regulations.

(6) Regulations under this section are subject to negative resolution procedure.

PART 34
OVERSEAS COMPANIES

Introductory

1044 Overseas companies

In the Companies Acts an "overseas company" means a company incorporated outside the United Kingdom.

1045 Company contracts and execution of documents by companies

(1) The Secretary of State may make provision by regulations applying sections 43 to 52 (formalities of doing business and other matters) to overseas companies, subject to such exceptions, adaptations or modifications as may be specified in the regulations.

(2) Regulations under this section are subject to negative resolution procedure.

Registration of particulars

1046 Duty to register particulars

(1) The Secretary of State may make provision by regulations requiring an overseas company—
(a) to deliver to the registrar for registration a return containing specified particulars, and
(b) to deliver to the registrar with the return specified documents.

(2) The regulations—
(a) must, in the case of a company other than a Gibraltar company, require the company to register particulars if the company opens a branch in the United Kingdom, and
(b) may, in the case of a Gibraltar company, require the company to register particulars if the company opens a branch in the United Kingdom, and
(c) may, in any case, require the registration of particulars in such other circumstances as may be specified.

(3) In subsection (2)—
"branch" means a branch within the meaning of the Eleventh Company Law Directive (89/666/EEC);
"Gibraltar company" means a company incorporated in Gibraltar.

(4) The regulations may provide that where a company has registered particulars under this section and any alteration is made—
(a) in the specified particulars, or
(b) in any document delivered with the return,
the company must deliver to the registrar for registration a return containing specified particulars of the alteration.

(5) The regulations may make provision—
(a) requiring the return under this section to be delivered for registration to the registrar for a specified part of the United Kingdom, and
(b) requiring it to be so delivered before the end of a specified period.

(6) The regulations may make different provision according to—
(a) the place where the company is incorporated, and
(b) the activities carried on (or proposed to be carried on) by it. This is without prejudice to the general power to make different provision for different cases.

(7) In this section "specified" means specified in the regulations.

(8) Regulations under this section are subject to affirmative resolution procedure.

1047 Registered name of overseas company

(1) Regulations under section 1046 (duty to register particulars) must require an overseas company that is required to register particulars to register its name.

(2) This may be—
(a) the company's corporate name (that is, its name under the law of the country or territory in which it is incorporated) or
(b) an alternative name specified in accordance with section 1048.

(3) Subject only to subsection (5), an EEA company may always register its corporate name.

(4) In any other case, the following provisions of Part 5 (a company's name) apply in relation to the registration of the name of an overseas company—
(a) section 53 (prohibited names);
(b) sections 54 to 56 (sensitive words and expressions);
(c) section 65 (inappropriate use of indications of company type or legal form);
(d) sections 66 to 74 (similarity to other names);
(e) section 75 (provision of misleading information etc);
(f) section 76 (misleading indication of activities).

(5) The provisions of section 57 (permitted characters etc) apply in every case.

(6) Any reference in the provisions mentioned in subsection (4) or (5) to a change of name shall be read as a reference to registration of a different name under section 1048.

1048 Registration under alternative name

(1) An overseas company that is required to register particulars under section 1046 may at any time deliver to the registrar for registration a statement specifying a name, other than its corporate name, under which it proposes to carry on business in the United Kingdom.

(2) An overseas company that has registered an alternative name may at any time deliver to the registrar of companies for registration a statement specifying a different name under which it proposes to carry on business in the United Kingdom (which may be its corporate name or a further alternative) in substitution for the name previously registered.

(3) The alternative name for the time being registered under this section is treated for all purposes of the law applying in the United Kingdom as the company's corporate name.

(4) This does not—

(a) affect the references in this section or section 1047 to the company's corporate name,

(b) affect any rights or obligation of the company, or

(c) render defective any legal proceedings by or against the company.

(5) Any legal proceedings that might have been continued or commenced against the company by its corporate name, or any name previously registered under this section, may be continued or commenced against it by its name for the time being so registered.

Other requirements

1049 Accounts and reports: general

(1) The Secretary of State may make provision by regulations requiring an overseas company that is required to register particulars under section 1046—

(a) to prepare the like accounts and directors' report, and

(b) to cause to be prepared such an auditor's report,

as would be required if the company were formed and registered under this Act.

(2) The regulations may for this purpose apply, with or without modifications, all or any of the provisions of—

Part 15 (accounts and reports), and

Part 16 (audit).

(3) The Secretary of State may make provision by regulations requiring an overseas company to deliver to the registrar copies of—

(a) the accounts and reports prepared in accordance with the regulations, or

(b) the accounts and reports that it is required to prepare and have audited under the law of the country in which it is incorporated.

(4) Regulations under this section are subject to negative resolution procedure.

1050 Accounts and reports: credit or financial institutions

(1) This section applies to a credit or financial institution—

(a) that is incorporated or otherwise formed outside the United Kingdom and Gibraltar,

(b) whose head office is outside the United Kingdom and Gibraltar, and

(c) that has a branch in the United Kingdom.

(2) In subsection (1) "branch" means a place of business that forms a legally dependent part of the institution and conducts directly all or some of the operations inherent in its business.

(3) The Secretary of State may make provision by regulations requiring an institution to which this section applies—

(a) to prepare the like accounts and directors' report, and

(b) to cause to be prepared such an auditor's report,

as would be required if the institution were a company formed and registered under this Act.

(4) The regulations may for this purpose apply, with or without modifications, all or any of the provisions of—

Part 15 (accounts and reports), and

Part 16 (audit).

(5) The Secretary of State may make provision by regulations requiring an institution to which this section applies to deliver to the registrar copies of—
(a) accounts and reports prepared in accordance with the regulations, or
(b) accounts and reports that it is required to prepare and have audited under the law of the country in which the institution has its head office.
(6) Regulations under this section are subject to negative resolution procedure.

1051 Trading disclosures

(1) The Secretary of State may by regulations make provision requiring overseas companies carrying on business in the United Kingdom—
(a) to display specified information in specified locations,
(b) to state specified information in specified descriptions of document or communication, and
(c) to provide specified information on request to those they deal with in the course of their business.
(2) The regulations—
(a) shall in every case require a company that has registered particulars under section 1046 to disclose the name registered by it under section 1047, and
(b) may make provision as to the manner in which any specified information is to be displayed, stated or provided.
(3) The regulations may make provision corresponding to that made by—
section 83 (civil consequences of failure to make required disclosure), and
section 84 (criminal consequences of failure to make required disclosure).
(4) In this section "specified" means specified in the regulations.
(5) Regulations under this section are subject to affirmative resolution procedure.

1052 Company charges

(1) The Secretary of State may by regulations make provision about the registration of specified charges over property in the United Kingdom of a registered overseas company.
(2) The power in subsection (1) includes power to make provision about—
(a) a registered overseas company that—
(i) has particulars registered in more than one part of the United Kingdom;
(ii) has property in more than one part of the United Kingdom;
(b) the circumstances in which property is to be regarded, for the purposes of the regulations, as being, or not being, in the United Kingdom or in a particular part of the United Kingdom;
(c) the keeping by a registered overseas company of records and registers about specified charges and their inspection;
(d) the consequences of a failure to register a charge in accordance with the regulations;
(e) the circumstances in which a registered overseas company ceases to be subject to the regulations.
(3) The regulations may for this purpose apply, with or without modifications, any of the provisions of Part 25 (company charges).
(4) The regulations may modify any reference in an enactment to Part 25, or to a particular provision of that Part, so as to include a reference to the regulations or to a specified provision of the regulations.
(5) Regulations under this section are subject to negative resolution procedure.
(6) In this section—
"registered overseas company" means an overseas company that has registered particulars under section 1046(1), and
"specified" means specified in the regulations.

1053 Other returns etc

(1) This section applies to overseas companies that are required to register particulars under section 1046.

(2) The Secretary of State may make provision by regulations requiring the delivery to the registrar of returns—

(a) by a company to which this section applies that—

(i) is being wound up, or

(ii) becomes or ceases to be subject to insolvency proceedings, or an arrangement or composition or any analogous proceedings;

(b) by the liquidator of a company to which this section applies.

(3) The regulations may specify—

(a) the circumstances in which a return is to be made,

(b) the particulars to be given in it, and

(c) the period within which it is to be made.

(4) The Secretary of State may make provision by regulations requiring notice to be given to the registrar of the appointment in relation to a company to which this section applies of a judicial factor (in Scotland).

(5) The regulations may include provision corresponding to any provision made by section 1154 of this Act (duty to notify registrar of certain appointments).

(6) Regulations under this section are subject to affirmative resolution procedure.

Supplementary

1054 Offences

(1) Regulations under this Part may specify the person or persons responsible for complying with any specified requirement of the regulations.

(2) Regulations under this Part may make provision for offences, including provision as to—

(a) the person or persons liable in the case of any specified contravention of the regulations, and

(b) circumstances that are, or are not, to be a defence on a charge of such an offence.

(3) The regulations must not provide—

(a) for imprisonment, or

(b) for the imposition on summary conviction of a fine exceeding level 5 on the standard scale and, for continued contravention, a daily default fine not exceeding one-tenth of level 5 on the standard scale.

(4) In this section "specified" means specified in the regulations.

1055 Disclosure of individual's residential address: protection from disclosure

Where regulations under section 1046 (overseas companies: duty to register particulars) require an overseas company to register particulars of an individual's usual residential address, they must contain provision corresponding to that made by Chapter 8 of Part 10 (directors' residential addresses: protection from disclosure).

1056 Requirement to identify persons authorised to accept service of documents

Regulations under section 1046 (overseas companies: duty to register particulars) must require an overseas company to register—

(a) particulars identifying every person resident in the United Kingdom authorised to accept service of documents on behalf of the company, or

(b) a statement that there is no such person.

1057 Registrar to whom returns, notices etc to be delivered

(1) This section applies to an overseas company that is required to register or has registered particulars under section 1046 in more than one part of the United Kingdom.

(2) The Secretary of State may provide by regulations that, in the case of such a company, anything authorised or required to be delivered to the registrar under this Part is to be delivered—

(a) to the registrar for each part of the United Kingdom in which the company is required to register or has registered particulars, or

(b) to the registrar for such part or parts of the United Kingdom as may be specified in or determined in accordance with the regulations.

(3) Regulations under this section are subject to negative resolution procedure.

1058 Duty to give notice of ceasing to have registrable presence

(1) The Secretary of State may make provision by regulations requiring an overseas company—

(a) if it has registered particulars following the opening of a branch, in accordance with regulations under section 1046(2)(a) or (b), to give notice to the registrar if it closes that branch;

(b) if it has registered particulars in other circumstances, in accordance with regulations under section 1046(2)(c), to give notice to the registrar if the circumstances that gave rise to the obligation to register particulars cease to obtain.

(2) The regulations must provide for the notice to be given to the registrar for the part of the United Kingdom to which the original return of particulars was delivered.

(3) The regulations may specify the period within which notice must be given.

(4) Regulations under this section are subject to negative resolution procedure.

1059 Application of provisions in case of relocation of branch

For the purposes of this Part—

(a) the relocation of a branch from one part of the United Kingdom to another counts as the closing of one branch and the opening of another;

(b) the relocation of a branch within the same part of the United Kingdom does not.

PART 35
THE REGISTRAR OF COMPANIES

Scheme of this Part

1059A Scheme of this Part

(1) The scheme of this Part is as follows.

(2) The following provisions apply generally (to the registrar, to any functions of the registrar, or to documents delivered to or issued by the registrar under any enactment, as the case may be)—

sections 1060(1) and (2) and 1061 to 1063 (the registrar),
sections 1068 to 1071 (delivery of documents to the registrar),
sections 1072 to 1076 (requirements for proper delivery),
sections 1080(1), (4) and (5) and 1092 (keeping and production of records),
section 1083 (preservation of original documents),
sections 1108 to 1110 (language requirements: transliteration),
sections 1111 and 1114 to 1119 (supplementary provisions).

(3) The following provisions apply in relation to companies (to companies or for the purposes of the Companies Acts, as the case may be)—

section 1060(3) and (4) (references to the registrar in the Companies Acts),
sections 1064 and 1065 (certificates of incorporation),
section 1066 (companies' registered numbers),
sections 1077 to 1079 (public notice of receipt of certain documents),
sections 1080(2) and (3), 1081, 1082 and 1084 (the register),
sections 1085 to 1091 (inspection of the register),
sections 1093 to 1098 (correction or removal of material on the register),
section 1106 (voluntary filing of translations),
sections 1112 and 1113 (supplementary provisions).

(4) The following provisions apply as indicated in the provisions concerned—

section 1067 (registered numbers of UK establishments of overseas companies),
sections 1099 to 1101 (the registrar's index of company names),
sections 1102 to 1105 and 1107 (language requirements: translation).

(5) Unless the context otherwise requires, the provisions of this Part apply to an overseas company as they apply to a company as defined in section 1.

The registrar

1060 The registrar

(1) There shall continue to be—

(a) a registrar of companies for England and Wales,

(b) a registrar of companies for Scotland, and

(c) a registrar of companies for Northern Ireland.

(2) The registrars shall be appointed by the Secretary of State.

(3) In the Companies Acts "the registrar of companies" and "the registrar" mean the registrar of companies for England and Wales, Scotland or Northern Ireland, as the case may require.

(4) References in the Companies Acts to registration in a particular part of the United Kingdom are to registration by the registrar for that part of the United Kingdom.

1061 The registrar's functions

(1) The registrar shall continue—

(a) to perform the functions conferred on the registrar by or under the Companies Acts or any other enactment, and

(b) to perform such functions on behalf of the Secretary of State, in relation to the registration of companies or other matters, as the Secretary of State may from time to time direct.

(2) . . .

(3) References in this Act to the functions of the registrar are to functions within subsection (1)(a) or (b).

1062 The registrar's official seal

The registrar shall have an official seal for the authentication of documents in connection with the performance of the registrar's functions.

1063 Fees payable to registrar

(1) The Secretary of State may make provision by regulations requiring the payment to the registrar of fees in respect of—

(a) the performance of any of the registrar's functions, or

(b) the provision by the registrar of services or facilities for purposes incidental to, or otherwise connected with, the performance of any of the registrar's functions.

(2) The matters for which fees may be charged include—

(a) the performance of a duty imposed on the registrar or the Secretary of State,

(b) the receipt of documents delivered to the registrar, and

(c) the inspection, or provision of copies, of documents kept by the registrar.

(3) The regulations may—

(a) provide for the amount of the fees to be fixed by or determined under the regulations;

(b) provide for different fees to be payable in respect of the same matter in different circumstances;

(c) specify the person by whom any fee payable under the regulations is to be paid;

(d) specify when and how fees are to be paid.

(4) Regulations under this section are subject to negative resolution procedure.

(5) In respect of the performance of functions or the provision of services or facilities—

(a) for which fees are not provided for by regulations, or

(b) in circumstances other than those for which fees are provided for by regulations,

the registrar may determine from time to time what fees (if any) are chargeable.

(6) Fees received by the registrar are to be paid into the Consolidated Fund.

(7) The Limited Partnerships Act 1907 is amended as follows—

(a) in section 16(1) (inspection of statements registered)—

(i) omit the words ", and there shall be paid for such inspection such fees as may be appointed by the Board of Trade, not exceeding 5p for each inspection", and
(ii) omit the words from "and there shall be paid for such certificate" to the end;

(b) in section 17 (power to make rules)—
(i) omit the words "(but as to fees with the concurrence of the Treasury)", and
(ii) omit paragraph (a).

Certificates of incorporation

1064 Public notice of issue of certificate of incorporation

(1) The registrar must cause to be published—
(a) in the Gazette, or
(b) in accordance with section 1116 (alternative means of giving public notice),
notice of the issue by the registrar of any certificate of incorporation of a company.

(2) The notice must state the name and registered number of the company and the date of issue of the certificate.

(3) This section applies to a certificate of incorporation issued under—
(a) section 80 (change of name),
(b) section 88 (Welsh companies), or
(c) any provision of Part 7 (re-registration),
as well as to the certificate issued on a company's formation.

1065 Right to certificate of incorporation

Any person may require the registrar to provide him with a copy of any certificate of incorporation of a company, signed by the registrar or authenticated by the registrar's seal.

Registered numbers

1066 Company's registered numbers

(1) The registrar shall allocate to every company a number, which shall be known as the company's registered number.

(2) Companies' registered numbers shall be in such form, consisting of one or more sequences of figures or letters, as the registrar may determine.

(3) The registrar may on adopting a new form of registered number make such changes of existing registered numbers as appear necessary.

(4) A change of a company's registered number has effect from the date on which the company is notified by the registrar of the change.

(5) For a period of three years beginning with that date any requirement to disclose the company's registered number imposed by regulations under section 82 or section 1051 (trading disclosures) is satisfied by the use of either the old number or the new.

(6) In this section "company" includes an overseas company whose particulars have been registered under section 1046, other than a company that appears to the registrar not to be required to register particulars under that section.

1067 Registered numbers of UK establishments of overseas company

(1) The registrar shall allocate to every UK establishment of an overseas company whose particulars are registered under section 1046 a number, which shall be known as the UK establishment's registered number.

(2) The registered numbers of UK establishments of overseas companies shall be in such form, consisting of one or more sequences of figures or letters, as the registrar may determine.

(3) The registrar may on adopting a new form of registered number make such changes of existing registered numbers as appear necessary.

(4) A change of the registered number of a UK establishment has effect from the date on which the company is notified by the registrar of the change.

(5) For a period of three years beginning with that date any requirement to disclose the UK establishment's registered number imposed by regulations under section 1051 (trading disclosures) is satisfied by the use of either the old number or the new.

(6) In this Part "establishment", in relation to an overseas company, means—

(a) a branch within the meaning of the Eleventh Company Law Directive (89/666/EEC), or

(b) a place of business that is not such a branch,

and "UK establishment" means an establishment in the United Kingdom.

Delivery of documents to the registrar

1068 Registrar's requirements as to form, authentication and manner of delivery

(1) The registrar may impose requirements as to the form, authentication and manner of delivery of documents required or authorised to be delivered to the registrar under any enactment.

(2) As regards the form of the document, the registrar may—

(a) require the contents of the document to be in a standard form;

(b) impose requirements for the purpose of enabling the document to be scanned or copied.

(3) As regards authentication, the registrar may—

(a) require the document to be authenticated by a particular person or a person of a particular description;

(b) specify the means of authentication;

(c) require the document to contain or be accompanied by the name or registered number (or both) of the company (or other body) to which it relates.

(4) As regards the manner of delivery, the registrar may specify requirements as to—

(a) the physical form of the document (for example, hard copy or electronic form);

(b) the means to be used for delivering the document (for example, by post or electronic means);

(c) the address to which the document is to be sent;

(d) in the case of a document to be delivered by electronic means, the hardware and software to be used, and technical specifications (for example, matters relating to protocol, security, anti-virus protection or encryption).

(5) The registrar must secure that as from 1st January 2007 all documents subject to the Directive disclosure requirements (see section 1078) may be delivered to the registrar by electronic means.

(6) The power conferred by this section does not authorise the registrar to require documents to be delivered by electronic means (see section 1069).

(7) Requirements imposed under this section must not be inconsistent with requirements imposed by any enactment with respect to the form, authentication or manner of delivery of the document concerned.

1069 Power to require delivery by electronic means

(1) The Secretary of State may make regulations requiring documents that are authorised or required to be delivered to the registrar to be delivered by electronic means.

(2) Any such requirement to deliver documents by electronic means is effective only if registrar's rules have been published with respect to the detailed requirements for such delivery.

(3) Regulations under this section are subject to affirmative resolution procedure.

1070 Agreement for delivery by electronic means

(1) The registrar may agree with a company (or other body) that documents relating to the company (or other body) that are required or authorised to be delivered to the registrar—

(a) will be delivered by electronic means, except as provided for in the agreement, and

(b) will conform to such requirements as may be specified in the agreement or specified by the registrar in accordance with the agreement.

(2) An agreement under this section may relate to all or any description of documents to be delivered to the registrar.

(3) Documents in relation to which an agreement is in force under this section must be delivered in accordance with the agreement.

1071 Document not delivered until received

(1) A document is not delivered to the registrar until it is received by the registrar.
(2) Provision may be made by registrar's rules as to when a document is to be regarded as received.

Requirements for proper delivery

1072 Requirements for proper delivery

(1) A document delivered to the registrar is not properly delivered unless all the following requirements are met—
  (a) the requirements of the provision under which the document is to be delivered to the registrar as regards—
    (i) the contents of the document, and
    (ii) form, authentication and manner of delivery;
  (b) any applicable requirements under—
  section 1068 (registrar's requirements as to form, authentication and manner of delivery),
  section 1069 (power to require delivery by electronic means), or
  section 1070 (agreement for delivery by electronic means);
  (c) any requirements of this Part as to the language in which the document is drawn up and delivered or as to its being accompanied on delivery by a certified translation into English;
  (d) in so far as it consists of or includes names and addresses, any requirements of this Part as to permitted characters, letters or symbols or as to its being accompanied on delivery by a certificate as to the transliteration of any element;
  (e) any applicable requirements under section 1111 (registrar's requirements as to certification or verification);
  (f) any requirement of regulations under section 1082 (use of unique identifiers);
  (g) any requirements as regards payment of a fee in respect of its receipt by the registrar.
(2) A document that is not properly delivered is treated for the purposes of the provision requiring or authorising it to be delivered as not having been delivered, subject to the provisions of section 1073 (power to accept documents not meeting requirements for proper delivery).

1073 Power to accept documents not meeting requirements for proper delivery

(1) The registrar may accept (and register) a document that does not comply with the requirements for proper delivery.
(2) A document accepted by the registrar under this section is treated as received by the registrar for the purposes of section 1077 (public notice of receipt of certain documents).
(3) No objection may be taken to the legal consequences of a document's being accepted (or registered) by the registrar under this section on the ground that the requirements for proper delivery were not met.
(4) The acceptance of a document by the registrar under this section does not affect—
  (a) the continuing obligation to comply with the requirements for proper delivery, or
  (b) subject as follows, any liability for failure to comply with those requirements.
(5) For the purposes of—
  (a) section 453 (civil penalty for failure to file accounts and reports), and
  (b) any enactment imposing a daily default fine for failure to deliver the document,
  the period after the document is accepted does not count as a period during which there is default in complying with the requirements for proper delivery.
(6) But if, subsequently—
  (a) the registrar issues a notice under section 1094(4) in respect of the document (notice of administrative removal from the register), and
  (b) the requirements for proper delivery are not complied with before the end of the period of 14 days after the issue of that notice,

any subsequent period of default does count for the purposes of those provisions.

1074 Documents containing unnecessary material

(1) This section applies where a document delivered to the registrar contains unnecessary material.

(2) "Unnecessary material" means material that—

(a) is not necessary in order to comply with an obligation under any enactment, and

(b) is not specifically authorised to be delivered to the registrar.

(3) For this purpose an obligation to deliver a document of a particular description, or conforming to certain requirements, is regarded as not extending to anything that is not needed for a document of that description or, as the case may be, conforming to those requirements.

(4) If the unnecessary material cannot readily be separated from the rest of the document, the document is treated as not meeting the requirements for proper delivery.

(5) If the unnecessary material can readily be separated from the rest of the document, the registrar may register the document either—

(a) with the omission of the unnecessary material, or

(b) as delivered.

1075 Informal correction of document

(1) A document delivered to the registrar may be corrected by the registrar if it appears to the registrar to be incomplete or internally inconsistent.

(2) This power is exercisable only—

(a) on instructions, and

(b) if the company (or other body) to which the document relates has given (and has not withdrawn) its consent to instructions being given under this section.

(3) The following requirements must be met as regards the instructions—

(a) the instructions must be given in response to an enquiry by the registrar;

(b) the registrar must be satisfied that the person giving the instructions is authorised to do so—

(i) by the person by whom the document was delivered, or

(ii) by the company (or other body) to which the document relates;

(c) the instructions must meet any requirements of registrar's rules as to—

(i) the form and manner in which they are given, and

(ii) authentication.

(4) The consent of the company (or other body) to instructions being given under this section (and any withdrawal of such consent)—

(a) may be in hard copy or electronic form, and

(b) must be notified to the registrar.

(5) This section applies in relation to documents delivered under Part 25 (company charges) by a person other than the company (or other body) as if the references to the company (or other body) were to the company (or other body) or the person by whom the document was delivered.

(6) A document that is corrected under this section is treated, for the purposes of any enactment relating to its delivery, as having been delivered when the correction is made.

(7) The power conferred by this section is not exercisable if the document has been registered under section 1073 (power to accept documents not meeting requirements for proper delivery).

1076 Replacement of document not meeting requirements for proper delivery

(1) The registrar may accept a replacement for a document previously delivered that—

(a) did not comply with the requirements for proper delivery, or

(b) contained unnecessary material (within the meaning of section 1074).

(2) A replacement document must not be accepted unless the registrar is satisfied that it is delivered by—

(a) the person by whom the original document was delivered, or

(b) the company (or other body) to which the original document relates, and that it complies with the requirements for proper delivery.

(3) The power of the registrar to impose requirements as to the form and manner of delivery includes power to impose requirements as to the identification of the original document and the delivery of the replacement in a form and manner enabling it to be associated with the original.

(4) This section does not apply where the original document was delivered under Part 25 (company charges) (but see section 859M (rectification of register).

Public notice of receipt of certain documents

1077 Public notice of receipt of certain documents

(1) The registrar must cause to be published—

(a) in the Gazette, or

(b) in accordance with section 1116 (alternative means of giving public notice),

notice of the receipt by the registrar of any document that, on receipt, is subject to the Directive disclosure requirements (see section 1078).

(2) The notice must state the name and registered number of the company, the description of document and the date of receipt.

(3) The registrar is not required to cause notice of the receipt of a document to be published before the date of incorporation of the company to which the document relates.

1078 Documents subject to Directive disclosure requirements

(1) The documents subject to the "Directive disclosure requirements" are as follows.

The requirements referred to are those of Article 3 of the First Company Law Directive (68/151/EEC), as amended, extended and applied.

(2) In the case of every company—

Constitutional documents

1 The company's memorandum and articles.

2 Any amendment of the company's articles (including every resolution or agreement required to be embodied in or annexed to copies of the company's articles issued by the company).

3 After any amendment of the company's articles, the text of the articles as amended.

4 Any notice of a change of the company's name.

Directors

1 The statement of proposed officers required on formation of the company.

2 Notification of any change among the company's directors.

3 Notification of any change in the particulars of directors required to be delivered to the registrar.

Accounts, reports and returns

1 All documents required to be delivered to the registrar under section 441 (annual accounts and reports).

1A All documents delivered to the registrar under sections 394A(2)(e), 448A(2)(e) and 479A(2)(e) (qualifying subsidiary companies: conditions for exemption from the audit, preparation and filing of individual accounts).

2 The company's annual return.

Registered office

Notification of any change of the company's registered office.

Winding up

1 Copy of any winding-up order in respect of the company.

2 Notice of the appointment of liquidators.

3 Order for the dissolution of a company on a winding up.

4 Return by a liquidator of the final meeting of a company on a winding up.

(3) In the case of a public company—

Share capital

1 Any statement of capital and initial shareholdings.
2 Any return of allotment and the statement of capital accompanying it.
3 Copy of any resolution under section 570 or 571 (disapplication of pre-emption rights).
4 Copy of any report under section 593 or 599 as to the value of a non-cash asset.
5 Statement of capital accompanying notice given under section 625 (notice by company of redenomination of shares).
6 Statement of capital accompanying notice given under section 627 (notice by company of reduction of capital in connection with redenomination of shares).
7 Notice delivered under section 636 (notice of new name of class of shares) or 637 (notice of variation of rights attached to shares).
8 Statement of capital accompanying order delivered under section 649 (order of court confirming reduction of capital).
9 Notification (under section 689) of the redemption of shares and the statement of capital accompanying it.
10 Statement of capital accompanying return delivered under section 708 (notice of cancellation of shares on purchase of own shares) or 730 (notice of cancellation of shares held as treasury shares).
11 Any statement of compliance delivered under section 762 (statement that company meets conditions for issue of trading certificate).

Mergers and divisions

1 Copy of any draft of the terms of a scheme required to be delivered to the registrar under section 906 or 921.
2 Copy of any order under section 899 or 900 in respect of a compromise or arrangement to which Part 27 (mergers and divisions of public companies) applies.

(4) Where a private company re-registers as a public company (see section 96)—
(a) the last statement of capital relating to the company received by the registrar under any provision of the Companies Acts becomes subject to the Directive disclosure requirements, and
(b) section 1077 (public notice of receipt of certain documents) applies as if the statement had been received by the registrar when the re-registration takes effect.

(5) In the case of an overseas company, such particulars, returns and other documents required to be delivered under Part 34 as may be specified by the Secretary of State by regulations.

(6) Regulations under subsection (5) are subject to negative resolution procedure.

1079 Effect of failure to give public notice

(1) A company is not entitled to rely against other persons on the happening of any event to which this section applies unless—
(a) the event has been officially notified at the material time, or
(b) the company shows that the person concerned knew of the event at the material time.

(2) The events to which this section applies are—
(a) an amendment of the company's articles,
(b) a change among the company's directors,
(c) (as regards service of any document on the company) a change of the company's registered office,
(d) the making of a winding-up order in respect of the company, or
(e) the appointment of a liquidator in a voluntary winding up of the company.

(3) If the material time falls—
(a) on or before the 15th day after the date of official notification, or
(b) where the 15th day was not a working day, on or before the next day that was,

the company is not entitled to rely on the happening of the event as against a person who shows that he was unavoidably prevented from knowing of the event at that time.

(4) "Official notification" means—

(a) in relation to an amendment of the company's articles, notification in accordance with section 1077 (public notice of receipt by registrar of certain documents) of the amendment and the amended text of the articles;

(b) in relation to anything else stated in a document subject to the Directive disclosure requirements, notification of that document in accordance with that section;

(c) in relation to the appointment of a liquidator in a voluntary winding up, notification of that event in accordance with section 109 of the Insolvency Act 1986 or Article 95 of the Insolvency (Northern Ireland) Order 1989.

The register

1080 The register

(1) The registrar shall continue to keep records of—

(a) the information contained in documents delivered to the registrar under any enactment, and

(b) certificates issued by the registrar under any enactment.

(2) The records relating to companies are referred to collectively in the Companies Acts as "the register".

(3) Information deriving from documents subject to the Directive disclosure requirements (see section 1078) that are delivered to the registrar on or after 1st January 2007 must be kept by the registrar in electronic form.

(4) Subject to that, information contained in documents delivered to the registrar may be recorded and kept in any form the registrar thinks fit, provided it is possible to inspect it and produce a copy of it.

This is sufficient compliance with any duty of the registrar to keep, file or register the document or to record the information contained in it.

(5) The records kept by the registrar must be such that information relating to a company or other registered body is associated with that body, in such manner as the registrar may determine, so as to enable all the information relating to the body to be retrieved.

1081 Annotation of the register

(1) The registrar must place a note in the register recording—

(a) the date on which a document is delivered to the registrar;

(b) if a document is corrected under section 1075, the nature and date of the correction;

(c) if a document is replaced (whether or not material derived from it is removed), the fact that it has been replaced and the date of delivery of the replacement;

(d) if material is removed—

(i) what was removed (giving a general description of its contents),

(ii) under what power, and

(iii) the date on which that was done;

(e) if a document is rectified under section 859M, the nature and date of rectification;

(f) if a document is replaced under section 859N, the fact that it has been replaced and the date of delivery of the replacement.

(2) The Secretary of State may make provision by regulations—

(a) authorising or requiring the registrar to annotate the register in such other circumstances as may be specified in the regulations, and

(b) as to the contents of any such annotation.

(3) No annotation is required in the case of a document that by virtue of section 1072(2) (documents not meeting requirements for proper delivery) is treated as not having been delivered.

(4) A note may be removed if it no longer serves any useful purpose.

(5) Any duty or power of the registrar with respect to annotation of the register is subject to the court's power under section 1097 (powers of court on ordering removal of material from the register) to direct—

(a) that a note be removed from the register, or

(b) that no note shall be made of the removal of material that is the subject of the court's order.

(6) Notes placed in the register in accordance with subsection (1), or in pursuance of regulations under subsection (2), are part of the register for all purposes of the Companies Acts.

(7) Regulations under this section are subject to negative resolution procedure.

1082 Allocation of unique identifiers

(1) The Secretary of State may make provision for the use, in connection with the register, of reference numbers ("unique identifiers") to identify each person who—

(a) is a director of a company,

(b) is secretary (or a joint secretary) of a company, or

(c) in the case of an overseas company whose particulars are registered under section 1046, holds any such position as may be specified for the purposes of this section by regulations under that section.

(2) The regulations may—

(a) provide that a unique identifier may be in such form, consisting of one or more sequences of letters or numbers, as the registrar may from time to time determine;

(b) make provision for the allocation of unique identifiers by the registrar;

(c) require there to be included, in any specified description of documents delivered to the registrar, as well as a statement of the person's name—

(i) a statement of the person's unique identifier, or

(ii) a statement that the person has not been allocated a unique identifier;

(d) enable the registrar to take steps where a person appears to have more than one unique identifier to discontinue the use of all but one of them.

(3) The regulations may contain provision for the application of the scheme in relation to persons appointed, and documents registered, before the commencement of this Act.

(4) The regulations may make different provision for different descriptions of person and different descriptions of document.

(5) Regulations under this section are subject to affirmative resolution procedure.

1083 Preservation of original documents

(1) The originals of documents delivered to the registrar in hard copy form must be kept for three years after they are received by the registrar, after which they may be destroyed provided the information contained in them has been recorded.

This is subject to section 1087(3) (extent of obligation to retain material not available for public inspection).

(2) The registrar is under no obligation to keep the originals of documents delivered in electronic form, provided the information contained in them has been recorded.

(3) This section applies to documents held by the registrar when this section comes into force as well as to documents subsequently received.

1084 Records relating to companies that have been dissolved etc

(1) This section applies where—

(a) a company is dissolved,

(b) an overseas company ceases to have any connection with the United Kingdom by virtue of which it is required to register particulars under section 1046, or

(c) a credit or financial institution ceases to be within section 1050 (overseas institutions required to file accounts with the registrar).

(2) At any time after two years from the date on which it appears to the registrar that—

(a) the company has been dissolved,

(b) the overseas company has ceased to have any connection with the United Kingdom by virtue of which it is required to register particulars under section 1046, or
(c) the credit or financial institution has ceased to be within section 1050 (overseas institutions required to file accounts with the registrar),

the registrar may direct that records relating to the company or institution may be removed to the Public Record Office or, as the case may be, the Public Record Office of Northern Ireland.

(3) Records in respect of which such a direction is given shall be disposed of under the enactments relating to that Office and the rules made under them.

(4) In subsection (1)(a) "company" includes a company provisionally or completely registered under the Joint Stock Companies Act 1844.

(5) This section does not extend to Scotland.

Inspection etc of the register

1085 Inspection of the register

(1) Any person may inspect the register.

(2) The right of inspection extends to the originals of documents delivered to the registrar in hard copy form if, and only if, the record kept by the registrar of the contents of the document is illegible or unavailable.
The period for which such originals are to be kept is limited by section 1083(1).

(3) This section has effect subject to section 1087 (material not available for public inspection).

1086 Right to copy of material on the register

(1) Any person may require a copy of any material on the register.

(2) The fee for any such copy of material derived from a document subject to the Directive disclosure requirements (see section 1078), whether in hard copy or electronic form, must not exceed the administrative cost of providing it.

(3) This section has effect subject to section 1087 (material not available for public inspection).

1087 Material not available for public inspection

(1) The following material must not be made available by the registrar for public inspection—
(a) the contents of any document sent to the registrar containing views expressed pursuant to section 56 (comments on proposal by company to use certain words or expressions in company name);
(b) protected information within section 242(1) (directors' residential addresses: restriction on disclosure by registrar) or any corresponding provision of regulations under section 1046 (overseas companies);
(ba) representations received by the registrar in response to a notice under—
(i) section 245(2) (notice of proposal to put director's usual residential address on the public record), or
(ii) any corresponding provision of regulations under section 1046 (overseas companies);
(c) any application to the registrar under section 1024 (application for administrative restoration to the register) that has not yet been determined or was not successful;
(d) any document received by the registrar in connection with the giving or withdrawal of consent under section 1075 (informal correction of documents);
(e) any application or other document delivered to the registrar under section 1088 (application to make address unavailable for public inspection) and any address in respect of which such an application is successful;
(f) any application or other document delivered to the registrar under section 1095 (application for rectification of register);
(g) any court order under section 1096 (rectification of the register under court order) that the court has directed under section 1097 (powers of court on ordering removal of material from the register) is not to be made available for public inspection;

(h) ...

(i) any e-mail address, identification code or password deriving from a document delivered for the purpose of authorising or facilitating electronic filing procedures or providing information by telephone;

(j) the contents of any documents held by the registrar pending a decision of the Regulator of Community Interest Companies under—

(i) section 36A of the Companies (Audit, Investigations and Community Enterprise) Act 2004 (eligibility for registration as community interest company),

(ii) section 38 of that Act (eligibility for conversion to community interest company), or

(iii) section 55 of that Act (eligibility for conversion from community interest company to charity),

and that the registrar is not later required to record;

(k) any other material excluded from public inspection by or under any other enactment.

(2) A restriction applying by reference to material deriving from a particular description of document does not affect the availability for public inspection of the same information contained in material derived from another description of document in relation to which no such restriction applies.

(3) Material to which this section applies need not be retained by the registrar for longer than appears to the registrar reasonably necessary for the purposes for which the material was delivered to the registrar.

1088 Application to registrar to make address unavailable for public inspection

(1) The Secretary of State may make provision by regulations requiring the registrar, on application, to make an address on the register unavailable for public inspection.

(2) The regulations may make provision as to—

(a) who may make an application,

(b) the grounds on which an application may be made,

(c) the information to be included in and documents to accompany an application,

(d) the notice to be given of an application and of its outcome, and

(e) how an application is to be determined.

(3) Provision under subsection (2)(e) may in particular—

(a) confer a discretion on the registrar;

(b) provide for a question to be referred to a person other than the registrar for the purposes of determining the application.

(4) An application must specify the address to be removed from the register and indicate where on the register it is.

(5) The regulations may provide—

(a) that an address is not to be made unavailable for public inspection under this section unless replaced by a service address, and

(b) that in such a case the application must specify a service address.

(6) Regulations under this section are subject to affirmative resolution procedure.

1089 Form of application for inspection or copy

(1) The registrar may specify the form and manner in which application is to be made for—

(a) inspection under section 1085, or

(b) a copy under section 1086.

(2) As from 1st January 2007, applications in respect of documents subject to the Directive disclosure requirements may be submitted to the registrar in hard copy or electronic form, as the applicant chooses.

This does not affect the registrar's power under subsection (1) above to impose requirements in respect of other matters.

1090 Form and manner in which copies to be provided

(1) The following provisions apply as regards the form and manner in which copies are to be provided under section 1086.

(2) As from 1st January 2007, copies of documents subject to the Directive disclosure requirements must be provided in hard copy or electronic form, as the applicant chooses.
This is subject to the following proviso.

(3) The registrar is not obliged by subsection (2) to provide copies in electronic form of a document that was delivered to the registrar in hard copy form if—
(a) the document was delivered to the registrar on or before 31st December 1996, or
(b) the document was delivered to the registrar on or before 31st December 2006 and ten years or more elapsed between the date of delivery and the date of receipt of the first application for a copy on or after 1st January 2007.

(4) Subject to the preceding provisions of this section, the registrar may determine the form and manner in which copies are to be provided.

1091 Certification of copies as accurate

(1) Copies provided under section 1086 in hard copy form must be certified as true copies unless the applicant dispenses with such certification.

(2) Copies so provided in electronic form must not be certified as true copies unless the applicant expressly requests such certification.

(3) A copy provided under section 1086, certified by the registrar (whose official position it is unnecessary to prove) to be an accurate record of the contents of the original document, is in all legal proceedings admissible in evidence—
(a) as of equal validity with the original document, and
(b) as evidence (in Scotland, sufficient evidence) of any fact stated in the original document of which direct oral evidence would be admissible.

(4) The Secretary of State may make provision by regulations as to the manner in which such a certificate is to be provided in a case where the copy is provided in electronic form.

(5) Except in the case of documents that are subject to the Directive disclosure requirements (see section 1078), copies provided by the registrar may, instead of being certified in writing to be an accurate record, be sealed with the registrar's official seal.

1092 Issue of process for production of records kept by the registrar

(1) No process for compelling the production of a record kept by the registrar shall issue from any court except with the permission of the court.

(2) Any such process shall bear on it a statement that it is issued with the permission of the court.

Correction or removal of material on the register

1093 Registrar's notice to resolve inconsistency on the register

(1) Where it appears to the registrar that the information contained in a document delivered to the registrar is inconsistent with other information on the register, the registrar may give notice to the company to which the document relates—
(a) stating in what respects the information contained in it appears to be inconsistent with other information on the register, and
(b) requiring the company to take steps to resolve the inconsistency.

(2) The notice must—
(a) state the date on which it is issued, and
(b) require the delivery to the registrar, within 14 days after that date, of such replacement or additional documents as may be required to resolve the inconsistency.

(3) If the necessary documents are not delivered within the period specified, an offence is committed by—
(a) the company, and
(b) every officer of the company who is in default.

(4) A person guilty of an offence under subsection (3) is liable on summary conviction to a fine not exceeding level 5 on the standard scale and, for continued contravention, a daily default fine not exceeding one-tenth of level 5 on the standard scale.

1094 Administrative removal of material from the register

(1) The registrar may remove from the register anything that there was power, but no duty, to include.

(2) This power is exercisable, in particular, so as to remove—

(a) unnecessary material within the meaning of section 1074, and

(b) material derived from a document that has been replaced under—

section 1076 (replacement of document not meeting requirements for proper delivery), or

section 1093 (notice to remedy inconsistency on the register).

(3) This section does not authorise the removal from the register of—

(a) anything whose registration has had legal consequences in relation to the company as regards—

(i) its formation,

(ii) a change of name,

(iii) its re-registration,

(iv) its becoming or ceasing to be a community interest company,

(v) a reduction of capital,

(vi) a change of registered office,

(vii) the registration of a charge, or

(viii) its dissolution;

(b) an address that is a person's registered address for the purposes of section 1140 (service of documents on directors, secretaries and others).

(4) On or before removing any material under this section (otherwise than at the request of the company) the registrar must give notice—

(a) to the person by whom the material was delivered (if the identity, and name and address of that person are known), or

(b) to the company to which the material relates (if notice cannot be given under paragraph (a) and the identity of that company is known).

(5) The notice must—

(a) state what material the registrar proposes to remove, or has removed, and on what grounds, and

(b) state the date on which it is issued.

1095 Rectification of register on application to registrar

(1) The Secretary of State may make provision by regulations requiring the registrar, on application, to remove from the register material of a description specified in the regulations that—

(a) derives from anything invalid or ineffective or that was done without the authority of the company, or

(b) is factually inaccurate, or is derived from something that is factually inaccurate or forged.

(2) The regulations may make provision as to—

(a) who may make an application,

(b) the information to be included in and documents to accompany an application,

(c) the notice to be given of an application and of its outcome,

(d) a period in which objections to an application may be made, and

(e) how an application is to be determined.

(3) An application must—

(a) specify what is to be removed from the register and indicate where on the register it is, and

(b) be accompanied by a statement that the material specified in the application complies with this section and the regulations.

(4) If no objections are made to the application, the registrar may accept the statement as sufficient evidence that the material specified in the application should be removed from the register.

(5) Where anything is removed from the register under this section the registration of which had legal consequences as mentioned in section 1094(3), any person appearing to the court to have a sufficient interest may apply to the court for such consequential orders as appear just with respect to the legal effect (if any) to be accorded to the material by virtue of its having appeared on the register.

(6) Regulations under this section are subject to affirmative resolution procedure.

1096 Rectification of the register under court order

(1) The registrar shall remove from the register any material—

(a) that derives from anything that the court has declared to be invalid or ineffective, or to have been done without the authority of the company, or

(b) that a court declares to be factually inaccurate, or to be derived from something that is factually inaccurate, or forged,

and that the court directs should be removed from the register.

(2) The court order must specify what is to be removed from the register and indicate where on the register it is.

(3) The court must not make an order for the removal from the register of anything the registration of which had legal consequences as mentioned in section 1094(3) unless satisfied—

(a) that the presence of the material on the register has caused, or may cause, damage to the company, and

(b) that the company's interest in removing the material outweighs any interest of other persons in the material continuing to appear on the register.

(4) Where in such a case the court does make an order for removal, it may make such consequential orders as appear just with respect to the legal effect (if any) to be accorded to the material by virtue of its having appeared on the register.

(5) A copy of the court's order must be sent to the registrar for registration.

(6) This section does not apply where the court has other, specific, powers to deal with the matter, for example under—

(a) the provisions of Part 15 relating to the revision of defective accounts and reports, or

(b) section 859M (rectification of register).

1097 Powers of court on ordering removal of material from the register

(1) Where the court makes an order for the removal of anything from the register under section 1096 (rectification of the register), it may give directions under this section.

(2) It may direct that any note on the register that is related to the material that is the subject of the court's order shall be removed from the register.

(3) It may direct that its order shall not be available for public inspection as part of the register.

(4) It may direct—

(a) that no note shall be made on the register as a result of its order, or

(b) that any such note shall be restricted to such matters as may be specified by the court.

(5) The court shall not give any direction under this section unless it is satisfied—

(a) that—

(i) the presence on the register of the note or, as the case may be, of an unrestricted note, or

(ii) the availability for public inspection of the court's order,

may cause damage to the company, and

(b) that the company's interest in non-disclosure outweighs any interest of other persons in disclosure.

1098 Public notice of removal of certain material from the register

(1) The registrar must cause to be published—

(a) in the Gazette, or

(b) in accordance with section 1116 (alternative means of giving public notice),

notice of the removal from the register of any document subject to the Directive disclosure requirements (see section 1078) or of any material derived from such a document.

(2) The notice must state the name and registered number of the company, the description of document and the date of receipt.

The registrar's index of company names

1099 The registrar's index of company names

(1) The registrar of companies must keep an index of the names of the companies and other bodies to which this section applies.

This is "the registrar's index of company names".

(2) This section applies to—

(a) UK-registered companies;

(b) any body to which any provision of the Companies Acts applies by virtue of regulations under section 1043 (unregistered companies); and

(c) overseas companies that have registered particulars with the registrar under section 1046, other than companies that appear to the registrar not to be required to do so.

(3) This section also applies to—

(a) limited partnerships registered in the United Kingdom;

(b) limited liability partnerships incorporated in the United Kingdom;

(c) European Economic Interest Groupings registered in the United Kingdom;

(d) open-ended investment companies authorised in the United Kingdom;

(e) societies registered under the *Industrial and Provident Societies Act 1965* or the Industrial and Provident Societies Act (Northern Ireland) 1969.

(4) The Secretary of State may by order amend subsection (3)—

(a) by the addition of any description of body;

(b) by the deletion of any description of body.

(5) Any such order is subject to negative resolution procedure.

Note. The words "Industrial and Provident Societies Act 1965" in subsection (3)(e) are substituted by the words "Co-operative and Community Benefit Societies and Credit Unions Act 1965" by the Co-operative and Community Benefit Societies and Credit Unions Act 2010, s. 2, as from a day to be appointed.

1100 Right to inspect index

Any person may inspect the registrar's index of company names.

1101 Power to amend enactments relating to bodies other than companies

(1) The Secretary of State may by regulations amend the enactments relating to any description of body for the time being within section 1099(3) (bodies other than companies whose names are to be entered in the registrar's index), so as to—

(a) require the registrar to be provided with information as to the names of bodies registered, incorporated, authorised or otherwise regulated under those enactments, and

(b) make provision in relation to such bodies corresponding to that made by—

section 66 (company name not to be the same as another in the index), and

sections 67 and 68 (power to direct change of company name in case of similarity to existing name).

(2) Regulations under this section are subject to affirmative resolution procedure.

Language requirements: translation

1102 Application of language requirements

(1) The provisions listed below apply to all documents required to be delivered to the registrar under any provision of—

(a) the Companies Acts, or

(b) the Insolvency Act 1986 or the Insolvency (Northern Ireland) Order 1989.

(2) The Secretary of State may make provision by regulations applying all or any of the listed provisions, with or without modifications, in relation to documents delivered to the registrar under any other enactment.

(3) The provisions are—
section 1103 (documents to be drawn up and delivered in English),
section 1104 (documents relating to Welsh companies),
section 1105 (documents that may be drawn up and delivered in other languages),
section 1107 (certified translations).

(4) Regulations under this section are subject to negative resolution procedure.

1103 Documents to be drawn up and delivered in English

(1) The general rule is that all documents required to be delivered to the registrar must be drawn up and delivered in English.

(2) This is subject to—
section 1104 (documents relating to Welsh companies) and
section 1105 (documents that may be drawn up and delivered in other languages).

1104 Documents relating to Welsh companies

(1) Documents relating to a Welsh company may be drawn up and delivered to the registrar in Welsh.

(2) On delivery to the registrar any such document must be accompanied by a certified translation into English, unless it is—

(a) of a description excepted from that requirement by regulations made by the Secretary of State, or

(b) in a form prescribed in Welsh (or partly in Welsh and partly in English) by virtue of section 26 of the Welsh Language Act 1993.

(3) Where a document is properly delivered to the registrar in Welsh without a certified translation into English, the registrar must obtain such a translation if the document is to be available for public inspection.

The translation is treated as if delivered to the registrar in accordance with the same provision as the original.

(4) A Welsh company may deliver to the registrar a certified translation into Welsh of any document in English that relates to the company and is or has been delivered to the registrar.

(5) Section 1105 (which requires certified translations into English of documents delivered to the registrar in another language) does not apply to a document relating to a Welsh company that is drawn up and delivered in Welsh.

1105 Documents that may be drawn up and delivered in other languages

(1) Documents to which this section applies may be drawn up and delivered to the registrar in a language other than English, but when delivered to the registrar they must be accompanied by a certified translation into English.

(2) This section applies to—

(a) agreements required to be forwarded to the registrar under Chapter 3 of Part 3 (agreements affecting the company's constitution);

(b) documents required to be delivered under section 400(2)(e) or section 401(2)(f) (company included in accounts of larger group: required to deliver copy of group accounts);

(c) certified copies delivered under Part 25 (company charges);

(d) documents of any other description specified in regulations made by the Secretary of State.

(3) Regulations under this section are subject to negative resolution procedure.

1106 Voluntary filing of translations

(1) A company may deliver to the registrar one or more certified translations of any document relating to the company that is or has been delivered to the registrar.

(2) The Secretary of State may by regulations specify—

(a) the languages, and

(b) the descriptions of document,

in relation to which this facility is available.

(3) The regulations must provide that it is available as from 1st January 2007—

(a) in relation to all the official languages of the European Union, and

(b) in relation to all documents subject to the Directive disclosure requirements (see section 1078).

(4) The power of the registrar to impose requirements as to the form and manner of delivery includes power to impose requirements as to the identification of the original document and the delivery of the translation in a form and manner enabling it to be associated with the original.

(5) Regulations under this section are subject to negative resolution procedure.

(6) This section does not apply where the original document was delivered to the registrar before this section came into force.

1107 Certified translations

(1) In this Part a "certified translation" means a translation certified to be a correct translation.

(2) In the case of any discrepancy between the original language version of a document and a certified translation—

(a) the company may not rely on the translation as against a third party, but

(b) a third party may rely on the translation unless the company shows that the third party had knowledge of the original.

(3) A "third party" means a person other than the company or the registrar.

Language requirements: transliteration

1108 Transliteration of names and addresses: permitted characters

(1) Names and addresses in a document delivered to the registrar must contain only letters, characters and symbols (including accents and other diacritical marks) that are permitted.

(2) The Secretary of State may make provision by regulations—

(a) as to the letters, characters and symbols (including accents and other diacritical marks) that are permitted, and

(b) permitting or requiring the delivery of documents in which names and addresses have not been transliterated into a permitted form.

(3) Regulations under this section are subject to negative resolution procedure.

1109 Transliteration of names and addresses: voluntary transliteration into Roman characters

(1) Where a name or address is or has been delivered to the registrar in a permitted form using other than Roman characters, the company (or other body) to which the document relates may deliver to the registrar a transliteration into Roman characters.

(2) The power of the registrar to impose requirements as to the form and manner of delivery includes power to impose requirements as to the identification of the original document and the delivery of the transliteration in a form and manner enabling it to be associated with the original.

1110 Transliteration of names and addresses: certification

(1) The Secretary of State may make provision by regulations requiring the certification of transliterations and prescribing the form of certification.

(2) Different provision may be made for compulsory and voluntary transliterations.

(3) Regulations under this section are subject to negative resolution procedure.

Supplementary provisions

1111 Registrar's requirements as to certification or verification

(1) Where a document required or authorised to be delivered to the registrar under any enactment is required—

(a) to be certified as an accurate translation or transliteration, or

(b) to be certified as a correct copy or verified,

the registrar may impose requirements as to the person, or description of person, by whom the certificate or verification is to be given.

(2) The power conferred by section 1068 (registrar's requirements as to form, authentication and manner of delivery) is exercisable in relation to the certificate or verification as if it were a separate document.

(3) Requirements imposed under this section must not be inconsistent with requirements imposed by any enactment with respect to the certification or verification of the document concerned.

1112 General false statement offence

(1) It is an offence for a person knowingly or recklessly—

(a) to deliver or cause to be delivered to the registrar, for any purpose of the Companies Acts, a document, or

(b) to make to the registrar, for any such purpose, a statement,

that is misleading, false or deceptive in a material particular.

(2) A person guilty of an offence under this section is liable—

(a) on conviction on indictment, to imprisonment for a term not exceeding two years or a fine (or both);

(b) on summary conviction—

(i) in England and Wales, to imprisonment for a term not exceeding twelve months or to a fine not exceeding the statutory maximum (or both);

(ii) in Scotland or Northern Ireland, to imprisonment for a term not exceeding six months, or to a fine not exceeding the statutory maximum (or both).

1113 Enforcement of company's filing obligations

(1) This section applies where a company has made default in complying with any obligation under the Companies Acts—

(a) to deliver a document to the registrar, or

(b) to give notice to the registrar of any matter.

(2) The registrar, or any member or creditor of the company, may give notice to the company requiring it to comply with the obligation.

(3) If the company fails to make good the default within 14 days after service of the notice, the registrar,

or any member or creditor of the company, may apply to the court for an order directing the company, and any specified officer of it, to make good the default within a specified time.

(4) The court's order may provide that all costs (in Scotland, expenses) of or incidental to the application are to be borne by the company or by any officers of it responsible for the default.

(5) This section does not affect the operation of any enactment making it an offence, or imposing a civil penalty, for the default.

1114 Application of provisions about documents and delivery

(1) In this Part—

(a) "document" means information recorded in any form, and

(b) references to delivering a document include forwarding, lodging, registering, sending, producing or submitting it or (in the case of a notice) giving it.

(2) Except as otherwise provided, this Part applies in relation to the supply to the registrar of information otherwise than in documentary form as it applies in relation to the delivery of a document.

1115 Supplementary provisions relating to electronic communications

(1) Registrar's rules may require a company (or other body) to give any necessary consents to the use of electronic means for communications by the registrar to the company (or other body) as a condition of making use of any facility to deliver material to the registrar by electronic means.

(2) A document that is required to be signed by the registrar or authenticated by the registrar's seal shall, if sent by electronic means, be authenticated in such manner as may be specified by registrar's rules.

1116 Alternative to publication in the Gazette

(1) Notices that would otherwise need to be published by the registrar in the Gazette may instead be published by such means as may from time to time be approved by the registrar in accordance with regulations made by the Secretary of State.

(2) The Secretary of State may make provision by regulations as to what alternative means may be approved.

(3) The regulations may, in particular—
- (a) require the use of electronic means;
- (b) require the same means to be used—
  - (i) for all notices or for all notices of specified descriptions, and
  - (ii) whether the company (or other body) to which the notice relates is registered in England and Wales, Scotland or Northern Ireland;
- (c) impose conditions as to the manner in which access to the notices is to be made available.

(4) Regulations under this section are subject to negative resolution procedure.

(5) Before starting to publish notices by means approved under this section the registrar must publish at least one notice to that effect in the Gazette.

(6) Nothing in this section prevents the registrar from giving public notice both in the Gazette and by means approved under this section.
In that case, the requirement of public notice is met when notice is first given by either means.

1117 Registrar's rules

(1) Where any provision of this Part enables the registrar to make provision, or impose requirements, as to any matter, the registrar may make such provision or impose such requirements by means of rules under this section.
This is without prejudice to the making of such provision or the imposing of such requirements by other means.

(2) Registrar's rules—
- (a) may make different provision for different cases, and
- (b) may allow the registrar to disapply or modify any of the rules.

(3) The registrar must—
- (a) publicise the rules in a manner appropriate to bring them to the notice of persons affected by them, and
- (b) make copies of the rules available to the public (in hard copy or electronic form).

1118 Payments into the Consolidated Fund

Nothing in the Companies Acts or any other enactment as to the payment of receipts into the Consolidated Fund shall be read as affecting the operation in relation to the registrar of section 3(1) of the Government Trading Funds Act 1973.

1119 Contracting out of registrar's functions

(1) Where by virtue of an order made under section 69 of the Deregulation and Contracting Out Act 1994 a person is authorised by the registrar to accept delivery of any class of documents that are under any enactment to be delivered to the registrar, the registrar may direct that documents of that class shall be delivered to a specified address of the authorised person.
Any such direction must be printed and made available to the public (with or without payment).

(2) A document of that class that is delivered to an address other than the specified address is treated as not having been delivered.

(3) Registrar's rules are not subordinate legislation for the purposes of section 71 of the Deregulation and Contracting Out Act 1994 (functions excluded from contracting out).

1120 . . .

PART 36
OFFENCES UNDER THE COMPANIES ACTS

Liability of officer in default

1121 Liability of officer in default

(1) This section has effect for the purposes of any provision of the Companies Acts to the effect that, in the event of contravention of an enactment in relation to a company, an offence is committed by every officer of the company who is in default.

(2) For this purpose "officer" includes—
- (a) any director, manager or secretary, and
- (b) any person who is to be treated as an officer of the company for the purposes of the provision in question.

(3) An officer is "in default" for the purposes of the provision if he authorises or permits, participates in, or fails to take all reasonable steps to prevent, the contravention.

1122 Liability of company as officer in default

(1) Where a company is an officer of another company, it does not commit an offence as an officer in default unless one of its officers is in default.

(2) Where any such offence is committed by a company the officer in question also commits the offence and is liable to be proceeded against and punished accordingly.

(3) In this section "officer" and "in default" have the meanings given by section 1121.

1123 Application to bodies other than companies

(1) Section 1121 (liability of officers in default) applies to a body other than a company as it applies to a company.

(2) As it applies in relation to a body corporate other than a company—
- (a) the reference to a director of the company shall be read as referring—
  - (i) where the body's affairs are managed by its members, to a member of the body,
  - (ii) in any other case, to any corresponding officer of the body, and
- (b) the reference to a manager or secretary of the company shall be read as referring to any manager, secretary or similar officer of the body.

(3) As it applies in relation to a partnership—
- (a) the reference to a director of the company shall be read as referring to a member of the partnership, and
- (b) the reference to a manager or secretary of the company shall be read as referring to any manager, secretary or similar officer of the partnership.

(4) As it applies in relation to an unincorporated body other than a partnership—
- (a) the reference to a director of the company shall be read as referring—
  - (i) where the body's affairs are managed by its members, to a member of the body,
  - (ii) in any other case, to a member of the governing body, and
- (b) the reference to a manager or secretary of the company shall be read as referring to any manager, secretary or similar officer of the body.

Offences under the Companies Act 1985

1124 Amendments of the Companies Act 1985

Schedule 3 contains amendments of the Companies Act 1985 relating to offences.

General provisions

1125 Meaning of "daily default fine"

(1) This section defines what is meant in the Companies Acts where it is provided that a person guilty of an offence is liable on summary conviction to a fine not exceeding a specified amount "and, for continued contravention, a daily default fine" not exceeding a specified amount.

(2) This means that the person is liable on a second or subsequent summary conviction of the offence to a fine not exceeding the latter amount for each day on which the contravention is continued (instead of being liable to a fine not exceeding the former amount).

1126 Consents required for certain prosecutions

(1) This section applies to proceedings for an offence under any of the following provisions—
section 458, 460 or 949 of this Act (offences of unauthorised disclosure of information);
section 953 of this Act (failure to comply with rules about takeover bid documents);
section 448, 449, 450, 451 or 453A of the Companies Act 1985 (offences in connection with company investigations);
section 798 of this Act or section 455 of the Companies Act 1985 (offence of attempting to evade restrictions on shares).

(2) No such proceedings are to be brought in England and Wales except by or with the consent of—
(a) in the case of an offence under—
(i) section 458, 460 or 949 of this Act,
(ii) section 953 of this Act, or
(iii) section 448, 449, 450, 451 or 453A of the Companies Act 1985, the Secretary of State or the Director of Public Prosecutions;
(b) in the case of an offence under section 798 of this Act or section 455 of the Companies Act 1985, the Secretary of State.

(3) No such proceedings are to be brought in Northern Ireland except by or with the consent of—
(a) in the case of an offence under—
(i) section 458, 460 or 949 of this Act,
(ii) section 953 of this Act, or
(iii) section 448, 449, 450, 451 or 453A of the Companies Act 1985,
the Secretary of State or the Director of Public Prosecutions for Northern Ireland;
(b) in the case of an offence under section 798 of this Act or section 455 of the Companies Act 1985, the Secretary of State.

1127 Summary proceedings: venue

(1) Summary proceedings for any offence under the Companies Acts may be taken—
(a) against a body corporate, at any place at which the body has a place of business, and
(b) against any other person, at any place at which he is for the time being.

(2) This is without prejudice to any jurisdiction exercisable apart from this section.

1128 Summary proceedings: time limit for proceedings

(1) An information relating to an offence under the Companies Acts that is triable by a magistrates' court in England and Wales may be so tried if it is laid—
(a) at any time within three years after the commission of the offence, and
(b) within twelve months after the date on which evidence sufficient in the opinion of the Director of Public Prosecutions or the Secretary of State (as the case may be) to justify the proceedings comes to his knowledge.

(2) Summary proceedings in Scotland for an offence under the Companies Acts—
(a) must not be commenced after the expiration of three years from the commission of the offence;
(b) subject to that, may be commenced at any time—
(i) within twelve months after the date on which evidence sufficient in the Lord Advocate's opinion to justify the proceedings came to his knowledge, or
(ii) where such evidence was reported to him by the Secretary of State, within twelve months after the date on which it came to the knowledge of the latter.

Section 136(3) of the Criminal Procedure (Scotland) Act 1995 (date when proceedings deemed to be commenced) applies for the purposes of this subsection as for the purposes of that section.

(3) A magistrates' court in Northern Ireland has jurisdiction to hear and determine a complaint charging the commission of a summary offence under the Companies Acts provided that the complaint is made—
(a) within three years from the time when the offence was committed, and
(b) within twelve months from the date on which evidence sufficient in the opinion of the Director of Public Prosecutions for Northern Ireland or the Secretary of State (as the case may be) to justify the proceedings comes to his knowledge.

(4) For the purposes of this section a certificate of the Director of Public Prosecutions, the Lord Advocate, the Director of Public Prosecutions for Northern Ireland or the Secretary of State (as the case may be) as to the date on which such evidence as is referred to above came to his notice is conclusive evidence.

1129 Legal professional privilege

In proceedings against a person for an offence under the Companies Acts, nothing in those Acts is to be taken to require any person to disclose any information that he is entitled to refuse to disclose on grounds of legal professional privilege (in Scotland, confidentiality of communications).

1130 Proceedings against unincorporated bodies

(1) Proceedings for an offence under the Companies Acts alleged to have been committed by an unincorporated body must be brought in the name of the body (and not in that of any of its members).

(2) For the purposes of such proceedings—
(a) any rules of court relating to the service of documents have effect as if the body were a body corporate, and
(b) the following provisions apply as they apply in relation to a body corporate—
(i) in England and Wales, section 33 of the Criminal Justice Act 1925 and Schedule 3 to the Magistrates' Courts Act 1980,
(ii) in Scotland, sections 70 and 143 of the Criminal Procedure (Scotland) Act 1995,
(iii) in Northern Ireland, section 18 of the Criminal Justice Act (Northern Ireland) 1945 and Article 166 of and Schedule 4 to the Magistrates' Courts (Northern Ireland) Order 1981.

(3) A fine imposed on an unincorporated body on its conviction of an offence under the Companies Acts must be paid out of the funds of the body.

1131 Imprisonment on summary conviction in England and Wales: transitory provision

(1) This section applies to any provision of the Companies Acts that provides that a person guilty of an offence is liable on summary conviction in England and Wales to imprisonment for a term not exceeding twelve months.

(2) In relation to an offence committed before the commencement of section 154(1) of the Criminal Justice Act 2003, for "twelve months" substitute "six months".

Production and inspection of documents

1132 Production and inspection of documents where offence suspected

(1) An application under this section may be made—
(a) in England and Wales, to a judge of the High Court by the Director of Public Prosecutions, the Secretary of State or a chief officer of police;
(b) in Scotland, to one of the Lords Commissioners of Justiciary by the Lord Advocate;
(c) in Northern Ireland, to the High Court by the Director of Public Prosecutions for Northern Ireland, the Department of Enterprise, Trade and Investment or a chief superintendent of the Police Service of Northern Ireland.

(2) If on an application under this section there is shown to be reasonable cause to believe—

(a) that any person has, while an officer of a company, committed an offence in connection with the management of the company's affairs, and

(b) that evidence of the commission of the offence is to be found in any documents in the possession or control of the company,

an order under this section may be made.

(3) The order may—

(a) authorise any person named in it to inspect the documents in question, or any of them, for the purpose of investigating and obtaining evidence of the offence, or

(b) require the secretary of the company, or such other officer of it as may be named in the order, to produce the documents (or any of them) to a person named in the order at a place so named.

(4) This section applies also in relation to documents in the possession or control of a person carrying on the business of banking, so far as they relate to the company's affairs, as it applies to documents in the possession or control of the company, except that no such order as is referred to in subsection (3) (b) may be made by virtue of this subsection.

(5) The decision under this section of a judge of the High Court, any of the Lords Commissioners of Justiciary or the High Court is not appealable.

(6) In this section "document" includes information recorded in any form.

Supplementary

1133 Transitional provision

The provisions of this Part except section 1132 do not apply to offences committed before the commencement of the relevant provision.

PART 37

COMPANIES: SUPPLEMENTARY PROVISIONS

Company records

1134 Meaning of "company records"

In this Part "company records" means—

(a) any register, index, accounting records, agreement, memorandum, minutes or other document required by the Companies Acts to be kept by a company, and

(b) any register kept by a company of its debenture holders.

1135 Form of company records

(1) Company records—

(a) may be kept in hard copy or electronic form, and

(b) may be arranged in such manner as the directors of the company think fit,

provided the information in question is adequately recorded for future reference.

(2) Where the records are kept in electronic form, they must be capable of being reproduced in hard copy form.

(3) If a company fails to comply with this section, an offence is committed by every officer of the company who is in default.

(4) A person guilty of an offence under this section is liable on summary conviction to a fine not exceeding level 3 on the standard scale and, for continued contravention, a daily default fine not exceeding one-tenth of level 3 on the standard scale.

(5) Any provision of an instrument made by a company before 12th February 1979 that requires a register of holders of the company's debentures to be kept in hard copy form is to be read as requiring it to be kept in hard copy or electronic form.

1136 Regulations about where certain company records to be kept available for inspection

(1) The Secretary of State may make provision by regulations specifying places other than a company's registered office at which company records required to be kept available for inspection under a relevant provision may be so kept in compliance with that provision.

(2) The "relevant provisions" are—
section 114 (register of members);
section 162 (register of directors);
section 228 (directors' service contracts);
section 237 (directors' indemnities);
section 275 (register of secretaries);
section 358 (records of resolutions etc);
section 702 (contracts relating to purchase of own shares);
section 720 (documents relating to redemption or purchase of own shares out of capital by private company);
section 743 (register of debenture holders);
section 805 (report to members of outcome of investigation by public company into interests in its shares);
section 809 (register of interests in shares disclosed to public company);
section 859Q (instruments creating charges).

(3) The regulations may specify a place by reference to the company's principal place of business, the part of the United Kingdom in which the company is registered, the place at which the company keeps any other records available for inspection or in any other way.

(4) The regulations may provide that a company does not comply with a relevant provision by keeping company records available for inspection at a place specified in the regulations unless conditions specified in the regulations are met.

(5) The regulations—
(a) need not specify a place in relation to each relevant provision;
(b) may specify more than one place in relation to a relevant provision.

(6) A requirement under a relevant provision to keep company records available for inspection is not complied with by keeping them available for inspection at a place specified in the regulations unless all the company's records subject to the requirement are kept there.

(7) Regulations under this section are subject to negative resolution procedure.

1137 Regulations about inspection of records and provision of copies

(1) The Secretary of State may make provision by regulations as to the obligations of a company that is required by any provision of the Companies Acts—
(a) to keep available for inspection any company records, or
(b) to provide copies of any company records.

(2) A company that fails to comply with the regulations is treated as having refused inspection or, as the case may be, having failed to provide a copy.

(3) The regulations may—
(a) make provision as to the time, duration and manner of inspection, including the circumstances in which and extent to which the copying of information is permitted in the course of inspection, and
(b) define what may be required of the company as regards the nature, extent and manner of extracting or presenting any information for the purposes of inspection or the provision of copies.

(4) Where there is power to charge a fee, the regulations may make provision as to the amount of the fee and the basis of its calculation.

(5) Nothing in any provision of this Act or in the regulations shall be read as preventing a company—
(a) from affording more extensive facilities than are required by the regulations, or
(b) where a fee may be charged, from charging a lesser fee than that prescribed or none at all.

(6) Regulations under this section are subject to negative resolution procedure.

1138 Duty to take precautions against falsification

(1) Where company records are kept otherwise than in bound books, adequate precautions must be taken—

(a) to guard against falsification, and

(b) to facilitate the discovery of falsification.

(2) If a company fails to comply with this section, an offence is committed by every officer of the company who is in default.

(3) A person guilty of an offence under this section is liable on summary conviction to a fine not exceeding level 3 on the standard scale and, for continued contravention, a daily default fine not exceeding one-tenth of level 3 on the standard scale.

(4) This section does not apply to the documents required to be kept under—

(a) section 228 (copy of director's service contract or memorandum of its terms); or

(b) section 237 (qualifying indemnity provision).

Service addresses

1139 Service of documents on company

(1) A document may be served on a company registered under this Act by leaving it at, or sending it by post to, the company's registered office.

(2) A document may be served on an overseas company whose particulars are registered under section 1046—

(a) by leaving it at, or sending it by post to, the registered address of any person resident in the United Kingdom who is authorised to accept service of documents on the company's behalf, or

(b) if there is no such person, or if any such person refuses service or service cannot for any other reason be effected, by leaving it at or sending by post to any place of business of the company in the United Kingdom.

(3) For the purposes of this section a person's "registered address" means any address for the time being shown as a current address in relation to that person in the part of the register available for public inspection.

(4) Where a company registered in Scotland or Northern Ireland carries on business in England and Wales, the process of any court in England and Wales may be served on the company by leaving it at, or sending it by post to, the company's principal place of business in England and Wales, addressed to the manager or other head officer in England and Wales of the company.

Where process is served on a company under this subsection, the person issuing out the process must send a copy of it by post to the company's registered office.

(5) Further provision as to service and other matters is made in the company communications provisions (see section 1143).

1140 Service of documents on directors, secretaries and others

(1) A document may be served on a person to whom this section applies by leaving it at, or sending it by post to, the person's registered address.

(2) This section applies to—

(a) a director or secretary of a company;

(b) in the case of an overseas company whose particulars are registered under section 1046, a person holding any such position as may be specified for the purposes of this section by regulations under that section;

(c) a person appointed in relation to a company as—

(i) a judicial factor (in Scotland),

(ii) an interim manager appointed under section 76 of the Charities Act 2011, or

(iii) a manager appointed under section 47 of the Companies (Audit, Investigations and Community Enterprise) Act 2004.

(3) This section applies whatever the purpose of the document in question.

It is not restricted to service for purposes arising out of or in connection with the appointment or position mentioned in subsection (2) or in connection with the company concerned.

(4) For the purposes of this section a person's "registered address" means any address for the time being shown as a current address in relation to that person in the part of the register available for public inspection.

(5) If notice of a change of that address is given to the registrar, a person may validly serve a document at the address previously registered until the end of the period of 14 days beginning with the date on which notice of the change is registered.

(6) Service may not be effected by virtue of this section at an address—

(a) if notice has been registered of the termination of the appointment in relation to which the address was registered and the address is not a registered address of the person concerned in relation to any other appointment;

(b) in the case of a person holding any such position as is mentioned in subsection (2)(b), if the overseas company has ceased to have any connection with the United Kingdom by virtue of which it is required to register particulars under section 1046.

(7) Further provision as to service and other matters is made in the company communications provisions (see section 1143).

(8) Nothing in this section shall be read as affecting any enactment or rule of law under which permission is required for service out of the jurisdiction.

1141 Service addresses

(1) In the Companies Acts a "service address", in relation to a person, means an address at which documents may be effectively served on that person.

(2) The Secretary of State may by regulations specify conditions with which a service address must comply.

(3) Regulations under this section are subject to negative resolution procedure.

1142 Requirement to give service address

Any obligation under the Companies Acts to give a person's address is, unless otherwise expressly provided, to give a service address for that person.

Sending or supplying documents or information

1143 The company communications provisions

(1) The provisions of sections 1144 to 1148 and Schedules 4 and 5 ("the company communications provisions") have effect for the purposes of any provision of the Companies Acts that authorises or requires documents or information to be sent or supplied by or to a company.

(2) The company communications provisions have effect subject to any requirements imposed, or contrary provision made, by or under any enactment.

(3) In particular, in their application in relation to documents or information to be sent or supplied to the registrar, they have effect subject to the provisions of Part 35.

(4) For the purposes of subsection (2), provision is not to be regarded as contrary to the company communications provisions by reason only of the fact that it expressly authorises a document or information to be sent or supplied in hard copy form, in electronic form or by means of a website.

1144 Sending or supplying documents or information

(1) Documents or information to be sent or supplied to a company must be sent or supplied in accordance with the provisions of Schedule 4.

(2) Documents or information to be sent or supplied by a company must be sent or supplied in accordance with the provisions of Schedule 5.

(3) The provisions referred to in subsection (2) apply (and those referred to in subsection (1) do not apply) in relation to documents or information that are to be sent or supplied by one company to another.

1145 Right to hard copy version

(1) Where a member of a company or a holder of a company's debentures has received a document or information from the company otherwise than in hard copy form, he is entitled to require the company to send him a version of the document or information in hard copy form.

(2) The company must send the document or information in hard copy form within 21 days of receipt of the request from the member or debenture holder.

(3) The company may not make a charge for providing the document or information in that form.

(4) If a company fails to comply with this section, an offence is committed by the company and every officer of it who is in default.

(5) A person guilty of an offence under this section is liable on summary conviction to a fine not exceeding level 3 on the standard scale and, for continued contravention, a daily default fine not exceeding one-tenth of level 3 on the standard scale.

1146 Requirement of authentication

(1) This section applies in relation to the authentication of a document or information sent or supplied by a person to a company.

(2) A document or information sent or supplied in hard copy form is sufficiently authenticated if it is signed by the person sending or supplying it.

(3) A document or information sent or supplied in electronic form is sufficiently authenticated—

(a) if the identity of the sender is confirmed in a manner specified by the company, or

(b) where no such manner has been specified by the company, if the communication contains or is accompanied by a statement of the identity of the sender and the company has no reason to doubt the truth of that statement.

(4) Where a document or information is sent or supplied by one person on behalf of another, nothing in this section affects any provision of the company's articles under which the company may require reasonable evidence of the authority of the former to act on behalf of the latter.

1147 Deemed delivery of documents and information

(1) This section applies in relation to documents and information sent or supplied by a company.

(2) Where—

(a) the document or information is sent by post (whether in hard copy or electronic form) to an address in the United Kingdom, and

(b) the company is able to show that it was properly addressed, prepaid and posted,

it is deemed to have been received by the intended recipient 48 hours after it was posted.

(3) Where—

(a) the document or information is sent or supplied by electronic means, and

(b) the company is able to show that it was properly addressed,

it is deemed to have been received by the intended recipient 48 hours after it was sent.

(4) Where the document or information is sent or supplied by means of a website, it is deemed to have been received by the intended recipient—

(a) when the material was first made available on the website, or

(b) if later, when the recipient received (or is deemed to have received) notice of the fact that the material was available on the website.

(5) In calculating a period of hours for the purposes of this section, no account shall be taken of any part of a day that is not a working day.

(6) This section has effect subject to—

(a) in its application to documents or information sent or supplied by a company to its members, any contrary provision of the company's articles;

(b) in its application to documents or information sent or supplied by a company to its debentures holders, any contrary provision in the instrument constituting the debentures;

(c) in its application to documents or information sent or supplied by a company to a person otherwise than in his capacity as a member or debenture holder, any contrary provision in an agreement between the company and that person.

1148 Interpretation of company communications provisions

(1) In the company communications provisions—
"address" includes a number or address used for the purposes of sending or receiving documents or information by electronic means;
"company" includes any body corporate;
"document" includes summons, notice, order or other legal process and registers.

(2) References in the company communications provisions to provisions of the Companies Acts authorising or requiring a document or information to be sent or supplied include all such provisions, whatever expression is used, and references to documents or information being sent or supplied shall be construed accordingly.

(3) References in the company communications provisions to documents or information being sent or supplied by or to a company include references to documents or information being sent or supplied by or to the directors of a company acting on behalf of the company.

Requirements as to independent valuation

1149 Application of valuation requirements

The provisions of sections 1150 to 1153 apply to the valuation and report required by—
section 93 (re-registration as public company: recent allotment of shares for non-cash consideration);
section 593 (allotment of shares of public company in consideration of non-cash asset);
section 599 (transfer of non-cash asset to public company).

1150 Valuation by qualified independent person

(1) The valuation and report must be made by a person ("the valuer") who—
(a) is eligible for appointment as a statutory auditor (see section 1212), and
(b) meets the independence requirement in section 1151.

(2) However, where it appears to the valuer to be reasonable for the valuation of the consideration, or part of it, to be made by (or for him to accept a valuation made by) another person who—
(a) appears to him to have the requisite knowledge and experience to value the consideration or that part of it, and
(b) is not an officer or employee of—
(i) the company, or
(ii) any other body corporate that is that company's subsidiary or holding company or a subsidiary of that company's holding company,
or a partner of or employed by any such officer or employee,
he may arrange for or accept such a valuation, together with a report which will enable him to make his own report under this section.

(3) The references in subsection (2) (b) to an officer or employee do not include an auditor.

(4) Where the consideration or part of it is valued by a person other than the valuer himself, the latter's report must state that fact and shall also—
(a) state the former's name and what knowledge and experience he has to carry out the valuation, and
(b) describe so much of the consideration as was valued by the other person, and the method used to value it, and specify the date of that valuation.

1151 The independence requirement

(1) A person meets the independence requirement for the purposes of section 1150 only if—
(a) he is not—
(i) an officer or employee of the company, or
(ii) a partner or employee of such a person, or a partnership of which such a person is a partner;
(b) he is not—
(i) an officer or employee of an associated undertaking of the company, or

(ii) a partner or employee of such a person, or a partnership of which such a person is a partner; and

(c) there does not exist between—

(i) the person or an associate of his, and

(ii) the company or an associated undertaking of the company, a connection of any such description as may be specified by regulations made by the Secretary of State.

(2) An auditor of the company is not regarded as an officer or employee of the company for this purpose.

(3) In this section—

"associated undertaking" means—

(a) a parent undertaking or subsidiary undertaking of the company, or

(b) a subsidiary undertaking of a parent undertaking of the company; and

"associate" has the meaning given by section 1152.

(4) Regulations under this section are subject to negative resolution procedure.

1152 Meaning of "associate"

(1) This section defines "associate" for the purposes of section 1151 (valuation: independence requirement).

(2) In relation to an individual, "associate" means—

(a) that individual's spouse or civil partner or minor child or step-child,

(b) any body corporate of which that individual is a director, and

(c) any employee or partner of that individual.

(3) In relation to a body corporate, "associate" means—

(a) any body corporate of which that body is a director,

(b) any body corporate in the same group as that body, and

(c) any employee or partner of that body or of any body corporate in the same group.

(4) In relation to a partnership that is a legal person under the law by which it is governed, "associate" means—

(a) any body corporate of which that partnership is a director,

(b) any employee of or partner in that partnership, and

(c) any person who is an associate of a partner in that partnership.

(5) In relation to a partnership that is not a legal person under the law by which it is governed, "associate" means any person who is an associate of any of the partners.

(6) In this section, in relation to a limited liability partnership, for "director" read "member".

1153 Valuer entitled to full disclosure

(1) A person carrying out a valuation or making a report with respect to any consideration proposed to be accepted or given by a company, is entitled to require from the officers of the company such information and explanation as he thinks necessary to enable him to—

(a) carry out the valuation or make the report, and

(b) provide any note required by section 596(3) or 600(3) (note required where valuation carried out by another person).

(2) A person who knowingly or recklessly makes a statement to which this subsection applies that is misleading, false or deceptive in a material particular commits an offence.

(3) Subsection (2) applies to a statement—

(a) made (whether orally or in writing) to a person carrying out a valuation or making a report, and

(b) conveying or purporting to convey any information or explanation which that person requires, or is entitled to require, under subsection (1).

(4) A person guilty of an offence under subsection (2) is liable—

(a) on conviction on indictment, to imprisonment for a term not exceeding two years or a fine (or both);

(b) on summary conviction—

(i) in England and Wales, to imprisonment for a term not exceeding twelve months or to a fine not exceeding the statutory maximum (or both);

(ii) in Scotland or Northern Ireland, to imprisonment for a term not exceeding six months, or to a fine not exceeding the statutory maximum (or both).

Notice of appointment of certain officers

1154 Duty to notify registrar of certain appointments etc

(1) Notice must be given to the registrar of the appointment in relation to a company of—

(a) a judicial factor (in Scotland),

(b) an interim manager appointed under section 76 of the Charities Act 2011, or

(c) a manager appointed under section 47 of the Companies (Audit, Investigations and Community Enterprise) Act 2004.

(2) The notice must be given—

(a) in the case of appointment of a judicial factor, by the judicial factor;

(b) in the case of appointment of an interim manager under section 76 of the Charities Act 2011, by the Charity Commission;

(c) in the case of appointment of a manager under section 47 of the Companies (Audit, Investigations and Community Enterprise) Act 2004, by the Regulator of Community Interest Companies.

(3) The notice must specify an address at which service of documents (including legal process) may be effected on the person appointed.

Notice of a change in the address for service may be given to the registrar by the person appointed.

(4) Where notice has been given under this section of the appointment of a person, notice must also be given to the registrar of the termination of the appointment. This notice must be given by the person specified in subsection (2).

1155 Offence of failure to give notice

(1) If a judicial factor fails to give notice of his appointment in accordance with section 1154 within the period of 14 days after the appointment he commits an offence.

(2) A person guilty of an offence under this section is liable on summary conviction to a fine not exceeding level 5 on the standard scale and, for continued contravention, a daily default fine not exceeding one-tenth of level 5 on the standard scale.

Courts and legal proceedings

1156 Meaning of "the court"

(1) Except as otherwise provided, in the Companies Acts "the court" means—

(a) in England and Wales, the High Court or (subject to subsection (3)) a county court;

(b) in Scotland, the Court of Session or the sheriff court;

(c) in Northern Ireland, the High Court.

(2) The provisions of the Companies Acts conferring jurisdiction on "the court" as defined above have effect subject to any enactment or rule of law relating to the allocation of jurisdiction or distribution of business between courts in any part of the United Kingdom.

(3) The Lord Chancellor may, with the concurrence of the Lord Chief Justice, by order—

(a) exclude a county court from having jurisdiction under the Companies Acts, and

(b) for the purposes of that jurisdiction attach that court's district, or any part of it, to another county court.

(4) The Lord Chief Justice may nominate a judicial office holder (as defined in section 109(4) of the Constitutional Reform Act 2005) to exercise his functions under subsection (3).

1157 Power of court to grant relief in certain cases

(1) If in proceedings for negligence, default, breach of duty or breach of trust against—

(a) an officer of a company, or

(b) a person employed by a company as auditor (whether he is or is not an officer of the company),

it appears to the court hearing the case that the officer or person is or may be liable but that he acted honestly and reasonably, and that having regard to all the circumstances of the case (including those connected with his appointment) he ought fairly to be excused, the court may relieve him, either wholly or in part, from his liability on such terms as it thinks fit.

(2) If any such officer or person has reason to apprehend that a claim will or might be made against him in respect of negligence, default, breach of duty or breach of trust—

(a) he may apply to the court for relief, and

(b) the court has the same power to relieve him as it would have had if it had been a court before which proceedings against him for negligence, default, breach of duty or breach of trust had been brought.

(3) Where a case to which subsection (1) applies is being tried by a judge with a jury, the judge, after hearing the evidence, may, if he is satisfied that the defendant (in Scotland, the defender) ought in pursuance of that subsection to be relieved either in whole or in part from the liability sought to be enforced against him, withdraw the case from the jury and forthwith direct judgment to be entered for the defendant (in Scotland, grant decree of absolvitor) on such terms as to costs (in Scotland, expenses) or otherwise as the judge may think proper.

PART 38
COMPANIES: INTERPRETATION

Meaning of "UK-registered company"

1158 Meaning of "UK-registered company"

In the Companies Acts "UK-registered company" means a company registered under this Act.

The expression does not include an overseas company that has registered particulars under section 1046.

Meaning of "subsidiary" and related expressions

1159 Meaning of "subsidiary" etc

(1) A company is a "subsidiary" of another company, its "holding company", if that other company—

(a) holds a majority of the voting rights in it, or

(b) is a member of it and has the right to appoint or remove a majority of its board of directors, or

(c) is a member of it and controls alone, pursuant to an agreement with other members, a majority of the voting rights in it,

or if it is a subsidiary of a company that is itself a subsidiary of that other company.

(2) A company is a "wholly-owned subsidiary" of another company if it has no members except that other and that other's wholly-owned subsidiaries or persons acting on behalf of that other or its wholly-owned subsidiaries.

(3) Schedule 6 contains provisions explaining expressions used in this section and otherwise supplementing this section.

(4) In this section and that Schedule "company" includes any body corporate.

1160 Meaning of "subsidiary" etc: power to amend

(1) The Secretary of State may by regulations amend the provisions of section 1159 (meaning of "subsidiary" etc) and Schedule 6 (meaning of "subsidiary" etc: supplementary provisions) so as to alter the meaning of the expressions "subsidiary", "holding company" or "wholly-owned subsidiary".

(2) Regulations under this section are subject to negative resolution procedure.

(3) Any amendment made by regulations under this section does not apply for the purposes of enactments outside the Companies Acts unless the regulations so provide.

(4) So much of section 23(3) of the Interpretation Act 1978 as applies section 17(2)(a) of that Act (effect of repeal and re-enactment) to deeds, instruments and documents other than enactments does not apply in relation to any repeal and re-enactment effected by regulations under this section.

Meaning of "undertaking" and related expressions

1161 Meaning of "undertaking" and related expressions

(1) In the Companies Acts "undertaking" means—

(a) a body corporate or partnership, or

(b) an unincorporated association carrying on a trade or business, with or without a view to profit.

(2) In the Companies Acts references to shares—

(a) in relation to an undertaking with capital but no share capital, are to rights to share in the capital of the undertaking; and

(b) in relation to an undertaking without capital, are to interests—

(i) conferring any right to share in the profits or liability to contribute to the losses of the undertaking, or

(ii) giving rise to an obligation to contribute to the debts or expenses of the undertaking in the event of a winding up.

(3) Other expressions appropriate to companies shall be construed, in relation to an undertaking which is not a company, as references to the corresponding persons, officers, documents or organs, as the case may be, appropriate to undertakings of that description.

This is subject to provision in any specific context providing for the translation of such expressions.

(4) References in the Companies Acts to "fellow subsidiary undertakings" are to undertakings which are subsidiary undertakings of the same parent undertaking but are not parent undertakings or subsidiary undertakings of each other.

(5) In the Companies Acts "group undertaking", in relation to an undertaking, means an undertaking which is—

(a) a parent undertaking or subsidiary undertaking of that undertaking, or

(b) a subsidiary undertaking of any parent undertaking of that undertaking.

1162 Parent and subsidiary undertakings

(1) This section (together with Schedule 7) defines "parent undertaking" and "subsidiary undertaking" for the purposes of the Companies Acts.

(2) An undertaking is a parent undertaking in relation to another undertaking, a subsidiary undertaking, if—

(a) it holds a majority of the voting rights in the undertaking, or

(b) it is a member of the undertaking and has the right to appoint or remove a majority of its board of directors, or

(c) it has the right to exercise a dominant influence over the undertaking—

(i) by virtue of provisions contained in the undertaking's articles, or

(ii) by virtue of a control contract, or

(d) it is a member of the undertaking and controls alone, pursuant to an agreement with other shareholders or members, a majority of the voting rights in the undertaking.

(3) For the purposes of subsection (2) an undertaking shall be treated as a member of another undertaking—

(a) if any of its subsidiary undertakings is a member of that undertaking, or

(b) if any shares in that other undertaking are held by a person acting on behalf of the undertaking or any of its subsidiary undertakings.

(4) An undertaking is also a parent undertaking in relation to another undertaking, a subsidiary undertaking, if—

(a) it has the power to exercise, or actually exercises, dominant influence or control over it, or

(b) it and the subsidiary undertaking are managed on a unified basis.

(5) A parent undertaking shall be treated as the parent undertaking of undertakings in relation to which any of its subsidiary undertakings are, or are to be treated as, parent undertakings; and references to its subsidiary undertakings shall be construed accordingly.

(6) Schedule 7 contains provisions explaining expressions used in this section and otherwise supplementing this section.

(7) In this section and that Schedule references to shares, in relation to an undertaking, are to allotted shares.

Other definitions

1163 "Non-cash asset"

(1) In the Companies Acts "non-cash asset" means any property or interest in property, other than cash.

For this purpose "cash" includes foreign currency.

(2) A reference to the transfer or acquisition of a non-cash asset includes—

(a) the creation or extinction of an estate or interest in, or a right over, any property, and

(b) the discharge of a liability of any person, other than a liability for a liquidated sum.

1164 Meaning of "banking company" and "banking group"

(1) This section defines "banking company" and "banking group" for the purposes of the Companies Acts.

(2) "Banking company" means a person who has permission under Part 4A of the Financial Services and Markets Act 2000 to accept deposits, other than—

(a) a person who is not a company, and

(b) a person who has such permission only for the purpose of carrying on another regulated activity in accordance with permission under that Part.

(3) The definition in subsection (2) must be read with section 22 of that Act, any relevant order under that section and Schedule 2 to that Act.

(4) References to a banking group are to a group where the parent company is a banking company or where—

(a) the parent company's principal subsidiary undertakings are wholly or mainly credit institutions, and

(b) the parent company does not itself carry on any material business apart from the acquisition, management and disposal of interests in subsidiary undertakings.

"Group" here means a parent undertaking and its subsidiary undertakings.

(5) For the purposes of subsection (4)—

(a) a parent company's principal subsidiary undertakings are the subsidiary undertakings of the company whose results or financial position would principally affect the figures shown in the group accounts, and

(b) the management of interests in subsidiary undertakings includes the provision of services to such undertakings.

1165 Meaning of "insurance company" and related expressions

(1) This section defines "insurance company", "authorised insurance company", "insurance group" and "insurance market activity" for the purposes of the Companies Acts.

(2) An "authorised insurance company" means a person (whether incorporated or not) who has permission under Part 4A of the Financial Services and Markets Act 2000 to effect or carry out contracts of insurance.

(3) An "insurance company" means—

(a) an authorised insurance company, or

(b) any other person (whether incorporated or not) who—

(i) carries on insurance market activity, or

(ii) may effect or carry out contracts of insurance under which the benefits provided by that person are exclusively or primarily benefits in kind in the event of accident to or breakdown of a vehicle.

(4) Neither expression includes a friendly society within the meaning of the Friendly Societies Act 1992.

(5) References to an insurance group are to a group where the parent company is an insurance company or where—

(a) the parent company's principal subsidiary undertakings are wholly or mainly insurance companies, and

(b) the parent company does not itself carry on any material business apart from the acquisition, management and disposal of interests in subsidiary undertakings.

"Group" here means a parent undertaking and its subsidiary undertakings.

(6) For the purposes of subsection (5)—

(a) a parent company's principal subsidiary undertakings are the subsidiary undertakings of the company whose results or financial position would principally affect the figures shown in the group accounts, and

(b) the management of interests in subsidiary undertakings includes the provision of services to such undertakings.

(7) "Insurance market activity" has the meaning given in section 316(3) of the Financial Services and Markets Act 2000.

(8) References in this section to contracts of insurance and to the effecting or carrying out of such contracts must be read with section 22 of that Act, any relevant order under that section and Schedule 2 to that Act.

1166 "Employees' share scheme"

For the purposes of the Companies Acts an employees' share scheme is a scheme for encouraging or facilitating the holding of shares in or debentures of a company by or for the benefit of—

(a) the bona fide employees or former employees of—

(i) the company,

(ii) any subsidiary of the company, or

(iii) the company's holding company or any subsidiary of the company's holding company, or

(b) the spouses, civil partners, surviving spouses, surviving civil partners, or minor children or step-children of such employees or former employees.

1167 Meaning of "prescribed"

In the Companies Acts "prescribed" means prescribed (by order or by regulations) by the Secretary of State.

1168 Hard copy and electronic form and related expressions

(1) The following provisions apply for the purposes of the Companies Acts.

(2) A document or information is sent or supplied in hard copy form if it is sent or supplied in a paper copy or similar form capable of being read.

References to hard copy have a corresponding meaning.

(3) A document or information is sent or supplied in electronic form if it is sent or supplied—

(a) by electronic means (for example, by e-mail or fax), or

(b) by any other means while in an electronic form (for example, sending a disk by post).

References to electronic copy have a corresponding meaning.

(4) A document or information is sent or supplied by electronic means if it is—

(a) sent initially and received at its destination by means of electronic equipment for the processing (which expression includes digital compression) or storage of data, and

(b) entirely transmitted, conveyed and received by wire, by radio, by optical means or by other electromagnetic means.

References to electronic means have a corresponding meaning.

(5) A document or information authorised or required to be sent or supplied in electronic form must be sent or supplied in a form, and by a means, that the sender or supplier reasonably considers will enable the recipient—

(a) to read it, and

(b) to retain a copy of it.

(6) For the purposes of this section, a document or information can be read only if—

(a) it can be read with the naked eye, or

(b) to the extent that it consists of images (for example photographs, pictures, maps, plans or drawings), it can be seen with the naked eye.

(7) The provisions of this section apply whether the provision of the Companies Acts in question uses the words "sent" or "supplied" or uses other words (such as "deliver", "provide", "produce" or, in the case of a notice, "give") to refer to the sending or supplying of a document or information.

1169 Dormant companies

(1) For the purposes of the Companies Acts a company is "dormant" during any period in which it has no significant accounting transaction.

(2) A "significant accounting transaction" means a transaction that is required by section 386 to be entered in the company's accounting records.

(3) In determining whether or when a company is dormant, there shall be disregarded—

(a) any transaction arising from the taking of shares in the company by a subscriber to the memorandum as a result of an undertaking of his in connection with the formation of the company;

(b) any transaction consisting of the payment of—

(i) a fee to the registrar on a change of the company's name,

(ii) a fee to the registrar on the re-registration of the company,

(iii) a penalty under section 453 (penalty for failure to file accounts), or

(iv) a fee to the registrar for the registration of an annual return.

(4) Any reference in the Companies Acts to a body corporate other than a company being dormant has a corresponding meaning.

1170 Meaning of "EEA State" and related expressions

In the Companies Acts—

"EEA State" has the meaning given by Schedule 1 to the Interpretation Act 1978;

"EEA company" and "EEA undertaking" mean a company or undertaking governed by the law of an EEA State.

1170A Receiver or manager and certain related references

(1) Any reference in the Companies Acts to a receiver or manager of the property of a company, or to a receiver of it, includes a receiver or manager or (as the case may be) a receiver of part only of that property and a receiver only of the income arising from the property or from part of it.

(2) Any reference in the Companies Acts to the appointment of a receiver or manager under powers contained in an instrument includes an appointment made under powers that by virtue of an enactment are implied in and have effect as if contained in an instrument.

1170B Meaning of "contributory"

(1) In the Companies Acts "contributory" means every person liable to contribute to the assets of a company in the event of its being wound up.

(2) For the purposes of all proceedings for determining, and all proceedings prior to the final determination of, the persons who are to be deemed contributories, the expression includes any person alleged to be a contributory.

(3) The reference in subsection (1) to persons liable to contribute to the assets does not include a person so liable by virtue of a declaration by the court under—

(a) section 213 of the Insolvency Act 1986 or Article 177 of the Insolvency (Northern Ireland) Order 1989 (fraudulent trading), or

(b) section 214 of that Act or Article 178 of that Order (wrongful trading).

1171 The former Companies Acts

In the Companies Acts—

"the former Companies Acts" means—

(a) the Joint Stock Companies Acts, the Companies Act 1862, the Companies (Consolidation) Act 1908, the Companies Act 1929, the Companies Act (Northern Ireland) 1932, the Companies Acts 1948 to 1983, the Companies Act (Northern Ireland) 1960, the Companies (Northern Ireland) Order 1986 and the Companies Consolidation (Consequential Provisions) (Northern Ireland) Order 1986, and

(b) the provisions of the Companies Act 1985 and the Companies Consolidation (Consequential Provisions) Act 1985 that are no longer in force;

"the Joint Stock Companies Acts" means the Joint Stock Companies Act 1856, the Joint Stock Companies Acts 1856, 1857, the Joint Stock Banking Companies Act 1857, and the Act to enable Joint Stock Banking Companies to be formed on the principle of limited liability, but does not include the Joint Stock Companies Act 1844.

General

1172 References to requirements of this Act

References in the company law provisions of this Act to the requirements of this Act include the requirements of regulations and orders made under it.

1173 Minor definitions: general

(1) In the Companies Acts—

"body corporate" and "corporation" include a body incorporated outside the United Kingdom, but do not include—

(a) a corporation sole, or

(b) a partnership that, whether or not a legal person, is not regarded as a body corporate under the law by which it is governed;

"credit institution" means a credit institution as defined in Article 4.1 of Directive 2006/48/EC of the European Parliament and of the Council relating to the taking up and pursuit of the business of credit institutions as last amended by Directive 2009/111/EC;

"financial institution" means a financial institution within the meaning of Article 1.1 of the Council Directive on the obligations of branches established in a Member State of credit and financial institutions having their head offices outside that Member State regarding the publication of annual accounting documents (the Bank Branches Directive, 89/ 117/ EEC);

"firm" means any entity, whether or not a legal person, that is not an individual and includes a body corporate, a corporation sole and a partnership or other unincorporated association;

"the Gazette" means—

(a) as respects companies registered in England and Wales, the London Gazette,

(b) as respects companies registered in Scotland, the Edinburgh Gazette, and

(c) as respects companies registered in Northern Ireland, the Belfast Gazette;

"hire-purchase agreement" has the same meaning as in the Consumer Credit Act 1974;

"officer", in relation to a body corporate, includes a director, manager or secretary;

"parent company" means a company that is a parent undertaking (see section 1162 and Schedule 7);

"regulated activity" has the meaning given in section 22 of the Financial Services and Markets Act 2000;

"regulated market" has the same meaning as in Directive 2004/39/EC of the European Parliament and of the Council on markets in financial instruments (see Article 4.1(14));

"working day", in relation to a company, means a day that is not a Saturday or Sunday, Christmas Day, Good Friday or any day that is a bank holiday under the Banking and Financial Dealings Act 1971 in the part of the United Kingdom where the company is registered.

(2) In relation to an EEA State that has not implemented Directive 2004/39/EC of the European Parliament and of the Council on markets in financial instruments, the following definition of "regulated market" has effect in place of that in subsection (1)—

"regulated market" has the same meaning as it has in Council Directive 93/22/ EEC on investment services in the securities field.

1174 Index of defined expressions

Schedule 8 contains an index of provisions defining or otherwise explaining expressions used in the Companies Acts.

PART 39
COMPANIES: MINOR AMENDMENTS

1175 Removal of special provisions about accounts and audit of charitable companies

(1) Part 7 of the Companies Act 1985 and Part 8 of the Companies (Northern Ireland) Order 1986 (accounts and audit) are amended in accordance with Schedule 9 to this Act so as to remove the special provisions about companies that are charities.

(2) In that Schedule—

Part 1 contains repeals and consequential amendments of provisions of the Companies Act 1985;

Part 2 contains repeals and consequential amendments of provisions of the Companies (Northern Ireland) Order 1986.

1176 Power of Secretary of State to bring civil proceedings on company's behalf

(1) Section 438 of the Companies Act 1985 (power of Secretary of State to bring civil proceedings on company's behalf) shall cease to have effect.

(2) In section 439 of that Act (expenses of investigating company's affairs)—

(a) in subsection (2) omit ", or is ordered to pay the whole or any part of the costs of proceedings brought under section 438,";

(b) omit subsections (3) and (7) (which relate to section 438);

(c) in subsection (8)—

(i) for "subsections (2) and (3)" substitute "subsection (2)", and

(ii) omit "; and any such liability imposed by subsection (2) is (subject as mentioned above) a liability also to indemnify all persons against liability under subsection (3)".

(3) In section 453(1A) of that Act (investigation of overseas companies: provisions not applicable), omit paragraph (b) (which relates to section 438).

(4) Nothing in this section affects proceedings brought under section 438 before the commencement of this section.

1177 Repeal of certain provisions about company directors

The following provisions of Part 10 of the Companies Act 1985 shall cease to have effect—

section 311 (prohibition on tax-free payments to directors);

sections 323 and 327 (prohibition on directors dealing in share options); sections 324 to 326 and 328 to 329, and Parts 2 to 4 of Schedule 13 (register of directors' interests);

sections 343 and 344 (special procedure for disclosure by banks).

1178 Repeal of requirement that certain companies publish periodical statement

The following provisions shall cease to have effect—

section 720 of the Companies Act 1985 (certain companies to publish periodical statement), and

Schedule 23 to that Act (form of statement under section 720).

1179 Repeal of requirement that Secretary of State prepare annual report

Section 729 of the Companies Act 1985 (annual report to Parliament by Secretary of State on matters within the Companies Acts) shall cease to have effect.

1180 Repeal of certain provisions about company charges

Part 4 of the Companies Act 1989 (registration of company charges), which has not been brought into force, is repealed.

1181 Access to constitutional documents of RTE and RTM companies

(1) The Secretary of State may by order—

(a) amend Chapter 1 of Part 1 of the Leasehold Reform, Housing and Urban Development Act 1993 for the purpose of facilitating access to the provisions of the articles or any other constitutional document of RTE companies;

(b) amend Chapter 1 of Part 2 of the Commonhold and Leasehold Reform Act 2002 (leasehold reform) for the purpose of facilitating access to the provisions of the articles or any other constitutional document of RTM companies.

(2) References in subsection (1) to provisions of a company's articles or any other constitutional document include any provisions included in those documents by virtue of any enactment.

(3) An order under this section is subject to negative resolution procedure.

(4) In this section—

"RTE companies" has the same meaning as in Chapter 1 of Part 1 of the Leasehold Reform, Housing and Urban Development Act 1993;

"RTM companies" has the same meaning as in Chapter 1 of Part 2 of the Commonhold and Leasehold Reform Act 2002.

PART 40
COMPANY DIRECTORS: FOREIGN DISQUALIFICATION ETC

Introductory

1182 Persons subject to foreign restrictions

(1) This section defines what is meant by references in this Part to a person being subject to foreign restrictions.

(2) A person is subject to foreign restrictions if under the law of a country or territory outside the United Kingdom—

(a) he is, by reason of misconduct or unfitness, disqualified to any extent from acting in connection with the affairs of a company,

(b) he is, by reason of misconduct or unfitness, required—

(i) to obtain permission from a court or other authority, or

(ii) to meet any other condition,

before acting in connection with the affairs of a company, or

(c) he has, by reason of misconduct or unfitness, given undertakings to a court or other authority of a country or territory outside the United Kingdom—

(i) not to act in connection with the affairs of a company, or

(ii) restricting the extent to which, or the way in which, he may do so.

(3) The references in subsection (2) to acting in connection with the affairs of a company are to doing any of the following—

(a) being a director of a company,

(b) acting as receiver of a company's property, or

(c) being concerned or taking part in the promotion, formation or management of a company.

(4) In this section—

(a) "company" means a company incorporated or formed under the law of the country or territory in question, and

(b) in relation to such a company—

"director" means the holder of an office corresponding to that of director of a UK company; and

"receiver" includes any corresponding officer under the law of that country or territory.

1183 Meaning of "the court" and "UK company"

In this Part—

"the court" means—

(a) in England and Wales, the High Court or a county court;

(b) in Scotland, the Court of Session or the sheriff court;

(c) in Northern Ireland, the High Court;

"UK company" means a company registered under this Act.

Power to disqualify

1184 Disqualification of persons subject to foreign restrictions

(1) The Secretary of State may make provision by regulations disqualifying a person subject to foreign restrictions from—

(a) being a director of a UK company,

(b) acting as receiver of a UK company's property, or

(c) in any way, whether directly or indirectly, being concerned or taking part in the promotion, formation or management of a UK company.

(2) The regulations may provide that a person subject to foreign restrictions—

(a) is disqualified automatically by virtue of the regulations, or

(b) may be disqualified by order of the court on the application of the Secretary of State.

(3) The regulations may provide that the Secretary of State may accept an undertaking (a "disqualification undertaking") from a person subject to foreign restrictions that he will not do anything which would be in breach of a disqualification under subsection (1).

(4) In this Part—

(a) a "person disqualified under this Part" is a person—

(i) disqualified as mentioned in subsection (2) (a) or (b), or

(i) who has given and is subject to a disqualification undertaking;

(b) references to a breach of a disqualification include a breach of a disqualification undertaking.

(5) The regulations may provide for applications to the court by persons disqualified under this Part for permission to act in a way which would otherwise be in breach of the disqualification.

(6) The regulations must provide that a person ceases to be disqualified under this Part on his ceasing to be subject to foreign restrictions.

(7) Regulations under this section are subject to affirmative resolution procedure.

1185 Disqualification regulations: supplementary

(1) Regulations under section 1184 may make different provision for different cases and may in particular distinguish between cases by reference to—

(a) the conduct on the basis of which the person became subject to foreign restrictions;

(b) the nature of the foreign restrictions;

(c) the country or territory under whose law the foreign restrictions were imposed.

(2) Regulations under section 1184(2)(b) or (5) (provision for applications to the court)—

(a) must specify the grounds on which an application may be made;

(b) may specify factors to which the court shall have regard in determining an application.

(3) The regulations may, in particular, require the court to have regard to the following factors—

(a) whether the conduct on the basis of which the person became subject to foreign restrictions would, if done in relation to a UK company, have led a court to make a disqualification order on an application under the Company Directors Disqualification Act 1986 or the Company Directors Disqualification (Northern Ireland) Order 2002;

(b) in a case in which the conduct on the basis of which the person became subject to foreign restrictions would not be unlawful if done in relation to a UK company, the fact that the person acted unlawfully under foreign law;

(c) whether the person's activities in relation to UK companies began after he became subject to foreign restrictions;
(d) whether the person's activities (or proposed activities) in relation to UK companies are undertaken (or are proposed to be undertaken) outside the United Kingdom.

(4) Regulations under section 1184(3) (provision as to undertakings given to the Secretary of State) may include provision allowing the Secretary of State, in determining whether to accept an undertaking, to take into account matters other than criminal convictions notwithstanding that the person may be criminally liable in respect of those matters.

(5) Regulations under section 1184(5) (provision for application to court for permission to act) may include provision—
(a) entitling the Secretary of State to be represented at the hearing of the application, and
(b) as to the giving of evidence or the calling of witnesses by the Secretary of State at the hearing of the application.

1186 Offence of breach of disqualification

(1) Regulations under section 1184 may provide that a person disqualified under this Part who acts in breach of the disqualification commits an offence.

(2) The regulations may provide that a person guilty of such an offence is liable—
(a) on conviction on indictment, to imprisonment for a term not exceeding two years or a fine (or both);
(b) on summary conviction—
(i) in England and Wales, to imprisonment for a term not exceeding twelve months or to a fine not exceeding the statutory maximum (or both);
(ii) in Scotland or Northern Ireland, to imprisonment for a term not exceeding six months, or to a fine not exceeding the statutory maximum (or both).

(3) In relation to an offence committed before the commencement of section 154(1) of the Criminal Justice Act 2003, for "twelve months" in subsection (2) (b) (i) substitute "six months".

Power to make persons liable for company's debts

1187 Personal liability for debts of company

(1) The Secretary of State may provide by regulations that a person who, at a time when he is subject to foreign restrictions—
(a) is a director of a UK company, or
(b) is involved in the management of a UK company,
is personally responsible for all debts and other liabilities of the company incurred during that time.

(2) A person who is personally responsible by virtue of this section for debts and other liabilities of a company is jointly and severally liable in respect of those debts and liabilities with—
(a) the company, and
(b) any other person who (whether by virtue of this section or otherwise) is so liable.

(3) For the purposes of this section a person is involved in the management of a company if he is concerned, whether directly or indirectly, or takes part, in the management of the company.

(4) The regulations may make different provision for different cases and may in particular distinguish between cases by reference to—
(a) the conduct on the basis of which the person became subject to foreign restrictions;
(b) the nature of the foreign restrictions;
(c) the country or territory under whose law the foreign restrictions were imposed.

(5) Regulations under this section are subject to affirmative resolution procedure.

Power to require statements to be sent to the registrar of companies

1188 Statements from persons subject to foreign restrictions

(1) The Secretary of State may make provision by regulations requiring a person who—

(a) is subject to foreign restrictions, and
(b) is not disqualified under this Part,

to send a statement to the registrar if he does anything that, if done by a person disqualified under this Part, would be in breach of the disqualification.

(2) The statement must include such information as may be specified in the regulations relating to—
(a) the person's activities in relation to UK companies, and
(b) the foreign restrictions to which the person is subject.

(3) The statement must be sent to the registrar within such period as may be specified in the regulations.

(4) The regulations may make different provision for different cases and may in particular distinguish between cases by reference to—
(a) the conduct on the basis of which the person became subject to foreign restrictions;
(b) the nature of the foreign restrictions;
(c) the country or territory under whose law the foreign restrictions were imposed.

(5) Regulations under this section are subject to affirmative resolution procedure.

1189 Statements from persons disqualified

(1) The Secretary of State may make provision by regulations requiring a statement or notice sent to the registrar of companies under any of the provisions listed below that relates (wholly or partly) to a person who—
(a) is a person disqualified under this Part, or
(b) is subject to a disqualification order or disqualification undertaking under the Company Directors Disqualification Act 1986 or the Company Directors Disqualification (Northern Ireland) Order 2002,

to be accompanied by an additional statement.

(2) The provisions referred to above are—
(a) section 12 (statement of a company's proposed officers),
(b) section 167(2) (notice of person having become director), and
(c) section 276 (notice of a person having become secretary or one of joint secretaries).

(3) The additional statement is a statement that the person has obtained permission from a court, on an application under section 1184(5) or (as the case may be) for the purposes of section 1(1)(a) of the Company Directors Disqualification Act 1986 or Article 3(1) of the Company Directors Disqualification (Northern Ireland) Order 2002, to act in the capacity in question.

(4) Regulations under this section are subject to affirmative resolution procedure.

1190 Statements: whether to be made public

(1) Regulations under section 1188 or 1189 (statements required to be sent to registrar) may provide that a statement sent to the registrar of companies under the regulations is to be treated as a record relating to a company for the purposes of section 1080 (the companies register).

(2) The regulations may make provision as to the circumstances in which such a statement is to be, or may be—
(a) withheld from public inspection, or
(b) removed from the register.

(3) The regulations may, in particular, provide that a statement is not to be withheld from public inspection or removed from the register unless the person to whom it relates provides such information, and satisfies such other conditions, as may be specified.

(4) The regulations may provide that section 1081 (note of removal of material from the register) does not apply, or applies with such modifications as may be specified, in the case of material removed from the register under the regulations.

(5) In this section "specified" means specified in the regulations.

1191 Offences

(1) Regulations under section 1188 or 1189 may provide that it is an offence for a person—

(a) to fail to comply with a requirement under the regulations to send a statement to the registrar;
(b) knowingly or recklessly to send a statement under the regulations to the registrar that is misleading, false or deceptive in a material particular.

(2) The regulations may provide that a person guilty of such an offence is liable—
(a) on conviction on indictment, to imprisonment for a term not exceeding two years or a fine (or both);
(b) on summary conviction—
(i) in England and Wales, to imprisonment for a term not exceeding twelve months or to a fine not exceeding the statutory maximum (or both);
(ii) in Scotland or Northern Ireland, to imprisonment for a term not exceeding six months, or to a fine not exceeding the statutory maximum (or both).

(3) In relation to an offence committed before the commencement of section 154(1) of the Criminal Justice Act 2003, for "twelve months" in subsection (2) (b) (i) substitute "six months".

PART 41
BUSINESS NAMES

CHAPTER 1
RESTRICTED OR PROHIBITED NAMES

Introductory

1192 Application of this Chapter

(1) This Chapter applies to any person carrying on business in the United Kingdom.

(2) The provisions of this Chapter do not prevent—
(a) an individual carrying on business under a name consisting of his surname without any addition other than a permitted addition, or
(b) individuals carrying on business in partnership under a name consisting of the surnames of all the partners without any addition other than a permitted addition.

(3) The following are the permitted additions—
(a) in the case of an individual, his forename or initial;
(b) in the case of a partnership—
(i) the forenames of individual partners or the initials of those forenames, or
(ii) where two or more individual partners have the same surname, the addition of "s" at the end of that surname;
(c) in either case, an addition merely indicating that the business is carried on in succession to a former owner of the business.

Sensitive words or expressions

1193 Name suggesting connection with government or public authority

(1) A person must not, without the approval of the Secretary of State, carry on business in the United Kingdom under a name that would be likely to give the impression that the business is connected with—
(a) Her Majesty's Government, any part of the Scottish administration, the Welsh Assembly Government or Her Majesty's Government in Northern Ireland,
(b) any local authority, or
(c) any public authority specified for the purposes of this section by regulations made by the Secretary of State.

(2) For the purposes of this section—
"local authority" means—
(a) a local authority within the meaning of the Local Government Act 1972, the Common Council of the City of London or the Council of the Isles of Scilly,

(b) a council constituted under section 2 of the Local Government etc. (Scotland) Act 1994, or

(c) a district council in Northern Ireland;

"public authority" includes any person or body having functions of a public nature.

(3) Regulations under this section are subject to affirmative resolution procedure.

(4) A person who contravenes this section commits an offence.

(5) Where an offence under this section is committed by a body corporate, an offence is also committed by every officer of the body who is in default.

(6) A person guilty of an offence under this section is liable on summary conviction to a fine not exceeding level 3 on the standard scale and, for continued contravention, a daily default fine not exceeding one-tenth of level 3 on the standard scale.

1194 Other sensitive words or expressions

(1) A person must not, without the approval of the Secretary of State, carry on business in the United Kingdom under a name that includes a word or expression for the time being specified in regulations made by the Secretary of State under this section.

(2) Regulations under this section are subject to approval after being made.

(3) A person who contravenes this section commits an offence.

(4) Where an offence under this section is committed by a body corporate, an offence is also committed by every officer of the body who is in default.

(5) A person guilty of an offence under this section is liable on summary conviction to a fine not exceeding level 3 on the standard scale and, for continued contravention, a daily default fine not exceeding one-tenth of level 3 on the standard scale.

1195 Requirement to seek comments of government department or other relevant body

(1) The Secretary of State may by regulations under—

(a) section 1193 (name suggesting connection with government or public authority), or

(b) section 1194 (other sensitive words or expressions),

require that, in connection with an application for the approval of the Secretary of State under that section, the applicant must seek the view of a specified Government department or other body.

(2) Where such a requirement applies, the applicant must request the specified department or other body (in writing) to indicate whether (and if so why) it has any objections to the proposed name.

(3) He must submit to the Secretary of State a statement that such a request has been made and a copy of any response received from the specified body.

(4) If these requirements are not complied with, the Secretary of State may refuse to consider the application for approval.

(5) In this section "specified" means specified in the regulations.

1196 Withdrawal of Secretary of State's approval

(1) This section applies to approval given for the purposes of—

section 1193 (name suggesting connection with government or public authority), or

section 1194 (other sensitive words or expressions).

(2) If it appears to the Secretary of State that there are overriding considerations of public policy that require such approval to be withdrawn, the approval may be withdrawn by notice in writing given to the person concerned.

(3) The notice must state the date as from which approval is withdrawn.

Misleading names

1197 Name containing inappropriate indication of company type or legal form

(1) The Secretary of State may make provision by regulations prohibiting a person from carrying on business in the United Kingdom under a name consisting of or containing specified words, expressions or other indications—

(a) that are associated with a particular type of company or form of organisation, or

(b) that are similar to words, expressions or other indications associated with a particular type of company or form of organisation.

(2) The regulations may prohibit the use of words, expressions or other indications—

(a) in a specified part, or otherwise than in a specified part, of a name;

(b) in conjunction with, or otherwise than in conjunction with, such other words, expressions or indications as may be specified.

(3) In this section "specified" means specified in the regulations.

(4) Regulations under this section are subject to negative resolution procedure.

(5) A person who uses a name in contravention of regulations under this section commits an offence.

(6) Where an offence under this section is committed by a body corporate, an offence is also committed by every officer of the body who is in default.

(7) A person guilty of an offence under this section is liable on summary conviction to a fine not exceeding level 3 on the standard scale and, for continued contravention, a daily default fine not exceeding one-tenth of level 3 on the standard scale.

1198 Name giving misleading indication of activities

(1) A person must not carry on business in the United Kingdom under a name that gives so misleading an indication of the nature of the activities of the business as to be likely to cause harm to the public.

(2) A person who uses a name in contravention of this section commits an offence.

(3) Where an offence under this section is committed by a body corporate, an offence is also committed by every officer of the body who is in default.

(4) A person guilty of an offence under this section is liable on summary conviction to a fine not exceeding level 3 on the standard scale and, for continued contravention, a daily default fine not exceeding one-tenth of level 3 on the standard scale.

Supplementary

1199 Savings for existing lawful business names

(1) This section has effect in relation to—

sections 1192 to 1196 (sensitive words or expressions), and

section 1197 (inappropriate indication of company type or legal form).

(2) Those sections do not apply to the carrying on of a business by a person who—

(a) carried on the business immediately before the date on which this Chapter came into force, and

(b) continues to carry it on under the name that immediately before that date was its lawful business name.

(3) Where—

(a) a business is transferred to a person on or after the date on which this Chapter came into force, and

(b) that person carries on the business under the name that was its lawful business name immediately before the transfer,

those sections do not apply in relation to the carrying on of the business under that name during the period of twelve months beginning with the date of the transfer.

(4) In this section "lawful business name", in relation to a business, means a name under which the business was carried on without contravening—

(a) section 2(1) of the Business Names Act 1985 or Article 4(1) of the Business Names (Northern Ireland) Order 1986, or

(b) after this Chapter has come into force, the provisions of this Chapter.

CHAPTER 2
DISCLOSURE REQUIRED IN CASE OF INDIVIDUAL OR PARTNERSHIP

Introductory

1200 Application of this Chapter

(1) This Chapter applies to an individual or partnership carrying on business in the United Kingdom under a business name.

References in this Chapter to "a person to whom this Chapter applies" are to such an individual or partnership.

(2) For the purposes of this Chapter a "business name" means a name other than—

(a) in the case of an individual, his surname without any addition other than a permitted addition;

(b) in the case of a partnership—

(i) the surnames of all partners who are individuals, and

(ii) the corporate names of all partners who are bodies corporate, without any addition other than a permitted addition.

(3) The following are the permitted additions—

(a) in the case of an individual, his forename or initial;

(b) in the case of a partnership—

(i) the forenames of individual partners or the initials of those forenames, or

(ii) where two or more individual partners have the same surname, the addition of "s" at the end of that surname;

(c) in either case, an addition merely indicating that the business is carried on in succession to a former owner of the business.

1201 Information required to be disclosed

(1) The "information required by this Chapter" is—

(a) in the case of an individual, the individual's name;

(b) in the case of a partnership, the name of each member of the partnership;

and, in relation to each person so named, an address at which service of any document relating in any way to the business will be effective.

(2) If the individual or partnership has a place of business in the United Kingdom, the address must be in the United Kingdom.

(3) If the individual or partnership does not have a place of business in the United Kingdom, the address must be an address at which service of documents can be effected by physical delivery and the delivery of documents is capable of being recorded by the obtaining of an acknowledgement of delivery.

Disclosure requirements

1202 Disclosure required: business documents etc

(1) A person to whom this Chapter applies must state the information required by this Chapter, in legible characters, on all—

(a) business letters,

(b) written orders for goods or services to be supplied to the business,

(c) invoices and receipts issued in the course of the business, and

(d) written demands for payment of debts arising in the course of the business.

This subsection has effect subject to section 1203 (exemption for large partnerships if certain conditions met).

(2) A person to whom this Chapter applies must secure that the information required by this Chapter is immediately given, by written notice, to any person with whom anything is done or discussed in the course of the business and who asks for that information.

(3) The Secretary of State may by regulations require that such notices be given in a specified form.

(4) Regulations under this section are subject to negative resolution procedure.

1203 Exemption for large partnerships if certain conditions met

(1) Section 1202(1) (disclosure required in business documents) does not apply in relation to a document issued by a partnership of more than 20 persons if the following conditions are met.

(2) The conditions are that—

(a) the partnership maintains at its principal place of business a list of the names of all the partners,

(b) no partner's name appears in the document, except in the text or as a signatory, and

(c) the document states in legible characters the address of the partnership's principal place of business and that the list of the partners' names is open to inspection there.

(3) Where a partnership maintains a list of the partners' names for the purposes of this section, any person may inspect the list during office hours.

(4) Where an inspection required by a person in accordance with this section is refused, an offence is committed by any member of the partnership concerned who without reasonable excuse refused the inspection or permitted it to be refused.

(5) A person guilty of an offence under subsection (4) is liable on summary conviction to a fine not exceeding level 3 on the standard scale and, for continued contravention, a daily default fine not exceeding one-tenth of level 3 on the standard scale.

1204 Disclosure required: business premises

(1) A person to whom this Chapter applies must, in any premises—

(a) where the business is carried on, and

(b) to which customers of the business or suppliers of goods or services to the business have access,

display in a prominent position, so that it may easily be read by such customers or suppliers, a notice containing the information required by this Chapter.

(2) The Secretary of State may by regulations require that such notices be displayed in a specified form.

(3) Regulations under this section are subject to negative resolution procedure.

Consequences of failure to make required disclosure

1205 Criminal consequences of failure to make required disclosure

(1) A person who without reasonable excuse fails to comply with the requirements of—
section 1202 (disclosure required: business documents etc), or
section 1204 (disclosure required: business premises),
commits an offence.

(2) Where an offence under this section is committed by a body corporate, an offence is also committed by every officer of the body who is in default.

(3) A person guilty of an offence under this section is liable on summary conviction to a fine not exceeding level 3 on the standard scale and, for continued contravention, a daily default fine not exceeding one-tenth of level 3 on the standard scale.

(4) References in this section to the requirements of section 1202 or 1204 include the requirements of regulations under that section.

1206 Civil consequences of failure to make required disclosure

(1) This section applies to any legal proceedings brought by a person to whom this Chapter applies to enforce a right arising out of a contract made in the course of a business in respect of which he was, at the time the contract was made, in breach of section 1202(1) or (2) (disclosure in business documents etc) or section 1204(1) (disclosure at business premises).

(2) The proceedings shall be dismissed if the defendant (in Scotland, the defender) to the proceedings shows—

(a) that he has a claim against the claimant (pursuer) arising out of the contract that he has been unable to pursue by reason of the latter's breach of the requirements of this Chapter, or

(b) that he has suffered some financial loss in connection with the contract by reason of the claimant's (pursuer's) breach of those requirements,

unless the court before which the proceedings are brought is satisfied that it is just and equitable to permit the proceedings to continue.

(3) References in this section to the requirements of this Chapter include the requirements of regulations under this Chapter.

(4) This section does not affect the right of any person to enforce such rights as he may have against another person in any proceedings brought by that person.

CHAPTER 3
SUPPLEMENTARY

1207 Application of general provisions about offences

The provisions of sections 1121 to 1123 (liability of officer in default) and 1125 to 1131 (general provisions about offences) apply in relation to offences under this Part as in relation to offences under the Companies Acts.

1208 Interpretation

In this Part—

"business" includes a profession;

"initial" includes any recognised abbreviation of a name;

"partnership" means—

(a) a partnership within the Partnership Act 1890, or

(b) a limited partnership registered under the Limited Partnerships Act 1907,

or a firm or entity of a similar character formed under the law of a country or territory outside the United Kingdom;

"surname", in relation to a peer or person usually known by a British title different from his surname, means the title by which he is known.

PART 42
STATUTORY AUDITORS

CHAPTER 1
INTRODUCTORY

1209 Main purposes of Part

The main purposes of this Part are—

(a) to secure that only persons who are properly supervised and appropriately qualified are appointed as statutory auditors, and

(b) to secure that audits by persons so appointed are carried out properly, with integrity and with a proper degree of independence.

1210 Meaning of "statutory auditor" etc

(1) In this Part "statutory auditor" means—

(a) a person appointed as auditor under Part 16 of this Act,

(b) a person appointed as auditor under section 77 of or Schedule 11 to the Building Societies Act 1986,

(c) a person appointed as auditor of an insurer that is a friendly society under section 72 of or Schedule 14 to the Friendly Societies Act 1992,

(d) . . .

(e) a person appointed as auditor for the purposes of regulation 5 of the Insurance Accounts Directive (Lloyd's Syndicate and Aggregate Accounts) Regulations 2008 or appointed to report on the "aggregate accounts" within the meaning of those Regulations,

(f) a person appointed as auditor of an insurance undertaking for the purposes of the Insurance Accounts Directive (Miscellaneous Insurance Undertakings) Regulations 2008,

(g) a person appointed as auditor of a bank for the purposes of the Bank Accounts Directive (Miscellaneous Banks) Regulations 2008,

(h) a person appointed as auditor of a prescribed person under a prescribed enactment authorising or requiring the appointment;

and the expressions "statutory audit" and "statutory audit work" are to be construed accordingly.

(2) In this Part "audited person" means the person in respect of whom a statutory audit is conducted.

(3) In subsection (1)—

"bank" means a person who—

(a) is a credit institution within the meaning given by Article 4.1 of Directive 2006/48/EC of the European Parliament and of the Council relating to the taking up and pursuit of the business of credit institutions as last amended by Directive 2009/111/EC, and

(b) is a company or a firm as defined in Article 54 of the Treaty on the Functioning of the European Union;

"friendly society" means a friendly society within the meaning of the Friendly Societies Act 1992;

. . .

"insurer" means a person who is an insurance undertaking within the meaning given by Article 2.1 of Council Directive 1991/674/EEC on the annual accounts and consolidated accounts of insurance undertakings;

"prescribed" means prescribed, or of a description prescribed, by order made by the Secretary of State for the purposes of subsection (1)(h).

(4) An order under this section is subject to negative resolution procedure.

1211 Eligibility for appointment as a statutory auditor: overview

A person is eligible for appointment as a statutory auditor only if the person is so eligible—

(a) by virtue of Chapter 2 (individuals and firms), or

(b) by virtue of Chapter 3 (Comptroller and Auditor General, etc).

CHAPTER 2
INDIVIDUALS AND FIRMS

Eligibility for appointment

1212 Individuals and firms: eligibility for appointment as a statutory auditor

(1) An individual or firm is eligible for appointment as a statutory auditor if the individual or firm—

(a) is a member of a recognised supervisory body, and

(b) is eligible for appointment under the rules of that body.

(2) In the cases to which section 1222 applies (individuals retaining only 1967 Act authorisation) a person's eligibility for appointment as a statutory auditor is restricted as mentioned in that section.

1213 Effect of ineligibility

(1) No person may act as statutory auditor of an audited person if he is ineligible for appointment as a statutory auditor.

(2) If at any time during his term of office a statutory auditor becomes ineligible for appointment as a statutory auditor, he must immediately—

(a) resign his office (with immediate effect), and

(b) give notice in writing to the audited person that he has resigned by reason of his becoming ineligible for appointment.

(3) A person is guilty of an offence if—
(a) he acts as a statutory auditor in contravention of subsection (1), or
(b) he fails to give the notice mentioned in paragraph (b) of subsection (2) in accordance with that subsection.

(4) A person guilty of an offence under subsection (3) is liable—
(a) on conviction on indictment, to a fine;
(b) on summary conviction, to a fine not exceeding the statutory maximum.

(5) A person is guilty of an offence if—
(a) he has been convicted of an offence under subsection (3)(a) or this subsection, and
(b) he continues to act as a statutory auditor in contravention of subsection (1) after the conviction.

(6) A person is guilty of an offence if—
(a) he has been convicted of an offence under subsection (3)(b) or this subsection, and
(b) he continues, after the conviction, to fail to give the notice mentioned in subsection (2)(b).

(7) A person guilty of an offence under subsection (5) or (6) is liable—
(a) on conviction on indictment, to a fine;
(b) on summary conviction, to a fine not exceeding one-tenth of the statutory maximum for each day on which the act or the failure continues.

(8) In proceedings against a person for an offence under this section it is a defence for him to show that he did not know and had no reason to believe that he was, or had become, ineligible for appointment as a statutory auditor.

Independence requirement

1214 Independence requirement

(1) A person may not act as statutory auditor of an audited person if one or more of subsections (2), (3) and (4) apply to him.

(2) This subsection applies if the person is—
(a) an officer or employee of the audited person, or
(b) a partner or employee of such a person, or a partnership of which such a person is a partner.

(3) This subsection applies if the person is—
(a) an officer or employee of an associated undertaking of the audited person, or
(b) a partner or employee of such a person, or a partnership of which such a person is a partner.

(4) This subsection applies if there exists, between—
(a) the person or an associate of his, and
(b) the audited person or an associated undertaking of the audited person,
a connection of any such description as may be specified by regulations made by the Secretary of State.

(5) An auditor of an audited person is not to be regarded as an officer or employee of the person for the purposes of subsections (2) and (3).

(6) In this section "associated undertaking", in relation to an audited person, means—
(a) a parent undertaking or subsidiary undertaking of the audited person, or
(b) a subsidiary undertaking of a parent undertaking of the audited person.

(7) Regulations under subsection (4) are subject to negative resolution procedure.

1215 Effect of lack of independence

(1) If at any time during his term of office a statutory auditor becomes prohibited from acting by section 1214(1), he must immediately—
(a) resign his office (with immediate effect), and
(b) give notice in writing to the audited person that he has resigned by reason of his lack of independence.

(2) A person is guilty of an offence if—
(a) he acts as a statutory auditor in contravention of section 1214(1), or

(b) he fails to give the notice mentioned in paragraph (b) of subsection (1) in accordance with that subsection.

(3) A person guilty of an offence under subsection (2) is liable—
(a) on conviction on indictment, to a fine;
(b) on summary conviction, to a fine not exceeding the statutory maximum.

(4) A person is guilty of an offence if—
(a) he has been convicted of an offence under subsection (2)(a) or this subsection, and
(b) he continues to act as a statutory auditor in contravention of section 1214(1) after the conviction.

(5) A person is guilty of an offence if—
(a) he has been convicted of an offence under subsection (2)(b) or this subsection, and
(b) after the conviction, he continues to fail to give the notice mentioned in subsection (1)(b).

(6) A person guilty of an offence under subsection (4) or (5) is liable—
(a) on conviction on indictment, to a fine;
(b) on summary conviction, to a fine not exceeding one-tenth of the statutory maximum for each day on which the act or the failure continues.

(7) In proceedings against a person for an offence under this section it is a defence for him to show that he did not know and had no reason to believe that he was, or had become, prohibited from acting as statutory auditor of the audited person by section 1214(1).

Effect of appointment of a partnership

1216 Effect of appointment of a partnership

(1) This section applies where a partnership constituted under the law of—
(a) England and Wales,
(b) Northern Ireland, or
(c) any other country or territory in which a partnership is not a legal person,
is by virtue of this Chapter appointed as statutory auditor of an audited person.

(2) Unless a contrary intention appears, the appointment is an appointment of the partnership as such and not of the partners.

(3) Where the partnership ceases, the appointment is to be treated as extending to—
(a) any appropriate partnership which succeeds to the practice of that partnership, or
(b) any other appropriate person who succeeds to that practice having previously carried it on in partnership.

(4) For the purposes of subsection (3)—
(a) a partnership is to be regarded as succeeding to the practice of another partnership only if the members of the successor partnership are substantially the same as those of the former partnership, and
(b) a partnership or other person is to be regarded as succeeding to the practice of a partnership only if it or he succeeds to the whole or substantially the whole of the business of the former partnership.

(5) Where the partnership ceases and the appointment is not treated under subsection (3) as extending to any partnership or other person, the appointment may with the consent of the audited person be treated as extending to an appropriate partnership, or other appropriate person, who succeeds to—
(a) the business of the former partnership, or
(b) such part of it as is agreed by the audited person is to be treated as comprising the appointment.

(6) For the purposes of this section, a partnership or other person is "appropriate" if it or he—
(a) is eligible for appointment as a statutory auditor by virtue of this Chapter, and
(b) is not prohibited by section 1214(1) from acting as statutory auditor of the audited person.

Supervisory bodies

1217 Supervisory bodies

(1) In this Part a "supervisory body" means a body established in the United Kingdom (whether a body corporate or an unincorporated association) which maintains and enforces rules as to—

(a) the eligibility of persons for appointment as a statutory auditor, and

(b) the conduct of statutory audit work,

which are binding on persons seeking appointment or acting as a statutory auditor … because they are members of that body …

(1A) The rules referred to in paragraphs 9(3)(b) (confidentiality of information) and 10C(3)(a) and (b) (bar on appointment as director or other officer) of Schedule 10 must also be binding on persons who—

(a) have sought appointment or acted as a statutory auditor, and

(b) have been members of the body at any time after the commencement of this Part.

(2) In this Part references to the members of a supervisory body are to the persons who, whether or not members of the body, are subject to its rules in seeking appointment or acting as a statutory auditor.

(3) In this Part references to the rules of a supervisory body are to the rules (whether or not laid down by the body itself) which the body has power to enforce and which are relevant for the purposes of this Part.

This includes rules relating to the admission or expulsion of members of the body, so far as relevant for the purposes of this Part.

(4) Schedule 10 has effect with respect to the recognition of supervisory bodies for the purposes of this Part.

1218 Exemption from liability for damages

(1) No person within subsection (2) is to be liable in damages for anything done or omitted in the discharge or purported discharge of functions to which this subsection applies.

(2) The persons within this subsection are—

(a) any recognised supervisory body,

(b) any officer or employee of a recognised supervisory body, and

(c) any member of the governing body of a recognised supervisory body.

(3) Subsection (1) applies to the functions of a recognised supervisory body so far as relating to, or to matters arising out of, any of the following—

(a) rules, practices, powers and arrangements of the body to which the requirements of Part 2 of Schedule 10 apply;

(b) the obligations with which paragraph 20 of that Schedule requires the body to comply;

(c) any guidance issued by the body;

(d) the obligations imposed on the body by or by virtue of this Part.

(4) The reference in subsection (3)(c) to guidance issued by a recognised supervisory body is a reference to any guidance or recommendation which is—

(a) issued or made by it to all or any class of its members or persons seeking to become members, and

(b) relevant for the purposes of this Part,

including any guidance or recommendation relating to the admission or expulsion of members of the body, so far as relevant for the purposes of this Part.

(5) Subsection (1) does not apply—

(a) if the act or omission is shown to have been in bad faith, or

(b) so as to prevent an award of damages in respect of the act or omission on the ground that it was unlawful as a result of section 6(1) of the Human Rights Act 1998 (acts of public authorities incompatible with Convention rights).

Professional qualifications

1219 Appropriate qualifications

(1) A person holds an appropriate qualification for the purposes of this Chapter if and only if—

(a) he holds a recognised professional qualification obtained in the United Kingdom,

(b) immediately before the commencement of this Chapter, he—

(i) held an appropriate qualification for the purposes of Part 2 of the Companies Act 1989 (eligibility for appointment as company auditor) by virtue of section 31(1)(a) or (c) of that Act, or

(ii) was treated as holding an appropriate qualification for those purposes by virtue of section 31(2), (3) or (4) of that Act,

(c) immediately before the commencement of this Chapter, he—

(i) held an appropriate qualification for the purposes of Part III of the Companies (Northern Ireland) Order 1990 by virtue of Article 34(1)(a) or (c) of that Order, or

(ii) was treated as holding an appropriate qualification for those purposes by virtue of Article 34(2), (3) or (4) of that Order,

(d) he is within subsection (2), or

(e) …

(f) subject to any direction under section 1221(5), he is regarded for the purposes of this Chapter as holding an approved third country qualification.

(2) A person is within this subsection if—

(a) before 1st January 1990, he began a course of study or practical training leading to a professional qualification in accountancy offered by a body established in the United Kingdom,

(b) he obtained that qualification on or after 1st January 1990 and before 1st January 1996, and

(c) the Secretary of State approves his qualification as an appropriate qualification for the purposes of this Chapter.

(3) The Secretary of State may approve a qualification under subsection (2)(c) only if he is satisfied that, at the time the qualification was awarded, the body concerned had adequate arrangements to ensure that the qualification was awarded only to persons educated and trained to a standard equivalent to that required, at that time, in the case of a recognised professional qualification under Part 2 of the Companies Act 1989 (eligibility for appointment as company auditor).

1220 Qualifying bodies and recognised professional qualifications

(1) In this Part a "qualifying body" means a body established in the United Kingdom (whether a body corporate or an unincorporated association) which offers a professional qualification in accountancy.

(2) In this Part references to the rules of a qualifying body are to the rules (whether or not laid down by the body itself) which the body has power to enforce and which are relevant for the purposes of this Part.

This includes, so far as so relevant, rules relating to—

(a) admission to or expulsion from a course of study leading to a qualification,

(b) the award or deprivation of a qualification, or

(c) the approval of a person for the purposes of giving practical training or the withdrawal of such approval.

(3) Schedule 11 has effect with respect to the recognition for the purposes of this Part of a professional qualification offered by a qualifying body.

1221 Approval of third country qualifications

(1) The Secretary of State may declare that the following are to be regarded for the purposes of this Chapter as holding an approved third country qualification—

(a) persons who are qualified to audit accounts under the law of a specified third country, or

(b) persons who hold a specified professional qualification in accountancy obtained in a specified third country.

(1A) A declaration under subsection (1)(a) or (b) must be expressed to be subject to the requirement that any person to whom the declaration relates must pass an aptitude test in accordance with subsection (7A), unless an aptitude test is not required (see subsection (7B)).

(2) A declaration under subsection (1)(b) may be expressed to be subject to the satisfaction of any specified requirement or requirements.

(3) The Secretary of State may make a declaration under subsection (1) only if he is satisfied that—
- (a) in the case of a declaration under subsection (1)(a), the fact that the persons in question are qualified to audit accounts under the law of the specified third country, or
- (b) in the case of a declaration under subsection (1)(b), the specified professional qualification taken with any requirement or requirements to be specified under subsection (2),

affords an assurance of professional competence equivalent to that afforded by a recognised professional qualification.

(4) The Secretary of State may make a declaration under subsection (1) only if he is satisfied that the treatment that the persons who are the subject of the declaration will receive as a result of it is comparable to the treatment which is, or is likely to be, afforded in the specified third country or a part of it to—
- (a) in the case of a declaration under subsection (1)(a), some or all persons who are eligible to be appointed as a statutory auditor, and
- (b) in the case of a declaration under subsection (1)(b), some or all persons who hold a corresponding recognised professional qualification.

(5) The Secretary of State may direct that persons holding an approved third country qualification are not to be treated as holding an appropriate qualification for the purposes of this Chapter unless they hold such additional educational qualifications as the Secretary of State may specify for the purpose of ensuring that such persons have an adequate knowledge of the law and practice in the United Kingdom relevant to the audit of accounts.

(6) The Secretary of State may give different directions in relation to different approved third country qualifications.

(7) The Secretary of State may, if he thinks fit, having regard to the considerations mentioned in subsections (3) and (4), withdraw a declaration under subsection (1) in relation to—
- (a) persons becoming qualified to audit accounts under the law of the specified third country after such date as he may specify, or
- (b) persons obtaining the specified professional qualification after such date as he may specify.

(7A) An aptitude test required for the purposes of subsection (1A)—
- (a) must test the person's knowledge of subjects—
  - (i) that are covered by a recognised professional qualification,
  - (ii) that are not covered by the professional qualification already held by the person, and
  - (iii) the knowledge of which is essential for the pursuit of the profession of statutory auditor;
- (b) may test the person's knowledge of rules of professional conduct;
- (c) must not test the person's knowledge of any other matters.

(7B) No aptitude test is required for the purposes of subsection (1A) if the subjects that are covered by a recognised professional qualification and the knowledge of which is essential for the pursuit of the profession of statutory auditor are covered by the professional qualification already held by the person.

(8) The Secretary of State may, if he thinks fit, having regard to the considerations mentioned in subsections (3) and (4), vary or revoke a requirement specified under subsection (2) from such date as he may specify.

(9) …

1222 Eligibility of individuals retaining only 1967 Act authorisation

(1) A person whose only appropriate qualification is based on his retention of an authorisation originally granted by the Board of Trade or the Secretary of State under section 13(1) of the Companies Act 1967 is eligible only for appointment as auditor of an unquoted company.

(2) A company is "unquoted" if, at the time of the person's appointment, neither the company, nor any parent undertaking of which it is a subsidiary undertaking, is a quoted company within the meaning of section 385(2).

(3) References to a person eligible for appointment as a statutory auditor by virtue of this Part in enactments relating to eligibility for appointment as auditor of a person other than a company do not include a person to whom this section applies.

Information

1223 Matters to be notified to the Secretary of State

(1) The Secretary of State may require a recognised supervisory body or a recognised qualifying body—

(a) to notify him immediately of the occurrence of such events as he may specify in writing and to give him such information in respect of those events as is so specified;

(b) to give him, at such times or in respect of such periods as he may specify in writing, such information as is so specified.

(2) The notices and information required to be given must be such as the Secretary of State may reasonably require for the exercise of his functions under this Part.

(3) The Secretary of State may require information given under this section to be given in a specified form or verified in a specified manner.

(4) Any notice or information required to be given under this section must be given in writing unless the Secretary of State specifies or approves some other manner.

1223A Notification of matters relevant to other EEA States

(1) A recognised supervisory body must notify the Secretary of State of—

(a) any withdrawal of a notifiable person's eligibility for appointment as a statutory auditor; and

(b) the reasons for the withdrawal.

(2) A recognised supervisory body must also notify the Secretary of State of any reasonable grounds it has for suspecting that—

(a) a person has contravened the law of the United Kingdom, or any other EEA State or part of an EEA State, implementing the Audit Directive, and

(b) the act or omission constituting that contravention took place on the territory of an EEA State other than the United Kingdom.

(3) In this section "notifiable person" means a member of the recognised supervisory body in question—

(a) who is also an EEA auditor; and

(b) in respect of whom the EEA competent authority is not the recognised supervisory body itself.

1224 The Secretary of State's power to call for information

(1) The Secretary of State may by notice in writing require a person within subsection (2) to give him such information as he may reasonably require for the exercise of his functions under this Part.

(2) The persons within this subsection are—

(a) any recognised supervisory body,

(b) any recognised qualifying body, and

(c) any person eligible for appointment as a statutory auditor by virtue of this Chapter.

(3) The Secretary of State may require that any information which he requires under this section is to be given within such reasonable time and verified in such manner as he may specify.

1224A Restrictions on disclosure

(1) This section applies to information (in whatever form)—

(a) relating to the private affairs of an individual, or

(b) relating to any particular business,

that is provided to a body to which this section applies in connection with the exercise of its functions under this Part or sections 522 to 524 (notification to appropriate audit authority of resignation or removal of auditor).

(2) This section applies to—

(a) a recognised supervisory body,

(b) a recognised qualifying body,

(c) a body performing functions for the purposes of arrangements within paragraph 23(1) (independent monitoring of certain audits), paragraph 23A(1) (independent monitoring of third country audits) or paragraph 24(1) (independent investigation of public interest cases) of Schedule 10,

(d) the Independent Supervisor,

(e) the Secretary of State, and

(f) a body designated by the Secretary of State under section 1252 (delegation of the Secretary of State's functions).

(3) No such information may, during the lifetime of the individual or so long as the business continues to be carried on, be disclosed without the consent of that individual or (as the case may be) the person for the time being carrying on that business.

(4) Subsection (3) does not apply to any disclosure of information that—

(a) is made for the purpose of facilitating the carrying out by the body of any of its functions,

(b) is made to a person specified in Part 1 of Schedule 11A,

(c) is of a description specified in Part 2 of that Schedule, or

(d) is made in accordance with Part 3 of that Schedule.

(5) Subsection (3) does not apply to—

(a) the disclosure by an EEA competent authority of information disclosed to it by the body in reliance on subsection (4);

(b) the disclosure of such information by anyone who has obtained it directly or indirectly from an EEA competent authority.

(6) This section does not prohibit the disclosure of information if the information is or has been available to the public from any other source.

(7) Nothing in this section authorises the making of a disclosure in contravention of the Data Protection Act 1998.

1224B Offence of disclosure in contravention of section 1224A

(1) A person who discloses information in contravention of section 1224A (restrictions on disclosure) is guilty of an offence, unless—

(a) he did not know, and had no reason to suspect, that the information had been provided as mentioned in section 1224A(1), or

(b) he took all reasonable steps and exercised all due diligence to avoid the commission of the offence.

(2) A person guilty of an offence under this section is liable—

(a) on conviction on indictment, to imprisonment for a term not exceeding two years or a fine (or both);

(b) on summary conviction—

(i) in Scotland, to imprisonment for a term not exceeding 12 months or to a fine not exceeding the statutory maximum, or to both;

(ii) in England and Wales or Northern Ireland, to imprisonment for a term not exceeding three months or to a fine not exceeding the statutory maximum, or to both.

Enforcement

1225 Enforcement: general

(1) This section applies if at any time it appears to the Secretary of State—

(a) in the case of a recognised supervisory body, that any requirement of Part 2 or 3 of Schedule 10 is not satisfied,

(b) in the case of a recognised professional qualification offered by a recognised qualifying body, that any requirement of Part 2 of Schedule 11 is not satisfied, or

(c) that a recognised supervisory body or a recognised qualifying body has not complied with an obligation imposed on it by or by virtue of this Part (other than an obligation to pay a financial penalty under section 1225D).

(2) The Secretary of State may do any one or more of the following—

(a) give a direction to the body under section 1225A;

(b) make an application to the court in respect of the body under section 1225C;

(c) impose a financial penalty on the body under section 1225D.

(3) Subsection (2) is without prejudice to the powers of the Secretary of State under paragraph 3 of Schedule 10 and paragraph 3 of Schedule 11 (revocation of recognition orders).

1225A Directions: general

(1) A direction under this section is one directing a body to take such steps as the Secretary of State considers will—

(a) secure that the requirement in question is satisfied or the obligation in question is complied with, or

(b) mitigate the effect, or prevent the recurrence, of the failure to satisfy the requirement or comply with the obligation.

(2) A direction under this section—

(a) may only require a body to take steps which it has power to take;

(b) may require a body to refrain from taking a particular course of action.

(3) The power to give a direction under this section is subject to any provision made by or under any other enactment.

(4) The Secretary of State may take such steps as the Secretary of State considers appropriate to monitor the extent to which a direction under this section is being, or has been, complied with.

1225B Directions: supplementary

(1) Before giving a direction to a body under section 1225A, the Secretary of State must give the body a notice (a "notice of proposed direction") accompanied by a copy of the proposed direction.

(2) A notice of proposed direction must—

(a) state that the Secretary of State proposes to give the body a direction in the form of the accompanying draft,

(b) identify the requirement or obligation in question and state why it appears to the Secretary of State that the requirement is not satisfied or the obligation has not been complied with,

(c) specify a period within which the body may make written representations with respect to the proposal.

(3) The period specified under subsection (2)(c)—

(a) must begin with the date on which the notice of proposed direction is given to the body, and

(b) must not be less than 14 days.

(4) Written representations made by the body within the period specified under subsection (2)(c) must be considered by the Secretary of State.

(5) After considering any such representations or, in their absence, on the expiry of the period specified under subsection (2)(c), the Secretary of State must decide whether to give the body the proposed direction.

(6) The Secretary of State must give notice of the decision (a "direction decision notice") to the body.

(7) Where the Secretary of State decides to give the proposed direction, the direction decision notice must—
(a) contain the direction,
(b) state the time at which the direction is to take effect, and
(c) specify the Secretary of State's reasons for the decision to give the direction.

(8) Where the Secretary of State decides to give the proposed direction, the Secretary of State must publish the direction decision notice in such manner as the Secretary of State considers appropriate for bringing the direction to the attention of persons likely to be affected.

(9) The Secretary of State may revoke a direction given to a body under section 1225A and, where doing so, must—
(a) give the body notice of the revocation, and
(b) publish the notice in the same manner as the direction decision notice was published.

1225C Compliance orders

(1) If on an application under this section in respect of a body, the court decides that a requirement is not satisfied or an obligation has not been complied with, the court may, subject to subsection (2), order the body to take such steps as it considers will secure that the requirement is satisfied or the obligation is complied with.

(2) Where the obligation is an obligation to comply with a direction under section 1225A, the court may not order compliance with the direction unless it also decides that—
(a) the requirement in respect of which the direction was given is not satisfied, or
(b) the obligation in respect of which the direction was given has not been complied with.

(3) In this section, "the court" means the High Court or, in Scotland, the Court of Session.

1225D Financial penalties: general

(1) A financial penalty imposed on a body under this section is a financial penalty of such amount as the Secretary of State considers appropriate, subject to subsection (2).

(2) In deciding what amount is appropriate the Secretary of State—
(a) must have regard to the nature of the requirement which is not satisfied or the obligation which has not been complied with; and
(b) must not take into account the Secretary of State's costs in discharging functions under this Part.

(3) A financial penalty under this section is payable to the Secretary of State.

(4) In sections 1225E to 1225G, references to a penalty are to a financial penalty under this section.

1225E Financial penalties: supplementary

(1) Before imposing a penalty on a body, the Secretary of State must give the body a notice (a "notice of proposed penalty")—
(a) stating that the Secretary of State proposes to impose a penalty and the amount of the penalty proposed,
(b) identifying the requirement or obligation in question and stating why it appears to the Secretary of State that the requirement is not satisfied or the obligation has not been complied with, and
(c) specifying a period within which the body may make written representations with respect to the proposed penalty.

(2) The period specified under subsection (1)(c)—
(a) must begin with the date on which the notice of proposed penalty is given to the body, and
(b) must not be less than 21 days.

(3) Written representations made by the body before the end of the period specified under subsection (1)(c) must be considered by the Secretary of State.

(4) After considering any such representations or, in their absence, on the expiry of the period specified under subsection (1)(c), the Secretary of State must decide—
(a) whether to impose a penalty, and

(b) where the Secretary of State decides to do so, whether to reduce the proposed amount of the penalty.

(5) The Secretary of State must give notice of the decision (a "penalty decision notice") to the body.

(6) Where the Secretary of State decides to impose a penalty, the penalty decision notice must—

(a) state that the Secretary of State has imposed a penalty on the body and its amount,

(b) identify the requirement or obligation in question and state—

(i) why it appears to the Secretary of State that the requirement is not satisfied or the obligation has not been complied with, or

(ii) where, by that time, the requirement is satisfied or the obligation has been complied with, why it appeared to the Secretary of State when giving the notice of proposed penalty that the requirement was not satisfied or the obligation had not been complied with, and

(c) specify a time by which the penalty is required to be paid.

(7) The time specified under subsection (6)(c) must be at least 3 months after the date on which the penalty decision notice is given to the body.

(8) Where the Secretary of State decides to impose a penalty, the Secretary of State must publish the penalty decision notice and must do so in such manner as the Secretary of State considers appropriate for bringing the penalty to the attention of persons likely to be affected.

(9) The Secretary of State may rescind a penalty imposed on a body under section 1225D and, where doing so, must—

(a) give the body notice of the rescission, and

(b) publish the notice in the same manner as the penalty decision notice was published.

1225F Appeals against financial penalties

(1) A body on which a penalty is imposed may appeal to the court on one or more of the appeal grounds.

(2) The appeal grounds are—

(a) that, before the giving of the notice under section 1225E(1), the requirement in respect of which the penalty was imposed was satisfied or the obligation in respect of which the penalty was imposed had been complied with;

(b) that, where the penalty was imposed in respect of a failure to comply with a direction under section 1225A, before the giving of the notice under section 1225B(6), the requirement in respect of which the direction was given was satisfied or the obligation in respect of which the direction was given had been complied with;

(c) that any of the requirements of section 1225E have not been complied with in relation to the imposition of the penalty and the interests of the body have been substantially prejudiced by the non-compliance;

(d) that the amount of the penalty is unreasonable;

(e) that it was unreasonable of the Secretary of State to require the penalty imposed to be paid by the time specified in the notice under section 1225E(5).

(3) An appeal under subsection (1) must be made within the period of 3 months beginning with the day on which the notice under section 1225E(5) is given to the body in respect of the penalty.

(4) On any such appeal, where the court considers it appropriate to do so in all the circumstances of the case and is satisfied of one or more of the appeal grounds, the court may—

(a) quash the penalty,

(b) substitute a penalty of such lesser amount as the court considers appropriate, or

(c) in the case of the appeal ground in subsection (2)(e), substitute a later time for the time specified in the notice under section 1225E(5).

(5) Where the court substitutes a penalty of a lesser amount, it may require the payment of interest on the substituted penalty, accruing from the time specified in the notice under section 1225E(5) or such later time as the court considers just and equitable.

(6) Where the court substitutes a later time for the time specified in the notice under section 1225E(5), it may require the payment of interest on the penalty, accruing from the substituted time or such later time as the court considers just and equitable.

(7) Where the court dismisses the appeal, it may require the payment of interest on the penalty, accruing from the time specified in the notice under section 1225E(5).

(8) Where the court requires the payment of interest under this section, the interest is payable at such rate as the court considers just and equitable.

(9) Except as provided by this section, the validity of a penalty is not to be questioned by any legal proceedings whatever.

(10) In this section "the court" means the High Court or, in Scotland, the Court of Session.

1225G Recovery of financial penalties

(1) If the whole or any part of a penalty is not paid by the time by which it is required to be paid, the unpaid balance from time to time carries interest at the rate for the time being specified in section 17 of the Judgments Act 1838 (c. 110) (unless a different rate is specified by the court under section 1225F(8)).

(2) If an appeal is made under section 1225F in relation to a penalty, the penalty is not required to be paid until the appeal has been determined or withdrawn.

(3) Subsection (2) does not prevent the court from specifying that interest is to accrue from an earlier date under section 1225F.

(4) Where a penalty, or any portion of it, has not been paid by the time when it is required to be paid and—

(a) no appeal relating to the penalty has been made under section 1225F during the period within which such an appeal can be made, or

(b) an appeal has been made under that section and has been determined or withdrawn,

the Secretary of State may recover from the body, as a debt due to the Secretary of State, any of the penalty and any interest which has not been paid.

CHAPTER 3
AUDITORS GENERAL

Eligibility for appointment

1226 Auditors General: eligibility for appointment as a statutory auditor

(1) In this Part "Auditor General" means—

(a) the Comptroller and Auditor General,

(b) the Auditor General for Scotland,

(c) the Auditor General for Wales, or

(d) the Comptroller and Auditor General for Northern Ireland.

(2) An Auditor General is eligible for appointment as a statutory auditor.

(3) Subsection (2) is subject to any suspension notice having effect under section 1234 (notices suspending eligibility for appointment as a statutory auditor).

Conduct of audits

1227 Individuals responsible for audit work on behalf of Auditors General

An Auditor General must secure that each individual responsible for statutory audit work on behalf of that Auditor General is eligible for appointment as a statutory auditor by virtue of Chapter 2.

The Independent Supervisor

1228 Appointment of the Independent Supervisor

(1) The Secretary of State must appoint a body ("the Independent Supervisor") to discharge the function mentioned in section 1229(1) ("the supervision function").

(2) An appointment under this section must be made by order.

(3) The order has the effect of making the body appointed under subsection (1) designated under section 5 of the Freedom of Information Act 2000 (further powers to designate public authorities).

(4) A body may be appointed under this section only if it is a body corporate or an unincorporated association which appears to the Secretary of State—

(a) to be willing and able to discharge the supervision function, and

(b) to have arrangements in place relating to the discharge of that function which are such as to be likely to ensure that the conditions in subsection (5) are met.

(5) The conditions are—

(a) that the supervision function will be exercised effectively, and

(b) where the order is to contain any requirements or other provisions specified under subsection (6), that that function will be exercised in accordance with any such requirements or provisions.

(6) An order under this section may contain such requirements or other provisions relating to the exercise of the supervision function by the Independent Supervisor as appear to the Secretary of State to be appropriate.

(7) An order under this section is subject to negative resolution procedure.

Supervision of Auditors General

1229 Supervision of Auditors General by the Independent Supervisor

(1) The Independent Supervisor must supervise the performance by each Auditor General of his functions as a statutory auditor.

(2) The Independent Supervisor must discharge that duty by—

(a) establishing supervision arrangements itself, or

(b) entering into supervision arrangements with one or more bodies.

(2A) If the Independent Supervisor enters into supervision arrangements with one or more bodies, it must oversee the effective operation of those supervision arrangements.

(3) For this purpose "supervision arrangements" are arrangements established by the Independent Supervisor or entered into by the Independent Supervisor with a body, for the purposes of this section, in accordance with which the Independent Supervisor or the body does … the following—

(a) determines standards relating to professional integrity and independence which must be applied by an Auditor General in statutory audit work;

(b) determines technical standards which must be applied by an Auditor General in statutory audit work and the manner in which those standards are to be applied in practice;

(c) monitors the performance of statutory audits carried out by an Auditor General;

(d) investigates any matter arising from the performance by an Auditor General of a statutory audit;

(e) holds disciplinary hearings in respect of an Auditor General which appear to be desirable following the conclusion of such investigations;

(f) decides whether (and, if so, what) disciplinary action should be taken against an Auditor General to whom such a hearing related.

(3A) The requirements of paragraphs 9 to 10A and 12 to 15 of Schedule 10 (requirements for recognition of a supervisory body) apply in relation to supervision arrangements as they apply in relation to the rules, practices and arrangements of supervisory bodies.

(4) The Independent Supervisor may enter into supervision arrangements with a body despite any relationship that may exist between the Independent Supervisor and that body.

(5) The Independent Supervisor must notify each Auditor General in writing of any supervision arrangements that it establishes or enters into under this section.

(5A) The Independent Supervisor must, at least once in every calendar year, deliver to the Secretary of State a summary of the results of any inspections conducted for the purposes of subsection (3)(c).

(6) Supervision arrangements within subsection (3)(f) may, in particular, provide for the payment by an Auditor General of a fine to any person.

(7) Any fine received by the Independent Supervisor under supervision arrangements is to be paid into the Consolidated Fund.

1230 Duties of Auditors General in relation to supervision arrangements

(1) Each Auditor General must—

(a) comply with any standards of the kind mentioned in subsection (3)(a) or (b) of section 1229 determined under the supervision arrangements,

(b) take such steps as may be reasonably required of that Auditor General to enable his performance of statutory audits to be monitored by means of inspections carried out under the supervision arrangements, and

(c) comply with any decision of the kind mentioned in subsection (3)(f) of that section made under the supervision arrangements.

(2) Each Auditor General must—

(a) if the Independent Supervisor has established supervision arrangements, pay to the Independent Supervisor;

(b) if the Independent Supervisor has entered into supervision arrangements with a body, pay to that body,

such proportion of the costs incurred by the Independent Supervisor or body for the purposes of the arrangements as the Independent Supervisor may notify to him in writing.

(3) Expenditure under subsection (2) is—

(a) . . .

(b) in the case of expenditure of the Comptroller and Auditor General for Northern Ireland, to be regarded as expenditure of the Northern Ireland Audit Office for the purposes of Article 6(1) of the Audit (Northern Ireland) Order 1987.

(4) In this section "the supervision arrangements" means the arrangements established or entered into under section 1229.

Reporting requirement

1231 Reports by the Independent Supervisor

(1) The Independent Supervisor must, at least once in each calendar year, prepare a report on the discharge of its functions.

(2) The Independent Supervisor must give a copy of each report prepared under subsection (1) to—

(a) the Secretary of State;

(b) the First Minister in Scotland;

(c) the First Minister and the deputy First Minister in Northern Ireland;

(d) the First Minister for Wales.

(3) The Secretary of State must lay before each House of Parliament a copy of each report received by him under subsection (2)(a).

(3A) The First Minister for Wales must lay before the National Assembly for Wales a copy of each report received by him under subsection (2)(d).

(4) In relation to a calendar year during which an appointment of a body as the Independent Supervisor is made or revoked by an order under section 1228, this section applies with such modifications as may be specified in the order.

Information

1232 Matters to be notified to the Independent Supervisor

(1) The Independent Supervisor may require an Auditor General—

(a) to notify the Independent Supervisor immediately of the occurrence of such events as it may specify in writing and to give it such information in respect of those events as is so specified;

(b) to give the Independent Supervisor, at such times or in respect of such periods as it may specify in writing, such information as is so specified.

(2) The notices and information required to be given must be such as the Independent Supervisor may reasonably require for the exercise of the functions conferred on it by or by virtue of this Part.

(3) The Independent Supervisor may require information given under this section to be given in a specified form or verified in a specified manner.

(4) Any notice or information required to be given under this section must be given in writing unless the Independent Supervisor specifies or approves some other manner.

1233 The Independent Supervisor's power to call for information

(1) The Independent Supervisor may by notice in writing require an Auditor General to give it such information as it may reasonably require for the exercise of the functions conferred on it by or by virtue of this Part.

(2) The Independent Supervisor may require that any information which it requires under this section is to be given within such reasonable time and verified in such manner as it may specify.

Enforcement

1234 Suspension notices

(1) The Independent Supervisor may issue—

(a) a notice (a "suspension notice") suspending an Auditor General's eligibility for appointment as a statutory auditor in relation to all persons, or any specified person or persons, indefinitely or until a date specified in the notice;

(b) a notice amending or revoking a suspension notice previously issued to an Auditor General.

(2) In determining whether it is appropriate to issue a notice under subsection (1), the Independent Supervisor must have regard to—

(a) the Auditor General's performance of the obligations imposed on him by or by virtue of this Part, and

(b) the Auditor General's performance of his functions as a statutory auditor.

(3) A notice under subsection (1) must—

(a) be in writing, and

(b) state the date on which it takes effect (which must be after the period of three months beginning with the date on which it is issued).

(4) Before issuing a notice under subsection (1), the Independent Supervisor must—

(a) give written notice of its intention to do so to the Auditor General, and

(b) publish the notice mentioned in paragraph (a) in such manner as it thinks appropriate for bringing it to the attention of any other persons who are likely to be affected.

(5) A notice under subsection (4) must—

(a) state the reasons for which the Independent Supervisor proposes to act, and

(b) give particulars of the rights conferred by subsection (6).

(6) A person within subsection (7) may, within the period of three months beginning with the date of service or publication of the notice under subsection (4) or such longer period as the Independent Supervisor may allow, make written representations to the Independent Supervisor and, if desired, oral representations to a person appointed for that purpose by the Independent Supervisor.

(7) The persons within this subsection are—

(a) the Auditor General, and

(b) any other person who appears to the Independent Supervisor to be affected.

(8) The Independent Supervisor must have regard to any representations made in accordance with subsection (6) in determining—

(a) whether to issue a notice under subsection (1), and

(b) the terms of any such notice.

(9) If in any case the Independent Supervisor considers it appropriate to do so in the public interest it may issue a notice under subsection (1), without regard to the restriction in subsection (3)(b), even if—

(a) no notice has been given or published under subsection (4), or

(b) the period of time for making representations in pursuance of such a notice has not expired.

(10) On issuing a notice under subsection (1), the Independent Supervisor must—

(a) give a copy of the notice to the Auditor General, and

(b) publish the notice in such manner as it thinks appropriate for bringing it to the attention of persons likely to be affected.

(11) In this section "specified" means specified in, or of a description specified in, the suspension notice in question.

1235 Effect of suspension notices

(1) An Auditor General must not act as a statutory auditor at any time when a suspension notice issued to him in respect of the audited person has effect.

(2) If at any time during an Auditor General's term of office as a statutory auditor a suspension notice issued to him in respect of the audited person takes effect, he must immediately—

(a) resign his office (with immediate effect), and

(b) give notice in writing to the audited person that he has resigned by reason of his becoming ineligible for appointment.

(3) A suspension notice does not make an Auditor General ineligible for appointment as a statutory auditor for the purposes of section 1213 (effect of ineligibility: criminal offences).

1236 Compliance orders

(1) If at any time it appears to the Independent Supervisor that an Auditor General has failed to comply with an obligation imposed on him by or by virtue of this Part, the Independent Supervisor may make an application to the court under this section.

(2) If on an application under this section the court decides that the Auditor General has failed to comply with the obligation in question, it may order the Auditor General to take such steps as the court directs for securing that the obligation is complied with.

(3) In this section "the court" means the High Court or, in Scotland, the Court of Session.

Proceedings

1237 Proceedings involving the Independent Supervisor

(1) If the Independent Supervisor is an unincorporated association, any relevant proceedings may be brought by or against it in the name of any body corporate whose constitution provides for the establishment of the body.

(2) For this purpose "relevant proceedings" means proceedings brought in or in connection with the exercise of any function by the body as the Independent Supervisor.

(3) Where an appointment under section 1228 is revoked, the revoking order may make such provision as the Secretary of State thinks fit with respect to pending proceedings.

Grants

1238 Grants to the Independent Supervisor

In section 16 of the Companies (Audit, Investigations and Community Enterprise) Act 2004 (grants to bodies concerned with accounting standards etc), after subsection (2)(k) insert—

"(ka) exercising functions of the Independent Supervisor appointed under Chapter 3 of Part 42 of the Companies Act 2006;".

CHAPTER 4
THE REGISTER OF AUDITORS ETC

1239 The register of auditors

(1) The Secretary of State must make regulations requiring the keeping of a register of—
(a) the persons eligible for appointment as a statutory auditor, and
(b) third country auditors (see Chapter 5) who apply to be registered in the specified manner and in relation to whom specified requirements are met.

(2) The regulations must require each person's entry in the register to contain—
(a) his name and address,
(b) in the case of an individual eligible for appointment as a statutory auditor, the specified information relating to any firm on whose behalf he is responsible for statutory audit work,
(c) in the case of a firm eligible for appointment as a statutory auditor, the specified information relating to the individuals responsible for statutory audit work on its behalf,
(d) in the case of an individual or firm eligible for appointment as a statutory auditor by virtue of Chapter 2, the name of the relevant supervisory body, …
(e) in the case of a firm eligible for appointment as a statutory auditor by virtue of Chapter 2 …, the information mentioned in subsection (3), and
(f) in the case of a third country auditor which is a firm, the name and address of each person who is—
(i) an owner or shareholder of the firm, or
(ii) a member of the firm's administrative or management body,
and may require each person's entry to contain other specified information.

(3) The information referred to in subsection (2)(e) is—
(a) in relation to a body corporate, except where paragraph (b) applies, the name and address of each person who is a director of the body or holds any shares in it;
(b) in relation to a limited liability partnership, the name and address of each member of the partnership;
(c) in relation to a corporation sole, the name and address of the individual for the time being holding the office by the name of which he is the corporation sole;
(d) in relation to a partnership, the name and address of each partner.

(4) The regulations may provide that different parts of the register are to be kept by different persons.

(5) The regulations may impose such obligations as the Secretary of State thinks fit on—
(a) recognised supervisory bodies,
(b) any body designated by order under section 1252 (delegation of Secretary of State's functions),
(c) persons eligible for appointment as a statutory auditor,
(d) third country auditors,
(e) any person with whom arrangements are made by one or more recognised supervisory bodies, or by any body designated by order under section 1252, with respect to the keeping of the register, or
(f) the Independent Supervisor appointed under section 1228.

(6) The regulations may include—
(a) provision requiring that specified entries in the register be open to inspection at times and places specified or determined in accordance with the regulations;
(b) provision enabling a person to require a certified copy of specified entries in the register;
(c) provision authorising the charging of fees for inspection, or the provision of copies, of such reasonable amount as may be specified or determined in accordance with the regulations.

(7) The Secretary of State may direct in writing that the requirements imposed by the regulations …, or such of those requirements as are specified in the direction, are not to apply, in whole or in part, in relation to a particular registered third country auditor or class of registered third country auditors.

(8) The obligations imposed by regulations under this section on such persons as are mentioned in subsection (5)(b) or (e) are enforceable on the application of the Secretary of State by injunction or, in Scotland, by an order under section 45 of the Court of Session Act 1988.

(9) In this section "specified" means specified by regulations under this section.

(10) Regulations under this section are subject to negative resolution procedure.

1240 Information to be made available to public

(1) The Secretary of State may make regulations requiring a person eligible for appointment as a statutory auditor, or a member of a specified class of such persons, to keep and make available to the public specified information, including information regarding—

(a) the person's ownership and governance,

(b) the person's internal controls with respect to the quality and independence of its audit work,

(c) the person's turnover, and

(d) the audited persons of whom the person has acted as statutory auditor.

(2) Regulations under this section may—

(a) impose such obligations as the Secretary of State thinks fit on persons eligible for appointment as a statutory auditor;

(b) require the information to be made available to the public in a specified manner.

(3) In this section "specified" means specified by regulations under this section.

(4) Regulations under this section are subject to negative resolution procedure.

CHAPTER 5
REGISTERED THIRD COUNTRY AUDITORS

Introductory

1241 Meaning of "registered third country auditor" and "UK-traded non-EEA company"

(1) In this Part—

"registered third country auditor" means a third country auditor who is entered in the register kept in accordance with regulations under section 1239(1).

(2) In this Part "UK-traded non-EEA company" means a body corporate—

(a) which is incorporated or formed under the law of a third country,

(b) whose transferable securities are admitted to trading on a regulated market situated or operating in the United Kingdom, and

(c) which has not been excluded, or is not of a description of bodies corporate which has been excluded, from this definition by an order made by the Secretary of State.

(3) For this purpose—

"regulated market" has the meaning given by Article 4.1(14) of Directive 2004/39/EC of the European Parliament and of the Council on markets in financial instruments;

"transferable securities" has the meaning given by Article 4.1(18) of that Directive.

(4) An order under this section is subject to negative resolution procedure.

Duties

1242 Duties of registered third country auditors

(1) A registered third country auditor who audits the accounts of a UK-traded non-EEA company must participate in—

(a) arrangements within paragraph 1 of Schedule 12 (arrangements for independent monitoring of audits . . .), and

(b) arrangements within paragraph 2 of that Schedule (arrangements for independent investigation for disciplinary purposes of public interest cases).

(2) A registered third country auditor must—

(a) take such steps as may be reasonably required of it to enable its performance of audits of accounts of UK-traded non-EEA companies to be monitored by means of inspections carried out under the arrangements mentioned in subsection (1)(a), and

(b) comply with any decision as to disciplinary action to be taken against it made under the arrangements mentioned in subsection (1)(b).

(3) Schedule 12 makes further provision with respect to the arrangements in which registered third country auditors are required to participate.

(4) The Secretary of State may direct in writing that subsections (1) to (3) are not to apply, in whole or in part, in relation to—

(a) a particular registered third country auditor or class of registered third country auditors;

(b) audits of the accounts of a particular UK-traded non-EEA company or class of UK-traded non-EEA companies;

(c) audits by a particular registered third country auditor or class of registered third country auditors of the accounts of a particular UK-traded non-EEA company or class of UK-traded non-EEA companies.

Information

1243 Matters to be notified to the Secretary of State

(1) The Secretary of State may require a registered third country auditor—

(a) to notify him immediately of the occurrence of such events as he may specify in writing and to give him such information in respect of those events as is so specified;

(b) to give him, at such times or in respect of such periods as he may specify in writing, such information as is so specified.

(2) The notices and information required to be given must be such as the Secretary of State may reasonably require for the exercise of his functions under this Part.

(3) The Secretary of State may require information given under this section to be given in a specified form or verified in a specified manner.

(4) Any notice or information required to be given under this section must be given in writing unless the Secretary of State specifies or approves some other manner.

1244 The Secretary of State's power to call for information

(1) The Secretary of State may by notice in writing require a registered third country auditor to give him such information as he may reasonably require for the exercise of his functions under this Part.

(2) The Secretary of State may require that any information which he requires under this section is to be given within such reasonable time and verified in such manner as he may specify.

Enforcement

1245 Compliance orders

(1) If at any time it appears to the Secretary of State that a registered third country auditor has failed to comply with an obligation imposed on him by or by virtue of this Part, the Secretary of State may make an application to the court under this section.

(2) If on an application under this section the court decides that the auditor has failed to comply with the obligation in question, it may order the auditor to take such steps as the court directs for securing that the obligation is complied with.

(3) In this section "the court" means the High Court or, in Scotland, the Court of Session.

1246 Removal of third country auditors from the register of auditors

(1) The Secretary of State may, by regulations, confer on the person keeping the register in accordance with regulations under section 1239(1) power to remove a third country auditor from the register.

(2) Regulations under this section must require the person keeping the register, in determining whether to remove a third country auditor from the register, to have regard to the auditor's compliance with obligations imposed on him by or by virtue of this Part.

(3) Where provision is made under section 1239(4) (different parts of the register to be kept by different persons), references in this section to the person keeping the register are to the person keeping that part of the register which relates to third country auditors.

(4) Regulations under this section are subject to negative resolution procedure.

1247 Grants to bodies concerned with arrangements under Schedule 12

In section 16 of the Companies (Audit, Investigations and Community Enterprise) Act 2004 (grants to bodies concerned with accounting standards etc), after subsection (2)(ka) (inserted by section 1238) insert—

"(kb) establishing, maintaining or carrying out arrangements within paragraph 1 or 2 of Schedule 12 to the Companies Act 2006;".

CHAPTER 6
SUPPLEMENTARY AND GENERAL

Power to require second company audit

1248 Secretary of State's power to require second audit of a company

(1) This section applies where a person appointed as statutory auditor of a company was not an appropriate person for any part of the period during which the audit was conducted.

(2) The Secretary of State may direct the company concerned to retain an appropriate person—

(a) to conduct a second audit of the relevant accounts, or

(b) to review the first audit and to report (giving his reasons) whether a second audit is needed.

(3) For the purposes of subsections (1) and (2) a person is "appropriate" if he—

(a) is eligible for appointment as a statutory auditor or, if the person is an Auditor General, for appointment as statutory auditor of the company, and

(b) is not prohibited by section 1214(1) (independence requirement) from acting as statutory auditor of the company.

(4) The Secretary of State must send a copy of a direction under subsection (2) to the registrar of companies.

(5) The company is guilty of an offence if—

(a) it fails to comply with a direction under subsection (2) within the period of 21 days beginning with the date on which it is given, or

(b) it has been convicted of a previous offence under this subsection and the failure to comply with the direction which led to the conviction continues after the conviction.

(6) The company must—

(a) send a copy of a report under subsection (2)(b) to the registrar of companies, and

(b) if the report states that a second audit is needed, take such steps as are necessary for the carrying out of that audit.

(7) The company is guilty of an offence if—

(a) it fails to send a copy of a report under subsection (2)(b) to the registrar within the period of 21 days beginning with the date on which it receives it,

(b) in a case within subsection (6)(b), it fails to take the steps mentioned immediately it receives the report, or

(c) it has been convicted of a previous offence under this subsection and the failure to send a copy of the report, or take the steps, which led to the conviction continues after the conviction.

(8) A company guilty of an offence under this section is liable on summary conviction—

(a) in a case within subsection (5)(a) or (7)(a) or (b), to a fine not exceeding level 5 on the standard scale, and

(b) in a case within subsection (5)(b) or (7)(c), to a fine not exceeding one-tenth of level 5 on the standard scale for each day on which the failure continues.

(9) In this section "registrar of companies" has the meaning given by section 1060.

1249 Supplementary provision about second audits

(1) If a person accepts an appointment, or continues to act, as statutory auditor of a company at a time when he knows he is not an appropriate person, the company may recover from him any costs incurred by it in complying with the requirements of section 1248.

For this purpose "appropriate" is to be construed in accordance with subsection (3) of that section.

(2) Where a second audit is carried out under section 1248, any statutory or other provision applying in relation to the first audit applies also, in so far as practicable, in relation to the second audit.

(3) A direction under section 1248(2) is, on the application of the Secretary of State, enforceable by injunction or, in Scotland, by an order under section 45 of the Court of Session Act 1988.

False and misleading statements

1250 Misleading, false and deceptive statements

(1) A person is guilty of an offence if—

(a) for the purposes of or in connection with any application under this Part, or

(b) in purported compliance with any requirement imposed on him by or by virtue of this Part,

he knowingly or recklessly furnishes information which is misleading, false or deceptive in a material particular.

(2) It is an offence for a person whose name does not appear on the register of auditors kept under regulations under section 1239 in an entry made under subsection (1)(a) of that section to describe himself as a registered auditor or so to hold himself out as to indicate, or be reasonably understood to indicate, that he is a registered auditor.

(3) It is an offence for a person whose name does not appear on the register of auditors kept under regulations under that section in an entry made under subsection (1)(b) of that section to describe himself as a registered third country auditor or so to hold himself out as to indicate, or be reasonably understood to indicate, that he is a registered third country auditor.

(4) It is an offence for a body which is not a recognised supervisory body or a recognised qualifying body to describe itself as so recognised or so to describe itself or hold itself out as to indicate, or be reasonably understood to indicate, that it is so recognised.

(5) A person guilty of an offence under subsection (1) is liable—

(a) on conviction on indictment, to imprisonment for a term not exceeding two years or to a fine (or both);

(b) on summary conviction—

(i) in England and Wales, to imprisonment for a term not exceeding twelve months or to a fine not exceeding the statutory maximum (or both),

(ii) in Scotland or Northern Ireland, to imprisonment for a term not exceeding six months or to a fine not exceeding the statutory maximum (or both).

In relation to an offence committed before the commencement of section 154(1) of the Criminal Justice Act 2003, for "twelve months" in paragraph (b)(i) substitute "six months".

(6) Subject to subsection (7), a person guilty of an offence under subsection (2), (3) or (4) is liable on summary conviction—

(a) in England and Wales, to imprisonment for a term not exceeding 51 weeks or to a fine not exceeding level 5 on the standard scale (or both),

(b) in Scotland or Northern Ireland, to imprisonment for a term not exceeding six months or to a fine not exceeding level 5 on the standard scale (or both).

In relation to an offence committed before the commencement of section 281(5) of the Criminal Justice Act 2003, for "51 weeks" in paragraph (a) substitute "six months".

(7) Where a contravention of subsection (2), (3) or (4) involves a public display of the offending description, the maximum fine that may be imposed is an amount equal to level 5 on the standard scale multiplied by the number of days for which the display has continued.

(8) It is a defence for a person charged with an offence under subsection (2), (3) or (4) to show that he took all reasonable precautions and exercised all due diligence to avoid the commission of the offence.

Fees

1251 Fees

(1) An applicant for a recognition order under this Part must pay such fee in respect of his application as the Secretary of State may by regulations prescribe; and no application is to be regarded as duly made unless this subsection is complied with.

(2) The Secretary of State may by regulations prescribe periodical fees to be paid by—
(a) every recognised supervisory body,
(b) every recognised qualifying body,
(c) every Auditor General, and
(d) every registered third country auditor.

(3) Fees received by the Secretary of State by virtue of this Part are to be paid into the Consolidated Fund.

(4) Regulations under this section are subject to negative resolution procedure.

Duty of Secretary of State to Report on Inspections

1251A Duty of the Secretary of State to report on inspections

The Secretary of State must, at least once in every calendar year, publish a report containing a summary of the results of inspections that are delivered to him—
(a) by the Independent Supervisor under section 1229(5A);
(b) by a recognised supervisory body under paragraph 13(9) of Schedule 10.

1252 Delegation of the Secretary of State's functions

(1) The Secretary of State may make an order under this section (a "delegation order") for the purpose of enabling functions of the Secretary of State under this Part to be exercised by a body designated by the order.

(2) The body designated by a delegation order may be either—
(a) a body corporate which is established by the order, or
(b) subject to section 1253, a body (whether a body corporate or an unincorporated association) which is already in existence ("an existing body").

(3) A delegation order has the effect of making the body designated by the order designated under section 5 of the Freedom of Information Act 2000 (further powers to designate public authorities).

(4) A delegation order has the effect of transferring to the body designated by it all functions of the Secretary of State under this Part—
(a) subject to such exceptions and reservations as may be specified in the order, and
(b) except—
(i) his functions in relation to the body itself, and
(ii) his functions under section 1228 (appointment of Independent Supervisor).

(5) A delegation order may confer on the body designated by it such other functions supplementary or incidental to those transferred as appear to the Secretary of State to be appropriate.

(6) Any transfer of functions under the following provisions must be subject to the reservation that the functions remain exercisable concurrently by the Secretary of State—
(a) section 1224 (power to call for information from recognised bodies etc);
(b) section 1244 (power to call for information from registered third country auditors);
(c) section 1254 (directions to comply with international obligations).

(7) Any transfer of—

(a) the function of refusing to make a declaration under section 1221(1) (approval of third country qualifications) on the grounds referred to in section 1221(4) (lack of comparable treatment), or

(b) the function of withdrawing such a declaration under section 1221(7) on those grounds,

must be subject to the reservation that the function is exercisable only with the consent of the Secretary of State.

(8) A delegation order may be amended or, if it appears to the Secretary of State that it is no longer in the public interest that the order should remain in force, revoked by a further order under this section.

(9) Where functions are transferred or resumed, the Secretary of State may by order confer or, as the case may be, take away such other functions supplementary or incidental to those transferred or resumed as appear to him to be appropriate.

(10) Where a delegation order is made, Schedule 13 has effect with respect to—

(a) the status of the body designated by the order in exercising functions of the Secretary of State under this Part,

(b) the constitution and proceedings of the body where it is established by the order,

(c) the exercise by the body of certain functions transferred to it, and

(d) other supplementary matters.

(11) An order under this section which has the effect of transferring or resuming any functions is subject to affirmative resolution procedure.

(12) Any other order under this section is subject to negative resolution procedure.

1253 Delegation of functions to an existing body

(1) The Secretary of State's power to make a delegation order under section 1252 which designates an existing body is exercisable in accordance with this section.

(2) The Secretary of State may make such a delegation order if it appears to him that—

(a) the body is able and willing to exercise the functions that would be transferred by the order, and

(b) the body has arrangements in place relating to the exercise of those functions which are such as to be likely to ensure that the conditions in subsection (3) are met.

(3) The conditions are—

(a) that the functions in question will be exercised effectively, and

(b) where the delegation order is to contain any requirements or other provisions specified under subsection (4), that those functions will be exercised in accordance with any such requirements or provisions.

(4) The delegation order may contain such requirements or other provision relating to the exercise of the functions by the designated body as appear to the Secretary of State to be appropriate.

(5) An existing body—

(a) may be designated by a delegation order under section 1252, and

(b) may accordingly exercise functions of the Secretary of State in pursuance of the order,

despite any involvement of the body in the exercise of any functions under arrangements within paragraph 21 to 22B, 23(1) or 24(1) of Schedule 10 or paragraph 1 or 2 of Schedule 12.

Cooperation with Foreign Competent Authorities

1253A Requests to foreign competent authorities

The Secretary of State may request from an EEA competent authority or a third country competent authority such assistance, information or investigation as he may reasonably require in connection with the exercise of his functions under this Part.

1253B Requests from EEA competent authorities

(1) The Secretary of State must take all necessary steps to—

(a) ensure that an investigation is carried out, or

(b) provide any other assistance or information,

if requested to do so by an EEA competent authority in accordance with Article 36 of the Audit Directive (cooperation between Member State authorities).

(2) Within 28 days following the date on which he receives the request, the Secretary of State must—
- (a) provide the assistance or information required by the EEA competent authority under subsection (1)(b), or
- (b) notify the EEA competent authority which made the request of the reasons why he has not done so.

(3) But the Secretary of State need not take steps to comply with a request under subsection (1) if—
- (a) he considers that complying with the request may prejudice the sovereignty, security or public order of the United Kingdom;
- (b) legal proceedings have been brought in the United Kingdom (whether continuing or not) in relation to the persons and matters to which the request relates; or
- (c) disciplinary action has been taken by a recognised supervisory body in relation to the persons and matters to which the request relates.

1253C Notification to competent authorities of other EEA States

(1) The Secretary of State must notify the relevant EEA competent authority if he receives notice from a recognised supervisory body under section 1223A(1) (notification of withdrawal of eligibility for appointment) of the withdrawal of a person's eligibility for appointment as a statutory auditor.

(2) In subsection (1) "the relevant EEA competent authority" means the EEA competent authority which has approved the person concerned in accordance with the Audit Directive to carry out audits of annual accounts or consolidated accounts required by EU law.

(3) The notification under subsection (1) must include the name of the person concerned and the reasons for the withdrawal of his eligibility for appointment as statutory auditor.

(4) The Secretary of State must notify the relevant EEA competent authority if he has reasonable grounds for suspecting that—
- (a) a person has contravened the law of the United Kingdom, or any other EEA State or part of an EEA State, implementing the Audit Directive, and
- (b) the act or omission constituting that contravention took place on the territory of an EEA State other than the United Kingdom.

(5) In subsection (4) "the relevant EEA competent authority" means the EEA competent authority for the EEA State in which the suspected contravention took place.

(6) The notification under subsection (4) must include the name of the person concerned and the grounds for the Secretary of State's suspicion.

Transfer of Papers to Third Countries

1253D Restriction on transfer of audit working papers to third countries

(1) Audit working papers must not be transferred to a third country competent authority except in accordance with—
- (a) section 1253DA (transfer by Secretary of State),
- (b) section 1253DB (transfer by statutory auditor with approval of Secretary of State), or
- (c) section 1253DC (transfer by statutory auditor for purposes of investigation of auditor).

(2) The following are approved third country competent authorities for the purposes of this Part—
- (a) the Australian Securities and Investments Commission;
- (b) the Canadian Public Accountability Board;
- (c) the Certified Public Accountants and Auditing Oversight Board of Japan;
- (d) the Financial Services Agency of Japan;
- (e) the Federal Audit Oversight Authority of Switzerland;
- *(f) the Public Company Accounting Oversight Board of the United States of America;*
- *(g) the Securities and Exchange Commission of the United States of America.*

(3) Nothing in the sections referred to in subsection (1) authorises the making of a disclosure in contravention of the Data Protection Act 1998.

Note. Subsection (2)(f), (g) are repealed by S.I. 2010/2537, reg. 4(1), as from 31 July 2013.

1253DA Transfer by Secretary of State

(1) The Secretary of State may transfer audit working papers to an approved third country competent authority if the following conditions are met (but see also section 1253DD).

(2) The first condition is that the authority has made a request to the Secretary of State for the transfer of the audit working papers.

(3) The second condition is that the audit working papers relate to audits of companies that—

(a) have issued securities in the third country in which the authority is established, or

(b) form part of a group issuing statutory consolidated accounts in that third country.

(4) The third condition is that the authority has entered into arrangements with the Secretary of State in accordance with section 1253E.

1253DB Transfer by statutory auditor with approval of Secretary of State

(1) A statutory auditor may transfer audit working papers to an approved third country competent authority if the transfer is made—

(a) with the prior approval of the Secretary of State, and

(b) in accordance with rules of a recognised supervisory body meeting the requirements of paragraph 16AA of Schedule 10.

(2) The Secretary of State must not approve a transfer of audit working papers to an approved third country competent authority for the purposes of this section unless the following conditions are met (see also section 1253DD).

(3) The first condition is that the authority has made a request to the Secretary of State for the transfer of the audit working papers.

(4) The second condition is that the audit working papers relate to audits of companies that—

(a) have issued securities in the third country in which the authority is established, or

(b) form part of a group issuing statutory consolidated accounts in that third country.

(5) The third condition is that the authority has entered into arrangements with the Secretary of State in accordance with section 1253E.

1253DC Transfer by statutory auditor for purposes of investigation of auditor

A statutory auditor may transfer audit working papers to a third country competent authority if the transfer is made—

(a) for the purposes of an investigation of an auditor or audit firm, and

(b) in accordance with rules of a recognised supervisory body meeting the requirements of paragraph 16AB of Schedule 10.

1253DD Agreement of EEA competent authority

(1) This section applies where—

(a) an approved third country competent authority makes a request to the Secretary of State for the transfer of audit working papers which relate to the audit of the consolidated accounts of a group, and

(b) the audit working papers that are the subject of the request—

(i) have been created by the auditor of a subsidiary that is located in another EEA State in relation to the audit of that subsidiary, and

(ii) are in the possession of a statutory auditor.

(2) In the case of a transfer by the Secretary of State under section 1253DA, the transfer must not take place unless the EEA competent authority responsible for the auditor of the subsidiary has given its express agreement to the transfer.

(3) In the case of a transfer by a statutory auditor under section 1253DB, the Secretary of State must not approve the transfer unless the EEA competent authority responsible for the auditor of the subsidiary has given its express agreement to the transfer.

1253DE Transfer by means of inspection

(1) This section applies in the case of a transfer of audit working papers if—

(a) it is a transfer to *an approved third country competent authority listed in section 1253D(2)(a), (f) or (g)*,

(b) it is a transfer under section 1253DA or 1253DB, and

(c) it is to take place by means of an inspection in the United Kingdom by *the authority.*

(2) The Secretary of State must participate in the inspection.

(3) The inspection must be under the leadership of the Secretary of State unless the Secretary of State otherwise permits.

Note. This section is amended as follows by S.I. 2010/2537, reg. 4, as from 31 July 2013: in subsection (1)(a), the words "an approved third country competent authority listed in section 1253D(2)(a), (f) or (g)" are substituted by the words "the Australian Securities and Investments Commission"; and in subsection (1)(c), the words "the authority" are substituted by the words "the Commission".

1253E Working arrangements for transfer of papers

(1) The Secretary of State may enter into arrangements with a third country competent authority relating to the transfer of audit working papers—

(a) from the third country competent authority or a third country auditor regulated by that authority to the Secretary of State, and

(b) from the Secretary of State or a statutory auditor to the third country competent authority.

(2) The arrangements must provide that a request by the Secretary of State or the third country competent authority for a transfer mentioned in subsection (1) must be accompanied by a statement explaining the reasons for the request.

(3) The arrangements must—

(a) provide that the Secretary of State may not use audit working papers obtained from the third country competent authority or a third country auditor regulated by that authority except in connection with one or more of the functions mentioned in subsection (4), and

(b) include comparable provision in relation to audit working papers obtained by the third country competent authority from the Secretary of State or a statutory auditor.

(4) Those functions are—

(a) quality assurance functions which meet requirements equivalent to those of Article 29 of the Audit Directive (quality assurance);

(b) investigation or disciplinary functions which meet requirements equivalent to those of Article 30 of the Audit Directive (investigations and penalties);

(c) public oversight functions which meet requirements equivalent to those of Article 32 of the Audit Directive (principles of public oversight).

(5) The arrangements must—

(a) provide that the Secretary of State, a person exercising the functions of the Secretary of State and persons employed or formerly employed in discharging those functions must be subject to obligations of confidentiality as to personal data, professional secrets and sensitive commercial information contained in audit working papers transferred to the Secretary of State, and

(b) provide that the third country competent authority and persons involved in exercising its functions are subject to comparable obligations in relation to audit working papers transferred to the authority.

(6) The arrangements must—

(a) provide that the Secretary of State may refuse, or direct a statutory auditor to refuse, a request from the third country competent authority for a transfer of audit working papers in a case mentioned in subsection (7)(a) or (b), and

(b) provide that the third country competent authority has comparable rights in relation to a request from the Secretary of State.

(7) Those cases are—

(a) where the transfer of the papers would adversely affect the sovereignty, security or public order of the European Union or of the United Kingdom;

(b) where legal proceedings have been brought in the United Kingdom (whether continuing or not) in relation to the persons and matters to which the request relates.

(8) Arrangements with *an approved third country competent authority listed in section 1253D(2)(a), (f) or (g)* must—

(a) provide that any contact between a statutory auditor and *the authority* relating to a relevant transfer of audit working papers to *the authority* must take place via the Secretary of State, and

(b) include comparable provision in relation to transfers of audit working papers to the Secretary of State.

(9) "Relevant transfer" means any transfer other than a transfer by a statutory auditor under section 1253DC.

Note. This section is amended as follows by S.I. 2010/2537, reg. 4, as from 31 July 2013: in subsection (8), the words "an approved third country competent authority listed in section 1253D(2)(a), (f) or (g)" are substituted by the words "the Australian Securities and Investments Commission"; and in paragraph (a) of that subsection, the words "the authority" in both places they occur are substituted by the words "the Commission".

1253F Publication of working arrangements

If the Secretary of State enters into working arrangements in accordance with section 1253E, he must publish on a website without undue delay—

(a) the name of the third country competent authority with which he has entered into such arrangements, and

(b) the country or territory in which it is established.

International obligations

1254 Directions to comply with international obligations

(1) If it appears to the Secretary of State—

(a) that any action proposed to be taken by a recognised supervisory body or a recognised qualifying body, the Independent Supervisor or a body designated by order under section 1252, would be incompatible with EU obligations or any other international obligations of the United Kingdom, or

(b) that any action which that body has power to take is required for the purpose of implementing any such obligations,

he may direct the body not to take or, as the case may be, to take the action in question.

(2) A direction may include such supplementary or incidental requirements as the Secretary of State thinks necessary or expedient.

(3) A direction under this section given to the Independent Supervisor or a body designated by order under section 1252 is enforceable on the application of the Secretary of State by injunction or, in Scotland, by an order under section 45 of the Court of Session Act 1988.

General provision relating to offences

1255 Offences by bodies corporate, partnerships and unincorporated associations

(1) Where an offence under this Part committed by a body corporate is proved to have been committed with the consent or connivance of, or to be attributable to any neglect on the part of, an officer of the body, or a person purporting to act in any such capacity, he as well as the body corporate is guilty of the offence and liable to be proceeded against and punished accordingly.

(2) Where an offence under this Part committed by a partnership is proved to have been committed with the consent or connivance of, or to be attributable to any neglect on the part of, a partner, he as well as the partnership is guilty of the offence and liable to be proceeded against and punished accordingly.

(3) Where an offence under this Part committed by an unincorporated association (other than a partnership) is proved to have been committed with the consent or connivance of, or to be attributable to any neglect on the part of, any officer of the association or any member of its governing body, he as well as the association is guilty of the offence and liable to be proceeded against and punished accordingly.

1256 Time limits for prosecution of offences

(1) An information relating to an offence under this Part which is triable by a magistrates" court in England and Wales may be so tried if it is laid at any time within the period of twelve months beginning with the date on which evidence sufficient in the opinion of the Director of Public Prosecutions or the Secretary of State to justify the proceedings comes to his knowledge.

(2) Proceedings in Scotland for an offence under this Part may be commenced at any time within the period of twelve months beginning with the date on which evidence sufficient in the Lord Advocate's opinion to justify proceedings came to his knowledge or, where such evidence was reported to him by the Secretary of State, within the period of twelve months beginning with the date on which it came to the knowledge of the Secretary of State.

(3) For the purposes of subsection (2) proceedings are to be deemed to be commenced on the date on which a warrant to apprehend or cite the accused is granted, if the warrant is executed without undue delay.

(4) A complaint charging an offence under this Part which is triable by a magistrates" court in Northern Ireland may be so tried if it is made at any time within the period of twelve months beginning with the date on which evidence sufficient in the opinion of the Director of Public Prosecutions for Northern Ireland or the Secretary of State to justify the proceedings comes to his knowledge.

(5) This section does not authorise—

(a) in the case of proceedings in England and Wales, the trial of an information laid,

(b) in the case of proceedings in Scotland, the commencement of proceedings, or

(c) in the case of proceedings in Northern Ireland, the trial of a complaint made,

more than three years after the commission of the offence.

(6) For the purposes of this section a certificate of the Director of Public Prosecutions, the Lord Advocate, the Director of Public Prosecutions for Northern Ireland or the Secretary of State as to the date on which such evidence as is referred to above came to his knowledge is conclusive evidence.

(7) Nothing in this section affects proceedings within the time limits prescribed by section 127(1) of the Magistrates' Courts Act 1980, section 331 of the Criminal Procedure (Scotland) Act 1975 or Article 19 of the Magistrates' Courts (Northern Ireland) Order 1981 (the usual time limits for criminal proceedings).

1257 Jurisdiction and procedure in respect of offences

(1) Summary proceedings for an offence under this Part may, without prejudice to any jurisdiction exercisable apart from this section, be taken—

(a) against a body corporate or unincorporated association at any place at which it has a place of business, and

(b) against an individual at any place where he is for the time being.

(2) Proceedings for an offence alleged to have been committed under this Part by an unincorporated association must be brought in the name of the association (and not in that of any of its members), and for the purposes of any such proceedings any rules of court relating to the service of documents apply as in relation to a body corporate.

(3) Section 33 of the Criminal Justice Act 1925 and Schedule 3 to the Magistrates' Courts Act 1980 (procedure on charge of offence against a corporation) apply in a case in which an unincorporated association is charged in England and Wales with an offence under this Part as they apply in the case of a corporation.

(4) Section 18 of the Criminal Justice Act (Northern Ireland) 1945 and Article 166 and Schedule 4 to the Magistrates' Courts (Northern Ireland) Order 1981 (procedure on charge of offence against a

corporation) apply in a case in which an unincorporated association is charged in Northern Ireland with an offence under this Part as they apply in the case of a corporation.

(5) In relation to proceedings on indictment in Scotland for an offence alleged to have been committed under this Part by an unincorporated association, section 70 of the Criminal Procedure (Scotland) Act 1995 (proceedings on indictment against bodies corporate) applies as if the association were a body corporate.

(6) A fine imposed on an unincorporated association on its conviction of such an offence must be paid out of the funds of the association.

Notices etc

1258 Service of notices

(1) This section has effect in relation to any notice, direction or other document required or authorised by or by virtue of this Part to be given to or served on any person other than the Secretary of State.

(2) Any such document may be given to or served on the person in question—

(a) by delivering it to him,

(b) by leaving it at his proper address, or

(c) by sending it by post to him at that address.

(3) Any such document may—

(a) in the case of a body corporate, be given to or served on an officer of that body;

(b) in the case of a partnership, be given to or served on any partner;

(c) in the case of an unincorporated association other than a partnership, be given to or served on any member of the governing body of that association.

(4) For the purposes of this section and section 7 of the Interpretation Act 1978 (service of documents by post) in its application to this section, the proper address of any person is his last known address (whether of his residence or of a place where he carries on business or is employed) and also—

(a) in the case of a person who is eligible under the rules of a recognised supervisory body for appointment as a statutory auditor and who does not have a place of business in the United Kingdom, the address of that body;

(b) in the case of a body corporate or an officer of that body, the address of the registered or principal office of that body in the United Kingdom;

(c) in the case of an unincorporated association other than a partnership or a member of its governing body, its principal office in the United Kingdom.

1259 Documents in electronic form

(1) This section applies where—

(a) section 1258 authorises the giving or sending of a notice, direction or other document by its delivery to a particular person ("the recipient"), and

(b) the notice, direction or other document is transmitted to the recipient—

(i) by means of an electronic communications network, or

(ii) by other means but in a form that requires the use of apparatus by the recipient to render it intelligible.

(2) The transmission has effect for the purposes of this Part as a delivery of the notice, direction or other document to the recipient, but only if the recipient has indicated to the person making the transmission his willingness to receive the notice, direction or other document in the form and manner used.

(3) An indication to a person for the purposes of subsection (2)—

(a) must be given to the person in such manner as he may require,

(b) may be a general indication or an indication that is limited to notices, directions or other documents of a particular description,

(c) must state the address to be used,

(d) must be accompanied by such other information as the person requires for the making of the transmission, and

(e) may be modified or withdrawn at any time by a notice given to the person in such manner as he may require.

(4) In this section "electronic communications network" has the same meaning as in the Communications Act 2003.

Interpretation

1260 Meaning of "associate"

(1) In this Part "associate", in relation to a person, is to be construed as follows.

(2) In relation to an individual, "associate" means—

(a) that individual's spouse, civil partner or minor child or step-child,

(b) any body corporate of which that individual is a director, and

(c) any employee or partner of that individual.

(3) In relation to a body corporate, "associate" means—

(a) any body corporate of which that body is a director,

(b) any body corporate in the same group as that body, and

(c) any employee or partner of that body or of any body corporate in the same group.

(4) In relation to a partnership constituted under the law of Scotland, or any other country or territory in which a partnership is a legal person, "associate" means—

(a) any body corporate of which that partnership is a director,

(b) any employee of or partner in that partnership, and

(c) any person who is an associate of a partner in that partnership.

(5) In relation to a partnership constituted under the law of England and Wales or Northern Ireland, or the law of any other country or territory in which a partnership is not a legal person, "associate" means any person who is an associate of any of the partners.

(6) In subsections (2)(b), (3)(a) and (4)(a), in the case of a body corporate which is a limited liability partnership, "director" is to be read as "member".

1261 Minor definitions

(1) In this Part, unless a contrary intention appears—

"address" means—

(a) in relation to an individual, his usual residential or business address;

(b) in relation to a firm, its registered or principal office in the United Kingdom;

"the Audit Directive" means Directive 2006/43/EC of the European Parliament and of the Council on statutory audits of annual accounts and consolidated accounts, amending Council Directives 78/660/EEC and 83/349/EEC and repealing Council Directive 84/253/EEC, as amended at any time before 1st January 2009;

"audit working papers" means any documents which—

(a) are or have been held by a statutory auditor, an EEA auditor or a third country auditor, and

(b) are related to the conduct of an audit conducted by that auditor;

"company" means any company or other body the accounts of which must be audited in accordance with Part 16;

"director", in relation to a body corporate, includes any person occupying in relation to it the position of a director (by whatever name called) and any person in accordance with whose directions or instructions (not being advice given in a professional capacity) the directors of the body are accustomed to act;

"EEA auditor" means an individual or firm approved in accordance with the Audit Directive by an EEA competent authority to carry out audits of annual accounts or consolidated accounts required by European Union law;

"EEA competent authority" means a competent authority within the meaning of Article 2.10 of the Audit Directive of an EEA State other than the United Kingdom;

"firm" means any entity, whether or not a legal person, which is not an individual and includes a body corporate, a corporation sole and a partnership or other unincorporated association;

"group", in relation to a body corporate, means the body corporate, any other body corporate which is its holding company or subsidiary and any other body corporate which is a subsidiary of that holding company;

"holding company" and "subsidiary" are to be read in accordance with section 1159 and Schedule 6;

"officer", in relation to a body corporate, includes a director, a manager, a secretary or, where the affairs of the body are managed by its members, a member;

"parent undertaking" and "subsidiary undertaking" are to be read in accordance with section 1162 and Schedule 7;

"third country" means a country or territory that is not an EEA State or part of an EEA State;

"third country auditor" means a person, other than a person eligible for appointment as a statutory auditor, who is eligible to conduct audits of the accounts of bodies corporate incorporated or formed under the law of a third country in accordance with the law of that country;

"third country competent authority" means a body established in a third country exercising functions related to the regulation or oversight of auditors;

"transfer", in relation to audit working papers, includes physical and electronic transfer and allowing access to such papers.

(2) For the purposes of this Part a body is to be regarded as "established in the United Kingdom" if and only if—

(a) it is incorporated or formed under the law of the United Kingdom or a part of the United Kingdom, or

(b) its central management and control are exercised in the United Kingdom;

and any reference to a qualification "obtained in the United Kingdom" is to a qualification obtained from such a body.

(2A) For the purposes of this Part, Gibraltar shall be treated as if it were an EEA State.

(3) The Secretary of State may by regulations make such modifications of this Part as appear to him to be necessary or appropriate for the purposes of its application in relation to any firm, or description of firm, which is not a body corporate or a partnership.

(4) Regulations under subsection (3) are subject to negative resolution procedure.

1262 Index of defined expressions

The following Table shows provisions defining or otherwise explaining expressions used in this Part (other than provisions defining or explaining an expression used only in the same section)—

Expression	Provision
address	section 1261(1)
appropriate qualification	section 1219
approved third country competent authority	section 1253D(2)
associate	section 1260
Audit Directive	section 1261(1)
audit working papers	section 1261(1)
audited person	section 1210(2)
Auditor General	section 1226(1)
company	section 1261(1)
delegation order	section 1252(1)
director (of a body corporate)	section 1261(1)
EEA auditor	section 1261(1)
EEA competent authority	section 1261(1)
enactment	section 1293
established in the United Kingdom	section 1261(2)
firm	section 1261(1)
group (in relation to a body corporate)	section 1261(1)

holding company	section 1261(1)
main purposes of this Part	section 1209
member (of a supervisory body)	section 1217(2)
obtained in the United Kingdom	section 1261(2)
officer	section 1261(1)
parent undertaking	section 1261(1)
qualifying body	section 1220(1)
recognised, in relation to a professional qualification	section 1220(3) and Schedule 11
recognised, in relation to a qualifying body	paragraph 1(2) of Schedule 11
recognised, in relation to a supervisory body	section 1217(4) and Schedule 10
registered third country auditor	section 1241(1)
rules of a qualifying body	section 1220(2)
rules of a supervisory body	section 1217(3)
statutory auditor, statutory audit and statutory audit work	section 1210(1)
subsidiary	section 1261(1)
supervisory body	section 1217(1)
subsidiary undertaking	section 1261(1)
third country	section 1261(1)
third country auditor …	section 1261(1)
third country competent authority	section 1261(1)
transfer (in relation to audit working papers)	section 1261(1)
UK-traded non-EEA company	section 1241(2)

Miscellaneous and general

1263 Power to make provision in consequence of changes affecting accountancy bodies

(1) The Secretary of State may by regulations make such amendments of enactments as appear to him to be necessary or expedient in consequence of any change of name, merger or transfer of engagements affecting—

(a) a recognised supervisory body or recognised qualifying body, or

(b) a body of accountants referred to in, or approved, authorised or otherwise recognised for the purposes of, any other enactment.

(2) Regulations under this section are subject to negative resolution procedure.

1264 Consequential amendments

Schedule 14 contains consequential amendments relating to this Part.

PART 43
TRANSPARENCY OBLIGATIONS AND RELATED MATTERS

Introductory

1265 The transparency obligations directive

In Part 6 of the Financial Services and Markets Act 2000 (which makes provision about official listing, prospectus requirements for transferable securities, etc), in section 103(1) (interpretation), at the appropriate place insert—

> ""the transparency obligations directive" means Directive 2004/ 109/EC of the European Parliament and of the Council relating to the harmonisation of transparency requirements in relation to information about issuers whose securities are admitted to trading on a regulated market;".

Transparency obligations

1266 Transparency rules

(1) After section 89 of the Financial Services and Markets Act 2000 insert—

"Transparency obligations

89A Transparency rules

(1) The competent authority may make rules for the purposes of the transparency obligations directive.

(2) The rules may include provision for dealing with any matters arising out of or related to any provision of the transparency obligations directive.

(3) The competent authority may also make rules—

(a) for the purpose of ensuring that voteholder information in respect of voting shares traded on a UK market other than a regulated market is made public or notified to the competent authority;

(b) providing for persons who hold comparable instruments (see section 89F(1) (c)) in respect of voting shares to be treated, in the circumstances specified in the rules, as holding some or all of the voting rights in respect of those shares.

(4) Rules under this section may, in particular, make provision—

(a) specifying how the proportion of—

(i) the total voting rights in respect of shares in an issuer, or

(ii) the total voting rights in respect of a particular class of shares in an issuer,

held by a person is to be determined;

(b) specifying the circumstances in which, for the purposes of any determination of the voting rights held by a person ("P") in respect of voting shares in an issuer, any voting rights held, or treated by virtue of subsection (3)(b) as held, by another person in respect of voting shares in the issuer are to be regarded as held by P;

(c) specifying the nature of the information which must be included in any notification;

(d) about the form of any notification;

(e) requiring any notification to be given within a specified period;

(f) specifying the manner in which any information is to be made public and the period within which it must be made public;

(g) specifying circumstances in which any of the requirements imposed by rules under this section does not apply.

(5) Rules under this section are referred to in this Part as "transparency rules".

(6) Nothing in sections 89B to 89G affects the generality of the power to make rules under this section.

89B Provision of voteholder information

(1) Transparency rules may make provision for voteholder information in respect of voting shares to be notified, in circumstances specified in the rules—

(a) to the issuer, or

(b) to the public,

or to both.

(2) Transparency rules may make provision for voteholder information notified to the issuer to be notified at the same time to the competent authority.

(3) In this Part "voteholder information" in respect of voting shares means information relating to the proportion of voting rights held by a person in respect of the shares.

(4) Transparency rules may require notification of voteholder information relating to a person—

(a) initially, not later than such date as may be specified in the rules for the purposes of the first indent of Article 30.2 of the transparency obligations directive, and

(b) subsequently, in accordance with the following provisions.

(5) Transparency rules under subsection (4) (b) may require notification of voteholder information relating to a person only where there is a notifiable change in the proportion of—

(a) the total voting rights in respect of shares in the issuer, or

(b) the total voting rights in respect of a particular class of share in the issuer, held by the person.

(6) For this purpose there is a "notifiable change" in the proportion of voting rights held by a person when the proportion changes—

(a) from being a proportion less than a designated proportion to a proportion equal to or greater than that designated proportion,

(b) from being a proportion equal to a designated proportion to a proportion greater or less than that designated proportion, or

(c) from being a proportion greater than a designated proportion to a proportion equal to or less than that designated proportion.

(7) In subsection (6) "designated" means designated by the rules.

89C Provision of information by issuers of transferable securities

(1) Transparency rules may make provision requiring the issuer of transferable securities, in circumstances specified in the rules—

(a) to make public information to which this section applies, or

(b) to notify to the competent authority information to which this section applies,

(c) or to do both.

(2) In the case of every issuer, this section applies to—

(a) information required by Article 4 of the transparency obligations directive;

(b) information relating to the rights attached to the transferable securities, including informationabout the terms and conditions of those securities which could indirectly affect those rights; and

(c) information about new loan issues and about any guarantee or security in connection with any such issue.

(3) In the case of an issuer of debt securities, this section also applies to information required by Article 5 of the transparency obligations directive.

(4) In the case of an issuer of shares, this section also applies to—

(a) information required by Article 5 of the transparency obligations directive;

(b) information required by Article 6 of that directive;

(c) voteholder information—

(i) notified to the issuer, or

(ii) relating to the proportion of voting rights held by the issuer in respect of shares in the issuer;

(d) information relating to the issuer's capital; and

(e) information relating to the total number of voting rights in respect of shares or shares of a particular class.

89D Notification of voting rights held by issuer

(1) Transparency rules may require notification of voteholder information relating to the proportion of voting rights held by an issuer in respect of voting shares in the issuer—

(a) initially, not later than such date as may be specified in the rules for the purposes of the second indent of Article 30.2 of the transparency obligations directive, and

(b) subsequently, in accordance with the following provisions.

(2) Transparency rules under subsection (1) (b) may require notification of voteholder information relating to the proportion of voting rights held by an issuer in respect of voting shares in the issuer only where there is a notifiable change in the proportion of—

(a) the total voting rights in respect of shares in the issuer, or

(b) the total voting rights in respect of a particular class of share in the issuer, held by the issuer.

(3) For this purpose there is a "notifiable change" in the proportion of voting rights held by a person when the proportion changes—

(a) from being a proportion less than a designated proportion to a proportion equal to or greater than that designated proportion,
(b) from being a proportion equal to a designated proportion to a proportion greater or less than that designated proportion, or
(c) from being a proportion greater than a designated proportion to a proportion equal to or less than that designated proportion.

(4) In subsection (3) "designated" means designated by the rules.

89E Notification of proposed amendment of issuer's constitution

Transparency rules may make provision requiring an issuer of transferable securities that are admitted to trading on a regulated market to notify a proposed amendment to its constitution—
(a) to the competent authority, and
(b) to the market on which the issuer's securities are admitted,
at times and in circumstances specified in the rules.

89F Transparency rules: interpretation etc

(1) For the purposes of sections 89A to 89G—
(a) the voting rights in respect of any voting shares are the voting rights attached to those shares,
(b) a person is to be regarded as holding the voting rights in respect of the shares—
(i) if, by virtue of those shares, he is a shareholder within the meaning of Article 2.1(e) of the transparency obligations directive;
(ii) if, and to the extent that, he is entitled to acquire, dispose of or exercise those voting rights in one or more of the cases mentioned in Article 10(a) to (h) of the transparency obligations directive;
(iii) if he holds, directly or indirectly, a financial instrument which results in an entitlement to acquire the shares and is an Article 13 instrument, and
(c) a person holds a "comparable instrument" in respect of voting shares if he holds, directly or indirectly, a financial instrument in relation to the shares which has similar economic effects to an Article 13 instrument (whether or not the financial instrument results in an entitlement to acquire the shares).

(2) Transparency rules under section 89A(3)(b) may make different provision for different descriptions of comparable instrument.

(3) For the purposes of sections 89A to 89G two or more persons may, at the same time, each be regarded as holding the same voting rights.

(4) In those sections—
"Article 13 instrument" means a financial instrument of a type determined by the European Commission under Article 13.2 of the transparency obligations directive;
"UK market" means a market that is situated or operating in the United Kingdom;
"voting shares" means shares of an issuer to which voting rights are attached.

89G Transparency rules: other supplementary provisions

(1) Transparency rules may impose the same obligations on a person who has applied for the admission of transferable securities to trading on a regulated market without the issuer's consent as they impose on an issuer of transferable securities.

(2) Transparency rules that require a person to make information public may include provision authorising the competent authority to make the information public in the event that the person fails to do so.

(3) The competent authority may make public any information notified to the authority in accordance with transparency rules.

(4) Transparency rules may make provision by reference to any provision of any rules made by the Panel on Takeovers and Mergers under Part 28 of the Companies Act 2006.

(5) Sections 89A to 89F and this section are without prejudice to any other power conferred by this Part to make Part 6 rules.".

(2) The effectiveness for the purposes of section 155 of the Financial Services and Markets Act 2000 (consultation on proposed rules) of things done by the Financial Services Authority before this section comes into force with a view to making transparency rules (as defined in the provisions to be inserted in that Act by subsection (1) above) is not affected by the fact that those provisions were not then in force.

1267 Competent authority's power to call for information

In Part 6 of the Financial Services and Markets Act 2000 after the sections inserted by section 1266 above insert—

"Power of competent authority to call for information

89H Competent authority's power to call for information

(1) The competent authority may by notice in writing given to a person to whom this section applies require him—

(a) to provide specified information or information of a specified description, or

(b) to produce specified documents or documents of a specified description.

(2) This section applies to—

(a) an issuer in respect of whom transparency rules have effect;

(b) a voteholder;

(c) an auditor of—

(i) an issuer to whom this section applies, or

(ii) a voteholder;

(d) a person who controls a voteholder;

(e) a person controlled by a voteholder;

(f) a director or other similar officer of an issuer to whom this section applies;

(g) a director or other similar officer of a voteholder or, where the affairs of a voteholder are managed by its members, a member of the voteholder.

(3) This section applies only to information and documents reasonably required in connection with the exercise by the competent authority of functions conferred on it by or under sections 89A to 89G (transparency rules).

(4) Information or documents required under this section must be provided or produced—

(a) before the end of such reasonable period as may be specified, and

(b) at such place as may be specified.

(5) If a person claims a lien on a document, its production under this section does not affect the lien.

89I Requirements in connection with call for information

(1) The competent authority may require any information provided under section 89H to be provided in such form as it may reasonably require.

(2) The competent authority may require—

(a) any information provided, whether in a document or otherwise, to be verified in such manner as it may reasonably require;

(b) any document produced to be authenticated in such manner as it may reasonably require.

(3) If a document is produced in response to a requirement imposed under section 89H, the competent authority may—

(a) take copies of or extracts from the document; or

(b) require the person producing the document, or any relevant person, to provide an explanation of the document.

(4) In subsection (3)(b) "relevant person", in relation to a person who is required to produce a document, means a person who—

(a) has been or is a director or controller of that person;

(b) has been or is an auditor of that person;

(c) has been or is an actuary, accountant or lawyer appointed or instructed by that person; or

(d) has been or is an employee of that person.

(5) If a person who is required under section 89H to produce a document fails to do so, the competent authority may require him to state, to the best of his knowledge and belief, where the document is.

89J Power to call for information: supplementary provisions

(1) The competent authority may require an issuer to make public any information provided to the authority under section 89H.

(2) If the issuer fails to comply with a requirement under subsection (1), the competent authority may, after seeking representations from the issuer, make the information public.

(3) In sections 89H and 89I (power of competent authority to call for information)—

"control" and "controlled" have the meaning given by subsection (4) below;

"specified" means specified in the notice;

"voteholder" means a person who—

(a) holds voting rights in respect of any voting shares for the purposes of sections 89A to 89G (transparency rules), or

(b) is treated as holding such rights by virtue of rules under section 89A(3)(b).

(4) For the purposes of those sections a person ("A") controls another person ("B") if—

(a) A holds a majority of the voting rights in B,

(b) A is a member of B and has the right to appoint or remove a majority of the members of the board of directors (or, if there is no such board, the equivalent management body) of B,

(c) A is a member of B and controls alone, pursuant to an agreement with other shareholders or members, a majority of the voting rights in B, or

(d) A has the right to exercise, or actually exercises, dominant influence or control over B.

(5) For the purposes of subsection (4)(b)—

(a) any rights of a person controlled by A, and

(b) any rights of a person acting on behalf of A or a person controlled by A,

are treated as held by A.".

1268 Powers exercisable in case of infringement of transparency obligation

In Part 6 of the Financial Services and Markets Act 2000, after the sections inserted by section 1267 above insert—

"Powers exercisable in case of infringement of transparency obligation

89K Public censure of issuer

(1) If the competent authority finds that an issuer of securities admitted to trading on a regulated market is failing or has failed to comply with an applicable transparency obligation, it may publish a statement to that effect.

(2) If the competent authority proposes to publish a statement, it must give the issuer a warning notice setting out the terms of the proposed statement.

(3) If, after considering any representations made in response to the warning notice, the competent authority decides to make the proposed statement, it must give the issuer a decision notice setting out the terms of the statement.

(4) A notice under this section must inform the issuer of his right to refer the matter to the Tribunal (see section 89N) and give an indication of the procedure on such a reference.

(5) In this section "transparency obligation" means an obligation under—

(a) a provision of transparency rules, or
(b) any other provision made in accordance with the transparency obligations directive.

(6) In relation to an issuer whose home State is a member State other than the United Kingdom, any reference to an applicable transparency obligation must be read subject to section 100A(2).

89L Power to suspend or prohibit trading of securities

(1) This section applies to securities admitted to trading on a regulated market.

(2) If the competent authority has reasonable grounds for suspecting that an applicable transparency obligation has been infringed by an issuer, it may—
(a) suspend trading in the securities for a period not exceeding 10 days,
(b) prohibit trading in the securities, or
(c) make a request to the operator of the market on which the issuer's securities are traded—
(i) to suspend trading in the securities for a period not exceeding 10 days, or
(ii) to prohibit trading in the securities.

(3) If the competent authority has reasonable grounds for suspecting that a provision required by the transparency obligations directive has been infringed by a voteholder of an issuer, it may—
(a) prohibit trading in the securities, or
(b) make a request to the operator of the market on which the issuer's securities are traded to prohibit trading in the securities.

(4) If the competent authority finds that an applicable transparency obligation has been infringed, it may require the market operator to prohibit trading in the securities.

(5) In this section "transparency obligation" means an obligation under—
(a) a provision contained in transparency rules, or
(b) any other provision made in accordance with the transparency obligations directive.

(6) In relation to an issuer whose home State is a member State other than the United Kingdom, any reference to an applicable transparency obligation must be read subject to section 100A(2).

89M Procedure under section 89L

(1) A requirement under section 89L takes effect—
(a) immediately, if the notice under subsection (2) states that that is the case;
(b) in any other case, on such date as may be specified in the notice.

(2) If the competent authority—
(a) proposes to exercise the powers in section 89L in relation to a person, or
(b) exercises any of those powers in relation to a person with immediate effect,
it must give that person written notice.

(3) The notice must—
(a) give details of the competent authority's action or proposed action;
(b) state the competent authority's reasons for taking the action in question and choosing the date on which it took effect or takes effect;
(c) inform the recipient that he may make representations to the competent authority within such period as may be specified by the notice (whether or not he had referred the matter to the Tribunal);
(d) inform him of the date on which the action took effect or takes effect;
(e) inform him of his right to refer the matter to the Tribunal (see section 89N) and give an indication of the procedure on such a reference.

(4) The competent authority may extend the period within which representations may be made to it.

(5) If, having considered any representations made to it, the competent authority decides to maintain, vary or revoke its earlier decision, it must give written notice to that effect to the person mentioned in subsection (2).

89N Right to refer matters to the Tribunal

A person—

(a) to whom a decision notice is given under section 89K (public censure), or

(b) to whom a notice is given under section 89M (procedure in connection with suspension or prohibition of trading),

may refer the matter to the Tribunal.".

Other matters

1269 Corporate governance rules

In Part 6 of the Financial Services and Markets Act 2000, after the sections inserted by section 1268 above insert—

"Corporate governance

89O Corporate governance rules

(1) The competent authority may make rules ("corporate governance rules")—

(a) for the purpose of implementing, enabling the implementation of or dealing with matters arising out of or related to, any Community obligation relating to the corporate governance of issuers who have requested or approved admission of their securities to trading on a regulated market;

(b) about corporate governance in relation to such issuers for the purpose of implementing, or dealing with matters arising out of or related to, any Community obligation.

(2) "Corporate governance", in relation to an issuer, includes—

(a) the nature, constitution or functions of the organs of the issuer;

(b) the manner in which organs of the issuer conduct themselves;

(c) the requirements imposed on organs of the issuer;

(d) the relationship between the different organs of the issuer;

(e) the relationship between the organs of the issuer and the members of the issuer or holders of the issuer's securities.

(3) The burdens and restrictions imposed by rules under this section on foreign-traded issuers must not be greater than the burdens and restrictions imposed on UK-traded issuers by—

(a) rules under this section, and

(b) listing rules.

(4) For this purpose—

"foreign-traded issuer" means an issuer who has requested or approved admission of the issuer's securities to trading on a regulated market situated or operating outside the United Kingdom;

"UK-traded issuer" means an issuer who has requested or approved admission of the issuer's securities to trading on a regulated market situated or operating in the United Kingdom.

(5) This section is without prejudice to any other power conferred by this Part to make Part 6 rules.".

1270 Liability for false or misleading statements in certain publications

In Part 6 of the Financial Services and Markets Act 2000, after section 90 insert—

"90A Compensation for statements in certain publications

(1) The publications to which this section applies are—

(a) any reports and statements published in response to a requirement imposed by a provision implementing Article 4, 5 or 6 of the transparency obligations directive, and

(b) any preliminary statement made in advance of a report or statement to be published in response to a requirement imposed by a provision implementing Article 4 of that directive, to the extent that it contains information that it is intended—

(i) will appear in the report or statement, and

(ii) will be presented in the report or statement in substantially the same form as that in which it is presented in the preliminary statement.

(2) The securities to which this section applies are—

(a) securities that are traded on a regulated market situated or operating in the United Kingdom, and

(b) securities that—

(i) are traded on a regulated market situated or operating outside the United Kingdom, and

(ii) are issued by an issuer for which the United Kingdom is the home Member State within the meaning of Article 2.1(i) of the transparency obligations directive.

(3) The issuer of securities to which this section applies is liable to pay compensation to a person who has—

(a) acquired such securities issued by it, and

(b) suffered loss in respect of them as a result of—

(i) any untrue or misleading statement in a publication to which this section applies, or

(ii) the omission from any such publication of any matter required to be included in it.

(4) The issuer is so liable only if a person discharging managerial responsibilities within the issuer in relation to the publication—

(a) knew the statement to be untrue or misleading or was reckless as to whether it was untrue or misleading, or

(b) knew the omission to be dishonest concealment of a material fact.

(5) A loss is not regarded as suffered as a result of the statement or omission in the publication unless the person suffering it acquired the relevant securities—

(a) in reliance on the information in the publication, and

(b) at a time when, and in circumstances in which, it was reasonable for him to rely on that information.

(6) Except as mentioned in subsection (8)—

(a) the issuer is not subject to any other liability than that provided for by this section in respect of loss suffered as a result of reliance by any person on—

(i) an untrue or misleading statement in a publication to which this section applies, or

(ii) the omission from any such publication of any matter required to be included in it, and

(b) a person other than the issuer is not subject to any liability, other than to the issuer, in respect of any such loss.

(7) Any reference in subsection (6) to a person being subject to a liability includes a reference to another person being entitled as against him to be granted any civil remedy or to rescind or repudiate an agreement.

(8) This section does not affect—

(a) the powers conferred by section 382 and 384 (powers of the court to make a restitution order and of the Authority to require restitution);

(i) liability for a civil penalty;

(ii) liability for a criminal offence.

(9) For the purposes of this section—

(a) the following are persons "discharging managerial responsibilities" in relation to a publication—

(i) any director of the issuer (or person occupying the position of director, by whatever name called),

(ii) in the case of an issuer whose affairs are managed by its members, any member of the issuer,

(iii) in the case of an issuer that has no persons within sub-paragraph (i) or (ii), any senior executive of the issuer having responsibilities in relation to the publication;

(b) references to the acquisition by a person of securities include his contracting to acquire them or any interest in them.

90B Power to make further provision about liability for published information

(1) The Treasury may by regulations make provision about the liability of issuers of securities traded on a regulated market, and other persons, in respect of information published to holders of securities, to the market or to the public generally.

(2) Regulations under this section may amend any primary or subordinate legislation, including any provision of, or made under, this Act.".

1271 Exercise of powers where UK is host member State

In Part 6 of the Financial Services and Markets Act 2000, after section 100 insert—

"100A Exercise of powers where UK is host member state

(1) This section applies to the exercise by the competent authority of any power under this Part exercisable in case of infringement of—

(a) a provision of prospectus rules or any other provision made in accordance with the prospectus directive, or

(b) a provision of transparency rules or any other provision made in accordance with the transparency obligations directive,

in relation to an issuer whose home State is a member State other than the United Kingdom.

(2) The competent authority may act in such a case only in respect of the infringement of a provision required by the relevant directive.

Any reference to an applicable provision or applicable transparency obligation shall be read accordingly.

(3) If the authority finds that there has been such an infringement, it must give a notice to that effect to the competent authority of the person's home State requesting it—

(a) to take all appropriate measures for the purpose of ensuring that the person remedies the situation that has given rise to the notice, and

(b) to inform the authority of the measures it proposes to take or has taken or the reasons for not taking such measures.

(4) The authority may not act further unless satisfied—

(a) that the competent authority of the person's home State has failed or refused to take measures for the purpose mentioned in subsection (3)(a), or

(b) that the measures taken by that authority have proved inadequate for that purpose.

This does not affect exercise of the powers under section 87K(2), 87L(2) or (3) or 89L(2) or (3) (powers to protect market).

(5) If the authority is so satisfied, it must, after informing the competent authority of the person's home State, take all appropriate measures to protect investors.

(6) In such a case the authority must inform the Commission of the measures at the earliest opportunity.".

1272 Transparency obligations and related matters: minor and consequential amendments

(1) Schedule 15 to this Act makes minor and consequential amendments in connection with the provision made by this Part.

(2) In that Schedule—

Part 1 contains amendments of the Financial Services and Markets Act 2000;

Part 2 contains amendments of the Companies (Audit, Investigations and Community Enterprise) Act 2004.

1273 Corporate governance regulations

(1) The Secretary of State may make regulations—

(a) for the purpose of implementing, enabling the implementation of or dealing with matters arising out of or related to, any EU obligation relating to the corporate governance of issuers who have requested or approved admission of their securities to trading on a regulated market;

(b) about corporate governance in relation to such issuers for the purpose of implementing, or dealing with matters arising out of or related to, any EU obligation.

(2) "Corporate governance", in relation to an issuer, includes—

(a) the nature, constitution or functions of the organs of the issuer;

(b) the manner in which organs of the issuer conduct themselves;

(c) the requirements imposed on organs of the issuer;

(d) the relationship between different organs of the issuer;

(e) the relationship between the organs of the issuer and the members of the issuer or holders of the issuer's securities.

(3) The regulations may—

(a) make provision by reference to any specified code on corporate governance that may be issued from time to time by a specified body;

(b) create new criminal offences (subject to subsection (4));

(c) make provision excluding liability in damages in respect of things done or omitted for the purposes of, or in connection with, the carrying on, or purported carrying on, of any specified activities.

"Specified" here means specified in the regulations.

(4) The regulations may not create a criminal offence punishable by a greater penalty than—

(a) on indictment, a fine;

(b) on summary conviction, a fine not exceeding the statutory maximum or (if calculated on a daily basis) £100 a day.

(5) Regulations under this section are subject to negative resolution procedure.

(6) In this section "issuer", "securities" and "regulated market" have the samemeaning as in Part 6 of the Financial Services and Markets Act 2000.

PART 44
MISCELLANEOUS PROVISIONS

Regulation of actuaries etc

1274 Grants to bodies concerned with actuarial standards etc

(1) Section 16 of the Companies (Audit, Investigations and Community Enterprise) Act 2004 (grants to bodies concerned with accounting standards etc) is amended as follows.

(2) In subsection (2) (matters carried on by bodies eligible for grants) for paragraph (l) substitute—

"(l) issuing standards to be applied in actuarial work;

(m) issuing standards in respect of matters to be contained in reports or other communications required to be produced or made by actuaries or in accordance with standards within paragraph (l);

(n) investigating departures from standards within paragraph (l) or (m);

(o) taking steps to secure compliance with standards within paragraph (l) or (m);

(p) carrying out investigations into public interest cases arising in connection with the performance of actuarial functions by members of professional actuarial bodies;

(q) holding disciplinary hearings relating to members of professional actuarial bodies following the conclusion of investigations within paragraph (p);

(r) deciding whether (and, if so, what) disciplinary action should be taken against members of professional actuarial bodies to whom hearings within paragraph (q) related;

(s) supervising the exercise by professional actuarial bodies of regulatory functions in relation to their members;

(t) overseeing or directing any of the matters mentioned above.".

(3) In subsection (5) (definitions) at the appropriate places insert—

""professional actuarial body" means—

(a) the Institute of Actuaries, or

(b) the Faculty of Actuaries in Scotland,

and the "members" of a professional actuarial body include persons who, although not members of the body, are subject to its rules in performing actuarial functions;"

""regulatory functions", in relation to professional actuarial bodies, means any of the following—

(a) investigatory or disciplinary functions exercised by such bodies in relation to the performance by their members of actuarial functions,

(b) the setting by such bodies of standards in relation to the performance by their members of actuarial functions, and

(c) the determining by such bodies of requirements in relation to the education and training of their members;".

1275 Levy to pay expenses of bodies concerned with actuarial standards etc

(1) Section 17 of the Companies (Audit, Investigations and Community Enterprise) Act 2004 (levy to pay expenses of bodies concerned with accounting standards etc) is amended in accordance with subsections (2) to (5).

(2) In subsection (3)(a) after "to which" insert ", or persons within subsection (3A) to whom,".

(3) After subsection (3) insert—

"(3A) The following persons are within this subsection—

(a) the administrators of a public service pension scheme (within the meaning of section 1 of the Pension Schemes Act 1993);

(b) the trustees or managers of an occupational or personal pension scheme (within the meaning of that section).".

(4) After subsection (4) (b) insert—

"(c) make different provision for different cases.".

(5) After subsection (12) insert—

"(13) If a draft of any regulations to which subsection (10) applies would, apart from this subsection, be treated for the purposes of the standing orders of either House of Parliament as a hybrid instrument, it is to proceed in that House as if it were not such an instrument.".

(6) The above amendments have effect in relation to any exercise of the power to make regulations under section 17 of the Companies (Audit, Investigations and Community Enterprise) Act 2004 after this section comes into force, regardless of when the expenses to be met by the levy in respect of which the regulations are made were incurred.

(7) In Schedule 3 to the Pensions Act 2004 (disclosure of information held by the Pensions Regulator), in the entry relating to the Secretary of State, in the second column, for "or" at the end of paragraph (g) substitute—

"(ga) Section 17 of the Companies (Audit, Investigations and Community Enterprise) Act 2004 (levy to pay expenses of bodies concerned with accounting standards, actuarial standards etc), or".

1276 Application of provisions to Scotland and Northern Ireland

(1) Section 16 of the Companies (Audit, Investigations and Community Enterprise) Act 2004 (grants to bodies concerned with accounting standards etc) is amended as follows.

(2) For subsection (6) (application of section to Scotland) substitute—

"(6) In their application to Scotland, subsection (2)(a) to (t) are to be read as referring only to matters provision relating to which would be outside the legislative competence of the Scottish Parliament.".

(3) In subsection (2) in paragraph (c), after "1985" insert "or the 1986 Order".

(4) In subsection (5)—

(a) in the definition of "company" after "1985" insert "or the 1986 Order",

(b) in the definition of "subsidiary" after "1985" insert "or Article 4 of the 1986 Order", and

(c) after that definition insert—

""the 1986 Order" means the Companies (Northern Ireland) Order 1986.".

(5) In section 66 of that Act (extent), in subsection (2) (provisions extending to Northern Ireland, as well as England and Wales and Scotland) for "17" substitute "16 to 18".

Information as to exercise of voting rights by institutional investors

1277 Power to require information about exercise of voting rights

(1) The Treasury or the Secretary of State may make provision by regulations requiring institutions to which this section applies to provide information about the exercise of voting rights attached to shares to which this section applies.

(2) This power is exercisable in accordance with—
section 1278 (institutions to which information provisions apply),
section 1279 (shares to which information provisions apply), and
section 1280 (obligations with respect to provision of information).

(3) In this section and the sections mentioned above—

(a) references to a person acting on behalf of an institution include—

(i) any person to whom authority has been delegated by the institution to take decisions as to any matter relevant to the subject matter of the regulations, and

(ii) such other persons as may be specified; and

(b) "specified" means specified in the regulations.

(4) The obligation imposed by regulations under this section is enforceable by civil proceedings brought by—

(a) any person to whom the information should have been provided, or

(b) a specified regulatory authority.

(5) Regulations under this section may make different provision for different descriptions of institution, different descriptions of shares and for other different circumstances.

(6) Regulations under this section are subject to affirmative resolution procedure.

1278 Institutions to which information provisions apply

(1) The institutions to which section 1277 applies are—

(a) unit trust schemes within the meaning of the Financial Services and Markets Act 2000 in respect of which an order is in force under section 243 of that Act;

(b) open-ended investment companies incorporated by virtue of regulations under section 262 of that Act;

(c) companies approved for the purposes of Chapter 4 of Part 24 of the Corporation Tax Act 2010 (investment trusts);

(d) pension schemes as defined in section 1(5) of the Pension Schemes Act 1993 or the Pension Schemes (Northern Ireland) Act 1993;

(e) undertakings authorised under the Financial Services and Markets Act 2000 to carry on long-term insurance business (that is, the activity of effecting or carrying out contracts of long-term insurance within the meaning of the Financial Services and Markets (Regulated Activities) Order 2001;

(f) collective investment schemes that are recognised by virtue of section 270 of that Act (schemes authorised in designated countries or territories).

(2) Regulations under that section may—

(a) provide that the section applies to other descriptions of institution;

(b) provide that the section does not apply to a specified description of institution.

(3) The regulations must specify by whom, in the case of any description of institution, the duty imposed by the regulations is to be fulfilled.

1279 Shares to which information provisions apply

(1) The shares to which section 1277 applies are shares—

(a) of a description traded on a specified market, and

(b) in which the institution has, or is taken to have, an interest.

Regulations under that section may provide that the section does not apply to shares of a specified description.

(2) For this purpose an institution has an interest in shares if the shares, or a depositary certificate in respect of them, are held by it, or on its behalf.

A "depositary certificate" means an instrument conferring rights (other than options)—

(a) in respect of shares held by another person, and

(b) the transfer of which may be effected without the consent of that person.

(3) Where an institution has an interest—

(a) in a specified description of collective investment scheme (within the meaning of the Financial Services and Markets Act 2000, or

(b) in any other specified description of scheme or collective investment vehicle,

it is taken to have an interest in any shares in which that scheme or vehicle has or is taken to have an interest.

(4) For this purpose a scheme or vehicle is taken to have an interest in shares if it would be regarded as having such an interest in accordance with subsection (2) if it was an institution to which section 1277 applied.

1280 Obligations with respect to provision of information

(1) Regulations under section 1277 may require the provision of specified information about—

(a) the exercise or non-exercise of voting rights by the institution or any person acting on its behalf,

(b) any instructions given by the institution or any person acting on its behalf as to the exercise or non-exercise of voting rights, and

(c) any delegation by the institution or any person acting on its behalf of any functions in relation to the exercise or non-exercise of voting rights or the giving of such instructions.

(2) The regulations may require information to be provided in respect of specified occasions or specified periods.

(3) Where instructions are given to act on the recommendations or advice of another person, the regulations may require the provision of information about what recommendations or advice were given.

(4) The regulations may require information to be provided—

(a) in such manner as may be specified, and

(b) to such persons as may be specified, or to the public, or both.

(5) The regulations may provide—

(a) that an institution may discharge its obligations under the regulations by referring to information disclosed by a person acting on its behalf, and

(b) that in such a case it is sufficient, where that other person acts on behalf of more than one institution, that the reference is to information given in aggregated form, that is—

(i) relating to the exercise or non-exercise by that person of voting rights on behalf of more than one institution, or

(ii) relating to the instructions given by that person in respect of the exercise or non-exercise of voting rights on behalf of more than one institution, or

(iii) relating to the delegation by that person of functions in relation to the exercise or non-exercise of voting rights, or the giving of instructions in respect of the exercise or non-exercise of voting rights, on behalf of more than one institution.

(6) References in this section to instructions are to instructions of any description, whether general or specific, whether binding or not and whether or not acted upon.

Disclosure of information under the Enterprise Act 2002

1281 Disclosure of information under the Enterprise Act 2002

In Part 9 of the Enterprise Act 2002 (information), after section 241 insert—

"241A Civil proceedings

(1) A public authority which holds prescribed information to which section 237 applies may disclose that information to any person—

(a) for the purposes of, or in connection with, prescribed civil proceedings (including prospective proceedings) in the United Kingdom or elsewhere, or

(b) for the purposes of obtaining legal advice in relation to such proceedings, or

(c) otherwise for the purposes of establishing, enforcing or defending legal rights that are or may be the subject of such proceedings.

(2) Subsection (1) does not apply to—

(a) information which comes to a public authority in connection with an investigation under Part 4, 5 or 6 of the 1973 Act or under section 11 of the Competition Act 1980;

(b) competition information within the meaning of section 351 of the Financial Services and Markets Act 2000;

(c) information which comes to a public authority in connection with an investigation under Part 3 or 4 or section 174 of this Act;

(d) information which comes to a public authority in connection with an investigation under the Competition Act 1998.

(3) In subsection (1) "prescribed" means prescribed by order of the Secretary of State.

(4) An order under this section—

(a) may prescribe information, or civil proceedings, for the purposes of this section by reference to such factors as appear to the Secretary of State to be appropriate;

(b) may prescribe for the purposes of this section all information, or civil proceedings, or all information or civil proceedings not falling within one or more specified exceptions;

(c) must be made by statutory instrument subject to annulment in pursuance of a resolution of either House of Parliament.

(5) Information disclosed under this section must not be used by the person to whom it is disclosed for any purpose other than those specified in subsection (1).".

Expenses of winding up

1282 Payment of expenses of winding up

(1) In Chapter 8 of Part 4 of the Insolvency Act 1986 (winding up of companies: provisions of general application), before section 176A (under the heading *"Property subject to floating charge")* insert—

"176ZA Payment of expenses of winding up (England and Wales)

(1) The expenses of winding up in England and Wales, so far as the assets of the company available for payment of general creditors are insufficient to meet them, have priority

over any claims to property comprised in or subject to any floating charge created by the company and shall be paid out of any such property accordingly.

(2) In subsection (1)—

(a) the reference to assets of the company available for payment of general creditors does not include any amount made available under section 176A(2)(a);

(b) the reference to claims to property comprised in or subject to a floating charge is to the claims of—

(i) the holders of debentures secured by, or holders of, the floating charge, and

(ii) any preferential creditors entitled to be paid out of that property in priority to them.

(3) Provision may be made by rules restricting the application of subsection (1), in such circumstances as may be prescribed, to expenses authorised or approved—

(a) by the holders of debentures secured by, or holders of, the floating charge and by any preferential creditors entitled to be paid in priority to them, or

(b) by the court.

(4) References in this section to the expenses of the winding up are to all expenses properly incurred in the winding up, including the remuneration of the liquidator.".

(2) In Chapter 8 of Part 5 of the Insolvency (Northern Ireland) Order 1989 (winding up of companies: provisions of general application), before Article 150A (under the heading *"Property subject to floating charge")* insert—

"150ZA Payment of expenses of winding up

(1) The expenses of winding up, so far as the assets of the company available for payment of general creditors are insufficient to meet them, have priority over any claims to property comprised in or subject to any floating charge created by the company and shall be paid out of any such property accordingly.

(2) In paragraph (1)—

(a) the reference to assets of the company available for payment of general creditors does not include any amount made available under Article 150A(2)(a);

(b) the reference to claims to property comprised in or subject to a floating charge is to the claims of—

(i) the holders of debentures secured by, or holders of, the floating charge, and

(ii) any preferential creditors entitled to be paid out of that property in priority to them.

(3) Provision may be made by rules restricting the application of paragraph (1), in such circumstances as may be prescribed, to expenses authorised or approved—

(a) by the holders of debentures secured by, or holders of, the floating charge and by any preferential creditors entitled to be paid in priority to them, or

(b) by the Court.

(4) References in this Article to the expenses of the winding up are to all expenses properly incurred in the winding up, including the remuneration of the liquidator.".

Commonhold associations

1283 Amendment of memorandum or articles of commonhold association

In paragraph 3(1) of Schedule 3 to the Commonhold and Leasehold Reform Act 2002 (alteration of memorandum or articles by commonhold association to be of no effect until altered version registered with Land Registry) for "An alteration of the memorandum or articles of association" substitute "Where a commonhold association alters its memorandum or articles at a time when the land specified in its memorandum is commonhold land, the alteration".

PART 45
NORTHERN IRELAND

1284 Extension of Companies Acts to Northern Ireland

(1) The Companies Acts as defined by this Act (see section 2) extend to Northern Ireland.

(2) The Companies (Northern Ireland) Order 1986, the Companies Consolidation (Consequential Provisions) (Northern Ireland) Order 1986 and Part 3 of the Companies (Audit, Investigations and Community Enterprise) Order 2005 shall cease to have effect accordingly.

1285 Extension of GB enactments relating to SEs

(1) The enactments in force in Great Britain relating to SEs extend to Northern Ireland.

(2) The following enactments shall cease to have effect accordingly—

(a) the European Public Limited-Liability Company Regulations (Northern Ireland) 2004, and

(b) the European Public Limited-Liability Company (Fees) Regulations (Northern Ireland) 2004.

(3) In this section "SE" means a European Public Limited-Liability Company (or Societas Europaea) within the meaning of Council Regulation 2157/2001/EC of 8 October 2001 on the Statute for a European Company.

1286 Extension of GB enactments relating to certain other forms of business organisation

(1) The enactments in force in Great Britain relating to—

(a) limited liability partnerships,

(b) limited partnerships,

(c) open-ended investment companies, and

(d) European Economic Interest Groupings,

extend to Northern Ireland.

(2) The following enactments shall cease to have effect accordingly—

(a) the Limited Liability Partnerships Act (Northern Ireland) 2002;

(b) the Limited Partnerships Act 1907 as it formerly had effect in Northern Ireland;

(c) the Open-Ended Investment Companies Act (Northern Ireland) 2002;

(d) the European Economic Interest Groupings Regulations (Northern Ireland) 1989.

1287 Extension of enactments relating to business names

(1) The provisions of Part 41 of this Act (business names) extend to Northern Ireland.

(2) The Business Names (Northern Ireland) Order 1986 shall cease to have effect accordingly.

PART 46
GENERAL SUPPLEMENTARY PROVISIONS

Regulations and orders

1288 Regulations and orders: statutory instrument

Except as otherwise provided, regulations and orders under this Act shall be made by statutory instrument.

1289 Regulations and orders: negative resolution procedure

Where regulations or orders under this Act are subject to "negative resolution procedure" the statutory instrument containing the regulations or order shall be subject to annulment in pursuance of a resolution of either House of Parliament.

1290 Regulations and orders: affirmative resolution procedure

Where regulations or orders under this Act are subject to "affirmative resolution procedure" the regulations or order must not be made unless a draft of the statutory instrument containing them has been laid before Parliament and approved by a resolution of each House of Parliament.

1291 Regulations and orders: approval after being made

(1) Regulations or orders under this Act that are subject to "approval after being made"—
(a) must be laid before Parliament after being made, and
(b) cease to have effect at the end of 28 days beginning with the day on which they were made unless during that period they are approved by resolution of each House.

(2) In reckoning the period of 28 days no account shall be taken of any time during which Parliament is dissolved or prorogued or during which both Houses are adjourned for more than four days.

(3) The regulations or order ceasing to have effect does not affect—
(a) anything previously done under them or it, or
(b) the making of new regulations or a new order.

1292 Regulations and orders: supplementary

(1) Regulations or orders under this Act may—
(a) make different provision for different cases or circumstances,
(b) include supplementary, incidental and consequential provision, and
(c) make transitional provision and savings.

(2) Any provision that may be made by regulations under this Act may be made by order; and any provision that may be made by order under this Act may be made by regulations.

(3) Any provision that may be made by regulations or order under this Act for which no Parliamentary procedure is prescribed may be made by regulations or order subject to negative or affirmative resolution procedure.

(4) Any provision that may be made by regulations or order under this Act subject to negative resolution procedure may be made by regulations or order subject to affirmative resolution procedure.

Meaning of "enactment"

1293 Meaning of "enactment"

In this Act, unless the context otherwise requires, "enactment" includes—
(a) an enactment contained in subordinate legislation within the meaning of the Interpretation Act 1978,
(b) an enactment contained in, or in an instrument made under, an Act of the Scottish Parliament, and
(c) an enactment contained in, or in an instrument made under, Northern Ireland legislation within the meaning of the Interpretation Act 1978.

Consequential and transitional provisions

1294 Power to make consequential amendments etc

(1) The Secretary of State or the Treasury may by order make such provision amending, repealing or revoking any enactment to which this section applies as they consider necessary or expedient in consequence of any provision made by or under this Act.

(2) This section applies to—
(a) any enactment passed or made before the passing of this Act,
(b) any enactment contained in this Act or in subordinate legislation made under it, and
(c) any enactment passed or made before the end of the session after that in which this Act is passed.

(3) Without prejudice to the generality of the power conferred by subsection (1), orders under this section may—
(a) make provision extending to other forms of organisation any provision made by or under this Act in relation to companies, or
(b) make provision corresponding to that made by or under this Act in relation to companies,
(c) in either case with such adaptations or other modifications as appear to the Secretary of State or the Treasury to be necessary or expedient.

(4) The references in subsection (3) to provision made by this Act include provision conferring power to make provision by regulations, orders or other subordinate legislation.

(5) Amendments and repeals made under this section are additional, and without prejudice, to those made by or under any other provision of this Act.

(6) Orders under this section are subject to affirmative resolution procedure.

1295 Repeals

The enactments specified in Schedule 16, which include enactments that are no longer of practical utility, are repealed to the extent specified.

1296 Power to make transitional provision and savings

(1) The Secretary of State or the Treasury may by order make such transitional provision and savings as they consider necessary or expedient in connection with the commencement of any provision made by or under this Act.

(2) An order may, in particular, make such adaptations of provisions brought into force as appear to be necessary or expedient in consequence of other provisions of this Act not yet having come into force.

(3) Transitional provision and savings made under this section are additional, and without prejudice, to those made by or under any other provision of this Act.

(4) Orders under this section are subject to negative resolution procedure.

1297 Continuity of the law

(1) This section applies where any provision of this Act re-enacts (with or without modification) an enactment repealed by this Act.

(2) The repeal and re-enactment does not affect the continuity of the law.

(3) Anything done (including subordinate legislation made), or having effect as if done, under or for the purposes of the repealed provision that could have been done under or for the purposes of the corresponding provision of this Act, if in force or effective immediately before the commencement of that corresponding provision, has effect thereafter as if done under or for the purposes of that corresponding provision.

(4) Any reference (express or implied) in this Act or any other enactment, instrument or document to a provision of this Act shall be construed (so far as the context permits) as including, as respects times, circumstances or purposes in relation to which the corresponding repealed provision had effect, a reference to that corresponding provision.

(5) Any reference (express or implied) in any enactment, instrument or document to a repealed provision shall be construed (so far as the context permits), as respects times, circumstances and purposes in relation to which the corresponding provision of this Act has effect, as being or (according to the context) including a reference to the corresponding provision of this Act.

(6) This section has effect subject to any specific transitional provision or saving contained in this Act.

(7) References in this section to this Act include subordinate legislation made under this Act.

(8) In this section "subordinate legislation" has the same meaning as in the Interpretation Act 1978.

PART 47
FINAL PROVISIONS

1298 Short title

The short title of this Act is the Companies Act 2006.

1299 Extent

Except as otherwise provided (or the context otherwise requires), the provisions of this Act extend to the whole of the United Kingdom.

1300 Commencement

(1) The following provisions come into force on the day this Act is passed—

(a) Part 43 (transparency obligations and related matters), except the amendment in paragraph 11(2) of Schedule 15 of the definition of "regulated market" in Part 6 of the Financial Services and Markets Act 2000,

(b) in Part 44 (miscellaneous provisions)—
section 1274 (grants to bodies concerned with actuarial standards etc), and
section 1276 (application of provisions to Scotland and Northern Ireland),

(c) Part 46 (general supplementary provisions), except section 1295 and Schedule 16 (repeals), and

(d) this Part.

(2) The other provisions of this Act come into force on such day as may be appointed by order of the Secretary of State or the Treasury.

SCHEDULES

SCHEDULE 1

Sections 254 and 255

CONNECTED PERSONS: REFERENCES TO AN INTEREST IN SHARES OR DEBENTURES

Introduction

1 (1) The provisions of this Schedule have effect for the interpretation of references in sections 254 and 255 (directors connected with or controlling a body corporate) to an interest in shares or debentures.

(2) The provisions are expressed in relation to shares but apply to debentures as they apply to shares.

General provisions

2 (1) A reference to an interest in shares includes any interest of any kind whatsoever in shares.

(2) Any restraints or restrictions to which the exercise of any right attached to the interest is or may be subject shall be disregarded.

(3) It is immaterial that the shares in which a person has an interest are not identifiable.

(4) Persons having a joint interest in shares are deemed each of them to have that interest.

Rights to acquire shares

3 (1) A person is taken to have an interest in shares if he enters into a contract to acquire them.

(2) A person is taken to have an interest in shares if—

(a) he has a right to call for delivery of the shares to himself or to his order, or

(b) he has a right to acquire an interest in shares or is under an obligation to take an interest in shares,

whether the right or obligation is conditional or absolute.

(3) Rights or obligations to subscribe for shares are not to be taken for the purposes of sub-paragraph (2) to be rights to acquire or obligations to take an interest in shares.

(4) A person ceases to have an interest in shares by virtue of this paragraph—

(a) on the shares being delivered to another person at his order—

(i) in fulfilment of a contract for their acquisition by him, or

(ii) in satisfaction of a right of his to call for their delivery;

(b) on a failure to deliver the shares in accordance with the terms of such a contract or on which such a right falls to be satisfied;

(c) on the lapse of his right to call for the delivery of shares.

Right to exercise or control exercise of rights

4 (1) A person is taken to have an interest in shares if, not being the registered holder, he is entitled—

(a) to exercise any right conferred by the holding of the shares, or

(b) to control the exercise of any such right.

(2) For this purpose a person is taken to be entitled to exercise or control the exercise of a right conferred by the holding of shares if he—

(a) has a right (whether subject to conditions or not) the exercise of which would make him so entitled, or

(b) is under an obligation (whether or not so subject) the fulfilment of which would make him so entitled.

(3) A person is not by virtue of this paragraph taken to be interested in shares by reason only that—

(a) he has been appointed a proxy to exercise any of the rights attached to the shares, or

(b) he has been appointed by a body corporate to act as its representative at any meeting of a company or of any class of its members.

Bodies corporate

5 (1) A person is taken to be interested in shares if a body corporate is interested in them and—

(a) the body corporate or its directors are accustomed to act in accordance with his directions or instructions, or

(b) he is entitled to exercise or control the exercise of more than one-half of the voting power at general meetings of the body corporate.

(2) For the purposes of sub-paragraph (1)(b) where—

(a) a person is entitled to exercise or control the exercise of more than one-half of the voting power at general meetings of a body corporate, and

(b) that body corporate is entitled to exercise or control the exercise of any of the voting power at general meetings of another body corporate,

the voting power mentioned in paragraph (b) above is taken to be exercisable by that person.

Trusts

6 (1) Where an interest in shares is comprised in property held on trust, every beneficiary of the trust is taken to have an interest in shares, subject as follows.

(2) So long as a person is entitled to receive, during the lifetime of himself or another, income from trust property comprising shares, an interest in the shares in reversion or remainder or (as regards Scotland) in fee shall be disregarded.

(3) A person is treated as not interested in shares if and so long as he holds them—

(a) under the law in force in any part of the United Kingdom, as a bare trustee or as a custodian trustee, or

(b) under the law in force in Scotland, as a simple trustee.

(4) There shall be disregarded any interest of a person subsisting by virtue of—

(a) an authorised unit trust scheme (within the meaning of section 237 of the Financial Services and Markets Act 2000;

(b) a scheme made under section 22 or 22A of the Charities Act 1960, section 25 of the Charities Act (Northern Ireland) 1964, section 24 or 25 of the Charities Act 1993 or section 96 or 100 of the Charities Act 2011, section 11 of the Trustee Investments Act 1961 or section 42 of the Administration of Justice Act 1982; or

(c) the scheme set out in the Schedule to the Church Funds Investment Measure 1958.

(5) There shall be disregarded any interest—

(a) of the Church of Scotland General Trustees or of the Church of Scotland Trust in shares held by them;

(b) of any other person in shares held by those Trustees or that Trust otherwise than as simple trustees.

"The Church of Scotland General Trustees" are the body incorporated by the order confirmed by the Church of Scotland (General Trustees) Order Confirmation Act 1921, and "the Church of Scotland Trust" is the body incorporated by the order confirmed by the Church of Scotland Trust Order Confirmation Act 1932.

SCHEDULE 2

Section 948

SPECIFIED PERSONS, DESCRIPTIONS OF DISCLOSURES ETC FOR THE PURPOSES OF SECTION 948

PART 1
SPECIFIED PERSONS

(A) UNITED KINGDOM

1 The Secretary of State.

2 The Department of Enterprise, Trade and Investment for Northern Ireland.

3 The Treasury.

4 The Bank of England.
5 The Financial Conduct Authority.
5A The Prudential Regulation Authority.
6 The Commissioners for Her Majesty's Revenue and Customs.
7 The Lord Advocate.
8 The Director of Public Prosecutions.
9 The Director of Public Prosecutions for Northern Ireland.
10 A constable.
11 A procurator fiscal.
12 The Scottish Ministers.

(B) JERSEY

1 The Minister for Economic Development.
2 The Minister for Treasury and Resources.
3 The Jersey Financial Services Commission.
4 The Comptroller of Income Tax.
5 The Agent of the Impôts.
6 Her Majesty's Attorney General for Jersey.
7 The Viscount.
8 A police officer (within the meaning of the Interpretation (Jersey) Law 1954: see Part 1 of the Schedule to that Law).

(C) GUERNSEY

1 The Commerce and Employment Department.
2 The Treasury and Resources Department.
3 The Guernsey Financial Services Commission.
4 The Director of Income Tax.
5 The Chief Officer of Customs and Excise.
6 Her Majesty's Procureur.
7 A police officer (within the meaning of the Companies (Guernsey) Law 2008: see section 532 of that Law).

(D) ISLE OF MAN

1— (1) The members and officers of each of the Departments constituted by section 1(1) of the Government Departments Act 1987 (an Act of Tynwald: c 13).
(2) In sub-paragraph (1) "member" has the same meaning as it has by virtue of section 7(1) of that Act.
2 The Treasury of the Isle of Man.
3 The Financial Supervision Commission of the Isle of Man.
4 Her Majesty's Attorney General of the Isle of Man.
5 A constable (within the meaning of the Interpretation Act 1976 (an Act of Tynwald: c 11): see section 3 of that Act).

PART 2
SPECIFIED DESCRIPTIONS OF DISCLOSURES

(A) UNITED KINGDOM

1 A disclosure for the purpose of enabling or assisting a person authorised under section 457 of this Act (revision of defective accounts: persons authorised to apply to court) to exercise their functions.

2 A disclosure for the purpose of enabling or assisting an inspector appointed under Part 14 of the Companies Act 1985 (c 6) (investigation of companies and their affairs, etc) to exercise their functions.

3 A disclosure for the purpose of enabling or assisting a person authorised under section 447 of the Companies Act 1985 (power to require production of documents) or section 84 of the Companies Act 1989 (c 40) (exercise of powers by officer etc) to exercise their functions.

4 A disclosure for the purpose of enabling or assisting a person appointed under section 167 of the Financial Services and Markets Act 2000 (c 8) (general investigations) to conduct an investigation to exercise their functions.

5 A disclosure for the purpose of enabling or assisting a person appointed under section 168 of the Financial Services and Markets Act 2000 (investigations in particular cases) to conduct an investigation to exercise their functions.

6 A disclosure for the purpose of enabling or assisting a person appointed under section 169(1)(b) of the Financial Services and Markets Act 2000 (investigation in support of overseas regulator) to conduct an investigation to exercise their functions.

7 A disclosure for the purpose of enabling or assisting the body corporate responsible for administering the scheme referred to in section 225 of the Financial Services and Markets Act 2000 (the ombudsman scheme) to exercise its functions.

8 A disclosure for the purpose of enabling or assisting a person appointed under paragraph 4 or 5 of Schedule 17 to the Financial Services and Markets Act 2000 (the panel of ombudsmen or the Chief Ombudsman) to exercise their functions.

9 A disclosure for the purpose of enabling or assisting a person appointed under regulations made under section 262(1) and (2)(k) of the Financial Services and Markets Act 2000 (investigations into open-ended investment companies) to conduct an investigation to exercise their functions.

10 A disclosure for the purpose of enabling or assisting a person appointed under section 284 of the Financial Services and Markets Act 2000 (investigations into affairs of certain collective investment schemes) to conduct an investigation to exercise their functions.

11 A disclosure for the purpose of enabling or assisting the investigator appointed under section 84 of the Financial Services Act 2012 (arrangements for investigation of complaints) to exercise their functions.

12 A disclosure for the purpose of enabling or assisting a person appointed by the Treasury to hold an inquiry into matters relating to financial services (including an inquiry under section 69 of the Financial Services Act 2012) to exercise their functions.

13 A disclosure for the purpose of enabling or assisting the Secretary of State or the Treasury to exercise any of their functions under any of the following—

(a) the Companies Acts;

(b) the Insolvency Act 1986 (c 45);

(c) the Company Directors Disqualification Act 1986 (c 46);

(d) Part 3 (investigations and powers to obtain information) or 7 (financial markets and insolvency) of the Companies Act 1989 (c 40);

(e) Part 5 of the Criminal Justice Act 1993 (c 36) (insider dealing);

(f) the Financial Services and Markets Act 2000;

(g) Part 42 of this Act (statutory auditors).

14 A disclosure for the purpose of enabling or assisting the Scottish Ministers to exercise their functions under the enactments relating to insolvency.

15 A disclosure for the purpose of enabling or assisting the Department of Enterprise, Trade and Investment for Northern Ireland to exercise any powers conferred on it by the enactments relating to companies or insolvency.

16 A disclosure for the purpose of enabling or assisting a person appointed or authorised by the Department of Enterprise, Trade and Investment for Northern Ireland under the enactments relating to companies or insolvency to exercise their functions.

17 A disclosure for the purpose of enabling or assisting an official receiver (including the Accountant in Bankruptcy in Scotland and the Official Assignee in Northern Ireland) to exercise their functions under the enactments relating to insolvency.

18 A disclosure for the purpose of enabling or assisting the Insolvency Practitioners Tribunal to exercise its functions under the Insolvency Act 1986 (c 45).

19 A disclosure for the purpose of enabling or assisting a body that is for the time being a recognised professional body for the purposes of section 391 of the Insolvency Act 1986 (recognised professional bodies) to exercise its functions as such.

20 A disclosure for the purpose of enabling or assisting the Pensions Regulator to exercise the functions conferred on it by or by virtue of any of the following—

(a) the Pension Schemes Act 1993 (c 48);
(b) the Pensions Act 1995 (c 26);
(c) the Welfare Reform and Pensions Act 1999 (c 30);
(d) the Pensions Act 2004 (c 35);
(e) any enactment in force in Northern Ireland corresponding to any of those enactments.

21 A disclosure for the purpose of enabling or assisting the Board of the Pension Protection Fund to exercise the functions conferred on it by or by virtue of Part 2 of the Pensions Act 2004 or any enactment in force in Northern Ireland corresponding to that Part.

22 A disclosure for the purpose of enabling or assisting the Bank of England to exercise its functions.

23 A disclosure for the purpose of enabling or assisting the Commissioners for Her Majesty's Revenue and Customs to exercise their functions.

24 A disclosure for the purpose of enabling or assisting organs of the Society of Lloyd's (being organs constituted by or under the Lloyd's Act 1982 (c. xiv)) to exercise their functions under or by virtue of the Lloyd's Acts 1871 to 1982.

25 A disclosure for the purpose of enabling or assisting the Office of Fair Trading to exercise its functions under any of the following—

(a) the Fair Trading Act 1973 (c 41);
(b) the Consumer Credit Act 1974 (c 39);
(c) the Estate Agents Act 1979 (c 38);
(d) the Competition Act 1980 (c 21);
(e) the Competition Act 1998 (c 41);
(f) the Financial Services and Markets Act 2000 (c 8);
(g) the Enterprise Act 2002 (c 40);
(h) the Unfair Terms in Consumer Contracts Regulations 1999 (SI 1999/2083);
(i) the Business Protection from Misleading Marketing Regulations 2008 (SI 2008/1276);
(j) the Consumer Protection from Unfair Trading Regulations 2008 (SI 2008/1277).

26 A disclosure for the purpose of enabling or assisting the Competition Commission to exercise its functions under any of the following—

(a) the Fair Trading Act 1973;
(b) the Competition Act 1980;
(c) the Competition Act 1998;
(d) the Enterprise Act 2002.

27 A disclosure with a view to the institution of, or otherwise for the purposes of, proceedings before the Competition Appeal Tribunal.

28 A disclosure for the purpose of enabling or assisting an enforcer under Part 8 of the Enterprise Act 2002 (enforcement of consumer legislation) to exercise their functions under that Part.

29 A disclosure for the purpose of enabling or assisting the Charity Commission to exercise its functions.

30 A disclosure for the purpose of enabling or assisting the Attorney General to exercise their functions in connection with charities.

31 A disclosure for the purpose of enabling or assisting the National Lottery Commission to exercise its functions under sections 5 to 10 and 15 of the National Lottery etc Act 1993 (c 39) (licensing and power of Secretary of State to require information).

32 A disclosure by the National Lottery Commission to the Comptroller and Auditor General for the purpose of enabling or assisting the Comptroller and Auditor General to carry out an examination under Part 2 of the National Audit Act 1983 (c 44) into the economy, effectiveness and efficiency with which the National Lottery Commission has used its resources in discharging its functions under sections 5 to 10 of the National Lottery etc Act 1993.

33 A disclosure for the purpose of enabling or assisting a qualifying body under the Unfair Terms in Consumer Contracts Regulations 1999 (SI 1999/2083) to exercise its functions under those Regulations.

34 A disclosure for the purpose of enabling or assisting an enforcement authority under the Consumer Protection (Distance Selling) Regulations 2000 (SI 2000/2334) to exercise its functions under those Regulations.

35 A disclosure for the purpose of enabling or assisting an enforcement authority under the Financial Services (Distance Marketing) Regulations 2004 (SI 2004/2095) to exercise its functions under those Regulations.

36 A disclosure for the purpose of enabling or assisting a local weights and measures authority in England and Wales to exercise its functions under section 230(2) of the Enterprise Act 2002 (c 40) (notice of intention to prosecute, etc).

37 A disclosure for the purpose of enabling or assisting the Financial Conduct Authority or the Prudential Regulation Authority to exercise its functions under any of the following—

(a) the legislation relating to friendly societies or to industrial and provident societies;
(b) the Building Societies Act 1986 (c 53);
(c) Part 7 of the Companies Act 1989 (c 40) (financial markets and insolvency);
(d) the Financial Services and Markets Act 2000 (c 8).

38 ...

39 A disclosure for the purpose of enabling or assisting a body corporate established in accordance with section 212(1) of the Financial Services and Markets Act 2000 (compensation scheme manager) to exercise its functions.

40— (1) A disclosure for the purpose of enabling or assisting a recognised investment exchange or a recognised clearing house to exercise its functions as such.

(2) In sub-paragraph (1) “recognised investment exchange” and “recognised clearing house” have the same meaning as in section 285 of the Financial Services and Markets Act 2000.

41 A disclosure for the purpose of enabling or assisting a person approved under the Uncertificated Securities Regulations 2001 (SI 2001/3755) as an operator of a relevant system (within the meaning of those Regulations) to exercise their functions.

42 A disclosure for the purpose of enabling or assisting a body designated under section 326(1) of the Financial Services and Markets Act 2000 (designated professional bodies) to exercise its functions in its capacity as a body designated under that section.

43 A disclosure with a view to the institution of, or otherwise for the purposes of, civil proceedings arising under or by virtue of the Financial Services and Markets Act 2000.

44 A disclosure for the purpose of enabling or assisting a body designated by order under section 1252 of this Act (delegation of functions of Secretary of State) to exercise its functions under Part 42 of this Act (statutory auditors).

45 A disclosure for the purpose of enabling or assisting a recognised supervisory or qualifying body, within the meaning of Part 42 of this Act, to exercise its functions as such.

46 A disclosure for the purpose of enabling or assisting the Regulator of Community Interest Companies to exercise functions under the Companies (Audit, Investigations and Community Enterprise) Act 2004 (c 27).

47 A disclosure for the purpose of enabling or assisting a person authorised by the Secretary of State under Part 2, 3 or 4 of the Proceeds of Crime Act 2002 (c 29) to exercise their functions.

48 A disclosure with a view to the institution of, or otherwise for the purposes of, proceedings on an application under section 6, 7 or 8 of the Company Directors Disqualification Act 1986 (c 46) (disqualification for unfitness).

49 A disclosure with a view to the institution of, or otherwise for the purposes of, proceedings before the Upper Tribunal in respect of—

(a) a decision of the Financial Conduct Authority;

(aa) a decision of the Prudential Regulation Authority;

(b) a decision of the Bank of England; or

(c) a decision of a person relating to the assessment of any compensation or consideration under the Banking (Special Provisions) Act 2008 or the Banking Act 2009.

50 A disclosure for the purposes of proceedings before a tribunal in relation to a decision of the Pensions Regulator.

51 A disclosure for the purpose of enabling or assisting a body appointed under section 14 of the Companies (Audit, Investigations and Community Enterprise) Act 2004 (supervision of periodic accounts and reports of issuers of listed securities) to exercise functions mentioned in subsection (2) of that section.

52— (1) A disclosure with a view to the institution of, or otherwise for the purposes of, disciplinary proceedings relating to the performance by a lawyer, auditor, accountant, valuer or actuary of their professional duties.

(2) In sub-paragraph (1) "lawyer" means—

(a) a person who for the purposes of the Legal Services Act 2007 (c 29) is an authorised person in relation to an activity that constitutes a reserved legal activity (within the meaning of that Act),

(b) a solicitor or barrister in Northern Ireland,

(c) a solicitor or advocate in Scotland, or

(d) a person who is a member, and entitled to practise as such, of a legal profession regulated in a jurisdiction outside the United Kingdom.

(3) Until the coming into force of section 18 of the Legal Services Act 2007, the following is substituted for paragraph (a) of sub-paragraph (2) above—

"(a) a solicitor or barrister in England and Wales,".

53— (1) A disclosure with a view to the institution of, or otherwise for the purposes of, disciplinary proceedings relating to the performance by a public servant of their duties.

(2) In sub-paragraph (1) "public servant" means—

(a) an officer or employee of the Crown, or

(b) an officer or employee of any public or other authority for the time being designated for the purposes of this paragraph by the Secretary of State by order subject to negative resolution procedure.

(B) JERSEY

1 A disclosure for the purpose of enabling or assisting an inspector appointed under Part 19 of the Companies (Jersey) Law 1991 to exercise their functions.

2 A disclosure for the purpose of enabling or assisting a person appointed under Article 33 of the Financial Services (Jersey) Law 1998 to exercise their functions.

3 A disclosure for the purpose of enabling or assisting an inspector appointed under Article 22 of the Collective Investment Funds (Jersey) Law 1988 to exercise their functions.

4 A disclosure for the purpose of enabling or assisting the Minister for Economic Development to exercise functions under any of the following—

(a) the Bankruptcy Désastre (Jersey) Law 1990;

(b) the Companies (Jersey) Law 1991;

(c) the Financial Services (Jersey) Law 1998.

5 A disclosure for the purpose of enabling or assisting the Comptroller of Income Tax to exercise their functions.

6 A disclosure for the purpose of enabling or assisting the Agent of the Impôts to exercise their functions.

7 A disclosure for the purpose of enabling or assisting the Jersey Competition Regulatory Authority to exercise its functions.

8 A disclosure for the purpose of enabling or assisting Her Majesty's Attorney General for Jersey to exercise their functions in connection with charities.

9 A disclosure for the purpose of enabling or assisting Her Majesty's Attorney General for Jersey to exercise their functions under the Distance Selling (Jersey) Law 2007.

10 A disclosure for the purpose of enabling or assisting the Viscount to exercise their functions in relation to désastre or in relation to Part 2 of the Proceeds of Crime (Jersey) Law 1999.

11 A disclosure with a view to the institution of, or otherwise for the purposes of, proceedings on an application under Article 78 of the Companies (Jersey) Law 1991 (disqualification orders).

12— (1) A disclosure with a view to the institution of, or otherwise for the purposes of, disciplinary proceedings relating to the performance by a solicitor, advocate, foreign lawyer, auditor, accountant, valuer or actuary of their professional duties.

(2) In sub-paragraph (1)—

(a) "solicitor" means a person who has been admitted as a solicitor under the Advocates and Solicitors (Jersey) Law 1997;

(b) "advocate" means a person who has been admitted to the Bar under that Law; and

(c) "foreign lawyer" means a person who has not been admitted as mentioned in paragraph (a) or (b) but is a member, and entitled to practise as such, of a legal profession regulated within a jurisdiction outside Jersey.

13— (1) A disclosure with a view to the institution of, or otherwise for the purposes of, disciplinary proceedings relating to the performance by a public servant of their duties.

(2) In sub-paragraph (1) "public servant" means—

(a) an individual who holds office under, or is employed by, the Crown,

(b) a member, officer or employee of the States of Jersey or an officer or employee in an administration of the States of Jersey,

(c) a member, officer or employee of the Jersey Financial Services Commission, or

(d) any person exercising public functions who is declared by Order of the Minister for Economic Development to be a public servant for the purposes of paragraph 25 of the Schedule to the Companies (Takeovers and Mergers Panel) (Jersey) Law 2009.

(C) GUERNSEY

1 A disclosure for the purpose of enabling or assisting the Registrar of Companies appointed under the Companies (Guernsey) Law 2008 to exercise their functions under that Law.

2 A disclosure for the purpose of enabling or assisting a person appointed under—

(a) section 27E or 41I of the Protection of Investors (Bailiwick of Guernsey) Law 1987,

(b) section 27 of the Banking Supervision (Bailiwick of Guernsey) Law 1994,

(c) section 10 of the Company Securities (Insider Dealing) (Bailiwick of Guernsey) Law 1996,

(d) section 24 of the Regulation of Fiduciaries, Administration Businesses and Company Directors (Bailiwick of Guernsey) Law 2000,

(e) section 69 of the Insurance Business (Bailiwick of Guernsey) Law 2002,

(f) section 46 of the Insurance Managers and Insurance Intermediaries (Bailiwick of Guernsey) Law 2002,

(g) section 19 of the Registration of Non-Regulated Financial Services Business (Bailiwick of Guernsey) Law 2008, to exercise their functions.

3 A disclosure for the purpose of enabling or assisting Her Majesty's Procureur to exercise their functions in connection with charities.

4 A disclosure for the purpose of enabling or assisting the Guernsey Banking Deposit Compensation Scheme, established under section 46 of the Banking Supervision (Bailiwick of

Guernsey) Law 1987 by the Banking Deposit Compensation Scheme (Bailiwick of Guernsey) Ordinance 2008, to exercise its functions.

5 A disclosure for the purpose of enabling or assisting any supervisory body or professional oversight body to exercise its functions under Part XVIA of the Companies (Guernsey) Law 2008 (regulation of auditors).

6 A disclosure with a view to the institution of, or otherwise for the purposes of, proceedings on an application under Part XXV of the Companies (Guernsey) Law 2008 (disqualification orders).

7— (1) A disclosure with a view to the institution of, or otherwise for the purposes of, disciplinary proceedings relating to the performance by an Advocate of the Royal Court, foreign lawyer, auditor, accountant, valuer or actuary of their professional duties.

(2) In sub-paragraph (1) "foreign lawyer" means a person who has not been admitted as an Advocate of the Royal Court, but is a member, and entitled to practise as such, of a legal profession regulated within a jurisdiction outside Guernsey.

8— (1) A disclosure with a view to the institution of, or otherwise for the purposes of, disciplinary proceedings relating to the performance by a public servant of their duties.

(2) In sub-paragraph (1) "public servant" means—

(a) an officer or employee of the Crown,

(b) a member, officer or employee of the States of Guernsey,

(c) a member, officer or employee of the Guernsey Financial Services Commission, or

(d) any person exercising public functions who is declared by regulations of the Commerce and Employment Department to be a public servant for the purposes of paragraph 17 of Schedule 6 to the Companies (Guernsey) Law 2008.

(D) ISLE OF MAN

1 A disclosure for the purpose of enabling or assisting an inspector appointed by the High Court of the Isle of Man under the enactments of the Isle of Man relating to companies to discharge their functions.

2 A disclosure for the purpose of enabling or assisting a person conducting an investigation under—

(a) section 16 of the Collective Investment Schemes Act 2008 (an Act of Tynwald: c 7);

(b) Schedule 2 to the Financial Services Act 2008 (an Act of Tynwald: c 8); or

(c) Schedule 5 to the Insurance Act 2008 (an Act of Tynwald: c 16),

to exercise their functions.

3 A disclosure for the purpose of enabling or assisting the Financial Supervision Commission of the Isle of Man to exercise any of its functions.

4 A disclosure for the purpose of enabling or assisting an auditor of a permitted person (within the meaning of the Financial Services Act 2008 (an Act of Tynwald)) to exercise their functions.

5 A disclosure for the purpose of enabling or assisting the Office of Fair Trading of the Isle of Man to exercise its functions under Schedule 4 to the Financial Services Act 2008 (an Act of Tynwald) in relation to a financial services dispute within the meaning of paragraph 1(1) of that Schedule.

6 A disclosure for the purpose of enabling or assisting an adjudicator appointed under paragraph 4 of Schedule 4 to the Financial Services Act 2008 (an Act of Tynwald) to exercise their functions.

7 A disclosure for the purpose of enabling or assisting the body administering a scheme under section 25 of the Financial Services Act 2008 (an Act of Tynwald) (compensation schemes) to exercise its functions under the scheme.

8 A disclosure with a view to the institution of, or otherwise for the purposes of, civil proceedings arising under or by virtue of the Financial Services Act 2008 (an Act of Tynwald).

9 A disclosure for the purpose of enabling or assisting—

(a) the Insurance and Pensions Authority of the Isle of Man; or

(b) the Retirement Benefits Schemes Supervisor of the Isle of Man,

to exercise its functions under the Retirement Benefits Schemes Act 2000 (an Act of Tynwald: c 14).

10 A disclosure for the purpose of enabling or assisting the Assessor of Income Tax to exercise their functions under enactments of the Isle of Man relating to income tax.

11 A disclosure for the purpose of enabling or assisting the Office of Fair Trading of the Isle of Man to exercise its functions under any of the following—
(a) the Unsolicited Goods and Services (Isle of Man) Act 1974 (an Act of Tynwald: c 5);
(b) the Moneylenders Act 1991 (an Act of Tynwald: c 6);
(c) the Consumer Protection Act 1991 (an Act of Tynwald: c 11);
(d) the Fair Trading Act 1996 (an Act of Tynwald: c 15).

12 A disclosure for the purpose of enabling or assisting the Department of Local Government and the Environment of the Isle of Man to exercise its functions under the Estate Agents Act 1975 (an Act of Tynwald: c 6) or the Estate Agents Act 1999 (an Act of Tynwald: c 7).

13 A disclosure for the purpose of enabling or assisting Her Majesty's Attorney General of the Isle of Man to exercise their functions in connection with charities.

14 A disclosure for the purpose of enabling or assisting the Treasury of the Isle of Man to exercise its functions under the enactments of the Isle of Man relating to companies, insurance companies or insolvency.

15 A disclosure for the purpose of enabling or assisting an official receiver appointed in the Isle of Man to exercise their functions under the enactments of the Isle of Man relating to insolvency.

16— (1) A disclosure with a view to the institution of, or otherwise for the purposes of, disciplinary proceedings relating to the performance by an advocate, registered legal practitioner, auditor, accountant, valuer or actuary of their professional duties.

(2) In sub-paragraph (1)—

"advocate" means a person who is qualified to act as an advocate in any court in the Island in accordance with section 7 of the Advocates Act 1976 (an Act of Tynwald: c 27);

"registered legal practitioner" means a legal practitioner within the meaning of section 10 of the Legal Practitioners Registration Act 1986 (an Act of Tynwald: c 15) who is registered within the meaning of that Act.

17— (1) A disclosure with a view to the institution of, or otherwise for the purposes of, disciplinary proceedings relating to the performance by a public servant of their duties.

(2) In sub-paragraph (1) "public servant" means—
(a) an officer or employee of the Crown, or
(b) an officer or employee of any public or other authority for the time being designated for the purposes of this paragraph by order made by the Council of Ministers of the Isle of Man.

(E) GENERAL

1 A disclosure for the purpose of enabling or assisting—
(a) the European Central Bank, or
(b) the central bank of any country or territory outside the British Islands,
to exercise its functions.

2— (1) A disclosure for the purpose of enabling or assisting an overseas regulatory authority to exercise its regulatory functions.

(2) In sub-paragraph (1) "overseas regulatory authority" and "regulatory functions" have the same meaning as in section 82 of the Companies Act 1989 (assistance for overseas regulatory authorities).

3 A disclosure with a view to the institution of, or otherwise for the purposes of, criminal proceedings in the British Islands or elsewhere.

4 A disclosure for the purpose of the provision of a summary or collection of information framed in such a way as not to enable the identity of any person to whom the information relates to be ascertained.

5 A disclosure in pursuance of any EU obligation.

PART 3
OVERSEAS REGULATORY BODIES

1— (1) A disclosure is made in accordance with this Part of this Schedule if—

(a) it is made to a person or body exercising relevant functions under legislation in a country or territory outside the British Islands, and

(b) it is made for the purpose of enabling or assisting that person or body to exercise those functions.

(2) "Relevant functions" for this purpose are functions of a public nature that appear to the Panel to be similar to its own functions or those of the Financial Conduct Authority or the Prudential Regulation Authority or similar to the regulatory functions of the Bank of England.

2 In determining whether to disclose information to a person or body in accordance with this Part of this Schedule, the Panel must have regard to the following considerations—

(a) whether the use that the person or body is likely to make of the information is sufficiently important to justify making the disclosure;

(b) whether the person or body has adequate arrangements to prevent the information from being used or further disclosed, otherwise than—

(i) for the purposes of carrying out the functions mentioned in paragraph 1(1)(a), or

(ii) for other purposes substantially similar to those for which information disclosed to the Panel could be used or further disclosed.

SCHEDULE 3

Section 1124

AMENDMENTS OF REMAINING PROVISIONS OF THE COMPANIES ACT 1985 RELATING TO OFFENCES

Failure to give information about interests in shares etc

1 (1) In subsection (3) of section 444 of the Companies Act 1985 (failure to give information requested by Secretary of State relating to interests in shares etc) for "is liable to imprisonment or a fine, or both" substitute "commits an offence".

(2) At the end of that section add—

"(4) A person guilty of an offence under this section is liable—

(a) on conviction on indictment, to imprisonment for a term not exceeding two years or a fine (or both);

(b) on summary conviction—

(i) in England and Wales, to imprisonment for a term not exceeding twelve months or to a fine not exceeding the statutory maximum (or both) and, for continued contravention, a daily default fine not exceeding one-fiftieth of the statutory maximum;

(ii) in Scotland or Northern Ireland, to imprisonment for a term not exceeding six months, or to a fine not exceeding the statutory maximum (or both) and, for continued contravention, a daily default fine not exceeding one-fiftieth of the statutory maximum.".

Obstruction of rights conferred by a warrant or failure to comply with requirement under section 448

2 (1) In section 448(7) of the Companies Act 1985 (obstruction of rights conferred by or by virtue of warrant for entry and search of premises) omit the words "and liable to a fine." to the end.

(2) After that provision insert—

"(7A) A person guilty of an offence under this section is liable—

(a) on conviction on indictment, to a fine;

(b) on summary conviction, to a fine not exceeding the statutory maximum.".

Wrongful disclosure of information to which section 449 applies

3 (1) Section 449 of the Companies Act 1985 (wrongful disclosure of information obtained in course of company investigation) is amended as follows.

(2) For subsection (6)(a) and (b) substitute "is guilty of an offence."

(3) After subsection (6) insert—

"(6A) A person guilty of an offence under this section is liable—

(a) on conviction on indictment, to imprisonment for a term not exceeding two years or a fine (or both);

(b) on summary conviction—

(i) in England and Wales, to imprisonment for a term not exceeding twelve months or to a fine not exceeding the statutory maximum (or both);

(ii) in Scotland or Northern Ireland, to imprisonment for a term not exceeding six months, or to a fine not exceeding the statutory maximum (or both).".

(2) Omit subsection (7).

Destruction, mutilation etc of company documents

4 (1) For subsection (3) of section 450 of the Companies Act 1985 (offence of destroying, etc company documents) substitute—

"(3) A person guilty of an offence under this section is liable—

(a) on conviction on indictment, to imprisonment for a term not exceeding seven years or a fine (or both);

(b) on summary conviction—

(i) in England and Wales, to imprisonment for a term not exceeding twelve months or to a fine not exceeding the statutory maximum (or both);

(ii) in Scotland or Northern Ireland, to imprisonment for a term not exceeding six months, or to a fine not exceeding the statutory maximum (or both).".

(2) Omit subsection (4) of that section.

Provision of false information in purported compliance with section 447

5 (1) For subsection (2) of section 451 of the Companies Act 1985 (provision of false information in response to requirement under section 447) substitute—

"(2) A person guilty of an offence under this section is liable—

(a) on conviction on indictment, to imprisonment for a term not exceeding two years or a fine (or both);

(b) on summary conviction—

(i) in England and Wales, to imprisonment for a term not exceeding twelve months or to a fine not exceeding the statutory maximum (or both);

(ii) in Scotland or Northern Ireland, to imprisonment for a term not exceeding six months, or to a fine not exceeding the statutory maximum (or both).".

(2) Omit subsection (3) of that section.

Obstruction of inspector, etc exercising power to enter and remain on premises

6 (1) Section 453A of the Companies Act 1985 (obstruction of inspector etc exercising power to enter and remain on premises) is amended as follows.

(2) For subsection (5)(a) and (b) substitute "is guilty of an offence."

(3) After subsection (5) insert—

"(5A) A person guilty of an offence under this section is liable—

(a) on conviction on indictment, to a fine;

(b) on summary conviction, to a fine not exceeding the statutory maximum.".

(4) Omit subsection (6).

Attempted evasion of restrictions under Part 15

7 (1) In subsection (1) of section 455 of the Companies Act 1985 (attempted evasion of restrictions under Part 15) for "is liable to a fine if he" substitute "commits an offence if he".

(2) In subsection (2) of that section for the words "the company" to the end substitute "an offence is committed by—

(a) the company, and

(b) every officer of the company who is in default."

(3) After that subsection insert—

"(2A) A person guilty of an offence under this section is liable—

(a) on conviction on indictment, to a fine;

(b) on summary conviction, to a fine not exceeding the statutory maximum.".

SCHEDULE 4

Section 1144(1)

DOCUMENTS AND INFORMATION SENT OR SUPPLIED TO A COMPANY

PART 1
INTRODUCTION

Application of Schedule

1 (1) This Schedule applies to documents or information sent or supplied to a company.

(2) It does not apply to documents or information sent or supplied by another company (see section 1144(3) and Schedule 5).

PART 2
COMMUNICATIONS IN HARD COPY FORM

Introduction

2 A document or information is validly sent or supplied to a company if it is sent or supplied in hard copy form in accordance with this Part of this Schedule.

Method of communication in hard copy form

3 (1) A document or information in hard copy form may be sent or supplied by hand or by post to an address (in accordance with paragraph 4).

(2) For the purposes of this Schedule, a person sends a document or information by post if he posts a prepaid envelope containing the document or information.

Address for communications in hard copy form

4 A document or information in hard copy form may be sent or supplied—

(a) to an address specified by the company for the purpose;

(b) to the company's registered office;

(c) to an address to which any provision of the Companies Acts authorises the document or information to be sent or supplied.

PART 3
COMMUNICATIONS IN ELECTRONIC FORM

Introduction

5 A document or information is validly sent or supplied to a company if it is sent or supplied in electronic form in accordance with this Part of this Schedule.

Conditions for use of communications in electronic form

6 A document or information may only be sent or supplied to a company in electronic form if—

(a) the company has agreed (generally or specifically) that the document or information may be sent or supplied in that form (and has not revoked that agreement), or

(b) the company is deemed to have so agreed by a provision in the Companies Acts.

Address for communications in electronic form

7 (1) Where the document or information is sent or supplied by electronic means, it may only be sent or supplied to an address—

(a) specified for the purpose by the company (generally or specifically), or

(b) deemed by a provision in the Companies Acts to have been so specified.

(2) Where the document or information is sent or supplied in electronic form by hand or by post, it must be sent or supplied to an address to which it could be validly sent if it were in hard copy form.

PART 4
OTHER AGREED FORMS OF COMMUNICATION

8 A document or information that is sent or supplied to a company otherwise than in hard copy form or electronic form is validly sent or supplied if it is sent or supplied in a form or manner that has been agreed by the company.

SCHEDULE 5 Section 1144(2)
COMMUNICATIONS BY A COMPANY

PART 1
INTRODUCTION

Application of this Schedule

1 This Schedule applies to documents or information sent or supplied by a company.

PART 2
COMMUNICATIONS IN HARD COPY FORM

Introduction

2 A document or information is validly sent or supplied by a company if it is sent or supplied in hard copy form in accordance with this Part of this Schedule.

Method of communication in hard copy form

3 (1) A document or information in hard copy form must be—

(a) handed to the intended recipient, or

(b) sent or supplied by hand or by post to an address (in accordance with paragraph 4).

(2) For the purposes of this Schedule, a person sends a document or information by post if he posts a prepaid envelope containing the document or information.

Address for communications in hard copy form

4 (1) A document or information in hard copy form may be sent or supplied by the company—

(a) to an address specified for the purpose by the intended recipient;

(b) to a company at its registered office;

(c) to a person in his capacity as a member of the company at his address as shown in the company's register of members;

(d) to a person in his capacity as a director of the company at his address as shown in the company's register of directors;

(e) to an address to which any provision of the Companies Acts authorises the document or information to be sent or supplied.

(2) Where the company is unable to obtain an address falling within sub-paragraph (1), the document or information may be sent or supplied to the intended recipient's last address known to the company.

PART 3
COMMUNICATIONS IN ELECTRONIC FORM

Introduction

5 A document or information is validly sent or supplied by a company if it is sent in electronic form in accordance with this Part of this Schedule.

Agreement to communications in electronic form

6 A document or information may only be sent or supplied by a company in electronic form—

(a) to a person who has agreed (generally or specifically) that the document or information may be sent or supplied in that form (and has not revoked that agreement), or

(b) to a company that is deemed to have so agreed by a provision in the Companies Acts.

Address for communications in electronic form

7 (1) Where the document or information is sent or supplied by electronic means, it may only be sent or supplied to an address—

(a) specified for the purpose by the intended recipient (generally or specifically), or

(b) where the intended recipient is a company, deemed by a provision of the Companies Acts to have been so specified.

(2) Where the document or information is sent or supplied in electronic form by hand or by post, it must be—

(a) handed to the intended recipient, or

(b) sent or supplied to an address to which it could be validly sent if it were in hard copy form.

PART 4
COMMUNICATIONS BY MEANS OF A WEBSITE

Use of website

8 A document or information is validly sent or supplied by a company if it is made available on a website in accordance with this Part of this Schedule.

Agreement to use of website

9 A document or information may only be sent or supplied by the company to a person by being made available on a website if the person—

(a) has agreed (generally or specifically) that the document or information may be sent or supplied to him in that manner, or

(b) is taken to have so agreed under—

(i) paragraph 10 (members of the company etc), or

(ii) paragraph 11 (debenture holders),

and has not revoked that agreement.

Deemed agreement of members of company etc to use of website

10 (1) This paragraph applies to a document or information to be sent or supplied to a person—

(a) as a member of the company, or

(b) as a person nominated by a member in accordance with the company's articles to enjoy or exercise all or any specified rights of the member in relation to the company, or

(c) as a person nominated by a member under section 146 to enjoy information rights.

(2) To the extent that—

(a) the members of the company have resolved that the company may send or supply documents or information to members by making them available on a website, or

(b) the company's articles contain provision to that effect,

a person in relation to whom the following conditions are met is taken to have agreed that the company may send or supply documents or information to him in that manner.

(3) The conditions are that—

(a) the person has been asked individually by the company to agree that the company may send or supply documents or information generally, or the documents or information in question, to him by means of a website, and

(b) the company has not received a response within the period of 28 days beginning with the date on which the company's request was sent.

(4) A person is not taken to have so agreed if the company's request—

(a) did not state clearly what the effect of a failure to respond would be, or

(b) was sent less than twelve months after a previous request made to him for the purposes of this paragraph in respect of the same or a similar class of documents or information.

(5) Chapter 3 of Part 3 (resolutions affecting a company's constitution) applies to a resolution under this paragraph.

Deemed agreement of debenture holders to use of website

11 (1) This paragraph applies to a document or information to be sent or supplied to a person as holder of a company's debentures.

(2) To the extent that—

(a) the relevant debenture holders have duly resolved that the company may send or supply documents or information to them by making them available on a website, or

(b) the instrument creating the debenture in question contains provision to that effect,

a debenture holder in relation to whom the following conditions are met is taken to have agreed that the company may send or supply documents or information to him in that manner.

(3) The conditions are that—

(a) the debenture holder has been asked individually by the company to agree that the company may send or supply documents or information generally, or the documents or information in question, to him by means of a website, and

(b) the company has not received a response within the period of 28 days beginning with the date on which the company's request was sent.

(4) A person is not taken to have so agreed if the company's request—

(a) did not state clearly what the effect of a failure to respond would be, or

(b) was sent less than twelve months after a previous request made to him for the purposes of this paragraph in respect of the same or a similar class of documents or information.

(5) For the purposes of this paragraph—

(a) the relevant debenture holders are the holders of debentures of the company ranking *pari passu* for all purposes with the intended recipient, and

(b) a resolution of the relevant debenture holders is duly passed if they agree in accordance with the provisions of the instruments creating the debentures.

Availability of document or information

12 (1) A document or information authorised or required to be sent or supplied by means of a website must be made available in a form, and by a means, that the company reasonably considers will enable the recipient—

(a) to read it, and

(b) to retain a copy of it.

(2) For this purpose a document or information can be read only if—

(a) it can be read with the naked eye, or

(b) to the extent that it consists of images (for example photographs, pictures, maps, plans or drawings), it can be seen with the naked eye.

Notification of availability

13 (1) The company must notify the intended recipient of—

(a) the presence of the document or information on the website,

(b) the address of the website,

(c) the place on the website where it may be accessed, and

(d) how to access the document or information.

(2) The document or information is taken to be sent—

(a) on the date on which the notification required by this paragraph is sent, or

(b) if later, the date on which the document or information first appears on the website after that notification is sent.

Period of availability on website

14 (1) The company must make the document or information available on the website throughout—

(a) the period specified by any applicable provision of the Companies Acts, or

(b) if no such period is specified, the period of 28 days beginning with the date on which the notification required under paragraph 13 is sent to the person in question.

(2) For the purposes of this paragraph, a failure to make a document or information available on a website throughout the period mentioned in sub-paragraph (1) shall be disregarded if—

(a) it is made available on the website for part of that period, and

(b) the failure to make it available throughout that period is wholly attributable to circumstances that it would not be reasonable to have expected the company to prevent or avoid.

PART 5
OTHER AGREED FORMS OF COMMUNICATION

15 A document or information that is sent or supplied otherwise than in hard copy or electronic form or by means of a website is validly sent or supplied if it is sent or supplied in a form or manner that has been agreed by the intended recipient.

PART 6
SUPPLEMENTARY PROVISIONS

Joint holders of shares or debentures

16 (1) This paragraph applies in relation to documents or information to be sent or supplied to joint holders of shares or debentures of a company.

(2) Anything to be agreed or specified by the holder must be agreed or specified by all the joint holders.

(3) Anything authorised or required to be sent or supplied to the holder may be sent or supplied either—

(a) to each of the joint holders, or

(b) to the holder whose name appears first in the register of members or the relevant register of debenture holders.

(4) This paragraph has effect subject to anything in the company's articles.

Death or bankruptcy of holder of shares

17 (1) This paragraph has effect in the case of the death or bankruptcy of a holder of a company's shares.

(2) Documents or information required or authorised to be sent or supplied to the member may be sent or supplied to the persons claiming to be entitled to the shares in consequence of the death or bankruptcy—

(a) by name, or

(b) by the title of representatives of the deceased, or trustee of the bankrupt, or by any like description,

at the address in the United Kingdom supplied for the purpose by those so claiming.

(3) Until such an address has been so supplied, a document or information may be sent or supplied in any manner in which it might have been sent or supplied if the death or bankruptcy had not occurred.

(4) This paragraph has effect subject to anything in the company's articles.

(5) References in this paragraph to the bankruptcy of a person include—

(a) the sequestration of the estate of a person;

(b) a person's estate being the subject of a protected trust deed (within the meaning of the Bankruptcy (Scotland) Act 1985).

In such a case the reference in sub-paragraph (2)(b) to the trustee of the bankrupt is to be read as the permanent or interim trustee (within the meaning of that Act) on the sequestrated estate or, as the case may be, the trustee under the protected deed.

SCHEDULE 6

Section 1159

MEANING OF "SUBSIDIARY" ETC: SUPPLEMENTARY PROVISIONS

Introduction

1 The provisions of this Part of this Schedule explain expressions used in section 1159 (meaning of "subsidiary" etc) and otherwise supplement that section.

Voting rights in a company

2 In section 1159(1) (a) and (c) the references to the voting rights in a company are to the rights conferred on shareholders in respect of their shares or, in the case of a company not having a share capital, on members, to vote at general meetings of the company on all, or substantially all, matters.

Right to appoint or remove a majority of the directors

3 (1) In section 1159(1)(b) the reference to the right to appoint or remove a majority of the board of directors is to the right to appoint or remove directors holding a majority of the voting rights at meetings of the board on all, or substantially all, matters.

(2) A company shall be treated as having the right to appoint to a directorship if—

(a) a person's appointment to it follows necessarily from his appointment as director of the company, or

(b) the directorship is held by the company itself.

(3) A right to appoint or remove which is exercisable only with the consent or concurrence of another person shall be left out of account unless no other person has a right to appoint or, as the case may be, remove in relation to that directorship.

Rights exercisable only in certain circumstances or temporarily incapable of exercise

4 (1) Rights which are exercisable only in certain circumstances shall be taken into account only—

(a) when the circumstances have arisen, and for so long as they continue to obtain, or

(b) when the circumstances are within the control of the person having the rights.

(2) Rights which are normally exercisable but are temporarily incapable of exercise shall continue to be taken into account.

Rights held by one person on behalf of another

5 Rights held by a person in a fiduciary capacity shall be treated as not held by him.

6 (1) Rights held by a person as nominee for another shall be treated as held by the other.

(2) Rights shall be regarded as held as nominee for another if they are exercisable only on his instructions or with his consent or concurrence.

Rights attached to shares held by way of security

7 Rights attached to shares held by way of security shall be treated as held by the person providing the security—

(a) where apart from the right to exercise them for the purpose of preserving the value of the security, or of realising it, the rights are exercisable only in accordance with his instructions, and

(b) where the shares are held in connection with the granting of loans as part of normal business activities and apart from the right to exercise them for the purpose of preserving the value of the security, or of realising it, the rights are exercisable only in his interests.

Rights attributed to holding company

8 (1) Rights shall be treated as held by a holding company if they are held by any of its subsidiary companies.

(2) Nothing in paragraph 6 or 7 shall be construed as requiring rights held by a holding company to be treated as held by any of its subsidiaries.

(3) For the purposes of paragraph 7 rights shall be treated as being exercisable in accordance with the instructions or in the interests of a company if they are exercisable in accordance with the instructions of or, as the case may be, in the interests of—

(a) any subsidiary or holding company of that company, or

(b) any subsidiary of a holding company of that company.

Disregard of certain rights

9 The voting rights in a company shall be reduced by any rights held by the company itself.

Supplementary

10 References in any provision of paragraphs 5 to 9 to rights held by a person include rights falling to be treated as held by him by virtue of any other provision of those paragraphs but not rights which by virtue of any such provision are to be treated as not held by him.

SCHEDULE 7

Section 1162

PARENT AND SUBSIDIARY UNDERTAKINGS: SUPPLEMENTARY PROVISIONS

Introduction

1 The provisions of this Schedule explain expressions used in section 1162 (parent and subsidiary undertakings) and otherwise supplement that section.

Voting rights in an undertaking

2 (1) In section 1162(2)(a) and (d) the references to the voting rights in an undertaking are to the rights conferred on shareholders in respect of their shares or, in the case of an undertaking not having a share capital, on members, to vote at general meetings of the undertaking on all, or substantially all, matters.

(2) In relation to an undertaking which does not have general meetings at which matters are decided by the exercise of voting rights the references to holding a majority of the voting rights in the undertaking shall be construed as references to having the right under the constitution of the undertaking to direct the overall policy of the undertaking or to alter the terms of its constitution.

Right to appoint or remove a majority of the directors

3 (1) In section 1162(2)(b) the reference to the right to appoint or remove a majority of the board of directors is to the right to appoint or remove directors holding a majority of the voting rights at meetings of the board on all, or substantially all, matters.

(2) An undertaking shall be treated as having the right to appoint to a directorship if—

(a) a person's appointment to it follows necessarily from his appointment as director of the undertaking, or

(b) the directorship is held by the undertaking itself.

(3) A right to appoint or remove which is exercisable only with the consent or concurrence of another person shall be left out of account unless no other person has a right to appoint or, as the case may be, remove in relation to that directorship.

Right to exercise dominant influence

4 (1) For the purposes of section 1162(2) (c) an undertaking shall not be regarded as having the right to exercise a dominant influence over another undertaking unless it has a right to give directions with respect to the operating and financial policies of that other undertaking which its directors are obliged to comply with whether or not they are for the benefit of that other undertaking.

(2) A "control contract" means a contract in writing conferring such a right which—

(a) is of a kind authorised by the articles of the undertaking in relation to which the right is exercisable, and

(b) is permitted by the law under which that undertaking is established.

(3) This paragraph shall not be read as affecting the construction of section 1162(4)(a).

Rights exercisable only in certain circumstances or temporarily incapable of exercise

5 (1) Rights which are exercisable only in certain circumstances shall be taken into account only—

(a) when the circumstances have arisen, and for so long as they continue to obtain, or

(b) when the circumstances are within the control of the person having the rights.

(2) Rights which are normally exercisable but are temporarily incapable of exercise shall continue to be taken into account.

Rights held by one person on behalf of another

6 Rights held by a person in a fiduciary capacity shall be treated as not held by him.

7 (1) Rights held by a person as nominee for another shall be treated as held by the other.

(2) Rights shall be regarded as held as nominee for another if they are exercisable only on his instructions or with his consent or concurrence.

Rights attached to shares held by way of security

8 Rights attached to shares held by way of security shall be treated as held by the person providing the security—

(a) where apart from the right to exercise them for the purpose of preserving the value of the security, or of realising it, the rights are exercisable only in accordance with his instructions, and

(b) where the shares are held in connection with the granting of loans as part of normal business activities and apart from the right to exercise them for the purpose of preserving the value of the security, or of realising it, the rights are exercisable only in his interests.

Rights attributed to parent undertaking

9 (1) Rights shall be treated as held by a parent undertaking if they are held by any of its subsidiary undertakings.

(2) Nothing in paragraph 7 or 8 shall be construed as requiring rights held by a parent undertaking to be treated as held by any of its subsidiary undertakings.

(3) For the purposes of paragraph 8 rights shall be treated as being exercisable in accordance with the instructions or in the interests of an undertaking if they are exercisable in accordance with the instructions of or, as the case may be, in the interests of any group undertaking.

Disregard of certain rights

10 The voting rights in an undertaking shall be reduced by any rights held by the undertaking itself.

Supplementary

11 References in any provision of paragraphs 6 to 10 to rights held by a person include rights falling to be treated as held by him by virtue of any other provision of those paragraphs but not rights which by virtue of any such provision are to be treated as not held by him.

SCHEDULE 8 INDEX OF DEFINED EXPRESSIONS

Section 1174

abbreviated accounts (in Part 15)	sections 444(4) and 445(3)
accounting reference date and accounting reference period	section 391
accounting standards (in Part 15)	section 464
accounts meeting	section 437(3)
acquisition, in relation to a non-cash asset	section 1163(2)
address	
— generally in the Companies Acts	section 1142
— in the company communications provisions	section 1148(1)
affirmative resolution procedure, in relation to regulations and orders	section 1290
allotment (time of)	section 558
allotment of equity securities (in Chapter 3 of Part 17)	section 560(2) and (3)
allotted share capital and allotted shares	section 546(1)(b) and (2)
annual accounts (in Part 15)	section 471
annual accounts and reports (in Part 15)	section 471
annual general meeting	section 336
annual return	section 854
appropriate audit authority (in sections 522, 523 and 524)	section 525(1)
appropriate rate of interest	
— in Chapter 5 of Part 17	section 592
— in Chapter 6 of Part 17	section 609
approval after being made, in relation to regulations and orders	section 1291
arrangement	
— in Chapter 7 of Part 17	section 616(1)
— in Part 26	section 895(2)
articles	section 18
associate (in Chapter 3 of Part 28)	section 988
associated bodies corporate and associated company (in Part 10)	section 256
authenticated, in relation to a document or information sent or supplied to a company	section 1146
authorised group, of members of a company (in Part 14)	section 370(3)
authorised insurance company	section 1165(2)

authorised minimum (in relation to share capital of public company)	section 763
available profits (in Chapter 5 of Part 18)	section 711 and 712
banking company and banking group	section 1164
body corporate	section 1173(1)
called-up share capital	section 547
capital redemption reserve	section 733
capitalisation in relation to a company's profits (in Part 23)	section 853(3)
cash (in relation to paying up or allotting shares)	section 583
cause of action, in relation to derivative proceedings (in Chapter 2 of Part 11)	section 265(7)
certified translation (in Part 35)	section 1107
charge (in Chapter A1 of Part 25)	section 859A
circulation date, in relation to a written resolution (in Part 13)	section 290
class of shares	section 629
the Companies Acts	section 2
Companies Act accounts	sections 395(1)(a) and 403(2)(a)
Companies Act group accounts	section 403(2)(a)
Companies Act individual accounts	section 395(1)
companies involved in the division (in Part 27)	section 919(2)
company	
— generally in the Companies Acts	section 1
— in Chapter 7 of Part 17	section 616(1)
— in Chapter A1 of Part 25	section 859A
...	...
— in Part 26	section 895(2)
— in Chapter 3 of Part 28	section 991(1)
— in the company communications provisions	section 1148(1)
the company communications provisions	section 1143
the company law provisions of this Act	section 2(2)
company records (in Part 37)	section 1134
connected with, in relation to a director (in Part 10)	sections 252 to 254
constitution, of a company	section
— generally in the Companies Acts	section 17
— in Part 10	section 257
contributory	section 1170B
controlling, of a body corporate by a director (in Part 10)	section 255
corporate governance statement and separate corporate governance statement	
— in Part 15	section 472A
— in Part 16	section 538A
corporation	section 1173(1)
the court	section 1156
credit institution	section 1173(1)
credit transaction (in Chapter 4 of Part 10)	section 202

creditor (in Chapter 1 of Part 31)	section 1011
daily default fine	section 1125
date of the offer (in Chapter 3 of Part 28)	section 991(1)
debenture	section 738
derivative claim (in Chapter 1 of Part 11)	section 260
derivative proceedings (in Chapter 2 of Part 11)	section 265
Directive disclosure requirements	section 1078
director	
— generally in the Companies Acts	section 250
— in Chapter 8 of Part 10	section 240(3)
— in Chapter 1 of Part 11	section 260(5)
— in Chapter 2 of Part 11	section 265(7)
— in Part 14	section 379(1)
directors' remuneration report	section 420
directors' report	section 415
distributable profits	
— in Chapter 2 of Part 18	section 683(1)
— elsewhere in Part 18	section 736
distribution	
— in Chapter 2 of Part 18	section 683(1)
— in Part 23	section 829
division (in Part 27)	section 919
document	
— in Part 35	section 1114(1)
— in the company communications provisions	section 1148(1)
dormant, in relation to a company or other body corporate	section 1169
EEA State and related expressions	section 1170
electronic form, electronic copy, electronic means	
— generally in the Companies Acts	section 1168(3) and (4)
— in relation to communications to a company	Part 3 of Schedule 4
— in relation to communications by a company	Part 3 of Schedule 5
eligible members, in relation to a written resolution	section 289
e-money issuer	
— in Part 15	section 474(1)
— in Part 16	section 539
employees' share scheme	section 1166
employer and employee (in Chapter 1 of Part 18)	section 676
enactment	section 1293
equity securities (in Chapter 3 of Part 17)	section 560(1)
equity share capital	section 548
equity shares (in Chapter 7 of Part 17)	section 616(1)
establishment of an overseas company (in Part 35)	section 1067(6)
existing company (in Part 27)	section 902(2)
fellow subsidiary undertakings	section 1161(4)

financial assistance (in Chapter 2 of Part 18)	section 677
financial institution	section 1173(1)
financial year, of a company	section 390
firm	section 1173(1)
fixed assets (in Part 23)	section 853
the former Companies Acts	section 1171
the Gazette	section 1173(1)
group (in Part 15)	section 474(1)
group undertaking	section 1161(5)
hard copy form and hard copy	
— generally in the Companies Acts	section 1168(2)
— in relation to communications to a company	Part 2 of Schedule 4
— in relation to communications by a company	Part 2 of Schedule 5
hire-purchase agreement	section 1173(1)
holder of shares (in Chapter 3 of Part 17)	section 574
holding company	section 1159 (and see section 1160 and Schedule 6)
IAS accounts	sections395(1)(b) and 403(1) and (2)(b)
IAS group accounts	section 403(1) and (2)(b)
IAS individual accounts	section 395(1)(b)
IAS Regulation (in Part 15)	section 474(1)
included in the consolidation, in relation to group accounts (in Part 15)	section 474(1)
individual accounts	section 394
information rights (in Part 9)	section 146(3)
insurance company	section 1165(3)
insurance group	section 1165(5)
insurance market activity	section 1165(7)
interest in shares (for the purposes of Part 22)	sections 820 to 825
international accounting standards (in Part 15)	section 474(1)
investment company (in Part 23)	section 833
...	
issued share capital and issued shares	section 546(1)(a) and (2)
the issuing company (in Chapter 7 of Part 17)	section 610(6)
the Joint Stock Companies Acts	section 1171
liabilities (in Part 27)	section 941
liability, references to incurring, reducing or discharging (in Chapter 2 of Part 18)	section 683(2)
limited by guarantee	section 3(3)
limited by shares	section 3(2)
limited company	section 3
the main register (of members) (in Chapter 3 of Part 8)	section 131(1)
major audit (in sections 522 and 525)	section 525(2)
market purchase, by a company of its own shares (in Chapter 4 of Part 18)	section 694(4)

member, of a company	
— generally in the Companies Acts	section 112
— in Chapter 1 of Part 11	section 260(5)
— in Chapter 2 of Part 11	section 265(7)
memorandum of association	section 8
merger (in Part 27)	section 904
merging companies (in Part 27)	section 904(2)
merger by absorption (in Part 27)	section 904(1)(a)
merger by formation of a new company (in Part 27)	section 904(1)(b)
MiFID investment firm	
—in Part 15	section 474(1)
—in Part 16	section 539
negative resolution procedure, in relation to regulations and orders	section 1289
net assets (in Part 7)	section 92
new company (in Part 27)	section 902(2)
non-cash asset	section 1163
non-voting shares (in Chapter 3 of Part 28)	section 991(1)
. . .	
number, in relation to shares	section 540(4)(b)
off-market purchase, by a company of its own shares (in Chapter 4 of Part 18)	section 693(2)
offer period (in Chapter 2 of Part 28)	section 971(1)
offer to the public (in Chapter 1 of Part 20)	section 756
offeror	
— in Chapter 2 of Part 28	section 971(1)
— in Chapter 3 of Part 28	section 991(1)
officer, in relation to a body corporate	section 1173(1)
officer in default	section 1121
official seal, of registrar	section 1062
opted-in company (in Chapter 2 of Part 28)	section 971(1)
opting-in resolution (in Chapter 2 of Part 28)	section 966(1)
opting-out resolution (in Chapter 2 of Part 28)	section 966(5)
ordinary resolution	section 282
ordinary shares (in Chapter 3 of Part 17)	section 560(1)
organisation (in Part 14)	section 379(1)
other relevant transactions or arrangements (in Chapter 4 of Part 10)	section 210
overseas company	section 1044
overseas branch register	section 129(1)
paid up	section 583
the Panel (in Part 28)	section 942
parent company	section 1173(1)
parent undertaking	section 1162 (and see Schedule 7)
payment for loss of office (in Chapter 4 of Part 10)	section 215

pension scheme (in Chapter 1 of Part 18)	section 675
period for appointing auditors, in relation to a private company	section 485(2)
period for filing, in relation to accounts and reports for a financial year	section 442
permissible capital payment (in Chapter 5 of Part 18)	section 710
political donation (in Part 14)	section 364
political expenditure (in Part 14)	section 365
political organisation (in Part 14)	section 363(2)
prescribed	section 1167
private company	section 4
profit and loss account (in Part 15)	section 474(1) and (2)
profits and losses (in Part 23)	section 853(2)
profits available for distribution (for the purposes of Part 23)	section 830(2)
property (in Part 27)	section 941
protected information (in Chapter 8 of Part 10)	section 240
provision for entrenchment, in relation to a company's articles	section 22
public company	section 4
publication, in relation to accounts and reports (in sections 433 to 435)	section 436
qualified, in relation to an auditor's report etc (in Part 16)	section 539
qualifying shares (in Chapter 6 of Part 18)	section 724(2)
qualifying third party indemnity provision (in Chapter 7 of Part 10)	section 234
qualifying pension scheme indemnity provision (in Chapter 7 of Part 10)	section 235
quasi-loan (in Chapter 4 of Part 10)	section 199
quoted company	
— in Part 13	section 361
— in Part 15	section 385
— in Chapter 5 of Part 16	section 531 (and section 385)
realised profits and losses (in Part 23)	section 853(4)
receiver or manager (and certain related references)	section 1170A
redeemable shares	section 684(1)
redenominate	section 622(1)
redenomination reserve	section 628
the register	section 1080
...	...
register of directors	section 162
register of directors' residential addresses	section 165
register of members	section 113
register of secretaries	section 275
...	...
registered number, of a company (or an overseas company)	section 1066 (and section 1059A(5))
registered number, of a UK establishment of an overseas company	section 1067
registered office, of a company	section 86
registrar and registrar of companies	section 1060
registrar's index of company names	section 1099

registrar's rules	section 1117
registration in a particular part of the United Kingdom	section 1060(4)
regulated activity	
— generally in the Companies Acts	section 1173(1)
— in Part 15	section 474(1)
regulated market	section 1173(1)
relevant accounts (in Part 23)	section 836(2)
requirements for proper delivery (in Part 35)	section 1072 (and see section 1073)
requirements of this Act	section 1172
return period (in Part 24)	section 855(4)
securities (and related expressions)	
— in Chapter 1 of Part 20	section 755(5)
— in Chapter 2 of Part 21	section 783
senior statutory auditor	section 504
sent or supplied, in relation to documents or information (in the company communications provisions)	section 1148(2) and (3)
service address	section 1141
service contract, of a director (in Part 10)	section 227
shadow director	section 251
share	
— generally in the Companies Acts	section 540 (and see section 1161(2))
— in Part 22	section 792
— in section 1162 and Schedule 7	section 1162(7)
share capital, company having a	section 545
share exchange ratio	
— in Chapter 2 of Part 27	section 905(2)
— in Chapter 3 of Part 27	section 920(2)
share premium account	section 610(1)
share warrant	section 779(1)
small companies exemption (in relation to directors' report)	section 415A
small companies regime (for accounts)	section 381
solvency statement (in sections 641 to 644)	section 643
special notice, in relation to a resolution	section 312
special resolution	section 283
statutory accounts	section 434(3)
subsidiary	section 1159 (and see section 1160 and Schedule 6)
subsidiary undertaking	section 1162 (and see Schedule 7)
summary financial statement	section 426
takeover bid (in Chapter 2 of Part 28)	section 971(1)
takeover offer (in Chapter 3 of Part 28)	section 974
the Takeovers Directive	

— in Chapter 1 of Part 28	section 943(8)
— in Chapter 2 of Part 28	section 971(1)
traded company (in Part 13)	section 360C
. . .	
trading certificate	section 761(1)
transfer, in relation to a non-cash asset	section 1163(2)
treasury shares	section 724(5)
turnover	
— in Part 15	section 474(1)
— in Part 16	section 539
UCITS management company	
— in Part 15	section 474(1)
— in Part 16	section 539
UK establishment of an overseas company (in Part 35)	section 1067(6)
UK-registered company	section 1158
uncalled share capital	section 547
unconditional, in relation to a contract to acquire shares (in Chapter 3 of Part 28)	section 991(2)
undistributable reserves	section 831(4)
undertaking	section 1161(1)
unique identifier	section 1082
unlimited company	section 3
unquoted company (in Part 15)	section 385
voting rights	
— in Chapter 2 of Part 28	section 971(1)
— in Chapter 3 of Part 28	section 991(1)
— in section 1159 and Schedule 6	paragraph 2 of Schedule 6
— in section 1162 and Schedule 7	paragraph 2 of Schedule 7
voting shares	
— in Chapter 2 of Part 28	section 971(1)
— in Chapter 3 of Part 28	section 991(1)
website, communication by a company by means of	section Part 4 of Schedule 5
Welsh company	section 88
wholly-owned subsidiary	section 1159(2) (and see section 1160 and Schedule 6)
working day, in relation to a company	section 1173(1)
written resolution	section 288

SCHEDULE 9

Section 1175

REMOVAL OF SPECIAL PROVISIONS ABOUT ACCOUNTS AND AUDIT OF CHARITABLE COMPANIES

PART 1
THE COMPANIES ACT 1985 (C 6)

1. In section 240 (requirements in connection with publication of accounts)—
   (a) in subsection (1) omit from "or, as the case may be," to "section 249A(2)";
   (b) in subsection (3)(c) omit from "and, if no such report" to "any financial year";
   (c) after subsection (3)(c) insert ", and";
   (d) omit subsection (3)(e) and the ", and" preceding it;
   (e) in the closing words of subsection (3) omit from "or any report" to "section 249A(2)".
2. In section 245 (voluntary revision of annual accounts or directors' report), in subsection (4)(b) omit "or reporting accountant".
3. In section 249A (exemptions from audit)—
   (a) omit subsections (2), (3A) and (4);
   (b) in subsection (6) for "figures for turnover or gross income" substitute "figure for turnover";
   (c) in subsection (6A) omit "or (2)";
   (d) in subsection (7) omit the definition of "gross income" and the ", and" preceding it.
4. In section 249B (cases where exemptions not available)—
   (a) in the opening words of subsection (1) omit "or (2)";
   (b) in subsection (1C)(b) omit from "where the company referred to" to "is not a charity";
   (c) in subsection (3) omit "or (2)";
   (d) in subsection (4), in the opening words and in paragraph (a), omit "or (2)".
5. Omit section 249C (report required for purposes of section 249A(2)).
6. Omit section 249D (the reporting accountant).
7. In section 249E (effect of exemptions) omit subsection (2).
8. In section 262A (index of defined expressions) omit the entry for "reporting accountant".

PART 2
THE COMPANIES (NORTHERN IRELAND) ORDER 1986 (SI 1986/1032(NI 6)

9. In Article 248 (requirements in connection with publication of accounts)—
   (a) in paragraph (1) omit from "or, as the case may be," to "Article 257A(2)";
   (b) in paragraph (3)(c) omit from "and, if no such report" to "any such financial year";
   (c) after paragraph (3)(c) insert ", and";
   (d) omit paragraph (3)(e) and the word ", and" preceding it;
   (e) in the closing words of paragraph (3) omit from "or any report" to "Article 257A(2)".
10. In Article 253 (voluntary revision of annual accounts or directors' report), in paragraph (4)(b) omit "or reporting accountant".
11. In Article 257A (exemptions from audit)—
   (a) omit paragraphs (2), (3A) and (4);
   (b) in paragraph (6) for "figures for turnover or gross income" substitute "figure for turnover";
   (c) in paragraph (6A) omit "or (2)";
   (d) in paragraph (7) omit the definition of "gross income" and the ", and" preceding it.
12. In Article 257B (cases where exemptions not available)—
   (a) in the opening words of paragraph (1) omit "or (2)";
   (b) in paragraph (1C)(b) omit from "where the company referred to" to "is not a charity";
   (c) in paragraph (3) omit "or (2)";
   (d) in paragraph (4), in the opening words and in sub-paragraph (a), omit "or (2)".
13. Omit Article 257C (report required for purposes of Article 257A(2).
14. Omit Article 257D (the reporting accountant).

15. In Article 257E (effect of exemptions) omit paragraph (2).

16. In Article 270A (index of defined expressions) omit the entry for "reporting accountant".

SCHEDULE 10 Section 1217

RECOGNISED SUPERVISORY BODIES

PART 1

GRANT AND REVOCATION OF RECOGNITION OF A SUPERVISORY BODY

Application for recognition of supervisory body

1. (1) A supervisory body may apply to the Secretary of State for an order declaring it to be a recognised supervisory body for the purposes of this Part of this Act ("a recognition order").

(2) Any such application must be—

(a) made in such manner as the Secretary of State may direct, and

(b) accompanied by such information as the Secretary of State may reasonably require for the purpose of determining the application.

(3) At any time after receiving an application and before determining it the Secretary of State may require the applicant to furnish additional information.

(4) The directions and requirements given or imposed under sub-paragraphs (2) and (3) may differ as between different applications.

(5) The Secretary of State may require any information to be furnished under this paragraph to be in such form or verified in such manner as he may specify.

(6) Every application must be accompanied by—

(a) a copy of the applicant's rules, and

(b) a copy of any guidance issued by the applicant in writing.

(7) The reference in sub-paragraph (6)(b) to guidance issued by the applicant is a reference to any guidance or recommendation—

(a) issued or made by it to all or any class of its members or persons seeking to become members,

(b) relevant for the purposes of this Part, and

(c) intended to have continuing effect,

including any guidance or recommendation relating to the admission or expulsion of members of the body, so far as relevant for the purposes of this Part.

Grant and refusal of recognition

2. (1) The Secretary of State may, on an application duly made in accordance with paragraph 1 and after being furnished with all such information as he may require under that paragraph, make or refuse to make a recognition order in respect of the applicant.

(2) The Secretary of State may make a recognition order only if it appears to him, from the information furnished by the body and having regard to any other information in his possession, that the requirements of Part 2 of this Schedule are satisfied in the case of that body.

(3) The Secretary of State may refuse to make a recognition order in respect of a body if he considers that its recognition is unnecessary having regard to the existence of one or more other bodies which—

(a) maintain and enforce rules as to the appointment and conduct of statutory auditors, and

(b) have been or are likely to be recognised.

(4) Where the Secretary of State refuses an application for a recognition order he must give the applicant a written notice to that effect—

(a) specifying which requirements, in the opinion of the Secretary of State, are not satisfied, or

(b) stating that the application is refused on the ground mentioned in sub-paragraph (3).

(5) A recognition order must state the date on which it takes effect.

Revocation of recognition

3. (1) A recognition order may be revoked by a further order made by the Secretary of State if at any time it appears to him—

(a) that any requirement of Part 2 or 3 of this Schedule is not satisfied in the case of the body to which the recognition order relates ("the recognised body"),

(b) that the body has failed to comply with any obligation imposed on it by or by virtue of this Part of this Act, or

(c) that the continued recognition of the body is undesirable having regard to the existence of one or more other bodies which have been or are to be recognised.

(2) An order revoking a recognition order must state the date on which it takes effect, which must be after the period of three months beginning with the date on which the revocation order is made.

(3) Before revoking a recognition order the Secretary of State must—

(a) give written notice of his intention to do so to the recognised body,

(b) take such steps as he considers reasonably practicable for bringing the notice to the attention of the members of the body, and

(c) publish the notice in such manner as he thinks appropriate for bringing it to the attention of any other persons who are in his opinion likely to be affected.

(4) A notice under sub-paragraph (3) must—

(a) state the reasons for which the Secretary of State proposes to act, and

(b) give particulars of the rights conferred by sub-paragraph (5).

(5) A person within sub-paragraph (6) may, within the period of three months beginning with the date of service or publication of the notice under sub-paragraph (3) or such longer period as the Secretary of State may allow, make written representations to the Secretary of State and, if desired, oral representations to a person appointed for that purpose by the Secretary of State.

(6) The persons within this sub-paragraph are—

(a) the recognised body on which a notice is served under sub-paragraph (3),

(b) any member of the body, and

(c) any other person who appears to the Secretary of State to be affected.

(7) The Secretary of State must have regard to any representations made in accordance with sub-paragraph (5) in determining whether to revoke the recognition order.

(8) If in any case the Secretary of State considers it essential to do so in the public interest he may revoke a recognition order without regard to the restriction imposed by sub-paragraph (2), even if—

(a) no notice has been given or published under sub-paragraph (3), or

(b) the period of time for making representations in pursuance of such a notice has not expired.

(9) An order revoking a recognition order may contain such transitional provision as the Secretary of State thinks necessary or expedient.

(10) A recognition order may be revoked at the request or with the consent of the recognised body and any such revocation is not subject to—

(a) the restrictions imposed by sub-paragraphs (1) and (2), or

(b) the requirements of sub-paragraphs (3) to (5) and (7).

(11) On making an order revoking a recognition order in respect of a body the Secretary of State must—

(a) give written notice of the making of the order to the body,

(b) take such steps as he considers reasonably practicable for bringing the making of the order to the attention of the members of the body, and

(c) publish a notice of the making of the order in such manner as he thinks appropriate for bringing it to the attention of any other persons who are in his opinion likely to be affected.

Transitional provision

4. A recognition order made and not revoked under—
(a) paragraph 2(1) of Schedule 11 to the Companies Act 1989, or
(b) paragraph 2(1) of Schedule 11 to the Companies (Northern Ireland) Order 1990,
before the commencement of this Chapter of this Part of this Act is to have effect after the commencement of this Chapter as a recognition order made under paragraph 2(1) of this Schedule.

Orders not statutory instruments

5. Orders under this Part of this Schedule shall not be made by statutory instrument.

PART 2
REQUIREMENTS FOR RECOGNITION OF A SUPERVISORY BODY

Holding of appropriate qualification

6. (1) The body must have rules to the effect that a person is not eligible for appointment as a statutory auditor unless—
(a) in the case of an individual other than an EEA auditor, he holds an appropriate qualification,
(aa) in the case of an individual who is an EEA auditor—
(i) he holds an appropriate qualification,
(ii) he has been authorised on or before 5 April 2008 to practise the profession of company auditor pursuant to the European Communities (Recognition of Professional Qualifications) (First General System) Regulations 2005 and has fulfilled any requirements imposed pursuant to regulation 6 of those Regulations, or
(iii) he has passed an aptitude test in accordance with sub-paragraph (2), unless an aptitude test is not required (see sub-paragraph (2A)),
(b) in the case of a firm—
(i) each individual responsible for statutory audit work on behalf of the firm is eligible for appointment as a statutory auditor, and
(ii) the firm is controlled by qualified persons (see paragraph 7 below).
(2) The aptitude test—
(a) must test the person's knowledge of subjects—
(i) that are covered by a recognised professional qualification,
(ii) that are not covered by the professional qualification already held by the person, and
(iii) the knowledge of which is essential for the pursuit of the profession of statutory auditor;
(b) may test the person's knowledge of rules of professional conduct;
(c) must not test the person's knowledge of any other matters.
(2A) No aptitude test is required if the subjects that are covered by a recognised professional qualification and the knowledge of which is essential for the pursuit of the profession of statutory auditor are covered by the professional qualification already held by the person.
(3) A firm which has ceased to comply with the conditions mentioned in sub-paragraph (1)(b) may be permitted to remain eligible for appointment as a statutory auditor for a period of not more than three months.

7. (1) This paragraph explains what is meant in paragraph 6(1)(b) by a firm being "controlled by qualified persons".

(2) In this paragraph references to a person being qualified are—
(a) in relation to an individual, to his holding—
(i) an appropriate qualification, or
(ii) a corresponding qualification to audit accounts under the law of an EEA State, or part of an EEA State, other than the United Kingdom;
(b) in relation to a firm, to its—
(i) being eligible for appointment as a statutory auditor, or
(ii) being eligible for a corresponding appointment as an auditor under the law of an EEA State, or part of an EEA State, other than the United Kingdom.

(3) A firm is to be treated as controlled by qualified persons if, and only if—
(a) a majority of the members of the firm are qualified persons, and
(b) where the firm's affairs are managed by a board of directors, committee or other management body, a majority of that body are qualified persons or, if the body consists of two persons only, at least one of them is a qualified person.

(4) A majority of the members of a firm means—
(a) where under the firm's constitution matters are decided upon by the exercise of voting rights, members holding a majority of the rights to vote on all, or substantially all, matters;
(b) in any other case, members having such rights under the constitution of the firm as enable them to direct its overall policy or alter its constitution.

(5) A majority of the members of the management body of a firm means—
(a) where matters are decided at meetings of the management body by the exercise of voting rights, members holding a majority of the rights to vote on all, or substantially all, matters at such meetings;
(b) in any other case, members having such rights under the constitution of the firm as enable them to direct its overall policy or alter its constitution.

(6) Paragraphs 5 to 11 of Schedule 7 to this Act (rights to be taken into account and attribution of rights) apply for the purposes of this paragraph.

Auditors to be fit and proper persons

8. (1) The body must have adequate rules and practices designed to ensure that the persons eligible under its rules for appointment as a statutory auditor are fit and proper persons to be so appointed.

(2) The matters which the body may take into account for this purpose in relation to a person must include—
(a) any matter relating to any person who is or will be employed by or associated with him for the purposes of or in connection with statutory audit work;
(b) in the case of a body corporate, any matter relating to—
(i) any director or controller of the body,
(ii) any other body corporate in the same group, or
(iii) any director or controller of any such other body; and
(c) in the case of a partnership, any matter relating to—
(i) any of the partners,
(ii) any director or controller of any of the partners,
(iii) any body corporate in the same group as any of the partners, or
(iv) any director or controller of any such other body.

(3) Where the person is a limited liability partnership, in sub-paragraph (2)(b) "director" is to be read as "member".

(4) In sub-paragraph (2)(b) and (c) "controller", in relation to a body corporate, means a person who either alone or with an associate or associates is entitled to exercise or control the exercise of 15% or more of the rights to vote on all, or substantially all, matters at general meetings of the body or another body corporate of which it is a subsidiary.

Professional integrity and independence

9. (1) The body must have adequate rules and practices designed to ensure that—

(a) statutory audit work is conducted properly and with integrity, …

(b) persons are not appointed as statutory auditors in circumstances in which they have an interest likely to conflict with the proper conduct of the audit,

(c) persons appointed as statutory auditors take steps to safeguard their independence from any significant threats to it,

(d) persons appointed as statutory auditors record any such threats and the steps taken to safeguard the proper conduct of the audit from them, and

(e) remuneration received or receivable by a statutory auditor in respect of statutory audit work is not—

(i) influenced or determined by the statutory auditor providing other services to the audited person, or

(ii) on a contingent fee basis.

(2) The body must participate in arrangements within paragraph 21, and the rules and practices mentioned in sub-paragraph (1) must include provision requiring compliance with any standards for the time being determined under such arrangements.

(3) The body must also have adequate rules and practices designed to ensure that—

(a) no firm is eligible under its rules for appointment as a statutory auditor unless the firm has arrangements to prevent any person from being able to exert any influence over the way in which a statutory audit is conducted in circumstances in which that influence would be likely to affect the independence or integrity of the audit;

(b) any rule of law relating to the confidentiality of information received in the course of statutory audit work by persons appointed as statutory auditors is complied with; and

(c) a person ceasing to hold office as a statutory auditor makes available to his successor in that office all relevant information which he holds in relation to that office.

(4) The rules referred to in sub-paragraph (3)(b) (confidentiality of information) must apply to persons who are no longer members of the body as they apply to members and any fine imposed in the enforcement of those rules shall be recoverable by the body as a debt due to it from the person obliged to pay it.

Technical standards

10. (1) The body must have rules and practices as to—

(a) the technical standards to be applied in statutory audit work, and

(b) the manner in which those standards are to be applied in practice.

(2) The body must participate in arrangements within paragraph 22, and the rules and practices mentioned in sub-paragraph (1) must include provision requiring compliance with any standards for the time being determined under such arrangements.

Technical standards for group audits

10A. (1) The body must have rules and practices as to technical standards ensuring that group auditors—

(a) review for the purposes of a group audit the audit work conducted by other persons, and

(b) record that review.

(2) The body must participate in arrangements within paragraph 22, and the rules and practices mentioned in sub-paragraph (1) must include provision requiring compliance with any standards for the time being determined under such arrangements.

(3) The body must also have rules and practices ensuring that group auditors—

(a) retain copies of any documents necessary for the purposes of the review that they have received from third country auditors who are not covered by working arrangements under section 1253E, or

(b) agree with those third country auditors proper and unrestricted access to those documents on request.

(4) The body's rules and practices must ensure that group auditors make those documents available on request to—

(a) the body;

(b) any other body with which the body has entered into arrangements for the purposes of paragraph 23, 23A or 24 (independent arrangements for monitoring and investigation);

(c) the Secretary of State.

(5) The body may provide that the rules and practices referred to in sub-paragraphs (3) and (4) do not apply if, after taking all reasonable steps, a group auditor is unable to obtain the copies of the documents or the access to the documents necessary for the review.

(6) If the body does so provide, its rules and practices must ensure that the group auditor records—

(a) the steps taken to obtain copies of or access to those documents,

(b) the reasons why the copies or access could not be obtained, and

(c) any evidence of those steps or those reasons.

(7) In this paragraph—

"group auditor" means a person appointed as statutory auditor to conduct an audit of group accounts;

"group" has the same meaning as in Part 15 of this Act (see section 474).

Public interest entity reporting requirements

10B. (1) The body must have adequate rules and practices designed to ensure that persons appointed as statutory auditors of public interest entities report to the entity's audit committee (if it has one) at least once in each calendar year at any time during which they hold the office of statutory auditor.

(2) The report must include—

(a) a statement in writing confirming the person's independence from the public interest entity;

(b) a description of any services provided by the person to the public interest entity other than in his capacity as statutory auditor;

(c) a description of any significant threats to the person's independence;

(d) an explanation of the steps taken by the person to safeguard his independence from those threats;

(e) a description of any material weaknesses arising from the statutory audit in the public interest entity's internal control in relation to the preparation of accounts; and

(f) any other significant matters arising from the statutory audit.

(3) The body must participate in arrangements within paragraph 22A (arrangements for setting standards), and the rules and practices mentioned in sub-paragraph (1) must include provision requiring compliance with any standards for the time being determined under such arrangements.

(4) In this paragraph, "audit committee" means a body which performs the functions referred to in Article 41.2 of the Audit Directive or equivalent functions.

Public interest entity independence requirements

10C. (1) The body must have adequate rules and practices designed to ensure that—

(a) an individual does not accept an appointment by a public interest entity as statutory auditor if—

(i) he has been the statutory auditor of the entity for a continuous period of more than seven years, and

(ii) less than two years have passed since he was last the statutory auditor of the entity;

(b) where a firm has been appointed by a public interest entity as statutory auditor, an individual may not be a key audit partner if—

(i) he has been a key audit partner in relation to audits of the entity for a continuous period of more than seven years, and

(ii) less than two years have passed since he was last the key audit partner in relation to an audit of the entity.

(2) The body must participate in arrangements within paragraph 22B (arrangements for setting standards), and the rules and practices mentioned in sub-paragraph (1) must include provision requiring compliance with any standards for the time being determined under such arrangements.

(3) The body must also have adequate rules and practices designed to ensure that—

(a) an individual who has been appointed by a public interest entity as statutory auditor may not be appointed as a director or other officer of the entity during a period of two years commencing on the date on which his appointment as statutory auditor ended;

(b) a key audit partner of a firm which has been appointed by a public interest entity as statutory auditor may not be appointed as a director or other officer of the entity during a period of two years commencing on the date on which his work as key audit partner ended.

(4) The rules referred to in sub-paragraph (3) must apply to persons who are no longer members of the body as they apply to members and any fine imposed in the enforcement of those rules shall be recoverable by the body as a debt due to it from the person obliged to pay it.

(5) An auditor of a public interest entity is not to be regarded as an officer of the entity for the purposes of sub-paragraph (3)(a) and (b).

(6) For the purposes of this paragraph—

(a) a "key audit partner" is an individual identified by a firm appointed as statutory auditor as being primarily responsible for the statutory audit; and

(b) a key audit partner of a firm appointed as statutory auditor of a parent undertaking or a material subsidiary undertaking of a public interest entity is to be treated as if he were a key audit partner of the firm appointed as statutory auditor of the public interest entity.

Procedures for maintaining competence

11. The body must have rules and practices designed to ensure that persons eligible under its rules for appointment as a statutory auditor continue to maintain an appropriate level of competence in the conduct of statutory audits.

Monitoring and enforcement

12. (1) The body must—

(a) have adequate resources for the effective monitoring and enforcement of compliance with its rules, and

(b) ensure that those resources may not be influenced improperly by the persons monitored.

(1A) The body must—

(a) have adequate arrangements for the effective monitoring and enforcement of compliance with its rules, and

(b) ensure that those arrangements operate independently of the persons monitored.

(2) The arrangements for monitoring may make provision for that function to be performed on behalf of the body (and without affecting its responsibility) by any other body or person who is able and willing to perform it.

(3) The arrangements for enforcement must include provision for—

(a) sanctions which include—

(i) the withdrawal of eligibility for appointment as a statutory auditor; and

(ii) any other disciplinary measures necessary to ensure the effective enforcement of the body's rules; and

(b) the body making available to the public information relating to steps it has taken to ensure the effective enforcement of its rules.

Monitoring of audits

13. (1) The body must—

(a) . . . have adequate arrangements for enabling the performance by its members of statutory audit functions, other than statutory audit functions in respect of major audits, to be monitored by means of inspections;

(b) in the case of members of the body who perform any statutory audit functions in respect of major audits—

(i) participate in arrangements within paragraph 23(1); and

(ii) have rules and practices designed to ensure that a sanction determined under paragraph 23(1)(b) is to be treated as if it were a sanction which the body had determined under arrangements for enforcement within paragraph 12(1A);

(ba) in the case of members of the body who perform any third country audit functions, participate in arrangements within paragraph 23A(1); and

(c) have rules designed to ensure that members of the body take such steps as may reasonably be required of them to enable their performance of any statutory audit functions or third country audit functions to be monitored by means of inspections.

(2) Any monitoring of members of the body under the arrangements within paragraph 23(1) or 23A(1) is to be regarded (so far as their performance of statutory audit functions in respect of major audits, or of third country audit functions, is concerned) as monitoring of compliance with the body's rules for the purposes of paragraph 12(1) and (1A).

(3) The arrangements referred to in sub-paragraph (1)(a) must include an inspection which is conducted in relation to each person eligible for appointment as a statutory auditor at least once every six years.

(4) The inspection must be conducted by persons who—

(a) have an appropriate professional education;

(b) have experience of—

(i) statutory audit work, or

(ii) equivalent work on the audit of accounts under the law of an EEA State, or part of an EEA State, other than the United Kingdom;

(c) have received adequate training in the conduct of inspections;

(d) do not have any interests likely to conflict with the proper conduct of the inspection.

(5) The inspection must review one or more statutory audits in which the person to whom the inspection relates has participated.

(6) The inspection must include an assessment of—

(a) the person's compliance with the body's rules established for the purposes of paragraphs 9 (professional integrity and independence), 10 (technical standards), 10A (technical standards for group audits) and 10C (public interest entity independence requirements);

(b) the resources allocated by the person to statutory audit work;

(c) in the case of an inspection in relation to a firm, its internal quality control system;

(d) the remuneration received by the person in respect of statutory audit work.

(7) An inspection conducted in relation to a firm may be treated as an inspection of all individuals responsible for statutory audit work on behalf of that firm, if the firm has a common quality assurance policy with which each such individual is required to comply.

(8) The main conclusions of the inspection must be recorded in a report which is made available to—

(a) the person to whom the inspection relates, and

(b) the body.

(9) The body must, at least once in every calendar year, deliver to the Secretary of State a summary of the results of inspections conducted under this paragraph.

(10) In this paragraph—

"major audit" means a statutory audit conducted in respect of—

(a) a public interest entity, or

(b) any other person in whose financial condition there is a major public interest;

"statutory audit function" means any function performed as a statutory auditor;

"third country audit function" means any function related to the audit of a UK-traded non-EEA company.

Membership, eligibility and discipline

14. The rules and practices of the body relating to—

(a) the admission and expulsion of members,

(b) the grant and withdrawal of eligibility for appointment as a statutory auditor, and

(c) the discipline it exercises over its members,

must be fair and reasonable and include adequate provision for appeals.

Investigation of complaints

15. (1) The body must have effective arrangements for the investigation of complaints against—

(a) persons who are eligible under its rules for appointment as a statutory auditor, and

(b) the body in respect of matters arising out of its functions as a supervisory body.

(2) The arrangements mentioned in sub-paragraph (1) may make provision for the whole or part of that function to be performed by and to be the responsibility of a body or person independent of the body itself.

Independent investigation for disciplinary purposes of public interest cases

16. (1) The body must—

(a) participate in arrangements within paragraph 24(1), and

(b) have rules and practices designed to ensure that, where the designated persons have decided that any particular disciplinary action should be taken against a member of the body following the conclusion of an investigation under such arrangements, that decision is to be treated as if it were a decision made by the body in disciplinary proceedings against the member.

(2) In sub-paragraph (1) "the designated persons" means the persons who, under the arrangements, have the function of deciding whether (and if so, what) disciplinary action should be taken against a member of the body in the light of an investigation carried out under the arrangements.

Transfer of papers to third countries

16A. (1) The body must have adequate rules and practices designed to ensure that a person eligible under its rules for appointment as a statutory auditor transfers audit working papers to a third country competent authority only in accordance with the requirements of—

(a) paragraph 16AA (transfer to approved third country competent authority), or

(b) paragraph 16AB (transfer for purposes of investigation).

(2) The body must also have adequate rules and practices designed to ensure that a person eligible under its rules for appointment as a statutory auditor must refuse to transfer audit

working papers to a third country competent authority if the Secretary of State directs under section 1253E(6) that such a transfer should not take place.

Transfer to approved third country competent authority

16AA. The requirements of this paragraph are that—

(a) the transfer is to an approved third country competent authority, and

(b) the Secretary of State has approved the transfer.

Transfer for purposes of investigation of auditor

16AB. (1) The requirements of this paragraph are that—

(a) the transfer to the third country competent authority is made for the purposes of an investigation of an auditor or audit firm, and

(b) the following conditions are met.

(2) The first condition is that the authority has requested the audit working papers for the purposes of an investigation which has been initiated by itself or another third country competent authority established in the same third country.

(3) The second condition is that the audit working papers relate to audits of companies that—

(a) have issued securities in that third country, or

(b) form part of a group issuing statutory consolidated accounts in that third country.

(4) The third condition is that, where the authority has made the request for the audit working papers directly to the statutory auditor, the authority has given the Secretary of State advance notice of the request, indicating the reasons for it.

(5) The fourth condition is that the authority has entered into arrangements with the Secretary of State in accordance with section 1253E.

Meeting of claims arising out of audit work

17. (1) The body must have adequate rules or arrangements designed to ensure that persons eligible under its rules for appointment as a statutory auditor take such steps as may reasonably be expected of them to secure that they are able to meet claims against them arising out of statutory audit work.

(2) This may be achieved by professional indemnity insurance or other appropriate arrangements.

Register of auditors and other information to be made available

18. The body must have rules requiring persons eligible under its rules for appointment as a statutory auditor to comply with any obligations imposed on them by—

(a) requirements under section 1224 (Secretary of State's power to call for information);

(b) regulations under section 1239 (the register of auditors);

(c) regulations under section 1240 (information to be made available to the public).

Taking account of costs of compliance

19. The body must have satisfactory arrangements for taking account, in framing its rules, of the cost to those to whom the rules would apply of complying with those rules and any other controls to which they are subject.

Promotion and maintenance of standards

20. The body must be able and willing—

(a) to promote and maintain high standards of integrity in the conduct of statutory audit work, and

(b) to co-operate, by the sharing of information and otherwise, with the Secretary of State and any other authority, body or person having responsibility in the United Kingdom for the qualification, supervision or regulation of auditors.

Interpretation

20A. In this Part of this Schedule—

"public interest entity" means an issuer—

(a) whose transferable securities are admitted to trading on a regulated market; and

(b) the audit of which is a statutory audit (see section 1210(1));

"issuer" and "regulated market" have the same meaning as in Part 6 of the Financial Services and Markets Act 2000 (see sections 102A to 103); and

"transferable securities" means anything which is a transferable security for the purposes of Directive 2004/39/EC of the European Parliament and of the Council on markets in financial instruments.

PART 3
ARRANGEMENTS IN WHICH RECOGNISED SUPERVISORY BODIES ARE REQUIRED TO PARTICIPATE

Arrangements for setting standards relating to professional integrity and independence

21. The arrangements referred to in paragraph 9(2) are appropriate arrangements—

(a) for the determining of standards for the purposes of the rules and practices mentioned in paragraph 9(1), and

(b) for ensuring that the determination of those standards is done independently of the body.

Arrangements for setting technical standards

22. The arrangements referred to in paragraphs 10(2) and 10A(2) are appropriate arrangements—

(a) for the determining of standards for the purposes of the rules and practices mentioned in paragraphs 10(1) and 10A(1) respectively, and

(b) for ensuring that the determination of those standards is done independently of the body.

Arrangements for setting standards relating to public interest entity reporting requirements

22A. The arrangements referred to in paragraph 10B(3) are appropriate arrangements—

(a) for the determining of standards for the purposes of the rules and practices mentioned in paragraph 10B(1), and

(b) for ensuring that the determination of those standards is done independently of the body.

Arrangements for setting standards relating to public interest entity independence requirements

22B. The arrangements referred to in paragraph 10C(2) are appropriate arrangements—

(a) for the determining of standards for the purposes of the rules and practices mentioned in paragraph 10C(1), and

(b) for ensuring that the determination of those standards is done independently of the body.

Arrangements for independent monitoring of audits of listed companies and other major bodies

23. (1) The arrangements referred to in paragraph 13(1)(b)(i) are appropriate arrangements—

(a) for enabling the performance by members of the supervisory body of statutory audit functions in respect of major audits to be monitored by means of inspections carried out under the arrangements;

(b) for enabling the body performing the inspections to determine sanctions (including those mentioned in paragraph 12(3)(a)) against members of the supervisory body where, pursuant to an inspection, it concludes that the members have not complied with the supervisory body's rules in so far as they are relevant to the performance of statutory audit functions; and

(c) for ensuring that the carrying out of such inspections and the determination of such sanctions are done independently of the supervisory body.

(1A) Subject to sub-paragraph (1C), the arrangements referred to in sub-paragraph (1) must include provision for an inspection conducted in relation to each person eligible for appointment as a statutory auditor at least once every three years.

(1B) Sub-paragraphs (4) to (9) of paragraph 13 apply in relation to inspections under sub-paragraph (1A) as they apply in relation to inspections under that paragraph.

(1C) The arrangements referred to in sub-paragraph (1) may provide that the body performing the inspections may decide that all or part of the inspection referred to in sub-paragraph (1A) is not required in the case of a member of a supervisory body who performs statutory audit functions in respect of ten or fewer major audits per year.

(1D) If—

(a) the arrangements make the provision referred to in sub-paragraph (1C), and

(b) the body performing the inspections decides that all of an inspection is not required in relation to a member,

the supervisory body must ensure that the arrangements referred to in paragraph 13(1)(a) apply in relation to that member, subject to the modification specified in sub-paragraph (1F).

(1E) If—

(a) the arrangements make the provision referred to in sub-paragraph (1C), and

(b) the body performing the inspections decides that part of an inspection is not required in relation to a member,

the supervisory body must ensure that the arrangements referred to in paragraph 13(1)(a) apply in relation to that part of the inspection of that member, subject to the modification specified in sub-paragraph (1F).

(1F) For the purposes of sub-paragraphs (1D) and (1E), paragraph 13(3) applies with the substitution of "three years" for "six years".

(2) In this paragraph "major audit" and "statutory audit function" have the same meaning as in paragraph 13.

Arrangements for independent monitoring of third country audits

23A. (1) The arrangements referred to in paragraph 13(1)(ba) are appropriate arrangements—

(a) for enabling the performance by members of the body of third country audit functions to be monitored by means of inspections carried out under the arrangements, and

(b) for ensuring that the carrying out of such monitoring and inspections is done independently of the body.

(2) Those arrangements must provide that the body performing the inspections--

(a) may decide that an inspection referred to in sub-paragraph (1) is not required, or that part of an inspection is not required, in relation to a member, and

(b) may direct that the arrangements referred to in sub-paragraph (3) apply in relation to the member or apply to such extent as may be specified in the direction.

(3) The supervisory body must have adequate arrangements for enabling the performance by its members of third country audit functions to be monitored by means of inspections for cases where a direction is given under sub-paragraph (2)(b).

(4) In this paragraph "third country audit function" means any function related to the audit of a UK-traded non-EEA company.

Arrangements for independent investigation for disciplinary purposes of public interest cases

24. (1) The arrangements referred to in paragraph 16(1) are appropriate arrangements—

(a) for the carrying out of investigations into public interest cases arising in connection with the performance of statutory audit functions or third country audit functions by members of the body,

(b) where it appears to be desirable following the conclusion of such investigations—

(i) for the holding, subject to sub-paragraph (1A), of disciplinary hearings relating to members of the body,

(ii) unless the interests of justice otherwise require, for any such hearings to be held in public, and

(iii) for decisions to be made as to whether (and, if so, what) disciplinary action should be taken against the members of the body, and

(c) for ensuring that the carrying out of those investigations, the holding of those hearings and the making of those decisions are done independently of the body.

(1A) The arrangements may provide that decisions to take disciplinary action, and decisions as to what that action should be, may be made in respect of a member of the body without the holding of a disciplinary hearing relating to that member where the member agrees in writing that such a hearing need not be held.

(2) In this paragraph—

"public interest cases" means matters which raise or appear to raise important issues affecting the public interest;

"statutory audit function" means any function performed as a statutory auditor;

"third country audit function" means any function related to the audit of a UK-traded non-EEA company.

Supplementary: arrangements to operate independently of body

25. (1) This paragraph applies for the purposes of—

(a) paragraph 21(b),

(b) paragraph 22(b),

(c) paragraph 23(1)(c), . . .

(ca) paragraph 23A(1)(b), or

(d) paragraph 24(1)(c).

(2) Arrangements are not to be regarded as appropriate for the purpose of ensuring that a thing is done independently of the body unless they are designed to ensure that the body—

(a) will have no involvement in the appointment or selection of any of the persons who are to be responsible for doing that thing, and

(b) will not otherwise be involved in the doing of that thing.

(3) Sub-paragraph (2) imposes a minimum requirement and does not preclude the possibility that additional criteria may need to be satisfied in order for the arrangements to be regarded as appropriate for the purpose in question.

Supplementary: funding of arrangements

26. The body must pay any of the costs of maintaining any arrangements within paragraph 21, 22, 23, 23A or 24 which the arrangements provide are to be paid by it.

Supplementary: scope of arrangement

27. Arrangements may qualify as arrangements within any of paragraphs 21, 22, 23, 23A and 24 even though the matters for which they provide are more extensive in any respect than those mentioned in the applicable paragraph.

SCHEDULE 11

Section 1220

RECOGNISED PROFESSIONAL QUALIFICATIONS

PART 1

GRANT AND REVOCATION OF RECOGNITION OF A PROFESSIONAL QUALIFICATION

Application for recognition of professional qualification

1. (1) A qualifying body may apply to the Secretary of State for an order declaring a qualification offered by it to be a recognised professional qualification for the purposes of this Part of this Act ("a recognition order").

(2) In this Part of this Act "a recognised qualifying body" means a qualifying body offering a recognised professional qualification.

(3) Any application must be—

(a) made in such manner as the Secretary of State may direct, and

(b) accompanied by such information as the Secretary of State may reasonably require for the purpose of determining the application.

(4) At any time after receiving an application and before determining it the Secretary of State may require the applicant to furnish additional information.

(5) The directions and requirements given or imposed under sub-paragraphs (3) and (4) may differ as between different applications.

(6) The Secretary of State may require any information to be furnished under this paragraph to be in such form or verified in such manner as he may specify.

(7) In the case of examination standards, the verification required may include independent moderation of the examinations over such a period as the Secretary of State considers necessary.

(8) Every application must be accompanied by—

(a) a copy of the applicant's rules, and

(b) a copy of any guidance issued by the applicant in writing.

(9) The reference in sub-paragraph (8)(b) to guidance issued by the applicant is a reference to any guidance or recommendation—

(a) issued or made by it to all or any class of persons holding or seeking to hold a qualification, or approved or seeking to be approved by the body for the purposes of giving practical training,

(b) relevant for the purposes of this Part of this Act, and

(c) intended to have continuing effect,

including any guidance or recommendation relating to a matter within sub-paragraph (10).

(10) The matters within this sub-paragraph are—

(a) admission to or expulsion from a course of study leading to a qualification,

(b) the award or deprivation of a qualification, and

(c) the approval of a person for the purposes of giving practical training or the withdrawal of such an approval,

so far as relevant for the purposes of this Part of this Act.

Grant and refusal of recognition

2. (1) The Secretary of State may, on an application duly made in accordance with paragraph 1 and after being furnished with all such information as he may require under that paragraph, make or refuse to make a recognition order in respect of the qualification in relation to which the application was made.

(2) The Secretary of State may make a recognition order only if it appears to him, from the information furnished by the applicant and having regard to any other information in his possession, that the requirements of Part 2 of this Schedule are satisfied in relation to the qualification.

(3) Where the Secretary of State refuses an application for a recognition order he must give the applicant a written notice to that effect specifying which requirements, in his opinion, are not satisfied.

(4) A recognition order must state the date on which it takes effect.

Revocation of recognition

3. (1) A recognition order may be revoked by a further order made by the Secretary of State if at any time it appears to him—

(a) that any requirement of Part 2 of this Schedule is not satisfied in relation to the qualification to which the recognition order relates, or

(b) that the qualifying body has failed to comply with any obligation imposed on it by or by virtue of this Part of this Act.

(2) An order revoking a recognition order must state the date on which it takes effect, which must be after the period of three months beginning with the date on which the revocation order is made.

(3) Before revoking a recognition order the Secretary of State must—

(a) give written notice of his intention to do so to the qualifying body,

(b) take such steps as he considers reasonably practicable for bringing the notice to the attention of persons holding the qualification or in the course of studying for it, and

(c) publish the notice in such manner as he thinks appropriate for bringing it to the attention of any other persons who are in his opinion likely to be affected.

(4) A notice under sub-paragraph (3) must—

(a) state the reasons for which the Secretary of State proposes to act, and

(b) give particulars of the rights conferred by sub-paragraph (5).

(5) A person within sub-paragraph (6) may, within the period of three months beginning with the date of service or publication or such longer period as the Secretary of State may allow, make written representations to the Secretary of State and, if desired, oral representations to a person appointed for that purpose by the Secretary of State.

(6) The persons within this sub-paragraph are—

(a) the qualifying body on which a notice is served under sub-paragraph (3),

(b) any person holding the qualification or in the course of studying for it, and

(c) any other person who appears to the Secretary of State to be affected.

(7) The Secretary of State must have regard to any representations made in accordance with sub-paragraph (5) in determining whether to revoke the recognition order.

(8) If in any case the Secretary of State considers it essential to do so in the public interest he may revoke a recognition order without regard to the restriction imposed by sub-paragraph (2), even if—

(a) no notice has been given or published under sub-paragraph (3), or

(b) the period of time for making representations in pursuance of such a notice has not expired.

(9) An order revoking a recognition order may contain such transitional provision as the Secretary of State thinks necessary or expedient.

(10) A recognition order may be revoked at the request or with the consent of the qualifying body and any such revocation is not subject to—

(a) the restrictions imposed by sub-paragraphs (1) and (2), or

(b) the requirements of sub-paragraphs (3) to (5) and (7).

(11) On making an order revoking a recognition order the Secretary of State must—

(a) give written notice of the making of the order to the qualifying body,

(b) take such steps as he considers reasonably practicable for bringing the making of the order to the attention of persons holding the qualification or in the course of studying for it, and

(c) publish a notice of the making of the order in such manner as he thinks appropriate for bringing it to the attention of any other persons who are in his opinion likely to be affected.

Transitional provision

4. A recognition order made and not revoked under—

(a) paragraph 2(1) of Schedule 12 to the Companies Act 1989, or

(b) paragraph 2(1) of Schedule 12 to the Companies (Northern Ireland) Order 1990,

before the commencement of this Chapter of this Part of this Act is to have effect after the commencement of this Chapter as a recognition order made under paragraph 2(1) of this Schedule.

Orders not statutory instruments

5. Orders under this Part of this Schedule shall not be made by statutory instrument.

PART 2
REQUIREMENTS FOR RECOGNITION OF A PROFESSIONAL QUALIFICATION

Entry requirements

6. (1) The qualification must only be open to persons who—
(a) have attained university entrance level, or
(b) have a sufficient period of professional experience.

(2) In relation to a person who has not been admitted to a university or other similar establishment in the United Kingdom, "attaining university entrance level" means—
(a) being educated to such a standard as would entitle him to be considered for such admission on the basis of—
(i) academic or professional qualifications obtained in the United Kingdom and recognised by the Secretary of State to be of an appropriate standard, or
(ii) academic or professional qualifications obtained outside the United Kingdom which the Secretary of State considers to be of an equivalent standard, or
(b) being assessed, on the basis of written tests of a kind appearing to the Secretary of State to be adequate for the purpose (with or without oral examination), as of such a standard of ability as would entitle him to be considered for such admission.

(3) The assessment, tests and oral examination referred to in sub-paragraph (2)(b) may be conducted by—
(a) the qualifying body, or
(b) some other body approved by the Secretary of State.

(4) The reference in sub-paragraph (1)(b) to "a sufficient period of professional experience" is to not less than seven years' experience in a professional capacity in the fields of finance, law and accountancy.

Requirement for theoretical instruction or professional experience

7. (1) The qualification must be restricted to persons who—
(a) have completed a course of theoretical instruction in the subjects prescribed for the purposes of paragraph 8, or
(b) have a sufficient period of professional experience.

(2) The reference in sub-paragraph (1)(b) to "a sufficient period of professional experience" is to not less than seven years' experience in a professional capacity in the fields of finance, law and accountancy.

Examination

8. (1) The qualification must be restricted to persons who have passed an examination (at least part of which is in writing) testing—
(a) theoretical knowledge of the subjects prescribed for the purposes of this paragraph by regulations made by the Secretary of State, and
(b) ability to apply that knowledge in practice,

and requiring a standard of attainment at least equivalent to that required to obtain a degree from a university or similar establishment in the United Kingdom.

(2) The qualification may be awarded to a person without his theoretical knowledge of a subject being tested by examination if he has passed a university or other examination of equivalent standard in that subject or holds a university degree or equivalent qualification in it.

(3) The qualification may be awarded to a person without his ability to apply his theoretical knowledge of a subject in practice being tested by examination if he has received practical training in that subject which is attested by an examination or diploma recognised by the Secretary of State for the purposes of this paragraph.

(4) Regulations under this paragraph are subject to negative resolution procedure.

Practical training

9. (1) The qualification must be restricted to persons who have completed at least three years' practical training of which—

(a) part was spent being trained in statutory audit work, and

(b) a substantial part was spent being trained in statutory audit work or other audit work of a description approved by the Secretary of State as being similar to statutory audit work.

(2) For the purpose of sub-paragraph (1) "statutory audit work" includes the work of a person appointed as the auditor of a person under the law of a country or territory outside the United Kingdom where it appears to the Secretary of State that the law and practice with respect to the audit of accounts is similar to that in the United Kingdom.

(3) The training must be given by persons approved by the body offering the qualification as persons whom the body is satisfied, in the light of undertakings given by them and the supervision to which they are subject (whether by the body itself or some other body or organisation), will provide adequate training.

(4) At least two-thirds of the training must be given by a person—

(a) eligible for appointment as a statutory auditor, or

(b) eligible for a corresponding appointment as an auditor under the law of an EEA State, or part of an EEA State, other than the United Kingdom.

Supplementary provision with respect to a sufficient period of professional experience

10. (1) Periods of theoretical instruction in the fields of finance, law and accountancy may be deducted from the required period of professional experience, provided the instruction—

(a) lasted at least one year, and

(b) is attested by an examination recognised by the Secretary of State for the purposes of this paragraph;

but the period of professional experience may not be so reduced by more than four years.

(2) The period of professional experience together with the practical training required in the case of persons satisfying the requirement in paragraph 7 by virtue of having a sufficient period of professional experience must not be shorter than the course of theoretical instruction referred to in that paragraph and the practical training required in the case of persons satisfying the requirement of that paragraph by virtue of having completed such a course.

The body offering the qualification

11. (1) The body offering the qualification must have—

(a) rules and arrangements adequate to ensure compliance with the requirements of paragraphs 6 to 10, and

(b) adequate arrangements for the effective monitoring of its continued compliance with those requirements.

(2) The arrangements must include arrangements for monitoring—

(a) the standard of the body's examinations, and

(b) the adequacy of the practical training given by the persons approved by it for that purpose.

SCHEDULE 11A

SPECIFIED PERSONS, DESCRIPTIONS, DISCLOSURES ETC FOR THE PURPOSES OF SECTION 1224A

PART 1
SPECIFIED PERSONS

1. The Secretary of State.
2. The Department of Enterprise, Trade and Investment for Northern Ireland.
3. The Treasury.
4. The Bank of England.
5. The Financial Conduct Authority.
5A. The Prudential Regulation Authority.
6. The Commissioners for Her Majesty's Revenue and Customs.
7. The Lord Advocate.
8. The Director of Public Prosecutions.
9. The Director of Public Prosecutions for Northern Ireland.
10. A constable.
11. A procurator fiscal.
12. The Scottish Ministers.
13. A body designated by the Secretary of State under section 1252 (delegation of the Secretary of State's functions).
14. A recognised supervisory body.
15. A recognised qualifying body.
16. A body with which a recognised supervisory body is participating in arrangements for the purposes of paragraph 23 or 23A (independent monitoring of audits) or 24 (independent investigation for disciplinary purposes) of Schedule 10 to this Act.
17. The Independent Supervisor.

PART 2
SPECIFIED DESCRIPTIONS OF DISCLOSURES

18. A disclosure for the purpose of enabling or assisting a person authorised under section 457 of this Act (persons authorised to apply to court) to exercise his functions.
19. A disclosure for the purpose of enabling or assisting an inspector appointed under Part 14 of the Companies Act 1985 (investigation of companies and their affairs, etc) to exercise his functions.
20. A disclosure for the purpose of enabling or assisting a person authorised under section 447 of the Companies Act 1985 (power to require production of documents) or section 84 of the Companies Act 1989 (exercise of powers by officer etc) to exercise his functions.
21. A disclosure for the purpose of enabling or assisting a person appointed under section 167 of the Financial Services and Markets Act 2000 (general investigations) to conduct an investigation to exercise his functions.
22. A disclosure for the purpose of enabling or assisting a person appointed under section 168 of the Financial Services and Markets Act 2000 (investigations in particular cases) to conduct an investigation to exercise his functions.
23. A disclosure for the purpose of enabling or assisting a person appointed under section 169(1)(b) of the Financial Services and Markets Act 2000 (investigation in support of overseas regulator) to conduct an investigation to exercise his functions.
24. A disclosure for the purpose of enabling or assisting the body corporate responsible for administering the scheme referred to in section 225 of the Financial Services and Markets Act 2000 (the ombudsman scheme) to exercise its functions.

25. A disclosure for the purpose of enabling or assisting a person appointed under paragraph 4 (the panel of ombudsmen) or 5 (the Chief Ombudsman) of Schedule 17 to the Financial Services and Markets Act 2000 to exercise his functions.

26. A disclosure for the purpose of enabling or assisting a person appointed under regulations made under section 262(1) and (2)(k) of the Financial Services and Markets Act 2000 (investigations into open-ended investment companies) to conduct an investigation to exercise his functions.

27. A disclosure for the purpose of enabling or assisting a person appointed under section 284 of the Financial Services and Markets Act 2000 (investigations into affairs of certain collective investment schemes) to conduct an investigation to exercise his functions.

28. A disclosure for the purpose of enabling or assisting the investigator appointed under section 84 of the Financial Services Act 2012 (arrangements for investigation of complaints) to exercise his functions.

29. A disclosure for the purpose of enabling or assisting a person appointed by the Treasury to hold an inquiry into matters relating to financial services (including an inquiry under section 69 of the Financial Services Act 2012) to exercise his functions.

30. A disclosure for the purpose of enabling or assisting the Secretary of State or the Treasury to exercise any of their functions under any of the following—
- (a) the Companies Acts;
- (b) Part 5 of the Criminal Justice Act 1993 (insider dealing);
- (c) the Insolvency Act 1986;
- (d) the Company Directors Disqualification Act 1986;
- (e) Part 42 of this Act (statutory auditors)
- (f) Part 3 (investigations and powers to obtain information) or 7 (financial markets and insolvency) of the Companies Act 1989;
- (g) the Financial Services and Markets Act 2000.

31. A disclosure for the purpose of enabling or assisting the Scottish Ministers to exercise their functions under the enactments relating to insolvency.

32. A disclosure for the purpose of enabling or assisting the Department of Enterprise, Trade and Investment for Northern Ireland to exercise any powers conferred on it by the enactments relating to companies or insolvency.

33. A disclosure for the purpose of enabling or assisting a person appointed or authorised by the Department of Enterprise, Trade and Investment for Northern Ireland under the enactments relating to companies or insolvency to exercise his functions.

34. A disclosure for the purpose of enabling or assisting the Pensions Regulator to exercise the functions conferred on it by or by virtue of any of the following—
- (a) the Pension Schemes Act 1993;
- (b) the Pensions Act 1995;
- (c) the Welfare Reform and Pensions Act 1999;
- (d) the Pensions Act 2004;
- (e) any enactment in force in Northern Ireland corresponding to any of those enactments.

35. A disclosure for the purpose of enabling or assisting the Board of the Pension Protection Fund to exercise the functions conferred on it by or by virtue of Part 2 of the Pensions Act 2004 or any enactment in force in Northern Ireland corresponding to that Part.

36. A disclosure for the purpose of enabling or assisting—
- (a) the Bank of England,
- (b) the European Central Bank, or
- (c) the central bank of any country or territory outside the United Kingdom, to exercise its functions.

37. A disclosure for the purpose of enabling or assisting the Commissioners for Her Majesty's Revenue and Customs to exercise their functions.

38. A disclosure for the purpose of enabling or assisting organs of the Society of Lloyd's (being organs constituted by or under the Lloyd's Act 1982) to exercise their functions under or by virtue of the Lloyd's Acts 1871 to 1982.

39. A disclosure for the purpose of enabling or assisting the Office of Fair Trading to exercise its functions under any of the following—
   (a) the Fair Trading Act 1973;
   (b) the Consumer Credit Act 1974;
   (c) the Estate Agents Act 1979;
   (d) the Competition Act 1980;
   (e) the Competition Act 1998;
   (f) the Financial Services and Markets Act 2000;
   (g) the Enterprise Act 2002;
   (h) the Control of Misleading Advertisements Regulations 1988;
   (i) the Unfair Terms in Consumer Contracts Regulations 1999.

40. A disclosure for the purpose of enabling or assisting the Competition Commission to exercise its functions under any of the following—
   (a) the Fair Trading Act 1973;
   (b) the Competition Act 1980;
   (c) the Competition Act 1998;
   (d) the Enterprise Act 2002.

41. A disclosure with a view to the institution of, or otherwise for the purposes of, proceedings before the Competition Appeal Tribunal.

42. A disclosure for the purpose of enabling or assisting an enforcer under Part 8 of the Enterprise Act 2002 (enforcement of consumer legislation) to exercise its functions under that Part.

43. A disclosure for the purpose of enabling or assisting the Takeover Panel to perform any of its functions under Part 28 of this Act (takeovers etc).

44. A disclosure for the purpose of enabling or assisting the Charity Commission to exercise its functions.

45. A disclosure for the purpose of enabling or assisting the Attorney General to exercise his functions in connection with charities.

46. A disclosure for the purpose of enabling or assisting the National Lottery Commission to exercise its functions under sections 5 to 10 (licensing) and 15 (power of Secretary of State to require information) of the National Lottery etc Act 1993.

47. A disclosure by the National Lottery Commission to the Comptroller and Auditor General for the purpose of enabling or assisting the Comptroller and Auditor General to carry out an examination under Part 2 of the National Audit Act 1983 into the economy, effectiveness and efficiency with which the National Lottery Commission has used its resources in discharging its functions under sections 5 to 10 of the National Lottery etc Act 1993.

48. A disclosure for the purpose of enabling or assisting a qualifying body under the Unfair Terms in Consumer Contracts Regulations 1999 to exercise its functions under those Regulations.

49. A disclosure for the purpose of enabling or assisting an enforcement authority under the Consumer Protection (Distance Selling) Regulations 2000 to exercise its functions under those Regulations.

50. A disclosure for the purpose of enabling or assisting an enforcement authority under the Financial Services (Distance Marketing) Regulations 2004 to exercise its functions under those Regulations.

51. A disclosure for the purpose of enabling or assisting a local weights and measures authority in England and Wales to exercise its functions under section 230(2) of the Enterprise Act 2002 (notice of intention to prosecute, etc).

52. A disclosure for the purpose of enabling or assisting the Financial Conduct Authority or the Prudential Regulation Authority to exercise its functions under any of the following—
   (a) the legislation relating to friendly societies or to industrial and provident societies;

(b) the Building Societies Act 1986;
(c) Part 7 of the Companies Act 1989 (financial markets and insolvency);
(d) the Financial Services and Markets Act 2000.

53. ...

54. A disclosure for the purpose of enabling or assisting a body corporate established in accordance with section 212(1) of the Financial Services and Markets Act 2000 (compensation scheme manager) to exercise its functions.

55. A disclosure for the purpose of enabling or assisting a recognised investment exchange or a recognised clearing house to exercise its functions as such.
"Recognised investment exchange" and "recognised clearing house" have the same meaning as in section 285 of the Financial Services and Markets Act 2000.

56. A disclosure for the purpose of enabling or assisting a person approved under the Uncertificated Securities Regulations 2001 as an operator of a relevant system (within the meaning of those regulations) to exercise his functions.

57. A disclosure for the purpose of enabling or assisting a body designated under section 326(1) of the Financial Services and Markets Act 2000 (designated professional bodies) to exercise its functions in its capacity as a body designated under that section.

58. A disclosure with a view to the institution of, or otherwise for the purposes of, civil proceedings arising under or by virtue of the Financial Services and Markets Act 2000.

59. A disclosure for the purpose of enabling or assisting a body designated by order under section 1252 of this Act (delegation of functions of Secretary of State) to exercise its functions under Part 42 of this Act (statutory auditors).

60. A disclosure for the purpose of enabling or assisting a recognised supervisory or qualifying body, within the meaning of Part 42 of this Act, to exercise its functions as such.

61. A disclosure for the purpose of making available to an audited person information relating to a statutory audit of that person's accounts.

62. A disclosure for the purpose of making available to the public information relating to monitoring or inspections carried out under arrangements within paragraph 23(1) or 23A(1) of Schedule 10 to this Act (arrangements for independent monitoring of audits of listed companies and other major bodies and of UK-traded non-EEA companies), provided such information does not identify any audited person.

63. A disclosure for the purpose of enabling or assisting an official receiver (including the Accountant in Bankruptcy in Scotland and the Official Assignee in Northern Ireland) to exercise his functions under the enactments relating to insolvency.

64. A disclosure for the purpose of enabling or assisting the Insolvency Practitioners Tribunal to exercise its functions under the Insolvency Act 1986.

65. A disclosure for the purpose of enabling or assisting a body that is for the time being a recognised professional body for the purposes of section 391 of the Insolvency Act 1986 (recognised professional bodies) to exercise its functions as such.

66. A disclosure for the purpose of enabling or assisting an overseas regulatory authority to exercise its regulatory functions.
"Overseas regulatory authority" and "regulatory functions" have the same meaning as in section 82 of the Companies Act 1989.

67. A disclosure for the purpose of enabling or assisting the Regulator of Community Interest Companies to exercise functions under the Companies (Audit, Investigations and Community Enterprise) Act 2004.

68. A disclosure with a view to the institution of, or otherwise for the purposes of, criminal proceedings.

69. A disclosure for the purpose of enabling or assisting a person authorised by the Secretary of State under Part 2, 3 or 4 of the Proceeds of Crime Act 2002 to exercise his functions.

70. A disclosure with a view to the institution of, or otherwise for the purposes of, proceedings on an application under section 6, 7 or 8 of the Company Directors Disqualification Act 1986 (disqualification for unfitness).

71. A disclosure with a view to the institution of, or otherwise for the purposes of, proceedings before the Upper Tribunal in respect of—
(a) a decision of the Financial Conduct Authority;
(aa) a decision of the Prudential Regulation Authority;
(b) a decision of the Bank of England; or
(c) a decision of a person relating to the assessment of any compensation or consideration under the Banking (Special Provisions) Act 2008 or the Banking Act 2009.

72. A disclosure for the purposes of proceedings before the Financial Services Tribunal by virtue of the Financial Services and Markets Act 2000 (Transitional Provisions) (Partly Completed Procedures) Order 2001.

73. A disclosure for the purposes of proceedings before a tribunal in relation to a decision of the Pensions Regulator.

74. A disclosure for the purpose of enabling or assisting a body appointed under section 14 of the Companies (Audit, Investigations and Community Enterprise) Act 2004 (supervision of periodic accounts and reports of issuers of listed securities) to exercise functions mentioned in subsection (2) of that section.

75. A disclosure with a view to the institution of, or otherwise for the purposes of, disciplinary proceedings relating to the performance by a relevant lawyer, foreign lawyer, auditor, accountant, valuer or actuary of his professional duties.
In this paragraph—
"foreign lawyer" means a person (other than a relevant lawyer) who is a foreign lawyer within the meaning of section 89(9) of the Courts and Legal Services Act 1990;
"relevant lawyer" means—
(a) a person who, for the purposes of the Legal Services Act 2007, is an authorised person in relation to an activity which constitutes a reserved legal activity (within the meaning of that Act),
(b) a solicitor or barrister in Northern Ireland, or
(c) a solicitor or advocate in Scotland.

76. A disclosure with a view to the institution of, or otherwise for the purposes of, disciplinary proceedings relating to the performance by a public servant of his duties.
"Public servant" means an officer or employee of the Crown.

77. A disclosure for the purpose of the provision of a summary or collection of information framed in such a way as not to enable the identity of any person to whom the information relates to be ascertained.

78. A disclosure in pursuance of any EU obligation.

PART 3
OVERSEAS REGULATORY BODIES

79. A disclosure is made in accordance with this Part of this Schedule if it is made to an EEA competent authority in accordance with section 1253B (requests from EEA competent authorities).

80. A disclosure is made in accordance with this Part of this Schedule if it is—
(a) a transfer of audit working papers to a third country competent authority in accordance with rules imposed under paragraph 16A of Schedule 10 (transfer of papers to third countries), or
(b) a disclosure other than a transfer of audit working papers made to a third country competent authority for the purpose of enabling or assisting the authority to exercise its functions.

SCHEDULE 12 Section 1242

ARRANGEMENTS IN WHICH REGISTERED THIRD COUNTRY AUDITORS ARE REQUIRED TO PARTICIPATE

Arrangements for independent monitoring of audits of UK-traded non-EEA companies

1. (1) The arrangements referred to in section 1242(1)(a) are appropriate arrangements—
   (a) for enabling the performance by the registered third country auditor of functions related to the audit of UK-traded non-EEA companies to be monitored by means of inspections carried out under the arrangements, and
   (b) for ensuring that the carrying out of such monitoring and inspections is done independently of the registered third country auditor.
   (2) . . .

Arrangements for independent investigations for disciplinary purposes

2. (1) The arrangements referred to in section 1242(1)(b) are appropriate arrangements—
   (a) for the carrying out of investigations into matters arising in connection with the performance of functions related to the audit of UK-traded non-EEA companies by the registered third country auditor,
   (b) for the holding of disciplinary hearings relating to the registered third country auditor which appear to be desirable following the conclusion of such investigations,
   (c) for requiring such hearings to be held in public except where the interests of justice otherwise require,
   (d) for the persons before whom such hearings have taken place to decide whether (and, if so, what) disciplinary action should be taken against the registered third country auditor, and
   (e) for ensuring that the carrying out of those investigations, the holding of those hearings and the taking of those decisions are done independently of the registered third country auditor.
   (2) In this paragraph—
   "disciplinary action" includes the imposition of a fine; and
   . . .

Supplementary: arrangements to operate independently of third country auditor

3. (1) This paragraph applies for the purposes of—
   (a) paragraph 1(1)(b), or
   (b) paragraph 2(1)(e).
   (2) Arrangements are not to be regarded as appropriate for the purpose of ensuring that a thing is done independently of the registered third country auditor unless they are designed to ensure that the registered third country auditor—
   (a) will have no involvement in the appointment or selection of any of the persons who are to be responsible for doing that thing, and
   (b) will not otherwise be involved in the doing of that thing.
   (3) Sub-paragraph (2) imposes a minimum requirement and does not preclude the possibility that additional criteria may need to be satisfied in order for the arrangements to be regarded as appropriate for the purpose in question.

Supplementary: funding of arrangements

4. (1) The registered third country auditor must pay any of the costs of maintaining any relevant arrangements which the arrangements provide are to be paid by it.
   (2) For this purpose "relevant arrangements" are arrangements within paragraph 1 or 2 in which the registered third country auditor is obliged to participate.

Supplementary: scope of arrangements

5. Arrangements may qualify as arrangements within either of paragraphs 1 and 2 even though the matters for which they provide are more extensive in any respect than those mentioned in the applicable paragraph.

Specification of particular arrangements by the Secretary of State

6. (1) If there exist two or more sets of arrangements within paragraph 1 or within paragraph 2, the obligation of a registered third country auditor under section 1242(1)(a) or (b), as the case may be, is to participate in such set of arrangements as the Secretary of State may by order specify.

(2) An order under sub-paragraph (1) is subject to negative resolution procedure.

SCHEDULE 13

Section 1252

SUPPLEMENTARY PROVISIONS WITH RESPECT TO DELEGATION ORDER

Operation of this Schedule

1. (1) This Schedule has effect in relation to a body designated by a delegation order under section 1252 as follows—

(a) paragraphs 2 to 12 have effect in relation to the body where it is established by the order;

(b) paragraphs 2 and 6 to 11 have effect in relation to the body where it is an existing body;

(c) paragraph 13 has effect in relation to the body where it is an existing body that is an unincorporated association.

(2) In their operation in accordance with sub-paragraph (1)(b), paragraphs 2 and 6 apply only in relation to—

(a) things done by or in relation to the body in or in connection with the exercise of functions transferred to it by the delegation order, and

(b) functions of the body which are functions so transferred.

(3) Any power conferred by this Schedule to make provision by order is a power to make provision by an order under section 1252.

Status

2. The body is not to be regarded as acting on behalf of the Crown and its members, officers and employees are not to be regarded as Crown servants.

Name, members and chairman

3. (1) The body is to be known by such name as may be specified in the delegation order.

(2) The body is to consist of such persons (not being less than eight) as the Secretary of State may appoint after such consultation as he thinks appropriate.

(3) The chairman of the body is to be such person as the Secretary of State may appoint from among its members.

(4) The Secretary of State may make provision by order as to—

(a) the terms on which the members of the body are to hold and vacate office;

(b) the terms on which a person appointed as chairman is to hold and vacate the office of chairman.

Financial provisions

4. (1) The body must pay to its chairman and members such remuneration, and such allowances in respect of expenses properly incurred by them in the performance of their duties, as the Secretary of State may determine.

(2) As regards any chairman or member in whose case the Secretary of State so determines, the body must pay or make provision for the payment of—

(a) such pension, allowance or gratuity to or in respect of that person on his retirement or death, or

(b) such contributions or other payment towards the provision of such a pension, allowance or gratuity,

as the Secretary of State may determine.

(3) Where—

(a) a person ceases to be a member of the body otherwise than on the expiry of his term of office, and

(b) it appears to the Secretary of State that there are special circumstances which make it right for that person to receive compensation,

the body must make a payment to him by way of compensation of such amount as the Secretary of State may determine.

Proceedings

5. (1) The delegation order may contain such provision as the Secretary of State considers appropriate with respect to the proceedings of the body.

(2) The delegation order may, in particular—

(a) authorise the body to discharge any functions by means of committees consisting wholly or partly of members of the body;

(b) provide that the validity of proceedings of the body, or of any such committee, is not affected by any vacancy among the members or any defect in the appointment of any member.

Fees

6. (1) The body may retain fees payable to it.

(2) The fees must be applied for—

(a) meeting the expenses of the body in discharging its functions, and

(b) any purposes incidental to those functions.

(3) Those expenses include any expenses incurred by the body on such staff, accommodation, services and other facilities as appear to it to be necessary or expedient for the proper performance of its functions.

(4) In prescribing the amount of fees in the exercise of the functions transferred to it the body must prescribe such fees as appear to it sufficient to defray those expenses, taking one year with another.

(5) Any exercise by the body of the power to prescribe fees requires the approval of the Secretary of State.

(6) The Secretary of State may, after consultation with the body, by order vary or revoke any regulations prescribing fees made by the body.

Legislative functions

7. (1) Regulations or an order made by the body in the exercise of the functions transferred to it must be made by instrument in writing, but not by statutory instrument.

(2) The instrument must specify the provision of this Part of this Act under which it is made.

(3) The Secretary of State may by order impose such requirements as he thinks necessary or expedient as to the circumstances and manner in which the body must consult on any regulations or order it proposes to make.

(4) Nothing in this Part applies to make regulations or an order made by the body subject to negative resolution procedure or affirmative resolution procedure.

8. (1) Immediately after an instrument is made it must be printed and made available to the public with or without payment.

(2) A person is not to be taken to have contravened any regulation or order if he shows that at the time of the alleged contravention the instrument containing the regulation or order had not been made available as required by this paragraph.

9. (1) The production of a printed copy of an instrument purporting to be made by the body on which is endorsed a certificate signed by an officer of the body authorised by it for the purpose and stating—

(a) that the instrument was made by the body,

(b) that the copy is a true copy of the instrument, and

(c) that on a specified date the instrument was made available to the public as required by paragraph 8,

is evidence (or, in Scotland, sufficient evidence) of the facts stated in the certificate.

(2) A certificate purporting to be signed as mentioned in sub-paragraph (1) is to be deemed to have been duly signed unless the contrary is shown.

(3) Any person wishing in any legal proceedings to cite an instrument made by the body may require the body to cause a copy of it to be endorsed with such a certificate as is mentioned in this paragraph.

Report and accounts

10. (1) The body must, at least once in each calendar year for which the delegation order is in force, make a report to the Secretary of State on—

(a) the discharge of the functions transferred to it, and

(b) such other matters as the Secretary of State may by order require.

(2) The delegation order may modify sub-paragraph (1) as it has effect in relation to the calendar year in which the order comes into force or is revoked.

(3) The Secretary of State must lay before Parliament copies of each report received by him under this paragraph.

(4) The following provisions of this paragraph apply as follows—

(a) sub-paragraphs (5) and (6) apply only where the body is established by the order, and

(b) sub-paragraphs (7) and (8) apply only where the body is an existing body.

(5) The Secretary of State may, with the consent of the Treasury, give directions to the body with respect to its accounts and the audit of its accounts.

(6) A person may only be appointed as auditor of the body if he is eligible for appointment as a statutory auditor.

(7) Unless the body is a company to which section 394 (duty to prepare individual company accounts) applies, the Secretary of State may, with the consent of the Treasury, give directions to the body with respect to its accounts and the audit of its accounts.

(8) Whether or not the body is a company to which section 394 applies, the Secretary of State may direct that any provisions of this Act specified in the directions are to apply to the body, with or without any modifications so specified.

Other supplementary provisions

11. (1) The transfer of a function to a body designated by a delegation order does not affect anything previously done in the exercise of the function transferred; and the resumption of a function so transferred does not affect anything previously done in exercise of the function resumed.

(2) The Secretary of State may by order make such transitional and other supplementary provision as he thinks necessary or expedient in relation to the transfer or resumption of a function.

(3) The provision that may be made in connection with the transfer of a function includes, in particular, provision—

(a) for modifying or excluding any provision of this Part of this Act in its application to the function transferred;

(b) for applying to the body designated by the delegation order, in connection with the function transferred, any provision applying to the Secretary of State which is contained in or made under any other enactment;

(c) for the transfer of any property, rights or liabilities from the Secretary of State to that body;

(d) for the carrying on and completion by that body of anything in the process of being done by the Secretary of State when the order takes effect;

(e) for the substitution of that body for the Secretary of State in any instrument, contract or legal proceedings.

(4) The provision that may be made in connection with the resumption of a function includes, in particular, provision—

(a) for the transfer of any property, rights or liabilities from that body to the Secretary of State;

(b) for the carrying on and completion by the Secretary of State of anything in the process of being done by that body when the order takes effect;

(c) for the substitution of the Secretary of State for that body in any instrument, contract or legal proceedings.

12. Where a delegation order is revoked, the Secretary of State may by order make provision—

(a) for the payment of compensation to persons ceasing to be employed by the body established by the delegation order;

(b) as to the winding up and dissolution of the body.

13. (1) This paragraph applies where the body is an unincorporated association.

(2) Any relevant proceedings may be brought by or against the body in the name of any body corporate whose constitution provides for the establishment of the body.

(3) In sub-paragraph (2) "relevant proceedings" means proceedings brought in or in connection with the exercise of any transferred function.

(4) In relation to proceedings brought as mentioned in sub-paragraph (2), any reference in paragraph 11(3)(e) or (4)(c) to the body replacing or being replaced by the Secretary of State in any legal proceedings is to be read with the appropriate modifications.

SCHEDULE 14

Section 1264

STATUTORY AUDITORS: CONSEQUENTIAL AMENDMENTS

Companies (Audit, Investigations and Community Enterprise) Act 2004 (c 27)

1. (1) Section 16 of the Companies (Audit, Investigations and Community Enterprise) Act 2004 (grants to bodies concerned with accounting standards etc) is amended as follows.

(2) In subsection (2)—

(a) in paragraph (f) for "paragraph 17" to the end substitute "paragraph 21, 22, 23(1) or 24(1) of Schedule 10 to the Companies Act 2006;",

(b) in paragraph (g) for "Part 2 of that Act" substitute "Part 42 of that Act".

(3) In subsection (5), in the definition of "professional accountancy body"—

(a) in paragraph (a) for "Part 2 of the Companies Act 1989" substitute "Part 42 of the Companies Act 2006", and

(b) in paragraph (b) for "section 32" substitute "section 1220".

SCHEDULE 15

Section 1272

TRANSPARENCY OBLIGATIONS AND RELATED MATTERS: MINOR AND CONSEQUENTIAL AMENDMENTS

PART 1

AMENDMENTS OF THE FINANCIAL SERVICES AND MARKETS ACT 2000

1 Part 6 of the Financial Services and Markets Act 2000 (listing and other matters) is amended as follows.

2 ...

3 In section 73A (Part 6 Rules), after subsection (5) insert—

"(6) Transparency rules and corporate governance rules are not listing rules, disclosure rules or prospectus rules, but are Part 6 rules."

4 For the cross-heading before section 90 substitute *"Compensation for false or misleading statements etc"*.

5 For the heading to section 90 substitute **"Compensation for statements in listing particulars or prospectus"**.

6 (1) Section 91 (penalties for breach of Part 6 rules) is amended as follows.

(2) For subsection (1) substitute—

"(1) If the competent authority considers that—

(a) an issuer of listed securities, or

(b) an applicant for listing,

has contravened any provision of listing rules, it may impose on him a penalty of such amount as it considers appropriate.

(1ZA) If the competent authority considers that—

(a) an issuer who has requested or approved the admission of a financial instrument to trading on a regulated market,

(b) a person discharging managerial responsibilities within such an issuer, or

(c) a person connected with such a person discharging managerial responsibilities,

has contravened any provision of disclosure rules, it may impose on him a penalty of such amount as it considers appropriate.".

(3) After subsection (1A) insert—

"(1B) If the competent authority considers—

(a) that a person has contravened—

(i) a provision of transparency rules or a provision otherwise made in accordance with the transparency obligations directive, or

(ii) a provision of corporate governance rules, or

(b) that a person on whom a requirement has been imposed under section 89L (power to suspend or prohibit trading of securities in case of infringement of applicable transparency obligation), has contravened that requirement,

it may impose on the person a penalty of such amount as it considers appropriate.".

(4) In subsection (2) for "(1)(a), (1)(b)(i) or (1A)" substitute "(1), (1ZA)(a), (1A) or (1B)".

7 In section 96B (persons discharging managerial responsibilities and connected persons)—

(a) for the heading substitute **"Disclosure rules: persons responsible for compliance"**;

(b) in subsection (1) for "For the purposes of this Part" substitute "for the purposes of the provisions of this Part relating to disclosure rules".

8 In section 97(1) (appointment by the competent authority of persons to carry out investigations), for paragraphs (a) and (b) substitute—

"(a) there may have been a contravention of—

(i) a provision of this Part or of Part 6 rules, or

(ii) a provision otherwise made in accordance with the prospectus directive or the transparency obligations directive;

(b) a person who was at the material time a director of a person mentioned in section 91(1), (1ZA)(a), (1A) or (1B) has been knowingly concerned in a contravention by that person of—

(i) a provision of this Part or of Part 6 rules, or

(ii) a provision otherwise made in accordance with the prospectus directive or the transparency obligations directive;".

9 ...

10 (1) Section 102A (meaning of "securities" etc) is amended as follows.

(2) After subsection (3) insert—

"(3A) "Debt securities" has the meaning given in Article 2.1(b) of the transparency obligations directive.".

(3) In subsection (3) (meaning of "transferable securities") for "the investment services directive" substitute "Directive 2004/39/EC of the European Parliament and of the Council on markets in financial instruments".

(4) In subsection (6) (meaning of "issuer"), after paragraph (a) insert—

"(aa) in relation to transparency rules, means a legal person whose securities are admitted to trading on a regulated market or whose voting shares are admitted to trading on a UK market other than a regulated market, and in the case of depository receipts representing securities, the issuer is the issuer of the securities represented;".

11 (1) Section 103(1) (interpretation of Part 6) is amended as follows.

(2) In the definition of "regulated market" for "Article 1.13 of the investment services directive" substitute "Article 4.1(14) of Directive 2004/39/EC of the European Parliament and of the Council on markets in financial instruments".

(3) At the appropriate place insert—

""transparency rules" has the meaning given by section 89A(5);

"voteholder information" has the meaning given by section 89B(3);".

12 In section 429(2) (Parliamentary control of statutory instruments: affirmative procedure) of the Financial Services and Markets Act 2000 after "section" insert "90B or".

PART 2
AMENDMENTS OF THE COMPANIES (AUDIT, INVESTIGATIONS AND COMMUNITY ENTERPRISE) ACT 2004

13 Chapter 2 of Part 1 of the Companies (Audit, Investigations and Community Enterprise) Act 2004 (accounts and reports) is amended as follows.

14 (1) Section 14 (supervision of periodic accounts and reports of issuers of listed securities) is amended as follows.

(2) In subsection (2)(a)—

(a) for "listed" substitute "transferable";

(b) for "listing" substitute "Part 6".

(3) In subsection (3)(a)—

(a) for "listed" substitute "transferable";

(b) for "listing" substitute "Part 6".

(4) In subsection (7)(b) for "listed" substitute "transferable".

(5) In subsection (12)—

(a) for ""listed securities" and "listing rules" have" substitute ""Part 6 rules" has";

(b) for the definition of "issuer" substitute—

""issuer" has the meaning given by section 102A(6) of that Act;";

(c) in the definition of "periodic" for "listing" substitute "Part 6";

(d) at the end add—

""transferable securities" has the meaning given by section 102A(3) of that Act.".

15 (1) Section 15 (application of certain company law provisions to bodies appointed under section 14) is amended as follows.

(2) In subsection (5)(a)—

(a) for "listed" substitute "transferable";

(b) for "listing" substitute "Part 6".

(3) In subsection (5B)(a)—

(a) for "listed" substitute "transferable";

(b) for "listing" substitute "Part 6".

(4) In subsection (6)(b) for ""listing rules" and "security"" substitute ""Part 6 rules" and "transferable securities"".

SCHEDULE 16 Section 1295

REPEALS

Company law repeals (Great Britain)

Short title and chapter	*Extent of repeal*
Companies Act 1985	Sections 1 to 430F. In section 437— (a) in subsection (1), the second sentence, and (b) subsections (1B) and (1C). Section 438. In section 439— (a) in subsection (2), ", or is ordered to pay the whole or any part of the costs of proceedings brought under section 438", (b) subsections (3) and (7), and (c) in subsection (8), "; and any such liability imposed by subsection (2) is (subject as mentioned above) a liability also to indemnify all persons against liability under subsection (3)". Section 442(2). Section 446. In section 448(7), the words "and liable to a fine." to the end. Section 449 Section 450404. Section 4513. In section 4(1A)— (a) paragraph (b), and (b) paragraph (d) and the word "and" preceding it. Section 453A(6). Sections 458 to 461. Sections 651 to 746. Schedules 1 to 15B. Schedules 20 to 25.
Insolvency Act 1985	Schedule 6.

Short title and chapter	*Extent of repeal*
Insolvency Act 1986	In Schedule 13, in Part 1, the entries relating to the following provisions of the Companies Act 1985— (a) section 13(4), (b) section 44(7), (c) section 103(7), (d) section 131(7), (e) section 140(2), (f) section 156(3), (g) section 173(4), (h) section 196, (i) section 380(4), (j) section 461(6), (k) section 462(5), (l) section 463(2), (m) section 463(3), (n) section 464(6), (o) section 657(2), (p) section 658(1), and (q) section 711(2).
Building Societies Act 1986	Section 102C(5).
Finance Act 1988	In section 117(3), from the beginning to "that section";". In section 117(4), the words "and (3)".
Water Act 1989	In Schedule 25, paragraph 71(3).
Companies Act 1989	Sections 1 to 22. Section 56(5). Sections 57 and 58. Section 64(2). Section 66(3). Section 71. Sections 92 to 110. Sections 113 to 138. Section 139(1) to (3). Sections 141 to 143. Section 144(1) to (3) and (6). Section 207. Schedules 1 to 9. In Schedule 10, paragraphs 1 to 24. Schedules 15 to 17. In Schedule 18, paragraphs 32 to 38. In Schedule 19, paragraphs 1 to 9 and 11 to 21.
Age of Legal Capacity (Scotland) Act 1991	In Schedule 1, paragraph 39.
Water Consolidation (Consequential Provisions) Act 1991	In Schedule 1, paragraph 40(2).
Charities Act 1992	In Schedule 6, paragraph 11.
Charities Act 1993	In Schedule 6, paragraph 20.
Criminal Justice Act 1993	In Schedule 5, paragraph 4.
Welsh Language Act 1993	Section 30.
Pension Schemes Act 1993	In Schedule 8, paragraph 16.

Short title and chapter	*Extent of repeal*
Trade Marks Act 1994	In Schedule 4, in paragraph 1(2), the reference to the Companies Act 1985.
Deregulation and Contracting Out Act 1994	Section 13(1). Schedule 5. In Schedule 16, paragraphs 8 to 10.
Requirements of Writing (Scotland) Act 1995	In Schedule 4, paragraphs 51 to 56.
Criminal Procedure (Consequential Provisions) (Scotland) Act 1995	In Schedule 4, paragraph 56(3) and (4).
Disability Discrimination Act 1995	In Schedule 6, paragraph 4.
Financial Services and Markets Act 2000	Section 143. Section 263.
Limited Liability Partnerships Act 2000	In the Schedule, paragraph 1.
Political Parties, Elections and Referendums Act 2000	Sections 139 and 140. Schedule 19. In Schedule 23, paragraphs 12 and 13.
Criminal Justice and Police Act 2001	Section 45. In Schedule 2, paragraph 17.
Enterprise Act 2002	In Schedule 17, paragraphs 3 to 8.
Companies (Audit, Investigations and Community Enterprise) Act 2004	Sections 7 to 10. Section 11(1). Sections 12 and 13. Sections 19 and 20. Schedule 1. In Schedule 2, paragraphs 5 to 10, 22 to 24 and 26. In Schedule 6, paragraphs 1 to 9.
Civil Partnership Act 2004	In Schedule 27, paragraphs 99 to 105.
Constitutional Reform Act 2005	In Schedule 11, in paragraph 4(3), the reference to the Companies Act 1985.

Repeals and revocations relating to Northern Ireland

Companies (Northern Ireland) Order 1986	The whole Order.
Companies Consolidation (Consequential Provisions) (Northern Ireland) Order 1986	The whole Order.
Business Names (Northern Ireland) Order 1986	The whole Order.
Industrial Relations (Northern Ireland) Order 1987	Article 3.
Finance Act 1988	In section 117(3), the words from "and for" to the end.
Companies (Northern Ireland) Order 1989	The whole Order.
Insolvency (Northern Ireland) Order 1989	In Schedule 7, in the entry relating to Article 166(4), the word "office". In Schedule 9, Part I.
European Economic Interest Groupings Regulations (Northern Ireland) 1989	The whole Regulations.
Companies (Northern Ireland) Order 1990	The whole Order.

Short title and chapter	*Extent of repeal*
Companies (No. 2) (Northern Ireland) Order 1990	Parts II to IV. Part VI. Schedules 1 to 6.
Criminal Justice Act 1993	In Schedule 5, Part 2. Schedule 6.
Financial Provisions (Northern Ireland) Order	Article 15.
Deregulation and Contracting Out Act 1994	Section 13(2). Schedule 6.
Pensions (Northern Ireland) Order 1995	In Schedule 3, paragraph 7.
Deregulation and Contracting Out (Northern Ireland) Order 1996	Article 11. Schedule 2. In Schedule 5, paragraph 4.
Youth Justice and Criminal Evidence Act 1999	In Schedule 4, paragraph 18.
Limited Liability Partnerships Act (Northern Ireland) 2002	The whole Act.
Open-Ended Investment Companies Act (Northern Ireland)	The whole Act.
Company Directors Disqualification (Northern Ireland) Order 2002	In Schedule 3, paragraphs 3 to 5.
Companies(Audit, Investigations and Community Enterprise) Act 2004	Section 11(2). In Schedule 2, paragraphs 11 to 15.
Law Reform (Miscellaneous Provisions) (Northern Ireland) Order 2005	Article 4(2).
Companies(Audit, Investigations and Community Enterprise) (Northern Ireland) Order 2005	The whole Order.
Other repeals	
Limited Partnerships Act 1907	In section 16(1)— (a) the words ", and there shall be paid for such inspection such fees as may be appointed by the Board of Trade, not exceeding 5p for each inspection", and (b) the words from "and there shall be paid for such certificate" to the end. In section 17— (a) the words "(but as to fees with the concurrence of the Treasury)", and (b) paragraph (a).
Business Names Act 1985	The whole Act.
Companies Act 1989	Sections 24 to 54. Schedules 11 to 13.
Criminal Procedure (Consequential Provisions) (Scotland) Act 1995	In Schedule 4, paragraph 74(2).
Companies (Audit, Investigations and Community Enterprise) Act 2004	Sections 1 to 6. In Schedule 2, Part 1.
Civil Partnership Act 2004	In Schedule 27, paragraph 128.

Company Directors Disqualification Act 1986

1986 c. 46

An Act to consolidate certain enactments relating to the disqualification of persons from being directors of companies, and from being otherwise concerned with a company's affairs

[25th July 1986]

Preliminary

1. Disqualification orders: general

(1) In the circumstances specified below in this Act a court may, and under sections 6 and 9A shall, make against a person a disqualification order, that is to say an order that for a period specified in the order—

(a) he shall not be a director of a company, act as receiver of a company's property or in any way, whether directly or indirectly, be concerned or take part in the promotion, formation or management of a company unless (in each case) he has the leave of the court, and

(b) he shall not act as an insolvency practitioner.

(2) In each section of this Act which gives to a court power or, as the case may be, imposes on it the duty to make a disqualification order there is specified the maximum (and, in section 6, the minimum) period of disqualification which may or (as the case may be) must be imposed by means of the order and, unless the court otherwise orders, the period of disqualification so imposed shall begin at the end of the period of 21 days beginning with the date of the order.

(3) Where a disqualification order is made against a person who is already subject to such an order or to a disqualification undertaking, the periods specified in those orders or, as the case may be, in the order and the undertaking shall run concurrently.

(4) A disqualification order may be made on grounds which are or include matters other than criminal convictions, notwithstanding that the person in respect of whom it is to be made may be criminally liable in respect of those matters.

1A. Disqualification undertakings: general

(1) In the circumstances specified in sections 7 and 8 the Secretary of State may accept a disqualification undertaking, that is to say an undertaking by any person that, for a period specified in the undertaking, the person—

(a) will not be a director of a company, act as receiver of a company's property or in any way, whether directly or indirectly, be concerned or take part in the promotion, formation or management of a company unless (in each case) he has the leave of a court, and

(b) will not act as an insolvency practitioner.

(2) The maximum period which may be specified in a disqualification undertaking is 15 years; and the minimum period which may be specified in a disqualification undertaking under section 7 is two years.

(3) Where a disqualification undertaking by a person who is already subject to such an undertaking or to a disqualification order is accepted, the periods specified in those undertakings or (as the case may be) the undertaking and the order shall run concurrently.

(4) In determining whether to accept a disqualification undertaking by any person, the Secretary of State may take account of matters other than criminal convictions, notwithstanding that the person may be criminally liable in respect of those matters.

Disqualification for general misconduct in connection with companies

2. Disqualification on conviction of indictable offence

(1) The court may make a disqualification order against a person where he is convicted of an indictable offence (whether on indictment or summarily) in connection with the promotion,

formation, management, liquidation or striking off of a company, with the receivership of a company's property or with his being an administrative receiver of a company.

(2) "The court" for this purpose means—

(a) any court having jurisdiction to wind up the company in relation to which the offence was committed, or

(b) the court by or before which the person is convicted of the offence, or

(c) in the case of a summary conviction in England and Wales, any other magistrates' court acting in the same local justice area;

and for the purposes of this section the definition of "indictable offence" in Schedule 1 to the Interpretation Act 1978 applies for Scotland as it does for England and Wales.

(3) The maximum period of disqualification under this section is—

(a) where the disqualification order is made by a court of summary jurisdiction, 5 years, and

(b) in any other case, 15 years.

3. Disqualification for persistent breaches of companies legislation

(1) The court may make a disqualification order against a person where it appears to it that he has been persistently in default in relation to provisions of the companies legislation requiring any return, account or other document to be filed with, delivered or sent, or notice of any matter to be given, to the registrar of companies.

(2) On an application to the court for an order to be made under this section, the fact that a person has been persistently in default in relation to such provisions as are mentioned above may (without prejudice to its proof in any other manner) be conclusively proved by showing that in the 5 years ending with the date of the application he has been adjudged guilty (whether or not on the same occasion) of three or more defaults in relation to those provisions.

(3) A person is to be treated under subsection (2) as being adjudged guilty of a default in relation to any provision of that legislation if—

(a) he is convicted (whether on indictment or summarily) of an offence consisting in a contravention of or failure to comply with that provision (whether on his own part or on the part of any company), or

(b) a default order is made against him, that is to say an order under any of the following provisions—

(i) section 452 of the Companies Act 2006 (order requiring delivery of company accounts),

(ia) section 456 of that Act (order requiring preparation of revised accounts),

(ii) section 1113 of that Act (enforcement of company's filing obligations),

(iii) section 41 of the Insolvency Act 1986 (enforcement of receiver's or manager's duty to make returns), or

(iv) section 170 of that Act (corresponding provision for liquidator in winding up),

in respect of any such contravention of or failure to comply with that provision (whether on his own part or on the part of any company).

(4) In this section "the court" means any court having jurisdiction to wind up any of the companies in relation to which the offence or other default has been or is alleged to have been committed.

(4A) In this section "the companies legislation" means the Companies Acts and Parts 1 to 7 of the Insolvency Act 1986 (company insolvency and winding up).

(5) The maximum period of disqualification under this section is 5 years.

4. Disqualification for fraud, etc, in winding up

(1) The court may make a disqualification order against a person if, in the course of the winding up of a company, it appears that he—

(a) has been guilty of an offence for which he is liable (whether he has been convicted or not) under section 993 of the Companies Act 2006 (fraudulent trading), or

(b) has otherwise been guilty, while an officer or liquidator of the company receiver of the company's property or administrative receiver of the company, of any fraud in relation to the company or of any breach of his duty as such officer, liquidator, receiver or administrative receiver.

(2) In this section "the court" means any court having jurisdiction to wind up any of the companies in relation to which the offence or other default has been or is alleged to have been committed; and "officer" includes a shadow director.

(3) The maximum period of disqualification under this section is 15 years.

5. Disqualification on summary conviction

(1) An offence counting for the purposes of this section is one of which a person is convicted (either on indictment or summarily) in consequence of a contravention of, or failure to comply with, any provision of the companies legislation requiring a return, account or other document to be filed with, delivered or sent, or notice of any matter to be given, to the registrar of companies (whether the contravention or failure is on the person's own part or on the part of any company).

(2) Where a person is convicted of a summary offence counting for those purposes, the court by which he is convicted (or, in England and Wales, any other magistrates' court acting in the same local justice area) may make a disqualification order against him if the circumstances specified in the next subsection are present.

(3) Those circumstances are that, during the 5 years ending with the date of the conviction, the person has had made against him, or has been convicted of, in total not less than 3 default orders and offences counting for the purposes of this section; and those offences may include that of which he is convicted as mentioned in subsection (2) and any other offence of which he is convicted on the same occasion.

(4) For the purposes of this section—

(a) the definition of "summary offence" in Schedule 1 to the Interpretation Act 1978 applies for Scotland as for England and Wales, and

(b) "default order" means the same as in section 3(3)(b).

(4A) In this section "the companies legislation" means the Companies Acts and Parts 1 to 7 of the Insolvency Act 1986 (company insolvency and winding up).

(5) The maximum period of disqualification under this section is 5 years.

Disqualification for unfitness

6. Duty of court to disqualify unfit directors of insolvent companies

(1) The court shall make a disqualification order against a person in any case where, on an application under this section, it is satisfied—

(a) that he is or has been a director of a company which has at any time become insolvent (whether while he was a director or subsequently), and

(b) that his conduct as a director of that company (either taken alone or taken together with his conduct as a director of any other company or companies) makes him unfit to be concerned in the management of a company.

(2) For the purposes of this section and the next, a company becomes insolvent if—

(a) the company goes into liquidation at a time when its assets are insufficient for the payment of its debts and other liabilities and the expenses of the winding up,

(b) the company enters administration, or

(c) an administrative receiver of the company is appointed;

and references to a person's conduct as a director of any company or companies include, where that company or any of those companies has become insolvent, that person's conduct in relation to any matter connected with or arising out of the insolvency of that company.

(3) In this section and section 7(2), "the court" means—

(a) where the company in question is being or has been wound up by the court, that court,

(b) where the company in question is being or has been wound up voluntarily, any court which has or (as the case may be) had jurisdiction to wind it up,

(c) where neither paragraph (a) nor (b) applies but an administrator or administrative receiver has at any time been appointed in respect of the company in question, any court which has jurisdiction to wind it up.

(3A) Sections 117 and 120 of the Insolvency Act 1986 (jurisdiction) shall apply for the purposes of subsection (3) as if the references in the definitions of "registered office" to the presentation of the petition for winding up were references—

(a) in a case within paragraph (b) of that subsection, to the passing of the resolution for voluntary winding up,

(b) in a case within paragraph (c) of that subsection, to the appointment of the administrator or (as the case may be) administrative receiver.

(3B) Nothing in subsection (3) invalidates any proceedings by reason of their being taken in the wrong court; and proceedings—

(a) for or in connection with a disqualification order under this section, or

(b) in connection with a disqualification undertaking accepted under section 7,

may be retained in the court in which the proceedings were commenced, although it may not be the court in which they ought to have been commenced.

(3C) In this section and section 7, "director" includes a shadow director.

(4) Under this section the minimum period of disqualification is 2 years, and the maximum period is 15 years.

7. Disqualification order or undertaking; and reporting provisions

(1) If it appears to the Secretary of State that it is expedient in the public interest that a disqualification order under section 6 should be made against any person, an application for the making of such an order against that person may be made—

(a) by the Secretary of State, or

(b) if the Secretary of State so directs in the case of a person who is or has been a director of a company which is being or has been wound up by the court in England and Wales, by the official receiver.

(2) Except with the leave of the court, an application for the making under that section of a disqualification order against any person shall not be made after the end of the period of 2 years beginning with the day on which the company of which that person is or has been a director became insolvent.

(2A) If it appears to the Secretary of State that the conditions mentioned in section 6(1) are satisfied as respects any person who has offered to give him a disqualification undertaking, he may accept the undertaking if it appears to him that it is expedient in the public interest that he should do so (instead of applying, or proceeding with an application, for a disqualification order).

(3) If it appears to the office-holder responsible under this section, that is to say—

(a) in the case of a company which is being wound up by the court in England and Wales, the official receiver,

(b) in the case of a company which is being wound up otherwise, the liquidator,

(c) in the case of a company which is in administration, the administrator, or

(d) in the case of a company of which there is an administrative receiver, that receiver,

that the conditions mentioned in section 6(1) are satisfied as respects a person who is or has been a director of that company, the office-holder shall forthwith report the matter to the Secretary of State.

(4) The Secretary of State or the official receiver may require the liquidator, administrator or administrative receiver of a company, or the former liquidator, administrator or administrative receiver of a company—

(a) to furnish him with such information with respect to any person's conduct as a director of the company, and

(b) to produce and permit inspection of such books, papers and other records relevant to that person's conduct as such a director, as the Secretary of State or the official receiver may reasonably require for the purpose of determining whether to exercise, or of exercising, any function of his under this section.

8. Disqualification after investigation of company

(1) If it appears to the Secretary of State from investigative material that it is expedient in the public interest that a disqualification order should be made against a person who is, or has been, a director or shadow director of a company, he may apply to the court for such an order.

(1A) "Investigative material" means—

(a) a report made by inspectors under—

(i) section 437 of the Companies Act 1985, or

(ii) section 167, 168, 169 or 284 of the Financial Services and Markets Act 2000; and

(b) information or documents obtained under—

(i) section 437, 446E, 447, 448, 451A or 453A of the Companies Act 1985;

(ii) section 2 of the Criminal Justice Act 1987;

(iii) section 28 of the Criminal Law (Consolidation) (Scotland) Act 1995;

(iv) section 83 of the Companies Act 1989; or

(v) section 165, 171, 172, 173 or 175 of the Financial Services and Markets Act 2000.

(2) The court may make a disqualification order against a person where, on an application under this section, it is satisfied that his conduct in relation to the company makes him unfit to be concerned in the management of a company.

(2A) Where it appears to the Secretary of State from such report, information or documents that, in the case of a person who has offered to give him a disqualification undertaking—

(a) the conduct of the person in relation to a company of which the person is or has been a director or shadow director makes him unfit to be concerned in the management of a company, and

(b) it is expedient in the public interest that he should accept the undertaking (instead of applying, or proceeding with an application, for a disqualification order),

he may accept the undertaking.

(3) In this section "the court" means the High Court or, in Scotland, the Court of Session.

(4) The maximum period of disqualification under this section is 15 years.

8A. Variation etc of disqualification undertaking

(1) The court may, on the application of a person who is subject to a disqualification undertaking—

(a) reduce the period for which the undertaking is to be in force, or

(b) provide for it to cease to be in force.

(2) On the hearing of an application under subsection (1), the Secretary of State shall appear and call the attention of the court to any matters which seem to him to be relevant, and may himself give evidence or call witnesses.

(2A) Subsection (2) does not apply to an application in the case of an undertaking given under section 9B, and in such a case on the hearing of the application whichever of the OFT or a specified regulator (within the meaning of section 9E) accepted the undertaking—

(a) must appear and call the attention of the court to any matters which appear to it or him (as the case may be) to be relevant;

(b) may give evidence or call witnesses.

(3) In this section "the court"—

(a) in the case of an undertaking given under section 9B means the High Court or (in Scotland) the Court of Session;

(b) in any other case has the same meaning as in section 7(2) or 8 (as the case may be).

9. Matters for determining unfitness of directors

(1) Where it falls to a court to determine whether a person's conduct as a director … of any particular company or companies makes him unfit to be concerned in the management of a company, the court shall, as respects his conduct as a director of that company or, as the case may be, each of those companies, have regard in particular—

(a) to the matters mentioned in Part I of Schedule 1 to this Act, and
(b) where the company has become insolvent, to the matters mentioned in Part II of that Schedule;

and references in that Schedule to the director and the company are to be read accordingly.

(1A) In determining whether he may accept a disqualification undertaking from any person the Secretary of State shall, as respects the person's conduct as a director of any company concerned, have regard in particular—
(a) to the matters mentioned in Part I of Schedule 1 to this Act, and
(b) where the company has become insolvent, to the matters mentioned in Part II of that Schedule;

and references in that Schedule to the director and the company are to be read accordingly.

(2) Section 6(2) applies for the purposes of this section and Schedule 1 as it applies for the purposes of sections 6 and 7 and in this section and that Schedule "director" includes a shadow director.

(3) . . .

(4) The Secretary of State may by order modify any of the provisions of Schedule 1; and such an order may contain such transitional provisions as may appear to the Secretary of State necessary or expedient.

(5) The power to make orders under this section is exercisable by statutory instrument subject to annulment in pursuance of a resolution of either House of Parliament.

Disqualification for competition infringements

9A. Competition disqualification order

(1) The court must make a disqualification order against a person if the following two conditions are satisfied in relation to him.

(2) The first condition is that an undertaking which is a company of which he is a director commits a breach of competition law.

(3) The second condition is that the court considers that his conduct as a director makes him unfit to be concerned in the management of a company.

(4) An undertaking commits a breach of competition law if it engages in conduct which infringes any of the following—
(a) the Chapter 1 prohibition (within the meaning of the Competition Act 1998) (prohibition on agreements, etc preventing, restricting or distorting competition);
(b) the Chapter 2 prohibition (within the meaning of that Act) (prohibition on abuse of a dominant position);
(c) Article 101 of the Treaty on the Functioning of the European Union (prohibition on agreements, etc preventing, restricting or distorting competition);
(d) Article 102 of that Treaty (prohibition on abuse of a dominant position).

(5) For the purpose of deciding under subsection (3) whether a person is unfit to be concerned in the management of a company the court—
(a) must have regard to whether subsection (6) applies to him;
(b) may have regard to his conduct as a director of a company in connection with any other breach of competition law;
(c) must not have regard to the matters mentioned in Schedule 1.

(6) This subsection applies to a person if as a director of the company—
(a) his conduct contributed to the breach of competition law mentioned in subsection (2);
(b) his conduct did not contribute to the breach but he had reasonable grounds to suspect that the conduct of the undertaking constituted the breach and he took no steps to prevent it;
(c) he did not know but ought to have known that the conduct of the undertaking constituted the breach.

(7) For the purposes of subsection (6)(a) it is immaterial whether the person knew that the conduct of the undertaking constituted the breach.

(8) For the purposes of subsection (4)(a) or (c) references to the conduct of an undertaking are references to its conduct taken with the conduct of one or more other undertakings.

(9) The maximum period of disqualification under this section is 15 years.

(10) An application under this section for a disqualification order may be made by the OFT or by a specified regulator.

(11) Section 60 of the Competition Act 1998 (consistent treatment of questions arising under United Kingdom and EU law) applies in relation to any question arising by virtue of subsection (4)(a) or (b) above as it applies in relation to any question arising under Part 1 of that Act.

9B. Competition undertakings

(1) This section applies if—

(a) the OFT or a specified regulator thinks that in relation to any person an undertaking which is a company of which he is a director has committed or is committing a breach of competition law,

(b) the OFT or the specified regulator thinks that the conduct of the person as a director makes him unfit to be concerned in the management of a company, and

(c) the person offers to give the OFT or the specified regulator (as the case may be) a disqualification undertaking.

(2) The OFT or the specified regulator (as the case may be) may accept a disqualification undertaking from the person instead of applying for or proceeding with an application for a disqualification order.

(3) A disqualification undertaking is an undertaking by a person that for the period specified in the undertaking he will not—

(a) be a director of a company;

(b) act as receiver of a company's property;

(c) in any way, whether directly or indirectly, be concerned or take part in the promotion, formation or management of a company;

(d) act as an insolvency practitioner.

(4) But a disqualification undertaking may provide that a prohibition falling within subsection (3)(a) to (c) does not apply if the person obtains the leave of the court.

(5) The maximum period which may be specified in a disqualification undertaking is 15 years.

(6) If a disqualification undertaking is accepted from a person who is already subject to a disqualification undertaking under this Act or to a disqualification order the periods specified in those undertakings or the undertaking and the order (as the case may be) run concurrently.

(7) Subsections (4) to (8) of section 9A apply for the purposes of this section as they apply for the purposes of that section but in the application of subsection (5) of that section the reference to the court must be construed as a reference to the OFT or a specified regulator (as the case may be).

9C. Competition investigations

(1) If the OFT or a specified regulator has reasonable grounds for suspecting that a breach of competition law has occurred it or he (as the case may be) may carry out an investigation for the purpose of deciding whether to make an application under section 9A for a disqualification order.

(2) For the purposes of such an investigation sections 26 to 30 of the Competition Act 1998 apply to the OFT and the specified regulators as they apply to the OFT for the purposes of an investigation under section 25 of that Act.

(3) Subsection (4) applies if as a result of an investigation under this section the OFT or a specified regulator proposes to apply under section 9A for a disqualification order.

(4) Before making the application the OFT or regulator (as the case may be) must—

(a) give notice to the person likely to be affected by the application, and

(b) give that person an opportunity to make representations.

9D. Co-ordination

(1) The Secretary of State may make regulations for the purpose of co-ordinating the performance of functions under sections 9A to 9C (relevant functions) which are exercisable concurrently by two or more persons.

(2) Section 54(5) to (7) of the Competition Act 1998 (c. 41) applies to regulations made under this section as it applies to regulations made under that section and for that purpose in that section—

(a) references to Part 1 functions must be read as references to relevant functions;

(b) references to a regulator must be read as references to a specified regulator;

(c) a competent person also includes any of the specified regulators.

(3) The power to make regulations under this section must be exercised by statutory instrument subject to annulment in pursuance of a resolution of either House of Parliament.

(4) Such a statutory instrument may—

(a) contain such incidental, supplemental, consequential and transitional provision as the Secretary of State thinks appropriate;

(b) make different provision for different cases.

9E. Interpretation

(1) This section applies for the purposes of sections 9A to 9D.

(2) Each of the following is a specified regulator for the purposes of a breach of competition law in relation to a matter in respect of which he or it has a function—

(a) the Office of Communications;

(b) the Gas and Electricity Markets Authority;

(c) the Water Services Regulation Authority;

(d) the Office of Rail Regulation;

(e) the Civil Aviation Authority;

(f) Monitor.

(3) The court is the High Court or (in Scotland) the Court of Session.

(4) Conduct includes omission.

(5) Director includes shadow director.

Other cases of disqualification

10. Participation in wrongful trading

(1) Where the court makes a declaration under section 213 or 214 of the Insolvency Act 1986 that a person is liable to make a contribution to a company's assets, then, whether or not an application for such an order is made by any person, the court may, if it thinks fit, also make a disqualification order against the person to whom the declaration relates.

(2) The maximum period of disqualification under this section is 15 years.

11. Undischarged bankrupts

(1) It is an offence for a person to act as director of a company or directly or indirectly to take part in or be concerned in the promotion, formation or management of a company, without the leave of the court, at a time when—

(a) he is an undischarged bankrupt,

(aa) a moratorium period under a debt relief order applies in relation to him, or

(b) a bankruptcy restrictions order or a debt relief restrictions order is in force in respect of him.

(2) For this purpose, the court is—

(a) in the case of a person adjudged bankrupt or, in Scotland, whose estate was sequestrated, the court by which the person was adjudged bankrupt or sequestration of the person's estate was awarded,

(b) in the case of a person in respect of whom a court made a debt relief restrictions order (under Schedule 4ZB of the Insolvency Act 1986), the court by which the order was made, and

(c) in the case of any other person, the court to which the person would make an application under section 251M(1) of the Insolvency Act 1986 (if the person were dissatisfied as mentioned there).

(3) In England and Wales, the leave of the court shall not be given unless notice of intention to apply for it has been served on the official receiver; and it is the latter's duty, if he is of opinion that it is contrary to the public interest that the application should be granted, to attend on the hearing of the application and oppose it.

(4) In this section "company" includes a company incorporated outside Great Britain that has an established place of business in Great Britain.

12. *Failure to pay under county court administration order*

(1) The following has effect where a court under section 429 of the Insolvency Act revokes an administration order under Part VI of the County Courts Act 1984.

(2) A person to whom *that section applies by virtue of the order under section 429(2)(b)* shall not, except with the leave of the court which made the order, act as director or liquidator of, or directly or indirectly take part or be concerned in the promotion, formation or management of, a company.

Note. This section is amended as follows by the Tribunals, Courts and Enforcement Act 2007, ss. 106(2), 146, Sch. 16, para. 5, Sch. 23, Pt. 5, as from a day to be appointed: the section heading is substituted by the words "Disabilities on revocation of administration order"; subsection (1) is repealed; and in subsection (2) the italicized words are repealed and substituted by the words "section 429 of the Insolvency Act 1986 applies by virtue of an order under subsection (2) of that section".

12A. Northern Irish disqualification orders

A person subject to a disqualification order under the Company Directors Disqualification (Northern Ireland) Order 2002—

(a) shall not be a director of a company, act as receiver of a company's property or in any way, whether directly or indirectly, be concerned or take part in the promotion, formation or management of a company unless (in each case) he has the leave of the High Court of Northern Ireland, and

(b) shall not act as an insolvency practitioner.

12B. Northern Irish disqualification undertakings

A person subject to a disqualification undertaking under the Company Directors Disqualification (Northern Ireland) Order 2002—

(a) shall not be a director of a company, act as receiver of a company's property or in any way, whether directly or indirectly, be concerned or take part in the promotion, formation or management of a company unless (in each case) he has the leave of the High Court of Northern Ireland, and

(b) shall not act as an insolvency practitioner.

Consequences of contravention

13. Criminal penalties

(1) If a person acts in contravention of a disqualification order or disqualification undertaking or in contravention of section 12(2), 12A or 12B, or is guilty of an offence under section 11, he is liable—

(a) on conviction on indictment, to imprisonment for not more than 2 years or a fine, or both; and

(b) on summary conviction, to imprisonment for not more than 6 months or a fine not exceeding the statutory maximum, or both.

14. Offences by body corporate

(1) Where a body corporate is guilty of an offence of acting in contravention of a disqualification order or disqualification undertaking or in contravention of section 12A or 12B, and it is proved that the offence occurred with the consent or connivance of, or was attributable to any neglect on

the part of any director, manager, secretary or other similar officer of the body corporate, or any person who was purporting to act in any such capacity he, as well as the body corporate, is guilty of the offence and liable to be proceeded against and punished accordingly.

(2) Where the affairs of a body corporate are managed by its members, subsection (1) applies in relation to the acts and defaults of a member in connection with his functions of management as if he were a director of the body corporate.

15. Personal liability for company's debts where person acts while disqualified

(1) A person is personally responsible for all the relevant debts of a company if at any time—

(a) in contravention of a disqualification order or disqualification undertaking or in contravention of section 11, 12A or 12B of this Act he is involved in the management of the company, or

(b) as a person who is involved in the management of the company, he acts or is willing to act on instructions given without the leave of the court by a person whom he knows at that time—

(i) to be the subject of a disqualification order made or disqualification undertaking accepted under this Act or under the Company Directors Disqualification (Northern Ireland) Order 2002, or

(ii) to be an undischarged bankrupt.

(2) Where a person is personally responsible under this section for the relevant debts of a company, he is jointly and severally liable in respect of those debts with the company and any other person who, whether under this section or otherwise, is so liable.

(3) For the purposes of this section the relevant debts of a company are—

(a) in relation to a person who is personally responsible under paragraph (a) of subsection (1), such debts and other liabilities of the company as are incurred at a time when that person was involved in the management of the company, and

(b) in relation to a person who is personally responsible under paragraph (b) of that subsection, such debts and other liabilities of the company as are incurred at a time when that person was acting or was willing to act on instructions given as mentioned in that paragraph.

(4) For the purposes of this section, a person is involved in the management of a company if he is a director of the company or if he is concerned, whether directly or indirectly, or takes part, in the management of the company.

(5) For the purposes of this section a person who, as a person involved in the management of a company, has at any time acted on instructions given without the leave of the court by a person whom he knew at that time—

(a) to be the subject of a disqualification order made or disqualification undertaking accepted under this Act or under the Company Directors Disqualification (Northern Ireland) Order 2002, or

(b) to be an undischarged bankrupt,

is presumed, unless the contrary is shown, to have been willing at any time thereafter to act on any instructions given by that person.

Supplementary provisions

16. Application for disqualification order

(1) A person intending to apply for the making of a disqualification order by the court having jurisdiction to wind up a company shall give not less than 10 days' notice of his intention to the person against whom the order is sought; and on the hearing of the application the last-mentioned person may appear and himself give evidence or call witnesses.

(2) An application to a court with jurisdiction to wind up companies for the making against any person of a disqualification order under any of sections 2 to 4 may be made by the Secretary of State or the official receiver, or by the liquidator or any past or present member or creditor of any company in relation to which that person has committed or is alleged to have committed an offence or other default.

(3) On the hearing of any application under this Act made by a person falling within subsection (4), the applicant shall appear and call the attention of the court to any matters which seem to him to be relevant, and may himself give evidence or call witnesses.

(4) The following fall within this subsection—

(a) the Secretary of State;

(b) the official receiver;

(c) the OFT;

(d) the liquidator;

(e) a specified regulator (within the meaning of section 9E).

17. Application for leave under an order or undertaking

(1) Where a person is subject to a disqualification order made by a court having jurisdiction to wind up companies, any application for leave for the purposes of section 1(1)(a) shall be made to that court.

(2) Where—

(a) a person is subject to a disqualification order made under section 2 by a court other than a court having jurisdiction to wind up companies, or

(b) a person is subject to a disqualification order made under section 5,

any application for leave for the purposes of section 1(1)(a) shall be made to any court which, when the order was made, had jurisdiction to wind up the company (or, if there is more than one such company, any of the companies) to which the offence (or any of the offences) in question related.

(3) Where a person is subject to a disqualification undertaking accepted at any time under section 7 or 8, any application for leave for the purposes of section 1A(1)(a) shall be made to any court to which, if the Secretary of State had applied for a disqualification order under the section in question at that time, his application could have been made.

(3A) Where a person is subject to a disqualification undertaking accepted at any time under section 9B any application for leave for the purposes of section 9B(4) must be made to the High Court or (in Scotland) the Court of Session.

(4) But where a person is subject to two or more disqualification orders or undertakings (or to one or more disqualification orders and to one or more disqualification undertakings), any application for leave for the purposes of section 1(1)(a), 1A(1)(a) or 9B(4) shall be made to any court to which any such application relating to the latest order to be made, or undertaking to be accepted, could be made.

(5) On the hearing of an application for leave for the purposes of section 1(1)(a) or 1A(1)(a), the Secretary of State shall appear and call the attention of the court to any matters which seem to him to be relevant, and may himself give evidence or call witnesses.

(6) Subsection (5) does not apply to an application for leave for the purposes of section 1(1)(a) if the application for the disqualification order was made under section 9A.

(7) In such a case and in the case of an application for leave for the purposes of section 9B(4) on the hearing of the application whichever of the OFT or a specified regulator (within the meaning of section 9E) applied for the order or accepted the undertaking (as the case may be)—

(a) must appear and draw the attention of the court to any matters which appear to it or him (as the case may be) to be relevant;

(b) may give evidence or call witnesses.

18. Register of disqualification orders and undertakings

(1) The Secretary of State may make regulations requiring officers of courts to furnish him with such particulars as the regulations may specify of cases in which—

(a) a disqualification order is made, or

(b) any action is taken by a court in consequence of which such an order or a disqualification undertaking is varied or ceases to be in force, or

(c) leave is granted by a court for a person subject to such an order to do any thing which otherwise the order prohibits him from doing, or

(d) leave is granted by a court for a person subject to such an undertaking to do anything which otherwise the undertaking prohibits him from doing;

and the regulations may specify the time within which, and the form and manner in which, such particulars are to be furnished.

(2) The Secretary of State shall, from the particulars so furnished, continue to maintain the register of orders, and of cases in which leave has been granted as mentioned in subsection (1)(c), . . .

(2A) The Secretary of State must include in the register such particulars as he considers appropriate of—

(a) disqualification undertakings accepted by him under section 7 or 8;

(b) disqualification undertakings accepted by the OFT or a specified regulator under section 9B;

(c) cases in which leave has been granted as mentioned in subsection (1)(d).

(3) When an order or undertaking of which entry is made in the register ceases to be in force, the Secretary of State shall delete the entry from the register and all particulars relating to it which have been furnished to him under this section or any previous corresponding provision and, in the case of a disqualification undertaking, any other particulars he has included in the register.

(4) The register shall be open to inspection on payment of such fee as may be specified by the Secretary of State in regulations.

(4A) Regulations under this section may extend the preceding provisions of this section, to such extent and with such modifications as may be specified in the regulations, to disqualification orders . . . or disqualification undertakings made under the Company Directors Disqualification (Northern Ireland) Order 2002.

(5) Regulations under this section shall be made by statutory instrument subject to annulment in pursuance of a resolution of either House of Parliament.

19. Special savings from repealed enactments

Schedule 2 to this Act has effect—

(a) in connection with certain transitional cases arising under sections 93 and 94 of the Companies Act 1981, so as to limit the power to make a disqualification order, or to restrict the duration of an order, by reference to events occurring or things done before the sections came into force,

(b) to preserve orders made under section 28 of the Companies Act 1976 (repealed by the Act of 1981), and

(c) to preclude any applications for a disqualification order under section 6 or 8, where the relevant company went into liquidation before 28th April 1986.

Miscellaneous and general

20. Admissibility in evidence of statements

(1) In any proceedings (whether or not under this Act), any statement made in pursuance of a requirement imposed by or under sections 6 to 10, 15 or 19(c) of, or Schedule 1 to, this Act, or by or under rules made for the purposes of this Act under the Insolvency Act 1986, may be used in evidence against any person making or concurring in making the statement.

(2) However, in criminal proceedings in which any such person is charged with an offence to which this subsection applies—

(a) no evidence relating to the statement may be adduced, and

(b) no question relating to it may be asked,

by or on behalf of the prosecution, unless evidence relating to it is adduced, or a question relating to it is asked, in the proceedings by or on behalf of that person.

(3) Subsection (2) applies to any offence other than—

(a) an offence which is—

(i) created by rules made for the purposes of this Act under the Insolvency Act 1986, and

(ii) designated for the purposes of this subsection by such rules or by regulations made by the Secretary of State;

(b) an offence which is—

(i) created by regulations made under any such rules, and

(ii) designated for the purposes of this subsection by such regulations;

(c) an offence under section 5 of the Perjury Act 1911 (false statements made otherwise than on oath); or

(d) an offence under section 44(2) of the Criminal Law (Consolidation) (Scotland) Act 1995 (false statements made otherwise than on oath).

(4) Regulations under subsection (3)(a)(ii) shall be made by statutory instrument and, after being made, shall be laid before each House of Parliament.

20A. Legal professional privilege

In proceedings against a person for an offence under this Act nothing in this Act is to be taken to require any person to disclose any information that he is entitled to refuse to disclose on grounds of legal professional privilege (in Scotland, confidentiality of communications).

21. Interaction with Insolvency Act 1986

(1) References in this Act to the official receiver, in relation to the winding up of a company or the bankruptcy of an individual, are to any person who, by virtue of section 399 of the Insolvency Act 1986, is authorised to act as the official receiver in relation to that winding up or bankruptcy; and, in accordance with section 401(2) of that Act, references in this Act to an official receiver includes a person appointed as his deputy.

(2) Sections 1A, 6 to 10, 13, 14, 15, 19(c) and 20 of, and Schedule 1 to, this Act and sections 1 and 17 of this Act as they apply for the purposes of those provisions are deemed included in Parts I to VII of the Insolvency Act 1986 for the purposes of the following sections of that Act—

section 411 (power to make insolvency rules);

section 414 (fees orders);

section 420 (orders extending provisions about insolvent companies to insolvent partnerships);

section 422 (modification of such provisions in their application to recognised banks); . . .

. . .

(3) Section 434 of that Act (Crown application) applies to sections 1A, 6 to 10, 13, 14, 15, 19(c) and 20 of, and Schedule 1 to, this Act and sections 1 and 17 of this Act as they apply for the purposes of those provisions as it does to the provisions of that Act which are there mentioned.

(4) For the purposes of summary proceedings in Scotland, section 431 of that Act applies to summary proceedings for an offence under section 11 or 13 of this Act as it applies to summary proceedings for an offence under Parts I to VII of that Act.

21A. Bank insolvency

Section 121 of the Banking Act 2009 provides for this Act to apply in relation to bank insolvency as it applies in relation to liquidation.

21B. Bank administration

Section 155 of the Banking Act 2009 provides for this Act to apply in relation to bank administration as it applies in relation to liquidation.

21C. Building society insolvency and special administration

Section 90E of the Building Societies Act 1986 provides for this Act to apply in relation to building society insolvency and building society special administration as it applies in relation to liquidation.

22. Interpretation

(1) This section has effect with respect to the meaning of expressions used in this Act, and applies unless the context otherwise requires.

(2) "Company" means—

(a) a company registered under the Companies Act 2006 in Great Britain, or
(b) a company that may be wound up under Part 5 of the Insolvency Act 1986 (unregistered companies).

(3) Section 247 in Part VII of the Insolvency Act 1986 (interpretation for the first Group of Parts to that Act) applies as regards references to a company's insolvency and to its going into liquidation; and "administrative receiver" has the meaning given by section 251 of that Act and references to acting as an insolvency practitioner are to be read in accordance with section 388 of that Act.

(4) "Director" includes any person occupying the position of director, by whatever name called … .

(5) "Shadow director", in relation to a company, means a person in accordance with whose directions or instructions the directors of the company are accustomed to act (but so that a person is not deemed a shadow director by reason only that the directors act on advice given by him in a professional capacity).

(6) "Body corporate" and "officer" have the same meaning as in the Companies Acts (see section 1173(1) of the Companies Act 2006).

(7) "The Companies Acts" has the meaning given by section 2(1) of the Companies Act 2006.

(8) Any reference to provisions, or a particular provision, of the Companies Acts or the Insolvency Act 1986 includes the corresponding provisions or provision of corresponding earlier legislation.

(9) Subject to the provisions of this section, expressions that are defined for the purposes of the Companies Acts (see section 1174 of, and Schedule 8 to, the Companies Act 2006) have the same meaning in this Act.

(10) Any reference to acting as receiver—
(a) includes acting as manager or as both receiver and manager, but
(b) does not include acting as administrative receiver;
and "receivership" is to be read accordingly.

22A. Application of Act to building societies

(1) This Act applies to building societies as it applies to companies.

(2) References in this Act to a company, or to a director or an officer of a company include, respectively, references to a building society within the meaning of the Building Societies Act 1986 or to a director or officer, within the meaning of that Act, of a building society.

(3) In relation to a building society the definition of "shadow director" in section 22(5) applies with the substitution of "building society" for "company".

(4) In the application of Schedule 1 to the directors of a building society, references to provisions of the Companies Act 2006 or the Insolvency Act 1986 include references to the corresponding provisions of the Building Societies Act 1986.

22B. Application of Act to incorporated friendly societies

(1) This Act applies to incorporated friendly societies as it applies to companies.

(2) References in this Act to a company, or to a director or an officer of a company include, respectively, references to an incorporated friendly society within the meaning of the Friendly Societies Act 1992 or to a member of the committee of management or officer, within the meaning of the Act, of an incorporated friendly society.

(3) In relation to an incorporated friendly society every reference to a shadow director shall be omitted.

(4) In the application of Schedule 1 to the members of the committee of management of an incorporated friendly society, references to provisions of the Companies Act 2006 or the Insolvency Act 1986 include references to the corresponding provisions of the Friendly Societies Act 1992.

22C. Application of Act to NHS foundation trusts

(1) This Act applies to NHS foundation trusts as it applies to companies within the meaning of this Act.

(2) References in this Act to a company, or to a director or officer of a company, include, respectively, references to an NHS foundation trust or to a director or officer of the trust; but references to shadow directors are omitted.

(3) In the application of Schedule 1 to the directors of an NHS foundation trust, references to the provisions of the Companies Act 2006 or the Insolvency Act 1986 include references to the corresponding provisions of Chapter 5 of Part 2 of the National Health Service Act 2006.

22D. Application of Act to open-ended investment companies

(1) This Act applies to open-ended investment companies with the following modifications.

(2) In section 8(1) (disqualification after investigation), the reference to investigative material shall be read as including a report made by inspectors under regulations made by virtue of section 262(2)(k) of the Financial Services and Markets Act 2000.

(3) In the application of Part 1 of Schedule 1 (matters for determining unfitness of directors: matters applicable in all cases) in relation to a director of an open-ended investment company, a reference to a provision of the Companies Act 2006 is to be taken to be a reference to the corresponding provision of the Open-Ended Investment Companies Regulations 2001 or of rules made under regulation 6 of those Regulations.

(4) In this section "open-ended investment company" has the meaning given by section 236 of the Financial Services and Markets Act 2000.

22E. Application of Act to societies registered under the Industrial and Provident Societies Act 1965

(1) In this section "registered society" means a society registered or deemed to be registered under the Industrial and Provident Societies Act 1965 ("the 1965 Act").

(2) This Act applies to registered societies as it applies to companies.

(3) Accordingly, in this Act—

(a) references to a company include a registered society, and

(b) references to a director or an officer of a company include a member of the committee or an officer of a registered society.

In paragraph (b) "committee" and "officer" have the same meaning as in the 1965 Act: see section 74(1) of that Act.

(4) As they apply in relation to registered societies, the provisions of this Act have effect with the following modifications—

(a) in section 2(1) (disqualification on conviction of indictable offence), the reference to striking off includes cancellation of the registration of a society under the 1965 Act;

(b) in section 3 (disqualification for persistent breaches) and section 5 (disqualification on summary conviction), references to the companies legislation shall be read as references to the legislation relating to registered societies;

(c) in section 8(1) (disqualification after investigation), the reference to investigative material shall be read as including—

(i) any report made under section 47 or 49(1) of the 1965 Act (inspection of books or appointment of inspector), and

(ii) any information, books, accounts or other documents obtained under section 48 of the 1965 Act;

(d) references to the registrar shall be read as references to the Financial Services Authority;

(e) references to a shadow director shall be disregarded.

(5) In the application of Schedule 1 to the members of the committee of a registered society, references to provisions of the Companies Act 2006 shall be read as including references to the corresponding provisions of the legislation relating to registered societies.

(6) In this section "the legislation relating to registered societies" means the Industrial and Provident Societies Acts 1965 to 2003, the Credit Unions Act 1979 and the Co-operative and Community Benefit Societies and Credit Unions Act 2010.

Note. This section is inserted by the Co-operative and Community Benefit Societies and Credit Unions Act 2010, s. 3, as from a day to be appointed. The following amendments are also made by section 2 of the 2010

Act, as from a day to be appointed: references to "Co-operative and Community Benefit Societies and Credit Unions Act 1965" are substituted for "Industrial and Provident Societies Act 1965" in the section heading and subsection (1); and "Co-operative and Community Benefit Societies and Credit Unions Acts 1965" is substituted for "Industrial and Provident Societies Acts 1965" in subsection (6).

22F Application of Act to charitable incorporated organisations

(1) This Act applies to charitable incorporated organisations ("CIOs") as it applies to companies.

(2) Accordingly, in this Act—

(a) references to a company are to be read as including references to a CIO;

(b) references to a director or an officer of a company are to be read as including references to a charity trustee of a CIO; and

(c) any reference to the Insolvency Act 1986 is to be read as including a reference to that Act as it applies to CIOs.

(3) As they apply in relation to CIOs, the provisions of this Act have effect with the following modifications—

(a) in section 2(1), the reference to striking off is to be read as including a reference to dissolution;

(b) in section 4(1)(a), the reference to an offence under section 993 of the Companies Act 2006 is to be read as including a reference to an offence under regulation 60 of the Charitable Incorporated Organisations (General) Regulations 2012 (fraudulent trading);

(c) sections 9A to 9E are to be disregarded;

(d) references to any of sections 9A to 9E are to be disregarded;

(e) references to a shadow director are to be disregarded.

(4) In the application of Schedule 1 to the charity trustees of a CIO, references to the provisions of the Companies Act 2006 are to be read as including references to the corresponding provisions (if any) of the Charities Act 2011 and regulations made under that Act.

(5) In this section "charity trustees" has the meaning given by section 177 of the Charities Act 2011.

23. Transitional provisions, savings, repeals

(1) The transitional provisions and savings in Schedule 3 to this Act have effect, and are without prejudice to anything in the Interpretation Act 1978 with regard to the effect of repeals.

(2) The enactments specified in the second column of Schedule 4 to this Act are repealed to the extent specified in the third column of that Schedule.

24. Extent

(1) This Act extends to England and Wales and to Scotland.

(2) Nothing in this Act extends to Northern Ireland.

25. Commencement

This Act comes into force simultaneously with the Insolvency Act 1986.

26. Citation

This Act may be cited as the Company Directors Disqualification Act 1986.

SCHEDULE 1

Section 9

MATTERS FOR DETERMINING UNFITNESS OF DIRECTORS

PART I

MATTERS APPLICABLE IN ALL CASES

1. Any misfeasance or breach of any fiduciary or other duty by the director in relation to the company, including in particular any breach by the director of a duty under Chapter 2 of Part 10 of the Companies Act 2006 (general duties of directors) owed to the company.

2. Any misapplication or retention by the director of, or any conduct by the director giving rise to an obligation to account for, any money or other property of the company.
3. The extent of the director's responsibility for the company entering into any transaction liable to be set aside under Part XVI of the Insolvency Act 1986 (provisions against debt avoidance).
4. The extent of the director's responsibility for any failure by the company to comply with any of the following provisions of the Companies Act 2006—
   (a) section 113 (register of members);
   (b) section 114 (register to be kept available for inspection);
   (c) section 162 (register of directors);
   (d) section 165 (register of directors' residential addresses);
   (e) section 167 (duty to notify registrar of changes: directors);
   (f) section 275 (register of secretaries);
   (g) section 276 (duty to notify registrar of changes: secretaries);
   (h) section 386 (duty to keep accounting records);
   (i) section 388 (where and for how long accounting records to be kept);
   (j) section 854 (duty to make annual returns);
   (k) section 860 (duty to register charges);
   (l) section 878 (duty to register charges: companies registered in Scotland).
5. The extent of the director's responsibility for any failure by the directors of the company to comply with the following provisions of the Companies Act 2006—
   (a) section 394 or 399 (duty to prepare annual accounts);
   (b) section 414 or 450 (approval and signature of abbreviated accounts); or
   (c) section 433 (name of signatory to be stated in published copy of accounts).

5A. . . .

PART II
MATTERS APPLICABLE WHERE COMPANY HAS BECOME INSOLVENT

6. The extent of the director's responsibility for the causes of the company becoming insolvent.
7. The extent of the director's responsibility for any failure by the company to supply any goods or services which have been paid for (in whole or in part).
8. The extent of the director's responsibility for the company entering into any transaction or giving any preference, being a transaction or preference—
   (a) liable to be set aside under section 127 or sections 238 to 240 of the Insolvency Act 1986, or
   (b) challengeable under section 242 or 243 of that Act or under any rule of law in Scotland.
9. The extent of the director's responsibility for any failure by the directors of the company to comply with section 98 of the Insolvency Act 1986 (duty to call creditors' meeting in creditors' voluntary winding up).
10. Any failure by the director to comply with any obligation imposed on him by or under any of the following provisions of the Insolvency Act 1986—
   (a) paragraph 47 of Schedule B1 (company's statement of affairs in administration);
   (b) section 47 (statement of affairs to administrative receiver);
   (c) section 66 (statement of affairs in Scottish receivership);
   (d) section 99 (directors' duty to attend meeting; statement of affairs in creditors' voluntary winding up);
   (e) section 131 (statement of affairs in winding up by the court);
   (f) section 234 (duty of any one with company property to deliver it up);
   (g) section 235 (duty to co-operate with liquidator, etc).

SCHEDULE 2

Section 19

SAVINGS FROM COMPANIES ACT 1981 SS 93, 94, AND INSOLVENCY ACT 1985 SCHEDULE 9

1. Sections 2 and 4(1)(b) do not apply in relation to anything done before 15th June 1982 by a person in his capacity as liquidator of a company or as receiver or manager of a company's property.
2. Subject to paragraph 1—
   (a) section 2 applies in a case where a person is convicted on indictment of an offence which he committed (and, in the case of a continuing offence, has ceased to commit) before 15th June 1982; but in such a case a disqualification order under that section shall not be made for a period in excess of 5 years;
   (b) that section does not apply in a case where a person is convicted summarily—
      (i) in England and Wales, if he had consented so to be tried before that date, or
      (ii) in Scotland, if the summary proceedings commenced before that date.
3. Subject to paragraph 1, section 4 applies in relation to an offence committed or other thing done before 15th June 1982; but a disqualification order made on the grounds of such an offence or other thing done shall not be made for a period in excess of 5 years.
4. The powers of a court under section 5 are not exercisable in a case where a person is convicted of an offence which he committed (and, in the case of a continuing offence, had ceased to commit) before 15th June 1982.
5. For purposes of section 3(1) and section 5, no account is to be taken of any offence which was committed, or any default order which was made, before 1st June 1977.
6. An order made under section 28 of the Companies Act 1976 has effect as if made under section 3 of this Act; and an application made before 15th June 1982 for such an order is to be treated as an application for an order under the section last mentioned.
7. Where—
   (a) an application is made for a disqualification order under section 6 of this Act by virtue of paragraph (a) of subsection (2) of that section, and
   (b) the company in question went into liquidation before 28th April 1986 (the coming into force of the provision replaced by section 6),

   the court shall not make an order under that section unless it could have made a disqualification order under section 300 of the Companies Act 1985 as it had effect immediately before the date specified in sub-paragraph (b) above.
8. An application shall not be made under section 8 of this Act in relation to a report made or information or documents obtained before 28th April 1986.

SCHEDULE 3

Section 23(1)

TRANSITIONAL PROVISIONS AND SAVINGS

1. In this Schedule, "the former enactments" means so much of the Companies Act 1985, and so much of the Insolvency Act 1986, as is repealed and replaced by this Act; and "the appointed day" means the day on which this Act comes into force.
2. So far as anything done or treated as done under or for the purposes of any provision of the former enactments could have been done under or for the purposes of the corresponding provision of this Act, it is not invalidated by the repeal of that provision but has effect as if done under or for the purposes of the corresponding provision; and any order, regulation, rule or other instrument made or having effect under any provision of the former enactments shall, insofar as its effect is preserved by this paragraph, be treated for all purposes as made and having effect under the corresponding provision.
3. Where any period of time specified in a provision of the former enactments is current immediately before the appointed day, this Act has effect as if the corresponding provision had

been in force when the period began to run; and (without prejudice to the foregoing) any period of time so specified and current is deemed for the purposes of this Act—

(a) to run from the date or event from which it was running immediately before the appointed day, and

(b) to expire (subject to any provision of this Act for its extension) whenever it would have expired if this Act had not been passed;

and any rights, priorities, liabilities, reliefs, obligations, requirements, powers, duties or exemptions dependent on the beginning, duration or end of such a period as above mentioned shall be under this Act as they were or would have been under the former enactments.

4. Where in any provision of this Act there is a reference to another such provision, and the first-mentioned provision operates, or is capable of operating, in relation to things done or omitted, or events occurring or not occurring, in the past (including in particular past acts of compliance with any enactment, failures of compliance, contraventions, offences and convictions of offences) the reference to the other provision is to be read as including a reference to the corresponding provision of the former enactments.

5. Offences committed before the appointed day under any provision of the former enactments may, notwithstanding any repeal by this Act, be prosecuted and punished after that day as if this Act had not passed.

6. A reference in any enactment, instrument or document (whether express or implied, and in whatever phraseology) to a provision of the former enactments (including the corresponding provision of any yet earlier enactment) is to be read, where necessary to retain for the enactment, instrument or document the same force and effect as it would have had but for the passing of this Act, as, or as including, a reference to the corresponding provision by which it is replaced in this Act.

Corporate Manslaughter and Corporate Homicide Act 2007

2007 c. 19

An Act to create a new offence that, in England and Wales or Northern Ireland, is to be called corporate manslaughter and, in Scotland, is to be called corporate homicide; and to make provision in connection with that offence.

[26th July 2007]

Corporate manslaughter and corporate homicide

1. The offence

(1) An organisation to which this section applies is guilty of an offence if the way in which its activities are managed or organised—
- (a) causes a person's death, and
- (b) amounts to a gross breach of a relevant duty of care owed by the organisation to the deceased.

(2) The organisations to which this section applies are—
- (a) a corporation;
- (b) a department or other body listed in Schedule 1;
- (c) a police force;
- (d) a partnership, or a trade union or employers' association, that is an employer.

(3) An organisation is guilty of an offence under this section only if the way in which its activities are managed or organised by its senior management is a substantial element in the breach referred to in subsection (1).

(4) For the purposes of this Act—
- (a) "relevant duty of care" has the meaning given by section 2, read with sections 3 to 7;
- (b) a breach of a duty of care by an organisation is a "gross" breach if the conduct alleged to amount to a breach of that duty falls far below what can reasonably be expected of the organisation in the circumstances;
- (c) "senior management", in relation to an organisation, means the persons who play significant roles in—
  - (i) the making of decisions about how the whole or a substantial part of its activities are to be managed or organised, or
  - (ii) the actual managing or organising of the whole or a substantial part of those activities.

(5) The offence under this section is called—
- (a) corporate manslaughter, in so far as it is an offence under the law of England and Wales or Northern Ireland;
- (b) corporate homicide, in so far as it is an offence under the law of Scotland.

(6) An organisation that is guilty of corporate manslaughter or corporate homicide is liable on conviction on indictment to a fine.

(7) The offence of corporate homicide is indictable only in the High Court of Justiciary.

2. Meaning of "relevant duty of care"

(1) A "relevant duty of care", in relation to an organisation, means any of the following duties owed by it under the law of negligence—
- (a) a duty owed to its employees or to other persons working for the organisation or performing services for it;
- (b) a duty owed as occupier of premises;
- (c) a duty owed in connection with—
  - (i) the supply by the organisation of goods or services (whether for consideration or not),
  - (ii) the carrying on by the organisation of any construction or maintenance operations,

(iii) the carrying on by the organisation of any other activity on a commercial basis, or
(iv) the use or keeping by the organisation of any plant, vehicle or other thing;
(d) a duty owed to a person who, by reason of being a person within subsection (2), is someone for whose safety the organisation is responsible.

(2) A person is within this subsection if—
(a) he is detained at a custodial institution or in a custody area at a court, a police station or customs premises;
(aa) he is detained in service custody premises;
(b) he is detained at a removal centre or short-term holding facility;
(c) he is being transported in a vehicle, or being held in any premises, in pursuance of prison escort arrangements or immigration escort arrangements;
(d) he is living in secure accommodation in which he has been placed;
(e) he is a detained patient.

(3) Subsection (1) is subject to sections 3 to 7.

(4) A reference in subsection (1) to a duty owed under the law of negligence includes a reference to a duty that would be owed under the law of negligence but for any statutory provision under which liability is imposed in place of liability under that law.

(5) For the purposes of this Act, whether a particular organisation owes a duty of care to a particular individual is a question of law.
The judge must make any findings of fact necessary to decide that question.

(6) For the purposes of this Act there is to be disregarded—
(a) any rule of the common law that has the effect of preventing a duty of care from being owed by one person to another by reason of the fact that they are jointly engaged in unlawful conduct;
(b) any such rule that has the effect of preventing a duty of care from being owed to a person by reason of his acceptance of a risk of harm.

(7) In this section—
"construction or maintenance operations" means operations of any of the following descriptions—
(a) construction, installation, alteration, extension, improvement, repair, maintenance, decoration, cleaning, demolition or dismantling of—
(i) any building or structure,
(ii) anything else that forms, or is to form, part of the land, or
(iii) any plant, vehicle or other thing;
(b) operations that form an integral part of, or are preparatory to, or are for rendering complete, any operations within paragraph (a);

"custodial institution" means a prison, a young offender institution, a secure training centre, a young offenders institution, a young offenders centre, a juvenile justice centre or a remand centre;
"customs premises" means premises wholly or partly occupied by persons designated under section 3 (general customs officials) or 11 (customs revenue officials) of the Borders, Citizenship and Immigration Act 2009;
"detained patient" means—
(a) a person who is detained in any premises under—
(i) Part 2 or 3 of the Mental Health Act 1983 ("the 1983 Act"), or
(ii) Part 2 or 3 of the Mental Health (Northern Ireland) Order 1986 ("the 1986 Order");
(b) a person who (otherwise than by reason of being detained as mentioned in paragraph (a)) is deemed to be in legal custody by—
(i) section 137 of the 1983 Act,
(ii) Article 131 of the 1986 Order, or
(iii) article 11 of the Mental Health (Care and Treatment) (Scotland) Act 2003 (Consequential Provisions) Order 2005;

(c) a person who is detained in any premises, or is otherwise in custody, under the Mental Health (Care and Treatment) (Scotland) Act 2003 or Part 6 of the Criminal Procedure (Scotland) Act 1995 or who is detained in a hospital under section 200 of that Act of 1995;

"immigration escort arrangements" means arrangements made under section 156 of the Immigration and Asylum Act 1999;

"the law of negligence" includes—

(a) in relation to England and Wales, the Occupiers' Liability Act 1957, the Defective Premises Act 1972 and the Occupiers' Liability Act 1984;

(b) in relation to Scotland, the Occupiers' Liability (Scotland) Act 1960;

(c) in relation to Northern Ireland, the Occupiers' Liability Act (Northern Ireland) 1957, the Defective Premises (Northern Ireland) Order 1975, the Occupiers' Liability (Northern Ireland) Order 1987 and the Defective Premises (Landlord's Liability) Act (Northern Ireland) 2001;

"prison escort arrangements" means arrangements made under section 80 of the Criminal Justice Act 1991 or under section 102 or 118 of the Criminal Justice and Public Order Act 1994;

"removal centre" and "short-term holding facility" have the meaning given by section 147 of the Immigration and Asylum Act 1999;

"secure accommodation" means accommodation, not consisting of or forming part of a custodial institution, provided for the purpose of restricting the liberty of persons under the age of 18;

"service custody premises" has the meaning given by section 300(7) of the Armed Forces Act 2006.

Companies (Tables A to F) Regulations 1985

S.I. 1985/805

1. These Regulations may be cited as the Companies (Tables A to F) Regulations 1985 and shall come into operation on 1st July 1985.
2. The regulations in Table A and the forms in Tables B, C, D, E and F in the Schedule to these Regulations shall be the regulations and forms of memorandum and articles of association for the purposes of sections 3 and 8 of the Companies Act 1985.

3. …

SCHEDULE

Regulation 2

TABLE A
REGULATIONS FOR MANAGEMENT OF A COMPANY LIMITED BY SHARES

INTERPRETATION

1. In these regulations—

   "the Act" means the Companies Act 1985 including any statutory modification or re-enactment thereof for the time being in force.

   "the articles" means the articles of the company.

   "clear days" in relation to the period of a notice means that period excluding the day when the notice is given or deemed to be given and the day for which it is given or on which it is to take effect.

   "communication" means the same as in the Electronic Communications Act 2000.

   "electronic communication" means the same as in the Electronic Communications Act 2000.

   "executed" includes any mode of execution.

   "office" means the registered office of the company.

   "the holder" in relation to shares means the member whose name is entered in the register of members as the holder of the shares.

   "the seal" means the common seal of the company.

   "secretary" means the secretary of the company or any other person appointed to perform the duties of the secretary of the company, including a joint, assistant or deputy secretary.

   "the United Kingdom" means Great Britain and Northern Ireland.

   Unless the context otherwise requires, words or expressions contained in these regulations bear the same meaning as in the Act but excluding any statutory modification thereof not in force when these regulations become binding on the company.

SHARE CAPITAL

2. Subject to the provisions of the Act and without prejudice to any rights attached to any existing shares, any share may be issued with such rights or restrictions as the company may by ordinary resolution determine.
3. Subject to the provisions of the Act, shares may be issued which are to be redeemed or are to be liable to be redeemed at the option of the company or the holder on such terms and in such manner as may be provided by the articles.

4. The company may exercise the powers of paying commissions conferred by the Act. Subject to the provisions of the Act, any such commission may be satisfied by the payment of cash or by the allotment of fully or partly paid shares or partly in one way and partly in the other.

5. Except as required by law, no person shall be recognised by the company as holding any share upon any trust and (except as otherwise provided by the articles or by law) the company shall not be bound by or recognise any interest in any share except an absolute right to the entirety thereof in the holder.

SHARE CERTIFICATES

6. Every member, upon becoming the holder of any shares, shall be entitled without payment to one certificate for all the shares of each class held by him (and, upon transferring a part of his holding of shares of any class, to a certificate for the balance of such holding) or several certificates each for one or more of his shares of any class, to a certificate for the balance of such holding) or several certificates each for one or more of his shares upon payment for every certificate after the first of such reasonable sum as the directors may determine. Every certificate shall be sealed with the seal and shall specify the number, class and distinguishing numbers (if any) of the shares to which it relates and the amount or respective amounts paid up thereon. The company shall not be bound to issue more than one certificate for shares held jointly by several persons and delivery of a certificate to one joint holder shall be a sufficient delivery to all of them.

7. If a share certificate is defaced, worn-out, lost or destroyed, it may be renewed on such terms (if any) as to evidence and indemnity and payment of the expenses reasonably incurred by the company in investigating evidence as the directors may determine but otherwise free of charge, and (in the case of defacement or wearing-out) on delivery up of the old certificate.

LIEN

8. The company shall have a first and paramount lien on every share (not being a fully paid share) for all moneys (whether presently payable or not) payable at a fixed time or called in respect of that share. The directors may at any time declare any share to be wholly or in part exempt from the provisions of this regulation. The company's lien on a share shall extend to any amount payable in respect of it.

9. The company may sell in such manner as the directors determine any shares on which the company has a lien if a sum in respect of which the lien exists is presently payable and is not paid within fourteen clear days after notice has been given to the holder of the share or to the person entitled to it in consequence of the death or bankruptcy of the holder, demanding payment and stating that if the notice is not complied with the shares may be sold.

10. To give effect to a sale the directors may authorise some person to execute an instrument of transfer of the shares sold to, or in accordance with the directions of, the purchaser. The title of the transferee to the shares shall not be affected by any irregularity in or invalidity of the proceedings in reference to the sale.

11. The net proceeds of the sale, after payment of the costs, shall be applied in payment of so much of the sum for which the lien exists as is presently payable, and any residue shall (upon surrender to the company for cancellation of the certificate for the shares sold and subject to a like lien for any moneys not presently payable as existed upon the shares before the sale) be paid to the person entitled to the shares at the date of the sale.

CALLS ON SHARES AND FORFEITURE

12. Subject to the terms of allotment, the directors may make calls upon the members in respect of any moneys unpaid on their shares (whether in respect of nominal value or premium) and each member shall (subject to receiving at least fourteen clear days' notice specifying when and where payment is to be made) pay to the company as required by the notice the amount called on his

shares. A call may be required to be paid by instalments. A call may, before receipt by the company of any sum due thereunder, be revoked in whole or part and payment of a call may be postponed in whole or part. A person upon whom a call is made shall remain liable for calls made upon him notwithstanding the subsequent transfer of the shares in respect whereof the call was made.

13. A call shall be deemed to have been made at the time when the resolution of the directors authorising the call was passed.

14. The joint holders of a share shall be jointly and severally liable to pay all calls in respect thereof.

15. If a call remains unpaid after it has become due and payable the person from whom it is due and payable shall pay interest on the amount unpaid from the day it became due and payable until it is paid at the rate fixed by the terms of allotment of the share or in the notice of the call or, if no rate is fixed, at the appropriate rate (as defined by the Act) but the directors may waive payment of the interest wholly or in part.

16. An amount payable in respect of a share on allotment or at any fixed date, whether in respect of nominal value or premium or as an instalment of a call, shall be deemed to be a call and if it is not paid the provisions of the articles shall apply as if that amount had become due and payable by virtue of a call.

17. Subject to the terms of allotment, the directors may make arrangements on the issue of shares for a difference between the holders in the amounts and times of payment of calls on their shares.

18. If a call remains unpaid after it has become due and payable the directors may give to the person from whom it is due not less than fourteen clear days' notice requiring payment of the amount unpaid together with any interest which may have accrued. The notice shall name the place where payment is to be made and shall state that if the notice is not complied with the shares in respect of which the call was made will be liable to be forfeited.

19. If the notice is not complied with any share in respect of which it was given may, before the payment required by the notice has been made, be forfeited by a resolution of the directors and the forfeiture shall include all dividends or other moneys payable in respect of the forfeited shares and not paid before the forfeiture.

20. Subject to the provisions of the Act, a forfeited share may be sold, re-alloted or otherwise disposed of on such terms and in such manner as the directors determine either to the person who was before the forfeiture the holder or to any other person and at any time before sale, re-allotment or other disposition, the forfeiture may be cancelled on such terms as the directors think fit. Where for the purposes of its disposal a forfeited share is to be transferred to any person the directors may authorise some person to execute an instrument of transfer of the share to that person.

21. A person any of whose shares have been forfeited shall cease to be a member in respect of them and shall surrender to the company for cancellation the certificate for the shares forfeited but shall remain liable to the company for all moneys which at the date of forfeiture were presently payable by him to the company in respect of those shares with interest at the rate at which interest was payable on those moneys before the forfeiture or, if no interest was so payable, at the appropriate rate (as defined in the Act) from the date of forfeiture until payment but the directors may waive payment wholly or in part or enforce payment without any allowance for the value of the shares at the time of forfeiture or for any consideration received on their disposal.

22. A statutory declaration by a director or the secretary that a share has been forfeited on a specified date shall be conclusive evidence of the facts stated in it as against all persons claiming to be entitled to the share and the declaration shall (subject to the execution of an instrument of transfer if necessary) constitute a good title to the share and the person to whom the share is disposed of shall not be bound to see to the application of the consideration, if any, nor shall his title to the share be affected by any irregularity in or invalidity of the proceedings in reference to the forfeiture or disposal of the share.

TRANSFER OF SHARES

23. The instrument of transfer of a share may be in any usual form or in any other form which the directors may approve and shall be executed by or on behalf of the transferor and, unless the share is fully paid, by or on behalf of the transferee.

24. The directors may refuse to register the transfer of a share which is not fully paid to a person of whom they do not approve and they may refuse to register the transfer of a share on which the company has a lien. They may also refuse to register a transfer unless—
(a) it is lodged at the office or at such other place as the directors may appoint and is accompanied by the certificate for the shares to which it relates and such other evidence as the directors may reasonably require to show the right of the transferor to make the transfer;
(b) it is in respect of only one class of shares; and
(c) it is in favour of not more than four transferees.

25. If the directors refuse to register a transfer of a share, they shall within two months after the date on which the transfer was lodged with the company send to the transferee notice of the refusal.

26. The registration of transfers of shares or of transfers of any class of shares may be suspended at such times and for such periods (not exceeding thirty days in any year) as the directors may determine.

27. No fee shall be charged for the registration of any instrument of transfer or other document relating to or affecting the title to any share.

28. The company shall be entitled to retain any instrument of transfer which is registered, but any instrument of transfer which the directors refuse to register shall be returned to the person lodging it when notice of the refusal is given.

TRANSMISSION OF SHARES

29. If a member dies the survivor or survivors where he was a joint holder, and his personal representatives where he was a sole holder or the only survivor of joint holders, shall be the only persons recognised by the company as having any title to his interest; but nothing herein contained shall release the estate of a deceased member from any liability in respect of any share which had been jointly held by him.

30. A person becoming entitled to a share in consequence of the death or bankruptcy of a member may, upon such evidence being produced as the directors may properly require, elect either to become the holder of the share or to have some person nominated by him registered as the transferee. If he elects to become the holder he shall give notice to the company to that effect. If he elects to have another person registered he shall execute an instrument of transfer of the share to that person. All the articles relating to the transfer of shares shall apply to the notice or instrument of transfer as if it were an instrument of transfer executed by the member and the death or bankruptcy of the member had not occurred.

31. A person becoming entitled to a share in consequence of the death or bankruptcy of a member shall have the rights to which he would be entitled if he were the holder of the share, except that he shall not, before being registered as the holder of the share, be entitled in respect of it to attend or vote at any meeting of the company or at any separate meeting of the holders of any class of shares in the company.

ALTERATION OF SHARE CAPITAL

32. The company may by ordinary resolution—
(a) increase its share capital by new shares of such amount as the resolution prescribes;
(b) consolidate and divide all or any of its share capital into shares of larger amount than its existing shares;
(c) subject to the provisions of the Act, sub-divide its shares, or any of them, into shares of smaller amount and the resolution may determine that, as between the shares resulting from

the sub-division, any of them may have any preference or advantage as compared with the others; and

(d) cancel shares which, at the date of the passing of the resolution, have not been taken or agreed to be taken by any person and diminish the amount of its share capital by the amount of the shares so cancelled.

33. Whenever as a result of a consolidation of shares any members would become entitled to fractions of a share, the directors may, on behalf of those members, sell the shares representing the fractions for the best price reasonably obtainable to any person (including, subject to the provisions of the Act, the company) and distribute the net proceeds of sale in due proportion among those members, and the directors may authorise some person to execute an instrument of transfer of the shares to, or in accordance with the directions of, the purchaser. The transferee shall not be bound to see to the application of the purchase money nor shall his title to the shares be affected by any irregularity in or invalidity of the proceedings in reference to the sale.

34. Subject to the provisions of the Act, the company may by special resolution reduce its share capital, any capital redemption reserve and any share premium account in any way.

PURCHASE OF OWN SHARES

35. Subject to the provisions of the Act, the company may purchase its own shares (including any redeemable shares) and, if it is a private company, make a payment in respect of the redemption or purchase of its own shares otherwise than out of distributable profits of the company or the proceeds of a fresh issue of shares.

GENERAL MEETINGS

36. All general meetings other than annual general meetings shall be called extraordinary general meetings.

37. The directors may call general meetings and, on the requisition of members pursuant to the provisions of the Act, shall forthwith proceed to convene an extraordinary general meeting for a date not later than eight weeks after receipt of the requisition. If there are not within the United Kingdom sufficient directors to call a general meeting, any director or any member of the company may call a general meeting.

NOTICE OF GENERAL MEETINGS

38. An annual general meeting and an extraordinary general meeting called for the passing of a special resolution or a resolution appointing a person as a director shall be called by at least twenty-one clear days' notice. All other extraordinary general meetings shall be called by at least fourteen clear days' notice but a general meeting may be called by shorter notice if is so agreed—

(a) in the case of an annual general meeting, by all the members entitled to attend and vote thereat; and

(b) in the case of any other meeting by a majority in number of the members having a right to attend and vote being a majority together holding not less than ninety-five per cent in nominal value of the shares giving that right.

The notice shall specify the time and place of the meeting and the general nature of the business to be transacted and, in the case of an annual general meeting, shall specify the meeting as such. Subject to the provisions of the articles and to any restrictions imposed on any shares, the notice shall be given to all the members, to all persons entitled to a share in consequence of the death or bankruptcy of a member and to the directors and auditors.

39. The accidental omission to give notice of a meeting to, or the non-receipt of notice of a meeting by, any person entitled to receive notice shall not invalidate the proceedings at that meeting.

PROCEEDINGS AT GENERAL MEETINGS

40. No business shall be transacted at any meeting unless a quorum is present. Two persons entitled to vote upon the business to be transacted, each being a member or a proxy for a member or a duly authorised representative of a corporation, shall be a quorum.

41. If such a quorum is not present within half an hour from the time appointed for the meeting, or if during a meeting such a quorum ceases to be present, the meeting shall stand adjourned to the same day in the next week at the same time and place or to such time and place as the directors may determine.

42. The chairman, if any, of the board of directors or in his absence some other director nominated by the directors shall preside as chairman of the meeting, but if neither the chairman nor such other director (if any) be present within fifteen minutes after the time appointed for holding the meeting and willing to act, the directors present shall elect one of their number to be chairman and, if there is only one director present and willing to act, he shall be chairman.

43. If no director is willing to act as chairman, or if no director is present within fifteen minutes after the time appointed for holding the meeting, the members present and entitled to vote shall choose one of their number to be chairman.

44. A director shall, notwithstanding that he is not a member, be entitled to attend and speak at any general meeting and at any separate meeting of the holders of any class of shares in the company.

45. The chairman may, with the consent of a meeting at which a quorum is present (and shall if so directed by the meeting), adjourn the meeting from time to time and from place to place, but no business shall be transacted at an adjourned meeting other than business which might properly have been transacted at the meeting had the adjournment not taken place. When a meeting is adjourned for fourteen days or more, at least seven clear days' notice shall be given specifying the time and place of the adjourned meeting and the general nature of the business to be transacted. Otherwise it shall not be necessary to give any such notice.

46. A resolution put to the vote of a meeting shall be decided on a show of hands unless before, or on the declaration of the result of, the show of hands a poll is duly demanded. Subject to the provisions of the Act, a poll may be demanded—

(a) by the chairman; or

(b) by at least two members having the right to vote at the meeting; or

(c) by a member or members representing not less than one-tenth of the total voting rights of all the members having the right to vote at the meeting; or

(d) by a member or members holding shares conferring a right to vote at the meeting being shares on which an aggregate sum has been paid up equal to not less than one-tenth of the total sum paid up on all the shares conferring that right;

and a demand by a person as proxy for a member shall be the same as a demand by the member.

47. Unless a poll is duly demanded a declaration by the chairman that a resolution has been carried or carried unanimously, or by a particular majority, or lost, or not carried by a particular majority and an entry to that effect in the minutes of the meeting shall be conclusive evidence of the fact without proof of the number or proportion of the votes recorded in favour of or against the resolution.

48. The demand for a poll may, before the poll is taken, be withdrawn but only with the consent of the chairman and a demand so withdrawn shall not be taken to have invalidated the result of a show of hands declared before the demand was made.

49. A poll shall be taken as the chairman directs and he may appoint scrutineers (who need not be members) and fix a time and place for declaring the result of the poll. The result of the poll shall be deemed to be the resolution of the meeting at which the poll was demanded.

50. In the case of an equality of votes, whether on a show of hands or on a poll, the chairman shall be entitled to a casting vote in addition to any other vote he may have.

51. A poll demanded on the election of a chairman or on a question of adjournment shall be taken forthwith. A poll demanded on any other question shall be taken either forthwith or at such time and place as the chairman directs not being more than thirty days after the poll is demanded. The

demand for a poll shall not prevent the continuance of a meeting for the transaction of any business other than the question on which the poll was demanded. If a poll is demanded before the declaration of the result of a show of hands and the demand is duly withdrawn, the meeting shall continue as if the demand had not been made.

52. No notice need be given of a poll not taken forthwith if the time and place at which it is to be taken are announced at the meeting at which it is demanded. In any other case at least seven clear days' notice shall be given specifying the time and place at which the poll is to be taken.

53. A resolution in writing executed by or on behalf of each member who would have been entitled to vote upon it if it had been proposed at a general meeting at which he was present shall be as effectual as if it had been passed at a general meeting duly convened and held and may consist of several instruments in the like form each executed by or on behalf of one or more members.

VOTES OF MEMBERS

54. Subject to any rights or restrictions attached to any shares, on a show of hands every member who (being an individual) is present in person or (being a corporation) is present by a duly authorised representative, not being himself a member entitled to vote, shall have one vote and on a poll every member shall have one vote for every share of which he is the holder.

55. In the case of joint holders the vote of the senior who tenders a vote, whether in person or by proxy, shall be accepted to the exclusion of the votes of the other joint holders; and seniority shall be determined by the order in which the names of the holders stand in the register of members.

56. A member in respect of whom an order has been made by any court having jurisdiction (whether in the United Kingdom or elsewhere) in matters concerning mental disorder may vote, whether on a show of hands or on a poll, by his receiver, curator bonis or other person authorised in that behalf appointed by that court, and any such receiver, curator bonis or other person may, on a poll, vote by proxy. Evidence to the satisfaction of the directors of the authority of the person claiming to exercise the right to vote shall be deposited at the office, or at such other place as is specified in accordance with the articles for the deposit of instruments of proxy, not less than 48 hours before the time appointed for holding the meeting or adjourned meeting at which the right to vote is to be exercised and in default the right to vote shall not be exercisable.

57. No member shall vote at any general meeting or at any separate meeting of the holders of any class of shares in the company, either in person or by proxy, in respect of any share held by him unless all moneys presently payable by him in respect of that share have been paid.

58. No objection shall be raised to the qualification of any voter except at the meeting or adjourned meeting at which the vote objected to is tendered, and every vote not disallowed at the meeting shall be valid. Any objection made in due time shall be referred to the chairman whose decision shall be final and conclusive.

59. On a poll votes may be given either personally or by proxy. A member may appoint more than one proxy to attend on the same occasion.

60. The appointment of a proxy shall be …, executed by or on behalf of the appointor and shall be in the following form (or in a form as near thereto as circumstances allow or in any other form which is usual or which the directors may approve)—

"………. PLC/Limited ………. I/We, ………., of ………., being a member/members of the above-named company, hereby appoint ………. of ………., or failing him, ………. of ………., as my/our proxy to vote in my/our names and on my/our behalf at the annual/extraordinary general meeting of the company to be held on ………. 19 ………., and at any adjournment thereof.

Signed on ………. 19 ………."

61. Where it is desired to afford members an opportunity of instructing the proxy how he shall act the appointment of a proxy shall be in the following form (or in a form as near thereto as circumstances allow or in any other form which is usual or which the directors may approve)—

"………. PLC/Limited ………. I/We, ………., of ………., being a member/members of the above-named company, hereby appoint ………. of ………., or failing him ……….

of .. .., as my/our proxy to vote in my/our names and on my/our behalf at the annual/ extraordinary general meeting of the company, to be held on .. .. 19 , ..., and at any adjournment thereof.

This form is to be used in respect of the resolutions mentioned below as follows:

Resolution No. 1 *for *against

Resolution No. 2 *for *against.

*Strike out whichever is not desired.

Unless otherwise instructed, the proxy may vote as he thinks fit or abstain from voting.

Signed this .. .. day of .. .. 19 .. .."

62. The appointment of a proxy and any authority under which it is executed or a copy of such authority certified notarially or in some other way approved by the directors may—

(a) in the case of an instrument in writing be deposited at the office or at such other place within the United kingdom as is specified in the notice convening the meeting or in any instrument of proxy sent out by the company in relation to the meeting not less than 48 hours before the time for holding the meeting or adjourned meeting at which the person named in the instrument proposes to vote; or

(aa) in the case of an appointment contained in an electronic communication, where an address has been specified for the purpose of receiving electronic communications—

(i) in the notice convening the meeting, or

(ii) in any instrument of proxy sent out by the company in relation to the meeting, or

(iii) in any invitation contained in an electronic communication to appoint a proxy issued by the company in relation to the meeting,

be received at such address not less than 48 hours before the time for holding the meeting or adjourned meeting at which the person named in the appointment proposes to vote;

(b) in the case of a poll taken more than 48 hours after it is demanded, be deposited or received as aforesaid after the poll has been demanded and not less than 24 hours before the time appointed for the taking of the poll; or

(c) where the poll is not taken forthwith but is taken not more than 48 hours after it was demanded, be delivered at the meeting at which the poll was demanded to the chairman or to the secretary or to any director;

and an appointment of proxy which is not deposited, delivered or received in a manner so permitted shall be invalid.

In this regulation and the next, "address", in relation to electronic communications, includes any number or address used for the purposes of such communications.

63. A vote given or poll demanded by proxy or by the duly authorised representative of a corporation shall be valid notwithstanding the previous determination of the authority of the person voting or demanding a poll unless notice of the determination was received by the company at the office or at such other place at which the instrument of proxy was duly deposited or, where the appointment of the proxy was contained in an electronic communication, at the address at which such appointment was duly received before the commencement of the meeting or adjourned meeting at which the vote is given or the poll demanded or (in the case of a poll taken otherwise than on the same day as the meeting or adjourned meeting) the time appointed for taking the poll.

NUMBER OF DIRECTORS

64. Unless otherwise determined by ordinary resolution, the number of directors (other than alternate directors) shall not be subject to any maximum but shall be not less than two.

ALTERNATE DIRECTORS

65. Any director (other than an alternate director) may appoint any other director, or any other person approved by resolution of the directors and willing to act, to be an alternate director and may remove from office an alternate director so appointed by him.

66. An alternate director shall be entitled to receive notice of all meetings of directors and of all meetings of committees of directors of which his appointor is a member, to attend and vote at any such meeting at which the director appointing him is not personally present and generally to perform all the functions of his appointor as a director in his absence but shall not be entitled to receive any remuneration from the company for his services as an alternate director. But it shall not be necessary to give notice of such a meeting to an alternate director who is absent from the United Kingdom.

67. An alternate director shall cease to be an alternate director if his appointor ceases to be a director; but, if a director retires by rotation or otherwise but is reappointed or deemed to have been reappointed at the meeting at which he retires, any appointment of an alternate director made by him which was in force immediately prior to his retirement shall continue after his reappointment.

68. Any appointment or removal of an alternate director shall be by notice to the company signed by the director making or revoking the appointment or in any other manner approved by the directors.

69. Save as otherwise provided in the articles, an alternate director shall be deemed for all purposes to be a director and shall alone be responsible for his own acts and defaults and he shall not be deemed to be the agent of the director appointing him.

POWERS OF DIRECTORS

70. Subject to the provisions of the Act, the memorandum and the articles and to any directions given by special resolution, the business of the company shall be managed by the directors who may exercise all the powers of the company. No alteration of the memorandum or articles and no such direction shall invalidate any prior act of the directors which would have been valid if that alteration had not been made or that direction had not been given. The powers given by this regulation shall not be limited by any special power given to the directors by the articles and a meeting of directors at which a quorum is present may exercise all powers exercisable by the directors.

71. The directors may, by power of attorney or otherwise, appoint any person to be the agent of the company for such purposes and on such conditions as they determine, including authority for the agent to delegate all or any of his powers.

DELEGATION OF DIRECTORS' POWERS

72. The directors may delegate any of their powers to any committee consisting of one or more directors. They may also delegate to any managing director or any director holding any other executive office such of their powers as they consider desirable to be exercised by him. Any such delegation may be made subject to any conditions the directors may impose, and either collaterally with or to the exclusion of their own powers and may be revoked or altered. Subject to any such conditions, the proceedings of a committee with two or more members shall be governed by the articles regulating the proceedings of directors so far as they are capable of applying.

APPOINTMENT AND RETIREMENT OF DIRECTORS

73. At the first annual general meeting all the directors shall retire from office, and at every subsequent annual general meeting one-third of the directors who are subject to retirement by rotation or, if their number is not three or a multiple of three, the number nearest to one-third shall retire from office; but, if there is only one director who is subject to retirement by rotation, he shall retire.

74. Subject to the provisions of the Act, the directors to retire by rotation shall be those who have been longest in office since their last appointment or reappointment, but as between persons who

became or were last reappointed directors on the same day those to retire shall (unless they otherwise agree among themselves) be determined by lot.

75. If the company, at the meeting at which a director retires by rotation, does not fill the vacancy the retiring director shall, if willing to act, be deemed to have been reappointed unless at the meeting it is resolved not to fill the vacancy or unless a resolution for the reappointment of the director is put to the meeting and lost.

76. No person other than a director retiring by rotation shall be appointed or reappointed a director at any general meeting unless—
(a) he is recommended by the directors; or
(b) not less than fourteen nor more than thirty-five clear days before the date appointed for the meeting, notice executed by a member qualified to vote at the meeting has been given to the company of the intention to propose that person for appointment or reappointment stating the particulars which would, if he were so appointed or reappointed, be required to be included in the company's register of directors together with notice executed by that person of his willingness to be appointed or reappointed.

77. Not less than seven nor more than twenty-eight clear days before the date appointed for holding a general meeting notice shall be given to all who are entitled to receive notice of the meeting of any person (other than a director retiring by rotation at the meeting) who is recommended by the directors for appointment or reappointment as a director at the meeting or in respect of whom notice has been duly given to the company of the intention to propose him at the meeting for appointment or reappointment as a director. The notice shall give the particulars of that person which would, if he were so appointed or reappointed, be required to be included in the company's register of directors.

78. Subject as aforesaid, the company may by ordinary resolution appoint a person who is willing to act to be a director either to fill a vacancy or as an additional director and may also determine the rotation in which any additional directors are to retire.

79. The directors may appoint a person who is willing to act to be a director, either to fill a vacancy or as an additional director, provided that the appointment does not cause the number of directors to exceed any number fixed by or in accordance with the articles as the maximum number of directors. A director so appointed shall hold office only until the next following annual general meeting and shall not be taken into account in determining the directors who are to retire by rotation at the meeting. If not reappointed at such annual general meeting, he shall vacate office at the conclusion thereof.

80. Subject as aforesaid, a director who retires at an annual general meeting may, if willing to act, be reappointed. If he is not reappointed, he shall retain office until the meeting appoints someone in his place, or if it does not do so, until the end of the meeting.

DISQUALIFICATION AND REMOVAL OF DIRECTORS

81. The office of a director shall be vacated if—
(a) he ceases to be a director by virtue of any provision of the Act or he becomes prohibited by law from being a director; or
(b) he becomes bankrupt or makes any arrangement or composition with his creditors generally; or
(c) he is, or may be, suffering from mental disorder and either—
(i) he is admitted to hospital in pursuance of an application for admission for treatment under the Mental Health Act 1983 or, in Scotland, an application for admission under the Mental Health (Scotland) Act 1960, or
(ii) an order is made by a court having jurisdiction (whether in the United Kingdom or elsewhere) in matters concerning mental disorder for his detention or for the appointment of a receiver, curator bonis or other person to exercise powers with respect to his property or affairs; or
(d) he resigns his office by notice to the company; or

(e) he shall for more than six consecutive months have been absent without permission of the directors from meetings of directors held during that period and the directors resolve that his office be vacated.

REMUNERATION OF DIRECTORS

82. The directors shall be entitled to such remuneration as the company may by ordinary resolution determine and, unless the resolution provides otherwise, the remuneration shall be deemed to accrue from day to day.

DIRECTORS' EXPENSES

83. The directors may be paid all travelling, hotel, and other expenses properly incurred by them in connection with their attendance at meetings of directors or committees of directors or general meetings or separate meetings of the holders of any class of shares or of debentures of the company or otherwise in connection with the discharge of their duties.

DIRECTORS' APPOINTMENTS AND INTERESTS

84. Subject to the provisions of the Act, the directors may appoint one or more of their number to the office of managing director or to any other executive office under the company and may enter into an agreement or arrangement with any director for his employment by the company or for the provision by him of any services outside the scope of the ordinary duties of a director. Any such appointment, agreement or arrangement may be made upon such terms as the directors determine and they may remunerate any such director for his services as they think fit. Any appointment of a director to an executive office shall terminate if he ceases to be a director but without prejudice to any claim to damages for breach of the contract of service between the director and the company. A managing director and a director holding any other executive office shall not be subject to retirement by rotation.

85. Subject to the provisions of the Act, and provided that he has disclosed to the directors the nature and extent of any material interest of his, a director notwithstanding his office—

(a) may be a party to, or otherwise interested in, any transaction or arrangement with the company or in which the company is otherwise interested;

(b) may be a director or other officer of, or employed by, or a party to any transaction or arrangement with, or otherwise interested in, any body corporate promoted by the company or in which the company is otherwise interested; and

(c) shall not, by reason of his office, be accountable to the company for any benefit which he derives from any such office or employment or from any such transaction or arrangement or from any interest in any such body corporate and no such transaction or arrangement shall be liable to be avoided on the ground of any such interest or benefit.

86. For the purposes of regulation 85—

(a) a general notice given to the directors that a director is to be regarded as having an interest of the nature and extent specified in the notice in any transaction or arrangement in which a specified person or class of persons is interested shall be deemed to be a disclosure that the director has an interest in any such transaction of the nature and extent so specified; and

(b) an interest of which a director has no knowledge and of which it is unreasonable to expect him to have knowledge shall not be treated as an interest of his.

DIRECTORS' GRATUITIES AND PENSIONS

87. The directors may provide benefits, whether by the payment of gratuities or pensions or by insurance or otherwise, for any director who has held but no longer holds any executive office or employment with the company or with any body corporate which is or has been a subsidiary of

the company or a predecessor in business of the company or of any such subsidiary, and for any member of his family (including a spouse and a former spouse) or any person who is or was dependent on him, and may (as well before as after he ceases to hold such office or employment) contribute to any fund and pay premiums for the purchase or provision of any such benefit.

PROCEEDINGS OF DIRECTORS

88. Subject to the provisions of the articles, the directors may regulate their proceedings as they think fit. A director may, and the secretary at the request of a director shall, call a meeting of the directors. It shall not be necessary to give notice of a meeting to a director who is absent from the United Kingdom. Questions arising at a meeting shall be decided by a majority of votes. In the case of an equality of votes, the chairman shall have a second or casting vote. A director who is also an alternate director shall be entitled in the absence of his appointor to a separate vote on behalf of his appointor in addition to his own vote.

89. The quorum for the transaction of the business of the directors may be fixed by the directors and unless so fixed at any other number shall be two. A person who holds office only as an alternate director shall, if his appointor is not present, be counted in the quorum.

90. The continuing directors or a sole continuing director may act notwithstanding any vacancies in their number, but, if the number of directors is less than the number fixed as the quorum, the continuing directors or director may act only for the purpose of filling vacancies or of calling a general meeting.

91. The directors may appoint one of their number to be the chairman of the board of directors and may at any time remove him from that office. Unless he is unwilling to do so, the director so appointed shall preside at every meeting of directors at which he is present. But if there is no director holding that office, or if the director holding it is unwilling to preside or is not present within five minutes after the time appointed for the meeting, the directors present may appoint one of their number to be chairman of the meeting.

92. All acts done by a meeting of directors, or of a committee of directors, or by a person acting as a director shall, notwithstanding that it be afterwards discovered that there was a defect in the appointment of any director or that any of them were disqualified from holding office, or had vacated office, or were not entitled to vote, be as valid as if every such person had been duly appointed and was qualified and had continued to be a director and had been entitled to vote.

93. A resolution in writing signed by all the directors entitled to receive notice of a meeting of directors or of a committee of directors shall be as valid and effectual as it if had been passed at a meeting of directors or (as the case may be) a committee of directors duly convened and held and may consist of several documents in the like form each signed by one or more directors; but a resolution signed by an alternate director need not also be signed by his appointor and, if it is signed by a director who has appointed an alternate director, it need not be signed by the alternate director in that capacity.

94. Save as otherwise provided by the articles, a director shall not vote at a meeting of directors or of a committee of directors on any resolution concerning a matter in which he has, directly or indirectly, an interest or duty which is material and which conflicts or may conflict with the interests of the company unless his interest or duty arises only because the case falls within one or more of the following paragraphs—

(a) the resolution relates to the giving to him of a guarantee, security, or indemnity in respect of money lent to, or an obligation incurred by him for the benefit of, the company or any of its subsidiaries;

(b) the resolution relates to the giving to a third party of a guarantee, security, or indemnity in respect of an obligation of the company or any of its subsidiaries for which the director has assumed responsibility in whole or part and whether alone or jointly with others under a guarantee or indemnity or by the giving of security;

(c) his interest arises by virtue of his subscribing or agreeing to subscribe for any shares, debentures, or other securities of the company or any of its subsidiaries, or by virtue of his being, or intending to become, a participant in the underwriting or sub-underwriting of an offer of any such shares, debentures, or other securities by the company or any of its subsidiaries for subscription, purchase or exchange;

(d) the resolution relates in any way to a retirement benefits scheme which has been approved, or is conditional upon approval, by the Board of Inland Revenue for taxation purposes.

For the purposes of this regulation, an interest of a person who is, for any purpose of the Act (excluding any statutory modification thereof not in force when this regulation becomes binding on the company), connected with a director shall be treated as an interest of the director and, in relation to an alternate director, an interest of his appointor shall be treated as an interest of the alternate director without prejudice to any interest which the alternate director has otherwise.

95. A director shall not be counted in the quorum present at a meeting in relation to a resolution on which he is not entitled to vote.

96. The company may by ordinary resolution suspend or relax to any extent, either generally or in respect of any particular matter, any provision of the articles prohibiting a director from voting at a meeting of directors or of a committee of directors.

97. Where proposals are under consideration concerning the appointment of two or more directors to offices or employments with the company or any body corporate in which the company is interested the proposals may be divided and considered in relation to each director separately and (provided he is not for another reason precluded from voting) each of the directors concerned shall be entitled to vote and be counted in the quorum in respect of each resolution except that concerning his own appointment.

98. If a question arises at a meeting of directors or of a committee of directors as to the right of a director to vote, the question may, before the conclusion of the meeting, be referred to the chairman of the meeting and his ruling in relation to any director other than himself shall be final and conclusive.

SECRETARY

99. Subject to the provisions of the Act, the secretary shall be appointed by the directors for such term, at such remuneration and upon such conditions as they may think fit; and any secretary so appointed may be removed by them.

MINUTES

100. The directors shall cause minutes to be made in books kept for the purpose—

(a) of all appointments of officers made by the directors; and

(b) of all proceedings at meetings of the company, of the holders of any class of shares in the company, and of the directors, and of committees of directors, including the names of the directors present at each such meeting.

THE SEAL

101. The seal shall only be used by the authority of the directors or of a committee of directors authorised by the directors. The directors may determine who shall sign any instrument to which the seal is affixed and unless otherwise so determined it shall be signed by a director and by the secretary or by a second director.

DIVIDENDS

102. Subject to the provisions of the Act, the company may by ordinary resolution declare dividends in accordance with the respective rights of the members, but no dividend shall exceed the amount recommended by the directors.

103. Subject to the provisions of the Act, the directors may pay interim dividends if it appears to them that they are justified by the profits of the company available for distribution. If the share capital is divided into different classes, the directors may pay interim dividends on shares which confer deferred or non-preferred rights with regard to dividend as well as on shares which confer preferential rights with regard to dividend, but no interim dividend shall be paid on shares carrying deferred or non-preferred rights if, at the time of payment, any preferential dividend is in arrear. The directors may also pay at intervals settled by them any dividend payable at a fixed rate if it appears to them that the profits available for distribution justify the payment. Provided the directors act in good faith they shall not incur any liability to the holders of shares conferring preferred rights for any loss they may suffer by the lawful payment of an interim dividend on any shares having deferred or non-preferred rights.

104. Except as otherwise provided by the rights attached to shares, all dividends shall be declared and paid according to the amounts paid up on the shares on which the dividend is paid. All dividends shall be apportioned and paid proportionately to the amounts paid up on the shares during any portion or portions of the period in respect of which the dividend is paid; but, if any share is issued on terms providing that it shall rank for dividend as from a particular date, that share shall rank for dividend accordingly.

105. A general meeting declaring a dividend may, upon the recommendation of the directors, direct that it shall be satisfied wholly or partly by the distribution of assets and, where any difficulty arises in regard to the distribution, the directors may settle the same and in particular may issue fractional certificates and fix the value for distribution of any assets and may determine that cash shall be paid to any member upon the footing of the value so fixed in order to adjust the rights of members and may vest any assets in trustees.

106. Any dividend or other moneys payable in respect of a share may be paid by cheque sent by post to the registered address of the person entitled or, if two or more persons are the holders of the share or are jointly entitled to it by reason of the death or bankruptcy of the holder, to the registered address of that one of those persons who is first named in the register of members or to such person and to such address as the person or persons entitled may in writing direct. Every cheque shall be made payable to the order of the person or persons entitled or to such other person as the person or persons entitled may in writing direct and payment of the cheque shall be a good discharge to the company. Any joint holder or other person jointly entitled to a share as aforesaid may give receipts for any dividend or other moneys payable in respect of the share.

107. No dividend or other moneys payable in respect of a share shall bear interest against the company unless otherwise provided by the rights attached to the share.

108. Any dividend which has remained unclaimed for twelve years from the date when it became due for payment shall, if the directors so resolve, be forfeited and cease to remain owing by the company.

ACCOUNTS

109. No member shall (as such) have any right of inspecting any accounting records or other book or document of the company except as conferred by statute or authorised by the directors or by ordinary resolution of the company.

CAPITALISATION OF PROFITS

110. The directors may with the authority of an ordinary resolution of the company—

(a) subject as hereinafter provided, resolve to capitalise any undivided profits of the company not required for paying any preferential dividend (whether or not they are available for distribution) or any sum standing to the credit of the company's share premium account or capital redemption reserve;

(b) appropriate the sum resolved to be capitalised to the members who would have been entitled to it if it were distributed by way of dividend and in the same proportions and apply such sum on their behalf either in or towards paying up the amounts, if any, for the time being unpaid on any shares held by them respectively, or in paying up in full unissued shares or debentures of the company of a nominal amount equal to that sum, and allot the shares or debentures credited as fully paid to those members, or as they may direct, in those proportions, or partly in one way and partly in the other: but the share premium account, the capital redemption reserve, and any profits which are not available for distribution may, for the purposes of this regulation, only be applied in paying up unissued shares to be allotted to members credited as fully paid;

(c) make such provision by the issue of fractional certificates or by payment in cash or otherwise as they determine in the case of shares or debentures becoming distributable under this regulation in fractions; and

(d) authorise any person to enter on behalf of all the members concerned into an agreement with the company providing for the allotment to them respectively, credited as fully paid, of any shares or debentures to which they are entitled upon such capitalisation, any agreement made under such authority being binding on all such members.

NOTICES

111. Any notice to be given to or by any person pursuant to the articles (other than a notice calling a meeting of the directors) shall be in writing or shall be given using electronic communications to an address for the time being notified for that purpose to the person giving the notice.

In this regulation, "address", in relation to electronic communications, includes any number or address used for the purposes of such communications.

112. The company may give any notice to a member either personally or by sending it by post in a prepaid envelope addressed to the member at his registered address or by leaving it at that address or by giving it using electronic communications to an address for the time being notified to the company by the member. In the case of joint holders of a share, all notices shall be given to the joint holder whose name stands first in the register of members in respect of the joint holding and notice so given shall be sufficient notice to all the joint holders. A member whose registered address is not within the United Kingdom and who gives to the company an address within the United Kingdom at which notices may be given to him, or an address to which notices may be sent using electronic communications, shall be entitled to have notices given to him at that address, but otherwise no such member shall be entitled to receive any notice from the company.

In this regulation and the next, "address", in relation to electronic communications, includes any number or address used for the purposes of such communications.

113. A member present, either in person or by proxy, at any meeting of the company or of the holders of any class of shares in the company shall be deemed to have received notice of the meeting and, where requisite, of the purposes for which it was called.

114. Every person who becomes entitled to a share shall be bound by any notice in respect of that share which, before his name is entered in the register of members, has been duly given to a person from whom he derives his title.

115. Proof that an envelope containing a notice was properly addressed, prepaid and posted shall be conclusive evidence that that the notice was given. Proof that a notice contained in an electronic communication was sent in accordance with guidance issued by the Institute of Chartered Secretaries and Administrators shall be conclusive evidence that the notice was given. A notice shall, … be deemed to be given at the expiration of 48 hours after the envelope containing it was posted or, in the case of a notice contained in an electronic communication, at the expiration of 48 hours after the time it was sent.

116. A notice may be given by the company to the persons entitled to a share in consequence of the death or bankruptcy of a member by sending or delivering it, in any manner authorised by the articles for the giving of notice to a member, addressed to them by name, or by the title of representatives of the deceased, or trustee of the bankrupt or by any like description at the address, if any, within the United Kingdom supplied for that purpose by the persons claiming to

be so entitled. Until such an address has been supplied, a notice may be given in any manner in which it might have been given if the death or bankruptcy had not occurred.

WINDING UP

117. If the company is wound up, the liquidator may, with the sanction of an extraordinary resolution of the company and any other sanction required by the Act, divide among the members in specie the whole or any part of the assets of the company and may, for that purpose, value any assets and determine how the division shall be carried out as between the members or different classes of members. The liquidator may, with the like sanction, vest the whole or any part of the assets in trustees upon such trusts for the benefit of the members as he with the like sanction determines, but no member shall be compelled to accept any assets upon which there is a liability.

INDEMNITY

118. Subject to the provisions of the Act but without prejudice to any indemnity to which a director may otherwise be entitled, every director or other officer or auditor of the company shall be indemnified out of the assets of the company against any liability incurred by him in defending any proceedings, whether civil or criminal, in which judgment is given in his favour or in which he is acquitted or in connection with any application in which relief is granted to him by the court from liability for negligence, default, breach of duty or breach of trust in relation to the affairs of the company.

TABLE B
A PRIVATE COMPANY LIMITED BY SHARES
MEMORANDUM OF ASSOCIATION

1. The company's name is "The South Wales Motor Transport Company cyfyngedig".
2. The company's registered office is to be situated in Wales.
3. The company's objects are the carriage of passengers and goods in motor vehicles between such places as the company may from time to time determine and the doing of all such other things as are incidental or conducive to the attainment of that object.
4. The liability of the members is limited.
5. The company's share capital is £50,000 divided into 50,000 shares of £1 each.

We, the subscribers to this memorandum of association, wish to be formed into a company pursuant to this memorandum; and we agree to take the number of shares shown opposite our respective names.

Names and Addresses of Subscribers	Number of shares taken by each Subsciber
1. Thomas Jones, 138 Mountfield Street,Tredegar.	1
2. Mary Evans, 19 Merthyr Road, Aberystwyth.	1
	Total shares taken 2

Dated . . . . 19 . . . .
Witness to the above signatures,
Anne Brown, "Woodlands", Fieldside Road, Bryn Mawr.

. . .

Companies (Model Articles) Regulations 2008

S.I. 2008/3229

1. Citation and Commencement

These Regulations may be cited as the Companies (Model Articles) Regulations 2008 and come into force on 1st October 2009.

2. Model articles for private companies limited by shares

Schedule 1 to these Regulations prescribes the model articles of association for private companies limited by shares.

3. Model articles for private companies limited by guarantee

Schedule 2 to these Regulations prescribes the model articles of association for private companies limited by guarantee.

4. Model articles for public companies

Schedule 3 to these Regulations prescribes the model articles of association for public companies.

SCHEDULE 1

Regulation 2

MODEL ARTICLES FOR PRIVATE COMPANIES LIMITED BY SHARES

PART 1
INTERPRETATION AND LIMITATION OF LIABILITY

1. Defined terms

In the articles, unless the context requires otherwise—

"articles" means the company's articles of association;

"bankruptcy" includes individual insolvency proceedings in a jurisdiction other than England and Wales or Northern Ireland which have an effect similar to that of bankruptcy;

"chairman" has the meaning given in article 12;

"chairman of the meeting" has the meaning given in article 39;

"Companies Acts" means the Companies Acts (as defined in section 2 of the Companies Act 2006), in so far as they apply to the company;

"director" means a director of the company, and includes any person occupying the position of director, by whatever name called;

"distribution recipient" has the meaning given in article 31;

"document" includes, unless otherwise specified, any document sent or supplied in electronic form;

"electronic form" has the meaning given in section 1168 of the Companies Act 2006;

"fully paid" in relation to a share, means that the nominal value and any premium to be paid to the company in respect of that share have been paid to the company;

"hard copy form" has the meaning given in section 1168 of the Companies Act 2006;

"holder" in relation to shares means the person whose name is entered in the register of members as the holder of the shares;

"instrument" means a document in hard copy form;

"ordinary resolution" has the meaning given in section 282 of the Companies Act 2006;

"paid" means paid or credited as paid;

"participate", in relation to a directors' meeting, has the meaning given in article 10;

"proxy notice" has the meaning given in article 45;

"shareholder" means a person who is the holder of a share;

"shares" means shares in the company;

"special resolution" has the meaning given in section 283 of the Companies Act 2006;

"subsidiary" has the meaning given in section 1159 of the Companies Act 2006;

"transmittee" means a person entitled to a share by reason of the death or bankruptcy of a shareholder or otherwise by operation of law; and

"writing" means the representation or reproduction of words, symbols or other information in a visible form by any method or combination of methods, whether sent or supplied in electronic form or otherwise.

Unless the context otherwise requires, other words or expressions contained in these articles bear the same meaning as in the Companies Act 2006 as in force on the date when these articles become binding on the company.

2. Liability of members

The liability of the members is limited to the amount, if any, unpaid on the shares held by them.

PART 2
DIRECTORS

Directors' Powers and Responsibilities

3. Directors' general authority

Subject to the articles, the directors are responsible for the management of the company's business, for which purpose they may exercise all the powers of the company.

4. Shareholders' reserve power

(1) The shareholders may, by special resolution, direct the directors to take, or refrain from taking, specified action.

(2) No such special resolution invalidates anything which the directors have done before the passing of the resolution.

5. Directors may delegate

(1) Subject to the articles, the directors may delegate any of the powers which are conferred on them under the articles—

(a) to such person or committee;

(b) by such means (including by power of attorney);

(c) to such an extent;

(d) in relation to such matters or territories; and

(e) on such terms and conditions;

as they think fit.

(2) If the directors so specify, any such delegation may authorise further delegation of the directors' powers by any person to whom they are delegated.

(3) The directors may revoke any delegation in whole or part, or alter its terms and conditions.

6. Committees

(1) Committees to which the directors delegate any of their powers must follow procedures which are based as far as they are applicable on those provisions of the articles which govern the taking of decisions by directors.

(2) The directors may make rules of procedure for all or any committees, which prevail over rules derived from the articles if they are not consistent with them.

Decision-Making by Directors

7. Directors to take decisions collectively

(1) The general rule about decision-making by directors is that any decision of the directors must be either a majority decision at a meeting or a decision taken in accordance with article 8.

(2) If—

(a) the company only has one director, and

(b) no provision of the articles requires it to have more than one director,

the general rule does not apply, and the director may take decisions without regard to any of the provisions of the articles relating to directors' decision-making.

8. Unanimous decisions

(1) A decision of the directors is taken in accordance with this article when all eligible directors indicate to each other by any means that they share a common view on a matter.

(2) Such a decision may take the form of a resolution in writing, copies of which have been signed by each eligible director or to which each eligible director has otherwise indicated agreement in writing.

(3) References in this article to eligible directors are to directors who would have been entitled to vote on the matter had it been proposed as a resolution at a directors' meeting.

(4) A decision may not be taken in accordance with this article if the eligible directors would not have formed a quorum at such a meeting.

9. Calling a directors' meeting

(1) Any director may call a directors' meeting by giving notice of the meeting to the directors or by authorising the company secretary (if any) to give such notice.

(2) Notice of any directors' meeting must indicate—

(a) its proposed date and time;

(b) where it is to take place; and

(c) if it is anticipated that directors participating in the meeting will not be in the same place, how it is proposed that they should communicate with each other during the meeting.

(3) Notice of a directors' meeting must be given to each director, but need not be in writing.

(4) Notice of a directors' meeting need not be given to directors who waive their entitlement to notice of that meeting, by giving notice to that effect to the company not more than 7 days after the date on which the meeting is held. Where such notice is given after the meeting has been held, that does not affect the validity of the meeting, or of any business conducted at it.

10. Participation in directors' meetings

(1) Subject to the articles, directors participate in a directors' meeting, or part of a directors' meeting, when—

(a) the meeting has been called and takes place in accordance with the articles, and

(b) they can each communicate to the others any information or opinions they have on any particular item of the business of the meeting.

(2) In determining whether directors are participating in a directors' meeting, it is irrelevant where any director is or how they communicate with each other.

(3) If all the directors participating in a meeting are not in the same place, they may decide that the meeting is to be treated as taking place wherever any of them is.

11. Quorum for directors' meetings

(1) At a directors' meeting, unless a quorum is participating, no proposal is to be voted on, except a proposal to call another meeting.

(2) The quorum for directors' meetings may be fixed from time to time by a decision of the directors, but it must never be less than two, and unless otherwise fixed it is two.

(3) If the total number of directors for the time being is less than the quorum required, the directors must not take any decision other than a decision—

(a) to appoint further directors, or

(b) to call a general meeting so as to enable the shareholders to appoint further directors.

12. Chairing of directors' meetings

(1) The directors may appoint a director to chair their meetings.

(2) The person so appointed for the time being is known as the chairman.

(3) The directors may terminate the chairman's appointment at any time.

(4) If the chairman is not participating in a directors' meeting within ten minutes of the time at which it was to start, the participating directors must appoint one of themselves to chair it.

13. Casting vote

(1) If the numbers of votes for and against a proposal are equal, the chairman or other director chairing the meeting has a casting vote.

(2) But this does not apply if, in accordance with the articles, the chairman or other director is not to be counted as participating in the decision-making process for quorum or voting purposes.

14. Conflicts of interest

(1) If a proposed decision of the directors is concerned with an actual or proposed transaction or arrangement with the company in which a director is interested, that director is not to be counted as participating in the decision-making process for quorum or voting purposes.

(2) But if paragraph (3) applies, a director who is interested in an actual or proposed transaction or arrangement with the company is to be counted as participating in the decision-making process for quorum and voting purposes.

(3) This paragraph applies when—

(a) the company by ordinary resolution disapplies the provision of the articles which would otherwise prevent a director from being counted as participating in the decision-making process;

(b) the director's interest cannot reasonably be regarded as likely to give rise to a conflict of interest; or

(c) the director's conflict of interest arises from a permitted cause.

(4) For the purposes of this article, the following are permitted causes—

(a) a guarantee given, or to be given, by or to a director in respect of an obligation incurred by or on behalf of the company or any of its subsidiaries;

(b) subscription, or an agreement to subscribe, for shares or other securities of the company or any of its subsidiaries, or to underwrite, sub-underwrite, or guarantee subscription for any such shares or securities; and

(c) arrangements pursuant to which benefits are made available to employees and directors or former employees and directors of the company or any of its subsidiaries which do not provide special benefits for directors or former directors.

(5) For the purposes of this article, references to proposed decisions and decision-making processes include any directors' meeting or part of a directors' meeting.

(6) Subject to paragraph (7), if a question arises at a meeting of directors or of a committee of directors as to the right of a director to participate in the meeting (or part of the meeting) for voting or quorum purposes, the question may, before the conclusion of the meeting, be referred to the chairman whose ruling in relation to any director other than the chairman is to be final and conclusive.

(7) If any question as to the right to participate in the meeting (or part of the meeting) should arise in respect of the chairman, the question is to be decided by a decision of the directors at that meeting, for which purpose the chairman is not to be counted as participating in the meeting (or that part of the meeting) for voting or quorum purposes.

15. Records of decisions to be kept

The directors must ensure that the company keeps a record, in writing, for at least 10 years from the date of the decision recorded, of every unanimous or majority decision taken by the directors.

16. Directors' discretion to make further rules

Subject to the articles, the directors may make any rule which they think fit about how they take decisions, and about how such rules are to be recorded or communicated to directors.

Appointment of Directors

17. Methods of appointing directors

(1) Any person who is willing to act as a director, and is permitted by law to do so, may be appointed to be a director—

(a) by ordinary resolution, or

(b) by a decision of the directors.

(2) In any case where, as a result of death, the company has no shareholders and no directors, the personal representatives of the last shareholder to have died have the right, by notice in writing, to appoint a person to be a director.

(3) For the purposes of paragraph (2), where 2 or more shareholders die in circumstances rendering it uncertain who was the last to die, a younger shareholder is deemed to have survived an older shareholder.

18. Termination of director's appointment

A person ceases to be a director as soon as—

(a) that person ceases to be a director by virtue of any provision of the Companies Act 2006 or is prohibited from being a director by law;

(b) a bankruptcy order is made against that person;

(c) a composition is made with that person's creditors generally in satisfaction of that person's debts;

(d) a registered medical practitioner who is treating that person gives a written opinion to the company stating that that person has become physically or mentally incapable of acting as a director and may remain so for more than three months;

(e) by reason of that person's mental health, a court makes an order which wholly or partly prevents that person from personally exercising any powers or rights which that person would otherwise have;

(f) notification is received by the company from the director that the director is resigning from office, and such resignation has taken effect in accordance with its terms.

Note. Subparagraph (e) is revoked by the Mental Health (Discrimination) Act 2013, s. 3(1)(a), as from 28 April 2013.

19. Directors' remuneration

(1) Directors may undertake any services for the company that the directors decide.

(2) Directors are entitled to such remuneration as the directors determine—

(a) for their services to the company as directors, and

(b) for any other service which they undertake for the company.

(3) Subject to the articles, a director's remuneration may—

(a) take any form, and

(b) include any arrangements in connection with the payment of a pension, allowance or gratuity, or any death, sickness or disability benefits, to or in respect of that director.

(4) Unless the directors decide otherwise, directors' remuneration accrues from day to day.

(5) Unless the directors decide otherwise, directors are not accountable to the company for any remuneration which they receive as directors or other officers or employees of the company's subsidiaries or of any other body corporate in which the company is interested.

20. Directors' expenses

The company may pay any reasonable expenses which the directors properly incur in connection with their attendance at—

(a) meetings of directors or committees of directors,

(b) general meetings, or

(c) separate meetings of the holders of any class of shares or of debentures of the company,

or otherwise in connection with the exercise of their powers and the discharge of their responsibilities in relation to the company.

PART 3
SHARES AND DISTRIBUTIONS

Shares

21. All shares to be fully paid up

(1) No share is to be issued for less than the aggregate of its nominal value and any premium to be paid to the company in consideration for its issue.

(2) This does not apply to shares taken on the formation of the company by the subscribers to the company's memorandum.

22. Powers to issue different classes of share

(1) Subject to the articles, but without prejudice to the rights attached to any existing share, the company may issue shares with such rights or restrictions as may be determined by ordinary resolution.

(2) The company may issue shares which are to be redeemed, or are liable to be redeemed at the option of the company or the holder, and the directors may determine the terms, conditions and manner of redemption of any such shares.

23. Company not bound by less than absolute interests

Except as required by law, no person is to be recognised by the company as holding any share upon any trust, and except as otherwise required by law or the articles, the company is not in any way to be bound by or recognise any interest in a share other than the holder's absolute ownership of it and all the rights attaching to it.

24. Share certificates

(1) The company must issue each shareholder, free of charge, with one or more certificates in respect of the shares which that shareholder holds.

(2) Every certificate must specify—

(a) in respect of how many shares, of what class, it is issued;

(b) the nominal value of those shares;

(c) that the shares are fully paid; and

(d) any distinguishing numbers assigned to them.

(3) No certificate may be issued in respect of shares of more than one class.

(4) If more than one person holds a share, only one certificate may be issued in respect of it.

(5) Certificates must—

(a) have affixed to them the company's common seal, or

(b) be otherwise executed in accordance with the Companies Acts.

25. Replacement share certificates

(1) If a certificate issued in respect of a shareholder's shares is—

(a) damaged or defaced, or

(b) said to be lost, stolen or destroyed,

that shareholder is entitled to be issued with a replacement certificate in respect of the same shares.

(2) A shareholder exercising the right to be issued with such a replacement certificate—

(a) may at the same time exercise the right to be issued with a single certificate or separate certificates;

(b) must return the certificate which is to be replaced to the company if it is damaged or defaced; and

(c) must comply with such conditions as to evidence, indemnity and the payment of a reasonable fee as the directors decide.

26. Share transfers

(1) Shares may be transferred by means of an instrument of transfer in any usual form or any other form approved by the directors, which is executed by or on behalf of the transferor.

(2) No fee may be charged for registering any instrument of transfer or other document relating to or affecting the title to any share.

(3) The company may retain any instrument of transfer which is registered.

(4) The transferor remains the holder of a share until the transferee's name is entered in the register of members as holder of it.

(5) The directors may refuse to register the transfer of a share, and if they do so, the instrument of transfer must be returned to the transferee with the notice of refusal unless they suspect that the proposed transfer may be fraudulent.

27. Transmission of shares

(1) If title to a share passes to a transmittee, the company may only recognise the transmittee as having any title to that share.

(2) A transmittee who produces such evidence of entitlement to shares as the directors may properly require—

(a) may, subject to the articles, choose either to become the holder of those shares or to have them transferred to another person, and

(b) subject to the articles, and pending any transfer of the shares to another person, has the same rights as the holder had.

(3) But transmittees do not have the right to attend or vote at a general meeting, or agree to a proposed written resolution, in respect of shares to which they are entitled, by reason of the holder's death or bankruptcy or otherwise, unless they become the holders of those shares.

28. Exercise of transmittees' rights

(1) Transmittees who wish to become the holders of shares to which they have become entitled must notify the company in writing of that wish.

(2) If the transmittee wishes to have a share transferred to another person, the transmittee must execute an instrument of transfer in respect of it.

(3) Any transfer made or executed under this article is to be treated as if it were made or executed by the person from whom the transmittee has derived rights in respect of the share, and as if the event which gave rise to the transmission had not occurred.

29. Transmittees bound by prior notices

If a notice is given to a shareholder in respect of shares and a transmittee is entitled to those shares, the transmittee is bound by the notice if it was given to the shareholder before the transmittee's name has been entered in the register of members.

Dividends and Other Distributions

30. Procedure for declaring dividends

(1) The company may by ordinary resolution declare dividends, and the directors may decide to pay interim dividends.

(2) A dividend must not be declared unless the directors have made a recommendation as to its amount. Such a dividend must not exceed the amount recommended by the directors.

(3) No dividend may be declared or paid unless it is in accordance with shareholders' respective rights.

(4) Unless the shareholders' resolution to declare or directors' decision to pay a dividend, or the terms on which shares are issued, specify otherwise, it must be paid by reference to each shareholder's holding of shares on the date of the resolution or decision to declare or pay it.

(5) If the company's share capital is divided into different classes, no interim dividend may be paid on shares carrying deferred or non-preferred rights if, at the time of payment, any preferential dividend is in arrear.

(6) The directors may pay at intervals any dividend payable at a fixed rate if it appears to them that the profits available for distribution justify the payment.

(7) If the directors act in good faith, they do not incur any liability to the holders of shares conferring preferred rights for any loss they may suffer by the lawful payment of an interim dividend on shares with deferred or non-preferred rights.

31. Payment of dividends and other distributions

(1) Where a dividend or other sum which is a distribution is payable in respect of a share, it must be paid by one or more of the following means—

(a) transfer to a bank or building society account specified by the distribution recipient either in writing or as the directors may otherwise decide;

(b) sending a cheque made payable to the distribution recipient by post to the distribution recipient at the distribution recipient's registered address (if the distribution recipient is a holder of the share), or (in any other case) to an address specified by the distribution recipient either in writing or as the directors may otherwise decide;

(c) sending a cheque made payable to such person by post to such person at such address as the distribution recipient has specified either in writing or as the directors may otherwise decide; or

(d) any other means of payment as the directors agree with the distribution recipient either in writing or by such other means as the directors decide.

(2) In the articles, "the distribution recipient" means, in respect of a share in respect of which a dividend or other sum is payable—

(a) the holder of the share; or

(b) if the share has two or more joint holders, whichever of them is named first in the register of members; or

(c) if the holder is no longer entitled to the share by reason of death or bankruptcy, or otherwise by operation of law, the transmittee.

32. No interest on distributions

The company may not pay interest on any dividend or other sum payable in respect of a share unless otherwise provided by—

(a) the terms on which the share was issued, or

(b) the provisions of another agreement between the holder of that share and the company.

33. Unclaimed distributions

(1) All dividends or other sums which are—

(a) payable in respect of shares, and

(b) unclaimed after having been declared or become payable,

may be invested or otherwise made use of by the directors for the benefit of the company until claimed.

(2) The payment of any such dividend or other sum into a separate account does not make the company a trustee in respect of it.

(3) If—

(a) twelve years have passed from the date on which a dividend or other sum became due for payment, and

(b) the distribution recipient has not claimed it,

the distribution recipient is no longer entitled to that dividend or other sum and it ceases to remain owing by the company.

34. Non-cash distributions

(1) Subject to the terms of issue of the share in question, the company may, by ordinary resolution on the recommendation of the directors, decide to pay all or part of a dividend or other distribution payable in respect of a share by transferring non-cash assets of equivalent value (including, without limitation, shares or other securities in any company).

(2) For the purposes of paying a non-cash distribution, the directors may make whatever arrangements they think fit, including, where any difficulty arises regarding the distribution—

(a) fixing the value of any assets;

(b) paying cash to any distribution recipient on the basis of that value in order to adjust the rights of recipients; and

(c) vesting any assets in trustees.

35. Waiver of distributions

Distribution recipients may waive their entitlement to a dividend or other distribution payable in respect of a share by giving the company notice in writing to that effect, but if—

(a) the share has more than one holder, or

(b) more than one person is entitled to the share, whether by reason of the death or bankruptcy of one or more joint holders, or otherwise,

the notice is not effective unless it is expressed to be given, and signed, by all the holders or persons otherwise entitled to the share.

Capitalisation of Profits

36. Authority to capitalise and appropriation of capitalised sums

(1) Subject to the articles, the directors may, if they are so authorised by an ordinary resolution—

(a) decide to capitalise any profits of the company (whether or not they are available for distribution) which are not required for paying a preferential dividend, or any sum standing to the credit of the company's share premium account or capital redemption reserve; and

(b) appropriate any sum which they so decide to capitalise (a "capitalised sum") to the persons who would have been entitled to it if it were distributed by way of dividend (the "persons entitled") and in the same proportions.

(2) Capitalised sums must be applied—

(a) on behalf of the persons entitled, and

(b) in the same proportions as a dividend would have been distributed to them.

(3) Any capitalised sum may be applied in paying up new shares of a nominal amount equal to the capitalised sum which are then allotted credited as fully paid to the persons entitled or as they may direct.

(4) A capitalised sum which was appropriated from profits available for distribution may be applied in paying up new debentures of the company which are then allotted credited as fully paid to the persons entitled or as they may direct.

(5) Subject to the articles the directors may—

(a) apply capitalised sums in accordance with paragraphs (3) and (4) partly in one way and partly in another;

(b) make such arrangements as they think fit to deal with shares or debentures becoming distributable in fractions under this article (including the issuing of fractional certificates or the making of cash payments); and

(c) authorise any person to enter into an agreement with the company on behalf of all the persons entitled which is binding on them in respect of the allotment of shares and debentures to them under this article.

PART 4
DECISION-MAKING BY SHAREHOLDERS

Organisation of General Meetings

37. Attendance and speaking at general meetings

(1) A person is able to exercise the right to speak at a general meeting when that person is in a position to communicate to all those attending the meeting, during the meeting, any information or opinions which that person has on the business of the meeting.

(2) A person is able to exercise the right to vote at a general meeting when—

(a) that person is able to vote, during the meeting, on resolutions put to the vote at the meeting, and

(b) that person's vote can be taken into account in determining whether or not such resolutions are passed at the same time as the votes of all the other persons attending the meeting.

(3) The directors may make whatever arrangements they consider appropriate to enable those attending a general meeting to exercise their rights to speak or vote at it.

(4) In determining attendance at a general meeting, it is immaterial whether any two or more members attending it are in the same place as each other.

(5) Two or more persons who are not in the same place as each other attend a general meeting if their circumstances are such that if they have (or were to have) rights to speak and vote at that meeting, they are (or would be) able to exercise them.

38. Quorum for general meetings

No business other than the appointment of the chairman of the meeting is to be transacted at a general meeting if the persons attending it do not constitute a quorum.

39. Chairing general meetings

(1) If the directors have appointed a chairman, the chairman shall chair general meetings if present and willing to do so.

(2) If the directors have not appointed a chairman, or if the chairman is unwilling to chair the meeting or is not present within ten minutes of the time at which a meeting was due to start—

(a) the directors present, or

(b) (if no directors are present), the meeting,

must appoint a director or shareholder to chair the meeting, and the appointment of the chairman of the meeting must be the first business of the meeting.

(3) The person chairing a meeting in accordance with this article is referred to as "the chairman of the meeting".

40. Attendance and speaking by directors and non-shareholders

(1) Directors may attend and speak at general meetings, whether or not they are shareholders.

(2) The chairman of the meeting may permit other persons who are not—

(a) shareholders of the company, or

(b) otherwise entitled to exercise the rights of shareholders in relation to general meetings,

to attend and speak at a general meeting.

41. Adjournment

(1) If the persons attending a general meeting within half an hour of the time at which the meeting was due to start do not constitute a quorum, or if during a meeting a quorum ceases to be present, the chairman of the meeting must adjourn it.

(2) The chairman of the meeting may adjourn a general meeting at which a quorum is present if—

(a) the meeting consents to an adjournment, or

(b) it appears to the chairman of the meeting that an adjournment is necessary to protect the safety of any person attending the meeting or ensure that the business of the meeting is conducted in an orderly manner.

(3) The chairman of the meeting must adjourn a general meeting if directed to do so by the meeting.

(4) When adjourning a general meeting, the chairman of the meeting must—

(a) either specify the time and place to which it is adjourned or state that it is to continue at a time and place to be fixed by the directors, and

(b) have regard to any directions as to the time and place of any adjournment which have been given by the meeting.

(5) If the continuation of an adjourned meeting is to take place more than 14 days after it was adjourned, the company must give at least 7 clear days' notice of it (that is, excluding the day of the adjourned meeting and the day on which the notice is given)—

(a) to the same persons to whom notice of the company's general meetings is required to be given, and

(b) containing the same information which such notice is required to contain.

(6) No business may be transacted at an adjourned general meeting which could not properly have been transacted at the meeting if the adjournment had not taken place.

Voting at General Meetings

42. Voting: general

A resolution put to the vote of a general meeting must be decided on a show of hands unless a poll is duly demanded in accordance with the articles.

43. Errors and disputes

(1) No objection may be raised to the qualification of any person voting at a general meeting except at the meeting or adjourned meeting at which the vote objected to is tendered, and every vote not disallowed at the meeting is valid.

(2) Any such objection must be referred to the chairman of the meeting, whose decision is final.

44. Poll votes

(1) A poll on a resolution may be demanded—

(a) in advance of the general meeting where it is to be put to the vote, or

(b) at a general meeting, either before a show of hands on that resolution or immediately after the result of a show of hands on that resolution is declared.

(2) A poll may be demanded by—

(a) the chairman of the meeting;

(b) the directors;

(c) two or more persons having the right to vote on the resolution; or

(d) a person or persons representing not less than one tenth of the total voting rights of all the shareholders having the right to vote on the resolution.

(3) A demand for a poll may be withdrawn if—

(a) the poll has not yet been taken, and

(b) the chairman of the meeting consents to the withdrawal.

(4) Polls must be taken immediately and in such manner as the chairman of the meeting directs.

45. Content of proxy notices

(1) Proxies may only validly be appointed by a notice in writing (a "proxy notice") which—

(a) states the name and address of the shareholder appointing the proxy;

(b) identifies the person appointed to be that shareholder's proxy and the general meeting in relation to which that person is appointed;

(c) is signed by or on behalf of the shareholder appointing the proxy, or is authenticated in such manner as the directors may determine; and

(d) is delivered to the company in accordance with the articles and any instructions contained in the notice of the general meeting to which they relate.

(2) The company may require proxy notices to be delivered in a particular form, and may specify different forms for different purposes.

(3) Proxy notices may specify how the proxy appointed under them is to vote (or that the proxy is to abstain from voting) on one or more resolutions.

(4) Unless a proxy notice indicates otherwise, it must be treated as—

(a) allowing the person appointed under it as a proxy discretion as to how to vote on any ancillary or procedural resolutions put to the meeting, and

(b) appointing that person as a proxy in relation to any adjournment of the general meeting to which it relates as well as the meeting itself.

46. Delivery of proxy notices

(1) A person who is entitled to attend, speak or vote (either on a show of hands or on a poll) at a general meeting remains so entitled in respect of that meeting or any adjournment of it, even though a valid proxy notice has been delivered to the company by or on behalf of that person.

(2) An appointment under a proxy notice may be revoked by delivering to the company a notice in writing given by or on behalf of the person by whom or on whose behalf the proxy notice was given.

(3) A notice revoking a proxy appointment only takes effect if it is delivered before the start of the meeting or adjourned meeting to which it relates.

(4) If a proxy notice is not executed by the person appointing the proxy, it must be accompanied by written evidence of the authority of the person who executed it to execute it on the appointor's behalf.

47. Amendments to resolutions

(1) An ordinary resolution to be proposed at a general meeting may be amended by ordinary resolution if—

(a) notice of the proposed amendment is given to the company in writing by a person entitled to vote at the general meeting at which it is to be proposed not less than 48 hours before the meeting is to take place (or such later time as the chairman of the meeting may determine), and

(b) the proposed amendment does not, in the reasonable opinion of the chairman of the meeting, materially alter the scope of the resolution.

(2) A special resolution to be proposed at a general meeting may be amended by ordinary resolution, if—

(a) the chairman of the meeting proposes the amendment at the general meeting at which the resolution is to be proposed, and

(b) the amendment does not go beyond what is necessary to correct a grammatical or other non-substantive error in the resolution.

(3) If the chairman of the meeting, acting in good faith, wrongly decides that an amendment to a resolution is out of order, the chairman's error does not invalidate the vote on that resolution.

PART 5
ADMINISTRATIVE ARRANGEMENTS

48. Means of communication to be used

(1) Subject to the articles, anything sent or supplied by or to the company under the articles may be sent or supplied in any way in which the Companies Act 2006 provides for documents or information which are authorised or required by any provision of that Act to be sent or supplied by or to the company.

(2) Subject to the articles, any notice or document to be sent or supplied to a director in connection with the taking of decisions by directors may also be sent or supplied by the means by which that director has asked to be sent or supplied with such notices or documents for the time being.

(3) A director may agree with the company that notices or documents sent to that director in a particular way are to be deemed to have been received within a specified time of their being sent, and for the specified time to be less than 48 hours.

49. Company seals

(1) Any common seal may only be used by the authority of the directors.

(2) The directors may decide by what means and in what form any common seal is to be used.

(3) Unless otherwise decided by the directors, if the company has a common seal and it is affixed to a document, the document must also be signed by at least one authorised person in the presence of a witness who attests the signature.

(4) For the purposes of this article, an authorised person is—

(a) any director of the company;

(b) the company secretary (if any); or

(c) any person authorised by the directors for the purpose of signing documents to which the common seal is applied.

50. No right to inspect accounts and other records

Except as provided by law or authorised by the directors or an ordinary resolution of the company, no person is entitled to inspect any of the company's accounting or other records or documents merely by virtue of being a shareholder.

51. Provision for employees on cessation of business

The directors may decide to make provision for the benefit of persons employed or formerly employed by the company or any of its subsidiaries (other than a director or former director or shadow director) in connection with the cessation or transfer to any person of the whole or part of the undertaking of the company or that subsidiary.

Directors' Indemnity and Insurance

52. Indemnity

(1) Subject to paragraph (2), a relevant director of the company or an associated company may be indemnified out of the company's assets against—

(a) any liability incurred by that director in connection with any negligence, default, breach of duty or breach of trust in relation to the company or an associated company,

(b) any liability incurred by that director in connection with the activities of the company or an associated company in its capacity as a trustee of an occupational pension scheme (as defined in section 235(6) of the Companies Act 2006),

(c) any other liability incurred by that director as an officer of the company or an associated company.

(2) This article does not authorise any indemnity which would be prohibited or rendered void by any provision of the Companies Acts or by any other provision of law.

(3) In this article—

(a) companies are associated if one is a subsidiary of the other or both are subsidiaries of the same body corporate, and

(b) a "relevant director" means any director or former director of the company or an associated company.

53. Insurance

(1) The directors may decide to purchase and maintain insurance, at the expense of the company, for the benefit of any relevant director in respect of any relevant loss.

(2) In this article—

(a) a "relevant director" means any director or former director of the company or an associated company,

(b) a "relevant loss" means any loss or liability which has been or may be incurred by a relevant director in connection with that director's duties or powers in relation to the company, any associated company or any pension fund or employees' share scheme of the company or associated company, and

(c) companies are associated if one is a subsidiary of the other or both are subsidiaries of the same body corporate.

SCHEDULE 3

Regulation 4

MODEL ARTICLES FOR PUBLIC COMPANIES

PART 1

INTERPRETATION AND LIMITATION OF LIABILITY

1. Defined terms

In the articles, unless the context requires otherwise—

"alternate" or "alternate director" has the meaning given in article 25;

"appointor" has the meaning given in article 25;

"articles" means the company's articles of association;

"bankruptcy" includes individual insolvency proceedings in a jurisdiction other than England and Wales or Northern Ireland which have an effect similar to that of bankruptcy;

"call" has the meaning given in article 54;

"call notice" has the meaning given in article 54;

"certificate" means a paper certificate (other than a share warrant) evidencing a person's title to specified shares or other securities;

"certificated" in relation to a share, means that it is not an uncertificated share or a share in respect of which a share warrant has been issued and is current;

"chairman" has the meaning given in article 12;

"chairman of the meeting" has the meaning given in article 31;

"Companies Acts" means the Companies Acts (as defined in section 2 of the Companies Act 2006), in so far as they apply to the company;

"company's lien" has the meaning given in article 52;

"director" means a director of the company, and includes any person occupying the position of director, by whatever name called;

"distribution recipient" has the meaning given in article 72;

"document" includes, unless otherwise specified, any document sent or supplied in electronic form;

"electronic form" has the meaning given in section 1168 of the Companies Act 2006;

"fully paid" in relation to a share, means that the nominal value and any premium to be paid to the company in respect of that share have been paid to the company;

"hard copy form" has the meaning given in section 1168 of the Companies Act 2006;

"holder" in relation to shares means the person whose name is entered in the register of members as the holder of the shares, or, in the case of a share in respect of which a share warrant has been issued (and not cancelled), the person in possession of that warrant;

"instrument" means a document in hard copy form;

"lien enforcement notice" has the meaning given in article 53;

"member" has the meaning given in section 112 of the Companies Act 2006;

"ordinary resolution" has the meaning given in section 282 of the Companies Act 2006;

"paid" means paid or credited as paid;

"participate", in relation to a directors' meeting, has the meaning given in article 9;

"partly paid" in relation to a share means that part of that share's nominal value or any premium at which it was issued has not been paid to the company;

"proxy notice" has the meaning given in article 38;
"securities seal" has the meaning given in article 47;
"shares" means shares in the company;
"special resolution" has the meaning given in section 283 of the Companies Act 2006;
"subsidiary" has the meaning given in section 1159 of the Companies Act 2006;
"transmittee" means a person entitled to a share by reason of the death or bankruptcy of a shareholder or otherwise by operation of law;
"uncertificated" in relation to a share means that, by virtue of legislation (other than section 778 of the Companies Act 2006) permitting title to shares to be evidenced and transferred without a certificate, title to that share is evidenced and may be transferred without a certificate; and
"writing" means the representation or reproduction of words, symbols or other information in a visible form by any method or combination of methods, whether sent or supplied in electronic form or otherwise.

Unless the context otherwise requires, other words or expressions contained in these articles bear the same meaning as in the Companies Act 2006 as in force on the date when these articles become binding on the company.

2. Liability of members

The liability of the members is limited to the amount, if any, unpaid on the shares held by them.

PART 2
DIRECTORS

Directors' Powers and Responsibilities

3. Directors' general authority

Subject to the articles, the directors are responsible for the management of the company's business, for which purpose they may exercise all the powers of the company.

4. Members' reserve power

(1) The members may, by special resolution, direct the directors to take, or refrain from taking, specified action.

(2) No such special resolution invalidates anything which the directors have done before the passing of the resolution.

5. Directors may delegate

(1) Subject to the articles, the directors may delegate any of the powers which are conferred on them under the articles—

(a) to such person or committee;
(b) by such means (including by power of attorney);
(c) to such an extent;
(d) in relation to such matters or territories; and
(e) on such terms and conditions;

as they think fit.

(2) If the directors so specify, any such delegation may authorise further delegation of the directors' powers by any person to whom they are delegated.

(3) The directors may revoke any delegation in whole or part, or alter its terms and conditions.

6. Committees

(1) Committees to which the directors delegate any of their powers must follow procedures which are based as far as they are applicable on those provisions of the articles which govern the taking of decisions by directors.

(2) The directors may make rules of procedure for all or any committees, which prevail over rules derived from the articles if they are not consistent with them.

Decision-Making by Directors

7. Directors to take decisions collectively

Decisions of the directors may be taken—

(a) at a directors' meeting, or

(b) in the form of a directors' written resolution.

8. Calling a directors' meeting

(1) Any director may call a directors' meeting.

(2) The company secretary must call a directors' meeting if a director so requests.

(3) A directors' meeting is called by giving notice of the meeting to the directors.

(4) Notice of any directors' meeting must indicate—

(a) its proposed date and time;

(b) where it is to take place; and

(c) if it is anticipated that directors participating in the meeting will not be in the same place, how it is proposed that they should communicate with each other during the meeting.

(5) Notice of a directors' meeting must be given to each director, but need not be in writing.

(6) Notice of a directors' meeting need not be given to directors who waive their entitlement to notice of that meeting, by giving notice to that effect to the company not more than 7 days after the date on which the meeting is held. Where such notice is given after the meeting has been held, that does not affect the validity of the meeting, or of any business conducted at it.

9. Participation in directors' meetings

(1) Subject to the articles, directors participate in a directors' meeting, or part of a directors' meeting, when—

(a) the meeting has been called and takes place in accordance with the articles, and

(b) they can each communicate to the others any information or opinions they have on any particular item of the business of the meeting.

(2) In determining whether directors are participating in a directors' meeting, it is irrelevant where any director is or how they communicate with each other.

(3) If all the directors participating in a meeting are not in the same place, they may decide that the meeting is to be treated as taking place wherever any of them is.

10. Quorum for directors' meetings

(1) At a directors' meeting, unless a quorum is participating, no proposal is to be voted on, except a proposal to call another meeting.

(2) The quorum for directors' meetings may be fixed from time to time by a decision of the directors, but it must never be less than two, and unless otherwise fixed it is two.

11. Meetings where total number of directors less than quorum

(1) This article applies where the total number of directors for the time being is less than the quorum for directors' meetings.

(2) If there is only one director, that director may appoint sufficient directors to make up a quorum or call a general meeting to do so.

(3) If there is more than one director—

(a) a directors' meeting may take place, if it is called in accordance with the articles and at least two directors participate in it, with a view to appointing sufficient directors to make up a quorum or calling a general meeting to do so, and

(b) if a directors' meeting is called but only one director attends at the appointed date and time to participate in it, that director may appoint sufficient directors to make up a quorum or call a general meeting to do so.

12. Chairing directors' meetings

(1) The directors may appoint a director to chair their meetings.

(2) The person so appointed for the time being is known as the chairman.

(3) The directors may appoint other directors as deputy or assistant chairmen to chair directors' meetings in the chairman's absence.

(4) The directors may terminate the appointment of the chairman, deputy or assistant chairman at any time.

(5) If neither the chairman nor any director appointed generally to chair directors' meetings in the chairman's absence is participating in a meeting within ten minutes of the time at which it was to start, the participating directors must appoint one of themselves to chair it.

13. Voting at directors' meetings: general rules

(1) Subject to the articles, a decision is taken at a directors' meeting by a majority of the votes of the participating directors.

(2) Subject to the articles, each director participating in a directors' meeting has one vote.

(3) Subject to the articles, if a director has an interest in an actual or proposed transaction or arrangement with the company—

(a) that director and that director's alternate may not vote on any proposal relating to it, but

(b) this does not preclude the alternate from voting in relation to that transaction or arrangement on behalf of another appointor who does not have such an interest.

14. Chairman's casting vote at directors' meetings

(1) If the numbers of votes for and against a proposal are equal, the chairman or other director chairing the meeting has a casting vote.

(2) But this does not apply if, in accordance with the articles, the chairman or other director is not to be counted as participating in the decision-making process for quorum or voting purposes.

15. Alternates voting at directors' meetings

A director who is also an alternate director has an additional vote on behalf of each appointor who is—

(a) not participating in a directors' meeting, and

(b) would have been entitled to vote if they were participating in it.

16. Conflicts of interest

(1) If a directors' meeting, or part of a directors' meeting, is concerned with an actual or proposed transaction or arrangement with the company in which a director is interested, that director is not to be counted as participating in that meeting, or part of a meeting, for quorum or voting purposes.

(2) But if paragraph (3) applies, a director who is interested in an actual or proposed transaction or arrangement with the company is to be counted as participating in a decision at a directors' meeting, or part of a directors' meeting, relating to it for quorum and voting purposes.

(3) This paragraph applies when—

(a) the company by ordinary resolution disapplies the provision of the articles which would otherwise prevent a director from being counted as participating in, or voting at, a directors' meeting;

(b) the director's interest cannot reasonably be regarded as likely to give rise to a conflict of interest; or

(c) the director's conflict of interest arises from a permitted cause.

(4) For the purposes of this article, the following are permitted causes—

(a) a guarantee given, or to be given, by or to a director in respect of an obligation incurred by or on behalf of the company or any of its subsidiaries;

(b) subscription, or an agreement to subscribe, for shares or other securities of the company or any of its subsidiaries, or to underwrite, sub-underwrite, or guarantee subscription for any such shares or securities; and

(c) arrangements pursuant to which benefits are made available to employees and directors or former employees and directors of the company or any of its subsidiaries which do not provide special benefits for directors or former directors.

(5) Subject to paragraph (6), if a question arises at a meeting of directors or of a committee of directors as to the right of a director to participate in the meeting (or part of the meeting) for voting or quorum purposes, the question may, before the conclusion of the meeting, be referred to the chairman whose ruling in relation to any director other than the chairman is to be final and conclusive.

(6) If any question as to the right to participate in the meeting (or part of the meeting) should arise in respect of the chairman, the question is to be decided by a decision of the directors at that meeting, for which purpose the chairman is not to be counted as participating in the meeting (or that part of the meeting) for voting or quorum purposes.

17. Proposing directors' written resolutions

(1) Any director may propose a directors' written resolution.

(2) The company secretary must propose a directors' written resolution if a director so requests.

(3) A directors' written resolution is proposed by giving notice of the proposed resolution to the directors.

(4) Notice of a proposed directors' written resolution must indicate—

(a) the proposed resolution, and

(b) the time by which it is proposed that the directors should adopt it.

(5) Notice of a proposed directors' written resolution must be given in writing to each director.

(6) Any decision which a person giving notice of a proposed directors' written resolution takes regarding the process of adopting that resolution must be taken reasonably in good faith.

18. Adoption of directors' written resolutions

(1) A proposed directors' written resolution is adopted when all the directors who would have been entitled to vote on the resolution at a directors' meeting have signed one or more copies of it, provided that those directors would have formed a quorum at such a meeting.

(2) It is immaterial whether any director signs the resolution before or after the time by which the notice proposed that it should be adopted.

(3) Once a directors' written resolution has been adopted, it must be treated as if it had been a decision taken at a directors' meeting in accordance with the articles.

(4) The company secretary must ensure that the company keeps a record, in writing, of all directors' written resolutions for at least ten years from the date of their adoption.

19. Directors' discretion to make further rules

Subject to the articles, the directors may make any rule which they think fit about how they take decisions, and about how such rules are to be recorded or communicated to directors.

Appointment of Directors

20. Methods of appointing directors

Any person who is willing to act as a director, and is permitted by law to do so, may be appointed to be a director—

(a) by ordinary resolution, or

(b) by a decision of the directors.

21. Retirement of directors by rotation

(1) At the first annual general meeting all the directors must retire from office.

(2) At every subsequent annual general meeting any directors—

(a) who have been appointed by the directors since the last annual general meeting, or

(b) who were not appointed or reappointed at one of the preceding two annual general meetings,

must retire from office and may offer themselves for reappointment by the members.

22. Termination of director's appointment

A person ceases to be a director as soon as—

(a) that person ceases to be a director by virtue of any provision of the Companies Act 2006 or is prohibited from being a director by law;

(b) a bankruptcy order is made against that person;

(c) a composition is made with that person's creditors generally in satisfaction of that person's debts;

(d) a registered medical practitioner who is treating that person gives a written opinion to the company stating that that person has become physically or mentally incapable of acting as a director and may remain so for more than three months;

(e) by reason of that person's mental health, a court makes an order which wholly or partly prevents that person from personally exercising any powers or rights which that person would otherwise have;

(f) notification is received by the company from the director that the director is resigning from office as director, and such resignation has taken effect in accordance with its terms.

Note. Subparagraph (e) is revoked by the Mental Health (Discrimination) Act 2013, s. 3(1)(c), as from 28 April 2013.

23. Directors' remuneration

(1) Directors may undertake any services for the company that the directors decide.

(2) Directors are entitled to such remuneration as the directors determine—

(a) for their services to the company as directors, and

(b) for any other service which they undertake for the company.

(3) Subject to the articles, a director's remuneration may—

(a) take any form, and

(b) include any arrangements in connection with the payment of a pension, allowance or gratuity, or any death, sickness or disability benefits, to or in respect of that director.

(4) Unless the directors decide otherwise, directors' remuneration accrues from day to day.

(5) Unless the directors decide otherwise, directors are not accountable to the company for any remuneration which they receive as directors or other officers or employees of the company's subsidiaries or of any other body corporate in which the company is interested.

24. Directors' expenses

The company may pay any reasonable expenses which the directors properly incur in connection with their attendance at—

(a) meetings of directors or committees of directors,

(b) general meetings, or

(c) separate meetings of the holders of any class of shares or of debentures of the company,

or otherwise in connection with the exercise of their powers and the discharge of their responsibilities in relation to the company.

Alternate Directors

25. Appointment and removal of alternates

(1) Any director (the "appointor") may appoint as an alternate any other director, or any other person approved by resolution of the directors, to—

(a) exercise that director's powers, and
(b) carry out that director's responsibilities,

in relation to the taking of decisions by the directors in the absence of the alternate's appointor.

(2) Any appointment or removal of an alternate must be effected by notice in writing to the company signed by the appointor, or in any other manner approved by the directors.

(3) The notice must—
(a) identify the proposed alternate, and
(b) in the case of a notice of appointment, contain a statement signed by the proposed alternate that the proposed alternate is willing to act as the alternate of the director giving the notice.

26. Rights and responsibilities of alternate directors

(1) An alternate director has the same rights, in relation to any directors' meeting or directors' written resolution, as the alternate's appointor.

(2) Except as the articles specify otherwise, alternate directors—
(a) are deemed for all purposes to be directors;
(b) are liable for their own acts and omissions;
(c) are subject to the same restrictions as their appointors; and
(d) are not deemed to be agents of or for their appointors.

(3) A person who is an alternate director but not a director—
(a) may be counted as participating for the purposes of determining whether a quorum is participating (but only if that person's appointor is not participating), and
(b) may sign a written resolution (but only if it is not signed or to be signed by that person's appointor).

No alternate may be counted as more than one director for such purposes.

(4) An alternate director is not entitled to receive any remuneration from the company for serving as an alternate director except such part of the alternate's appointor's remuneration as the appointor may direct by notice in writing made to the company.

27. Termination of alternate directorship

An alternate director's appointment as an alternate terminates—
(a) when the alternate's appointor revokes the appointment by notice to the company in writing specifying when it is to terminate;
(b) on the occurrence in relation to the alternate of any event which, if it occurred in relation to the alternate's appointor, would result in the termination of the appointor's appointment as a director;
(c) on the death of the alternate's appointor; or
(d) when the alternate's appointor's appointment as a director terminates, except that an alternate's appointment as an alternate does not terminate when the appointor retires by rotation at a general meeting and is then re-appointed as a director at the same general meeting.

PART 3
DECISION-MAKING BY MEMBERS

Organisation of General Meetings

28. Members can call general meeting if not enough directors

If—
(a) the company has fewer than two directors, and
(b) the director (if any) is unable or unwilling to appoint sufficient directors to make up a quorum or to call a general meeting to do so,

then two or more members may call a general meeting (or instruct the company secretary to do so) for the purpose of appointing one or more directors.

29. Attendance and speaking at general meetings

(1) A person is able to exercise the right to speak at a general meeting when that person is in a position to communicate to all those attending the meeting, during the meeting, any information or opinions which that person has on the business of the meeting.

(2) A person is able to exercise the right to vote at a general meeting when—

(a) that person is able to vote, during the meeting, on resolutions put to the vote at the meeting, and

(b) that person's vote can be taken into account in determining whether or not such resolutions are passed at the same time as the votes of all the other persons attending the meeting.

(3) The directors may make whatever arrangements they consider appropriate to enable those attending a general meeting to exercise their rights to speak or vote at it.

(4) In determining attendance at a general meeting, it is immaterial whether any two or more members attending it are in the same place as each other.

(5) Two or more persons who are not in the same place as each other attend a general meeting if their circumstances are such that if they have (or were to have) rights to speak and vote at that meeting, they are (or would be) able to exercise them.

30. Quorum for general meetings

No business other than the appointment of the chairman of the meeting is to be transacted at a general meeting if the persons attending it do not constitute a quorum.

31. Chairing general meetings

(1) If the directors have appointed a chairman, the chairman shall chair general meetings if present and willing to do so.

(2) If the directors have not appointed a chairman, or if the chairman is unwilling to chair the meeting or is not present within ten minutes of the time at which a meeting was due to start—

(a) the directors present, or

(b) (if no directors are present), the meeting,

must appoint a director or member to chair the meeting, and the appointment of the chairman of the meeting must be the first business of the meeting.

(3) The person chairing a meeting in accordance with this article is referred to as "the chairman of the meeting".

32. Attendance and speaking by directors and non-members

(1) Directors may attend and speak at general meetings, whether or not they are members.

(2) The chairman of the meeting may permit other persons who are not—

(a) members of the company, or

(b) otherwise entitled to exercise the rights of members in relation to general meetings,

to attend and speak at a general meeting.

33. Adjournment

(1) If the persons attending a general meeting within half an hour of the time at which the meeting was due to start do not constitute a quorum, or if during a meeting a quorum ceases to be present, the chairman of the meeting must adjourn it.

(2) The chairman of the meeting may adjourn a general meeting at which a quorum is present if—

(a) the meeting consents to an adjournment, or

(b) it appears to the chairman of the meeting that an adjournment is necessary to protect the safety of any person attending the meeting or ensure that the business of the meeting is conducted in an orderly manner.

(3) The chairman of the meeting must adjourn a general meeting if directed to do so by the meeting.

(4) When adjourning a general meeting, the chairman of the meeting must—
(a) either specify the time and place to which it is adjourned or state that it is to continue at a time and place to be fixed by the directors, and
(b) have regard to any directions as to the time and place of any adjournment which have been given by the meeting.

(5) If the continuation of an adjourned meeting is to take place more than 14 days after it was adjourned, the company must give at least 7 clear days' notice of it (that is, excluding the day of the adjourned meeting and the day on which the notice is given)—
(a) to the same persons to whom notice of the company's general meetings is required to be given, and
(b) containing the same information which such notice is required to contain.

(6) No business may be transacted at an adjourned general meeting which could not properly have been transacted at the meeting if the adjournment had not taken place.

Voting at General Meetings

34. Voting: general

A resolution put to the vote of a general meeting must be decided on a show of hands unless a poll is duly demanded in accordance with the articles.

35. Errors and disputes

(1) No objection may be raised to the qualification of any person voting at a general meeting except at the meeting or adjourned meeting at which the vote objected to is tendered, and every vote not disallowed at the meeting is valid.

(2) Any such objection must be referred to the chairman of the meeting whose decision is final.

36. Demanding a poll

(1) A poll on a resolution may be demanded—
(a) in advance of the general meeting where it is to be put to the vote, or
(b) at a general meeting, either before a show of hands on that resolution or immediately after the result of a show of hands on that resolution is declared.

(2) A poll may be demanded by—
(a) the chairman of the meeting;
(b) the directors;
(c) two or more persons having the right to vote on the resolution; or
(d) a person or persons representing not less than one tenth of the total voting rights of all the members having the right to vote on the resolution.

(3) A demand for a poll may be withdrawn if—
(a) the poll has not yet been taken, and
(b) the chairman of the meeting consents to the withdrawal.

37. Procedure on a poll

(1) Subject to the articles, polls at general meetings must be taken when, where and in such manner as the chairman of the meeting directs.

(2) The chairman of the meeting may appoint scrutineers (who need not be members) and decide how and when the result of the poll is to be declared.

(3) The result of a poll shall be the decision of the meeting in respect of the resolution on which the poll was demanded.

(4) A poll on—
(a) the election of the chairman of the meeting, or
(b) a question of adjournment,
must be taken immediately.

(5) Other polls must be taken within 30 days of their being demanded.

(6) A demand for a poll does not prevent a general meeting from continuing, except as regards the question on which the poll was demanded.

(7) No notice need be given of a poll not taken immediately if the time and place at which it is to be taken are announced at the meeting at which it is demanded.

(8) In any other case, at least 7 days' notice must be given specifying the time and place at which the poll is to be taken.

38. Content of proxy notices

(1) Proxies may only validly be appointed by a notice in writing (a "proxy notice") which—
- (a) states the name and address of the member appointing the proxy;
- (b) identifies the person appointed to be that member's proxy and the general meeting in relation to which that person is appointed;
- (c) is signed by or on behalf of the member appointing the proxy, or is authenticated in such manner as the directors may determine; and
- (d) is delivered to the company in accordance with the articles and any instructions contained in the notice of the general meeting to which they relate.

(2) The company may require proxy notices to be delivered in a particular form, and may specify different forms for different purposes.

(3) Proxy notices may specify how the proxy appointed under them is to vote (or that the proxy is to abstain from voting) on one or more resolutions.

(4) Unless a proxy notice indicates otherwise, it must be treated as—
- (a) allowing the person appointed under it as a proxy discretion as to how to vote on any ancillary or procedural resolutions put to the meeting, and
- (b) appointing that person as a proxy in relation to any adjournment of the general meeting to which it relates as well as the meeting itself.

39. Delivery of proxy notices

(1) Any notice of a general meeting must specify the address or addresses ("proxy notification address") at which the company or its agents will receive proxy notices relating to that meeting, or any adjournment of it, delivered in hard copy or electronic form.

(2) A person who is entitled to attend, speak or vote (either on a show of hands or on a poll) at a general meeting remains so entitled in respect of that meeting or any adjournment of it, even though a valid proxy notice has been delivered to the company by or on behalf of that person.

(3) Subject to paragraphs (4) and (5), a proxy notice must be delivered to a proxy notification address not less than 48 hours before the general meeting or adjourned meeting to which it relates.

(4) In the case of a poll taken more than 48 hours after it is demanded, the notice must be delivered to a proxy notification address not less than 24 hours before the time appointed for the taking of the poll.

(5) In the case of a poll not taken during the meeting but taken not more than 48 hours after it was demanded, the proxy notice must be delivered—
- (a) in accordance with paragraph (3), or
- (b) at the meeting at which the poll was demanded to the chairman, secretary or any director.

(6) An appointment under a proxy notice may be revoked by delivering a notice in writing given by or on behalf of the person by whom or on whose behalf the proxy notice was given to a proxy notification address.

(7) A notice revoking a proxy appointment only takes effect if it is delivered before—
- (a) the start of the meeting or adjourned meeting to which it relates, or
- (b) (in the case of a poll not taken on the same day as the meeting or adjourned meeting) the time appointed for taking the poll to which it relates.

(8) If a proxy notice is not signed by the person appointing the proxy, it must be accompanied by written evidence of the authority of the person who executed it to execute it on the appointor's behalf.

40. Amendments to resolutions

(1) An ordinary resolution to be proposed at a general meeting may be amended by ordinary resolution if—

(a) notice of the proposed amendment is given to the company secretary in writing by a person entitled to vote at the general meeting at which it is to be proposed not less than 48 hours before the meeting is to take place (or such later time as the chairman of the meeting may determine), and

(b) the proposed amendment does not, in the reasonable opinion of the chairman of the meeting, materially alter the scope of the resolution.

(2) A special resolution to be proposed at a general meeting may be amended by ordinary resolution, if—

(a) the chairman of the meeting proposes the amendment at the general meeting at which the resolution is to be proposed, and

(b) the amendment does not go beyond what is necessary to correct a grammatical or other non-substantive error in the resolution.

(3) If the chairman of the meeting, acting in good faith, wrongly decides that an amendment to a resolution is out of order, the chairman's error does not invalidate the vote on that resolution.

Restrictions on Members' Rights

41. No voting of shares on which money owed to company

No voting rights attached to a share may be exercised at any general meeting, at any adjournment of it, or on any poll called at or in relation to it, unless all amounts payable to the company in respect of that share have been paid.

Application of Rules to Class Meetings

42. Class meetings

The provisions of the articles relating to general meetings apply, with any necessary modifications, to meetings of the holders of any class of shares.

PART 4
SHARES AND DISTRIBUTIONS

Issue of Shares

43. Powers to issue different classes of share

(1) Subject to the articles, but without prejudice to the rights attached to any existing share, the company may issue shares with such rights or restrictions as may be determined by ordinary resolution.

(2) The company may issue shares which are to be redeemed, or are liable to be redeemed at the option of the company or the holder, and the directors may determine the terms, conditions and manner of redemption of any such shares.

44. Payment of commissions on subscription for shares

(1) The company may pay any person a commission in consideration for that person—

(a) subscribing, or agreeing to subscribe, for shares, or

(b) procuring, or agreeing to procure, subscriptions for shares.

(2) Any such commission may be paid—

(a) in cash, or in fully paid or partly paid shares or other securities, or partly in one way and partly in the other, and

(b) in respect of a conditional or an absolute subscription.

Interests in Shares

45. Company not bound by less than absolute interests

Except as required by law, no person is to be recognised by the company as holding any share upon any trust, and except as otherwise required by law or the articles, the company is not in any way to be bound by or recognise any interest in a share other than the holder's absolute ownership of it and all the rights attaching to it.

Share Certificates

46. Certificates to be issued except in certain cases

(1) The company must issue each member with one or more certificates in respect of the shares which that member holds.

(2) This article does not apply to—

(a) uncertificated shares;

(b) shares in respect of which a share warrant has been issued; or

(c) shares in respect of which the Companies Acts permit the company not to issue a certificate.

(3) Except as otherwise specified in the articles, all certificates must be issued free of charge.

(4) No certificate may be issued in respect of shares of more than one class.

(5) If more than one person holds a share, only one certificate may be issued in respect of it.

47. Contents and execution of share certificates

(1) Every certificate must specify—

(a) in respect of how many shares, of what class, it is issued;

(b) the nominal value of those shares;

(c) the amount paid up on them; and

(d) any distinguishing numbers assigned to them.

(2) Certificates must—

(a) have affixed to them the company's common seal or an official seal which is a facsimile of the company's common seal with the addition on its face of the word "Securities" (a "securities seal"), or

(b) be otherwise executed in accordance with the Companies Acts.

48. Consolidated share certificates

(1) When a member's holding of shares of a particular class increases, the company may issue that member with—

(a) a single, consolidated certificate in respect of all the shares of a particular class which that member holds, or

(b) a separate certificate in respect of only those shares by which that member's holding has increased.

(2) When a member's holding of shares of a particular class is reduced, the company must ensure that the member is issued with one or more certificates in respect of the number of shares held by the member after that reduction. But the company need not (in the absence of a request from the member) issue any new certificate if—

(a) all the shares which the member no longer holds as a result of the reduction, and

(b) none of the shares which the member retains following the reduction,

were, immediately before the reduction, represented by the same certificate.

(3) A member may request the company, in writing, to replace—

(a) the member's separate certificates with a consolidated certificate, or

(b) the member's consolidated certificate with two or more separate certificates representing such proportion of the shares as the member may specify.

(4) When the company complies with such a request it may charge such reasonable fee as the directors may decide for doing so.

(5) A consolidated certificate must not be issued unless any certificates which it is to replace have first been returned to the company for cancellation.

49. Replacement share certificates

(1) If a certificate issued in respect of a member's shares is—

(a) damaged or defaced, or

(b) said to be lost, stolen or destroyed,

that member is entitled to be issued with a replacement certificate in respect of the same shares.

(2) A member exercising the right to be issued with such a replacement certificate—

(a) may at the same time exercise the right to be issued with a single certificate or separate certificates;

(b) must return the certificate which is to be replaced to the company if it is damaged or defaced; and

(c) must comply with such conditions as to evidence, indemnity and the payment of a reasonable fee as the directors decide.

Shares not Held in Certificated Form

50. Uncertificated shares

(1) In this article, "the relevant rules" means—

(a) any applicable provision of the Companies Acts about the holding, evidencing of title to, or transfer of shares other than in certificated form, and

(b) any applicable legislation, rules or other arrangements made under or by virtue of such provision.

(2) The provisions of this article have effect subject to the relevant rules.

(3) Any provision of the articles which is inconsistent with the relevant rules must be disregarded, to the extent that it is inconsistent, whenever the relevant rules apply.

(4) Any share or class of shares of the company may be issued or held on such terms, or in such a way, that—

(a) title to it or them is not, or must not be, evidenced by a certificate, or

(b) it or they may or must be transferred wholly or partly without a certificate.

(5) The directors have power to take such steps as they think fit in relation to—

(a) the evidencing of and transfer of title to uncertificated shares (including in connection with the issue of such shares);

(b) any records relating to the holding of uncertificated shares;

(c) the conversion of certificated shares into uncertificated shares; or

(d) the conversion of uncertificated shares into certificated shares.

(6) The company may by notice to the holder of a share require that share—

(a) if it is uncertificated, to be converted into certificated form, and

(b) if it is certificated, to be converted into uncertificated form,

to enable it to be dealt with in accordance with the articles.

(7) If—

(a) the articles give the directors power to take action, or require other persons to take action, in order to sell, transfer or otherwise dispose of shares, and

(b) uncertificated shares are subject to that power, but the power is expressed in terms which assume the use of a certificate or other written instrument,

the directors may take such action as is necessary or expedient to achieve the same results when exercising that power in relation to uncertificated shares.

(8) In particular, the directors may take such action as they consider appropriate to achieve the sale, transfer, disposal, forfeiture, re-allotment or surrender of an uncertificated share or otherwise to enforce a lien in respect of it.

(9) Unless the directors otherwise determine, shares which a member holds in uncertificated form must be treated as separate holdings from any shares which that member holds in certificated form.

(10) A class of shares must not be treated as two classes simply because some shares of that class are held in certificated form and others are held in uncertificated form.

51. Share warrants

(1) The directors may issue a share warrant in respect of any fully paid share.

(2) Share warrants must be—

(a) issued in such form, and

(b) executed in such manner,

as the directors decide.

(3) A share represented by a share warrant may be transferred by delivery of the warrant representing it.

(4) The directors may make provision for the payment of dividends in respect of any share represented by a share warrant.

(5) Subject to the articles, the directors may decide the conditions on which any share warrant is issued. In particular, they may—

(a) decide the conditions on which new warrants are to be issued in place of warrants which are damaged or defaced, or said to have been lost, stolen or destroyed;

(b) decide the conditions on which bearers of warrants are entitled to attend and vote at general meetings;

(c) decide the conditions subject to which bearers of warrants may surrender their warrant so as to hold their shares in certificated or uncertificated form instead; and

(d) vary the conditions of issue of any warrant from time to time,

and the bearer of a warrant is subject to the conditions and procedures in force in relation to it, whether or not they were decided or specified before the warrant was issued.

(6) Subject to the conditions on which the warrants are issued from time to time, bearers of share warrants have the same rights and privileges as they would if their names had been included in the register as holders of the shares represented by their warrants.

(7) The company must not in any way be bound by or recognise any interest in a share represented by a share warrant other than the absolute right of the bearer of that warrant to that warrant.

Partly Paid Shares

52. Company's lien over partly paid shares

(1) The company has a lien ("the company's lien") over every share which is partly paid for any part of—

(a) that share's nominal value, and

(b) any premium at which it was issued,

which has not been paid to the company, and which is payable immediately or at some time in the future, whether or not a call notice has been sent in respect of it.

(2) The company's lien over a share—

(a) takes priority over any third party's interest in that share, and

(b) extends to any dividend or other money payable by the company in respect of that share and (if the lien is enforced and the share is sold by the company) the proceeds of sale of that share.

(3) The directors may at any time decide that a share which is or would otherwise be subject to the company's lien shall not be subject to it, either wholly or in part.

53. Enforcement of the company's lien

(1) Subject to the provisions of this article, if—

(a) a lien enforcement notice has been given in respect of a share, and

(b) the person to whom the notice was given has failed to comply with it,

the company may sell that share in such manner as the directors decide.

(2) A lien enforcement notice—

(a) may only be given in respect of a share which is subject to the company's lien, in respect of which a sum is payable and the due date for payment of that sum has passed;

(b) must specify the share concerned;

(c) must require payment of the sum payable within 14 days of the notice;

(d) must be addressed either to the holder of the share or to a person entitled to it by reason of the holder's death, bankruptcy or otherwise; and

(e) must state the company's intention to sell the share if the notice is not complied with.

(3) Where shares are sold under this article—

(a) the directors may authorise any person to execute an instrument of transfer of the shares to the purchaser or a person nominated by the purchaser, and

(b) the transferee is not bound to see to the application of the consideration, and the transferee's title is not affected by any irregularity in or invalidity of the process leading to the sale.

(4) The net proceeds of any such sale (after payment of the costs of sale and any other costs of enforcing the lien) must be applied—

(a) first, in payment of so much of the sum for which the lien exists as was payable at the date of the lien enforcement notice,

(b) second, to the person entitled to the shares at the date of the sale, but only after the certificate for the shares sold has been surrendered to the company for cancellation or a suitable indemnity has been given for any lost certificates, and subject to a lien equivalent to the company's lien over the shares before the sale for any money payable in respect of the shares after the date of the lien enforcement notice.

(5) A statutory declaration by a director or the company secretary that the declarant is a director or the company secretary and that a share has been sold to satisfy the company's lien on a specified date—

(a) is conclusive evidence of the facts stated in it as against all persons claiming to be entitled to the share, and

(b) subject to compliance with any other formalities of transfer required by the articles or by law, constitutes a good title to the share.

54. Call notices

(1) Subject to the articles and the terms on which shares are allotted, the directors may send a notice (a "call notice") to a member requiring the member to pay the company a specified sum of money (a "call") which is payable in respect of shares which that member holds at the date when the directors decide to send the call notice.

(2) A call notice—

(a) may not require a member to pay a call which exceeds the total sum unpaid on that member's shares (whether as to the share's nominal value or any amount payable to the company by way of premium);

(b) must state when and how any call to which it relates it is to be paid; and

(c) may permit or require the call to be paid by instalments.

(3) A member must comply with the requirements of a call notice, but no member is obliged to pay any call before 14 days have passed since the notice was sent.

(4) Before the company has received any call due under a call notice the directors may—

(a) revoke it wholly or in part, or

(b) specify a later time for payment than is specified in the notice,

by a further notice in writing to the member in respect of whose shares the call is made.

55. Liability to pay calls

(1) Liability to pay a call is not extinguished or transferred by transferring the shares in respect of which it is required to be paid.

(2) Joint holders of a share are jointly and severally liable to pay all calls in respect of that share.

(3) Subject to the terms on which shares are allotted, the directors may, when issuing shares, provide that call notices sent to the holders of those shares may require them—

(a) to pay calls which are not the same, or

(b) to pay calls at different times.

56. When call notice need not be issued

(1) A call notice need not be issued in respect of sums which are specified, in the terms on which a share is issued, as being payable to the company in respect of that share (whether in respect of nominal value or premium)—

(a) on allotment;

(b) on the occurrence of a particular event; or

(c) on a date fixed by or in accordance with the terms of issue.

(2) But if the due date for payment of such a sum has passed and it has not been paid, the holder of the share concerned is treated in all respects as having failed to comply with a call notice in respect of that sum, and is liable to the same consequences as regards the payment of interest and forfeiture.

57. Failure to comply with call notice: automatic consequences

(1) If a person is liable to pay a call and fails to do so by the call payment date—

(a) the directors may issue a notice of intended forfeiture to that person, and

(b) until the call is paid, that person must pay the company interest on the call from the call payment date at the relevant rate.

(2) For the purposes of this article—

(a) the "call payment date" is the time when the call notice states that a call is payable, unless the directors give a notice specifying a later date, in which case the "call payment date" is that later date;

(b) the "relevant rate" is—

(i) the rate fixed by the terms on which the share in respect of which the call is due was allotted;

(ii) such other rate as was fixed in the call notice which required payment of the call, or has otherwise been determined by the directors; or

(iii) if no rate is fixed in either of these ways, 5 per cent per annum.

(3) The relevant rate must not exceed by more than 5 percentage points the base lending rate most recently set by the Monetary Policy Committee of the Bank of England in connection with its responsibilities under Part 2 of the Bank of England Act 1998.

(4) The directors may waive any obligation to pay interest on a call wholly or in part.

58. Notice of intended forfeiture

A notice of intended forfeiture—

(a) may be sent in respect of any share in respect of which a call has not been paid as required by a call notice;

(b) must be sent to the holder of that share or to a person entitled to it by reason of the holder's death, bankruptcy or otherwise;

(c) must require payment of the call and any accrued interest by a date which is not less than 14 days after the date of the notice;

(d) must state how the payment is to be made; and

(e) must state that if the notice is not complied with, the shares in respect of which the call is payable will be liable to be forfeited.

59. Directors' power to forfeit shares

If a notice of intended forfeiture is not complied with before the date by which payment of the call is required in the notice of intended forfeiture, the directors may decide that any share in respect of which it was given is forfeited, and the forfeiture is to include all dividends or other moneys payable in respect of the forfeited shares and not paid before the forfeiture.

60. Effect of forfeiture

(1) Subject to the articles, the forfeiture of a share extinguishes—
 (a) all interests in that share, and all claims and demands against the company in respect of it, and
 (b) all other rights and liabilities incidental to the share as between the person whose share it was prior to the forfeiture and the company.

(2) Any share which is forfeited in accordance with the articles—
 (a) is deemed to have been forfeited when the directors decide that it is forfeited;
 (b) is deemed to be the property of the company; and
 (c) may be sold, re-allotted or otherwise disposed of as the directors think fit.

(3) If a person's shares have been forfeited—
 (a) the company must send that person notice that forfeiture has occurred and record it in the register of members;
 (b) that person ceases to be a member in respect of those shares;
 (c) that person must surrender the certificate for the shares forfeited to the company for cancellation;
 (d) that person remains liable to the company for all sums payable by that person under the articles at the date of forfeiture in respect of those shares, including any interest (whether accrued before or after the date of forfeiture); and
 (e) the directors may waive payment of such sums wholly or in part or enforce payment without any allowance for the value of the shares at the time of forfeiture or for any consideration received on their disposal.

(4) At any time before the company disposes of a forfeited share, the directors may decide to cancel the forfeiture on payment of all calls and interest due in respect of it and on such other terms as they think fit.

61. Procedure following forfeiture

(1) If a forfeited share is to be disposed of by being transferred, the company may receive the consideration for the transfer and the directors may authorise any person to execute the instrument of transfer.

(2) A statutory declaration by a director or the company secretary that the declarant is a director or the company secretary and that a share has been forfeited on a specified date—
 (a) is conclusive evidence of the facts stated in it as against all persons claiming to be entitled to the share, and
 (b) subject to compliance with any other formalities of transfer required by the articles or by law, constitutes a good title to the share.

(3) A person to whom a forfeited share is transferred is not bound to see to the application of the consideration (if any) nor is that person's title to the share affected by any irregularity in or invalidity of the process leading to the forfeiture or transfer of the share.

(4) If the company sells a forfeited share, the person who held it prior to its forfeiture is entitled to receive from the company the proceeds of such sale, net of any commission, and excluding any amount which—
 (a) was, or would have become, payable, and
 (b) had not, when that share was forfeited, been paid by that person in respect of that share,

but no interest is payable to such a person in respect of such proceeds and the company is not required to account for any money earned on them.

62. Surrender of shares

(1) A member may surrender any share—

(a) in respect of which the directors may issue a notice of intended forfeiture;

(b) which the directors may forfeit; or

(c) which has been forfeited.

(2) The directors may accept the surrender of any such share.

(3) The effect of surrender on a share is the same as the effect of forfeiture on that share.

(4) A share which has been surrendered may be dealt with in the same way as a share which has been forfeited.

Transfer and Transmission of Shares

63. Transfers of certificated shares

(1) Certificated shares may be transferred by means of an instrument of transfer in any usual form or any other form approved by the directors, which is executed by or on behalf of—

(a) the transferor, and

(b) (if any of the shares is partly paid) the transferee.

(2) No fee may be charged for registering any instrument of transfer or other document relating to or affecting the title to any share.

(3) The company may retain any instrument of transfer which is registered.

(4) The transferor remains the holder of a certificated share until the transferee's name is entered in the register of members as holder of it.

(5) The directors may refuse to register the transfer of a certificated share if—

(a) the share is not fully paid;

(b) the transfer is not lodged at the company's registered office or such other place as the directors have appointed;

(c) the transfer is not accompanied by the certificate for the shares to which it relates, or such other evidence as the directors may reasonably require to show the transferor's right to make the transfer, or evidence of the right of someone other than the transferor to make the transfer on the transferor's behalf;

(d) the transfer is in respect of more than one class of share; or

(e) the transfer is in favour of more than four transferees.

(6) If the directors refuse to register the transfer of a share, the instrument of transfer must be returned to the transferee with the notice of refusal unless they suspect that the proposed transfer may be fraudulent.

64. Transfer of uncertificated shares

A transfer of an uncertificated share must not be registered if it is in favour of more than four transferees.

65. Transmission of shares

(1) If title to a share passes to a transmittee, the company may only recognise the transmittee as having any title to that share.

(2) Nothing in these articles releases the estate of a deceased member from any liability in respect of a share solely or jointly held by that member.

66. Transmittees' rights

(1) A transmittee who produces such evidence of entitlement to shares as the directors may properly require—

(a) may, subject to the articles, choose either to become the holder of those shares or to have them transferred to another person, and

(b) subject to the articles, and pending any transfer of the shares to another person, has the same rights as the holder had.

(2) But transmittees do not have the right to attend or vote at a general meeting in respect of shares to which they are entitled, by reason of the holder's death or bankruptcy or otherwise, unless they become the holders of those shares

67. Exercise of transmittees' rights

(1) Transmittees who wish to become the holders of shares to which they have become entitled must notify the company in writing of that wish.

(2) If the share is a certificated share and a transmittee wishes to have it transferred to another person, the transmittee must execute an instrument of transfer in respect of it.

(3) If the share is an uncertificated share and the transmittee wishes to have it transferred to another person, the transmittee must—

(a) procure that all appropriate instructions are given to effect the transfer, or

(b) procure that the uncertificated share is changed into certificated form and then execute an instrument of transfer in respect of it.

(4) Any transfer made or executed under this article is to be treated as if it were made or executed by the person from whom the transmittee has derived rights in respect of the share, and as if the event which gave rise to the transmission had not occurred.

68. Transmittees bound by prior notices

If a notice is given to a member in respect of shares and a transmittee is entitled to those shares, the transmittee is bound by the notice if it was given to the member before the transmittee's name has been entered in the register of members.

Consolidation of Shares

69. Procedure for disposing of fractions of shares

(1) This article applies where—

(a) there has been a consolidation or division of shares, and

(b) as a result, members are entitled to fractions of shares.

(2) The directors may—

(a) sell the shares representing the fractions to any person including the company for the best price reasonably obtainable;

(b) in the case of a certificated share, authorise any person to execute an instrument of transfer of the shares to the purchaser or a person nominated by the purchaser; and

(c) distribute the net proceeds of sale in due proportion among the holders of the shares.

(3) Where any holder's entitlement to a portion of the proceeds of sale amounts to less than a minimum figure determined by the directors, that member's portion may be distributed to an organisation which is a charity for the purposes of the law of England and Wales, Scotland or Northern Ireland.

(4) The person to whom the shares are transferred is not obliged to ensure that any purchase money is received by the person entitled to the relevant fractions.

(5) The transferee's title to the shares is not affected by any irregularity in or invalidity of the process leading to their sale.

Distributions

70. Procedure for declaring dividends

(1) The company may by ordinary resolution declare dividends, and the directors may decide to pay interim dividends.

(2) A dividend must not be declared unless the directors have made a recommendation as to its amount. Such a dividend must not exceed the amount recommended by the directors.

(3) No dividend may be declared or paid unless it is in accordance with members' respective rights.

(4) Unless the members' resolution to declare or directors' decision to pay a dividend, or the terms on which shares are issued, specify otherwise, it must be paid by reference to each member's holding of shares on the date of the resolution or decision to declare or pay it.

(5) If the company's share capital is divided into different classes, no interim dividend may be paid on shares carrying deferred or non-preferred rights if, at the time of payment, any preferential dividend is in arrear.

(6) The directors may pay at intervals any dividend payable at a fixed rate if it appears to them that the profits available for distribution justify the payment.

(7) If the directors act in good faith, they do not incur any liability to the holders of shares conferring preferred rights for any loss they may suffer by the lawful payment of an interim dividend on shares with deferred or non-preferred rights.

71. Calculation of dividends

(1) Except as otherwise provided by the articles or the rights attached to shares, all dividends must be—

(a) declared and paid according to the amounts paid up on the shares on which the dividend is paid, and

(b) apportioned and paid proportionately to the amounts paid up on the shares during any portion or portions of the period in respect of which the dividend is paid.

(2) If any share is issued on terms providing that it ranks for dividend as from a particular date, that share ranks for dividend accordingly.

(3) For the purposes of calculating dividends, no account is to be taken of any amount which has been paid up on a share in advance of the due date for payment of that amount.

72. Payment of dividends and other distributions

(1) Where a dividend or other sum which is a distribution is payable in respect of a share, it must be paid by one or more of the following means—

(a) transfer to a bank or building society account specified by the distribution recipient either in writing or as the directors may otherwise decide;

(b) sending a cheque made payable to the distribution recipient by post to the distribution recipient at the distribution recipient's registered address (if the distribution recipient is a holder of the share), or (in any other case) to an address specified by the distribution recipient either in writing or as the directors may otherwise decide;

(c) sending a cheque made payable to such person by post to such person at such address as the distribution recipient has specified either in writing or as the directors may otherwise decide; or

(d) any other means of payment as the directors agree with the distribution recipient either in writing or by such other means as the directors decide.

(2) In the articles, "the distribution recipient" means, in respect of a share in respect of which a dividend or other sum is payable—

(a) the holder of the share; or

(b) if the share has two or more joint holders, whichever of them is named first in the register of members; or

(c) if the holder is no longer entitled to the share by reason of death or bankruptcy, or otherwise by operation of law, the transmittee.

73. Deductions from distributions in respect of sums owed to the company

(1) If—

(a) a share is subject to the company's lien, and

(b) the directors are entitled to issue a lien enforcement notice in respect of it,

they may, instead of issuing a lien enforcement notice, deduct from any dividend or other sum payable in respect of the share any sum of money which is payable to the company in respect of that share to the extent that they are entitled to require payment under a lien enforcement notice.

(2) Money so deducted must be used to pay any of the sums payable in respect of that share.

(3) The company must notify the distribution recipient in writing of—

(a) the fact and amount of any such deduction;

(b) any non-payment of a dividend or other sum payable in respect of a share resulting from any such deduction; and

(c) how the money deducted has been applied.

74. No interest on distributions

The company may not pay interest on any dividend or other sum payable in respect of a share unless otherwise provided by—

(a) the terms on which the share was issued, or

(b) the provisions of another agreement between the holder of that share and the company.

75. Unclaimed distributions

(1) All dividends or other sums which are—

(a) payable in respect of shares, and

(b) unclaimed after having been declared or become payable,

may be invested or otherwise made use of by the directors for the benefit of the company until claimed.

(2) The payment of any such dividend or other sum into a separate account does not make the company a trustee in respect of it.

(3) If—

(a) twelve years have passed from the date on which a dividend or other sum became due for payment, and

(b) the distribution recipient has not claimed it,

the distribution recipient is no longer entitled to that dividend or other sum and it ceases to remain owing by the company.

76. Non-cash distributions

(1) Subject to the terms of issue of the share in question, the company may, by ordinary resolution on the recommendation of the directors, decide to pay all or part of a dividend or other distribution payable in respect of a share by transferring non-cash assets of equivalent value (including, without limitation, shares or other securities in any company).

(2) If the shares in respect of which such a non-cash distribution is paid are uncertificated, any shares in the company which are issued as a non-cash distribution in respect of them must be uncertificated.

(3) For the purposes of paying a non-cash distribution, the directors may make whatever arrangements they think fit, including, where any difficulty arises regarding the distribution—

(a) fixing the value of any assets;

(b) paying cash to any distribution recipient on the basis of that value in order to adjust the rights of recipients; and

(c) vesting any assets in trustees.

77. Waiver of distributions

Distribution recipients may waive their entitlement to a dividend or other distribution payable in respect of a share by giving the company notice in writing to that effect, but if—

(a) the share has more than one holder, or

(b) more than one person is entitled to the share, whether by reason of the death or bankruptcy of one or more joint holders, or otherwise,

the notice is not effective unless it is expressed to be given, and signed, by all the holders or persons otherwise entitled to the share.

Capitalisation of Profits

78. Authority to capitalise and appropriation of capitalised sums

(1) Subject to the articles, the directors may, if they are so authorised by an ordinary resolution—

(a) decide to capitalise any profits of the company (whether or not they are available for distribution) which are not required for paying a preferential dividend, or any sum standing to the credit of the company's share premium account or capital redemption reserve; and

(b) appropriate any sum which they so decide to capitalise (a "capitalised sum") to the persons who would have been entitled to it if it were distributed by way of dividend (the "persons entitled") and in the same proportions.

(2) Capitalised sums must be applied—

(a) on behalf of the persons entitled, and

(b) in the same proportions as a dividend would have been distributed to them.

(3) Any capitalised sum may be applied in paying up new shares of a nominal amount equal to the capitalised sum which are then allotted credited as fully paid to the persons entitled or as they may direct.

(4) A capitalised sum which was appropriated from profits available for distribution may be applied—

(a) in or towards paying up any amounts unpaid on existing shares held by the persons entitled, or

(b) in paying up new debentures of the company which are then allotted credited as fully paid to the persons entitled or as they may direct.

(5) Subject to the articles the directors may—

(a) apply capitalised sums in accordance with paragraphs (3) and (4) partly in one way and partly in another;

(b) make such arrangements as they think fit to deal with shares or debentures becoming distributable in fractions under this article (including the issuing of fractional certificates or the making of cash payments); and

(c) authorise any person to enter into an agreement with the company on behalf of all the persons entitled which is binding on them in respect of the allotment of shares and debentures to them under this article.

PART 5

MISCELLANEOUS PROVISIONS

Communications

79. Means of communication to be used

(1) Subject to the articles, anything sent or supplied by or to the company under the articles may be sent or supplied in any way in which the Companies Act 2006 provides for documents or information which are authorised or required by any provision of that Act to be sent or supplied by or to the company.

(2) Subject to the articles, any notice or document to be sent or supplied to a director in connection with the taking of decisions by directors may also be sent or supplied by the means by which that director has asked to be sent or supplied with such notices or documents for the time being.

(3) A director may agree with the company that notices or documents sent to that director in a particular way are to be deemed to have been received within a specified time of their being sent, and for the specified time to be less than 48 hours.

80. Failure to notify contact details

(1) If—

(a) the company sends two consecutive documents to a member over a period of at least 12 months, and

(b) each of those documents is returned undelivered, or the company receives notification that it has not been delivered,

that member ceases to be entitled to receive notices from the company.

(2) A member who has ceased to be entitled to receive notices from the company becomes entitled to receive such notices again by sending the company—

(a) a new address to be recorded in the register of members, or

(b) if the member has agreed that the company should use a means of communication other than sending things to such an address, the information that the company needs to use that means of communication effectively.

Administrative Arrangements

81. Company seals

(1) Any common seal may only be used by the authority of the directors.

(2) The directors may decide by what means and in what form any common seal or securities seal is to be used.

(3) Unless otherwise decided by the directors, if the company has a common seal and it is affixed to a document, the document must also be signed by at least one authorised person in the presence of a witness who attests the signature.

(4) For the purposes of this article, an authorised person is—

(a) any director of the company;

(b) the company secretary; or

(c) any person authorised by the directors for the purpose of signing documents to which the common seal is applied.

(5) If the company has an official seal for use abroad, it may only be affixed to a document if its use on that document, or documents of a class to which it belongs, has been authorised by a decision of the directors.

(6) If the company has a securities seal, it may only be affixed to securities by the company secretary or a person authorised to apply it to securities by the company secretary.

(7) For the purposes of the articles, references to the securities seal being affixed to any document include the reproduction of the image of that seal on or in a document by any mechanical or electronic means which has been approved by the directors in relation to that document or documents of a class to which it belongs.

82. Destruction of documents

(1) The company is entitled to destroy—

(a) all instruments of transfer of shares which have been registered, and all other documents on the basis of which any entries are made in the register of members, from six years after the date of registration;

(b) all dividend mandates, variations or cancellations of dividend mandates, and notifications of change of address, from two years after they have been recorded;

(c) all share certificates which have been cancelled from one year after the date of the cancellation;

(d) all paid dividend warrants and cheques from one year after the date of actual payment; and

(e) all proxy notices from one year after the end of the meeting to which the proxy notice relates.

(2) If the company destroys a document in good faith, in accordance with the articles, and without notice of any claim to which that document may be relevant, it is conclusively presumed in favour of the company that—

(a) entries in the register purporting to have been made on the basis of an instrument of transfer or other document so destroyed were duly and properly made;

(b) any instrument of transfer so destroyed was a valid and effective instrument duly and properly registered;

(c) any share certificate so destroyed was a valid and effective certificate duly and properly cancelled; and

(d) any other document so destroyed was a valid and effective document in accordance with its recorded particulars in the books or records of the company.

(3) This article does not impose on the company any liability which it would not otherwise have if it destroys any document before the time at which this article permits it to do so.

(4) In this article, references to the destruction of any document include a reference to its being disposed of in any manner.

83. No right to inspect accounts and other records

Except as provided by law or authorised by the directors or an ordinary resolution of the company, no person is entitled to inspect any of the company's accounting or other records or documents merely by virtue of being a member.

84. Provision for employees on cessation of business

The directors may decide to make provision for the benefit of persons employed or formerly employed by the company or any of its subsidiaries (other than a director or former director or shadow director) in connection with the cessation or transfer to any person of the whole or part of the undertaking of the company or that subsidiary.

Directors' Indemnity and Insurance

85. Indemnity

(1) Subject to paragraph (2), a relevant director of the company or an associated company may be indemnified out of the company's assets against—

(a) any liability incurred by that director in connection with any negligence, default, breach of duty or breach of trust in relation to the company or an associated company,

(b) any liability incurred by that director in connection with the activities of the company or an associated company in its capacity as a trustee of an occupational pension scheme (as defined in section 235(6) of the Companies Act 2006),

(c) any other liability incurred by that director as an officer of the company or an associated company.

(2) This article does not authorise any indemnity which would be prohibited or rendered void by any provision of the Companies Acts or by any other provision of law.

(3) In this article—

(a) companies are associated if one is a subsidiary of the other or both are subsidiaries of the same body corporate, and

(b) a "relevant director" means any director or former director of the company or an associated company.

86. Insurance

(1) The directors may decide to purchase and maintain insurance, at the expense of the company, for the benefit of any relevant director in respect of any relevant loss.

(2) In this article—

(a) a "relevant director" means any director or former director of the company or an associated company,

(b) a "relevant loss" means any loss or liability which has been or may be incurred by a relevant director in connection with that director's duties or powers in relation to the company, any associated company or any pension fund or employees' share scheme of the company or associated company, and

(c) companies are associated if one is a subsidiary of the other or both are subsidiaries of the same body corporate.

Companies (Trading Disclosures) Regulations 2008

S.I. 2008/495

1. Citation, commencement and interpretation

(1) These Regulations may be cited as the Companies (Trading Disclosures) Regulations 2008 and come into force on 1st October 2008.

(2) In these Regulations—

(a) "the Act" means the Companies Act 2006;

(b) "company record" means—

(i) any register, index, accounting records, agreement, memorandum, minutes or other document required by the Companies Acts to be kept by a company; and

(ii) any register kept by a company of its debenture holders;

(c) "inspection place" means any location, other than a company's registered office, at which a company keeps available for inspection any company record which it is required under the Companies Acts to keep available for inspection;

(d) a reference to any type of document is a reference to a document of that type in hard copy, electronic or any other form; and

(e) in relation to a company, a reference to "its websites" includes a reference to any part of a website relating to that company which that company has caused or authorised to appear.

2. Legibility of displays and disclosures

Any display or disclosure of information required by these Regulations must be in characters that can be read with the naked eye.

3. Requirement to display registered name at registered office and inspection place

(1) A company shall display its registered name at—

(a) its registered office; and

(b) any inspection place.

(2) But paragraph (1) does not apply to any company which has at all times since its incorporation been dormant.

(3) Paragraph (1) shall also not apply to the registered office or an inspection place of a company where—

(a) in respect of that company, a liquidator, administrator or administrative receiver has been appointed; and

(b) the registered office or inspection place is also a place of business of that liquidator, administrator or administrative receiver.

4. Requirement to display registered name at other business locations

(1) This regulation applies to a location other than a company's registered office or any inspection place.

(2) A company shall display its registered name at any such location at which it carries on business.

(3) But paragraph (2) shall not apply to a location which is primarily used for living accommodation.

(4) Paragraph (2) shall also not apply to any location at which business is carried on by a company where—

(a) in respect of that company, a liquidator, administrator or administrative receiver has been appointed; and

(b) the location is also a place of business of that liquidator, administrator or administrative receiver.

(5) Paragraph (2) shall also not apply to any location at which business is carried on by a company of which every director who is an individual is a relevant director.

(6) In this regulation—

(a) "administrative receiver" has the meaning given—
(i) in England and Wales or Scotland, by section 251 of the Insolvency Act 1986, and
(ii) in Northern Ireland, by Article 5 of the Insolvency (Northern Ireland) Order 1989;
(b) "credit reference agency" has the meaning given in section 243(7) of the Act;
(c) "protected information" has the meaning given in section 240 of the Act; and
(d) "relevant director" means an individual in respect of whom the registrar is required by regulations made pursuant to section 243(4) of the Act to refrain from disclosing protected information to a credit reference agency.

5. Manner of display of registered name

(1) This regulation applies where a company is required to display its registered name at any office, place or location.
(2) The registered name shall be so positioned that it may be easily seen by any visitor to that office, place or location.
(3) The registered name shall be displayed continuously but where any such office, place or location is shared by six or more companies, each such company is only required to display its registered name for at least fifteen continuous seconds at least once in every three minutes.

6. Registered name to appear in communications

(1) Every company shall disclose its registered name on—
(a) its business letters, notices and other official publications;
(b) its bills of exchange, promissory notes, endorsements and order forms;
(c) cheques purporting to be signed by or on behalf of the company;
(d) orders for money, goods or services purporting to be signed by or on behalf of the company;
(e) its bills of parcels, invoices and other demands for payment, receipts and letters of credit;
(f) its applications for licences to carry on a trade or activity; and
(g) all other forms of its business correspondence and documentation.
(2) Every company shall disclose its registered name on its websites.

7. Further particulars to appear in business letters, order forms and websites

(1) Every company shall disclose the particulars set out in paragraph (2) on—
(a) its business letters;
(b) its order forms; and
(c) its websites.
(2) The particulars are—
(a) the part of the United Kingdom in which the company is registered;
(b) the company's registered number;
(c) the address of the company's registered office;
(d) in the case of a limited company exempt from the obligation to use the word "limited" as part of its registered name under section 60 of the Act, the fact that it is a limited company;
(e) in the case of a community interest company which is not a public company, the fact that it is a limited company; and
(f) in the case of an investment company within the meaning of section 833 of the Act, the fact that it is such a company.
(3) If, in the case of a company having a share capital, there is a disclosure as to the amount of share capital on—
(a) its business letters;
(b) its order forms; or
(c) its websites,
that disclosure must be to paid up share capital.

8. Disclosure of names of directors

(1) Where a company's business letter includes the name of any director of that company, other than in the text or as a signatory, the letter must disclose the name of every director of that company.

(2) In paragraph (1), "name" has the following meanings—

(a) in the case of a director who is an individual, "name" has the meaning given in section 163(2) of the Act; and

(b) in the case of a director who is a body corporate or a firm that is a legal person under the law by which it is governed, "name" means corporate name or firm name.

9. Disclosures relating to registered office and inspection place

(1) A company shall disclose—

(a) the address of its registered office;

(b) any inspection place; and

(c) the type of company records which are kept at that office or place,

to any person it deals with in the course of business who makes a written request to the company for that information.

(2) The company shall send a written response to that person within five working days of the receipt of that request.

10. Offence

(1) Where a company fails, without reasonable excuse, to comply with any requirement in regulations 2 to 9, an offence is committed by—

(a) the company; and

(b) every officer of the company who is in default.

(2) A person guilty of an offence under paragraph (1) is liable on summary conviction to—

(a) a fine not exceeding level 3 on the standard scale; and

(b) for continued contravention, a daily default fine not exceeding one-tenth of level 3 on the standard scale.

(3) For the purposes of this regulation a shadow director is to be treated as an officer of the company.

11. Revocation

(1) The Companies (Registrar, Languages and Trading Disclosures) Regulations 2006 are amended as follows.

(2) Revoke regulation 6 and Schedules 1 and 2.

Small Companies and Groups (Accounts and Directors' Report) Regulations 2008

S.I. 2008/409

PART 1
INTRODUCTION

1. Citation and interpretation

(1) These Regulations may be cited as the Small Companies and Groups (Accounts and Directors' Report) Regulations 2008.

(2) In these Regulations "the 2006 Act" means the Companies Act 2006.

2. Commencement and application

(1) These Regulations come into force on 6th April 2008.

(2) They apply in relation to financial years beginning on or after 6th April 2008.

(3) They apply to companies which are subject to the small companies regime under Part 15 of the 2006 Act (see section 381 of that Act).

PART 2
FORM AND CONTENT OF INDIVIDUAL ACCOUNTS

3. Companies Act individual accounts

(1) Companies Act individual accounts under section 396 of the 2006 Act (Companies Act: individual accounts) must comply with the provisions of Schedule 1 to these Regulations as to the form and content of the balance sheet and profit and loss account, and additional information to be provided by way of notes to the accounts.

(2) The profit and loss account of a company that falls within section 408 of the 2006 Act (individual profit and loss account where group accounts prepared) need not contain the information specified in paragraphs 59 to 61 of Schedule 1 to these Regulations (information supplementing the profit and loss account).

(3) Accounts are treated as having complied with any provision of Schedule 1 to these Regulations if they comply instead with the corresponding provision of Schedule 1 to the Large and Medium-Sized Companies and Groups (Accounts and Reports) Regulations 2008.

4. Information about related undertakings (Companies Act or IAS individual accounts)

(1) Companies Act or IAS individual accounts must comply with the provisions of Schedule 2 to these Regulations as to information about related undertakings to be given in notes to the company's accounts.

(2) Information otherwise required to be given by Schedule 2 to these Regulations need not be disclosed with respect to an undertaking that—

(a) is established under the law of a country outside the United Kingdom, or

(b) carries on business outside the United Kingdom,

if the conditions specified in section 409(4) of the 2006 Act are met (see section 409(5) of the 2006 Act for disclosure required where advantage taken of this exemption).

This paragraph does not apply in relation to the information required by paragraphs 4 and 8 of Schedule 2 to these Regulations.

5. Information about directors' benefits: remuneration (Companies Act or IAS individual accounts)

Companies Act or IAS individual accounts must comply with the provisions of Schedule 3 to these Regulations as to information about directors' remuneration to be given in notes to the company's accounts.

6. Accounts for delivery to registrar of companies (Companies Act individual accounts)

(1) The directors of a company for which they are preparing Companies Act individual accounts may deliver to the registrar of companies under section 444 of the 2006 Act (filing obligations of companies subject to small companies regime) a copy of a balance sheet which complies with Schedule 4 to these Regulations rather than Schedule 1.

(2) Companies Act individual accounts delivered to the registrar need not give the information required by—

(a) paragraph 4 of Schedule 2 to these Regulations (shares of company held by subsidiary undertakings), or

(b) Schedule 3 to these Regulations (directors' benefits).

PART 3
DIRECTORS' REPORT

7. Directors' report

The report which the directors of a company are required to prepare under section 415 of the 2006 Act (duty to prepare directors' report) must disclose the matters specified in Schedule 5 to these Regulations.

PART 4
FORM AND CONTENT OF GROUP ACCOUNTS

8. Companies Act group accounts

(1) Where the directors of a parent company which—

(a) is subject to the small companies regime, and

(b) has prepared Companies Act individual accounts in accordance with regulation 3,

prepare Companies Act group accounts under section 398 of the 2006 Act (option to prepare group accounts), those accounts must comply with the provisions of Part 1 of Schedule 6 to these Regulations as to the form and content of the consolidated balance sheet and consolidated profit and loss account, and additional information to be provided by way of notes to the accounts.

(2) Accounts are treated as having complied with any provision of Part 1 of Schedule 6 if they comply instead with the corresponding provision of Schedule 6 to the Large and Medium-Sized Companies and Groups (Accounts and Reports) Regulations 2008.

9. Information about directors' benefits: remuneration (Companies Act or IAS group accounts)

Companies Act or IAS group accounts must comply with the provisions of Schedule 3 to these Regulations as to information about directors' remuneration to be given in notes to the company's accounts.

10. Information about related undertakings (Companies Act or IAS group accounts)

(1) Companies Act or IAS group accounts must comply with the provisions of Part 2 of Schedule 6 to these Regulations as to information about related undertakings to be given in notes to the company's accounts.

(2) Information otherwise required to be given by Part 2 of Schedule 6 need not be disclosed with respect to an undertaking that—

(a) is established under the law of a country outside the United Kingdom, or

(b) carries on business outside the United Kingdom,

if the conditions specified in section 409(4) of the 2006 Act are met (see section 409(5) of the 2006 Act for disclosure required where advantage taken of this exemption).

This paragraph does not apply in relation to the information required by paragraphs 26 and 35 of Schedule 6 to these Regulations.

11. Accounts for delivery to registrar of companies (Companies Act group accounts)

Companies Act group accounts delivered to the registrar of companies under section 444 of the 2006 Act need not give the information required by—

(a) Schedule 3 to these Regulations (directors' benefits), or

(b) paragraph 25 of Schedule 6 to these Regulations (shares of company held by subsidiary undertakings).

PART 5
INTERPRETATION

12. Definition of "provisions"

Schedule 7 to these Regulations defines "provisions" for the purpose of these Regulations and for the purposes of—

(a) section 677(3)(a) (Companies Act accounts: relevant provisions for purposes of financial assistance) in Part 18 of the 2006 Act,

(b) section 712(2)(b)(i) (Companies Act accounts: relevant provisions to determine available profits for redemption or purchase by private company out of capital) in that Part, . . .

(c) section 836(1)(b)(i) (Companies Act accounts: relevant provisions for distribution purposes) in Part 23 of that Act, and

(d) section 841(2)(a) (Companies Act accounts: provisions to be treated as realised losses) in that Part.

13. General interpretation

Schedule 8 to these Regulations contains general definitions for the purposes of these Regulations.

SCHEDULE 1

Regulation 3(1)

COMPANIES ACT INDIVIDUAL ACCOUNTS

PART 1
GENERAL RULES AND FORMATS

SECTION A
GENERAL RULES

1.— (1) Subject to the following provisions of this Schedule—

(a) every balance sheet of a company must show the items listed in either of the balance sheet formats in Section B of this Part, and

(b) every profit and loss account must show the items listed in any one of the profit and loss account formats in Section B.

(2) References in this Schedule to the items listed in any of the formats in Section B are to those items read together with any of the notes following the formats which apply to those items.

(3) The items must be shown in the order and under the headings and sub-headings given in the particular format used, but—

(a) the notes to the formats may permit alternative positions for any particular items, and

(b) the heading or sub-heading for any item does not have to be distinguished by any letter or number assigned to that item in the format used.

2.— (1) Where in accordance with paragraph 1 a company's balance sheet or profit and loss account for any financial year has been prepared by reference to one of the formats in Section B, the company's directors must use the same format in preparing Companies Act individual accounts for subsequent financial years, unless in their opinion there are special reasons for a change.

(2) Particulars of any such change must be given in a note to the accounts in which the new format is first used, and the reasons for the change must be explained.

3.— (1) Any item required to be shown in a company's balance sheet or profit and loss account may be shown in greater detail than required by the particular format used.

(2) The balance sheet or profit and loss account may include an item representing or covering the amount of any asset or liability, income or expenditure not otherwise covered by any of the items listed in the format used, save that none of the following may be treated as assets in any balance sheet—

(a) preliminary expenses,

(b) expenses of, and commission on, any issue of shares or debentures, and

(c) costs of research.

4.— (1) Where the special nature of the company's business requires it, the company's directors must adapt the arrangement, headings and sub-headings otherwise required in respect of items given an Arabic number in the balance sheet or profit and loss account format used.

(2) The directors may combine items to which Arabic numbers are given in any of the formats in Section B if—

(a) their individual amounts are not material to assessing the state of affairs or profit or loss of the company for the financial year in question, or

(b) the combination facilitates that assessment.

(3) Where sub-paragraph (2)(b) applies, the individual amounts of any items which have been combined must be disclosed in a note to the accounts.

5.— (1) Subject to sub-paragraph (2), the directors must not include a heading or sub-heading corresponding to an item in the balance sheet or profit and loss account format used if there is no amount to be shown for that item for the financial year to which the balance sheet or profit and loss account relates.

(2) Where an amount can be shown for the item in question for the immediately preceding financial year that amount must be shown under the heading or sub-heading required by the format for that item.

6. Every profit and loss account must show the amount of a company's profit or loss on ordinary activities before taxation.

7.— (1) For every item shown in the balance sheet or profit and loss account the corresponding amount for the immediately preceding financial year must also be shown.

(2) Where that corresponding amount is not comparable with the amount to be shown for the item in question in respect of the financial year to which the balance sheet or profit and loss account relates, the former amount may be adjusted, and particulars of the non-comparability and of any adjustment must be disclosed in a note to the accounts.

8. Amounts in respect of items representing assets or income may not be set off against amounts in respect of items representing liabilities or expenditure (as the case may be), or vice versa.

9. The company's directors must, in determining how amounts are presented within items in the profit and loss account and balance sheet, have regard to the substance of the reported transaction or arrangement, in accordance with generally accepted accounting principles or practice.

SECTION B
THE REQUIRED FORMATS FOR ACCOUNTS

Balance sheet formats

Format 1

A Called up share capital not paid (1)

B Fixed assets

I Intangible assets

1 Goodwill (2)
2 Other intangible assets (3)
II Tangible assets
1 Land and buildings
2 Plant and machinery etc
III Investments
1 Shares in group undertakings and participating interests
2 Loans to group undertakings in which the company has a participating interest
3 Other investments other than loans
4 Other investments (4)
C Current assets
I Stocks
1 Stocks
2 Payments on account
II Debtors (5)
1 Trade debtors
2 Amounts owed by group undertakings in which the company has a participating interest
3 Other debtors (1)
III Investments
1 Shares in group undertakings
2 Other investments (4)
IV Cash at bank and in hand
D Prepayments and accrued income (6)
E Creditors: amounts falling due within one year
1 Bank loans and overdrafts
2 Trade creditors
3 Amounts owed to group undertakings and undertakings in which the company has a participating interest
4 Other creditors (7)
F Net current assets (liabilities) (8)
G Total assets less current liabilities
H Creditors: amounts falling due after more than one year
1 Bank loans and overdrafts
2 Trade creditors
3 Amounts owed to group undertakings and undertakings in which the company has a participating interest
4 Other creditors (7)
I Provisions for liabilities
J Accruals and deferred income (7)
K Capital and reserves
I Called up share capital (9)
II Share premium account
III Revaluation reserve
IV Other reserves
V Profit and loss account

Balance sheet formats

Format 2

ASSETS
A Called up share capital not paid (1)
B Fixed assets

I Intangible assets
 1 Goodwill (2)
 2 Other intangible assets (3)
II Tangible assets
 1 Land and buildings
 2 Plant and machinery etc
III Investments
 1 Shares in group undertakings and participating interests
 2 Loans to group undertakings and undertakings in which the company has a participating interest
 3 Other investments other than loans
 4 Other investments (4)

C Current assets
I Stocks
 1 Stocks
 2 Payments on account
II Debtors (5)
 1 Trade debtors
 2 Amounts owed by group undertakings and undertakings in which the company has a participating interest
 3 Other debtors (1)
III Investments
 1 Shares in group undertakings
 2 Other investments (4)
IV Cash at bank and in hand

D Prepayments and accrued income (6)

LIABILITIES

A Capital and reserves
I Called up share capital (9)
II Share premium account
III Revaluation reserve
IV Other reserves
V Profit and loss account

B Provisions for liabilities

C Creditors (10)
 1 Bank loans and overdrafts
 2 Trade creditors
 3 Amounts owed to group undertakings and undertakings in which the company has a participating interest
 4 Other creditors (7)

D Accruals and deferred income (7)

Notes on the balance sheet formats

(1) Called up share capital not paid
(Formats 1 and 2, items A and C II 3)
This item may either be shown at item A or included under item C II 3 in Format 1 or 2.

(2) Goodwill
(Formats 1 and 2, item B I 1)
Amounts representing goodwill are only to be included to the extent that the goodwill was acquired for valuable consideration.

(3) Other intangible assets
(Formats 1 and 2, item B I 2)

Amounts in respect of concessions, patents, licences, trade marks and similar rights and assets must only be included in a company's balance sheet under this item if either—

(a) the assets were acquired for valuable consideration and are not required to be shown under goodwill, or

(b) the assets in question were created by the company itself.

(4) Other investments

(Formats 1 and 2, items B III 4 and C III 2)

Where amounts in respect of own shares held are included under either of these items, the nominal value of such shares must be shown separately.

(5) Debtors

(Formats 1 and 2, items C II 1 to 3)

The amount falling due after more than one year must be shown separately for each item included under debtors unless the aggregate amount of debtors falling due after more than one year is disclosed in the notes to the accounts.

(6) Prepayments and accrued income

(Formats 1 and 2, item D)

This item may alternatively be included under item C II 3 in Format 1 or 2.

(7) Other creditors

(Format 1, items E 4, H 4 and J and Format 2, items C 4 and D.)

There must be shown separately—

(a) the amount of any convertible loans, and

(b) the amount for creditors in respect of taxation and social security.

Payments received on account of orders must be included in so far as they are not shown as deductions from stocks.

In Format 1, accruals and deferred income may be shown under item J or included under item E 4 or H 4, or both (as the case may require). In Format 2, accruals and deferred income may be shown under item D or within item C 4 under Liabilities.

(8) Net current assets (liabilities)

(Format 1, item F)

In determining the amount to be shown under this item any prepayments and accrued income must be taken into account wherever shown.

(9) Called up share capital

(Format 1, item K I and format 2, item A I)

The amount of allotted share capital and the amount of called up share capital which has been paid up must be shown separately.

(10) Creditors

(Format 2, items C 1 to 4)

Amounts falling due within one year and after one year must be shown separately for each of these items and for the aggregate of all of these items unless the aggregate amount of creditors falling due within one year and the aggregate amount of creditors falling due after more than one year is disclosed in the notes to the accounts.

Profit and loss account formats

Format 1

(see note (14) below)

1 Turnover

2 Cost of sales (11)

3 Gross profit or loss

4 Distribution costs (11)

5 Administrative expenses (11)

6 Other operating income

7 Income from shares in group undertakings

8 Income from participating interests
9 Income from other fixed asset investments (12)
10 Other interest receivable and similar income (12)
11 Amounts written off investments
12 Interest payable and similar charges (13)
13 Tax on profit or loss on ordinary activities
14 Profit or loss on ordinary activities after taxation
15 Extraordinary income
16 Extraordinary charges
17 Extraordinary profit or loss
18 Tax on extraordinary profit or loss
19 Other taxes not shown under the above items
20 Profit or loss for the financial year

Profit and loss account formats

Format 2

1 Turnover
2 Change in stocks of finished goods and in work in progress
3 Own work capitalised
4 Other operating income
5 (a) Raw materials and consumables
 (b) Other external charges
6 Staff costs
 (a) wages and salaries
 (b) social security costs
 (c) other pension costs
7 (a) Depreciation and other amounts written off tangible and intangible fixed assets
 (b) Exceptional amounts written off current assets
8 Other operating charges
9 Income from shares in group undertakings
10 Income from participating interests
11 Income from other fixed asset investments (12)
12 Other interest receivable and similar income (12)
13 Amounts written off investments
14 Interest payable and similar charges (13)
15 Tax on profit or loss on ordinary activities
16 Profit or loss on ordinary activities after taxation
17 Extraordinary income
18 Extraordinary charges
19 Extraordinary profit or loss
20 Tax on extraordinary profit or loss
21 Other taxes not shown under the above items
22 Profit or loss for the financial year

Profit and loss account formats

Format 3
(see note (14) below)

A Charges
 1 Cost of sales (11)
 2 Distribution costs (11)
 3 Administrative expenses (11)
 4 Amounts written off investments

5 Interest payable and similar charges (13)
6 Tax on profit or loss on ordinary activities
7 Profit or loss on ordinary activities after taxation
8 Extraordinary charges
9 Tax on extraordinary profit or loss
10 Other taxes not shown under the above items
11 Profit or loss for the financial year

B Income

1 Turnover
2 Other operating income
3 Income from shares in group undertakings
4 Income from participating interests
5 Income from other fixed asset investments (12)
6 Other interest receivable and similar income (12)
7 Profit or loss on ordinary activities after taxation
8 Extraordinary income
9 Profit or loss for the financial year

Profit and loss account formats

Format 4

A Charges

1 Reduction in stocks of finished goods and in work in progress
2 (a) Raw materials and consumables
(b) Other external charges
3 Staff costs
(a) wages and salaries
(b) social security costs
(c) other pension costs
4 (a) Depreciation and other amounts written off tangible and intangible fixed assets
(b) Exceptional amounts written off current assets
5 Other operating charges
6 Amounts written off investments
7 Interest payable and similar charges (13)
8 Tax on profit or loss on ordinary activities
9 Profit or loss on ordinary activities after taxation
10 Extraordinary charges
11 Tax on extraordinary profit or loss
12 Other taxes not shown under the above items
13 Profit or loss for the financial year

B Income

1 Turnover
2 Increase in stocks of finished goods and in work in progress
3 Own work capitalised
4 Other operating income
5 Income from shares in group undertakings
6 Income from participating interests
7 Income from other fixed asset investments (12)
8 Other interest receivable and similar income (12)
9 Profit or loss on ordinary activities after taxation
10 Extraordinary income
11 Profit or loss for the financial year

Notes on the profit and loss account formats

(11) Cost of sales: distribution costs: administrative expenses
(Format 1, items 2, 4 and 5 and format 3, items A 1, 2 and 3)
These items must be stated after taking into account any necessary provisions for depreciation or diminution in value of assets.

(12) Income from other fixed asset investments: other interest receivable and similar income
(Format 1, items 9 and 10; format 2, items 11 and 12; format 3, items B 5 and 6 and format 4, items B 7 and 8)
Income and interest derived from group undertakings must be shown separately from income and interest derived from other sources.

(13) Interest payable and similar charges
(Format 1, item 12; format 2, item 14; format 3, item A 5 and format 4, item A 7)
The amount payable to group undertakings must be shown separately.

(14) Formats 1 and 3
The amount of any provisions for depreciation and diminution in value of tangible and intangible fixed assets falling to be shown under items 7(a) and A 4(a) respectively in Formats 2 and 4 must be disclosed in a note to the accounts in any case where the profit and loss account is prepared using Format 1 or Format 3.

PART 2
ACCOUNTING PRINCIPLES AND RULES

SECTION A
ACCOUNTING PRINCIPLES

Preliminary

10.— (1) The amounts to be included in respect of all items shown in a company's accounts must be determined in accordance with the principles set out in this Section.

(2) But if it appears to the company's directors that there are special reasons for departing from any of those principles in preparing the company's accounts in respect of any financial year they may do so, in which case particulars of the departure, the reasons for it and its effect must be given in a note to the accounts.

Accounting principles

11. The company is presumed to be carrying on business as a going concern.

12. Accounting policies must be applied consistently within the same accounts and from one financial year to the next.

13. The amount of any item must be determined on a prudent basis, and in particular—

(a) only profits realised at the balance sheet date are to be included in the profit and loss account, and

(b) all liabilities which have arisen in respect of the financial year to which the accounts relate or a previous financial year must be taken into account, including those which only become apparent between the balance sheet date and the date on which it is signed on behalf of the board of directors in accordance with section 414 of the 2006 Act (approval and signing of accounts).

14. All income and charges relating to the financial year to which the accounts relate must be taken into account, without regard to the date of receipt or payment.

15. In determining the aggregate amount of any item, the amount of each individual asset or liability that falls to be taken into account must be determined separately.

SECTION B
HISTORICAL COST ACCOUNTING RULES

Preliminary

16. Subject to Sections C and D of this Part of this Schedule, the amounts to be included in respect of all items shown in a company's accounts must be determined in accordance with the rules set out in this Section.

Fixed assets

General rules

17.— (1) The amount to be included in respect of any fixed asset must be its purchase price or production cost.

(2) This is subject to any provision for depreciation or diminution in value made in accordance with paragraphs 18 to 20.

Rules for depreciation and diminution in value

18. In the case of any fixed asset which has a limited useful economic life, the amount of—

(a) its purchase price or production cost, or

(b) where it is estimated that any such asset will have a residual value at the end of the period of its useful economic life, its purchase price or production cost less that estimated residual value,

must be reduced by provisions for depreciation calculated to write off that amount systematically over the period of the asset's useful economic life.

19.— (1) Where a fixed asset investment falling to be included under item B.III of either of the balance sheet formats set out in Part 1 of this Schedule has diminished in value, provisions for diminution in value may be made in respect of it and the amount to be included in respect of it may be reduced accordingly.

(2) Provisions for diminution in value must be made in respect of any fixed asset which has diminished in value if the reduction in its value is expected to be permanent (whether its useful economic life is limited or not), and the amount to be included in respect of it must be reduced accordingly.

(3) Any provisions made under sub-paragraph (1) or (2) which are not shown in the profit and loss account must be disclosed (either separately or in aggregate) in a note to the accounts.

20.— (1) Where the reasons for which any provision was made in accordance with paragraph 19 have ceased to apply to any extent, that provision must be written back to the extent that it is no longer necessary.

(2) Any amounts written back in accordance with sub-paragraph (1) which are not shown in the profit and loss account must be disclosed (either separately or in aggregate) in a note to the accounts.

Development costs

21.— (1) Notwithstanding that an item in respect of "development costs" is included under "fixed assets" in the balance sheet formats set out in Part 1 of this Schedule, an amount may only be included in a company's balance sheet in respect of development costs in special circumstances.

(2) If any amount is included in a company's balance sheet in respect of development costs the following information must be given in a note to the accounts—

(a) the period over which the amount of those costs originally capitalised is being or is to be written off, and

(b) the reasons for capitalising the development costs in question.

Goodwill

22.— (1) The application of paragraphs 17 to 20 in relation to goodwill (in any case where goodwill is treated as an asset) is subject to the following.

(2) Subject to sub-paragraph (3), the amount of the consideration for any goodwill acquired by a company must be reduced by provisions for depreciation calculated to write off that amount systematically over a period chosen by the directors of the company.

(3) The period chosen must not exceed the useful economic life of the goodwill in question.

(4) In any case where any goodwill acquired by a company is shown or included as an asset in the company's balance sheet there must be disclosed in a note to the accounts—

(a) the period chosen for writing off the consideration for that goodwill, and

(b) the reasons for choosing that period.

Current assets

23. Subject to paragraph 24, the amount to be included in respect of any current asset must be its purchase price or production cost.

24.— (1) If the net realisable value of any current asset is lower than its purchase price or production cost, the amount to be included in respect of that asset must be the net realisable value.

(2) Where the reasons for which any provision for diminution in value was made in accordance with sub-paragraph (1) have ceased to apply to any extent, that provision must be written back to the extent that it is no longer necessary.

Miscellaneous and supplementary provisions

Excess of money owed over value received as an asset item

25.— (1) Where the amount repayable on any debt owed by a company is greater than the value of the consideration received in the transaction giving rise to the debt, the amount of the difference may be treated as an asset.

(2) Where any such amount is so treated—

(a) it must be written off by reasonable amounts each year and must be completely written off before repayment of the debt, and

(b) if the current amount is not shown as a separate item in the company's balance sheet, it must be disclosed in a note to the accounts.

Assets included at a fixed amount

26.— (1) Subject to sub-paragraph (2), assets which fall to be included—

(a) amongst the fixed assets of a company under the item "tangible assets", or

(b) amongst the current assets of a company under the item "raw materials and consumables",

may be included at a fixed quantity and value.

(2) Sub-paragraph (1) applies to assets of a kind which are constantly being replaced where—

(a) their overall value is not material to assessing the company's state of affairs, and

(b) their quantity, value and composition are not subject to material variation.

Determination of purchase price or production cost

27.— (1) The purchase price of an asset is to be determined by adding to the actual price paid any expenses incidental to its acquisition.

(2) The production cost of an asset is to be determined by adding to the purchase price of the raw materials and consumables used the amount of the costs incurred by the company which are directly attributable to the production of that asset.

(3) In addition, there may be included in the production cost of an asset—

(a) a reasonable proportion of the costs incurred by the company which are only indirectly attributable to the production of that asset, but only to the extent that they relate to the period of production, and

(b) interest on capital borrowed to finance the production of that asset, to the extent that it accrues in respect of the period of production, provided, however, in a case within paragraph (b), that the inclusion of the interest in determining the cost of that asset and the amount of the interest so included is disclosed in a note to the accounts.

(4) In the case of current assets distribution costs may not be included in production costs.

28.— (1) The purchase price or production cost of—

(a) any assets which fall to be included under any item shown in a company's balance sheet under the general item "stocks", and

(b) any assets which are fungible assets (including investments),

may be determined by the application of any of the methods mentioned in sub-paragraph (2) in relation to any such assets of the same class, provided that the method chosen is one which appears to the directors to be appropriate in the circumstances of the company.

(2) Those methods are—

(a) the method known as "first in, first out" (FIFO),

(b) the method known as "last in, first out" (LIFO),

(c) a weighted average price, and

(d) any other method similar to any of the methods mentioned above.

(3) For the purposes of this paragraph, assets of any description must be regarded as fungible if assets of that description are substantially indistinguishable one from another.

Substitution of original stated amount where price or cost unknown

29.— (1) This paragraph applies where—

(a) there is no record of the purchase price or production cost of any asset of a company or of any price, expenses or costs relevant for determining its purchase price or production cost in accordance with paragraph 27, or

(b) any such record cannot be obtained without unreasonable expense or delay.

(2) In such a case, the purchase price or production cost of the asset must be taken, for the purposes of paragraphs 17 to 24, to be the value ascribed to it in the earliest available record of its value made on or after its acquisition or production by the company.

SECTION C
ALTERNATIVE ACCOUNTING RULES

Preliminary

30.— (1) The rules set out in Section B are referred to below in this Schedule as the historical cost accounting rules.

(2) Those rules, with the omission of paragraphs 16, 22 and 26 to 29, are referred to below in this Part of this Schedule as the depreciation rules; and references below in this Schedule to the historical cost accounting rules do not include the depreciation rules as they apply by virtue of paragraph 33.

31. Subject to paragraphs 33 to 35, the amounts to be included in respect of assets of any description mentioned in paragraph 32 may be determined on any basis so mentioned.

Alternative accounting rules

32.— (1) Intangible fixed assets, other than goodwill, may be included at their current cost.

(2) Tangible fixed assets may be included at a market value determined as at the date of their last valuation or at their current cost.

(3) Investments of any description falling to be included under item B III of either of the balance sheet formats set out in Part 1 of this Schedule may be included either—

(a) at a market value determined as at the date of their last valuation, or

(b) at a value determined on any basis which appears to the directors to be appropriate in the circumstances of the company.

But in the latter case particulars of the method of valuation adopted and of the reasons for adopting it must be disclosed in a note to the accounts.

(4) Investments of any description falling to be included under item C III of either of the balance sheet formats set out in Part 1 of this Schedule may be included at their current cost.

(5) Stocks may be included at their current cost.

Application of the depreciation rules

33.— (1) Where the value of any asset of a company is determined on any basis mentioned in paragraph 32, that value must be, or (as the case may require) be the starting point for determining, the amount to be included in respect of that asset in the company's accounts, instead of its purchase price or production cost or any value previously so determined for that asset.

The depreciation rules apply accordingly in relation to any such asset with the substitution for any reference to its purchase price or production cost of a reference to the value most recently determined for that asset on any basis mentioned in paragraph 32.

(2) The amount of any provision for depreciation required in the case of any fixed asset by paragraphs 18 to 20 as they apply by virtue of sub-paragraph (1) is referred to below in this paragraph as the adjusted amount, and the amount of any provision which would be required by any of those paragraphs in the case of that asset according to the historical cost accounting rules is referred to as the historical cost amount.

(3) Where sub-paragraph (1) applies in the case of any fixed asset the amount of any provision for depreciation in respect of that asset—

(a) included in any item shown in the profit and loss account in respect of amounts written off assets of the description in question, or

(b) taken into account in stating any item so shown which is required by note (11) of the notes on the profit and loss account formats set out in Part 1 of this Schedule to be stated after taking into account any necessary provision for depreciation or diminution in value of assets included under it,

may be the historical cost amount instead of the adjusted amount, provided that the amount of any difference between the two is shown separately in the profit and loss account or in a note to the accounts.

Additional information to be provided in case of departure from historical cost accounting rules

34.— (1) This paragraph applies where the amounts to be included in respect of assets covered by any items shown in a company's accounts have been determined on any basis mentioned in paragraph 32.

(2) The items affected and the basis of valuation adopted in determining the amounts of the assets in question in the case of each such item must be disclosed in a note to the accounts.

(3) In the case of each balance sheet item affected (except stocks) either—

(a) the comparable amounts determined according to the historical cost accounting rules, or

(b) the differences between those amounts and the corresponding amounts actually shown in the balance sheet in respect of that item,

must be shown separately in the balance sheet or in a note to the accounts.

(4) In sub-paragraph (3), references in relation to any item to the comparable amounts determined as there mentioned are references to—

(a) the aggregate amount which would be required to be shown in respect of that item if the amounts to be included in respect of all the assets covered by that item were determined according to the historical cost accounting rules, and

(b) the aggregate amount of the cumulative provisions for depreciation or diminution in value which would be permitted or required in determining those amounts according to those rules.

Revaluation reserve

35.— (1) With respect to any determination of the value of an asset of a company on any basis mentioned in paragraph 32, the amount of any profit or loss arising from that determination (after allowing, where appropriate, for any provisions for depreciation or diminution in value made otherwise than by reference to the value so determined and any adjustments of any such provisions made in the light of that determination) must be credited or (as the case may be) debited to a separate reserve ("the revaluation reserve").

(2) The amount of the revaluation reserve must be shown in the company's balance sheet under a separate sub-heading in the position given for the item "revaluation reserve" in Format 1 or 2 of the balance sheet formats set out in Part 1 of this Schedule, but need not be shown under that name.

(3) An amount may be transferred—

(a) from the revaluation reserve—

(i) to the profit and loss account, if the amount was previously charged to that account or represents realised profit, or

(ii) on capitalisation,

(b) to or from the revaluation reserve in respect of the taxation relating to any profit or loss credited or debited to the reserve.

The revaluation reserve must be reduced to the extent that the amounts transferred to it are no longer necessary for the purposes of the valuation method used.

(4) In sub-paragraph (3)(a)(ii) "capitalisation", in relation to an amount standing to the credit of the revaluation reserve, means applying it in wholly or partly paying up unissued shares in the company to be allotted to members of the company as fully or partly paid shares.

(5) The revaluation reserve must not be reduced except as mentioned in this paragraph.

(6) The treatment for taxation purposes of amounts credited or debited to the revaluation reserve must be disclosed in a note to the accounts.

SECTION D
FAIR VALUE ACCOUNTING

Inclusion of financial instruments at fair value

36.— (1) Subject to sub-paragraphs (2) to (5), financial instruments (including derivatives) may be included at fair value.

(2) Sub-paragraph (1) does not apply to financial instruments that constitute liabilities unless—

(a) they are held as part of a trading portfolio,

(b) they are derivatives, or

(c) they are financial instruments falling within sub-paragraph (4).

(3) Unless they are financial instruments falling within sub-paragraph (4), sub-paragraph (1) does not apply to—

(a) financial instruments (other than derivatives) held to maturity,

(b) loans and receivables originated by the company and not held for trading purposes,

(c) interests in subsidiary undertakings, associated undertakings and joint ventures,

(d) equity instruments issued by the company,

(e) contracts for contingent consideration in a business combination, or

(f) other financial instruments with such special characteristics that the instruments, according to generally accepted accounting principles or practice, should be accounted for differently from other financial instruments.

(4) Financial instruments that, under international accounting standards adopted by the European Commission on or before 5th September 2006 in accordance with the IAS Regulation, may be included in accounts at fair value, may be so included, provided that the disclosures required by such accounting standards are made.

(5) If the fair value of a financial instrument cannot be determined reliably in accordance with paragraph 37, sub-paragraph (1) does not apply to that financial instrument.

(6) In this paragraph—

"associated undertaking" has the meaning given by paragraph 19 of Schedule 6 to these Regulations;

"joint venture" has the meaning given by paragraph 18 of that Schedule.

Determination of fair value

37.— (1) The fair value of a financial instrument is its value determined in accordance with this paragraph.

(2) If a reliable market can readily be identified for the financial instrument, its fair value is determined by reference to its market value.

(3) If a reliable market cannot readily be identified for the financial instrument but can be identified for its components or for a similar instrument, its fair value is determined by reference to the market value of its components or of the similar instrument.

(4) If neither sub-paragraph (2) nor (3) applies, the fair value of the financial instrument is a value resulting from generally accepted valuation models and techniques.

(5) Any valuation models and techniques used for the purposes of sub-paragraph (4) must ensure a reasonable approximation of the market value.

Hedged items

38. A company may include any assets and liabilities, or identified portions of such assets or liabilities, that qualify as hedged items under a fair value hedge accounting system at the amount required under that system.

Other assets that may be included at fair value

39.— (1) This paragraph applies to—

(a) investment property, and

(b) living animals and plants,

that, under international accounting standards, may be included in accounts at fair value.

(2) Such investment property and such living animals and plants may be included at fair value, provided that all such investment property or, as the case may be, all such living animals and plants are so included where their fair value can reliably be determined.

(3) In this paragraph, "fair value" means fair value determined in accordance with relevant international accounting standards.

Accounting for changes in value

40.— (1) This paragraph applies where a financial instrument is valued in accordance with paragraph 36 or 38 or an asset is valued in accordance with paragraph 39.

(2) Notwithstanding paragraph 13 in this Part of this Schedule, and subject to sub-paragraphs (3) and (4), a change in the value of the financial instrument or of the investment property or living animal or plant must be included in the profit and loss account.

(3) Where—

(a) the financial instrument accounted for is a hedging instrument under a hedge accounting system that allows some or all of the change in value not to be shown in the profit and loss account, or

(b) the change in value relates to an exchange difference arising on a monetary item that forms part of a company's net investment in a foreign entity,

the amount of the change in value must be credited to or (as the case may be) debited from a separate reserve ("the fair value reserve").

(4) Where the instrument accounted for—

(a) is an available for sale financial asset, and

(b) is not a derivative,

the change in value may be credited to or (as the case may be) debited from the fair value reserve.

The fair value reserve

41.— (1) The fair value reserve must be adjusted to the extent that the amounts shown in it are no longer necessary for the purposes of paragraph 40(3) or (4).

(2) The treatment for taxation purposes of amounts credited or debited to the fair value reserve must be disclosed in a note to the accounts.

PART 3
NOTES TO THE ACCOUNTS

Preliminary

42. Any information required in the case of any company by the following provisions of this Part of this Schedule must (if not given in the company's accounts) be given by way of a note to the accounts.

Reserves and dividends

43. There must be stated—

(a) any amount set aside or proposed to be set aside to, or withdrawn or proposed to be withdrawn from, reserves,

(b) the aggregate amount of dividends paid in the financial year (other than those for which a liability existed at the immediately preceding balance sheet date),

(c) the aggregate amount of dividends that the company is liable to pay at the balance sheet date, and

(d) the aggregate amount of dividends that are proposed before the date of approval of the accounts, and not otherwise disclosed under sub-paragraph (b) or (c).

Disclosure of accounting policies

44. The accounting policies adopted by the company in determining the amounts to be included in respect of items shown in the balance sheet and in determining the profit or loss of the company must be stated (including such policies with respect to the depreciation and diminution in value of assets).

Information supplementing the balance sheet

45. Paragraphs 46 to 58 require information which either supplements the information given with respect to any particular items shown in the balance sheet or is otherwise relevant to assessing the company's state of affairs in the light of the information so given.

Share capital

46.— (1) Where shares of more than one class have been allotted, the number and aggregate nominal value of shares of each class allotted must be given.

(2) In the case of any part of the allotted share capital that consists of redeemable shares, the following information must be given—

(a) the earliest and latest dates on which the company has power to redeem those shares,

(b) whether those shares must be redeemed in any event or are liable to be redeemed at the option of the company or of the shareholder, and

(c) whether any (and, if so, what) premium is payable on redemption.

47. If the company has allotted any shares during the financial year, the following information must be given—

(a) the classes of shares allotted, and

(b) as respects each class of shares, the number allotted, their aggregate nominal value, and the consideration received by the company for the allotment.

Fixed assets

48.— (1) In respect of each item which is or would but for paragraph 4(2)(b) be shown under the general item "fixed assets" in the company's balance sheet the following information must be given—

(a) the appropriate amounts in respect of that item as at the date of the beginning of the financial year and as at the balance sheet date respectively,

(b) the effect on any amount shown in the balance sheet in respect of that item of—

(i) any revision of the amount in respect of any assets included under that item made during that year on any basis mentioned in paragraph 32,
(ii) acquisitions during that year of any assets,
(iii) disposals during that year of any assets, and
(iv) any transfers of assets of the company to and from that item during that year.

(2) The reference in sub-paragraph (1)(a) to the appropriate amounts in respect of any item as at any date there mentioned is a reference to amounts representing the aggregate amounts determined, as at that date, in respect of assets falling to be included under that item on either of the following bases, that is to say—
(a) on the basis of purchase price or production cost (determined in accordance with paragraphs 27 and 28), or
(b) on any basis mentioned in paragraph 32,
(leaving out of account in either case any provisions for depreciation or diminution in value).

(3) In respect of each item within sub-paragraph (1) there must also be stated—
(a) the cumulative amount of provisions for depreciation or diminution in value of assets included under that item as at each date mentioned in sub-paragraph (1)(a),
(b) the amount of any such provisions made in respect of the financial year,
(c) the amount of any adjustments made in respect of any such provisions during that year in consequence of the disposal of any assets, and
(d) the amount of any other adjustments made in respect of any such provisions during that year.

49. Where any fixed assets of the company (other than listed investments) are included under any item shown in the company's balance sheet at an amount determined on any basis mentioned in paragraph 32, the following information must be given—
(a) the years (so far as they are known to the directors) in which the assets were severally valued and the several values, and
(b) in the case of assets that have been valued during the financial year, the names of the persons who valued them or particulars of their qualifications for doing so and (whichever is stated) the bases of valuation used by them.

Investments

50.— (1) In respect of the amount of each item which is or would but for paragraph 4(2)(b) be shown in the company's balance sheet under the general item "investments" (whether as fixed assets or as current assets) there must be stated how much of that amount is ascribable to listed investments.

(2) Where the amount of any listed investments is stated for any item in accordance with sub-paragraph (1), the following amounts must also be stated—
(a) the aggregate market value of those investments where it differs from the amount so stated, and
(b) both the market value and the stock exchange value of any investments of which the former value is, for the purposes of the accounts, taken as being higher than the latter.

Information about fair value of assets and liabilities

51.— (1) This paragraph applies where financial instruments have been valued in accordance with paragraph 36 or 38.

(2) There must be stated—
(a) the significant assumptions underlying the valuation models and techniques used where the fair value of the instruments has been determined in accordance with paragraph 37(4),
(b) for each category of financial instrument, the fair value of the instruments in that category and the changes in value—
(i) included in the profit and loss account, or

(ii) credited to or (as the case may be) debited from the fair value reserve, in respect of those instruments, and

(c) for each class of derivatives, the extent and nature of the instruments, including significant terms and conditions that may affect the amount, timing and certainty of future cash flows.

(3) Where any amount is transferred to or from the fair value reserve during the financial year, there must be stated in tabular form—

(a) the amount of the reserve as at the date of the beginning of the financial year and as at the balance sheet date respectively,

(b) the amount transferred to or from the reserve during that year, and

(c) the source and application respectively of the amounts so transferred.

52.— (1) This paragraph applies if—

(a) the company has financial fixed assets that could be included at fair value by virtue of paragraph 36,

(b) the amount at which those items are included under any item in the company's accounts is in excess of their fair value, and

(c) the company has not made provision for diminution in value of those assets in accordance with paragraph 19(1) of this Schedule.

(2) There must be stated—

(a) the amount at which either the individual assets or appropriate groupings of those individual assets are included in the company's accounts,

(b) the fair value of those assets or groupings, and

(c) the reasons for not making a provision for diminution in value of those assets, including the nature of the evidence that provides the basis for the belief that the amount at which they are stated in the accounts will be recovered.

Information where investment property and living animals and plants included at fair value

53.— (1) This paragraph applies where the amounts to be included in a company's accounts in respect of investment property or living animals and plants have been determined in accordance with paragraph 39.

(2) The balance sheet items affected and the basis of valuation adopted in determining the amounts of the assets in question in the case of each such item must be disclosed in a note to the accounts.

(3) In the case of investment property, for each balance sheet item affected there must be shown, either separately in the balance sheet or in a note to the accounts—

(a) the comparable amounts determined according to the historical cost accounting rules, or

(b) the differences between those amounts and the corresponding amounts actually shown in the balance sheet in respect of that item.

(4) In sub-paragraph (3), references in relation to any item to the comparable amounts determined in accordance with that sub-paragraph are to—

(a) the aggregate amount which would be required to be shown in respect of that item if the amounts to be included in respect of all the assets covered by that item were determined according to the historical cost accounting rules, and

(b) the aggregate amount of the cumulative provisions for depreciation or diminution in value which would be permitted or required in determining those amounts according to those rules.

Reserves and provisions

54.— (1) This paragraph applies where any amount is transferred—

(a) to or from any reserves, or

(b) to any provision for liabilities, or

(c) from any provision for liabilities otherwise than for the purpose for which the provision was established,

and the reserves or provisions are or would but for paragraph 4(2)(b) be shown as separate items in the company's balance sheet.

(2) The following information must be given in respect of the aggregate of reserves or provisions included in the same item—

(a) the amount of the reserves or provisions as at the date of the beginning of the financial year and as at the balance sheet date respectively,

(b) any amounts transferred to or from the reserves or provisions during that year, and

(c) the source and application respectively of any amounts so transferred.

(3) Particulars must be given of each provision included in the item "other provisions" in the company's balance sheet in any case where the amount of that provision is material.

Details of indebtedness

55.— (1) For the aggregate of all items shown under "creditors" in the company's balance sheet there must be stated the aggregate of the following amounts—

(a) the amount of any debts included under "creditors" which are payable or repayable otherwise than by instalments and fall due for payment or repayment after the end of the period of five years beginning with the day next following the end of the financial year, and

(b) in the case of any debts so included which are payable or repayable by instalments, the amount of any instalments which fall due for payment after the end of that period.

(2) In respect of each item shown under "creditors" in the company's balance sheet there must be stated the aggregate amount of any debts included under that item in respect of which any security has been given by the company.

(3) References above in this paragraph to an item shown under "creditors" in the company's balance sheet include references, where amounts falling due to creditors within one year and after more than one year are distinguished in the balance sheet—

(a) in a case within sub-paragraph (1), to an item shown under the latter of those categories, and

(b) in a case within sub-paragraph (2), to an item shown under either of those categories.

References to items shown under "creditors" include references to items which would but for paragraph 4(2)(b) be shown under that heading.

56. If any fixed cumulative dividends on the company's shares are in arrear, there must be stated—

(a) the amount of the arrears, and

(b) the period for which the dividends or, if there is more than one class, each class of them are in arrear.

Guarantees and other financial commitments

57.— (1) Particulars must be given of any charge on the assets of the company to secure the liabilities of any other person, including, where practicable, the amount secured.

(2) The following information must be given with respect to any other contingent liability not provided for—

(a) the amount or estimated amount of that liability,

(b) its legal nature, and

(c) whether any valuable security has been provided by the company in connection with that liability and if so, what.

(3) There must be stated, where practicable, the aggregate amount or estimated amount of contracts for capital expenditure, so far as not provided for.

(4) Particulars must be given of—

(a) any pension commitments included under any provision shown in the company's balance sheet, and

(b) any such commitments for which no provision has been made, and where any such commitment relates wholly or partly to pensions payable to past directors of the company separate particulars must be given of that commitment so far as it relates to such pensions.

(5) Particulars must also be given of any other financial commitments that—

(a) have not been provided for, and

(b) are relevant to assessing the company's state of affairs.

(6) Commitments within any of sub-paragraphs (1) to (5) which are undertaken on behalf of or for the benefit of—

(a) any parent undertaking or fellow subsidiary undertaking, or

(b) any subsidiary undertaking of the company,

must be stated separately from the other commitments within that sub-paragraph, and commitments within paragraph (a) must also be stated separately from those within paragraph (b).

Miscellaneous matters

58. Particulars must be given of any case where the purchase price or production cost of any asset is for the first time determined under paragraph 29.

Information supplementing the profit and loss account

59. Paragraphs 60 and 61 require information which either supplements the information given with respect to any particular items shown in the profit and loss account or otherwise provides particulars of income or expenditure of the company or of circumstances affecting the items shown in the profit and loss account (see regulation 3(2) for exemption for companies falling within section 408 of the 2006 Act).

Particulars of turnover

60.— (1) If the company has supplied geographical markets outside the United Kingdom during the financial year in question, there must be stated the percentage of its turnover that, in the opinion of the directors, is attributable to those markets.

(2) In analysing for the purposes of this paragraph the source of turnover, the directors of the company must have regard to the manner in which the company's activities are organised.

Miscellaneous matters

61.— (1) Where any amount relating to any preceding financial year is included in any item in the profit and loss account, the effect must be stated.

(2) Particulars must be given of any extraordinary income or charges arising in the financial year.

(3) The effect must be stated of any transactions that are exceptional by virtue of size or incidence though they fall within the ordinary activities of the company.

Sums denominated in foreign currencies

62. Where any sums originally denominated in foreign currencies have been brought into account under any items shown in the balance sheet format or profit and loss account formats, the basis on which those sums have been translated into sterling (or the currency in which the accounts are drawn up) must be stated.

Dormant companies acting as agents

63. Where the directors of a company take advantage of the exemption conferred by section 480 of the 2006 Act (dormant companies: exemption from audit), and the company has during the financial year in question acted as an agent for any person, the fact that it has so acted must be stated.

SCHEDULE 2 Regulation 4

INFORMATION ABOUT RELATED UNDERTAKINGS WHERE COMPANY NOT PREPARING GROUP ACCOUNTS (COMPANIES ACT OR IAS INDIVIDUAL ACCOUNTS)

PART 1
REQUIRED DISCLOSURES

Subsidiary undertakings

1.— (1) The following information must be given where at the end of the financial year the company has subsidiary undertakings.

(2) The name of each subsidiary undertaking must be stated.

(3) There must be stated with respect to each subsidiary undertaking—

(a) if it is incorporated outside the United Kingdom, the country in which it is incorporated,

(b) if it is unincorporated, the address of its principal place of business.

Holdings in subsidiary undertakings

2.— (1) There must be stated in relation to shares of each class held by the company in a subsidiary undertaking—

(a) the identity of the class, and

(b) the proportion of the nominal value of the shares of that class represented by those shares.

(2) The shares held by or on behalf of the company itself must be distinguished from those attributed to the company which are held by or on behalf of a subsidiary undertaking.

Financial information about subsidiary undertakings

3.— (1) There must be disclosed with respect to each subsidiary undertaking—

(a) the aggregate amount of its capital and reserves as at the end of its relevant financial year, and

(b) its profit or loss for that year.

(2) That information need not be given if the company would (if it were not subject to the small companies regime) be exempt by virtue of section 400 or 401 of the 2006 Act (parent company included in accounts of larger group) from the requirement to prepare group accounts.

(3) That information need not be given if the company's investment in the subsidiary undertaking is included in the company's accounts by way of the equity method of valuation.

(4) That information need not be given if—

(a) the subsidiary undertaking is not required by any provision of the 2006 Act to deliver a copy of its balance sheet for its relevant financial year and does not otherwise publish that balance sheet in the United Kingdom or elsewhere, and

(b) the company's holding is less than 50% of the nominal value of the shares in the undertaking.

(5) Information otherwise required by this paragraph need not be given if it is not material.

(6) For the purposes of this paragraph the "relevant financial year" of a subsidiary undertaking is—

(a) if its financial year ends with that of the company, that year, and

(b) if not, its financial year ending last before the end of the company's financial year.

Shares of company held by subsidiary undertakings

4.— (1) The number, description and amount of the shares in the company held by or on behalf of its subsidiary undertakings must be disclosed.

(2) Sub-paragraph (1) does not apply in relation to shares in the case of which the subsidiary undertaking is concerned as personal representative or, subject as follows, as trustee.

(3) The exception for shares in relation to which the subsidiary undertaking is concerned as trustee does not apply if the company, or any subsidiary undertaking of the company, is beneficially interested under the trust, otherwise than by way of security only for the purposes of a transaction entered into by it in the ordinary course of a business which includes the lending of money.

(4) Part 2 of this Schedule has effect for the interpretation of the reference in sub-paragraph (3) to a beneficial interest under a trust.

Significant holdings in undertakings other than subsidiary undertakings

5.— (1) The information required by paragraphs 6 and 7 must be given where at the end of the financial year the company has a significant holding in an undertaking which is not a subsidiary undertaking of the company.

(2) A holding is significant for this purpose if—

(a) it amounts to 20% or more of the nominal value of any class of shares in the undertaking, or

(b) the amount of the holding (as stated or included in the company's accounts) exceeds 20% of the amount (as so stated) of the company's assets.

6.— (1) The name of the undertaking must be stated.

(2) There must be stated—

(a) if the undertaking is incorporated outside the United Kingdom, the country in which it is incorporated,

(b) if it is unincorporated, the address of its principal place of business.

(3) There must also be stated—

(a) the identity of each class of shares in the undertaking held by the company, and

(b) the proportion of the nominal value of the shares of that class represented by those shares.

7.— (1) There must also be stated—

(a) the aggregate amount of the capital and reserves of the undertaking as at the end of its relevant financial year, and

(b) its profit or loss for that year.

(2) That information need not be given if—

(a) the company would (if it were not subject to the small companies regime) be exempt by virtue of section 400 or 401 of the 2006 Act (parent company included in accounts of larger group) from the requirement to prepare group accounts, and

(b) the investment of the company in all undertakings in which it has such a holding as is mentioned in sub-paragraph (1) is shown, in aggregate, in the notes to the accounts by way of the equity method of valuation.

(3) That information need not be given in respect of an undertaking if—

(a) the undertaking is not required by any provision of the 2006 Act to deliver to the registrar a copy of its balance sheet for its relevant financial year and does not otherwise publish that balance sheet in the United Kingdom or elsewhere, and

(b) the company's holding is less than 50% of the nominal value of the shares in the undertaking.

(4) Information otherwise required by this paragraph need not be given if it is not material.

(5) For the purposes of this paragraph the "relevant financial year" of an undertaking is—

(a) if its financial year ends with that of the company, that year, and

(b) if not, its financial year ending last before the end of the company's financial year.

Membership of certain undertakings

8.— (1) The information required by this paragraph must be given where at the end of the financial year the company is a member of a qualifying undertaking.

(2) There must be stated—

(a) the name and legal form of the undertaking, and

(b) the address of the undertaking's registered office (whether in or outside the United Kingdom) or, if it does not have such an office, its head office (whether in or outside the United Kingdom).

(3) Where the undertaking is a qualifying partnership there must also be stated either—

(a) that a copy of the latest accounts of the undertaking has been or is to be appended to the copy of the company's accounts sent to the registrar under section 444 of the 2006 Act, or

(b) the name of at least one body corporate (which may be the company) in whose group accounts the undertaking has been or is to be dealt with on a consolidated basis.

(4) Information otherwise required by sub-paragraph (2) need not be given if it is not material.

(5) Information otherwise required by sub-paragraph (3)(b) need not be given if the notes to the company's accounts disclose that advantage has been taken of the exemption conferred by regulation 7 of the Partnerships (Accounts) Regulations 2008.

(6) In this paragraph—

"dealt with on a consolidated basis", "member" and "qualifying partnership" have the same meanings as in the Partnerships (Accounts) Regulations 2008;

"qualifying undertaking" means—

(a) a qualifying partnership, or

(b) an unlimited company each of whose members is—

(i) a limited company,

(ii) another unlimited company each of whose members is a limited company, or

(iii) a Scottish partnership each of whose members is a limited company,

and references in this paragraph to a limited company, another unlimited company or a Scottish partnership include a comparable undertaking incorporated in or formed under the law of a country or territory outside the United Kingdom.

Parent undertaking drawing up accounts for larger group

9.— (1) Where the company is a subsidiary undertaking, the following information must be given with respect to the parent undertaking of—

(a) the largest group of undertakings for which group accounts are drawn up and of which the company is a member, and

(b) the smallest such group of undertakings.

(2) The name of the parent undertaking must be stated.

(3) There must be stated—

(a) if the undertaking is incorporated outside the United Kingdom, the country in which it is incorporated,

(b) if it is unincorporated, the address of its principal place of business.

(4) If copies of the group accounts referred to in sub-paragraph (1) are available to the public, there must also be stated the addresses from which copies of the accounts can be obtained.

Identification of ultimate parent company

10.— (1) Where the company is a subsidiary undertaking, the following information must be given with respect to the company (if any) regarded by the directors as being the company's ultimate parent company.

(2) The name of that company must be stated.

(3) If that company is incorporated outside the United Kingdom, the country in which it is incorporated must be stated (if known to the directors).

(4) In this paragraph "company" includes any body corporate.

Construction of references to shares held by company

11.— (1) References in this Part of this Schedule to shares held by a company are to be construed as follows.

(2) For the purposes of paragraphs 2 and 3 (information about subsidiary undertakings)—

(a) there must be attributed to the company any shares held by a subsidiary undertaking, or by a person acting on behalf of the company or a subsidiary undertaking; but

(b) there must be treated as not held by the company any shares held on behalf of a person other than the company or a subsidiary undertaking.

(3) For the purposes of paragraphs 5 to 7 (information about undertakings other than subsidiary undertakings)—

(a) there must be attributed to the company shares held on its behalf by any person; but

(b) there must be treated as not held by a company shares held on behalf of a person other than the company.

(4) For the purposes of any of those provisions, shares held by way of security must be treated as held by the person providing the security—

(a) where apart from the right to exercise them for the purpose of preserving the value of the security, or of realising it, the rights attached to the shares are exercisable only in accordance with his instructions, and

(b) where the shares are held in connection with the granting of loans as part of normal business activities and apart from the right to exercise them for the purpose of preserving the value of the security, or of realising it, the rights attached to the shares are exercisable only in his interests.

PART 2
INTERPRETATION OF REFERENCES TO "BENEFICIAL INTEREST"

Introduction

12.— (1) References in this Schedule to a beneficial interest are to be interpreted in accordance with the following provisions.

(2) This Part of this Schedule applies in relation to debentures as it applies in relation to shares.

Residual interests under pension and employees' share schemes

13.— (1) Where shares in an undertaking are held on trust for the purposes of a pension scheme or an employees' share scheme, there must be disregarded any residual interest of the undertaking or any of its subsidiary undertakings (the "residual beneficiary") that has not vested in possession.

(2) A "residual interest" means a right to receive any of the trust property in the event of—

(a) all the liabilities arising under the scheme having been satisfied or provided for, or

(b) the residual beneficiary ceasing to participate in the scheme, or

(c) the trust property at any time exceeding what is necessary for satisfying the liabilities arising or expected to arise under the scheme.

(3) In sub-paragraph (2)—

(a) references to a right include a right dependent on the exercise of a discretion vested by the scheme in the trustee or any other person, and

(b) references to liabilities arising under a scheme include liabilities that have resulted or may result from the exercise of any such discretion.

(4) For the purposes of this paragraph a residual interest vests in possession—

(a) in a case within sub-paragraph (2)(a), on the occurrence of the event there mentioned, whether or not the amount of the property receivable pursuant to the right mentioned in that sub-paragraph is then ascertained,

(b) in a case within sub-paragraph (2)(b) or (c), when the residual beneficiary becomes entitled to require the trustee to transfer to it any of the property receivable pursuant to that right.

Employer's charges and other rights of recovery

14.— (1) Where shares in an undertaking are held on trust there must be disregarded—

(a) if the trust is for the purposes of a pension scheme, any such rights as are mentioned in sub-paragraph (2),

(b) if the trust is for the purposes of an employees' share scheme, any such rights as are mentioned in paragraph (a) of that sub-paragraph,

being rights of the undertaking or any of its subsidiary undertakings.

(2) The rights referred to are—

(a) any charge or lien on, or set-off against, any benefit or other right or interest under the scheme for the purpose of enabling the employer or former employer of a member of the scheme to obtain the discharge of a monetary obligation due to him from the member,

(b) any right to receive from the trustee of the scheme, or as trustee of the scheme to retain, an amount that can be recovered or retained under section 61 of the Pension Schemes Act 1993 or section 57 of the Pension Schemes (Northern Ireland) Act 1993 (deduction of contributions equivalent premium from refund of scheme contributions) or otherwise, as reimbursement or partial reimbursement for any contributions equivalent premium paid in connection with the scheme under Chapter 3 of Part 3 of that Act.

Trustee's right to expenses, remuneration, indemnity etc

15.— (1) Where an undertaking is a trustee, there must be disregarded any rights which the undertaking has in its capacity as trustee.

(2) This includes in particular—

(a) any right to recover its expenses or be remunerated out of the trust property, and

(b) any right to be indemnified out of that property for any liability incurred by reason of any act or omission of the undertaking in the performance of its duties as trustee.

Meaning of "pension scheme"

16.— (1) In this Part of this Schedule "pension scheme" means any scheme for the provision of benefits consisting of or including relevant benefits for or in respect of employees or former employees.

(2) For this purpose "relevant benefits" means any pension, lump sum, gratuity or other like benefit given or to be given on retirement or on death or in anticipation of retirement or, in connection with past service, after retirement or death.

Application of provisions to directors

17. In paragraphs 14(2) and 16, "employee" and "employer" are to be read as if a director of an undertaking were employed by it.

SCHEDULE 3

Regulations 5 and 9

INFORMATION ABOUT DIRECTORS' BENEFITS: REMUNERATION (COMPANIES ACT OR IAS ACCOUNTS)

PART 1

INFORMATION REQUIRED TO BE DISCLOSED

Total amount of directors' remuneration etc

1.— (1) There must be shown the overall total of the following amounts—

(a) the amount of remuneration paid to or receivable by directors in respect of qualifying services;

(b) the amount of money paid to or receivable by directors, and the net value of assets (other than money, share options or shares) received or receivable by directors, under long term incentive schemes in respect of qualifying services; and

(c) the value of any company contributions—

(i) paid, or treated as paid, to a pension scheme in respect of directors' qualifying services, and

(ii) by reference to which the rate or amount of any money purchase benefits that may become payable will be calculated.

(2) There must be shown the number of directors (if any) to whom retirement benefits are accruing in respect of qualifying services—

(a) under money purchase schemes, and

(b) under defined benefit schemes.

Compensation to directors for loss of office

2.— (1) There must be shown the aggregate amount of any payments made to directors or past directors for loss of office.

(2) "Payment for loss of office" has the same meaning as in section 215 of the 2006 Act.

Sums paid to third parties in respect of directors' services

3.— (1) There must be shown the aggregate amount of any consideration paid to or receivable by third parties for making available the services of any person—

(a) as a director of the company, or

(b) while director of the company—

(i) as director of any of its subsidiary undertakings, or

(ii) otherwise in connection with the management of the affairs of the company or any of its subsidiary undertakings.

(2) In sub-paragraph (1)—

(a) the reference to consideration includes benefits otherwise than in cash, and

(b) in relation to such consideration the reference to its amount is to the estimated money value of the benefit.

The nature of any such consideration must be disclosed.

(3) For the purposes of this paragraph a "third party" means a person other than—

(a) the director himself or a person connected with him or body corporate controlled by him, or

(b) the company or any of its subsidiary undertakings.

PART 2
SUPPLEMENTARY PROVISIONS

General nature of obligations

4.— (1) This Schedule requires information to be given only so far as it is contained in the company's books and papers or the company has the right to obtain it from the persons concerned.

(2) For the purposes of this Schedule any information is treated as shown if it is capable of being readily ascertained from other information which is shown.

Provisions as to amounts to be shown

5.— (1) The following provisions apply with respect to the amounts to be shown under this Schedule.

(2) The amount in each case includes all relevant sums, whether paid by or receivable from the company, any of the company's subsidiary undertakings or any other person.

(3) References to amounts paid to or receivable by a person include amounts paid to or receivable by a person connected with him or a body corporate controlled by him (but not so as to require an amount to be counted twice).

(4) Except as otherwise provided, the amounts to be shown for any financial year are—

(a) the sums receivable in respect of that year (whenever paid) or,

(b) in the case of sums not receivable in respect of a period, the sums paid during that year.

(5) Sums paid by way of expenses allowance that are charged to United Kingdom income tax after the end of the relevant financial year must be shown in a note to the first accounts in

which it is practicable to show them and must be distinguished from the amounts to be shown apart from this provision.

(6) Where it is necessary to do so for the purpose of making any distinction required in complying with this Schedule, the directors may apportion payments between the matters in respect of which they have been paid or are receivable in such manner as they think appropriate.

Exclusion of sums liable to be accounted for to company etc

6.— (1) The amounts to be shown under this Schedule do not include any sums that are to be accounted for—

(a) to the company or any of its subsidiary undertakings, or

(b) by virtue of sections 219 and 222(3) of the 2006 Act (payments in connection with share transfers: duty to account), to persons who sold their shares as a result of the offer made.

(2) Where—

(a) any such sums are not shown in a note to the accounts for the relevant financial year on the ground that the person receiving them is liable to account for them, and

(b) the liability is afterwards wholly or partly released or is not enforced within a period of two years,

those sums, to the extent to which the liability is released or not enforced, must be shown in a note to the first accounts in which it is practicable to show them and must be distinguished from the amounts to be shown apart from this provision.

Meaning of "remuneration"

7.— (1) In this Schedule "remuneration" of a director includes—

(a) salary, fees and bonuses, sums paid by way of expenses allowance (so far as they are chargeable to United Kingdom income tax), and

(b) subject to sub-paragraph (2), the estimated money value of any other benefits received by him otherwise than in cash.

(2) The expression does not include—

(a) the value of any share options granted to a director or the amount of any gains made on the exercise of any such options,

(b) any company contributions paid, or treated as paid, in respect of him under any pension scheme or any benefits to which he is entitled under any such scheme, or

(c) any money or other assets paid to or received or receivable by him under any long term incentive scheme.

Meaning of "long term incentive scheme"

8.— (1) In this Schedule "long term incentive scheme" means an agreement or arrangement—

(a) under which money or other assets may become receivable by a director, and

(b) which includes one or more qualifying conditions with respect to service or performance which cannot be fulfilled within a single financial year.

(2) For this purpose the following must be disregarded—

(a) bonuses the amount of which falls to be determined by reference to service or performance within a single financial year;

(b) compensation for loss of office, payments for breach of contract and other termination payments; and

(c) retirement benefits.

Meaning of "shares" and "share option" and related expressions

9.— In this Schedule—

(a) "shares" means shares (whether allotted or not) in the company, or any undertaking which is a group undertaking in relation to the company, and includes a share warrant as defined by section 779(1) of the 2006 Act; and

(b) "share option" means a right to acquire shares.

Meaning of "pension scheme" and related expressions

10.— (1) In this Schedule—

pension scheme" means a retirement benefits scheme as defined by section 611 of the Income and Corporation Taxes Act 1988; and

"retirement benefits" has the meaning given by section 612(1) of that Act.

(2) In this Schedule, "company contributions", in relation to a pension scheme and a director, means any payments (including insurance premiums) made, or treated as made, to the scheme in respect of the director by a person other than the director.

(3) In this Schedule, in relation to a director—

"defined benefits" means retirement benefits payable under a pension scheme that are not money purchase benefits;

"defined benefit scheme" means a pension scheme that is not a money purchase scheme;

"money purchase benefits" means retirement benefits payable under a pension scheme the rate or amount of which is calculated by reference to payments made, or treated as made, by the director or by any other person in respect of the director and which are not average salary benefits; and

"money purchase scheme" means a pension scheme under which all of the benefits that may become payable to or in respect of the director are money purchase benefits.

(4) Where a pension scheme provides for any benefits that may become payable to or in respect of any director to be whichever are the greater of—

(a) money purchase benefits as determined by or under the scheme; and

(b) defined benefits as so determined,

the company may assume for the purposes of this paragraph that those benefits will be money purchase benefits, or defined benefits, according to whichever appears more likely at the end of the financial year.

(5) For the purpose of determining whether a pension scheme is a money purchase or defined benefit scheme, any death in service benefits provided for by the scheme are to be disregarded.

References to subsidiary undertakings

11.— (1) Any reference in this Schedule to a subsidiary undertaking of the company, in relation to a person who is or was, while a director of the company, a director also, by virtue of the company's nomination (direct or indirect) of any other undertaking, includes that undertaking, whether or not it is or was in fact a subsidiary undertaking of the company.

(2) Any reference to a subsidiary undertaking of the company—

(a) for the purposes of paragraph 1 (remuneration etc) is to an undertaking which is a subsidiary undertaking at the time the services were rendered, and

(b) for the purposes of paragraph 2 (compensation for loss of office) is to a subsidiary undertaking immediately before the loss of office as director.

Other minor definitions

12.— (1) In this Schedule—

"net value", in relation to any assets received or receivable by a director, means value after deducting any money paid or other value given by the director in respect of those assets;

"qualifying services", in relation to any person, means his services as a director of the company, and his services while director of the company—

(a) as director of any of its subsidiary undertakings; or

(b) otherwise in connection with the management of the affairs of the company or any of its subsidiary undertakings.

(2) For the purposes of this Schedule, remuneration paid or receivable or share options granted in respect of a person's accepting office as a director are treated as emoluments paid or receivable or share options granted in respect of his services as a director.

SCHEDULE 4 Regulation 6(1)

COMPANIES ACT ABBREVIATED ACCOUNTS FOR DELIVERY TO REGISTRAR OF COMPANIES

PART 1
THE REQUIRED BALANCE SHEET FORMATS

1.— (1) A company may deliver to the registrar a copy of the balance sheet showing the items listed in either of the balance sheet formats set out below, in the order and under the headings and sub-headings given in the format adopted, but in other respects corresponding to the full balance sheet.

(2) The copy balance sheet must contain in a prominent position a statement that it has been prepared in accordance with the provisions applicable to companies subject to the small companies regime.

Balance sheet formats

Format 1

A Called up share capital not paid
B Fixed assets
  I Intangible assets
  II Tangible assets
  III Investments
C Current assets
  I Stocks
  II Debtors (1)
  III Investments
  IV Cash at bank and in hand
D Prepayments and accrued income
E Creditors: amounts falling due within one year
F Net current assets (liabilities)
G Total assets less current liabilities
H Creditors: amounts falling due after more than one year
I Provisions for liabilities
J Accruals and deferred income
K Capital and reserves
  I Called up share capital
  II Share premium account
  III Revaluation reserve
  IV Other reserves
  V Profit and loss account

Balance sheet formats

Format 2

ASSETS
A Called up share capital not paid
B Fixed assets
  I Intangible assets
  II Tangible assets
  III Investments
C Current assets
  I Stocks
  II Debtors (1)

III Investments
IV Cash at bank and in hand
D Prepayments and accrued income

LIABILITIES

A Capital and reserves
I Called up share capital
II Share premium account
III Revaluation reserve
IV Other reserves
V Profit and loss account
B Provisions for liabilities
C Creditors (2)
D Accruals and deferred income

Notes on the balance sheet formats

(1) Debtors

(Formats 1 and 2, items C II)

The aggregate amount of debtors falling due after more than one year must be shown separately, unless it is disclosed in the notes to the accounts.

(2) Creditors

(Format 2, Liabilities item C)

The aggregate amount of creditors falling due within one year and of creditors falling due after more than one year must be shown separately, unless it is disclosed in the notes to the accounts.

PART 2
NOTES TO THE ACCOUNTS

Preliminary

2. Any information required in the case of any company by the following provisions of this Part of this Schedule must (if not given in the company's accounts) be given by way of a note to those accounts.

Disclosure of accounting policies

3. The accounting policies adopted by the company in determining the amounts to be included in respect of items shown in the balance sheet and in determining the profit or loss of the company must be stated (including such policies with respect to the depreciation and diminution in value of assets).

Information Supplementing the Balance Sheet

Share capital and debentures

4.— (1) Where shares of more than one class have been allotted, the number and aggregate nominal value of shares of each class allotted must be given.

(2) In the case of any part of the allotted share capital that consists of redeemable shares, the following information must be given—

(a) the earliest and latest dates on which the company has power to redeem those shares,

(b) whether those shares must be redeemed in any event or are liable to be redeemed at the option of the company or of the shareholder, and

(c) whether any (and, if so, what) premium is payable on redemption.

5. If the company has allotted any shares during the financial year, the following information must be given—

(a) the classes of shares allotted, and

(b) as respects each class of shares, the number allotted, their aggregate nominal value, and the consideration received by the company for the allotment.

Fixed assets

6.— (1) In respect of each item to which a letter or Roman number is assigned under the general item "fixed assets" in the company's balance sheet the following information must be given—

(a) the appropriate amounts in respect of that item as at the date of the beginning of the financial year and as at the balance sheet date respectively,

(b) the effect on any amount shown in the balance sheet in respect of that item of—

(i) any revision of the amount in respect of any assets included under that item made during that year on any basis mentioned in paragraph 32 of Schedule 1 to these Regulations,

(ii) acquisitions during that year of any assets,

(iii) disposals during that year of any assets, and

(iv) any transfers of assets of the company to and from that item during that year.

(2) The reference in sub-paragraph (1)(a) to the appropriate amounts in respect of any item as at any date there mentioned is a reference to amounts representing the aggregate amounts determined, as at that date, in respect of assets falling to be included under that item on either of the following bases, that is to say—

(a) on the basis of purchase price or production cost (determined in accordance with paragraphs 27 and 28 of Schedule 1 to these Regulations), or

(b) on any basis mentioned in paragraph 32 of that Schedule, (leaving out of account in either case any provisions for depreciation or diminution in value).

(3) In respect of each item within sub-paragraph (1) there must also be stated—

(a) the cumulative amount of provisions for depreciation or diminution in value of assets included under that item as at each date mentioned in sub-paragraph (1)(a),

(b) the amount of any such provisions made in respect of the financial year,

(c) the amount of any adjustments made in respect of any such provisions during that year in consequence of the disposal of any assets, and

(d) the amount of any other adjustments made in respect of any such provisions during that year.

Financial fixed assets

7.— (1) This paragraph applies if—

(a) the company has financial fixed assets that could be included at fair value by virtue of paragraph 36 of Schedule 1 to these Regulations,

(b) the amount at which those items are included under any item in the company's accounts is in excess of their fair value, and

(c) the company has not made provision for diminution in value of those assets in accordance with paragraph 19(1) of that Schedule.

(2) There must be stated—

(a) the amount at which either the individual assets or appropriate groupings of those individual assets are included in the company's accounts,

(b) the fair value of those assets or groupings, and

(c) the reasons for not making a provision for diminution in value of those assets, including the nature of the evidence that provides the basis for the belief that the amount at which they are stated in the accounts will be recovered.

Details of indebtedness

8.— (1) For the aggregate of all items shown under "creditors" in the company's balance sheet there must be stated the aggregate of the following amounts—

(a) the amount of any debts included under "creditors" which are payable or repayable otherwise than by instalments and fall due for payment or repayment after the end of the period of five years beginning with the day next following the end of the financial year, and

(b) in the case of any debts so included which are payable or repayable by instalments, the amount of any instalments which fall due for payment after the end of that period.

(2) In respect of each item shown under "creditors" in the company's balance sheet there must be stated the aggregate amount of any debts included under that item in respect of which any security has been given by the company.

Sums denominated in foreign currencies

9. Where sums originally denominated in foreign currencies have been brought into account under any items shown in the balance sheet or profit and loss account, the basis on which those sums have been translated into sterling (or the currency in which the accounts are drawn up) must be stated.

Dormant companies acting as agents

10. Where the directors of a company take advantage of the exemption conferred by section 480 of the 2006 Act (dormant companies: exemption from audit), and the company has during the financial year in question acted as an agent for any person, the fact that it has so acted must be stated.

SCHEDULE 5 Regulation 7

MATTERS TO BE DEALT WITH IN DIRECTORS' REPORT

Introduction

1. In addition to the information required by section 416 of the 2006 Act, the directors' report must contain the following information.

Political donations and expenditure

2.— (1) If—

(a) the company (not being the wholly-owned subsidiary of a company incorporated in the United Kingdom) has in the financial year—

(i) made any political donation to any political party or other political organisation,

(ii) made any political donation to any independent election candidate, or

(iii) incurred any political expenditure, and

(b) the amount of the donation or expenditure, or (as the case may be) the aggregate amount of all donations and expenditure falling within paragraph (a), exceeded £2000,

the directors' report for the year must contain the following particulars.

(2) Those particulars are—

(a) as respects donations falling within sub-paragraph (1)(a)(i) or (ii)—

(i) the name of each political party, other political organisation or independent election candidate to whom any such donation has been made, and

(ii) the total amount given to that party, organisation or candidate by way of such donations in the financial year; and

(b) as respects expenditure falling within sub-paragraph (1)(a)(iii), the total amount incurred by way of such expenditure in the financial year.

(3) If—

(a) at the end of the financial year the company has subsidiaries which have, in that year, made any donations or incurred any such expenditure as is mentioned in sub-paragraph (1)(a), and

(b) it is not itself the wholly-owned subsidiary of a company incorporated in the United Kingdom,

the directors' report for the year is not, by virtue of sub-paragraph (1), required to contain the particulars specified in sub-paragraph (2).

But, if the total amount of any such donations or expenditure (or both) made or incurred in that year by the company and the subsidiaries between them exceeds £2000, the directors' report for the year must contain those particulars in relation to each body by whom any such donation or expenditure has been made or incurred.

(4) Any expression used in this paragraph which is also used in Part 14 of the 2006 Act (control of political donations and expenditure) has the same meaning as in that Part.

3.— (1) If the company (not being the wholly-owned subsidiary of a company incorporated in the United Kingdom) has in the financial year made any contribution to a non-EU political party, the directors' report for the year must contain—

(a) a statement of the amount of the contribution, or

(b) (if it has made two or more such contributions in the year) a statement of the total amount of the contributions.

(2) If—

(a) at the end of the financial year the company has subsidiaries which have, in that year, made any such contributions as are mentioned in sub-paragraph (1), and

(b) it is not itself the wholly-owned subsidiary of a company incorporated in the United Kingdom,

the directors' report for the year is not, by virtue of sub-paragraph (1), required to contain any such statement as is there mentioned, but it must instead contain a statement of the total amount of the contributions made in the year by the company and the subsidiaries between them.

(3) In this paragraph, "contribution", in relation to an organisation, means—

(a) any gift of money to the organisation (whether made directly or indirectly);

(b) any subscription or other fee paid for affiliation to, or membership of, the organisation; or

(c) any money spent (otherwise than by the organisation or a person acting on its behalf) in paying any expenses incurred directly or indirectly by the organisation.

(4) In this paragraph, "non-EU political party" means any political party which carries on, or proposes to carry on, its activities wholly outside the member States.

Charitable donations

4.— (1) If—

(a) the company (not being the wholly-owned subsidiary of a company incorporated in the United Kingdom) has in the financial year given money for charitable purposes, and

(b) the money given exceeded £2000 in amount,

the directors' report for the year must contain, in the case of each of the purposes for which money has been given, a statement of the amount of money given for that purpose.

(2) If—

(a) at the end of the financial year the company has subsidiaries which have, in that year, given money for charitable purposes, and

(b) it is not itself the wholly owned subsidiary of a company incorporated in the United Kingdom,

sub-paragraph (1) does not apply to the company.

But, if the amount given in that year for charitable purposes by the company and the subsidiaries between them exceeds £2000, the directors' report for the year must contain, in the case of each of the purposes for which money has been given by the company and the subsidiaries between them, a statement of the amount of money given for that purpose.

(3) Money given for charitable purposes to a person who, when it was given, was ordinarily resident outside the United Kingdom is to be left out of account for the purposes of this paragraph.

(4) For the purposes of this paragraph, "charitable purposes" means purposes which are exclusively charitable, and as respects Scotland a purpose is charitable if it is listed in section 7(2) of the Charities and Trustee Investment (Scotland) Act 2005.

Disclosure concerning employment etc of disabled persons

5.— (1) This paragraph applies to the directors' report where the average number of persons employed by the company in each week during the financial year exceeded 250.

(2) That average number is the quotient derived by dividing, by the number of weeks in the financial year, the number derived by ascertaining, in relation to each of those weeks, the number of persons who, under contracts of service, were employed in the week (whether throughout it or not) by the company, and adding up the numbers ascertained.

(3) The directors' report must in that case contain a statement describing such policy as the company has applied during the financial year—

(a) for giving full and fair consideration to applications for employment by the company made by disabled persons, having regard to their particular aptitudes and abilities,

(b) for continuing the employment of, and for arranging appropriate training for, employees of the company who have become disabled persons during the period when they were employed by the company, and

(c) otherwise for the training, career development and promotion of disabled persons employed by the company.

(4) In this paragraph—

(a) "employment" means employment other than employment to work wholly or mainly outside the United Kingdom, and "employed" and "employee" are to be construed accordingly; and

(b) "disabled person" means the same as in the Disability Discrimination Act 1995.

Disclosure required by company acquiring its own shares etc

6.— (1) This paragraph applies where shares in a company—

(a) are purchased by the company or are acquired by it by forfeiture or surrender in lieu of forfeiture, or in pursuance of any of the following provisions (acquisition of own shares by company limited by shares)—

(i) section 143(3) of the Companies Act 1985,

(ii) Article 153(3) of the Companies (Northern Ireland) Order 1986, or

(iii) section 659 of the 2006 Act, or

(b) are acquired by another person in circumstances where paragraph (c) or (d) of any of the following provisions applies (acquisition by company's nominee, or by another with company financial assistance, the company having a beneficial interest)—

(i) section 146(1) of the Companies Act 1985,

(ii) Article 156(1) of the Companies (Northern Ireland) Order 1986, or

(iii) section 662(1) of the 2006 Act, or

(c) are made subject to a lien or other charge taken (whether expressly or otherwise) by the company and permitted by any of the following provisions (exceptions from general rule against a company having a lien or charge on its own shares)—

(i) section 150(2) or (4) of the Companies Act 1985,

(ii) Article 160(2) or (4) of the Companies (Northern Ireland) Order 1986, or

(iii) section 670(2) or (4) of the 2006 Act.

(2) The directors' report for a financial year must state—

(a) the number and nominal value of the shares so purchased, the aggregate amount of the consideration paid by the company for such shares and the reasons for their purchase;

(b) the number and nominal value of the shares so acquired by the company, acquired by another person in such circumstances and so charged respectively during the financial year;

(c) the maximum number and nominal value of shares which, having been so acquired by the company, acquired by another person in such circumstances or so charged (whether or not during that year) are held at any time by the company or that other person during that year;

(d) the number and nominal value of the shares so acquired by the company, acquired by another person in such circumstances or so charged (whether or not during that year) which are disposed of by the company or that other person or cancelled by the company during that year;
(e) where the number and nominal value of the shares of any particular description are stated in pursuance of any of the preceding sub-paragraphs, the percentage of the called-up share capital which shares of that description represent;
(f) where any of the shares have been so charged the amount of the charge in each case; and
(g) where any of the shares have been disposed of by the company or the person who acquired them in such circumstances for money or money's worth the amount or value of the consideration in each case.

SCHEDULE 6
Regulations 8(1) and 10

GROUP ACCOUNTS

PART 1
FORM AND CONTENT OF COMPANIES ACT GROUP ACCOUNTS

General rules

1.— (1) Subject to sub-paragraphs (1) and (2), group accounts must comply so far as practicable with the provisions of Schedule 1 to these Regulations (Companies Act individual accounts) as if the undertakings included in the consolidation ("the group") were a single company.

(2) For item B III in each balance sheet format set out in that Schedule substitute—
"B III Investments
1 Shares in group undertakings
2 Interests in associated undertakings
3 Other participating interests
4 Loans to group undertakings and undertakings in which a participating interest is held
5 Other investments other than loans
6 Others".

(3) In the profit and loss account formats replace the items headed "Income from participating interests", that is—
(a) in Format 1, item 8,
(b) in Format 2, item 10,
(c) in Format 3, item B 4, and
(d) in Format 4, item B 6,
by two items: "Income from interests in associated undertakings" and "Income from other participating interests".

2.— (1) The consolidated balance sheet and profit and loss account must incorporate in full the information contained in the individual accounts of the undertakings included in the consolidation, subject to the adjustments authorised or required by the following provisions of this Schedule and to such other adjustments (if any) as may be appropriate in accordance with generally accepted accounting principles or practice.

(2) If the financial year of a subsidiary undertaking included in the consolidation does not end with that of the parent company, the group accounts must be made up—
(a) from the accounts of the subsidiary undertaking for its financial year last ending before the end of the parent company's financial year, provided that year ended no more than three months before that of the parent company, or
(b) from interim accounts prepared by the subsidiary undertaking as at the end of the parent company's financial year.

3.— (1) Where assets and liabilities to be included in the group accounts have been valued or otherwise determined by undertakings according to accounting rules differing from those used for the group accounts, the values or amounts must be adjusted so as to accord with the rules used for the group accounts.

(2) If it appears to the directors of the parent company that there are special reasons for departing from sub-paragraph (1) they may do so, but particulars of any such departure, the reasons for it and its effect must be given in a note to the accounts.

(3) The adjustments referred to in this paragraph need not be made if they are not material for the purpose of giving a true and fair view.

4. Any differences of accounting rules as between a parent company's individual accounts for a financial year and its group accounts must be disclosed in a note to the latter accounts and the reasons for the difference given.

5. Amounts that in the particular context of any provision of this Schedule are not material may be disregarded for the purposes of that provision.

Elimination of group transactions

6.— (1) Debts and claims between undertakings included in the consolidation, and income and expenditure relating to transactions between such undertakings, must be eliminated in preparing the group accounts.

(2) Where profits and losses resulting from transactions between undertakings included in the consolidation are included in the book value of assets, they must be eliminated in preparing the group accounts.

(3) The elimination required by sub-paragraph (2) may be effected in proportion to the group's interest in the shares of the undertakings.

(4) Sub-paragraphs (1) and (2) need not be complied with if the amounts concerned are not material for the purpose of giving a true and fair view.

Acquisition and merger accounting

7.— (1) The following provisions apply where an undertaking becomes a subsidiary undertaking of the parent company.

(2) That event is referred to in those provisions as an "acquisition", and references to the "undertaking acquired" are to be construed accordingly.

8. An acquisition must be accounted for by the acquisition method of accounting unless the conditions for accounting for it as a merger are met and the merger method of accounting is adopted.

9.— (1) The acquisition method of accounting is as follows.

(2) The identifiable assets and liabilities of the undertaking acquired must be included in the consolidated balance sheet at their fair values as at the date of acquisition.

(3) The income and expenditure of the undertaking acquired must be brought into the group accounts only as from the date of the acquisition.

(4) There must be set off against the acquisition cost of the interest in the shares of the undertaking held by the parent company and its subsidiary undertakings the interest of the parent company and its subsidiary undertakings in the adjusted capital and reserves of the undertaking acquired.

(5) The resulting amount if positive must be treated as goodwill, and if negative as a negative consolidation difference.

10.— (1) The conditions for accounting for an acquisition as a merger are—

(a) that at least 90% of the nominal value of the relevant shares in the undertaking acquired (excluding any shares in the undertaking held as treasury shares) is held by or on behalf of the parent company and its subsidiary undertakings,

(b) that the proportion referred to in paragraph (a) was attained pursuant to an arrangement providing for the issue of equity shares by the parent company or one or more of its subsidiary undertakings,

(c) that the fair value of any consideration other than the issue of equity shares given pursuant to the arrangement by the parent company and its subsidiary undertakings did not exceed 10% of the nominal value of the equity shares issued, and

(d) that adoption of the merger method of accounting accords with generally accepted accounting principles or practice.

(2) The reference in sub-paragraph (1)(a) to the "relevant shares" in an undertaking acquired is to those carrying unrestricted rights to participate both in distributions and in the assets of the undertaking upon liquidation.

11.— (1) The merger method of accounting is as follows.

(2) The assets and liabilities of the undertaking acquired must be brought into the group accounts at the figures at which they stand in the undertaking's accounts, subject to any adjustment authorised or required by this Schedule.

(3) The income and expenditure of the undertaking acquired must be included in the group accounts for the entire financial year, including the period before the acquisition.

(4) The group accounts must show corresponding amounts relating to the previous financial year as if the undertaking acquired had been included in the consolidation throughout that year.

(5) There must be set off against the aggregate of—

(a) the appropriate amount in respect of qualifying shares issued by the parent company or its subsidiary undertakings in consideration for the acquisition of shares in the undertaking acquired, and

(b) the fair value of any other consideration for the acquisition of shares in the undertaking acquired,

determined as at the date when those shares were acquired, the nominal value of the issued share capital of the undertaking acquired held by the parent company and its subsidiary undertakings.

(6) The resulting amount must be shown as an adjustment to the consolidated reserves.

(7) In sub-paragraph (5)(a) "qualifying shares" means—

(a) shares in relation to which any of the following provisions applies (merger relief), and in respect of which the appropriate amount is the nominal value—

(i) section 131 of the Companies Act 1985,

(ii) Article 141 of the Companies (Northern Ireland) Order 1986, or

(iii) section 612 of the 2006 Act, or

(b) shares in relation to which any of the following provisions applies (group reconstruction relief),

and in respect of which the appropriate amount is the nominal value together with any minimum premium value within the meaning of that section—

(i) section 132 of the Companies Act 1985,

(ii) Article 142 of the Companies (Northern Ireland) Order 1986, or

(iii) section 611 of the 2006 Act.

12.— (1) Where a group is acquired, paragraphs 9 to 11 apply with the following adaptations.

(2) References to shares of the undertaking acquired are to be construed as references to shares of the parent undertaking of the group.

(3) Other references to the undertaking acquired are to be construed as references to the group; and

references to the assets and liabilities, income and expenditure and capital and reserves of the undertaking acquired must be construed as references to the assets and liabilities, income and expenditure and capital and reserves of the group after making the set-offs and other adjustments required by this Schedule in the case of group accounts.

13.— (1) The following information with respect to acquisitions taking place in the financial year must be given in a note to the accounts.

(2) There must be stated—

(a) the name of the undertaking acquired or, where a group was acquired, the name of the parent undertaking of that group, and

(b) whether the acquisition has been accounted for by the acquisition or the merger method of accounting;

and in relation to an acquisition which significantly affects the figures shown in the group accounts, the following further information must be given.

(3) The composition and fair value of the consideration for the acquisition given by the parent company and its subsidiary undertakings must be stated.

(4) Where the acquisition method of accounting has been adopted, the book values immediately prior to the acquisition, and the fair values at the date of acquisition, of each class of assets and liabilities of the undertaking or group acquired must be stated in tabular form, including a statement of the amount of any goodwill or negative consolidation difference arising on the acquisition, together with an explanation of any significant adjustments made.

(5) In ascertaining for the purposes of sub-paragraph (4) the profit or loss of a group, the book values and fair values of assets and liabilities of a group or the amount of the assets and liabilities of a group, the set-offs and other adjustments required by this Schedule in the case of group accounts must be made.

14.— (1) There must also be stated in a note to the accounts the cumulative amount of goodwill resulting from acquisitions in that and earlier financial years which has been written off otherwise than in the consolidated profit and loss account for that or any earlier financial year.

(2) That figure must be shown net of any goodwill attributable to subsidiary undertakings or businesses disposed of prior to the balance sheet date.

15. Where during the financial year there has been a disposal of an undertaking or group which significantly affects the figure shown in the group accounts, there must be stated in a note to the accounts—

(a) the name of that undertaking or, as the case may be, of the parent undertaking of that group, and

(b) the extent to which the profit or loss shown in the group accounts is attributable to profit or loss of that undertaking or group.

16. The information required by paragraph 13, 14 or 15 need not be disclosed with respect to an undertaking which—

(a) is established under the law of a country outside the United Kingdom, or

(b) carries on business outside the United Kingdom,

if in the opinion of the directors of the parent company the disclosure would be seriously prejudicial to the business of that undertaking or to the business of the parent company or any of its subsidiary undertakings and the Secretary of State agrees that the information should not be disclosed.

Minority interests

17.— (1) The formats set out in Schedule 1 to these Regulations have effect in relation to group accounts with the following additions.

(2) In the Balance Sheet Formats there must be shown, as a separate item and under an appropriate heading, the amount of capital and reserves attributable to shares in subsidiary undertakings included in the consolidation held by or on behalf of persons other than the parent company and its subsidiary undertakings.

(3) In the Profit and Loss Account Formats there must be shown, as a separate item and under an appropriate heading—

(a) the amount of any profit or loss on ordinary activities, and

(b) the amount of any profit or loss on extraordinary activities,

attributable to shares in subsidiary undertakings included in the consolidation held by or on behalf of persons other than the parent company and its subsidiary undertakings.

(4) For the purposes of paragraph 4 of Schedule 1 (power to adapt or combine items)—

(a) the additional item required by sub-paragraph (2) is treated as one to which a letter is assigned, and
(b) the additional items required by sub-paragraph (3)(a) and (b) are treated as ones to which an Arabic number is assigned.

Joint ventures

18.— (1) Where an undertaking included in the consolidation manages another undertaking jointly with one or more undertakings not included in the consolidation, that other undertaking ("the joint venture") may, if it is not—
(a) a body corporate, or
(b) a subsidiary undertaking of the parent company,
be dealt with in the group accounts by the method of proportional consolidation.
(2) The provisions of this Schedule relating to the preparation of consolidated accounts apply, with any necessary modifications, to proportional consolidation under this paragraph.

Associated undertakings

19.— (1) An "associated undertaking" means an undertaking in which an undertaking included in the consolidation has a participating interest and over whose operating and financial policy it exercises a significant influence, and which is not—
(a) a subsidiary undertaking of the parent company, or
(b) a joint venture dealt with in accordance with paragraph 18.
(2) Where an undertaking holds 20% or more of the voting rights in another undertaking, it is presumed to exercise such an influence over it unless the contrary is shown.
(3) The voting rights in an undertaking means the rights conferred on shareholders in respect of their shares or, in the case of an undertaking not having a share capital, on members, to vote at general meetings of the undertaking on all, or substantially all, matters.
(4) The provisions of paragraphs 5 to 11 of Schedule 7 to the 2006 Act (parent and subsidiary undertakings: rights to be taken into account and attribution of rights) apply in determining for the purposes of this paragraph whether an undertaking holds 20% or more of the voting rights in another undertaking.

20.— (1) The interest of an undertaking in an associated undertaking, and the amount of profit or loss attributable to such an interest, must be shown by the equity method of accounting (including dealing with any goodwill arising in accordance with paragraphs 17 to 20 and 22 of Schedule 1 to these Regulations).
(2) Where the associated undertaking is itself a parent undertaking, the net assets and profits or losses to be taken into account are those of the parent and its subsidiary undertakings (after making any consolidation adjustments).
(3) The equity method of accounting need not be applied if the amounts in question are not material for the purpose of giving a true and fair view.

PART 2
INFORMATION ABOUT RELATED UNDERTAKINGS WHERE COMPANY PREPARING GROUP ACCOUNTS (COMPANIES ACT OR IAS GROUP ACCOUNTS)

Introduction and interpretation

21. In this Part of this Schedule "the group" means the group consisting of the parent company and its subsidiary undertakings.

Subsidiary undertakings

22.— (1) The following information must be given with respect to the undertakings that are subsidiary undertakings of the parent company at the end of the financial year.
(2) The name of each undertaking must be stated.
(3) There must be stated—

(a) if the undertaking is incorporated outside the United Kingdom, the country in which it is incorporated,

(b) if it is unincorporated, the address of its principal place of business.

(4) It must also be stated whether the subsidiary undertaking is included in the consolidation and, if it is not, the reasons for excluding it from consolidation must be given.

(5) It must be stated with respect to each subsidiary undertaking by virtue of which of the conditions specified in section 1162(2) or (4) of the 2006 Act it is a subsidiary undertaking of its immediate parent undertaking.

That information need not be given if the relevant condition is that specified in subsection (2)(a) of that section (holding of a majority of the voting rights) and the immediate parent undertaking holds the same proportion of the shares in the undertaking as it holds voting rights.

Holdings in subsidiary undertakings

23.— (1) The following information must be given with respect to the shares of a subsidiary undertaking held—

(a) by the parent company, and

(b) by the group,

and the information under paragraphs (a) and (b) must (if different) be shown separately.

(2) There must be stated—

(a) the identity of each class of shares held, and

(b) the proportion of the nominal value of the shares of that class represented by those shares.

Financial information about subsidiary undertakings not included in the consolidation

24.— (1) There must be shown with respect to each subsidiary undertaking not included in the consolidation—

(a) the aggregate amount of its capital and reserves as at the end of its relevant financial year, and

(b) its profit or loss for that year.

(2) That information need not be given if the group's investment in the undertaking is included in the accounts by way of the equity method of valuation or if—

(a) the undertaking is not required by any provision of the 2006 Act to deliver a copy of its balance sheet for its relevant financial year and does not otherwise publish that balance sheet in the United Kingdom or elsewhere, and

(b) the holding of the group is less than 50% of the nominal value of the shares in the undertaking.

(3) Information otherwise required by this paragraph need not be given if it is not material.

(4) For the purposes of this paragraph the "relevant financial year" of a subsidiary undertaking is—

(a) if its financial year ends with that of the company, that year, and

(b) if not, its financial year ending last before the end of the company's financial year.

Shares of company held by subsidiary undertakings

25.— (1) The number, description and amount of the shares in the company held by or on behalf of its subsidiary undertakings must be disclosed.

(2) Sub-paragraph (1) does not apply in relation to shares in the case of which the subsidiary undertaking is concerned as personal representative or, subject as follows, as trustee.

(3) The exception for shares in relation to which the subsidiary undertaking is concerned as trustee does not apply if the company or any of its subsidiary undertakings is beneficially interested under the trust, otherwise than by way of security only for the purposes of a transaction entered into by it in the ordinary course of a business which includes the lending of money.

(4) Part 2 of Schedule 2 to these Regulations has effect for the interpretation of the reference in sub-paragraph (3) to a beneficial interest under a trust.

Joint ventures

26.— (1) The following information must be given where an undertaking is dealt with in the consolidated accounts by the method of proportional consolidation in accordance with paragraph 18 of this Schedule (joint ventures)—

(a) the name of the undertaking,

(b) the address of the principal place of business of the undertaking,

(c) the factors on which joint management of the undertaking is based, and

(d) the proportion of the capital of the undertaking held by undertakings included in the consolidation.

(2) Where the financial year of the undertaking did not end with that of the company, there must be stated the date on which a financial year of the undertaking last ended before that date.

Associated undertakings

27.— (1) The following information must be given where an undertaking included in the consolidation has an interest in an associated undertaking.

(2) The name of the associated undertaking must be stated.

(3) There must be stated—

(a) if the undertaking is incorporated outside the United Kingdom, the country in which it is incorporated,

(b) if it is unincorporated, the address of its principal place of business.

(4) The following information must be given with respect to the shares of the undertaking held—

(a) by the parent company, and

(b) by the group,

and the information under paragraphs (a) and (b) must be shown separately.

(5) There must be stated—

(a) the identity of each class of shares held, and

(b) the proportion of the nominal value of the shares of that class represented by those shares.

(6) In this paragraph "associated undertaking" has the meaning given by paragraph 19 of this Schedule; and the information required by this paragraph must be given notwithstanding that paragraph 20(3) of this Schedule (materiality) applies in relation to the accounts themselves.

Other significant holdings of parent company or group

28.— (1) The information required by paragraphs 29 and 30 must be given where at the end of the financial year the parent company has a significant holding in an undertaking which is not one of its subsidiary undertakings and does not fall within paragraph 26 (joint ventures) or paragraph 27 (associated undertakings).

(2) A holding is significant for this purpose if—

(a) it amounts to 20% or more of the nominal value of any class of shares in the undertaking, or

(b) the amount of the holding (as stated or included in the company's individual accounts) exceeds 20% of the amount of its assets (as so stated).

29.— (1) The name of the undertaking must be stated.

(2) There must be stated—

(a) if the undertaking is incorporated outside the United Kingdom, the country in which it is incorporated,

(b) if it is unincorporated, the address of its principal place of business.

(3) The following information must be given with respect to the shares of the undertaking held by the parent company.

(4) There must be stated—

(a) the identity of each class of shares held, and
(b) the proportion of the nominal value of the shares of that class represented by those shares.

30.— (1) There must also be stated—
(a) the aggregate amount of the capital and reserves of the undertaking as at the end of its relevant financial year, and
(b) its profit or loss for that year.

(2) That information need not be given in respect of an undertaking if—
(a) the undertaking is not required by any provision of the 2006 Act to deliver a copy of its balance sheet for its relevant financial year and does not otherwise publish that balance sheet in the United Kingdom or elsewhere, and
(b) the company's holding is less than 50% of the nominal value of the shares in the undertaking.

(3) Information otherwise required by this paragraph need not be given if it is not material.

(4) For the purposes of this paragraph the "relevant financial year" of an undertaking is—
(a) if its financial year ends with that of the company, that year, and
(b) if not, its financial year ending last before the end of the company's financial year.

31.— (1) The information required by paragraphs 32 and 33 must be given where at the end of the financial year the group has a significant holding in an undertaking which is not a subsidiary undertaking of the parent company and does not fall within paragraph 26 (joint ventures) or paragraph 27 (associated undertakings).

(2) A holding is significant for this purpose if—
(a) it amounts to 20% or more of the nominal value of any class of shares in the undertaking, or
(b) the amount of the holding (as stated or included in the group accounts) exceeds 20% of the amount of the group's assets (as so stated).

32.— (1) The name of the undertaking must be stated.

(2) There must be stated—
(a) if the undertaking is incorporated outside the United Kingdom, the country in which it is incorporated,
(b) if it is unincorporated, the address of its principal place of business.

(3) The following information must be given with respect to the shares of the undertaking held by the group.

(4) There must be stated—
(a) the identity of each class of shares held, and
(b) the proportion of the nominal value of the shares of that class represented by those shares.

33.— (1) There must also be stated—
(a) the aggregate amount of the capital and reserves of the undertaking as at the end of its relevant financial year, and
(b) its profit or loss for that year.

(2) That information need not be given if—
(a) the undertaking is not required by any provision of the 2006 Act to deliver a copy of its balance sheet for its relevant financial year and does not otherwise publish that balance sheet in the United Kingdom or elsewhere, and
(b) the holding of the group is less than 50% of the nominal value of the shares in the undertaking.

(3) Information otherwise required by this paragraph need not be given if it is not material.

(4) For the purposes of this paragraph the "relevant financial year" of an outside undertaking is—
(a) if its financial year ends with that of the parent company, that year, and

(b) if not, its financial year ending last before the end of the parent company's financial year.

Parent company's or group's membership of certain undertakings

34.— (1) The information required by this paragraph must be given where at the end of the financial year the parent company or group is a member of a qualifying undertaking.

(2) There must be stated—

(a) the name and legal form of the undertaking, and

(b) the address of the undertaking's registered office (whether in or outside the United Kingdom) or, if it does not have such an office, its head office (whether in or outside the United Kingdom).

(3) Where the undertaking is a qualifying partnership there must also be stated either—

(a) that a copy of the latest accounts of the undertaking has been or is to be appended to the copy of the company's accounts sent to the registrar under section 444 of the 2006 Act, or

(b) the name of at least one body corporate (which may be the company) in whose group accounts the undertaking has been or is to be dealt with on a consolidated basis.

(4) Information otherwise required by sub-paragraph (2) need not be given if it is not material.

(5) Information otherwise required by sub-paragraph (3)(b) need not be given if the notes to the company's accounts disclose that advantage has been taken of the exemption conferred by regulation 7 of the Partnerships (Accounts) Regulations 2008.

(6) In this paragraph—

"dealt with on a consolidated basis", "member" and "qualifying partnership" have the same meanings as in the Partnerships (Accounts) Regulations 2008;

"qualifying undertaking" means—

(a) a qualifying partnership, or

(b) an unlimited company each of whose members is—

(i) a limited company,

(ii) another unlimited company each of whose members is a limited company, or

(iii) a Scottish partnership each of whose members is a limited company,

and references in this paragraph to a limited company, another unlimited company or a Scottish partnership include a comparable undertaking incorporated in or formed under the law of a country or territory outside the United Kingdom.

Parent undertaking drawing up accounts for larger group

35.— (1) Where the parent company is itself a subsidiary undertaking, the following information must be given with respect to that parent undertaking of the company which heads—

(a) the largest group of undertakings for which group accounts are drawn up and of which that company is a member, and

(b) the smallest such group of undertakings.

(2) The name of the parent undertaking must be stated.

(3) There must be stated—

(a) if the undertaking is incorporated outside the United Kingdom, the country in which it is incorporated,

(b) if it is unincorporated, the address of its principal place of business.

(4) If copies of the group accounts referred to in sub-paragraph (1) are available to the public, there must also be stated the addresses from which copies of the accounts can be obtained.

Identification of ultimate parent company

36.— (1) Where the parent company is itself a subsidiary undertaking, the following information must be given with respect to the company (if any) regarded by the directors as being that company's ultimate parent company.

(2) The name of that company must be stated.

(3) If that company is incorporated outside the United Kingdom, the country in which it is incorporated must be stated (if known to the directors).

(4) In this paragraph "company" includes any body corporate.

Construction of references to shares held by parent company or group

37.— (1) References in this Part of this Schedule to shares held by the parent company or the group are to be construed as follows.

(2) For the purposes of paragraphs 23, 27(4) and (5) and 28 to 30 (information about holdings in subsidiary and other undertakings)—

(a) there must be attributed to the parent company shares held on its behalf by any person; but

(b) there must be treated as not held by the parent company shares held on behalf of a person other than the company.

(3) References to shares held by the group are to any shares held by or on behalf of the parent company or any of its subsidiary undertakings; but any shares held on behalf of a person other than the parent company or any of its subsidiary undertakings are not to be treated as held by the group.

(4) Shares held by way of security must be treated as held by the person providing the security—

(a) where apart from the right to exercise them for the purpose of preserving the value of the security, or of realising it, the rights attached to the shares are exercisable only in accordance with his instructions, and

(b) where the shares are held in connection with the granting of loans as part of normal business activities and apart from the right to exercise them for the purpose of preserving the value of the security, or of realising it, the rights attached to the shares are exercisable only in his interests.

SCHEDULE 7

Regulation 12

INTERPRETATION OF TERM "PROVISIONS"

PART 1

MEANING FOR PURPOSES OF THESE REGULATIONS

Definition of "Provisions"

1.— (1) In these Regulations, references to provisions for depreciation or diminution in value of assets are to any amount written off by way of providing for depreciation or diminution in value of assets.

(2) Any reference in the profit and loss account formats set out in Part 1 of Schedule 1 to these Regulations to the depreciation of, or amounts written off, assets of any description is to any provision for depreciation or diminution in value of assets of that description.

2. References in these Regulations to provisions for liabilities are to any amount retained as reasonably necessary for the purpose of providing for any liability the nature of which is clearly defined and which is either likely to be incurred, or certain to be incurred but uncertain as to amount or as to the date on which it will arise.

PART 2

MEANING FOR PURPOSES OF PARTS 18 AND 23 OF THE 2006 ACT

Financial assistance for purchase of own shares

3. The specified provisions for the purposes of section 677(3)(a) of the 2006 Act (Companies Act accounts: relevant provisions for purposes of financial assistance) are provisions for liabilities within paragraph 2 of this Schedule.

Redemption or purchase by private company out of capital

4. The specified provisions for the purposes of section 712(2)(b)(i) of the 2006 Act (Companies Act accounts: relevant provisions to determine available profits for redemption or purchase out of capital) are provisions of any of the kinds mentioned in paragraphs 1 and 2 of this Schedule.

Justification of distribution by references to accounts

5. The specified provisions for the purposes of section 836(1)(b)(i) of the 2006 Act (Companies Act accounts: relevant provisions for distribution purposes) are provisions of any of the kinds mentioned in paragraphs 1 and 2 of this Schedule.

Realised losses

6. The specified provisions for the purposes of section 841(2)(a) of the 2006 Act (Companies Act accounts: treatment of provisions as realised losses) are provisions of any of the kinds mentioned in paragraphs 1 and 2 of this Schedule.

SCHEDULE 8

Regulation 13

GENERAL INTERPRETATION

Financial instruments

1. References to "derivatives" include commodity-based contracts that give either contracting party the right to settle in cash or in some other financial instrument, except where such contracts—
   (a) were entered into for the purpose of, and continue to meet, the company's expected purchase, sale or usage requirements,
   (b) were designated for such purpose at their inception, and
   (c) are expected to be settled by delivery of the commodity.

2.— (1) The expressions listed in sub-paragraph (2) have the same meaning as they have in Council Directive 78/660/EEC on the annual accounts of certain types of companies.

(2) Those expressions are "available for sale financial asset", "business combination", "commodity-based contracts", "derivative", "equity instrument", "exchange difference", "fair value hedge accounting system", "financial fixed asset", "financial instrument", "foreign entity", "hedge accounting", "hedge accounting system", "hedged items", "hedging instrument", "held for trading purposes", "held to maturity", "monetary item", "receivables", "reliable market" and "trading portfolio".

Fixed and current assets

3. "Fixed assets" means assets of a company which are intended for use on a continuing basis in the company's activities, and "current assets" means assets not intended for such use.

Historical cost accounting rules

4. References to the historical cost accounting rules are to be read in accordance with paragraph 30 of Schedule 1 to these Regulations.

Listed investments

5.— (1) "Listed investment" means an investment as respects which there has been granted a listing on—
   (a) a recognised investment exchange other than an overseas investment exchange, or
   (b) a stock exchange of repute outside the United Kingdom.

(2) "Recognised investment exchange" and "overseas investment exchange" have the meaning given in Part 18 of the Financial Services and Markets Act 2000.

Loans

6. A loan is treated as falling due for repayment, and an instalment of a loan is treated as falling due for payment, on the earliest date on which the lender could require repayment or (as the case may be) payment, if he exercised all options and rights available to him.

Materiality

7. Amounts which in the particular context of any provision of Schedule 1 to these Regulations are not material may be disregarded for the purposes of that provision.

Participating interests

8.— (1) A "participating interest" means an interest held by an undertaking in the shares of another undertaking which it holds on a long-term basis for the purpose of securing a contribution to its activities by the exercise of control or influence arising from or related to that interest.

(2) A holding of 20% or more of the shares of the undertaking is to be presumed to be a participating interest unless the contrary is shown.

(3) The reference in sub-paragraph (1) to an interest in shares includes—

(a) an interest which is convertible into an interest in shares, and

(b) an option to acquire shares or any such interest,

and an interest or option falls within paragraph (a) or (b) notwithstanding that the shares to which it relates are, until the conversion or the exercise of the option, unissued.

(4) For the purposes of this paragraph an interest held on behalf of an undertaking is to be treated as held by it.

(5) In the balance sheet and profit and loss formats set out in Part 1 of Schedule 1 and Part 1 of Schedule 4 to these Regulations, "participating interest" does not include an interest in a group undertaking.

(6) For the purpose of this paragraph as it applies in relation to the expression "participating interest"—

(a) in those formats as they apply in relation to group accounts, and

(b) in paragraph 19 of Schedule 6 (group accounts: undertakings to be accounted for as associated undertakings),

the references in sub-paragraphs (1) to (4) to the interest held by, and the purposes and activities of, the undertaking concerned are to be construed as references to the interest held by, and the purposes and activities of, the group (within the meaning of paragraph 1 of that Schedule).

Purchase price

9. "Purchase price", in relation to an asset of a company or any raw materials or consumables used in the production of such an asset, includes any consideration (whether in cash or otherwise) given by the company in respect of that asset or those materials or consumables, as the case may be.

Realised profits and losses

10. "Realised profits" and "realised losses" have the same meaning as in section 853(4) and (5) of the 2006 Act.

Staff costs

11.— (1) "Social security costs" means any contributions by the company to any state social security or pension scheme, fund or arrangement.

(2) "Pension costs" includes—

(a) any costs incurred by the company in respect of any pension scheme established for the purpose of providing pensions for persons currently or formerly employed by the company,

(b) any sums set aside for the future payment of pensions directly by the company to current or former employees, and

(c) any pensions paid directly to such persons without having first been set aside.

(3) Any amount stated in respect of the item "social security costs" or in respect of the item "wages and salaries" in the company's profit and loss account must be determined by reference to payments made or costs incurred in respect of all persons employed by the company during the financial year under contracts of service.

Large and Medium-sized Companies and Groups (Accounts and Reports) Regulations 2008

S.I. 2008/410

PART 1
INTRODUCTION

1. Citation and interpretation

(1) These Regulations may be cited as the Large and Medium-sized Companies and Groups (Accounts and Reports) Regulations 2008.

(2) In these Regulations "the 2006 Act" means the Companies Act 2006.

2. Commencement and application

(1) These Regulations come into force on 6th April 2008.

(2) Subject to paragraph (3), they apply in relation to financial years beginning on or after 6th April 2008.

(3) The requirement for disclosure in paragraph 4 of Schedule 8 to these Regulations (directors' remuneration report: disclosure relating to consideration of conditions in company and group) applies in relation to financial years beginning on or after 6th April 2009.

(4) These Regulations apply to companies other than those which are subject to the small companies regime under Part 15 of the 2006 Act.

PART 2
FORM AND CONTENT OF ACCOUNTS

3. Companies Act individual accounts (companies other than banking and insurance companies)

(1) Subject to regulation 4, the directors of a company—

(a) for which they are preparing Companies Act individual accounts under section 396 of the 2006 Act (Companies Act: individual accounts), and

(b) which is not a banking company or an insurance company,

must comply with the provisions of Schedule 1 to these Regulations as to the form and content of the balance sheet and profit and loss account, and additional information to be provided by way of notes to the accounts.

(2) The profit and loss account of a company that falls within section 408 of the 2006 Act (individual profit and loss account where group accounts prepared) need not contain the information specified in paragraphs 65 to 69 of Schedule 1 to these Regulations (information supplementing the profit and loss account).

4. Medium-sized companies: exemptions for Companies Act individual accounts

(1) This regulation applies to a company—

(a) which qualifies as medium-sized in relation to a financial year under section 465 of the 2006 Act, and

(b) the directors of which are preparing Companies Act individual accounts under section 396 of that Act for that year.

(2) The individual accounts for the year need not comply with the following provisions of Schedule 1 to these Regulations—

(a) paragraph 45 (disclosure with respect to compliance with accounting standards), and

(b) paragraph 72 (related party transactions).

(3) The directors of the company may deliver to the registrar of companies a copy of the accounts for the year—

(a) which includes a profit and loss account in which the following items listed in the profit and loss account formats set out in Schedule 1 are combined as one item—
items 2, 3 and 6 in format 1;
items 2 to 5 in format 2;
items A.1 and B.2 in format 3;
items A.1, A.2 and B.2 to B.4 in format 4;

(b) which does not contain the information required by paragraph 68 of Schedule 1 (particulars of turnover).

5. Companies Act individual accounts: banking companies

(1) The directors of a company—

(a) for which they are preparing Companies Act individual accounts under section 396 of the 2006 Act, and

(b) which is a banking company,

must comply with the provisions of Schedule 2 to these Regulations as to the form and content of the balance sheet and profit and loss account, and additional information to be provided by way of notes to the accounts.

(2) The profit and loss account of a banking company that falls within section 408 of the 2006 Act (individual profit and loss account where group accounts prepared) need not contain the information specified in paragraphs 85 to 91 of Schedule 2 to these Regulations (information supplementing the profit and loss account).

(3) Accounts prepared in accordance with this regulation must contain a statement that they are prepared in accordance with the provisions of these Regulations relating to banking companies.

6. Companies Act individual accounts: insurance companies

(1) The directors of a company—

(a) for which they are preparing Companies Act individual accounts under section 396 of the 2006 Act, and

(b) which is an insurance company,

must comply with the provisions of Schedule 3 to these Regulations as to the form and content of the balance sheet and profit and loss account, and additional information to be provided by way of notes to the accounts.

(2) The profit and loss account of a company that falls within section 408 of the 2006 Act (individual profit and loss account where group accounts prepared) need not contain the information specified in paragraphs 83 to 89 of Schedule 3 to these Regulations (information supplementing the profit and loss account).

(3) Accounts prepared in accordance with this regulation must contain a statement that they are prepared in accordance with the provisions of these Regulations relating to insurance companies.

7. Information about related undertakings (Companies Act or IAS individual or group accounts)

(1) Companies Act or IAS individual or group accounts must comply with the provisions of Schedule 4 to these Regulations as to information about related undertakings to be given in notes to the company's accounts.

(2) In Schedule 4—

Part 1 contains provisions applying to all companies
Part 2 contains provisions applying only to companies not required to prepare group accounts
Part 3 contains provisions applying only to companies required to prepare group accounts
Part 4 contains additional disclosures for banking companies and groups
Part 5 contains interpretative provisions.

(3) Information otherwise required to be given by Schedule 4 need not be disclosed with respect to an undertaking that—

(a) is established under the law of a country outside the United Kingdom, or

(b) carries on business outside the United Kingdom,

if the conditions specified in section 409(4) of the 2006 Act are met (see section 409(5) of the 2006 Act for disclosure required where advantage taken of this exemption).

This paragraph does not apply in relation to the information otherwise required by paragraph 3, 7 or 21 of Schedule 4.

8. Information about directors' benefits: remuneration (Companies Act or IAS individual or group accounts: quoted and unquoted companies)

(1) Companies Act or IAS individual or group accounts must comply with the provisions of Schedule 5 to these Regulations as to information about directors' remuneration to be given in notes to the company's accounts.

(2) In Schedule 5—

Part 1 contains provisions applying to quoted and unquoted companies,

Part 2 contains provisions applying only to unquoted companies, and

Part 3 contains supplementary provisions.

9. Companies Act group accounts

(1) Subject to paragraphs (2) and (3), where the directors of a parent company prepare Companies Act group accounts under section 403 of the 2006 Act (group accounts: applicable accounting framework), those accounts must comply with the provisions of Part 1 of Schedule 6 to these Regulations as to the form and content of the consolidated balance sheet and consolidated profit and loss account, and additional information to be provided by way of notes to the accounts.

(2) The directors of the parent company of a banking group preparing Companies Act group accounts must do so in accordance with the provisions of Part 1 of Schedule 6 as modified by Part 2 of that Schedule.

(3) The directors of the parent company of an insurance group preparing Companies Act group accounts must do so in accordance with the provisions of Part 1 of Schedule 6 as modified by Part 3 of that Schedule.

(4) Accounts prepared in accordance with paragraph (2) or (3) must contain a statement that they are prepared in accordance with the provisions of these Regulations relating to banking groups or to insurance groups, as the case may be.

PART 3
DIRECTORS' REPORT

10. Directors' report

(1) The report which the directors of a company are required to prepare under section 415 of the 2006 Act (duty to prepare directors' report) must disclose the matters specified in Schedule 7 to these Regulations.

(2) In Schedule 7—

Part 1 relates to matters of a general nature, including changes in asset values and contributions for political and charitable purposes,

Part 2 relates to the acquisition by a company of its own shares or a charge on them,

Part 3 relates to the employment, training and advancement of disabled persons,

Part 4 relates to the involvement of employees in the affairs, policy and performance of the company, and

Part 5 relates to the company's policy and practice on the payment of creditors.

PART 4
DIRECTORS' REMUNERATION REPORT

11. Directors' remuneration report (quoted companies)

(1) The remuneration report which the directors of a quoted company are required to prepare under section 420 of the 2006 Act (duty to prepare directors' remuneration report) must contain the

information specified in Schedule 8 to these Regulations, and must comply with any requirement of that Schedule as to how information is to be set out in the report.

(2) In Schedule 8—

Part 1 is introductory,

Part 2 relates to information about remuneration committees, performance related remuneration, consideration of conditions elsewhere in company and group and liabilities in respect of directors' contracts,

Part 3 relates to detailed information about directors' remuneration (information included under Part 3 is required to be reported on by the auditor (see subsection (3)), and

Part 4 contains interpretative and supplementary provisions.

(3) For the purposes of section 497 in Part 16 of the 2006 Act (auditor's report on auditable part of directors' remuneration report), "the auditable part" of a directors' remuneration report is the part containing the information required by Part 3 of Schedule 8 to these Regulations.

PART 5
INTERPRETATION

12. Definition of "provisions"

Schedule 9 to these Regulations defines "provisions" for the purposes of these Regulations and for the purposes of—

(a) section 677(3)(a) (Companies Act accounts: relevant provisions for purposes of financial assistance) in Part 18 of the 2006 Act,

(b) section 712(2)(b)(i) (Companies Act accounts: relevant provisions to determine available profits for redemption or purchase by private company out of capital) in that Part, …

(c) sections 831(3)(a) (Companies Act accounts: net asset restriction on public company distributions), 832(4)(a) (Companies Act accounts: investment companies distributions) and 836(1)(b)(i) (Companies Act accounts: relevant provisions for distribution purposes) in Part 23 of that Act, and

(d) section 841(2)(a) (Companies Act accounts: provisions to be treated as realised losses) in that Part.

13. General interpretation

Schedule 10 to these Regulations contains general definitions for the purposes of these Regulations.

SCHEDULE 1 Regulation 3(1)
COMPANIES ACT INDIVIDUAL ACCOUNTS: COMPANIES WHICH ARE NOT BANKING OR INSURANCE COMPANIES

PART 1
GENERAL RULES AND FORMATS

SECTION A
GENERAL RULES

1.— (1) Subject to the following provisions of this Schedule—

(a) every balance sheet of a company must show the items listed in either of the balance sheet formats in Section B of this Part, and

(b) every profit and loss account must show the items listed in any one of the profit and loss account formats in Section B.

(2) References in this Schedule to the items listed in any of the formats in Section B are to those items read together with any of the notes following the formats which apply to those items.

(3) The items must be shown in the order and under the headings and sub-headings given in the particular format used, but—

(a) the notes to the formats may permit alternative positions for any particular items, and

(b) the heading or sub-heading for any item does not have to be distinguished by any letter or number assigned to that item in the format used.

2.— (1) Where in accordance with paragraph 1 a company's balance sheet or profit and loss account for any financial year has been prepared by reference to one of the formats in Section B, the company's directors must use the same format in preparing Companies Act individual accounts for subsequent financial years, unless in their opinion there are special reasons for a change.

(2) Particulars of any such change must be given in a note to the accounts in which the new format is first used, and the reasons for the change must be explained.

3.— (1) Any item required to be shown in a company's balance sheet or profit and loss account may be shown in greater detail than required by the particular format used.

(2) The balance sheet or profit and loss account may include an item representing or covering the amount of any asset or liability, income or expenditure not otherwise covered by any of the items listed in the format used, save that none of the following may be treated as assets in any balance sheet—

(a) preliminary expenses,

(b) expenses of, and commission on, any issue of shares or debentures, and

(c) costs of research.

4.— (1) Where the special nature of the company's business requires it, the company's directors must adapt the arrangement, headings and sub-headings otherwise required in respect of items given an Arabic number in the balance sheet or profit and loss account format used.

(2) The directors may combine items to which Arabic numbers are given in any of the formats in Section B if—

(a) their individual amounts are not material to assessing the state of affairs or profit or loss of the company for the financial year in question, or

(b) the combination facilitates that assessment.

(3) Where sub-paragraph (2)(b) applies, the individual amounts of any items which have been combined must be disclosed in a note to the accounts.

5.— (1) Subject to sub-paragraph (2), the directors must not include a heading or sub-heading corresponding to an item in the balance sheet or profit and loss account format used if there is no amount to be shown for that item for the financial year to which the balance sheet or profit and loss account relates.

(2) Where an amount can be shown for the item in question for the immediately preceding financial year that amount must be shown under the heading or sub-heading required by the format for that item.

6. Every profit and loss account must show the amount of a company's profit or loss on ordinary activities before taxation.

7.— (1) For every item shown in the balance sheet or profit and loss account the corresponding amount for the immediately preceding financial year must also be shown.

(2) Where that corresponding amount is not comparable with the amount to be shown for the item in question in respect of the financial year to which the balance sheet or profit and loss account relates, the former amount may be adjusted, and particulars of the non-comparability and of any adjustment must be disclosed in a note to the accounts.

8. Amounts in respect of items representing assets or income may not be set off against amounts in respect of items representing liabilities or expenditure (as the case may be), or vice versa.

9. The company's directors must, in determining how amounts are presented within items in the profit and loss account and balance sheet, have regard to the substance of the reported transaction or arrangement, in accordance with generally accepted accounting principles or practice.

SECTION B
THE REQUIRED FORMATS FOR ACCOUNTS

Balance sheet formats

Format 1

A Called up share capital not paid (1)
B Fixed assets
I Intangible assets
1 Development costs
2 Concessions, patents, licences, trade marks and similar rights and assets (2)
3 Goodwill (3)
4 Payments on account
II Tangible assets
1 Land and buildings
2 Plant and machinery
3 Fixtures, fittings, tools and equipment
4 Payments on account and assets in course of construction
III Investments
1 Shares in group undertakings
2 Loans to group undertakings
3 Participating interests
4 Loans to undertakings in which the company has a participating interest
5 Other investments other than loans
6 Other loans
7 Own shares (4)
C Current assets
I Stocks
1 Raw materials and consumables
2 Work in progress
3 Finished goods and goods for resale
4 Payments on account
II Debtors (5)
1 Trade debtors
2 Amounts owed by group undertakings
3 Amounts owed by undertakings in which the company has a participating interest
4 Other debtors
5 Called up share capital not paid (1)
6 repayments and accrued income (6)
III Investments
1 Shares in group undertakings
2 Own shares (4)
3 Other investments
IV Cash at bank and in hand
D Prepayments and accrued income (6)
E Creditors: amounts falling due within one year
1 Debenture loans (7)
2 Bank loans and overdrafts
3 Payments received on account (8)
4 Trade creditors
5 Bills of exchange payable
6 Amounts owed to group undertakings
7 Amounts owed to undertakings in which the company has a participating interest

8 Other creditors including taxation and social security (9)
9 Accruals and deferred income (10)
F Net current assets (liabilities) (11)
G Total assets less current liabilities
H Creditors: amounts falling due after more than one year
1 Debenture loans (7)
2 Bank loans and overdrafts
3 Payments received on account (8)
4 Trade creditors
5 Bills of exchange payable
6 Amounts owed to group undertakings
7 Amounts owed to undertakings in which the company has a participating interest
8 Other creditors including taxation and social security (9)
9 Accruals and deferred income (10)
I Provisions for liabilities
1 Pensions and similar obligations
2 Taxation, including deferred taxation
3 Other provisions
J Accruals and deferred income (10)
K Capital and reserves
I Called up share capital (12)
II Share premium account
III Revaluation reserve
IV Other reserves
1 Capital redemption reserve
2 Reserve for own shares
3 Reserves provided for by the articles of association
4 Other reserves
V Profit and loss account

Balance sheet formats

Format 2

ASSETS
A Called up share capital not paid (1)
B Fixed assets
I Intangible assets
1 Development costs
2 Concessions, patents, licences, trade marks and similar rights and assets (2)
3 Goodwill (3)
4 Payments on account
II Tangible assets
1 Land and buildings
2 Plant and machinery
3 Fixtures, fittings, tools and equipment
4 Payments on account and assets in course of construction
III Investments
1 Shares in group undertakings
2 Loans to group undertakings
3 Participating interests
4 Loans to undertakings in which the company has a participating interest
5 Other investments other than loans
6 Other loans

7 Own shares (4)

C Current assets

I Stocks

1 Raw materials and consumables

2 work in progress

3 Finished goods and goods for resale

4 Payments on account

II Debtors (5)

1 Trade debtors

2 Amounts owed by group undertakings

3 Amounts owed by undertakings in which the company has a participating interest

4 Other debtors

5 Called up share capital not paid (1)

6 Prepayments and accrued income (6)

III Investments

1 Shares in group undertakings

2 Own shares (4)

3 Other investments

IV Cash at bank and in hand

D Prepayments and accrued income (6)

LIABILITIES

A Capital and reserves

I Called up share capital (12)

II Share premium account

III Revaluation reserve

IV Other reserves

1 Capital redemption reserve

2 Reserve for own shares

3 Reserves provided for by the articles of association

4 Other reserves

V Profit and loss account

B Provisions for liabilities

1 Pensions and similar obligations

2 Taxation, including deferred taxation

3 Other provisions

C Creditors (13)

1 Debenture loans (7)

2 Bank loans and overdrafts

3 Payments received on account (8)

4 Trade creditors

5 Bills of exchange payable

6 Amounts owed to group undertakings

7 Amounts owed to undertakings in which the company has a participating interest

8 Other creditors including taxation and social security (9)

9 Accruals and deferred income (10)

D Accruals and deferred income (10)

Notes on the balance sheet formats

(1) Called up share capital not paid
(Formats 1 and 2, items A and CII.5)
This item may be shown in either of the two positions given in formats 1 and 2.

(2) Concessions, patents, licences, trade marks and similar rights and assets
(Formats 1 and 2, item B.I.2)

Amounts in respect of assets are only to be included in a company's balance sheet under this item if either—

(a) the assets were acquired for valuable consideration and are not required to be shown under goodwill, or

(b) the assets in question were created by the company itself.

(3) Goodwill

(Formats 1 and 2, item B.I.3)

Amounts representing goodwill are only to be included to the extent that the goodwill was acquired for valuable consideration.

(4) Own shares

(Formats 1 and 2, items B.III.7 and CIII.2)

The nominal value of the shares held must be shown separately.

(5) Debtors

(Formats 1 and 2, items CII.1 to 6)

The amount falling due after more than one year must be shown separately for each item included under debtors.

(6) Prepayments and accrued income

(Formats 1 and 2, items CII.6 and D)

This item may be shown in either of the two positions given in formats 1 and 2.

(7) Debenture loans

(Format 1, items E.1 and H.1 and format 2, item C1)

The amount of any convertible loans must be shown separately.

(8) Payments received on account

(Format 1, items E.3 and H.3 and format 2, item C3)

Payments received on account of orders must be shown for each of these items in so far as they are not shown as deductions from stocks.

(9) Other creditors including taxation and social security

(Format 1, items E.8 and H.8 and format 2, item C8)

The amount for creditors in respect of taxation and social security must be shown separately from the amount for other creditors.

(10) Accruals and deferred income

(Format 1, items E.9, H.9 and J and format 2, items C9 and D)

The two positions given for this item in format 1 at E.9 and H.9 are an alternative to the position at J, but if the item is not shown in a position corresponding to that at J it may be shown in either or both of the other two positions (as the case may require).

The two positions given for this item in format 2 are alternatives.

(11) Net current assets (liabilities)

(Format 1, item F)

In determining the amount to be shown for this item any amounts shown under "prepayments and accrued income" must be taken into account wherever shown.

(12) Called up share capital

(Format 1, item K.I and format 2, item A.I)

The amount of allotted share capital and the amount of called up share capital which has been paid up must be shown separately.

(13) Creditors

(Format 2, items C1 to 9)

Amounts falling due within one year and after one year must be shown separately for each of these items and for the aggregate of all of these items.

Profit and loss account formats

Format 1
(see note (14) below)

1 Turnover
2 Cost of sales (14)
3 Gross profit or loss
4 Distribution costs (14)
5 Administrative expenses (14)
6 Other operating income
7 Income from shares in group undertakings
8 Income from participating interests
9 Income from other fixed asset investments (15)
10 Other interest receivable and similar income (15)
11 Amounts written off investments
12 Interest payable and similar charges (16)
13 Tax on profit or loss on ordinary activities
14 Profit or loss on ordinary activities after taxation
15 Extraordinary income
16 Extraordinary charges
17 Extraordinary profit or loss
18 Tax on extraordinary profit or loss
19 Other taxes not shown under the above items
20 Profit or loss for the financial year

Profit and loss account formats

Format 2

1 Turnover
2 Change in stocks of finished goods and in work in progress
3 Own work capitalised
4 Other operating income
5 (a) Raw materials and consumables
(b) Other external charges
6 Staff costs
(a) wages and salaries
(b) social security costs
(c) other pension costs
7 (a) Depreciation and other amounts written off tangible and intangible fixed assets
(b) Exceptional amounts written off current assets
8 Other operating charges
9 Income from shares in group undertakings
10 Income from participating interests
11 Income from other fixed asset investments (15)
12 Other interest receivable and similar income (15)
13 Amounts written off investments
14 Interest payable and similar charges (16)
15 Tax on profit or loss on ordinary activities
16 Profit or loss on ordinary activities after taxation
17 Extraordinary income
18 Extraordinary charges
19 Extraordinary profit or loss
20 Tax on extraordinary profit or loss

21 Other taxes not shown under the above items
22 Profit or loss for the financial year

Profit and loss account formats

Format 3
(see note (14) below)

A Charges
1 Cost of sales (14)
2 Distribution costs (14)
3 Administrative expenses (14)
4 Amounts written off investments
5 Interest payable and similar charges (16)
6 Tax on profit or loss on ordinary activities
7 Profit or loss on ordinary activities after taxation
8 Extraordinary charges
9 Tax on extraordinary profit or loss
10 Other taxes not shown under the above items
11 Profit or loss for the financial year

B Income
1 Turnover
2 Other operating income
3 Income from shares in group undertakings
4 Income from participating interests
5 Income from other fixed asset investments (15)
6 Other interest receivable and similar income (15)
7 Profit or loss on ordinary activities after taxation
8 Extraordinary income
9 Profit or loss for the financial year

Profit and loss account formats

Format 4

A Charges
1 Reduction in stocks of finished goods and in work in progress
2 (a) Raw materials and consumables
(b) Other external charges
3 Staff costs
(a) wages and salaries
(b) social security costs
(c) other pension costs
4 (a) Depreciation and other amounts written off tangible and intangible fixed assets
(b) Exceptional amounts written off current assets
5 Other operating charges
6 Amounts written off investments
7 Interest payable and similar charges (16)
8 Tax on profit or loss on ordinary activities
9 Profit or loss on ordinary activities after taxation
10 Extraordinary charges
11 Tax on extraordinary profit or loss
12 Other taxes not shown under the above items
13 Profit or loss for the financial year

B Income
1 Turnover

2 Increase in stocks of finished goods and in work in progress
3 Own work capitalised
4 Other operating income
5 Income from shares in group undertakings
6 Income from participating interests
7 Income from other fixed asset investments (15)
8 Other interest receivable and similar income (15)
9 Profit or loss on ordinary activities after taxation
10 Extraordinary income
11 Profit or loss for the financial year

Notes on the profit and loss account formats

(14) Cost of sales: distribution costs: administrative expenses
(Format 1, items 2, 4 and 5 and format 3, items A.1, 2 and 3)
These items must be stated after taking into account any necessary provisions for depreciation or diminution in value of assets.

(15) Income from other fixed asset investments: other interest receivable and similar income
(Format 1, items 9 and 10; format 2, items 11 and 12; format 3, items B.5 and 6 and format 4, items B.7 and 8)
Income and interest derived from group undertakings must be shown separately from income and interest derived from other sources.

(16) Interest payable and similar charges
(Format 1, item 12; format 2, item 14; format 3, item A.5 and format 4, item A.7)
The amount payable to group undertakings must be shown separately.

(17) Formats 1 and 3
The amount of any provisions for depreciation and diminution in value of tangible and intangible fixed assets falling to be shown under items 7(a) and A.4(a) respectively in formats 2 and 4 must be disclosed in a note to the accounts in any case where the profit and loss account is prepared using format 1 or format 3.

PART 2
ACCOUNTING PRINCIPLES AND RULES

SECTION A
ACCOUNTING PRINCIPLES

Preliminary

10.— (1) The amounts to be included in respect of all items shown in a company's accounts must be determined in accordance with the principles set out in this Section.

(2) But if it appears to the company's directors that there are special reasons for departing from any of those principles in preparing the company's accounts in respect of any financial year they may do so, in which case particulars of the departure, the reasons for it and its effect must be given in a note to the accounts.

Accounting principles

11. The company is presumed to be carrying on business as a going concern.

12. Accounting policies must be applied consistently within the same accounts and from one financial year to the next.

13. The amount of any item must be determined on a prudent basis, and in particular—

(a) only profits realised at the balance sheet date are to be included in the profit and loss account, and

(b) all liabilities which have arisen in respect of the financial year to which the accounts relate or a previous financial year must be taken into account, including those which only become apparent between the balance sheet date and the date on which it is signed on behalf of the board of directors in accordance with section 414 of the 2006 Act (approval and signing of accounts).

14. All income and charges relating to the financial year to which the accounts relate must be taken into account, without regard to the date of receipt or payment.

15. In determining the aggregate amount of any item, the amount of each individual asset or liability that falls to be taken into account must be determined separately.

SECTION B
HISTORICAL COST ACCOUNTING RULES

Preliminary

16. Subject to Sections C and D of this Part of this Schedule, the amounts to be included in respect of all items shown in a company's accounts must be determined in accordance with the rules set out in this Section.

Fixed assets

General rules

17.— (1) The amount to be included in respect of any fixed asset must be its purchase price or production cost.

(2) This is subject to any provision for depreciation or diminution in value made in accordance with paragraphs 18 to 20.

Rules for depreciation and diminution in value

18. In the case of any fixed asset which has a limited useful economic life, the amount of—

(a) its purchase price or production cost, or

(b) where it is estimated that any such asset will have a residual value at the end of the period of its useful economic life, its purchase price or production cost less that estimated residual value, must be reduced by provisions for depreciation calculated to write off that amount systematically over the period of the asset's useful economic life.

19.— (1) Where a fixed asset investment falling to be included under item B.III of either of the balance sheet formats set out in Part 1 of this Schedule has diminished in value, provisions for diminution in value may be made in respect of it and the amount to be included in respect of it may be reduced accordingly.

(2) Provisions for diminution in value must be made in respect of any fixed asset which has diminished in value if the reduction in its value is expected to be permanent (whether its useful economic life is limited or not), and the amount to be included in respect of it must be reduced accordingly.

(3) Any provisions made under sub-paragraph (1) or (2) which are not shown in the profit and loss account must be disclosed (either separately or in aggregate) in a note to the accounts.

20.— (1) Where the reasons for which any provision was made in accordance with paragraph 19 have ceased to apply to any extent, that provision must be written back to the extent that it is no longer necessary.

(2) Any amounts written back in accordance with sub-paragraph (1) which are not shown in the profit and loss account must be disclosed (either separately or in aggregate) in a note to the accounts.

Development costs

21.— (1) Notwithstanding that an item in respect of "development costs" is included under "fixed assets" in the balance sheet formats set out in Part 1 of this Schedule, an amount may only be included in a company's balance sheet in respect of development costs in special circumstances.

(2) If any amount is included in a company's balance sheet in respect of development costs the following information must be given in a note to the accounts—

(a) the period over which the amount of those costs originally capitalised is being or is to be written off, and
(b) the reasons for capitalising the development costs in question.

Goodwill

22.— (1) The application of paragraphs 17 to 20 in relation to goodwill (in any case where goodwill is treated as an asset) is subject to the following.
(2) Subject to sub-paragraph (3), the amount of the consideration for any goodwill acquired by a company must be reduced by provisions for depreciation calculated to write off that amount systematically over a period chosen by the directors of the company.
(3) The period chosen must not exceed the useful economic life of the goodwill in question.
(4) In any case where any goodwill acquired by a company is shown or included as an asset in the company's balance sheet there must be disclosed in a note to the accounts—
(a) the period chosen for writing off the consideration for that goodwill, and
(b) the reasons for choosing that period.

Current assets

23. Subject to paragraph 24, the amount to be included in respect of any current asset must be its purchase price or production cost.

24.— (1) If the net realisable value of any current asset is lower than its purchase price or production cost, the amount to be included in respect of that asset must be the net realisable value.
(2) Where the reasons for which any provision for diminution in value was made in accordance with sub-paragraph (1) have ceased to apply to any extent, that provision must be written back to the extent that it is no longer necessary.

Miscellaneous and supplementary provisions

Excess of money owed over value received as an asset item

25.— (1) Where the amount repayable on any debt owed by a company is greater than the value of the consideration received in the transaction giving rise to the debt, the amount of the difference may be treated as an asset.
(2) Where any such amount is so treated—
(a) it must be written off by reasonable amounts each year and must be completely written off before repayment of the debt, and
(b) if the current amount is not shown as a separate item in the company's balance sheet, it must be disclosed in a note to the accounts.

Assets included at a fixed amount

26.— (1) Subject to sub-paragraph (2) , assets which fall to be included—
(a) amongst the fixed assets of a company under the item "tangible assets", or
(b) amongst the current assets of a company under the item "raw materials and consumables",
may be included at a fixed quantity and value.
(2) Sub-paragraph (1) applies to assets of a kind which are constantly being replaced where—
(a) their overall value is not material to assessing the company's state of affairs, and
(b) their quantity, value and composition are not subject to material variation.

Determination of purchase price or production cost

27.— (1) The purchase price of an asset is to be determined by adding to the actual price paid any expenses incidental to its acquisition.
(2) The production cost of an asset is to be determined by adding to the purchase price of the raw materials and consumables used the amount of the costs incurred by the company which are directly attributable to the production of that asset.
(3) In addition, there may be included in the production cost of an asset—

(a) a reasonable proportion of the costs incurred by the company which are only indirectly attributable to the production of that asset, but only to the extent that they relate to the period of production, and

(b) interest on capital borrowed to finance the production of that asset, to the extent that it accrues in respect of the period of production,

provided, however, in a case within paragraph (b), that the inclusion of the interest in determining the cost of that asset and the amount of the interest so included is disclosed in a note to the accounts.

(4) In the case of current assets distribution costs may not be included in production costs.

28.— (1) The purchase price or production cost of—

(a) any assets which fall to be included under any item shown in a company's balance sheet under the general item "stocks", and

(b) any assets which are fungible assets (including investments),

may be determined by the application of any of the methods mentioned in sub-paragraph (2) in relation to any such assets of the same class, provided that the method chosen is one which appears to the directors to be appropriate in the circumstances of the company.

(2) Those methods are—

(a) the method known as "first in, first out" (FIFO),

(b) the method known as "last in, first out" (LIFO),

(c) a weighted average price, and

(d) any other method similar to any of the methods mentioned above.

(3) Where in the case of any company—

(a) the purchase price or production cost of assets falling to be included under any item shown in the company's balance sheet has been determined by the application of any method permitted by this paragraph, and

(b) the amount shown in respect of that item differs materially from the relevant alternative amount given below in this paragraph,

the amount of that difference must be disclosed in a note to the accounts.

(4) Subject to sub-paragraph (5), for the purposes of sub-paragraph (3)(b), the relevant alternative amount, in relation to any item shown in a company's balance sheet, is the amount which would have been shown in respect of that item if assets of any class included under that item at an amount determined by any method permitted by this paragraph had instead been included at their replacement cost as at the balance sheet date.

(5) The relevant alternative amount may be determined by reference to the most recent actual purchase price or production cost before the balance sheet date of assets of any class included under the item in question instead of by reference to their replacement cost as at that date, but only if the former appears to the directors of the company to constitute the more appropriate standard of comparison in the case of assets of that class.

Substitution of original stated amount where price or cost unknown

29.— (1) This paragraph applies where—

(a) there is no record of the purchase price or production cost of any asset of a company or of any price, expenses or costs relevant for determining its purchase price or production cost in accordance with paragraph 27, or

(b) any such record cannot be obtained without unreasonable expense or delay.

(2) In such a case, the purchase price or production cost of the asset must be taken, for the purposes of paragraphs 17 to 24, to be the value ascribed to it in the earliest available record of its value made on or after its acquisition or production by the company.

SECTION C
ALTERNATIVE ACCOUNTING RULES

Preliminary

30.— (1) The rules set out in Section B are referred to below in this Schedule as the historical cost accounting rules.

(2) Those rules, with the omission of paragraphs 16, 22 and 26 to 29, are referred to below in this Part of this Schedule as the depreciation rules; and references below in this Schedule to the historical cost accounting rules do not include the depreciation rules as they apply by virtue of paragraph 33.

31. Subject to paragraphs 33 to 35, the amounts to be included in respect of assets of any description mentioned in paragraph 32 may be determined on any basis so mentioned.

Alternative accounting rules

32.— (1) Intangible fixed assets, other than goodwill, may be included at their current cost.

(2) Tangible fixed assets may be included at a market value determined as at the date of their last valuation or at their current cost.

(3) Investments of any description falling to be included under item B III of either of the balance sheet formats set out in Part 1 of this Schedule may be included either—

(a) at a market value determined as at the date of their last valuation, or

(b) at a value determined on any basis which appears to the directors to be appropriate in the circumstances of the company.

But in the latter case particulars of the method of valuation adopted and of the reasons for adopting it must be disclosed in a note to the accounts.

(4) Investments of any description falling to be included under item C III of either of the balance sheet formats set out in Part 1 of this Schedule may be included at their current cost.

(5) Stocks may be included at their current cost.

Application of the depreciation rules

33.— (1) Where the value of any asset of a company is determined on any basis mentioned in paragraph 32, that value must be, or (as the case may require) be the starting point for determining, the amount to be included in respect of that asset in the company's accounts, instead of its purchase price or production cost or any value previously so determined for that asset.

The depreciation rules apply accordingly in relation to any such asset with the substitution for any reference to its purchase price or production cost of a reference to the value most recently determined for that asset on any basis mentioned in paragraph 32.

(2) The amount of any provision for depreciation required in the case of any fixed asset by paragraphs 18 to 20 as they apply by virtue of sub-paragraph (1) is referred to below in this paragraph as the adjusted amount, and the amount of any provision which would be required by any of those paragraphs in the case of that asset according to the historical cost accounting rules is referred to as the historical cost amount.

(3) Where sub-paragraph (1) applies in the case of any fixed asset the amount of any provision for depreciation in respect of that asset—

(a) included in any item shown in the profit and loss account in respect of amounts written off assets of the description in question, or

(b) taken into account in stating any item so shown which is required by note (14) of the notes on the profit and loss account formats set out in Part 1 of this Schedule to be stated after taking into account any necessary provision for depreciation or diminution in value of assets included under it, may be the historical cost amount instead of the adjusted amount, provided that the amount of any difference between the two is shown separately in the profit and loss account or in a note to the accounts.

Additional information to be provided in case of departure from historical cost accounting rules

34.— (1) This paragraph applies where the amounts to be included in respect of assets covered by any items shown in a company's accounts have been determined on any basis mentioned in paragraph 32.

(2) The items affected and the basis of valuation adopted in determining the amounts of the assets in question in the case of each such item must be disclosed in a note to the accounts.

(3) In the case of each balance sheet item affected (except stocks) either—

(a) the comparable amounts determined according to the historical cost accounting rules, or

(b) the differences between those amounts and the corresponding amounts actually shown in the balance sheet in respect of that item,

must be shown separately in the balance sheet or in a note to the accounts.

(4) In sub-paragraph (3), references in relation to any item to the comparable amounts determined as there mentioned are references to—

(a) the aggregate amount which would be required to be shown in respect of that item if the amounts to be included in respect of all the assets covered by that item were determined according to the historical cost accounting rules, and

(b) the aggregate amount of the cumulative provisions for depreciation or diminution in value which would be permitted or required in determining those amounts according to those rules.

Revaluation reserve

35.— (1) With respect to any determination of the value of an asset of a company on any basis mentioned in paragraph 32, the amount of any profit or loss arising from that determination (after allowing, where appropriate, for any provisions for depreciation or diminution in value made otherwise than by reference to the value so determined and any adjustments of any such provisions made in the light of that determination) must be credited or (as the case may be) debited to a separate reserve ("the revaluation reserve").

(2) The amount of the revaluation reserve must be shown in the company's balance sheet under a separate sub-heading in the position given for the item "revaluation reserve" in format 1 or 2 of the balance sheet formats set out in Part 1 of this Schedule, but need not be shown under that name.

(3) An amount may be transferred—

(a) from the revaluation reserve—

(i) to the profit and loss account, if the amount was previously charged to that account or represents realised profit, or

(ii) on capitalisation,

(b) to or from the revaluation reserve in respect of the taxation relating to any profit or loss credited or debited to the reserve.

The revaluation reserve must be reduced to the extent that the amounts transferred to it are no longer necessary for the purposes of the valuation method used.

(4) In sub-paragraph (3)(a)(ii) "capitalisation", in relation to an amount standing to the credit of the revaluation reserve, means applying it in wholly or partly paying up unissued shares in the company to be allotted to members of the company as fully or partly paid shares.

(5) The revaluation reserve must not be reduced except as mentioned in this paragraph.

(6) The treatment for taxation purposes of amounts credited or debited to the revaluation reserve must be disclosed in a note to the accounts.

SECTION D
FAIR VALUE ACCOUNTING

Inclusion of financial instruments at fair value

36.— (1) Subject to sub-paragraphs (2) to (5), financial instruments (including derivatives) may be included at fair value.

(2) Sub-paragraph (1) does not apply to financial instruments that constitute liabilities unless—

(a) they are held as part of a trading portfolio,

(b) they are derivatives, or

(c) they are financial instruments falling within sub-paragraph (4).

(3) Unless they are financial instruments falling within sub-paragraph (4), sub-paragraph (1) does not apply to—

(a) financial instruments (other than derivatives) held to maturity,

(b) loans and receivables originated by the company and not held for trading purposes,

(c) interests in subsidiary undertakings, associated undertakings and joint ventures,

(d) equity instruments issued by the company,

(e) contracts for contingent consideration in a business combination, or

(f) other financial instruments with such special characteristics that the instruments, according to generally accepted accounting principles or practice, should be accounted for differently from other financial instruments.

(4) Financial instruments that, under international accounting standards adopted by the European Commission on or before 5th September 2006 in accordance with the IAS Regulation, may be included in accounts at fair value, may be so included, provided that the disclosures required by such accounting standards are made.

(5) If the fair value of a financial instrument cannot be determined reliably in accordance with paragraph 37, sub-paragraph (1) does not apply to that financial instrument.

(6) In this paragraph—

"associated undertaking" has the meaning given by paragraph 19 of Schedule 6 to these Regulations;

"joint venture" has the meaning given by paragraph 18 of that Schedule.

Determination of fair value

37.— (1) The fair value of a financial instrument is its value determined in accordance with this paragraph.

(2) If a reliable market can readily be identified for the financial instrument, its fair value is determined by reference to its market value.

(3) If a reliable market cannot readily be identified for the financial instrument but can be identified for its components or for a similar instrument, its fair value is determined by reference to the market value of its components or of the similar instrument.

(4) If neither sub-paragraph (2) nor (3) applies, the fair value of the financial instrument is a value resulting from generally accepted valuation models and techniques.

(5) Any valuation models and techniques used for the purposes of sub-paragraph (4) must ensure a reasonable approximation of the market value.

Hedged items

38. A company may include any assets and liabilities, or identified portions of such assets or liabilities, that qualify as hedged items under a fair value hedge accounting system at the amount required under that system.

Other assets that may be included at fair value

39.— (1) This paragraph applies to—

(a) investment property, and

(b) living animals and plants,

that, under international accounting standards, may be included in accounts at fair value.

(2) Such investment property and such living animals and plants may be included at fair value, provided that all such investment property or, as the case may be, all such living animals and plants are so included where their fair value can reliably be determined.

(3) In this paragraph, "fair value" means fair value determined in accordance with relevant international accounting standards.

Accounting for changes in value

40.— (1) This paragraph applies where a financial instrument is valued in accordance with paragraph 36 or 38 or an asset is valued in accordance with paragraph 39.

(2) Notwithstanding paragraph 13 in this Part of this Schedule, and subject to sub-paragraphs (3) and (4), a change in the value of the financial instrument or of the investment property or living animal or plant must be included in the profit and loss account.

(3) Where—

(a) the financial instrument accounted for is a hedging instrument under a hedge accounting system that allows some or all of the change in value not to be shown in the profit and loss account, or

(b) the change in value relates to an exchange difference arising on a monetary item that forms part of a company's net investment in a foreign entity,

the amount of the change in value must be credited to or (as the case may be) debited from a separate reserve ("the fair value reserve").

(4) Where the instrument accounted for—

(a) is an available for sale financial asset, and

(b) is not a derivative,

the change in value may be credited to or (as the case may be) debited from the fair value reserve.

The fair value reserve

41.— (1) The fair value reserve must be adjusted to the extent that the amounts shown in it are no longer necessary for the purposes of paragraph 40(3) or (4).

(2) The treatment for taxation purposes of amounts credited or debited to the fair value reserve must be disclosed in a note to the accounts.

PART 3
NOTES TO THE ACCOUNTS

Preliminary

42. Any information required in the case of any company by the following provisions of this Part of this Schedule must (if not given in the company's accounts) be given by way of a note to the accounts.

GENERAL

Reserves and dividends

43. There must be stated—

(a) any amount set aside or proposed to be set aside to, or withdrawn or proposed to be withdrawn from, reserves,

(b) the aggregate amount of dividends paid in the financial year (other than those for which a liability existed at the immediately preceding balance sheet date),

(c) the aggregate amount of dividends that the company is liable to pay at the balance sheet date, and

(d) the aggregate amount of dividends that are proposed before the date of approval of the accounts, and not otherwise disclosed under sub-paragraph (b) or (c).

Disclosure of accounting policies

44. The accounting policies adopted by the company in determining the amounts to be included in respect of items shown in the balance sheet and in determining the profit or loss of the company must be stated (including such policies with respect to the depreciation and diminution in value of assets).

45. It must be stated whether the accounts have been prepared in accordance with applicable accounting standards and particulars of any material departure from those standards and the reasons for it must be given (see regulation 4(2) for exemption for medium-sized companies).

Information supplementing the balance sheet

46. Paragraphs 47 to 64 require information which either supplements the information given with respect to any particular items shown in the balance sheet or is otherwise relevant to assessing the company's state of affairs in the light of the information so given.

Share capital and debentures

47.— (1) The following information must be given with respect to the company's share capital—

(a) where shares of more than one class have been allotted, the number and aggregate nominal value of shares of each class allotted, and

(b) where shares are held as treasury shares, the number and aggregate nominal value of the treasury shares and, where shares of more than one class have been allotted, the number and aggregate nominal value of the shares of each class held as treasury shares.

(2) In the case of any part of the allotted share capital that consists of redeemable shares, the following information must be given—

(a) the earliest and latest dates on which the company has power to redeem those shares,

(b) whether those shares must be redeemed in any event or are liable to be redeemed at the option of the company or of the shareholder, and

(c) whether any (and, if so, what) premium is payable on redemption.

48. If the company has allotted any shares during the financial year, the following information must be given—

(a) the classes of shares allotted, and

(b) as respects each class of shares, the number allotted, their aggregate nominal value, and the consideration received by the company for the allotment.

49.— (1) With respect to any contingent right to the allotment of shares in the company the following particulars must be given—

(a) the number, description and amount of the shares in relation to which the right is exercisable,

(b) the period during which it is exercisable, and

(c) the price to be paid for the shares allotted.

(2) In sub-paragraph (1) "contingent right to the allotment of shares" means any option to subscribe for shares and any other right to require the allotment of shares to any person whether arising on the conversion into shares of securities of any other description or otherwise.

50.— (1) If the company has issued any debentures during the financial year to which the accounts relate, the following information must be given—

(a) the classes of debentures issued, and

(b) as respects each class of debentures, the amount issued and the consideration received by the company for the issue.

(2) Where any of the company's debentures are held by a nominee of or trustee for the company, the nominal amount of the debentures and the amount at which they are stated in the accounting records kept by the company in accordance with section 386 of the 2006 Act (duty to keep accounting records) must be stated.

Fixed assets

51.— (1) In respect of each item which is or would but for paragraph 4(2)(b) be shown under the general item "fixed assets" in the company's balance sheet the following information must be given—

(a) the appropriate amounts in respect of that item as at the date of the beginning of the financial year and as at the balance sheet date respectively,

(b) the effect on any amount shown in the balance sheet in respect of that item of—

(i) any revision of the amount in respect of any assets included under that item made during that year on any basis mentioned in paragraph 32,

(ii) acquisitions during that year of any assets,

(iii) disposals during that year of any assets, and

(iv) any transfers of assets of the company to and from that item during that year.

(2) The reference in sub-paragraph (1)(a) to the appropriate amounts in respect of any item as at any date there mentioned is a reference to amounts representing the aggregate amounts determined, as at that date, in respect of assets falling to be included under that item on either of the following bases, that is to say—

(a) on the basis of purchase price or production cost (determined in accordance with paragraphs 27 and 28), or

(b) on any basis mentioned in paragraph 32,

(leaving out of account in either case any provisions for depreciation or diminution in value).

(3) In respect of each item within sub-paragraph (1) there must also be stated—

(a) the cumulative amount of provisions for depreciation or diminution in value of assets included under that item as at each date mentioned in sub-paragraph (1)(a),

(b) the amount of any such provisions made in respect of the financial year,

(c) the amount of any adjustments made in respect of any such provisions during that year in consequence of the disposal of any assets, and

(d) the amount of any other adjustments made in respect of any such provisions during that year.

52. Where any fixed assets of the company (other than listed investments) are included under any item shown in the company's balance sheet at an amount determined on any basis mentioned in paragraph 32, the following information must be given—

(a) the years (so far as they are known to the directors) in which the assets were severally valued and the several values, and

(b) in the case of assets that have been valued during the financial year, the names of the persons who valued them or particulars of their qualifications for doing so and (whichever is stated) the bases of valuation used by them.

53. In relation to any amount which is or would but for paragraph 4(2)(b) be shown in respect of the item "land and buildings" in the company's balance sheet there must be stated—

(a) how much of that amount is ascribable to land of freehold tenure and how much to land of leasehold tenure, and

(b) how much of the amount ascribable to land of leasehold tenure is ascribable to land held on long lease and how much to land held on short lease.

Investments

54.— (1) In respect of the amount of each item which is or would but for paragraph 4(2)(b) be shown in the company's balance sheet under the general item "investments" (whether as fixed assets or as current assets) there must be stated how much of that amount is ascribable to listed investments.

(2) Where the amount of any listed investments is stated for any item in accordance with sub-paragraph (1), the following amounts must also be stated—

(a) the aggregate market value of those investments where it differs from the amount so stated, and

(b) both the market value and the stock exchange value of any investments of which the former value is, for the purposes of the accounts, taken as being higher than the latter.

Information about fair value of assets and liabilities

55.— (1) This paragraph applies where financial instruments have been valued in accordance with paragraph 36 or 38.

(2) There must be stated—

(a) the significant assumptions underlying the valuation models and techniques used where the fair value of the instruments has been determined in accordance with paragraph 37(4),

(b) for each category of financial instrument, the fair value of the instruments in that category and the changes in value—

(i) included in the profit and loss account, or

(ii) credited to or (as the case may be) debited from the fair value reserve,

in respect of those instruments, and

(c) for each class of derivatives, the extent and nature of the instruments, including significant terms and conditions that may affect the amount, timing and certainty of future cash flows.

(3) Where any amount is transferred to or from the fair value reserve during the financial year, there must be stated in tabular form—

(a) the amount of the reserve as at the date of the beginning of the financial year and as at the balance sheet date respectively,

(b) the amount transferred to or from the reserve during that year, and

(c) the source and application respectively of the amounts so transferred.

56. Where the company has derivatives that it has not included at fair value, there must be stated for each class of such derivatives—

(a) the fair value of the derivatives in that class, if such a value can be determined in accordance with paragraph 37, and

(b) the extent and nature of the derivatives.

57.— (1) This paragraph applies if—

(a) the company has financial fixed assets that could be included at fair value by virtue of paragraph 36,

(b) the amount at which those items are included under any item in the company's accounts is in excess of their fair value, and

(c) the company has not made provision for diminution in value of those assets in accordance with paragraph 19(1) of this Schedule.

(2) There must be stated—

(a) the amount at which either the individual assets or appropriate groupings of those individual assets are included in the company's accounts,

(b) the fair value of those assets or groupings, and

(c) the reasons for not making a provision for diminution in value of those assets, including the nature of the evidence that provides the basis for the belief that the amount at which they are stated in the accounts will be recovered.

Information where investment property and living animals and plants included at fair value

58.— (1) This paragraph applies where the amounts to be included in a company's accounts in respect of investment property or living animals and plants have been determined in accordance with paragraph 39.

(2) The balance sheet items affected and the basis of valuation adopted in determining the amounts of the assets in question in the case of each such item must be disclosed in a note to the accounts.

(3) In the case of investment property, for each balance sheet item affected there must be shown, either separately in the balance sheet or in a note to the accounts—

(a) the comparable amounts determined according to the historical cost accounting rules, or

(b) the differences between those amounts and the corresponding amounts actually shown in the balance sheet in respect of that item.

(4) In sub-paragraph (3), references in relation to any item to the comparable amounts determined in accordance with that sub-paragraph are to—

(a) the aggregate amount which would be required to be shown in respect of that item if the amounts to be included in respect of all the assets covered by that item were determined according to the historical cost accounting rules, and

(b) the aggregate amount of the cumulative provisions for depreciation or diminution in value which would be permitted or required in determining those amounts according to those rules.

Reserves and provisions

59.— (1) This paragraph applies where any amount is transferred—

(a) to or from any reserves, or

(b) to any provision for liabilities, or

(c) from any provision for liabilities otherwise than for the purpose for which the provision was established,

and the reserves or provisions are or would but for paragraph 4(2)(b) be shown as separate items in the company's balance sheet.

(2) The following information must be given in respect of the aggregate of reserves or provisions included in the same item—

(a) the amount of the reserves or provisions as at the date of the beginning of the financial year and as at the balance sheet date respectively,

(b) any amounts transferred to or from the reserves or provisions during that year, and

(c) the source and application respectively of any amounts so transferred.

(3) Particulars must be given of each provision included in the item "other provisions" in the company's balance sheet in any case where the amount of that provision is material.

Provision for taxation

60. The amount of any provision for deferred taxation must be stated separately from the amount of any provision for other taxation.

Details of indebtedness

61.— (1) For the aggregate of all items shown under "creditors" in the company's balance sheet there must be stated the aggregate of the following amounts—

(a) the amount of any debts included under "creditors" which are payable or repayable otherwise than by instalments and fall due for payment or repayment after the end of the period of five years beginning with the day next following the end of the financial year, and

(b) in the case of any debts so included which are payable or repayable by instalments, the amount of any instalments which fall due for payment after the end of that period.

(2) Subject to sub-paragraph (3), in relation to each debt falling to be taken into account under sub-paragraph (1), the terms of payment or repayment and the rate of any interest payable on the debt must be stated.

(3) If the number of debts is such that, in the opinion of the directors, compliance with sub-paragraph (2) would result in a statement of excessive length, it is sufficient to give a general indication of the terms of payment or repayment and the rates of any interest payable on the debts.

(4) In respect of each item shown under "creditors" in the company's balance sheet there must be stated—

(a) the aggregate amount of any debts included under that item in respect of which any security has been given by the company, and

(b) an indication of the nature of the securities so given.

(5) References above in this paragraph to an item shown under "creditors" in the company's balance sheet include references, where amounts falling due to creditors within one year and after more than one year are distinguished in the balance sheet—

(a) in a case within sub-paragraph (1), to an item shown under the latter of those categories, and

(b) in a case within sub-paragraph (4), to an item shown under either of those categories.

References to items shown under "creditors" include references to items which would but for paragraph 4(2)(b) be shown under that heading.

62. If any fixed cumulative dividends on the company's shares are in arrear, there must be stated—

(a) the amount of the arrears, and

(b) the period for which the dividends or, if there is more than one class, each class of them are in arrear.

Guarantees and other financial commitments

63.— (1) Particulars must be given of any charge on the assets of the company to secure the liabilities of any other person, including, where practicable, the amount secured.

(2) The following information must be given with respect to any other contingent liability not provided for—

(a) the amount or estimated amount of that liability,

(b) its legal nature, and

(c) whether any valuable security has been provided by the company in connection with that liability and if so, what.

(3) There must be stated, where practicable, the aggregate amount or estimated amount of contracts for capital expenditure, so far as not provided for.

(4) Particulars must be given of—

(a) any pension commitments included under any provision shown in the company's balance sheet, and

(b) any such commitments for which no provision has been made,

and where any such commitment relates wholly or partly to pensions payable to past directors of the company separate particulars must be given of that commitment so far as it relates to such pensions.

(5) Particulars must also be given of any other financial commitments that—

(a) have not been provided for, and

(b) are relevant to assessing the company's state of affairs.

Miscellaneous matters

64.— (1) Particulars must be given of any case where the purchase price or production cost of any asset is for the first time determined under paragraph 29.

(2) Where any outstanding loans made under the authority of section 682(2)(b), (c) or (d) of the 2006 Act (various cases of financial assistance by a company for purchase of its own shares) are included under any item shown in the company's balance sheet, the aggregate amount of those loans must be disclosed for each item in question.

Information supplementing the profit and loss account

65. Paragraphs 66 to 69 require information which either supplements the information given with respect to any particular items shown in the profit and loss account or otherwise provides particulars of income or expenditure of the company or of circumstances affecting the items shown in the profit and loss account (see regulation 3(2) for exemption for companies falling within section 408 of the 2006 Act (individual profit and loss account where group accounts prepared)).

Separate statement of certain items of income and expenditure

66.— (1) Subject to sub-paragraph (2), there must be stated the amount of the interest on or any similar charges in respect of bank loans and overdrafts, and loans of any other kind made to the company.

(2) Sub-paragraph (1) does not apply to interest or charges on loans to the company from group undertakings, but, with that exception, it applies to interest or charges on all loans, whether made on the security of debentures or not.

Particulars of tax

67.— (1) Particulars must be given of any special circumstances which affect liability in respect of taxation of profits, income or capital gains for the financial year or liability in respect of taxation of profits, income or capital gains for succeeding financial years.

(2) The following amounts must be stated—

(a) the amount of the charge for United Kingdom corporation tax,

(b) if that amount would have been greater but for relief from double taxation, the amount which it would have been but for such relief,

(c) the amount of the charge for United Kingdom income tax, and

(d) the amount of the charge for taxation imposed outside the United Kingdom of profits, income and (so far as charged to revenue) capital gains.

These amounts must be stated separately in respect of each of the amounts which is or would but for paragraph 4(2)(b) be shown under the items "tax on profit or loss on ordinary activities" and "tax on extraordinary profit or loss" in the profit and loss account.

Particulars of turnover

68.— (1) If in the course of the financial year the company has carried on business of two or more classes that, in the opinion of the directors, differ substantially from each other, the amount of the turnover attributable to each class must be stated and the class described (see regulation 4(3)(b) for exemption for medium-sized companies in accounts delivered to registrar).

(2) If in the course of the financial year the company has supplied markets that, in the opinion of the directors, differ substantially from each other, the amount of the turnover attributable to each such market must also be stated.

In this paragraph "market" means a market delimited by geographical bounds.

(3) In analysing for the purposes of this paragraph the source (in terms of business or in terms of market) of turnover, the directors of the company must have regard to the manner in which the company's activities are organised.

(4) For the purposes of this paragraph—

(a) classes of business which, in the opinion of the directors, do not differ substantially from each other must be treated as one class, and

(b) markets which, in the opinion of the directors, do not differ substantially from each other must be treated as one market,

and any amounts properly attributable to one class of business or (as the case may be) to one market which are not material may be included in the amount stated in respect of another.

(5) Where in the opinion of the directors the disclosure of any information required by this paragraph would be seriously prejudicial to the interests of the company, that information need not be disclosed, but the fact that any such information has not been disclosed must be stated.

Miscellaneous matters

69.— (1) Where any amount relating to any preceding financial year is included in any item in the profit and loss account, the effect must be stated.

(2) Particulars must be given of any extraordinary income or charges arising in the financial year.

(3) The effect must be stated of any transactions that are exceptional by virtue of size or incidence though they fall within the ordinary activities of the company.

Sums denominated in foreign currencies

70. Where any sums originally denominated in foreign currencies have been brought into account under any items shown in the balance sheet format or profit and loss account formats, the basis on which those sums have been translated into sterling (or the currency in which the accounts are drawn up) must be stated.

Dormant companies acting as agents

71. Where the directors of a company take advantage of the exemption conferred by section 480 of the 2006 Act (dormant companies: exemption from audit), and the company has during the financial year in question acted as an agent for any person, the fact that it has so acted must be stated.

Related party transactions

72.— (1) Particulars may be given of transactions which the company has entered into with related parties, and must be given if such transactions are material and have not been concluded under normal market conditions (see regulation 4(2) for exemption for medium-sized companies).

(2) The particulars of transactions required to be disclosed by sub-paragraph (1) must include—

(a) the amount of such transactions,

(b) the nature of the related party relationship, and

(c) other information about the transactions necessary for an understanding of the financial position of the company.

(3) Information about individual transactions may be aggregated according to their nature, except where separate information is necessary for an understanding of the effects of related party transactions on the financial position of the company.

(4) Particulars need not be given of transactions entered into between two or more members of a group, provided that any subsidiary undertaking which is a party to the transaction is wholly-owned by such a member.

(5) In this paragraph, "related party" has the same meaning as in international accounting standards.

PART 4
SPECIAL PROVISION WHERE COMPANY IS A PARENT COMPANY OR SUBSIDIARY UNDERTAKING

Company's own accounts: guarantees and other financial commitments in favour of group undertakings

73. Commitments within any of sub-paragraphs (1) to (5) of paragraph 63 (guarantees and other financial commitments) which are undertaken on behalf of or for the benefit of—

(a) any parent undertaking or fellow subsidiary undertaking, or

(b) any subsidiary undertaking of the company,

must be stated separately from the other commitments within that paragraph, and commitments within paragraph (a) must also be stated separately from those within paragraph (b).

PART 5
SPECIAL PROVISIONS WHERE THE COMPANY IS AN INVESTMENT COMPANY

74.— (1) Paragraph 35 does not apply to the amount of any profit or loss arising from a determination of the value of any investments of an investment company on any basis mentioned in paragraph 32(3).

(2) Any provisions made by virtue of paragraph 19(1) or (2) in the case of an investment company in respect of any fixed asset investments need not be charged to the company's profit and loss account provided they are either—

(a) charged against any reserve account to which any amount excluded by sub-paragraph (1) from the requirements of paragraph 35 has been credited, or

(b) shown as a separate item in the company's balance sheet under the sub-heading "other reserves".

(3) For the purposes of this paragraph, as it applies in relation to any company, "fixed asset investment" means any asset falling to be included under any item shown in the company's balance sheet under the subdivision "investments" under the general item "fixed assets".

75.— (1) Any distribution made by an investment company which reduces the amount of its net assets to less than the aggregate of its called-up share capital and undistributable reserves shall be disclosed in a note to the company's accounts.

(2) For purposes of this paragraph, a company's net assets are the aggregate of its assets less the aggregate of its liabilities (including any provision for liabilities within paragraph 2 of Schedule 9 to these Regulations that is made in Companies Act accounts and any provision that is made in IAS accounts); and "undistributable reserves" has the meaning given by section 831(4) of the 2006 Act.

(3) A company shall be treated as an investment company for the purposes of this Part of this Schedule in relation to any financial year of the company if—

(a) during the whole of that year it was an investment company as defined by section 833 of the 2006 Act, and

(b) it was not at any time during that year prohibited from making a distribution by virtue of section 832 of the 2006 Act due to either or both of the conditions specified in section 832(5)(a) or (b) (no distribution where capital profits have been distributed etc) not being met.

SCHEDULE 2

Regulation 5(1)

BANKING COMPANIES: COMPANIES ACT INDIVIDUAL ACCOUNTS

PART 1
GENERAL RULES AND FORMATS

SECTION A
GENERAL RULES

1. Subject to the following provisions of this Part of this Schedule—

(a) every balance sheet of a company must show the items listed in the balance sheet format set out in Section B of this Part, and

(b) every profit and loss account must show the items listed in either of the profit and loss account formats in Section B.

2.— (1) References in this Part of this Schedule to the items listed in any of the formats set out in Section B, are to those items read together with any of the notes following the formats which apply to those items.

(2) The items must be shown in the order and under the headings and sub-headings given in the particular format used, but—

(a) the notes to the formats may permit alternative positions for any particular items,

(b) the heading or sub-heading for any item does not have to be distinguished by any letter or number assigned to that item in the format used, and

(c) where the heading of an item in the format used contains any wording in square brackets, that wording may be omitted if not applicable to the company.

3.— (1) Where in accordance with paragraph 1 a company's profit and loss account for any financial year has been prepared by reference to one of the formats in Section B, the company's directors must use the same format in preparing the profit and loss account for subsequent financial years, unless in their opinion there are special reasons for a change.

(2) Particulars of any change must be given in a note to the accounts in which the new format is first used, and the reasons for the change must be explained.

4.— (1) Any item required to be shown in a company's balance sheet or profit and loss account may be shown in greater detail than required by the particular format used.

(2) The balance sheet or profit and loss account may include an item representing or covering the amount of any asset or liability, income or expenditure not specifically covered by any of the items listed in the format used, save that none of the following may be treated as assets in any balance sheet—

(a) preliminary expenses,

(b) expenses of, and commission on, any issue of shares or debentures, and

(c) costs of research.

5.— (1) Items to which lower case letters are assigned in any of the formats in Section B may be combined in a company's accounts for any financial year if—

(a) their individual amounts are not material for the purpose of giving a true and fair view, or

(b) the combination facilitates the assessment of the state of affairs or profit or loss of the company for that year.

(2) Where sub-paragraph (1)(b) applies, the individual amounts of any items so combined must be disclosed in a note to the accounts and any notes required by this Schedule to the items so combined must, notwithstanding the combination, be given.

6.— (1) Subject to sub-paragraph (2), the directors must not include a heading or sub-heading corresponding to an item in the balance sheet or profit and loss account format used if there is no amount to be shown for that item for the financial year to which the balance sheet or profit and loss account relates.

(2) Where an amount can be shown for the item in question for the immediately preceding financial year, that amount must be shown under the heading or sub-heading required by the format for that item.

7.— (1) For every item shown in the balance sheet or profit and loss account the corresponding amount for the immediately preceding financial year must also be shown.

(2) Where that corresponding amount is not comparable with the amount to be shown for the item in question in respect of the financial year to which the balance sheet or profit and loss account relates, the former amount may be adjusted, and particulars of the non-comparability and of any adjustment must be disclosed in a note to the accounts.

8.— (1) Subject to the following provisions of this paragraph and without prejudice to note (6) to the balance sheet format, amounts in respect of items representing assets or income may not be set off against amounts in respect of items representing liabilities or expenditure (as the case may be), or vice versa.

(2) Charges required to be included in profit and loss account format 1, items 11(a) and 11(b) or format 2, items A7(a) and A7(b) may be set off against income required to be included in format 1, items 12(a) and 12(b) or format 2, items B5(a) and B5(b) and the resulting figure shown as a single item (in format 2 at position A7 if negative and at position B5 if positive).

(3) Charges required to be included in profit and loss account format 1, item 13 or format 2, item A8 may also be set off against income required to be included in format 1, item 14 or format 2, item B6 and the resulting figure shown as a single item (in format 2 at position A8 if negative and at position B6 if positive).

9.— (1) Assets must be shown under the relevant balance sheet headings even where the company has pledged them as security for its own liabilities or for those of third parties or has otherwise assigned them as security to third parties.

(2) A company may not include in its balance sheet assets pledged or otherwise assigned to it as security unless such assets are in the form of cash in the hands of the company.

(3) Assets acquired in the name of and on behalf of third parties must not be shown in the balance sheet.

10. The company's directors must, in determining how amounts are presented within items in the profit and loss account and balance sheet, have regard to the substance of the reported transaction or arrangement, in accordance with generally accepted accounting principles or practice.

SECTION B
THE REQUIRED FORMATS

Balance sheet format

ASSETS

1 Cash and balances at central [or post office] banks (1)
2 Treasury bills and other eligible bills (20)
  (a) Treasury bills and similar securities (2)
  (b) Other eligible bills (3)
3 Loans and advances to banks (4), (20)
  (a) Repayable on demand
  (b) Other loans and advances
4 Loans and advances to customers (5), (20)
5 Debt securities [and other fixed-income securities] (6), (20)
  (a) Issued by public bodies
  (b) Issued by other issuers
6 Equity shares [and other variable-yield securities]
7 Participating interests
8 Shares in group undertakings
9 Intangible fixed assets (7)
10 Tangible fixed assets (8)
11 Called up capital not paid (9)
12 Own shares (10)
13 Other assets
14 Called up capital not paid (9)
15 Prepayments and accrued income

Total assets

LIABILITIES

1 Deposits by banks (11), (20)
  (a) Repayable on demand
  (b) With agreed maturity dates or periods of notice
2 Customer accounts (12), (20)
  (a) Repayable on demand
  (b) With agreed maturity dates or periods of notice
3 Debt securities in issue (13), (20)
  (a) Bonds and medium term notes
  (b) Others
4 Other liabilities
5 Accruals and deferred income
6 Provisions for liabilities
  (a) Provisions for pensions and similar obligations
  (b) Provisions for tax
  (c) Other provisions
7 Subordinated liabilities (14), (20)
8 Called up share capital (15)
9 Share premium account
10 Reserves

(a) Capital redemption reserve
(b) Reserve for own shares
(c) Reserves provided for by the articles of association
(d) Other reserves
11 Revaluation reserve
12 Profit and loss account
Total liabilities
MEMORANDUM ITEMS
1 Contingent liabilities (16)
(1) Acceptances and endorsements
(2) Guarantees and assets pledged as collateral security (17)
(3) Other contingent liabilities
2 Commitments (18)
(1) Commitments arising out of sale and option to resell transactions (19)
(2) Other commitments

Notes on the balance sheet format and memorandum items

(1) Cash and balances at central [or post office] banks
(Assets item 1)
Cash is to comprise all currency including foreign notes and coins.
Only those balances which may be withdrawn without notice and which are deposited with central or post office banks of the country or countries in which the company is established may be included in this item.
All other claims on central or post office banks must be shown under assets items 3 or 4.

(2) Treasury bills and other eligible bills: Treasury bills and similar securities
(Assets item 2(a))
Treasury bills and similar securities are to comprise treasury bills and similar debt instruments issued by public bodies which are eligible for refinancing with central banks of the country or countries in which the company is established. Any treasury bills or similar debt instruments not so eligible must be included under assets item 5(a).

(3) Treasury bills and other eligible bills: Other eligible bills
(Assets item 2(b))
Other eligible bills are to comprise all bills purchased to the extent that they are eligible, under national law, for refinancing with the central banks of the country or countries in which the company is established.

(4) Loans and advances to banks
(Assets item 3)
Loans and advances to banks are to comprise all loans and advances to domestic or foreign credit institutions made by the company arising out of banking transactions. However loans and advances to credit institutions represented by debt securities or other fixed-income securities must be included under assets item 5 and not this item.

(5) Loans and advances to customers
(Assets item 4)
Loans and advances to customers are to comprise all types of assets in the form of claims on domestic and foreign customers other than credit institutions. However loans and advances represented by debt securities or other fixed-income securities must be included under assets item 5 and not this item.

(6) Debt securities [and other fixed-income securities]
(Assets item 5)
This item is to comprise transferable debt securities and any other transferable fixed-income securities issued by credit institutions, other undertakings or public bodies. Debt securities and other fixed-income securities issued by public bodies are, however, only to be included in this item if they may not be shown under assets item 2.

Where a company holds its own debt securities these must not be included under this item but must be deducted from liabilities item 3(a) or (b), as appropriate.

Securities bearing interest rates that vary in accordance with specific factors, for example the interest rate on the inter-bank market or on the Euromarket, are also to be regarded as fixed-income securities to be included under this item.

(7) Intangible fixed assets

(Assets item 9)

This item is to comprise—

(a) development costs,
(b) concessions, patents, licences, trade marks and similar rights and assets,
(c) goodwill, and
(d) payments on account.

Amounts are, however, to be included in respect of (b) only if the assets were acquired for valuable consideration or the assets in question were created by the company itself.

Amounts representing goodwill are only to be included to the extent that the goodwill was acquired for valuable consideration.

The amount of any goodwill included in this item must be disclosed in a note to the accounts.

(8) Tangible fixed assets

(Assets item 10)

This item is to comprise—

(a) land and buildings,
(b) plant and machinery,
(c) fixtures and fittings, tools and equipment, and
(d) payments on account and assets in the course of construction.

The amount included in this item with respect to land and buildings occupied by the company for its own activities must be disclosed in a note to the accounts.

(9) Called up capital not paid

(Assets items 11 and 14)

The two positions shown for this item are alternatives.

(10) Own shares

(Assets item 12)

The nominal value of the shares held must be shown separately under this item.

(11) Deposits by banks

(Liabilities item 1)

Deposits by banks are to comprise all amounts arising out of banking transactions owed to other domestic or foreign credit institutions by the company. However liabilities in the form of debt securities and any liabilities for which transferable certificates have been issued must be included under liabilities item 3 and not this item.

(12) Customer accounts

(Liabilities item 2)

This item is to comprise all amounts owed to creditors that are not credit institutions. However liabilities in the form of debt securities and any liabilities for which transferable certificates have been issued must be shown under liabilities item 3 and not this item.

(13) Debt securities in issue

(Liabilities item 3)

This item is to include both debt securities and debts for which transferable certificates have been issued, including liabilities arising out of own acceptances and promissory notes. (Only acceptances which a company has issued for its own refinancing and in respect of which it is the first party liable are to be treated as own acceptances.)

(14) Subordinated liabilities

(Liabilities item 7)

This item is to comprise all liabilities in respect of which there is a contractual obligation that, in the event of winding up or bankruptcy, they are to be repaid only after the claims of other creditors have been met.

This item must include all subordinated liabilities, whether or not a ranking has been agreed between the subordinated creditors concerned.

(15) Called up share capital

(Liabilities item 8)

The amount of allotted share capital and the amount of called up share capital which has been paid up must be shown separately.

(16) Contingent liabilities

(Memorandum item 1)

This item is to include all transactions whereby the company has underwritten the obligations of a third party.

Liabilities arising out of the endorsement of rediscounted bills must be included in this item. Acceptances other than own acceptances must also be included.

(17) Contingent liabilities: Guarantees and assets pledged as collateral security

(Memorandum item 1(2))

This item is to include all guarantee obligations incurred and assets pledged as collateral security on behalf of third parties, particularly in respect of sureties and irrevocable letters of credit.

(18) Commitments

(Memorandum item 2)

This item is to include every irrevocable commitment which could give rise to a credit risk.

(19) Commitments: Commitments arising out of sale and option to resell transactions

(Memorandum item 2(1))

This item is to comprise commitments entered into by the company in the context of sale and option to resell transactions.

(20) Claims on, and liabilities to, undertakings in which a participating interest is held or group undertakings

(Assets items 2 to 5, liabilities items 1 to 3 and 7)

The following information must be given either by way of subdivision of the relevant items or by way of notes to the accounts.

The amount of the following must be shown for each of assets items 2 to 5—

(a) claims on group undertakings included therein, and

(b) claims on undertakings in which the company has a participating interest included therein.

The amount of the following must be shown for each of liabilities items 1, 2, 3 and 7—

(i) liabilities to group undertakings included therein, and

(ii) liabilities to undertakings in which the company has a participating interest included therein.

Special rules

Subordinated assets

11.— (1) The amount of any assets that are subordinated must be shown either as a subdivision of any relevant asset item or in the notes to the accounts; in the latter case disclosure must be by reference to the relevant asset item or items in which the assets are included.

(2) In the case of assets items 2 to 5 in the balance sheet format, the amounts required to be shown by note (20) to the format as sub-items of those items must be further subdivided so as to show the amount of any claims included therein that are subordinated.

(3) For this purpose, assets are subordinated if there is a contractual obligation to the effect that, in the event of winding up or bankruptcy, they are to be repaid only after the claims of other creditors have been met, whether or not a ranking has been agreed between the subordinated creditors concerned.

Syndicated loans

12.— (1) Where a company is a party to a syndicated loan transaction the company must include only that part of the total loan which it itself has funded.

(2) Where a company is a party to a syndicated loan transaction and has agreed to reimburse (in whole or in part) any other party to the syndicate any funds advanced by that party or any interest thereon upon the occurrence of any event, including the default of the borrower, any additional liability by reason of such a guarantee must be included as a contingent liability in Memorandum item 1(2).

Sale and repurchase transactions

13.— (1) The following rules apply where a company is a party to a sale and repurchase transaction.

(2) Where the company is the transferor of the assets under the transaction—

(a) the assets transferred must, notwithstanding the transfer, be included in its balance sheet,

(b) the purchase price received by it must be included in its balance sheet as an amount owed to the transferee, and

(c) the value of the assets transferred must be disclosed in a note to its accounts.

(3) Where the company is the transferee of the assets under the transaction, it must not include the assets transferred in its balance sheet but the purchase price paid by it to the transferor must be so included as an amount owed by the transferor.

Sale and option to resell transactions

14.— (1) The following rules apply where a company is a party to a sale and option to resell transaction.

(2) Where the company is the transferor of the assets under the transaction, it must not include in its balance sheet the assets transferred but it must enter under Memorandum item 2 an amount equal to the price agreed in the event of repurchase.

(3) Where the company is the transferee of the assets under the transaction it must include those assets in its balance sheet.

Managed funds

15.— (1) For the purposes of this paragraph, "managed funds" are funds which the company administers in its own name but on behalf of others and to which it has legal title.

(2) The company must, in any case where claims and obligations arising in respect of managed funds fall to be treated as claims and obligations of the company, adopt the following accounting treatment.

(3) Claims and obligations representing managed funds are to be included in the company's balance sheet, with the notes to the accounts disclosing the total amount included with respect to such assets and liabilities in the balance sheet and showing the amount included under each relevant balance sheet item in respect of such assets or (as the case may be) liabilities.

Profit and loss account formats

Format 1

Vertical layout

1 Interest receivable (1)

(1) Interest receivable and similar income arising from debt securities [and other fixed-income securities]

(2) Other interest receivable and similar income

2 Interest payable (2)

3 Dividend income

(a) Income from equity shares [and other variable-yield securities]

(b) Income from participating interests

(c) Income from shares in group undertakings
4 Fees and commissions receivable (3)
5 Fees and commissions payable (4)
6 Dealing [profits] [losses] (5)
7 Other operating income
8 Administrative expenses
(a) Staff costs
(i) Wages and salaries
(ii) Social security costs
(iii) Other pension costs
(b) Other administrative expenses
9 Depreciation and amortisation (6)
10 Other operating charges
11 Provisions
(a) Provisions for bad and doubtful debts (7)
(b) Provisions for contingent liabilities and commitments (8)
12 Adjustments to provisions
(a) Adjustments to provisions for bad and doubtful debts (9)
(b) Adjustments to provisions for contingent liabilities and commitments (10)
13 Amounts written off fixed asset investments (11)
14 Adjustments to amounts written off fixed asset investments (12)
15 [Profit] [loss] on ordinary activities before tax
16 Tax on [profit] [loss] on ordinary activities
17 [Profit] [loss] on ordinary activities after tax
18 Extraordinary income
19 Extraordinary charges
20 Extraordinary [profit] [loss]
21 Tax on extraordinary [profit] [loss]
22 Extraordinary [profit] [loss] after tax
23 Other taxes not shown under the preceding items
24 [Profit] [loss] for the financial year

Profit and loss account formats

Format 2

Horizontal layout
A Charges
1 Interest payable (2)
2 Fees and commissions payable (4)
3 Dealing losses (5)
4 Administrative expenses
(a) Staff costs
(i) Wages and salaries
(ii) Social security costs
(iii) Other pension costs
(b) Other administrative expenses
5 Depreciation and amortisation (6)
6 Other operating charges
7 Provisions
(a) Provisions for bad and doubtful debts (7)
(b) Provisions for contingent liabilities and commitments (8)
8 Amounts written off fixed asset investments (11)
9 Profit on ordinary activities before tax

10 Tax on [profit] [loss] on ordinary activities
11 Profit on ordinary activities after tax
12 Extraordinary charges
13 Tax on extraordinary [profit] [loss]
14 Extraordinary loss after tax
15 Other taxes not shown under the preceding items
16 Profit for the financial year

B Income

1 Interest receivable (1)

(1) Interest receivable and similar income arising from debt securities [and other fixed-income securities]

(2) Other interest receivable and similar income

2 Dividend income

(a) Income from equity shares [and other variable-yield securities]

(b) Income from participating interests

(c) Income from shares in group undertakings

3 Fees and commissions receivable (3)
4 Dealing profits (5)
5 Adjustments to provisions

(a) Adjustments to provisions for bad and doubtful debts (9)

(b) Adjustments to provisions for contingent liabilities and commitments (10)

6 Adjustments to amounts written off fixed asset investments (12)
7 Other operating income
8 Loss on ordinary activities before tax
9 Loss on ordinary activities after tax
10 Extraordinary income
11 Extraordinary profit after tax
12 Loss for the financial year

Notes on the profit and loss account formats

(1) Interest receivable

(Format 1, item 1; format 2, item B1)

This item is to include all income arising out of banking activities, including—

(a) income from assets included in assets items 1 to 5 in the balance sheet format, however calculated,

(b) income resulting from covered forward contracts spread over the actual duration of the contract and similar in nature to interest, and

(c) fees and commissions receivable similar in nature to interest and calculated on a time basis or by reference to the amount of the claim (but not other fees and commissions receivable).

(2) Interest payable

(Format 1, item 2; format 2, item A1)

This item is to include all expenditure arising out of banking activities, including—

(a) charges arising out of liabilities included in liabilities items 1, 2, 3 and 7 in the balance sheet format, however calculated,

(b) charges resulting from covered forward contracts, spread over the actual duration of the contract and similar in nature to interest, and

(c) fees and commissions payable similar in nature to interest and calculated on a time basis or by reference to the amount of the liability (but not other fees and commissions payable).

(3) Fees and commissions receivable

(Format 1, item 4; format 2, item B3)

Fees and commissions receivable are to comprise income in respect of all services supplied by the company to third parties, but not fees or commissions required to be included under interest receivable (format 1, item 1; format 2, item B1).

In particular the following fees and commissions receivable must be included (unless required to be included under interest receivable)—

(a) fees and commissions for guarantees, loan administration on behalf of other lenders and securities transactions,

(b) fees, commissions and other income in respect of payment transactions, account administration charges and commissions for the safe custody and administration of securities,

(c) fees and commissions for foreign currency transactions and for the sale and purchase of coin and precious metals, and

(d) fees and commissions charged for brokerage services in connection with savings and insurance contracts and loans.

(4) Fees and commissions payable

(Format 1, item 5; format 2, item A2)

Fees and commissions payable are to comprise charges for all services rendered to the company by third parties but not fees or commissions required to be included under interest payable (format 1, item 2; format 2, item A1).

In particular the following fees and commissions payable must be included (unless required to be included under interest payable)—

(a) fees and commissions for guarantees, loan administration and securities transactions;

(b) fees, commissions and other charges in respect of payment transactions, account administration charges and commissions for the safe custody and administration of securities;

(c) fees and commissions for foreign currency transactions and for the sale and purchase of coin and precious metals; and

(d) fees and commissions for brokerage services in connection with savings and insurance contracts and loans.

(5) Dealing [profits] [losses]

(Format 1, item 6; format 2, items B4 and A3)

This item is to comprise—

(a) the net profit or net loss on transactions in securities which are not held as financial fixed assets together with amounts written off or written back with respect to such securities, including amounts written off or written back as a result of the application of paragraph 33(1),

(b) the net profit or loss on exchange activities, save in so far as the profit or loss is included in interest receivable or interest payable (format 1, items 1 or 2; format 2, items B1 or A1), and

(c) the net profits and losses on other dealing operations involving financial instruments, including precious metals.

(6) Depreciation and amortisation

(Format 1, item 9; format 2, item A5)

This item is to comprise depreciation and other amounts written off in respect of balance sheet assets items 9 and 10.

(7) Provisions: Provisions for bad and doubtful debts

(Format 1, item 11(a); format 2, item A7(a))

Provisions for bad and doubtful debts are to comprise charges for amounts written off and for provisions made in respect of loans and advances shown under balance sheet assets items 3 and 4.

(8) Provisions: Provisions for contingent liabilities and commitments

(Format 1, item 11(b); format 2, item A7(b))

This item is to comprise charges for provisions for contingent liabilities and commitments of a type which would, if not provided for, be shown under Memorandum items 1 and 2.

(9) Adjustments to provisions: Adjustments to provisions for bad and doubtful debts

(Format 1, item 12(a); format 2, item B5(a))

This item is to include credits from the recovery of loans that have been written off, from other advances written back following earlier write offs and from the reduction of provisions previously made with respect to loans and advances.

(10) Adjustments to provisions: Adjustments to provisions for contingent liabilities and commitments (Format 1, item 12(b); format 2, item B5(b))

This item comprises credits from the reduction of provisions previously made with respect to contingent liabilities and commitments.

(11) Amounts written off fixed asset investments
(Format 1, item 13; format 2, item A8)

Amounts written off fixed asset investments are to comprise amounts written off in respect of assets which are transferable securities held as financial fixed assets, participating interests and shares in group undertakings and which are included in assets items 5 to 8 in the balance sheet format.

(12) Adjustments to amounts written off fixed asset investments
(Format 1, item 14; format 2, item B6)

Adjustments to amounts written off fixed asset investments are to include amounts written back following earlier write offs and provisions in respect of assets which are transferable securities held as financial fixed assets, participating interests and group undertakings and which are included in assets items 5 to 8 in the balance sheet format.

PART 2
ACCOUNTING PRINCIPLES AND RULES

SECTION A
ACCOUNTING PRINCIPLES

Preliminary

16.— (1) The amounts to be included in respect of all items shown in a company's accounts must be determined in accordance with the principles set out in this Section.

(2) But if it appears to the company's directors that there are special reasons for departing from any of those principles in preparing the company's accounts in respect of any financial year they may do so, in which case particulars of the departure, the reasons for it and its effect must be given in a note to the accounts.

Accounting principles

17. The company is presumed to be carrying on business as a going concern.

18. Accounting policies must be applied consistently within the same accounts and from one financial year to the next.

19. The amount of any item must be determined on a prudent basis, and in particular—

(a) only profits realised at the balance sheet date are to be included in the profit and loss account, and

(b) all liabilities which have arisen in respect of the financial year to which the accounts relate or a previous financial year must be taken into account, including those which only become apparent between the balance sheet date and the date on which it is signed on behalf of the board of directors in accordance with section 414 of the 2006 Act (approval and signing of accounts).

20. All income and charges relating to the financial year to which the accounts relate must be taken into account, without regard to the date of receipt or payment.

21. In determining the aggregate amount of any item, the amount of each individual asset or liability that falls to be taken into account must be determined separately.

SECTION B
HISTORICAL COST ACCOUNTING RULES

Preliminary

22. Subject to Sections C and D of this Part of this Schedule, the amounts to be included in respect of all items shown in a company's accounts must be determined in accordance with the rules set out in this Section.

Fixed assets

General rules

23.— (1) The amount to be included in respect of any fixed asset is its cost.

(2) This is subject to any provision for depreciation or diminution in value made in accordance with paragraphs 24 to 26.

Rules for depreciation and diminution in value

24. In the case of any fixed asset which has a limited useful economic life, the amount of—

(a) its cost, or

(b) where it is estimated that any such asset will have a residual value at the end of the period of its useful economic life, its cost less that estimated residual value,

must be reduced by provisions for depreciation calculated to write off that amount systematically over the period of the asset's useful economic life.

25.— (1) Where a fixed asset investment to which sub-paragraph (2) applies has diminished in value, provisions for diminution in value may be made in respect of it and the amount to be included in respect of it may be reduced accordingly.

(2) This sub-paragraph applies to fixed asset investments of a description falling to be included under assets item 7 (participating interests) or 8 (shares in group undertakings) in the balance sheet format, or any other holding of securities held as a financial fixed asset.

(3) Provisions for diminution in value must be made in respect of any fixed asset which has diminished in value if the reduction in its value is expected to be permanent (whether its useful economic life is limited or not), and the amount to be included in respect of it must be reduced accordingly.

(4) Any provisions made under this paragraph which are not shown in the profit and loss account must be disclosed (either separately or in aggregate) in a note to the accounts.

26.— (1) Where the reasons for which any provision was made in accordance with paragraph 25 have ceased to apply to any extent, that provision must be written back to the extent that it is no longer necessary.

(2) Any amounts written back in accordance with sub-paragraph (1) which are not shown in the profit and loss account must be disclosed (either separately or in aggregate) in a note to the accounts.

Development costs

27.— (1) Notwithstanding that amounts representing "development costs" may be included under assets item 9 in the balance sheet format, an amount may only be included in a company's balance sheet in respect of development costs in special circumstances.

(2) If any amount is included in a company's balance sheet in respect of development costs the following information must be given in a note to the accounts—

(a) the period over which the amount of those costs originally capitalised is being or is to be written off, and

(b) the reasons for capitalising the development costs in question.

Goodwill

28.— (1) The application of paragraphs 23 to 26 in relation to goodwill (in any case where goodwill is treated as an asset) is subject to the following.

(2) Subject to sub-paragraph (3), the amount of the consideration for any goodwill acquired by a company must be reduced by provisions for depreciation calculated to write off that amount systematically over a period chosen by the directors of the company.

(3) The period chosen must not exceed the useful economic life of the goodwill in question.

(4) In any case where any goodwill acquired by a company is included as an asset in the company's balance sheet there must be disclosed in a note to the accounts—

(a) the period chosen for writing off the consideration for that goodwill, and

(b) the reasons for choosing that period.

Treatment of fixed assets

29.— (1) Assets included in assets items 9 (intangible fixed assets) and 10 (tangible fixed assets) in the balance sheet format must be valued as fixed assets.

(2) Other assets falling to be included in the balance sheet must be valued as fixed assets where they are intended for use on a continuing basis in the company's activities.

Financial fixed assets

30.— (1) Debt securities, including fixed-income securities, held as financial fixed assets must be included in the balance sheet at an amount equal to their maturity value plus any premium, or less any discount, on their purchase, subject to the following provisions of this paragraph.

(2) The amount included in the balance sheet with respect to such securities purchased at a premium must be reduced each financial year on a systematic basis so as to write the premium off over the period to the maturity date of the security and the amounts so written off must be charged to the profit and loss account for the relevant financial years.

(3) The amount included in the balance sheet with respect to such securities purchased at a discount must be increased each financial year on a systematic basis so as to extinguish the discount over the period to the maturity date of the security and the amounts by which the amount is increased must be credited to the profit and loss account for the relevant years.

(4) The notes to the accounts must disclose the amount of any unamortized premium or discount not extinguished which is included in the balance sheet by virtue of sub-paragraph (1).

(5) For the purposes of this paragraph "premium" means any excess of the amount paid for a security over its maturity value and "discount" means any deficit of the amount paid for a security over its maturity value.

Current assets

31. The amount to be included in respect of loans and advances, debt or other fixed-income securities and equity shares or other variable yield securities not held as financial fixed assets must be their cost, subject to paragraphs 32 and 33.

32.— (1) If the net realisable value of any asset referred to in paragraph 31 is lower than its cost, the amount to be included in respect of that asset is the net realisable value.

(2) Where the reasons for which any provision for diminution in value was made in accordance with sub-paragraph (1) have ceased to apply to any extent, that provision must be written back to the extent that it is no longer necessary.

33.— (1) Subject to paragraph 32, the amount to be included in the balance sheet in respect of transferable securities not held as financial fixed assets may be the higher of their cost or their market value at the balance sheet date.

(2) The difference between the cost of any securities included in the balance sheet at a valuation under sub-paragraph (1) and their market value must be shown (in aggregate) in the notes to the accounts.

Miscellaneous and supplementary provisions

Excess of money owed over value received as an asset item

34.— (1) Where the amount repayable on any debt owed by a company is greater than the value of the consideration received in the transaction giving rise to the debt, the amount of the difference may be treated as an asset.

(2) Where any such amount is so treated—

(a) it must be written off by reasonable amounts each year and must be completely written off before repayment of the debt, and

(b) if the current amount is not shown as a separate item in the company's balance sheet, it must be disclosed in a note to the accounts.

Determination of cost

35.— (1) The cost of an asset that has been acquired by the company is to be determined by adding to the actual price paid any expenses incidental to its acquisition.

(2) The cost of an asset constructed by the company is to be determined by adding to the purchase price of the raw materials and consumables used the amount of the costs incurred by the company which are directly attributable to the construction of that asset.

(3) In addition, there may be included in the cost of an asset constructed by the company—

(a) a reasonable proportion of the costs incurred by the company which are only indirectly attributable to the construction of that asset, but only to the extent that they relate to the period of construction, and

(b) interest on capital borrowed to finance the construction of that asset, to the extent that it accrues in respect of the period of construction,

provided, however, in a case within paragraph (b), that the inclusion of the interest in determining the cost of that asset and the amount of the interest so included is disclosed in a note to the accounts.

36.— (1) The cost of any assets which are fungible assets (including investments), may be determined by the application of any of the methods mentioned in sub-paragraph (2) in relation to any such assets of the same class, provided that the method chosen is one which appears to the directors to be appropriate in the circumstances of the company.

(2) Those methods are—

(a) the method known as "first in, first out" (FIFO),

(b) the method known as "last in, first out" (LIFO),

(c) a weighted average price, and

(d) any other method similar to any of the methods mentioned above.

(3) Where in the case of any company—

(a) the cost of assets falling to be included under any item shown in the company's balance sheet has been determined by the application of any method permitted by this paragraph, and

(b) the amount shown in respect of that item differs materially from the relevant alternative amount given below in this paragraph,

the amount of that difference must be disclosed in a note to the accounts.

(4) Subject to sub-paragraph (5), for the purposes of sub-paragraph (3)(b), the relevant alternative amount, in relation to any item shown in a company's balance sheet, is the amount which would have been shown in respect of that item if assets of any class included under that item at an amount determined by any method permitted by this paragraph had instead been included at their replacement cost as at the balance sheet date.

(5) The relevant alternative amount may be determined by reference to the most recent actual purchase price before the balance sheet date of assets of any class included under the item in question instead of by reference to their replacement cost as at that date, but only if the former appears to the directors of the company to constitute the more appropriate standard of comparison in the case of assets of that class.

Substitution of original stated amount where price or cost unknown

37.— (1) This paragraph applies where—

(a) there is no record of the purchase price of any asset acquired by a company or of any price, expenses or costs relevant for determining its cost in accordance with paragraph 35, or

(b) any such record cannot be obtained without unreasonable expense or delay.

(2) In such a case, its cost is to be taken, for the purposes of paragraphs 23 to 33, to be the value ascribed to it in the earliest available record of its value made on or after its acquisition by the company.

SECTION C
ALTERNATIVE ACCOUNTING RULES

Preliminary

38.— (1) The rules set out in Section B are referred to below in this Schedule as the historical cost accounting rules.

(2) Paragraphs 23 to 26 and 30 to 34 are referred to below in this Section as the depreciation rules; and references below in this Schedule to the historical cost accounting rules do not include the depreciation rules as they apply by virtue of paragraph 41.

39. Subject to paragraphs 41 to 43, the amounts to be included in respect of assets of any description mentioned in paragraph 40 may be determined on any basis so mentioned.

Alternative accounting rules

40.— (1) Intangible fixed assets, other than goodwill, may be included at their current cost.

(2) Tangible fixed assets may be included at a market value determined as at the date of their last valuation or at their current cost.

(3) Investments of any description falling to be included under assets items 7 (participating interests) or 8 (shares in group undertakings) of the balance sheet format and any other securities held as financial fixed assets may be included either—

(a) at a market value determined as at the date of their last valuation, or

(b) at a value determined on any basis which appears to the directors to be appropriate in the circumstances of the company.

But in the latter case particulars of the method of valuation adopted and of the reasons for adopting it must be disclosed in a note to the accounts.

(4) Securities of any description not held as financial fixed assets (if not valued in accordance with paragraph 33) may be included at their current cost.

Application of the depreciation rules

41.— (1) Where the value of any asset of a company is determined in accordance with paragraph 40, that value must be, or (as the case may require) be the starting point for determining, the amount to be included in respect of that asset in the company's accounts, instead of its cost or any value previously so determined for that asset.

The depreciation rules apply accordingly in relation to any such asset with the substitution for any reference to its cost of a reference to the value most recently determined for that asset in accordance with paragraph 40.

(2) The amount of any provision for depreciation required in the case of any fixed asset by paragraphs 24 to 26 as they apply by virtue of sub-paragraph (1) is referred to below in this paragraph as the adjusted amount, and the amount of any provision which would be required by any of those paragraphs in the case of that asset according to the historical cost accounting rules is referred to as the historical cost amount.

(3) Where sub-paragraph (1) applies in the case of any fixed asset the amount of any provision for depreciation in respect of that asset included in any item shown in the profit and loss account in respect of amounts written off assets of the description in question may be the

historical cost amount instead of the adjusted amount, provided that the amount of any difference between the two is shown separately in the profit and loss account or in a note to the accounts.

Additional information to be provided in case of departure from historical cost accounting rules

42.— (1) This paragraph applies where the amounts to be included in respect of assets covered by any items shown in a company's accounts have been determined in accordance with paragraph 40.

(2) The items affected and the basis of valuation adopted in determining the amounts of the assets in question in the case of each such item must be disclosed in a note to the accounts.

(3) In the case of each balance sheet item affected either—

(a) the comparable amounts determined according to the historical cost accounting rules, or

(b) the differences between those amounts and the corresponding amounts actually shown in the balance sheet in respect of that item, must be shown separately in the balance sheet or in a note to the accounts.

(4) In sub-paragraph (3), references in relation to any item to the comparable amounts determined as there mentioned are references to—

(a) the aggregate amount which would be required to be shown in respect of that item if the amounts to be included in respect of all the assets covered by that item were determined according to the historical cost accounting rules, and

(b) the aggregate amount of the cumulative provisions for depreciation or diminution in value which would be permitted or required in determining those amounts according to those rules.

Revaluation reserve

43.— (1) With respect to any determination of the value of an asset of a company in accordance with paragraph 40, the amount of any profit or loss arising from that determination (after allowing, where appropriate, for any provisions for depreciation or diminution in value made otherwise than by reference to the value so determined and any adjustments of any such provisions made in the light of that determination) must be credited or (as the case may be) debited to a separate reserve ("the revaluation reserve").

(2) The amount of the revaluation reserve must be shown in the company's balance sheet under liabilities item 11 in the balance sheet format, but need not be shown under that name.

(3) An amount may be transferred—

(a) from the revaluation reserve—

(i) to the profit and loss account, if the amount was previously charged to that account or represents realised profit, or

(ii) on capitalisation,

(b) to or from the revaluation reserve in respect of the taxation relating to any profit or loss credited or debited to the reserve.

The revaluation reserve must be reduced to the extent that the amounts transferred to it are no longer necessary for the purposes of the valuation method used.

(4) In sub-paragraph (3)(a)(ii) "capitalisation", in relation to an amount standing to the credit of the revaluation reserve, means applying it in wholly or partly paying up unissued shares in the company to be allotted to members of the company as fully or partly paid shares.

(5) The revaluation reserve must not be reduced except as mentioned in this paragraph.

(6) The treatment for taxation purposes of amounts credited or debited to the revaluation reserve must be disclosed in a note to the accounts.

SECTION D
FAIR VALUE ACCOUNTING

Inclusion of financial instruments at fair value

44.— (1) Subject to sub-paragraphs (2) to (5), financial instruments (including derivatives) may be included at fair value.

(2) Sub-paragraph (1) does not apply to financial instruments that constitute liabilities unless—

(a) they are held as part of a trading portfolio,

(b) they are derivatives, or

(c) they are financial instruments falling within sub-paragraph (4).

(3) Unless they are financial instruments falling within sub-paragraph (4), sub-paragraph (1) does not apply to—

(a) financial instruments (other than derivatives) held to maturity,

(b) loans and receivables originated by the company and not held for trading purposes,

(c) interests in subsidiary undertakings, associated undertakings and joint ventures,

(d) equity instruments issued by the company,

(e) contracts for contingent consideration in a business combination, or

(f) other financial instruments with such special characteristics that the instruments, according to generally accepted accounting principles or practice, should be accounted for differently from other financial instruments.

(4) Financial instruments that, under international accounting standards adopted by the European Commission on or before 5th September 2006 in accordance with the IAS Regulation, may be included in accounts at fair value, may be so included, provided that the disclosures required by such accounting standards are made.

(5) If the fair value of a financial instrument cannot be determined reliably in accordance with paragraph 45, sub-paragraph (1) does not apply to that financial instrument.

(6) In this paragraph—

"associated undertaking" has the meaning given by paragraph 19 of Schedule 6 to these Regulations;

"joint venture" has the meaning given by paragraph 18 of that Schedule.

Determination of fair value

45.— (1) The fair value of a financial instrument is its value determined in accordance with this paragraph.

(2) If a reliable market can readily be identified for the financial instrument, its fair value is determined by reference to its market value.

(3) If a reliable market cannot readily be identified for the financial instrument but can be identified for its components or for a similar instrument, its fair value is determined by reference to the market value of its components or of the similar instrument.

(4) If neither sub-paragraph (2) nor (3) applies, the fair value of the financial instrument is a value resulting from generally accepted valuation models and techniques.

(5) Any valuation models and techniques used for the purposes of sub-paragraph (4) must ensure a reasonable approximation of the market value.

Hedged items

46. A company may include any assets and liabilities, or identified portions of such assets or liabilities, that qualify as hedged items under a fair value hedge accounting system at the amount required under that system.

Other assets that may be included at fair value

47.— (1) This paragraph applies to—

(a) investment property, and

(b) living animals and plants,

that, under international accounting standards, may be included in accounts at fair value.

(2) Such investment property and such living animals and plants may be included at fair value, provided that all such investment property or, as the case may be, all such living animals and plants are so included where their fair value can reliably be determined.

(3) In this paragraph, "fair value" means fair value determined in accordance with relevant international accounting standards.

Accounting for changes in value

48.— (1) This paragraph applies where a financial instrument is valued in accordance with paragraph 44 or 46 or an asset is valued in accordance with paragraph 47.

(2) Notwithstanding paragraph 19 in this Part of this Schedule, and subject to sub-paragraphs (3) and (4), a change in the value of the financial instrument or of the investment property or living animal or plant must be included in the profit and loss account.

(3) Where—

(a) the financial instrument accounted for is a hedging instrument under a hedge accounting system that allows some or all of the change in value not to be shown in the profit and loss account, or

(b) the change in value relates to an exchange difference arising on a monetary item that forms part of a company's net investment in a foreign entity,

the amount of the change in value must be credited to or (as the case may be) debited from a separate reserve ("the fair value reserve").

(4) Where the instrument accounted for—

(a) is an available for sale financial asset, and

(b) is not a derivative,

the change in value may be credited to or (as the case may be) debited from the fair value reserve.

The fair value reserve

49.— (1) The fair value reserve must be adjusted to the extent that the amounts shown in it are no longer necessary for the purposes of paragraph 48(3) or (4).

(2) The treatment for taxation purposes of amounts credited or debited to the fair value reserve must be disclosed in a note to the accounts.

Assets and liabilities denominated in foreign currencies

50.— (1) Subject to the following sub-paragraphs, amounts to be included in respect of assets and liabilities denominated in foreign currencies must be in sterling (or the currency in which the accounts are drawn up) after translation at an appropriate spot rate of exchange prevailing at the balance sheet date.

(2) An appropriate rate of exchange prevailing on the date of purchase may however be used for assets held as financial fixed assets and assets to be included under assets items 9 (intangible fixed assets) and 10 (tangible fixed assets) in the balance sheet format, if they are not covered or not specifically covered in either the spot or forward currency markets.

(3) An appropriate spot rate of exchange prevailing at the balance sheet date must be used for translating uncompleted spot exchange transactions.

(4) An appropriate forward rate of exchange prevailing at the balance sheet date must be used for translating uncompleted forward exchange transactions.

(5) This paragraph does not apply to any assets or liabilities held, or any transactions entered into, for hedging purposes or to any assets or liabilities which are themselves hedged.

51.— (1) Subject to sub-paragraph (2), any difference between the amount to be included in respect of an asset or liability under paragraph 50 and the book value, after translation into sterling (or the currency in which the accounts are drawn up) at an appropriate rate, of that asset or liability must be credited or, as the case may be, debited to the profit and loss account.

(2) In the case, however, of assets held as financial fixed assets, of assets to be included under assets items 9 (intangible fixed assets) and 10 (tangible fixed assets) in the balance sheet

format and of transactions undertaken to cover such assets, any such difference may be deducted from or credited to any non-distributable reserve available for the purpose.

PART 3
NOTES TO THE ACCOUNTS

Preliminary

52. Any information required in the case of any company by the following provisions of this Part of this Schedule must (if not given in the company's accounts) be given by way of a note to the accounts.

General

Disclosure of accounting policies

53. The accounting policies adopted by the company in determining the amounts to be included in respect of items shown in the balance sheet and in determining the profit or loss of the company must be stated (including such policies with respect to the depreciation and diminution in value of assets).

54. It must be stated whether the accounts have been prepared in accordance with applicable accounting standards and particulars of any material departure from those standards and the reasons for it must be given.

Sums denominated in foreign currencies

55. Where any sums originally denominated in foreign currencies have been brought into account under any items shown in the balance sheet format or profit and loss account formats, the basis on which those sums have been translated into sterling (or the currency in which the accounts are drawn up) must be stated.

Reserves and dividends

56. There must be stated—

(a) any amount set aside or proposed to be set aside to, or withdrawn or proposed to be withdrawn from, reserves,

(b) the aggregate amount of dividends paid in the financial year (other than those for which a liability existed at the immediately preceding balance sheet date),

(c) the aggregate amount of dividends that the company is liable to pay at the balance sheet date, and

(d) the aggregate amount of dividends that are proposed before the date of approval of the accounts, and not otherwise disclosed under sub-paragraph (b) or (c).

Information supplementing the balance sheet

57. Paragraphs 58 to 84 require information which either supplements the information given with respect to any particular items shown in the balance sheet or is otherwise relevant to assessing the company's state of affairs in the light of the information so given.

Share capital and debentures

58.— (1) Where shares of more than one class have been allotted, the number and aggregate nominal value of shares of each class allotted must be given.

(2) In the case of any part of the allotted share capital that consists of redeemable shares, the following information must be given—

(a) the earliest and latest dates on which the company has power to redeem those shares,

(b) whether those shares must be redeemed in any event or are liable to be redeemed at the option of the company or of the shareholder, and

(c) whether any (and, if so, what) premium is payable on redemption.

59. If the company has allotted any shares during the financial year, the following information must be given—

(a) the classes of shares allotted, and

(b) as respects each class of shares, the number allotted, their aggregate nominal value and the consideration received by the company for the allotment.

60.— (1) With respect to any contingent right to the allotment of shares in the company the following particulars must be given—

(a) the number, description and amount of the shares in relation to which the right is exercisable,

(b) the period during which it is exercisable, and

(c) the price to be paid for the shares allotted.

(2) In sub-paragraph (1) "contingent right to the allotment of shares" means any option to subscribe for shares and any other right to require the allotment of shares to any person whether arising on the conversion into shares of securities of any other description or otherwise.

61.— (1) If the company has issued any debentures during the financial year to which the accounts relate, the following information must be given—

(a) the classes of debentures issued, and

(b) as respects each class of debentures, the amount issued and the consideration received by the company for the issue.

(2) Where any of the company's debentures are held by a nominee of or trustee for the company, the nominal amount of the debentures and the amount at which they are stated in the accounting records kept by the company in accordance with section 386 of the 2006 Act (duty to keep accounting records) must be stated.

Fixed assets

62.— (1) In respect of any fixed assets of the company included in any assets item in the company's balance sheet the following information must be given by reference to each such item—

(a) the appropriate amounts in respect of those assets included in the item as at the date of the beginning of the financial year and as at the balance sheet date respectively,

(b) the effect on any amount shown included in the item in respect of those assets of—

(i) any determination during that year of the value to be ascribed to any of those assets in accordance with paragraph 40,

(ii) acquisitions during that year of any fixed assets,

(iii) disposals during that year of any fixed assets, and

(iv) any transfers of fixed assets of the company to and from that item during that year.

(2) The reference in sub-paragraph (1)(a) to the appropriate amounts in respect of any fixed assets (included in an assets item) as at any date there mentioned is a reference to amounts representing the aggregate amounts determined, as at that date, in respect of fixed assets falling to be included under the item on either of the following bases—

(a) on the basis of cost (determined in accordance with paragraphs 35 and 36), or

(b) on any basis permitted by paragraph 40,

(leaving out of account in either case any provisions for depreciation or diminution in value).

(3) In addition, in respect of any fixed assets of the company included in any assets item in the company's balance sheet, there must be stated (by reference to each such item)—

(a) the cumulative amount of provisions for depreciation or diminution in value of those assets included under that item as at each date mentioned in sub-paragraph (1)(a),

(b) the amount of any such provisions made in respect of the financial year,

(c) the amount of any adjustments made in respect of any such provisions during that year in consequence of the disposal of any of those assets, and

(d) the amount of any other adjustments made in respect of any such provisions during that year.

(4) The requirements of this paragraph need not be complied with to the extent that a company takes advantage of the option of setting off charges and income afforded by paragraph 8(3) in Part 1 of this Schedule.

63. Where any fixed assets of the company (other than listed investments) are included under any item shown in the company's balance sheet at an amount determined in accordance with paragraph 40, the following information must be given—

(a) the years (so far as they are known to the directors) in which the assets were severally valued and the several values, and

(b) in the case of assets that have been valued during the financial year, the names of the persons who valued them or particulars of their qualifications for doing so and (whichever is stated) the bases of valuation used by them.

64. In relation to any amount which is included under assets item 10 in the balance sheet format (tangible fixed assets) with respect to land and buildings there must be stated—

(a) how much of that amount is ascribable to land of freehold tenure and how much to land of leasehold tenure, and

(b) how much of the amount ascribable to land of leasehold tenure is ascribable to land held on long lease and how much to land held on short lease.

65. There must be disclosed separately the amount of—

(a) any participating interests, and

(b) any shares in group undertakings that are held in credit institutions.

Information about fair value of assets and liabilities

66.— (1) This paragraph applies where financial instruments have been valued in accordance with paragraph 44 or 46.

(2) There must be stated—

(a) the significant assumptions underlying the valuation models and techniques used where the fair value of the instruments has been determined in accordance with paragraph 45(4),

(b) for each category of financial instrument, the fair value of the instruments in that category and the changes in value—

(i) included in the profit and loss account, or

(ii) credited to or (as the case may be) debited from the fair value reserve,

in respect of those instruments, and

(c) for each class of derivatives, the extent and nature of the instruments, including significant terms and conditions that may affect the amount, timing and certainty of future cash flows.

(3) Where any amount is transferred to or from the fair value reserve during the financial year, there must be stated in tabular form—

(a) the amount of the reserve as at the date of the beginning of the financial year and as at the balance sheet date respectively,

(b) the amount transferred to or from the reserve during that year, and

(c) the source and application respectively of the amounts so transferred.

67. Where the company has derivatives that it has not included at fair value, there must be stated for each class of such derivatives—

(a) the fair value of the derivatives in that class, if such a value can be determined in accordance with paragraph 45, and

(b) the extent and nature of the derivatives.

68.— (1) This paragraph applies if—

(a) the company has financial fixed assets that could be included at fair value by virtue of paragraph 44,

(b) the amount at which those items are included under any item in the company's accounts is in excess of their fair value, and

(c) the company has not made provision for diminution in value of those assets in accordance with paragraph 25(1) in Part 2 of this Schedule.

(2) There must be stated—

(a) the amount at which either the individual assets or appropriate groupings of those individual assets are included in the company's accounts,

(b) the fair value of those assets or groupings, and

(c) the reasons for not making a provision for diminution in value of those assets, including the nature of the evidence that provides the basis for the belief that the amount at which they are stated in the accounts will be recovered.

Information where investment property and living animals and plants included at fair value

69.— (1) This paragraph applies where the amounts to be included in a company's accounts in respect of investment property or living animals and plants have been determined in accordance with paragraph 47.

(2) The balance sheet items affected and the basis of valuation adopted in determining the amounts of the assets in question in the case of each such item must be disclosed in a note to the accounts.

(3) In the case of investment property, for each balance sheet item affected there must be shown, either separately in the balance sheet or in a note to the accounts—

(a) the comparable amounts determined according to the historical cost accounting rules, or

(b) the differences between those amounts and the corresponding amounts actually shown in the balance sheet in respect of that item.

(4) In sub-paragraph (3), references in relation to any item to the comparable amounts determined in accordance with that sub-paragraph are to—

(a) the aggregate amount which would be required to be shown in respect of that item if the amounts to be included in respect of all the assets covered by that item were determined according to the historical cost accounting rules, and

(b) the aggregate amount of the cumulative provisions for depreciation or diminution in value which would be permitted or required in determining those amounts according to those rules.

Reserves and provisions

70.— (1) This paragraph applies where any amount is transferred—

(a) to or from any reserves, or

(b) to any provision for liabilities, or

(c) from any provision for liabilities otherwise than for the purpose for which the provision was established,

and the reserves or provisions are or would but for paragraph 5(1) in Part 1 of this Schedule be shown as separate items in the company's balance sheet.

(2) The following information must be given in respect of the aggregate of reserves or provisions included in the same item—

(a) the amount of the reserves or provisions as at the date of the beginning of the financial year and as at the balance sheet date respectively,

(b) any amounts transferred to or from the reserves or provisions during that year, and

(c) the source and application respectively of any amounts so transferred.

(3) Particulars must be given of each provision included in liabilities item 6.(c) (other provisions) in the company's balance sheet in any case where the amount of that provision is material.

Provision for taxation

71. The amount of any provision for deferred taxation must be stated separately from the amount of any provision for other taxation.

Maturity analysis

72.— (1) A company must disclose separately for each of assets items 3.(b) and 4 and liabilities items 1.(b), 2.(b) and 3.(b) the aggregate amount of the loans and advances and liabilities included in those items broken down into the following categories—

(a) those repayable in not more than three months,

(b) those repayable in more than three months but not more than one year,

(c) those repayable in more than one year but not more than five years,

(d) those repayable in more than five years,

from the balance sheet date.

(2) A company must also disclose the aggregate amounts of all loans and advances falling within assets item 4 (loans and advances to customers) which are—

(a) repayable on demand, or

(b) are for an indeterminate period, being repayable upon short notice.

(3) For the purposes of sub-paragraph (1), where a loan or advance or liability is repayable by instalments, each such instalment is to be treated as a separate loan or advance or liability.

Debt and other fixed-income securities

73. A company must disclose the amount of debt and fixed-income securities included in assets item 5 (debt securities [and other fixed-income securities]) and the amount of such securities included in liabilities item 3.(a) (bonds and medium term notes) that (in each case) will become due within one year of the balance sheet date.

Subordinated liabilities

74.— (1) The following information must be disclosed in relation to any borrowing included in liabilities item 7 (subordinated liabilities) that exceeds 10% of the total for that item—

(a) its amount,

(b) the currency in which it is denominated,

(c) the rate of interest and the maturity date (or the fact that it is perpetual),

(d) the circumstances in which early repayment may be demanded,

(e) the terms of the subordination, and

(f) the existence of any provisions whereby it may be converted into capital or some other form of liability and the terms of any such provisions.

(2) The general terms of any other borrowings included in liabilities item 7 must also be stated.

Fixed cumulative dividends

75. If any fixed cumulative dividends on the company's shares are in arrear, there must be stated—

(a) the amount of the arrears, and

(b) the period for which the dividends or, if there is more than one class, each class of them are in arrear.

Details of assets charged

76.— (1) There must be disclosed, in relation to each liabilities and memorandum item of the balance sheet format—

(a) the aggregate amount of any assets of the company which have been charged to secure any liability or potential liability included under that item,

(b) the aggregate amount of the liabilities or potential liabilities so secured, and

(c) an indication of the nature of the security given.

(2) Particulars must also be given of any other charge on the assets of the company to secure the liabilities of any other person, including, where practicable, the amount secured.

Guarantees and other financial commitments

77.— (1) There must be stated, where practicable, the aggregate amount or estimated amount of contracts for capital expenditure, so far as not provided for.

(2) Particulars must be given of—

(a) any pension commitments included under any provision shown in the company's balance sheet, and
(b) any such commitments for which no provision has been made,

and where any such commitment relates wholly or partly to pensions payable to past directors of the company separate particulars must be given of that commitment so far as it relates to such pensions.

(3) Particulars must also be given of any other financial commitments, including any contingent liabilities, that—
(a) have not been provided for,
(b) have not been included in the memorandum items in the balance sheet format, and
(c) are relevant to assessing the company's state of affairs.

(4) Commitments within any of the preceding sub-paragraphs undertaken on behalf of or for the benefit of—
(a) any parent company or fellow subsidiary undertaking of the company, or
(b) any subsidiary undertaking of the company,

must be stated separately from the other commitments within that sub-paragraph (and commitments within paragraph (a) must be stated separately from those within paragraph (b)).

(5) There must be disclosed the nature and amount of any contingent liabilities and commitments included in Memorandum items 1 and 2 which are material in relation to the company's activities.

Memorandum items: Group undertakings

78.— (1) With respect to contingent liabilities required to be included under Memorandum item 1 in the balance sheet format, there must be stated in a note to the accounts the amount of such contingent liabilities incurred on behalf of or for the benefit of—
(a) any parent undertaking or fellow subsidiary undertaking, or
(b) any subsidiary undertaking,

of the company; in addition the amount incurred in respect of the undertakings referred to in paragraph (a) must be stated separately from the amount incurred in respect in respect of the undertakings referred to in paragraph (b).

(2) With respect to commitments required to be included under Memorandum item 2 in the balance sheet format, there must be stated in a note to the accounts the amount of such commitments undertaken on behalf of or for the benefit of—
(a) any parent undertaking or fellow subsidiary undertaking, or
(b) any subsidiary undertaking,

of the company; in addition the amount incurred in respect of the undertakings referred to in paragraph (a) must be stated separately from the amount incurred in respect of the undertakings referred to in paragraph (b).

Transferable securities

79.— (1) There must be disclosed for each of assets items 5 to 8 in the balance sheet format the amount of transferable securities included under those items that are listed and the amount of those that are unlisted.

(2) In the case of each amount shown in respect of listed securities under sub-paragraph (1), there must also be disclosed the aggregate market value of those securities, if different from the amount shown.

(3) There must also be disclosed for each of assets items 5 and 6 the amount of transferable securities included under those items that are held as financial fixed assets and the amount of those that are not so held, together with the criterion used by the directors to distinguish those held as financial fixed assets.

Leasing transactions

80. The aggregate amount of all property (other than land) leased by the company to other persons must be disclosed, broken down so as to show the aggregate amount included in each relevant balance sheet item.

Assets and liabilities denominated in a currency other than sterling (or the currency in which the accounts are drawn up)

81.— (1) The aggregate amount, in sterling (or the currency in which the accounts are drawn up), of all assets denominated in a currency other than sterling (or the currency used) together with the aggregate amount, in sterling (or the currency used), of all liabilities so denominated, is to be disclosed.

(2) For the purposes of this paragraph an appropriate rate of exchange prevailing at the balance sheet date must be used to determine the amounts concerned.

Sundry assets and liabilities

82. Where any amount shown under either of the following items is material, particulars must be given of each type of asset or liability included in that item, including an explanation of the nature of the asset or liability and the amount included with respect to assets or liabilities of that type—

(a) assets item 13 (other assets),

(b) liabilities item 4 (other liabilities).

Unmatured forward transactions

83.— (1) The following must be disclosed with respect to unmatured forward transactions outstanding at the balance sheet date—

(a) the categories of such transactions, by reference to an appropriate system of classification,

(b) whether, in the case of each such category, they have been made, to any material extent, for the purpose of hedging the effects of fluctuations in interest rates, exchange rates and market prices or whether they have been made, to any material extent, for dealing purposes.

(2) Transactions falling within sub-paragraph (1) must include all those in relation to which income or expenditure is to be included in—

(a) format 1, item 6 or format 2, items B4 or A3 (dealing [profits][losses]),

(b) format 1, items 1 or 2, or format 2, items B1 or A1, by virtue of notes (1)(b) and (2)(b) to the profit and loss account formats (forward contracts, spread over the actual duration of the contract and similar in nature to interest).

Miscellaneous matters

84.— (1) Particulars must be given of any case where the cost of any asset is for the first time determined under paragraph 37 in Part 2 of this Schedule.

(2) Where any outstanding loans made under the authority of section 682(2)(b), (c) or (d) of the 2006 Act (various cases of financial assistance by a company for purchase of its own shares) are included under any item shown in the company's balance sheet, the aggregate amount of those loans must be disclosed for each item in question.

Information supplementing the profit and loss account

85. Paragraphs 86 to 91 require information which either supplements the information given with respect to any particular items shown in the profit and loss account or otherwise provides particulars of income or expenditure of the company or of circumstances affecting the items shown in the profit and loss account (see regulation 5(2) for exemption for companies falling within section 408 of the 2006 Act (individual profit and loss account where group accounts prepared)).

Particulars of tax

86.— (1) Particulars must be given of any special circumstances which affect liability in respect of taxation of profits, income or capital gains for the financial year or liability in respect of taxation of profits, income or capital gains for succeeding financial years.

(2) The following amounts must be stated—

(a) the amount of the charge for United Kingdom corporation tax,

(b) if that amount would have been greater but for relief from double taxation, the amount which it would have been but for such relief,

(c) the amount of the charge for United Kingdom income tax, and

(d) the amount of the charge for taxation imposed outside the United Kingdom of profits, income and (so far as charged to revenue) capital gains.

These amounts must be stated separately in respect of each of the amounts which is shown under the following items in the profit and loss account, that is to say format 1 item 16, format 2 item A10 (tax on [profit][loss] on ordinary activities) and format 1 item 21, format 2 item A13 (tax on extraordinary [profit][loss]).

Particulars of income

87.— (1) A company must disclose, with respect to income included in the following items in the profit and loss account formats, the amount of that income attributable to each of the geographical markets in which the company has operated during the financial year—

(a) format 1 item 1, format 2 item B1 (interest receivable),

(b) format 1 item 3, format 2 item B2 (dividend income),

(c) format 1 item 4, format 2 item B3 (fees and commissions receivable),

(d) format 1 item 6, format 2 item B4 (dealing profits), and

(e) format 1 item 7, format 2 item B7 (other operating income).

(2) In analysing for the purposes of this paragraph the source of any income, the directors must have regard to the manner in which the company's activities are organised.

(3) For the purposes of this paragraph, markets which do not differ substantially from each other shall be treated as one market.

(4) Where in the opinion of the directors the disclosure of any information required by this paragraph would be seriously prejudicial to the interests of the company, that information need not be disclosed, but the fact that any such information has not been disclosed must be stated.

Management and agency services

88. A company providing any management and agency services to customers must disclose that fact, if the scale of such services provided is material in the context of its business as a whole.

Subordinated liabilities

89. Any amounts charged to the profit and loss account representing charges incurred during the year with respect to subordinated liabilities must be disclosed.

Sundry income and charges

90. Where any amount to be included in any of the following items is material, particulars must be given of each individual component of the figure, including an explanation of their nature and amount—

(a) in format 1—

(i) items 7 and 10 (other operating income and charges),

(ii) items 18 and 19 (extraordinary income and charges);

(b) in format 2—

(i) items A6 and B7 (other operating charges and income),

(ii) items A12 and B10 (extraordinary charges and income).

Miscellaneous matters

91.— (1) Where any amount relating to any preceding financial year is included in any item in the profit and loss account, the effect must be stated.

(2) The effect must be stated of any transactions that are exceptional by virtue of size or incidence though they fall within the ordinary activities of the company.

Related party transactions

92.— (1) Particulars may be given of transactions which the company has entered into with related parties, and must be given if such transactions are material and have not been concluded under normal market conditions.

(2) The particulars of transactions required to be disclosed by sub-paragraph (1) must include—

(a) the amount of such transactions,

(b) the nature of the related party relationship, and

(c) other information about the transactions necessary for an understanding of the financial position of the company.

(3) Information about individual transactions may be aggregated according to their nature, except where separate information is necessary for an understanding of the effects of related party transactions on the financial position of the company.

(4) Particulars need not be given of transactions entered into between two or more members of a group, provided that any subsidiary undertaking which is a party to the transaction is wholly-owned by such a member.

(5) In this paragraph, "related party" has the same meaning as in international accounting standards.

PART 4
INTERPRETATION OF THIS SCHEDULE

Definitions for this Schedule

93. The following definitions apply for the purposes of this Schedule.

Financial fixed assets

94. "Financial fixed assets" means loans and advances and securities held as fixed assets; participating interests and shareholdings in group undertakings are to be regarded as financial fixed assets.

Financial instruments

95. For the purposes of this Schedule, references to "derivatives" include commodity-based contracts that give either contracting party the right to settle in cash or in some other financial instrument, except when such contracts—

(a) were entered into for the purpose of, and continue to meet, the company's expected purchase, sale or usage requirements,

(b) were designated for such purpose at their inception, and

(c) are expected to be settled by delivery of the commodity.

96.— (1) The expressions listed in sub-paragraph (2) have the same meaning in paragraphs 44 to 49, 66 to 68 and 95 of this Schedule as they have in Council Directives 78/660/EEC on the annual accounts of certain types of companies and 86/635/EEC on the annual accounts and consolidated accounts of banks and other financial institutions.

(2) Those expressions are "available for sale financial asset", "business combination", "commodity-based contracts", "derivative", "equity instrument", "exchange difference", "fair value hedge accounting system", "financial fixed asset", "financial instrument", "foreign entity", "hedge accounting", "hedge accounting system", "hedged items", "hedging instrument", "held for trading purposes", "held to maturity", "monetary item", "receivables", "reliable market" and "trading portfolio".

Repayable on demand

97. "Repayable on demand", in connection with deposits, loans or advances, means that they can at any time be withdrawn or demanded without notice or that a maturity or period of notice of not more than 24 hours or one working day has been agreed for them.

Sale and repurchase transaction

98.— (1) "Sale and repurchase transaction" means a transaction which involves the transfer by a credit institution or customer ("the transferor") to another credit institution or customer ("the transferee") of assets subject to an agreement that the same assets, or (in the case of fungible assets) equivalent assets, will subsequently be transferred back to the transferor at a specified price on a date specified or to be specified by the transferor.

(2) The following are not to be regarded as sale and repurchase transactions for the purposes of sub-paragraph (1)—

(a) forward exchange transactions,

(b) options,

(c) transactions involving the issue of debt securities with a commitment to repurchase all or part of the issue before maturity, or

(d) any similar transactions.

Sale and option to resell transaction

99. "Sale and option to resell transaction" means a transaction which involves the transfer by a credit institution or customer ("the transferor") to another credit institution or customer ("the transferee") of assets subject to an agreement that the transferee is entitled to require the subsequent transfer of the same assets, or (in the case of fungible assets) equivalent assets, back to the transferor at the purchase price or another price agreed in advance on a date specified or to be specified.

SCHEDULE 3 Regulation 6(1)

INSURANCE COMPANIES: COMPANIES ACT INDIVIDUAL ACCOUNTS

PART 1
GENERAL RULES AND FORMATS

SECTION A
GENERAL RULES

1.— (1) Subject to the following provisions of this Schedule—

(a) every balance sheet of a company must show the items listed in the balance sheet format in Section B of this Part, and

(b) every profit and loss account must show the items listed in the profit and loss account format in Section B.

(2) References in this Schedule to the items listed in any of the formats in Section B are to those items read together with any of the notes following the formats which apply to those items.

(3) The items must be shown in the order and under the headings and sub-headings given in the particular format, but—

(a) the notes to the formats may permit alternative positions for any particular items, and

(b) the heading or sub-heading for any item does not have to be distinguished by any letter or number assigned to that item in the format used.

2.— (1) Any item required to be shown in a company's balance sheet or profit and loss account may be shown in greater detail than required by the particular format.

(2) The balance sheet or profit and loss account may include an item representing or covering the amount of any asset or liability, income or expenditure not specifically covered by any of the items listed in the formats set out in Section B, save that none of the following may be treated as assets in any balance sheet—

(a) preliminary expenses,

(b) expenses of, and commission on, any issue of shares or debentures, and

(c) costs of research.

3.— (1) The directors may combine items to which Arabic numbers are given in the balance sheet format set out in Section B (except for items concerning technical provisions and the reinsurers' share of technical provisions), and items to which lower case letters in parentheses are given in the profit and loss account format so set out (except for items within items I.1 and 4 and II.1, 5 and 6) if—

(a) their individual amounts are not material for the purpose of giving a true and fair view, or

(b) the combination facilitates the assessment of the state of affairs or profit or loss of the company for the financial year in question.

(2) Where sub-paragraph (1)(b) applies—

(a) the individual amounts of any items which have been combined must be disclosed in a note to the accounts, and

(b) any notes required by this Schedule to the items so combined must, notwithstanding the combination, be given.

4.— (1) Subject to sub-paragraph (2), the directors must not include a heading or sub-heading corresponding to an item in the balance sheet or profit and loss account format used if there is no amount to be shown for that item for the financial year to which the balance sheet or profit and loss account relates.

(2) Where an amount can be shown for the item in question for the immediately preceding financial year that amount must be shown under the heading or sub-heading required by the format for that item.

5.— (1) For every item shown in the balance sheet or profit and loss account the corresponding amount for the immediately preceding financial year must also be shown.

(2) Where that corresponding amount is not comparable with the amount to be shown for the item in question in respect of the financial year to which the balance sheet or profit and loss account relates, the former amount may be adjusted, and particulars of the non-comparability and of any adjustment must be disclosed in a note to the accounts.

6. Subject to the provisions of this Schedule, amounts in respect of items representing assets or income may not be set off against amounts in respect of items representing liabilities or expenditure (as the case may be), or vice versa.

7.— (1) The provisions of this Schedule which relate to long-term business apply, with necessary modifications, to business which consists of effecting or carrying out relevant contracts of general insurance which—

(a) is transacted exclusively or principally according to the technical principles of long-term business, and

(b) is a significant amount of the business of the company.

(2) For the purposes of paragraph (1), a contract of general insurance is a relevant contract if the risk insured against relates to—

(a) accident, or

(b) sickness.

(3) Sub-paragraph (2) must be read with—

(a) section 22 of the Financial Services and Markets Act 2000,

(b) the Financial Services and Markets Act 2000 (Regulated Activities) Order 2001, and

(c) Schedule 2 to that Act.

8. The company's directors must, in determining how amounts are presented within items in the profit and loss account and balance sheet, have regard to the substance of the reported transaction or arrangement, in accordance with generally accepted accounting principles or practice.

SECTION B
THE REQUIRED FORMATS

9.— (1) Where in respect of any item to which an Arabic number is assigned in the balance sheet or profit and loss account format, the gross amount and reinsurance amount or reinsurers' share are required to be shown, a sub-total of those amounts must also be given.

(2) Where in respect of any item to which an Arabic number is assigned in the profit and loss account format, separate items are required to be shown, then a separate sub-total of those items must also be given in addition to any sub-total required by sub-paragraph (1).

10.— (1) In the profit and loss account format set out below—

(a) the heading "Technical account—General business" is for business which consists of effecting or carrying out contracts of general business; and

(b) the heading "Technical account—Long-term business" is for business which consists of effecting or carrying out contracts of long-term insurance.

(2) In sub-paragraph (1), references to—

(a) contracts of general or long-term insurance, and

(b) the effecting or carrying out of such contracts,

must be read with section 22 of the Financial Services and Markets Act 2000, the Financial Services and Markets Act 2000 (Regulated Activities) Order 2001, and Schedule 2 to that Act.

Balance sheet format

ASSETS

A Called up share capital not paid (1)

B Intangible assets

1 Development costs

2 Concessions, patents, licences, trade marks and similar rights and assets (2)

3 Goodwill (3)

4 Payments on account

C Investments

I Land and buildings (4)

II Investments in group undertakings and participating interests

1 Shares in group undertakings

2 Debt securities issued by, and loans to, group undertakings

3 Participating interests

4 Debt securities issued by, and loans to, undertakings in which the company has a participating interest

III Other financial investments

1 Shares and other variable-yield securities and units in unit trusts

2 Debt securities and other fixed-income securities (5)

3 Participation in investment pools (6)

4 Loans secured by mortgages (7)

5 Other loans (7)

6 Deposits with credit institutions (8)

7 Other (9)

IV Deposits with ceding undertakings (10)

D Assets held to cover linked liabilities (11)

Da Reinsurers' share of technical provisions (12)

1 Provision for unearned premiums

2 Long-term business provision

3 Claims outstanding

4 Provisions for bonuses and rebates

5 Other technical provisions

6 Technical provisions for unit-linked liabilities

E Debtors (13)

I Debtors arising out of direct insurance operations

1 Policyholders

2 Intermediaries

II Debtors arising out of reinsurance operations

III Other debtors

IV Called up share capital not paid (1)

F Other assets

I Tangible assets

1 Plant and machinery

2 Fixtures, fittings, tools and equipment

3 Payments on account (other than deposits paid on land and buildings) and assets (other than buildings) in course of construction

II Stocks

1 Raw materials and consumables

2 Work in progress

3 Finished goods and goods for resale

4 Payments on account

III Cash at bank and in hand

IV Own shares (14)

V Other (15)

G Prepayments and accrued income

I Accrued interest and rent (16)

II Deferred acquisition costs (17)

III Other prepayments and accrued income

LIABILITIES

A Capital and reserves

I Called up share capital or equivalent funds

II Share premium account

III Revaluation reserve

IV Reserves

1 Capital redemption reserve

2 Reserve for own shares

3 Reserves provided for by the articles of association

4 Other reserves

V Profit and loss account

B Subordinated liabilities (18)

Ba Fund for future appropriations (19)

C Technical provisions

1 Provision for unearned premiums (20)

(a) gross amount

(b) reinsurance amount (12)

2 Long-term business provision (20), (21), (26)

(a) gross amount

(b) reinsurance amount (12)

3 Claims outstanding (22)

(a) gross amount

(b) reinsurance amount (12)

4 Provision for bonuses and rebates (23)

(a) gross amount

(b) reinsurance amount (12)

5 Equalisation provision (24)
6 Other technical provisions (25)
(a) gross amount
(b) reinsurance amount (12)
D Technical provisions for linked liabilities (26)
(a) gross amount
(b) reinsurance amount (12)
E Provisions for other risks
1 Provisions for pensions and similar obligations
2 Provisions for taxation
3 Other provisions
F Deposits received from reinsurers (27)
G Creditors (28)
I Creditors arising out of direct insurance operations
II Creditors arising out of reinsurance operations
III Debenture loans (29)
IV Amounts owed to credit institutions
V Other creditors including taxation and social security
H Accruals and deferred income

Notes on the balance sheet format

(1) Called up share capital not paid
(Assets items A and E.IV)
This item may be shown in either of the positions given in the format.

(2) Concessions, patents, licences, trade marks and similar rights and assets
(Assets item B.2)
Amounts in respect of assets are only to be included in a company's balance sheet under this item if either—
(a) the assets were acquired for valuable consideration and are not required to be shown under goodwill, or
(b) the assets in question were created by the company itself.

(3) Goodwill
(Assets item B.3)
Amounts representing goodwill are only to be included to the extent that the goodwill was acquired for valuable consideration.

(4) Land and buildings
(Assets item CI)
The amount of any land and buildings occupied by the company for its own activities must be shown separately in the notes to the accounts.

(5) Debt securities and other fixed-income securities
(Assets item CIII.2)
This item is to comprise transferable debt securities and any other transferable fixed-income securities issued by credit institutions, other undertakings or public bodies, in so far as they are not covered by assets item CII.2 or CII.4.
Securities bearing interest rates that vary in accordance with specific factors, for example the interest rate on the inter-bank market or on the Euromarket, are also to be regarded as debt securities and other fixed-income securities and so be included under this item.

(6) Participation in investment pools
(Assets item CIII.3)
This item is to comprise shares held by the company in joint investments constituted by several undertakings or pension funds, the management of which has been entrusted to one of those undertakings or to one of those pension funds.

(7) Loans secured by mortgages and other loans

(Assets items CIII.4 and CIII.5)

Loans to policyholders for which the policy is the main security are to be included under "Other loans" and their amount must be disclosed in the notes to the accounts. Loans secured by mortgage are to be shown as such even where they are also secured by insurance policies. Where the amount of "Other loans" not secured by policies is material, an appropriate breakdown must be given in the notes to the accounts.

(8) Deposits with credit institutions

(Assets item CIII.6)

This item is to comprise sums the withdrawal of which is subject to a time restriction. Sums deposited with no such restriction must be shown under assets item F.III even if they bear interest.

(9) Other (Assets item CIII.7)

This item is to comprise those investments which are not covered by assets items CIII.1 to 6. Where the amount of such investments is significant, they must be disclosed in the notes to the accounts.

(10) Deposits with ceding undertakings

(Assets item CIV)

Where the company accepts reinsurance this item is to comprise amounts, owed by the ceding undertakings and corresponding to guarantees, which are deposited with those ceding undertakings or with third parties or which are retained by those undertakings.

These amounts may not be combined with other amounts owed by the ceding insurer to the reinsurer or set off against amounts owed by the reinsurer to the ceding insurer.

Securities deposited with ceding undertakings or third parties which remain the property of the company must be entered in the company's accounts as an investment, under the appropriate item.

(11) Assets held to cover linked liabilities

(Assets item D)

In respect of long-term business, this item is to comprise investments made pursuant to long- term policies under which the benefits payable to the policyholder are wholly or partly to be determined by reference to the value of, or the income from, property of any description (whether or not specified in the contract) or by reference to fluctuations in, or in an index of, the value of property of any description (whether or not so specified).

This item is also to comprise investments which are held on behalf of the members of a tontine and are intended for distribution among them.

(12) Reinsurance amounts

(Assets item Da: liabilities items C1(b), 2(b), 3(b), 4(b) and 6(b) and D(b))

The reinsurance amounts may be shown either under assets item Da or under liabilities items C1(b), 2(b), 3(b), 4(b) and 6(b) and D(b).

The reinsurance amounts are to comprise the actual or estimated amounts which, under contractual reinsurance arrangements, are deducted from the gross amounts of technical provisions.

As regards the provision for unearned premiums, the reinsurance amounts must be calculated according to the methods referred to in paragraph 50 below or in accordance with the terms of the reinsurance policy.

(13) Debtors

(Assets item E)

Amounts owed by group undertakings and undertakings in which the company has a participating interest must be shown separately as sub-items of assets items E.I, II and III.

(14) Own shares

(Assets item F.IV)

The nominal value of the shares must be shown separately under this item.

(15) Other

(Assets item F.V)

This item is to comprise those assets which are not covered by assets items F.I to IV. Where such assets are material they must be disclosed in the notes to the accounts.

(16) Accrued interest and rent

(Assets item G.I)

This item is to comprise those items that represent interest and rent that have been earned up to the balance-sheet date but have not yet become receivable.

(17) Deferred acquisition costs

(Assets item G.II)

This item is to comprise the costs of acquiring insurance policies which are incurred during a financial year but relate to a subsequent financial year ("deferred acquisition costs"), except in so far as—

(a) allowance has been made in the computation of the long-term business provision made under paragraph 52 below and shown under liabilities item C2 or D in the balance sheet, for—

(i) the explicit recognition of such costs, or

(ii) the implicit recognition of such costs by virtue of the anticipation of future income from which such costs may prudently be expected to be recovered, or

(b) allowance has been made for such costs in respect of general business policies by a deduction from the provision for unearned premiums made under paragraph 50 below and shown under liabilities item CI in the balance sheet.

Deferred acquisition costs arising in general business must be distinguished from those arising in long-term business.

In the case of general business, the amount of any deferred acquisition costs must be established on a basis compatible with that used for unearned premiums.

There must be disclosed in the notes to the accounts—

(c) how the deferral of acquisition costs has been treated (unless otherwise expressly stated in the accounts), and

(d) where such costs are included as a deduction from the provisions at liabilities item CI, the amount of such deduction, or

(e) where the actuarial method used in the calculation of the provisions at liabilities item C2 or D has made allowance for the explicit recognition of such costs, the amount of the costs so recognised.

(18) Subordinated liabilities

(Liabilities item B)

This item is to comprise all liabilities in respect of which there is a contractual obligation that, in the event of winding up or of bankruptcy, they are to be repaid only after the claims of all other creditors have been met (whether or not they are represented by certificates).

(19) Fund for future appropriations

(Liabilities item Ba)

This item is to comprise all funds the allocation of which either to policyholders or to shareholders has not been determined by the end of the financial year.

Transfers to and from this item must be shown in item II.12a in the profit and loss account.

(20) Provision for unearned premiums

(Liabilities item C1)

In the case of long-term business the provision for unearned premiums may be included in liabilities item C2 rather than in this item.

The provision for unearned premiums is to comprise the amount representing that part of gross premiums written which is estimated to be earned in the following financial year or to subsequent financial years.

(21) Long-term business provision

(Liabilities item C2)

This item is to comprise the actuarially estimated value of the company's liabilities (excluding technical provisions included in liabilities item D), including bonuses already declared and after deducting the actuarial value of future premiums.

This item is also to comprise claims incurred but not reported, plus the estimated costs of settling such claims.

(22) Claims outstanding
(Liabilities item C3)

This item is to comprise the total estimated ultimate cost to the company of settling all claims arising from events which have occurred up to the end of the financial year (including, in the case of general business, claims incurred but not reported) less amounts already paid in respect of such claims.

(23) Provision for bonuses and rebates
(Liabilities item C4)

This item is to comprise amounts intended for policyholders or contract beneficiaries by way of bonuses and rebates as defined in Note (5) on the profit and loss account format to the extent that such amounts have not been credited to policyholders or contract beneficiaries or included in liabilities item Ba or in liabilities item C2.

(24) Equalisation provision
(Liabilities item C5)

This item is to comprise the amount of any equalisation reserve maintained in respect of general business by the company, in accordance with the rules in section 1.4 of the Prudential Sourcebook for Insurers made by the Financial Services Authority under Part 10 of the Financial Services and Markets Act 2000.

This item is also to comprise any amounts which, in accordance with Council Directive 87/343/EEC of 22nd June 1987, are required to be set aside by a company to equalise fluctuations in loss ratios in future years or to provide for special risks.

A company which otherwise constitutes reserves to equalise fluctuations in loss ratios in future years or to provide for special risks must disclose that fact in the notes to the accounts.

(25) Other technical provisions
(Liabilities item C6)

This item is to comprise, inter alia, the provision for unexpired risks as defined in paragraph 91 below.

Where the amount of the provision for unexpired risks is significant, it must be disclosed separately either in the balance sheet or in the notes to the accounts.

(26) Technical provisions for linked liabilities
(Liabilities item D)

This item is to comprise technical provisions constituted to cover liabilities relating to investment in the context of long-term policies under which the benefits payable to policyholders are wholly or partly to be determined by reference to the value of, or the income from, property of any description (whether or not specified in the contract) or by reference to fluctuations in, or in an index of, the value of property of any description (whether or not so specified).

Any additional technical provisions constituted to cover death risks, operating expenses or other risks (such as benefits payable at the maturity date or guaranteed surrender values) must be included under liabilities item C2.

This item must also comprise technical provisions representing the obligations of a tontine's organiser in relation to its members.

(27) Deposits received from reinsurers
(Liabilities item F)

Where the company cedes reinsurance, this item is to comprise amounts deposited by or withheld from other insurance undertakings under reinsurance contracts. These amounts may not be merged with other amounts owed to or by those other undertakings.

Where the company cedes reinsurance and has received as a deposit securities which have been transferred to its ownership, this item is to comprise the amount owed by the company by virtue of the deposit.

(28) Creditors
(Liabilities item G)
Amounts owed to group undertakings and undertakings in which the company has a participating interest must be shown separately as sub-items.

(29) Debenture loans
(Liabilities item G.III)
The amount of any convertible loans must be shown separately.

Additional items

11.— (1) Every balance sheet of a company which carries on long-term business must show separately as an additional item the aggregate of any amounts included in liabilities item A (capital and reserves) which are required not to be treated as realised profits under section 843 of the 2006 Act.

(2) A company which carries on long-term business must show separately, in the balance sheet or in the notes to the accounts, the total amount of assets representing the long-term fund valued in accordance with the provisions of this Schedule.

Managed funds

12.— (1) For the purposes of this paragraph "managed funds" are funds of a group pension fund—

(a) the management of which constitutes long-term insurance business, and
(b) which the company administers in its own name but on behalf of others, and
(c) to which it has legal title.

(2) The company must, in any case where assets and liabilities arising in respect of managed funds fall to be treated as assets and liabilities of the company, adopt the following accounting treatment: assets and liabilities representing managed funds are to be included in the company's balance sheet, with the notes to the accounts disclosing the total amount included with respect to such assets and liabilities in the balance sheet and showing the amount included under each relevant balance sheet item in respect of such assets or (as the case may be) liabilities.

Deferred acquisition costs

13. The costs of acquiring insurance policies which are incurred during a financial year but which relate to a subsequent financial year must be deferred in a manner specified in Note (17) on the balance sheet format.

Profit and loss account format

I Technical account—General business

1 Earned premiums, net of reinsurance
(a) gross premiums written (1)
(b) outward reinsurance premiums (2)
(c) change in the gross provision for unearned premiums
(d) change in the provision for unearned premiums, reinsurers' share

2 Allocated investment return transferred from the non-technical account (item III.6) (10)

2a Investment income (8) (10)
(a) income from participating interests, with a separate indication of that derived from group undertakings
(b) income from other investments, with a separate indication of that derived from group undertakings
(aa) income from land and buildings
(bb) income from other investments
(c) value re-adjustments on investments

(d) gains on the realisation of investments
3 Other technical income, net of reinsurance
4 Claims incurred, net of reinsurance (4)
(a) claims paid
(aa) gross amount
(bb) reinsurers' share
(b) change in the provision for claims
(aa) gross amount
(bb) reinsurers' share
5 Changes in other technical provisions, net of reinsurance, not shown under other headings
6 Bonuses and rebates, net of reinsurance (5)
7 Net operating expenses
(a) acquisition costs (6)
(b) change in deferred acquisition costs
(c) administrative expenses (7)
(d) reinsurance commissions and profit participation
8 Other technical charges, net of reinsurance
8a Investment expenses and charges (8)
(a) investment management expenses, including interest
(b) value adjustments on investments
(c) losses on the realisation of investments
9 Change in the equalisation provision
10 Sub-total (balance on the technical account for general business) (item III.1)

II Technical account—Long-term business
1 Earned premiums, net of reinsurance
(a) gross premiums written (1)
(b) outward reinsurance premiums (2)
(c) change in the provision for unearned premiums, net of reinsurance (3)
2 Investment income (8) (10)
(a) income from participating interests, with a separate indication of that derived from group undertakings
(b) income from other investments, with a separate indication of that derived from group undertakings
(aa) income from land and buildings
(bb) income from other investments
(c) value re-adjustments on investments
(d) gains on the realisation of investments
3 Unrealised gains on investments (9)
4 Other technical income, net of reinsurance
5 Claims incurred, net of reinsurance (4)
(a) claims paid
(aa) gross amount
(bb) reinsurers' share
(b) change in the provision for claims
(aa) gross amount
(bb) reinsurers' share
6 Change in other technical provisions, net of reinsurance, not shown under other headings
(a) Long-term business provision, net of reinsurance (3)
(aa) gross amount
(bb) reinsurers' share
(b) other technical provisions, net of reinsurance
7 Bonuses and rebates, net of reinsurance (5)

8 Net operating expenses
(a) acquisition costs (6)
(b) change in deferred acquisition costs
(c) administrative expenses (7)
(d) reinsurance commissions and profit participation
9 Investment expenses and charges (8)
(a) investment management expenses, including interest
(b) value adjustments on investments
(c) losses on the realisation of investments
10 Unrealised losses on investments (9)
11 Other technical charges, net of reinsurance
11a Tax attributable to the long-term business
12 Allocated investment return transferred to the non-technical account (item III.4)
12a Transfers to or from the fund for future appropriations
13 Sub-total (balance on the technical account—long-term business) (item III.2)

III Non-technical account
1 Balance on the general business technical account (item I.10)
2 Balance on the long-term business technical account (item II.13)
2a Tax credit attributable to balance on the long-term business technical account
3 Investment income (8)
(a) income from participating interests, with a separate indication of that derived from group undertakings
(b) income from other investments, with a separate indication of that derived from group undertakings
(aa) income from land and buildings
(bb) income from other investments
(c) value re-adjustments on investments
(d) gains on the realisation of investments
3a Unrealised gains on investments (9)
4 Allocated investment return transferred from the long-term business technical account (item II.12) (10)
5 Investment expenses and charges (8)
(a) investment management expenses, including interest
(b) value adjustments on investments
(c) losses on the realisation of investments
5a Unrealised losses on investments (9)
6 Allocated investment return transferred to the general business technical account (item I.2) (10)
7 Other income
8 Other charges, including value adjustments
8a Profit or loss on ordinary activities before tax
9 Tax on profit or loss on ordinary activities
10 Profit or loss on ordinary activities after tax
11 Extraordinary income
12 Extraordinary charges
13 Extraordinary profit or loss
14 Tax on extraordinary profit or loss
15 Other taxes not shown under the preceding items
16 Profit or loss for the financial year

Notes on the profit and loss account format

(1) Gross premiums written
(General business technical account: item I.1.(a)

Long-term business technical account: item II.1.(a))

This item is to comprise all amounts due during the financial year in respect of insurance contracts entered into regardless of the fact that such amounts may relate in whole or in part to a later financial year, and must include inter alia—

(i) premiums yet to be determined, where the premium calculation can be done only at the end of the year;

(ii) single premiums, including annuity premiums, and, in long-term business, single premiums resulting from bonus and rebate provisions in so far as they must be considered as premiums under the terms of the contract;

(iii) additional premiums in the case of half-yearly, quarterly or monthly payments and additional payments from policyholders for expenses borne by the company;

(iv) in the case of co-insurance, the company's portion of total premiums;

(v) reinsurance premiums due from ceding and retroceding insurance undertakings, including portfolio entries, after deduction of cancellations and portfolio withdrawals credited to ceding and retroceding insurance undertakings.

The above amounts must not include the amounts of taxes or duties levied with premiums.

(2) Outward reinsurance premiums

(General business technical account: item I.1.(b)

Long-term business technical account: item II.1.(b))

This item is to comprise all premiums paid or payable in respect of outward reinsurance contracts entered into by the company. Portfolio entries payable on the conclusion or amendment of outward reinsurance contracts must be added; portfolio withdrawals receivable must be deducted.

(3) Change in the provision for unearned premiums, net of reinsurance

(Long-term business technical account: items II.1.(c) and II.6.(a))

In the case of long-term business, the change in unearned premiums may be included either in item II.1.(c) or in item II.6.(a) of the long-term business technical account.

(4) Claims incurred, net of reinsurance

(General business technical account: item I.4.

Long-term business technical account: item II.5)

This item is to comprise all payments made in respect of the financial year with the addition of the provision for claims (but after deducting the provision for claims for the preceding financial year).

These amounts must include annuities, surrenders, entries and withdrawals of loss provisions to and from ceding insurance undertakings and reinsurers and external and internal claims management costs and charges for claims incurred but not reported such as are referred to in paragraphs 53(2) and 55 below.

Sums recoverable on the basis of subrogation and salvage (within the meaning of paragraph 53 below) must be deducted.

Where the difference between—

(a) the loss provision made at the beginning of the year for outstanding claims incurred in previous years, and

(b) the payments made during the year on account of claims incurred in previous years and the loss provision shown at the end of the year for such outstanding claims, is material, it must be shown in the notes to the accounts, broken down by category and amount.

(5) Bonuses and rebates, net of reinsurance

(General business technical account: item I.6.

Long-term business technical account: item II.7)

Bonuses are to comprise all amounts chargeable for the financial year which are paid or payable to policyholders and other insured parties or provided for their benefit, including amounts used to increase technical provisions or applied to the reduction of future premiums, to the extent that such amounts represent an allocation of surplus or profit arising on business as a whole or a section of business, after deduction of amounts provided in previous years which are no longer required.

Rebates are to comprise such amounts to the extent that they represent a partial refund of premiums resulting from the experience of individual contracts.

Where material, the amount charged for bonuses and that charged for rebates must be disclosed separately in the notes to the accounts.

(6) Acquisition costs

(General business technical account: item I.7.(a).

Long-term business technical account: item II.8.(a))

This item is to comprise the costs arising from the conclusion of insurance contracts. They must cover both direct costs, such as acquisition commissions or the cost of drawing up the insurance document or including the insurance contract in the portfolio, and indirect costs, such as advertising costs or the administrative expenses connected with the processing of proposals and the issuing of policies.

In the case of long-term business, policy renewal commissions must be included under item II.8.(c) in the long-term business technical account.

(7) Administrative expenses

(General business technical account: item I.7.(c).

Long-term business technical account: item II.8.(c))

This item must include the costs arising from premium collection, portfolio administration, handling of bonuses and rebates, and inward and outward reinsurance. They must in particular include staff costs and depreciation provisions in respect of office furniture and equipment in so far as these need not be shown under acquisition costs, claims incurred or investment charges.

Item II.8.(c) must also include policy renewal commissions.

(8) Investment income, expenses and charges

(General business technical account: items I.2a and 8a.

Long-term business technical account: items II.2 and 9.

Non-technical account: items III.3 and 5)

Investment income, expenses and charges must, to the extent that they arise in the long-term fund, be disclosed in the long-term business technical account. Other investment income, expenses and charges must either be disclosed in the non-technical account or attributed between the appropriate technical and non-technical accounts. Where the company makes such an attribution it must disclose the basis for it in the notes to the accounts.

(9) Unrealised gains and losses on investments

(Long-term business technical account: items II.3 and 10.

Non-technical account: items III.3a and 5a)

In the case of investments attributed to the long-term fund, the difference between the valuation of the investments and their purchase price or, if they have previously been valued, their valuation as at the last balance sheet date, may be disclosed (in whole or in part) in item II.3 or II.10 (as the case may be) of the long-term business technical account, and in the case of investments shown as assets under assets item D (assets held to cover linked liabilities) must be so disclosed.

In the case of other investments, the difference between the valuation of the investments and their purchase price or, if they have previously been valued, their valuation as at the last balance sheet date, may be disclosed (in whole or in part) in item III.3a or III.5a (as the case may require) of the non-technical account.

(10) Allocated investment return

(General business technical account: item I.2.

Long-term business technical account: item II.2.

Non-technical account: items III.4 and 6)

The allocated return may be transferred from one part of the profit and loss account to another.

Where part of the investment return is transferred to the general business technical account, the transfer from the non-technical account must be deducted from item III.6 and added to item I.2.

Where part of the investment return disclosed in the long-term business technical account is transferred to the non-technical account, the transfer to the non-technical account shall be deducted from item II.12 and added to item III.4.

The reasons for such transfers (which may consist of a reference to any relevant statutory requirement) and the bases on which they are made must be disclosed in the notes to the accounts.

PART 2
ACCOUNTING PRINCIPLES AND RULES
SECTION A
ACCOUNTING PRINCIPLES

Preliminary

14. The amounts to be included in respect of all items shown in a company's accounts must be determined in accordance with the principles set out in this Section.

15. But if it appears to the company's directors that there are special reasons for departing from any of those principles in preparing the company's accounts in respect of any financial year they may do so, in which case particulars of the departure, the reasons for it and its effect must be given in a note to the accounts.

Accounting principles

16. The company is presumed to be carrying on business as a going concern.

17. Accounting policies must be applied consistently within the same accounts and from one financial year to the next.

18. The amount of any item must be determined on a prudent basis, and in particular—
   (a) subject to note (9) on the profit and loss account format, only profits realised at the balance sheet date are to be included in the profit and loss account, and
   (b) all liabilities which have arisen in respect of the financial year to which the accounts relate or a previous financial year must be taken into account, including those which only become apparent between the balance sheet date and the date on which it is signed on behalf of the board of directors in accordance with section 414 of the 2006 Act (approval and signing of accounts).

19. All income and charges relating to the financial year to which the accounts relate are to be taken into account, without regard to the date of receipt or payment.

20. In determining the aggregate amount of any item, the amount of each individual asset or liability that falls to be taken into account must be determined separately.

Valuation

21.— (1) The amounts to be included in respect of assets of any description mentioned in paragraph 22 (valuation of assets: general) must be determined either—
   (a) in accordance with that paragraph and paragraph 24 (but subject to paragraphs 27 to 29), or
   (b) so far as applicable to an asset of that description, in accordance with Section C (valuation at fair value).

(2) The amounts to be included in respect of assets of any description mentioned in paragraph 24 (alternative valuation of fixed-income securities) may be determined—
   (a) in accordance with that paragraph (but subject to paragraphs 27 to 29), or
   (b) so far as applicable to an asset of that description, in accordance with Section C

(3) The amounts to be included in respect of assets which—
   (a) are not assets of a description mentioned in paragraph 22 or 23, but
   (b) are assets of a description to which Section C is applicable,

may be determined in accordance with that Section.

(4) Subject to sub-paragraphs (1) to (3), the amounts to be included in respect of all items shown in a company's accounts are determined in accordance with Section C

SECTION B
CURRENT VALUE ACCOUNTING RULES

Valuation of assets: general

22.— (1) Subject to paragraph 24, investments falling to be included under assets item C (investments) must be included at their current value calculated in accordance with paragraphs 25 and 26.

(2) Investments falling to be included under assets item D (assets held to cover linked liabilities) must be shown at their current value calculated in accordance with paragraphs 25 and 26.

23.— (1) Intangible assets other than goodwill may be shown at their current cost.

(2) Assets falling to be included under assets items F.I (tangible assets) and F.IV (own shares) in the balance sheet format may be shown at their current value calculated in accordance with paragraphs 25 and 26 or at their current cost.

(3) Assets falling to be included under assets item F.II (stocks) may be shown at current cost.

Alternative valuation of fixed-income securities

24.— (1) This paragraph applies to debt securities and other fixed-income securities shown as assets under assets items CII (investments in group undertakings and participating interests) and CIII (other financial investments).

(2) Securities to which this paragraph applies may either be valued in accordance with paragraph 22 or their amortised value may be shown in the balance sheet, in which case the provisions of this paragraph apply.

(3) Subject to sub-paragraph (4), where the purchase price of securities to which this paragraph applies exceeds the amount repayable at maturity, the amount of the difference—

(a) must be charged to the profit and loss account, and

(b) must be shown separately in the balance sheet or in the notes to the accounts.

(4) The amount of the difference referred to in sub-paragraph (3) may be written off in instalments so that it is completely written off when the securities are repaid, in which case there must be shown separately in the balance sheet or in the notes to the accounts the difference between the purchase price (less the aggregate amount written off) and the amount repayable at maturity.

(5) Where the purchase price of securities to which this paragraph applies is less than the amount repayable at maturity, the amount of the difference must be released to income in instalments over the period remaining until repayment, in which case there must be shown separately in the balance sheet or in the notes to the accounts the difference between the purchase price (plus the aggregate amount released to income) and the amount repayable at maturity.

(6) Both the purchase price and the current value of securities valued in accordance with this paragraph must be disclosed in the notes to the accounts.

(7) Where securities to which this paragraph applies which are not valued in accordance with paragraph 22 are sold before maturity, and the proceeds are used to purchase other securities to which this paragraph applies, the difference between the proceeds of sale and their book value may be spread uniformly over the period remaining until the maturity of the original investment.

Meaning of "current value"

25.— (1) Subject to sub-paragraph (5), in the case of investments other than land and buildings, current value means market value determined in accordance with this paragraph.

(2) In the case of listed investments, market value means the value on the balance sheet date or, when the balance sheet date is not a stock exchange trading day, on the last stock exchange trading day before that date.

(3) Where a market exists for unlisted investments, market value means the average price at which such investments were traded on the balance sheet date or, when the balance sheet date is not a trading day, on the last trading day before that date.

(4) Where, on the date on which the accounts are drawn up, listed or unlisted investments have been sold or are to be sold within the short term, the market value must be reduced by the actual or estimated realisation costs.

(5) Except where the equity method of accounting is applied, all investments other than those referred to in sub-paragraphs (2) and (3) must be valued on a basis which has prudent regard to the likely realisable value.

26.— (1) In the case of land and buildings, current value means the market value on the date of valuation, where relevant reduced as provided in sub-paragraphs (4) and (5).

(2) Market value means the price at which land and buildings could be sold under private contract between a willing seller and an arm's length buyer on the date of valuation, it being assumed that the property is publicly exposed to the market, that market conditions permit orderly disposal and that a normal period, having regard to the nature of the property, is available for the negotiation of the sale.

(3) The market value must be determined through the separate valuation of each land and buildings item, carried out at least every five years in accordance with generally recognised methods of valuation.

(4) Where the value of any land and buildings item has diminished since the preceding valuation under sub-paragraph (3), an appropriate value adjustment must be made.

(5) The lower value arrived at under sub-paragraph (4) must not be increased in subsequent balance sheets unless such increase results from a new determination of market value arrived at in accordance with sub-paragraphs (2) and (3).

(6) Where, on the date on which the accounts are drawn up, land and buildings have been sold or are to be sold within the short term, the value arrived at in accordance with sub-paragraphs (2) and (4) must be reduced by the actual or estimated realisation costs.

(7) Where it is impossible to determine the market value of a land and buildings item, the value arrived at on the basis of the principle of purchase price or production cost is deemed to be its current value.

Application of the depreciation rules

27.— (1) Where—

(a) the value of any asset of a company is determined in accordance with paragraph 22 or 23, and

(b) in the case of a determination under paragraph 22, the asset falls to be included under assets item CI, that value must be, or (as the case may require) must be the starting point for determining, the amount to be included in respect of that asset in the company's accounts, instead of its cost or any value previously so determined for that asset.

Paragraphs 36 to 41 and 43 apply accordingly in relation to any such asset with the substitution for any reference to its cost of a reference to the value most recently determined for that asset in accordance with paragraph 22 or 23 (as the case may be).

(2) The amount of any provision for depreciation required in the case of any asset by paragraph 37 or 38 as it applies by virtue of sub-paragraph (1) is referred to below in this paragraph as the adjusted amount, and the amount of any provision which would be required by that paragraph in the case of that asset according to the historical cost accounting rules is referred to as the historical cost amount.

(3) Where sub-paragraph (1) applies in the case of any asset the amount of any provision for depreciation in respect of that asset included in any item shown in the profit and loss account in respect of amounts written off assets of the description in question may be the historical cost amount instead of the adjusted amount, provided that the amount of any

difference between the two is shown separately in the profit and loss account or in a note to the accounts.

Additional information to be provided

28.— (1) This paragraph applies where the amounts to be included in respect of assets covered by any items shown in a company's accounts have been determined in accordance with paragraph 22 or 23.

(2) The items affected and the basis of valuation adopted in determining the amounts of the assets in question in the case of each such item must be disclosed in a note to the accounts.

(3) The purchase price of investments valued in accordance with paragraph 22 must be disclosed in the notes to the accounts.

(4) In the case of each balance sheet item valued in accordance with paragraph 23 either—

(a) the comparable amounts determined according to the historical cost accounting rules (without any provision for depreciation or diminution in value), or

(b) the differences between those amounts and the corresponding amounts actually shown in the balance sheet in respect of that item,

must be shown separately in the balance sheet or in a note to the accounts.

(5) In sub-paragraph (4), references in relation to any item to the comparable amounts determined as there mentioned are references to—

(a) the aggregate amount which would be required to be shown in respect of that item if the amounts to be included in respect of all the assets covered by that item were determined according to the historical cost accounting rules, and

(b) the aggregate amount of the cumulative provisions for depreciation or diminution in value which would be permitted or required in determining those amounts according to those rules.

Revaluation reserve

29.— (1) Subject to sub-paragraph (7) , with respect to any determination of the value of an asset of a company in accordance with paragraph 22 or 23, the amount of any profit or loss arising from that determination (after allowing, where appropriate, for any provisions for depreciation or diminution in value made otherwise than by reference to the value so determined and any adjustments of any such provisions made in the light of that determination) must be credited or (as the case may be) debited to a separate reserve ("the revaluation reserve").

(2) The amount of the revaluation reserve must be shown in the company's balance sheet under liabilities item A.III, but need not be shown under the name "revaluation reserve".

(3) An amount may be transferred—

(a) from the revaluation reserve—

(i) to the profit and loss account, if the amount was previously charged to that account or represents realised profit, or

(ii) on capitalisation,

(b) to or from the revaluation reserve in respect of the taxation relating to any profit or loss credited or debited to the reserve.

The revaluation reserve must be reduced to the extent that the amounts transferred to it are no longer necessary for the purposes of the valuation method used.

(4) In sub-paragraph (3)(a)(ii) "capitalisation", in relation to an amount standing to the credit of the revaluation reserve, means applying it in wholly or partly paying up unissued shares in the company to be allotted to members of the company as fully or partly paid shares.

(5) The revaluation reserve must not be reduced except as mentioned in this paragraph.

(6) The treatment for taxation purposes of amounts credited or debited to the revaluation reserve must be disclosed in a note to the accounts.

(7) This paragraph does not apply to the difference between the valuation of investments and their purchase price or previous valuation shown in the long-term business technical

account or the non-technical account in accordance with note (9) on the profit and loss account format.

SECTION C
VALUATION AT FAIR VALUE

Inclusion of financial instruments at fair value

30.— (1) Subject to sub-paragraphs (2) to (5), financial instruments (including derivatives) may be included at fair value.

(2) Sub-paragraph (1) does not apply to financial instruments that constitute liabilities unless—

(a) they are held as part of a trading portfolio,

(b) they are derivatives, or

(c) they are financial instruments falling within paragraph (4).

(3) Except where they fall within paragraph (4), or fall to be included under assets item D (assets held to cover linked liabilities), sub-paragraph (1) does not apply to—

(a) financial instruments (other than derivatives) held to maturity,

(b) loans and receivables originated by the company and not held for trading purposes,

(c) interests in subsidiary undertakings, associated undertakings and joint ventures,

(d) equity instruments issued by the company,

(e) contracts for contingent consideration in a business combination, or

(f) other financial instruments with such special characteristics that the instruments, according to generally accepted accounting principles or practice, should be accounted for differently from other financial instruments.

(4) Financial instruments that, under international accounting standards adopted by the European Commission on or before 5th September 2006 in accordance with the IAS Regulation, may be included in accounts at fair value, may be so included, provided that the disclosures required by such accounting standards are made.

(5) If the fair value of a financial instrument cannot be determined reliably in accordance with paragraph 31, sub-paragraph (1) does not apply to that financial instrument.

(6) In this paragraph—

"associated undertaking" has the meaning given by paragraph 19 of Schedule 6 to these Regulations; and

"joint venture" has the meaning given by paragraph 18 of that Schedule.

Determination of fair value

31.— (1) The fair value of a financial instrument is its value determined in accordance with this paragraph.

(2) If a reliable market can readily be identified for the financial instrument, its fair value is determined by reference to its market value.

(3) If a reliable market cannot readily be identified for the financial instrument but can be identified for its components or for a similar instrument, its fair value is determined by reference to the market value of its components or of the similar instrument.

(4) If neither sub-paragraph (2) nor (3) applies, the fair value of the financial instrument is a value resulting from generally accepted valuation models and techniques.

(5) Any valuation models and techniques used for the purposes of sub-paragraph (4) must ensure a reasonable approximation of the market value.

Hedged items

32. A company may include any assets and liabilities, or identified portions of such assets or liabilities, that qualify as hedged items under a fair value hedge accounting system at the amount required under that system.

Other assets that may be included at fair value

33.— (1) This paragraph applies to—

(a) investment property, and
(b) living animals and plants,
that, under international accounting standards, may be included in accounts at fair value.

(2) Such investment property and such living animals and plants may be included at fair value, provided that all such investment property or, as the case may be, all such living animals and plants are so included where their fair value can reliably be determined.

(3) In this paragraph, "fair value" means fair value determined in accordance with relevant international accounting standards.

Accounting for changes in value

34.— (1) This paragraph applies where a financial instrument is valued in accordance with paragraph 30 or 32 or an asset is valued in accordance with paragraph 33.

(2) Notwithstanding paragraph 18 in this Part of this Schedule, and subject to sub-paragraphs (3) and (4), a change in the value of the financial instrument or of the investment property or living animal or plant must be included in the profit and loss account.

(3) Where—
(a) the financial instrument accounted for is a hedging instrument under a hedge accounting system that allows some or all of the change in value not to be shown in the profit and loss account, or
(b) the change in value relates to an exchange difference arising on a monetary item that forms part of a company's net investment in a foreign entity,
the amount of the change in value must be credited to or (as the case may be) debited from a separate reserve ("the fair value reserve").

(4) Where the instrument accounted for—
(a) is an available for sale financial asset, and
(b) is not a derivative,
the change in value may be credited to or (as the case may be) debited from the fair value reserve.

The fair value reserve

35.— (1) The fair value reserve must be adjusted to the extent that the amounts shown in it are no longer necessary for the purposes of paragraph 34(3) or (4).

(2) The treatment for taxation purposes of amounts credited or debited to the fair value reserve must be disclosed in a note to the accounts.

SECTION D
HISTORICAL COST ACCOUNTING RULES

Valuation of assets

General rules

36.— (1) The rules in this Section are "the historical cost accounting rules".

(2) Subject to any provision for depreciation or diminution in value made in accordance with paragraph 37 or 38, the amount to be included in respect of any asset in the balance sheet format is its cost.

37. In the case of any asset included under assets item B (intangible assets), CI (land and buildings), F.I (tangible assets) or F.II (stocks) which has a limited useful economic life, the amount of—
(a) its cost, or
(b) where it is estimated that any such asset will have a residual value at the end of the period of its useful economic life, its cost less that estimated residual value,
must be reduced by provisions for depreciation calculated to write off that amount systematically over the period of the asset's useful economic life.

38.— (1) This paragraph applies to any asset included under assets item B (intangible assets), C (investments), F.I (tangible assets) or F.IV (own shares).

(2) Where an asset to which this paragraph applies has diminished in value, provisions for diminution in value may be made in respect of it and the amount to be included in respect of it may be reduced accordingly.

(3) Provisions for diminution in value must be made in respect of any asset to which this paragraph applies if the reduction in its value is expected to be permanent (whether its useful economic life is limited or not), and the amount to be included in respect of it must be reduced accordingly.

(4) Any provisions made under sub-paragraph (2) or (3) which are not shown in the profit and loss account must be disclosed (either separately or in aggregate) in a note to the accounts.

39.— (1) Where the reasons for which any provision was made in accordance with paragraph 38 have ceased to apply to any extent, that provision must be written back to the extent that it is no longer necessary.

(2) Any amounts written back in accordance with sub-paragraph (1) which are not shown in the profit and loss account must be disclosed (either separately or in aggregate) in a note to the accounts.

40.— (1) This paragraph applies to assets included under assets items E.I, II and III (debtors) and F.III (cash at bank and in hand) in the balance sheet.

(2) If the net realisable value of an asset to which this paragraph applies is lower than its cost the amount to be included in respect of that asset is the net realisable value.

(3) Where the reasons for which any provision for diminution in value was made in accordance with sub-paragraph (2) have ceased to apply to any extent, that provision must be written back to the extent that it is no longer necessary.

Development costs

41.— (1) Notwithstanding that amounts representing "development costs" may be included under assets item B (intangible assets) in the balance sheet format, an amount may only be included in a company's balance sheet in respect of development costs in special circumstances.

(2) If any amount is included in a company's balance sheet in respect of development costs the following information must be given in a note to the accounts—

(a) the period over which the amount of those costs originally capitalised is being or is to be written off, and

(b) the reasons for capitalising the development costs in question.

Goodwill

42.— (1) The application of paragraphs 36 to 39 in relation to goodwill (in any case where goodwill is treated as an asset) is subject to the following.

(2) Subject to sub-paragraph (3), the amount of the consideration for any goodwill acquired by a company must be reduced by provisions for depreciation calculated to write off that amount systematically over a period chosen by the directors of the company.

(3) The period chosen must not exceed the useful economic life of the goodwill in question.

(4) In any case where any goodwill acquired by a company is included as an asset in the company's balance sheet, there must be disclosed in a note to the accounts—

(a) the period chosen for writing off the consideration for that goodwill, and

(b) the reasons for choosing that period.

Miscellaneous and supplementary provisions

Excess of money owed over value received as an asset item

43.— (1) Where the amount repayable on any debt owed by a company is greater than the value of the consideration received in the transaction giving rise to the debt, the amount of the difference may be treated as an asset.

(2) Where any such amount is so treated—

(a) it must be written off by reasonable amounts each year and must be completely written off before repayment of the debt, and

(b) if the current amount is not shown as a separate item in the company's balance sheet, it must be disclosed in a note to the accounts.

Assets included at a fixed amount

44.— (1) Subject to sub-paragraph (2), assets which fall to be included under assets item F.I (tangible assets) in the balance sheet format may be included at a fixed quantity and value.

(2) Sub-paragraph (1) applies to assets of a kind which are constantly being replaced where—

(a) their overall value is not material to assessing the company's state of affairs, and

(b) their quantity, value and composition are not subject to material variation.

Determination of cost

45.— (1) The cost of an asset that has been acquired by the company is to be determined by adding to the actual price paid any expenses incidental to its acquisition.

(2) The cost of an asset constructed by the company is to be determined by adding to the purchase price of the raw materials and consumables used the amount of the costs incurred by the company which are directly attributable to the construction of that asset.

(3) In addition, there may be included in the cost of an asset constructed by the company—

(a) a reasonable proportion of the costs incurred by the company which are only indirectly attributable to the construction of that asset, but only to the extent that they relate to the period of construction, and

(b) interest on capital borrowed to finance the construction of that asset, to the extent that it accrues in respect of the period of construction,

provided, however, in a case within paragraph (b), that the inclusion of the interest in determining the cost of that asset and the amount of the interest so included is disclosed in a note to the accounts.

46.— (1) The cost of any assets which are fungible assets may be determined by the application of any of the methods mentioned in sub-paragraph (2) in relation to any such assets of the same class, provided that the method chosen is one which appears to the directors to be appropriate in the circumstances of the company.

(2) Those methods are—

(a) the method known as "first in, first out" (FIFO),

(b) the method known as "last in, first out" (LIFO),

(c) a weighted average price, and

(d) any other method similar to any of the methods mentioned above.

(3) Where in the case of any company—

(a) the cost of assets falling to be included under any item shown in the company's balance sheet has been determined by the application of any method permitted by this paragraph, and

(b) the amount shown in respect of that item differs materially from the relevant alternative amount given below in this paragraph,

the amount of that difference must be disclosed in a note to the accounts.

(4) Subject to sub-paragraph (5), for the purposes of sub-paragraph (3)(b), the relevant alternative amount, in relation to any item shown in a company's balance sheet, is the amount which would have been shown in respect of that item if assets of any class included under that item at an amount determined by any method permitted by this paragraph had instead been included at their replacement cost as at the balance sheet date.

(5) The relevant alternative amount may be determined by reference to the most recent actual purchase price before the balance sheet date of assets of any class included under the item in question instead of by reference to their replacement cost as at that date, but only if the former appears to the directors of the company to constitute the more appropriate standard of comparison in the case of assets of that class.

Substitution of original amount where price or cost unknown

47.— (1) This paragraph applies where—

(a) there is no record of the purchase price of any asset acquired by a company or of any price, expenses or costs relevant for determining its cost in accordance with paragraph 45, or

(b) any such record cannot be obtained without unreasonable expense or delay.

(2) In such a case, the cost of the asset must be taken, for the purposes of paragraphs 36 to 42, to be the value ascribed to it in the earliest available record of its value made on or after its acquisition by the company.

SECTION E
RULES FOR DETERMINING PROVISIONS

Preliminary

48. Provisions which are to be shown in a company's accounts are to be determined in accordance with this Section.

Technical provisions

49. The amount of technical provisions must at all times be sufficient to cover any liabilities arising out of insurance contracts as far as can reasonably be foreseen.

Provision for unearned premiums

50.— (1) The provision for unearned premiums must in principle be computed separately for each insurance contract, save that statistical methods (and in particular proportional and flat rate methods) may be used where they may be expected to give approximately the same results as individual calculations.

(2) Where the pattern of risk varies over the life of a contract, this must be taken into account in the calculation methods.

Provision for unexpired risks

51. The provision for unexpired risks (as defined in paragraph 91) must be computed on the basis of claims and administrative expenses likely to arise after the end of the financial year from contracts concluded before that date, in so far as their estimated value exceeds the provision for unearned premiums and any premiums receivable under those contracts.

Long-term business provision

52.— (1) The long-term business provision must in principle be computed separately for each long-term contract, save that statistical or mathematical methods may be used where they may be expected to give approximately the same results as individual calculations.

(2) A summary of the principal assumptions in making the provision under sub-paragraph (1) must be given in the notes to the accounts.

(3) The computation must be made annually by a Fellow of the Institute or Faculty of Actuaries on the basis of recognised actuarial methods, with due regard to the actuarial principles laid down in Directive 2002/83/EC of the European Parliament and of the Council of 5th November 2002 concerning life assurance.

Provisions for claims outstanding

General business

53.— (1) A provision must in principle be computed separately for each claim on the basis of the costs still expected to arise, save that statistical methods may be used if they result in an adequate provision having regard to the nature of the risks.

(2) This provision must also allow for claims incurred but not reported by the balance sheet date, the amount of the allowance being determined having regard to past experience as to the number and magnitude of claims reported after previous balance sheet dates.

(3) All claims settlement costs (whether direct or indirect) must be included in the calculation of the provision.

(4) Recoverable amounts arising out of subrogation or salvage must be estimated on a prudent basis and either deducted from the provision for claims outstanding (in which case if the amounts are material they must be shown in the notes to the accounts) or shown as assets.

(5) In sub-paragraph (4), "subrogation" means the acquisition of the rights of policy holders with respect to third parties, and "salvage" means the acquisition of the legal ownership of insured property.

(6) Where benefits resulting from a claim must be paid in the form of annuity, the amounts to be set aside for that purpose must be calculated by recognised actuarial methods, and paragraph 54 does not apply to such calculations.

(7) Implicit discounting or deductions, whether resulting from the placing of a current value on a provision for an outstanding claim which is expected to be settled later at a higher figure or otherwise effected, is prohibited.

54.— (1) Explicit discounting or deductions to take account of investment income is permitted, subject to the following conditions—

(a) the expected average interval between the date for the settlement of claims being discounted and the accounting date must be at least four years;

(b) the discounting or deductions must be effected on a recognised prudential basis;

(c) when calculating the total cost of settling claims, the company must take account of all factors that could cause increases in that cost;

(d) the company must have adequate data at its disposal to construct a reliable model of the rate of claims settlements;

(e) the rate of interest used for the calculation of present values must not exceed a rate prudently estimated to be earned by assets of the company which are appropriate in magnitude and nature to cover the provisions for claims being discounted during the period necessary for the payment of such claims, and must not exceed either—

(i) a rate justified by the performance of such assets over the preceding five years, or

(ii) a rate justified by the performance of such assets during the year preceding the balance sheet date.

(2) When discounting or effecting deductions, the company must, in the notes to the accounts, disclose—

(a) the total amount of provisions before discounting or deductions,

(b) the categories of claims which are discounted or from which deductions have been made,

(c) for each category of claims, the methods used, in particular the rates used for the estimates referred to in sub-paragraph (1)(d) and (e), and the criteria adopted for estimating the period that will elapse before the claims are settled.

Long-term business

55. The amount of the provision for claims must be equal to the sums due to beneficiaries, plus the costs of settling claims.

Equalisation reserves

56. The amount of any equalisation reserve maintained in respect of general business by the company, in accordance with the rules in section 1.4 of the Prudential Sourcebook for Insurers made by the Financial Services Authority under Part 10 of the Financial Services and Markets Act 2000, must be determined in accordance with such rules.

Accounting on a non-annual basis

57.— (1) Either of the methods described in paragraphs 58 and 59 may be applied where, because of the nature of the class or type of insurance in question, information about premiums receivable or claims payable (or both) for the underwriting years is insufficient when the accounts are drawn up for reliable estimates to be made.

(2) The use of either of the methods referred to in sub-paragraph (1) must be disclosed in the notes to the accounts together with the reasons for adopting it.

(3) Where one of the methods referred to in sub-paragraph (1) is adopted, it must be applied systematically in successive years unless circumstances justify a change.

(4) In the event of a change in the method applied, the effect on the assets, liabilities, financial position and profit or loss must be stated in the notes to the accounts.

(5) For the purposes of this paragraph and paragraph 58, "underwriting year" means the financial year in which the insurance contracts in the class or type of insurance in question commenced.

58.— (1) The excess of the premiums written over the claims and expenses paid in respect of contracts commencing in the underwriting year shall form a technical provision included in the technical provision for claims outstanding shown in the balance sheet under liabilities item C3.

(2) The provision may also be computed on the basis of a given percentage of the premiums written where such a method is appropriate for the type of risk insured.

(3) If necessary, the amount of this technical provision must be increased to make it sufficient to meet present and future obligations.

(4) The technical provision constituted under this paragraph must be replaced by a provision for claims outstanding estimated in accordance with paragraph 53 as soon as sufficient information has been gathered and not later than the end of the third year following the underwriting year.

(5) The length of time that elapses before a provision for claims outstanding is constituted in accordance with sub-paragraph (4) must be disclosed in the notes to the accounts.

59.— (1) The figures shown in the technical account or in certain items within it must relate to a year which wholly or partly precedes the financial year (but by no more than 12 months).

(2) The amounts of the technical provisions shown in the accounts must if necessary be increased to make them sufficient to meet present and future obligations.

(3) The length of time by which the earlier year to which the figures relate precedes the financial year and the magnitude of the transactions concerned must be disclosed in the notes to the accounts.

PART 3
NOTES TO THE ACCOUNTS

Preliminary

60. Any information required in the case of any company by the following provisions of this Part of this Schedule must (if not given in the company's accounts) be given by way of a note to the accounts.

General

Disclosure of accounting policies

61. The accounting policies adopted by the company in determining the amounts to be included in respect of items shown in the balance sheet and in determining the profit or loss of the company must be stated (including such policies with respect to the depreciation and diminution in value of assets).

62. It must be stated whether the accounts have been prepared in accordance with applicable accounting standards and particulars of any material departure from those standards and the reasons for it must be given.

Sums denominated in foreign currencies

63. Where any sums originally denominated in foreign currencies have been brought into account under any items shown in the balance sheet or profit and loss account format, the basis on which those sums have been translated into sterling (or the currency in which the accounts are drawn up) must be stated.

Reserves and dividends

64. There must be stated—

(a) any amount set aside or proposed to be set aside to, or withdrawn or proposed to be withdrawn from, reserves,

(b) the aggregate amount of dividends paid in the financial year (other than those for which a liability existed at the immediately preceding balance sheet date),

(c) the aggregate amount of dividends that the company is liable to pay at the balance sheet date, and

(d) the aggregate amount of dividends that are proposed before the date of approval of the accounts,

and not otherwise disclosed under sub-paragraph (b) or (c).

Information Supplementing the Balance Sheet

Share capital and debentures

65.— (1) Where shares of more than one class have been allotted, the number and aggregate nominal value of shares of each class allotted must be given.

(2) In the case of any part of the allotted share capital that consists of redeemable shares, the following information must be given—

(a) the earliest and latest dates on which the company has power to redeem those shares,

(b) whether those shares must be redeemed in any event or are liable to be redeemed at the option of the company or of the shareholder, and

(c) whether any (and, if so, what) premium is payable on redemption.

66. If the company has allotted any shares during the financial year, the following information must be given—

(a) the classes of shares allotted, and

(b) as respects each class of shares, the number allotted, their aggregate nominal value and the consideration received by the company for the allotment.

67.— (1) With respect to any contingent right to the allotment of shares in the company the following particulars must be given—

(a) the number, description and amount of the shares in relation to which the right is exercisable,

(b) the period during which it is exercisable, and

(c) the price to be paid for the shares allotted.

(2) In sub-paragraph (1) "contingent right to the allotment of shares" means any option to subscribe for shares and any other right to require the allotment of shares to any person whether arising on the conversion into shares of securities of any other description or otherwise.

68.— (1) If the company has issued any debentures during the financial year to which the accounts relate, the following information must be given—

(a) the classes of debentures issued, and

(b) as respects each class of debentures, the amount issued and the consideration received by the company for the issue.

(2) Where any of the company's debentures are held by a nominee of or trustee for the company, the nominal amount of the debentures and the amount at which they are stated in the accounting records kept by the company in accordance with section 386 of the 2006 Act (duty to keep accounting records) must be stated.

Assets

69.— (1) In respect of any assets of the company included in assets items B (intangible assets), CI (land and buildings) and CII (investments in group undertakings and participating interests) in the company's balance sheet the following information must be given by reference to each such item—

(a) the appropriate amounts in respect of those assets included in the item as at the date of the beginning of the financial year and as at the balance sheet date respectively,

(b) the effect on any amount included in assets item B in respect of those assets of—

(i) any determination during that year of the value to be ascribed to any of those assets in accordance with paragraph 23,

(ii) acquisitions during that year of any assets,

(iii) disposals during that year of any assets, and

(iv) any transfers of assets of the company to and from the item during that year.

(2) The reference in sub-paragraph (1)(a) to the appropriate amounts in respect of any assets (included in an assets item) as at any date there mentioned is a reference to amounts representing the aggregate amounts determined, as at that date, in respect of assets falling to be included under the item on either of the following bases—

(a) on the basis of cost (determined in accordance with paragraphs 45 and 46), or

(b) on any basis permitted by paragraph 22 or 23 ,

(leaving out of account in either case any provisions for depreciation or diminution in value).

(3) In addition, in respect of any assets of the company included in any assets item in the company's balance sheet, there must be stated (by reference to each such item)—

(a) the cumulative amount of provisions for depreciation or diminution in value of those assets included under the item as at each date mentioned in sub-paragraph (1)(a),

(b) the amount of any such provisions made in respect of the financial year,

(c) the amount of any adjustments made in respect of any such provisions during that year in consequence of the disposal of any of those assets, and

(d) the amount of any other adjustments made in respect of any such provisions during that year.

70. Where any assets of the company (other than listed investments) are included under any item shown in the company's balance sheet at an amount determined on any basis mentioned in paragraph 22 or 23, the following information must be given—

(a) the years (so far as they are known to the directors) in which the assets were severally valued and the several values, and

(b) in the case of assets that have been valued during the financial year, the names of the persons who valued them or particulars of their qualifications for doing so and (whichever is stated) the bases of valuation used by them.

71. In relation to any amount which is included under assets item CI (land and buildings) there must be stated—

(a) how much of that amount is ascribable to land of freehold tenure and how much to land of leasehold tenure, and

(b) how much of the amount ascribable to land of leasehold tenure is ascribable to land held on long lease and how much to land held on short lease.

Investments

72. In respect of the amount of each item which is shown in the company's balance sheet under assets item C (investments) there must be stated how much of that amount is ascribable to listed investments.

Information about fair value of assets and liabilities

73.— (1) This paragraph applies where financial instruments have been valued in accordance with paragraph 30 or 32.

(2) The items affected and the basis of valuation adopted in determining the amounts of the financial instruments must be disclosed.

(3) The purchase price of the financial instruments must be disclosed.

(4) There must be stated—

(a) the significant assumptions underlying the valuation models and techniques used, where the fair value of the instruments has been determined in accordance with paragraph 31(4),

(b) for each category of financial instrument, the fair value of the instruments in that category and the changes in value—

(i) included in the profit and loss account, or

(ii) credited to or (as the case may be) debited from the fair value reserve,

in respect of those instruments, and

(c) for each class of derivatives, the extent and nature of the instruments, including significant terms and conditions that may affect the amount, timing and certainty of future cash flows.

(5) Where any amount is transferred to or from the fair value reserve during the financial year, there must be stated in tabular form—

(a) the amount of the reserve as at the date of the beginning of the financial year and as at the balance sheet date respectively,

(b) the amount transferred to or from the reserve during that year, and

(c) the source and application respectively of the amounts so transferred.

74. Where the company has derivatives that it has not included at fair value, there must be stated for each class of such derivatives—

(a) the fair value of the derivatives in that class, if such a value can be determined in accordance with paragraph 31, and

(b) the extent and nature of the derivatives.

75.— (1) This paragraph applies if—

(a) the company has financial fixed assets that could be included at fair value by virtue of paragraph 30,

(b) the amount at which those assets are included under any item in the company's accounts is in excess of their fair value, and

(c) the company has not made provision for diminution in value of those assets in accordance with paragraph 38(2) of this Schedule.

(2) There must be stated—

(a) the amount at which either the individual assets or appropriate groupings of those individual assets are included in the company's accounts,

(b) the fair value of those assets or groupings, and

(c) the reasons for not making a provision for diminution in value of those assets, including the nature of the evidence that provides the basis for the belief that the amount at which they are stated in the accounts will be recovered.

Information where investment property and living animals and plants included at fair value

76.— (1) This paragraph applies where the amounts to be included in a company's accounts in respect of investment property or living animals and plants have been determined in accordance with paragraph 33.

(2) The balance sheet items affected and the basis of valuation adopted in determining the amounts of the assets in question in the case of each such item must be disclosed in a note to the accounts.

(3) In the case of investment property, for each balance sheet item affected there must be shown, either separately in the balance sheet or in a note to the accounts—

(a) the comparable amounts determined according to the historical cost accounting rules, or

(b) the differences between those amounts and the corresponding amounts actually shown in the balance sheet in respect of that item.

(4) In sub-paragraph (3), references in relation to any item to the comparable amounts determined in accordance with that sub-paragraph are to—

(a) the aggregate amount which would be required to be shown in respect of that item if the amounts to be included in respect of all the assets covered by that item were determined according to the historical cost accounting rules, and

(b) the aggregate amount of the cumulative provisions for depreciation or diminution in value which would be permitted or required in determining those amounts according to those rules.

Reserves and provisions

77.— (1) This paragraph applies where any amount is transferred—

(a) to or from any reserves,

(b) to any provisions for other risks, or

(c) from any provisions for other risks otherwise than for the purpose for which the provision was established,

and the reserves or provisions are or would but for paragraph 3(1) be shown as separate items in the company's balance sheet.

(2) The following information must be given in respect of the aggregate of reserves or provisions included in the same item—

(a) the amount of the reserves or provisions as at the date of the beginning of the financial year and as at the balance sheet date respectively,

(b) any amounts transferred to or from the reserves or provisions during that year, and

(c) the source and application respectively of any amounts so transferred.

(3) Particulars must be given of each provision included in liabilities item E.3 (other provisions) in the company's balance sheet in any case where the amount of that provision is material.

Provision for taxation

78. The amount of any provision for deferred taxation must be stated separately from the amount of any provision for other taxation.

Details of indebtedness

79.— (1) In respect of each item shown under "creditors" in the company's balance sheet there must be stated the aggregate of the following amounts—

(a) the amount of any debts included under that item which are payable or repayable otherwise than by instalments and fall due for payment or repayment after the end of the period of five years beginning with the day next following the end of the financial year, and

(b) in the case of any debts so included which are payable or repayable by instalments, the amount of any instalments which fall due for payment after the end of that period.

(2) Subject to sub-paragraph (3), in relation to each debt falling to be taken into account under sub-paragraph (1), the terms of payment or repayment and the rate of any interest payable on the debt must be stated.

(3) If the number of debts is such that, in the opinion of the directors, compliance with sub-paragraph (2) would result in a statement of excessive length, it is sufficient to give a general indication of the terms of payment or repayment and the rates of any interest payable on the debts.

(4) In respect of each item shown under "creditors" in the company's balance sheet there must be stated—

(a) the aggregate amount of any debts included under that item in respect of which any security has been given by the company, and

(b) an indication of the nature of the securities so given.

(5) References above in this paragraph to an item shown under "creditors" in the company's balance sheet include references, where amounts falling due to creditors within one year and after more than one year are distinguished in the balance sheet—
(a) in a case within sub-paragraph (1), to an item shown under the latter of those categories, and
(b) in a case within sub-paragraph (4), to an item shown under either of those categories.
References to items shown under "creditors" include references to items which would but for paragraph 3(1)(b) be shown under that heading.

80. If any fixed cumulative dividends on the company's shares are in arrear, there must be stated—
(a) the amount of the arrears, and
(b) the period for which the dividends or, if there is more than one class, each class of them are in arrear.

Guarantees and other financial commitments

81.— (1) Particulars must be given of any charge on the assets of the company to secure the liabilities of any other person, including, where practicable, the amount secured.
(2) The following information must be given with respect to any other contingent liability not provided for (other than a contingent liability arising out of an insurance contract)—
(a) the amount or estimated amount of that liability,
(b) its legal nature, and
(c) whether any valuable security has been provided by the company in connection with that liability and if so, what.
(3) There must be stated, where practicable, the aggregate amount or estimated amount of contracts for capital expenditure, so far as not provided for.
(4) Particulars must be given of—
(a) any pension commitments included under any provision shown in the company's balance sheet, and
(b) any such commitments for which no provision has been made,
and where any such commitment relates wholly or partly to pensions payable to past directors of the company separate particulars must be given of that commitment so far as it relates to such pensions.
(5) Particulars must also be given of any other financial commitments, other than commitments arising out of insurance contracts, that—
(a) have not been provided for, and
(b) are relevant to assessing the company's state of affairs.
(6) Commitments within any of the preceding sub-paragraphs undertaken on behalf of or for the benefit of—
(a) any parent undertaking or fellow subsidiary undertaking, or
(b) any subsidiary undertaking of the company,
must be stated separately from the other commitments within that sub-paragraph, and commitments within paragraph (a) must also be stated separately from those within paragraph (b).

Miscellaneous matters

82.— (1) Particulars must be given of any case where the cost of any asset is for the first time determined under paragraph 47.
(2) Where any outstanding loans made under the authority of section 682(2)(b), (c) or (d) of the 2006 Act (various cases of financial assistance by a company for purchase of its own shares) are included under any item shown in the company's balance sheet, the aggregate amount of those loans must be disclosed for each item in question.

Information supplementing the profit and loss account

Separate statement of certain items of income and expenditure

83.— (1) Subject to sub-paragraph (2), there must be stated the amount of the interest on or any similar charges in respect of—

(a) bank loans and overdrafts, and

(b) loans of any other kind made to the company.

(2) Sub-paragraph (1) does not apply to interest or charges on loans to the company from group undertakings, but, with that exception, it applies to interest or charges on all loans, whether made on the security of debentures or not.

Particulars of tax

84.— (1) Particulars must be given of any special circumstances which affect liability in respect of taxation of profits, income or capital gains for the financial year or liability in respect of taxation of profits, income or capital gains for succeeding financial years.

(2) The following amounts must be stated—

(a) the amount of the charge for United Kingdom corporation tax,

(b) if that amount would have been greater but for relief from double taxation, the amount which it would have been but for such relief,

(c) the amount of the charge for United Kingdom income tax, and

(d) the amount of the charge for taxation imposed outside the United Kingdom of profits, income and (so far as charged to revenue) capital gains.

Those amounts must be stated separately in respect of each of the amounts which is shown under the following items in the profit and loss account, that is to say item III.9 (tax on profit or loss on ordinary activities) and item III.14 (tax on extraordinary profit or loss).

Particulars of business

85.— (1) As regards general business a company must disclose—

(a) gross premiums written,

(b) gross premiums earned,

(c) gross claims incurred,

(d) gross operating expenses, and

(e) the reinsurance balance.

(2) The amounts required to be disclosed by sub-paragraph (1) must be broken down between direct insurance and reinsurance acceptances, if reinsurance acceptances amount to 10 per cent or more of gross premiums written.

(3) Subject to sub-paragraph (4), the amounts required to be disclosed by sub-paragraphs (1) and (2) with respect to direct insurance must be further broken down into the following groups of classes—

(a) accident and health,

(b) motor (third party liability),

(c) motor (other classes),

(d) marine, aviation and transport,

(e) fire and other damage to property,

(f) third-party liability,

(g) credit and suretyship,

(h) legal expenses,

(i) assistance, and

(j) miscellaneous,

where the amount of the gross premiums written in direct insurance for each such group exceeds 10 million Euros.

(4) The company must in any event disclose the amounts relating to the three largest groups of classes in its business.

86.— (1) As regards long-term business, the company must disclose—

(a) gross premiums written, and
(b) the reinsurance balance.

(2) Subject to sub-paragraph (3)—
(a) gross premiums written must be broken down between those written by way of direct insurance and those written by way of reinsurance, and
(b) gross premiums written by way of direct insurance must be broken down—
(i) between individual premiums and premiums under group contracts,
(ii) between periodic premiums and single premiums, and
(iii) between premiums from non-participating contracts, premiums from participating contracts and premiums from contracts where the investment risk is borne by policyholders.

(3) Disclosure of any amount referred to in sub-paragraph (2)(a) or (2)(b)(i), (ii) or (iii) is not required if it does not exceed 10 per cent of the gross premiums written or (as the case may be) of the gross premiums written by way of direct insurance.

87.— (1) Subject to sub-paragraph (2), there must be disclosed as regards both general and long-term business the total gross direct insurance premiums resulting from contracts concluded by the company—
(a) in the member State of its head office,
(b) in the other member States, and
(c) in other countries.

(2) Disclosure of any amount referred to in sub-paragraph (1) is not required if it does not exceed 5 per cent of total gross premiums.

Commissions

88. There must be disclosed the total amount of commissions for direct insurance business accounted for in the financial year, including acquisition, renewal, collection and portfolio management commissions.

Miscellaneous matters

89.— (1) Where any amount relating to any preceding financial year is included in any item in the profit and loss account, the effect must be stated.

(2) Particulars must be given of any extraordinary income or charges arising in the financial year.

(3) The effect must be stated of any transactions that are exceptional by virtue of size or incidence though they fall within the ordinary activities of the company.

Related party transactions

90.— (1) Particulars may be given of transactions which the company has entered into with related parties, and must be given if such transactions are material and have not been concluded under normal market conditions.

(2) The particulars of transactions required to be disclosed by sub-paragraph (1) must include—
(a) the amount of such transactions,
(b) the nature of the related party relationship, and
(c) other information about the transactions necessary for an understanding of the financial position of the company.

(3) Information about individual transactions may be aggregated according to their nature, except where separate information is necessary for an understanding of the effects of related party transactions on the financial position of the company.

(4) Particulars need not be given of transactions entered into between two or more members of a group,
provided that any subsidiary undertaking which is a party to the transaction is wholly-owned by such a member.

(5) In this paragraph, "related party" has the same meaning as in international accounting standards.

PART 4
INTERPRETATION OF THIS SCHEDULE

Definitions for this Schedule

91. The following definitions apply for the purposes of this Schedule and its interpretation—

"general business" means business which consists of effecting or carrying out contracts of general insurance;

"long-term business" means business which consists of effecting or carrying out contracts of long-term insurance;

"long-term fund" means the fund or funds maintained by a company in respect of its long-term business in accordance with rule 1.5.22 in the Prudential Sourcebook for Insurers made by the Financial Services Authority under Part 10 of the Financial Services and Markets Act 2000;

"policyholder" has the meaning given by article 3 of the Financial Services and Markets Act 2000 (Meaning of "Policy" and "Policyholder") Order 2001;

"provision for unexpired risks" means the amount set aside in addition to unearned premiums in respect of risks to be borne by the company after the end of the financial year, in order to provide for all claims and expenses in connection with insurance contracts in force in excess of the related unearned premiums and any premiums receivable on those contracts.

SCHEDULE 4

Regulation 7

INFORMATION ON RELATED UNDERTAKINGS REQUIRED WHETHER PREPARING COMPANIES ACT OR IAS ACCOUNTS

PART 1
PROVISIONS APPLYING TO ALL COMPANIES

Subsidiary undertakings

1.— (1) The following information must be given where at the end of the financial year the company has subsidiary undertakings.

(2) The name of each subsidiary undertaking must be stated.

(3) There must be stated with respect to each subsidiary undertaking—

(a) if it is incorporated outside the United Kingdom, the country in which it is incorporated,

(b) if it is unincorporated, the address of its principal place of business.

Financial information about subsidiary undertakings

2.— (1) There must be disclosed with respect to each subsidiary undertaking not included in consolidated accounts by the company—

(a) the aggregate amount of its capital and reserves as at the end of its relevant financial year, and

(b) its profit or loss for that year.

(2) That information need not be given if the company is exempt by virtue of section 400 or 401 of the 2006 Act from the requirement to prepare group accounts (parent company included in accounts of larger group).

(3) That information need not be given if the company's investment in the subsidiary undertaking is included in the company's accounts by way of the equity method of valuation.

(4) That information need not be given if—

(a) the subsidiary undertaking is not required by any provision of the 2006 Act to deliver a copy of its balance sheet for its relevant financial year and does not otherwise publish that balance sheet in the United Kingdom or elsewhere, and

(b) the company's holding is less than 50% of the nominal value of the shares in the undertaking.

(5) Information otherwise required by this paragraph need not be given if it is not material.

(6) For the purposes of this paragraph the "relevant financial year" of a subsidiary undertaking is—

(a) if its financial year ends with that of the company, that year, and

(b) if not, its financial year ending last before the end of the company's financial year.

Shares and debentures of company held by subsidiary undertakings

3.— (1) The number, description and amount of the shares in the company held by or on behalf of its subsidiary undertakings must be disclosed.

(2) Sub-paragraph (1) does not apply in relation to shares in the case of which the subsidiary undertaking is concerned as personal representative or, subject as follows, as trustee.

(3) The exception for shares in relation to which the subsidiary undertaking is concerned as trustee does not apply if the company, or any of its subsidiary undertakings, is beneficially interested under the trust, otherwise than by way of security only for the purposes of a transaction entered into by it in the ordinary course of a business which includes the lending of money.

(4) Part 5 of this Schedule has effect for the interpretation of the reference in sub-paragraph (3) to a beneficial interest under a trust.

Significant holdings in undertakings other than subsidiary undertakings

4.— (1) The information required by paragraphs 5 and 6 must be given where at the end of the financial year the company has a significant holding in an undertaking which is not a subsidiary undertaking of the company, and which does not fall within paragraph 18 (joint ventures) or 19 (associated undertakings).

(2) A holding is significant for this purpose if—

(a) it amounts to 20% or more of the nominal value of any class of shares in the undertaking, or

(b) the amount of the holding (as stated or included in the company's individual accounts) exceeds one-fifth of the amount (as so stated) of the company's assets.

5.— (1) The name of the undertaking must be stated.

(2) There must be stated—

(a) if the undertaking is incorporated outside the United Kingdom, the country in which it is incorporated,

(b) if it is unincorporated, the address of its principal place of business.

(3) There must also be stated—

(a) the identity of each class of shares in the undertaking held by the company, and

(b) the proportion of the nominal value of the shares of that class represented by those shares.

6.— (1) Subject to paragraph 14, there must also be stated—

(a) the aggregate amount of the capital and reserves of the undertaking as at the end of its relevant financial year, and

(b) its profit or loss for that year.

(2) That information need not be given in respect of an undertaking if—

(a) the undertaking is not required by any provision of the 2006 Act to deliver a copy of its balance sheet for its relevant financial year and does not otherwise publish that balance sheet in the United Kingdom or elsewhere, and

(b) the company's holding is less than 50% of the nominal value of the shares in the undertaking.

(3) Information otherwise required by this paragraph need not be given if it is not material.

(4) For the purposes of this paragraph the "relevant financial year" of an undertaking is—

(a) if its financial year ends with that of the company, that year, and

(b) if not, its financial year ending last before the end of the company's financial year.

Membership of certain undertakings

7.— (1) The information required by this paragraph must be given where at the end of the financial year the company is a member of a qualifying undertaking.

(2) There must be stated—

(a) the name and legal form of the undertaking, and

(b) the address of the undertaking's registered office (whether in or outside the United Kingdom) or, if it does not have such an office, its head office (whether in or outside the United Kingdom).

(3) Where the undertaking is a qualifying partnership there must also be stated either—

(a) that a copy of the latest accounts of the undertaking has been or is to be appended to the copy of the company's accounts sent to the registrar under section 444 of the 2006 Act, or

(b) the name of at least one body corporate (which may be the company) in whose group accounts the undertaking has been or is to be dealt with on a consolidated basis.

(4) Information otherwise required by sub-paragraph (2) need not be given if it is not material.

(5) Information otherwise required by sub-paragraph (3)(b) need not be given if the notes to the company's accounts disclose that advantage has been taken of the exemption conferred by regulation 7 of the Partnerships (Accounts) Regulations 2008.

(6) In this paragraph—

"dealt with on a consolidated basis", "member" and "qualifying partnership" have the same meanings as in the Partnerships (Accounts) Regulations 2008;

"qualifying undertaking" means—

(a) a qualifying partnership, or

(b) an unlimited company each of whose members is—

(i) a limited company,

(ii) another unlimited company each of whose members is a limited company, or

(iii) a Scottish partnership each of whose members is a limited company,

and references in this paragraph to a limited company, another unlimited company or a Scottish partnership include a comparable undertaking incorporated in or formed under the law of a country or territory outside the United Kingdom.

Parent undertaking drawing up accounts for larger group

8.— (1) Where the company is a subsidiary undertaking, the following information must be given with respect to the parent undertaking of—

(a) the largest group of undertakings for which group accounts are drawn up and of which the company is a member, and

(b) the smallest such group of undertakings.

(2) The name of the parent undertaking must be stated.

(3) There must be stated—

(a) if the undertaking is incorporated outside the United Kingdom, the country in which it is incorporated,

(b) if it is unincorporated, the address of its principal place of business.

(4) If copies of the group accounts referred to in sub-paragraph (1) are available to the public, there must also be stated the addresses from which copies of the accounts can be obtained.

Identification of ultimate parent company

9.— (1) Where the company is a subsidiary undertaking, the following information must be given with respect to the company (if any) regarded by the directors as being the company's ultimate parent company.

(2) The name of that company must be stated.

(3) If that company is incorporated outside the United Kingdom, the country in which it is incorporated must be stated (if known to the directors).

(4) In this paragraph "company" includes any body corporate.

PART 2
COMPANIES NOT REQUIRED TO PREPARE GROUP ACCOUNTS

Reason for not preparing group accounts

10.— (1) The reason why the company is not required to prepare group accounts must be stated.

(2) If the reason is that all the subsidiary undertakings of the company fall within the exclusions provided for in section 405 of the 2006 Act (Companies Act group accounts: subsidiary undertakings included in the consolidation), it must be stated with respect to each subsidiary undertaking which of those exclusions applies.

Holdings in subsidiary undertakings

11.— (1) There must be stated in relation to shares of each class held by the company in a subsidiary undertaking—

(a) the identity of the class, and

(b) the proportion of the nominal value of the shares of that class represented by those shares.

(2) The shares held by or on behalf of the company itself must be distinguished from those attributed to the company which are held by or on behalf of a subsidiary undertaking.

Financial years of subsidiary undertakings

12. Where—

(a) disclosure is made under paragraph 2(1) with respect to a subsidiary undertaking, and

(b) that undertaking's financial year does not end with that of the company,

there must be stated in relation to that undertaking the date on which its last financial year ended (last before the end of the company's financial year).

Exemption from giving information about significant holdings in non-subsidiary undertakings

13.— (1) The information otherwise required by paragraph 6 (significant holdings in undertakings other than subsidiary undertaking) need not be given if—

(a) the company is exempt by virtue of section 400 or 401 of the 2006 Act from the requirement to prepare group accounts (parent company included in accounts of larger group), and

(b) the investment of the company in all undertakings in which it has such a holding as is mentioned in sub-paragraph (1) is shown, in aggregate, in the notes to the accounts by way of the equity method of valuation.

Construction of references to shares held by company

14.— (1) References in Parts 1 and 2 of this Schedule to shares held by a company are to be construed as follows.

(2) For the purposes of paragraphs 2, 11 and 12 (information about subsidiary undertakings)—

(a) there must be attributed to the company any shares held by a subsidiary undertaking, or by a person acting on behalf of the company or a subsidiary undertaking; but

(b) there must be treated as not held by the company any shares held on behalf of a person other than the company or a subsidiary undertaking.

(3) For the purposes of paragraphs 4 to 6 (information about undertakings other than subsidiary undertakings)—

(a) there must be attributed to the company shares held on its behalf by any person; but

(b) there must be treated as not held by a company shares held on behalf of a person other than the company.

(4) For the purposes of any of those provisions, shares held by way of security must be treated as held by the person providing the security—

(a) where apart from the right to exercise them for the purpose of preserving the value of the security, or of realising it, the rights attached to the shares are exercisable only in accordance with that person's instructions, and

(b) where the shares are held in connection with the granting of loans as part of normal business activities and apart from the right to exercise them for the purpose of preserving the value of the security, or of realising it, the rights attached to the shares are exercisable only in that person's interests.

PART 3
COMPANIES REQUIRED TO PREPARE GROUP ACCOUNTS

Introductory

15. In this Part of this Schedule "the group" means the group consisting of the parent company and its subsidiary undertakings.

Subsidiary undertakings

16.— (1) In addition to the information required by paragraph 2, the following information must also be given with respect to the undertakings which are subsidiary undertakings of the parent company at the end of the financial year.

(2) It must be stated whether the subsidiary undertaking is included in the consolidation and, if it is not, the reasons for excluding it from consolidation must be given.

(3) It must be stated with respect to each subsidiary undertaking by virtue of which of the conditions specified in section 1162(2) or (4) of the 2006 Act it is a subsidiary undertaking of its immediate parent undertaking.

That information need not be given if the relevant condition is that specified in subsection (2)(a) of that section (holding of a majority of the voting rights) and the immediate parent undertaking holds the same proportion of the shares in the undertaking as it holds voting rights.

Holdings in subsidiary undertakings

17.— (1) The following information must be given with respect to the shares of a subsidiary undertaking held—

(a) by the parent company, and

(b) by the group,

and the information under paragraphs (a) and (b) must (if different) be shown separately.

(2) There must be stated—

(a) the identity of each class of shares held, and

(b) the proportion of the nominal value of the shares of that class represented by those shares.

Joint ventures

18.— (1) The following information must be given where an undertaking is dealt with in the consolidated accounts by the method of proportional consolidation in accordance with paragraph 18 of Schedule 6 to these Regulations (joint ventures)—

(a) the name of the undertaking,

(b) the address of the principal place of business of the undertaking,

(c) the factors on which joint management of the undertaking is based, and

(d) the proportion of the capital of the undertaking held by undertakings included in the consolidation.

(2) Where the financial year of the undertaking did not end with that of the company, there must be stated the date on which a financial year of the undertaking last ended before that date.

Associated undertakings

19.— (1) The following information must be given where an undertaking included in the consolidation has an interest in an associated undertaking.

(2) The name of the associated undertaking must be stated.

(3) There must be stated—

(a) if the undertaking is incorporated outside the United Kingdom, the country in which it is incorporated,

(b) if it is unincorporated, the address of its principal place of business.

(4) The following information must be given with respect to the shares of the undertaking held—

(a) by the parent company, and

(b) by the group,

and the information under paragraphs (a) and (b) must be shown separately.

(5) There must be stated—

(a) the identity of each class of shares held, and

(b) the proportion of the nominal value of the shares of that class represented by those shares.

(6) In this paragraph "associated undertaking" has the meaning given by paragraph 19 of Schedule 6 to these Regulations; and the information required by this paragraph must be given notwithstanding that paragraph 21(3) of that Schedule (materiality) applies in relation to the accounts themselves.

Requirement to give information about other significant holdings of parent company or group

20.— (1) The information required by paragraphs 5 and 6 must also be given where at the end of the financial year the group has a significant holding in an undertaking which is not a subsidiary undertaking of the parent company and does not fall within paragraph 18 (joint ventures) or 19 (associated undertakings), as though the references to the company in those paragraphs were a reference to the group.

(2) A holding is significant for this purpose if—

(a) it amounts to 20% or more of the nominal value of any class of shares in the undertaking, or

(b) the amount of the holding (as stated or included in the group accounts) exceeds one-fifth of the amount of the group's assets (as so stated).

(3) For the purposes of those paragraphs as applied to a group the "relevant financial year" of an outside undertaking is—

(a) if its financial year ends with that of the parent company, that year, and

(b) if not, its financial year ending last before the end of the parent company's financial year.

Group's membership of certain undertakings

21. The information required by paragraph 7 must also be given where at the end of the financial year the group is a member of a qualifying undertaking.

Construction of references to shares held by parent company or group

22.— (1) References in Parts 1 and 3 of this Schedule to shares held by that parent company or group are to be construed as follows.

(2) For the purposes of paragraphs 4 to 6, 17, 19(4) and (5) and 12 (information about holdings in subsidiary and other undertakings)—

(a) there must be attributed to the parent company shares held on its behalf by any person; but

(b) there must be treated as not held by the parent company shares held on behalf of a person other than the company.

(3) References to shares held by the group are to any shares held by or on behalf of the parent company or any of its subsidiary undertakings; but any shares held on behalf of a person other than the parent company or any of its subsidiary undertakings are not to be treated as held by the group.

(4) Shares held by way of security must be treated as held by the person providing the security—

(a) where apart from the right to exercise them for the purpose of preserving the value of the security, or of realising it, the rights attached to the shares are exercisable only in accordance with his instructions, and

(b) where the shares are held in connection with the granting of loans as part of normal business activities and apart from the right to exercise them for the purpose of preserving the value of the security, or of realising it, the rights attached to the shares are exercisable only in his interests.

PART 4
ADDITIONAL DISCLOSURES FOR BANKING COMPANIES AND GROUPS

23.— (1) This paragraph applies where accounts are prepared in accordance with the special provisions of Schedules 2 and 6 relating to banking companies or groups.

(2) The information required by paragraph 5 of this Schedule, modified where applicable by paragraph 20 (information about significant holdings of the company or group in undertakings other than subsidiary undertakings) need only be given in respect of undertakings (otherwise falling within the class of undertakings in respect of which disclosure is required) in which the company or group has a significant holding amounting to 20 % or more of the nominal value of the shares in the undertaking.

In addition any information required by those paragraphs may be omitted if it is not material.

(3) Paragraphs 14(3) and (4) and 22(3) and (4) of this Schedule apply with necessary modifications for the purposes of this paragraph.

PART 5
INTERPRETATION OF REFERENCES TO "BENEFICIAL INTEREST"

Residual interests under pension and employees' share schemes

24.— (1) Where shares in an undertaking are held on trust for the purposes of a pension scheme or an employees' share scheme, there must be disregarded any residual interest which has not vested in possession, being an interest of the undertaking or any of its subsidiary undertakings.

(2) In this paragraph a "residual interest" means a right of the undertaking in question (the "residual beneficiary") to receive any of the trust property in the event of—

(a) all the liabilities arising under the scheme having been satisfied or provided for, or

(b) the residual beneficiary ceasing to participate in the scheme, or

(c) the trust property at any time exceeding what is necessary for satisfying the liabilities arising or expected to arise under the scheme.

(3) In sub-paragraph (2) references to a right include a right dependent on the exercise of a discretion vested by the scheme in the trustee or any other person; and references to liabilities arising under a scheme include liabilities that have resulted or may result from the exercise of any such discretion.

(4) For the purposes of this paragraph a residual interest vests in possession—

(a) in a case within sub-paragraph (2)(a), on the occurrence of the event there mentioned, whether or not the amount of the property receivable pursuant to the right mentioned in that sub-paragraph is then ascertained,

(b) in a case within sub-paragraph (2)(b) or (c), when the residual beneficiary becomes entitled to require the trustee to transfer to that beneficiary any of the property receivable pursuant to that right.

Employer's charges and other rights of recovery

25.— (1) Where shares in an undertaking are held on trust there must be disregarded—

(a) if the trust is for the purposes of a pension scheme, any such rights as are mentioned in sub-paragraph (2),

(b) if the trust is for the purposes of an employees' share scheme, any such rights as are mentioned in paragraph (a) of that sub-paragraph,

being rights of the undertaking or any of its subsidiary undertakings.

(2) The rights referred to are—

(a) any charge or lien on, or set-off against, any benefit or other right or interest under the scheme for the purpose of enabling the employer or former employer of a member of the scheme to obtain the discharge of a monetary obligation due to him from the member, and

(b) any right to receive from the trustee of the scheme, or as trustee of the scheme to retain, an amount that can be recovered or retained under section 61 of the Pension Schemes Act 1993 or section 57 of the Pension Schemes (Northern Ireland) Act 1993 (deduction of contributions equivalent premium from refund of scheme contributions) or otherwise as reimbursement or partial reimbursement for any contributions equivalent premium paid in connection with the scheme under Chapter 3 of Part 3 of that Act.

Trustee's right to expenses, remuneration, indemnity etc

26. Where an undertaking is a trustee, there must be disregarded any rights which the undertaking has in its capacity as trustee including, in particular, any right to recover its expenses or be remunerated out of the trust property and any right to be indemnified out of that property for any liability incurred by reason of any act or omission of the undertaking in the performance of its duties as trustee.

Supplementary

27.— (1) This Schedule applies in relation to debentures as it applies in relation to shares.

(2) "Pension scheme" means any scheme for the provision of benefits consisting of or including relevant benefits for or in respect of employees or former employees; and "relevant benefits" means any pension, lump sum, gratuity or other like benefit given or to be given on retirement or on death or in anticipation of retirement or, in connection with past service, after retirement or death.

(3) In sub-paragraph (2) of this paragraph and in paragraph 25(2) "employee" and "employer" are to be read as if a director of an undertaking were employed by it.

SCHEDULE 5

Regulation 8

INFORMATION ABOUT BENEFITS OF DIRECTORS

PART 1

PROVISIONS APPLYING TO QUOTED AND UNQUOTED COMPANIES

Total amount of directors' remuneration etc

1.— (1) There must be shown—

(a) the aggregate amount of remuneration paid to or receivable by directors in respect of qualifying services;

(b) the aggregate of the amount of gains made by directors on the exercise of share options;

(c) the aggregate of the amount of money paid to or receivable by directors, and the net value of assets (other than money and share options) received or receivable by directors, under long term incentive schemes in respect of qualifying services; and

(d) the aggregate value of any company contributions—

(i) paid, or treated as paid, to a pension scheme in respect of directors' qualifying services, and

(ii) by reference to which the rate or amount of any money purchase benefits that may become payable will be calculated.

(2) There must be shown the number of directors (if any) to whom retirement benefits are accruing in respect of qualifying services—
(a) under money purchase schemes, and
(b) under defined benefit schemes.

(3) In the case of a company which is not a quoted company and whose equity share capital is not listed on the market known as AIM—
(a) sub-paragraph (1) has effect as if paragraph (b) were omitted and, in paragraph (c), "assets" did not include shares; and
(b) the number of each of the following (if any) must be shown, namely—
(i) the directors who exercised share options, and
(ii) the directors in respect of whose qualifying services shares were received or receivable under long term incentive schemes.

PART 2
PROVISIONS APPLYING ONLY TO UNQUOTED COMPANIES

Details of highest paid director's emoluments etc

2.— (1) Where the aggregates shown under paragraph 1(1)(a), (b) and (c) total £200,000 or more, there must be shown—
(a) so much of the total of those aggregates as is attributable to the highest paid director, and
(b) so much of the aggregate mentioned in paragraph 1(1)(d) as is so attributable.

(2) Where sub-paragraph (1) applies and the highest paid director has performed qualifying services during the financial year by reference to which the rate or amount of any defined benefits that may become payable will be calculated, there must also be shown—
(a) the amount at the end of the year of his accrued pension, and
(b) where applicable, the amount at the end of the year of his accrued lump sum.

(3) Subject to sub-paragraph (4), where sub-paragraph (1) applies in the case of a company which is not a listed company, there must also be shown—
(a) whether the highest paid director exercised any share options, and
(b) whether any shares were received or receivable by that director in respect of qualifying services under a long term incentive scheme.

(4) Where the highest paid director has not been involved in any of the transactions specified in sub-paragraph (3), that fact need not be stated.

Excess retirement benefits of directors and past directors

3.— (1) Subject to sub-paragraph (2), there must be shown the aggregate amount of—
(a) so much of retirement benefits paid to or receivable by directors under pension schemes, and
(b) so much of retirement benefits paid to or receivable by past directors under such schemes,

as (in each case) is in excess of the retirement benefits to which they were respectively entitled on the date on which the benefits first became payable or 31st March 1997, whichever is the later.

(2) Amounts paid or receivable under a pension scheme need not be included in the aggregate amount if—
(a) the funding of the scheme was such that the amounts were or, as the case may be, could have been paid without recourse to additional contributions, and
(b) amounts were paid to or receivable by all pensioner members of the scheme on the same basis.

(3) In sub-paragraph (2), "pensioner member", in relation to a pension scheme, means any person who is entitled to the present payment of retirement benefits under the scheme.

(4) In this paragraph—

(a) references to retirement benefits include benefits otherwise than in cash, and

(b) in relation to so much of retirement benefits as consists of a benefit otherwise than in cash, references to their amount are to the estimated money value of the benefit, and the nature of any such benefit must also be disclosed.

Compensation to directors for loss of office

4.— (1) There must be shown the aggregate amount of any compensation to directors or past directors in respect of loss of office.

(2) This includes compensation received or receivable by a director or past director—

(a) for loss of office as director of the company, or

(b) for loss, while director of the company or on or in connection with his ceasing to be a director of it, of—

(i) any other office in connection with the management of the company's affairs, or

(ii) any office as director or otherwise in connection with the management of the affairs of any subsidiary undertaking of the company.

(3) In this paragraph references to compensation for loss of office include—

(a) compensation in consideration for, or in connection with, a person's retirement from office, and

(b) where such a retirement is occasioned by a breach of the person's contract with the company or with a subsidiary undertaking of the company—

(i) payments made by way of damages for the breach, or

(ii) payments made by way of settlement or compromise of any claim in respect of the breach.

(4) In this paragraph—

(a) references to compensation include benefits otherwise than in cash, and

(b) in relation to such compensation references to its amount are to the estimated money value of the benefit.

The nature of any such compensation must be disclosed.

Sums paid to third parties in respect of directors' services

5.— (1) There must be shown the aggregate amount of any consideration paid to or receivable by third parties for making available the services of any person—

(a) as a director of the company, or

(b) while director of the company—

(i) as director of any of its subsidiary undertakings, or

(ii) otherwise in connection with the management of the affairs of the company or any of its subsidiary undertakings.

(2) In sub-paragraph (1)—

(a) the reference to consideration includes benefits otherwise than in cash, and

(b) in relation to such consideration the reference to its amount is to the estimated money value of the benefit.

The nature of any such consideration must be disclosed.

(3) For the purposes of this paragraph a "third party" means a person other than—

(a) the director himself or a person connected with him or a body corporate controlled by him, or

(b) the company or any of its subsidiary undertakings.

PART 3
SUPPLEMENTARY PROVISIONS

General nature of obligations

6.— (1) This Schedule requires information to be given only so far as it is contained in the company's books and papers or the company has the right to obtain it from the persons concerned.

(2) For the purposes of this Schedule any information is treated as shown if it is capable of being readily ascertained from other information which is shown.

Provisions as to amounts to be shown

7.— (1) The following provisions apply with respect to the amounts to be shown under this Schedule.

(2) The amount in each case includes all relevant sums, whether paid by or receivable from the company, any of the company's subsidiary undertakings or any other person.

(3) References to amounts paid to or receivable by a person include amounts paid to or receivable by a person connected with him or a body corporate controlled by him (but not so as to require an amount to be counted twice).

(4) Except as otherwise provided, the amounts to be shown for any financial year are—

(a) the sums receivable in respect of that year (whenever paid), or

(b) in the case of sums not receivable in respect of a period, the sums paid during that year.

(5) Sums paid by way of expenses allowance that are charged to United Kingdom income tax after the end of the relevant financial year must be shown in a note to the first accounts in which it is practicable to show them and must be distinguished from the amounts to be shown apart from this provision.

(6) Where it is necessary to do so for the purpose of making any distinction required in complying with this Schedule, the directors may apportion payments between the matters in respect of which they have been paid or are receivable in such manner as they think appropriate.

Exclusion of sums liable to be accounted for to company etc

8.— (1) The amounts to be shown under this Schedule do not include any sums that are to be accounted for—

(a) to the company or any of its subsidiary undertakings, or

(b) by virtue of sections 219 and 222(3) of the 2006 Act (payments in connection with share transfers: duty to account) to persons who sold their shares as a result of the offer made.

(2) Where—

(a) any such sums are not shown in a note to the accounts for the relevant financial year on the ground that the person receiving them is liable to account for them, and

(b) the liability is afterwards wholly or partly released or is not enforced within a period of two years, those sums, to the extent to which the liability is released or not enforced, must be shown in a note to the first accounts in which it is practicable to show them and must be distinguished from the amounts to be shown apart from this provision.

Meaning of "remuneration"

9.— (1) In this Schedule "remuneration" of a director includes—

(a) salary, fees and bonuses, sums paid by way of expenses allowance (so far as they are chargeable to United Kingdom income tax), and

(b) subject to sub-paragraph (2), the estimated money value of any other benefits received by the director otherwise than in cash.

(2) The expression does not include—

(a) the value of any share options granted to the director or the amount of any gains made on the exercise of any such options,

(b) any company contributions paid, or treated as paid, under any pension scheme or any benefits to which the director is entitled under any such scheme, or

(c) any money or other assets paid to or received or receivable by the director under any long term incentive scheme.

Meaning of "highest paid director"

10. In this Schedule, "the highest paid director" means the director to whom is attributable the greatest part of the total of the aggregates shown under paragraph 1(1)(a), (b) and (c).

Meaning of "long term incentive scheme"

11.— (1) In this Schedule "long term incentive scheme" means an agreement or arrangement—

(a) under which money or other assets may become receivable by a director, and

(b) which includes one or more qualifying conditions with respect to service or performance which cannot be fulfilled within a single financial year.

(2) For this purpose the following must be disregarded—

(a) bonuses the amount of which falls to be determined by reference to service or performance within a single financial year;

(b) compensation for loss of office, payments for breach of contract and other termination payments; and

(c) retirement benefits.

Meaning of "shares" and "share option" and related expressions

12. In this Schedule—

(a) "shares" means shares (whether allotted or not) in the company, or any undertaking which is a group undertaking in relation to the company, and includes a share warrant as defined by section 779(1) of the 2006 Act; and

(b) "share option" means a right to acquire shares.

Meaning of "pension scheme" and related expressions

13.— (1) In this Schedule—

"pension scheme" means a retirement benefits scheme as defined by section 611 of the Income and Corporation Taxes Act 1988; and

"retirement benefits" has the meaning given by section 612(1) of that Act.

(2) In this Schedule "accrued pension" and "accrued lump sum", in relation to any pension scheme and any director, mean respectively the amount of the annual pension, and the amount of the lump sum, which would be payable under the scheme on his attaining normal pension age if—

(a) he had left the company's service at the end of the financial year,

(b) there was no increase in the general level of prices in the United Kingdom during the period beginning with the end of that year and ending with his attaining that age,

(c) no question arose of any commutation of the pension or inverse commutation of the lump sum, and

(d) any amounts attributable to voluntary contributions paid by the director to the scheme, and any money purchase benefits which would be payable under the scheme, were disregarded.

(3) In this Schedule, "company contributions", in relation to a pension scheme and a director, means any payments (including insurance premiums) made, or treated as made, to the scheme in respect of the director by a person other than the director.

(4) In this Schedule, in relation to a director—

"defined benefits" means retirement benefits payable under a pension scheme that are not money purchase benefits;

"defined benefit scheme" means a pension scheme that is not a money purchase scheme;

"money purchase benefits" means retirement benefits payable under a pension scheme the rate or amount of which is calculated by reference to payments made, or treated as made, by the director or by any other person in respect of the director and which are not average salary benefits; and

"money purchase scheme" means a pension scheme under which all of the benefits that may become payable to or in respect of the director are money purchase benefits.

(5) In this Schedule, "normal pension age", in relation to any pension scheme and any director, means the age at which the director will first become entitled to receive a full pension on retirement of an amount determined without reduction to take account of its payment before a later age (but disregarding any entitlement to pension upon retirement in the event of illness, incapacity or redundancy).

(6) Where a pension scheme provides for any benefits that may become payable to or in respect of any director to be whichever are the greater of—

(a) money purchase benefits as determined by or under the scheme; and

(b) defined benefits as so determined,

the company may assume for the purposes of this paragraph that those benefits will be money purchase benefits, or defined benefits, according to whichever appears more likely at the end of the financial year.

(7) For the purpose of determining whether a pension scheme is a money purchase or defined benefit scheme, any death in service benefits provided for by the scheme are to be disregarded.

References to subsidiary undertakings

14.— (1) Any reference in this Schedule to a subsidiary undertaking of the company, in relation to a person who is or was, while a director of the company, a director also, by virtue of the company's nomination (direct or indirect) of any other undertaking, includes that undertaking, whether or not it is or was in fact a subsidiary undertaking of the company.

(2) Any reference to a subsidiary undertaking of the company—

(a) for the purposes of paragraph 1 (remuneration etc) is to an undertaking which is a subsidiary undertaking at the time the services were rendered, and

(b) for the purposes of paragraph 4 (compensation for loss of office) is to a subsidiary undertaking immediately before the loss of office as director.

Other minor definitions

15.— (1) In this Schedule—

"net value", in relation to any assets received or receivable by a director, means value after deducting any money paid or other value given by the director in respect of those assets;

"qualifying services", in relation to any person, means his services as a director of the company, and his services while director of the company—

(a) as director of any of its subsidiary undertakings; or

(b) otherwise in connection with the management of the affairs of the company or any of its subsidiary undertakings.

(2) References in this Schedule to a person being "connected" with a director, and to a director "controlling" a body corporate, are to be construed in accordance with sections 252 to 255 of the 2006 Act.

(3) For the purposes of this Schedule, remuneration paid or receivable or share options granted in respect of a person's accepting office as a director are treated as emoluments paid or receivable or share options granted in respect of his services as a director.

SCHEDULE 6

Regulation 9

COMPANIES ACT GROUP ACCOUNTS

PART 1

GENERAL RULES

General rules

1.— (1) Group accounts must comply so far as practicable with the provisions of Schedule 1 to these Regulations as if the undertakings included in the consolidation ("the group") were a single company (see Parts 2 and 3 of this Schedule for modifications for banking and insurance groups).

(2) Where the parent company is treated as an investment company for the purposes of Part 5 of Schedule 1 (special provisions for investment companies) the group must be similarly treated.

2.— (1) The consolidated balance sheet and profit and loss account must incorporate in full the information contained in the individual accounts of the undertakings included in the consolidation, subject to the adjustments authorised or required by the following provisions of this Schedule and to such other adjustments (if any) as may be appropriate in accordance with generally accepted accounting principles or practice.

(2) If the financial year of a subsidiary undertaking included in the consolidation does not end with that of the parent company, the group accounts must be made up—

(a) from the accounts of the subsidiary undertaking for its financial year last ending before the end of the parent company's financial year, provided that year ended no more than three months before that of the parent company, or

(b) from interim accounts prepared by the subsidiary undertaking as at the end of the parent company's financial year.

3.— (1) Where assets and liabilities to be included in the group accounts have been valued or otherwise determined by undertakings according to accounting rules differing from those used for the group accounts, the values or amounts must be adjusted so as to accord with the rules used for the group accounts.

(2) If it appears to the directors of the parent company that there are special reasons for departing from sub-paragraph (1) they may do so, but particulars of any such departure, the reasons for it and its effect must be given in a note to the accounts.

(3) The adjustments referred to in this paragraph need not be made if they are not material for the purpose of giving a true and fair view.

4. Any differences of accounting rules as between a parent company's individual accounts for a financial year and its group accounts must be disclosed in a note to the latter accounts and the reasons for the difference given.

5. Amounts that in the particular context of any provision of this Schedule are not material may be disregarded for the purposes of that provision.

Elimination of group transactions

6.— (1) Debts and claims between undertakings included in the consolidation, and income and expenditure relating to transactions between such undertakings, must be eliminated in preparing the group accounts.

(2) Where profits and losses resulting from transactions between undertakings included in the consolidation are included in the book value of assets, they must be eliminated in preparing the group accounts.

(3) The elimination required by sub-paragraph (2) may be effected in proportion to the group's interest in the shares of the undertakings.

(4) Sub-paragraphs (1) and (2) need not be complied with if the amounts concerned are not material for the purpose of giving a true and fair view.

Acquisition and merger accounting

7.— (1) The following provisions apply where an undertaking becomes a subsidiary undertaking of the parent company.

(2) That event is referred to in those provisions as an "acquisition", and references to the "undertaking acquired" are to be construed accordingly.

8. An acquisition must be accounted for by the acquisition method of accounting unless the conditions for accounting for it as a merger are met and the merger method of accounting is adopted.

9.— (1) The acquisition method of accounting is as follows.

(2) The identifiable assets and liabilities of the undertaking acquired must be included in the consolidated balance sheet at their fair values as at the date of acquisition.

(3) The income and expenditure of the undertaking acquired must be brought into the group accounts only as from the date of the acquisition.

(4) There must be set off against the acquisition cost of the interest in the shares of the undertaking held by the parent company and its subsidiary undertakings the interest of the parent company and its subsidiary undertakings in the adjusted capital and reserves of the undertaking acquired.

(5) The resulting amount if positive must be treated as goodwill, and if negative as a negative consolidation difference.

10.— (1) The conditions for accounting for an acquisition as a merger are—

(a) that at least 90% of the nominal value of the relevant shares in the undertaking acquired (excluding any shares in the undertaking held as treasury shares) is held by or on behalf of the parent company and its subsidiary undertakings,

(b) that the proportion referred to in paragraph (a) was attained pursuant to an arrangement providing for the issue of equity shares by the parent company or one or more of its subsidiary undertakings,

(c) that the fair value of any consideration other than the issue of equity shares given pursuant to the arrangement by the parent company and its subsidiary undertakings did not exceed 10% of the nominal value of the equity shares issued, and

(d) that adoption of the merger method of accounting accords with generally accepted accounting principles or practice.

(2) The reference in sub-paragraph (1)(a) to the "relevant shares" in an undertaking acquired is to those carrying unrestricted rights to participate both in distributions and in the assets of the undertaking upon liquidation.

11.— (1) The merger method of accounting is as follows.

(2) The assets and liabilities of the undertaking acquired must be brought into the group accounts at the figures at which they stand in the undertaking's accounts, subject to any adjustment authorised or required by this Schedule.

(3) The income and expenditure of the undertaking acquired must be included in the group accounts for the entire financial year, including the period before the acquisition.

(4) The group accounts must show corresponding amounts relating to the previous financial year as if the undertaking acquired had been included in the consolidation throughout that year.

(5) There must be set off against the aggregate of—

(a) the appropriate amount in respect of qualifying shares issued by the parent company or its subsidiary undertakings in consideration for the acquisition of shares in the undertaking acquired, and

(b) the fair value of any other consideration for the acquisition of shares in the undertaking acquired, determined as at the date when those shares were acquired,

the nominal value of the issued share capital of the undertaking acquired held by the parent company and its subsidiary undertakings.

(6) The resulting amount must be shown as an adjustment to the consolidated reserves.

(7) In sub-paragraph (5)(a) "qualifying shares" means—

(a) shares in relation to which any of the following provisions applies (merger relief), and in respect of which the appropriate amount is the nominal value—

(i) section 131 of the Companies Act 1985,

(ii) Article 141 of the Companies (Northern Ireland) Order 1986, or

(iii) section 612 of the 2006 Act, or

(b) shares in relation to which any of the following provisions applies (group reconstruction relief),

and in respect of which the appropriate amount is the nominal value together with any minimum premium value within the meaning of that section—

(i) section 132 of the Companies Act 1985,

(ii) Article 142 of the Companies (Northern Ireland) Order 1986, or

(iii) section 611 of the 2006 Act.

12.— (1) Where a group is acquired, paragraphs 9 to 11 apply with the following adaptations.

(2) References to shares of the undertaking acquired are to be construed as references to shares of the parent undertaking of the group.

(3) Other references to the undertaking acquired are to be construed as references to the group; and references to the assets and liabilities, income and expenditure and capital and reserves of the undertaking acquired must be construed as references to the assets and liabilities, income and expenditure and capital and reserves of the group after making the set-offs and other adjustments required by this Schedule in the case of group accounts.

13.— (1) The following information with respect to acquisitions taking place in the financial year must be given in a note to the accounts.

(2) There must be stated—

(a) the name of the undertaking acquired or, where a group was acquired, the name of the parent undertaking of that group, and

(b) whether the acquisition has been accounted for by the acquisition or the merger method of accounting;

and in relation to an acquisition which significantly affects the figures shown in the group accounts, the following further information must be given.

(3) The composition and fair value of the consideration for the acquisition given by the parent company and its subsidiary undertakings must be stated.

(4) Where the acquisition method of accounting has been adopted, the book values immediately prior to the acquisition, and the fair values at the date of acquisition, of each class of assets and liabilities of the undertaking or group acquired must be stated in tabular form, including a statement of the amount of any goodwill or negative consolidation difference arising on the acquisition, together with an explanation of any significant adjustments made.

(5) In ascertaining for the purposes of sub-paragraph (4) the profit or loss of a group, the book values and fair values of assets and liabilities of a group or the amount of the assets and liabilities of a group, the set-offs and other adjustments required by this Schedule in the case of group accounts must be made.

14.— (1) There must also be stated in a note to the accounts the cumulative amount of goodwill resulting from acquisitions in that and earlier financial years which has been written off otherwise than in the consolidated profit and loss account for that or any earlier financial year.

(2) That figure must be shown net of any goodwill attributable to subsidiary undertakings or businesses disposed of prior to the balance sheet date.

15. Where during the financial year there has been a disposal of an undertaking or group which significantly affects the figure shown in the group accounts, there must be stated in a note to the accounts—

(a) the name of that undertaking or, as the case may be, of the parent undertaking of that group, and

(b) the extent to which the profit or loss shown in the group accounts is attributable to profit or loss of that undertaking or group.

16. The information required by paragraph 13, 14 or 15 need not be disclosed with respect to an undertaking which—

(a) is established under the law of a country outside the United Kingdom, or

(b) carries on business outside the United Kingdom,

if in the opinion of the directors of the parent company the disclosure would be seriously prejudicial to the business of that undertaking or to the business of the parent company or any of its subsidiary undertakings and the Secretary of State agrees that the information should not be disclosed.

Minority interests

17.— (1) The formats set out in Schedule 1 to these Regulations have effect in relation to group accounts with the following additions.

(2) In the balance sheet formats there must be shown, as a separate item and under an appropriate heading, the amount of capital and reserves attributable to shares in subsidiary undertakings included in the consolidation held by or on behalf of persons other than the parent company and its subsidiary undertakings.

(3) In the profit and loss account formats there must be shown, as a separate item and under an appropriate heading—

(a) the amount of any profit or loss on ordinary activities, and

(b) the amount of any profit or loss on extraordinary activities,

attributable to shares in subsidiary undertakings included in the consolidation held by or on behalf of persons other than the parent company and its subsidiary undertakings.

(4) For the purposes of paragraph 4(1) and (2) of Schedule 1 (power to adapt or combine items)—

(a) the additional item required by sub-paragraph (2) above is treated as one to which a letter is assigned, and

(b) the additional items required by sub-paragraph (3)(a) and (b) above are treated as ones to which an Arabic number is assigned.

Joint ventures

18.— (1) Where an undertaking included in the consolidation manages another undertaking jointly with one or more undertakings not included in the consolidation, that other undertaking ("the joint venture") may, if it is not—

(a) a body corporate, or

(b) a subsidiary undertaking of the parent company,

be dealt with in the group accounts by the method of proportional consolidation.

(2) The provisions of this Schedule relating to the preparation of consolidated accounts apply, with any necessary modifications, to proportional consolidation under this paragraph.

Associated undertakings

19.— (1) An "associated undertaking" means an undertaking in which an undertaking included in the consolidation has a participating interest and over whose operating and financial policy it exercises a significant influence, and which is not—

(a) a subsidiary undertaking of the parent company, or

(b) a joint venture dealt with in accordance with paragraph 18.

(2) Where an undertaking holds 20% or more of the voting rights in another undertaking, it is presumed to exercise such an influence over it unless the contrary is shown.

(3) The voting rights in an undertaking means the rights conferred on shareholders in respect of their shares or, in the case of an undertaking not having a share capital, on members, to vote at general meetings of the undertaking on all, or substantially all, matters.

(4) The provisions of paragraphs 5 to 11 of Schedule 7 to the 2006 Act (parent and subsidiary undertakings: rights to be taken into account and attribution of rights) apply in determining for the purposes of this paragraph whether an undertaking holds 20% or more of the voting rights in another undertaking.

20.— (1) The formats set out in Schedule 1 to these Regulations have effect in relation to group accounts with the following modifications.

(2) In the balance sheet formats replace the items headed "Participating interests", that is—

(a) in format 1, item B.III.3, and

(b) in format 2, item B.III.3 under the heading "ASSETS",

by two items: "Interests in associated undertakings" and "Other participating interests".

(3) In the profit and loss account formats replace the items headed "Income from participating interests", that is—

(a) in format 1, item 8,
(b) in format 2, item 10,
(c) in format 3, item B.4, and
(d) in format 4, item B.6,

by two items: "Income from interests in associated undertakings" and "Income from other participating interests".

21.— (1) The interest of an undertaking in an associated undertaking, and the amount of profit or loss attributable to such an interest, must be shown by the equity method of accounting (including dealing with any goodwill arising in accordance with paragraphs 17 to 20 and 22 of Schedule 1 to these Regulations).

(2) Where the associated undertaking is itself a parent undertaking, the net assets and profits or losses to be taken into account are those of the parent and its subsidiary undertakings (after making any consolidation adjustments).

(3) The equity method of accounting need not be applied if the amounts in question are not material for the purpose of giving a true and fair view.

Related party transactions

22. Paragraph 72 of Schedule 1 to these Regulations applies to transactions which the parent company, or other undertakings included in the consolidation, have entered into with related parties, unless they are intra group transactions.

PART 2
MODIFICATIONS FOR BANKING GROUPS

General application of provisions applicable to individual accounts

23. In its application to banking groups, Part 1 of this Schedule has effect with the following modifications.

24. In paragraph 1 of this Schedule—
(a) the reference in sub-paragraph (1) to the provisions of Schedule 1 to these Regulations is to be construed as a reference to the provisions of Schedule 2 to these Regulations, and
(b) sub-paragraph (2) is to be omitted.

Minority interests and associated undertakings

25.— (1) This paragraph adapts paragraphs 17 and 20 (which require items in respect of "Minority interests" and associated undertakings to be added to the formats set out in Schedule 1 to these Regulations) to the formats prescribed by Schedule 2 to these Regulations.

(2) In paragraph 17—
(a) in sub-paragraph (1), for the reference to Schedule 1 to these Regulations, substitute a reference to Schedule 2, and
(b) paragraph 17(4) is not to apply, but for the purposes of paragraph 5(1) of Part I of Schedule 2 to these Regulations (power to combine items) the additional items required by the foregoing provisions of this paragraph are to be treated as items to which a letter is assigned.

(3) Paragraph 20(2) is to apply with respect to a balance sheet prepared under Schedule 2 to these Regulations as if it required assets item 7 (participating interests) in the balance sheet format to be replaced by the two replacement items referred to in that paragraph.

(4) Paragraph 20(3) is not to apply, but the following items in the profit and loss account formats—
(a) format 1 item 3(b) (income from participating interests),
(b) format 2 item B2(b) (income from participating interests),

are replaced by the following—
(i) "Income from participating interests other than associated undertakings", to be shown at position 3(b) in format 1 and position B2(b) in format 2, and
(ii) "Income from associated undertakings", to be shown at an appropriate position.

26. In paragraph 21(1) of this Schedule, for the references to paragraphs 17 to 20 and 22 of Schedule 1 to these Regulations substitute references to paragraphs 23 to 26 and 28 of Schedule 2 to these Regulations.

Related party transactions

27. In paragraph 22 of this Schedule, for the reference to paragraph 72 of Schedule 1 to these Regulations substitute a reference to paragraph 92 of Schedule 2 to these Regulations.

Foreign currency translation

28. Any difference between—

(a) the amount included in the consolidated accounts for the previous financial year with respect to any undertaking included in the consolidation or the group's interest in any associated undertaking, together with the amount of any transactions undertaken to cover any such interest, and

(b) the opening amount for the financial year in respect of those undertakings and in respect of any such transactions, arising as a result of the application of paragraph 50 of Schedule 2 to these Regulations may be credited to (where (a) is less than (b)), or deducted from (where (a) is greater than (b)), (as the case may be) consolidated reserves.

29. Any income and expenditure of undertakings included in the consolidation and associated undertakings in a foreign currency may be translated for the purposes of the consolidated accounts at the average rates of exchange prevailing during the financial year.

Information as to undertaking in which shares held as a result of financial assistance operation

30.— (1) The following provisions apply where the parent company of a banking group has a subsidiary undertaking which—

(a) is a credit institution of which shares are held as a result of a financial assistance operation with a view to its reorganisation or rescue, and

(b) is excluded from consolidation under section 405(3)(c) of the 2006 Act (interest held with a view to resale).

(2) Information as to the nature and terms of the operations must be given in a note to the group accounts, and there must be appended to the copy of the group accounts delivered to the registrar in accordance with section 441 of the 2006 Act a copy of the undertaking's latest individual accounts and, if it is a parent undertaking, its latest group accounts.

If the accounts appended are required by law to be audited, a copy of the auditor's report must also be appended.

(3) Any requirement of Part 35 of the 2006 Act as to the delivery to the registrar of a certified translation into English must be met in relation to any document required to be appended by sub-paragraph (2).

(4) The above requirements are subject to the following qualifications—

(a) an undertaking is not required to prepare for the purposes of this paragraph accounts which would not otherwise be prepared, and if no accounts satisfying the above requirements are prepared none need be appended;

(b) the accounts of an undertaking need not be appended if they would not otherwise be required to be published, or made available for public inspection, anywhere in the world, but in that case the reason for not appending the accounts must be stated in a note to the consolidated accounts.

(5) Where a copy of an undertaking's accounts is required to be appended to the copy of the group accounts delivered to the registrar, that fact must be stated in a note to the group accounts.

PART 3
MODIFICATIONS FOR INSURANCE GROUPS

General application of provisions applicable to individual accounts

31. In its application to insurance groups, Part 1 of this Schedule has effect with the following modifications.

32. In paragraph 1 of this Schedule—
   (a) the reference in sub-paragraph (1) to the provisions of Schedule 1 to these Regulations is to be construed as a reference to the provisions of Schedule 3 to these Regulations, and
   (b) sub-paragraph (2) is to be omitted.

Financial years of subsidiary undertakings

33. In paragraph 2(2)(a), for "three months" substitute "six months".

Assets and liabilities to be included in group accounts

34. In paragraph 3, after sub-paragraph (1) insert—
"(1A)Sub-paragraph (1) is not to apply to those liabilities items the valuation of which by the undertakings included in a consolidation is based on the application of provisions applying only to insurance undertakings, nor to those assets items changes in the values of which also affect or establish policyholders' rights.
(1B) Where sub-paragraph (1A) applies, that fact must be disclosed in the notes to the consolidated accounts.".

Elimination of group transactions

35. For sub-paragraph (4) of paragraph 6 substitute—
"(4) Sub-paragraphs (1) and (2) need not be complied with—
   (a) where a transaction has been concluded according to normal market conditions and a policyholder has rights in respect of the transaction, or
   (b) if the amounts concerned are not material for the purpose of giving a true and fair view.
(5) Where advantage is taken of sub-paragraph (4)(a) that fact must be disclosed in the notes to the accounts, and where the transaction in question has a material effect on the assets, liabilities, financial position and profit or loss of all the undertakings included in the consolidation that fact must also be so disclosed.".

Minority interests

36. In paragraph 17—
   (a) in sub-paragraph (1), for the reference to Schedule 1 to these Regulations, substitute a reference to Schedule 3, and
   (b) for sub-paragraph (4) substitute—
   "(4) Paragraph 3(1) of Schedule 3 to these Regulations (power to combine items) does not apply in relation to the additional items required by the above provisions of this paragraph.".

Associated undertakings

37. In paragraph 20—
   (a) in sub-paragraph (1), for the reference to Schedule 1 to these Regulations substitute a reference to Schedule 3 to these Regulations, and
   (b) for sub-paragraphs (2) and (3) substitute—
   "(2) In the balance sheet format, replace asset item CII.3 (participating interests) with two items, "Interests in associated undertakings" and "Other participating interests".
   (3) In the profit and loss account format, replace items II.2.(a) and III.3.(a) (income from participating interests, with a separate indication of that derived from group undertakings) with—

(a) "Income from participating interests other than associated undertakings, with a separate indication of that derived from group undertakings", to be shown as items II.2.(a) and III.3.(a), and

(b) "Income from associated undertakings", to be shown as items II.2.(aa) and III.3.(aa).".

38. In paragraph 21(1) of this Schedule, for the references to paragraphs 17 to 20 and 22 of Schedule 1 to these Regulations, substitute references to paragraphs 36 to 39 and 42 of Schedule 3 to these Regulations.

Related party transactions

39. In paragraph 22 of this Schedule, for the reference to paragraph 72 of Schedule 1 to these Regulations substitute a reference to paragraph 90 of Schedule 3 to these Regulations.

Modifications of Schedule 3 to these Regulations for purposes of paragraph 31

40.— (1) For the purposes of paragraph 31 of this Schedule, Schedule 3 to these Regulations is to be modified as follows.

(2) The information required by paragraph 11 (additional items) need not be given.

(3) In the case of general business, investment income, expenses and charges may be disclosed in the non-technical account rather than in the technical account.

(4) In the case of subsidiary undertakings which are not authorised to carry on long-term business in the United Kingdom, notes (8) and (9) to the profit and loss account format have effect as if references to investment income, expenses and charges arising in the long-term fund or to investments attributed to the long-term fund were references to investment income, expenses and charges or (as the case may be) investments relating to long-term business.

(5) In the case of subsidiary undertakings which do not have a head office in the United Kingdom, the computation required by paragraph 52 must be made annually by an actuary or other specialist in the field on the basis of recognised actuarial methods.

(6) The information required by paragraphs 85 to 88 need not be shown.

SCHEDULE 7

Regulation 10

MATTERS TO BE DEALT WITH IN DIRECTORS' REPORT

PART 1

MATTERS OF A GENERAL NATURE

Introduction

1. In addition to the information required by section 416 of the 2006 Act, the directors' report must contain the following information.

Asset values

2.— (1) If, in the case of such of the fixed assets of the company as consist in interests in land, their market value (as at the end of the financial year) differs substantially from the amount at which they are included in the balance sheet, and the difference is, in the directors' opinion, of such significance as to require that the attention of members of the company or of holders of its debentures should be drawn to it, the report must indicate the difference with such degree of precision as is practicable.

(2) In relation to a group directors' report sub-paragraph (1) has effect as if the reference to the fixed assets of the company was a reference to the fixed assets of the company and of its subsidiary undertakings included in the consolidation.

Political donations and expenditure

3.— (1) If—

(a) the company (not being the wholly-owned subsidiary of a company incorporated in the United Kingdom) has in the financial year—
   (i) made any political donation to any political party or other political organisation,
   (ii) made any political donation to any independent election candidate, or
   (iii) incurred any political expenditure, and
(b) the amount of the donation or expenditure, or (as the case may be) the aggregate amount of all donations and expenditure falling within paragraph (a), exceeded £2000, the directors' report for the year must contain the following particulars.

(2) Those particulars are—
(a) as respects donations falling within sub-paragraph (1)(a)(i) or (ii)—
   (i) the name of each political party, other political organisation or independent election candidate to whom any such donation has been made, and
   (ii) the total amount given to that party, organisation or candidate by way of such donations in the financial year; and
(b) as respects expenditure falling within sub-paragraph (1)(a)(iii), the total amount incurred by way of such expenditure in the financial year.

(3) If—
(a) at the end of the financial year the company has subsidiaries which have, in that year, made any donations or incurred any such expenditure as is mentioned in sub-paragraph (1)(a), and
(b) it is not itself the wholly-owned subsidiary of a company incorporated in the United Kingdom,

the directors' report for the year is not, by virtue of sub-paragraph (1), required to contain the particulars specified in sub-paragraph (2).

But, if the total amount of any such donations or expenditure (or both) made or incurred in that year by the company and the subsidiaries between them exceeds £2000, the directors' report for the year must contain those particulars in relation to each body by whom any such donation or expenditure has been made or incurred.

(4) Any expression used in this paragraph which is also used in Part 14 of the 2006 Act (control of political donations and expenditure) has the same meaning as in that Part.

4.— (1) If the company (not being the wholly-owned subsidiary of a company incorporated in the United Kingdom) has in the financial year made any contribution to a non-EU political party, the directors' report for the year must contain—
(a) a statement of the amount of the contribution, or
(b) (if it has made two or more such contributions in the year) a statement of the total amount of the contributions.

(2) If—
(a) at the end of the financial year the company has subsidiaries which have, in that year, made any such contributions as are mentioned in sub-paragraph (1), and
(b) it is not itself the wholly-owned subsidiary of a company incorporated in the United Kingdom,

the directors' report for the year is not, by virtue of sub-paragraph (1), required to contain any such statement as is there mentioned, but it must instead contain a statement of the total amount of the contributions made in the year by the company and the subsidiaries between them.

(3) In this paragraph, "contribution", in relation to an organisation, means—
(a) any gift of money to the organisation (whether made directly or indirectly);
(b) any subscription or other fee paid for affiliation to, or membership of, the organisation; or
(c) any money spent (otherwise than by the organisation or a person acting on its behalf) in paying any expenses incurred directly or indirectly by the organisation.

(4) In this paragraph, "non-EU political party" means any political party which carries on, or proposes to carry on, its activities wholly outside the member States.

Charitable donations

5.— (1) If—

(a) the company (not being the wholly-owned subsidiary of a company incorporated in the United Kingdom) has in the financial year given money for charitable purposes, and

(b) the money given exceeded £2000 in amount,

the directors' report for the year must contain, in the case of each of the purposes for which money has been given, a statement of the amount of money given for that purpose.

(2) If—

(a) at the end of the financial year the company has subsidiaries which have, in that year, given money for charitable purposes, and

(b) it is not itself the wholly owned subsidiary of a company incorporated in the United Kingdom, sub-paragraph (1) does not apply to the company.

But, if the amount given in that year for charitable purposes by the company and the subsidiaries between them exceeds £2000, the directors' report for the year must contain, in the case of each of the purposes for which money has been given by the company and the subsidiaries between them, a statement of the amount of money given for that purpose.

(3) Money given for charitable purposes to a person who, when it was given, was ordinarily resident outside the United Kingdom is to be left out of account for the purposes of this paragraph.

(4) For the purposes of this paragraph, "charitable purposes" means purposes which are exclusively charitable, and as respects Scotland a purpose is charitable if it is listed in section 7(2) of the Charities and Trustee Investment (Scotland) Act 2005.

Financial instruments

6.— (1) In relation to the use of financial instruments by a company, the directors' report must contain an indication of—

(a) the financial risk management objectives and policies of the company, including the policy for hedging each major type of forecasted transaction for which hedge accounting is used, and

(b) the exposure of the company to price risk, credit risk, liquidity risk and cash flow risk,

unless such information is not material for the assessment of the assets, liabilities, financial position and profit or loss of the company.

(2) In relation to a group directors' report sub-paragraph (1) has effect as if the references to the company were references to the company and its subsidiary undertakings included in the consolidation.

(3) In sub-paragraph (1) the expressions "hedge accounting", "price risk", "credit risk", "liquidity risk" and "cash flow risk" have the same meaning as they have in Council Directive 78/660/EEC on the annual accounts of certain types of companies, and in Council Directive 83/349/EEC on consolidated accounts.

Miscellaneous

7.— (1) The directors' report must contain—

(a) particulars of any important events affecting the company which have occurred since the end of the financial year,

(b) an indication of likely future developments in the business of the company,

(c) an indication of the activities (if any) of the company in the field of research and development, and

(d) (unless the company is an unlimited company) an indication of the existence of branches (as defined in section 1046(3) of the 2006 Act) of the company outside the United Kingdom.

(2) In relation to a group directors' report paragraphs (a), (b) and (c) of sub-paragraph (1) have effect as if the references to the company were references to the company and its subsidiary undertakings included in the consolidation.

PART 2
DISCLOSURE REQUIRED BY COMPANY ACQUIRING ITS OWN SHARES ETC

8. This Part of this Schedule applies where shares in a company—
   (a) are purchased by the company or are acquired by it by forfeiture or surrender in lieu of forfeiture, or in pursuance of any of the following provisions (acquisition of own shares by company limited by shares)—
      (i) section 143(3) of the Companies Act 1985,
      (ii) Article 153(3) of the Companies (Northern Ireland) Order 1986, or
      (iii) section 659 of the 2006 Act, or
   (b) are acquired by another person in circumstances where paragraph (c) or (d) of any of the following provisions applies (acquisition by company's nominee, or by another with company financial assistance, the company having a beneficial interest)—
      (i) section 146(1) of the Companies Act 1985,
      (ii) Article 156(1) of the Companies (Northern Ireland) Order 1986, or
      (iii) section 662(1) of the 2006 Act applies, or
   (c) are made subject to a lien or other charge taken (whether expressly or otherwise) by the company and permitted by any of the following provisions (exceptions from general rule against a company having a lien or charge on its own shares)—
      (i) section 150(2) or (4) of the Companies Act 1985,
      (ii) Article 160(2) or (4) of the Companies (Northern Ireland) Order 1986, or
      (iii) section 670(2) or (4) of the 2006 Act.

9. The directors' report for a financial year must state—
   (a) the number and nominal value of the shares so purchased, the aggregate amount of the consideration paid by the company for such shares and the reasons for their purchase;
   (b) the number and nominal value of the shares so acquired by the company, acquired by another person in such circumstances and so charged respectively during the financial year;
   (c) the maximum number and nominal value of shares which, having been so acquired by the company, acquired by another person in such circumstances or so charged (whether or not during that year) are held at any time by the company or that other person during that year;
   (d) the number and nominal value of the shares so acquired by the company, acquired by another person in such circumstances or so charged (whether or not during that year) which are disposed of by the company or that other person or cancelled by the company during that year;
   (e) where the number and nominal value of the shares of any particular description are stated in pursuance of any of the preceding sub-paragraphs, the percentage of the called-up share capital which shares of that description represent;
   (f) where any of the shares have been so charged the amount of the charge in each case; and
   (g) where any of the shares have been disposed of by the company or the person who acquired them in such circumstances for money or money's worth the amount or value of the consideration in each case.

PART 3
DISCLOSURE CONCERNING EMPLOYMENT ETC OF DISABLED PERSONS

10.— (1) This Part of this Schedule applies to the directors' report where the average number of persons employed by the company in each week during the financial year exceeded 250.

(2) That average number is the quotient derived by dividing, by the number of weeks in the financial year, the number derived by ascertaining, in relation to each of those weeks, the

number of persons who, under contracts of service, were employed in the week (whether throughout it or not) by the company, and adding up the numbers ascertained.

(3) The directors' report must in that case contain a statement describing such policy as the company has applied during the financial year—

(a) for giving full and fair consideration to applications for employment by the company made by disabled persons, having regard to their particular aptitudes and abilities,

(b) for continuing the employment of, and for arranging appropriate training for, employees of the company who have become disabled persons during the period when they were employed by the company, and

(c) otherwise for the training, career development and promotion of disabled persons employed by the company.

(4) In this Part—

(a) "employment" means employment other than employment to work wholly or mainly outside the United Kingdom, and "employed" and "employee" are to be construed accordingly; and

(b) "disabled person" means the same as in the Disability Discrimination Act 1995.

PART 4
EMPLOYEE INVOLVEMENT

11.— (1) This Part of this Schedule applies to the directors' report where the average number of persons employed by the company in each week during the financial year exceeded 250.

(2) That average number is the quotient derived by dividing, by the number of weeks in the financial year, the number derived by ascertaining, in relation to each of those weeks, the number of persons who, under contracts of service, were employed in the week (whether throughout it or not) by the company, and adding up the numbers ascertained.

(3) The directors' report must in that case contain a statement describing the action that has been taken during the financial year to introduce, maintain or develop arrangements aimed at—

(a) providing employees systematically with information on matters of concern to them as employees,

(b) consulting employees or their representatives on a regular basis so that the views of employees can be taken into account in making decisions which are likely to affect their interests,

(c) encouraging the involvement of employees in the company's performance through an employees' share scheme or by some other means,

(d) achieving a common awareness on the part of all employees of the financial and economic factors affecting the performance of the company.

(4) In sub-paragraph (3) "employee" does not include a person employed to work wholly or mainly outside the United Kingdom; and for the purposes of sub-paragraph (2) no regard is to be had to such a person.

PART 5
POLICY AND PRACTICE ON PAYMENT OF CREDITORS

12.— (1) This Part of this Schedule applies to the directors' report for a financial year if—

(a) the company was at any time within the year a public company, or

(b) the company did not qualify as small or medium-sized in relation to the year by virtue of section 382 or 465 of the 2006 Act and was at any time within the year a member of a group of which the parent company was a public company.

(2) The report must state, with respect to the next following financial year—

(a) whether in respect of some or all of its suppliers it is the company's policy to follow any code or standard on payment practice and, if so, the name of the code or standard and the place where information about, and copies of, the code or standard can be obtained,

(b) whether in respect of some or all of its suppliers it is the company's policy—

(i) to settle the terms of payment with those suppliers when agreeing the terms of each transaction,

(ii) to ensure that those suppliers are made aware of the terms of payment, and

(iii) to abide by the terms of payment,

(c) where the company's policy is not as mentioned in paragraph (a) or (b) in respect of some or all of its suppliers, what its policy is with respect to the payment of those suppliers;

and if the company's policy is different for different suppliers or classes of suppliers, the report must identify the suppliers to which the different policies apply.

In this sub-paragraph references to the company's suppliers are references to persons who are or may become its suppliers.

(3) The report must also state the number of days which bears to the number of days in the financial year the same proportion as X bears to Y where—

X = the aggregate of the amounts which were owed to trade creditors at the end of the year; and

Y = the aggregate of the amounts in which the company was invoiced by suppliers during the year.

(4) For the purposes of sub-paragraphs (2) and (3) a person is a supplier of the company at any time if—

(a) at that time, he is owed an amount in respect of goods or services supplied, and

(b) that amount would be included under the heading corresponding to item E.4 (trade creditors) in format 1 if—

(i) the company's accounts fell to be prepared as at that time,

(ii) those accounts were prepared in accordance with Schedule 1 to these Regulations, and

(iii) that format were adopted.

(5) For the purpose of sub-paragraph (3), the aggregate of the amounts which at the end of the financial year were owed to trade creditors is taken to be—

(a) where in the company's accounts format 1 of the balance sheet formats set out in Part 1 of Schedule 1 to these Regulations is adopted, the amount shown under the heading corresponding to item E.4 (trade creditors) in that format,

(b) where format 2 is adopted, the amount which, under the heading corresponding to item C4 (trade creditors) in that format, is shown as falling due within one year, and

(c) where the company's accounts are prepared in accordance with Schedule 2 or 3 to these Regulations or the company's accounts are IAS accounts, the amount which would be shown under the heading corresponding to item E.4 (trade creditors) in format 1 if the company's accounts were prepared in accordance with Schedule 1 and that format were adopted.

PART 6
DISCLOSURE REQUIRED BY CERTAIN PUBLICLY-TRADED COMPANIES

13.— (1) This Part of this Schedule applies to the directors' report for a financial year if the company had securities carrying voting rights admitted to trading on a regulated market at the end of that year.

(2) The report must contain detailed information, by reference to the end of that year, on the following matters—

(a) the structure of the company's capital, including in particular—

(i) the rights and obligations attaching to the shares or, as the case may be, to each class of shares in the company, and

(ii) where there are two or more such classes, the percentage of the total share capital represented by each class;

(b) any restrictions on the transfer of securities in the company, including in particular—

(i) limitations on the holding of securities, and

(ii) requirements to obtain the approval of the company, or of other holders of securities in the company, for a transfer of securities;

(c) in the case of each person with a significant direct or indirect holding of securities in the company, such details as are known to the company of—

(i) the identity of the person,

(ii) the size of the holding, and

(iii) the nature of the holding;

(d) in the case of each person who holds securities carrying special rights with regard to control of the company—

(i) the identity of the person, and

(ii) the nature of the rights;

(e) where—

(i) the company has an employees' share scheme, and

(ii) shares to which the scheme relates have rights with regard to control of the company that are not exercisable directly by the employees, how those rights are exercisable;

(f) any restrictions on voting rights, including in particular—

(i) limitations on voting rights of holders of a given percentage or number of votes,

(ii) deadlines for exercising voting rights, and

(iii) arrangements by which, with the company's co-operation, financial rights carried by securities are held by a person other than the holder of the securities;

(g) any agreements between holders of securities that are known to the company and may result in restrictions on the transfer of securities or on voting rights;

(h) any rules that the company has about—

(i) appointment and replacement of directors, or

(ii) amendment of the company's articles of association;

(i) the powers of the company's directors, including in particular any powers in relation to the issuing or buying back by the company of its shares;

(j) any significant agreements to which the company is a party that take effect, alter or terminate upon a change of control of the company following a takeover bid, and the effects of any such agreements;

(k) any agreements between the company and its directors or employees providing for compensation for loss of office or employment (whether through resignation, purported redundancy or otherwise) that occurs because of a takeover bid.

(3) For the purposes of sub-paragraph (2)(a) a company's capital includes any securities in the company that are not admitted to trading on a regulated market.

(4) For the purposes of sub-paragraph (2)(c) a person has an indirect holding of securities if—

(a) they are held on his behalf, or

(b) he is able to secure that rights carried by the securities are exercised in accordance with his wishes.

(5) Sub-paragraph (2)(j) does not apply to an agreement if—

(a) disclosure of the agreement would be seriously prejudicial to the company, and

(b) the company is not under any other obligation to disclose it.

(6) In this paragraph—

"securities" means shares or debentures;

"takeover bid" has the same meaning as in the Takeovers Directive;

"the Takeovers Directive" means Directive 2004/25/EC of the European Parliament and of the Council;

"voting rights" means rights to vote at general meetings of the company in question, including rights that arise only in certain circumstances.

14. The directors' report must also contain any necessary explanatory material with regard to information that is required to be included in the report by this Part.

SCHEDULE 8

Regulation 11

QUOTED COMPANIES: DIRECTORS' REMUNERATION REPORT

PART 1
INTRODUCTORY

1.— (1) In the directors' remuneration report for a financial year ("the relevant financial year") there must be shown the information specified in Parts 2 and 3.

(2) Information required to be shown in the report for or in respect of a particular person must be shown in the report in a manner that links the information to that person identified by name.

PART 2
INFORMATION NOT SUBJECT TO AUDIT

Consideration by the directors of matters relating to directors' remuneration

2.— (1) If a committee of the company's directors has considered matters relating to the directors' remuneration for the relevant financial year, the directors' remuneration report must—

(a) name each director who was a member of the committee at any time when the committee was considering any such matter;

(b) name any person who provided to the committee advice, or services, that materially assisted the committee in their consideration of any such matter;

(c) in the case of any person named under paragraph (b), who is not a director of the company, state—

(i) the nature of any other services that that person has provided to the company during the relevant financial year; and

(ii) whether that person was appointed by the committee.

(2) In sub-paragraph (1)(b) "person" includes (in particular) any director of the company who does not fall within sub-paragraph (1)(a).

Statement of company's policy on directors' remuneration

3.— (1) The directors' remuneration report must contain a statement of the company's policy on directors' remuneration for the following financial year and for financial years subsequent to that.

(2) The policy statement must include—

(a) for each director, a detailed summary of any performance conditions to which any entitlement of the director—

(i) to share options, or

(ii) under a long term incentive scheme,

is subject;

(b) an explanation as to why any such performance conditions were chosen;

(c) a summary of the methods to be used in assessing whether any such performance conditions are met and an explanation as to why those methods were chosen;

(d) if any such performance condition involves any comparison with factors external to the company—

(i) a summary of the factors to be used in making each such comparison, and

(ii) if any of the factors relates to the performance of another company, of two or more other companies or of an index on which the securities of a company or companies are listed, the identity of that company, of each of those companies or of the index;

(e) a description of, and an explanation for, any significant amendment proposed to be made to the terms and conditions of any entitlement of a director to share options or under a long term incentive scheme; and

(f) if any entitlement of a director to share options, or under a long term incentive scheme, is not subject to performance conditions, an explanation as to why that is the case.

(3) The policy statement must, in respect of each director's terms and conditions relating to remuneration, explain the relative importance of those elements which are, and those which are not, related to performance.

(4) The policy statement must summarise, and explain, the company's policy on—

(a) the duration of contracts with directors, and

(b) notice periods, and termination payments, under such contracts.

(5) In sub-paragraphs (2) and (3), references to a director are to any person who serves as a director of the company at any time in the period beginning with the end of the relevant financial year and ending with the date on which the directors' remuneration report is laid before the company in general meeting.

Statement of consideration of conditions elsewhere in company and group

4. The directors' remuneration report must contain a statement of how pay and employment conditions of employees of the company and of other undertakings within the same group as the company were taken into account when determining directors' remuneration for the relevant financial year.

Performance graph

5.— (1) The directors' remuneration report must—

(a) contain a line graph that shows for each of—

(i) a holding of shares of that class of the company's equity share capital whose listing, or admission to dealing, has resulted in the company falling within the definition of "quoted company", and

(ii) a hypothetical holding of shares made up of shares of the same kinds and number as those by reference to which a broad equity market index is calculated,

a line drawn by joining up points plotted to represent, for each of the financial years in the relevant period, the total shareholder return on that holding; and

(b) state the name of the index selected for the purposes of the graph and set out the reasons for selecting that index.

(2) For the purposes of sub-paragraphs (1) and (4), "relevant period" means the five financial years of which the last is the relevant financial year.

(3) Where the relevant financial year—

(a) is the company's second, third or fourth financial year, sub-paragraph (2) has effect with the substitution of "two", "three" or "four" (as the case may be) for "five"; and

(b) is the company's first financial year, "relevant period", for the purposes of sub-paragraphs (1) and (4), means the relevant financial year.

(4) For the purposes of sub-paragraph (1), the "total shareholder return" for a relevant period on a holding of shares must be calculated using a fair method that—

(a) takes as its starting point the percentage change over the period in the market price of the holding;

(b) involves making—

(i) the assumptions specified in sub-paragraph (5) as to reinvestment of income, and

(ii) the assumption specified in sub-paragraph (7) as to the funding of liabilities, and

(c) makes provision for any replacement of shares in the holding by shares of a different description;

and the same method must be used for each of the holdings mentioned in sub-paragraph (1).

(5) The assumptions as to reinvestment of income are—

(a) that any benefit in the form of shares of the same kind as those in the holding is added to the holding at the time the benefit becomes receivable; and

(b) that any benefit in cash, and an amount equal to the value of any benefit not in cash and not falling within paragraph (a), is applied at the time the benefit becomes receivable in the purchase at their market price of shares of the same kind as those in the holding and that the shares purchased are added to the holding at that time.

(6) In sub-paragraph (5) "benefit" means any benefit (including, in particular, any dividend) receivable in respect of any shares in the holding by the holder from the company of whose share capital the shares form part.

(7) The assumption as to the funding of liabilities is that, where the holder has a liability to the company of whose capital the shares in the holding form part, shares are sold from the holding—

(a) immediately before the time by which the liability is due to be satisfied, and

(b) in such numbers that, at the time of the sale, the market price of the shares sold equals the amount of the liability in respect of the shares in the holding that are not being sold.

(8) In sub-paragraph (7) "liability" means a liability arising in respect of any shares in the holding or from the exercise of a right attached to any of those shares.

Service contracts

6.— (1) The directors' remuneration report must contain, in respect of the contract of service or contract for services of each person who has served as a director of the company at any time during the relevant financial year, the following information—

(a) the date of the contract, the unexpired term and the details of any notice periods;

(b) any provision for compensation payable upon early termination of the contract; and

(c) such details of other provisions in the contract as are necessary to enable members of the company to estimate the liability of the company in the event of early termination of the contract.

(2) The directors' remuneration report must contain an explanation for any significant award made to a person in the circumstances described in paragraph 15.

PART 3
INFORMATION SUBJECT TO AUDIT

Amount of each director's emoluments and compensation in the relevant financial year

7.— (1) The directors' remuneration report must for the relevant financial year show, for each person who has served as a director of the company at any time during that year, each of the following—

(a) the total amount of salary and fees paid to or receivable by the person in respect of qualifying services;

(b) the total amount of bonuses so paid or receivable;

(c) the total amount of sums paid by way of expenses allowance that are—

(i) chargeable to United Kingdom income tax (or would be if the person were an individual), and

(ii) paid to or receivable by the person in respect of qualifying services;

(d) the total amount of—

(i) any compensation for loss of office paid to or receivable by the person, and

(ii) any other payments paid to or receivable by the person in connection with the termination of qualifying services;

(e) the total estimated value of any benefits received by the person otherwise than in cash that—

(i) do not fall within any of paragraphs (a) to (d) or paragraphs 8 to 12,

(ii) are emoluments of the person, and

(iii) are received by the person in respect of qualifying services; and

(f) the amount that is the total of the sums mentioned in paragraphs (a) to (e).

(2) The directors' remuneration report must show, for each person who has served as a director of the company at any time during the relevant financial year, the amount that for the financial year preceding the relevant financial year is the total of the sums mentioned in paragraphs (a) to (e) of sub-paragraph (1).

(3) The directors' remuneration report must also state the nature of any element of a remuneration package which is not cash.

(4) The information required by sub-paragraphs (1) and (2) must be presented in tabular form.

Share options

8.— (1) The directors' remuneration report must contain, in respect of each person who has served as a director of the company at any time in the relevant financial year, the information specified in paragraph 9.

(2) Sub-paragraph (1) is subject to paragraph 10 (aggregation of information to avoid excessively lengthy reports).

(3) The information specified in sub-paragraphs (a) to (c) of paragraph 9 must be presented in tabular form in the report.

(4) In paragraph 9 "share option", in relation to a person, means a share option granted in respect of qualifying services of the person.

9. The information required by sub-paragraph (1) of paragraph 8 in respect of such a person as is mentioned in that sub-paragraph is—

(a) the number of shares that are subject to a share option—

(i) at the beginning of the relevant financial year or, if later, on the date of the appointment of the person as a director of the company, and

(ii) at the end of the relevant financial year or, if earlier, on the cessation of the person's appointment as a director of the company,

in each case differentiating between share options having different terms and conditions;

(b) information identifying those share options that have been awarded in the relevant financial year, those that have been exercised in that year, those that in that year have expired unexercised and those whose terms and conditions have been varied in that year;

(c) for each share option that is unexpired at any time in the relevant financial year—

(i) the price paid, if any, for its award,

(ii) the exercise price,

(iii) the date from which the option may be exercised, and

(iv) the date on which the option expires;

(d) a description of any variation made in the relevant financial year in the terms and conditions of a share option;

(e) a summary of any performance criteria upon which the award or exercise of a share option is conditional, including a description of any variation made in such performance criteria during the relevant financial year;

(f) for each share option that has been exercised during the relevant financial year, the market price of the shares, in relation to which it is exercised, at the time of exercise; and

(g) for each share option that is unexpired at the end of the relevant financial year—

(i) the market price at the end of that year, and

(ii) the highest and lowest market prices during that year,

of each share that is subject to the option.

10.— (1) If, in the opinion of the directors of the company, disclosure in accordance with paragraphs 8 and 9 would result in a disclosure of excessive length then, (subject to sub-paragraphs (2) and (3))—

(a) information disclosed for a person under paragraph 9(a) need not differentiate between share options having different terms and conditions;

(b) for the purposes of disclosure in respect of a person under paragraph 9(c)(i) and (ii) and (g),

share options may be aggregated and (instead of disclosing prices for each share option) disclosure may be made of weighted average prices of aggregations of share options;

(c) for the purposes of disclosure in respect of a person under paragraph 9(c)(iii) and (iv), share options may be aggregated and (instead of disclosing dates for each share option) disclosure may be made of ranges of dates for aggregation of share options.

(2) Sub-paragraph (1)(b) and (c) does not permit the aggregation of—

(a) share options in respect of shares whose market price at the end of the relevant financial year is below the option exercise price, with

(b) share options in respect of shares whose market price at the end of the relevant financial year is equal to, or exceeds, the option exercise price.

(3) Sub-paragraph (1) does not apply (and accordingly, full disclosure must be made in accordance with paragraphs 8 and 9) in respect of share options that during the relevant financial year have been awarded or exercised or had their terms and conditions varied.

Long term incentive schemes

11.— (1) The directors' remuneration report must contain, in respect of each person who has served as a director of the company at any time in the relevant financial year, the information specified in paragraph 12.

(2) Sub-paragraph (1) does not require the report to contain share option details that are contained in the report in compliance with paragraphs 8 to 10.

(3) The information specified in paragraph 12 must be presented in tabular form in the report.

(4) For the purposes of paragraph 12—

(a) "scheme interest", in relation to a person, means an interest under a long term incentive scheme that is an interest in respect of which assets may become receivable under the scheme in respect of qualifying services of the person; and

(b) such an interest "vests" at the earliest time when—

(i) it has been ascertained that the qualifying conditions have been fulfilled, and

(ii) the nature and quantity of the assets receivable under the scheme in respect of the interest have been ascertained.

(5) In this Schedule "long term incentive scheme" means any agreement or arrangement under which money or other assets may become receivable by a person and which includes one or more qualifying conditions with respect to service or performance that cannot be fulfilled within a single financial year, and for this purpose the following must be disregarded, namely—

(a) any bonus the amount of which falls to be determined by reference to service or performance within a single financial year;

(b) compensation in respect of loss of office, payments for breach of contract and other termination payments; and

(c) retirement benefits.

12.— (1) The information required by sub-paragraph (1) of paragraph 11 in respect of such a person as is mentioned in that sub-paragraph is—

(a) details of the scheme interests that the person has at the beginning of the relevant financial year or if later on the date of the appointment of the person as a director of the company;

(b) details of the scheme interests awarded to the person during the relevant financial year;

(c) details of the scheme interests that the person has at the end of the relevant financial year or if earlier on the cessation of the person's appointment as a director of the company;

(d) for each scheme interest within paragraphs (a) to (c)—

(i) the end of the period over which the qualifying conditions for that interest have to be fulfilled (or if there are different periods for different conditions, the end of whichever of those periods ends last); and

(ii) a description of any variation made in the terms and conditions of the scheme interests during the relevant financial year; and

(e) for each scheme interest that has vested in the relevant financial year—

(i) the relevant details (see sub-paragraph (3)) of any shares,

(ii) the amount of any money, and

(iii) the value of any other assets,

that have become receivable in respect of the interest.

(2) The details that sub-paragraph (1)(b) requires of a scheme interest awarded during the relevant financial year include, if shares may become receivable in respect of the interest, the following—

(a) the number of those shares;

(b) the market price of each of those shares when the scheme interest was awarded; and

(c) details of qualifying conditions that are conditions with respect to performance.

(3) In sub-paragraph (1)(e)(i) "the relevant details", in relation to any shares that have become receivable in respect of a scheme interest, means—

(a) the number of those shares;

(b) the date on which the scheme interest was awarded;

(c) the market price of each of those shares when the scheme interest was awarded;

(d) the market price of each of those shares when the scheme interest vested; and

(e) details of qualifying conditions that were conditions with respect to performance.

Pensions

13.— (1) The directors' remuneration report must, for each person who has served as a director of the company at any time during the relevant financial year, contain the information in respect of pensions that is specified in sub-paragraphs (2) and (3).

(2) Where the person has rights under a pension scheme that is a defined benefit scheme in relation to the person and any of those rights are rights to which he has become entitled in respect of qualifying services of his—

(a) details—

(i) of any changes during the relevant financial year in the person's accrued benefits under the scheme, and

(ii) of the person's accrued benefits under the scheme as at the end of that year;

(b) the transfer value, calculated in accordance with regulations 7 to 7E of the Occupational Pension Schemes (Transfer Values) Regulations 1996, of the person's accrued benefits under the scheme at the end of the relevant financial year;

(c) the transfer value of the person's accrued benefits under the scheme that in compliance with paragraph (b) was contained in the directors' remuneration report for the previous financial year or, if there was no such report or no such value was contained in that report, the transfer value, calculated in such a manner as is mentioned in paragraph (b), of the person's accrued benefits under the scheme at the beginning of the relevant financial year;

(d) the amount obtained by subtracting—

(i) the transfer value of the person's accrued benefits under the scheme that is required to be contained in the report by paragraph (c), from

(ii) the transfer value of those benefits that is required to be contained in the report by paragraph (b),

and then subtracting from the result of that calculation the amount of any contributions made to the scheme by the person in the relevant financial year.

(3) Where—

(a) the person has rights under a pension scheme that is a money purchase scheme in relation to the person, and

(b) any of those rights are rights to which he has become entitled in respect of qualifying services of his,

details of any contribution to the scheme in respect of the person that is paid or payable by the company for the relevant financial year or paid by the company in that year for another financial year.

Excess retirement benefits of directors and past directors

14.— (1) Subject to sub-paragraph (3), the directors' remuneration report must show in respect of each person who has served as a director of the company—

(a) at any time during the relevant financial year, or

(b) at any time before the beginning of that year,

the amount of so much of retirement benefits paid to or receivable by the person under pension schemes as is in excess of the retirement benefits to which he was entitled on the date on which the benefits first became payable or 31st March 1997, whichever is the later.

(2) In subsection (1) "retirement benefits" means retirement benefits to which the person became entitled in respect of qualifying services of his.

(3) Amounts paid or receivable under a pension scheme need not be included in an amount required to be shown under sub-paragraph (1) if—

(a) the funding of the scheme was such that the amounts were or, as the case may be, could have been paid without recourse to additional contributions; and

(b) amounts were paid to or receivable by all pensioner members of the scheme on the same basis; and in this sub-paragraph "pensioner member", in relation to a pension scheme, means any person who is entitled to the present payment of retirement benefits under the scheme.

(4) In this paragraph—

(a) references to retirement benefits include benefits otherwise than in cash; and

(b) in relation to so much of retirement benefits as consists of a benefit otherwise than in cash,

references to their amount are to the estimated money value of the benefit, and the nature of any such benefit must also be shown in the report.

Compensation for past directors

15. The directors' remuneration report must contain details of any significant award made in the relevant financial year to any person who was not a director of the company at the time the award was made but had previously been a director of the company, including (in particular) compensation in respect of loss of office and pensions but excluding any sums which have already been shown in the report under paragraph 7(1)(d).

Sums paid to third parties in respect of a director's services

16.— (1) The directors' remuneration report must show, in respect of each person who served as a director of the company at any time during the relevant financial year, the aggregate amount of any consideration paid to or receivable by third parties for making available the services of the person—

(a) as a director of the company, or

(b) while director of the company—

(i) as director of any of its subsidiary undertakings, or

(ii) as director of any other undertaking of which he was (while director of the company) a director by virtue of the company's nomination (direct or indirect), or

(iii) otherwise in connection with the management of the affairs of the company or any such other undertaking.

(2) The reference to consideration includes benefits otherwise than in cash; and in relation to such consideration the reference to its amount is to the estimated money value of the benefit.

The nature of any such consideration must be shown in the report.

(3) The reference to third parties is to persons other than—

(a) the person himself or a person connected with him or a body corporate controlled by him, and

(b) the company or any such other undertaking as is mentioned in sub-paragraph (1)(b)(ii).

PART 4
INTERPRETATION AND SUPPLEMENTARY

17.— (1) In this Schedule—

"amount", in relation to a gain made on the exercise of a share option, means the difference between—

(a) the market price of the shares on the day on which the option was exercised; and

(b) the price actually paid for the shares;

"company contributions", in relation to a pension scheme and a person, means any payments (including insurance premiums) made, or treated as made, to the scheme in respect of the person by anyone other than the person;

"defined benefit scheme", in relation to a person, means a pension scheme which is not a money purchase scheme in relation to the person;

"emoluments" of a person—

(a) includes salary, fees and bonuses, sums paid by way of expenses allowance (so far as they are chargeable to United Kingdom income tax or would be if the person were an individual), but

(b) does not include any of the following, namely—

(i) the value of any share options granted to him or the amount of any gains made on the exercise of any such options;

(ii) any company contributions paid, or treated as paid, in respect of him under any pension scheme or any benefits to which he is entitled under any such scheme; or

(iii) any money or other assets paid to or received or receivable by him under any long term incentive scheme;

"long term incentive scheme" has the meaning given by paragraph 11(5);

"money purchase benefits", in relation to a person, means retirement benefits the rate or amount of which is calculated by reference to payments made, or treated as made, by the person or by any other person in respect of that person and which are not average salary benefits;

"money purchase scheme", in relation to a person, means a pension scheme under which all of the benefits that may become payable to or in respect of the person are money purchase benefits in relation to the person;

"pension scheme" means a retirement benefits scheme within the meaning given by section 611 of the Income and Corporation Taxes Act 1988;

"qualifying services", in relation to any person, means his services as a director of the company, and his services at any time while he is a director of the company—

(a) as a director of an undertaking that is a subsidiary undertaking of the company at that time;

(b) as a director of any other undertaking of which he is a director by virtue of the company's nomination (direct or indirect); or

(c) otherwise in connection with the management of the affairs of the company or any such subsidiary undertaking or any such other undertaking;

"retirement benefits" means relevant benefits within the meaning given by section 612(1) of the Income and Corporation Taxes Act 1988;

"shares" means shares (whether allotted or not) in the company, or any undertaking which is a group undertaking in relation to the company, and includes a share warrant as defined by section 779(1) of the 2006 Act;

"share option" means a right to acquire shares;

"value", in relation to shares received or receivable on any day by a person who is or has been a director of the company, means the market price of the shares on that day.

(2) In this Schedule "compensation in respect of loss of office" includes compensation received or receivable by a person for—

(a) loss of office as director of the company, or

(b) loss, while director of the company or on or in connection with his ceasing to be a director of it, of—

(i) any other office in connection with the management of the company's affairs, or

(ii) any office as director or otherwise in connection with the management of the affairs of any undertaking that, immediately before the loss, is a subsidiary undertaking of the company or an undertaking of which he is a director by virtue of the company's nomination (direct or indirect);

(c) compensation in consideration for, or in connection with, a person's retirement from office; and

(d) where such a retirement is occasioned by a breach of the person's contract with the company or with an undertaking that, immediately before the breach, is a subsidiary undertaking of the company or an undertaking of which he is a director by virtue of the company's nomination (direct or indirect)—

(i) payments made by way of damages for the breach; or

(ii) payments made by way of settlement or compromise of any claim in respect of the breach.

(3) References in this Schedule to compensation include benefits otherwise than in cash; and in relation to such compensation references in this Schedule to its amounts are to the estimated money value of the benefit.

(4) References in this Schedule to a person being "connected" with a director, and to a director "controlling" a body corporate, are to be construed in accordance with sections 252 to 255 of the 2006 Act.

18.— (1) For the purposes of this Schedule emoluments paid or receivable or share options granted in respect of a person's accepting office as a director are to be treated as emoluments paid or receivable or share options granted in respect of his services as a director.

(2) Where a pension scheme provides for any benefits that may become payable to or in respect of a person to be whichever are the greater of—

(a) such benefits determined by or under the scheme as are money purchase benefits in relation to the person; and

(b) such retirement benefits determined by or under the scheme to be payable to or in respect of the person as are not money purchase benefits in relation to the person,

the company may assume for the purposes of this Schedule that those benefits will be money purchase benefits in relation to the person, or not, according to whichever appears more likely at the end of the relevant financial year.

(3) In determining for the purposes of this Schedule whether a pension scheme is a money purchase scheme in relation to a person or a defined benefit scheme in relation to a person, any death in service benefits provided for by the scheme are to be disregarded.

19.— (1) The following applies with respect to the amounts to be shown under this Schedule.

(2) The amount in each case includes all relevant sums paid by or receivable from—

(a) the company; and

(b) the company's subsidiary undertakings; and

(c) any other person,

except sums to be accounted for to the company or any of its subsidiary undertakings or any other undertaking of which any person has been a director while director of the company, by virtue of section 219 of the 2006 Act (payment in connection with share transfer:

requirement of members' approval), to past or present members of the company or any of its subsidiaries or any class of those members.

(3) Reference to amounts paid to or receivable by a person include amounts paid to or receivable by a person connected with him or a body corporate controlled by him (but not so as to require an amount to be counted twice).

20.— (1) The amounts to be shown for any financial year under Part 3 of this Schedule are the sums receivable in respect of that year (whenever paid) or, in the case of sums not receivable in respect of a period, the sums paid during that year.

(2) But where—

(a) any sums are not shown in the directors' remuneration report for the relevant financial year on the ground that the person receiving them is liable to account for them as mentioned in paragraph 19(2), but the liability is thereafter wholly or partly released or is not enforced within a period of 2 years; or

(b) any sums paid by way of expenses allowance are charged to United Kingdom income tax after the end of the relevant financial year or, in the case of any such sums paid otherwise than to an individual, it does not become clear until the end of the relevant financial year that those sums would be charged to such tax were the person an individual,

those sums must, to the extent to which the liability is released or not enforced or they are charged as mentioned above (as the case may be), be shown in the first directors' remuneration report in which it is practicable to show them and must be distinguished from the amounts to be shown apart from this provision.

21. Where it is necessary to do so for the purpose of making any distinction required by the preceding paragraphs in an amount to be shown in compliance with this Part of this Schedule, the directors may apportion any payments between the matters in respect of which these have been paid or are receivable in such manner as they think appropriate.

22. The Schedule requires information to be given only so far as it is contained in the company's books and papers, available to members of the public or the company has the right to obtain it.

SCHEDULE 9

Regulation 12

INTERPRETATION OF TERM "PROVISIONS"

PART 1

MEANING FOR PURPOSES OF THESE REGULATIONS

Definition of "Provisions"

1.— (1) In these Regulations, references to provisions for depreciation or diminution in value of assets are to any amount written off by way of providing for depreciation or diminution in value of assets.

(2) Any reference in the profit and loss account formats or the notes to them set out in Schedule 1, 2 or 3 to these Regulations to the depreciation of, or amounts written off, assets of any description is to any provision for depreciation or diminution in value of assets of that description.

2. References in these Regulations to provisions for liabilities or, in the case of insurance companies, to provisions for other risks are to any amount retained as reasonably necessary for the purpose of providing for any liability the nature of which is clearly defined and which is either likely to be incurred, or certain to be incurred but uncertain as to amount or as to the date on which it will arise.

PART 2
MEANING FOR PURPOSES OF PARTS 18 AND 23 OF THE 2006 ACT

Financial assistance for purchase of own shares

3. The specified provisions for the purposes of section 677(3)(a) of the 2006 Act (Companies Act accounts: relevant provisions for purposes of financial assistance) are provisions within paragraph 2 of this Schedule.

Redemption or purchase by private company out of capital

4. The specified provisions for the purposes of section 712(2)(b)(i) of the 2006 Act (Companies Act accounts: relevant provisions to determine available profits for redemption or purchase out of capital) are provisions of any of the kinds mentioned in paragraphs 1 and 2 of this Schedule.

Net asset restriction on public companies distributions

5. The specified provisions for the purposes of section 831(3)(a) of the 2006 Act (Companies Act accounts: net asset restriction on public company distributions) are—
   (a) provisions within paragraph 2 of this Schedule, and
   (b) in the case of an insurance company, any amount included under liabilities items Ba (fund for future appropriations), C (technical provisions) and D (technical provisions for linked liabilities) in a balance sheet drawn up in accordance with Schedule 3 to these Regulations.

Distributions by investment companies

6. The specified provisions for the purposes of section 832(4)(a) of the 2006 Act (Companies Act accounts: investment companies distributions) are provisions within paragraph 2 of this Schedule.

Justification of distribution by references to accounts

7. The specified provisions for the purposes of section 836(1)(b)(i) of the 2006 Act (Companies Act accounts: relevant provisions for distribution purposes)—
   (a) are provisions of any of the kinds mentioned in paragraphs 1 and 2 of this Schedule, and
   (b) in the case of an insurance company, any amount included under liabilities items Ba (fund for future appropriations), C (technical provisions) and D (technical provisions for linked liabilities) in a balance sheet drawn up in accordance with Schedule 3 to these Regulations.

Realised losses

8. The specified provisions for the purposes of section 841(2)(a) of the 2006 Act (Companies Act accounts: treatment of provisions as realised losses) are provisions of any of the kinds mentioned in paragraphs 1 and 2 of this Schedule.

SCHEDULE 10
Regulation 13

GENERAL INTERPRETATION

Capitalisation

1. "Capitalisation", in relation to work or costs, means treating that work or those costs as a fixed asset.

Financial instruments

2. Save in Schedule 2 to these Regulations, references to "derivatives" include commodity-based contracts that give either contracting party the right to settle in cash or in some other financial instrument, except where such contracts—
   (a) were entered into for the purpose of, and continue to meet, the company's expected purchase, sale or usage requirements,
   (b) were designated for such purpose at their inception, and
   (c) are expected to be settled by delivery of the commodity (for banking companies, see the definition in paragraph 94 of Schedule 2 to these Regulations).

3.— (1) Save in Schedule 2 to these Regulations, the expressions listed in sub-paragraph (2) have the same meaning as they have in Council Directive 78/660/EEC on the annual accounts of certain types of companies and 91/674/EEC on the annual accounts and consolidated accounts of insurance undertakings (for banking companies, see the definition in paragraph 96 of Schedule 2 to these Regulations).

(2) Those expressions are "available for sale financial asset", "business combination", "commodity-based contracts", "derivative", "equity instrument", "exchange difference", "fair value hedge accounting system", "financial fixed asset", "financial instrument", "foreign entity", "hedge accounting", "hedge accounting system", "hedged items", "hedging instrument", "held for trading purposes", "held to maturity", "monetary item", "receivables", "reliable market" and "trading portfolio".

Fixed and current assets

4. "Fixed assets" means assets of a company which are intended for use on a continuing basis in the company's activities, and "current assets" means assets not intended for such use.

Fungible assets

5. "Fungible assets" means assets of any description which are substantially indistinguishable one from another.

Historical cost accounting rules

6. References to the historical cost accounting rules are to be read in accordance with paragraph 30 of Schedule 1, paragraph 38 of Schedule 2 and paragraph 36(1) of Schedule 3 to these Regulations.

Leases

7.— (1) "Long lease" means a lease in the case of which the portion of the term for which it was granted remaining unexpired at the end of the financial year is not less than 50 years.

(2) "Short lease" means a lease which is not a long lease.

(3) "Lease" includes an agreement for a lease.

Listed investments

8.— (1) "Listed investment" means an investment as respects which there has been granted a listing on—

(a) a recognised investment exchange other than an overseas investment exchange, or

(b) a stock exchange of repute outside the United Kingdom.

(2) "Recognised investment exchange" and "overseas investment exchange" have the meaning given in Part 18 of the Financial Services and Markets Act 2000.

Loans

9. A loan or advance (including a liability comprising a loan or advance) is treated as falling due for repayment, and an instalment of a loan or advance is treated as falling due for payment, on the earliest date on which the lender could require repayment or (as the case may be) payment, if he exercised all options and rights available to him.

Materiality

10. Amounts which in the particular context of any provision of Schedules 1, 2 or 3 to these Regulations are not material may be disregarded for the purposes of that provision.

Participating interests

11.— (1) A "participating interest" means an interest held by an undertaking in the shares of another undertaking which it holds on a long-term basis for the purpose of securing a contribution to its activities by the exercise of control or influence arising from or related to that interest.

(2) A holding of 20% or more of the shares of the undertaking is to be presumed to be a participating interest unless the contrary is shown.

(3) The reference in sub-paragraph (1) to an interest in shares includes—

(a) an interest which is convertible into an interest in shares, and

(b) an option to acquire shares or any such interest,

and an interest or option falls within paragraph (a) or (b) notwithstanding that the shares to which it relates are, until the conversion or the exercise of the option, unissued.

(4) For the purposes of this regulation an interest held on behalf of an undertaking is to be treated as held by it.

(5) In the balance sheet and profit and loss formats set out in Schedules 1, 2 and 3 to these Regulations, "participating interest" does not include an interest in a group undertaking.

(6) For the purpose of this regulation as it applies in relation to the expression "participating interest"—

(a) in those formats as they apply in relation to group accounts, and

(b) in paragraph 19 of Schedule 6 (group accounts: undertakings to be accounted for as associated undertakings),

the references in sub-paragraphs (1) to (4) to the interest held by, and the purposes and activities of, the undertaking concerned are to be construed as references to the interest held by, and the purposes and activities of, the group (within the meaning of paragraph 1 of that Schedule).

Purchase price

12. "Purchase price", in relation to an asset of a company or any raw materials or consumables used in the production of such an asset, includes any consideration (whether in cash or otherwise) given by the company in respect of that asset or those materials or consumables, as the case may be.

Realised profits and realised losses

13. "Realised profits" and "realised losses" have the same meaning as in section 853(4) and (5) of the 2006 Act.

Staff costs

14.— (1) "Social security costs" means any contributions by the company to any state social security or pension scheme, fund or arrangement.

(2) "Pension costs" includes—

(a) any costs incurred by the company in respect of any pension scheme established for the purpose of providing pensions for persons currently or formerly employed by the company,

(b) any sums set aside for the future payment of pensions directly by the company to current or former employees, and

(c) any pensions paid directly to such persons without having first been set aside.

(3) Any amount stated in respect of the item "social security costs" or in respect of the item "wages and salaries" in the company's profit and loss account must be determined by reference to payments made or costs incurred in respect of all persons employed by the company during the financial year under contracts of service.

Scots land tenure

15. In the application of these Regulations to Scotland, "land of freehold tenure" means land in respect of which the company is the owner; "land of leasehold tenure" means land of which the company is the tenant under a lease.

Companies Act 2006 (Commencement No. 8, Transitional Provisions and Savings) Order 2008

S.I. 2008/2860

1. Citation and commencement

(1) This Order may be cited as the Companies Act 2006 (Commencement No 8, Transitional Provisions and Savings) Order 2008.

(2) This Order comes into force on 1st October 2009.

2. Interpretation

In this Order—

"the 1985 Act" means the Companies Act 1985;

"the 1986 Order" means the Companies (Northern Ireland) Order 1986;

"existing company" means a company that immediately before 1st October 2009 was formed and registered under the 1985 Act or the 1986 Order or was an existing company for the purposes of that Act or Order;

"transitional company" means a company that is formed and registered, or re-registered, under the 1985 Act or the 1986 Order on or after 1st October 2009 by virtue of paragraph 2(3) or 22(3) of Schedule 2 to this Order.

3. Provisions of the Companies Act 2006 coming into force on 1st October 2009

The following provisions of the Companies Act 2006 come into force on 1st October 2009—

(a) in Part 1 (general introductory provisions)—
section 1 (companies);
sections 3 to 6 (types of company);

(b) Part 2 (sections 7 to 16) (company formation);

(c) in Part 3 (a company's constitution)—
section 17 (a company's constitution);
sections 18 to 21, 22(1), (3) and (4) and 23 to 28 (articles of association);
sections 31 to 38 (other provisions relating to a company's constitution);

(d) in Part 4 (a company's capacity and related matters)—
sections 39 to 42 (capacity of company and power of directors to bind it);
sections 43 and 45 to 47 (formalities of doing business under the law of England and Wales or Northern Ireland);
section 48 (formalities of doing business under the law of Scotland);
sections 49 to 52 (other matters);

(e) in Part 5 (a company's name)—
sections 53 to 57 (general requirements);
sections 58 to 65 (indications of company type or legal form);
sections 66 to 68 (similarity to other names);
sections 75 and 76 (powers of Secretary of State in relation to company names);
sections 77 to 81 (change of name);

(f) Part 6 (sections 86 to 88) (a company's registered office);

(g) Part 7 (sections 89 to 111) (re-registration as a means of altering a company's status);

(h) in Part 8 (a company's members)—
section 112 (the members of a company);
sections 113 to 115 and 120 and 122 to 127 (register of members);
sections 129 to 135 (overseas branch registers);
sections 136 to 144 (prohibition on subsidiary being member of its holding company);

(i) in Part 10 (a company's directors)—
sections 162 to 167 (register of directors);
sections 240 to 246 (directors' residential addresses: protection from disclosure);
section 247 (power to make provision for employees on cessation or transfer of business);
(j) in Part 12 (company secretaries), sections 275 to 279 (register of secretaries);
(k) in Part 17 (a company's share capital)—
sections 540 to 543 and 545 to 548 (shares and share capital);
sections 549 to 559 (allotment of shares: general provisions);
sections 560 to 577 (allotment of equity securities: shareholders' right of pre-emption);
sections 578 and 579 (public companies: allotment where issue not fully subscribed);
sections 580 to 592 (payment for shares);
sections 593 to 609 (public companies: independent valuation of non-cash consideration);
sections 610 to 616 (share premiums);
sections 617 to 628 (alteration of share capital);
sections 629 to 640 (classes of share and class rights);
sections 641(1)(b) and 645 to 653 (reduction of share capital confirmed by the court);
sections 655 to 657 (miscellaneous and supplementary provisions);
(l) Part 18 (sections 658 to 737) (acquisition by limited company of its own shares);
(m) Part 24 (sections 854 to 859) (a company's annual return);
(n) Part 25 (sections 860 to 894) (company charges);
(o) Part 31 (sections 1000 to 1034) (dissolution and restoration to the register);
(p) in Part 33 (UK companies not formed under companies legislation), sections 1040 to 1042 (companies not formed under companies legislation but authorised to register);
(q) Part 34 (sections 1044 to 1059) (overseas companies);
(r) in Part 35 (the registrar of companies)—
sections 1060 to 1062 (the registrar);
section 1063 (fees payable to registrar), so far as not already in force;
sections 1064 to 1067 (certificates of incorporation and registered numbers);
sections 1068(1) to (4), (6) and (7) and 1069 to 1071 (delivery of documents to the registrar);
sections 1072 to 1076 (requirements for proper delivery);
sections 1081 to 1084 (the register);
sections 1093 to 1098 (correction or removal of material on the register);
sections 1099 to 1101 (the registrar's index of company names);
sections 1108 to 1110 (language requirements: transliteration);
sections 1112 to 1120 (supplementary provisions);
(s) in Part 36 (offences under the Companies Acts)—
sections 1121 to 1123 (liability of officer in default);
section 1125 (meaning of "daily default fine");
sections 1127 to 1133 (other provisions);
(t) in Part 37 (companies: supplementary provisions)—
sections 1134 to 1136, 1137(2), (3) and (5)(a) and 1138 (company records);
sections 1139 to 1142 (service addresses);
sections 1149 to 1153 (requirements as to independent valuation);
sections 1154 and 1155 (notice of appointment of certain officers);
section 1156 (meaning of "the court");
(u) in Part 38 (companies: interpretation)—
section 1158 (meaning of "UK-registered company");

sections 1159 and 1160 and Schedule 6 (meaning of "subsidiary" and related expressions);
section 1163 (meaning of "non-cash asset");
section 1166 (meaning of "employees' share scheme");
sections 1168, 1171, 1173 (so far as not already in force) and 1174 and Schedule 8 (other definitions etc);

(v) in Part 39 (companies: minor amendments)—
section 1180 (repeal of certain provisions about company charges);
section 1181 (access to constitutional documents of RTE and RTM companies);

(w) Part 40 (sections 1182 to 1191) (company directors: foreign disqualification);

(x) Part 41 (sections 1192 to 1208) (business names);

(y) in Part 44 (miscellaneous provisions)—
section 1275 (levy to pay expenses of bodies concerned with actuarial standards etc);
section 1283 (commonhold associations);

(z) Part 45 (sections 1284 to 1287) (Northern Ireland).

4. Repeals

Section 1295 of, and Schedule 16 to, the Companies Act 2006 (repeals) come into force on 1st October 2009 so far as relating to the repeal of the provisions specified in Schedule 1 to this Order.

5. Transitional provisions and savings

Schedule 2 to this Order contains transitional provisions and savings relating to the provisions (and repeals) brought into force by this Order.

6. Revocation of spent transitional adaptations

(1) The following provisions (which make transitional adaptations that are no longer needed as a result of this Order) are revoked—

(a) Schedule 1 to the Companies Act 2006 (Commencement No 1, Transitional Provisions and Savings) Order 2006;

(b) Schedule 1 to the Companies Act 2006 (Commencement No 2, Consequential Amendments, Transitional Provisions and Savings) Order 2007;

(c) Schedule 1 to the Companies Act 2006 (Commencement No 3, Consequential Amendments, Transitional Provisions and Savings) Order 2007;

(d) Schedule 1 to the Companies Act 2006 (Commencement No 5, Transitional Provisions and Savings) Order 2007;

(e) paragraph 1 of Schedule 3 to the Companies Act 2006 (Commencement No 6, Saving and Commencement Nos 3 and 5 (Amendment)) Order 2008;

(f) articles 3 to 5 of the Companies Act 2006 (Commencement No 7, Transitional Provisions and Savings) Order 2008.

(2) The revocations have effect subject to any relevant transitional provision or saving in Schedule 2 to this Order.

7. Prosecution of offences in transitional cases

(1) Where a provision creating an offence is repealed and re-enacted without modification by or under the Companies Act 2006—

(a) an offence committed before the commencement of the new law is to be charged under the old law,

(b) an offence committed after the commencement of the new law is to be charged under the new law, and

(c) an offence committed partly before and partly after the commencement of the new law is to be charged under the new law and not under the old.

(2) For this purpose an offence is committed partly before and partly after the commencement of the new law if a relevant event occurs before commencement and another relevant event occurs after commencement.

(3) A "relevant event" means an act, omission or other event (including any result of one or more acts or omissions) proof of which is required for conviction of the offence.

(4) This article is without prejudice to section 1297(2) of the Companies Act 2006 (continuity of the law).

8. General saving

The provisions of this Order do not affect the operation of section 1297 of the Companies Act 2006 (continuity of the law) except as expressly provided.

SCHEDULE 1 Article 4

REPEALS COMING INTO FORCE ON 1ST OCTOBER 2009

PART 1

GREAT BRITAIN

Short title and chapter	*Extent of repeal brought into force*
	Sections 1 to 28. Section 29(1) to (3), (5) and (6). Sections 30 to 36. Section 36A(1) and (3). Sections 36AA to 40. Sections 43 to 55. Section 62 (so far as not previously repealed). Sections 80 and 80A. Sections 82 to 116. Sections 119 to 124. Section 125(1) to (5), (7) and (8). Sections 126 to 182. Sections 287 to 291. Sections 306 to 308. Section 322A. Section 350. Sections 352 to 355. Sections 357 to 365. Sections 379A and 380. Sections 395 to 424. Sections 651 to 706. Section 707A(2) to (4). Section 707B. Section 708(1) to (4). Sections 710 and 710A. Section 711A. Sections 713 and 714. Section 715A. Sections 718 and 719. Sections 721 to 725 and 726(1). Section 728. Section 730(1) to (4). Sections 730A and 731.

Short title and chapter	*Extent of repeal brought into force*
	Sections 735 to 740. Section 742. Sections 743 to 745. Schedules 1 and 2. Paragraph 2 of Schedule 3 (so far as not previously repealed). Schedule 14. Schedules 20 to 22. Schedule 24. Schedule 25.
Business Names Act 1985 (c 7)	The whole Act.
. . .	
Insolvency Act 1985 (c 65)	In Schedule 6, paragraphs 10, 46 and 47.
Insolvency Act 1986 (c 45)	In Schedule 13, the entries relating to the following provisions of the Companies Act 1985— (a) section 13(4); (b) section 44(7); (c) section 103(7); (d) section 131(7);(e) section 140(2); (f) section 173(4); (g) section 657(2); (h) section 658(1).
Building Societies Act 1986 (c 53)	Section 102C(5).
Companies Act 1989 (c 40)	Sections 92 to 110. Section 115(1). Section 116(1) and (2). Section 117. Section 123(5). Section 125(1). Sections 126 to 129. Section 130(1) to (5) and (7). Sections 131 to 133. Section 136. Section 139(1) to (3). Sections 141 to 143. Section 144(1) and (3). In Schedule 10, paragraphs 1, 9 to 18 and 24. Schedules 15 to 17. In Schedule 18, paragraphs 32 to 38. In Schedule 19, paragraphs 1 to 7, 11 to 17 and 19 to 21.
Charities Act 1993 (c 10)	In Schedule 6, paragraph 20.
Criminal Justice Act 1993 (c 36)	In Schedule 5, paragraph 4.
Pension Schemes Act 1993 (c 48)	In Schedule 8, paragraph 16.

Short title and chapter	*Extent of repeal brought into force*
Trade Marks Act 1994 (c 26)	In Schedule 4, in paragraph 1(2), the entries relating to sections 392 and 410 of the Companies Act 1985.
Deregulation and Contracting Out Act 1994 (c 40)	Section 13(1). Schedule 5. In Schedule 16, paragraphs 8 to 10.
Requirements of Writing (Scotland) Act 1995 (c 7)	In Schedule 4, paragraphs 51 to 54.
Criminal Procedure (Consequential Provisions) (Scotland) Act 1995 (c 40)	In Schedule 4, paragraph 56(4).
Limited Liability Partnerships Act 2000 (c 12)	In the Schedule, paragraph 1.
Political Parties, Elections and Referendums Act 2000 (c 41)	Section 139(2).
Criminal Justice and Police Act 2001 (c 16)	Section 45. In Schedule 2, paragraph 17.
Enterprise Act 2002 (c 40)	In Schedule 17, paragraphs 3, 7 and 8.
Companies (Audit, Investigations and Community Enterprise) Act 2004 (c 27)	Sections 19(1) and 20. In Schedule 6, paragraphs 1 to 9.
Civil Partnership Act 2004 (c 33)	In Schedule 27, paragraph 104.

PART 2
NORTHERN IRELAND

Short title and chapter	*Extent of repeal or revocation brought into force*
Companies (Northern Ireland) Order 1986 (SI 1986/1032 (NI 6))	Articles 1 to 8. Article 10. Article 11. Articles 12 to 38. Article 39(1) to (3), (5) and (6). Articles 40 to 46. Article 46A(1) and (3). Articles 46B to 50. Articles 53 to 65. Article 72 (so far as not previously revoked). Articles 90 and 90A. Articles 92 to 126. Articles 129 to 134. Article 135(1) to (5), (7) and (8).

Short title and chapter	*Extent of repeal or revocation brought into force*
	Articles 136 to 192. Articles 295 to 299. Articles 314 to 316. Article 330A. Article 358. Articles 360 to 363. Articles 365 to 373. Articles 387A and 388. Articles 402 to 417J. Articles 424 to 450. Articles 602 to 655. Article 656A(2) to (4). Article 656B. Article 657. Articles 659 and 659A. Articles 662 and 663. Article 664A. Articles 667 and 668. Articles 670 to 673. Article 676. Articles 678 and 679. Article 681. Schedules 1 and 2. Paragraph 2 of Schedule 3 (so far as not previously revoked). Schedule 14. Schedules 20 to 21. Schedules 23 and 24.
Business Names (Northern Ireland) Order 1986 (SI 1986/1033 (NI 7))	The whole Order.
Companies Consolidation (Consequential Provisions) (Northern Ireland) Order 1986 (SI 1986/1035 (NI 9))	The whole Order.
Companies (Northern Ireland) Order 1989 (SI 1989/2404 (NI 18))	Articles 1 to 2A. Article 26. Articles 35 and 36. Schedules 4 and 5.
Insolvency (Northern Ireland) Order 1989 (SI 1989/2405 (NI 19))	In Schedule 9, Part 1.
European Economic Interest Groupings Regulations (Northern Ireland) 1989 (SR (NI) 1989/216)	The whole Regulations.

Short title and chapter	*Extent of repeal or revocation brought into force*
Companies (Northern Ireland) Order 1990 (SI 1990/593 (NI 5))	Articles 1 and 2. Articles 25 and 26. Article 57. Schedule 10. Schedule 15.
Companies (No 2) (Northern Ireland) Order 1990 (SI 1990/1504 (NI 10))	Articles 3 to 5. Articles 7 to 20. Articles 28 to 42. Articles 44 to 46. Articles 49 to 53. Articles 59 to 61. Article 62(1) to (3) and (5). Articles 63 to 68. Articles 70 and 71. Articles 74 to 78. Schedule 1. In Schedule 2, paragraphs 1 and 2. Schedules 4 to 6.
Criminal Justice Act 1993 (c 36)	In Schedule 5, Part 2.
Financial Provisions (Northern Ireland) Order 1993 (SI 1993/1252 (NI 5))	Article 15.
Deregulation and Contracting Out Act 1994 (c 40)	Section 13(2). Schedule 6.
Pensions (Northern Ireland) Order 1995 (SI 1995/3213 (NI 22))	In Schedule 3, paragraph 7.
Deregulation and Contracting Out (Northern Ireland) Order 1996 (SI 1996/1632 (NI 11))	In Schedule 5, paragraph 4.
Youth Justice and Criminal Evidence Act 1999 (c 23)	In Schedule 4, paragraph 18.
Limited Liability Partnerships Act (Northern Ireland) 2002 (c 12 (NI))	The whole Act.
Open-Ended Investment Companies Act (Northern Ireland) 2002 (c 13 (NI))	The whole Act.
Company Directors Disqualification (Northern Ireland) Order 2002 (SI 2002/3150 (NI 4))	In Schedule 3, paragraphs 3 to 5.

Short title and chapter	*Extent of repeal or revocation brought into force*
Companies (Audit, Investigations and Community Enterprise) (Northern Ireland) Order 2005 (SI 2005/1967 (NI 17))	The provisions of the Order that remain in force.

SCHEDULE 2

Article 5

TRANSITIONAL PROVISIONS AND SAVINGS

1. General saving for existing companies etc

(1) Nothing in the Companies Act 2006 affects—

(a) the registration or re-registration of a company under the former Companies Acts, or the continued existence of a company by virtue of such registration or re-registration, or

(b) the application in relation to an existing company of—

(i) Table B in the Joint Stock Companies Act 1856,

(ii) Table A in any of the former Companies Acts, or

(iii) the Companies (Tables A to F) Regulations 1985 or the Companies (Tables A to F) Regulations (Northern Ireland) 1986.

(2) Section 1297(3) of the Companies Act 2006 (continuity of the law: things done under old law to be treated as done under the corresponding provision of the new law) applies—

(a) in relation to a company to which section 675(1) of the 1985 Act or Article 625(1) of the 1986 Order applied (application of Act or Order to companies formed and registered under earlier companies legislation) as if the company had been formed and registered under Part 1 of the 1985 Act or Part 2 of the 1986 Order;

(b) in relation to a company to which section 676(1) of the 1985 Act or Article 626(1) of the 1986 Order applied (application of Act or Order to companies registered but not formed under earlier companies legislation) as if the company had been registered under Chapter 2 of Part 22 of the 1985 Act or Chapter 2 of Part 22 of the 1986 Order;

(c) in relation to a company to which section 677(1) of the 1985 Act or Article 627(1) of the 1986 Order applied (application of Act or Order to companies re-registered under earlier companies legislation) as if the company had been re-registered under Part 2 of the 1985 Act or Part 3 of the 1986 Order.

(3) Nothing in this paragraph or in section 1297(3) of the Companies Act 2006 shall be read as affecting any reference to the date on which a company was registered or re-registered.

2. Company formation (ss 7 to 16)

(1) Sections 7 to 16 of the Companies Act 2006 (company formation) apply to applications for registration received by the registrar on or after 1st October 2009.

(2) Any application for registration under those provisions received by the registrar before that date shall not be entertained.

(3) The corresponding provisions of the 1985 Act or 1986 Order continue to apply to an application for registration if—

(a) it is received by the registrar, and

(b) the requirements as to registration are met in relation to it,

before 1st October 2009.

(4) Any application for registration under that Act or Order in relation to which the requirements as to registration are not met before that date shall be treated as withdrawn.

(5) For the purposes of section 1297(3) of the Companies Act 2006 (continuity of the law) as it applies to treat a company formed and registered under Part 1 of the 1985 Act or Part 2 of the 1986 Order as if formed and registered under the corresponding provisions of the

Companies Act 2006, the registration of a company on an application to which sub-paragraph (3) above applies is to be regarded as in force and effective immediately before the commencement of Part 1 of the Companies Act 2006.

(6) In the definition of "company" in section 1 of the Companies Act 2006—

(a) the reference to a company formed and registered after the commencement of Part 1 of that Act shall be read as a reference to a company formed and registered on an application to which sub-paragraph (1) above applies, and

(b) the reference to a company formed and registered under the 1985 Act or 1986 Order immediately before the commencement of Part 1 of the Companies Act 2006 includes a company formed and registered on an application to which sub-paragraph (3) above applies.

3. Articles of association (ss 18 to 20)

(1) Sections 7 and 8 of the 1985 Act or Articles 18 and 19 of the 1986 Order (articles of association) apply, and sections 18 to 20 of the Companies Act 2006 do not apply, to a company formed and registered under the 1985 Act or 1986 Order on an application to which paragraph 2(3) above applies.

(2) Nothing in section 18(3) of the Companies Act 2006 (articles to be contained in single document divided into consecutively numbered paragraphs) is to be read as affecting the operation of section 28 of that Act (under which certain provisions are to be treated as part of a company's articles).

4. Amendment of provisions of articles (ss 21 and 22)

(1) The power conferred by section 21(1) of the Companies Act 2006 (amendment of company's articles by special resolution) does not apply—

(a) to provisions of the articles of an existing company that were not capable of being so amended immediately before 1st October 2009; or

(b) to provisions of the articles of a transitional company that were not capable of being so amended under the company's constitution on its registration or re-registration (as the case may be).

(2) The power conferred by section 22(3)(a) of that Act (amendment of entrenched provisions of articles by agreement of all the members of the company) does not apply—

(a) to provisions of the articles of an existing company that were not capable of being so amended immediately before 1st October 2009; or

(b) to provisions of the articles of a transitional company that were not capable of being so amended under the company's constitution on its registration or re-registration (as the case may be).

(3) References in this paragraph to provisions of the articles of an existing or transitional company include provisions of the company's memorandum that are to be treated by virtue of section 28 of that Act as provisions of its articles.

(4) A special resolution passed before 1st October 2009 removing or amending with effect from that date any provision that as from that date is treated by virtue of section 28 of that Act as a provision of the company's articles, has effect as if passed on that date.

5. Notice to registrar of existence of restrictions on amendment of articles (s 23)

Section 23(1)(a) of the Companies Act 2006 (notice to registrar of fact that company's articles on formation contain provision for entrenchment) does not apply to a transitional company.

6. Registrar to be sent copy of amended articles (s 26)

(1) Section 26 of the Companies Act 2006 (registrar to be sent copy of amended articles) applies in relation to amendments taking effect on or after 1st October 2009.

(2) Section 18(2) and (3) of the 1985 Act or Article 29(2) and (3) of the 1986 Order continue to apply in relation to amendments taking effect before that date.

7. Provisions of memorandum treated as provisions of articles (s 28)

(1) Section 28 of the Companies Act 2006 (existing companies: provisions of memorandum treated as provisions of articles) applies not only to an existing company but also to a transitional company.

(2) In its application to a transitional company the reference to provisions that were contained in the company's memorandum immediately before the commencement of Part 3 shall be read as a reference to provisions that are contained in the company's memorandum on its registration or re-registration (as the case may be).

(3) Subject to sub-paragraphs (1) and (2), in subsection (1) of that section—

(a) "before the commencement of this Part" means before 1st October 2009, and

(b) "after the commencement of this Part" means on or after that date.

8. Nothing in section 28 of the Companies Act 2006 requires a company to give notice to the registrar of an alteration of its articles.

9. (1) A company whose articles are deemed by virtue of section 28 of the Companies Act 2006 to contain provisions formerly in its memorandum may comply with any obligation to send a person a copy of its articles—

(a) by appending to a copy of the other provisions of the articles a copy of the provisions of its old-style memorandum that are deemed to be provisions of the articles, or

(b) by sending together with a copy of the other provisions of the articles a copy of its old-style memorandum indicating the provisions that are deemed to be provisions of the articles.

(2) References in sub-paragraph (1) to a company's "old-style memorandum" are—

(a) in the case of an existing company, to its memorandum of association as it stood immediately before 1st October 2009;

(b) in the case of a transitional company, to its memorandum of association as it stood on its registration or re-registration (as the case may be) apart from the operation of section 28.

10. Nothing in the Companies Act 2006 shall be read as enabling a company to amend or omit provisions of its articles that were formerly in its memorandum so as to change its status as a limited or unlimited company otherwise than in accordance with the relevant provisions of Part 7 of that Act (re-registration as a means of changing company's status).

11. Constitutional documents to be provided to members (s 32)

(1) Section 32 of the Companies Act 2006 (constitutional documents to be provided to members) applies where the request is received by the company on or after 1st October 2009.

(2) Section 19 of the 1985 Act or Article 30 of the 1986 Order continues to apply where the request was received by the company before that date.

12. Notice to registrar where company's constitution altered by enactment (s 34)

(1) Section 34 of the Companies Act 2006 (notice to registrar where company's constitution altered by enactment) applies where the enactment in question comes into force on or after 1st October 2009.

(2) Section 18(1) and (3) of the 1985 Act or Article 29(1) and (3) of the 1986 Order continue to apply in relation to alterations made by statutory provisions coming into force before that date.

13. Notice to registrar where company's constitution altered by order (s 35)

Section 35 of the Companies Act 2006 (notice to registrar where company's constitution altered by order) applies in relation to orders made on or after 1st October 2009.

14. Documents to be incorporated in or accompany copies of articles issued by company (s 36)

(1) Section 36 of the Companies Act 2006 (documents to be incorporated in or accompany copies of articles issued by company) applies to copies of a company's articles issued on or after 1st October 2009.

(2) Section 380(2), (6) and (7) of the 1985 Act or Article 388(2), (6) and (7) of the 1986 Order continue to apply to copies issued before that date.

15. A company's capacity (s 39)

(1) Section 39 of the Companies Act 2006 (a company's capacity) applies to acts of a company done on or after 1st October 2009.

(2) Section 35 of the 1985 Act or Article 45 of the 1986 Order continues to apply to acts of a company done before that date.

16. Execution of deeds or other documents by attorney (s 47)

(1) Section 47 of the Companies Act 2006 (execution of deeds or other documents by attorney) applies where the instrument empowering a person to act as a company's attorney is executed on or after 1st October 2009.

(2) Section 38 of the 1985 Act or Article 48 of the 1986 Order continues to have effect where the power to act as a company's attorney was conferred before that date (including in relation to instruments executed by the attorney on behalf of the company on or after that date).

17. A company's name (ss 53 to 81)

(1) The following provisions of the Companies Act 2006 do not affect the continued registration of a company by a name by which it was duly registered—

(a) in the case of an existing company, immediately before 1st October 2009, or

(b) in the case of a transitional company, on its registration or re-registration (as the case may be).

(2) The provisions are—

(a) section 54 (name suggesting connection with government or public authority);

(b) section 55 (other sensitive words or expressions);

(c) section 57 (permitted characters etc);

(d) section 65 (inappropriate use of indications of company type or legal form);

(e) section 66 (name not to be the same as another in registrar's index).

18. (1) Sections 54 to 56 of the Companies Act 2006 (sensitive words and expressions) apply to applications for approval received by the Secretary of State on or after 1st October 2009.

(2) Section 29 of the 1985 Act or Article 39 of the 1986 Order continues to apply in relation to applications received by the Secretary of State or the Department of Enterprise, Trade and Investment in Northern Ireland before that date.

19. (1) Sections 77(1)(a) and 78 of the Companies Act 2006 (change of name by special resolution), and sections 80 and 81 of that Act so far as relating to a change of name by special resolution, apply where—

(a) the resolution is passed on or after 1st October 2009, or

(b) the resolution is passed before that date but no copy of the resolution is received by the registrar under section 30 of that Act (resolution affecting a company's constitution) before that date.

(2) Section 28(1), (6) and (7) of the 1985 Act or Article 38(1), (6) and (7) of the 1986 Order continue to apply to resolutions of which a copy is received by the registrar before that date.

20. The provisions of section 31(2) to (4) and (6) of the 1985 Act or Article 41(2) to (4) and (6) of the 1986 Order (power to direct company to change its name so that it ends with "limited") continue to apply where a direction under section 31(2) or Article 41(2) was given before 1st October 2009.

21. The provisions of section 32 of the 1985 Act or Article 42 of the 1986 Order (power to require company to abandon misleading name) continue to apply in relation to a direction under that section or Article given before 1st October 2009.

22. Re-registration as a means of altering a company's status (ss 89 to 108)

(1) Sections 89 to 108 of the Companies Act 2006 (re-registration as a means of altering a company's status) apply to applications for re-registration received by the registrar on or after 1st October 2009.

(2) Any application for re-registration under those provisions received by the registrar before that date shall not be entertained.

(3) The corresponding provisions of the 1985 Act or 1986 Order continue to apply to an application for re-registration if—

(a) it is received by the registrar, and

(b) the requirements for re-registration are met in relation to it,

before 1st October 2009.

(4) Any application for re-registration under that Act or Order in relation to which the requirements as to re-registration are not met before that date shall be treated as withdrawn.

(5) On an application to which sub-paragraph (1) above applies a resolution agreed to, or other thing done, before 1st October 2009 may be relied on for the purpose of meeting the requirements of the Companies Act 2006.

(6) For the purposes of section 1297(3) of the Companies Act 2006 (continuity of the law) as it applies to treat a company re-registered under the 1985 Act or the 1986 Order as if re-registered under the corresponding provisions of the Companies Act 2006, the re-registration of a company on an application to which sub-paragraph (3) above applies is to be regarded as in force and effective immediately before the commencement of Part 7 of the Companies Act 2006.

23. Register of members: information as to state of register and index (s 120)

Section 120 of the Companies Act 2006 (information as to state of register or index) applies where a person—

(a) inspects a company's register of members or index of members' names on or after 1st October 2009, or

(b) is provided by a company on or after that date with a copy of the company's register of members or any part of it,

whether the person's request to inspect, or be provided with a copy, was made before, on or after that date.

24. Repeal of minimum membership requirement

The repeal of section 24 of the 1985 Act or Article 34 of the 1986 Order (minimum membership for carrying on business) does not affect any liability under that section or Article for debts of the company contracted before 1st October 2009.

25. Registers of directors and secretaries (ss 162 and 275)

On and after 1st October 2009 the register of directors and secretaries kept by a company under section 288(1) of the 1985 Act or Article 296(1) of the 1986 Order shall be treated as two separate registers—

(a) a register of directors kept under and for the purposes of section 162 of the Companies Act 2006, and

(b) a register of secretaries kept under and for the purposes of section 275 of that Act.

26. Particulars to be registered (ss 163, 164 and 166 and 277 to 279)

(1) Subject to the following provisions, an existing company need not comply with any provision of the Companies Act 2006 requiring the company's register of directors or

secretaries to contain particulars additional to those required by the 1985 Act or the 1986 Order until the earlier of—

(a) the date to which the company makes up its first annual return made up to a date on or after 1st October 2009, and

(b) the last date to which the company should have made up that return.

(2) Sub-paragraph (1) does not apply in relation to a director or secretary of whom particulars are first registered on or after 1st October 2009 (whether the director or secretary was appointed before, on or after that date).

(3) Sub-paragraph (1) ceases to apply in relation to a director or secretary whose registered particulars fall to be altered on or after 1st October 2009 because they have changed (whether the change occurred before, on or after that date).

(4) This paragraph does not affect the particulars required to be included in the company's annual return.

27. (1) In the case of an existing company—

(a) the relevant existing address of a director or secretary is deemed, on and after 1st October 2009, to be a service address, and

(b) any entry in the company's register of directors or secretaries stating that address is treated, on and after that date, as complying with the obligation in section 163(1)(b) or 277(1)(b) of the Companies Act 2006 to state a service address.

(2) The relevant existing address is—

(a) the address that immediately before 1st October 2009 appeared in the company's register of directors and secretaries as having been notified to the company under section 289(1A) or 290(1A) of the 1985 Act (service address notified by individual applying for confidentiality order in respect of usual residential address), or

(b) if no such address appeared, the address that immediately before that date appeared in the company's register of directors and secretaries as the director's or secretary's usual residential address.

(3) Any notification of a change of a relevant existing address occurring before 1st October 2009 that is received by the company on or after that date is treated as being or, as the case may be, including notification of a change of service address.

(4) The operation of this paragraph does not give rise to any duty to notify the registrar under section 167 or 276 of the Companies Act 2006 (duty to notify registrar of changes in particulars contained in register).

28. (1) An existing company must remove from its register of directors on 1st October 2009 any entry relating to a shadow director.

(2) Section 167 of the Companies Act 2006 (duty to notify registrar of changes) applies as if the shadow director had ceased to be a director on that date.

29. The removal by an existing company from its register of directors or secretaries on or after 1st October 2009 of particulars required by the 1985 Act or the 1986 Order but not required by the Companies Act 2006 does not give rise to any duty to notify the registrar under section 167 or 276 of the Companies Act 2006 (duty to notify registrar of changes in particulars contained in register).

30. Register of directors' residential addresses (s 165)

(1) The duty of a company to keep a register of directors' residential addresses has effect on and after 1st October 2009.

(2) The entry on that register of information that immediately before that date was contained in the company's register of directors and secretaries does not give rise to any duty to notify the registrar under section 167 of the Companies Act 2006 (duty to notify registrar of changes in particulars contained in register).

31. Duty to notify registrar of changes (ss 167 and 276)

(1) Sections 167 and 276 of the Companies Act 2006 (duty to notify registrar of changes) apply in relation to—

(a) a change among a company's directors or in its secretaries, or

(b) a change in the particulars contained in the register,

occurring on or after 1st October 2009.

(2) Sections 288(2), (4) and (6), 289 and 290 of the 1985 Act or Articles 296(2), (4) and (6), 297 and 298 of the 1986 Order (notification to registrar of changes) continue to apply in relation to a change occurring before that date.

32. Directors and secretaries: entries on the register of companies

(1) The registrar may make such entries in the register as appear to be appropriate having regard to paragraphs 26 to 30 and the information appearing on the register immediately before 1st October 2009 or notified to the registrar in accordance with paragraph 31(2).

(2) In particular, the registrar may record as a service address—

(a) a relevant existing address (within the meaning of paragraph 27), or

(b) in the case of a company formed and registered on an application to which paragraph 2(3) applies, an address notified to the registrar in connection with that application as a director's or secretary's usual residential address.

(3) Any notification of a change of a relevant existing address occurring before 1st October 2009 that is received by the registrar on or after that date is treated as being or, as the case may be, including notification of a change of service address.

33. Directors' residential addresses: protection from disclosure (ss 240 to 246)

Where a director's usual residential address appears as a service address—

(a) in the company's register of directors by virtue of paragraph 27, or

(b) in the register of companies by virtue of paragraph 32,

that address is not protected information for the purposes of Chapter 8 of Part 10 of the Companies Act 2006.

34. (1) Section 242(1) of the Companies Act 2006 (duty of registrar to omit protected information from material available for inspection) does not apply—

(a) to material delivered to the registrar before 1st October 2009, or

(b) to material delivered to the registrar on or after 1st October 2009 by virtue of paragraph 31(2) (notification of change occurring before that date).

(2) In section 242(2)(b) of the Companies Act 2006 (exclusion of material registered before commencement) the reference to things registered before Chapter 8 of Part 10 of that Act comes into force is treated as including anything registered as a result of a notification in accordance with paragraph 31(2) (notification on or after 1st October 2009 of change occurring before that date).

(3) Sub-paragraphs (1) and (2) have effect subject to paragraph 36 below (which provides for the continued protection of information formerly protected by a confidentiality order).

35. In determining under section 245(1) of the Companies Act 2006 whether to put a director's usual residential address on the public record, the registrar may take into account only—

(a) communications sent by the registrar on or after 1st October 2009, and

(b) evidence as to the effectiveness of service coming to the registrar's attention on or after that date.

36. Continuation of protection afforded by confidentiality orders under the 1985 Act

(1) A director or secretary in relation to whom a confidentiality order under section 723B of the 1985 Act was in force immediately before 1st October 2009 is treated on and after that date as if—

(a) they had made an application under section 1088 of the Companies Act 2006 (application to make address unavailable for public inspection) in respect of any address that immediately before that date was contained in "confidential records" as defined in section 723D(3) of the 1985 Act, and

(b) that application had been determined by the registrar in their favour.

(2) The provisions of regulations under section 1088 relating to decisions of the registrar in favour of an applicant (in particular, as to the duration and revocation of such a decision) apply accordingly.

(3) As those regulations apply in accordance with this paragraph any reference to an offence under section 1112 of the Companies Act 2006 (false statement) shall be read as a reference to an offence under regulations under section 723E(1)(a) of the 1985 Act in relation to the application for the confidentiality order.

37. (1) A director in relation to whom a confidentiality order under section 723B of the 1985 Act was in force immediately before 1st October 2009 is treated on and after that date as if—

(a) they had made an application under section 243(4) of the Companies Act 2006 (application to prevent disclosure of protected information by registrar to credit reference agency), and

(b) that application had been determined by the registrar in their favour.

(2) The provisions of regulations under section 243(4) relating to decisions of the registrar in favour of an applicant (in particular, as to the duration and revocation of such a decision) apply accordingly.

(3) As those regulations apply in accordance with this paragraph any reference to an offence under section 1112 (false statement) shall be read as a reference to an offence under regulations under section 723E(1)(a) of the 1985 Act in relation to the application for the confidentiality order.

38. Where a confidentiality order under section 723B of the 1985 Act was in force immediately before 1st October 2009 in relation to a director or secretary of a company—

(a) section 162(5) and (8) of the Companies Act 2006 (inspection of company's register of directors), or

(b) section 275(5) and (8) of that Act (inspection of company's register of secretaries),

do not apply in relation to the part of the company's register containing particulars of the usual residential address of the individual that before that date were protected from disclosure by section 288(5A) of the 1985 Act.

39. Effect of pending application for confidentiality order

(1) Section 723B(3) to (8) of the 1985 Act (application for confidentiality order) continue to apply in relation to an application for a confidentiality order made before 1st October 2009.

(2) Paragraphs 36 to 38 (continuation of protection afforded by confidentiality orders) apply to a person in respect of whom such an application has been made, and has not been determined or withdrawn, as to a person in relation to whom a confidentiality order was in force immediately before that date.

(3) If the application is dismissed or withdrawn, those paragraphs cease to apply.

(4) If the application is successful those paragraphs continue to apply as in the case of an individual in relation to whom a confidentiality order was in force immediately before 1st October 2009.

40. Power to make provision for employees on cessation or transfer of business (s 247)

(1) Section 247 of the Companies Act 2006 (power to make provision for employees on cessation or transfer of business) applies to provision made on or after 1st October 2009 (subject to sub-paragraph (2)(b)).

(2) Section 719 of the 1985 Act or Article 668 of the 1986 Order continues to apply—

(a) to provision made before that date, and

(b) to anything sanctioned in accordance with subsection (3) of that section or paragraph (3) of that Article before that date.

41. Conversion of shares into stock (s 540(2) and (3))

(1) Section 540(2) of the Companies Act 2006 (prohibition on conversion of shares into stock) does not affect the conversion of shares into stock in pursuance of a resolution of the company in general meeting passed, or a written resolution agreed to, before 1st October 2009.

(2) The reference in section 540(3) (reconversion) to stock created before the commencement of Part 17 of that Act includes stock created in pursuance of such a resolution.

(3) Section 122(1)(b) and (2) of the 1985 Act or Article 132(1)(b) and (2) of the 1986 Order (notice to registrar of conversion) continue to apply in relation to the conversion of shares into stock under such a resolution.

42. Saving for provisions as to amount of authorised share capital

(1) This paragraph applies to any provision of a company's memorandum as to the amount of a company's authorised share capital that is in force immediately before 1st October 2009, as altered by anything done by virtue of section 121 of the 1985 Act or Article 131 of the 1986 Order (alteration of share capital) and in force immediately before that date.

(2) Any such provision—

(a) is treated on and after 1st October 2009 as a provision of the company's articles setting the maximum amount of shares that may be allotted by the company, and

(b) may be amended or revoked by the company by ordinary resolution.

(3) Chapter 3 of Part 3 of the Companies Act 2006 (resolutions and agreements affecting a company's constitution) applies to any such resolution.

(4) Nothing in sub-paragraph (2) affects the power of a company by special resolution to adopt new articles, with effect from 1st October 2009 or any later date, that make no provision as to the maximum number of shares that may be allotted by the company.

(5) Any such resolution as is mentioned in sub-paragraph (2) or (4) that is passed before 1st October 2009 is treated as passed on that date.

(6) An amendment of a company's articles on or after 1st October 2009 authorising the directors to allot shares in excess of the amount allowed by any such provision as is mentioned in sub-paragraph (1) has effect although not expressed as amending or revoking it.

43. Power of directors to allot shares etc: private company with only one class of shares (s 550)

(1) Section 550 of the Companies Act 2006 (power of directors to allot shares etc: private company with only one class of shares) applies to an existing or transitional company only if the members of the company have resolved that the directors should have the powers given by that section.

(2) A resolution under this paragraph may be an ordinary resolution (even if it takes the form of an alteration of the company's articles).

(3) Chapter 3 of Part 3 of the Companies Act 2006 (resolutions and agreements affecting a company's constitution) applies to any such resolution.

(4) Any such resolution passed before 1st October 2009 is treated as if passed on that date.

(5) Once the members of the company have resolved as mentioned in sub-paragraph (1), the application of section 550 in relation to the company is not affected by any subsequent resolution, except one altering the company's articles so as to prohibit (to any extent) exercise of the powers mentioned in the section.

44. For the purposes of section 550 of the Companies Act 2006 provisions of the articles of an existing or transitional company—

(a) authorising the directors to allot shares in accordance with section 80 of the 1985 Act or Article 90 of the 1986 Order, or

(b) added following an elective resolution under section 80A of the 1985 Act or Article 90A of the 1986 Order and authorising the directors to allot shares,

are not to be treated as provisions prohibiting the directors from exercising the powers conferred by section 550 in cases to which the authority does not extend.

45. Power of directors to allot shares etc: authorisation by company (s 551)

An authorisation in force immediately before 1st October 2009 under section 80 or 80A of the 1985 Act or Article 90 or 90A of the 1986 Order has effect on and after that date as if given under section 551 of the Companies Act 2006 (power of directors to allot shares etc: authorisation by company).

46. Registration of allotment (s 554)

Section 554 of the Companies Act 2006 (registration of allotment) applies to shares allotted on or after 1st October 2009.

47. Return of allotment (ss 555 to 557)

(1) Section 555 of the Companies Act 2006 (return of allotment by limited company) applies to shares allotted on or after 1st October 2009.

(2) Section 88 of the 1985 Act or Article 98 of the 1986 Order continues to apply to shares allotted before that date.

48. (1) Section 556 of the Companies Act 2006 (return of allotment by unlimited company allotting new class of shares) applies to shares allotted on or after 1st October 2009.

(2) Section 128(1), (2) and (5) of the 1985 Act or Article 138(1), (2) and (5) of the 1986 Order continue to apply to shares allotted before that date.

49. Existing shareholders' right of pre-emption (ss 561 to 577)

(1) Section 561 of the Companies Act 2006 (prohibition on allotment unless offers made to existing shareholders) applies to the allotment of shares on or after 1st October 2009.

(2) Where that section applies—

(a) section 562 of that Act (communication of pre-emption offers to shareholders) applies to offers made on or after 1st October 2009, and

(b) section 90 of the 1985 Act or Article 100 of the 1986 Order continues to apply to offers made before that date,

and the requirements of section 561 may be met by offers within paragraph (a) or (b) above.

(3) Section 563 of the Companies Act 2006 (consequences of contravention) applies where section 561 applies and the reference to section 562 of that Act shall be read accordingly as including a reference to section 90 of the 1985 Act or Article 100 of the 1986 Order.

50. (1) This paragraph applies where provision made by virtue of section 91 of the 1985 Act or Article 101 of the 1986 Order (exclusion of requirements by private company) excluding the requirements of section 89 or 90 or Article 99 or 100 is in force immediately before 1st October 2009.

(2) That provision has effect on and after that date as if it was or, as the case may be, included provision made by virtue of section 567 of the Companies Act 2006 excluding the corresponding requirements of section 561 or 562 of that Act.

51. (1) Section 568 of the Companies Act 2006 (exclusion of statutory pre-emption right where articles confer corresponding right) applies to the allotment of shares on or after 1st October 2009.

(2) The reference in section 568(3) to section 562 of that Act (communication of pre-emption offers to shareholders) shall be read in relation to offers made before 1st October 2009 as a reference to section 90 of the 1985 Act or Article 100 of the 1986 Order.

(3) Section 563 of the Companies Act 2006 (consequences of contravention) applies in relation to such an offer as if the reference to section 562 of that Act were a reference to section 90 of the 1985 Act or Article 100 of the 1986 Order.

52. (1) This paragraph applies where provision excluding or modifying section 89(1) of the 1985 Act or Article 99(1) of the 1986 Order has been made by virtue of section 95(1) of the 1985 Act or Article 105(1) of the 1986 Order and is in force immediately before 1st October 2009.

(2) The provision has effect on and after that date as if it had been made by virtue of section 570 of the Companies Act 2006 (disapplication of pre-emption rights: directors acting under general authorisation) and excluded, or made corresponding modifications of, section 561 of that Act.

(3) The power conferred to allot equity securities may accordingly be renewed under section 570(3).

53. (1) This paragraph applies where a special resolution excluding or modifying section 89(1) of the 1985 Act or Article 99(1) of the 1986 Order has been passed by virtue of section 95(2) of the 1985 Act or Article 105(2) of the 1986 Order and is in force immediately before 1st October 2009.

(2) The resolution has effect on and after that date as if it had been passed by virtue of section 571 of the Companies Act 2006 (disapplication of pre-emption rights by special resolution) and excluded, or made corresponding modifications of, section 561 of that Act.

(3) The resolution may accordingly be renewed under section 571(3).

54. (1) It is immaterial whether the directors' statement required before a resolution can be proposed under section 571 of the Companies Act 2006 (disapplication of pre-emption rights by special resolution) is made, or is sent, submitted or circulated as required by subsection (7) of that section before, on or after 1st October 2009.

(2) Section 572 of that Act (criminal liability for false statement) applies to a directors' statement that is sent, submitted or circulated to a member on or after 1st October 2009.

(3) Section 95(6) of the 1985 Act or Article 105(6) of the 1986 Order applies to a directors' statement that is circulated or supplied to a member before that date.

55. (1) This paragraph applies where provision excluding or modifying section 89(1) of the 1985 Act or Article 99(1) of the 1986 Order has been made by virtue of section 95(2A) of the 1985 Act or Article 105(2A) of the 1986 Order and is in force immediately before 1st October 2009.

(2) The provision has effect on and after that date as if it had been made by virtue of section 573 of the Companies Act 2006 (disapplication of pre-emption rights: sale of treasury shares) and excluded, or made corresponding modifications of, section 561 of that Act.

(3) The power conferred to allot equity securities may accordingly be renewed under section 570(3) or, as the case may be, section 571(3).

56. Public companies: allotment where issue not fully subscribed (ss 578 and 579)

(1) Sections 578 and 579 of the Companies Act 2006 (public companies: allotment where issue not fully subscribed) apply where the offer is made on or after 1st October 2009, unless a prospectus has been issued before that date.

(2) Sections 84 and 85 of the 1985 Act or Articles 94 and 95 of the 1986 Order continue to apply where the offer was made, or a prospectus issued, before that date.

(3) In the case of an offer made or a prospectus issued on more than one day, the references in this paragraph to the date on which it is made or issued are to the first day on which it was made or issued.

(4) References in this paragraph to a prospectus being issued are to its being made available to the public in accordance with Part 6 of the Financial Services and Markets Act 2000.

57. Meaning of "cash consideration" for shares (ss 583 and 607)

(1) Section 583(3)(e) of the Companies Act 2006 (meaning of "cash consideration for shares": other means equivalent to payment in cash) applies only in relation to consideration received in pursuance of an obligation entered into on or after 1st October 2009.

(2) Section 607 of that Act (penalty for contravention of provisions about valuation of non-cash consideration) applies in relation to consideration received in pursuance of an obligation entered into on or after that date.

(3) Section 114 of the 1985 Act or Article 124 of the 1986 Order continues to apply in relation to consideration received in pursuance of an obligation entered into before that date.

58. Power of court to grant relief (ss 589 and 606)

In section 589(3) and (4) and section 606(2) and (3) of the Companies Act 2006 (power of court to grant relief from liabilities in connection with payment for shares: matters to be taken into account), the words from "having regard to" to the end of the subsection shall be omitted in relation to a decision whether to grant relief in respect of a liability for interest arising before 1st October 2009.

59. Sub-division or consolidation of shares (s 618)

The repeal of section 122(1)(a) and (d) and (2) of the 1985 Act or Article 132(1)(a) and (d) and (2) of the 1986 Order (notice to registrar of consolidation and division, or sub-division, of shares) does not affect the operation of those provisions in relation to a consolidation and division, or sub-division, of shares effected before 1st October 2009.

60. Reconversion of stock into shares (s 620)

The repeal of section 122(1)(c) and (2) of the 1985 Act or Article 132(1)(c) and (2) of the 1986 Order (notice to registrar of reconversion of stock into shares) does not affect the operation of those provisions in relation to a reconversion effected before 1st October 2009.

61. Variation of class rights: companies without a share capital (ss 631 and 634)

Nothing in section 631 or 634 of the Companies Act 2006 (variation of class rights by company without a share capital) affects a variation of class rights made (in accordance with provision in the company's memorandum or articles) before 1st October 2009.

62. Notice of name or other designation of class of shares (s 636)

(1) Section 636 of the Companies Act 2006 (notice of name or other designation of class of shares) applies where the new name or other designation is assigned on or after 1st October 2009.

(2) Section 128(4) and (5) of the 1985 Act or Article 138(4) and (5) of the 1986 Order continue to apply where the new name or other designation was assigned before that date.

63. Notice of particulars of variation of rights attached to shares (s 637)

(1) Section 637 of the Companies Act 2006 (notice of particulars of variation of rights attached to shares) applies where the variation is made on or after 1st October 2009.

(2) Section 128(3) and (5) of the 1985 Act or Article 138(3) and (5) of the 1986 Order continue to apply where the variation was made before that date.

64. Notice of new class of members (s 638)

(1) Section 638 of the Companies Act 2006 (notice of new class of members) applies where a new class of members is created on or after 1st October 2009.

(2) Section 129(1) and (4) of the 1985 Act or Article 139(1) and (4) of the 1986 Order continue to apply where a new class of members was created before that date.

65. Notice of name or other designation of class of members (s 639)

(1) Section 639 of the Companies Act 2006 (notice of name or other designation of class of members) applies where the name or other designation, or new name or other designation, is assigned on or after 1st October 2009.

(2) Section 129(3) and (4) of the 1985 Act or Article 139(3) and (4) of the 1986 Order continue to apply where the name or other designation, or new name or other designation, was assigned before that date.

66. Notice of particulars of variation of class rights (s 640)

(1) Section 640 of the Companies Act 2006 (notice of particulars of variation of class rights) applies where the variation is made on or after 1st October 2009.

(2) Section 129(2) and (4) of the 1985 Act or Article 139(2) and (4) of the 1986 Order continue to apply where the variation was made before that date.

67. Repeal of provisions about reserve liability and reserve capital

The repeal of—

(a) section 120 of the 1985 Act or Article 130 of the 1986 Order (reserve liability of limited company), or

(b) section 124 of the 1985 Act or Article 134 of the 1986 Order (reserve capital of unlimited company),

does not affect the validity of any resolution under those provisions that is in force immediately before 1st October 2009.

68. Reduction of capital confirmed by the court (ss 645 to 653)

(1) Sections 645 to 651 of the Companies Act 2006 (reduction of capital confirmed by the court) apply where an application to the court is made under section 645(1) on or after 1st October 2009.

(2) It is immaterial for the purposes of such an application whether the resolution for reducing share capital was agreed to before, on or after 1st October 2009.

(3) The corresponding provisions of the 1985 Act or the 1986 Order continue to apply where an application to the court has been made under section 136 of that Act or Article 146 of that Order before that date.

(4) For the purposes of an application under section 645(1) any amendments of a company's memorandum contained in a resolution agreed to before 1st October 2009 are treated as amendments of the company's articles.

69. (1) Nothing in section 652 of the Companies Act 2006 (liability of members following reduction of capital) as it applies in relation to a reduction of capital confirmed by the court, or in section 653 of that Act (liability to creditor in case of omission from list of creditors), applies in relation to a reduction of capital in pursuance of an application to the court made before 1st October 2009.

(2) The provisions of section 140 of the 1985 Act or Article 150 of the 1986 Order continue to apply in relation to such a reduction.

70. Cancellation of shares in public company held by or for the company (ss 662 to 668)

(1) Section 662 of the Companies Act 2006 (duty to cancel shares in public company held by or for the company) applies where an event mentioned in section 662(1) or 668(1)(a) to (d) occurs on or after 1st October 2009.

(2) Section 662 also applies where an event mentioned in section 146(1) or 148(1)(a) to (d) of the 1985 Act or Article 156(1) or 158(1)(a) to (d) of the 1986 Order occurred before 1st October 2009, unless before that date—

(a) the company has complied with section 146(2) or Article 156(2), or

(b) the period for compliance specified in section 146(3) or Article 156(3) has expired.

(3) The provisions of the 1985 Act or 1986 Order continue to apply in those cases where section 662 does not apply.

71. (1) Section 663 of the Companies Act 2006 (notice of cancellation of shares in public company held by or for the company) applies where the shares referred to in subsection (1) of that section are cancelled on or after 1st October 2009.

(2) Section 122(1)(f) and (2) of the 1985 Act or Article 132(1)(f) and (2) of the 1986 Order continue to apply where the shares referred to in section 122(1)(f) or Article 132(1)(f) are cancelled before that date.

72. (1) Sections 664 to 667 of the Companies Act 2006 (re-registration as private company in consequence of cancellation) apply in any case where section 662 of that Act applies (see paragraph 70(1) and (2) above).

(2) The corresponding provisions of the 1985 Act or 1986 Order continue to apply in any other case.

(3) For the purposes of an application under section 664 made by virtue of paragraph 70(2) above a resolution agreed to before 1st October 2009 under section 147(2) of the 1985 Act or Article 157(2) of the 1986 Order may be treated as if agreed to under section 664(1) and (2) (and as if amendments of the company's memorandum were amendments of its articles).

73. Redeemable shares (ss 684 to 689)

(1) Section 686(2) of the Companies Act 2006 (terms allowing for payment on date later than redemption date) applies—

(a) to shares issued on or after 1st October 2009, and

(b) to shares issued before that date where the terms of redemption have been amended on or after that date to allow for payment on a date later than the redemption date.

(2) So much of section 159(3) of the 1985 Act or Article 169(3) of the 1986 Order as requires payment on redemption continues to apply in any other case.

74. (1) Section 689 of the Companies Act 2006 (notice to registrar of redemption) applies where shares are redeemed on or after 1st October 2009.

(2) Section 122(1)(e) and (2) of the 1985 Act or Article 132(1)(e) and (2) of the 1986 Order continue to apply where shares are redeemed before that date.

75. Purchase of own shares (ss 690 to 708)

Where immediately before 1st October 2009 a resolution is in force having been passed under any provision of—

(a) section 164 of the 1985 Act or Article 174 of the 1986 Order (authority for off-market purchase),

(b) section 165 of the 1985 Act or Article 175 of the 1986 Order (authority for contingent purchase contract),

(c) section 166 of the 1985 Act or Article 176 of the 1986 Order (authority for market purchase), or

(d) section 167(2) of the 1985 Act or Article 177(2) of the 1986 Order (release of company's right to purchase own shares),

the resolution has effect on and after that date as if passed under the corresponding provision of the Companies Act 2006 and may be varied, revoked or renewed from time to time accordingly.

76. (1) Sections 693(1)(a) and 694 of the Companies Act 2006 (purchase of own shares: authority for off-market purchase) apply—

(a) to contracts entered into on or after 1st October 2009, and

(b) to contracts entered into before that date that—

(i) provide that no shares may be purchased in pursuance of the contract until its terms have been authorised by a special resolution of the company, and

(ii) are authorised by a special resolution passed on or after that date.

(2) Sections 164 and 165 of the 1985 Act or Articles 174 and 175 of the 1986 Order continue to apply to any other contract entered into before that date.

77. (1) Sections 707 and 708 of the Companies Act 2006 (return to registrar of purchase of own shares and notice of cancellation) apply in relation to shares delivered to the company on or after 1st October 2009.

(2) Section 169 of the 1985 Act or Article 179 of the 1986 Order continues to apply in relation to shares delivered to the company before that date.

78. Power of private company to redeem or purchase own shares out of capital (ss 709 to 723)

(1) Sections 709 to 723 of the Companies Act 2006 (redemption or purchase by private company out of capital) apply where the directors' statement referred to in section 714 is made on or after 1st October 2009.

(2) Sections 171 to 178 of the 1985 Act or Articles 181 to 188 of the 1986 Order continue to apply where the statutory declaration required by section 173(3) or Article 183(3) was made before that date.

79. Treasury shares: disposal (s 727)

(1) Section 727(1)(a) of the Companies Act 2006 (treasury shares: disposal) applies where the contract for the sale of the shares is entered into on or after 1st October 2009.

(2) Section 162D(1)(a) of the 1985 Act or Article 172D(1)(a) of the 1986 Order continues to apply where the contract for the sale of the shares was entered into before that date.

80. Treasury shares: notice of cancellation (s 730)

(1) Section 730 of the Companies Act 2006 (treasury shares: notice of cancellation) applies to shares cancelled on or after 1st October 2009.

(2) Section 169A of the 1985 Act or Article 179A of the 1986 Order continues to apply to shares cancelled before that date.

81. Annual returns (ss 854 to 859)

(1) Sections 854 to 859 of the Companies Act 2006 (a company's annual return) apply to annual returns made up to a date on or after 1st October 2009.

(2) Sections 363 to 365 of the 1985 Act or Articles 371 to 373 of the 1986 Order continue to apply to annual returns made up to a date before 1st October 2009.

(3) Any reference in the Companies Act 2006 to a company's last return, or to a return delivered in accordance with Part 24 of that Act, shall be read as including (so far as necessary to ensure the continuity of the law) a return made up to a date before 1st October 2009 or delivered in accordance with the 1985 Act or the 1986 Order.

82. Company charges (ss 860 to 894)

(1) Sections 860 and 878 of the Companies Act 2006 (charges created by company) apply to charges created on or after 1st October 2009.

(2) The corresponding provisions of the 1985 Act or the 1986 Order continue to apply to charges created before that date.

83. (1) Sections 862 and 880 of the Companies Act 2006 (charges existing on property acquired) apply to property acquired on or after 1st October 2009.

(2) Sections 400 and 416 of the 1985 Act or Article 407 of the 1986 Order continue to apply to property acquired before that date.

84. (1) Sections 863 and 882 of the Companies Act 2006 (charge in series of debentures) apply where the first debenture of the series is executed on or after 1st October 2009.

(2) The corresponding provisions of the 1985 Act or the 1986 Order continue to apply where the first debenture of the series is executed before that date.

85. (1) Section 868 of the Companies Act 2006 (Northern Ireland: registration of certain charges etc affecting land) applies where the date of registration of the charge in the Land Registry is on or after 1st October 2009.

(2) Article 408 of the 1986 Order continues to apply where the date of registration of the charge in the Land Registry is before that date.

86. (1) Section 871 of the Companies Act 2006 (notice to registrar of appointment of receiver or manager etc) applies where the order or appointment is made, or the receiver or manager ceases to act, on or after 1st October 2009.

(2) Section 405 of the 1985 Act or Article 413 of the 1986 Order continues to apply where the order or appointment is made, or the receiver or manager ceases to act, before that date.

87. (1) Sections 872 and 887 of the Companies Act 2006 (entries of satisfaction and release) apply to statements delivered to the registrar on or after 1st October 2009.

(2) Section 403 or 419 of the 1985 Act or Article 411 of the 1986 Order continues to apply where the relevant statutory declaration, statement or application and statutory declaration or statement is received by the registrar before that date.

88. Property of dissolved company (ss 1012 to 1023)

(1) Sections 1012 to 1023 of the Companies Act 2006 (property of dissolved company) apply in relation to the property of a company dissolved on or after 1st October 2009.

(2) Subject to paragraph 88A, the corresponding provisions of the 1985 Act or 1986 Order continue to apply in relation to the property of a company dissolved before that date.

88A. (1) Section 1013 of the Companies Act 2006 (Crown disclaimer of property vesting as bona vacantia) applies in relation to property of a company dissolved before 1st October 2009 if at that date—

(a) no period has begun to run in relation to the property under section 656(3)(a) or (b) of the 1985 Act or Article 607(3)(a) or (b) of the 1986 Order (period within which notice of disclaimer must be executed), and

(b) the right to disclaim has not ceased to be exercisable in relation to the property by virtue of section 656(2) of the 1985 Act or Article 607(2) of the 1986 Order (waiver of right to disclaim).

(2) In section 1013 as it applies by virtue of this paragraph the references to property vesting under section 1012 shall be read as references to its vesting under section 654 of the 1985 Act or Article 605 of the 1986 Order (or corresponding earlier provisions).

(3) Where section 1013 applies by virtue of this paragraph—

(a) the other provisions of sections 1012 to 1022 of the Companies Act 2006 apply accordingly, and

(b) the corresponding provisions of the 1985 Act or 1986 Order do not apply.

89. Saving for applications to court made before 1st October 2009

The repeal of—

(a) section 651 of the 1985 Act or Article 602 of the 1986 Order (power of court to declare dissolution of company void), or

(b) section 653 of the 1985 Act or Article 604 of the 1986 Order (objection to striking off by person aggrieved),

does not affect an application made under that section or Article before 1st October 2009.

90. Application to court for restoration to the register (ss 1029 to 1032)

Sections 1029 to 1032 of the Companies Act 2006 (restoration to register by the court) apply whether the company was dissolved or struck off the register before, on or after 1st October 2009.

91. (1) The following provisions apply where the company was dissolved or struck off the register before 1st October 2009.

(2) In section 1029 (application to court for restoration to register), the references in subsection (1) to enactments under which a company may have been dissolved or struck off include corresponding earlier enactments (and for this purpose sections 1000 and 1003 of that Act are regarded as corresponding to sections 652 and 652A of the 1985 Act and Articles 603 and 603A of the 1986 Order).

(3) No application under section 1029 may be made if an application in respect of the same dissolution or striking off has been made under section 653 of the 1985 Act or Article 604 of the 1986 Order (objection to striking off by person aggrieved), and has not been withdrawn.

(4) Section 1030(4) (general time limit of six years) does not enable an application to be made in respect of a company dissolved before 1st October 2007, subject to sub-paragraphs (5) and (6).

(5) If the company was struck off under section 652 or 652A of the 1985 Act or Article 603 or 603A of the 1986 Order, section 1030(4) does not prevent an application being made at any time before—

(a) 1st October 2015 (that is, six years after commencement), or

(b) the expiration of the period of 20 years from publication in the Gazette of notice under the relevant section or Article, whichever occurs first.

(6) Section 1030(5) (extension of period for application where application for administrative restoration refused) applies in relation to the time limit under sub-paragraph (5) above as in relation to the time limit in section 1030(4).

92. Effect of restoration to the register where property has vested as bona vacantia (s 1034)

(1) Section 1034 of the Companies Act 2006 (effect of restoration to the register where property has vested as bona vacantia) applies whenever the company was dissolved.

(2) The following provisions apply where the company was dissolved before 1st October 2009.

(3) The reference in section 1034(1) to section 1012 (property of dissolved company to be bona vacantia) shall be read as a reference to section 654 of the 1985 Act or Article 605 of the 1986 Order (or corresponding earlier provisions).

(4) No deduction is to be made under section 1034(3) (deduction of reasonable costs of Crown representative from amount payable to company) from consideration realised before 1st October 2009.

93. Registration of companies not formed under companies legislation (ss 1040 to 1042)

(1) The provisions of Chapter 1 of Part 33 of the Companies Act 2006 (registration of companies not formed under companies legislation) apply to applications for registration received by the registrar on or after 1st October 2009.

(2) Any application for registration under those provisions received by the registrar before that date shall not be entertained.

(3) The provisions of Chapter 2 of Part 22 of the 1985 Act or Chapter 2 of Part 22 of the 1986 Order continue to apply to an application for registration if—

(a) it is received by the registrar, and

(b) the requirements as to registration are met in relation to it,

before 1st October 2009.

(4) Any application for registration under that Act or Order in relation to which the requirements as to registration are not met before that date shall be treated as withdrawn.

(5) On an application to which sub-paragraph (1) above applies a resolution agreed to, or other thing done, before 1st October 2009 may be relied on for the purpose of meeting the requirements of the Companies Act 2006.

(6) For the purposes of section 1297(3) of the Companies Act 2006 (continuity of the law) as it applies to treat the registration of a company under Chapter 2 of Part 22 of the 1985 Act or Chapter 2 of Part 22 of the 1986 Order as if done under the corresponding provision of the Companies Act 2006, the registration of a company on an application to which sub-paragraph (3) above applies is to be regarded as in force and effective immediately before the commencement of Chapter 1 of Part 33 of the Companies Act 2006.

94. Fees payable to registrar (s 1063)

Any regulations under section 708 of the 1985 Act or Article 657 of the 1986 Order (fees payable to registrar) that are in force immediately before 1st October 2009 have effect on or after that date as if made under section 1063 of the Companies Act 2006.

95. Certificates of incorporation (ss 1064 and 1065)

Section 1064 of the Companies Act 2006 (public notice of issue of certificate of incorporation) applies—

(a) to certificates of incorporation issued under that Act, and

(b) to certificates of incorporation issued under the 1985 Act or 1986 Order on or after 1st October 2009.

96. Section 1065 of the Companies Act 2006 (right to be provided with copy of certificate of incorporation) applies to certificates of incorporation whenever issued.

97. Delivery of documents to the registrar (ss 1068 to 1076)

(1) Sections 1068 and 1069 of the Companies Act 2006 (registrar's requirements as to form, authentication and manner of delivery and power to require delivery by electronic means) apply to documents delivered to the registrar on or after 1st October 2009 other than those delivered in pursuance of an obligation arising before that date.

(2) Where the obligation to deliver a document to the registrar arose before 1st October 2009, the provisions that would have applied if the document had been delivered before that date continue to apply.

98. Section 1070 of the Companies Act 2006 (agreement for delivery by electronic means) applies to all documents delivered to the registrar on or after 1st October 2009.

99. (1) Section 1071 of the Companies Act 2006 (document not delivered until received) applies in relation to the delivery of documents to the registrar on or after 1st October 2009 other than those delivered in pursuance of an obligation arising before that date.

(2) Where the obligation to deliver a document to the registrar arose before 1st October 2009, the provisions that would have applied if the document had been delivered before that date continue to apply.

100. (1) Sections 1072 to 1074 of the Companies Act 2006 (requirements for proper delivery) apply to documents delivered to the registrar on or after 1st October 2009 other than those delivered in pursuance of an obligation arising before that date.

(2) Where the obligation to deliver a document to the registrar arose before 1st October 2009, the provisions that would have applied if the document had been delivered before that date (and the registrar's former practice with respect to the requirements for proper delivery and documents containing unnecessary material) continue to apply.

101. (1) Section 1075 of the Companies Act 2006 (informal correction of document) applies to documents delivered to the registrar on or after 1st October 2009 other than those delivered in pursuance of an obligation arising before that date.

(2) Where the obligation to deliver a document to the registrar arose before 1st October 2009, the provisions that would have applied if the document had been delivered before that date (and the registrar's former practice with respect to documents requiring correction) continue to apply.

102. Section 1076 of the Companies Act 2006 (replacement of document not meeting requirements for proper delivery) applies to documents to which sections 1072 to 1074 of that Act apply (see paragraph 100 above).

103. Documents subject to Directive disclosure requirements (s 1078)

(1) This paragraph has effect in relation to section 1078 of the Companies Act 2006 (documents subject to the Directive disclosure requirements) and the adaptations of that section made by paragraph 5 of Schedule 1 to the Companies Act 2006 (Commencement No 1, Transitional Provisions and Savings) Order 2006.

(2) The adaptations continue to have effect in relation to documents delivered to the registrar on or after 1st October 2009 in pursuance of provisions of the 1985 Act or 1986 Order.

(3) Documents subject to the Directive disclosure requirements by virtue of any such adaptation remain subject to the Directive disclosure requirements notwithstanding that the adaptation has ceased to have effect.

104. Effect of failure to give public notice (s 1079)

In section 1079 of the Companies Act 2006 (effect of failure to give public notice) the references to an amendment of the company's articles include an amendment before 1st October 2009 of the company's memorandum.

105. Annotation of the register (s 1081)

(1) Section 1081 of the Companies Act 2006 (annotation of the register) applies in relation to—

(a) documents delivered to the registrar on or after 1st October 2009 other than those delivered in pursuance of an obligation arising before that date, and

(b) certificates issued by the registrar on or after 1st October 2009 other than those issued in response to a document delivered to the registrar before that date or in pursuance of an obligation arising before that date,

and in relation to the content of, and material derived from, such documents and certificates.

(2) The provisions applicable before 1st October 2009 (and the registrar's former practice with respect to annotation of the register) continue to apply in relation to—

(a) documents delivered to the registrar before that date, or in pursuance of an obligation arising before that date, and

(b) certificates issued by the registrar before that date or in response to a document delivered to the registrar before that date or in pursuance of an obligation arising before that date, and in relation to the content of, and material derived from, such documents and certificates.

106. Registrar's notice to resolve inconsistency on the register (s 1093)

(1) Section 1093 of the Companies Act 2006 (registrar's notice to resolve inconsistency on the register) applies where—

(a) a document is delivered to the registrar on or after 1st October 2009 otherwise than in pursuance of an obligation arising before that date, and

(b) it appears to the registrar that the information contained in the document is inconsistent with other information on the register.

(2) The provisions applicable before 1st October 2009 (and the registrar's former practice with respect to inconsistencies on the register) continue to apply in relation to documents delivered to the registrar before that date or in pursuance of an obligation arising before that date.

107. Removal of material from the register (ss 1094 to 1098)

(1) This paragraph applies to—

(a) sections 1094 to 1097 of the Companies Act 2006 (removal of material from the register), and

(b) section 1098 of that Act (public notice of removal of certain material from the register).

(2) Those provisions apply in relation to—

(a) documents delivered to the registrar on or after 1st October 2009 other than those delivered in pursuance of an obligation arising before that date, and

(b) certificates issued by the registrar on or after 1st October 2009, other than those issued in response to a document delivered to the registrar before that date or in pursuance of an obligation arising before that date,

and in relation to the content of, and material derived from, such documents and certificates.

(3) The provisions applicable before 1st October 2009 (and the registrar's former practice with respect to removal of material from the register) continue to apply in relation to—

(a) documents delivered to the registrar before that date, or in pursuance of an obligation arising before that date, and

(b) certificates issued by the registrar before that date or in response to a document delivered to the registrar before that date or in pursuance of an obligation arising before that date,

and in relation to the content of, and material derived from, such documents or certificates.

108. Language requirements: transliteration (ss 1108 to 1110)

Sections 1108 to 1110 of the Companies Act 2006 (transliteration of names and addresses) apply in relation to all documents delivered to the registrar on or after 1st October 2009.

109. General false statement offence (s 1112)

Section 1112 of the Companies Act 2006 (general false statement offence) applies to all documents delivered, and statements made, on or after 1st October 2009.

110. Resolution to alter company's objects agreed to before 1st October 2009

(1) The repeal of sections 4 to 6 of the 1985 Act or Articles 15 to 17 of the 1986 Order (resolution to alter company's objects: procedure for objecting to alteration) does not affect the application of those provisions in relation to a resolution agreed to before 1st October 2009.

(2) Where an application is made under section 5 of the 1985 Act or Article 16 of the 1986 Order (application to court for cancellation of alteration) and on or after 1st October 2009—

(a) the alteration is confirmed (either wholly or in part) by the court, or

(b) the court by order alters the company's memorandum under section 5(5) or Article 16(5) (alteration in consequence of provision for purchase by company of shares of members of the company),

the alteration has effect, in accordance with section 28 of the Companies Act 2006 (provisions of memorandum treated as provisions of articles), as an alteration of the company's articles of association.

111. Provision and authentication by registrar of documents sent by electronic means

(1) The repeal of section 710A of the 1985 Act or Article 659A of the 1986 Order (provision and authentication by registrar of documents in non-legible form) does not affect the application of those provisions on or after 1st October 2009 in relation to saved provisions of that Act or Order.

(2) Section 1115(2) of the Companies Act 2006 (authentication in manner specified by registrar's rules) does not apply to a document in relation to which section 710A(2) of the 1985 Act or Article 659A(2) of the 1986 Order applies.

112. Notice of appointment of certain officers (ss 1154 and 1155)

Sections 1154 and 1155 of the Companies Act 2006 (duty to notify registrar of certain appointments etc) apply in relation to appointments made on or after 1st October 2009.

113. Amendment of memorandum or articles of commonhold association (s 1283)

Section 1283 of the Companies Act 2006 (amendment of memorandum or articles of commonhold association) applies to amendments made on or after 1st October 2009.

114. Extension of provisions to Northern Ireland (s 1284)

(1) The extension to Northern Ireland by section 1284 of the Companies Act 2006 of Parts 14 and 15 of the 1985 Act (company investigations) has effect to enable the exercise of the powers conferred by those Parts in relation to companies registered in Northern Ireland, and otherwise in relation to Northern Ireland, on and after 1st October 2009.

(2) Parts 15 and 16 of the 1986 Order, and any other provision of that Order having effect for the purposes of Part 15, continue to apply (subject to sub-paragraph (3) below)—

(a) in relation to inspectors appointed under Part 15 before 1st October 2009 and matters arising in connection with or in consequence of any such appointment or any report of inspectors so appointed;

(b) in relation to any exercise before 1st October 2009 of any power of the Department of Enterprise, Trade and Investment in Northern Ireland not within paragraph (a), and matters arising in connection with or in consequence of any such exercise.

(3) A direction in force immediately before 1st October 2009 under Article 438(1A) or 449(1A) of the 1986 Order (direction limiting or relaxing restrictions on shares) shall continue in force and have effect on and after that date as if made under the corresponding provision of Part 14 of the 1985 Act, and the provisions of Part 15 of that Act shall apply accordingly.

114A. Company or business name suggesting connection with Welsh Assembly Government

(1) The repeal of section 26(2)(a) of the 1985 Act or section 2(1)(a) of the Business Names Act 1985 does not affect the operation of that provision in relation to names suggesting a connection with the Welsh Assembly Government.

(2) In section 26(2)(a) of the 1985 Act as it has effect by virtue of paragraph (1) above, the reference to registration under that Act shall be read as a reference to registration under the Companies Act 2006 in England and Wales or Scotland.

(3) The other provisions of the Business Names Act 1985 continue to have effect for the purposes of section 2(1)(a) of that Act as it has effect by virtue of paragraph (1) above.

(4) Paragraphs (1) to (3) above shall cease to have effect on the coming into force of amendments of the Companies Act 2006 having the effect of extending section 54(1)(a) (company names) or, as the case may be, section 1193(1)(a) (business names) of that Act to names suggesting a connection with the Welsh Assembly Government.

115. Saving for provisions as to form or manner in which documents to be delivered

(1) Any saving in this Schedule for the effect of a provision of the 1985 Act or 1986 Order requiring use of a prescribed form extends to the form and the power under which it is prescribed.

(2) Any saving in this Schedule for the effect of a provision of the 1985 Act or 1986 Order requiring a document to be delivered to the registrar extends to section 707B of the 1985 Act or Article 656B of the 1986 Order (delivery to the registrar using electronic communications) so far as relating to the provision in question and the delivery of documents under it.

116. Savings for provisions relating to offences

(1) The repeal of any provision of the 1985 Act or 1986 Order creating an offence does not affect the continued operation of that provision in relation to an offence committed before 1st October 2009.

(2) Any saving in this Schedule for the effect of a provision of the 1985 Act or 1986 Order that creates an offence extends to the entry relating to that provision in Schedule 24 to that Act or Schedule 23 to that Order (punishment of offences).

(3) References in this paragraph to provisions of the 1985 Act or 1986 Order include provisions of regulations or orders made under that Act or Order.

Companies (Shares and Share Capital) Order 2009

S.I. 2009/388

1. Citation, commencement and interpretation

(1) This Order may be cited as the Companies (Shares and Share Capital) Order 2009 and shall come into force on 1st October 2009.

(2) In this Order, a reference to a section is a reference to a section of the Companies Act 2006.

2. Statements of capital, and returns of allotment by unlimited companies: prescribed particulars of the rights attached to shares

(1) The particulars in paragraph (3) are prescribed for the purposes of the provisions in paragraph (2).

(2) The provisions are—

(a) section 10(2)(c)(i);
(b) section 32(2)(c)(i);
(c) section 108(3)(c)(i);
(d) section 555(4)(c)(i);
(e) section 556(3);
(f) section 619(3)(c)(i);
(g) section 621(3)(c)(i);
(h) section 625(3)(c)(i);
(i) section 627(3)(c)(i);
(j) section 644(2)(c)(i);
(k) section 649(2)(c)(i);
(l) section 663(3)(c)(i);
(m) section 689(3)(c)(i);
(n) section 708(3)(c)(i); and
(o) section 730(5)(c)(i).

(3) The particulars are—

(a) particulars of any voting rights attached to the shares, including rights that arise only in certain circumstances;
(b) particulars of any rights attached to the shares, as respects dividends, to participate in a distribution;
(c) particulars of any rights attached to the shares, as respects capital, to participate in a distribution (including on winding up); and
(d) whether the shares are to be redeemed or are liable to be redeemed at the option of the company or the shareholder.

3. Prescribed information for a return of an allotment by a limited company

(1) The information in paragraph (2) is prescribed for the purposes of section 555(3)(a) (information to be contained in a return of an allotment by a limited company).

(2) The information is—

(a) the number of shares allotted;
(b) the amount paid up and the amount (if any) unpaid on each allotted share (whether on account of the nominal value of the share or by way of premium); and
(c) where the shares are allotted as fully or partly paid up (as to their nominal value or any premium on them) otherwise than in cash, the consideration for the allotment.

4. Shares deemed paid up in or allotted for cash, and sale of treasury shares for a cash consideration: meaning of cash consideration

(1) The creation of an obligation on the part of a settlement bank to make a relevant payment in respect of the allotment of a share to a system-member by means of a relevant system is to be regarded as a means of payment falling within section 583(3)(e).

(2) The creation of an obligation on the part of a settlement bank to make a relevant payment in respect of the payment up of a share by a system-member by means of a relevant system is to be regarded as a means of payment falling within section 583(3)(e).

(3) The creation of an obligation on the part of a settlement bank to make a relevant payment in respect of the transfer by a company to a system-member, by means of a relevant system, of a share held by the company as a treasury share is to be regarded as a means of payment falling within section 727(2)(e).

(4) In this article—

(a) the expressions "Operator", "relevant system", "rules", "settlement bank", "system-member" and "uncertificated" have the meanings given in the Uncertificated Securities Regulations 2001; and

(b) "relevant payment" means a payment in accordance with the rules and practices of an Operator of a relevant system.

5. Redemption or purchase of own shares out of capital by a private company: prescribed form of, and information with respect to the nature of the company's business to be contained in, a directors' statement

(1) The directors' statement required by section 714 (directors' statement to be made where a private company makes a payment out of capital for the redemption or purchase of its own shares) must—

(a) be in writing;

(b) indicate that it is a directors' statement made under that section; and

(c) be signed by each of the company's directors.

(2) The statement must state—

(a) whether the company's business includes that of a banking company; and

(b) whether its business includes that of an insurance company.

Companies (Reduction of Share Capital) Order 2008

S.I. 2008/1915

1. (1) This Order may be cited as the Companies (Reduction of Share Capital) Order 2008 and comes into force on 1st October 2008.

(2) In this Order, "the Act" means the Companies Act 2006.

2. A solvency statement under section 643 of the Act must—

(a) be in writing,

(b) indicate that it is a solvency statement for the purposes of section 642 of the Act, and

(c) be signed by each of the directors.

3. (1) If an unlimited company reduces its share capital—

(a) the prohibition in section 654(1) of the Act does not apply, and

(b) a reserve arising from the reduction is to be treated for the purposes of Part 23 of the Act as a realised profit.

(2) If a private company limited by shares reduces its share capital and the reduction is supported by a solvency statement but has not been the subject of an application to the court for an order confirming it—

(a) the prohibition in section 654(1) of the Act does not apply, and

(b) a reserve arising from the reduction is to be treated for the purposes of Part 23 of the Act as a realised profit.

(3) If a limited company having a share capital reduces its share capital and the reduction is confirmed by order of the court—

(a) the prohibition in section 654(1) of the Act does not apply, and

(b) a reserve arising from the reduction is to be treated for the purposes of Part 23 of the Act as a realised profit unless the court orders otherwise under section 648(1) of the Act.

(4) This article is without prejudice to any contrary provision of—

(a) an order of, or undertaking given to, the court,

(b) the resolution for, or any other resolution relevant to, the reduction of share capital, or

(c) the company's memorandum or articles of association.

Companies (Registration) Regulations 2008

S.I. 2008/3014

The prohibition

1. Citation, commencement and interpretation

(1) These Regulations may be cited as the Companies (Registration) Regulations 2008 and come into force on 1st October 2009.

(2) In these Regulations "the Act" means the Companies Act 2006.

2. Memorandum of association

For the purposes of section 8 of the Act—

(a) the memorandum of association of a company having a share capital shall be in the form set out in Schedule 1; and

(b) the memorandum of association of a company not having a share capital shall be in the form set out in Schedule 2.

3. Statement of capital and initial shareholdings

For the purposes of section 10(3) of the Act, the statement of capital and initial shareholdings shall contain the name and address of each subscriber to the memorandum of association.

4. Statement of guarantee

For the purposes of section 11(2) of the Act, the statement of guarantee shall contain the name and address of each subscriber to the memorandum of association.

5. Form of assent for re-registration of private limited company as unlimited

The form set out in Schedule 3 is the form prescribed for the purposes of section 103(2)(a) of the Act.

6. Form of assent for re-registration of public company as private and unlimited

The form set out in Schedule 4 is the form prescribed for the purposes of section 110(2)(a) of the Act.

SCHEDULE 1

Regulation 2(a)

COMPANY HAVING A SHARE CAPITAL

Memorandum of association of [*insert name of company*]

Each subscriber to this memorandum of association wishes to form a company under the Companies Act 2006 and agrees to become a member of the company and to take at least one share.

Name of each subscriber	*Authentication by each subscriber*

Dated

SCHEDULE 2

Regulation 2(b)

COMPANY NOT HAVING A SHARE CAPITAL

Memorandum of association of [*insert name of company*]

Each subscriber to this memorandum of association wishes to form a company under the Companies Act 2006 and agrees to become a member of the company.

Name of each subscriber	*Authentication by each subscriber*

Dated

SCHEDULE 3 Regulation 5

Form of assents for re-registration of private limited company as unlimited

Assent to private limited company being re-registered as unlimited

In accordance with section 103(2)(a) of the Companies Act 2006

Company number

Company name

Each member of the company assents to the company being re-registered as unlimited

Member's name in full

Authentication of member (or person lawfully authorised to authenticate on the member's behalf) Date

Member's name in full

Authentication of member (or person lawfully authorised to authenticate on the member's behalf) Date

Member's name in full

Authentication of member (or person lawfully authorised to authenticate on the member's behalf) Date

Member's name in full

Authentication of member (or person lawfully authorised to authenticate on the member's behalf) Date

Please enter in the opposite box the number of continuation sheets attached (if any)

SCHEDULE 4 Regulation 6

Form of assents for re-registration of public company as private and unlimited

Assent by each member to public company being re-registered as private and unlimited

In accordance with section 110(2)(a) of the Companies Act 2006

Company number

Company name

Each member of the company assents to the company being re-registered as unlimited

Member's name in full

Authentication of member (or person lawfully authorised to authenticate on the member's behalf) Date

Member's name in full

Authentication of member (or person lawfully authorised to authenticate on the member's behalf) Date

Member's name in full

Authentication of member (or person lawfully authorised to authenticate on the member's behalf) Date

Member's name in full

Authentication of member (or person lawfully authorised to authenticate on the member's behalf) Date

Please enter in the opposite box the number of continuation sheets attached (if any)

Stock Transfer Act 1963

1963 c. 18

An Act to amend the law with respect to the transfer of securities

[10th July 1963]

1. Simplified transfer of securities

(1) Registered securities to which this section applies may be transferred by means of an instrument under hand in the form set out in Schedule 1 to this Act (in this Act referred to as a stock transfer), executed by the transferor only and specifying (in addition to the particulars of the consideration, of the description and number or amount of the securities, and of the person by whom the transfer is made) the full name and address of the transferee.

(2) The execution of a stock transfer need not be attested; and where such a transfer has been executed for the purpose of a stock exchange transaction, the particulars of the consideration and of the transferee may either be inserted in that transfer or, as the case may require, supplied by means of separate instruments in the form set out in Schedule 2 to this Act (in this Act referred to as brokers transfers), identifying the stock transfer and specifying the securities to which each such instrument relates and the consideration paid for those securities.

(3) Nothing in this section shall be construed as affecting the validity of any instrument which would be effective to transfer securities apart from this section; and any instrument purporting to be made in any form which was common or usual before the commencement of this Act, or in any other form authorised or required for that purpose apart from this section, shall be sufficient, whether or not it is completed in accordance with the form, if it complies with the requirements as to execution and contents which apply to a stock transfer.

(4) This section applies to fully paid up registered securities of any description, being—

(a) securities issued by any company as defined in section 1(1) of the Companies Act 2006 except a company limited by guarantee or an unlimited company;

(b) securities issued by any body (other than a company as so defined) incorporated in Great Britain by or under any enactment or by Royal Charter except a building society within the meaning of the Building Societies Act 1986 or a society registered under the Industrial and Provident Societies Act 1893;

(c) securities issued by the Government of the United Kingdom, except stock or bonds in the National Savings Stock Register …, and except national savings certificates;

(d) securities issued by any local authority;

(e) units of an authorised unit trust scheme or a recognised scheme within the meaning of Part 17 of the Financial Services and Markets Act 2000;

(f) shares issued by an open-ended investment company within the meaning of the Open-Ended Investment Companies Regulations 2001.

2. Supplementary provisions as to simplified transfer

(1) Section 1 of this Act shall have effect in relation to the transfer of any securities to which that section applies notwithstanding anything to the contrary in any enactment or instrument relating to the transfer of those securities; but nothing in that section affects—

(a) any right to refuse to register a person as the holder of any securities on any ground other than the form in which those securities purport to be transferred to him: or

(b) any enactment or rule of law regulating the execution of documents by companies or other bodies corporate, or any articles of association or other instrument regulating the execution of documents by any particular company or body corporate.

(2) Subject to the provisions of this section, any enactment or instrument relating to the transfer of securities to which section 1 of this Act applies shall, with any necessary modifications, apply in relation to an instrument of transfer authorised by that section as it applies in relation to an

instrument of transfer to which it applies apart from this subsection; and without prejudice to the generality of the foregoing provision, the references to an instrument of transfer in section 775 of the Companies Act 2006 (certification of instrument of transfer) shall be construed as including a reference to a brokers transfer.

(3) In relation to the transfer of securities by means of a stock transfer and a brokers transfer—

(a) any reference in any enactment or instrument (including in particular section 770(1)(a) of the Companies Act 2006 (registration of transfer) …) to the delivery or lodging of an instrument (or proper instrument) of transfer shall be construed as a reference to the delivery or lodging of the stock transfer and the brokers transfer;

(b) any such reference to the date on which an instrument of transfer is delivered or lodged shall be construed as a reference to the data by which the later of those transfers to be delivered or lodged has been delivered or lodged; and

(c) subject to the foregoing provisions of this subsection, the brokers transfer (and not the stock transfer) shall be deemed to be the conveyance or transfer for the purposes of the enactments relating to stamp duty.

(4) …

Note. Subsection (3)(c) is repealed by the Finance Act 1990, s. 132, Sch. 19, Pt. VI, as from a day to be appointed.

3. Additional provisions as to transfer forms

(1) References in this Act to the forms set out in Schedule 1 and Schedule 2 include references to forms substantially corresponding to those forms respectively.

(2) The Treasury may by order amend the said Schedules either by altering the forms set out therein or by substituting different forms for those forms or by the addition of forms for use as alternatives to those forms; and references in this Act to the forms set out in those Schedules (including references in this section) shall be construed accordingly.

(3) Any order under subsection (2) of this section which substitutes a different form for a form set out in Schedule 1 to this Act may direct that subsection (3) of section 1 of this Act shall apply, with any necessary modifications, in relation to the form for which that form is substituted as it applies to any form which was common or usual before the commencement of this Act.

(4) Any order of the Treasury under this section shall be made by statutory instrument, and may be varied or revoked by a subsequent order; and any statutory instrument made by virtue of this section shall be subject to annulment in pursuance of a resolution of either House of Parliament.

(5) An order under subsection (2) of this section may—

(a) provide for forms on which some of the particulars mentioned in subsection (1) of section 1 of this Act are not required to be specified;

(b) provide for that section to have effect, in relation to such forms as are mentioned in the preceding paragraph or other forms specified in the order, subject to such amendments as are so specified (which may include an amendment of the reference in subsection (1) of that section to an instrument under hand);

(c) provide for all or any of the provisions of the order to have effect in such cases only as are specified in the order.

4. Interpretation

(1) In this Act the following expressions have the meanings hereby respectively assigned to them, that is to say—

"local authority" means, in relation to England and Wales,

(a) a billing authority or a precepting authority, as defined in section 69 of the Local Government Finance Act 1992;

(aa) a fire and rescue authority in Wales constituted by a scheme under section 2 of the Fire and Rescue Services Act 2004 or a scheme to which section 4 of that Act applies;

(b) a levying body within the meaning of section 74 of the Local Government Finance Act 1988; and

(c) a body as regards which section 75 of that Act applies,

and, in relation to Scotland, a county council, a town council and any statutory authority, commissioners or trustees to whom section 270 of the Local Government (Scotland) Act 1947 applies;

"registered securities" means transferable securities the holders of which are entered in a register (whether maintained in Great Britain or not); "securities" means shares, stock, debentures, debenture stock, loan stock, bonds, units of a collective investment scheme within the meaning of the Financial Services and Markets Act 2000, and other securities of any description;

"stock exchange transaction" means a sale and purchase of securities in which each of the parties is a member of a stock exchange acting in the ordinary course of his business as such or is acting through the agency of such a member;

"stock exchange" means the Stock Exchange, London, and any other stock exchange (whether in Great Britain or not) which is declared by order of the Treasury to be a recognised stock exchange for the purposes of this Act.

(2) Any order of the Treasury under this section shall be made by statutory instrument, and may be varied or revoked by a subsequent order.

5. Application to Northern Ireland

(1) This Act, so far as it applies to things done outside Great Britain, extends to Northern Ireland.

(2) Without prejudice to subsection (1) of this section, the provisions of this Act affecting securities issued by the Government of the United Kingdom shall apply to any such securities entered in a register maintained in Northern Ireland.

(3) …

(4) Except as provided by this section, this Act shall not extend to Northern Ireland.

6. Short title and commencement

(1) This Act may be cited as the Stock Transfer Act 1963.

(2) Subsection (3) of section 5 of this Act shall come into force on the passing of this Act, and the remaining provisions of this Act shall come into force on such date as the Treasury may by order made by statutory instrument direct.

SCHEDULES

SCHEDULE 1

STOCK TRANSFER FORM

Certificate lodged with the Registrar

Consideration Money £..............................

(For completion by the Registrar/ Stock Exchange)

Name of Undertaking.		
Description of Security.		
Number or amount of Shares, Stock or other security and, in figures column only, number and denomination of units, if any.	**Words**	**Figures** **(units of)**
Name(s) of registered holder(s) should be given in full: the address should be given where there is only one holder. **If the transfer is not made by the registered holder(s) insert also the name(s) and capacity (eg, Executor(s)), of the person(s) making the transfer.**	**in the name(s) of**	

Delete words in italics except for stock exchange transactions.

I/We hereby transfer the above security out of the name(s) aforesaid to the person(s) named below ***or to the several persons named in Parts 2 of Brokers Transfer Forms relating to the above security:***
Signature(s) of transferor(s)

1 .... 3 ....

2 .... 4 ....

A body corporate should execute this transfer under its common seal or otherwise in accordance with applicable statutory requirements.

Stamp of Selling Broker(s) or, for transactions which are not stock exchange transactions, of Agent(s), if any, acting for the Transferor(s).

Date

Full name(s), full postal address(es) (including County or, if applicable, Postal District number) of the person(s) to whom the security is transferred. **Please state title, if any, or whether Mr, Mrs or Miss.** **Please complete in type or in Block Capitals.**	

I/We request that such entries be made in the register as are necessary to give effect to this transfer.

Stamp of Buying Broker(s) (if any).	**Stamp or name and address of person lodging this form (if other than the Buying Broker(s)).**

Reference to the Registrar in this form means the registrar or registration agent of the undertaking, not the Registrar of Companies at Companies House.

(Endorsement for use only in stock exchange transactions)

The security represented by the transfer overleaf has been sold as follows:–

....*Shares/Stock*	....*Shares/Stock*
....*Shares/Stock*	....*Shares/Stock*
....*Shares/Stock*	....*Shares/Stock*
....*Shares/Stock*	....*Shares/Stock*
....*Shares/Stock*	....*Shares/Stock*
....*Shares/Stock*	....*Shares/Stock*

Balance (if any) due to Selling Broker(s)

Amount of Certificate(s)

Brokers Transfer Forms for above amount certified

Stamp of certifying Stock Exchange

Stamp of Selling Broker(s)

TALISMAN SOLD TRANSFER

This transfer is exempt from Transfer Stamp Duty

Above this line for Registrar's use only

Bargain Reference No:

Certificate lodged with Registrar

Name of Undertaking

Description of Security

(for completion by the Registrars/ Stock Exchange)

Amount of Stock or number of Stock units or shares or other security in words

Figures

In the name(s) of

Account Designation (if any)

Name(s) of registered holder(s) should be given in full; the address should be given where there is only one holder.

If the transfer is not made by the registered holder(s) insert also the name(s) and capacity (e.g. Executor(s)) of the person(s) making the transfer.

I/We hereby transfer the above security out of the name(s) aforesaid into the name of and request the necessary entries to be made in the register.

Balance Certificate Required for (amount or number in figures)

Bodies corporate should affix their common seal and each signatory should state his/her representative capacity (e.g. 'Company Secretary' 'Director') agaist his/her signature

Stamp of Lodging Agent

PLEASE SIGN HERE ⇨

1 ________________

2 ________________

3 ________________

4 ________________

Date

is lodging this transfer at the direction and on behalf of the Lodging Agent whose stamp appears herein ("the Original Lodging Agent") and does not in any manner or to any extent warrant or represent the validity, genuineness or correctness of the transfer instructions contained herein or the genuineness of the signature(s) of the transferor(s) The Original Lodging Agent be delivering this transfer to authorises to lodge this transfer for registration and agrees to be deemed for all purposes to be the person(s) actually lodging this transfer for registration

INSP Code (if applicable)

Transfer Number

TALISMAN BOUGHT TRANSFER

Above this line for Registrar's use only

Name of Undertaking

Rate

Description of Security

Stamp Duty	Bargain Date	Settlement	Price	Transfer Consideration	Figures

Amount of Stock or Number of Stock Units or Shares or Other Security in Words

Hundred Millions	Ten Millions	Millions	Hundred Thousands	Ten Thousands	Thousands	Hundreds	Tens	Units

Transferee Details

Account Designation

Apportionment Date

Registrar	Batch	Company	Security	Bargain Reference	Firm	Transfer Number	Quantity

hereby transfers the above security to the person(s) named under "Transferee Details" and requests the necessary entries to be made in the register. It confirms that the price and transfer consideration have been derived from information supplied by Member Firms

is lodging this transfer at the direction and on behalf of the Member Firm whose code number appears herein ('the Original Lodging Agent') and does not in any manner or to any extent warrant or represent the validity or correctness of the transfer instructions contained herein. The Original Lodging Agent by instructing to deliver this transfer for registration agrees to be deemed for all purposes to be the person(s) actually lodging this transfer for registration

It is hereby certified on behalf of The Stock Exchange that the Stamp Duty indicated hereon has been or will be accounted for to the Commissioners of Inland Revenue pursuant to an agreement under Section 33 of the Finance Act 1970 as amended.

Dated

Above this line for Registrar's use

TRANSFER

Counter Location Stamp	Barcode or reference **RN**

Above this line for completion by the depositing system-user only.

	Consideration Money	Certificate(s) lodged with Registrar (To be completed by Registrar)
Name of Undertaking.		
Description of Security.		
Please complete form in type or in block capitals.	Amount of shares or other security in words	Figures
Name(s) of registered holder(s) should be given in full; the address should be given where there is only one holder. If the transfer is not made by the registered holder(s) insert also the name(s) and capacity (e.g. executor(s)) of the person(s) making the transfer.	In the name(s) of	Designation (if any) Balance certificate(s) required
Please Sign Here →	I/We hereby transfer the above security out of the name(s) aforesaid into the name(s) of the system-member set out below and request that the necessary entries be made in the undertaking's own register of members. Signature(s) of transferor(s) 1. 2. 3. 4. A body corporate should execute this transfer under its common seal or otherwise in accordance with applicable statutory requirements.	Stamp of depositing system-user Date
Full name(s) of the person(s) to whom the security is transferred. Such person(s) must be a system-member.		Participant ID Member Account ID
	is delivering this transfer at the direction and on behalf of the depositing system-user whose stamp appears herein and does not in any manner or to any extent warrant or represent the validity, genuineness or correctness of the transfer instructions contained herein or the genuineness of the signature(s) of the transferor(s). The depositing system-user by delivering this transfer to authorises to deliver this transfer for registration and agrees to be deemed for all purposes to be the person(s) actually so delivering this transfer for registration.	
Reference to the Registrar in this form means the registrar or registration agent of the undertaking, not the Registrar of Companies at Companies House.		

Theft Act 1968

19. False statements by company directors, etc

(1) Where an officer of a body corporate or unincorporated association (or person purporting to act as such), with intent to deceive members or creditors of the body corporate or association about its affairs, publishes or concurs in publishing a written statement or account which to his knowledge is or may be misleading, false or deceptive in a material particular, he shall on conviction on indictment be liable to imprisonment for a term not exceeding seven years.

(2) For purposes of this section a person who has entered into a security for the benefit of a body corporate or association is to be treated as a creditor of it.

(3) Where the affairs of a body corporate or association are managed by its members, this section shall apply to any statement which a member publishes or concurs in publishing in connection with his functions of management as if he were an officer of the body corporate or association.

Companies (Tables A to F) Regulations 1985 as amended by S.I. 2007/2541 and S.I. 2007/2826

TABLE A
REGULATIONS FOR MANAGEMENT OF A (PRIVATE) COMPANY LIMITED BY SHARES

INTERPRETATION

1. In these regulations—

   "the Act" means the Companies Act 1985 including any statutory modification or re-enactment thereof for the time being in force and any provisions of the Companies Act 2006 for the time being in force.

   "the articles" means the articles of the company.

   "clear days" in relation to the period of a notice means that period excluding the day when the notice is given or deemed to be given and the day for which it is given or on which it is to take effect.

   "communication" means the same as in the Electronic Communications Act 2000.

   "electronic communication" means the same as in the Electronic Communications Act 2000.

   "executed" includes any mode of execution.

   "office" means the registered office of the company.

   "the holder" in relation to shares means the member whose name is entered in the register of members as the holder of the shares.

   "the seal" means the common seal of the company.

   "secretary" means the secretary of the company or any other person appointed to perform the duties of the secretary of the company, including a joint, assistant or deputy secretary.

   "the United Kingdom" means Great Britain and Northern Ireland.

   Unless the context otherwise requires, words or expressions contained in these regulations bear the same meaning as in the Act but excluding any statutory modification thereof not in force when these regulations become binding on the company.

SHARE CAPITAL

2. Subject to the provisions of the Act and without prejudice to any rights attached to any existing shares, any share may be issued with such rights or restrictions as the company may by ordinary resolution determine.
3. Subject to the provisions of the Act, shares may be issued which are to be redeemed or are to be liable to be redeemed at the option of the company or the holder on such terms and in such manner as may be provided by the articles.
4. The company may exercise the powers of paying commissions conferred by the Act. Subject to the provisions of the Act, any such commission may be satisfied by the payment of cash or by the allotment of fully or partly paid shares or partly in one way and partly in the other.
5. Except as required by law, no person shall be recognised by the company as holding any share upon any trust and (except as otherwise provided by the articles or by law) the company shall not be bound by or recognise any interest in any share except an absolute right to the entirety thereof in the holder.

SHARE CERTIFICATES

6. Every member, upon becoming the holder of any shares, shall be entitled without payment to one certificate for all the shares of each class held by him (and, upon transferring a part of his holding

of shares of any class, to a certificate for the balance of such holding) or several certificates each for one or more of his shares of any class, to a certificate for the balance of such holding) or several certificates each for one or more of his shares upon payment for every certificate after the first of such reasonable sum as the directors may determine. Every certificate shall be sealed with the seal and shall specify the number, class and distinguishing numbers (if any) of the shares to which it relates and the amount or respective amounts paid up thereon. The company shall not be bound to issue more than one certificate for shares held jointly by several persons and delivery of a certificate to one joint holder shall be a sufficient delivery to all of them.

7. If a share certificate is defaced, worn-out, lost or destroyed, it may be renewed on such terms (if any) as to evidence and indemnity and payment of the expenses reasonably incurred by the company in investigating evidence as the directors may determine but otherwise free of charge, and (in the case of defacement or wearing-out) on delivery up of the old certificate.

LIEN

8. The company shall have a first and paramount lien on every share (not being a fully paid share) for all moneys (whether presently payable or not) payable at a fixed time or called in respect of that share. The directors may at any time declare any share to be wholly or in part exempt from the provisions of this regulation. The company's lien on a share shall extend to any amount payable in respect of it.

9. The company may sell in such manner as the directors determine any shares on which the company has a lien if a sum in respect of which the lien exists is presently payable and is not paid within fourteen clear days after notice has been given to the holder of the share or to the person entitled to it in consequence of the death or bankruptcy of the holder, demanding payment and stating that if the notice is not complied with the shares may be sold.

10. To give effect to a sale the directors may authorise some person to execute an instrument of transfer of the shares sold to, or in accordance with the directions of, the purchaser. The title of the transferee to the shares shall not be affected by any irregularity in or invalidity of the proceedings in reference to the sale.

11. The net proceeds of the sale, after payment of the costs, shall be applied in payment of so much of the sum for which the lien exists as is presently payable, and any residue shall (upon surrender to the company for cancellation of the certificate for the shares sold and subject to a like lien for any moneys not presently payable as existed upon the shares before the sale) be paid to the person entitled to the shares at the date of the sale.

CALLS ON SHARES AND FORFEITURE

12. Subject to the terms of allotment, the directors may make calls upon the members in respect of any moneys unpaid on their shares (whether in respect of nominal value or premium) and each member shall (subject to receiving at least fourteen clear days' notice specifying when and where payment is to be made) pay to the company as required by the notice the amount called on his shares. A call may be required to be paid by instalments. A call may, before receipt by the company of any sum due thereunder, be revoked in whole or part and payment of a call may be postponed in whole or part. A person upon whom a call is made shall remain liable for calls made upon him notwithstanding the subsequent transfer of the shares in respect whereof the call was made.

13. A call shall be deemed to have been made at the time when the resolution of the directors authorising the call was passed.

14. The joint holders of a share shall be jointly and severally liable to pay all calls in respect thereof.

15. If a call remains unpaid after it has become due and payable the person from whom it is due and payable shall pay interest on the amount unpaid from the day it became due and payable until it is paid at the rate fixed by the terms of allotment of the share or in the notice of the call or, if no rate

is fixed, at the appropriate rate (as defined by the Act) but the directors may waive payment of the interest wholly or in part.

16. An amount payable in respect of a share on allotment or at any fixed date, whether in respect of nominal value or premium or as an instalment of a call, shall be deemed to be a call and if it is not paid the provisions of the articles shall apply as if that amount had become due and payable by virtue of a call.

17. Subject to the terms of allotment, the directors may make arrangements on the issue of shares for a difference between the holders in the amounts and times of payment of calls on their shares.

18. If a call remains unpaid after it has become due and payable the directors may give to the person from whom it is due not less than fourteen clear days' notice requiring payment of the amount unpaid together with any interest which may have accrued. The notice shall name the place where payment is to be made and shall state that if the notice is not complied with the shares in respect of which the call was made will be liable to be forfeited.

19. If the notice is not complied with any share in respect of which it was given may, before the payment required by the notice has been made, be forfeited by a resolution of the directors and the forfeiture shall include all dividends or other moneys payable in respect of the forfeited shares and not paid before the forfeiture.

20. Subject to the provisions of the Act, a forfeited share may be sold, re-alloted or otherwise disposed of on such terms and in such manner as the directors determine either to the person who was before the forfeiture the holder or to any other person and at any time before sale, re-allotment or other disposition, the forfeiture may be cancelled on such terms as the directors think fit. Where for the purposes of its disposal a forfeited share is to be transferred to any person the directors may authorise some person to execute an instrument of transfer of the share to that person.

21. A person any of whose shares have been forfeited shall cease to be a member in respect of them and shall surrender to the company for cancellation the certificate for the shares forfeited but shall remain liable to the company for all moneys which at the date of forfeiture were presently payable by him to the company in respect of those shares with interest at the rate at which interest was payable on those moneys before the forfeiture or, if no interest was so payable, at the appropriate rate (as defined in the Act) from the date of forfeiture until payment but the directors may waive payment wholly or in part or enforce payment without any allowance for the value of the shares at the time of forfeiture or for any consideration received on their disposal.

22. A statutory declaration by a director or the secretary that a share has been forfeited on a specified date shall be conclusive evidence of the facts stated in it as against all persons claiming to be entitled to the share and the declaration shall (subject to the execution of an instrument of transfer if necessary) constitute a good title to the share and the person to whom the share is disposed of shall not be bound to see to the application of the consideration, if any, nor shall his title to the share be affected by any irregularity in or invalidity of the proceedings in reference to the forfeiture or disposal of the share.

TRANSFER OF SHARES

23. The instrument of transfer of a share may be in any usual form or in any other form which the directors may approve and shall be executed by or on behalf of the transferor and, unless the share is fully paid, by or on behalf of the transferee.

24. The directors may refuse to register the transfer of a share which is not fully paid to a person of whom they do not approve and they may refuse to register the transfer of a share on which the company has a lien. They may also refuse to register a transfer unless—

(a) it is lodged at the office or at such other place as the directors may appoint and is accompanied by the certificate for the shares to which it relates and such other evidence as the directors may reasonably require to show the right of the transferor to make the transfer;

(b) it is in respect of only one class of shares; and

(c) it is in favour of not more than four transferees.

25. If the directors refuse to register a transfer of a share, they shall within two months after the date on which the transfer was lodged with the company send to the transferee notice of the refusal.

26. The registration of transfers of shares or of transfers of any class of shares may be suspended at such times and for such periods (not exceeding thirty days in any year) as the directors may determine.

27. No fee shall be charged for the registration of any instrument of transfer or other document relating to or affecting the title to any share.

28. The company shall be entitled to retain any instrument of transfer which is registered, but any instrument of transfer which the directors refuse to register shall be returned to the person lodging it when notice of the refusal is given.

TRANSMISSION OF SHARES

29. If a member dies the survivor or survivors where he was a joint holder, and his personal representatives where he was a sole holder or the only survivor of joint holders, shall be the only persons recognised by the company as having any title to his interest; but nothing herein contained shall release the estate of a deceased member from any liability in respect of any share which had been jointly held by him.

30. A person becoming entitled to a share in consequence of the death or bankruptcy of a member may, upon such evidence being produced as the directors may properly require, elect either to become the holder of the share or to have some person nominated by him registered as the transferee. If he elects to become the holder he shall give notice to the company to that effect. If he elects to have another person registered he shall execute an instrument of transfer of the share to that person. All the articles relating to the transfer of shares shall apply to the notice or instrument of transfer as if it were an instrument of transfer executed by the member and the death or bankruptcy of the member had not occurred.

31. A person becoming entitled to a share in consequence of the death or bankruptcy of a member shall have the rights to which he would be entitled if he were the holder of the share, except that he shall not, before being registered as the holder of the share, be entitled in respect of it to attend or vote at any meeting of the company or at any separate meeting of the holders of any class of shares in the company.

ALTERATION OF SHARE CAPITAL

32. The company may by ordinary resolution—
   (a) increase its share capital by new shares of such amount as the resolution prescribes;
   (b) consolidate and divide all or any of its share capital into shares of larger amount than its existing shares;
   (c) subject to the provisions of the Act, sub-divide its shares, or any of them, into shares of smaller amount and the resolution may determine that, as between the shares resulting from the sub-division, any of them may have any preference or advantage as compared with the others; and
   (d) cancel shares which, at the date of the passing of the resolution, have not been taken or agreed to be taken by any person and diminish the amount of its share capital by the amount of the shares so cancelled.

33. Whenever as a result of a consolidation of shares any members would become entitled to fractions of a share, the directors may, on behalf of those members, sell the shares representing the fractions for the best price reasonably obtainable to any person (including, subject to the provisions of the Act, the company) and distribute the net proceeds of sale in due proportion among those members, and the directors may authorise some person to execute an instrument of transfer of the shares to, or in accordance with the directions of, the purchaser. The transferee shall not be bound to see to the application of the purchase money nor shall his title to the shares be affected by any irregularity in or invalidity of the proceedings in reference to the sale.

34. Subject to the provisions of the Act, the company may by special resolution reduce its share capital, any capital redemption reserve and any share premium account in any way.

PURCHASE OF OWN SHARES

35. Subject to the provisions of the Act, the company may purchase its own shares (including any redeemable shares) and, if it is a private company, make a payment in respect of the redemption or purchase of its own shares otherwise than out of distributable profits of the company or the proceeds of a fresh issue of shares.

GENERAL MEETINGS

37. The directors may call general meetings and, on the requisition of members pursuant to the provisions of the Act, shall forthwith proceed to convene a general meeting in accordance with the provisions of the Act. If there are not within the United Kingdom sufficient directors to call a general meeting, any director or any member of the company may call a general meeting.

NOTICE OF GENERAL MEETINGS

38. General meetings shall be called by at least fourteen clear days' notice but a general meeting may be called by shorter notice if is so agreed by a majority in number of the members having a right to attend and vote being a majority together holding not less than ninety per cent in nominal value of the shares giving that right.

The notice shall specify the time and place of the meeting and the general nature of the business to be transacted.

Subject to the provisions of the articles and to any restrictions imposed on any shares, the notice shall be given to all the members, to all persons entitled to a share in consequence of the death or bankruptcy of a member and to the directors and auditors.

39. The accidental omission to give notice of a meeting to, or the non-receipt of notice of a meeting by, any person entitled to receive notice shall not invalidate the proceedings at that meeting.

PROCEEDINGS AT GENERAL MEETINGS

40. No business shall be transacted at any meeting unless a quorum is present. Save in the case of a company wth a single member two persons entitled to vote upon the business to be transacted, each being a member or a proxy for a member or a duly authorised representative of a corporation, shall be a quorum.

41. If such a quorum is not present within half an hour from the time appointed for the meeting, or if during a meeting such a quorum ceases to be present, the meeting shall stand adjourned to the same day in the next week at the same time and place or to such time and place as the directors may determine.

42. The chairman, if any, of the board of directors or in his absence some other director nominated by the directors shall preside as chairman of the meeting, but if neither the chairman nor such other director (if any) be present within fifteen minutes after the time appointed for holding the meeting and willing to act, the directors present shall elect one of their number to be chairman and, if there is only one director present and willing to act, he shall be chairman.

43. If no director is willing to act as chairman, or if no director is present within fifteen minutes after the time appointed for holding the meeting, the members present and entitled to vote shall choose one of their number to be chairman.

44. A director shall, notwithstanding that he is not a member, be entitled to attend and speak at any general meeting and at any separate meeting of the holders of any class of shares in the company.

45. The chairman may, with the consent of a meeting at which a quorum is present (and shall if so directed by the meeting), adjourn the meeting from time to time and from place to place, but no

business shall be transacted at an adjourned meeting other than business which might properly have been transacted at the meeting had the adjournment not taken place. When a meeting is adjourned for fourteen days or more, at least seven clear days' notice shall be given specifying the time and place of the adjourned meeting and the general nature of the business to be transacted. Otherwise it shall not be necessary to give any such notice.

46. A resolution put to the vote of a meeting shall be decided on a show of hands unless before, or on the declaration of the result of, the show of hands a poll is duly demanded. Subject to the provisions of the Act, a poll may be demanded—
   (a) by the chairman; or
   (b) by at least two members having the right to vote at the meeting; or
   (c) by a member or members representing not less than one-tenth of the total voting rights of all the members having the right to vote at the meeting; or
   (d) by a member or members holding shares conferring a right to vote at the meeting being shares on which an aggregate sum has been paid up equal to not less than one-tenth of the total sum paid up on all the shares conferring that right;

   and a demand by a person as proxy for a member shall be the same as a demand by the member.

47. Unless a poll is duly demanded a declaration by the chairman that a resolution has been carried or carried unanimously, or by a particular majority, or lost, or not carried by a particular majority and an entry to that effect in the minutes of the meeting shall be conclusive evidence of the fact without proof of the number or proportion of the votes recorded in favour of or against the resolution.

48. The demand for a poll may, before the poll is taken, be withdrawn but only with the consent of the chairman and a demand so withdrawn shall not be taken to have invalidated the result of a show of hands declared before the demand was made.

49. A poll shall be taken as the chairman directs and he may appoint scrutineers (who need not be members) and fix a time and place for declaring the result of the poll. The result of the poll shall be deemed to be the resolution of the meeting at which the poll was demanded.

51. A poll demanded on the election of a chairman or on a question of adjournment shall be taken forthwith. A poll demanded on any other question shall be taken either forthwith or at such time and place as the chairman directs not being more than thirty days after the poll is demanded. The demand for a poll shall not prevent the continuance of a meeting for the transaction of any business other than the question on which the poll was demanded. If a poll is demanded before the declaration of the result of a show of hands and the demand is duly withdrawn, the meeting shall continue as if the demand had not been made.

52. No notice need be given of a poll not taken forthwith if the time and place at which it is to be taken are announced at the meeting at which it is demanded. In any other case at least seven clear days' notice shall be given specifying the time and place at which the poll is to be taken.

VOTES OF MEMBERS

54. Subject to any rights or restrictions attached to any shares, on a show of hands every member who (being an individual) is present in person or by proxy or (being a corporation) is present by a duly authorised representative or by proxy, unless the proxy (in either case) or the representative is himself a member entitled to vote, shall have one vote and on a poll every member shall have one vote for every share of which he is the holder.

55. In the case of joint holders the vote of the senior who tenders a vote, whether in person or by proxy, shall be accepted to the exclusion of the votes of the other joint holders; and seniority shall be determined by the order in which the names of the holders stand in the register of members.

56. A member in respect of whom an order has been made by any court having jurisdiction (whether in the United Kingdom or elsewhere) in matters concerning mental disorder may vote, whether on a show of hands or on a poll, by his receiver, curator bonis or other person authorised in that behalf appointed by that court, and any such receiver, curator bonis or other person may, on a poll, vote by proxy. Evidence to the satisfaction of the directors of the authority of the person

claiming to exercise the right to vote shall be deposited at the office, or at such other place as is specified in accordance with the articles for the deposit of instruments of proxy, not less than 48 hours before the time appointed for holding the meeting or adjourned meeting at which the right to vote is to be exercised and in default the right to vote shall not be exercisable.

57. No member shall vote at any general meeting or at any separate meeting of the holders of any class of shares in the company, either in person or by proxy, in respect of any share held by him unless all moneys presently payable by him in respect of that share have been paid.

58. No objection shall be raised to the qualification of any voter except at the meeting or adjourned meeting at which the vote objected to is tendered, and every vote not disallowed at the meeting shall be valid. Any objection made in due time shall be referred to the chairman whose decision shall be final and conclusive.

59. On a poll votes may be given either personally or by proxy. A member may appoint more than one proxy to attend on the same occasion.

60. The appointment of a proxy shall be executed by or on behalf of the appointor and shall be in the following form (or in a form as near thereto as circumstances allow or in any other form which is usual or which the directors may approve)—

" .. .. PLC/Limited .. .. I/We, ..., of .. .., being a member/members of the above-named company, hereby appoint .. .. of .. .., or failing him, ... of .. .., as my/our proxy to vote in my/our names and on my/our behalf at the general meeting of the company to be held on .. .. 19 .. .., and at any adjournment thereof.

Signed on .. .. 19 .. .."

61. Where it is desired to afford members an opportunity of instructing the proxy how he shall act the appointment of a proxy shall be in the following form (or in a form as near thereto as circumstances allow or in any other form which is usual or which the directors may approve)—

".. .. .. PLC/Limited .. .. I/We, ..., of .. .., being a member/members of the above-named company, hereby appoint .. .. of .. .., or failing him .. .. of .. .., as my/our proxy to vote in my/our names and on my/our behalf at the general meeting of the company, to be held on .. .. 19 , ..., and at any adjournment thereof.

This form is to be used in respect of the resolutions mentioned below as follows:

Resolution No. 1 *for *against

Resolution No. 2 *for *against.

*Strike out whichever is not desired.

Unless otherwise instructed, the proxy may vote as he thinks fit or abstain from voting.

Signed this .. .. day of .. .. 19 .. .."

62. The appointment of a proxy and any authority under which it is executed or a copy of such authority certified notarially or in some other way approved by the directors may—

(a) in the case of an instrument in writing be deposited at the office or at such other place within the United kingdom as is specified in the notice convening the meeting or in any instrument of proxy sent out by the company in relation to the meeting not less than 48 hours before the time for holding the meeting or adjourned meeting at which the person named in the instrument proposes to vote; or

(aa) in the case of an appointment contained in an electronic communication, where an address has been specified for the purpose of receiving electronic communications—

(i) in the notice convening the meeting, or

(ii) in any instrument of proxy sent out by the company in relation to the meeting, or

(iii) in any invitation contained in an electronic communication to appoint a proxy issued by the company in relation to the meeting,

be received at such address not less than 48 hours before the time for holding the meeting or adjourned meeting at which the person named in the appointment proposes to vote;

(b) in the case of a poll taken more than 48 hours after it is demanded, be deposited or received as aforesaid after the poll has been demanded and not less than 24 hours before the time appointed for the taking of the poll; or

(c) where the poll is not taken forthwith but is taken not more than 48 hours after it was demanded, be delivered at the meeting at which the poll was demanded to the chairman or to the secretary or to any director;

and an appointment of proxy which is not deposited, delivered or received in a manner so permitted shall be invalid.

In this regulation and the next, "address", in relation to electronic communications, includes any number or address used for the purposes of such communications.

63. A vote given or poll demanded by proxy or by the duly authorised representative of a corporation shall be valid notwithstanding the previous determination of the authority of the person voting or demanding a poll unless notice of the determination was received by the company at the office or at such other place at which the instrument of proxy was duly deposited or, where the appointment of the proxy was contained in an electronic communication, at the address at which such appointment was duly received before the commencement of the meeting or adjourned meeting at which the vote is given or the poll demanded or (in the case of a poll taken otherwise than on the same day as the meeting or adjourned meeting) the time appointed for taking the poll.

NUMBER OF DIRECTORS

64. Unless otherwise determined by ordinary resolution, the number of directors (other than alternate directors) shall not be subject to any maximum but shall be not less than two.

ALTERNATE DIRECTORS

65. Any director (other than an alternate director) may appoint any other director, or any other person approved by resolution of the directors and willing to act, to be an alternate director and may remove from office an alternate director so appointed by him.

66. An alternate director shall be entitled to receive notice of all meetings of directors and of all meetings of committees of directors of which his appointor is a member, to attend and vote at any such meeting at which the director appointing him is not personally present and generally to perform all the functions of his appointor as a director in his absence but shall not be entitled to receive any remuneration from the company for his services as an alternate director. But it shall not be necessary to give notice of such a meeting to an alternate director who is absent from the United Kingdom.

67. An alternate director shall cease to be an alternate director if his appointor ceases to be a director; but, if a director retires by rotation or otherwise but is reappointed or deemed to have been reappointed at the meeting at which he retires, any appointment of an alternate director made by him which was in force immediately prior to his retirement shall continue after his reappointment.

68. Any appointment or removal of an alternate director shall be by notice to the company signed by the director making or revoking the appointment or in any other manner approved by the directors.

69. Save as otherwise provided in the articles, an alternate director shall be deemed for all purposes to be a director and shall alone be responsible for his own acts and defaults and he shall not be deemed to be the agent of the director appointing him.

POWERS OF DIRECTORS

70. Subject to the provisions of the Act, the memorandum and the articles and to any directions given by special resolution, the business of the company shall be managed by the directors who may exercise all the powers of the company. No alteration of the memorandum or articles and no such direction shall invalidate any prior act of the directors which would have been valid if that alteration had not been made or that direction had not been given. The powers given by this regulation shall not be limited by any special power given to the directors by the articles and a

meeting of directors at which a quorum is present may exercise all powers exercisable by the directors.

71. The directors may, by power of attorney or otherwise, appoint any person to be the agent of the company for such purposes and on such conditions as they determine, including authority for the agent to delegate all or any of his powers.

DELEGATION OF DIRECTORS' POWERS

72. The directors may delegate any of their powers to any committee consisting of one or more directors. They may also delegate to any managing director or any director holding any other executive office such of their powers as they consider desirable to be exercised by him. Any such delegation may be made subject to any conditions the directors may impose, and either collaterally with or to the exclusion of their own powers and may be revoked or altered. Subject to any such conditions, the proceedings of a committee with two or more members shall be governed by the articles regulating the proceedings of directors so far as they are capable of applying.

APPOINTMENT AND RETIREMENT OF DIRECTORS

76. No person shall be appointed or reappointed a director at any general meeting unless—
(a) he is recommended by the directors; or
(b) not less than fourteen nor more than thirty-five clear days before the date appointed for the meeting, notice executed by a member qualified to vote at the meeting has been given to the company of the intention to propose that person for appointment or reappointment stating the particulars which would, if he were so appointed or reappointed, be required to be included in the company's register of directors together with notice executed by that person of his willingness to be appointed or reappointed.

77. Not less than seven nor more than twenty-eight clear days before the date appointed for holding a general meeting notice shall be given to all who are entitled to receive notice of the meeting of any person who is recommended by the directors for appointment or reappointment as a director at the meeting or in respect of whom notice has been duly given to the company of the intention to propose him at the meeting for appointment or reappointment as a director. The notice shall give the particulars of that person which would, if he were so appointed or reappointed, be required to be included in the company's register of directors.

78. The company may by ordinary resolution appoint a person who is willing to act to be a director either to fill a vacancy or as an additional director and may also determine the rotation in which any additional directors are to retire.

79. The directors may appoint a person who is willing to act to be a director, either to fill a vacancy or as an additional director, provided that the appointment does not cause the number of directors to exceed any number fixed by or in accordance with the articles as the maximum number of directors.

DISQUALIFICATION AND REMOVAL OF DIRECTORS

81. The office of a director shall be vacated if—
(a) he ceases to be a director by virtue of any provision of the Act or he becomes prohibited by law from being a director; or
(b) he becomes bankrupt or makes any arrangement or composition with his creditors generally; or
(c) he is, or may be, suffering from mental disorder and either—
(i) he is admitted to hospital in pursuance of an application for admission for treatment under the Mental Health Act 1983 or, in Scotland, an application for admission under the Mental Health (Scotland) Act 1960, or

(ii) an order is made by a court having jurisdiction (whether in the United Kingdom or elsewhere) in matters concerning mental disorder for his detention or for the appointment of a receiver, curator bonis or other person to exercise powers with respect to his property or affairs; or

(d) he resigns his office by notice to the company; or

(e) he shall for more than six consecutive months have been absent without permission of the directors from meetings of directors held during that period and the directors resolve that his office be vacated.

REMUNERATION OF DIRECTORS

82. The directors shall be entitled to such remuneration as the company may by ordinary resolution determine and, unless the resolution provides otherwise, the remuneration shall be deemed to accrue from day to day.

DIRECTORS' EXPENSES

83. The directors may be paid all travelling, hotel, and other expenses properly incurred by them in connection with their attendance at meetings of directors or committees of directors or general meetings or separate meetings of the holders of any class of shares or of debentures of the company or otherwise in connection with the discharge of their duties.

DIRECTORS' APPOINTMENTS AND INTERESTS

84. Subject to the provisions of the Act, the directors may appoint one or more of their number to the office of managing director or to any other executive office under the company and may enter into an agreement or arrangement with any director for his employment by the company or for the provision by him of any services outside the scope of the ordinary duties of a director. Any such appointment, agreement or arrangement may be made upon such terms as the directors determine and they may remunerate any such director for his services as they think fit. Any appointment of a director to an executive office shall terminate if he ceases to be a director but without prejudice to any claim to damages for breach of the contract of service between the director and the company. A managing director and a director holding any other executive office shall not be subject to retirement by rotation.

85. Subject to the provisions of the Act, and provided that he has disclosed to the directors the nature and extent of any material interest of his, a director notwithstanding his office—

(a) may be a party to, or otherwise interested in, any transaction or arrangement with the company or in which the company is otherwise interested;

(b) may be a director or other officer of, or employed by, or a party to any transaction or arrangement with, or otherwise interested in, any body corporate promoted by the company or in which the company is otherwise interested; and

(c) shall not, by reason of his office, be accountable to the company for any benefit which he derives from any such office or employment or from any such transaction or arrangement or from any interest in any such body corporate and no such transaction or arrangement shall be liable to be avoided on the ground of any such interest or benefit.

86. For the purposes of regulation 85—

(a) a general notice given to the directors that a director is to be regarded as having an interest of the nature and extent specified in the notice in any transaction or arrangement in which a specified person or class of persons is interested shall be deemed to be a disclosure that the director has an interest in any such transaction of the nature and extent so specified; and

(b) an interest of which a director has no knowledge and of which it is unreasonable to expect him to have knowledge shall not be treated as an interest of his.

DIRECTORS' GRATUITIES AND PENSIONS

87. The directors may provide benefits, whether by the payment of gratuities or pensions or by insurance or otherwise, for any director who has held but no longer holds any executive office or employment with the company or with any body corporate which is or has been a subsidiary of the company or a predecessor in business of the company or of any such subsidiary, and for any member of his family (including a spouse and a former spouse) or any person who is or was dependent on him, and may (as well before as after he ceases to hold such office or employment) contribute to any fund and pay premiums for the purchase or provision of any such benefit.

PROCEEDINGS OF DIRECTORS

88. Subject to the provisions of the articles, the directors may regulate their proceedings as they think fit. A director may, and the secretary at the request of a director shall, call a meeting of the directors. It shall not be necessary to give notice of a meeting to a director who is absent from the United Kingdom. Questions arising at a meeting shall be decided by a majority of votes. In the case of an equality of votes, the chairman shall have a second or casting vote. A director who is also an alternate director shall be entitled in the absence of his appointor to a separate vote on behalf of his appointor in addition to his own vote.

89. The quorum for the transaction of the business of the directors may be fixed by the directors and unless so fixed at any other number shall be two. A person who holds office only as an alternate director shall, if his appointor is not present, be counted in the quorum.

90. The continuing directors or a sole continuing director may act notwithstanding any vacancies in their number, but, if the number of directors is less than the number fixed as the quorum, the continuing directors or director may act only for the purpose of filling vacancies or of calling a general meeting.

91. The directors may appoint one of their number to be the chairman of the board of directors and may at any time remove him from that office. Unless he is unwilling to do so, the director so appointed shall preside at every meeting of directors at which he is present. But if there is no director holding that office, or if the director holding it is unwilling to preside or is not present within five minutes after the time appointed for the meeting, the directors present may appoint one of their number to be chairman of the meeting.

92. All acts done by a meeting of directors, or of a committee of directors, or by a person acting as a director shall, notwithstanding that it be afterwards discovered that there was a defect in the appointment of any director or that any of them were disqualified from holding office, or had vacated office, or were not entitled to vote, be as valid as if every such person had been duly appointed and was qualified and had continued to be a director and had been entitled to vote.

93. A resolution in writing signed by all the directors entitled to receive notice of a meeting of directors or of a committee of directors shall be as valid and effectual as it if had been passed at a meeting of directors or (as the case may be) a committee of directors duly convened and held and may consist of several documents in the like form each signed by one or more directors; but a resolution signed by an alternate director need not also be signed by his appointor and, if it is signed by a director who has appointed an alternate director, it need not be signed by the alternate director in that capacity.

94. Save as otherwise provided by the articles, a director shall not vote at a meeting of directors or of a committee of directors on any resolution concerning a matter in which he has, directly or indirectly, an interest or duty which is material and which conflicts or may conflict with the interests of the company unless his interest or duty arises only because the case falls within one or more of the following paragraphs—

(a) the resolution relates to the giving to him of a guarantee, security, or indemnity in respect of money lent to, or an obligation incurred by him for the benefit of, the company or any of its subsidiaries;

(b) the resolution relates to the giving to a third party of a guarantee, security, or indemnity in respect of an obligation of the company or any of its subsidiaries for which the director has assumed responsibility in whole or part and whether alone or jointly with others under a guarantee or indemnity or by the giving of security;

(c) his interest arises by virtue of his subscribing or agreeing to subscribe for any shares, debentures, or other securities of the company or any of its subsidiaries, or by virtue of his being, or intending to become, a participant in the underwriting or sub-underwriting of an offer of any such shares, debentures, or other securities by the company or any of its subsidiaries for subscription, purchase or exchange;

(d) the resolution relates in any way to a retirement benefits scheme which has been approved, or is conditional upon approval, by the Board of Inland Revenue for taxation purposes.

For the purposes of this regulation, an interest of a person who is, for any purpose of the Act (excluding any statutory modification thereof not in force when this regulation becomes binding on the company), connected with a director shall be treated as an interest of the director and, in relation to an alternate director, an interest of his appointor shall be treated as an interest of the alternate director without prejudice to any interest which the alternate director has otherwise.

95. A director shall not be counted in the quorum present at a meeting in relation to a resolution on which he is not entitled to vote.

96. The company may by ordinary resolution suspend or relax to any extent, either generally or in respect of any particular matter, any provision of the articles prohibiting a director from voting at a meeting of directors or of a committee of directors.

97. Where proposals are under consideration concerning the appointment of two or more directors to offices or employments with the company or any body corporate in which the company is interested the proposals may be divided and considered in relation to each director separately and (provided he is not for another reason precluded from voting) each of the directors concerned shall be entitled to vote and be counted in the quorum in respect of each resolution except that concerning his own appointment.

98. If a question arises at a meeting of directors or of a committee of directors as to the right of a director to vote, the question may, before the conclusion of the meeting, be referred to the chairman of the meeting and his ruling in relation to any director other than himself shall be final and conclusive.

SECRETARY

99. Subject to the provisions of the Act, the secretary shall be appointed by the directors for such term, at such remuneration and upon such conditions as they may think fit; and any secretary so appointed may be removed by them.

MINUTES

100. The directors shall cause minutes to be made in books kept for the purpose—

(a) of all appointments of officers made by the directors; and

(b) of all proceedings at meetings of the company, of the holders of any class of shares in the company, and of the directors, and of committees of directors, including the names of the directors present at each such meeting.

THE SEAL

101. The seal shall only be used by the authority of the directors or of a committee of directors authorised by the directors. The directors may determine who shall sign any instrument to which the seal is affixed and unless otherwise so determined it shall be signed by a director and by the secretary or by a second director.

DIVIDENDS

102. Subject to the provisions of the Act, the company may by ordinary resolution declare dividends in accordance with the respective rights of the members, but no dividend shall exceed the amount recommended by the directors.

103. Subject to the provisions of the Act, the directors may pay interim dividends if it appears to them that they are justified by the profits of the company available for distribution. If the share capital is divided into different classes, the directors may pay interim dividends on shares which confer deferred or non-preferred rights with regard to dividend as well as on shares which confer preferential rights with regard to dividend, but no interim dividend shall be paid on shares carrying deferred or non-preferred rights if, at the time of payment, any preferential dividend is in arrear. The directors may also pay at intervals settled by them any dividend payable at a fixed rate if it appears to them that the profits available for distribution justify the payment. Provided the directors act in good faith they shall not incur any liability to the holders of shares conferring preferred rights for any loss they may suffer by the lawful payment of an interim dividend on any shares having deferred or non-preferred rights.

104. Except as otherwise provided by the rights attached to shares, all dividends shall be declared and paid according to the amounts paid up on the shares on which the dividend is paid. All dividends shall be apportioned and paid proportionately to the amounts paid up on the shares during any portion or portions of the period in respect of which the dividend is paid; but, if any share is issued on terms providing that it shall rank for dividend as from a particular date, that share shall rank for dividend accordingly.

105. A general meeting declaring a dividend may, upon the recommendation of the directors, direct that it shall be satisfied wholly or partly by the distribution of assets and, where any difficulty arises in regard to the distribution, the directors may settle the same and in particular may issue fractional certificates and fix the value for distribution of any assets and may determine that cash shall be paid to any member upon the footing of the value so fixed in order to adjust the rights of members and may vest any assets in trustees.

106. Any dividend or other moneys payable in respect of a share may be paid by cheque sent by post to the registered address of the person entitled or, if two or more persons are the holders of the share or are jointly entitled to it by reason of the death or bankruptcy of the holder, to the registered address of that one of those persons who is first named in the register of members or to such person and to such address as the person or persons entitled may in writing direct. Every cheque shall be made payable to the order of the person or persons entitled or to such other person as the person or persons entitled may in writing direct and payment of the cheque shall be a good discharge to the company. Any joint holder or other person jointly entitled to a share as aforesaid may give receipts for any dividend or other moneys payable in respect of the share.

107. No dividend or other moneys payable in respect of a share shall bear interest against the company unless otherwise provided by the rights attached to the share.

108. Any dividend which has remained unclaimed for twelve years from the date when it became due for payment shall, if the directors so resolve, be forfeited and cease to remain owing by the company.

ACCOUNTS

109. No member shall (as such) have any right of inspecting any accounting records or other book or document of the company except as conferred by statute or authorised by the directors or by ordinary resolution of the company.

CAPITALISATION OF PROFITS

110. The directors may with the authority of an ordinary resolution of the company—

(a) subject as hereinafter provided, resolve to capitalise any undivided profits of the company not required for paying any preferential dividend (whether or not they are available for distribution) or any sum standing to the credit of the company's share premium account or capital redemption reserve;

(b) appropriate the sum resolved to be capitalised to the members who would have been entitled to it if it were distributed by way of dividend and in the same proportions and apply such sum on their behalf either in or towards paying up the amounts, if any, for the time being unpaid on any shares held by them respectively, or in paying up in full unissued shares or debentures of the company of a nominal amount equal to that sum, and allot the shares or debentures credited as fully paid to those members, or as they may direct, in those proportions, or partly in one way and partly in the other: but the share premium account, the capital redemption reserve, and any profits which are not available for distribution may, for the purposes of this regulation, only be applied in paying up unissued shares to be allotted to members credited as fully paid;

(c) make such provision by the issue of fractional certificates or by payment in cash or otherwise as they determine in the case of shares or debentures becoming distributable under this regulation in fractions; and

(d) authorise any person to enter on behalf of all the members concerned into an agreement with the company providing for the allotment to them respectively, credited as fully paid, of any shares or debentures to which they are entitled upon such capitalisation, any agreement made under such authority being binding on all such members.

NOTICES

111. Any notice to be given to or by any person pursuant to the articles (other than a notice calling a meeting of the directors) shall be in writing or shall be given using electronic communications to an address for the time being notified for that purpose to the person giving the notice.

In this regulation, "address", in relation to electronic communications, includes any number or address used for the purposes of such communications.

112. The company may give any notice to a member either personally or by sending it by post in a prepaid envelope addressed to the member at his registered address or by leaving it at that address or by giving it using electronic communications to an address for the time being notified to the company by the member. In the case of joint holders of a share, all notices shall be given to the joint holder whose name stands first in the register of members in respect of the joint holding and notice so given shall be sufficient notice to all the joint holders. A member whose registered address is not within the United Kingdom and who gives to the company an address within the United Kingdom at which notices may be given to him, or an address to which notices may be sent using electronic communications, shall be entitled to have notices given to him at that address, but otherwise no such member shall be entitled to receive any notice from the company.

In this regulation and the next, "address", in relation to electronic communications, includes any number or address used for the purposes of such communications.

113. A member present, either in person or by proxy, at any meeting of the company or of the holders of any class of shares in the company shall be deemed to have received notice of the meeting and, where requisite, of the purposes for which it was called.

114. Every person who becomes entitled to a share shall be bound by any notice in respect of that share which, before his name is entered in the register of members, has been duly given to a person from whom he derives his title.

115. Proof that an envelope containing a notice was properly addressed, prepaid and posted shall be conclusive evidence that that the notice was given. Proof that a notice contained in an electronic communication was sent in accordance with guidance issued by the Institute of Chartered Secretaries and Administrators shall be conclusive evidence that the notice was given. A notice shall be deemed to be given at the expiration of 48 hours after the envelope containing it was

posted or, in the case of a notice contained in an electronic communication, at the expiration of 48 hours after the time it was sent.

116. A notice may be given by the company to the persons entitled to a share in consequence of the death or bankruptcy of a member by sending or delivering it, in any manner authorised by the articles for the giving of notice to a member, addressed to them by name, or by the title of representatives of the deceased, or trustee of the bankrupt or by any like description at the address, if any, within the United Kingdom supplied for that purpose by the persons claiming to be so entitled. Until such an address has been supplied, a notice may be given in any manner in which it might have been given if the death or bankruptcy had not occurred.

WINDING UP

117. If the company is wound up, the liquidator may, with the sanction of a special resolution of the company and any other sanction required by the Act, divide among the members in specie the whole or any part of the assets of the company and may, for that purpose, value any assets and determine how the division shall be carried out as between the members or different classes of members. The liquidator may, with the like sanction, vest the whole or any part of the assets in trustees upon such trusts for the benefit of the members as he with the like sanction determines, but no member shall be compelled to accept any assets upon which there is a liability.

INDEMNITY

118. Subject to the provisions of the Act but without prejudice to any indemnity to which a director may otherwise be entitled, every director or other officer or auditor of the company shall be indemnified out of the assets of the company against any liability incurred by him in defending any proceedings, whether civil or criminal, in which judgment is given in his favour or in which he is acquitted or in connection with any application in which relief is granted to him by the court from liability for negligence, default, breach of duty or breach of trust in relation to the affairs of the company.

Partnership Act 1890

1890 c. 39

An Act to declare and amend the Law of Partnership

[14th August 1890]

Nature of Partnership

1. Definition of Partnership

(1) Partnership is the relation which subsists between persons carrying on a business in common with a view of profit.

(2) But the relation between members of any company or association which is—

(a) registered under the Companies Act 2006, or

(b) Formed or incorporated by or in pursuance of any other Act of Parliament or letters patent, or Royal Charter …

(c) …

is not a partnership within the meaning of this Act.

2. Rules for determining existence of partnership

In determining whether a partnership does or does not exist, regard shall be had to the following rules:

(1) Joint tenancy, tenancy in common, joint property, common property, or part ownership does not of itself create a partnership as to anything so held or owned, whether the tenants or owners do or do not share any profits made by the use thereof.

(2) The sharing of gross returns does not of itself create a partnership, whether the persons sharing such returns have or have not a joint or common right or interest in any property from which or from the use of which the returns are derived.

(3) The receipt by a person of a share of the profits of a business is *prima facie* evidence that he is a partner in the business, but receipt of such a share, or of a payment contingent on or varying with the profits of a business, does not of itself make him a partner in the business; and in particular—

(a) The receipt by a person of a debt or other liquidated amount by instalments or otherwise out of the accruing profits of a business does not of itself make him a partner in the business or liable as such:

(b) A contract for the remuneration of a servant or agent of a person engaged in a business by a share of the profits of the business does not of itself make the servant or agent a partner in the business or liable as such:

(c) A person being the widow, widower, surviving civil partner or child of a deceased partner, and receiving by way of annuity a portion of the profits made in the business in which the deceased person was a partner, is not by reason only of such receipt a partner in the business or liable as such:

(d) The advance of money by way of loan to a person engaged or about to engage in any business on a contract with that person that the lender shall receive a rate of interest varying with the profits, or shall receive a share of the profits arising from carrying on the business, does not of itself make the lender a partner with the person or persons carrying on the business or liable as such. Provided that the contract is in writing, and signed by or on behalf of all the parties thereto:

(e) A person receiving by way of annuity or otherwise a portion of the profits of a business in consideration of the sale by him of the goodwill of the business is not by reason only of such receipt a partner in the business or liable as such.

3. Postponement of rights of person lending or selling in consideration of share of profits in case of insolvency

In the event of any person to whom money has been advanced by way of loan upon such a contract as is mentioned in the last foregoing section, or of any buyer of a goodwill in consideration of a share of the profits of the business, being adjudged a bankrupt, entering into an arrangement to pay his creditors less than 100p in the pound, or dying in insolvent circumstances, the lender of the loan shall not be entitled to recover anything in respect of his loan, and the seller of the goodwill shall not be entitled to recover anything in respect of the share of profits contracted for, until the claims of the other creditors of the borrower or buyer for valuable consideration in money or money's worth have been satisfied.

4. Meaning of firm

(1) Persons who have entered into partnership with one another are for the purposes of this Act called collectively a firm, and the name under which their business is carried on is called the firm-name.

(2) In Scotland a firm is a legal person distinct from the partners of whom it is composed, but an individual partner may be charged on a decree or diligence directed against the firm, and on payment of the debts is entitled to relief pro rata from the firm and its other members.

Relations of Partners to persons dealing with them

5. Power of partner to bind the firm

Every partner is an agent of the firm and his other partners for the purpose of the business of the partnership; and the acts of every partner who does any act for carrying on in the usual way business of the kind carried on by the firm of which he is a member bind the firm and his partners, unless the partner so acting has in fact no authority to act for the firm in the particular matter, and the person with whom he is dealing either knows that he has no authority, or does not know or believe him to be a partner.

6. Partners bound by acts on behalf of firm

An act or instrument relating to the business of the firm done or executed in the firm-name, or in any other manner showing an intention to bind the firm, by any person thereto authorised, whether a partner or not, is binding on the firm and all the partners.

Provided that this section shall not affect any general rule of law relating to the execution of deeds or negotiable instruments.

7. Partner using credit of firm for private purposes

Where one partner pledges the credit of the firm for a purpose apparently not connected with the firm's ordinary course of business, the firm is not bound, unless he is in fact specially authorised by the other partners; but this section does not affect any personal liability incurred by an individual partner.

8. Effect of notice that firm will not be bound by acts of partner

If it has been agreed between the partners that any restriction shall be placed on the power of any one or more of them to bind the firm, no act done in contravention of the agreement is binding on the firm with respect to persons having notice of the agreement.

9. Liability of partners

Every partner in a firm is liable jointly with the other partners, and in Scotland severally also, for all debts and obligations of the firm incurred while he is a partner; and after his death his estate is also severally liable in a due course of administration for such debts and obligations, so far as they remain unsatisfied, but subject in England or Ireland to the prior payment of his separate debts.

10. Liability of the firm for wrongs

Where, by any wrongful act or omission of any partner acting in the ordinary course of the business of the firm, or with the authority of his co-partners, loss or injury is caused to any person not being a partner in the firm, or any penalty is incurred, the firm is liable therefor to the same extent as the partner so acting or omitting to act.

11. Misapplication of money or property received for or in custody of the firm

In the following cases; namely—

(a) Where one partner acting within the scope of his apparent authority receives the money or property of a third person and misapplies it; and

(b) Where a firm in the course of its business receives money or property of a third person, and the money or property so received is misapplied by one or more of the partners while it is in the custody of the firm;

the firm is liable to make good the loss.

12. Liability for wrongs joint and several

Every partner is liable jointly with his co-partners and also severally for everything for which the firm while he is a partner therein becomes liable under either of the two last preceding sections.

13. Improper employment of trust-property for partnership purposes

If a partner, being a trustee, improperly employs trust-property in the business or on the account of the partnership, no other partner is liable for the trust property to the persons beneficially interested therein:

Provided as follows:—

(1) This section shall not affect any liability incurred by any partner by reason of his having notice of a breach of trust; and

(2) Nothing in this section shall prevent trust money from being followed and recovered from the firm if still in its possession or under its control.

14. Persons liable by "holding out"

(1) Every one who by words spoken or written or by conduct represents himself, or who knowingly suffers himself to be represented, as a partner in a particular firm, is liable as a partner to any one who has on the faith of any such representation given credit to the firm, whether the representation has or has not been made or communicated to the person so giving credit by or with the knowledge of the apparent partner making the representation or suffering it to be made.

(2) Provided that where after a partner's death the partnership business is continued in the old firm's name, the continued use of that name or of the deceased partner's name as part thereof shall not of itself make his executors or administrators estate or effects liable for any partnership debts contracted after his death.

15. Admissions and representation of partners

An admission or representation made by any partner concerning the partnership affairs, and in the ordinary course of its business, is evidence against the firm.

16. Notice to acting partner to be notice to the firm

Notice to any partner who habitually acts in the partnership business of any matter relating to partnership affairs operates as notice to the firm, except in the case of a fraud on the firm committed by or with the consent of that partner.

17. Liabilities of incoming and outgoing partners

(1) A person who is admitted as a partner into an existing firm does not thereby become liable to the creditors of the firm for anything done before he became a partner.

(2) A partner who retires from a firm does not thereby cease to be liable for partnership debts or obligations incurred before his retirement.

(3) A retiring partner may be discharged from any existing liabilities, by an agreement to that effect between himself and the members of the firm as newly constituted and the creditors, and this agreement may be either expressed or inferred as a fact from the course of dealing between the creditors and the firm as newly constituted.

18. Revocation of continuing guaranty by change in firm

A continuing guaranty or cautionary obligation given either to a firm or to a third person in respect of the transactions of a firm is, in the absence of agreement to the contrary, revoked as to future transactions by any change in the constitution of the firm to which, or of the firm in respect of the transactions of which, the guaranty or obligation was given.

Relations of Partners to one another

19. Variation by consent of terms of partnership

The mutual rights and duties of partners, whether ascertained by agreement or defined by this Act, may be varied by the consent of all the partners, and such consent may be either express or inferred from a course of dealing.

20. Partnership property

(1) All property and rights and interests in property originally brought into the partnership stock or acquired, whether by purchase or otherwise, on account of the firm, or for the purposes and in the course of the partnership business, are called in this Act partnership property, and must be held and applied by the partners exclusively for the purposes of the partnership and in accordance with the partnership agreement.

(2) Provided that the legal estate or interest in any land, or in Scotland the title to and interest in any heritable estate, which belongs to the partnership shall devolve according to the nature and tenure thereof, and the general rules of law thereto applicable, but in trust, so far as necessary, for the persons beneficially interested in the land under this section.

(3) Where co-owners of an estate or interest in any land, or in Scotland of any heritable estate, not being itself partnership property, are partners as to profits made by the use of that land or estate, and purchase other land or estate out of the profits to be used in like manner, the land or estate so purchased belongs to them, in the absence of an agreement to the contrary, not as partners, but as co-owners for the same respective estates and interests as are held by them in the land or estate first mentioned at the date of the purchase.

21. Property bought with partnership money

Unless the contrary intention appears, property bought with money belonging to the firm is deemed to have been bought on account of the firm.

22. ...

23. Procedure against partnership property for a partner's separate judgement debt

(1) … A writ of execution shall not issue against any partnership property except on a judgment against the firm.

(2) The High Court, or a judge thereof, …, or a county court, may, on the application by summons of any judgment creditor of a partner, make an order charging that partner's interest in the partnership property and profits with payment of the amount of the judgment debt and interest thereon, and may by the same or a subsequent order appoint a receiver of that partner's share of profits (whether already declared or accruing), and of any other money which may be coming to him in respect of the partnership, and direct all accounts and inquiries, and give all other orders and directions which might have been directed or given if the charge had been made in favour of the judgment creditor by the partner, or which the circumstances of the case may require.

(3) The other partner or partners shall be at liberty at any time to redeem the interest charged, or in case of a sale being directed, to purchase the same.

(4) …

(5) This section shall not apply to Scotland.

24. Rules as to interests and duties of partners subject to special agreement

The interests of partners in the partnership property and their rights and duties in relation to the partnership shall be determined, subject to any agreement express or implied between the partners, by the following rules:

(1) All the partners are entitled to share equally in the capital and profits of the business, and must contribute equally towards the losses whether of capital or otherwise sustained by the firm.

(2) The firm must indemnify every partner in respect of payments made and personal liabilities incurred by him—

(a) In the ordinary and proper conduct of the business of the firm; or,

(b) In or about anything necessarily done for the preservation of the business or property of the firm.

(3) A partner making, for the purpose of the partnership, any actual payment or advance beyond the amount of capital which he has agreed to subscribe, is entitled to interest at the rate of five per cent. per annum from the date of the payment or advance.

(4) A partner is not entitled, before the ascertainment of profits, to interest on the capital subscribed by him.

(5) Every partner may take part in the management of the partnership business.

(6) No partner shall be entitled to remuneration for acting in the partnership business.

(7) No person may be introduced as a partner without the consent of all existing partners.

(8) Any difference arising as to ordinary matters connected with the partnership business may be decided by a majority of the partners, but no change may be made in the nature of the partnership business without the consent of all existing partners.

(9) The partnership books are to be kept at the place of business of the partnership (or the principal place, if there is more than one), and every partner may, when he thinks fit, have access to and inspect and copy any of them.

25. Expulsion of partner

No majority of the partners can expel any partner unless a power to do so has been conferred by express agreement between the partners.

26. Retirement from partnership at will

(1) Where no fixed term has been agreed upon for the duration of the partnership, any partner may determine the partnership at any time on giving notice of his intention so to do to all the other partners.

(2) Where the partnership has originally been constituted by deed, a notice in writing, signed by the partner giving it, shall be sufficient for this purpose.

27. Where partnership for term is continued over, continuance on old terms presumed

(1) Where a partnership entered into for a fixed term is continued after the term has expired, and without any express new agreement, the rights and duties of the partners remain the same as they were at the expiration of the term, so far as is consistent with the incidents of a partnership at will.

(2) A continuance of the business by the partners or such of them as habitually acted therein during the term, without any settlement or liquidation of the partnership affairs, is presumed to be a continuance of the partnership.

28. Duty of partners to render accounts, etc

Partners are bound to render true accounts and full information of all things affecting the partnership to any partner or his legal representatives.

29. Accountability of partners for private profits

(1) Every partner must account to the firm for any benefit derived by him without the consent of the other partners from any transaction concerning the partnership, or from any use by him of the partnership property name or business connexion.

(2) This section applies also to transactions undertaken after a partnership has been dissolved by the death of a partner, and before the affairs thereof have been completely wound up, either by any surviving partner or by the representatives of the deceased partner.

30. Duty of partner not to compete with firm

If a partner, without the consent of the other partners, carries on any business of the same nature as and competing with that of the firm, he must account for and pay over to the firm all profits made by him in that business.

31. Rights of assignee of share in partnership

(1) An assignment by any partner of his share in the partnership, either absolute or by way of mortgage or redeemable charge, does not, as against the other partners, entitle the assignee, during the continuance of the partnership, to interfere in the management or administration of the partnership business or affairs, or to require any accounts of the partnership transactions, or to inspect the partnership books, but entitles the assignee only to receive the share of profits to which the assigning partner would otherwise be entitled, and the assignee must accept the account of profits agreed to by the partners.

(2) In case of a dissolution of the partnership, whether as respects all the partners or as respects the assigning partner, the assignee is entitled to receive the share of the partnership assets to which the assigning partner is entitled as between himself and the other partners, and, for the purpose of ascertaining that share, to an account as from the date of the dissolution.

Dissolution of Partnership, and its consequences

32. Dissolution by expiration or notice

Subject to any agreement between the partners, a partnership is dissolved—

(a) If entered into for a fixed term, by the expiration of that term:

(b) If entered into for a single adventure or undertaking, by the termination of that adventure or undertaking:

(c) If entered into for an undefined time, by any partner giving notice to the other or others of his intention to dissolve the partnership.

In the last-mentioned case the partnership is dissolved as from the date mentioned in the notice as the date of dissolution, or, if no date is so mentioned, as from the date of the communication of the notice.

33. Dissolution by bankruptcy, death or charge

(1) Subject to any agreement between the partners, every partnership is dissolved as regards all the partners by the death or bankruptcy of any partner.

(2) A partnership may, at the option of the other partners, be dissolved if any partner suffers his share of the partnership property to be charged under this Act for his separate debt.

34. Dissolution by illegality of partnership

A partnership is in every case dissolved by the happening of any event which makes it unlawful for the business of the firm to be carried on or for the members of the firm to carry it on in partnership.

35. Dissolution by the Court

On application by a partner the Court may decree a dissolution of the partnership in any of the following cases:

(a) …

(b) When a partner, other than the partner suing, becomes in any other way permanently incapable of performing his part of the partnership contract:

(c) When a partner, other than the partner suing, has been guilty of such conduct as, in the opinion of the Court, regard being had to the nature of the business, is calculated to prejudicially affect the carrying on of the business:

(d) When a partner, other than the partner suing, wilfully or persistently commits a breach of the partnership agreement, or otherwise so conducts himself in matters relating to the partnership business that it is not reasonably practicable for the other partner or partners to carry on the business in partnership with him:

(e) When the business of the partnership can only be carried on at a loss:

(f) Whenever in any case circumstances have arisen which, in the opinion of the Court, render it just and equitable that the partnership be dissolved.

36. Rights of persons dealing with firm against apparent members of firm

(1) Where a person deals with a firm after a change in its constitution he is entitled to treat all apparent members of the old firm as still being members of the firm until he has notice of the change.

(2) An advertisement in the London Gazette as to a firm whose principal place of business is in England or Wales, in the Edinburgh Gazette as to a firm whose principal place of business is in Scotland, and in the Belfast Gazette as to a firm whose principal place of business is in Ireland, shall be notice as to persons who had not dealings with the firm before the date of the dissolution or change so advertised.

(3) The estate of a partner who dies, or who becomes bankrupt, or of a partner who, not having been known to the person dealing with the firm to be a partner, retires from the firm, is not liable for partnership debts contracted after the date of the death, bankruptcy, or retirement respectively.

37. Right of partners to notify dissolution

On the dissolution of a partnership or retirement of a partner any partner may publicly notify the same, and may require the other partner or partners to concur for that purpose in all necessary or proper acts, if any, which cannot be done without his or their concurrence.

38. Continuing authority of partners for purposes of winding up

After the dissolution of a partnership the authority of each partner to bind the firm, and the other rights and obligations of the partners, continue notwithstanding the dissolution so far as may be necessary to wind up the affairs of the partnership, and to complete transactions begun but unfinished at the time of the dissolution, but not otherwise.

Provided that the firm is in no case bound by the acts of a partner who has become bankrupt; but this proviso does not affect the liability of any person who has after the bankruptcy represented himself or knowingly suffered himself to be represented as a partner of the bankrupt.

39. Rights of partners as to application of partnership property

On the dissolution of a partnership every partner is entitled, as against the other partners in the firm, and all persons claiming through them in respect of their interests as partners, to have the property of the partnership applied in payment of the debts and liabilities of the firm, and to have the surplus assets after such payment applied in payment of what may be due to the partners respectively after deducting what may be due from them as partners to the firm; and for that purpose any partner or his representatives may on the termination of the partnership apply to the Court to wind up the business and affairs of the firm.

40. Apportionment of premium where partnership prematurely dissolved

Where one partner has paid a premium to another on entering into a partnership for a fixed term, and the partnership is dissolved before the expiration of that term otherwise than by the death of a partner, the Court may order the repayment of the premium, or of such part thereof as it thinks just, having regard to the terms of the partnership contract and to the length of time during which the partnership has continued; unless

(a) the dissolution is, in the judgment of the Court, wholly or chiefly due to the misconduct of the partner who paid the premium; or

(b) the partnership has been dissolved by an agreement containing no provision for a return of any part of the premium.

41. Rights where partnership dissolved for fraud or misrepresentation

Where a partnership contract is rescinded on the ground of the fraud or misrepresentation of one of the parties thereto, the party entitled to rescind is, without prejudice to any other right, entitled—

(a) to a lien on, or right of retention of, the surplus of the partnership assets, after satisfying the partnership liabilities, for any sum of money paid by him for the purchase of a share in the partnership and for any capital contributed by him, and is

(b) to stand in the place of the creditors of the firm for any payments made by him in respect of the partnership liabilities, and

(c) to be indemnified by the person guilty of the fraud or making the representation against all the debts and liabilities of the firm.

42. Right of outgoing partner in certain cases to share profits made after dissolution

(1) Where any member of a firm has died or otherwise ceased to be a partner, and the surviving or continuing partners carry on the business of the firm with its capital or assets without any final settlement of accounts as between the firm and the outgoing partner or his estate, then, in the absence of any agreement to the contrary, the outgoing partner or his estate is entitled at the option of himself or his representatives to such share of the profits made since the dissolution as the Court may find to be attributable to the use of his share of the partnership assets, or to interest at the rate of five per cent. per annum on the amount of his share of the partnership assets.

(2) Provided that where by the partnership contract an option is given to surviving or continuing partners to purchase the interest of a deceased or outgoing partner, and that option is duly exercised, the estate of the deceased partner, or the outgoing partner or his estate, as the case may be, is not entitled to any further or other share of profits; but if any partner assuming to act in exercise of the option does not in all material respects comply with the terms thereof, he is liable to account under the foregoing provisions of this section.

43. Retiring or deceased partner's share to be a debt

Subject to any agreement between the partners, the amount due from surviving or continuing partners to an outgoing partner or the representatives of a deceased partner in respect of the outgoing or deceased partner's share is a debt accruing at the date of the dissolution or death.

44. Rule for distribution of assets on final settlement of accounts

In settling accounts between the partners after a dissolution of partnership, the following rules shall, subject to any agreement, be observed:

(a) Losses, including losses and deficiencies of capital, shall be paid first out of profits, next out of capital, and lastly, if necessary, by the partners individually in the proportion in which they were entitled to share profits:

(b) The assets of the firm including the sums, if any, contributed by the partners to make up losses or deficiencies of capital, shall be applied in the following manner and order:

1. In paying the debts and liabilities of the firm to persons who are not partners therein:
2. In paying to each partner rateably what is due from the firm to him for advances as distinguished from capital:
3. In paying to each partner rateably what is due from the firm to him in respect of capital:
4. The ultimate residue, if any, shall be divided among the partners in the proportion in which profits are divisible.

Supplemental

45. Definitions of "court" and "business"

In this Act, unless the contrary intention appears,—

The expression "court" includes every court and judge having jurisdiction in the case:

The expression "business" includes every trade, occupation, or profession.

46. Saving for rules of equity and common law

The rules of equity and of common law applicable to partnership shall continue in force except so far as they are inconsistent with the express provisions of this Act.

47. Provision as to bankruptcy in Scotland

(1) In the application of this Act to Scotland the bankruptcy of a firm or of an individual shall mean sequestration under the Bankruptcy (Scotland) Acts, and also in the case of an individual the issue against him of a decree of cessio bonorum.

(2) Nothing in this Act shall alter the rules of the law of Scotland relating to the bankruptcy of a firm or of the individual partners thereof.

48, 49. ...

50. Short title

This Act may be cited as the Partnership Act 1890.

SCHEDULE

...

Limited Partnerships Act 1907

7 Edward 7, c. 24

An Act to establish Limited Partnership

[28th August 1907]

1. Short title

This Act may be cited for all purposes as the Limited Partnerships Act 1907.

3. Interpretation of terms

In the construction of this Act the following words and expressions shall have the meanings respectively assigned to them in this section, unless there be something in the subject or context repugnant to such construction:

"Firm," "firm name," and "business" have the same meanings as in the Partnership Act 1890.

"General partner" shall mean any partner who is not a limited partner as defined by this Act.

4. Definition and constitution of limited partnership

(1) Limited partnerships may be formed in the manner and subject to the conditions by this Act provided.

(2) A limited partnership … must consist of one or more persons called general partners, who shall be liable for all debts and obligations of the firm, and one or more persons to be called limited partners, who shall at the time of entering into such partnership contribute thereto a sum or sums as capital or property valued at a stated amount, and who shall not be liable for the debts or obligations of the firm beyond the amount so contributed.

(3) A limited partner shall not during the continuance of the partnership, either directly or indirectly, draw out or receive back any part of his contribution, and if he does so draw out or receive back any such part shall be liable for the debts and obligations of the firm up to the amount so drawn out or received back.

(4) A body corporate may be a limited partner.

5. Registration of limited partnership required

Every limited partnership must be registered as such in accordance with the provisions of this Act, . . .

6. Modifications of general law in case of limited partnerships

(1) A limited partner shall not take part in the management of the partnership business, and shall not have power to bind the firm:

Provided that a limited partner may by himself or his agent at any time inspect the books of the firm and examine into the state and prospects of the partnership business, and may advise with the partner thereon.

If a limited partner takes part in the management of the partnership business he shall be liable for all debts and obligations of the firm incurred while he so takes part in the management as though he were a general partner.

(2) A limited partnership shall not be dissolved by the death or bankruptcy of a limited partner, and the lunacy of a limited partner shall not be a ground for dissolution of the partnership by the court unless the lunatic's share cannot be otherwise ascertained and realised.

(3) In the event of the dissolution of a limited partnership its affairs shall be wound up by the general partners unless the court otherwise orders.

(4) …

(5) Subject to any agreement expressed or implied between the partners—

(a) Any difference arising as to ordinary matters connected with the partnership business may be decided by a majority of the general partners

(b) A limited partner may, with the consent of the general partners, assign his share in the partnership, and upon such an assignment the assignee shall become a limited partner with all the rights of the assignor

(c) The other partners shall not be entitled to dissolve the partnership by reason of any limited partner suffering his share to be charged for his separate debt

(d) A person be may introduced as a partner without the consent of the existing limited partners

(e) A limited partner shall not be entitled to dissolve the partnership by notice.

7. Law as to private partnerships to apply where not excluded by this Act 53 & 54 Vict. Ch. 39

Subject to the provisions of this Act, the Partnership Act 1890, and the rules of equity and of common law applicable to partnerships, except so far as they are inconsistent with the express provisions of the last-mentioned Act, shall apply to limited partnerships.

8. Duty to register

The registrar shall register a limited partnership if an application is made to the registrar in accordance with section 8A.

8A. Application for registration

(1) An application for registration must—

(a) specify the firm name, complying with section 8B, under which the limited partnership is to be registered,

(b) contain the details listed in subsection (2),

(c) be signed or otherwise authenticated by or on behalf of each partner, and

(d) be made to the registrar for the part of the United Kingdom in which the principal place of business of the limited partnership is to be situated.

(2) The required details are—

(a) the general nature of the partnership business,

(b) the name of each general partner,

(c) the name of each limited partner,

(d) the amount of the capital contribution of each limited partner (and whether the contribution is paid in cash or in another specified form),

(e) the address of the proposed principal place of business of the limited partnership, and

(f) the term (if any) for which the limited partnership is to be entered into (beginning with the date of registration).

8B. Name of limited partnership

(1) This section sets out conditions which must be satisfied by the firm name of a limited partnership as specified in the application for registration.

(2) The name must end with—

(a) the words "limited partnership" (upper or lower case, or any combination), or

(b) the abbreviation "LP" (upper or lower case, or any combination, with or without punctuation).

(3) But if the principal place of business of a limited partnership is to be in Wales, its firm name may end with—

(a) the words "partneriaeth cyfyngedig" (upper or lower case, or any combination), or

(b) the abbreviation "PC" (upper or lower case, or any combination, with or without punctuation).

8C. Certificate of registration

(1) On registering a limited partnership the registrar shall issue a certificate of registration.

(2) The certificate must be—

(a) signed by the registrar, or

(b) authenticated with the registrar's seal.

(3) The certificate must state—

(a) the firm name of the limited partnership given in the application for registration,
(b) the limited partnership's registration number,
(c) the date of registration, and
(d) that the limited partnership is registered as a limited partnership under this Act.

(4) The certificate is conclusive evidence that a limited partnership came into existence on the date of registration.

9. Registration of changes in partnerships

(1) If during the continuance of a limited partnership any change is made or occurs in—
(a) the firm name
(b) the general nature of the business
(c) the principal place of business;
(d) the partners or the name of any partner;
(e) the term or character of the partnership;
(f) the sum contributed by any limited partner;
(g) the liability of any partner by reason of his becoming a limited instead of a general partner or a general instead of a limited partner

a statement, signed by the firm, specifying the nature of the change shall within seven days be sent by post or delivered to the Registrar . . .

(2) If default is made in compliance with the requirements of this section each of the general partners shall on conviction under the Magistrates Courts Acts 1980 be liable to a fine not exceeding one pound for each day during which the default continues.

10. Advertisement in Gazette of statement of general partner becoming a limited partner and of assignment of share of limited partner

(1) Notice of any arrangement or transaction under which any person will cease to be a general partner in any firm, and will become a limited partner in that firm, or under which the share of a limited partner in a firm will be assigned to any person, shall be forthwith advertised in the Gazette, and until notice of the arrangement or transaction is so advertised, the arrangement or transaction shall, for the purposes of this Act, be deemed to be of no effect.

(2) For the purposes of this section, the expression "the Gazette" means—
In the case of a limited partnership registered in England, the London Gazette
In the case of a limited partnership registered in Scotland, the Edinburgh Gazette
In the case of a limited partnership registered in Northern Ireland, the Belfast Gazette.

13. Registrar to file statement and issue certificate of registration

On receiving any statement made in pursuance of this Act the Registrar shall cause the same to be filed, and he shall send by post to the firm from whom such statement shall have been received a certificate of the registration thereof.

14. Register and index to be kept

. . . the Registrar shall keep . . . a register and an index of all the limited partnerships registered as aforesaid, and of all the statements registered in relation to such partnerships.

15. The registrar

(1) The registrar of companies is the registrar of limited partnerships.

(2) In this Act—
(a) references to the registrar in relation to the registration of a limited partnership are to the registrar to whom the application for registration is to be made (see section 8A(1)(d));
(b) references to registration in a particular part of the United Kingdom are to registration by the registrar for that part of the United Kingdom;
(c) references to the registrar in relation to any other matter relating to a limited partnership are to the registrar for the part of the United Kingdom in which the partnership is registered.

16. Inspection of statements registered

(1) Any person may inspect the statements filed by the Registrar . . .; and any person may require a certificate of the registration of any limited partnership, or a copy of or extract from any registered statement, to be certified by the Registrar . . .

(2) A certificate of registration, or a copy of or extract from any statement registered under this Act, if duly certified to be a true copy under the hand of the Registrar . . . (whom it shall not be necessary to prove to be the Registrar . . .) shall, in all legal proceedings, civil or criminal, and in all cases whatsoever be received in evidence.

17. Power to Board of Trade to make rules

The Board of Trade may make rules ... concerning any of the following matters—

(a) ...

(b) The duties or additional duties to be performed by the Registrar for the purposes of this Act.

(c) The performance by assistant Registrars and other officers of acts by this Act required to be done by the Registrar.

(d) The forms to be used for the purposes of this Act.

(e) Generally the conduct and regulation of registration under this Act and any matters incidental thereto.

Limited Liability Partnerships Act 2000

2000 c. 12

An Act to make provision for limited liability partnerships

[20th July 2000]

Introductory

1. **Limited liability partnerships**

(1) There shall be a new form of legal entity to be known as a limited liability partnership.

(2) A limited liability partnership is a body corporate (with legal personality separate from that of its members) which is formed by being incorporated under this Act; and—

(a) in the following provisions of this Act (except in the phrase "oversea limited liability partnership"), and

(b) in any other enactment (except where provision is made to the contrary or the context otherwise requires),

references to a limited liability partnership are to such a body corporate.

(3) A limited liability partnership has unlimited capacity.

(4) The members of a limited liability partnership have such liability to contribute to its assets in the event of its being wound up as is provided for by virtue of this Act.

(5) Accordingly, except as far as otherwise provided by this Act or any other enactment, the law relating to partnerships does not apply to a limited liability partnership.

(6) The Schedule (which makes provision about the names and registered offices of limited liability partnerships) has effect.

Incorporation

2. **Incorporation document etc**

(1) For a limited liability partnership to be incorporated—

(a) two or more persons associated for carrying on a lawful business with a view to profit must have subscribed their names to an incorporation document,

(b) the incorporation document or a copy of it must have been delivered to the registrar, and

(c) there must have been so delivered a statement . . . made by either a solicitor engaged in the formation of the limited liability partnership or anyone who subscribed his name to the incorporation document, that the requirement imposed by paragraph (a) has been complied with.

(2) The incorporation document must—

(a) . . .

(b) state the name of the limited liability partnership,

(c) state whether the registered office of the limited liability partnership is to be situated in England and Wales, in Wales, in Scotland or in Northern Ireland,

(d) state the address of that registered office,

(e) give the required particulars of each of the persons who are to be members of the limited liability partnership on incorporation, and

(f) either specify which of those persons are to be designated members or state that every person who from time to time is a member of the limited liability partnership is a designated member.

(2ZA) The required particulars mentioned in subsection (2)(e) are the particulars required to be stated in the LLP's register of members and register of members' residential addresses.

(2A), (2B) . . .

(3) If a person makes a false statement under subsection (1)(c) which he—

(a) knows to be false, or

(b) does not believe to be true,

he commits an offence.

(4) A person guilty of an offence under subsection (3) is liable—

(a) on summary conviction, to imprisonment for a period not exceeding six months or a fine not exceeding the statutory maximum, or to both, or

(b) on conviction on indictment, to imprisonment for a period not exceeding two years or a fine, or to both.

3. Incorporation by registration

(1) The registrar, if satisfied that the requirements of section 2 are complied with, shall—

(a) register the documents delivered under that section, and

(b) give a certificate that the limited liability partnership is incorporated.

(1A) The certificate must state—

(a) the name and registered number of the limited liability partnership,

(b) the date of its incorporation, and

(c) whether the limited liability partnership's registered office is situated in England and Wales (or in Wales), in Scotland or in Northern Ireland.

(2) The registrar may accept the statement delivered under paragraph (c) of subsection (1) of section 2 as sufficient evidence that the requirement imposed by paragraph (a) of that subsection has been complied with.

(3) The certificate shall either be signed by the registrar or be authenticated by his official seal.

(4) The certificate is conclusive evidence that the requirements of section 2 are complied with and that the limited liability partnership is incorporated by the name specified in the incorporation document.

Membership

4. Members

(1) On the incorporation of a limited liability partnership its members are the persons who subscribed their names to the incorporation document (other than any who have died or been dissolved).

(2) Any other person may become a member of a limited liability partnership by and in accordance with an agreement with the existing members.

(3) A person may cease to be a member of a limited liability partnership (as well as by death or dissolution) in accordance with an agreement with the other members or, in the absence of agreement with the other members as to cessation of membership, by giving reasonable notice to the other members.

(4) A member of a limited liability partnership shall not be regarded for any purpose as employed by the limited liability partnership unless, if he and the other members were partners in a partnership, he would be regarded for that purpose as employed by the partnership.

4A. Minimum membership for carrying on business

(1) This section applies where a limited liability partnership carries on business without having at least two members, and does so for more than 6 months.

(2) A person who, for the whole or any part of the period that it so carries on business after those 6 months—

(a) is a member of the limited liability partnership, and

(b) knows that it is carrying on business with only one member,

is liable (jointly and severally with the limited liability partnership) for the payment of the limited liability partnership's debts contracted during the period or, as the case may be, that part of it.

5. Relationship of members etc

(1) Except as far as otherwise provided by this Act or any other enactment, the mutual rights and duties of the members of a limited liability partnership, and the mutual rights and duties of a limited liability partnership and its members, shall be governed—

(a) by agreement between the members, or between the limited liability partnership and its members, or

(b) in the absence of agreement as to any matter, by any provision made in relation to that matter by regulations under section 15(c).

(2) An agreement made before the incorporation of a limited liability partnership between the persons who subscribe their names to the incorporation document may impose obligations on the limited liability partnership (to take effect at any time after its incorporation).

6. Members as agents

(1) Every member of a limited liability partnership is the agent of the limited liability partnership.

(2) But a limited liability partnership is not bound by anything done by a member in dealing with a person if—

(a) the member in fact has no authority to act for the limited liability partnership by doing that thing, and

(b) the person knows that he has no authority or does not know or believe him to be a member of the limited liability partnership.

(3) Where a person has ceased to be a member of a limited liability partnership, the former member is to be regarded (in relation to any person dealing with the limited liability partnership) as still being a member of the limited liability partnership unless—

(a) the person has notice that the former member has ceased to be a member of the limited liability partnership, or

(b) notice that the former member has ceased to be a member of the limited liability partnership has been delivered to the registrar.

(4) Where a member of a limited liability partnership is liable to any person (other than another member of the limited liability partnership) as a result of a wrongful act or omission of his in the course of the business of the limited liability partnership or with its authority, the limited liability partnership is liable to the same extent as the member.

7. Ex-members

(1) This section applies where a member of a limited liability partnership has either ceased to be a member or—

(a) has died,

(b) has become bankrupt or had his estate sequestrated or has been wound up,

(c) has granted a trust deed for the benefit of his creditors, or

(d) has assigned the whole or any part of his share in the limited liability partnership (absolutely or by way of charge or security).

(2) In such an event the former member or—

(a) his personal representative,

(b) his trustee in bankruptcy or permanent or interim trustee (within the meaning of the Bankruptcy (Scotland) Act 1985) or liquidator,

(c) his trustee under the trust deed for the benefit of his creditors, or

(d) his assignee,

may not interfere in the management or administration of any business or affairs of the limited liability partnership.

(3) But subsection (2) does not affect any right to receive an amount from the limited liability partnership in that event.

8. Designated members

(1) If the incorporation document specifies who are to be designated members—

(a) they are designated members on incorporation, and

(b) any member may become a designated member by and in accordance with an agreement with the other members,

and a member may cease to be a designated member in accordance with an agreement with the other members.

(2) But if there would otherwise be no designated members, or only one, every member is a designated member.

(3) If the incorporation document states that every person who from time to time is a member of the limited liability partnership is a designated member, every member is a designated member.

(4) A limited liability partnership may at any time deliver to the registrar—

(a) notice that specified members are to be designated members, or

(b) notice that every person who from time to time is a member of the limited liability partnership is a designated member,

and, once it is delivered, subsection (1) (apart from paragraph (a)) and subsection (2), or subsection (3), shall have effect as if that were stated in the incorporation document.

(5) . . .

(6) A person ceases to be a designated member if he ceases to be a member.

9. Registration of membership changes

(1) A limited liability partnership must ensure that—

(a) where a person becomes or ceases to be a member or designated member, notice is delivered to the registrar within fourteen days, and

(b) where there is any change in the particulars contained in its register of members or its register of members' residential addresses, notice is delivered to the registrar within 14 days.

(2) Where all the members from time to time of a limited liability partnership are designated members, subsection (1)(a) does not require notice that a person has become or ceased to be a designated member as well as a member.

(3) A notice delivered under subsection (1) that relates to a person becoming a member or designated member must contain—

(a) a statement that the member or designated member consents to acting in that capacity, and

(b) in the case of a person becoming a member, a statement of the particulars of the new member that are required to be included in the limited liability partnership's register of members and its register of residential addresses.

(3ZA) Where—

(a) a limited liability partnership gives notice of a change of a member's service address as stated in its register of members, and

(b) the notice is not accompanied by notice of any resulting change in the particulars contained in its register of members' residential addresses,

the notice must be accompanied by a statement that no such change is required.

(3A), (3B) . . .

(4) If a limited liability partnership fails to comply with this section, the partnership and every designated member commits an offence.

(5) But it is a defence for a designated member charged with an offence under subsection (4) to prove that he took all reasonable steps for securing that this section was complied with.

(6) A person guilty of an offence under subsection (4) is liable on summary conviction to a fine not exceeding level 5 on the standard scale.

Taxation

10, 11. ...

12. Stamp duty

(1) Stamp duty shall not be chargeable on an instrument by which property is conveyed or transferred by a person to a limited liability partnership in connection with its incorporation within the period of one year beginning with the date of incorporation if the following two conditions are satisfied.

(2) The first condition is that at the relevant time the person—

(a) is a partner in a partnership comprised of all the persons who are or are to be members of the limited liability partnership (and no-one else), or

(b) holds the property conveyed or transferred as nominee or bare trustee for one or more of the partners in such a partnership.

(3) The second condition is that—

(a) the proportions of the property conveyed or transferred to which the persons mentioned in subsection (2)(a) are entitled immediately after the conveyance or transfer are the same as those to which they were entitled at the relevant time, or

(b) none of the differences in those proportions has arisen as part of a scheme or arrangement of which the main purpose, or one of the main purposes, is avoidance of liability to any duty or tax.

(4) For the purposes of subsection (2) a person holds property as bare trustee for a partner if the partner has the exclusive right (subject only to satisfying any outstanding charge, lien or other right of the trustee to resort to the property for payment of duty, taxes, costs or other outgoings) to direct how the property shall be dealt with.

(5) In this section "the relevant time" means—

(a) if the person who conveyed or transferred the property to the limited liability partnership acquired the property after its incorporation, immediately after he acquired the property, and

(b) in any other case, immediately before its incorporation.

(6) An instrument in respect of which stamp duty is not chargeable by virtue of subsection (1) shall not be taken to be duly stamped unless—

(a) it has, in accordance with section 12 of the Stamp Act 1891, been stamped with a particular stamp denoting that it is not chargeable with any duty or that it is duly stamped, or

(b) it is stamped with the duty to which it would be liable apart from that subsection.

13. ...

Regulations

14. Insolvency and winding up

(1) Regulations shall make provision about the insolvency and winding up of limited liability partnerships by applying or incorporating, with such modifications—

(a) in relation to a limited liability partnership registered in Great Britain, Parts 1 to 4, 6 and 7 of the Insolvency Act 1986;

(b) in relation to a limited liability partnership registered in Northern Ireland, Parts 2 to 5 and 7 of the Insolvency (Northern Ireland) Order 1989, and so much of Part 1 of that Order as applies for the purposes of those Parts.

(2) Regulations may make other provision about the insolvency and winding up of limited liability partnerships, and provision about the insolvency and winding up of oversea limited liability partnerships, by—

(a) applying or incorporating, with such modifications as appear appropriate, any law relating to the insolvency or winding up of companies or other corporations which would not otherwise have effect in relation to them, or

(b) providing for any law relating to the insolvency or winding up of companies or other corporations which would otherwise have effect in relation to them not to apply to them or to apply to them with such modifications as appear appropriate.

(3) In this Act "oversea limited liability partnership" means a body incorporated or otherwise established outside the United Kingdom and having such connection with the United Kingdom, and such other features, as regulations may prescribe.

15. Application of company law etc

Regulations may make provision about limited liability partnerships and oversea limited liability partnerships (not being provision about insolvency or winding up) by—

(a) applying or incorporating, with such modifications as appear appropriate, any law relating to companies or other corporations which would not otherwise have effect in relation to them,

(b) providing for any law relating to companies or other corporations which would otherwise have effect in relation to them not to apply to them or to apply to them with such modifications as appear appropriate, or

(c) applying or incorporating, with such modifications as appear appropriate, any law relating to partnerships.

16. Consequential amendments

(1) Regulations may make in any enactment such amendments or repeals as appear appropriate in consequence of this Act or regulations made under it.

(2) The regulations may, in particular, make amendments and repeals affecting companies or other corporations or partnerships

17. General

(1) In this Act "regulations" means regulations made by the Secretary of State by statutory instrument.

(2) Regulations under this Act may in particular—

(a) make provisions for dealing with non-compliance with any of the regulations (including the creation of criminal offences),

(b) impose fees (which shall be paid into the Consolidated Fund), and

(c) provide for the exercise of functions by persons prescribed by the regulations.

(3) Regulations under this Act may—

(a) contain any appropriate consequential, incidental, supplementary or transitional provisions or savings, and

(b) make different provision for different purposes.

(4) No regulations to which this subsection applies shall be made unless a draft of the statutory instrument containing the regulations (whether or not together with other provisions) has been laid before, and approved by a resolution of, each House of Parliament.

(5) Subsection (4) applies to—

(a) regulations under section 14(2) not consisting entirely of the application or incorporation (with or without modifications) of provisions contained in or made under the Insolvency Act 1986 or the Insolvency (Northern Ireland) Order 1989,

(b) regulations under section 15 not consisting entirely of the application or incorporation (with or without modifications) of provisions contained in or made under the following provisions of the Companies Act 2006 (c 46)—

Part 4 (a company's capacity and related matters);
Part 5 (a company's name);
Part 6 (a company's registered office);
Chapters 1 and 8 of Part 10 (register of directors);
Part 15 (accounts and reports);
Part 16 (audit);
Part 19 (debentures);
Part 21 (certification and transfer of securities);
Part 24 (a company's annual return);
Part 25 (company charges);
Part 26 (arrangements and reconstructions);
Part 29 (fraudulent trading);
Part 30 (protection of members against unfair prejudice);
Part 31 (dissolution and restoration to the register);
Part 35 (the registrar of companies);
Part 36 (offences under the Companies Acts);
Part 37 (supplementary provisions);
Part 38 (interpretation),

(c) regulations under section 14 or 15 making provision about oversea limited liability partnerships, and

(d) regulations under section 16.

(6) A statutory instrument containing regulations under this Act shall (unless a draft of it has been approved by a resolution of each House of Parliament) be subject to annulment in pursuance of a resolution of either House of Parliament.

Supplementary

18. Interpretation

In this Act—

. . .

"business" includes every trade, profession and occupation,

"designated member" shall be construed in accordance with section 8,

"enactment" includes subordinate legislation (within the meaning of the Interpretation Act 1978),

"incorporation document" shall be construed in accordance with section 2,

"limited liability partnership" has the meaning given by section 1(2),

"member" shall be construed in accordance with section 4,

"modifications" includes additions and omissions,

"name", in relation to a member of a limited liability partnership, means—

(a) if an individual, his forename and surname (or, in the case of a peer or other person usually known by a title, his title instead of or in addition to either or both his forename and surname), and

(b) if a corporation or Scottish firm, its corporate or firm name,

"oversea limited liability partnership" has the meaning given by section 14(3),

"the registrar" means—

(a) if the registered office of the limited liability partnership is, or is to be, in England and Wales (or Wales), the registrar of companies for England and Wales,

(b) if the registered office of the limited liability partnership is, or is to be, in Scotland, the registrar of companies for Scotland, and

(c) if the registered office of the limited liability partnership is, or is to be, in Northern Ireland, the registrar of companies for Northern Ireland;

"regulations" has the meaning given by section 17(1).

19. Commencement, extent and short title

(1) The preceding provisions of this Act shall come into force on such day as the Secretary of State may by order made by statutory instrument appoint; and different days may be appointed for different purposes.

(2) The Secretary of State may by order made by statutory instrument make any transitional provisions and savings which appear appropriate in connection with the coming into force of any provision of this Act.

(3) For the purposes of the Scotland Act 1998 this Act shall be taken to be a pre-commencement enactment within the meaning of that Act.

(4) This Act extends to the whole of the United Kingdom.

(5) This Act may be cited as the Limited Liability Partnerships Act 2000.

SCHEDULE

NAMES AND REGISTERED OFFICES

Section 1

PART I
NAMES

1. …

Name to indicate status

2.— (1) The name of a limited liability partnership must end with—
(a) the expression "limited liability partnership", or
(b) the abbreviation "llp" or "LLP".
(2) But if the incorporation document for a limited liability partnership states that the registered office is to be situated in Wales, its name must end with—
(a) one of the expressions "limited liability partnership" and "partneriaeth atebolrwydd cyfyngedig", or
(b) one of the abbreviations "llp", "LLP", "pac" and "PAC".

Registration of names

3. …

Change of name

4.— (1) A limited liability partnership may change its name at any time.
(2) The name of a limited liability partnership may also be changed—
(a) on the determination of a new name by a company names adjudicator under section 73 of the Companies Act 2006 (C 46) as applied to limited liability partnerships (powers of adjudicator on upholding objection to name);
(b) on the determination of a new name by the court under section 74 of the Companies Act 2006 as so applied (appeal against decision of company names adjudicator);
(c) under section 1033 as so applied (name on restoration to the register).

Notification of change of name

5.— (1) Where a limited liability partnership changes its name it shall deliver notice of the change to the registrar.
(2) …
(3) Where the registrar receives notice of a change of name he shall (unless the new name is one by which a limited liability partnership may not be registered)—
(a) enter the new name on the register in place of the former name, and
(b) issue a certificate of the change of name.
(4) The change of name has effect from the date on which the certificate is issued.

Effect of change of name

6. A change of name by a limited liability partnership does not—
(a) affect any of its rights or duties,
(b) render defective any legal proceedings by or against it,
and any legal proceedings that might have been commenced or continued against it by its former name may be commenced or continued against it by its new name.

Improper use of "limited liability partnership" etc

7.— (1) If any person carries on a business under a name or title which includes as the last words—

(a) the expression “limited liability partnership” or “partneriaeth atebolrwydd cyfyngedig”, or

(b) any contraction or imitation of either of those expressions,

that person, unless a limited liability partnership or oversea limited liability partnership, commits an offence.

(2) A person guilty of an offence under sub-paragraph (1) is liable on summary conviction to a fine not exceeding level 3 on the standard scale.

8. . . .

PART II

. . .

Limited Liability Partnerships Regulations 2001

S.I. 2001/1090

PART I

CITATION, COMMENCEMENT AND INTERPRETATION

1. Citation and commencement

These Regulations may be cited as the Limited Liability Partnerships Regulations 2001 and shall come into force on 6th April 2001.

2. Interpretation

In these Regulations—

"the 1985 Act" means the Companies Act 1985;

"the 1986 Act" means the Insolvency Act 1986;

"the 2000 Act" means the Financial Services and Markets Act 2000;

"devolved", in relation to the provisions of the 1986 Act, means the provisions of the 1986 Act which are listed in Schedule 4 and, in their application to Scotland, concern wholly or partly, matters which are set out in Section C 2 of Schedule 5 to the Scotland Act 1998 as being exceptions to the reservations made in that Act in the field of insolvency;

"limited liability partnership agreement", in relation to a limited liability partnership, means any agreement express or implied between the members of the limited liability partnership or between the limited liability partnership and the members of the limited liability partnership which determines the mutual rights and duties of the members, and their rights and duties in relation to the limited liability partnership;

"the principal Act" means the Limited Liability Partnerships Act 2000; and

"shadow member", in relation to limited liability partnerships, means a person in accordance with whose directions or instructions the members of the limited liability partnership are accustomed to act (but so that a person is not deemed a shadow member by reason only that the members of the limited partnership act on advice given by him in a professional capacity).

2A. Application of provisions

(1) The provisions of these Regulations applying—

(a) the Company Directors Disqualification Act 1986, or

(b) provisions of the Insolvency Act 1986,

have effect only in relation to limited liability partnerships registered in Great Britain.

(2) The other provisions of these Regulations have effect in relation to limited liability partnerships registered in any part of the United Kingdom.

. . .

PART III

COMPANIES ACT 1985 AND COMPANY DIRECTORS DISQUALIFICATION ACT 1986

4. Application of certain provisions of the 1985 Act and of the provisions of the Company Directors Disqualification Act 1986 to limited liability partnerships

(1) The provisions of the 1985 Act specified in the first column of Part I of Schedule 2 to these Regulations shall apply to limited liability partnerships, except where the context otherwise requires, with the following modifications—

(a) references to a company shall include references to a limited liability partnership;

(b) . . .

(c) references to the Insolvency Act 1986 shall include references to that Act as it applies to limited liability partnerships by virtue of Part IV of these Regulations;

(d) references in a provision of the 1985 Act to—

(i) other provisions of that Act, or

(ii) provisions of the Companies Act 2006,

shall include references to those provisions as they apply to limited liability partnerships;

(e), (f) . . .

(g) references to a director of a company or to an officer of a company shall include references to a member of a limited liability partnership;

(h) the modifications, if any, specified in the second column of Part I of Schedule 2 opposite the provision specified in the first column; and

(i) such further modifications as the context requires for the purpose of giving effect to that legislation as applied by these Regulations.

(2) The provisions of the Company Director Disqualification Act 1986 shall apply to limited liability partnerships, except where the context otherwise requires, with the following modifications—

(a) references to a company shall include references to a limited liability partnership;

(b) references to the Companies Acts shall include references to the principal Act and regulations made thereunder;

(c) references to the Insolvency Act 1986 shall include references to that Act as it applies to limited liability partnerships by virtue of Part IV of these Regulations;

(d) references in a provision of the 1985 Act to other provisions of that Act shall include references to those other provisions as they apply to limited liability partnerships by virtue of these Regulations;

(e) . . .

(f) references to a shadow director shall include references to a shadow member;

(g) references to a director of a company or to an officer of a company shall include references to a member of a limited liability partnership;

(h) the modifications, if any, specified in the second column of Part II of Schedule 2 opposite the provision specified in the first column; and

(i) such further modifications as the context requires for the purpose of giving effect to that legislation as applied by these Regulations.

PART IV

WINDING UP AND INSOLVENCY

5. Application of the 1986 Act to limited liability partnerships

(1) Subject to paragraphs (2) and (3), the following provisions of the 1986 Act, shall apply to limited liability partnerships—

(a) Parts I, II, III, IV, VI and VII of the First Group of Parts (company insolvency; companies winding up),

(b) the Third Group of Parts (miscellaneous matters bearing on both company and individual insolvency; general interpretation; final provisions).

(2) The provisions of the 1986 Act referred to in paragraph (1) shall apply to limited liability partnerships, except where the context otherwise requires, with the following modifications—

(a) references to a company shall include references to a limited liability partnership;

(b) references to a director or to an officer of a company shall include references to a member of a limited liability partnership;

(c) references to a shadow director shall include references to a shadow member;

(d) references to the Companies Acts, the Company Directors Disqualification Act 1986, the Companies Act 1989 or to any provisions of those Acts or to any provisions of the 1986 Act shall include references to those Acts or provisions as they apply to limited liability partnerships by virtue of the principal Act;

(e) references . . . to the articles of association of a company shall include references to the limited liability partnership agreement of a limited liability partnership;

(f) the modifications set out in Schedule 3 to these Regulations; and

(g) such further modifications as the context requires for the purpose of giving effect to that legislation as applied by these Regulations.

(3) In the application of this regulation to Scotland, the provisions of the 1986 Act referred to in paragraph (1) shall not include the provisions listed in Schedule 4 to the extent specified in that Schedule.

PART V

FINANCIAL SERVICES AND MARKETS

6. Application of provisions contained in Parts XV and XXIV of the 2000 Act to limited liability partnerships

(1) Subject to paragraph (2), sections 215(3),(4) and (6), 356, 359(1) to (4), 361 to 365, 367, 370 and 371 of the 2000 Act shall apply to limited liability partnerships.

(2) The provisions of the 2000 Act referred to in paragraph (1) shall apply to limited liability partnerships, except where the context otherwise requires, with the following modifications—

(a) references to a company shall include references to a limited liability partnership;

(b) references to body shall include references to a limited liability partnership; and

(c) references to the 1985 Act, the 1986 Act or to any of the provisions of those Acts shall include references to those Acts or provisions as they apply to limited liability partnerships by virtue of the principal Act.

PART VI

DEFAULT PROVISION

7. Default provision for limited liability partnerships

The mutual rights and duties of the members and the mutual rights and duties of the limited liability partnership and the members shall be determined, subject to the provisions of the general law and to the terms of any limited liability partnership agreement, by the following rules:

(1) All the members of a limited liability partnership are entitled to share equally in the capital and profits of the limited liability partnership.

(2) The limited liability partnership must indemnify each member in respect of payments made and personal liabilities incurred by him—

(a) in the ordinary and proper conduct of the business of the limited liability partnership; or

(b) in or about anything necessarily done for the preservation of the business or property of the limited liability partnership.

(3) Every member may take part in the management of the limited liability partnership.

(4) No member shall be entitled to remuneration for acting in the business or management of the limited liability partnership.

(5) No person may be introduced as a member or voluntarily assign an interest in a limited liability partnership without the consent of all existing members.

(6) Any difference arising as to ordinary matters connected with the business of the limited liability partnership may be decided by a majority of the members, but no change may be made in the nature of the business of the limited liability partnership without the consent of all the members.

(7) The books and records of the limited liability partnership are to be made available for inspection at the registered office of the limited liability partnership or at such other place as the members think fit and every member of the limited liability partnership may when he thinks fit have access to and inspect and copy any of them.

(8) Each member shall render true accounts and full information of all things affecting the limited liability partnership to any member or his legal representatives.

(9) If a member, without the consent of the limited liability partnership, carries on any business of the same nature as and competing with the limited liability partnership, he must account for and pay over to the limited liability partnership all profits made by him in that business.

(10) Every member must account to the limited liability partnership for any benefit derived by him without the consent of the limited liability partnership from any transaction concerning the limited liability partnership, or from any use by him of the property of the limited liability partnership, name or business connection.

8. Expulsion

No majority of the members can expel any member unless a power to do so has been conferred by express agreement between the members.

PART VII

MISCELLANEOUS

9. General and consequential amendments

(1) Subject to paragraph (2), the enactments mentioned in Schedule 5 shall have effect subject to the amendments specified in that Schedule.

(2) In the application of this regulation to Scotland—

(a) paragraph 15 of Schedule 5 which amends section 110 of the 1986 Act shall not extend to Scotland; and

(b) paragraph 22 of Schedule 5 which applies to limited liability partnerships the culpable officer provisions in existing primary legislation shall not extend to Scotland insofar as it relates to matters which have not been reserved by Schedule 5 to the Scotland Act 1998.

10. Application of subordinate legislation

(1) The subordinate legislation specified in Schedule 6 shall apply as from time to time in force to limited liability partnerships and—

(a) in the case of the subordinate legislation listed in Part I of that Schedule with such modifications as the context requires for the purpose of giving effect to the provisions of the Companies Act 1985 which are applied by these Regulations;

(b) in the case of the subordinate legislation listed in Part II of that Schedule with such modifications as the context requires for the purpose of giving effect to the provisions of the Insolvency Act 1986 which are applied by these Regulations; and

(c) in the case of the subordinate legislation listed in Part III of that Schedule with such modifications as the context requires for the purpose of giving effect to the provisions of . . . the Company Directors Disqualification Act 1986 which are applied by these Regulations.

(2) In the case of any conflict between any provision of the subordinate legislation applied by paragraph (1) and any provision of these Regulations, the latter shall prevail.

SCHEDULES

. . .

SCHEDULE 2

Regulation 4

PART I

MODIFICATIONS TO PROVISIONS OF THE 1985 ACT APPLIED TO LIMITED LIABILITY PARTNERSHIPS

Provisions	Modifications
Formalities of Carrying on Business	
. . .	
Investigation of companies and their affairs: Requisition of documents	
431 (investigation of a company on its own application or that of its members)	For subsection (2) substitute the following: "(2)—The appointment may be made on the application of the limited liability partnership or on the application of not less than one-fifth in number of those who appear from notifications made to the registrar of companies to be currently members of the limited liability partnership."
432 (other company investigations) subsection (4)	For the words "but to whom shares in the company have been transferred or transmitted by operation of law"substitute "but to whom a member's share in the limited liability partnership has been transferred or transmitted by operation of law."
433 (inspectors' powers during investigation)	
434 (production of documents and evidence to inspectors)	
436 (obstruction of inspectors treated as contempt of court)	
437 (inspectors' reports)	
. . .	
439 (expenses of investigating a company's affairs) subsection (5)	Omit paragraph (b) together with the word "or"at the end of paragraph (a).
441 (inspectors' report to be evidence)	
446A (general powers to give directions)	
446B (direction to terminate investigation)	
446C (resignation and revocation of appointment)	
446D (appointment of replacement inspectors)	
446E (obtaining information from former inspectors etc)	
447 (Secretary of State's power to require production of documents)	
447A (information provided: evidence)	
448 (entry and search of premises)	
448A (protection in relation to certain disclosures: information provided to Secretary of State)	

Provisions	Modifications
449 (provision for security of information obtained)	
450 (punishment for destroying, mutilating etc company documents)	Omit subsection (1A).
451 (punishment for furnishing false information)	
451A (disclosure of information by Secretary of State or inspector)	In subsection (1), for the words "sections 434 to 446E"substitute "sections 434 to 441 and 446E". Omit subsection (5).
452 (privileged information)	In subsection (1), for the words "sections 431 to 446E"substitute "sections 431 to 441 and 446E". In subsection (1A), for the words "sections 434, 443 or 446"substitute "section 434".
453A (power to enter and remain on premises)	In subsection (7), for the words "section 431, 432 or 442" substitute "section 431 or 432".
453B (power to enter and remain on premises: proceural)	
453C (failure to comply with certain requirements)	
. . .	
Floating charges and Receivers (Scotland)	
464 (ranking of floating charges)	In subsection (1), for the words "section 462"substitute "the law of Scotland".
466 (alteration of floating charges)	Omit subsections (1), (2), (3) and (6).
486 (interpretation for Part XVIII generally)	For the current definition of "company"substitute""company"means a limited liability partnership;" Omit the definition of "Register of Sasines".
487 (extent of Part XVIII)	
. . .	
Schedule 15C (security of information obtained: specified persons)	
Schedule 15D (security of information obtained: specified disclosures)	
. . .	

PART II
MODIFICATIONS TO THECOMPANY DIRECTORS DISQUALIFICATION ACT 1986

Part II of Schedule I	After paragraph 8 insert— "8A The extent of the member's and shadow members' responsibility for events leading to a member or shadow member, whether himself or some other member or shadow member, being declared by the court to be liable to make a contribution to the assets of the limited liability partnership under section 214A of the Insolvency Act 1986."

SCHEDULE 3
MODIFICATIONS TO THE 1986 ACT

Regulation 5

Provisions	**Modifications**
Section 1 (those who may propose an arrangement)	
subsection (1)	For "The directors of a company" substitute "A limited liability partnership" and delete "to the company and".
subsection (3)	At the end add "but where a proposal is so made it must also be made to the limited liability partnership".
Section 1A (moratorium)	
subsection (1)	For "the directors of an eligible company intend" substitute "an eligible limited liability partnership intends". For "they" substitute "it".

The following modifications to sections 2 to 7 apply where a proposal under section 1 has been made by the limited liability partnership.

Provisions	Modifications
Section 2 (procedure where the nominee is not the liquidator or administrator)	
subsection (1)	For "the directors do" substitute "the limited liability partnership does".
subsection (2)	In paragraph (aa) for "meetings of the company and of it creditors" substitute "a meeting of the creditors of the limited liability partnership"; In paragraph (b) for the first "meetings" substitute "a meeting" and for the second "meetings" substitute "meeting".
subsection (3)	For "the person intending to make the proposal" substitute "the designated members of the limited liability partnership".
subsection (4)	In paragraph (a) for "the person intending to make the proposal" substitute "the designated members of the limited liability partnership". In paragraph (b) for "that person" substitute "those designated members".
Section 3 (summoning of meetings)	
subsection (1)	For "such meetings as are mentioned in section 2(2)" substitute "a meeting of creditors" and for "those meetings" substitute "that meeting".
subsection (2)	Delete subsection (2).
Section 4 (decisions of meetings)	
subsection (1)	For "meetings" substitute "meeting".
subsection (5)	For "each of the meetings" substitute "the meeting".
new subsection (5A)	Insert a new subsection (5A) as follows—

Provisions	Modifications
	"(5A) If modifications to the proposal are proposed at the meeting the chairman of the meeting shall, before the conclusion of the meeting, ascertain from the limited liability partnership whether or not it accepts the proposed modifications; and if at that conclusion the limited liability partnership has failed to respond to a proposed modification it shall be presumed not to have agreed to it."
subsection (6)	For "either" substitute "the"; after "the result of the meeting", in the first place where it occurs, insert "(including, where modifications to the proposal were proposed at the meeting, the response to those proposed modifications made by the limited liability partnership)"; and at the end add "and to the limited liability partnership".
Section 4A (approval of arrangement)	
subsection (2)	Omit "—(a)". For "both meetings" substitute "the meeting". Omit the words from ", or" to "that section".
subsection (3)	Omit.
subsection (4)	Omit.
subsection (5)	Omit.
subsection (6)	Omit.
Section 5 (effect of approval)	
. . .	. . .
subsection (4)	For "each of the reports" substitute "the report".
Section 6 (challenge of decisions)	
subsection (1)	For . . . "either of the meetings" substitute "the meeting".
subsection (2)	For "either of the meetings" substitute "the meeting" and after paragraph (aa) add a new paragraph (ab) as follows— "(ab) any member of the limited liability partnership; and". Omit the word "and" at the end of paragraph (b) and omit paragraph (c).
subsection (3)	For "each of the reports" substitute "the report".
subsection (4)	For subsection (4) substitute the following— "(4) Where on such an application the court is satisfied as to either of the grounds mentioned in subsection (1), it may do one or both of the following, namely— (a) revoke or suspend any decision approving the voluntary arrangement which has effect under section 4A; (b) give a direction to any person for the summoning of a further meeting to consider any revised proposal the limited liability partnership may make or, in a case falling within subsection (1)(b), a further meeting to consider the original proposal.".

Provisions	**Modifications**
subsection (5)	For . . . "meetings" substitute "a meeting" . . . and for "person who made the original proposal" substitute "limited liability partnership".
Section 6A (false representations, etc)	
subsection (1)	Omit "members or".
Section 7 (implementation of proposal)	. . .
subsection (2)	In paragraph (a) omit "one or both of" and for "meetings" substitute "meeting".

The following modifications to sections 2 and 3 apply where a proposal under section 1 has been made, the limited liability partnership is in administration, by the administrator or, where the limited liability partnership is being wound up, by the liquidator.

Section 2 (procedure where the nominee is not the liquidator or administrator)	
subsection (2)	In paragraph (a) for "meetings of the company" substitute "meetings of the members of the limited liability partnership".
Section 3 (summoning of meetings)	
subsection (2)	For "meetings of the company" substitute "a meeting of the members of the limited liability partnership".
. . .	. . .
Section 73 (alternative modes of winding up)	
subsection (1)	Delete ", within the meaning given to that expression by section 735 of the Companies Act,".
Section 74 (liability as contributories of present and past members)	For section 74 there shall be substituted the following— "74. When a limited liability partnership is wound up every present and past member of the limited liability partnership who has agreed with the other members or with the limited liability partnership that he will, in circumstances which have arisen, be liable to contribute to the assets of the limited liability partnership in the event that the limited liability partnership goes into liquidation is liable, to the extent that he has so agreed, to contribute to its assets to any amount sufficient for payment of its debts and liabilities, and the expenses of the winding up, and for the adjustment of the rights of the contributories among themselves. However, a past member shall only be liable if the obligation arising from such agreement survived his ceasing to be a member of the limited liability partnership."
Section 75 to 78	Delete sections 75 to 78.
Section 79 (meaning of "contributory")	
subsection (1)	In subsection (1) for "every person" substitute "(a) every present member of the limited liability partnership and (b) every past member of the limited liability partnership".
subsection (2)	After "section 214 (wrongful trading)" insert "or 214A (adjustment of withdrawals)".

Provisions	Modifications
subsection (3)	Delete subsection (3).
Section 83 (companies registered under Companies Act, Part XXII, Chapter II)	Delete section 83.
Section 84 (circumstances in which company may be wound up voluntarily)	
subsection (1)	For subsection (1) substitute the following— "(1) A limited liability partnership may be wound up voluntarily when it determines that it is to be wound up voluntarily."
subsection (2)	Omit subsection (2).
subsection (2A)	For "company passes a resolution for voluntary winding up" substitute "limited liability partnership determines that it is to be wound up voluntarily" and for "resolution" where it appears for the second time substitute "determination".
subsection (2B)	For "resolution for voluntary winding up may be passed only" substitute "determination to wind up voluntarily may only be made" and in sub-paragraph (b), for "passing of the resolution" substitute "making of the determination".
subsection (3)	For subsection (3) substitute the following— "(3) Within 15 days after a limited liability partnership has determined that it be wound up there shall be forwarded to the registrar of companies either a printed copy or else a copy in some other form approved by the registrar of the determination."
subsection (5)	After subsection (4) insert a new subsection (5)— "(5) If a limited liability partnership fails to comply with this regulation the limited liability partnership and every designated member of it who is in default is liable on summary conviction to a fine not exceeding level 3 on the standard scale."
Section 85 (notice of resolution to wind up)	
subsection (1)	For subsection (1) substitute the following— "(1) When a limited liability partnership has determined that it shall be wound up voluntarily, it shall within 14 days after the making of the determination give notice of the determination by advertisement in the Gazette."
Section 86 (commencement of winding up)	Substitute the following new section— "86. A voluntary winding up is deemed to commence at the time when the limited liability partnership determines that it be wound up voluntarily.".
Section 87 (effect on business and status of company)	
subsection (2)	In subsection (2), for "articles" substitute "limited liability partnership agreement".
Section 88 (avoidance of share transfers, etc after winding-up resolution)	For "shares" substitute "the interest of any member in the property of the limited liability partnership".

Provisions	Modifications
Section 89 (statutory declaration of solvency)	For "director(s)" wherever it appears in section 89 substitute "designated member(s)";
subsection (2)	For paragraph (a) substitute the following— "(a) it is made within the 5 weeks immediately preceding the date when the limited liability partnership determined that it be wound up voluntarily or on that date but before the making of the determination, and".
subsection (3)	For "the resolution for winding up is passed" substitute "the limited liability partnership determined that it be wound up voluntarily".
subsection (5)	For "in pursuance of a resolution passed" substitute "voluntarily".
Section 90 (distinction between "members" and "creditors" voluntary winding up)	For "directors'" substitute "designated members'".
Section 91 (appointment of liquidator)	
subsection (1)	Delete "in general meeting".
subsection (2)	For the existing wording substitute "(2) On the appointment of a liquidator the powers of the members of the limited liability partnership shall cease except to the extent that a meeting of the members of the limited liability partnership summoned for the purpose or the liquidator sanctions their continuance." After subsection (2) insert— "(3) Subsections (3) and (4) of section 92 shall apply for the purposes of this section as they apply for the purposes of that section."
Section 92 (power to fill vacancy in office of liquidator)	
subsection (1)	For "the company in general meeting" substitute "a meeting of the members of the limited liability partnership summoned for the purpose".
subsection (2)	For "a general meeting" substitute "a meeting of the members of the limited liability partnership".
subsection (3)	In subsection (3), for "articles" substitute "limited liability partnership agreement".
new subsection (4)	Add a new subsection (4) as follows— "(4) The quorum required for a meeting of the members of the limited liability partnership shall be any quorum required by the limited liability partnership agreement for meetings of the members of the limited liability partnership and if no requirement for a quorum has been agreed upon the quorum shall be 2 members."
Section 93 (general company meeting at each year's end)	
subsection (1)	For "a general meeting of the company" substitute "a meeting of the members of the limited liability partnership".
new subsection (4)	Add a new subsection (4) as follows—

Provisions	Modifications
	"(4) subsections (3) and (4) of section 92 shall apply for the purposes of this section as they apply for the purposes of that section."
Section 94 (final meeting prior to dissolution)	
subsection (1)	For "a general meeting of the company" substitute "a meeting of the members of the limited liability partnership".
new subsection (5A)	Add a new subsection (5A) as follows— "(5A) Subsections (3) and (4) of section 92 shall apply for the purposes of this section as they apply for the purposes of that section."
subsection (6)	For "a general meeting of the company" substitute "a meeting of the members of the limited liability partnership".
Section 95 (effect of company's insolvency)	
subsection (1)	For "directors'" substitute "designated members'".
subsection (7)	For subsection (7) substitute the following— "(7) In this section "the relevant period" means the period of 6 months immediately preceding the date on which the limited liability partnership determined that it be wound up voluntarily."
Section 96 (conversion to creditors' voluntary winding up)	
paragraph (a)	For "directors'" substitute "designated members'".
paragraph (b)	Substitute a new paragraph (b) as follows— "(b) the creditors' meeting was the meeting mentioned in section 98 in the next Chapter;".
Section 98 (meeting of creditors)	
subsection (1)	For paragraph (a) substitute the following— "(a) cause a meeting of its creditors to be summoned for a day not later than the 14th day after the day on which the limited liability partnership determines that it be wound up voluntarily;".
subsection (5)	For "were sent the notices summoning the company meeting at which it was resolved that the company be wound up voluntarily" substitute "the limited liability partnership determined that it be wound up voluntarily".
Section 99 (directors to lay statement of affairs before creditors)	
subsection (1)	For "the directors of the company" substitute "the designated members" and for "the director so appointed" substitute "the designated member so appointed".
subsection (2)	For "directors" substitute "designated members".
subsection (3)	For "directors" substitute "designated members" and for "director" substitute "designated member".
Section 100 (appointment of liquidator)	

Provisions	Modifications
subsection (1)	For "The creditors and the company at their respective meetings mentioned in section 98" substitute "The creditors at their meeting mentioned in section 98 and the limited liability partnership".
subsection (3)	Delete "director,".
Section 101 (appointment of liquidation committee)	
subsection (2)	For subsection (2) substitute the following— "(2) If such a committee is appointed, the limited liability partnership may, when it determines that it be wound up voluntarily or at any time thereafter, appoint such number of persons as they think fit to act as members of the committee, not exceeding 5."
Section 105 (meetings of company and creditors at each year's end)	
subsection (1)	For "a general meeting of the company" substitute "a meeting of the members of the limited liability partnership".
new subsection (5)	Add a new subsection (5) as follows— "(5) Subsections (3) and (4) of section 92 shall apply for the purposes of this section as they apply for the purposes of that section."
Section 106 (final meeting prior to dissolution)	
subsection (1)	For "a general meeting of the company" substitute "a meeting of the members of the limited liability partnership".
new subsection (5A)	After subsection (5) insert a new subsection (5A) as follows— "5A) Subsections (3) and (4) of section 92 shall apply for the purposes of this section as they apply for the purposes of that section."
subsection (6)	For "a general meeting of the company" substitute "a meeting of the members of the limited liability partnership".
Section 110 (acceptance of shares, etc, as consideration for sale of company property)	For the existing section substitute the following: "(1) This section applies, in the case of a limited liability partnership proposed to be, or being, wound up voluntarily, where the whole or part of the limited liability partnership's business or property is proposed to be transferred or sold to another company whether or not it is a company within the meaning of the Companies Act ("the transferee company") or to a limited liability partnership ("the transferee limited liability partnership").

Provisions	Modifications
	(2) With the requisite sanction, the liquidator of the limited liability partnership being, or proposed to be, wound up ("the transferor limited liability partnership") may receive, in compensation or part compensation for the transfer or sale, shares, policies or other like interests in the transferee company or the transferee limited liability partnership for distribution among the members of the transferor limited liability partnership. (3) The sanction required under subsection (2) is— (a) in the case of a members' voluntary winding up, that of a determination of the limited liability partnership at a meeting of the members of the limited liability partnership conferring either a general authority on the liquidator or an authority in respect of any particular arrangement, (subsections (3) and (4) of section 92 to apply for this purpose as they apply for the purposes of that section), and (b) in the case of a creditor's voluntary winding up, that of either court or the liquidation committee. (4) Alternatively to subsection (2), the liquidator may (with the sanction) enter into any other arrangement whereby the members of the transferor limited liability partnership may, in lieu of receiving cash, shares, policies or other like interests (or in addition thereto), participate in the profits, or receive any other benefit from the transferee company or the transferee limited liability partnership. (5) A sale or arrangement in pursuance of this section is binding on members of the transferor limited liability partnership. (6) A determination by the limited liability partnership is not invalid for the purposes of this section by reason that it is made before or concurrently with a determination by the limited liability partnership that it be wound up voluntarily or for appointing liquidators; but, if an order is made within a year for winding up the limited liability partnership by the court, the determination by the limited liability partnership is not valid unless sanctioned by the court."
Section 111 (dissent from arrangement under section 110) subsections (1)–(3)	For subsections (1)–(3) substitute the following— "(1) This section applies in the case of a voluntary winding up where, for the purposes of section 110(2) or (4), a determination of the limited liability partnership has provided the sanction requisite for the liquidator under that section.

Provisions	Modifications
	(2) If a member of the transferor limited liability partnership who did not vote in favour of providing the sanction required for the liquidator under section 110 expresses his dissent from it in writing addressed to the liquidator and left at the registered office of the limited liability partnership within 7 days after the date on which that sanction was given, he may require the liquidator either to abstain from carrying the arrangement so sanctioned into effect or to purchase his interest at a price to be determined by agreement or arbitration under this section. (3) If the liquidator elects to purchase the member's interest, the purchase money must be paid before the limited liability partnership is dissolved and be raised by the liquidator in such manner as may be determined by the limited liability partnership."
subsection (4)	Omit subsection (4).
Section 117 (high court and county court jurisdiction)	
subsection (2)	Delete "Where the amount of a company's share capital paid up or credited as paid up does not exceed £120,000, then (subject to this section)".
subsection (3)	Delete subsection (3).
Section 120 (court of session and sheriff court jurisdiction)	
subsection (3)	Delete "Where the amount of a company's share capital paid up or credited as paid up does not exceed £120,000,".
subsection (5)	Delete subsection (5).
Section 122 (circumstances in which company may be wound up by the court)	
subsection (1)	For subsection (1) substitute the following— "(1) A limited liability partnership may be wound up by the court if— (a) the limited liability partnership has determined that the limited liability partnership be wound up by the court, (b) the limited liability partnership does not commence its business within a year from its incorporation or suspends its business for a whole year, (c) the number of members is reduced below two, (d) the limited liability partnership is unable to pay its debts, . . . (da) at the time at which a moratorium for the limited liability partnership under section 1A comes to an end, no voluntary arrangement approved under Part I has effect in relation to the limited liability partnership,

Provisions	Modifications
	(e) the court is of the opinion that it is just and equitable that the limited liability partnership should be wound up."
Section 124 (application for winding up)	
subsections (2), (3)and (4)(a)	Delete these subsections.
subsection (3A)	For "122(1)(fa)" substitute "122(1)(da)".
Section 124A (petition for winding-up on grounds of public interest)	
subsection (1)	Omit paragraphs (b) and (bb).
Section 126 (power to stay or restrain proceedings against company)	
subsection (2)	Delete subsection (2).
Section 127 (avoidance of property dispositions, etc)	
subsection (1)	For "any transfer of shares" substitute "any transfer by a member of the limited liability partnership of his interest in the property of the limited liability partnership".
Section 129 (commencement of winding up by the court)	
subsection (1)	For "a resolution has been passed by the company" substitute "a determination has been made" and for "at the time of the passing of the resolution" substitute "at the time of that determination".
Section 130 (consequences of winding-up order)	
subsection (3)	Delete subsection (3).
Section 148 (settlement of list of contributories and application of assets)	
subsection (1)	Delete ", with power to rectify the register of members in all cases where rectification is required in pursuance of the Companies Act or this Act,".
Section 149 (debts due from contributory to company)	
subsection (1)	Delete "the Companies Act or".
subsection (2)	Delete subsection (2).
subsection (3)	Delete ", whether limited or unlimited,".
Section 160 (delegation of powers to liquidator (England and Wales))	
subsection (1)	In subsection (1)(b) delete "and the rectifying of the register of members".
subsection (2)	For subsection (2) substitute the following— "(2) But the liquidator shall not make any call without the special leave of the court or the sanction of the liquidation committee."
Section 165 (voluntary winding up)	
subsection (2)	In paragraph (a) for "an extraordinary resolution of the company" substitute "a determination by a meeting of the members of the limited liability partnership".
subsection (4)	For paragraph (c) substitute the following—

Provisions	Modifications
	"(c) summon meetings of the members of the limited liability partnership for the purpose of obtaining their sanction or for any other purpose he may think fit."
new subsection (4A)	Insert a new subsection (4A) as follows— "(4A) Subsections (3) and (4) of section 92 shall apply for the purposes of this section as they apply for the purposes of that section."
Section 166 (creditors' voluntary winding up)	
subsection (5)	In paragraph (b) for "directors" substitute "designated members".
Section 171 (removal, etc (voluntary winding up))	
subsection (2)	For paragraph (a) substitute the following— "(a) in the case of a members' voluntary winding up, by a meeting of the members of the limited liability partnership summoned specially for that purpose, or".
subsection (6)	In paragraph (a) for "final meeting of the company" substitute "final meeting of the members of the limited liability partnership" and in paragraph (b) for "final meetings of the company" substitute "final meetings of the members of the limited liability partnership".
new subsection (7)	Insert a new subsection (7) as follows— "(7) Subsections (3) and (4) of section 92 are to apply for the purposes of this section as they apply for the purposes of that section."
Section 173 (release (voluntary winding up))	
subsection (2)	In paragraph (a) for "a general meeting of the company" substitute "a meeting of the members of the limited liability partnership".
Section 183 (effect of execution or attachment (England and Wales))	
subsection (2)	Delete paragraph (a).
Section 184 (duties of sheriff (England and Wales))	
subsection (1)	For "a resolution for voluntary winding up has been passed" substitute "the limited liability partnership has determined that it be wound up voluntarily".
subsection (4)	Delete "or of a meeting having been called at which there is to be proposed a resolution for voluntary winding up," and "or a resolution is passed (as the case may be)".
Section 187 (power to make over assets to employees)	Delete section 187.
Section 194 (resolutions passed at adjourned meetings)	After "contributories" insert "or of the members of a limited liability partnership".
Section 195 (meetings to ascertain wishes of creditors or contributories)	
subsection (3)	Delete "the Companies Act or".

Provisions	Modifications
Section 206 (fraud, etc in anticipation of winding up)	
subsection (1)	For "passes a resolution for voluntary winding up" substitute "makes a determination that it be wound up voluntarily".
Section 207 (transactions in fraud of creditors)	
subsection (1)	For "passes a resolution for voluntary winding up" substitute "makes a determination that it be wound up voluntarily".
Section 210 (material omissions from statement relating to company's affairs)	
subsection (2)	For "passed a resolution for voluntary winding up" substitute "made a determination that it be wound up voluntarily".
Section 214 (wrongful trading)	
subsection (2)	Delete from "but the court shall not" to the end of the subsection.
After section 214	Insert the following new section 214A "214A. Adjustment of withdrawals (1) This section has effect in relation to a person who is or has been a member of a limited liability partnership where, in the course of the winding up of that limited liability partnership, it appears that subsection (2) of this section applies in relation to that person. (2) This subsection applies in relation to a person if— (a) within the period of two years ending with the commencement of the winding up, he was a member of the limited liability partnership who withdrew property of the limited liability partnership, whether in the form of a share of profits, salary, repayment of or payment of interest on a loan to the limited liability partnership or any other withdrawal of property, and (b) it is proved by the liquidator to the satisfaction of the court that at the time of the withdrawal he knew or had reasonable ground for believing that the limited liability partnership— (i) was at the time of the withdrawal unable to pay its debts within the meaning of section 123, or (ii) would become so unable to pay its debts after the assets of the limited liability partnership had been depleted by that withdrawal taken together with all other withdrawals (if any) made by any members contemporaneously with that withdrawal or in contemplation when that withdrawal was made.

Provisions	Modifications
	(3) Where this section has effect in relation to any person the court, on the application of the liquidator, may declare that that person is to be liable to make such contribution (if any) to the limited liability partnership's assets as the court thinks proper. (4) The court shall not make a declaration in relation to any person the amount of which exceeds the aggregate of the amounts or values of all the withdrawals referred to in subsection (2) made by that person within the period of two years referred to in that subsection. (5) The court shall not make a declaration under this section with respect to any person unless that person knew or ought to have concluded that after each withdrawal referred to in subsection (2) there was no reasonable prospect that the limited liability partnership would avoid going into insolvent liquidation. (6) For the purposes of subsection (5) the facts which a member ought to know or ascertain and the conclusions which he ought to reach are those which would be known, ascertained, or reached by a reasonably diligent person having both: (a) the general knowledge, skill and experience that may reasonably be expected of a person carrying out the same functions as are carried out by that member in relation to the limited liability partnership, and (b) the general knowledge, skill and experience that that member has. (7) For the purposes of this section a limited liability partnership goes into insolvent liquidation if it goes into liquidation at a time when its assets are insufficient for the payment of its debts and other liabilities and the expenses of the winding up. (8) In this section "member" includes a shadow member. (9) This section is without prejudice to section 214."
Section 215 (proceedings under ss 213, 214)	
subsection (1)	Omit the word "or" between the words "213" and "214" and insert after "214" "or 214A".
subsection (2)	For "either section" substitute "any of those sections".
subsection (4)	For "either section" substitute "any of those sections".
subsection (5)	For "Sections 213 and 214" substitute "Sections 213, 214 or 214A".
Section 218 (prosecution of delinquent officers and members of company)	

Provisions	Modifications
subsection (1)	For "officer, or any member, of the company" substitute "member of the limited liability partnership".
subsections (3), (4) and (6)	For "officer of the company, or any member of it," substitute "officer or member of the limited liability partnership".
. . .	. . .
Section 247 ("insolvency" and "go into liquidation")	
subsection (2)	For "passes a resolution for voluntary winding up" substitute "makes a determination that it be wound up voluntarily" and for "passing such a resolution" substitute "making such a determination".
subsection (3)	For "resolution for voluntary winding up" substitute "determination to wind up voluntarily".
Section 249 ("connected with a company")	For the existing words substitute "For the purposes of any provision in this Group of Parts, a person is connected with a company (including a limited liability partnership) if— (a) he is a director or shadow director of a company or an associate of such a director or shadow director (including a member or a shadow member of a limited liability partnership or an associate of such a member or shadow member); or (b) he is an associate of the company or of the limited liability partnership."
Section 250 ("member" of a company)	Delete section 250.
Section 251 (expressions used generally)	Delete the word "and" appearing after the definition of "the rules" and insert the word "and" after the definition of "shadow director". After the definition of "shadow director" insert the following— ""shadow member", in relation to a limited liability partnership, means a person in accordance with whose directions or instructions the members of the limited liability partnership are accustomed to act (but so that a person is not deemed a shadow member by reason only that the members of the limited liability partnership act on advice given by him in a professional capacity);".
Section 386 (categories of preferential debts)	
subsection (1)	In subsection (1), omit the words "or an individual".
subsection (2)	In subsection (2), omit the words "or the individual".
Section 387 ("the relevant date")	In paragraph (ab) for "passed a resolution for voluntary winding up" substitute "made a determination that it be wound up voluntarily".

Provisions	Modifications
subsection (3)	In paragraph (c) for "passing of the resolution for the winding up of the company" substitute "making of the determination by the limited liability partnership that it be wound up voluntarily".
subsection (5)	Omit subsection (5).
subsection (6)	Omit subsection (6).
Section 388 (meaning of "act as insolvency practitioner")	
subsection (2)	Omit subsection (2).
subsection (3)	Omit subsection (3).
subsection (4)	Delete ""company" means a company within the meaning given by section 735(1) of the Companies Act or a company which may be wound up under Part V of this Act (unregistered companies);" and delete ""interim trustee" and "permanent trustee" mean the same as the Bankruptcy (Scotland) Act 1985".
Section 389 (acting without qualification an offence)	
subsection (1)	Omit the words "or an individual".
Section 389A (authorisation of nominees and supervisors)	
subsection (1)	Omit "or Part VIII".
Section 402 (official petitioner)	Delete section 402.
Section 412 (individual insolvency rules (England and Wales))	Delete section 412.
Section 415 (Fees orders (individual insolvency proceedings in England and Wales))	Delete section 415.
Section 416 (monetary limits (companies winding up))	
subsection (1)	In subsection (1), omit the words "section 117(2) (amount of company's share capital determining whether county court has jurisdiction to wind it up);" and the words "section 120(3) (the equivalent as respects sheriff court jurisdiction in Scotland);".
subsection (3)	In subsection (3), omit the words "117(2), 120(3) or".
Section 418 (monetary limits (bankruptcy))	Delete section 418.
Section 420 (insolvent partnerships)	Delete section 420.
Section 421 (insolvent estates of deceased persons)	Delete section 421.
Section 422 (recognised banks, etc)	Delete section 422.
Section 426A (disqualification from Parliament (England and Wales))	Omit.
Section 426B (devolution)	Omit.
Section 426C (irrelevance of privilege)	Omit.
Section 427 (parliamentary disqualification)	Delete section 427.
Section 429 (disabilities on revocation or administration order against an individual)	Delete section 429.
Section 432 (offences by bodies corporate)	
subsection (2)	Delete "secretary or".

Provisions	Modifications
Section 435 (meaning of "associate")	
new subsection (3A)	Insert a new subsection (3A) as follows— "(3A) A member of a limited liability partnership is an associate of that limited liability partnership and of every other member of that limited liability partnership and of the husband or wife or civil partner or relative of every other member of that limited liability partnership.".
subsection (11)	For subsection (11) there shall be substituted "(11) In this section "company" includes any body corporate (whether incorporated in Great Britain or elsewhere); and references to directors and other officers of a company and to voting power at any general meeting of a company have effect with any necessary modifications."
Section 436 (expressions used generally)	The following expressions and definitions shall be added to the section— "designated member" has the same meaning as it has in the Limited Liability Partnerships Act 2000; "limited liability partnership" means a limited liability partnership formed and registered under the Limited Liability Partnerships Act 2000; "limited liability partnership agreement", in relation to a limited liability partnership, means any agreement, express or implied, made between the members of the limited liability partnership or between the limited liability partnership and the members of the limited liability partnership which determines the mutual rights and duties of the members, and their rights and duties in relation to the limited liability partnership.
Section 437 (transitional provisions, and savings)	Delete section 437.
Section 440 (extent (Scotland))	
subsection (2)	In subsection (2), omit paragraph (b).
Section 441 (extent (Northern Ireland))	Delete section 441.
Section 442 (extent (other territories))	Delete section 442.
Schedule A1	
Paragraph 6	
sub-paragraph (1)	For "directors of a company wish" substitute "limited liability partnership wishes". For "they" substitute "the designated members of the limited liability partnership".
sub-paragraph (2)	For "directors" substitute "the designated members of the limited liability partnership". In sub-paragraph (c), for "meetings of the company and" substitute "a meeting of".
Paragraph 7	
sub-paragraph (1)	For "directors of a company" substitute "designated members of the limited liability partnership".

Provisions	Modifications
	In sub-paragraph (e)(iii), for "meetings of the company and" substitute "a meeting of".
Paragraph 8	
sub-paragraph (2)	For "meetings" substitute "meeting". For "are" substitute "is". Omit the words in parenthesis.
sub-paragraph (3)	For "either of those meetings" substitute "the meeting". For "those meetings were" substitute "that meeting was". Omit the words in parenthesis.
sub-paragraph (4)	For "either" substitute "the".
sub-paragraph (6)(c)	For "one or both of the meetings" substitute "the meeting".
Paragraph 9	
sub-paragraph (1)	For "directors" substitute "designated members of the limited liability partnership".
sub-paragraph (2)	For "directors" substitute "designated members of the limited liability partnership".
Paragraph 12	
sub-paragraph (1)(b)	Omit.
sub-paragraph (1)(c)	For "resolution may be passed" substitute "determination that it may be wound up may be made".
sub-paragraph (2)	For "transfer of shares" substitute "any transfer by a member of the limited liability partnership of his interest in the property of the limited liability partnership".
Paragraph 20	
sub-paragraph (8)	For "directors" substitute "designated members of the limited liability partnership".
sub-paragraph (9)	For "directors" substitute "designated members of the limited liability partnership".
Paragraph 24	
sub-paragraph (2)	For "directors" substitute "designated members of the limited liability partnership".
Paragraph 25	
sub-paragraph (2)(c)	For "directors" substitute "designated members of the limited liability partnership".
Paragraph 26	
sub-paragraph (1)	Omit ", director".
Paragraph 29	
sub-paragraph (1)	For "meetings of the company and its creditors" substitute "a meeting of the creditors of the limited liability partnership".
Paragraph 30	
sub-paragraph (1)	For "meetings" substitute "meeting".
new sub-paragraph (2A)	Insert new sub-paragraph (2A) as follows—

Provisions	Modifications
	"(2A) If modifications to the proposal are proposed at the meeting the chairman of the meeting shall, before the conclusion of the meeting, ascertain from the limited liability partnership whether or not it accepts the proposed modifications; and if at that conclusion the limited liability partnership has failed to respond to a proposed modification it shall be presumed not to have agreed to it.".
sub-paragraph (3)	For "either" substitute "the".
	After "the result of the meeting" in the first place where it occurs insert " (including, where modifications to the proposal were proposed at the meeting, the response to those proposed modifications made by the limited liability partnership)".
	At the end add "and to the limited liability partnership".
Paragraph 31	
sub-paragraph (1)	For "meetings" substitute "meeting".
sub-paragraph (7)	For "directors of the company" substitute "designated members of the limited liability partnership".
	For "meetings (or either of them)" substitute "meeting".
	For "directors" substitute "limited liability partnership".
	For "those meetings" substitute "that meeting".
Paragraph 32	
sub-paragraph (2)	For sub-paragraphs (a) and (b) substitute "with the day on which the meeting summoned under paragraph 29 is first held.".
Paragraph 36	
sub-paragraph (2)	For sub-paragraph (2) substitute—
	"(2) The decision has effect if, in accordance with the rules, it has been taken by the creditors' meeting summoned under paragraph 29.".
sub-paragraph (3)	Omit.
sub-paragraph (4)	Omit.
sub-paragraph (5)	Omit.
Paragraph 37	
sub-paragraph (5)	For "each of the reports of the meetings" substitute "the report of the meeting".
Paragraph 38	
sub-paragraph (1)(a)	For "one or both of the meetings" substitute "the meeting".
sub-paragraph (1)(b)	For "either of those meetings" substitute "the meeting".
sub-paragraph (2)(a)	For "either of the meetings" substitute "the meeting".
	After sub-paragraph (2)(a) insert new (aa) as follows—

Provisions	Modifications
	"(aa) any member of the limited liability partnership;".
sub-paragraph (2)(b)	Omit "creditors'".
sub-paragraph (3)(a)	For "each of the reports" substitute "the report".
sub-paragraph (3)(b)	Omit "creditors'".
sub-paragraph (4)(a)(ii)	Omit "in question".
sub-paragraph (4)(b)(i)	For "further meetings" substitute "a further meeting" and for "directors" substitute "limited liability partnership".
sub-paragraph (4)(b)(ii)	Omit "company or (as the case may be) creditors'".
sub-paragraph (5)	For "directors do" substitute "limited liability partnerships does".
Paragraph 39	
sub-paragraph (1)	For "one or both of the meetings" substitute "the meeting".
Schedule B1	
Paragraph 2	
sub-paragraph (c)	For "company or its directors" substitute "limited liability partnership".
Paragraph 8	
sub-paragraph (1)(a)	For "resolution for voluntary winding up" substitute "determination to wind up voluntarily".
Paragraph 9	Omit.
Paragraph 12	
sub-paragraph (1)(b)	Omit.
Paragraph 22	For sub-paragraph (1) substitute— "(1) A limited liability partnership may appoint an administrator.". Omit sub-paragraph (2).
Paragraph 23	
sub-paragraph (1)(b)	Omit "or its directors".
Paragraph 42	
sub-paragraph (2)	For "resolution may be passed for the winding up of" substitute "determination to wind up voluntarily may be made by".
Paragraph 61	For paragraph 61 substitute—" "61. The administrator has power to prevent any person from taking part in the management of the business of the limited liability partnership and to appoint any person to be a manager of that business.".
Paragraph 62	At the end add the following— "Subsections (3) and (4) of section 92 shall apply for the purposes of this paragraph as they apply for the purposes of that section.".
Paragraph 83	
sub-paragraph (6)(b)	For "resolution for voluntary winding up" substitute "determination to wind up voluntarily".
sub-paragraph (8)(b)	For "passing of the resolution for voluntary winding up" substitute "determination to wind up voluntarily".

Provisions	Modifications
sub-paragraph (8)(e)	For "passing of the resolution for voluntary winding up" substitute "determination to wind up voluntarily".
Paragraph 87	
sub-paragraph (2)(b)	Insert at the end "or".
sub-paragraph (2)(c)	Omit ", or".
sub-paragraph (2)(d)	Omit the words from "(d)" to "company".
Paragraph 89	
sub-paragraph (2)(b)	Insert at the end "or".
sub-paragraph (2)(c)	Omit ", or".
sub-paragraph (2)(d)	Omit the words from "(d)" to "company".
Paragraph 91	
sub-paragraph (1)(c)	Omit.
Paragraph 94	Omit.
Paragraph 95	For "to 94" substitute "and 93".
Paragraph 97	
sub-paragraph (1)(a)	Omit "or directors".
Paragraph 103	
sub-paragraph (5)	Omit.
Paragraph 105	Omit.
Schedule 1	
Paragraph 19	For paragraph 19 substitute the following— "19. Power to enforce any rights the limited liability partnership has against the members under the terms of the limited liability partnership agreement."
Schedule 10	
Section 6A(1)	In the entry relating to section 6A omit "members' or".
Section 85(2)	In the entry relating to section 85(2) for "resolution for voluntary winding up" substitute "making of determination for voluntary winding up".
Section 89(4)	In the entry relating to section 89(4) for "Director" substitute "Designated member".
Section 93(3)	In the entry relating to section 93(3) for "general meeting of the company" substitute "meeting of members of the limited liability partnership".
Section 99(3)	In the entries relating to section 99(3) for "director" and "directors" where they appear substitute "designated member" or "designated members" as appropriate.
Section 105(3)	In the entry relating to section 105(3) for "company general meeting" substitute "meeting of the members of the limited liability partnership".
Section 106(6)	In the entry relating to section 106(6) for "final meeting of the company" substitute "final meeting of the members of the limited liability partnership".
Sections 353(1) to 362	Delete the entries relating to sections 353(1) to 362 inclusive.
Section 429(5)	Delete the entry relating to section 429(5).
Schedule A1, paragraph 9(2)	For "Directors" substitute "Designated Members".

Provisions	Modifications
Schedule A1, paragraph 20(9)	For "Directors" substitute "Designated Members".
Schedule B1, paragraph 27(4)	Omit "or directors".
Schedule B1, paragraph 29(7)	Omit "or directors".
Schedule B1, paragraph 32	Omit "or directors".

SCHEDULE 4

Regulation 5(3)

The provisions listed in this Schedule are not applied to Scotland to the extent specified below:

Sections 50 to 52;

Section 53(1) and (2), to the extent that those subsections do not relate to the requirement for a copy of the instrument and notice being forwarded to the registrar of companies;

Section 53(4) (6) and (7);

Section 54(1), (2), (3) (to the extent that that subsection does not relate to the requirement for a copy of the interlocutor to be sent to the registrar of companies), and subsections (5), (6) and (7);

Sections 55 to 58;

Section 60, other than subsection (1);

Section 61, including subsections (6) and (7) to the extent that those subsections do not relate to anything to be done or which may be done to or by the registrar of companies;

Section 62, including subsection (5) to the extent that that subsection does not relate to anything to be done or which may be done to or by the registrar of companies;

Sections 63 to 66;

Section 67, including subsections (1) and (8) to the extent that those subsections do not relate to anything to be done or which may be done to the registrar of companies;

Section 68;

Section 69, including subsections (1) and (2) to the extent that those subsections do not relate to anything to be done or which may be done by the registrar of companies;

Sections 70 and 71;

Subsection 84(3), to the extent that it does not concern the copy of the resolution being forwarded to the registrar of companies within 15 days;

Sections 91 to 93;

Section 94, including subsections (3) and (4) to the extent that those subsections do not relate to the liquidator being required to send to the registrar of companies a copy of the account and a return of the final meeting;

Section 95;

Section 97;

Sections 100 to 102;

Sections 104 to 105;

Section 106, including subsections (3), (4) and (5) to the extent that those subsections do not relate to the liquidator being required to send to the registrar of companies a copy of the account of winding up and a return of the final meeting/quorum;

Sections 109 to 111;

Section 112, including subsection (3) to the extent that that subsection does not relate to the liquidator being required to send to the registrar a copy of the order made by the court;

Sections 113 to 115;

Sections 126 to 128;

Section 130(1) to the extent that that subsection does not relate to a copy of the order being forwarded by the court to the registrar;

Section 131;

Sections 133 to 135;

Sections 138 to 140;

Sections 142 to 146;
Section 147, including subsection (3) to the extent that that subsection does not relate to a copy of the order being forwarded by the company to the registrar;
Section 162 to the extent that that section concerns the matters set out in Section C.2 of Schedule 5 to the Scotland Act 1998 as being exceptions to the insolvency reservation;
Sections 163 to 167;
Section 169;
Section 170, including subsection (2) to the extent that that subsection does not relate to an application being made by the registrar to make good the default;
Section 171;
Section 172, including subsection (8) to the extent that that subsection does not relate to the liquidator being required to give notice to the registrar;
Sections 173 and 174;
Section 177;
Sections 185 to 189;
Sections 191 to 194;
Section 196 to the extent that that section applies to the specified devolved functions of Part IV of the Insolvency Act 1986;
Section 199;
Section 200 to the extent that it applies to the specified devolved functions of Part IV of the First Group of Parts of the 1986 Act;
Sections 206 to 215;
Section 218 subsections (1), (2), (4) and (6);
Section 231 to 232 to the extent that the sections apply to administrative receivers, liquidators and provisional liquidators;
Section 233, to the extent that that section applies in the case of the appointment of an administrative receiver, of a voluntary arrangement taking effect, of a company going into liquidation or where a provisional liquidator is appointed;
Section 234 to the extent that that section applies to situations other than those where an administration order applies;
Section 235 to the extent that that section applies to situations other than those where an administration order applies;
Sections 236 to 237 to the extent that those sections apply to situations other than administration orders and winding up;
Sections 242 to 243;
Section 244 to the extent that that section applies in circumstances other than a company which is subject to an administration order;
Section 245;
Section 251, to the extent that that section contains definitions which apply only to devolved matters;
Section 416(1) and (4), to the extent that those subsections apply to section 206(1)(a) and (b) in connection with the offence provision relating to the winding up of a limited liability partnership;
Schedule 2;
Schedule 3;
Schedule 4;
Schedule 8, to the extent that that Schedule does not apply to voluntary arrangements or administrations within the meaning of Parts I and II of the 1986 Act.

In addition, Schedule 10, which concerns punishment of offences under the Insolvency Act 1986, lists various sections of the Insolvency Act 1986 which create an offence. The following sections, which are listed in Schedule 10, are devolved in their application to Scotland:
Section 51(4);
Section 51(5);

Sections 53(2) to 62(5) to the extent that those subsections relate to matters other than delivery to the registrar of companies;
Section 64(2);
Section 65(4);
Section 66(6);
Section 67(8) to the extent that that subsection relates to matters other than delivery to the registrar of companies;
Section 93(3);
Section 94(4) to the extent that that subsection relates to matters other than delivery to the registrar of companies;
Section 94(6);
Section 95(8);
Section 105(3);
Section 106(4) to the extent that that subsection relates to matters other than delivery to the registrar of companies;
Section 106(6);
Section 109(2);
Section 114(4);
Section 131(7);
Section 164;
Section 166(7);
Section 188(2);
Section 192(2);
Sections 206 to 211; and
Section 235(5) to the extent that it relates to matters other than administration orders.

SCHEDULE 5

GENERAL AND CONSEQUENTIAL AMENDMENTS IN OTHER LEGISLATION

Regulation 9

…

SCHEDULE 6

APPLICATION OF SUBORDINATE LEGISLATION

Regulation 10

PART I

REGULATIONS MADE UNDER THE 1985 ACT

…

7. The Companies Act 1985 (Power to Enter and Remain on Premises: Procedural) Regulations 2005

PART II

REGULATIONS MADE UNDER THE 1986 ACT

1. Insolvency Practitioners Regulations 1990
2. The Insolvency Practitioners (Recognised Professional Bodies) Order 1986

3. The Insolvency Rules 1986 and the Insolvency (Scotland) Rules 1986 (except in so far as they relate to the exceptions to the reserved matters specified in section C 2 of Part II of Schedule 5 to the Scotland Act 1998)
4. The Insolvency Fees Order 1986
5. The Co-operation of Insolvency Courts (Designation of Relevant Countries and Territories) Order 1986
6. The Co-operation of Insolvency Courts (Designation of Relevant Countries and Territories) Order 1996
7. The Co-operation of Insolvency Courts (Designation of Relevant Country) Order 1998
8. Insolvency Proceedings (Monetary Limits) Order 1986
9. Insolvency Practitioners Tribunal (Conduct of Investigations) Rules 1986
10. Insolvency Regulations 1994
11. Insolvency (Amendment) Regulations 2000

PART III

REGULATIONS MADE UNDER OTHER LEGISLATION

1. . . .
2. The Companies (Disqualification Orders) Regulations 1986
3. The Insolvent Companies (Disqualification of Unfit Directors) Proceedings Rules 1987
4. The Contracting Out (Functions of the Official Receiver) Order 1995
5. The Uncertificated Securities Regulations 1995
6. The Insolvent Companies (Reports on Conduct of Directors) Rules 1996
7. The Insolvent Companies (Reports on Conduct of Directors) (Scotland) Rules 1996

Limited Liability Partnerships (Application of Companies Act 2006) Regulations 2009

S.I. 2009/1804

PART 1
GENERAL INTRODUCTORY PROVISIONS

1. Citation

These Regulations may be cited as the Limited Liability Partnerships (Application of Companies Act 2006) Regulations 2009.

2.

(1) The provisions of these Regulations come into force as follows.

(2) Regulations 8, 64, 77, 80 and 81 of, and paragraphs 6 and 7 of Schedule 3 to, these Regulations come into force on the day after the Regulations are made for the purpose of enabling the exercise of powers to make regulations or orders by statutory instrument.

(3) Otherwise, the Regulations come into force on 1st October 2009.

3.

(1) In these Regulations "LLP" means a limited liability partnership registered under the Limited Liability Partnerships Act 2000.

(2) In these Regulations, unless the context otherwise requires—

(a) any reference to a numbered Part, section or Schedule is to the Part, section or Schedule so numbered in the Companies Act 2006;

(b) references in provisions applied to LLPs—

(i) to provisions of the Companies Act 2006, or

(ii) to provisions of instruments made under that Act,

are to those provisions as applied to LLPs by these Regulations or by the Limited Liability Partnerships (Accounts and Audit) (Application of Companies Act 2006) Regulations 2008;

(c) references in provisions applied to LLPs to provisions of the Insolvency Act 1986 or the Insolvency (Northern Ireland) Order 1989 are to those provisions as applied to LLPs by the Limited Liability Partnerships Regulations 2001 or the Limited Liability Partnerships Regulations (Northern Ireland) 2004.

PART 2
FORMALITIES OF DOING BUSINESS

Formalities of doing business under the law of England and Wales or Northern Ireland

4.

Sections 43 to 47 apply to LLPs, modified so that they read as follows—

"43. LLP contracts

(1) Under the law of England and Wales or Northern Ireland a contract may be made—

(a) by an LLP, by writing under its common seal, or

(b) on behalf of an LLP, by a person acting under its authority, express or implied.

(2) This is without prejudice to section 6 of the Limited Liability Partnerships Act 2000 (c 12) (members as agents).

(3) Any formalities required by law in the case of a contract made by an individual also apply, unless a contrary intention appears, to a contract made by or on behalf of an LLP.

44. Execution of documents

(1) Under the law of England and Wales or Northern Ireland a document is executed by an LLP—

(a) by the affixing of its common seal, or

(b) by signature in accordance with the following provisions.

(2) A document is validly executed by an LLP if it is signed on behalf of the LLP—

(a) by two members, or

(b) by a member of the LLP in the presence of a witness who attests the signature.

(3) A document signed in accordance with subsection (2) and expressed, in whatever words, to be executed by the LLP has the same effect as if executed under the common seal of the LLP.

(4) In favour of a purchaser a document is deemed to have been duly executed by an LLP if it purports to be signed in accordance with subsection (2).

A "purchaser" means a purchaser in good faith for valuable consideration and includes a lessee, mortgagee or other person who for valuable consideration acquires an interest in property.

(5) Where a document is to be signed by a person on behalf of more than one LLP, or on behalf of an LLP and a company, it is not duly signed by that person for the purposes of this section unless he signs it separately in each capacity.

(6) References in this section to a document being (or purporting to be) signed by a member are to be read, in a case where that member is a firm, as references to its being (or purporting to be) signed by an individual authorised by the firm to sign on its behalf.

(7) This section applies to a document that is (or purports to be) executed by an LLP in the name of or on behalf of another person whether or not that person is also an LLP.

45. Common seal

(1) An LLP may have a common seal, but need not have one.

(2) An LLP which has a common seal shall have its name engraved in legible characters on the seal.

(3) If an LLP fails to comply with subsection (2) an offence is committed by—

(a) the LLP, and

(b) every member of the LLP who is in default.

(4) A member of an LLP, or a person acting on behalf of an LLP, commits an offence if he uses, or authorises the use of, a seal purporting to be a seal of the LLP on which its name is not engraved as required by subsection (2).

(5) A person guilty of an offence under this section is liable on summary conviction to a fine not exceeding level 3 on the standard scale.

(6) This section does not form part of the law of Scotland.

46. Execution of deeds

(1) A document is validly executed by an LLP as a deed for the purposes of section 1(2)(b) of the Law of Property (Miscellaneous Provisions) Act 1989 (c 34) and for the purposes of the law of Northern Ireland if, and only if—

(a) it is duly executed by the LLP, and

(b) it is delivered as a deed.

(2) For the purposes of subsection (1)(b) a document is presumed to be delivered upon its being executed, unless a contrary intention is proved.

47. Execution of deeds or other documents by attorney

(1) Under the law of England and Wales or Northern Ireland an LLP may, by instrument executed as a deed, empower a person, either generally or in respect of specified matters, as its attorney to execute deeds or other documents on its behalf.

(2) A deed or other document so executed, whether in the United Kingdom or elsewhere, has effect as if executed by the LLP.".

Formalities of doing business under the law of Scotland

5.

Section 48 applies to LLPs, modified so that it reads as follows—

"48. Execution of documents by LLPs: Scotland

(1) The following provisions form part of the law of Scotland only.

(2) Notwithstanding the provisions of any enactment, an LLP need not have a common seal.

(3) For the purposes of any enactment—

(a) providing for a document to be executed by an LLP by affixing its common seal, or

(b) referring (in whatever terms) to a document so executed,

a document signed or subscribed by or on behalf of the LLP in accordance with the provisions of the Requirements of Writing (Scotland) Act 1995 (c 7) has effect as if so executed.".

Official seal for use abroad

6.

Section 49 applies to LLPs, modified so that it reads as follows—

"49. Official seal for use abroad

(1) An LLP that has a common seal may have an official seal for use outside the United Kingdom.

(2) The official seal must be a facsimile of the LLP's common seal, with the addition on its face of the place or places where it is to be used.

(3) The official seal when duly affixed to a document has the same effect as the LLP's common seal.

This subsection does not extend to Scotland.

(4) An LLP having an official seal for use outside the United Kingdom may—

(a) by writing under its common seal, or

(b) as respects Scotland, by writing subscribed in accordance with the Requirements of Writing (Scotland) Act 1995,

authorise any person appointed for the purpose to affix the official seal to any deed or other document to which the LLP is party.

(5) As between the LLP and a person dealing with such an agent, the agent's authority continues—

(a) during the period mentioned in the instrument conferring the authority, or

(b) if no period is mentioned, until notice of the revocation or termination of the agent's authority has been given to the person dealing with him.

(6) The person affixing the official seal must certify in writing on the deed or other document to which the seal is affixed the date on which, and place at which, it is affixed.".

Other matters

7.

Sections 51 and 52 apply to LLPs, modified so that they read as follows—

"51. Pre-incorporation contracts, deeds and obligations

(1) A contract that purports to be made by or on behalf of an LLP at a time when the LLP has not been formed has effect, subject to any agreement to the contrary, as one made with the person purporting to act for the LLP or as agent for it, and he is personally liable on the contract accordingly.

(2) Subsection (1) applies—

(a) to the making of a deed under the law of England and Wales or Northern Ireland, and

(b) to the undertaking of an obligation under the law of Scotland,

as it applies to the making of a contract.

52. Bills of exchange and promissory notes

A bill of exchange or promissory note is deemed to have been made, accepted or endorsed on behalf of an LLP if made, accepted or endorsed in the name of, or by or on behalf or on account of, the LLP by a person acting under its authority.".

PART 3
AN LLP'S NAME

CHAPTER 1
GENERAL REQUIREMENTS

Prohibited names and sensitive words and expressions

8.

Sections 53 to 56 apply to LLPs, modified so that they read as follows—

"53. Prohibited names

An LLP must not be registered under the Limited Liability Partnerships Act 2000 (c 12) by a name if, in the opinion of the Secretary of State—

(a) its use by the LLP would constitute an offence, or

(b) it is offensive.

54. Names suggesting connection with government or public authority

(1) The approval of the Secretary of State is required for an LLP to be registered under the Limited Liability Partnerships Act 2000 (c 12) by a name that would be likely to give the impression that the LLP is connected with—

(a) Her Majesty's Government, any part of the Scottish Administration, the Welsh Assembly Government or Her Majesty's Government in Northern Ireland,

(b) a local authority, or

(c) any public authority specified for the purposes of this section by regulations made by the Secretary of State.

(2) For the purposes of this section—

"local authority" means—

(a) a local authority within the meaning of the Local Government Act 1972 (c 70), the Common Council of the City of London or the Council of the Isles of Scilly,

(b) a council constituted under section 2 of the Local Government etc (Scotland) Act 1994 (c 39), or

(c) a district council in Northern Ireland;

"public authority" includes any person or body having functions of a public nature.

(3) Regulations under this section are subject to affirmative resolution procedure.

55. Other sensitive words or expressions

(1) The approval of the Secretary of State is required for an LLP to be registered under the Limited Liability Partnerships Act 2000 (c 12) by a name that includes a word or expression for the time being specified in regulations made by the Secretary of State under this section.

(2) Regulations under this section are subject to approval after being made.

56. Duty to seek comments of government department or other specified body

(1) The Secretary of State may by regulations under—

(a) section 54 (name suggesting connection with government or public authority), or

(b) section 55 (other sensitive words or expressions),

require that, in connection with an application for the approval of the Secretary of State under that section, the applicant must seek the view of a specified Government department or other body.

(2) Where such a requirement applies, the applicant must request the specified department or other body (in writing) to indicate whether (and if so why) it has any objections to the proposed name.

(3) Where a request under this section is made in connection with an application for the registration of an LLP under the Limited Liability Partnerships Act 2000 (c 12), the application must—

(a) include a statement that a request under this section has been made, and

(b) be accompanied by a copy of any response received.

(4) Where a request under this section is made in connection with a change in an LLP's name, the notice of the change sent to the registrar must—

(a) include a statement by a designated member of the LLP that a request under this section has been made, and

(b) be accompanied by a copy of any response received.

(5) In this section "specified" means specified in the regulations.".

Permitted characters etc

9.

Section 57 applies to LLPs, modified so that it reads as follows—

"57. Permitted characters etc

(1) The provisions of the Company and Business Names (Miscellaneous Provisions) Regulations 2009 (SI 2009/1085) relating to the characters, signs or symbols and punctuation that may be used in a registered name apply to LLPs.

(2) Those provisions are—

(a) regulation 2 and Schedule 1, and

(b) any other provisions of those Regulations having effect for the purpose of those provisions.

(3) In those provisions as they apply to LLPs—

(a) for "company" substitute "LLP", and

(b) for "the Act" substitute "the Limited Liability Partnerships Act 2000".

(4) An LLP may not be registered under the Limited Liability Partnerships Act 2000 (c 12) by a name that consists of or includes anything that is not permitted in accordance with the provisions applied by this section.".

Inappropriate use of indications of company type or legal form

10.

Section 65 applies to LLPs, modified so that it reads as follows—

"65. Inappropriate use of indications of company type or legal form

(1) The provisions of the Company and Business Names (Miscellaneous Provisions) Regulations 2009 (SI 2009/1085) relating to inappropriate use of indications of company type or legal form apply to LLPs.

(2) Those provisions are—

(a) regulation 4 and Schedule 2, and

(b) any other provisions of those Regulations having effect for the purpose of those provisions.

(3) As applied to LLPs regulation 4 is modified so as to read as follows—

"4

(1) An LLP must not be registered under the Limited Liability Partnerships Act 2000 (c 12) by a name that includes in any part of the name—

(a) an expression or abbreviation specified in inverted commas in paragraph 3(a) to (o) or (r) to (v) in Schedule 2 (other than the abbreviation "LLP" or "PAC" (with or without full stops) at the end of its name), or

(b) an expression or abbreviation specified as similar.

(2) An LLP must not be registered under the Limited Liability Partnerships Act 2000 by a name that includes immediately before the expression "LIMITED LIABILITY PARTNERSHIP" OR "PARTNERIAETH ATEBOLRWYDD CYFYNGEDIG" or the

abbreviations "LLP" or "PAC" an abbreviation specified in inverted commas in paragraph 3(v) of that Schedule (or any abbreviation specified as similar)".".

CHAPTER 2
SIMILARITY TO OTHER NAMES

Similarity to other name on registrar's index

11

Sections 66 to 68 apply to LLPs, modified so that they read as follows—

"66. Name not to be the same as another in the index

(1) An LLP must not be registered under the Limited Liability Partnerships Act 2000 (c 12) by a name that is the same as another name appearing in the registrar's index of company names.

(2) The provisions of the Company and Business Names (Miscellaneous Provisions) Regulations 2009 (SI 2009/1085) supplementing this section apply to LLPs.

(3) Those provisions are—

(a) regulation 7 and Schedule 3 (matters that are to be disregarded and words, expressions, signs and symbols that are to be regarded as the same),

(b) regulation 8 (consent to registration of a name which is the same as another in the registrar's index of company names), and

(c) any other provisions of those Regulations having effect for the purpose of those provisions.

(4) In regulation 8 as applied to LLPs—

(a) for "a company" or "the company" substitute "an LLP" or "the LLP",

(b) for "Company Y" substitute "LLP Y", and

(c) in paragraph (1), for "the Act" substitute "the Limited Liability Partnerships Act 2000".

67. Power to direct change of name in case of similarity to existing name

The Secretary of State may direct an LLP to change its name if it has been registered in a name that is the same as or, in the opinion of the Secretary of State, too like—

(a) a name appearing at the time of the registration in the registrar's index of company names, or

(b) a name that should have appeared in that index at that time.

68. Direction to change names: supplementary provisions

(1) The following provisions have effect in relation to a direction under section 67 (power to direct change of name in case of similarity to existing name).

(2) Any such direction—

(a) must be given within twelve months of the LLP's registration by the name in question, and

(b) must specify the period within which the LLP is to change its name.

(3) The Secretary of State may by a further direction extend that period.
Any such direction must be given before the end of the period for the time being specified.

(4) A direction under section 67 or this section must be in writing.

(5) If an LLP fails to comply with the direction, an offence is committed by—

(a) the LLP, and

(b) every designated member of the LLP who is in default.

(6) A person guilty of an offence under this section is liable on summary conviction to a fine not exceeding level 3 on the standard scale and, for continued contravention, a daily default fine not exceeding one-tenth of level 3 on the standard scale.".

Similarity to other name in which person has goodwill

12

Sections 69 to 74 apply to LLPs, modified so that they read as follows—

"69. Objection to LLP's registered name

(1) A person ("the applicant") may object to an LLP's registered name on the ground—

(a) that it is the same as a name associated with the applicant in which he has goodwill, or

(b) that it is sufficiently similar to such a name that its use in the United Kingdom would be likely to mislead by suggesting a connection between the LLP and the applicant.

(2) The objection must be made by application to a company names adjudicator (see section 70).

(3) The LLP concerned shall be the primary respondent to the application.
Any of its members may be joined as respondents.

(4) If the ground specified in subsection (1)(a) or (b) is established, it is for the respondents to show—

(a) that the name was registered before the commencement of the activities on which the applicant relies to show goodwill; or

(b) that the LLP—

(i) is operating under the name, or

(ii) is proposing to do so and has incurred substantial start-up costs in preparation, or

(iii) was formerly operating under the name and is now dormant; or

(c) that the name was registered in the ordinary course of an LLP formation business and the LLP is available for sale to the applicant on the standard terms of that business; or

(d) that the name was adopted in good faith; or

(e) that the interests of the applicant are not adversely affected to any significant extent.

If none of those is shown, the objection shall be upheld.

(5) If the facts mentioned in subsection (4)(a), (b) or (c) are established, the objection shall nevertheless be upheld if the applicant shows that the main purpose of the respondents (or any of them) in registering the name was to obtain money (or other consideration) from the applicant or prevent him from registering the name.

(6) If the objection is not upheld under subsection (4) or (5), it shall be dismissed.

(7) In this section "goodwill" includes reputation of any description.

70. Company names adjudicators

(1) The Secretary of State shall appoint persons to be company names adjudicators.

(2) The persons appointed must have such legal or other experience as, in the Secretary of State's opinion, makes them suitable for appointment.

(3) An adjudicator—

(a) holds office in accordance with the terms of his appointment,

(b) is eligible for re-appointment when his term of office ends,

(c) may resign at any time by notice in writing given to the Secretary of State, and

(d) may be dismissed by the Secretary of State on the ground of incapacity or misconduct.

(4) One of the adjudicators shall be appointed Chief Adjudicator.
He shall perform such functions as the Secretary of State may assign to him.

(5) The other adjudicators shall undertake such duties as the Chief Adjudicator may determine.

(6) The Secretary of State may—

(a) appoint staff for the adjudicators;

(b) pay remuneration and expenses to the adjudicators and their staff;

(c) defray other costs arising in relation to the performance by the adjudicators of their functions;

(d) compensate persons for ceasing to be adjudicators.

71. Procedural rules

(1) The Company Names Adjudicator Rules 2008 (SI 2008/1738) apply to LLPs.

(2) As they apply to LLPs, omit—

(a) in rule 3(6) (persons joined as respondent), the reference to a director of the primary respondent;

(b) rule 13(2) (registered office treated as address for service).

72. Decision of adjudicator to be made available to public

(1) A company names adjudicator must, within 90 days of determining an application under section 69, make his decision and his reasons for it available to the public.

(2) He may do so by means of a website or by such other means as appear to him to be appropriate.

73. Order requiring name to be changed

(1) If an application under section 69 is upheld, the adjudicator shall make an order—

(a) requiring the respondent LLP to change its name to one that is not an offending name, and

(b) requiring all the respondents—

(i) to take all such steps as are within their power to make, or facilitate the making, of that change, and

(ii) not to cause or permit any steps to be taken calculated to result in another LLP being registered with a name that is an offending name.

(2) An "offending name" means a name that, by reason of its similarity to the name associated with the applicant in which he claims goodwill, would be likely—

(a) to be the subject of a direction under section 67 (power of Secretary of State to direct change of name), or

(b) to give rise to a further application under section 69.

(3) The order must specify a date by which the respondent LLP's name is to be changed and may be enforced—

(a) in England and Wales or Northern Ireland, in the same way as an order of the High Court;

(b) in Scotland, in the same way as a decree of the Court of Session.

(4) If the respondent LLP's name is not changed in accordance with the order by the specified date, the adjudicator may determine a new name for the LLP.

(5) If the adjudicator determines a new name for the respondent LLP he must give notice of his determination—

(a) to the applicant,

(b) to the respondents, and

(c) to the registrar.

(6) For the purposes of this section an LLP's name is changed when the change takes effect in accordance with paragraph 5(4) in Part 1 of the Schedule to the Limited Liability Partnerships Act 2000 (c 12) (on the issue of the certificate of the change of name).

74. Appeal from adjudicator's decision

(1) An appeal lies to the court from any decision of a company names adjudicator to uphold or dismiss an application under section 69.

(2) Notice of appeal against a decision upholding an application must be given before the date specified in the adjudicator's order by which the respondent LLP's name is to be changed.

(3) If notice of appeal is given against a decision upholding an application, the effect of the adjudicator's order is suspended.

(4) If on appeal the court—

(a) affirms the decision of the adjudicator to uphold the application, or

(b) reverses the decision of the adjudicator to dismiss the application,

the court may (as the case may require) specify the date by which the adjudicator's order is to be complied with, remit the matter to the adjudicator or make any order or determination that the adjudicator might have made.

(5) If the court determines a new name for the LLP it must give notice of the determination—
   (a) to the parties to the appeal, and
   (b) to the registrar.”.

CHAPTER 3
OTHER POWERS OF THE SECRETARY OF STATE

Provision of misleading information etc

13.

Sections 75 and 76 apply to LLPs, modified so that they read as follows—

“75. Provision of misleading information etc

(1) If it appears to the Secretary of State—
   (a) that misleading information has been given for the purposes of an LLP’s registration by a particular name, or
   (b) that an undertaking or assurance has been given for that purpose and has not been fulfilled, the Secretary of State may direct the LLP to change its name.

(2) Any such direction—
   (a) must be given within five years of the LLP’s registration by that name, and
   (b) must specify the period within which the LLP is to change its name.

(3) The Secretary of State may by a further direction extend the period within which the LLP is to change its name.

Any such direction must be given before the end of the period for the time being specified.

(4) A direction under this section must be in writing.

(5) If an LLP fails to comply with a direction under this section, an offence is committed by—
   (a) the LLP, and
   (b) every designated member of the LLP who is in default.

(6) A person guilty of an offence under this section is liable on summary conviction to a fine not exceeding level 3 on the standard scale and, for continued contravention, a daily default fine not exceeding one-tenth of level 3 on the standard scale.

76. Misleading indication of activities

(1) If in the opinion of the Secretary of State the name by which an LLP is registered gives so misleading an indication of the nature of its activities as to be likely to cause harm to the public, the Secretary of State may direct the LLP to change its name.

(2) The direction must be in writing.

(3) The direction must be complied with within a period of six weeks from the date of the direction or such longer period as the Secretary of State may think fit to allow.

This does not apply if an application is duly made to the court under the following provisions.

(4) The LLP may apply to the court to set the direction aside.

The application must be made within the period of three weeks from the date of the direction.

(5) The court may set the direction aside or confirm it.

If the direction is confirmed, the court shall specify the period within which the direction is to be complied with.

(6) If an LLP fails to comply with a direction under this section, an offence is committed by—
   (a) the LLP, and
   (b) every designated member of the LLP who is in default.

(7) A person guilty of an offence under this section is liable on summary conviction to a fine not exceeding level 3 on the standard scale and, for continued contravention, a daily default fine not exceeding one-tenth of level 3 on the standard scale.”.

CHAPTER 4
TRADING DISCLOSURES

Requirement to disclose LLP name etc

14.

Sections 82 and 83 apply to LLPs, modified so that they read as follows—

"82. Requirement to disclose LLP name etc

(1) The Companies (Trading Disclosures) Regulations 2008 (SI 2008/495 apply to LLPs.

(2) As they apply to LLPs—

(a) read references to a company as references to an LLP;

(b) read references to a director as references to a member of an LLP;

(c) read references to an officer of a company as references to a designated member of an LLP;

(d) in regulation 7 (further particulars to appear in business letters, order forms and websites), for paragraphs (2)(d) to (f) and (3) substitute—

"(d) in the case of an LLP whose name ends with the abbreviation "llp", "LLP", "pac" or "PAC", the fact that it is an LLP or a partneriaeth atebolrwydd cyfyngedig".";

(e) in regulation 8 (disclosure of names of members)—

(i) at the beginning of paragraph (1) insert "Subject to paragraph (3)," and

(ii) after paragraph (2) insert—

"(3) Paragraph (1) does not apply in relation to any document issued by an LLP with more than 20 members which maintains at its principal place of business a list of the names of all the members if the document states in legible characters the address of the principal place of business of the LLP and that the list of the members' names is open to inspection at that place.

(4) Where an LLP maintains a list of the members' names for the purposes of paragraph (3), any person may inspect the list during office hours.";

(f) omit regulation 10(3) (offences: shadow directors).

83. Civil consequences of failure to make required disclosure

(1) This section applies to any legal proceedings brought by an LLP to which section 82 applies (requirement to disclose LLP name etc) to enforce a right arising out of a contract made in the course of a business in respect of which the LLP was, at the time the contract was made, in breach of the Companies (Trading Disclosures) Regulations 2008 (SI 2008/495).

(2) The proceedings shall be dismissed if the defendant (in Scotland, the defender) to the proceedings shows—

(a) that he has a claim against the claimant (pursuer) arising out of the contract that he has been unable to pursue by reason of the latter's breach of the regulations, or

(b) that he has suffered some financial loss in connection with the contract by reason of the claimant's (pursuer's) breach of the regulations,

unless the court before which the proceedings are brought is satisfied that it is just and equitable to permit the proceedings to continue.

(3) This section does not affect the right of any person to enforce such rights as he may have against another person in any proceedings brought by that person.".

15.

Section 85 applies to LLPs, modified so that it reads as follows—

"85. Minor variations in form of name to be left out of account

(1) For the purposes of this Chapter, in considering an LLP's name no account is to be taken of—

(a) whether upper or lower case characters (or a combination of the two) are used,

(b) whether diacritical marks or punctuation are present or absent, provided there is no real likelihood of names differing only in those respects being taken to be different names.

(2) This does not affect the operation of provisions of the Company and Business Names (Miscellaneous Provisions) Regulations 2009 (SI 2009/1085) permitting only specified characters or punctuation.".

PART 4
AN LLP'S REGISTERED OFFICE

General

16.

Sections 86 and 87 apply to LLPs, modified so that they read as follows—

"86. An LLP's registered office

(1) An LLP must at all times have a registered office situated in England and Wales (or in Wales), in Scotland or in Northern Ireland, to which all communications and notices may be addressed.

(2) On the incorporation of an LLP the situation of its registered office shall be that stated in the incorporation document.

87. Change of address of registered office

(1) An LLP may change the address of its registered office by giving notice to the registrar.

(2) The change takes effect upon the notice being registered by the registrar, but until the end of the period of 14 days beginning with the date on which it is registered a person may validly serve any document on the LLP at the address previously registered.

(3) For the purposes of any duty of an LLP—

(a) to keep available for inspection at its registered office any register, index or other document, or

(b) to mention the address of its registered office in any document,

an LLP that has given notice to the registrar of a change in the address of its registered office may act on the change as from such date, not more than 14 days after the notice is given, as it may determine.

(4) Where an LLP unavoidably ceases to perform at its registered office any such duty as is mentioned in subsection (3)(a) in circumstances in which it was not practicable to give prior notice to the registrar of a change in the address of its registered office, but—

(a) resumes performance of that duty at other premises as soon as practicable, and

(b) gives notice accordingly to the registrar of a change in the situation of its registered office within 14 days of doing so, it is not to be treated as having failed to comply with that duty.".

Welsh LLPs

17.

Section 88 applies to LLPs, modified so that it reads as follows—

"88. Welsh LLPs

(1) In this Act a "Welsh LLP" means an LLP as to which it is stated in the register that its registered office is to be situated in Wales.

(2) An LLP—

(a) whose registered office is in Wales, and

(b) as to which it is stated in the register that its registered office is to be situated in England and Wales,

may determine that the register be amended so that it states that the LLP's registered office is to be situated in Wales.

(3) An LLP—

(a) whose registered office is in Wales, and

(b) as to which it is stated in the register that its registered office is to be situated in Wales,

may determine that the register be amended so that it states that the LLP's registered office is to be situated in England and Wales.

(4) Where an LLP makes a determination under this section it must give notice to the registrar, who shall—

(a) amend the register accordingly, and

(b) issue a new certificate of incorporation altered to meet the circumstances of the case.".

PART 5
AN LLP'S MEMBERS

CHAPTER 1
REGISTER OF MEMBERS

Requirements for register of members

18.

Sections 162 to 165 apply to LLPs, modified so that they read as follows—

"162 Register of members

(1) Every LLP must keep a register of its members.

(2) The register must contain the required particulars (see sections 163 and 164) of each person who is a member of the LLP.

(3) The register must be kept available for inspection—

(a) at the LLP's registered office, or

(b) at a place specified in Part 2 of the Companies (Company Records) Regulations 2008 (SI 2008/3006).

(4) The LLP must give notice to the registrar—

(a) of the place at which the register is kept available for inspection, and

(b) of any change in that place,

unless it has at all times been kept at the LLP's registered office.

(5) The register must be open to the inspection—

(a) of any member of the LLP without charge, and

(b) of any other person on payment of the fee prescribed by regulation 2(a) of the Companies (Fees for Inspection of Company Records) Regulations 2008 (SI 2008/3007).

(6) If default is made in complying with subsection (1), (2) or (3) or if default is made for 14 days in complying with subsection (4), or if an inspection required under subsection (5) is refused, an offence is committed by—

(a) the LLP, and

(b) every designated member of the LLP who is in default.

(7) A person guilty of an offence under this section is liable on summary conviction to a fine not exceeding level 5 on the standard scale and, for continued contravention, a daily default fine not exceeding one-tenth of level 5 on the standard scale.

(8) In the case of a refusal of inspection of the register, the court may by order compel an immediate inspection of it.

163. Particulars of members to be registered: individuals

(1) An LLP's register of members must contain the following particulars in the case of an individual—

(a) name and any former name;

(b) a service address;

(c) the country or state (or part of the United Kingdom) in which he is usually resident;

(d) date of birth;

(e) whether he is a designated member.

(2) For the purposes of this section "name" means a person's Christian name (or other forename) and surname, except that in the case of—

(a) a peer, or
(b) an individual usually known by a title,
the title may be stated instead of his Christian name (or other forename)and surname or in addition to either or both of them.

(3) For the purposes of this section a "former name" means a name by which the individual was formerly known for business purposes.
Where a person is or was formerly known by more than one such name, each of them must be stated.

(4) It is not necessary for the register to contain particulars of a former name in the following cases—
(a) in the case of a peer or an individual normally known by a British title, where the name is one by which the person was known previous to the adoption of or succession to the title;
(b) in the case of any person, where the former name—
(i) was changed or disused before the person attained the age of 16 years, or
(ii) has been changed or disused for 20 years or more.

(5) A person's service address may be stated to be "The LLP's registered office".

164. Particulars of members to be registered: corporate members and firms

An LLP's register of members must contain the following particulars in the case of a body corporate, or a firm that is a legal person under the law by which it is governed—
(a) corporate or firm name;
(b) registered or principal office;
(c) in the case of an EEA company to which the First Company Law Directive (68/151/EEC) applies, particulars of—
(i) the register in which the company file mentioned in Article 3 of that Directive is kept (including details of the relevant state), and
(ii) the registration number in that register;
(d) in any other case, particulars of—
(i) the legal form of the company or firm and the law by which it is governed, and
(ii) if applicable, the register in which it is entered (including details of the state) and its registration number in that register;
(e) whether it is a designated member.

165. Register of members' residential addresses

(1) Every LLP must keep a register of members' residential addresses.

(2) The register must state the usual residential address of each of the LLP's members.

(3) If a member's usual residential address is the same as his service address (as stated in the LLP's register of members), the register of members' residential addresses need only contain an entry to that effect.
This does not apply if his service address is stated to be "The LLP's registered office".

(4) If default is made in complying with this section, an offence is committed by—
(a) the LLP, and
(b) every designated member of the LLP who is in default.

(5) A person guilty of an offence under this section is liable on summary conviction to a fine not exceeding level 5 on the standard scale and, for continued contravention, a daily default fine not exceeding one-tenth of level 5 on the standard scale.

(6) This section applies only to members who are individuals, not where the member is a body corporate or a firm that is a legal person under the law by which it is governed.".

CHAPTER 2
MEMBERS' RESIDENTIAL ADDRESSES: PROTECTION FROM DISCLOSURE

Members' residential addresses: protection from disclosure

19.

Sections 240 to 246 apply to LLPs, modified so that they read as follows—

"240. Protected information

(1) This Chapter makes provision for protecting, in the case of an LLP member who is an individual—
   (a) information as to his usual residential address;
   (b) the information that his service address is his usual residential address.

(2) That information is referred to in this Chapter as "protected information".

(3) Information does not cease to be protected information on the individual ceasing to be a member of the LLP.

References in this Chapter to a member include, to that extent, a former member.

241. Protected information: restriction on use or disclosure by LLP

(1) An LLP must not use or disclose protected information about any of its members, except—
   (a) for communicating with the member concerned,
   (b) in order to comply with any requirement of this Act or of the Limited Liability Partnerships Act 2000 (c 12) as to particulars to be sent to the registrar, or
   (c) in accordance with section 244 (disclosure under court order).

(2) Subsection (1) does not prohibit any use or disclosure of protected information with the consent of the member concerned.

242. Protected information: restriction on use or disclosure by registrar

(1) The registrar must omit protected information from the material on the register that is available for inspection where—
   (a) it is contained in a document delivered to him in which such information is required to be stated, and
   (b) in the case of a document having more than one part, it is contained in a part of the document in which such information is required to be stated.

(2) The registrar is not obliged—
   (a) to check other documents or (as the case may be) other parts of the document to ensure the absence of protected information, or
   (b) to omit from the material that is available for public inspection anything registered before 1st October 2009.

(3) The registrar must not use or disclose protected information except—
   (a) as permitted by section 243 (permitted use or disclosure by registrar), or
   (b) in accordance with section 244 (disclosure under court order).

243. Permitted use or disclosure by the registrar

(1) The registrar may use protected information for communicating with the member in question.

(2) The registrar may disclose protected information—
   (a) to a public authority specified for the purposes of this section, or
   (b) to a credit reference agency.

(3) The provisions of the Companies (Disclosure of Address) Regulations 2009 (SI 2009/214) relating to disclosure of protected information under this section apply to LLPs.

(4) The provisions are—
   (a) Part 2 (disclosure of protected information),
   (b) Part 4 (matters relating to applications), so far as relating to disclosure under this section, and
   (c) any other provisions of the Regulations having effect for the purposes of those provisions.

(5) As those provisions apply to LLPs—

(a) references to provisions of the Companies Act 1985 (c 6), the Insolvency Act 1986 (c 45), the Companies (Northern Ireland) Order 1986 (SI 1986/1032 (NI 6)) or the Insolvency (Northern Ireland) Order 1989 (SI 1989/2405 (NI 9)) are to those provisions as applied to LLPs by the Limited Liability Partnerships Regulations 2001 (SI 2001/1090) or the Limited Liability Partnerships Regulations (Northern Ireland) 2004 (SR (NI) 2004 No 307);

(b) read references to a company or proposed company as references to an LLP or proposed LLP;

(c) read references to a director as references to a member of an LLP;

(d) read references to a subscriber to a memorandum of association as references to a proposed member of a proposed LLP;

(e) in regulation 1(2), for the definition of "former name" substitute—

""former name" means a name by which an individual was formerly known and which has been notified to the registrar under section 2 or 9 of the Limited Liability Partnerships Act 2000;".

(6) In this section—

"credit reference agency" means a person carrying on a business comprising the furnishing of information relevant to the financial standing of individuals, being information collected by the agency for that purpose; and

"public authority" includes any person or body having functions of a public nature.

244. Disclosure under court order

(1) The court may make an order for the disclosure of protected information by the LLP or by the registrar if—

(a) there is evidence that service of documents at a service address other than the member's usual residential address is not effective to bring them to the notice of the member, or

(b) it is necessary or expedient for the information to be provided in connection with the enforcement of an order or decree of the court,

and the court is otherwise satisfied that it is appropriate to make the order.

(2) An order for disclosure by the registrar is to be made only if the LLP—

(a) does not have the member's usual residential address, or

(b) has been dissolved.

(3) The order may be made on the application of a liquidator, creditor or member of the LLP, or any other person appearing to the court to have a sufficient interest.

(4) The order must specify the persons to whom, and purposes for which, disclosure is authorised.

245. Circumstances in which registrar may put address on the public record

(1) The registrar may put a member's usual residential address on the public record if—

(a) communications sent by the registrar to the member and requiring a response within a specified period remain unanswered, or

(b) there is evidence that service of documents at a service address provided in place of the member's usual residential address is not effective to bring them to the notice of the member.

(2) The registrar must give notice of the proposal—

(a) to the member, and

(b) to every LLP of which the registrar has been notified that the individual is a member.

(3) The notice must—

(a) state the grounds on which it is proposed to put the member's usual residential address on the public record, and

(b) specify a period within which representations may be made before that is done.

(4) It must be sent to the member at his usual residential address, unless it appears to the registrar that service at that address may be ineffective to bring it to the individual's notice, in which case it may be sent to any service address provided in place of that address.

(5) The registrar must take account of any representations received within the specified period.

(6) What is meant by putting the address on the public record is explained in section 246.

246. Putting the address on the public record

(1) The registrar, on deciding in accordance with section 245 that a member's usual residential address is to be put on the public record, shall proceed as if notice of a change of registered particulars had been given—

(a) stating that address as the member's service address, and

(b) stating that the member's usual residential address is the same as his service address.

(2) The registrar must give notice of having done so—

(a) to the member, and

(b) to the LLP.

(3) On receipt of the notice the LLP must—

(a) enter the member's usual residential address in its register of members as his service address, and

(b) state in its register of members' residential addresses that his usual residential address is the same as his service address.

(4) If the LLP has been notified by the member in question of a more recent address as his usual residential address, it must—

(a) enter that address in its register of members as the member's service address, and

(b) give notice to the registrar as on a change of registered particulars.

(5) If an LLP fails to comply with subsection (3) or (4), an offence is committed by—

(a) the LLP, and

(b) every designated member of the LLP who is in default.

(6) A person guilty of an offence under subsection (5) is liable on summary conviction to a fine not exceeding level 5 on the standard scale and, for continued contravention, a daily default fine not exceeding one-tenth of level 5 on the standard scale.

(7) A member whose usual residential address has been put on the public record by the registrar under this section may not register a service address other than his usual residential address for a period of five years from the date of the registrar's decision.".

PART 6
DEBENTURES

General provisions

20.

Sections 738 to 742 apply to LLPs, modified so that they read as follows—

"738. Meaning of "debenture"

In this Act "debenture" includes debenture stock, bonds and any other securities of an LLP, whether or not constituting a charge on the assets of the LLP.

739. Perpetual debentures

(1) A condition contained in debentures, or in a deed for securing debentures, is not invalid by reason only that the debentures are made—

(a) irredeemable, or

(b) redeemable only—

(i) on the happening of a contingency (however remote), or

(ii) on the expiration of a period (however long),

any rule of equity to the contrary notwithstanding.

(2) Subsection (1) applies to debentures whenever issued and to deeds whenever executed.

740. Enforcement of contract to subscribe for debentures

A contract with an LLP to take up and pay for debentures of the LLP may be enforced by an order for specific performance.

741. Registration of allotment of debentures

(1) An LLP must register an allotment of debentures as soon as practicable and in any event within two months after the date of the allotment.

(2) If an LLP fails to comply with this section, an offence is committed by—
  (a) the LLP, and
  (b) every member of the LLP who is in default.

(3) A person guilty of an offence under this section is liable on summary conviction to a fine not exceeding level 3 on the standard scale and, for continued contravention, a daily default fine not exceeding one-tenth of level 3 on the standard scale.

(4) For the duties of the LLP as to the issue of the debentures, or certificates of debenture stock, see Part 21 (certification and transfer of securities).

742. Debentures to bearer (Scotland)

Notwithstanding anything in the statute of the Scots Parliament of 1696, chapter 25, debentures to bearer issued in Scotland are valid and binding according to their terms.".

21.

Sections 743 to 748 apply to LLPs, modified so that they read as follows—

"743. Register of debenture holders

(1) Any register of debenture holders of an LLP that is kept by the LLP must be kept available for inspection—
  (a) at the LLP's registered office, or
  (b) at a place specified in Part 2 of the Companies (Company Records) Regulations 2008 (SI 2008/3006).

(2) An LLP must give notice to the registrar of the place where any such register is kept available for inspection and of any change in that place.

(3) No such notice is required if the register has, at all times since it came into existence, been kept available for inspection at the LLP's registered office.

(4) If an LLP makes default for 14 days in complying with subsection (2), an offence is committed by—
  (a) the LLP, and
  (b) every member of the LLP who is in default.

(5) A person guilty of an offence under this section is liable on summary conviction to a fine not exceeding level 3 on the standard scale and, for continued contravention, a daily default fine not exceeding one-tenth of level 3 on the standard scale.

(6) References in this section to a register of debenture holders include a duplicate—
  (a) of a register of debenture holders that is kept outside the United Kingdom, or
  (b) of any part of such a register.

744. Register of debenture holders: right to inspect and require copy

(1) Every register of debenture holders of an LLP must, except when duly closed, be open to the inspection—
  (a) of the registered holder of any such debentures, or any member of the LLP, without charge, and
  (b) of any other person on payment of the fee prescribed by regulation 2 of the Companies (Fees for Inspection and Copying of Company Records) (No 2) Regulations 2007 (SI 2007/3535).

(2) Any person may require a copy of the register, or any part of it, on payment of the fee prescribed by regulation 3 of the Companies (Fees for Inspection and Copying of Company Records) (No 2) Regulations 2007 (SI 2007/3535).

(3) A person seeking to exercise either of the rights conferred by this section must make a request to the LLP to that effect.

(4) The request must contain the following information—
(a) in the case of an individual, his name and address;
(b) in the case of an organisation, the name and address of an individual responsible for making the request on behalf of the organisation;
(c) the purpose for which the information is to be used; and
(d) whether the information will be disclosed to any other person, and if so—
(i) where that person is an individual, his name and address,
(ii) where that person is an organisation, the name and address of an individual responsible for receiving the information on its behalf, and
(iii) the purpose for which the information is to be used by that person.

(5) For the purposes of this section a register is "duly closed" if it is closed in accordance with provision contained—
(a) in the debentures,
(b) in the case of debenture stock in the stock certificates, or
(c) in the trust deed or other document securing the debentures or debenture stock.
The total period for which a register is closed in any year must not exceed 30 days.

(6) References in this section to a register of debenture holders include a duplicate—
(a) of a register of debenture holders that is kept outside the United Kingdom, or
(b) of any part of such a register.

745. Register of debenture holders: response to request for inspection or copy

(1) Where an LLP receives a request under section 744 (register of debenture holders: right to inspect and require copy), it must within five working days either—
(a) comply with the request, or
(b) apply to the court.

(2) If it applies to the court it must notify the person making the request.

(3) If on an application under this section the court is satisfied that the inspection or copy is not sought for a proper purpose—
(a) it shall direct the LLP not to comply with the request, and
(b) it may further order that the LLP's costs (in Scotland, expenses) on the application be paid in whole or in part by the person who made the request, even if he is not a party to the application.

(4) If the court makes such a direction and it appears to the court that the LLP is or may be subject to other requests made for a similar purpose (whether made by the same person or different persons), it may direct that the LLP is not to comply with any such request.
The order must contain such provision as appears to the court appropriate to identify the requests to which it applies.

(5) If on an application under this section the court does not direct the LLP not to comply with the request, the LLP must comply with the request immediately upon the court giving its decision or, as the case may be, the proceedings being discontinued.

746. Register of debenture holders: refusal of inspection or default in providing copy

(1) If an inspection required under section 744 (register of debenture holders: right to inspect and require copy) is refused or default is made in providing a copy required under that section, otherwise than in accordance with an order of the court, an offence is committed by—
(a) the LLP, and
(b) every member of the LLP who is in default.

(2) A person guilty of an offence under this section is liable on summary conviction to a fine not exceeding level 3 on the standard scale and, for continued contravention, a daily default fine not exceeding one-tenth of level 3 on the standard scale.

(3) In the case of any such refusal or default the court may by order compel an immediate inspection or, as the case may be, direct that the copy required be sent to the person requesting it.

747. Register of debenture holders: offences in connection with request for or disclosure of information

(1) It is an offence for a person knowingly or recklessly to make in a request under section 744 (register of debenture holders: right to inspect and require copy) a statement that is misleading, false or deceptive in a material particular.

(2) It is an offence for a person in possession of information obtained by exercise of either of the rights conferred by that section—

(a) to do anything that results in the information being disclosed to another person, or

(b) to fail to do anything with the result that the information is disclosed to another person,

knowing, or having reason to suspect, that person may use the information for a purpose that is not a proper purpose.

(3) A person guilty of an offence under this section is liable—

(a) on conviction on indictment, to imprisonment for a term not exceeding two years or a fine (or both);

(b) on summary conviction—

(i) in England and Wales or Scotland, to imprisonment for a term not exceeding twelve months or to a fine not exceeding the statutory maximum (or both);

(ii) in Northern Ireland, to imprisonment for a term not exceeding six months, or to a fine not exceeding the statutory maximum (or both).

748. Time limit for claims arising from entry in register

(1) Liability incurred by an LLP—

(a) from the making or deletion of an entry in the register of debenture holders, or

(b) from a failure to make or delete any such entry,

is not enforceable more than ten years after the date on which the entry was made or deleted or, as the case may be, the failure first occurred.

(2) This is without prejudice to any lesser period of limitation (and, in Scotland, to any rule that the obligation giving rise to the liability prescribes before the expiry of that period).".

Supplementary provisions

22.

Sections 749 and 750 apply to LLPs, modified so that they read as follows—

"749. Right of debenture holder to copy of deed

(1) Any holder of debentures of an LLP is entitled, on request and on payment of the fee prescribed by regulation 4 of the Companies (Fees for Inspection and Copying of Company Records) (No 2) Regulations 2007 (SI 2007/3535), to be provided with a copy of any trust deed for securing the debentures.

(2) If default is made in complying with this section, an offence is committed by every member of the LLP who is in default.

(3) A person guilty of an offence under this section is liable on summary conviction to a fine not exceeding level 3 on the standard scale and, for continued contravention, a daily default fine not exceeding one-tenth of level 3 on the standard scale.

(4) In the case of any such default the court may direct that the copy required be sent to the person requiring it.

750. Liability of trustees of debentures

(1) Any provision contained in—

(a) a trust deed for securing an issue of debentures, or

(b) any contract with the holders of debentures secured by a trust deed,

is void in so far as it would have the effect of exempting a trustee of the deed from, or indemnifying him against, liability for breach of trust where he fails to show the degree of care and diligence required of him as trustee, having regard to the provisions of the trust deed conferring on him any powers, authorities or discretions.

(2) Subsection (1) does not invalidate—
  (a) a release otherwise validly given in respect of anything done or omitted to be done by a trustee before the giving of the release;
  (b) any provision enabling such a release to be given—
    (i) on being agreed to by a majority of not less than 75% in value of the debenture holders present and voting in person or, where proxies are permitted, by proxy at a meeting summoned for the purpose, and
    (ii) either with respect to specific acts or omissions or on the trustee dying or ceasing to act.".

23.

Sections 752 to 754 apply to LLPs, modified so that they read as follows—

"752. Power to re-issue redeemed debentures

(1) Where an LLP has redeemed debentures previously issued, then unless—
  (a) provision to the contrary (express or implied) is contained in any contract made by the LLP, or
  (b) the LLP has, by making a determination to that effect or by some other act, manifested its intention that the debentures shall be cancelled,

the LLP may re-issue the debentures, either by re-issuing the same debentures or by issuing new debentures in their place.

This subsection is deemed always to have had effect.

(2) On a re-issue of redeemed debentures the person entitled to the debentures has (and is deemed always to have had) the same priorities as if the debentures had never been redeemed.

(3) The re-issue of a debenture or the issue of another debenture in its place under this section is treated as the issue of a new debenture for the purposes of stamp duty.

It is not so treated for the purposes of any provision limiting the amount or number of debentures to be issued.

(4) A person lending money on the security of a debenture re-issued under this section which appears to be duly stamped may give the debenture in evidence in any proceedings for enforcing his security without payment of the stamp duty or any penalty in respect of it, unless he had notice (or, but for his negligence, might have discovered) that the debenture was not duly stamped.

In that case the LLP is liable to pay the proper stamp duty and penalty.

753. Deposit of debentures to secure advances

Where an LLP has deposited any of its debentures to secure advances from time to time on current account or otherwise, the debentures are not treated as redeemed by reason only of the LLP's account having ceased to be in debit while the debentures remained so deposited.

754. Priorities where debentures secured by floating charge

(1) This section applies where debentures of an LLP registered in England and Wales or Northern Ireland are secured by a charge that, as created, was a floating charge.

(2) If possession is taken, by or on behalf of the holders of the debentures, of any property comprised in or subject to the charge, and the LLP is not at that time in the course of being wound up, the LLP's preferential debts shall be paid out of assets coming to the hands of the persons taking possession in priority to any claims for principal or interest in respect of the debentures.

(3) "Preferential debts" means the categories of debts listed in Schedule 6 to the Insolvency Act 1986 (c 45) or Schedule 4 to the Insolvency (Northern Ireland) Order 1989 (SI 1989/2405 (NI 19)).

For the purposes of those Schedules "the relevant date" is the date of possession being taken as mentioned in subsection (2).

(4) Payments under this section shall be recouped, as far as may be, out of the assets of the LLP available for payment of general creditors.".

PART 7
CERTIFICATION AND TRANSFER OF DEBENTURES

Issue of certificates etc on allotment

24.

Section 769 applies to LLPs, modified so that it reads as follows—

"769. Duty of LLP as to issue of certificates etc on allotment

(1) An LLP must, within two months after the allotment of any of its debentures or debenture stock, complete and have ready for delivery—

(a) the debentures allotted, or

(b) the certificates of the debenture stock allotted.

(2) Subsection (1) does not apply—

(a) if the conditions of issue of the debentures or debenture stock provide otherwise, or

(b) in the case of allotment to a financial institution (see section 778).

(3) If default is made in complying with subsection (1) an offence is committed by every member of the LLP who is in default.

(4) A person guilty of an offence under subsection (3) is liable on summary conviction to a fine not exceeding level 3 on the standard scale and, for continued contravention, a daily default fine not exceeding one-tenth of level 3 on the standard scale.".

Transfer of debentures

25

Sections 770 and 771 apply to LLPs, modified so that they read as follows—

"770. Registration of transfer

(1) An LLP may not register a transfer of debentures of the LLP unless—

(a) a proper instrument of transfer has been delivered to it, or

(b) the transfer is an exempt transfer within the Stock Transfer Act 1982 (c 41).

(2) Subsection (1) does not affect any power of the LLP to register as debenture holder a person to whom the right to any debentures of the LLP has been transmitted by operation of law.

771. Procedure on transfer being lodged

(1) When a transfer of debentures of an LLP has been lodged with the LLP, the LLP must either—

(a) register the transfer, or

(b) give the transferee notice of refusal to register the transfer, together with its reasons for the refusal,

as soon as practicable and in any event within two months after the date on which the transfer is lodged with it.

(2) If the LLP refuses to register the transfer, it must provide the transferee with such further information about the reasons for the refusal as the transferee may reasonably request. This does not include copies of minutes of meetings of members.

(3) If an LLP fails to comply with this section, an offence is committed by—

(a) the LLP, and

(b) every member of the LLP who is in default.

(4) A person guilty of an offence under this section is liable on summary conviction to a fine not exceeding level 3 on the standard scale and, for continued contravention, a daily default fine not exceeding one-tenth of level 3 on the standard scale.

(5) This section does not apply in relation to the transmission of debentures by operation of law.".

26.

Sections 774 and 775 apply to LLPs, modified so that they read as follows—

"774. Evidence of grant of probate etc

The production to an LLP of any document that is by law sufficient evidence of the grant of—

(a) probate of the will of a deceased person,

(b) letters of administration of the estate of a deceased person, or

(c) confirmation as executor of a deceased person,

shall be accepted by the LLP as sufficient evidence of the grant.

775. Certification of instrument of transfer

(1) The certification by an LLP of an instrument of transfer of any debentures of the LLP is to be taken as a representation by the LLP to any person acting on the faith of the certification that there have been produced to the LLP such documents as on their face show a prima facie title to the debentures in the transferor named in the instrument.

(2) The certification is not to be taken as a representation that the transferor has any title to the debentures.

(3) Where a person acts on the faith of a false certification by an LLP made negligently, the LLP is under the same liability to him as if the certification had been made fraudulently.

(4) For the purposes of this section—

(a) an instrument of transfer is certificated if it bears the words "certificate lodged" (or words to the like effect);

(b) the certification of an instrument of transfer is made by an LLP if—

(i) the person issuing the instrument is a person authorised to issue certificated instruments of transfer on the LLP's behalf, and

(ii) the certification is signed by a person authorised to certificate transfers on the LLP's behalf or by a member or employee of the LLP or by an officer or employee of a body corporate so authorised;

(c) a certification is treated as signed by a person if—

(i) it purports to be authenticated by his signature or initials (whether handwritten or not), and

(ii) it is not shown that the signature or initials was or were placed there neither by himself nor by a person authorised to use the signature or initials for the purpose of certificating transfers on the LLP's behalf.".

Issue of certificates etc on transfer

27.

Section 776 applies to LLPs, modified so that it reads as follows—

"776. Duty of LLP as to issue of certificates etc on transfer

(1) An LLP must, within two months after the date on which a transfer of any of its debentures or debenture stock is lodged with the LLP, complete and have ready for delivery—

(a) the debentures transferred, or

(b) the certificates of the debenture stock transferred.

(2) For this purpose a "transfer" means—

(a) a transfer duly stamped and otherwise valid, or

(b) an exempt transfer within the Stock Transfer Act 1982 (c 41),

but does not include a transfer that the LLP is for any reason entitled to refuse to register and does not register.

(3) Subsection (1) does not apply—

(a) if the conditions of issue of the debentures or debenture stock provide otherwise, or

(b) in the case of a transfer to a financial institution (see section 778).

(4) If default is made in complying with subsection (1) an offence is committed by every member of the LLP who is in default.

(5) A person guilty of an offence under this section is liable on summary conviction to a fine not exceeding level 3 on the standard scale and, for continued contravention, a daily default fine not exceeding one-tenth of level 3 on the standard scale.".

Issue of certificates etc on allotment or transfer to financial institution

28.

Section 778 applies to LLPs, modified so that it reads as follows—

"778. Issue of certificates etc: allotment or transfer to financial institution

(1) An LLP—

(a) of which debentures are allotted to a financial institution,

(b) of which debenture stock is allotted to a financial institution, or

(c) with which a transfer for transferring debentures or debenture stock to a financial institution is lodged,

is not required in consequence of that allotment or transfer to comply with section 769(1) or 776(1) (duty of LLP as to issue of certificates etc).

(2) A "financial institution" means—

(a) a recognised clearing house acting in relation to a recognised investment exchange, or

(b) a nominee of—

(i) a recognised clearing house acting in that way, or

(ii) a recognised investment exchange,

designated for the purposes of this section in the rules of the recognised investment exchange in question.

(3) Expressions used in subsection (2) have the same meaning as in Part 18 of the Financial Services and Markets Act 2000 (c 8).".

Supplementary provisions

29.

Section 782 is applied to LLPs, modified so that it reads as follows—

"782. Issue of certificates etc: court order to make good default

(1) If an LLP on which a notice has been served requiring it to make good any default in complying with—

(a) section 769(1) (duty of LLP as to issue of certificates etc on allotment), or

(b) section 776(1) (duty of LLP as to issue of certificates etc on transfer),

fails to make good the default within ten days after service of the notice, the person entitled to have the certificates or the debentures delivered to him may apply to the court.

(2) The court may on such an application make an order directing the LLP and any member of it to make good the default within such time as may be specified in the order.

(3) The order may provide that all costs (in Scotland, expenses) of and incidental to the application are to be borne by the LLP or by a member of it responsible for the default.".

PART 8
AN LLP'S ANNUAL RETURN

Contents and delivery of LLP's annual return

30.

Sections 854, 855 and 855A apply to LLPs, modified so that they read as follows—

"854. Duty to deliver annual returns

(1) Every LLP must deliver to the registrar successive annual returns each of which is made up to a date not later than the date that is from time to time the LLP's return date.

(2) The LLP's return date is—

(a) the anniversary of the LLP's incorporation, or

(b) if the LLP's last return delivered in accordance with this Part was made up to a different date, the anniversary of that date.

(3) Each return must—

(a) contain the information required by or under the following provisions of this Part, and

(b) be delivered to the registrar within 28 days after the date to which it is made up.

855. Contents of annual return: general

(1) Every annual return must state the date to which it is made up and contain the following information—

(a) the address of the LLP's registered office;

(b) the required particulars of the members of the LLP (see section 855A);

(c) if any LLP records are kept at a place other than the LLP's registered office, the address of that place and the records that are kept there.

(2) In this Part, "return period", in relation to an annual return, means the period beginning immediately after the date to which the last return was made up (or, in the case of the first return, with the incorporation of the LLP) and ending with the date to which the return is made up.

855A. Required particulars of members

(1) For the purposes of section 855(1)(b) the required particulars of a member are—

(a) where the member is an individual, the particulars required by section 163 to be entered in the register of members (subject to subsection (2) below); and

(b) where the member is a body corporate or a firm that is a legal person under the law by which it is governed, the particulars required by section 164 to be entered in the register of members.

(2) The former name of a member who is an individual is a required particular in relation to an annual return only if the member was known by the name for business purposes during the return period.".

31.

Section 858 applies to LLPs, modified so that it reads as follows—

"858. Failure to deliver annual return

(1) If an LLP fails to deliver an annual return before the end of the period of 28 days after a return date, an offence is committed by—

(a) the LLP, and

(b) subject to subsection (4), every designated member of the LLP.

(2) A person guilty of an offence under subsection (1) is liable on summary conviction to a fine not exceeding level 5 on the standard scale and, for continued contravention, a daily default fine not exceeding one-tenth of level 5 on the standard scale.

(3) The contravention continues until such time as an annual return made up to that return date is delivered by the LLP to the registrar.

(4) It is a defence for a designated member charged with an offence under subsection (1)(b) to prove that he took all reasonable steps to avoid the commission or continuation of the offence.

(5) In the case of continued contravention, an offence is also committed by every designated member of the LLP who did not commit an offence under subsection (1) in relation to the initial contravention but is in default in relation to the continued contravention.

A person guilty of an offence under this subsection is liable on summary conviction to a fine not exceeding one-tenth of level 5 on the standard scale for each day on which the contravention continues and he is in default.".

PART 9
LLP CHARGES

CHAPTER 1
LLPS REGISTERED IN ENGLAND AND WALES OR IN NORTHERN IRELAND

Requirement to register LLP charges

32.

Sections 860 to 862 apply to LLPs, modified so that they read as follows—

"860. Charges created by an LLP

(1) An LLP that creates a charge to which this section applies must deliver the required particulars of the charge, together with the instrument (if any) by which the charge is created or evidenced, to the registrar for registration before the end of the period allowed for registration.

(2) The required particulars are those prescribed by regulation 2 of the Companies (Particulars of Company Charges) Regulations 2008 (SI 2008/2996).

(3) Registration of a charge to which this section applies may instead be effected on the application of a person interested in it.

(4) Where registration is effected on the application of some person other than the LLP, that person is entitled to recover from the LLP the amount of any fees properly paid by him to the registrar on registration.

(5) If an LLP fails to comply with subsection (1), an offence is committed by—

(a) the LLP, and

(b) every member of it who is in default.

(6) A person guilty of an offence under this section is liable—

(a) on conviction on indictment, to a fine;

(b) on summary conviction, to a fine not exceeding the statutory maximum.

(7) Subsection (5) does not apply if registration of the charge has been effected on the application of some other person.

(8) This section applies to the following charges—

(a) a charge on land or any interest in land, other than a charge for any rent or other periodical sum issuing out of land,

(b) a charge created or evidenced by an instrument which, if executed by an individual, would require registration as a bill of sale,

(c) a charge for the purposes of securing any issue of debentures,

(d) a charge on book debts of the LLP,

(e) a floating charge on the LLP's property or undertaking,

(f) a charge on a ship or aircraft, or any share in a ship,

(g) a charge on goodwill or on any intellectual property.

861. Charges which have to be registered: supplementary

(1) The holding of debentures entitling the holder to a charge on land is not, for the purposes of section 860(8)(a), an interest in the land.

(2) It is immaterial for the purposes of this Chapter where land subject to a charge is situated.

(3) The deposit by way of security of a negotiable instrument given to secure the payment of book debts is not, for the purposes of section 860(8)(d), a charge on those book debts.

(4) For the purposes of section 860(8)(g), "intellectual property" means—

(a) any patent, trade mark, registered design, copyright or design right;

(b) any licence under or in respect of any such right.

(5) In this Chapter—

"charge" includes mortgage, and

"LLP" means an LLP registered in England and Wales or in Northern Ireland.

862. Charges existing on property acquired

(1) This section applies where an LLP acquires property which is subject to a charge of a kind which would, if it had been created by the LLP after the acquisition of the property, have been required to be registered under this Chapter.

(2) The LLP must deliver the required particulars of the charge, together with a certified copy of the instrument (if any) by which the charge is created or evidenced, to the registrar for registration.

(3) The required particulars are those prescribed by regulation 4 of the Companies (Particulars of Company Charges) Regulations 2008 (SI 2008/2996).

(4) Subsection (2) must be complied with before the end of the period allowed for registration.

(5) If default is made in complying with this section, an offence is committed by—
   (a) the LLP, and
   (b) every member of it who is in default.
(6) A person guilty of an offence under this section is liable—
   (a) on conviction on indictment, to a fine;
   (b) on summary conviction, to a fine not exceeding the statutory maximum.".

Special rules about debentures

33.

Sections 863 to 865 apply to LLPs, modified so that they read as follows—

"863. Charge in series of debentures

(1) Where a series of debentures containing, or giving by reference to another instrument, any charge to the benefit of which debenture holders of that series are entitled pari passu is created by an LLP, it is for the purposes of section 860(1) sufficient if the required particulars, together with the deed containing the charge (or, if there is no such deed, one of the debentures of the series), are delivered to the registrar before the end of the period allowed for registration.
(2) The following are the required particulars—
   (a) the total amount secured by the whole series, and
   (b) the dates of the determinations of the LLP authorising the issue of the series and the date of the covering deed (if any) by which the series is created or defined, and
   (c) a general description of the property charged, and
   (d) the names of the trustees (if any) for the debenture holders.
(3) Particulars of the date and amount of each issue of debentures of a series of the kind mentioned in subsection (1) must be sent to the registrar for entry in the register of charges.
(4) Failure to comply with subsection (3) does not affect the validity of the debentures issued.
(5) Subsections (3) to (7) of section 860 apply for the purposes of this section as they apply for the purposes of that section, but as if references to the registration of a charge were references to the registration of a series of debentures.

864. Additional registration requirement for commission etc in relation to debentures

(1) Where any commission, allowance or discount has been paid or made either directly or indirectly by an LLP to a person in consideration of his—
   (a) subscribing or agreeing to subscribe, whether absolutely or conditionally, for debentures in an LLP, or
   (b) procuring or agreeing to procure subscriptions, whether absolute or conditional, for such debentures, the particulars required to be sent for registration under section 860 shall include particulars as to the amount or rate per cent. of the commission, discount or allowance so paid or made.
(2) The deposit of debentures as security for a debt of the LLP is not, for the purposes of this section, treated as the issue of debentures at a discount.
(3) Failure to comply with this section does not affect the validity of the debentures issued.

865. Endorsement of certificate on debentures

(1) The LLP shall cause a copy of every certificate of registration given under section 869 to be endorsed on every debenture or certificate of debenture stock which is issued by the LLP, and the payment of which is secured by the charge so registered.
(2) But this does not require an LLP to cause a certificate of registration of any charge so given to be endorsed on any debenture or certificate of debenture stock issued by the LLP before the charge was created.
(3) If a person knowingly and wilfully authorises or permits the delivery of a debenture or certificate of debenture stock which under this section is required to have endorsed on it a copy of a certificate of registration, without the copy being so endorsed upon it, he commits an offence.

(4) A person guilty of an offence under this section is liable on summary conviction to a fine not exceeding level 3 on the standard scale.".

Charges in other jurisdictions

34.

Sections 866 and 867 apply to LLPs, modified so that they read as follows—

"866. Charges created in, or over property in, jurisdictions outside the United Kingdom

(1) Where a charge is created outside the United Kingdom comprising property situated outside the United Kingdom, the delivery to the registrar of a verified copy of the instrument by which the charge is created or evidenced has the same effect for the purposes of this Chapter as the delivery of the instrument itself.

(2) Where a charge is created in the United Kingdom but comprises property outside the United Kingdom, the instrument creating or purporting to create the charge may be sent for registration under section 860 even if further proceedings may be necessary to make the charge valid or effectual according to the law of the country in which the property is situated.

867. Charges created in, or over property in, another United Kingdom jurisdiction

(1) Subsection (2) applies where—

(a) a charge comprises property situated in a part of the United Kingdom other than the part in which the LLP is registered, and

(b) registration in that other part is necessary to make the charge valid or effectual under the law of that part of the United Kingdom.

(2) The delivery to the registrar of a verified copy of the instrument by which the charge is created or evidenced, together with a certificate stating that the charge was presented for registration in that other part of the United Kingdom on the date on which it was so presented has, for the purposes of this Chapter, the same effect as the delivery of the instrument itself.".

Orders charging land: Northern Ireland

35.

Section 868 applies to LLPs, modified so that it reads as follows—

"868. Northern Ireland: registration of certain charges etc affecting land

(1) Where a charge imposed by an order under Article 46 of the 1981 Order or notice of such a charge is registered in the Land Registry against registered land or any estate in registered land of an LLP, the Registrar of Titles shall as soon as may be cause two copies of the order made under Article 46 of that Order or of any notice under Article 48 of that Order to be delivered to the registrar.

(2) Where a charge imposed by an order under Article 46 of the 1981 Order is registered in the Registry of Deeds against any unregistered land or estate in land of an LLP, the Registrar of Deeds shall as soon as may be cause two copies of the order to be delivered to the registrar.

(3) On delivery of copies under this section, the registrar shall—

(a) register one of them in accordance with section 869, and

(b) not later than 7 days from that date of delivery, cause the other copy together with a certificate of registration under section 869(5) to be sent to the LLP against which judgment was given.

(4) Where a charge to which subsection (1) or (2) applies is vacated, the Registrar of Titles or, as the case may be, the Registrar of Deeds shall cause a certified copy of the certificate of satisfaction lodged under Article 132(1) of the 1981 Order to be delivered to the registrar for entry of a memorandum of satisfaction in accordance with section 872.

(5) In this section—

"the 1981 Order" means the Judgments Enforcement (Northern Ireland) Order 1981 (SI 1981/226 (NI 6));

"the Registrar of Deeds" means the registrar appointed under the Registration of Deeds Act (Northern Ireland) 1970 (c 25);

"Registry of Deeds" has the same meaning as in the Registration of Deeds Acts;

"Registration of Deeds Acts" means the Registration of Deeds Act (Northern Ireland) 1970 and every statutory provision for the time being in force amending that Act or otherwise relating to the registry of deeds, or the registration of deeds, orders or other instruments or documents in such registry;

"the Land Registry" and "the Registrar of Titles" are to be construed in accordance with section 1 of the Land Registration Act (Northern Ireland) 1970 (c 18);

"registered land" and "unregistered land" have the same meaning as in Part 3 of the Land Registration Act (Northern Ireland) 1970.".

The register of charges

36.

Sections 869 to 873 apply to LLPs, modified so that they read as follows—

"869. Register of charges to be kept by registrar

(1) The registrar shall keep, with respect to each LLP, a register of all the charges requiring registration under this Chapter.

(2) In the case of a charge to the benefit of which holders of a series of debentures are entitled, the registrar shall enter in the register the required particulars specified in section 863(2).

(3) In the case of a charge imposed by the Enforcement of Judgments Office under Article 46 of the Judgments Enforcement (Northern Ireland) Order 1981, the registrar shall enter in the register the date on which the charge became effective.

(4) In the case of any other charge, the registrar shall enter in the register the following particulars—

(a) if it is a charge created by an LLP, the date of its creation and, if it is a charge which was existing on property acquired by the LLP, the date of the acquisition,

(b) the amount secured by the charge,

(c) short particulars of the property charged, and

(d) the persons entitled to the charge.

(5) The registrar shall give a certificate of the registration of any charge registered in pursuance of this Chapter, stating the amount secured by the charge.

(6) The certificate—

(a) shall be signed by the registrar or authenticated by the registrar's official seal, and

(b) is conclusive evidence that the requirements of this Chapter as to registration have been satisfied.

(7) The register kept in pursuance of this section shall be open to inspection by any person.

870. The period allowed for registration

(1) The period allowed for registration of a charge created by an LLP is—

(a) 21 days beginning with the day after the day on which the charge is created, or

(b) if the charge is created outside the United Kingdom, 21 days beginning with the day after the day on which the instrument by which the charge is created or evidenced (or a copy of it) could, in due course of post (and if despatched with due diligence) have been received in the United Kingdom.

(2) The period allowed for registration of a charge to which property acquired by an LLP is subject is—

(a) 21 days beginning with the day after the day on which the acquisition is completed, or

(b) if the property is situated and the charge was created outside the United Kingdom, 21 days beginning with the day after the day on which the instrument by which the charge is created or evidenced (or a copy of it) could, in due course of post (and if despatched with due diligence) have been received in the United Kingdom.

(3) The period allowed for registration of particulars of a series of debentures as a result of section 863 is—

(a) if there is a deed containing the charge mentioned in section 863(1), 21 days beginning with the day after the day on which that deed is executed, or

(b) if there is no such deed, 21 days beginning with the day after the day on which the first debenture of the series is executed.

871. Registration of enforcement of security

(1) If a person obtains an order for the appointment of a receiver or manager of an LLP's property, or appoints such a receiver or manager under powers contained in an instrument, he shall within 7 days of the order or of the appointment under those powers, give notice of the fact to the registrar.

(2) Where a person appointed receiver or manager of an LLP's property under powers contained in an instrument ceases to act as such receiver or manager, he shall, on so ceasing, give the registrar notice to that effect.

(3) The registrar must enter a fact of which he is given notice under this section in the register of charges.

(4) A person who makes default in complying with the requirements of this section commits an offence.

(5) A person guilty of an offence under this section is liable on summary conviction to a fine not exceeding level 3 on the standard scale and, for continued contravention, a daily default fine not exceeding one-tenth of level 3 on the standard scale.

872. Entries of satisfaction and release

(1) Subsection (2) applies if a statement is delivered to the registrar verifying with respect to a registered charge—

(a) that the debt for which the charge was given has been paid or satisfied in whole or in part, or

(b) that part of the property or undertaking charged has been released from the charge or has ceased to form part of the LLP's property or undertaking.

(2) The registrar may enter on the register a memorandum of satisfaction in whole or in part, or of the fact part of the property or undertaking has been released from the charge or has ceased to form part of the LLP's property or undertaking (as the case may be).

(3) Where the registrar enters a memorandum of satisfaction in whole, the registrar shall if required send the LLP a copy of it.

873. Rectification of register of charges

(1) Subsection (2) applies if the court is satisfied—

(a) that the failure to register a charge before the end of the period allowed for registration, or the omission or mis-statement of any particular with respect to any such charge or in a memorandum of satisfaction—

(i) was accidental or due to inadvertence or to some other sufficient cause, or

(ii) is not of a nature to prejudice the position of creditors of the LLP, or

(b) that on other grounds it is just and equitable to grant relief.

(2) The court may, on the application of the LLP or a person interested, and on such terms and conditions as seem to the court just and expedient, order that the period allowed for registration shall be extended or, as the case may be, that the omission or mis-statement shall be rectified.".

Avoidance of certain charges

37.

Section 874 applies to LLPs, modified so that it reads as follows—

"874. Consequence of failure to register charges created by an LLP

(1) If an LLP creates a charge to which section 860 applies, the charge is void (so far as any security on the LLP's property or undertaking is conferred by it) against—

(a) a liquidator of the LLP,
(b) an administrator of the LLP, and
(c) a creditor of the LLP,
unless that section is complied with.
(2) Subsection (1) is subject to the provisions of this Chapter.
(3) Subsection (1) is without prejudice to any contract or obligation for repayment of the money secured by the charge; and when a charge becomes void under this section, the money secured by it immediately becomes payable.".

LLPs' records and registers

38.

Sections 875 to 877 apply to LLPs, modified so that they read as follows—

"875. LLPs to keep copies of instruments creating charges

(1) An LLP must keep available for inspection a copy of every instrument creating a charge requiring registration under this Chapter, including any document delivered to the LLP under section 868(3)(b) (Northern Ireland: orders imposing charges affecting land).
(2) In the case of a series of uniform debentures, a copy of one of the debentures of the series is sufficient.

876. LLP's register of charges

(1) Every LLP shall keep available for inspection a register of charges and enter in it—
(a) all charges specifically affecting property of the LLP, and
(b) all floating charges on the whole or part of the LLP's property or undertaking.
(2) The entry shall in each case give a short description of the property charged, the amount of the charge and, except in the cases of securities to bearer, the names of the persons entitled to it.
(3) If a member of the LLP knowingly and wilfully authorises or permits the omission of an entry required to be made in pursuance of this section, he commits an offence.
(4) A person guilty of an offence under this section is liable—
(a) on conviction on indictment, to a fine;
(b) on summary conviction, to a fine not exceeding the statutory maximum.

877. Instruments creating charges and register of charges to be available for inspection

(1) This section applies to—
(a) documents required to be kept available for inspection under section 875 (copies of instruments creating charges), and
(b) an LLP's register of charges kept in pursuance of section 876.
(2) The documents and register must be kept available for inspection—
(a) at the LLP's registered office, or
(b) at a place specified in Part 2 of the Companies (Company Records) Regulations 2008 (SI 2008/3006).
(3) The LLP must give notice to the registrar—
(a) of the place at which the documents and register are kept available for inspection, and
(b) of any change in that place,
unless they have at all times been kept at the LLP's registered office.
(4) The documents and register shall be open to the inspection—
(a) of any creditor or member of the LLP without charge, and
(b) of any other person on payment of the fee prescribed by regulation 2(c) of the Companies (Fees for Inspection of Company Records) Regulations 2008 (SI 2008/3007).
(5) If default is made for 14 days in complying with subsection (3) or an inspection required under subsection (4) is refused, an offence is committed by—
(a) the LLP, and
(b) every member of the LLP who is in default.

(6) A person guilty of an offence under this section is liable on summary conviction to a fine not exceeding level 3 on the standard scale and, for continued contravention, a daily default fine not exceeding one-tenth of level 3 on the standard scale.

(7) If an inspection required under subsection (4) is refused the court may by order compel an immediate inspection.".

CHAPTER 2
LLPS REGISTERED IN SCOTLAND

Charges requiring registration

39.

Sections 878 to 881 apply to LLPs, modified so that they read as follows—

"878. Charges created by an LLP

(1) An LLP that creates a charge to which this section applies must deliver the required particulars of the charge, together with a copy certified as a correct copy of the instrument (if any) by which the charge is created or evidenced, to the registrar for registration before the end of the period allowed for registration.

(2) The required particulars are those prescribed by regulation 3 of the Companies (Particulars of Company Charges) Regulations 2008 (SI 2008/2996).

(3) Registration of a charge to which this section applies may instead be effected on the application of a person interested in it.

(4) Where registration is effected on the application of some person other than the LLP, that person is entitled to recover from the LLP the amount of any fees properly paid by him to the registrar on the registration.

(5) If an LLP fails to comply with subsection (1), an offence is committed by—
(a) the LLP, and
(b) every member of the LLP who is in default.

(6) A person guilty of an offence under this section is liable—
(a) on conviction on indictment, to a fine;
(b) on summary conviction, to a fine not exceeding the statutory maximum.

(7) Subsection (5) does not apply if registration of the charge has been effected on the application of some other person.

(8) This section applies to the following charges—
(a) a charge on land or any interest in such land, other than a charge for any rent or other periodical sum payable in respect of the land,
(b) a security over incorporeal moveable property of any of the following categories—
(i) goodwill,
(ii) a patent or a licence under a patent,
(iii) a trade mark,
(iv) a copyright or a licence under a copyright,
(v) a registered design or a licence in respect of such a design,
(vi) a design right or a licence under a design right, and
(vii) the book debts (whether book debts of the LLP or assigned to it),
(c) a security over a ship or aircraft or any share in a ship,
(d) a floating charge.

879. Charges which have to be registered: supplementary

(1) A charge on land, for the purposes of section 878(8)(a), includes a charge created by a heritable security within the meaning of section 9(8) of the Conveyancing and Feudal Reform (Scotland) Act 1970 (c 35).

(2) The holding of debentures entitling the holder to a charge on land is not, for the purposes of section 878(8)(a), deemed to be an interest in land.

(3) It is immaterial for the purposes of this Chapter where land subject to a charge is situated.

(4) The deposit by way of security of a negotiable instrument given to secure the payment of book debts is not, for the purposes of section 878(8)(b)(vii), to be treated as a charge on those book debts.

(5) References in this Chapter to the date of the creation of a charge are—

(a) in the case of a floating charge, the date on which the instrument creating the floating charge was executed by the LLP creating the charge, and

(b) in any other case, the date on which the right of the person entitled to the benefit of the charge was constituted as a real right.

(6) In this Chapter "LLP" means an LLP registered in Scotland.

880. Duty to register charges existing on property acquired

(1) Subsection (2) applies where an LLP acquires any property which is subject to a charge of any kind as would, if it had been created by the LLP after the acquisition of the property, have been required to be registered under this Chapter.

(2) The LLP must deliver the required particulars of the charge, together with a copy (certified to be a correct copy) of the instrument (if any) by which the charge was created or is evidenced, to the registrar for registration before the end of the period allowed for registration.

(3) The required particulars are those prescribed by regulation 4 of the Companies (Particulars of Company Charges) Regulations 2008 (SI 2008/2996).

(4) If default is made in complying with this section, an offence is committed by—

(a) the LLP, and

(b) every member of it who is in default.

(5) A person guilty of an offence under this section is liable—

(a) on conviction on indictment, to a fine;

(b) on summary conviction, to a fine not exceeding the statutory maximum.

881. Charge by way of ex facie absolute disposition, etc

(1) For the avoidance of doubt, it is hereby declared that, in the case of a charge created by way of an ex facie absolute disposition or assignation qualified by a back letter or other agreement, or by a standard security qualified by an agreement, compliance with section 878(1) does not of itself render the charge unavailable as security for indebtedness incurred after the date of compliance.

(2) Where the amount secured by a charge so created is purported to be increased by a further back letter or agreement, a further charge is held to have been created by the ex facie absolute disposition or assignation or (as the case may be) by the standard security, as qualified by the further back letter or agreement.

(3) In that case, the provisions of this Chapter apply to the further charge as if—

(a) references in this Chapter (other than in this section) to a charge were references to the further charge, and

(b) references to the date of the creation of a charge were references to the date on which the further back letter or agreement was executed.".

Special rules about debentures

40.

Sections 882 and 883 apply to LLPs, modified so that they read as follows—

"882. Charge in series of debentures

(1) Where a series of debentures containing, or giving by reference to any other instrument, any charge to the benefit of which the debenture-holders of that series are entitled pari passu, is created by an LLP, it is sufficient for purposes of section 878 if the required particulars, together with a copy of the deed containing the charge (or, if there is no such deed, of one of the debentures of the series) are delivered to the registrar before the end of the period allowed for registration.

(2) The following are the required particulars—

(a) the total amount secured by the whole series,

(b) the dates of the determinations of the LLP authorising the issue of the series and the date of the covering deed (if any) by which the security is created or defined,

(c) a general description of the property charged,

(d) the names of the trustees (if any) for the debenture-holders, and

(e) in the case of a floating charge, a statement of any provisions of the charge and of any instrument relating to it which prohibit or restrict or regulate the power of the LLP to grant further securities ranking in priority to, or pari passu with, the floating charge, or which vary or otherwise regulate the order of ranking of the floating charge in relation to subsisting securities.

(3) Where more than one issue is made of debentures in the series, particulars of the date and amount of each issue of debentures of the series must be sent to the registrar for entry in the register of charges.

(4) Failure to comply with subsection (3) does not affect the validity of any of those debentures.

(5) Subsections (3) to (7) of section 878 apply for the purposes of this section as they apply for the purposes of that section but as if for the reference to the registration of the charge there was substituted a reference to the registration of the series of debentures.

883. Additional registration requirement for commission etc in relation to debentures

(1) Where any commission, allowance or discount has been paid or made either directly or indirectly by an LLP to a person in consideration of his—

(a) subscribing or agreeing to subscribe, whether absolutely or conditionally, for debentures in an LLP, or

(b) procuring or agreeing to procure subscriptions, whether absolute or conditional, for such debentures,

the particulars required to be sent for registration under section 878 shall include particulars as to the amount or rate per cent. of the commission, discount or allowance so paid or made.

(2) The deposit of debentures as security for a debt of the LLP is not, for the purposes of this section, treated as the issue of debentures at a discount.

(3) Failure to comply with this section does not affect the validity of the debentures issued.".

Charges on property outside the United Kingdom

41.

Section 884 applies to LLPs, modified so that it reads as follows—

"884. Charges on property outside United Kingdom

Where a charge is created in the United Kingdom but comprises property outside the United Kingdom, the copy of the instrument creating or purporting to create the charge may be sent for registration under section 878 even if further proceedings may be necessary to make the charge valid or effectual according to the law of the country in which the property is situated.".

The register of charges

42.

Sections 885 to 888 apply to LLPs, modified so that they read as follows—

"885. Register of charges to be kept by registrar

(1) The registrar shall keep, with respect to each LLP, a register of all the charges requiring registration under this Chapter.

(2) In the case of a charge to the benefit of which holders of a series of debentures are entitled, the registrar shall enter in the register the required particulars specified in section 882(2).

(3) In the case of any other charge, the registrar shall enter in the register the following particulars—

(a) if it is a charge created by an LLP, the date of its creation and, if it is a charge which was existing on property acquired by the LLP, the date of the acquisition,

(b) the amount secured by the charge,

(c) short particulars of the property charged,
(d) the persons entitled to the charge, and
(e) in the case of a floating charge, a statement of any of the provisions of the charge and of any instrument relating to it which prohibit or restrict or regulate the LLP's power to grant further securities ranking in priority to, or pari passu with, the floating charge, or which vary or otherwise regulate the order of ranking of the floating charge in relation to subsisting securities.

(4) The registrar shall give a certificate of the registration of any charge registered in pursuance of this Chapter, stating—
(a) the name of the LLP and the person first-named in the charge among those entitled to the benefit of the charge (or, in the case of a series of debentures, the name of the holder of the first such debenture issued), and
(b) the amount secured by the charge.

(5) The certificate—
(a) shall be signed by the registrar or authenticated by the registrar's official seal, and
(b) is conclusive evidence that the requirements of this Chapter as to registration have been satisfied.

(6) The register kept in pursuance of this section shall be open to inspection by any person.

886. The period allowed for registration

(1) The period allowed for registration of a charge created by an LLP is—
(a) 21 days beginning with the day after the day on which the charge is created, or
(b) if the charge is created outside the United Kingdom, 21 days beginning with the day after the day on which a copy of the instrument by which the charge is created or evidenced could, in due course of post (and if despatched with due diligence) have been received in the United Kingdom.

(2) The period allowed for registration of a charge to which property acquired by an LLP is subject is—
(a) 21 days beginning with the day after the day on which the transaction is settled, or
(b) if the property is situated and the charge was created outside the United Kingdom, 21 days beginning with the day after the day on which a copy of the instrument by which the charge is created or evidenced could, in due course of post (and if despatched with due diligence) have been received in the United Kingdom.

(3) The period allowed for registration of particulars of a series of debentures as a result of section 882 is—
(a) if there is a deed containing the charge mentioned in section 882(1), 21 days beginning with the day after the day on which that deed is executed, or
(b) if there is no such deed, 21 days beginning with the day after the day on which the first debenture of the series is executed.

887. Entries of satisfaction and relief

(1) Subsection (2) applies if a statement is delivered to the registrar verifying with respect to any registered charge—
(a) that the debt for which the charge was given has been paid or satisfied in whole or in part, or
(b) that part of the property charged has been released from the charge or has ceased to form part of the LLP's property.

(2) If the charge is a floating charge, the statement must be accompanied by either—
(a) a statement by the creditor entitled to the benefit of the charge, or a person authorised by him for the purpose, verifying that the statement mentioned in subsection (1) is correct, or
(b) a direction obtained from the court, on the ground that the statement by the creditor mentioned in paragraph (a) could not be readily obtained, dispensing with the need for that statement.

(3) The registrar may enter on the register a memorandum of satisfaction (in whole or in part) regarding the fact contained in the statement mentioned in subsection (1).

(4) Where the registrar enters a memorandum of satisfaction in whole, he shall, if required, furnish the LLP with a copy of the memorandum.

(5) Nothing in this section requires the LLP to submit particulars with respect to the entry in the register of a memorandum of satisfaction where the LLP, having created a floating charge over all or any part of its property, disposes of part of the property subject to the floating charge.

888. Rectification of register of charges

(1) Subsection (2) applies if the court is satisfied—

(a) that the failure to register a charge before the end of the period allowed for registration, or the omission or mis-statement of any particular with respect to any such charge or in a memorandum of satisfaction—

(i) was accidental or due to inadvertence or to some other sufficient cause, or

(ii) is not of a nature to prejudice the position of creditors of the LLP, or

(b) that on other grounds it is just and equitable to grant relief.

(2) The court may, on the application of the LLP or a person interested, and on such terms and conditions as seem to the court just and expedient, order that the period allowed for registration shall be extended or, as the case may be, that the omission or mis-statement shall be rectified.".

43.

Section 889 applies to LLPs, modified so that it reads as follows—

"889. Charges void unless registered

(1) If an LLP creates a charge to which section 878 applies, the charge is void (so far as any security on the LLP's property or any part of it is conferred by the charge) against—

(a) the liquidator of the LLP,

(b) an administrator of the LLP, and

(c) any creditor of the LLP,

unless that section is complied with.

(2) Subsection (1) is without prejudice to any contract or obligation for repayment of the money secured by the charge; and when a charge becomes void under this section the money secured by it immediately becomes payable.".

44.

Sections 890 to 892 apply to LLPs, modified so that they read as follows—

"890. Copies of instruments creating charges to be kept by LLP

(1) Every LLP shall cause a copy of every instrument creating a charge requiring registration under this Chapter to be kept available for inspection.

(2) In the case of a series of uniform debentures, a copy of one debenture of the series is sufficient.

891. LLP's register of charges

(1) Every LLP shall keep available for inspection a register of charges and enter in it all charges specifically affecting property of the LLP, and all floating charges on any property of the LLP.

(2) There shall be given in each case a short description of the property charged, the amount of the charge and, except in the case of securities to bearer, the names of the persons entitled to it.

(3) If a member of the LLP knowingly and wilfully authorises or permits the omission of an entry required to be made in pursuance of this section, he commits an offence.

(4) A person guilty of an offence under this section is liable—

(a) on conviction on indictment, to a fine;

(b) on summary conviction, to a fine not exceeding the statutory maximum.

892. Instruments creating charges and register of charges to be available for inspection

(1) This section applies to—

(a) documents required to be kept available for inspection under section 890 (copies of instruments creating charges), and

(b) an LLP's register of charges kept in pursuance of section 891.

(2) The documents and register must be kept available for inspection—

(a) at the LLP's registered office, or

(b) at a place specified in Part 2 of the Companies (Company Records) Regulations 2008 (SI 2008/3006).

(3) The LLP must give notice to the registrar—

(a) of the place at which the documents and register are kept available for inspection, and

(b) of any change in that place,

unless they have at all times been kept at the LLP's registered office.

(4) The documents and register shall be open to the inspection—

(a) of any creditor or member of the LLP without charge, and

(b) of any other person on payment of the fee prescribed by regulation 2(d) of the Companies (Fees for Inspection of Company Records) Regulations (SI 2008/3007).

(5) If default is made for 14 days in complying with subsection (3) or an inspection required under subsection (4) is refused, an offence is committed by—

(a) the LLP, and

(b) every member of the LLP who is in default.

(6) A person guilty of an offence under this section is liable on summary conviction to a fine not exceeding level 3 on the standard scale and, for continued contravention, a daily default fine not exceeding one-tenth of level 3 on the standard scale.

(7) If an inspection required under subsection (4) is refused the court may by order compel an immediate inspection.".

PART 10

ARRANGEMENTS, RECONSTRUCTIONS AND CROSS-BORDER MERGERS

Arrangements and reconstructions

45.

(1) Sections 895 to 900 apply to LLPs, modified so that they read as follows—

"895. Application of this Part

The provisions of this Part apply where a compromise or arrangement is proposed between an LLP and—

(a) its creditors, or any class of them, or

(b) its members, or any class of them.

896. Court order for holding of meeting

(1) The court may, on an application under this section, order a meeting of the creditors or class of creditors, or of the members of the LLP or class of members (as the case may be), to be summoned in such manner as the court directs.

(2) An application under this section may be made by—

(a) the LLP,

(b) any creditor or member of the LLP,

(c) if the LLP is being wound up, the liquidator, or

(d) if the LLP is in administration, the administrator.

897. Statement to be circulated or made available

(1) Where a meeting is summoned under section 896—

(a) every notice summoning the meeting that is sent to a creditor or member must be accompanied by a statement complying with this section, and

(b) every notice summoning the meeting that is given by advertisement must either—

(i) include such a statement, or

(ii) state where and how creditors or members entitled to attend the meeting may obtain copies of such a statement.

(2) The statement must—

(a) explain the effect of the compromise or arrangement, and

(b) in particular, state—

(i) any material interests of the members of the LLP (whether as members or as creditors of the LLP or otherwise), and

(ii) the effect on those interests of the compromise or arrangement, in so far as it is different from the effect on the like interests of other persons.

(3) Where the compromise or arrangement affects the rights of debenture holders of the LLP, the statement must give the like explanation as respects the trustees of any deed for securing the issue of the debentures as it is required to give as respects the LLP's members.

(4) Where a notice given by advertisement states that copies of an explanatory statement can be obtained by creditors or members entitled to attend the meeting, every such creditor or member is entitled, on making application in the manner indicated by the notice, to be provided by the LLP with a copy of the statement free of charge.

(5) If an LLP makes default in complying with any requirement of this section, an offence is committed by—

(a) the LLP, and

(b) every member of the LLP who is in default.

This is subject to subsection (7) below.

(6) For this purpose the following are treated as members of the LLP—

(a) a liquidator or administrator of the LLP, and

(b) a trustee of a deed for securing the issue of debentures of the LLP.

(7) A person is not guilty of an offence under this section if he shows that the default was due to the refusal of a member or trustee for debenture holders to supply the necessary particulars of his interests.

(8) A person guilty of an offence under this section is liable—

(a) on conviction on indictment, to a fine;

(b) on summary conviction, to a fine not exceeding the statutory maximum.

898. Duty of members and trustees to provide information

(1) It is the duty of—

(a) any member of the LLP, and

(b) any trustee for its debenture holders,

to give notice to the LLP of such matters relating to himself as may be necessary for the purposes of section 897 (explanatory statement to be circulated or made available).

(2) Any person who makes default in complying with this section commits an offence.

(3) A person guilty of an offence under this section is liable on summary conviction to a fine not exceeding level 3 on the standard scale.

899. Court sanction for compromise or arrangement

(1) If a majority in number representing 75% in value of the creditors or class of creditors or members or class of members (as the case may be), present and voting either in person or by proxy at the meeting summoned under section 896, agree a compromise or arrangement, the court may, on an application under this section, sanction the compromise or arrangement.

(2) An application under this section may be made by—

(a) the LLP,

(b) any creditor or member of the LLP,

(c) if the LLP is being wound up, the liquidator, or

(d) if the LLP is in administration, the administrator.

(3) A compromise or agreement sanctioned by the court is binding on—

(a) all creditors or the class of creditors or on the members or class of members (as the case may be), and

(b) the LLP or, in the case of an LLP in the course of being wound up, the liquidator and contributories of the LLP.

(4) The court's order has no effect until a copy of it has been delivered to the registrar.

900. Powers of court to facilitate reconstruction or amalgamation

(1) This section applies where application is made to the court under section 899 to sanction a compromise or arrangement and it is shown that—

(a) the compromise or arrangement is proposed for the purposes of, or in connection with, a scheme for the reconstruction of any LLP or LLPs, or the amalgamation of any two or more relevant bodies corporate (where one or more of them is an LLP), and

(b) under the scheme the whole or any part of the undertaking or the property of any LLP concerned in the scheme ("a transferor LLP") is to be transferred to another relevant body corporate ("the transferee body corporate").

(2) The court may, either by the order sanctioning the compromise or arrangement or by a subsequent order, make provision for all or any of the following matters—

(a) the transfer to the transferee body corporate of the whole or any part of the undertaking and of the property or liabilities of any transferor LLP;

(b) the allotting or appropriation by the transferee body corporate of any shares, debentures, policies or other like interests in that body corporate which under the compromise or arrangement are to be allotted or appropriated by that body corporate to or for any person;

(c) the continuation by or against the transferee body corporate of any legal proceedings pending by or against any transferor LLP;

(d) the dissolution, without winding up, of any transferor LLP;

(e) the provision to be made for any persons who, within such time and in such manner as the court directs, dissent from the compromise or arrangement;

(f) such incidental, consequential and supplemental matters as are necessary to secure that the reconstruction or amalgamation is fully and effectively carried out.

(3) If an order under this section provides for the transfer of property or liabilities—

(a) the property is by virtue of the order transferred to, and vests in, the transferee body corporate, and

(b) the liabilities are, by virtue of the order, transferred to and become liabilities of that body corporate.

(4) The property (if the order so directs) vests freed from any charge that is by virtue of the compromise or arrangement to cease to have effect.

(5) In this section—

"relevant body corporate" means an LLP or a company;

"property" includes property, rights and powers of every description; and

"liabilities" includes duties.

(6) Every body corporate in relation to which an order is made under this section must cause a copy of the order to be delivered to the registrar within seven days after its making.

(7) If default is made in complying with subsection (6) an offence is committed by—

(a) the LLP, and every member of the LLP who is in default, and

(b) the company, and every officer of the company who is in default.

(8) A person guilty of an offence under subsection (7) is liable on summary conviction to a fine not exceeding level 3 on the standard scale and, for continued contravention, a daily default fine not exceeding one-tenth of level 3 on the standard scale.".

(2) Section 323 of the Companies Act 2006 (representation of corporations at meetings) applies to a meeting of creditors of the LLP under section 896 or 899 of that Act.

Cross-border mergers

46.

(1) Parts 1 to 3 and 5 of the Companies (Cross-Border Mergers) Regulations 2007 apply to LLPs with the following modifications.

(2) The modifications are—

(a) for references to a company substitute references to an LLP (or other EEA body corporate);

(b) for references to a UK company, substitute references to a UK LLP;

(c) for references to an EEA company substitute references to an EEA body corporate;

(d) references to a transferor or transferee LLP include references to an EEA body corporate which is the transferor or transferee in a cross-border merger with a UK LLP;

(e) for references to the directors or officers of a company substitute references to the members of an LLP;

(f) for "share exchange ratio" substitute "the rights to be given to transferor members";

(g) in regulation 2 (meaning of "cross-border merger")—

(i) for paragraph (2)(f) substitute—

"(f) the consideration for the transfer is—

(i) members of the transferor LLP becoming members of the transferee LLP, and

(ii) if so agreed, a cash payment receivable by members of the transferor LLP.",

(ii) for paragraph (3)(a) to (c) substitute—

"(a) there is one transferor LLP, of which the only member is an existing transferee LLP;",

(iii) for paragraph (4)(c) substitute—

"(c) the consideration for the transfer is—

(i) members of the transferor LLP becoming members of the transferee LLP, and

(ii) if so agreed, a cash payment receivable by members of the transferor LLP.";

(h) in regulation 3(1) (interpretation)—

(i) for the definitions of "EEA company", "member" and "members' report" substitute respectively—

""EEA body corporate" means a body corporate governed by the law of an EEA State other than the United Kingdom;"

""member", in relation to a UK LLP, has the same meaning as in section 4 of the Limited Liability Partnerships Act 2000 (c 12);"

""members' report" means a report prepared and adopted in accordance with regulation 8 (members' report);",

(ii) omit the definitions of "the 1996 Act", "the Appeal Tribunal", "the CAC", "director", "dismissed" and "dismissal", "employee", "employee participation", "employee representatives", "share exchange ratio", "standard rules of employee participation", "treasury shares", "UK employee" and "UK members of the special negotiating body",

(iii) for the definition of "UK company" substitute—

""UK LLP" means a limited liability partnership registered and incorporated under the Limited Liability Partnerships Act 2000 other than a limited liability partnership which is being wound up;";

(i) omit regulation 5 (unregistered companies);

(j) in regulation 7 (draft terms of merger)—

(i) omit paragraphs (2)(c), (g) and (j) and (4),

(ii) for paragraph (2)(e) substitute—

"(e) the date from which being a member of the transferee LLP will entitle the member to participate in profits, and any special conditions affecting that entitlement;", and

(iii) paragraph (2)(i) only applies where the transferee body corporate is a company;

(k) in regulation 8 (members' report)—

(i) in paragraph (2)(b)(ii), omit "or as members", and

(ii) omit paragraphs (5) and (6);

(l) in regulation 9 (independent expert's report)—

(i) in paragraph (1)(b) for "90% or more (but not all) of the relevant securities" substitute "90% or more (but not all) of the voting rights at meetings of members",

(ii) omit paragraph (9);

(m) in regulation 10 (inspection of documents)—

(i) in paragraph (1), omit "and its employee representatives (or if there are no such representatives, the employees)", and

(ii) in paragraph (2), omit ", or any class of members,";

(n) in regulation 11 (power of court to summon meeting of members or creditors), in paragraphs (1)(a) and (2)(b) omit "or a class of members";

(o) in regulation 12 (public notice of receipt of registered documents)—

(i) omit paragraph (1)(c)(v),

(ii) in paragraph (1)(c)(vi) omit "other";

(p) in regulation 13 (approval of members in meeting)—

(i) in paragraph (1), for "75% in value, of each class of members of the UK merging company" substitute " 75% of the voting rights of the members of the UK merging LLP";

(ii) omit paragraph (2),

(iii) in paragraph (4)(c)(i)—

(aa) for "the paid up capital of the company which carried the right to vote at general meetings of the company (excluding any shares held as treasury shares)" substitute "the voting rights at meetings of members of the LLP", and

(bb) omit "each class of members";

(q) in regulation 16 (court approval of cross-border merger), omit paragraph (1)(f);

(r) omit regulation 19(2)(b) and the word "other" in regulation 19(2)(c);

(s) omit regulation 20 (obligations of transferee company with respect to articles etc);

(t) omit regulation 21(1)(a) and in regulation 21(1)(b) the word "other".

PART 11
FRAUDULENT TRADING

Offence of fraudulent trading

47.

Section 993 applies to LLPs, modified so that it reads as follows—

"993. Offence of fraudulent trading

(1) If any business of an LLP is carried on with intent to defraud creditors of the LLP or creditors of any other person, or for any fraudulent purpose, every person who is knowingly a party to the carrying on of the business in that manner commits an offence.

(2) This applies whether or not the LLP has been, or is in the course of being, wound up.

(3) A person guilty of an offence under this section is liable—

(a) on conviction on indictment, to imprisonment for a term not exceeding ten years or a fine (or both);

(b) on summary conviction—

(i) in England and Wales or Scotland, to imprisonment for a term not exceeding twelve months or a fine not exceeding the statutory maximum (or both);

(ii) in Northern Ireland, to imprisonment for a term not exceeding six months or a fine not exceeding the statutory maximum (or both).".

PART 12
PROTECTION OF MEMBERS AGAINST UNFAIR PREJUDICE
Main provisions

48.

Sections 994 to 996 apply to LLPs, modified so that they read as follows—

"994. Petition by LLP member

(1) A member of an LLP may apply to the court by petition for an order under this Part on the ground—
   (a) that the LLP's affairs are being or have been conducted in a manner that is unfairly prejudicial to the interests of members generally or of some part of its members (including at least himself), or
   (b) that an actual or proposed act or omission of the LLP (including an act or omission on its behalf) is or would be so prejudicial.

(2) For the purposes of subsection (1)(a), a removal of the LLP's auditor from office—
   (a) on grounds of divergence of opinions on accounting treatments or audit procedures, or
   (b) on any other improper grounds,

shall be treated as being unfairly prejudicial to the interests of some part of the LLP's members.

(3) The members of an LLP may by unanimous agreement exclude the right contained in subsection (1) either indefinitely or for such period as is specified in the agreement. The agreement must be recorded in writing.

995. Petition by Secretary of State

(1) This section applies to an LLP in respect of which—
   (a) the Secretary of State has received a report under section 437 of the Companies Act 1985 (c 6) (inspector's report);
   (b) the Secretary of State has exercised his powers under section 447 or 448 of that Act (powers to require documents and information or to enter and search premises);
   (c) the Secretary of State or the Financial Services Authority has exercised his or its powers under Part 11 of the Financial Services and Markets Act 2000 (c 8) (information gathering and investigations); or
   (d) the Secretary of State has received a report from an investigator appointed by him or the Financial Services Authority under that Part.

(2) If it appears to the Secretary of State that in the case of such an LLP—
   (a) the LLP's affairs are being or have been conducted in a manner that is unfairly prejudicial to the interests of members generally or of some part of its members, or
   (b) an actual or proposed act or omission of the LLP (including an act or omission on its behalf) is or would be so prejudicial,

he may apply to the court by petition for an order under this Part.

(3) The Secretary of State may do this in addition to, or instead of, presenting a petition for the winding up of the LLP.

996. Powers of the court under this Part

(1) If the court is satisfied that a petition under this Part is well founded, it may make such order as it thinks fit for giving relief in respect of the matters complained of.

(2) Without prejudice to the generality of subsection (1), the court's order may—
   (a) regulate the conduct of the LLP's affairs in the future;
   (b) require the LLP—
      (i) to refrain from doing or continuing an act complained of, or
      (ii) to do an act that the petitioner has complained it has omitted to do;
   (c) authorise civil proceedings to be brought in the name and on behalf of the LLP by such person or persons and on such terms as the court may direct;

(d) require the LLP or the members of the LLP not to make any, or any specified, alterations in the LLP agreement without the leave of the court;

(e) provide for the purchase of the rights and interests of any members in the LLP by other members or by the LLP itself.".

Supplementary provision

49.

Section 997 applies to LLPs as follows—

"997. Application of general rule-making powers

The power to make rules under section 411 of the Insolvency Act 1986 (c 45) or Article 359 of the Insolvency (Northern Ireland) Order 1989 (SI 1989/2405 (NI 19)), so far as relating to a winding-up petition, applies for the purposes of a petition under this Part.".

PART 13
DISSOLUTION AND RESTORATION TO THE REGISTER

CHAPTER 1
STRIKING OFF

Registrar's power to strike off defunct LLP

50.

Sections 1000 to 1002 apply to LLPs, modified so that they read as follows—

"1000. Power to strike off LLP not carrying on business or in operation

(1) If the registrar has reasonable cause to believe that an LLP is not carrying on business or in operation, the registrar may send to the LLP by post a letter inquiring whether the LLP is carrying on business or in operation.

(2) If the registrar does not within one month of sending the letter receive any answer to it, the registrar must within 14 days after the expiration of that month send to the LLP by post a registered letter referring to the first letter, and stating—

(a) that no answer to it has been received, and

(b) that if an answer is not received to the second letter within one month from its date, a notice will be published in the Gazette with a view to striking the LLP's name off the register.

(3) If the registrar—

(a) receives an answer to the effect that the LLP is not carrying on business or in operation, or

(b) does not within one month after sending the second letter receive any answer,

the registrar may publish in the Gazette, and send to the LLP by post, a notice that at the expiration of three months from the date of the notice the name of the LLP mentioned in it will, unless cause is shown to the contrary, be struck off the register and the LLP will be dissolved.

(4) At the expiration of the time mentioned in the notice the registrar may, unless cause to the contrary is previously shown by the LLP, strike its name off the register.

(5) The registrar must publish notice in the Gazette of the LLP's name having been struck off the register.

(6) On the publication of the notice in the Gazette the LLP is dissolved.

(7) However—

(a) the liability (if any) of every member of the LLP continues and may be enforced as if the LLP had not been dissolved, and

(b) nothing in this section affects the power of the court to wind up an LLP the name of which has been struck off the register.

1001. Duty to act in case of LLP being wound up

(1) If, in a case where an LLP is being wound up—

(a) the registrar has reasonable cause to believe—

(i) that no liquidator is acting, or

(ii) that the affairs of the LLP are fully wound up, and

(b) the returns required to be made by the liquidator have not been made for a period of six consecutive months,

the registrar must publish in the Gazette and send to the LLP or the liquidator (if any) a notice that at the expiration of three months from the date of the notice the name of the LLP mentioned in it will, unless cause is shown to the contrary, be struck off the register and the LLP will be dissolved.

(2) At the expiration of the time mentioned in the notice the registrar may, unless cause to the contrary is previously shown by the LLP, strike its name off the register.

(3) The registrar must publish notice in the Gazette of the LLP's name having been struck off the register.

(4) On the publication of the notice in the Gazette the LLP is dissolved.

(5) However—

(a) the liability (if any) of every member of the LLP continues and may be enforced as if the LLP had not been dissolved, and

(b) nothing in this section affects the power of the court to wind up an LLP the name of which has been struck off the register.

1002. Supplementary provisions as to service of letter or notice

(1) A letter or notice to be sent under section 1000 or 1001 to an LLP may be addressed to the LLP at its registered office or, if no office has been registered, to the care of some member of the LLP.

(2) If there is no member of the LLP whose name and address are known to the registrar, the letter or notice may be sent to each of the persons who subscribed the incorporation document (if their addresses are known to the registrar).

(3) A notice to be sent to a liquidator under section 1001 may be addressed to him at his last known place of business.".

Voluntary striking off

51.

Sections 1003 to 1011 apply to LLPs, modified so that they read as follows—

"1003. Striking off on application by LLP

(1) The registrar of companies may strike the LLP's name off the register on application by—

(a) a majority of the members of an LLP, or

(b) if there are only two such members, by both of them, or

(c) if there is only one remaining member of an LLP, by that member.

(2) The application must contain a declaration by the member or members making the application that neither section 1004 nor 1005 prevents the application from being made.

(3) The registrar may not strike an LLP off under this section until after the expiration of three months from the publication by the registrar in the Gazette of a notice—

(a) stating that the registrar may exercise the power under this section in relation to the LLP, and

(b) inviting any person to show cause why that should not be done.

(4) The registrar must publish notice in the Gazette of the LLP's name having been struck off.

(5) On the publication of the notice in the Gazette the LLP is dissolved.

(6) However—

(a) the liability (if any) of every member of the LLP continues and may be enforced as if the LLP had not been dissolved, and

(b) nothing in this section affects the power of the court to wind up an LLP the name of which has been struck off the register.

1004. Circumstances in which application not to be made: activities of LLP

(1) An application under section 1003 (application for voluntary striking off) on behalf of an LLP must not be made if, at any time in the previous three months, the LLP has—

(a) changed its name,

(b) traded or otherwise carried on business,

(c) made a disposal for value of property or rights that, immediately before ceasing to trade or otherwise carry on business, it held for the purpose of disposal for gain in the normal course of trading or otherwise carrying on business, or

(d) engaged in any other activity, except one which is—

(i) necessary or expedient for the purpose of making an application under that section, or deciding whether to do so,

(ii) necessary or expedient for the purpose of concluding the affairs of the LLP, or

(iii) necessary or expedient for the purpose of complying with any statutory requirement.

(2) For the purposes of this section, an LLP is not to be treated as trading or otherwise carrying on business by virtue only of the fact that it makes a payment in respect of a liability incurred in the course of trading or otherwise carrying on business.

(3) It is an offence for a person to make an application in contravention of this section.

(4) In proceedings for such an offence it is a defence for the accused to prove that he did not know, and could not reasonably have known, of the existence of the facts that led to the contravention.

(5) A person guilty of an offence under this section is liable—

(a) on conviction on indictment, to a fine;

(b) on summary conviction, to a fine not exceeding the statutory maximum.

1005. Circumstances in which application not to be made: proceedings pending

(1) An application under section 1003 (application for voluntary striking off) on behalf of an LLP must not be made at a time when—

(a) an application to the court under Part 26 has been made on behalf of the LLP for the sanctioning of a compromise or arrangement and the matter has not been finally concluded;

(b) a voluntary arrangement in relation to the LLP has been proposed under Part 1 of the Insolvency Act 1986 (c 45) or Part 2 of the Insolvency (Northern Ireland) Order 1989 (SI 1989/2405 (NI 19)) and the matter has not been finally concluded;

(c) the LLP is in administration under Part 2 of that Act or Part 3 of that Order;

(d) paragraph 44 of Schedule B1 to that Act or paragraph 45 of Schedule B1 to that Order applies (interim moratorium on proceedings where application to the court for an administration order has been made or notice of intention to appoint administrator has been filed);

(e) the LLP is being wound up under Part 4 of that Act or Part 5 of that Order, whether voluntarily or by the court, or a petition under that Part for winding up of the LLP by the court has been presented and not finally dealt with or withdrawn;

(f) there is a receiver or manager of the LLP's property;

(g) the LLP's estate is being administered by a judicial factor.

(2) For the purposes of subsection (1)(a), the matter is finally concluded if—

(a) the application has been withdrawn,

(b) the application has been finally dealt with without a compromise or arrangement being sanctioned by the court, or

(c) a compromise or arrangement has been sanctioned by the court and has, together with anything required to be done under any provision made in relation to the matter by order of the court, been fully carried out.

(3) For the purposes of subsection (1)(b), the matter is finally concluded if—

(a) no meeting is to be summoned under section 3 of the Insolvency Act 1986 (c 45) or Article 16 of the Insolvency (Northern Ireland) Order 1989,

(b) the meeting summoned under that section or Article fails to approve the arrangement with no, or the same, modifications,

(c) an arrangement approved by a meeting summoned under that section, or in consequence of a direction under section 6(4)(b) of that Act or Article 19(4)(b) of that Order, has been fully implemented, or

(d) the court makes an order under section 6(5) of that Act or Article 19(5) of that Order revoking approval given at a previous meeting and, if the court gives any directions under section 6(6) of that Act or Article 19(6) of that Order, the LLP has done whatever it is required to do under those directions.

(4) It is an offence for a person to make an application in contravention of this section.

(5) In proceedings for such an offence it is a defence for the accused to prove that he did not know, and could not reasonably have known, of the existence of the facts that led to the contravention.

(6) A person guilty of an offence under this section is liable—

(a) on conviction on indictment, to a fine;

(b) on summary conviction, to a fine not exceeding the statutory maximum.

1006. Copy of application to be given to members, employees etc

(1) A person who makes an application under section 1003 (application for voluntary striking off) on behalf of an LLP must secure that, within seven days from the day on which the application is made, a copy of it is given to every person who at any time on that day is—

(a) a member of the LLP,

(b) an employee of the LLP,

(c) a creditor of the LLP, or

(d) a manager or trustee of any pension fund established for the benefit of employees of the LLP.

(2) Subsection (1) does not require a copy of the application to be given to a member who is a party to the application.

(3) The duty imposed by this section ceases to apply if the application is withdrawn before the end of the period for giving the copy application.

(4) A person who fails to perform the duty imposed on him by this section commits an offence. If he does so with the intention of concealing the making of the application from the person concerned, he commits an aggravated offence.

(5) In proceedings for an offence under this section it is a defence for the accused to prove that he took all reasonable steps to perform the duty.

(6) A person guilty of an offence under this section (other than an aggravated offence) is liable—

(a) on conviction on indictment, to a fine;

(b) on summary conviction, to a fine not exceeding the statutory maximum.

(7) A person guilty of an aggravated offence under this section is liable—

(a) on conviction on indictment, to imprisonment for a term not exceeding seven years or a fine (or both);

(b) on summary conviction—

(i) in England and Wales or Scotland, to imprisonment for a term not exceeding twelve months or to a fine not exceeding the statutory maximum (or both);

(ii) in Northern Ireland, to imprisonment for a term not exceeding six months, or to a fine not exceeding the statutory maximum (or both).

1007. Copy of application to be given to new members, employees, etc

(1) This section applies in relation to any time after the day on which an LLP makes an application under section 1003 (application for voluntary striking off) and before the day on which the application is finally dealt with or withdrawn.

(2) A person who is a member of the LLP at the end of a day on which a person (other than himself) becomes—

(a) a member of the LLP,

(b) an employee of the LLP,

(c) a creditor of the LLP, or

(d) a manager or trustee of any pension fund established for the benefit of employees of the LLP,

must secure that a copy of the application is given to that person within seven days from that day.

(3) The duty imposed by this section ceases to apply if the application is finally dealt with or withdrawn before the end of the period for giving the copy application.

(4) A person who fails to perform the duty imposed on him by this section commits an offence. If he does so with the intention of concealing the making of the application from the person concerned, he commits an aggravated offence.

(5) In proceedings for an offence under this section it is a defence for the accused to prove—

(a) that at the time of the failure he was not aware of the fact that the LLP had made an application under section 1003, or

(b) that he took all reasonable steps to perform the duty.

(6) A person guilty of an offence under this section (other than an aggravated offence) is liable—

(a) on conviction on indictment, to a fine;

(b) on summary conviction, to a fine not exceeding the statutory maximum.

(7) A person guilty of an aggravated offence under this section is liable—

(a) on conviction on indictment, to imprisonment for a term not exceeding seven years or a fine (or both);

(b) on summary conviction—

(i) in England and Wales or Scotland, to imprisonment for a term not exceeding twelve months or to a fine not exceeding the statutory maximum (or both);

(ii) in Northern Ireland, to imprisonment for a term not exceeding six months, or to a fine not exceeding the statutory maximum (or both).

1008. Copy of application: provisions as to service of documents

(1) The following provisions have effect for the purposes of section 1006 (copy of application to be given to members, employees, etc), and section 1007 (copy of application to be given to new members, employees, etc).

(2) A document is treated as given to a person if it is—

(a) delivered to him, or

(b) left at his proper address, or

(c) sent by post to him at that address.

(3) For the purposes of subsection (2) and section 7 of the Interpretation Act 1978 (c 30) (service of documents by post) as it applies in relation to that subsection, the proper address of a person is—

(a) in the case of a firm incorporated or formed in the United Kingdom, its registered or principal office;

(b) in the case of a firm incorporated or formed outside the United Kingdom—

(i) if it has a place of business in the United Kingdom, its principal office in the United Kingdom, or

(ii) if it does not have a place of business in the United Kingdom, its registered or principal office;

(c) in the case of an individual, his last known address.

(4) In the case of a creditor of the LLP a document is treated as given to him if it is left or sent by post to him—

(a) at the place of business of his with which the LLP has had dealings by virtue of which he is a creditor of the LLP, or

(b) if there is more than one such place of business, at each of them.

1009. Circumstances in which application to be withdrawn

(1) This section applies where, at any time on or after the day on which an LLP makes an application under section 1003 (application for voluntary striking off) and before the day on which the application is finally dealt with or withdrawn—

(a) the LLP—

(i) changes its name,

(ii) trades or otherwise carries on business,

(iii) makes a disposal for value of any property or rights other than those which it was necessary or expedient for it to hold for the purpose of making, or proceeding with, an application under that section, or

(iv) engages in any activity, except one to which subsection (4) applies;

(b) an application is made to the court under Part 26 on behalf of the LLP for the sanctioning of a compromise or arrangement;

(c) a voluntary arrangement in relation to the LLP is proposed under Part 1 of the Insolvency Act 1986 (c 45) or Part 2 of the Insolvency (Northern Ireland) Order 1989 (SI 1989/2405 (NI 19));

(d) an application to the court for an administration order in respect of the LLP is made under paragraph 12 of Schedule B1 to that Act or paragraph 13 of Schedule B1 to that Order;

(e) an administrator is appointed in respect of the LLP under paragraph 14 or 22 of Schedule B1 to that Act or paragraph 15 or 23 of Schedule B1 to that Order, or a copy of notice of intention to appoint an administrator of the LLP under any of those provisions is filed with the court;

(f) there arise any of the circumstances in which, under section 84(1) of that Act or Article 70 of that Order, the LLP may be voluntarily wound up;

(g) a petition is presented for the winding up of the LLP by the court under Part 4 of that Act or Part 5 of that Order;

(h) a receiver or manager of the LLP's property is appointed; or

(i) a judicial factor is appointed to administer the LLP's estate.

(2) A person who, at the end of a day on which any of the events mentioned in subsection (1) occurs, is a member of the LLP must secure that the LLP's application is withdrawn forthwith.

(3) For the purposes of subsection (1)(a), an LLP is not treated as trading or otherwise carrying on business by virtue only of the fact that it makes a payment in respect of a liability incurred in the course of trading or otherwise carrying on business.

(4) The excepted activities referred to in subsection (1)(a)(iv) are any activity necessary or expedient for the purposes of—

(a) making, or proceeding with, an application under section 1003 (application for voluntary striking off),

(b) concluding affairs of the LLP that are outstanding because of what has been necessary or expedient for the purpose of making, or proceeding with, such an application, or

(c) complying with any statutory requirement.

(5) A person who fails to perform the duty imposed on him by this section commits an offence.

(6) In proceedings for an offence under this section it is a defence for the accused to prove—

(a) that at the time of the failure he was not aware of the fact that the LLP had made an application under section 1003, or

(b) that he took all reasonable steps to perform the duty.

(7) A person guilty of an offence under this section is liable—

(a) on conviction on indictment, to a fine;

(b) on summary conviction, to a fine not exceeding the statutory maximum.

1010. Withdrawal of application

An application under section 1003 is withdrawn by notice to the registrar.

1011. Meaning of "creditor"

In this Chapter "creditor" includes a contingent or prospective creditor.".

CHAPTER 2

PROPERTY OF DISSOLVED LLP

Property of dissolved LLP vesting as bona vacantia

52.

Sections 1012 to 1014 apply to LLPs, modified so that they read as follows—

"1012. Property of dissolved LLP to be bona vacantia

(1) When an LLP is dissolved, all property and rights whatsoever vested in or held on trust for the LLP immediately before its dissolution (including leasehold property, but not including property held by the LLP on trust for another person) are deemed to be bona vacantia and—

(a) accordingly belong to the Crown, or to the Duchy of Lancaster or to the Duke of Cornwall for the time being (as the case may be), and

(b) vest and may be dealt with in the same manner as other bona vacantia accruing to the Crown, to the Duchy of Lancaster or to the Duke of Cornwall.

(2) Subsection (1) has effect subject to the possible restoration of the LLP to the register under Chapter 3 (see section 1034).

1013. Crown disclaimer of property vesting as bona vacantia

(1) Where property vests in the Crown under section 1012, the Crown's title to it under that section may be disclaimed by a notice signed by the Crown representative, that is to say the Treasury Solicitor, or, in relation to property in Scotland, the Queen's and Lord Treasurer's Remembrancer.

(2) The right to execute a notice of disclaimer under this section may be waived by or on behalf of the Crown either expressly or by taking possession.

(3) A notice of disclaimer must be executed within three years after—

(a) the date on which the fact that the property may have vested in the Crown under section 1012 first comes to the notice of the Crown representative, or

(b) if ownership of the property is not established at that date, the end of the period reasonably necessary for the Crown representative to establish the ownership of the property.

(4) If an application in writing is made to the Crown representative by a person interested in the property requiring him to decide whether he will or will not disclaim, any notice of disclaimer must be executed within twelve months after the making of the application or such further period as may be allowed by the court.

(5) A notice of disclaimer under this section is of no effect if it is shown to have been executed after the end of the period specified by subsection (3) or (4).

(6) A notice of disclaimer under this section must be delivered to the registrar and retained and registered by him.

(7) Copies of it must be published in the Gazette and sent to any persons who have given the Crown representative notice that they claim to be interested in the property.

(8) This section applies to property vested in the Duchy of Lancaster or the Duke of Cornwall under section 1012 as if for references to the Crown and the Crown representative there were respectively substituted references to the Duchy of Lancaster and to the Solicitor to

that Duchy, or to the Duke of Cornwall and to the Solicitor to the Duchy of Cornwall, as the case may be.

1014. Effect of Crown disclaimer

(1) Where notice of disclaimer is executed under section 1013 as respects any property, that property is deemed not to have vested in the Crown under section 1012.

(2) The following sections contain provisions as to the effect of the Crown disclaimer—

sections 1015 to 1019 apply in relation to property in England and Wales or Northern Ireland;

sections 1020 to 1022 apply in relation to property in Scotland.".

Effect of Crown disclaimer: England and Wales and Northern Ireland

53.

Sections 1015 to 1019 apply to LLPs, modified so that they read as follows—

"1015. General effect of disclaimer

(1) The Crown's disclaimer operates so as to terminate, as from the date of the disclaimer, the rights, interests and liabilities of the LLP in or in respect of the property disclaimed.

(2) It does not, except so far as is necessary for the purpose of releasing the LLP from any liability, affect the rights or liabilities of any other person.

1016. Disclaimer of leaseholds

(1) The disclaimer of any property of a leasehold character does not take effect unless a copy of the disclaimer has been served (so far as the Crown representative is aware of their addresses) on every person claiming under the LLP as underlessee or mortgagee, and either—

(a) no application under section 1017 (power of court to make vesting order) is made with respect to that property before the end of the period of 14 days beginning with the day on which the last notice under this paragraph was served, or

(b) where such an application has been made, the court directs that the disclaimer shall take effect.

(2) Where the court gives a direction under subsection (1)(b) it may also, instead of or in addition to any order it makes under section 1017, make such order as it thinks fit with respect to fixtures, tenant's improvements and other matters arising out of the lease.

(3) In this section the "Crown representative" means—

(a) in relation to property vested in the Duchy of Lancaster, the Solicitor to that Duchy;

(b) in relation to property vested in the Duke of Cornwall, the Solicitor to the Duchy of Cornwall;

(c) in relation to property in Scotland, the Queen's and Lord Treasurer's Remembrancer;

(d) in relation to other property, the Treasury Solicitor.

1017. Power of court to make vesting order

(1) The court may on application by a person who—

(a) claims an interest in the disclaimed property, or

(b) is under a liability in respect of the disclaimed property that is not discharged by the disclaimer,

make an order under this section in respect of the property.

(2) An order under this section is an order for the vesting of the disclaimed property in, or its delivery to—

(a) a person entitled to it (or a trustee for such a person), or

(b) a person subject to such a liability as is mentioned in subsection (1)(b) (or a trustee for such a person).

(3) An order under subsection (2)(b) may only be made where it appears to the court that it would be just to do so for the purpose of compensating the person subject to the liability in respect of the disclaimer.

(4) An order under this section may be made on such terms as the court thinks fit.

(5) On a vesting order being made under this section, the property comprised in it vests in the person named in that behalf in the order without conveyance, assignment or transfer.

1018. Protection of persons holding under a lease

(1) The court must not make an order under section 1017 vesting property of a leasehold nature in a person claiming under the LLP as underlessee or mortgagee except on terms making that person—

(a) subject to the same liabilities and obligations as those to which the LLP was subject under the lease, or

(b) if the court thinks fit, subject to the same liabilities and obligations as if the lease had been assigned to him.

(2) Where the order relates to only part of the property comprised in the lease, subsection (1) applies as if the lease had comprised only the property comprised in the vesting order.

(3) A person claiming under the LLP as underlessee or mortgagee who declines to accept a vesting order on such terms is excluded from all interest in the property.

(4) If there is no person claiming under the LLP who is willing to accept an order on such terms, the court has power to vest the LLP's estate and interest in the property in any person who is liable (whether personally or in a representative character, and whether alone or jointly with the LLP) to perform the lessee's covenants in the lease.

(5) The court may vest that estate and interest in such a person freed and discharged from all estates, incumbrances and interests created by the LLP.

1019. Land subject to rentcharge

Where in consequence of the disclaimer land that is subject to a rentcharge vests in any person, neither he nor his successors in title are subject to any personal liability in respect of sums becoming due under the rentcharge, except sums becoming due after he, or some person claiming under or through him, has taken possession or control of the land or has entered into occupation of it.".

Effect of Crown disclaimer: Scotland

54.

Sections 1020 to 1022 apply to LLPs, modified so that they read as follows—

"1020. General effect of disclaimer

(1) The Crown's disclaimer operates to determine, as from the date of the disclaimer, the rights, interests and liabilities of the LLP, and the property of the LLP, in or in respect of the property disclaimed.

(2) It does not (except so far as is necessary for the purpose of releasing the LLP and its property from liability) affect the rights or liabilities of any other person.

1021. Power of court to make vesting order

(1) The court may—

(a) on application by a person who either claims an interest in disclaimed property or is under a liability not discharged by this Act in respect of disclaimed property, and

(b) on hearing such persons as it thinks fit,

make an order for the vesting of the property in or its delivery to any persons entitled to it, or to whom it may seem just that the property should be delivered by way of compensation for such liability, or a trustee for him.

(2) The order may be made on such terms as the court thinks fit.

(3) On a vesting order being made under this section, the property comprised in it vests accordingly in the person named in that behalf in the order, without conveyance or assignation for that purpose.

1022. Protection of persons holding under a lease

(1) Where the property disclaimed is held under a lease the court must not make a vesting order in favour of a person claiming under the LLP, whether—

(a) as sub-lessee, or

(b) as creditor in a duly registered or (as the case may be) recorded heritable security over a lease, except on the following terms.

(2) The person must by the order be made subject—

(a) to the same liabilities and obligations as those to which the LLP was subject under the lease in respect of the property, or

(b) if the court thinks fit, only to the same liabilities and obligations as if the lease had been assigned to him.

In either event (if the case so requires) the liabilities and obligations must be as if the lease had comprised only the property comprised in the vesting order.

(3) A sub-lessee or creditor declining to accept a vesting order on such terms is excluded from all interest in and security over the property.

(4) If there is no person claiming under the LLP who is willing to accept an order on such terms, the court has power to vest the LLP's estate and interest in the property in any person liable (either personally or in a representative character, and either alone or jointly with the LLP) to perform the lessee's obligations under the lease.

(5) The court may vest that estate and interest in such a person freed and discharged from all interests, rights and obligations created by the LLP in the lease or in relation to the lease.

(6) For the purposes of this section a heritable security—

(a) is duly recorded if it is recorded in the Register of Sasines, and

(b) is duly registered if registered in accordance with the Land Registration (Scotland) Act 1979 (c 33).".

Supplementary provisions

55.

Section 1023 applies to LLPs, modified so that it reads as follows—

"1023. Liability for rentcharge on LLP's land after dissolution

(1) This section applies where on the dissolution of an LLP land in England and Wales or Northern Ireland that is subject to a rentcharge vests by operation of law in the Crown or any other person ("the proprietor").

(2) Neither the proprietor nor his successors in title are subject to any personal liability in respect of sums becoming due under the rentcharge, except sums becoming due after the proprietor, or some person claiming under or through him, has taken possession or control of the land or has entered into occupation of it.".

CHAPTER 3
RESTORATION TO THE REGISTER

Administrative restoration to the register

56.

Sections 1024 to 1028 apply to LLPs, modified so that they read as follows—

"1024. Application for administrative restoration to the register

(1) An application may be made to the registrar to restore to the register an LLP that has been struck off the register under section 1000 or 1001 (power of registrar to strike off defunct LLP).

(2) An application under this section may be made whether or not the LLP has in consequence been dissolved.

(3) An application under this section may only be made by a former member of the LLP.

(4) An application under this section may not be made after the end of the period of six years from the date of the dissolution of the LLP.

For this purpose an application is made when it is received by the registrar.

1025. Requirements for administrative restoration

(1) On an application under section 1024 the registrar shall restore the LLP to the register if, and only if, the following conditions are met.

(2) The first condition is that the LLP was carrying on business or in operation at the time of its striking off.

(3) The second condition is that, if any property or right previously vested in or held on trust for the LLP has vested as bona vacantia, the Crown representative has signified to the registrar in writing consent to the LLP's restoration to the register.

(4) It is the applicant's responsibility to obtain that consent and to pay any costs (in Scotland, expenses) of the Crown representative—

(a) in dealing with the property during the period of dissolution, or

(b) in connection with the proceedings on the application,

that may be demanded as a condition of giving consent.

(5) The third condition is that the applicant has—

(a) delivered to the registrar such documents relating to the LLP as are necessary to bring up to date the records kept by the registrar, and

(b) paid any penalties under section 453 or corresponding earlier provisions (civil penalty for failure to deliver accounts) that were outstanding at the date of dissolution or striking off.

(6) The fourth condition is that the applicant has sent notice of the application under section 1024 to all those who were members of the LLP at the time of its striking off.

(7) In this section the "Crown representative" means—

(a) in relation to property vested in the Duchy of Lancaster, the Solicitor to that Duchy;

(b) in relation to property vested in the Duke of Cornwall, the Solicitor to the Duchy of Cornwall;

(c) in relation to property in Scotland, the Queen's and Lord Treasurer's Remembrancer;

(d) in relation to other property, the Treasury Solicitor.

1026. Application to be accompanied by statement of compliance

(1) An application under section 1024 (application for administrative restoration to the register) must be accompanied by a statement of compliance.

(2) The statement of compliance required is a statement—

(a) that the person making the application has standing to apply (see subsection (3) of that section), and

(b) that the requirements for administrative restoration (see section 1025) are met.

(3) The registrar may accept the statement of compliance as sufficient evidence of those matters.

11027. Registrar's decision on application for administrative restoration

(1) The registrar must give notice to the applicant of the decision on an application under section 1024 (application for administrative restoration to the register).

(2) If the decision is that the LLP should be restored to the register, the restoration takes effect as from the date that notice is sent.

(3) In the case of such a decision, the registrar must—

(a) enter on the register a note of the date as from which the LLP's restoration to the register takes effect, and

(b) cause notice of the restoration to be published in the Gazette.

(4) The notice under subsection (3)(b) must state—

(a) the name of the LLP or, if the LLP is restored to the register under a different name (see section 1033), that name and its former name,

(b) the LLP's registered number, and

(c) the date as from which the restoration of the LLP to the register takes effect.

1028. Effect of administrative restoration

(1) The general effect of administrative restoration to the register is that the LLP is deemed to have continued in existence as if it had not been dissolved or struck off the register.

(2) The LLP is not liable to a penalty under section 453 or any corresponding earlier provision (civil penalty for failure to deliver accounts) for a financial year in relation to which the period for filing accounts and reports ended—

(a) after the date of dissolution or striking off, and

(b) before the restoration of the LLP to the register.

(3) The court may give such directions and make such provision as seems just for placing the LLP and all other persons in the same position (as nearly as may be) as if the LLP had not been dissolved or struck off the register.

(4) An application to the court for such directions or provision may be made any time within three years after the date of restoration of the LLP to the register.".

Restoration to the register by the court

57.

Sections 1029 to 1032 apply to LLPs, modified so that they read as follows—

"1029. Application to court for restoration to the register

(1) An application may be made to the court to restore to the register an LLP—

(a) that has been dissolved under Chapter 9 of Part 4 of the Insolvency Act 1986 (c 45) or Chapter 9 of Part 5 of the Insolvency (Northern Ireland) Order 1989 (SI 1989/2405 (NI 19)) (dissolution of LLP after winding up),

(b) that is deemed to have been dissolved under paragraph 84(6) of Schedule B1 to that Act or paragraph 85(6) of Schedule B1 to that Order (dissolution of LLP following administration), or

(c) that has been struck off the register—

(i) under section 1000 or 1001 (power of registrar to strike off defunct LLP), or

(ii) under section 1003 (voluntary striking off),

whether or not the LLP has in consequence been dissolved.

(2) An application under this section may be made by—

(a) the Secretary of State,

(b) any person having an interest in land in which the LLP had a superior or derivative interest,

(c) any person having an interest in land or other property—

(i) that was subject to rights vested in the LLP, or

(ii) that was benefited by obligations owed by the LLP,

(d) any person who but for the LLP's dissolution would have been in a contractual relationship with it,

(e) any person with a potential legal claim against the LLP,

(f) any manager or trustee of a pension fund established for the benefit of employees of the LLP,

(g) any former member of the LLP (or the personal representatives of such a person),

(h) any person who was a creditor of the LLP at the time of its striking off or dissolution,

(i) any former liquidator of the LLP,

or by any other person appearing to the court to have an interest in the matter.

1030. When application to the court may be made

(1) An application to the court for restoration of an LLP to the register may be made at any time for the purpose of bringing proceedings against the LLP for damages for personal injury.

(2) No order shall be made on such an application if it appears to the court that the proceedings would fail by virtue of any enactment as to the time within which proceedings must be brought.

(3) In making that decision the court must have regard to its power under section 1032(3) (power to give consequential directions etc) to direct that the period between the dissolution (or striking off) of the LLP and the making of the order is not to count for the purposes of any such enactment.

(4) In any other case an application to the court for restoration of an LLP to the register may not be made after the end of the period of six years from the date of the dissolution of the LLP, subject as follows.

(5) In a case where—

(a) the LLP has been struck off the register under section 1000 or 1001 (power of registrar to strike off defunct LLP),

(b) an application to the registrar has been made under section 1024 (application for administrative restoration to the register) within the time allowed for making such an application, and

(c) the registrar has refused the application,

an application to the court under this section may be made within 28 days of notice of the registrar's decision being issued by the registrar, even if the period of six years mentioned in subsection (4) above has expired.

(6) For the purposes of this section—

(a) "personal injury" includes any disease and any impairment of a person's physical or mental condition; and

(b) references to damages for personal injury include—

(i) any sum claimed by virtue of section 1(2)(c) of the Law Reform (Miscellaneous Provisions) Act 1934 (c 41) or section 14(2)(c) of the Law Reform (Miscellaneous Provisions) Act (Northern Ireland) 1937 (1937 C 9 (NI)) (funeral expenses), and

(ii) damages under the Fatal Accidents Act 1976 (c 30), the Damages (Scotland) Act 1976 (c 13) or the Fatal Accidents (Northern Ireland) Order 1977 (SI 1977/1251 (NI 18)).

1031. Decision on application for restoration by the court

(1) On an application under section 1029 the court may order the restoration of the LLP to the register—

(a) if the LLP was struck off the register under section 1000 or 1001 (power of registrar to strike off defunct LLPs) and the LLP was, at the time of the striking off, carrying on business or in operation;

(b) if the LLP was struck off the register under section 1003 (voluntary striking off) and any of the requirements of sections 1004 to 1009 was not complied with;

(c) if in any other case the court considers it just to do so.

(2) If the court orders restoration of the LLP to the register, the restoration takes effect on a copy of the court's order being delivered to the registrar.

(3) The registrar must cause to be published in the Gazette notice of the restoration of the LLP to the register.

(4) The notice must state—

(a) the name of the LLP or, if the LLP is restored to the register under a different name (see section 1033), that name and its former name,

(b) the LLP's registered number, and

(c) the date on which the restoration took effect.

1032. Effect of court order for restoration to the register

(1) The general effect of an order by the court for restoration to the register is that the LLP is deemed to have continued in existence as if it had not been dissolved or struck off the register.

(2) The LLP is not liable to a penalty under section 453 or any corresponding earlier provision (civil penalty for failure to deliver accounts) for a financial year in relation to which the period for filing accounts and reports ended—
   (a) after the date of dissolution or striking off, and
   (b) before the restoration of the LLP to the register.

(3) The court may give such directions and make such provision as seems just for placing the LLP and all other persons in the same position (as nearly as may be) as if the LLP had not been dissolved or struck off the register.

(4) The court may also give directions as to—
   (a) the delivery to the registrar of such documents relating to the LLP as are necessary to bring up to date the records kept by the registrar,
   (b) the payment of the costs (in Scotland, expenses) of the registrar in connection with the proceedings for the restoration of the LLP to the register,
   (c) where any property or right previously vested in or held on trust for the LLP has vested as bona vacantia, the payment of the costs (in Scotland, expenses) of the Crown representative—
      (i) in dealing with the property during the period of dissolution, or
      (ii) in connection with the proceedings on the application.

(5) In this section the "Crown representative" means—
   (a) in relation to property vested in the Duchy of Lancaster, the Solicitor to that Duchy;
   (b) in relation to property vested in the Duke of Cornwall, the Solicitor to the Duchy of Cornwall;
   (c) in relation to property in Scotland, the Queen's and Lord Treasurer's Remembrancer;
   (d) in relation to other property, the Treasury Solicitor.".

Supplementary provisions

58.

Sections 1033 and 1034 apply to LLPs, modified so that they read as follows—

"1033. LLP's name on restoration

(1) An LLP is restored to the register with the name it had before it was dissolved or struck off the register, subject to the following provisions.

(2) If at the date of restoration the LLP could not be registered under its former name without contravening section 66 (name not to be the same as another in the registrar's index of names), it must be restored to the register—
   (a) under another name specified—
      (i) in the case of administrative restoration, in the application to the registrar, or
      (ii) in the case of restoration under a court order, in the court's order, or
   (b) as if its registered number was also its name.

References to an LLP's being registered in a name, and to registration in that context, shall be read as including the LLP's being restored to the register.

(3) If an LLP is restored to the register under a name specified in the application to the registrar, the provisions of—
   paragraph 5 of the Schedule to the Limited Liability Partnerships Act 2000 (c 12) (change of name: registration and issue of certificate of change of name), and
   paragraph 6 of that Schedule (change of name: effect),
apply as if the application to the registrar were notice of a change of name.

(4) If an LLP is restored to the register under a name specified in the court's order, the provisions of—
   paragraph 5 of the Schedule to the Limited Liability Partnerships Act 2000 (c 12) (change of name: registration and issue of certificate of change of name), and
   paragraph 6 of that Schedule (change of name: effect),
apply as if the copy of the court order delivered to the registrar were notice of a change a name.

(5) If the LLP is restored to the register as if its registered number was also its name—
(a) the LLP must change its name within 14 days after the date of the restoration,
(b) the change may be made by determination of the members,
(c) the LLP must give notice to the registrar of the change, and
(d) paragraphs 5 and 6 of the Schedule to the Limited Liability Partnerships Act 2000 (c 12) apply as regards the registration and effect of the change.
(6) If the LLP fails to comply with subsection (5)(a) or (c) an offence is committed by—
(a) the LLP, and
(b) every designated member of the LLP who is in default.
(7) A person guilty of an offence under subsection (6) is liable on summary conviction to a fine not exceeding level 5 on the standard scale and, for continued contravention, a daily default fine not exceeding one-tenth of level 5 on the standard scale.

1034. Effect of restoration to the register where property has vested as bona vacantia

(1) The person in whom any property or right is vested by section 1012 (property of dissolved LLP to be bona vacantia) may dispose of, or of an interest in, that property or right despite the fact that the LLP may be restored to the register under this Chapter.
(2) If the LLP is restored to the register—
(a) the restoration does not affect the disposition (but without prejudice to its effect in relation to any other property or right previously vested in or held on trust for the LLP), and
(b) the Crown or, as the case may be, the Duke of Cornwall shall pay to the LLP an amount equal to—
(i) the amount of any consideration received for the property or right or, as the case may be, the interest in it, or
(ii) the value of any such consideration at the time of the disposition,

or, if no consideration was received an amount equal to the value of the property, right or interest disposed of, as at the date of the disposition.
(3) There may be deducted from the amount payable under subsection (2)(b) the reasonable costs of the Crown representative in connection with the disposition (to the extent that they have not been paid as a condition of administrative restoration or pursuant to a court order for restoration).
(4) Where a liability accrues under subsection (2) in respect of any property or right which before the restoration of the LLP to the register had accrued as bona vacantia to the Duchy of Lancaster, the Attorney General of that Duchy shall represent Her Majesty in any proceedings arising in connection with that liability.
(5) Where a liability accrues under subsection (2) in respect of any property or right which before the restoration of the LLP to the register had accrued as bona vacantia to the Duchy of Cornwall, such persons as the Duke of Cornwall (or other possessor for the time being of the Duchy) may appoint shall represent the Duke (or other possessor) in any proceedings arising out of that liability.
(6) In this section the "Crown representative" means—
(a) in relation to property vested in the Duchy of Lancaster, the Solicitor to that Duchy;
(b) in relation to property vested in the Duke of Cornwall, the Solicitor to the Duchy of Cornwall;
(c) in relation to property in Scotland, the Queen's and Lord Treasurer's Remembrancer;
(d) in relation to other property, the Treasury Solicitor.".

PART 14
OVERSEAS LLPS

Trading disclosures

59.

Section 1051 applies to LLPs, modified so that it reads as follows—

"1051. Trading disclosures

(1) The following provisions of Part 7 of the Overseas Companies Regulations 2009 (SI 2009/1801) (trading disclosures) apply to LLPs—

(a) regulation 58(2);

(b) regulation 59;

(c) regulations 61 and 62;

(d) regulation 66;

(e) regulation 67(1) and (2).

(2) As those provisions apply to LLPs—

(a) for references to an overseas company substitute references to an overseas LLP;

(b) for references to an officer of a company substitute references to a member of an LLP;

(c) for regulation 61(1) substitute—

"(1) Every overseas LLP must display the name of the LLP and the country in which it is incorporated or otherwise established at every location where it carries on business in the United Kingdom.";

(d) for the introductory words to regulation 62 substitute—

"Every overseas LLP must state the LLP's name and the country in which it is incorporated on all—"

(3) For the purposes of paragraph (2)(a) above, "overseas LLP" means a body incorporated or otherwise established outside the United Kingdom whose name under its law of incorporation or establishment includes (or when translated into English includes) the words "limited liability partnership" or the abbreviation "llp" or "LLP".".

PART 15
THE REGISTRAR OF COMPANIES

Provisions of general application

60.

(1) The application to LLPs by the following regulations of certain provisions of Part 35 of the Companies Act 2006 is without prejudice to the application in relation to LLPs of the provisions of that Part that are of general application.

(2) Those provisions are—

sections 1060(1) and (2) and 1061 to 1063 (the registrar),
sections 1068 to 1071 (delivery of documents to the registrar),
sections 1072 to 1076 (requirements for proper delivery),
sections 1080(1), (4) and (5) and 1092 (keeping and production of records),
section 1083 (preservation of original documents),
sections 1108 to 1110 (language requirements: transliteration),
sections 1111 and 1114 to 1119 (supplementary provisions).

Certificates of incorporation

61.

Sections 1064 and 1065 apply to LLPs, modified so that they read as follows—

"1064. Public notice of issue of certificate of incorporation

(1) The registrar must cause to be published—

(a) in the Gazette, or

(b) in accordance with section 1116 (alternative means of giving public notice),

notice of the issue by the registrar of any certificate of incorporation of an LLP.

(2) The notice must state the name and registered number of the LLP and the date of issue of the certificate.

(3) This section applies to a certificate issued under—

(a) paragraph 5 of the Schedule to the Limited Liability Partnerships Act 2000 (c 12) (change of name: registration and issue of certificate of change of name), or

(b) section 88(4) of this Act (Welsh LLPs),

as well as to the certificate issued on an LLP's formation.

1065. Right to certificate of incorporation

Any person may require the registrar to provide him with a copy of any certificate of incorporation of an LLP, signed by the registrar or authenticated by the registrar's seal.".

Registered numbers

62.

Section 1066 applies to LLPs, modified so that it reads as follows—

"1066. LLP's registered numbers

(1) The registrar shall allocate to every LLP a number, which shall be known as the LLP's registered number.

(2) LLPs' registered numbers shall be in such form, consisting of one or more sequences of figures or letters, as the registrar may determine.

(3) The registrar may on adopting a new form of registered number make such changes of existing registered numbers as appear necessary.

(4) A change of an LLP's registered number has effect from the date on which the LLP is notified by the registrar of the change.

(5) For a period of three years beginning with that date any requirement to disclose the LLP's registered number imposed by section 82 or section 1051 (trading disclosures) is satisfied by the use of either the old number or the new.".

Public notice of receipt of certain documents

63.

Sections 1077 to 1079 apply to LLPs, modified so that they read as follows—

"1077. Public notice of receipt of certain documents

(1) The registrar must cause to be published—

(a) in the Gazette, or

(b) in accordance with section 1116 (alternative means of giving public notice),

notice of the receipt by the registrar of any document specified in section 1078.

(2) The notice must state the name and registered number of the LLP, the description of document and the date of receipt.

(3) The registrar is not required to cause notice of the receipt of a document to be published before the date of incorporation of the LLP to which the document relates.

1078. The section 1077 documents

The following documents are specified for the purposes of section 1077—

Constitutional documents

1. The LLP's incorporation document.
2. Any notice delivered under section 8(4) of the Limited Liability Partnerships Act 2000 (c 12).
3. Any notice of the change of the LLP's name.

Members

1. Notification of any change in the membership of the LLP.

2. Notification of any change in the particulars of members required to be delivered to the registrar.

Accounts and returns

1. All documents required to be delivered to the registrar under section 441 (annual accounts).

1A. All documents delivered to the registrar under sections 394A(2)(e), 448A(2)(e) and 479A(2)(e) (qualifying subsidiaries: conditions for exemptions from the audit, preparation and filing of individual accounts).

2. The LLP's annual return.

Registered office

Notification of any change of the LLP's registered office.

Winding up

1. Copy of any winding-up order in respect of the LLP.
2. Notice of the appointment of liquidators.
3. Order for the dissolution of an LLP on a winding up.
4. Return by a liquidator of the final meeting of an LLP on a winding up.

1079. Effect of failure to give public notice

(1) An LLP is not entitled to rely against other persons on the happening of any event to which this section applies unless—

(a) the event has been officially notified at the material time, or

(b) the LLP shows that the person concerned knew of the event at the material time.

(2) The events to which this section applies are—

(a) (as regards service of any document on the LLP) a change of the LLP's registered office,

(b) the making of a winding-up order in respect of the LLP, or

(c) the appointment of a liquidator in a voluntary winding up of the LLP.

(3) If the material time falls—

(a) on or before the 15th day after the date of official notification, or

(b) where the 15th day was not a working day, on or before the next day that was,

the LLP is not entitled to rely on the happening of the event as against a person who shows that he was unavoidably prevented from knowing of the event at that time.

(4) "Official notification" means—

(a) in relation to anything stated in a document specified in section 1078, notification of that document in accordance with section 1077;

(b) in relation to the appointment of a liquidator in a voluntary winding up, notification of that event in accordance with section 109 of the Insolvency Act 1986 (c 45) or Article 95 of the Insolvency (Northern Ireland) Order 1989 (SI 1989/2405 (NI 19)).".

The register

64.

Sections 1081 and 1082 apply to LLPs, modified so that they read as follows—

"1081. Annotation of the register

(1) The registrar must place a note in the register recording—

(a) the date on which a document is delivered to the registrar;

(b) if a document is corrected under section 1075, the nature and date of the correction;

(c) if a document is replaced (whether or not material derived from it is removed), the fact that it has been replaced and the date of delivery of the replacement;

(d) if material is removed—

(i) what was removed (giving a general description of its contents),

(ii) under what power, and

(iii) the date on which that was done.

(2) Regulation 3 of the Registrar of Companies and Applications for Striking Off Regulations 2009 (SI 2009/1803) applies to LLPs as regards—

(a) other circumstances in which the registrar is required or authorised to annotate the register, and

(b) the contents of any such annotation.

(3) No annotation is required in the case of a document that by virtue of section 1072(2) (documents not meeting requirements for proper delivery) is treated as not having been delivered.

(4) A note may be removed if it no longer serves any useful purpose.

(5) Any duty or power of the registrar with respect to annotation of the register is subject to the court's power under section 1097 (powers of court on ordering removal of material from the register) to direct—

(a) that a note be removed from the register, or

(b) that no note shall be made of the removal of material that is the subject of the court's order.

(6) Notes placed in the register in accordance with subsection (1), or in pursuance of the provision referred to in subsection (2), are part of the register for all purposes of the Companies Acts and the Limited Liability Partnerships Act 2000.

1082. Allocation of unique identifiers

(1) The Secretary of State may make provision for the use, in connection with the register, of reference numbers ("unique identifiers") to identify each person who is a member of an LLP.

(2) The regulations may—

(a) provide that a unique identifier may be in such form, consisting of one or more sequences of letters or numbers, as the registrar may from time to time determine;

(b) make provision for the allocation of unique identifiers by the registrar;

(c) require there to be included, in any specified description of documents delivered to the registrar, as well as a statement of the person's name—

(i) a statement of the person's unique identifier, or

(ii) a statement that the person has not been allocated a unique identifier;

(d) enable the registrar to take steps where a person appears to have more than one unique identifier to discontinue the use of all but one of them.

(3) The regulations may contain provision for the application of the scheme in relation to persons appointed, and documents registered, before the commencement of this Act.

(4) The regulations may make different provision for different descriptions of person and different descriptions of document.

(5) Regulations under this section are subject to affirmative resolution procedure.".

65.

Section 1084 applies to LLPs, modified so that it reads as follows—

"1084. Records relating to LLPs that have been dissolved

(1) This section applies where an LLP is dissolved.

(2) At any time after two years from the date on which it appears to the registrar that the LLP has been dissolved, the registrar may direct that records relating to the LLP may be removed to the Public Record Office or, as the case may be, the Public Record Office of Northern Ireland.

(3) Records in respect of which such a direction is given shall be disposed of under the enactments relating to that Office and the rules made under them.

(4) This section does not extend to Scotland.".

66.

Sections 1085 to 1091 apply to LLPs, modified so that they read as follows—

"1085. Inspection of the register

(1) Any person may inspect the register.

(2) The right of inspection extends to the originals of documents delivered to the registrar in hard copy form if, and only if, the record kept by the registrar of the contents of the document is illegible or unavailable.

The period for which such originals are to be kept is limited by section 1083(1).

(3) This section has effect subject to section 1087 (material not available for public inspection).

1086. Right to copy of material not on the register

(1) Any person may require a copy of any material on the register.

(2) The fee for any such copy of material derived from a document specified for the purposes of section 1077, whether in hard copy or electronic form, must not exceed the administrative cost of providing it.

(3) This section has effect subject to section 1087 (material not available for public inspection).

1087. Material not available for public inspection

(1) The following material must not be made available by the registrar for public inspection—

(a) the contents of any document sent to the registrar containing views expressed pursuant to section 56 (comments on proposal by LLP to use certain words or expressions in LLP name);

(b) protected information within section 242(1) (members' residential addresses: restriction on disclosure by registrar);

(c) representations received by the registrar in response to a notice under section 245(2) (notice of proposal to put member's usual residential address on the public record);

(d) any application to the registrar under section 1024 (application for administrative restoration to the register) that has not yet been determined or was not successful;

(e) any document received by the registrar in connection with the giving or withdrawal of consent under section 1075 (informal correction of documents);

(f) any application or other document delivered to the registrar under section 1088 (application to make address unavailable for public inspection) and any address in respect of which such an application is successful;

(g) any application or other document delivered to the registrar under section 1095 (application for rectification of register);

(h) any court order under section 1096 (rectification of the register under court order) that the court has directed under section 1097 (powers of court on ordering removal of material from the register) is not to be made available for public inspection;

(i) the contents of—

(i) any instrument creating or evidencing a charge, or

(ii) any certified or verified copy of an instrument creating or evidencing a charge,

delivered to the registrar under Part 25 (LLP charges);

(j) any e-mail address, identification code or password deriving from a document delivered for the purpose of authorising or facilitating electronic filing procedures or providing information by telephone;

(k) any other material excluded from public inspection by or under any other enactment.

(2) A restriction applying by reference to material deriving from a particular description of document does not affect the availability for public inspection of the same information contained in material derived from another description of document in relation to which no such restriction applies.

(3) Material to which this section applies need not be retained by the registrar for longer than appears to the registrar reasonably necessary for the purposes for which the material was delivered to the registrar.

1088. Application to registrar to make address unavailable for public inspection

(1) The provisions of the Companies (Disclosure of Address) Regulations 2009 (SI 2009/214) relating to applications to make an address unavailable for inspection under this section apply to LLPs.

(2) The provisions are—

(a) Part 3 (disclosure of protected information),

(b) Part 4 (matters relating to applications), so far as relating to applications to make an address unavailable for inspection under this section, and

(c) any other provisions of the Regulations having effect for the purposes of those provisions.

(3) As those provisions apply to LLPs—

(a) references in the regulations to provisions of the Companies Act 1985 (c 6) or the Companies (Northern Ireland) Order 1986 (SI 1986/1032 (NI 6)) are to those provisions as applied to LLPs by the Limited Liability Partnerships Regulations 2001 (SI 2001/1090) or the Limited Liability Partnerships Regulations (Northern Ireland) 2004 (SR (NI) 2004 No 307);

(b) read references to a company as references to an LLP;

(c) read references to a director as references to a member of an LLP;

(d) omit all references to secretaries or permanent representatives;

(e) in regulation 1(2) for the definition of "former name" substitute—

""former name" means a name by which the individual was formerly known and which has been notified to the registrar under section 2 or 9 of the Limited Liability Partnerships Act 2000;";

(f) in regulation 9, for paragraph (1) substitute—

"(1) A section 1088 application may be made to the registrar by an individual whose usual residential address was placed on the register either—

(a) under section 288 (register of members) or 363 (duty to deliver annual returns) of the 1985 Act;

(b) under Article 296 or 371 of the 1986 Order;

(c) under section 2 (incorporation document etc) or 9 (registration of membership changes) of the Limited Liability Partnerships Act 2000; or

(d) as a service address under section 855 (contents of annual return) of the Act,

in respect of that usual residential address where it was placed on the register on or after 1st January 2003;"; and

(g) omit regulation 10.

1089. Form of application for inspection or copy

The registrar may specify the form and manner in which application is to be made for—

(a) inspection under section 1085, or

(b) a copy under section 1086.

1090. Form and manner in which copies to be provided

The registrar may determine the form and manner in which copies are to be provided.

1091. Certification of copies as accurate

(1) Copies provided under section 1086 in hard copy form must be certified as true copies unless the applicant dispenses with such certification.

(2) Copies so provided in electronic form must not be certified as true copies unless the applicant expressly requests such certification.

(3) A copy provided under section 1086, certified by the registrar (whose official position it is unnecessary to prove) to be an accurate record of the contents of the original document, is in all legal proceedings admissible in evidence—

(a) as of equal validity with the original document, and

(b) as evidence (in Scotland, sufficient evidence) of any fact stated in the original document of which direct oral evidence would be admissible.

(4) Regulation 2 of the Companies (Registrar, Languages and Trading Disclosures) Regulations 2006 (SI 2006/3429) (certification of electronic copies by registrar) applies where the copy is provided in electronic form.

(5) Copies provided by the registrar may, instead of being certified in writing to be an accurate record, be sealed with the registrar's official seal.".

Correction or removal of material on the register

67.

Sections 1093 to 1098 apply to LLPs, modified so that they read as follows—

"1093. Registrar's notice to resolve inconsistency on the register

(1) Where it appears to the registrar that the information contained in a document delivered to the registrar is inconsistent with other information on the register, the registrar may give notice to the LLP to which the document relates—

(a) stating in what respects the information contained in it appears to be inconsistent with other information on the register, and

(b) requiring the LLP to take steps to resolve the inconsistency.

(2) The notice must—

(a) state the date on which it is issued, and

(b) require the delivery to the registrar, within 14 days after that date, of such replacement or additional documents as may be required to resolve the inconsistency.

(3) If the necessary documents are not delivered within the period specified, an offence is committed by—

(a) the LLP, and

(b) every member of the LLP who is in default.

(4) A person guilty of an offence under subsection (3) is liable on summary conviction to a fine not exceeding level 5 on the standard scale and, for continued contravention, a daily default fine not exceeding one-tenth of level 5 on the standard scale.

1094. Administrative removal of material from the register

(1) The registrar may remove from the register anything that there was power, but no duty, to include.

(2) This power is exercisable, in particular, so as to remove—

(a) unnecessary material within the meaning of section 1074, and

(b) material derived from a document that has been replaced under—

section 1076 (replacement of document not meeting requirements for proper delivery), or

section 1093 (notice to remedy inconsistency on the register).

(3) This section does not authorise the removal from the register of—

(a) anything whose registration has had legal consequences in relation to the LLP as regards—

(i) its formation,

(ii) a change of name,

(iii) a change of registered office,

(iv) a change in the situation of a registered office,

(v) the registration of a charge, or

(vi) its dissolution;

(b) an address that is a person's registered address for the purposes of section 1140 (service of documents on members and others).

(4) On or before removing any material under this section (otherwise than at the request of the LLP) the registrar must give notice—

(a) to the person by whom the material was delivered (if the identity, and name and address of that person are known), or

(b) to the LLP to which the material relates (if notice cannot be given under paragraph (a) and the identity of that LLP is known).

(5) The notice must—

(a) state what material the registrar proposes to remove, or has removed, and on what grounds, and
(b) state the date on which it is issued.

1095. Rectification of register on application to registrar

(1) The provisions of the Registrar of Companies and Applications for Striking Off Regulations 2009 (SI 2009/1803) requiring the registrar, on application, to remove from the register material that—
(a) derives from anything invalid or ineffective or that was done without authority, or
(b) is factually inaccurate, or is derived from something that is factually inaccurate or forged, apply to LLPs.

(2) Those provisions are—
(a) regulations 4 and 5, and
(b) any other provisions of the regulations having effect for the purposes of those provisions.

(2A) In those provisions as they apply to LLPs—
(a) for "company" substitute "LLP", and for "relevant company form" substitute "relevant LLP form";
(b) omit all references to overseas companies and overseas company forms;
(c) omit all references to secretaries;
(d) in regulation 4—
(i) for paragraph (3) substitute—
"(3) A "relevant LLP form" is—
(a) a standard form required for giving notice under section 87 of the Companies Act 2006 (change of address of registered office) or section 9 of the Limited Liability Partnerships Act 2000 (c 12) (changes relating to members); or
(b) so much of a standard form required for delivering an application under section 2 of the Limited Liability Partnerships Act 2000 (incorporation document etc) as is required for the statement of those who are to be members of the LLP referred to in section 2(2)(e).",
(ii) omit paragraphs (4) and (6),
(iii) in paragraph (7) omit "or (6)", and
(iv) in paragraph (8)(a), for "(2), (3), (4) or (5)" substitute "(2) or (3)";
(e) in regulation 5—
(i) in paragraph (1)(b), omit "or (6)",
(ii) in paragraphs (2)(b) and (3)(b), for "director or secretary of the company" substitute "designated member of the LLP",
(iii) omit paragraphs (4) to (7) and (16),
(iv) in paragraphs (8), (11), (12) and (14)(c), for "(2), (3), (4) or (5)" substitute "(2) or (3)"; and
(v) omit paragraph (8)(b) and (c).

(3) An application must—
(a) specify what is to be removed from the register and indicate where on the register it is, and
(b) be accompanied by a statement that the material specified in the application complies with this section and the regulations.

(4) If no objections are made to the application, the registrar may accept the statement as sufficient evidence that the material specified in the application should be removed from the register.

(5) Where anything is removed from the register under this section the registration of which had legal consequences as mentioned in section 1094(3), any person appearing to the court to

have a sufficient interest may apply to the court for such consequential orders as appear just with respect to the legal effect (if any) to be accorded to the material by virtue of its having appeared on the register.

1096. Rectification of the register under court order

(1) The registrar shall remove from the register any material—

(a) that derives from anything that the court has declared to be invalid or ineffective, or to have been done without the authority of the LLP, or

(b) that a court declares to be factually inaccurate, or to be derived from something that is factually inaccurate, or forged,

and that the court directs should be removed from the register.

(2) The court order must specify what is to be removed from the register and indicate where on the register it is.

(3) The court must not make an order for the removal from the register of anything the registration of which had legal consequences as mentioned in section 1094(3) unless satisfied—

(a) that the presence of the material on the register has caused, or may cause, damage to the LLP, and

(b) that the LLP's interest in removing the material outweighs any interest of other persons in the material continuing to appear on the register.

(4) Where in such a case the court does make an order for removal, it may make such consequential orders as appear just with respect to the legal effect (if any) to be accorded to the material by virtue of its having appeared on the register.

(5) A copy of the court's order must be sent to the registrar for registration.

(6) This section does not apply where the court has other, specific, powers to deal with the matter, for example under—

(a) the provisions of Part 15 relating to the revision of defective accounts, or

(b) section 873 or 888 (rectification of the register of charges).

1097. Powers of court on ordering removal of material from the register

(1) Where the court makes an order for the removal of anything from the register under section 1096 (rectification of the register), it may give directions under this section.

(2) It may direct that any note on the register that is related to the material that is the subject of the court's order shall be removed from the register.

(3) It may direct that its order shall not be available for public inspection as part of the register.

(4) It may direct—

(a) that no note shall be made on the register as a result of its order, or

(b) that any such note shall be restricted to such matters as may be specified by the court.

(5) The court shall not give any direction under this section unless it is satisfied—

(a) that—

(i) the presence on the register of the note or, as the case may be, of an unrestricted note, or

(ii) the availability for public inspection of the court's order,

may cause damage to the LLP, and

(b) that the LLP's interest in non-disclosure outweighs any interest of other persons in disclosure.

1098. Public notice of removal of certain material from the register

(1) The registrar must cause to be published—

(a) in the Gazette, or

(b) in accordance with section 1116 (alternative means of giving public notice),

notice of the removal from the register of any document specified in section 1078 or of any material derived from such a document.

(2) The notice must state the name and registered number of the LLP, the description of document and the date of receipt.".

Language requirements: translation

68.

Sections 1103 to 1107 apply to LLPs, modified so that they read as follows—

"1103. Documents to be drawn up and delivered in English

(1) The general rule is that all documents required to be delivered to the registrar must be drawn up and delivered in English.

(2) This is subject to—
section 1104 (documents relating to Welsh LLPs) and
section 1105 (documents that may be drawn up and delivered in other languages).

1104. Documents relating to Welsh LLPs

(1) Documents relating to a Welsh LLP may be drawn up and delivered to the registrar in Welsh.

(2) On delivery to the registrar any such document must be accompanied by a certified translation into English, unless they are—

(a) annual accounts and auditors' reports required to be delivered to the registrar under Part 15,

(b) revised accounts, and any auditor's report on such revised accounts, required to be delivered to the registrar by the Companies (Revision of Defective Accounts and Reports) Regulations 2008 (SI 2008/373), or

(c) in a form prescribed in Welsh (or partly in Welsh and partly in English) by virtue of section 26 of the Welsh Language Act 1993 (c 38),

(d) documents to be delivered to the registrar under sections 394A(2)(e), 448A(2)(e) and 479A(2)(e) (qualifying subsidiaries: conditions for exemptions from the audit, preparation and filing of individual accounts).

(3) Where a document is properly delivered to the registrar in Welsh without a certified translation into English, the registrar must obtain such a translation if the document is to be available for public inspection.
The translation is treated as if delivered to the registrar in accordance with the same provision as the original.

(4) A Welsh LLP may deliver to the registrar a certified translation into Welsh of any document in English that relates to the LLP and is or has been delivered to the registrar.

(5) Section 1105 (which requires certified translations into English of documents delivered to the registrar in another language) does not apply to a document relating to a Welsh LLP that is drawn up and delivered in Welsh.

1105. Documents that may be drawn up and delivered in other languages

(1) Documents to which this section applies may be drawn up and delivered to the registrar in a language other than English, but when delivered to the registrar they must be accompanied by a certified translation into English.

(2) This section applies to—

(a) documents required to be delivered under section 400(2)(e) or section 401(2)(f) (LLP included in accounts of larger group: required to deliver copy of group accounts);

(b) instruments or copy instruments required to be delivered under Part 25 (LLP charges);

(c) any order made by a competent court in the United Kingdom or elsewhere;

(d) copies of the consolidated accounts, the auditor's report and the consolidated annual report to be delivered to the registrar under sections 394A(2)(e), 448A(2)(e) and 479A(2)(e) (qualifying subsidiaries: conditions for exemption from the audit, preparation and filing of individual accounts).

1106. Voluntary filing of translations

(1) An LLP may deliver to the registrar one or more certified translations of any document relating to the LLP that is or has been delivered to the registrar.

(2) The facility described in subsection (1) is available in relation to—

(a) all the official languages of the European Union, and

(b) all the documents specified by section 1078.

(3) The power of the registrar to impose requirements as to the form and manner of delivery includes power to impose requirements as to the identification of the original document and the delivery of the translation in a form and manner enabling it to be associated with the original.

(4) This section does not apply where the original document was delivered to the registrar before this section came into force.

1107. Certified translations

(1) In this Part a "certified translation" means a translation certified to be a correct translation.

(2) In the case of any discrepancy between the original language version of a document and a certified translation—

(a) the LLP may not rely on the translation as against a third party, but

(b) a third party may rely on the translation unless the LLP shows that the third party had knowledge of the original.

(3) A "third party" means a person other than the LLP or the registrar.".

Supplementary provisions

69.

Sections 1112 and 1113 apply to LLPs, modified so that they read as follows—

"1112. General false statement offence

(1) It is an offence for a person knowingly or recklessly—

(a) to deliver or cause to be delivered to the registrar, for any purpose of this Act or the Limited Liability Partnerships Act 2000 (c 12), a document, or

(b) to make to the registrar, for any such purpose, a statement,

that is misleading, false or deceptive in a material particular.

(2) A person guilty of an offence under this section is liable—

(a) on conviction on indictment, to imprisonment for a term not exceeding two years or a fine (or both);

(b) on summary conviction—

(i) in England and Wales or Scotland, to imprisonment for a term not exceeding twelve months or to a fine not exceeding the statutory maximum (or both);

(ii) in Northern Ireland, to imprisonment for a term not exceeding six months, or to a fine not exceeding the statutory maximum (or both).

1113. Enforcement of LLP's filing obligations

(1) This section applies where an LLP has made default in complying with any obligation under this Act or the Limited Liability Partnerships Act 2000 (c 12)—

(a) to deliver a document to the registrar, or

(b) to give notice to the registrar of any matter.

(2) The registrar, or any member or creditor of the LLP, may give notice to the LLP requiring it to comply with the obligation.

(3) If the LLP fails to make good the default within 14 days after service of the notice, the registrar, or any member or creditor of the LLP, may apply to the court for an order directing the LLP, and any specified member of it, to make good the default within a specified time.

(4) The court's order may provide that all costs (in Scotland, expenses) of or incidental to the application are to be borne by the LLP or by any members of it responsible for the default.

(5) This section does not affect the operation of any enactment making it an offence, or imposing a civil penalty, for the default.".

PART 16
OFFENCES

Liability of member in default

70.

Sections 1121 and 1122 apply to LLPs for the purposes of these Regulations, modified so that they read as follows—

"1121. Liability of member in default

(1) This section has effect for the purposes of any provision of the Companies Acts to the effect that, in the event of contravention of an enactment in relation to an LLP, an offence is committed by every member or, as the case may be, every designated member of the LLP who is in default.

(2) A member or designated member is "in default" for the purposes of the provision if he authorises or permits, participates in, or fails to take all reasonable steps to prevent, the contravention.

1122. Liability of company or LLP as member in default

(1) Where a company or an LLP is a member or designated member of an LLP, it does not commit an offence as a member or designated member in default unless (in the case of a company) one of its officers is in default, or (in the case of a member LLP) one of its members is in default.

(2) Where any such offence is committed by a company or LLP the officer or member in question also commits the offence and is liable to be proceeded against and punished accordingly.

(3) In this section an officer or member is "in default" for the purposes of the provision if he authorises or permits, participates in, or fails to take all reasonable steps to prevent, the contravention.".

Daily default fine

71.

Section 1125 applies to LLPs for the purposes of these Regulations as follows—

"1125. Meaning of "daily default fine"

(1) This section defines what is meant in the Companies Acts where it is provided that a person guilty of an offence is liable on summary conviction to a fine not exceeding a specified amount "and, for continued contravention, a daily default fine" not exceeding a specified amount.

(2) This means that the person is liable on a second or subsequent summary conviction of the offence to a fine not exceeding the latter amount for each day on which the contravention is continued (instead of being liable to a fine not exceeding the former amount).".

Consents for certain prosecutions

72.

Section 1126 applies to LLPs, modified so that it reads as follows—

"1126. Consents required for certain prosecutions

(1) This section applies to proceedings for an offence under section 448, 449, 450, 451 or 453A of the Companies Act 1985, as applied to LLPs.

(2) No such proceedings are to be brought in England and Wales except by or with the consent of the Secretary of State or the Director of Public Prosecutions.

(3) No such proceedings are to be brought in Northern Ireland except by or with the consent of the Secretary of State or the Director of Public Prosecutions for Northern Ireland.".

73.

Sections 1127 to 1133 apply to LLPs for the purposes of these Regulations, modified so that they read as follows—

"1127. Summary proceedings: venue

(1) Summary proceedings for any offence under the Companies Acts may be taken—

(a) against a body corporate, at any place at which the body has a place of business, and

(b) against any other person, at any place at which he is for the time being.

(2) This is without prejudice to any jurisdiction exercisable apart from this section.

1128. Summary proceedings: time limit for proceedings

(1) An information relating to an offence under the Companies Acts that is triable by a magistrates' court in England and Wales may be so tried if it is laid—

(a) at any time within three years after the commission of the offence, and

(b) within twelve months after the date on which evidence sufficient in the opinion of the Director of Public Prosecutions or the Secretary of State (as the case may be) to justify the proceedings comes to his knowledge.

(2) Summary proceedings in Scotland for an offence under the Companies Acts—

(a) must not be commenced after the expiration of three years from the commission of the offence;

(b) subject to that, may be commenced at any time—

(i) within twelve months after the date on which evidence sufficient in the Lord Advocate's opinion to justify the proceedings came to his knowledge, or

(ii) where such evidence was reported to him by the Secretary of State, within twelve months after the date on which it came to the knowledge of the latter.

Section 136(3) of the Criminal Procedure (Scotland) Act 1995 (c 46) (date when proceedings deemed to be commenced) applies for the purposes of this subsection as for the purposes of that section.

(3) A magistrates' court in Northern Ireland has jurisdiction to hear and determine a complaint charging the commission of a summary offence under the Companies Acts provided that the complaint is made—

(a) within three years from the time when the offence was committed, and

(b) within twelve months from the date on which evidence sufficient in the opinion of the Director of Public Prosecutions for Northern Ireland or the Secretary of State (as the case may be) to justify the proceedings comes to his knowledge..

(4) For the purposes of this section a certificate of the Director of Public Prosecutions, the Lord Advocate, the Director of Public Prosecutions for Northern Ireland or the Secretary of State (as the case may be) as to the date on which such evidence as is referred to above came to his notice is conclusive evidence.

1129. Legal professional privilege

In proceedings against a person for an offence under the Companies Acts, nothing in those Acts is to be taken to require any person to disclose any information that he is entitled to refuse to disclose on grounds of legal professional privilege (in Scotland, confidentiality of communications).

1130. Proceedings against unincorporated bodies

(1) Proceedings for an offence under the Companies Acts alleged to have been committed by an unincorporated body must be brought in the name of the body (and not in that of any of its members).

(2) For the purposes of such proceedings—

(a) any rules of court relating to the service of documents have effect as if the body were a body corporate, and

(b) the following provisions apply as they apply in relation to a body corporate—

(i) in England and Wales, section 33 of the Criminal Justice Act 1925 (c 86) and Schedule 3 to the Magistrates' Courts Act 1980 (c 43),

(ii) in Scotland, sections 70 and 143 of the Criminal Procedure (Scotland) Act 1995 (c 46),

(iii) in Northern Ireland, section 18 of the Criminal Justice Act (Northern Ireland) 1945 (c 15 (NI)) and Article 166 of and Schedule 4 to the Magistrates' Courts (Northern Ireland) Order 1981 (SI 1981/1675 (NI 26)).

(3) A fine imposed on an unincorporated body on its conviction of an offence under the Companies Acts must be paid out of the funds of the body.

1131. Imprisonment on summary conviction in England and Wales: transitory provision

(1) This section applies to any provision of the Companies Acts that provides that a person guilty of an offence is liable on summary conviction in England and Wales to imprisonment for a term not exceeding twelve months.

(2) In relation to an offence committed before the commencement of section 154(1) of the Criminal Justice Act 2003 (c 44), for "twelve months" substitute "six months".

1132. Production and inspection of documents where offence suspected

(1) An application under this section may be made—

(a) in England and Wales, to a judge of the High Court by the Director of Public Prosecutions, the Secretary of State or a chief officer of police;

(b) in Scotland, to one of the Lords Commissioners of Justiciary by the Lord Advocate;

(c) in Northern Ireland, to the High Court by the Director of Public Prosecutions for Northern Ireland, the Department of Enterprise, Trade and Investment or a chief superintendent of the Police Service of Northern Ireland.

(2) If on an application under this section there is shown to be reasonable cause to believe—

(a) that any person has, while a member of an LLP, committed an offence in connection with the management of the LLP's affairs, and

(b) that evidence of the commission of the offence is to be found in any documents in the possession or control of the LLP,

an order under this section may be made.

(3) The order may—

(a) authorise any person named in it to inspect the documents in question, or any of them, for the purpose of investigating and obtaining evidence of the offence, or

(b) require such member of the LLP as may be named in the order, to produce the documents (or any of them) to a person named in the order at a place so named.

(4) This section applies also in relation to documents in the possession or control of a person carrying on the business of banking, so far as they relate to the LLP's affairs, as it applies to documents in the possession or control of the LLP, except that no such order as is referred to in subsection (3)(b) may be made by virtue of this subsection.

(5) The decision under this section of a judge of the High Court, any of the Lords Commissioners of Justiciary or the High Court is not appealable.

(6) In this section "document" includes information recorded in any form.

1133. Transitional provision

The provisions of this Part except section 1132 do not apply to offences committed before 1st October 2009.".

PART 17

SUPPLEMENTARY PROVISIONS AND INTERPRETATION

LLP records

74.

Sections 1134 to 1138 apply to LLPs, modified so that they read as follows—

"1134. Meaning of "LLP records"

In this Part "LLP records" means—

(a) any register, index, accounting records, agreement, memorandum, minutes or other document required by this Act to be kept by an LLP, and
(b) any register kept by an LLP of its debenture holders.

1135. Form of LLP records

(1) LLP records—
  (a) may be kept in hard copy or electronic form, and
  (b) may be arranged in such manner as the members of the LLP think fit,
  provided the information in question is adequately recorded for future reference.
(2) Where the records are kept in electronic form, they must be capable of being reproduced in hard copy form.
(3) If an LLP fails to comply with this section, an offence is committed by every member of the LLP who is in default.
(4) A person guilty of an offence under this section is liable on summary conviction to a fine not exceeding level 3 on the standard scale and, for continued contravention, a daily default fine not exceeding one-tenth of level 3 on the standard scale.

1136. Where certain LLP records to be kept available for inspection

(1) The provisions of the Companies (Company Records) Regulations 2008 (SI 2008/3006) relating to places other than the registered office at which records required to be kept available for inspection under a relevant provision may be so kept in compliance with that provision apply to LLPs.
(2) The "relevant provisions" are—
  section 162 (register of members);
  section 743 (register of debenture holders);
  section 877 (instruments creating charges and register of charges: England and Wales);
  section 892 (instruments creating charges and register of charges: Scotland).
(3) The provisions applied by subsection (1) are—
  (a) regulation 3, and
  (b) any other provision of the regulations having effect for the purposes of that provision.
(4) In the application of those provisions to LLPs for "company" substitute "LLP".

1137. Inspection of records and provision of copies

(1) The provisions of the Companies (Company Records) Regulations 2008 (SI 2008/3006) as to the obligations of an LLP that is required by any provision of this Act or of the Limited Liability Partnerships Act 2000 (c 12)—
  (a) to keep available for inspection any LLP records, or
  (b) to provide copies of any LLP records,
  apply to LLPs.
(2) Those provisions are—
  (a) Part 3 (inspection of records),
  (b) Part 4 (provision of copies of records), and
  (c) any other provision of the regulations having effect for the purposes of those provisions.
(3) As those provisions apply to LLPs—
  (a) for "a company" or "the company" substitute "an LLP" or "the LLP";
  (b) for "company record" substitute "LLP record";
  (c) in regulation 4 (inspection: private company)—
    (i) for the reference in paragraph (1) to a private company substitute a reference to an LLP,
    (ii) for sub-paragraph (b) substitute—
      "(b) that person gives the LLP at least 10 working days' notice of the specified day.";
  (d) omit paragraphs (2) and (3); and
  (e) omit regulation 5 (inspection: public company).

(4) An LLP that fails to comply with the regulations is treated as having refused inspection or, as the case may be, having failed to provide a copy.

(5) Nothing in any provision of this Act or in the regulations shall be read as preventing an LLP—

(a) from affording more extensive facilities than are required by the regulations, or

(b) where a fee may be charged, from charging a lesser fee than that prescribed or none at all.

1138. Duty to take precautions against falsification

(1) Where LLP records are kept otherwise than in bound books, adequate precautions must be taken—

(a) to guard against falsification, and

(b) to facilitate the discovery of falsification.

(2) If an LLP fails to comply with this section, an offence is committed by every member of the LLP who is in default.

(3) A person guilty of an offence under this section is liable on summary conviction to a fine not exceeding level 3 on the standard scale and, for continued contravention, a daily default fine not exceeding one-tenth of level 3 on the standard scale.".

Service addresses

75.

Sections 1139 to 1142 apply to LLPs, modified so that they read as follows—

"1139. Service of documents on LLP

(1) A document may be served on an LLP by leaving it at, or sending it by post to, the LLP's registered office.

(2) Where an LLP registered in Scotland or Northern Ireland carries on business in England and Wales,

the process of any court in England and Wales may be served on the LLP by leaving it at, or sending it by post to, the LLP's principal place of business in England and Wales, addressed to the manager or a designated member in England and Wales of the LLP.

Where process is served on an LLP under this subsection, the person issuing out the process must send a copy of it by post to the LLP's registered office.

1140. Service of documents on members and others

(1) A document may be served on—

(a) a member of an LLP, or

(b) a person appointed in relation to an LLP as a judicial factor (in Scotland),

by leaving it at, or sending it by post to, the member's or factor's registered address.

(2) This section applies whatever the purpose of the document in question.

(3) For the purposes of this section a person's "registered address" means any address for the time being shown as a current address in relation to that person in the part of the register available for public inspection.

(4) If notice of a change of that address is given to the registrar, a person may validly serve a document at the address previously registered until the end of the period of 14 days beginning with the date on which notice of the change is registered.

(5) Service may not be effected by virtue of this section at an address if notice has been registered of the cessation of the membership or (as the case may be) termination of the appointment in relation to which the address was registered and the address is not a registered address of the person concerned in relation to any other appointment.

(6) Nothing in this section shall be read as affecting any enactment or rule of law under which permission is required for service out of the jurisdiction.

1141. Service addresses

(1) In this Act a "service address", in relation to a person, means an address at which documents may be effectively served on that person.

(2) The service address must be a place where—
(a) the service of documents can be effected by physical delivery; and
(b) the delivery of documents is capable of being recorded by the obtaining of an acknowledgment of delivery.

1142. Requirement to give service address

Any obligation under this Act to give a person's address is, unless otherwise expressly provided, to give a service address for that person.".

Notice of appointment of judicial factor

76.

Sections 1154 and 1155 apply to LLPs, modified so that they read as follows—

"1154. Duty to notify registrar of appointment of judicial factor

(1) Notice must be given to the registrar of the appointment in relation to an LLP of a judicial factor (in Scotland).
(2) The notice must be given by the judicial factor.
(3) The notice must specify an address at which service of documents (including legal process) may be effected on the judicial factor.
Notice of a change in the address for service may be given to the registrar by the judicial factor.
(4) Where notice has been given under this section of the appointment of a judicial factor, notice must also be given to the registrar by the judicial factor of the termination of the appointment.

1155. Offence of failure to give notice

(1) If a judicial factor fails to give notice of his appointment in accordance with section 1154 within the period of 14 days after the appointment he commits an offence.
(2) A person guilty of an offence under this section is liable on summary conviction to a fine not exceeding level 5 on the standard scale and, for continued contravention, a daily default fine not exceeding one-tenth of level 5 on the standard scale.".

Courts and legal proceedings

77.

Sections 1156 and 1157 apply to LLPs for the purposes of these Regulations, modified so that they read as follows—

"1156. Meaning of "the court"

(1) Except as otherwise provided, in this Act "the court" means—
(a) in England and Wales, the High Court or (subject to subsection (3)) a county court;
(b) in Scotland, the Court of Session or the sheriff court;
(c) in Northern Ireland, the High Court.
(2) The provisions of the Companies Acts conferring jurisdiction on "the court" as defined above have effect subject to any enactment or rule of law relating to the allocation of jurisdiction or distribution of business between courts in any part of the United Kingdom.
(3) The Lord Chancellor may, with the concurrence of the Lord Chief Justice, by order—
(a) exclude a county court from having jurisdiction under this Act, and
(b) for the purposes of that jurisdiction attach that court's district, or any part of it, to another county court.
(4) The Lord Chief Justice may nominate a judicial office holder (as defined in section 109(4) of the Constitutional Reform Act 2005 (c 4)) to exercise his functions under subsection (3).

1157. Power of court to grant relief in certain cases

(1) If in proceedings for negligence, default, breach of duty or breach of trust against—
(a) a member of an LLP, or
(b) a person employed by an LLP as auditor,

it appears to the court hearing the case that the member or person is or may be liable but that he acted honestly and reasonably, and that having regard to all the circumstances of the case (including those connected with his appointment) he ought fairly to be excused, the court may relieve him, either wholly or in part, from his liability on such terms as it thinks fit.

(2) If any such member or person has reason to apprehend that a claim will or might be made against him in respect of negligence, default, breach of duty or breach of trust—

(a) he may apply to the court for relief, and

(b) the court has the same power to relieve him as it would have had if it had been a court before which proceedings against him for negligence, default, breach of duty or breach of trust had been brought.

(3) Where a case to which subsection (1) applies is being tried by a judge with a jury, the judge, after hearing the evidence, may, if he is satisfied that the defendant (in Scotland, the defender) ought in pursuance of that subsection to be relieved either in whole or in part from the liability sought to be enforced against him, withdraw the case from the jury and forthwith direct judgment to be entered for the defendant (in Scotland, grant decree of absolvitor) on such terms as to costs (in Scotland, expenses) or otherwise as the judge may think proper.".

Requirements of this Act

78.

Section 1172 applies to LLPs for the purposes of these Regulations, modified so that it reads as follows—

"1172. References to requirements of this Act

References in the provisions of this Act applied to LLPs to the requirements of this Act include the requirements of regulations and orders made under it.".

Minor definitions

79.

Section 1173 applies to LLPs for the purposes of these Regulations, modified so that it reads as follows—

"1173. Minor definitions: general

(1) In this Act—

"body corporate" and "corporation" include a body incorporated outside the United Kingdom, but do not include—

(a) a corporation sole, or

(b) a partnership that, whether or not a legal person, is not regarded as a body corporate under the law by which it is governed;

"the Companies Acts" is to be construed in accordance with section 2;

"firm" means any entity, whether or not a legal person, that is not an individual and includes a body corporate, a corporation sole and a partnership or other unincorporated association;

"the Gazette" means—

(a) as respects LLPs registered in England and Wales, the London Gazette,

(b) as respects LLPs registered in Scotland, the Edinburgh Gazette, and

(c) as respects LLPs registered in Northern Ireland, the Belfast Gazette;

"LLP" means a limited liability partnership registered under the Limited Liability Partnerships Act 2000 (c 12);

"LLP agreement" means any agreement, express or implied, between the members of the LLP or between the LLP and the members of the LLP which determines the mutual rights and duties of the members, and their rights and duties in relation to the LLP;

"officer", in relation to a body corporate, includes a director, manager or secretary;

"working day", in relation to an LLP, means a day that is not a Saturday or Sunday, Christmas Day, Good Friday or any day that is a bank holiday under the Banking and Financial Dealings Act 1971 (c 80) in the part of the United Kingdom where the LLP is registered.

(2) In this Act, unless the context otherwise requires, "enactment" includes—

(a) an enactment contained in subordinate legislation within the meaning of the Interpretation Act 1978 (c 30),

(b) an enactment contained in, or in an instrument made under, an Act of the Scottish Parliament, and

(c) an enactment contained in, or in an instrument made under, Northern Ireland legislation within the meaning of the Interpretation Act 1978.".

Regulations and orders

80.

Sections 1288 to 1290 apply to LLPs for the purposes of these Regulations, modified so that they read as follows—

"1288. Regulations and orders: statutory instrument

Except as otherwise provided, regulations and orders under this Act shall be made by statutory instrument.

1289. Regulations: negative resolution procedure

Where regulations under this Act are subject to "negative resolution procedure" the statutory instrument containing the regulations shall be subject to annulment in pursuance of a resolution of either House of Parliament.

1290. Regulations: affirmative resolution procedure

Where regulations under this Act are subject to "affirmative resolution procedure" the regulations must not be made unless a draft of the statutory instrument containing them has been laid before Parliament and approved by a resolution of each House of Parliament.".

81.

Section 1292 applies to LLPs for the purposes of these Regulations, modified so that it reads as follows—

"1292. Regulations and orders: supplementary

(1) Regulations or orders under this Act may—

(a) make different provision for different cases or circumstances,

(b) include supplementary, incidental and consequential provision, and

(c) make transitional provision and savings.

(2) Any provision that may be made by regulations under this Act may be made by order; and any provision that may be made by order under this Act may be made by regulations.

(3) Any provision that may be made by regulations or order under this Act for which no Parliamentary procedure is prescribed may be made by regulations subject to negative or affirmative resolution procedure.

(4) Any provision that may be made by regulations under this Act subject to negative resolution procedure may be made by regulations subject to affirmative resolution procedure.".

Continuity of the law

82.

Section 1297 applies to LLPs, modified so that it reads as follows—

"1297. Continuity of the law

(1) This section applies where any provision of this Act applied to LLPs re-enacts (with or without modification) an enactment repealed by this Act which was applied to LLPs.

(2) The repeal and re-enactment does not affect the continuity of the law.

(3) Anything done (including subordinate legislation made and applied to LLPs), or having effect as if done, under or for the purposes of the repealed provision as applied to LLPs that could have been done under or for the purposes of the corresponding provision of this Act as applied to LLPs, if in force or effective immediately before the commencement of that corresponding provision, has effect thereafter as if done under or for the purposes of that corresponding provision.

(4) Any reference (express or implied) in this Act or any other enactment, instrument or document to a provision of this Act as applied to LLPs shall be construed (so far as the context permits) as including, as respects times, circumstances or purposes in relation to which the corresponding repealed provision had effect, a reference to that corresponding provision.

(5) Any reference (express or implied) in any enactment, instrument or document to a repealed provision which was applied to LLPs shall be construed (so far as the context permits), as respects times, circumstances and purposes in relation to which the corresponding provision of this Act applied to LLPs has effect, as being or (according to the context) including a reference to the corresponding provision of this Act.

(6) This section has effect subject to any specific transitional provision or saving contained in this Act as applied to LLPs.

(7) References in this section to this Act as applied to LLPs include subordinate legislation made under this Act as so applied.

(8) In this section "subordinate legislation" has the same meaning as in the Interpretation Act 1978 (c. 30).".

Company and Business Names (Miscellaneous Provisions) Regulations 2009

S.I. 2009/1085

PART 1
INTRODUCTORY

1. Citation, commencement and interpretation

(1) These Regulations may be cited as the Company and Business Names (Miscellaneous Provisions) Regulations 2009 and come into force on 1st October 2009.

(2) In these Regulations—

"the Act" means the Companies Act 2006;

"expression or abbreviation specified as similar" has the meaning given in paragraph 4 of Schedule 2 and "abbreviation specified as similar" has the meaning that would be given to it in that paragraph if that paragraph made no reference to "expressions";

"permitted characters" has the meaning given in regulation 2(1);

"word or abbreviation specified as similar" has the meaning given in paragraph 2 of Schedule 2; and

"word specified as similar" has the meaning given in paragraph 2 of Schedule 2.

(3) For the purposes of computing the number of permitted characters in regulation 2(4) and paragraph 7 of Schedule 3 (but not in regulation 2(3)), any blank space between one permitted character and another in the name shall be counted as though it was a permitted character.

PART 2
COMPANY NAMES

2. Permitted characters

(1) This regulation sets out the characters, signs, symbols and punctuation that may be used in the name of a company registered under the Act ("the permitted characters").

(2) The following permitted characters may be used in any part of the name—

(a) any character, sign or symbol set out in table 1 in Schedule 1;

(b) 0, 1, 2, 3, 4, 5, 6, 7, 8 or 9;

(c) full stop, comma, colon, semi-colon or hyphen; and

(d) any other punctuation referred to in column 1 of table 2 in Schedule 1 but only in one of the forms set out opposite that punctuation in column 2 of that table.

(3) The signs and symbols set out in table 3 in Schedule 1 are permitted characters that may be used but not as one of the first three permitted characters of the name.

(4) The name must not consist of more than 160 permitted characters.

3. Exemption from requirement as to use of "limited"

(1) A private company limited by guarantee is exempt from the requirement of section 59 of the Act (requirement to have name ending with "limited" or permitted alternative) so long as it meets the following two conditions.

(2) The first condition is that the objects of that company are the promotion or regulation of commerce, art, science, education, religion, charity or any profession, and anything incidental or conducive to any of those objects.

(3) The second condition is that the company's articles—

(a) require its income to be applied in promoting its objects;

(b) prohibit the payment of dividends, or any return of capital, to its members; and

(c) require all the assets that would otherwise be available to its members generally to be transferred on its winding up either—
   (i) to another body with objects similar to its own; or
   (ii) to another body the objects of which are the promotion of charity and anything incidental or conducive thereto,

(whether or not the body is a member of the company).

4. Inappropriate indication of company type or legal form: generally applicable provisions

(1) A company must not be registered under the Act by a name that includes, otherwise than at the end of the name, an expression or abbreviation specified in inverted commas in paragraph 3(a) to (f) of Schedule 2 (or any expression or abbreviation specified as similar).

(2) A company must not be registered under the Act by a name that includes in any part of the name an expression or abbreviation specified in inverted commas in paragraph 3(g) or (h) of Schedule 2 (or any expression or abbreviation specified as similar) unless that company is a RTE company within the meaning of section 4A of the Leasehold Reform, Housing and Urban Development Act 1993.

(3) A company must not be registered under the Act by a name that includes in any part of the name an expression or abbreviation specified in inverted commas in paragraph 3(i) or (j) of Schedule 2 (or any expression or abbreviation specified as similar) unless that company is a RTM company within the meaning of section 73 of the Commonhold and Leasehold Reform Act 2002.

(4) A company must not be registered under the Act by a name that includes in any part of the name an expression or abbreviation specified in inverted commas in paragraph 3(k) to (u) of Schedule 2 (or any expression or abbreviation specified as similar).

(5) A company must not be registered under the Act by a name that includes immediately before an expression or abbreviation specified in inverted commas in paragraph 3(a) to (j) of Schedule 2 an abbreviation specified in inverted commas in paragraph 3(v) of that Schedule (or any abbreviation specified as similar).

(6) Paragraph (1) is subject to regulations 5(b) and 6(b).

5. Inappropriate indication of company type or legal form: company exempt from requirement to have name ending in "limited"

A company which is exempt from the requirement of section 59 of the Act (requirement to have name ending with "limited" or permitted alternative) under section 60 of the Act must not be registered under the Act by a name that concludes with—

(a) a word specified in inverted commas in paragraph 1(c) or (d) of Schedule 2 (or any word specified as similar); or

(b) an expression or abbreviation specified in inverted commas in paragraph 3(a) to (f) or (v) of Schedule 2 (or any expression or abbreviation specified as similar).

6. Inappropriate indication of company type or legal form: unlimited company

An unlimited company must not be registered under the Act by a name that concludes with—

(a) a word or abbreviation specified in inverted commas in paragraph 1(a) or (b) of Schedule 2 (or any word or abbreviation specified as similar); or

(b) an expression or abbreviation specified in inverted commas in paragraph 3(a) to (f) or (v) of Schedule 2 (or any expression or abbreviation specified as similar).

7. Name not to be the same as another in the registrar's index of company names

For the purposes of section 66 of the Act (determining whether a name to be registered under the Act is the same as another name appearing in the registrar's index of company names) Schedule 3 has effect for setting out—

(a) the matters that are to be disregarded; and

(b) the words, expressions, signs and symbols that are to be regarded as the same.

8. Consent to registration of a name which is the same as another in the registrar's index of company names

(1) A company may be registered under the Act by a proposed same name if the conditions in paragraph (2) are met.

(2) The conditions are—

(a) the company or other body whose name already appears in the registrar's index of company names ("Body X") consents to the proposed same name being the name of a company ("Company Y");

(b) Company Y forms, or is to form, part of the same group as Body X; and

(c) Company Y provides to the registrar a copy of a statement made by Body X indicating—

(i) the consent of Body X as referred to in sub-paragraph (a); and

(ii) that Company Y forms, or is to form, part of the same group as Body X.

(3) If the proposed same name is to be taken by a company which has not yet been incorporated, the copy of such statement must be provided to the registrar instead by the person who delivers to the registrar the application for registration of the company (and the reference in paragraph (1) to the conditions in paragraph (2) shall be read accordingly).

(4) The registrar may accept the statement referred to in paragraph (2)(c) as sufficient evidence that the conditions referred to in paragraph (2)(a) and (b) have been met.

(5) If the consent referred to in paragraph (2)(a) is given by Body X, a subsequent withdrawal of that consent does not affect the registration of Company Y by that proposed same name.

(6) In this regulation—

(a) "group" has the meaning given in section 474(1) of the Act; and

(b) "proposed same name" means a name which is, due to the application of regulation 7 and Schedule 3, considered the same as a name appearing in the registrar's index of company names and differs from that name appearing in the index only by one of the matters set out in inverted commas in paragraph 4 of Schedule 3.

PART 3
OVERSEAS COMPANY NAMES

9. Interpretation and permitted characters

Regulations 1(2) and (3) and 2 apply to the name of an overseas company which is registered by that company under Part 34 of the Act (overseas companies) as they apply to the name of a company formed and registered under the Act.

10. Inappropriate indication of company type or legal form

(1) An overseas company must not be registered under the Act by a name that concludes with a word or abbreviation specified in inverted commas in paragraph 1(a) or (b) of Schedule 2 (or any word or abbreviation specified as similar) unless the liability of the members of the company is limited by its constitution.

(2) An overseas company must not be registered under the Act by a name that concludes with a word specified in inverted commas in paragraph 1(c) or (d) of Schedule 2 (or any word specified as similar) unless the liability of the members of the company is not limited by its constitution.

(3) An overseas company must not be registered under the Act by a name that includes in any part of the name an expression or abbreviation specified in inverted commas in paragraph 3 of Schedule 2 (or any expression or abbreviation specified as similar).

11. Name not to be the same as another in the registrar's index of company names

Regulation 7 applies to the name of an overseas company which is registered by that company under Part 34 of the Act as it applies to the name of a company formed and registered under the Act.

12. Consent to registration of a name which is the same as another in the registrar's index of company names

(1) Regulation 8 applies to the proposed same name of an overseas company as it applies to the proposed same name of a company formed and registered under the Act.

(2) In this regulation "proposed same name" has the same meaning as in regulation 8.

PART 4
BUSINESS NAMES

13. "Limited" and permitted alternatives

(1) A person must not carry on business in the United Kingdom under a name that concludes with any word or abbreviation set out in inverted commas in paragraph 1(a) or (b) of Schedule 2 unless that person is—

(a) a company or an overseas company registered in the United Kingdom by that name;

(b) an overseas company incorporated with that name; …

(c) a society registered under the Industrial and Provident Societies Act 1965 or the Industrial and Provident Societies Act (Northern Ireland) 1969 by that name;

(d) an incorporated friendly society (as defined in section 116 of the Friendly Societies Act 1992) which has that name; or

(e) a company to which section 1040 of the Companies Act 2006 (companies authorised to register under the Companies Act 2006) applies which has that name.

(2) A person must not carry on business in the United Kingdom under a name that concludes with any word or abbreviation specified as similar to any word or abbreviation set out in inverted commas in paragraph 1(a) or (b) of Schedule 2.

14. Other indications of legal form

(1) A person must not carry on business in the United Kingdom under a name that includes any expression or abbreviation set out in inverted commas in paragraph 3 of Schedule 2 unless that person is such a company, partnership, grouping or organisation as is indicated in that expression or abbreviation.

(2) A person must not carry on business in the United Kingdom under a name that includes any expression or abbreviation specified as similar to any expression or abbreviation set out in inverted commas in paragraph 3 of Schedule 2.

15. Transitional provisions

(1) Regulation 14 does not apply to the carrying on of a business under a name by a person who—

(a) carried on that business under that name immediately before these Regulations came into force; and

(b) continues to carry it on under that name,

if it was lawful for the business to be carried on under that name immediately before these Regulations came into force.

(2) Regulation 14 does not apply to the carrying on of a business under a name by a person to whom the business is transferred on or after the date on which these Regulations came into force—

(a) where that person continues to carry on the business under that name; and

(b) where it was lawful for the business to be carried on under that name immediately before the transfer,

during the period of 12 months beginning with the date of the transfer.

SCHEDULE 1

CHARACTERS, SIGNS, SYMBOLS AND PUNCTUATION

Regulation 2

Table 1

Characters, signs and symbols				
A	B	C	D	E
F	G	H	I	J
K	L	M	N	O
P	Q	R	S	T
U	V	W	X	Y
Z	&	@	£	$
€	¥			

Table 2

Type of punctuation	*Punctuation mark*
Apostrophe	‘
	’
	'
Bracket	(
	)
	[
	]
	{
	}
	<
	>
Exclamation mark	!
Guillemet	«
	»
Inverted comma	“
	”
	"
Question mark	?
Solidus	\
	/

Table 3

Signs and symbols
*
=
#
%
+

SCHEDULE 2

SPECIFIED WORDS, EXPRESSIONS AND ABBREVIATIONS

Regulations 1, 4 to 6, 10, 13 and 14

1. The words and abbreviations specified are—
   (a) "LIMITED" or (with or without full stops) the abbreviation "LTD";
   (b) "CYFYNGEDIG" or (with or without full stops) the abbreviation "CYF";
   (c) "UNLIMITED"; and
   (d) "ANGHYFYNGEDIG".
2. The words and abbreviations specified as similar to the words and abbreviations set out in inverted commas in paragraph 1(a) and (b) and the words specified as similar to the words set out in inverted commas in paragraph 1(c) and (d) are any in which—
   (a) one or more characters has been omitted;
   (b) one or more characters, signs, symbols or punctuation has been added; or
   (c) each of one or more characters has been substituted by one or more other characters, signs, symbols or punctuation,

   in such a way as to be likely to mislead the public as to the legal form of a company or business if included in the registered name of the company or in a business name.
3. The expressions and abbreviations specified are—
   (a) "PUBLIC LIMITED COMPANY" or (with or without full stops) the abbreviation "PLC";
   (b) "CWMNI CYFYNGEDIG CYHOEDDUS" or (with or without full stops) the abbreviation "CCC";
   (c) "COMMUNITY INTEREST COMPANY" or (with or without full stops) the abbreviation "CIC";
   (d) "CWMNI BUDDIANT CYMUNEDOL" or (with or without full stops) the abbreviation "CBC";
   (e) "COMMUNITY INTEREST PUBLIC LIMITED COMPANY" or (with or without full stops) the abbreviation "COMMUNITY INTEREST PLC";
   (f) "CWMNI BUDDIANT CYMUNEDOL CYHOEDDUS CYFYNGEDIG" or (with or without full stops) the abbreviation "CWMNI BUDDIANT CYMUNEDOL CCC";
   (g) "RIGHT TO ENFRANCHISEMENT" or (with or without full stops) the abbreviation "RTE";
   (h) "HAWL I RYDDFREINIAD";
   (i) "RIGHT TO MANAGE" or (with or without full stops) the abbreviation "RTM";
   (j) "CWMNI RTM CYFYNGEDIG";
   (k) "EUROPEAN ECONOMIC INTEREST GROUPING" or (with or without full stops) the abbreviation "EEIG";
   (l) "INVESTMENT COMPANY WITH VARIABLE CAPITAL";
   (m) "CWMNI BUDDSODDI A CHYFALAF NEWIDIOL";
   (n) "LIMITED PARTNERSHIP";
   (o) "PARTNERIAETH CYFYNGEDIG";

(p) "LIMITED LIABILITY PARTNERSHIP";
(q) "PARTNERIAETH ATEBOLRWYDD CYFYNGEDIG";
(r) "OPEN-ENDED INVESTMENT COMPANY";
(s) "CWMNI BUDDSODDIANT PENAGORED";
(t) "CHARITABLE INCORPORATED ORGANISATION";
(u) "SEFDYDLIAD ELUSENNOL CORFFOREDIG"; …
(ua) "INDUSTRIAL AND PROVIDENT SOCIETY"; and
(v) the following abbreviations (with or without full stops) of the expressions specified in sub-paragraphs (n), (o), (p), (q), (t) and (u) respectively, namely "LP", "PC", "LLP", "PAC", "CIO" and "SEC".

4. The expressions and abbreviations specified as similar to the expressions and abbreviations set out in inverted commas in paragraph 3 are any in which—
(a) one or more characters has been omitted;
(b) one or more characters, signs, symbols or punctuation has been added; or
(c) each of one or more characters has been substituted by one or more other characters, signs, symbols or punctuation,

in such a way as to be likely to mislead the public as to the legal form of a company or business if included in the registered name of the company or in a business name.

SCHEDULE 3

NAME SAME AS ANOTHER IN THE REGISTRAR'S INDEX OF COMPANY NAMES

Regulations 7 and 8

1. In determining whether a name is the same as another name appearing in the registrar's index of company names the provisions in this Schedule are to be applied in the order set out in the Schedule.

2. Disregard any word, expression or abbreviation set out in inverted commas in Schedule 2 where it appears at the end of the name.

3.— (1) Taking the name remaining after the application of paragraph 2, regard each of the words, expressions, signs and symbols set out in inverted commas in any of the paragraphs of sub-paragraph (2) ("relevant matters") as the same as the other relevant matters set out in that paragraph where each relevant matter—
(a) is preceded by and followed by a blank space; or
(b) where the relevant matter is at the beginning of the name, where it is followed by a blank space.

(2) The words, expressions, signs and symbols are—
(a) "AND" and "&";
(b) "PLUS" and "+";
(c) "0", "ZERO" and "O";
(d) "1" and "ONE";
(e) "2", "TWO", "TO" and "TOO";
(f) "3" and "THREE";
(g) "4", "FOUR" and "FOR";
(h) "5" and "FIVE";
(i) "6" and "SIX";
(j) "7" and "SEVEN";
(k) "8" and "EIGHT";
(l) "9" and "NINE";
(m) "£" and "POUND";
(n) " EUR " and "EURO";
(o) "$" and "DOLLAR";
(p) "¥" and "YEN";

(q) "%", "PER CENT", "PERCENT", "PER CENTUM" and "PERCENTUM"; and
(r) "@" and "AT".

4.— (1) Taking the name remaining after the application of paragraphs 2 and 3, disregard at the end of the name the matters set out in inverted commas in sub-paragraph (2) (or any combination of such matters) where the matter (or combination) is preceded by the following punctuation or symbol in inverted commas—
(a) a blank space;
(b) a full stop; or
(c) "@".

(2) The matters are—
(a) "BIZ";
(b) "CO";
(c) "CO UK";
(d) "CO.UK";
(e) "COM";
(f) "COMPANY";
(g) "EU";
(h) "EXPORTS";
(i) "GB";
(j) "GREAT BRITAIN";
(k) "GROUP";
(l) "HOLDINGS";
(m) "IMPORTS";
(n) "INTERNATIONAL";
(o) "NET";
(p) "NI";
(q) "NORTHERN IRELAND";
(r) "ORG";
(s) "ORG UK";
(t) "ORG.UK";
(u) "SERVICES";
(v) "UK";
(w) "UNITED KINGDOM";
(x) "WALES";
(y) "ALLFORION";
(z) "CWMNI";
(aa) "CYM";
(bb) "CYMRU";
(cc) "CYNHEILIAID";
(dd) "CYRDDAU";
(ee) "DALIADAU";
(ff) "DU";
(gg) "GRWP";
(hh) "GWASANAETHAU";
(ii) "MEWNFORION";
(jj) "PF";
(kk) "PRYDAIN FAWR";
(ll) "RHYNGWLADOL";
(mm) "RYNGWLADOL"; and
(nn) "Y DEYRNAS UNEDIG".

5. Taking the name remaining after the application of paragraphs 2 to 4, disregard the following matters in any part of the name—

(a) any punctuation set out in regulation 2(2)(c) or in column 2 of table 2 in Schedule 1; and
(b) the following symbols set out in inverted commas—
(i) "*";
(ii) "=“; and
(iii) "#".

6. Taking the name remaining after the application of paragraphs 2 to 5, disregard the letter "S" at the end of the name.

7. Taking the name remaining after the application of paragraphs 2 to 6, disregard any permitted character after the first 60 permitted characters of the name.

8. Taking the name remaining after the application of paragraphs 2 to 7, disregard the following matters or any combination of the following matters set out in inverted commas where they appear at the beginning of the name—
(a) "@";
(b) "THE" (but only where followed by a blank space); and
(c) "WWW".

9. Taking the name remaining after the application of paragraphs 2 to 8, disregard blank spaces between permitted characters.

Company, Limited Liability Partnership and Business Names (Sensitive Words and Expressions) Regulations 2009

S.I. 2009/2615

1. Citation and commencement

These Regulations may be cited as the Company, Limited Liability Partnership and Business Names (Sensitive Words and Expressions) Regulations 2009 and come into force on 1st October 2009.

2. Interpretation

(1) In these Regulations "the 2006 Act" means the Companies Act 2006.

(2) Any reference in these Regulations to section 55 or 88 of the 2006 Act includes a reference to that section as applied by regulation 8 or 17 of the Limited Liability Partnerships (Application of Companies Act 2006) Regulations 2009.

3. Specified words and expressions applicable to sections 55 and 1194 of the 2006 Act

(1) The following words and expressions are specified for the purposes of sections 55(1) and 1194(1) of the 2006 Act—

(a) the words and expressions set out in Part 1 of Schedule 1;

(b) the plural and possessive forms of those words and expressions, and, where relevant, the feminine form; and

(c) in the case of the words and expressions set out in Part 1 of Schedule 1 which are marked with an asterisk, the grammatically mutated forms of those words and expressions.

(2) For the purposes of section 55(1) of the 2006 Act any word or expression specified in Part 1 of Schedule 1 which contains an accent or other diacritical mark is to be read as though that accent or other diacritical mark were omitted.

4. Specified words and expressions applicable to section 55 of the 2006 Act

The following words and expressions are specified for the purposes of section 55(1) of the 2006 Act—

(a) the words and expressions set out in Part 2 of Schedule 1;

(b) the plural and possessive forms of those words and expressions, and, where relevant, the feminine form; and

(c) in the case of the words and expressions set out in Part 2 of Schedule 1 which are marked with an asterisk, the grammatically mutated forms of those words and expressions.

5. Applications where situation of registered office or principal place of business is irrelevant

In connection with an application for the approval of the Secretary of State under section 55 or 1194 of the 2006 Act in relation to a name that includes a word or expression specified in column (1) of Part 1 of Schedule 2 the applicant must seek the view of the Government department or other body set out opposite that word or expression in column (2) of Part 1 of Schedule 2.

6. Applications where situation of registered office or principal place of business is relevant

In connection with an application for the approval of the Secretary of State under section 55 or 1194 of the 2006 Act in relation to a name that includes a word or expression specified in column (1) of Part 2 of Schedule 2 the applicant must seek the view of a Government department or other body as follows—

(a) in the case of—

(i) a company or limited liability partnership that has already been registered, whose registered office is situated in England and Wales;
(ii) a proposed company or limited liability partnership that has not yet been registered under the 2006 Act, whose registered office is to be situated in England and Wales;
(iii) a business, whose principal place of business is or is to be situated in England; and
(iv) an overseas company (see section 1044 of the 2006 Act),

the Government department or other body set out in column (2) of Part 2 of Schedule 2 opposite that word or expression;

(b) in the case of—
(i) a company or limited liability partnership that has already been registered, that is a Welsh company or Welsh LLP (see section 88 of the 2006 Act);
(ii) a proposed company or limited liability partnership that has not yet been registered, that is to be a Welsh company or Welsh LLP; and
(iii) a business, whose principal place of business is or is to be situated in Wales,

the Government department or other body set out in column (3) of Part 2 of Schedule 2 opposite that word or expression;

(c) in the case of—
(i) a company or limited liability partnership that has already been registered, whose registered office is situated in Scotland;
(ii) a proposed company or limited liability partnership that has not yet been registered, whose registered office is to be situated in Scotland; and
(iii) a business, whose principal place of business is or is to be situated in Scotland,

the Government department or other body set out in column (4) of Part 2 of Schedule 2 opposite that word or expression; and

(d) in the case of—
(i) a company or limited liability partnership that has already been registered, whose registered office is situated in Northern Ireland;
(ii) a proposed company or limited liability partnership that has not yet been registered, whose registered office is to be situated in Northern Ireland; and
(iii) a business, whose principal place of business is or is to be situated in Northern Ireland,

the Government department or other body set out in column (5) of Part 2 of Schedule 2 opposite that word or expression.

7. The following Regulations are revoked—
(a) the Company and Business Names Regulations 1981,
(b) the Company and Business Names (Amendment) Regulations 1982,
(c) the Company and Business Names (Amendment) Regulations 1992,
(d) the Company and Business Names (Amendment) Regulations 1995,
(e) the Company and Business Names (Amendment) Regulations 2001, and
(f) the Company and Business Names (Amendment) (No 2) Regulations 2007.

SCHEDULE 1

Regulations 3 and 4

SPECIFIED WORDS AND EXPRESSIONS

PART 1
SPECIFIED WORDS AND EXPRESSIONS APPLICABLE TO SECTIONS 55(1) AND 1194(1) OF THE 2006 ACT

Abortion
Accredit
Accreditation
Accredited
Accrediting
Adjudicator
Association
Assurance
Assurer
Audit office
Auditor General
Authority
*Banc
Bank
Banking
Banknote
Benevolent
Board

*Breatannach
*Breatainn
*Brenhinol
*Brenin
*Brenhiniaeth
Britain
British
*Cenedlaethol
Chamber of
Charitable
Charity
Charter
Chartered
Child maintenance
Child support
*Coimisean
*Comhairle
*Comisiwn
Commission
Co-operative
Council
*Cyngor
Data protection
Dental
Dentistry
Disciplinary
Discipline
*Diùc
*Dug
Duke
Ei Fawrhydi
England
English
European
Federation
Friendly Society
Foundation
Fund
Giro
Government
Group
*Gwasanaeth iechyd
*Gwladol
Health centre
Health service
Health visitor
His Majesty
Holding
HPSS
HSC
Human rights
Inspectorate
Institute
Institution
Insurance
Insurer
International
Judicial appointment
King
Licensing
*Llywodraeth
Medical centre
Midwife
Midwifery
*Mòrachd
Mutual
National
NHS
Northern Ireland
Northern Irish
Nurse
Nursing
Oifis sgrùdaidh
*Oilthigh
Ombudsman
*Ombwdsmon
Oversight
*Parlamaid
Parliament
Parliamentarian
Parliamentary
Patent
Patentee
Police
Polytechnic
Post office
Pregnancy termination
*Prifysgol
Prince
*Prionnsa
*Prydain
*Prydeinig
Queen
Reassurance
Reassurer
Register
Registered
Registrar
Registration
Page 7
Registry
Regulation
Regulator
Reinsurance
Reinsurer
*Riaghaltas
*Rìgh
Rìoghachd Aonaichte
Rìoghail
Rìoghalachd
Royal
Royalty
Rule committee
Scotland
Scottish
Senedd
Sheffield
Siambr
Social service
Society
Special school
Standards
Stock exchange
Swyddfa archwilio
*Teyrnas Gyfunol
*Teyrnas Unedig
Trade union
Tribunal
Trust
*Tywysog
Underwrite
Underwriting
United Kingdom
University
Wales
Watchdog
Welsh
Windsor

Part 2
Specified Words and Expressions Applicable to Section 55(1) of the 2006 Act

Alba
Albannach
Na h-Alba
*Cymru
*Cymraeg
*Cymreig

SCHEDULE 2

Regulations 5 and 6

LIST OF GOVERNMENT DEPARTMENTS AND OTHER BODIES WHOSE VIEWS MUST BE SOUGHT

PART 1

APPLICATIONS WHERE SITUATION OF REGISTERED OFFICE OR PRINCIPAL PLACE OF BUSINESS IS IRRELEVANT

Column (1)	*Column (2)*
Word or expression specified under regulation 3	*Specified Government department or other body whose view must be sought*
Abortion	Department of Health
Accredit	Department for Business, Innovation & Skills
Accreditation	Department for Business, Innovation & Skills
Accredited	Department for Business, Innovation & Skills
Accrediting	Department for Business, Innovation & Skills
Assurance	Financial Services Authority
Assurer	Financial Services Authority
Banc	Financial Services Authority
Bank	Financial Services Authority
Banking	Financial Services Authority
Banknote	The Governor and Company of the Bank of England
Brenhinol	The Welsh Assembly Government
Brenin	The Welsh Assembly Government
Brenhiniaeth	The Welsh Assembly Government
Child maintenance	Department for Work and Pensions
Child support	Department for Work and Pensions
Data protection	Information Commissioner's Office
Dental General	Dental Council
Dentistry General	Dental Council
Diùc	The Scottish Executive
Dug	The Welsh Assembly Government
Ei Fawrhydi	The Welsh Assembly Government
Friendly Society	Financial Services Authority
Fund	Financial Services Authority
Gwasanaeth iechyd	The Welsh Assembly Government
Health visitor	Nursing & Midwifery Council
HPSS	Department of Health, Social Services and Public Safety
HSC	Department of Health, Social Services and Public Safety
Insurance	Financial Services Authority
Insurer	Financial Services Authority
Judicial appointment	Ministry of Justice
Llywodraeth	The Welsh Assembly Government

Column (1)	*Column (2)*
Medical centre	Department of Health, Social Services and Public Safety
Midwife	Nursing & Midwifery Council
Midwifery	Nursing & Midwifery Council
Mòrachd	The Scottish Executive
Mutual	Financial Services Authority
NHS	Department of Health
Nurse	Nursing & Midwifery Council
Nursing	Nursing & Midwifery Council
Oifis sgrùdaidh	Audit Scotland
Oilthigh	The Scottish Executive
Parlamaid	The Scottish Parliamentary Corporate Body
Parliament	The Corporate Officer of the House of Lords and The Corporate Officer of the House of Commons
Parliamentarian	The Corporate Officer of the House of Lords and The Corporate Officer of the House of Commons
Parliamentary	The Corporate Officer of the House of Lords and The Corporate Officer of the House of Commons
Patent	The Patent Office
Patentee	The Patent Office
Polytechnic	Department for Business, Innovation & Skills
Pregnancy termination	Department of Health
Prifysgol	The Welsh Assembly Government
Prionnsa	The Scottish Executive
Reassurance	Financial Services Authority
Reassurer	Financial Services Authority
Reinsurance	Financial Services Authority
Reinsurer	Financial Services Authority
Riaghaltas	The Scottish Executive
Rìgh	The Scottish Executive
Rìoghail	The Scottish Executive
Rìoghalachd	The Scottish Executive
Rule committee	Ministry of Justice
Senedd	The National Assembly for Wales
Sheffield	The Company of Cutlers in Hallamshire
Swyddfa archwilio	Auditor General for Wales
Tywysog	The Welsh Assembly Government
Underwrite	Financial Services Authority
Underwriting	Financial Services Authority

PART 2
APPLICATIONS WHERE SITUATION OF REGISTERED OFFICE OR PRINCIPAL PLACE OF BUSINESS IS RELEVANT

Column (1)	*Column (2)*	*Column (3)*	*Column (4)*	*Column (5)*
Word or expression specified under regulation 3	*Specified Government department or other body whose view must be sought*			
	under regulation 6(a)	*under regulation 6(b)*	*under regulation 6(c)*	*under regulation 6(d)*
Audit office	Comptroller & Auditor General	Auditor General for Wales	Audit Scotland	Northern Ireland Audit Office
Charitable Charity	The Charity Commission	The Charity Commission	Office of the Scottish Charity Regulator	The Charity Commission
Duke His Majesty King Prince Queen Royal Royalty Windsor	Ministry of Justice	The Welsh Assembly Government	The Scottish Executive	Ministry of Justice
Health centre Health service	Department of Health	The Welsh Assembly Government	The Scottish Executive	Department of Health, Social Services and Public Safety
Police	The Home Office	The Home Office	The Scottish Executive	Department of Justice in Northern Ireland
Special school	Department for Education	The Welsh Assembly Government	The Scottish Executive	Department of Education
University	Department for Business, Innovation & Skills	The Welsh Assembly Government	The Scottish Executive	Department for Employment and Learning

Insolvency Act 1986

1986 c. 45

An Act to consolidate the enactments relating to company insolvency and winding up (including the winding up of companies that are not insolvent, and of unregistered companies); enactments relating to the insolvency and bankruptcy of individuals; and other enactments bearing on those two subject matters, including the functions and qualification of insolvency practitioners, the public administration of insolvency, the penalisation and redress of malpractice and wrongdoing, and the avoidance of certain transactions at an undervalue

[25th July 1986]

THE FIRST GROUP OF PARTS
COMPANY INSOLVENCY; COMPANIES WINDING UP

PART I
COMPANY VOLUNTARY ARRANGEMENTS

The proposal

1. Those who may propose an arrangement

(1) The directors of a company (other than one which is in administration or being wound up) may make a proposal under this Part to the company and to its creditors for a composition in satisfaction of its debts or a scheme of arrangement of its affairs (from here on referred to, in either case, as a "voluntary arrangement").

(2) A proposal under this Part is one which provides for some person ("the nominee") to act in relation to the voluntary arrangement either as trustee or otherwise for the purpose of supervising its implementation; and the nominee must be a person who is qualified to act as an insolvency practitioner or authorised to act as nominee, in relation to the voluntary arrangement.

(3) Such a proposal may also be made—

(a) where the company is in administration, by the administrator, and

(b) where the company is being wound up, by the liquidator.

(4) In this Part "company" means—

(a) a company registered under the Companies Act 2006 in England and Wales or Scotland;

(b) a company incorporated in an EEA State other than the United Kingdom; or

(c) a company not incorporated in an EEA State but having its centre of main interests in a member State other than Denmark.

(5) In subsection (4), in relation to a company, "centre of main interests" has the same meaning as in the EC Regulation and, in the absence of proof to the contrary, is presumed to be the place of its registered office (within the meaning of that Regulation).

(6) If a company incorporated outside the United Kingdom has a principal place of business in Northern Ireland, no proposal under this Part shall be made in relation to it unless it also has a principal place of business in England and Wales or Scotland (or both in England and Wales or Scotland).

1A. Moratorium

(1) Where the directors of an eligible company intend to make a proposal for a voluntary arrangement, they may take steps to obtain a moratorium for the company.

(2) The provisions of Schedule A1 to this Act have effect with respect to—

(a) companies eligible for a moratorium under this section,

(b) the procedure for obtaining such a moratorium,

(c) the effects of such a moratorium, and

(d) the procedure applicable (in place of sections 2 to 6 and 7) in relation to the approval and implementation of a voluntary arrangement where such a moratorium is or has been in force.

2. Procedure where nominee is not the liquidator or administrator

(1) This section applies where the nominee under section 1 is not the liquidator or administrator of the company and the directors do not propose to take steps to obtain a moratorium under section 1A for the company.

(2) The nominee shall, within 28 days (or such longer period as the court may allow) after he is given notice of the proposal for a voluntary arrangement, submit a report to the court stating—

(a) whether, in his opinion, the proposed voluntary arrangement has a reasonable prospect of being approved and implemented,

(aa) whether, in his opinion, meetings of the company and of its creditors should be summoned to consider the proposal, and

(b) if in his opinion such meetings should be summoned, the date on which, and time and place at which, he proposes the meetings should be held.

(3) For the purposes of enabling the nominee to prepare his report, the person intending to make the proposal shall submit to the nominee—

(a) a document setting out the terms of the proposed voluntary arrangement, and

(b) a statement of the company's affairs containing—

(i) such particulars of its creditors and of its debts and other liabilities and of its assets as may be prescribed, and

(ii) such other information as may be prescribed.

(4) The court may—

(a) on an application made by the person intending to make the proposal, in a case where the nominee has failed to submit the report required by this section or has died, or

(b) on an application made by that person or the nominee, in a case where it is impracticable or inappropriate for the nominee to continue to act as such,

direct that the nominee be replaced as such by another person qualified to act as an insolvency practitioner, or authorised to act as nominee, in relation to the voluntary arrangement.

3. Summoning of meetings

(1) Where the nominee under section 1 is not the liquidator or administrator, and it has been reported to the court that such meetings as are mentioned in section 2(2) should be summoned, the person making the report shall (unless the court otherwise directs) summon those meetings for the time, date and place proposed in the report.

(2) Where the nominee is the liquidator or administrator, he shall summon meetings of the company and of its creditors to consider the proposal for such a time, date and place as he thinks fit.

(3) The persons to be summoned to a creditors' meeting under this section are every creditor of the company of whose claim and address the person summoning the meeting is aware.

Consideration and implementation of proposal

4. Decisions of meetings

(1) The meetings summoned under section 3 shall decide whether to approve the proposed voluntary arrangement (with or without modifications).

(2) The modifications may include one conferring the functions proposed to be conferred on the nominee on another person qualified to act as an insolvency practitioner or authorised to act as nominee, in relation to the voluntary arrangement.

But they shall not include any modification by virtue of which the proposal ceases to be a proposal such as is mentioned in section 1.

(3) A meeting so summoned shall not approve any proposal or modification which affects the right of a secured creditor of the company to enforce his security, except with the concurrence of the creditor concerned.

(4) Subject as follows, a meeting so summoned shall not approve any proposal or modification under which—

(a) any preferential debt of the company is to be paid otherwise than in priority to such of its debts as are not preferential debts, or

(b) a preferential creditor of the company is to be paid an amount in respect of a preferential debt that bears to that debt a smaller proportion than is borne to another preferential debt by the amount that is to be paid in respect of that other debt.

However, the meeting may approve such a proposal or modification with the concurrence of the preferential creditor concerned.

(5) Subject as above, each of the meetings shall be conducted in accordance with the rules.

(6) After the conclusion of either meeting in accordance with the rules, the chairman of the meeting shall report the result of the meeting to the court, and, immediately after reporting to the court, shall give notice of the result of the meeting to such persons as may be prescribed.

(7) References in this section to preferential debts and preferential creditors are to be read in accordance with section 386 in Part XII of this Act.

4A. Approval of arrangement

(1) This section applies to a decision, under section 4, with respect to the approval of a proposed voluntary arrangement.

(2) The decision has effect if, in accordance with the rules—

(a) it has been taken by both meetings summoned under section 3, or

(b) (subject to any order made under subsection (4)) it has been taken by the creditors' meeting summoned under that section.

(3) If the decision taken by the creditors' meeting differs from that taken by the company meeting, a member of the company may apply to the court.

(4) An application under subsection (3) shall not be made after the end of the period of 28 days beginning with—

(a) the day on which the decision was taken by the creditors' meeting, or

(b) where the decision of the company meeting was taken on a later day, that day.

(5) Where a member of a regulated company, within the meaning given by paragraph 44 of Schedule A1, applies to the court under subsection (3), the appropriate regulator is entitled to be heard on the application.

(5A) The "appropriate regulator" means—

(a) where the regulated company is a PRA-regulated company within the meaning of paragraph 44 of Schedule A1, the Financial Conduct Authority and the Prudential Regulation Authority, and

(b) in any other case, the Financial Conduct Authority.

(6) On an application under subsection (3), the court may—

(a) order the decision of the company meeting to have effect instead of the decision of the creditors' meeting, or

(b) make such other order as it thinks fit.

5. Effect of approval

(1) This section applies where a decision approving a voluntary arrangement has effect under section 4A.

(2) The … voluntary arrangement—

(a) takes effect as if made by the company at the creditors' meeting, and

(b) binds every person who in accordance with the rules—

(i) was entitled to vote at that meeting (whether or not he was present or represented at it), or

(ii) would have been so entitled if he had had notice of it,

as if he were a party to the voluntary arrangement.

(2A) If—

(a) when the arrangement ceases to have effect any amount payable under the arrangement to a person bound by virtue of subsection (2)(b)(ii) has not been paid, and

(b) the arrangement did not come to an end prematurely,

the company shall at that time become liable to pay to that person the amount payable under the arrangement.

(3) Subject as follows, if the company is being wound up or is in administration, the court may do one or both of the following, namely—

(a) by order stay or sist all proceedings in the winding up or provide for the appointment of the administrator to cease to have effect;

(b) give such directions with respect to the conduct of the winding up or the administration as it thinks appropriate for facilitating the implementation of the … voluntary arrangement.

(4) The court shall not make an order under subsection (3)(a)—

(a) at any time before the end of the period of 28 days beginning with the first day on which each of the reports required by section 4(6) has been made to the court, or

(b) at any time when an application under the next section or an appeal in respect of such an application is pending, or at any time in the period within which such an appeal may be brought.

(5) Where the company is in energy administration, the court shall not make an order or give a direction under subsection (3) unless—

(a) the court has given the Secretary of State or the Gas and Electricity Markets Authority a reasonable opportunity of making representations to it about the proposed order or direction; and

(b) the order or direction is consistent with the objective of the energy administration.

(6) In subsection (5) "in energy administration" and "objective of the energy administration" are to be construed in accordance with Schedule B1 to this Act, as applied by Part 1 of Schedule 20 to the Energy Act 2004.

6. Challenge of decisions

(1) Subject to this section, an application to the court may be made, by any of the persons specified below, on one or both of the following grounds, namely—

(a) that a voluntary arrangement which has effect under section 4A unfairly prejudices the interests of a creditor, member or contributory of the company;

(b) that there has been some material irregularity at or in relation to either of the meetings.

(2) The persons who may apply under subsection (1) are—

(a) a person entitled, in accordance with the rules, to vote at either of the meetings;

(aa) a person who would have been entitled, in accordance with the rules, to vote at the creditors' meeting if he had had notice of it;

(b) the nominee or any person who has replaced him under section 2(4) or 4(2); and

(c) if the company is being wound up or is in administration, the liquidator or administrator.

(2A) Subject to this section, where a voluntary arrangement in relation to a company in energy administration is approved at the meetings summoned under section 3, an application to the court may be made—

(a) by the Secretary of State, or

(b) with the consent of the Secretary of State, by the Gas and Electricity Markets Authority,

on the ground that the voluntary arrangement is not consistent with the achievement of the objective of the energy administration.

(3) An application under this section shall not be made—

(a) after the end of the period of 28 days beginning with the first day on which each of the reports required by section 4(6) has been made to the court, or

(b) in the case of a person who was not given notice of the creditors' meeting, after the end of the period of 28 days beginning with the day on which he became aware that the meeting had taken place, but (subject to that) an application made by a person within subsection (2)(aa) on the ground that the voluntary arrangement prejudices his interests may be made after the arrangement has ceased to have effect, unless it came to an end prematurely.

(4) Where on such an application the court is satisfied as to either of the grounds mentioned in subsection (1) or, in the case of an application under subsection (2A), as to the ground mentioned in that subsection, it may do one or both of the following, namely—

(a) revoke or suspend any decision approving the voluntary arrangement which has effect under section 4A or, in a case falling within subsection (1)(b), any decision taken by the meeting in question which has effect under that section;

(b) give a direction to any person for the summoning of further meetings to consider any revised proposal the person who made the original proposal may make or, in a case falling within subsection (1)(b), a further company or (as the case may be) creditors' meeting to reconsider the original proposal.

(5) Where at any time after giving a direction under subsection (4)(b) for the summoning of meetings to consider a revised proposal the court is satisfied that the person who made the original proposal does not intend to submit a revised proposal, the court shall revoke the direction and revoke or suspend any decision approving the voluntary arrangement which has effect under section 4A.

(6) In a case where the court, on an application under this section with respect to any meeting—

(a) gives a direction under subsection (4)(b), or

(b) revokes or suspends an approval under subsection (4)(a) or (5),

the court may give such supplemental directions as it thinks fit and, in particular, directions with respect to things done under the voluntary arrangement since it took effect.

(7) Except in pursuance of the preceding provisions of this section, a decision taken at a meeting summoned under section 3 is not invalidated by any irregularity at or in relation to the meeting.

(8) In this section "in energy administration" and "objective of the energy administration" are to be construed in accordance with Schedule B1 to this Act, as applied by Part 1 of Schedule 20 to the Energy Act 2004.

6A. False representations, etc

(1) If, for the purpose of obtaining the approval of the members or creditors of a company to a proposal for a voluntary arrangement, a person who is an officer of the company—

(a) makes any false representation, or

(b) fraudulently does, or omits to do, anything,

he commits an offence.

(2) Subsection (1) applies even if the proposal is not approved.

(3) For purposes of this section "officer" includes a shadow director.

(4) A person guilty of an offence under this section is liable to imprisonment or a fine, or both.

7. Implementation of proposal

(1) This section applies where a voluntary arrangement has effect under section 4A.

(2) The person who is for the time being carrying out in relation to the voluntary arrangement the functions conferred—

(a) on the nominee by virtue of the approval given at one or both of the meetings summoned under section 3,

(b) by virtue of section 2(4) or 4(2) on a person other than the nominee,

shall be known as the supervisor of the voluntary arrangement.

(3) If any of the company's creditors or any other person is dissatisfied by any act, omission or decision of the supervisor, he may apply to the court; and on the application the court may—

(a) confirm, reverse or modify any act or decision of the supervisor,

(b) give him directions, or

(c) make such other order as it thinks fit.

(4) The supervisor—

(a) may apply to the court for directions in relation to any particular matter arising under the voluntary arrangement, and
(b) is included among the persons who may apply to the court for the winding up of the company or for an administration order to be made in relation to it.

(5) The court may, whenever—
(a) it is expedient to appoint a person to carry out the functions of the supervisor, and
(b) it is inexpedient, difficult or impracticable for an appointment to be made without the assistance of the court,

make an order appointing a person who is qualified to act as an insolvency practitioner or authorised to act as supervisor, in relation to the voluntary arrangement, either in substitution for the existing supervisor or to fill a vacancy.

(6) The power conferred by subsection (5) is exercisable so as to increase the number of persons exercising the functions of supervisor or, where there is more than one person exercising those functions, so as to replace one or more of those persons.

7A. Prosecution of delinquent officers of company

(1) This section applies where a moratorium under section 1A has been obtained for a company or the approval of a voluntary arrangement in relation to a company has taken effect under section 4A or paragraph 36 of Schedule A1.

(2) If it appears to the nominee or supervisor that any past or present officer of the company has been guilty of any offence in connection with the moratorium or, as the case may be, voluntary arrangement for which he is criminally liable, the nominee or supervisor shall forthwith—
(a) report the matter to the appropriate authority, and
(b) provide the appropriate authority with such information and give the authority such access to and facilities for inspecting and taking copies of documents (being information or documents in the possession or under the control of the nominee or supervisor and relating to the matter in question) as the authority requires.

In this subsection, "the appropriate authority" means—
(i) in the case of a company registered in England and Wales, the Secretary of State, and
(ii) in the case of a company registered in Scotland, the Lord Advocate.

(3) Where a report is made to the Secretary of State under subsection (2), he may, for the purpose of investigating the matter reported to him and such other matters relating to the affairs of the company as appear to him to require investigation, exercise any of the powers which are exercisable by inspectors appointed under section 431 or 432 of the Companies Act 1985 to investigate a company's affairs.

(4) For the purpose of such an investigation any obligation imposed on a person by any provision of the Companies Acts to produce documents or give information to, or otherwise to assist, inspectors so appointed is to be regarded as an obligation similarly to assist the Secretary of State in his investigation.

(5) An answer given by a person to a question put to him in exercise of the powers conferred by subsection (3) may be used in evidence against him.

(6) However, in criminal proceedings in which that person is charged with an offence to which this subsection applies—
(a) no evidence relating to the answer may be adduced, and
(b) no question relating to it may be asked,

by or on behalf of the prosecution, unless evidence relating to it is adduced, or a question relating to it is asked, in the proceedings by or on behalf of that person.

(7) Subsection (6) applies to any offence other than—
(a) an offence under section 2 or 5 of the Perjury Act 1911 (false statements made on oath otherwise than in judicial proceedings or made otherwise than on oath), or
(b) an offence under section 44(1) or (2) of the Criminal Law (Consolidation) (Scotland) Act 1995 (false statements made on oath or otherwise than on oath).

(8) Where a prosecuting authority institutes criminal proceedings following any report under subsection (2), the nominee or supervisor, and every officer and agent of the company past and present (other than the defendant or defender), shall give the authority all assistance in connection with the prosecution which he is reasonably able to give.

For this purpose—

"agent" includes any banker or solicitor of the company and any person employed by the company as auditor, whether that person is or is not an officer of the company,

"prosecuting authority" means the Director of Public Prosecutions, the Lord Advocate or the Secretary of State.

(9) The court may, on the application of the prosecuting authority, direct any person referred to in subsection (8) to comply with that subsection if he has failed to do so.

7B. Arrangements coming to an end prematurely

For the purposes of this Part, a voluntary arrangement the approval of which has taken effect under section 4A or paragraph 36 of Schedule A1 comes to an end prematurely if, when it ceases to have effect, it has not been fully implemented in respect of all persons bound by the arrangement by virtue of section 5(2)(b)(i) or, as the case may be, paragraph 37(2)(b)(i) of Schedule A1.

PART II
ADMINISTRATION

8. Administration

Schedule B1 to this Act (which makes provision about the administration of companies) shall have effect.

9–27. …

PART III
RECEIVERSHIP

CHAPTER I
RECEIVERS AND MANAGERS (ENGLAND AND WALES)

Preliminary and general provisions

28. Extent of this Chapter

(1) In this Chapter "company" means a company registered under the Companies Act 2006 in England and Wales or Scotland.

(2) This Chapter does not apply to receivers appointed under Chapter 2 of this Part (Scotland).

29. Definitions

(1) It is hereby declared that, except where the context otherwise requires—

(a) any reference in . . . this Act to a receiver or manager of the property of a company, or to a receiver of it, includes a receiver or manager, or (as the case may be) a receiver of part only of that property and a receiver only of the income arising from the property or from part of it; and

(b) any reference in . . . this Act to the appointment of a receiver or manager under powers contained in an instrument includes an appointment made under powers which, by virtue of any enactment, are implied in and have effect as if contained in an instrument.

(2) In this Chapter "administrative receiver" means—

(a) a receiver or manager of the whole (or substantially the whole) of a company's property appointed by or on behalf of the holders of any debentures of the company secured by a charge which, as created, was a floating charge, or by such a charge and one or more other securities; or

(b) a person who would be such a receiver or manager but for the appointment of some other person as the receiver of part of the company's property.

30. Disqualification of body corporate from acting as receiver

A body corporate is not qualified for appointment as receiver of the property of a company, and any body corporate which acts as such a receiver is liable to a fine.

31. Disqualification of bankrupt or person in respect of whom a debt relief order is made

(1) A person commits an offence if he acts as receiver or manager of the property of a company on behalf of debenture holders while—

(a) he is an undischarged bankrupt,

(aa) a moratorium period under a debt relief order applies in relation to him,

(b) a bankruptcy restrictions order or a debt relief restrictions order is in force in respect of him.

(2) A person guilty of an offence under subsection (1) shall be liable to imprisonment, a fine or both.

(3) This section does not apply to a receiver or manager acting under an appointment made by the court.

32. Power for court to appoint official receiver

Where application is made to the court to appoint a receiver on behalf of the debenture holders or other creditors of a company which is being wound up by the court, the official receiver may be appointed.

Receivers and managers appointed out of court

33. Time for which appointment is effective

(1) The appointment of a person as a receiver or manager of a company's property under powers contained in an instrument—

(a) is of no effect unless it is accepted by that person before the end of the business day next following that on which the instrument of appointment is received by him or on his behalf, and

(b) subject to this, is deemed to be made at the time at which the instrument of appointment is so received.

(2) This section applies to the appointment of two or more persons as joint receivers or managers of a company's property under powers contained in an instrument, subject to such modifications as may be prescribed by the rules.

34. Liability for invalid appointment

Where the appointment of a person as the receiver or manager of a company's property under powers contained in an instrument is discovered to be invalid (whether by virtue of the invalidity of the instrument or otherwise), the court may order the person by whom or on whose behalf the appointment was made to indemnify the person appointed against any liability which arises solely by reason of the invalidity of the appointment.

35. Application to court for directions

(1) A receiver or manager of the property of a company appointed under powers contained in an instrument, or the persons by whom or on whose behalf a receiver or manager has been so appointed, may apply to the court for directions in relation to any particular matter arising in connection with the performance of the functions of the receiver or manager.

(2) On such an application, the court may give such directions, or may make such order declaring the rights of persons before the court or otherwise, as it thinks just.

36. Court's power to fix remuneration

(1) The court may, on an application made by the liquidator of a company, by order fix the amount to be paid by way of remuneration to a person who, under powers contained in an instrument, has been appointed receiver or manager of the company's property.

(2) The court's power under subsection (1), where no previous order has been made with respect thereto under the subsection—

(a) extends to fixing the remuneration for any period before the making of the order or the application for it,

(b) is exercisable notwithstanding that the receiver or manager has died or ceased to act before the making of the order or the application, and

(c) where the receiver or manager has been paid or has retained for his remuneration for any period before the making of the order any amount in excess of that so fixed for that period, extends to requiring him or his personal representatives to account for the excess or such part of it as may be specified in the order.

But the power conferred by paragraph (c) shall not be exercised as respects any period before the making of the application for the order under this section, unless in the court's opinion there are special circumstances making it proper for the power to be exercised.

(3) The court may from time to time on an application made either by the liquidator or by the receiver or manager, vary or amend an order made under subsection (1).

37. Liability for contracts, etc

(1) A receiver or manager appointed under powers conferred in an instrument (other than an administrative receiver) is, to the same extent as if he had been appointed by order of the court—

(a) personally liable on any contract entered into by him in the performance of his functions (except in so far as the contract otherwise provides) and on any contract of employment adopted by him in the performance of those functions, and

(b) entitled in respect of that liability to indemnity out of the assets.

(2) For the purposes of subsection (1)(a), the receiver or manager is not to be taken to have adopted a contract of employment by reason of anything done or omitted to be done within 14 days after his appointment.

(3) Subsection (1) does not limit any right to indemnity which the receiver or manager would have apart from it, nor limit his liability on contracts entered into without authority, nor confer any right to indemnity in respect of that liability.

(4) Where at any time the receiver or manager so appointed vacates office—

(a) his remuneration and any expenses properly incurred by him, and

(b) any indemnity to which he is entitled out of the assets of the company,

shall be charged on and paid out of any property of the company which is in his custody or under his control at that time in priority to any charge or other security held by the person by or on whose behalf he was appointed.

38. Receivership accounts to be delivered to registrar

(1) Except in the case of an administrative receiver, every receiver or manager of a company's property who has been appointed under powers contained in an instrument shall deliver to the registrar of companies for registration the requisite accounts of his receipts and payments.

(2) The accounts shall be delivered within one month (or such longer period as the registrar may allow) after the expiration of 12 months from the date of his appointment and of every subsequent period of 6 months, and also within one month after he ceases to act as receiver or manager.

(3) The requisite accounts shall be an abstract in the prescribed form showing—

(a) receipts and payments during the relevant period of 12 or 6 months, or

(b) where the receiver or manager ceases to act, receipts and payments during the period from the end of the period of 12 or 6 months to which the last preceding abstract related (or, if no preceding abstract has been delivered under this section, from the date of his appointment) up to the date of his so ceasing, and the aggregate amount of receipts and payments during all preceding periods since his appointment.

(4) In this section "prescribed" means prescribed by regulations made by statutory instrument by the Secretary of State.

(5) A receiver or manager who makes default in complying with this section is liable to a fine and, for continued contravention, to a daily default fine.

Provisions applicable to every receivership

39. Notification that receiver or manager appointed

(1) Where a receiver or manager of the property of a company has been appointed—

(a) every invoice, order for goods or services, business letter or order form (whether in hard copy, electronic or any other form) issued by or on behalf of the company or the receiver or manager or the liquidator of the company; and

(b) all the company's websites,

must contain a statement that a receiver or manager has been appointed.

(2) If default is made in complying with this section, the company and any of the following persons, who knowingly and wilfully authorises or permits the default, namely, any officer of the company, any liquidator of the company and any receiver or manager, is liable to a fine.

40. Payment of debts out of assets subject to floating charge

(1) The following applies, in the case of a company, where a receiver is appointed on behalf of the holders of any debentures of the company secured by a charge which, as created, was a floating charge.

(2) If the company is not at the time in course of being wound up, its preferential debts (within the meaning given to that expression by section 386 in Part XII) shall be paid out of the assets coming to the hands of the receiver in priority to any claims for principal or interest in respect of the debentures.

(3) Payments made under this section shall be recouped, as far as may be, out of the assets of the company available for payment of general creditors.

41. Enforcement of duty to make returns

(1) If a receiver or manager of a company's property—

(a) having made default in filing, delivering or making any return, account or other document, or in giving any notice, which a receiver or manager is by law required to file, deliver, make or give, fails to make good the default within 14 days after the service on him of a notice requiring him to do so, or

(b) having been appointed under powers contained in an instrument, has, after being required at any time by the liquidator of the company to do so, failed to render proper accounts of his receipts and payments and to vouch them and pay over to the liquidator the amount properly payable to him,

the court may, on an application made for the purpose, make an order directing the receiver or manager (as the case may be) to make good the default within such time as may be specified in the order.

(2) In the case of the default mentioned in subsection (1)(a), application to the court may be made by any member or creditor of the company or by the registrar of companies; and in the case of the default mentioned in subsection (1)(b), the application shall be made by the liquidator. In either case the court's order may provide that all costs of and incidental to the application shall be borne by the receiver or manager, as the case may be.

(3) Nothing in this section prejudices the operation of any enactment imposing penalties on receivers in respect of any such default as is mentioned in subsection (1).

Administrative receivers: general

42. General powers

(1) The powers conferred on the administrative receiver of a company by the debentures by virtue of which he was appointed are deemed to include (except in so far as they are inconsistent with any of the provisions of those debentures) the powers specified in Schedule 1 to this Act.

(2) In the application of Schedule 1 to the administrative receiver of a company—

(a) the words "he" and "him" refer to the administrative receiver, and
(b) references to the property of the company are to the property of which he is or, but for the appointment of some other person as the receiver of part of the company's property, would be the receiver or manager.

(3) A person dealing with the administrative receiver in good faith and for value is not concerned to inquire whether the receiver is acting within his powers.

43. Power to dispose of charged property, etc

(1) Where, on an application by the administrative receiver, the court is satisfied that the disposal (with or without other assets) of any relevant property which is subject to a security would be likely to promote a more advantageous realisation of the company's assets than would otherwise be effected, the court may by order authorise the administrative receiver to dispose of the property as if it were not subject to the security.

(2) Subsection (1) does not apply in the case of any security held by the person by or on whose behalf the administrative receiver was appointed, or of any security to which a security so held has priority.

(3) It shall be a condition of an order under this section that—
(a) the net proceeds of the disposal, and
(b) where those proceeds are less than such amount as may be determined by the court to be the net amount which would be realised on a sale of the property in the open market by a willing vendor, such sums as may be required to make good the deficiency,

shall be applied towards discharging the sums secured by the security.

(4) Where a condition imposed in pursuance of subsection (3) relates to two or more securities, that condition shall require the net proceeds of the disposal and, where paragraph (b) of that subsection applies, the sums mentioned in that paragraph to be applied towards discharging the sums secured by those securities in the order of their priorities.

(5) A copy of an order under this section shall, within 14 days of the making of the order, be sent by the administrative receiver to the registrar of companies.

(6) If the administrative receiver without reasonable excuse fails to comply with subsection (5), he is liable to a fine and, for continued contravention, to a daily default fine.

(7) In this section "relevant property", in relation to the administrative receiver, means the property of which he is or, but for the appointment of some other person as the receiver of part of the company's property, would be the receiver or manager.

44. Agency and liability for contracts

(1) The administrative receiver of a company—
(a) is deemed to be the company's agent, unless and until the company goes into liquidation;
(b) is personally liable on any contract entered into by him in the carrying out of his functions (except in so far as the contract otherwise provides) and, to the extent of any qualifying liability, on any contract of employment adopted by him in the carrying out of those functions; and
(c) is entitled in respect of that liability to an indemnity out of the assets of the company.

(2) For the purposes of subsection (1)(b) the administrative receiver is not to be taken to have adopted a contract of employment by reason of anything done or omitted to be done within 14 days after his appointment.

(2A) For the purposes of subsection (1)(b), a liability under a contract of employment is a qualifying liability if—
(a) it is a liability to pay a sum by way of wages or salary or contribution to an occupational pension scheme,
(b) it is incurred while the administrative receiver is in office, and
(c) it is in respect of services rendered wholly or partly after the adoption of the contract.

(2B) Where a sum payable in respect of a liability which is a qualifying liability for the purposes of subsection (1)(b) is payable in respect of services rendered partly before and partly after the adoption of the contract, liability under subsection (1)(b) shall only extend to so much of the sum as is payable in respect of services rendered after the adoption of the contract.

(2C) For the purposes of subsections (2A) and (2B)—

(a) wages or salary payable in respect of a period of holiday or absence from work through sickness or other good cause are deemed to be wages or (as the case may be) salary in respect of services rendered in that period, and

(b) a sum payable in lieu of holiday is deemed to be wages or (as the case may be) salary in respect of services rendered in the period by reference to which the holiday entitlement arose.

(2D) In subsection (2C)(a), the reference to wages or salary payable in respect of a period of holiday includes any sums which, if they had been paid, would have been treated for the purposes of the enactments relating to social security as earnings in respect of that period.

(3) This section does not limit any right to indemnity which the administrative receiver would have apart from it, nor limit his liability on contracts entered into or adopted without authority, nor confer any right to indemnity in respect of that liability.

45. Vacation of office

(1) An administrative receiver of a company may at any time be removed from office by order of the court (but not otherwise) and may resign his office by giving notice of his resignation in the prescribed manner to such persons as may be prescribed.

(2) An administrative receiver shall vacate office if he ceases to be qualified to act as an insolvency practitioner in relation to the company.

(3) Where at any time an administrative receiver vacates office—

(a) his remuneration and any expenses properly incurred by him, and

(b) any indemnity to which he is entitled out of the assets of the company,

shall be charged on and paid out of any property of the company which is in his custody or under his control at that time in priority to any security held by the person by or on whose behalf he was appointed.

(4) Where an administrative receiver vacates office otherwise than by death, he shall, within 14 days after his vacation of office, send a notice to that effect to the registrar of companies.

(5) If an administrative receiver without reasonable excuse fails to comply with subsection (4), he is liable to a fine *and, for continued contravention, to a daily default fine.*

Note. The italicized words in subsection (5) are repealed by the Companies Act 1989, ss. 107, 212, Sch. 16, para. 3(3), Sch. 24, as from a day to be appointed.

Administrative receivers:
ascertainment and investigation of company's affairs

46. Information to be given by administrative receiver

(1) Where an administrative receiver is appointed, he shall—

(a) forthwith send to the company and publish in the prescribed manner a notice of his appointment, and

(b) within 28 days after his appointment, unless the court otherwise directs, send such a notice to all the creditors of the company (so far as he is aware of their addresses).

(2) This section and the next do not apply in relation to the appointment of an administrative receiver to act—

(a) with an existing administrative receiver, or

(b) in place of an administrative receiver dying or ceasing to act,

except that, where they apply to an administrative receiver who dies or ceases to act before they have been fully complied with, the references in this section and the next to the administrative receiver include (subject to the next subsection) his successor and any continuing administrative receiver.

(3) If the company is being wound up, this section and the next apply notwithstanding that the administrative receiver and the liquidator are the same person, but with any necessary modifications arising from that fact.

(4) If the administrative receiver without reasonable excuse fails to comply with this section, he is liable to a fine and, for continued contravention, to a daily default fine.

47. Statement of affairs to be submitted

(1) Where an administrative receiver is appointed, he shall forthwith require some or all of the persons mentioned below to make out and submit to him a statement in the prescribed form as to the affairs of the company.

(2) A statement submitted under this section shall be verified by a statement of truth by the persons required to submit it and shall show—

(a) particulars of the company's assets, debts and liabilities;
(b) the names and addresses of its creditors;
(c) the securities held by them respectively;
(d) the dates when the securities were respectively given; and
(e) such further or other information as may be prescribed.

(3) The persons referred to in subsection (1) are—

(a) those who are or have been officers of the company;
(b) those who have taken part in the company's formation at any time within one year before the date of the appointment of the administrative receiver;
(c) those who are in the company's employment, or have been in its employment within that year, and are in the administrative receiver's opinion capable of giving the information required;
(d) those who are or have been within that year officers of or in the employment of a company which is, or within that year was, an officer of the company.

In this subsection "employment" includes employment under a contract for services.

(4) Where any persons are required under this section to submit a statement of affairs to the administrative receiver, they shall do so (subject to the next subsection) before the end of the period of 21 days beginning with the day after that on which the prescribed notice of the requirement is given to them by the administrative receiver.

(5) The administrative receiver, if he thinks fit, may—

(a) at any time release a person from an obligation imposed on him under subsection (1) or (2), or
(b) either when giving notice under subsection (4) or subsequently, extend the period so mentioned;

and where the administrative receiver has refused to exercise a power conferred by this subsection, the court, if it thinks fit, may exercise it.

(6) If a person without reasonable excuse fails to comply with any obligation imposed under this section, he is liable to a fine and, for continued contravention, to a daily default fine.

48. Report by administrative receiver

(1) Where an administrative receiver is appointed, he shall, within 3 months (or such longer period as the court may allow) after his appointment, send to the registrar of companies, to any trustees for secured creditors of the company and (so far as he is aware of their addresses) to all such creditors a report as to the following matters, namely—

(a) the events leading up to his appointment, so far as he is aware of them;
(b) the disposal or proposed disposal by him of any property of the company and the carrying on or proposed carrying on by him of any business of the company;
(c) the amounts of principal and interest payable to the debenture holders by whom or on whose behalf he was appointed and the amounts payable to preferential creditors; and
(d) the amount (if any) likely to be available for the payment of other creditors.

(2) The administrative receiver shall also, within 3 months (or such longer period as the court may allow) after his appointment, either—

(a) send a copy of the report (so far as he is aware of their addresses) to all unsecured creditors of the company; or

(b) publish in the prescribed manner a notice stating an address to which unsecured creditors of the company should write for copies of the report to be sent to them free of charge,

and (in either case), unless the court otherwise directs, lay a copy of the report before a meeting of the company's unsecured creditors summoned for the purpose on not less than 14 days' notice.

(3) The court shall not give a direction under subsection (2) unless—

(a) the report states the intention of the administrative receiver to apply for the direction, and

(b) a copy of the report is sent to the persons mentioned in paragraph (a) of that subsection, or a notice is published as mentioned in paragraph (b) of that subsection, not less than 14 days before the hearing of the application.

(4) Where the company has gone or goes into liquidation, the administrative receiver—

(a) shall, within 7 days after his compliance with subsection (1) or, if later, the nomination or appointment of the liquidator, send a copy of the report to the liquidator, and

(b) where he does so within the time limited for compliance with subsection (2), is not required to comply with that subsection.

(5) A report under this section shall include a summary of the statement of affairs made out and submitted to the administrative receiver under section 47 and of his comments (if any) upon it.

(6) Nothing in this section is to be taken as requiring any such report to include any information the disclosure of which would seriously prejudice the carrying out by the administrative receiver of his functions.

(7) Section 46(2) applies for the purposes of this section also.

(8) If the administrative receiver without reasonable excuse fails to comply with this section, he is liable to a fine and, for continued contravention, to a default fine.

49. Committee of creditors

(1) Where a meeting of creditors is summoned under section 48, the meeting may, if it thinks fit, establish a committee ("the creditors' committee") to exercise the functions conferred on it by or under this Act.

(2) If such a committee is established, the committee may, on giving not less than 7 days' notice, require the administrative receiver to attend before it at any reasonable time and furnish it with such information relating to the carrying out by him of his functions as it may reasonably require.

CHAPTER II
RECEIVERS (SCOTLAND)

50. Extent of this Chapter

This Chapter extends to Scotland only.

51. Power to appoint receiver

(1) It is competent under the law of Scotland for the holder of a floating charge over all or any part of the property (including uncalled capital), which may from time to time be comprised in the property and undertaking of an incorporated company (whether a company registered under the Companies Act 2006 or not)—

(a) which the Court of Session has jurisdiction to wind up; or

(b) where paragraph (a) does not apply, in respect of which a court of a member state other than the United Kingdom has under the EU Regulation jurisdiction to open insolvency proceedings,

to appoint a receiver of such part of the property of the company as is subject to the charge.

(2) It is competent under the law of Scotland for the court, on the application of the holder of such a floating charge, to appoint a receiver of such part of the property of the company as is subject to the charge.

(2ZA) But, in relation to a company mentioned in subsection (1)(b), a receiver may be appointed under subsection (1) or (2) only in respect of property situated in Scotland.

(2A) Subsections (1) and (2) are subject to section 72A.

(3) The following are disqualified from being appointed as receiver—

(a) a body corporate;

(b) an undischarged bankrupt; and

(ba) a person subject to a bankruptcy restrictions order;

(c) a firm according to the law of Scotland.

(4) A body corporate or a firm according to the law of Scotland which acts as a receiver is liable to a fine.

(5) An undischarged bankrupt or a person subject to a bankruptcy restrictions order who so acts is liable to imprisonment or a fine, or both.

(6) In this section, "receiver" includes joint receivers; and

"bankruptcy restrictions order" means—

(a) a bankruptcy restrictions order made under section 56A of the Bankruptcy (Scotland) Act 1985;

(b) a bankruptcy restrictions undertaking entered into under section 56G of that Act;

(c) a bankruptcy restrictions order made under paragraph 1 of Schedule 4A to this Act; or

(d) a bankruptcy restrictions undertaking entered into under paragraph 7 of that Schedule.

"the EU Regulation" is the Regulation of the Council of the European Union published as Council Regulation (EC) No 1346/2000 on insolvency proceedings;

"court" is to be construed in accordance with Article 2(d) of the EU Regulation;

"insolvency proceedings" is to be construed in accordance with Article 2(a) of the EU Regulation.

52. Circumstances justifying appointment

(1) A receiver may be appointed under section 51(1) by the holder of the floating charge on the occurrence of any event which, by the provisions of the instrument creating the charge, entitles the holder of the charge to make that appointment and, in so far as not otherwise provided for by the instrument, on the occurrence of any of the following events, namely—

(a) the expiry of a period of 21 days after the making of a demand for payment of the whole or any part of the principal sum secured by the charge, without payment having been made;

(b) the expiry of a period of 2 months during the whole of which interest due and payable under the charge has been in arrears;

(c) the making of an order or the passing of a resolution to wind up the company;

(d) the appointment of a receiver by virtue of any other floating charge created by the company.

(2) A receiver may be appointed by the court under section 51(2) on the occurrence of any event which, by the provisions of the instrument creating the floating charge, entitles the holder of the charge to make that appointment and, in so far as not otherwise provided for by the instrument, on the occurrence of any of the following events, namely—

(a) where the court, on the application of the holder of the charge, pronounces itself satisfied that the position of the holder of the charge is likely to be prejudiced if no such appointment is made;

(b) any of the events referred to in paragraphs (a) to (c) of subsection (1).

53. Mode of appointment by holder of charge

(1) The appointment of a receiver by the holder of the floating charge under section 51(1) shall be by means of an instrument subscribed in accordance with the Requirements of Writing (Scotland) Act 1995 ("the instrument of appointment"), a copy (certified in the prescribed manner to be a correct copy) whereof shall be delivered by or on behalf of the person making the appointment to

the registrar of companies for registration within 7 days of its execution and shall be accompanied by a notice in the prescribed form.

(2) If any person without reasonable excuse makes default in complying with the requirements of subsection (1), he is liable to a fine *and, for continued contravention, to a daily default fine.*

(3) …

(4) If the receiver is to be appointed by the holders of a series of secured debentures, the instrument of appointment may be executed on behalf of the holders of the floating charge by any person authorised by resolution of the debenture-holders to execute the instrument.

(5) On receipt of the certified copy of the instrument of appointment in accordance with subsection (1), the registrar shall, on payment of the prescribed fee, enter the particulars of the appointment in the register.

(6) The appointment of a person as a receiver by an instrument of appointment in accordance with subsection (1)—

(a) is of no effect unless it is accepted by that person before the end of the business day next following that on which the instrument of appointment is received by him or on his behalf, and

(b) subject to paragraph (a), is deemed to be made on the day on and at the time at which the instrument of appointment is so received, as evidenced by a written docquet by that person or on his behalf;

and this subsection applies to the appointment of joint receivers subject to such modifications as may be prescribed.

(7) On the appointment of a receiver under this section, the floating charge by virtue of which he was appointed attaches to the property then subject to the charge; and such attachment has effect as if the charge was a fixed security over the property to which it has attached.

Note. The italicized words in subsection (2) are repealed by the Companies Act 1989, ss. 107, 212, Sch. 16, para. 3(3), Sch. 24, as from a day to be appointed.

54. Appointment by court

(1) Application for the appointment of a receiver by the court under section 51(2) shall be by petition to the court, which shall be served on the company.

(2) On such an application, the court shall, if it thinks fit, issue an interlocutor making the appointment of the receiver.

(3) A copy (certified by the clerk of the court to be a correct copy) of the court's interlocutor making the appointment shall be delivered by or on behalf of the petitioner to the registrar of companies for registration, accompanied by a notice in the prescribed form, within 7 days of the date of the interlocutor or such longer period as the court may allow.

If any person without reasonable excuse makes default in complying with the requirements of this subsection, he is liable to a fine *and, for continued contravention, to a daily default fine.*

(4) On receipt of the certified copy interlocutor in accordance with subsection (3), the registrar shall, on payment of the prescribed fee, enter the particulars of the appointment in the register.

(5) The receiver is to be regarded as having been appointed on the date of his being appointed by the court.

(6) On the appointment of a receiver under this section, the floating charge by virtue of which he was appointed attaches to the property then subject to the charge; and such attachment has effect as if the charge were a fixed security over the property to which it has attached.

(7) In making rules of court for the purposes of this section, the Court of Session shall have regard to the need for special provision for cases which appear to the court to require to be dealt with as a matter of urgency.

Note. The italicized words in subsection (3) are repealed by the Companies Act 1989, ss. 107, 212, Sch. 16, para. 3(3), Sch. 24, as from a day to be appointed.

55. Powers of receiver

(1) Subject to the next subsection, a receiver has in relation to such part of the property of the company as is attached by the floating charge by virtue of which he was appointed, the powers, if any, given to him by the instrument creating that charge.

(2) In addition, the receiver has under this Chapter the powers as respects that property (in so far as these are not inconsistent with any provision contained in that instrument) which are specified in Schedule 2 to this Act.

(3) Subsections (1) and (2) apply—

(a) subject to the rights of any person who has effectually executed diligence on all or any part of the property of the company prior to the appointment of the receiver, and

(b) subject to the rights of any person who holds over all or any part of the property of the company a fixed security or floating charge having priority over, or ranking pari passu with, the floating charge by virtue of which the receiver was appointed.

(4) A person dealing with a receiver in good faith and for value is not concerned to enquire whether the receiver is acting within his powers.

56. Precedence among receivers

(1) Where there are two or more floating charges subsisting over all or any part of the property of the company, a receiver may be appointed under this Chapter by virtue of each such charge; but a receiver appointed by, or on the application of, the holder of a floating charge having priority of ranking over any other floating charge by virtue of which a receiver has been appointed has the powers given to a receiver by section 55 and Schedule 2 to the exclusion of any other receiver.

(2) Where two or more floating charges rank with one another equally, and two or more receivers have been appointed by virtue of such charges, the receivers so appointed are deemed to have been appointed as joint receivers.

(3) Receivers appointed, or deemed to have been appointed, as joint receivers shall act jointly unless the instrument of appointment or respective instruments of appointment otherwise provide.

(4) Subject to subsection (5) below, the powers of a receiver appointed by, or on the application of, the holder of a floating charge are suspended by, and as from the date of, the appointment of a receiver by, or on the application of, the holder of a floating charge having priority of ranking over that charge to such extent as may be necessary to enable the receiver second mentioned to exercise his powers under section 55 and Schedule 2; and any powers so suspended take effect again when the floating charge having priority of ranking ceases to attach to the property then subject to the charge, whether such cessation is by virtue of section 62(6) or otherwise.

(5) The suspension of the powers of a receiver under subsection (4) does not have the effect of requiring him to release any part of the property (including any letters or documents) of the company from his control until he receives from the receiver superseding him a valid indemnity (subject to the limit of the value of such part of the property of the company as is subject to the charge by virtue of which he was appointed) in respect of any expenses, charges and liabilities he may have incurred in the performance of his functions as receiver.

(6) The suspension of the powers of a receiver under subsection (4) does not cause the floating charge by virtue of which he was appointed to cease to attach to the property to which it attached by virtue of section 53(7) or 54(6).

(7) Nothing in this section prevents the same receiver being appointed by virtue of two or more floating charges.

57. Agency and liability of receiver for contracts

(1) A receiver is deemed to be the agent of the company in relation to such property of the company as is attached by the floating charge by virtue of which he was appointed.

(1A) Without prejudice to subsection (1), a receiver is deemed to be the agent of the company in relation to any contract of employment adopted by him in the carrying out of his functions.

(2) A receiver (including a receiver whose powers are subsequently suspended under section 56) is personally liable on any contract entered into by him in the performance of his functions, except

in so far as the contract otherwise provides, and, to the extent of any qualifying liability, on any contract of employment adopted by him in the carrying out of those functions.

(2A) For the purposes of subsection (2), a liability under a contract of employment is a qualifying liability if—

(a) it is a liability to pay a sum by way of wages or salary or contribution to an occupational pension scheme,

(b) it is incurred while the receiver is in office, and

(c) it is in respect of services rendered wholly or partly after the adoption of the contract.

(2B) Where a sum payable in respect of a liability which is a qualifying liability for the purposes of subsection (2) is payable in respect of services rendered partly before and partly after the adoption of the contract, liability under that subsection shall only extend to so much of the sum as is payable in respect of services rendered after the adoption of the contract.

(2C) For the purposes of subsections (2A) and (2B)—

(a) wages or salary payable in respect of a period of holiday or absence from work through sickness or other good cause are deemed to be wages or (as the case may be) salary in respect of services rendered in that period, and

(b) a sum payable in lieu of holiday is deemed to be wages or (as the case may be) salary in respect of services rendered in the period by reference to which the holiday entitlement arose.

(2D) In subsection (2C)(a), the reference to wages or salary payable in respect of a period of holiday includes any sums which, if they had been paid, would have been treated for the purposes of the enactments relating to social security as earnings in respect of that period.

(3) A receiver who is personally liable by virtue of subsection (2) is entitled to be indemnified out of the property in respect of which he was appointed.

(4) Any contract entered into by or on behalf of the company prior to the appointment of a receiver continues in force (subject to its terms) notwithstanding that appointment, but the receiver does not by virtue only of his appointment incur any personal liability on any such contract.

(5) For the purposes of subsection (2), a receiver is not to be taken to have adopted a contract of employment by reason of anything done or omitted to be done within 14 days after his appointment.

(6) This section does not limit any right to indemnity which the receiver would have apart from it, nor limit his liability on contracts entered into or adopted without authority, nor confer any right to indemnity in respect of that liability.

(7) Any contract entered into by a receiver in the performance of his functions continues in force (subject to its terms) although the powers of the receiver are subsequently suspended under section 56.

58. Remuneration of receiver

(1) The remuneration to be paid to a receiver is to be determined by agreement between the receiver and the holder of the floating charge by virtue of which he was appointed.

(2) Where the remuneration to be paid to the receiver has not been determined under subsection (1), or where it has been so determined but is disputed by any of the persons mentioned in paragraphs (a) to (d) below, it may be fixed instead by the Auditor of the Court of Session on application made to him by—

(a) the receiver;

(b) the holder of any floating charge or fixed security over all or any part of the property of the company;

(c) the company; or

(d) the liquidator of the company.

(3) Where the receiver has been paid or has retained for his remuneration for any period before the remuneration has been fixed by the Auditor of the Court of Session under subsection (2) any amount in excess of the remuneration so fixed for that period, the receiver or his personal representatives shall account for the excess.

59. Priority of debts

(1) Where a receiver is appointed and the company is not at the time of the appointment in course of being wound up, the debts which fall under subsection (2) of this section shall be paid out of any assets coming to the hands of the receiver in priority to any claim for principal or interest by the holder of the floating charge by virtue of which the receiver was appointed.

(2) Debts falling under this subsection are preferential debts (within the meaning given by section 386 in Part XII) which, by the end of a period of 6 months after advertisement by the receiver for claims in the Edinburgh Gazette and in a newspaper circulating in the district where the company carries on business either—

(i) have been intimated to him, or

(ii) have become known to him.

(3) Any payments made under this section shall be recouped as far as may be out of the assets of the company available for payment of ordinary creditors.

60. Distribution of moneys

(1) Subject to the next section, and to the rights of any of the following categories of persons (which rights shall, except to the extent otherwise provided in any instrument, have the following order of priority), namely—

(a) the holder of any fixed security which is over property subject to the floating charge and which ranks prior to, or pari passu with, the floating charge;

(b) all persons who have effectually executed diligence on any part of the property of the company which is subject to the charge by virtue of which the receiver was appointed;

(c) creditors in respect of all liabilities, charges and expenses incurred by or on behalf of the receiver;

(d) the receiver in respect of his liabilities, expenses and remuneration, and any indemnity to which he is entitled out of the property of the company; and

(e) the preferential creditors entitled to payment under section 59,

the receiver shall pay moneys received by him to the holder of the floating charge by virtue of which the receiver was appointed in or towards satisfaction of the debt secured by the floating charge.

(2) Any balance of moneys remaining after the provisions of subsection (1) and section 61 below have been satisfied shall be paid in accordance with their respective rights and interests to the following persons, as the case may require—

(a) any other receiver;

(b) the holder of a fixed security which is over property subject to the floating charge;

(c) the company or its liquidator, as the case may be.

(3) Where any question arises as to the person entitled to a payment under this section, or where a receipt or a discharge of a security cannot be obtained in respect of any such payment, the receiver shall consign the amount of such payment in any joint stock bank of issue in Scotland in name of the Accountant of Court for behoof of the person or persons entitled thereto.

61. Disposal of interest in property

(1) Where the receiver sells or disposes, or is desirous of selling or disposing, of any property or interest in property of the company which is subject to the floating charge by virtue of which the receiver was appointed and which is—

(a) subject to any security or interest of, or burden or encumbrance in favour of, a creditor the ranking of which is prior to, or pari passu with, or postponed to the floating charge, or

(b) property or an interest in property affected or attached by effectual diligence executed by any person,

and the receiver is unable to obtain the consent of such creditor or, as the case may be, such person to such a sale or disposal, the receiver may apply to the court for authority to sell or dispose of the property or interest in property free of such security, interest, burden, encumbrance or diligence.

(1A) For the purposes of subsection (1) above, an inhibition which takes effect after the creation of the floating charge by virtue of which the receiver was appointed is not an effectual diligence.

(1B) For the purposes of subsection (1) above, an arrestment is an effectual diligence only where it is executed before the floating charge, by virtue of which the receiver was appointed, attaches to the property comprised in the company's property and undertaking.

(2) Subject to the next subsection, on such an application the court may, if it thinks fit, authorise the sale or disposal of the property or interest in question free of such security, interest, burden, encumbrance or diligence, and such authorisation may be on such terms or conditions as the court thinks fit.

(3) In the case of an application where a fixed security over the property or interest in question which ranks prior to the floating charge has not been met or provided for in full, the court shall not authorise the sale or disposal of the property or interest in question unless it is satisfied that the sale or disposal would be likely to provide a more advantageous realisation of the company's assets than would otherwise be effected.

(4) It shall be a condition of an authorisation to which subsection (3) applies that—

(a) the net proceeds of the disposal, and

(b) where those proceeds are less than such amount as may be determined by the court to be the net amount which would be realised on a sale of the property or interest in the open market by a willing seller, such sums as may be required to make good the deficiency,

shall be applied towards discharging the sums secured by the fixed security.

(5) Where a condition imposed in pursuance of subsection (4) relates to two or more such fixed securities, that condition shall require the net proceeds of the disposal and, where paragraph (b) of that subsection applies, the sums mentioned in that paragraph to be applied towards discharging the sums secured by those fixed securities in the order of their priorities.

(6) A copy of an authorisation under subsection (2) . . . shall, within 14 days of the granting of the authorisation, be sent by the receiver to the registrar of companies.

(7) If the receiver without reasonable excuse fails to comply with subsection (6), he is liable to a fine and, for continued contravention, to a daily default fine.

(8) Where any sale or disposal is effected in accordance with the authorisation of the court under subsection (2), the receiver shall grant to the purchaser or disponee an appropriate document of transfer or conveyance of the property or interest in question, and that document has the effect, or, where recording, intimation or registration of that document is a legal requirement for completion of title to the property or interest, then that recording, intimation or registration (as the case may be) has the effect, of—

(a) disencumbering the property or interest of the security, interest, burden or encumbrance affecting it, and

(b) freeing the property or interest from the diligence executed upon it.

(9) Nothing in this section prejudices the right of any creditor of the company to rank for his debt in the winding up of the company.

Note. Subsection (1B) is inserted by the Bankruptcy and Diligence etc. (Scotland) Act 2007, s. 226(1), Sch. 5, para. 14, as from a day to be appointed.

62. Cessation of appointment of receiver

(1) A receiver may be removed from office by the court under subsection (3) below and may resign his office by giving notice of his resignation in the prescribed manner to such persons as may be prescribed.

(2) A receiver shall vacate office if he ceases to be qualified to act as an insolvency practitioner in relation to the company.

(3) Subject to the next subsection, a receiver may, on application to the court by the holder of the floating charge by virtue of which he was appointed, be removed by the court on cause shown.

(4) Where at any time a receiver vacates office—

(a) his remuneration and any expenses properly incurred by him, and

(b) any indemnity to which he is entitled out of the property of the company, shall be paid out of the property of the company which is subject to the floating charge and shall have priority as provided for in section 60(1).

(5) When a receiver ceases to act as such otherwise than by death he shall, and, when a receiver is removed by the court, the holder of the floating charge by virtue of which he was appointed shall, within 14 days of the cessation or removal (as the case may be) give the registrar of companies notice to that effect, and the registrar shall enter the notice in the register.

If the receiver or the holder of the floating charge (as the case may require) makes default in complying with the requirements of this subsection, he is liable to a fine *and, for continued contravention, to a daily default fine.*

(6) If by the expiry of a period of one month following upon the removal of the receiver or his ceasing to act as such no other receiver has been appointed, the floating charge by virtue of which the receiver was appointed—

(a) thereupon ceases to attach to the property then subject to the charge, and

(b) again subsists as a floating charge;

and for the purposes of calculating the period of one month under this subsection no account shall be taken of any period during which the company is in administration, under Part II of this Act …

Note. The italicized words in subsection (5) are repealed by the Companies Act 1989, ss. 107, 212, Sch. 16, para. 3(3), Sch. 24, as from a day to be appointed.

63. Powers of court

(1) The court on the application of—

(a) the holder of a floating charge by virtue of which a receiver was appointed, or

(b) a receiver appointed under section 51,

may give directions to the receiver in respect of any matter arising in connection with the performance by him of his functions.

(2) Where the appointment of a person as a receiver by the holder of a floating charge is discovered to be invalid (whether by virtue of the invalidity of the instrument or otherwise), the court may order the holder of the floating charge to indemnify the person appointed against any liability which arises solely by reason of the invalidity of the appointment.

64. Notification that receiver appointed

(1) Where a receiver has been appointed—

(a) every invoice, order for goods or services, business letter or order form (whether in hard copy, electronic or any other form) issued by or on behalf of the company or the receiver or the liquidator of the company; and

(b) all the company's websites,

must contain a statement that a receiver has been appointed.

(2) If default is made in complying with the requirements of this section, the company and any of the following persons who knowingly and wilfully authorises or permits the default, namely any officer of the company, any liquidator of the company and any receiver, is liable to a fine.

65. Information to be given by receiver

(1) Where a receiver is appointed, he shall—

(a) forthwith send to the company and publish notice of his appointment, and

(b) within 28 days after his appointment, unless the court otherwise directs, send such notice to all the creditors of the company (so far as he is aware of their addresses).

(2) This section and the next do not apply in relation to the appointment of a receiver to act—

(a) with an existing receiver, or

(b) in place of a receiver who has died or ceased to act,

except that, where they apply to a receiver who dies or ceases to act before they have been fully complied with, the references in this section and the next to the receiver include (subject to subsection (3) of this section) his successor and any continuing receiver.

(3) If the company is being wound up, this section and the next apply notwithstanding that the receiver and the liquidator are the same person, but with any necessary modifications arising from that fact.

(4) If a person without reasonable excuse fails to comply with this section, he is liable to a fine and, for continued contravention, to a daily default fine.

66. Company's statement of affairs

(1) Where a receiver of a company is appointed, the receiver shall forthwith require some or all of the persons mentioned in subsection (3) below to make out and submit to him a statement in the prescribed form as to the affairs of the company.

(2) A statement submitted under this section shall be verified by affidavit by the persons required to submit it and shall show—

(a) particulars of the company's assets, debts and liabilities;
(b) the names and addresses of its creditors;
(c) the securities held by them respectively;
(d) the dates when the securities were respectively given; and
(e) such further or other information as may be prescribed.

(3) The persons referred to in subsection (1) are—

(a) those who are or have been officers of the company;
(b) those who have taken part in the company's formation at any time within one year before the date of the appointment of the receiver;
(c) those who are in the company's employment or have been in its employment within that year, and are in the receiver's opinion capable of giving the information required;
(d) those who are or have been within that year officers of or in the employment of a company which is, or within that year was, an officer of the company.

In this subsection "employment" includes employment under a contract for services.

(4) Where any persons are required under this section to submit a statement of affairs to the receiver they shall do so (subject to the next subsection) before the end of the period of 21 days beginning with the day after that on which the prescribed notice of the requirement is given to them by the receiver.

(5) The receiver, if he thinks fit, may—

(a) at any time release a person from an obligation imposed on him under subsection (1) or (2), or
(b) either when giving the notice mentioned in subsection (4) or subsequently extend the period so mentioned,

and where the receiver has refused to exercise a power conferred by this subsection, the court, if it thinks fit, may exercise it.

(6) If a person without reasonable excuse fails to comply with any obligation imposed under this section, he is liable to a fine and, for continued contravention, to a daily default fine.

67. Report by receiver

(1) Where a receiver is appointed under section 51, he shall within 3 months (or such longer period as the court may allow) after his appointment, send to the registrar of companies, to the holder of the floating charge by virtue of which he was appointed and to any trustees for secured creditors of the company and (so far as he is aware of their addresses) to all such creditors a report as to the following matters, namely—

(a) the events leading up to his appointment, so far as he is aware of them;
(b) the disposal or proposed disposal by him of any property of the company and the carrying on or proposed carrying on by him of any business of the company;
(c) the amounts of principal and interest payable to the holder of the floating charge by virtue of which he was appointed and the amounts payable to preferential creditors; and
(d) the amount (if any) likely to be available for the payment of other creditors.

(2) The receiver shall also, within 3 months (or such longer period as the court may allow) after his appointment, either—

(a) send a copy of the report (so far as he is aware of their addresses) to all unsecured creditors of the company, or

(b) publish in the prescribed manner a notice stating an address to which unsecured creditors of the company should write for copies of the report to be sent to them free of charge,

and (in either case), unless the court otherwise directs, lay a copy of the report before a meeting of the company's unsecured creditors summoned for the purpose on not less than 14 days' notice.

(3) The court shall not give a direction under subsection (2) unless—

(a) the report states the intention of the receiver to apply for the direction; and

(b) a copy of the report is sent to the persons mentioned in paragraph (a) of that subsection, or a notice is published as mentioned in paragraph (b) of that subsection, not less than 14 days before the hearing of the application.

(4) Where the company has gone or goes into liquidation, the receiver—

(a) shall, within 7 days after his compliance with subsection (1) or, if later, the nomination or appointment of the liquidator, send a copy of the report to the liquidator, and

(b) where he does so within the time limited for compliance with subsection (2), is not required to comply with that subsection.

(5) A report under this section shall include a summary of the statement of affairs made out and submitted under section 66 and of his comments (if any) on it.

(6) Nothing in this section shall be taken as requiring any such report to include any information the disclosure of which would seriously prejudice the carrying out by the receiver of his functions.

(7) Section 65(2) applies for the purposes of this section also.

(8) If a person without reasonable excuse fails to comply with this section, he is liable to a fine and, for continued contravention, to a daily default fine.

(9) In this section "secured creditor", in relation to a company, means a creditor of the company who holds in respect of his debt a security over property of the company, and "unsecured creditor" shall be construed accordingly.

68. Committee of creditors

(1) Where a meeting of creditors is summoned under section 67, the meeting may, if it thinks fit, establish a committee ("the creditors' committee") to exercise the functions conferred on it by or under this Act.

(2) If such a committee is established, the committee may on giving not less than 7 days' notice require the receiver to attend before it at any reasonable time and furnish it with such information relating to the carrying out by him of his functions as it may reasonably require.

69. Enforcement of receiver's duty to make returns, etc

(1) If any receiver—

(a) having made default in filing, delivering or making any return, account or other document, or in giving any notice, which a receiver is by law required to file, deliver, make or give, fails to make good the default within 14 days after the service on him of a notice requiring him to do so; or

(b) has, after being required at any time by the liquidator of the company so to do, failed to render proper accounts of his receipts and payments and to vouch the same and to pay over to the liquidator the amount properly payable to him,

the court may, on an application made for the purpose, make an order directing the receiver to make good the default within such time as may be specified in the order.

(2) In the case of any such default as is mentioned in subsection (1)(a), an application for the purposes of this section may be made by any member or creditor of the company or by the registrar of companies; and, in the case of any such default as is mentioned in subsection (1)(b), the application shall be made by the liquidator; and, in either case, the order may provide that all expenses of and incidental to the application shall be borne by the receiver.

(3) Nothing in this section prejudices the operation of any enactments imposing penalties on receivers in respect of any such default as is mentioned in subsection (1).

70. Interpretation for Chapter II

(1) In this Chapter, unless the contrary intention appears, the following expressions have the following meanings respectively assigned to them—

"company" means an incorporated company (whether or not a company registered under the Companies Act 2006) which the Court of Session has jurisdiction to wind up;

"fixed security", in relation to any property of a company, means any security, other than a floating charge or a charge having the nature of a floating charge, which on the winding up of the company in Scotland would be treated as an effective security over that property, and (without prejudice to that generality) includes a security over that property, being a heritable security within the meaning of the Conveyancing and Feudal Reform (Scotland) Act 1970;

"instrument of appointment" has the meaning given by section 53(1);

"prescribed" means prescribed by regulations made under this Chapter by the Secretary of State;

"receiver" means a receiver of such part of the property of the company as is subject to the floating charge by virtue of which he has been appointed under section 51;

"the register" has the meaning given by section 1080 of the Companies Act 2006;

"secured debenture" means a bond, debenture, debenture stock or other security which, either itself or by reference to any other instrument, creates a floating charge over all or any part of the property of the company, but does not include a security which creates no charge other than a fixed security; and

"series of secured debentures" means two or more secured debentures created as a series by the company in such a manner that the holders thereof are entitled pari passu to the benefit of the floating charge.

(2) Where a floating charge, secured debenture or series of secured debentures has been created by the company, then, except where the context otherwise requires, any reference in this Chapter to the holder of the floating charge shall—

(a) where the floating charge, secured debenture or series of secured debentures provides for a receiver to be appointed by any person or body, be construed as a reference to that person or body;

(b) where, in the case of a series of secured debentures, no such provision has been made therein but—

(i) there are trustees acting for the debenture-holders under and in accordance with a trust deed, be construed as a reference to those trustees, and

(ii) where no such trustees are acting, be construed as a reference to—

(aa) a majority in nominal value of those present or represented by proxy and voting at a meeting of debenture-holders at which the holders of at least one-third in nominal value of the outstanding debentures of the series are present or so represented, or

(bb) where no such meeting is held, the holders of at least one-half in nominal value of the outstanding debentures of the series.

(3) Any reference in this Chapter to a floating charge, secured debenture, series of secured debentures or instrument creating a charge includes, except where the context otherwise requires, a reference to that floating charge, debenture, series of debentures or instrument as varied by any instrument.

(4) References in this Chapter to the instrument by which a floating charge was created are, in the case of a floating charge created by words in a bond or other written acknowledgement, references to the bond or, as the case may be, the other written acknowledgement.

71. Prescription of forms etc; regulations

(1) The notice referred to in section 62(5), and the notice referred to in section 65(1)(a) shall be in such form as may be prescribed.

(2) Any power conferred by this Chapter on the Secretary of State to make regulations is exercisable by statutory instrument; and a statutory instrument made in the exercise of the power so conferred to prescribe a fee is subject to annulment in pursuance of a resolution of either House of Parliament.

CHAPTER III
RECEIVERS' POWERS IN GREAT BRITAIN AS A WHOLE

72. Cross-border operation of receivership provisions

(1) A receiver appointed under the law of either part of Great Britain in respect of the whole or any part of any property or undertaking of a company and in consequence of the company having created a charge which, as created, was a floating charge may exercise his powers in the other part of Great Britain so far as their exercise is not inconsistent with the law applicable there.

(2) In subsection (1) "receiver" includes a manager and a person who is appointed both receiver and manager.

CHAPTER IV
PROHIBITION OF APPOINTMENT OF ADMINISTRATIVE RECEIVER

72A. Floating charge holder not to appoint administrative receiver

(1) The holder of a qualifying floating charge in respect of a company's property may not appoint an administrative receiver of the company.

(2) In Scotland, the holder of a qualifying floating charge in respect of a company's property may not appoint or apply to the court for the appointment of a receiver who on appointment would be an administrative receiver of property of the company.

(3) In subsections (1) and (2)—

"holder of a qualifying floating charge in respect of a company's property" has the same meaning as in paragraph 14 of Schedule B1 to this Act, and

"administrative receiver" has the meaning given by section 251.

(4) This section applies—

(a) to a floating charge created on or after a date appointed by the Secretary of State by order made by statutory instrument, and

(b) in spite of any provision of an agreement or instrument which purports to empower a person to appoint an administrative receiver (by whatever name).

(5) An order under subsection (4)(a) may—

(a) make provision which applies generally or only for a specified purpose;

(b) make different provision for different purposes;

(c) make transitional provision.

(6) This section is subject to the exceptions specified in sections 72B to 72GA.

72B. First exception: capital market

(1) Section 72A does not prevent the appointment of an administrative receiver in pursuance of an agreement which is or forms part of a capital market arrangement if—

(a) a party incurs or, when the agreement was entered into was expected to incur, a debt of at least £50 million under the arrangement, and

(b) the arrangement involves the issue of a capital market investment.

(2) In subsection (1)—

"capital market arrangement" means an arrangement of a kind described in paragraph 1 of Schedule 2A, and

"capital market investment" means an investment of a kind described in paragraph 2 or 3 of that Schedule.

72C. Second exception: public-private partnership

(1) Section 72A does not prevent the appointment of an administrative receiver of a project company of a project which—
- (a) is a public-private partnership project, and
- (b) includes step-in rights.

(2) In this section "public-private partnership project" means a project—
- (a) the resources for which are provided partly by one or more public bodies and partly by one or more private persons, or
- (b) which is designed wholly or mainly for the purpose of assisting a public body to discharge a function.

(3) In this section—

"step-in rights" has the meaning given by paragraph 6 of Schedule 2A, and

"project company" has the meaning given by paragraph 7 of that Schedule.

72D. Third exception: utilities

(1) Section 72A does not prevent the appointment of an administrative receiver of a project company of a project which—
- (a) is a utility project, and
- (b) includes step-in rights.

(2) In this section—
- (a) "utility project" means a project designed wholly or mainly for the purpose of a regulated business,
- (b) "regulated business" means a business of a kind listed in paragraph 10 of Schedule 2A,
- (c) "step-in rights" has the meaning given by paragraph 6 of that Schedule, and
- (d) "project company" has the meaning given by paragraph 7 of that Schedule.

72DA. Exception in respect of urban regeneration projects

(1) Section 72A does not prevent the appointment of an administrative receiver of a project company of a project which—
- (a) is designed wholly or mainly to develop land which at the commencement of the project is wholly or partly in a designated disadvantaged area outside Northern Ireland, and
- (b) includes step-in rights.

(2) In subsection (1) "develop" means to carry out—
- (a) building operations,
- (b) any operation for the removal of substances or waste from land and the levelling of the surface of the land, or
- (c) engineering operations in connection with the activities mentioned in paragraph (a) or (b).

(3) In this section—

"building" includes any structure or erection, and any part of a building as so defined, but does not include plant and machinery comprised in a building,

"building operations" includes—
- (a) demolition of buildings,
- (b) filling in of trenches,
- (c) rebuilding,
- (d) structural alterations of, or additions to, buildings, and
- (e) other operations normally undertaken by a person carrying on business as a builder,

"designated disadvantaged area" means an area designated as a disadvantaged area under section 92 of the Finance Act 2001,

"engineering operations" includes the formation and laying out of means of access to highways,

"project company" has the meaning given by paragraph 7 of Schedule 2A,

"step-in rights" has the meaning given by paragraph 6 of that Schedule, "substance" means any natural or artificial substance whether in solid or liquid form or in the form of a gas or vapour, and

"waste" includes any waste materials, spoil, refuse or other matter deposited on land.

72E. Fourth exception: project finance

(1) Section 72A does not prevent the appointment of an administrative receiver of a project company of a project which—

(a) is a financed project, and

(b) includes step-in rights.

(2) In this section—

(a) a project is "financed" if under an agreement relating to the project a project company incurs, or when the agreement is entered into is expected to incur, a debt of at least £50 million for the purposes of carrying out the project,

(b) "project company" has the meaning given by paragraph 7 of Schedule 2A, and

(c) "step-in rights" has the meaning given by paragraph 6 of that Schedule.

72F. Fifth exception: financial market

Section 72A does not prevent the appointment of an administrative receiver of a company by virtue of—

(a) a market charge within the meaning of section 173 of the Companies Act 1989,

(b) a system-charge within the meaning of the Financial Markets and Insolvency Regulations 1996,

(c) a collateral security charge within the meaning of the Financial Markets and Insolvency (Settlement Finality) Regulations 1999.

72G. Sixth exception: social landlords

Section 72A does not prevent the appointment of an administrative receiver of a company which is—

(a) a private registered provider of social housing, or

(b) registered as a social landlord under Part I of the Housing Act 1996 (c 52) or under Part 2 of the Housing (Scotland) Act 2010 (asp 17).

72GA. Exception in relation to protected railway companies etc

Section 72A does not prevent the appointment of an administrative receiver of—

(a) a company holding an appointment under Chapter I of Part II of the Water Industry Act 1991,

(b) a protected railway company within the meaning of section 59 of the Railways Act 1993 (including that section as it has effect by virtue of section 19 of the Channel Tunnel Rail Link Act 1996), or

(c) a licence company within the meaning of section 26 of the Transport Act 2000.

72H. Sections 72A to 72G: supplementary

(1) Schedule 2A (which supplements sections 72B to 72G) shall have effect.

(2) The Secretary of State may by order—

(a) insert into this Act provision creating an additional exception to section 72A(1) or (2);

(b) provide for a provision of this Act which creates an exception to section 72A(1) or (2) to cease to have effect;

(c) amend section 72A in consequence of provision made under paragraph (a) or (b);

(d) amend any of sections 72B to 72G;

(e) amend Schedule 2A.

(3) An order under subsection (2) must be made by statutory instrument.

(4) An order under subsection (2) may make—

(a) provision which applies generally or only for a specified purpose;

(b) different provision for different purposes;

(c) consequential or supplementary provision;
(d) transitional provision.

(5) An order under subsection (2)—
(a) in the case of an order under subsection (2)(e), shall be subject to annulment in pursuance of a resolution of either House of Parliament,
(b) in the case of an order under subsection (2)(d) varying the sum specified in section 72B(1)(a) or 72E(2)(a) (whether or not the order also makes consequential or transitional provision), shall be subject to annulment in pursuance of a resolution of either House of Parliament, and
(c) in the case of any other order under subsection (2)(a) to (d), may not be made unless a draft has been laid before and approved by resolution of each House of Parliament.

PART IV
WINDING UP OF COMPANIES REGISTERED UNDER THE COMPANIES ACTS

CHAPTER I
PRELIMINARY

Introductory

73. Scheme of this Part

(1) This Part applies to the winding up of a company registered under the Companies Act 2006 in England and Wales or Scotland.
(2) The winding up may be either—
(a) voluntary (see Chapters 2 to 5), or
(b) by the court (see Chapter 6).
(3) This Chapter and Chapters 7 to 10 relate to winding up generally, except where otherwise stated.

Contributories

74. Liability as contributories of present and past members

(1) When a company is wound up, every present and past member is liable to contribute to its assets to any amount sufficient for payment of its debts and liabilities, and the expenses of the winding up, and for the adjustment of the rights of the contributories among themselves.
(2) This is subject as follows—
(a) a past member is not liable to contribute if he has ceased to be a member for one year or more before the commencement of the winding up;
(b) a past member is not liable to contribute in respect of any debt or liability of the company contracted after he ceased to be a member;
(c) a past member is not liable to contribute, unless it appears to the court that the existing members are unable to satisfy the contributions required to be made by them . . .;
(d) in the case of a company limited by shares, no contribution is required from any member exceeding the amount (if any) unpaid on the shares in respect of which he is liable as a present or past member;
(e) nothing in the Companies Acts or this Act invalidates any provision contained in a policy of insurance or other contract whereby the liability of individual members on the policy or contract is restricted, or whereby the funds of the company are alone made liable in respect of the policy or contract;
(f) a sum due to any member of the company (in his character of a member) by way of dividends, profits or otherwise is not deemed to be a debt of the company, payable to that member in a case of competition between himself and any other creditor not a member of the company, but any such sum may be taken into account for the purpose of the final adjustment of the rights of the contributories among themselves.

(3) In the case of a company limited by guarantee, no contribution is required from any member exceeding the amount undertaken to be contributed by him to the company's assets in the event of its being wound up; but if it is a company with a share capital, every member of it is liable (in addition to the amount so undertaken to be contributed to the assets), to contribute to the extent of any sums unpaid on shares held by him.

75. . . .

76. Liability of past directors and shareholders

(1) This section applies where a company is being wound up and—

(a) it has under Chapter 5 of Part 18 of the Companies Act 2006 (acquisition by limited company of its own shares: redemption or purchase by private company out of capital) made a payment out of capital in respect of the redemption or purchase of any of its own shares (the payment being referred to below as "the relevant payment"), and

(b) the aggregate amount of the company's assets and the amounts paid by way of contribution to its assets (apart from this section) is not sufficient for payment of its debts and liabilities, and the expenses of the winding up.

(2) If the winding up commenced within one year of the date on which the relevant payment was made, then—

(a) the person from whom the shares were redeemed or purchased, and

(b) the directors who signed the statement made in accordance with section 714(1) to (3) of the Companies Act 2006 for purposes of the redemption or purchase (except a director who shows that he had reasonable grounds for forming the opinion set out in the statement),

are, so as to enable that insufficiency to be met, liable to contribute to the following extent to the company's assets.

(3) A person from whom any of the shares were redeemed or purchased is liable to contribute an amount not exceeding so much of the relevant payment as was made by the company in respect of his shares; and the directors are jointly and severally liable with that person to contribute that amount.

(4) A person who has contributed any amount to the assets in pursuance of this section may apply to the court for an order directing any other person jointly and severally liable in respect of that amount to pay him such amount as the court thinks just and equitable.

(5) Section 74 does not apply in relation to liability accruing by virtue of this section.

(6) . . .

77. Limited company formerly unlimited

(1) This section applies in the case of a company being wound up which was at some former time registered as unlimited but has re-registered as a limited company.

(2) Notwithstanding section 74(2)(a) above, a past member of the company who was a member of it at the time of re-registration, if the winding up commences within the period of 3 years beginning with the day on which the company was re-registered, is liable to contribute to the assets of the company in respect of debts and liabilities contracted before that time.

(3) If no persons who were members of the company at that time are existing members of it, a person who at that time was a present or past member is liable to contribute as above notwithstanding that the existing members have satisfied the contributions required to be made by them . . .

This applies subject to section 74(2)(a) above and to subsection (2) of this section, but notwithstanding section 74(2)(c).

(4) Notwithstanding section 74(2)(d) and (3), there is no limit on the amount which a person who, at that time, was a past or present member of the company is liable to contribute as above.

78. Unlimited company formerly limited

(1) This section applies in the case of a company being wound up which was at some former time registered as limited but has been re-registered as unlimited . . .

(2) A person who, at the time when the application for the company to be re-registered was lodged, was a past member of the company and did not after that again become a member of it is not liable to contribute to the assets of the company more than he would have been liable to contribute had the company not been re-registered.

79. Meaning of "contributory"

(1) In this Act . . . the expression "contributory" means every person liable to contribute to the assets of a company in the event of its being wound up, and for the purposes of all proceedings for determining, and all proceedings prior to the final determination of, the persons who are to be deemed contributories, includes any person alleged to be a contributory.

(2) The reference in subsection (1) to persons liable to contribute to the assets does not include a person so liable by virtue of a declaration by the court under section 213 (imputed responsibility for company's fraudulent trading) or section 214 (wrongful trading) in Chapter X of this Part.

(3) A reference in a company's articles to a contributory does not (unless the context requires) include a person who is a contributory only by virtue of section 76.

. . .

80. Nature of contributory's liability

The liability of a contributory creates a debt (in England and Wales in the nature of an ordinary contract debt) accruing due from him at the time when his liability commenced, but payable at the times when calls are made for enforcing the liability.

81. Contributories in case of death of a member

(1) If a contributory dies either before or after he has been placed on the list of contributories, his personal representatives, and the heirs and legatees of heritage of his heritable estate in Scotland, are liable in a due course of administration to contribute to the assets of the company in discharge of his liability and are contributories accordingly.

(2) Where the personal representatives are placed on the list of contributories, the heirs or legatees of heritage need not be added, but they may be added as and when the court thinks fit.

(3) If in England and Wales the personal representatives make default in paying any money ordered to be paid by them, proceedings may be taken for administering the estate of the deceased contributory and for compelling payment out of it of the money due.

82. Effect of contributory's bankruptcy

(1) The following applies if a contributory becomes bankrupt, either before or after he has been placed on the list of contributories.

(2) His trustee in bankruptcy represents him for all purposes of the winding up, and is a contributory accordingly.

(3) The trustee may be called on to admit to proof against the bankrupt's estate, or otherwise allow to be paid out of the bankrupt's assets in due course of law, any money due from the bankrupt in respect of his liability to contribute to the company's assets.

(4) There may be proved against the bankrupt's estate the estimated value of his liability to future calls as well as calls already made.

83. Companies registered but not formed under the Companies Act 2006

(1) The following applies in the event of a company being wound up which is registered but not formed under the Companies Act 2006.

(2) Every person is a contributory, in respect of the company's debts and liabilities contracted before registration, who is liable—

(a) to pay, or contribute to the payment of, any debt or liability so contracted, or

(b) to pay, or contribute to the payment of, any sum for the adjustment of the rights of the members among themselves in respect of any such debt or liability, or

(c) to pay, or contribute to the amount of, the expenses of winding up the company, so far as relates to the debts or liabilities above-mentioned.

(3) Every contributory is liable to contribute to the assets of the company, in the course of the winding up, all sums due from him in respect of any such liability.

(4) In the event of the death, bankruptcy or insolvency of any contributory, provisions of this Act, with respect to the personal representatives, to the heirs and legatees of heritage of the heritable estate in Scotland of deceased contributories and to the trustees of bankrupt or insolvent contributories respectively, apply.

CHAPTER II
VOLUNTARY WINDING UP
(INTRODUCTORY AND GENERAL)

Resolutions for, and commencement of, voluntary winding up

84. Circumstances in which company may be wound up voluntarily

(1) A company may be wound up voluntarily—

(a) when the period (if any) fixed for the duration of the company by the articles expires, or the event (if any) occurs, on the occurrence of which the articles provide that the company is to be dissolved, and the company in general meeting has passed a resolution requiring it to be wound up voluntarily;

(b) if the company resolves by special resolution that it be wound up voluntarily;

(c) ...

(2) In this Act the expression "a resolution for voluntary winding up" means a resolution passed under either of the paragraphs of subsection (1).

(2A) Before a company passes a resolution for voluntary winding up it must give written notice of the resolution to the holder of any qualifying floating charge to which section 72A applies.

(2B) Where notice is given under subsection (2A) a resolution for voluntary winding up may be passed only—

(a) after the end of the period of five business days beginning with the day on which the notice was given, or

(b) if the person to whom the notice was given has consented in writing to the passing of the resolution.

(3) Chapter 3 of Part 3 of the Companies Act 2006 (resolutions affecting a company's constitution) applies to a resolution under paragraph (a) of subsection (1) as well as a special resolution under paragraph (b).

(4) This section has effect subject to section 43 of the Commonhold and Leasehold Reform Act 2002.

85. Notice of resolution to wind up

(1) When a company has passed a resolution for voluntary winding up, it shall, within 14 days after the passing of the resolution, give notice of the resolution by advertisement in the Gazette.

(2) If default is made in complying with this section, the company and every officer of it who is in default is liable to a fine and, for continued contravention, to a daily default fine.

For the purposes of this subsection the liquidator is deemed an officer of the company.

86. Commencement of winding up

A voluntary winding up is deemed to commence at the time of the passing of the resolution for voluntary winding up.

Consequences of resolution to wind up

87. Effect on business and status of company

(1) In case of a voluntary winding up, the company shall from the commencement of the winding up cease to carry on its business, except so far as may be required for its beneficial winding up.

(2) However, the corporate state and corporate powers of the company, notwithstanding anything to the contrary in its articles, continue until the company is dissolved.

88. Avoidance of share transfers, etc after winding-up resolution

Any transfer of shares, not being a transfer made to or with the sanction of the liquidator, and any alteration in the status of the company's members, made after the commencement of a voluntary winding up, is void.

Declaration of solvency

89. Statutory declaration of solvency

(1) Where it is proposed to wind up a company voluntarily, the directors (or, in the case of a company having more than two directors, the majority of them) may at a directors' meeting make a statutory declaration to the effect that they have made a full inquiry into the company's affairs and that, having done so, they have formed the opinion that the company will be able to pay its debts in full, together with interest at the official rate (as defined in section 251), within such period, not exceeding 12 months from the commencement of the winding up, as may be specified in the declaration.

(2) Such a declaration by the directors has no effect for purposes of this Act unless—
(a) it is made within the 5 weeks immediately preceding the date of the passing of the resolution for winding up, or on that date but before the passing of the resolution, and
(b) it embodies a statement of the company's assets and liabilities as at the latest practicable date before the making of the declaration.

(3) The declaration shall be delivered to the registrar of companies before the expiration of 15 days immediately following the date on which the resolution for winding up is passed.

(4) A director making a declaration under this section without having reasonable grounds for the opinion that the company will be able to pay its debts in full, together with interest at the official rate, within the period specified is liable to imprisonment or a fine, or both.

(5) If the company is wound up in pursuance of a resolution passed within 5 weeks after the making of the declaration, and its debts (together with interest at the official rate) are not paid or provided for in full within the period specified, it is to be presumed (unless the contrary is shown) that the director did not have reasonable grounds for his opinion.

(6) If a declaration required by subsection (3) to be delivered to the registrar is not so delivered within the time prescribed by that subsection, the company and every officer in default is liable to a fine and, for continued contravention, to a daily default fine.

90. Distinction between "members'" and "creditors'" voluntary winding up

A winding up in the case of which a directors' statutory declaration under section 89 has been made is a "members' voluntary winding up"; and a winding up in the case of which such a declaration has not been made is a "creditors' voluntary winding up".

CHAPTER III
MEMBERS' VOLUNTARY WINDING UP

91. Appointment of liquidator

(1) In a members' voluntary winding up, the company in general meeting shall appoint one or more liquidators for the purpose of winding up the company's affairs and distributing its assets.

(2) On the appointment of a liquidator all the powers of the directors cease, except so far as the company in general meeting or the liquidator sanctions their continuance.

92. Power to fill vacancy in office of liquidator

(1) If a vacancy occurs by death, resignation or otherwise in the office of liquidator appointed by the company, the company in general meeting may, subject to any arrangement with its creditors, fill the vacancy.

(2) For that purpose a general meeting may be convened by any contributory or, if there were more liquidators than one, by the continuing liquidators.

(3) The meeting shall be held in manner provided by this Act or by the articles, or in such manner as may, on application by any contributory or by the continuing liquidators, be determined by the court.

92A. Progress report to company at year's end (England and Wales)

(1) Subject to sections 96 and 102, in the event of the winding up of a company registered in England and Wales continuing for more than one year, the liquidator must—
(a) for each prescribed period produce a progress report relating to the prescribed matters; and
(b) within such period commencing with the end of the period referred to in paragraph (a) as may be prescribed send a copy of the progress report to—
(i) the members of the company; and
(ii) such other persons as may be prescribed.

(2) A liquidator who fails to comply with this section is liable to a fine.

93. General company meeting at each year's end (Scotland)

(1) Subject to sections 96 and 102, in the event of the winding up of a company registered in Scotland continuing for more than one year, the liquidator shall summon a general meeting of the company at the end of the first year from the commencement of the winding up, and of each succeeding year, or at the first convenient date within 3 months from the end of the year or such longer period as the Secretary of State may allow.

(2) The liquidator shall lay before the meeting an account of his acts and dealings, and of the conduct of the winding up, during the preceding year.

(3) If the liquidator fails to comply with this section, he is liable to a fine.

94. Final meeting prior to dissolution

(1) As soon as the company's affairs are fully wound up, the liquidator shall make up an account of the winding up, showing how it has been conducted and the company's property has been disposed of, and thereupon shall call a general meeting of the company for the purpose of laying before it the account, and giving an explanation of it.

(2) The meeting shall be called by advertisement in the Gazette, specifying its time, place and object and published at least one month before the meeting.

(3) Within one week after the meeting, the liquidator shall send to the registrar of companies a copy of the account, and shall make a return to him of the holding of the meeting and of its date.

(4) If the copy is not sent or the return is not made in accordance with subsection (3), the liquidator is liable to a fine and, for continued contravention, to a daily default fine.

(5) If a quorum is not present at the meeting, the liquidator shall, in lieu of the return mentioned above, make a return that the meeting was duly summoned and that no quorum was present; and upon such a return being made, the provisions of subsection (3) as to the making of the return are deemed complied with.

(6) If the liquidator fails to call a general meeting of the company as required by subsection (1), he is liable to a fine.

95. Effect of company's insolvency

(1) This section applies where the liquidator is of the opinion that the company will be unable to pay its debts in full (together with interest at the official rate) within the period stated in the directors' declaration under section 89.

(2) In the case of the winding up of a company registered in Scotland, the liquidator shall—
(a) summon a meeting of creditors for a day not later than the 28th day after the day on which he formed that opinion;
(b) send notices of the creditors' meeting to the creditors by post not less than 7 days before the day on which that meeting is to be held;
(c) cause notice of the creditors' meeting to be advertised once in the Gazette and once at least in 2 newspapers circulating in the relevant locality (that is to say the locality in which the

company's principal place of business in Great Britain was situated during the relevant period); and

(d) during the period before the day on which the creditors' meeting is to be held, furnish creditors free of charge with such information concerning the affairs of the company as they may reasonably require;

and the notice of the creditors' meeting shall state the duty imposed by paragraph (d) above.

(2A) In the case of the winding up of a company registered in England and Wales, the liquidator—

(a) shall summon a meeting of creditors for a day not later than the 28th day after the day on which he formed that opinion;

(b) shall send notices of the creditors' meeting to the creditors … not less than 7 days before the day on which that meeting is to be held;

(c) shall cause notice of the creditors' meeting to be advertised once in the Gazette;

(d) may cause notice of the meeting to be advertised in such other manner as he thinks fit; and

(e) shall during the period before the day on which the creditors' meeting is to be held, furnish creditors free of charge with such information concerning the affairs of the company as they may reasonably require;

and the notice of the creditors' meeting shall state the duty imposed by paragraph (e) above.

(3) The liquidator shall also—

(a) make out a statement in the prescribed form as to the affairs of the company;

(b) lay that statement before the creditors' meeting; and

(c) attend and preside at that meeting.

(4) The statement as to the affairs of the company . . . shall show—

(a) particulars of the company's assets, debts and liabilities;

(b) the names and addresses of the company's creditors;

(c) the securities held by them respectively;

(d) the dates when the securities were respectively given; and

(e) such further or other information as may be prescribed.

(4A) The statement as to the affairs of the company shall be verified by the liquidator—

(a) in the case of a winding up of a company registered in England and Wales, by a statement of truth; and

(b) in the case of a winding up of a company registered in Scotland, by affidavit.

(5) Where the company's principal place of business in Great Britain was situated in different localities at different times during the relevant period, the duty imposed by subsection (2)(c) applies separately in relation to each of those localities.

(6) Where the company had no place of business in Great Britain during the relevant period, references in subsections (2)(c) and (5) to the company's principal place of business in Great Britain are replaced by references to its registered office.

(7) In this section "the relevant period" means the period of 6 months immediately preceding the day on which were sent the notices summoning the company meeting at which it was resolved that the company be wound up voluntarily.

(8) If the liquidator without reasonable excuse fails to comply with this section, he is liable to a fine.

96. Conversion to creditors' voluntary winding up

As from the day on which the creditors' meeting is held under section 95, this Act has effect as if—

(a) the directors' declaration under section 89 had not been made; and

(b) the creditors' meeting and the company meeting at which it was resolved that the company be wound up voluntarily were the meetings mentioned in section 98 in the next Chapter;

and accordingly the winding up becomes a creditors' voluntary winding up.

CHAPTER IV
CREDITORS' VOLUNTARY WINDING UP

97. Application of this Chapter

(1) Subject as follows, this Chapter applies in relation to a creditors' voluntary winding up.

(2) Sections 98 and 99 do not apply where, under section 96 in Chapter III, a members' voluntary winding up has become a creditors' voluntary winding up.

98. Meeting of creditors

(1) In the case of the winding up of a company registered in Scotland, the company shall—
- (a) cause a meeting of its creditors to be summoned for a day not later than the 14th day after the day on which there is to be held the company meeting at which the resolution for voluntary winding up is to be proposed;
- (b) cause the notices of the creditors' meeting to be sent by post to the creditors not less than 7 days before the day on which that meeting is to be held; and
- (c) cause notice of the creditors' meeting to be advertised once in the Gazette and once at least in two newspapers circulating in the relevant locality (that is to say the locality in which the company's principal place of business in Great Britain was situated during the relevant period).

(1A) In the case of the winding up of a company registered in England and Wales, the company—
- (a) shall cause a meeting of its creditors to be summoned for a day not later than the 14th day after the day on which there is to be held the company meeting at which the resolution for voluntary winding up is to be proposed;
- (b) shall cause the notices of the creditors' meeting to be sent … to the creditors not less than 7 days before the day on which that meeting is to be held;
- (c) shall cause notice of the creditors' meeting to be advertised once in the Gazette; and
- (d) may cause notice of the meeting to be advertised in such other manner as the directors think fit.

(2) The notice of the creditors' meeting shall state either—
- (a) the name and address of a person qualified to act as an insolvency practitioner in relation to the company who, during the period before the day on which that meeting is to be held, will furnish creditors free of charge with such information concerning the company's affairs as they may reasonably require; or
- (b) a place in the relevant locality where, on the two business days falling next before the day on which that meeting is to be held, a list of the names and addresses of the company's creditors will be available for inspection free of charge.

(3) Where the company's principal place of business in Great Britain was situated in different localities at different times during the relevant period, the duties imposed by subsections (1)(c) and (2)(b) above apply separately in relation to each of those localities.

(4) Where the company had no place of business in Great Britain during the relevant period, references in subsections (1)(c) and (3) to the company's principal place of business in Great Britain are replaced by references to its registered office.

(5) In this section "the relevant period" means the period of 6 months immediately preceding the day on which were sent the notices summoning the company meeting at which it was resolved that the company be wound up voluntarily.

(6) If the company without reasonable excuse fails to comply with subsection (1), (1A) or (2), it is guilty of an offence and liable to a fine.

99. Directors to lay statement of affairs before creditors

(1) The directors of the company shall—
- (a) make out a statement in the prescribed form as to the affairs of the company;
- (b) cause that statement to be laid before the creditors' meeting under section 98; and
- (c) appoint one of their number to preside at that meeting;

and it is the duty of the director so appointed to attend the meeting and preside over it.

(2) The statement as to the affairs of the company . . . shall show—

(a) particulars of the company's assets, debts and liabilities;

(b) the names and addresses of the company's creditors;

(c) the securities held by them respectively;

(d) the dates when the securities were respectively given; and

(e) such further or other information as may be prescribed.

(2A) The statement as to the affairs of the company shall be verified by some or all of the directors—

(a) in the case of a winding up of a company registered in England and Wales, by a statement of truth; and

(b) in the case of a winding up of a company registered in Scotland, by affidavit.

(3) If—

(a) the directors without reasonable excuse fail to comply with subsection (1), (2) or (2A); or

(b) any director without reasonable excuse fails to comply with subsection (1), so far as requiring him to attend and preside at the creditors' meeting,

the directors are or (as the case may be) the director is guilty of an offence and liable to a fine.

100. Appointment of liquidator

(1) The creditors and the company at their respective meetings mentioned in section 98 may nominate a person to be liquidator for the purpose of winding up the company's affairs and distributing its assets.

(2) The liquidator shall be the person nominated by the creditors or, where no person has been so nominated, the person (if any) nominated by the company.

(3) In the case of different persons being nominated, any director, member or creditor of the company may, within 7 days after the date on which the nomination was made by the creditors, apply to the court for an order either—

(a) directing that the person nominated as liquidator by the company shall be liquidator instead of or jointly with the person nominated by the creditors, or

(b) appointing some other person to be liquidator instead of the person nominated by the creditors.

(4) The court shall grant an application under subsection (3) made by the holder of a qualifying floating charge in respect of the company's property (within the meaning of paragraph 14 of Schedule B1) unless the court thinks it right to refuse the application because of the particular circumstances of the case.

Note. Subsection (4) is inserted by the Enterprise Act 2002, s. 248(3), Sch. 17, paras. 9, 14, as from a day to be appointed.

101. Appointment of liquidation committee

(1) The creditors at the meeting to be held under section 98 or at any subsequent meeting may, if they think fit, appoint a committee ("the liquidation committee") of not more than 5 persons to exercise the functions conferred on it by or under this Act.

(2) If such a committee is appointed, the company may, either at the meeting at which the resolution for voluntary winding up is passed or at any time subsequently in general meeting, appoint such number of persons as they think fit to act as members of the committee, not exceeding 5.

(3) However, the creditors may, if they think fit, resolve that all or any of the persons so appointed by the company ought not to be members of the liquidation committee; and if the creditors so resolve—

(a) the persons mentioned in the resolution are not then, unless the court otherwise directs, qualified to act as members of the committee; and

(b) on any application to the court under this provision the court may, if it thinks fit, appoint other persons to act as such members in place of the persons mentioned in the resolution.

(4) In Scotland, the liquidation committee has, in addition to the powers and duties conferred and imposed on it by this Act, such of the powers and duties of commissioners on a bankrupt estate as may be conferred and imposed on liquidation committees by the rules.

102. Creditors' meeting where winding up converted under s 96

Where, in the case of a winding up which was, under section 96 in Chapter III, converted to a creditors' voluntary winding up, a creditors' meeting is held in accordance with section 95, any appointment made or committee established by that meeting is deemed to have been made or established by a meeting held in accordance with section 98 in this Chapter.

103. Cesser of directors' powers

On the appointment of a liquidator, all the powers of the directors cease, except so far as the liquidation committee (or, if there is no such committee, the creditors) sanction their continuance.

104. Vacancy in office of liquidator

If a vacancy occurs, by death, resignation or otherwise, in the office of a liquidator (other than a liquidator appointed by, or by the direction of, the court) the creditors may fill the vacancy.

104A. Progress report to company and creditors at year's end (England and Wales)

(1) If the winding up of a company registered in England and Wales continues for more than one year, the liquidator must—

(a) for each prescribed period produce a progress report relating to the prescribed matters; and

(b) within such period commencing with the end of the period referred to in paragraph (a) as may be prescribed send a copy of the progress report to—

(i) the members and creditors of the company; and

(ii) such other persons as may be prescribed.

(2) A liquidator who fails to comply with this section is liable to a fine.

105. Meetings of company and creditors at each year's end (Scotland)

(1) If the winding up of a company registered in Scotland continues for more than one year, the liquidator shall summon a general meeting of the company and a meeting of the creditors at the end of the first year from the commencement of the winding up, and of each succeeding year, or at the first convenient date within 3 months from the end of the year or such longer period as the Secretary of State may allow.

(2) The liquidator shall lay before each of the meetings an account of his acts and dealings and of the conduct of the winding up during the preceding year.

(3) If the liquidator fails to comply with this section, he is liable to a fine.

(4) Where under section 96 a members' voluntary winding up has become a creditors' voluntary winding up, and the creditors' meeting under section 95 is held 3 months or less before the end of the first year from the commencement of the winding up, the liquidator is not required by this section to summon a meeting of creditors at the end of that year.

106. Final meeting prior to dissolution

(1) As soon as the company's affairs are fully wound up, the liquidator shall make up an account of the winding up, showing how it has been conducted and the company's property has been disposed of, and thereupon shall call a general meeting of the company and a meeting of the creditors for the purpose of laying the account before the meetings and giving an explanation of it.

(2) Each such meeting shall be called by advertisement in the Gazette specifying the time, place and object of the meeting, and published at least one month before it.

(3) Within one week after the date of the meetings (or, if they are not held on the same date, after the date of the later one) the liquidator shall send to the registrar of companies a copy of the account, and shall make a return to him of the holding of the meetings and of their dates.

(4) If the copy is not sent or the return is not made in accordance with subsection (3), the liquidator is liable to a fine and, for continued contravention, to a daily default fine.

(5) However, if a quorum is not present at either such meeting, the liquidator shall, in lieu of the return required by subsection (3), make a return that the meeting was duly summoned and that no quorum was present; and upon such return being made the provisions of that subsection as to the making of the return are, in respect of that meeting, deemed complied with.

(6) If the liquidator fails to call a general meeting of the company or a meeting of the creditors as required by this section, he is liable to a fine.

CHAPTER V
PROVISIONS APPLYING TO BOTH KINDS OF VOLUNTARY WINDING UP

107. Distribution of company's property

Subject to the provisions of this Act as to preferential payments, the company's property in a voluntary winding up shall on the winding up be applied in satisfaction of the company's liabilities pari passu and, subject to that application, shall (unless the articles otherwise provide) be distributed among the members according to their rights and interests in the company.

108. Appointment or removal of liquidator by the court

(1) If from any cause whatever there is no liquidator acting, the court may appoint a liquidator.

(2) The court may, on cause shown, remove a liquidator and appoint another.

109. Notice by liquidator of his appointment

(1) The liquidator shall, within 14 days after his appointment, publish in the Gazette and deliver to the registrar of companies for registration a notice of his appointment in the form prescribed by statutory instrument made by the Secretary of State.

(2) If the liquidator fails to comply with this section, he is liable to a fine and, for continued contravention, to a daily default fine.

110. Acceptance of shares, etc, as consideration for sale of company property

(1) This section applies, in the case of a company proposed to be, or being, wound up voluntarily, where the whole or part of the company's business or property is proposed to be transferred or sold—

(a) to another company ("the transferee company"), whether or not the latter is a company registered under the Companies Act 2006, or

(b) to a limited liability partnership (the "transferee limited liability partnership").

(2) With the requisite sanction, the liquidator of the company being, or proposed to be, wound up ("the transferor company") may receive, in compensation or part compensation for the transfer or sale—

(a) in the case of the transferee company, shares, policies or other like interests in the transferee company for distribution among the members of the transferor company, or

(b) in the case of the transferee limited liability partnership, membership in the transferee limited liability partnership for distribution among the members of the transferor company.

(3) The sanction requisite under subsection (2) is—

(a) in the case of a members' voluntary winding up, that of a special resolution of the company, conferring either a general authority on the liquidator or an authority in respect of any particular arrangement, and

(b) in the case of a creditors' voluntary winding up, that of either the court or the liquidation committee.

(4) Alternatively to subsection (2), the liquidator may (with that sanction) enter into any other arrangement whereby the members of the transferor company may—

(a) in the case of the transferee company, in lieu of receiving cash, shares, policies or other like interests (or in addition thereto) participate in the profits of, or receive any other benefit from, the transferee company, or

(b) in the case of the transferee limited liability partnership, in lieu of receiving cash or membership (or in addition thereto), participate in some other way in the profits of, or receive any other benefit from, the transferee limited liability partnership.

(5) A sale or arrangement in pursuance of this section is binding on members of the transferor company.

(6) A special resolution is not invalid for purposes of this section by reason that it is passed before or concurrently with a resolution for voluntary winding up or for appointing liquidators; but, if an order is made within a year for winding up the company by the court, the special resolution is not valid unless sanctioned by the court.

111. Dissent from arrangement under s 110

(1) This section applies in the case of a voluntary winding up where, for the purposes of section 110(2) or (4), there has been passed a special resolution of the transferor company providing the sanction requisite for the liquidator under that section.

(2) If a member of the transferor company who did not vote in favour of the special resolution expresses his dissent from it in writing, addressed to the liquidator and left at the company's registered office within 7 days after the passing of the resolution, he may require the liquidator either to abstain from carrying the resolution into effect or to purchase his interest at a price to be determined by agreement or by arbitration under this section.

(3) If the liquidator elects to purchase the member's interest, the purchase money must be paid before the company is dissolved and be raised by the liquidator in such manner as may be determined by special resolution.

(4) For purposes of an arbitration under this section, the provisions of the Companies Clauses Consolidation Act 1845 or, in the case of a winding up in Scotland, the Companies Clauses Consolidation (Scotland) Act 1845 with respect to the settlement of disputes by arbitration are incorporated with this Act, and—

(a) in the construction of those provisions this Act is deemed the special Act and "the company" means the transferor company, and

(b) any appointment by the incorporated provisions directed to be made under the hand of the secretary or any two of the directors may be made in writing by the liquidator (or, if there is more than one liquidator, then any two or more of them).

112. Reference of questions to court

(1) The liquidator or any contributory or creditor may apply to the court to determine any question arising in the winding up of a company, or to exercise, as respects the enforcing of calls or any other matter, all or any of the powers which the court might exercise if the company were being wound up by the court.

(2) The court, if satisfied that the determination of the question or the required exercise of power will be just and beneficial, may accede wholly or partially to the application on such terms and conditions as it thinks fit, or may make such other order on the application as it thinks just.

(3) A copy of an order made by virtue of this section staying the proceedings in the winding up shall forthwith be forwarded by the company, or otherwise as may be prescribed, to the registrar of companies, who shall enter it in his records relating to the company.

113. Court's power to control proceedings (Scotland)

If the court, on the application of the liquidator in the winding up of a company registered in Scotland, so directs, no action or proceeding shall be proceeded with or commenced against the company except by leave of the court and subject to such terms as the court may impose.

114. No liquidator appointed or nominated by company

(1) This section applies where, in the case of a voluntary winding up, no liquidator has been appointed or nominated by the company.

(2) The powers of the directors shall not be exercised, except with the sanction of the court or (in the case of a creditors' voluntary winding up) so far as may be necessary to secure compliance with

sections 98 (creditors' meeting) and 99 (statement of affairs), during the period before the appointment or nomination of a liquidator of the company.

(3) Subsection (2) does not apply in relation to the powers of the directors—

(a) to dispose of perishable goods and other goods the value of which is likely to diminish if they are not immediately disposed of, and

(b) to do all such other things as may be necessary for the protection of the company's assets.

(4) If the directors of the company without reasonable excuse fail to comply with this section, they are liable to a fine.

115. Expenses of voluntary winding up

All expenses properly incurred in the winding up, including the remuneration of the liquidator, are payable out of the company's assets in priority to all other claims.

116. Saving for certain rights

The voluntary winding up of a company does not bar the right of any creditor or contributory to have it wound up by the court; but in the case of an application by a contributory the court must be satisfied that the rights of the contributories will be prejudiced by a voluntary winding up.

CHAPTER VI
WINDING UP BY THE COURT

Jurisdiction (England and Wales)

117. High Court and county court jurisdiction

(1) The High Court has jurisdiction to wind up any company registered in England and Wales.

(2) Where the amount of a company's share capital paid up or credited as paid up does not exceed £120,000, then (subject to this section) the county court of the district in which the company's registered office is situated has concurrent jurisdiction with the High Court to wind up the company.

(3) The money sum for the time being specified in subsection (2) is subject to increase or reduction by order under section 416 in Part XV.

(4) The Lord Chancellor may, with the concurrence of the Lord Chief Justice, by order in a statutory instrument exclude a county court from having winding-up jurisdiction, and for the purposes of that jurisdiction may attach its district, or any part thereof, to any other county court, and may by statutory instrument revoke or vary any such order.

In exercising the powers of this section, the Lord Chancellor shall provide that a county court is not to have winding-up jurisdiction unless it has for the time being jurisdiction for the purposes of Parts VIII to XI of this Act (individual insolvency).

(5) Every court in England and Wales having winding-up jurisdiction has for the purposes of that jurisdiction all the powers of the High Court; and every prescribed officer of the court shall perform any duties which an officer of the High Court may discharge by order of a judge of that court or otherwise in relation to winding up.

(6) For the purposes of this section, a company's "registered office" is the place which has longest been its registered office during the 6 months immediately preceding the presentation of the petition for winding up.

(7) This section is subject to Article 3 of the EC Regulation (jurisdiction under EC Regulation).

(8) The Lord Chief Justice may nominate a judicial office holder (as defined in section 109(4) of the Constitutional Reform Act 2005) to exercise his functions under this section.

118. Proceedings taken in wrong court

(1) Nothing in section 117 invalidates a proceeding by reason of its being taken in the wrong court.

(2) The winding up of a company by the court in England and Wales, or any proceedings in the winding up, may be retained in the court in which the proceedings were commenced, although it may not be the court in which they ought to have been commenced.

119. Proceedings in county court; case stated for High Court

(1) If any question arises in any winding-up proceedings in a county court which all the parties to the proceedings, or which one of them and the judge of the court, desire to have determined in the first instance in the High Court, the judge shall state the facts in the form of a special case for the opinion of the High Court.

(2) Thereupon the special case and the proceedings (or such of them as may be required) shall be transmitted to the High Court for the purposes of the determination.

Jurisdiction (Scotland)

120. Court of Session and sheriff court jurisdiction

(1) The Court of Session has jurisdiction to wind up any company registered in Scotland.

(2) When the Court of Session is in vacation, the jurisdiction conferred on that court by this section may (subject to the provisions of this Part) be exercised by the judge acting as vacation judge …

(3) Where the amount of a company's share capital paid up or credited as paid up does not exceed £120,000, the sheriff court of the sheriffdom in which the company's registered office is situated has concurrent jurisdiction with the Court of Session to wind up the company; but—

(a) the Court of Session may, if it thinks expedient having regard to the amount of the company's assets to do so—

(i) remit to sheriff court any petition presented to the Court of Session for winding up such a company, or

(ii) require such a petition presented to a sheriff court to be remitted to the Court of Session; and

(b) the Court of Session may require any such petition as above-mentioned presented to one sheriff court to be remitted to another sheriff court; and

(c) in a winding up in the sheriff court the sheriff may submit a stated case for the opinion of the Court of Session on any question of law arising in that winding up.

(4) For purposes of this section, the expression "registered office" means the place which has longest been the company's registered office during the 6 months immediately preceding the presentation of the petition for winding up.

(5) The money sum for the time being specified in subsection (3) is subject to increase or reduction by order under section 416 in Part XV.

(6) This section is subject to Article 3 of the EC Regulation (jurisdiction under EC Regulation).

121. Power to remit winding up to Lord Ordinary

(1) The Court of Session may, by Act of Sederunt, make provision for the taking of proceedings in a winding up before one of the Lords Ordinary; and, where provision is so made, the Lord Ordinary has, for the purposes of the winding up, all the powers and jurisdiction of the court.

(2) However, the Lord Ordinary may report to the Inner House any matter which may arise in the course of a winding up.

Grounds and effect of winding-up petition

122. Circumstances in which company may be wound up by the court

(1) A company may be wound up by the court if—

(a) the company has by special resolution resolved that the company be wound up by the court,

(b) being a public company which was registered as such on its original incorporation, the company has not been issued with a trading certificate under section 761 of the Companies Act 2006 (requirement as to minimum share capital) and more than a year has expired since it was so registered,

(c) it is an old public company, within the meaning of Schedule 3 to the Companies Act 2006 (Consequential Amendments, Transitional Provisions and Savings) Order 2009,

(d) the company does not commence its business within a year from its incorporation or suspends its business for a whole year,

(e) . . .

(f) the company is unable to pay its debts,

(fa) at the time at which a moratorium for the company under section 1A comes to an end, no voluntary arrangement approved under Part I has effect in relation to the company,

(g) the court is of the opinion that it is just and equitable that the company should be wound up.

(2) In Scotland, a company which the Court of Session has jurisdiction to wind up may be wound up by the Court if there is subsisting a floating charge over property comprised in the company's property and undertaking, and the court is satisfied that the security of the creditor entitled to the benefit of the floating charge is in jeopardy.

For this purpose a creditor's security is deemed to be in jeopardy if the Court is satisfied that events have occurred or are about to occur which render it unreasonable in the creditor's interests that the company should retain power to dispose of the property which is subject to the floating charge.

123. Definition of inability to pay debts

(1) A company is deemed unable to pay its debts—

(a) if a creditor (by assignment or otherwise) to whom the company is indebted in a sum exceeding £750 then due has served on the company, by leaving it at the company's registered office, a written demand (in the prescribed form) requiring the company to pay the sum so due and the company has for 3 weeks thereafter neglected to pay the sum or to secure or compound for it to the reasonable satisfaction of the creditor, or

(b) if, in England and Wales, execution or other process issued on a judgment, decree or order of any court in favour of a creditor of the company is returned unsatisfied in whole or in part, or

(c) if, in Scotland, the inducia e of a charge for payment on an extract decree, or an extract registered bond, or an extract registered protest, have expired without payment being made, or

(d) if, in Northern Ireland, a certificate of unenforceability has been granted in respect of a judgment against the company, or

(e) if it is proved to the satisfaction of the court that the company is unable to pay its debts as they fall due.

(2) A company is also deemed unable to pay its debts if it is proved to the satisfaction of the court that the value of the company's assets is less than the amount of its liabilities, taking into account its contingent and prospective liabilities.

(3) The money sum for the time being specified in subsection (1)(a) is subject to increase or reduction by order under section 416 in Part XV.

124. Application for winding up

(1) Subject to the provisions of this section, an application to the court for the winding up of a company shall be by petition presented either by the company, or the directors, or by any creditor or creditors (including any contingent or prospective creditor or creditors), contributory or contributories, or by a liquidator (within the meaning of Article 2(b) of the EC Regulation) appointed in proceedings by virtue of Article 3(1) of the EC Regulation or a temporary administrator (within the meaning of Article 38 of the EC Regulation) or by the designated officer for a magistrates' court in the exercise of the power conferred by section 87A of the Magistrates' Courts Act 1980 (enforcement of fines imposed on companies), or by all or any of those parties, together or separately.

(2) Except as mentioned below, a contributory is not entitled to present a winding-up petition unless either—

(a) the number of members is reduced below 2, or

(b) the shares in respect of which he is a contributory, or some of them, either were originally allotted to him, or have been held by him, and registered in his name, for at least 6 months during the 18 months before the commencement of the winding up, or have devolved on him through the death of a former holder.

(3) A person who is liable under section 76 to contribute to a company's assets in the event of its being wound up may petition on either of the grounds set out in section 122(1)(f) and (g), and subsection (2) above does not then apply; but unless the person is a contributory otherwise than under section 76, he may not in his character as contributory petition on any other ground.

. . .

(3A) A winding-up petition on the ground set out in section 122(1)(fa) may only be presented by one or more creditors.

(4) A winding-up petition may be presented by the Secretary of State—

(a) if the ground of the petition is that in section 122(1)(b) or (c), or

(b) in a case falling within section 124A or 124B below.

(4AA) A winding up petition may be presented by the Financial Services Authority in a case falling within section 124C(1) or (2).

(4A) A winding-up petition may be presented by the Regulator of Community Interest Companies in a case falling within section 50 of the Companies (Audit, Investigations and Community Enterprise) Act 2004.

(5) Where a company is being wound up voluntarily in England and Wales, a winding-up petition may be presented by the official receiver attached to the court as well as by any other person authorised in that behalf under the other provisions of this section; but the court shall not make a winding-up order on the petition unless it is satisfied that the voluntary winding up cannot be continued with due regard to the interests of the creditors or contributories.

124A. Petition for winding up on grounds of public interest

(1) Where it appears to the Secretary of State from—

(a) any report made or information obtained under Part XIV (except section 448A) of the Companies Act 1985 (company investigations, &c.),

(b) any report made by inspectors under—

(i) section 167, 168, 169 or 284 of the Financial Services and Markets Act 2000, or

(ii) where the company is an open-ended investment company (within the meaning of that Act), regulations made as a result of section 262(2)(k) of that Act,

(bb) any information or documents obtained under section 165, 171, 172, 173 or 175 of that Act,

(c) any information obtained under section 2 of the Criminal Justice Act 1987 or section 52 of the Criminal Justice (Scotland) Act 1987 (fraud investigations), or

(d) any information obtained under section 83 of the Companies Act 1989 (powers exercisable for purpose of assisting overseas regulatory authorities),

that it is expedient in the public interest that a company should be wound up, he may present a petition for it to be wound up if the court thinks it just and equitable for it to be so.

(2) This section does not apply if the company is already being wound up by the court.

124B. Petition for winding up of SE

(1) Where—

(a) an SE whose registered office is in Great Britain is not in compliance with Article 7 of Council Regulation (EC) No 2157/2001 on the Statute for a European company (the "EC Regulation") (location of head office and registered office), and

(b) it appears to the Secretary of State that the SE should be wound up, he may present a petition for it to be wound up if the court thinks it is just and equitable for it to be so.

(2) This section does not apply if the SE is already being wound up by the court.

(3) In this section "SE" has the same meaning as in the EC Regulation.

124C. Petition for winding up of SCE

(1) Where, in the case of an SCE whose registered office is in Great Britain—

(a) there has been such a breach as is mentioned in Article 73(1) of Council Regulation (EC) No 1435/2003 on the Statute for a European Cooperative Society (SCE) (the "European

Cooperative Society Regulation") (winding up by the court or other competent authority), and

(b) it appears to the Financial Services Authority that the SCE should be wound up,

the Authority may present a petition for the SCE to be wound up if the court thinks it is just and equitable for it to be so.

(2) Where, in the case of an SCE whose registered office is in Great Britain—

(a) the SCE is not in compliance with Article 6 of the European Cooperative Society Regulation (location of head office and registered office, and

(b) it appears to the Financial Service Authority that the SCE should be wound up,

the Authority may present a petition for the SCE to be wound up if the court thinks it is just and equitable for it to be so.

(3) This section does not apply if the SCE is already being wound up by the court.

(4) In this section "SCE" has the same meaning as in the European Cooperative Society Regulation.

125. Powers of court on hearing of petition

(1) On hearing a winding-up petition the court may dismiss it, or adjourn the hearing conditionally or unconditionally, or make an interim order, or any other order that it thinks fit; but the court shall not refuse to make a winding-up order on the ground only that the company's assets have been mortgaged to an amount equal to or in excess of those assets, or that the company has no assets.

(2) If the petition is presented by members of the company as contributories on the ground that it is just and equitable that the company should be wound up, the court, if it is of opinion—

(a) that the petitioners are entitled to relief either by winding up the company or by some other means, and

(b) that in the absence of any other remedy it would be just and equitable that the company should be wound up,

shall make a winding-up order; but this does not apply if the court is also of the opinion both that some other remedy is available to the petitioners and that they are acting unreasonably in seeking to have the company wound up instead of pursuing that other remedy.

126. Power to stay or restrain proceedings against company

(1) At any time after the presentation of a winding-up petition, and before a winding-up order has been made, the company, or any creditor or contributory, may—

(a) where any action or proceeding against the company is pending in the High Court or Court of Appeal in England and Wales or Northern Ireland, apply to the court in which the action or proceeding is pending for a stay of proceedings therein, and

(b) where any other action or proceeding is pending against the company, apply to the court having jurisdiction to wind up the company to restrain further proceedings in the action or proceeding;

and the court to which application is so made may (as the case may be) stay, sist or restrain the proceedings accordingly on such terms as it thinks fit.

(2) In the case of a company registered but not formed under the Companies Act 2006, where the application to stay, sist or restrain is by a creditor, this section extends to actions and proceedings against any contributory of the company.

127. Avoidance of property dispositions, etc

(1) In a winding up by the court, any disposition of the company's property, and any transfer of shares, or alteration in the status of the company's members, made after the commencement of the winding up is, unless the court otherwise orders, void.

(2) This section has no effect in respect of anything done by an administrator of a company while a winding-up petition is suspended under paragraph 40 of Schedule B1.

128. Avoidance of attachments, etc

(1) Where a company registered in England and Wales is being wound up by the court, any attachment, sequestration, distress or execution put in force against the estate or effects of the company after the commencement of the winding up is void.

(2) This section, so far as relates to any estate or effects of the company situated in England and Wales, applies in the case of a company registered in Scotland as it applies in the case of a company registered in England and Wales.

Commencement of winding up

129. Commencement of winding up by the court

(1) If, before the presentation of a petition for the winding up of a company by the court, a resolution has been passed by the company for voluntary winding up, the winding up of the company is deemed to have commenced at the time of the passing of the resolution; and unless the court, on proof of fraud or mistake, directs otherwise, all proceedings taken in the voluntary winding up are deemed to have been validly taken.

(1A) Where the court makes a winding-up order by virtue of paragraph 13(1)(e) of Schedule B1, the winding up is deemed to commence on the making of the order.

(2) In any other case, the winding up of a company by the court is deemed to commence at the time of the presentation of the petition for winding up.

130. Consequences of winding-up order

(1) On the making of a winding-up order, a copy of the order must forthwith be forwarded by the company (or otherwise as may be prescribed) to the registrar of companies, who shall enter it in his records relating to the company.

(2) When a winding-up order has been made or a provisional liquidator has been appointed, no action or proceeding shall be proceeded with or commenced against the company or its property, except by leave of the court and subject to such terms as the court may impose.

(3) When an order has been made for winding up a company registered but not formed under the Companies Act 2006, no action or proceeding shall be commenced or proceeded with against the company or its property or any contributory of the company, in respect of any debt of the company, except by leave of the court, and subject to such terms as the court may impose.

(4) An order for winding up a company operates in favour of all the creditors and of all contributories of the company as if made on the joint petition of a creditor and of a contributory.

Investigation procedures

131. Company's statement of affairs

(1) Where the court has made a winding-up order or appointed a provisional liquidator, the official receiver may require some or all of the persons mentioned in subsection (3) below to make out and submit to him a statement in the prescribed form as to the affairs of the company.

(2) The statement . . . shall show—

(a) particulars of the company's assets, debts and liabilities;

(b) the names and addresses of the company's creditors;

(c) the securities held by them respectively;

(d) the dates when the securities were respectively given; and

(e) such further or other information as may be prescribed or as the official receiver may require.

(2A) The statement shall be verified by the persons required to submit it—

(a) in the case of an appointment of a provisional liquidator or a winding up by the court in England and Wales, by a statement of truth; and

(b) in the case of an appointment of a provisional liquidator or a winding up by the court in Scotland, by affidavit.

(3) The persons referred to in subsection (1) are—

(a) those who are or have been officers of the company;
(b) those who have taken part in the formation of the company at any time within one year before the relevant date;
(c) those who are in the company's employment, or have been in its employment within that year, and are in the official receiver's opinion capable of giving the information required;
(d) those who are or have been within that year officers of, or in the employment of, a company which is, or within that year was, an officer of the company.

(4) Where any persons are required under this section to submit a statement of affairs to the official receiver, they shall do so (subject to the next subsection) before the end of the period of 21 days beginning with the day after that on which the prescribed notice of the requirement is given to them by the official receiver.

(5) The official receiver, if he thinks fit, may—
(a) at any time release a person from an obligation imposed on him under subsection (1) or (2) above; or
(b) either when giving the notice mentioned in subsection (4) or subsequently, extend the period so mentioned;

and where the official receiver has refused to exercise a power conferred by this subsection, the court, if it thinks fit, may exercise it.

(6) In this section—
"employment" includes employment under a contract for services; and
"the relevant date" means—
(a) in a case where a provisional liquidator is appointed, the date of his appointment; and
(b) in a case where no such appointment is made, the date of the winding-up order.

(7) If a person without reasonable excuse fails to comply with any obligation imposed under this section, he is liable to a fine and, for continued contravention, to a daily default fine.

(8) In the application of this section to Scotland references to the official receiver are to the liquidator or, in a case where a provisional liquidator is appointed, the provisional liquidator.

132. Investigation by official receiver

(1) Where a winding-up order is made by the court in England and Wales, it is the duty of the official receiver to investigate—
(a) if the company has failed, the causes of the failure; and
(b) generally, the promotion, formation, business, dealings and affairs of the company,

and to make such report (if any) to the court as he thinks fit.

(2) The report is, in any proceedings, prima facie evidence of the facts stated in it.

133. Public examination of officers

(1) Where a company is being wound up by the court, the official receiver or, in Scotland, the liquidator may at any time before the dissolution of the company apply to the court for the public examination of any person who—
(a) is or has been an officer of the company; or
(b) has acted as liquidator or administrator of the company or as receiver or manager or, in Scotland, receiver of its property; or
(c) not being a person falling within paragraph (a) or (b), is or has been concerned, or has taken part, in the promotion, formation or management of the company.

(2) Unless the court otherwise orders, the official receiver or, in Scotland, the liquidator shall make an application under subsection (1) if he is requested in accordance with the rules to do so by—
(a) one-half, in value, of the company's creditors; or
(b) three-quarters, in value, of the company's contributories.

(3) On an application under subsection (1), the court shall direct that a public examination of the person to whom the application relates shall be held on a day appointed by the court; and that person shall attend on that day and be publicly examined as to the promotion, formation or

management of the company or as to the conduct of its business and affairs, or his conduct or dealings in relation to the company.

(4) The following may take part in the public examination of a person under this section and may question that person concerning the matters mentioned in subsection (3), namely—

(a) the official receiver;

(b) the liquidator of the company;

(c) any person who has been appointed as special manager of the company's property or business;

(d) any creditor of the company who has tendered a proof or, in Scotland, submitted a claim in the winding up;

(e) any contributory of the company.

134. Enforcement of s 133

(1) If a person without reasonable excuse fails at any time to attend his public examination under section 133, he is guilty of a contempt of court and liable to be punished accordingly.

(2) In a case where a person without reasonable excuse fails at any time to attend his examination under section 133 or there are reasonable grounds for believing that a person has absconded, or is about to abscond, with a view to avoiding or delaying his examination under that section, the court may cause a warrant to be issued to a constable or prescribed officer of the court—

(a) for the arrest of that person; and

(b) for the seizure of any books, papers, records, money or goods in that person's possession.

(3) In such a case the court may authorise the person arrested under the warrant to be kept in custody, and anything seized under such a warrant to be held, in accordance with the rules, until such time as the court may order.

Appointment of liquidator

135. Appointment and powers of provisional liquidator

(1) Subject to the provisions of this section, the court may, at any time after the presentation of a winding-up petition, appoint a liquidator provisionally.

(2) In England and Wales, the appointment of a provisional liquidator may be made at any time before the making of a winding-up order; and either the official receiver or any other fit person may be appointed.

(3) In Scotland, such an appointment may be made at any time before the first appointment of liquidators.

(4) The provisional liquidator shall carry out such functions as the court may confer on him.

(5) When a liquidator is provisionally appointed by the court, his powers may be limited by the order appointing him.

136. Functions of official receiver in relation to office of liquidator

(1) The following provisions of this section have effect, subject to section 140 below, on a winding-up order being made by the court in England and Wales.

(2) The official receiver, by virtue of his office, becomes the liquidator of the company and continues in office until another person becomes liquidator under the provisions of this Part.

(3) The official receiver is, by virtue of his office, the liquidator during any vacancy.

(4) At any time when he is the liquidator of the company, the official receiver may summon separate meetings of the company's creditors and contributories for the purpose of choosing a person to be liquidator of the company in place of the official receiver.

(5) It is the duty of the official receiver—

(a) as soon as practicable in the period of 12 weeks beginning with the day on which the winding-up order was made, to decide whether to exercise his power under subsection (4) to summon meetings, and

(b) if in pursuance of paragraph (a) he decides not to exercise that power, to give notice of his decision, before the end of that period, to the court and to the company's creditors and contributories, and

(c) (whether or not he has decided to exercise that power) to exercise his power to summon meetings under subsection (4) if he is at any time requested, in accordance with the rules, to do so by one-quarter, in value, of the company's creditors;

and accordingly, where the duty imposed by paragraph (c) arises before the official receiver has performed a duty imposed by paragraph (a) or (b), he is not required to perform the latter duty.

(6) A notice given under subsection (5)(b) to the company's creditors shall contain an explanation of the creditors' power under subsection (5)(c) to require the official receiver to summon meetings of the company's creditors and contributories.

137. Appointment by Secretary of State

(1) In a winding up by the court in England and Wales the official receiver may, at any time when he is the liquidator of the company, apply to the Secretary of State for the appointment of a person as liquidator in his place.

(2) If meetings are held in pursuance of a decision under section 136(5)(a), but no person is chosen to be liquidator as a result of those meetings, it is the duty of the official receiver to decide whether to refer the need for an appointment to the Secretary of State.

(3) On an application under subsection (1), or a reference made in pursuance of a decision under subsection (2), the Secretary of State shall either make an appointment or decline to make one.

(4) Where a liquidator has been appointed by the Secretary of State under subsection (3), the liquidator shall give notice of his appointment to the company's creditors or, if the court so allows, shall advertise his appointment in accordance with the directions of the court.

(5) In that notice or advertisement the liquidator shall—

(a) state whether he proposes to summon a general meeting of the company's creditors under section 141 below for the purpose of determining (together with any meeting of contributories) whether a liquidation committee should be established under that section, and

(b) if he does not propose to summon such a meeting, set out the power of the company's creditors under that section to require him to summon one.

138. Appointment of liquidator in Scotland

(1) Where a winding-up order is made by the court in Scotland, a liquidator shall be appointed by the court at the time when the order is made.

(2) The liquidator so appointed (here referred to as "the interim liquidator") continues in office until another person becomes liquidator in his place under this section or the next.

(3) The interim liquidator shall (subject to the next subsection) as soon as practicable in the period of 28 days beginning with the day on which the winding-up order was made or such longer period as the court may allow, summon separate meetings of the company's creditors and contributories for the purpose of choosing a person (who may be the person who is the interim liquidator) to be liquidator of the company in place of the interim liquidator.

(4) If it appears to the interim liquidator, in any case where a company is being wound up on grounds including its inability to pay its debts, that it would be inappropriate to summon under subsection (3) a meeting of the company's contributories, he may summon only a meeting of the company's creditors for the purpose mentioned in that subsection.

(5) If one or more meetings are held in pursuance of this section but no person is appointed or nominated by the meeting or meetings, the interim liquidator shall make a report to the court which shall appoint either the interim liquidator or some other person to be liquidator of the company.

(6) A person who becomes liquidator of the company in place of the interim liquidator shall, unless he is appointed by the court, forthwith notify the court of that fact.

139. Choice of liquidator at meetings of creditors and contributories

(1) This section applies where a company is being wound up by the court and separate meetings of the company's creditors and contributories are summoned for the purpose of choosing a person to be liquidator of the company.

(2) The creditors and the contributories at their respective meetings may nominate a person to be liquidator.

(3) The liquidator shall be the person nominated by the creditors or, where no person has been so nominated, the person (if any) nominated by the contributories.

(4) In the case of different persons being nominated, any contributory or creditor may, within 7 days after the date on which the nomination was made by the creditors, apply to the court for an order either—

(a) appointing the person nominated as liquidator by the contributories to be a liquidator instead of, or jointly with, the person nominated by the creditors; or

(b) appointing some other person to be liquidator instead of the person nominated by the creditors.

140. Appointment by the court following administration or voluntary arrangement

(1) Where a winding-up order is made immediately upon the appointment of an administrator ceasing to have effect, the court may appoint as liquidator of the company the person whose appointment as administrator has ceased to have effect.

(2) Where a winding-up order is made at a time when there is a supervisor of a voluntary arrangement approved in relation to the company under Part I, the court may appoint as liquidator of the company the person who is the supervisor at the time when the winding-up order is made.

(3) Where the court makes an appointment under this section, the official receiver does not become the liquidator as otherwise provided by section 136(2), and he has no duty under section 136(5)(a) or (b) in respect of the summoning of creditors' or contributories' meetings.

Liquidation committees

141. Liquidation committee (England and Wales)

(1) Where a winding-up order has been made by the court in England and Wales and separate meetings of creditors and contributories have been summoned for the purpose of choosing a person to be liquidator, those meetings may establish a committee ("the liquidation committee") to exercise the functions conferred on it by or under this Act.

(2) The liquidator (not being the official receiver) may at any time, if he thinks fit, summon separate general meetings of the company's creditors and contributories for the purpose of determining whether such a committee should be established and, if it is so determined, of establishing it.

The liquidator (not being the official receiver) shall summon such a meeting if he is requested, in accordance with the rules, to do so by one-tenth, in value, of the company's creditors.

(3) Where meetings are summoned under this section, or for the purpose of choosing a person to be liquidator, and either the meeting of creditors or the meeting of contributories decides that a liquidation committee should be established, but the other meeting does not so decide or decides that a committee should not be established, the committee shall be established in accordance with the rules, unless the court otherwise orders.

(4) The liquidation committee is not to be able or required to carry out its functions at any time when the official receiver is liquidator; but at any such time its functions are vested in the Secretary of State except to the extent that the rules otherwise provide.

(5) Where there is for the time being no liquidation committee, and the liquidator is a person other than the official receiver, the functions of such a committee are vested in the Secretary of State except to the extent that the rules otherwise provide.

142. Liquidation committee (Scotland)

(1) Where a winding-up order has been made by the court in Scotland and separate meetings of creditors and contributories have been summoned for the purpose of choosing a person to be

liquidator or, under section 138(4), only a meeting of creditors has been summoned for that purpose, those meetings or (as the case may be) that meeting may establish a committee ("the liquidation committee") to exercise the functions conferred on it by or under this Act.

(2) The liquidator may at any time, if he thinks fit, summon separate general meetings of the company's creditors and contributories for the purpose of determining whether such a committee should be established and, if it is so determined, of establishing it.

(3) The liquidator, if appointed by the court otherwise than under section 139(4)(a), is required to summon meetings under subsection (2) if he is requested, in accordance with the rules, to do so by one-tenth, in value, of the company's creditors.

(4) Where meetings are summoned under this section, or for the purpose of choosing a person to be liquidator, and either the meeting of creditors or the meeting of contributories decides that a liquidation committee should be established, but the other meeting does not so decide or decides that a committee should not be established, the committee shall be established in accordance with the rules, unless the court otherwise orders.

(5) Where in the case of any winding up there is for the time being no liquidation committee, the functions of such a committee are vested in the court except to the extent that the rules otherwise provide.

(6) In addition to the powers and duties conferred and imposed on it by this Act, a liquidation committee has such of the powers and duties of commissioners in a sequestration as may be conferred and imposed on such committees by the rules.

The liquidator's functions

143. General functions in winding up by the court

(1) The functions of the liquidator of a company which is being wound up by the court are to secure that the assets of the company are got in, realised and distributed to the company's creditors and, if there is a surplus, to the persons entitled to it.

(2) It is the duty of the liquidator of a company which is being wound up by the court in England and Wales, if he is not the official receiver—

(a) to furnish the official receiver with such information,

(b) to produce to the official receiver, and permit inspection by the official receiver of, such books, papers and other records, and

(c) to give the official receiver such other assistance,

as the official receiver may reasonably require for the purposes of carrying out his functions in relation to the winding up.

144. Custody of company's property

(1) When a winding-up order has been made, or where a provisional liquidator has been appointed, the liquidator or the provisional liquidator (as the case may be) shall take into his custody or under his control all the property and things in action to which the company is or appears to be entitled.

(2) In a winding up by the court in Scotland, if and so long as there is no liquidator, all the property of the company is deemed to be in the custody of the court.

145. Vesting of company property in liquidator

(1) When a company is being wound up by the court, the court may on the application of the liquidator by order direct that all or any part of the property of whatsoever description belonging to the company or held by trustees on its behalf shall vest in the liquidator by his official name; and thereupon the property to which the order relates vests accordingly.

(2) The liquidator may, after giving such indemnity (if any) as the court may direct, bring or defend in his official name any action or other legal proceeding which relates to that property or which it is necessary to bring or defend for the purpose of effectually winding up the company and recovering its property.

146. Duty to summon final meeting

(1) Subject to the next subsection, if it appears to the liquidator of a company which is being wound by the court that the winding up of the company is for practical purposes complete and the liquidator is not the official receiver, the liquidator shall summon a final general meeting of the company's creditors which—

(a) shall receive the liquidator's report of the winding up, and

(b) shall determine whether the liquidator should have his release under section 174 in Chapter VII of this Part.

(2) The liquidator may, if he thinks fit, give the notice summoning the final general meeting at the same time as giving notice of any final distribution of the company's property but, if summoned for an earlier date, that meeting shall be adjourned (and, if necessary, further adjourned) until a date on which the liquidator is able to report to the meeting that the winding up of the company is for practical purposes complete.

(3) In the carrying out of his functions in the winding up it is the duty of the liquidator to retain sufficient sums from the company's property to cover the expenses of summoning and holding the meeting required by this section.

General powers of court

147. Power to stay or sist winding up

(1) The court may at any time after an order for winding up, on the application either of the liquidator or the official receiver or any creditor or contributory, and on proof to the satisfaction of the court that all proceedings in the winding up ought to be stayed or sisted, make an order staying or sisting the proceedings, either altogether or for a limited time, on such terms and conditions as the court thinks fit.

(2) The court may, before making an order, require the official receiver to furnish to it a report with respect to any facts or matters which are in his opinion relevant to the application.

(3) A copy of every order made under this section shall forthwith be forwarded by the company, or otherwise as may be prescribed, to the registrar of companies, who shall enter it in his records relating to the company.

148. Settlement of list of contributories and application of assets

(1) As soon as may be after making a winding-up order, the court shall settle a list of contributories, with power to rectify the register of members in all cases where rectification is required . . ., and shall cause the company's assets to be collected, and applied in discharge of its liabilities.

(2) If it appears to the court that it will not be necessary to make calls on or adjust the rights of contributories, the court may dispense with the settlement of a list of contributories.

(3) In settling the list, the court shall distinguish between persons who are contributories in their own right and persons who are contributories as being representatives of or liable for the debts of others.

149. Debts due from contributory to company

(1) The court may, at any time after making a winding-up order, make an order on any contributory for the time being on the list of contributories to pay, in manner directed by the order, any money due from him (or from the estate of the person who he represents) to the company, exclusive of any money payable by him or the estate by virtue of any call . . .

(2) The court in making such an order may—

(a) in the case of an unlimited company, allow to the contributory by way of set-off any money due to him or the estate which he represents from the company on any independent dealing or contract with the company, but not any money due to him as a member of the company in respect of any dividend or profit, and

(b) in the case of a limited company, make to any director or manager whose liability is unlimited or to his estate the like allowance.

(3) In the case of any company, whether limited or unlimited, when all the creditors are paid in full (together with interest at the official rate), any money due on any account whatever to a contributory from the company may be allowed to him by way of set-off against any subsequent call.

150. Power to make calls

(1) The court may, at any time after making a winding-up order, and either before or after it has ascertained the sufficiency of the company's assets, make calls on all or any of the contributories for the time being settled on the list of the contributories to the extent of their liability, for payment of any money which the court considers necessary to satisfy the company's debts and liabilities, and the expenses of winding up, and for the adjustment of the rights of the contributories among themselves, and make an order for payment of any calls so made.

(2) In making a call the court may take into consideration the probability that some of the contributories may partly or wholly fail to pay it.

151. Payment into bank of money due to company

(1) The court may order any contributory, purchaser or other person from whom money is due to the company to pay the amount due into the Bank of England (or any branch of it) to the account of the liquidator instead of to the liquidator, and such an order may be enforced in the same manner as if it had directed payment to the liquidator.

(2) All money and securities paid or delivered into the Bank of England (or branch) in the event of a winding up by the court are subject in all respects to the orders of the court.

152. Order on contributory to be conclusive evidence

(1) An order made by the court on a contributory is conclusive evidence that the money (if any) thereby appearing to be due or ordered to be paid is due, but subject to any right of appeal.

(2) All other pertinent matters stated in the order are to be taken as truly stated as against all persons and in all proceedings except proceedings in Scotland against the heritable estate of a deceased contributory; and in that case the order is only prima facie evidence for the purpose of charging his heritable estate, unless his heirs or legatees of heritage were on the list of contributories at the time of the order being made.

153. Power to exclude creditors not proving in time

The court may fix a time or times within which creditors are to prove their debts or claims or to be excluded from the benefit of any distribution made before those debts are proved.

154. Adjustment of rights of contributories

The court shall adjust the rights of the contributories among themselves and distribute any surplus among the persons entitled to it.

155. Inspection of books by creditors, etc

(1) The court may, at any time after making a winding-up order, make such order for inspection of the company's books and papers by creditors and contributories as the court thinks just; and any books and papers in the company's possession may be inspected by creditors and contributories accordingly, but not further or otherwise.

(2) Nothing in this section excludes or restricts any statutory rights of a government department or person acting under the authority of a government department.

(3) For the purposes of subsection (2) above, references to a government department shall be construed as including references to any part of the Scottish Administration.

156. Payment of expenses of winding up

The court may, in the event of the assets being insufficient to satisfy the liabilities, make an order as to the payment out of the assets of the expenses incurred in the winding up in such order of priority as the court thinks just.

157. Attendance at company meetings (Scotland)

In the winding up by the court of a company registered in Scotland, the court has power to require the attendance of any officer of the company at any meeting of creditors or of contributories, or of a liquidation committee, for the purpose of giving information as to the trade, dealings, affairs or property of the company.

158. Power to arrest absconding contributory

The court, at any time either before or after making a winding-up order, on proof of probable cause for believing that a contributory is about to quit the United Kingdom or otherwise to abscond or to remove or conceal any of his property for the purpose of evading payment of calls, may cause the contributory to be arrested and his books and papers and movable personal property to be seized and him and them to be kept safely until such time as the court may order.

159. Powers of court to be cumulative

Powers conferred on the court by this Act are in addition to, and not in restriction of, any existing powers of instituting proceedings against a contributory or debtor of the company, or the estate of any contributory or debtor, for the recovery of any call or other sums.

160. Delegation of powers to liquidator (England and Wales)

(1) Provision may be made by rules for enabling or requiring all or any of the powers and duties conferred and imposed on the court in England and Wales . . . in respect of the following matters—

(a) the holding and conducting of meetings to ascertain the wishes of creditors and contributories,

(b) the settling of lists of contributories and the rectifying of the register of members where required, and the collection and application of the assets,

(c) the payment, delivery, conveyance, surrender or transfer of money, property, books or papers to the liquidator,

(d) the making of calls,

(e) the fixing of a time within which debts and claims must be proved,

to be exercised or performed by the liquidator as an officer of the court, and subject to the court's control.

(2) But the liquidator shall not, without the special leave of the court, rectify the register of members, and shall not make any call without either that special leave or the sanction of the liquidation committee.

Enforcement of, and appeal from, orders

161. Orders for calls on contributories (Scotland)

(1) In Scotland, where an order, interlocutor or decree has been made for winding up a company by the court, it is competent to the court, on production by the liquidators of a list certified by them of the names of the contributories liable in payment of any calls, and of the amount due by each contributory, and of the date when that amount became due, to pronounce forthwith a decree against those contributories for payment of the sums so certified to be due, with interest from that date until payment (at 5 per cent. per annum) in the same way and to the same effect as if they had severally consented to registration for execution, on a charge of 6 days, of a legal obligation to pay those calls and interest.

(2) The decree may be extracted immediately, and no suspension of it is competent, except on caution or consignation, unless with special leave of the court.

162. Appeals from orders in Scotland

(1) Subject to the provisions of this section and to rules of court, an appeal from any order or decision made or given in the winding up of a company by the court in Scotland under this Act lies in the same manner and subject to the same conditions as an appeal from an order or decision of the court in cases within its ordinary jurisdiction.

(2) In regard to orders or judgments pronounced by the judge acting as vacation judge … —

(a) none of the orders specified in Part I of Schedule 3 to this Act are subject to review, reduction, suspension or stay of execution, and

(b) every other order or judgment (except as mentioned below) may be submitted to review by the Inner House by reclaiming motion enrolled within 14 days from the date of the order or judgment.

(3) However, an order being one of those specified in Part II of that Schedule shall, from the date of the order and notwithstanding that it has been submitted to review as above, be carried out and receive effect until the Inner House have disposed of the matter.

(4) In regard to orders or judgments pronounced in Scotland by a Lord Ordinary before whom proceedings in a winding up are being taken, any such order or judgment may be submitted to review by the Inner House by reclaiming motion enrolled within 14 days from its date; but should it not be so submitted to review during session, the provisions of this section in regard to orders or judgments pronounced by the judge acting as vacation judge apply.

(5) Nothing in this section affects provisions of the Companies Acts or this Act in reference to decrees in Scotland for payment of calls in the winding up of companies, whether voluntary or by the court.

CHAPTER VII
LIQUIDATORS

Preliminary

163. Style and title of liquidators

The liquidator of a company shall be described—

(a) where a person other than the official receiver is liquidator, by the style of "the liquidator" of the particular company, or

(b) where the official receiver is liquidator, by the style of "the official receiver and liquidator" of the particular company;

and in neither case shall he be described by an individual name.

164. Corrupt inducement affecting appointment

A person who gives, or agrees or offers to give, to any member or creditor of a company any valuable consideration with a view to securing his own appointment or nomination, or to securing or preventing the appointment or nomination of some person other than himself, as the company's liquidator is liable to a fine.

Liquidator's powers and duties

165. Voluntary winding up

(1) This section has effect where a company is being wound up voluntarily, but subject to section 166 below in the case of a creditors' voluntary winding up.

(2) The liquidator may—

(a) in the case of a member's voluntary winding up, with the sanction of a special resolution of the company, and

(b) in the case of a creditors' voluntary winding up, with the sanction of the court or the liquidation committee (or, if there is no such committee, a meeting of the company's creditors),

exercise any of the powers specified in Part I of Schedule 4 to this Act (payment of debts, compromise of claims, etc).

(3) The liquidator may, without sanction, exercise either of the powers specified in Part II of that Schedule (institution and defence of proceedings; carrying on the business of the company) and any of the general powers specified in Part III of that Schedule.

(4) The liquidator may—

(a) exercise the court's power of settling a list of contributories (which list is prima facie evidence of the liability of the persons named in it to be contributories),

(b) exercise the court's power of making calls,

(c) summon general meetings of the company for the purpose of obtaining its sanction by special resolution or for any other purpose he may think fit.

(5) The liquidator shall pay the company's debts and adjust the rights of the contributories among themselves.

(6) Where the liquidator in exercise of the powers conferred on him by this Act disposes of any property of the company to a person who is connected with the company (within the meaning of section 249 in Part VII), he shall, if there is for the time being a liquidation committee, give notice to the committee of that exercise of his powers.

166. Creditors' voluntary winding up

(1) This section applies where, in the case of a creditors' voluntary winding up, a liquidator has been nominated by the company.

(1A) The exercise by the liquidator of the power specified in paragraph 6 of Schedule 4 to this Act (power to sell any of the company's property) shall not be challengeable on the ground of any prior inhibition.

(2) The powers conferred on the liquidator by section 165 shall not be exercised, except with the sanction of the court, during the period before the holding of the creditors' meeting under section 98 in Chapter IV.

(3) Subsection (2) does not apply in relation to the power of the liquidator—

(a) to take into his custody or under his control all the property to which the company is or appears to be entitled;

(b) to dispose of perishable goods and other goods the value of which is likely to diminish if they are not immediately disposed of; and

(c) to do all such other things as may be necessary for the protection of the company's assets.

(4) The liquidator shall attend the creditors' meeting held under section 98 and shall report to the meeting on any exercise by him of his powers (whether or not under this section or under section 112 or 165).

(5) If default is made—

(a) by the company in complying with subsection (1), (1A) or (2) of section 98, or

(b) by the directors in complying with subsection (1), (2) or (2A) of section 99,

the liquidator shall, within 7 days of the relevant day, apply to the court for directions as to the manner in which that default is to be remedied.

(6) "The relevant day" means the day on which the liquidator was nominated by the company or the day on which he first became aware of the default, whichever is the later.

(7) If the liquidator without reasonable excuse fails to comply with this section, he is liable to a fine.

167. Winding up by the court

(1) Where a company is being wound up by the court, the liquidator may—

(a) with the sanction of the court or the liquidation committee, exercise any of the powers specified in Parts I and II of Schedule 4 to this Act (payment of debts; compromise of claims, etc; institution and defence of proceedings; carrying on of the business of the company), and

(b) with or without that sanction, exercise any of the general powers specified in Part III of that Schedule.

(2) Where the liquidator (not being the official receiver), in exercise of the powers conferred on him by this Act—

(a) disposes of any property of the company to a person who is connected with the company (within the meaning of section 249 in Part VII), or

(b) employs a solicitor to assist him in the carrying out of his functions, he shall, if there is for the time being a liquidation committee, give notice to the committee of that exercise of his powers.

(3) The exercise by the liquidator in a winding up by the court of the powers conferred by this section is subject to the control of the court, and any creditor or contributory may apply to the court with respect to any exercise or proposed exercise of any of those powers.

168. Supplementary powers (England and Wales)

(1) This section applies in the case of a company which is being wound up by the court in England and Wales.

(2) The liquidator may summon general meetings of the creditors or contributories for the purpose of ascertaining their wishes; and it is his duty to summon meetings at such times as the creditors or contributories by resolution (either at the meeting appointing the liquidator or otherwise) may direct, or whenever requested in writing to do so by one-tenth in value of the creditors or contributories (as the case may be).

(3) The liquidator may apply to the court (in the prescribed manner) for directions in relation to any particular matter arising in the winding up.

(4) Subject to the provisions of this Act, the liquidator shall use his own discretion in the management of the assets and their distribution among the creditors.

(5) If any person is aggrieved by an act or decision of the liquidator, that person may apply to the court; and the court may confirm, reverse or modify the act or decision complained of, and make such order in the case as it thinks just.

(5A) Where at any time after a winding-up petition has been presented to the court against any person (including an insolvent partnership or other body which may be wound up under Part V of the Act as an unregistered company), whether by virtue of the provisions of the Insolvent Partnerships Order 1994 or not, the attention of the court is drawn to the fact that the person in question is a member of an insolvent partnership, the court may make an order as to the future conduct of the insolvency proceedings and any such order may apply any provisions of that Order with any necessary modifications.

(5B) Any order or directions under subsection (5A) may be made or given on the application of the official receiver, any responsible insolvency practitioner, the trustee of the partnership or any other interested person and may include provisions as to the administration of the joint estate of the partnership, and in particular how it and the separate estate of any member are to be administered.

(5C) Where the court makes an order for the winding up of an insolvent partnership under—

(a) section 72(1)(a) of the Financial Services Act 1986;

(b) section 92(1)(a) of the Banking Act 1987; or

(c) section 367(3)(a) of the Financial Services and Markets Act 2000,

the court may make an order as to the future conduct of the winding up proceedings, and any such order may apply any provisions of the Insolvent Partnerships Order 1994 with any necessary modifications.

169. Supplementary powers (Scotland)

(1) In the case of a winding up in Scotland, the court may provide by order that the liquidator may, where there is no liquidation committee, exercise any of the following powers, namely—

(a) to bring or defend any action or other legal proceeding in the name and on behalf of the company, or

(b) to carry on the business of the company so far as may be necessary for its beneficial winding up,

without the sanction or intervention of the court.

(2) In a winding up by the court in Scotland, the liquidator has (subject to the rules) the same powers as a trustee on a bankrupt estate.

170. Enforcement of liquidator's duty to make returns, etc

(1) If a liquidator who has made any default—

(a) in filing, delivering or making any return, account or other document, or
(b) in giving any notice which he is by law required to file, deliver, make or give,

fails to make good the default within 14 days after the service on him of a notice requiring him to do so, the court has the following powers.

(2) On an application made by any creditor or contributory of the company, or by the registrar of companies, the court may make an order directing the liquidator to make good the default within such time as may be specified in the order.

(3) The court's order may provide that all costs of and incidental to the application shall be borne by the liquidator.

(4) Nothing in this section prejudices the operation of any enactment imposing penalties on a liquidator in respect of any such default as is mentioned above.

Removal; vacation of office

171. Removal, etc (voluntary winding up)

(1) This section applies with respect to the removal from office and vacation of office of the liquidator of a company which is being wound up voluntarily.

(2) Subject to the next subsection, the liquidator may be removed from office only by an order of the court or—

(a) in the case of a members' voluntary winding up, by a general meeting of the company summoned specially for that purpose, or
(b) in the case of a creditors' voluntary winding up, by a general meeting of the company's creditors summoned specially for that purpose in accordance with the rules.

(3) Where the liquidator was appointed by the court under section 108 in Chapter V, a meeting such as is mentioned in subsection (2) above shall be summoned for the purpose of replacing him only if he thinks fit or the court so directs or the meeting is requested, in accordance with the rules—

(a) in the case of a members' voluntary winding up, by members representing not less than one-half of the total voting rights of all the members having at the date of the request a right to vote at the meeting, or
(b) in the case of a creditors' voluntary winding up, by not less than one-half, in value, of the company's creditors.

(4) A liquidator shall vacate office if he ceases to be a person who is qualified to act as an insolvency practitioner in relation to the company.

(5) A liquidator may, in the prescribed circumstances, resign his office by giving notice of his resignation to the registrar of companies.

(6) Where—

(a) in the case of a members' voluntary winding up, a final meeting of the company has been held under section 94 in Chapter III, or
(b) in the case of a creditors' voluntary winding up, final meetings of the company and of the creditors have been held under section 106 in Chapter IV,

the liquidator whose report was considered at the meeting or meetings shall vacate office as soon as he has complied with subsection (3) of that section and has given notice to the registrar of companies that the meeting or meetings have been held and of the decisions (if any) of the meeting or meetings.

172. Removal, etc (winding up by the court)

(1) This section applies with respect to the removal from office and vacation of office of the liquidator of a company which is being wound up by the court, or of a provisional liquidator.

(2) Subject as follows, the liquidator may be removed from office only by an order of the court or by a general meeting of the company's creditors summoned specially for that purpose in accordance with the rules; and a provisional liquidator may be removed from office only by an order of the court.

(3) Where—

(a) the official receiver is liquidator otherwise than in succession under section 136(3) to a person who held office as a result of a nomination by a meeting of the company's creditors or contributories, or

(b) the liquidator was appointed by the court otherwise than under section 139(4)(a) or 140(1), or was appointed by the Secretary of State,

a general meeting of the company's creditors shall be summoned for the purpose of replacing him only if he thinks fit, or the court so directs, or the meeting is requested, in accordance with the rules, by not less that one-quarter, in value, of the creditors.

(4) If appointed by the Secretary of State, the liquidator may be removed from office by a direction of the Secretary of State.

(5) A liquidator or provisional liquidator, not being the official receiver, shall vacate office if he ceases to be a person who is qualified to act as an insolvency practitioner in relation to the company.

(6) A liquidator may, in the prescribed circumstances, resign his office by giving notice of his resignation to the court.

(7) Where an order is made under section 204 (early dissolution in Scotland) for the dissolution of the company, the liquidator shall vacate office when the dissolution of the company takes effect in accordance with that section.

(8) Where a final meeting has been held under section 146 (liquidator's report on completion of winding up), the liquidator whose report was considered at the meeting shall vacate office as soon as he has given notice to the court and the registrar of companies that the meeting has been held and of the decisions (if any) of the meeting.

Release of liquidator

173. Release (voluntary winding up)

(1) This section applies with respect to the release of the liquidator of a company which is being wound up voluntarily.

(2) A person who has ceased to be a liquidator shall have his release with effect from the following time, that is to say—

(a) in the case of a person who has been removed from office by a general meeting of the company or by a general meeting of the company's creditors that has not resolved against his release or who has died, the time at which notice is given to the registrar of companies in accordance with the rules that that person has ceased to hold office;

(b) in the case of a person who has been removed from office by a general meeting of the company's creditors that has resolved against his release, or by the court, or who has vacated office under section 171(4) above, such time as the Secretary of State may, on the application of that person, determine;

(c) in the case of a person who has resigned, such time as may be prescribed;

(d) in the case of a person who has vacated office under subsection (6)(a) of section 171, the time at which he vacated office;

(e) in the case of a person who has vacated office under subsection (6)(b) of that section—

(i) if the final meeting of the creditors referred to in that subsection has resolved against that person's release, such time as the Secretary of State may, on an application by that person, determine, and

(ii) if that meeting has not resolved against that person's release, the time at which he vacated office.

(3) In the application of subsection (2) to the winding up of a company registered in Scotland, the references to a determination by the Secretary of State as to the time from which a person who has ceased to be liquidator shall have his release are to be read as references to such a determination by the Accountant of Court.

(4) Where a liquidator has his release under subsection (2), he is, with effect from the time specified in that subsection, discharged from all liability both in respect of acts or omissions of his in the winding up and otherwise in relation to his conduct as liquidator.

But nothing in this section prevents the exercise, in relation to a person who has had his release under subsection (2), of the court's powers under section 212 of this Act (summary remedy against delinquent directors, liquidators, etc).

174. Release (winding up by the court)

(1) This section applies with respect to the release of the liquidator of a company which is being wound up by the court, or of a provisional liquidator.

(2) Where the official receiver has ceased to be liquidator and a person becomes liquidator in his stead, the official receiver has his release with effect from the following time, that is to say—

(a) in a case where that person was nominated by a general meeting of creditors or contributories, or was appointed by the Secretary of State, the time at which the official receiver gives notice to the court that he has been replaced;

(b) in a case where that person is appointed by the court, such time as the court may determine.

(3) If the official receiver while he is a liquidator gives notice to the Secretary of State that the winding up is for practical purposes complete, he has his release with effect from such time as the Secretary of State may determine.

(4) A person other than the official receiver who has ceased to be a liquidator has his release with effect from the following time, that is to say—

(a) in the case of a person who has been removed from office by a general meeting of creditors that has not resolved against his release or who has died, the time at which notice is given to the court in accordance with the rules that that person has ceased to hold office;

(b) in the case of a person who has been removed from office by a general meeting of creditors that has resolved against his release, or by the court or the Secretary of State, or who has vacated office under section 172(5) or (7), such time as the Secretary of State may, on an application by that person, determine;

(c) in the case of a person who has resigned, such time as may be prescribed;

(d) in the case of a person who has vacated office under section 172(8)—

(i) if the final meeting referred to in that subsection has resolved against that person's release, such time as the Secretary of State may, on an application by that person, determine, and

(ii) if that meeting has not so resolved, the time at which that person vacated office.

(5) A person who has ceased to hold office as a provisional liquidator has his release with effect from such time as the court may, on an application by him, determine.

(6) Where the official receiver or a liquidator or provisional liquidator has his release under this section, he is, with effect from the time specified in the preceding provisions of this section, discharged from all liability both in respect of acts or omissions of his in the winding up and otherwise in relation to his conduct as liquidator or provisional liquidator.

But nothing in this section prevents the exercise, in relation to a person who has had his release under this section, of the court's powers under section 212 (summary remedy against delinquent directors, liquidators, etc).

(7) In the application of this section to a case where the order for winding up has been made by the court in Scotland, the references to a determination by the Secretary of State as to the time from which a person who has ceased to be liquidator has his release are to such a determination by the Accountant of Court.

CHAPTER VIII
PROVISIONS OF GENERAL APPLICATION IN WINDING UP

Preferential debts

175. Preferential debts (general provision)

(1) In a winding up the company's preferential debts (within the meaning given by section 386 in Part XII) shall be paid in priority to all other debts.

(2) Preferential debts—

(a) rank equally among themselves after the expenses of the winding up and shall be paid in full, unless the assets are insufficient to meet them, in which case they abate in equal proportions; and

(b) so far as the assets of the company available for payment of general creditors are insufficient to meet them, have priority over the claims of holders of debentures secured by, or holders of, any floating charge created by the company, and shall be paid accordingly out of any property comprised in or subject to that charge.

176. Preferential charge on goods distrained

(1) This section applies where a company is being wound up by the court in England and Wales, and is without prejudice to section 128 (avoidance of attachments, etc).

(2) Where any person (whether or not a landlord or person entitled to rent) has distrained upon the goods or effects of the company in the period of 3 months ending with the date of the winding-up order, those goods or effects, or the proceeds of their sale, shall be charged for the benefit of the company with the preferential debts of the company to the extent that the company's property is for the time being insufficient for meeting them.

(3) Where by virtue of a charge under subsection (2) any person surrenders any goods or effects to a company or makes a payment to a company, that person ranks, in respect of the amount of the proceeds of sale of those goods or effects by the liquidator or (as the case may be) the amount of the payment, as a preferential creditor of the company, except as against so much of the company's property as is available for the payment of preferential creditors by virtue of the surrender or payment.

Property subject to floating charge

176ZA. Payment of expenses of winding up (England and Wales)

(1) The expenses of winding up in England and Wales, so far as the assets of the company available for payment of general creditors are insufficient to meet them, have priority over any claims to property comprised in or subject to any floating charge created by the company and shall be paid out of any such property accordingly.

(2) In subsection (1)—

(a) the reference to assets of the company available for payment of general creditors does not include any amount made available under section 176A(2)(a);

(b) the reference to claims to property comprised in or subject to a floating charge is to the claims of—

(i) the holders of debentures secured by, or holders of, the floating charge, and

(ii) any preferential creditors entitled to be paid out of that property in priority to them.

(3) Provision may be made by rules restricting the application of subsection (1), in such circumstances as may be prescribed, to expenses authorised or approved—

(a) by the holders of debentures secured by, or holders of, the floating charge and by any preferential creditors entitled to be paid in priority to them, or

(b) by the court.

(4) References in this section to the expenses of the winding up are to all expenses properly incurred in the winding up, including the remuneration of the liquidator.

176A. Share of assets for unsecured creditors

(1) This section applies where a floating charge relates to property of a company—

(a) which has gone into liquidation,

(b) which is in administration,

(c) of which there is a provisional liquidator, or

(d) of which there is a receiver.

(2) The liquidator, administrator or receiver—

(a) shall make a prescribed part of the company's net property available for the satisfaction of unsecured debts, and

(b) shall not distribute that part to the proprietor of a floating charge except in so far as it exceeds the amount required for the satisfaction of unsecured debts.

(3) Subsection (2) shall not apply to a company if—

(a) the company's net property is less than the prescribed minimum, and

(b) the liquidator, administrator or receiver thinks that the cost of making a distribution to unsecured creditors would be disproportionate to the benefits.

(4) Subsection (2) shall also not apply to a company if or in so far as it is disapplied by—

(a) a voluntary arrangement in respect of the company, or

(b) a compromise or arrangement agreed under Part 26 of the Companies Act 2006 (arrangements and reconstructions).

(5) Subsection (2) shall also not apply to a company if—

(a) the liquidator, administrator or receiver applies to the court for an order under this subsection on the ground that the cost of making a distribution to unsecured creditors would be disproportionate to the benefits, and

(b) the court orders that subsection (2) shall not apply.

(6) In subsections (2) and (3) a company's net property is the amount of its property which would, but for this section, be available for satisfaction of claims of holders of debentures secured by, or holders of, any floating charge created by the company.

(7) An order under subsection (2) prescribing part of a company's net property may, in particular, provide for its calculation—

(a) as a percentage of the company's net property, or

(b) as an aggregate of different percentages of different parts of the company's net property.

(8) An order under this section—

(a) must be made by statutory instrument, and

(b) shall be subject to annulment pursuant to a resolution of either House of Parliament.

(9) In this section—

"floating charge" means a charge which is a floating charge on its creation and which is created after the first order under subsection (2)(a) comes into force, and

"prescribed" means prescribed by order by the Secretary of State.

(10) An order under this section may include transitional or incidental provision.

Special managers

177. Power to appoint special manager

(1) Where a company has gone into liquidation or a provisional liquidator has been appointed, the court may, on an application under this section, appoint any person to be the special manager of the business or property of the company.

(2) The application may be made by the liquidator or provisional liquidator in any case where it appears to him that the nature of the business or property of the company, or the interests of the company's creditors or contributories or members generally, require the appointment of another person to manage the company's business or property.

(3) The special manager has such powers as may be entrusted to him by the court.

(4) The court's power to entrust powers to the special manager includes power to direct that any provision of this Act that has effect in relation to the provisional liquidator or liquidator of a company shall have the like effect in relation to the special manager for the purposes of the carrying out by him of any of the functions of the provisional liquidator or liquidator.

(5) The special manager shall—

(a) give such security or, in Scotland, caution as may be prescribed;

(b) prepare and keep such accounts as may be prescribed; and

(c) produce those accounts in accordance with the rules to the Secretary of State or to such other persons as may be prescribed.

Disclaimer (England and Wales only)

178. Power to disclaim onerous property

(1) This and the next two sections apply to a company that is being wound up in England and Wales.

(2) Subject as follows, the liquidator may, by the giving of the prescribed notice, disclaim any onerous property and may do so notwithstanding that he has taken possession of it, endeavoured to sell it, or otherwise exercised rights of ownership in relation to it.

(3) The following is onerous property for the purposes of this section—

(a) any unprofitable contract, and

(b) any other property of the company which is unsaleable or not readily saleable or is such that it may give rise to a liability to pay money or perform any other onerous act.

(4) A disclaimer under this section—

(a) operates so as to determine, as from the date of the disclaimer, the rights, interests and liabilities of the company in or in respect of the property disclaimed; but

(b) does not, except so far as is necessary for the purpose of releasing the company from any liability, affect the rights or liabilities of any other person.

(5) A notice of disclaimer shall not be given under this section in respect of any property if—

(a) a person interested in the property has applied in writing to the liquidator or one of his predecessors as liquidator requiring the liquidator or that predecessor to decide whether he will disclaim or not, and

(b) the period of 28 days beginning with the day on which that application was made, or such longer period as the court may allow, has expired without a notice of disclaimer having been given under this section in respect of that property.

(6) Any person sustaining loss or damage in consequence of the operation of a disclaimer under this section is deemed a creditor of the company to the extent of the loss or damage and accordingly may prove for the loss or damage in the winding up.

179. Disclaimer of leaseholds

(1) The disclaimer under section 178 of any property of a leasehold nature does not take effect unless a copy of the disclaimer has been served (so far as the liquidator is aware of their addresses) on every person claiming under the company as underlessee or mortgagee and either—

(a) no application under section 181 below is made with respect to that property before the end of the period of 14 days beginning with the day on which the last notice served under this subsection was served; or

(b) where such an application has been made, the court directs that the disclaimer shall take effect.

(2) Where the court gives a direction under subsection (1)(b) it may also, instead of or in addition to any order it makes under section 181, make such orders with respect to fixtures, tenant's improvements and other matters arising out of the lease as it thinks fit.

180. Land subject to rentcharge

(1) The following applies where, in consequence of the disclaimer under section 178 of any land subject to a rentcharge, that land vests by operation of law in the Crown or any other person (referred to in the next subsection as "the proprietor").

(2) The proprietor and the successors in title of the proprietor are not subject to any personal liability in respect of any sums becoming due under the rentcharge except sums becoming due after the proprietor, or some person claiming under or through the proprietor, has taken possession or control of the land or has entered into occupation of it.

181. Powers of court (general)

(1) This section and the next apply where the liquidator has disclaimed property under section 178.

(2) An application under this section may be made to the court by—

(a) any person who claims an interest in the disclaimed property, or

(b) any person who is under any liability in respect of the disclaimed property, not being a liability discharged by the disclaimer.

(3) Subject as follows, the court may on the application make an order, on such terms as it thinks fit, for the vesting of the disclaimed property in, or for its delivery to—

(a) a person entitled to it or a trustee for such a person, or

(b) a person subject to such a liability as is mentioned in subsection (2)(b) or a trustee for such a person.

(4) The court shall not make an order under subsection (3)(b) except where it appears to the court that it would be just to do so for the purpose of compensating the person subject to the liability in respect of the disclaimer.

(5) The effect of any order under this section shall be taken into account in assessing for the purpose of section 178(6) the extent of any loss or damage sustained by any person in consequence of the disclaimer.

(6) An order under this section vesting property in any person need not be completed by conveyance, assignment or transfer.

182. Powers of court (leaseholds)

(1) The court shall not make an order under section 181 vesting property of a leasehold nature in any person claiming under the company as underlessee or mortgagee except on terms making that person—

(a) subject to the same liabilities and obligations as the company was subject to under the lease at the commencement of the winding up, or

(b) if the court thinks fit, subject to the same liabilities and obligations as that person would be subject to if the lease had been assigned to him at the commencement of the winding up.

(2) For the purposes of an order under section 181 relating to only part of any property comprised in a lease, the requirements of subsection (1) apply as if the lease comprised only the property to which the order relates.

(3) Where subsection (1) applies and no person claiming under the company as underlessee or mortgagee is willing to accept an order under section 181 on the terms required by virtue of that subsection, the court may, by order under that section, vest the company's estate or interest in the property in any person who is liable (whether personally or in a representative capacity, and whether alone or jointly with the company) to perform the lessee's covenants in the lease.
The court may vest that estate and interest in such a person freed and discharged from all estates, incumbrances and interests created by the company.

(4) Where subsection (1) applies and a person claiming under the company as underlessee or mortgagee declines to accept an order under section 181, that person is excluded from all interest in the property.

Execution, attachment and the Scottish equivalents

183. Effect of execution or attachment (England and Wales)

(1) Where a creditor has issued execution against the goods or land of a company or has attached any debt due to it, and the company is subsequently wound up, he is not entitled to retain the benefit of the execution or attachment against the liquidator unless he has completed the execution or attachment before the commencement of the winding up.

(2) However—

(a) if a creditor has had notice of a meeting having been called at which a resolution for voluntary winding up is to be proposed, the date on which he had notice is substituted, for the purpose of subsection (1), for the date of commencement of the winding up;

(b) a person who purchases in good faith under a sale by the enforcement officer or other officer charged with the execution of the writ any goods of a company on which execution has been levied in all cases acquires a good title to them against the liquidator; and

(c) the rights conferred by subsection (1) on the liquidator may be set aside by the court in favour of the creditor to such extent and subject to such terms as the court thinks fit.

(3) For the purposes of this Act—
(a) an execution against goods is completed by seizure and sale, or by the making of a charging order under section 1 of the Charging Orders Act 1979;
(b) an attachment of a debt is completed by receipt of the debt; and
(c) an execution against land is completed by seizure, by the appointment of a receiver, or by the making of a charging order under section 1 of the Act above-mentioned.

(4) In this section "goods" includes all chattels personal; and "enforcement officer" means an individual who is authorised to act as an enforcement officer under the Courts Act 2003.

(5) This section does not apply in the case of a winding up in Scotland.

184. Duties of officers charged with execution of writs and other processes (England and Wales)

(1) The following applies where a company's goods are taken in execution and, before their sale or the completion of the execution (by the receipt or recovery of the full amount of the levy), notice is served on the enforcement officer, or other officer, charged with execution of the writ or other process, that a provisional liquidator has been appointed or that a winding-up order has been made, or that a resolution for voluntary winding up has been passed.

(2) The enforcement officer or other officer shall, on being so required, deliver the goods and any money seized or received in part satisfaction of the execution to the liquidator; but the costs of execution are a first charge on the goods or money so delivered, and the liquidator may sell the goods, or a sufficient part of them, for the purpose of satisfying the charge.

(3) If under an execution in respect of a judgment for a sum exceeding £500 a company's goods are sold or money is paid in order to avoid sale, the enforcement officer or other officer shall deduct the costs of the execution from the proceeds of sale or the money paid and retain the balance for 14 days.

(4) If within that time notice is served on the enforcement officer or other officer of a petition for the winding up of the company having been presented, or of a meeting having been called at which there is to be proposed a resolution for voluntary winding up, and an order is made or a resolution passed (as the case may be), the enforcement officer or other officer shall pay the balance to the liquidator, who is entitled to retain it as against the execution creditor.

(5) The rights conferred by this section on the liquidator may be set aside by the court in favour of the creditor to such extent and subject to such terms as the court thinks fit.

(6) In this section, "goods" includes all chattels personal; and "enforcement officer" means an individual who is authorised to act as an enforcement officer under the Courts Act 2003.

(7) The money sum for the time being specified in subsection (3) is subject to increase or reduction by order under section 416 in Part XV.

(8) This section does not apply in the case of a winding up in Scotland.

185. Effect of diligence (Scotland)

(1) In the winding up of a company registered in Scotland, the following provisions of the Bankruptcy (Scotland) Act 1985—
(a) subsections (1) to (6), *(8A) to (8F) and (10)* of section 37 (effect of sequestration on diligence); and
(b) subsections (3), (4), (7) and (8) of section 39 (realisation of estate),

apply, so far as consistent with this Act, in like manner as they apply in the sequestration of a debtor's estate, with the substitutions specified below and with any other necessary modifications.

(2) The substitutions to be made in those sections of the Act of 1985 are as follows—
(a) for references to the debtor, substitute references to the company;
(b) for references to the sequestration, substitute references to the winding up;
(c) for references to the date of sequestration, substitute references to the commencement of the winding up of the company; and
(d) for references to the . . . trustee, substitute references to the liquidator.

(3) In this section, "the commencement of the winding up of the company" means, where it is being wound up by the court, the day on which the winding-up order is made.

(4) This section, so far as relating to any estate or effects of the company situated in Scotland, applies in the case of a company registered in England and Wales as in the case of one registered in Scotland.

Note. The italicized words in subsection (1)(a) are inserted by the Bankruptcy and Diligence etc. (Scotland) Act 2007, s. 226, Sch. 5, para. 14, as from a day to be appointed.

Miscellaneous matters

186. Rescission of contracts by the court

(1) The court may, on the application of a person who is, as against the liquidator, entitled to the benefit or subject to the burden of a contract made with the company, make an order rescinding the contract on such terms as to payment by or to either party of damages for the non-performance of the contract, or otherwise as the court thinks just.

(2) Any damages payable under the order to such a person may be proved by him as a debt in the winding up.

187. Power to make over assets to employees

(1) On the winding up of a company (whether by the court or voluntarily), the liquidator may, subject to the following provisions of this section, make any payment which the company has, before the commencement of the winding up, decided to make under section 247 of the Companies Act 2006 (power to provide for employees or former employees on cessation or transfer of business).

(2) The liquidator may, after the winding up has commenced, make any such provision as is mentioned in section 247(1) if—

(a) the company's liabilities have been fully satisfied and provision has been made for the expenses of the winding up,

(b) the exercise of the power has been sanctioned by a resolution of the company, and

(c) any requirements of the company's articles as to the exercise of the power conferred by section 247(1) are complied with.

(3) Any payment which may be made by a company under this section (that is, a payment after the commencement of its winding up) may be made out of the company's assets which are available to the members on the winding up.

(4) On a winding up by the court, the exercise by the liquidator of his powers under this section is subject to the court's control, and any creditor or contributory may apply to the court with respect to any exercise or proposed exercise of the power.

(5) Subsections (1) and (2) above have effect notwithstanding anything in any rule of law or in section 107 of this Act (property of company after satisfaction of liabilities to be distributed among members).

188. Notification that company is in liquidation

(1) When a company is being wound up, whether by the court or voluntarily—

(a) every invoice, order for goods or services, business letter or order form (whether in hard copy, electronic or any other form) issued by or on behalf of the company, or a liquidator of the company or a receiver or manager of the company's property. . ., and

(b) all the company's websites,

must contain a statement that the company is being wound up.

(2) If default is made in complying with this section, the company and any of the following persons who knowingly and wilfully authorises or permits the default, namely, any officer of the company, any liquidator of the company and any receiver or manager, is liable to a fine.

189. Interest on debts

(1) In a winding up interest is payable in accordance with this section on any debt proved in the winding up, including so much of any such debt as represents interest on the remainder.

(2) Any surplus remaining after the payment of the debts proved in a winding up shall, before being applied for any other purpose, be applied in paying interest on those debts in respect of the periods during which they have been outstanding since the company went into liquidation.

(3) All interest under this section ranks equally, whether or not the debts on which it is payable rank equally.

(4) The rate of interest payable under this section in respect of any debt ("the official rate" for the purposes of any provision of this Act in which that expression is used) is whichever is the greater of—

(a) the rate specified in section 17 of the Judgments Act 1838 on the day on which the company went into liquidation, and

(b) the rate applicable to that debt apart from the winding up.

(5) In the application of this section to Scotland—

(a) references to a debt proved in a winding up have effect as references to a claim accepted in a winding up, and

(b) the reference to section 17 of the Judgments Act 1838 has effect as a reference to the rules.

190. Documents exempt from stamp duty

(1) In the case of a winding up by the court, or of a creditors' voluntary winding up, the following has effect as regards exemption from duties chargeable under the enactments relating to stamp duties.

(2) If the company is registered in England and Wales, the following documents are exempt from stamp duty—

(a) every assurance relating solely to freehold or leasehold property, or to any estate, right or interest in, any real or personal property, which forms part of the company's assets and which, after the execution of the assurance, either at law or in equity, is or remains part of those assets, and

(b) every writ, order, certificate, or other instrument or writing relating solely to the property of any company which is being wound up as mentioned in subsection (1), or to any proceeding under such a winding up.

"Assurance" here includes deed, conveyance, assignment and surrender.

(3) If the company is registered in Scotland, the following documents are exempt from stamp duty—

(a) every conveyance relating solely to property which forms part of the company's assets and which, after the execution of the conveyance, is or remains the company's property for the benefit of its creditors,

(b) any articles of roup or sale, submission and every other instrument and writing whatsoever relating solely to the company's property, and

(c) every deed or writing forming part of the proceedings in the winding up.

"Conveyance" here includes assignation, instrument, discharge, writing and deed.

191. Company's books to be evidence

Where a company is being wound up, all books and papers of the company and of the liquidators are, as between the contributories of the company, prima facie evidence of the truth of all matters purporting to be recorded in them.

192. Information as to pending liquidations

(1) If the winding up of a company is not concluded within one year after its commencement, the liquidator shall, at such intervals as may be prescribed, until the winding up is concluded, send to the registrar of companies a statement in the prescribed form and containing the prescribed particulars with respect to the proceedings in, and position of, the liquidation.

(2) If a liquidator fails to comply with this section, he is liable to a fine and, for continued contravention, to a daily default fine.

193. Unclaimed dividends (Scotland)

(1) The following applies where a company registered in Scotland has been wound up, and is about to be dissolved.

(2) The liquidator shall lodge in an appropriate bank or institution as defined in section 73(1) of the Bankruptcy (Scotland) Act 1985 (not being a bank or institution in or of which the liquidator is acting partner, manager, agent or cashier) in the name of the Accountant of Court the whole

unclaimed dividends and unapplied or undistributable balances, and the deposit receipts shall be transmitted to the Accountant of Court.

(3) The provisions of section 58 of the Bankruptcy (Scotland) Act 1985 (so far as consistent with this Act and the Companies Acts) apply with any necessary modifications to sums lodged in a bank or institution under this section as they apply to sums deposited under section 57 of the Act first mentioned.

194. Resolutions passed at adjourned meetings

Where a resolution is passed at an adjourned meeting of a company's creditors or contributories, the resolution is treated for all purposes as having been passed on the date on which it was in fact passed, and not as having been passed on any earlier date.

195. Meetings to ascertain wishes of creditors or contributories

(1) The court may—

(a) as to all matters relating to the winding up of a company, have regard to the wishes of the creditors or contributories (as proved to it by any sufficient evidence), and

(b) if it thinks fit, for the purpose of ascertaining those wishes, direct meetings of the creditors or contributories to be called, held and conducted in such manner as the court directs, and appoint a person to act as chairman of any such meeting and report the result of it to the court.

(2) In the case of creditors, regard shall be had to the value of each creditor's debt.

(3) In the case of contributories, regard shall be had to the number of votes conferred on each contributory . . .

196. Judicial notice of court documents

In all proceedings under this Part, all courts, judges and persons judicially acting, and all officers, judicial or ministerial, of any court, or employed in enforcing the process of any court shall take judicial notice—

(a) of the signature of any officer of the High Court or of a county court in England and Wales, or of the Court of Session or a sheriff court in Scotland, or of the High Court in Northern Ireland, and also

(b) of the official seal or stamp of the several offices of the High Court in England and Wales or Northern Ireland, or of the Court of Session, appended to or impressed on any document made, issued or signed under the provisions of this Act or the Companies Acts, or any official copy of such a document.

197. Commission for receiving evidence

(1) When a company is wound up in England and Wales or in Scotland, the court may refer the whole or any part of the examination of witnesses—

(a) to a specified county court in England and Wales, or

(b) to the sheriff principal for a special sheriffdom in Scotland, or

(c) to the High Court in Northern Ireland or a specified Northern Ireland County Court,

("specified" meaning specified in the order of the winding-up court).

(2) Any person exercising jurisdiction as a judge of the court to which the reference is made (or, in Scotland, the sheriff principal to whom it is made) shall then, by virtue of this section, be a commissioner for the purpose of taking the evidence of those witnesses.

(3) The judge or sheriff principal has in the matter referred the same power of summoning and examining witnesses, of requiring the production and delivery of documents, of punishing defaults by witnesses, and of allowing costs and expenses to witnesses, as the court which made the winding-up order.

These powers are in addition to any which the judge or sheriff principal might lawfully exercise apart from this section.

(4) The examination so taken shall be returned or reported to the court which made the order in such manner as that court requests.

(5) This section extends to Northern Ireland.

198. Court order for examination of persons in Scotland

(1) The court may direct the examination in Scotland of any person for the time being in Scotland (whether a contributory of the company or not), in regard to the trade, dealings, affairs or property of any company in course of being wound up, or of any person being a contributory of the company, so far as the company may be interested by reason of his being a contributory.

(2) The order or commission to take the examination shall be directed to the sheriff principal of the sheriffdom in which the person to be examined is residing or happens to be for the time; and the sheriff principal shall summon the person to appear before him at a time and place to be specified in the summons for examination on oath as a witness or as a haver, and to produce any books or papers called for which are in his possession or power.

(3) The sheriff principal may take the examination either orally or on written interrogatories, and shall report the same in writing in the usual form to the court, and shall transmit with the report the books and papers produced, if the originals are required and specified by the order or commission, or otherwise copies or extracts authenticated by the sheriff.

(4) If a person so summoned fails to appear at the time and place specified, or refuses to be examined or to make the production required, the sheriff principal shall proceed against him as a witness or haver duly cited; and failing to appear or refusing to give evidence or make production may be proceeded against by the law of Scotland.

(5) The sheriff principal is entitled to such fees, and the witness is entitled to such allowances, as sheriffs principal when acting as commissioners under appointment from the Court or Session and as witnesses and havers are entitled to in the like cases according to the law and practice of Scotland.

(6) If any objection is stated to the sheriff principal by the witness, either on the ground of his incompetency as a witness, or as to the production required, or on any other ground, the sheriff principal may, if he thinks fit, report the objection to the court, and suspend the examination of the witness until it has been disposed of by the court.

199. Costs of application for leave to proceed (Scottish companies)

Where a petition or application for leave to proceed with an action or proceeding against a company which is being wound up in Scotland is unopposed and is granted by the court, the costs of the petition or application shall, unless the court otherwise directs, be added to the amount of the petitioner's or applicant's claim against the company.

200. Affidavits etc in United Kingdom and overseas

(1) An affidavit required to be sworn under or for the purposes of this Part may be sworn in the United Kingdom, or elsewhere in Her Majesty's dominions, before any court, judge or person lawfully authorised to take and receive affidavits, or before any of Her Majesty's consuls or vice-consuls in any place outside Her dominions.

(2) All courts, judges, justices, commissioners and persons acting judicially shall take judicial notice of the seal or stamp or signature (as the case may be) of any such court, judge, person, consul or vice-consul attached, appended or subscribed to any such affidavit, or to any other document to be used for the purposes of this Part.

CHAPTER IX
DISSOLUTION OF COMPANIES AFTER WINDING UP

201. Dissolution (voluntary winding up)

(1) This section applies, in the case of a company wound up voluntarily, where the liquidator has sent to the registrar of companies his final account and return under section 94 (members' voluntary) or section 106 (creditors' voluntary).

(2) The registrar on receiving the account and return shall forthwith register them; and on the expiration of 3 months from the registration of the return the company is deemed to be dissolved.

(3) However, the court may, on the application of the liquidator or any other person who appears to the court to be interested, make an order deferring the date at which the dissolution of the company is to take effect for such time as the court thinks fit.

(4) It is the duty of the person on whose application an order of the court under this section is made within 7 days after the making of the order to deliver to the registrar a copy of the order for registration; and if that person fails to do so he is liable to a fine and, for continued contravention, to a daily default fine.

202. Early dissolution (England and Wales)

(1) This section applies where an order for the winding up of a company has been made by the court in England and Wales.

(2) The official receiver, if—

(a) he is the liquidator of the company, and

(b) it appears to him—

(i) that the realisable assets of the company are insufficient to cover the expenses of the winding up, and

(ii) that the affairs of the company do not require any further investigation,

may at any time apply to the registrar of companies for the early dissolution of the company.

(3) Before making that application, the official receiver shall give not less than 28 days' notice of his intention to do so to the company's creditors and contributories and, if there is an administrative receiver of the company, to that receiver.

(4) With the giving of that notice the official receiver ceases (subject to any directions under the next section) to be required to perform any duties imposed on him in relation to the company, its creditors or contributories by virtue of any provision of this Act, apart from a duty to make an application under subsection (2) of this section.

(5) On the receipt of the official receiver's application under subsection (2) the registrar shall forthwith register it and, at the end of the period of 3 months beginning with the day of the registration of the application, the company shall be dissolved.

However, the Secretary of State may, on the application of the official receiver or any other person who appears to the Secretary of State to be interested, give directions under section 203 at any time before the end of that period.

203. Consequence of notice under s 202

(1) Where a notice has been given under section 202(3), the official receiver or any creditor or contributory of the company, or the administrative receiver of the company (if there is one) may apply to the Secretary of State for directions under this section.

(2) The grounds on which that application may be made are—

(a) that the realisable assets of the company are sufficient to cover the expenses of the winding up;

(b) that the affairs of the company do require further investigation; or

(c) that for any other reason the early dissolution of the company is inappropriate.

(3) Directions under this section—

(a) are directions making such provision as the Secretary of State thinks fit for enabling the winding up of the company to proceed as if no notice had been given under section 202(3), and

(b) may, in the case of an application under section 202(5), include a direction deferring the date at which the dissolution of the company is to take effect for such period as the Secretary of State thinks fit.

(4) An appeal to the court lies from any decision of the Secretary of State on an application for directions under this section.

(5) It is the duty of the person on whose application any directions are given under this section, or in whose favour an appeal with respect to an application for such directions is determined, within 7 days after the giving of the directions or the determination of the appeal, to deliver to the registrar of companies for registration such a copy of the directions or determination as is prescribed.

(6) If a person without reasonable excuse fails to deliver a copy as required by subsection (5), he is liable to a fine and, for continued contravention, to a daily default fine.

204. Early dissolution (Scotland)

(1) This section applies where a winding-up order has been made by the court in Scotland.

(2) If after a meeting or meetings under section 138 (appointment of liquidator in Scotland) it appears to the liquidator that the realisable assets of the company are insufficient to cover the expenses of the winding up, he may apply to the court for an order that the company be dissolved.

(3) Where the liquidator makes that application, if the court is satisfied that the realisable assets of the company are insufficient to cover the expenses of the winding up and it appears to the court appropriate to do so, the court shall make an order that the company be dissolved in accordance with this section.

(4) A copy of the order shall within 14 days from its date be forwarded by the liquidator to the registrar of companies, who shall forthwith register it; and, at the end of the period of 3 months beginning with the day of the registration of the order, the company shall be dissolved.

(5) The court may, on an application by any person who appears to the court to have an interest, order that the date at which the dissolution of the company is to take effect shall be deferred for such period as the court thinks fit.

(6) It is the duty of the person on whose application an order is made under subsection (5), within 7 days after the making of the order, to deliver to the registrar of companies such a copy of the order as is prescribed.

(7) If the liquidator without reasonable excuse fails to comply with the requirements of subsection (4), he is liable to a fine and, for continued contravention, to a daily default fine.

(8) If a person without reasonable excuse fails to deliver a copy as required by subsection (6), he is liable to a fine and, for continued contravention, to a daily default fine.

205. Dissolution otherwise than under ss 202–204

(1) This section applies where the registrar of companies receives—
  (a) a notice served for the purposes of section 172(8) (final meeting of creditors and vacation of office by liquidator), or
  (b) a notice from the official receiver that the winding up of a company by the court is complete.

(2) The registrar shall, on receipt of the notice, forthwith register it; and, subject as follows, at the end of the period of 3 months beginning with the day of the registration of the notice, the company shall be dissolved.

(3) The Secretary of State may, on the application of the official receiver or any other person who appears to the Secretary of State to be interested, give a direction deferring the date at which the dissolution of the company is to take effect for such period as the Secretary of State thinks fit.

(4) An appeal to the court lies from any decision of the Secretary of State on an application for a direction under subsection (3).

(5) Subsection (3) does not apply in a case where the winding-up order was made by the court in Scotland, but in such a case the court may, on an application by any person appearing to the court to have an interest, order that the date at which the dissolution of the company is to take effect shall be deferred for such period as the court thinks fit.

(6) It is the duty of the person—
  (a) on whose application a direction is given under subsection (3);
  (b) in whose favour an appeal with respect to an application for such a direction is determined; or
  (c) on whose application an order is made under subsection (5),

within 7 days after the giving of the direction, the determination of the appeal or the making of the order, to deliver to the registrar for registration such a copy of the direction, determination or order as is prescribed.

(7) If a person without reasonable excuse fails to deliver a copy as required by subsection (6), he is liable to a fine and, for continued contravention to a daily default fine.

CHAPTER X
MALPRACTICE BEFORE AND DURING LIQUIDATION; PENALISATION OF COMPANIES AND COMPANY OFFICERS; INVESTIGATIONS AND PROSECUTIONS

Offences of fraud, deception, etc

206. Fraud, etc in anticipation of winding up

(1) When a company is ordered to be wound up by the court, or passes a resolution for voluntary winding up, any person, being a past or present officer of the company, is deemed to have committed an offence if, within the 12 months immediately preceding the commencement of the winding up, he has—

(a) concealed any part of the company's property to the value of £500 or more, or concealed any debt due to or from the company, or

(b) fraudulently removed any part of the company's property to the value of £500 or more, or

(c) concealed, destroyed, mutilated or falsified any book or paper affecting or relating to the company's property or affairs, or

(d) made any false entry in any book or paper affecting or relating to the company's property or affairs, or

(e) fraudulently parted with, altered or made any omission in any document affecting or relating to the company's property or affairs, or

(f) pawned, pledged or disposed of any property of the company which has been obtained on credit and has not been paid for (unless the pawning, pledging or disposal was in the ordinary way of the company's business).

(2) Such a person is deemed to have committed an offence if within the period above mentioned he has been privy to the doing by others of any of the things mentioned in paragraphs (c), (d) and (e) of subsection (1); and he commits an offence if, at any time after the commencement of the winding up, he does any of the things mentioned in paragraphs (a) to (f) of that subsection, or is privy to the doing by others of any of the things mentioned in paragraphs (c) to (e) of it.

(3) For purposes of this section, "officer" includes a shadow director.

(4) It is a defence—

(a) for a person charged under paragraph (a) or (f) of subsection (1) (or under subsection (2) in respect of the things mentioned in either of those two paragraphs) to prove that he had no intent to defraud, and

(b) for a person charged under paragraph (c) or (d) of subsection (1) (or under subsection (2) in respect of the things mentioned in either of those two paragraphs) to prove that he had no intent to conceal the state of affairs of the company or to defeat the law.

(5) Where a person pawns, pledges or disposes of any property in circumstances which amount to an offence under subsection (1)(f), every person who takes in pawn or pledge, or otherwise receives, the property knowing it to be pawned, pledged or disposed of in such circumstances, is guilty of an offence.

(6) A person guilty of an offence under this section is liable to imprisonment or a fine, or both.

(7) The money sums specified in paragraphs (a) and (b) of subsection (1) are subject to increase or reduction by order under section 416 in Part XV.

207. Transactions in fraud of creditors

(1) When a company is ordered to be wound up by the court or passes a resolution for voluntary winding up, a person is deemed to have committed an offence if he, being at the time an officer of the company—

(a) has made or caused to be made any gift or transfer of, or charge on, or has caused or connived at the levying of any execution against, the company's property, or

(b) has concealed or removed any part of the company's property since, or within 2 months before, the date of any unsatisfied judgment or order for the payment of money obtained against the company.

(2) A person is not guilty of an offence under this section—

(a) by reason of conduct constituting an offence under subsection (1)(a) which occurred more than 5 years before the commencement of the winding up, or

(b) if he proves that, at the time of the conduct constituting the offence, he had no intent to defraud the company's creditors.

(3) A person guilty of an offence under this section is liable to imprisonment or a fine, or both.

208. Misconduct in course of winding up

(1) When a company is being wound up, whether by the court or voluntarily, any person, being a past or present officer of the company, commits an offence if he—

(a) does not to the best of his knowledge and belief fully and truly discover to the liquidator all the company's property, and how and to whom and for what consideration and when the company disposed of any part of that property (except such part as has been disposed of in the ordinary way of the company's business), or

(b) does not deliver up to the liquidator (or as he directs) all such part of the company's property as is in his custody or under his control, and which he is required by law to deliver up, or

(c) does not deliver up to the liquidator (or as he directs) all books and papers in his custody or under his control belonging to the company and which he is required by law to deliver up, or

(d) knowing or believing that a false debt has been proved by any person in the winding up, fails to inform the liquidator as soon as practicable, or

(e) after the commencement of the winding up, prevents the production of any book or paper affecting or relating to the company's property or affairs.

(2) Such a person commits an offence if after the commencement of the winding up he attempts to account for any part of the company's property by fictitious losses or expenses; and he is deemed to have committed that offence if he has so attempted at any meeting of the company's creditors within the 12 months immediately preceding the commencement of the winding up.

(3) For purposes of this section, "officer" includes a shadow director.

(4) It is a defence—

(a) for a person charged under paragraph (a), (b) or (c) of subsection (1) to prove that he had no intent to defraud, and

(b) for a person charged under paragraph (e) of that subsection to prove that he had no intent to conceal the state of affairs of the company or to defeat the law.

(5) A person guilty of an offence under this section is liable to imprisonment or a fine, or both.

209. Falsification of company's books

(1) When a company is being wound up, an officer or contributory of the company commits an offence if he destroys, mutilates, alters or falsifies any books, papers or securities, or makes or is privy to the making of any false or fraudulent entry in any register, book of account or document belonging to the company with intent to defraud or deceive any person.

(2) A person guilty of an offence under this section is liable to imprisonment or a fine, or both.

210. Material omissions from statement relating to company's affairs

(1) When a company is being wound up, whether by the court or voluntarily, any person, being a past or present officer of the company, commits an offence if he makes any material omission in any statement relating to the company's affairs.

(2) When a company has been ordered to be wound up by the court, or has passed a resolution for voluntary winding up, any such person is deemed to have committed that offence if, prior to the winding up, he has made any material omission in any such statement.

(3) For purposes of this section, "officer" includes a shadow director.

(4) It is a defence for a person charged under this section to prove that he had no intent to defraud.

(5) A person guilty of an offence under this section is liable to imprisonment or a fine, or both.

211. False representations to creditors

(1) When a company is being wound up, whether by the court or voluntarily, any person, being a past or present officer of the company—

(a) commits an offence if he makes any false representation or commits any other fraud for the purpose of obtaining the consent of the company's creditors or any of them to an agreement with reference to the company's affairs or to the winding up, and

(b) is deemed to have committed that offence if, prior to the winding up, he has made any false representation, or committed any other fraud, for that purpose.

(2) For purposes of this section, "officer" includes a shadow director.

(3) A person guilty of an offence under this section is liable to imprisonment or a fine, or both.

Penalisation of directors and officers

212. Summary remedy against delinquent directors, liquidators, etc

(1) This section applies if in the course of the winding up of a company it appears that a person who—

(a) is or has been an officer of the company,

(b) has acted as liquidator… or administrative receiver of the company, or

(c) not being a person falling within paragraph (a) or (b), is or has been concerned, or has taken part, in the promotion, formation or management of the company,

has misapplied or retained, or become accountable for, any money or other property of the company, or been guilty of any misfeasance or breach of any fiduciary or other duty in relation to the company.

(2) The reference in subsection (1) to any misfeasance or breach of any fiduciary or other duty in relation to the company includes, in the case of a person who has acted as liquidator … of the company, any misfeasance or breach of any fiduciary or other duty in connection with the carrying out of his functions as liquidator … of the company.

(3) The court may, on the application of the official receiver or the liquidator, or of any creditor or contributory, examine into the conduct of the person falling within subsection (1) and compel him—

(a) to repay, restore or account for the money or property or any part of it, with interest at such rate as the court thinks just, or

(b) to contribute such sum to the company's assets by way of compensation in respect of the misfeasance or breach of fiduciary or other duty as the court thinks just.

(4) The power to make an application under subsection (3) in relation to a person who has acted as liquidator … of the company is not exercisable, except with the leave of the court, after he has had his release.

(5) The power of a contributory to make an application under subsection (3) is not exercisable except with the leave of the court, but is exercisable notwithstanding that he will not benefit from any order the court may make on the application.

213. Fraudulent trading

(1) If in the course of the winding up of a company it appears that any business of the company has been carried on with intent to defraud creditors of the company or creditors of any other person, or for any fraudulent purpose, the following has effect.

(2) The court, on the application of the liquidator may declare that any persons who were knowingly parties to the carrying on of the business in the manner above-mentioned are to be liable to make such contributions (if any) to the company's assets as the court thinks proper.

214. Wrongful trading

(1) Subject to subsection (3) below, if in the course of the winding up of a company it appears that subsection (2) of this section applies in relation to a person who is or has been a director of the company, the court, on the application of the liquidator, may declare that that person is to be liable to make such contribution (if any) to the company's assets as the court thinks proper.

(2) This subsection applies in relation to a person if—

(a) the company has gone into insolvent liquidation,

(b) at some time before the commencement of the winding up of the company, that person knew or ought to have concluded that there was no reasonable prospect that the company would avoid going into insolvent liquidation, and

(c) that person was a director of the company at that time;

but the court shall not make a declaration under this section in any case where the time mentioned in paragraph (b) above was before 28th April 1986.

(3) The court shall not make a declaration under this section with respect to any person if it is satisfied that after the condition specified in subsection (2)(b) was first satisfied in relation to him that person took every step with a view to minimising the potential loss to the company's creditors as (assuming him to have known that there was no reasonable prospect that the company would avoid going into insolvent liquidation) he ought to have taken.

(4) For the purposes of subsections (2) and (3), the facts which a director of a company ought to know or ascertain, the conclusions which he ought to reach and the steps which he ought to take are those which would be known or ascertained, or reached or taken, by a reasonably diligent person having both—

(a) the general knowledge, skill and experience that may reasonably be expected of a person carrying out the same functions as are carried out by that director in relation to the company, and

(b) the general knowledge, skill and experience that that director has.

(5) The reference in subsection (4) to the functions carried out in relation to a company by a director of the company includes any functions which he does not carry out but which have been entrusted to him.

(6) For the purposes of this section a company goes into insolvent liquidation if it goes into liquidation at a time when its assets are insufficient for the payment of its debts and other liabilities and the expenses of the winding up.

(7) In this section "director" includes a shadow director.

(8) This section is without prejudice to section 213.

215. Proceedings under ss 213, 214

(1) On the hearing of an application under section 213 or 214, the liquidator may himself give evidence or call witnesses.

(2) Where under either section the court makes a declaration, it may give such further directions as it thinks proper for giving effect to the declaration; and in particular, the court may—

(a) provide for the liability of any person under the declaration to be a charge on any debt or obligation due from the company to him, or on any mortgage or charge or any interest in a mortgage or charge on assets of the company held by or vested in him, or any person on his behalf, or any person claiming as assignee from or through the person liable or any person acting on his behalf, and

(b) from time to time make such further order as may be necessary for enforcing any charge imposed under this subsection.

(3) For the purposes of subsection (2), "assignee"—

(a) includes a person to whom or in whose favour, by the directions of the person made liable, the debt, obligation, mortgage or charge was created, issued or transferred or the interest created, but

(b) does not include an assignee for valuable consideration (not including consideration by way of marriage or the formation of a civil partnership) given in good faith and without notice of any of the matters on the ground of which the declaration is made.

(4) Where the court makes a declaration under either section in relation to a person who is a creditor of the company, it may direct that the whole or any part of any debt owed by the company to that person and any interest thereon shall rank in priority after all other debts owed by the company and after any interest on those debts.

(5) Sections 213 and 214 have effect notwithstanding that the person concerned may be criminally liable in respect of matters on the ground of which the declaration under the section is to be made.

216. Restriction on re-use of company names

(1) This section applies to a person where a company ("the liquidating company") has gone into insolvent liquidation on or after the appointed day and he was a director or shadow director of the company at any time in the period of 12 months ending with the day before it went into liquidation.

(2) For the purposes of this section, a name is a prohibited name in relation to such a person if—

(a) it is a name by which the liquidating company was known at any time in that period of 12 months, or

(b) it is a name which is so similar to a name falling within paragraph (a) as to suggest an association with that company.

(3) Except with leave of the court or in such circumstances as may be prescribed, a person to whom this section applies shall not at any time in the period of 5 years beginning with the day on which the liquidating company went into liquidation—

(a) be a director of any other company that is known by a prohibited name, or

(b) in any way, whether directly or indirectly, be concerned or take part in the promotion, formation or management of any such company, or

(c) in any way, whether directly or indirectly, be concerned or take part in the carrying on of a business carried on (otherwise than by a company) under a prohibited name.

(4) If a person acts in contravention of this section, he is liable to imprisonment or a fine, or both.

(5) In subsection (3) "the court" means any court having jurisdiction to wind up companies; and on an application for leave under that subsection, the Secretary of State or the official receiver may appear and call the attention of the court to any matters which seem to him to be relevant.

(6) References in this section, in relation to any time, to a name by which a company is known are to the name of the company at that time or to any name under which the company carries on business at that time.

(7) For the purposes of this section a company goes into insolvent liquidation if it goes into liquidation at a time when its assets are insufficient for the payment of its debts and other liabilities and the expenses of the winding up.

(8) In this section "company" includes a company which may be wound up under Part V of this Act.

217. Personal liability for debts, following contravention of s 216

(1) A person is personally responsible for all the relevant debts of a company if at any time—

(a) in contravention of section 216, he is involved in the management of the company, or

(b) as a person who is involved in the management of the company, he acts or is willing to act on instructions given (without the leave of the court) by a person whom he knows at that time to be in contravention in relation to the company of section 216.

(2) Where a person is personally responsible under this section for the relevant debts of a company, he is jointly and severally liable in respect of those debts with the company and any other person who, whether under this section or otherwise, is so liable.

(3) For the purposes of this section the relevant debts of a company are—

(a) in relation to a person who is personally responsible under paragraph (a) of subsection (1), such debts and other liabilities of the company as are incurred at a time when that person was involved in the management of the company, and

(b) in relation to a person who is personally responsible under paragraph (b) of that subsection, such debts and other liabilities of the company as are incurred at a time when that person was acting or was willing to act on instructions given as mentioned in that paragraph.

(4) For the purposes of this section, a person is involved in the management of a company if he is a director of the company or if he is concerned, whether directly or indirectly, or takes part, in the management of the company.

(5) For the purposes of this section a person who, as a person involved in the management of a company, has at any time acted on instructions given (without the leave of the court) by a person whom he knew at that time to be in contravention in relation to the company of section 216 is presumed, unless the contrary is shown, to have been willing at any time thereafter to act on any instructions given by that person.

(6) In this section "company" includes a company which may be wound up under Part V.

Investigation and prosecution of malpractice

218. Prosecution of delinquent officers and members of company

(1) If it appears to the court in the course of a winding up by the court that any past or present officer, or any member, of the company has been guilty of any offence in relation to the company for which he is criminally liable, the court may (either on the application of a person interested in the winding up or of its own motion) direct the liquidator to refer the matter

(a) in the case of a winding up in England and Wales, to the Secretary of State, and

(b) in the case of a winding up in Scotland, to the Lord Advocate.

(2) …

(3) If in the case of a winding up by the court in England and Wales it appears to the liquidator, not being the official receiver, that any past or present officer of the company, or any member of it, has been guilty of an offence in relation to the company for which he is criminally liable, the liquidator shall report the matter to the official receiver.

(4) If it appears to the liquidator in the course of a voluntary winding up that any past or present officer of the company, or any member of it, has been guilty of an offence in relation to the company for which he is criminally liable, he shall forthwith report the matter—

(a) in the case of a winding up in England and Wales, to the Secretary of State, and

(b) in the case of a winding up in Scotland, to the Lord Advocate,

and shall furnish to the Secretary of State or (as the case may be) the Lord Advocate such information and give to him such access to and facilities for inspecting and taking copies of documents (being information or documents in the possession or under the control of the liquidator and relating to the matter in question) as the Secretary of State or (as the case may be) the Lord Advocate requires.

(5) Where a report is made to the Secretary of State under subsection (4) he may, for the purpose of investigating the matter reported to him and such other matters relating to the affairs of the company as appear to him to require investigation, exercise any of the powers which are exercisable by inspectors appointed under section 431 or 432 of the Companies Act 1985 to investigate a company's affairs.

(6) If it appears to the court in the course of a voluntary winding up that—

(a) any past or present officer of the company, or any member of it, has been guilty as above-mentioned, and

(b) no report with respect to the matter has been made by the liquidator … under subsection (4), the court may (on the application of any person interested in the winding up or of its own motion) direct the liquidator to make such a report.

On a report being made accordingly, this section has effect as though the report had been made in pursuance of subsection (4).

219. Obligations arising under s 218

(1) For the purpose of an investigation by the Secretary of State in consequence of a report made to him under section 218(4), any obligation imposed on a person by any provision of the Companies Act 1985 to produce documents or give information to, or otherwise to assist, inspectors appointed as mentioned in section 218(5) is to be regarded as an obligation similarly to assist the Secretary of State in his investigation.

(2) An answer given by a person to a question put to him in exercise of the powers conferred by section 218(5) may be used in evidence against him.

(2A) However, in criminal proceedings in which that person is charged with an offence to which this subsection applies—

(a) no evidence relating to the answer may be adduced, and

(b) no question relating to it may be asked,

by or on behalf of the prosecution, unless evidence relating to it is adduced, or a question relating to it is asked, in the proceedings by or on behalf of that person.

(2B) Subsection (2A) applies to any offence other than—

(a) an offence under section 2 or 5 of the Perjury Act 1911 (false statements made on oath otherwise than in judicial proceedings or made otherwise than on oath), or

(b) an offence under section 44(1) or (2) of the Criminal Law (Consolidation) (Scotland) Act 1995 (false statements made on oath or otherwise than on oath).

(3) Where criminal proceedings are instituted by the Director of Public Prosecutions, the Lord Advocate or the Secretary of State following any report or reference under section 218, it is the duty of the liquidator and every officer and agent of the company past and present (other than the defendant or defender) to give to the Director of Public Prosecutions, the Lord Advocate or the Secretary of State (as the case may be) all assistance in connection with the prosecution which he is reasonably able to give.

For this purpose "agent" includes any banker or solicitor of the company and any person employed by the company as auditor, whether that person is or is not an officer of the company.

(4) If a person fails or neglects to give assistance in the manner required by subsection (3), the court may, on the application of the Director of Public Prosecutions, the Lord Advocate or the Secretary of State (as the case may be) direct the person to comply with that subsection; and if the application is made with respect to a liquidator, the court may (unless it appears that the failure or neglect to comply was due to the liquidator not having in his hands sufficient assets of the company to enable him to do so) direct that the costs shall be borne by the liquidator personally.

PART V
WINDING UP OF UNREGISTERED COMPANIES

220. Meaning of "unregistered company"

For the purposes of this Part "unregistered company" includes any association and any company, with the exception of a company registered under the Companies Act 2006 in any part of the United Kingdom.

221. Winding up of unregistered companies

(1) Subject to the provisions of this Part, any unregistered company may be wound up under this Act; and all the provisions of this Act . . . about winding up apply to an unregistered company with the exceptions and additions mentioned in the following subsections.

(2) If an unregistered company has a principal place of business situated in Northern Ireland, it shall not be wound up under this Part unless it has a principal place of business situated in England and Wales or Scotland, or in both England and Wales and Scotland.

(3) For the purpose of determining a court's winding-up jurisdiction, an unregistered company is deemed—
(a) to be registered in England and Wales or Scotland, according as its principal place of business is situated in England and Wales or Scotland, or
(b) if it has a principal place of business situated in both countries, to be registered in both countries;

and the principal place of business situated in that part of Great Britain in which proceedings are being instituted is, for all purposes of the winding up, deemed to be the registered office of the company.

(4) No unregistered company shall be wound up under this Act voluntarily, except in accordance with the EC Regulation.

(5) The circumstances in which an unregistered company may be wound up are as follows—
(a) if the company is dissolved, or has ceased to carry on business, or is carrying on business only for the purpose of winding up its affairs;
(b) if the company is unable to pay its debts;
(c) if the court is of opinion that it is just and equitable that the company should be wound up.

(6) …

(7) In Scotland, an unregistered company which the Court of Session has jurisdiction to wind up may be wound up by the court if there is subsisting a floating charge over property comprised in the company's property and undertaking, and the court is satisfied that the security of the creditor entitled to the benefit of the floating charge is in jeopardy.

For this purpose a creditor's security is deemed to be in jeopardy if the court is satisfied that events have occurred or are about to occur which render it unreasonable in the creditor's interests that the company should retain power to dispose of the property which is subject to the floating charge.

222. Inability to pay debts: unpaid creditor for £750 or more

(1) An unregistered company is deemed (for the purposes of section 221) unable to pay its debts if there is a creditor, by assignment or otherwise, to whom the company is indebted in a sum exceeding £750 then due and—
(a) the creditor has served on the company, by leaving at its principal place of business, or by delivering to the secretary or some director, manager or principal officer of the company, or by otherwise serving in such manner as the court may approve or direct, a written demand in the prescribed form requiring the company to pay the sum due, and
(b) the company has for 3 weeks after the service of the demand neglected to pay the sum or to secure or compound for it to the creditor's satisfaction.

(2) The money sum for the time being specified in subsection (1) is subject to increase or reduction by regulations under section 417 in Part XV; but no increase in the sum so specified affects any case in which the winding-up petition was presented before the coming into force of the increase.

223. Inability to pay debts: debt remaining unsatisfied after action brought

An unregistered company is deemed (for the purposes of section 221) unable to pay its debts if an action or other proceeding has been instituted against any member for any debt or demand due, or claimed to be due, from the company, or from him in his character of member, and—
(a) notice in writing of the institution of the action or proceeding has been served on the company by leaving it at the company's principal place of business (or by delivering it to the secretary, or some director, manager or principal officer of the company, or by otherwise serving it in such manner as the court may approve or direct), and
(b) the company has not within 3 weeks after service of the notice paid, secured or compounded for the debt or demand, or procured the action or proceeding to be stayed or sisted, or indemnified the defendant or defender to his reasonable satisfaction against the action or proceeding, and against all costs, damages and expenses to be incurred by him because of it.

224. Inability to pay debts: other cases

(1) An unregistered company is deemed (for purposes of section 221) unable to pay its debts—

(a) if in England and Wales execution or other process issued on a judgment, decree or order obtained in any court in favour of a creditor against the company, or any member of it as such, or any person authorised to be sued as nominal defendant on behalf of the company, is returned unsatisfied;

(b) if in Scotland the induciae of a charge for payment on an extract decree, or an extract registered bond, or an extract registered protest, have expired without payment being made;

(c) if in Northern Ireland a certificate of unenforceability has been granted in respect of any judgment, decree or order obtained as mentioned in paragraph (a);

(d) if it is otherwise proved to the satisfaction of the court that the company is unable to pay its debts as they fall due.

(2) An unregistered company is also deemed unable to pay its debts if it is proved to the satisfaction of the court that the value of the company's assets is less than the amount of its liabilities, taking into account its contingent and prospective liabilities.

225. Company incorporated outside Great Britain may be wound up though dissolved

(1) Where a company incorporated outside Great Britain which has been carrying on business in Great Britain ceases to carry on business in Great Britain, it may be wound up as an unregistered company under this Act, notwithstanding that it has been dissolved or otherwise ceased to exist as a company under or by virtue of the laws of the country under which it was incorporated.

(2) This section is subject to the EC Regulation.

226. Contributories in winding up of unregistered company

(1) In the event of an unregistered company being wound up, every person is deemed a contributory who is liable to pay or contribute to the payment of any debt or liability of the company, or to pay or contribute to the payment of any sum for the adjustment of the rights of members among themselves, or to pay or contribute to the payment of the expenses of winding up the company.

(2) Every contributory is liable to contribute to the company's assets all sums due from him in respect of any such liability as is mentioned above.

(3) In the case of an unregistered company engaged in or formed for working mines within the stannaries, a past member is not liable to contribute to the assets if he has ceased to be a member for 2 years or more either before the mine ceased to be worked or before the date of the winding-up order.

(4) . . .

227. Power of court to stay, sist or restrain proceedings

The provisions of this Part with respect to staying, sisting or restraining actions and proceedings against a company at any time after the presentation of a petition for winding up and before the making of a winding-up order extend, in the case of an unregistered company, where the application to stay, sist or restrain is presented by a creditor, to actions and proceedings against any contributory of the company.

228. Actions stayed on winding-up order

Where an order has been made for winding up an unregistered company, no action or proceeding shall be proceeded with or commenced against any contributory of the company in respect of any debt of the company, except by leave of the court, and subject to such terms as the court may impose.

229. Provisions of this Part to be cumulative

(1) The provisions of this Part with respect to unregistered companies are in addition to and not in restriction of any provisions in Part IV with respect to winding up companies by the court; and the court or liquidator may exercise any powers or do any act in the case of unregistered companies

which might be exercised or done by it or him in winding up companies registered under the Companies Act 2006 in England and Wales or Scotland.

(2) …

PART VI
MISCELLANEOUS PROVISIONS APPLYING TO COMPANIES WHICH ARE INSOLVENT OR IN LIQUIDATION

Office-holders

230. Holders of office to be qualified insolvency practitioners

(1) …

(2) Where an administrative receiver of a company is appointed, he must be a person who is so qualified.

(3) Where a company goes into liquidation, the liquidator must be a person who is so qualified.

(4) Where a provisional liquidator is appointed, he must be a person who is so qualified.

(5) Subsections (3) and (4) are without prejudice to any enactment under which the official receiver is to be, or may be, liquidator or provisional liquidator.

231. Appointment to office of two or more persons

(1) This section applies if an appointment or nomination of any person to the office of … administrative receiver, liquidator or provisional liquidator—

(a) relates to more than one person, or

(b) has the effect that the office is to be held by more than one person.

(2) The appointment or nomination shall declare whether any act required or authorised under any enactment to be done by the … administrative receiver, liquidator or provisional liquidator is to be done by all or any one or more of the persons for the time being holding the office in question.

232. Validity of office-holder's acts

The acts of an individual as … administrative receiver, liquidator or provisional liquidator of a company are valid notwithstanding any defect in his appointment, nomination or qualifications.

Management by administrators, liquidators, etc

233. Supplies of gas, water, electricity, etc

(1) This section applies in the case of a company where—

(a) the company enters administration, or

(b) an administrative receiver is appointed, or

(ba) a moratorium under section 1A is in force, or

(c) a voluntary arrangement approved under Part I, has taken effect, or

(d) the company goes into liquidation, or

(e) a provisional liquidator is appointed;

and "the office-holder" means the administrator, the administrative receiver, the nominee, the supervisor of the voluntary arrangement, the liquidator or the provisional liquidator, as the case may be.

(2) If a request is made by or with the concurrence of the office-holder for the giving, after the effective date, of any of the supplies mentioned in the next subsection, the supplier—

(a) may make it a condition of the giving of the supply that the office-holder personally guarantees the payment of any charges in respect of the supply, but

(b) shall not make it a condition of the giving of the supply, or do anything which has the effect of making it a condition of the giving of the supply, that any outstanding charges in respect of a supply given to the company before the effective date are paid.

(3) The supplies referred to in subsection (2) are—

(a) a supply of gas by a gas supplier within the meaning of Part I of the Gas Act 1986;

(b) a supply of electricity by an electricity supplier within the meaning of Part I of the Electricity Act 1989;

(c) a supply of water by a water undertaker or, in Scotland, Scottish Water,

(d) a supply of communications services by a provider of a public electronic communications service.

(4) "The effective date" for the purposes of this section is whichever is applicable of the following dates—

(a) the date on which the company entered administration,

(b) the date on which the administrative receiver was appointed (or, if he was appointed in succession to another administrative receiver, the date on which the first of his predecessors was appointed),

(ba) the date on which the moratorium came into force,

(c) the date on which the voluntary arrangement took effect,

(d) the date on which the company went into liquidation,

(e) the date on which the provisional liquidator was appointed.

(5) The following applies to expressions used in subsection (3)—

(a)–(c)…

(d) "communications services" do not include electronic communications services to the extent that they are used to broadcast or otherwise transmit programme services (within the meaning of the Communications Act 2003).

234. Getting in the company's property

(1) This section applies in the case of a company where—

(a) the company enters administration, or

(b) an administrative receiver is appointed, or

(c) the company goes into liquidation, or

(d) a provisional liquidator is appointed;

and "the office-holder" means the administrator, the administrative receiver, the liquidator or the provisional liquidator, as the case may be.

(2) Where any person has in his possession or control any property, books, papers or records to which the company appears to be entitled, the court may require that person forthwith (or within such period as the court may direct) to pay, deliver, convey, surrender or transfer the property, books, papers or records to the office-holder.

(3) Where the office-holder—

(a) seizes or disposes of any property which is not property of the company, and

(b) at the time of seizure or disposal believes, and has reasonable grounds for believing, that he is entitled (whether in pursuance of an order of the court or otherwise) to seize or dispose of that property,

the next subsection has effect.

(4) In that case the office-holder—

(a) is not liable to any person in respect of any loss or damage resulting from the seizure or disposal except in so far as that loss or damage is caused by the office-holder's own negligence, and

(b) has a lien on the property, or the proceeds of its sale, for such expenses as were incurred in connection with the seizure or disposal.

235. Duty to co-operate with office-holder

(1) This section applies as does section 234; and it also applies, in the case of a company in respect of which a winding-up order has been made by the court in England and Wales, as if references to the office-holder included the official receiver, whether or not he is the liquidator.

(2) Each of the persons mentioned in the next subsection shall—

(a) give to the office-holder such information concerning the company and its promotion, formation, business, dealings, affairs or property as the office-holder may at any time after the effective date reasonably require, and

(b) attend on the office-holder at such times as the latter may reasonably require.

(3) The persons referred to above are—

(a) those who are or have at any time been officers of the company,

(b) those who have taken part in the formation of the company at any time within one year before the effective date,

(c) those who are in the employment of the company, or have been in its employment (including employment under a contract for services) within that year, and are in the office-holder's opinion capable of giving information which he requires,

(d) those who are, or have within that year been, officers of, or in the employment (including employment under a contract for services) of, another company which is, or within that year was, an officer of the company in question, and

(e) in the case of a company being wound up by the court, any person who has acted as administrator, administrative receiver or liquidator of the company.

(4) For the purposes of subsections (2) and (3), "the effective date" is whichever is applicable of the following dates—

(a) the date on which the company entered administration,

(b) the date on which the administrative receiver was appointed or, if he was appointed in succession to another administrative receiver, the date on which the first of his predecessors was appointed,

(c) the date on which the provisional liquidator was appointed, and

(d) the date on which the company went into liquidation.

(5) If a person without reasonable excuse fails to comply with any obligation imposed by this section, he is liable to a fine and, for contravention, to a daily default fine.

236. Inquiry into company's dealings, etc

(1) This section applies as does section 234; and it also applies in the case of a company in respect of which a winding-up order has been made by the court in England and Wales as if references to the office-holder included the official receiver, whether or not he is the liquidator.

(2) The court may, on the application of the office-holder, summon to appear before it—

(a) any officer of the company,

(b) any person known or suspected to have in his possession any property of the company or supposed to be indebted to the company, or

(c) any person whom the court thinks capable of giving information concerning the promotion, formation, business, dealings, affairs or property of the company.

(3) The court may require any such person as is mentioned in subsection (2)(a) to (c) to submit to the court an account of his dealings with the company or to produce any books, papers or other records in his possession or under his control relating to the company or the matters mentioned in paragraph (c) of the subsection.

(3A) An account submitted to the court under subsection (3) must be contained in—

(a) a witness statement verified by a statement of truth (in England and Wales), and

(b) an affidavit (in Scotland).

(4) The following applies in a case where—

(a) a person without reasonable excuse fails to appear before the court when he is summoned to do so under this section, or

(b) there are reasonable grounds for believing that a person has absconded, or is about to abscond, with a view to avoiding his appearance before the court under this section.

(5) The court may, for the purpose of bringing that person and anything in his possession before the court, cause a warrant to be issued to a constable or prescribed officer of the court—

(a) for the arrest of that person, and

(b) for the seizure of any books, papers, records, money or goods in that person's possession.

(6) The court may authorise a person arrested under such a warrant to be kept in custody, and anything seized under such a warrant to be held, in accordance with the rules, until that person is brought before the court under the warrant or until such other time as the court may order.

237. Court's enforcement powers under s 236

(1) If it appears to the court, on consideration of any evidence obtained under section 236 or this section, that any person has in his possession any property of the company, the court may, on the application of the office-holder, order that person to deliver the whole or any part of the property to the office-holder at such time, in such manner and on such terms as the court thinks fit.

(2) If it appears to the court, on consideration of any evidence so obtained, that any person is indebted to the company, the court may, on the application of the office-holder, order that person to pay to the office-holder, at such time and in such manner as the court may direct, the whole or any part of the amount due, whether in full discharge of the debt or otherwise, as the court thinks fit.

(3) The court may, if it thinks fit, order that any person who if within the jurisdiction of the court would be liable to be summoned to appear before it under section 236 or this section shall be examined in any part of the United Kingdom where he may for the time being be, or in a place outside the United Kingdom.

(4) Any person who appears or is brought before the court under section 236 or this section may be examined on oath, either orally or (except in Scotland) by interrogatories, concerning the company or the matters mentioned in section 236(2)(c).

Adjustment of prior transactions (administration and liquidation)

238. Transactions at an undervalue (England and Wales)

(1) This section applies in the case of a company where—

(a) the company enters administration, or

(b) the company goes into liquidation;

and "the office-holder" means the administrator or the liquidator, as the case may be.

(2) Where the company has at a relevant time (defined in section 240) entered into a transaction with any person at an undervalue, the office-holder may apply to the court for an order under this section.

(3) Subject as follows, the court shall, on such an application, make such order as it thinks fit for restoring the position to what it would have been if the company had not entered into that transaction.

(4) For the purposes of this section and section 241, a company enters into a transaction with a person at an undervalue if—

(a) the company makes a gift to that person or otherwise enters into a transaction with that person on terms that provide for the company to receive no consideration, or

(b) the company enters into a transaction with that person for a consideration the value of which, in money or money's worth, is significantly less than the value, in money or money's worth, of the consideration provided by the company.

(5) The court shall not make an order under this section in respect of a transaction at an undervalue if it is satisfied—

(a) that the company which entered into the transaction did so in good faith and for the purpose of carrying on its business, and

(b) that at the time it did so there were reasonable grounds for believing that the transaction would benefit the company.

239. Preferences (England and Wales)

(1) This section applies as does section 238.

(2) Where the company has at a relevant time (defined in the next section) given a preference to any person, the office-holder may apply to the court for an order under this section.

(3) Subject as follows, the court shall, on such an application, make such order as it thinks fit for restoring the position to what it would have been if the company had not given that preference.

(4) For the purposes of this section and section 241, a company gives a preference to a person if—
 (a) that person is one of the company's creditors or a surety or guarantor for any of the company's debts or other liabilities, and
 (b) the company does anything or suffers anything to be done which (in either case) has the effect of putting that person into a position which, in the event of the company going into insolvent liquidation, will be better than the position he would have been in if that thing had not been done.

(5) The court shall not make an order under this section in respect of a preference given to any person unless the company which gave the preference was influenced in deciding to give it by a desire to produce in relation to that person the effect mentioned in subsection (4)(b).

(6) A company which has given a preference to a person connected with the company (otherwise than by reason only of being its employee) at the time the preference was given is presumed, unless the contrary is shown, to have been influenced in deciding to give it by such a desire as is mentioned in subsection (5).

(7) The fact that something has been done in pursuance of the order of a court does not, without more, prevent the doing or suffering of that thing from constituting the giving of a preference.

240. "Relevant time" under ss 238, 239

(1) Subject to the next subsection, the time at which a company enters into a transaction at an undervalue or gives a preference is a relevant time if the transaction is entered into, or the preference given—
 (a) in the case of a transaction at an undervalue or of a preference which is given to a person who is connected with the company (otherwise than by reason only of being its employee), at a time in the period of 2 years ending with the onset of insolvency (which expression is defined below),
 (b) in the case of a preference which is not such a transaction and is not so given, at a time in the period of 6 months ending with the onset of insolvency, …
 (c) in either case, at a time between the making of an administration application in respect of the company and the making of an administration order on that application, and
 (d) in either case, at a time between the filing with the court of a copy of notice of intention to appoint an administrator under paragraph 14 or 22 of Schedule B1 and the making of an appointment under that paragraph.

(2) Where a company enters into a transaction at an undervalue or gives a preference at a time mentioned in subsection (1)(a) or (b), that time is not a relevant time for the purposes of section 238 or 239 unless the company—
 (a) is at that time unable to pay its debts within the meaning of section 123 in Chapter VI of Part IV, or
 (b) becomes unable to pay its debts within the meaning of that section in consequence of the transaction or preference;

but the requirements of this subsection are presumed to be satisfied, unless the contrary is shown, in relation to any transaction at an undervalue which is entered into by a company with a person who is connected with the company.

(3) For the purposes of subsection (1), the onset of insolvency is—
 (a) in a case where section 238 or 239 applies by reason of an administrator of a company being appointed by administration order, the date on which the administration application is made,
 (b) in a case where section 238 or 239 applies by reason of an administrator of a company being appointed under paragraph 14 or 22 of Schedule B1 following filing with the court of a copy of a notice of intention to appoint under that paragraph, the date on which the copy of the notice is filed,
 (c) in a case where section 238 or 239 applies by reason of an administrator of a company being appointed otherwise than as mentioned in paragraph (a) or (b), the date on which the appointment takes effect,

(d) in a case where section 238 or 239 applies by reason of a company going into liquidation either following conversion of administration into winding up by virtue of Article 37 of the EC Regulation or at the time when the appointment of an administrator ceases to have effect, the date on which the company entered administration (or, if relevant, the date on which the application for the administration order was made or a copy of the notice of intention to appoint was filed), and

(e) in a case where section 238 or 239 applies by reason of a company going into liquidation at any other time, the date of the commencement of the winding up.

241. Orders under ss 238, 239

(1) Without prejudice to the generality of sections 238(3) and 239(3), an order under either of those sections with respect to a transaction or preference entered into or given by a company may (subject to the next subsection)—

(a) require any property transferred as part of the transaction, or in connection with the giving of the preference, to be vested in the company,

(b) require any property to be so vested if it represents in any person's hands the application either of the proceeds of sale of property so transferred or of money so transferred,

(c) release or discharge (in whole or in part) any security given by the company,

(d) require any person to pay, in respect of benefits received by him from the company, such sums to the office-holder as the court may direct,

(e) provide for any surety or guarantor whose obligations to any person were released or discharged (in whole or in part) under the transaction, or by the giving of the preference, to be under such new or revived obligations to that person as the court thinks appropriate,

(f) provide for security to be provided for the discharge of any obligation imposed by or arising under the order, for such an obligation to be charged on any property and for the security or charge to have the same priority as a security or charge released or discharged (in whole or in part) under the transaction or by the giving of the preference, and

(g) provide for the extent to which any person whose property is vested by the order in the company, or on whom obligations are imposed by the order, is to be able to prove in the winding up of the company for debts or other liabilities which arose from, or were released or discharged (in whole or in part) under or by, the transaction or the giving of the preference.

(2) An order under section 238 or 239 may affect the property of, or impose any obligation on, any person whether or not he is the person with whom the company in question entered into the transaction or (as the case may be) the person to whom the preference was given; but such an order—

(a) shall not prejudice any interest in property which was acquired from a person other than the company and was acquired in good faith and for value, or prejudice any interest deriving from such an interest, and

(b) shall not require a person who received a benefit from the transaction or preference in good faith and for value to pay a sum to the office-holder, except where that person was a party to the transaction or the payment is to be in respect of a preference given to that person at a time when he was a creditor of the company.

(2A) Where a person has acquired an interest in property from a person other than the company in question, or has received a benefit from the transaction or preference, and at the time of that acquisition or receipt—

(a) he had notice of the relevant surrounding circumstances and of the relevant proceedings, or

(b) he was connected with, or was an associate of, either the company in question or the person with whom that company entered into the transaction or to whom that company gave the preference,

then, unless the contrary is shown, it shall be presumed for the purposes of paragraph (a) or (as the case may be) paragraph (b) of subsection (2) that the interest was acquired or the benefit was received otherwise than in good faith.

(3) For the purposes of subsection (2A)(a), the relevant surrounding circumstances are (as the case may require)—
- (a) the fact that the company in question entered into the transaction at an undervalue; or
- (b) the circumstances which amounted to the giving of the preference by the company in question;

and subsections (3A) to (3C) have effect to determine whether, for those purposes, a person has notice of the relevant proceedings.

(3A) Where section 238 or 239 applies by reason of a company's entering administration, a person has notice of the relevant proceedings if he has notice that—
- (a) an administration application has been made,
- (b) an administration order has been made,
- (c) a copy of a notice of intention to appoint an administrator under paragraph 14 or 22 of Schedule B1 has been filed, or
- (d) notice of the appointment of an administrator has been filed under paragraph 18 or 29 of that Schedule.

(3B) Where section 238 or 239 applies by reason of a company's going into liquidation at the time when the appointment of an administrator of the company ceases to have effect, a person has notice of the relevant proceedings if he has notice that—
- (a) an administration application has been made,
- (b) an administration order has been made,
- (c) a copy of a notice of intention to appoint an administrator under paragraph 14 or 22 of Schedule B1 has been filed,
- (d) notice of the appointment of an administrator has been filed under paragraph 18 or 29 of that Schedule, or
- (e) the company has gone into liquidation.

(3C) In a case where section 238 or 239 applies by reason of the company in question going into liquidation at any other time, a person has notice of the relevant proceedings if he has notice—
- (a) where the company goes into liquidation on the making of a winding-up order, of the fact that the petition on which the winding-up order is made has been presented or of the fact that the company has gone into liquidation;
- (b) in any other case, of the fact that the company has gone into liquidation.

(4) The provisions of sections 238 to 241 apply without prejudice to the availability of any other remedy, even in relation to a transaction or preference which the company had no power to enter into or give.

242. Gratuitous alienations (Scotland)

(1) Where this subsection applies and—
- (a) the winding up of a company has commenced, an alienation by the company is challengeable by—
  - (i) any creditor who is a creditor by virtue of a debt incurred on or before the date of such commencement, or
  - (ii) the liquidator;
- (b) a company enters administration, an alienation by the company is challengeable by the administrator.

(2) Subsection (1) applies where—
- (a) by the alienation, whether before or after 1st April 1986 (the coming into force of section 75 of the Bankruptcy (Scotland) Act 1985), any part of the company's property is transferred or any claim or right of the company is discharged or renounced, and
- (b) the alienation takes place on a relevant day.

(3) For the purposes of subsection (2)(b), the day on which an alienation takes place is the day on which it becomes completely effectual; and in that subsection "relevant day" means, if the alienation has the effect of favouring—

(a) a person who is an associate (within the meaning of the Bankruptcy (Scotland) Act 1985) of the company, a day not earlier than 5 years before the date on which—

(i) the winding up of the company commences, or

(ii) as the case may be, the company enters administration; or

(b) any other person, a day not earlier than 2 years before that date.

(4) On a challenge being brought under subsection (1), the court shall grant decree of reduction or for such restoration of property to the company's assets or other redress as may be appropriate; but the court shall not grant such a decree if the person seeking to uphold the alienation establishes—

(a) that immediately, or at any other time, after the alienation the company's assets were greater than its liabilities, or

(b) that the alienation was made for adequate consideration, or

(c) that the alienation—

(i) was a birthday, Christmas or other conventional gift, or

(ii) was a gift made, for a charitable purpose, to a person who is not an associate of the company,

which, having regard to all the circumstances, it was reasonable for the company to make.

Provided that this subsection is without prejudice to any right or interest acquired in good faith and for value from or through the transferee in the alienation.

(5) In subsection (4) above, "charitable purpose" means any charitable, benevolent or philanthropic purpose, whether or not it is charitable within the meaning of any rule of law.

(6) For the purposes of the foregoing provisions of this section, an alienation in implementation of a prior obligation is deemed to be one for which there was no consideration or no adequate consideration to the extent that the prior obligation was undertaken for no consideration or no adequate consideration.

(7) A liquidator and an administrator have the same right as a creditor has under any rule of law to challenge an alienation of a company made for no consideration or no adequate consideration.

(8) This section applies to Scotland only.

243. Unfair preferences (Scotland)

(1) Subject to subsection (2) below, subsection (4) below applies to a transaction entered into by a company, whether before or after 1st April 1986, which has the effect of creating a preference in favour of a creditor to the prejudice of the general body of creditors, being a preference created not earlier than 6 months before the commencement of the winding up of the company or the company enters administration.

(2) Subsection (4) below does not apply to any of the following transactions—

(a) a transaction in the ordinary course of trade or business;

(b) a payment in cash for a debt which when it was paid had become payable, unless the transaction was collusive with the purpose of prejudicing the general body of creditors;

(c) a transaction whereby the parties to it undertake reciprocal obligations (whether the performance by the parties of their respective obligations occurs at the same time or at different times) unless the transaction was collusive as aforesaid;

(d) the granting of a mandate by a company authorising an arrestee to pay over the arrested funds or part thereof to the arrester where—

(i) there has been a decree for payment or a warrant for summary diligence, and

(ii) the decree or warrant has been preceded by an arrestment on the dependence of the action or followed by an arrestment in execution.

(3) For the purposes of subsection (1) above, the day on which a preference was created is the day on which the preference became completely effectual.

(4) A transaction to which this subsection applies is challengeable by—

(a) in the case of a winding up—

(i) any creditor who is a creditor by virtue of a debt incurred on or before the date of commencement of the winding up, or

(ii) the liquidator; and

(b) where the company has entered administration, the administrator.

(5) On a challenge being brought under subsection (4) above, the court, if satisfied that the transaction challenged is a transaction to which this section applies, shall grant decree of reduction or for such restoration of property to the company's assets or other redress as may be appropriate:

Provided that this subsection is without prejudice to any right or interest acquired in good faith and for value from or through the creditor in whose favour the preference was created.

(6) A liquidator and an administrator have the same right as a creditor has under any rule of law to challenge a preference created by a debtor.

(7) This section applies to Scotland only.

244. Extortionate credit transactions

(1) This section applies as does section 238, and where the company is, or has been, a party to a transaction for, or involving, the provision of credit to the company.

(2) The court may, on the application of the office-holder, make an order with respect to the transaction if the transaction is or was extortionate and was entered into in the period of 3 years ending with the day on which the company entered administration or went into liquidation.

(3) For the purposes of this section a transaction is extortionate if, having regard to the risk accepted by the person providing the credit—

(a) the terms of it are or were such as to require grossly exorbitant payments to be made (whether unconditionally or in certain contingencies) in respect of the provision of the credit, or

(b) it otherwise grossly contravened ordinary principles of fair dealing;

and it shall be presumed, unless the contrary is proved, that a transaction with respect to which an application is made under this section is or, as the case may be, was extortionate.

(4) An order under this section with respect to any transaction may contain such one or more of the following as the court thinks fit, that is to say—

(a) provision setting aside the whole or part of any obligation created by the transaction,

(b) provision otherwise varying the terms of the transaction or varying the terms on which any security for the purposes of the transaction is held,

(c) provision requiring any person who is or was a party to the transaction to pay to the office-holder any sums paid to that person, by virtue of the transaction, by the company,

(d) provision requiring any person to surrender to the office-holder any property held by him as security for the purposes of the transaction,

(e) provision directing accounts to be taken between any persons.

(5) The powers conferred by this section are exercisable in relation to any transaction concurrently with any powers exercisable in relation to that transaction as a transaction at an undervalue or under section 242 (gratuitous alienations in Scotland).

245. Avoidance of certain floating charges

(1) This section applies as does section 238, but applies to Scotland as well as to England and Wales.

(2) Subject as follows, a floating charge on the company's undertaking or property created at a relevant time is invalid except to the extent of the aggregate of—

(a) the value of so much of the consideration for the creation of the charge as consists of money paid, or goods or services supplied, to the company at the same time as, or after, the creation of the charge,

(b) the value of so much of that consideration as consists of the discharge or reduction, at the same time as, or after the creation of the charge, of any debt of the company, and

(c) the amount of such interest (if any) as is payable on the amount falling within paragraph (a) or (b) in pursuance of any agreement under which the money was so paid, the goods or services were so supplied or the debt was so discharged or reduced.

(3) Subject to the next subsection, the time at which a floating charge is created by a company is a relevant time for the purposes of this section if the charge is created—

(a) in the case of a charge which is created in favour of a person who is connected with the company, at a time in the period of 2 years ending with the onset of insolvency,
(b) in the case of a charge which is created in favour of any other person, at a time in the period of 12 months ending with the onset of insolvency, …
(c) in either case, at a time between the making of an administration application in respect of the company and the making of an administration order on that application, or
(d) in either case, at a time between the filing with the court of a copy of notice of intention to appoint an administrator under paragraph 14 or 22 of Schedule B1 and the making of an appointment under that paragraph.

(4) Where a company creates a floating charge at a time mentioned in subsection (3)(b) and the person in favour of whom the charge is created is not connected with the company, that time is not a relevant time for the purposes of this section unless the company—
(a) is at that time unable to pay its debts within the meaning of section 123 in Chapter VI of Part IV, or
(b) becomes unable to pay its debts within the meaning of that section in consequence of the transaction under which the charge is created.

(5) For the purposes of subsection (3), the onset of insolvency is—
(a) in a case where this section applies by reason of an administrator of a company being appointed by administration order, the date on which the administration application is made,
(b) in a case where this section applies by reason of an administrator of a company being appointed under paragraph 14 or 22 of Schedule B1 following filing with the court of a copy of notice of intention to appoint under that paragraph, the date on which the copy of the notice is filed,
(c) in a case where this section applies by reason of an administrator of a company being appointed otherwise than as mentioned in paragraph (a) or (b), the date on which the appointment takes effect, and
(d) in a case where this section applies by reason of a company going into liquidation, the date of the commencement of the winding up.

(6) For the purposes of subsection (2)(a) the value of any goods or services supplied by way of consideration for a floating charge is the amount in money which at the time they were supplied could reasonably have been expected to be obtained for supplying the goods or services in the ordinary course of business and on the same terms (apart from the consideration) as those on which they were supplied to the company.

246. Unenforceability of liens on books, etc

(1) This section applies in the case of a company where—
(a) the company enters administration, or
(b) the company goes into liquidation, or
(c) a provisional liquidator is appointed;

and "the office-holder" means the administrator, the liquidator or the provisional liquidator, as the case may be.

(2) Subject as follows, a lien or other right to retain possession of any of the books, papers or other records of the company is unenforceable to the extent that its enforcement would deny possession of any books, papers or other records to the office-holder.

(3) This does not apply to a lien on documents which give a title to property and are held as such.

Remote attendance at meetings

246A. Remote attendance at meetings

(1) Subject to subsection (2), this section applies to—
(a) any meeting of the creditors of a company summoned under this Act or the rules, or
(b) any meeting of the members or contributories of a company summoned by the office-holder under this Act or the rules, other than a meeting of the members of a company in a members' voluntary winding up.

(2) This section does not apply where—
(a) a company is being wound up in Scotland, or
(b) a receiver is appointed under section 51 in Chapter 2 of Part 3.

(3) Where the person summoning a meeting ("the convener") considers it appropriate, the meeting may be conducted and held in such a way that persons who are not present together at the same place may attend it.

(4) Where a meeting is conducted and held in the manner referred to in subsection (3), a person attends the meeting if that person is able to exercise any rights which that person may have to speak and vote at the meeting.

(5) For the purposes of this section—
(a) a person is able to exercise the right to speak at a meeting when that person is in a position to communicate to all those attending the meeting, during the meeting, any information or opinions which that person has on the business of the meeting; and
(b) a person is able to exercise the right to vote at a meeting when—
(i) that person is able to vote, during the meeting, on resolutions put to the vote at the meeting, and
(ii) that person's vote can be taken into account in determining whether or not such resolutions are passed at the same time as the votes of all the other persons attending the meeting.

(6) The convener of a meeting which is to be conducted and held in the manner referred to in subsection (3) shall make whatever arrangements the convener considers appropriate to—
(a) enable those attending the meeting to exercise their rights to speak or vote, and
(b) ensure the identification of those attending the meeting and the security of any electronic means used to enable attendance.

(7) Where in the reasonable opinion of the convener—
(a) a meeting will be attended by persons who will not be present together at the same place, and
(b) it is unnecessary or inexpedient to specify a place for the meeting,

any requirement under this Act or the rules to specify a place for the meeting may be satisfied by specifying the arrangements the convener proposes to enable persons to exercise their rights to speak or vote.

(8) In making the arrangements referred to in subsection (6) and in forming the opinion referred to in subsection (7)(b), the convener must have regard to the legitimate interests of the creditors, members or contributories and others attending the meeting in the efficient despatch of the business of the meeting.

(9) If—
(a) the notice of a meeting does not specify a place for the meeting,
(b) the convener is requested in accordance with the rules to specify a place for the meeting, and
(c) that request is made—
(i) in the case of a meeting of creditors or contributories, by not less than ten percent in value of the creditors or contributories, or
(ii) in the case of a meeting of members, by members representing not less than ten percent of the total voting rights of all the members having at the date of the request a right to vote at the meeting,

it shall be the duty of the convener to specify a place for the meeting.

(10) In this section, "the office-holder", in relation to a company, means—
(a) its liquidator, provisional liquidator, administrator, or administrative receiver, or
(b) where a voluntary arrangement in relation to the company is proposed or has taken effect under Part 1, the nominee or the supervisor of the voluntary arrangement.

Use of websites

246B. Use of websites

(1) Subject to subsection (2), where any provision of this Act or the rules requires the office-holder to give, deliver, furnish or send a notice or other document or information to any person, that requirement is satisfied by making the notice, document or information available on a website—

(a) in accordance with the rules, and

(b) in such circumstances as may be prescribed.

(2) This section does not apply where—

(a) a company is being wound up in Scotland, or

(b) a receiver is appointed under section 51 in Chapter 2 of Part 3.

(3) In this section, "the office-holder" means—

(a) the liquidator, provisional liquidator, administrator, or administrative receiver of a company, or

(b) where a voluntary arrangement in relation to a company is proposed or has taken effect under Part 1, the nominee or the supervisor of the voluntary arrangement.

PART VII
INTERPRETATION FOR FIRST GROUP OF PARTS

247. "Insolvency" and "go into liquidation"

(1) In this Group of Parts, except in so far as the context otherwise requires, "insolvency", in relation to a company, includes the approval of a voluntary arrangement under Part I, or the appointment of an administrator or administrative receiver.

(2) For the purposes of any provision in this Group of Parts, a company goes into liquidation if it passes a resolution for voluntary winding up or an order for its winding up is made by the court at a time when it has not already gone into liquidation by passing such a resolution.

(3) The reference to a resolution for voluntary winding up in subsection (2) includes a reference to a resolution which is deemed to occur by virtue of—

(a) paragraph 83(6)(b) of Schedule B1, or

(b) an order made following conversion of administration or a voluntary arrangement into winding up by virtue of Article 37 of the EC Regulation.

248. "Secured creditor", etc

In this Group of Parts, except in so far as the context otherwise requires—

(a) "secured creditor", in relation to a company, means a creditor of the company who holds in respect of his debt a security over property of the company, and "unsecured creditor" is to be read accordingly; and

(b) "security" means—

(i) in relation to England and Wales, any mortgage, charge, lien or other security, and

(ii) in relation to Scotland, any security (whether heritable or moveable), any floating charge and any right of lien or preference and any right of retention (other than a right of compensation or set off).

249. "Connected" with a company

For the purposes of any provision in this Group of Parts, a person is connected with a company if—

(a) he is a director or shadow director of the company or an associate of such a director or shadow director, or

(b) he is an associate of the company;

and "associate" has the meaning given by section 435 in Part XVIII of this Act.

250. "Member" of a company

For the purposes of any provision in this Group of Parts, a person who is not a member of a company but to whom shares in the company have been transferred, or transmitted by operation of law, is to be regarded as a member of the company, and references to a member or members are to be read accordingly.

251. Expressions used generally

In this Group of Parts, except in so far as the context otherwise requires—

"administrative receiver" means—

(a) an administrative receiver as defined by section 29(2) in Chapter I of Part III, or

(b) a receiver appointed under section 51 in Chapter II of that Part in a case where the whole (or substantially the whole) of the company's property is attached by the floating charge;

"agent" does not include a person's counsel acting as such;

"books and papers" and "books or papers" includes accounts, deeds, writing and documents;

"business day" means any day other than a Saturday, a Sunday, Christmas Day, Good Friday or a day which is a bank holiday in any part of Great Britain;

"chattel leasing agreement" means an agreement for the bailment or, in Scotland, the hiring of goods which is capable of subsisting for more than 3 months;

"contributory" has the meaning given by section 79;

"the court", in relation to a company, means a court having jurisdiction to wind up the company;

"director" includes any person occupying the position of director, by whatever name called;

"document" includes summons, notice, order and other legal process, and registers;

"floating charge" means a charge which, as created, was a floating charge and includes a floating charge within section 462 of the Companies Act (Scottish floating charges);

"the Gazette" means—

(a) as respects companies registered in England and Wales, the London Gazette;

(b) as respects companies registered in Scotland, the Edinburgh Gazette;

"officer", in relation to a body corporate, includes a director, manager or secretary;

"the official rate", in relation to interest, means the rate payable under section 189(4);

"prescribed" means prescribed by the rules;

"receiver", in the expression "receiver or manager", does not include a receiver appointed under section 51 in Chapter II of Part III;

"retention of title agreement" means an agreement for the sale of goods to a company, being an agreement—

(a) which does not constitute a charge on the goods, but

(b) under which, if the seller is not paid and the company is wound up, the seller will have priority over all other creditors of the company as respects the goods or any property representing the goods;

"the rules" means rules under section 411 in Part XV; and

"shadow director", in relation to a company, means a person in accordance with whose directions or instructions the directors of the company are accustomed to act (but so that a person is not deemed a shadow director by reason only that the directors act on advice given by him in a professional capacity).

THE SECOND GROUP OF PARTS
INSOLVENCY OF INDIVIDUALS; BANKRUPTCY

PART VIIA
DEBT RELIEF ORDERS

Preliminary

251A. Debt relief orders

(1) An individual who is unable to pay his debts may apply for an order under this Part ("a debt relief order") to be made in respect of his qualifying debts.

(2) In this Part "qualifying debt" means (subject to subsection (3)) a debt which—

(a) is for a liquidated sum payable either immediately or at some certain future time; and

(b) is not an excluded debt.

(3) A debt is not a qualifying debt to the extent that it is secured.

(4) In this Part "excluded debt" means a debt of any description prescribed for the purposes of this subsection.

Applications for a debt relief order

251B. Making of application

(1) An application for a debt relief order must be made to the official receiver through an approved intermediary.

(2) The application must include—

(a) a list of the debts to which the debtor is subject at the date of the application, specifying the amount of each debt (including any interest, penalty or other sum that has become payable in relation to that debt on or before that date) and the creditor to whom it is owed;

(b) details of any security held in respect of any of those debts; and

(c) such other information about the debtor's affairs (including his creditors, debts and liabilities and his income and assets) as may be prescribed.

(3) The rules may make further provision as to—

(a) the form of an application for a debt relief order;

(b) the manner in which an application is to be made; and

(c) information and documents to be supplied in support of an application.

(4) For the purposes of this Part an application is not to be regarded as having been made until—

(a) the application has been submitted to the official receiver; and

(b) any fee required in connection with the application by an order under section 415 has been paid to such person as the order may specify.

251C. Duty of official receiver to consider and determine application

(1) This section applies where an application for a debt relief order is made.

(2) The official receiver may stay consideration of the application until he has received answers to any queries raised with the debtor in relation to anything connected with the application.

(3) The official receiver must determine the application by—

(a) deciding whether to refuse the application;

(b) if he does not refuse it, by making a debt relief order in relation to the specified debts he is satisfied were qualifying debts of the debtor at the application date;

but he may only refuse the application if he is authorised or required to do so by any of the following provisions of this section.

(4) The official receiver may refuse the application if he considers that—

(a) the application does not meet all the requirements imposed by or under section 251B;

(b) any queries raised with the debtor have not been answered to the satisfaction of the official receiver within such time as he may specify when they are raised;

(c) the debtor has made any false representation or omission in making the application or on supplying any information or documents in support of it.

(5) The official receiver must refuse the application if he is not satisfied that—

(a) the debtor is an individual who is unable to pay his debts;

(b) at least one of the specified debts was a qualifying debt of the debtor at the application date;

(c) each of the conditions set out in Part 1 of Schedule 4ZA is met.

(6) The official receiver may refuse the application if he is not satisfied that each condition specified in Part 2 of Schedule 4ZA is met.

(7) If the official receiver refuses an application he must give reasons for his refusal to the debtor in the prescribed manner.

(8) In this section "specified debt" means a debt specified in the application.

251D. Presumptions applicable to the determination of an application

(1) The following presumptions are to apply to the determination of an application for a debt relief order.

(2) The official receiver must presume that the debtor is an individual who is unable to pay his debts at the determination date if—

(a) that appears to the official receiver to be the case at the application date from the information supplied in the application and he has no reason to believe that the information supplied is incomplete or inaccurate; and

(b) he has no reason to believe that, by virtue of a change in the debtor's financial circumstances since the application date, the debtor may be able to pay his debts.

(3) The official receiver must presume that a specified debt (of the amount specified in the application and owed to the creditor so specified) is a qualifying debt at the application date if—

(a) that appears to him to be the case from the information supplied in the application; and

(b) he has no reason to believe that the information supplied is incomplete or inaccurate.

(4) The official receiver must presume that the condition specified in paragraph 1 of Schedule 4ZA is met if—

(a) that appears to him to be the case from the information supplied in the application;

(b) any prescribed verification checks relating to the condition have been made; and

(c) he has no reason to believe that the information supplied is incomplete or inaccurate.

(5) The official receiver must presume that any other condition specified in Part 1 or 2 of Schedule 4ZA is met if—

(a) that appears to him to have been the case as at the application date from the information supplied in the application and he has no reason to believe that the information supplied is incomplete or inaccurate;

(b) any prescribed verification checks relating to the condition have been made; and

(c) he has no reason to believe that, by virtue of a change in circumstances since the application date, the condition may no longer be met.

(6) References in this section to information supplied in the application include information supplied to the official receiver in support of the application.

(7) In this section "specified debt" means a debt specified in the application.

Making and effect of debt relief order

251E. Making of debt relief orders

(1) This section applies where the official receiver makes a debt relief order on determining an application under section 251C

(2) The order must be made in the prescribed form.

(3) The order must include a list of the debts which the official receiver is satisfied were qualifying debts of the debtor at the application date, specifying the amount of the debt at that time and the creditor to whom it was then owed.

(4) The official receiver must—

(a) give a copy of the order to the debtor; and

(b) make an entry for the order in the register containing the prescribed information about the order or the debtor.

(5) The rules may make provision as to other steps to be taken by the official receiver or the debtor on the making of the order.

(6) Those steps may include in particular notifying each creditor to whom a qualifying debt specified in the order is owed of—

(a) the making of the order and its effect,

(b) the grounds on which a creditor may object under section 251K, and

(c) any other prescribed information.

(7) In this Part the date on which an entry relating to the making of a debt relief order is first made in the register is referred to as "the effective date".

251F. Effect of debt relief order on other debt management arrangements

(1) This section applies if—

(a) a debt relief order is made, and

(b) immediately before the order is made, other debt management arrangements are in force in respect of the debtor.

(2) The other debt management arrangements cease to be in force when the debt relief order is made.

(3) In this section "other debt management arrangements" means—

(a) an administration order under Part 6 of the County Courts Act 1984;

(b) an enforcement restriction order under Part 6A of that Act;

(c) a debt repayment plan arranged in accordance with a debt management scheme that is approved under Chapter 4 of Part 5 of the Tribunals, Courts and Enforcement Act 2007.

251G. Moratorium from qualifying debts

(1) A moratorium commences on the effective date for a debt relief order in relation to each qualifying debt specified in the order ("a specified qualifying debt").

(2) During the moratorium, the creditor to whom a specified qualifying debt is owed—

(a) has no remedy in respect of the debt, and

(b) may not—

(i) commence a creditor's petition in respect of the debt, or

(ii) otherwise commence any action or other legal proceedings against the debtor for the debt,

except with the permission of the court and on such terms as the court may impose.

(3) If on the effective date a creditor to whom a specified qualifying debt is owed has any such petition, action or other proceeding as mentioned in subsection (2)(b) pending in any court, the court may—

(a) stay the proceedings on the petition, action or other proceedings (as the case may be), or

(b) allow them to continue on such terms as the court thinks fit.

(4) In subsection (2)(a) and (b) references to the debt include a reference to any interest, penalty or other sum that becomes payable in relation to that debt after the application date.

(5) Nothing in this section affects the right of a secured creditor of the debtor to enforce his security.

251H. The moratorium period

(1) The moratorium relating to the qualifying debts specified in a debt relief order continues for the period of one year beginning with the effective date for the order, unless—

(a) the moratorium terminates early; or

(b) the moratorium period is extended by the official receiver under this section or by the court under section 251M.

(2) The official receiver may only extend the moratorium period for the purpose of—

(a) carrying out or completing an investigation under section 251K;

(b) taking any action he considers necessary (whether as a result of an investigation or otherwise) in relation to the order; or

(c) in a case where he has decided to revoke the order, providing the debtor with the opportunity to make arrangements for making payments towards his debts.

(3) The official receiver may not extend the moratorium period for the purpose mentioned in subsection (2)(a) without the permission of the court.

(4) The official receiver may not extend the moratorium period beyond the end of the period of three months beginning after the end of the initial period of one year mentioned in subsection (1).

(5) The moratorium period may be extended more than once, but any extension (whether by the official receiver or by the court) must be made before the moratorium would otherwise end.

(6) References in this Part to a moratorium terminating early are to its terminating before the end of what would otherwise be the moratorium period, whether on the revocation of the order or by virtue of any other enactment.

251I. Discharge from qualifying debts

(1) Subject as follows, at the end of the moratorium applicable to a debt relief order the debtor is discharged from all the qualifying debts specified in the order (including all interest, penalties and other sums which may have become payable in relation to those debts since the application date).

(2) Subsection (1) does not apply if the moratorium terminates early.

(3) Subsection (1) does not apply in relation to any qualifying debt which the debtor incurred in respect of any fraud or fraudulent breach of trust to which the debtor was a party.

(4) The discharge of the debtor under subsection (1) does not release any other person from—

(a) any liability (whether as partner or co-trustee of the debtor or otherwise) from which the debtor is released by the discharge; or

(b) any liability as surety for the debtor or as a person in the nature of such a surety.

(5) If the order is revoked by the court under section 251M after the end of the moratorium period, the qualifying debts specified in the order shall (so far as practicable) be treated as though subsection (1) had never applied to them.

Duties of debtor

251J. Providing assistance to official receiver etc

(1) The duties in this section apply to a debtor at any time after the making of an application by him for a debt relief order.

(2) The debtor must—

(a) give to the official receiver such information as to his affairs,

(b) attend on the official receiver at such times, and

(c) do all such other things,

as the official receiver may reasonably require for the purpose of carrying out his functions in relation to the application or, as the case may be, the debt relief order made as a result of the application.

(3) The debtor must notify the official receiver as soon as reasonably practicable if he becomes aware of—

(a) any error in, or omission from, the information supplied to the official receiver in, or in support of, the application;

(b) any change in his circumstances between the application date and the determination date that would affect (or would have affected) the determination of the application.

(4) The duties under subsections (2) and (3) apply after (as well as before) the determination of the application, for as long as the official receiver is able to exercise functions of the kind mentioned in subsection (2).

(5) If a debt relief order is made as a result of the application, the debtor must notify the official receiver as soon as reasonably practicable if—

(a) there is an increase in his income during the moratorium period applicable to the order;

(b) he acquires any property or any property is devolved upon him during that period;

(c) he becomes aware of any error in or omission from any information supplied by him to the official receiver after the determination date.

(6) A notification under subsection (3) or (5) must give the prescribed particulars (if any) of the matter being notified.

Objections, investigations and revocation

251K. Objections and investigations

(1) Any person specified in a debt relief order as a creditor to whom a specified qualifying debt is owed may object to—

(a) the making of the order;

(b) the inclusion of the debt in the list of the debtor's qualifying debts; or

(c) the details of the debt specified in the order.

(2) An objection under subsection (1) must be—

(a) made during the moratorium period relating to the order and within the prescribed period for objections;
(b) made to the official receiver in the prescribed manner;
(c) based on a prescribed ground;
(d) supported by any information and documents as may be prescribed;

and the prescribed period mentioned in paragraph (a) must not be less than 28 days after the creditor in question has been notified of the making of the order.

(3) The official receiver must consider every objection made to him under this section.

(4) The official receiver may—
(a) as part of his consideration of an objection, or
(b) on his own initiative,

carry out an investigation of any matter that appears to the official receiver to be relevant to the making of any decision mentioned in subsection (5) in relation to a debt relief order or the debtor.

(5) The decisions to which an investigation may be directed are—
(a) whether the order should be revoked or amended under section 251L;
(b) whether an application should be made to the court under section 251M; or
(c) whether any other steps should be taken in relation to the debtor.

(6) The power to carry out an investigation under this section is exercisable after (as well as during) the moratorium relating to the order.

(7) The official receiver may require any person to give him such information and assistance as he may reasonably require in connection with an investigation under this section.

(8) Subject to anything prescribed in the rules as to the procedure to be followed in carrying out an investigation under this section, an investigation may be carried out by the official receiver in such manner as he thinks fit.

251L. Power of official receiver to revoke or amend a debt relief order

(1) The official receiver may revoke or amend a debt relief order during the applicable moratorium period in the circumstances provided for by this section.

(2) The official receiver may revoke the order on the ground that—
(a) any information supplied to him by the debtor—
(i) in, or in support of, the application, or
(ii) after the determination date,
was incomplete, incorrect or otherwise misleading;
(b) the debtor has failed to comply with a duty under section 251J;
(c) a bankruptcy order has been made in relation to the debtor; or
(d) the debtor has made a proposal under Part 8 (or has notified the official receiver of his intention to do so).

(3) The official receiver may revoke the order on the ground that he should not have been satisfied—
(a) that the debts specified in the order were qualifying debts of the debtor as at the application date;
(b) that the conditions specified in Part 1 of Schedule 4ZA were met;
(c) that the conditions specified in Part 2 of that Schedule were met or that any failure to meet such a condition did not prevent his making the order.

(4) The official receiver may revoke the order on the ground that either or both of the conditions in paragraphs 7 and 8 of Schedule 4ZA (monthly surplus income and property) are not met at any time after the order was made.

For this purpose those paragraphs are to be read as if references to the determination date were references to the time in question.

(5) Where the official receiver decides to revoke the order, he may revoke it either—
(a) with immediate effect, or
(b) with effect from such date (not more than three months after the date of the decision) as he may specify.

(6) In considering when the revocation should take effect the official receiver must consider (in the light of the grounds on which the decision to revoke was made and all the other circumstances of the case) whether the debtor ought to be given the opportunity to make arrangements for making payments towards his debts.

(7) If the order has been revoked with effect from a specified date the official receiver may, if he thinks it appropriate to do so at any time before that date, revoke the order with immediate effect.

(8) The official receiver may amend a debt relief order for the purpose of correcting an error in or omission from anything specified in the order.

(9) But subsection (8) does not permit the official receiver to add any debts that were not specified in the application for the debt relief order to the list of qualifying debts.

(10) The rules may make further provision as to the procedure to be followed by the official receiver in the exercise of his powers under this section.

Role of the court

251M. Powers of court in relation to debt relief orders

(1) Any person may make an application to the court if he is dissatisfied by any act, omission or decision of the official receiver in connection with a debt relief order or an application for such an order.

(2) The official receiver may make an application to the court for directions or an order in relation to any matter arising in connection with a debt relief order or an application for such an order.

(3) The matters referred to in subsection (2) include, among other things, matters relating to the debtor's compliance with any duty arising under section 251J.

(4) An application under this section may, subject to anything in the rules, be made at any time.

(5) The court may extend the moratorium period applicable to a debt relief order for the purposes of determining an application under this section.

(6) On an application under this section the court may dismiss the application or do one or more of the following—

(a) quash the whole or part of any act or decision of the official receiver;

(b) give the official receiver directions (including a direction that he reconsider any matter in relation to which his act or decision has been quashed under paragraph (a));

(c) make an order for the enforcement of any obligation on the debtor arising by virtue of a duty under section 251J;

(d) extend the moratorium period applicable to the debt relief order;

(e) make an order revoking or amending the debt relief order;

(f) make an order under section 251N; or

(g) make such other order as the court thinks fit.

(7) An order under subsection (6)(e) for the revocation of a debt relief order—

(a) may be made during the moratorium period applicable to the debt relief order or at any time after that period has ended;

(b) may be made on the court's own motion if the court has made a bankruptcy order in relation to the debtor during that period;

(c) may provide for the revocation of the order to take effect on such terms and at such a time as the court may specify.

(8) An order under subsection (6)(e) for the amendment of a debt relief order may not add any debts that were not specified in the application for the debt relief order to the list of qualifying debts.

251N. Inquiry into debtor's dealings and property

(1) An order under this section may be made by the court on the application of the official receiver.

(2) An order under this section is an order summoning any of the following persons to appear before the court—

(a) the debtor;

(b) the debtor's spouse or former spouse or the debtor's civil partner or former civil partner;

(c) any person appearing to the court to be able to give information or assistance concerning the debtor or his dealings, affairs and property.

(3) The court may require a person falling within subsection (2)(c)—

(a) to provide a written account of his dealings with the debtor; or

(b) to produce any documents in his possession or under his control relating to the debtor or to the debtor's dealings, affairs or property.

(4) Subsection (5) applies where a person fails without reasonable excuse to appear before the court when he is summoned to do so by an order under this section.

(5) The court may cause a warrant to be issued to a constable or préscribed officer of the court—

(a) for the arrest of that person, and

(b) for the seizure of any records or other documents in that person's possession.

(6) The court may authorise a person arrested under such a warrant to be kept in custody, and anything seized under such a warrant to be held, in accordance with the rules, until that person is brought before the court under the warrant or until such other time as the court may order.

Offences

251O. False representations and omissions

(1) A person who makes an application for a debt relief order is guilty of an offence if he knowingly or recklessly makes any false representation or omission in making the application or providing any information or documents to the official receiver in support of the application.

(2) A person who makes an application for a debt relief order is guilty of an offence if—

(a) he intentionally fails to comply with a duty under section 251J(3) in connection with the application; or

(b) he knowingly or recklessly makes any false representation or omission in providing any information to the official receiver in connection with such a duty or otherwise in connection with the application.

(3) It is immaterial for the purposes of an offence under subsection (1) or (2) whether or not a debt relief order is made as a result of the application.

(4) A person in respect of whom a debt relief order is made is guilty of an offence if—

(a) he intentionally fails to comply with a duty under section 251J(5) in connection with the order; or

(b) he knowingly or recklessly makes any false representation or omission in providing information to the official receiver in connection with such a duty or otherwise in connection with the performance by the official receiver of functions in relation to the order.

(5) It is immaterial for the purposes of an offence under subsection (4)—

(a) whether the offence is committed during or after the moratorium period; and

(b) whether or not the order is revoked after the conduct constituting the offence takes place.

251P. Concealment or falsification of documents

(1) A person in respect of whom a debt relief order is made is guilty of an offence if, during the moratorium period in relation to that order—

(a) he does not provide, at the request of the official receiver, all his books, papers and other records of which he has possession or control and which relate to his affairs;

(b) he prevents the production to the official receiver of any books, papers or other records relating to his affairs;

(c) he conceals, destroys, mutilates or falsifies, or causes or permits the concealment, destruction, mutilation or falsification of, any books, papers or other records relating his affairs;

(d) he makes, or causes or permits the making of, any false entries in any book, document or record relating to his affairs; or

(e) he disposes of, or alters or makes any omission in, or causes or permits the disposal, altering or making of any omission in, any book, document or record relating to his affairs.

(2) A person in respect of whom a debt relief order is made is guilty of an offence if—

(a) he did anything falling within paragraphs (c) to (e) of subsection (1) during the period of 12 months ending with the application date; or

(b) he did anything falling within paragraphs (b) to (e) of subsection (1) after that date but before the effective date.

(3) A person is not guilty of an offence under this section if he proves that, in respect of the conduct constituting the offence, he had no intent to defraud or to conceal the state of his affairs.

(4) In its application to a trading record subsection (2)(a) has effect as if the reference to 12 months were a reference to two years.

(5) In subsection (4) "trading record" means a book, document or record which shows or explains the transactions or financial position of a person's business, including—

(a) a periodic record of cash paid and received,

(b) a statement of periodic stock-taking, and

(c) except in the case of goods sold by way of retail trade, a record of goods sold and purchased which identifies the buyer and seller or enables them to be identified.

(6) It is immaterial for the purposes of an offence under this section whether or not the debt relief order in question is revoked after the conduct constituting the offence takes place (but no offence is committed under this section by virtue of conduct occurring after the order is revoked).

251Q. Fraudulent disposal of property

(1) A person in respect of whom a debt relief order is made is guilty of an offence if he made or caused to be made any gift or transfer of his property during the period between—

(a) the start of the period of two years ending with the application date; and

(b) the end of the moratorium period.

(2) The reference in subsection (1) to making a transfer of any property includes causing or conniving at the levying of any execution against that property.

(3) A person is not guilty of an offence under this section if he proves that, in respect of the conduct constituting the offence, he had no intent to defraud or to conceal the state of his affairs.

(4) For the purposes of subsection (3) a person is to be taken to have proved that he had no such intent if—

(a) sufficient evidence is adduced to raise an issue as to whether he had such intent; and

(b) the contrary is not proved beyond reasonable doubt.

(5) It is immaterial for the purposes of this section whether or not the debt relief order in question is revoked after the conduct constituting an offence takes place (but no offence is committed by virtue of conduct occurring after the order is revoked).

251R. Fraudulent dealing with property obtained on credit

(1) A person in respect of whom a debt relief order is made is guilty of an offence if during the relevant period he disposed of any property which he had obtained on credit and, at the time he disposed of it, had not paid for it.

(2) Any other person is guilty of an offence if during the relevant period he acquired or received property from a person in respect of whom a debt relief order was made (the "debtor") knowing or believing—

(a) that the debtor owed money in respect of the property, and

(b) that the debtor did not intend, or was unlikely to be able, to pay the money he so owed.

(3) In subsections (1) and (2) "relevant period" means the period between—

(a) the start of the period of two years ending with the application date; and

(b) the determination date.

(4) A person is not guilty of an offence under subsection (1) or (2) if the disposal, acquisition or receipt of the property was in the ordinary course of a business carried on by the debtor at the time of the disposal, acquisition or receipt.

(5) In determining for the purposes of subsection (4) whether any property is disposed of, acquired or received in the ordinary course of a business carried on by the debtor, regard may be had, in particular, to the price paid for the property.

(6) A person is not guilty of an offence under subsection (1) if he proves that, in respect of the conduct constituting the offence, he had no intent to defraud or to conceal the state of his affairs.

(7) In this section references to disposing of property include pawning or pledging it; and references to acquiring or receiving property shall be read accordingly.

(8) It is immaterial for the purposes of this section whether or not the debt relief order in question is revoked after the conduct constituting an offence takes place (but no offence is committed by virtue of conduct occurring after the order is revoked).

251S. Obtaining credit or engaging in business

(1) A person in respect of whom a debt relief order is made is guilty of an offence if, during the relevant period—

(a) he obtains credit (either alone or jointly with any other person) without giving the person from whom he obtains the credit the relevant information about his status; or

(b) he engages directly or indirectly in any business under a name other than that in which the order was made without disclosing to all persons with whom he enters into any business transaction the name in which the order was made.

(2) For the purposes of subsection (1)(a) the relevant information about a person's status is the information that—

(a) a moratorium is in force in relation to the debt relief order,

(b) a debt relief restrictions order is in force in respect of him, or

(c) both a moratorium and a debt relief restrictions order is in force,

as the case may be.

(3) In subsection (1) "relevant period" means—

(a) the moratorium period relating to the debt relief order, or

(b) the period for which a debt relief restrictions order is in force in respect of the person in respect of whom the debt relief order is made, as the case may be.

(4) Subsection (1)(a) does not apply if the amount of the credit is less than the prescribed amount (if any).

(5) The reference in subsection (1)(a) to a person obtaining credit includes the following cases—

(a) where goods are bailed to him under a hire-purchase agreement, or agreed to be sold to him under a conditional sale agreement;

(b) where he is paid in advance (in money or otherwise) for the supply of goods or services.

251T. Offences: supplementary

(1) Proceedings for an offence under this Part may only be instituted by the Secretary of State or by or with the consent of the Director of Public Prosecutions.

(2) It is not a defence in proceedings for an offence under this Part that anything relied on, in whole or in part, as constituting the offence was done outside England and Wales.

(3) A person guilty of an offence under this Part is liable to imprisonment or a fine, or both (but see section 430).

Supplementary

251U. Approved intermediaries

(1) In this Part "approved intermediary" means an individual for the time being approved by a competent authority to act as an intermediary between a person wishing to make an application for a debt relief order and the official receiver.

(2) In this section "competent authority" means a person or body for the time being designated by the Secretary of State for the purposes of granting approvals under this section.

(3) Designation as a competent authority may be limited so as to permit the authority only to approve persons of a particular description.

(4) The Secretary of State may by regulations make provision as to—

(a) the procedure for designating persons or bodies as competent authorities;

(b) descriptions of individuals who are ineligible to be approved under this section;

(c) the procedure for granting approvals under this section;
(d) the withdrawal of designations or approvals under this section;
and provision made under paragraph (a) or (c) may include provision requiring the payment of fees.

(5) The rules may make provision about the activities to be carried out by an approved intermediary in connection with an application for a debt relief order, which may in particular include—
(a) assisting the debtor in making the application;
(b) checking that the application has been properly completed;
(c) sending the application to the official receiver.

(6) The rules may also make provision about other activities to be carried out by approved intermediaries.

(7) An approved intermediary may not charge a debtor any fee in connection with an application for a debt relief order.

(8) An approved intermediary is not liable to any person in damages for anything done or omitted to be done when acting (or purporting to act) as an approved intermediary in connection with a particular application by a debtor for a debt relief order.

(9) Subsection (8) does not apply if the act or omission was in bad faith.

(10) Regulations under subsection (4) shall be made by statutory instrument subject to annulment in pursuance of a resolution of either House of Parliament.

251V. Debt relief restrictions orders and undertakings

Schedule 4ZB (which makes provision about debt relief restrictions orders and debt relief restrictions undertakings) has effect.

251W. Register of debt relief orders etc

The Secretary of State must maintain a register of matters relating to—
(a) debt relief orders;
(b) debt relief restrictions orders; and
(c) debt relief restrictions undertakings.

251X. Interpretation

(1) In this Part—

"the application date", in relation to a debt relief order or an application for a debt relief order, means the date on which the application for the order is made to the official receiver;

"approved intermediary" has the meaning given in section 251U(1);

"debt relief order" means an order made by the official receiver under this Part;

"debtor" means—
(a) in relation to an application for a debt relief order, the applicant; and
(b) in relation to a debt relief order, the person in relation to whom the order is made;

"debt relief restrictions order" and "debt relief restrictions undertaking" means an order made, or an undertaking accepted, under Schedule 4ZB;

"the determination date", in relation to a debt relief order or an application for a debt relief order, means the date on which the application for the order is determined by the official receiver;

"the effective date" has the meaning given in section 251E(7);

"excluded debt" is to be construed in accordance with section 251A;

"moratorium" and "moratorium period" are to be construed in accordance with sections 251G and 251H;

"qualifying debt", in relation to a debtor, has the meaning given in section 251A(2);

"the register" means the register maintained under section 251W;

"specified qualifying debt" has the meaning given in section 251G(1).

(2) In this Part references to a creditor specified in a debt relief order as the person to whom a qualifying debt is owed by the debtor include a reference to any person to whom the right to claim the whole or any part of the debt has passed, by assignment or operation of law, after the date of the application for the order.

PART VIII
INDIVIDUAL VOLUNTARY ARRANGEMENTS

Moratorium for insolvent debtor

252. Interim order of court

(1) In the circumstances specified below, the court may in the case of a debtor (being an individual) make an interim order under this section.

(2) An interim order has the effect that, during the period for which it is in force—

(a) no bankruptcy petition relating to the debtor may be presented or proceeded with,

(aa) no landlord or other person to whom rent is payable may exercise any right of forfeiture by peaceable re-entry in relation to premises let to the debtor in respect of a failure by the debtor to comply with any term or condition of his tenancy of such premises, except with the leave of the court, and

(b) no other proceedings, and no execution or other legal process, may be commenced or continued and no distress may be levied against the debtor or his property except with the leave of the court.

253. Application for interim order

(1) Application to the court for an interim order may be made where the debtor intends to make a proposal under this Part, that is, a proposal to his creditors for a composition in satisfaction of his debts or a scheme of arrangement of his affairs (from here on referred to, in either case, as a "voluntary arrangement").

(2) The proposal must provide for some person ("the nominee") to act in relation to the voluntary arrangement either as trustee or otherwise for the purpose of supervising its implementation and the nominee must be a person who is qualified to act as an insolvency practitioner, or authorised to act as nominee, in relation to the voluntary arrangement.

(3) Subject as follows, the application may be made—

(a) if the debtor is an undischarged bankrupt, by the debtor, the trustee of his estate, or the official receiver, and

(b) in any other case, by the debtor.

(4) An application shall not be made under subsection (3)(a) unless the debtor has given notice of the proposal to the official receiver and, if there is one, the trustee of his estate.

(5) An application shall not be made while a bankruptcy petition presented by the debtor is pending, if the court has, under section 273 below, appointed an insolvency practitioner to inquire into the debtor's affairs and report.

254. Effect of application

(1) At any time when an application under section 253 for an interim order is pending,

(a) no landlord or other person to whom rent is payable may exercise any right of forfeiture by peaceable re-entry in relation to premises let to the debtor in respect of a failure by the debtor to comply with any term or condition of his tenancy of such premises, except with the leave of the court, and

(b) the court may forbid the levying of any distress on the debtor's property or its subsequent sale, or both, and stay any action, execution or other legal process against the property or person of the debtor.

(2) Any court in which proceedings are pending against an individual may, on proof that an application under that section has been made in respect of that individual, either stay the proceedings or allow them to continue on such terms as it thinks fit.

255. Cases in which interim order can be made

(1) The court shall not make an interim order on an application under section 253 unless it is satisfied—

(a) that the debtor intends to make a proposal under this Part;

(b) that on the day of the making of the application the debtor was an undischarged bankrupt or was able to petition for his own bankruptcy;

(c) that no previous application has been made by the debtor for an interim order in the period of 12 months ending with that day; and

(d) that the nominee under the debtor's proposal … is willing to act in relation to the proposal.

(2) The court may make an order if it thinks that it would be appropriate to do so for the purpose of facilitating the consideration and implementation of the debtor's proposal.

(3) Where the debtor is an undischarged bankrupt, the interim order may contain provision as to the conduct of the bankruptcy, and the administration of the bankrupt's estate, during the period for which the order is in force.

(4) Subject as follows, the provision contained in an interim order by virtue of subsection (3) may include provision staying proceedings in the bankruptcy or modifying any provision in this Group of Parts, and any provision of the rules in their application to the debtor's bankruptcy.

(5) An interim order shall not, in relation to a bankrupt, make provision relaxing or removing any of the requirements of provisions in this Group of Parts, or of the rules, unless the court is satisfied that that provision is unlikely to result in any significant diminution in, or in the value of, the debtor's estate for the purposes of the bankruptcy.

(6) Subject to the following provisions of this Part, and interim order made on an application under section 253 ceases to have effect at the end of the period of 14 days beginning with the day after the making of the order.

256. Nominee's report on debtor's proposal

(1) Where an interim order has been made on an application under section 253, the nominee shall, before the order ceases to have effect, submit a report to the court stating—

(a) whether, in his opinion, the voluntary arrangement which the debtor is proposing has a reasonable prospect of being approved and implemented,

(aa) whether, in his opinion, a meeting of the debtor's creditors should be summoned to consider the debtor's proposal, and

(b) if in his opinion such a meeting should be summoned, the date on which, and time and place at which, he proposes the meeting should be held.

(2) For the purpose of enabling the nominee to prepare his report the debtor shall submit to the nominee—

(a) a document setting out the terms of the voluntary arrangement which the debtor is proposing, and

(b) a statement of his affairs containing—

(i) such particulars of his creditors and of his debts and other liabilities and of his assets as may be prescribed, and

(ii) such other information as may be prescribed.

(3) The court may—

(a) on an application made by the debtor in a case where the nominee has failed to submit the report required by this section or has died, or

(b) on an application made by the debtor or the nominee in a case where it is impracticable or inappropriate for the nominee to continue to act as such,

direct that the nominee shall be replaced as such by another person qualified to act as an insolvency practitioner, or authorised to act as nominee, in relation to the voluntary arrangement.

(3A) The court may, on an application made by the debtor in a case where the nominee has failed to submit the report required by this section, direct that the interim order shall continue, or (if it has ceased to have effect) be renewed, for such further period as the court may specify in the direction.

(4) The court may, on the application of the nominee, extend the period for which the interim order has effect so as to enable the nominee to have more time to prepare his report.

(5) If the court is satisfied on receiving the nominee's report that a meeting of the debtor's creditors should be summoned to consider the debtor's proposal, the court shall direct that the period for

which the interim order has effect shall be extended, for such further period as it may specify in the direction, for the purpose of enabling the debtor's proposal to be considered by his creditors in accordance with the following provisions of this Part.

(6) The court may discharge the interim order if it is satisfied, on the application of the nominee—

(a) that the debtor has failed to comply with his obligations under subsection (2), or

(b) that for any other reason it would be inappropriate for a meeting of the debtor's creditors to be summoned to consider the debtor's proposal.

Procedure where no interim order made

256A. Debtor's proposal and nominee's report

(1) This section applies where a debtor (being an individual)—

(a) intends to make a proposal under this Part (but an interim order has not been made in relation to the proposal and no application for such an order is pending), and

(b) if he is an undischarged bankrupt, has given notice of the proposal to the official receiver and, if there is one, the trustee of his estate,

unless a bankruptcy petition presented by the debtor is pending and the court has, under section 273, appointed an insolvency practitioner to inquire into the debtor's affairs and report.

(2) For the purpose of enabling the nominee to prepare a report under subsection (3), the debtor shall submit to the nominee—

(a) a document setting out the terms of the voluntary arrangement which the debtor is proposing, and

(b) a statement of his affairs containing—

(i) such particulars of his creditors and of his debts and other liabilities and of his assets as may be prescribed, and

(ii) such other information as may be prescribed.

(3) If the nominee is of the opinion that the debtor is an undischarged bankrupt, or is able to petition for his own bankruptcy, the nominee shall, within 14 days (or such longer period as the court may allow) after receiving the document and statement mentioned in subsection (2), submit a report to the debtor's creditors stating—

(a) whether, in his opinion, the voluntary arrangement which the debtor is proposing has a reasonable prospect of being approved and implemented,

(b) whether, in his opinion, a meeting of the debtor's creditors should be summoned to consider the debtor's proposal, and

(c) if in his opinion such a meeting should be summoned, the date on which, and time and place at which, he proposes the meeting should be held.

(4) The court may—

(a) on an application made by the debtor in a case where the nominee has failed to submit the report required by this section or has died, or

(b) on an application made by the debtor or the nominee in a case where it is impracticable or inappropriate for the nominee to continue to act as such,

direct that the nominee shall be replaced as such by another person qualified to act as an insolvency practitioner, or authorised to act as nominee, in relation to the voluntary arrangement.

(5) The court may, on an application made by the nominee, extend the period within which the nominee is to submit his report.

Creditors' meeting

257. Summoning of creditors' meeting

(1) Where it has been reported to the court under section 256 or to the debtor's creditors under section 256A that a meeting of debtor's creditors should be summoned, the nominee (or the nominee's replacement under section 256(3) or 256A(4)) shall summon that meeting for the time, date and place proposed in the nominee's report unless, in the case of a report to which section 256 applies, the court otherwise directs.

(2) The persons to be summoned to the meeting are every creditor of the debtor of whose claim and address the person summoning the meeting is aware.

(3) For this purpose the creditors of a debtor who is an undischarged bankrupt include—

(a) every person who is a creditor of the bankrupt in respect of a bankruptcy debt, and

(b) every person who would be such a creditor if the bankruptcy had commenced on the day on which notice of the meeting is given.

Consideration and implementation of debtor's proposal

258. Decisions of creditors' meeting

(1) A creditors' meeting summoned under section 257 shall decide whether to approve the proposed voluntary arrangement.

(2) The meeting may approve the proposed voluntary arrangement with modifications, but shall not do so unless the debtor consents to each modification.

(3) The modifications subject to which the proposed voluntary arrangement may be approved may include one conferring the functions proposed to be conferred on the nominee on another person qualified to act as an insolvency practitioner or authorised to act as nominee, in relation to the voluntary arrangement.

But they shall not include any modification by virtue of which the proposal ceases to be a proposal under this Part.

(4) The meeting shall not approve any proposal or modification which affects the right of a secured creditor of the debtor to enforce his security, except with the concurrence of the creditor concerned.

(5) Subject as follows, the meeting shall not approve any proposal or modification under which—

(a) any preferential debt of the debtor is to be paid otherwise than in priority to such of his debts as are not preferential debts, or

(b) a preferential creditor of the debtor is to be paid an amount in respect of a preferential debt that bears to that debt a smaller proportion than is borne to another preferential debt by the amount that is to be paid in respect of that other debt.

However, the meeting may approve such a proposal or modification with the concurrence of the preferential creditor concerned.

(6) Subject as above, the meeting shall be conducted in accordance with the rules.

(7) In this section "preferential debt" has the meaning given by section 386 in Part XII; and "preferential creditor" is to be construed accordingly.

259. Report of decisions to court

(1) After the conclusion in accordance with the rules of the meeting summoned under section 257, the chairman of the meeting shall—

(a) give notice of the result of the meeting to such persons as may be prescribed, and

(b) where the meeting was summoned under section 257 pursuant to a report to the court under section 256(1)(aa), report the result of it to the court.

(2) If the report is that the meeting has declined (with or without modifications) to approve the voluntary arrangement proposed under section 256, the court may discharge any interim order which is in force in relation to the debtor.

260. Effect of approval

(1) This section has effect where the meeting summoned under section 257 approves the proposed voluntary arrangement (with or without modifications).

(2) The approved arrangement—

(a) takes effect as if made by the debtor at the meeting, and

(b) binds every person who in accordance with the rules—

(i) was entitled to vote at the meeting (whether or not he was present or represented at it), or

(ii) would have been so entitled if he had had notice of it, as if he were a party to the arrangement.

(2A) If—

(a) when the arrangement ceases to have effect any amount payable under the arrangement to a person bound by virtue of subsection (2)(b)(ii) has not been paid, and

(b) the arrangement did not come to an end prematurely,

the debtor shall at that time become liable to pay to that person the amount payable under the arrangement.

(3) The Deeds of Arrangement Act 1914 does not apply to the approved voluntary arrangement.

(4) Any interim order in force in relation to the debtor immediately before the end of the period of 28 days beginning with the day on which the report with respect to the creditors' meeting was made, to the court under section 259 ceases to have effect at the end of that period.

This subsection applies except to such extent as the court may direct for the purposes of any application under section 262 below.

(5) Where proceedings on a bankruptcy petition have been stayed by an interim order which ceases to have effect under subsection (4), the petition is deemed, unless the court otherwise orders, to have been dismissed.

261. Additional effect on undischarged bankrupt

(1) This section applies where—

(a) the creditors' meeting summoned under section 257 approves the proposed voluntary arrangement (with or without modifications), and

(b) the debtor is an undischarged bankrupt.

(2) Where this section applies the court shall annul the bankruptcy order on an application made—

(a) by the bankrupt, or

(b) where the bankrupt has not made an application within the prescribed period, by the official receiver.

(3) An application under subsection (2) may not be made—

(a) during the period specified in section 262(3)(a) during which the decision of the creditors' meeting can be challenged by application under section 262,

(b) while an application under that section is pending, or

(c) while an appeal in respect of an application under that section is pending or may be brought.

(4) Where this section applies the court may give such directions about the conduct of the bankruptcy and the administration of the bankrupt's estate as it thinks appropriate for facilitating the implementation of the approved voluntary arrangement.

262. Challenge of meeting's decision

(1) Subject to this section, an application to the court may be made, by any of the persons specified below, on one or both of the following grounds, namely—

(a) that a voluntary arrangement approved by a creditors' meeting summoned under section 257 unfairly prejudices the interests of a creditor of the debtor;

(b) that there has been some material irregularity at or in relation to such a meeting.

(2) The persons who may apply under this section are—

(a) the debtor;

(b) a person who—

(i) was entitled, in accordance with the rules, to vote at the creditors' meeting, or

(ii) would have been so entitled if he had had notice of it;

(c) the nominee (or his replacement under section 256(3), 256A(4) or 258(3)); and

(d) if the debtor is an undischarged bankrupt, the trustee of his estate or the official receiver.

(3) An application under this section shall not be made—

(a) after the end of the period of 28 days beginning with the day on which the report of the creditors' meeting was made to the court under section 259, or

(b) in the case of a person who was not given notice of the creditors' meeting, after the end of the period of 28 days beginning with the day on which he became aware that the meeting had taken place,

but (subject to that) an application made by a person within subsection (2)(b)(ii) on the ground that the arrangement prejudices his interests may be made after the arrangement has ceased to have effect, unless it has come to an end prematurely.

(4) Where on an application under this section the court is satisfied as to either of the grounds mentioned in subsection (1), it may do one or both of the following, namely—

(a) revoke or suspend any approval given by the meeting;

(b) give a direction to any person for the summoning of a further meeting of the debtor's creditors to consider any revised proposal he may make or, in a case falling within subsection (1)(b), to reconsider his original proposal.

(5) Where at any time after giving a direction under subsection (4)(b) for the summoning of a meeting to consider a revised proposal the court is satisfied that the debtor does not intend to submit such a proposal, the court shall revoke the direction and revoke or suspend any approval given at the previous meeting.

(6) Where the court gives a direction under subsection (4)(b), it may also give a direction continuing or, as the case may require, renewing, for such period as may be specified in the direction, the effect in relation to the debtor of any interim order.

(7) In any case where the court, on an application made under this section with respect to a creditors' meeting, gives a direction under subsection (4)(b) or revokes or suspends an approval under subsection (4)(a) or (5), the court may give such supplemental directions as it thinks fit and, in particular, directions with respect to—

(a) things done since the meeting under any voluntary arrangement approved by the meeting, and

(b) such things done since the meeting as could not have been done if an interim order had been in force in relation to the debtor when they were done.

(8) Except in pursuance of the preceding provisions of this section, an approval given at a creditors' meeting summoned under section 257 is not invalidated by any irregularity at or in relation to the meeting.

262A. False representations etc

(1) If for the purpose of obtaining the approval of his creditors to a proposal for a voluntary arrangement, the debtor—

(a) makes any false representation, or

(b) fraudulently does, or omits to do, anything,

he commits an offence.

(2) Subsection (1) applies even if the proposal is not approved.

(3) A person guilty of an offence under this section is liable to imprisonment or a fine, or both.

262B. Prosecution of delinquent debtors

(1) This section applies where a voluntary arrangement approved by a creditors' meeting summoned under section 257 has taken effect.

(2) If it appears to the nominee or supervisor that the debtor has been guilty of any offence in connection with the arrangement for which he is criminally liable, he shall forthwith—

(a) report the matter to the Secretary of State, and

(b) provide the Secretary of State with such information and give the Secretary of State such access to and facilities for inspecting and taking copies of documents (being information or documents in his possession or under his control and relating to the matter in question) as the Secretary of State requires.

(3) Where a prosecuting authority institutes criminal proceedings following any report under subsection (2), the nominee or, as the case may be, supervisor shall give the authority all assistance in connection with the prosecution which he is reasonably able to give.

For this purpose, "prosecuting authority" means the Director of Public Prosecutions or the Secretary of State.

(4) The court may, on the application of the prosecuting authority, direct a nominee or supervisor to comply with subsection (3) if he has failed to do so.

262C. Arrangements coming to an end prematurely

For the purposes of this Part, a voluntary arrangement approved by a creditors' meeting summoned under section 257 comes to an end prematurely if, when it ceases to have effect, it has not been fully implemented in respect of all persons bound by the arrangement by virtue of section 260(2)(b)(i).

263. Implementation and supervision of approved voluntary arrangement

(1) This section applies where a voluntary arrangement approved by a creditors' meeting summoned under section 257 has taken effect.

(2) The person who is for the time being carrying out, in relation to the voluntary arrangement, the functions conferred by virtue of the approval on the nominee (or his replacement under section 256(3), 256A(4) or 258(3)) shall be known as the supervisor of the voluntary arrangement.

(3) If the debtor, any of his creditors or any other person is dissatisfied by any act, omission or decision of the supervisor, he may apply to the court; and on such an application the court may—

(a) confirm, reverse or modify any act or decision of the supervisor,

(b) give him directions, or

(c) make such other order as it thinks fit.

(4) The supervisor may apply to the court for directions in relation to any particular matter arising under the voluntary arrangement.

(5) The court may, whenever—

(a) it is expedient to appoint a person to carry out the functions of the supervisor, and

(b) it is inexpedient, difficult or impracticable for an appointment to be made without the assistance of the court,

make an order appointing a person who is qualified to act as an insolvency practitioner or authorised to act as supervisor, in relation to the voluntary arrangement, either in substitution for the existing supervisor or to fill a vacancy.

This is without prejudice to section 41(2) of the Trustee Act 1925 (power of court to appoint trustees of deeds of arrangement).

(6) The power conferred by subsection (5) is exercisable so as to increase the number of persons exercising the functions of the supervisor or, where there is more than one person exercising those functions, so as to replace one or more of those persons.

Fast-track voluntary arrangement

263A. Availability

Section 263B applies where an individual debtor intends to make a proposal to his creditors for a voluntary arrangement and—

(a) the debtor is an undischarged bankrupt,

(b) the official receiver is specified in the proposal as the nominee in relation to the voluntary arrangement, and

(c) no interim order is applied for under section 253.

263B. Decision

(1) The debtor may submit to the official receiver—

(a) a document setting out the terms of the voluntary arrangement which the debtor is proposing, and

(b) a statement of his affairs containing such particulars as may be prescribed of his creditors, debts, other liabilities and assets and such other information as may be prescribed.

(2) If the official receiver thinks that the voluntary arrangement proposed has a reasonable prospect of being approved and implemented, he may make arrangements for inviting creditors to decide whether to approve it.

(3) For the purposes of subsection (2) a person is a "creditor" only if—

(a) he is a creditor of the debtor in respect of a bankruptcy debt, and

(b) the official receiver is aware of his claim and his address.

(4) Arrangements made under subsection (2)—

(a) must include the provision to each creditor of a copy of the proposed voluntary arrangement,

(b) must include the provision to each creditor of information about the criteria by reference to which the official receiver will determine whether the creditors approve or reject the proposed voluntary arrangement, and

(c) may not include an opportunity for modifications to the proposed voluntary arrangement to be suggested or made.

(5) Where a debtor submits documents to the official receiver under subsection (1) no application under section 253 for an interim order may be made in respect of the debtor until the official receiver has—

(a) made arrangements as described in subsection (2), or

(b) informed the debtor that he does not intend to make arrangements (whether because he does not think the voluntary arrangement has a reasonable prospect of being approved and implemented or because he declines to act).

263C. Result

As soon as is reasonably practicable after the implementation of arrangements under section 263B(2) the official receiver shall notify the Secretary of State whether the proposed voluntary arrangement has been approved or rejected.

263D. Approval of voluntary arrangement

(1) This section applies where the official receiver notifies the Secretary of State under section 263C that a proposed voluntary arrangement has been approved.

(2) The voluntary arrangement—

(a) takes effect,

(b) binds the debtor, and

(c) binds every person who was entitled to participate in the arrangements made under section 263B(2).

(3) The court shall annul the bankruptcy order in respect of the debtor on an application made by the official receiver.

(4) An application under subsection (3) may not be made—

(a) during the period specified in section 263F(3) during which the voluntary arrangement can be challenged by application under section 263F(2),

(b) while an application under that section is pending, or

(c) while an appeal in respect of an application under that section is pending or may be brought.

(5) The court may give such directions about the conduct of the bankruptcy and the administration of the bankrupt's estate as it thinks appropriate for facilitating the implementation of the approved voluntary arrangement.

(6) The Deeds of Arrangement Act 1914 does not apply to the voluntary arrangement.

(7) A reference in this Act or another enactment to a voluntary arrangement approved under this Part includes a reference to a voluntary arrangement which has effect by virtue of this section.

263E. Implementation

Section 263 shall apply to a voluntary arrangement which has effect by virtue of section 263D(2) as it applies to a voluntary arrangement approved by a creditors' meeting.

263F. Revocation

(1) The court may make an order revoking a voluntary arrangement which has effect by virtue of section 263D(2) on the ground—

(a) that it unfairly prejudices the interests of a creditor of the debtor, or

(b) that a material irregularity occurred in relation to the arrangements made under section 263B(2).

(2) An order under subsection (1) may be made only on the application of—

(a) the debtor,

(b) a person who was entitled to participate in the arrangements made under section 263B(2),

(c) the trustee of the bankrupt's estate, or

(d) the official receiver.

(3) An application under subsection (2) may not be made after the end of the period of 28 days beginning with the date on which the official receiver notifies the Secretary of State under section 263C.

(4) But a creditor who was not made aware of the arrangements under section 263B(2) at the time when they were made may make an application under subsection (2) during the period of 28 days beginning with the date on which he becomes aware of the voluntary arrangement.

263G. Offences

(1) Section 262A shall have effect in relation to obtaining approval to a proposal for a voluntary arrangement under section 263D.

(2) Section 262B shall have effect in relation to a voluntary arrangement which has effect by virtue of section 263D(2) (for which purposes the words "by a creditors' meeting summoned under section 257" shall be disregarded).

PART IX
BANKRUPTCY

CHAPTER I
BANKRUPTCY PETITIONS; BANKRUPTCY ORDERS

Preliminary

264. Who may present a bankruptcy petition

(1) A petition for a bankruptcy order to be made against an individual may be presented to the court in accordance with the following provisions of this Part—

(a) by one of the individual's creditors or jointly by more than one of them,

(b) by the individual himself,

(ba) by a temporary administrator (within the meaning of Article 38 of the EC Regulation),

(bb) by a liquidator (within the meaning of Article 2(b) of the EC Regulation) appointed in proceedings by virtue of Article 3(1) of the EC Regulation,

(c) by the supervisor of, or any person (other than the individual) who is for the time being bound by, a voluntary arrangement proposed by the individual and approved under Part VIII, *or*

(d) where a criminal bankruptcy order has been made against the individual, by the Official Petitioner or by any person specified in the order in pursuance of section 39(3)(b) of the Powers of Criminal Courts Act 1973.

(2) Subject to those provisions, the court may make a bankruptcy order on any such petition.

Note. Subsection (1)(d) and the italicized word preceding it are repealed by the Criminal Justice Act 1988, s. 170(2), Sch. 16, as from a day to be appointed.

265. Conditions to be satisfied in respect of debtor

(1) A bankruptcy petition shall not be presented to the court under section 264(1)(a) or (b) unless the debtor—

(a) is domiciled in England and Wales,
(b) is personally present in England and Wales on the day on which the petition is presented, or
(c) at any time in the period of 3 years ending with that day—
(i) has been ordinarily resident, or has had a place of residence, in England and Wales, or
(ii) has carried on business in England and Wales.

(2) The reference in subsection (1)(c) to an individual carrying on business includes—
(a) the carrying on of business by a firm or partnership of which the individual is a member, and
(b) the carrying on of business by an agent or manager for the individual or for such a firm or partnership.

(3) This section is subject to Article 3 of the EC Regulation.

266. Other preliminary conditions

(1) Where a bankruptcy petition relating to an individual is presented by a person who is entitled to present a petition under two or more paragraphs of section 264(1), the petition is to be treated for the purposes of this Part as a petition under such one of those paragraphs as may be specified in the petition.

(2) A bankruptcy petition shall not be withdrawn without the leave of the court.

(3) The court has a general power, if it appears to it appropriate to do so on the grounds that there has been a contravention of the rules or for any other reason, to dismiss a bankruptcy petition or to stay proceedings on such a petition; and, where it stays proceedings on a petition, it may do so on such terms and conditions as it thinks fit.

(4) Without prejudice to subsection (3), where a petition under section 264(1)(a), (b) or (c) in respect of an individual is pending at a time when a criminal bankruptcy order is made against him, or is presented after such an order has been so made, the court may on the application of the Official Petitioner dismiss the petition if it appears to it appropriate to do so.

Note. Subsection (4) is repealed by the Criminal Justice Act 1988, s. 170(2), Sch. 16, as from a day to be appointed.

Creditor's petition

267. Grounds of creditor's petition

(1) A creditor's petition must be in respect of one or more debts owed by the debtor, and the petitioning creditor or each of the petitioning creditors must be a person to whom the debt or (as the case may be) at least one of the debts is owed.

(2) Subject to the next three sections, a creditor's petition may be presented to the court in respect of a debt or debts only if, at the time the petition is presented—
(a) the amount of the debt, or the aggregate amount of the debts, is equal to or exceeds the bankruptcy level,
(b) the debt, or each of the debts, is for a liquidated sum payable to the petitioning creditor, or one or more of the petitioning creditors, either immediately or at some certain, future time, and is unsecured,
(c) the debt, or each of the debts, is a debt which the debtor appears either to be unable to pay or to have no reasonable prospect of being able to pay, and
(d) there is no outstanding application to set aside a statutory demand served (under section 268 below) in respect of the debt or any of the debts.

(3) A debt is not to be regarded for the purposes of subsection (2) as a debt for a liquidated sum by reason only that the amount of the debt is specified in a criminal bankruptcy order.

(4) "The bankruptcy level" is £750; but the Secretary of State may by order in a statutory instrument substitute any amount specified in the order for that amount or (as the case may be) for the amount which by virtue of such an order is for the time being the amount of the bankruptcy level.

(5) An order shall not be made under subsection (4) unless a draft of it has been laid before, and approved by a resolution of, each House of Parliament.

Note. Subsection (3) is repealed by the Criminal Justice Act 1988, s. 170(2), Sch. 16, as from a day to be appointed.

268. Definition of "inability to pay", etc; the statutory demand

(1) For the purposes of section 267(2)(c), the debtor appears to be unable to pay a debt if, but only if, the debt is payable immediately and either—

(a) the petitioning creditor to whom the debt is owed has served on the debtor a demand (known as "the statutory demand") in the prescribed form requiring him to pay the debt or to secure or compound for it to the satisfaction of the creditor, at least 3 weeks have elapsed since the demand was served and the demand has been neither complied with nor set aside in accordance with the rules, or

(b) execution or other process issued in respect of the debt on a judgment or order of any court in favour of the petitioning creditor, or one or more of the petitioning creditors to whom the debt is owed, has been returned unsatisfied in whole or in part.

(2) For the purposes of section 267(2)(c) the debtor appears to have no reasonable prospect of being able to pay a debt if, but only if, the debt is not immediately payable and—

(a) the petitioning creditor to whom it is owed has served on the debtor a demand (also known as "the statutory demand") in the prescribed form requiring him to establish to the satisfaction of the creditor that there is a reasonable prospect that the debtor will be able to pay the debt when it falls due,

(b) at least 3 weeks have elapsed since the demand was served, and

(c) the demand has been neither complied with nor set aside in accordance with the rules.

269. Creditor with security

(1) A debt which is the debt, or one of the debts, in respect of which a creditor's petition is presented need not be unsecured if either—

(a) the petition contains a statement by the person having the right to enforce the security that he is willing, in the event of a bankruptcy order being made, to give up his security for the benefit of all the bankrupt's creditors, or

(b) the petition is expressed not to be made in respect of the secured part of the debt and contains a statement by that person of the estimated value at the date of the petition of the security for the secured part of the debt.

(2) In a case falling within subsection (1)(b) the secured and unsecured parts of the debt are to be treated for the purposes of sections 267 and 270 as separate debts.

270. Expedited petition

In the case of a creditor's petition presented wholly or partly in respect of a debt which is the subject of a statutory demand under section 268, the petition may be presented before the end of the 3-week period there mentioned if there is a serious possibility that the debtor's property or the value of any of his property will be significantly diminished during that period and the petition contains a statement to that effect.

271. Proceedings on creditor's petition

(1) The court shall not make a bankruptcy order on a creditor's petition unless it is satisfied that the debt, or one of the debts, in respect of which the petition was presented is either—

(a) a debt which, having been payable at the date of the petition or having since become payable, has been neither paid nor secured or compounded for, or

(b) a debt which the debtor has no reasonable prospect of being able to pay when it falls due.

(2) In a case in which the petition contains such a statement as is required by section 270, the court shall not make a bankruptcy order until at least 3 weeks have elapsed since the service of any statutory demand under section 268.

(3) The court may dismiss the petition if it is satisfied that the debtor is able to pay all his debts or is satisfied—

(a) that the debtor has made an offer to secure or compound for a debt in respect of which the petition is presented,

(b) that the acceptance of that offer would have required the dismissal of the petition, and

(c) that the offer has been unreasonably refused;

and, in determining for the purposes of this subsection whether the debtor is able to pay all his debts, the court shall take into account his contingent and prospective liabilities.

(4) In determining for the purposes of this section what constitutes a reasonable prospect that a debtor will be able to pay a debt when it falls due, it is to be assumed that the prospect given by the facts and other matters known to the creditor at the time he entered into the transaction resulting in the debt was a reasonable prospect.

(5) Nothing in sections 267 to 271 prejudices the power of the court, in accordance with the rules, to authorise a creditor's petition to be amended by the omission of any creditor or debt and to be proceeded with as if things done for the purposes of those sections had been done only by or in relation to the remaining creditors or debts.

Debtor's petition

272. Grounds of debtor's petition

(1) A debtor's petition may be presented to the court only on the grounds that the debtor is unable to pay his debts.

(2) The petition shall be accompanied by a statement of the debtor's affairs containing—

(a) such particulars of the debtor's creditors and of his debts and other liabilities and of his assets as may be prescribed, and

(b) such other information as may be prescribed.

273. Appointment of insolvency practitioner by the court

(1) Subject to the next section, on the hearing of a debtor's petition the court shall not make a bankruptcy order if it appears to the court—

(a) that if a bankruptcy order were made the aggregate amount of the bankruptcy debts, so far as unsecured, would be less than the small bankruptcies level,

(b) that if a bankruptcy order were made, the value of the bankrupt's estate would be equal to or more than the minimum amount,

(c) that within the period of 5 years ending with the presentation of the petition the debtor has neither been adjudged bankrupt nor made a composition with his creditors in satisfaction of his debts or a scheme of arrangement of his affairs, and

(d) that it would be appropriate to appoint a person to prepare a report under section 274.

"The minimum amount" and "the small bankruptcies level" mean such amounts as may for the time being be prescribed for the purposes of this section.

(2) Where on the hearing of the petition, it appears to the court as mentioned in subsection (1), the court shall appoint a person who is qualified to act as an insolvency practitioner in relation to the debtor—

(a) to prepare a report under the next section, and

(b) subject to section 258(3) in Part VIII, to act in relation to any voluntary arrangement to which the report relates either as trustee or otherwise for the purpose of supervising its implementation.

274. Action on report of insolvency practitioner

(1) A person appointed under section 273 shall inquire into the debtor's affairs and, within such period as the court may direct, shall submit a report to the court stating whether the debtor is willing, for the purposes of Part VIII, to make a proposal for a voluntary arrangement.

(2) A report which states that the debtor is willing as above mentioned shall also state—

(a) whether, in the opinion of the person making the report, a meeting of the debtor's creditors should be summoned to consider the proposal, and

(b) if in that person's opinion such a meeting should be summoned, the date on which, and time and place at which, he proposes the meeting should be held.

(3) On considering a report under this section the court may—

(a) without any application, make an interim order under section 252, if it thinks that it is appropriate to do so for the purpose of facilitating the consideration and implementation of the debtor's proposal, or

(b) if it thinks it would be inappropriate to make such an order, make a bankruptcy order.

(4) An interim order made by virtue of this section ceases to have effect at the end of such period as the court may specify for the purpose of enabling the debtor's proposal to be considered by his creditors in accordance with the applicable provisions of Part VIII.

(5) Where it has been reported to the court under this section that a meeting of the debtor's creditors should be summoned, the person making the report shall, unless the court otherwise directs, summon that meeting for the time, date and place proposed in his report.

The meeting is then deemed to have been summoned under section 257 in Part VIII, and subsections (2) and (3) of that section, and sections 258 to 263 apply accordingly.

274A. Debtor who meets conditions for a debt relief order

(1) This section applies where, on the hearing of a debtor's petition—

(a) it appears to the court that a debt relief order would be made in relation to the debtor if, instead of presenting the petition, he had made an application under Part 7A; and

(b) the court does not appoint an insolvency practitioner under section 273.

(2) If the court thinks it would be in the debtor's interests to apply for a debt relief order instead of proceeding on the petition, the court may refer the debtor to an approved intermediary (within the meaning of Part 7A) for the purposes of making an application for a debt relief order.

(3) Where a reference is made under subsection (2) the court shall stay proceedings on the petition on such terms and conditions as it thinks fit; but if following the reference a debt relief order is made in relation to the debtor the court shall dismiss the petition.

275. …

Other cases for special consideration

276. Default in connection with voluntary arrangement

(1) The court shall not make a bankruptcy order on a petition under section 264(1)(c) (supervisor of, or person bound by, voluntary arrangement proposed and approved) unless it is satisfied—

(a) that the debtor has failed to comply with his obligations under the voluntary arrangement, or

(b) that information which was false or misleading in any material particular or which contained material omissions—

(i) was contained in any statement of affairs or other document supplied by the debtor under Part VIII to any person, or

(ii) was otherwise made available by the debtor to his creditors at or in connection with a meeting summoned under that Part, or

(c) that the debtor has failed to do all such things as may for the purposes of the voluntary arrangement have been reasonably required of him by the supervisor of the arrangement.

(2) Where a bankruptcy order is made on a petition under section 264(1)(c), any expenses properly incurred as expenses of the administration of the voluntary arrangement in question shall be a first charge on the bankrupt's estate.

277. Petition based on criminal bankruptcy order

(1) Subject to section 266(3), the court shall make a bankruptcy order on a petition under section 264(1)(d) on production of a copy of the criminal bankruptcy order on which the petition is based.

This does not apply if it appears to the court that the criminal bankruptcy order has been rescinded on appeal.

(2) *Subject to the provisions of this Part, the fact that an appeal is pending against any conviction by virtue of which a criminal bankruptcy order was made does not affect any proceedings on a petition under section 264(1)(d) based on that order.*

(3) *For the purposes of this section, an appeal against a conviction is pending—*

(a) *in any case, until the expiration of the period of 28 days beginning with the date of conviction;*

(b) *if notice of appeal to the Court of Appeal is given during that period and during that period the appellant notifies the official receiver of it, until the determination of the appeal and thereafter for so long as an appeal to the Supreme Court is pending within the meaning of subsection (4).*

(4) *For the purposes of subsection (3)(b) an appeal to the Supreme Court shall be treated as pending until any application for leave to appeal is disposed of and, if leave to appeal is granted, until the appeal is disposed of; and for the purposes of this subsection an application for leave to appeal shall be treated as disposed of at the expiration of the time within which it may be made, if it is not made within that time.*

Note. This section is repealed by the Criminal Justice Act 1988, s. 170(2), Sch. 16, as from a day to be appointed.

Commencement and duration of bankruptcy; discharge

278. Commencement and continuance

The bankruptcy of an individual against whom a bankruptcy order has been made—

(a) commences with the day on which the order is made, and

(b) continues until the individual is discharged under the following provisions of this Chapter.

279. Duration

(1) A bankrupt is discharged from bankruptcy at the end of the period of one year beginning with the date on which the bankruptcy commences.

(2) If before the end of that period the official receiver files with the court a notice stating that investigation of the conduct and affairs of the bankrupt under section 289 is unnecessary or concluded, the bankrupt is discharged when the notice is filed.

(3) On the application of the official receiver or the trustee of a bankrupt's estate, the court may order that the period specified in subsection (1) shall cease to run until—

(a) the end of a specified period, or

(b) the fulfilment of a specified condition.

(4) The court may make an order under subsection (3) only if satisfied that the bankrupt has failed or is failing to comply with an obligation under this Part.

(5) In subsection (3)(b) "condition" includes a condition requiring that the court be satisfied of something.

(6) In the case of an individual who is adjudged bankrupt on a petition under section 264(1)(d)—

(a) subsections (1) to (5) shall not apply, and

(b) the bankrupt is discharged from bankruptcy by an order of the court under section 280.

(7) This section is without prejudice to any power of the court to annul a bankruptcy order.

280. Discharge by order of the court

(1) An application for an order of the court discharging an individual from bankruptcy in a case falling within section 279(6) may be made by the bankrupt at any time after the end of the period of 5 years beginning with the date on which the bankruptcy commences.

(2) On an application under this section the court may—

(a) refuse to discharge the bankrupt from bankruptcy,

(b) make an order discharging him absolutely, or

(c) make an order discharging him subject to such conditions with respect to any income which may subsequently become due to him, or with respect to property devolving upon him, or acquired by him, after his discharge, as may be specified in the order.

(3) The court may provide for an order falling within subsection (2)(b) or (c) to have immediate effect or to have its effect suspended for such period, or until the fulfilment of such conditions (including a condition requiring the court to be satisfied as to any matter), as may be specified in the order.

281. Effect of discharge

(1) Subject as follows, where a bankrupt is discharged, the discharge releases him from all the bankruptcy debts, but has no effect—

(a) on the functions (so far as they remain to be carried out) of the trustee of his estate, or

(b) on the operation, for the purposes of the carrying out of those functions, of the provisions of this Part;

and, in particular, discharge does not affect the right of any creditor of the bankrupt to prove in the bankruptcy for any debt from which the bankrupt is released.

(2) Discharge does not affect the right of any secured creditor of the bankrupt to enforce his security for the payment of a debt from which the bankrupt is released.

(3) Discharge does not release the bankrupt from any bankruptcy debt which he incurred in respect of, or forbearance in respect of which was secured by means of, any fraud or fraudulent breach of trust to which he was a party.

(4) Discharge does not release the bankrupt from any liability in respect of a fine imposed for an offence or from any liability under a recognisance except, in the case of a penalty imposed for an offence under an enactment relating to the public revenue or of a recognisance, with the consent of the Treasury.

(4A) In subsection (4) the reference to a fine includes a reference to a confiscation order under Part 2, 3 or 4 of the Proceeds of Crime Act 2002.

(5) Discharge does not, except to such extent and on such conditions as the court may direct, release the bankrupt from any bankruptcy debt which—

(a) consists in a liability to pay damages for negligence, nuisance or breach of a statutory, contractual or other duty, or to pay damages by virtue of Part I of the Consumer Protection Act 1987, being in either case damages in respect of personal injuries to any person, or

(b) arises under any order made in family proceedings or under a *maintenance assessment [maintenance calculation]* made under the Child Support Act 1991 ... .

(6) Discharge does not release the bankrupt from such other bankruptcy debts, not being debts provable in his bankruptcy, as are prescribed.

(7) Discharge does not release any person other than the bankrupt from any liability (whether as partner or co-trustee of the bankrupt or otherwise) from which the bankrupt is released by the discharge, or from any liability as surety for the bankrupt or as a person in the nature of such a surety.

(8) In this section—

"family proceedings" means—

(a) family proceedings within the meaning of the Magistrates' Courts Act 1980 and any proceedings which would be such proceedings but for section 65(1)(ii) of that Act (proceedings for variation of order for periodical payments); and

(b) family proceedings within the meaning of Part V of the Matrimonial and Family Proceedings Act 1984;

"fine" means the same as in the Magistrates' Courts Act 1980; and

"personal injuries" includes death and any disease or other impairment of a person's physical or mental condition.

Note. The words "maintenance assessment" in subsection (5)(b) are repealed and the subsequent italicized words in square brackets are substituted by the Child Support, Pensions and Social Security Act 2000, s. 26, Sch. 3, para. 6, from 3 March 2003 in relation to certain cases (see S.I. 2003/192) and as from a day to be appointed otherwise.

281A. Post-discharge restrictions

Schedule 4A to this Act (bankruptcy restrictions order and bankruptcy restrictions undertaking) shall have effect.

282. Court's power to annul bankruptcy order

(1) The court may annul a bankruptcy order if it at any time appears to the court—

(a) that, on the grounds existing at the time the order was made, the order ought not to have been made, or

(b) that, to the extent required by the rules, the bankruptcy debts and the expenses of the bankruptcy have all, since the making of the order, been either paid or secured for to the satisfaction of the court.

(2) The court may annul a bankruptcy order made against an individual on a petition under paragraph (a), (b) or (c) of section 264(1) if it at any time appears to the court, on an application by the Official Petitioner—

(a) that the petition was pending at a time when a criminal bankruptcy order was made against the individual or was presented after such an order was so made, and

(b) no appeal is pending (within the meaning of section 277) against the individual's conviction of any offence by virtue of which the criminal bankruptcy order was made;

and the court shall annul a bankruptcy order made on a petition under section 264(1)(d) if it at any time appears to the court that the criminal bankruptcy order on which the petition was based has been rescinded in consequence of an appeal.

(3) The court may annul a bankruptcy order whether or not the bankrupt has been discharged from the bankruptcy.

(4) Where the court annuls a bankruptcy order (whether under this section or under section 261 or 263D in Part VIII)—

(a) any sale or other disposition of property, payment made or other thing duly done, under any provision in this Group of Parts, by or under the authority of the official receiver or a trustee of the bankrupt's estate or by the court is valid, but

(b) if any of the bankrupt's estate is then vested, under any such provision, in such a trustee, it shall vest in such person as the court may appoint or, in default of any such appointment, revert to the bankrupt on such terms (if any) as the court may direct;

and the court may include in its order such supplemental provisions as may be authorised by the rules.

(5) …

Note. Subsection (2) is repealed by the Criminal Justice Act 1988, s. 170(2), Sch. 16, as from a day to be appointed.

CHAPTER II
PROTECTION OF BANKRUPT'S ESTATE AND INVESTIGATION OF HIS AFFAIRS

283. Definition of bankrupt's estate

(1) Subject as follows, a bankrupt's estate for the purposes of any of this Group of Parts comprises—

(a) all property belonging to or vested in the bankrupt at the commencement of the bankruptcy, and

(b) any property which by virtue of any of the following provisions of this Part is comprised in that estate or is treated as falling within the preceding paragraph.

(2) Subsection (1) does not apply to—

(a) such tools, books, vehicles and other items of equipment as are necessary to the bankrupt for use personally by him in his employment, business or vocation;

(b) such clothing, bedding, furniture, household equipment and provisions as are necessary for satisfying the basic domestic needs of the bankrupt and his family.

This subsection is subject to section 308 in Chapter IV (certain excluded property reclaimable by trustee).

(3) Subsection (1) does not apply to—

(a) property held by the bankrupt on trust for any other person, or

(b) the right of nomination to a vacant ecclesiastical benefice.

(3A) Subject to section 308A in Chapter IV, subsection (1) does not apply to—

(a) a tenancy which is an assured tenancy or an assured agricultural occupancy, within the meaning of Part I of the Housing Act 1988, and the terms of which inhibit an assignment as mentioned in section 127(5) of the Rent Act 1977, or

(b) a protected tenancy, within the meaning of the Rent Act 1977, in respect of which, by virtue of any provision of Part IX of that Act, no premium can lawfully be required as a condition of assignment, or

(c) a tenancy of a dwelling-house by virtue of which the bankrupt is, within the meaning of the Rent (Agriculture) Act 1976, a protected occupier of the dwelling-house, and the terms of which inhibit an assignment as mentioned in section 127(5) of the Rent Act 1977, or

(d) a secure tenancy, within the meaning of Part IV of the Housing Act 1985, which is not capable of being assigned, except in the cases mentioned in section 91(3) of that Act.

(4) References in any of this Group of Parts to property, in relation to a bankrupt, include references to any power exercisable by him over or in respect of property except in so far as the power is exercisable over or in respect of property not for the time being comprised in the bankrupt's estate and—

(a) is so exercisable at a time after either the official receiver has had his release in respect of that estate under section 299(2) in Chapter III or a meeting summoned by the trustee of that estate under section 331 in Chapter IV has been held, or

(b) cannot be so exercised for the benefit of the bankrupt;

and a power exercisable over or in respect of property is deemed for the purposes of any of this Group of Parts to vest in the person entitled to exercise it at the time of the transaction or event by virtue of which it is exercisable by that person (whether or not it becomes so exercisable at that time).

(5) For the purposes of any such provision in this Group of Parts, property comprised in a bankrupt's estate is so comprised subject to the rights of any person other than the bankrupt (whether as a secured creditor of the bankrupt or otherwise) in relation thereto, but disregarding—

(a) any rights in relation to which a statement such as is required by section 269(1)(a) was made in the petition on which the bankrupt was adjudged bankrupt, and

(b) any rights which have been otherwise given up in accordance with the rules.

(6) This section has effect subject to the provisions of any enactment not contained in this Act under which any property is to be excluded from a bankrupt's estate.

283A. Bankrupt's home ceasing to form part of estate

(1) This section applies where property comprised in the bankrupt's estate consists of an interest in a dwelling-house which at the date of the bankruptcy was the sole or principal residence of—

(a) the bankrupt,

(b) the bankrupt's spouse or civil partner, or

(c) a former spouse or former civil partner of the bankrupt.

(2) At the end of the period of three years beginning with the date of the bankruptcy the interest mentioned in subsection (1) shall—

(a) cease to be comprised in the bankrupt's estate, and

(b) vest in the bankrupt (without conveyance, assignment or transfer).

(3) Subsection (2) shall not apply if during the period mentioned in that subsection—

(a) the trustee realises the interest mentioned in subsection (1),

(b) the trustee applies for an order for sale in respect of the dwelling-house,

(c) the trustee applies for an order for possession of the dwelling-house,

(d) the trustee applies for an order under section 313 in Chapter IV in respect of that interest, or

(e) the trustee and the bankrupt agree that the bankrupt shall incur a specified liability to his estate (with or without the addition of interest from the date of the agreement) in consideration of which the interest mentioned in subsection (1) shall cease to form part of the estate.

(4) Where an application of a kind described in subsection (3)(b) to (d) is made during the period mentioned in subsection (2) and is dismissed, unless the court orders otherwise the interest to which the application relates shall on the dismissal of the application—

(a) cease to be comprised in the bankrupt's estate, and

(b) vest in the bankrupt (without conveyance, assignment or transfer).

(5) If the bankrupt does not inform the trustee or the official receiver of his interest in a property before the end of the period of three months beginning with the date of the bankruptcy, the period of three years mentioned in subsection (2)—

(a) shall not begin with the date of the bankruptcy, but

(b) shall begin with the date on which the trustee or official receiver becomes aware of the bankrupt's interest.

(6) The court may substitute for the period of three years mentioned in subsection (2) a longer period—

(a) in prescribed circumstances, and

(b) in such other circumstances as the court thinks appropriate.

(7) The rules may make provision for this section to have effect with the substitution of a shorter period for the period of three years mentioned in subsection (2) in specified circumstances (which may be described by reference to action to be taken by a trustee in bankruptcy).

(8) The rules may also, in particular, make provision—

(a) requiring or enabling the trustee of a bankrupt's estate to give notice that this section applies or does not apply;

(b) about the effect of a notice under paragraph (a);

(c) requiring the trustee of a bankrupt's estate to make an application to the Chief Land Registrar.

(9) Rules under subsection (8)(b) may, in particular—

(a) disapply this section;

(b) enable a court to disapply this section;

(c) make provision in consequence of a disapplication of this section;

(d) enable a court to make provision in consequence of a disapplication of this section;

(e) make provision (which may include provision conferring jurisdiction on a court or tribunal) about compensation.

284. Restrictions on dispositions of property

(1) Where a person is adjudged bankrupt, any disposition of property made by that person in the period to which this section applies is void except to the extent that it is or was made with the consent of the court, or is or was subsequently ratified by the court.

(2) Subsection (1) applies to a payment (whether in cash or otherwise) as it applies to a disposition of property and, accordingly, where any payment is void by virtue of that subsection, the person paid shall hold the sum paid for the bankrupt as part of his estate.

(3) This section applies to the period beginning with the day of the presentation of the petition for the bankruptcy order and ending with the vesting, under Chapter IV of this Part, of the bankrupt's estate in a trustee.

(4) The preceding provisions of this section do not give a remedy against any person—

(a) in respect of any property or payment which he received before the commencement of the bankruptcy in good faith, for value and without notice that the petition had been presented, or

(b) in respect of any interest in property which derives from an interest in respect of which there is, by virtue of this subsection, no remedy.

(5) Where after the commencement of his bankruptcy the bankrupt has incurred a debt to a banker or other person by reason of the making of a payment which is void under this section, that debt is deemed for the purposes of any of this Group of Parts to have been incurred before the commencement of the bankruptcy unless—

(a) that banker or person had notice of the bankruptcy before the debt was incurred, or

(b) it is not reasonably practicable for the amount of the payment to be recovered from the person to whom it was made.

(6) A disposition of property is void under this section notwithstanding that the property is not or, as the case may be, would not be comprised in the bankrupt's estate; but nothing in this section affects any disposition made by a person of property held by him on trust for any other person.

285. Restriction on proceedings and remedies

(1) At any time when proceedings on a bankruptcy petition are pending or an individual has been adjudged bankrupt the court may stay any action, execution or other legal process against the property or person of the debtor or, as the case may be, of the bankrupt.

(2) Any court in which proceedings are pending against any individual may, on proof that a bankruptcy petition has been presented in respect of that individual or that he is an undischarged bankrupt, either stay the proceedings or allow them to continue on such terms as it thinks fit.

(3) After the making of a bankruptcy order no person who is a creditor of the bankrupt in respect of a debt provable in the bankruptcy shall—

(a) have any remedy against the property or person of the bankrupt in respect of that debt, or

(b) before the discharge of the bankrupt, commence any action or other legal proceedings against the bankrupt except with the leave of the court and on such terms as the court may impose.

This is subject to sections 346 (enforcement procedures) and 347 (limited right to distress).

(4) Subject as follows, subsection (3) does not affect the right of a secured creditor of the bankrupt to enforce his security.

(5) Where any goods of an undischarged bankrupt are held by any person by way of pledge, pawn or other security, the official receiver may, after giving notice in writing of his intention to do so, inspect the goods.

Where such a notice has been given to any person, that person is not entitled, without leave of the court, to realise his security unless he has given the trustee of the bankrupt's estate a reasonable opportunity of inspecting the goods and of exercising the bankrupt's right of redemption.

(6) References in this section to the property or goods of the bankrupt are to any of his property or goods, whether or not comprised in his estate.

286. Power to appoint interim receiver

(1) The court may, if it is shown to be necessary for the protection of the debtor's property, at any time after the presentation of a bankruptcy petition and before making a bankruptcy order, appoint the official receiver to be interim receiver of the debtor's property.

(2) Where the court has, on a debtor's petition, appointed an insolvency practitioner under section 273 and it is shown to the court as mentioned in subsection (1) of this section, the court may, without making a bankruptcy order, appoint that practitioner, instead of the official receiver, to be interim receiver of the debtor's property.

(3) The court may by an order appointing any person to be an interim receiver direct that his powers shall be limited or restricted in any respect; but, save as so directed, an interim receiver has, in relation to the debtor's property, all the rights, powers, duties and immunities of a receiver and manager under the next section.

(4) An order of the court appointing any person to be an interim receiver shall require that person to take immediate possession of the debtor's property or, as the case may be, the part of it to which his powers as interim receiver are limited.

(5) Where an interim receiver has been appointed, the debtor shall give him such inventory of his property and such other information, and shall attend on the interim receiver at such times, as the latter may for the purpose of carrying out his functions under this section reasonably require.

(6) Where an interim receiver is appointed, section 285(3) applies for the period between the appointment and the making of a bankruptcy order on the petition, or the dismissal of the petition, as if the appointment were the making of such an order.

(7) A person ceases to be interim receiver of a debtor's property if the bankruptcy petition relating to the debtor is dismissed, if a bankruptcy order is made on the petition or if the court by order otherwise terminates the appointment.

(8) References in this section to the debtor's property are to all his property, whether or not it would be comprised in his estate if he were adjudged bankrupt.

287. Receivership pending appointment of trustee

(1) Between the making of a bankruptcy order and the time at which the bankrupt's estate vests in a trustee under Chapter IV of this Part, the official receiver is the receiver and (subject to section 370 (special manager)) the manager of the bankrupt's estate and is under a duty to act as such.

(2) The function of the official receiver while acting as receiver or manager of the bankrupt's estate under this section is to protect the estate; and for this purpose—

(a) he has the same powers as if he were a receiver or manager appointed by the High Court, and

(b) he is entitled to sell or otherwise dispose of any perishable goods comprised in the estate and any other goods so comprised the value of which is likely to diminish if they are not disposed of.

(3) The official receiver while acting as receiver or manager of the estate under this section—

(a) shall take all such steps as he thinks fit for protecting any property which may be claimed for the estate by the trustee of that estate,

(b) is not, except in pursuance of directions given by the Secretary of State, required to do anything that involves his incurring expenditure,

(c) may, if he thinks fit (and shall, if so directed by the court) at any time summon a general meeting of the bankrupt's creditors.

(4) Where—

(a) the official receiver acting as receiver or manager of the estate under this section seizes or disposes of any property which is not comprised in the estate, and

(b) at the time of the seizure or disposal the official receiver believes, and has reasonable grounds for believing, that he is entitled (whether in pursuance of an order of the court or otherwise) to seize or dispose of that property,

the official receiver is not to be liable to any person in respect of any loss or damage resulting from the seizure or disposal except in so far as that loss or damage is caused by his negligence; and he has a lien on the property, or the proceeds of its sale, for such of the expenses of the bankruptcy as were incurred in connection with the seizure or disposal.

(5) This section does not apply where by virtue of section 297 (appointment of trustee; special cases) the bankrupt's estate vests in a trustee immediately on the making of the bankruptcy order.

288. Statement of affairs

(1) Where a bankruptcy order has been made otherwise than on a debtor's petition, the bankrupt shall submit a statement of his affairs to the official receiver before the end of the period of 21 days beginning with the commencement of the bankruptcy.

(2) The statement of affairs shall contain—

(a) such particulars of the bankrupt's creditors and of his debts and other liabilities and of his assets as may be prescribed, and

(b) such other information as may be prescribed.

(3) The official receiver may, if he thinks fit—

(a) release the bankrupt from his duty under subsection (1), or

(b) extend the period specified in that subsection;

and where the official receiver has refused to exercise a power conferred by this section, the court, if it thinks fit, may exercise it.

(4) A bankrupt who—

(a) without reasonable excuse fails to comply with the obligation imposed by this section, or

(b) without reasonable excuse submits a statement of affairs that does not comply with the prescribed requirements,

is guilty of a contempt of court and liable to be punished accordingly (in addition to any other punishment to which he may be subject).

289. Investigatory duties of official receiver

(1) The official receiver shall—

(a) investigate the conduct and affairs of each bankrupt (including his conduct and affairs before the making of the bankruptcy order), and

(b) make such report (if any) to the court as the official receiver thinks fit.

(2) Subsection (1) shall not apply to a case in which the official receiver thinks an investigation under that subsection unnecessary.

(3) Where a bankrupt makes an application for discharge under section 280—

(a) the official receiver shall make a report to the court about such matters as may be prescribed, and

(b) the court shall consider the report before determining the application.

(4) A report by the official receiver under this section shall in any proceedings be prima facie evidence of the facts stated in it.

290. Public examination of bankrupt

(1) Where a bankruptcy order has been made, the official receiver may at any time before the discharge of the bankrupt apply to the court for the public examination of the bankrupt.

(2) Unless the court otherwise orders, the official receiver shall make an application under subsection (1) if notice requiring him to do so is given to him, in accordance with the rules, by one of the bankrupt's creditors with the concurrence of not less than one-half, in value, of those creditors (including the creditor giving notice).

(3) On an application under subsection (1), the court shall direct that a public examination of the bankrupt shall be held on a day appointed by the court; and the bankrupt shall attend on that day and be publicly examined as to his affairs, dealings and property.

(4) The following may take part in the public examination of the bankrupt and may question him concerning his affairs, dealings and property and the causes of his failure, namely—

(a) the official receiver and, in the case of an individual adjudged bankrupt on a petition under section 264(1)(d), the Official Petitioner,

(b) the trustee of the bankrupt's estate, if his appointment has taken effect,

(c) any person who has been appointed as special manager of the bankrupt's estate or business,

(d) any creditor of the bankrupt who has tendered a proof in the bankruptcy.

(5) If a bankrupt without reasonable excuse fails at any time to attend his public examination under this section he is guilty of a contempt of court and liable to be punished accordingly (in addition to any other punishment to which he may be subject).

291. Duties of bankrupt in relation to official receiver

(1) Where a bankruptcy order has been made, the bankrupt is under a duty—

(a) to deliver possession of his estate to the official receiver, and

(b) to deliver up to the official receiver all books, papers and other records of which he has possession or control and which relate to his estate and affairs (including any which would be privileged from disclosure in any proceedings).

(2) In the case of any part of the bankrupt's estate which consists of things possession of which cannot be delivered to the official receiver, and in the case of any property that may be claimed

for the bankrupt's estate by the trustee, it is the bankrupt's duty to do all such things as may reasonably be required by the official receiver for the protection of those things or that property.

(3) Subsections (1) and (2) do not apply where by virtue of section 297 below the bankrupt's estate vests in a trustee immediately on the making of the bankruptcy order.

(4) The bankrupt shall give the official receiver such inventory of his estate and such other information, and shall attend on the official receiver at such times, as the official receiver may reasonably require—

(a) for a purpose of this Chapter, or

(b) in connection with the making of a bankruptcy restrictions order.

(5) Subsection (4) applies to a bankrupt after his discharge.

(6) If the bankrupt without reasonable excuse fails to comply with any obligation imposed by this section, he is guilty of a contempt of court and liable to be punished accordingly (in addition to any other punishment to which he may be subject).

CHAPTER III
TRUSTEES IN BANKRUPTCY

Tenure of office as trustee

292. Power to make appointments

(1) The power to appoint a person as trustee of a bankrupt's estate (whether the first such trustee or a trustee appointed to fill any vacancy) is exercisable—

(a) … by a general meeting of the bankrupt's creditors;

(b) under section 295(2), 296(2) or 300(6) below in this Chapter, by the Secretary of State; or

(c) under section 297, by the court.

(2) No person may be appointed as trustee of a bankrupt's estate unless he is, at the time of the appointment, qualified to act as an insolvency practitioner in relation to the bankrupt.

(3) Any power to appoint a person as trustee of a bankrupt's estate includes power to appoint two or more persons as joint trustees; but such an appointment must make provision as to the circumstances in which the trustees must act together and the circumstances in which one or more of them may act for the others.

(4) The appointment of any person as trustee takes effect only if that person accepts the appointment in accordance with the rules. Subject to this, the appointment of any person as trustee takes effect at the time specified in his certificate of appointment.

(5) This section is without prejudice to the provisions of this Chapter under which the official receiver is, in certain circumstances, to be trustee of the estate.

293. Summoning of meeting to appoint first trustee

(1) Where a bankruptcy order has been made … it is the duty of the official receiver, as soon as practicable in the period of 12 weeks beginning with the day on which the order was made, to decide whether to summon a general meeting of the bankrupt's creditors for the purpose of appointing a trustee of the bankrupt's estate.

This section does not apply where the bankruptcy order was made on a petition under section 264(1)(d) (criminal bankruptcy); and it is subject to the provision made in sections 294(3) and 297(6) below.

(2) Subject to the next section, if the official receiver decides not to summon such a meeting, he shall, before the end of the period of 12 weeks above mentioned, give notice of his decision to the court and to every creditor of the bankrupt who is known to the official receiver or is identified in the bankrupt's statement of affairs.

(3) As from the giving to the court of a notice under subsection (2), the official receiver is the trustee of the bankrupt's estate.

Note. The italicized words in subsection (1) are repealed by the Criminal Justice Act 1988, s. 170(2), Sch. 16, as from a day to be appointed.

294. Power of creditors to requisition meeting

(1) Where in the case of any bankruptcy—

(a) the official receiver has not yet summoned, or has decided not to summon, a general meeting of the bankrupt's creditors for the purpose of appointing the trustee, …

any creditor of the bankrupt may request the official receiver to summon such a meeting for that purpose.

(2) If such a request appears to the official receiver to be made with the concurrence of not less than one-quarter, in value, of the bankrupt's creditors (including the creditor making the request), it is the duty of the official receiver to summon the requested meeting.

(3) Accordingly, where the duty imposed by subsection (2) has arisen, the official receiver is required neither to reach a decision for the purposes of section 293(1) nor (if he has reached one) to serve any notice under section 293(2).

295. Failure of meeting to appoint trustee

(1) If a meeting summoned under section 293 or 294 is held but no appointment of a person as trustee is made, it is the duty of the official receiver to decide whether to refer the need for an appointment to the Secretary of State.

(2) On a reference made in pursuance of that decision, the Secretary of State shall either make an appointment or decline to make one.

(3) If—

(a) the official receiver decides not to refer the need for an appointment to the Secretary of State, or

(b) on such a reference the Secretary of State declines to make an appointment,

the official receiver shall give notice of his decision or, as the case may be, of the Secretary of State's decision to the court.

(4) As from the giving of notice under subsection (3) in a case in which no notice has been given under section 293(2), the official receiver shall be trustee of the bankrupt's estate.

296. Appointment of trustee by Secretary of State

(1) At any time when the official receiver is the trustee of a bankrupt's estate by virtue of any provision of this Chapter (other than section 297(1) below) he may apply to the Secretary of State for the appointment of a person as trustee instead of the official receiver.

(2) On an application under subsection (1) the Secretary of State shall either make an appointment or decline to make one.

(3) Such an application may be made notwithstanding that the Secretary of State has declined to make an appointment either on a previous application under subsection (1) or on a reference under section 295 or under section 300(4) below.

(4) Where the trustee of a bankrupt's estate has been appointed by the Secretary of State (whether under this section or otherwise), the trustee shall give notice to the bankrupt's creditors of his appointment or, if the court so allows, shall advertise his appointment in accordance with the court's directions.

(5) In that notice or advertisement the trustee shall—

(a) state whether he proposes to summon a general meeting of the bankrupt's creditors for the purposes of establishing a creditor's committee under section 301, and

(b) if he does not propose to summon such a meeting, set out the power of the creditors under this Part to require him to summon one.

297. Special cases

(1) Where a bankruptcy order is made on a petition under section 264(1)(d) (criminal bankruptcy), the official receiver shall be trustee of the bankrupt's estate.

(2), (3) …

(4) Where a bankruptcy order is made in a case in which an insolvency practitioner's report has been submitted to the court under section 274 …, the court, if it thinks fit, may on making the order appoint the person who made the report as trustee.

(5) Where a bankruptcy order is made (whether or not on a petition under section 264(1)(c)) at a time when there is a supervisor of a voluntary arrangement approved in relation to the bankrupt under Part VIII, the court, if it thinks fit, may on making the order appoint the supervisor of the arrangement as trustee.

(6) Where an appointment is made under subsection (4) or (5) of this section, the official receiver is not under the duty imposed by section 293(1) (to decide whether or not to summon a meeting of creditors).

(7) Where the trustee of a bankrupt's estate has been appointed by the court, the trustee shall give notice to the bankrupt's creditors of his appointment or, if the court so allows, shall advertise his appointment in accordance with the directions of the court.

(8) In that notice or advertisement he shall—

(a) state whether he proposes to summon a general meeting of the bankrupt's creditors for the purpose of establishing a creditor's committee under section 301 below, and

(b) if he does not propose to summon such a meeting, set out the power of the creditors under this Part to require him to summon one.

Note. Subsection (1) is repealed by the Criminal Justice Act 1988, s. 170(2), Sch. 16, as from a day to be appointed.

298. Removal of trustee; vacation of office

(1) Subject as follows, the trustee of a bankrupt's estate may be removed from office only by an order of the court or by a general meeting of the bankrupt's creditors summoned specially for that purpose in accordance with the rules.

(2) Where the official receiver is trustee by virtue of section 297(1), he shall not be removed from office under this section.

(3) …

(4) Where the official receiver is trustee by virtue of section 293(3) or 295(4) or a trustee is appointed by the Secretary of State or (otherwise than under section 297(5)) by the court, a general meeting of the bankrupt's creditors shall be summoned for the purpose of replacing the trustee only if—

(a) the trustee thinks fit, or

(b) the court so directs, or

(c) the meeting is requested by one of the bankrupt's creditors with the concurrence of not less than one-quarter, in value, of the creditors (including the creditor making the request).

(5) If the trustee was appointed by the Secretary of State, he may be removed by a direction of the Secretary of State.

(6) The trustee (not being the official receiver) shall vacate office if he ceases to be a person who is for the time being qualified to act as an insolvency practitioner in relation to the bankrupt.

(7) The trustee may, in the prescribed circumstances, resign his office by giving notice of his resignation to the court.

(8) The trustee shall vacate office on giving notice to the court that a final meeting has been held under section 331 in Chapter IV and of the decision (if any) of that meeting.

(9) The trustee shall vacate office if the bankruptcy order is annulled.

299. Release of trustee

(1) Where the official receiver has ceased to be the trustee of a bankrupt's estate and a person is appointed in his stead, the official receiver shall have his release with effect from the following time, that is to say—

(a) where that person is appointed by a general meeting of the bankrupt's creditors or by the Secretary of State, the time at which the official receiver gives notice to the court that he has been replaced, and

(b) where that person is appointed by the court, such time as the court may determine.

(2) If the official receiver while he is the trustee gives notice to the Secretary of State that the administration of the bankrupt's estate in accordance with Chapter IV of this Part is for practical purposes complete, he shall have his release with effect from such time as the Secretary of State may determine.

(3) A person other than the official receiver who has ceased to be the trustee shall have his release with effect from the following time, that is to say—

(a) in the case of a person who has been removed from office by a general meeting of the bankrupt's creditors that has not resolved against his release or who has died, the time at which notice is given to the court in accordance with the rules that that person has ceased to hold office;

(b) in the case of a person who has been removed from office by a general meeting of the bankrupt's creditors that has resolved against his release, or by the court, or by the Secretary of State, or who has vacated office under section 298(6), such time as the Secretary of State may, on an application by that person, determine;

(c) in the case of a person who has resigned, such time as may be prescribed;

(d) in the case of a person who has vacated office under section 298(8)—

(i) if the final meeting referred to in that subsection has resolved against that person's release, such time as the Secretary of State may, on an application by that person, determine; and

(ii) if that meeting has not so resolved, the time at which the person vacated office.

(4) Where a bankruptcy order is annulled, the trustee at the time of the annulment has his release with effect from such time as the court may determine.

(5) Where the official receiver or the trustee has his release under this section, he shall, with effect from the time specified in the preceding provisions of this section, be discharged from all liability both in respect of acts or omissions of his in the administration of the estate and otherwise in relation to his conduct as trustee.

But nothing in this section prevents the exercise, in relation to a person who has had his release under this section, of the court's powers under section 304.

300. Vacancy in office of trustee

(1) This section applies where the appointment of any person as trustee of a bankrupt's estate fails to take effect or, such an appointment having taken effect, there is otherwise a vacancy in the office of trustee.

(2) The official receiver shall be trustee until the vacancy is filled.

(3) The official receiver may summon a general meeting of the bankrupt's creditors for the purpose of filling the vacancy and shall summon such a meeting if required to do so in pursuance of section 314(7) (creditors' requisition).

(4) If at the end of the period of 28 days beginning with the day on which the vacancy first came to the official receiver's attention he has not summoned, and is not proposing to summon, a general meeting of creditors for the purpose of filling the vacancy, he shall refer the need for an appointment to the Secretary of State.

(5) …

(6) On a reference to the Secretary of State under subsection (4) … the Secretary of State shall either make an appointment or decline to make one.

(7) If on a reference under subsection (4) … no appointment is made, the official receiver shall continue to be trustee of the bankrupt's estate, but without prejudice to his power to make a further reference.

(8) References in this section to a vacancy include a case where it is necessary, in relation to any property which is or may be comprised in a bankrupt's estate, to revive the trusteeship of that estate after the holding of a final meeting summoned under section 331 or the giving by the official receiver of notice under section 299(2).

Control of trustee

301. Creditors' committee

(1) Subject as follows, a general meeting of a bankrupt's creditors (whether summoned under the preceding provisions of this Chapter or otherwise) may, in accordance with the rules, establish a committee (known as "the creditors' committee") to exercise the functions conferred on it by or under this Act.

(2) A general meeting of the bankrupt's creditors shall not establish such a committee, or confer any functions on such a committee, at any time when the official receiver is the trustee of the bankrupt's estate, except in connection with an appointment made by that meeting of a person to be trustee instead of the official receiver.

302. Exercise by Secretary of State of functions of creditors' committee

(1) The creditors' committee is not to be able or required to carry out its functions at any time when the official receiver is trustee of the bankrupt's estate; but at any such time the functions of the committee under this Act shall be vested in the Secretary of State, except to the extent that the rules otherwise provide.

(2) Where in the case of any bankruptcy there is for the time being no creditors' committee and the trustee of the bankrupt's estate is a person other than the official receiver, the functions of such a committee shall be vested in the Secretary of State, except to the extent that the rules otherwise provide.

303. General control of trustee by the court

(1) If a bankrupt or any of his creditors or any other person is dissatisfied by any act, omission or decision of a trustee of the bankrupt's estate, he may apply to the court; and on such an application the court may confirm, reverse or modify any act or decision of the trustee, may give him directions or may make such other order as it thinks fit.

(2) The trustee of a bankrupt's estate may apply to the court for directions in relation to any particular matter arising under the bankruptcy.

(2A) Where at any time after a bankruptcy petition has been presented to the court against any person, whether under the provisions of the Insolvent Partnerships Order 1994 or not, the attention of the court is drawn to the fact that the person in question is a member of an insolvent partnership, the court may make an order as to the future conduct of the insolvency proceedings and any such order may apply any provisions of that Order with any necessary modifications.

(2B) Where a bankruptcy petition has been presented against more than one individual in the circumstances mentioned in subsection (2A) above, the court may give such directions for consolidating the proceedings, or any of them, as it thinks just.

(2C) Any order or directions under subsection (2A) or (2B) may be made or given on the application of the official receiver, any responsible insolvency practitioner, the trustee of the partnership or any other interested person and may include provisions as to the administration of the joint estate of the partnership, and in particular how it and the separate estate of any member are to be administered.

304. Liability of trustee

(1) Where on an application under this section the court is satisfied—

(a) that the trustee of a bankrupt's estate has misapplied or retained, or become accountable for, any money or other property comprised in the bankrupt's estate, or

(b) that a bankrupt's estate has suffered any loss in consequence of any misfeasance or breach of fiduciary or other duty by a trustee of the estate in the carrying out of his functions,

the court may order the trustee, for the benefit of the estate, to repay, restore or account for money or other property (together with interest at such rate as the court thinks just) or, as the case may require, to pay such sum by way of compensation in respect of the misfeasance or breach of fiduciary or other duty as the court thinks just.

This is without prejudice to any liability arising apart from this section.

(2) An application under this section may be made by the official receiver, the Secretary of State, a creditor of the bankrupt or (whether or not there is, or is likely to be, a surplus for the purposes of section 330(5) (final distribution)) the bankrupt himself.

But the leave of the court is required for the making of an application if it is to be made by the bankrupt or if it is to be made after the trustee has had his release under section 299.

(3) Where—

(a) the trustee seizes or disposes of any property which is not comprised in the bankrupt's estate, and

(b) at the time of the seizure or disposal the trustee believes, and has reasonable grounds for believing, that he is entitled (whether in pursuance of an order of the court or otherwise) to seize or dispose of that property,

the trustee is not liable to any person (whether under this section or otherwise) in respect of any loss or damage resulting from the seizure or disposal except in so far as that loss or damage is caused by the negligence of the trustee; and he has a lien on the property, or the proceeds of its sale, for such of the expenses of the bankruptcy as were incurred in connection with the seizure or disposal.

CHAPTER IV
ADMINISTRATION BY TRUSTEE

Preliminary

305. General functions of trustee

(1) This Chapter applies in relation to any bankruptcy where either—

(a) the appointment of a person as trustee of a bankrupt's estate takes effect, or

(b) the official receiver becomes trustee of a bankrupt's estate.

(2) The function of the trustee is to get in, realise and distribute the bankrupt's estate in accordance with the following provisions of this Chapter; and in the carrying out of that function and in the management of the bankrupt's estate the trustee is entitled, subject to those provisions, to use his own discretion.

(3) It is the duty of the trustee, if he is not the official receiver—

(a) to furnish the official receiver with such information,

(b) to produce to the official receiver, and permit inspection by the official receiver of, such books, papers and other records, and

(c) to give the official receiver such other assistance,

as the official receiver may reasonably require for the purpose of enabling him to carry out his functions in relation to the bankruptcy.

(4) The official name of the trustee shall be "the trustee of the estate of .. .., a bankrupt" (inserting the name of the bankrupt); be he may be referred to as "the trustee in bankruptcy" of the particular bankrupt.

Acquisition, control and realisation of bankrupt's estate

306. Vesting of bankrupt's estate in trustee

(1) The bankrupt's estate shall vest in the trustee immediately on his appointment taking effect or, in the case of the official receiver, on his becoming trustee.

(2) Where any property which is, or is to be, comprised in the bankrupt's estate vests in the trustee (whether under this section or under any other provision of this Part), it shall so vest without any conveyance, assignment or transfer.

306A. Property subject to restraint order

(1) This section applies where—

(a) property is excluded from the bankrupt's estate by virtue of section 417(2)(a) of the Proceeds of Crime Act 2002 (property subject to a restraint order),

(b) an order under section *50, . . . 128 or 198* of that Act has not been made in respect of the property, *and*

(c) the restraint order is discharged*; and*

(d) immediately after the discharge of the restraint order the property is not detained under or by virtue of section 44A, 47J, 122A, 127J, 193A or 195J of that Act.

(2) On the discharge of the restraint order the property vests in the trustee as part of the bankrupt's estate.

(2) The property vests in the trustee as part of the bankrupt's estate.

(3) But subsection (2) does not apply to the proceeds of property realised by a management receiver under section 49(2)(d) or 197(2)(d) of that Act (realisation of property to meet receiver's remuneration and expenses).

Note. This section is amended as follows by the Policing and Crime Act 2009, s. 112, Sch. 7, Pt. 6, paras. 53, 54, Sch. 8, Pt. 4, as from a day to be appointed: the italicized words "section 50, 128 or 198" in subsection (1)(b) are substituted by the words "section 50, 67A, 128, 131A, 198 or 215A"; the word "and" at the end of subsection (1)(b) is repealed; subsection (1)(d) and word "; and" immediately preceding it are inserted; and subsection (2) is substituted.

306AA. Property released from detention

(1) This section applies where—

(a) property is excluded from the bankrupt's estate by virtue of section 417(2)(b) of the Proceeds of Crime Act 2002 (property detained under certain provisions),

(b) no order is in force in respect of the property under section 41, 50, 120, 128, 190 or 198 of that Act, and

(c) the property is released.

(2) The property vests in the trustee as part of the bankrupt's estate.

Note. This section is inserted by the Policing and Crime Act 2009, s. 112(1), Sch. 7, Pt. 6, paras. 53, 55, as from a day to be appointed.

306B. Property in respect of which receivership or administration order made

(1) This section applies where—

(a) property is excluded from the bankrupt's estate by virtue of section *417(2)(b), (c) or (d)* of the Proceeds of Crime Act 2002 (property in respect of which an order for the appointment of a receiver or administrator under certain provisions of that Act is in force),

(b) a confiscation order is made under section 6, 92 or 156 of that Act,

(c) the amount payable under the confiscation order is fully paid, and

(d) any of the property remains in the hands of the receiver or administrator (as the case may be).

(2) The property vests in the trustee as part of the bankrupt's estate.

Note. The italicized words in subsection (1)(a) are substituted by the words "section 417(2)(c)" by the Policing and Crime Act 2009, s. 112(1), Sch. 7, Pt. 6, paras. 53, 56, as from a day to be appointed.

306BA. Property in respect of which realisation order made

(1) This section applies where—

(a) property is excluded from the bankrupt's estate by virtue of section 417(2)(d) of the Proceeds of Crime Act 2002 (property in respect of which an order has been made authorising realisation of the property by an appropriate officer),

(b) a confiscation order is made under section 6, 92 or 156 of that Act,

(c) the amount payable under the confiscation order is fully paid, and

(d) any of the property remains in the hands of the appropriate officer.

(2) The property vests in the trustee as part of the bankrupt's estate.

Note. This section is inserted by the Policing and Crime Act 2009, s. 112(1), Sch. 7, Pt. 6, paras. 53, 57, as from a day to be appointed.

306C. Property subject to certain orders where confiscation order discharged or quashed

(1) This section applies where—

(a) property is excluded from the bankrupt's estate by virtue of section 417(2)(a), (b), (c) or (d) of the Proceeds of Crime Act 2002 (property in respect of which a restraint order or an order for the appointment of a receiver or administrator under that Act is in force),

(b) a confiscation order is made under section 6, 92 or 156 of that Act, and

(c) the confiscation order is discharged under section 30, 114 or 180 of that Act (as the case may be) or quashed under that Act or in pursuance of any enactment relating to appeals against conviction or sentence.

(2) Any such property in the hands of a receiver appointed under Part 2 or 4 of that Act or an administrator appointed under Part 3 of that Act vests in the trustee as part of the bankrupt's estate.

(3) But subsection (2) does not apply to the proceeds of property realised by a management receiver under section 49(2)(d) or 197(2)(d) of that Act (realisation of property to meet receiver's remuneration and expenses).

307. After-acquired property

(1) Subject to this section and section 309, the trustee may by notice in writing claim for the bankrupt's estate any property which has been acquired by, or has devolved upon, the bankrupt since the commencement of the bankruptcy.

(2) A notice under this section shall not served in respect of—

(a) any property falling within subsection (2) or (3) of section 283 in Chapter II,

(aa) any property vesting in the bankrupt by virtue of section 283A in Chapter II,

(b) any property which by virtue of any other enactment is excluded from the bankrupt's estate, or

(c) without prejudice to section 280(2)(c) (order of court on application for discharge), any property which is acquired by or, devolves upon, the bankrupt after his discharge.

(3) Subject to the next subsection, upon the service on the bankrupt of a notice under this section the property to which the notice relates shall vest in the trustee as part of the bankrupt's estate; and the trustee's title to that property has relation back to the time at which the property was acquired by, or devolved upon, the bankrupt.

(4) Where, whether before or after service of a notice under this section—

(a) a person acquires property in good faith, for value and without notice of the bankruptcy, or

(b) a banker enters into a transaction in good faith and without such notice,

the trustee is not in respect of that property or transaction entitled by virtue of this section to any remedy against that person or banker, or any person whose title to any property derives from that person or banker.

(5) References in this section to property do not include any property which, as part of the bankrupt's income, may be the subject of an income payments order under section 310.

308. Vesting in trustee of certain items of excess value

(1) Subject to section 309, where—

(a) property is excluded by virtue of section 283(2) (tools of trade, household effects, etc) from the bankrupt's estate, and

(b) it appears to the trustee that the realisable value of the whole or any part of that property exceeds the cost of a reasonable replacement for that property or that part of it,

the trustee may by notice in writing claim that property or, as the case may be, that part of it for the bankrupt's estate.

(2) Upon the service on the bankrupt of a notice under this section, the property to which the notice relates vests in the trustee as part of the bankrupt's estate; and, except against a purchaser in good faith, for value and without notice of the bankruptcy, the trustee's title to that property has relation back to the commencement of the bankruptcy.

(3) The trustee shall apply funds comprised in the estate to the purchase by or on behalf of the bankrupt of a reasonable replacement for any property vested in the trustee under this section; and the duty imposed by this subsection has priority over the obligation of the trustee to distribute the estate.

(4) For the purposes of this section property is a reasonable replacement for other property if it is reasonably adequate for meeting the needs met by the other property.

308A. Vesting in trustee of certain tenancies

Upon the service on the bankrupt by the trustee of a notice in writing under this section, any tenancy—

(a) which is excluded by virtue of section 283(3A) from the bankrupt's estate, and

(b) to which the notice relates,

vests in the trustee as part of the bankrupt's estate; and, except against a purchaser in good faith, for value and without notice of the bankruptcy, the trustee's title to that tenancy has relation back to the commencement of the bankruptcy.

309. Time-limit for notice under s 307 or 308

(1) Except with the leave of the court, a notice shall not be served—

(a) under section 307, after the end of the period of 42 days beginning with the day on which it first came to the knowledge of the trustee that the property in question had been acquired by, or had devolved upon, the bankrupt;

(b) under section 308 or section 308A, after the end of the period of 42 days beginning with the day on which the property or tenancy in question first came to the knowledge of the trustee.

(2) For the purposes of this section—

(a) anything which comes to the knowledge of the trustee is deemed in relation to any successor of his as trustee to have come to the knowledge of the successor at the same time; and

(b) anything which comes (otherwise than under paragraph (a)) to the knowledge of a person before he is the trustee is deemed to come to his knowledge on his appointment taking effect or, in the case of the official receiver, on his becoming trustee.

310. Income payments orders

(1) The court may, … make an order ("an income payments order") claiming for the bankrupt's estate so much of the income of the bankrupt during the period for which the order is in force as may be specified in the order.

(1A) An income payments order may be made only on an application instituted—

(a) by the trustee, and

(b) before the discharge of the bankrupt.

(2) The court shall not make an income payments order the effect of which would be to reduce the income of the bankrupt when taken together with any payments to which subsection (8) applies below what appears to the court to be necessary for meeting the reasonable domestic needs of the bankrupt and his family.

(3) An income payments order shall, in respect of any payment of income to which it is to apply, either—

(a) require the bankrupt to pay the trustee an amount equal to so much of that payment as is claimed by the order, or

(b) require the person making the payment to pay so much of it as is so claimed to the trustee, instead of to the bankrupt.

(4) Where the court makes an income payments order it may, if it thinks fit, discharge or vary any attachment of earnings order that is for the time being in force to secure payments by the bankrupt.

(5) Sums received by the trustee under an income payments order form part of the bankrupt's estate.

(6) An income payments order must specify the period during which it is to have effect; and that period—

(a) may end after the discharge of the bankrupt, but

(b) may not end after the period of three years beginning with the date on which the order is made.

(6A) An income payments order may (subject to subsection (6)(b)) be varied on the application of the trustee or the bankrupt (whether before or after discharge).

(7) For the purposes of this section the income of the bankrupt comprises every payment in the nature of income which is from time to time made to him or to which he from time to time becomes entitled, including any payment in respect of the carrying on of any business or in respect of any office or employment and (despite anything in section 11 or 12 of the Welfare Reform and Pensions Act 1999) any payment under a pension scheme but excluding any payment to which subsection (8) applies.

(8) This subsection applies to—

(a) payments by way of guaranteed minimum pension; ...

(b) ...

(9) In this section, "guaranteed minimum pension" has the same meaning as in the Pension Schemes Act 1993.

310A. Income payments agreement

(1) In this section "income payments agreement" means a written agreement between a bankrupt and his trustee or between a bankrupt and the official receiver which provides—

(a) that the bankrupt is to pay to the trustee or the official receiver an amount equal to a specified part or proportion of the bankrupt's income for a specified period, or

(b) that a third person is to pay to the trustee or the official receiver a specified proportion of money due to the bankrupt by way of income for a specified period.

(2) A provision of an income payments agreement of a kind specified in subsection (1)(a) or (b) may be enforced as if it were a provision of an income payments order.

(3) While an income payments agreement is in force the court may, on the application of the bankrupt, his trustee or the official receiver, discharge or vary an attachment of earnings order that is for the time being in force to secure payments by the bankrupt.

(4) The following provisions of section 310 shall apply to an income payments agreement as they apply to an income payments order—

(a) subsection (5) (receipts to form part of estate), and

(b) subsections (7) to (9) (meaning of income).

(5) An income payments agreement must specify the period during which it is to have effect; and that period—

(a) may end after the discharge of the bankrupt, but

(b) may not end after the period of three years beginning with the date on which the agreement is made.

(6) An income payments agreement may (subject to subsection (5)(b)) be varied—

(a) by written agreement between the parties, or

(b) by the court on an application made by the bankrupt, the trustee or the official receiver.

(7) The court—

(a) may not vary an income payments agreement so as to include provision of a kind which could not be included in an income payments order, and

(b) shall grant an application to vary an income payments agreement if and to the extent that the court thinks variation necessary to avoid the effect mentioned in section 310(2).

311. Acquisition by trustee of control

(1) The trustee shall take possession of all books, papers and other records which relate to the bankrupt's estate or affairs and which belong to him or are in his possession or under his control (including any which would be privileged from disclosure in any proceedings).

(2) In relation to, and for the purpose of acquiring or retaining possession of, the bankrupt's estate, the trustee is in the same position as if he were a receiver of property appointed by the High Court; and the court may, on his application, enforce such acquisition or retention accordingly.

(3) Where any part of the bankrupt's estate consists of stock or shares in a company, shares in a ship or any other property transferable in the books of a company, office or person, the trustee may exercise the right to transfer the property to the same extent as the bankrupt might have exercised it if he had not become bankrupt.

(4) Where any part of the estate consists of things in action, they are deemed to have been assigned to the trustee; but notice of the deemed assignment need not be given except in so far as it is necessary, in a case where the deemed assignment is from the bankrupt himself, for protecting the priority of the trustee.

(5) Where any goods comprised in the estate are held by any person by way of pledge, pawn or other security and no notice has been served in respect of those goods by the official receiver under subsection (5) of section 285 (restriction on realising security), the trustee may serve such a notice in respect of the goods; and whether or not a notice has been served under this subsection or that subsection, the trustee may, if he thinks fit, exercise the bankrupt's right of redemption in respect of any such goods.

(6) A notice served by the trustee under subsection (5) has the same effect as a notice served by the official receiver under section 285(5).

312. Obligation to surrender control to trustee

(1) The bankrupt shall deliver up to the trustee possession of any property, books, papers or other records of which he has possession or control and of which the trustee is required to take possession.

This is without prejudice to the general duties of the bankrupt under section 333 in this Chapter.

(2) If any of the following is in possession of any property, books, papers or other records of which the trustee is required to take possession, namely—

(a) the official receiver,

(b) a person who has ceased to be trustee of the bankrupt's estate, or

(c) a person who has been the supervisor of a voluntary arrangement approved in relation to the bankrupt under Part VIII,

the official receiver or, as the case may be, that person shall deliver up possession of the property, books, papers or records to the trustee.

(3) Any banker or agent of the bankrupt or any other person who holds any property to the account of, or for, the bankrupt shall pay or deliver to the trustee all property in his possession or under his control which forms part of the bankrupt's estate and which he is not by law entitled to retain as against the bankrupt or trustee.

(4) If any person without reasonable excuse fails to comply with any obligation imposed by this section, he is guilty of a contempt of court and liable to be punished accordingly (in addition to any other punishment to which he may be subject).

313. Charge on bankrupt's home

(1) Where any property consisting of an interest in a dwelling house which is occupied by the bankrupt or by his spouse or former spouse or by his civil partner or former civil partner is comprised in the bankrupt's estate and the trustee is, for any reason, unable for the time being to realise that property, the trustee may apply to the court for an order imposing a charge on the property for the benefit of the bankrupt's estate.

(2) If on an application under this section the court imposes a charge on any property, the benefit of that charge shall be comprised in the bankrupt's estate and is enforceable, up to the charged value from time to time, for the payment of any amount which is payable otherwise than to the bankrupt out of the estate and of interest on that amount at the prescribed rate.

(2A) In subsection (2) the charged value means—

(a) the amount specified in the charging order as the value of the bankrupt's interest in the property at the date of the order, plus

(b) interest on that amount from the date of the charging order at the prescribed rate.

(2B) In determining the value of an interest for the purposes of this section the court shall disregard any matter which it is required to disregard by the rules.

(3) An order under this section made in respect of property vested in the trustee shall provide, in accordance with the rules, for the property to cease to be comprised in the bankrupt's estate and, subject to the charge (and any prior charge), to vest in the bankrupt.

(4) Subsection (1), (2), (4), (5) and (6) of section 3 of the Charging Orders Act 1979 (supplemental provisions with respect to charging orders) have effect in relation to orders under this section as in relation to charging orders under that Act.

(5) But an order under section 3(5) of that Act may not vary a charged value.

313A. Low value home: application for sale, possession or charge

(1) This section applies where—

(a) property comprised in the bankrupt's estate consists of an interest in a dwelling-house which at the date of the bankruptcy was the sole or principal residence of—

(i) the bankrupt,

(ii) the bankrupt's spouse or civil partner, or

(iii) a former spouse or former civil partner of the bankrupt, and

(b) the trustee applies for an order for the sale of the property, for an order for possession of the property or for an order under section 313 in respect of the property.

(2) The court shall dismiss the application if the value of the interest is below the amount prescribed for the purposes of this subsection.

(3) In determining the value of an interest for the purposes of this section the court shall disregard any matter which it is required to disregard by the order which prescribes the amount for the purposes of subsection (2).

314. Powers of trustee

(1) The trustee may—

(a) with the permission of the creditors' committee or the court, exercise any of the powers specified in Part I of Schedule 5 to this Act, and

(b) without that permission, exercise any of the general powers specified in Part II of that Schedule.

(2) With the permission of the creditors' committee or the court, the trustee may appoint the bankrupt—

(a) to superintend the management of his estate or any part of it,

(b) to carry on his business (if any) for the benefit of his creditors, or

(c) in any other respect to assist in administering the estate in such manner and on such terms as the trustee may direct.

(3) A permission given for the purposes of subsection (1)(a) or (2) shall not be a general permission but shall relate to a particular proposed exercise of the power in question; and a person dealing with the trustee in good faith and for value is not to be concerned to enquire whether any permission required in either case has been given.

(4) Where the trustee has done anything without the permission required by subsection (1)(a) or (2), the court or the creditors' committee may, for the purpose of enabling him to meet his expenses out of the bankrupt's estate, ratify what the trustee has done.

But the committee shall not do so unless it is satisfied that the trustee has acted in a case of urgency and has sought its ratification without undue delay.

(5) Part III of Schedule 5 to this Act has effect with respect to the things which the trustee is able to do for the purposes of, or in connection with, the exercise of any of his powers under any of this Group of Parts.

(6) Where the trustee (not being the official receiver) in exercise of the powers conferred on him by any provision in this Group of Parts—

(a) disposes of any property comprised in the bankrupt's estate to an associate of the bankrupt, or

(b) employs a solicitor,

he shall, if there is for the time being a creditors' committee, give notice to the committee of that exercise of his powers.

(7) Without prejudice to the generality of subsection (5) and Part III of Schedule 5, the trustee may, if he thinks fit, at any time summon a general meeting of the bankrupt's creditors.

Subject to the preceding provisions in this Group of Parts, he shall summon such a meeting if he is requested to do so by a creditor of the bankrupt and the request is made with the concurrence of not less than one-tenth, in value, of the bankrupt's creditors (including the creditor making the request).

(8) Nothing in this Act is to be construed as restricting the capacity of the trustee to exercise any of his powers outside England and Wales.

Disclaimer of onerous property

315. Disclaimer (general power)

(1) Subject as follows, the trustee may, by the giving of the prescribed notice, disclaim any onerous property and may do so notwithstanding that he has taken possession of it, endeavoured to sell it or otherwise exercised rights of ownership in relation to it.

(2) The following is onerous property for the purposes of this section, that is to say—

(a) any unprofitable contract, and

(b) any other property comprised in the bankrupt's estate which is unsaleable or not readily saleable, or is such that it may give rise to a liability to pay money or perform any other onerous act.

(3) A disclaimer under this section—

(a) operates so as to determine, as from the date of the disclaimer, the rights, interests and liabilities of the bankrupt and his estate in or in respect of the property disclaimed, and

(b) discharges the trustee from all personal liability in respect of that property as from the commencement of his trusteeship,

but does not, except so far as is necessary for the purpose of releasing the bankrupt, the bankrupt's estate and the trustee from any liability, affect the rights or liabilities of any other person.

(4) A notice of disclaimer shall not be given under this section in respect of any property that has been claimed for the estate under section 307 (after-acquired property) or 308 (personal property of bankrupt exceeding reasonable replacement value) or 308A, except with the leave of the court.

(5) Any person sustaining loss or damage in consequence of the operation of a disclaimer under this section is deemed to be a creditor of the bankrupt to the extent of the loss or damage and accordingly may prove for the loss or damage as a bankruptcy debt.

316. Notice requiring trustee's decision

(1) Notice of disclaimer shall not be given under section 315 in respect of any property if—

(a) a person interested in the property has applied in writing to the trustee or one of his predecessors as trustee requiring the trustee or that predecessor to decide whether he will disclaim or not, and

(b) the period of 28 days beginning with the day on which that application was made has expired without a notice of disclaimer having been given under section 315 in respect of that property.

(2) The trustee is deemed to have adopted any contract which by virtue of this section he is not entitled to disclaim.

317. Disclaimer of leaseholds

(1) The disclaimer of any property of a leasehold nature does not take effect unless a copy of the disclaimer has been served (so far as the trustee is aware of their addresses) on every person claiming under the bankrupt as underlessee or mortgagee and either—

(a) no application under section 320 below is made with respect to the property before the end of the period of 14 days beginning with the day on which the last notice served under this subsection was served, or

(b) where such an application has been made, the court directs that the disclaimer is to take effect.

(2) Where the court gives a direction under subsection (1)(b) it may also, instead of or in addition to any order it makes under section 320, make such orders with respect to fixtures, tenant's improvements and other matters arising out of the lease as it thinks fit.

318. Disclaimer of dwelling house

Without prejudice to section 317, the disclaimer of any property in a dwelling house does not take effect unless a copy of the disclaimer has been served (so far as the trustee is aware of their addresses) on every person in occupation of or claiming a right to occupy the dwelling house and either—

(a) no application under section 320 is made with respect to the property before the end of the period of 14 days beginning with the day on which the last notice served under this section was served, or

(b) where such an application has been made, the court directs that the disclaimer is to take effect.

319. Disclaimer of land subject to rentcharge

(1) The following applies where, in consequence of the disclaimer under section 315 of any land subject to a rentcharge, that land vests by operation of law in the Crown or any other person (referred to in the next subsection as "the proprietor").

(2) The proprietor, and the successors in title of the proprietor, are not subject to any personal liability in respect of any sums becoming due under the rentcharge, except sums becoming due after the proprietor, or some person claiming under or through the proprietor, has taken possession or control of the land or has entered into occupation of it.

320. Court order vesting disclaimed property

(1) This section and the next apply where the trustee has disclaimed property under section 315.

(2) An application may be made to the court under this section by—

(a) any person who claims an interest in the disclaimed property,

(b) any person who is under any liability in respect of the disclaimed property, not being a liability discharged by the disclaimer, or

(c) where the disclaimed property is property in a dwelling-house, any person who at the time when the bankruptcy petition was presented was in occupation of or entitled to occupy the dwelling house.

(3) Subject as follows in this section and the next, the court may, on an application under this section, make an order on such terms as it thinks fit for the vesting of the disclaimed property in, or for its delivery to—

(a) a person entitled to it or a trustee for such a person,

(b) a person subject to such a liability as is mentioned in subsection (2)(b) or a trustee for such a person, or

(c) where the disclaimed property is property in a dwelling-house, any person who at the time when the bankruptcy petition was presented was in occupation of or entitled to occupy the dwelling house.

(4) The court shall not make an order by virtue of subsection (3)(b) except where it appears to the court that it would be just to do so for the purpose of compensating the person subject to the liability in respect of the disclaimer.

(5) The effect of any order under this section shall be taken into account in assessing for the purposes of section 315(5) the extent of any loss or damage sustained by any person in consequence of the disclaimer.

(6) An order under this section vesting property in any person need not be completed by any conveyance, assignment or transfer.

321. Order under s 320 in respect of leaseholds

(1) The court shall not make an order under section 320 vesting property of a leasehold nature in any person, except on terms making that person—

(a) subject to the same liabilities and obligations as the bankrupt was subject to under the lease on the day the bankruptcy petition was presented, or

(b) if the court thinks fit, subject to the same liabilities and obligations as that person would be subject to if the lease had been assigned to him on that day.

(2) For the purposes of an order under section 320 relating to only part of any property comprised in a lease, the requirements of subsection (1) apply as if the lease comprised only the property to which the order relates.

(3) Where subsection (1) applies and no person is willing to accept an order under section 320 on the terms required by that subsection, the court may (by order under section 320) vest the estate or interest of the bankrupt in the property in any person who is liable (whether personally or in a representative capacity and whether alone or jointly with the bankrupt) to perform the lessee's covenants in the lease.

The court may by virtue of this subsection vest that estate and interest in such a person freed and discharged from all estates, incumbrances and interests created by the bankrupt.

(4) Where subsection (1) applies and a person declines to accept any order under section 320, that person shall be excluded from all interest in the property.

Distribution of bankrupt's estate

322. Proof of debts

(1) Subject to this section and the next, the proof of any bankruptcy debt by a secured or unsecured creditor of the bankrupt and the admission or rejection of any proof shall take place in accordance with the rules.

(2) Where a bankruptcy debt bears interest, that interest is provable as part of the debt except in so far as it is payable in respect of any period after the commencement of the bankruptcy.

(3) The trustee shall estimate the value of any bankruptcy debt which, by reason of its being subject to any contingency or contingencies or for any other reason, does not bear a certain value.

(4) Where the value of a bankruptcy debt is estimated by the trustee under subsection (3) or, by virtue of section 303 in Chapter III, by the court, the amount provable in the bankruptcy in respect of the debt is the amount of the estimate.

323. Mutual credit and set-off

(1) This section applies where before the commencement of the bankruptcy there have been mutual credits, mutual debts or other mutual dealings between the bankrupt and any creditor of the bankrupt proving or claiming to prove for a bankruptcy debt.

(2) An account shall be taken of what is due from each party to the other in respect of the mutual dealings and the sums due from one party shall be set off against the sums due from the other.

(3) Sums due from the bankrupt to another party shall not be included in the account taken under subsection (2) if that other party had notice at the time they became due that a bankruptcy petition relating to the bankrupt was pending.

(4) Only the balance (if any) of the account taken under subsection (2) is provable as a bankruptcy debt or, as the case may be, to be paid to the trustee as part of the bankrupt's estate.

324. Distribution by means of dividend

(1) Whenever the trustee has sufficient funds in hand for the purpose he shall, subject to the retention of such sums as may be necessary for the expenses of the bankruptcy, declare and distribute dividends among the creditors in respect of the bankruptcy debts which they have respectively proved.

(2) The trustee shall give notice of his intention to declare and distribute a dividend.

(3) Where the trustee has declared a dividend, he shall give notice of the dividend and of how it is proposed to distribute it; and a notice given under this subsection shall contain the prescribed particulars of the bankrupt's estate.

(4) In the calculation and distribution of a dividend the trustee shall make provision—

(a) for any bankruptcy debts which appear to him to be due to persons who, by reason of the distance of their place of residence, may not have had sufficient time to tender and establish their proofs,

(b) for any bankruptcy debts which are the subject of claims which have not yet been determined, and

(c) for disputed proofs and claims.

325. Claims by unsatisfied creditors

(1) A creditor who has not proved his debt before the declaration of any dividend is not entitled to disturb, by reason that he has not participated in it, the distribution of that dividend or any other dividend declared before his debt was proved, but—

(a) when he has proved that debt he is entitled to be paid, out of any money for the time being available for the payment of any further dividend, any dividend or dividends which he has failed to receive; and

(b) any dividend or dividends payable under paragraph (a) shall be paid before that money is applied to the payment of any such further dividend.

(2) No action lies against the trustee for a dividend, but if the trustee refuses to pay a dividend the court may, if it thinks fit, order him to pay it and also to pay, out of his own money—

(a) interest on the dividend, at the rate for the time being specified in section 17 of the Judgments Act 1838, from the time it was withheld, and

(b) the costs of the proceedings in which the order to pay is made.

326. Distribution of property in specie

(1) Without prejudice to sections 315 to 319 (disclaimer), the trustee may, with the permission of the creditors' committee, divide in its existing form amongst the bankrupt's creditors, according to its estimated value, any property which from its peculiar nature or other special circumstances cannot be readily or advantageously sold.

(2) A permission given for the purposes of subsection (1) shall not be a general permission but shall relate to a particular proposed exercise of the power in question; and a person dealing with the trustee in good faith and for value is not to be concerned to enquire whether any permission required by subsection (1) has been given.

(3) Where the trustee has done anything without the permission required by subsection (1), the court or the creditors' committee may, for the purpose of enabling him to meet his expenses out of the bankrupt's estate, ratify what the trustee has done.

But the committee shall not do so unless it is satisfied that the trustee acted in a case of urgency and has sought its ratification without undue delay.

327. Distribution in criminal bankruptcy

Where the bankruptcy order was made on a petition under section 264(1)(d) (criminal bankruptcy), no distribution shall be made under sections 324 to 326 so long as an appeal is pending (within the meaning of section 277) against the bankrupt's conviction of any offence by virtue of which the criminal bankruptcy order on which the petition was based was made.

Note. This section is repealed by the Criminal Justice Act 1988, s. 170(2), Sch. 16, as from a day to be appointed.

328. Priority of debts

(1) In the distribution of the bankrupt's estate, his preferential debts (within the meaning given by section 386 in Part XII) shall be paid in priority to other debts.

(2) Preferential debts rank equally between themselves after the expenses of the bankruptcy and shall be paid in full unless the bankrupt's estate is insufficient for meeting them, in which case they abate in equal proportions between themselves.

(3) Debts which are neither preferential debts nor debts to which the next section applies also rank equally between themselves and, after the preferential debts, shall be paid in full unless the bankrupt's estate is insufficient for meeting them, in which case they abate in equal proportions between themselves.

(4) Any surplus remaining after the payment of the debts that are preferential or rank equally under subsection (3) shall be applied in paying interest on those debts in respect of the periods during which they have been outstanding since the commencement of the bankruptcy; and interest on preferential debts ranks equally with interest on debts other than preferential debts.

(5) The rate of interest payable under subsection (4) in respect of any debt is whichever is the greater of the following—

(a) the rate specified in section 17 of the Judgments Act 1838 at the commencement of the bankruptcy, and

(b) the rate applicable to that debt apart from the bankruptcy.

(6) This section and the next are without prejudice to any provision of this Act or any other Act under which the payment of any debt or the making of any other payment is, in the event of bankruptcy, to have a particular priority or to be postponed.

329. Debts to spouse or civil partner

(1) This section applies to bankruptcy debts owed in respect of credit provided by a person who (whether or not the bankrupt's spouse or civil partner at the time the credit was provided) was the bankrupt's spouse or civil partner at the commencement of the bankruptcy.

(2) Such debts—

(a) rank in priority after the debts and interest required to be paid in pursuance of section 328(3) and (4), and

(b) are payable with interest at the rate specified in section 328(5) in respect of the period during which they have been outstanding since the commencement of the bankruptcy;

and the interest payable under paragraph (b) has the same priority as the debts on which it is payable.

330. Final distribution

(1) When the trustee has realised all the bankrupt's estate or so much of it as can, in the trustee's opinion, be realised without needlessly protracting the trusteeship, he shall give notice in the prescribed manner either—

(a) of his intention to declare a final dividend, or

(b) that no dividend, or further dividend, will be declared.

(2) The notice under subsection (1) shall contain the prescribed particulars and shall require claims against the bankrupt's estate to be established by a date ("the final date") specified in the notice.

(3) The court may, on the application of any person, postpone the final date.

(4) After the final date, the trustee shall—

(a) defray any outstanding expenses of the bankruptcy out of the bankrupt's estate, and

(b) if he intends to declare a final dividend, declare and distribute that dividend without regard to the claim of any person in respect of a debt not already proved in the bankruptcy.

(5) If a surplus remains after payment in full and with interest of all the bankrupt's creditors and the payment of the expenses of the bankruptcy, the bankrupt is entitled to the surplus.

(6) Subsection (5) is subject to Article 35 of the EC Regulation (surplus in secondary proceedings to be transferred to main proceedings).

331. Final meeting

(1) Subject as follows in this section and the next, this section applies where—

(a) it appears to the trustee that the administration of the bankrupt's estate in accordance with this Chapter is for practical purposes complete, and

(b) the trustee is not the official receiver.

(2) The trustee shall summon a final general meeting of the bankrupt's creditors which—

(a) shall receive the trustee's report of his administration of the bankrupt's estate, and

(b) shall determine whether the trustee should have his release under section 299 in Chapter III.

(3) The trustee may, if he thinks fit, give the notice summoning the final general meeting at the same time as giving notice under section 330(1); but, if summoned for an earlier date, that meeting shall be adjourned (and, if necessary, further adjourned) until a date on which the trustee is able to report to the meeting that the administration of the bankrupt's estate is for practical purposes complete.

(4) In the administration of the estate it is the trustee's duty to retain sufficient sums from the estate to cover the expenses of summoning and holding the meeting required by this section.

332. Saving for bankrupt's home

(1) This section applies where—

(a) there is comprised in the bankrupt's estate property consisting of an interest in a dwelling house which is occupied by the bankrupt or by his spouse or former spouse or by his civil partner or former civil partner, and

(b) the trustee has been unable for any reason to realise that property.

(2) The trustee shall not summon a meeting under section 331 unless either—

(a) the court has made an order under section 313 imposing a charge on that property for the benefit of the bankrupt's estate, or

(b) the court has declined, on an application under that section, to make such an order, or

(c) the Secretary of State has issued a certificate to the trustee stating that it would be inappropriate or inexpedient for such an application to be made in the case in question.

Supplemental

333. Duties of bankrupt in relation to trustee

(1) The bankrupt shall—

(a) give to the trustee such information as to his affairs,

(b) attend on the trustee at such times, and

(c) do all such other things,

as the trustee may for the purposes of carrying out his functions under any of this Group of Parts reasonably require.

(2) Where at any time after the commencement of the bankruptcy any property is acquired by, or devolves upon, the bankrupt or there is an increase of the bankrupt's income, the bankrupt shall, within the prescribed period, give the trustee notice of the property or, as the case may be, of the increase.

(3) Subsection (1) applies to a bankrupt after his discharge.

(4) If the bankrupt without reasonable excuse fails to comply with any obligation imposed by this section, he is guilty of a contempt of court and liable to be punished accordingly (in addition to any other punishment to which he may be subject).

334. Stay of distribution in case of second bankruptcy

(1) This section and the next apply where a bankruptcy order is made against an undischarged bankrupt; and in both sections—

(a) "the later bankruptcy" means the bankruptcy arising from that order,

(b) "the earlier bankruptcy" means the bankruptcy (or, as the case may be, most recent bankruptcy) from which the bankrupt has not been discharged at the commencement of the later bankruptcy, and

(c) "the existing trustee" means the trustee (if any) of the bankrupt's estate for the purposes of the earlier bankruptcy.

(2) Where the existing trustee has been given the prescribed notice of the presentation of the petition for the later bankruptcy, any distribution or other disposition by him of anything to which the next

subsection applies, if made after the giving of the notice, is void except to the extent that it was made with the consent of the court or is or was subsequently ratified by the court.

This is without prejudice to section 284 (restrictions on dispositions of property following bankruptcy order).

(3) This subsection applies to—

(a) any property which is vested in the existing trustee under section 307(3) (after-acquired property);

(b) any money paid to the existing trustee in pursuance of an income payments order under section 310; and

(c) any property or money which is, or in the hands of the existing trustee represents, the proceeds of sale or application of property or money falling within paragraph (a) or (b) of this subsection.

335. Adjustment between earlier and later bankruptcy estates

(1) With effect from the commencement of the later bankruptcy anything to which section 334(3) applies which, immediately before the commencement of that bankruptcy, is comprised in the bankrupt's estate for the purposes of the earlier bankruptcy is to be treated as comprised in the bankrupt's estate for the purposes of the later bankruptcy and, until there is a trustee of that estate, is to be dealt with by the existing trustee in accordance with the rules.

(2) Any sums which in pursuance of an income payments order under section 310 are payable after the commencement of the later bankruptcy to the existing trustee shall form part of the bankrupt's estate for the purposes of the later bankruptcy; and the court may give such consequential directions for the modification of the order as it thinks fit.

(3) Anything comprised in a bankrupt's estate by virtue of subsection (1) or (2) is so comprised subject to a first charge in favour of the existing trustee for any bankruptcy expenses incurred by him in relation thereto.

(4) Except as provided above and in section 334, property which is, or by virtue of section 308 (personal property of bankrupt exceeding reasonable replacement value) or section 308A (vesting in trustee of certain tenancies) is capable of being, comprised in the bankrupt's estate for the purposes of the earlier bankruptcy, or of any bankruptcy prior to it, shall not be comprised in his estate for the purposes of the later bankruptcy.

(5) The creditors of the bankrupt in the earlier bankruptcy and the creditors of the bankrupt in any bankruptcy prior to the earlier one, are not to be creditors of his in the later bankruptcy in respect of the same debts; but the existing trustee may prove in the later bankruptcy for—

(a) the unsatisfied balance of the debts (including any debt under this subsection) provable against the bankrupt's estate in the earlier bankruptcy;

(b) any interest payable on that balance; and

(c) any unpaid expenses of the earlier bankruptcy.

(6) Any amount provable under subsection (5) ranks in priority after all the other debts provable in the later bankruptcy and after interest on those debts and, accordingly, shall not be paid unless those debts and that interest have first been paid in full.

CHAPTER V
EFFECT OF BANKRUPTCY ON CERTAIN RIGHTS, TRANSACTIONS, ETC

Rights under trusts of land

335A. Rights under trusts of land

(1) Any application by a trustee of a bankrupt's estate under section 14 of the Trusts of Land and Appointment of Trustees Act 1996 (powers of court in relation to trusts of land) for an order under that section for the sale of land shall be made to the court having jurisdiction in relation to the bankruptcy.

(2) On such an application the court shall make such order as it thinks just and reasonable having regard to—

(a) the interests of the bankrupt's creditors;

(b) where the application is made in respect of land which includes a dwelling house which is or has been the home of the bankrupt or the bankrupt's spouse or civil partner or former spouse or former civil partner—

(i) the conduct of the spouse, civil partner, former spouse or former civil partner, so far as contributing to the bankruptcy,

(ii) the needs and financial resources of the spouse, civil partner, former spouse or former civil partner, and

(iii) the needs of any children; and

(c) all the circumstances of the case other than the needs of the bankrupt.

(3) Where such an application is made after the end of the period of one year beginning with the first vesting under Chapter IV of this Part of the bankrupt's estate in a trustee, the court shall assume, unless the circumstances of the case are exceptional, that the interests of the bankrupt's creditors outweigh all other considerations.

(4) The powers conferred on the court by this section are exercisable on an application whether it is made before or after the commencement of this section.

Rights of occupation

336. Rights of occupation etc of bankrupt's spouse or civil partner

(1) Nothing occurring in the initial period of the bankruptcy (that is to say, the period beginning with the day of the presentation of the petition for the bankruptcy order and ending with the vesting of the bankrupt's estate in a trustee) is to be taken as having given rise to any home rights under Part IV of the Family Law Act 1996 in relation to a dwelling house comprised in the bankrupt's estate.

(2) Where a spouse's or civil partner's home rights under the Act of 1996 are a charge on the estate or interest of the other spouse or civil partner, or of trustees for the other spouse or civil partner, and the other spouse or civil partner is adjudged bankrupt—

(a) the charge continues to subsist notwithstanding the bankruptcy and, subject to the provisions of that Act, binds the trustee of the bankrupt's estate and persons deriving title under that trustee, and

(b) any application for an order under section 33 of that Act shall be made to the court having jurisdiction in relation to the bankruptcy.

(3) ...

(4) On such an application as is mentioned in subsection (2) ... the court shall make such order under section 33 of the Act of 1996 … as it thinks just and reasonable having regard to—

(a) the interests of the bankrupt's creditors,

(b) the conduct of the spouse or former spouse or civil partner or former civil partner, so far as contributing to the bankruptcy,

(c) the needs and financial resources of the spouse or former spouse or civil partner or former civil partner,

(d) the needs of any children, and

(e) all the circumstances of the case other than the needs of the bankrupt.

(5) Where such an application is made after the end of the period of one year beginning with the first vesting under Chapter IV of this Part of the bankrupt's estate in a trustee, the court shall assume, unless the circumstances of the case are exceptional, that the interests of the bankrupt's creditors outweigh all other considerations.

337. Rights of occupation of bankrupt

(1) This section applies where—

(a) a person who is entitled to occupy a dwelling house by virtue of a beneficial estate or interest is adjudged bankrupt, and

(b) any persons under the age of 18 with whom that person had at some time occupied that dwelling house had their home with that person at the time when the bankruptcy petition was presented and at the commencement of the bankruptcy.

(2) Whether or not the bankrupt's spouse or civil partner (if any) has home rights under Part IV of the Family Law Act 1996—

(a) the bankrupt has the following rights as against the trustee of his estate—

(i) if in occupation, a right not to be evicted or excluded from the dwelling house or any part of it, except with the leave of the court,

(ii) if not in occupation, a right with the leave of the court to enter into and occupy the dwelling house, and

(b) the bankrupt's rights are a charge, having the like priority as an equitable interest created immediately before the commencement of the bankruptcy, on so much of his estate or interest in the dwelling house as vests in the trustee.

(3) The Act of 1996 has effect, with the necessary modifications, as if—

(a) the rights conferred by paragraph (a) of subsection (2) were home rights under that Act,

(b) any application for such leave as is mentioned in that paragraph were an application for an order under section 33 of that Act, and

(c) any charge under paragraph (b) of that subsection on the estate or interest of the trustee were a charge under that Act on the estate or interest of a spouse or civil partner.

(4) Any application for leave such as is mentioned in subsection (2)(a) or otherwise by virtue of this section for an order under section 33 of the Act of 1996 shall be made to the court having jurisdiction in relation to the bankruptcy.

(5) On such an application the court shall make such order under section 33 of the Act of 1996 as it thinks just and reasonable having regard to the interests of the creditors, to the bankrupt's financial resources, to the needs of the children and to all the circumstances of the case other than the needs of the bankrupt.

(6) Where such an application is made after the end of the period of one year beginning with the vesting (under Chapter IV of this Part) of the bankrupt's estate in a trustee, the court shall assume, unless the circumstances of the case are exceptional, that the interests of the bankrupt's creditors outweigh all other considerations.

338. Payments in respect of premises occupied by bankrupt

Where any premises comprised in a bankrupt's estate are occupied by him (whether by virtue of the preceding section or otherwise) on condition that he makes payments towards satisfying any liability arising under a mortgage of the premises or otherwise towards the outgoings of the premises, the bankrupt does not, by virtue of those payments, acquire any interest in the premises.

Adjustment of prior transactions, etc

339. Transactions at an undervalue

(1) Subject as follows in this section and sections 341 and 342, where an individual is adjudged bankrupt and he has at a relevant time (defined in section 341) entered into a transaction with any person at an undervalue, the trustee of the bankrupt's estate may apply to the court for an order under this section.

(2) The court shall, on such an application, make such order as it thinks fit for restoring the position to what it would have been if that individual had not entered into that transaction.

(3) For the purposes of this section and sections 341 and 342, an individual enters into a transaction with a person at an undervalue if—

(a) he makes a gift to that person or he otherwise enters into a transaction with that person on terms that provide for him to receive no consideration,

(b) he enters into a transaction with that person in consideration of marriage or the formation of a civil partnership, or

(c) he enters into a transaction with that person for a consideration the value of which, in money or money's worth, is significantly less than the value, in money or money's worth, of the consideration provided by the individual.

340. Preferences

(1) Subject as follows in this and the next two sections, where an individual is adjudged bankrupt and he has at a relevant time (defined in section 341) given a preference to any person, the trustee of the bankrupt's estate may apply to the court for an order under this section.

(2) The court shall, on such an application, make such order as it thinks fit for restoring the position to what it would have been if that individual had not given that preference.

(3) For the purposes of this and the next two sections, an individual gives a preference to a person if—

(a) that person is one of the individual's creditors or a surety or guarantor for any of his debts or other liabilities, and

(b) the individual does anything or suffers anything to be done which (in either case) has the effect of putting that person into a position which, in the event of the individual's bankruptcy, will be better than the position he would have been in if that thing had not been done.

(4) The court shall not make an order under this section in respect of a preference given to any person unless the individual who gave the preference was influenced in deciding to give it by a desire to produce in relation to that person the effect mentioned in subsection (3)(b) above.

(5) An individual who has given a preference to a person who, at the time the preference was given, was an associate of his (otherwise than by reason only of being his employee) is presumed, unless the contrary is shown, to have been influenced in deciding to give it by such a desire as is mentioned in subsection (4).

(6) The fact that something has been done in pursuance of the order of a court does not, without more, prevent the doing or suffering of that thing from constituting the giving of a preference.

341. "Relevant time" under ss 339, 340

(1) Subject as follows, the time at which an individual enters into a transaction at an undervalue or gives a preference is a relevant time if the transaction is entered into or the preference given—

(a) in the case of a transaction at an undervalue, at a time in the period of 5 years ending with the day of the presentation of the bankruptcy petition on which the individual is adjudged bankrupt,

(b) in the case of a preference which is not a transaction at an undervalue and is given to a person who is an associate of the individual (otherwise than by reason only of being his employee), at a time in the period of 2 years ending with that day, and

(c) in any other case of a preference which is not a transaction at an undervalue, at a time in the period of 6 months ending with that day.

(2) Where an individual enters into a transaction at an undervalue or gives a preference at a time mentioned in paragraph (a), (b) or (c) of subsection (1) (not being, in the case of a transaction at an undervalue, a time less than 2 years before the end of the period mentioned in paragraph (a)), that time is not a relevant time for the purposes of sections 339 and 340 unless the individual—

(a) is insolvent at that time, or

(b) becomes insolvent in consequence of the transaction or preference;

but the requirements of this subsection are presumed to be satisfied, unless the contrary is shown, in relation to any transaction at an undervalue which is entered into by an individual with a person who is an associate of his (otherwise than by reason only of being his employee).

(3) For the purposes of subsection (2), an individual is insolvent if—

(a) he is unable to pay his debts as they fall due, or

(b) the value of his assets is less than the amount of his liabilities, taking into account his contingent and prospective liabilities.

(4) *A transaction entered into or preference given by a person who is subsequently adjudged bankrupt on a petition under section 264(1)(d) (criminal bankruptcy) is to be treated as having been entered into or given at a relevant time for the purposes of sections 339 and 340 if it was entered into or given at any time on or after the date specified for the purposes of this subsection in the criminal bankruptcy order on which the petition was based.*

(5) *No order shall be made under section 339 or 340 by virtue of subsection (4) of this section where an appeal is pending (within the meaning of section 277) against the individual's conviction of any offence by virtue of which the criminal bankruptcy order was made.*

Note. Subsections (4) and (5) are repealed by the Criminal Justice Act 1988, s. 170(2), Sch. 16, as from a day to be appointed.

342. Orders under ss 339, 340

(1) Without prejudice to the generality of section 339(2) or 340(2), an order under either of those sections with respect to a transaction or preference entered into or given by an individual who is subsequently adjudged bankrupt may (subject as follows)—

(a) require any property transferred as part of the transaction, or in connection with the giving of the preference, to be vested in the trustee of the bankrupt's estate as part of that estate;

(b) require any property to be so vested if it represents in any person's hands the application either of the proceeds of sale of property so transferred or of money so transferred;

(c) release or discharge (in whole or in part) any security given by the individual;

(d) require any person to pay, in respect of benefits received by him from the individual, such sums to the trustee of his estate as the court may direct;

(e) provide for any surety or guarantor whose obligations to any person were released or discharged (in whole or in part) under the transaction or by the giving of the preference to be under such new or revived obligations to that person as the court thinks appropriate;

(f) provide for security to be provided for the discharge of any obligation imposed by or arising under the order, for such an obligation to be charged on any property and for the security or charge to have the same priority as a security or charge released or discharged (in whole or in part) under the transaction or by the giving of the preference; and

(g) provide for the extent to which any person whose property is vested by the order in the trustee of the bankrupt's estate, or on whom obligations are imposed by the order, is to be able to prove in the bankruptcy for debts or other liabilities which arose from, or were released or discharged (in whole or in part) under or by, the transaction or the giving of the preference.

(2) An order under section 339 or 340 may affect the property of, or impose any obligation on, any person whether or not he is the person with whom the individual in question entered into the transaction or, as the case may be, the person to whom the preference was given; but such an order—

(a) shall not prejudice any interest in property which was acquired from a person other than that individual and was acquired in good faith and for value, or prejudice any interest deriving from such an interest, and

(b) shall not require a person who received a benefit from the transaction or preference in good faith and for value to pay a sum to the trustee of the bankrupt's estate, except where he was a party to the transaction or the payment is to be in respect of a preference given to that person at a time when he was a creditor of that individual.

(2A) Where a person has acquired an interest in property from a person other than the individual in question, or has received a benefit from the transaction or preference, and at the time of that acquisition or receipt—

(a) he had notice of the relevant surrounding circumstances and of the relevant proceedings, or

(b) he was an associate of, or was connected with, either the individual in question or the person with whom that individual entered into the transaction or to whom that individual gave the preference, then, unless the contrary is shown, it shall be presumed for the purposes of paragraph (a) or (as the case may be) paragraph (b) of subsection (2) that the interest was acquired or the benefit was received otherwise than in good faith.

(3) Any sums required to be paid to the trustee in accordance with an order under section 339 or 340 shall be comprised in the bankrupt's estate.

(4) For the purposes of subsection (2A)(a), the relevant surrounding circumstances are (as the case may require)—

(a) the fact that the individual in question entered into the transaction at an undervalue; or

(b) the circumstances which amounted to the giving of the preference by the individual in question.

(5) For the purposes of subsection (2A)(a), a person has notice of the relevant proceedings if he has notice—

(a) of the fact that the petition on which the individual in question is adjudged bankrupt has been presented; or

(b) of the fact that the individual in question has been adjudged bankrupt.

(6) Section 249 in Part VII of this Act shall apply for the purposes of subsection (2A)(b) as it applies for the purposes of the first Group of Parts.

342A. Recovery of excessive pension contributions

(1) Where an individual who is adjudged bankrupt—

(a) has rights under an approved pension arrangement, or

(b) has excluded rights under an unapproved pension arrangement,

the trustee of the bankrupt's estate may apply to the court for an order under this section.

(2) If the court is satisfied—

(a) that the rights under the arrangement are to any extent, and whether directly or indirectly, the fruits of relevant contributions, and

(b) that the making of any of the relevant contributions ("the excessive contributions") has unfairly prejudiced the individual's creditors,

the court may make such order as it thinks fit for restoring the position to what it would have been had the excessive contributions not been made.

(3) Subsection (4) applies where the court is satisfied that the value of the rights under the arrangement is, as a result of rights of the individual under the arrangement or any other pension arrangement having at any time become subject to a debit under section 29(1)(a) of the Welfare Reform and Pensions Act 1999 (debits giving effect to pension-sharing), less than it would otherwise have been.

(4) Where this subsection applies—

(a) any relevant contributions which were represented by the rights which became subject to the debit shall, for the purposes of subsection (2), be taken to be contributions of which the rights under the arrangement are the fruits, and

(b) where the relevant contributions represented by the rights under the arrangement (including those so represented by virtue of paragraph (a)) are not all excessive contributions, relevant contributions which are represented by the rights under the arrangement otherwise than by virtue of paragraph (a) shall be treated as excessive contributions before any which are so represented by virtue of that paragraph.

(5) In subsections (2) to (4) "relevant contributions" means contributions to the arrangement or any other pension arrangement—

(a) which the individual has at any time made on his own behalf, or

(b) which have at any time been made on his behalf.

(6) The court shall, in determining whether it is satisfied under subsection (2)(b), consider in particular—

(a) whether any of the contributions were made for the purpose of putting assets beyond the reach of the individual's creditors or any of them, and

(b) whether the total amount of any contributions—

(i) made by or on behalf of the individual to pension arrangements, and
(ii) represented (whether directly or indirectly) by rights under approved pension arrangements or excluded rights under unapproved pension arrangements,

is an amount which is excessive in view of the individual's circumstances when those contributions were made.

(7) For the purposes of this section and sections 342B and 342C ("the recovery provisions"), rights of an individual under an unapproved pension arrangement are excluded rights if they are rights which are excluded from his estate by virtue of regulations under section 12 of the Welfare Reform and Pensions Act 1999.

(8) In the recovery provisions—

"approved pension arrangement" has the same meaning as in section 11 of the Welfare Reform and Pensions Act 1999;

"unapproved pension arrangement" has the same meaning as in section 12 of that Act.

342B. Orders under section 342A

(1) Without prejudice to the generality of section 342A(2), an order under section 342A may include provision—

(a) requiring the person responsible for the arrangement to pay an amount to the individual's trustee in bankruptcy,
(b) adjusting the liabilities of the arrangement in respect of the individual,
(c) adjusting any liabilities of the arrangement in respect of any other person that derive, directly or indirectly, from rights of the individual under the arrangement,
(d) for the recovery by the person responsible for the arrangement (whether by deduction from any amount which that person is ordered to pay or otherwise) of costs incurred by that person in complying in the bankrupt's case with any requirement under section 342C(1) or in giving effect to the order.

(2) In subsection (1), references to adjusting the liabilities of the arrangement in respect of a person include (in particular) reducing the amount of any benefit or future benefit to which that person is entitled under the arrangement.

(3) In subsection (1)(c), the reference to liabilities of the arrangement does not include liabilities in respect of a person which result from giving effect to an order or provision falling within section 28(1) of the Welfare Reform and Pensions Act 1999 (pension sharing orders and agreements).

(4) The maximum amount which the person responsible for an arrangement may be required to pay by an order under section 342A is the lesser of—

(a) the amount of the excessive contributions, and
(b) the value of the individual's rights under the arrangement (if the arrangement is an approved pension arrangement) or of his excluded rights under the arrangement (if the arrangement is an unapproved pension arrangement).

(5) An order under section 342A which requires the person responsible for an arrangement to pay an amount ("the restoration amount") to the individual's trustee in bankruptcy must provide for the liabilities of the arrangement to be correspondingly reduced.

(6) For the purposes of subsection (5), liabilities are correspondingly reduced if the difference between—

(a) the amount of the liabilities immediately before the reduction, and
(b) the amount of the liabilities immediately after the reduction,

is equal to the restoration amount.

(7) An order under section 342A in respect of an arrangement—

(a) shall be binding on the person responsible for the arrangement, and
(b) overrides provisions of the arrangement to the extent that they conflict with the provisions of the order.

342C. Orders under section 342A: supplementary

(1) The person responsible for—

(a) an approved pension arrangement under which a bankrupt has rights,
(b) an unapproved pension arrangement under which a bankrupt has excluded rights, or
(c) a pension arrangement under which a bankrupt has at any time had rights,

shall, on the bankrupt's trustee in bankruptcy making a written request, provide the trustee with such information about the arrangement and rights as the trustee may reasonably require for, or in connection with, the making of applications under section 342A.

(2) Nothing in—

(a) any provision of section 159 of the Pension Schemes Act 1993 or section 91 of the Pensions Act 1995 (which prevent assignment and the making of orders that restrain a person from receiving anything which he is prevented from assigning),
(b) any provision of any enactment (whether passed or made before or after the passing of the Welfare Reform and Pensions Act 1999) corresponding to any of the provisions mentioned in paragraph (a), or
(c) any provision of the arrangement in question corresponding to any of those provisions,

applies to a court exercising its powers under section 342A.

(3) Where any sum is required by an order under section 342A to be paid to the trustee in bankruptcy, that sum shall be comprised in the bankrupt's estate.

(4) Regulations may, for the purposes of the recovery provisions, make provision about the calculation and verification of—

(a) any such value as is mentioned in section 342B(4)(b);
(b) any such amounts as are mentioned in section 342B(6)(a) and (b).

(5) The power conferred by subsection (4) includes power to provide for calculation or verification—

(a) in such manner as may, in the particular case, be approved by a prescribed person; or
(b) in accordance with guidance from time to time prepared by a prescribed person.

(6) References in the recovery provisions to the person responsible for a pension arrangement are to—

(a) the trustees, managers or provider of the arrangement, or
(b) the person having functions in relation to the arrangement corresponding to those of a trustee, manager or provider.

(7) In this section and sections 342A and 342B—

"prescribed" means prescribed by regulations;
"the recovery provisions" means this section and sections 342A and 342B;
"regulations" means regulations made by the Secretary of State.

(8) Regulations under the recovery provisions may—

(a) make different provision for different cases;
(b) contain such incidental, supplemental and transitional provisions as appear to the Secretary of State necessary or expedient.

(9) Regulations under the recovery provisions shall be made by statutory instrument subject to annulment in pursuance of a resolution of either House of Parliament.

342D. Recovery of excessive contributions in pension-sharing cases

(1) For the purposes of sections 339, 341 and 342, a pension-sharing transaction shall be taken—

(a) to be a transaction, entered into by the transferor with the transferee, by which the appropriate amount is transferred by the transferor to the transferee; and
(b) to be capable of being a transaction entered into at an undervalue only so far as it is a transfer of so much of the appropriate amount as is recoverable.

(2) For the purposes of sections 340 to 342, a pension-sharing transaction shall be taken—

(a) to be something (namely a transfer of the appropriate amount to the transferee) done by the transferor; and
(b) to be capable of being a preference given to the transferee only so far as it is a transfer of so much of the appropriate amount as is recoverable.

(3) If on an application under section 339 or 340 any question arises as to whether, or the extent to which, the appropriate amount in the case of a pension-sharing transaction is recoverable, the question shall be determined in accordance with subsections (4) to (8).

(4) The court shall first determine the extent (if any) to which the transferor's rights under the shared arrangement at the time of the transaction appear to have been (whether directly or indirectly) the fruits of contributions ("personal contributions")—

(a) which the transferor has at any time made on his own behalf, or

(b) which have at any time been made on the transferor's behalf,

to the shared arrangement or any other pension arrangement.

(5) Where it appears that those rights were to any extent the fruits of personal contributions, the court shall then determine the extent (if any) to which those rights appear to have been the fruits of personal contributions whose making has unfairly prejudiced the transferor's creditors ("the unfair contributions").

(6) If it appears to the court that the extent to which those rights were the fruits of the unfair contributions is such that the transfer of the appropriate amount could have been made out of rights under the shared arrangement which were not the fruits of the unfair contributions, then the appropriate amount is not recoverable.

(7) If it appears to the court that the transfer could not have been wholly so made, then the appropriate amount is recoverable to the extent to which it appears to the court that the transfer could not have been so made.

(8) In making the determination mentioned in subsection (5) the court shall consider in particular—

(a) whether any of the personal contributions were made for the purpose of putting assets beyond the reach of the transferor's creditors or any of them, and

(b) whether the total amount of any personal contributions represented, at the time the pension-sharing transaction was made, by rights under pension arrangements is an amount which is excessive in view of the transferor's circumstances when those contributions were made.

(9) In this section and sections 342E and 342F—

"appropriate amount", in relation to a pension-sharing transaction, means the appropriate amount in relation to that transaction for the purposes of section 29(1) of the Welfare Reform and Pensions Act 1999 (creation of pension credits and debits);

"pension-sharing transaction" means an order or provision falling within section 28(1) of the Welfare Reform and Pensions Act 1999 (orders and agreements which activate pension-sharing);

"shared arrangement", in relation to a pension-sharing transaction, means the pension arrangement to which the transaction relates;

"transferee", in relation to a pension-sharing transaction, means the person for whose benefit the transaction is made;

"transferor", in relation to a pension-sharing transaction, means the person to whose rights the transaction relates.

342E. Orders under section 339 or 340 in respect of pension-sharing transactions

(1) This section and section 342F apply if the court is making an order under section 339 or 340 in a case where—

(a) the transaction or preference is, or is any part of, a pension-sharing transaction, and

(b) the transferee has rights under a pension arrangement ("the destination arrangement", which may be the shared arrangement or any other pension arrangement) that are derived, directly or indirectly, from the pension-sharing transaction.

(2) Without prejudice to the generality of section 339(2) or 340(2), or of section 342, the order may include provision—

(a) requiring the person responsible for the destination arrangement to pay an amount to the transferor's trustee in bankruptcy,

(b) adjusting the liabilities of the destination arrangement in respect of the transferee,

(c) adjusting any liabilities of the destination arrangement in respect of any other person that derive, directly or indirectly, from rights of the transferee under the destination arrangement,

(d) for the recovery by the person responsible for the destination arrangement (whether by deduction from any amount which that person is ordered to pay or otherwise) of costs incurred by that person in complying in the transferor's case with any requirement under section 342F(1) or in giving effect to the order,

(e) for the recovery, from the transferor's trustee in bankruptcy, by the person responsible for a pension arrangement, of costs incurred by that person in complying in the transferor's case with any requirement under section 342F(2) or (3).

(3) In subsection (2), references to adjusting the liabilities of the destination arrangement in respect of a person include (in particular) reducing the amount of any benefit or future benefit to which that person is entitled under the arrangement.

(4) The maximum amount which the person responsible for the destination arrangement may be required to pay by the order is the smallest of—

(a) so much of the appropriate amount as, in accordance with section 342D, is recoverable,

(b) so much (if any) of the amount of the unfair contributions (within the meaning given by section 342D(5)) as is not recoverable by way of an order under section 342A containing provision such as is mentioned in section 342B(1)(a), and

(c) the value of the transferee's rights under the destination arrangement so far as they are derived, directly or indirectly, from the pension-sharing transaction.

(5) If the order requires the person responsible for the destination arrangement to pay an amount ("the restoration amount") to the transferor's trustee in bankruptcy it must provide for the liabilities of the arrangement to be correspondingly reduced.

(6) For the purposes of subsection (5), liabilities are correspondingly reduced if the difference between—

(a) the amount of the liabilities immediately before the reduction, and

(b) the amount of the liabilities immediately after the reduction,

is equal to the restoration amount.

(7) The order—

(a) shall be binding on the person responsible for the destination arrangement, and

(b) overrides provisions of the destination arrangement to the extent that they conflict with the provisions of the order.

342F. Orders under section 339 or 340 in pension-sharing cases: supplementary

(1) On the transferor's trustee in bankruptcy making a written request to the person responsible for the destination arrangement, that person shall provide the trustee with such information about—

(a) the arrangement,

(b) the transferee's rights under it, and

(c) where the destination arrangement is the shared arrangement, the transferor's rights under it,

as the trustee may reasonably require for, or in connection with, the making of applications under sections 339 and 340.

(2) Where the shared arrangement is not the destination arrangement, the person responsible for the shared arrangement shall, on the transferor's trustee in bankruptcy making a written request to that person, provide the trustee with such information about—

(a) the arrangement, and

(b) the transferor's rights under it,

as the trustee may reasonably require for, or in connection with, the making of applications under sections 339 and 340.

(3) On the transferor's trustee in bankruptcy making a written request to the person responsible for any intermediate arrangement, that person shall provide the trustee with such information about—

(a) the arrangement, and

(b) the transferee's rights under it,

as the trustee may reasonably require for, or in connection with, the making of applications under sections 339 and 340.

(4) In subsection (3) "intermediate arrangement" means a pension arrangement, other than the shared arrangement or the destination arrangement, in relation to which the following conditions are fulfilled—

(a) there was a time when the transferee had rights under the arrangement that were derived (directly or indirectly) from the pension-sharing transaction, and

(b) the transferee's rights under the destination arrangement (so far as derived from the pension-sharing transaction) are to any extent derived (directly or indirectly) from the rights mentioned in paragraph (a).

(5) Nothing in—

(a) any provision of section 159 of the Pension Schemes Act 1993 or section 91 of the Pensions Act 1995 (which prevent assignment and the making of orders which restrain a person from receiving anything which he is prevented from assigning),

(b) any provision of any enactment (whether passed or made before or after the passing of the Welfare Reform and Pensions Act 1999) corresponding to any of the provisions mentioned in paragraph (a), or

(c) any provision of the destination arrangement corresponding to any of those provisions,

applies to a court exercising its powers under section 339 or 340.

(6) Regulations may, for the purposes of sections 339 to 342, sections 342D and 342E and this section, make provision about the calculation and verification of—

(a) any such value as is mentioned in section 342E(4)(c);

(b) any such amounts as are mentioned in section 342E(6)(a) and (b).

(7) The power conferred by subsection (6) includes power to provide for calculation or verification—

(a) in such manner as may, in the particular case, be approved by a prescribed person; or

(b) in accordance with guidance from time to time prepared by a prescribed person.

(8) In section 342E and this section, references to the person responsible for a pension arrangement are to—

(a) the trustees, managers or provider of the arrangement, or

(b) the person having functions in relation to the arrangement corresponding to those of a trustee, manager or provider.

(9) In this section—

"prescribed" means prescribed by regulations;

"regulations" means regulations made by the Secretary of State.

(10) Regulations under this section may—

(a) make different provision for different cases;

(b) contain such incidental, supplemental and transitional provisions as appear to the Secretary of State necessary or expedient.

(11) Regulations under this section shall be made by statutory instrument subject to annulment in pursuance of a resolution of either House of Parliament.

343. Extortionate credit transactions

(1) This section applies where a person is adjudged bankrupt who is or has been a party to a transaction for, or involving, the provision to him of credit.

(2) The court may, on the application of the trustee of the bankrupt's estate, make an order with respect to the transaction if the transaction is or was extortionate and was not entered into more than 3 years before the commencement of the bankruptcy.

(3) For the purposes of this section a transaction is extortionate if, having regard to the risk accepted by the person providing the credit—

(a) the terms of it are or were such as to require grossly exorbitant payments to be made (whether unconditionally or in certain contingencies) in respect of the provision of the credit, or

(b) it otherwise grossly contravened ordinary principles of fair dealing;

and it shall be presumed, unless the contrary is proved, that a transaction with respect to which an application is made under this section is or, as the case may be, was extortionate.

(4) An order under this section with respect to any transaction may contain such one or more of the following as the court thinks fit, that is to say—

(a) provision setting aside the whole or part of any obligation created by the transaction;

(b) provision otherwise varying the terms of the transaction or varying the terms on which any security for the purposes of the transaction is held;

(c) provision requiring any person who is or was party to the transaction to pay to the trustee any sums paid to that person, by virtue of the transaction, by the bankrupt;

(d) provision requiring any person to surrender to the trustee any property held by him as security for the purposes of the transaction;

(e) provision directing accounts to be taken between any persons.

(5) Any sums or property required to be paid or surrendered to the trustee in accordance with an order under this section shall be comprised in the bankrupt's estate.

(6) ...

The powers conferred by this section are exercisable in relation to any transaction concurrently with any powers exercisable under this Act in relation to that transaction as a transaction at an undervalue.

344. Avoidance of general assignment of book debts

(1) The following applies where a person engaged in any business makes a general assignment to another person of his existing or future book debts, or any class of them, and is subsequently adjudged bankrupt.

(2) The assignment is void against the trustee of the bankrupt's estate as regards book debts which were not paid before the presentation of the bankruptcy petition, unless the assignment has been registered under the Bills of Sale Act 1878.

(3) For the purposes of subsections (1) and (2)—

(a) "assignment" includes an assignment by way of security or charge on book debts, and

(b) "general assignment" does not include—

(i) an assignment of book debts due at the date of the assignment from specified debtors or of debts becoming due under specified contracts, or

(ii) an assignment of book debts included either in a transfer of a business made in good faith and for value or in an assignment of assets for the benefit of creditors generally.

(4) For the purposes of registration under the Act of 1878 an assignment of book debts is to be treated as if it were a bill of sale given otherwise than by way of security for the payment of a sum of money; and the provisions of that Act with respect to the registration of bills of sale apply accordingly with such necessary modifications as may be made by rules under that Act.

345. Contracts to which bankrupt is a party

(1) The following applies where a contract has been made with a person who is subsequently adjudged bankrupt.

(2) The court may, on the application of any other party to the contract, make an order discharging obligations under the contract on such terms as to payment by the applicant or the bankrupt of damages for non-performance or otherwise as appear to the court to be equitable.

(3) Any damages payable by the bankrupt by virtue of an order of the court under this section are provable as a bankruptcy debt.

(4) Where an undischarged bankrupt is a contractor in respect of any contract jointly with any person, that person may sue or be sued in respect of the contract without the joinder of the bankrupt.

346. Enforcement procedures

(1) Subject to section 285 in Chapter II (restrictions on proceedings and remedies) and to the following provisions of this section, where the creditor of any person who is adjudged bankrupt has, before the commencement of the bankruptcy—

(a) issued execution against the goods or land of that person, or
(b) attached a debt due to that person from another person,

that creditor is not entitled, as against the official receiver or trustee of the bankrupt's estate, to retain the benefit of the execution or attachment, or any sums paid to avoid it, unless the execution or attachment was completed, or the sums were paid, before the commencement of the bankruptcy.

(2) Subject as follows, where any goods of a person have been taken in execution, then, if before the completion of the execution notice is given to the enforcement officer or other officer charged with the execution that that person has been adjudged bankrupt—

(a) the enforcement officer or other officer shall on request deliver to the official receiver or trustee of the bankrupt's estate the goods and any money seized or recovered in part satisfaction of the execution, but
(b) the costs of the execution are a first charge on the goods or money so delivered and the official receiver or trustee may sell the goods or a sufficient part of them for the purpose of satisfying the charge.

(3) Subject to subsection (6) below, where—

(a) under an execution in respect of a judgment for a sum exceeding such sum as may be prescribed for the purposes of this subsection, the goods of any person are sold or money is paid in order to avoid a sale, and
(b) before the end of the period of 14 days beginning with the day of the sale or payment the enforcement officer or other officer charged with the execution is given notice that a bankruptcy petition has been presented in relation to that person, and
(c) a bankruptcy order is or has been made on that petition,

the balance of the proceeds of sale or money paid, after deducting the costs of execution, shall (in priority to the claim of the execution creditor) be comprised in the bankrupt's estate.

(4) Accordingly, in the case of an execution in respect of a judgment for a sum exceeding the sum prescribed for the purposes of subsection (3), the enforcement officer or other officer charged with the execution—

(a) shall not dispose of the balance mentioned in subsection (3) at any time within the period of 14 days so mentioned or while there is pending a bankruptcy petition of which he has been given notice under that subsection, and
(b) shall pay that balance, where by virtue of that subsection it is comprised in the bankrupt's estate, to the official receiver or (if there is one) to the trustee of that estate.

(5) For the purposes of this section—

(a) an execution against goods is completed by seizure and sale or by the making of a charging order under section 1 of the Charging Orders Act 1979;
(b) an execution against land is completed by seizure, by the appointment of a receiver or by the making of a charging order under that section;
(c) an attachment of a debt is completed by the receipt of the debt.

(6) The rights conferred by subsections (1) to (3) on the official receiver or the trustee may, to such extent and on such terms as it thinks fit, be set aside by the court in favour of the creditor who has issued the execution or attached the debt.

(7) Nothing in this section entitles the trustee of a bankrupt's estate to claim goods from a person who has acquired them in good faith under a sale by an enforcement officer or other officer charged with an execution.

(8) Neither subsection (2) nor subsection (3) applies in relation to any execution against property which has been acquired by or has devolved upon the bankrupt since the commencement of the bankruptcy, unless, at the time the execution is issued or before it is completed—

(a) the property has been or is claimed for the bankrupt's estate under section 307 (after-acquired property), and
(b) a copy of the notice given under that section has been or is served on the enforcement officer or other officer charged with the execution.

(9) In this section "enforcement officer" means an individual who is authorised to act as an enforcement officer under the Courts Act 2003.

347. Distress, etc

(1) *The right of any landlord or other person to whom rent is payable to distrain upon the goods and effects of an undischarged bankrupt for rent due to him from the bankrupt is available* (subject to sections 252(2)(b) and 254(1) above and subsection (5) below) against goods and effects comprised in the bankrupt's estate, but only for 6 months' rent accrued due before the commencement of the bankruptcy.

(2) *Where a landlord or other person to whom rent is payable has distrained for rent upon the goods and effects of* an individual to whom a bankruptcy petition relates and a bankruptcy order is subsequently made on that petition, any amount recovered by way of *that distress* which—

(a) is in excess of the amount which by virtue of subsection (1) would have been recoverable after the commencement of the bankruptcy, or

(b) is in respect of rent for a period or part of a period after *the distress was levied,*

shall be held for the bankrupt as part of his estate.

(3) Where any person (whether or not a landlord or person entitled to rent) has distrained upon the goods or effects of an individual who is adjudged bankrupt before the end of the period of 3 months beginning with the distraint, so much of those goods or effects, or of the proceeds of their sale, as is not held for the bankrupt under subsection (2) shall be charged for the benefit of the bankrupt's estate with the preferential debts of the bankrupt to the extent that the bankrupt's estate is for the time being insufficient for meeting those debts.

(4) Where by virtue of any charge under subsection (3) any person surrenders any goods or effects to the trustee of a bankrupt's estate or makes a payment to such a trustee, that person ranks, in respect of the amount of the proceeds of the sale of those goods or effects by the trustee or, as the case may be, the amount of the payment, as a preferential creditor of the bankrupt, except as against so much of the bankrupt's estate as is available for the payment of preferential creditors by virtue of the surrender or payment.

(5) *A landlord or other person to whom rent is payable is not at any time after the discharge of a bankrupt entitled to distrain upon* any goods or effects comprised in the bankrupt's estate.

(6) Where in the case of any execution—

(a) a landlord is (apart from this section) entitled under section 1 of the Landlord and Tenant Act 1709 or section 102 of the County Courts Act 1984 (claims for rent where goods seized in execution) to claim for an amount not exceeding one year's rent, and

(b) the person against whom the execution is levied is adjudged bankrupt before the notice of claim is served on the enforcement officer, or other officer charged with the execution,

the right of the landlord to claim under that section is restricted to a right to claim for an amount not exceeding 6 months' rent and does not extend to any rent payable in respect of a period after the notice of claim is so served.

(7) Nothing in subsection (6) imposes any liability on an enforcement officer or other officer charged with an execution to account to the official receiver or the trustee of a bankrupt's estate for any sums paid by him to a landlord at any time before the enforcement officer or other officer was served with notice of the bankruptcy order in question.

But this subsection is without prejudice to the liability of the landlord.

(8) Subject to sections 252(2)(b) and 254(1) above nothing in this Group of Parts affects any right to distrain otherwise than for rent; and any such right is at any time exercisable without restriction against property comprised in a bankrupt's estate, even if that right is expressed by any enactment to be exercisable in like manner as a right to distrain for rent.

(9) Any right to distrain against property comprised in a bankrupt's estate is exercisable notwithstanding that the property has vested in the trustee.

(10) The provisions of this section are without prejudice to a landlord's right in a bankruptcy to prove for any bankruptcy debt in respect of rent.

(11) *In this section "enforcement officer" means an individual who is authorised to act as an enforcement officer under the Courts Act 2003.*

Note. The following amendments are made by the Tribunals, Courts and Enforcement Act 2007, ss. 86, 146, Sch. 14, para. 44, Sch. 23, Pt. 4, as from a day to be appointed: in subsection (1), the italicized words "The right of any landlord or other person to whom rent is payable to distrain upon the goods and effects of an undischarged bankrupt for rent due to him from the bankrupt is available" are repealed and substituted by the words "CRAR (the power of commercial rent arrears recovery under section 72(1) of the Tribunals, Courts and Enforcement Act 2007) is exercisable where the tenant is an undischarged bankrupt"; in subsection (2), the italicized words "Where a landlord or other person to whom rent is payable has distrained for rent upon the goods and effects of" are repealed and substituted by the words "Where CRAR has been exercised to recover rent from", the words "that distress" are repealed and substituted by the words "CRAR", and the italicized words "the distress was levied" are repealed and substituted by the words "goods were taken control of under CRAR"; in subsection (5), the italicized words "A landlord or other person to whom rent is payable is not at any time after the discharge of a bankrupt entitled to distrain upon" are repealed and substituted by the words "CRAR is not exercisable at any time after the discharge of a bankrupt against"; and subsections (6), (7), and (11) are repealed.

348. Apprenticeships, etc

(1) This section applies where—

(a) a bankruptcy order is made in respect of an individual to whom another individual was an apprentice or articled clerk at the time when the petition on which the order was made was presented, and

(b) the bankrupt or the apprentice or clerk gives notice to the trustee terminating the apprenticeship or articles.

(2) Subject to subsection (6) below, the indenture of apprenticeship or, as the case may be, the articles of agreement shall be discharged with effect from the commencement of the bankruptcy.

(3) If any money has been paid by or on behalf of the apprentice or clerk to the bankrupt as a fee, the trustee may, on an application made by or on behalf of the apprentice or clerk, pay such sum to the apprentice or clerk as the trustee thinks reasonable, having regard to—

(a) the amount of the fee,

(b) the proportion of the period in respect of which the fee was paid that has been served by the apprentice or clerk before the commencement of the bankruptcy, and

(c) the other circumstances of the case.

(4) The power of the trustee to make a payment under subsection (3) has priority over his obligation to distribute the bankrupt's estate.

(5) Instead of making a payment under subsection (3), the trustee may, if it appears to him expedient to do so on an application made by or on behalf of the apprentice or clerk, transfer the indenture or articles to a person other than the bankrupt.

(6) Where a transfer is made under subsection (5), subsection (2) has effect only as between the apprentice or clerk and the bankrupt.

349. Unenforceability of liens on books, etc

(1) Subject as follows, a lien or other right to retain possession of any of the books, papers or other records of a bankrupt is unenforceable to the extent that its enforcement would deny possession of any books, papers or other records to the official receiver or the trustee of the bankrupt's estate.

(2) Subsection (1) does not apply to a lien on documents which give a title to property and are held as such.

349A. Arbitration agreements to which bankrupt is party

(1) This section applies where a bankrupt had become party to a contract containing an arbitration agreement before the commencement of his bankruptcy.

(2) If the trustee in bankruptcy adopts the contract, the arbitration agreement is enforceable by or against the trustee in relation to matters arising from or connected with the contract.

(3) If the trustee in bankruptcy does not adopt the contract and a matter to which the arbitration agreement applies requires to be determined in connection with or for the purposes of the bankruptcy proceedings—

(a) the trustee with the consent of the creditors' committee, or

(b) any other party to the agreement,

may apply to the court which may, if it thinks fit in all the circumstances of the case, order that the matter be referred to arbitration in accordance with the arbitration agreement.

(4) In this section—

"arbitration agreement" has the same meaning as in Part I of the Arbitration Act 1996; and

"the court" means the court which has jurisdiction in the bankruptcy proceedings.

CHAPTER VI
BANKRUPTCY OFFENCES

Preliminary

350. Scheme of this Chapter

(1) Subject to section 360(3) below, this Chapter applies where the court has made a bankruptcy order on a bankruptcy petition.

(2) This Chapter applies whether or not the bankruptcy order is annulled, but proceedings for an offence under this Chapter shall not be instituted after the annulment.

(3) Without prejudice to his liability in respect of a subsequent bankruptcy, the bankrupt is not guilty of an offence under this Chapter in respect of anything done after his discharge; but nothing in this Group of Parts prevents the institution of proceedings against a discharged bankrupt for an offence committed before his discharge.

(3A) Subsection (3) is without prejudice to any provision of this Chapter which applies to a person in respect of whom a bankruptcy restrictions order is in force.

(4) It is not a defence in proceedings for an offence under this Chapter that anything relied on, in whole or in part, as constituting that offence was done outside England and Wales.

(5) Proceedings for an offence under this Chapter or under the rules shall not be instituted except by the Secretary of State or by or with the consent of the Director of Public Prosecutions.

(6) A person guilty of an offence under this Chapter is liable to imprisonment or a fine, or both.

351. Definitions

In the following provisions of this Chapter—

(a) references to property comprised in the bankrupt's estate or to property possession of which is required to be delivered up to the official receiver or the trustee of the bankrupt's estate include any property which would be such property if a notice in respect of it were given under section 307 (after-acquired property), section 308 (personal property and effects of bankrupt having more than replacement value) or section 308A (vesting in trustee of certain tenancies);

(b) "the initial period" means the period between the presentation of the bankruptcy petition and the commencement of the bankruptcy; and

(c) a reference to a number of months or years before petition is to that period ending with the presentation of the bankruptcy petition.

352. Defence of innocent intention

Where in the case of an offence under any provision of this Chapter it is stated that this section applies, a person is not guilty of the offence if he proves that, at the time of the conduct constituting the offence, he had no intent to defraud or to conceal the state of his affairs.

Wrongdoing by the bankrupt before and after bankruptcy

353. Non-disclosure

(1) The bankrupt is guilty of an offence if—

(a) he does not to the best of his knowledge and belief disclose all the property comprised in his estate to the official receiver or the trustee, or

(b) he does not inform the official receiver or the trustee of any disposal of any property which but for the disposal would be so comprised, stating how, when, to whom and for what consideration the property was disposed of.

(2) Subsection (1)(b) does not apply to any disposal in the ordinary course of a business carried on by the bankrupt or to any payment of the ordinary expenses of the bankrupt or his family.

(3) Section 352 applies to this offence.

354. Concealment of property

(1) The bankrupt is guilty of an offence if—

(a) he does not deliver up possession to the official receiver or trustee, or as the official receiver or trustee may direct, of such part of the property comprised in his estate as is in his possession or under his control and possession of which he is required by law so to deliver up,

(b) he conceals any debt due to or from him or conceals any property the value of which is not less than the prescribed amount and possession of which he is required to deliver up to the official receiver or trustee, or

(c) in the 12 months before petition, or in the initial period, he did anything which would have been an offence under paragraph (b) above if the bankruptcy order had been made immediately before he did it.

Section 352 applies to this offence.

(2) The bankrupt is guilty of an offence if he removes, or in the initial period removed, any property the value of which was not less than the prescribed amount and possession of which he has or would have been required to deliver up to the official receiver or the trustee.

Section 352 applies to this offence.

(3) The bankrupt is guilty of an offence if he without reasonable excuse fails, on being required to do so by the official receiver, the trustee or the court—

(a) to account for the loss of any substantial part of his property incurred in the 12 months before petition or in the initial period, or

(b) to give a satisfactory explanation of the manner in which such a loss was incurred.

355. Concealment of books and papers; falsification

(1) The bankrupt is guilty of an offence if he does not deliver up possession to the official receiver or the trustee, or as the official receiver or trustee may direct, of all books, papers and other records of which he has possession or control and which relate to his estate or his affairs.

Section 352 applies to this offence.

(2) The bankrupt is guilty of an offence if—

(a) he prevents, or in the initial period prevented, the production of any books, papers or records relating to his estate or affairs;

(b) he conceals, destroys, mutilates or falsifies, or causes or permits the concealment, destruction, mutilation or falsification of, any books, papers or other records relating to his estate or affairs;

(c) he makes, or causes or permits the making of, any false entries in any book, document or record relating to his estate or affairs; or

(d) in the 12 months before petition, or in the initial period, he did anything which would have been an offence under paragraph (b) or (c) above if the bankruptcy order had been made before he did it.

Section 352 applies to this offence.

(3) The bankrupt is guilty of an offence if—

(a) he disposes of, or alters or makes any omission in, or causes or permits the disposal, altering or making of any omission in, any book, document or record relating to his estate or affairs, or

(b) in the 12 months before petition, or in the initial period, he did anything which would have been an offence under paragraph (a) if the bankruptcy order had been made before he did it.

Section 352 applies to this offence.

(4) In their application to a trading record subsections (2)(d) and (3)(b) shall have effect as if the reference to 12 months were a reference to two years.

(5) In subsection (4) "trading record" means a book, document or record which shows or explains the transactions or financial position of a person's business, including—

(a) a periodic record of cash paid and received,

(b) a statement of periodic stock-taking, and

(c) except in the case of goods sold by way of retail trade, a record of goods sold and purchased which identifies the buyer and seller or enables them to be identified.

356. False statements

(1) The bankrupt is guilty of an offence if he makes or has made any material omission in any statement made under any provision in this Group of Parts and relating to his affairs.

Section 352 applies to this offence.

(2) The bankrupt is guilty of an offence if—

(a) knowing or believing that a false debt has been proved by any person under the bankruptcy, he fails to inform the trustee as soon as practicable; or

(b) he attempts to account for any part of his property by fictitious losses or expenses; or

(c) at any meeting of his creditors in the 12 months before petition or (whether or not at such a meeting) at any time in the initial period, he did anything which would have been an offence under paragraph (b) if the bankruptcy order had been made before he did it; or

(d) he is, or at any time has been, guilty of any false representation or other fraud for the purpose of obtaining the consent of his creditors, or any of them, to an agreement with reference to his affairs or to his bankruptcy.

357. Fraudulent disposal of property

(1) The bankrupt is guilty of an offence if he makes or causes to be made, or has in the period of 5 years ending with the commencement of the bankruptcy made or caused to be made, any gift or transfer of, or any charge on, his property.

Section 352 applies to this offence.

(2) The reference to making a transfer of or charge on any property includes causing or conniving at the levying of any execution against that property.

(3) The bankrupt is guilty of an offence if he conceals or removes, or has at any time before the commencement of the bankruptcy concealed or removed, any part of his property after, or within 2 months before, the date on which a judgment or order for the payment of money has been obtained against him, being a judgment or order which was not satisfied before the commencement of the bankruptcy.

Section 352 applies to this offence.

358. Absconding

The bankrupt is guilty of an offence if—

(a) he leaves, or attempts or makes preparations to leave, England and Wales with any property the value of which is not less than the prescribed amount and possession of which he is required to deliver up to the official receiver or the trustee, or

(b) in the 6 months before petition, or in the initial period, he did anything which would have been an offence under paragraph (a) if the bankruptcy order had been made immediately before he did it.

Section 352 applies to this offence.

359. Fraudulent dealing with property obtained on credit

(1) The bankrupt is guilty of an offence if, in the 12 months before petition, or in the initial period, he disposed of any property which he had obtained on credit and, at the time he disposed of it, had not paid for.

Section 352 applies to this offence.

(2) A person is guilty of an offence if, in the 12 months before petition or in the initial period, he acquired or received property from the bankrupt knowing or believing—

(a) that the bankrupt owed money in respect of the property, and

(b) that the bankrupt did not intend, or was unlikely to be able, to pay the money he so owed.

(3) A person is not guilty of an offence under subsection (1) or (2) if the disposal, acquisition or receipt of the property was in the ordinary course of a business carried on by the bankrupt at the time of the disposal, acquisition or receipt.

(4) In determining for the purposes of this section whether any property is disposed of, acquired or received in the ordinary course of a business carried on by the bankrupt, regard may be had, in particular, to the price paid for the property.

(5) In this section references to disposing of property include pawning or pledging it; and references to acquiring or receiving property shall be read accordingly.

360. Obtaining credit; engaging in business

(1) The bankrupt is guilty of an offence if—

(a) either alone or jointly with any other person, he obtains credit to the extent of the prescribed amount or more without giving the person from whom he obtains it the relevant information about his status; or

(b) he engages (whether directly or indirectly) in any business under a name other than that in which he was adjudged bankrupt without disclosing to all persons with whom he enters into any business transaction the name in which he was so adjudged.

(2) The reference to the bankrupt obtaining credit includes the following cases—

(a) where goods are bailed to him under a hire-purchase agreement, or agreed to be sold to him under a conditional sale agreement, and

(b) where he is paid in advance (whether in money or otherwise) for the supply of goods or services.

(3) A person whose estate has been sequestrated in Scotland, or who has been adjudged bankrupt in Northern Ireland, is guilty of an offence if, before his discharge, he does anything in England and Wales which would be an offence under subsection (1) if he were an undischarged bankrupt and the sequestration of his estate or the adjudication in Northern Ireland were an adjudication under this Part.

(4) For the purposes of subsection (1)(a), the relevant information about the status of the person in question is the information that he is an undischarged bankrupt or, as the case may be, that his estate has been sequestrated in Scotland and that he has not been discharged.

(5) This section applies to the bankrupt after discharge while a bankruptcy restrictions order is in force in respect of him.

(6) For the purposes of subsection (1)(a) as it applies by virtue of subsection (5), the relevant information about the status of the person in question is the information that a bankruptcy restrictions order is in force in respect of him.

361, 362.…

CHAPTER VII
POWERS OF COURT IN BANKRUPTCY

363. General control of court

(1) Every bankruptcy is under the general control of the court and, subject to the provisions in this Group of Parts, the court has full power to decide all questions of priorities and all other questions, whether of law or fact, arising in any bankruptcy.

(2) Without prejudice to any other provision in this Group of Parts, an undischarged bankrupt or a discharged bankrupt whose estate is still being administered under Chapter IV of this Part shall do

all such things as he may be directed to do by the court for the purposes of his bankruptcy or, as the case may be, the administration of that estate.

(3) The official receiver or the trustee of a bankrupt's estate may at any time apply to the court for a direction under subsection (2).

(4) If any person without reasonable excuse fails to comply with any obligation imposed on him by subsection (2), he is guilty of a contempt of court and liable to be punished accordingly (in addition to any other punishment to which he may be subject).

364. Power of arrest

(1) In the cases specified in the next subsection the court may cause a warrant to be issued to a constable or prescribed officer of the court—

(a) for the arrest of a debtor to whom a bankruptcy petition relates or of an undischarged bankrupt, or of a discharged bankrupt whose estate is still being administered under Chapter IV of this Part, and

(b) for the seizure of any books, papers, records, money or goods in the possession of a person arrested under the warrant,

and may authorise a person arrested under such a warrant to be kept in custody, and anything seized under such a warrant to be held, in accordance with the rules, until such time as the court may order.

(2) The powers conferred by subsection (1) are exercisable in relation to a debtor or undischarged or discharged bankrupt if, at any time after the presentation of the bankruptcy petition relating to him or the making of the bankruptcy order against him, it appears to the court—

(a) that there are reasonable grounds for believing that he has absconded, or is about to abscond, with a view to avoiding or delaying the payment of any of his debts or his appearance to a bankruptcy petition or to avoiding, delaying or disrupting any proceedings in bankruptcy against him or any examination of his affairs, or

(b) that he is about to remove his goods with a view to preventing or delaying possession being taken of them by the official receiver or the trustee of his estate, or

(c) that there are reasonable grounds for believing that he has concealed or destroyed, or is about to conceal or destroy, any of his goods or any books, papers or records which might be of use to his creditors in the course of his bankruptcy or in connection with the administration of his estate, or

(d) that he has, without the leave of the official receiver or the trustee of his estate, removed any goods in his possession which exceed in value such sum as may be prescribed for the purposes of this paragraph, or

(e) that he has failed, without reasonable excuse, to attend any examination ordered by the court.

365. Seizure of bankrupt's property

(1) At any time after a bankruptcy order has been made, the court may, on the application of the official receiver or the trustee of the bankrupt's estate, issue a warrant authorising the person to whom it is directed to seize any property comprised in the bankrupt's estate which is, or any books, papers or records relating to the bankrupt's estate or affairs which are, in the possession or under the control of the bankrupt or any other person who is required to deliver the property, books, papers or records to the official receiver or trustee.

(2) Any person executing a warrant under this section may, for the purpose of seizing any property comprised in the bankrupt's estate or any books, papers or records relating to the bankrupt's estate or affairs, break open any premises where the bankrupt or anything that may be seized under the warrant is or is believed to be and any receptacle of the bankrupt which contains or is believed to contain anything that may be so seized.

(3) If, after a bankruptcy order has been made, the court is satisfied that any property comprised in the bankrupt's estate is, or any books, papers or records relating to the bankrupt's estate or affairs are, concealed in any premises not belonging to him, it may issue a warrant authorising any

constable or prescribed officer of the court to search those premises for the property, books, papers or records.

(4) A warrant under subsection (3) shall not be executed except in the prescribed manner and in accordance with its terms.

366. Inquiry into bankrupt's dealings and property

(1) At any time after a bankruptcy order has been made the court may, on the application of the official receiver or the trustee of the bankrupt's estate, summon to appear before it—

(a) the bankrupt or the bankrupt's spouse or former spouse or civil partner or former civil partner,

(b) any person known or believed to have any property comprised in the bankrupt's estate in his possession or to be indebted to the bankrupt,

(c) any person appearing to the court to be able to give information concerning the bankrupt or the bankrupt's dealings, affairs or property.

The court may require any such person as is mentioned in paragraph (b) or (c) to submit a witness statement verified by a statement of truth to the court containing an account of his dealings with the bankrupt or to produce any documents in his possession or under his control relating to the bankrupt or the bankrupt's dealings, affairs or property.

(2) Without prejudice to section 364, the following applies in a case where—

(a) a person without reasonable excuse fails to appear before the court when he is summoned to do so under this section, or

(b) there are reasonable grounds for believing that a person has absconded, or is about to abscond, with a view to avoiding his appearance before the court under this section.

(3) The court may, for the purpose of bringing that person and anything in his possession before the court, cause a warrant to be issued to a constable or prescribed officer of the court—

(a) for the arrest of that person, and

(b) for the seizure of any books, papers, records, money or goods in that person's possession.

(4) The court may authorise a person arrested under such a warrant to be kept in custody, and anything seized under such a warrant to be held, in accordance with the rules, until that person is brought before the court under the warrant or until such other time as the court may order.

367. Court's enforcement powers under s 366

(1) If it appears to the court, on consideration of any evidence obtained under section 366 or this section, that any person has in his possession any property comprised in the bankrupt's estate, the court may, on the application of the official receiver or the trustee of the bankrupt's estate, order that person to deliver the whole or any part of the property to the official receiver or the trustee at such time, in such manner and on such terms as the court thinks fit.

(2) If it appears to the court, on consideration of any evidence obtained under section 366 or this section, that any person is indebted to the bankrupt, the court may, on the application of the official receiver or the trustee of the bankrupt's estate, order that person to pay to the official receiver or trustee, at such time and in such manner as the court may direct, the whole or part of the amount due, whether in full discharge of the debt or otherwise as the court thinks fit.

(3) The court may, if it thinks fit, order that any person who if within the jurisdiction of the court would be liable to be summoned to appear before it under section 366 shall be examined in any part of the United Kingdom where he may be for the time being, or in any place outside the United Kingdom.

(4) Any person who appears or is brought before the court under section 366 or this section may be examined on oath, either orally or by interrogatories, concerning the bankrupt or the bankrupt's dealings, affairs and property.

368. Provision corresponding to s 366, where interim receiver appointed

Sections 366 and 367 apply where an interim receiver has been appointed under section 286 as they apply where a bankruptcy order has been made, as if—

(a) references to the official receiver or the trustee were to the interim receiver, and

(b) references to the bankrupt and to his estate were (respectively) to the debtor and his property.

369. Order for production of documents by inland revenue

(1) For the purposes of an examination under section 290 (public examination of bankrupt) or proceedings under sections 366 to 368, the court may, on the application of the official receiver or the trustee of the bankrupt's estate, order an inland revenue official to produce to the court—

(a) any return, account or accounts submitted (whether before or after the commencement of the bankruptcy) by the bankrupt to any inland revenue official,

(b) any assessment or determination made (whether before or after the commencement of the bankruptcy) in relation to the bankrupt by any inland revenue official, or

(c) any correspondence (whether before or after the commencement of the bankruptcy) between the bankrupt and any inland revenue official.

(2) Where the court has made an order under subsection (1) for the purposes of any examination or proceedings, the court may, at any time after the document to which the order relates is produced to it, by order authorise the disclosure of the document, or of any part of its contents, to the official receiver, the trustee of the bankrupt's estate or the bankrupt's creditors.

(3) The court shall not address an order under subsection (1) to an inland revenue official unless it is satisfied that that official is dealing, or has dealt, with the affairs of the bankrupt.

(4) Where any document to which an order under subsection (1) relates is not in the possession of the official to whom the order is addressed, it is the duty of that official to take all reasonable steps to secure possession of it and, if he fails to do so, to report the reasons for his failure to the court.

(5) Where any document to which an order under subsection (1) relates is in the possession of an inland revenue official other than the one to whom the order is addressed, it is the duty of the official in possession of the document, at the request of the official to whom the order is addressed, to deliver it to the official making the request.

(6) In this section "inland revenue official" means any inspector or collector of taxes appointed by the Commissioners of Inland Revenue or any person appointed by the Commissioners to serve in any other capacity.

(7) This section does not apply for the purposes of an examination under sections 366 and 367 which takes place by virtue of section 368 (interim receiver).

370. Power to appoint special manager

(1) The court may, on an application under this section, appoint any person to be the special manager—

(a) of a bankrupt's estate, or

(b) of the business of an undischarged bankrupt, or

(c) of the property or business of a debtor in whose case the official receiver has been appointed interim receiver under section 286.

(2) An application under this section may be made by the official receiver or the trustee of the bankrupt's estate in any case where it appears to the official receiver or trustee that the nature of the estate, property or business, or the interests of the creditors generally, require the appointment of another person to manage the estate, property or business.

(3) A special manager appointed under this section has such powers as may be entrusted to him by the court.

(4) The power of the court under subsection (3) to entrust powers to a special manager includes power to direct that any provision in this Group of Parts that has effect in relation to the official receiver, interim receiver or trustee shall have the like effect in relation to the special manager for the purposes of the carrying out by the special manager of any of the functions of the official receiver, interim receiver or trustee.

(5) A special manager appointed under this section shall—

(a) give such security as may be prescribed,

(b) prepare and keep such accounts as may be prescribed, and

(c) produce those accounts in accordance with the rules to the Secretary of State or to such other persons as may be prescribed.

371. Re-direction of bankrupt's letters, etc

(1) Where a bankruptcy order has been made, the court may from time to time, on the application of the official receiver or the trustee of the bankrupt's estate, order a postal operator (within the meaning of Part 3 of the Postal Services Act 2011) to re-direct and send or deliver to the official receiver or trustee or otherwise any postal packet (within the meaning of that Act) which would otherwise be sent or delivered by the operator concerned to the bankrupt at such place or places as may be specified in the order.

(2) An order under this section has effect for such period, not exceeding 3 months, as may be specified in the order.

PART X
INDIVIDUAL INSOLVENCY: GENERAL PROVISIONS

372. Supplies of gas, water, electricity, etc

(1) This section applies where on any day ("the relevant day")—

(a) a bankruptcy order is made against an individual or an interim receiver of an individual's property is appointed, or

(b) a voluntary arrangement proposed by an individual is approved under Part VIII, or

(c) a deed of arrangement is made for the benefit of an individual's creditors;

and in this section "the office-holder" means the official receiver, the trustee in bankruptcy, the interim receiver, the supervisor of the voluntary arrangement or the trustee under the deed of arrangement, as the case may be.

(2) If a request falling within the next subsection is made for the giving after the relevant day of any of the supplies mentioned in subsection (4), the supplier—

(a) may make it a condition of the giving of the supply that the office-holder personally guarantees the payment of any charges in respect of the supply, but

(b) shall not make it a condition of the giving of the supply, or do anything which has the effect of making it a condition of the giving of the supply, that any outstanding charges in respect of a supply given to the individual before the relevant day are paid.

(3) A request falls within this subsection if it is made—

(a) by or with the concurrence of the office-holder, and

(b) for the purposes of any business which is or has been carried on by the individual, by a firm or partnership of which the individual is or was a member, or by an agent or manager for the individual or for such a firm or partnership.

(4) The supplies referred to in subsection (2) are—

(a) a supply of gas by a gas supplier within the meaning of Part I of the Gas Act 1986;

(b) a supply of electricity by an electricity supplier within the meaning of Part I of the Electricity Act 1989;

(c) a supply of water by a water undertaker,

(d) a supply of communications services by a provider of a public electronic communications service.

(5) The following applies to expressions used in subsection (4)—

(a) …

(b) … and

(c) "communications services" do not include electronic communications services to the extent that they are used to broadcast or otherwise transmit programme services (within the meaning of the Communications Act 2003).

373. Jurisdiction in relation to insolvent individuals

(1) The High Court and the county courts have jurisdiction throughout England and Wales for the purposes of the Parts in this Group.

(2) For the purposes of those Parts, a county court has, in addition to its ordinary jurisdiction, all the powers and jurisdiction of the High Court; and the orders of the court may be enforced accordingly in the prescribed manner.

(3) Jurisdiction for the purposes of those Parts is exercised—

(a) by the High Court or the Central London County Court in relation to the proceedings which, in accordance with the rules, are allocated to the London insolvency district, and

(b) by each county court in relation to the proceedings which are so allocated to the insolvency district of that court.

(4) Subsection (3) is without prejudice to the transfer of proceedings from one court to another in the manner prescribed by the rules; and nothing in that subsection invalidates any proceedings on the grounds that they were initiated or continued in the wrong court.

374. Insolvency districts

(1) The Lord Chancellor may, with the concurrence of the Lord Chief Justice, by order designate the areas which are for the time being to be comprised, for the purposes of the Parts in this Group, in the London Insolvency district and the insolvency district of each county court; and an order under this section may—

(a) exclude any county court from having jurisdiction for the purposes of those Parts, or

(b) confer jurisdiction for those purposes on any county court which has not previously had that jurisdiction.

(2) An order under this section may contain such incidental, supplemental and transitional provisions as may appear to the Lord Chancellor and the Lord Chief Justice necessary or expedient.

(3) An order under this section shall be made by statutory instrument and, after being made, shall be laid before each House of Parliament.

(4) Subject to any order under this section—

(a) the district which, immediately before the appointed day, is the London bankruptcy district becomes, on that day, the London insolvency district;

(b) any district which immediately before that day is the bankruptcy district of a county court becomes, on that day, the insolvency district of that court, and

(c) any county court which immediately before that day is excluded from having jurisdiction in bankruptcy is excluded, on and after that day, from having jurisdiction for the purposes of the Parts in this Group.

(5) The Lord Chief Justice may nominate a judicial office holder (as defined in section 109(4) of the Constitutional Reform Act 2005) to exercise his functions under this section.

375. Appeals etc from courts exercising insolvency jurisdiction

(1) Every court having jurisdiction for the purposes of the Parts in this Group may review, rescind or vary any order made by it in the exercise of that jurisdiction.

(2) An appeal from a decision made in the exercise of jurisdiction for the purposes of those Parts by a county court or by a registrar in bankruptcy of the High Court lies to a single judge of the High Court; and an appeal from a decision of that judge on such an appeal lies… to the Court of Appeal.

(3) A county court is not, in the exercise of its jurisdiction for the purposes of those Parts, to be subject to be restrained by the order of any other court, and no appeal lies from its decision in the exercise of that jurisdiction except as provided by this section.

376. Time-limits

Where by any provision in this Group of Parts or by the rules the time for doing anything is limited, the court may extend the time, either before or after it has expired, on such terms, if any, as it thinks fit.

377. Formal defects

The acts of a person as the trustee of a bankrupt's estate or as a special manager, and the acts of the creditors' committee established for any bankruptcy, are valid notwithstanding any defect in the appointment, election or qualifications of the trustee or manager or, as the case may be, of any member of the committee.

378. Exemption from stamp duty

Stamp duty shall not be charged on—

(a) any document, being a deed, conveyance, assignment, surrender, admission or other assurance relating solely to property which is comprised in a bankrupt's estate and which, after the execution of that document, is or remains at law or in equity the property of the bankrupt or of the trustee of that estate,

(b) any writ, order, certificate or other instrument relating solely to the property of a bankrupt or to any bankruptcy proceedings.

379. Annual report

As soon as practicable after the end of 1986 and each subsequent calendar year, the Secretary of State shall prepare and lay before each House of Parliament a report about the operation during that year of so much of this Act as is comprised in this Group of Parts, and about proceedings in the course of that year under the Deeds of Arrangement Act 1914.

Remote attendance at meetings

379A. Remote attendance at meetings

(1) Where—

(a) a bankruptcy order is made against an individual or an interim receiver of an individual's property is appointed, or

(b) a voluntary arrangement in relation to an individual is proposed or is approved under Part 8,

this section applies to any meeting of the individual's creditors summoned under this Act or the rules.

(2) Where the person summoning a meeting ("the convener") considers it appropriate, the meeting may be conducted and held in such a way that persons who are not present together at the same place may attend it.

(3) Where a meeting is conducted and held in the manner referred to in subsection (2), a person attends the meeting if that person is able to exercise any rights which that person may have to speak and vote at the meeting.

(4) For the purposes of this section—

(a) a person exercises the right to speak at a meeting when that person is in a position to communicate to all those attending the meeting, during the meeting, any information or opinions which that person has on the business of the meeting; and

(b) a person exercises the right to vote at a meeting when—

(i) that person is able to vote, during the meeting, on resolutions put to the vote at the meeting, and

(ii) that person's vote can be taken into account in determining whether or not such resolutions are passed at the same time as the votes of all the other persons attending the meeting.

(5) The convener of a meeting which is to be conducted and held in the manner referred to in subsection (2) may make whatever arrangements the convener considers appropriate to—

(a) enable those attending the meeting to exercise their rights to speak or vote, and

(b) ensure the identification of those attending the meeting and the security of any electronic means used to enable attendance.

(6) Where in the reasonable opinion of the convener—

(a) a meeting will be attended by persons who will not be present together at the same place, and

(b) it is unnecessary or inexpedient to specify a place for the meeting, any requirement under this Act or the rules to specify a place for the meeting may be satisfied by specifying the arrangements the convener proposes to enable persons to exercise their rights to speak or vote.

(7) In making the arrangements referred to in subsection (5) and in forming the opinion referred to in subsection (6)(b), the convener must have regard to the legitimate interests of the creditors and others attending the meeting in the efficient despatch of the business of the meeting.

(8) If—

(a) the notice of a meeting does not specify a place for the meeting,

(b) the convener is requested in accordance with the rules to specify a place for the meeting, and

(c) that request is made by not less than ten percent in value of the creditors,

it shall be the duty of the convener to specify a place for the meeting.

Use of websites

379B. Use of websites

(1) This section applies where—

(a) a bankruptcy order is made against an individual or an interim receiver of an individual's property is appointed, or

(b) a voluntary arrangement in relation to an individual is proposed or is approved under Part 8,

and "the office-holder" means the official receiver, the trustee in bankruptcy, the interim receiver, the nominee or the supervisor of the voluntary arrangement, as the case may be.

(2) Where any provision of this Act or the rules requires the office-holder to give, deliver, furnish or send a notice or other document or information to any person, that requirement is satisfied by making the notice, document or information available on a website—

(a) in accordance with the rules, and

(b) in such circumstances as may be prescribed.

PART XI
INTERPRETATION FOR SECOND GROUP OF PARTS

380. Introductory

The next five sections have effect for the interpretation of the provisions of this Act which are comprised in this Group of Parts; and where a definition is provided for a particular expression, it applies except so far as the context otherwise requires.

381. "Bankrupt" and associated terminology

(1) "Bankrupt" means an individual who has been adjudged bankrupt and, in relation to a bankruptcy order, it means the individual adjudged bankrupt by that order.

(2) "Bankruptcy order" means an order adjudging an individual bankrupt.

(3) "Bankruptcy petition" means a petition to the court for a bankruptcy order.

382. "Bankruptcy debt", "liability"

(1) "Bankruptcy debt", in relation to a bankrupt, means (subject to the next subsection) any of the following—

(a) any debt or liability to which he is subject at the commencement of the bankruptcy,

(b) any debt or liability to which he may become subject after the commencement of the bankruptcy (including after his discharge from bankruptcy) by reason of any obligation incurred before the commencement of the bankruptcy,

(c) any amount specified in pursuance of section 39(3)(c) of the Powers of Criminal Courts Act 1973 in any criminal bankruptcy order made against him before the commencement of the bankruptcy, and

(d) any interest provable as mentioned in section 322(2) in Chapter IV of Part IX.

(2) In determining for the purposes of any provision in this Group of Parts whether any liability in tort is a bankruptcy debt, the bankrupt is deemed to become subject to that liability by reason of an obligation incurred at the time when the cause of action accrued.

(3) For the purposes of references in this Group of Parts to a debt or liability, it is immaterial whether the debt or liability is present or future, whether it is certain or contingent or whether its amount is fixed or liquidated, or is capable of being ascertained by fixed rules or as a matter of opinion; and references in this Group of Parts to owing a debt are to be read accordingly.

(4) In this Group of Parts, except in so far as the context otherwise requires, "liability" means (subject to subsection (3) above) a liability to pay money or money's worth, including any liability under an enactment, any liability for breach of trust, any liability in contract, tort or bailment and any liability arising out of an obligation to make restitution.

(5) Liability under the Child Support Act 1991 to pay child support maintenance to any person is not a debt or liability for the purposes of Part 8.

Note. Subsection (1)(c) is repealed by the Criminal Justice Act 1988, s. 170(2), Sch. 16, as from a day to be appointed.

383. "Creditor", "security", etc

(1) "Creditor"—

(a) in relation to a bankrupt, means a person to whom any of the bankruptcy debts is owed *(being, in the case of an amount falling within paragraph (c) of the definition in section 382(1) of "bankruptcy debt", the person in respect of whom that amount is specified in the criminal bankruptcy order in question)*, and

(b) in relation to an individual to whom a bankruptcy petition relates, means a person who would be a creditor in the bankruptcy if a bankruptcy order were made on that petition.

(2) Subject to the next two subsections and any provision of the rules requiring a creditor to give up his security for the purposes of proving a debt, a debt is secured for the purposes of this Group of Parts to the extent that the person to whom the debt is owed holds any security for the debt (whether a mortgage, charge, lien or other security) over any property of the person by whom the debt is owed.

(3) Where a statement such as is mentioned in section 269(1)(a) in Chapter I of Part IX has been made by a secured creditor for the purposes of any bankruptcy petition and a bankruptcy order is subsequently made on that petition, the creditor is deemed for the purposes of the Parts in this Group to have given up the security specified in the statement.

(4) In subsection (2) the reference to a security does not include a lien on books, papers or other records, except to the extent that they consist of documents which give a title to property and are held as such.

Note. The italicized words in subsection (1)(a) are repealed by the Criminal Justice Act 1988, s. 170(2), Sch. 16, as from a day to be appointed.

384. "Prescribed" and "the rules"

(1) Subject to the next subsection and sections 342C(7) and 342F(9) in Chapter V of Part IX, "prescribed" means prescribed by the rules; and "the rules" means rules made under section 412 in Part XV.

(2) References in this Group of Parts to the amount prescribed for the purposes of any of the following provisions—

section 251S(4);
section 273;
section 313A;
section 346(3);
section 354(1) and (2);
section 358;
section 360(1);
section 361(2); . . .

section 364(2)(d),
paragraphs 6 to 8 of Schedule 4ZA.
and references in those provisions to the prescribed amount are to be read in accordance with section 418 in Part XV and orders made under that section.

385. Miscellaneous definitions

(1) The following definitions have effect—

"the court", in relation to any matter, means the court to which, in accordance with section 373 in Part X and the rules, proceedings with respect to that matter are allocated or transferred;

"creditor's petition" means a bankruptcy petition under section 264(1)(a);

"criminal bankruptcy order" means an order under section 39(1) of the Powers of Criminal Courts Act 1973;

"debt" is to be construed in accordance with section 382(3);

"the debtor"—

(za) in relation to a debt relief order or an application for such an order, has the same meaning as in Part 7A,

(a) in relation to a proposal for the purposes of Part VIII, means the individual making or intending to make that proposal, and

(b) in relation to a bankruptcy petition, means the individual to whom the petition relates;

"debtor's petition" means a bankruptcy petition presented by the debtor himself under section 264(1)(b);

"debt relief order" means an order made by the official receiver under Part 7A;

"dwelling house" includes any building or part of a building which is occupied as a dwelling and any yard, garden, garage or outhouse belonging to the dwelling house and occupied with it;

"estate", in relation to a bankrupt is to be construed in accordance with section 283 in Chapter II of Part IX;

"family", in relation to a bankrupt, means the persons (if any) who are living with him and are dependent on him;

"insolvency administration order" means an order for the administration in bankruptcy of the insolvent estate of a deceased debtor (being an individual at the date of his death);

"insolvency administration petition" means a petition for an insolvency administration order;

"the Rules" means the Insolvency Rules 1986;

"secured" and related expressions are to be construed in accordance with section 383; and

"the trustee", in relation to a bankruptcy and the bankrupt, means the trustee of the bankrupt's estate.

(2) References in this Group of Parts to a person's affairs include his business, if any.

Note. The italicized definition of "criminal bankruptcy order" in subsection (1) is repealed by the Criminal Justice Act 1988, s. 170(2), Sch. 16, as from a day to be appointed.

THE THIRD GROUP OF PARTS
MISCELLANEOUS MATTERS BEARING ON BOTH COMPANY AND INDIVIDUAL INSOLVENCY; GENERAL INTERPRETATION; FINAL PROVISIONS

PART XII
PREFERENTIAL DEBTS IN COMPANY AND INDIVIDUAL INSOLVENCY

386. Categories of preferential debts

(1) A reference in this Act to the preferential debts of a company or an individual is to the debts listed in Schedule 6 to this Act (contributions to occupational pension schemes; remuneration, &c of

employees; levies on coal and steel production); and references to preferential creditors are to be read accordingly.

(2) In that Schedule "the debtor" means the company or the individual concerned.

(3) Schedule 6 is to be read with Schedule 4 to the Pension Schemes Act 1993 (occupational pension scheme contributions).

387. "The relevant date"

(1) This section explains references in Schedule 6 to the relevant date (being the date which determines the existence and amount of a preferential debt).

(2) For the purposes of section 4 in Part I (meetings to consider company voluntary arrangement), the relevant date in relation to a company which is not being wound up is—

(a) if the company is in administration, the date on which it entered administration, and

(b) if the company is not in administration, the date on which the voluntary arrangement takes effect.

(2A) For the purposes of paragraph 31 of Schedule A1 (meetings to consider company voluntary arrangement where a moratorium under section 1A is in force), the relevant date in relation to a company is the date of filing.

(3) In relation to a company which is being wound up, the following applies—

(a) if the winding up is by the court, and the winding-up order was made immediately upon the discharge of an administration order, the relevant date is the date on which the company entered administration;

(aa) if the winding up is by the court and the winding-up order was made following conversion of administration into winding up by virtue of Article 37 of the EC Regulation, the relevant date is the date on which the company entered administration;

(ab) if the company is deemed to have passed a resolution for voluntary winding up by virtue of an order following conversion of administration into winding up under Article 37 of the EC Regulation, the relevant date is the date on which the company entered administration;

(b) if the case does not fall within paragraph (a), (aa) or (ab) and the company—

(i) is being wound up by the court, and

(ii) had not commenced to be wound up voluntarily before the date of the making of the winding-up order,

the relevant date is the date of the appointment (or first appointment) of a provisional liquidator or, if no such appointment has been made, the date of the winding-up order;

(ba) if the case does not fall within paragraph (a), (aa), (ab) or (b) and the company is being wound up following administration pursuant to paragraph 83 of Schedule B1, the relevant date is the date on which the company entered administration;

(c) if the case does not fall within paragraph (a), (aa), (ab), (b) or (ba), the relevant date is the date of the passing of the resolution for the winding up of the company.

(3A) In relation to a company which is in administration (and to which no other provision of this section applies) the relevant date is the date on which the company enters administration.

(4) In relation to a company in receivership (where section 40 or, as the case may be, section 59 applies), the relevant date is—

(a) in England and Wales, the date of the appointment of the receiver by debenture-holders, and

(b) in Scotland, the date of the appointment of the receiver under section 53(6) or (as the case may be) 54(5).

(5) For the purposes of section 258 in Part VIII (individual voluntary arrangements), the relevant date is, in relation to a debtor who is not an undischarged bankrupt—

(a) where an interim order has been made under section 252 with respect to his proposal, the date of that order, and

(b) in any other case, the date on which the voluntary arrangement takes effect.

(6) In relation to a bankrupt, the following applies—

(a) where at the time the bankruptcy order was made there was an interim receiver appointed under section 286, the relevant date is the date on which the interim receiver was first appointed after the presentation of the bankruptcy petition;

(b) otherwise, the relevant date is the date of the making of the bankruptcy order.

PART XIII
INSOLVENCY PRACTITIONERS AND THEIR QUALIFICATION

Restrictions on unqualified persons acting as liquidator, trustee in bankruptcy, etc

388. Meaning of "act as insolvency practitioner"

(1) A person acts as an insolvency practitioner in relation to a company by acting—

(a) as its liquidator, provisional liquidator, administrator or administrative receiver, or

(b) where a voluntary arrangement in relation to the company is proposed or approved under Part I, as nominee or supervisor.

(2) A person acts as an insolvency practitioner in relation to an individual by acting—

(a) as his trustee in bankruptcy or interim receiver of his property or as permanent or interim trustee in the sequestration of his estate; or

(b) as trustee under a deed which is a deed of arrangement made for the benefit of his creditors or, in Scotland, a trust deed for his creditors; or

(c) where a voluntary arrangement in relation to the individual is proposed or approved under Part VIII, as nominee or supervisor; or

(d) in the case of a deceased individual to the administration of whose estate this section applies by virtue of an order under section 421 (application of provisions of this Act to insolvent estates of deceased persons), as administrator of that estate.

(2A) A person acts as an insolvency practitioner in relation to an insolvent partnership by acting—

(a) as its liquidator, provisional liquidator or administrator, or

(b) as trustee of the partnership under article 11 of the Insolvent Partnerships Order 1994, or

(c) where a voluntary arrangement in relation to the insolvent partnership is proposed or approved under Part I of the Act, as nominee or supervisor.

(2B) In relation to a voluntary arrangement proposed under Part I or VIII, a person acts as nominee if he performs any of the functions conferred on nominees under the Part in question.

(3) References in this section to an individual include, except in so far as the context otherwise requires, references ... to any debtor within the meaning of the Bankruptcy (Scotland) Act 1985.

(4) In this section—

"administrative receiver" has the meaning given by section 251 in Part VII;

"company" means—

(a) a company registered under the Companies Act 2006 in England and Wales or Scotland, or

(b) a company that may be wound up under Part 5 of this Act (unregistered companies);

"interim trustee" and "permanent trustee" mean the same as in the Bankruptcy (Scotland) Act 1985.

(5) Nothing in this section applies to anything done by—

(a) the official receiver; or

(b) the Accountant in Bankruptcy (within the meaning of the Bankruptcy (Scotland) Act 1985).

(6) Nothing in this section applies to anything done (whether in the United Kingdom or elsewhere) in relation to insolvency proceedings under the EC Regulation in a member State other than the United Kingdom.

389. Acting without qualification an offence

(1) A person who acts as an insolvency practitioner in relation to a company or an individual at a time when he is not qualified to do so is liable to imprisonment or a fine, or to both.

(1A) This section is subject to section 389A.

(2) This section does not apply to the official receiver or the Accountant in Bankruptcy (within the meaning of the Bankruptcy (Scotland) Act 1985.

389A. Authorisation of nominees and supervisors

(1) Section 389 does not apply to a person acting, in relation to a voluntary arrangement proposed or approved under Part I or Part VIII, as nominee or supervisor if he is authorised so to act.

(2) For the purposes of subsection (1) and those Parts, an individual to whom subsection (3) does not apply is authorised to act as nominee or supervisor in relation to such an arrangement if—

(a) he is a member of a body recognised for the purpose by the Secretary of State or of a body recognised for the purpose of Article 348A(2)(a) of the Insolvency (Northern Ireland) Order 1989 by the Department of Enterprise, Trade and Investment for Northern Ireland, and

(b) there is in force security (in Scotland, caution) for the proper performance of his functions and that security or caution meets the prescribed requirements with respect to his so acting in relation to the arrangement.

(3) This subsection applies to a person if—

(a) he has been adjudged bankrupt or sequestration of his estate has been awarded and (in either case) he has not been discharged,

(aa) a moratorium period under a debt relief order applies in relation to him (under Part 7A of this Act),

(b) he is subject to a disqualification order made or a disqualification undertaking accepted under the Company Directors Disqualification Act 1986 or the Company Directors Disqualification (Northern Ireland) Order 2002,

(c) he is a patient within the meaning of ... section 329(1) of the Mental Health (Care and Treatment) (Scotland) Act 2003, or

(d) he lacks capacity (within the meaning of the Mental Capacity Act 2005) to act as nominee or supervisor.

(4) The Secretary of State may by order declare a body which appears to him to fall within subsection (5) to be a recognised body for the purposes of subsection (2)(a).

(5) A body may be recognised if it maintains and enforces rules for securing that its members—

(a) are fit and proper persons to act as nominees or supervisors, and

(b) meet acceptable requirements as to education and practical training and experience.

(6) For the purposes of this section, a person is a member of a body only if he is subject to its rules when acting as nominee or supervisor (whether or not he is in fact a member of the body).

(7) An order made under subsection (4) in relation to a body may be revoked by a further order if it appears to the Secretary of State that the body no longer falls within subsection (5).

(8) An order of the Secretary of State under this section has effect from such date as is specified in the order; and any such order revoking a previous order may make provision for members of the body in question to continue to be treated as members of a recognised body for a specified period after the revocation takes effect.

389B. Official receiver as nominee or supervisor

(1) The official receiver is authorised to act as nominee or supervisor in relation to a voluntary arrangement approved under Part VIII provided that the debtor is an undischarged bankrupt when the arrangement is proposed.

(2) The Secretary of State may by order repeal the proviso in subsection (1).

(3) An order under subsection (2)—

(a) must be made by statutory instrument, and

(b) shall be subject to annulment in pursuance of a resolution of either House of Parliament.

The requisite qualification, and the means of obtaining it

390. Persons not qualified to act as insolvency practitioners

(1) A person who is not an individual is not qualified to act as an insolvency practitioner.

(2) A person is not qualified to act as an insolvency practitioner at any time unless at that time—

(a) he is authorised so to act by virtue of membership of a professional body recognised under section 391 below, being permitted so to act by or under the rules of that body, or
(b) he holds an authorisation granted by a competent authority under section 393; or
(c) he holds an authorisation granted by the Department of Enterprise, Trade and Investment for Northern Ireland under Article 352 of the Insolvency (Northern Ireland) Order 1989.

(3) A person is not qualified to act as an insolvency practitioner in relation to another person at any time unless—
(a) there is in force at that time security or, in Scotland, caution for the proper performance of his functions, and
(b) that security or caution meets the prescribed requirements with respect to his so acting in relation to that other person.

(4) A person is not qualified to act as an insolvency practitioner at any time if at that time—
(a) he has been adjudged bankrupt or sequestration of his estate has been awarded and (in either case) he has not been discharged,
(aa) a moratorium period under a debt relief order applies in relation of him,
(b) he is subject to a disqualification order made or a disqualification undertaking accepted under the Company Directors Disqualification Act 1986 or the Company Directors Disqualification (Northern Ireland) Order 2002,
(c) he is a patient within the meaning of ... section 329(1) of the Mental Health (Care and Treatment) (Scotland) Act 2003 or has had a guardian appointed to him under the Adults with Incapacity (Scotland) Act 2000 (asp 4), or
(d) he lacks capacity (within the meaning of the Mental Capacity Act 2005) to act as an insolvency practitioner.

(5) A person is not qualified to act as an insolvency practitioner while a bankruptcy restrictions order or a debt relief restrictions order is in force in respect of him.

391. Recognised professional bodies

(1) The Secretary of State may by order declare a body which appears to him to fall within subsection (2) below to be a recognised professional body for the purposes of this section.

(2) A body may be recognised if it regulates the practice of a profession and maintains and enforces rules for securing that such of its members as are permitted by or under the rules to act as insolvency practitioners—
(a) are fit and proper persons so to act, and
(b) meet acceptable requirements as to education and practical training and experience.

(3) References to members of a recognised professional body are to persons who, whether members of that body or not, are subject to its rules in the practice of the profession in question.
The reference in section 390(2) above to membership of a professional body recognised under this section is to be read accordingly.

(4) An order made under subsection (1) in relation to a professional body may be revoked by a further order if it appears to the Secretary of State that the body no longer falls within subsection (2).

(5) An order of the Secretary of State under this section has effect from such date as is specified in the order; and any such order revoking a previous order may make provision whereby members of the body in question continue to be treated as authorised to act as insolvency practitioners for a specified period after the revocation takes effect.

392. Authorisation by competent authority

(1) Application may be made to a competent authority for authorisation to act as an insolvency practitioner.

(2) The competent authorities for this purpose are—
(a) in relation to a case of any description specified in directions given by the Secretary of State, the body or person so specified in relation to cases of that description, and
(b) in relation to a case not falling within paragraph (a), the Secretary of State.

(3) The application—

(a) shall be made in such manner as the competent authority may direct,

(b) shall contain or be accompanied by such information as that authority may reasonably require for the purpose of determining the application, and

(c) shall be accompanied by the prescribed fee;

and the authority may direct that notice of the making of the application shall be published in such manner as may be specified in the direction.

(4) At any time after receiving the application and before determining it the authority may require the applicant to furnish additional information.

(5) Directions and requirements given or imposed under subsection (3) or (4) may differ as between different applications.

(6) Any information to be furnished to the competent authority under this section shall, if it so requires, be in such form or verified in such manner as it may specify.

(7) An application may be withdrawn before it is granted or refused.

(8) Any sums received under this section by a competent authority other than the Secretary of State may be retained by the authority; and any sums so received by the Secretary of State shall be paid into the Consolidated Fund.

(9) Subsection (3)(c) shall not have effect in respect of an application made to the Secretary of State (but this subsection is without prejudice to section 415A).

393. Grant, refusal and withdrawal of authorisation

(1) The competent authority may, on an application duly made in accordance with section 392 and after being furnished with all such information as it may require under that section, grant or refuse the application.

(2) The authority shall grant the application if it appears to it from the information furnished by the applicant and having regard to such other information, if any, as it may have—

(a) that the applicant is a fit and proper person to act as an insolvency practitioner, and

(b) that the applicant meets the prescribed requirements with respect to education and practical training and experience.

(3) An authorisation granted under this section, if not previously withdrawn, continues in force for one year.

(3A) But where an authorisation is granted under this section the competent authority must, before its expiry (and without a further application made in accordance with section 392) grant a further authorisation under this section taking effect immediately after the expiry of the previous authorisation, unless it appears to the authority that the subject of the authorisation no longer complies with subsection (2)(a) and (b).

(4) An authorisation granted under this section may be withdrawn by the competent authority if it appears to it—

(a) that the holder of the authorisation is no longer a fit and proper person to act as an insolvency practitioner, or

(b) without prejudice to paragraph (a), that the holder—

(i) has failed to comply with any provision of this Part or of any regulations made under this Part or Part XV, or

(ii) in purported compliance with any such provision, has furnished the competent authority with false, inaccurate or misleading information.

(5) An authorisation granted under this section may be withdrawn by the competent authority at the request or with the consent of the holder of the authorisation.

(6) Where an authorisation granted under this section is withdrawn—

(a) subsection (3A) does not require a further authorisation to be granted, or

(b) if a further authorisation has already been granted at the time of the withdrawal, the further authorisation is also withdrawn.

394. Notices

(1) Where a competent authority grants an authorisation under section 393, it shall give written notice of that fact to the applicant, specifying the date on which the authorisation takes effect.

(2) Where the authority proposes to refuse an application, or to withdraw an authorisation under section 393(4), it shall give the applicant or holder of the authorisation written notice of its intention to do so, setting out particulars of the grounds on which it proposes to act.

(3) In the case of a proposed withdrawal the notice shall state the date on which it is proposed that the withdrawal should take effect.

(4) A notice under subsection (2) shall give particulars of the rights exercisable under the next two sections by a person on whom the notice is served.

395. Right to make representations

(1) A person on whom a notice is served under section 394(2) may within 14 days after the date of service make written representations to the competent authority.

(2) The competent authority shall have regard to any representations so made in determining whether to refuse the application or withdraw the authorisation, as the case may be.

396. Reference to Tribunal

(1) The Insolvency Practitioners Tribunal ("the Tribunal") continues in being; and the provisions of Schedule 7 apply to it.

(2) Where a person is served with a notice under section 394(2), he may—

(a) at any time within 28 days after the date of service of the notice, or

(b) at any time after the making by him of representations under section 395 and before the end of the period of 28 days after the date of the service on him of a notice by the competent authority that the authority does not propose to alter its decision in consequence of the representations,

give written notice to the authority requiring the case to be referred to the Tribunal.

(3) Where a requirement is made under subsection (2), then, unless the competent authority—

(a) has decided or decides to grant the application or, as the case may be, not to withdraw the authorisation, and

(b) within 7 days after the date of the making of the requirement, gives written notice of that decision to the person by whom the requirement was made,

it shall refer the case to the Tribunal.

397. Action of Tribunal on reference

(1) On a reference under section 396 the Tribunal shall—

(a) investigate the case, and

(b) make a report to the competent authority stating what would in their opinion be the appropriate decision in the matter and the reasons for that opinion,

and it is the duty of the competent authority to decide the matter accordingly.

(2) The Tribunal shall send a copy of the report to the applicant or, as the case may be, the holder of the authorisation; and the competent authority shall serve him with a written notice of the decision made by it in accordance with the report.

(3) The competent authority may, if he thinks fit, publish the report of the Tribunal.

398. Refusal or withdrawal without reference to Tribunal

Where in the case of any proposed refusal or withdrawal of an authorisation either—

(a) the period mentioned in section 396(2)(a) has expired without the making of any requirement under that subsection or of any representations under section 395, or

(b) the competent authority has given a notice such as is mentioned in section 396(2)(b) and the period so mentioned has expired without the making of any such requirement,

the competent authority may give written notice of the refusal or withdrawal to the person concerned in accordance with the proposal in the notice given under section 394(2).

PART XIV
PUBLIC ADMINISTRATION (ENGLAND AND WALES)

Official receivers

399. Appointment, etc of official receivers

(1) For the purposes of this Act the official receiver, in relation to any bankruptcy, winding up, individual voluntary arrangement, debt relief order or application for such an order, is any person who by virtue of the following provisions of this section or section 401 below is authorised to act as the official receiver in relation to that bankruptcy, winding up, individual voluntary arrangement, debt relief order or application for such an order.

(2) The Secretary of State may (subject to the approval of the Treasury as to numbers) appoint persons to the office of official receiver, and a person appointed to that office (whether under this section or section 70 of the Bankruptcy Act 1914)—

(a) shall be paid out of money provided by Parliament such salary as the Secretary of State may with the concurrence of the Treasury direct,

(b) shall hold office on such other terms and conditions as the Secretary of State may with the concurrence of the Treasury direct, and

(c) may be removed from office by a direction of the Secretary of State.

(3) Where a person holds the office of official receiver, the Secretary of State shall from time to time attach him either to the High Court or to a county court having jurisdiction for the purposes of the second Group of Parts of this Act.

(4) Subject to any directions under subsection (6) below, an official receiver attached to a particular court is the person authorised to act as the official receiver in relation to every bankruptcy, winding up, individual voluntary arrangement, debt relief order or application for such an order falling within the jurisdiction of that court.

(5) The Secretary of State shall ensure that there is, at all times, at least one official receiver attached to the High Court and at least one attached to each county court having jurisdiction for the purposes of the second Group of Parts; but he may attach the same official receiver to two or more different courts.

(6) The Secretary of State may give directions with respect to the disposal of the business of official receivers, and such directions may, in particular—

(a) authorise an official receiver attached to one court to act as the official receiver in relation to any case or description of cases falling within the jurisdiction of another court;

(b) provide, where there is more than one official receiver authorised to act as the official receiver in relation to cases falling within the jurisdiction of any court, for the distribution of their business between or among themselves.

(7) A person who at the coming into force of section 222 of the Insolvency Act 1985 (replaced by this section) is an official receiver attached to a court shall continue in office after the coming into force of that section as an official receiver attached to that court under this section.

400. Functions and status of official receivers

(1) In addition to any functions conferred on him by this Act, a person holding the office of official receiver shall carry out such other functions as may from time to time be conferred on him by the Secretary of State.

(2) In the exercise of the functions of his office a person holding the office of official receiver shall act under the general directions of the Secretary of State and shall also be an officer of the court in relation to which he exercises those functions.

(3) Any property vested in his official capacity in a person holding the office of official receiver shall, on his dying, ceasing to hold office or being otherwise succeeded in relation to the bankruptcy or winding up in question by another official receiver, vest in his successor without any conveyance, assignment or transfer.

401. Deputy official receivers and staff

(1) The Secretary of State may, if he thinks it expedient to do so in order to facilitate the disposal of the business of the official receiver attached to any court, appoint an officer of his department to act as deputy to that official receiver.

(2) Subject to any directions given by the Secretary of State under section 399 or 400, a person appointed to act as deputy to an official receiver has, on such conditions and for such period as may be specified in the terms of his appointment, the same status and functions as the official receiver to whom he is appointed deputy.

Accordingly, references in this Act (except section 399(1) to (5)) to an official receiver include a person appointed to act as his deputy.

(3) An appointment made under subsection (1) may be terminated at any time by the Secretary of State.

(4) The Secretary of State may, subject to the approval of the Treasury as to numbers and remuneration and as to the other terms and conditions of the appointments, appoint officers of his department to assist official receivers in the carrying out of their functions.

The Official Petitioner

402. Official Petitioner

(1) There continues to be an officer known as the Official Petitioner for the purpose of discharging, in relation to cases in which a criminal bankruptcy order is made, the functions assigned to him by or under this Act; and the Director of Public Prosecutions continues, by virtue of his office, to be the Official Petitioner.

(2) The functions of the Official Petitioner include the following—

(a) to consider whether, in a case in which a criminal bankruptcy order is made, it is in the public interest that he should himself present a petition under section 264(1)(d) of this Act;

(b) to present such a petition in any case where he determines that it is in the public interest for him to do so;

(c) to make payments, in such cases as he may determine, towards expenses incurred by other persons in connection with proceedings in pursuance of such a petition; and

(d) to exercise, so far as he considers it in the public interest to do so, any of the powers conferred on him by or under this Act.

(3) Any functions of the Official Petitioner may be discharged on his behalf by any person acting with his authority.

(4) Neither the Official Petitioner nor any person acting with his authority is liable to any action or proceeding in respect of anything done or omitted to be done in the discharge, or purported discharge, of the functions of the Official Petitioner.

(5) In this section "criminal bankruptcy order" means an order under section 39(1) of the Powers of Criminal Courts Act 1973.

Note. This section is repealed by the Criminal Justice Act 1988, s. 170(2), Sch. 16, as from a day to be appointed.

Insolvency Service finance, accounting and investment

403. Insolvency Services Account

(1) All money received by the Secretary of State in respect of proceedings under this Act as it applies to England and Wales shall be paid into the Insolvency Services Account kept by the Secretary of State with the Bank of England; and all payments out of money standing to the credit of the Secretary of State in that account shall be made by the Bank of England in such manner as he may direct.

(2) Whenever the cash balance standing to the credit of the Insolvency Services Account is in excess of the amount which in the opinion of the Secretary of State is required for the time being to answer demands in respect of bankrupts' estates or companies' estates, the Secretary of State shall—

(a) notify the excess to the National Debt Commissioners, and
(b) pay into the Insolvency Services Investment Account ("the Investment Account") kept by the Commissioners with the Bank of England the whole or any part of the excess as the Commissioners may require for investment in accordance with the following provisions of this Part.

(3) Whenever any part of the money so invested is, in the opinion of the Secretary of State, required to answer any demand in respect of bankrupt's estates or companies' estates, he shall notify to the National Debt Commissioners the amount so required and the Commissioners—
(a) shall thereupon repay to the Secretary of State such sum as may be required to the credit of the Insolvency Services Account, and
(b) for that purpose may direct the sale of such part of the securities in which the money has been invested as may be necessary.

404. Investment Account

Any money standing to the credit of the Investment Account (including any money received by the National Debt Commissioners by way of interest on or proceeds of any investment under this section) may be invested by the Commissioners, in accordance with such directions as may be given by the Treasury, in any manner for the time being specified in Part II of Schedule 1 to the Trustee Investments Act 1961.

405. …

406. Interest on money received by liquidators or trustees in bankruptcy and invested

Where under rules made by virtue of paragraph 16 of Schedule 8 to this Act (investment of money received by company liquidators) or paragraph 21 of Schedule 9 to this Act (investment of money received by trustee in bankruptcy) a company or a bankrupt's estate has become entitled to any sum by way of interest, the Secretary of State shall certify that sum and the amount of tax payable on it to the National Debt Commissioners; and the Commissioners shall pay, out of the Investment Account—
(a) into the Insolvency Services Account, the sum so certified less the amount of tax so certified, and
(b) to the Commissioners of Inland Revenue, the amount of tax so certified.

407. Unclaimed dividends and undistributed balances

(1) The Secretary of State shall from time to time pay into the Consolidated Fund out of the Insolvency Services Account so much of the sums standing to the credit of that Account as represents—
(a) dividends which were declared before such date as the Treasury may from time to time determine and have not been claimed, and
(b) balances ascertained before that date which are too small to be divided among the persons entitled to them.

(2) For the purposes of this section the sums standing to the credit of the Insolvency Services Account are deemed to include any sums paid out of that Account and represented by any sums or securities standing to the credit of the Investment Account.

(3) The Secretary of State may require the National Debt Commissioners to pay out of the Investment Account into the Insolvency Services Account the whole or part of any sum which he is required to pay out of that account under subsection (1); and the Commissioners may direct the sale of such securities standing to the credit of the Investment Account as may be necessary for that purpose.

408. Adjustment of balances

(1) The Treasury may direct the payment out of the Consolidated Fund of sums into—
(a) the Insolvency Services Account;
(b) the Investment Account.

(2) The Treasury shall certify to the House of Commons the reason for any payment under subsection (1).

(3) The Secretary of State may pay sums out of the Insolvency Services Account into the Consolidated Fund.

(4) The National Debt Commissioners may pay sums out of the Investment Account into the Consolidated Fund.

409. Annual financial statement and audit

(1) The National Debt Commissioners shall for each year ending on 31st March prepare a statement of the sums credited and debited to the Investment Account in such form and manner as the Treasury may direct and shall transmit it to the Comptroller and Auditor General before the end of November next following the year.

(2) The Secretary of State shall for each year ending 31st March prepare a statement of the sums received or paid by him under section 403 above in such form and manner as the Treasury may direct and shall transmit each statement to the Comptroller and Auditor General before the end of November next following the year.

(3) Every such statement shall include such additional information as the Treasury may direct.

(4) The Comptroller and Auditor General shall examine, certify and report on every such statement and shall lay copies of it, and of his report, before Parliament.

Supplementary

410. Extent of this Part

This Part of this Act extends to England and Wales only.

PART XV
SUBORDINATE LEGISLATION

General insolvency rules

411. Company insolvency rules

(1) Rules may be made—

(a) in relation to England and Wales, by the Lord Chancellor with the concurrence of the Secretary of State and, in the case of rules that affect court procedure, with the concurrence of the Lord Chief Justice, or

(b) in relation to Scotland, by the Secretary of State,

for the purpose of giving effect to Parts I to VII of this Act or the EC Regulation.

(1A) Rules may also be made for the purpose of giving effect to Part 2 of the Banking Act 2009 (bank insolvency orders); and rules for that purpose shall be made—

(a) in relation to England and Wales, by the Lord Chancellor with the concurrence of—

(i) the Treasury, and

(ii) in the case of rules that affect court procedure, the Lord Chief Justice, or

(b) in relation to Scotland, by the Treasury.

(1B) Rules may also be made for the purpose of giving effect to Part 3 of the Banking Act 2009 (bank administration); and rules for that purpose shall be made—

(a) in relation to England and Wales, by the Lord Chancellor with the concurrence of—

(i) the Treasury, and

(ii) in the case of rules that affect court procedure, the Lord Chief Justice, or

(b) in relation to Scotland, by the Treasury.

(2) Without prejudice to the generality of subsection (1), (1A) or (1B) or to any provision of those Parts by virtue of which rules under this section may be made with respect to any matter, rules under this section may contain—

(a) any such provision as is specified in Schedule 8 to this Act or corresponds to provision contained immediately before the coming into force of section 106 of the Insolvency Act

1985 in rules made, or having effect as if made, under section 663(1) or (2) of the Companies Act 1985 (old winding-up rules), and

(b) such incidental, supplemental and transitional provisions as may appear to the Lord Chancellor or, as the case may be, the Secretary of State or the Treasury necessary or expedient.

(2A) For the purposes of subsection (2), a reference in Schedule 8 to this Act to doing anything under or for the purposes of a provision of this Act includes a reference to doing anything under or for the purposes of the EC Regulation (in so far as the provision of this Act relates to a matter to which the EC Regulation applies).

(2B) Rules under this section for the purpose of giving effect to the EC Regulation may not create an offence of a kind referred to in paragraph 1(1)(d) of Schedule 2 to the European Communities Act 1972.

(2C) For the purposes of subsection (2), a reference in Schedule 8 to this Act to doing anything under or for the purposes of a provision of this Act includes a reference to doing anything under or for the purposes of Part 2 of the Banking Act 2009.

(2D) For the purposes of subsection (2), a reference in Schedule 8 to this Act to doing anything under or for the purposes of a provision of this Act includes a reference to doing anything under or for the purposes of Part 3 of the Banking Act 2009.

(3) In Schedule 8 to this Act "liquidator" includes a provisional liquidator or bank liquidator or administrator; and references above in this section to Parts I to VII of this Act or Part 2 or 3 of the Banking Act 2009 are to be read as including the Companies Acts so far as relating to, and to matters connected with or arising out of, the insolvency or winding up of companies.

(3A) In this section references to Part 2 or 3 of the Banking Act 2009 include references to those Parts as applied to building societies (see section 90C of the Building Societies Act 1986).

(4) Rules under this section shall be made by statutory instrument subject to annulment in pursuance of a resolution of either House of Parliament.

(5) Regulations made by the Secretary of State or the Treasury under a power conferred by rules under this section shall be made by statutory instrument and, after being made, shall be laid before each House of Parliament.

(6) Nothing in this section prejudices any power to make rules of court.

(7) The Lord Chief Justice may nominate a judicial office holder (as defined in section 109(4) of the Constitutional Reform Act 2005) to exercise his functions under this section.

412. Individual insolvency rules (England and Wales)

(1) The Lord Chancellor may, with the concurrence of the Secretary of State and, in the case of rules that affect court procedure, with the concurrence of the Lord Chief Justice, make rules for the purpose of giving effect to Parts 7A to 11 of this Act or the EC Regulation.

(2) Without prejudice to the generality of subsection (1), or to any provision of those Parts by virtue of which rules under this section may be made with respect to any matter, rules under this section may contain—

(a) any such provision as is specified in Schedule 9 to this Act or corresponds to provision contained immediately before the appointed day in rules made under section 132 of the Bankruptcy Act 1914; and

(b) such incidental, supplemental and transitional provisions as may appear to the Lord Chancellor necessary or expedient.

(2A) For the purposes of subsection (2), a reference in Schedule 9 to this Act to doing anything under or for the purposes of a provision of this Act includes a reference to doing anything under or for the purposes of the EC Regulation (in so far as the provision of this Act relates to a matter to which the EC Regulation applies).

(2B) Rules under this section for the purpose of giving effect to the EC Regulation may not create an offence of a kind referred to in paragraph 1(1)(d) of Schedule 2 to the European Communities Act 1972.

(3) Rules under this section shall be made by statutory instrument subject to annulment in pursuance of a resolution of either House of Parliament.

(4) Regulations made by the Secretary of State under a power conferred by rules under this section shall be made by statutory instrument and, after being made, shall be laid before each House of Parliament.

(5) Nothing in this section prejudices any power to make rules of court.

(6) The Lord Chief Justice may nominate a judicial office holder (as defined in section 109(4) of the Constitutional Reform Act 2005) to exercise his functions under this section.

413. Insolvency Rules Committee

(1) The committee established under section 10 of the Insolvency Act 1976 (advisory committee on bankruptcy and winding-up rules) continues to exist for the purpose of being consulted under this section.

(2) The Lord Chancellor shall consult the committee before making any rules under section 411 or 412 other than rules which contain a statement that the only provision made by the rules is provision applying rules made under section 411, with or without modifications, for the purposes of provision made by any of sections 23 to 26 of the Water Industry Act 1991 or Schedule 3 to that Act or by any of sections 59 to 65 of, or Schedule 6 or 7 to, the Railways Act 1993.

(3) Subject to the next subsection, the committee shall consist of—

(a) a judge of the High Court attached to the Chancery Division;

(b) a circuit judge;

(c) a registrar in bankruptcy of the High Court;

(d) the registrar of a county court;

(e) a practising barrister;

(f) a practising solicitor; and

(g) a practising accountant;

and the appointment of any person as a member of the committee shall be made in accordance with subsection (3A) or (3B).

(3A) The Lord Chief Justice must appoint the persons referred to in paragraphs (a) to (d) of subsection (3), after consulting the Lord Chancellor.

(3B) The Lord Chancellor must appoint the persons referred to in paragraphs (e) to (g) of subsection (3), after consulting the Lord Chief Justice.

(4) The Lord Chancellor may appoint as additional members of the committee any persons appearing to him to have qualifications or experience that would be of value to the committee in considering any matter with which it is concerned.

(5) The Lord Chief Justice may nominate a judicial office holder (as defined in section 109(4) of the Constitutional Reform Act 2005) to exercise his functions under this section.

Fees orders

414. Fees orders (company insolvency proceedings)

(1) There shall be paid in respect of—

(a) proceedings under any of Parts I to VII of this Act, and

(b) the performance by the official receiver or the Secretary of State of functions under those Parts,

such fees as the competent authority may with the sanction of the Treasury by order direct.

(2) That authority is—

(a) in relation to England and Wales, the Lord Chancellor, and

(b) in relation to Scotland, the Secretary of State.

(3) The Treasury may by order direct by whom and in what manner the fees are to be collected and accounted for.

(4) The Lord Chancellor may, with the sanction of the Treasury, by order provide for sums to be deposited, by such persons, in such manner and in such circumstances as may be specified in the order, by way of security for fees payable by virtue of this section.

(5) An order under this section may contain such incidental, supplemental and transitional provisions as may appear to the Lord Chancellor, the Secretary of State or (as the case may be) the Treasury necessary or expedient.

(6) An order under this section shall be made by statutory instrument and, after being made, shall be laid before each House of Parliament.

(7) Fees payable by virtue of this section shall be paid into the Consolidated Fund.

(8) References in subsection (1) to Parts I to VII of this Act are to be read as including the Companies Acts so far as relating to, and to matters connected with or arising out of, the insolvency or winding up of companies.

(8A) This section applies in relation to Part 2 of the Banking Act 2009 (bank insolvency) as in relation to Parts I to VII of this Act.

(8B) This section applies in relation to Part 3 of the Banking Act 2009 (bank administration) as in relation to Parts I to VII of this Act.

(8C) In subsections (8A) and (8B) the reference to Parts 2 and 3 of the Banking Act 2009 include references to those Parts as applied to building societies (see section 90C of the Building Societies Act 1986).

(9) Nothing in this section prejudices any power to make rules of court; and the application of this section to Scotland is without prejudice to section 2 of the Courts of Law Fees (Scotland) Act 1895.

415. Fees orders (individual insolvency proceedings in England and Wales)

(1) There shall be paid in respect of—

(za) the costs of persons acting as approved intermediaries under Part 7A,

(a) proceedings under Parts 7A to 11 of this Act, and

(b) the performance by the official receiver or the Secretary of State of functions under those Parts,

such fees as the Lord Chancellor may with the sanction of the Treasury by order direct.

(2) The Treasury may by order direct by whom and in what manner the fees are to be collected and accounted for.

(3) The Lord Chancellor may, with the sanction of the Treasury, by order provide for sums to be deposited, by such persons, in such manner and in such circumstances as may be specified in the order, by way of security for—

(a) fees payable by virtue of this section, and

(b) fees payable to any person who has prepared an insolvency practitioner's report under section 274 in Chapter I of Part IX.

(4) An order under this section may contain such incidental, supplemental and transitional provisions as may appear to the Lord Chancellor or, as the case may be, the Treasury, necessary or expedient.

(5) An order under this section shall be made by statutory instrument and, after being made, shall be laid before each House of Parliament.

(6) Fees payable by virtue of this section shall be paid into the Consolidated Fund.

(7) Nothing in this section prejudices any power to make rules of court.

415A. Fees orders (general)

(A1) The Secretary of State—

(a) may by order require a person or body to pay a fee in connection with the grant or maintenance of a designation of that person or body as a competent authority under section 251U, and

(b) may refuse to grant, or may withdraw, any such designation where a fee is not paid.

(1) The Secretary of State—

(a) may by order require a body to pay a fee in connection with the grant or maintenance of recognition of the body under section 391, and

(b) may refuse recognition, or revoke an order of recognition under section 391(1) by a further order, where a fee is not paid.

(2) The Secretary of State—

(a) may by order require a person to pay a fee in connection with the grant or maintenance of authorisation of the person under section 393, and

(b) may disregard an application or withdraw an authorisation where a fee is not paid.

(3) The Secretary of State may by order require the payment of fees in respect of—

(a) the operation of the Insolvency Services Account;

(b) payments into and out of that Account.

(4) The following provisions of section 414 apply to fees under this section as they apply to fees under that section—

(a) subsection (3) (manner of payment),

(b) subsection (5) (additional provision),

(c) subsection (6) (statutory instrument),

(d) subsection (7) (payment into Consolidated Fund), and

(e) subsection (9) (saving for rules of court).

Specification, increase and reduction of money sums relevant in the operation of this Act

416. Monetary limits (companies winding up)

(1) The Secretary of State may by order in a statutory instrument increase or reduce any of the money sums for the time being specified in the following provisions in the first Group of Parts—

section 117(2) (amount of company's share capital determining whether county court has jurisdiction to wind it up);

section 120(3) (the equivalent as respects sheriff court jurisdiction in Scotland);

section 123(1)(a) (minimum debt for service of demand on company by unpaid creditor);

section 184(3) (minimum value of judgment, affecting sheriff's duties on levying execution);

section 206(1)(a) and (b) (minimum value of company property concealed or fraudulently removed, affecting criminal liability of company's officer).

(2) An order under this section may contain such transitional provisions as may appear to the Secretary of State necessary or expedient.

(3) No order under this section increasing or reducing any of the money sums for the time being specified in section 117(2), 120(3), or 123(1)(a) shall be made unless a draft of the order has been laid before and approved by a resolution of each House of Parliament.

(4) A statutory instrument containing an order under this section, other than an order to which subsection (3) applies, is subject to annulment in pursuance of a resolution of either House of Parliament.

417. Money sum in s 222

The Secretary of State may by regulations in a statutory instrument increase or reduce the money sum for the time being specified in section 222(1) (minimum debt for service of demand on unregistered company by unpaid creditor); but such regulations shall not be made unless a draft of the statutory instrument containing them has been approved by resolution of each House of Parliament.

417A. Money sums (company moratorium)

(1) The Secretary of State may by order increase or reduce any of the money sums for the time being specified in the following provisions of Schedule A1 to this Act—

paragraph 17(1) (maximum amount of credit which company may obtain without disclosure of moratorium);

paragraph 41(4) (minimum value of company property concealed or fraudulently removed, affecting criminal liability of company's officer).

(2) An order under this section may contain such transitional provisions as may appear to the Secretary of State necessary or expedient.

(3) An order under this section shall be made by statutory instrument subject to annulment in pursuance of a resolution of either House of Parliament.

418. Monetary limits (bankruptcy)

(1) The Secretary of State may by order prescribe amounts for the purposes of the following provisions in the second Group of Parts—

section 251S(4) (maximum amount of credit which a person in respect of whom a debt relief order is made may obtain without disclosure of his status);

section 273 (minimum value of debtor's estate determining whether immediate bankruptcy order should be made; small bankruptcies level);

section 313A (value of property below which application for sale, possession or charge to be dismissed);

section 346(3) (minimum amount of judgment, determining whether amount recovered on sale of debtor's goods is to be treated as part of his estate in bankruptcy);

section 354(1) and (2) (minimum amount of concealed debt, or value of property concealed or removed, determining criminal liability under the section);

section 358 (minimum value of property taken by a bankrupt out of England and Wales, determining his criminal liability);

section 360(1) (maximum amount of credit which bankrupt may obtain without disclosure of his status);

section 361(2) (exemption of bankrupt from criminal liability for failure to keep proper accounts, if unsecured debts not more than the prescribed minimum);

section 364(2)(d) (minimum value of goods removed by the bankrupt, determining his liability to arrest);

paragraphs 6 to 8 of Schedule 4ZA (maximum amount of a person's debts monthly surplus income and property for purposes of obtaining a debt relief order);

and references in the second Group of Parts to the amount prescribed for the purposes of any of those provisions, and references in those provisions to the prescribed amount, are to be construed accordingly.

(2) An order under this section may contain such transitional provisions as may appear to the Secretary of State necessary or expedient.

(3) An order under this section shall be made by statutory instrument subject to annulment in pursuance of a resolution of either House of Parliament.

Insolvency practice

419. Regulations for purposes of Part XIII

(1) The Secretary of State may make regulations for the purpose of giving effect to Part XIII of this Act; and "prescribed" in that Part means prescribed by regulations made by the Secretary of State.

(2) Without prejudice to the generality of subsection (1) or to any provision of that Part by virtue of which regulations may be made with respect to any matter, regulations under this section may contain—

(a) provision as to the matters to be taken into account in determining whether a person is a fit and proper person to act as an insolvency practitioner;

(b) provision prohibiting a person from so acting in prescribed cases, being cases in which a conflict of interest will or may arise;

(c) provision imposing requirements with respect to—

(i) the preparation and keeping by a person who acts as an insolvency practitioner of prescribed books, accounts and other records, and

(ii) the production of those books, accounts and records to prescribed persons;

(d) provision conferring power on prescribed persons—

(i) to require any person who acts or has acted as an insolvency practitioner to answer any inquiry in relation to a case in which he is so acting or has so acted, and

(ii) to apply to a court to examine such a person or any other person on oath concerning such a case;

(e) provision making non-compliance with any of the regulations a criminal offence; and

(f) such incidental, supplemental and transitional provisions as may appear to the Secretary of State necessary or expedient.

(3) Any power conferred by Part XIII or this Part to make regulations, rules or orders is exercisable by statutory instrument subject to annulment by resolution of either House of Parliament.

(4) Any rule or regulation under Part XIII or this Part may make different provision with respect to different cases or descriptions of cases, including different provision for different areas.

Other order-making powers

420. Insolvent partnerships

(1) The Lord Chancellor may, by order made with the concurrence of the Secretary of State and the Lord Chief Justice, provide that such provisions of this Act as may be specified in the order shall apply in relation to insolvent partnerships with such modifications as may be so specified.

(1A) An order under this section may make provision in relation to the EC Regulation.

(1B) But provision made by virtue of this section in relation to the EC Regulation may not create an offence of a kind referred to in paragraph 1(1)(d) of Schedule 2 to the European Communities Act 1972.

(2) An order under this section may make different provision for different cases and may contain such incidental, supplemental and transitional provisions as may appear to the Lord Chancellor and the Lord Chief Justice necessary or expedient.

(3) An order under this section shall be made by statutory instrument subject to annulment in pursuance of a resolution of either House of Parliament.

(4) The Lord Chief Justice may nominate a judicial office holder (as defined in section 109(4) of the Constitutional Reform Act 2005) to exercise his functions under this section.

421. Insolvent estates of deceased persons

(1) The Lord Chancellor may, by order made with the concurrence of the Secretary of State and the Lord Chief Justice, provide that such provisions of this Act as may be specified in the order shall apply in relation to the administration of the insolvent estates of deceased persons with such modifications as may be so specified.

(1A) An order under this section may make provision in relation to the EC Regulation.

(1B) But provision made by virtue of this section in relation to the EC Regulation may not create an offence of a kind referred to in paragraph 1(1)(d) of Schedule 2 to the European Communities Act 1972.

(2) An order under this section may make different provision for different cases and may contain such incidental, supplemental and transitional provisions as may appear to the Lord Chancellor and the Lord Chief Justice necessary or expedient.

(3) An order under this section shall be made by statutory instrument subject to annulment in pursuance of a resolution of either House of Parliament.

(4) For the purposes of this section the estate of a deceased person is insolvent if, when realised, it will be insufficient to meet in full all the debts and other liabilities to which it is subject.

(5) The Lord Chief Justice may nominate a judicial office holder (as defined in section 109(4) of the Constitutional Reform Act 2005) to exercise his functions under this section.

421A. Insolvent estates: joint tenancies

(1) This section applies where—

(a) an insolvency administration order has been made in respect of the insolvent estate of a deceased person,

(b) the petition for the order was presented after the commencement of this section and within the period of five years beginning with the day on which he died, and

(c) immediately before his death he was beneficially entitled to an interest in any property as joint tenant.

(2) For the purpose of securing that debts and other liabilities to which the estate is subject are met, the court may, on an application by the trustee appointed pursuant to the insolvency administration order, make an order under this section requiring the survivor to pay to the trustee an amount not exceeding the value lost to the estate.

(3) In determining whether to make an order under this section, and the terms of such an order, the court must have regard to all the circumstances of the case, including the interests of the deceased's creditors and of the survivor; but, unless the circumstances are exceptional, the court must assume that the interests of the deceased's creditors outweigh all other considerations.

(4) The order may be made on such terms and conditions as the court thinks fit.

(5) Any sums required to be paid to the trustee in accordance with an order under this section shall be comprised in the estate.

(6) The modifications of this Act which may be made by an order under section 421 include any modifications which are necessary or expedient in consequence of this section.

(7) In this section, "survivor" means the person who, immediately before the death, was beneficially entitled as joint tenant with the deceased or, if the person who was so entitled dies after the making of the insolvency administration order, his personal representatives.

(8) If there is more than one survivor—

(a) an order under this section may be made against all or any of them, but

(b) no survivor shall be required to pay more than so much of the value lost to the estate as is properly attributable to him.

(9) In this section—

"insolvency administration order" has the same meaning as in any order under section 421 having effect for the time being,

"value lost to the estate" means the amount which, if paid to the trustee, would in the court's opinion restore the position to what it would have been if the deceased had been adjudged bankrupt immediately before his death.

422. Formerly authorised banks

(1) The Secretary of State may by order made with the concurrence of the Treasury and after consultation with the Financial Conduct Authority and the Prudential Regulation Authority provide that specified provisions in the first Group of Parts shall apply with specified modifications in relation to any person who—

(a) has a liability in respect of a deposit which he accepted in accordance with the Banking Act 1979 or 1987, but

(b) does not have permission under Part 4A of the Financial Services and Markets Act 2000 (regulated activities) to accept deposits.

(1A) Subsection (1)(b) shall be construed in accordance with—

(a) section 22 of the Financial Services and Markets Act 2000 (classes of regulated activity and categories of investment),

(b) any relevant order under that section, and

(c) Schedule 2 to that Act (regulated activities).

(2) An order under this section may make different provision for different cases and may contain such incidental, supplemental and transitional provisions as may appear to the Secretary of State necessary or expedient.

(3) An order under this section shall be made by statutory instrument subject to annulment in pursuance of a resolution of either House of Parliament.

PART XVI
PROVISIONS AGAINST DEBT AVOIDANCE
(ENGLAND AND WALES ONLY)

423. Transactions defrauding creditors

(1) This section relates to transactions entered into at an undervalue; and a person enters into such a transaction with another person if—

(a) he makes a gift to the other person or he otherwise enters into a transaction with the other on terms that provide for him to receive no consideration;

(b) he enters into a transaction with the other in consideration of marriage or the formation of a civil partnership; or

(c) he enters into a transaction with the other for a consideration the value of which, in money or money's worth, is significantly less than the value, in money or money's worth, of the consideration provided by himself.

(2) Where a person has entered into such a transaction, the court may, if satisfied under the next subsection, make such order as it thinks fit for—

(a) restoring the position to what it would have been if the transaction had not been entered into, and

(b) protecting the interests of persons who are victims of the transaction.

(3) In the case of a person entering into such a transaction, an order shall only be made if the court is satisfied that it was entered into by him for the purpose—

(a) of putting assets beyond the reach of a person who is making, or may at some time make, a claim against him, or

(b) of otherwise prejudicing the interests of such a person in relation to the claim which he is making or may make.

(4) In this section "the court" means the High Court or—

(a) if the person entering into the transaction is an individual, any other court which would have jurisdiction in relation to a bankruptcy petition relating to him;

(b) if that person is a body capable of being wound up under Part IV or V of this Act, any other court having jurisdiction to wind it up.

(5) In relation to a transaction at an undervalue, references here and below to a victim of the transaction are to a person who is, or is capable of being, prejudiced by it; and in the following two sections the person entering into the transaction is referred to as "the debtor".

424. Those who may apply for an order under s 423

(1) An application for an order under section 423 shall not be made in relation to a transaction except—

(a) in a case where the debtor has been adjudged bankrupt or is a body corporate which is being wound up or is in administration, by the official receiver, by the trustee of the bankrupt's estate or the liquidator or administrator of the body corporate or (with the leave of the court) by a victim of the transaction;

(b) in a case where a victim of the transaction is bound by a voluntary arrangement approved under Part I or Part VIII of this Act, by the supervisor of the voluntary arrangement or by any person who (whether or not so bound) is such a victim; or

(c) in any other case, by a victim of the transaction.

(2) An application made under any of the paragraphs of subsection (1) is to be treated as made on behalf of every victim of the transaction.

425. Provision which may be made by order under s 423

(1) Without prejudice to the generality of section 423, an order made under that section with respect to a transaction may (subject as follows)—

(a) require any property transferred as part of the transaction to be vested in any person, either absolutely or for the benefit of all the persons on whose behalf the application for the order is treated as made;

(b) require any property to be so vested if it represents, in any person's hands, the application either of the proceeds of sale of property so transferred or of money so transferred;

(c) release or discharge (in whole or in part) any security given by the debtor;

(d) require any person to pay to any other person in respect of benefits received from the debtor such sums as the court may direct;

(e) provide for any surety or guarantor whose obligations to any person were released or discharged (in whole or in part) under the transaction to be under such new or revived obligations as the court thinks appropriate;

(f) provide for security to be provided for the discharge of any obligation imposed by or arising under the order, for such an obligation to be charged on any property and for such security or charge to have the same priority as a security or charge released or discharged (in whole or in part) under the transaction.

(2) An order under section 423 may affect the property of, or impose any obligation on, any person whether or not he is the person with whom the debtor entered into the transaction; but such an order—

(a) shall not prejudice any interest in property which was acquired from a person other than the debtor and was acquired in good faith, for value and without notice of the relevant circumstances, or prejudice any interest deriving from such an interest, and

(b) shall not require a person who received a benefit from the transaction in good faith, for value and without notice of the relevant circumstances to pay any sum unless he was a party to the transaction.

(3) For the purposes of this section the relevant circumstances in relation to a transaction are the circumstances by virtue of which an order under section 423 may be made in respect of the transaction.

(4) In this section "security" means any mortgage, charge, lien or other security.

PART XVII
MISCELLANEOUS AND GENERAL

426. Co-operation between courts exercising jurisdiction in relation to insolvency

(1) An order made by a court in any part of the United Kingdom in the exercise of jurisdiction in relation to insolvency law shall be enforced in any other part of the United Kingdom as if it were made by a court exercising the corresponding jurisdiction in that other part.

(2) However, without prejudice to the following provisions of this section, nothing in subsection (1) requires a court in any part of the United Kingdom to enforce, in relation to property situated in that part, any order made by a court in any other part of the United Kingdom.

(3) The Secretary of State, with the concurrence in relation to property situated in England and Wales of the Lord Chancellor, may by order make provision for securing that a trustee or assignee under the insolvency law of any part of the United Kingdom has, with such modifications as may be specified in the order, the same rights in relation to any property situated in another part of the United Kingdom as he would have in the corresponding circumstances if he were a trustee or assignee under the insolvency law of that other part.

(4) The courts having jurisdiction in relation to insolvency law in any part of the United Kingdom shall assist the courts having the corresponding jurisdiction in any other part of the United Kingdom or any relevant country or territory.

(5) For the purposes of subsection (4) a request made to a court in any part of the United Kingdom by a court in any other part of the United Kingdom or in a relevant country or territory is authority for the court to which the request is made to apply, in relation to any matters specified in the request, the insolvency law which is applicable by either court in relation to comparable matters falling within its jurisdiction.

In exercising its discretion under this subsection, a court shall have regard in particular to the rules of private international law.

(6) Where a person who is a trustee or assignee under the insolvency law of any part of the United Kingdom claims property situated in any other part of the United Kingdom (whether by virtue of an order under subsection (3) or otherwise), the submission of that claim to the court exercising jurisdiction in relation to insolvency law in that other part shall be treated in the same manner as a request made by a court for the purpose of subsection (4).

(7) Section 38 of the Criminal Law Act 1977 (execution of warrant of arrest throughout the United Kingdom) applies to a warrant which, in exercise of any jurisdiction in relation to insolvency law, is issued in any part of the United Kingdom for the arrest of a person as it applies to a warrant issued in that part of the United Kingdom for the arrest of a person charged with an offence.

(8) Without prejudice to any power to make rules of court, any power to make provision by subordinate legislation for the purpose of giving effect in relation to companies or individuals to the insolvency law of any part of the United Kingdom includes power to make provision for the purpose of giving effect in that part to any provision made by or under the preceding provisions of this section.

(9) An order under subsection (3) shall be made by statutory instrument subject to annulment in pursuance of a resolution of either House of Parliament.

(10) In this section "insolvency law" means—

(a) in relation to England and Wales, provision extending to England and Wales and made by or under this Act or sections 1A, 6 to 10, 12 to 15, 19(c) and 20 (with Schedule 1) of the Company Directors Disqualification Act 1986 and sections 1 to 17 of that Act as they apply for the purposes of those provisions of that Act;

(b) in relation to Scotland, provision extending to Scotland and made by or under this Act, sections 1A, 6 to 10, 12 to 15, 19(c) and 20 (with Schedule 1) of the Company Directors Disqualification Act 1986 and sections 1 to 17 of that Act as they apply for the purposes of those provisions of that Act, Part XVIII of the Companies Act or the Bankruptcy (Scotland) Act 1985;

(c) in relation to Northern Ireland, provision made by or under the Insolvency (Northern Ireland) Order 1989 *or Part II of the Companies (Northern Ireland) Order 1989* [*or the Company Directors Disqualification (Northern Ireland) Order 2002*];

(d) in relation to any relevant country or territory, so much of the law of that country or territory as corresponds to provisions falling within any of the foregoing paragraphs;

and references in this subsection to any enactment include, in relation to any time before the coming into force of that enactment the corresponding enactment in force at that time.

(11) In this section "relevant country or territory" means—

(a) any of the Channel Islands or the Isle of Man, or

(b) any country or territory designated for the purposes of this section by the Secretary of State by order made by statutory instrument.

(12) In the application of this section to Northern Ireland—

(a) for any reference to the Secretary of State there is substituted a reference to the Department of Economic Development in Northern Ireland;

(b) in subsection (3) for the words "another part of the United Kingdom" and the words "that other part" there are substituted the words "Northern Ireland";

(c) for subsection (9) there is substituted the following subsection—

"(9) An order made under subsection (3) by the Department of Economic Development in Northern Ireland shall be a statutory rule for the purposes of the Statutory Rules (Northern Ireland) Order 1979 and shall be subject to negative resolution within the meaning of section 41(6) of the Interpretation Act (Northern Ireland) 1954.".

(13) Section 129 of the Banking Act 2009 provides for provisions of that Act about bank insolvency to be "insolvency law" for the purposes of this section.

(14) Section 165 of the Banking Act 2009 provides for provisions of that Act about bank administration to be "insolvency law" for the purposes of this section.

Note. The italicized words "or Part II of the Companies (Northern Ireland) Order 1989" in subsection (10)(c) are repealed and the subsequent italicized words in square brackets are substituted by S.I. 2002/3150, art. 26(2), Sch. 3, para. 2, as from a day to be appointed.

426A. Disqualification from Parliament (England and Wales and Northern Ireland)

(1) A person in respect of whom a bankruptcy restrictions order or a debt relief restrictions order has effect shall be disqualified—

(a) from membership of the House of Commons,

(b) from sitting or voting in the House of Lords, and

(c) from sitting or voting in a committee of the House of Lords or a joint committee of both Houses.

(2) If a member of the House of Commons becomes disqualified under this section, his seat shall be vacated.

(3) If a person who is disqualified under this section is returned as a member of the House of Commons, his return shall be void.

(4) No writ of summons shall be issued to a member of the House of Lords who is disqualified under this section.

(5) If a court makes a bankruptcy restrictions order or interim order, or a debt relief restrictions order or an interim debt relief restrictions order, in respect of a member of the House of Commons or the House of Lords the court shall notify the Speaker of that House.

(6) If the Secretary of State accepts a bankruptcy restrictions undertaking or a debt relief restrictions undertaking made by a member of the House of Commons or the House of Lords, the Secretary of State shall notify the Speaker of that House.

(7) If the Department of Enterprise, Trade and Investment for Northern Ireland accepts a bankruptcy restrictions undertaking made by a member of the House of Commons or the House of Lords under Schedule 2A to the Insolvency (Northern Ireland) Order 1989, the Department shall notify the Speaker of that House.

(8) In this section a reference to a bankruptcy restrictions order or an interim order includes a reference to a bankruptcy restrictions order or an interim order made under Schedule 2A to the Insolvency (Northern Ireland) Order 1989.

426B. Devolution

(1) If a court in England and Wales makes a bankruptcy restrictions order or interim order in respect of a member of the Scottish Parliament, the Northern Ireland Assembly or the National Assembly for Wales, or makes a debt relief restrictions order or interim debt relief restrictions order in respect of such a member, the court shall notify the presiding officer of that body.

(1A) If the High Court in Northern Ireland makes a bankruptcy restrictions order or interim order under Schedule 2A to the Insolvency (Northern Ireland) Order 1989 in respect of a member of the Scottish Parliament or the National Assembly for Wales, the Court shall notify the presiding officer of that body.

(2) If the Secretary of State accepts a bankruptcy restrictions undertaking or a debt relief restrictions undertaking made by a member of the Scottish Parliament, the Northern Ireland Assembly or the National Assembly for Wales, the Secretary of State shall notify the presiding officer of that body.

(3) If the Department of Enterprise, Trade and Investment for Northern Ireland accepts a bankruptcy restrictions undertaking made by a member of the Scottish Parliament or the National Assembly for Wales under Schedule 2A to the Insolvency (Northern Ireland) Order 1989, the Department shall notify the presiding officer of that body.

426C. Irrelevance of privilege

(1) An enactment about insolvency applies in relation to a member of the House of Commons or the House of Lords irrespective of any Parliamentary privilege.

(2) In this section "enactment" includes a provision made by or under—
(a) an Act of the Scottish Parliament, or
(b) Northern Ireland legislation.

427. Disqualification from Parliament (Scotland ...)

(1) Where a ... court in Scotland awards sequestration of an individual's estate, the individual is disqualified—
(a) for sitting or voting in the House of Lords,
(b) for being elected to, or sitting or voting in, the House of Commons, and
(c) for sitting or voting in a committee of either House.

(2) Where an individual is disqualified under this section, the disqualification ceases—
(a) except where the award is recalled or reduced without the individual having been first discharged, on the discharge of the individual, and
(b) in the excepted case, on the ..., recall or reduction, as the case may be.

(3) No writ of summons shall be issued to any lord of Parliament who is for the time being disqualified under this section for sitting and voting in the House of Lords.

(4) Where a member of the House of Commons who is disqualified under this section continues to be so disqualified until the end of the period of 6 months beginning with the day of the ... award, his seat shall be vacated at the end of that period.

(5) A court which makes an ... award such as is mentioned in subsection (1) in relation to any lord of Parliament or member of the House of Commons shall forthwith certify the ... award to the Speaker of the House of Lords or, as the case may be, to the Speaker of the House of Commons.

(6) Where a court has certified an ... award to the Speaker of the House of Commons under subsection (5), then immediately after it becomes apparent which of the following certificates is applicable, the court shall certify to the Speaker of the House of Commons—
(a) that the period of 6 months beginning with the day of the ... award has expired without the ... award having been ... recalled or reduced, or
(b) that the ... award has been ... recalled or reduced before the end of that period.

(6A) Subsections (4) to (6) have effect in relation to a member of the Scottish Parliament but as if—
(a) references to the House of Commons were to the Parliament and references to the Speaker were to the Presiding Officer, and
(b) in subsection (4), for "under this section" there were substituted "under section 15(1)(b) of the Scotland Act 1998 by virtue of this section".

(6B) Subsections (4) to (6) have effect in relation to a member of the National Assembly for Wales but as if—
(a) references to the House of Commons were to the Assembly and references to the Speaker were to the presiding officer, and
(b) in subsection (4), for "under this section" there were substituted "under section 16(2) of the Government of Wales Act 2006 by virtue of this section".

(6C) Subsections (4) to (6) have effect in relation to a member of the Northern Ireland Assembly but as if—
(a) references to the House of Commons were to the Assembly and references to the Speaker were to the Presiding Officer; and
(b) in subsection (4), for "under this section" there were substituted "under section 36(4) of the Northern Ireland Act 1998 by virtue of this section".

(7) …

428. Exemptions from Restrictive Trade Practices Act

(1), (2) …

(3) In this section "insolvency services" means the services of persons acting as insolvency practitioners or carrying out under the law of Northern Ireland functions corresponding to those mentioned in section 388(1) or (2) in Part XIII, in their capacity as such….

429. Disabilities on revocation of administration order against an individual

(1) The following applies where a person fails to make any payment which he is required to make by virtue of an administration order under Part VI of the County Courts Act 1984.

(2) The court which is administering that person's estate under the order may, if it thinks fit—

(a) revoke the administration order, and

(b) make an order directing that this section and section 12 of the Company Directors Disqualification Act 1986 shall apply to the person for such period, not exceeding one year, as may be specified in the order.

(1) This section applies if a county court revokes an administration order made in respect of an individual ("the debtor") on one of the relevant grounds.

(2) The court may, at the time it revokes the administration order, make an order directing that this section and section 12 of the Company Directors Disqualification Act 1986 shall apply to the debtor for such period, not exceeding one year, as may be specified in the order.

(2A) Each of the following is a relevant ground—

(a) the debtor had failed to make two payments (whether consecutive or not) required by the order;

(b) at the time the order was made—

(i) the total amount of the debtor's qualifying debts was more than the prescribed maximum for the purposes of Part 6 of the 1984 Act, but

(ii) because of information provided, or not provided, by the debtor, that amount was thought to be less than, or the same as, the prescribed maximum.

(3) *A person* to whom this section so applies shall not—

(a) either alone or jointly with another person, obtain credit to the extent of the amount prescribed for the purposes of section 360(1)(a) or more, or

(b) enter into any transaction in the course of or for the purposes of any business in which he is directly or indirectly engaged,

without disclosing to the person from whom he obtains the credit, or (as the case may be) with whom the transaction is entered into, the fact that this section applies to him.

(4) The reference in subsection (3) to *a person* obtaining credit includes—

(a) a case where goods are bailed or hired to him under a hire-purchase agreement or agreed to be sold to him under a conditional sale agreement, and

(b) a case where he is paid in advance (whether in money or otherwise) for the supply of goods or services.

(5) *A person* who contravenes this section is guilty of an offence and liable to imprisonment or a fine, or both.

Note. Subsections (1), (2) are substituted by the italicized subsections (1), (2), (2A), and the italicized words "a person" in subsections (3)–(5) are substituted by the words "an individual", by the Tribunals, Courts and Enforcement Act 2007, s. 106, Sch. 16, para.3, as from a day to be appointed.

430. Provision introducing Schedule of punishments

(1) Schedule 10 to this Act has effect with respect to the way in which offences under this Act are punishable on conviction.

(2) In relation to an offence under a provision of this Act specified in the first column of the Schedule (the general nature of the offence being described in the second column), the third column shows whether the offence is punishable on conviction on indictment, or on summary conviction, or either in the one way or the other.

(3) The fourth column of the Schedule shows, in relation to an offence, the maximum punishment by way of fine or imprisonment under this Act which may be imposed on a person convicted of the offence in the way specified in relation to it in the third column (that is to say, on indictment or summarily) a reference to a period of years or months being to a term of imprisonment of that duration.

(4) The fifth column shows, (in relation to an offence for which there is an entry in that column) that a person convicted of the offence after continued contravention is liable to a daily default fine; that is to say, he is liable on a second or subsequent conviction of the offence to the fine specified

in that column for each day on which the contravention is continued (instead of the penalty specified for the offence in the fourth column of the Schedule).

(5) For the purpose of any enactment in this Act whereby an officer of a company who is in default is liable to a fine or penalty, the expression "officer who is in default" means any officer of the company who knowingly and wilfully authorises or permits the default, refusal or contravention mentioned in the enactment.

431. Summary proceedings

(1) Summary proceedings for any offence under any of Parts I to VII of this Act may (without prejudice to any jurisdiction exercisable apart from this subsection) be taken against a body corporate at any place at which the body has a place of business, and against any other person at any place at which he is for the time being.

(2) Notwithstanding anything in section 127(1) of the Magistrates' Courts Act 1980, an information relating to such an offence which is triable by a magistrates' court in England and Wales may be so tried if it is laid at any time within 3 years after the commission of the offence and within 12 months after the date on which evidence sufficient in the opinion of the Director of Public Prosecutions or the Secretary of State (as the case may be) to justify the proceedings comes to his knowledge.

(3) Summary proceedings in Scotland for such an offence shall not be commenced after the expiration of 3 years from the commission of the offence.

Subject to this (and notwithstanding anything in section 136 of the Criminal Procedure (Scotland) Act 1995), such proceedings may (in Scotland) be commenced at any time within 12 months after the date on which evidence sufficient in the Lord Advocate's opinion to justify the proceedings came to his knowledge or, where such evidence was reported to him by the Secretary of State, within 12 months after the date on which it came to the knowledge of the latter; and subsection (3) of that section applies for the purpose of this subsection as it applies for the purpose of that section.

(4) For purposes of this section, a certificate of the Director of Public Prosecutions, the Lord Advocate or the Secretary of State (as the case may be) as to the date on which such evidence as is referred to above came to his knowledge is conclusive evidence.

432. Offences by bodies corporate

(1) This section applies to offences under this Act other than those excepted by subsection (4).

(2) Where a body corporate is guilty of an offence to which this section applies and the offence is proved to have been committed with the consent or connivance of, or to be attributable to any neglect on the part of, any director, manager, secretary or other similar officer of the body corporate or any person who was purporting to act in any such capacity he, as well as the body corporate, is guilty of the offence and liable to be proceeded against and punished accordingly.

(3) Where the affairs of a body corporate are managed by its members, subsection (2) applies in relation to the acts and defaults of a member in connection with his functions of management as if he were a director of the body corporate.

(4) The offences excepted from this section are those under sections 30, 39, 51, 53, 54, 62, 64, 66, 85, 89, 164, 188, 201, 206, 207, 208, 209, 210 and 211 and those under paragraphs 16(2), 17(3)(a), 18(3)(a), 19(3)(a), 22(1) and 23(1)(a) of Schedule A1.

433. Admissibility in evidence of statements of affairs, etc

(1) In any proceedings (whether or not under this Act)—

(a) a statement of affairs prepared for the purposes of any provision of this Act which is derived from the Insolvency Act 1985,

(aa) a statement made in pursuance of a requirement imposed by or under Part 2 of the Banking Act 2009 (bank insolvency),

(ab) a statement made in pursuance of a requirement imposed by or under Part 3 of that Act (bank administration), and

(b) any other statement made in pursuance of a requirement imposed by or under any such provision or by or under rules made under this Act, may be used in evidence against any person making or concurring in making the statement.

(2) However, in criminal proceedings in which any such person is charged with an offence to which this subsection applies—

(a) no evidence relating to the statement may be adduced, and

(b) no question relating to it may be asked,

by or on behalf of the prosecution, unless evidence relating to it is adduced, or a question relating to it is asked, in the proceedings by or on behalf of that person.

(3) Subsection (2) applies to any offence other than—

(a) an offence under section 22(6), 47(6), 48(8), 66(6), 67(8), 95(8), 98(6), 99(3)(a), 131(7), 192(2), 208(1)(a) or (d) or (2), 210, 235(5), 353(1), 354(1)(b) or (3) or 356(1) or (2)(a) or (b) or paragraph 4(3)(a) of Schedule 7;

(b) an offence which is—

(i) created by rules made under this Act, and

(ii) designated for the purposes of this subsection by such rules or by regulations made by the Secretary of State;

(c) an offence which is—

(i) created by regulations made under any such rules, and

(ii) designated for the purposes of this subsection by such regulations;

(d) an offence under section 1, 2 or 5 of the Perjury Act 1911 (false statements made on oath or made otherwise than on oath); or

(e) an offence under section 44(1) or (2) of the Criminal Law (Consolidation) (Scotland) Act 1995 (false statements made on oath or otherwise than on oath).

(4) Regulations under subsection (3)(b)(ii) shall be made by statutory instrument and, after being made, shall be laid before each House of Parliament.

434. Crown application

For the avoidance of doubt it is hereby declared that provisions of this Act which derive from the Insolvency Act 1985 bind the Crown so far as affecting or relating to the following matters, namely—

(a) remedies against, or against the property of, companies or individuals;

(b) priorities of debts;

(c) transactions at an undervalue or preferences;

(d) voluntary arrangements approved under Part I or Part VIII, and

(e) discharge from bankruptcy.

PART 17A
SUPPLEMENTARY PROVISIONS

434A. Introductory

The provisions of this Part have effect for the purposes of—

(a) the First Group of Parts, and

(b) sections 411, 413, 414, 416 and 417 in Part 15.

434B. Representation of corporations at meetings

(1) If a corporation is a creditor or debenture-holder, it may by resolution of its directors or other governing body authorise a person or persons to act as its representative or representatives—

(a) at any meeting of the creditors of a company held in pursuance of this Act or of rules made under it, or

(b) at any meeting of a company held in pursuance of the provisions contained in a debenture or trust deed.

(2) Where the corporation authorises only one person, that person is entitled to exercise the same powers on behalf of the corporation as the corporation could exercise if it were an individual creditor or debenture-holder.

(3) Where the corporation authorises more than one person, any one of them is entitled to exercise the same powers on behalf of the corporation as the corporation could exercise if it were an individual creditor or debenture-holder.

(4) Where the corporation authorises more than one person and more than one of them purport to exercise a power under subsection (3)—

(a) if they purport to exercise the power in the same way, the power is treated as exercised in that way;

(b) if they do not purport to exercise the power in the same way, the power is treated as not exercised.

434C. Legal professional privilege

In proceedings against a person for an offence under this Act nothing in this Act is to be taken to require any person to disclose any information that he is entitled to refuse to disclose on grounds of legal professional privilege (in Scotland, confidentiality of communications).

434D. Enforcement of company's filing obligations

(1) This section applies where a company has made default in complying with any obligation under this Act—

(a) to deliver a document to the registrar, or

(b) to give notice to the registrar of any matter.

(2) The registrar, or any member or creditor of the company, may give notice to the company requiring it to comply with the obligation.

(3) If the company fails to make good the default within 14 days after service of the notice, the registrar, or any member or creditor of the company, may apply to the court for an order directing the company, and any specified officer of it, to make good the default within a specified time.

(4) The court's order may provide that all costs (in Scotland, expenses) of or incidental to the application are to be borne by the company or by any officers of it responsible for the default.

(5) This section does not affect the operation of any enactment imposing penalties on a company or its officers in respect of any such default.

434E. Application of filing obligations to overseas companies

The provisions of this Act requiring documents to be forwarded or delivered to, or filed with, the registrar of companies apply in relation to an overseas company that is required to register particulars under section 1046 of the Companies Act 2006 as they apply in relation to a company registered under that Act in England and Wales or Scotland.

PART XVIII
INTERPRETATION

435. Meaning of "associate"

(1) For the purposes of this Act any question whether a person is an associate of another person is to be determined in accordance with the following provisions of this section (any provision that a person is an associate of another person being taken to mean that they are associates of each other).

(2) A person is an associate of an individual if that person is—

(a) the individual's husband or wife or civil partner,

(b) a relative of—

(i) the individual, or

(ii) the individual's husband or wife or civil partner, or

(c) the husband or wife or civil partner of a relative of—

(i) the individual, or

(ii) the individual's husband or wife or civil partner.

(3) A person is an associate of any person with whom he is in partnership, and of the husband or wife or civil partner or a relative of any individual with whom he is in partnership; and a Scottish firm is an associate of any person who is a member of the firm.

(4) A person is an associate of any person whom he employs or by whom he is employed.

(5) A person in his capacity as trustee of a trust other than—

(a) a trust arising under any of the second Group of Parts or the Bankruptcy (Scotland) Act 1985, or

(b) a pension scheme or an employees' share scheme . . .,

is an associate of another person if the beneficiaries of the trust include, or the terms of the trust confer a power that may be exercised for the benefit of, that other person or an associate of that other person.

(6) A company is an associate of another company—

(a) if the same person has control of both, or a person has control of one and persons who are his associates, or he and persons who are his associates, have control of the other, or

(b) if a group of two or more persons has control of each company, and the groups either consist of the same persons or could be regarded as consisting of the same persons by treating (in one or more cases) a member of either group as replaced by a person of whom he is an associate.

(7) A company is an associate of another person if that person has control of it or if that person and persons who are his associates together have control of it.

(8) For the purposes of this section a person is a relative of an individual if he is that individual's brother, sister, uncle, aunt, nephew, niece, lineal ancestor or lineal descendant, treating—

(a) any relationship of the half blood as a relationship of the whole blood and the stepchild or adopted child of any person as his child, and

(b) an illegitimate child as the legitimate child of his mother and reputed father;

and references in this section to a husband or wife include a former husband or wife and a reputed husband or wife and references to a civil partner include a former civil partner and a reputed civil partner.

(9) For the purposes of this section any director or other officer of a company is to be treated as employed by that company.

(10) For the purposes of this section a person is to be taken as having control of a company if—

(a) the directors of the company or of another company which has control of it (or any of them) are accustomed to act in accordance with his directions or instructions, or

(b) he is entitled to exercise, or control the exercise of, one third or more of the voting power at any general meeting of the company or of another company which has control of it;

and where two or more persons together satisfy either of the above conditions, they are to be taken as having control of the company.

(11) In this section "company" includes any body corporate (whether incorporated in Great Britain or elsewhere); and references to directors and other officers of a company and to voting power at any general meeting of a company have effect with any necessary modifications.

436. Expressions used generally

(1) In this Act, except in so far as the context otherwise requires (and subject to Parts VII and XI)—

. . .

"the appointed day" means the day on which this Act comes into force under section 443;

"associate" has the meaning given by section 435;

"body corporate" includes a body incorporated outside Great Britain, but does not include—

(a) a corporation sole, or

(b) a partnership that, whether or not a legal person, is not regarded as a body corporate under the law by which it is governed;

"business" includes a trade or profession;

. . .

"the Companies Acts" means the Companies Acts (as defined in section 2 of the Companies Act 2006) as they have effect in Great Britain;

"conditional sale agreement" and "hire-purchase agreement" have the same meanings as in the Consumer Credit Act 1974;

"distress" includes use of the procedure in Schedule 12 to the Tribunals, Courts and Enforcement Act 2007, and references to levying distress, seizing goods and related expressions shall be construed accordingly;

. . .

"the EC Regulation" means Council Regulation (EC) No 1346/2000;

"EEA State" means a state that is a Contracting Party to the Agreement on the European Economic Area signed at Oporto on 2nd May 1992 as adjusted by the Protocol signed at Brussels on 17th March 1993;

"employees' share scheme" means a scheme for encouraging or facilitating the holding of shares in or debentures of a company by or for the benefit of—

(a) the bona fide employees or former employees of—
  (i) the company,
  (ii) any subsidiary of the company, or
  (iii) the company's holding company or any subsidiary of the company's holding company, or

(b) the spouses, civil partners, surviving spouses, surviving civil partners, or minor children or step-children of such employees or former employees;

"modifications" includes additions, alterations and omissions and cognate expressions shall be construed accordingly;

. . .

"property" includes money, goods, things in action, land and every description of property wherever situated and also obligations and every description of interest, whether present or future or vested or contingent, arising out of, or incidental to, property;

"records" includes computer records and other non-documentary records;

. . .

"subordinate legislation" has the same meaning as in the Interpretation Act 1978; and

"transaction" includes a gift, agreement or arrangement, and references to entering into a transaction shall be construed accordingly.

. . .

(2) The following expressions have the same meaning in this Act as in the Companies Acts—

"articles", in relation to a company (see section 18 of the Companies Act 2006);

"debenture" (see section 738 of that Act);

"holding company" (see sections 1159 and 1160 of, and Schedule 6 to, that Act);

"the Joint Stock Companies Acts" (see section 1171 of that Act);

"overseas company" (see section 1044 of that Act);

"paid up" (see section 583 of that Act);

"private company" and "public company" (see section 4 of that Act);

"registrar of companies" (see section 1060 of that Act);

"share" (see section 540 of that Act);

"subsidiary" (see sections 1159 and 1160 of, and Schedule 6 to, that Act).

Note. The definition "distress" is inserted by the Tribunals, Courts and Enforcement Act 2007, s. 62(3), Sch. 13, para. 85, as from a day to be appointed.

436A. Proceedings under EC Regulation: modified definition of property

In the application of this Act to proceedings by virtue of Article 3 of the EC Regulation, a reference to property is a reference to property which may be dealt with in the proceedings.

436B. References to things in writing

(1) A reference in this Act to a thing in writing includes that thing in electronic form.

(2) Subsection (1) does not apply to the following provisions—

(a) section 53 (mode of appointment by holder of charge),

(b) section 67(2) (report by receiver),

(c) section 70(4) (reference to instrument creating a charge),

(d) section 111(2) (dissent from arrangement under s 110),

(e) in the case of a winding up of a company registered in Scotland, section 111(4),

(f) section 123(1) (definition of inability to pay debts),

(g) section 198(3) (duties of sheriff principal as regards examination),

(h) section 222(1) (inability to pay debts: unpaid creditor for £750 or more), and

(i) section 223 (inability to pay debts: debt remaining unsatisfied after action brought).

PART XIX
FINAL PROVISIONS

437. Transitional provisions, and savings

The transitional provisions and savings set out in Schedule 11 to this Act shall have effect, the Schedule comprising the following Parts—

Part I: company insolvency and winding up (matters arising before appointed day, and continuance of proceedings in certain cases as before that day);

Part II: individual insolvency (matters so arising, and continuance of bankruptcy proceedings in certain cases as before that day);

Part III: transactions entered into before the appointed day and capable of being affected by orders of the court under Part XVI of this Act;

Part IV: insolvency practitioners acting as such before the appointed day; and

Part V: general transitional provisions and savings required consequentially on, and in connection with, the repeal and replacement by this Act and the Company Directors Disqualification Act 1986 of provisions of the Companies Act 1985, the greater part of the Insolvency Act 1985 and other enactments.

438. Repeals

The enactments specified in the second column of Schedule 12 to this Act are repealed to the extent specified in the third column of that Schedule.

439. Amendment of enactments

(1) The Companies Act is amended as shown in Parts I and II of Schedule 13 to this Act, being amendments consequential on this Act and the Company Directors Disqualification Act 1986.

(2) The enactments specified in the first column of Schedule 14 to this Act (being enactments which refer, or otherwise relate, to those which are repealed and replaced by this Act or the Company Directors Disqualification Act 1986) are amended as shown in the second column of that Schedule.

(3) The Lord Chancellor may by order make such consequential modifications of any provision contained in any subordinate legislation made before the appointed day and such transitional provisions in connection with those modifications as appear to him necessary or expedient in respect of—

(a) any reference in that subordinate legislation to the Bankruptcy Act 1914;

(b) any reference in that subordinate legislation to any enactment repealed by Part III or IV of Schedule 10 to the Insolvency Act 1985; or

(c) any reference in that subordinate legislation to any matter provided for under the Act of 1914 or under any enactment so repealed.

(4) An order under this section shall be made by statutory instrument subject to annulment in pursuance of a resolution of either House of Parliament.

440. Extent (Scotland)

(1) Subject to the next subsection, provisions of this Act contained in the first Group of Parts extend to Scotland except where otherwise stated.

(2) The following provisions of this Act do not extend to Scotland—
- (a) in the first Group of Parts—
  section 43;
  sections 238 to 241; and
  section 246;
- (b) the second Group of Parts;
- (c) in the third Group of Parts—
  sections 399 to 402,
  sections 412, 413, 415, 415A(3), 418, 420 and 421,
  sections 423 to 425, and
  section 429(1) and (2); and
- (d) in the Schedules—
  Parts II and III of Schedule 11; and
  Schedules 12 and 14 so far as they repeal or amend enactments which extend to England and Wales only.

Note. In subsection (2)(c), the italicized words "section 429(1) and (2)" are repealed and substituted by the words "section 429(1) to (2A)" by the Tribunals, Courts and Enforcement Act 2007, s. 106, Sch. 16, para. 4, as from a day to be appointed.

441. Extent (Northern Ireland)

(1) The following provisions of this Act extend to Northern Ireland—
- (a) sections 197, 426, 426A, 426B, 427 and 428; and
- (b) so much of section 439 and Schedule 14 as relates to enactments which extend to Northern Ireland.

(2) Subject as above, and to any provision expressly relating to companies incorporated elsewhere than in Great Britain, nothing in this Act extends to Northern Ireland or applies to or in relation to companies registered or incorporated in Northern Ireland.

442. Extent (other territories)

Her Majesty may, by Order in Council, direct that such of the provisions of this Act as are specified in the Order, being provisions formerly contained in the Insolvency Act 1985, shall extend to any of the Channel Islands or any colony with such modifications as may be so specified.

443. Commencement

This Act comes into force on the day appointed under section 236(2) of the Insolvency Act 1985 for the coming into force of Part III of that Act (individual insolvency and bankruptcy), immediately after that Part of that Act comes into force for England and Wales.

444. Citation

This Act may be cited as the Insolvency Act 1986.

SCHEDULE A1

MORATORIUM WHERE DIRECTORS PROPOSE VOLUNTARY ARRANGEMENT

PART I
INTRODUCTORY

Interpretation

1. In this Schedule—

"the beginning of the moratorium" has the meaning given by paragraph 8(1),

"the date of filing" means the date on which the documents for the time being referred to in paragraph 7(1) are filed or lodged with the court,

"hire-purchase agreement" includes a conditional sale agreement, a chattel leasing agreement and a retention of title agreement, "market contract" and "market charge" have the meanings given by Part VII of the Companies Act 1989,

…

"moratorium" means a moratorium under section 1A,

"the nominee" includes any person for the time being carrying out the functions of a nominee under this Schedule,

…

"the settlement finality regulations" means the Financial Markets and Insolvency (Settlement Finality) Regulations 1999,

"system-charge" has the meaning given by the Financial Markets and Insolvency Regulations 1996.

Eligible companies

2.— (1) A company is eligible for a moratorium if it meets the requirements of paragraph 3, unless—

(a) it is excluded from being eligible by virtue of paragraph 4, or

(b) it falls within sub-paragraph (2).

(2) A company falls within this sub-paragraph if—

(a) it effects or carries out contracts of insurance, but is not exempt from the general prohibition, within the meaning of section 19 of the Financial Services and Markets Act 2000, in relation to that activity,

(b) it has permission under Part IV of that Act to accept deposits,

(bb) it has a liability in respect of a deposit which it accepted in accordance with the Banking Act 1979 or 1987,

(c) it is a party to a market contract … or any of its property is subject to a market charge … or a system-charge, or

(d) it is a participant (within the meaning of the settlement finality regulations) or any of its property is subject to a collateral security charge (within the meaning of those regulations).

(3) Paragraphs (a), (b) and (bb) of sub-paragraph (2) must be read with—

(a) section 22 of the Financial Services and Markets Act 2000;

(b) any relevant order under that section; and

(c) Schedule 2 to that Act.

3.— (1) A company meets the requirements of this paragraph if the qualifying conditions are met—

(a) in the year ending with the date of filing, or

(b) in the financial year of the company which ended last before that date.

(2) For the purposes of sub-paragraph (1)—

(a) the qualifying conditions are met by a company in a period if, in that period, it satisfies two or more of the requirements for being a small company specified for the time being in section 382(3) of the Companies Act 2006, and

(b) a company's financial year is to be determined in accordance with that Act.

(3) Section 382(4), (5) and (6) of that Act apply for the purposes of this paragraph as they apply for the purposes of that section.

(4) A company does not meet the requirements of this paragraph if it is a parent company of a group of companies which does not qualify as a small group or a medium-sized group in relation to the financial year of the company which ended last before the date of filing.

(5) For the purposes of sub-paragraph (4)—

(a) "group" has the same meaning as in Part 15 of the Companies Act 2006 (see section 474(1) of that Act); and

(b) a group qualifies as small in relation to a financial year if it so qualifies under section 383(2) to (7) of that Act, and qualifies as medium-sized in relation to a financial year if it so qualifies under section 466(2) to (7) of that Act.

(6) Expressions used in this paragraph that are defined expressions in Part 15 of the Companies Act 2006 (accounts and reports) have the same meaning in this paragraph as in that Part.

4.— (1) A company is excluded from being eligible for a moratorium if, on the date of filing—

(a) the company is in administration,

(b) the company is being wound up,

(c) there is an administrative receiver of the company,

(d) a voluntary arrangement has effect in relation to the company,

(e) there is a provisional liquidator of the company,

(f) a moratorium has been in force for the company at any time during the period of 12 months ending with the date of filing and—

(i) no voluntary arrangement had effect at the time at which the moratorium came to an end, or

(ii) a voluntary arrangement which had effect at any time in that period has come to an end prematurely,

(fa) an administrator appointed under paragraph 22 of Schedule B1 has held office in the period of 12 months ending with the date of filing, or

(g) a voluntary arrangement in relation to the company which had effect in pursuance of a proposal under section 1(3) has come to an end prematurely and, during the period of 12 months ending with the date of filing, an order under section 5(3)(a) has been made.

(2) Sub-paragraph (1)(b) does not apply to a company which, by reason of a winding-up order made after the date of filing, is treated as being wound up on that date.

Capital market arrangement

4A. A company is also excluded from being eligible for a moratorium if, on the date of filing, it is a party to an agreement which is or forms part of a capital market arrangement under which—

(i) a party has incurred, or when the agreement was entered into was expected to incur, a debt of at least £10 million under the arrangement, and

(ii) the arrangement involves the issue of a capital market investment.

Public private partnership

4B. A company is also excluded from being eligible for a moratorium if, on the date of filing, it is a project company of a project which—

(i) is a public-private partnership project, and

(ii) includes step-in rights.

Liability under an arrangement

4C.— (1) A company is also excluded from being eligible for a moratorium if, on the date of filing, it has incurred a liability under an agreement of £10 million or more.

(2) Where the liability in sub-paragraph (1) is a contingent liability under or by virtue of a guarantee or an indemnity or security provided on behalf of another person, the amount of that liability is the full amount of the liability in relation to which the guarantee, indemnity or security is provided.

(3) In this paragraph—

(a) the reference to "liability" includes a present or future liability whether, in either case, it is certain or contingent,

(b) the reference to "liability" includes a reference to a liability to be paid wholly or partly in foreign currency (in which case the sterling equivalent shall be calculated as at the time when the liability is incurred).

Interpretation of capital market arrangement

4D.— (1) For the purposes of paragraph 4A an arrangement is a capital market arrangement if—

(a) it involves a grant of security to a person holding it as trustee for a person who holds a capital market investment issued by a party to the arrangement, or
(b) at least one party guarantees the performance of obligations of another party, or
(c) at least one party provides security in respect of the performance of obligations of another party, or
(d) the arrangement involves an investment of a kind described in articles 83 to 85 of the Financial Services and Markets Act 2000 (Regulated Activities) Order 2001 (options, futures and contracts for differences).

(2) For the purposes of sub-paragraph (1)—
(a) a reference to holding as trustee includes a reference to holding as nominee or agent,
(b) a reference to holding for a person who holds a capital market investment includes a reference to holding for a number of persons at least one of whom holds a capital market investment, and
(c) a person holds a capital market investment if he has a legal or beneficial interest in it.

(3) In paragraph 4A, 4C, 4J and this paragraph—
"agreement" includes an agreement or undertaking effected by—
(a) contract,
(b) deed, or
(c) any other instrument intended to have effect in accordance with the law of England and Wales, Scotland or another jurisdiction, and
"party" to an arrangement includes a party to an agreement which—
(a) forms part of the arrangement,
(b) provides for the raising of finance as part of the arrangement, or
(c) is necessary for the purposes of implementing the arrangement.

Capital market investment

4E.— (1) For the purposes of paragraphs 4A and 4D, an investment is a capital market investment if—
(a) it is within article 77 or 77A of the Financial Services and Markets Act 2000 (Regulated Activities) Order 2001 (debt instruments) and
(b) it is rated, listed or traded or designed to be rated, listed or traded.

(2) In sub-paragraph (1)—
"listed" means admitted to the official list within the meaning given by section 103(1) of the Financial Services and Markets Act 2000 (interpretation),
"rated" means rated for the purposes of investment by an internationally recognised rating agency,
"traded" means admitted to trading on a market established under the rules of a recognised investment exchange or on a foreign market.

(3) In sub-paragraph (2)—
"foreign market" has the same meaning as "relevant market" in article 67(2) of the Financial Services and Markets Act 2000 (Financial Promotion) Order 2001 (foreign markets),
"recognised investment exchange" has the meaning given by section 285 of the Financial Services and Markets Act 2000 (recognised investment exchange).

4F.— (1) For the purposes of paragraphs 4A and 4D an investment is also a capital market investment if it consists of a bond or commercial paper issued to one or more of the following—
(a) an investment professional within the meaning of article 19(5) of the Financial Services and Markets Act 2000 (Financial Promotion) Order 2001,
(b) a person who is, when the agreement mentioned in paragraph 4A is entered into, a certified high net worth individual in relation to a communication within the meaning of article 48(2) of that order,
(c) a person to whom article 49(2) of that order applies (high net worth company, &c.),

(d) a person who is, when the agreement mentioned in paragraph 4A is entered into, a certified sophisticated investor in relation to a communication within the meaning of article 50(1) of that order, and

(e) a person in a State other than the United Kingdom who under the law of that State is not prohibited from investing in bonds or commercial paper.

(2) For the purposes of sub-paragraph (1)—

(a) in applying article 19(5) of the Financial Services and Markets Act 2000 (Financial Promotion) Order 2001 for the purposes of sub-paragraph (1)(a)—

(i) in article 19(5)(b), ignore the words after "exempt person",

(ii) in article 19(5)(c)(i), for the words from "the controlled activity" to the end substitute "a controlled activity", and

(iii) in article 19(5)(e) ignore the words from "where the communication" to the end, and

(b) in applying article 49(2) of that order for the purposes of sub-paragraph (1)(c), ignore article 49(2)(e).

(3) In sub-paragraph (1)—

"bond" shall be construed in accordance with article 77 of the Financial Services and Markets Act 2000 (Regulated Activities) Order 2001, and includes any instrument falling within article 77A of that Order, and

"commercial paper" has the meaning given by article 9(3) of that order.

Debt

4G. The debt of at least £10 million referred to in paragraph 4A—

(a) may be incurred at any time during the life of the capital market arrangement, and

(b) may be expressed wholly or partly in a foreign currency (in which case the sterling equivalent shall be calculated as at the time when the arrangement is entered into).

Interpretation of project company

4H.— (1) For the purposes of paragraph 4B a company is a "project company" of a project if—

(a) it holds property for the purpose of the project,

(b) it has sole or principal responsibility under an agreement for carrying out all or part of the project,

(c) it is one of a number of companies which together carry out the project,

(d) it has the purpose of supplying finance to enable the project to be carried out, or

(e) it is the holding company of a company within any of paragraphs (a) to (d).

(2) But a company is not a "project company" of a project if—

(a) it performs a function within sub-paragraph (1)(a) to (d) or is within sub-paragraph (1)(e), but

(b) it also performs a function which is not—

(i) within sub-paragraph (1)(a) to (d),

(ii) related to a function within sub-paragraph (1)(a) to (d), or

(iii) related to the project.

(3) For the purposes of this paragraph a company carries out all or part of a project whether or not it acts wholly or partly through agents.

Public-private partnership project

4I.— (1) In paragraph 4B "public-private partnership project" means a project—

(a) the resources for which are provided partly by one or more public bodies and partly by one or more private persons, or

(b) which is designed wholly or mainly for the purpose of assisting a public body to discharge a function.

(2) In sub-paragraph (1) "resources" includes—

(a) funds (including payment for the provision of services or facilities),

(b) assets,
(c) professional skill,
(d) the grant of a concession or franchise, and
(e) any other commercial resource.

(3) In sub-paragraph (1) "public body" means—
(a) a body which exercises public functions,
(b) a body specified for the purposes of this paragraph by the Secretary of State, and
(c) a body within a class specified for the purposes of this paragraph by the Secretary of State.

(4) A specification under sub-paragraph (3) may be—
(a) general, or
(b) for the purpose of the application of paragraph 4B to a specified case.

Step-in rights

4J.— (1) For the purposes of paragraph 4B a project has "step-in rights" if a person who provides finance in connection with the project has a conditional entitlement under an agreement to—
(i) assume sole or principal responsibility under an agreement for carrying out all or part of the project, or
(ii) make arrangements for carrying out all or part of the project.

(2) In sub-paragraph (1) a reference to the provision of finance includes a reference to the provision of an indemnity.

"Person"

4K. For the purposes of paragraphs 4A to 4J, a reference to a person includes a reference to a partnership or another unincorporated group of persons.

5. The Secretary of State may by regulations modify the qualifications for eligibility of a company for a moratorium.

PART II
OBTAINING A MORATORIUM

Nominee's statement

6.— (1) Where the directors of a company wish to obtain a moratorium, they shall submit to the nominee—
(a) a document setting out the terms of the proposed voluntary arrangement,
(b) a statement of the company's affairs containing—
(i) such particulars of its creditors and of its debts and other liabilities and of its assets as may be prescribed, and
(ii) such other information as may be prescribed, and
(c) any other information necessary to enable the nominee to comply with sub-paragraph (2) which he requests from them.

(2) The nominee shall submit to the directors a statement in the prescribed form indicating whether or not, in his opinion—
(a) the proposed voluntary arrangement has a reasonable prospect of being approved and implemented,
(b) the company is likely to have sufficient funds available to it during the proposed moratorium to enable it to carry on its business, and
(c) meetings of the company and its creditors should be summoned to consider the proposed voluntary arrangement.

(3) In forming his opinion on the matters mentioned in sub-paragraph (2), the nominee is entitled to rely on the information submitted to him under sub-paragraph (1) unless he has reason to doubt its accuracy.

(4) The reference in sub-paragraph (2)(b) to the company's business is to that business as the company proposes to carry it on during the moratorium.

Documents to be submitted to court

7.— (1) To obtain a moratorium the directors of a company must file (in Scotland, lodge) with the court—

(a) a document setting out the terms of the proposed voluntary arrangement,

(b) a statement of the company's affairs containing—

(i) such particulars of its creditors and of its debts and other liabilities and of its assets as may be prescribed, and

(ii) such other information as may be prescribed,

(c) a statement that the company is eligible for a moratorium,

(d) a statement from the nominee that he has given his consent to act, and

(e) a statement from the nominee that, in his opinion—

(i) the proposed voluntary arrangement has a reasonable prospect of being approved and implemented,

(ii) the company is likely to have sufficient funds available to it during the proposed moratorium to enable it to carry on its business, and

(iii) meetings of the company and its creditors should be summoned to consider the proposed voluntary arrangement.

(2) Each of the statements mentioned in sub-paragraph (1)(b) to (e), except so far as it contains the particulars referred to in paragraph (b)(i), must be in the prescribed form.

(3) The reference in sub-paragraph (1)(e)(ii) to the company's business is to that business as the company proposes to carry it on during the moratorium.

(4) The Secretary of State may by regulations modify the requirements of this paragraph as to the documents required to be filed (in Scotland, lodged) with the court in order to obtain a moratorium.

Duration of moratorium

8.— (1) A moratorium comes into force when the documents for the time being referred to in paragraph 7(1) are filed or lodged with the court and references in this Schedule to "the beginning of the moratorium" shall be construed accordingly.

(2) A moratorium ends at the end of the day on which the meetings summoned under paragraph 29(1) are first held (or, if the meetings are held on different days, the later of those days), unless it is extended under paragraph 32.

(3) If either of those meetings has not first met before the end of the period of 28 days beginning with the day on which the moratorium comes into force, the moratorium ends at the end of the day on which those meetings were to be held (or, if those meetings were summoned to be held on different days, the later of those days), unless it is extended under paragraph 32.

(4) If the nominee fails to summon either meeting within the period required by paragraph 29(1), the moratorium ends at the end of the last day of that period.

(5) If the moratorium is extended (or further extended) under paragraph 32, it ends at the end of the day to which it is extended (or further extended).

(6) Sub-paragraphs (2) to (5) do not apply if the moratorium comes to an end before the time concerned by virtue of—

(a) paragraph 25(4) (effect of withdrawal by nominee of consent to act),

(b) an order under paragraph 26(3), 27(3) or 40 (challenge of actions of nominee or directors), or

(c) a decision of one or both of the meetings summoned under paragraph 29.

(7) If the moratorium has not previously come to an end in accordance with sub-paragraphs (2) to (6), it ends at the end of the day on which a decision under paragraph 31 to approve a voluntary arrangement takes effect under paragraph 36.

(8) The Secretary of State may by order increase or reduce the period for the time being specified in sub-paragraph (3).

Notification of beginning of moratorium

9.— (1) When a moratorium comes into force, the directors shall notify the nominee of that fact forthwith.

(2) If the directors without reasonable excuse fail to comply with sub-paragraph (1), each of them is liable to imprisonment or a fine, or both.

10.— (1) When a moratorium comes into force, the nominee shall, in accordance with the rules—

(a) advertise that fact forthwith, and

(b) notify the registrar of companies, the company and any petitioning creditor of the company of whose claim he is aware of that fact.

(2) In sub-paragraph (1)(b), "petitioning creditor" means a creditor by whom a winding-up petition has been presented before the beginning of the moratorium, as long as the petition has not been dismissed or withdrawn.

(3) If the nominee without reasonable excuse fails to comply with sub-paragraph (1)(a) or (b), he is liable to a fine.

Notification of end of moratorium

11.— (1) When a moratorium comes to an end, the nominee shall, in accordance with the rules—

(a) advertise that fact forthwith, and

(b) notify the court, the registrar of companies, the company and any creditor of the company of whose claim he is aware of that fact.

(2) If the nominee without reasonable excuse fails to comply with sub-paragraph (1)(a) or (b), he is liable to a fine.

PART III
EFFECTS OF MORATORIUM

Effect on creditors, etc

12.— (1) During the period for which a moratorium is in force for a company—

(a) no petition may be presented for the winding up of the company,

(b) no meeting of the company may be called or requisitioned except with the consent of the nominee or the leave of the court and subject (where the court gives leave) to such terms as the court may impose,

(c) no resolution may be passed or order made for the winding up of the company,

(d) no administration application may be made in respect of the company,

(da) no administrator of the company may be appointed under paragraph 14 or 22 of Schedule B1,

(e) no administrative receiver of the company may be appointed,

(f) no landlord or other person to whom rent is payable may exercise any right of forfeiture by peaceable re-entry in relation to premises let to the company in respect of a failure by the company to comply with any term or condition of its tenancy of such premises, except with the leave of the court and subject to such terms as the court may impose,

(g) no other steps may be taken to enforce any security over the company's property, or to repossess goods in the company's possession under any hire-purchase agreement, except with the leave of the court and subject to such terms as the court may impose, and

(h) no other proceedings and no execution or other legal process may be commenced or continued, and no distress may be levied, against the company or its property except with the leave of the court and subject to such terms as the court may impose.

(2) Where a petition, other than an excepted petition, for the winding up of the company has been presented before the beginning of the moratorium, section 127 shall not apply in relation to any disposition of property, transfer of shares or alteration in status made during the moratorium or at a time mentioned in paragraph 37(5)(a).

(3) In the application of sub-paragraph (1)(h) to Scotland, the reference to execution being commenced or continued includes a reference to diligence being carried out or continued, and the reference to distress being levied is omitted.

(4) Paragraph (a) of sub-paragraph (1) does not apply to an excepted petition and, where such a petition has been presented before the beginning of the moratorium or is presented during the moratorium, paragraphs (b) and (c) of that sub-paragraph do not apply in relation to proceedings on the petition.

(5) For the purposes of this paragraph, "excepted petition" means a petition under—

(a) section 124A or 124B of this Act,

(b) section 72 of the Financial Services Act 1986 on the ground mentioned in subsection (1)(b) of that section, or

(c) section 92 of the Banking Act 1987 on the ground mentioned in subsection (1)(b) of that section,

(d) section 367 of the Financial Services and Markets Act 2000 on the ground mentioned in subsection (3)(b) of that section.

13.— (1) This paragraph applies where there is an uncrystallised floating charge on the property of a company for which a moratorium is in force.

(2) If the conditions for the holder of the charge to give a notice having the effect mentioned in sub-paragraph (4) are met at any time, the notice may not be given at that time but may instead be given as soon as practicable after the moratorium has come to an end.

(3) If any other event occurs at any time which (apart from this sub-paragraph) would have the effect mentioned in sub-paragraph (4), then—

(a) the event shall not have the effect in question at that time, but

(b) if notice of the event is given to the company by the holder of the charge as soon as is practicable after the moratorium has come to an end, the event is to be treated as if it had occurred when the notice was given.

(4) The effect referred to in sub-paragraphs (2) and (3) is—

(a) causing the crystallisation of the floating charge, or

(b) causing the imposition, by virtue of provision in the instrument creating the charge, of any restriction on the disposal of any property of the company.

(5) Application may not be made for leave under paragraph 12(1)(g) or (h) with a view to obtaining—

(a) the crystallisation of the floating charge, or

(b) the imposition, by virtue of provision in the instrument creating the charge, of any restriction on the disposal of any property of the company.

14. Security granted by a company at a time when a moratorium is in force in relation to the company may only be enforced if, at that time, there were reasonable grounds for believing that it would benefit the company.

Effect on company

15.— (1) Paragraphs 16 to 23 apply in relation to a company for which a moratorium is in force.

(2) The fact that a company enters into a transaction in contravention of any of paragraphs 16 to 22 does not—

(a) make the transaction void, or

(b) make it to any extent unenforceable against the company.

Company invoices, etc

16.— (1) Every invoice, order for goods or services, business letter or order form (whether in hard copy, electronic or any other form) issued by or on behalf of the company, and all the company's websites, must also contain the nominee's name and a statement that the moratorium is in force for the company.

(2) If default is made in complying with sub-paragraph (1), the company and (subject to sub-paragraph (3)) any officer of the company is liable to a fine.

(3) An officer of the company is only liable under sub-paragraph (2) if, without reasonable excuse, he authorises or permits the default.

Obtaining credit during moratorium

17.— (1) The company may not obtain credit to the extent of £250 or more from a person who has not been informed that a moratorium is in force in relation to the company.

(2) The reference to the company obtaining credit includes the following cases—

(a) where goods are bailed (in Scotland, hired) to the company under a hire-purchase agreement, or agreed to be sold to the company under a conditional sale agreement, and

(b) where the company is paid in advance (whether in money or otherwise) for the supply of goods or services.

(3) Where the company obtains credit in contravention of sub-paragraph (1)—

(a) the company is liable to a fine, and

(b) if any officer of the company knowingly and wilfully authorised or permitted the contravention, he is liable to imprisonment or a fine, or both.

(4) The money sum specified in sub-paragraph (1) is subject to increase or reduction by order under section 417A in Part XV.

Disposals and payments

18.— (1) Subject to sub-paragraph (2), the company may only dispose of any of its property if—

(a) there are reasonable grounds for believing that the disposal will benefit the company, and

(b) the disposal is approved by the committee established under paragraph 35(1) or, where there is no such committee, by the nominee.

(2) Sub-paragraph (1) does not apply to a disposal made in the ordinary way of the company's business.

(3) If the company makes a disposal in contravention of sub-paragraph (1) otherwise than in pursuance of an order of the court—

(a) the company is liable to a fine, and

(b) if any officer of the company authorised or permitted the contravention, without reasonable excuse, he is liable to imprisonment or a fine, or both.

19.— (1) Subject to sub-paragraph (2), the company may only make any payment in respect of any debt or other liability of the company in existence before the beginning of the moratorium if—

(a) there are reasonable grounds for believing that the payment will benefit the company, and

(b) the payment is approved by the committee established under paragraph 35(1) or, where there is no such committee, by the nominee.

(2) Sub-paragraph (1) does not apply to a payment required by paragraph 20(6).

(3) If the company makes a payment in contravention of sub-paragraph (1) otherwise than in pursuance of an order of the court—

(a) the company is liable to a fine, and

(b) if any officer of the company authorised or permitted the contravention, without reasonable excuse, he is liable to imprisonment or a fine, or both.

Disposal of charged property, etc

20.— (1) This paragraph applies where—

(a) any property of the company is subject to a security, or

(b) any goods are in the possession of the company under a hire-purchase agreement.

(2) If the holder of the security consents, or the court gives leave, the company may dispose of the property as if it were not subject to the security.

(3) If the owner of the goods consents, or the court gives leave, the company may dispose of the goods as if all rights of the owner under the hire-purchase agreement were vested in the company.

(4) Where property subject to a security which, as created, was a floating charge is disposed of under sub-paragraph (2), the holder of the security has the same priority in respect of any property of the company directly or indirectly representing the property disposed of as he would have had in respect of the property subject to the security.

(5) Sub-paragraph (6) applies to the disposal under sub-paragraph (2) or (as the case may be) sub-paragraph (3) of—

(a) any property subject to a security other than a security which, as created, was a floating charge, or

(b) any goods in the possession of the company under a hire-purchase agreement.

(6) It shall be a condition of any consent or leave under sub-paragraph (2) or (as the case may be) sub-paragraph (3) that—

(a) the net proceeds of the disposal, and

(b) where those proceeds are less than such amount as may be agreed, or determined by the court, to be the net amount which would be realised on a sale of the property or goods in the open market by a willing vendor, such sums as may be required to make good the deficiency,

shall be applied towards discharging the sums secured by the security or payable under the hire-purchase agreement.

(7) Where a condition imposed in pursuance of sub-paragraph (6) relates to two or more securities, that condition requires—

(a) the net proceeds of the disposal, and

(b) where paragraph (b) of sub-paragraph (6) applies, the sums mentioned in that paragraph,

to be applied towards discharging the sums secured by those securities in the order of their priorities.

(8) Where the court gives leave for a disposal under sub-paragraph (2) or (3), the directors shall, within 14 days after leave is given, send a copy of the order giving leave to the registrar of companies.

(9) If the directors without reasonable excuse fail to comply with sub-paragraph (8), they are liable to a fine.

21.— (1) Where property is disposed of under paragraph 20 in its application to Scotland, the company shall grant to the disponee an appropriate document of transfer or conveyance of the property, and

(a) that document, or

(b) where any recording, intimation or registration of the document is a legal requirement for completion of title to the property, that recording, intimation or registration,

has the effect of disencumbering the property of, or (as the case may be) freeing the property from, the security.

(2) Where goods in the possession of the company under a hire-purchase agreement are disposed of under paragraph 20 in its application to Scotland, the disposal has the effect of extinguishing, as against the disponee, all rights of the owner of the goods under the agreement.

22.— (1) If the company—

(a) without any consent or leave under paragraph 20, disposes of any of its property which is subject to a security otherwise than in accordance with the terms of the security,

(b) without any consent or leave under paragraph 20, disposes of any goods in the possession of the company under a hire-purchase agreement otherwise than in accordance with the terms of the agreement, or

(c) fails to comply with any requirement imposed by paragraph 20 or 21,

it is liable to a fine.

(2) If any officer of the company, without reasonable excuse, authorises or permits any such disposal or failure to comply, he is liable to imprisonment or a fine, or both.

Market contracts, etc

23.— (1) If the company enters into any transaction to which this paragraph applies—

(a) the company is liable to a fine, and

(b) if any officer of the company, without reasonable excuse, authorised or permitted the company to enter into the transaction, he is liable to imprisonment or a fine, or both.

(2) A company enters into a transaction to which this paragraph applies if it—

(a) enters into a market contract, …

(b) gives a transfer order,

(c) grants a market charge … or a system-charge, or

(d) provides any collateral security.

(3) The fact that a company enters into a transaction in contravention of this paragraph does not—

(a) make the transaction void, or

(b) make it to any extent unenforceable by or against the company.

(4) Where during the moratorium a company enters into a transaction to which this paragraph applies, nothing done by or in pursuance of the transaction is to be treated as done in contravention of paragraphs 12(1)(g), 14 or 16 to 22.

(5) Paragraph 20 does not apply in relation to any property which is subject to a market charge, … a system-charge or a collateral security charge.

(6) In this paragraph, "transfer order", "collateral security" and "collateral security charge" have the same meanings as in the settlement finality regulations.

PART IV
NOMINEES

Monitoring of company's activities

24.— (1) During a moratorium, the nominee shall monitor the company's affairs for the purpose of forming an opinion as to whether—

(a) the proposed voluntary arrangement or, if he has received notice of proposed modifications under paragraph 31(7), the proposed arrangement with those modifications has a reasonable prospect of being approved and implemented, and

(b) the company is likely to have sufficient funds available to it during the remainder of the moratorium to enable it to continue to carry on its business.

(2) The directors shall submit to the nominee any information necessary to enable him to comply with sub-paragraph (1) which he requests from them.

(3) In forming his opinion on the matters mentioned in sub-paragraph (1), the nominee is entitled to rely on the information submitted to him under sub-paragraph (2) unless he has reason to doubt its accuracy.

(4) The reference in sub-paragraph (1)(b) to the company's business is to that business as the company proposes to carry it on during the remainder of the moratorium.

Withdrawal of consent to act

25.— (1) The nominee may only withdraw his consent to act in the circumstances mentioned in this paragraph.

(2) The nominee must withdraw his consent to act if, at any time during a moratorium—

(a) he forms the opinion that—

(i) the proposed voluntary arrangement or, if he has received notice of proposed modifications under paragraph 31(7), the proposed arrangement with those modifications no longer has a reasonable prospect of being approved or implemented, or

(ii) the company will not have sufficient funds available to it during the remainder of the moratorium to enable it to continue to carry on its business,

(b) he becomes aware that, on the date of filing, the company was not eligible for a moratorium, or

(c) the directors fail to comply with their duty under paragraph 24(2).

(3) The reference in sub-paragraph (2)(a)(ii) to the company's business is to that business as the company proposes to carry it on during the remainder of the moratorium.

(4) If the nominee withdraws his consent to act, the moratorium comes to an end.

(5) If the nominee withdraws his consent to act he must, in accordance with the rules, notify the court, the registrar of companies, the company and any creditor of the company of whose claim he is aware of his withdrawal and the reason for it.

(6) If the nominee without reasonable excuse fails to comply with sub-paragraph (5), he is liable to a fine.

Challenge of nominee's actions, etc

26.— (1) If any creditor, director or member of the company, or any other person affected by a moratorium, is dissatisfied by any act, omission or decision of the nominee during the moratorium, he may apply to the court.

(2) An application under sub-paragraph (1) may be made during the moratorium or after it has ended.

(3) On an application under sub-paragraph (1) the court may—

(a) confirm, reverse or modify any act or decision of the nominee,

(b) give him directions, or

(c) make such other order as it thinks fit.

(4) An order under sub-paragraph (3) may (among other things) bring the moratorium to an end and make such consequential provision as the court thinks fit.

27.— (1) Where there are reasonable grounds for believing that—

(a) as a result of any act, omission or decision of the nominee during the moratorium, the company has suffered loss, but

(b) the company does not intend to pursue any claim it may have against the nominee,

any creditor of the company may apply to the court.

(2) An application under sub-paragraph (1) may be made during the moratorium or after it has ended.

(3) On an application under sub-paragraph (1) the court may—

(a) order the company to pursue any claim against the nominee,

(b) authorise any creditor to pursue such a claim in the name of the company, or

(c) make such other order with respect to such a claim as it thinks fit,

unless the court is satisfied that the act, omission or decision of the nominee was in all the circumstances reasonable.

(4) An order under sub-paragraph (3) may (among other things)—

(a) impose conditions on any authority given to pursue a claim,

(b) direct the company to assist in the pursuit of a claim,

(c) make directions with respect to the distribution of anything received as a result of the pursuit of a claim,

(d) bring the moratorium to an end and make such consequential provision as the court thinks fit.

(5) On an application under sub-paragraph (1) the court shall have regard to the interests of the members and creditors of the company generally.

Replacement of nominee by court

28.— (1) The court may—

(a) on an application made by the directors in a case where the nominee has failed to comply with any duty imposed on him under this Schedule or has died, or

(b) on an application made by the directors or the nominee in a case where it is impracticable or inappropriate for the nominee to continue to act as such,

direct that the nominee be replaced as such by another person qualified to act as an insolvency practitioner, or authorised to act as nominee, in relation to the voluntary arrangement.

(2) A person may only be appointed as a replacement nominee under this paragraph if he submits to the court a statement indicating his consent to act.

PART V
CONSIDERATION AND IMPLEMENTATION OF VOLUNTARY ARRANGEMENT

Summoning of meetings

29.— (1) Where a moratorium is in force, the nominee shall summon meetings of the company and its creditors for such a time, date (within the period for the time being specified in paragraph 8(3)) and place as he thinks fit.

(2) The persons to be summoned to a creditors' meeting under this paragraph are every creditor of the company of whose claim the nominee is aware.

Conduct of meetings

30.— (1) Subject to the provisions of paragraphs 31 to 35, the meetings summoned under paragraph 29 shall be conducted in accordance with the rules.

(2) A meeting so summoned may resolve that it be adjourned (or further adjourned).

(3) After the conclusion of either meeting in accordance with the rules, the chairman of the meeting shall report the result of the meeting to the court, and, immediately after reporting to the court, shall give notice of the result of the meeting to such persons as may be prescribed.

Approval of voluntary arrangement

31.— (1) The meetings summoned under paragraph 29 shall decide whether to approve the proposed voluntary arrangement (with or without modifications).

(2) The modifications may include one conferring the functions proposed to be conferred on the nominee on another person qualified to act as an insolvency practitioner, or authorised to act as nominee, in relation to the voluntary arrangement.

(3) The modifications shall not include one by virtue of which the proposal ceases to be a proposal such as is mentioned in section 1.

(4) A meeting summoned under paragraph 29 shall not approve any proposal or modification which affects the right of a secured creditor of the company to enforce his security, except with the concurrence of the creditor concerned.

(5) Subject to sub-paragraph (6), a meeting so summoned shall not approve any proposal or modification under which—

(a) any preferential debt of the company is to be paid otherwise than in priority to such of its debts as are not preferential debts, or

(b) a preferential creditor of the company is to be paid an amount in respect of a preferential debt that bears to that debt a smaller proportion than is borne to another preferential debt by the amount that is to be paid in respect of that other debt.

(6) The meeting may approve such a proposal or modification with the concurrence of the preferential creditor concerned.

(7) The directors of the company may, before the beginning of the period of seven days which ends with the meetings (or either of them) summoned under paragraph 29 being held, give

notice to the nominee of any modifications of the proposal for which the directors intend to seek the approval of those meetings.

(8) References in this paragraph to preferential debts and preferential creditors are to be read in accordance with section 386 in Part XII of this Act.

Extension of moratorium

32.— (1) Subject to sub-paragraph (2), a meeting summoned under paragraph 29 which resolves that it be adjourned (or further adjourned) may resolve that the moratorium be extended (or further extended), with or without conditions.

(2) The moratorium may not be extended (or further extended) to a day later than the end of the period of two months which begins—

(a) where both meetings summoned under paragraph 29 are first held on the same day, with that day,

(b) in any other case, with the day on which the later of those meetings is first held.

(3) At any meeting where it is proposed to extend (or further extend) the moratorium, before a decision is taken with respect to that proposal, the nominee shall inform the meeting—

(a) of what he has done in order to comply with his duty under paragraph 24 and the cost of his actions for the company, and

(b) of what he intends to do to continue to comply with that duty if the moratorium is extended (or further extended) and the expected cost of his actions for the company.

(4) Where, in accordance with sub-paragraph (3)(b), the nominee informs a meeting of the expected cost of his intended actions, the meeting shall resolve whether or not to approve that expected cost.

(5) If a decision not to approve the expected cost of the nominee's intended actions has effect under paragraph 36, the moratorium comes to an end.

(6) A meeting may resolve that a moratorium which has been extended (or further extended) be brought to an end before the end of the period of the extension (or further extension).

(7) The Secretary of State may by order increase or reduce the period for the time being specified in sub-paragraph (2).

33.— (1) The conditions which may be imposed when a moratorium is extended (or further extended) include a requirement that the nominee be replaced as such by another person qualified to act as an insolvency practitioner, or authorised to act as nominee, in relation to the voluntary arrangement.

(2) A person may only be appointed as a replacement nominee by virtue of sub-paragraph (1) if he submits to the court a statement indicating his consent to act.

(3) At any meeting where it is proposed to appoint a replacement nominee as a condition of extending (or further extending) the moratorium—

(a) the duty imposed by paragraph 32(3)(b) on the nominee shall instead be imposed on the person proposed as the replacement nominee, and

(b) paragraphs 32(4) and (5) and 36(1)(e) apply as if the references to the nominee were to that person.

34.— (1) If a decision to extend, or further extend, the moratorium takes effect under paragraph 36, the nominee shall, in accordance with the rules, notify the registrar of companies and the court.

(2) If the moratorium is extended, or further extended, by virtue of an order under paragraph 36(5), the nominee shall, in accordance with the rules, send a copy of the order to the registrar of companies.

(3) If the nominee without reasonable excuse fails to comply with this paragraph, he is liable to a fine.

Moratorium committee

35.— (1) A meeting summoned under paragraph 29 which resolves that the moratorium be extended (or further extended) may, with the consent of the nominee, resolve that a committee be established to exercise the functions conferred on it by the meeting.

(2) The meeting may not so resolve unless it has approved an estimate of the expenses to be incurred by the committee in the exercise of the proposed functions.

(3) Any expenses, not exceeding the amount of the estimate, incurred by the committee in the exercise of its functions shall be reimbursed by the nominee.

(4) The committee shall cease to exist when the moratorium comes to an end.

Effectiveness of decisions

36.— (1) Sub-paragraph (2) applies to references to one of the following decisions having effect, that is, a decision, under paragraph 31, 32 or 35, with respect to—

(a) the approval of a proposed voluntary arrangement,

(b) the extension (or further extension) of a moratorium,

(c) the bringing of a moratorium to an end,

(d) the establishment of a committee, or

(e) the approval of the expected cost of a nominee's intended actions.

(2) The decision has effect if, in accordance with the rules—

(a) it has been taken by both meetings summoned under paragraph 29, or

(b) (subject to any order made under sub-paragraph (5)) it has been taken by the creditors' meeting summoned under that paragraph.

(3) If a decision taken by the creditors' meeting under any of paragraphs 31, 32 or 35 with respect to any of the matters mentioned in sub-paragraph (1) differs from one so taken by the company meeting with respect to that matter, a member of the company may apply to the court.

(4) An application under sub-paragraph (3) shall not be made after the end of the period of 28 days beginning with—

(a) the day on which the decision was taken by the creditors' meeting, or

(b) where the decision of the company meeting was taken on a later day, that day.

(5) On an application under sub-paragraph (3), the court may—

(a) order the decision of the company meeting to have effect instead of the decision of the creditors' meeting, or

(b) make such other order as it thinks fit.

Effect of approval of voluntary arrangement

37.— (1) This paragraph applies where a decision approving a voluntary arrangement has effect under paragraph 36.

(2) The approved voluntary arrangement—

(a) takes effect as if made by the company at the creditors' meeting, and

(b) binds every person who in accordance with the rules—

(i) was entitled to vote at that meeting (whether or not he was present or represented at it), or

(ii) would have been so entitled if he had had notice of it,

as if he were a party to the voluntary arrangement.

(3) If—

(a) when the arrangement ceases to have effect any amount payable under the arrangement to a person bound by virtue of sub-paragraph (2)(b)(ii) has not been paid, and

(b) the arrangement did not come to an end prematurely,

the company shall at that time become liable to pay to that person the amount payable under the arrangement.

(4) Where a petition for the winding up of the company, other than an excepted petition within the meaning of paragraph 12, was presented before the beginning of the moratorium, the court shall dismiss the petition.

(5) The court shall not dismiss a petition under sub-paragraph (4)—

(a) at any time before the end of the period of 28 days beginning with the first day on which each of the reports of the meetings required by paragraph 30(3) has been made to the court, or

(b) at any time when an application under paragraph 38 or an appeal in respect of such an application is pending, or at any time in the period within which such an appeal may be brought.

Challenge of decisions

38.— (1) Subject to the following provisions of this paragraph, any of the persons mentioned in sub-paragraph (2) may apply to the court on one or both of the following grounds—

(a) that a voluntary arrangement approved at one or both of the meetings summoned under paragraph 29 and which has taken effect unfairly prejudices the interests of a creditor, member or contributory of the company,

(b) that there has been some material irregularity at or in relation to either of those meetings.

(2) The persons who may apply under this paragraph are—

(a) a person entitled, in accordance with the rules, to vote at either of the meetings,

(b) a person who would have been entitled, in accordance with the rules, to vote at the creditors' meeting if he had had notice of it, and

(c) the nominee.

(3) An application under this paragraph shall not be made—

(a) after the end of the period of 28 days beginning with the first day on which each of the reports required by paragraph 30(3) has been made to the court, or

(b) in the case of a person who was not given notice of the creditors' meeting, after the end of the period of 28 days beginning with the day on which he became aware that the meeting had taken place,

but (subject to that) an application made by a person within sub-paragraph (2)(b) on the ground that the arrangement prejudices his interests may be made after the arrangement has ceased to have effect, unless it came to an end prematurely.

(4) Where on an application under this paragraph the court is satisfied as to either of the grounds mentioned in sub-paragraph (1), it may do any of the following—

(a) revoke or suspend—

(i) any decision approving the voluntary arrangement which has effect under paragraph 36, or

(ii) in a case falling within sub-paragraph (1)(b), any decision taken by the meeting in question which has effect under that paragraph,

(b) give a direction to any person—

(i) for the summoning of further meetings to consider any revised proposal for a voluntary arrangement which the directors may make, or

(ii) in a case falling within sub-paragraph (1)(b), for the summoning of a further company or (as the case may be) creditors' meeting to reconsider the original proposal.

(5) Where at any time after giving a direction under sub-paragraph (4)(b)(i) the court is satisfied that the directors do not intend to submit a revised proposal, the court shall revoke the direction and revoke or suspend any decision approving the voluntary arrangement which has effect under paragraph 36.

(6) Where the court gives a direction under sub-paragraph (4)(b), it may also give a direction continuing or, as the case may require, renewing, for such period as may be specified in the direction, the effect of the moratorium.

(7) Sub-paragraph (8) applies in a case where the court, on an application under this paragraph—
(a) gives a direction under sub-paragraph (4)(b), or
(b) revokes or suspends a decision under sub-paragraph (4)(a) or (5).

(8) In such a case, the court may give such supplemental directions as it thinks fit and, in particular, directions with respect to—
(a) things done under the voluntary arrangement since it took effect, and
(b) such things done since that time as could not have been done if a moratorium had been in force in relation to the company when they were done.

(9) Except in pursuance of the preceding provisions of this paragraph, a decision taken at a meeting summoned under paragraph 29 is not invalidated by any irregularity at or in relation to the meeting.

Implementation of voluntary arrangement

39.— (1) This paragraph applies where a voluntary arrangement approved by one or both of the meetings summoned under paragraph 29 has taken effect.

(2) The person who is for the time being carrying out in relation to the voluntary arrangement the functions conferred—
(a) by virtue of the approval of the arrangement, on the nominee, or
(b) by virtue of paragraph 31(2), on a person other than the nominee,
shall be known as the supervisor of the voluntary arrangement.

(3) If any of the company's creditors or any other person is dissatisfied by any act, omission or decision of the supervisor, he may apply to the court.

(4) On an application under sub-paragraph (3) the court may—
(a) confirm, reverse or modify any act or decision of the supervisor,
(b) give him directions, or
(c) make such other order as it thinks fit.

(5) The supervisor—
(a) may apply to the court for directions in relation to any particular matter arising under the voluntary arrangement, and
(b) is included among the persons who may apply to the court for the winding up of the company or for an administration order to be made in relation to it.

(6) The court may, whenever—
(a) it is expedient to appoint a person to carry out the functions of the supervisor, and
(b) it is inexpedient, difficult or impracticable for an appointment to be made without the assistance of the court,
make an order appointing a person who is qualified to act as an insolvency practitioner, or authorised to act as supervisor, in relation to the voluntary arrangement, either in substitution for the existing supervisor or to fill a vacancy.

(7) The power conferred by sub-paragraph (6) is exercisable so as to increase the number of persons exercising the functions of supervisor or, where there is more than one person exercising those functions, so as to replace one or more of those persons.

PART VI
MISCELLANEOUS

Challenge of directors' actions

40.— (1) This paragraph applies in relation to acts or omissions of the directors of a company during a moratorium.

(2) A creditor or member of the company may apply to the court for an order under this paragraph on the ground—
(a) that the company's affairs, business and property are being or have been managed by the directors in a manner which is unfairly prejudicial to the interests of its creditors or

members generally, or of some part of its creditors or members (including at least the petitioner), or

(b) that any actual or proposed act or omission of the directors is or would be so prejudicial.

(3) An application for an order under this paragraph may be made during or after the moratorium.

(4) On an application for an order under this paragraph the court may—

(a) make such order as it thinks fit for giving relief in respect of the matters complained of,

(b) adjourn the hearing conditionally or unconditionally, or

(c) make an interim order or any other order that it thinks fit.

(5) An order under this paragraph may in particular—

(a) regulate the management by the directors of the company's affairs, business and property during the remainder of the moratorium,

(b) require the directors to refrain from doing or continuing an act complained of by the petitioner, or to do an act which the petitioner has complained they have omitted to do,

(c) require the summoning of a meeting of creditors or members for the purpose of considering such matters as the court may direct,

(d) bring the moratorium to an end and make such consequential provision as the court thinks fit.

(6) In making an order under this paragraph the court shall have regard to the need to safeguard the interests of persons who have dealt with the company in good faith and for value.

(7) Sub-paragraph (8) applies where—

(a) the appointment of an administrator has effect in relation to the company and that appointment was in pursuance of—

(i) an administration application made, or

(ii) a notice of intention to appoint filed,

before the moratorium came into force, or

(b) the company is being wound up in pursuance of a petition presented before the moratorium came into force.

(8) No application for an order under this paragraph may be made by a creditor or member of the company; but such an application may be made instead by the administrator or (as the case may be) the liquidator.

Offences

41.— (1) This paragraph applies where a moratorium has been obtained for a company.

(2) If, within the period of 12 months ending with the day on which the moratorium came into force, a person who was at the time an officer of the company—

(a) did any of the things mentioned in paragraphs (a) to (f) of sub-paragraph (4), or

(b) was privy to the doing by others of any of the things mentioned in paragraphs (c), (d) and (e) of that sub-paragraph,

he is to be treated as having committed an offence at that time.

(3) If, at any time during the moratorium, a person who is an officer of the company—

(a) does any of the things mentioned in paragraphs (a) to (f) of sub-paragraph (4), or

(b) is privy to the doing by others of any of the things mentioned in paragraphs (c), (d) and (e) of that sub-paragraph,

he commits an offence.

(4) Those things are—

(a) concealing any part of the company's property to the value of £500 or more, or concealing any debt due to or from the company, or

(b) fraudulently removing any part of the company's property to the value of £500 or more, or

(c) concealing, destroying, mutilating or falsifying any book or paper affecting or relating to the company's property or affairs, or

(d) making any false entry in any book or paper affecting or relating to the company's property or affairs, or

(e) fraudulently parting with, altering or making any omission in any document affecting or relating to the company's property or affairs, or

(f) pawning, pledging or disposing of any property of the company which has been obtained on credit and has not been paid for (unless the pawning, pledging or disposal was in the ordinary way of the company's business).

(5) For the purposes of this paragraph, "officer" includes a shadow director.

(6) It is a defence—

(a) for a person charged under sub-paragraph (2) or (3) in respect of the things mentioned in paragraph (a) or (f) of sub-paragraph (4) to prove that he had no intent to defraud, and

(b) for a person charged under sub-paragraph (2) or (3) in respect of the things mentioned in paragraph (c) or (d) of sub-paragraph (4) to prove that he had no intent to conceal the state of affairs of the company or to defeat the law.

(7) Where a person pawns, pledges or disposes of any property of a company in circumstances which amount to an offence under sub-paragraph (2) or (3), every person who takes in pawn or pledge, or otherwise receives, the property knowing it to be pawned, pledged or disposed of in circumstances which—

(a) would, if a moratorium were obtained for the company within the period of 12 months beginning with the day on which the pawning, pledging or disposal took place, amount to an offence under sub-paragraph (2), or

(b) amount to an offence under sub-paragraph (3),

commits an offence.

(8) A person guilty of an offence under this paragraph is liable to imprisonment or a fine, or both.

(9) The money sums specified in paragraphs (a) and (b) of sub-paragraph (4) are subject to increase or reduction by order under section 417A in Part XV.

42.— (1) If, for the purpose of obtaining a moratorium, or an extension of a moratorium, for a company, a person who is an officer of the company—

(a) makes any false representation, or

(b) fraudulently does, or omits to do, anything,

he commits an offence.

(2) Sub-paragraph (1) applies even if no moratorium or extension is obtained.

(3) For the purposes of this paragraph, "officer" includes a shadow director.

(4) A person guilty of an offence under this paragraph is liable to imprisonment or a fine, or both.

Void provisions in floating charge documents

43.— (1) A provision in an instrument creating a floating charge is void if it provides for—

(a) obtaining a moratorium, or

(b) anything done with a view to obtaining a moratorium (including any preliminary decision or investigation),

to be an event causing the floating charge to crystallise or causing restrictions which would not otherwise apply to be imposed on the disposal of property by the company or a ground for the appointment of a receiver.

(2) In sub-paragraph (1), "receiver" includes a manager and a person who is appointed both receiver and manager.

Functions of the Financial Conduct Authority and Prudential Regulation Authority

44.— (1) This Schedule has effect in relation to a moratorium for a regulated company with the modifications in sub-paragraphs (2) to (16) below.

(2) Any notice or other document required by virtue of this Schedule to be sent to a creditor of a regulated company must also be sent to the appropriate regulator.

(3) The appropriate regulator is entitled to be heard on any application to the court for leave under paragraph 20(2) or 20(3) (disposal of charged property, etc).

(4) Where paragraph 26(1) (challenge of nominee's actions, etc) applies, the persons who may apply to the court include the appropriate regulator.

(5) If a person other than a regulator applies to the court under that paragraph, the appropriate regulator is entitled to be heard on the application.

(6) Where paragraph 27(1) (challenge of nominee's actions, etc) applies, the persons who may apply to the court include the the appropriate regulator.

(7) If a person other than a regulator applies to the court under that paragraph, the appropriate regulator is entitled to be heard on the application.

(8) The persons to be summoned to a creditors' meeting under paragraph 29 include the appropriate regulator.

(9) A person appointed for the purpose by the appropriate regulator is entitled to attend and participate in (but not to vote at)—
   (a) any creditors' meeting summoned under that paragraph,
   (b) any meeting of a committee established under paragraph 35 (moratorium committee).

(10) The appropriate regulator is entitled to be heard on any application under paragraph 36(3) (effectiveness of decisions).

(11) Where paragraph 38(1) (challenge of decisions) applies, the persons who may apply to the court include the appropriate regulator.

(12) If a person other than a regulator applies to the court under that paragraph, the appropriate regulator is entitled to be heard on the application.

(13) Where paragraph 39(3) (implementation of voluntary arrangement) applies, the persons who may apply to the court include the appropriate regulator.

(14) If a person other than a regulator applies to the court under that paragraph, the appropriate regulator is entitled to be heard on the application.

(15) Where paragraph 40(2) (challenge of directors' actions) applies, the persons who may apply to the court include the appropriate regulator.

(16) If a person other than a regulator applies to the court under that paragraph, the appropriate regulator is entitled to be heard on the application.

(16A) If either regulator makes an application to the court under any of the provisions mentioned in sub-paragraphs (5), (7), (12), (14) or (16) in relation to a PRA-regulated company, the other regulator is entitled to be heard on the application.

(17) This paragraph does not prejudice any right the appropriate regulator has (apart from this paragraph) as a creditor of a regulated company.

(17A) The "appropriate regulator" means—
   (a) for the purposes of sub-paragraphs (2) to (8) and (10) to (17)—
      (i) where the regulated company is a PRA-regulated company, each of the Financial Conduct Authority and the Prudential Regulation Authority, and
      (ii) in any other case, the Financial Conduct Authority;
   (b) for the purposes of sub-paragraph (9)—
      (i) where the regulated company is a PRA-regulated company, the Financial Conduct Authority or the Prudential Regulation Authority, and
      (ii) in any other case, the Financial Conduct Authority.

(18) In this paragraph—

"PRA-authorised person" has the meaning given by section 2B(5) of the Financial Services and Markets Act 2000;

"PRA-regulated activity" has the meaning given by section 22A of the Financial Services and Markets Act 2000;

"PRA-regulated company" means a regulated company which—

(a) is, or has been, a PRA-authorised person,
(b) is, or has been, an appointed representative within the meaning given by section 39 of the Financial Services and Markets Act 2000, whose principal (or one of whose principals) is, or was, a PRA-authorised person, or
(c) is carrying on, or has carried on, a PRA-regulated activity in contravention of the general prohibition;

"regulated company" means a company which—

(a) is, or has been, an authorised person within the meaning given by section 31 of the Financial Services and Markets Act 2000,
(b) is, or has been, an appointed representative within the meaning given by section 39 of that Act, or
(c) is carrying on, or has carried on, a regulated activity, within the meaning given by section 22 of that Act, in contravention of the general prohibition within the meaning given by section 19 of that Act;

"regulator" means the Financial Conduct Authority or the Prudential Regulation Authority.

Subordinate legislation

45.— (1) Regulations or an order made by the Secretary of State under this Schedule may make different provision for different cases.

(2) Regulations so made may make such consequential, incidental, supplemental and transitional provision as may appear to the Secretary of State necessary or expedient.

(3) Any power of the Secretary of State to make regulations under this Schedule may be exercised by amending or repealing any enactment contained in this Act (including one contained in this Schedule) or contained in the Company Directors Disqualification Act 1986.

(4) Regulations (except regulations under paragraph 5) or an order made by the Secretary of State under this Schedule shall be made by statutory instrument subject to annulment in pursuance of a resolution of either House of Parliament.

(5) Regulations under paragraph 5 of this Schedule are to be made by statutory instrument and shall only be made if a draft containing the regulations has been laid before and approved by resolution of each House of Parliament.

SCHEDULE B1

ADMINISTRATION

Section 8

ARRANGEMENT OF SCHEDULE

NATURE OF ADMINISTRATION

Administration

1.— (1) For the purposes of this Act "administrator" of a company means a person appointed under this Schedule to manage the company's affairs, business and property.

(2) For the purposes of this Act—

(a) a company is "in administration" while the appointment of an administrator of the company has effect,

(b) a company "enters administration" when the appointment of an administrator takes effect,

(c) a company ceases to be in administration when the appointment of an administrator of the company ceases to have effect in accordance with this Schedule, and

(d) a company does not cease to be in administration merely because an administrator vacates office (by reason of resignation, death or otherwise) or is removed from office.

2. A person may be appointed as administrator of a company—

(a) by administration order of the court under paragraph 10,

(b) by the holder of a floating charge under paragraph 14, or

(c) by the company or its directors under paragraph 22.

Purpose of administration

3.— (1) The administrator of a company must perform his functions with the objective of—

(a) rescuing the company as a going concern, or

(b) achieving a better result for the company's creditors as a whole than would be likely if the company were wound up (without first being in administration), or

(c) realising property in order to make a distribution to one or more secured or preferential creditors.

(2) Subject to sub-paragraph (4), the administrator of a company must perform his functions in the interests of the company's creditors as a whole.

(3) The administrator must perform his functions with the objective specified in sub-paragraph (1)(a) unless he thinks either—

(a) that it is not reasonably practicable to achieve that objective, or

(b) that the objective specified in sub-paragraph (1)(b) would achieve a better result for the company's creditors as a whole.

(4) The administrator may perform his functions with the objective specified in sub-paragraph (1)(c) only if—

(a) he thinks that it is not reasonably practicable to achieve either of the objectives specified in sub-paragraph (1)(a) and (b), and

(b) he does not unnecessarily harm the interests of the creditors of the company as a whole.

4. The administrator of a company must perform his functions as quickly and efficiently as is reasonably practicable.

Status of administrator

5. An administrator is an officer of the court (whether or not he is appointed by the court).

General restrictions

6. A person may be appointed as administrator of a company only if he is qualified to act as an insolvency practitioner in relation to the company.

7. A person may not be appointed as administrator of a company which is in administration (subject to the provisions of paragraphs 90 to 97 and 100 to 103 about replacement and additional administrators).

8.— (1) A person may not be appointed as administrator of a company which is in liquidation by virtue of—

(a) a resolution for voluntary winding up, or
(b) a winding-up order.
(2) Sub-paragraph (1)(a) is subject to paragraph 38.
(3) Sub-paragraph (1)(b) is subject to paragraphs 37 and 38.

9.— (1) A person may not be appointed as administrator of a company which—
(a) has a liability in respect of a deposit which it accepted in accordance with the Banking Act 1979 or 1987, but
(b) is not an authorised deposit taker.
(2) A person may not be appointed as administrator of a company which effects or carries out contracts of insurance.
(3) But sub-paragraph (2) does not apply to a company which—
(a) is exempt from the general prohibition in relation to effecting or carrying out contracts of insurance, or
(b) is an authorised deposit taker effecting or carrying out contracts of insurance in the course of a banking business.
(4) In this paragraph—
"authorised deposit taker" means a person with permission under Part IV of the Financial Services and Markets Act 2000 to accept deposits, and
"the general prohibition" has the meaning given by section 19 of that Act.
(5) This paragraph shall be construed in accordance with—
(a) section 22 of the Financial Services and Markets Act 2000 (classes of regulated activity and categories of investment),
(b) any relevant order under that section, and
(c) Schedule 2 to that Act (regulated activities).

APPOINTMENT OF ADMINISTRATOR BY COURT

Administration order

10. An administration order is an order appointing a person as the administrator of a company.

Conditions for making order

11. The court may make an administration order in relation to a company only if satisfied—
(a) that the company is or is likely to become unable to pay its debts, and
(b) that the administration order is reasonably likely to achieve the purpose of administration.

Administration application

12.— (1) An application to the court for an administration order in respect of a company (an "administration application") may be made only by—
(a) the company,
(b) the directors of the company,
(c) one or more creditors of the company,
(d) designated officer for a magistrates' court in the exercise of the power conferred by section 87A of the Magistrates' Courts Act 1980 (fine imposed on company), or
(e) a combination of persons listed in paragraphs (a) to (d).
(2) As soon as is reasonably practicable after the making of an administration application the applicant shall notify—
(a) any person who has appointed an administrative receiver of the company,
(b) any person who is or may be entitled to appoint an administrative receiver of the company,
(c) any person who is or may be entitled to appoint an administrator of the company under paragraph 14, and
(d) such other persons as may be prescribed.
(3) An administration application may not be withdrawn without the permission of the court.

(4) In sub-paragraph (1) "creditor" includes a contingent creditor and a prospective creditor.

(5) Sub-paragraph (1) is without prejudice to section 7(4)(b).

Powers of court

13.— (1) On hearing an administration application the court may—

(a) make the administration order sought;

(b) dismiss the application;

(c) adjourn the hearing conditionally or unconditionally;

(d) make an interim order;

(e) treat the application as a winding-up petition and make any order which the court could make under section 125;

(f) make any other order which the court thinks appropriate.

(2) An appointment of an administrator by administration order takes effect—

(a) at a time appointed by the order, or

(b) where no time is appointed by the order, when the order is made.

(3) An interim order under sub-paragraph (1)(d) may, in particular—

(a) restrict the exercise of a power of the directors or the company;

(b) make provision conferring a discretion on the court or on a person qualified to act as an insolvency practitioner in relation to the company.

(4) This paragraph is subject to paragraph 39.

APPOINTMENT OF ADMINISTRATOR BY HOLDER OF FLOATING CHARGE

Power to appoint

14.— (1) The holder of a qualifying floating charge in respect of a company's property may appoint an administrator of the company.

(2) For the purposes of sub-paragraph (1) a floating charge qualifies if created by an instrument which—

(a) states that this paragraph applies to the floating charge,

(b) purports to empower the holder of the floating charge to appoint an administrator of the company,

(c) purports to empower the holder of the floating charge to make an appointment which would be the appointment of an administrative receiver within the meaning given by section 29(2), or

(d) purports to empower the holder of a floating charge in Scotland to appoint a receiver who on appointment would be an administrative receiver.

(3) For the purposes of sub-paragraph (1) a person is the holder of a qualifying floating charge in respect of a company's property if he holds one or more debentures of the company secured—

(a) by a qualifying floating charge which relates to the whole or substantially the whole of the company's property,

(b) by a number of qualifying floating charges which together relate to the whole or substantially the whole of the company's property, or

(c) by charges and other forms of security which together relate to the whole or substantially the whole of the company's property and at least one of which is a qualifying floating charge.

Restrictions on power to appoint

15.— (1) A person may not appoint an administrator under paragraph 14 unless—

(a) he has given at least two business days' written notice to the holder of any prior floating charge which satisfies paragraph 14(2), or

(b) the holder of any prior floating charge which satisfies paragraph 14(2) has consented in writing to the making of the appointment.

(2) One floating charge is prior to another for the purposes of this paragraph if—
(a) it was created first, or
(b) it is to be treated as having priority in accordance with an agreement to which the holder of each floating charge was party.

(3) Sub-paragraph (2) shall have effect in relation to Scotland as if the following were substituted for paragraph (a)—
"(a) it has priority of ranking in accordance with section 464(4)(b) of the Companies Act 1985,".

16. An administrator may not be appointed under paragraph 14 while a floating charge on which the appointment relies is not enforceable.

17. An administrator of a company may not be appointed under paragraph 14 if—
(a) a provisional liquidator of the company has been appointed under section 135, or
(b) an administrative receiver of the company is in office.

Notice of appointment

18.— (1) A person who appoints an administrator of a company under paragraph 14 shall file with the court—
(a) a notice of appointment, and
(b) such other documents as may be prescribed.

(2) The notice of appointment must include a statutory declaration by or on behalf of the person who makes the appointment—
(a) that the person is the holder of a qualifying floating charge in respect of the company's property,
(b) that each floating charge relied on in making the appointment is (or was) enforceable on the date of the appointment, and
(c) that the appointment is in accordance with this Schedule.

(3) The notice of appointment must identify the administrator and must be accompanied by a statement by the administrator—
(a) that he consents to the appointment,
(b) that in his opinion the purpose of administration is reasonably likely to be achieved, and
(c) giving such other information and opinions as may be prescribed.

(4) For the purpose of a statement under sub-paragraph (3) an administrator may rely on information supplied by directors of the company (unless he has reason to doubt its accuracy).

(5) The notice of appointment and any document accompanying it must be in the prescribed form.

(6) A statutory declaration under sub-paragraph (2) must be made during the prescribed period.

(7) A person commits an offence if in a statutory declaration under sub-paragraph (2) he makes a statement—
(a) which is false, and
(b) which he does not reasonably believe to be true.

Commencement of appointment

19. The appointment of an administrator under paragraph 14 takes effect when the requirements of paragraph 18 are satisfied.

20. A person who appoints an administrator under paragraph 14—
(a) shall notify the administrator and such other persons as may be prescribed as soon as is reasonably practicable after the requirements of paragraph 18 are satisfied, and
(b) commits an offence if he fails without reasonable excuse to comply with paragraph (a).

Invalid appointment: indemnity

21.— (1) This paragraph applies where—

(a) a person purports to appoint an administrator under paragraph 14, and
(b) the appointment is discovered to be invalid.

(2) The court may order the person who purported to make the appointment to indemnify the person appointed against liability which arises solely by reason of the appointment's invalidity.

APPOINTMENT OF ADMINISTRATOR BY COMPANY OR DIRECTORS

Power to appoint

22.— (1) A company may appoint an administrator.

(2) The directors of a company may appoint an administrator.

Restrictions on power to appoint

23.— (1) This paragraph applies where an administrator of a company is appointed—
(a) under paragraph 22, or
(b) on an administration application made by the company or its directors.

(2) An administrator of the company may not be appointed under paragraph 22 during the period of 12 months beginning with the date on which the appointment referred to in sub-paragraph (1) ceases to have effect.

24.— (1) If a moratorium for a company under Schedule A1 ends on a date when no voluntary arrangement is in force in respect of the company, this paragraph applies for the period of 12 months beginning with that date.

(2) This paragraph also applies for the period of 12 months beginning with the date on which a voluntary arrangement in respect of a company ends if—
(a) the arrangement was made during a moratorium for the company under Schedule A1, and
(b) the arrangement ends prematurely (within the meaning of section 7B).

(3) While this paragraph applies, an administrator of the company may not be appointed under paragraph 22.

25. An administrator of a company may not be appointed under paragraph 22 if—
(a) a petition for the winding up of the company has been presented and is not yet disposed of,
(b) an administration application has been made and is not yet disposed of, or
(c) an administrative receiver of the company is in office.

Notice of intention to appoint

26.— (1) A person who proposes to make an appointment under paragraph 22 shall give at least five business days' written notice to—
(a) any person who is or may be entitled to appoint an administrative receiver of the company, and
(b) any person who is or may be entitled to appoint an administrator of the company under paragraph 14.

(2) A person who proposes to make an appointment under paragraph 22 shall also give such notice as may be prescribed to such other persons as may be prescribed.

(3) A notice under this paragraph must—
(a) identify the proposed administrator, and
(b) be in the prescribed form.

27.— (1) A person who gives notice of intention to appoint under paragraph 26 shall file with the court as soon as is reasonably practicable a copy of—
(a) the notice, and
(b) any document accompanying it.

(2) The copy filed under sub-paragraph (1) must be accompanied by a statutory declaration made by or on behalf of the person who proposes to make the appointment—
(a) that the company is or is likely to become unable to pay its debts,

(b) that the company is not in liquidation, and

(c) that, so far as the person making the statement is able to ascertain, the appointment is not prevented by paragraphs 23 to 25, and

(d) to such additional effect, and giving such information, as may be prescribed.

(3) A statutory declaration under sub-paragraph (2) must—

(a) be in the prescribed form, and

(b) be made during the prescribed period.

(4) A person commits an offence if in a statutory declaration under sub-paragraph (2) he makes a statement—

(a) which is false, and

(b) which he does not reasonably believe to be true.

28.— (1) An appointment may not be made under paragraph 22 unless the person who makes the appointment has complied with any requirement of paragraphs 26 and 27 and—

(a) the period of notice specified in paragraph 26(1) has expired, or

(b) each person to whom notice has been given under paragraph 26(1) has consented in writing to the making of the appointment.

(2) An appointment may not be made under paragraph 22 after the period of ten business days beginning with the date on which the notice of intention to appoint is filed under paragraph 27(1).

Notice of appointment

29.— (1) A person who appoints an administrator of a company under paragraph 22 shall file with the court—

(a) a notice of appointment, and

(b) such other documents as may be prescribed.

(2) The notice of appointment must include a statutory declaration by or on behalf of the person who makes the appointment—

(a) that the person is entitled to make an appointment under paragraph 22,

(b) that the appointment is in accordance with this Schedule, and

(c) that, so far as the person making the statement is able to ascertain, the statements made and information given in the statutory declaration filed with the notice of intention to appoint remain accurate.

(3) The notice of appointment must identify the administrator and must be accompanied by a statement by the administrator—

(a) that he consents to the appointment,

(b) that in his opinion the purpose of administration is reasonably likely to be achieved, and

(c) giving such other information and opinions as may be prescribed.

(4) For the purpose of a statement under sub-paragraph (3) an administrator may rely on information supplied by directors of the company (unless he has reason to doubt its accuracy).

(5) The notice of appointment and any document accompanying it must be in the prescribed form.

(6) A statutory declaration under sub-paragraph (2) must be made during the prescribed period.

(7) A person commits an offence if in a statutory declaration under sub-paragraph (2) he makes a statement—

(a) which is false, and

(b) which he does not reasonably believe to be true.

30. In a case in which no person is entitled to notice of intention to appoint under paragraph 26(1) (and paragraph 28 therefore does not apply)—

(a) the statutory declaration accompanying the notice of appointment must include the statements and information required under paragraph 27(2), and

(b) paragraph 29(2)(c) shall not apply.

Commencement of appointment

31. The appointment of an administrator under paragraph 22 takes effect when the requirements of paragraph 29 are satisfied.

32. A person who appoints an administrator under paragraph 22—

(a) shall notify the administrator and such other persons as may be prescribed as soon as is reasonably practicable after the requirements of paragraph 29 are satisfied, and

(b) commits an offence if he fails without reasonable excuse to comply with paragraph (a).

33. If before the requirements of paragraph 29 are satisfied the company enters administration by virtue of an administration order or an appointment under paragraph 14—

(a) the appointment under paragraph 22 shall not take effect, and

(b) paragraph 32 shall not apply.

Invalid appointment: indemnity

34.— (1) This paragraph applies where—

(a) a person purports to appoint an administrator under paragraph 22, and

(b) the appointment is discovered to be invalid.

(2) The court may order the person who purported to make the appointment to indemnify the person appointed against liability which arises solely by reason of the appointment's invalidity.

ADMINISTRATION APPLICATION—SPECIAL CASES

Application by holder of floating charge

35.— (1) This paragraph applies where an administration application in respect of a company—

(a) is made by the holder of a qualifying floating charge in respect of the company's property, and

(b) includes a statement that the application is made in reliance on this paragraph.

(2) The court may make an administration order—

(a) whether or not satisfied that the company is or is likely to become unable to pay its debts, but

(b) only if satisfied that the applicant could appoint an administrator under paragraph 14.

Intervention by holder of floating charge

36.— (1) This paragraph applies where—

(a) an administration application in respect of a company is made by a person who is not the holder of a qualifying floating charge in respect of the company's property, and

(b) the holder of a qualifying floating charge in respect of the company's property applies to the court to have a specified person appointed as administrator (and not the person specified by the administration applicant).

(2) The court shall grant an application under sub-paragraph (1)(b) unless the court thinks it right to refuse the application because of the particular circumstances of the case.

Application where company in liquidation

37.— (1) This paragraph applies where the holder of a qualifying floating charge in respect of a company's property could appoint an administrator under paragraph 14 but for paragraph 8(1)(b).

(2) The holder of the qualifying floating charge may make an administration application.

(3) If the court makes an administration order on hearing an application made by virtue of sub-paragraph (2)—

(a) the court shall discharge the winding-up order,

(b) the court shall make provision for such matters as may be prescribed,

(c) the court may make other consequential provision,

(d) the court shall specify which of the powers under this Schedule are to be exercisable by the administrator, and

(e) this Schedule shall have effect with such modifications as the court may specify.

38.— (1) The liquidator of a company may make an administration application.

(2) If the court makes an administration order on hearing an application made by virtue of sub-paragraph (1)—

(a) the court shall discharge any winding-up order in respect of the company,

(b) the court shall make provision for such matters as may be prescribed,

(c) the court may make other consequential provision,

(d) the court shall specify which of the powers under this Schedule are to be exercisable by the administrator, and

(e) this Schedule shall have effect with such modifications as the court may specify.

Effect of administrative receivership

39.— (1) Where there is an administrative receiver of a company the court must dismiss an administration application in respect of the company unless—

(a) the person by or on behalf of whom the receiver was appointed consents to the making of the administration order,

(b) the court thinks that the security by virtue of which the receiver was appointed would be liable to be released or discharged under sections 238 to 240 (transaction at under-value and preference) if an administration order were made,

(c) the court thinks that the security by virtue of which the receiver was appointed would be avoided under section 245 (avoidance of floating charge) if an administration order were made, or

(d) the court thinks that the security by virtue of which the receiver was appointed would be challengeable under section 242 (gratuitous alienations) or 243 (unfair preferences) or under any rule of law in Scotland.

(2) Sub-paragraph (1) applies whether the administrative receiver is appointed before or after the making of the administration application.

EFFECT OF ADMINISTRATION

Dismissal of pending winding-up petition

40.— (1) A petition for the winding up of a company—

(a) shall be dismissed on the making of an administration order in respect of the company, and

(b) shall be suspended while the company is in administration following an appointment under paragraph 14.

(2) Sub-paragraph (1)(b) does not apply to a petition presented under—

(a) section 124A (public interest), or

(aa) section 124B (SEs),

(b) section 367 of the Financial Services and Markets Act 2000 (petition by Financial Conduct Authority or Prudential Regulation Authority).

(3) Where an administrator becomes aware that a petition was presented under a provision referred to in sub-paragraph (2) before his appointment, he shall apply to the court for directions under paragraph 63.

Dismissal of administrative or other receiver

41.— (1) When an administration order takes effect in respect of a company any administrative receiver of the company shall vacate office.

(2) Where a company is in administration, any receiver of part of the company's property shall vacate office if the administrator requires him to.

(3) Where an administrative receiver or receiver vacates office under sub-paragraph (1) or (2)—
 (a) his remuneration shall be charged on and paid out of any property of the company which was in his custody or under his control immediately before he vacated office, and
 (b) he need not take any further steps under section 40 or 59.

(4) In the application of sub-paragraph (3)(a)—
 (a) "remuneration" includes expenses properly incurred and any indemnity to which the administrative receiver or receiver is entitled out of the assets of the company,
 (b) the charge imposed takes priority over security held by the person by whom or on whose behalf the administrative receiver or receiver was appointed, and
 (c) the provision for payment is subject to paragraph 43.

Moratorium on insolvency proceedings

42.— (1) This paragraph applies to a company in administration.

(2) No resolution may be passed for the winding up of the company.

(3) No order may be made for the winding up of the company.

(4) Sub-paragraph (3) does not apply to an order made on a petition presented under—
 (a) section 124A (public interest), or
 (aa) section 124B (SEs),
 (b) section 367 of the Financial Services and Markets Act 2000 (petition by Financial Conduct Authority or Prudential Regulation Authority).

(5) If a petition presented under a provision referred to in sub-paragraph (4) comes to the attention of the administrator, he shall apply to the court for directions under paragraph 63.

Moratorium on other legal process

43.— (1) This paragraph applies to a company in administration.

(2) No step may be taken to enforce security over the company's property except—
 (a) with the consent of the administrator, or
 (b) with the permission of the court.

(3) No step may be taken to repossess goods in the company's possession under a hire-purchase agreement except—
 (a) with the consent of the administrator, or
 (b) with the permission of the court.

(4) A landlord may not exercise a right of forfeiture by peaceable re-entry in relation to premises let to the company except—
 (a) with the consent of the administrator, or
 (b) with the permission of the court.

(5) In Scotland, a landlord may not exercise a right of irritancy in relation to premises let to the company except—
 (a) with the consent of the administrator, or
 (b) with the permission of the court.

(6) No legal process (including legal proceedings, execution, distress and diligence) may be instituted or continued against the company or property of the company except—
 (a) with the consent of the administrator, or
 (b) with the permission of the court.

(6A) An administrative receiver of the company may not be appointed.

(7) Where the court gives permission for a transaction under this paragraph it may impose a condition on or a requirement in connection with the transaction.

(8) In this paragraph "landlord" includes a person to whom rent is payable.

Interim moratorium

44.— (1) This paragraph applies where an administration application in respect of a company has been made and—

(a) the application has not yet been granted or dismissed, or

(b) the application has been granted but the administration order has not yet taken effect.

(2) This paragraph also applies from the time when a copy of notice of intention to appoint an administrator under paragraph 14 is filed with the court until—

(a) the appointment of the administrator takes effect, or

(b) the period of five business days beginning with the date of filing expires without an administrator having been appointed.

(3) Sub-paragraph (2) has effect in relation to a notice of intention to appoint only if it is in the prescribed form.

(4) This paragraph also applies from the time when a copy of notice of intention to appoint an administrator is filed with the court under paragraph 27(1) until—

(a) the appointment of the administrator takes effect, or

(b) the period specified in paragraph 28(2) expires without an administrator having been appointed.

(5) The provisions of paragraphs 42 and 43 shall apply (ignoring any reference to the consent of the administrator).

(6) If there is an administrative receiver of the company when the administration application is made, the provisions of paragraphs 42 and 43 shall not begin to apply by virtue of this paragraph until the person by or on behalf of whom the receiver was appointed consents to the making of the administration order.

(7) This paragraph does not prevent or require the permission of the court for—

(a) the presentation of a petition for the winding up of the company under a provision mentioned in paragraph 42(4),

(b) the appointment of an administrator under paragraph 14,

(c) the appointment of an administrative receiver of the company, or

(d) the carrying out by an administrative receiver (whenever appointed) of his functions.

Publicity

45.— (1) While a company is in administration, every business document issued by or on behalf of the company or the administrator, and all the company's websites, must state—

(a) the name of the administrator, and

(b) that the affairs, business and property of the company are being managed by the administrator.

(2) Any of the following persons commits an offence if without reasonable excuse the person authorises or permits a contravention of sub-paragraph (1)—

(a) the administrator,

(b) an officer of the company, and

(c) the company.

(3) In sub-paragraph (1) "business document" means—

(a) an invoice,

(b) an order for goods or services,

(c) a business letter, and

(d) an order form,

whether in hard copy, electronic or any other form.

PROCESS OF ADMINISTRATION

Announcement of administrator's appointment

46.— (1) This paragraph applies where a person becomes the administrator of a company.

(2) As soon as is reasonably practicable the administrator shall—

(a) send a notice of his appointment to the company, and

(b) publish a notice of his appointment in the prescribed manner.

(3) As soon as is reasonably practicable the administrator shall—

(a) obtain a list of the company's creditors, and

(b) send a notice of his appointment to each creditor of whose claim and address he is aware.

(4) The administrator shall send a notice of his appointment to the registrar of companies before the end of the period of 7 days beginning with the date specified in sub-paragraph (6).

(5) The administrator shall send a notice of his appointment to such persons as may be prescribed before the end of the prescribed period beginning with the date specified in sub-paragraph (6).

(6) The date for the purpose of sub-paragraphs (4) and (5) is—

(a) in the case of an administrator appointed by administration order, the date of the order,

(b) in the case of an administrator appointed under paragraph 14, the date on which he receives notice under paragraph 20, and

(c) in the case of an administrator appointed under paragraph 22, the date on which he receives notice under paragraph 32.

(7) The court may direct that sub-paragraph (3)(b) or (5)—

(a) shall not apply, or

(b) shall apply with the substitution of a different period.

(8) A notice under this paragraph must—

(a) contain the prescribed information, and

(b) be in the prescribed form.

(9) An administrator commits an offence if he fails without reasonable excuse to comply with a requirement of this paragraph.

Statement of company's affairs

47.— (1) As soon as is reasonably practicable after appointment the administrator of a company shall by notice in the prescribed form require one or more relevant persons to provide the administrator with a statement of the affairs of the company.

(2) The statement must—

(a) be verified by a statement of truth in accordance with Civil Procedure Rules,

(b) be in the prescribed form,

(c) give particulars of the company's property, debts and liabilities,

(d) give the names and addresses of the company's creditors,

(e) specify the security held by each creditor,

(f) give the date on which each security was granted, and

(g) contain such other information as may be prescribed.

(3) In sub-paragraph (1) "relevant person" means—

(a) a person who is or has been an officer of the company,

(b) a person who took part in the formation of the company during the period of one year ending with the date on which the company enters administration,

(c) a person employed by the company during that period, and

(d) a person who is or has been during that period an officer or employee of a company which is or has been during that year an officer of the company.

(4) For the purpose of sub-paragraph (3) a reference to employment is a reference to employment through a contract of employment or a contract for services.

(5) In Scotland, a statement of affairs under sub-paragraph (1) must be a statutory declaration made in accordance with the Statutory Declarations Act 1835 (and sub-paragraph (2)(a) shall not apply).

48.— (1) A person required to submit a statement of affairs must do so before the end of the period of 11 days beginning with the day on which he receives notice of the requirement.

(2) The administrator may—
(a) revoke a requirement under paragraph 47(1), or
(b) extend the period specified in sub-paragraph (1) (whether before or after expiry).

(3) If the administrator refuses a request to act under sub-paragraph (2)—
(a) the person whose request is refused may apply to the court, and
(b) the court may take action of a kind specified in sub-paragraph (2).

(4) A person commits an offence if he fails without reasonable excuse to comply with a requirement under paragraph 47(1).

Administrator's proposals

49.— (1) The administrator of a company shall make a statement setting out proposals for achieving the purpose of administration.

(2) A statement under sub-paragraph (1) must, in particular—
(a) deal with such matters as may be prescribed, and
(b) where applicable, explain why the administrator thinks that the objective mentioned in paragraph 3(1)(a) or (b) cannot be achieved.

(3) Proposals under this paragraph may include—
(a) a proposal for a voluntary arrangement under Part I of this Act (although this paragraph is without prejudice to section 4(3));
(b) a proposal for a compromise or arrangement to be sanctioned under Part 26 of the Companies Act 2006 (arrangements and reconstructions).

(4) The administrator shall send a copy of the statement of his proposals—
(a) to the registrar of companies,
(b) to every creditor of the company of whose claim and address he is aware, and
(c) to every member of the company of whose address he is aware.

(5) The administrator shall comply with sub-paragraph (4)—
(a) as soon as is reasonably practicable after the company enters administration, and
(b) in any event, before the end of the period of eight weeks beginning with the day on which the company enters administration.

(6) The administrator shall be taken to comply with sub-paragraph (4)(c) if he publishes in the prescribed manner a notice undertaking to provide a copy of the statement of proposals free of charge to any member of the company who applies in writing to a specified address.

(7) An administrator commits an offence if he fails without reasonable excuse to comply with sub-paragraph (5).

(8) A period specified in this paragraph may be varied in accordance with paragraph 107.

Creditors' meeting

50.— (1) In this Schedule "creditors' meeting" means a meeting of creditors of a company summoned by the administrator—
(a) in the prescribed manner, and
(b) giving the prescribed period of notice to every creditor of the company of whose claim and address he is aware.

(2) A period prescribed under sub-paragraph (1)(b) may be varied in accordance with paragraph 107.

(3) A creditors' meeting shall be conducted in accordance with the rules.

Requirement for initial creditors' meeting

51.— (1) Each copy of an administrator's statement of proposals sent to a creditor under paragraph 49(4)(b) must be accompanied by an invitation to a creditors' meeting (an "initial creditors' meeting").

(2) The date set for an initial creditors' meeting must be—
(a) as soon as is reasonably practicable after the company enters administration, and

(b) in any event, within the period of ten weeks beginning with the date on which the company enters administration.

(3) An administrator shall present a copy of his statement of proposals to an initial creditors' meeting.

(4) A period specified in this paragraph may be varied in accordance with paragraph 107.

(5) An administrator commits an offence if he fails without reasonable excuse to comply with a requirement of this paragraph.

52.— (1) Paragraph 51(1) shall not apply where the statement of proposals states that the administrator thinks—

(a) that the company has sufficient property to enable each creditor of the company to be paid in full,

(b) that the company has insufficient property to enable a distribution to be made to unsecured creditors other than by virtue of section 176A(2)(a), or

(c) that neither of the objectives specified in paragraph 3(1)(a) and (b) can be achieved.

(2) But the administrator shall summon an initial creditors' meeting if it is requested—

(a) by creditors of the company whose debts amount to at least 10% of the total debts of the company,

(b) in the prescribed manner, and

(c) in the prescribed period.

(3) A meeting requested under sub-paragraph (2) must be summoned for a date in the prescribed period.

(4) The period prescribed under sub-paragraph (3) may be varied in accordance with paragraph 107.

Business and result of initial creditors' meeting

53.— (1) An initial creditors' meeting to which an administrator's proposals are presented shall consider them and may—

(a) approve them without modification, or

(b) approve them with modification to which the administrator consents.

(2) After the conclusion of an initial creditors' meeting the administrator shall as soon as is reasonably practicable report any decision taken to—

(a) the court,

(b) the registrar of companies, and

(c) such other persons as may be prescribed.

(3) An administrator commits an offence if he fails without reasonable excuse to comply with sub-paragraph (2).

Revision of administrator's proposals

54.— (1) This paragraph applies where—

(a) an administrator's proposals have been approved (with or without modification) at an initial creditors' meeting,

(b) the administrator proposes a revision to the proposals, and

(c) the administrator thinks that the proposed revision is substantial.

(2) The administrator shall—

(a) summon a creditors' meeting,

(b) send a statement in the prescribed form of the proposed revision with the notice of the meeting sent to each creditor,

(c) send a copy of the statement, within the prescribed period, to each member of the company of whose address he is aware, and

(d) present a copy of the statement to the meeting.

(3) The administrator shall be taken to have complied with sub-paragraph (2)(c) if he publishes a notice undertaking to provide a copy of the statement free of charge to any member of the company who applies in writing to a specified address.

(4) A notice under sub-paragraph (3) must be published—

(a) in the prescribed manner, and

(b) within the prescribed period.

(5) A creditors' meeting to which a proposed revision is presented shall consider it and may—

(a) approve it without modification, or

(b) approve it with modification to which the administrator consents.

(6) After the conclusion of a creditors' meeting the administrator shall as soon as is reasonably practicable report any decision taken to—

(a) the court,

(b) the registrar of companies, and

(c) such other persons as may be prescribed.

(7) An administrator commits an offence if he fails without reasonable excuse to comply with sub-paragraph (6).

Failure to obtain approval of administrator's proposals

55.— (1) This paragraph applies where an administrator reports to the court that—

(a) an initial creditors' meeting has failed to approve the administrator's proposals presented to it, or

(b) a creditors' meeting has failed to approve a revision of the administrator's proposals presented to it.

(2) The court may—

(a) provide that the appointment of an administrator shall cease to have effect from a specified time;

(b) adjourn the hearing conditionally or unconditionally;

(c) make an interim order;

(d) make an order on a petition for winding up suspended by virtue of paragraph 40(1)(b);

(e) make any other order (including an order making consequential provision) that the court thinks appropriate.

Further creditors' meetings

56.— (1) The administrator of a company shall summon a creditors' meeting if—

(a) it is requested in the prescribed manner by creditors of the company whose debts amount to at least 10% of the total debts of the company, or

(b) he is directed by the court to summon a creditors' meeting.

(2) An administrator commits an offence if he fails without reasonable excuse to summon a creditors' meeting as required by this paragraph.

Creditors' committee

57.— (1) A creditors' meeting may establish a creditors' committee.

(2) A creditors' committee shall carry out functions conferred on it by or under this Act.

(3) A creditors' committee may require the administrator—

(a) to attend on the committee at any reasonable time of which he is given at least seven days' notice, and

(b) to provide the committee with information about the exercise of his functions.

Correspondence instead of creditors' meeting

58.— (1) Anything which is required or permitted by or under this Schedule to be done at a creditors' meeting may be done by correspondence between the administrator and creditors—

(a) in accordance with the rules, and

(b) subject to any prescribed condition.

(2) A reference in this Schedule to anything done at a creditors' meeting includes a reference to anything done in the course of correspondence in reliance on sub-paragraph (1).

(3) A requirement to hold a creditors' meeting is satisfied by conducting correspondence in accordance with this paragraph.

FUNCTIONS OF ADMINISTRATOR

General powers

59.— (1) The administrator of a company may do anything necessary or expedient for the management of the affairs, business and property of the company.

(2) A provision of this Schedule which expressly permits the administrator to do a specified thing is without prejudice to the generality of sub-paragraph (1).

(3) A person who deals with the administrator of a company in good faith and for value need not inquire whether the administrator is acting within his powers.

60. The administrator of a company has the powers specified in Schedule 1 to this Act.

61. The administrator of a company—

(a) may remove a director of the company, and

(b) may appoint a director of the company (whether or not to fill a vacancy).

62. The administrator of a company may call a meeting of members or creditors of the company.

63. The administrator of a company may apply to the court for directions in connection with his functions.

64.— (1) A company in administration or an officer of a company in administration may not exercise a management power without the consent of the administrator.

(2) For the purpose of sub-paragraph (1)—

(a) "management power" means a power which could be exercised so as to interfere with the exercise of the administrator's powers,

(b) it is immaterial whether the power is conferred by an enactment or an instrument, and

(c) consent may be general or specific.

Distribution

65.— (1) The administrator of a company may make a distribution to a creditor of the company.

(2) Section 175 shall apply in relation to a distribution under this paragraph as it applies in relation to a winding up.

(3) A payment may not be made by way of distribution under this paragraph to a creditor of the company who is neither secured nor preferential unless the court gives permission.

66. The administrator of a company may make a payment otherwise than in accordance with paragraph 65 or paragraph 13 of Schedule 1 if he thinks it likely to assist achievement of the purpose of administration.

General duties

67. The administrator of a company shall on his appointment take custody or control of all the property to which he thinks the company is entitled.

68.— (1) Subject to sub-paragraph (2), the administrator of a company shall manage its affairs, business and property in accordance with—

(a) any proposals approved under paragraph 53,

(b) any revision of those proposals which is made by him and which he does not consider substantial, and

(c) any revision of those proposals approved under paragraph 54.

(2) If the court gives directions to the administrator of a company in connection with any aspect of his management of the company's affairs, business or property, the administrator shall comply with the directions.

(3) The court may give directions under sub-paragraph (2) only if—

(a) no proposals have been approved under paragraph 53,

(b) the directions are consistent with any proposals or revision approved under paragraph 53 or 54,

(c) the court thinks the directions are required in order to reflect a change in circumstances since the approval of proposals or a revision under paragraph 53 or 54, or

(d) the court thinks the directions are desirable because of a misunderstanding about proposals or a revision approved under paragraph 53 or 54.

Administrator as agent of company

69. In exercising his functions under this Schedule the administrator of a company acts as its agent.

Charged property: floating charge

70.— (1) The administrator of a company may dispose of or take action relating to property which is subject to a floating charge as if it were not subject to the charge.

(2) Where property is disposed of in reliance on sub-paragraph (1) the holder of the floating charge shall have the same priority in respect of acquired property as he had in respect of the property disposed of.

(3) In sub-paragraph (2) "acquired property" means property of the company which directly or indirectly represents the property disposed of.

Charged property: non-floating charge

71.— (1) The court may by order enable the administrator of a company to dispose of property which is subject to a security (other than a floating charge) as if it were not subject to the security.

(2) An order under sub-paragraph (1) may be made only—

(a) on the application of the administrator, and

(b) where the court thinks that disposal of the property would be likely to promote the purpose of administration in respect of the company.

(3) An order under this paragraph is subject to the condition that there be applied towards discharging the sums secured by the security—

(a) the net proceeds of disposal of the property, and

(b) any additional money required to be added to the net proceeds so as to produce the amount determined by the court as the net amount which would be realised on a sale of the property at market value.

(4) If an order under this paragraph relates to more than one security, application of money under sub-paragraph (3) shall be in the order of the priorities of the securities.

(5) An administrator who makes a successful application for an order under this paragraph shall send a copy of the order to the registrar of companies before the end of the period of 14 days starting with the date of the order.

(6) An administrator commits an offence if he fails to comply with sub-paragraph (5) without reasonable excuse.

Hire-purchase property

72.— (1) The court may by order enable the administrator of a company to dispose of goods which are in the possession of the company under a hire-purchase agreement as if all the rights of the owner under the agreement were vested in the company.

(2) An order under sub-paragraph (1) may be made only—

(a) on the application of the administrator, and

(b) where the court thinks that disposal of the goods would be likely to promote the purpose of administration in respect of the company.

(3) An order under this paragraph is subject to the condition that there be applied towards discharging the sums payable under the hire-purchase agreement—

(a) the net proceeds of disposal of the goods, and

(b) any additional money required to be added to the net proceeds so as to produce the amount determined by the court as the net amount which would be realised on a sale of the goods at market value.

(4) An administrator who makes a successful application for an order under this paragraph shall send a copy of the order to the registrar of companies before the end of the period of 14 days starting with the date of the order.

(5) An administrator commits an offence if he fails without reasonable excuse to comply with sub-paragraph (4).

Protection for secured or preferential creditor

73.— (1) An administrator's statement of proposals under paragraph 49 may not include any action which—

(a) affects the right of a secured creditor of the company to enforce his security,

(b) would result in a preferential debt of the company being paid otherwise than in priority to its non-preferential debts, or

(c) would result in one preferential creditor of the company being paid a smaller proportion of his debt than another.

(2) Sub-paragraph (1) does not apply to—

(a) action to which the relevant creditor consents,

(b) a proposal for a voluntary arrangement under Part I of this Act (although this sub-paragraph is without prejudice to section 4(3)), ...

(c) a proposal for a compromise or arrangement to be sanctioned under Part 26 of the Companies Act 2006 (arrangements and reconstructions), or

(d) a proposal for a cross-border merger within the meaning of regulation 2 of the Companies (Cross-Border Mergers) Regulations 2007.

(3) The reference to a statement of proposals in sub-paragraph (1) includes a reference to a statement as revised or modified.

Challenge to administrator's conduct of company

74.— (1) A creditor or member of a company in administration may apply to the court claiming that—

(a) the administrator is acting or has acted so as unfairly to harm the interests of the applicant (whether alone or in common with some or all other members or creditors), or

(b) the administrator proposes to act in a way which would unfairly harm the interests of the applicant (whether alone or in common with some or all other members or creditors).

(2) A creditor or member of a company in administration may apply to the court claiming that the administrator is not performing his functions as quickly or as efficiently as is reasonably practicable.

(3) The court may—

(a) grant relief;

(b) dismiss the application;

(c) adjourn the hearing conditionally or unconditionally;

(d) make an interim order;

(e) make any other order it thinks appropriate.

(4) In particular, an order under this paragraph may—

(a) regulate the administrator's exercise of his functions;

(b) require the administrator to do or not do a specified thing;

(c) require a creditors' meeting to be held for a specified purpose;

(d) provide for the appointment of an administrator to cease to have effect;

(e) make consequential provision.

(5) An order may be made on a claim under sub-paragraph (1) whether or not the action complained of—

(a) is within the administrator's powers under this Schedule;

(b) was taken in reliance on an order under paragraph 71 or 72.

(6) An order may not be made under this paragraph if it would impede or prevent the implementation of—
(a) a voluntary arrangement approved under Part I,
(b) a compromise or arrangement sanctioned under Part 26 of the Companies Act 2006 (arrangements and reconstructions), ...
(ba) a cross-border merger within the meaning of regulation 2 of the Companies (Cross-Border Mergers) Regulations 2007, or
(c) proposals or a revision approved under paragraph 53 or 54 more than 28 days before the day on which the application for the order under this paragraph is made.

Misfeasance

75.— (1) The court may examine the conduct of a person who—
(a) is or purports to be the administrator of a company, or
(b) has been or has purported to be the administrator of a company.
(2) An examination under this paragraph may be held only on the application of—
(a) the official receiver,
(b) the administrator of the company,
(c) the liquidator of the company,
(d) a creditor of the company, or
(e) a contributory of the company.
(3) An application under sub-paragraph (2) must allege that the administrator—
(a) has misapplied or retained money or other property of the company,
(b) has become accountable for money or other property of the company,
(c) has breached a fiduciary or other duty in relation to the company, or
(d) has been guilty of misfeasance.
(4) On an examination under this paragraph into a person's conduct the court may order him—
(a) to repay, restore or account for money or property;
(b) to pay interest;
(c) to contribute a sum to the company's property by way of compensation for breach of duty or misfeasance.
(5) In sub-paragraph (3) "administrator" includes a person who purports or has purported to be a company's administrator.
(6) An application under sub-paragraph (2) may be made in respect of an administrator who has been discharged under paragraph 98 only with the permission of the court.

ENDING ADMINISTRATION

Automatic end of administration

76.— (1) The appointment of an administrator shall cease to have effect at the end of the period of one year beginning with the date on which it takes effect.
(2) But—
(a) on the application of an administrator the court may by order extend his term of office for a specified period, and
(b) an administrator's term of office may be extended for a specified period not exceeding six months by consent.

77.— (1) An order of the court under paragraph 76—
(a) may be made in respect of an administrator whose term of office has already been extended by order or by consent, but
(b) may not be made after the expiry of the administrator's term of office.
(2) Where an order is made under paragraph 76 the administrator shall as soon as is reasonably practicable notify the registrar of companies.

(3) An administrator who fails without reasonable excuse to comply with sub-paragraph (2) commits an offence.

78.— (1) In paragraph 76(2)(b) "consent" means consent of—

(a) each secured creditor of the company, and

(b) if the company has unsecured debts, creditors whose debts amount to more than 50% of the company's unsecured debts, disregarding debts of any creditor who does not respond to an invitation to give or withhold consent.

(2) But where the administrator has made a statement under paragraph 52(1)(b) "consent" means—

(a) consent of each secured creditor of the company, or

(b) if the administrator thinks that a distribution may be made to preferential creditors, consent of—

(i) each secured creditor of the company, and

(ii) preferential creditors whose debts amount to more than 50% of the preferential debts of the company, disregarding debts of any creditor who does not respond to an invitation to give or withhold consent.

(3) Consent for the purposes of paragraph 76(2)(b) may be—

(a) written, or

(b) signified at a creditors' meeting.

(4) An administrator's term of office—

(a) may be extended by consent only once,

(b) may not be extended by consent after extension by order of the court, and

(c) may not be extended by consent after expiry.

(5) Where an administrator's term of office is extended by consent he shall as soon as is reasonably practicable—

(a) file notice of the extension with the court, and

(b) notify the registrar of companies.

(6) An administrator who fails without reasonable excuse to comply with sub-paragraph (5) commits an offence.

Court ending administration on application of administrator

79.— (1) On the application of the administrator of a company the court may provide for the appointment of an administrator of the company to cease to have effect from a specified time.

(2) The administrator of a company shall make an application under this paragraph if—

(a) he thinks the purpose of administration cannot be achieved in relation to the company,

(b) he thinks the company should not have entered administration, or

(c) a creditors' meeting requires him to make an application under this paragraph.

(3) The administrator of a company shall make an application under this paragraph if—

(a) the administration is pursuant to an administration order, and

(b) the administrator thinks that the purpose of administration has been sufficiently achieved in relation to the company.

(4) On an application under this paragraph the court may—

(a) adjourn the hearing conditionally or unconditionally;

(b) dismiss the application;

(c) make an interim order;

(d) make any order it thinks appropriate (whether in addition to, in consequence of or instead of the order applied for).

Termination of administration where objective achieved

80.— (1) This paragraph applies where an administrator of a company is appointed under paragraph 14 or 22.

(2) If the administrator thinks that the purpose of administration has been sufficiently achieved in relation to the company he may file a notice in the prescribed form—

(a) with the court, and

(b) with the registrar of companies.

(3) The administrator's appointment shall cease to have effect when the requirements of sub-paragraph (2) are satisfied.

(4) Where the administrator files a notice he shall within the prescribed period send a copy to every creditor of the company of whose claim and address he is aware.

(5) The rules may provide that the administrator is taken to have complied with sub-paragraph (4) if before the end of the prescribed period he publishes in the prescribed manner a notice undertaking to provide a copy of the notice under sub-paragraph (2) to any creditor of the company who applies in writing to a specified address.

(6) An administrator who fails without reasonable excuse to comply with sub-paragraph (4) commits an offence.

Court ending administration on application of creditor

81.— (1) On the application of a creditor of a company the court may provide for the appointment of an administrator of the company to cease to have effect at a specified time.

(2) An application under this paragraph must allege an improper motive—

(a) in the case of an administrator appointed by administration order, on the part of the applicant for the order, or

(b) in any other case, on the part of the person who appointed the administrator.

(3) On an application under this paragraph the court may—

(a) adjourn the hearing conditionally or unconditionally;

(b) dismiss the application;

(c) make an interim order;

(d) make any order it thinks appropriate (whether in addition to, in consequence of or instead of the order applied for).

Public interest winding-up

82.— (1) This paragraph applies where a winding-up order is made for the winding up of a company in administration on a petition presented under—

(a) section 124A (public interest), or

(aa) section 124B (SEs),

(b) section 367 of the Financial Services and Markets Act 2000 (petition by Financial Conduct Authority or Prudential Regulation Authority).

(2) This paragraph also applies where a provisional liquidator of a company in administration is appointed following the presentation of a petition under any of the provisions listed in sub-paragraph (1).

(3) The court shall order—

(a) that the appointment of the administrator shall cease to have effect, or

(b) that the appointment of the administrator shall continue to have effect.

(4) If the court makes an order under sub-paragraph (3)(b) it may also—

(a) specify which of the powers under this Schedule are to be exercisable by the administrator, and

(b) order that this Schedule shall have effect in relation to the administrator with specified modifications.

Moving from administration to creditors' voluntary liquidation

83.— (1) This paragraph applies in England and Wales where the administrator of a company thinks—

(a) that the total amount which each secured creditor of the company is likely to receive has been paid to him or set aside for him, and

(b) that a distribution will be made to unsecured creditors of the company (if there are any).

(2) This paragraph applies in Scotland where the administrator of a company thinks—

(a) that each secured creditor of the company will receive payment in respect of his debt, and

(b) that a distribution will be made to unsecured creditors (if there are any).

(3) The administrator may send to the registrar of companies a notice that this paragraph applies.

(4) On receipt of a notice under sub-paragraph (3) the registrar shall register it.

(5) If an administrator sends a notice under sub-paragraph (3) he shall as soon as is reasonably practicable—

(a) file a copy of the notice with the court, and

(b) send a copy of the notice to each creditor of whose claim and address he is aware.

(6) On the registration of a notice under sub-paragraph (3)—

(a) the appointment of an administrator in respect of the company shall cease to have effect, and

(b) the company shall be wound up as if a resolution for voluntary winding up under section 84 were passed on the day on which the notice is registered.

(7) The liquidator for the purposes of the winding up shall be—

(a) a person nominated by the creditors of the company in the prescribed manner and within the prescribed period, or

(b) if no person is nominated under paragraph (a), the administrator.

(8) In the application of Part IV to a winding up by virtue of this paragraph—

(a) section 85 shall not apply,

(b) section 86 shall apply as if the reference to the time of the passing of the resolution for voluntary winding up were a reference to the beginning of the date of registration of the notice under sub-paragraph (3),

(c) section 89 does not apply,

(d) sections 98, 99 and 100 shall not apply,

(e) section 129 shall apply as if the reference to the time of the passing of the resolution for voluntary winding up were a reference to the beginning of the date of registration of the notice under sub-paragraph (3), and

(f) any creditors' committee which is in existence immediately before the company ceases to be in administration shall continue in existence after that time as if appointed as a liquidation committee under section 101.

Moving from administration to dissolution

84.— (1) If the administrator of a company thinks that the company has no property which might permit a distribution to its creditors, he shall send a notice to that effect to the registrar of companies.

(2) The court may on the application of the administrator of a company disapply sub-paragraph (1) in respect of the company.

(3) On receipt of a notice under sub-paragraph (1) the registrar shall register it.

(4) On the registration of a notice in respect of a company under sub-paragraph (1) the appointment of an administrator of the company shall cease to have effect.

(5) If an administrator sends a notice under sub-paragraph (1) he shall as soon as is reasonably practicable—

(a) file a copy of the notice with the court, and

(b) send a copy of the notice to each creditor of whose claim and address he is aware.

(6) At the end of the period of three months beginning with the date of registration of a notice in respect of a company under sub-paragraph (1) the company is deemed to be dissolved.

(7) On an application in respect of a company by the administrator or another interested person the court may—

(a) extend the period specified in sub-paragraph (6),

(b) suspend that period, or

(c) disapply sub-paragraph (6).

(8) Where an order is made under sub-paragraph (7) in respect of a company the administrator shall as soon as is reasonably practicable notify the registrar of companies.

(9) An administrator commits an offence if he fails without reasonable excuse to comply with sub-paragraph (5).

Discharge of administration order where administration ends

85.— (1) This paragraph applies where—

(a) the court makes an order under this Schedule providing for the appointment of an administrator of a company to cease to have effect, and

(b) the administrator was appointed by administration order.

(2) The court shall discharge the administration order.

Notice to Companies Registrar where administration ends

86.— (1) This paragraph applies where the court makes an order under this Schedule providing for the appointment of an administrator to cease to have effect.

(2) The administrator shall send a copy of the order to the registrar of companies within the period of 14 days beginning with the date of the order.

(3) An administrator who fails without reasonable excuse to comply with sub-paragraph (2) commits an offence.

REPLACING ADMINISTRATOR

Resignation of administrator

87.— (1) An administrator may resign only in prescribed circumstances.

(2) Where an administrator may resign he may do so only—

(a) in the case of an administrator appointed by administration order, by notice in writing to the court,

(b) in the case of an administrator appointed under paragraph 14, by notice in writing to the holder of the floating charge by virtue of which the appointment was made,

(c) in the case of an administrator appointed under paragraph 22(1), by notice in writing to the company, or

(d) in the case of an administrator appointed under paragraph 22(2), by notice in writing to the directors of the company.

Removal of administrator from office

88. The court may by order remove an administrator from office.

Administrator ceasing to be qualified

89.— (1) The administrator of a company shall vacate office if he ceases to be qualified to act as an insolvency practitioner in relation to the company.

(2) Where an administrator vacates office by virtue of sub-paragraph (1) he shall give notice in writing—

(a) in the case of an administrator appointed by administration order, to the court,

(b) in the case of an administrator appointed under paragraph 14, to the holder of the floating charge by virtue of which the appointment was made,

(c) in the case of an administrator appointed under paragraph 22(1), to the company, or

(d) in the case of an administrator appointed under paragraph 22(2), to the directors of the company.

(3) An administrator who fails without reasonable excuse to comply with sub-paragraph (2) commits an offence.

Supplying vacancy in office of administrator

90. Paragraphs 91 to 95 apply where an administrator—

(a) dies,

(b) resigns,

(c) is removed from office under paragraph 88, or

(d) vacates office under paragraph 89.

91.— (1) Where the administrator was appointed by administration order, the court may replace the administrator on an application under this sub-paragraph made by—

(a) a creditors' committee of the company,

(b) the company,

(c) the directors of the company,

(d) one or more creditors of the company, or

(e) where more than one person was appointed to act jointly or concurrently as the administrator, any of those persons who remains in office.

(2) But an application may be made in reliance on sub-paragraph (1)(b) to (d) only where—

(a) there is no creditors' committee of the company,

(b) the court is satisfied that the creditors' committee or a remaining administrator is not taking reasonable steps to make a replacement, or

(c) the court is satisfied that for another reason it is right for the application to be made.

92. Where the administrator was appointed under paragraph 14 the holder of the floating charge by virtue of which the appointment was made may replace the administrator.

93.— (1) Where the administrator was appointed under paragraph 22(1) by the company it may replace the administrator.

(2) A replacement under this paragraph may be made only—

(a) with the consent of each person who is the holder of a qualifying floating charge in respect of the company's property, or

(b) where consent is withheld, with the permission of the court.

94.— (1) Where the administrator was appointed under paragraph 22(2) the directors of the company may replace the administrator.

(2) A replacement under this paragraph may be made only—

(a) with the consent of each person who is the holder of a qualifying floating charge in respect of the company's property, or

(b) where consent is withheld, with the permission of the court.

95. The court may replace an administrator on the application of a person listed in paragraph 91(1) if the court—

(a) is satisfied that a person who is entitled to replace the administrator under any of paragraphs 92 to 94 is not taking reasonable steps to make a replacement, or

(b) that for another reason it is right for the court to make the replacement.

Substitution of administrator: competing floating charge-holder

96.— (1) This paragraph applies where an administrator of a company is appointed under paragraph 14 by the holder of a qualifying floating charge in respect of the company's property.

(2) The holder of a prior qualifying floating charge in respect of the company's property may apply to the court for the administrator to be replaced by an administrator nominated by the holder of the prior floating charge.

(3) One floating charge is prior to another for the purposes of this paragraph if—

(a) it was created first, or

(b) it is to be treated as having priority in accordance with an agreement to which the holder of each floating charge was party.

(4) Sub-paragraph (3) shall have effect in relation to Scotland as if the following were substituted for paragraph (a)—

"(a) it has priority of ranking in accordance with section 464(4)(b) of the Companies Act 1985,".

Substitution of administrator appointed by company or directors: creditors' meeting

97.— (1) This paragraph applies where—

(a) an administrator of a company is appointed by a company or directors under paragraph 22, and

(b) there is no holder of a qualifying floating charge in respect of the company's property.

(2) A creditors' meeting may replace the administrator.

(3) A creditors' meeting may act under sub-paragraph (2) only if the new administrator's written consent to act is presented to the meeting before the replacement is made.

Vacation of office: discharge from liability

98.— (1) Where a person ceases to be the administrator of a company (whether because he vacates office by reason of resignation, death or otherwise, because he is removed from office or because his appointment ceases to have effect) he is discharged from liability in respect of any action of his as administrator.

(2) The discharge provided by sub-paragraph (1) takes effect—

(a) in the case of an administrator who dies, on the filing with the court of notice of his death,

(b) in the case of an administrator appointed under paragraph 14 or 22, at a time appointed by resolution of the creditors' committee or, if there is no committee, by resolution of the creditors, or

(c) in any case, at a time specified by the court.

(3) For the purpose of the application of sub-paragraph (2)(b) in a case where the administrator has made a statement under paragraph 52(1)(b), a resolution shall be taken as passed if (and only if) passed with the approval of—

(a) each secured creditor of the company, or

(b) if the administrator has made a distribution to preferential creditors or thinks that a distribution may be made to preferential creditors—

(i) each secured creditor of the company, and

(ii) preferential creditors whose debts amount to more than 50% of the preferential debts of the company, disregarding debts of any creditor who does not respond to an invitation to give or withhold approval.

(4) Discharge—

(a) applies to liability accrued before the discharge takes effect, and

(b) does not prevent the exercise of the court's powers under paragraph 75.

Vacation of office: charges and liabilities

99.— (1) This paragraph applies where a person ceases to be the administrator of a company (whether because he vacates office by reason of resignation, death or otherwise, because he is removed from office or because his appointment ceases to have effect).

(2) In this paragraph—

"the former administrator" means the person referred to in sub-paragraph (1), and

"cessation" means the time when he ceases to be the company's administrator.

(3) The former administrator's remuneration and expenses shall be—

(a) charged on and payable out of property of which he had custody or control immediately before cessation, and

(b) payable in priority to any security to which paragraph 70 applies.

(4) A sum payable in respect of a debt or liability arising out of a contract entered into by the former administrator or a predecessor before cessation shall be—

(a) charged on and payable out of property of which the former administrator had custody or control immediately before cessation, and

(b) payable in priority to any charge arising under sub-paragraph (3).

(5) Sub-paragraph (4) shall apply to a liability arising under a contract of employment which was adopted by the former administrator or a predecessor before cessation; and for that purpose—

(a) action taken within the period of 14 days after an administrator's appointment shall not be taken to amount or contribute to the adoption of a contract,

(b) no account shall be taken of a liability which arises, or in so far as it arises, by reference to anything which is done or which occurs before the adoption of the contract of employment, and

(c) no account shall be taken of a liability to make a payment other than wages or salary.

(6) In sub-paragraph (5)(c) "wages or salary" includes—

(a) a sum payable in respect of a period of holiday (for which purpose the sum shall be treated as relating to the period by reference to which the entitlement to holiday accrued),

(b) a sum payable in respect of a period of absence through illness or other good cause,

(c) a sum payable in lieu of holiday,

(d) in respect of a period, a sum which would be treated as earnings for that period for the purposes of an enactment about social security, and

(e) a contribution to an occupational pension scheme.

GENERAL

Joint and concurrent administrators

100.— (1) In this Schedule—

(a) a reference to the appointment of an administrator of a company includes a reference to the appointment of a number of persons to act jointly or concurrently as the administrator of a company, and

(b) a reference to the appointment of a person as administrator of a company includes a reference to the appointment of a person as one of a number of persons to act jointly or concurrently as the administrator of a company.

(2) The appointment of a number of persons to act as administrator of a company must specify—

(a) which functions (if any) are to be exercised by the persons appointed acting jointly, and

(b) which functions (if any) are to be exercised by any or all of the persons appointed.

101.— (1) This paragraph applies where two or more persons are appointed to act jointly as the administrator of a company.

(2) A reference to the administrator of the company is a reference to those persons acting jointly.

(3) But a reference to the administrator of a company in paragraphs 87 to 99 of this Schedule is a reference to any or all of the persons appointed to act jointly.

(4) Where an offence of omission is committed by the administrator, each of the persons appointed to act jointly—

(a) commits the offence, and

(b) may be proceeded against and punished individually.

(5) The reference in paragraph 45(1)(a) to the name of the administrator is a reference to the name of each of the persons appointed to act jointly.

(6) Where persons are appointed to act jointly in respect of only some of the functions of the administrator of a company, this paragraph applies only in relation to those functions.

102.— (1) This paragraph applies where two or more persons are appointed to act concurrently as the administrator of a company.

(2) A reference to the administrator of a company in this Schedule is a reference to any of the persons appointed (or any combination of them).

103.— (1) Where a company is in administration, a person may be appointed to act as administrator jointly or concurrently with the person or persons acting as the administrator of the company.

(2) Where a company entered administration by administration order, an appointment under sub-paragraph (1) must be made by the court on the application of—

(a) a person or group listed in paragraph 12(1)(a) to (e), or

(b) the person or persons acting as the administrator of the company.

(3) Where a company entered administration by virtue of an appointment under paragraph 14, an appointment under sub-paragraph (1) must be made by—

(a) the holder of the floating charge by virtue of which the appointment was made, or

(b) the court on the application of the person or persons acting as the administrator of the company.

(4) Where a company entered administration by virtue of an appointment under paragraph 22(1), an appointment under sub-paragraph (1) above must be made either by the court on the application of the person or persons acting as the administrator of the company or—

(a) by the company, and

(b) with the consent of each person who is the holder of a qualifying floating charge in respect of the company's property or, where consent is withheld, with the permission of the court.

(5) Where a company entered administration by virtue of an appointment under paragraph 22(2), an appointment under sub-paragraph (1) must be made either by the court on the application of the person or persons acting as the administrator of the company or—

(a) by the directors of the company, and

(b) with the consent of each person who is the holder of a qualifying floating charge in respect of the company's property or, where consent is withheld, with the permission of the court.

(6) An appointment under sub-paragraph (1) may be made only with the consent of the person or persons acting as the administrator of the company.

Presumption of validity

104. An act of the administrator of a company is valid in spite of a defect in his appointment or qualification.

Majority decision of directors

105. A reference in this Schedule to something done by the directors of a company includes a reference to the same thing done by a majority of the directors of a company.

Penalties

106.— (1) A person who is guilty of an offence under this Schedule is liable to a fine (in accordance with section 430 and Schedule 10).

(2) A person who is guilty of an offence under any of the following paragraphs of this Schedule is liable to a daily default fine (in accordance with section 430 and Schedule 10)—

(a) paragraph 20,

(b) paragraph 32,

(c) paragraph 46,

(d) paragraph 48,

(e) paragraph 49,

(f) paragraph 51,

(g) paragraph 53,

(h) paragraph 54,

(i) paragraph 56,

(j) paragraph 71,
(k) paragraph 72,
(l) paragraph 77,
(m) paragraph 78,
(n) paragraph 80,
(o) paragraph 84,
(p) paragraph 86, and
(q) paragraph 89.

Extension of time limit

107.— (1) Where a provision of this Schedule provides that a period may be varied in accordance with this paragraph, the period may be varied in respect of a company—
(a) by the court, and
(b) on the application of the administrator.
(2) A time period may be extended in respect of a company under this paragraph—
(a) more than once, and
(b) after expiry.

108.— (1) A period specified in paragraph 49(5), 50(1)(b) or 51(2) may be varied in respect of a company by the administrator with consent.
(2) In sub-paragraph (1) "consent" means consent of—
(a) each secured creditor of the company, and
(b) if the company has unsecured debts, creditors whose debts amount to more than 50% of the company's unsecured debts, disregarding debts of any creditor who does not respond to an invitation to give or withhold consent.
(3) But where the administrator has made a statement under paragraph 52(1)(b) "consent" means—
(a) consent of each secured creditor of the company, or
(b) if the administrator thinks that a distribution may be made to preferential creditors, consent of—
(i) each secured creditor of the company, and
(ii) preferential creditors whose debts amount to more than 50% of the total preferential debts of the company, disregarding debts of any creditor who does not respond to an invitation to give or withhold consent.
(4) Consent for the purposes of sub-paragraph (1) may be—
(a) written, or
(b) signified at a creditors' meeting.
(5) The power to extend under sub-paragraph (1)—
(a) may be exercised in respect of a period only once,
(b) may not be used to extend a period by more than 28 days,
(c) may not be used to extend a period which has been extended by the court, and
(d) may not be used to extend a period after expiry.

109. Where a period is extended under paragraph 107 or 108, a reference to the period shall be taken as a reference to the period as extended.

Amendment of provision about time

110.— (1) The Secretary of State may by order amend a provision of this Schedule which—
(a) requires anything to be done within a specified period of time,
(b) prevents anything from being done after a specified time, or
(c) requires a specified minimum period of notice to be given.
(2) An order under this paragraph—
(a) must be made by statutory instrument, and
(b) shall be subject to annulment in pursuance of a resolution of either House of Parliament.

Interpretation

111.— (1) In this Schedule—

"administrative receiver" has the meaning given by section 251,

"administrator" has the meaning given by paragraph 1 and, where the context requires, includes a reference to a former administrator,

. . .

"correspondence" includes correspondence by telephonic or other electronic means,

"creditors' meeting" has the meaning given by paragraph 50,

"enters administration" has the meaning given by paragraph 1,

"floating charge" means a charge which is a floating charge on its creation,

"in administration" has the meaning given by paragraph 1,

"hire-purchase agreement" includes a conditional sale agreement, a chattel leasing agreement and a retention of title agreement,

"holder of a qualifying floating charge" in respect of a company's property has the meaning given by paragraph 14,

"market value" means the amount which would be realised on a sale of property in the open market by a willing vendor,

"the purpose of administration" means an objective specified in paragraph 3, and

"unable to pay its debts" has the meaning given by section 123.

(1A) In this Schedule, "company" means—

(a) a company registered under the Companies Act 2006 in England and Wales or Scotland,

(b) a company incorporated in an EEA State other than the United Kingdom, or

(c) a company not incorporated in an EEA State but having its centre of main interests in a member State other than Denmark.

(1B) In sub-paragraph (1A), in relation to a company, "centre of main interests" has the same meaning as in the EC Regulation and, in the absence of proof to the contrary, is presumed to be the place of its registered office (within the meaning of that Regulation).

(2) . . .

(3) In this Schedule a reference to action includes a reference to inaction.

Non-UK companies

111A. A company incorporated outside the United Kingdom that has a principal place of business in Northern Ireland may not enter administration under this Schedule unless it also has a principal place of business in England and Wales or Scotland (or both in England and Wales and in Scotland).

Scotland

112. In the application of this Schedule to Scotland—

(a) a reference to filing with the court is a reference to lodging in court, and

(b) a reference to a charge is a reference to a right in security.

113. Where property in Scotland is disposed of under paragraph 70 or 71, the administrator shall grant to the disponee an appropriate document of transfer or conveyance of the property, and—

(a) that document, or

(b) recording, intimation or registration of that document (where recording, intimation or registration of the document is a legal requirement for completion of title to the property),

has the effect of disencumbering the property of or, as the case may be, freeing the property from, the security.

114. In Scotland, where goods in the possession of a company under a hire-purchase agreement are disposed of under paragraph 72, the disposal has the effect of extinguishing as against the disponee all rights of the owner of the goods under the agreement.

115.— (1) In Scotland, the administrator of a company may make, in or towards the satisfaction of the debt secured by the floating charge, a payment to the holder of a floating charge which has attached to the property subject to the charge.

(2) In Scotland, where the administrator thinks that the company has insufficient property to enable a distribution to be made to unsecured creditors other than by virtue of section 176A(2)(a), he may file a notice to that effect with the registrar of companies.

(3) On delivery of the notice to the registrar of companies, any floating charge granted by the company shall, unless it has already so attached, attach to the property which is subject to the charge and that attachment shall have effect as if each floating charge is a fixed security over the property to which it has attached.

116. In Scotland, the administrator in making any payment in accordance with paragraph 115 shall make such payment subject to the rights of any of the following categories of persons (which rights shall, except to the extent provided in any instrument, have the following order of priority)—

(a) the holder of any fixed security which is over property subject to the floating charge and which ranks prior to, or pari passu with, the floating charge,

(b) creditors in respect of all liabilities and expenses incurred by or on behalf of the administrator,

(c) the administrator in respect of his liabilities, expenses and remuneration and any indemnity to which he is entitled out of the property of the company,

(d) the preferential creditors entitled to payment in accordance with paragraph 65,

(e) the holder of the floating charge in accordance with the priority of that charge in relation to any other floating charge which has attached, and

(f) the holder of a fixed security, other than one referred to in paragraph (a), which is over property subject to the floating charge.

SCHEDULE 1

POWERS OF ADMINISTRATOR OR ADMINISTRATIVE RECEIVER

Sections 14, 42

1. Power to take possession of, collect and get in the property of the company and, for that purpose, to take such proceedings as may seem to him expedient.
2. Power to sell or otherwise dispose of the property of the company by public auction or private contract or, in Scotland, to sell, ... hire out or otherwise dispose of the property of the company by public roup or private bargain.
3. Power to raise or borrow money and grant security therefor over the property of the company.
4. Power to appoint a solicitor or accountant or other professionally qualified person to assist him in the performance of his functions.
5. Power to bring or defend any action or other legal proceedings in the name and on behalf of the company.
6. Power to refer to arbitration any question affecting the company.
7. Power to effect and maintain insurances in respect of the business and property of the company.
8. Power to use the company's seal.
9. Power to do all acts and to execute in the name and on behalf of the company any deed, receipt or other document.
10. Power to draw, accept, make and endorse any bill of exchange or promissory note in the name and on behalf of the company.
11. Power to appoint any agent to do any business which he is unable to do himself or which can more conveniently be done by an agent and power to employ and dismiss employees.
12. Power to do all such things (including the carrying out of works) as may be necessary for the realisation of the property of the company.

13. Power to make any payment which is necessary or incidental to the performance of his functions.
14. Power to carry on the business of the company.
15. Power to establish subsidiaries of the company.
16. Power to transfer to subsidiaries of the company the whole or any part of the business and property of the company.
17. Power to grant or accept a surrender of a lease or tenancy of any of the property of the company, and to take a lease or tenancy of any property required or convenient for the business of the company.
18. Power to make any arrangement or compromise on behalf of the company.
19. Power to call up any uncalled capital of the company.
20. Power to rank and claim in the bankruptcy, insolvency, sequestration or liquidation of any person indebted to the company and to receive dividends, and to accede to trust deeds for the creditors of any such person.
21. Power to present or defend a petition for the winding up of the company.
22. Power to change the situation of the company's registered office.
23. Power to do all other things incidental to the exercise of the foregoing powers.

SCHEDULE 2

POWERS OF A SCOTTISH RECEIVER (ADDITIONAL TO THOSE CONFERRED ON HIM BY THE INSTRUMENT OF CHARGE)

Section 55

1. Power to take possession of, collect and get in the property from the company or a liquidator thereof or any other person, and for that purpose, to take such proceedings as may seem to him expedient.
2. Power to sell, . . . hire out or otherwise dispose of the property by public roup or private bargain and with or without advertisement.
3. Power to raise or borrow money and grant security therefor over the property.
4. Power to appoint a solicitor or accountant or other professionally qualified person to assist him in the performance of his functions.
5. Power to bring or defend any action or other legal proceedings in the name and on behalf of the company.
6. Power to refer to arbitration all questions affecting the company.
7. Power to effect and maintain insurances in respect of the business and property of the company.
8. Power to use the company's seal.
9. Power to do all acts and to execute in the name and on behalf of the company any deed, receipt or other document.
10. Power to draw, accept, make and endorse any bill of exchange or promissory note in the name and on behalf of the company.
11. Power to appoint any agent to do any business which he is unable to do himself or which can more conveniently be done by an agent, and power to employ and dismiss employees.
12. Power to do all such things (including the carrying out of works), as may be necessary for the realisation of the property.
13. Power to make any payment which is necessary or incidental to the performance of his functions.
14. Power to carry on the business of the company or any part of it.
15. Power to grant or accept a surrender of a lease or tenancy of any of the property, and to take a lease or tenancy of any property required or convenient for the business of the company.
16. Power to make any arrangement or compromise on behalf of the company.
17. Power to call up any uncalled capital of the company.
18. Power to establish subsidiaries of the company.

19. Power to transfer to subsidiaries of the company the business of the company or any part of it and any of the property.
20. Power to rank and claim in the bankruptcy, insolvency, sequestration or liquidation of any person or company indebted to the company and to receive dividends, and to accede to trust deeds for creditors of any such person.
21. Power to present or defend a petition for the winding up of the company.
22. Power to change the situation of the company's registered office.
23. Power to do all other things incidental to the exercise of the powers mentioned in section 55(1) of this Act or above in this Schedule.

SCHEDULE 2A

EXCEPTIONS TO PROHIBITION ON APPOINTMENT OF ADMINISTRATIVE RECEIVER: SUPPLEMENTARY PROVISIONS

Section 72H(1)

Capital market arrangement

1.— (1) For the purposes of section 72B an arrangement is a capital market arrangement if—
(a) it involves a grant of security to a person holding it as trustee for a person who holds a capital market investment issued by a party to the arrangement, or
(aa) it involves a grant of security to—
(i) a party to the arrangement who issues a capital market investment, or
(ii) a person who holds the security as trustee for a party to the arrangement in connection with the issue of a capital market investment, or
(ab) it involves a grant of security to a person who holds the security as trustee for a party to the arrangement who agrees to provide finance to another party, or
(b) at least one party guarantees the performance of obligations of another party, or
(c) at least one party provides security in respect of the performance of obligations of another party, or
(d) the arrangement involves an investment of a kind described in articles 83 to 85 of the Financial Services and Markets Act 2000 (Regulated Activities) Order 2001 (options, futures and contracts for differences).

(2) For the purposes of sub-paragraph (1)—
(a) a reference to holding as trustee includes a reference to holding as nominee or agent,
(b) a reference to holding for a person who holds a capital market investment includes a reference to holding for a number of persons at least one of whom holds a capital market investment, and
(c) a person holds a capital market investment if he has a legal or beneficial interest in it, and
(d) the reference to the provision of finance includes the provision of an indemnity.

(3) In section 72B(1) and this paragraph "party" to an arrangement includes a party to an agreement which—
(a) forms part of the arrangement,
(b) provides for the raising of finance as part of the arrangement, or
(c) is necessary for the purposes of implementing the arrangement.

Capital market investment

2.— (1) For the purposes of section 72B an investment is a capital market investment if it—
(a) is within article 77 or 77A of the Financial Services and Markets Act 2000 (Regulated Activities) Order 2001 (debt instruments), and
(b) is rated, listed or traded or designed to be rated, listed or traded.

(2) In sub-paragraph (1)—

"rated" means rated for the purposes of investment by an internationally recognised rating agency,

"listed" means admitted to the official list within the meaning given by section 103(1) of the Financial Services and Markets Act 2000 (interpretation), and

"traded" means admitted to trading on a market established under the rules of a recognised investment exchange or on a foreign market.

(3) In sub-paragraph (2)—

"recognised investment exchange" has the meaning given by section 285 of the Financial Services and Markets Act 2000 (recognised investment exchange), and

"foreign market" has the same meaning as "relevant market" in article 67(2) of the Financial Services and Markets Act 2000 (Financial Promotion) Order 2001 (foreign markets).

3.— (1) An investment is also a capital market investment for the purposes of section 72B if it consists of a bond or commercial paper issued to one or more of the following—

(a) an investment professional within the meaning of article 19(5) of the Financial Services and Markets Act 2000 (Financial Promotion) Order 2001,

(b) a person who is, when the agreement mentioned in section 72B(1) is entered into, a certified high net worth individual in relation to a communication within the meaning of article 48(2) of that order,

(c) a person to whom article 49(2) of that order applies (high net worth company, &c),

(d) a person who is, when the agreement mentioned in section 72B(1) is entered into, a certified sophisticated investor in relation to a communication within the meaning of article 50(1) of that order, and

(e) a person in a State other than the United Kingdom who under the law of that State is not prohibited from investing in bonds or commercial paper.

(2) In sub-paragraph (1)—

"bond" shall be construed in accordance with article 77 of the Financial Services and Markets Act 2000 (Regulated Activities) Order 2001, and includes any instrument falling within article 77A of that Order, and

"commercial paper" has the meaning given by article 9(3) of that order.

(3) For the purposes of sub-paragraph (1)—

(a) in applying article 19(5) of the Financial Promotion Order for the purposes of sub-paragraph (1)(a)—

(i) in article 19(5)(b), ignore the words after "exempt person",

(ii) in article 19(5)(c)(i), for the words from "the controlled activity" to the end substitute "a controlled activity", and

(iii) in article 19(5)(e) ignore the words from "where the communication" to the end, and

(b) in applying article 49(2) of that order for the purposes of sub-paragraph (1)(c), ignore article 49(2)(e).

"Agreement"

4. For the purposes of sections 72B and 72E and this Schedule "agreement" includes an agreement or undertaking effected by—

(a) contract,

(b) deed, or

(c) any other instrument intended to have effect in accordance with the law of England and Wales, Scotland or another jurisdiction.

Debt

5. The debt of at least £50 million referred to in section 72B(1)(a) or 72E(2)(a)—

(a) may be incurred at any time during the life of the capital market arrangement or financed project, and

(b) may be expressed wholly or partly in foreign currency (in which case the sterling equivalent shall be calculated as at the time when the arrangement is entered into or the project begins).

Step-in rights

6.— (1) For the purposes of sections 72C to 72E a project has "step-in rights" if a person who provides finance in connection with the project has a conditional entitlement under an agreement to—

(a) assume sole or principal responsibility under an agreement for carrying out all or part of the project, or

(b) make arrangements for carrying out all or part of the project.

(2) In sub-paragraph (1) a reference to the provision of finance includes a reference to the provision of an indemnity.

Project company

7.— (1) For the purposes of sections 72C to 72E a company is a "project company" of a project if—

(a) it holds property for the purpose of the project,

(b) it has sole or principal responsibility under an agreement for carrying out all or part of the project,

(c) it is one of a number of companies which together carry out the project,

(d) it has the purpose of supplying finance to enable the project to be carried out, or

(e) it is the holding company of a company within any of paragraphs (a) to (d).

(2) But a company is not a "project company" of a project if—

(a) it performs a function within sub-paragraph (1)(a) to (d) or is within sub-paragraph (1)(e), but

(b) it also performs a function which is not—

(i) within sub-paragraph (1)(a) to (d),

(ii) related to a function within sub-paragraph (1)(a) to (d), or

(iii) related to the project.

(3) For the purposes of this paragraph a company carries out all or part of a project whether or not it acts wholly or partly through agents.

"Resources"

8. In section 72C "resources" includes—

(a) funds (including payment for the provision of services or facilities),

(b) assets,

(c) professional skill,

(d) the grant of a concession or franchise, and

(e) any other commercial resource.

"Public body"

9.— (1) In section 72C "public body" means—

(a) a body which exercises public functions,

(b) a body specified for the purposes of this paragraph by the Secretary of State, and

(c) a body within a class specified for the purposes of this paragraph by the Secretary of State.

(2) A specification under sub-paragraph (1) may be—

(a) general, or

(b) for the purpose of the application of section 72C to a specified case.

Regulated business

10.— (1) For the purposes of section 72D a business is regulated if it is carried on—

(a) . . .

(b) in reliance on a licence under section 7 , 7A or 7B of the Gas Act 1986 (transport and supply of gas),

(c) in reliance on a licence granted by virtue of section 41C of that Act (power to prescribe additional licensable activity),

(d) in reliance on a licence under section 6 of the Electricity Act 1989 (supply of electricity),

(e) by a water undertaker,

(f) by a sewerage undertaker,

(g) by a universal service provider within the meaning of Part 3 of the Postal Services Act 2011,

(h) by a Post Office company within the meaning of Part 1 of that Act,

(i) . . .

(j) in reliance on a licence under section 8 of the Railways Act 1993 (railway services),

(k) in reliance on a licence exemption under section 7 of that Act (subject to sub-paragraph (2) below),

(l) by the operator of a system of transport which is deemed to be a railway for a purpose of Part I of that Act by virtue of section 81(2) of that Act (tramways, &c), . . .

(m) by the operator of a vehicle carried on flanged wheels along a system within paragraph (l), or

(n) in reliance on a European licence granted pursuant to a provision contained in any instrument made for the purpose of implementing Council Directive 1995/18/EC dated 19th June 1995 on the licensing of railway undertakings, as amended by Directive 2001/13/EC dated 26th February 2001 and Directive 2004/49/EC dated 29th April 2004, both of the European Parliament and of the Council, or pursuant to any action taken by an EEA State for that purpose.

(2) Sub-paragraph (1)(k) does not apply to the operator of a railway asset on a railway unless on some part of the railway there is a permitted line speed exceeding 40 kilometres per hour.

(2A) For the purposes of section 72D a business is also regulated to the extent that it consists in the provision of a public electronic communications network or a public electronic communications service.

(2B) In sub-paragraph (1)(n), an "EEA State" means a member State, Norway, Iceland or Liechtenstein.

"Person"

11. A reference to a person in this Schedule includes a reference to a partnership or another unincorporated group of persons.

SCHEDULE 3

ORDERS IN COURSE OF WINDING UP PRONOUNCED IN VACATION (SCOTLAND)

Section 162

PART I
ORDERS WHICH ARE TO BE FINAL

Orders under section 153, as to the time for proving debts and claims.

Orders under section 195 as to meetings for ascertaining wishes of creditors or contributories.

Orders under section 198, as to the examination of witnesses in regard to the property or affairs of a company.

PART II
ORDERS WHICH ARE TO TAKE EFFECT UNTIL MATTER DISPOSED OF BY INNER HOUSE

Orders under section 126(1), 130(2) or (3), 147, 227 or 228, restraining or permitting the commencement or the continuance of legal proceedings.
Orders under section 135(5), limiting the powers of provisional liquidators.
Orders under section 108, appointing a liquidator to fill a vacancy.
Orders under section 167 or 169, sanctioning the exercise of any powers by a liquidator, other than the powers specified in paragraphs 1, 2 and 3 of Schedule 4 to this Act.
Orders under section 158, as to the arrest and detention of an absconding contributory and his property.

SCHEDULE 4

POWERS OF LIQUIDATOR IN A WINDING UP

Sections 165, 167

PART I
POWERS EXERCISABLE WITH SANCTION

1. Power to pay any class of creditors in full.
2. Power to make any compromise or arrangement with creditors or persons claiming to be creditors, or having or alleging themselves to have any claim (present or future, certain or contingent, ascertained or sounding only in damages) against the company, or whereby the company may be rendered liable.
3. In the case of a winding up in Scotland, power to compromise, on such terms as may be agreed—
   (a) all calls and liabilities to calls, all debts and liabilities capable of resulting in debts, and all claims (present or future, certain or contingent, ascertained or sounding only in damages) subsisting or supposed to subsist between the company and a contributory or alleged contributory or other debtor or person apprehending liability to the company, and
   (b) all questions in any way relating to or affecting the assets or the winding up of the company,

   and take any security for the discharge of any such call, debt, liability or claim and give a complete discharge in respect of it.

3A. Power to bring legal proceedings under section 213, 214, 238, 239, 242, 243 or 423.

PART II
POWERS EXERCISABLE WITHOUT SANCTION IN VOLUNTARY WINDING UP, WITH SANCTION IN WINDING UP BY THE COURT

4. Power to bring or defend any action or other legal proceeding in the name and on behalf of the company.
5. Power to carry on the business of the company so far as may be necessary for its beneficial winding up.

PART III
POWERS EXERCISABLE WITHOUT SANCTION IN ANY WINDING UP

6. Power to sell any of the company's property by public auction or private contract with power to transfer the whole of it to any person or to sell the same in parcels.

6A. In the case of a winding up in England and Wales, power to compromise, on such terms as may be agreed—

(a) all calls and liabilities to calls, all debts and liabilities capable of resulting in debts, and all claims (present or future, certain or contingent, ascertained or sounding only in damages) subsisting or supposed to subsist between the company and a contributory or alleged contributory or other debtor or person apprehending liability to the company, and

(b) subject to paragraph 2 in Part 1 of this Schedule, all questions in any way relating to or affecting the assets or the winding up of the company,

and take any security for the discharge of any such call, debt, liability or claim and give a complete discharge in respect of it.

7. Power to do all acts and execute, in the name and on behalf of the company, all deeds, receipts and other documents and for that purpose to use, when necessary, the company's seal.

8. Power to prove, rank and claim in the bankruptcy, insolvency or sequestration of any contributory for any balance against his estate, and to receive dividends in the bankruptcy, insolvency or sequestration in respect of that balance, as a separate debt due from the bankrupt or insolvent, and rateably with the other separate creditors.

9. Power to draw, accept, make and indorse any bill of exchange or promissory note in the name and on behalf of the company, with the same effect with respect to the company's liability as if the bill or note had been drawn, accepted, made or indorsed by or on behalf of the company in the course of its business.

10. Power to raise on the security of the assets of the company any money requisite.

11. Power to take out in his official name letters of administration to any deceased contributory, and to do in his official name any other act necessary for obtaining payment of any money due from a contributory or his estate which cannot conveniently be done in the name of the company. In all such cases the money due is deemed, for the purpose of enabling the liquidator to take out the letters of administration or recover the money, to be due to the liquidator himself.

12. Power to appoint an agent to do any business which the liquidator is unable to do himself.

13. Power to do all such other things as may be necessary for winding up the company's affairs and distributing its assets.

SCHEDULE 4ZA

CONDITIONS FOR MAKING A DEBT RELIEF ORDER

PART 1
CONDITIONS WHICH MUST BE MET

Connection with England and Wales

1.— (1) The debtor—

(a) is domiciled in England and Wales on the application date; or

(b) at any time during the period of three years ending with that date—

(i) was ordinarily resident, or had a place of residence, in England and Wales; or

(ii) carried on business in England and Wales.

(2) The reference in sub-paragraph (1)(b)(ii) to the debtor carrying on business includes—

(a) the carrying on of business by a firm or partnership of which he is a member;

(b) the carrying on of business by an agent or manager for him or for such a firm or partnership.

Debtor's previous insolvency history

2. The debtor is not, on the determination date—

(a) an undischarged bankrupt;

(b) subject to an interim order or voluntary arrangement under Part 8; or

(c) subject to a bankruptcy restrictions order or a debt relief restrictions order.

3. A debtor's petition for the debtor's bankruptcy under Part 9—

(a) has not been presented by the debtor before the determination date;

(b) has been so presented, but proceedings on the petition have been finally disposed of before that date; or

(c) has been so presented and proceedings in relation to the petition remain before the court at that date, but the court has referred the debtor under section 274A(2) for the purposes of making an application for a debt relief order.

4. A creditor's petition for the debtor's bankruptcy under Part 9—

(a) has not been presented against the debtor at any time before the determination date;

(b) has been so presented, but proceedings on the petition have been finally disposed of before that date; or

(c) has been so presented and proceedings in relation to the petition remain before the court at that date, but the person who presented the petition has consented to the making of an application for a debt relief order.

5. A debt relief order has not been made in relation to the debtor in the period of six years ending with the determination date.

Limit on debtor's overall indebtedness

6.— (1) The total amount of the debtor's debts on the determination date, other than unliquidated debts and excluded debts, does not exceed the prescribed amount.

(2) For this purpose an unliquidated debt is a debt that is not for a liquidated sum payable to a creditor either immediately or at some future certain time.

Limit on debtor's monthly surplus income

7.— (1) The debtor's monthly surplus income (if any) on the determination date does not exceed the prescribed amount.

(2) For this purpose "monthly surplus income" is the amount by which a person's monthly income exceeds the amount necessary for the reasonable domestic needs of himself and his family.

(3) The rules may—

(a) make provision as to how the debtor's monthly surplus income is to be determined;

(b) provide that particular descriptions of income are to be excluded for the purposes of this paragraph.

Limit on value of debtor's property

8.— (1) The total value of the debtor's property on the determination date does not exceed the prescribed amount.

(2) The rules may—

(a) make provision as to how the value of a person's property is to be determined;

(b) provide that particular descriptions of property are to be excluded for the purposes of this paragraph.

PART 2
OTHER CONDITIONS

9.— (1) The debtor has not entered into a transaction with any person at an undervalue during the period between—

(a) the start of the period of two years ending with the application date; and

(b) the determination date.

(2) For this purpose a debtor enters into a transaction with a person at an undervalue if—

(a) he makes a gift to that person or he otherwise enters into a transaction with that person on terms that provide for him to receive no consideration;

(b) he enters into a transaction with that person in consideration of marriage or the formation of a civil partnership; or

(c) he enters into a transaction with that person for a consideration the value of which, in money or money's worth, is significantly less than the value, in money or money's worth, of the consideration provided by the individual.

10.— (1) The debtor has not given a preference to any person during the period between—

(a) the start of the period of two years ending with the application date; and

(b) the determination date.

(2) For this purpose a debtor gives a preference to a person if—

(a) that person is one of the debtor's creditors to whom a qualifying debt is owed or is a surety or guarantor for any such debt, and

(b) the debtor does anything or suffers anything to be done which (in either case) has the effect of putting that person into a position which, in the event that a debt relief order is made in relation to the debtor, will be better than the position he would have been in if that thing had not been done.

SCHEDULE 4ZB

DEBT RELIEF RESTRICTIONS ORDERS AND UNDERTAKINGS

Debt relief restrictions order

1.— (1) A debt relief restrictions order may be made by the court in relation to a person in respect of whom a debt relief order has been made.

(2) An order may be made only on the application of—

(a) the Secretary of State, or

(b) the official receiver acting on a direction of the Secretary of State.

Grounds for making order

2.— (1) The court shall grant an application for a debt relief restrictions order if it thinks it appropriate to do so having regard to the conduct of the debtor (whether before or after the making of the debt relief order).

(2) The court shall, in particular, take into account any of the following kinds of behaviour on the part of the debtor—

(a) failing to keep records which account for a loss of property by the debtor, or by a business carried on by him, where the loss occurred in the period beginning two years before the application date for the debt relief order and ending with the date of the application for the debt relief restrictions order;

(b) failing to produce records of that kind on demand by the official receiver;

(c) entering into a transaction at an undervalue in the period beginning two years before the application date for the debt relief order and ending with the date of the determination of that application;

(d) giving a preference in the period beginning two years before the application date for the debt relief order and ending with the date of the determination of that application;

(e) making an excessive pension contribution;

(f) a failure to supply goods or services that were wholly or partly paid for;

(g) trading at a time, before the date of the determination of the application for the debt relief order, when the debtor knew or ought to have known that he was himself to be unable to pay his debts;

(h) incurring, before the date of the determination of the application for the debt relief order, a debt which the debtor had no reasonable expectation of being able to pay;

(i) failing to account satisfactorily to the court or the official receiver for a loss of property or for an insufficiency of property to meet his debts;

(j) carrying on any gambling, rash and hazardous speculation or unreasonable extravagance which may have materially contributed to or increased the extent of his inability to pay his debts before the application date for the debt relief order or which took place between that date and the date of the determination of the application for the debt relief order;

(k) neglect of business affairs of a kind which may have materially contributed to or increased the extent of his inability to pay his debts;

(l) fraud or fraudulent breach of trust;

(m) failing to co-operate with the official receiver.

(3) The court shall also, in particular, consider whether the debtor was an undischarged bankrupt at some time during the period of six years ending with the date of the application for the debt relief order.

(4) For the purposes of sub-paragraph (2)—

"excessive pension contribution" shall be construed in accordance with section 342A;

"preference" shall be construed in accordance with paragraph 10(2) of Schedule 4ZA;

"undervalue" shall be construed in accordance with paragraph 9(2) of that Schedule.

Timing of application for order

3. An application for a debt relief restrictions order in respect of a debtor may be made—

(a) at any time during the moratorium period relating to the debt relief order in question, or

(b) after the end of that period, but only with the permission of the court.

Duration of order

4.— (1) A debt relief restrictions order—

(a) comes into force when it is made, and

(b) ceases to have effect at the end of a date specified in the order.

(2) The date specified in a debt relief restrictions order under sub-paragraph (1)(b) must not be—

(a) before the end of the period of two years beginning with the date on which the order is made, or

(b) after the end of the period of 15 years beginning with that date.

Interim debt relief restrictions order

5.— (1) This paragraph applies at any time between—

(a) the institution of an application for a debt relief restrictions order, and

(b) the determination of the application.

(2) The court may make an interim debt relief restrictions order if the court thinks that—

(a) there are prima facie grounds to suggest that the application for the debt relief restrictions order will be successful, and

(b) it is in the public interest to make an interim debt relief restrictions order.

(3) An interim debt relief restrictions order may only be made on the application of—

(a) the Secretary of State, or

(b) the official receiver acting on a direction of the Secretary of State.

(4) An interim debt relief restrictions order—

(a) has the same effect as a debt relief restrictions order, and

(b) comes into force when it is made.

(5) An interim debt relief restrictions order ceases to have effect—

(a) on the determination of the application for the debt relief restrictions order,

(b) on the acceptance of a debt relief restrictions undertaking made by the debtor, or

(c) if the court discharges the interim debt relief restrictions order on the application of the person who applied for it or of the debtor.

6.— (1) This paragraph applies to a case in which both an interim debt relief restrictions order and a debt relief restrictions order are made.

(2) Paragraph 4(2) has effect in relation to the debt relief restrictions order as if a reference to the date of that order were a reference to the date of the interim debt relief restrictions order.

Debt relief restrictions undertaking

7.— (1) A debtor may offer a debt relief restrictions undertaking to the Secretary of State.

(2) In determining whether to accept a debt relief restrictions undertaking the Secretary of State shall have regard to the matters specified in paragraph 2(2) and (3).

8. A reference in an enactment to a person in respect of whom a debt relief restrictions order has effect (or who is "the subject of" a debt relief restrictions order) includes a reference to a person in respect of whom a debt relief restrictions undertaking has effect.

9.— (1) A debt relief restrictions undertaking—

(a) comes into force on being accepted by the Secretary of State, and

(b) ceases to have effect at the end of a date specified in the undertaking.

(2) The date specified under sub-paragraph (1)(b) must not be—

(a) before the end of the period of two years beginning with the date on which the undertaking is accepted, or

(b) after the end of the period of 15 years beginning with that date.

(3) On an application by the debtor the court may—

(a) annul a debt relief restrictions undertaking;

(b) provide for a debt relief restrictions undertaking to cease to have effect before the date specified under sub-paragraph (1)(b).

Effect of revocation of debt relief order

10. Unless the court directs otherwise, the revocation at any time of a debt relief order does not—

(a) affect the validity of any debt relief restrictions order, interim debt relief restrictions order or debt relief restrictions undertaking which is in force in respect of the debtor;

(b) prevent the determination of any application for a debt relief restrictions order, or an interim debt relief restrictions order, in relation to the debtor that was instituted before that time;

(c) prevent the acceptance of a debt relief restrictions undertaking that was offered before that time; or

(d) prevent the institution of an application for a debt relief restrictions order or interim debt relief restrictions order in respect of the debtor, or the offer or acceptance of a debt relief restrictions undertaking by the debtor, after that time.

SCHEDULE 4A

BANKRUPTCY RESTRICTIONS ORDER AND UNDERTAKING

Section 281A

Bankruptcy restrictions order

1.— (1) A bankruptcy restrictions order may be made by the court.

(2) An order may be made only on the application of—

(a) the Secretary of State, or

(b) the official receiver acting on a direction of the Secretary of State.

Grounds for making order

2.— (1) The court shall grant an application for a bankruptcy restrictions order if it thinks it appropriate having regard to the conduct of the bankrupt (whether before or after the making of the bankruptcy order).

(2) The court shall, in particular, take into account any of the following kinds of behaviour on the part of the bankrupt—

(a) failing to keep records which account for a loss of property by the bankrupt, or by a business carried on by him, where the loss occurred in the period beginning 2 years before petition and ending with the date of the application;

(b) failing to produce records of that kind on demand by the official receiver or the trustee;
(c) entering into a transaction at an undervalue;
(d) giving a preference;
(e) making an excessive pension contribution;
(f) a failure to supply goods or services which were wholly or partly paid for which gave rise to a claim provable in the bankruptcy;
(g) trading at a time before commencement of the bankruptcy when the bankrupt knew or ought to have known that he was himself to be unable to pay his debts;
(h) incurring, before commencement of the bankruptcy, a debt which the bankrupt had no reasonable expectation of being able to pay;
(i) failing to account satisfactorily to the court, the official receiver or the trustee for a loss of property or for an insufficiency of property to meet bankruptcy debts;
(j) carrying on any gambling, rash and hazardous speculation or unreasonable extravagance which may have materially contributed to or increased the extent of the bankruptcy or which took place between presentation of the petition and commencement of the bankruptcy;
(k) neglect of business affairs of a kind which may have materially contributed to or increased the extent of the bankruptcy;
(l) fraud or fraudulent breach of trust;
(m) failing to cooperate with the official receiver or the trustee.

(3) The court shall also, in particular, consider whether the bankrupt was an undischarged bankrupt at some time during the period of six years ending with the date of the bankruptcy to which the application relates.

(4) For the purpose of sub-paragraph (2)—
"before petition" shall be construed in accordance with section 351(c),
"excessive pension contribution" shall be construed in accordance with section 342A,
"preference" shall be construed in accordance with section 340, and
"undervalue" shall be construed in accordance with section 339.

Timing of application for order

3.— (1) An application for a bankruptcy restrictions order in respect of a bankrupt must be made—
(a) before the end of the period of one year beginning with the date on which the bankruptcy commences, or
(b) with the permission of the court.

(2) The period specified in sub-paragraph (1)(a) shall cease to run in respect of a bankrupt while the period set for his discharge is suspended under section 279(3).

Duration of order

4.— (1) A bankruptcy restrictions order—
(a) shall come into force when it is made, and
(b) shall cease to have effect at the end of a date specified in the order.

(2) The date specified in a bankruptcy restrictions order under sub-paragraph (1)(b) must not be—
(a) before the end of the period of two years beginning with the date on which the order is made, or
(b) after the end of the period of 15 years beginning with that date.

Interim bankruptcy restrictions order

5.— (1) This paragraph applies at any time between—
(a) the institution of an application for a bankruptcy restrictions order, and
(b) the determination of the application.

(2) The court may make an interim bankruptcy restrictions order if the court thinks that—

(a) there are prima facie grounds to suggest that the application for the bankruptcy restrictions order will be successful, and

(b) it is in the public interest to make an interim order.

(3) An interim order may be made only on the application of—

(a) the Secretary of State, or

(b) the official receiver acting on a direction of the Secretary of State.

(4) An interim order—

(a) shall have the same effect as a bankruptcy restrictions order, and

(b) shall come into force when it is made.

(5) An interim order shall cease to have effect—

(a) on the determination of the application for the bankruptcy restrictions order,

(b) on the acceptance of a bankruptcy restrictions undertaking made by the bankrupt, or

(c) if the court discharges the interim order on the application of the person who applied for it or of the bankrupt.

6.— (1) This paragraph applies to a case in which both an interim bankruptcy restrictions order and a bankruptcy restrictions order are made.

(2) Paragraph 4(2) shall have effect in relation to the bankruptcy restrictions order as if a reference to the date of that order were a reference to the date of the interim order.

Bankruptcy restrictions undertaking

7.— (1) A bankrupt may offer a bankruptcy restrictions undertaking to the Secretary of State.

(2) In determining whether to accept a bankruptcy restrictions undertaking the Secretary of State shall have regard to the matters specified in paragraph 2(2) and (3).

8. A reference in an enactment to a person in respect of whom a bankruptcy restrictions order has effect (or who is "the subject of" a bankruptcy restrictions order) includes a reference to a person in respect of whom a bankruptcy restrictions undertaking has effect.

9.— (1) A bankruptcy restrictions undertaking—

(a) shall come into force on being accepted by the Secretary of State, and

(b) shall cease to have effect at the end of a date specified in the undertaking.

(2) The date specified under sub-paragraph (1)(b) must not be—

(a) before the end of the period of two years beginning with the date on which the undertaking is accepted, or

(b) after the end of the period of 15 years beginning with that date.

(3) On an application by the bankrupt the court may—

(a) annul a bankruptcy restrictions undertaking;

(b) provide for a bankruptcy restrictions undertaking to cease to have effect before the date specified under sub-paragraph (1)(b).

Effect of annulment of bankruptcy order

10. Where a bankruptcy order is annulled under section 282(1)(a) or (2)—

(a) any bankruptcy restrictions order, interim order or undertaking which is in force in respect of the bankrupt shall be annulled,

(b) no new bankruptcy restrictions order or interim order may be made in respect of the bankrupt, and

(c) no new bankruptcy restrictions undertaking by the bankrupt may be accepted.

11. Where a bankruptcy order is annulled under section 261, 263D or 282(1)(b)—

(a) the annulment shall not affect any bankruptcy restrictions order, interim order or undertaking in respect of the bankrupt,

(b) the court may make a bankruptcy restrictions order in relation to the bankrupt on an application instituted before the annulment,

(c) the Secretary of State may accept a bankruptcy restrictions undertaking offered before the annulment, and

(d) an application for a bankruptcy restrictions order or interim order in respect of the bankrupt may not be instituted after the annulment.

Registration

12. The Secretary of State shall maintain a register of—
(a) bankruptcy restrictions orders,
(b) interim bankruptcy restrictions orders, and
(c) bankruptcy restrictions undertakings.

SCHEDULE 5

POWERS OF TRUSTEE IN BANKRUPTCY

Section 314

PART I
POWERS EXERCISABLE WITH SANCTION

1. Power to carry on any business of the bankrupt so far as may be necessary for winding it up beneficially and so far as the trustee is able to do so without contravening any requirement imposed by or under any enactment.
2. Power to bring, institute or defend any action or legal proceedings relating to the property comprised in the bankrupt's estate.
2A. Power to bring legal proceedings under section 339, 340 or 423.
3. Power to accept as the consideration for the sale of any property comprised in the bankrupt's estate a sum of money payable at a future time subject to such stipulations as to security or otherwise as the creditors' committee or the court thinks fit.
4. Power to mortgage or pledge any part of the property comprised in the bankrupt's estate for the purpose of raising money for the payment of his debts.
5. Power, where any right, option or other power forms part of the bankrupt's estate, to make payments or incur liabilities with a view to obtaining, for the benefit of the creditors, any property which is the subject of the right, option or power.
6. . . .
7. Power to make such compromise or other arrangement as may be thought expedient with creditors, or persons claiming to be creditors, in respect of bankruptcy debts.
8. Power to make such compromise or other arrangement as may be thought expedient with respect to any claim arising out of or incidental to the bankrupt's estate made or capable of being made on the trustee by any person . . .

PART II
GENERAL POWERS

9. Power to sell any part of the property for the time being comprised in the bankrupt's estate, including the goodwill and book debts of any business.
9A. Power to refer to arbitration, or compromise on such terms as may be agreed, any debts, claims or liabilities subsisting or supposed to subsist between the bankrupt and any person who may have incurred any liability to the bankrupt.
9B. Power to make such compromise or other arrangement as may be thought expedient with respect to any claim arising out of or incidental to the bankrupt's estate made or capable of being made by the trustee on any person.
10. Power to give receipts for any money received by him, being receipts which effectually discharge the person paying the money from all responsibility in respect of its application.
11. Power to prove, rank, claim and draw a dividend in respect of such debts due to the bankrupt as are comprised in his estate.

12. Power to exercise in relation to any property comprised in the bankrupt's estate any powers the capacity to exercise which is vested in him under Parts VIII to XI of this Act.

13. Power to deal with any property comprised in the estate to which the bankrupt is beneficially entitled as tenant in tail in the same manner as the bankrupt might have dealt with it.

PART III
ANCILLARY POWERS

14. For the purposes of, or in connection with, the exercise of any of his powers under Parts VIII to XI of this Act, the trustee may, by his official name—
   (a) hold property of every description,
   (b) make contracts,
   (c) sue and be sued,
   (d) enter into engagements binding on himself and, in respect of the bankrupt's estate, on his successors in office,
   (e) employ an agent,
   (f) execute any power of attorney, deed or other instrument;

and he may do any other act which is necessary or expedient for the purposes of or in connection with the exercise of those powers.

SCHEDULE 6

THE CATEGORIES OF PREFERENTIAL DEBTS

Section 386

1–7. …

Category 4:
Contributions to occupational pension schemes, etc

8. Any sum which is owed by the debtor and is a sum to which Schedule 4 to the Pension Schemes Act 1993 applies (contributions to occupational pension schemes and state scheme premiums).

Category 5:
Remuneration, etc, of employees

9. So much of any amount which—
   (a) is owed by the debtor to a person who is or has been an employee of the debtor, and
   (b) is payable by way of remuneration in respect of the whole or any part of the period of 4 months next before the relevant date,

as does not exceed so much as may be prescribed by order made by the Secretary of State.

10. An amount owed by way of accrued holiday remuneration, in respect of any period of employment before the relevant date, to a person whose employment by the debtor has been terminated, whether before, on or after that date.

11. So much of any sum owed in respect of money advanced for the purpose as has been applied for the payment of a debt which, if it had not been paid, would have been a debt falling within paragraph 9 or 10.

12. So much of any amount which—
   (a) is ordered (whether before or after the relevant date) to be paid by the debtor under the Reserve Forces (Safeguard of Employment) Act 1985, and
   (b) is so ordered in respect of a default made by the debtor before that date in the discharge of his obligations under that Act,

as does no exceed such amount as may be prescribed by order made by the Secretary of State.

Interpretation for Category 5

13.— (1) For the purposes of paragraphs 9 to 12, a sum is payable by the debtor to a person by way of remuneration in respect of any period if—

(a) it is paid as wages or salary (whether payable for time or for piece work or earned wholly or partly by way of commission) in respect of services rendered to the debtor in that period, or

(b) it is an amount falling within the following sub-paragraph and is payable by the debtor in respect of that period.

(2) An amount falls within this sub-paragraph if it is—

(a) a guarantee payment under Part III of the Employment Rights Act 1996 (employee without work to do);

(b) any payment for time off under section 53 (time off to look for work or arrange training) or section 56 (time off for ante-natal care) of that Act or under section 169 of the Trade Union and Labour Relations (Consolidation) Act 1992 (time off for carrying out trade union duties etc);

(c) remuneration on suspension on medical grounds, or on maternity grounds, under Part VII of the Employment Rights Act 1996; or

(d) remuneration under a protective award under section 189 of the Trade Union and Labour Relations (Consolidation) Act 1992 (redundancy dismissal with compensation).

14.— (1) This paragraph relates to a case in which a person's employment has been terminated by or in consequence of his employer going into liquidation or being adjudged bankrupt or (his employer being a company not in liquidation) by or in consequence of—

(a) a receiver being appointed as mentioned in section 40 of this Act (debenture-holders secured by floating charge), or

(b) the appointment of a receiver under section 53(6) or 54(5) of this Act (Scottish company with property subject to floating charge), or

(c) the taking of possession by debenture-holders (so secured), as mentioned in section 754 of the Companies Act 2006.

(2) For the purposes of paragraphs 9 to 12, holiday remuneration is deemed to have accrued to that person in respect of any period of employment if, by virtue of his contract of employment or of any enactment that remuneration would have accrued in respect of that period if his employment had continued until he became entitled to be allowed the holiday.

(3) The reference in sub-paragraph (2) to any enactment includes an order or direction made under an enactment.

15. Without prejudice to paragraphs 13 and 14—

(a) any remuneration payable by the debtor to a person in respect of a period of holiday or of absence from work through sickness or other good cause is deemed to be wages or (as the case may be) salary in respect of services rendered to the debtor in that period, and

(b) references here and in those paragraphs to remuneration in respect of a period of holiday include any sums which, if they had been paid, would have been treated for the purposes of the enactments to social security as earnings in respect of that period.

Category 6:
Levies on coal and steel production

15A. Any sums due at the relevant date from the debtor in respect of—

(a) the levies on the production of coal and steel referred to in Articles 49 and 50 of the E.C.S.C. Treaty, or

(b) any surcharge for delay provided for in Article 50(3) of that Treaty and Article 6 of Decision 3/52 of the High Authority of the Coal and Steel Community.

Orders

16. An order under paragraph 9 or 12—

(a) may contain such transitional provisions as may appear to the Secretary of State necessary or expedient;

(b) shall be made by statutory instrument subject to annulment in pursuance of a resolution of either House of Parliament.

SCHEDULE 7

INSOLVENCY PRACTITIONERS TRIBUNAL

Section 396

Panels of members

1.— (1) The Secretary of State shall draw up and from time to time revise—

(a) a panel of persons who

(i) satisfy the judicial-appointment eligibility condition on a 5-year basis;

(ii) are advocates or solicitors in Scotland of at least 5 years' standing,

and are nominated for the purpose by the Lord Chancellor or the Lord President of the Court of Session, and

(b) a panel of persons who are experienced in insolvency matters;

and the members of the Tribunal shall be selected from those panels in accordance with this Schedule.

(2) The power to revise the panels includes power to terminate a person's membership of either of them, and is accordingly to that extent subject to section 7 of the Tribunals and Inquiries Act 1992 (which makes it necessary to obtain the concurrence of the Lord Chancellor and the Lord President of the Court of Session to dismissals in certain cases).

Remuneration of members

2. The Secretary of State may out of money provided by Parliament pay to members of the Tribunal such remuneration as he may with the approval of the Treasury determine; and such expenses of the Tribunal as the Secretary of State and the Treasury may approve shall be defrayed by the Secretary of State out of money so provided.

Sittings of Tribunal

3.— (1) For the purposes of carrying out their functions in relation to any cases referred to them, the Tribunal may sit either as a single tribunal or in two or more divisions.

(2) The functions of the Tribunal in relation to any case referred to them shall be exercised by three members consisting of—

(a) a chairman selected by the Secretary of State from the panel drawn up under paragraph 1(1)(a) above, and

(b) two other members selected by the Secretary of State from the panel drawn up under paragraph 1(1)(b).

Procedure of Tribunal

4.— (1) Any investigation by the Tribunal shall be so conducted as to afford a reasonable opportunity for representations to be made to the Tribunal by or on behalf of the person whose case is the subject of the investigation.

(2) For the purposes of any such investigation, the Tribunal—

(a) may by summons require any person to attend, at such time and place as is specified in the summons, to give evidence or to produce any books, papers and other records in his possession or under his control which the Tribunal consider it necessary for the purposes of the investigation to examine, and

(b) may take evidence on oath, and for the purpose administer oaths, or may, instead of administering an oath, require the person examined to make and subscribe a declaration of the truth of the matter respecting which he is examined;

but no person shall be required, in obedience to such a summons, to go more than ten miles from his place of residence, unless the necessary expenses of his attendance are paid or tendered to him.

(3) Every person who—

(a) without reasonable excuse fails to attend in obedience to a summons issued under this paragraph, or refuses to give evidence, or

(b) intentionally alters, suppresses, conceals or destroys or refuses to produce any document which he may be required to produce for the purpose of an investigation by the Tribunal,

is liable to a fine.

(4) Subject to the provisions of this paragraph, the Secretary of State may make rules for regulating the procedure on any investigation by the Tribunal.

(5) In their application to Scotland, sub-paragraphs (2) and (3) above have effect as if for any reference to a summons there were substituted a reference to a notice in writing.

SCHEDULE 8

PROVISIONS CAPABLE OF INCLUSION IN COMPANY INSOLVENCY RULES

Section 411

Courts

1. Provision for supplementing, in relation to the insolvency or winding up of companies, any provision made by or under section 117 of this Act (jurisdiction in relation to winding up).

2.— (1) Provision for regulating the practice and procedure of any court exercising jurisdiction for the purposes of Parts I to VII of this Act or the Companies Acts so far as relating to, and to matters connected with or arising out of, the insolvency or winding up of companies, being any provision that could be made by rules of court.

(2) Rules made by virtue of this paragraph about the consequence of failure to comply with practice or procedure may, in particular, include provision about the termination of administration.

Notices, etc

3. Provision requiring notice of any proceedings in connection with or arising out of the insolvency or winding up of a company to be given or published in the manner prescribed by the rules.

4. Provision with respect to the form, manner of serving, contents and proof of any petition, application, order, notice, statement or other document required to be presented, made, given, published or prepared under any enactment or subordinate legislation relating to, or to matters connected with or arising out of, the insolvency or winding up of companies.

5. Provisions specifying the persons to whom any notice is to be given.

Registration of voluntary arrangements

6. Provision for the registration of voluntary arrangements approved under Part I of this Act, including provision for the keeping and inspection of a register.

Provisional liquidator

7. Provision as to the manner in which a provisional liquidator appointed under section 135 is to carry out his functions.

Conduct of insolvency

8. Provision with respect to the certification of any person as, and as to the proof that a person is, the liquidator, administrator or administrative receiver of a company.

9. The following provision with respect to meetings of a company's creditors, contributories or members—

(a) provision as to the manner of summoning a meeting (including provision as to how any power to require a meeting is to be exercised, provision as to the manner of determining the value of any debt or contribution for the purposes of any such power and provision making the exercise of any such power subject to the deposit of a sum sufficient to cover the expenses likely to be incurred in summoning and holding a meeting);

(b) provision specifying the time and place at which a meeting may be held and the period of notice required for a meeting;

(c) provision as to the procedure to be followed at a meeting (including the manner in which decisions may be reached by a meeting and the manner in which the value of any vote at a meeting is to be determined);

(d) provision for requiring a person who is or has been an officer of the company to attend a meeting;

(e) provision creating, in the prescribed circumstances, a presumption that a meeting has been duly summoned and held;

(f) provision as to the manner of proving the decisions of a meeting.

10. (1) Provision as to the functions, membership and proceedings of a committee established under section 49, 68, 101, 141 or 142 of, or paragraph 57 of Schedule B1 to, this Act.

(2) The following provision with respect to the establishment of a committee under section 101, 141 or 142 of this Act, that is to say—

(a) provision for resolving differences between a meeting of the company's creditors and a meeting of its contributories or members;

(b) provision authorising the establishment of the committee without a meeting of contributories in a case where a company is being wound up on grounds including its inability to pay its debts; and

(c) provision modifying the requirements of this Act with respect to the establishment of the committee in a case where a winding-up order has been made immediately upon the discharge of an administration order.

11. Provision as to the manner in which any requirement that may be imposed on a person under any of Parts I to VII of this Act by the official receiver, the liquidator, administrator or administrative receiver of a company or a special manager appointed under section 177 is to be so imposed.

12. Provision as to the debts that may be proved in a winding up, as to the manner and conditions of proving a debt and as to the manner and expenses of establishing the value of any debt or security.

13. Provision with respect to the manner of the distribution of the property of a company that is being wound up, including provision with respect to unclaimed funds and dividends.

14. Provision which, with or without modifications, applies in relation to the winding up of companies any enactment contained in Parts VIII to XI of this Act or in the Bankruptcy (Scotland) Act 1985.

14A. Provision about the application of section 176A of this Act which may include, in particular—

(a) provision enabling a receiver to institute winding up proceedings;

(b) provision requiring a receiver to institute winding up proceedings.

Administration

14B. Provision which—

(a) applies in relation to administration, with or without modifications, a provision of Parts IV to VII of this Act, or

(b) serves a purpose in relation to administration similar to a purpose that may be served by the rules in relation to winding up by virtue of a provision of this Schedule.

Financial provisions

15. Provision as to the amount, or manner of determining the amount, payable to the liquidator, administrator or administrative receiver of a company or a special manager appointed under section 177, by way of remuneration for the carrying out of functions in connection with or arising out of the insolvency or winding up of a company.

16. Provision with respect to the manner in which moneys received by the liquidator of a company in the course of carrying out his functions as such are to be invested or otherwise handled and with respect to the payment of interest on sums which, in pursuance of rules made by virtue of this paragraph, have been paid into the Insolvency Services Account.

16A. Provision enabling the Secretary of State to set the rate of interest paid on sums which have been paid into the Insolvency Services Account.

17. Provision as to the fees, costs, charges and other expenses that may be treated as the expenses of a winding up.

18. Provision as to the fees, costs, charges and other expenses that may be treated as properly incurred by the administrator or administrative receiver of a company.

19. Provision as to the fees, costs, charges and other expenses that may be incurred for any of the purposes of Part I of this Act or in the administration of any voluntary arrangement approved under that Part.

Information and records

20. Provision requiring registrars and other officers of courts having jurisdiction in England and Wales in relation to, or to matters connected with or arising out of, the insolvency or winding up of companies—
    (a) to keep books and other records with respect to the exercise of that jurisdiction, and
    (b) to make returns to the Secretary of State of the business of those courts.

21. Provision requiring a creditor, member or contributory, or such a committee as is mentioned in paragraph 10 above, to be supplied (on payment in prescribed cases of the prescribed fee) with such information and with copies of such documents as may be prescribed.

22. Provision as to the manner in which public examinations under sections 133 and 134 of this Act and proceedings under sections 236 and 237 are to be conducted, as to the circumstances in which records of such examinations or proceedings are to be made available to prescribed persons and as to the costs of such examinations and proceedings.

23. Provision imposing requirements with respect to—
    (a) the preparation and keeping by the liquidator, administrator or administrative receiver of a company, or by the supervisor of a voluntary arrangement approved under Part I of this Act, of prescribed books, accounts and other records;
    (b) the production of those books, accounts and records for inspection by prescribed persons;
    (c) the auditing of accounts kept by the liquidator, administrator or administrative receiver of a company, or the supervisor of such a voluntary arrangement; and
    (d) the issue by the administrator or administrative receiver of a company of such a certificate as is mentioned in section 22(3)(b) of the Value Added Tax Act 1983 (refund of tax in cases of bad debts) and the supply of copies of the certificate to creditors of the company.

24. Provision requiring the person who is the supervisor of a voluntary arrangement approved under Part I, when it appears to him that the voluntary arrangement has been fully implemented and that nothing remains to be done by him under the arrangement—
    (a) to give notice of that fact to persons bound by the voluntary arrangement, and
    (b) to report to those persons on the carrying out of the functions conferred on the supervisor of the arrangement.

25. Provision as to the manner in which the liquidator of a company is to act in relation to the books, papers and other records of the company, including provision authorising their disposal.

26. Provision imposing requirements in connection with the carrying out of functions under section 7(3) of the Company Directors Disqualification Act 1986 (including, in particular, requirements with respect to the making of periodic returns).

General

27. Provision conferring power on the Secretary of State or the Treasury to make regulations with respect to so much of any matter that may be provided for in the rules as relates to the carrying out of the functions of the liquidator, administrator or administrative receiver of a company.

28. Provision conferring a discretion on the court.
29. Provision conferring power on the court to make orders for the purpose of securing compliance with obligations imposed by or under section 47, 66, 131, 143(2) or 235 of, or paragraph 47 of Schedule B1 to, this Act or section 7(4) of the Company Directors Disqualification Act 1986.
30. Provision making non-compliance with any of the rules a criminal offence.
31. Provision making different provision for different cases or descriptions of cases, including different provisions for different areas.

SCHEDULE 9

PROVISIONS CAPABLE OF INCLUSION IN INDIVIDUAL INSOLVENCY RULES

Section 412

Courts

1. Provision with respect to the arrangement and disposition of the business under Parts 7A to 11 of this Act of courts having jurisdiction for the purpose of those Parts, including provision for the allocation of proceedings under those Parts to particular courts and for the transfer of such proceedings from one court to another.
2. Provision for enabling a registrar in bankruptcy of the High Court or a registrar of a county court having jurisdiction for the purposes of those Parts to exercise such of the jurisdiction conferred for those purposes on the High Court or, as the case may be, that county court as may be prescribed.
3. Provision for regulating the practice and procedure of any court exercising jurisdiction for the purposes of those Parts, being any provision that could be made by rules of court.
4. Provision conferring rights of audience, in courts exercising jurisdiction for the purposes of those Parts, on the official receiver and on solicitors.

Notices, etc

5. Provision requiring notice of any proceedings under Parts 7A to 11 of this Act or of any matter relating to or arising out of a proposal under Part VIII or a bankruptcy to be given or published in the prescribed manner.
6. Provision with respect to the form, manner of serving, contents and proof of any petition, application, order, notice, statement or other document required to be presented, made, given, published or prepared under any enactment contained in Parts 7A to 11 or subordinate legislation under those Parts or Part XV (including provision requiring prescribed matters to be verified by affidavit).
7. Provision specifying the persons to whom any notice under Parts VIII to XI is to be given.

Debt relief orders

7A. Provision as to the manner in which the official receiver is to carry out his functions under Part 7A.

7B. Provision as to the manner in which any requirement that may be imposed by the official receiver on a person under Part 7A is to take effect.

7C. Provision modifying the application of Part 7A in relation to an individual who has died at a time when a moratorium period under a debt relief order applies in relation to him.

Debt relief restrictions orders and undertakings

7D. Provision about debt relief restrictions orders, interim orders and undertakings, including provision about evidence.

Register of debt relief orders and debt relief restrictions orders etc

7E. Provision about the register required to be maintained by section 251W and the information to be contained in it, including provision—

(a) enabling the amalgamation of the register with another register;
(b) enabling inspection of the register by the public.

Registration of voluntary arrangements

8. Provision for the registration of voluntary arrangements approved under Part VIII of this Act, including provision for the keeping and inspection of a register.

Official receiver acting on voluntary arrangement

8A. Provision about the official receiver acting as nominee or supervisor in relation to a voluntary arrangement under Part VIII of this Act, including—
(a) provision requiring the official receiver to act in specified circumstances;
(b) provision about remuneration;
(c) provision prescribing terms or conditions to be treated as forming part of a voluntary arrangement in relation to which the official receiver acts as nominee or supervisor;
(d) provision enabling those terms or conditions to be varied or excluded, in specified circumstances or subject to specified conditions, by express provision in an arrangement.

Interim receiver

9. Provision as to the manner in which an interim receiver appointed under section 286 is to carry out his functions, including any such provision as is specified in relation to the trustee of a bankrupt's estate in paragraph 21 or 27 below.

Receiver or manager

10. Provision as to the manner in which the official receiver is to carry out his functions as receiver or manager of a bankrupt's estate under section 287, including any such provision as is specified in relation to the trustee of a bankrupt's estate in paragraph 21 or 27 below.

Administration of individual insolvency

11. Provision with respect to the certification of the appointment of any person as trustee of a bankrupt's estate and as to the proof of that appointment.

12. The following provision with respect to meetings of creditors—
(a) provision as to the manner of summoning a meeting (including provision as to how any power to require a meeting is to be exercised, provision as to the manner of determining the value of any debt for the purposes of any such power and provision making the exercise of any such power subject to the deposit of a sum sufficient to cover the expenses likely to be incurred in summoning and holding a meeting);
(b) provision specifying the time and place at which a meeting may be held and the period of notice required for a meeting;
(c) provision as to the procedure to be followed at such a meeting (including the manner in which decisions may be reached by a meeting and the manner in which the value of any vote at a meeting is to be determined);
(d) provision for requiring a bankrupt or debtor to attend a meeting;
(e) provision creating, in the prescribed circumstances, a presumption that a meeting has been duly summoned and held; and
(f) provision as to the manner of proving the decisions of a meeting.

13. Provision as to the functions, membership and proceedings of a creditors' committee established under section 301.

14. Provision as to the manner in which any requirement that may be imposed on a person under Parts VIII to XI of this Act by the official receiver, the trustee of a bankrupt's estate or a special manager appointed under section 370 is to be so imposed and, in the case of any requirement imposed under section 305(3) (information etc to be given by the trustee to the official receiver), provision conferring power on the court to make orders for the purpose of securing compliance with that requirement.

15. Provision as to the manner in which any requirement imposed by virtue of section 310(3) (compliance with income payments order) is to take effect.

16. Provision as to the terms and conditions that may be included in a charge under section 313 (dwelling house forming part of bankrupt's estate).

17. Provision as to the debts that may be proved in any bankruptcy, as to the manner and conditions of proving a debt and as to the manner and expenses of establishing the value of any debt or security.

18. Provision with respect to the manner of the distribution of a bankrupt's estate, including provision with respect to unclaimed funds and dividends.

19. Provision modifying the application of Parts VIII to XI of this Act in relation to a debtor or bankrupt who has died.

Financial provisions

20. Provision as to the amount, or manner of determining the amount, payable to an interim receiver, the trustee of a bankrupt's estate or a special manager appointed under section 370 by way of remuneration for the performance of functions in connection with or arising out of the bankruptcy of any person.

21. Provision with respect to the manner in which moneys received by the trustee of a bankrupt's estate in the course of carrying out his functions as such are to be invested or otherwise handled and with respect to the payment of interest on sums which, in pursuance of rules made by virtue of this paragraph, have been paid into the Insolvency Services Account.

21A. Provision enabling the Secretary of State to set the rate of interest paid on sums which have been paid into the Insolvency Services Account.

22. Provision as to the fees, costs, charges and other expenses that may be treated as the expenses of a bankruptcy.

23. Provision as to the fees, costs, charges and other expenses that may be incurred for any of the purposes of Part VIII of this Act or in the administration of any voluntary arrangement approved under that Part.

Information and records

24. Provision requiring registrars and other officers of courts having jurisdiction for the purposes of Parts VIII to XI—
    (a) to keep books and other records with respect to the exercise of that jurisdiction and of jurisdiction under the Deeds of Arrangement Act 1914, and
    (b) to make returns to the Secretary of State of the business of those courts.

25. Provision requiring a creditor or a committee established under section 301 to be supplied (on payment in prescribed cases of the prescribed fee) with such information and with copies of such documents as may be prescribed.

26. Provision as to the manner in which public examinations under section 290 and proceedings under sections 366 to 368 are to be conducted, as to the circumstances in which records of such examinations and proceedings are to be made available to prescribed persons and as to the costs of such examinations and proceedings.

27. Provision imposing requirements with respect to—
    (a) the preparation and keeping by the trustee of a bankrupt's estate, or the supervisor of a voluntary arrangement approved under Part VIII, of prescribed books, accounts and other records;
    (b) the production of those books, accounts and records for inspection by prescribed persons; and
    (c) the auditing of accounts kept by the trustee of a bankrupt's estate or the supervisor of such a voluntary arrangement.

28. Provision requiring the person who is the supervisor of a voluntary arrangement approved under Part VIII, when it appears to him that the voluntary arrangement has been fully implemented and that nothing remains to be done by him under it—

(a) to give notice of that fact to persons bound by the voluntary arrangement, and
(b) to report to those persons on the carrying out of the functions conferred on the supervisor of it.

29. Provision as to the manner in which the trustee of a bankrupt's estate is to act in relation to the books, papers and other records of the bankrupt, including provision authorising their disposal.

Bankruptcy restrictions orders and undertakings

29A. Provision about bankruptcy restrictions orders, interim orders and undertakings, including—
(a) provision about evidence;
(b) provision enabling the amalgamation of the register mentioned in paragraph 12 of Schedule 4A with another register;
(c) provision enabling inspection of that register by the public.

General

30. Provision conferring power on the Secretary of State to make regulations with respect to so much of any matter that may be provided for in the rules as relates to the carrying out of the functions of an interim receiver appointed under section 286, of the official receiver while acting as a receiver or manager under section 287 or of a trustee of a bankrupt's estate.

31. Provision conferring a discretion on the court.

32. Provision making non-compliance with any of the rules a criminal offence.

33. Provision making different provision for different cases, including different provision for different areas.

SCHEDULE 10

PUNISHMENT OF OFFENCES UNDER THIS ACT

Section 430

Section of Act creating offence	*General nature of offence*	*Mode of prosecution*	*Punishment*	*Daily default fine (where applicable)*
6A(1)	False representation or fraud for purpose of obtaining members' or creditors' approval of proposed voluntary arrangement.	1. On indictment	7 years or a fine, or both.	
		2. Summary	6 months or the statutory maximum, or both.	
		…		
30	Body corporate acting as receiver.	1. On indictment	A fine.	
		2. Summary	The statutory maximum.	

Section of Act creating offence	*General nature of offence*	*Mode of prosecution*	*Punishment*	*Daily default fine (where applicable)*
31	… bankrupt or person in respect of whom a debt relief order is made acting as receiver or manager.	1. On indictment	2 years or a fine, or both.	
		2. Summary	6 months or the statutory maximum, or both.	
38(5)	Receiver failing to deliver accounts to registrar.	Summary	One-fifth of the statutory maximum.	One-fiftieth of the statutory maximum.
39(2)	Company and others failing to state in correspondence that receiver appointed.	Summary	One-fifth of the statutory maximum.	
43(6)	Administrative receiver failing to file . . . copy of order permitting disposal of charged property.	Summary	One-fifth of the statutory maximum.	One-fiftieth of the statutory maximum.
45(5)	Administrative receiver failing to file notice of vacation of office.	Summary	One-fifth of the statutory maximum.	*One-fiftieth of the statutory maximum.*
46(4)	Administrative receiver failing to give notice of his appointment.	Summary	One-fifth of the statutory maximum.	One-fiftieth of the statutory maximum.
47(6)	Failure to comply with provisions relating to statement of affairs, where administrative receiver appointed.	1. On indictment	A fine.	
		2. Summary	The statutory maximum.	One-tenth of the statutory maximum.
48(8)	Administrative receiver failing to comply with requirements as to his report.	Summary	One-fifth of the statutory maximum.	One-fiftieth of the statutory maximum.
51(4)	Body corporate or Scottish firm acting as receiver.	1. On indictment	A fine.	
		2. Summary	The statutory maximum.	
51(5)	Undischarged bankrupt acting as receiver (Scotland).	1. On indictment	2 years or a fine, or both.	

Section of Act creating offence	*General nature of offence*	*Mode of prosecution*	*Punishment*	*Daily default fine (where applicable)*
		2. Summary	6 months or the statutory maximum, or both.	
53(2)	Failing to deliver to registrar copy of instrument of appointment of receiver.	Summary	One-fifth of the statutory maximum.	*One-fiftieth of the statutory maximum.*
54(3)	Failing to deliver to registrar the court's interlocutor appointing receiver.	Summary	One-fifth of the statutory maximum.	*One-fiftieth of the statutory maximum.*
61(7)	Receiver failing to send to registrar certified copy of court order authorising disposal of charged property.	Summary	One-fifth of the statutory maximum.	One-fiftieth of the statutory maximum.
62(5)	Failing to give notice to registrar of cessation or removal of receiver.	Summary	One-fifth of the statutory maximum.	*One-fiftieth of the statutory maximum.*
64(2)	Company and others failing to state on correspondence etc that receiver appointed.	Summary	One-fifth of the statutory maximum.	
65(4)	Receiver failing to send or publish notice of his appointment.	Summary	One-fifth of the statutory maximum.	One-fiftieth of the statutory maximum.
66(6)	Failing to comply with provisions concerning statement of affairs, where receiver appointed.	1. On indictment	A fine.	
		2. Summary	The statutory maximum.	One-tenth of the statutory maximum.
67(8)	Receiver failing to comply with requirements as to his report.	Summary	One-fifth of the statutory maximum.	One-fiftieth of the statutory maximum.
85(2)	Company failing to give notice in Gazette of resolution for voluntary winding up.	Summary	One-fifth of the statutory maximum.	One-fiftieth of the statutory maximum.

Section of Act creating offence	*General nature of offence*	*Mode of prosecution*	*Punishment*	*Daily default fine (where applicable)*
89(4)	Director making statutory declaration of company's solvency without reasonable grounds for his opinion.	1. On indictment	2 years or a fine, or both.	
		2. Summary	6 months or the statutory maximum, or both.	
89(6)	Declaration under section 89 not delivered to registrar within prescribed time.	Summary	One-fifth of the statutory maximum.	One-fiftieth of the statutory maximum.
92A(2)	Liquidator failing to send progress report to members at year's end	Summary	Level 3 on the standard scale.	
93(3)	Liquidator failing to summon general meeting of company at each year's end.	Summary	One-fifth of the statutory maximum.	
94(4)	Liquidator failing to send to registrar a copy of account of winding up and return of final meeting.	Summary	One-fifth of the statutory maximum.	One-fiftieth of the statutory maximum.
94(6)	Liquidator failing to call final meeting.	Summary	One-fifth of the statutory maximum.	
95(8)	Liquidator failing to comply with s 95, where company insolvent.	Summary	The statutory maximum.	
98(6)	Company failing to comply with s. 98 in respect of summoning and giving notice of creditors' meeting.	1. On indictment	A fine.	
		2. Summary	The statutory maximum.	
99(3)	Directors failing to attend and lay statement in prescribed form before creditors' meeting.	1. On indictment	A fine.	
		2. Summary	The statutory maximum.	

Section of Act creating offence	*General nature of offence*	*Mode of prosecution*	*Punishment*	*Daily default fine (where applicable)*
104A(2)	Liquidator failing to send progress report to members and creditors at year's end	Summary	Level 3 on the standard scale.	
105(3)	Liquidator failing to summon company general meeting and creditors' meeting at each year's end.	Summary	One-fifth of the statutory maximum.	
106(4)	Liquidator failing to send to registrar account of winding up and return of final meetings.	Summary	One-fifth of the statutory maximum.	One-fiftieth of the statutory maximum.
106(6)	Liquidator failing to call final meeting of company or creditors.	Summary	One-fifth of the statutory maximum.	
109(2)	Liquidator failing to publish notice of his appointment.	Summary	One-fifth of the statutory maximum.	One-fiftieth of the statutory maximum.
114(4)	Directors exercising powers in breach of s 114, where no liquidator.	Summary	The statutory maximum.	
131(7)	Failing to comply with requirements as to statement of affairs, where liquidator appointed.	1. On indictment	A fine.	
		2. Summary	The statutory maximum.	One-tenth of the statutory maximum.
164	Giving, offering etc corrupt inducement affecting appointment of liquidator.	1. On indictment	A fine.	
		2. Summary	The statutory maximum.	
166(7)	Liquidator failing to comply with requirements of s 166 in creditors' voluntary winding up.	Summary	The statutory maximum.	
188(2)	Default in compliance with s 188 as to notification that company being wound up.	Summary	One-fifth of the statutory maximum.	
192(2)	Liquidator failing to notify registrar as to progress of winding up.	Summary	One-fifth of the statutory maximum.	One-fiftieth of the statutory maximum.

Section of Act creating offence	*General nature of offence*	*Mode of prosecution*	*Punishment*	*Daily default fine (where applicable)*
201(4)	Failing to deliver to registrar . . . copy of court order deferring dissolution.	Summary	One-fifth of the statutory maximum.	One-fiftieth of the statutory maximum.
203(6)	Failing to deliver to registrar copy of directions or result of appeal under s 203.	Summary	One-fifth of the statutory maximum.	One-fiftieth of the statutory maximum.
204(7)	Liquidator failing to deliver to registrar copy of court order for early dissolution.	Summary	One-fifth of the statutory maximum.	One-fiftieth of the statutory maximum.
204(8)	Failing to deliver to registrar copy of court order deferring early dissolution.	Summary	One-fifth of the statutory maximum.	One-fiftieth of the statutory maximum.
205(7)	Failing to deliver to registrar copy of Secretary of State's directions or court order deferring dissolution.	Summary	One-fifth of the statutory maximum.	One-fiftieth of the statutory maximum.
206(1)	Fraud etc in anticipation of winding up.	1. On indictment	7 years or a fine, or both.	
		2. Summary	6 months or the statutory maximum, or both.	
206(2)	Privity to fraud in anticipation of winding up; fraud, or privity to fraud, after commencement of winding up.	1. On indictment	7 years or a fine, or both.	
		2. Summary	6 months or the statutory maximum, or both.	
206(5)	Knowingly taking in pawn or pledge, or otherwise receiving, company property.	1. On indictment	7 years or a fine, or both.	
		2. Summary	6 months or the statutory maximum, or both.	

Section of Act creating offence	*General nature of offence*	*Mode of prosecution*	*Punishment*	*Daily default fine (where applicable)*
207	Officer of company entering into transaction in fraud of company's creditors.	1. On indictment	2 years or a fine, or both.	
		2. Summary	6 months or the statutory maximum, or both.	
208	Officer of company misconducting himself in course of winding up.	1. On indictment	7 years or a fine, or both.	
		2. Summary	6 months or the statutory maximum, or both.	
209	Officer or contributory destroying, falsifying, etc company's books.	1. On indictment	7 years or a fine, or both.	
		2. Summary	6 months or the statutory maximum, or both.	
210	Officer of company making material omission from statement relating to company's affairs.	1. On indictment	7 years or a fine, or both.	
		2. Summary	6 months or the statutory maximum, or both.	
211	False representation or fraud for purpose of obtaining creditors' consent to an agreement in connection with winding up.	1. On indictment	7 years or a fine, or both.	
		2. Summary	6 months or the statutory maximum, or both.	
216(4)	Contravening restrictions on re-use of name of company in insolvent liquidation.	1. On indictment	2 years or a fine, or both.	

Section of Act creating offence	*General nature of offence*	*Mode of prosecution*	*Punishment*	*Daily default fine (where applicable)*
		2. Summary	6 months or the statutory maximum, or both.	
235(5)	Failing to co-operate with office-holder.	1. On indictment.	A fine.	
		2. Summary	The statutory maximum.	One-tenth of the statutory maximum.
251O(1)	False representations or omissions in making an application for a debt relief order.	1 On indictment	7 years or a fine, or both.	
		2 Summary	12 months or the statutory maximum, or both.	
251O(2)(a)	Failing to comply with duty in connection with an application for a debt relief order.	1 On indictment	2 years or a fine, or both.	
		2 Summary	12 months or the statutory maximum, or both.	
251O(2)(b)	False representations or omissions in connection with duty in relation to an application for a debt relief order.	1 On indictment	7 years or a fine, or both.	
		2 Summary	12 months or the statutory maximum, or both.	
251O(4)(a)	Failing to comply with duty in connection with a debt relief order.	1 On indictment	2 years or a fine, or both.	
		2 Summary	12 months or the statutory maximum, or both.	

Section of Act creating offence	*General nature of offence*	*Mode of prosecution*	*Punishment*	*Daily default fine (where applicable)*
251O(4)(b)	False representations or omissions in connection with a duty in relation to a debt relief order.	1 On indictment	7 years or a fine, or both.	
		2 Summary	12 months or the statutory maximum, or both.	
251P(1)	Failing to deliver books, records and papers to official receiver, concealing or destroying them or making false entries in them by person in respect of whom a debt relief order is made.	1 On indictment	7 years or a fine, or both.	
		2 Summary	12 months or the statutory maximum, or both.	
251P(2)	Person in respect of whom debt relief order is made doing anything falling within paragraphs (c) to (e) of section 251P(1) during the period of 12 months ending with the application date or doing anything falling within paragraphs (b) to (e) of section 251P(1) after that date but before the effective date.	1 On indictment	7 years or a fine, or both.	
		2 Summary	12 months or the statutory maximum, or both.	
251Q(1)	Fraudulent disposal of property by person in respect of whom a debt relief order is made.	1 On indictment	2 years or a fine, or both.	
		2 Summary	12 months or the statutory maximum, or both.	

Section of Act creating offence	*General nature of offence*	*Mode of prosecution*	*Punishment*	*Daily default fine (where applicable)*
251R(1)	Disposal of property that is not paid for by person in respect of whom a debt relief order is made.	1 On indictment	7 years or a fine, or both.	
		2 Summary	12 months or the statutory maximum, or both.	
251R(2)	Obtaining property in respect of which money is owed by a person in respect of whom a debt relief order is made.	1 On indictment	7 years or a fine, or both.	
		2 Summary	12 months or the statutory maximum, or both.	
251S(1)	Person in respect of whom a debt relief order is made obtaining credit or engaging in business without disclosing his status or name.	1 On indictment	2 years or a fine, or both.	
		2 Summary	12 months or the statutory maximum, or both.	
262A(1)	False representation or fraud for purpose of obtaining creditors' approval of proposed voluntary arrangement.	1. On indictment	7 years or a fine, or both.	
		2. Summary	6 months or the statutory maximum, or both.	
353(1)	Bankrupt failing to disclose property or disposals to official receiver or trustee.	1. On indictment	7 years or a fine, or both.	
		2. Summary	6 months or the statutory maximum, or both.	

Section of Act creating offence	*General nature of offence*	*Mode of prosecution*	*Punishment*	*Daily default fine (where applicable)*
354(1)	Bankrupt failing to deliver property to, or concealing property from, official receiver or trustee.	1. On indictment	7 years or a fine, or both.	
		2. Summary	6 months or the statutory maximum, or both.	
354(2)	Bankrupt removing property which he is required to deliver to official receiver or trustee.	1. On indictment	7 years or a fine, or both.	
		2. Summary	6 months or the statutory maximum, or both.	
354(3)	Bankrupt failing to account for loss of substantial part of property.	1. On indictment	2 years or a fine, or both.	
		2. Summary	6 months or the statutory maximum, or both.	
355(1)	Bankrupt failing to deliver books, papers and records to official receiver or trustee.	1. On indictment	7 years or a fine, or both.	
		2. Summary	6 months or the statutory maximum, or both.	
355(2)	Bankrupt concealing, destroying etc books, papers or records, or making false entries in them.	1. On indictment	7 years or a fine, or both.	
		2. Summary	6 months or the statutory maximum, or both.	
355(3)	Bankrupt disposing of, or altering, books, papers or records relating to his estate or affairs.	1. On indictment	7 years or a fine, or both.	

Section of Act creating offence	*General nature of offence*	*Mode of prosecution*	*Punishment*	*Daily default fine (where applicable)*
		2. Summary	6 months or the statutory maximum, or both.	
356(1)	Bankrupt making material omission in statement relating to his affairs.	1. On indictment	7 years or a fine, or both.	
		2. Summary	6 months or the statutory maximum, or both.	
356(2)	Bankrupt making false statement, or failing to inform trustee, where false debt proved.	1. On indictment	7 years or a fine, or both.	
		2. Summary	6 months or the statutory maximum, or both.	
357	Bankrupt fraudulently disposing of property.	1. On indictment	2 years or a fine, or both.	
		2. Summary	6 months or the statutory maximum, or both.	
358	Bankrupt absconding with property he is required to deliver to official receiver or trustee.	1. On indictment	2 years or a fine, or both.	
		2. Summary	6 months or the statutory maximum, or both.	
359(1)	Bankrupt disposing of property obtained on credit and not paid for.	1. On indictment	7 years or a fine, or both.	
		2. Summary	6 months or the statutory maximum, or both.	
359(2)	Obtaining property in respect of which money is owed by a bankrupt.	1. On indictment	7 years or a fine, or both.	

Section of Act creating offence	General nature of offence	Mode of prosecution	Punishment	Daily default fine (where applicable)
		2. Summary	6 months or the statutory maximum, or both.	
360(1)	Bankrupt obtaining credit or engaging in business without disclosing his status or name in which he was made bankrupt.	1. On indictment	2 years or a fine, or both.	
		2. Summary	6 months or the statutory maximum, or both.	
360(3)	Person made bankrupt in Scotland or Northern Ireland obtaining credit, etc in England and Wales.	1. On indictment	2 years or a fine, or both.	
		2. Summary	6 months or the statutory maximum, or both.	
		…		
389	Acting as insolvency practitioner when not qualified.	1. On indictment	2 years or a fine, or both.	
		2. Summary	6 months or the statutory maximum or both.	
429(5)	Contravening s 429 in respect of disabilities imposed by county court on revocation of administration order.	1. On indictment	2 years or a fine, or both.	
		2. Summary	6 months or the statutory maximum, or both.	
Sch A1, para 9(2)	Directors failing to notify nominee of beginning of moratorium.	1. On indictment	2 years or a fine, or both.	
		2. Summary	6 months or the statutory maximum, or both.	

Section of Act creating offence	*General nature of offence*	*Mode of prosecution*	*Punishment*	*Daily default fine (where applicable)*
Sch A1, para 10(3)	Nominee failing to advertise or notify beginning of moratorium.	Summary	One-fifth of the statutory maximum.	
Sch A1, para 11(2)	Nominee failing to advertise or notify end of moratorium.	Summary	One-fifth of the statutory maximum.	
Sch A1, para 16(2)	Company and officers failing to state in correspondence etc that moratorium in force.	Summary	One-fifth of the statutory maximum.	
Sch A1, para 17(3)(a)	Company obtaining credit without disclosing existence of moratorium.	1. On indictment	A fine.	
		2. Summary	The statutory maximum.	
Sch A1, para 17(3)(b)	Obtaining credit for company without disclosing existence of moratorium.	1. On indictment	2 years or a fine, or both.	
		2. Summary	6 months or the statutory maximum, or both.	
Sch A1, para 18(3)(a)	Company disposing of property otherwise than in ordinary way of business.	1. On indictment	A fine.	
		2. Summary	The statutory maximum.	
Sch A1, para 18(3)(b)	Authorising or permitting disposal of company property.	1. On indictment	2 years or a fine, or both.	
		2. Summary	6 months or the statutory maximum, or both.	
Sch A1, para 19(3)(a)	Company making payments in respect of liabilities existing before beginning of moratorium.	1. On indictment	A fine.	
		2. Summary	The statutory maximum.	
Sch A1, para 19(3)(b)	Authorising or permitting such a payment.	1. On indictment	2 years or a fine, or both.	

Section of Act creating offence	*General nature of offence*	*Mode of prosecution*	*Punishment*	*Daily default fine (where applicable)*
		2. Summary	6 months or the statutory maximum, or both.	
Sch A1, para. 20(9)	Directors failing to send to registrar . . . copy of court order permitting disposal of charged property.	Summary	One-fifth of the statutory maximum.	
Sch A1, para 22(1)	Company disposing of charged property.	1. On indictment	A fine.	
		2. Summary	The statutory maximum.	
Sch A1, para 22(2)	Authorising or permitting such a disposal.	1. On indictment	2 years or a fine, or both.	
		2. Summary	6 months or the statutory maximum, or both.	
Sch A1, para 23(1)(a)	Company entering into market contract, etc.	1. On indictment	A fine.	
		2. Summary	The statutory maximum.	
Sch A1, para 23(1)(b)	Authorising or permitting company to do so.	1. On indictment	2 years or a fine, or both.	
		2. Summary	6 months or the statutory maximum, or both.	
Sch A1, para 25(6)	Nominee failing to give notice of withdrawal of consent to act.	Summary	One-fifth of the statutory maximum.	
Sch A1, para 34(3)	Nominee failing to give notice of extension of moratorium.	Summary	One-fifth of the statutory maximum.	
Sch A1, para 41(2)	Fraud or privity to fraud in anticipation of moratorium.	1. On indictment	7 years or a fine, or both.	
		2. Summary	6 months or the statutory maximum, or both.	

Section of Act creating offence	*General nature of offence*	*Mode of prosecution*	*Punishment*	*Daily default fine (where applicable)*
Sch A1, para 41(3)	Fraud or privity to fraud during moratorium.	1. On indictment	7 years or a fine, or both.	
		2. Summary	6 months or the statutory maximum, or both.	
Sch A1, para 41(7)	Knowingly taking in pawn or pledge, or otherwise receiving, company property.	1. On indictment	7 years or a fine, or both.	
		2. Summary	6 months or the statutory maximum, or both.	
Sch A1, para 42(1)	False representation or fraud for purpose of obtaining or extending moratorium.	1. On indictment	7 years or a fine, or both.	
		2. Summary	6 months or the statutory maximum, or both.	
Sch B1, para 18(7)	Making false statement in statutory declaration where administrator appointed by holder of floating charge.	1. On indictment	2 years, or a fine or both.	
		2. Summary	6 months, or the statutory maximum or both.	
Sch B1, para 20	Holder of floating charge failing to notify administrator or others of commencement of appointment.	1. On indictment	2 years, or a fine or both.	
		2. Summary	6 months, or the statutory maximum or both.	One-tenth of the statutory maximum.
Sch B1, para 27(4)	Making false statement in statutory declaration where appointment of administrator proposed by company or directors.	1. On indictment	2 years, or a fine or both.	

Section of Act creating offence	*General nature of offence*	*Mode of prosecution*	*Punishment*	*Daily default fine (where applicable)*
		2. Summary	6 months, or the statutory maximum or both.	
Sch B1, para 29(7)	Making false statement in statutory declaration where administrator appointed by company or directors.	1. On indictment	2 years, or a fine or both.	
		2. Summary	6 months, or the statutory maximum or both.	
Sch B1, para 32	Company or directors failing to notify administrator or others of commencement of appointment.	1. On indictment	2 years, or a fine or both.	One-tenth of the statutory maximum.
		2. Summary	6 months, or the statutory maximum or both.	
Sch B1, para 45(2)	Administrator, company or officer failing to state in business document that administrator appointed.	Summary	One-fifth of the statutory maximum.	
Sch B1, para 46(9)	Administrator failing to give notice of his appointment.	Summary	One-fifth of the statutory maximum.	One-fiftieth of the statutory maximum.
Sch B1, para 48(4)	Failing to comply with provisions about statement of affairs where administrator appointed.	1. On indictment	A fine.	
		2. Summary	The statutory maximum.	One-tenth of the statutory maximum.
Sch B1, para 49(7)	Administrator failing to send out statement of his proposals.	Summary	One-fifth of the statutory maximum.	One-fiftieth of the statutory maximum.
Sch B1, para 51(5)	Administrator failing to arrange initial creditors' meeting.	Summary	One-fifth of the statutory maximum.	One-fiftieth of the statutory maximum.
Sch B1, para 53(3)	Administrator failing to report decision taken at initial creditors' meeting.	Summary	One-fifth of the statutory maximum.	One-fiftieth of the statutory maximum.

Section of Act creating offence	*General nature of offence*	*Mode of prosecution*	*Punishment*	*Daily default fine (where applicable)*
Sch B1, para 54(7)	Administrator failing to report decision taken at creditors' meeting summoned to consider revised proposal.	Summary	One-fifth of the statutory maximum.	One-fiftieth of the statutory maximum.
Sch B1, para 56(2)	Administrator failing to summon creditors' meeting.	Summary	One-fifth of the statutory maximum.	One-fiftieth of the statutory maximum.
Sch B1, para 71(6)	Administrator failing to file court order enabling disposal of charged property.	Summary	One-fifth of the statutory maximum.	One-fiftieth of the statutory maximum.
Sch B1, para 72(5)	Administrator failing to file court order enabling disposal of hire-purchase property.	Summary	One-fifth of the statutory maximum.	One-fiftieth of the statutory maximum.
Sch B1, para 77(3)	Administrator failing to notify Registrar of Companies of automatic end of administration.	Summary	One-fifth of the statutory maximum.	One-fiftieth of the statutory maximum.
Sch B1, para 78(6)	Administrator failing to give notice of extension by consent of term of office.	Summary	One-fifth of the statutory maximum.	One-fiftieth of the statutory maximum.
Sch B1, para 80(6)	Administrator failing to give notice of termination of administration where objective achieved.	Summary	One-fifth of the statutory maximum.	One-fiftieth of the statutory maximum.
Sch B1, para 84(9)	Administrator failing to comply with provisions where company moves to dissolution.	Summary	One-fifth of the statutory maximum.	One-fiftieth of the statutory maximum.
Sch B1, para 86(3)	Administrator failing to notify Registrar of Companies where court terminates administration.	Summary	One-fifth of the statutory maximum.	One-fiftieth of the statutory maximum.
Sch B1, para 89(3)	Administrator failing to give notice on ceasing to be qualified.	Summary	One-fifth of the statutory maximum.	One-fiftieth of the statutory maximum.

Section of Act creating offence	General nature of offence	Mode of prosecution	Punishment	Daily default fine (where applicable)
Sch 7, para 4(3)	Failure to attend and give evidence to Insolvency Practitioners Tribunal; suppressing, concealing, etc relevant documents.	Summary	Level 3 on the standard scale within the meaning given by section 75 of the Criminal Justice Act 1982.	

Note. The italicized words in the entries for "45(5)", "53(2)", "54(3)" and "62(5)" are repealed by the Companies Act 1989, s. 212, Sch. 24, as from a day to be appointed.

SCHEDULE 11

TRANSITIONAL PROVISIONS AND SAVINGS

Section 437

PART I
COMPANY INSOLVENCY AND WINDING UP

Administration orders

1.— (1) Where any right to appoint an administrative receiver of a company is conferred by any debentures or floating charge created before the appointed day, the conditions precedent to the exercise of that right are deemed to include the presentation of a petition applying for an administration order to be made in relation to the company.

(2) "Administrative receiver" here has the meaning assigned by section 251.

Receivers and managers (England and Wales)

2.— (1) In relation to any receiver or manager of a company's property who was appointed before the appointed day, the new law does not apply; and the relevant provisions of the former law continue to have effect.

(2) "The new law" here means Chapter I of Part III, and Part VI, of this Act; and "the former law" means the Companies Act 1985 and so much of this Act as replaces provisions of that Act (without the amendments in paragraphs 15 to 17 of Schedule 6 to the Insolvency Act 1985, or the associated repeals made by that Act), and any provision of the Insolvency Act 1985 which was in force before the appointed day.

(3) This paragraph is without prejudice to the power conferred by this Act under which rules under section 411 may make transitional provision in connection with the coming into force of those rules; and such provision may apply those rules in relation to the receiver or manager of a company's property notwithstanding that he was appointed before the coming into force of the rules or section 411.

Receivers (Scotland)

3.— (1) In relation to any receiver appointed under section 467 of the Companies Act 1985 before the appointed day, the new law does not apply and the relevant provisions of the former law continue to have effect.

(2) "The new law" here means Chapter II of Part III, and Part VI, of this Act; and "the former law" means the Companies Act 1985 and so much of this Act as replaces provisions of that Act (without the amendments in paragraphs 18 to 22 of Schedule 6 to the Insolvency Act

1985 or the associated repeals made by that Act), and any provision of the Insolvency Act 1985 which was in force before the appointed day.

(3) This paragraph is without prejudice to the power conferred by this Act under which rules under section 411 may make transitional provision in connection with the coming into force of those rules; and such provision may apply those rules in relation to a receiver appointed under section 467 notwithstanding that he was appointed before the coming into force of the rules or section 411.

Winding up already in progress

4.— (1) In relation to any winding up which has commenced, or is treated as having commenced, before the appointed day, the new law does not apply, and the former law continues to have effect, subject to the following paragraphs.

(2) "The new law" here means any provisions in the first Group of Parts of this Act which replace sections 66 to 87 and 89 to 105 of the Insolvency Act 1985; and "the former law" means Parts XX and XXI of the Companies Act 1985 (without the amendments in paragraphs 23 to 52 of Schedule 6 to the Insolvency Act 1985, or the associated repeals made by that Act).

Statement of affairs

5.— (1) Where a winding up by the court in England and Wales has commenced, or is treated as having commenced, before the appointed day, the official receiver or (on appeal from a refusal by him) the court may, at any time on or after that day—

(a) release a person from an obligation imposed on him by or under section 528 of the Companies Act 1985 (statement of affairs), or

(b) extend the period specified in subsection (6) of that section.

(2) Accordingly, on and after the appointed day, section 528(6) has effect in relation to a winding up to which this paragraph applies with the omission of the words from "or within" onwards.

Provisions relating to liquidator

6.— (1) This paragraph applies as regards the liquidator in the case of a winding up by the court in England and Wales commenced, or treated as having commenced, before the appointed day.

(2) The official receiver may, at any time when he is liquidator of the company, apply to the Secretary of State for the appointment of a liquidator in his (the official receiver's) place; and on any such application the Secretary of State shall either make an appointment or decline to make one.

(3) Where immediately before the appointed day the liquidator of the company has not made an application under section 545 of the Companies Act 1985 (release of liquidators), then—

(a) except where the Secretary of State otherwise directs, sections 146(1) and (2) and 172(8) of this Act apply, and section 545 does not apply, in relation to any liquidator of that company who holds office on or at any time after the appointed day and is not the official receiver;

(b) section 146(3) applies in relation to the carrying out at any time after that day by any liquidator of the company of any of his functions; and

(c) a liquidator in relation to whom section 172(8) has effect by virtue of this paragraph has his release with effect from the time specified in section 174(4)(d) of this Act.

(4) Subsection (6) of section 174 of this Act has effect for the purposes of sub-paragraph (3)(c) above as it has for the purposes of that section, but as if the reference to section 212 were to section 631 of the Companies Act 1985.

(5) The liquidator may employ a solicitor to assist him in the carrying out of his functions without the permission of the committee of inspection; but if he does so employ a solicitor he shall inform the committee of inspection that he has done so.

Winding up under supervision of the court

7. The repeals in Part II of Schedule 10 to the Insolvency Act 1985 of references (in the Companies Act 1985 and elsewhere) to a winding up under the supervision of the court do not affect the operation of the enactments in which the references are contained in relation to any case in which an order under section 606 of the Companies Act 1985 (power to order winding up under supervision) was made before the appointed day.

Saving for power to make rules

8.— (1) Paragraphs 4 to 7 are without prejudice to the power conferred by this Act under which rules made under section 411 may make transitional provision in connection with the coming into force of those rules.

(2) Such provision may apply those rules in relation to a winding up notwithstanding that the winding up commenced, or is treated as having commenced, before the coming into force of the rules or section 411.

Setting aside of preferences and other transactions

9.— (1) Where a provision in Part VI of this Act applies in relation to a winding up or in relation to a case in which an administration order has been made, a preference given, floating charge created or other transaction entered into before the appointed day shall not be set aside under that provision except to the extent that it could have been set aside under the law in force immediately before that day, assuming for this purpose that any relevant administration order had been a winding-up order.

(2) The references above to setting aside a preference, floating charge or other transaction include the making of an order which varies or reverses any effect of a preference, floating charge or other transaction.

PART II
INDIVIDUAL INSOLVENCY

Bankruptcy (general)

10.— (1) Subject to the following provisions of this Part of this Schedule, so much of this Act as replaces Part III of the Insolvency Act 1985 does not apply in relation to any case in which a petition in bankruptcy was presented, or a receiving order or adjudication in bankruptcy was made, before the appointed day.

(2) In relation to any such case as is mentioned above, the enactments specified in Schedule 8 to that Act, so far as they relate to bankruptcy, and those specified in Parts III and IV of Schedule 10 to that Act, so far as they so relate, have effect without the amendments and repeals specified in those Schedules.

(3) Where any subordinate legislation made under an enactment referred to in sub-paragraph (2) is in force immediately before the appointed day, that subordinate legislation continues to have effect on and after that day in relation to any such case as is mentioned in sub-paragraph (1).

11.— (1) In relation to any such case as is mentioned in paragraph 10(1) the references in any enactment or subordinate legislation to a petition, order or other matter which is provided for under the Bankruptcy Act 1914 and corresponds to a petition, order or other matter provided for under provisions of this Act replacing Part III of the Insolvency Act 1985 continue on and after the appointed day to have effect as references to the petition, order or matter provided for by the Act of 1914; but otherwise those references have effect on and after that day as references to the petition, order or matter provided for by those provisions of this Act.

(2) Without prejudice to sub-paragraph (1), in determining for the purposes of section 279 of this Act (period of bankruptcy) or paragraph 13 below whether any person was an

undischarged bankrupt at a time before the appointed day, an adjudication in bankruptcy and an annulment of a bankruptcy under the Act of 1914 are to be taken into account in the same way, respectively, as a bankruptcy order under the provisions of this Act replacing Part III of the Insolvency Act 1985 and the annulment under section 282 of this Act of such an order.

12. Transactions entered into before the appointed day have effect on and after that day as if references to acts of bankruptcy in the provisions for giving effect to those transactions continued to be references to acts of bankruptcy within the meaning of the Bankruptcy Act 1914, but as if such acts included failure to comply with a statutory demand served under section 268 of this Act.

Discharge from old bankruptcy

13.— (1) Where a person—

(a) was adjudged bankrupt before the appointed day or is adjudged bankrupt on or after that day on a petition presented before that day, and

(b) that person was not an undischarged bankrupt at any time in the period of 15 years ending with the adjudication,

that person is deemed (if not previously discharged) to be discharged from his bankruptcy for the purposes of the Bankruptcy Act 1914 at the end of the discharge period.

(2) Subject to sub-paragraph (3) below, the discharge period for the purposes of this paragraph is—

(a) in the case of a person adjudged bankrupt before the appointed day, the period of 3 years beginning with that day, and

(b) in the case of a person who is adjudged bankrupt on or after that day on a petition presented before that day, the period of 3 years beginning with the date of the adjudication.

(3) Where the court exercising jurisdiction in relation to a bankruptcy to which this paragraph applies is satisfied, on the application of the official receiver, that the bankrupt has failed, or is failing, to comply with any of his obligations under the Bankruptcy Act 1914, any rules made under that Act or any such rules as are mentioned in paragraph 19(1) below, the court may order that the discharge period shall cease to run for such period, or until the fulfilment of such conditions (including a condition requiring the court to be satisfied as to any matter) as may be specified in the order.

Provisions relating to trustee

14.— (1) This paragraph applies as regards the trustee in the case of a person adjudged bankrupt before the appointed day, or adjudged bankrupt on or after that day on a petition presented before that day.

(2) The official receiver may at any time when he is the trustee of the bankrupt's estate apply to the Secretary of State for the appointment of a person as trustee instead of the official receiver; and on any such application the Secretary of State shall either make an appointment or decline to make one.

(3) Where on the appointed day the trustee of a bankrupt's estate has not made an application under section 93 of the Bankruptcy Act 1914 (release of trustee), then—

(a) except where the Secretary of State otherwise directs, sections 298(8), 304 and 331(1) to (3) of this Act apply, and section 93 of the Act of 1914 does not apply, in relation to any trustee of the bankrupt's estate who holds office on or at any time after the appointed day and is not the official receiver;

(b) section 331(4) of this Act applies in relation to the carrying out at any time on or after the appointed day by the trustee of the bankrupt's estate of any of his functions; and

(c) a trustee in relation to whom section 298(8) of this Act has effect by virtue of this paragraph has his release with effect from the time specified in section 299(3)(d).

(4) Subsection (5) of section 299 has effect for the purposes of sub-paragraph (3)(c) as it has for the purposes of that section.

(5) In the application of subsection (3) of section 331 in relation to a case by virtue of this paragraph, the reference in that subsection to section 330(1) has effect as a reference to section 67 of the Bankruptcy Act 1914.

(6) The trustee of the bankrupt's estate may employ a solicitor to assist him in the carrying out of his functions without the permission of the committee of inspection; but if he does so employ a solicitor, he shall inform the committee of inspection that he has done so.

Copyright

15. Where a person who is adjudged bankrupt on a petition presented on or after the appointed day is liable, by virtue of a transaction entered into before that day, to pay royalties or a share of the profits to any person in respect of any copyright or interest in copyright comprised in the bankrupt's estate, section 60 of the Bankruptcy Act 1914 (limitation on trustee's powers in relation to copyright) applies in relation to the trustee of that estate as it applies in relation to a trustee in bankruptcy under the Act of 1914.

Second bankruptcy

16.— (1) Sections 334 and 335 of this Act apply with the following modifications where the earlier bankruptcy (within the meaning of section 334) is a bankruptcy in relation to which the Act of 1914 applies instead of the second Group of Parts in this Act, that is to say—

(a) references to property vested in the existing trustee under section 307(3) of this Act have effect as references to such property vested in that trustee as was acquired by or devolved on the bankrupt after the commencement (within the meaning of the Act of 1914) of the earlier bankruptcy; and

(b) references to an order under section 310 of this Act have effect as references to an order under section 51 of the Act of 1914.

(2) Section 39 of the Act of 1914 (second bankruptcy) does not apply where a person who is an undischarged bankrupt under that Act is adjudged bankrupt under this Act.

Setting aside of preferences and other transactions

17.— (1) A preference given, assignment made or other transaction entered into before the appointed day shall not be set aside under any of sections 339 to 344 of this Act except to the extent that it could have been set aside under the law in force immediately before that day.

(2) References in sub-paragraph (1) to setting aside a preference, assignment or other transaction include the making of any order which varies or reverses any effect of a preference, assignment or other transaction.

Bankruptcy offences

18.— (1) Where a bankruptcy order is made under this Act on or after the appointed day, a person is not guilty of an offence under Chapter VI of Part IX in respect of anything done before that day; but, notwithstanding the repeal by the Insolvency Act 1985 of the Bankruptcy Act 1914, is guilty of an offence under the Act of 1914 in respect of anything done before the appointed day which would have been an offence under that Act if the making of the bankruptcy order had been the making of a receiving order under that Act.

(2) Subsection (5) of section 350 of this Act applies (instead of sections 157(2), 158(2), 161 and 165 of the Act of 1914) in relation to proceedings for an offence under that Act which are instituted (whether by virtue of sub-paragraph (1) or otherwise) after the appointed day.

Power to make rules

19.— (1) The preceding provisions of this Part of this Schedule are without prejudice to the power conferred by this Act under which rules under section 412 may make transitional provision in connection with the coming into force of those rules; and such provision may apply those rules in relation to a bankruptcy notwithstanding that it arose from a petition presented before either the coming into force of the rules or the appointed day.

(2) Rules under section 412 may provide for such notices served before the appointed day as may be prescribed to be treated for the purposes of this Act as statutory demands served under section 268.

PART III
TRANSITIONAL EFFECT OF PART XVI

20.— (1) A transaction entered into before the appointed day shall not be set aside under Part XVI of this Act except to the extent that it could have been set aside under the law in force immediately before that day.

(2) References above to setting aside a transaction include the making of any order which varies or reverses any effect of a transaction.

PART IV
INSOLVENCY PRACTITIONERS

21. Where an individual began to act as an insolvency practitioner in relation to any person before the appointed day, nothing in section 390(2) or (3) prevents that individual from being qualified to act as an insolvency practitioner in relation to that person.

PART V
GENERAL TRANSITIONAL PROVISIONS AND SAVINGS

Interpretation for this Part

22. In this Part of this Schedule, "the former enactments" means so much of the Companies Act 1985 as is repealed and replaced by this Act, the Insolvency Act 1985 and the other enactments repealed by this Act.

General saving for past acts and events

23. So far as anything done or treated as done under or for the purposes of any provision of the former enactments could have been done under or for the purposes of the corresponding provision of this Act, it is not invalidated by the repeal of that provision but has effect as if done under or for the purposes of the corresponding provision; and any order, regulation, rule or other instrument made or having effect under any provision of the former enactments shall, insofar as its effect is preserved by this paragraph, be treated for all purposes as made and having effect under the corresponding provision.

Periods of time

24. Where any period of time specified in a provision of the former enactments is current immediately before the appointed day, this Act has effect as if the corresponding provision had been in force when the period began to run; and (without prejudice to the foregoing) any period of time so specified and current is deemed for the purposes of this Act—

(a) to run from the date or event from which it was running immediately before the appointed day, and

(b) to expire (subject to any provision of this Act for its extension) whenever it would have expired if this Act had not been passed;

and any rights, priorities, liabilities, reliefs, obligations, requirements, powers, duties or exemptions dependent on the beginning, duration or end of such a period as above mentioned shall be under this Act as they were or would have been under the former enactments.

Internal cross-references in this Act

25. Where in any provision of this Act there is a reference to another such provision, and the first-mentioned provision operates, or is capable of operating, in relation to things done or omitted, or events occurring or not occurring, in the past (including in particular past acts of compliance with

any enactment, failures of compliance, contraventions, offences and convictions of offences), the reference to the other provision is to be read as including a reference to the corresponding provision of the former enactments.

Punishment of offences

26.— (1) Offences committed before the appointed day under any provision of the former enactments may, notwithstanding any repeal by this Act, be prosecuted and punished after that day as if this Act had not passed.

(2) A contravention of any provision of the former enactments committed before the appointed day shall not be visited with any severer punishment under or by virtue of this Act than would have been applicable under that provision at the time of the contravention; but where an offence for the continuance of which a penalty was provided has been committed under any provision of the former enactments, proceedings may be taken under this Act in respect of the continuance of the offence on and after the appointed day in the like manner as if the offence had been committed under the corresponding provision of this Act.

References elsewhere to the former enactments

27.— (1) A reference in any enactment, instrument or document (whether express or implied, and in whatever phraseology) to a provision of the former enactments (including the corresponding provision of any yet earlier enactment) is to be read, where necessary to retain for the enactment, instrument or document the same force and effect as it would have had but for the passing of this Act, as, or as including, a reference to the corresponding provision by which it is replaced in this Act.

(2) The generality of the preceding sub-paragraph is not affected by any specific conversion of references made by this Act, nor by the inclusion in any provision of this Act of a reference (whether express or implied, and in whatever phraseology) to the provision of the former enactments corresponding to that provision, or to a provision of the former enactments which is replaced by a corresponding provision of this Act.

Saving for power to repeal provisions in section 51

28. The Secretary of State may by order in a statutory instrument repeal subsections (3) to (5) of section 51 of this Act and the entries in Schedule 10 relating to subsections (4) and (5) of that section.

Saving for Interpretation Act 1978 ss 16, 17

29. Nothing in this Schedule is to be taken as prejudicing sections 16 and 17 of the Interpretation Act 1978 (savings from, and effect of, repeals); and for the purposes of section 17(2) of that Act (construction of references to enactments repealed and replaced, etc), so much of section 18 of the Insolvency Act 1985 as is replaced by a provision of this Act is deemed to have been replaced by this Act and not by the Company Directors Disqualification Act 1986.

SCHEDULES 12–14

...

Financial Services and Markets Act 2000

2000 c. 8

An Act to make provision about the regulation of financial services and markets; to provide for the transfer of certain statutory functions relating to building societies, friendly societies, industrial and provident societies and certain other mutual societies; and for connected purposes

[14th June 2000]

PART 1A
THE REGULATORS

CHAPTER 1
THE FINANCIAL CONDUCT AUTHORITY

The Financial Conduct Authority

1A. The Financial Conduct Authority

(1) The body corporate previously known as the Financial Services Authority is renamed as the Financial Conduct Authority.

(2) The Financial Conduct Authority is in this Act referred to as "the FCA".

(3) The FCA is to have the functions conferred on it by or under this Act.

(4) The FCA must comply with the requirements as to its constitution set out in Schedule 1ZA.

(5) Schedule 1ZA also makes provision about the status of the FCA and the exercise of certain of its functions.

(6) References in this Act or any other enactment to functions conferred on the FCA by or under this Act include references to functions conferred on the FCA by or under—

(a) the Insolvency Act 1986,
(b) the Banking Act 2009,
(c) the Financial Services Act 2012, or
(d) a qualifying EU provision that is specified, or of a description specified, for the purposes of this subsection by the Treasury by order.

The FCA's general duties

1B. The FCA's general duties

(1) In discharging its general functions the FCA must, so far as is reasonably possible, act in a way which—

(a) is compatible with its strategic objective, and
(b) advances one or more of its operational objectives.

(2) The FCA's strategic objective is: ensuring that the relevant markets (see section 1F) function well.

(3) The FCA's operational objectives are—

(a) the consumer protection objective (see section 1C);
(b) the integrity objective (see section 1D);
(c) the competition objective (see section 1E).

(4) The FCA must, so far as is compatible with acting in a way which advances the consumer protection objective or the integrity objective, discharge its general functions in a way which promotes effective competition in the interests of consumers.

(5) In discharging its general functions the FCA must have regard to—

(a) the regulatory principles in section 3B, and
(b) the importance of taking action intended to minimise the extent to which it is possible for a business carried on—

(i) by an authorised person or a recognised investment exchange, or
(ii) in contravention of the general prohibition,

to be used for a purpose connected with financial crime.

(6) For the purposes of this Chapter, the FCA's general functions are—

(a) its function of making rules under this Act (considered as a whole),
(b) its function of preparing and issuing codes under this Act (considered as a whole),
(c) its functions in relation to the giving of general guidance under this Act (considered as a whole), and
(d) its function of determining the general policy and principles by reference to which it performs particular functions under this Act.

(7) Except to the extent that an order under section 50 of the Financial Services Act 2012 (orders relating to mutual societies functions) so provides, the FCA's general functions do not include functions that are transferred functions within the meaning of section 52 of that Act.

(8) "General guidance" has the meaning given in section 139B(5).

1C. The consumer protection objective

(1) The consumer protection objective is: securing an appropriate degree of protection for consumers.

(2) In considering what degree of protection for consumers may be appropriate, the FCA must have regard to—

(a) the differing degrees of risk involved in different kinds of investment or other transaction;
(b) the differing degrees of experience and expertise that different consumers may have;
(c) the needs that consumers may have for the timely provision of information and advice that is accurate and fit for purpose;
(d) the general principle that consumers should take responsibility for their decisions;
(e) the general principle that those providing regulated financial services should be expected to provide consumers with a level of care that is appropriate having regard to the degree of risk involved in relation to the investment or other transaction and the capabilities of the consumers in question;
(f) the differing expectations that consumers may have in relation to different kinds of investment or other transaction;
(g) any information which the consumer financial education body has provided to the FCA in the exercise of the consumer financial education function;
(h) any information which the scheme operator of the ombudsman scheme has provided to the FCA pursuant to section 232A.

1D. The integrity objective

(1) The integrity objective is: protecting and enhancing the integrity of the UK financial system.

(2) The "integrity" of the UK financial system includes—

(a) its soundness, stability and resilience,
(b) its not being used for a purpose connected with financial crime,
(c) its not being affected by behaviour that amounts to market abuse,
(d) the orderly operation of the financial markets, and
(e) the transparency of the price formation process in those markets.

1E. The competition objective

(1) The competition objective is: promoting effective competition in the interests of consumers in the markets for—

(a) regulated financial services, or
(b) services provided by a recognised investment exchange in carrying on regulated activities in respect of which it is by virtue of section 285(2) exempt from the general prohibition.

(2) The matters to which the FCA may have regard in considering the effectiveness of competition in the market for any services mentioned in subsection (1) include—

(a) the needs of different consumers who use or may use those services, including their need for information that enables them to make informed choices,

(b) the ease with which consumers who may wish to use those services, including consumers in areas affected by social or economic deprivation, can access them,
(c) the ease with which consumers who obtain those services can change the person from whom they obtain them,
(d) the ease with which new entrants can enter the market, and
(e) how far competition is encouraging innovation.

Interpretation of terms used in relation to FCA's general duties

1F. Meaning of "relevant markets" in strategic objective

In section 1B(2) "the relevant markets" means—
(a) the financial markets,
(b) the markets for regulated financial services (see section 1H(2)), and
(c) the markets for services that are provided by persons other than authorised persons in carrying on regulated activities but are provided without contravening the general prohibition.

1G. Meaning of "consumer"

(1) In sections 1B to 1E "consumers" means persons who—
(a) use, have used or may use—
(i) regulated financial services, or
(ii) services that are provided by persons other than authorised persons but are provided in carrying on regulated activities,
(b) have relevant rights or interests in relation to any of those services,
(c) have invested, or may invest, in financial instruments,
(d) have relevant rights or interests in relation to financial instruments, or
(e) have rights, interests or obligations that are affected by the level of a regulated benchmark.

(2) A person ("P") has a "relevant right or interest" in relation to any services within subsection (1)(a) if P has a right or interest—
(a) which is derived from, or is otherwise attributable to, the use of the services by others, or
(b) which may be adversely affected by the use of the services by persons acting on P's behalf or in a fiduciary capacity in relation to P.

(3) If a person is providing a service within subsection (1)(a) as trustee, the persons who are, have been or may be beneficiaries of the trust are to be treated as persons who use, have used or may use the service.

(4) A person who deals with another person ("B") in the course of B providing a service within subsection (1)(a) is to be treated as using the service.

(5) A person ("P") has a "relevant right or interest" in relation to any financial instrument if P has—
(a) a right or interest which is derived from, or is otherwise attributable to, investment in the instrument by others, or
(b) a right or interest which may be adversely affected by the investment in the instrument by persons acting on P's behalf or in a fiduciary capacity in relation to P.

1H. Further interpretative provisions for sections 1B to 1G

(1) The following provisions have effect for the interpretation of sections 1B to 1G.

(2) "Regulated financial services" means services provided—
(a) by authorised persons in carrying on regulated activities;
(b) by authorised persons in carrying on a consumer credit business in connection with the accepting of deposits;
(c) by authorised persons in communicating, or approving the communication by others of, invitations to engage in investment activity;
(d) by authorised persons who are investment firms, or credit institutions, in providing relevant ancillary services;
(e) by persons acting as appointed representatives;

(f) by payment service providers in providing payment services;
(g) by electronic money issuers in issuing electronic money;
(h) by sponsors to issuers of securities;
(i) by primary information providers to persons who issue financial instruments.

(3) "Financial crime" includes any offence involving—
(a) fraud or dishonesty,
(b) misconduct in, or misuse of information relating to, a financial market,
(c) handling the proceeds of crime, or
(d) the financing of terrorism.

(4) "Offence" includes an act or omission which would be an offence if it had taken place in the United Kingdom.

(5) "Issuer", except in the expression "electronic money issuer", has the meaning given in section 102A(6).

(6) "Financial instrument" has the meaning given in section 102A(4).

(7) "Securities" has the meaning given in section 102A(2).

(7A) "Regulated benchmark" means a benchmark, as defined in section 22(6), in relation to which any provision made under section 22(1A)(b) has effect.

(8) In this section—
"accepting", in relation to deposits, includes agreeing to accept;
"consumer credit business" has the same meaning as in the Consumer Credit Act 1974;
"credit institution" means—
(a) a credit institution authorised under the banking consolidation directive, or
(b) an institution which would satisfy the requirements for authorisation as a credit institution under that directive if it had its registered office (or if it does not have a registered office, its head office) in an EEA State;

"electronic money" has the same meaning as in the Electronic Money Regulations 2011;
"electronic money issuer" means a person who is an electronic money issuer as defined in regulation 2(1) of the Electronic Money Regulations 2011 other than a person falling within paragraph (f), (g) or (j) of the definition;
"engage in investment activity" has the meaning given in section 21;
"financial instrument" has the meaning given in section 102A(4);
"payment services" has the same meaning as in the Payment Services Regulations 2009;
"payment service provider" means a person who is a payment service provider as defined in regulation 2(1) of the Payment Services Regulations 2009 other than a person falling within paragraph (g) or (h) of the definition;
"primary information provider" has the meaning given in section 89P(2);
"relevant ancillary service" means any service of a kind mentioned in Section B of Annex I to the markets in financial instruments directive the provision of which does not involve the carrying on of a regulated activity;
"sponsor" has the meaning given in section 88(2).

1I. Meaning of "the UK financial system"

In this Act "the UK financial system" means the financial system operating in the United Kingdom and includes—
(a) financial markets and exchanges,
(b) regulated activities, and
(c) other activities connected with financial markets and exchanges.

Power to amend objectives

1J. Power to amend objectives

The Treasury may by order amend any of the following provisions—
(a) in section 1E(1), paragraphs (a) and (b),
(b) section 1G, and

(c) section 1H(2) and (5) to (8).

Guidance about objectives

1K. Guidance about objectives

(1) The general guidance given by the FCA under section 139A must include guidance about how it intends to advance its operational objectives in discharging its general functions in relation to different categories of authorised person or regulated activity.

(2) Before giving or altering any guidance complying with subsection (1), the FCA must consult the PRA.

Supervision, monitoring and enforcement

1L. Supervision, monitoring and enforcement

(1) The FCA must maintain arrangements for supervising authorised persons.

(2) The FCA must maintain arrangements designed to enable it to determine whether persons other than authorised persons are complying—

(a) with requirements imposed on them by or under this Act, in cases where the FCA is the appropriate regulator for the purposes of Part 14 (disciplinary measures), or

(b) with requirements imposed on them by any qualifying EU provision that is specified, or of a description specified, for the purposes of this subsection by the Treasury by order.

(3) The FCA must also maintain arrangements for enforcing compliance by persons other than authorised persons with relevant requirements, within the meaning of Part 14, in cases where the FCA is the appropriate regulator for the purposes of any provision of that Part.

Arrangements for consulting practitioners and consumers

1M. The FCA's general duty to consult

The FCA must make and maintain effective arrangements for consulting practitioners and consumers on the extent to which its general policies and practices are consistent with its general duties under section 1B.

1N. The FCA Practitioner Panel

(1) Arrangements under section 1M must include the establishment and maintenance of a panel of persons (to be known as "the FCA Practitioner Panel") to represent the interests of practitioners.

(2) The FCA must appoint one of the members of the FCA Practitioner Panel to be its chair.

(3) The Treasury's approval is required for the appointment or dismissal of the chair.

(4) The FCA must appoint to the FCA Practitioner Panel such—

(a) persons representing authorised persons, and

(b) persons representing recognised investment exchanges,

as it considers appropriate.

(5) The FCA may appoint to the FCA Practitioner Panel such other persons as it considers appropriate.

1O. The Smaller Business Practitioner Panel

(1) Arrangements under section 1M must include the establishment and maintenance of a panel of persons (to be known as "the Smaller Business Practitioner Panel") to represent the interests of eligible practitioners.

(2) "Eligible practitioners" means authorised persons of a description specified in a statement maintained by the FCA.

(3) The FCA must appoint one of the members of the Smaller Business Practitioner Panel to be its chair.

(4) The Treasury's approval is required for the appointment or dismissal of the chair.

(5) The FCA must appoint to the Smaller Business Practitioner Panel such—

(a) individuals who are eligible practitioners, and

(b) persons representing eligible practitioners,

as it considers appropriate.

(6) The FCA may appoint to the Smaller Business Practitioner Panel such other persons as it considers appropriate.

(7) In making the appointments, the FCA must have regard to the desirability of ensuring the representation of eligible practitioners carrying on a range of regulated activities.

(8) The FCA may revise the statement maintained under subsection (2).

(9) The FCA must—

(a) give the Treasury a copy of the statement or revised statement without delay, and

(b) publish the statement as for the time being in force in such manner as it thinks fit.

1P. The Markets Practitioner Panel

(1) Arrangements under section 1M must include the establishment and maintenance of a panel of persons (to be known as "the Markets Practitioner Panel") to represent the interests of practitioners who are likely to be affected by the exercise by the FCA of its functions relating to markets, including its functions under Parts 6, 8A and 18.

(2) The FCA must appoint one of the members of the Markets Practitioner Panel to be its chair.

(3) The Treasury's approval is required for the appointment or dismissal of the chair.

(4) The FCA must appoint to the Markets Practitioner Panel such persons to represent the interests of persons within subsection (5) as it considers appropriate.

(5) The persons within this subsection are—

(a) authorised persons,

(b) persons who issue financial instruments,

(c) sponsors, as defined in section 88(2),

(d) recognised investment exchanges, and

(e) primary information providers, as defined in section 89P(2).

(6) The FCA may appoint to the Markets Practitioner Panel such other persons as it considers appropriate.

1Q. The Consumer Panel

(1) Arrangements under section 1M must include the establishment and maintenance of a panel of persons (to be known as "the Consumer Panel") to represent the interests of consumers.

(2) The FCA must appoint one of the members of the Consumer Panel to be its chair.

(3) The Treasury's approval is required for the appointment or dismissal of the chair.

(4) The FCA may appoint to the Consumer Panel such consumers, or persons representing the interests of consumers, as it considers appropriate.

(5) The FCA must secure that membership of the Consumer Panel is such as to give a fair degree of representation to those who are using, or are or may be contemplating using, services otherwise than in connection with businesses carried on by them.

(6) Sections 425A and 425B (meaning of "consumers") apply for the purposes of this section, but the references to consumers in this section do not include consumers who are authorised persons.

1R. Duty to consider representations made by the Panels

(1) The FCA must consider representations that are made to it in accordance with arrangements made under section 1M.

(2) The FCA must from time to time publish in such manner as it thinks fit responses to the representations.

Reviews

1S. Reviews

(1) The Treasury may appoint an independent person to conduct a review of the economy, efficiency and effectiveness with which the FCA has used its resources in discharging its functions.

(2) A review may be limited by the Treasury to such functions of the FCA (however described) as the Treasury may specify in appointing the person to conduct it.

(3) A review is not to be concerned with the merits of the FCA's general policy or principles in complying with its general duties under section 1B(1) and (4).

(4) On completion of a review, the person conducting it must make a written report to the Treasury—
   (a) setting out the result of the review, and
   (b) making such recommendations (if any) as the person considers appropriate.

(5) A copy of the report must be—
   (a) laid before Parliament, and
   (b) published in such manner as the Treasury consider appropriate.

(6) Any expenses reasonably incurred in the conduct of the review are to be met by the Treasury out of money provided by Parliament.

(7) "Independent" means appearing to the Treasury to be independent of the FCA.

1T. Right to obtain documents and information

(1) A person conducting a review under section 1S—
   (a) has a right of access at any reasonable time to all such documents as the person may reasonably require for the purposes of the review, and
   (b) may require any person holding or accountable for any such document to provide such information and explanation as are reasonably necessary for that purpose.

(2) Subsection (1) applies only to documents in the custody of or under the control of the FCA.

(3) An obligation imposed on a person as a result of the exercise of the powers conferred by subsection (1) is enforceable by injunction or, in Scotland, by an order for specific performance under section 45 of the Court of Session Act 1988.

CHAPTER 2
THE PRUDENTIAL REGULATION AUTHORITY

The Prudential Regulation Authority

2A. The Prudential Regulation Authority

(1) The body corporate originally incorporated as the Prudential Regulation Authority Limited is renamed as the Prudential Regulation Authority.

(2) The Prudential Regulation Authority is in this Act referred to as "the PRA".

(3) The PRA is to have the functions conferred on it by or under this Act.

(4) The PRA must comply with the requirements as to its constitution set out in Schedule 1ZB.

(5) Schedule 1ZB also confers on the Bank of England functions in relation to the PRA and makes provision about the status of the PRA and the exercise of certain of its functions.

(6) References in this Act or any other enactment to functions conferred on the PRA by or under this Act include references to functions conferred on the PRA by or under—
   (a) the Insolvency Act 1986,
   (b) the Banking Act 2009,
   (c) the Financial Services Act 2012, or
   (d) a qualifying EU provision that is specified, or of a description specified, for the purposes of this subsection by the Treasury by order.

The PRA's general duties

2B. The PRA's general objective

(1) In discharging its general functions the PRA must, so far as is reasonably possible, act in a way which advances its general objective.

(2) The PRA's general objective is: promoting the safety and soundness of PRA-authorised persons.

(3) That objective is to be advanced primarily by—
   (a) seeking to ensure that the business of PRA-authorised persons is carried on in a way which avoids any adverse effect on the stability of the UK financial system, and

(b) seeking to minimise the adverse effect that the failure of a PRA-authorised person could be expected to have on the stability of the UK financial system.

(4) The adverse effects mentioned in subsection (3) may, in particular, result from the disruption of the continuity of financial services.

(5) In this Act "PRA-authorised person" means an authorised person who has permission—

(a) given under Part 4A, or

(b) resulting from any other provision of this Act,

to carry on regulated activities that consist of or include one or more PRA-regulated activities (see section 22A).

(6) Subsection (1) is subject to sections 2C and 2D.

2C. Insurance objective

(1) In discharging its general functions so far as relating to a PRA-regulated activity relating to the effecting or carrying out of contracts of insurance or PRA-authorised persons carrying on that activity, the PRA must, so far as is reasonably possible, act in a way—

(a) which is compatible with its general objective and its insurance objective, and

(b) which the PRA considers most appropriate for the purpose of advancing those objectives.

(2) The PRA's insurance objective is: contributing to the securing of an appropriate degree of protection for those who are or may become policyholders.

(3) This section applies only if the effecting or carrying out of contracts of insurance as principal is to any extent a PRA-regulated activity.

2D. Power to provide for additional objectives

(1) Subsection (2) applies to an order under section 22A which—

(a) is made at any time after the coming into force of the first order under that section, and

(b) contains a statement by the Treasury that, in their opinion, the effect (or one of the effects) of the proposed order is that an activity would become a PRA-regulated activity.

(2) An order to which this subsection applies may specify an additional objective ("the specified objective") in relation to specified activities that become PRA-regulated activities by virtue of the order ("the additional activities").

(3) In discharging its general functions so far as relating to the additional activities or PRA-authorised persons carrying on those activities, the PRA must, so far as is reasonably possible, act in a way—

(a) which is compatible with its general objective and the specified objective, and

(b) which the PRA considers most appropriate for the purpose of advancing those objectives.

2E. Strategy

(1) The PRA must—

(a) determine its strategy in relation to its objectives, and

(b) from time to time review, and if necessary revise, the strategy.

(2) Before determining or revising its strategy, the PRA must consult the court of directors of the Bank of England about a draft of the strategy or of the revisions.

(3) The PRA must determine its strategy within 12 months of the coming into force of this section.

(4) The PRA must carry out and complete a review of its strategy before the end of each relevant period.

(5) The relevant period is 12 months beginning with the date on which the previous review was completed, except that in the case of the first review the relevant period is the period of 12 months beginning with the date on which the strategy was determined under subsection (3).

(6) The PRA must publish its strategy.

(7) If the strategy is revised the PRA must publish the revised strategy.

(8) Publication under subsection (6) or (7) is to be in such manner as the PRA thinks fit.

2F. Interpretation of references to objectives

In this Act, a reference, in relation to any function of the PRA, to the objectives of the PRA is a reference to its general objective but—

(a) so far as the function is exercisable in relation to the activity of effecting or carrying out contracts of insurance, or PRA-authorised persons carrying on that activity, is a reference to its general objective and its insurance objective;

(b) so far as the function is exercisable in relation to an activity to which an objective specified by order by virtue of section 2D(2) relates, or PRA-authorised persons carrying on that activity, is a reference to its general objective and the objective specified by the order.

2G. Limit on effect of sections 2B to 2D

Nothing in sections 2B to 2D is to be regarded as requiring the PRA to ensure that no PRA-authorised person fails.

2H. Duty to have regard to regulatory principles

(1) In discharging its general functions, the PRA must also have regard to—

(a) the regulatory principles in section 3B, and

(b) the need to minimise any adverse effect on competition in the relevant markets that may result from the manner in which the PRA discharges those functions.

(2) In subsection (1)(b) "the relevant markets" means the markets for services provided by PRA-authorised persons in carrying on regulated activities.

2I. Guidance about objectives

(1) The PRA must give, and from time to time review, guidance about how it intends to advance its objectives in discharging its general functions in relation to different categories of PRA-authorised person or PRA-regulated activity.

(2) Before giving or altering any guidance complying with subsection (1), the PRA must consult the FCA.

(3) The PRA must publish the guidance as for the time being in force.

2J. Interpretation of Chapter 2

(1) For the purposes of this Chapter, the PRA's general functions are—

(a) its function of making rules under this Act (considered as a whole),

(b) its function of preparing and issuing codes under this Act (considered as a whole), and

(c) its function of determining the general policy and principles by reference to which it performs particular functions under this Act.

(2) Except to the extent that an order under section 50 of the Financial Services Act 2012 (orders relating to mutual societies functions) so provides, the PRA's general functions do not include functions that are transferred functions within the meaning of section 52 of that Act.

(3) For the purposes of this Chapter, the cases in which a PRA-authorised person ("P") is to be regarded as failing include those where—

(a) P enters insolvency,

(b) any of the stabilisation options in Part 1 of the Banking Act 2009 is achieved in relation to P, or

(c) P falls to be taken for the purposes of the compensation scheme to be unable, or likely to be unable, to satisfy claims against P.

(4) In subsection (3)(a) "insolvency" includes—

(a) bankruptcy,

(b) liquidation,

(c) bank insolvency,

(d) administration,

(e) bank administration,

(f) receivership,

(g) a composition between P and P's creditors, and

(h) a scheme of arrangement of P's affairs.

Supervision

2K. Arrangements for supervision of PRA-authorised persons

The PRA must maintain arrangements for supervising PRA-authorised persons.

Arrangements for consulting practitioners

2L. The PRA's general duty to consult

The PRA must make and maintain effective arrangements for consulting PRA-authorised persons or, where appropriate, persons appearing to the PRA to represent the interests of such persons on the extent to which its general policies and practices are consistent with its general duties under sections 2B to 2H.

2M. The PRA Practitioner Panel

(1) Arrangements under section 2L must include the establishment and maintenance of a panel of persons (to be known as "the PRA Practitioner Panel") to represent the interests of practitioners.

(2) The PRA must appoint one of the members of the PRA Practitioner Panel to be its chair.

(3) The Treasury's approval is required for the appointment or dismissal of the chair.

(4) The PRA must appoint to the PRA Practitioner Panel such persons representing PRA-authorised persons as it considers appropriate.

(5) The PRA may appoint to the PRA Practitioner Panel such other persons as it considers appropriate.

2N. Duty to consider representations

(1) The PRA must consider representations that are made to it in accordance with arrangements made under section 2L.

(2) The PRA must from time to time publish in such manner as it thinks fit responses to the representations.

Reviews

2O. Reviews

(1) The Treasury may appoint an independent person to conduct a review of the economy, efficiency and effectiveness with which the PRA has used its resources in discharging its functions.

(2) A review may be limited by the Treasury to such functions of the PRA (however described) as the Treasury may specify in appointing the person to conduct it.

(3) A review is not to be concerned with the merits of the PRA's general policy or principles in pursuing the PRA's objectives.

(4) On completion of a review, the person conducting it must make a written report to the Treasury—

(a) setting out the result of the review, and

(b) making such recommendations (if any) as the person considers appropriate.

(5) A copy of the report must be—

(a) laid before Parliament, and

(b) published in such manner as the Treasury consider appropriate.

(6) Any expenses reasonably incurred in the conduct of the review are to be met by the Treasury out of money provided by Parliament.

(7) "Independent" means appearing to the Treasury to be independent of the PRA.

2P. Right to obtain documents and information

(1) A person conducting a review under section 2O—

(a) has a right of access at any reasonable time to all such documents as the person may reasonably require for the purposes of the review, and

(b) may require any person holding or accountable for any such document to provide such information and explanation as are reasonably necessary for that purpose.

(2) Subsection (1) applies only to documents in the custody of or under the control of the PRA.

(3) An obligation imposed on a person as a result of the exercise of the powers conferred by subsection (1) is enforceable by injunction or, in Scotland, by an order for specific performance under section 45 of the Court of Session Act 1988.

CHAPTER 3
FURTHER PROVISIONS RELATING TO FCA AND PRA

Introductory

3A. Meaning of "regulator"

(1) This section has effect for the interpretation of this Act.

(2) The FCA and the PRA are the "regulators", and references to a regulator are to be read accordingly.

(3) Subsection (2) does not affect—

(a) the meaning of the following expressions—
"home state regulator";
"host state regulator";
"overseas regulator"; or

(b) the meaning of "the appropriate regulator" in Part 18 (recognised investment exchanges and clearing houses).

Regulatory principles

3B. Regulatory principles to be applied by both regulators

(1) In relation to the regulators, the regulatory principles referred to in section 1B(5)(a) and 2H(1)(a) are as follows—

(a) the need to use the resources of each regulator in the most efficient and economic way;

(b) the principle that a burden or restriction which is imposed on a person, or on the carrying on of an activity, should be proportionate to the benefits, considered in general terms, which are expected to result from the imposition of that burden or restriction;

(c) the desirability of sustainable growth in the economy of the United Kingdom in the medium or long term;

(d) the general principle that consumers should take responsibility for their decisions;

(e) the responsibilities of the senior management of persons subject to requirements imposed by or under this Act, including those affecting consumers, in relation to compliance with those requirements;

(f) the desirability where appropriate of each regulator exercising its functions in a way that recognises differences in the nature of, and objectives of, businesses carried on by different persons subject to requirements imposed by or under this Act;

(g) the desirability in appropriate cases of each regulator publishing information relating to persons on whom requirements are imposed by or under this Act, or requiring such persons to publish information, as a means of contributing to the advancement by each regulator of its objectives;

(h) the principle that the regulators should exercise their functions as transparently as possible.

(2) "Consumer" has the meaning given in section 1G.

(3) "Objectives", in relation to the FCA, means operational objectives.

(4) The Treasury may by order amend subsection (2).

Corporate governance

3C. Duty to follow principles of good governance

In managing its affairs, each regulator must have regard to such generally accepted principles of good corporate governance as it is reasonable to regard as applicable to it.

Relationship between FCA and PRA

3D. Duty of FCA and PRA to ensure co-ordinated exercise of functions

(1) The regulators must co-ordinate the exercise of their respective functions conferred by or under this Act with a view to ensuring—

(a) that each regulator consults the other regulator (where not otherwise required to do so) in connection with any proposed exercise of a function in a way that may have a material adverse effect on the advancement by the other regulator of any of its objectives;

(b) that where appropriate each regulator obtains information and advice from the other regulator in connection with the exercise of its functions in relation to matters of common regulatory interest in cases where the other regulator may be expected to have relevant information or relevant expertise;

(c) that where either regulator exercises functions in relation to matters of common regulatory interest, both regulators comply with their respective duties under section 1B(5)(a) or 2H(1)(a), so far as relating to the regulatory principles in section 3B(1)(a) and (b).

(2) The duty in subsection (1) applies only to the extent that compliance with the duty—

(a) is compatible with the advancement by each regulator of any of its objectives, and

(b) does not impose a burden on the regulators that is disproportionate to the benefits of compliance.

(3) A function conferred on either regulator by or under this Act relates to matters of common regulatory interest if—

(a) the other regulator exercises similar or related functions in relation to the same persons,

(b) the other regulator exercises functions which relate to different persons but relate to similar subject-matter, or

(c) its exercise could affect the advancement by the other regulator of any of its objectives.

(4) "Objectives", in relation to the FCA, means operational objectives.

3E. Memorandum of understanding

(1) The regulators must prepare and maintain a memorandum which describes in general terms—

(a) the role of each regulator in relation to the exercise of functions conferred by or under this Act which relate to matters of common regulatory interest, and

(b) how the regulators intend to comply with section 3D in relation to the exercise of such functions.

(2) The memorandum may in particular contain provisions about how the regulators intend to comply with section 3D in relation to—

(a) applications for Part 4A permission;

(b) the variation of permission;

(c) the imposition of requirements;

(d) the obtaining and disclosure of information;

(e) cases where a PRA-authorised person is a member of a group whose other members include one or more other authorised persons (whether or not PRA-authorised persons);

(f) functions under Schedule 3 (EEA passport rights) and Schedule 4 (Treaty rights);

(g) the making of rules;

(h) directions under section 138A (modification or waiver of rules);

(i) powers to appoint competent persons under Part 11 (information gathering and investigations) to conduct investigations on their behalf;

(j) functions under Part 12 (control over authorised persons);

(k) functions under Part 13 (incoming firms: intervention by regulator);

(l) functions under Part 19 (Lloyd's);

(m) functions under section 347 (record of authorised persons etc.);

(n) functions under Part 24 (insolvency);

(o) fees payable to either regulator.

(3) The memorandum must contain provision about the co-ordination by the regulators of—

(a) the exercise of their functions relating to membership of, and their relations with, the European Supervisory Authorities (namely, the European Banking Authority, the European Insurance and Occupational Pensions Authority and the European Securities and Markets Authority),

(b) their relations with regulatory bodies outside the United Kingdom, and

(c) the exercise of their functions in relation to the compensation scheme.

(4) The regulators must review the memorandum at least once in each calendar year.

(5) The regulators must give the Treasury a copy of the memorandum and any revised memorandum.

(6) The Treasury must lay before Parliament a copy of any document received by them under this section.

(7) The regulators must ensure that the memorandum as currently in force is published in the way appearing to them to be best calculated to bring it to the attention of the public.

(8) The memorandum need not relate to any aspect of compliance with section 3D if the regulators consider—

(a) that publication of information about that aspect would be against the public interest, or

(b) that that aspect is a technical or operational matter not affecting the public.

(9) The reference in subsection (1)(a) to matters of common regulatory interest is to be read in accordance with section 3D(3).

3F. With-profits insurance policies

(1) The regulators must prepare and maintain a memorandum which describes in general terms—

(a) the role of each regulator in relation to the exercise of functions conferred by or under this Act so far as they relate to with-profits insurers, and

(b) how the regulators intend to comply with section 3D in relation to the exercise of those functions so far as they relate to the effecting or carrying out of with-profits policies by with-profits insurers.

(2) The memorandum required by this section may be combined with the memorandum required by section 3E.

(3) If the memorandum required by this section is contained in a separate document, the PRA and the FCA must publish the memorandum as currently in force in such manner as they think fit.

(4) Subsections (1) to (3) apply only if the effecting or carrying out of with-profits policies is a PRA-regulated activity.

(5) For the purposes of this section—

(a) a "with-profits policy" is a contract of insurance under which the policyholder is eligible to receive a financial benefit at the discretion of the insurer;

(b) a "with-profits insurer" is a PRA-authorised person who has a Part 4A permission, or permission resulting from any other provision of this Act, relating to the effecting or carrying out of with-profits policies (whether or not the permission also relates to contracts of insurance of other kinds).

(6) The Treasury may by order amend the definition of "with-profits policy" applying for the purposes of this section.

3G. Power to establish boundary between FCA and PRA responsibilities

(1) The Treasury may by order specify matters that, in relation to the exercise by either regulator of its functions relating to PRA-authorised persons, are to be, or are to be primarily, the responsibility of one regulator rather than the other.

(2) The order may—

(a) provide that one regulator is or is not to have regard to specified matters when exercising specified functions;

(b) require one regulator to consult the other.

3H. Parliamentary control of orders under section 3G

(1) No order may be made under section 3G unless—

(a) a draft of the order has been laid before Parliament and approved by a resolution of each House, or
(b) subsection (3) applies.

(2) Subsection (3) applies if an order under section 3G contains a statement that the Treasury are of the opinion that, by reason of urgency, it is necessary to make the order without a draft being so laid and approved.

(3) Where this subsection applies the order—
(a) must be laid before Parliament after being made, and
(b) ceases to have effect at the end of the relevant period unless before the end of that period the order is approved by a resolution of each House of Parliament (but without that affecting anything done under the order or the power to make a new order).

(4) The "relevant period" is a period of 28 days beginning with the day on which the order is made.

(5) In calculating the relevant period no account is to be taken of any time during which Parliament is dissolved or prorogued or during which both Houses are adjourned for more than 4 days.

Power of PRA to restrain proposed action by FCA

3I. Power of PRA to require FCA to refrain from specified action

(1) Where the first, second and third conditions are met, the PRA may give a direction under this section to the FCA.

(2) The first condition is that the FCA is proposing—
(a) to exercise any of its regulatory powers in relation to PRA-authorised persons generally, a class of PRA-authorised persons or a particular PRA-authorised person, or
(b) to exercise any of its insolvency powers in relation to—
(i) a PRA-authorised person,
(ii) an appointed representative whose principal, or one of whose principals, is a PRA-authorised person, or
(iii) a person who is carrying on a PRA-regulated activity in contravention of the general prohibition.

(3) In subsection (2)—
(a) "regulatory powers", in relation to the FCA, means its powers in relation to the regulation of authorised persons, other than its powers in relation to consent for the purposes of section 55F or 55I or its powers under Part 24;
(b) "insolvency powers", in relation to the FCA, means its powers under Part 24.

(4) The second condition is that the PRA is of the opinion that the exercise of the power in the manner proposed may—
(a) threaten the stability of the UK financial system, or
(b) result in the failure of a PRA-authorised person in a way that would adversely affect the UK financial system.

(5) The third condition is that the PRA is of the opinion that the giving of the direction is necessary in order to avoid the possible consequence falling within subsection (4).

(6) A direction under this section is a direction requiring the FCA not to exercise the power or not to exercise it in a specified manner.

(7) The direction may be expressed to have effect during a specified period or until revoked.

(8) The FCA is not required to comply with a direction under this section if or to the extent that in the opinion of the FCA compliance would be incompatible with any EU obligation or any other international obligation of the United Kingdom.

(9) The reference in subsection (4)(b) to the "failure" of a PRA-authorised person is to be read in accordance with section 2J(3) and (4).

3J. Power of PRA in relation to with-profits policies

(1) Where the first, second and third conditions are met, the PRA may give a direction under this section to the FCA.

(2) The first condition is that the FCA is proposing to exercise any of its regulatory powers in relation to with-profits insurers, a class of with-profits insurers or a particular with-profits insurer.

(3) In subsection (2) "regulatory powers", in relation to the FCA, means its powers in relation to the regulation of authorised persons, including its powers under Part 24 (insolvency) but not its powers in relation to consent for the purposes of section 55F or 55I.

(4) The second condition is that the proposed exercise of the power relates to the provision of financial benefits under with-profits policies at the discretion of the insurer, or affects or may affect the amount, timing or distribution of financial benefits that are so provided or the entitlement to future benefits that are so provided.

(5) The third condition is that the PRA is of the opinion that the giving of the direction is desirable in order to advance the PRA's general objective or its insurance objective.

(6) A direction under this section is a direction requiring the FCA not to exercise the power or not to exercise it in a specified manner.

(7) The direction may be expressed to have effect during a specified period or until revoked.

(8) The FCA is not required to comply with a direction under this section if or to the extent that in the opinion of the FCA compliance would be incompatible with any EU obligation or any other international obligation of the United Kingdom.

(9) Subsections (1) to (8) apply only if the effecting or carrying out of with-profits policies is a PRA-regulated activity.

(10) In this section "with-profits insurer" and "with-profits policy" have the same meaning as they have for the purposes of section 3F.

3K. Revocation of directions under section 3I or 3J

(1) The PRA may at any time by notice to the FCA revoke a direction under section 3I or 3J.

(2) The revocation of a direction under section 3I or 3J does not affect the validity of anything previously done in accordance with it.

3L. Further provisions about directions under section 3I or 3J

(1) Before giving a direction under section 3I or 3J, the PRA must consult the FCA.

(2) A direction under section 3I or 3J must be given or confirmed in writing, and must be accompanied by a statement of the reasons for giving it.

(3) A notice revoking a direction under section 3I or 3J must be given or confirmed in writing.

(4) The PRA must—

(a) publish the direction and statement, or the notice, in such manner as it thinks fit, and

(b) where the direction or notice relates to a particular authorised person or a particular with-profits insurer, give a copy of the direction and statement, or the notice, to that person.

(5) The PRA must give the Treasury a copy of—

(a) a direction under section 3I;

(b) a statement relating to such a direction;

(c) a notice revoking such a direction.

(6) The Treasury must lay before Parliament any document received by them under subsection (5).

(7) Subsection (4) does not apply where the PRA, after consulting the Treasury, decides that compliance with that subsection would be against the public interest, and at any time when this subsection excludes the application of subsection (4) in relation to a direction under section 3I, subsection (6) also does not apply.

(8) Where the PRA decides that compliance with subsection (4) would be against the public interest, it must from time to time review that decision and if it subsequently decides that compliance is no longer against the public interest it must—

(a) comply with that subsection, and

(b) in the case of a direction under section 3I, notify the Treasury for the purposes of subsection (6).

Directions relating to consolidated supervision

3M. Directions relating to consolidated supervision of groups

(1) This section applies where one of the regulators ("the supervising regulator"), but not the other, is the competent authority for the purpose of consolidated supervision that is required in relation to some or all of the members of a group ("the relevant group") in pursuance of any of the relevant directives.

(2) "Consolidated supervision" includes supplementary supervision.

(3) The "relevant directives" are—

(a) the banking consolidation directive;

(b) Directive 2002/87/EC of the European Parliament and of the Council on the supplementary supervision of credit institutions, insurance undertakings and investment firms in a financial conglomerate;

(c) Directive 2006/49/EC on the capital adequacy of investment firms and credit institutions;

(d) Directive 2009/138/EC of the European Parliament and the Council of 25 November 2009 on the taking-up and pursuit of the business of Insurance and Reinsurance (Solvency II).

(4) The supervising regulator may, if it considers it necessary to do so for the effective consolidated supervision of the relevant group, give the other regulator a direction under this section.

(5) A direction under this section is a direction requiring the other regulator to exercise, or not to exercise, a relevant function in a specified manner in relation to authorised persons who are members of the relevant group.

(6) The direction may relate to members of the relevant group other than the members in respect of which consolidated supervision is required.

(7) A "relevant function", in relation to either regulator, is a function conferred by or under this Act which relates to the regulation of authorised persons, but does not include—

(a) the regulator's function of making rules under this Act;

(b) its function of preparing and issuing codes under this Act;

(c) its function of determining the general policy and principles by reference to which it performs particular functions;

(d) the FCA's functions in relation to the giving of general guidance;

(e) the PRA's functions in relation to the giving of guidance under section 2I;

(f) the FCA's functions in relation to consent for the purposes of section 55F or 55I.

(8) The direction may not require the regulator to which it is given ("the directed regulator") to do anything that it has no power to do, but the direction is relevant to the exercise of any discretion conferred on the directed regulator.

(9) The directed regulator must comply with the direction as soon as practicable, but this is subject to subsections (10) and (11).

(10) The directed regulator is not required to comply with a direction under this section if or to the extent that in its opinion compliance would be incompatible with any EU obligation or any other international obligation of the United Kingdom.

(11) Directions given by the FCA under this section are subject to any directions given to the FCA under section 3I or 3J.

3N. Revocation of directions under section 3M

(1) The supervising regulator may at any time by notice to the other regulator revoke a direction under section 3M.

(2) The revocation of the direction does not affect the validity of anything previously done in accordance with it.

(3) Expressions defined for the purposes of section 3M have the same meaning in this section.

3O. Further provisions about directions under section 3M

(1) Before giving a direction under section 3M, the supervising regulator must consult the other regulator.

(2) A direction under section 3M must be given or confirmed in writing, and must be accompanied by a statement of the reasons for giving it.

(3) A notice revoking a direction under section 3M must be given or confirmed in writing.

(4) The regulator to which a direction under section 3M is given must give a copy of the direction and statement to each of the authorised persons to whom the direction relates.

(5) The supervising regulator must publish the direction and statement, or the notice, in such manner as it thinks fit.

(6) But subsection (4) or (5) does not apply in a case where the regulator on which the duty is imposed considers that compliance with that subsection would be against the public interest.

(7) In a case where a regulator decides that compliance with subsection (4) or (5) would be against the public interest, the regulator must from time to time review that decision and if it subsequently decides that compliance is no longer against the public interest it must comply with the subsection.

(8) Expressions defined for the purposes of section 3M have the same meaning in this section.

3P. Consultation by regulator complying with direction

(1) If the directed regulator is required by this Act to consult any person other than the supervising regulator before exercising the relevant function to which the direction relates, the directed regulator must give the supervising regulator copies of any written representations received from the persons consulted.

(2) Expressions defined for the purposes of section 3M have the same meaning in this section.

Co-operation with Bank of England

3Q. Co-operation by FCA and PRA with Bank of England

(1) Each regulator must take such steps as it considers appropriate to co-operate with the Bank of England in connection with—

(a) the pursuit by the Bank of its Financial Stability Objective, and

(b) the Bank's compliance with its duties under sections 58 and 59 of the Financial Services Act 2012 (duty to notify Treasury of possible need for public funds and of subsequent changes).

(2) Co-operation under subsection (1) may include the sharing of information that the regulator is not prevented from disclosing.

Arrangements for provision of services

3R. Arrangements for provision of services

(1) The regulators may enter into arrangements with each other for the provision of services by one of them to the other.

(2) Either regulator may enter into arrangements with the Bank of England for the provision of services—

(a) by the Bank to the regulator, or

(b) by the regulator to the Bank.

(3) Either regulator may enter into arrangements with any of the bodies specified in subsection (4) for the provision of services by the regulator to that body.

(4) Those bodies are—

(a) the consumer financial education body (see section 3S(2)),

(b) the scheme manager (see section 212(1)), and

(c) the scheme operator (see section 225(2)).

(5) The FCA may enter into arrangements with—

(a) a local weights and measures authority in England, Wales or Scotland, or

(b) the Department of Enterprise, Trade and Investment in Northern Ireland,

for the provision by the authority or department to the FCA of services which relate to activities to which this subsection applies.

(6) Subsection (5) applies to activities that are regulated activities by virtue of—

(a) an order made under section 22(1) in relation to an investment of a kind falling within paragraph 23 or 23B of Schedule 2, or

(b) an order made under section 22(1A)(a).

(7) Arrangements under this section are to be on such terms as may be agreed by the parties.

Enhancing public understanding of financial matters etc.

3S. The consumer financial education body

(1) The consumer financial education body continues to have the consumer financial education function.

(2) The "consumer financial education body" means the body corporate originally established by the Financial Services Authority under section 6A of this Act (as it had effect before the passing of the Financial Services Act 2012).

(3) The consumer financial education function is to enhance—

(a) the understanding and knowledge of members of the public of financial matters (including the UK financial system), and

(b) the ability of members of the public to manage their own financial affairs.

(4) The consumer financial education function includes, in particular—

(a) promoting awareness of the benefits of financial planning;

(b) promoting awareness of the financial advantages and disadvantages in relation to particular decisions relating to different kinds of goods or services;

(c) promoting awareness of the benefits and risks associated with different kinds of financial dealing (which includes informing the FCA and other bodies of those benefits and risks);

(d) the publication of educational materials or the carrying out of other educational activities;

(e) the provision of information and advice to members of the public;

(f) assisting members of the public with the management of debt;

(g) working with other organisations which provide debt services, with a view to improving—

(i) the availability to the public of those services;

(ii) the quality of the services provided;

(iii) consistency in the services available, in the way in which they are provided and in the advice given.

(5) In subsection (4) "debt services" means debt advice or assistance with the management of debt.

(6) Schedule 1A makes further provision about the consumer financial education body.

PART II

REGULATED AND PROHIBITED ACTIVITIES

The general prohibition

19. The general prohibition

(1) No person may carry on a regulated activity in the United Kingdom, or purport to do so, unless he is—

(a) an authorised person; or

(b) an exempt person.

(2) The prohibition is referred to in this Act as the general prohibition.

Requirement for permission

20. Authorised persons acting without permission

(1) If an authorised person other than a PRA-authorised person carries on a regulated activity in the United Kingdom, or purports to do so, otherwise than in accordance with permission—

(a) given to that person under Part 4A, or

(b) resulting from any other provision of this Act,

he is to be taken to have contravened a requirement imposed on him by the FCA under this Act.

(1A) If a PRA-authorised person carries on a regulated activity in the United Kingdom, or purports to do so, otherwise than in accordance with permission given to the person under Part 4A or resulting from any other provision of this Act, the person is to be taken to have contravened—

(a) a requirement imposed by the FCA, and

(b) a requirement imposed by the PRA.

(2) A contravention within subsection (1) or (1A)—

(a) does not, except as provided by section 23(1A), make a person guilty of an offence,

(b) does not, except as provided by section 26A, make any transaction void or unenforceable, and

(c) does not, except as provided by subsection (3), give rise to any right of action for breach of statutory duty.

(3) In prescribed cases a contravention within subsection (1) or (1A) is actionable at the suit of a person who suffers loss as a result of the contravention, subject to the defences and other incidents applying to actions for breach of statutory duty.

(4) Subsections (1) and (1A) are subject to section 39(1D).

(5) References in this Act to an authorised person acting in contravention of this section are references to the person acting in a way that results in a contravention within subsection (1) or (1A).

Financial promotion

21. Restrictions on financial promotion

(1) A person ("A") must not, in the course of business, communicate an invitation or inducement to engage in investment activity.

(2) But subsection (1) does not apply if—

(a) A is an authorised person; or

(b) the content of the communication is approved for the purposes of this section by an authorised person.

(3) In the case of a communication originating outside the United Kingdom, subsection (1) applies only if the communication is capable of having an effect in the United Kingdom.

(4) The Treasury may by order specify circumstances in which a person is to be regarded for the purposes of subsection (1) as—

(a) acting in the course of business;

(b) not acting in the course of business.

(5) The Treasury may by order specify circumstances (which may include compliance with financial promotion rules) in which subsection (1) does not apply.

(6) An order under subsection (5) may, in particular, provide that subsection (1) does not apply in relation to communications—

(a) of a specified description;

(b) originating in a specified country or territory outside the United Kingdom;

(c) originating in a country or territory which falls within a specified description of country or territory outside the United Kingdom; or

(d) originating outside the United Kingdom.

(7) The Treasury may by order repeal subsection (3).

(8) "Engaging in investment activity" means—

(a) entering or offering to enter into an agreement the making or performance of which by either party constitutes a controlled activity; or

(b) exercising any rights conferred by a controlled investment to acquire, dispose of, underwrite or convert a controlled investment.

(9) An activity is a controlled activity if—

(a) it is an activity of a specified kind or one which falls within a specified class of activity; and

(b) it relates to an investment of a specified kind, or to one which falls within a specified class of investment.

(10) An investment is a controlled investment if it is an investment of a specified kind or one which falls within a specified class of investment.

(11) Schedule 2 (except paragraph 26) applies for the purposes of subsections (9) and (10) with references to section 22 being read as references to each of those subsections.

(12) Nothing in Schedule 2, as applied by subsection (11), limits the powers conferred by subsection (9) or (10).

(13) "Communicate" includes causing a communication to be made.

(14) "Investment" includes any asset, right or interest.

(15) "Specified" means specified in an order made by the Treasury.

Regulated activities

22. Regulated activities

(1) An activity is a regulated activity for the purposes of this Act if it is an activity of a specified kind which is carried on by way of business and—

(a) relates to an investment of a specified kind; or

(b) in the case of an activity of a kind which is also specified for the purposes of this paragraph, is carried on in relation to property of any kind.

(1A) An activity is also a regulated activity for the purposes of this Act if it is an activity of a specified kind which is carried on by way of business and relates to—

(a) information about a person's financial standing, or

(b) the setting of a specified benchmark.

(2) Schedule 2 makes provision supplementing this section.

(3) Nothing in Schedule 2 limits the powers conferred by subsection (1) or (1A).

(4) "Investment" includes any asset, right or interest.

(5) "Specified" means specified in an order made by the Treasury.

(6) "Benchmark" means an index, rate or price that—

(a) is determined from time to time by reference to the state of the market,

(b) is made available to the public (whether free of charge or on payment), and

(c) is used for reference for purposes that include one or more of the following—

(i) determining the interest payable, or other sums due, under loan agreements or under other contracts relating to investments;

(ii) determining the price at which investments may be bought or sold or the value of investments;

(iii) measuring the performance of investments.

22A. Designation of activities requiring prudential regulation by PRA

(1) The Treasury may by order specify the regulated activities that are "PRA-regulated activities" for the purposes of this Act.

(2) An order under subsection (1) may—

(a) provide for exceptions;

(b) confer powers on the Treasury or either regulator;

(c) authorise the making of rules or other instruments by either regulator for purposes of, or connected with, any relevant provision;

(d) make provision in respect of any information or document which in the opinion of the Treasury or either regulator is relevant for purposes of, or connected with, any relevant provision;

(e) make such consequential, transitional, or supplemental provision as the Treasury consider appropriate for purposes of, or connected with, any relevant provision.

(3) Provision made as a result of subsection (2)(e) may amend any primary or subordinate legislation, including any provision of, or made under, this Act.

(4) "Relevant provision" means this section or any provision made under this section.

22B. Parliamentary control in relation to certain orders under section 22A

(1) This section applies to the first order made under section 22A(1).

(2) This section also applies to any subsequent order made under section 22A(1) which—

(a) contains a statement by the Treasury that, in their opinion, the effect (or one of the effects) of the proposed order would be—

(i) that an activity would become a PRA-regulated activity, or

(ii) that a PRA-regulated activity would become a regulated activity that is not a PRA-regulated activity, or

(b) amends primary legislation.

(3) No order to which this section applies may be made unless—

(a) a draft of the order has been laid before Parliament and approved by a resolution of each House, or

(b) subsection (5) applies.

(4) Subsection (5) applies if an order to which this section applies contains a statement that the Treasury are of the opinion that, by reason of urgency, it is necessary to make the order without a draft being so laid and approved.

(5) Where this subsection applies the order—

(a) must be laid before Parliament after being made, and

(b) ceases to have effect at the end of the relevant period unless before the end of that period the order is approved by a resolution of each House of Parliament (but without that affecting anything done under the order or the power to make a new order).

(6) The "relevant period" is a period of 28 days beginning with the day on which the order is made.

(7) In calculating the relevant period no account is to be taken of any time during which Parliament is dissolved or prorogued or during which both Houses are adjourned for more than 4 days.

Offences

23. Contravention of the general prohibition or section 20(1) or (1A)

(1) A person who contravenes the general prohibition is guilty of an offence and liable—

(a) on summary conviction, to imprisonment for a term not exceeding six months or a fine not exceeding the statutory maximum, or both;

(b) on conviction on indictment, to imprisonment for a term not exceeding two years or a fine, or both.

(1A) An authorised person ("A") is guilty of an offence if A carries on a credit-related regulated activity in the United Kingdom, or purports to do so, otherwise than in accordance with permission—

(a) given to that person under Part 4A, or

(b) resulting from any other provision of this Act.

(1B) In this Act "credit-related regulated activity" means a regulated activity of a kind designated by the Treasury by order.

(1C) The Treasury may designate a regulated activity under subsection (1B) only if the activity involves a person—

(a) entering into or administering an agreement under which the person provides another person with credit,

(b) exercising or being able to exercise the rights of the lender under an agreement under which another person provides a third party with credit, or

(c) taking steps to procure payment of debts due under an agreement under which another person is provided with credit.

(1D) But a regulated activity may not be designated under subsection (1B) if the agreement in question is one under which the obligation of the borrower is secured on land.

(1E) "Credit" includes any cash loan or other financial accommodation.

(1F) A person guilty of an offence under subsection (1A) is liable—

(a) on summary conviction, to imprisonment for a term not exceeding the applicable maximum term or a fine not exceeding the statutory maximum, or both;

(b) on conviction on indictment, to imprisonment for a term not exceeding two years, or a fine, or both.

(1G) The "applicable maximum term" is—

(a) in England and Wales, 12 months (or 6 months, if the offence was committed before the commencement of section 154(1) of the Criminal Justice Act 2003);

(b) in Scotland, 12 months;

(c) in Northern Ireland, 6 months.

(2) In this Act "an authorisation offence" means an offence under this section.

(3) In proceedings for an authorisation offence it is a defence for the accused to show that he took all reasonable precautions and exercised all due diligence to avoid committing the offence.

(4) Subsection (1A) is subject to section 39(1D).

(5) No proceedings may be brought against a person in respect of an offence under subsection (1A) in a case where either regulator has taken action under section 205, 206 or 206A in relation to the alleged contravention within section 20(1) or (1A).

23A. Parliamentary control in relation to certain orders under section 23

(1) This section applies to the first order made under section 23(1B).

(2) This section also applies to any subsequent order made under section 23(1B) which contains a statement by the Treasury that, in their opinion, the effect (or one of the effects) of the proposed order would be that an activity would become a credit-related regulated activity.

(3) An order to which this section applies may not be made unless a draft of the order has been laid before Parliament and approved by a resolution of each House.

24. False claims to be authorised or exempt

(1) A person who is neither an authorised person nor, in relation to the regulated activity in question, an exempt person is guilty of an offence if he—

(a) describes himself (in whatever terms) as an authorised person;

(b) describes himself (in whatever terms) as an exempt person in relation to the regulated activity; or

(c) behaves, or otherwise holds himself out, in a manner which indicates (or which is reasonably likely to be understood as indicating) that he is—

(i) an authorised person; or

(ii) an exempt person in relation to the regulated activity.

(2) In proceedings for an offence under this section it is a defence for the accused to show that he took all reasonable precautions and exercised all due diligence to avoid committing the offence.

(3) A person guilty of an offence under this section is liable on summary conviction to imprisonment for a term not exceeding six months or a fine not exceeding level 5 on the standard scale, or both.

(4) But where the conduct constituting the offence involved or included the public display of any material, the maximum fine for the offence is level 5 on the standard scale multiplied by the number of days for which the display continued.

25. Contravention of section 21

(1) A person who contravenes section 21(1) is guilty of an offence and liable—

(a) on summary conviction, to imprisonment for a term not exceeding six months or a fine not exceeding the statutory maximum, or both;

(b) on conviction on indictment, to imprisonment for a term not exceeding two years or a fine, or both.

(2) In proceedings for an offence under this section it is a defence for the accused to show—

(a) that he believed on reasonable grounds that the content of the communication was prepared, or approved for the purposes of section 21, by an authorised person; or

(b) that he took all reasonable precautions and exercised all due diligence to avoid committing the offence.

Enforceability of agreements

26. Agreements made by unauthorised persons

(1) An agreement made by a person in the course of carrying on a regulated activity in contravention of the general prohibition is unenforceable against the other party.

(2) The other party is entitled to recover—

(a) any money or other property paid or transferred by him under the agreement; and

(b) compensation for any loss sustained by him as a result of having parted with it.

(3) "Agreement" means an agreement—

(a) made after this section comes into force; and

(b) the making or performance of which constitutes, or is part of, the regulated activity in question.

(4) This section does not apply if the regulated activity is accepting deposits.

26A. Agreements relating to credit

(1) An agreement that is made by an authorised person in contravention of section 20 is unenforceable against the other party if the agreement is entered into in the course of carrying on a credit-related regulated activity involving matters falling within section 23(1C)(a).

(2) The other party is entitled to recover—

(a) any money or other property paid or transferred by that party under the agreement, and

(b) compensation for any loss sustained by that party as a result of having parted with it.

(3) In subsections (1) and (2) "agreement" means an agreement—

(a) which is made after this section comes into force, and

(b) the making or performance of which constitutes, or is part of, the credit-related regulated activity.

(4) If the administration of an agreement involves the carrying on of a credit-related regulated activity, the agreement may not be enforced by a person for the time being exercising the rights of the lender under the agreement unless that person has permission, given under Part 4A or resulting from any other provision of this Act, in relation to that activity.

(5) If the taking of steps to procure payment of debts due under an agreement involves the carrying on of a credit-related regulated activity, the agreement may not be enforced by a person for the time being exercising the rights of the lender under the agreement unless the agreement is enforced in accordance with permission—

(a) given under Part 4A to the person enforcing the agreement, or

(b) resulting from any other provision of this Act.

27. Agreements made through unauthorised persons

(1) This section applies to an agreement that—

(a) is made by an authorised person ("the provider") in the course of carrying on a regulated activity,

(b) is not made in contravention of the general prohibition,

(c) if it relates to a credit-related regulated activity, is not made in contravention of section 20, and

(d) is made in consequence of something said or done by another person ("the third party") in the course of—

(i) a regulated activity carried on by the third party in contravention of the general prohibition, or

(ii) a credit-related regulated activity carried on by the third party in contravention of section 20.

(1A) The agreement is unenforceable against the other party.

(2) The other party is entitled to recover—

(a) any money or other property paid or transferred by him under the agreement; and

(b) compensation for any loss sustained by him as a result of having parted with it.

(3) "Agreement" means an agreement—

(a) made after this section comes into force; and
(b) the making or performance of which constitutes, or is part of, the regulated activity in question carried on by the provider.

(4) This section does not apply if the regulated activity is accepting deposits.

28. Agreements made unenforceable by section 26 or 27: general cases

(1) This section applies to an agreement which is unenforceable because of section 26 or 27, other than an agreement entered into in the course of carrying on a credit-related regulated activity.

(2) The amount of compensation recoverable as a result of that section is—
(a) the amount agreed by the parties; or
(b) on the application of either party, the amount determined by the court.

(3) If the court is satisfied that it is just and equitable in the circumstances of the case, it may allow—
(a) the agreement to be enforced; or
(b) money and property paid or transferred under the agreement to be retained.

(4) In considering whether to allow the agreement to be enforced or (as the case may be) the money or property paid or transferred under the agreement to be retained the court must—
(a) if the case arises as a result of section 26, have regard to the issue mentioned in subsection (5); or
(b) if the case arises as a result of section 27, have regard to the issue mentioned in subsection (6).

(5) The issue is whether the person carrying on the regulated activity concerned reasonably believed that he was not contravening the general prohibition by making the agreement.

(6) The issue is whether the provider knew that the third party was (in carrying on the regulated activity) contravening the general prohibition.

(7) If the person against whom the agreement is unenforceable—
(a) elects not to perform the agreement, or
(b) as a result of this section, recovers money paid or other property transferred by him under the agreement,

he must repay any money and return any other property received by him under the agreement.

(8) If property transferred under the agreement has passed to a third party, a reference in section 26 or 27 or this section to that property is to be read as a reference to its value at the time of its transfer under the agreement.

(9) The commission of an authorisation offence does not make the agreement concerned illegal or invalid to any greater extent than is provided by section 26 or 27.

28A. Credit-related agreements made unenforceable by section 26, 26A or 27

(1) This section applies to an agreement that—
(a) is entered into in the course of carrying on a credit-related regulated activity, and
(b) is unenforceable because of section 26, 26A or 27.

(2) The amount of compensation recoverable as a result of that section is—
(a) the amount agreed by the parties, or
(b) on the application of either party, the amount specified in a written notice given by the FCA to the applicant.

(3) If on application by the relevant firm the FCA is satisfied that it is just and equitable in the circumstances of the case, it may by written notice to the applicant allow—
(a) the agreement to be enforced, or
(b) money paid or property transferred under the agreement to be retained.

(4) In considering whether to allow the agreement to be enforced or (as the case may be) the money or property paid or transferred under the agreement to be retained the FCA must—
(a) if the case arises as a result of section 26 or 26A, have regard to the issue mentioned in subsection (5), or
(b) if the case arises as a result of section 27, have regard to the issue mentioned in subsection (6).

(5) The issue is whether the relevant firm reasonably believed that by making the agreement the relevant firm was neither contravening the general prohibition nor contravening section 20.

(6) The issue is whether the provider knew that the third party was (in carrying on the credit-related regulated activity) either contravening the general prohibition or contravening section 20.

(7) An application to the FCA under this section by the relevant firm may relate to specified agreements or to agreements of a specified description or made at a specified time.

(8) "The relevant firm" means—

(a) in a case falling within section 26, the person in breach of the general prohibition;

(b) in a case falling within section 26A or 27, the authorised person concerned.

(9) If the FCA thinks fit, it may when acting under subsection (2)(b) or (3)—

(a) limit the determination in its notice to specified agreements, or agreements of a specified description or made at a specified time;

(b) make the determination in its notice conditional on the doing of specified acts by the applicant.

28B. Decisions under section 28A: procedure

(1) A notice under section 28A(2)(b) or (3) must—

(a) give the FCA's reasons for its determination, and

(b) give an indication of—

(i) the right to have the matter referred to the Tribunal that is conferred by subsection (3), and

(ii) the procedure on such a reference.

(2) The FCA must, so far as it is reasonably practicable to do so, give a copy of the notice to any other person who appears to it to be affected by the determination to which the notice relates.

(3) A person who is aggrieved by the determination of an application under section 28A(2)(b) or (3) may refer the matter to the Tribunal.

29. Accepting deposits in breach of general prohibition

(1) This section applies to an agreement between a person ("the depositor") and another person ("the deposit-taker") made in the course of the carrying on by the deposit-taker of accepting deposits in contravention of the general prohibition.

(2) If the depositor is not entitled under the agreement to recover without delay any money deposited by him, he may apply to the court for an order directing the deposit-taker to return the money to him.

(3) The court need not make such an order if it is satisfied that it would not be just and equitable for the money deposited to be returned, having regard to the issue mentioned in subsection (4).

(4) The issue is whether the deposit-taker reasonably believed that he was not contravening the general prohibition by making the agreement.

(5) "Agreement" means an agreement—

(a) made after this section comes into force; and

(b) the making or performance of which constitutes, or is part of, accepting deposits.

30. Enforceability of agreements resulting from unlawful communications

(1) In this section—

"unlawful communication" means a communication in relation to which there has been a contravention of section 21(1);

"controlled agreement" means an agreement the making or performance of which by either party constitutes a controlled activity for the purposes of that section; and

"controlled investment" has the same meaning as in section 21.

(2) If in consequence of an unlawful communication a person enters as a customer into a controlled agreement, it is unenforceable against him and he is entitled to recover—

(a) any money or other property paid or transferred by him under the agreement; and

(b) compensation for any loss sustained by him as a result of having parted with it.

(3) If in consequence of an unlawful communication a person exercises any rights conferred by a controlled investment, no obligation to which he is subject as a result of exercising them is enforceable against him and he is entitled to recover—

(a) any money or other property paid or transferred by him under the obligation; and

(b) compensation for any loss sustained by him as a result of having parted with it.

(4) But the court may allow—

(a) the agreement or obligation to be enforced, or

(b) money or property paid or transferred under the agreement or obligation to be retained,

if it is satisfied that it is just and equitable in the circumstances of the case.

(5) In considering whether to allow the agreement or obligation to be enforced or (as the case may be) the money or property paid or transferred under the agreement to be retained the court must have regard to the issues mentioned in subsections (6) and (7).

(6) If the applicant made the unlawful communication, the issue is whether he reasonably believed that he was not making such a communication.

(7) If the applicant did not make the unlawful communication, the issue is whether he knew that the agreement was entered into in consequence of such a communication.

(8) "Applicant" means the person seeking to enforce the agreement or obligation or retain the money or property paid or transferred.

(9) Any reference to making a communication includes causing a communication to be made.

(10) The amount of compensation recoverable as a result of subsection (2) or (3) is—

(a) the amount agreed between the parties; or

(b) on the application of either party, the amount determined by the court.

(11) If a person elects not to perform an agreement or an obligation which (by virtue of subsection (2) or (3)) is unenforceable against him, he must repay any money and return any other property received by him under the agreement.

(12) If (by virtue of subsection (2) or (3)) a person recovers money paid or property transferred by him under an agreement or obligation, he must repay any money and return any other property received by him as a result of exercising the rights in question.

(13) If any property required to be returned under this section has passed to a third party, references to that property are to be read as references to its value at the time of its receipt by the person required to return it.

PART III
AUTHORISATION AND EXEMPTION

Authorisation

31. Authorised persons

(1) The following persons are authorised for the purposes of this Act—

(a) a person who has a Part 4A permission to carry on one or more regulated activities;

(b) an EEA firm qualifying for authorisation under Schedule 3;

(c) a Treaty firm qualifying for authorisation under Schedule 4;

(d) a person who is otherwise authorised by a provision of, or made under, this Act.

(2) In this Act "authorised person" means a person who is authorised for the purposes of this Act.

...

PART VI
OFFICIAL LISTING

...

72, 73. ...

Rules

73A. Part 6 Rules

(1) The FCA may make rules ("Part 6 rules") for the purposes of this Part.

(2) Provisions of Part 6 rules expressed to relate to the official list are referred to in this Part as "listing rules".

(3) Provisions of Part 6 rules expressed to relate to disclosure of information in respect of financial instruments which have been admitted to trading on a regulated market or for which a request for admission to trading on such a market has been made, are referred to in this Part as "disclosure rules".

(4) Provisions of Part 6 rules expressed to relate to transferable securities are referred to in this Part as "prospectus rules".

(5) In relation to prospectus rules, the purposes of this Part include the purposes of the prospectus directive.

(6) Transparency rules and corporate governance rules are not listing rules, disclosure rules or prospectus rules, but are Part 6 rules.

The official list

74. The official list

(1) The FCA must maintain the official list.

(2) The FCA may admit to the official list such securities and other things as it considers appropriate.

(3) But—

(a) nothing may be admitted to the official list except in accordance with this Part; and

(b) the Treasury may by order provide that anything which falls within a description or category specified in the order may not be admitted to the official list.

(4) . . .

(5) In the following provisions of this Part—

. . .

"listing" means being included in the official list in accordance with this Part.

Listing

75. Applications for listing

(1) Admission to the official list may be granted only on an application made to the FCA in such manner as may be required by listing rules.

(2) No application for listing may be entertained by the FCA unless it is made by, or with the consent of, the issuer of the securities concerned.

(3) No application for listing may be entertained by the FCA in respect of securities which are to be issued by a body of a prescribed kind.

(4) The FCA may not grant an application for listing unless it is satisfied that—

(a) the requirements of listing rules (so far as they apply to the application), and

(b) any other requirements imposed by the FCA in relation to the application,

are complied with.

(5) An application for listing may be refused if, for a reason relating to the issuer, the FCA considers that granting it would be detrimental to the interests of investors.

(6) An application for listing securities which are already officially listed in another EEA State may be refused if the issuer has failed to comply with any obligations to which he is subject as a result of that listing.

76. Decision on application

(1) The FCA must notify the applicant of its decision on an application for listing—

(a) before the end of the period of six months beginning with the date on which the application is received; or

(b) if within that period the FCA has required the applicant to provide further information in connection with the application, before the end of the period of six months beginning with the date on which that information is provided.

(2) If the FCA fails to comply with subsection (1), it is to be taken to have decided to refuse the application.

(3) If the FCA decides to grant an application for listing, it must give the applicant written notice.

(4) If the FCA proposes to refuse an application for listing, it must give the applicant a warning notice.

(5) If the FCA decides to refuse an application for listing, it must give the applicant a decision notice.

(6) If the FCA decides to refuse an application for listing, the applicant may refer the matter to the Tribunal.

(7) If securities are admitted to the official list, their admission may not be called in question on the ground that any requirement or condition for their admission has not been complied with.

77. Discontinuance and suspension of listing

(1) The FCA may, in accordance with listing rules, discontinue the listing of any securities if satisfied that there are special circumstances which preclude normal regular dealings in them.

(2) The FCA may, in accordance with listing rules, suspend the listing of any securities.

(2A) The FCA may discontinue under subsection (1) or suspend under subsection (2) the listing of any securities on its own initiative or on the application of the issuer of those securities.

(3) If securities are suspended under subsection (2) they are to be treated, for the purposes of section 96 and paragraph 23(6) of Schedule 1ZA, as still being listed.

(4) This section applies to securities whenever they were admitted to the official list.

(5) If the FCA discontinues or suspends the listing of any securities, on its own initiative, the issuer may refer the matter to the Tribunal.

78. Discontinuance or suspension: procedure

(1) A discontinuance or suspension by the FCA on its own initiative takes effect—

(a) immediately, if the notice under subsection (2) states that that is the case;

(b) in any other case, on such date as may be specified in that notice.

(2) If on its own initiative the FCA—

(a) proposes to discontinue or suspend the listing of securities, or

(b) discontinues or suspends the listing of securities with immediate effect,

it must give the issuer of the securities written notice.

(3) The notice must—

(a) give details of the discontinuance or suspension;

(b) state the FCA's reasons for the discontinuance or suspension and for choosing the date on which it took effect or takes effect;

(c) inform the issuer of the securities that he may make representations to the FCA within such period as may be specified in the notice (whether or not he has referred the matter to the Tribunal);

(d) inform him of the date on which the discontinuance or suspension took effect or will take effect; and

(e) inform him of his right to refer the matter to the Tribunal.

(4) The FCA may extend the period within which representations may be made to it.

(5) If, having considered any representations made by the issuer of the securities, the FCA decides—

(a) to discontinue or suspend the listing of the securities, or

(b) if the discontinuance or suspension has taken effect, not to cancel it,

the FCA must give the issuer of the securities written notice.

(6) A notice given under subsection (5) must inform the issuer of the securities of his right to refer the matter to the Tribunal.

(7) If a notice informs a person of his right to refer a matter to the Tribunal, it must give an indication of the procedure on such a reference.

(8) If the FCA decides—

(a) not to discontinue or suspend the listing of the securities, or

(b) if the discontinuance or suspension has taken effect, to cancel it, the FCA must give the issuer of the securities written notice.

(9) The effect of cancelling a discontinuance is that the securities concerned are to be readmitted, without more, to the official list.

(10) If the FCA has suspended the listing of securities on its own initiative and proposes to refuse an application by the issuer of the securities for the cancellation of the suspension, it must give him a warning notice.

(11) The FCA must, having considered any representations made in response to the warning notice—

(a) if it decides to refuse the application, give the issuer of the securities a decision notice;

(b) if it grants the application, give him written notice of its decision.

(12) If the FCA decides to refuse an application for the cancellation of the suspension of listed securities, the applicant may refer the matter to the Tribunal.

(13) "Discontinuance" means a discontinuance of listing under section 77(1).

(14) "Suspension" means a suspension of listing under section 77(2).

78A. Discontinuance or suspension at the request of the issuer: procedure

(1) A discontinuance or suspension by the FCA on the application of the issuer of the securities takes effect—

(a) immediately, if the notification under subsection (2) so provides;

(b) in any other case, on such date as may be provided for in that notification.

(2) If the FCA discontinues or suspends the listing of securities on the application of the issuer of the securities it must notify the issuer (whether in writing or otherwise).

(3) The notification must—

(a) notify the issuer of the date on which the discontinuance or suspension took effect or will take effect, and

(b) notify the issuer of such other matters (if any) as are specified in listing rules.

(4) If the FCA proposes to refuse an application by the issuer of the securities for the discontinuance or suspension of the listing of the securities, it must give him a warning notice.

(5) The FCA must, having considered any representations made in response to the warning notice, if it decides to refuse the application, give the issuer of the securities a decision notice.

(6) If the FCA decides to refuse an application by the issuer of the securities for the discontinuance or suspension of the listing of the securities, the issuer may refer the matter to the Tribunal.

(7) If the FCA has suspended the listing of securities on the application of the issuer of the securities and proposes to refuse an application by the issuer for the cancellation of the suspension, it must give him a warning notice.

(8) The FCA must, having considered any representations made in response to the warning notice—

(a) if it decides to refuse the application for the cancellation of the suspension, give the issuer of the securities a decision notice;

(b) if it grants the application, give him written notice of its decision.

(9) If the FCA decides to refuse an application for the cancellation of the suspension of listed securities, the applicant may refer the matter to the Tribunal.

(10) "Discontinuance" means a discontinuance of listing under section 77(1).

(11) "Suspension" means a suspension of listing under section 77(2).

Listing particulars

79. Listing particulars and other documents

(1) Listing rules may provide that securities . . . of a kind specified in the rules may not be admitted to the official list unless—

(a) listing particulars have been submitted to, and approved by, the FCA and published; or

(b) in such cases as may be specified by listing rules, such document (other than listing particulars or a prospectus of a kind required by listing rules) as may be so specified has been published.

(2) "Listing particulars" means a document in such form and containing such information as may be specified in listing rules.

(3) For the purposes of this Part, the persons responsible for listing particulars are to be determined in accordance with regulations made by the Treasury.

(3A) Listing rules made under subsection (1) may not specify securities of a kind for which an approved prospectus is required as a result of section 85.

(4) Nothing in this section affects the FCA's general power to make listing rules.

80. General duty of disclosure in listing particulars

(1) Listing particulars submitted to the FCA under section 79 must contain all such information as investors and their professional advisers would reasonably require, and reasonably expect to find there, for the purpose of making an informed assessment of—

(a) the assets and liabilities, financial position, profits and losses, and prospects of the issuer of the securities; and

(b) the rights attaching to the securities.

(2) That information is required in addition to any information required by—

(a) listing rules, or

(b) the FCA,

as a condition of the admission of the securities to the official list.

(3) Subsection (1) applies only to information—

(a) within the knowledge of any person responsible for the listing particulars; or

(b) which it would be reasonable for him to obtain by making enquiries.

(4) In determining what information subsection (1) requires to be included in listing particulars, regard must be had (in particular) to—

(a) the nature of the securities and their issuer;

(b) the nature of the persons likely to consider acquiring them;

(c) the fact that certain matters may reasonably be expected to be within the knowledge of professional advisers of a kind which persons likely to acquire the securities may reasonably be expected to consult; and

(d) any information available to investors or their professional advisers as a result of requirements imposed on the issuer of the securities by a recognised investment exchange, by listing rules or by or under any other enactment.

81. Supplementary listing particulars

(1) If at any time after the preparation of listing particulars which have been submitted to the FCA under section 79 and before the commencement of dealings in the securities concerned following their admission to the official list—

(a) there is a significant change affecting any matter contained in those particulars the inclusion of which was required by—

(i) section 80,

(ii) listing rules, or

(iii) the FCA, or

(b) a significant new matter arises, the inclusion of information in respect of which would have been so required if it had arisen when the particulars were prepared,

the issuer must, in accordance with listing rules, submit supplementary listing particulars of the change or new matter to the FCA, for its approval and, if they are approved, publish them.

(2) "Significant" means significant for the purpose of making an informed assessment of the kind mentioned in section 80(1).

(3) If the issuer of the securities is not aware of the change or new matter in question, he is not under a duty to comply with subsection (1) unless he is notified of the change or new matter by a person responsible for the listing particulars.

(4) But it is the duty of any person responsible for those particulars who is aware of such a change or new matter to give notice of it to the issuer.

(5) Subsection (1) applies also as respects matters contained in any supplementary listing particulars previously published under this section in respect of the securities in question.

82. Exemptions from disclosure

(1) The FCA may authorise the omission from listing particulars of any information, the inclusion of which would otherwise be required by section 80 or 81, on the ground—

(a) that its disclosure would be contrary to the public interest;

(b) that its disclosure would be seriously detrimental to the issuer; or

(c) in the case of securities of a kind specified in listing rules, that its disclosure is unnecessary for persons of the kind who may be expected normally to buy or deal in securities of that kind.

(2) But—

(a) no authority may be granted under subsection (1)(b) in respect of essential information; and

(b) no authority granted under subsection (1)(b) extends to any such information.

(3) The Secretary of State or the Treasury may issue a certificate to the effect that the disclosure of any information (including information that would otherwise have to be included in listing particulars for which they are themselves responsible) would be contrary to the public interest.

(4) The FCA is entitled to act on any such certificate in exercising its powers under subsection (1)(a).

(5) This section does not affect any powers of the FCA under listing rules made as a result of section 101(2).

(6) "Essential information" means information which a person considering acquiring securities of the kind in question would be likely to need in order not to be misled about any facts which it is essential for him to know in order to make an informed assessment.

(7) "Listing particulars" includes supplementary listing particulars.

83. . . .

Transferable securities: public offers and admission to trading

84. Matters which may be dealt with by prospectus rules

(1) Prospectus rules may make provision as to—

(a) the required form and content of a prospectus (including a summary);

(b) the cases in which a summary need not be included in a prospectus;

(c) the languages which may be used in a prospectus (including a summary);

(d) the determination of the persons responsible for a prospectus;

(e) the manner in which applications to the FCA for the approval of a prospectus are to be made.

(2) Prospectus rules may also make provision as to—

(a) the period of validity of a prospectus;

(b) the disclosure of the maximum price or of the criteria or conditions according to which the final offer price is to be determined, if that information is not contained in a prospectus;

(c) the disclosure of the amount of the transferable securities which are to be offered to the public or of the criteria or conditions according to which that amount is to be determined, if that information is not contained in a prospectus;

(d) the required form and content of other summary documents (including the languages which may be used in such a document);

(e) the ways in which a prospectus that has been approved by the FCA may be made available to the public;

(f) the disclosure, publication or other communication of such information as the FCA may reasonably stipulate;

(g) the principles to be observed in relation to advertisements in connection with an offer of transferable securities to the public or admission of transferable securities to trading on a regulated market and the enforcement of those principles;

(h) the suspension of trading in transferable securities where continued trading would be detrimental to the interests of investors;

(i) elections under section 87 or under Article 2.1(m)(iii) of the prospectus directive as applied for the purposes of this Part by section 102C.

(3) ...

(4) Prospectus rules may make provision for the purpose of dealing with matters arising out of or related to any provision of the prospectus directive.

(5) In relation to cases where the home State in relation to an issuer of transferable securities is an EEA State other than the United Kingdom, prospectus rules may make provision for the recognition of elections made in relation to such securities under the law of that State in accordance with Article 1.3 or 2.1(m)(iii) of the prospectus directive.

(6) In relation to a document relating to transferable securities issued by an issuer incorporated in a non-EEA State and drawn up in accordance with the law of that State, prospectus rules may make provision as to the approval of that document as a prospectus.

(7) Nothing in this section affects the FCA's general power to make prospectus rules.

85. Prohibition of dealing etc in transferable securities without approved prospectus

(1) It is unlawful for transferable securities to which this subsection applies to be offered to the public in the United Kingdom unless an approved prospectus has been made available to the public before the offer is made.

(2) It is unlawful to request the admission of transferable securities to which this subsection applies to trading on a regulated market situated or operating in the United Kingdom unless an approved prospectus has been made available to the public before the request is made.

(3) A person who contravenes subsection (1) or (2) is guilty of an offence and liable—
- (a) on summary conviction, to imprisonment for a term not exceeding 3 months or a fine not exceeding the statutory maximum or both;
- (b) on conviction on indictment, to imprisonment for a term not exceeding 2 years or a fine or both.

(4) A contravention of subsection (1) or (2) is actionable, at the suit of a person who suffers loss as a result of the contravention, subject to the defences and other incidents applying to actions for breach of statutory duty.

(5) Subsection (1) applies to all transferable securities other than—
- (a) those listed in Schedule 11A;
- (b) such other transferable securities as may be specified in prospectus rules.

(6) Subsection (2) applies to all transferable securities other than—
- (a) those listed in Part 1 of Schedule 11A;
- (b) such other transferable securities as may be specified in prospectus rules.

(7) "Approved prospectus" means, in relation to transferable securities to which this section applies, a prospectus approved by the competent authority of the home State in relation to the issuer of the securities.

86. Exempt offers to the public

(1) A person does not contravene section 85(1) if—
- (a) the offer is made to or directed at qualified investors only;
- (b) the offer is made to or directed at fewer than 150 persons, other than qualified investors, per EEA State;
- (c) the minimum consideration which may be paid by any person for transferable securities acquired by him pursuant to the offer is at least 100,000 euros (or an equivalent amount);
- (d) the transferable securities being offered are denominated in amounts of at least 100,000 euros (or equivalent amounts); ...
- (e) the total consideration for the transferable securities being in the EEA States offered cannot exceed 100,000 euros (or an equivalent amount); or
- (f) the offer falls within subsection (1A).

(1A) An offer ("the current offer") falls within this subsection if the transferable securities are being sold or placed through a financial intermediary where—
- (a) the transferable securities have previously been the subject of one or more offers to the public;

(b) in respect of one or more of those previous offers any of paragraphs (a) to (e) of subsection (1) applied;

(c) a prospectus is available for the securities which has been approved by the FCA no earlier than 12 months before the date the current offer is made; and

(d) the issuer or other person who was responsible for drawing up the prospectus has given written consent to the use of the prospectus for the purpose of the current offer.

(2) Where—

(a) a person who is not a qualified investor ("the client") has engaged a qualified investor falling within point (1) of Section I of Annex II to the markets in financial instruments directive to act as his agent, and

(b) the terms on which the qualified investor is engaged enable him to make decisions concerning the acceptance of offers of transferable securities on the client's behalf without reference to the client,

an offer made to or directed at the qualified investor is not to be regarded for the purposes of subsection (1) as also having been made to or directed at the client.

(3) For the purposes of subsection (1)(b), the making of an offer of transferable securities to—

(a) trustees of a trust,

(b) members of a partnership in their capacity as such, or

(c) two or more persons jointly,

is to be treated as the making of an offer to a single person.

(4) In determining whether subsection (1)(e) is satisfied in relation to an offer ("offer A"), offer A is to be taken together with any other offer of transferable securities of the same class made by the same person which—

(a) was open at any time within the period of 12 months ending with the date on which offer A is first made; and

(b) had previously satisfied subsection (1)(e).

(5) For the purposes of this section, an amount (in relation to an amount denominated in euros) is an "equivalent amount" if it is an amount of equal value denominated wholly or partly in another currency or unit of account.

(6) The equivalent is to be calculated at the latest practicable date before (but in any event not more than 3 working days before) the date on which the offer is first made.

(7) "Qualified investor", in relation to an offer of transferable securities, means—

(a) a person described in points (1) to (4) of Section I of Annex II to the markets in financial instruments directive, other than a person who, before the making of the offer, has agreed in writing with the relevant firm (or each of the relevant firms) to be treated as a non-professional client in accordance with the final paragraph of Section I of Annex II to that directive;

(b) a person who has made a request to one or more relevant firms to be treated as a professional client in accordance with Section II of Annex II to that directive and has not subsequently, but before the making of the offer, agreed in writing with that relevant firm (or each of those relevant firms) to be treated as a non-professional client in accordance with the final paragraph of Section I of Annex II to that directive;

(c) a person who is an eligible counterparty in accordance with Article 24 of that directive and has not, before the making of the offer, agreed in writing with the relevant firm (or each of the relevant firms) to be treated as a non-professional client in accordance with the final paragraph of Section I of Annex II to that directive; or

(d) a person whom any relevant firm is authorised to continue to treat as a professional client in accordance with Article 71(6) of that directive.

(8) In subsection (7) "relevant firm" means an investment firm or credit institution acting in connection with the offer.

(9) Investment firms and credit institutions which are authorised persons must communicate their classification of their clients as being or not being qualified investors on request to an issuer

subject to complying with the Data Protection Act 1998 or any directly applicable EU legislation relating to data protection.

(10) In subsections (8) and (9), "credit institution" means—
(a) a credit institution authorised under the banking consolidation directive; or
(b) an institution which would satisfy the requirements for authorisation as a credit institution under that directive if it had its registered office (or if it does not have one, its head office) in an EEA State.

87. Election to have prospectus

(1) A person who proposes—
(a) to issue transferable securities to which this section applies,
(b) to offer to the public transferable securities to which this section applies, or
(c) to request the admission to a regulated market of transferable securities to which this section applies,

may elect, in accordance with prospectus rules, to have a prospectus in relation to the securities.

(2) If a person makes such an election, the provisions of this Part and of prospectus rules apply in relation to those transferable securities as if, in relation to an offer of the securities to the public or the admission of the securities to trading on a regulated market, they were transferable securities for which an approved prospectus would be required as a result of section 85.

(3) Listing rules made under section 79 do not apply to securities which are the subject of an election.

(4) The transferable securities to which this section applies are those which fall within any of the following paragraphs of Schedule 11A—
(a) paragraph 2,
(b) paragraph 4,
(c) paragraph 8, or
(d) paragraph 9,

where the United Kingdom is the home State in relation to the issuer of the securities.

Approval of prospectus

87A. Criteria for approval of prospectus by FCA

(1) The FCA may not approve a prospectus unless it is satisfied that—
(a) the United Kingdom is the home State in relation to the issuer of the transferable securities to which it relates,
(b) the prospectus contains the necessary information, and
(c) all of the other requirements imposed by or in accordance with this Part or the prospectus directive have been complied with (so far as those requirements apply to a prospectus for the transferable securities in question).

(2) The necessary information is the information necessary to enable investors to make an informed assessment of—
(a) the assets and liabilities, financial position, profits and losses, and prospects of the issuer of the transferable securities and of any guarantor; and
(b) the rights attaching to the transferable securities.

(2A) If, in the case of transferable securities to which section 87 applies, the prospectus states that the guarantor is a specified EEA State, the prospectus is not required to include other information about the guarantor.

(3) The necessary information must be presented in a form which is comprehensible and easy to analyse.

(4) The necessary information must be prepared having regard to the particular nature of the transferable securities and their issuer.

(5) The prospectus must include a summary (unless the transferable securities in question are ones in relation to which prospectus rules provide that a summary is not required).

(6) The summary must convey concisely, in non-technical language and in an appropriate structure, the key information relevant to the securities which are the subject of the prospectus and, when

read with the rest of the prospectus, must be an aid to investors considering whether to invest in the securities.

(7) Where the prospectus for which approval is sought does not include the final offer price or the amount of transferable securities to be offered to the public, the applicant must, as soon as that element is finalised—

(a) inform, in writing, the FCA and any competent authority of any EEA State which the applicant has requested be supplied with a certificate of approval under section 87I; and

(b) make that information available, in writing, to prospective investors.

(7A) The document containing the final offer price or the amount of transferable securities to be offered to the public may only contain information that relates to the securities note and must not be used to supplement the prospectus.

(8) "Prospectus" (except in subsection (5)) includes a supplementary prospectus.

(9) "the key information" means the information which is essential to enable investors to understand the transferable securities to which the prospectus relates and to decide whether to consider the offer further.

(10) The key information must include—

(a) the essential characteristics of, and risks associated with, the issuer and any guarantor, including their assets, liabilities and financial positions;

(b) the essential characteristics of, and risks associated with, investment in the transferable securities, including any rights attaching to the securities;

(c) the general terms of the offer, including an estimate of the expenses charged to an investor by the issuer and the person offering the securities to the public, if not the issuer;

(d) details of the admission to trading; and

(e) the reasons for the offer and proposed use of the proceeds.

87B. Exemptions from disclosure

(1) The FCA may authorise the omission from a prospectus of any information, the inclusion of which would otherwise be required, on the ground—

(a) that its disclosure would be contrary to the public interest;

(b) that its disclosure would be seriously detrimental to the issuer, provided that the omission would be unlikely to mislead the public with regard to any facts or circumstances which are essential for an informed assessment of the kind mentioned in section 87A(2); or

(c) that the information is only of minor importance for a specific offer to the public or admission to trading on a regulated market and unlikely to influence an informed assessment of the kind mentioned in section 87A(2).

(2) The Secretary of State or the Treasury may issue a certificate to the effect that the disclosure of any information would be contrary to the public interest.

(3) The FCA is entitled to act on any such certificate in exercising its powers under subsection (1)(a).

(4) This section does not affect any powers of the FCA under prospectus rules.

(5) "Prospectus" includes a supplementary prospectus.

87C. Consideration of application for approval

(1) The FCA must notify the applicant of its decision on an application for approval of a prospectus before the end of the period for consideration.

(2) The period for consideration—

(a) begins with the first working day after the date on which the application is received; but

(b) if the FCA gives a notice under subsection (4), is to be treated as beginning with the first working day after the date on which the notice is complied with.

(3) The period for consideration is—

(a) except in the case of a new issuer, 10 working days; or

(b) in that case, 20 working days.

(4) The FCA may by notice in writing require a person who has applied for approval of a prospectus to provide—

(a) specified documents or documents of a specified description, or

(b) specified information or information of a specified description.

(5) No notice under subsection (4) may be given after the end of the period, beginning with the first working day after the date on which the application is received, of—

(a) except in the case of a new issuer, 10 working days; or

(b) in that case, 20 working days.

(6) Subsection (4) applies only to information and documents reasonably required in connection with the exercise by the FCA of its functions in relation to the application.

(7) The FCA may require any information provided under this section to be provided in such form as it may reasonably require.

(8) The FCA may require—

(a) any information provided, whether in a document or otherwise, to be verified in such manner, or

(b) any document produced to be authenticated in such manner,

as it may reasonably require.

(9) The FCA must notify the applicant of its decision on an application for approval of a supplementary prospectus before the end of the period of 7 working days beginning with the date on which the application is received; and subsections (4) and (6) to (8) apply to such an application as they apply to an application for approval of a prospectus.

(10) The FCA's failure to comply with subsection (1) or (9) does not constitute approval of the application in question.

(11) "New issuer" means an issuer of transferable securities which—

(a) does not have transferable securities admitted to trading on any regulated market; and

(b) has not previously offered transferable securities to the public.

87D. Procedure for decision on application for approval

(1) If the FCA approves a prospectus, it must give the applicant written notice.

(2) If the FCA proposes to refuse to approve a prospectus, it must give the applicant written notice.

(3) The notice must state the FCA's reasons for the proposed refusal.

(4) If the FCA decides to refuse to approve a prospectus, it must give the applicant written notice.

(5) The notice must—

(a) give the FCA's reasons for refusing the application; and

(b) inform the applicant of his right to refer the matter to the Tribunal.

(6) If the FCA refuses to approve a prospectus, the applicant may refer the matter to the Tribunal.

(7) In this section "prospectus" includes a supplementary prospectus.

Transfer of application for approval of a prospectus

87E. Transfer by FCA

(1) The FCA may transfer an application for the approval of a prospectus or a supplementary prospectus to the competent authority of another EEA State ("the transferee authority").

(2) Before doing so, the FCA must obtain the agreement of the transferee authority and notify ESMA.

(3) The FCA must inform the applicant of the transfer within 3 working days beginning with the first working day after the date of the transfer.

(4) On making a transfer under subsection (1), the FCA ceases to have functions under this Part in relation to the application transferred.

87F. Transfer to FCA

(1) Where the FCA agrees to the transfer to it of an application for the approval of a prospectus made to the competent authority of another EEA State—

(a) the United Kingdom is to be treated for the purposes of this Part as the home State in relation to the issuer of the transferable securities to which the prospectus relates, and

(b) this Part applies to the application as if it had been made to the FCA but with the modification in subsection (2).

(2) Section 87C applies as if the date of the transfer were the date on which the application was received by the FCA.

Supplementary prospectus

87G. Supplementary prospectus

(1) Subsection (2) applies if, during the relevant period, there arises or is noted a significant new factor, material mistake or inaccuracy relating to the information included in a prospectus approved by the FCA.

(2) The person on whose application the prospectus was approved must, in accordance with prospectus rules, submit a supplementary prospectus containing details of the new factor, mistake or inaccuracy to the FCA for its approval.

(3) The relevant period begins when the prospectus is approved and ends—

(a) with the closure of the offer of the transferable securities to which the prospectus relates; or

(b) when trading in those securities on a regulated market begins.

(3A) But where the prospectus relates both to an offer of transferable securities to the public and the admission of those securities to trading on a regulated market, subsection (3) does not apply and the relevant period begins when the prospectus is approved and ends with the later of—

(a) the closure of the offer to the public to which the prospectus relates, or

(b) the time when trading in those securities on a regulated markets begins.

(4) "Significant" means significant for the purposes of making an informed assessment of the kind mentioned in section 87A(2).

(5) Any person responsible for the prospectus who is aware of any new factor, mistake or inaccuracy which may require the submission of a supplementary prospectus in accordance with subsection (2) must give notice of it to—

(a) the issuer of the transferable securities to which the prospectus relates, and

(b) the person on whose application the prospectus was approved.

(6) A supplementary prospectus must provide sufficient information to correct any mistake or inaccuracy which gave rise to the need for it.

(7) Subsection (1) applies also to information contained in any supplementary prospectus published under this section.

Passporting

87H. Prospectus approved in another EEA State

(1) A prospectus approved by the competent authority of an EEA State other than the United Kingdom is not an approved prospectus for the purposes of section 85 unless that authority has notified ESMA and provided the FCA with—

(a) a certificate of approval;

(b) a copy of the prospectus as approved; and

(c) if requested by the FCA, a translation of the summary of the prospectus.

(2) A document is not a certificate of approval unless it states that the prospectus—

(a) has been drawn up in accordance with the prospectus directive; and

(b) has been approved, in accordance with that directive, by the competent authority providing the certificate.

(3) A document is not a certificate of approval unless it states whether (and, if so, why) the competent authority providing it authorised, in accordance with the prospectus directive, the omission from the prospectus of information which would otherwise have been required to be included.

(3A) The FCA must publish on its website a list of certificates of approval provided to it in accordance with this section.

(3B) The list referred to in subsection (3A) must—

(a) be kept up-to-date,

(b) retain items on it for a period of at least 12 months, and

(c) include hyperlinks to any certificate of approval and prospectus published on the website of—
(i) the competent authority of the EEA State which provided the certificate,
(ii) the issuer, or
(iii) the regulated market where admission to trading is sought.

(4) "Prospectus" includes a supplementary prospectus.

87I. Provision of information to host Member State

(1) The FCA must, if requested to do so, supply the competent authority of a specified EEA State with—
(a) a certificate of approval;
(b) a copy of the specified prospectus (as approved by the FCA); and
(c) a translation of the summary of the specified prospectus (if the request states that one has been requested by the ... competent authority).

(1A) If the FCA supplies a certificate of approval to the competent authority of the specified EEA State, it must also supply a copy of that certificate to—
(a) the person who made the request under this section; and
(b) ESMA.

(2) Only the following may make a request under this section—
(a) the issuer of the transferable securities to which the specified prospectus relates;
(b) a person who wishes to offer the transferable securities to which the specified prospectus relates to the public in an EEA State other than (or as well as) the United Kingdom;
(c) a person requesting the admission of the transferable securities to which the specified prospectus relates to a regulated market situated or operating in an EEA State other than (or as well as) the United Kingdom.

(3) A certificate of approval must state that the prospectus—
(a) has been drawn up in accordance with this Part and the prospectus directive; and
(b) has been approved, in accordance with those provisions, by the FCA.

(4) A certificate of approval must state whether (and, if so, why) the FCA authorised, in accordance with section 87B, the omission from the prospectus of information which would otherwise have been required to be included.

(5) The FCA must comply with a request under this section—
(a) if the prospectus has been approved before the request is made, within 3 working days beginning with the date the request is received; or
(b) if the request is submitted with an application for the approval of the prospectus, on the first working day after the date on which it approves the prospectus.

(6) "Prospectus" includes a supplementary prospectus.

(7) "Specified" means specified in a request made for the purposes of this section.

Transferable securities: powers of FCA

87J. Requirements imposed as condition of approval

(1) As a condition of approving a prospectus, the FCA may by notice in writing—
(a) require the inclusion in the prospectus of such supplementary information necessary for investor protection as the FCA may specify;
(b) require a person controlling, or controlled by, the applicant to provide specified information or documents;
(c) require an auditor or manager of the applicant to provide specified information or documents;
(d) require a financial intermediary commissioned to assist either in carrying out the offer to the public of the transferable securities to which the prospectus relates or in requesting their admission to trading on a regulated market, to provide specified information or documents.

(2) "Specified" means specified in the notice.

(3) "Prospectus" includes a supplementary prospectus.

87K. Power to suspend or prohibit offer to the public

(1) This section applies where a person ("the offeror") has made an offer of transferable securities to the public in the United Kingdom ("the offer").

(2) If the FCA has reasonable grounds for suspecting that an applicable provision has been infringed, it may—

(a) require the offeror to suspend the offer for a period not exceeding 10 working days;

(b) require a person not to advertise the offer, or to take such steps as the FCA may specify to suspend any existing advertisement of the offer, for a period not exceeding 10 working days.

(3) If the FCA has reasonable grounds for suspecting that it is likely that an applicable provision will be infringed, it may require the offeror to withdraw the offer.

(4) If the FCA finds that an applicable provision has been infringed, it may require the offeror to withdraw the offer.

(5) "An applicable provision" means—

(a) a provision of this Part,

(b) a provision contained in prospectus rules,

(c) any other provision made in accordance with the prospectus directive,

applicable in relation to the offer.

87L. Power to suspend or prohibit admission to trading on a regulated market

(1) This section applies where a person has requested the admission of transferable securities to trading on a regulated market situated or operating in the United Kingdom.

(2) If the FCA has reasonable grounds for suspecting that an applicable provision has been infringed and the securities have not yet been admitted to trading on the regulated market in question, it may—

(a) require the person requesting admission to suspend the request for a period not exceeding 10 working days;

(b) require a person not to advertise the securities to which it relates, or to take such steps as the FCA may specify to suspend any existing advertisement in connection with those securities, for a period not exceeding 10 working days.

(3) If the FCA has reasonable grounds for suspecting that an applicable provision has been infringed and the securities have been admitted to trading on the regulated market in question, it may—

(a) require the market operator to suspend trading in the securities for a period not exceeding 10 working days;

(b) require a person not to advertise the securities, or to take such steps as the FCA may specify to suspend any existing advertisement in connection with those securities, for a period not exceeding 10 working days.

(4) If the FCA finds that an applicable provision has been infringed, it may require the market operator to prohibit trading in the securities on the regulated market in question.

(5) "An applicable provision" means—

(a) a provision of this Part,

(b) a provision contained in prospectus rules,

(c) any other provision made in accordance with the prospectus directive,

applicable in relation to the admission of the transferable securities to trading on the regulated market in question.

87M. Public censure of issuer

(1) If the FCA finds that—

(a) an issuer of transferable securities,

(b) a person offering transferable securities to the public, or

(c) a person requesting the admission of transferable securities to trading on a regulated market,

is failing or has failed to comply with his obligations under an applicable provision, it may publish a statement to that effect.

(2) If the FCA proposes to publish a statement, it must give the person a warning notice setting out the terms of the proposed statement.

(3) If, after considering any representations made in response to the warning notice, the FCA decides to make the proposed statement, it must give the person a decision notice setting out the terms of the statement.

(4) "An applicable provision" means—

(a) a provision of this Part,

(b) a provision contained in prospectus rules,

(c) any other provision made in accordance with the prospectus directive,

applicable to a prospectus in relation to the transferable securities in question.

(5) "Prospectus" includes a supplementary prospectus.

87N. Right to refer matters to the Tribunal

(1) A person to whom a decision notice is given under section 87M may refer the matter to the Tribunal.

(2) A person to whom a notice is given under section 87O may refer the matter to the Tribunal.

87O. Procedure under sections 87K and 87L

(1) A requirement under section 87K or 87L takes effect—

(a) immediately, if the notice under subsection (2) states that that is the case;

(b) in any other case, on such date as may be specified in that notice.

(2) If the FCA—

(a) proposes to exercise the powers in section 87K or 87L in relation to a person, or

(b) exercises any of those powers in relation to a person with immediate effect,

it must give that person written notice.

(3) The notice must—

(a) give details of the FCA's action or proposed action;

(b) state the FCA's reasons for taking the action in question and choosing the date on which it took effect or takes effect;

(c) inform the recipient that he may make representations to the FCA within such period as may be specified by the notice (whether or not he has referred the matter to the Tribunal);

(d) inform him of the date on which the action took effect or takes effect; and

(e) inform him of his right to refer the matter to the Tribunal.

(4) The FCA may extend the period within which representations may be made to it.

(5) If, having considered any representations made to it, the FCA decides to maintain, vary or revoke its earlier decision, it must give written notice to that effect to the person mentioned in subsection (2).

(6) A notice given under subsection (5) must inform that person, where relevant, of his right to refer the matter to the Tribunal.

(7) If a notice informs a person of his right to refer a matter to the Tribunal, it must give an indication of the procedure on such a reference.

(8) If a notice under this section relates to the exercise of the power conferred by section 87L(3), the notice must also be given to the person at whose request the transferable securities were admitted to trading on the regulated market.

87P. Exercise of powers at request of competent authority of another EEA State

(1) This section applies if—

(a) the competent authority of an EEA State other than the United Kingdom has approved a prospectus,

(b) the transferable securities to which the prospectus relates have been offered to the public in the United Kingdom or their admission to trading on a regulated market has been requested, and

(c) that competent authority makes a request that the FCA assist it in the performance of its functions under the law of that State in connection with the prospectus directive.

(2) For the purpose of complying with the request mentioned in subsection (1)(c), the powers conferred by sections 87K and 87L may be exercised as if the prospectus were one which had been approved by the FCA.

(3) Section 87N does not apply to an exercise of those powers as a result of this section.

(4) Section 87O does apply to such an exercise of those powers but with the omission of subsections (3)(e), (6) and (7).

Rights of investors

87Q. Right of investor to withdraw

(1) Where a person agrees to buy or subscribe for transferable securities in circumstances where the final offer price or the amount of transferable securities to be offered to the public is not included in the prospectus, he may withdraw his acceptance before the end of the withdrawal period.

(2) The withdrawal period—

(a) begins with the investor's acceptance; and

(b) ends at the end of the second working day after the date on which the FCA is informed of the information in accordance with section 87A(7).

(3) Subsection (1) does not apply if the prospectus contains—

(a) in the case of the amount of transferable securities to be offered to the public, the criteria or conditions (or both) according to which that element will be determined, or

(b) in the case of price, the criteria or conditions (or both) according to which that element will be determined or the maximum price.

(4) A person ("P") may withdraw P's acceptance of an offer of transferable securities to the public before the specified time where the conditions in subsection (5) are satisfied.

(5) The conditions are that—

(a) a prospectus which relates to an offer of transferable securities to the public has been published;

(b) a supplementary prospectus has been published;

(c) prior to the publication of the supplementary prospectus, P agreed to buy or subscribe for transferable securities to which the offer relates; and

(d) the significant new factor, material mistake or inaccuracy referred to in section 87G(1) which caused the supplementary prospectus to be published arose before delivery of the securities.

(6) The specified time is—

(a) the end of the second working day after the day on which the supplementary prospectus was published; or

(b) such later time as may be specified in the supplementary prospectus.

...

87R. ...

Sponsors

88. Sponsors

(1) Listing rules may require a person to make arrangements with a sponsor for the performance by the sponsor of such services in relation to him as may be specified in the rules.

(2) "Sponsor" means a person approved by the FCA for the purposes of the rules.

(3) Listing rules made by virtue of subsection (1) may—

(a) provide for the FCA to maintain a list of sponsors;

(b) specify services which must be performed by a sponsor;

(c) impose requirements on a sponsor in relation to the provision of services or specified services;

(d) specify the circumstances in which a person is qualified for being approved as a sponsor;

(e) provide for limitations or other restrictions to be imposed on the services to which an approval relates (whether or not the approval has already been granted);

(f) provide for the approval of a sponsor to be suspended on the application of the sponsor.

(4) If the FCA proposes—

(a) to refuse a person's application under sponsor rules,

(aa) to impose limitations or other restrictions on the services to which a person's approval relates, or

(b) to cancel a person's approval as a sponsor otherwise than at his request,

it must give him a warning notice.

(5) If, after considering any representations made in response to the warning notice, the FCA decides—

(a) to grant the application under sponsor rules,

(aa) not to impose limitations or other restrictions on the services to which a person's approval relates, or

(b) not to cancel the approval,

it must give the person concerned, and any person to whom a copy of the warning notice was given, written notice of its decision.

(6) If, after considering any representations made in response to the warning notice, the FCA decides—

(a) to refuse to grant the application under sponsor rules,

(aa) to impose limitations or other restrictions on the services to which a person's approval relates, or

(b) to cancel the approval,

it must give the person concerned a decision notice.

(7) A person to whom a decision notice is given under this section may refer the matter to the Tribunal.

(8) In this section any reference to an application under sponsor rules means—

(a) an application for approval as a sponsor,

(b) an application for the suspension of an approval as a sponsor,

(c) an application for the withdrawal of the suspension of an approval as a sponsor, or

(d) an application for the withdrawal or variation of a limitation or other restriction on the services to which a sponsor's approval relates.

88A. Disciplinary powers: contravention of s 88(3)(c) or (e)

(1) The FCA may take action against a sponsor under this section if it considers that the sponsor has contravened a requirement or restriction imposed on the sponsor by rules made as a result of section 88(3)(c) or (e).

(2) If the FCA is entitled to take action under this section against a sponsor, it may do one or more of the following—

(a) impose a penalty on the sponsor of such amount as it considers appropriate;

(b) suspend, for such period as it considers appropriate, the sponsor's approval;

(c) impose, for such period as it considers appropriate, such limitations or other restrictions in relation to the performance of services to which the sponsor's approval relates as it considers appropriate;

(d) publish a statement to the effect that the sponsor has contravened a requirement or restriction imposed on the sponsor by rules made as a result of section 88(3)(c) or (e).

(3) The period for which a suspension or restriction is to have effect may not exceed 12 months.

(4) A suspension may relate only to the performance in specified circumstances of a service to which the approval relates.

(5) A restriction may, in particular, be imposed so as to require the sponsor to take, or refrain from taking, specified action.

(6) The FCA may—

(a) withdraw a suspension or restriction; or

(b) vary a suspension or restriction so as to reduce the period for which it has effect or otherwise to limit its effect.

(7) The FCA may not take action against a sponsor under this section after the end of the limitation period unless, before the end of that period, it has given a warning notice to the sponsor under section 88B(1).

(8) "The limitation period" means the period of 3 years beginning with the first day on which the FCA knew that the sponsor had contravened the requirement or restriction.

(9) For this purpose the FCA is to be treated as knowing that a sponsor has contravened a requirement or restriction if it has information from which that can reasonably be inferred.

88B. Action under s 88A: procedure and right to refer to Tribunal

(1) If the FCA proposes to take action against a sponsor under section 88A, it must give the sponsor a warning notice.

(2) A warning notice about a proposal to impose a penalty must state the amount of the penalty.

(3) A warning notice about a proposal—

(a) to suspend an approval, or

(b) to impose a restriction in relation to the performance of a service,

must state the period for which the suspension or restriction is to have effect.

(4) A warning notice about a proposal to publish a statement must set out the terms of the statement.

(5) If the FCA decides to take action against a sponsor under section 88A, it must give the sponsor a decision notice.

(6) A decision notice about the imposition of a penalty must state the amount of the penalty.

(7) A decision notice about—

(a) the suspension of an approval, or

(b) the imposition of a restriction in relation to the performance of a service,

must state the period for which the suspension or restriction is to have effect.

(8) A decision notice about the publication of a statement must set out the terms of the statement.

(9) If the FCA decides to take action against a sponsor under section 88A, the sponsor may refer the matter to the Tribunal.

88C. Action under s 88A: statement of policy

(1) The FCA must prepare and issue a statement of its policy with respect to—

(a) the imposition of penalties, suspensions or restrictions under section 88A,

(b) the amount of penalties under that section, and

(c) the period for which suspensions or restrictions under that section are to have effect.

(2) The FCA's policy in determining what the amount of a penalty should be, or what the period for which a suspension or restriction is to have effect should be, must include having regard to—

(a) the seriousness of the contravention in question in relation to the nature of the requirement concerned,

(b) the extent to which that contravention was deliberate or reckless, and

(c) whether the sponsor concerned is an individual.

(3) The FCA may at any time alter or replace a statement issued under this section.

(4) If a statement issued under this section is altered or replaced, the FCA must issue the altered or replacement statement.

(5) In exercising, or deciding whether to exercise, its power under section 88A in the case of any particular contravention, the FCA must have regard to any statement of policy published under this section and in force at a time when the contravention in question occurred.

(6) A statement issued under this section must be published by the FCA in the way appearing to the FCA to be best calculated to bring it to the attention of the public.

(7) The FCA may charge a reasonable fee for providing a person with a copy of the statement.

(8) The FCA must, without delay, give the Treasury a copy of any statement which it publishes under this section.

88D. Statement of policy under s 88C: procedure

(1) Before issuing a statement under section 88C, the FCA must publish a draft of the proposed statement in the way appearing to the FCA to be best calculated to bring it to the attention of the public.

(2) The draft must be accompanied by notice that representations about the proposal may be made to the FCA within a specified time.

(3) Before issuing the proposed statement, the FCA must have regard to any representations made to it in accordance with subsection (2).

(4) If the FCA issues the proposed statement it must publish an account, in general terms, of—

(a) the representations made to it in accordance with subsection (2), and

(b) its response to them.

(5) If the statement differs from the draft published under subsection (1) in a way which is, in the opinion of the FCA, significant, the FCA must (in addition to complying with subsection (4)) publish details of the difference.

(6) The FCA may charge a reasonable fee for providing a person with a copy of a draft published under subsection (1).

(7) This section also applies to a proposal to alter or replace a statement.

88E. Powers exercisable to advance operational objectives

(1) The FCA may take action against a sponsor under this section if it considers that it is desirable to do so in order to advance one or more of its operational objectives.

(2) If the FCA is entitled to take action under this section against a sponsor, it may—

(a) suspend, for such period as it considers appropriate, the sponsor's approval, or

(b) impose, for such period as it considers appropriate, such limitations or other restrictions in relation to the performance of services to which the sponsor's approval relates as it considers appropriate.

(3) A suspension may relate only to the performance in specified circumstances of a service to which the approval relates.

(4) A restriction may, in particular, be imposed so as to require the sponsor to take, or refrain from taking, specified action.

(5) The FCA may—

(a) withdraw a suspension or restriction, or

(b) vary a suspension or restriction so as to reduce the period for which it has effect or otherwise to limit its effect.

(6) A person against whom the FCA takes action under this section may refer the matter to the Tribunal.

88F. Action under s 88E: procedure

(1) Action against a sponsor under section 88E takes effect—

(a) immediately, if the notice given under subsection (3) so provides, or

(b) on such later date as may be specified in the notice.

(2) If the FCA—

(a) proposes to take action against a sponsor under that section, or

(b) takes action against a sponsor under that section with immediate effect,

it must give the sponsor written notice.

(3) The notice must—

(a) give details of the action,

(b) state the FCA's reasons for taking the action and for its determination as to when the action takes effect,

(c) inform the sponsor that the sponsor may make representations to the FCA within such period as may be specified in the notice (whether or not the matter has been referred to the Tribunal),

(d) inform the sponsor of when the action takes effect,

(e) inform the sponsor of the right to refer the matter to the Tribunal, and
(f) give an indication of the procedure on such a reference.

(4) The FCA may extend the period allowed under the notice for making representations.

(5) If the FCA decides—
(a) to take the action in the way proposed, or
(b) if the action has taken effect, not to rescind it,
the FCA must give the sponsor written notice.

(6) If the FCA decides—
(a) not to take the action in the way proposed,
(b) to take action under section 88E that differs from the action originally proposed, or
(c) to rescind action which has taken effect,
the FCA must give the sponsor written notice.

(7) A notice under subsection (5) must—
(a) inform the sponsor of the right to refer the matter to the Tribunal, and
(b) give an indication of the procedure on such a reference.

(8) A notice under subsection (6)(b) must comply with subsection (3).

89. ...

Transparency obligations

89A. Transparency rules

(1) The FCA may make rules for the purposes of the transparency obligations directive.

(2) The rules may include provision for dealing with any matters arising out of or related to any provision of the transparency obligations directive.

(3) The FCA may also make rules—
(a) for the purpose of ensuring that voteholder information in respect of voting shares traded on a UK market other than a regulated market is made public or notified to the FCA;
(b) providing for persons who hold comparable instruments (see section 89F(1)(c)) in respect of voting shares to be treated, in the circumstances specified in the rules, as holding some or all of the voting rights in respect of those shares.

(4) Rules under this section may, in particular, make provision—
(a) specifying how the proportion of—
(i) the total voting rights in respect of shares in an issuer, or
(ii) the total voting rights in respect of a particular class of shares in an issuer,
held by a person is to be determined;
(b) specifying the circumstances in which, for the purposes of any determination of the voting rights held by a person ("P") in respect of voting shares in an issuer, any voting rights held, or treated by virtue of subsection (3)(b) as held, by another person in respect of voting shares in the issuer are to be regarded as held by P;
(c) specifying the nature of the information which must be included in any notification;
(d) about the form of any notification;
(e) requiring any notification to be given within a specified period;
(f) specifying the manner in which any information is to be made public and the period within which it must be made public;
(g) specifying circumstances in which any of the requirements imposed by rules under this section does not apply.

(5) Rules under this section are referred to in this Part as "transparency rules".

(6) Nothing in sections 89B to 89G affects the generality of the power to make rules under this section.

89B. Provision of voteholder information

(1) Transparency rules may make provision for voteholder information in respect of voting shares to be notified, in circumstances specified in the rules—

(a) to the issuer, or
(b) to the public,
or to both.

(2) Transparency rules may make provision for voteholder information notified to the issuer to be notified at the same time to the FCA.

(3) In this Part "voteholder information" in respect of voting shares means information relating to the proportion of voting rights held by a person in respect of the shares.

(4) Transparency rules may require notification of voteholder information relating to a person—
(a) initially, not later than such date as may be specified in the rules for the purposes of the first indent of Article 30.2 of the transparency obligations directive, and
(b) subsequently, in accordance with the following provisions.

(5) Transparency rules under subsection (4)(b) may require notification of voteholder information relating to a person only where there is a notifiable change in the proportion of—
(a) the total voting rights in respect of shares in the issuer, or
(b) the total voting rights in respect of a particular class of share in the issuer,
held by the person.

(6) For this purpose there is a "notifiable change" in the proportion of voting rights held by a person when the proportion changes—
(a) from being a proportion less than a designated proportion to a proportion equal to or greater than that designated proportion,
(b) from being a proportion equal to a designated proportion to a proportion greater or less than that designated proportion, or
(c) from being a proportion greater than a designated proportion to a proportion equal to or less than that designated proportion.

(7) In subsection (6) "designated" means designated by the rules.

89C. Provision of information by issuers of transferable securities

(1) Transparency rules may make provision requiring the issuer of transferable securities, in circumstances specified in the rules—
(a) to make public information to which this section applies, or
(b) to notify to the FCA information to which this section applies,
or to do both.

(2) In the case of every issuer, this section applies to—
(a) information required by Article 4 of the transparency obligations directive;
(b) information relating to the rights attached to the transferable securities, including information about the terms and conditions of those securities which could indirectly affect those rights; and
(c) information about new loan issues and about any guarantee or security in connection with any such issue.

(3) In the case of an issuer of debt securities, this section also applies to information required by Article 5 of the transparency obligations directive.

(4) In the case of an issuer of shares, this section also applies to—
(a) information required by Article 5 of the transparency obligations directive;
(b) information required by Article 6 of that directive;
(c) voteholder information—
(i) notified to the issuer, or
(ii) relating to the proportion of voting rights held by the issuer in respect of shares in the issuer;
(d) information relating to the issuer's capital; and
(e) information relating to the total number of voting rights in respect of shares or shares of a particular class.

89D. Notification of voting rights held by issuer

(1) Transparency rules may require notification of voteholder information relating to the proportion of voting rights held by an issuer in respect of voting shares in the issuer—

(a) initially, not later than such date as may be specified in the rules for the purposes of the second indent of Article 30.2 of the transparency obligations directive, and

(b) subsequently, in accordance with the following provisions.

(2) Transparency rules under subsection (1)(b) may require notification of voteholder information relating to the proportion of voting rights held by an issuer in respect of voting shares in the issuer only where there is a notifiable change in the proportion of—

(a) the total voting rights in respect of shares in the issuer, or

(b) the total voting rights in respect of a particular class of share in the issuer,

held by the issuer.

(3) For this purpose there is a "notifiable change" in the proportion of voting rights held by a person when the proportion changes—

(a) from being a proportion less than a designated proportion to a proportion equal to or greater than that designated proportion,

(b) from being a proportion equal to a designated proportion to a proportion greater or less than that designated proportion, or

(c) from being a proportion greater than a designated proportion to a proportion equal to or less than that designated proportion.

(4) In subsection (3) "designated" means designated by the rules.

89E. Notification of proposed amendment of issuer's constitution

Transparency rules may make provision requiring an issuer of transferable securities that are admitted to trading on a regulated market to notify a proposed amendment to its constitution—

(a) to the FCA, and

(b) to the market on which the issuer's securities are admitted,

at times and in circumstances specified in the rules.

89F. Transparency rules: interpretation etc

(1) For the purposes of sections 89A to 89G—

(a) the voting rights in respect of any voting shares are the voting rights attached to those shares,

(b) a person is to be regarded as holding the voting rights in respect of the shares—

(i) if, by virtue of those shares, he is a shareholder within the meaning of Article 2.1(e) of the transparency obligations directive;

(ii) if, and to the extent that, he is entitled to acquire, dispose of or exercise those voting rights in one or more of the cases mentioned in Article 10(a) to (h) of the transparency obligations directive;

(iii) if he holds, directly or indirectly, a financial instrument which results in an entitlement to acquire the shares and is an Article 13 instrument, and

(c) a person holds a "comparable instrument" in respect of voting shares if he holds, directly or indirectly, a financial instrument in relation to the shares which has similar economic effects to an Article 13 instrument (whether or not the financial instrument results in an entitlement to acquire the shares).

(2) Transparency rules under section 89A(3)(b) may make different provision for different descriptions of comparable instrument.

(3) For the purposes of sections 89A to 89G two or more persons may, at the same time, each be regarded as holding the same voting rights.

(4) In those sections—

"Article 13 instrument" means a financial instrument of a type determined by the European Commission under Article 13.2 of the transparency obligations directive;

"financial instrument" has the meaning given in Article 4.1(17) of Directive 2004/39/EC on markets in financial instruments;

"UK market" means a market that is situated or operating in the United Kingdom;

"voting shares" means shares of an issuer to which voting rights are attached.

89G. Transparency rules: other supplementary provisions

(1) Transparency rules may impose the same obligations on a person who has applied for the admission of transferable securities to trading on a regulated market without the issuer's consent as they impose on an issuer of transferable securities.

(2) Transparency rules that require a person to make information public may include provision authorising the FCA to make the information public in the event that the person fails to do so.

(3) The FCA may make public any information notified to the FCA in accordance with transparency rules.

(4) Transparency rules may make provision by reference to any provision of any rules made by the Panel on Takeovers and Mergers under Part 28 of the Companies Act 2006.

(5) Sections 89A to 89F and this section are without prejudice to any other power conferred by this Part to make Part 6 rules.

Power of FCA to call for information

89H. FCA's power to call for information

(1) The FCA may by notice in writing given to a person to whom this section applies require him—
- (a) to provide specified information or information of a specified description, or
- (b) to produce specified documents or documents of a specified description.

(2) This section applies to—
- (a) an issuer in respect of whom transparency rules have effect;
- (b) a voteholder;
- (c) an auditor of—
  - (i) an issuer to whom this section applies, or
  - (ii) a voteholder;
- (d) a person who controls a voteholder;
- (e) a person controlled by a voteholder;
- (f) a director or other similar officer of an issuer to whom this section applies;
- (g) a director or other similar officer of a voteholder or, where the affairs of a voteholder are managed by its members, a member of the voteholder.

(3) This section applies only to information and documents reasonably required in connection with the exercise by the FCA of functions conferred on it by or under sections 89A to 89G (transparency rules).

(4) Information or documents required under this section must be provided or produced—
- (a) before the end of such reasonable period as may be specified, and
- (b) at such place as may be specified.

(5) If a person claims a lien on a document, its production under this section does not affect the lien.

89I. Requirements in connection with call for information

(1) The FCA may require any information provided under section 89H to be provided in such form as it may reasonably require.

(2) The FCA may require—
- (a) any information provided, whether in a document or otherwise, to be verified in such manner as it may reasonably require;
- (b) any document produced to be authenticated in such manner as it may reasonably require.

(3) If a document is produced in response to a requirement imposed under section 89H, the FCA may—
- (a) take copies of or extracts from the document; or

(b) require the person producing the document, or any relevant person, to provide an explanation of the document.

(4) In subsection (3)(b) "relevant person", in relation to a person who is required to produce a document, means a person who—

(a) has been or is a director or controller of that person;

(b) has been or is an auditor of that person;

(c) has been or is an actuary, accountant or lawyer appointed or instructed by that person; or

(d) has been or is an employee of that person.

(5) If a person who is required under section 89H to produce a document fails to do so, the FCA may require him to state, to the best of his knowledge and belief, where the document is.

89J. Power to call for information: supplementary provisions

(1) The FCA may require an issuer to make public any information provided to the authority under section 89H.

(2) If the issuer fails to comply with a requirement under subsection (1), the FCA may, after seeking representations from the issuer, make the information public.

(3) In sections 89H and 89I (power of FCA to call for information)—

"control" and "controlled" have the meaning given by subsection (4) below;

"specified" means specified in the notice;

"voteholder" means a person who—

(a) holds voting rights in respect of any voting shares for the purposes of sections 89A to 89G (transparency rules), or

(b) is treated as holding such rights by virtue of rules under section 89A(3)(b).

(4) For the purposes of those sections a person ("A") controls another person ("B") if—

(a) A holds a majority of the voting rights in B,

(b) A is a member of B and has the right to appoint or remove a majority of the members of the board of directors (or, if there is no such board, the equivalent management body) of B,

(c) A is a member of B and controls alone, pursuant to an agreement with other shareholders or members, a majority of the voting rights in B, or

(d) A has the right to exercise, or actually exercises, dominant influence or control over B.

(5) For the purposes of subsection (4)(b)—

(a) any rights of a person controlled by A, and

(b) any rights of a person acting on behalf of A or a person controlled by A,

are treated as held by A.

Powers exercisable in case of infringement of transparency obligation

89K. Public censure of issuer

(1) If the FCA finds that an issuer of securities admitted to trading on a regulated market is failing or has failed to comply with an applicable transparency obligation, it may publish a statement to that effect.

(2) If the FCA proposes to publish a statement, it must give the issuer a warning notice setting out the terms of the proposed statement.

(3) If, after considering any representations made in response to the warning notice, the FCA decides to make the proposed statement, it must give the issuer a decision notice setting out the terms of the statement.

(4) A notice under this section must inform the issuer of his right to refer the matter to the Tribunal (see section 89N) and give an indication of the procedure on such a reference.

(5) In this section "transparency obligation" means an obligation under—

(a) a provision of transparency rules, or

(b) any other provision made in accordance with the transparency obligations directive.

(6) In relation to an issuer whose home State is a member State other than the United Kingdom, any reference to an applicable transparency obligation must be read subject to section 100A(2).

89L. Power to suspend or prohibit trading of securities

(1) This section applies to securities admitted to trading on a regulated market.

(2) If the FCA has reasonable grounds for suspecting that an applicable transparency obligation has been infringed by an issuer, it may—

(a) suspend trading in the securities for a period not exceeding 10 days,

(b) prohibit trading in the securities, or

(c) make a request to the operator of the market on which the issuer's securities are traded—

(i) to suspend trading in the securities for a period not exceeding 10 days, or

(ii) to prohibit trading in the securities.

(3) If the FCA has reasonable grounds for suspecting that a provision required by the transparency obligations directive has been infringed by a voteholder of an issuer, it may—

(a) prohibit trading in the securities, or

(b) make a request to the operator of the market on which the issuer's securities are traded to prohibit trading in the securities.

(4) If the FCA finds that an applicable transparency obligation has been infringed, it may require the market operator to prohibit trading in the securities.

(5) In this section "transparency obligation" means an obligation under—

(a) a provision contained in transparency rules, or

(b) any other provision made in accordance with the transparency obligations directive.

(6) In relation to an issuer whose home State is a member State other than the United Kingdom, any reference to an applicable transparency obligation must be read subject to section 100A(2).

89M. Procedure under section 89L

(1) A requirement under section 89L takes effect—

(a) immediately, if the notice under subsection (2) states that that is the case;

(b) in any other case, on such date as may be specified in the notice.

(2) If the FCA—

(a) proposes to exercise the powers in section 89L in relation to a person, or

(b) exercises any of those powers in relation to a person with immediate effect,

it must give that person written notice.

(3) The notice must—

(a) give details of the FCA's action or proposed action;

(b) state the FCA's reasons for taking the action in question and choosing the date on which it took effect or takes effect;

(c) inform the recipient that he may make representations to the FCA within such period as may be specified by the notice (whether or not he had referred the matter to the Tribunal);

(d) inform him of the date on which the action took effect or takes effect;

(e) inform him of his right to refer the matter to the Tribunal (see section 89N) and give an indication of the procedure on such a reference.

(4) The FCA may extend the period within which representations may be made to it.

(5) If, having considered any representations made to it, the FCA decides to maintain, vary or revoke its earlier decision, it must give written notice to that effect to the person mentioned in subsection (2).

89N. Right to refer matters to the Tribunal

A person—

(a) to whom a decision notice is given under section 89K (public censure), or

(b) to whom a notice is given under section 89M (procedure in connection with suspension or prohibition of trading),

may refer the matter to the Tribunal.

Corporate governance

89O. Corporate governance rules

(1) The FCA may make rules ("corporate governance rules")—

(a) for the purpose of implementing, enabling the implementation of or dealing with matters arising out of or related to, any EU obligation relating to the corporate governance of issuers who have requested or approved admission of their securities to trading on a regulated market;

(b) about corporate governance in relation to such issuers for the purpose of implementing, or dealing with matters arising out of or related to, any EU obligation.

(2) "Corporate governance", in relation to an issuer, includes—

(a) the nature, constitution or functions of the organs of the issuer;

(b) the manner in which organs of the issuer conduct themselves;

(c) the requirements imposed on organs of the issuer;

(d) the relationship between the different organs of the issuer;

(e) the relationship between the organs of the issuer and the members of the issuer or holders of the issuer's securities.

(3) The burdens and restrictions imposed by rules under this section on foreign-traded issuers must not be greater than the burdens and restrictions imposed on UK-traded issuers by—

(a) rules under this section, and

(b) listing rules.

(4) For this purpose—

"foreign-traded issuer" means an issuer who has requested or approved admission of the issuer's securities to trading on a regulated market situated or operating outside the United Kingdom;

"UK-traded issuer" means an issuer who has requested or approved admission of the issuer's securities to trading on a regulated market situated or operating in the United Kingdom.

(5) This section is without prejudice to any other power conferred by this Part to make Part 6 rules.

Primary information providers

89P. Primary information providers

(1) Part 6 rules may require issuers of financial instruments to use primary information providers for the purpose of giving information of a specified description to a market of a specified description.

(2) "Primary information provider" means a person approved by the FCA for the purposes of this section.

(3) "Specified" means specified in the Part 6 rules.

(4) Part 6 rules made by virtue of subsection (1) may—

(a) provide for the FCA to maintain a list of providers;

(b) impose requirements on a provider in relation to the giving of information or of information of a specified description;

(c) specify the circumstances in which a person is qualified for being approved as a provider;

(d) provide for limitations or other restrictions to be imposed on the giving of information to which an approval relates (whether or not the approval has already been granted);

(e) provide for the approval of a provider to be suspended on the application of the provider.

(5) If the FCA proposes—

(a) to refuse a person's application under information provider rules,

(b) to impose limitations or other restrictions on the giving of information to which a person's approval relates, or

(c) to cancel a person's approval as a provider otherwise than at the person's request,

it must give the person a warning notice.

(6) If the FCA decides—

(a) to grant the application under information provider rules,

(b) not to impose limitations or other restrictions on the giving of information to which a person's approval relates, or

(c) not to cancel the approval,

it must give the person concerned written notice of its decision.

(7) If the FCA decides—

(a) to refuse to grant the application under information provider rules,

(b) to impose limitations or other restrictions on the giving of information to which a person's approval relates, or

(c) to cancel the approval,

it must give the person concerned a decision notice.

(8) A person to whom a decision notice is given under this section may refer the matter to the Tribunal.

(9) In this section any reference to an application under information provider rules means—

(a) an application for approval as a provider,

(b) an application for the suspension of an approval as a provider,

(c) an application for the withdrawal of the suspension of an approval as a provider, or

(d) an application for the withdrawal or variation of a limitation or other restriction on the giving of information to which a provider's approval relates.

89Q. Disciplinary powers: contravention of s 89P(4)(b) or (d)

(1) The FCA may take action against a provider under this section if it considers that the provider has contravened a requirement or restriction imposed on the provider by rules made as a result of section 89P(4)(b) or (d).

(2) If the FCA is entitled to take action under this section against a provider, it may do one or more of the following—

(a) impose a penalty on the provider of such amount as it considers appropriate;

(b) suspend, for such period as it considers appropriate, the provider's approval;

(c) impose, for such period as it considers appropriate, such limitations or other restrictions in relation to the giving by the provider of information as it considers appropriate;

(d) publish a statement to the effect that the provider has contravened a requirement or restriction imposed on the provider by rules made as a result of section 89P(4)(b) or (d).

(3) The period for which a suspension or restriction is to have effect may not exceed 12 months.

(4) A suspension may relate only to the giving of information in specified circumstances.

(5) A restriction may, in particular, be imposed so as to require the provider to take, or refrain from taking, specified action.

(6) The FCA may—

(a) withdraw a suspension or restriction, or

(b) vary a suspension or restriction so as to reduce the period for which it has effect or otherwise to limit its effect.

(7) The FCA may not take action against a provider under this section after the end of the limitation period unless, before the end of that period, it has given a warning notice to the provider under section 89R(1).

(8) "The limitation period" means the period of 3 years beginning with the first day on which the FCA knew that the provider had contravened the requirement or restriction.

(9) For this purpose the FCA is to be treated as knowing that a provider has contravened a requirement or restriction if it has information from which that can reasonably be inferred.

89R. Action under s 89Q: procedure and right to refer to Tribunal

(1) If the FCA proposes to take action against a provider under section 89Q, it must give the provider a warning notice.

(2) A warning notice about a proposal to impose a penalty must state the amount of the penalty.

(3) A warning notice about a proposal—

(a) to suspend an approval, or

(b) to impose a restriction in relation to the giving of information,

must state the period for which the suspension or restriction is to have effect.

(4) A warning notice about a proposal to publish a statement must set out the terms of the statement.

(5) If the FCA decides to take action against a provider under section 89Q, it must give the provider a decision notice.

(6) A decision notice about the imposition of a penalty must state the amount of the penalty.

(7) A decision notice about—

(a) the suspension of an approval, or

(b) the imposition of a restriction in relation to the giving of information,

must state the period for which the suspension or restriction is to have effect.

(8) A decision notice about the publication of a statement must set out the terms of the statement.

(9) If the FCA decides to take action against a provider under section 89Q, the provider may refer the matter to the Tribunal.

89S. Action under s 89Q: statement of policy

(1) The FCA must prepare and issue a statement of its policy with respect to—

(a) the imposition of penalties, suspensions or restrictions under section 89Q,

(b) the amount of penalties under that section,

(c) the period for which suspensions or restrictions under that section are to have effect, and

(d) the matters in relation to which suspensions or restrictions under that section are to have effect.

(2) The FCA's policy in determining what the amount of a penalty should be, or what the period for which a suspension or restriction is to have effect should be, must include having regard to—

(a) the seriousness of the contravention in question in relation to the nature of the requirement concerned,

(b) the extent to which that contravention was deliberate or reckless, and

(c) whether the provider concerned is an individual.

(3) The FCA may at any time alter or replace a statement issued under this section.

(4) If a statement issued under this section is altered or replaced, the FCA must issue the altered or replacement statement.

(5) In exercising, or deciding whether to exercise, its power under section 89Q in the case of any particular contravention, the FCA must have regard to any statement of policy published under this section and in force at a time when the contravention in question occurred.

(6) A statement issued under this section must be published by the FCA in the way appearing to the FCA to be best calculated to bring it to the attention of the public.

(7) The FCA may charge a reasonable fee for providing a person with a copy of the statement.

(8) The FCA must, without delay, give the Treasury a copy of any statement which it publishes under this section.

89T. Statement of policy under s 89S: procedure

(1) Before issuing a statement under section 89S, the FCA must publish a draft of the proposed statement in the way appearing to the FCA to be best calculated to bring it to the attention of the public.

(2) The draft must be accompanied by notice that representations about the proposal may be made to the FCA within a specified time.

(3) Before issuing the proposed statement, the FCA must have regard to any representations made to it in accordance with subsection (2).

(4) If the FCA issues the proposed statement it must publish an account, in general terms, of—

(a) the representations made to it in accordance with subsection (2); and

(b) its response to them.

(5) If the statement differs from the draft published under subsection (1) in a way which is, in the opinion of the FCA, significant, the FCA must (in addition to complying with subsection (4)) publish details of the difference.

(6) The FCA may charge a reasonable fee for providing a person with a copy of a draft published under subsection (1).

(7) This section also applies to a proposal to alter or replace a statement.

89U. Powers exercisable to advance operational objectives

(1) The FCA may take action against a provider under this section if it considers that it is desirable to do so in order to advance one or more of its operational objectives.

(2) If the FCA is entitled to take action under this section against a provider, it may—

(a) suspend, for such period as it considers appropriate, the provider's approval, or

(b) impose, for such period as it considers appropriate, such limitations or other restrictions in relation to the giving by the provider of information as it considers appropriate.

(3) A suspension may relate only to the giving of information in specified circumstances.

(4) A restriction may, in particular, be imposed so as to require the provider to take, or refrain from taking, specified action.

(5) The FCA may—

(a) withdraw a suspension or restriction, or

(b) vary a suspension or restriction so as to reduce the period for which it has effect or otherwise to limit its effect.

(6) A person against whom the FCA takes action under this section may refer the matter to the Tribunal.

89V. Action under s 89U: procedure

(1) Action against a provider under section 89U takes effect—

(a) immediately, if the notice given under subsection (2) so provides, or

(b) on such later date as may be specified in the notice.

(2) If the FCA—

(a) proposes to take action against a provider under that section, or

(b) takes action against a provider under that section with immediate effect,

it must give the provider written notice.

(3) The notice must—

(a) give details of the action,

(b) state the FCA's reasons for taking the action and for its determination as to when the action takes effect,

(c) inform the provider that the provider may make representations to the FCA within such period as may be specified in the notice (whether or not the matter has been referred to the Tribunal),

(d) inform the provider of when the action takes effect,

(e) inform the provider of the right to refer the matter to the Tribunal, and

(f) give an indication of the procedure on such a reference.

(4) The FCA may extend the period allowed under the notice for making representations.

(5) If the FCA decides—

(a) to take the action in the way proposed, or

(b) if the action has taken effect, not to rescind it,

the FCA must give the provider written notice.

(6) If the FCA decides—

(a) not to take the action in the way proposed,

(b) to take action under section 89U that differs from the action originally proposed, or

(c) to rescind action which has taken effect,

the FCA must give the provider written notice.

(7) A notice under subsection (5) must—

(a) inform the provider of the right to refer the matter to the Tribunal, and

(b) give an indication of the procedure on such a reference.

(8) A notice under subsection (6)(b) must comply with subsection (3).

Compensation for false or misleading statements etc

90. Compensation for statements in listing particulars or prospectus

(1) Any person responsible for listing particulars is liable to pay compensation to a person who has—
(a) acquired securities to which the particulars apply; and
(b) suffered loss in respect of them as a result of—
(i) any untrue or misleading statement in the particulars; or
(ii) the omission from the particulars of any matter required to be included by section 80 or 81.

(2) Subsection (1) is subject to exemptions provided by Schedule 10.

(3) If listing particulars are required to include information about the absence of a particular matter, the omission from the particulars of that information is to be treated as a statement in the listing particulars that there is no such matter.

(4) Any person who fails to comply with section 81 is liable to pay compensation to any person who has—
(a) acquired securities of the kind in question; and
(b) suffered loss in respect of them as a result of the failure.

(5) Subsection (4) is subject to exemptions provided by Schedule 10.

(6) This section does not affect any liability which may be incurred apart from this section.

(7) References in this section to the acquisition by a person of securities include references to his contracting to acquire them or any interest in them.

(8) No person shall, by reason of being a promoter of a company or otherwise, incur any liability for failing to disclose information which he would not be required to disclose in listing particulars in respect of a company's securities—
(a) if he were responsible for those particulars; or
(b) if he is responsible for them, which he is entitled to omit by virtue of section 82.

(9) The reference in subsection (8) to a person incurring liability includes a reference to any other person being entitled as against that person to be granted any civil remedy or to rescind or repudiate an agreement.

(10) "Listing particulars", in subsection (1) and Schedule 10, includes supplementary listing particulars.

(11) This section applies in relation to a prospectus as it applies to listing particulars, with the following modifications—
(a) references in this section or in Schedule 10 to listing particulars, supplementary listing particulars or sections 80, 81 or 82 are to be read, respectively, as references to a prospectus, supplementary prospectus and sections 87A, 87G and 87B;
(b) references in Schedule 10 to admission to the official list are to be read as references to admission to trading on a regulated market;
(c) in relation to a prospectus, "securities" means "transferable securities".

(12) A person is not to be subject to civil liability solely on the basis of a summary in a prospectus unless the summary, when read with the rest of the prospectus—
(a) is misleading, inaccurate or inconsistent; or
(b) does not provide key information (as defined in section 87A(9) and (10)),
and in this subsection a summary includes any translation of it.

90ZA. Liability for key investor information

(1) A person is not to be subject to civil liability solely on the basis of the key investor information produced in relation to a collective investment scheme or a sub-fund of such a scheme in accordance with rules or other provisions implementing Chapter IX of the UCITS directive, or of any translation of that information, unless the key investor information is misleading, inaccurate or inconsistent with the relevant parts of the prospectus published for that collective investment scheme or sub-fund in accordance with rules made by the FCA under section 248 of this Act.

(2) In this section, a reference to a sub-fund of a collective investment scheme is a reference to a part of the property of the collective investment scheme which forms a separate pool where—

(a) the collective investment scheme provides arrangements for separate pooling of the contributions of the participants and the profits and income out of which payments are made to them; and

(b) the participants are entitled to exchange rights in one pool for rights in another.

90A. Liability of issuers in connection with published information

Schedule 10A makes provision about the liability of issuers of securities to pay compensation to persons who have suffered loss as a result of—

(a) a misleading statement or dishonest omission in certain published information relating to the securities, or

(b) a dishonest delay in publishing such information.

90B. Power to make further provision about liability for published information

(1) The Treasury may by regulations make provision about the liability of issuers of securities traded on a regulated market, and other persons, in respect of information published to holders of securities, to the market or to the public generally.

(2) Regulations under this section may amend any primary or subordinate legislation, including any provision of, or made under, this Act.

Penalties

91. Penalties for breach of Part 6 rules

(1) If the FCA considers that—

(a) an issuer of listed securities, or

(b) an applicant for listing,

has contravened any provision of listing rules, it may impose on him a penalty of such amount as it considers appropriate.

(1ZA) If the FCA considers that—

(a) an issuer who has requested or approved the admission of a financial instrument to trading on a regulated market,

(b) a person discharging managerial responsibilities within such an issuer, or

(c) a person connected with such a person discharging managerial responsibilities,

has contravened any provision of disclosure rules, it may impose on him a penalty of such amount as it considers appropriate.

(1A) If the FCA considers that—

(a) an issuer of transferable securities,

(b) a person offering transferable securities to the public or requesting their admission to trading on a regulated market,

(c) an applicant for the approval of a prospectus in relation to transferable securities,

(d) a person on whom a requirement has been imposed under section 87K or 87L, or

(e) any other person to whom a provision of the prospectus directive applies,

has contravened a provision of this Part or of prospectus rules, or a provision otherwise made in accordance with the prospectus directive or a requirement imposed on him under such a provision, it may impose on him a penalty of such amount as it considers appropriate.

(1B) If the FCA considers—

(a) that a person has contravened—

(i) a provision of transparency rules or a provision otherwise made in accordance with the transparency obligations directive, or

(ii) a provision of corporate governance rules, or

(b) that a person on whom a requirement has been imposed under section 89L (power to suspend or prohibit trading of securities in case of infringement of applicable transparency obligation), has contravened that requirement, it may impose on the person a penalty of such amount as it considers appropriate.

(2) If, in the case of a contravention by a person referred to in subsection (1), (1ZA)(a), (1A) or (1B) ("P"), the FCA considers that another person who was at the material time a director of P was knowingly concerned in the contravention, it may impose upon him a penalty of such amount as it considers appropriate.

(3) If the FCA is entitled to impose a penalty on a person under this section in respect of a particular matter it may, instead of imposing a penalty on him in respect of that matter, publish a statement censuring him.

(4) Nothing in this section prevents the FCA from taking any other steps which it has power to take under this Part.

(5) A penalty under this section is payable to the FCA.

(6) The FCA may not take action against a person under this section after the end of the period of 3 years beginning with the first day on which it knew of the contravention unless proceedings against that person, in respect of the contravention, were begun before the end of that period.

(7) For the purposes of subsection (6)—

(a) the FCA is to be treated as knowing of a contravention if it has information from which the contravention can reasonably be inferred; and

(b) proceedings against a person in respect of a contravention are to be treated as begun when a warning notice is given to him under section 92.

92. Warning notices

(1) If the FCA proposes to take action against a person under section 91, it must give him a warning notice.

(2) A warning notice about a proposal to impose a penalty must state the amount of the proposed penalty.

(3) A warning notice about a proposal to publish a statement must set out the terms of the proposed statement.

(4) If the FCA decides to take action against a person under section 91, it must give him a decision notice.

(5) A decision notice about the imposition of a penalty must state the amount of the penalty.

(6) A decision notice about the publication of a statement must set out the terms of the statement.

(7) If the FCA decides to take action against a person under section 91, he may refer the matter to the Tribunal.

93. Statement of policy

(1) The FCA must prepare and issue a statement ("its policy statement") of its policy with respect to—

(a) the imposition of penalties under section 91; and

(b) the amount of penalties under that section.

(2) The FCA's policy in determining what the amount of a penalty should be must include having regard to—

(a) the seriousness of the contravention in question in relation to the nature of the requirement contravened;

(b) the extent to which that contravention was deliberate or reckless; and

(c) whether the person on whom the penalty is to be imposed is an individual.

(3) The FCA may at any time alter or replace its policy statement.

(4) If its policy statement is altered or replaced, the FCA must issue the altered or replacement statement.

(5) In exercising, or deciding whether to exercise, its power under section 91 in the case of any particular contravention, the FCA must have regard to any policy statement published under this section and in force at the time when the contravention in question occurred.

(6) The FCA must publish a statement issued under this section in the way appearing to the FCA to be best calculated to bring it to the attention of the public.

(7) The FCA may charge a reasonable fee for providing a person with a copy of the statement.

(8) The FCA must, without delay, give the Treasury a copy of any policy statement which it publishes under this section.

94. Statements of policy: procedure

(1) Before issuing a statement under section 93, the FCA must publish a draft of the proposed statement in the way appearing to the FCA to be best calculated to bring it to the attention of the public.

(2) The draft must be accompanied by notice that representations about the proposal may be made to the FCA within a specified time.

(3) Before issuing the proposed statement, the FCA must have regard to any representations made to it in accordance with subsection (2).

(4) If the FCA issues the proposed statement it must publish an account, in general terms, of—

(a) the representations made to it in accordance with subsection (2); and

(b) its response to them.

(5) If the statement differs from the draft published under subsection (1) in a way which is, in the opinion of the FCA, significant, the competent authority must (in addition to complying with subsection (4)) publish details of the difference.

(6) The FCA may charge a reasonable fee for providing a person with a copy of a draft published under subsection (1).

(7) This section also applies to a proposal to alter or replace a statement.

...

95. ...

Miscellaneous

96. Obligations of issuers of listed securities

(1) Listing rules may—

(a) specify requirements to be complied with by issuers of listed securities; and

(b) make provision with respect to the action that may be taken by the FCA in the event of non-compliance.

(2) If the rules require an issuer to publish information, they may include provision authorising the FCA to publish it in the event of his failure to do so.

(3) This section applies whenever the listed securities were admitted to the official list.

96A. Disclosure of information requirements

(1) Disclosure rules must include provision specifying the disclosure of information requirements to be complied with by—

(a) issuers who have requested or approved admission of their financial instruments to trading on a regulated market in the United Kingdom;

(b) persons acting on behalf of or for the account of such issuers;

(c) persons discharging managerial responsibilities within an issuer—

(i) who is registered in the United Kingdom and who has requested or approved admission of its shares to trading on a regulated market; or

(ii) who is not registered in the United Kingdom or any other EEA State but who has requested or approved admission of its shares to trading on a regulated market and whose home State is the United Kingdom;

(d) persons connected to such persons discharging managerial responsibilities.

(2) The rules must in particular—

(a) require an issuer to publish specified inside information;

(b) require an issuer to publish any significant change concerning information it has already published in accordance with paragraph (a);

(c) allow an issuer to delay the publication of inside information in specified circumstances;

(d) require an issuer (or a person acting on his behalf or for his account) who discloses inside information to a third party to publish that information without delay in specified circumstances;

(e) require an issuer (or person acting on his behalf or for his account) to draw up a list of those persons working for him who have access to inside information relating directly or indirectly to that issuer; and

(f) require persons discharging managerial responsibilities within an issuer falling within subsection (1)(c)(i) or (ii), and persons connected to such persons discharging managerial responsibilities, to disclose transactions conducted on their own account in shares of the issuer, or derivatives or any other financial instrument relating to those shares.

(3) Disclosure rules may make provision with respect to the action that may be taken by the FCA in respect of non-compliance.

96B. Disclosure rules: persons responsible for compliance

(1) For the purposes of the provisions of this Part relating to disclosure rules, a "person discharging managerial responsibilities within an issuer" means—

(a) a director of an issuer falling within section 96A(1)(c)(i) or (ii); or

(b) a senior executive of such an issuer who—

(i) has regular access to inside information relating, directly or indirectly, to the issuer, and

(ii) has power to make managerial decisions affecting the future development and business prospects of the issuer.

(2) Schedule 11B (connected persons) has effect for the purposes of the provisions of this Part relating to disclosure rules.

96C. Suspension of trading

(1) The FCA may, in accordance with disclosure rules, suspend trading in a financial instrument.

(2) If the FCA does so, the issuer of that financial instrument may refer the matter to the Tribunal.

(3) The provisions relating to suspension of listing of securities in section 78 apply to the suspension of trading in a financial instrument and the references to listing and securities are to be read as references to trading and financial instruments respectively for the purposes of this section.

97. Appointment by FCA of persons to carry out investigations

(1) Subsection (2) applies if it appears to the FCA that there are circumstances suggesting that—

(a) there may have been a contravention of—

(i) a provision of this Part or of Part 6 rules, or

(ii) a provision otherwise made in accordance with the prospectus directive or the transparency obligations directive;

(b) a person who was at the material time a director of a person mentioned in section 91(1), (1ZA)(a), (1A) or (1B) has been knowingly concerned in a contravention by that person of—

(i) a provision of this Part or of Part 6 rules, or

(ii) a provision otherwise made in accordance with the prospectus directive or the transparency obligations directive;

(c) . . .

(d) there may have been a contravention of section 85 or 87G.

(2) The FCA may appoint one or more competent persons to conduct an investigation on its behalf.

(3) Part XI applies to an investigation under subsection (2) as if—

(a) the investigator were appointed under section 167(1);

(b) references to the investigating authority in relation to him were to the FCA;

(c) references to the offences mentioned in section 168 were to those mentioned in subsection (1)(d);

(d) references to an authorised person were references to the person under investigation.

98–100. . . .

100A. Exercise of powers where UK is host member state

(1) This section applies to the exercise by the FCA of any power under this Part exercisable in case of infringement of—

(a) a provision of prospectus rules or any other provision made in accordance with the prospectus directive, or

(b) a provision of transparency rules or any other provision made in accordance with the transparency obligations directive,

in relation to an issuer whose home State is a member State other than the United Kingdom.

(2) The FCA may act in such a case only in respect of the infringement of a provision required by the relevant directive.

Any reference to an applicable provision or applicable transparency obligation shall be read accordingly.

(3) If the FCA finds that there has been such an infringement, it must—

(a) give a notice to that effect to the competent authority of the person's home State requesting it—

(i) to take all appropriate measures for the purpose of ensuring that the person remedies the situation that has given rise to the notice, and

(ii) to inform the FCA of the measures it proposes to take or has taken or the reasons for not taking such measures, and

(b) notify ESMA.

(4) The FCA may not act further unless satisfied—

(a) that the competent authority of the person's home State has failed or refused to take measures for the purpose mentioned in subsection (3)(a), or

(b) that the measures taken by that authority have proved inadequate for that purpose.

This does not affect exercise of the powers under section 87K(2), 87L(2) or (3) or 89L(2) or (3) (powers to protect market).

(5) If the FCA is so satisfied, it must, after informing the competent authority of the person's home State and ESMA, take all appropriate measures to protect investors.

(6) In such a case the FCA must inform the Commission and ESMA of the measures at the earliest opportunity.

101. Part 6 rules: general provisions

(1) ...

(2) Part 6 rules may authorise the FCA to dispense with or modify the application of the rules in particular cases and by reference to any circumstances.

(3)–(8) ...

102. ...

Interpretative provisions

102A. Meaning of "securities" etc.

(1) This section applies for the purposes of this Part.

(2) "Securities" means (except in section 74(2) and the expression "transferable securities") anything which has been, or may be, admitted to the official list.

(3) "Transferable securities" means anything which is a transferable security for the purposes of Directive 2004/39/EC of the European Parliament and of the Council on markets in financial instruments, other than money-market instruments for the purposes of that directive which have a maturity of less than 12 months.

(3A) "Debt securities" has the meaning given in Article 2.1(b) of the transparency obligations directive.

(4) "Financial instrument" has (except in section 89F) the meaning given in Article 1.3 of Directive 2003/6/EC of the European Parliament and of the Council of 28 January 2003 on insider dealing

and market manipulation (as modified by Article 69 of Directive 2004/39/EC on markets in financial instruments).

(5) "Non-equity transferable securities" means all transferable securities that are not equity securities; and for this purpose "equity securities" has the meaning given in Article 2.1(b) of the prospectus directive.

(6) "Issuer"—

(a) in relation to an offer of transferable securities to the public or admission of transferable securities to trading on a regulated market for which an approved prospectus is required as a result of section 85, means a legal person who issues or proposes to issue the transferable securities in question,

(aa) in relation to transparency rules, means a legal person whose securities are admitted to trading on a regulated market or whose voting shares are admitted to trading on a UK market other than a regulated market, and in the case of depository receipts representing securities, the issuer is the issuer of the securities represented;

(b) in relation to anything else which is or may be admitted to the official list, has such meaning as may be prescribed by the Treasury, and

(c) in any other case, means a person who issues financial instruments.

102B. Meaning of "offer of transferable securities to the public" etc.

(1) For the purposes of this Part there is an offer of transferable securities to the public if there is a communication to any person which presents sufficient information on—

(a) the transferable securities to be offered, and

(b) the terms on which they are offered,

to enable an investor to decide to buy or subscribe for the securities in question.

(2) For the purposes of this Part, to the extent that an offer of transferable securities is made to a person in the United Kingdom it is an offer of transferable securities to the public in the United Kingdom.

(3) The communication may be made—

(a) in any form;

(b) by any means.

(4) Subsection (1) includes the placing of securities through a financial intermediary.

(5) Subsection (1) does not include a communication in connection with trading on—

(a) a regulated market;

(b) a multilateral trading facility; or

(c) a market prescribed by an order under section 130A(3).

(6) "Multilateral trading facility" means a multilateral system, operated by an investment firm ... or a market operator, which brings together multiple third-party buying and selling interests in financial instruments in accordance with non-discretionary rules so as to result in a contract.

102C. Meaning of "home State" in relation to transferable securities

In this Part, in relation to an issuer of transferable securities, the "home-State" is the EEA State which is the "home Member State" for the purposes of the prospectus directive (which is to be determined in accordance with Article 2.1(m) of that directive).

103. Interpretation of this Part

(1) In this Part, save where the context otherwise requires—

"disclosure rules" has the meaning given in section 73A;

"inside information" has the meaning given in section 118C;

"listed securities" means anything which has been admitted to the official list;

"listing" has the meaning given in section 74(5);

"listing particulars" has the meaning given in section 79(2);

"listing rules" has the meaning given in section 73A;

"market operator" means a person who manages or operates the business of a regulated market;

"offer of transferable securities to the public" has the meaning given in section 102B;

"the official list" means the list maintained by the FCA as that list has effect for the time being;
"Part 6 rules" has the meaning given in section 73A;
"the prospectus directive" means Directive 2003/71/EC of the European Parliament and of the Council of 4 November 2003 on the prospectus to be published when securities are offered to the public or admitted to trading as amended by Directive 2010/73/EU of the European Parliament and of the Council of 24 November 2010 and by Directive 2010/78/EU of the European Parliament and of the Council of 24 November 2010;
"prospectus rules" has the meaning given in section 73A;
"regulated market" has the meaning given in Article 4.1(14) of Directive 2004/39/EC of the European Parliament and of the Council on markets in financial instruments;
"supplementary prospectus" has the meaning given in section 87G;
"the transparency obligations directive" means Directive 2004/ 109/EC of the European Parliament and of the Council relating to the harmonisation of transparency requirements in rela-tion to information about issuers whose securities are admitted to trading on a regulated market as amended by Directive 2010/73/EU of the European Parliament and of the Council of 24 November 2010 and by Directive 2010/78/EU of the European Parliament and of the Council of 24 November 2010;
"transparency rules" has the meaning given by section 89A(5);
"voteholder information" has the meaning given by section 89B(3);
"working day" means any day other that a Saturday, a Sunday, Christmas Day, Good Friday or a day which is a bank holiday under the Banking and Financial Dealings Act 1971 in any part of the United Kingdom.

(2), (3) ...

...

PART VIII
PENALTIES FOR MARKET ABUSE

Market abuse

118. Market abuse

(1) For the purposes of this Act, market abuse is behaviour (whether by one person alone or by two or more persons jointly or in concert) which—
(a) occurs in relation to—
(i) qualifying investments admitted to trading on a prescribed market,
(ii) qualifying investments in respect of which a request for admission to trading on such a market has been made, or
(iii) in the case of subsection (2) or (3) behaviour, investments which are related investments in relation to such qualifying investments, and
(b) falls within any one or more of the types of behaviour set out in subsections (2) to (8).

(2) The first type of behaviour is where an insider deals, or attempts to deal, in a qualifying investment or related investment on the basis of inside information relating to the investment in question.

(3) The second is where an insider discloses inside information to another person otherwise than in the proper course of the exercise of his employment, profession or duties.

(4) The third is where the behaviour (not falling within subsection (2) or (3))—
(a) is based on information which is not generally available to those using the market but which, if available to a regular user of the market, would be, or would be likely to be, regarded by him as relevant when deciding the terms on which transactions in qualifying investments should be effected, and
(b) is likely to be regarded by a regular user of the market as a failure on the part of the person concerned to observe the standard of behaviour reasonably expected of a person in his position in relation to the market.

(5) The fourth is where the behaviour consists of effecting transactions or orders to trade (otherwise than for legitimate reasons and in conformity with accepted market practices on the relevant market) which—

(a) give, or are likely to give, a false or misleading impression as to the supply of, or demand for, or as to the price of, one or more qualifying investments, or

(b) secure the price of one or more such investments at an abnormal or artificial level.

(6) The fifth is where the behaviour consists of effecting transactions or orders to trade which employ fictitious devices or any other form of deception or contrivance.

(7) The sixth is where the behaviour consists of the dissemination of information by any means which gives, or is likely to give, a false or misleading impression as to a qualifying investment by a person who knew or could reasonably be expected to have known that the information was false or misleading.

(8) The seventh is where the behaviour (not falling within subsection (5), (6) or (7))—

(a) is likely to give a regular user of the market a false or misleading impression as to the supply of, demand for or price or value of, qualifying investments, or

(b) would be, or would be likely to be, regarded by a regular user of the market as behaviour that would distort, or would be likely to distort, the market in such an investment,

and the behaviour is likely to be regarded by a regular user of the market as a failure on the part of the person concerned to observe the standard of behaviour reasonably expected of a person in his position in relation to the market.

(9) Subsections (4) and (8) and the definition of "regular user" in section 130A(3) cease to have effect on 31 December 2014 and subsection (1)(b) is then to be read as no longer referring to those subsections.

118A. Supplementary provision about certain behaviour

(1) Behaviour is to be taken into account for the purposes of this Part only if it occurs—

(a) in the United Kingdom, or

(b) in relation to—

(i) qualifying investments which are admitted to trading on a prescribed market situated in, or operating in, the United Kingdom,

(ii) qualifying investments for which a request for admission to trading on such a prescribed market has been made, or

(iii) in the case of section 118(2) and (3), investments which are related investments in relation to such qualifying investments.

(2) For the purposes of subsection (1), as it applies in relation to section 118(4) and (8), a prescribed market accessible electronically in the United Kingdom is to be treated as operating in the United Kingdom.

(3) For the purposes of section 118(4) and (8), the behaviour that is to be regarded as occurring in relation to qualifying investments includes behaviour which—

(a) occurs in relation to anything that is the subject matter, or whose price or value is expressed by reference to the price or value of the qualifying investments, or

(b) occurs in relation to investments (whether or not they are qualifying investments) whose subject matter is the qualifying investments.

(4) For the purposes of section 118(7), the dissemination of information by a person acting in the capacity of a journalist is to be assessed taking into account the codes governing his profession unless he derives, directly or indirectly, any advantage or profits from the dissemination of the information.

(5) Behaviour does not amount to market abuse for the purposes of this Act if—

(a) it conforms with a rule which includes a provision to the effect that behaviour conforming with the rule does not amount to market abuse,

(b) it conforms with the relevant provisions of Commission Regulation (EC) No. 2273/2003 of 22 December 2003 implementing Directive 2003/6/EC of the European Parliament and of the Council as regards exemptions for buy-back programmes and stabilisation of financial instruments, or

(c) it is done by a person acting on behalf of a public authority in pursuit of monetary policies or policies with respect to exchange rates or the management of public debt or foreign exchange reserves.

(6) Subsections (2) and (3) cease to have effect on 31 December 2014.

118B. Insiders

For the purposes of this Part an insider is any person who has inside information—

(a) as a result of his membership of an administrative, management or supervisory body of an issuer of qualifying investments,

(b) as a result of his holding in the capital of an issuer of qualifying investments,

(c) as a result of having access to the information through the exercise of his employment, profession or duties,

(d) as a result of his criminal activities, or

(e) which he has obtained by other means and which he knows, or could reasonably be expected to know, is inside information.

118C. Inside information

(1) This section defines "inside information" for the purposes of this Part.

(2) In relation to qualifying investments, or related investments, which are not commodity derivatives, inside information is information of a precise nature which—

(a) is not generally available,

(b) relates, directly or indirectly, to one or more issuers of the qualifying investments or to one or more of the qualifying investments, and

(c) would, if generally available, be likely to have a significant effect on the price of the qualifying investments or on the price of related investments.

(3) In relation to qualifying investments or related investments which are commodity derivatives, inside information is information of a precise nature which—

(a) is not generally available,

(b) relates, directly or indirectly, to one or more such derivatives, and

(c) users of markets on which the derivatives are traded would expect to receive in accordance with any accepted market practices on those markets.

(4) In relation to a person charged with the execution of orders concerning any qualifying investments or related investments, inside information includes information conveyed by a client and related to the client's pending orders which—

(a) is of a precise nature,

(b) is not generally available,

(c) relates, directly or indirectly, to one or more issuers of qualifying investments or to one or more qualifying investments, and

(d) would, if generally available, be likely to have a significant effect on the price of those qualifying investments or the price of related investments.

(5) Information is precise if it—

(a) indicates circumstances that exist or may reasonably be expected to come into existence or an event that has occurred or may reasonably be expected to occur, and

(b) is specific enough to enable a conclusion to be drawn as to the possible effect of those circumstances or that event on the price of qualifying investments or related investments.

(6) Information would be likely to have a significant effect on price if and only if it is information of a kind which a reasonable investor would be likely to use as part of the basis of his investment decisions.

(7) For the purposes of subsection (3)(c), users of markets on which investments in commodity derivatives are traded are to be treated as expecting to receive information relating directly or

indirectly to one or more such derivatives in accordance with any accepted market practices, which is—

(a) routinely made available to the users of those markets, or

(b) required to be disclosed in accordance with any statutory provision, market rules, or contracts or customs on the relevant underlying commodity market or commodity derivatives market.

(8) Information which can be obtained by research or analysis conducted by, or on behalf of, users of a market is to be regarded, for the purposes of this Part, as being generally available to them.

The code

119. The code

(1) The FCA must prepare and issue a code containing such provisions as the FCA considers will give appropriate guidance to those determining whether or not behaviour amounts to market abuse.

(2) The code may among other things specify—

(a) descriptions of behaviour that, in the opinion of the FCA, amount to market abuse;

(b) descriptions of behaviour that, in the opinion of the FCA, do not amount to market abuse;

(c) factors that, in the opinion of the FCA, are to be taken into account in determining whether or not behaviour amounts to market abuse;

(d) descriptions of behaviour that are accepted market practices in relation to one or more specified markets;

(e) descriptions of behaviour that are not accepted market practices in relation to one or more specified markets.

(2A) In determining, for the purposes of subsections (2)(d) and (2)(e) or otherwise, what are and what are not accepted market practices, the FCA must have regard to the factors and procedures laid down in Articles 2 and 3 respectively of Commission Directive 2004/72/EC of 29 April 2004 implementing Directive 2003/6/EC of the European Parliament and of the Council.

(3) The code may make different provision in relation to persons, cases or circumstances of different descriptions.

(4) The FCA may at any time alter or replace the code.

(5) If the code is altered or replaced, the altered or replacement code must be issued by the FCA.

(6) A code issued under this section must be published by the FCA in the way appearing to the FCA to be best calculated to bring it to the attention of the public.

(7) The FCA must, without delay, give the Treasury a copy of any code published under this section.

(8) The FCA may charge a reasonable fee for providing a person with a copy of the code.

120. Provisions included in the FCA's code by reference to the City Code

(1) The FCA may include in a code issued by it under section 119 ("the FCA's code") provision to the effect that in its opinion behaviour conforming with the City Code—

(a) does not amount to market abuse;

(b) does not amount to market abuse in specified circumstances; or

(c) does not amount to market abuse if engaged in by a specified description of person.

(2) But the Treasury's approval is required before any such provision may be included in the FCA's code.

(3) If the FCA's code includes provision of a kind authorised by subsection (1), the FCA must keep itself informed of the way in which the Panel on Takeovers and Mergers interprets and administers the relevant provisions of the City Code.

(4) "City Code" means the City Code on Takeovers and Mergers issued by the Panel as it has effect at the time when the behaviour occurs.

(5) "Specified" means specified in the FCA's code.

121. Codes: procedure

(1) Before issuing a code under section 119, the FCA must publish a draft of the proposed code in the way appearing to the FCA to be best calculated to bring it to the attention of the public.

(2) The draft must be accompanied by—

(a) a cost benefit analysis; and

(b) notice that representations about the proposal may be made to the FCA within a specified time.

(3) Before issuing the proposed code, the FCA must have regard to any representations made to it in accordance with subsection (2)(b).

(4) If the FCA issues the proposed code it must publish an account, in general terms, of—

(a) the representations made to it in accordance with subsection (2)(b); and

(b) its response to them.

(5) If the code differs from the draft published under subsection (1) in a way which is, in the opinion of the FCA, significant—

(a) the FCA must (in addition to complying with subsection (4)) publish details of the difference; and

(b) those details must be accompanied by a cost benefit analysis.

(6) Subsections (1) to (5) do not apply if the FCA considers that there is an urgent need to publish the code.

(7) Neither subsection (2)(a) nor subsection (5)(b) applies if the FCA considers—

(a) that, making the appropriate comparison, there will be no increase in costs; or

(b) that, making that comparison, there will be an increase in costs but the increase will be of minimal significance.

(8) The FCA may charge a reasonable fee for providing a person with a copy of a draft published under subsection (1).

(9) This section also applies to a proposal to alter or replace a code.

(10) "Cost benefit analysis" means—

(a) an analysis of the costs together with an analysis of the benefits that will arise—

(i) if the proposed code is issued, or

(ii) if subsection (5)(b) applies, from the code that has been issued, and

(b) subject to subsection (10A), an estimate of those costs and of those benefits.

(10A) If, in the opinion of the FCA—

(a) the costs or benefits referred to in subsection (10) cannot reasonably be estimated, or

(b) it is not reasonably practicable to produce an estimate,

the cost benefit analysis need not estimate them, but must include a statement of the FCA's opinion and an explanation of it.

(11) "The appropriate comparison" means—

(a) in relation to subsection (2)(a), a comparison between the overall position if the code is issued and the overall position if it is not issued;

(b) in relation to subsection (5)(b), a comparison between the overall position after the issuing of the code and the overall position before it was issued.

122. Effect of the code

(1) If a person behaves in a way which is described (in the code in force under section 119 at the time of the behaviour) as behaviour that, in the FCA's opinion, does not amount to market abuse that behaviour of his is to be taken, for the purposes of this Act, as not amounting to market abuse.

(2) Otherwise, the code in force under section 119 at the time when particular behaviour occurs may be relied on so far as it indicates whether or not that behaviour should be taken to amount to market abuse.

Power to impose penalties

123. Power to impose penalties in cases of market abuse

(1) If the FCA is satisfied that a person ("A")—

(a) is or has engaged in market abuse, or

(b) by taking or refraining from taking any action has required or encouraged another person or persons to engage in behaviour which, if engaged in by A, would amount to market abuse,

it may impose on him a penalty of such amount as it considers appropriate.

(2) But the FCA may not impose a penalty on a person if, having considered any representations made to it in response to a warning notice, there are reasonable grounds for it to be satisfied that—

(a) he believed, on reasonable grounds, that his behaviour did not fall within paragraph (a) or (b) of subsection (1), or

(b) he took all reasonable precautions and exercised all due diligence to avoid behaving in a way which fell within paragraph (a) or (b) of that subsection.

(3) If the FCA is entitled to impose a penalty on a person under this section it may, instead of imposing a penalty on him, publish a statement to the effect that he has engaged in market abuse.

Statement of policy

124. Statement of policy

(1) The FCA must prepare and issue a statement of its policy with respect to—

(a) the imposition of penalties under section 123; and

(b) the amount of penalties under that section.

(2) The FCA's policy in determining what the amount of a penalty should be must include having regard to—

(a) whether the behaviour in respect of which the penalty is to be imposed had an adverse effect on the market in question and, if it did, how serious that effect was;

(b) the extent to which that behaviour was deliberate or reckless; and

(c) whether the person on whom the penalty is to be imposed is an individual.

(3) A statement issued under this section must include an indication of the circumstances in which the FCA is to be expected to regard a person as—

(a) having a reasonable belief that his behaviour did not amount to market abuse; or

(b) having taken reasonable precautions and exercised due diligence to avoid engaging in market abuse.

(4) The FCA may at any time alter or replace a statement issued under this section.

(5) If a statement issued under this section is altered or replaced, the FCA must issue the altered or replacement statement.

(6) In exercising, or deciding whether to exercise, its power under section 123 in the case of any particular behaviour, the FCA must have regard to any statement published under this section and in force at the time when the behaviour concerned occurred.

(7) A statement issued under this section must be published by the FCA in the way appearing to the FCA to be best calculated to bring it to the attention of the public.

(8) The FCA may charge a reasonable fee for providing a person with a copy of a statement published under this section.

(9) The FCA must, without delay, give the Treasury a copy of any statement which it publishes under this section.

125. Statement of policy: procedure

(1) Before issuing a statement of policy under section 124, the FCA must publish a draft of the proposed statement in the way appearing to the FCA to be best calculated to bring it to the attention of the public.

(2) The draft must be accompanied by notice that representations about the proposal may be made to the FCA within a specified time.

(3) Before issuing the proposed statement, the FCA must have regard to any representations made to it in accordance with subsection (2).

(4) If the FCA issues the proposed statement it must publish an account, in general terms, of—

(a) the representations made to it in accordance with subsection (2); and

(b) its response to them.

(5) If the statement differs from the draft published under subsection (1) in a way which is, in the opinion of the FCA, significant, the FCA must (in addition to complying with subsection (4)) publish details of the difference.

(6) The FCA may charge a reasonable fee for providing a person with a copy of a draft published under subsection (1).

(7) This section also applies to a proposal to alter or replace a statement.

Procedure

126. Warning notices

(1) If the FCA proposes to take action against a person under section 123, it must give him a warning notice.

(2) A warning notice about a proposal to impose a penalty must state the amount of the proposed penalty.

(3) A warning notice about a proposal to publish a statement must set out the terms of the proposed statement.

127. Decision notices and right to refer to Tribunal

(1) If the FCA decides to take action against a person under section 123, it must give him a decision notice.

(2) A decision notice about the imposition of a penalty must state the amount of the penalty.

(3) A decision notice about the publication of a statement must set out the terms of the statement.

(4) If the FCA decides to take action against a person under section 123, that person may refer the matter to the Tribunal.

Miscellaneous

128. Suspension of investigations

(1) If the FCA considers it desirable or expedient because of the exercise or possible exercise of a power relating to market abuse, it may direct a recognised investment exchange or recognised clearing house—

(a) to terminate, suspend or limit the scope of any inquiry which the exchange or clearing house is conducting under its rules; or

(b) not to conduct an inquiry which the exchange or clearing house proposes to conduct under its rules.

(2) A direction under this section—

(a) must be given to the exchange or clearing house concerned by notice in writing; and

(b) is enforceable, on the application of the FCA, by injunction or, in Scotland, by an order under section 45 of the Court of Session Act 1988.

(3) The FCA's powers relating to market abuse are its powers—

(a) to impose penalties under section 123; or

(b) to appoint a person to conduct an investigation under section 168 in a case falling within subsection (2)(d) of that section.

129. Power of court to impose penalty in cases of market abuse

(1) The FCA may on an application to the court under section 381 or 383 request the court to consider whether the circumstances are such that a penalty should be imposed on the person to whom the application relates.

(2) The court may, if it considers it appropriate, make an order requiring the person concerned to pay to the FCA a penalty of such amount as it considers appropriate.

130. Guidance

(1) The Treasury may from time to time issue written guidance for the purpose of helping relevant authorities to determine the action to be taken in cases where behaviour occurs which is behaviour—

(a) with respect to which the power in section 123 appears to be exercisable; and

(b) which appears to involve the commission of an offence under Part 7 of the Financial Services Act 2012 or Part V of the Criminal Justice Act 1993 (insider dealing).

(2) The Treasury must obtain the consent of the Attorney General and the Secretary of State before issuing any guidance under this section.

(3) In this section "relevant authorities"—

(a) in relation to England and Wales, means the Secretary of State, the FCA, the Director of the Serious Fraud Office and the Director of Public Prosecutions;

(b) in relation to Northern Ireland, means the Secretary of State, the FCA, the Director of the Serious Fraud Office and the Director of Public Prosecutions for Northern Ireland.

(4) Subsections (1) to (3) do not apply to Scotland.

(5) In relation to Scotland, the Lord Advocate may from time to time, after consultation with the Treasury, issue written guidance for the purpose of helping the FCA to determine the action to be taken in cases where behaviour mentioned in subsection (1) occurs.

130A. Interpretation and supplementary provision

(1) The Treasury may by order specify (whether by name or description)—

(a) the markets which are prescribed markets for the purposes of specified provisions of this Part, and

(b) the investments that are qualifying investments in relation to the prescribed markets.

(2) An order may prescribe different investments or descriptions of investment in relation to different markets or descriptions of market.

(3) In this Part—

"accepted market practices" means practices that are reasonably expected in the financial market or markets in question and are accepted by the FCA or, in the case of a market situated in another EEA State, the competent authority of that EEA State within the meaning of Directive 2003/6/EC of the European Parliament and of the Council of 28 January 2003 on insider dealing and market manipulation (market abuse),

"behaviour" includes action or inaction,

"dealing", in relation to an investment, means acquiring or disposing of the investment whether as principal or agent or directly or indirectly, and includes agreeing to acquire or dispose of the investment, and entering into and bringing to an end a contract creating it,

"investment" is to be read with section 22 and Schedule 2,

"regular user", in relation to a particular market, means a reasonable person who regularly deals on that market in investments of the kind in question,

"related investment", in relation to a qualifying investment, means an investment whose price or value depends on the price or value of the qualifying investment.

(4) Any reference in this Act to a person engaged in market abuse is to a person engaged in market abuse either alone or with one or more other persons.

131. Effect on transactions

The imposition of a penalty under this Part does not make any transaction void or unenforceable.

131A. Protected Disclosures

(1) A disclosure which satisfies the following three conditions is not to be taken to breach any restriction on the disclosure of information (however imposed).

(2) The first condition is that the information or other matter—

(a) causes the person making the disclosure (the discloser) to know or suspect, or

(b) gives him reasonable grounds for knowing or suspecting, that another person has engaged in market abuse.

(3) The second condition is that the information or other matter disclosed came to the discloser in the course of his trade, profession, business or employment.

(4) The third condition is that the disclosure is made to the FCA or to a nominated officer as soon as is practicable after the information or other matter comes to the discloser.

(5) A disclosure to a nominated officer is a disclosure which is made to a person nominated by the discloser's employer to receive disclosures under this section, and is made in the course of the discloser's employment and in accordance with the procedure established by the employer for the purpose.

(6) For the purposes of this section, references to a person's employer include any body, association or organisation (including a voluntary organisation) in connection with whose activities the person exercises a function (whether or not for gain or reward) and references to employment must be construed accordingly.

...

PART XVIII
RECOGNISED INVESTMENT EXCHANGES AND CLEARING HOUSES

CHAPTER I
EXEMPTION

General

285. Exemption for recognised investment exchanges and clearing houses

(1) In this Act—
- (a) "recognised investment exchange" means an investment exchange in relation to which a recognition order is in force; ...
- (b) "recognised clearing house" means—
  - (i) a central counterparty in relation to which a recognition order is in force (in this Part referred to as a "recognised central counterparty"), or
  - (ii) a clearing house which provides clearing services in the United Kingdom without doing so as a central counterparty, and in relation to which a recognition order is in force;
- (c) "EEA central counterparty" means a person established in an EEA State other than the United Kingdom who has been authorised by the competent authority of that State as a central counterparty pursuant to Article 17 of the EMIR regulation; and
- (d) "third country central counterparty" means a person established in a State which is not an EEA State who has been recognised by ESMA as a central counterparty pursuant to Article 25 of the EMIR regulation.

(2) A recognised investment exchange is exempt from the general prohibition as respects any regulated activity—
- (a) which is carried on as a part of the exchange's business as an investment exchange; or
- (b) which is carried on for the purposes of, or in connection with, the provision by the exchange of services designed to facilitate the provision of clearing services by another person.

(3) A recognised clearing house which is not a recognised central counterparty is exempt from the general prohibition as respects any regulated activity—
- (a) which is carried on for the purposes of, or in connection with, the provision of clearing services by the clearing house, or
- (b) which is carried on for the purposes of, or in connection with, the provision by the clearing house of services designed to facilitate the provision of clearing services by another person.

(3A) A recognised central counterparty is exempt from the general prohibition as respects any regulated activity which is carried on for the purposes of, or in connection with, the services or activities specified in its recognition order.

(3B) An EEA central counterparty is exempt from the general prohibition as respects any regulated activity which is carried on for the purposes of, or in connection with, the services or activities specified in its authorisation granted pursuant to Article 17 of the EMIR regulation.

(3C) A third country central counterparty is exempt from the general prohibition as respects any regulated activity which is carried on for the purposes of, or in connection with, the services or activities specified in its recognition by ESMA pursuant to Article 25 of the EMIR regulation.

(4) The Treasury may by order amend paragraph (b) of subsection (2) or (3).

285A. Powers exercisable in relation to recognised investment exchanges and clearing houses

(1) For the purposes of this Part, the FCA is "the appropriate regulator" in relation to recognised investment exchanges.

(2) For the purposes of this Part, the Bank of England is "the appropriate regulator" in relation to recognised clearing houses.

(3) In Schedule 17A—

(a) Part 1 makes provision for a memorandum of understanding between the appropriate regulators and the PRA with respect to the exercise of their functions in relation to recognised investment exchanges and clearing houses;

(b) Part 2 applies certain provisions of this Act in relation to the Bank of England in consequence of the conferring of functions on the Bank under this Part of this Act;

(c) Part 3 makes provision relating to the winding up, administration or insolvency of recognised clearing houses; and

(d) Part 4 makes provision about fees.

286. Qualification for recognition

(1) The Treasury may make regulations setting out the requirements—

(a) which must be satisfied by an investment exchange or clearing house if it is to qualify as a body in respect of which the appropriate regulator may make a recognition order under this Part; and

(b) which, if a recognition order is made, it must continue to satisfy if it is to remain a recognised body.

(2) But if regulations contain provision as to the default rules of an investment exchange or clearing house, or as to proceedings taken under such rules by such a body, they require the approval of the Secretary of State.

(3) "Default rules" means rules of an investment exchange or clearing house which provide for the taking of action in the event of a person's appearing to be unable, or likely to become unable, to meet his obligations in respect of one or more market contracts connected with the exchange or clearing house.

(4) "Market contract" means—

(a) a contract to which Part VII of the Companies Act 1989 applies as a result of section 155 of that Act or a contract to which Part V of the Companies (No 2) (Northern Ireland) Order 1990 applies as a result of Article 80 of that Order; and

(b) such other kind of contract as may be prescribed.

(4A) If regulations under subsection (1) require an investment exchange to make information available to the public in accordance with—

(a) Article 29.1 of the markets in financial instruments directive and the Commission Regulation, or

(b) Article 44.1 of that directive and that Regulation,

the regulations may authorise the FCA to waive the requirement in the circumstances specified in the relevant provisions.

(4B) The "relevant provisions" for the purposes of subsection (4A) are—

(a) in a case falling within paragraph (a) of that subsection, Article 29.2 of the markets in financial instruments directive and the Commission Regulation, and

(b) in a case falling within paragraph (b) of that subsection, Article 44.2 of that directive and that Regulation.

(4C) If regulations under subsection (1) require an investment exchange to make information available to the public in accordance with—

(a) Article 30.1 of the markets in financial instruments directive and the Commission Regulation, or

(b) Article 45.1 of that directive and that Regulation,

the regulations may authorise the FCA to defer the requirement in the circumstances specified, and subject to the requirements contained, in the relevant provisions.

(4D) The "relevant provisions" for the purposes of subsection (4C) are—

(a) in a case falling within paragraph (a) of that subsection, Article 30.2 of the markets in financial instruments directive and the Commission Regulation, and

(b) in a case falling within paragraph (b) of that subsection, Article 45.2 of that directive and that Regulation.

(4E) "The Commission Regulation" means Commission Regulation 1287/2006 of 10 August 2006.

(4F) Regulations under subsection (1) may confer power on the appropriate regulator to make rules for the purposes of the regulations or of any specified provision made by the regulations.

(5) Requirements resulting from this section are referred to in this Part as "recognition requirements".

(6) In the case of an investment exchange, requirements resulting from this section are in addition to requirements which must be satisfied by the exchange as a result of section 290(1A) before the FCA may make a recognition order declaring the exchange to be a recognised investment exchange.

Applications for recognition

287. Application by an investment exchange

(1) Any body corporate or unincorporated association may apply to the FCA for an order declaring it to be a recognised investment exchange for the purposes of this Act.

(2) The application must be made in such manner as the FCA may direct and must be accompanied by—

(a) a copy of the applicant's rules;

(b) a copy of any guidance issued by the applicant;

(c) the required particulars; and

(d) such other information as the FCA may reasonably require for the purpose of determining the application.

(3) The required particulars are—

(a) particulars of any arrangements which the applicant has made, or proposes to make, for the provision by another person of clearing services in respect of transactions effected on the exchange;

(b) if the applicant proposes to provide services falling within section 285(2)(b) in respect of transactions other than those effected on the exchange, particulars of the criteria which the applicant will apply when determining to whom it will provide those services;

(c) a programme of operations which includes the types of business the applicant proposes to undertake and the applicant's proposed organisational structure;

(d) such particulars of the persons who effectively direct the business and operations of the exchange as the FCA may reasonably require;

(e) such particulars of the ownership of the exchange, and in particular of the identity and scale of interests of the persons who are in a position to exercise significant influence over the management of the exchange, whether directly or indirectly, as the FCA may reasonably require.

(4) Subsection (3)(c) to (e) does not apply to an application by an overseas applicant.

288. Application by a clearing house

(1) A body corporate or unincorporated association which is established in the United Kingdom may, where it intends to provide clearing services as a central counterparty, apply to the Bank of England in accordance with Article 17 of the EMIR regulation for an order granting authorisation for the purposes of that Article and declaring it to be a recognised central counterparty for the purposes of this Act.

(1A) A body corporate or unincorporated association may, where it intends to provide clearing services in the United Kingdom without doing so as a central counterparty, apply to the Bank of England for an order declaring it to be for the purposes of this Act a recognised clearing house which is not a recognised central counterparty.

(2) An application under subsection (1A) must be made in such manner as the Bank of England may direct and must be accompanied by—

(a) a copy of the applicant's rules;

(b) a copy of any guidance issued by the applicant;

(c) the required particulars; and

(d) such other information as the Bank may reasonably require for the purpose of determining the application.

(3) The required particulars are—

(a) if the applicant makes, or proposes to make, clearing arrangements with a recognised investment exchange, particulars of those arrangements;

(b) if the applicant proposes to provide clearing services or services falling within section 285(3)(b) for persons other than recognised investment exchanges, particulars of the criteria which it will apply when determining to whom it will provide those services.

289. Applications: supplementary

(1) At any time after receiving an application and before determining it, the appropriate regulator may require the applicant to provide such further information as it reasonably considers necessary to enable it to determine the application.

(2) Information which the appropriate regulator requires in connection with an application must be provided in such form, or verified in such manner, as the appropriate regulator may direct.

(3) Different directions may be given, or requirements imposed, by the appropriate regulator with respect to different applications.

(4) In relation to an application under section 288(1), this section does not apply to information which can be required under Article 17 of the EMIR regulation.

290. Recognition orders

(1) If it appears to the appropriate regulator that the applicant satisfies the recognition requirements applicable in its case, the regulator may—

(a) where the application is made under section 287, make a recognition order declaring the applicant to be a recognised investment exchange;

(b) where the application is made under section 288(1) and Article 17 of the EMIR regulation allows authorisation to be granted, make a recognition order ("a central counterparty recognition order") granting authorisation for the purposes of that Article and declaring the applicant to be a recognised central counterparty; or

(c) where the application is made under section 288(1A), make a recognition order declaring the applicant to be a recognised clearing house which is not a recognised central counterparty.

(1A) In the case of an application for an order declaring the applicant to be a recognised investment exchange, the reference in subsection (1) to the recognition requirements applicable in its case includes a reference to requirements contained in any directly applicable Community regulation made under the markets in financial instruments directive.

(1B) In the case mentioned in subsection (1A), the application must be determined by the FCA before the end of the period of six months beginning with the date on which it receives the completed application.

(1C) Subsection (1B) does not apply in the case of an application by an overseas applicant.

(1D) A central counterparty recognition order must specify the services or activities linked to clearing which the applicant may provide or perform and the classes of financial instruments covered by the order.

(2) …

(3) In considering an application made under section 287 or 288(1A), the appropriate regulator may have regard to any information which it considers is relevant to the application.

(4) A recognition order must specify a date on which it is to take effect.

(5) Section 298 has effect in relation to a decision to refuse to make a recognition order in respect of an investment exchange or a clearing house which is not a central counterparty—

(a) as it has effect in relation to a decision to revoke such an order; and

(b) as if references to a recognised body were references to the applicant.

(6) ...

(7) Where—

(a) a body corporate or unincorporated association has made an application under section 288(1), and

(b) the Bank of England has determined that application in accordance with Article 17 of the EMIR regulation,

any previous recognition order under section 290(1)(c) or 292(2)(b) shall cease to be valid.

290ZA. Variation of central counterparty recognition order

(1) On an application made to it in accordance with Article 15 of the EMIR regulation, the Bank of England may in accordance with Article 17 of that regulation vary a central counterparty recognition order by specifying an additional service or activity or class of financial instruments.

(2) Where Article 20(5) of the EMIR regulation applies, the Bank of England may vary a central counterparty recognition order by removing a service or activity or class of financial instruments from those specified in the order.

(3) The Bank of England may at any time vary a central counterparty recognition order for the purpose of correcting an error in, or omission from, the order.

290A. Refusal of recognition on ground of excessive regulatory provision

(1) The appropriate regulator must not make a recognition order if it appears to it that an existing or proposed regulatory provision of the applicant in connection with—

(a) the applicant's business as an investment exchange, ...

(b) the provision by the applicant of clearing services, or

(c) the provision by the applicant of services falling within section 285(2)(b) or (3)(b),

imposes or will impose an excessive requirement on the persons affected (directly or indirectly) by it.

(2) The reference in section 290(1) (making of recognition order) to satisfying the applicable recognition requirements shall be read accordingly.

(3) Expressions used in subsection (1) above that are defined for the purposes of section 300A (power of appropriate regulator to disallow excessive regulatory provision) have the same meaning as in that section.

(4) The provisions of section 300A(3) and (4) (determination whether regulatory provision excessive) apply for the purposes of this section as for the purposes of section 300A.

(5) Section 298 has effect in relation to a decision under this section to refuse a recognition order in respect of an investment exchange or a clearing house which is not a central counterparty—

(a) as it has effect in relation to a decision to revoke such an order, and

(b) as if references to a recognised body were references to the applicant.

(6) This section does not apply to an application for recognition as an overseas investment exchange, an overseas clearing house or a recognised central counterparty.

291. Liability in relation to recognised body's regulatory functions

(1) A recognised body and its officers and staff are not to be liable in damages for anything done or omitted in the discharge of the recognised body's regulatory functions unless it is shown that the act or omission was in bad faith.

(2) But subsection (1) does not prevent an award of damages made in respect of an act or omission on the ground that the act or omission was unlawful as a result of section 6(1) of the Human Rights Act 1998.

(3) "Regulatory functions" means the functions of the recognised body so far as relating to, or to matters arising out of, the obligations to which the body is subject under or by virtue of this Act.

292. Overseas investment exchanges and overseas clearing houses

(1) An application under section 287 or 288(1A) by an overseas applicant must contain the address of a place in the United Kingdom for the service on the applicant of notices or other documents required or authorised to be served on it under this Act.

(2) If it appears to the appropriate regulator that an overseas applicant satisfies the requirements of subsection (3) it may make a recognition order declaring the applicant to be—

(a) a recognised investment exchange;

(b) a recognised clearing house which is not a central counterparty.

(3) The requirements are that—

(a) investors are afforded protection equivalent to that which they would be afforded if the body concerned were required to comply with recognition requirements, other than any such requirements which are expressed in regulations under section 286 not to apply for the purposes of this paragraph;

(b) there are adequate procedures for dealing with a person who is unable, or likely to become unable, to meet his obligations in respect of one or more market contracts connected with the investment exchange or clearing house;

(c) the applicant is able and willing to co-operate with the appropriate regulator by the sharing of information and in other ways;

(d) adequate arrangements exist for co-operation between the appropriate regulator and those responsible for the supervision of the applicant in the country or territory in which the applicant's head office is situated.

(4) In considering whether it is satisfied as to the requirements mentioned in subsection (3)(a) and (b), the appropriate regulator is to have regard to—

(a) the relevant law and practice of the country or territory in which the applicant's head office is situated;

(b) the rules and practices of the applicant.

(5) In relation to an overseas applicant and a body or association declared to be a recognised investment exchange or recognised clearing house by a recognition order made by virtue of subsection (2)—

(a) the reference in section 313(2) to recognition requirements is to be read as a reference to matters corresponding to the matters in respect of which provision is made in the recognition requirements;

(b) sections 296(1) and 297(2) have effect as if the requirements mentioned in section 296(1)(a) and section 297(2)(a) were those of subsection (3)(a), (b), and (c) of this section;

(c) section 297(2) has effect as if the grounds on which a recognition order may be revoked under that provision included the ground that in the opinion of the appropriate regulator arrangements of the kind mentioned in subsection (3)(d) no longer exist.

(6) Where a recognised clearing house is authorised as an EEA central counterparty or recognised as a third country central counterparty, any previous recognition order under section 290(1)(c) or 292(2)(b) shall cease to be valid.

Publication of information by recognised investment exchange

292A. Publication of information by recognised investment exchange

(1) A recognised investment exchange must as soon as practicable after a recognition order is made in respect of it publish such particulars of the ownership of the exchange as the FCA may reasonably require.

(2) The particulars published under subsection (1) must include particulars of the identity and scale of interests of the persons who are in a position to exercise significant influence over the management of the exchange, whether directly or indirectly.

(3) If an ownership transfer takes place in relation to a recognised investment exchange, the exchange must as soon as practicable after becoming aware of the transfer publish such particulars relating to the transfer as the FCA may reasonably require.

(4) "Ownership transfer", in relation to an exchange, means a transfer of ownership which gives rise to a change in the persons who are in a position to exercise significant influence over the management of the exchange, whether directly or indirectly.

(5) A recognised investment exchange must publish such particulars of any decision it makes to suspend or remove a financial instrument from trading on a regulated market operated by it as the FCA may reasonably require.

(6) The FCA may determine the manner of publication under subsections (1), (3) and (5) and the timing of publication under subsection (5).

(7) This section does not apply to an overseas investment exchange.

…

PART XX
PROVISION OF FINANCIAL SERVICES BY MEMBERS OF THE PROFESSIONS

325. FCA's general duty

(1) The FCA must keep itself informed about—

(a) the way in which designated professional bodies supervise and regulate the carrying on of exempt regulated activities by members of the professions in relation to which they are established;

(b) the way in which such members are carrying on exempt regulated activities.

(2) In this Part—

"exempt regulated activities" means regulated activities which may, as a result of this Part, be carried on by members of a profession which is supervised and regulated by a designated professional body without breaching the general prohibition; and

"members", in relation to a profession, means persons who are entitled to practise the profession in question and, in practising it, are subject to the rules of the body designated in relation to that profession, whether or not they are members of that body.

(3) The FCA must keep under review the desirability of exercising any of its powers under this Part.

(4) Each designated professional body must co-operate with the FCA, by the sharing of information and in other ways, in order to enable the FCA to perform its functions under this Part.

326. Designation of professional bodies

(1) The Treasury may by order designate bodies for the purposes of this Part.

(2) A body designated under subsection (1) is referred to in this Part as a designated professional body.

(3) The Treasury may designate a body under subsection (1) only if they are satisfied that—

(a) the basic condition, and

(b) one or more of the additional conditions,

are met in relation to it.

(4) The basic condition is that the body has rules applicable to the carrying on by members of the profession in relation to which it is established of regulated activities which, if the body were to be designated, would be exempt regulated activities.

(5) The additional conditions are that—

(a) the body has power under any enactment to regulate the practice of the profession;

(b) being a member of the profession is a requirement under any enactment for the exercise of particular functions or the holding of a particular office;

(c) the body has been recognised for the purpose of any enactment other than this Act and the recognition has not been withdrawn;

(d) the body is established in an EEA State other than the United Kingdom and in that State—

(i) the body has power corresponding to that mentioned in paragraph (a);

(ii) there is a requirement in relation to the body corresponding to that mentioned in paragraph (b); or

(iii) the body is recognised in a manner corresponding to that mentioned in paragraph (c).

(6) "Enactment" includes an Act of the Scottish Parliament, Northern Ireland legislation and subordinate legislation (whether made under an Act, an Act of the Scottish Parliament or Northern Ireland legislation).

(7) "Recognised" means recognised by—

(a) a Minister of the Crown;

(b) the Scottish Ministers;

(c) a Northern Ireland Minister;

(d) a Northern Ireland department or its head.

327. Exemption from the general prohibition

(1) The general prohibition does not apply to the carrying on of a regulated activity by a person ("P") if—

(a) the conditions set out in subsections (2) to (7) are satisfied; and

(b) there is not in force—

(i) a direction under section 328, or

(ii) an order under section 329,

which prevents this subsection from applying to the carrying on of that activity by him.

(2) P must be—

(a) a member of a profession; or

(b) controlled or managed by one or more such members.

(3) P must not receive from a person other than his client any pecuniary reward or other advantage, for which he does not account to his client, arising out of his carrying on of any of the activities.

(4) The manner of the provision by P of any service in the course of carrying on the activities must be incidental to the provision by him of professional services.

(5) P must not carry on, or hold himself out as carrying on, a regulated activity other than—

(a) one which rules made as a result of section 332(3) allow him to carry on; or

(b) one in relation to which he is an exempt person.

(6) The activities must not be of a description, or relate to an investment of a description, specified in an order made by the Treasury for the purposes of this subsection.

(7) The activities must be the only regulated activities carried on by P (other than regulated activities in relation to which he is an exempt person).

(8) "Professional services" means services—

(a) which do not constitute carrying on a regulated activity, and

(b) the provision of which is supervised and regulated by a designated professional body.

328. Directions in relation to the general prohibition

(1) The FCA may direct that section 327(1) is not to apply to the extent specified in the direction.

(2) A direction under subsection (1)—

(a) must be in writing;

(b) may be given in relation to different classes of person or different descriptions of regulated activity.

(3) A direction under subsection (1) must be published in the way appearing to the FCA to be best calculated to bring it to the attention of the public.

(4) The FCA may charge a reasonable fee for providing a person with a copy of the direction.

(5) The FCA must, without delay, give the Treasury a copy of any direction which it gives under this section.

(6) The FCA may exercise the power conferred by subsection (1) only if it is satisfied either—

(a) that it is desirable to do so in order to protect the interests of clients; or

(b) that it is necessary to do so in order to comply with an EU obligation imposed by the insurance mediation directive.

(7) In considering whether it is satisfied of the matter specified in subsection (6)(a), the FCA must have regard amongst other things to the effectiveness of any arrangements made by any designated professional body—

(a) for securing compliance with rules made under section 332(1);

(b) for dealing with complaints against its members in relation to the carrying on by them of exempt regulated activities;

(c) in order to offer redress to clients who suffer, or claim to have suffered, loss as a result of misconduct by its members in their carrying on of exempt regulated activities;

(d) for co-operating with the FCA under section 325(4).

(8) In this Part "clients" means—

(a) persons who use, have used or are or may be contemplating using, any of the services provided by a member of a profession in the course of carrying on exempt regulated activities;

(b) persons who have rights or interests which are derived from, or otherwise attributable to, the use of any such services by other persons; or

(c) persons who have rights or interests which may be adversely affected by the use of any such services by persons acting on their behalf or in a fiduciary capacity in relation to them.

(9) If a member of a profession is carrying on an exempt regulated activity in his capacity as a trustee, the persons who are, have been or may be beneficiaries of the trust are to be treated as persons who use, have used or are or may be contemplating using services provided by that person in his carrying on of that activity.

329. Orders in relation to the general prohibition

(1) Subsection (2) applies if it appears to the FCA that a person to whom, as a result of section 327(1), the general prohibition does not apply is not a fit and proper person to carry on regulated activities in accordance with that section.

(2) The FCA may make an order disapplying section 327(1) in relation to that person to the extent specified in the order.

(3) The FCA may, on the application of the person named in an order under subsection (1), vary or revoke it.

(4) "Specified" means specified in the order.

(5) If a partnership is named in an order under this section, the order is not affected by any change in its membership.

(6) If a partnership named in an order under this section is dissolved, the order continues to have effect in relation to any partnership which succeeds to the business of the dissolved partnership.

(7) For the purposes of subsection (6), a partnership is to be regarded as succeeding to the business of another partnership only if—

(a) the members of the resulting partnership are substantially the same as those of the former partnership; and

(b) succession is to the whole or substantially the whole of the business of the former partnership.

330. Consultation

(1) Before giving a direction under section 328(1), the FCA must publish a draft of the proposed direction.

(2) The draft must be accompanied by—

(a) a cost benefit analysis; and

(b) notice that representations about the proposed direction may be made to the FCA within a specified time.

(3) Before giving the proposed direction, the FCA must have regard to any representations made to it in accordance with subsection (2)(b).

(4) If the FCA gives the proposed direction it must publish an account, in general terms, of—

(a) the representations made to it in accordance with subsection (2)(b); and

(b) its response to them.

(5) If the direction differs from the draft published under subsection (1) in a way which is, in the opinion of the FCA, significant—

(a) the FCA must (in addition to complying with subsection (4)) publish details of the difference; and

(b) those details must be accompanied by a cost benefit analysis.

(6) Subsections (1) to (5) do not apply if the FCA considers that the delay involved in complying with them would prejudice the interests of consumers.

(7) Neither subsection (2)(a) nor subsection (5)(b) applies if the FCA considers—

(a) that, making the appropriate comparison, there will be no increase in costs; or

(b) that, making that comparison, there will be an increase in costs but the increase will be of minimal significance.

(8) The FCA may charge a reasonable fee for providing a person with a copy of a draft published under subsection (1).

(9) When the FCA is required to publish a document under this section it must do so in the way appearing to it to be best calculated to bring it to the attention of the public.

(10) "Cost benefit analysis" means—

(a) an analysis of the costs together with an analysis of the benefits that will arise—

(i) if the proposed direction is given, or

(ii) if subsection (5)(b) applies, from the direction that has been given, and

(b) subject to subsection (10A), an estimate of those costs and of those benefits.

(10A) If, in the opinion of the FCA—

(a) the costs or benefits referred to in subsection (10) cannot reasonably be estimated, or

(b) it is not reasonably practicable to produce an estimate,

the cost benefit analysis need not estimate them, but must include a statement of the FCA's opinion and an explanation of it.

(11) "The appropriate comparison" means—

(a) in relation to subsection (2)(a), a comparison between the overall position if the direction is given and the overall position if it is not given;

(b) in relation to subsection (5)(b), a comparison between the overall position after the giving of the direction and the overall position before it was given.

331. Procedure on making or varying orders under section 329

(1) If the FCA proposes to make an order under section 329, it must give the person concerned a warning notice.

(2) The warning notice must set out the terms of the proposed order.

(3) If the FCA decides to make an order under section 329, it must give the person concerned a decision notice.

(4) The decision notice must—

(a) name the person to whom the order applies;

(b) set out the terms of the order; and

(c) be given to the person named in the order.

(5) Subsections (6) to (8) apply to an application for the variation or revocation of an order under section 329.

(6) If the FCA decides to grant the application, it must give the applicant written notice of its decision.

(7) If the FCA proposes to refuse the application, it must give the applicant a warning notice.

(8) If the FCA decides to refuse the application, it must give the applicant a decision notice.

(9) A person—

(a) against whom the FCA have decided to make an order under section 329, or

(b) whose application for the variation or revocation of such an order the FCA had decided to refuse,

may refer the matter to the Tribunal.

(10) The FCA may not make an order under section 329 unless—
(a) the period within which the decision to make to the order may be referred to the Tribunal has expired and no such reference has been made; or
(b) if such a reference has been made, the reference has been determined.

332. Rules in relation to persons to whom the general prohibition does not apply

(1) The FCA may make rules applicable to persons to whom, as a result of section 327(1), the general prohibition does not apply.
(2) The power conferred by subsection (1) is to be exercised for the purpose of ensuring that clients are aware that such persons are not authorised persons.
(3) A designated professional body must make rules—
(a) applicable to members of the profession in relation to which it is established who are not authorised persons; and
(b) governing the carrying on by those members of regulated activities (other than regulated activities in relation to which they are exempt persons).
(4) Rules made in compliance with subsection (3) must be designed to secure that, in providing a particular professional service to a particular client, the member carries on only regulated activities which arise out of, or are complementary to, the provision by him of that service to that client.
(5) Rules made by a designated professional body under subsection (3) require the approval of the FCA.

333. False claims to be a person to whom the general prohibition does not apply

(1) A person who—
(a) describes himself (in whatever terms) as a person to whom the general prohibition does not apply, in relation to a particular regulated activity, as a result of this Part, or
(b) behaves, or otherwise holds himself out, in a manner which indicates (or which is reasonably likely to be understood as indicating) that he is such a person,
is guilty of an offence if he is not such a person.
(2) In proceedings for an offence under this section it is a defence for the accused to show that he took all reasonable precautions and exercised all due diligence to avoid committing the offence.
(3) A person guilty of an offence under this section is liable on summary conviction to imprisonment for a term not exceeding six months or a fine not exceeding level 5 on the standard scale, or both.
(4) But where the conduct constituting the offence involved or included the public display of any material, the maximum fine for the offence is level 5 on the standard scale multiplied by the number of days for which the display continued.

…

PART XXVII
OFFENCES

Miscellaneous offences

397. ...

398. Misleading FCA or PRA: residual cases

(1) A person who, in purported compliance with any requirement imposed by or under this Act, or by the short selling regulation, knowingly or recklessly gives a regulator information which is false or misleading in a material particular is guilty of an offence.
(2) Subsection (1) applies only to a requirement in relation to which no other provision of this Act creates an offence in connection with the giving of information.
(3) A person guilty of an offence under this section is liable—
(a) on summary conviction, to a fine not exceeding the statutory maximum;
(b) on conviction on indictment, to a fine.

399. Misleading the OFT

Section 44 of the Competition Act 1998 (offences connected with the provision of false or misleading information) applies in relation to any function of the Office of Fair Trading under this Act as if it were a function under Part I of that Act.

Bodies corporate and partnerships

400. Offences by bodies corporate etc

(1) If an offence under this Act committed by a body corporate is shown—

(a) to have been committed with the consent or connivance of an officer, or

(b) to be attributable to any neglect on his part,

the officer as well as the body corporate is guilty of the offence and liable to be proceeded against and punished accordingly.

(2) If the affairs of a body corporate are managed by its members, subsection (1) applies in relation to the acts and defaults of a member in connection with his functions of management as if he were a director of the body.

(3) If an offence under this Act committed by a partnership is shown—

(a) to have been committed with the consent or connivance of a partner, or

(b) to be attributable to any neglect on his part,

the partner as well as the partnership is guilty of the offence and liable to be proceeded against and punished accordingly.

(4) In subsection (3) "partner" includes a person purporting to act as a partner.

(5) "Officer", in relation to a body corporate, means—

(a) a director, member of the committee of management, chief executive, manager, secretary or other similar officer of the body, or a person purporting to act in any such capacity; and

(b) an individual who is a controller of the body.

(6) If an offence under this Act committed by an unincorporated association (other than a partnership) is shown—

(a) to have been committed with the consent or connivance of an officer of the association or a member of its governing body, or

(b) to be attributable to any neglect on the part of such an officer or member,

that officer or member as well as the association is guilty of the offence and liable to be proceeded against and punished accordingly.

(6A) References in this section to an offence under this Act include a reference to an offence under Part 7 of the Financial Services Act 2012 (offences relating to financial services).

(7) Regulations may provide for the application of any provision of this section, with such modifications as the Treasury consider appropriate, to a body corporate or unincorporated association formed or recognised under the law of a territory outside the United Kingdom.

Institution of proceedings

401. Proceedings for offences

(1) In this section "offence" means—

(a) an offence under this Act,

(b) an offence under subordinate legislation made under this Act, or

(c) an offence under Part 7 of the Financial Services Act 2012 (offences relating to financial services).

(2) Proceedings for an offence may be instituted in England and Wales only—

(a) by the appropriate regulator or the Secretary of State; or

(b) by or with the consent of the Director of Public Prosecutions.

(3) Proceedings for an offence may be instituted in Northern Ireland only—

(a) by the appropriate regulator or the Secretary of State; or

(b) by or with the consent of the Director of Public Prosecutions for Northern Ireland.

(3A) For the purposes of subsections (2)(a) and (3)(a), the PRA is the "appropriate regulator" in respect of each of the following offences—

(a) an offence under section 55P(10) where the contravention is of a requirement imposed by the PRA;

(b) an offence under section 56(4) where the prohibition order is made by the PRA;

(c) an offence under section 177(3) where the investigation is being, or is likely to be, conducted on behalf of the PRA;

(d) an offence under section 177(4) where the requirement is imposed by the PRA;

(e) an offence under section 177(6) where the warrant is issued as a result of information on oath given by the PRA or a person appointed by the PRA to conduct an investigation on its behalf;

(f) an offence under section 191F(1) where the notice should have been given to the PRA;

(g) an offence under any of section 191F(2) to (7) where the notice, approval or information was given to or by the PRA;

(h) an offence under section 366(3), unless the activity of effecting or carrying out long-term contracts of insurance is not to any extent a PRA-regulated activity;

(i) an offence under section 398(1) where the information was given to the PRA.

(3B) For the purposes of subsections (2)(a) and (3)(a), the FCA is the "appropriate regulator" in respect of any other offence.

(4) Except in Scotland, proceedings for an offence under section 203 may also be instituted by the Office of Fair Trading.

(5) In exercising its power to institute proceedings for an offence, the appropriate regulator must comply with any conditions or restrictions imposed in writing by the Treasury.

(6) Conditions or restrictions may be imposed under subsection (5) in relation to—

(a) proceedings generally; or

(b) such proceedings, or categories of proceedings, as the Treasury may direct.

402. Power of FCA to institute proceedings for certain other offences

(1) Except in Scotland, the FCA may institute proceedings for an offence under—

(a) Part V of the Criminal Justice Act 1993 (insider dealing); . . .

(b) prescribed regulations relating to money laundering; or

(c) Schedule 7 to the Counter-Terrorism Act 2008 (terrorist financing or money laundering).

(2) In exercising its power to institute proceedings for any such offence, the FCA must comply with any conditions or restrictions imposed in writing by the Treasury.

(3) Conditions or restrictions may be imposed under subsection (2) in relation to—

(a) proceedings generally; or

(b) such proceedings, or categories of proceedings, as the Treasury may direct.

403. Jurisdiction and procedure in respect of offences

(1) A fine imposed on an unincorporated association on its conviction of an offence is to be paid out of the funds of the association.

(2) Proceedings for an offence alleged to have been committed by an unincorporated association must be brought in the name of the association (and not in that of any of its members).

(3) Rules of court relating to the service of documents are to have effect as if the association were a body corporate.

(4) In proceedings for an offence brought against an unincorporated association—

(a) section 33 of the Criminal Justice Act 1925 and Schedule 3 to the Magistrates' Courts Act 1980 (procedure) apply as they do in relation to a body corporate;

(b) section 70 of the Criminal Procedure (Scotland) Act 1995 (procedure) applies as if the association were a body corporate;

(c) section 18 of the Criminal Justice (Northern Ireland) Act 1945 and Schedule 4 to the Magistrates' Courts (Northern Ireland) Order 1981 (procedure) apply as they do in relation to a body corporate.

(5) Summary proceedings for an offence may be taken—

(a) against a body corporate or unincorporated association at any place at which it has a place of business;

(b) against an individual at any place where he is for the time being.

(6) Subsection (5) does not affect any jurisdiction exercisable apart from this section.

(7) "Offence" means an offence under this Act or an offence under Part 7 of the Financial Services Act 2012 (offences relating to financial services).

…

PART XXX
SUPPLEMENTAL

426. Consequential and supplementary provision

(1) A Minister of the Crown may by order make such incidental, consequential, transitional or supplemental provision as he considers necessary or expedient for the general purposes, or any particular purpose, of this Act or in consequence of any provision made by or under this Act or for giving full effect to this Act or any such provision.

(2) An order under subsection (1) may, in particular, make provision—

(a) for enabling any person by whom any powers will become exercisable, on a date set by or under this Act, by virtue of any provision made by or under this Act to take before that date any steps which are necessary as a preliminary to the exercise of those powers;

(b) for applying (with or without modifications) or amending, repealing or revoking any provision of or made under an Act passed before this Act or in the same Session;

(c) dissolving any body corporate established by any Act passed, or instrument made, before the passing of this Act;

(d) for making savings, or additional savings, from the effect of any repeal or revocation made by or under this Act.

(3) Amendments made under this section are additional, and without prejudice, to those made by or under any other provision of this Act.

(4) No other provision of this Act restricts the powers conferred by this section.

427. Transitional provisions

(1) Subsections (2) and (3) apply to an order under section 426 which makes transitional provisions or savings.

(2) The order may, in particular—

(a) if it makes provision about the authorisation and permission of persons who before commencement were entitled to carry on any activities, also include provision for such persons not to be treated as having any authorisation or permission (whether on an application to the Authority or otherwise);

(b) make provision enabling the Authority to require persons of such descriptions as it may direct to re-apply for permissions having effect by virtue of the order;

(c) make provision for the continuation as rules of such provisions (including primary and subordinate legislation) as may be designated in accordance with the order by the Authority, including provision for the modification by the Authority of provisions designated;

(d) make provision about the effect of requirements imposed, liabilities incurred and any other things done before commencement, including provision for and about investigations, penalties and the taking or continuing of any other action in respect of contraventions;

(e) make provision for the continuation of disciplinary and other proceedings begun before commencement, including provision about the decisions available to bodies before which such proceedings take place and the effect of their decisions;

(f) make provision as regards the Authority's obligation to maintain a record under section 347 as respects persons in relation to whom provision is made by the order.

(3) The order may—

(a) confer functions on the Treasury, the Secretary of State, the Authority, the scheme manager, the scheme operator, members of the panel established under paragraph 4 of Schedule 17, the Competition Commission or the Office of Fair Trading;

(b) confer jurisdiction on the Tribunal;

(c) provide for fees to be charged in connection with the carrying out of functions conferred under the order;

(d) modify, exclude or apply (with or without modifications) any primary or subordinate legislation (including any provision of, or made under, this Act).

(4) In subsection (2) "commencement" means the commencement of such provisions of this Act as may be specified by the order.

428. Regulations and orders

(1) Any power to make an order which is conferred on a Minister of the Crown by this Act and any power to make regulations which is conferred by this Act is exercisable by statutory instrument.

(2) The Lord Chancellor's power to make rules under section 132 is exercisable by statutory instrument.

(3) Any statutory instrument made under this Act may—

(a) contain such incidental, supplemental, consequential and transitional provision as the person making it considers appropriate; and

(b) make different provision for different cases.

429. Parliamentary control of statutory instruments

(1) No order is to be made under—

(a) section 1J, 3B(4), 3F(6), 55C, 144(4), 192(b) or (e), 138K(6)(c), 192B(6), 204A(7), 213(1A), 236(5), 285(4), 380(12), 382(15), 384(13), 404G or 419, or

(b) ...

unless a draft of the order has been laid before Parliament and approved by a resolution of each House.

(2) No regulations are to be made under section 90B, 214A, 214B, 214D or 262 unless a draft of the regulations has been laid before Parliament and approved by a resolution of each House.

(3) An order to which, if it is made, subsection (4) or (5) will apply is not to be made unless a draft of the order has been laid before Parliament and approved by a resolution of each House.

(4) This subsection applies to an order under section 21 if—

(a) it is the first order to be made, or to contain provisions made, under section 21(4);

(b) it varies an order made under section 21(4) so as to make section 21(1) apply in circumstances in which it did not previously apply;

(c) it is the first order to be made, or to contain provision made, under section 21(5);

(d) it varies a previous order made under section 21(5) so as to make section 21(1) apply in circumstances in which it did not, as a result of that previous order, apply;

(e) it is the first order to be made, or to contain provisions made, under section 21(9) or (10);

(f) it adds one or more activities to those that are controlled activities for the purposes of section 21; or

(g) it adds one or more investments to those which are controlled investments for the purposes of section 21.

(5) This subsection applies to an order under section 38 if—

(a) it is the first order to be made, or to contain provisions made, under that section; or

(b) it contains provisions restricting or removing an exemption provided by an earlier order made under that section.

(6) An order containing a provision to which, if the order is made, subsection (7) will apply is not to be made unless a draft of the order has been laid before Parliament and approved by a resolution of each House.

(7) This subsection applies to a provision contained in an order if—

(a) it is the first to be made in the exercise of the power conferred by subsection (1) of section 326 or it removes a body from those for the time being designated under that subsection; or

(b) it is the first to be made in the exercise of the power conferred by subsection (6) of section 327 or it adds a description of regulated activity or investment to those for the time being specified for the purposes of that subsection.

(8) Any other statutory instrument made under this Act, apart from one made under section 3G(1), 137D(1)(b), 165A(2)(d), 192A(4) or 431(2) or to which section 22B or 23A or paragraph 26 of Schedule 2 applies, shall be subject to annulment in pursuance of a resolution of either House of Parliament.

430. Extent

(1) This Act, except Chapter IV of Part XVII, extends to Northern Ireland.

(2) Except where Her Majesty by Order in Council provides otherwise, the extent of any amendment or repeal made by or under this Act is the same as the extent of the provision amended or repealed.

(3) Her Majesty may by Order in Council provide for any provision of or made under this Act relating to a matter which is the subject of other legislation which extends to any of the Channel Islands or the Isle of Man to extend there with such modifications (if any) as may be specified in the Order.

431. Commencement

(1) The following provisions come into force on the passing of this Act—

(a) this section;

(b) sections 428, 430 and 433;

(c) paragraphs 1 and 2 of Schedule 21.

(2) The other provisions of this Act come into force on such day as the Treasury may by order appoint; and different days may be appointed for different purposes.

432. Minor and consequential amendments, transitional provisions and repeals

(1) Schedule 20 makes minor and consequential amendments.

(2) Schedule 21 makes transitional provisions.

(3) The enactments set out in Schedule 22 are repealed.

433. Short title

This Act may be cited as the Financial Services and Markets Act 2000.

SCHEDULE 1

...

SCHEDULE 1ZA

Section 1A THE FINANCIAL CONDUCT AUTHORITY

PART 1

GENERAL

Interpretation

1. In this Schedule—

"the Bank" means the Bank of England;

"functions", in relation to the FCA, means functions conferred on the FCA by or under any provision of this Act (see section 1A(6) which affects the meaning of references to such functions).

Constitution

2.— (1) The constitution of the FCA must provide for the FCA to have a governing body.

(2) The governing body must consist of—

(a) a chair appointed by the Treasury,

(b) a chief executive appointed by the Treasury,

(c) the Bank's Deputy Governor for prudential regulation,

(d) 2 members appointed jointly by the Secretary of State and the Treasury, and

(e) at least one other member appointed by the Treasury.

(3) The members referred to in sub-paragraph (2)(a), (c) and (d) are to be non-executive members.

(4) In exercising its powers under sub-paragraph (2)(e) to appoint executive or non-executive members,

the Treasury must secure that the majority of members of the governing body are non-executive members.

(5) An employee of the FCA may not be appointed as a non-executive member.

(6) In the following provisions of this Schedule an "appointed member" means a member of the governing body appointed under sub-paragraph (2)(a), (b), (d) or (e).

3.— (1) The terms of service of the appointed members are to be determined by the Treasury.

(2) In the case of a member appointed under paragraph 2(2)(d), the Treasury must consult the Secretary of State about the terms of service.

(3) Before appointing a person as an appointed member, the Treasury (or as the case requires the Treasury and the Secretary of State) must consider whether the person has any financial or other interests that could have a material effect on the extent of the functions as member that it would be proper for the person to discharge.

(4) The terms of service of an appointed member ("M") must be such as—

(a) to secure that M is not subject to direction by the Treasury or the Secretary of State,

(b) to require M not to act in accordance with the directions of any other person, and

(c) to prohibit M from acquiring any financial or other interests that have a material effect on the extent of the functions as member that it would be proper for M to discharge.

(5) If an appointed member is an employee of the FCA, the member's interest as employee is to be disregarded for the purposes of sub-paragraphs (3) and (4)(c) and paragraph 4(1)(b).

(6) A person who is an employee of the PRA is disqualified for appointment as an appointed member.

(7) The FCA may pay expenses to the Bank's Deputy Governor for prudential regulation in respect of that person's service as a member.

4.— (1) The Treasury may remove an appointed member from office—

(a) on the grounds of incapacity or serious misconduct, or

(b) on the grounds that in all the circumstances the member's financial or other interests are such as to have a material effect on the extent of the functions as member that it would be proper for the person to discharge.

(2) Before removing from office a member appointed under paragraph 2(2)(d), the Treasury must consult the Secretary of State.

5. The validity of any act of the FCA is not affected—

(a) by any vacancy in any of the offices mentioned in paragraph 2(2)(a), (b) or (c), or

(b) by a defect in the appointment of a person—

(i) to any of those offices, or

(ii) as an appointed member.

6. The Bank's Deputy Governor for prudential regulation must not take part in any discussion by or decision of the FCA which relates to—

(a) the exercise of the FCA's functions in relation to a particular person, or

(b) a decision not to exercise those functions.

Remuneration

7. The FCA must pay to the appointed members such remuneration as may be determined—

(a) in the case of the non-executive members, by the Treasury;

(b) in the case of the executive members, by the FCA.

Arrangements for discharging functions

8.— (1) The FCA may make arrangements for any of its functions to be discharged by a committee, sub-committee, officer or member of staff of the FCA, but subject to the following provisions.

(2) In exercising its legislative functions, the FCA must act through its governing body.

(3) For that purpose, the following are the FCA's legislative functions—

(a) making rules;

(b) issuing codes under section 64 or 119;

(c) issuing statements under—

(i) section 63C, 64, 69, 88C, 89S, 93, 124, 131J, 138N, 192H, 192N, 210 or 312J,

(ii) section 345D (whether as a result of section 345(2) or section 249(1)), or

(iii) section 80 of the Financial Services Act 2012;

(d) giving directions under section 316, 318 or 328.

(4) The function of issuing general guidance (as defined in section 139B(5)) may not be discharged by an officer or member of staff of the FCA.

Records

9. The FCA must maintain satisfactory arrangements for—

(a) recording decisions made in the exercise of its functions, and

(b) the safe-keeping of those records which it considers ought to be preserved.

Publication of record of meetings of governing body

10.— (1) The FCA must publish a record of each meeting of its governing body—

(a) before the end of the period of 6 weeks beginning with the day of the meeting, or

(b) if no meeting of the governing body is subsequently held during that period, before the end of the period of 2 weeks beginning with the day of the next meeting.

(2) The record must specify any decision taken at the meeting (including decisions to take no action) and must set out, in relation to each decision, a summary of the deliberations of the governing body.

(3) Sub-paragraphs (1) and (2) do not require the publication of information whose publication within the time required by sub-paragraph (1) would in the opinion of the governing body be against the public interest.

(4) Publication under this section is to be in such manner as the FCA thinks fit.

Annual report

11.— (1) At least once a year the FCA must make a report to the Treasury on—

(a) the discharge of its functions,

(b) the extent to which, in its opinion, its operational objectives have been advanced,

(c) the extent to which, in its opinion, it has acted compatibly with its strategic objective,

(d) how, in its opinion, it has complied with the duty in section 1B(4),

(e) its consideration of the matter mentioned in section 1B(5)(b),

(f) its consideration of the principles in section 3B,

(g) how it has complied with section 3D,

(h) any direction received under section 3I or 3J during the period to which the report relates,

(i) how it has complied with section 354A(1) so far as relating to co-operation with persons outside the United Kingdom, and

(j) such other matters as the Treasury may from time to time direct.

(2) Sub-paragraph (1) does not require the inclusion in the report of any information whose publication would in the opinion of the FCA be against the public interest.

(3) The report must be accompanied by—

(a) a statement of the remuneration of the appointed members of the governing body of the FCA during the period to which the report relates, and

(b) such other reports or information, prepared by such persons, as the Treasury may from time to time direct.

(4) The Treasury must lay before Parliament a copy of each report received by them under this paragraph.

Annual public meeting

12.— (1) Not later than 3 months after making a report under paragraph 11, the FCA must hold a public meeting ("the annual meeting") for the purposes of enabling that report to be considered.

(2) The FCA must organise the annual meeting so as to allow—

(a) a general discussion of the contents of the report which is being considered, and

(b) a reasonable opportunity for those attending the meeting to put questions to the FCA about the way in which it discharged, or failed to discharge, its functions during the period to which the report relates.

(3) But otherwise the annual meeting is to be organised and conducted in such a way as the FCA considers appropriate.

(4) The FCA must give reasonable notice of its annual meeting.

(5) That notice must—

(a) give details of the time and place at which the meeting is to be held,

(b) set out the proposed agenda for the meeting,

(c) indicate the proposed duration of the meeting,

(d) give details of the FCA's arrangements for enabling persons to attend, and

(e) be published by the FCA in the way appearing to it to be best calculated to bring the notice to the attention of the public.

(6) If the FCA proposes to alter any of the arrangements which have been included in the notice given under sub-paragraph (5), it must—

(a) give reasonable notice of the alteration, and

(b) publish that notice in the way appearing to the FCA to be best calculated to bring it to the attention of the public.

Report of annual meeting

13. Not later than one month after its annual meeting, the FCA must publish a report of the proceedings of the meeting.

Accounts and audit

14.— (1) The Treasury may—

(a) require the FCA to comply with any provisions of the Companies Act 2006 about accounts and their audit which would not otherwise apply to it, or

(b) direct that any provision of that Act about accounts and their audit is to apply to the FCA with such modifications as are specified in the direction, whether or not the provision would otherwise apply to the FCA.

(2) Compliance with any requirement under sub-paragraph (1)(a) or (b) is enforceable by injunction or, in Scotland, an order for specific performance under section 45 of the Court of Session Act 1988.

(3) Proceedings under sub-paragraph (2) may be brought only by the Treasury.

15.— (1) The FCA must send a copy of its annual accounts to the Comptroller and Auditor General as soon as is reasonably practicable.

(2) The Comptroller and Auditor General must—

(a) examine, certify and report on accounts received under this paragraph, and

(b) send a copy of the certified accounts and the report to the Treasury.

(3) The Treasury must lay the copy of the certified accounts and the report before Parliament.

(4) Except as provided by paragraph 14(1), the FCA is exempt from the requirements of Part 16 of the Companies Act 2006 (audit), and its balance sheet must contain a statement to that effect.

(5) In this paragraph "annual accounts" has the meaning given in section 471 of the Companies Act 2006.

PART 2
STATUS

Status

16. In relation to any of its functions—

(a) the FCA is not to be regarded as acting on behalf of the Crown, and

(b) its members, officers and staff are not to be regarded as Crown servants.

Exemption from requirement for use of "limited" in name of FCA

17. The FCA is to continue to be exempt from the requirements of the Companies Act 2006 relating to the use of "limited" as part of its name.

18. If the Secretary of State is satisfied that any action taken by the FCA makes it inappropriate for the exemption given by paragraph 17 to continue, the Secretary of State may, after consulting the Treasury, give a direction removing it.

PART 3
PENALTIES AND FEES

Penalties

19. In determining its policy with respect to the amounts of penalties to be imposed by it under this Act, the FCA must take no account of the expenses which it incurs, or expects to incur, in discharging its functions.

20.— (1) The FCA must in respect of each of its financial years pay to the Treasury its penalty receipts after deducting its enforcement costs.

(2) The FCA's "penalty receipts" in respect of a financial year are any amounts received by it during the year by way of penalties imposed under this Act.

(3) The FCA's "enforcement costs" in respect of a financial year are the expenses incurred by it during the year in connection with—

(a) the exercise, or consideration of the possible exercise, of any of its enforcement powers in particular cases, or

(b) the recovery of penalties imposed under this Act.

(4) For this purpose the FCA's enforcement powers are—

(a) its powers under any of the provisions mentioned in section 133(7A),

(b) its powers under section 56 (prohibition orders),

(c) its powers under Part 25 of this Act (injunctions and restitution),

(d) its powers under any other enactment specified by the Treasury by order,

(e) its powers in relation to the investigation of relevant offences, and

(f) its powers in England and Wales or Northern Ireland in relation to the prosecution of relevant offences.

(5) "Relevant offences" are—

(a) offences under FSMA 2000,

(b) offences under subordinate legislation made under that Act,

(c) offences falling within section 402(1) of that Act,

(d) offences under Part 7 of the Financial Services Act 2012, and

(e) any other offences specified by the Treasury by order.

(6) The Treasury may give directions to the FCA as to how the FCA is to comply with its duty under sub-paragraph (1).

(7) The directions may in particular—

(a) specify descriptions of expenditure that are, or are not, to be regarded as incurred in connection with either of the matters mentioned in sub-paragraph (3),

(b) relate to the calculation and timing of the deduction in respect of the FCA's enforcement costs, and

(c) specify the time when any payment is required to be made to the Treasury.

(8) The directions may also require the FCA to provide the Treasury at specified times with specified information relating to—

(a) penalties that the FCA has imposed under this Act, or

(b) the FCA's enforcement costs.

(9) The Treasury must pay into the Consolidated Fund any sums received by them under this paragraph.

21.— (1) The FCA must prepare and operate a scheme ("the financial penalty scheme") for ensuring that the amounts that, as a result of the deduction for which paragraph 20(1) provides, are retained by the FCA in respect of amounts paid to it by way of penalties imposed under this Act are applied for the benefit of regulated persons.

(2) "Regulated persons" means—

(a) authorised persons,

(b) recognised investment exchanges,

(c) issuers of securities admitted to the official list, and

(d) issuers who have requested or approved the admission of financial instruments to trading on a regulated market.

(3) The financial penalty scheme may, in particular, make different provision with respect to different classes of regulated person.

(4) The financial penalty scheme must ensure that those who have become liable to pay a penalty to the FCA in any financial year of the FCA do not receive any benefit under the scheme in the following financial year.

(5) Up-to-date details of the financial penalty scheme must be set out in a document ("the scheme details").

22.— (1) The scheme details must be published by the FCA in the way appearing to it to be best calculated to bring them to the attention of the public.

(2) Before making the financial penalty scheme, the FCA must publish a draft of the proposed scheme in the way appearing to the FCA to be best calculated to bring it to the attention of the public.

(3) The draft must be accompanied by notice that representations about the proposals may be made to the FCA within a specified time.

(4) Before making the scheme, the FCA must have regard to any representations made to it in accordance with sub-paragraph (3).

(5) If the FCA makes the proposed scheme, it must publish an account, in general terms, of—

(a) the representations made to it in accordance with sub-paragraph (3), and

(b) its response to them.

(6) If the scheme differs from the draft published under sub-paragraph (2) in a way which is, in the opinion of the FCA, significant, the FCA must (in addition to complying with sub-paragraph (5)) publish details of the difference.

(7) The FCA must, without delay, give the Treasury a copy of any scheme details published by it.

(8) The FCA may charge a reasonable fee for providing a person with a copy of—

(a) a draft published under sub-paragraph (2);

(b) scheme details.

(9) Sub-paragraphs (2) to (6) and (8)(a) also apply to a proposal to alter or replace the financial penalty scheme.

Fees

23.— (1) The FCA may make rules providing for the payment to it of such fees, in connection with the discharge of any of its qualifying functions, as it considers will (taking account of its expected income from fees and charges provided for by any other provision of this Act) enable it—

(a) to meet expenses incurred in carrying out its functions or for any incidental purpose,

(b) to repay the principal of, and pay any interest on, any relevant borrowing and to meet relevant commencement expenses, and

(c) to maintain adequate reserves.

(2) The "qualifying functions" of the FCA are—

(a) its functions under or as a result of this Act or any of the other Acts mentioned in section 1A(6), and

(b) its functions under or as a result of a qualifying EU provision that is specified, or of a description specified, for the purposes of this sub-paragraph by the Treasury by order.

(3) In sub-paragraph (1)(b)—

"relevant borrowing" means any money borrowed by the FCA which has been used for the purpose of meeting expenses incurred in relation to its assumption of functions under this Act, and

"relevant commencement expenses" means expenses incurred by the FCA—

(a) in preparation for the exercise of functions by the FCA under this Act, or

(b) for the purpose of facilitating the exercise by the FCA of those functions or otherwise in connection with their exercise by it.

(4) Neither section 1A(6)(d) nor the definition of "functions" in paragraph 1 applies for the purposes of sub-paragraph (2).

(5) For the purposes of sub-paragraph (3) it is irrelevant when the borrowing of the money, the incurring of the expenses or the assumption of functions took place (and, in particular, it is irrelevant if any of those things were done at a time when the FCA was known as the Financial Services Authority).

(6) In the case of rules made under Part 6 of this Act, the rules may, in particular, require the payment of fees in respect of—

(a) the continued inclusion of securities or persons in any list or register required to be kept by the FCA as a result of any provision made by or under that Part,

(b) access to any list or register within paragraph (a), and

(c) the continued admission of financial instruments to trading on a regulated market.

(7) In fixing the amount of any fee which is to be payable to the FCA, no account is to be taken of any sums which the FCA receives, or expects to receive, by way of penalties imposed by it under this Act.

(8) Any fee which is owed to the FCA under any provision made by or under this Act may be recovered as a debt due to the FCA.

Services for which fees may not be charged

24. The power conferred by paragraph 23 may not be used to require—

(a) a fee to be paid in respect of the discharge of any of the FCA's functions under paragraph 13, 14, 19 or 20 of Schedule 3, or

(b) a fee to be paid by any person whose application for approval under section 59 has been granted.

PART 4
MISCELLANEOUS

Exemption from liability in damages

25.— (1) None of the following is to be liable in damages for anything done or omitted in the discharge, or purported discharge, of the FCA's functions—

(a) the FCA;

(b) any person ("P") who is, or is acting as, a member, officer or member of staff of the FCA;

(c) any person who could be held vicariously liable for things done or omitted by P, but only in so far as the liability relates to P's conduct.

(2) Anything done or omitted by a person mentioned in sub-paragraph (1)(a) or (b) while acting, or purporting to act, as a result of an appointment under any of sections 166 to 169 is to be taken for the purposes of sub-paragraph (1) to have been done or omitted in the discharge, or as the case may be purported discharge, of the FCA's functions.

(3) Sub-paragraph (1) does not apply—

(a) if the act or omission is shown to have been in bad faith, or

(b) so as to prevent an award of damages made in respect of an act or omission on the ground that the act or omission was unlawful as a result of section 6(1) of the Human Rights Act 1998.

Accredited financial investigators

26. For the purposes of this Act anything done by an accredited financial investigator within the meaning of the Proceeds of Crime Act 2002 who—

(a) is, or is acting as, an officer of, or member of the staff of, the FCA, or

(b) is appointed by the FCA under section 97, 167 or 168 to conduct an investigation,

is to be treated as done in the exercise or discharge of a function of the FCA.

Amounts required by rules to be paid to the FCA

27. Any amount (other than a fee) which is required by rules to be paid to the FCA may be recovered as a debt due to the FCA.

SCHEDULE 1ZB

Section 2A

THE PRUDENTIAL REGULATION AUTHORITY

PART 1
GENERAL

Interpretation

1. In this Schedule—

"the Bank" means the Bank of England;

"functions", in relation to the PRA, means functions conferred on the PRA by or under any provision of this Act (see section 2A(6) which affects the meaning of references to such functions).

Constitution

2. The constitution of the PRA must provide—

(a) for the Governor of the Bank to be the chair of the PRA,

(b) for the Bank's Deputy Governor for prudential regulation to be the chief executive of the PRA, and

(c) for the PRA to have a governing body.

3. The governing body must consist of—

(a) the chair,

(b) the chief executive,

(c) the Bank's Deputy Governor for financial stability,

(d) the chief executive of the FCA, and

(e) other members (in this Schedule referred to as "appointed members").

4. The validity of any act of the PRA is not affected—

(a) by any vacancy resulting from a vacancy in the office of Governor of the Bank, Deputy Governor of the Bank for prudential regulation, Deputy Governor of the Bank for financial stability, or chief executive of the FCA, or

(b) by a defect in the appointment of a person—

(i) to any of those offices, or

(ii) as an appointed member.

5. The chief executive of the FCA must not take part in any discussion by or decision of the PRA which relates to—

(a) the exercise of the PRA's functions in relation to a particular person, or

(b) a decision not to exercise those functions.

Appointed members of governing body

6. The appointed members must be appointed by the court of directors of the Bank with the approval of the Treasury.

7. Paragraphs 8 to 12 apply to the exercise by the court of directors of the Bank of its power to appoint appointed members.

8. The court of directors must secure that the majority of the members of the governing body of the PRA are non-executive members.

9. For the purposes of paragraph 8, and for the purposes of the PRA's duty in section 3C (duty to follow principles of good governance) none of the following is a non-executive member—

(a) the members referred to in paragraph 3(a), (b) and c), and

(b) a member who is an employee of the PRA or of the Bank.

10. The court of directors must have regard to generally accepted principles of good practice relating to the making of public appointments.

11.— (1) Before appointing a person as an appointed member, the court of directors must consider whether the person has any financial or other interests that could have a material effect on the extent of the functions as member that it would be proper for the person to discharge.

(2) The terms on which an appointed member ("M") is appointed must be such as—

(a) to secure that M is not subject to direction by the Bank,

(b) to require M not to act in accordance with the directions of any other person, and

(c) to prohibit M from acquiring any financial or other interests that have a material effect on the extent of the functions as member that it would be proper for M to discharge.

(3) If M is an employee of the PRA, M's interest as employee is to be disregarded for the purposes of sub-paragraphs (1) and (2)(c) and paragraph 14.

12. An employee of the FCA is disqualified for appointment as an appointed member.

13. The PRA must pay to the Bank the amount of any expenses incurred by the Bank in connection with the appointment of appointed members.

14. The court of directors of the Bank may, with the approval of the Treasury, remove an appointed member from office—

(a) on the grounds of incapacity or serious misconduct, or

(b) on the grounds that in all the circumstances the member's financial or other interests are such as to have a material effect on the extent of the functions as member that it would be proper for the person to discharge.

Terms of service

15.— (1) The terms of service of the members of the governing body are to be determined by the Oversight

Committee of the Bank.

(2) The PRA must pay to the members of its governing body such remuneration as may be determined by that Committee.

Arrangements for discharging functions

16.— (1) The PRA may make arrangements for any of its functions to be discharged by a committee, sub-committee, officer or member of staff of the PRA, but subject to the following provision.

(2) In exercising its legislative functions or its functions under section 2E (strategy), the PRA must act through its governing body.

(3) For that purpose, the following are the PRA's legislative functions—

(a) making rules;

(b) issuing codes under section 64;

(c) issuing statements under—

(i) section 63C, 64, 69, 192H, 192N, 210 or 345D, or

(ii) section 80 of the Financial Services Act 2012;

(d) giving directions under section 316 or 318;

(e) issuing guidance under section 2I.

Records

17. The PRA must maintain satisfactory arrangements for—

(a) recording decisions made in the exercise of its functions, and

(b) the safe-keeping of those records which it considers ought to be preserved.

Budget

18.— (1) The PRA must, for each of its financial years, adopt an annual budget which has been approved by the Bank.

(2) The budget must be adopted before the start of the financial year to which it relates, except that the first budget must be adopted as soon as reasonably practicable after the coming into force of this paragraph.

(3) The PRA may, with the approval of the Bank, vary the budget for a financial year at any time after its adoption.

(4) The PRA must publish each budget, and each variation of a budget, in such manner as the PRA thinks fit.

Annual report

19.— (1) At least once a year the PRA must make a report to the Treasury on—

(a) the discharge of its functions,

(b) the extent to which, in its opinion, its objectives have been advanced,

(c) its consideration of the principles in section 3B and of the matter mentioned in section 2H(1)(b),

(d) how it has complied with section 3D,

(e) any direction given under section 3I or 3J during the period to which the report relates,

(f) how it has complied with section 354B(1) so far as relating to co-operation with persons outside the United Kingdom, and

(g) such other matters as the Treasury may from time to time direct.

(2) Sub-paragraph (1) does not require the inclusion in the report of any information whose publication would in the opinion of the PRA be against the public interest.

(3) The report must be accompanied by—

(a) a statement of the remuneration of the members of the governing body of the PRA during the period to which the report relates, and

(b) such other reports or information, prepared by such persons, as the Treasury may from time to time direct.

(4) The Treasury must lay before Parliament a copy of each report received by them under this paragraph.

Consultation about annual report

20.— (1) In relation to each report made under paragraph 19, the PRA must publish at the same time as the report an invitation to members of the public to make representations to the PRA, within the 3 months beginning with the date of publication—

(a) about the report,

(b) about the way in which the PRA has discharged, or failed to discharge, its functions during the period to which the report relates, and

(c) about the extent to which, in their opinion, the PRA's objectives have been advanced and the PRA has considered the regulatory principles in section 3B and the matter mentioned in section 2H(1)(b).

(2) The invitation must be published in the way appearing to it to be best calculated to bring the invitation to the attention of the public.

Report on consultation

21.— (1) The PRA must publish a report about its consultation in accordance with paragraph 20.

(2) The report must contain an account, in general terms, of any representations received in pursuance of the invitation published under that paragraph.

(3) The report must be published not later than 4 months after the date on which the report under paragraph 19 was published.

Accounts and audit

22.— (1) The Treasury may—

(a) require the PRA to comply with any provisions of the Companies Act 2006 about accounts and their audit which would not otherwise apply to it, or

(b) direct that any provision of that Act about accounts and their audit is to apply to the PRA with such modifications as are specified in the direction, whether or not the provision would otherwise apply to the PRA.

(2) Compliance with any requirement under sub-paragraph (1)(a) or (b) is enforceable by injunction or, in Scotland, an order for specific performance under section 45 of the Court of Session Act 1988.

(3) Proceedings under sub-paragraph (2) may be brought only by the Treasury.

23.— (1) The PRA must send a copy of its annual accounts to the Comptroller and Auditor General as soon as is reasonably practicable.

(2) The Comptroller and Auditor General must—

(a) examine, certify and report on accounts received under this paragraph, and

(b) send a copy of the certified accounts and the report to the Treasury.

(3) The Treasury must lay the copy of the certified accounts and the report before Parliament.

(4) The PRA must send a copy of the certified accounts and the report to the Bank.

(5) Except as provided by paragraph 22(1), the PRA is exempt from the requirements of Part 16 of the Companies Act 2006 (audit), and its balance sheet must contain a statement to that effect.

(6) In this paragraph "annual accounts" has the meaning given in section 471 of the Companies Act 2006.

PART 2
STATUS

Status

24. In relation to any of its functions—

(a) the PRA is not to be regarded as acting on behalf of the Crown, and

(b) its members, officers and staff are not to be regarded as Crown servants.

Exemption from requirement for use of "limited" in name of PRA

25. The PRA is to be exempt from the requirements of the Companies Act 2006 relating to the use of "limited" as part of its name.

26. If the Secretary of State is satisfied that any action taken by the PRA makes it inappropriate for the exemption given by paragraph 25 to continue, the Secretary of State may, after consulting the Treasury, give a direction removing it.

PART 3
PENALTIES AND FEES

Penalties

27. In determining its policy with respect to the amounts of penalties to be imposed by it under this Act, the PRA must take no account of the expenses which it incurs, or expects to incur, in discharging its functions.

28.— (1) The PRA must in respect of each of its financial years pay to the Treasury its penalty receipts after deducting its enforcement costs.

(2) The PRA's "penalty receipts" in respect of a financial year are any amounts received by it during the year by way of penalties imposed under this Act.

(3) The PRA's "enforcement costs" in respect of a financial year are the expenses incurred by it during the year in connection with—

(a) the exercise, or consideration of the possible exercise, of any of its enforcement powers in particular cases, or

(b) the recovery of penalties imposed under this Act.

(4) For this purpose the PRA's enforcement powers are—

(a) its powers under any of the provisions mentioned in section 133(7A),

(b) its powers under section 56 (prohibition orders),

(c) its powers under Part 25 of this Act (injunctions and restitution),

(d) its powers under any other enactment specified by the Treasury by order,

(e) its powers in relation to the investigation of relevant offences, and

(f) its powers in England and Wales or Northern Ireland in relation to the prosecution of relevant offences.

(5) "Relevant offences" are—

(a) offences under FSMA 2000,

(b) offences under subordinate legislation made under that Act, and

(c) any other offences specified by the Treasury by order.

(6) The Treasury may give directions to the PRA as to how the PRA is to comply with its duty under sub-paragraph (1).

(7) The directions may in particular—

(a) specify descriptions of expenditure that are, or are not, to be regarded as incurred in connection with either of the matters mentioned in sub-paragraph (3),

(b) relate to the calculation and timing of the deduction in respect of the PRA's enforcement costs, and

(c) specify the time when any payment is required to be made to the Treasury.

(8) The directions may also require the PRA to provide the Treasury at specified times with information relating to—

(a) penalties that the PRA has imposed under FSMA 2000, or

(b) the PRA's enforcement costs.

(9) The Treasury must pay into the Consolidated Fund any sums received by them under this paragraph.

29.— (1) The PRA must prepare and operate a scheme ("the financial penalty scheme") for ensuring that the amounts that, as a result of the deduction for which paragraph 28(1) provides, are retained by the PRA in respect of amounts paid to it by way of penalties imposed under this Act are applied for the benefit of PRA-authorised persons.

(2) The financial penalty scheme may, in particular, make different provision with respect to different classes of PRA-authorised person.

(3) The financial penalty scheme must ensure that those who have become liable to pay a penalty to the PRA in any financial year of the PRA do not receive any benefit under the scheme in the following financial year.

(4) Up-to-date details of the financial penalty scheme must be set out in a document ("the scheme details").

30.— (1) The scheme details must be published by the PRA in the way appearing to it to be best calculated to bring them to the attention of the public.

(2) Before making the financial penalty scheme, the PRA must publish a draft of the proposed scheme in the way appearing to the PRA to be best calculated to bring it to the attention of the public.

(3) The draft must be accompanied by notice that representations about the proposals may be made to the PRA within a specified time.

(4) Before making the scheme, the PRA must have regard to any representations made to it in accordance with sub-paragraph (3).

(5) If the PRA makes the proposed scheme, it must publish an account, in general terms, of—

(a) the representations made to it in accordance with sub-paragraph (3), and

(b) its response to them.

(6) If the scheme differs from the draft published under sub-paragraph (2) in a way which is, in the opinion of the PRA, significant, the PRA must (in addition to complying with sub-paragraph (5)) publish details of the difference.

(7) The PRA must, without delay, give the Treasury a copy of any scheme details published by it.

(8) The PRA may charge a reasonable fee for providing a person with a copy of—

(a) a draft published under sub-paragraph (2);

(b) scheme details.

(9) Sub-paragraphs (2) to (6) and (8)(a) also apply to a proposal to alter or replace the financial penalty scheme.

Fees

31.— (1) The PRA may make rules providing for the payment to it of such fees, in connection with the discharge of any of its qualifying functions, as it considers will (taking account of its expected income from fees and charges provided for by any other provision of this Act) enable it—

(a) to meet expenses incurred in carrying out its functions or for any incidental purpose,

(b) to repay the principal of, and pay any interest on, any relevant borrowing and to meet relevant commencement expenses, and

(c) to maintain adequate reserves.

(2) The "qualifying functions" of the PRA are—

(a) its functions under or as a result of this Act or any of the other Acts mentioned in section 2A(6), and

(b) its functions under or as a result of a qualifying EU provision that is specified, or of a description specified, for the purposes of this sub-paragraph by the Treasury by order.

(3) In sub-paragraph (1)(b)—

"relevant borrowing" means any money borrowed by the PRA which has been used for the purpose of meeting expenses incurred in relation to its assumption of functions under this Act, and

"relevant commencement expenses" means expenses incurred by the PRA, the FCA or the Bank—

(a) in preparation for the exercise of functions by the PRA under this Act, or

(b) for the purpose of facilitating the exercise by the PRA of those functions or otherwise in connection with their exercise by it.

(4) Neither section 2A(6)(d) nor the definition of "functions" in paragraph 1 applies for the purposes of sub-paragraph (2).

(5) For the purposes of sub-paragraph (3) it is irrelevant when the borrowing of the money, the incurring of the expenses or the assumption of functions took place (and, in particular, it is irrelevant if expenses were incurred by the FCA at a time when it was known as the Financial Services Authority).

(6) In fixing the amount of any fee which is to be payable to the PRA, no account is to be taken of any sums which the PRA receives, or expects to receive, by way of penalties imposed by it under this Act.

(7) Any fee which is owed to the PRA under any provision made by or under this Act may be recovered as a debt due to the PRA.

Services for which fees may not be charged

32. The power conferred by paragraph 31 may not be used to require—

(a) a fee to be paid in respect of the discharge of any of the PRA's functions under paragraph 13, 14, 19 or 20 of Schedule 3, or

(b) a fee to be paid by any person whose application for approval under section 59 has been granted.

PART 4
MISCELLANEOUS

Exemption from liability in damages

33.— (1) None of the following is to be liable in damages for anything done or omitted in the discharge, or purported discharge, of the PRA's functions—

(a) the PRA;

(b) any person ("P") who is, or is acting as, a member, officer or member of staff of the PRA;

(c) any person who could be held vicariously liable for things done or omitted by P, but only in so far as the liability relates to P's conduct.

(2) Anything done or omitted by a person mentioned in sub-paragraph (1)(a) or (b) while acting, or purporting to act, as a result of an appointment under any of sections 97, 166 to 169 and 284 is to be taken for the purposes of sub-paragraph (1) to have been done or omitted in the discharge, or as the case may be purported discharge, of the PRA's functions.

(3) Sub-paragraph (1) does not apply—

(a) if the act or omission is shown to have been in bad faith, or

(b) so as to prevent an award of damages made in respect of an act or omission on the ground that the act or omission was unlawful as a result of section 6(1) of the Human Rights Act 1998.

Accredited financial investigators

34. For the purposes of this Act anything done by an accredited financial investigator within the meaning of the Proceeds of Crime Act 2002 who—

(a) is, or is acting as, an officer of, or member of the staff of, the PRA, or

(b) is appointed by the PRA under section 167 or 168 to conduct an investigation,

is to be treated as done in the exercise or discharge of a function of the PRA.

Amounts required by rules to be paid to the PRA

35. Any amount (other than a fee) which is required by rules to be paid to the PRA may be recovered as a debt due to the PRA.

SCHEDULE 2

REGULATED ACTIVITIES

Section 22(2)

PART I
REGULATED ACTIVITIES: GENERAL

General

1. The matters with respect to which provision may be made under section 22(1) in respect of activities include, in particular, those described in general terms in this Part of this Schedule.

Dealing in investments

2.— (1) Buying, selling, subscribing for or underwriting investments or offering or agreeing to do so, either as a principal or as an agent.

(2) In the case of an investment which is a contract of insurance, that includes carrying out the contract.

Arranging deals in investments

3. Making, or offering or agreeing to make—

(a) arrangements with a view to another person buying, selling, subscribing for or underwriting a particular investment;

(b) arrangements with a view to a person who participates in the arrangements buying, selling, subscribing for or underwriting investments.

Deposit taking

4. Accepting deposits.

Safekeeping and administration of assets

5.— (1) Safeguarding and administering assets belonging to another which consist of or include investments or offering or agreeing to do so.

(2) Arranging for the safeguarding and administration of assets belonging to another, or offering or agreeing to do so.

Managing investments

6. Managing, or offering or agreeing to manage, assets belonging to another person where—

(a) the assets consist of or include investments; or

(b) the arrangements for their management are such that the assets may consist of or include investments at the discretion of the person managing or offering or agreeing to manage them.

Investment advice

7. Giving or offering or agreeing to give advice to persons on—

(a) buying, selling, subscribing for or underwriting an investment; or

(b) exercising any right conferred by an investment to acquire, dispose of, underwrite or convert an investment.

Establishing collective investment schemes

8. Establishing, operating or winding up a collective investment scheme, including acting as—

(a) trustee of a unit trust scheme;

(b) depositary of a collective investment scheme other than a unit trust scheme; or

(c) sole director of a body incorporated by virtue of regulations under section 262.

Using computer-based systems for giving investment instructions

9.— (1) Sending on behalf of another person instructions relating to an investment by means of a computer-based system which enables investments to be transferred without a written instrument.

(2) Offering or agreeing to send such instructions by such means on behalf of another person.

(3) Causing such instructions to be sent by such means on behalf of another person.

(4) Offering or agreeing to cause such instructions to be sent by such means on behalf of another person.

PART 1A
REGULATED ACTIVITIES: RECLAIM FUNDS

Activities of reclaim funds

9A.— (1) The matters with respect to which provision may be made under section 22(1) in respect of activities include, in particular, any of the activities of a reclaim fund.

(2) "Reclaim fund" has the meaning given by section 5(1) of the Dormant Bank and Building Society Accounts Act 2008.

PART II
INVESTMENTS

General

10. The matters with respect to which provision may be made under section 22(1) in respect of investments include, in particular, those described in general terms in this Part of this Schedule.

Securities

11.— (1) Shares or stock in the share capital of a company.

(2) "Company" includes—

(a) any body corporate (wherever incorporated), and

(b) any unincorporated body constituted under the law of a country or territory outside the United Kingdom,

other than an open-ended investment company.

Instruments creating or acknowledging indebtedness

12. Any of the following—

(a) debentures;

(b) debenture stock;

(c) loan stock;

(d) bonds;

(e) certificates of deposit;

(f) any other instruments creating or acknowledging a present or future indebtedness.

Government and public securities

13.— (1) Loan stock, bonds and other instruments—

(a) creating or acknowledging indebtedness; and

(b) issued by or on behalf of a government, local authority or public authority.

(2) "Government, local authority or public authority" means—

(a) the government of the United Kingdom, of Northern Ireland, or of any country or territory outside the United Kingdom;

(b) a local authority in the United Kingdom or elsewhere;

(c) any international organisation the members of which include the United Kingdom or another member State.

Instruments giving entitlement to investments

14.— (1) Warrants or other instruments entitling the holder to subscribe for any investment.

(2) It is immaterial whether the investment is in existence or identifiable.

Certificates representing securities

15. Certificates or other instruments which confer contractual or property rights—

(a) in respect of any investment held by someone other than the person on whom the rights are conferred by the certificate or other instrument; and

(b) the transfer of which may be effected without requiring the consent of that person.

Units in collective investment schemes

16.— (1) Shares in or securities of an open-ended investment company.

(2) Any right to participate in a collective investment scheme.

Options

17. Options to acquire or dispose of property.

Futures

18. Rights under a contract for the sale of a commodity or property of any other description under which delivery is to be made at a future date.

Contracts for differences

19. Rights under—

(a) a contract for differences; or

(b) any other contract the purpose or pretended purpose of which is to secure a profit or avoid a loss by reference to fluctuations in—

(i) the value or price of property of any description; or

(ii) an index or other factor designated for that purpose in the contract.

Contracts of insurance

20. Rights under a contract of insurance, including rights under contracts falling within head C of Schedule 2 to the Friendly Societies Act 1992.

Participation in Lloyd's syndicates

21.— (1) The underwriting capacity of a Lloyd's syndicate.

(2) A person's membership (or prospective membership) of a Lloyd's syndicate.

Deposits

22. Rights under any contract under which a sum of money (whether or not denominated in a currency) is paid on terms under which it will be repaid, with or without interest or a premium, and either on demand or at a time or in circumstances agreed by or on behalf of the person making the payment and the person receiving it.

Loans and other forms of credit

23.— (1) Rights under any contract under which one person provides another with credit.

(2) "Credit" includes any cash loan or other financial accommodation.

(3) "Cash" includes money in any form.

(4) It is immaterial for the purposes of sub-paragraph (1) whether or not the obligation of the borrower is secured on property of any kind.

Other finance arrangements involving land

23A.— (1) Rights under any arrangement for the provision of finance under which the person providing the finance either—

(a) acquires a major interest in land from the person to whom the finance is provided, or

(b) disposes of a major interest in land to that person,

as part of the arrangement.

(2) References in sub-paragraph (1) to a "major interest" in land are to—

(a) in relation to land in England or Wales—

(i) an estate in fee simple absolute, or

(ii) a term of years absolute,

whether subsisting at law or in equity;

(b) in relation to land in Scotland—

(i) the interest of an owner of land, or

(ii) the tenant's right over or interest in a property subject to a lease;

(c) in relation to land in Northern Ireland—

(i) any freehold estate, or

(ii) any leasehold estate,

whether subsisting at law or in equity.

(3) It is immaterial for the purposes of sub-paragraph (1) whether either party acquires or (as the case may be) disposes of the interest in land—

(a) directly, or

(b) indirectly.

Contracts for hire of goods

23B.— (1) Rights under a contract for the bailment or (in Scotland) hiring of goods to a person other than a body corporate.

(2) "Goods" has the meaning given in section 61(1) of the Sale of Goods Act 1979.

(3) It is immaterial for the purposes of sub-paragraph (1) whether the rights of the person to whom the goods are bailed or hired have been assigned to a body corporate.

Rights in investments

24. Any right or interest in anything which is an investment as a result of any other provision made under section 22(1).

PART IIA

REGULATED ACTIVITIES RELATING TO INFORMATION ABOUT PERSONS' FINANCIAL STANDING

General

24A. The matters with respect to which provision may be made under section 22(1A)(a) include, in particular, those described in general terms in this Part of this Schedule.

Providing credit reference services

24B. Furnishing persons with information that—

(a) is relevant to the financial standing of persons other than bodies corporate, and

(b) is collected for that purpose by the person furnishing it.

Providing credit information services

24C.— (1) Taking steps on behalf of a person other than a body corporate in connection with information relevant to that person's financial standing that is or may be held by a regulated person.

(2) "Regulated person" means—

(a) a person who is carrying on a regulated activity, or

(b) a person who is carrying on a business in respect of which a licence under section 21 of the Consumer Credit Act 1974 is required.

24D. Giving advice to a person other than a body corporate in relation to the taking of any steps of the kind mentioned in paragraph 24C(1).

PART IIB
REGULATED ACTIVITIES RELATING TO THE SETTING OF BENCHMARKS

General

24E. The matters with respect to which provisions may be made under section 22(1A)(b) include, in particular, those described in general terms in this Part of this Schedule.

Providing information

24F. Providing any information or expression of opinion that—
(a) is required by another person in connection with the determination of a benchmark, and
(b) is provided to that person for that purpose.

Administration

24G.— (1) Administering the arrangements for determining a benchmark.
(2) Collecting, analysing or processing information or expressions of opinion for the purpose of the determination of a benchmark.

Determining or publishing benchmark or publishing connected information

24H.— (1) Determining a benchmark.
(2) Publishing a benchmark or information connected with a benchmark.

PART III
SUPPLEMENTAL PROVISIONS

The order-making power

25.— (1) An order under section 22(1) or (1A) may—
(a) provide for exemptions;
(b) confer powers on the Treasury or either regulator;
(c) authorise the making of regulations or other instruments by the Treasury for purposes of, or connected with, any relevant provision;
(d) authorise the making of rules or other instruments by either regulator for purposes of, or connected with, any relevant provision;
(e) make provision in respect of any information or document which, in the opinion of the Treasury or either regulator, is relevant for purposes of, or connected with, any relevant provision;
(f) make such consequential, transitional or supplemental provision as the Treasury consider appropriate for purposes of, or connected with, any relevant provision.
(2) Provision made as a result of sub-paragraph (1)(f) may amend any primary or subordinate legislation, including any provision of, or made under, this Act.
(3) "Relevant provision" means any provision—
(a) of section 22 or this Schedule; or
(b) made under that section or this Schedule.

Parliamentary control

26.— (1) This paragraph applies to any order made under section 22(1) or (1A) which contains a statement by the Treasury that, in their opinion, the effect (or one of the effects) of the proposed order would be that an activity which is not a regulated activity would become a regulated activity.
(2) No order to which this paragraph applies may be made unless—
(a) a draft of the order has been laid before Parliament and approved by a resolution of each House, or
(b) sub-paragraph (4) applies.

(3) Sub-paragraph (4) applies if an order to which this paragraph applies also contains a statement that the Treasury are of the opinion that, by reason of urgency, it is necessary to make the order without a draft being so laid and approved.

(4) Where this sub-paragraph applies the order—

(a) must be laid before Parliament after being made, and

(b) ceases to have effect at the end of the relevant period unless before the end of that period the order is approved by a resolution of each House of Parliament (but without that affecting anything done under the order or the power to make a new order).

(5) The "relevant period" is a period of 28 days beginning with the day on which the order is made.

(6) In calculating the relevant period no account is to be taken of any time during which Parliament is dissolved or prorogued or during which both Houses are adjourned for more than 4 days.

Interpretation

27.— (1) In this Schedule—

"buying" includes acquiring for valuable consideration;

"offering" includes inviting to treat;

"property" includes currency of the United Kingdom or any other country or territory; and

"selling" includes disposing for valuable consideration.

(2) In sub-paragraph (1) "disposing" includes—

(a) in the case of an investment consisting of rights under a contract—

(i) surrendering, assigning or converting those rights; or

(ii) assuming the corresponding liabilities under the contract;

(b) in the case of an investment consisting of rights under other arrangements, assuming the corresponding liabilities under the contract or arrangements;

(c) in the case of any other investment, issuing or creating the investment or granting the rights or interests of which it consists.

(3) In this Schedule references to an instrument include references to any record (whether or not in the form of a document).

…

SCHEDULES 7–9

…

SCHEDULE 10

COMPENSATION: EXEMPTIONS

Section 90(2) and (5)

Statements believed to be true

1.— (1) In this paragraph "statement" means—

(a) any untrue or misleading statement in listing particulars; or

(b) the omission from listing particulars of any matter required to be included by section 80 or 81.

(2) A person does not incur any liability under section 90(1) for loss caused by a statement if he satisfies the court that, at the time when the listing particulars were submitted to the FCA, he reasonably believed (having made such enquiries, if any, as were reasonable) that—

(a) the statement was true and not misleading, or

(b) the matter whose omission caused the loss was properly omitted, and that one or more of the conditions set out in sub-paragraph (3) are satisfied.

(3) The conditions are that—

(a) he continued in his belief until the time when the securities in question were acquired;

(b) they were acquired before it was reasonably practicable to bring a correction to the attention of persons likely to acquire them;

(c) before the securities were acquired, he had taken all such steps as it was reasonable for him to have taken to secure that a correction was brought to the attention of those persons;

(d) he continued in his belief until after the commencement of dealings in the securities following their admission to the official list and they were acquired after such a lapse of time that he ought in the circumstances to be reasonably excused.

Statements by experts

2.— (1) In this paragraph "statement" means a statement included in listing particulars which—

(a) purports to be made by, or on the authority of, another person as an expert; and

(b) is stated to be included in the listing particulars with that other person's consent.

(2) A person does not incur any liability under section 90(1) for loss in respect of any securities caused by a statement if he satisfies the court that, at the time when the listing particulars were submitted to the FCA, he reasonably believed that the other person—

(a) was competent to make or authorise the statement, and

(b) had consented to its inclusion in the form and context in which it was included,

and that one or more of the conditions set out in sub-paragraph (3) are satisfied.

(3) The conditions are that—

(a) he continued in his belief until the time when the securities were acquired;

(b) they were acquired before it was reasonably practicable to bring the fact that the expert was not competent, or had not consented, to the attention of persons likely to acquire the securities in question;

(c) before the securities were acquired he had taken all such steps as it was reasonable for him to have taken to secure that that fact was brought to the attention of those persons;

(d) he continued in his belief until after the commencement of dealings in the securities following their admission to the official list and they were acquired after such a lapse of time that he ought in the circumstances to be reasonably excused.

Corrections of statements

3.— (1) In this paragraph "statement" has the same meaning as in paragraph 1.

(2) A person does not incur liability under section 90(1) for loss caused by a statement if he satisfies the court—

(a) that before the securities in question were acquired, a correction had been published in a manner calculated to bring it to the attention of persons likely to acquire the securities; or

(b) that he took all such steps as it was reasonable for him to take to secure such publication and reasonably believed that it had taken place before the securities were acquired.

(3) Nothing in this paragraph is to be taken as affecting paragraph 1.

Corrections of statements by experts

4.— (1) In this paragraph "statement" has the same meaning as in paragraph 2.

(2) A person does not incur liability under section 90(1) for loss caused by a statement if he satisfies the court—

(a) that before the securities in question were acquired, the fact that the expert was not competent or had not consented had been published in a manner calculated to bring it to the attention of persons likely to acquire the securities; or

(b) that he took all such steps as it was reasonable for him to take to secure such publication and reasonably believed that it had taken place before the securities were acquired.

(3) Nothing in this paragraph is to be taken as affecting paragraph 2.

Official statements

5. A person does not incur any liability under section 90(1) for loss resulting from—

(a) a statement made by an official person which is included in the listing particulars, or

(b) a statement contained in a public official document which is included in the listing particulars,

if he satisfies the court that the statement is accurately and fairly reproduced.

False or misleading information known about

6. A person does not incur any liability under section 90(1) or (4) if he satisfies the court that the person suffering the loss acquired the securities in question with knowledge—

(a) that the statement was false or misleading,

(b) of the omitted matter, or

(c) of the change or new matter,

as the case may be.

Belief that supplementary listing particulars not called for

7. A person does not incur any liability under section 90(4) if he satisfies the court that he reasonably believed that the change or new matter in question was not such as to call for supplementary listing particulars.

Meaning of "expert"

8. "Expert" includes any engineer, valuer, accountant or other person whose profession, qualifications or experience give authority to a statement made by him.

SCHEDULE 10A

LIABILITY OF ISSUERS IN CONNECTION WITH PUBLISHED INFORMATION

Section 90A

PART 1
SCOPE OF THIS SCHEDULE

Securities to which this Schedule applies

1.— (1) This Schedule applies to securities that are, with the consent of the issuer, admitted to trading on a securities market, where—

(a) the market is situated or operating in the United Kingdom, or

(b) the United Kingdom is the issuer's home State.

(2) For the purposes of this Schedule—

(a) an issuer of securities is not taken to have consented to the securities being admitted to trading on a securities market by reason only of having consented to their admission to trading on another market as a result of which they are admitted to trading on the first-mentioned market;

(b) an issuer who has accepted responsibility (to any extent) for any document prepared for the purposes of the admission of the securities to trading on a securities market (such as a prospectus or listing particulars) is taken to have consented to their admission to trading on that market.

(3) For the purposes of this Schedule the United Kingdom is the home State of an issuer—

(a) in the case of securities in relation to which the transparency obligations directive applies, if the United Kingdom is the home Member State for the purposes of that directive (see Article 2.1 of the directive);

(b) in any other case, if the issuer has its registered office (or, if it does not have a registered office, its head office) in the United Kingdom.

Published information to which this Schedule applies

4.— (1) This Schedule applies to information published by the issuer of securities to which this Schedule applies—

(a) by recognised means, or

(b) by other means where the availability of the information has been announced by the issuer by recognised means.

(2) It is immaterial whether the information is required to be published (by recognised means or otherwise).

(3) The following are "recognised means"—

(a) a recognised information service;

(b) other means required or authorised to be used to communicate information to the market in question, or to the public, when a recognised information service is unavailable.

(4) A "recognised information service" means—

(a) in relation to a securities market situated or operating in the EEA, a service used for the dissemination of information in accordance with Article 21 of the transparency obligations directive;

(b) in relation to a securities market situated or operating outside the EEA, a service used for the dissemination of information corresponding to that required to be disclosed under that directive; or

(c) in relation to any securities market, any other service used by issuers of securities for the dissemination of information required to be disclosed by the rules of the market.

PART 2

LIABILITY IN CONNECTION WITH PUBLISHED INFORMATION

Liability of issuer for misleading statement or dishonest omission

3.— (1) An issuer of securities to which this Schedule applies is liable to pay compensation to a person who—

(a) acquires, continues to hold or disposes of the securities in reliance on published information to which this Schedule applies, and

(b) suffers loss in respect of the securities as a result of—

(i) any untrue or misleading statement in that published information, or

(ii) the omission from that published information of any matter required to be included in it.

(2) The issuer is liable in respect of an untrue or misleading statement only if a person discharging managerial responsibilities within the issuer knew the statement to be untrue or misleading or was reckless as to whether it was untrue or misleading.

(3) The issuer is liable in respect of the omission of any matter required to be included in published information only if a person discharging managerial responsibilities within the issuer knew the omission to be a dishonest concealment of a material fact.

(4) A loss is not regarded as suffered as a result of the statement or omission unless the person suffering it acquired, continued to hold or disposed of the relevant securities—

(a) in reliance on the information in question, and

(b) at a time when, and in circumstances in which, it was reasonable for him to rely on it.

4.— An issuer of securities to which this Schedule applies is not liable under paragraph 3 to pay compensation to a person for loss suffered as a result of an untrue or misleading statement in, or omission from, published information to which this Schedule applies if—

(a) the published information is contained in listing particulars or a prospectus (or supplementary listing particulars or a supplementary prospectus), and

(b) the issuer is liable under section 90 (compensation for statements in listing particulars or prospectus) to pay compensation to the person in respect of the statement or omission.

Liability of issuer for dishonest delay in publishing information

5.— (1) An issuer of securities to which this Schedule applies is liable to pay compensation to a person who—

(a) acquires, continues to hold or disposes of the securities, and

(b) suffers loss in respect of the securities as a result of delay by the issuer in publishing information to which this Schedule applies.

(2) The issuer is liable only if a person discharging managerial responsibilities within the issuer acted dishonestly in delaying the publication of the information.

Meaning of dishonesty

6.— For the purposes of paragraphs 3(3) and 5(2) a person's conduct is regarded as dishonest if (and only if)—

(a) it is regarded as dishonest by persons who regularly trade on the securities market in question, and

(b) the person was aware (or must be taken to have been aware) that it was so regarded.

Exclusion of certain other liabilities

7.— (1) The issuer is not subject—

(a) to any liability other than that provided for by paragraph 3 in respect of loss suffered as a result of reliance by any person on—

(i) an untrue or misleading statement in published information to which this Schedule applies, or

(ii) the omission from any such published information of any matter required to be included in it;

(b) to any liability other than that provided for by paragraph 5 in respect of loss suffered as a result of delay in the publication of information to which this Schedule applies.

(2) A person other than the issuer is not subject to any liability, other than to the issuer, in respect of any such loss.

(3) This paragraph does not affect—

(a) civil liability—

(i) under section 90 (compensation for statements in listing particulars or prospectus),

(ii) under rules made by virtue of section 954 of the Companies Act 2006 (compensation),

(iii) for breach of contract,

(iv) under the Misrepresentation Act 1967, or

(v) arising from a person's having assumed responsibility, to a particular person for a particular purpose, for the accuracy or completeness of the information concerned;

(b) liability to a civil penalty; or

(c) criminal liability.

(4) This paragraph does not affect the powers conferred by sections 382 and 384 (powers of the court to make a restitution order and of the Authority to require restitution).

(5) References in this paragraph to liability, in relation to a person, include a reference to another person being entitled as against that person to be granted any civil remedy or to rescind or repudiate an agreement.

PART 3
SUPPLEMENTARY PROVISIONS

Interpretation

8.— (1) In this Schedule—

(a) "securities" means transferable securities within the meaning of Article 4.1.18 of the markets in financial instruments directive, other than money-market instruments as defined in Article 4.1.19 of that directive that have a maturity of less than 12 months (and includes instruments outside the EEA);

(b) "securities market" means—

(i) a regulated market as defined in Article 4.1.14 of the markets in financial instruments directive,

(ii) a multilateral trading facility as defined in Article 4.1.15 of the markets in financial instruments directive, or

(iii) a market or facility of a corresponding description outside the EEA.

(2) References in this Schedule to the issuer of securities are—

(a) in relation to a depositary receipt, derivative instrument or other financial instrument representing securities where the issuer of the securities represented has consented to the admission of the instrument to trading as mentioned in paragraph 1(1), to the issuer of the securities represented;

(b) in any other case, to the person who issued the securities.

(3) References in this Schedule to the acquisition or disposal of securities include—

(a) acquisition or disposal of any interest in securities, or

(b) contracting to acquire or dispose of securities or of any interest in securities,

except where what is acquired or disposed of (or contracted to be acquired or disposed of) is a depositary receipt, derivative instrument or other financial instrument representing securities.

(4) References to continuing to hold securities have a corresponding meaning.

(5) For the purposes of this Schedule the following are persons "discharging managerial responsibilities" within an issuer—

(a) any director of the issuer (or person occupying the position of director, by whatever name called);

(b) in the case of an issuer whose affairs are managed by its members, any member of the issuer;

(c) in the case of an issuer that has no persons within paragraph (a) or (b), any senior executive of the issuer having responsibilities in relation to the information in question or its publication.

(6) The following definitions (which apply generally for the purposes of Part 6 of this Act) do not apply for the purposes of this Schedule:

(a) section 102A(1), (2) and (6) (meaning of "securities" and "issuer");

(b) section 102C (meaning of "home State" in relation to transferable securities).

SCHEDULE 11

. . .

SCHEDULE 11A

TRANSFERABLE SECURITIES

Section 85(5)(a)

PART 1

1. Units (within the meaning in section 237(2)) in an open-ended collective investment scheme.

2. Non-equity transferable securities issued by
   - (a) the government of an EEA State;
   - (b) a local or regional authority of an EEA State;
   - (c) a public international body of which an EEA State is a member;
   - (d) the European Central Bank;
   - (e) the central bank of an EEA State.
3. Shares in the share capital of the central bank of an EEA State.
4. Transferable securities unconditionally and irrevocably guaranteed by the government, or a local or regional authority, of an EEA State.

5.— (1) Non-equity transferable securities, issued in a continuous or repeated manner by a credit institution, which satisfy the conditions in sub-paragraph (2).

(2) The conditions are that the transferable securities—
   - (a) are not subordinated, convertible or exchangeable;
   - (b) do not give a right to subscribe to or acquire other types of securities and are not linked to a derivative instrument;
   - (c) materialise reception of repayable deposits; and
   - (d) are covered by a deposit guarantee under directive 94/19/EC of the European Parliament and of the Council on deposit-guarantee schemes.

6. Non-fungible shares of capital—
   - (a) the main purpose of which is to provide the holder with a right to occupy any immoveable property, and
   - (b) which cannot be sold without that right being given up.

PART 2

7.— (1) Transferable securities issued by a body specified in sub-paragraph (2) if, and only if, the proceeds of the offer of the transferable securities to the public will be used solely for the purposes of the issuer's objectives.

(2) The bodies are
   - (a) a charity—
     - (i) as defined by section 1(1) of the Charities Act 2011, or
     - (ii) within the meaning of section 35 of the Charities Act (Northern Ireland) 1964;
   - (b) a body entered in the Scottish Charity Register;
   - (c) a housing association within the meaning of—
     - (i) section 5(1) of the Housing Act 1985,
     - (ii) section 1 of the Housing Associations Act 1985, or
     - (iii) Article 3 of the Housing (Northern Ireland) Order 1992;
   - (d) an industrial and provident society registered in accordance with—
     - (i) section 1(2)(b) of the *Industrial and Provident Societies Act 1965*, or
     - (ii) section 1(2)(b) of the Industrial and Provident Societies Act (Northern Ireland) 1969;
   - (e) a non-profit making association or body recognised by an EEA State with objectives similar to those of a body falling within any of sub-paragraphs (a) to (d).

8.— (1) Non-equity transferable securities, issued in a continuous or repeated manner by a credit institution, which satisfy the conditions in sub-paragraph (2).

(2) The conditions are—
   - (a) that the total consideration for the transferable securities being offered in the EEA States is less than 75,000,000 euros (or an equivalent amount); and
   - (b) those mentioned in paragraph 5(2)(a) and (b).

(3) In determining whether sub-paragraph (2)(a) is satisfied in relation to an offer ("offer A"), offer A is to be taken together with any other offer of transferable securities of the same class made by the same person which—

(a) was open at any time within the period of 12 months ending with the date on which offer A is first made; and

(b) had previously satisfied sub-paragraph (2)(a).

(4) For the purposes of this paragraph, an amount (in relation to an amount denominated in euros) is an "equivalent amount" if it is an amount of equal value denominated wholly or partly in another currency or unit of account.

(5) The equivalent is to be calculated at the latest practicable date before (but in any event not more than 3 working days before) the date on which the offer is first made.

(6) "Credit institution" means a credit institution as defined in Article 4(1) of the banking consolidation directive.

9.— (1) Transferable securities included in an offer where the total consideration for the transferable securities being offered in the EEA States is less than 5,000,000 euros (or an equivalent amount).

(2) Sub-paragraphs (3) to (5) of paragraph 8 apply for the purposes of this paragraph but with the references in sub-paragraph (3) to "sub-paragraph (2)(a)" being read as references to "paragraph 9(1)".

Note. The words "Industrial and Provident Societies Act 1965" in paragraph (2)(d)(i) of this Schedule are substituted by the words "Co-operative and Community Benefit Societies and Credit Unions Act 1965" by the Co-operative and Community Benefit Societies and Credit Unions Act 2010, s. 2, as from a day to be appointed.

SCHEDULE 11B
CONNECTED PERSONS

PART 1
MEANING OF "CONNECTED PERSON"

Introduction

1.— (1) In this Schedule "manager" means a person discharging managerial responsibilities within an issuer.

(2) This Schedule defines what is meant by references in the provisions of this Part relating to disclosure rules to a person being "connected" with a manager (or a manager being "connected" with a person).

Meaning of "connected person"

2.— (1) The following persons (and only those persons) are connected with a manager—

(a) members of the manager's family (see paragraph 3);

(b) a body corporate with which the manager is associated (as defined in paragraph 4);

(c) a person acting in his capacity as trustee of a trust—

(i) the beneficiaries of which include the manager or a person who by virtue of paragraph (a) or (b) is connected with him, or

(ii) the terms of which confer a power on the trustees that may be exercised for the benefit of the manager or any such person,

other than a trust for the purposes of an employees' share scheme or a pension scheme;

(d) a person acting in his capacity as partner—

(i) of the manager, or

(ii) of a person who, by virtue of paragraph (a), (b) or (c), is connected with that manager;

(e) a firm that is a legal person under the law by which it is governed and in which—

(i) the manager is a partner,

(ii) a partner is a person who, by virtue of paragraph (a), (b) or (c) is connected with the manager, or

(iii) a partner is a firm in which the manager is a partner or in which there is a partner who, by virtue of paragraph (a), (b) or (c), is connected with the director.

(2) References to a person connected with a manager do not include a person who is also a manager of the issuer in question.

Family members

3.— (1) This paragraph defines what is meant by references to members of a manager's family.

(2) The members of a manager's family are—

(a) the manager's spouse or civil partner;

(b) any relative of the manager who, on the date of the transaction in question, has shared the same household as the manager for at least 12 months;

(c) the manager's children or step-children under the age of 18.

Associated bodies corporate

4.— (1) This paragraph defines what is meant by a manager being "associated" with a body corporate.

(2) A manager is associated with a body corporate if, but only if—

(a) the manager, or a person connected with the manager, is a director or senior executive who has the power to make management decisions affecting the future development and business prospects of the body corporate; or

(b) the manager and the persons connected with the manager together—

(i) are interested in shares comprised in the equity share capital of that body corporate of a nominal value equal to at least 20% of that share capital, or

(ii) are entitled to exercise or control the exercise of more than 20% of the voting power at any general meeting of that body.

(3) The rules set out in Part 2 of this Schedule (references to interest in shares or debentures) apply for the purposes of this paragraph.

(4) References in this paragraph to voting power the exercise of which is controlled by a manager include voting power whose exercise is controlled by a body corporate controlled by the manager.

(5) Shares in a company held as treasury shares, and any voting rights attached to such shares, are disregarded for the purposes of this paragraph.

Control of a body corporate

5.— (1) This paragraph defines what is meant by a manager "controlling" a body corporate.

(2) A manager is taken to control a body corporate if, but only if—

(a) the manager or a person connected with the manager—

(i) is interested in any part of the equity share capital of that body, or

(ii) is entitled to exercise or control the exercise of any part of the voting power at any general meeting of that body, and

(b) the manager, the persons connected with the manager and the other managers of the issuer in question, together—

(i) are interested in more than 50% of that share capital, or

(ii) are entitled to exercise or control the exercise of more than 50% of that voting power.

(3) The rules set out in Part 2 of this Schedule (references to interest in shares or debentures) apply for the purposes of this paragraph.

(4) References in this paragraph to voting power the exercise of which is controlled by a manager include voting power whose exercise is controlled by a body corporate controlled by the manager.

(5) Shares in a company held as treasury shares, and any voting rights attached to such shares, are disregarded for the purposes of this paragraph.

Supplementary provisions

6. For the purposes of paragraphs 4 and 5 (associated bodies corporate and control of a body corporate)—

(a) a body corporate with which a manager is associated is not treated as connected with that manager unless it is also connected with that manager by virtue of sub-paragraph (1)(c) or (d) of that paragraph (connection as trustee or partner); and

(b) a trustee of a trust the beneficiaries of which include (or may include) a body corporate with which a manager is associated is not treated as connected with a manager by reason only of that fact.

PART 2
CONNECTED PERSONS: REFERENCES TO AN INTEREST IN SHARES OR DEBENTURES

Introduction

7.— (1) The provisions of this Part of this Schedule have effect for the interpretation of references in paragraphs 4 and 5 (associated bodies corporate and control of a body corporate) to an interest in shares or debentures.

(2) The provisions are expressed in relation to shares but apply to debentures as they apply to shares.

General provisions

8.— (1) A reference to an interest in shares includes any interest of any kind whatsoever in shares.

(2) Any restraints or restrictions to which the exercise of any right attached to the interest is or may be subject shall be disregarded.

(3) It is immaterial that the shares in which a person has an interest are not identifiable.

(4) Persons having a joint interest in shares are deemed each of them to have that interest.

Rights to acquire shares

9.— (1) A person who enters into a contract to acquire shares is taken to have an interest in the shares.

(2) A person who—

(a) has a right to call for delivery of shares to the person or to the person's order, or

(b) has a right to acquire an interest in shares or is under an obligation to take an interest in shares,

is taken to have an interest in the shares, whether the right or obligation is conditional or absolute.

(3) Rights or obligations to subscribe for shares are not to be taken for the purposes of sub-paragraph (2) to be rights to acquire or obligations to take an interest in shares.

(4) A person ("A") ceases to have an interest in shares by virtue of this paragraph—

(a) on the shares being delivered to another person at A's order—

(i) in fulfilment of a contract for their acquisition by A, or

(ii) in satisfaction of a right of A's to call for their delivery;

(b) on a failure to deliver the shares in accordance with the terms of such a contract or on which such a right falls to be satisfied;

(c) on the lapse of A's right to call for the delivery of shares.

Right to exercise or control exercise of rights

10.— (1) A person who, not being the registered holder, is entitled—

(a) to exercise any right conferred by the holding of the shares, or

(b) to control the exercise of any such right.

is taken to have an interest in the shares.

(2) For this purpose a person is taken to be entitled to exercise or control the exercise of a right conferred by the holding of shares who—

(a) has a right (whether subject to conditions or not) the exercise of which would make the person so entitled, or

(b) is under an obligation (whether or not so subject) the fulfilment of which would make the person so entitled.

(3) A person who—

(a) has been appointed a proxy to exercise any of the rights attached to the shares, or

(b) has been appointed by a body corporate to act as its representative at any meeting of a company or of any class of its members,

is not, by reason only of that fact, to be taken by virtue of this paragraph to be interested in the shares.

Bodies corporate

11.— (1) A person is taken to be interested in shares if a body corporate is interested in them and—

(a) the body corporate or its directors are accustomed to act in accordance with the person's directions or instructions, or

(b) the person is entitled to exercise or control the exercise of more than one-half of the voting power at general meetings of the body corporate.

(2) For the purposes of sub-paragraph (1)(b) where—

(a) a person is entitled to exercise or control the exercise of more than one-half of the voting power at general meetings of a body corporate, and

(b) that body corporate is entitled to exercise or control the exercise of any of the voting power at general meetings of another body corporate,

the voting power mentioned in paragraph (b) above is taken to be exercisable by that person.

Trusts

12.— (1) Where an interest in shares is comprised in property held on trust, every beneficiary of the trust is taken to have an interest in shares, subject as follows.

(2) So long as a person is entitled to receive, during the lifetime of that person or another, income from trust property comprising shares, an interest in the shares in reversion or remainder or (as regards Scotland) in fee shall be disregarded.

(3) A person is treated as not interested in shares if and so long as the person holds them—

(a) under the law in force in any part of the United Kingdom, as a bare trustee or as a custodian trustee, or

(b) under the law in force in Scotland, as a simple trustee.

(4) There shall be disregarded any interest of a person subsisting by virtue of—

(a) an authorised unit trust scheme (within the meaning of section 237 (other definitions));

(b) a scheme made under section 22 or 22A of the Charities Act 1960 (c 58), section 25 of the Charities Act (Northern Ireland) 1964 (c 33 (NI)) section 24 or 25 of the Charities Act 1993 or section 96 or 100 of the Charities Act 2011, section 11 of the Trustee Investments Act 1961 (c 62) or section 42 of the Administration of Justice Act 1982 (c 53); or

(c) the scheme set out in the Schedule to the Church Funds Investment Measure 1958 (1958 No 1).

(5) There shall be disregarded any interest—

(a) of the Church of Scotland General Trustees or of the Church of Scotland Trust in shares held by them;

(b) of any other person in shares held by those Trustees or that Trust otherwise than as simple trustees.

"The Church of Scotland General Trustees" are the body incorporated by the order confirmed by the Church of Scotland (General Trustees) Order Confirmation Act 1921 (1921 c xxv), and "the Church of Scotland Trust" is the body incorporated by the order confirmed by the Church of Scotland Trust Order Confirmation Act 1932 (1932 c xxi).

Financial Services and Markets Act 2000 (Regulated Activities) Order 2001

S.I. 2001/544

PART I
GENERAL

1. Citation

This Order may be cited as the Financial Services and Markets Act 2000 (Regulated Activities) Order 2001.

2. Commencement

(1) Except as provided by paragraph (2), this Order comes into force on the day on which section 19 of the Act comes into force.

(2) This Order comes into force—

(a) for the purposes of articles 59, 60 and 87 (funeral plan contracts) on 1st January 2002; and

(b) for the purposes of articles 61 to 63, 88, 90 and 91 (regulated mortgage contracts) on such a day as the Treasury may specify.

(3) Any day specified under paragraph (2)(b) must be caused to be notified in the London, Edinburgh and Belfast Gazettes published not later than one week before that day.

3. Interpretation

(1) In this Order—

"the Act" means the Financial Services and Markets Act 2000;

"agreement provider" has the meaning given by article 63J(3);

"agreement seller" has the meaning given by article 63J(3);

"aircraft operator" has the same meaning as in the emission allowance trading directive;

"annuities on human life" does not include superannuation allowances and annuities payable out of any fund applicable solely to the relief and maintenance of persons engaged, or who have been engaged, in any particular profession, trade or employment, or of the dependants of such persons;

"auction platform" means a platform on which auctions of greenhouse gas emissions allowances are held in accordance with the emission allowance auctioning regulation;

"buying" includes acquiring for valuable consideration;

"close relative" in relation to a person means—

(a) his spouse or civil partner;

(b) his children and step children, his parents and step-parents, his brothers and sisters and his step-brothers and step-sisters; and

(c) the spouse or civil partner of any person within sub-paragraph (b);

"the Commission Regulation" means Commission Regulation 1287/2006 of 10 August 2006;

"contract of general insurance" means any contract falling within Part I of Schedule 1;

"contract of insurance" means any contract of insurance which is a contract of long-term insurance or a contract of general insurance, and includes—

(a) fidelity bonds, performance bonds, administration bonds, bail bonds, customs bonds or similar contracts of guarantee, where these are—

(i) effected or carried out by a person not carrying on a banking business;

(ii) not effected merely incidentally to some other business carried on by the person effecting them; and

(iii) effected in return for the payment of one or more premiums;

(b) tontines;
(c) capital redemption contracts or pension fund management contracts, where these are effected or carried out by a person who—
   (i) does not carry on a banking business; and
   (ii) otherwise carries on a regulated activity of the kind specified by article 10(1) or (2);
(d) contracts to pay annuities on human life;
(e) contracts of a kind referred to in article 1(2)(e) of the first life insurance directive (collective insurance etc); and
(f) contracts of a kind referred to in article 1(3) of the first life insurance directive (social insurance);

but does not include a funeral plan contract (or a contract which would be a funeral plan contract but for the exclusion in article 60);

"contract of long-term insurance" means any contract falling within Part II of Schedule 1;

"contractually based investment" means—
(a) rights under a qualifying contract of insurance;
(b) any investment of the kind specified by any of articles 83, 84, 85 and 87; or
(c) any investment of the kind specified by article 89 so far as relevant to an investment falling within (a) or (b);

"credit institution" means—
(a) a credit institution authorised under the banking consolidation directive (as last amended by Directive 2009/111/EC) other than an institution to which Article 2.1 of the markets in financial instruments directive (the text of which is set out in Schedule 3) applies, or
(b) an institution which would satisfy the requirements for authorisation as a credit institution under that directive (other than an institution to which Article 2.1 of the markets in financial instruments directive would apply) if it had its registered office (or if it does not have a registered office, its head office) in an EEA State;

"deposit" has the meaning given by article 5;

"electronic money" has the meaning given by regulation 2(1) of the Electronic Money Regulations 2011;

"emission allowance auctioning regulation" means Commission Regulation (EU) No 1031/2010 of 12 November 2010 on the timing, administration and other aspects of auctioning of greenhouse gas emission allowances pursuant to the emission allowance trading directive;

"emission allowance trading directive" means Directive 2003/87/EC of the European Parliament and of the Council of 13 October 2003 establishing a scheme for greenhouse gas emission allowances trading within the Community;

"financial instrument" means any instrument listed in Section C of Annex I to the markets in financial instruments directive (the text of which is set out in Part 1 of Schedule 2) read with Chapter VI of the Commission Regulation (the text of which is set out in Part 2 of Schedule 2);

"funeral plan contract" has the meaning given by article 59;

"greenhouse gas emissions allowances" mean "allowances" as defined in Article 3(a) of the emission allowance trading directive;

"home Member State", in relation to an investment firm, has the meaning given by Article 4.1.20 of the markets in financial instruments directive, and in relation to a credit institution, has the meaning given by Article 4.7 of the banking consolidation directive;

"home purchase provider" has the meaning given by article 63F(3);

"home purchaser" has the meaning given by article 63F(3);

"instrument" includes any record whether or not in the form of a document;

"investment firm" means a person whose regular occupation or business is the provision or performance of investment services and activities on a professional basis but does not include—

(a) a person to whom the markets in financial instruments directive does not apply by virtue of Article 2 of that directive (the text of which is set out in Schedule 3);

(b) a person whose home Member State is an EEA State other than the United Kingdom and to whom, by reason of the fact that the State has given effect to Article 3 of that directive, that direc-tive does not apply by virtue of that Article;

(c) a person who does not have a home Member State and to whom (if he had his registered office in an EEA State, or, being a person other than a body corporate or a body corporate not hav-ing a registered office, if he had his head office in an EEA State) the markets in financial instruments directive would not apply by virtue of Article 2 of that directive;

"investment services and activities" means—

(a) any service provided to third parties listed in Section A of Annex 1 to the markets in financial instruments directive (the text of which is set out in Part 3 of Schedule 2) read with Article 52 of Commission Directive 2006/73/EC of 10 August 2006 (the text of which is set out in Part 4 of Schedule 2), including the reception, transmission or submission of a bid by an investment firm or credit institution on any auction platform, in relation to any financial instrument; or

(b) any activity listed in Section A of Annex 1 to that directive, in relation to any financial instrument;

"joint enterprise" means an enterprise into which two or more persons ("the participators") enter for commercial purposes related to a business or businesses (other than the business of engaging in a regulated activity) carried on by them; and, where a participator is a member of a group, each other member of the group is also to be regarded as a participator in the enterprise;

"local authority" means—

(a) in England and Wales, a local authority within the meaning of the Local Government Act 1972, the Greater London Authority, the Common Council of the City of London or the Council of the Isles of Scilly;

(b) in Scotland, a local authority within the meaning of the Local Government (Scotland) Act 1973;

(c) in Northern Ireland, a district council within the meaning of the Local Government Act (Northern Ireland) 1972;

"management company" has the meaning given by Article 2.1(b) of the UCITS directive;

"managing agent" means a person who is permitted by the Council of Lloyd's in the conduct of his business as an underwriting agent to perform for a member of Lloyd's one or more of the following functions—

(a) underwriting contracts of insurance at Lloyd's;

(b) reinsuring such contracts in whole or in part;

(c) paying claims on such contracts;

"market operator" means a market operator within the meaning of Article 4.1.13 of the markets in financial instruments directive, or a person who would be a market operator if he had his registered office, or if he does not have a registered office his head office, in an EEA State, but does not include—

(a) a person to whom the markets in financial instruments directive does not apply by virtue of Article 2 of that directive (the text of which is set out in Schedule 3);

(b) a person who does not have a home Member State to whom (if he had his registered office, or if he does not have a registered office his head office, in an EEA State) the markets in financial instruments directive would not apply by virtue of Article 2 of that directive;

"multilateral trading facility" means—
(a) a multilateral trading facility (within the meaning of Article 4.1.15 of the markets in financial instruments directive) operated by an investment firm, a credit institution or a market operator, or
(b) a facility which—
(i) is operated by an investment firm, a credit institution or market operator which does not have a home Member State, and
(ii) if its operator had a home Member State, would be a multilateral trading facility within the meaning of Article 4.1.15 of the markets in financial instruments directive;

"occupational pension scheme" has the meaning given by section 1 of the Pension Schemes Act 1993 but with paragraph (b) of the definition omitted;

"operator" has the same meaning as in the emission allowance trading directive;

"overseas person" means a person who—
(a) carries on activities of the kind specified by any of articles 14, 21, 25, 25A, 25B, 25C, 25D, 25E, 37, 39A, 40, 45, 51, 52, 53, 53A, 53B, 53C, 53D, 61, 63B, 63F and 63J or, so far as relevant to any of those articles, article 64 (or activities of a kind which would be so specified but for the exclusion in article 72); but
(b) does not carry on any such activities, or offer to do so, from a permanent place of business maintained by him in the United Kingdom;

"pension fund management contract" means a contract to manage the investments of pension funds (other than funds solely for the benefit of the officers or employees of the person effecting or carrying out the contract and their dependants or, in the case of a company, partly for the benefit of officers and employees and their dependants of its subsidiary or holding company or a subsidiary of its holding company); and for the purposes of this definition, "subsidiary" and "holding company" are to be construed in accordance with section 1159 of the Companies Act 2006;

"personal pension scheme" means a scheme or arrangement which is not an occupational pension scheme or a stakeholder pension scheme and which is comprised in one or more instruments or agreements, having or capable of having effect so as to provide benefits to or in respect of people—
(a) on retirement,
(b) on having reached a particular age, or
(c) on termination of service in an employment;

"plan provider" has the meaning given by paragraph (3) of article 63B, read with paragraphs (7) and (8) of that article;

"property" includes currency of the United Kingdom or any other country or territory;

"qualifying contract of insurance" means a contract of long-term insurance which is not—
(a) a reinsurance contract; nor
(b) a contract in respect of which the following conditions are met—
(i) the benefits under the contract are payable only on death or in respect of incapacity due to injury, sickness or infirmity;
(ii) ...
(iii) the contract has no surrender value, or the consideration consists of a single premium and the surrender value does not exceed that premium; and
(iv) the contract makes no provision for its conversion or extension in a manner which would result in it ceasing to comply with any of the above conditions;

"reception", "transmission" and "submission" have the same meaning in relation to a bid at an auction for an investment of the kind specified in article 82A as in the emission allowance auctioning regulation;

"regulated home purchase plan" has the meaning given by article 63F(3);

"regulated home reversion plan" has the meaning given by article 63B(3);

"regulated mortgage contract" has the meaning given by article 61(3);

"regulated sale and rent back agreement" has the meaning given by article 63J(3);

"relevant investment" means—

(a) rights under a qualifying contract of insurance;

(b) rights under any other contract of insurance;

(c) any investment of the kind specified by any of articles 83, 84, 85 and 87; or

(d) any investment of the kind specified by article 89 so far as relevant to an investment falling within (a) or (c);

"reversion seller" has the meaning given by article 63B(3);

"security" means (except where the context otherwise requires) any investment of the kind specified by any of articles 76 to 82 or, so far as relevant to any such investment, article 89;

"selling", in relation to any investment, includes disposing of the investment for valuable consideration, and for these purposes "disposing" includes—

(a) in the case of an investment consisting of rights under a contract—

(i) surrendering, assigning or converting those rights; or

(ii) assuming the corresponding liabilities under the contract;

(b) in the case of an investment consisting of rights under other arrangements, assuming the corresponding liabilities under the arrangements; and

(c) in the case of any other investment, issuing or creating the investment or granting the rights or interests of which it consists;

"stakeholder pension scheme" has the meaning given by section 1 of the Welfare Reform and Pensions Act 1999 in relation to Great Britain and has the meaning given by article 3 of the Welfare Reform and Pensions (Northern Ireland) Order 1999 in relation to Northern Ireland;

"syndicate" means one or more persons, to whom a particular syndicate number has been assigned by or under the authority of the Council of Lloyd's, carrying out or effecting contracts of insurance written at Lloyd's;

"trade repository" means a person registered with ESMA under Article 55 of Regulation (EU) 648/2012 of the European Parliament and of the Council of 4 July 2012 on OTC derivatives, central counterparties and trade repositories or a person recognised by ESMA under Article 77 of that Regulation;

"voting shares", in relation to a body corporate, means shares carrying voting rights attributable to share capital which are exercisable in all circumstances at any general meeting of that body corporate.

(2) For the purposes of this Order, a transaction is entered into through a person if he enters into it as agent or arranges, in a manner constituting the carrying on of an activity of the kind specified by article 25(1), 25A(1), 25B(1), 25C(1) or 25E(1), for it to be entered into by another person as agent or principal.

(3) For the purposes of this Order, a contract of insurance is to be treated as falling within Part II of Schedule 1, notwithstanding the fact that it contains related and subsidiary provisions such that it might also be regarded as falling within Part I of that Schedule, if its principal object is that of a contract falling within Part II and it is effected or carried out by an authorised person who has permission to effect or carry out contracts falling within paragraph I of Part II of Schedule 1.

PART II
SPECIFIED ACTIVITIES

CHAPTER I
GENERAL

4. Specified activities: general

(1) The following provisions of this Part specify kinds of activity for the purposes of section 22 of the Act (and accordingly any activity of one of those kinds, which is carried on by way of business,

and relates to an investment of a kind specified by any provision of Part III and applicable to that activity, is a regulated activity for the purposes of the Act).

(2) The kinds of activity specified by articles 51, 52 and 63N are also specified for the purposes of section 22(1)(b) of the Act (and accordingly any activity of one of those kinds, when carried on by way of business, is a regulated activity when carried on in relation to property of any kind).

(3) Subject to paragraph (4), each provision specifying a kind of activity is subject to the exclusions applicable to that provision (and accordingly any reference in this Order to an activity of the kind specified by a particular provision is to be read subject to any such exclusions).

(4) Where an investment firm or credit institution—

(a) provides or performs investment services and activities on a professional basis, and

(b) in doing so would be treated as carrying on an activity of a kind specified by a provision of this Part but for an exclusion in any of articles 15, 16, 19, 22, 23, 29, 38, 67, 68, 69, 70 and 72E,

that exclusion is to be disregarded and, accordingly, the investment firm or credit institution is to be treated as carrying on an activity of the kind specified by the provision in question.

(4A) Where a person, other than a person specified by Article 1.2 of the insurance mediation directive (the text of which is set out in Part 1 of Schedule 4)—

(a) for remuneration, takes up or pursues insurance mediation or reinsurance mediation in relation to a risk or commitment located in an EEA State, and

(b) in doing so would be treated as carrying on an activity of a kind specified by a provision of this Part but for an exclusion in any of articles 30, 66 and 67,

that exclusion is to be disregarded (and accordingly that person is to be treated as carrying on an activity of the kind specified by the provision in question).

(5) In this article—

"insurance mediation" has the meaning given by Article 2.3 of the insurance mediation directive, the text of which is set out in Part II of Schedule 4;

...

"reinsurance mediation" has the meaning given by Article 2.4 of the insurance mediation directive, the text of which is set out in Part III of Schedule 4.

CHAPTER II
ACCEPTING DEPOSITS

The activity

5. Accepting deposits

(1) Accepting deposits is a specified kind of activity if—

(a) money received by way of deposit is lent to others; or

(b) any other activity of the person accepting the deposit is financed wholly, or to a material extent, out of the capital of or interest on money received by way of deposit.

(2) In paragraph (1), "deposit" means a sum of money, other than one excluded by any of articles 6 to 9A, paid on terms—

(a) under which it will be repaid, with or without interest or premium, and either on demand or at a time or in circumstances agreed by or on behalf of the person making the payment and the person receiving it; and

(b) which are not referable to the provision of property (other than currency) or services or the giving of security.

(3) For the purposes of paragraph (2), money is paid on terms which are referable to the provision of property or services or the giving of security if, and only if—

(a) it is paid by way of advance or part payment under a contract for the sale, hire or other provision of property or services, and is repayable only in the event that the property or services is or are not in fact sold, hired or otherwise provided;

(b) it is paid by way of security for the performance of a contract or by way of security in respect of loss which may result from the non-performance of a contract; or

(c) without prejudice to sub-paragraph (b), it is paid by way of security for the delivery up or return of any property, whether in a particular state of repair or otherwise.

Exclusions

6. Sums paid by certain persons

(1) A sum is not a deposit for the purposes of article 5 if it is—

(a) paid by any of the following persons—

(i) the Bank of England, the central bank of an EEA State other than the United Kingdom, or the European Central Bank;

(ii) an authorised person who has permission to accept deposits, or to effect or carry out contracts of insurance;

(iii) an EEA firm falling within paragraph 5(b), (c) or (d) of Schedule 3 to the Act (other than one falling within paragraph (ii) above);

(iv) the National Savings Bank;

(v) a municipal bank, that is to say a company which was, immediately before the coming into force of this article, exempt from the prohibition in section 3 of the Banking Act 1987 by virtue of section 4(1) of, and paragraph 4 of Schedule 2 to, that Act;

(vi) Keesler Federal Credit Union;

(vii) a body of persons certified as a school bank by the National Savings Bank or by an authorised person who has permission to accept deposits;

(viii) a local authority;

(xi) any body which by virtue of any enactment has power to issue a precept to a local authority in England and Wales or a requisition to a local authority in Scotland, or to the expenses of which, by virtue of any enactment, a local authority in the United Kingdom is or can be required to contribute (and in this paragraph, "enactment" includes an enactment comprised in, or in an instrument made under, an Act of the Scottish Parliament);

(x) the European Union, the European Atomic Energy Community or the European Coal and Steel Community;

(xi) the European Investment Bank;

(xii) the International Bank for Reconstruction and Development;

(xiii) the International Finance Corporation;

(xiv) the International Monetary Fund;

(xv) the African Development Bank;

(xvi) the Asian Development Bank;

(xvii) the Caribbean Development Bank;

(xviii) the Inter-American Development Bank;

(xix) the European Bank for Reconstruction and Development;

(xx) the Council of Europe Development Bank;

(b) paid by a person other than one mentioned in sub-paragraph (a) in the course of carrying on a business consisting wholly or to a significant extent of lending money;

(c) paid by one company to another at a time when both are members of the same group or when the same individual is a majority shareholder controller of both of them; or

(d) paid by a person who, at the time when it is paid, is a close relative of the person receiving it or who is, or is a close relative of, a director or manager of that person or who is, or is a close relative of, a controller of that person.

(2) For the purposes of paragraph (1)(c), an individual is a majority shareholder controller of a company if he is a controller of the company by virtue of paragraph (a), (c), (e) or (g) of section 422(2) of the Act, and if in his case the greatest percentage of those referred to in those paragraphs is 50 or more.

(3) In the application of sub-paragraph (d) of paragraph (1) to a sum paid by a partnership, that sub-paragraph is to have effect as if, for the reference to the person paying the sum, there were substituted a reference to each of the partners.

7. Sums received by solicitors etc

(1) A sum is not a deposit for the purposes of article 5 if it is received by a practising solicitor acting in the course of his profession.

(2) In paragraph (1), "practising solicitor" means—

(a) a solicitor who is qualified to act as such under section 1 of the Solicitors Act 1974, article 4 of the Solicitors (Northern Ireland) Order 1976 or section 4 of the Solicitors (Scotland) Act 1980;

(b) a recognised body;

(c) a registered foreign lawyer in the course of providing professional services as a member of a multi-national partnership;

(d) a registered European lawyer; or

(e) a partner of a registered European lawyer who is providing professional services in accordance with—

(i) rules made under section 31 of the Solicitors Act 1974;

(ii) regulations made under article 26 of the Solicitors (Northern Ireland) Order 1976; or

(iii) rules made under section 34 of the Solicitors (Scotland) Act 1980.

(3) In this article—

(a) "a recognised body" means a body . . . recognised by—

(i) the Council of the Law Society under section 9 of the Administration of Justice Act 1985;

(ii) the Incorporated Law Society of Northern Ireland under article 26A of the Solicitors (Northern Ireland) Order 1976; or

(iii) the Council of the Law Society of Scotland under section 34 of the Solicitors (Scotland) Act 1980;

(b) "registered foreign lawyer" has the meaning given by section 89 of the Courts and Legal Services Act 1990 or, in Scotland, section 65 of the Solicitors (Scotland) Act 1980;

(c) "multi-national partnership" has the meaning given by section 89 of the Courts and Legal Services Act 1990 but, in Scotland, is a reference to a "multi-national practice" within the meaning of section 60A of the Solicitors (Scotland) Act 1980; and

(d) "registered European lawyer" has the meaning given by regulation 2(1) of the European Communities (Lawyer's Practice) Regulations 2000 or regulation 2(1) of the European Communities (Lawyer's Practice) (Scotland) Regulation 2000.

8. Sums received by persons authorised to deal etc

A sum is not a deposit for the purposes of article 5 if it is received by a person who is—

(a) an authorised person with permission to carry on an activity of the kind specified by any of articles 14, 21, 25, 37, 51 and 52, or

(b) an exempt person in relation to any such activity,

in the course of, or for the purpose of, carrying on any such activity (or any activity which would be such an activity but for any exclusion made by this Part) with or on behalf of the person by or on behalf of whom the sum is paid.

9. Sums received in consideration for the issue of debt securities

(1) Subject to paragraph (2), a sum is not a deposit for the purposes of article 5 if it is received by a person as consideration for the issue by him of any investment of the kind specified by article 77 or 78.

(2) The exclusion in paragraph (1) does not apply to the receipt by a person of a sum as consideration for the issue by him of commercial paper unless—

(a) the commercial paper is issued to persons—

(i) whose ordinary activities involve them in acquiring, holding, managing or disposing of investments (as principal or agent) for the purposes of their businesses; or

(ii) who it is reasonable to expect will acquire, hold, manage or dispose of investments (as principal or agent) for the purposes of their businesses; and

(b) the redemption value of the commercial paper is not less than £100,000 (or an amount of equivalent value denominated wholly or partly in a currency other than sterling), and no part of the commercial paper may be transferred unless the redemption value of that part is not less than £100,000 (or such an equivalent amount).

(3) In paragraph (2), "commercial paper" means an investment of the kind specified by article 77 or 78 having a maturity of less than one year from the date of issue.

9A. Sums received in exchange for electronic money

A sum is not a deposit for the purposes of article 5 if it is immediately exchanged for electronic money.

9AA. Information society services

Article 5 is subject to the exclusion in article 72A (information society services).

9AB. Funds received for payment services

(1) A sum is not a deposit for the purposes of article 5 if it is received by an authorised payment institution, an EEA authorised payment institution, a small payment institution, an electronic money institution or an EEA authorised electronic money institution from a payment service user with a view to the provision of payment services.

(2) For the purposes of paragraph (1), "authorised payment institution", "EEA authorised payment institution", "small payment institution", "payment services" and "payment service user" have the meanings given in the Payment Services Regulations 2009 and "electronic money institution" and "EEA authorised electronic money institution" have the meanings given in the Electronic Money Regulations 2011.

CHAPTER IIA
ELECTRONIC MONEY

The activity

9B. Issuing electronic money

Issuing electronic money by—

(a) a credit institution, a credit union or a municipal bank; or

(b) a person who is deemed to have been granted authorisation under regulation 74 of the Electronic Money Regulations 2011 or who falls within regulation 76(1) of those Regulations, is a specified kind of activity.

9BA.

Articles 9C to 9I and 9K apply only in the case of a person falling within regulation 76(1) of the Electronic Money Regulations 2011.

Exclusions

9C. Persons certified as small issuers etc

(1) There is excluded from article 9B the issuing of electronic money by a person to whom the FCA has given a certificate under this article (provided the certificate has not been revoked).

(2) An application for a certificate may be made by—

(a) a body corporate, or

(b) a partnership,

(other than a credit institution as defined in Article 4(1)(a) of the banking consolidation directive) which has its head office in the United Kingdom.

(3) The authority must, on the application of such a person ("A"), give A a certificate if it appears to the FCA that paragraph (4), (5) or (6) applies.

(4) This paragraph applies if—

(a) A does not issue electronic money except on terms that the electronic device on which the monetary value is stored is subject to a maximum storage amount of not more than 150 euro; and

(b) A's total liabilities with respect to the issuing of electronic money do not (or will not) usually exceed 5 million euro and do not (or will not) ever exceed 6 million euro.

(5) This paragraph applies if—

(a) the condition in paragraph (4)(a) is met;

(b) A's total liabilities with respect to the issuing of electronic money do not (or will not) exceed 10 million euro; and

(c) electronic money issued by A is accepted as a means of payment only by—

(i) subsidiaries of A which perform operational or other ancillary functions related to electronic money issued or distributed by A; or

(ii) other members of the same group as A (other than subsidiaries of A).

(6) This paragraph applies if—

(a) the conditions in paragraphs (4)(a) and (5)(b) are met; and

(b) electronic money issued by A is accepted as a means of payment, in the course of business, by not more than one hundred persons where—

(i) those persons accept such electronic money only at locations within the same premises or limited local area; or

(ii) those persons have a close financial or business relationship with A, such as a common marketing or distribution scheme.

(7) For the purposes of paragraph (6)(b)(i), locations are to be treated as situated within the same premises or limited local area if they are situated within—

(a) a shopping centre, airport, railway station, bus station, or campus of a university, polytechnic, college, school or similar educational establishment; or

(b) an area which does not exceed four square kilometres;

but sub-paragraphs (a) and (b) are illustrative only and are not to be treated as limiting the scope of paragraph (6)(b)(i).

(8) For the purposes of paragraph (6)(b)(ii), persons are not to be treated as having a close financial or business relationship with A merely because they participate in arrangements for the acceptance of electronic money issued by A.

(9) In this article, references to amounts in euro include references to equivalent amounts in sterling.

(10) A person to whom a certificate has been given under this article (and whose certificate has not been revoked) is referred to in this Chapter as a "certified person".

9D. Applications for certificates

The following provisions of the Act apply to applications to the FCA for certificates under 9C (and the determination of such applications) as they apply to applications for Part IV permissions (and the determination of such applications)—

(a) section 55U(1)(b) and (4) to (8);

(b) section 55V;

(c) section 55X(2) and (4)(f); and

(d) section 55Z3(1).

9E. Revocation of certificate on FCA's own initiative

(1) The FCA may revoke a certificate given to a person ("A") under article 9C if—

(a) it appears to it that A does not meet the relevant conditions, or has failed to meet the relevant conditions at any time since the certificate was given; or

(b) the person to whom the certificate was given has contravened any rule or requirement to which he is subject as a result of article 9G.

(2) For the purposes of paragraph (1), A meets the relevant conditions at any time if, at that time, paragraph (4), (5) or (6) of article 9C applies.

(3) Sections 55Z and 55Z3(2) of the Act apply to the revocation of a certificate under paragraph (1) as they apply to the cancellation of a Part IV permission on the FCA's own initiative, as if references in those sections to an authorised person were references to a certified person.

9F. Revocation of certificate on request

(1) A certified person ("B") may apply to the FCA for his certificate to be revoked, and the Authority must then revoke the certificate and give B written notice that it has done so.

(2) An application under paragraph (1) must be made in such manner as the FCA may direct.

(3) If—

(a) B has made an application under Part IV of the Act for permission to carry on a regulated activity of the kind specified by article 9B (or for variation of an existing permission so as to add a regulated activity of that kind), and

(b) on making an application for revocation of his certificate under paragraph (1), he requests that the revocation be conditional on the granting of his application under Part IV of the Act,

the revocation of B's certificate is to be conditional on the granting of his application under Part IV of the Act.

9G. Obtaining information from certified persons etc

(1) The FCA may make rules requiring certified persons to provide information to the Authority about their activities so far as relating to the issuing of electronic money, including the amount of their liabilities with respect to the issuing of electronic money.

(2) Section 138A of the Act (modification or waiver of rules) applies in relation to rules made under paragraph (1) as if references in that section to an authorised person were references to a certified person.

(3) Section 138D of the Act (actions for damages) applies in relation to a rule made under paragraph (1) as if the reference in subsection (1) of that section to an authorised person were a reference to a certified person.

(4) The FCA may, by notice in writing given to a certified person, require him—

(a) to provide specified information or information of a specified description; or

(b) to produce specified documents or documents of a specified description.

(5) Paragraph (4) applies only to information or documents reasonably required for the purposes of determining whether the certified person meets, or has met, the relevant conditions.

(6) Subsections (2), (5) and (6) of section 165 of the Act (Regulator's power to require information) apply to a requirement imposed under paragraph (4) as they apply to a requirement imposed under that section.

(7) Section 166 of the Act (reports by skilled persons) has effect as if—

(a) ...

(b) the reference in section 166(2)(a) of the Act to an authorised person included a reference to a certified person.

(8) Subsection (4) of section 168 of the Act (appointment of persons to carry out investigations in particular cases) has effect as if it provided for subsection (5) of that section to apply if it appears to the FCA that there are circumstances suggesting that a certified person may not meet, or may not have met, the relevant conditions.

(9) Sections 175 (information and documents: supplemental provisions), 176 (entry of premises under warrant) and 177 (offences) of the Act apply to a requirement imposed under paragraph (4) as they apply to a requirement imposed under section 165 of the Act (the reference in section 176(3)(a) to an authorised person being read as a reference to a certified person).

(10) In this article—

(a) "specified", in paragraph (4), means specified in the notice mentioned in that paragraph;

(b) a certified person ("A") meets the relevant conditions at any time if, at that time, paragraph (4), (5) or (6) of article 9C applies.

Supplemental

9H. Rules prohibiting the issue of electronic money at a discount

(1) The FCA may make rules applying to authorised persons with permission to carry on an activity of the kind specified by article 9B, prohibiting the issue of electronic money having a monetary value greater than the funds received.

(2) Section 138A of the Act (modification or waiver of rules) applies in relation to rules made under paragraph (1).

9I. False claims to be a certified person

A person who is not a certified person is to be treated as guilty of an offence under section 24 of the Act (false claims to be authorised or exempt) if he—

(a) describes himself (in whatever terms) as a certified person;

(b) behaves, or otherwise holds himself out, in a manner which indicates (or which is reasonably likely to be understood as indicating) that he is a certified person.

9J. Exclusion of electronic money from the compensation scheme

The compensation scheme established under Part XV of the Act is not to provide for the compensation of persons in respect of claims made in connection with any activity of the kind specified by article 9B.

9K. Record of certified persons

The record maintained by the FCA under section 347 of the Act (public record of authorised persons etc) must include every certified person.

9L. . . .

CHAPTER III
INSURANCE

The activities

10. Effecting and carrying out contracts of insurance

(1) Effecting a contract of insurance as principal is a specified kind of activity.

(2) Carrying out a contract of insurance as principal is a specified kind of activity.

Exclusions

11. Community co-insurers

(1) There is excluded from article 10(1) or (2) the effecting or carrying out of a contract of insurance by an EEA firm falling within paragraph 5(d) of Schedule 3 to the Act—

(a) other than through a branch in the United Kingdom; and

(b) pursuant to a Community co-insurance operation in which the firm is participating otherwise than as the leading insurer.

(2) In paragraph (1), "Community co-insurance operation" and "leading insurer" have the same meaning as in the Council Directive of 30 May 1978 on the co-ordination of laws, regulations and administrative provisions relating to Community co-insurance (No 78/473/EEC).

12. Breakdown insurance

(1) There is excluded from article 10(1) or (2) the effecting or carrying out, by a person who does not otherwise carry on an activity of the kind specified by that article, of a contract of insurance which—

(a) is a contract under which the benefits provided by that person ("the provider") are exclusively or primarily benefits in kind in the event of accident to or breakdown of a vehicle; and

(b) contains the terms mentioned in paragraph (2).

(2) Those terms are that—

(a) the assistance takes either or both of the forms mentioned in paragraph (3)(a) and (b);

(b) the assistance is not available outside the United Kingdom and the Republic of Ireland except where it is provided without the payment of additional premium by a person in the country concerned with whom the provider has entered into a reciprocal agreement; and

(c) assistance provided in the case of an accident or breakdown occurring in the United Kingdom or the Republic of Ireland is, in most circumstances, provided by the provider's servants.

(3) The forms of assistance are—

(a) repairs to the relevant vehicle at the place where the accident or breakdown has occurred; this assistance may also include the delivery of parts, fuel, oil, water or keys to the relevant vehicle;

(b) removal of the relevant vehicle to the nearest or most appropriate place at which repairs may be carried out, or to—

(i) the home, point of departure or original destination within the United Kingdom of the driver and passengers, provided the accident or breakdown occurred within the United Kingdom;

(ii) the home, point of departure or original destination within the Republic of Ireland of the driver and passengers, provided the accident or breakdown occurred within the Republic of Ireland or within Northern Ireland;

(iii) the home, point of departure or original destination within Northern Ireland of the driver and passengers, provided the accident or breakdown occurred within the Republic of Ireland;

and this form of assistance may include the conveyance of the driver or passengers of the relevant vehicle, with the vehicle, or (where the vehicle is to be conveyed only to the nearest or most appropriate place at which repairs may be carried out) separately, to the nearest location from which they may continue their journey by other means.

(4) A contract does not fail to meet the condition in paragraph (1)(a) solely because the provider may reimburse the person entitled to the assistance for all or part of any sums paid by him in respect of assistance either because he failed to identify himself as a person entitled to the assistance or because he was unable to get in touch with the provider in order to claim the assistance.

(5) In this article—

"the assistance" means the benefits to be provided under a contract of the kind mentioned in paragraph (1);

"breakdown" means an event—

(a) which causes the driver of the relevant vehicle to be unable to start a journey in the vehicle or involuntarily to bring the vehicle to a halt on a journey because of some malfunction of the vehicle or failure of it to function, and

(b) after which the journey cannot reasonably be commenced or continued in the relevant vehicle;

"the relevant vehicle" means the vehicle (including a trailer or caravan) in respect of which the assistance is required.

12A. Information society services

Article 10 is subject to the exclusion in article 72A (information society services), as qualified by paragraph (2) of that article.

Supplemental

13. Application of sections 327 and 332 of the Act to insurance market activities

(1) In sections 327(5) and (7) and 332(3)(b) of the Act (exemption from the general prohibition for members of the professions, and rules in relation to such persons), the references to "a regulated activity" and "regulated activities" do not include—

(a) any activity of the kind specified by article 10(1) or (2), where—

(i) P is a member of the Society; and

(ii) by virtue of section 316 of the Act (application of the Act to Lloyd's underwriting), the general prohibition does not apply to the carrying on by P of that activity; or

(b) any activity of the kind specified by article 10(2), where—

(i) P is a former underwriting member; and

(ii) the contract of insurance in question is one underwritten by P at Lloyd's.

(2) In paragraph (1)—

"member of the Society" has the same meaning as in Lloyd's Act 1982; and

"former underwriting member" has the meaning given by section 324(1) of the Act.

CHAPTER IV
DEALING IN INVESTMENTS AS PRINCIPAL

The activity

14. Dealing in investments as principal

(1) Buying, selling, subscribing for or underwriting securities or contractually based investments (other than investments of the kind specified by article 87, or article 89 so far as relevant to that article) as principal is a specified kind of activity.

(2) Paragraph (1) does not apply to a kind of activity to which article 25D applies.

Exclusions

15. Absence of holding out etc

(1) Subject to paragraph (3), a person ("A") does not carry on an activity of the kind specified by article 14 by entering into a transaction which relates to a security or is the assignment (or, in Scotland, the assignation) of a qualifying contract of insurance (or an investment of the kind specified by article 89, so far as relevant to such a contract), unless—

(a) A holds himself out as willing, as principal, to buy, sell or subscribe for investments of the kind to which the transaction relates at prices determined by him generally and continuously rather than in respect of each particular transaction;

(b) A holds himself out as engaging in the business of buying investments of the kind to which the transaction relates, with a view to selling them;

(c) A holds himself out as engaging in the business of underwriting investments of the kind to which the transaction relates; or

(d) A regularly solicits members of the public with the purpose of inducing them, as principals or agents, to enter into transactions constituting activities of the kind specified by article 14, and the transaction is entered into as a result of his having solicited members of the public in that manner.

(2) In paragraph (1)(d), "members of the public" means any persons other than—

(a) authorised persons or persons who are exempt persons in relation to activities of the kind specified by article 14;

(b) members of the same group as A;

(c) persons who are or who propose to become participators with A in a joint enterprise;

(d) any person who is solicited by A with a view to the acquisition by A of 20 per cent or more of the voting shares in a body corporate;

(e) if A (either alone or with members of the same group as himself) holds more than 20 per cent of the voting shares in a body corporate, any person who is solicited by A with a view to—

(i) the acquisition by A of further shares in the body corporate; or

(ii) the disposal by A of shares in the body corporate to the person solicited or to a member of the same group as the person solicited;

(f) any person who—

(i) is solicited by A with a view to the disposal by A of shares in a body corporate to the person solicited or to a member of the same group as that person; and

(ii) either alone or with members of the same group holds 20 per cent or more of the voting shares in the body corporate;

(g) any person whose head office is outside the United Kingdom, who is solicited by an approach made or directed to him at a place outside the United Kingdom and whose ordinary business involves him in carrying on activities of the kind specified by any of articles 14, 21, 25, 37, 40, 45, 51, 52 and 53 or (so far as relevant to any of those articles) article 64, or would do so apart from any exclusion from any of those articles made by this Order.

(3) This article does not apply where A enters into the transaction as bare trustee or, in Scotland, as nominee for another person and is acting on that other person's instructions (but the exclusion in article 66(1) applies if the conditions set out there are met).

(4) This article is subject to article 4(4).

16. Dealing in contractually based investments

(1) A person who is not an authorised person does not carry on an activity of the kind specified by article 14 by entering into a transaction relating to a contractually based investment—

(a) with or through an authorised person, or an exempt person acting in the course of a business comprising a regulated activity in relation to which he is exempt; or

(b) through an office outside the United Kingdom maintained by a party to the transaction, and with or through a person whose head office is situated outside the United Kingdom and whose ordinary business involves him in carrying on activities of the kind specified by any of articles 14, 21, 25, 37, 40, 45, 51, 52 and 53 or, so far as relevant to any of those articles, article 64 (or would do so apart from any exclusion from any of those articles made by this Order).

(2) This article is subject to article 4(4).

17. Acceptance of instruments creating or acknowledging indebtedness

(1) A person does not carry on an activity of the kind specified by article 14 by accepting an instrument creating or acknowledging indebtedness in respect of any loan, credit, guarantee or other similar financial accommodation or assurance which he has made, granted or provided.

(2) The reference in paragraph (1) to a person accepting an instrument includes a reference to a person becoming a party to an instrument otherwise than as a debtor or a surety.

18. Issue by a company of its own shares etc

(1) There is excluded from article 14 the issue by a company of its own shares or share warrants, and the issue by any person of his own debentures or debenture warrants.

(2) In this article—

(a) "company" means any body corporate other than an open-ended investment company;

(b) "shares" and "debentures" include any investment of the kind specified by article 76, 77 or 77A;

(c) "share warrants" and "debenture warrants" mean any investment of the kind specified by article 79 which relates to shares in the company concerned or, as the case may be, debentures issued by the person concerned.

18A. Dealing by a company in its own shares

(1) A company does not carry on an activity of the kind specified by article 14 by purchasing its own shares where section 724 of the Companies Act 2006 (Treasury shares) applies to the shares purchased.

(2) A company does not carry on an activity of the kind specified by article 14 by dealing in its own shares held as treasury shares, in accordance with section 727 (Treasury shares: disposal) or 729 (Treasury shares: cancellation) of that Act.

(3) In this article "shares held as treasury shares" has the same meaning as in that Act.

19. Risk management

(1) A person ("B") does not carry on an activity of the kind specified by article 14 by entering as principal into a transaction with another person ("C") if—

(a) the transaction relates to investments of the kind specified by any of articles 83 to 85 (or article 89 so far as relevant to any of those articles);

(b) neither B nor C is an individual;

(c) the sole or main purpose for which B enters into the transaction (either by itself or in combination with other such transactions) is that of limiting the extent to which a relevant business will be affected by any identifiable risk arising otherwise than as a result of the carrying on of a regulated activity; and

(d) the relevant business consists mainly of activities other than—

(i) regulated activities; or

(ii) activities which would be regulated activities but for any exclusion made by this Part.

(2) In paragraph (1), "relevant business" means a business carried on by—

(a) B;

(b) a member of the same group as B; or

(c) where B and another person are, or propose to become, participators in a joint enterprise, that other person.

(3) This article is subject to article 4(4).

20. Other exclusions

Article 14 is also subject to the exclusions in articles 66 (trustees etc), 68 (sale of goods and supply of services), 69 (groups and joint enterprises), 70 (sale of body corporate), 71 (employee share schemes), 72 (overseas persons) and 72A (information society services).

CHAPTER V
DEALING IN INVESTMENTS AS AGENT

The activity

21. Dealing in investments as agent

(1) Buying, selling, subscribing for or underwriting securities or relevant investments (other than investments of the kind specified by article 87, or article 89 so far as relevant to that article) as agent is a specified kind of activity.

(2) Paragraph (1) does not apply to a kind of activity to which article 25D applies.

Exclusions

22. Deals with or through authorised persons

(1) A person who is not an authorised person does not carry on an activity of the kind specified by article 21 by entering into a transaction as agent for another person ("the client") with or through an authorised person if—

(a) the transaction is entered into on advice given to the client by an authorised person; or

(b) it is clear, in all the circumstances, that the client, in his capacity as an investor, is not seeking and has not sought advice from the agent as to the merits of the client's entering into the transaction (or, if the client has sought such advice, the agent has declined to give it but has recommended that the client seek such advice from an authorised person).

(2) But the exclusion in paragraph (1) does not apply if—

(a) the transaction relates to a contract of insurance; or

(b) the agent receives from any person other than the client any pecuniary reward or other advantage, for which he does not account to the client, arising out of his entering into the transaction.

(3) This article is subject to article 4(4).

23. Risk management

(1) A person ("B") does not carry on an activity of the kind specified by article 21 by entering as agent for a relevant person into a transaction with another person ("C") if—

(a) the transaction relates to investments of the kind specified by any of articles 83 to 85 (or article 89 so far as relevant to any of those articles);

(b) neither B nor C is an individual;

(c) the sole or main purpose for which B enters into the transaction (either by itself or in combination with other such transactions) is that of limiting the extent to which a relevant business will be affected by any identifiable risk arising otherwise than as a result of the carrying on of a regulated activity; and

(d) the relevant business consists mainly of activities other than—

(i) regulated activities; or

(ii) activities which would be regulated activities but for any exclusion made by this Part.

(2) In paragraph (1), "relevant person" means—

(a) a member of the same group as B; or

(b) where B and another person are, or propose to become, participators in a joint enterprise, that other person;

and "relevant business" means a business carried on by a relevant person.

(3) This article is subject to article 4(4).

24. Other exclusions

Article 21 is also subject to the exclusions in articles 67 (profession or non-investment business), 68 (sale of goods and supply of services), 69 (groups and joint enterprises), 70 (sale of body corporate), 71 (employee share schemes), 72 (overseas persons), 72A (information society services), 72B (activities carried on by a provider of relevant goods or services) and 72D (large risks contracts where risk situated outside the EEA).

CHAPTER 5A
BIDDING IN EMISSIONS AUCTIONS

The activity

24A. Bidding in emissions auctions

(1) The reception, transmission or submission of a bid at an auction of an investment of the kind specified by article 82A conducted—

(a) on a recognised auction platform, or

(b) on any other auction platform which has been appointed under the emission allowance auctioning regulation,

is a specified kind of activity.

(2) An activity which falls within paragraph (1) (or would do so but for the exclusions in article 24B) does not form part of any other activity specified under any other article of this Order.

(3) In this article, "recognised auction platform" has the meaning given in regulation 1(3) of the Recognised Auction Platform Regulations 2011.

Exclusions

24B. Miscellaneous exclusions

(1) There is excluded from article 24A any activity carried on by—

(a) an operator or an aircraft operator having an operator holding account, in either case bidding on its own account, including any parent undertaking, subsidiary undertaking or affiliate undertaking forming part of the same group of undertakings as the operator or the aircraft operator;

(b) business groupings of persons listed in sub-paragraph (a) bidding on their own account or acting as an agent on behalf of their members; or

(c) public bodies or state-owned entities of the Member States that control any of the persons listed in sub-paragraph (a).

(2) There is excluded from article 24A the reception, transmission or submission of a bid by an investment firm or a credit institution on any auction platform on their own account for investments of the kind specified by article 82A which are not financial instruments.

(3) In this article, the expressions "parent undertaking", "subsidiary undertaking", "affiliate undertaking", "business grouping", "public bodies" and "state-owned entities" have the same meaning as in the emission allowance auctioning regulation.

CHAPTER VI
ARRANGING DEALS IN INVESTMENTS

The activities

25. Arranging deals in investments

(1) Making arrangements for another person (whether as principal or agent) to buy, sell, subscribe for or underwrite a particular investment which is—

(a) a security,

(b) a relevant investment, or

(c) an investment of the kind specified by article 86, or article 89 so far as relevant to that article,

is a specified kind of activity.

(2) Making arrangements with a view to a person who participates in the arrangements buying, selling, subscribing for or underwriting investments falling within paragraph (1)(a), (b) or (c) (whether as principal or agent) is also a specified kind of activity.

(3) Paragraphs (1) and (2) do not apply to a kind of activity to which article 25D applies.

25A. Arranging regulated mortgage contracts

(1) Making arrangements—

(a) for another person to enter into a regulated mortgage contract as borrower; or

(b) for another person to vary the terms of a regulated mortgage contract entered into by him as borrower after the coming into force of article 61, in such a way as to vary his obligations under that contract,

is a specified kind of activity.

(2) Making arrangements with a view to a person who participates in the arrangements entering into a regulated mortgage contract as borrower is also a specified kind of activity.

(3) In this article "borrower" has the meaning given by article 61(3)(a)(i).

25B. Arranging regulated home reversion plans

(1) Making arrangements—

(a) for another person to enter into a regulated home reversion plan as reversion seller or as plan provider; or

(b) for another person to vary the terms of a regulated home reversion plan, entered into on or after 6th April 2007 by him as reversion seller or as plan provider, in such a way as to vary his obligations under that plan,

is a specified kind of activity.

(2) Making arrangements with a view to a person who participates in the arrangements entering into a regulated home reversion plan as reversion seller or as plan provider is also a specified kind of activity.

25C. Arranging regulated home purchase plans

(1) Making arrangements—

(a) for another person to enter into a regulated home purchase plan as home purchaser; or

(b) for another person to vary the terms of a regulated home purchase plan, entered into on or after 6th April 2007 by him as home purchaser, in such a way as to vary his obligations under that plan,

is a specified kind of activity.

(2) Making arrangements with a view to a person who participates in the arrangements entering into a regulated home purchase plan as home purchaser is also a specified kind of activity.

25D. Operating a multilateral trading facility

(1) The operation of a multilateral trading facility on which MiFID instruments are traded is a specified kind of activity.

(2) In paragraph (1), "MiFID instrument" means any investment—

(a) of the kind specified by article 76, 77, 77A, 78, 79, 80, 81, 83, 84 or 85; or

(b) of the kind specified by article 89 so far as relevant to an investment falling within sub-paragraph (a),

that is a financial instrument.

25E. Arranging regulated sale and rent back agreements

(1) Making arrangements—

(a) for another person to enter into a regulated sale and rent back agreement as an agreement seller or as an agreement provider; or

(b) for another person ("A") to vary the terms of a regulated sale and rent back agreement, entered into on or after 1st July 2009 by A as agreement seller or agreement provider, in such a way as to vary A's obligations under that agreement,

is a specified kind of activity.

(2) Making arrangements with a view to a person who participates in the arrangements entering into a regulated sale and rent back agreement as agreement seller or agreement provider is also a specified kind of activity.

Exclusions

26. Arrangements not causing a deal

There are excluded from articles 25(1), 25A(1), 25B(1), 25C(1) and 25E(1) arrangements which do not or would not bring about the transaction to which the arrangements relate.

27. Enabling parties to communicate

A person does not carry on an activity of the kind specified by article 25(2), 25A(2), 25B(2), 25C(2) or 25E(2) merely by providing means by which one party to a transaction (or potential transaction) is able to communicate with other such parties.

28. Arranging transactions to which the arranger is a party

(1) There are excluded from article 25(1) any arrangements for a transaction into which the person making the arrangements enters or is to enter as principal or as agent for some other person.

(2) There are excluded from article 25(2) any arrangements which a person makes with a view to transactions into which he enters or is to enter as principal or as agent for some other person.

(3) But the exclusions in paragraphs (1) and (2) do not apply to arrangements made for or with a view to a transaction which relates to a contract of insurance, unless the person making the arrangements either—

(a) is the only policyholder; or

(b) as a result of the transaction, would become the only policyholder.

28A. Arranging contracts, plans or agreements to which the arranger is a party

(1) There are excluded from articles 25A(1), 25B(1), 25C(1) and 25E(1) any arrangements—

(a) for a contract, plan or agreement into which the person making the arrangements enters or is to enter; or

(b) for a variation of a contract, plan or agreement to which that person is (or is to become) a party.

(2) There are excluded from articles 25A(2), 25B(2), 25C(2) and 25E(2) any arrangements which a person makes with a view to contracts, plans or agreements into which he enters or is to enter.

29. Arranging deals with or through authorised persons

(1) There are excluded from articles 25(1) and (2), 25A(1) and (2), 25B(1) and (2), 25C(1) and (2) and 25E(1) and (2)arrangements made by a person ("A") who is not an authorised person for or with a view to a transaction which is or is to be entered into by a person ("the client") with or though an authorised person if—

(a) the transaction is or is to be entered into on advice to the client by an authorised person; or

(b) it is clear, in all the circumstances, that the client, in his capacity as an investor, borrower, reversion seller, plan provider, home purchaser, agreement provider or (as the case may be) agreement seller, is not seeking and has not sought advice from A as to the merits of the client's entering into the transaction (or, if the client has sought such advice, A has declined to give it but has recommended that the client seek such advice from an authorised person).

(2) But the exclusion in paragraph (1) does not apply if—

(a) the transaction relates, or would relate, to a contract of insurance; or

(b) A receives from any person other than the client any pecuniary reward or other advantage, for which he does not account to the client, arising out of his making the arrangements.

(3) This article is subject to article 4(4).

29A. Arrangements made in the course of administration by authorised person

(1) A person who is not an authorised person ("A") does not carry on an activity of the kind specified by article 25A(1)(b) as a result of—

(a) anything done by an authorised person ("B") in relation to a regulated mortgage contract which B is administering pursuant to an arrangement of the kind mentioned in article 62(a); or

(b) anything A does in connection with the administration of a regulated mortgage contract in circumstances falling within article 62(b).

(2) A person who is not an authorised person ("A") does not carry on an activity of the kind specified by article 25B(1)(b) as a result of—

(a) anything done by an authorised person ("B") in relation to a regulated home reversion plan which B is administering pursuant to an arrangement of the kind mentioned in article 63C(a); or

(b) anything A does in connection with the administration of a regulated home reversion plan in circumstances falling within article 63C(b).

(3) A person who is not an authorised person ("A") does not carry on an activity of the kind specified by article 25C(1)(b) as a result of—

(a) anything done by an authorised person ("B") in relation to a regulated home purchase plan which B is administering pursuant to an arrangement of the kind mentioned in article 63G(a); or

(b) anything A does in connection with the administration of a regulated home purchase plan in circumstances falling within article 63G(b).

(4) A person who is not an authorised person ("A") does not carry on an activity of the kind specified by article 25E(1)(b) as a result of—

(a) anything done by an authorised person ("B") in relation to a regulated sale and rent back agreement which B is administering pursuant to an arrangement of the kind mentioned in article 63K(a); or

(b) anything A does in connection with the administration of a regulated sale and rent back agreement in circumstances falling within article 63K(b).

30. Arranging transactions in connection with lending on the security of insurance policies

(1) There are excluded from article 25(1) and (2) arrangements made by a money-lender under which either—

(a) a relevant authorised person or a person acting on his behalf will introduce to the money-lender persons with whom the relevant authorised person has entered, or proposes to enter, into a relevant transaction, or will advise such persons to approach the money-lender, with a view to the money-lender lending money on the security of any contract effected pursuant to a relevant transaction;

(b) a relevant authorised person gives an assurance to the money-lender as to the amount which, on the security of any contract effected pursuant to a relevant transaction, will or may be received by the money-lender should the money-lender lend money to a person introduced to him pursuant to the arrangements.

(2) In paragraph (1)—

"money-lender" means a person who is—

(a) a money-lending company within the meaning of section 209 of the Companies Act 2006;

(b) a body corporate incorporated under the law of, or of any part of, the United Kingdom relating to building societies; or

(c) a person whose ordinary business includes the making of loans or the giving of guarantees in connection with loans;

"relevant authorised person" means an authorised person who has permission to effect contracts of insurance or to sell investments of the kind specified by article 89, so far as relevant to such contracts;

"relevant transaction" means the effecting of a contract of insurance or the sale of an investment of the kind specified by article 89, so far as relevant to such contracts.

(3) This article is subject to article 4(4A).

31. Arranging the acceptance of debentures in connection with loans

(1) There are excluded from article 25(1) and (2) arrangements under which a person accepts or is to accept, whether as principal or agent, an instrument creating or acknowledging indebtedness in respect of any loan, credit, guarantee or other similar financial accommodation or assurance which is, or is to be, made, granted or provided by that person or his principal.

(2) The reference in paragraph (1) to a person accepting an instrument includes a reference to a person becoming a party to an instrument otherwise than as a debtor or a surety.

32. Provision of finance

There are excluded from article 25(2) arrangements having as their sole purpose the provision of finance to enable a person to buy, sell, subscribe for or underwrite investments.

33. Introducing

There are excluded from articles 25(2), 25A(2), 25B(2), 25C(2) and 25E(2) arrangements where—

(a) they are arrangements under which persons ("clients") will be introduced to another person;

(b) the person to whom introductions are to be made is—

(i) an authorised person;

(ii) an exempt person acting in the course of a business comprising a regulated activity in relation to which he is exempt; or

(iii) a person who is not unlawfully carrying on regulated activities in the United Kingdom and whose ordinary business involves him in engaging in an activity of the kind specified by any of articles 14, 21, 25, 25A, 25B, 25C, 25E, 37, 39A, 40, 45, 51, 52, 53, 53A, 53B, 53C and 53D (or, so far as relevant to any of those articles, article 64), or would do so apart from any exclusion from any of those articles made by this Order;

...

(c) the introduction is made with a view to the provision of independent advice or the independent exercise of discretion in relation to investments generally or in relation to any class of investments to which the arrangements relate; and

(d) the arrangements are made with a view to a person entering into a transaction which does not relate to a contract of insurance.

33A. Introducing to authorised persons etc.

(1) There are excluded from article 25A(2) arrangements where—

(a) they are arrangements under which a client is introduced to a person ("N") who is—

(i) an authorised person who has permission to carry on a regulated activity of the kind specified by any of articles 25A, 53A, and 61(1),

(ii) an appointed representative who may carry on a regulated activity of the kind specified by either of articles 25A and 53A without contravening the general prohibition, or

(iii) an overseas person who carries on activities specified by any of articles 25A, 53A and 61(1); and

(b) the conditions mentioned in paragraph (2) are satisfied.

(1A) There are excluded from article 25B(2) arrangements where—

(a) they are arrangements under which a client is introduced to a person ("N") who is—

(i) an authorised person who has permission to carry on a regulated activity of the kind specified by any of articles 25B, 53B and 63B(1),

(ii) an appointed representative who may carry on a regulated activity of the kind specified by either of articles 25B and 53B without contravening the general prohibition, or

(iii) an overseas person who carries on activities specified by any of articles 25B, 53B and 63B(1); and

(b) the conditions mentioned in paragraph (2) are satisfied.

(1B) There are excluded from article 25C(2) arrangements where—

(a) they are arrangements under which a client is introduced to a person ("N") who is—

(i) an authorised person who has permission to carry on a regulated activity of the kind specified by any of articles 25C, 53C and 63F(1),

(ii) an appointed representative who may carry on a regulated activity of the kind specified by either of articles 25C and 53C without contravening the general prohibition, or

(iii) an overseas person who carries on activities specified by any of articles 25C, 53C and 63F(1); and

(b) the conditions mentioned in paragraph (2) are satisfied.

(1C) There are excluded from article 25E(2) arrangements where—

(a) they are arrangements under which a client is introduced to a person ("N") who is—

(i) an authorised person who has permission to carry on a regulated activity of the kind specified by any of articles 25E, 53D and 63J(1),

(ii) an appointed representative who may carry on a regulated activity of the kind specified by either of articles 25E or 53D without contravening the general prohibition, or

(iii) an overseas person who carries on activities specified by any of articles 25E, 53D and 63J(1); and

(b) the conditions mentioned in paragraph (2) are satisfied.

(2) Those conditions are—

(a) that the person making the introduction ("P") does not receive any money, other than money payable to P on his own account, paid by the client for or in connection with any transaction which the client enters into with or through N as a result of the introduction; and

(b) that before making the introduction P discloses to the client such of the information mentioned in paragraph (3) as applies to P.

(3) That information is—

(a) that P is a member of the same group as N;
(b) details of any payment which P will receive from N, by way of fee or commission, for introducing the client to N;
(c) an indication of any other reward or advantage received or to be received by P that arises out of his introducing clients to N.

(4) In this article, "client" means—
(a) for the purposes of paragraph (1), a borrower within the meaning given by article 61(3)(a)(i), or a person who is or may be contemplating entering into a regulated mortgage contract as such a borrower;
(b) for the purposes of paragraph (1A), a reversion seller, a plan provider or a person who is or may be contemplating entering into a regulated home reversion plan as a reversion seller or as a plan provider;
(c) for the purposes of paragraph (1B), a home purchaser or a person who is or may be contemplating entering into a regulated home purchase plan as a home purchaser;
(d) for the purposes of paragraph (1C), an agreement provider, an agreement seller or a person who is or may be contemplating entering into a regulated sale and rent back agreement as an agreement provider or agreement seller.

34. Arrangements for the issue of shares etc

(1) There are excluded from article 25(1) and (2)—
(a) arrangements made by a company for the purposes of issuing its own shares or share warrants; and
(b) arrangements made by any person for the purposes of issuing his own debentures or debenture warrants;

and for the purposes of article 25(1) and (2), a company is not, by reason of issuing its own shares or share warrants, and a person is not, by reason of issuing his own debentures or debenture warrants, to be treated as selling them.

(2) In paragraph (1), "company", "shares", "debentures", "share warrants" and "debenture warrants" have the meanings given by article 18(2).

35. International securities self-regulating organisations

(1) There are excluded from article 25(1) and (2) any arrangements made for the purposes of carrying out the functions of a body or association which is approved under this article as an international securities self-regulating organisation, whether the arrangements are made by the organisation itself or by a person acting on its behalf.

(2) The Treasury may approve as an international securities self-regulating organisation any body corporate or unincorporated association with respect to which the conditions mentioned in paragraph (3) appear to them to be met if, having regard to such matters affecting international trade, overseas earnings and the balance of payments or otherwise as they consider relevant, it appears to them that to do so would be desirable and not result in any undue risk to investors.

(3) The conditions are that—
(a) the body or association does not have its head office in the United Kingdom;
(b) the body or association is not eligible for recognition under section 287 or 288 of the Act (applications by investment exchanges and clearing houses) on the ground that (whether or not it has applied, and whether or not it would be eligible on other grounds) it is unable to satisfy the requirements of one or both of paragraphs (a) and (b) of section 292(3) of the Act (requirements for overseas investment exchanges and overseas clearing houses);
(ba) the body or association is also not eligible to become an EEA central counterparty (as defined in section 285(1)(c) of the Act) or a third country central counterparty (as defined in section 285(1)(d) of the Act);
(c) the body or association is able and willing to co-operate with the FCA and the PRA by the sharing of information and in other ways;

(d) adequate arrangements exist for co-operation between the FCA and the PRA and those responsible for the supervision of the body or association in the country or territory in which its head office is situated;

(e) the body or association has a membership composed of persons falling within any of the following categories, that is to say, authorised persons, exempt persons, and persons whose head offices are outside the United Kingdom and whose ordinary business involves them in engaging in activities which are activities of a kind specified by this Order (or would be apart from any exclusion made by this Part); and

(f) the body or association facilitates and regulates the activity of its members in the conduct of international securities business.

(4) In paragraph (3)(f), "international securities business" means the business of buying, selling, subscribing for or underwriting investments (or agreeing to do so), either as principal or agent, where—

(a) the investments are securities or relevant investments and are of a kind which, by their nature, and the manner in which the business is conducted, may be expected normally to be bought or dealt in by persons sufficiently expert to understand the risks involved; and

(b) either the transaction is international or each of the parties may be expected to be indifferent to the location of the other;

and, for the purposes of this definition, it is irrelevant that the investments may ultimately be bought otherwise than in the course of such business by persons not so expert.

(5) Any approval under this article is to be given by notice in writing; and the Treasury may by a further notice in writing withdraw any such approval if for any reason it appears to them that it is not appropriate to it to continue in force.

35A. Trade repositories

A trade repository does not carry on an activity of the kind specified by article 25(2) by carrying on its functions of centrally collecting and maintaining records of derivatives under Regulation (EU) 648/2012 of the European Parliament and of the Council of 4 July 2012 on OTC derivatives, central counterparties and trade repositories.

36. Other exclusions

(1) Article 25 is also subject to the exclusions in articles 66 (trustees etc), 67 (profession or non-investment business), 68 (sale of goods and supply of services), 69 (groups and joint enterprises), 70 (sale of body corporate), 71 (employee share schemes), 72 (overseas persons), 72A (information society services), 72B (activities carried on by a provider of relevant goods or services), 72C (provision of information about contracts of insurance on an incidental basis) and 72D (large risks contracts where risk situated outside the EEA).

(2) Articles 25A, 25B, 25C and 25E are also subject to the exclusions in articles 66 (trustees etc.), 67 (profession or non-investment business), 72 (overseas persons) and 72A (information society services).

(3) Article 25D is also subject to the exclusion in article 72 (overseas persons).

CHAPTER VII
MANAGING INVESTMENTS

The activity

37. Managing investments

Managing assets belonging to another person, in circumstances involving the exercise of discretion, is a specified kind of activity if—

(a) the assets consist of or include any investment which is a security or a contractually based investment; or

(b) the arrangements for their management are such that the assets may consist of or include such investments, and either the assets have at any time since 29th April 1988 done so, or the arrangements have at any time (whether before or after that date) been held out as arrangements under which the assets would do so.

Exclusions

38. Attorneys

(1) A person does not carry on an activity of the kind specified by article 37 if—

(a) he is a person appointed to manage the assets in question under a power of attorney; and

(b) all routine or day-to-day decisions, so far as relating to investments of a kind mentioned in article 37(a), are taken on behalf of that person by—

(i) an authorised person with permission to carry on activities of the kind specified by article 37; …

(ii) a person who is an exempt person in relation to activities of that kind; or

(iii) an overseas person.

This Article is subject to article 4(4).

39. Other exclusions

Article 37 is also subject to the exclusions in articles 66 (trustees etc), 68 (sale of goods and supply of services), 69 (groups and joint enterprises), 72A (information society services) and 72C (provision of information about contracts of insurance on an incidental basis).

CHAPTER VIIA

ASSISTING IN THE ADMINISTRATION AND PERFORMANCE OF A CONTRACT OF INSURANCE

The activity

39A. Assisting in the administration and performance of a contract of insurance

Assisting in the administration and performance of a contract of insurance is a specified kind of activity.

Exclusions

39B. Claims management on behalf of an insurer etc.

(1) A person does not carry on an activity of the kind specified by article 39A if he acts in the course of carrying on the activity of—

(a) expert appraisal;

(b) loss adjusting on behalf of a relevant insurer; or

(c) managing claims on behalf of a relevant insurer,

and that activity is carried on in the course of carrying on any profession or business.

(2) In this article—

(a) "relevant insurer" means—

(i) a person who has Part IV permission to carry on an activity of the kind specified by article 10;

(ii) a person to whom the general prohibition does not apply by virtue of section 316(1)(a) of the Act (members of the Society of Lloyd's);

(iii) an EEA firm falling within paragraph 5(d) of Schedule 3 to the Act (insurance undertaking); or

(iv) a relevant reinsurer;

(b) "relevant reinsurer" means a person whose main business consists of accepting risks ceded by—

(i) a person falling within sub-paragraph (i), (ii) or (iii) of the definition of "relevant insurer"; ...

(ii) an EEA firm falling within paragraph 5(da) of Schedule 3 to the Act (reinsurance undertaking); or

(iii) a person established outside the United Kingdom and not falling within paragraph (ii) who carries on an activity of the kind specified by article 10 by way of business.

39C. Other exclusions

Article 39A is also subject to the exclusions in articles 66 (trustees etc.), 67 (profession or non-investment business), 72A (information society services), 72B (activities carried on by a provider of relevant goods or services), 72C (provision of information about contracts of insurance on an incidental basis) and 72D (large risks contracts where risk situated outside the EEA).

CHAPTER VIII
SAFEGUARDING AND ADMINISTERING INVESTMENTS

The activity

40. Safeguarding and administering investments

(1) The activity consisting of both—

(a) the safeguarding of assets belonging to another, and

(b) the administration of those assets,

or arranging for one or more other persons to carry on that activity, is a specified kind of activity if the condition in sub-paragraph (a) or (b) of paragraph (2) is met.

(2) The condition is that—

(a) the assets consist of or include any investment which is a security or a contractually based investment; or

(b) the arrangements for their safeguarding and administration are such that the assets may consist of or include such investments, and either the assets have at any time since 1st June 1997 done so, or the arrangements have at any time (whether before or after that date) been held out as ones under which such investments would be safeguarded and administered.

(3) For the purposes of this article—

(a) it is immaterial that title to the assets safeguarded and administered is held in uncertificated form;

(b) it is immaterial that the assets safeguarded and administered may be transferred to another person, subject to a commitment by the person safeguarding and administering them, or arranging for their safeguarding and administration, that they will be replaced by equivalent assets at some future date or when so requested by the person to whom they belong.

Exclusions

41. Acceptance of responsibility by third party

(1) There are excluded from article 40 any activities which a person carries on pursuant to arrangements which—

(a) are ones under which a qualifying custodian undertakes to the person to whom the assets belong a responsibility in respect of the assets which is no less onerous than the qualifying custodian would have if the qualifying custodian were safeguarding and administering the assets; and

(b) are operated by the qualifying custodian in the course of carrying on in the United Kingdom an activity of the kind specified by article 40.

(2) In paragraph (1), "qualifying custodian" means a person who is—

(a) an authorised person who has permission to carry on an activity of the kind specified by article 40, or

(b) an exempt person acting in the course of a business comprising a regulated activity in relation to which he is exempt.

42. Introduction to qualifying custodians

(1) There are excluded from article 40 any arrangements pursuant to which introductions are made by a person ("P") to a qualifying custodian with a view to the qualifying custodian providing in the

United Kingdom a service comprising an activity of the kind specified by article 40, where the qualifying person (or other person who is to safeguard and administer the assets in question) is not connected with P.

(2) For the purposes of paragraph (1)—

(a) "qualifying custodian" has the meaning given by article 41(2); and

(b) a person is connected with P if either he is a member of the same group as P, or P is remunerated by him.

43. Activities not constituting administration

The following activities do not constitute the administration of assets for the purposes of article 40—

(a) providing information as to the number of units or the value of any assets safeguarded;

(b) converting currency;

(c) receiving documents relating to an investment solely for the purpose of onward transmission to, from or at the direction of the person to whom the investment belongs.

44. Other exclusions

Article 40 is also subject to the exclusions in articles 66 (trustees etc), 67 (profession or non-investment business), 68 (sale of goods and supply of services), 69 (groups and joint enterprises), 71 (employee share schemes), 72A (information society services) and 72C (provision of information about contracts of insurance on an incidental basis).

CHAPTER IX
SENDING DEMATERIALISED INSTRUCTIONS

The activities

45. Sending dematerialised instructions

(1) Sending, on behalf of another person, dematerialised instructions relating to a security or a contractually based investment is a specified kind of activity, where those instructions are sent by means of a relevant system in respect of which an Operator is approved under the 2001 Regulations.

(2) Causing dematerialised instructions relating to a security or a contractually based investment to be sent on behalf of another person by means of such a system is also a specified kind of activity where the person causing them to be sent is a system-participant.

(3) In this Chapter—

(a) "the 2001 Regulations" means the Uncertificated Securities Regulations 2001; and

(b) "dematerialised instruction", "Operator", "settlement bank" and "system-participant" have the meaning given by regulation 3 of the 2001 Regulations.

Exclusions

46. Instructions on behalf of participating issuers

There is excluded from article 45 the act of sending, or causing to be sent, a dematerialised instruction where the person on whose behalf the instruction is sent or caused to be sent is a participating issuer within the meaning of the 2001 Regulations.

47. Instructions on behalf of settlement banks

There is excluded from article 45 the act of sending, or causing to be sent, a dematerialised instruction where the person on whose behalf the instruction is sent or caused to be sent is a settlement bank in its capacity as such.

48. Instructions in connection with takeover offers

(1) There is excluded from article 45 of the act of sending, or causing to be sent, a dematerialised instruction where the person on whose behalf the instruction is sent or caused to be sent is an offeror making a takeover offer.

(2) In this article—

(a) "offeror" means, in the case of a takeover offer made by two or more persons jointly, the joint offers or any of them;

(b) "takeover offer" means—

(i) an offer to acquire shares (which in this sub-paragraph has the same meaning as in section 974 of the Companies Act 2006) in a body corporate incorporated in the United Kingdom which is a takeover offer within the meaning of Chapter 3 of Part 28 of that Act (or would be such an offer if that Part of that Act applied in relation to any body corporate);

(ii) an offer to acquire all or substantially all the shares, or all the shares of a particular class, in a body corporate incorporated outside the United Kingdom; or

(iii) an offer made to all the holders of shares, or shares of a particular class, in a body corporate to acquire a specified proportion of those shares;

but in determining whether an offer falls within paragraph (ii) there are to be disregarded any shares which the offeror or any associate of his (within the meaning of section 988 of the Companies Act 2006) holds or has contracted to acquire; and in determining whether an offer falls within paragraph (iii) the offeror, any such associate and any person whose shares the offeror or any such associate has contracted to acquire is not to be regarded as a holder of shares.

49. Instructions in the course of providing a network

There is excluded from article 45 the act of sending, or causing to be sent, a dematerialised instruction as a necessary part of providing a network, the purpose of which is to carry dematerialised instructions which are at all time properly authenticated (within the meaning of the 2001 Regulations).

50. Other exclusions

Article 45 is also subject to the exclusions in articles 66 (trustees etc), 69 (groups and joint enterprises) and 72A (information society services).

CHAPTER X
COLLECTIVE INVESTMENT SCHEMES

The activities

51. Establishing etc a collective investment scheme

(1) The following are specified kinds of activity—

(a) establishing, operating or winding up a collective investment scheme;

(b) acting as trustee of an authorised unit trust scheme;

(c) acting as the depositary or sole director of an open-ended investment company.

(2) In this article, "trustee", "authorised unit trust scheme" and "depositary" have the meaning given by section 237 of the Act.

Exclusion

51A. Information society services

Article 51 is subject to the exclusion in article 72A (information society services).

CHAPTER XI
... PENSION SCHEMES

The activities

52. Establishing etc a pension scheme

The following are specified kinds of activity—

(a) establishing, operating or winding up a stakeholder pension scheme;

(b) establishing, operating or winding up a personal pension scheme.

Exclusion

52A. Information society services

Article 52 is subject to the exclusion in article 72A (information society services).

CHAPTER XIA
PROVIDING BASIC ADVICE ON STAKEHOLDER PRODUCTS

The activity

52B. Providing basic advice on stakeholder products

(1) Providing basic advice to a retail consumer on a stakeholder product is a specified kind of activity.

(2) For the purposes of paragraph (1), a person ("P") provides basic advice when—

(a) he asks a retail consumer questions to enable him to assess whether a stakeholder product is appropriate for that consumer; and

(b) relying on the information provided by the retail consumer P assesses that a stakeholder product is appropriate for the retail consumer and—

(i) describes that product to that consumer;

(ii) gives a recommendation of that product to that consumer; and

(c) the retail consumer has indicated to P that he has understood the description and the recommendation in sub-paragraph (b).

(3) In this article—

"retail consumer" means any person who is advised by P on the merits of opening or buying a stakeholder product in the course of a business carried on by P and who does not receive the advice in the course of a business carried on by him;

"stakeholder product" means—

(a) an account which qualifies as a stakeholder child trust fund within the meaning given by the Child Trust Funds Regulations 2004;

(b) rights under a stakeholder pension scheme;

(c) an investment of a kind specified in regulations made by the Treasury.

CHAPTER XII
ADVISING ON INVESTMENTS

The activity

53. Advising on investments

Advising a person is a specified kind of activity if the advice is—

(a) given to the person in his capacity as an investor or potential investor, or in his capacity as agent for an investor or a potential investor; and

(b) advice on the merits of his doing any of the following (whether as principal or agent)—

(i) buying, selling, subscribing for or underwriting a particular investment which is a security or a relevant investment, or

(ii) exercising any right conferred by such an investment to buy, sell, subscribe for or underwrite such an investment.

53A. Advising on regulated mortgage contracts

(1) Advising a person is a specified kind of activity if the advice—

(a) is given to the person in his capacity as a borrower or potential borrower; and

(b) is advice on the merits of his doing any of the following—

(i) entering into a particular regulated mortgage contract, or

(ii) varying the terms of a regulated mortgage contract entered into by him after the coming into force of article 61 in such a way as to vary his obligations under that contract.

(2) In this article, "borrower" has the meaning given by article 61(3)(a)(i).

53B. Advising on regulated home reversion plans

Advising a person is a specified kind of activity if the advice—

(a) is given to the person in his capacity as—

(i) a reversion seller or potential reversion seller, or

(ii) a plan provider or potential plan provider; and

(b) is advice on the merits of his doing either of the following—

(i) entering into a particular regulated home reversion plan, or

(ii) varying the terms of a regulated home reversion plan, entered into on or after 6th April 2007 by him, in such a way as to vary his obligations under that plan.

53C. Advising on regulated home purchase plans

Advising a person is a specified kind of activity if the advice—

(a) is given to the person in his capacity as a home purchaser or potential home purchaser; and

(b) is advice on the merits of his doing either of the following—

(i) entering into a particular regulated home purchase plan, or

(ii) varying the terms of a regulated home purchase plan, entered into on or after 6th April 2007 by him, in such a way as to vary his obligations under that plan.

53D. Advising on regulated sale and rent back agreements

Advising a person is a specified kind of activity if the advice—

(a) is given to the person ("A") in A's capacity as—

(i) an agreement seller or potential agreement seller, or

(ii) an agreement provider or potential agreement provider; and

(b) is advice on the merits of A doing either of the following—

(i) entering into a particular regulated sale and rent back agreement; or

(ii) varying the terms of a regulated sale and rent back agreement entered into on or after 1st July 2009 by A as agreement seller or agreement provider, in such a way so as to vary A's obligations under that agreement.

Exclusions

54. Advice given in newspapers etc

(1) There is excluded from articles 53, 53A, 53B, 53C and 53D the giving of advice in writing or other legible form if the advice is contained in a newspaper, journal, magazine, or other periodical publication, or is given by way of a service comprising regularly updated news or information, if the principal purpose of the publication or service, taken as a whole and including any advertisements or other promotional material contained in it, is neither—

(a) that of giving advice of a kind mentioned in article 53, 53A, 53B, 53C or 53D, as the case may be; nor

(b) that of leading or enabling persons—

(i) to buy, sell, subscribe for or underwrite securities or contractually based investments, or (as the case may be),

(ii) to enter as borrower into regulated mortgage contracts, or vary the terms of regulated mortgage contracts entered into by them as borrower,

(iii) to enter as reversion seller or plan provider into regulated home reversion plans, or vary the terms of regulated home reversion plans entered into by them as reversion seller or plan provider,

(iv) to enter as home purchaser into regulated home purchase plans, or vary the terms of regulated home purchase plans entered into by them as home purchaser;

(v) to enter as agreement seller or agreement provider into regulated sale and rent back agreements, or vary the terms of regulated sale and rent back agreements entered into by them as agreement seller or agreement provider.

(2) There is also excluded from articles 53, 53A, 53B, 53C and 53D the giving of advice in any service consisting of the broadcast or transmission of television or radio programmes, if the principal purpose of the service, taken as a whole and including any advertisements or other promotional material contained in it, is neither of those mentioned in paragraph (1)(a) and (b).

(3) The FCA may, on the application of the proprietor of any such publication or service as is mentioned in paragraph (1) or (2), certify that it is of the nature described in that paragraph, and may revoke any such certificate if it considers that it is no longer justified.

(4) A certificate given under paragraph (3) and not revoked is conclusive evidence of the matters certified.

54A. Advice given in the course of administration by authorised person

(1) A person who is not an authorised person ("A") does not carry on an activity of the kind specified by article 53A by reason of—

(a) anything done by an authorised person ("B") in relation to a regulated mortgage contract which B is administering pursuant to arrangements of the kind mentioned in article 62(a); or

(b) anything A does in connection with the administration of a regulated mortgage contract in circumstances falling within article 62(b).

(2) A person who is not an authorised person ("A") does not carry on an activity of the kind specified by article 53B by reason of—

(a) anything done by an authorised person ("B") in relation to a regulated home reversion plan which B is administering pursuant to arrangements of the kind mentioned in article 63C(a); or

(b) anything A does in connection with the administration of a regulated home reversion plan in circumstances falling within article 63C(b).

(3) A person who is not an authorised person ("A") does not carry on an activity of the kind specified by article 53C by reason of—

(a) anything done by an authorised person ("B") in relation to a regulated home purchase plan which B is administering pursuant to arrangements of the kind mentioned in article 63G(a); or

(b) anything A does in connection with the administration of a regulated home purchase plan in circumstances falling within article 63G(b).

(4) A person who is not an authorised person ("A") does not carry on an activity of the kind specified by article 53D by reason of—

(a) anything done by an authorised person ("B") in relation to a regulated sale and rent back agreement which B is administering pursuant to arrangements of the kind mentioned in article 63K(a); or

(b) anything A does in connection with the administration of a regulated sale and rent back agreement in circumstances falling within article 63K(b).

55. Other exclusions

(1) Article 53 is also subject to the exclusions in articles 66 (trustees etc), 67, (profession or non-investment business), 68 (sale of goods and supply of services), 69 (groups and joint enterprises), 70 (sale of body corporate), 72 (overseas persons), 72A (information society services), 72B (activities carried on by a provider of relevant goods or services) and 72D (large risks contracts where risk situated outside the EEA).

(2) Articles 53A, 53B, 53C and 53D are also subject to the exclusions in articles 66 (trustees etc.), 67 (profession or non-investment business) and 72A (information society services).

CHAPTER XIII
LLOYD'S

The activities

56. Advice on syndicate participation at Lloyd's

Advising a person to become, or continue or cease to be, a member of a particular Lloyd's syndicate is a specified kind of activity.

57. Managing the underwriting capacity of a Lloyd's syndicate

Managing the underwriting capacity of a Lloyd's syndicate as a managing agent at Lloyd's is a specified kind of activity.

58. Arranging deals in contracts of insurance written at Lloyd's

The arranging, by the society incorporated by Lloyd's Act 1871 by the name of Lloyd's, of deals in contracts of insurance written at Lloyd's, is a specified kind of activity.

Exclusion

58A. Information society services

Articles 56 to 58 are subject to the exclusion in article 72A (information society services).

CHAPTER XIV
FUNERAL PLAN CONTRACTS

The activity

59. Funeral plan contracts

(1) Entering as provider into a funeral plan contract is a specified kind of activity.

(2) A "funeral plan contract" is a contract (other than one excluded by article 60) under which—

(a) a person ("the customer") makes one or more payments to another person ("the provider"); and

(b) the provider undertakes to provide, or secure that another person provides, a funeral in the United Kingdom for the customer (or some other person who is living at the date when the contract is entered into) on his death;

unless, at the time of entering into the contract, the customer and the provider intend or expect the funeral to occur within one month.

Exclusions

60. Plans covered by insurance or trust arrangements

(1) There is excluded from article 59 any contract under which—

(a) the provider undertakes to secure that sums paid by the customer under the contract will be applied towards a contract of whole life insurance on the life of the customer (or other person for whom the funeral is to be provided), effected and carried out by an authorised person who has permission to effect and carry out such contracts of insurance, for the purpose of providing the funeral; or

(b) the provider undertakes to secure that sums paid by the customer under the contract will be held on trust for the purpose of providing the funeral, and that the following requirements are or will be met with respect to the trust—

(i) the trust must be established by a written instrument;

(ii) more than half of the trustees must be unconnected with the provider;

(iii) the trustees must appoint, or have appointed, an independent fund manager who is an authorised person who has permission to carry on an activity of the kind specified by article 37, and who is a person who is unconnected with the provider, to manage the assets of the trust;

(iv) annual accounts must be prepared, and audited by a person who is eligible for appointment as a statutory auditor under Part 42 of the Companies Act 2006, with respect to the assets and liabilities of the trust; and

(v) the assets and liabilities of the trust must, at least once every three years, be determined, calculated and verified by an actuary who is a Fellow of the Institute of Actuaries or of the Faculty of Actuaries.

(2) For the purposes of paragraph (1)(b)(ii) and (iii), a person is unconnected with the provider if he is a person other than—

(a) the provider;

(b) a member of the same group as the provider;

(c) a director, other officer or employee of the provider, or of any member of the same group as the provider;

(d) a partner of the provider;

(e) a close relative of a person falling within sub-paragraph (a), (c) or (d); or

(f) an agent of any person falling within sub-paragraphs (a) to (e).

60A. Information society services

Article 59 is subject to the exclusion in article 72A (information society services).

CHAPTER XV
REGULATED MORTGAGE CONTRACTS

The activities

61. Regulated mortgage contracts

(1) Entering into a regulated mortgage contract as lender is a specified kind of activity.

(2) Administering a regulated mortgage contract is also a specified kind of activity, where the contract was entered into by way of business after the coming into force of this article.

(3) In this Chapter—

(a) a contract is a "regulated mortgage contract" if, at the time it is entered into, the following conditions are met—

(i) the contract is one under which a person ("the lender") provides credit to an individual or to trustees ("the borrower");

(ii) the contract provides for the obligation of the borrower to repay to be secured by a first legal mortgage on land (other than timeshare accommodation) in the United Kingdom;

(iii) at least 40% of that land is used, or is intended to be used, as or in connection with a dwelling by the borrower or (in the case of credit provided to trustees) by an individual who is a beneficiary of the trust, or by a related person;

but such a contract is not a regulated mortgage contract if it is a regulated home purchase plan;

(b) "administering" a regulated mortgage contract means either or both of—

(i) notifying the borrower of changes in interest rates or payments due under the contract, or of other matters of which the contract requires him to be notified; and

(ii) taking any necessary steps for the purposes of collecting or recovering payments due under the contract from the borrower;

but a person is not to be treated as administering a regulated mortgage contract merely because he has, or exercises, a right to take action for the purposes of enforcing the contract (or to require that such action is or is not taken);

(c) "credit" includes a cash loan, and any other form of financial accommodation.

(4) For the purposes of paragraph (3)(a)—

(a) a "first legal mortgage" means a legal mortgage ranking in priority ahead of all other mortgages (if any) affecting the land in question, where "mortgage" includes charge and (in Scotland) a heritable security;

(b) the area of any land which comprises a building or other structure containing two or more storeys is to be taken to be the aggregate of the floor areas of each of those storeys;

(c) "related person", in relation to the borrower or (in the case of credit provided to trustees) a beneficiary of the trust, means—

(i) that person's spouse or civil partner;

(ii) a person (whether or not of the opposite sex) whose relationship with that person has the characteristics of the relationship between husband and wife; or

(iii) that person's parent, brother, sister, child, grandparent or grandchild; and

(d) "timeshare accommodation" means overnight accommodation which is the subject of a timeshare contract within the meaning of the Timeshare, Holiday Products, Resale and Exchange Contracts Regulations 2010.

Exclusions

62. Arranging administration by authorised person

A person who is not an authorised person does not carry on an activity of the kind specified by article 61(2) in relation to a regulated mortgage contract where he—

(a) arranges for another person, being an authorised person with permission to carry on an activity of that kind, to administer the contract; or

(b) administers the contract himself during a period of not more than one month beginning with the day on which any such arrangement comes to an end.

63. Administration pursuant to agreement with authorised person

A person who is not an authorised person does not carry on an activity of the kind specified by article 61(2) in relation to a regulated mortgage contract where he administers the contract pursuant to an agreement with an authorised person who has permission to carry on an activity of that kind.

63A. Other exclusions

Article 61 is also subject to the exclusions in articles 66 (trustees etc), 72 (overseas persons) and 72A (information society services).

CHAPTER XVA
REGULATED HOME REVERSION PLANS

The activities

63B. Entering into and administering regulated home reversion plans

(1) Entering into a regulated home reversion plan as plan provider is a specified kind of activity.

(2) Administering a regulated home reversion plan is also a specified kind of activity where the plan was entered into on or after 6th April 2007.

(3) In this Chapter—

(a) a "regulated home reversion plan" is an arrangement comprised in one or more instruments or agreements, in relation to which the following conditions are met at the time it is entered into—

(i) the arrangement is one under which a person (the "plan provider") buys all or part of a qualifying interest in land (other than timeshare accommodation) in the United Kingdom from an individ-ual or trustees (the "reversion seller");

(ii) the reversion seller (if he is an individual) or an individual who is a beneficiary of the trust (if the reversion seller is a trustee), or a related person, is entitled under the arrangement to occupy at least 40% of the land in question as or in connection with a dwelling, and intends to do so; and

(iii) the arrangement specifies one or more qualifying termination events, on the occurrence of which that entitlement will end;

(b) "administering" a regulated home reversion plan means any of—
   (i) notifying the reversion seller of changes in payments due under the plan, or of other matters of which the plan requires him to be notified;
   (ii) taking any necessary steps for the purposes of making payments to the reversion seller under the plan; and
   (iii) taking any necessary steps for the purposes of collecting or recovering payments due under the plan from the reversion seller,

but a person is not to be treated as administering a regulated home reversion plan merely because he has, or exercises, a right to take action for the purposes of enforcing the plan (or to require that such action is or is not taken).

(4) For the purposes of paragraph (3)—
(a) the reference to a "qualifying interest" in land—
   (i) in relation to land in England or Wales, is to an estate in fee simple absolute or a term of years absolute, whether subsisting at law or in equity;
   (ii) in relation to land in Scotland, is to the interest of an owner in land or the tenant's right over or interest in a property subject to a lease;
   (iii) in relation to land in Northern Ireland, is to any freehold estate or any leasehold estate, whether subsisting at law or in equity;
(b) "timeshare accommodation" has the meaning given by section 1 of the Timeshare Act 1992;
(c) "related person" in relation to the reversion seller or, where the reversion seller is a trustee, a beneficiary of the trust, means—
   (i) that person's spouse or civil partner;
   (ii) a person (whether or not of the opposite sex) whose relationship with that person has the characteristics of the relationship between husband and wife; or
   (iii) that person's parent, brother, sister, child, grandparent or grandchild; and
(d) "qualifying termination event", in relation to a person's entitlement to occupy land, means—
   (i) the person becomes a resident of a care home;
   (ii) the person dies;
   (iii) the end of a specified period of at least twenty years beginning with the day on which the reversion seller entered into the arrangement.

(5) For the purposes of paragraph (3)(a)(ii), the area of any land which comprises a building or other structure containing two or more storeys is to be taken to be the aggregate of the floor areas of each of those storeys.

(6) For the purposes of the definition of "qualifying termination event" in paragraph (4), "care home"—
(a) in relation to England and Wales, has the meaning given by section 3 of the Care Standards Act 2000;
(b) in relation to Scotland, means accommodation provided by a "care home service" within the meaning of paragraph 2 of Schedule 12 to the Public Services Reform (Scotland) Act 2010;
(c) in relation to Northern Ireland, means—
   (i) a residential care home within the meaning of article 10 of the Health and Personal Social Services (Quality, Improvement and Regulation) (Northern Ireland) Order 2003; or
   (ii) a nursing home within the meaning of article 11 of that Order.

(7) In this Order—
(a) references to entering into a regulated home reversion plan as plan provider include acquiring any obligations or rights (including his interest in land) of the plan provider, under such a plan; but
(b) in relation to a person who acquires any such obligations or rights, an activity is a specified kind of activity for the purposes of articles 25B(1)(b) and 53B(b)(ii) and paragraph (2) only

if the plan was entered into by the plan provider (rather than the obligations or rights acquired) on or after 6th April 2007.

(8) Accordingly, references in this Order to a plan provider, other than in paragraph (7), include a person who acquires any such obligations or rights.

Exclusions

63C. Arranging administration by authorised person

A person who is not an authorised person does not carry on an activity of the kind specified by article 63B(2) in relation to a regulated home reversion plan where he—

(a) arranges for another person, being an authorised person with permission to carry on an activity of that kind, to administer the plan; or

(b) administers the plan himself during a period of not more than one month beginning with the day on which any such arrangement comes to an end.

63D. Administration pursuant to agreement with authorised person

A person who is not an authorised person does not carry on an activity of the kind specified by article 63B(2) in relation to a regulated home reversion plan where he administers the plan pursuant to an agreement with an authorised person who has permission to carry on an activity of that kind.

63E. Other exclusions

Article 63B is also subject to the exclusions in articles 66 (trustees etc), 72 (overseas persons) and 72A (information society services).

CHAPTER XVB
REGULATED HOME PURCHASE PLANS

The activities

63F. Entering into and administering regulated home purchase plans

(1) Entering into a regulated home purchase plan as home purchase provider is a specified kind of activity.

(2) Administering a regulated home purchase plan is also a specified kind of activity where the plan was entered into by way of business on or after 6th April 2007.

(3) In this Chapter—

(a) a "regulated home purchase plan" is an arrangement comprised in one or more instruments or agreements, in relation to which the following conditions are met at the time it is entered into—

(i) the arrangement is one under which a person (the "home purchase provider") buys a qualifying interest or an undivided share of a qualifying interest in land (other than timeshare accommo-dation) in the United Kingdom;

(ii) where an undivided share of a qualifying interest in land is bought, the interest is held on trust for the home purchase provider and the individual or trustees mentioned in paragraph (iii) as beneficial tenants in common;

(iii) the arrangement provides for the obligation of an individual or trustees (the "home purchaser") to buy the interest bought by the home purchase provider over the course of or at the end of a specified period; and

(iv) the home purchaser (if he is an individual) or an individual who is a beneficiary of the trust (if the home purchaser is a trustee), or a related person, is entitled under the arrangement to oc-cupy at least 40% of the land in question as or in connection with a dwelling during that period, and intends to do so;

(b) "administering" a regulated home purchase plan means either or both of—

(i) notifying the home purchaser of changes in payments due under the plan, or of other matters of which the plan requires him to be notified; and

(ii) taking any necessary steps for the purposes of collecting or recovering payments due under the plan from the home purchaser;

but a person is not to be treated as administering a regulated home purchase plan merely because he has, or exercises, a right to take action for the purposes of enforcing the plan or to require that such action is or is not taken.

(4) Article 63B(4)(a) to (c) applies for the purposes of paragraph (3)(a) with references to the "reversion seller" being read as references to the "home purchaser".

(5) Article 63B(5) applies for the purposes of paragraph (3)(a)(iv) with the reference to "paragraph (3)(a)(ii)" being read as a reference to "paragraph (3)(a)(iv)".

Exclusions

63G. Arranging administration by authorised person

A person who is not an authorised person does not carry on an activity of the kind specified by article 63F(2) in relation to a regulated home purchase plan where he—

(a) arranges for another person, being an authorised person with permission to carry on an activity of that kind, to administer the plan; or

(b) administers the plan himself during a period of not more than one month beginning with the day on which any such arrangement comes to an end.

63H. Administration pursuant to agreement with authorised person

A person who is not an authorised person does not carry on an activity of the kind specified by article 63F(2) in relation to a regulated home purchase plan where he administers the plan pursuant to an agreement with an authorised person who has permission to carry on an activity of that kind.

63I. Other exclusions

Article 63F is also subject to the exclusions in articles 66 (trustees etc), 72 (overseas persons) and 72A (information society services).

CHAPTER XVC
REGULATED SALE AND RENT BACK AGREEMENTS

The activities

63J. Entering into and administering regulated sale and rent back agreements

(1) Entering into a regulated sale and rent back agreement as an agreement provider is a specified kind of activity.

(2) Administering a regulated sale and rent back agreement is also a specified kind of activity when the agreement was entered into on or after 1st July 2009.

(3) In this Chapter—

(a) a "regulated sale and rent back agreement" is an arrangement comprised in one or more instruments or agreements, in relation to which the following conditions are met at the time it is entered into—

(i) the arrangement is one under which a person (the "agreement provider") buys all or part of the qualifying interest in land (other than timeshare accommodation) in the United Kingdom from an individual or trustees (the "agreement seller "); and

(ii) the agreement seller (if the agreement seller is an individual) or an individual who is the beneficiary of the trust (if the agreement seller is a trustee), or a related person, is entitled under the arrangement to occupy at least 40% of the land in question as or in connection with a dwelling, and intends to do so;

but such an arrangement is not a regulated sale and rent back agreement if it is a regulated home reversion plan;

(b) "administering" a regulated sale and rent back agreement means any of—
  (i) notifying the agreement seller of changes in payments due under the agreement, or of other matters of which the agreement requires the agreement seller to be notified;
  (ii) taking any necessary steps for the purpose of making payments to the agreement seller under the agreement; and
  (iii) taking any necessary steps for the purposes of collecting or recovering payments due under the agreement from the agreement seller,

but a person is not to be treated as administering a regulated sale and rent back agreement because that person has, or exercises, a right to take action for the purposes of enforcing the agreement (or to require that such action is or is not taken).

(4) For the purposes of paragraph (3)—
(a) the reference to a "qualifying interest" in land—
  (i) in relation to land in England and Wales, is to an estate in fee simple absolute or a term of years absolute, whether subsisting at law or in equity;
  (ii) in relation to land in Scotland, is to the interest of an owner in land or the tenant's right over or interest in a property subject to a lease;
  (iii) in relation to land in Northern Ireland, is to any freehold estate or any leasehold estate, whether subsisting at law or in equity;
(b) "timeshare accommodation" means overnight accommodation which is the subject of a timeshare contract within the meaning of the Timeshare, Holiday Products, Resale and Exchange Contracts Regulations 2010; and
(c) "related person" in relation to the agreement seller or, where the agreement seller is a trustee, a beneficiary of the trust, means—
  (i) that person's spouse or civil partner;
  (ii) a person (whether or not of the opposite sex) whose relationship with that person has the characteristic of the relationship between husband and wife;
  (iii) that person's parent, brother, sister, child, grandparent or grandchild.

(5) For the purposes of paragraph (3)(a)(ii), the area of any land which compromises a building or other structure containing two or more storeys is to be taken to be the aggregate of the floor areas of each of those storeys.

(6) In this Order—
(a) references to entering into a regulated sale and rent back agreement as agreement provider include acquiring any obligations or rights of the agreement provider, including the agreement provider's interest in land or interests under one or more of the instruments or agreements referred to in paragraph (3)(a); but
(b) in relation to a person who acquires any such obligations or rights, an activity is a specified kind of activity for the purposes of articles 25E(1)(b) and 53D(b)(ii) and paragraph (2) only if the agreement was entered into by the agreement provider (rather than the obligations or rights acquired) on or after 1st July 2009.

(7) Accordingly, references in this Order to an agreement provider, other than in paragraph (6), include a person who acquires any such obligations or rights.

Exclusions

63K. Arranging administration by authorised person

A person who is not an authorised person does not carry on an activity of the kind specified by article 63J(2) in relation to a regulated sale and rent back agreement where that person—
(a) arranges for another person, being an authorised person with permission to carry on an activity of that kind, to administer the agreement; or
(b) administers the agreement during a period of not more than one month beginning with the day on which any such arrangement comes to an end.

63L. Administration pursuant to agreement with authorised person

A person who is not an authorised person does not carry on an activity of the kind specified by article 63J(2) in relation to a regulated sale and rent back agreement where that person administers the agreement pursuant to an agreement with an authorised person who has permission to carry on activity of that kind.

63M. Other exclusions

Article 63J is also subject to the exclusions in article 66 (trustees etc), 72 (overseas persons) and 72A (information society services).

CHAPTER XVD
ACTIVITIES OF RECLAIM FUNDS

The activities

63N. Dormant account funds

(1) The following are specified kinds of activity—
(a) the meeting of repayment claims by a reclaim fund;
(b) the management of dormant account funds (including the investment of such funds) by a reclaim fund.

(2) In this article—
"account", "balance", "dormant" and "reclaim fund" have the same meaning as in Part 1 of the Dormant Bank and Building Society Accounts Act 2008 (transfer of balances in dormant accounts) (see section 6 of that Act);
"dormant account funds" and "repayment claims" have the same meaning as in section 5 of that Act;
"management of dormant account funds" means the acceptance of a transfer from a bank or building society of the balance of a dormant account, or a proportion of such a balance, and the management of those funds in such a way as to enable the reclaim fund to meet whatever repayment claims it is prudent to anticipate.

CHAPTER 15E
SPECIFIED BENCHMARKS

The activities

63O. Specified benchmarks

(1) The following are specified kinds of activity—
(a) providing information in relation to a specified benchmark;
(b) administering a specified benchmark.

(2) In this Chapter—
(a) "providing information" in relation to a specified benchmark means providing any information or expression of opinion that is—
(i) provided to, or for the purpose of passing to, a person who has permission to carry on the activity specified in paragraph (1)(b) in relation to that specified benchmark;
(ii) required in connection with the determination of the specified benchmark; and
(iii) provided for the purpose of determining the specified benchmark;
(b) "administering" a specified benchmark means—
(i) administering the arrangements for determining a specified benchmark;
(ii) collecting, analysing or processing information or expressions of opinion provided for the purpose of determining a specified benchmark;
(iii) determining a specified benchmark through the application of a formula or other method of calculation to the information or expressions of opinion provided for that purpose.

63P. Publicly available factual data and subscription services

A person does not carry on an activity of the kind specified by article 63O(1)(a) in relation to a specified benchmark where the information provided—

(a) consists solely of factual data obtained from a publicly available source; or

(b) is—

(i) compiled by a subscription service for purposes other than in connection with the determination of a specified benchmark;

(ii) provided to a person who has permission to carry on an activity of the kind specified by article 63O(1)(b) and who is a subscriber to the service; and

(iii) provided to such a person only in that person's capacity as a subscriber.

63Q. Administration of a specified benchmark by the FCA

(1) The FCA does not carry on the activity of the kind specified by article 63O(1)(b) in relation to a specified benchmark where the FCA administers the specified benchmark itself.

(2) Where a specified benchmark is administered by the FCA, the reference in article 63O(2)(a)(i) to a person who has permission to carry on the activity specified in 63O(1)(b) in relation to that specified benchmark is to be read as referring to the FCA.

63R. Schedule

Schedule 5 specifies benchmarks for the purposes of section 22(1A)(b) of the Act.

CHAPTER XVI
AGREEING TO CARRY ON ACTIVITIES

The activity

64. Agreeing to carry on specified kinds of activity

Agreeing to carry on an activity of the kind specified by any other provision of this Part (other than article 5, 9B, 10, 25D, 51, 52 and 63N) is a specified kind of activity.

Exclusions

65. Overseas persons etc

Article 64 is subject to the exclusions in articles 72 (overseas persons) and 72A (information society services).

CHAPTER XVII
EXCLUSIONS APPLYING TO SEVERAL SPECIFIED KINDS OF ACTIVITY

66. Trustees, nominees and personal representatives

(1) A person ("X") does not carry on an activity of the kind specified by article 14 where he enters into a transaction as bare trustee or, in Scotland, as nominee for another person ("Y") and—

(a) X is acting on Y's instructions; and

(b) X does not hold himself out as providing a service of buying and selling securities or contractually based investments.

(2) Subject to paragraph (7), there are excluded from articles 25(1) and (2), 25A(1) and (2), 25B(1) and (2), 25C(1) and (2) and 25E(1) and (2) arrangements made by a person acting as trustee or personal representative for or with a view to a transaction which is or is to be entered into—

(a) by that person and a fellow trustee or personal representative (acting in their capacity as such); or

(b) by a beneficiary under the trust, will or intestacy.

(3) Subject to paragraph (7), there is excluded from article 37 any activity carried on by a person acting as trustee or personal representative, unless—

(a) he holds himself out as providing a service comprising an activity of the kind specified by article 37; or

(b) the assets in question are held for the purposes of an occupational pension scheme, and, by virtue of article 4 of the Financial Services and Markets Act 2000 (Carrying on Regulated Activities by Way of Business) Order 2001, he is to be treated as carrying on that activity by way of business.

(3A) Subject to paragraph (7), there is excluded from article 39A any activity carried on by a person acting as trustee or personal representative, unless he holds himself out as providing a service comprising an activity of the kind specified by article 39A.

(4) Subject to paragraph (7), there is excluded from article 40 any activity carried on by a person acting as trustee or personal representative, unless he holds himself out as providing a service comprising an activity of the kind specified by article 40.

(4A) There is excluded from article 40 any activity carried on by a person acting as trustee which consists of arranging for one or more other persons to safeguard and administer trust assets where—

(a) that other person is a qualifying custodian; or

(b) that safeguarding and administration is also arranged by a qualifying custodian.

In this paragraph, "qualifying custodian" has the meaning given by article 41(2).

(5) A person does not, by sending or causing to be sent a dematerialised instruction (within the meaning of article 45), carry on an activity of the kind specified by that article if the instruction relates to an investment which that person holds as trustee or personal representative.

(6) Subject to paragraph (7), there is excluded from articles 53, 53A, 53B, 53C and 53D the giving of advice by a person acting as trustee or personal representative where he gives the advice to—

(a) a fellow trustee or personal representative for the purposes of the trust or the estate; or

(b) a beneficiary under the trust, will or intestacy concerning his interest in the trust fund or estate.

(6A) Subject to paragraph (7), a person acting as trustee or personal representative does not carry on an activity of the kind specified by article 61(1) or (2) where the borrower under the regulated mortgage contract in question is a beneficiary under the trust, will or intestacy.

(6B) Subject to paragraph (7), a person acting as trustee or personal representative does not carry on an activity of the kind specified by article 63B(1) or (2) where the reversion seller under the regulated home reversion plan in question is a beneficiary under the trust, will or intestacy.

(6C) Subject to paragraph (7), a person acting as trustee or personal representative does not carry on an activity of the kind specified by article 63F(1) or (2) where the home purchaser under the regulated home purchase plan in question is a beneficiary under the trust, will or intestacy.

(6D) Subject to paragraph (7), a person acting as a trustee or personal representative does not carry on an activity of the kind specified by article 63J(1) or (2) where the agreement seller under the regulated sale and rent back agreement is a beneficiary under the trust, will or intestacy.

(7) Paragraphs (2), (3), (3A), (4), (6), (6A), (6B), (6C) and (6D) do not apply if the person carrying on the activity is remunerated for what he does in addition to any remuneration he receives as trustee or personal representative, and for these purposes a person is not to be regarded as receiving additional remuneration merely because his remuneration is calculated by reference to time spent.

(8) This article is subject to article 4(4A).

67. Activities carried on in the course of a profession or non-investment business

(1) There is excluded from articles 21, 25(1) and (2), 25A, 25B, 25C, 25E, 39A, 40, 53, 53A, 53B, 53C and 53D any activity which—

(a) is carried on in the course of carrying on any profession or business which does not otherwise consist of the carrying on of regulated activities in the United Kingdom; and

(b) may reasonably be regarded as a necessary part of other services provided in the course of that profession or business.

(2) But the exclusion in paragraph (1) does not apply if the activity in question is remunerated separately from the other services.

(3) This article is subject to article 4(4) and (4A).

68. Activities carried on in connection with the sale of goods or supply of services

(1) Subject to paragraphs (9), (10) and (11), this article concerns certain activities carried on for the purposes of or in connection with the sale of goods or supply of services by a supplier to a customer, where—

"supplier" means a person whose main business is to sell goods or supply services and not to carry on any activities of the kind specified by any of articles 14, 21, 25, 37, 39A, 40, 45, 51, 52 and 53 and, where the supplier is a member of a group, also means any other member of that group; and

"customer" means a person, other than an individual, to whom a supplier sells goods or supplies services, or agrees to do so, and, where the customer is a member of a group, also means any other member of that group;

and in this article "related sale or supply" means a sale of goods or supply of services to the customer otherwise than by the supplier, but for or in connection with the same purpose as the sale or supply mentioned above.

(2) There is excluded from article 14 any transaction entered into by a supplier with a customer, if the transaction is entered into for the purposes of or in connection with the sale of goods or supply of services, or a related sale or supply.

(3) There is excluded from article 21 any transaction entered into by a supplier as agent for a customer, if the transaction is entered into for the purposes of or in connection with the sale of goods or supply of services, or a related sale or supply, and provided that—

(a) where the investment to which the transaction relates is a security, the supplier does not hold himself out (other than to the customer) as engaging in the business of buying securities of the kind to which the transaction relates with a view to selling them, and does not regularly solicit members of the public for the purpose of inducing them (as principals or agents) to buy, sell, subscribe for or underwrite securities;

(b) where the investment to which the transaction relates is a contractually based investment, the supplier enters into the transaction—

(i) with or through an authorised person, or an exempt person acting in the course of a business comprising a regulated activity in relation to which he is exempt; or

(ii) through an office outside the United Kingdom maintained by a party to the transaction, and with or through a person whose head office is situated outside the United Kingdom and whose ordinary business involves him in carrying on activities of the kind specified by any of articles 14, 21, 25, 37, 40, 45, 51, 52 and 53 or, so far as relevant to any of those articles, article 64, or would do so apart from any exclusion from any of those articles made by this Order.

(4) In paragraph (3)(a), "members of the public" has the meaning given by article 15(2), references to "A" being read as references to the supplier.

(5) There are excluded from article 25(1) and (2) arrangements made by a supplier for, or with a view to, a transaction which is or is to be entered into by a customer for the purposes of or in connection with the sale of goods or supply of services, or a related sale or supply.

(6) There is excluded from article 37 any activity carried on by a supplier where the assets in question—

(a) are those of a customer; and

(b) are managed for the purposes of or in connection with the sale of goods or supply of services, or a related sale or supply.

(7) There is excluded from article 40 any activity carried on by a supplier where the assets in question are or are to be safeguarded and administered for the purposes of or in connection with the sale of goods or supply of services, or a related sale or supply.

(8) There is excluded from article 53 the giving of advice by a supplier to a customer for the purposes of or in connection with the sale of goods or supply of services, or a related sale or supply, or to a person with whom the customer proposes to enter into a transaction for the purposes of or in connection with such a sale or supply or related sale or supply.

(9) Paragraphs (2), (3) and (5) do not apply in the case of a transaction for the sale or purchase of a contract of insurance, an investment of the kind specified by article 81, or an investment of the kind specified by article 89 so far as relevant to such a contract or such an investment.

(10) Paragraph (6) does not apply where the assets managed consist of qualifying contracts of insurance, investments of the kind specified by article 81, or investments of the kind specified by article 89 so far as relevant to such contracts or such investments.

(11) Paragraph (8) does not apply in the case of advice in relation to an investment which is a contract of insurance, is of the kind specified by article 81, or is of the kind specified by article 89 so far as relevant to such a contract or such an investment.

(12) This article is subject to article 4(4).

69. Groups and joint enterprises

(1) There is excluded from article 14 any transaction into which a person enters as principal with another person if that other person is also acting as principal and—

(a) they are members of the same group; or

(b) they are, or propose to become, participators in a joint enterprise and the transaction is entered into for the purposes of or in connection with that enterprise.

(2) There is excluded from article 21 any transaction into which a person enters as agent for another person if that other person is acting as principal, and the condition in paragraph (1)(a) or (b) is met, provided that—

(a) where the investment to which the transaction relates is a security, the agent does not hold himself out (other than to members of the same group or persons who are or propose to become participators with him in a joint enterprise) as engaging in the business of buying securities of the kind to which the transaction relates with a view to selling them, and does not regularly solicit members of the public for the purpose of inducing them (as principals or agents) to buy, sell, subscribe for or underwrite securities;

(b) where the investment to which the transaction relates is a contractually based investment, the agent enters into the transaction—

(i) with or through an authorised person, or an exempt person acting in the course of a business comprising a regulated activity in relation to which he is exempt; or

(ii) through an office outside the United Kingdom maintained by a party to the transaction, and with or through a person whose head office is situated outside the United Kingdom and whose ordinary business involves him in carrying on activities of the kind specified by any of articles 14, 21, 25, 37, 40, 45, 51, 52 and 53 or, so far as relevant to any of those articles, article 64, or would do so apart from any exclusion from any of those articles made by this Order.

(3) In paragraph (2)(a), "members of the public" has the meaning given by article 15(2), references to "A" being read as references to the agent.

(4) There are excluded from article 25(1) and (2) arrangements made by a person if—

(a) he is a member of a group and the arrangements in question are for, or with a view to, a transaction which is or is to be entered into, as principal, by another member of the same group; or

(b) he is or proposes to become a participator in a joint enterprise, and the arrangements in question are for, or with a view to, a transaction which is or is to be entered into, as principal, by another person who is or proposes to become a participator in that enterprise, for the purposes of or in connection with that enterprise.

(5) There is excluded from article 37 any activity carried on by a person if—

(a) he is a member of a group and the assets in question belong to another member of the same group; or

(b) he is or proposes to become a participator in a joint enterprise with the person to whom the assets belong, and the assets are managed for the purposes of or in connection with that enterprise.

(6) There is excluded from article 40 any activity carried on by a person if—

(a) he is a member of a group and the assets in question belong to another member of the same group; or

(b) he is or proposes to become a participator in a joint enterprise, and the assets in question—

(i) belong to another person who is or proposes to become a participator in that joint enterprise; and

(ii) are or are to be safeguarded and administered for the purposes of or in connection with that enterprise.

(7) A person who is a member of a group does not carry on an activity of the kind specified by article 45 where he sends a dematerialised instruction, or causes one to be sent, on behalf of another member of the same group, if the investment to which the instruction relates is one in respect of which a member of the same group is registered as holder in the appropriate register of securities, or will be so registered as a result of the instruction.

(8) In paragraph (7), "dematerialised instruction" and "register of securities" have the meaning given by regulation 3 of the Uncertificated Securities Regulations 2001.

(9) There is excluded from article 53 the giving of advice by a person if—

(a) he is a member of a group and gives the advice in question to another member of the same group; or

(b) he is, or proposes to become, a participator in a joint enterprise and the advice in question is given to another person who is, or proposes to become, a participator in that enterprise for the purposes of or in connection with that enterprise.

(10) Paragraph (2) does not apply to a transaction for the sale or purchase of a contract of insurance.

(11) Paragraph (4) does not apply to arrangements for, or with a view to, a transaction for the sale or purchase of a contract of insurance.

(12) Paragraph (9) does not apply where the advice relates to a transaction for the sale or purchase of a contract of insurance.

(13) This article is subject to article 4(4).

70. Activities carried on in connection with the sale of a body corporate

(1) A person does not carry on an activity of the kind specified by article 14 by entering as principal into a transaction if—

(a) the transaction is one to acquire or dispose of shares in a body corporate other than an open-ended investment company, or is entered into for the purposes of such an acquisition or disposal; and

(b) either—

(i) the conditions set out in paragraph (2) are met; or

(ii) those conditions are not met, but the object of the transaction may nevertheless reasonably be regarded as being the acquisition of day to day control of the affairs of the body corporate.

(2) The conditions mentioned in paragraph (1)(b) are that—

(a) the shares consist of or include 50 per cent or more of the voting shares in the body corporate; or

(b) the shares, together with any already held by the person acquiring them, consist of or include at least that percentage of such shares; and

(c) in either case, the acquisition or disposal is between parties each of whom is a body corporate, a partnership, a single individual or a group of connected individuals.

(3) In paragraph (2)(c), "a group of connected individuals" means—

(a) in relation to a party disposing of shares in a body corporate, a single group of persons each of whom is—

(i) a director or manager of the body corporate;

(ii) a close relative of any such director or manager;

(iii) a person acting as trustee for any person falling within paragraph (i) or (ii); and

(b) in relation to a party acquiring shares in a body corporate, a single group of persons each of whom is—

(i) a person who is or is to be a director or manager of the body corporate;

(ii) a close relative of any such person; or

(iii) a person acting as trustee for any person falling within paragraph (i) or (ii).

(4) A person does not carry on an activity of the kind specified by article 21 by entering as agent into a transaction of the kind described in paragraph (1).

(5) There are excluded from article 25(1) and (2) arrangements made for, or with a view to, a transaction of the kind described in paragraph (1).

(6) There is excluded from article 53 the giving of advice in connection with a transaction (or proposed transaction) of the kind described in paragraph (1).

(7) Paragraphs (4), (5) and (6) do not apply in the case of a transaction for the sale or purchase of a contract of insurance.

(8) This article is subject to article 4(4).

71. Activities carried on in connection with employee share schemes

(1) A person ("C"), a member of the same group as C or a relevant trustee does not carry on an activity of the kind specified by article 14 by entering as principal into a transaction the purpose of which is to enable or facilitate—

(a) transactions in shares in, or debentures issued by, C between, or for the benefit of, any of the persons mentioned in paragraph (2); or

(b) the holding of such shares or debentures by, or for the benefit of, such persons.

(2) The persons referred to in paragraph (1) are—

(a) the bona fide employees or former employees of C or of another member of the same group as C;

(b) the wives, husbands, widows, widowers, civil partners, surviving civil partners, or children or step-children under the age of eighteen of such employees or former employees.

(3) C, a member of the same group as C or a relevant trustee does not carry on an activity of the kind specified by article 21 by entering as agent into a transaction of the kind described in paragraph (1).

(4) There are excluded from article 25(1) or (2) arrangements made by C, a member of the same group as C or a relevant trustee if the arrangements in question are for, or with a view to, a transaction of the kind described in paragraph (1).

(5) There is excluded from article 40 any activity if the assets in question are, or are to be, safeguarded and administered by C, a member of the same group as C or a relevant trustee for the purpose of enabling or facilitating transactions of the kind described in paragraph (1).

(6) In this article—

(a) "shares" and "debentures" include—

(i) any investment of the kind specified by article 76, 77 or 77A;

(ii) any investment of the kind specified by article 79 or 80 so far as relevant to articles 76, 77 or 77A; and

(iii) any investment of the kind specified by article 89 so far as relevant to investments of the kind mentioned in paragraph (i) or (ii);

(b) "relevant trustee" means a person who, in pursuance of the arrangements made for the purpose mentioned in paragraph (1), holds, as trustee, shares in or debentures issued by C.

72. Overseas persons

(1) An overseas person does not carry on an activity of the kind specified by article 14 or 25D by—

(a) entering into a transaction as principal with or though an authorised person, or an exempt person acting in the course of a business comprising a regulated activity in relation to which he is exempt; or

(b) entering into a transaction as principal with a person in the United Kingdom, if the transaction is the result of a legitimate approach.

(2) An overseas person does not carry on an activity of the kind specified by article 21 or 25D by—

(a) entering into a transaction as agent for any person with or through an authorised person or an exempt person acting in the course of a business comprising a regulated activity in relation to which he is exempt; or

(b) entering into a transaction with another party ("X") as agent for any person ("Y"), other than with or through an authorised person or such an exempt person, unless—

(i) either X or Y is in the United Kingdom; and

(ii) the transaction is the result of an approach (other than a legitimate approach) made by or on behalf of, or to, whichever of X or Y is in the United Kingdom.

(3) There are excluded from article 25(1) or 25D arrangements made by an overseas person with an authorised person, or an exempt person acting in the course of a business comprising a regulated activity in relation to which he is exempt.

(4) There are excluded from article 25(2) or 25D arrangements made by an overseas person with a view to transactions which are, as respects transactions in the United Kingdom, confined to—

(a) transactions entered into by authorised persons as principal or agent; and

(b) transactions entered into by exempt persons, as principal or agent, in the course of business comprising regulated activities in relation to which they are exempt.

(5) There is excluded from article 53 the giving of advice by an overseas person as a result of a legitimate approach.

(5A) An overseas person does not carry on an activity of the kind specified by article 25A(1)(a), 25B(1)(a), 25C(1)(a) or 25E(1)(a) if each person who may be contemplating entering into the relevant type of agree-ment in the relevant capacity is non-resident.

(5B) There are excluded from articles 25A(1)(b), 25B(1)(b), 25C(1)(b) and 25E(1)(b) arrangements made by an overseas person to vary the terms of a qualifying agreement.

(5C) There are excluded from articles 25A(2), 25B(2), 25C(2) and 25E(2), arrangements made by an overseas person which are made solely with a view to non-resident persons who participate in those ar-rangements entering, in the relevant capacity, into the relevant type of agreement.

(5D) An overseas person does not carry on an activity of the kind specified in article 61(1), 63B(1), 63F(1) or 63J(1) by entering into a qualifying agreement.

(5E) An overseas person does not carry on an activity of the kind specified in article 61(2), 63B(2), 63F(2) or 63J(2) where he administers a qualifying agreement.

(5F) In paragraphs (5A) to (5E)—

(a) "non-resident" means not normally resident in the United Kingdom;

(b) "qualifying agreement" means—

(i) in relation to articles 25A and 61, a regulated mortgage contract where the borrower (or each borrower) is non-resident when he enters into it;

(ii) in relation to articles 25B and 63B, a regulated home reversion plan where the reversion seller (or each reversion seller) is non-resident when he enters into it;

(iii) in relation to articles 25C and 63F, a regulated home purchase plan where the home purchaser (or each home purchaser) is non-resident when he enters into it;

(iv) in relation to articles 25E and 63J, a regulated sale and rent back agreement where the agreement seller (or each agreement seller) is non-resident when the agreement seller enters into it;

(c) "the relevant capacity" means—

(i) in the case of a regulated mortgage contract, as borrower;

(ii) in the case of a regulated home reversion plan, as reversion seller or plan provider;

(iii) in the case of a regulated home purchase plan, as home purchaser;

(iv) in the case of a regulated sale and rent back agreement, as agreement seller or agreement provider;

(d) "the relevant type of agreement" means—

(i) in relation to article 25A, a regulated mortgage contract;
(ii) in relation to article 25B, a regulated home reversion plan;
(iii) in relation to article 25C, a regulated home purchase plan;
(iv) in relation to article 25E, a regulated sale and rent back agreement.

(6) There is excluded from article 64 any agreement made by an overseas person to carry on an activity of the kind specified by article 25(1) or (2), 37, 39A, 40 or 45 if the agreement is the result of a legitimate approach.

(7) In this article, "legitimate approach" means—
(a) an approach made to the overseas person which has not been solicited by him in any way, or has been solicited by him in a way which does not contravene section 21 of the Act; or
(b) an approach made by or on behalf of the overseas person in a way which does not contravene that section.

(8) Paragraphs (1) to (5) do not apply where the overseas person is an investment firm or credit institution—
(a) who is providing or performing investment services and activities on a professional basis; and
(b) whose home Member State is the United Kingdom.

(9) Paragraphs (1) to (5) do not apply where the overseas person is providing clearing services as a central counterparty (within the meaning of section 313(1) of the Act).

72A. Information society services

(1) There is excluded from this Part any activity consisting of the provision of an information society service from an EEA State other than the United Kingdom.

(2) The exclusion in paragraph (1) does not apply to the activity of effecting or carrying out a contract of insurance as principal, where—
(a) the activity is carried on by an undertaking which has received official authorisation in accordance with Article 4 of the life assurance consolidation directive or the first non-life insurance directive, and
(b) the insurance falls within the scope of any of the insurance directives.

72B. Activities carried on by a provider of relevant goods or services

(1) In this article—

"connected contract of insurance" means a contract of insurance which—
(a) is not a contract of long-term insurance;
(b) has a total duration (or would have a total duration were any right to renew conferred by the contract exercised) of five years or less;
(c) has an annual premium (or, where the premium is paid otherwise than by way of annual premium, the equivalent of an annual premium) of 500 euro or less, or the equivalent amount in sterling or other currency;
(d) covers the risk of—
(i) breakdown, loss of, or damage to, non-motor goods supplied by the provider; or
(ii) damage to, or loss of, baggage and other risks linked to the travel booked with the provider ("travel risks") in circumstances where—
(aa) the travel booked with the provider relates to attendance at an event organised or managed by that provider and the party seeking insurance is not an individual (acting in his private capacity) or a small business; or
(bb) the travel booked with the provider is only the hire of an aircraft, vehicle or vessel which does not provide sleeping accommodation;
(e) does not cover any liability risks (except, in the case of a contract which covers travel risks, where that cover is ancillary to the main cover provided by the contract);
(f) is complementary to the non-motor goods being supplied or service being provided by the provider; and

(g) is of such a nature that the only information that a person requires in order to carry on an activity of the kind specified by article 21, 25, 39A or 53 in relation to it is the cover provided by the contract;

"non-motor goods" means goods which are not mechanically propelled road vehicles;

"provider" means a person who supplies non-motor goods or provides services related to travel in the course of carrying on a profession or business which does not otherwise consist of the carrying on of regulated activities. For these purposes, the transfer of possession of an aircraft, vehicle or vessel under an agreement for hire which is not—

(a) a hire-purchase agreement within the meaning of section 189(1) of the Consumer Credit Act 1974, or

(b) any other agreement which contemplates that the property in those goods will also pass at some time in the future,

is the provision of a service related to travel, not a supply of goods;

"small business" means—

(a) subject to paragraph (b) a sole trader, body corporate, partnership or an unincorporated association which had a turnover in the last financial year of less than £1,000,000;

(b) where the business concerned is a member of a group within the meaning of section 474(1) of the Companies Act 2006, reference to its turnover means the combined turnover of the group;

"turnover" means the amounts derived from the provision of goods and services falling within the business's ordinary activities, after deduction of trade discounts, value added tax and any other taxes based on the amounts so derived.

(2) There is excluded from article 21 any transaction for the sale or purchase of a connected contract of insurance into which a provider enters as agent.

(3) There are excluded from article 25(1) and (2) any arrangements made by a provider for, or with a view to, a transaction for the sale or purchase of a connected contract of insurance.

(4) There is excluded from article 39A any activity carried on by a provider where the contract of insurance in question is a connected contract of insurance.

(5) There is excluded from article 53 the giving of advice by a provider in relation to a transaction for the sale or purchase of a connected contract of insurance.

(6) For the purposes of this article, a contract of insurance which covers travel risks is not to be treated as a contract of long-term insurance, notwithstanding the fact that it contains related and subsidiary provisions such that it might be regarded as a contract of long-term insurance, if the cover to which those provisions relate is ancillary to the main cover provided by the contract.

72C. Provision of information on an incidental basis

(1) There is excluded from articles 25(1) and (2) the making of arrangements for, or with a view to, a transaction for the sale or purchase of a contract of insurance or an investment of the kind specified by article 89, so far as relevant to such a contract, where that activity meets the conditions specified in paragraph (4).

(2) There is excluded from articles 37 and 40 any activity—

(a) where the assets in question are rights under a contract of insurance or an investment of the kind specified by article 89, so far as relevant to such a contract; and

(b) which meets the conditions specified in paragraph (4).

(3) There is excluded from article 39A any activity which meets the conditions specified in paragraph (4).

(4) The conditions specified in this paragraph are that the activity—

(a) consists of the provision of information to the policyholder or potential policyholder;

(b) is carried on by a person in the course of carrying on a profession or business which does not otherwise consist of the carrying on of regulated activities; and

(c) may reasonably be regarded as being incidental to that profession or business.

72D. Large risks contracts where risk situated outside the EEA

(1) There is excluded from articles 21, 25(1) and (2), 39A and 53 any activity which is carried on in relation to a large risks contract of insurance, to the extent that the risk or commitment covered by the contract is not situated in an EEA State.

(2) In this article, a "large risks contract of insurance" is a contract of insurance the principal object of which is to cover—

(a) risks falling within paragraph 4 (railway rolling stock), 5 (aircraft), 6 (ships), 7 (goods in transit), 11 (aircraft liability) or 12 (liability of ships) of Part 1 of Schedule 1;

(b) risks falling within paragraph 14 (credit) or 15 (suretyship) of that Part provided that the risks relate to a business carried on by the policyholder; or

(c) risks falling within paragraph 3 (land vehicles), 8 (fire and natural forces), 9 (damage to property), 10 (motor vehicle liability), 13 (general liability) or 16 (miscellaneous financial loss) of that Part provided that the risks relate to a business carried on by the policyholder and that the condition specified in paragraph (3) is met in relation to that business.

(3) The condition specified in this paragraph is that at least two of the three following criteria were met in the most recent financial year for which information is available—

(a) the balance sheet total of the business (within the meaning of section 382(5) or 465(5) of the Companies Act 2006) exceeded 6.2 million euro,

(b) the net turnover (within the meaning given to "turnover" by section 474(1) of the Companies Act 2006) exceeded 12.8 million euro,

(c) the number of employees (within the meaning given by sections 382(6) and 465(6) of the Companies Act 2006) exceeded 250,

and for a financial year which is a company's financial year but not in fact a year, the net turnover of the policyholder shall be proportionately adjusted.

(4) For the purposes of paragraph (3), where the policyholder is a member of a group for which consolidated accounts (within the meaning of the Seventh Company Law Directive) are drawn up, the question whether the condition specified by that paragraph is met is to be determined by reference to those accounts.

72E. Business Angel-led Enterprise Capital Funds

(1) A body corporate of a type specified in paragraph (7) does not carry on the activity of the kind specified by article 21 by entering as agent into a transaction on behalf of the participants of a Business Angel-led Enterprise Capital Fund.

(2) There are excluded from article 25(1) and (2) arrangements, made by a body corporate of a type specified in paragraph (7), for or with a view to a transaction which is or is to be entered into by or on behalf of the participants in a Business Angel-led Enterprise Capital Fund.

(3) There is excluded from article 37 any activity, carried on by a body corporate of a type specified in paragraph (7), which consists in the managing of assets belonging to the participants in a Business Angel-led Enterprise Capital Fund.

(4) There is excluded from article 40 any activity, carried on by a body corporate of a type specified in paragraph (7), in respect of assets belonging to the participants in a Business Angel-led Enterprise Capital Fund.

(5) A body corporate of a type specified in paragraph (7) does not carry on the activity of the kind specified in article 51(1)(a) where it carries on the activity of establishing, operating or winding up a Business Angel-led Enterprise Capital Fund.

(6) A body corporate of a type specified in paragraph (7) does not carry on the activity of the kind specified in article 53 where it is advising the participants in a Business Angel-led Enterprise Capital Fund on investments to be made by or on behalf of the participants of that Business Angel-led Enterprise Capital Fund.

(7) The type of body corporate specified is a limited company—

(i) which operates a Business Angel-led Enterprise Capital Fund; and

(ii) the members of which are participants in the Business Angel-led Enterprise Capital Fund operated by that limited company and between them have invested at least 50 per cent of the total investment in that Business Angel-led Enterprise Capital Fund excluding any investment made by the Secretary of State.

(8) For the purposes of paragraph (7), "a limited company" means a body corporate with limited liability which is a company or firm formed in accordance with the law of an EEA State and having its registered office, central administration or principal place of business within the territory of an EEA State.

(9) Nothing in this article has the effect of excluding a body corporate from the application of the Money Laundering Regulations 2007, in so far as those Regulations would have applied to it but for this article.

(10) Nothing in this article has the effect of excluding a body corporate from the application of section 397 of the Act (misleading statements and practices), in so far as that section would have applied to it but for this article.

(11) This article is subject to article 4(4).

72F. Interpretation

(1) For the purposes of this article and of article 72E—

"Business Angel-led Enterprise Capital Fund" means a collective investment scheme which—

(a) is established for the purpose of enabling participants to participate in or receive profits or income arising from the acquisition, holding, management or disposal of investments falling within one or more of—
  (i) article 76, being shares in an unlisted company;
  (ii) article 77, being instruments creating or acknowledging indebtedness in respect of an unlisted company;
  (iia) article 77A, being rights under an alternative finance investment bond issued by an unlisted company; and
  (iii) article 79, being warrants or other instruments entitling the holder to subscribe for shares in an unlisted company;

(b) has only the following as its participants—
  (i) the Secretary of State;
  (ii) a body corporate of a type specified in article 72E(7); and
  (iii) one or more persons each of whom at the time they became a participant was—
    (aa) a sophisticated investor;
    (bb) a high net worth individual;
    (cc) a high net worth company;
    (dd) a high net worth unincorporated association;
    (ee) a trustee of a high value trust; or
    (ff) a self-certified sophisticated investor;

(c) is prevented, by the arrangements by which it is established, from—
  (i) acquiring investments, other than those falling within paragraphs (i) to (iii) of sub-paragraph (a); and
  (ii) acquiring investments falling within paragraphs (i) to (iii) of sub-paragraph (a) in an unlisted company, where the aggregated cost of those investments exceeds £2 million, unless that acquisition is necessary to prevent or reduce the dilution of an existing share-holding in that unlisted company;

"high net worth company" means a body corporate which—

(a) falls within article 49(2)(a) of the Financial Services and Markets Act 2000 (Financial Promotion) Order 2001 (high net worth companies, unincorporated associations etc); and

(b) has executed a document (in a manner which binds the company) in the following terms:

"This company is a high net worth company and falls within article 49(2)(a) of the Financial Services and Markets Act 2000 (Financial Promotion) Order 2001. We understand that any Business Angel-led Enterprise Capital Fund (within the meaning of article 72F of the Financial Services and Markets Act 2000 (Regulated Activities) Order 2001), in which this company participates, or any person who operates that

Business Angel-led Enterprise Capital Fund, in which this company participates, will not be authorised under the Financial Services and Markets Act 2000 (and so will not have to satisfy the threshold conditions set out in Part I of Schedule 6 to that Act and will not be subject to Financial Services Authority rules such as those on holding client money). We understand that this means that redress through the Financial Services Authority, the Financial Ombudsman Scheme or the Financial Services Compensation Scheme will not be available. We also understand the risks associated in investing in a Business Angel-led Enterprise Capital Fund and are aware that it is open to us to seek advice from someone who is authorised under the Financial Services and Markets Act 2000 and who specialises in advising on this kind of investment."

"high net worth individual" means an individual who—

(a) is a "certified high net worth individual" within the meaning of article 48(2) of the Financial Services and Markets Act 2000 (Financial Promotion) Order 2001 (certified high net worth individuals); and

(b) has signed a statement in the following terms:

"I declare that I am a certified high net worth individual within the meaning of article 48(2) of the Financial Services and Markets Act 2000 (Financial Promotion) Order 2001 and that I understand that any Business Angel-led Enterprise Capital Fund (within the meaning of article 72F of the Financial Services and Markets Act 2000 (Regulated Activities) Order 2001), in which I participate, or any person who operates that Business Angel-led Enterprise Capital Fund, in which I participate, will not be authorised under the Financial Services and Markets Act 2000 (and so will not have to satisfy the threshold conditions set out in Part I of Schedule 6 to that Act and will not be subject to Financial Services Authority rules such as those on holding client money). I understand that this means that redress through the Financial Services Authority, the Financial Ombudsman Scheme or the Financial Services Compensation Scheme will not be available. I also understand the risks associated in investing in a Business Angel-led Enterprise Capital Fund and am aware that it is open to me to seek advice from someone who is authorised under the Financial Services and Markets Act 2000 and who specialises in advising on this kind of investment.";

"high net worth unincorporated association" means an unincorporated association—

(a) which falls within article 49(2)(b) of the Financial Services and Markets Act 2000 (Financial Promotion) Order 2001; and

(b) on behalf of which an officer of that association or a member of its governing body has signed a statement in the following terms:

"This unincorporated association is a high net worth unincorporated association and falls within article 49(2)(b) of the Financial Services and Markets Act 2000 (Financial Promotion) Order 2001. I understand that any Business Angel-led Enterprise Capital Fund (within the meaning of article 72F of the Financial Services and Markets Act 2000 (Regulated Activities) Order 2001), in which this association participates, or any person who operates that Business Angel-led Enterprise Capital Fund, in which this association participates, will not be authorised under the Financial Services and Markets Act 2000 (and so will not have to satisfy the threshold conditions set out in Part I of Schedule 6 to that Act and will not be subject to Financial Services Authority rules such as those on holding client money). I understand that this means that redress through the Financial Services Authority, the Financial Ombudsman Scheme or the Financial Services Compensation Scheme will not be available. I also understand the risks associated in investing in a Business Angel-led Enterprise Capital Fund and am aware that it is open to the association to seek advice from someone who is authorised under the Financial Services and Markets Act 2000 and who specialises in advising on this kind of investment.";

"high value trust" means a trust—

(a) where the aggregate value of the cash and investments which form a part of the trust's assets (before deducting the amount of its liabilities) is £10 million or more;

(b) on behalf of which a trustee has signed a statement in the following terms:

"This trust is a high value trust. I understand that any Business Angel-led Enterprise Capital Fund (within the meaning of article 72F of the Financial Services and Markets Act 2000 (Regulated Activities) Order 2001), in which this trust participates, or any person who operates that Business Angel-led Enterprise Capital Fund, in which this trust participates, will not be authorised under the Financial Services and Markets Act 2000 (and so will not have to satisfy the threshold conditions set out in Part I of Schedule 6 to that Act and will not be subject to Financial Services Authority rules such as those on holding client money). I understand that this means that redress through the Financial Services Authority, the Financial Ombudsman Scheme or the Financial Services Compensation Scheme will not be available. I also understand the risks associated in investing in a Business Angel-led Enterprise Capital Fund and am aware that it is open to the trust to seek advice from someone who is authorised under the Financial Services and Markets Act 2000 and who specialises in advising on this kind of investment.";

"self-certified sophisticated investor" means an individual who—

(a) is a "self-certified sophisticated investor" within the meaning of article 50A of the Financial Services and Markets Act 2000 (Financial Promotion) Order 2001;

(b) has signed a statement in the following terms:

"I declare that I am a self-certified sophisticated investor within the meaning of article 50A of the Financial Services and Markets Act 2000 (Financial Promotion) Order 2001 and that I understand that any Business Angel-led Enterprise Capital Fund (within the meaning of article 72F of the Financial Services and Markets Act 2000 (Regulated Activities) Order 2001), in which I participate, or any person who operates that Business Angel-led Enterprise Capital Fund, in which I participate, will not be authorised under the Financial Services and Markets Act 2000 (and so will not have to satisfy the threshold conditions set out in Part I of Schedule 6 to that Act and will not be subject to Financial Services Authority rules such as those on holding client money). I understand that this means that redress through the Financial Services Authority, the Financial Ombudsman Scheme or the Financial Services Compensation Scheme will not be available. I also understand the risks associated in investing in a Business Angel-led Enterprise Capital Fund and am aware that it is open to me to seek advice from someone who is authorised under the Financial Services and Markets Act 2000 and who specialises in advising on this kind of investment.";

"sophisticated investor" means an individual who—

(a) is a "certified sophisticated investor" within the meaning of article 50(1) of the Financial Services and Markets Act 2000 (Financial Promotion) Order 2001; and

(b) has signed a statement in the following terms:

"I declare that I am a certified sophisticated investor within the meaning of article 50(1) of the Financial Services and Markets Act 2000 (Financial Promotion) Order 2001 and that I understand that any Business Angel-led Enterprise Capital Fund (within the meaning of article 72F of the Financial Services and Markets Act 2000 (Regulated Activities) Order 2001), in which I participate, or any person who operates that Business Angel-led Enterprise Capital Fund, in which I participate, will not be authorised under the Financial Services and Markets Act 2000 (and so will not have to satisfy the threshold conditions set out in Part I of Schedule 6 to that Act and will not be subject to Financial Services Authority rules such as those on holding client money). I understand that this means that redress through the Financial Services Authority, the Financial Ombudsman Scheme or the Financial Services Compensation Scheme will not be available. I also understand the risks associated in investing in a

Business Angel-led Enterprise Capital Fund and am aware that it is open to me to seek advice from someone who is authorised under the Financial Services and Markets Act 2000 and who specialises in advising on this kind of investment.";

"unlisted company" has the meaning given by article 3 of the Financial Services and Markets Act 2000 (Financial Promotion) Order 2001.

(2) References in this Article and in Article 72E to a participant in a Business Angel-led Enterprise Capital Fund, doing things on behalf of such a participant and property belonging to such a participant are, respectively, references to that participant in that capacity, to doing things on behalf of that participant in that capacity or to the property of that participant held in that capacity.

PART III
SPECIFIED INVESTMENTS

73. Investments: general

The following kinds of investment are specified for the purposes of section 22 of the Act.

74. Deposits

A deposit.

74A. Electronic money

Electronic money.

75. Contracts of insurance

Rights under a contract of insurance.

76. Shares etc

(1) Shares or stock in the share capital of—

(a) any body corporate (wherever incorporated), and

(b) any unincorporated body constituted under the law of a country or territory outside the United Kingdom.

(2) Paragraph (1) includes—

(a) any shares of a class defined as deferred shares for the purposes of section 119 of the Building Societies Act 1986 or section 31A of the Credit Unions Act 1979; and

(b) any transferable shares in a body incorporated under the law of, or any part of, the United Kingdom relating to industrial and provident societies or credit unions, or in a body constituted under the law of another EEA State for purposes equivalent to those of such a body.

(3) But subject to paragraph (2) there are excluded from paragraph (1) shares or stock in the share capital of—

(a) an open-ended investment company;

(b) a building society incorporated under the law of, or any part of, the United Kingdom;

(c) a body incorporated under the law of, or any part of, the United Kingdom relating to industrial and provident societies or credit unions;

(d) any body constituted under the law of an EEA State for purposes equivalent to those of a body falling within sub-paragraph (b) or (c).

77. Instruments creating or acknowledging indebtedness

(1) Subject to paragraph (2), such of the following as do not fall within article . . . 78—

(a) debentures;

(b) debenture stock;

(c) loan stock;

(d) bonds;

(e) certificates of deposit;

(f) any other instrument creating or acknowledging indebtedness.

(2) If and to the extent that they would otherwise fall within paragraph (1), there are excluded from that paragraph—

(a) an instrument acknowledging or creating indebtedness for, or for money borrowed to defray, the consideration payable under a contract for the supply of goods or services;

(b) a cheque or other bill of exchange, a banker's draft or a letter of credit (but not a bill of exchange accepted by a banker);

(c) a banknote, a statement showing a balance on a current, deposit or savings account, a lease or other disposition of property, or a heritable security;

(d) a contract of insurance;

(e) . . .

(3) An instrument excluded from paragraph (1) of article 78 by paragraph (2)(b) of that article is not thereby to be taken to fall within paragraph (1) of this article.

77A. Alternative finance investment bonds

(1) Rights under an alternative finance investment bond, to the extent that they do not fall within article 77 or 78.

(2) For the purposes of this article, arrangements constitute an alternative finance investment bond if—

(a) the arrangements provide for a person ("the bond-holder") to pay a sum of money ("the capital") to another ("the bond-issuer");

(b) the arrangements identify assets, or a class of assets, which the bond-issuer will acquire for the purpose of generating income or gains directly or indirectly ("the bond assets");

(c) the arrangements specify a period at the end of which they cease to have effect ("the bond term");

(d) the bond-issuer undertakes under the arrangements—

(i) to make a repayment in respect of the capital ("the redemption payment") to the bond-holder during or at the end of the bond term (whether or not in instalments); and

(ii) to pay to the bond-holder other payments on one or more occasions during or at the end of the bond term ("the additional payments");

(e) the amount of the additional payments does not exceed an amount which would, at the time at which the bond is issued, be a reasonable commercial return on a loan of the capital; and

(f) the arrangements are a security admitted to—

(i) an official list (in accordance with the provisions of Directive 2001/34/EC of the European Parliament and of the Council on the admission of securities to official stock exchange listing and on information to be published on those securities); or

(ii) trading on a regulated market (within the meaning of Article 4.1(14) of Directive 2004/39/EC of the European Parliament and of the Council on markets in financial instruments) or on a recognised investment exchange (within the meaning of section 285 of the Act).

(3) For the purposes of paragraph (2)—

(a) the bond-issuer may acquire the bond assets before or after the arrangements take effect;

(b) the bond assets may be property of any kind, including rights in relation to property owned by someone other than the bond-issuer;

(c) the identification of the bond assets mentioned in paragraph (2)(b) and the undertakings mentioned in paragraph (2)(d) may (but need not) be described as, or accompanied by a document described as, a declaration of trust;

(d) the reference to a period in paragraph (2)(c) includes any period specified to end upon the redemption of the bond by the bond-issuer;

(e) the bond-holder may (but need not) be entitled under the arrangements to terminate them, or participate in terminating them, before the end of the bond term;

(f) the amount of the additional payments may be—

(i) fixed at the beginning of the bond term;

(ii) determined wholly or partly by reference to the value of or income generated by the bond assets; or

(iii) determined in some other way;

(g) if the amount of the additional payments is not fixed at the beginning of the bond term, the reference in paragraph (2)(e) to the amount of the additional payments is a reference to the maximum amount of the additional payments;

(h) the amount of the redemption payment may (but need not) be subject to reduction in the event of a fall in the value of the bond assets or in the rate of income generated by them; and

(i) entitlement to the redemption payment may (but need not) be capable of being satisfied (whether or not at the option of the bond-issuer or the bond-holder) by the issue or transfer of shares or other securities.

(4) An instrument excluded from paragraph (1) of article 78 by paragraph (2)(b) of that article is not thereby taken to fall within paragraph (1) of this article.

78. Government and public securities

(1) Subject to paragraph (2), loan stock, bonds and other instruments creating or acknowledging indebtedness, issued by or on behalf of any of the following—

(a) the government of the United Kingdom;

(b) the Scottish Administration;

(c) the Executive Committee of the Northern Ireland Assembly;

(d) the National Assembly for Wales;

(e) the government of any country or territory outside the United Kingdom;

(f) a local authority in the United Kingdom or elsewhere; or

(g) a body the members of which comprise—

(i) states including the United Kingdom or another EEA State; or

(ii) bodies whose members comprise states including the United Kingdom or another EEA State.

(2) Subject to paragraph (3), there are excluded from paragraph (1)—

(a) so far as applicable, the instruments mentioned in article 77(2)(a) to (d);

(b) any instrument creating or acknowledging indebtedness in respect of—

(i) money received by the Director of Savings as deposits or otherwise in connection with the business of the National Savings Bank;

(ii) money raised under the National Loans Act 1968 under the auspices of the Director of Savings or treated as so raised by virtue of section 11(3) of the National Debt Act 1972.

(3) Paragraph (2)(a) does not exclude an instrument which meets the requirements set out in sub-paragraphs (a) to (e) of article 77A(2).

79. Instruments giving entitlements to investments

(1) Warrants and other instruments entitling the holder to subscribe for any investment of the kind specified by article 76, 77, 77A or 78.

(2) It is immaterial whether the investment to which the entitlement relates is in existence or identifiable.

(3) An investment of the kind specified by this article is not to be regarded as falling within article 83, 84 or 85.

80. Certificates representing certain securities

(1) Subject to paragraph (2), certificates or other instruments which confer contractual or property rights (other than rights consisting of an investment of the kind specified by article 83)—

(a) in respect of any investment of the kind specified by any of articles 76 to 79, being an investment held by a person other than the person on whom the rights are conferred by the certificate or instrument; and

(b) the transfer of which may be effected without the consent of that person.

(2) There is excluded from paragraph (1) any certificate or other instrument which confers rights in respect of two or more investments issued by different persons, or in respect of two or more different investments of the kind specified by article 78 and issued by the same person.

81. Units in a collective investment scheme

Units in a collective investment scheme (within the meaning of Part XVII of the Act).

82. Rights under a pension scheme

(1) Rights under a stakeholder pension scheme.
(2) Rights under a personal pension scheme.

82A. Greenhouse gas emissions allowances

Greenhouse gas emissions allowances which are auctioned as financial instruments or as two-day spots within the meaning of Article 3.3 of the emission allowance auctioning regulation.

83. Options

(1) Options to acquire or dispose of—
- (a) a security or contractually based investment (other than one of a kind specified by this article);
- (b) currency of the United Kingdom or any other country or territory;
- (c) palladium, platinum, gold or silver; ...
- (d) an option to acquire or dispose of an investment of the kind specified by this article by virtue of paragraph (a), (b) or (c);
- (e) subject to paragraph (4), an option to acquire or dispose of an option to which paragraph 5, 6, 7 or 10 of Section C of Annex I to the markets in financial instruments directive (the text of which is set out in Part I of Schedule 2) applies].

(2) Subject to paragraph (4), options—
- (a) to which paragraph (1) does not apply;
- (b) which relate to commodities;
- (c) which may be settled physically; and
- (d) either—
  - (i) to which paragraph 5 or 6 of Section C of Annex I to the markets in financial instruments directive, the text of which is set out in Part 1 of Schedule 2, applies, or
  - (ii) which in accordance with Article 38 of the Commission Regulation (the text of which is set out in Part 2 of Schedule 2) are to be considered as having the characteristics of other derivative financial instruments and not being for commercial purposes, and to which paragraph 7 of Section C of Annex I to the markets in financial instruments directive applies.

(3) Subject to paragraph (4), options—
- (a) to which paragraph (1) does not apply;
- (b) which may be settled physically; and
- (c) to which paragraph 10 of Section C of Annex I to the markets in financial instruments directive (read with the Commission Regulation) applies.

(4) Paragraphs (1)(e), (2) and (3) only apply to options in relation to which—
- (a) an investment firm or credit institution is providing or performing investment services and activities on a professional basis,
- (b) a management company is providing, in accordance with Article 6(3) of the UCITS directive, the investment service specified in paragraph 4 or 5 of Section A, or the ancillary service specified in paragraph 1 of Section B, of Annex I to the markets in financial instruments directive, or
- (c) a market operator is providing the investment service specified in paragraph 8 of Section A of Annex I to the markets in financial instruments directive.

(5) Expressions used in paragraphs (1)(e), (2) and (3) and in the markets in financial instruments directive have the same meaning as in that directive.

84. Futures

(1) Subject to paragraph (2), rights under a contract for the sale of a commodity or property of any other description under which delivery is to be made at a future date and at a price agreed on when the contract is made.

(1A) Subject to paragraph (1D), futures—
(a) to which paragraph (1) does not apply;
(b) which relate to commodities;
(c) which may be settled physically; and
(d) to which paragraph 5 or 6 of Section C of Annex I to the markets in financial instruments directive applies.

(1B) Subject to paragraph (1D), futures and forwards—
(a) to which paragraph (1) does not apply;
(b) which relate to commodities;
(c) which may be settled physically;
(d) which in accordance with Article 38 of the Commission Regulation (the text of which is set out in Part 2 of Schedule 2) are to be considered as having the characteristics of other derivative financial instruments and not being for commercial purposes; and
(e) to which paragraph 7 of Section C of Annex I to the markets in financial instruments directive applies.

(1C) Subject to paragraph (1D), futures—
(a) to which paragraph (1) does not apply;
(b) which may be settled physically; and
(c) to which paragraph 10 of Section C of Annex I to the markets in financial instruments directive (read with the Commission Regulation) applies.

(1D) Paragraph (1A), (1B) and (1C) only apply to futures or forwards in relation to which—
(a) an investment firm or credit institution is providing or performing investment services and activities on a professional basis,
(b) a management company is providing, in accordance with Article 6(3) of the UCITS directive, the investment service specified in paragraph 4 or 5 of Section A, or the ancillary service specified in paragraph 1 of Section B, of Annex I to the markets in financial instruments directive, or
(c) a market operator is providing the investment service specified in paragraph 8 of Section A of Annex I to the markets in financial instruments directive.

(1E) Expressions used in paragraphs (1A) to (1C) and in the markets in financial instruments directive have the same meaning as in that directive.

(2) There are excluded from paragraph (1) rights under any contract which is made for commercial and not investment purposes.

(3) A contract is to be regarded as made for investment purposes if it is made or traded on a recognised investment exchange, or is made otherwise than on a recognised investment exchange but is expressed to be as traded on such an exchange or on the same terms as those on which an equivalent contract would be made on such an exchange.

(4) A contract not falling within paragraph (3) is to be regarded as made for commercial purposes if under the terms of the contract delivery is to be made within seven days, unless it can be shown that there existed an understanding that (notwithstanding the express terms of the contract) delivery would not be made within seven days.

(5) The following are indications that a contract not falling within paragraph (3) or (4) is made for commercial purposes and the absence of them is an indication that it is made for investment purposes—
(a) one or more of the parties is a producer of the commodity or other property, or uses it in his business;
(b) the seller delivers or intends to deliver the property or the purchaser takes or intends to take delivery of it.

(6) It is an indication that a contract is made for commercial purposes that the prices, the lot, the delivery date or other terms are determined by the parties for the purposes of the particular contract and not by reference (or not solely by reference) to regularly published prices, to standard lots or delivery dates or to standard terms.

(7) The following are indications that a contract is made for investment purposes—

(a) it is expressed to be as traded on an investment exchange;

(b) performance of the contract is ensured by an investment exchange or a clearing house;

(c) there are arrangements for the payment or provision of margin.

(8) For the purposes of paragraph (1), a price is to be taken to be agreed on when a contract is made—

(a) notwithstanding that it is left to be determined by reference to the price at which a contract is to be entered into on a market or exchange or could be entered into at a time and place specified in the contract; or

(b) in a case where the contract is expressed to be by reference to a standard lot and quality, notwithstanding that provision is made for a variation in the price to take account of any variation in quantity or quality on delivery.

85. Contracts for differences etc

(1) Subject to paragraph (2), rights under—

(a) a contract for differences; or

(b) any other contract the purpose or pretended purpose of which is to secure a profit or avoid a loss by reference to fluctuations in—

(i) the value or price of property of any description; or

(ii) an index or other factor designated for that purpose in the contract.

(2) There are excluded from paragraph (1)—

(a) rights under a contract if the parties intend that the profit is to be secured or the loss is to be avoided by one or more of the parties taking delivery of any property to which the contract relates;

(b) rights under a contract under which money is received by way of deposit on terms that any interest or other return to be paid on the sum deposited will be calculated by reference to fluctuations in an index or other factor;

(c) rights under any contract under which—

(i) money is received by the Director of Savings as deposits or otherwise in connection with the business of the National Savings Bank; or

(ii) money is raised under the National Loans Act 1968 under the auspices of the Director of Savings or treated as so raised by virtue of section 11(3) of the National Debt Act 1972;

(d) rights under a qualifying contract of insurance.

(3) Subject to paragraph (4), derivative instruments for the transfer of credit risk—

(a) to which neither article 83 nor paragraph (1) applies; and

(b) to which paragraph 8 of Section C of Annex I to the markets in financial instruments directive applies.

(4) Paragraph (3) only applies to derivatives in relation to which—

(a) an investment firm or credit institution is providing or performing investment services and activities on a professional basis,

(b) a management company is providing, in accordance with Article 6(3) of the UCITS directive, the investment service specified in paragraph 4 or 5 of Section A, or the ancillary service specified in paragraph 1 of Section B, of Annex I to the markets in financial instruments directive, or

(c) a market operator is providing the investment service specified in paragraph 8 of Section A of Annex I to the markets in financial instruments directive.

(5) "Derivative instruments for the transfer of credit risk" has the same meaning as in the markets in financial instruments directive.

86. Lloyd's syndicate capacity and syndicate membership

(1) The underwriting capacity of a Lloyd's syndicate.

(2) A person's membership (or prospective membership) of a Lloyd's syndicate.

87. Funeral plan contracts

Rights under a funeral plan contract.

88. Regulated mortgage contracts

Rights under a regulated mortgage contract.

88A. Regulated home reversion plans

Rights under a regulated home reversion plan.

88B. Regulated home purchase plans

Rights under a regulated home purchase plan.

88C. Regulated sale and rent back agreements

Rights under a regulated sale and rent back agreement.

89. Rights to or interests in investments

(1) Subject to paragraphs (2) to (4), any right to or interest in anything which is specified by any other provision of this Part (other than article 88, 88A, 88B or 88C).

(2) Paragraph (1) does not include interests under the trusts of an occupational pension scheme.

(3) Paragraph (1) does not include—

(a) rights to or interests in a contract of insurance of the kind referred to in paragraph (1)(a) of article 60; or

(b) interests under a trust of the kind referred to in paragraph (1)(b) of that article.

(4) Paragraph (1) does not include anything which is specified by any other provision of this Part.

PART IV
CONSEQUENTIAL PROVISIONS

Regulated mortgage contracts: consequential provisions

90, 91. …

PART V
UNATHORISED PERSONS CARRYING ON INSURANCE MEDIATION ACTIVITIES

92. Interpretation

In this Part—

"designated professional body" means a body which is for the time being designated by the Treasury under section 326 of the Act (designation of professional bodies);

"insurance mediation activity" means any regulated activity of the kind specified by article 21, 25(1) or (2), 39A or 53, or, so far as relevant to any of those articles, article 64, which is carried on in relation to a contract of insurance;

"the record" means the record maintained by the FCA under section 347 of the Act (public record of authorised persons etc.);

"recorded insurance intermediary" has the meaning given by article 93(4);

"a relevant member", in relation to a designated professional body, means a member (within the meaning of section 325(2) of the Act) of the profession in relation to which that designated professional body is established, or a person who is controlled or managed by one or more such members.

93. Duty to maintain a record of unauthorised persons carrying on insurance mediation activities

(1) Subject to articles 95 and 96, the FCA must include in the record every person who—

(a) as a result of information obtained by virtue of its rules or by virtue of a direction given, or requirement imposed, under section 55U(4) of the Act (procedure for applications under Part IV), appears to the FCA to fall within paragraph (2); or

(b) as a result of information obtained by virtue of article 94, appears to the FCA to fall within paragraph (3).

(2) A person falls within this paragraph if he is, or has entered into a contract by virtue of which he will be, an appointed representative who carries on any insurance mediation activity.

(3) A person falls within this paragraph if—

(a) he is a relevant member of a designated professional body who carries on, or is proposing to carry on, any insurance mediation activity; and

(b) the general prohibition does not (or will not) apply to the carrying on of those activities by virtue of section 327 of the Act (exemption from the general prohibition).

(4) In this Part, "recorded insurance intermediary" means a person who is included in the record by virtue of paragraph (1).

(5) The record must include—

(a) in the case of any recorded insurance intermediary, its address; and

(b) in the case of a recorded insurance intermediary which is not an individual, the name of the individuals who are responsible for the management of the business carried on by the intermediary, so far as it relates to insurance mediation activities.

94. Members of designated professional bodies

(1) A designated professional body must, by notice in writing, inform the FCA of—

(a) the name,

(b) the address, and

(c) in the case of a relevant member which is not an individual, the name of the individuals who are responsible for the management of the business carried on by the member, so far as it relates to insurance mediation activities,

of any relevant member who falls within paragraph (2).

(2) A relevant member of a designated professional body falls within this paragraph if, in accordance with the rules of that body, he carries on, or proposes to carry on any insurance mediation activity but does not have, and does not propose to apply for, Part IV permission on the basis that the general prohibition does not (or will not) apply to the carrying on of that activity by virtue of section 327 of the Act.

(3) A designated professional body must also, by notice in writing, inform the FCA of any change in relation to the matters specified in sub-paragraphs (a) to (c) of paragraph (1).

(4) A designated professional body must inform the FCA when a relevant member to whom paragraph (2) applies ceases, for whatever reason, to carry on insurance mediation activities.

(5) The FCA may give directions to a designated professional body as to the manner in which the information referred to in paragraphs (1), (3) and (4) must be provided.

95. Exclusion from record where not fit and proper to carry on insurance mediation activities

(1) If it appears to the FCA that a person who falls within article 93(2) (appointed representatives) ("AR") is not a fit and proper person to carry on insurance mediation activities, it may decide not to include him in the record or, if that person is already included in the record, to remove him from the record.

(2) Where the FCA proposes to make a determination under paragraph (1), it must give AR a warning notice.

(3) If the FCA makes a determination under paragraph (1), it must give AR a decision notice.

(4) If the FCA gives AR a decision notice under paragraph (3), AR may refer the matter to the Tribunal.

(5) The FCA may, on the application of AR, revoke a determination under paragraph (1).

(6) If the FCA decides to grant the application, it must give AR written notice of its decision.

(7) If the FCA proposes to refuse the application, it must give AR a warning notice.

(8) If the FCA decides to refuse the application, it must give AR a decision notice.

(9) If the FCA gives AR a decision notice under paragraph (8), AR may refer the matter to the Tribunal.

(10) Sections 393 and 394 of the Act (third party rights and access to FCA or PRA material) apply to a warning notice given in accordance with paragraph (2) or (7) and to a decision notice given in accordance with paragraph (3) or (8).

96. Exclusion from the record where FCA has exercised its powers under Part XX of the Act

(1) If a person who appears to the FCA to fall within article 93(3) (member of a designated professional body) falls within paragraph (2) or (3), the FCA must not include him in the record or, if that person is already included in the record, must remove him from the record.

(2) A person falls within this paragraph if, by virtue of a direction given by the FCA under section 328(1) of the Act (directions in relation to the general prohibition), section 327(1) of the Act does not apply in relation to the carrying on by him of any insurance mediation activity.

(3) A person falls within this paragraph if the FCA has made an order under section 329(2) of the Act (orders in relation to the general prohibition) disapplying section 327(1) of the Act in relation to the carrying on by him of any insurance mediation activity.

PART 6
MISCELLANEOUS

97. Disapplication of section 49(2) of the Act

In section 49 of the Act (persons connected with an applicant for Part 4 permission), after subsection (2) insert—

"(2A) But subsection (2) does not apply to the extent that the permission relates to—

(a) an insurance mediation activity (within the meaning given by paragraph 2(5) of Schedule 6); or

(b) a regulated activity involving a regulated mortgage contract.".

SCHEDULE 1
CONTRACTS OF INSURANCE

Article 3(1)

PART I
CONTRACTS OF GENERAL INSURANCE

1. Accident

Contracts of insurance providing fixed pecuniary benefits or benefits in the nature of indemnity (or a combination of both) against risks of the person insured or, in the case of a contract made by virtue of section 140, 140A or 140B of the Local Government Act 1972 (or, in Scotland, section 86(1) of the Local Government (Scotland) Act 1973), a person for whose benefit the contract is made—

(a) sustaining injury as the result of an accident or of an accident of a specified class; or

(b) dying as a result of an accident or of an accident of a specified class; or

(c) becoming incapacitated in consequence of disease or of disease of a specified class,

including contracts relating to industrial injury and occupational disease but excluding contracts falling within paragraph 2 of Part I of, or paragraph IV of Part II of, this Schedule.

2. Sickness

Contracts of insurance providing fixed pecuniary benefits or benefits in the nature of indemnity (or a combination of both) against risks of loss to the persons insured attributable to sickness or infirmity but excluding contracts falling within paragraph IV of Part II of this Schedule.

3. Land vehicles

Contracts of insurance against loss of or damage to vehicles used on land, including motor vehicles but excluding railway rolling stock.

4. Railway rolling stock

Contract of insurance against loss of or damage to railway rolling stock.

5. Aircraft

Contracts of insurance upon aircraft or upon the machinery, tackle, furniture or equipment of aircraft.

6. Ships

Contracts of insurance upon vessels used on the sea or on inland water, or upon the machinery, tackle, furniture or equipment of such vessels.

7. Goods in transit

Contracts of insurance against loss of or damage to merchandise, baggage and all other goods in transit, irrespective of the form of transport.

8. Fire and natural forces

Contracts of insurance against loss of or damage to property (other than property to which paragraphs 3 to 7 relate) due to fire, explosion, storm, natural forces other than storm, nuclear energy or land subsidence.

9. Damage to property

Contracts of insurance against loss of or damage to property (other than property to which paragraphs 3 to 7 relate) due to hail or frost or any other event (such as theft) other than those mentioned in paragraph 8.

10. Motor vehicle liability

Contracts of insurance against damage arising out of or in connection with the use of motor vehicles on land, including third-party risks and carrier's liability.

11. Aircraft liability

Contracts of insurance against damage arising out of or in connection with the use of aircraft, including third-party risks and carrier's liability.

12. Liability of ships

Contracts of insurance against damage arising out of or in connection with the use of vessels on the sea or on inland water, including third party risks and carrier's liability.

13. General liability

Contracts of insurance against risks of the persons insured incurring liabilities to third parties, the risks in question not being risks to which paragraph 10, 11 or 12 relates.

14. Credit

Contracts of insurance against risks of loss to the persons insured arising from the insolvency of debtors of theirs or from the failure (otherwise than through insolvency) of debtors of theirs to pay their debts when due.

15. Suretyship

(1) Contracts of insurance against the risks of loss to the persons insured arising from their having to perform contracts of guarantee entered into by them.

(2) Fidelity bonds, performance bonds, administration bonds, bail bonds or customs bonds or similar contracts of guarantee, where these are—

(a) effected or carried out by a person not carrying on a banking business;

(b) not effected merely incidentally to some other business carried on by the person effecting them; and

(c) effected in return for the payment of one or more premiums.

16. Miscellaneous financial loss

Contracts of insurance against any of the following risks, namely—

(a) risks of loss to the persons insured attributable to interruptions of the carrying on of business carried on by them or to reduction of the scope of business so carried on;

(b) risks of loss to the persons insured attributable to their incurring unforeseen expense (other than loss such as is covered by contracts falling within paragraph 18);

(c) risks which do not fall within sub-paragraph (a) or (b) and which are not of a kind such that contracts of insurance against them fall within any other provision of this Schedule.

17. Legal expenses

Contracts of insurance against risks of loss to the persons insured attributable to their incurring legal expenses (including costs of litigation).

18. Assistance

Contracts of insurance providing either or both of the following benefits, namely—

(a) assistance (whether in cash or in kind) for persons who get into difficulties while travelling, while away from home or while away from their permanent residence; or

(b) assistance (whether in cash or in kind) for persons who get into difficulties otherwise than as mentioned in sub-paragraph (a).

PART II
CONTRACTS OF LONG-TERM INSURANCE

I. Life and annuity

Contracts of insurance on human life or contracts to pay annuities on human life, but excluding (in each case) contracts within paragraph III.

II. Marriage and birth

Contract of insurance to provide a sum on marriage or the formation of a civil partnership or on the birth of a child, being contracts expressed to be in effect for a period of more than one year.

III. Linked long term

Contracts of insurance on human life or contracts to pay annuities on human life where the benefits are wholly or party to be determined by references to the value of, or the income from, property of any description (whether or not specified in the contracts) or by reference to fluctuations in, or in an index of, the value of property of any description (whether or not so specified).

IV. Permanent health

Contracts of insurance providing specified benefits against risks of persons becoming incapacitated in consequence of sustaining injury as a result of an accident or of an accident of a specified class or of sickness or infirmity, being contracts that—

(a) are expressed to be in effect for a period of not less than five years, or until the normal retirement age for the persons concerned, or without limit of time; and

(b) either are not expressed to be terminable by the insurer, or are expressed to be so terminable only in special circumstances mentioned in the contract.

V. Tontines

Tontines.

VI. Capital redemption contracts

Capital redemption contracts, where effected or carried out by a person who does not carry on a banking business, and otherwise carries on a regulated activity of the kind specified by article 10(1) or (2).

VII. Pension fund management

(a) Pension fund management contracts, and
(b) pension fund management contracts which are combined with contracts of insurance covering either conservation of capital or payment of a minimum interest,

where effected or carried out by a person who does not carry on a banking business, and otherwise carries on a regulated activity of the kind specified by article 10(1) or (2).

VIII. Collective insurance etc

Contracts of a kind referred to in article 1(2)(e) of the first life insurance directive.

IX. Social insurance

Contracts of a kind referred to in article 1(3) of the first life insurance directive.

SCHEDULE 2

SECTIONS A AND C OF ANNEX I TO THE MARKETS IN FINANCIAL INSTRUMENTS DIRECTIVE AND RELATED COMMUNITY SUBORDINATE LEGISLATION

Article 3(1)

PART 1

SECTION C OF ANNEX I TO THE MARKETS IN FINANCIAL INSTRUMENTS DIRECTIVE

Financial Instruments

1. Transferable securities;
2. Money-market instruments;
3. Units in collective investment undertakings;
4. Options, futures, swaps, forward rate agreements and any other derivative contracts relating to securities, currencies, interest rates or yields, or other derivatives instruments, financial indices or financial measures which may be settled physically or in cash;
5. Options, futures, swaps, forward rate agreements and any other derivative contracts relating to commodities that must be settled in cash or may be settled in cash at the option of one of the parties (otherwise than by reason of a default or other termination event);
6. Options, futures, swaps, and any other derivative contracts relating to commodities that can be physically settled provided that they are traded on a regulated market and/or an MTF;
7. Options, futures, swaps, forwards and any other derivative contracts relating to commodities, that can be physically settled not otherwise mentioned in C6 and not being for commercial purposes, which have the characteristics of other derivative financial instruments, having regard to whether, inter alia, they are cleared and settled through recognised clearing houses or are subject to regular margin calls;
8. Derivative instruments for the transfer of credit risk;
9. Financial contracts for differences;
10. Options, futures, swaps, forward rate agreements and any other derivative contracts relating to climatic variables, freight rates, emission allowances or inflation rates or other official economic statistics that must be settled in cash or may be settled in cash at the option of one of the parties (otherwise than by reason of a default or other termination event), as well as any other derivative contracts relating to assets, rights, obligations, indices and measures not otherwise mentioned in this Section, which have the characteristics of other derivative financial instruments, having regard to whether, inter alia, they are traded on a regulated market or an MTF, are cleared and settled through recognised clearing houses or are subject to regular margin calls.

PART 2

CHAPTER VI OF THE COMMISSION REGULATION

DERIVATIVE FINANCIAL INSTRUMENTS

Article 38

Characteristics of other derivative financial instruments

1. For the purposes of Section C(7) of Annex I to Directive 2004/39/EC, a contract which is not a spot contract within the meaning of paragraph 2 of this Article and which is not covered by paragraph 4 shall be considered as having the characteristics of other derivative financial instruments and not being for commercial purposes if it satisfies the following conditions:
   (a) it meets one of the following sets of criteria:
      (i) it is traded on a third country trading facility that performs a similar function to a regulated market or an MTF;
      (ii) it is expressly stated to be traded on, or is subject to the rules of, a regulated market, an MTF or such a third country trading facility;
      (iii) it is expressly stated to be equivalent to a contract traded on a regulated market, MTF or such a third country trading facility;
   (b) it is cleared by a clearing house or other entity carrying out the same functions as a central counterparty, or there are arrangements for the payment or provision of margin in relation to the contract;
   (c) it is standardised so that, in particular, the price, the lot, the delivery date or other terms are determined principally by reference to regularly published prices, standard lots or standard delivery dates.
2. A spot contract for the purposes of paragraph 1 means a contract for the sale of a commodity, asset or right, under the terms of which delivery is scheduled to be made within the longer of the following periods:
   (a) two trading days;
   (b) the period generally accepted in the market for that commodity, asset or right as the standard delivery period.

   However, a contract is not a spot contract if, irrespective of its explicit terms, there is an understanding between the parties to the contract that delivery of the underlying is to be postponed and not to be performed within the period mentioned in the first subparagraph.
3. For the purposes of Section C(10) of Annex I to Directive 2004/39/EC, a derivative contract relating to an underlying referred to in that Section or in Article 39 shall be considered to have the characteristics of other derivative financial instruments if one of the following conditions is satisfied:
   (a) that contract is settled in cash or may be settled in cash at the option of one or more of the parties, otherwise than by reason of a default or other termination event;
   (b) that contract is traded on a regulated market or an MTF;
   (c) the conditions laid down in paragraph 1 are satisfied in relation to that contract.
4. A contract shall be considered to be for commercial purposes for the purposes of Section C(7) of Annex I to Directive 2004/39/EC, and as not having the characteristics of other derivative financial instruments for the purposes of Sections C(7) and (10) of that Annex, if it is entered into with or by an operator or administrator of an energy transmission grid, energy balancing mechanism or pipeline network, and it is necessary to keep in balance the supplies and uses of energy at a given time.

Article 39

Derivatives Within Section C(10) of Annex I to Directive 2004/39/EC

In addition to derivative contracts of a kind referred to in Section C(10) of Annex I to Directive 2004/39/EC, a derivative contract relating to any of the following shall fall within that Section if it meets the criteria set out in that Section and in Article 38(3):

(a) telecommunications bandwidth;
(b) commodity storage capacity;
(c) transmission or transportation capacity relating to commodities, whether cable, pipeline or other means;
(d) an allowance, credit, permit, right or similar asset which is directly linked to the supply, distribution or consumption of energy derived from renewable resources;
(e) a geological, environmental or other physical variable;
(f) any other asset or right of a fungible nature, other than a right to receive a service, that is capable of being transferred;
(g) an index or measure related to the price or value of, or volume of transactions in any asset, right, service or obligation.

PART 3
SECTION A OF ANNEX I TO THE MARKETS IN FINANCIAL INSTRUMENTS DIRECTIVE

Investment Services and Activities

1. Reception and transmission of orders in relation to one or more financial instruments.
2. Execution of orders on behalf of clients.
3. Dealing on own account.
4. Portfolio management.
5. Investment advice.
6. Underwriting of financial instruments and/or placing of financial instruments on a firm commitment basis.
7. Placing of financial instruments without a firm commitment basis.
8. Operation of Multilateral Trading Facilities.

PART 4
ARTICLE 52 OF COMMISSION DIRECTIVE 2006/73/EC

Article 52
Investment Advice

For the purposes of the definition of "investment advice" in Article 4(1)(4) of Directive 2004/39/EC, a personal recommendation is a recommendation that is made to a person in his capacity as an investor or potential investor, or in his capacity as an agent for an investor or potential investor.

That recommendation must be presented as suitable for that person, or must be based on a consideration of the circumstances of that person, and must constitute a recommendation to take one of the following sets of steps:

(a) to buy, sell, subscribe for, exchange, redeem, hold or underwrite a particular financial instrument;
(b) to exercise or not to exercise any right conferred by a particular financial instrument to buy, sell, subscribe for, exchange, or redeem a financial instrument.

A recommendation is not a personal recommendation if it is issued exclusively through distribution channels or to the public.

SCHEDULE 3
ARTICLE 2 OF THE MARKETS IN FINANCIAL INSTRUMENTS DIRECTIVE

Article 3(1)

Article 2
Exemptions

1. This Directive shall not apply to:

(a) insurance undertakings as defined in Article 1 of Directive 73/239/EEC or assurance undertakings as defined in Article 1 of Directive 2002/83/EC or undertakings carrying on the reinsurance and retrocession activities referred to in Directive 64/225/EEC;

(b) persons which provide investment services exclusively for their parent undertakings, for their subsidiaries or for other subsidiaries of their parent undertakings;

(c) persons providing an investment service where that service is provided in an incidental manner in the course of a professional activity and that activity is regulated by legal or regulatory provisions or a code of ethics governing the profession which do not exclude the provision of that service;

(d) persons who do not provide any investment services or activities other than dealing on own account unless they are market makers or deal on own account outside a regulated market or an MTF on an organised, frequent and systematic basis by providing a system accessible to third parties in order to engage in dealings with them;

(e) persons which provide investment services consisting exclusively in the administration of employee-participation schemes;

(f) persons which provide investment services which only involve both administration of employee-participation schemes and the provision of investment services exclusively for their parent undertakings, for their subsidiaries or for other subsidiaries of their parent undertakings;

(g) the members of the European System of Central Banks and other national bodies performing similar functions and other public bodies charged with or intervening in the management of the public debt;

(h) collective investment undertakings and pension funds whether coordinated at Community level or not and the depositaries and managers of such undertakings;

(i) persons dealing on own account in financial instruments, or providing investment services in commodity derivatives or derivative contracts included in Annex I, Section C10 to the clients of their main business, provided this is an ancillary activity to their main business, when considered on a group basis, and that main business is not the provision of investment services within the meaning of this Directive or banking services under Directive 2000/12/EC;

(j) persons providing investment advice in the course of providing another professional activity not covered by this Directive provided that the provision of such advice is not specifically remunerated;

(k) persons whose main business consists of dealing on own account in commodities and/or commodity derivatives. This exception shall not apply where the persons that deal on own account in commodities and/or commodity derivatives are part of a group the main business of which is the provision of other investment services within the meaning of this Directive or banking services under Directive 2000/12/EC;

(l) firms which provide investment services and/or perform investment activities consisting exclusively in dealing on own account on markets in financial futures or options or other derivatives and on cash markets for the sole purpose of hedging positions on derivatives markets or which deal for the accounts of other members of those markets or make prices for them and which are guaranteed by clearing members of the same markets, where responsibility for ensuring the performance of contracts entered into by such firms is assumed by clearing members of the same markets;

(m) associations set up by Danish and Finnish pensions funds with the sole aim of managing the assets of pension funds that are members of those associations;

(n) 'agenti di cambio' whose activities and functions are governed by Article 201 of Italian Legislative Decree No 58 of 24 February 1998.

2. The rights conferred by this Directive shall not extend to the provision of services as counterparty in transactions carried out by public bodies dealing with public debt or by members of the European System of Central Banks performing their tasks as provided for by the Treaty and the

Statute of the European System of Central Banks and of the European Central Bank or performing equivalent functions under national provisions.

3. In order to take account of developments on financial markets, and to ensure the uniform application of this Directive, the Commission, acting in accordance with the procedure referred to in Article 64(2), may, in respect of exemptions (c), (i) and (k) define the criteria for determining when an activity is to be considered as ancillary to the main business on a group level as well as for determining when an activity is provided in an incidental manner."

SCHEDULE 4 Article 4

RELEVANT TEXT OF THE INSURANCE MEDIATION DIRECTIVE

PART 1

ARTICLE 1.2

"This Directive shall not apply to persons providing mediation services for insurance contracts if all the following conditions are met:

(a) the insurance contract only requires knowledge of the insurance cover that is provided;

(b) the insurance contract is not a life assurance contract;

(c) the insurance contract does not cover any liability risks;

(d) the principal professional activity of the person is other than insurance mediation;

(e) the insurance is complementary to the product or service supplied by any provider, where such insurance covers:

 (i) the risk of breakdown, loss of or damage to goods supplied by that provider; or

 (ii) damage to or loss of baggage and other risks linked to the travel booked with that provider, even if the insurance covers life assurance or liability risks, provided that the cover is ancillary to the main cover for the risks linked to that travel;

(f) the amount of the annual premium does not exceed EUR 500 and the total duration of the insurance contract, including any renewals, does not exceed five years."

PART II

ARTICLE 2.3

""Insurance mediation" means the activities of introducing, proposing or carrying out other work preparatory to the conclusion of contracts of insurance, or of concluding such contracts, or of assisting in the administration and performance of such contracts, in particular in the event of a claim.

These activities when undertaken by an insurance undertaking or an employee of an insurance undertaking who is acting under the responsibility of the insurance undertaking shall not be considered as insurance mediation.

The provision of information on an incidental basis in the context of another professional activity provided that the purpose of that activity is not to assist the customer in concluding or performing an insurance contract, the management of claims of an insurance undertaking on a professional basis, and loss adjusting and expert appraisal of claims shall also not be considered as insurance mediation."

PART III

ARTICLE 2.4

""Reinsurance mediation" means the activities of introducing, proposing or carrying out other work preparatory to the conclusion of contracts of reinsurance, or of concluding such contracts, or of assisting in the administration and performance of such contracts, in particular in the event of a claim.

These activities when undertaken by a reinsurance undertaking or an employee of a reinsurance undertaking who is acting under the responsibility of the reinsurance undertaking are not considered as reinsurance mediation.

The provision of information on an incidental basis in the context of another professional activity provided that the purpose of that activity is not to assist the customer in concluding or performing a reinsurance contract, the management of claims of a reinsurance undertaking on a professional basis, and loss adjusting and expert appraisal of claims shall also not be considered as reinsurance mediation."

SCHEDULE 5
SPECIFIED BENCHMARKS

Article 63R

The following benchmarks are specified:

1. The benchmarks that are known as the London Interbank Offered Rate, also known as LIBOR.

Financial Services and Markets Act 2000 (Prescribed Markets and Qualifying Investments) Order 2001

S.I. 2001/996

1. Citation

This Order may be cited as the Financial Services and Markets Act 2000 (Prescribed Markets and Qualifying Investments) Order 2001.

2. Commencement

This Order comes into force on the day on which section 123 of the Act (power to impose penalties in cases of market abuse) comes into force.

3. Interpretation

In this Order—

"the Act" means the Financial Services and Markets Act 2000;

"auctioned products" has the meaning given in Article 4 of Commission Regulation (EU) No 1031/2010 on the timing, administration and other aspects of auctioning of greenhouse gas emission allowances pursuant to Directive 2003/87/EC of the European Parliament and of the Council establishing a scheme for greenhouse gas emission allowances trading within the Community;

"emission allowance auctioning regulation" means Commission Regulation (EU) No 1031/2010 of 12 November 2010 on the timing, administration and other aspects of auctioning of greenhouse gas emission allowances pursuant to the emission allowance trading directive;

"recognised auction platform" means a recognised investment exchange in relation to which there is in force a recognition order made under regulation 2 of the Recognised Auction Platforms Regulations 2011 (recognition orders);

"regulated market" has the meaning given in Article 4.1.14 of the markets in financial instruments directive; and

"UK recognised investment exchange" means a body corporate or unincorporated association in respect of which there is in effect a recognition order made under section 290(1)(a) of the Act (recognition orders in respect of investment exchanges other than overseas investment exchanges).

4. Prescribed Markets and auction platforms

(1) There are prescribed, as markets to which subsections (2), (3), (5), (6) and (7) of section 118 apply—

(a) all markets which are established under the rules of a UK recognised investment exchange,

(b) the market known as OFEX,

(c) all other markets which are regulated markets.

(2) There are prescribed, as markets to which subsections (4) and (8) of section 118 apply—

(a) all markets which are established under the rules of a UK recognised investment exchange;

(b) the market known as OFEX.

(3) There are prescribed, as auction platforms to which subsections (2), (3), (5), (6) and (7) of section 118 (as modified by the Recognised Auction Platform Regulations 2011) apply, all recognised auction platforms, and all other auction platforms which have been appointed under the emission allowance auctioning regulation.

(4) There are prescribed, as auction platforms to which subsections (4) and (8) of section 118 (as modified by the Recognised Auction Platform Regulations 2011) apply, all recognised auction platforms.

(5) There are prescribed, as auction platforms to which subsection (8A) of section 118 as inserted by the modifications made to that section by the Recognised Auction Platforms Regulations 2011

applies, all auction platforms which have been appointed under the emission allowance auctioning regulation.

4A. ...

5. Qualifying Investments

(1) There are prescribed, as qualifying investments in relation to the markets prescribed by article 4, all financial instruments within the meaning given in Article 1(3) of Directive 2003/6/EC of the European Parliament and the Council of 28 January 2003 on insider dealing and market manipulation (market abuse) as modified by Article 69 of Directive 2004/39/EC on markets in financial instruments.

(2) There are prescribed, as qualifying investments in relation to the auction platforms prescribed by article 4(3) and (4), all auctioned products which are financial instruments within the meaning given in Article 4.1(17) of the market in financial instruments directive.

(3) There are prescribed, as qualifying investments in relation to the auction platforms prescribed by article 4(5), all auctioned products which are not financial instruments within the meaning given in Article 4.1(17) of the market in financial instruments directive.

Financial Services and Markets Act 2000 (Professions) (Non-Exempt Activities) Order 2001

S.I. 2001/1227

1. Citation and Commencement

(1) This Order may be cited as the Financial Services and Markets Act 2000 (Professions) (Non-Exempt Activities) Order 2001.

(2) Subject to paragraph (3), this Order comes into force on the day on which section 19 of the Act comes into force.

(3) This Order comes into force—

(a) for the purposes of article 4(g), on 1st January 2002; and

(b) for the purposes of article 6A, on such a day as the Treasury may specify.

(4) Any day specified under paragraph (3)(b) must be caused to be notified in the London, Edinburgh and Belfast Gazettes published not later than one week before that day.

2. Interpretation

(1) In this Order—

"the Act" means the Financial Services and Markets Act 2000;

"agreement provider" has the meaning given by paragraph (3) of article 63J of the Regulated Activities Order, read with paragraphs (6) and (7) of that article;

"agreement seller" has the meaning given by article 63J(3) of the Regulated Activities Order;

"home purchase provider" has the meaning given by article 63F(3) of the Regulated Activities Order;

"home purchaser" has the meaning given by article 63F(3) of the Regulated Activities Order;

"contract of insurance" has the meaning given by article 3(1) of the Regulated Activities Order;

"contractually based investment" has the meaning given by article 3(1) of the Regulated Activities Order;

"occupational pension scheme" and "personal pension scheme" have the meaning given by section 1 of the Pension Schemes Act 1993;

"plan provider" has the meaning given by paragraph (3) of article 63B of the Regulated Activities Order, read with paragraphs (7) and (8) of that article;

"record of insurance intermediaries" means the record maintained by the Authority under section 347 of the Act (the public record) by virtue of article 93 of the Regulated Activities Order (recorded insurance intermediaries);

"the Regulated Activities Order" means the Financial Services and Markets Act 2000 (Regulated Activities) Order 2001;

"regulated home purchase plan" has the meaning given by article 63F(3) of the Regulated Activities Order;

"regulated home reversion plan" has the meaning given by article 63B(3) of the Regulated Activities Order;

"regulated mortgage contract" has the meaning given by article 61 of the Regulated Activities Order;

"regulated sale and rent back agreement" has the meaning given by article 63J(3) of the Regulated Activities Order;

"relevant investment" has the meaning given by article 3(1) of the Regulated Activities Order;

"reversion seller" has the meaning given by article 63B(3) of the Regulated Activities Order;

"security" has the meaning given by article 3(1) of the Regulated Activities Order;

"syndicate" has the meaning given by article 3(1) of the Regulated Activities Order.

(2) For the purposes of this Order, a person is a member of a personal pension scheme if he is a person to or in respect of whom benefits are or may become payable under the scheme.

3. Activities to which exemption from the general prohibition does not apply

The activities in articles 4 to 8 are specified for the purposes of section 327(6) of the Act.

4.

An activity of the kind specified by any of the following provisions of the Regulated Activities Order—

(a) article 5 (accepting deposits);

(aa) article 9B (issuing electronic money);

(b) article 10 (effecting and carrying out contracts of insurance);

(c) article 14 (dealing in investments as principal);

(ca) article 24A (bidding in emissions auctions);

(d) article 51 (establishing etc. a collective investment scheme);

(e) article 52 (establishing etc. a ... pension scheme);

(ea) article 52B (providing basic advice on stakeholder products);

(f) article 57 (managing the underwriting capacity of a Lloyd's syndicate);

(g) article 59 (funeral plan contracts);

(h) …

4A.

An activity of the kind specified by article 21 or 25 of the Regulated Activities Order (dealing in investments as agent or arranging deals in investments) in so far as it—

(a) relates to a transaction for the sale or purchase of rights under a contract of insurance; and

(b) is carried on by a person who is not included in the record of insurance intermediaries.

5.

(1) An activity of the kind specified by article 37 of the Regulated Activities Order (managing investments) in so far as it consists of buying or subscribing for a security or contractually based investment.

(2) Paragraph (1) does not apply—

(a) if all routine or day to day decisions, so far as relating to that activity, are taken by an authorised person with permission to carry on that activity or by a person who is an exempt person in relation to such an activity; or

(b) to an activity undertaken in accordance with the advice of an authorised person with permission to give advice in relation to such an activity or a person who is an exempt person in relation to the giving of such advice.

5A.

An activity of the kind specified by article 39A of the Regulated Activities Order (assisting in the administration and performance of a contract of insurance) if it is carried on by a person who is not included in the record of insurance intermediaries.

6.

(1) An activity of the kind specified by article 53 of the Regulated Activities Order (advising on investments) where the advice in question falls within paragraph (2), (3) or (5).

(2) Subject to paragraph (4), advice falls within this paragraph in so far as—

(a) it is given to an individual (or his agent) other than where the individual acts—

(i) in connection with the carrying on of a business of any kind by himself or by an undertaking of which he is, or would become as a result of the transaction to which the advice relates, a controller; or

(ii) in his capacity as a trustee of an occupational pension scheme;

(b) it consists of a recommendation to buy or subscribe for a particular security or contractually based investment; and

(c) the transaction to which the advice relates would be made—

(i) with a person acting in the course of carrying on the business of buying, selling, subscribing for or underwriting the security or contractually based investment, whether as principal or agent;

(ii) on an investment exchange or any other market to which that investment is admitted for dealing; or

(iii) in response to an invitation to subscribe for such an investment which is, or is to be, admitted for dealing on an investment exchange or any other market.

(3) Subject to paragraph (4), advice falls within this paragraph in so far as it consists of a recommendation to a member of a personal pension scheme (or his agent) to dispose of any rights or interests which the member has in or under the scheme.

(4) Advice does not fall within paragraph (2) or (3) if it endorses a corresponding recommendation given to the individual (or, as the case may be, the member) by an authorised person with permission to give advice in relation to the proposed transaction or a person who is an exempt person in relation to the giving of such advice.

(5) Advice falls within this paragraph in so far as—

(a) it relates to a transaction for the sale or purchase of rights under a contract of insurance; and

(b) it is given by a person who is not included in the record of insurance intermediaries.

6A.

(1) An activity of the kind specified by article 53A of the Regulated Activities Order (advising on regulated mortgage contracts) where the advice in question falls within paragraph (2).

(2) Subject to paragraph (3), advice falls within this paragraph in so far as—

(a) it consists of a recommendation, given to an individual, to enter as borrower into a regulated mortgage contract with a particular person; and

(b) in entering into a regulated mortgage contract that person would be carrying on an activity of the kind specified by article 61(1) of the Regulated Activities Order (regulated mortgage contracts).

(3) Advice does not fall within paragraph (2) if it endorses a corresponding recommendation given to the individual by an authorised person with permission to carry on an activity of the kind specified by article 53A of the Regulated Activities Order or a person who is an exempt person in relation to an activity of that kind.

6B.

(1) An activity of the kind specified by article 61(1) or (2) of the Regulated Activities Order (regulated mortgage contracts).

(2) Paragraph (1) does not apply to an activity carried on by a person in his capacity as a trustee or personal representative where the borrower under the regulated mortgage contract in question is a beneficiary under the trust, will or intestacy.

6C.

(1) An activity of the kind specified by article 53B of the Regulated Activities Order (advising on regulated home reversion plans) where the advice in question falls within paragraph (2).

(2) Subject to paragraph (3), advice falls within this paragraph in so far as—

(a) it consists of a recommendation, given to an individual to enter as reversion seller or plan provider into a regulated home reversion plan with a particular person; and

(b) in entering into a regulated home reversion plan that person would be carrying on an activity of the kind specified by article 63B(1) of the Regulated Activities Order (regulated home reversion plans).

(3) Advice does not fall within paragraph (2) if it endorses a corresponding recommendation given to the individual by an authorised person with permission to carry on an activity of the kind specified by article 53B of the Regulated Activities Order or a person who is an exempt person in relation to an activity of that kind.

6D.

(1) An activity of the kind specified by article 63B(1) or (2) of the Regulated Activities Order (regulated home reversion plans).

(2) Paragraph (1) does not apply to an activity carried on by a person in his capacity as a trustee or personal representative where the reversion seller under the regulated home reversion plan in question is a beneficiary under the trust, will or intestacy.

6E.

(1) An activity of the kind specified by article 53C of the Regulated Activities Order (advising on regulated home purchase plans) where the advice in question falls within paragraph (2).

(2) Subject to paragraph (3), advice falls within this paragraph in so far as—

(a) it consists of a recommendation, given to an individual to enter as home purchaser into a regulated home purchase plan with a particular person; and

(b) in entering into a regulated home purchase plan that person would be carrying on an activity of the kind specified by article 63F(1) of the Regulated Activities Order (regulated home purchase plans).

(3) Advice does not fall within paragraph (2) if it endorses a corresponding recommendation given to the individual by an authorised person with permission to carry on an activity of the kind specified by article 53C of the Regulated Activities Order or a person who is an exempt person in relation to an activity of that kind.

6F.

(1) An activity of the kind specified by article 63F(1) or (2) of the Regulated Activities Order (regulated home purchase plans).

(2) Paragraph (1) does not apply to an activity carried on by a person in his capacity as a trustee or personal representative where the home purchaser under the regulated home purchase plan in question is a beneficiary under the trust, will or intestacy.

6G.

(1) An activity of the kind specified by article 53D of the Regulated Activities Order (advising on regulated sale and rent back agreements) where the advice in question falls within paragraph (2).

(2) Subject to paragraph (3), advice falls within this paragraph in so far as—

(a) it consists of a recommendation, given to an individual to enter as agreement seller or agreement provider into a regulated sale and rent back agreement with a particular person; and

(b) in entering into a regulated sale and rent back agreement that person would be carrying on an activity of the kind specified by article 63J(1) of the Regulated Activities Order (regulated sale and rent back agreements).

(3) Advice does not fall within paragraph (2) if it endorses a corresponding recommendation given to the individual by an authorised person with permission to carry on an activity of the kind specified by article 53D of the Regulated Activities Order or a person who is an exempt person in relation to an activity of that kind.

6H.

(1) An activity of the kind specified by article 63J(or (2) of the Regulated Activities Order (regulated sale and rent back agreements).

An activity of the kind specified by article 63J(1) or (2) of the Regulated Activities Order (regulated sale and rent back agreements).

(2) Paragraph (1) does not apply to an activity carried on by a person in his capacity as a trustee or personal representative where the agreement seller under the regulated sale and rent back agreement in question is a beneficiary under the trust, will or intestacy.

7.

(1) Advising a person to become a member of a particular Lloyd's syndicate.

(2) Paragraph (1) does not apply to advice which endorses that of an authorised person with permission to give such advice or a person who is an exempt person in relation to the giving of such advice.

8.

Agreeing to carry on any of the activities mentioned in articles 4 to 7 other than the activities mentioned in article 4(a), (aa), (b), (d) and (e).

Financial Services and Markets Act 2000 (Financial Promotion) Order 2005

S.I. 2005/1529

PART I

Citation, Commencement and Interpretation

1. Citation and commencement

This Order may be cited as the Financial Services and Markets Act 2000 (Financial Promotion) Order 2005 and comes into force on 1st July 2005.

2. Interpretation: general

(1) In this Order, except where the context otherwise requires—

. . .

"the 2006 Act" means the Companies Act 2006;

"the Act" means the Financial Services and Markets Act 2000;

"close relative" in relation to a person means—

(a) his spouse or civil partner;

(b) his children and step-children, his parents and step-parents, his brothers and sisters and his step-brothers and step-sisters; and

(c) the spouse or civil partner of any person within sub-paragraph (b);

"controlled activity" has the meaning given by article 4 and Schedule 1;

"controlled investment" has the meaning given by article 4 and Schedule 1;

"deposit" means a sum of money which is a deposit for the purposes of article 5 of the Regulated Activities Order;

"direct financial benefit" includes any commission, discount, remuneration or reduction in premium;

"equity share capital" has the meaning given in the 2006 Act (see section 548);

"financial promotion restriction" has the meaning given by article 5;

"government" means the government of the United Kingdom, the Scottish Administration, the Executive Committee of the Northern Ireland Assembly, the National Assembly for Wales and any government of any country or territory outside the United Kingdom;

"instrument" includes any record whether or not in the form of a document;

"international organisation" means any body the members of which comprise—

(a) states including the United Kingdom or another EEA State; or

(b) bodies whose members comprise states including the United Kingdom or another EEA State;

"overseas communicator" has the meaning given by article 30;

"previously overseas customer" has the meaning given by article 31;

"publication" means—

(a) a newspaper, journal, magazine or other periodical publication;

(b) a web site or similar system for the electronic display of information;

(c) any programme forming part of a service consisting of the broadcast or transmission of television or radio programmes;

(d) any teletext service, that — is to say a service consisting of television transmissions consisting of a succession of visual displays (with or without accompanying sound) capable of being selected and held for separate viewing or other use;

"qualifying contract of insurance" has the meaning given in the Regulated Activities Order;

"qualifying credit" has the meaning given by paragraph 10 of Schedule 1;

"the Regulated Activities Order" means the Financial Services and Markets Act 2000 (Regulated Activities) Order 2001;
"relevant insurance activity" has the meaning given by article 21;
"relevant investment activities" has the meaning given by article 30;
"solicited real time communication" has the meaning given by article 8;
"units", in a collective investment scheme, has the meaning given by Part XVII of the Act;
"unsolicited real time communication" has the meaning given by article 8.

(2) References to a person engaging in investment activity are to be construed in accordance with subsection (8) of section 21 of the Act; and for these purposes, "controlled activity" and "controlled investment" in that subsection have the meaning given in this Order.

3. Interpretation: unlisted companies

(1) In this Order, an "unlisted company" means a body corporate the shares in which are not—
(a) listed or quoted on an investment exchange whether in the United Kingdom or elsewhere;
(b) shares in respect of which information is, with the agreement or approval of any officer of the company, published for the purpose of facilitating deals in the shares indicating prices at which persons have dealt or are willing to deal in them other than persons who, at the time the information is published, are existing members of a relevant class; or
(c) subject to a marketing arrangement which accords to the company the facilities referred to in section 693(3)(b) of the 2006 Act.

(2) For the purpose of paragraph (1)(b), a person is to be regarded as a member of a relevant class if he was, at the relevant time—
(a) an existing member or debenture holder of the company;
(b) an existing employee of the company;
(c) a close relative of such a member or employee; or
(d) a trustee (acting in his capacity as such) of a trust, the principal beneficiary of which is a person within any of sub-paragraphs (a), (b) and (c).

(3) In this Order references to shares in and debentures of an unlisted company are references to—
(a) in the case of a body corporate which is a company within the meaning of the 2006 Act (see section 1), shares and debentures within the meaning of that Act (see sections 540(1) and (4) and 738);
(b) . . .
(c) in the case of any other body corporate, investments falling within paragraph 14, 15 or 15A of Schedule 1 to this Order.

PART II

Controlled Activities and Controlled Investments

4. Definition of controlled activities and controlled investments

(1) For the purposes of section 21(9) of the Act, a controlled activity is an activity which falls within any of paragraphs 1 to 11 of Schedule 1.

(2) For the purposes of section 21(10) of the Act, a controlled investment is an investment which falls within any of paragraphs 12 to 27 of Schedule 1.

PART III

Exemptions: Interpretation and Application

5. Interpretation: financial promotion restriction

In this Order, any reference to the financial promotion restriction is a reference to the restriction in section 21(1) of the Act.

6. Interpretation: communications

In this Order—

(a) any reference to a communication is a reference to the communication, in the course of business, of an invitation or inducement to engage in investment activity;

(b) any reference to a communication being made to another person is a reference to a communication being addressed, whether orally or in legible form, to a particular person or persons (for example where it is contained in a telephone call or letter);

(c) any reference to a communication being directed at persons is a reference to a communication being addressed to persons generally (for example where it is contained in a television broadcast or web site);

(d) "communicate" includes causing a communication to be made or directed;

(e) a "recipient" of a communication is the person to whom the communication is made or, in the case of a non-real time communication which is directed at persons generally, any person who reads or hears the communication;

(f) "electronic commerce communication" means a communication, the making of which constitutes the provision of an information society service;

(g) "incoming electronic commerce communication" means an electronic commerce communication made from an establishment in an EEA State other than the United Kingdom;

(h) "outgoing electronic commerce communication" means an electronic commerce communication made from an establishment in the United Kingdom to a person in an EEA State other than the United Kingdom.

7. Interpretation: real time communications

(1) In this Order, references to a real time communication are references to any communication made in the course of a personal visit, telephone conversation or other interactive dialogue.

(2) A non-real time communication is a communication not falling within paragraph (1).

(3) For the purposes of this Order, non-real time communications include communications made by letter or e-mail or contained in a publication.

(4) For the purposes of this Order, the factors in paragraph (5) are to be treated as indications that a communication is a non-real time communication.

(5) The factors are that—

(a) the communication is made to or directed at more than one recipient in identical terms (save for details of the recipient's identity);

(b) the communication is made or directed by way of a system which in the normal course constitutes or creates a record of the communication which is available to the recipient to refer to at a later time;

(c) the communication is made or directed by way of a system which in the normal course does not enable or require the recipient to respond immediately to it.

8. Interpretation: solicited and unsolicited real time communications

(1) A real time communication is solicited where it is made in the course of a personal visit, telephone call or other interactive dialogue if that call, visit or dialogue—

(a) was initiated by the recipient of the communication; or

(b) takes place in response to an express request from the recipient of the communication.

(2) A real time communication is unsolicited where it is made otherwise than as described in paragraph (1).

(3) For the purposes of paragraph (1)—

(a) a person is not to be treated as expressly requesting a call, visit or dialogue—

(i) because he omits to indicate that he does not wish to receive any or any further visits or calls or to engage in any or any further dialogue;

(ii) because he agrees to standard terms that state that such visits, calls or dialogue will take place, unless he has signified clearly that, in addition to agreeing to the terms, he is willing for them to take place;

(b) a communication is solicited only if it is clear from all the circumstances when the call, visit or dialogue is initiated or requested that during the course of the visit, call or dialogue communications will be made concerning the kind of controlled activities or investments to which the communications in fact made relate;

(c) it is immaterial whether the express request was made before or after this article comes into force.

(4) Where a real time communication is solicited by a recipient ("R"), it is treated as having also been solicited by any other person to whom it is made at the same time as it is made to R if that other recipient is—

(a) a close relative of R; or

(b) expected to engage in any investment activity jointly with R.

8A. Interpretation: outgoing electronic commerce communications

(1) For the purposes of the application of those articles to outgoing electronic commerce communications—

(a) any reference in article 48(7)(c), 50(1)(a) or (3)(e) or 52(3)(c) to an authorised person includes a reference to a person who is entitled, under the law of an EEA State other than the United Kingdom, to carry on regulated activities in that State;

(b) any reference in article 68(1) or 71 to rules or legislation includes a reference to provisions corresponding to those rules or legislation in the law of an EEA State other than the United Kingdom;

(c) any reference in article 49 to an amount in pounds sterling includes a reference to an equivalent amount in another currency.

(2) For the purposes of the application of article 49 to outgoing electronic commerce communications, any reference in section 831(2) and (3) of the 2006 Act to a body corporate or company includes a reference to a body corporate or company registered under the law of an EEA State other than the United Kingdom.

(3) For the purposes of the application of article 3 in respect of outgoing electronic commerce communications—

(a) any reference in section 693(3)(b) of the 2006 Act to a company includes a reference to a company registered under the law of an EEA State other than the United Kingdom;

(b) any reference in that section to an investment exchange includes a reference to an investment exchange which is recognised as an investment exchange under the law of an EEA State other than the United Kingdom.

9. Degree of prominence to be given to required indications

Where a communication must, if it is to fall within any provision of this Order, be accompanied by an indication of any matter, the indication must be presented to the recipient—

(a) in a way that can be easily understood; and

(b) in such manner as, depending on the means by which the communication is made or directed, is best calculated to bring the matter in question to the attention of the recipient and to allow him to consider it.

10. Application to qualifying contracts of insurance

(1) Nothing in this Order exempts from the application of the financial promotion restriction a communication which invites or induces a person to enter into a qualifying contract of insurance with a person who is not—

(a) an authorised person;

(b) an exempt person who is exempt in relation to effecting or carrying out contracts of insurance of the class to which the communication relates;

(c) a company which has its head office in an EEA State other than the United Kingdom and which is entitled under the law of that State to carry on there insurance business of the class to which the communication relates;

(d) a company which has a branch or agency in an EEA State other than the United Kingdom and is entitled under the law of that State to carry on there insurance business of the class to which the communication relates;

(e) a company authorised to carry on insurance business of the class to which the communication relates in any country or territory which is listed in Schedule 2.

(2) In this article, references to a class of insurance are references to the class of insurance contract described in Schedule 1 to the Regulated Activities Order into which the effecting or carrying out of the contract to which the communication relates would fall.

11. Combination of different exemptions

(1) In respect of a communication relating to—

(a) a controlled activity falling within paragraph 2 of Schedule 1 carried on in relation to a qualifying contract of insurance; or

(b) a controlled activity falling within any of paragraphs 3 to 11 of Schedule 1,

a person may rely on the application of one or more of the exemptions in Parts IV and VI.

(2) In respect of a communication relating to—

(a) an activity falling within paragraph 1 of Schedule 1; or

(b) a relevant insurance activity,

a person may rely on one or more of the exemptions in Parts IV and V; and, where a communication relates to any such activity and also to an activity mentioned in paragraph (1)(a) or (b), a person may rely on one or more of the exemptions in Parts IV and V in respect of the former activity and on one or more of the exemptions in Parts V and VI in respect of the latter activity.

PART IV

Exempt Communications: All Controlled Activities

12. Communications to overseas recipients

(1) Subject to paragraphs (2) and (7), the financial promotion restriction does not apply to any communication—

(a) which is made (whether from inside or outside the United Kingdom) to a person who receives the communication outside the United Kingdom; or

(b) which is directed (whether from inside or outside the United Kingdom) only at persons outside the United Kingdom.

(2) Paragraph (1) does not apply to an unsolicited real time communication unless—

(a) it is made from a place outside the United Kingdom; and

(b) it is made for the purposes of a business which is carried on outside the United Kingdom and which is not carried on in the United Kingdom.

(3) For the purposes of paragraph (1)(b)—

(a) if the conditions set out in paragraph (4)(a), (b), (c) and (d) are met, a communication directed from a place inside the United Kingdom is to be regarded as directed only at persons outside the United Kingdom;

(b) if the conditions set out in paragraph (4)(c) and (d) are met, a communication directed from a place outside the United Kingdom is to be regarded as directed only at persons outside the United Kingdom;

(c) in any other case where one or more of the conditions in paragraph (4)(a) to (e) are met, that fact is to be taken into account in determining whether or not a communication is to be regarded as directed only at persons outside the United Kingdom (but a communication may still be regarded as directed only at persons outside the United Kingdom even if none of the conditions in paragraph (4) is met).

(4) The conditions are that—

(a) the communication is accompanied by an indication that it is directed only at persons outside the United Kingdom;

(b) the communication is accompanied by an indication that it must not be acted upon by persons in the United Kingdom;

(c) the communication is not referred to in, or directly accessible from, any other communication made to a person or directed at persons in the United Kingdom by the person directing the communication;

(d) there are in place proper systems and procedures to prevent recipients in the United Kingdom (other than those to whom the communication might otherwise lawfully have been made by the person directing it or a member of the same group) engaging in the investment activity to which the communication relates with the person directing the communication, a close relative of his or a member of the same group;

(e) the communication is included in—

(i) a web site, newspaper, journal, magazine or periodical publication which is principally accessed in or intended for a market outside the United Kingdom;

(ii) a radio or television broadcast or teletext service transmitted principally for reception outside the United Kingdom.

(5) For the purpose of paragraph (1)(b), a communication may be treated as directed only at persons outside the United Kingdom even if—

(a) it is also directed, for the purposes of article 19(1)(b), at investment professionals falling within article 19(5) (but disregarding paragraph (6) of that article for this purpose);

(b) it is also directed, for the purposes of article 49(1)(b), at high net worth persons to whom article 49 applies (but disregarding paragraph (2)(e) of that article for this purpose) and it relates to a controlled activity to which article 49 applies;

(c) it is a communication to which article 31 applies.

(6) Where a communication falls within paragraph (5)(a) or (b)—

(a) the condition in paragraph (4)(a) is to be construed as requiring an indication that the communication is directed only at persons outside the United Kingdom or persons having professional experience in matters relating to investments or high net worth persons (as the case may be);

(b) the condition in paragraph (4)(b) is to be construed as requiring an indication that the communication must not be acted upon by persons in the United Kingdom except by persons who have professional experience in matters relating to investments or who are not high net worth persons (as the case may be);

(c) the condition in paragraph (4)(c) will not apply where the other communication referred to in that paragraph is made to a person or directed at a person in the United Kingdom to whom paragraph (5) applies.

(7) Paragraph (1) does not apply to an outgoing electronic commerce communication.

13. Communications from customers and potential customers

(1) The financial promotion restriction does not apply to any communication made by or on behalf of a person ("customer") to one other person ("supplier")—

(a) in order to obtain information about a controlled investment available from or a controlled service provided by the supplier; or

(b) in order that the customer can acquire a controlled investment from that supplier or be supplied with a controlled service by that supplier.

(2) For the purposes of paragraph (1), a controlled service is a service the provision of which constitutes engaging in a controlled activity by the supplier.

14. Follow up non-real time communications and solicited real time communications

(1) Where a person makes or directs a communication ("the first communication") which is exempt from the financial promotion restriction because, in compliance with the requirements of another provision of this Order, it is accompanied by certain indications or contains certain information, then the financial promotion restriction does not apply to any subsequent communication which complies with the requirements of paragraph (2).

(2) The requirements of this paragraph are that the subsequent communication—
(a) is a non-real time communication or a solicited real time communication;
(b) is made by, or on behalf of, the same person who made the first communication;
(c) is made to a recipient of the first communication;
(d) relates to the same controlled activity and the same controlled investment as the first communication; and
(e) is made within 12 months of the recipient receiving the first communication.

(3) The provisions of this article only apply in the case of a person who makes or directs a communication on behalf of another where the first communication is made by that other person.

(4) Where a person makes or directs a communication on behalf of another person in reliance on the exemption contained in this article the person on whose behalf the communication was made or directed remains responsible for the content of that communication.

(5) A communication made or directed before this article comes into force is to be treated as a first communication falling within paragraph (1) if it would have fallen within that paragraph had it been made or directed after this article comes into force.

15. Introductions

(1) If the requirements of paragraph (2) are met, the financial promotion restriction does not apply to any communication which is made with a view to or for the purposes of introducing the recipient to—
(a) an authorised person who carries on the controlled activity to which the communication relates; or
(b) an exempt person where the communication relates to a controlled activity which is also a regulated activity in relation to which he is an exempt person.

(2) The requirements of this paragraph are that—
(a) the maker of the communication ("A") is not a close relative of, nor a member of the same group as, the person to whom the introduction is, or is to be, made;
(b) A does not receive from any person other than the recipient any pecuniary reward or other advantage arising out of his making the introduction; and
(c) it is clear in all the circumstances that the recipient, in his capacity as an investor, is not seeking and has not sought advice from A as to the merits of the recipient engaging in investment activity (or, if the client has sought such advice, A has declined to give it, but has recommended that the recipient seek such advice from an authorised person).

16. Exempt persons

(1) The financial promotion restriction does not apply to any communication which—
(a) is a non-real time communication or a solicited real time communication;
(b) is made or directed by an exempt person; and
(c) is for the purposes of that exempt person's business of carrying on a controlled activity which is also a regulated activity in relation to which he is an exempt person.

(2) The financial promotion restriction does not apply to any unsolicited real time communication made by a person ("AR") who is an appointed representative (within the meaning of section 39(2) of the Act) where—
(a) the communication is made by AR in carrying on the business—
(i) for which his principal ("P") has accepted responsibility for the purposes of section 39 of the Act; and
(ii) in relation to which AR is exempt from the general prohibition by virtue of that section; and
(b) the communication is one which, if it were made by P, would comply with any rules made by the Authority under section 145 of the Act (financial promotion rules) which are relevant to a communication of that kind.

17. Generic promotions

The financial promotion restriction does not apply to any communication which—

(a) does not identify (directly or indirectly) a person who provides the controlled investment to which the communication relates; and

(b) does not identify (directly or indirectly) any person as a person who carries on a controlled activity in relation to that investment.

17A. Communications caused to be made or directed by unauthorised persons

(1) If a condition in paragraph (2) is met, the financial promotion restriction does not apply to a communication caused to be made or directed by an unauthorised person which is made or directed by an authorised person.

(2) The conditions in this paragraph are that—

(a) the authorised person prepared the content of the communication; or

(b) it is a real-time communication.

18. Mere conduits

(1) Subject to paragraph (4), the financial promotion restriction does not apply to any communication which is made or directed by a person who acts as a mere conduit for it.

(2) A person acts as a mere conduit for a communication if—

(a) he communicates it in the course of an activity carried on by him, the principal purpose of which is transmitting or receiving material provided to him by others;

(b) the content of the communication is wholly devised by another person; and

(c) the nature of the service provided by him in relation to the communication is such that he does not select, modify or otherwise exercise control over its content prior to its transmission or receipt.

(3) For the purposes of paragraph (2)(c) a person does not select, modify or otherwise exercise control over the content of a communication merely by removing or having the power to remove material—

(a) which is, or is alleged to be, illegal, defamatory or in breach of copyright;

(b) in response to a request to a body which is empowered by or under any enactment to make such a request; or

(c) when otherwise required to do so by law.

(4) Nothing in paragraph (1) prevents the application of the financial promotion restriction in so far as it relates to the person who has caused the communication to be made or directed.

(5) This article does not apply to an electronic commerce communication.

18A. Electronic commerce communications: mere conduits, caching and hosting

The financial promotion restriction does not apply to an electronic commerce communication in circumstances where—

(a) the making of the communication constitutes the provision of an information society service of a kind falling within paragraph 1 of Article 12, 13 or 14 of the electronic commerce directive ("mere conduit", "caching" and "hosting"); and

(b) the conditions mentioned in the paragraph in question, to the extent that they are applicable at the time of, or prior to, the making of the communication, are or have been met at that time.

19. Investment professionals

(1) The financial promotion restriction does not apply to any communication which—

(a) is made only to recipients whom the person making the communication believes on reasonable grounds to be investment professionals; or

(b) may reasonably be regarded as directed only at such recipients.

(2) For the purposes of paragraph (1)(b), if all the conditions set out in paragraph (4)(a) to (c) are met in relation to the communication, it is to be regarded as directed only at investment professionals.

(3) In any other case in which one or more of the conditions set out in paragraph (4)(a) to (c) are met, that fact is to be taken into account in determining whether the communication is directed only at

investment professionals (but a communication may still be regarded as so directed even if none of the conditions in paragraph (4) is met).

(4) The conditions are that—

(a) the communication is accompanied by an indication that it is directed at persons having professional experience in matters relating to investments and that any investment or investment activity to which it relates is available only to such persons or will be engaged in only with such persons;

(b) the communication is accompanied by an indication that persons who do not have professional experience in matters relating to investments should not rely on it;

(c) there are in place proper systems and procedures to prevent recipients other than investment professionals engaging in the investment activity to which the communication relates with the person directing the communication, a close relative of his or a member of the same group.

(5) "Investment professionals" means—

(a) an authorised person;

(b) an exempt person where the communication relates to a controlled activity which is a regulated activity in relation to which the person is exempt;

(c) any other person—

(i) whose ordinary activities involve him in carrying on the controlled activity to which the communication relates for the purpose of a business carried on by him; or

(ii) who it is reasonable to expect will carry on such activity for the purposes of a business carried on by him;

(d) a government, local authority (whether in the United Kingdom or elsewhere) or an international organisation;

(e) a person ("A") who is a director, officer or employee of a person ("B") falling within any of sub-paragraphs (a) to (d) where the communication is made to A in that capacity and where A's responsibilities when acting in that capacity involve him in the carrying on by B of controlled activities.

(6) For the purposes of paragraph (1), a communication may be treated as made only to or directed only at investment professionals even if it is also made to or directed at other persons to whom it may lawfully be communicated.

20. Communications by journalists

(1) Subject to paragraph (2), the financial promotion restriction does not apply to any non-real time communication if—

(a) the content of the communication is devised by a person acting in the capacity of a journalist;

(b) the communication is contained in a qualifying publication; and

(c) in the case of a communication requiring disclosure, one of the conditions in paragraph (2) is met.

(2) The conditions in this paragraph are that—

(a) the communication is accompanied by an indication explaining the nature of the author's financial interest or that of a member of his family (as the case may be);

(b) the authors are subject to proper systems and procedures which prevent the publication of communications requiring disclosure without the explanation referred to in sub-paragraph (a); or

(c) the qualifying publication in which the communication appears falls within the remit of—

(i) the Code of Practice issued by the Press Complaints Commission;

(ii) the OFCOM Broadcasting Code; or

(iii) the Producers' Guidelines issued by the British Broadcasting Corporation.

(3) For the purposes of this article, a communication requires disclosure if—

(a) an author of the communication or a member of his family is likely to obtain a financial benefit or avoid a financial loss if people act in accordance with the invitation or inducement contained in the communication;

(b) the communication relates to a controlled investment of a kind falling within paragraph (4); and

(c) the communication identifies directly a person who issues or provides the controlled investment to which the communication relates.

(4) A controlled investment falls within this paragraph if it is—

(a) an investment falling within paragraph 14 of Schedule 1 (shares or stock in share capital);

(b) an investment falling within paragraph 21 of that Schedule (options) to acquire or dispose of an investment falling within sub-paragraph (a);

(c) an investment falling within paragraph 22 of that Schedule (futures) being rights under a contract for the sale of an investment falling within sub-paragraph (a); or

(d) an investment falling within paragraph 23 of that Schedule (contracts for differences etc.) being rights under a contract relating to, or to fluctuations in, the value or price of an investment falling within sub-paragraph (a).

(5) For the purposes of this article—

(a) the authors of the communication are the person who devises the content of the communication and the person who is responsible for deciding to include the communication in the qualifying publication;

(b) a "qualifying publication" is a publication or service of the kind mentioned in paragraph (1) or (2) of article 54 of the Regulated Activities Order and which is of the nature described in that article, and for the purposes of this article, a certificate given under paragraph (3) of article 54 of that Order and not revoked is conclusive evidence of the matters certified;

(c) the members of a person's family are his spouse or civil partner and any children of his under the age of 18 years.

20A. Promotion broadcast by company director etc.

(1) The financial promotion restriction does not apply to a communication which is communicated as part of a qualifying service by a person ("D") who is a director or employee of an undertaking ("U") where—

(a) the communication invites or induces the recipient to acquire—

(i) a controlled investment of the kind falling within article 20(4) which is issued by U (or by an undertaking in the same group as U); or

(ii) a controlled investment issued or provided by an authorised person in the same group as U;

(b) the communication—

(i) comprises words which are spoken by D and not broadcast, transmitted or displayed in writing; or

(ii) is displayed in writing only because it forms part of an interactive dialogue to which D is a party and in the course of which D is expected to respond immediately to questions put by a recipient of the communication;

(c) the communication is not part of an organised marketing campaign; and

(d) the communication is accompanied by an indication that D is a director or employee (as the case may be) of U.

(2) For the purposes of this article, a "qualifying service" is a service—

(a) which is broadcast or transmitted in the form of television or radio programmes; or

(b) displayed on a web site (or similar system for the electronic display of information) comprising regularly updated news and information,

provided that the principal purpose of the service, taken as a whole and including any advertisements and other promotional material contained in it, is neither of the purposes described in article 54(1)(a) or (b) of the Regulated Activities Order.

(3) For the purposes of paragraph (2), a certificate given under article 54(3) of the Regulated Activities Order and not revoked is conclusive evidence of the matters certified.

20B. Incoming electronic commerce communications

(1) The financial promotion restriction does not apply to an incoming electronic commerce communication.

(2) Paragraph (1) does not apply to—

(a) a communication which constitutes an advertisement by the operator of a UCITS directive scheme of units in that scheme;

(b) a communication consisting of an invitation or inducement to enter into a contract of insurance, where—

(i) the communication is made by an undertaking which has received official authorisation in accordance with Article 4 of the life assurance consolidation directive or the first non-life insurance directive, and

(ii) the insurance falls within the scope of any of the insurance directives; or

(c) an unsolicited communication made by electronic mail.

(3) In this article, "UCITS directive scheme" means an undertaking for collective investment in transferable securities which is subject to Directive 2009/65/EC of the European Parliament and of the Council of 13th July 2009 on the co-ordination of laws, regulations and administrative provisions relating to undertakings for collective investment in transferable securities and has been authorised in accordance with Article 5 of that Directive.

(4) For the purposes of this article, a communication by electronic mail is to be regarded as unsolicited, unless it is made in response to an express request from the recipient of the communication.

PART V

Exempt Communications: Deposits and Insurance

21. Interpretation: relevant insurance activity

In this Part, a "relevant insurance activity" means a controlled activity falling within paragraph 2 of Schedule 1 carried on in relation to an investment falling within paragraph 13 of that Schedule where that investment is not a qualifying contract of insurance.

22. Deposits: non-real time communications

(1) If the requirements of paragraph (2) are met, the financial promotion restriction does not apply to any non-real time communication which relates to a controlled activity falling within paragraph 1 of Schedule 1.

(2) The requirements of this paragraph are that the communication is accompanied by an indication—

(a) of the full name of the person with whom the investment which is the subject of the communication is to be made ("deposit-taker");

(b) of the country or territory in which a deposit-taker that is a body corporate is incorporated (described as such);

(c) if different, of the country or territory in which the deposit-taker's principal place of business is situated (described as such);

(d) whether or not the deposit-taker is regulated in respect of his deposit-taking business;

(e) if the deposit-taker is so regulated, of the name of the regulator in the deposit-taker's principal place of business, or if there is more than one such regulator, the prudential regulator;

(f) whether any transaction to which the communication relates would, if entered into by the recipient and the deposit-taker, fall within the jurisdiction of any dispute resolution scheme or deposit guarantee scheme and if so, identifying each such scheme;

(g) the necessary capital information.

(3) In this article—

"full name", in relation to a person, means the name under which that person carries on business and, if different, that person's corporate name;

"liabilities" includes provisions where such provisions have not been deducted from the value of the assets;

"necessary capital information" means—

(a) in relation to a deposit-taker which is a body corporate, either the amount of its paid up capital and reserves, described as such, or a statement that the amount of its paid up capital and reserves exceeds a particular amount (stating it);

(b) in relation to a deposit-taker which is not a body corporate, either the amount of the total assets less liabilities (described as such) or a statement that the amount of its total assets exceeds a particular amount (stating it) and that its total liabilities do not exceed a particular amount (stating it).

23. Deposits: real time communications

The financial promotion restriction does not apply to any real time communication (whether solicited or unsolicited) which relates to an activity falling within paragraph 1 of Schedule 1.

24. Relevant insurance activity: non-real time communications

(1) If the requirements of paragraph (2) are met, the financial promotion restriction does not apply to any non-real time communication which relates to a relevant insurance activity.

(2) The requirements of this paragraph are that the communication is accompanied by an indication—

(a) of the full name of the person with whom the investment which is the subject of the communication is to be made ("the insurer");

(b) of the country or territory in which the insurer is incorporated (described as such);

(c) if different, of the country or territory in which the insurer's principal place of business is situated (described as such);

(d) whether or not the insurer is regulated in respect of its insurance business;

(e) if the insurer is so regulated, of the name of the regulator of the insurer in its principal place of business or, if there is more than one such regulator, the name of the prudential regulator;

(f) whether any transaction to which the communication relates would, if entered into by the recipient and the insurer, fall within the jurisdiction of any dispute resolution scheme or compensation scheme and if so, identifying each such scheme.

(3) In this article "full name", in relation to a person, means the name under which that person carries on business and, if different, that person's corporate name.

25. Relevant insurance activity: non-real time communications: reinsurance and large risks

(1) The financial promotion restriction does not apply to any non-real time communication which relates to a relevant insurance activity and concerns only—

(a) a contract of reinsurance; or

(b) a contract that covers large risks.

(2) "Large risks" means—

(a) risks falling within paragraph 4 (railway rolling stock), 5 (aircraft), 6 (ships), 7 (goods in transit), 11 (aircraft liability) or 12 (liability of ships) of Schedule 1 to the Regulated Activities Order;

(b) risks falling within paragraph 14 (credit) or 15 (suretyship) of that Schedule provided that the risks relate to a business carried on by the recipient;

(c) risks falling within paragraph 3 (land vehicles), 8 (fire and natural forces), 9 (damage to property), 10 (motor vehicle liability), 13 (general liability) or 16 (miscellaneous financial loss) of that Schedule provided that the risks relate to a business carried on by the recipient and that the condition specified in paragraph (3) is met in relation to that business.

(3) The condition specified in this paragraph is that at least two of the three following criteria were exceeded in the most recent financial year for which information is available prior to the making of the communication—

(a) the aggregate of the amounts shown as assets in the balance sheet of the business was 6.2 million euros;

(b) the net turnover (within the meaning given to "turnover" by section 474(1) of the 2006 Act) was 12.8 million euros;

(c) the number of employees (within the meaning given by section 465(6) of the 2006 Act) was 250;

and for a financial year which is a company's financial year but not in fact a year, the net turnover of the recipient shall be proportionately adjusted.

(4) For the purposes of paragraph (3), where the recipient is a member of a group for which consolidated accounts (within the meaning of the Seventh Company Law Directive) are drawn up, the question whether the condition met in that paragraph is met is to be determined by reference to those accounts.

26. Relevant insurance activity: real time communication

The financial promotion restriction does not apply to any real time communication (whether solicited or unsolicited) which relates to a relevant insurance activity.

PART VI

Exempt Communications: Certain Controlled Activities

27. Application of exemptions in this Part

Except where otherwise stated, the exemptions in this Part apply to communications which relate to—

(a) a controlled activity falling within paragraph 2 of Schedule 1 carried on in relation to a qualifying contract of insurance;

(b) controlled activities falling within any of paragraphs 3 to 11 of Schedule 1.

28. One off non-real time communications and solicited real time communications

(1) The financial promotion restriction does not apply to a one off communication which is either a non-real time communication or a solicited real time communication.

(2) If all the conditions set out in paragraph (3) are met in relation to a communication it is to be regarded as a one off communication. In any other case in which one or more of those conditions are met, that fact is to be taken into account in determining whether the communication is a one off communication (but a communication may still be regarded as a one off communication even if none of the conditions in paragraph (3) is met).

(3) The conditions are that—

(a) the communication is made only to one recipient or only to one group of recipients in the expectation that they would engage in any investment activity jointly;

(b) the identity of the product or service to which the communication relates has been determined having regard to the particular circumstances of the recipient;

(c) the communication is not part of an organised marketing campaign.

28A. One off unsolicited real time communications

(1) The financial promotion restriction does not apply to an unsolicited real time communication if the conditions in paragraph (2) are met.

(2) The conditions in this paragraph are that—

(a) the communication is a one off communication;

(b) the communicator believes on reasonable grounds that the recipient understands the risks associated with engaging in the investment activity to which the communication relates;

(c) at the time that the communication is made, the communicator believes on reasonable grounds that the recipient would expect to be contacted by him in relation to the investment activity to which the communication relates.

(3) Paragraphs (2) and (3) of article 28 apply in determining whether a communication is a one off communication for the purposes of this article as they apply for the purposes of article 28.

28B. Real time communications: introductions ...

(1) If the requirements of paragraph (2) are met, the financial promotion restriction does not apply to any real time communication which—

(a) relates to a controlled activity falling within paragraph 10, 10A, 10B, 10C, 10D, 10E, 10F, 10G, 10H, 10I, 10J or 10K of Schedule 1; and

(b) is made for the purpose of, or with a view to, introducing the recipient to a person ("N") who is—

(i) an authorised person who carries on the controlled activity to which the communication relates,

(ii) an appointed representative, where the controlled activity to which the communication relates is also a regulated activity in respect of which he is exempt from the general prohibition, or

(iii) an overseas person who carries on the controlled activity to which the communication relates.

(2) The requirements of this paragraph are that the maker of the communication ("M")—

(a) does not receive any money, other than money payable to M on his own account, paid by the recipient for or in connection with any transaction which the recipient enters into with or through N as a result of the introduction; and

(b) before making the introduction, discloses to the recipient such of the information mentioned in paragraph (3) as applies to M.

(3) That information is—

(a) that M is a member of the same group as N;

(b) details of any payment which M will receive from N, by way of fee or commission, for introducing the recipient to N;

(c) an indication of any other reward or advantage received or to be received by M that arises out of his making introductions to N.

(4) In this article, "overseas person" means a person who carries on controlled activities which fall within paragraph 10, 10A or 10B of Schedule 1, but who does not carry on any such activity, or offer to do so, from a permanent place of business maintained by him in the United Kingdom.

29. Communications required or authorised by enactments

(1) Subject to paragraph (2), the financial promotion restriction does not apply to any communication which is required or authorised by or under any enactment other than the Act.

(2) This article does not apply to a communication which relates to a controlled activity falling within paragraph 10, 10A or 10B of Schedule 1 or within paragraph 11 in so far as it relates to that activity.

30. Overseas communicators: solicited real time communications

(1) The financial promotion restriction does not apply to any solicited real time communication which is made by an overseas communicator from outside the United Kingdom in the course of or for the purposes of his carrying on the business of engaging in relevant investment activities outside the United Kingdom.

(2) In this article—

"overseas communicator" means a person who carries on relevant investment activities outside the United Kingdom but who does not carry on any such activity from a permanent place of business maintained by him in the United Kingdom;

"relevant investment activities" means controlled activities which fall within paragraphs 3 to 7 or 10 to 10B of Schedule 1 or, so far as relevant to any of those paragraphs, paragraph 11 of that Schedule.

31. Overseas communicators: non-real time communications to previously overseas customers

(1) The financial promotion restriction does not apply to any non-real time communication which is communicated by an overseas communicator from outside the United Kingdom to a previously overseas customer of his.

(2) In this article a "previously overseas customer" means a person with whom the overseas communicator has done business within the period of twelve months ending with the day on which the communication was received ("the earlier business") and where—

(a) at the time that the earlier business was done, the customer was neither resident in the United Kingdom nor had a place of business there; or

(b) at the time the earlier business was done, the overseas communicator had on a former occasion done business with the customer, being business of the same description as the business to which the communication relates, and on that former occasion the customer was neither resident in the United Kingdom nor had a place of business there.

(3) For the purposes of this article, an overseas communicator has done business with a customer if, in the course of carrying on his relevant investment activities outside the United Kingdom, he has—

(a) effected a transaction, or arranged for a transaction to be effected, with the customer;

(b) provided, outside the United Kingdom; a service to the customer as described in paragraph 6 of Schedule 1 (whether or not that paragraph was in force at the time the business was done); or

(c) given, outside the United Kingdom, any advice to the customer as described in paragraph 7 of that Schedule (whether or not that paragraph was in force at the time the business was done).

32. Overseas communicators: unsolicited real time communications to previously overseas customers

(1) If the requirements of paragraphs (2) and (3) are met, the financial promotion restriction does not apply to an unsolicited real time communication which is made by an overseas communicator from outside the United Kingdom to a previously overseas customer of his.

(2) The requirements of this paragraph are that the terms on which previous transactions and services had been effected or provided by the overseas communicator to the previously overseas customer were such that the customer would reasonably expect, at the time that the unsolicited real time communication is made, to be contacted by the overseas communicator in relation to the investment activity to which the communication relates.

(3) The requirements of this paragraph are that the previously overseas customer has been informed by the overseas communicator on an earlier occasion—

(a) that the protections conferred by or under the Act will not apply to any unsolicited real time communication which is made by the overseas communicator and which relates to that investment activity;

(b) that the protections conferred by or under the Act may not apply to any investment activity that may be engaged in as a result of the communication; and

(c) whether any transaction between them resulting from the communication would fall within the jurisdiction of any dispute resolution scheme or compensation scheme or, if there is no such scheme, of that fact.

33. Overseas communicators: unsolicited real time communications to knowledgeable customers

(1) If the requirements of paragraphs (2), (3) and (4) are met, the financial promotion restriction does not apply to an unsolicited real time communication which is made by an overseas communicator

from outside the United Kingdom in the course of his carrying on relevant investment activities outside the United Kingdom.

(2) The requirements of this paragraph are that the overseas communicator believes on reasonable grounds that the recipient is sufficiently knowledgeable to understand the risks associated with engaging in the investment activity to which the communication relates.

(3) The requirements of this paragraph are that, in relation to any particular investment activity, the recipient has been informed by the overseas communicator on an earlier occasion—

(a) that the protections conferred by or under the Act will not apply to any unsolicited real time communication which is made by him and which relates to that activity;

(b) that the protections conferred by or under the Act may not apply to any investment activity that may be engaged in as a result of the communication; and

(c) whether any transaction between them resulting from the communication would fall within the jurisdiction of any dispute resolution scheme or compensation scheme or, if there is no such scheme, of that fact.

(4) The requirements of this paragraph are that the recipient, after being given a proper opportunity to consider the information given to him in accordance with paragraph (3), has clearly signified that he understands the warnings referred to in paragraph (3)(a) and (b) and that he accepts that he will not benefit from the protections referred to.

34. Governments, central banks etc.

The financial promotion restriction does not apply to any communication which—

(a) is a non-real time communication or a solicited real time communication;

(b) is communicated by and relates only to controlled investments issued, or to be issued, by—

(i) any government;

(ii) any local authority (in the United Kingdom or elsewhere);

(iii) any international organisation;

(iv) the Bank of England;

(v) the European Central Bank;

(vi) the central bank of any country or territory outside the United Kingdom.

35. Industrial and provident societies

The financial promotion restriction does not apply to any communication which—

(a) is a non-real time communication or a solicited real time communication;

(b) is communicated by an industrial and provident society; and

(c) relates only to an investment falling within paragraph 15 or 15A of Schedule 1 issued, or to be issued, by the society in question.

36. Nationals of EEA States other than United Kingdom

The financial promotion restriction does not apply to any communication which—

(a) is a non-real time communication or a solicited real time communication;

(b) is communicated by a national of an EEA State other than the United Kingdom in the course of any controlled activity lawfully carried on by him in that State; and

(c) conforms with any rules made by the Authority under section 145 of the Act (financial promotion rules) which are relevant to a communication of that kind.

37. Financial markets

(1) The financial promotion restriction does not apply to any communication—

(a) which is a non-real time communication or a solicited real time communication;

(b) which is communicated by a relevant market; and

(c) to which paragraph (2) or (3) applies.

(2) This paragraph applies to a communication if—

(a) it relates only to facilities provided by the market; and

(b) it does not identify (directly or indirectly)—

(i) any particular investment issued, or to be issued, by or available from an identified person as one that may be traded or dealt in on the market; or

(ii) any particular person as a person through whom transactions on the market may be effected.

(3) This paragraph applies to a communication if—

(a) it relates only to a particular investment falling within paragraph 21, 22 or 23 of Schedule 1; and

(b) it identifies the investment as one that may be traded or dealt in on the market.

(4) "Relevant market" means a market which—

(a) meets the criteria specified in Part I of Schedule 3; or

(b) is specified in, or is established under the rules of an exchange specified in, Part II, III or IV of that Schedule.

38. Persons in the business of placing promotional material

The financial promotion restriction does not apply to any communication which is made to a person whose business it is to place, or arrange for the placing of, promotional material provided that it is communicated so that he can place or arrange for placing it.

39. Joint enterprises

(1) The financial promotion restriction does not apply to any communication which is made or directed by a participator in a joint enterprise to or at another participator in the same joint enterprise in connection with, or for the purposes of, that enterprise.

(2) "Joint enterprise" means an enterprise into which two or more persons ("the participators") enter for commercial purposes related to a business or businesses (other than the business of engaging in a controlled activity) carried on by them; and, where a participator is a member of a group, each other member of the group is also to be regarded as a participator in the enterprise.

(3) "Participator" includes potential participator.

40. Participants in certain recognised collective investment schemes

The financial promotion restriction does not apply to any non-real time communication or solicited real time communication which is made—

(a) by a person who is the operator of a scheme recognised under section 270 or 272 of the Act; and

(b) to persons in the United Kingdom who are participants in any such recognised scheme operated by the person making the communication,

and which relates only to such recognised schemes as are operated by that person or to units in such schemes.

41. Bearer instruments: promotions required or permitted by market rules

(1) The financial promotion restriction does not apply to any communication which—

(a) is a non-real time communication or a solicited real time communication;

(b) is communicated by a body corporate ("A") that is not an open-ended investment company;

(c) is made to or may reasonably be regarded as directed at persons entitled to bearer instruments issued by A, a parent undertaking of A or a subsidiary undertaking of A; and

(d) is required or permitted by the rules of a relevant market to be communicated to holders of instruments of a class which consists of or includes the bearer instruments in question.

(2) "Bearer instrument" means any of the following investments title to which is capable of being transferred by delivery—

(a) any investment falling within paragraph 14, 15 or 15A of Schedule 1;

(b) any investment falling within paragraph 17 or 18 of that Schedule which confers rights in respect of an investment falling within paragraph 14, 15 or 15A.

(3) For the purposes of this article, a bearer instrument falling within paragraph 17 or 18 of Schedule 1 is treated as issued by the person ("P") who issued the investment in respect of which the bearer instrument confers rights if it is issued by—

(a) an undertaking in the same group as P; or

(b) a person acting on behalf of, or pursuant to arrangements made with, P.

(4) "Relevant market", in relation to instruments of any particular class, means any market on which instruments of that class can be traded or dealt in and which—

(a) meets the criteria specified in Part I of Schedule 3; or

(b) is specified in, or established under the rules of an exchange specified in, Part II or III of that Schedule.

42. Bearer instruments: promotions to existing holders 42.

(1) The financial promotion restriction does not apply to any communication which—

(a) is a non-real time communication or a solicited real time communication;

(b) is communicated by a body corporate ("A") that is not an open-ended investment company;

(c) is made to or may reasonably be regarded as directed at persons entitled to bearer instruments issued by A, a parent undertaking of A or a subsidiary undertaking of A;

(d) relates only to instruments of a class which consists of or includes either the bearer instruments to which the communication relates or instruments in respect of which those bearer instruments confer rights; and

(e) is capable of being accepted or acted on only by persons who are entitled to instruments (whether or not bearer instruments) issued by A, a parent undertaking of A or a subsidiary undertaking of A.

(2) "Bearer instruments" has the meaning given by article 41.

(3) For the purposes of this article, an instrument falling within paragraph 17 or 18 of Schedule 1 is treated as issued by the person ("P") who issued the investment in respect of which the bearer instrument confers rights if it is issued by—

(a) an undertaking in the same group as P; or

(b) a person acting on behalf of, or pursuant to arrangements made with, P.

43. Members and creditors of certain bodies corporate

(1) The financial promotion restriction does not apply to any non-real time communication or solicited real time communication which is communicated—

(a) by, or on behalf of, a body corporate ("A") that is not an open-ended investment company; and

(b) to persons whom the person making or directing the communication believes on reasonable grounds to be persons to whom paragraph (2) applies,

and which relates only to a relevant investment which is issued or to be issued by A, or by an undertaking ("U") in the same group as A that is not an open-ended investment company.

(2) This paragraph applies to—

(a) a creditor or member of A or of U;

(b) a person who is entitled to a relevant investment which is issued, or to be issued, by A or by U;

(c) a person who is entitled, whether conditionally or unconditionally, to become a member of A or of U but who has not yet done so;

(d) a person who is entitled, whether conditionally or unconditionally, to have transferred to him title to a relevant investment which is issued by A or by U but has not yet acquired title to the investment.

(3) "Relevant investment" means—

(a) an investment falling within paragraph 14, 15 or 15A of Schedule 1;

(b) an investment falling within paragraph 17 or 18 of that Schedule so far as relating to any investments within sub-paragraph (a).

(4) For the purposes of this article, an investment falling within paragraph 17 or 18 of Schedule 1 is treated as issued by the person ("P") who issued the investment in respect of which the instrument confers rights if it is issued by—

(a) an undertaking in the same group as P; or

(b) a person acting on behalf of, or pursuant to arrangements made with, P.

44. Members and creditors of open-ended investment companies

(1) The financial promotion restriction does not apply to any communication which—

(a) is a non-real time communication or a solicited real time communication;

(b) is communicated by, or on behalf of, a body corporate ("A") that is an open-ended investment company;

(c) is communicated to persons whom the person making or directing the communication believes on reasonable grounds to be persons to whom paragraph (2) applies; and

(d) relates only to an investment falling within paragraph 15, 15A, 17 or 19 of Schedule 1 which is issued, or to be issued, by A.

(2) This paragraph applies to—

(a) a creditor or member of A;

(b) a person who is entitled to an investment falling within paragraph 15, 15A, 17 or 19 of Schedule 1 which is issued, or to be issued, by A;

(c) a person who is entitled, whether conditionally or unconditionally, to become a member of A but who has not yet done so;

(d) a person who is entitled, whether conditionally or unconditionally, to have transferred to him title to an investment falling within paragraph 15, 15A, 17 or 19 of Schedule 1 which is issued by A but has not yet acquired title to the investment.

(3) For the purposes of this article, an investment falling within paragraph 17 of Schedule 1 is treated as issued by the person ("P") who issued the investment in respect of which the instrument confers rights if it is issued by—

(a) an undertaking in the same group as P; or

(b) a person acting on behalf of, or pursuant to arrangements made with, P.

45. Group companies

The financial promotion restriction does not apply to any communication made by one body corporate in a group to another body corporate in the same group.

46. Qualifying credit to bodies corporate

The financial promotion restriction does not apply to any communication which relates to a controlled activity falling within paragraph 10, 10A or 10B of Schedule 1 (or within paragraph 11 so far as it relates to that activity) if the communication is—

(a) made to or directed at bodies corporate only; or

(b) accompanied by an indication that the qualifying credit to which it relates is only available to bodies corporate.

47. Persons in the business of disseminating information

(1) The financial promotion restriction does not apply to any communication which is made only to recipients whom the person making the communication believes on reasonable grounds to be persons to whom paragraph (2) applies.

(2) This paragraph applies to—

(a) a person who receives the communication in the course of a business which involves the dissemination through a publication of information concerning controlled activities;

(b) a person whilst acting in the capacity of director, officer or employee of a person falling within sub-paragraph (a) being a person whose responsibilities when acting in that capacity involve him in the business referred to in that sub-paragraph;

(c) any person to whom the communication may otherwise lawfully be made.

48. Certified high net worth individuals

(1) If the requirements of paragraphs (4) and (7) are met, the financial promotion restriction does not apply to any communication which—

(a) is a non-real time communication or a solicited real time communication;

(b) is made to an individual whom the person making the communication believes on reasonable grounds to be a certified high net worth individual, and

(c) relates only to one or more investments falling within paragraph (8).

(2) "Certified high net worth individual" means an individual who has signed, within the period of twelve months ending with the day on which the communication is made, a statement complying with Part I of Schedule 5.

(3) The validity of a statement signed for the purposes of paragraph (2) is not affected by a defect in the form or wording of the statement, provided that the defect does not alter the statement's meaning and that the words shown in bold type in Part I of Schedule 5 are so shown in the statement.

(4) The requirements of this paragraph are that either the communication is accompanied by the giving of a warning in accordance with paragraphs (5) and (6) or where, because of the nature of the communication, this is not reasonably practicable,—

(a) a warning in accordance with paragraph (5) is given to the recipient orally at the beginning of the communication together with an indication that he will receive the warning in legible form and that, before receipt of that warning, he should consider carefully any decision to engage in investment activity to which the communication relates; and

(b) a warning in accordance with paragraphs (5) and (6) (d) to (h) is sent to the recipient of the communication within two business days of the day on which the communication is made.

(5) The warning must be in the following terms—

" The content of this promotion has not been approved by an authorised person within the meaning of the Financial Services and Markets Act 2000. Reliance on this promotion for the purpose of engaging in any investment activity may expose an individual to a significant risk of losing all of the property or other assets invested.".

But where a warning is sent pursuant to paragraph (4)(b), for the words "this promotion" in both places where they occur there must be substituted wording which clearly identifies the promotion which is the subject of the warning.

(6) The warning must—

(a) be given at the beginning of the communication;

(b) precede any other written or pictorial matter;

(c) be in a font size consistent with the text forming the remainder of the communication;

(d) be indelible;

(e) be legible;

(f) be printed in black, bold type;

(g) be surrounded by a black border which does not interfere with the text of the warning; and

(h) not be hidden, obscured or interrupted by any other written or pictorial matter.

(7) The requirements of this paragraph are that the communication is accompanied by an indication—

(a) that it is exempt from the general restriction (in section 21 of the Act) on the communication of invitations or inducements to engage in investment activity on the ground that it is made to a certified high net worth individual;

(b) of the requirements that must be met for an individual to qualify as a certified high net worth individual; and

(c) that any individual who is in any doubt about the investment to which the communication relates should consult an authorised person specialising in advising on investments of the kind in question.

(8) An investment falls within this paragraph if—

(a) it is an investment falling within paragraph 14 of Schedule 1 being stock or shares in an unlisted company;

(b) it is an investment falling within paragraph 15 of Schedule 1 being an investment acknowledging the indebtedness of an unlisted company;

(ba) it is an investment falling within paragraph 15A of Schedule 1 being an investment constituting an alternative finance investment bond issued by an unlisted company;

(c) it is an investment falling within paragraph 17 or 18 of Schedule 1 conferring entitlement or rights with respect to investments falling within sub-paragraph (a) or (b);
(d) it comprises units in a collective investment scheme being a scheme which invests wholly or predominantly in investments falling within sub-paragraph (a) or (b);
(e) it is an investment falling within paragraph 21 of Schedule 1 being an option to acquire or dispose of an investment falling within sub-paragraph (a), (b) or (c);
(f) it is an investment falling within paragraph 22 of Schedule 1 being rights under a contract for the sale of an investment falling within sub-paragraph (a), (b) or (c);
(g) it is an investment falling within paragraph 23 of Schedule 1 being a contract relating to, or to fluctuations in value or price of, an investment falling within sub-paragraph (a), (b) or (c),

provided in each case that it is an investment under the terms of which the investor cannot incur a liability or obligation to pay or contribute more than he commits by way of investment.

(9) "Business day" means any day except a Saturday, a Sunday, Christmas Day, Good Friday or a day which is a bank holiday under the Banking and Financial Dealings Act 1971 in any part of the United Kingdom.

49. High net worth companies, unincorporated associations etc.

(1) The financial promotion restriction does not apply to any communication which—
(a) is made only to recipients whom the person making the communication believes on reasonable grounds to be persons to whom paragraph (2) applies; or
(b) may reasonably be regarded as directed only at persons to whom paragraph (2) applies.

(2) This paragraph applies to—
(a) any body corporate which has, or which is a member of the same group as an undertaking which has, a called-up share capital or net assets of not less than—
(i) if the body corporate has more than 20 members or is a subsidiary undertaking of an undertaking which has more than 20 members, £500,000;
(ii) otherwise, £5 million;
(b) any unincorporated association or partnership which has net assets of not less than £5 million;
(c) the trustee of a high value trust;
(d) any person ("A") whilst acting in the capacity of director, officer or employee of a person ("B") falling within any of sub-paragraphs (a) to (c) where A's responsibilities, when acting in that capacity, involve him in B's engaging in investment activity;
(e) any person to whom the communication may otherwise lawfully be made.

(3) For the purposes of paragraph (1)(b)—
(a) if all the conditions set out in paragraph (4)(a) to (c) are met, the communication is to be regarded as directed at persons to whom paragraph (2) applies;
(b) in any other case in which one or more of those conditions are met, that fact is to be taken into account in determining whether the communication is directed at persons to whom paragraph (2) applies (but a communication may still be regarded as so directed even if none of the conditions in paragraph (4) is met).

(4) The conditions are that—
(a) the communication includes an indication of the description of persons to whom it is directed and an indication of the fact that the controlled investment or controlled activity to which it relates is available only to such persons;
(b) the communication includes an indication that persons of any other description should not act upon it;
(c) there are in place proper systems and procedures to prevent recipients other than persons to whom paragraph (2) applies engaging in the investment activity to which the communication relates with the person directing the communication, a close relative of his or a member of the same group.

(5) "Called-up share capital" has the meaning given in the 2006 Act (see section 547).

(6) "High value trust" means a trust where the aggregate value of the cash and investments which form part of the trust's assets (before deducting the amount of its liabilities)—

(a) is £10 million or more; or

(b) has been £10 million or more at anytime during the year immediately preceding the date on which the communication in question was first made or directed.

(7) "Net assets" has the meaning given by section 831 of the 2006 Act.

50. Sophisticated investors

(1) "Certified sophisticated investor", in relation to any description of investment, means a person—

(a) who has a current certificate in writing or other legible form signed by an authorised person to the effect that he is sufficiently knowledgeable to understand the risks associated with that description of investment; and

(b) who has signed, within the period of twelve months ending with the day on which the communication is made, a statement in the following terms:

> "I make this statement so that I am able to receive promotions which are exempt from the restrictions on financial promotion in the Financial Services and Markets Act 2000. The exemption relates to certified sophisticated investors and I declare that I qualify as such in relation to investments of the following kind [list them]. I accept that the contents of promotions and other material that I receive may not have been approved by an authorised person and that their content may not therefore be subject to controls which would apply if the promotion were made or approved by an authorised person. I am aware that it is open to me to seek advice from someone who specialises in advising on this kind of investment.".

(1A) The validity of a statement signed in accordance with paragraph (1)(b) is not affected by a defect in the wording of the statement, provided that the defect does not alter the statement's meaning.

(2) If the requirements of paragraph (3) are met, the financial promotion restriction does not apply to any communication which—

(a) is made to a certified sophisticated investor;

(b) does not invite or induce the recipient to engage in investment activity with the person who has signed the certificate referred to in paragraph (1)(a); and

(c) relates only to a description of investment in respect of which that investor is certified.

(3) The requirements of this paragraph are that the communication is accompanied by an indication—

(a) that it is exempt from the general restriction (in section 21 of the Act) on the communication of invitations or inducements to engage in investment activity on the ground that it is made to a certified sophisticated investor;

(b) of the requirements that must be met for a person to qualify as a certified sophisticated investor;

(c) that the content of the communication has not been approved by an authorised person and that such approval is, unless this exemption or any other exemption applies, required by section 21 of the Act;

(d) that reliance on the communication for the purpose of engaging in any investment activity may expose the individual to a significant risk of losing all of the property invested or of incurring additional liability;

(e) that any person who is in any doubt about the investment to which the communication relates should consult an authorised person specialising in advising on investments of the kind in question.

(4) For the purposes of paragraph (1)(a), a certificate is current if it is signed and dated not more than three years before the date on which the communication is made.

50A. Self-certified sophisticated investors

(1) "Self-certified sophisticated investor" means an individual who has signed within the period of twelve months ending with the day on which the communication is made, a statement complying with Part II of Schedule 5.

(2) The validity of a statement signed for the purposes of paragraph (1) is not affected by a defect in the form or wording of the statement, provided that the defect does not alter the statement's meaning and that the words shown in bold type in Part II of Schedule 5 are so shown in the statement.

(3) If the requirements of paragraphs (4) and (7) are met, the financial promotion restriction does not apply to any communication which—

(a) is made to an individual whom the person making the communication believes on reasonable grounds to be a self-certified sophisticated investor; and

(b) relates only to one or more investments falling within paragraph (8).

(4) The requirements of this paragraph are that either the communication is accompanied by the giving of a warning in accordance with paragraphs (5) and (6) or where, because of the nature of the communication this is not reasonably practicable—

(a) a warning in accordance with paragraph (5) is given to the recipient orally at the beginning of the communication together with an indication that he will receive the warning in legible form and that, before receipt of that warning, he should consider carefully any decision to engage in investment activity to which the communication relates; and

(b) a warning in accordance with paragraphs (5) and (6) (d) to (h) is sent to the recipient of the communication within two business days of the day on which the communication is made.

(5) The warning must be in the following terms—

"The content of this promotion has not been approved by an authorised person within the meaning of the Financial Services and Markets Act 2000. Reliance on this promotion for the purpose of engaging in any investment activity may expose an individual to a significant risk of losing all of the property or other assets invested.".

But where a warning is sent pursuant to paragraph (4)(b), for the words "this promotion" in both places where they occur there must be substituted wording which clearly identifies the promotion which is the subject of the warning.

(6) The warning must—

(a) be given at the beginning of the communication;

(b) precede any other written or pictorial matter;

(c) be in a font size consistent with the text forming the remainder of the communication;

(d) be indelible;

(e) be legible;

(f) be printed in black, bold type;

(g) be surrounded by a black border which does not interfere with the text of the warning; and

(h) not be hidden, obscured or interrupted by any other written or pictorial matter.

(7) The requirements of this paragraph are that the communication is accompanied by an indication—

(a) that it is exempt from the general restriction (in section 21 of the Act) on the communication of invitations or inducements to engage in investment activity on the ground that it is made to a self-certified sophisticated investor;

(b) of the requirements that must be met for an individual to qualify as a self-certified sophisticated investor;

(c) that any individual who is in any doubt about the investment to which the communication relates should consult an authorised person specialising in advising on investments of the kind in question.

(8) An investment falls within this paragraph if—

(a) it is an investment falling within paragraph 14 of Schedule 1 being stock or shares in an unlisted company;

(b) it is an investment falling within paragraph 15 of Schedule 1 being an investment acknowledging the indebtedness of an unlisted company;

(ba) it is an investment falling within paragraph 15A of Schedule 1 being an investment constituting an alternative finance investment bond issued by an unlisted company;

(c) it is an investment falling within paragraph 17 or 18 of Schedule 1 conferring entitlement or rights with respect to investments falling within sub-paragraph (a) or (b);
(d) it comprises units in a collective investment scheme being a scheme which invests wholly or predominantly in investments falling within sub-paragraph (a) or (b);
(e) it is an investment falling within paragraph 21 of Schedule 1 being an option to acquire or dispose of an investment falling within sub-paragraph (a), (b) or (c);
(f) it is an investment falling within paragraph 22 of Schedule 1 being rights under a contract for the sale of an investment falling within sub-paragraph (a), (b) or (c);
(g) it is an investment falling within paragraph 23 of Schedule 1 being a contract relating to, or to fluctuations in value or price of, an investment falling within sub-paragraph (a), (b) or (c),

provided in each case that it is an investment under the terms of which the investor cannot incur a liability or obligation to pay or contribute more than he commits by way of investment.

(9) "Business day" means any day except a Saturday, a Sunday, Christmas Day, Good Friday or a day which is a bank holiday under the Banking and Financial Dealings Act 1971 in any part of the United Kingdom.

51. Associations of high net worth or sophisticated investors

The financial promotion restriction does not apply to any non-real time communication or solicited real time communication which—

(a) is made to an association, or to a member of an association, the membership of which the person making the communication believes on reasonable grounds comprises wholly or predominantly persons who are—
  (i) certified or self-certified high net worth individuals within the meaning of article 48;
  (ii) high net worth persons falling within article 49(2)(a) to (d);
  (iii) certified or self-certified sophisticated investors within the meaning of article 50 or 50A; and
(b) relates only to an investment under the terms of which a person cannot incur a liability or obligation to pay or contribute more than he commits by way of investment.

52. Common interest group of a company

(1) "Common interest group", in relation to a company, means an identified group of persons who at the time the communication is made might reasonably be regarded as having an existing and common interest with each other and that company in—
(a) the affairs of the company; and
(b) what is done with the proceeds arising from any investment to which the communication relates.

(2) If the requirements of paragraphs (3) and either (4) or (5) are met, the financial promotion restriction does not apply to any communication which—
(a) is a non-real time communication or a solicited real time communication;
(b) is made only to persons who are members of a common interest group of a company, or may reasonably be regarded as directed only at such persons; and
(c) relates to investments falling within paragraph 14, 15 or 15A of Schedule 1 which are issued, or to be issued, by that company.

(3) The requirements of this paragraph are that the communication is accompanied by an indication—
(a) that the directors of the company (or its promoters named in the communication) have taken all reasonable care to ensure that every statement of fact or opinion included in the communication is true and not misleading given the form and context in which it appears;
(b) that the directors of the company (or its promoters named in the communication) have not limited their liability with respect to the communication; and
(c) that any person who is in any doubt about the investment to which the communication relates should consult an authorised person specialising in advising on investments of the kind in question.

(4) The requirements of this paragraph are that the communication is accompanied by an indication—

(a) that the directors of the company (or its promoters named in the communication) have taken all reasonable care to ensure that any person belonging to the common interest group (and his professional advisers) can have access, at all reasonable times, to all the information that he or they would reasonably require, and reasonably expect to find, for the purpose of making an informed assessment of the assets and liabilities, financial position, profits and losses and prospects of the company and of the rights attaching to the investments in question; and

(b) describing the means by which such information can be accessed.

(5) The requirements of this paragraph are that the communication is accompanied by an indication that any person considering subscribing for the investments in question should regard any subscription as made primarily to assist the furtherance of the company's objectives (other than any purely financial objectives) and only secondarily, if at all, as an investment.

(6) For the purposes of paragraph (2)(b)—

(a) if all the conditions set out in paragraph (7) are met, the communication is to be regarded as directed at persons who are members of the common interest group;

(b) in any other case in which one or more of those conditions are met, that fact shall be taken into account in determining whether the communication is directed at persons who are members of the common interest group (but a communication may still be regarded as directed only at such persons even if none of the conditions in paragraph (7) is met).

(7) The conditions are that—

(a) the communication is accompanied by an indication that it is directed at persons who are members of the common interest group and that any investment or activity to which it relates is available only to such persons;

(b) the communication is accompanied by an indication that it must not be acted upon by persons who are not members of the common interest group;

(c) there are in place proper systems and procedures to prevent recipients other than members of the common interest group engaging in the investment activity to which the communication relates with the person directing the communication, a close relative of his or a member of the same group.

(8) Persons are not to be regarded as having an interest of the kind described in paragraph (1) if the only reason why they would be so regarded is that—

(a) they will have such an interest if they become members or creditors of the company;

(b) they all carry on a particular trade or profession; or

(c) they are persons with whom the company has an existing business relationship, whether by being its clients, customers, contractors, suppliers or otherwise.

53. Settlors, trustees and personal representatives

The financial promotion restriction does not apply to any communication which is made between—

(a) a person when acting as a settlor or grantor of a trust, a trustee or a personal representative; and

(b) a trustee of the trust, a fellow trustee or a fellow personal representative (as the case may be),

if the communication is made for the purposes of the trust or estate.

54. Beneficiaries of trust, will or intestacy

The financial promotion restriction does not apply to any communication which is made—

(a) between a person when acting as a settlor or grantor of a trust, trustee or personal representative and a beneficiary under the trust, will or intestacy; or

(b) between a beneficiary under a trust, will or intestacy and another beneficiary under the same trust, will or intestacy, if the communication relates to the management or distribution of that trust fund or estate.

55. Communications by members of professions

(1) The financial promotion restriction does not apply to a real time communication (whether solicited or unsolicited) which—

(a) is made by a person ("P") who carries on a regulated activity to which the general prohibition does not apply by virtue of section 327 of the Act; and

(b) is made to a recipient who has, prior to the communication being made, engaged P to provide professional services,

where the controlled activity to which the communication relates is an excluded activity which would be undertaken by P for the purposes of, and incidental to, the provision by him of professional services to or at the request of the recipient.

(2) "Professional services" has the meaning given in section 327 of the Act.

(3) An "excluded activity" is an activity to which the general prohibition would apply but for the application of—

(a) section 327 of the Act; or

(b) article 67 of the Regulated Activities Order.

55A. Non-real time communication by members of professions

(1) The financial promotion restriction does not apply to a non-real time communication which is—

(a) made by a person ("P") who carries on Part XX activities; and

(b) limited to what is required or permitted by paragraphs (2) and (3).

(2) The communication must be in the following terms—

"This [firm/company] is not authorised under the Financial Services and Markets Act 2000 but we are able in certain circumstances to offer a limited range of investment services to clients because we are members of [relevant designated professional body]. We can provide these investment services if they are an incidental part of the professional services we have been engaged to provide."

(3) The communication may in addition set out the Part XX activities which P is able to offer to his clients, provided it is clear that these are the investment services to which the statement in paragraph (2) relates.

(4) The validity of a communication made in accordance with paragraph (2) is not affected by a defect in the wording of it provided that the defect does not alter the communication's meaning.

(5) "Part XX activities" means the regulated activities to which the general prohibition does not apply when they are carried on by P by virtue of section 327 of the Act.

56. Remedy following report by Parliamentary Commissioner for Administration

The financial promotion restriction does not apply to any communication made or directed by a person for the purpose of enabling any injustice, stated by the Parliamentary Commissioner for Administration in a report under section 10 of the Parliamentary Commissioner Act 1967 to have occurred, to be remedied with respect to the recipient.

57. Persons placing promotional material in particular publications

The financial promotion restriction does not apply to any communication received by a person who receives the publication in which the communication is contained because he has himself placed an advertisement in that publication.

58. Acquisition of interest in premises run by management companies

(1) "Management company" means a company established for the purpose of—

(a) managing the common parts or fabric of premises used for residential or business purposes; or

(b) supplying services to such premises.

(2) The financial promotion restriction does not apply to any non-real time communication or solicited real time communication if it relates to an investment falling within paragraph 14 of Schedule 1 which—

(a) is issued, or to be issued, by a management company; and

(b) is to be acquired by any person in connection with the acquisition of an interest in the premises in question.

59. Annual accounts and directors' report

(1) If the requirements in paragraphs (2) to (5) are met, the financial promotion restriction does not apply to any communication by a body corporate (other than an open-ended investment company) which—

(a) consists of, or is accompanied by, the whole or any part of the annual accounts of a body corporate (other than an open-ended investment company); or

(b) is accompanied by any report which is prepared and approved by the directors of such a body corporate under—

(i) sections 415 and 419 of the 2006 Act; or

(ii) . . .

(iii) the law of an EEA State other than the United Kingdom which corresponds to the provisions mentioned in paragraph (i) . . .

(2) The requirements of this paragraph are that the communication—

(a) does not contain any invitation to persons to underwrite, subscribe for, or otherwise acquire or dispose of, a controlled investment; and

(b) does not advise persons to engage in any of the activities within sub-paragraph (a).

(3) The requirements of this paragraph are that the communication does not contain any invitation to persons to—

(a) effect any transaction with the body corporate (or with any named person) in the course of that body's (or person's) carrying on of any activity falling within any of paragraphs 3 to 11 of Schedule 1; or

(b) make use of any services provided by that body corporate (or by any named person) in the course of carrying on such activity.

(4) The requirements of this paragraph are that the communication does not contain any inducement relating to an investment other than one issued, or to be issued, by the body corporate (or another body corporate in the same group) which falls within—

(a) paragraph 14, 15 or 15A of Schedule 1; or

(b) paragraph 17 or 18 of that Schedule, so far as relating to any investments within sub-paragraph (a).

(5) The requirements of this paragraph are that the communication does not contain any reference to—

(a) the price at which investments issued by the body corporate have in the past been bought or sold; or

(b) the yield on such investments,

unless it is also accompanied by an indication that past performance cannot be relied on as a guide to future performance.

(6) For the purposes of paragraph (5)(b), a reference, in relation to an investment, to earnings, dividend or nominal rate of interest payable shall not be taken to be a reference to the yield on the investment.

(7) "Annual accounts" means—

(a) accounts produced by virtue of Part 15 of the 2006 Act (or of that Part as applied by virtue of any other enactment);

(b) . . .

(c) a summary financial statement prepared under section 426 of the 2006 Act;

(d) accounts produced in accordance with Chapter 3 of Part 5 of the Overseas Companies Regulations 2009 and filed with the registrar under section 441 of the 2006 Act as applied and modified by regulation 40 of those Regulations;

(e) accounts which are produced or published by virtue of the law of an EEA State other than the United Kingdom and which correspond to accounts within any of sub-paragraphs (a) to (d).

60. Participation in employee share schemes

(1) The financial promotion restriction does not apply to any communication by a person ("C"), a member of the same group as C or a relevant trustee where the communication is for the purposes of an employee share scheme and relates to any of the following investments issued, or to be issued, by C—

(a) investments falling within paragraph 14, 15 or 15A of Schedule 1;

(b) investments falling within paragraph 17 or 18 so far as relating to any investments within sub-paragraph (a); or

(c) investments falling within paragraph 21 or 27 so far as relating to any investments within sub-paragraph (a) or (b).

(2) "Employee share scheme", in relation to any investments issued by C, means arrangements made or to be made by C or by a person in the same group as C to enable or facilitate—

(a) transactions in the investments specified in paragraphs (1)(a) or (b) between or for the benefit of—

(i) the bona fide employees or former employees of C or of another member of the same group as C;

(ii) the wives, husbands, widows, widowers, civil partners, surviving civil partners or children or step-children under the age of eighteen of such employees or former employees; or

(b) the holding of those investments by, or for the benefit of, such persons.

(3) "Relevant trustee" means a person who, in pursuance of an actual or proposed employee share scheme, holds as trustee or will hold as trustee investments issued by C.

61. Sale of goods and supply of services 61

(1) In this article—

"supplier" means a person whose main business is to sell goods or supply services and not to carry on controlled activities falling within any of paragraphs 3 to 7 of Schedule 1 and, where the supplier is a member of a group, also means any other member of that group;

"customer" means a person, other than an individual, to whom a supplier sells goods or supplies services, or agrees to do so, and, where the customer is a member of a group, also means any other member of that group;

"a related sale or supply" means a sale of goods or supply of services to the customer otherwise than by the supplier, but for or in connection with the same purpose as the sale or supply mentioned above.

(2) The financial promotion restriction does not apply to any non-real time communication or any solicited real time communication made by a supplier to a customer of his for the purposes of, or in connection with, the sale of goods or supply of services or a related sale or supply.

(3) But the exemption in paragraph (2) does not apply if the communication relates to—

(a) a qualifying contract of insurance or units in a collective investment scheme; or

(b) investments falling within paragraph 27 of Schedule 1 so far as relating to investments within paragraph (a).

62. Sale of body corporate

(1) The financial promotion restriction does not apply to any communication by, or on behalf of, a body corporate, a partnership, a single individual or a group of connected individuals which relates to a transaction falling within paragraph (2).

(2) A transaction falls within this paragraph if—

(a) it is one to acquire or dispose of shares in a body corporate other than an open-ended investment company, or is entered into for the purposes of such an acquisition or disposal; and

(b) either—

(i) the conditions set out in paragraph (3) are met; or

(ii) those conditions are not met, but the object of the transaction may nevertheless reasonably be regarded as being the acquisition of day to day control of the affairs of the body corporate.

(3) The conditions mentioned in paragraph (2)(b) are that—

(a) the shares consist of or include 50 per cent or more of the voting shares in the body corporate; or

(b) the shares, together with any already held by the person acquiring them, consist of or include at least that percentage of such shares; and

(c) in either case, the acquisition or disposal is, or is to be, between parties each of whom is a body corporate, a partnership, a single individual or a group of connected individuals.

(4) "A group of connected individuals" means—

(a) in relation to a party disposing of shares in a body corporate, a single group of persons each of whom is—

(i) a director or manager of the body corporate;

(ii) a close relative of any such director or manager; or

(iii) a person acting as trustee for, or nominee of, any person falling within paragraph (i) or (ii); and

(b) in relation to a party acquiring shares in a body corporate, a single group of of persons each of whom is—

(i) a person who is or is to be a director or manager of the body corporate;

(ii) a close relative of any such person; or

(iii) a person acting as trustee for or nominee of any person falling within paragraph (i) or (ii).

(5) "Voting shares" in relation to a body corporate, means shares carrying voting rights attributable to share capital which are exercisable in all circumstances at any general meeting of that body corporate.

63. Takeovers of relevant unlisted companies: interpretation

(1) In this article and in articles 64, 65 and 66, a "relevant unlisted company", in relation to a takeover offer, means a company which is an unlisted company at the time that the offer is made and which has been an unlisted company throughout the period of ten years immediately preceding the date of the offer.

(2) In this article and in articles 64, 65 and 66, references to a takeover offer for a relevant unlisted company are references to an offer which meets the requirements of Part I of Schedule 4 and which is an offer—

(a) for all the shares in, or all the shares comprised in the equity or non-equity share capital of, a relevant unlisted company (other than any shares already held by or on behalf of the person making the offer); or

(b) for all the debentures of such a company (other than debentures already held by or on behalf of the person making the offer).

(3) Shares in or debentures of an unlisted company are to be regarded as being held by or on behalf of the person making the offer if the person who holds them, or on whose behalf they are held, has agreed that an offer should not be made in respect of them.

64. Takeovers of relevant unlisted companies

(1) If the requirements of paragraphs (2) and (3) are met, the financial promotion restriction does not apply to any communication which is communicated in connection with a takeover offer for a relevant unlisted company.

(2) The requirements of this paragraph are that the communication is accompanied by the material listed in Part II of Schedule 4.

(3) The requirements of this paragraph are that the material listed in Part III of Schedule 4 is available at a place in the United Kingdom at all times during normal office hours for inspection free of charge.

65. Takeovers of relevant unlisted companies: warrants etc.

The financial promotion restriction does not apply to any communication which—

(a) is communicated at the same time as, or after, a takeover offer for a relevant unlisted company is made; and

(b) relates to investments falling within paragraph 17 or 18 of Schedule 1 so far as relating to the shares in or debentures of the unlisted company which are the subject of the offer.

66. Takeovers of relevant unlisted companies: application forms

The financial promotion restriction does not apply to any communication made in connection with a takeover offer for a relevant unlisted company which is a form of application for—

(a) shares in or debentures of the unlisted company; or

(b) investments falling within paragraphs 17 or 18 of Schedule 1 so far as relating to the shares in or debentures of the company which are the subject of the offer.

67. Promotions required or permitted by market rules

(1) The financial promotion restriction does not apply to any communication which—

(a) is a non-real time communication or a solicited real time communication;

(b) relates to an investment which falls within any of paragraphs 14 to 18 of Schedule 1 and which is permitted to be traded or dealt in on a relevant market; and

(c) is required or permitted to be communicated by—

(i) the rules of the relevant market;

(ii) a body which regulates the market; or

(iii) a body which regulates offers or issues of investments to be traded on such a market.

(2) "Relevant market" means a market which—

(a) meets the criteria specified in Part I of Schedule 3; or

(b) is specified in, or established under the rules of an exchange specified in, Part II or III of that Schedule.

68. Promotions in connection with admission to certain EEA markets

(1) The financial promotion restriction does not apply to any communication—

(a) which is a non-real time communication or a solicited real time communication;

(b) which a relevant EEA market requires to be communicated before an investment can be admitted to trading on that market;

(c) which, if it were included in a prospectus issued in accordance with prospectus rules made under Part VI of the Act, would be required to be communicated by those rules; and

(d) which is not accompanied by any information other than information which is required or permitted to be published by the rules of that market.

(2) In this article "relevant EEA market" means any market on which investments can be traded or dealt in and which—

(a) meets the criteria specified in Part I of Schedule 3; or

(b) is specified in, or established under the rules of an exchange specified in, Part II of that Schedule.

69. Promotions of securities already admitted to certain markets

(1) In this article—

"relevant investment" means any investment falling within—

(a) paragraph 14, 15 or 15A of Schedule 1; or

(b) paragraph 17 or 18 of that Schedule so far as relating to any investment mentioned in sub-paragraph (a);

"relevant market" means any market on which investments can be traded and which—

(a) meets the criteria specified in Part I of Schedule 3; or

(b) is specified in, or established under, the rules of an exchange specified in, Part II or III of that Schedule.

(2) If the requirements of paragraph (3) are met, the financial promotion restriction does not apply to any communication which—

(a) is a non-real time communication or a solicited real time communication;

(b) is communicated by a body corporate ("A"), other than an open-ended investment company; and

(c) relates only to relevant investments issued, or to be issued, by A or by another body corporate in the same group,

if relevant investments issued by A or by any such body corporate are permitted to be traded on a relevant market.

(3) The requirements of this paragraph are that the communication—

(a) is not, and is not accompanied by, an invitation to engage in investment activity;

(b) is not, and is not accompanied by, an inducement relating to an investment other than one issued, or to be issued, by A (or another body corporate in the same group);

(c) is not, and is not accompanied by, an inducement relating to a relevant investment which refers to—

(i) the price at which relevant investments have been bought or sold in the past, or

(ii) the yield on such investments,

unless the inducement also contains an indication that past performance cannot be relied on as a guide to future performance.

(4) For the purposes of this article, an investment falling within paragraph 17 or 18 of Schedule 1 is treated as issued by the person ("P") who issued the investment in respect of which the investment confers rights if it is issued by—

(a) an undertaking in the same group as P; or

(b) a person acting on behalf of, or pursuant to, arrangements made with P.

(5) For the purposes of paragraph (3)(a), "engaging in investment activity" has the meaning given in section 21(8) of the Act; and for the purposes of paragraph (3)(c)(ii), a reference, in relation to an investment, to earnings, dividend or nominal rate of interest payable shall not be taken to be a reference to the yield on the investment.

70. Promotions included in listing particulars etc.

(1) The financial promotion restriction does not apply to any non-real time communication which is included in—

(a) listing particulars;

(b) supplementary listing particulars;

(c) a prospectus or supplementary prospectus approved—

(i) by the competent authority in accordance with Part 6 of the Act; or

(ii) by the competent authority of an EEA State other than the United Kingdom, provided the requirements of section 87H of the Act have been met,

or part of such a prospectus or supplementary prospectus; or

(d) any other document required or permitted to be published by listing rules or prospectus rules under Part VI of the Act (except an advertisement within the meaning of the prospectus directive).

(1A) The financial promotion restriction does not apply to any non-real time communication—

(a) comprising the final terms of an offer or the final offer price or amount of securities which will be offered to the public; and

(b) complying with Articles 5(4), 8(1) and 14(2) of the prospectus directive.

(2) In this article "listing particulars", "listing rules", "the prospectus directive" and "prospectus rules" have the meaning given by Part VI of the Act.

71. Material relating to prospectus for public offer of unlisted securities

(1) The financial promotion restriction does not apply to any non-real time communication relating to a prospectus or supplementary prospectus where the only reason for considering it to be an invitation or inducement is that it does one or more of the following—

(a) it states the name and address of the person by whom the transferable securities to which the prospectus or supplementary prospectus relates are to be offered;

(b) it gives other details for contacting that person;

(c) it states the nature and the nominal value of the transferable securities to which the prospectus or supplementary prospectus relates, the number offered and the price at which they are offered;

(d) it states that a prospectus or supplementary prospectus is or will be available (and, if it is not yet available, when it is expected to be);

(e) it gives instructions for obtaining a copy of the prospectus or supplementary prospectus.

(2) In this article—

(a) "transferable securities" has the same meaning as in section 102A(3) of the Act;

(b) references to a prospectus or supplementary prospectus are references to a prospectus or supplementary prospectus which is published in accordance with prospectus rules made under Part VI of the Act.

72. Pension products offered by employers

(1) If the requirements of paragraph (2) are met, the financial promotion restriction does not apply to any communication which is made by an employer to an employee in relation to a group personal pension scheme or a stakeholder pension scheme.

(2) The requirements of this paragraph are that—

(a) the employer will make a contribution to the group personal pension scheme or stakeholder pension scheme to which the communication relates in the event of the employee becoming a member of the scheme and the communication contains a statement informing the employee of this;

(b) the employer has not received, and will not receive, any direct financial benefit as a result of making the communication;

(c) the employer notifies the employee in writing prior to the employee becoming a member of the scheme of the amount of the contribution that the employer will make to the scheme in respect of that employee or the basis on which the contribution will be calculated; and

(d) in the case of a non-real time communication, the communication contains, or is accompanied by, a statement informing the employee of his right to seek advice from an authorised person or an appointed representative.

(3) . . .

(4) In this article—

"group personal pension scheme" means arrangements administered on a group basis under a personal pension scheme and which are available to employees of the same employer or of employers within a group;

"personal pension scheme" means a scheme or arrangement which is not an occupational pension scheme or a stakeholder pension scheme and which is comprised in one or more instruments or agreements, having or capable of having effect so as to provide benefits to or in respect of people—

(a) on retirement,

(b) on having reached a particular age, or

(c) on termination of service in an employment;

"stakeholder pension scheme" has the meaning given by section 1 of the Welfare Reform and Pensions Act 1999.

72A. Pension product offers communicated to employees by third parties

(1) If the requirements of paragraph (2) are met, the financial promotion restriction does not apply to any communication which is made to an employee by or on behalf of a person ("A") in relation to a group personal pension scheme or a stakeholder pension scheme.

(2) The requirements of this paragraph are that—

(a) the employer and A have entered into a written contract specifying the terms on which the communication may be made;

(b) in the case of a communication made by a person ("B") on behalf of A, A and B have also entered into a written contract specifying the terms on which the communication may be made;

(c) the employer has not received, and will not receive, any direct financial benefit as a result of the communication being made;

(d) the employer will make a contribution to the scheme in the event of the employee becoming a member of the scheme and the communication contains a statement informing the employee of this;

(e) in the case of a non-real time communication, the communication contains, or is accompanied by, a statement informing the employee of their right to seek advice from an authorised person or an appointed representative; and

(f) the employer or A notifies the employee in writing prior to the employee becoming a member of the scheme of—

(i) the amount of the contribution that the employer will make to the scheme in respect of that employee, or the basis on which the contribution will be calculated; and

(ii) any remuneration A or B has received, or will receive, as a consequence of the employee becoming a member of the scheme, or the basis on which any such remuneration will be calculated.

(3) In this article "group personal pension scheme" and "stakeholder pension scheme" have the meaning given by article 72(4).

72B. Insurance product offers communicated to employees by employers

(1) If the requirements of paragraph (2) are met, the financial promotion restriction does not apply to any communication which is made by an employer to an employee in relation to work-related insurance.

(2) The requirements of this paragraph are that—

(a) where the provider of the insurance is not the employer, the employer has not received, and will not receive, any direct financial benefit as a result of making the communication; and

(b) in the case of a non-real time communication, the communication contains, or is accompanied by, a statement informing the employee of their right to seek advice from an authorised person or an appointed representative.

(3) In this article "work-related insurance" includes—

(a) life assurance;

(b) long term disability insurance (also known as permanent health insurance); and

(c) accidental death, injury, critical illness, medical, dental, income protection or travel insurance.

72C. Insurance product offers communicated to employees by third parties

(1) If the requirements of paragraph (2) are met, the financial promotion restriction does not apply to any communication which is made to an employee by or on behalf of a person ("A") in relation to work-related insurance.

(2) The requirements of this paragraph are that—

(a) the employer and A have entered into a written contract specifying the terms on which the communication may be made;

(b) in the case of a communication made by a person ("B") on behalf of A, A and B have also entered into a written contract specifying the terms on which the communication may be made;

(c) the employer has not received, and will not receive, any direct financial benefit as a result of the communication being made;

(d) in the case of a non-real time communication, the communication contains, or is accompanied by, a statement informing the employee of their right to seek advice from an authorised person or an appointed representative; and

(e) the employer or A notifies the employee in writing prior to the employee entering into a contract for the work-related insurance of any remuneration A or B has received, or will receive, as a consequence of the employee entering into the contract, or the basis on which any such remuneration will be calculated.

(3) In this article "work-related insurance" has the meaning given by article 72B(3).

72D. Staff mortgage offers communicated to employees by employers

(1) If the requirements of paragraph (2) are met, the financial promotion restriction does not apply to any communication which is made by an employer to an employee in relation to a staff mortgage.

(2) The requirements of this paragraph are that—

(a) where the provider of the staff mortgage is an undertaking in the same group as the employer, the employer has not received, and will not receive, any direct financial benefit as a result of making the communication; and

(b) in the case of a non-real time communication, the communication contains or is accompanied by a statement informing the employee of their right to seek advice from an authorised person or an appointed representative.

(3) In this article, "staff mortgage" means a regulated mortgage contract between the employer, or an undertaking in the same group as the employer, as lender and the employee (alone or with another person) as borrower to defray money applied for any of the following purposes—

(a) acquiring any residential land which was intended, at the time of the acquisition, for occupation by the employee as their home;

(b) carrying out repairs or improvements to any residential land which was intended, at the time of taking out the loan, for occupation by the employee as their home; or

(c) payments in respect of a loan (whether of interest or capital).

(4) In this article, "borrower", "lender" and "regulated mortgage contract" have the meaning given by article 61(3)(a) (regulated mortgage contracts) of the Financial Services and Markets Act 2000 (Regulated Activities) Order 2001.

72E. Staff mortgage offers communicated to employees by third parties

(1) If the requirements of paragraph (2) are met, the financial promotion restriction does not apply to any communication which is made to an employee by or on behalf of a person ("A") in relation to a staff mortgage.

(2) The requirements of this paragraph are that—

(a) the employer and A have entered into a written contract specifying the terms on which the communication may be made;

(b) in the case of a communication made by a person ("B") on behalf of A, A and B have also entered into a written contract specifying the terms on which the communication may be made;

(c) where the provider of the staff mortgage is an undertaking in the same group as the employer, the employer has not received, and will not receive, any direct financial benefit as a result of the communication being made;

(d) in the case of a non-real time communication, the communication contains, or is accompanied by, a statement informing the employee of their right to seek advice from an authorised person or an appointed representative; and

(e) the employer or A notifies the employee in writing prior to the employee entering into the staff mortgage of any remuneration A or B has received, or will receive, as a consequence of the employee entering into the staff mortgage, or the basis on which any such remuneration will be calculated.

(3) In this article "staff mortgage" has the same meaning as in article 72D(3).

73. Advice centres

(1) If the requirements of paragraph (2) are met, the financial promotion restriction does not apply to any communication which is made by a person in the course of carrying out his duties as an adviser for, or employee of, an advice centre.

(2) The requirements of this paragraph are that the communication relates to—

(a) qualifying credit;

(b) rights under, or rights to or interests in rights under, qualifying contracts of insurance; ...

(c) a child trust fund;

(d) a regulated home reversion plan; . . .

(e) a regulated home purchase plan; or

(f) a regulated sale and rent back agreement.

(3) In this article—

"adequate professional indemnity insurance", in relation to an advice centre, means insurance providing cover that is adequate having regard to—

(a) the claims record of the centre;

(b) the financial resources of the centre; and

(c) the right of clients of the centre to be compensated for loss arising from the negligent provision of financial advice;

"advice centre" means a body which—

(a) gives advice which is free and in respect of which the centre does not receive any fee, commission or other reward;

(b) provides debt advice as its principal financial services activity; and

(c) in the case of a body which is not part of a local authority, holds adequate professional indemnity insurance or a guarantee providing comparable cover;

"child trust fund" has the meaning given by section 1(2) of the Child Trust Funds Act 2004;

"local authority" has the meaning given in article 2 of the Financial Services and Markets Act 2000 (Exemption) Order 2001.

SCHEDULE 1

Article 4

PART I

Controlled Activities

1. Accepting deposits

Accepting deposits is a controlled activity if—

(a) money received by way of deposit is lent to others; or

(b) any other activity of the person accepting the deposit is financed wholly, or to a material extent, out of the capital of or interest on money received by way of deposit,

and the person accepting the deposit holds himself out as accepting deposits on a day to day basis.

2. Effecting or carrying out contracts of insurance

(1) Effecting a contract of insurance as principal is a controlled activity.

(2) Carrying out a contract of insurance as principal is a controlled activity.

(3) There is excluded from sub-paragraph (1) or (2) the effecting or carrying out of a contract of insurance of the kind described in article 12 of the Regulated Activities Order by a person who does not otherwise carry on an activity falling within those sub-paragraphs.

3. Dealing in securities and contractually based investments

(1) Buying, selling, subscribing for or underwriting securities or contractually based investments (other than investments of the kind specified by paragraph 25, or paragraph 27 so far as relevant to that paragraph) as principal or agent is a controlled activity.

(2) A person does not carry on the activity in sub-paragraph (1) by accepting an instrument creating or acknowledging indebtedness in respect of any loan, credit, guarantee or other similar financial accommodation or assurance which he has made, granted or provided.

(3) The reference in sub-paragraph (2) to a person accepting an instrument includes a reference to a person becoming a party to an instrument otherwise than as a debtor or a surety.

4. Arranging deals in investments

(1) Making arrangements for another person (whether as principal or agent) to buy, sell, subscribe for or underwrite a particular investment which is—

(a) a security;

(b) a contractually based investment; or

(c) an investment of the kind specified by paragraph 24, or paragraph 27 so far as relevant to that paragraph,

is a controlled activity.

(2) Making arrangements with a view to a person who participates in the arrangements buying, selling, subscribing for or underwriting investments falling within sub-paragraph (1)(a), (b) or (c) (whether as principal or agent) is a controlled activity.

(3) A person does not carry on an activity falling within paragraph (2) merely by providing means by which one party to a transaction (or potential transaction) is able to communicate with other such parties.

4A. Operating a multilateral trading facility

Operating a multilateral trading facility on which MiFID instruments are traded is a controlled activity.

5. Managing investments

Managing assets belonging to another person, in circumstances involving the exercise of discretion, is a controlled activity if—

(a) the assets consist of or include any investment which is a security or a contractually based investment; or

(b) the arrangements for their management are such that the assets may consist of or include such investments, and either the assets have at any time since 29th April 1988 done so, or the arrangements have at any time (whether before or after that date) been held out as arrangements under which the assets would do so.

6. Safeguarding and administering investments

(1) The activity consisting of both—

(a) the safeguarding of assets belonging to another; and

(b) the administration of those assets,

or arranging for one or more other persons to carry on that activity, is a controlled activity if either the condition in paragraph (a) or (b) of sub-paragraph (2) is met.

(2) The condition is that—

(a) the assets consist of or include any investment which is a security or a contractually based investment; or

(b) the arrangements for their safeguarding and administration are such that the assets may consist of or include investments of the kind mentioned in sub-paragraph (a) and either the assets have at any time since 1st June 1997 done so, or the arrangements have at any time (whether before or after that date) been held out as ones under which such investments would be safeguarded and administered.

(3) For the purposes of this article—

(a) it is immaterial that title to the assets safeguarded and administered is held in uncertificated form;

(b) it is immaterial that the assets safeguarded and administered may be transferred to another person, subject to a commitment by the person safeguarding and administering them, or arranging for their safeguarding and administration, that they will be replaced by equivalent assets at some future date or when so requested by the person to whom they belong.

(4) For the purposes of this article, the following activities do not constitute the administration of assets—

(a) providing information as to the number of units or the value of any assets safeguarded;

(b) converting currency;

(c) receiving documents relating to an investment solely for the purpose of onward transmission to, from or at the direction of the person to whom the investment belongs.

7. Advising on investments

Advising a person is a controlled activity if the advice is—

(a) given to the person in his capacity as an investor or potential investor, or in his capacity as agent for an investor or a potential investor; and

(b) advice on the merits of his doing any of the following (whether as principal or agent)—

(i) buying, selling, subscribing for or underwriting a particular investment which is a security or a contractually based investment; or

(ii) exercising any right conferred by such an investment to buy, sell, subscribe for or underwrite such an investment.

8. Advising on syndicate participation at Lloyd's

Advising a person to become, or continue or cease to be, a member of a particular Lloyd's syndicate is a controlled activity.

9. Providing funeral plan contracts

(1) Entering as provider into a qualifying funeral plan contract is a controlled activity.

(2) A "qualifying funeral plan contract" is a contract under which—

(a) a person ("the customer") makes one or more payments to another person ("the provider");

(b) the provider undertakes to provide, or to secure that another person provides, a funeral in the United Kingdom for the customer (or some other person who is living at the date when the contract is entered into) on his death; and

(c) the provider is a person who carries on the regulated activity specified in article 59 of the Regulated Activities Order.

10. Providing qualifying credit

(1) Providing qualifying credit is a controlled activity.

(2) "Qualifying credit" is a credit provided pursuant to an agreement under which—

(a) the lender is a person who carries on the regulated activity specified in article 61 of the Regulated Activities Order; and

(b) the obligation of the borrower to repay is secured (in whole or in part) on land.

(3) "Credit" includes a cash loan and any other form of financial accommodation.

10A. Arranging qualifying credit etc.

Making arrangements—

(a) for another person to enter as borrower into an agreement for the provision of qualifying credit; or

(b) for a borrower under a regulated mortgage contract, within the meaning of article 61(3) of the Regulated Activities Order, entered into after the coming into force of that article, to vary the terms of that contract in such a way as to vary his obligations under that contract,

is a controlled activity.

10B. Advising on qualifying credit etc.

(1) Advising a person is a controlled activity if the advice is—

(a) given to the person in his capacity as a borrower or potential borrower; and

(b) advice on the merits of his doing any of the following—

(i) entering into an agreement for the provision of qualifying credit, or

(ii) varying the terms of a regulated mortgage contract entered into by him after the coming into force of article 61 of the Regulated Activities Order in such a way as to vary his obligations under that contract.

(2) In this paragraph, "borrower" and "regulated mortgage contract" have the meaning given by article 61(3) of the Regulated Activities Order.

10C. Providing a regulated home reversion plan

Entering into a regulated home reversion plan as plan provider is a controlled activity.

10D. Arranging a regulated home reversion plan

Making arrangements—

(a) for another person to enter as reversion seller or plan provider into a regulated home reversion plan; or

(b) for a reversion seller or a plan provider under a regulated home reversion plan, entered into on or after 6th April 2007 by him, to vary the terms of that plan in such a way as to vary his obligations under that plan,

is a controlled activity.

10E. Advising on a regulated home reversion plan

Advising a person is a controlled activity if the advice is—

(a) given to the person in his capacity as reversion seller, potential reversion seller, plan provider or potential plan provider; and

(b) advice on the merits of his doing either of the following—

(i) entering into a regulated home reversion plan, or

(ii) varying the terms of a regulated home reversion plan, entered into on or after 6th April 2007 by him, in such a way as to vary his obligations under that plan.

10F. Providing a regulated home purchase plan

Entering into a regulated home purchase plan as home purchase provider is a controlled activity.

10G. Arranging a regulated home purchase plan

Making arrangements—

(a) for another person to enter as home purchaser into a regulated home purchase plan; or

(b) for a home purchaser under a regulated home purchase plan, entered into on or after 6th April 2007 by him, to vary the terms of that plan in such a way as to vary his obligations under that plan,

is a controlled activity.

10H. Advising on a regulated home purchase plan

Advising a person is a controlled activity if the advice is—

(a) given to the person in his capacity as home purchaser or potential home purchaser; and

(b) advice on the merits of his doing either of the following—

(i) entering into a regulated home purchase plan, or

(ii) varying the terms of a regulated home purchase plan, entered into on or after 6th April 2007 by him, in such a way as to vary his obligations under that plan.

10I. Providing a regulated sale and rent back agreement

Entering into a regulated sale and rent back agreement as agreement provider is a controlled activity.

10J. Arranging a regulated sale and rent back agreement

Making arrangements—

(a) for another person to enter as agreement seller or agreement provider into a regulated sale and rent back agreement; or

(b) for an agreement seller or an agreement provider under a regulated sale and rent back agreement, entered into on or after 1st July 2009, to vary the terms of that plan in such a way as to vary the obligations of the agreement seller or the agreement provider under that plan,

is a controlled activity.

10K. Advising on a regulated sale and rent back agreement

Advising a person ("A") is a controlled activity if the advice is—

(a) given to A in A's capacity as agreement seller, potential agreement seller, agreement provider or potential agreement provider; and

(b) advice on the merits of A doing either of the following—

(i) entering into a regulated sale and rent back agreement, or

(ii) varying the terms of a regulated sale and rent back agreement, entered into on or after 1st July 2009 by A, in such a way as to vary A's obligations under that agreement.

11. Agreeing to carry on specified kinds of activity

Agreeing to carry on any controlled activity falling within any of paragraphs 3 to 10B (other than paragraph 4A) above is a controlled activity.

PART II

Controlled Investments

12. A deposit.

13. Rights under a contract of insurance.

14.

(1) Shares or stock in the share capital of—

(a) any body corporate (wherever incorporated);

(b) any unincorporated body constituted under the law of a country or territory outside the United Kingdom.

(2) Sub-paragraph (1) includes—

(a) any shares of a class defined as deferred shares for the purposes of section 119 of the Building Societies Act 1986;

(b) any transferable shares in a body incorporated under the law of, or any part of, the United Kingdom relating to industrial and provident societies or credit unions or in a body constituted under the law of another EEA State for purposes equivalent to those of such a body.

(3) But subject to sub-paragraph (2) there are excluded from sub-paragraph (1) shares or stock in the share capital of—

(a) an open-ended investment company;

(b) a building society incorporated under the law of, or any part of, the United Kingdom;

(c) any body incorporated under the law of, or any part of, the United Kingdom relating to industrial and provident societies or credit unions;

(d) any body constituted under the law of an EEA State for purposes equivalent to those of a body falling within paragraph (b) or (c).

15. Instruments creating or acknowledging indebtedness

(1) Subject to sub-paragraph (2), such of the following as do not fall within paragraph . . . 16—

(a) debentures;

(b) debenture stock;

(c) loan stock;

(d) bonds;
(e) certificates of deposit;
(f) any other instrument creating or acknowledging a present or future indebtedness.

(2) If and to the extent that they would otherwise fall within sub-paragraph (1), there are excluded from that sub-paragraph—
(a) any instrument acknowledging or creating indebtedness for, or for money borrowed to defray, the consideration payable under a contract for the supply of goods or services;
(b) a cheque or other bill of exchange, a banker's draft or a letter of credit (but not a bill of exchange accepted by a banker);
(c) a banknote, a statement showing a balance on a current, deposit or saving account, a lease or other disposition of property, a heritable security; and
(d) a contract of insurance;
(e) . . .

(3) An instrument excluded from sub-paragraph (1) of paragraph 16 by paragraph 16(2)(b) is not thereby to be taken to fall within sub-paragraph (1) of this paragraph.

15A. Alternative finance investment bonds

(1) Rights under an alternative finance investment bond, to the extent that they do not fall within paragraph 15 or 16.

(2) For the purposes of this paragraph, arrangements constitute an alternative finance investment bond if—
(a) the arrangements provide for a person ("the bond-holder") to pay a sum of money ("the capital") to another ("the bond-issuer");
(b) the arrangements identify assets, or a class of assets, which the bond-issuer will acquire for the purpose of generating income or gains directly or indirectly ("the bond assets");
(c) the arrangements specify a period at the end of which they cease to have effect ("the bond term");
(d) the bond-issuer undertakes under the arrangements—
(i) to make a repayment in respect of the capital ("the redemption payment") to the bond-holder during or at the end of the bond term (whether or not in instalments); and
(ii) to pay to the bond-holder other payments on one or more occasions during or at the end of the bond term ("the additional payments");
(e) the amount of the additional payments does not exceed an amount which would, at the time at which the bond is issued, be a reasonable commercial return on a loan of the capital; and
(f) the arrangements are a security admitted to—
(i) an official list (in accordance with the provisions of Directive 2001/34/EC of the European Parliament and of the Council on the admission of securities to official stock exchange listing and on information to be published on those securities); or
(ii) trading on a regulated market (within the meaning of Article 4.1(14) of Directive 2004/39/EC of the European Parliament and of the Council on markets in financial instruments) or on a recognised investment exchange (within the meaning of section 285 of the Act).

(3) For the purposes of sub-paragraph (2)—
(a) the bond-issuer may acquire the bond assets before or after the arrangements take effect;
(b) the bond assets may be property of any kind, including rights in relation to property owned by someone other than the bond-issuer;
(c) the identification of the bond assets mentioned in sub-paragraph (2)(b) and the undertakings mentioned in sub-paragraph (2)(d) may (but need not) be described as, or accompanied by a document described as, a declaration of trust;
(d) the reference to a period in sub-paragraph (2)(c) includes any period specified to end upon the redemption of the bond by the bond-issuer;
(e) the bond-holder may (but need not) be entitled under the arrangements to terminate them, or participate in terminating them, before the end of the bond term;

(f) the amount of the additional payments may be—
  (i) fixed at the beginning of the bond term;
  (ii) determined wholly or partly by reference to the value of or income generated by the bond assets; or
  (iii) determined in some other way;

(g) if the amount of the additional payments is not fixed at the beginning of the bond term, the reference in sub-paragraph (2)(e) to the amount of the additional payments is a reference to the maximum amount of the additional payments;

(h) the amount of the redemption payment may (but need not) be subject to reduction in the event of a fall in the value of the bond assets or in the rate of income generated by them; and

(i) entitlement to the redemption payment may (but need not) be capable of being satisfied (whether or not at the option of the bond-issuer or the bond-holder) by the issue or transfer of shares or other securities.

(4) An instrument excluded from sub-paragraph (1) of paragraph 16 by sub-paragraph (2)(b) of that paragraph is not thereby taken to fall within sub-paragraph (1) of this paragraph.

16. Government and public securities

(1) Subject to sub-paragraph (2), loan stock, bonds and other instruments—
  (a) creating or acknowledging indebtedness; and
  (b) issued by or on behalf of a government, local authority (whether in the United Kingdom or elsewhere) or international organisation.

(2) Subject to sub-paragraph (3), there are excluded from sub-paragraph (1)—
  (a) so far as applicable, the instruments mentioned in paragraph 15(2)(a) to (d);
  (b) any instrument creating or acknowledging indebtedness in respect of—
    (i) money received by the Director of Savings as deposits or otherwise in connection with the business of the National Savings Bank;
    (ii) money raised under the National Loans Act 1968 under the auspices of the Director of Savings or treated as so raised by virtue of section 11(3) of the National Debt Act 1972.

(3) Sub-paragraph (2)(a) does not exclude an instrument which meets the requirements set out in paragraphs (a) to (e) of paragraph 15A(2).

17. Instruments giving entitlements to investments

(1) Warrants and other instruments entitling the holder to subscribe for any investment falling within paragraph 14, 15 or 16.

(2) It is immaterial whether the investment to which the entitlement relates is in existence or identifiable.

(3) An investment falling within this paragraph shall not be regarded as falling within paragraph 21, 22 or 23.

18. Certificates representing certain securities

(1) Subject to sub-paragraph (2), certificates or other instruments which confer contractual or property rights (other than rights consisting of an investment of the kind specified by paragraph 21)—
  (a) in respect of any investment of the kind specified by any of paragraphs 14 to 17 being an investment held by a person other than the person on whom the rights are conferred by the certificate or instrument; and
  (b) the transfer of which may be effected without the consent of that person.

(2) There is excluded from sub-paragraph (1) any instrument which confers rights in respect of two or more investments issued by different persons, or in respect of two or more different investments of the kind specified by paragraph 16 and issued by the same person.

19. Units in a collective investment scheme

Units in a collective investment scheme.

20. Rights under a pension scheme

(1) Rights under a stakeholder pension scheme.

(2) Rights under a personal pension scheme.

(3) "Stakeholder pension scheme" and "personal pension scheme" have the meanings given by article 72(4).

21. Options

(1) Options to acquire or dispose of—

(a) a security or contractually based investment (other than one of a kind specified in this paragraph);

(b) currency of the United Kingdom or of any other country or territory;

(c) palladium, platinum, gold or silver; ...

(d) an option to acquire or dispose of an investment falling within this paragraph by virtue of sub-paragraph (a), (b) or (c);

(e) subject to sub-paragraph (4), an option to acquire or dispose of an option to which paragraph 5, 6, 7 or 10 of Section C of Annex I to the markets in financial instruments directive applies

(2) Subject to sub-paragraph (4), options—

(a) to which sub-paragraph (1) does not apply;

(b) which relate to commodities;

(c) which may be settled physically; and

(d) either—

(i) to which paragraph 5 or 6 of Section C of Annex I to the markets in financial instruments directive applies, or

(ii) which in accordance with Article 38 of the Commission Regulation are to be considered as having the characteristics of other derivative financial instruments and not being for commercial purposes, and to which paragraph 7 of Section C of Annex I to the markets in financial instruments directive applies.

(3) Subject to sub-paragraph (4), options—

(a) to which sub-paragraph (1) does not apply;

(b) which may be settled physically; and

(c) to which paragraph 10 of Section C of Annex I to the markets in financial instruments directive (read with the Commission Regulation) applies.

(4) Sub-paragraphs (1)(e), (2) and (3) only apply to options in relation to which—

(a) an investment firm or credit institution is providing or performing investment services and activities on a professional basis,

(b) a management company is providing, in accordance with Article 6(3) of the UCITS directive, the investment service specified in paragraph 4 or 5 of Section A, or the ancillary service specified in paragraph 1 of Section B, of Annex I to the markets in financial instruments directive, or

(c) a market operator is providing the investment service specified in paragraph 8 of Section A of Annex I to the markets in financial instruments directive.

(5) Expressions used in sub-paragraphs (1)(e), (2) and (3) and in the markets in financial instruments directive have the same meaning as in that directive.

22. Futures

(1) Subject to sub-paragraph (2), rights under a contract for the sale of a commodity or property of any other description under which delivery is to be made at a future date and at a price agreed on when the contract is made.

(1A) Subject to sub-paragraph (1D), futures—

(a) to which sub-paragraph (1) does not apply;

(b) which relate to commodities;

(c) which may be settled physically; and

(d) to which paragraph 5 or 6 of Section C of Annex I to the markets in financial instruments directive applies.

(1B) Subject to sub-paragraph (1D), futures and forwards—

(a) to which sub-paragraph (1) does not apply;

(b) which relate to commodities;

(c) which may be settled physically;

(d) which in accordance with Article 38 of the Commission Regulation are to be considered as having the characteristics of other derivative financial instruments and not being for commercial purposes; and

(e) to which paragraph 7 of Section C of Annex I to the markets in financial instruments directive applies.

(1C) Subject to sub-paragraph (1D), futures—

(a) to which sub-paragraph (1) does not apply;

(b) which may be settled physically; and

(c) to which paragraph 10 of Section C of Annex I to the markets in financial instruments directive (read with the Commission Regulation) applies.

(1D) Sub-paragraphs (1A), (1B) and (1C) only apply to futures or forwards in relation to which—

(a) an investment firm or credit institution is providing or performing investment services and activities on a professional basis,

(b) a management company is providing, in accordance with Article 5(3) of the UCITS directive, the investment service specified in paragraph 4 or 5 of Section A, or the ancillary service specified in paragraph 1 of Section B, of Annex I to the markets in financial instruments directive, or

(c) a market operator is providing the investment service specified in paragraph 8 of Section A of Annex I to the markets in financial instruments directive.

(1E) Expressions used in sub-paragraphs (1A) to (1C) and in the markets in financial instruments directive have the same meaning as in that directive.

(2) There are excluded from sub-paragraph (1) rights under any contract which is made for commercial and not investment purposes.

(3) For the purposes of sub-paragraph (2), in considering whether a contract is to be regarded as made for investment purposes or for commercial purposes, the indicators set out in article 84 of the Regulated Activities Order shall be applied in the same way as they are applied for the purposes of that article.

23. Contracts for differences etc.

(1) Subject to sub-paragraph (2), rights under—

(a) a contract for differences; or

(b) any other contract the purpose or pretended purpose of which is to secure a profit or avoid a loss by reference to fluctuations in—

(i) the value or price of property of any description;

(ii) an index or other factor designated for that purpose in the contract.

(2) There are excluded from sub-paragraph (1)—

(a) rights under a contract if the parties intend that the profit is to be secured or the loss is to be avoided by one or more of the parties taking delivery of any property to which the contract relates;

(b) rights under a contract under which money is received by way of deposit on terms that any interest or other return to be paid on the sum deposited will be calculated by reference to fluctuations in an index or other factor;

(c) rights under any contract under which—

(i) money is received by the Director of Savings as deposits or otherwise in connection with the business of the National Savings Bank; or

(ii) money is raised under the National Loans Act 1968 under the auspices of the Director of Savings or treated as so raised by virtue of section 11(3) of the National Debt Act 1972;

(d) rights under a qualifying contract of insurance.

(3) Subject to sub-paragraph (4), derivative instruments for the transfer of credit risk—

(a) to which neither paragraph 21 nor sub-paragraph (1) applies; and

(b) to which paragraph 8 of Section C of Annex I to the markets in financial instruments directive applies.

(4) Sub-paragraph (3) only applies to derivatives in relation to which—

(a) an investment firm or credit institution is providing or performing investment services and activities on a professional basis,

(b) a management company is providing, in accordance with Article 5(3) of the UCITS directive, the investment service specified in paragraph 4 or 5 of Section A, or the ancillary service specified in paragraph 1 of Section B, of Annex I to the markets in financial instruments directive, or

(c) a market operator is providing the investment service specified in paragraph 8 of Section A of Annex I to the markets in financial instruments directive.

(5) "Derivative instruments for the transfer of credit risk" has the same meaning as in the markets in financial instruments directive.

24. Lloyd's syndicate capacity and syndicate membership

(1) The underwriting capacity of a Lloyd's syndicate.

(2) A person's membership (or prospective membership) of a Lloyd's syndicate.

25. Funeral plan contracts

Rights under a qualifying funeral plan contract.

26. Agreements for qualifying credit

Rights under an agreement for qualifying credit.

26A. Regulated home reversion plans

Rights under a regulated home reversion plan.

26B. Regulated home purchase plans

Rights under a regulated home purchase plan.

26C. Regulated sale and rent back agreement

Rights under a regulated sale and rent back agreement.

27. Rights to or interests in investments

(1) Subject to sub-paragraphs (2) and (3), any right to or interest in anything which is specified by any other provision of this Part of this Schedule (other than paragraph 26, 26A, 26B or 26C).

(2) Sub-paragraph (1) does not apply to interests under the trusts of an occupational pension scheme.

(2A) Sub-paragraph (1) does not apply to any right or interest acquired as a result of entering into a funeral plan contract (and for this purpose a "funeral plan contract" is a contract of a kind described in paragraph 9(2)(a) and (b)).

(3) Sub-paragraph (1) does not apply to anything which falls within any other provision of this Part of this Schedule.

28. Interpretation

In this Schedule—

"agreement provider" has the meaning given in paragraph (3) of article 63J of the Regulated Activities Order, read with paragraphs (6) and (7) of that article;

"agreement seller" has the meaning given in article 63J(3) of the Regulated Activities Order;

"buying" includes acquiring for valuable consideration;

"Commission Regulation" means Commission Regulation 1287/2006 of 10 August 2006;
"contract of insurance" has the meaning given in the Regulated Activities Order;
"contractually based investment" means—

(a) rights under a qualifying contract of insurance;
(b) any investment of the kind specified by any of paragraphs 21, 22, 23 and 25;
(c) any investment of the kind specified by paragraph 27 so far as relevant to an investment falling within (a) or (b);

"credit institution" has the meaning given in the Regulated Activities Order;
"home purchase provider" and "home purchaser" have the meanings given in article 63F(3) of the Regulated Activities Order;
"investment firm" has the meaning given in the Regulated Activities Order;
"investment services and activities" has the meaning given in the Regulated Activities Order;
"management company" has the meaning given in the Regulated Activities Order;
"market operator" has the meaning given in the Regulated Activities Order;
"MiFID instrument" has the meaning given in article 25D(2) of the Regulated Activities Order;
"multilateral trading facility" has the meaning given in the Regulated Activities Order;
"occupational pension scheme" has the meaning given by section 1 of the Pension Schemes Act 1993 but with paragraph (b) of the definition omitted;
"plan provider" has the meaning given by paragraph (3) of article 63B of the Regulated Activities Order, read with paragraphs (7) and (8) of that article;
"property" includes currency of the United Kingdom or any other country or territory;
"qualifying funeral plan contract" has the meaning given by paragraph 9;
"regulated home purchase plan" has the meaning given in article 63F(3) of the Regulated Activities Order;
"regulated home reversion plan" and "reversion seller" have the meanings given in article 63B(3) of the Regulated Activities Order;
"regulated sale and rent back agreement" has the meaning given in article 63J(3) of the Regulated Activities Order;
"security" means a controlled investment falling within any of paragraphs 14 to 20 or, so far as relevant to any such investment, paragraph 27;
"selling", in relation to any investment, includes disposing of the investment for valuable consideration, and for these purposes "disposing" includes—

(a) in the case of an investment consisting of rights under a contract—
    (i) surrendering, assigning or converting those rights; or
    (ii) assuming the corresponding liabilities under the contract;
(b) in the case of an investment consisting of rights under other arrangements, assuming the corresponding liabilities under the arrangements; and
(c) in the case of any other investment, issuing or creating the investment or granting the rights or interests of which it consists;

"syndicate" has the meaning given in the Regulated Activities Order.

SCHEDULE 2

Article 10

COUNTRIES AND TERRITORIES

1. The Bailiwick of Guernsey.

2. The Isle of Man.

3. The Commonwealth of Pennsylvania.

4. The State of Iowa.

5. The Bailiwick of Jersey.

SCHEDULE 3

Articles 37, 41, 67, 68 and 69

MARKETS AND EXCHANGES

PART I

Criteria for Relevant EEA Markets

The criteria are—

(a) the head office of the market must be situated in an EEA State; and

(b) the market must be subject to requirements in the EEA State in which its head office is situated as to—

(i) the manner in which it operates;

(ii) the means by which access may be had to the facilities it provides;

(iii) the conditions to be satisfied before an investment may be traded or dealt in by means of its facilities;

(iv) the reporting and publication of transactions effected by means of its facilities.

PART II

Certain Investment Exchanges Operating Relevant EEA Markets

Aktietorget I Norden (Sweden).
Amsterdam Options Exchange (Netherlands).
Athens Stock Exchange (Greece).
Athens Derivative Exchange (Greece).
Barcelona Stock Exchange (Spain).
Bavarian Stock Exchange (Germany).
Belgian Secondary Market for Treasury Certificates (Belgium).
Berlin-Bremen Stock Exchange (Germany).
Bilbao Stock Exchange (Spain).
Böag Borsen AG (Germany).
Bratislava Stock Exchange (Slovakia).
Bucharest Stock Exchange (Romania).
Budapest Stock Exchange (Hungary).
Bulgaria Stock Exchange (Bulgaria).
Copenhagen Stock Exchange (Denmark).
Cyprus Stock Exchange (Cyprus).
Danish Authorised Market Place (Denmark).
Dusseldorf Stock Market (Germany).
EDX (UK).
Eurex Deutschland (Germany).
Euronext Amsterdam (Netherlands).
Euronext Brussels (Belgium).
Euronext Lisbon (Portugal).
Euronext Paris (France).
Frankfurt Stock Exchange (Germany).
Helsinki Stock Exchange and Securities and Derivatives Exchange (Finland).
Irish Stock Exchange (Ireland).
Italian and Foreign Government Bonds Market (Italy).
Italian Stock Exchange (Italy).
Ljubliana Stock Exchange (Slovenia).
London International Financial Futures and Options Exchange (UK).
London Stock Exchange (UK).

Luxembourg Stock Exchange (Luxembourg).
Madrid Stock Exchange (Spain)
Malta Stock Exchange (Malta).
Market for Public Debt (Spain).
MEFF Renta Variable Futures Options Exchange (Spain).
MEFF Renta Fija Equity Futures Exchange (Spain).
MTS Italy (Italy).
MTS Poland (Poland).
MTS Portugal (Portugal).
National Stock Exchange of Lithuania (Lithuania).
Nordic Growth Market (Sweden).
PLUS (UK).
Prague Stock Exchange (Czech Republic).
Riga Stock Exchange (Latvia).
ShareMark (UK).
Stockholm Stock Exchange (Sweden).
Stuttgart Stock Exchange (Germany).
Tallinn Stock Exchange (Estonia).
Valencia Stock Exchange (Spain).
Vienna Stock Exchange (Austria).
Virt-x (UK).
Warsaw Stock Exchange (Poland).

PART III

Certain Non-EEA Investment Exchanges Operating Relevant Markets

America Stock Exchange.
Australian Stock Exchange.
Basler Effektenbourse.
Boston Stock Exchange.
Bourse de Geneve.
Buenos Aires Stock Exchange.
Canadian Venture Exchange.
Chicago Board Options Exchange.
Chicago Stock Exchange.
Effektenborsenverein Zurich.
Fukuoka Stock Exchange.
Hiroshima Stock Exchange.
Iceland Stock Exchange.
Johannesburg Stock Exchange.
Korean Stock Exchange.
Kuala Lumpur Stock Exchange.
Kyoto Stock Exchange.
Midwest Stock Exchange.
Montreal Stock Exchange.
Nagoya Stock Exchange.
NASDAQ.
National Stock Exchange.
New York Stock Exchange.
New Zealand Stock Exchange Limited.
Niigita Stock Exchange.
Osaka Stock Exchange.
Oslo Stock Exchange.

Pacific Stock Exchange.
Philadelphia Stock Exchange.
Sapporo Stock Exchange.
Singapore Stock Exchange.
Stock Exchange of Hong Kong Limited.
Stock Exchange of Thailand.
Tokyo Stock Exchange.
Toronto Stock Exchange.

PART IV

Other Relevant Markets

American Commodity Exchange.
Australian Financial Futures Market.
Chicago Board of Trade.
Chicago Mercantile Exchange.
Chicago Rice and Cotton Exchange.
Commodity Exchange Inc.
Eurex US.
Eurex Zurich.
International Securities Market Association.
International Petroleum Exchange.
Kansas City Board of Trade.
London Metal Exchange.
Minneapolis Grain Exchange.
New York Board of Trade.
New York Futures Exchange.
New York Mercantile Exchange.
New Zealand Futures Exchange.
Pacific Commodity Exchange.
Philadelphia Board of Trade.
Singapore International Monetary Exchange.
Sydney Futures Exchange.
Toronto Futures Exchange.

SCHEDULE 4

Articles 63 and 64

TAKEOVERS OF RELEVANT UNLISTED COMPANIES

PART I

Requirements Relating to the Offer

1. The terms of the offer must be recommended by all the directors of the company other than any director who is—

(a) the person by whom, or on whose behalf, an offer is made ("offeror"); or

(b) a director of the offeror.

2. (1) This paragraph applies to an offer for debentures or for non-equity share capital.

(2) Where, at the date of the offer, shares carrying 50 per cent or less of the voting rights attributable to the equity share capital are held by or on behalf of the offeror, the offer must include or be accompanied by an offer made by the offeror for the rest of the shares comprised in the equity share capital.

3. (1) This paragraph applies to an offer for shares comprised in the equity share capital. (2) Where, at the date of the offer, shares which carry 50 per cent or less of the categories of voting rights described in sub-paragraph (3) are held by or on behalf of the offeror, it must be a condition of the offer that sufficient shares will be acquired or agreed to be acquired by the offeror pursuant to or during the offer so as to result in shares carrying more than 50 per cent of one or both categories of relevant voting rights being held by him or on his behalf.

(3) The categories of voting rights mentioned in sub-paragraph (2) are—

(a) voting rights exercisable in general meetings of the company;

(b) voting rights attributable to the equity share capital.

4. (1) Subject to sub-paragraph (2), the offer must be open for acceptance by every recipient for the period of at least 21 days beginning with the day after the day on which the invitation or inducement in question was first communicated to recipients of the offer.

(2) Sub-paragraph (1) does not apply if the offer is totally withdrawn and all persons are released from any obligation incurred under it.

5. The acquisition of the shares or debentures to which the offer relates must not be conditional upon the recipients approving, or consenting, to any payment or other benefit being made or given to any director or former director of the company in connection with, or as compensation or consideration for—

(a) his ceasing to be a director;

(b) his ceasing to hold any office held in conjunction with any directorship; or

(c) in the case of a former director, his ceasing to hold any office which he held in conjunction with his former directorship and which he continued to hold after ceasing to be a director.

6. The consideration for the shares or debentures must be—

(a) cash; or

(b) in the case of an offeror which is a body corporate other than an open-ended investment company, either cash or shares in, or debentures of, the body corporate or any combination of such cash, shares or debentures.

PART II

Accompanying Material

7. An indication of the identity of the offeror and, if the offer is being made on behalf of another person, the identity of that person.

8. An indication of the fact that the terms of the offer are recommended by all directors of the company other than (if that is the case) any director who is the offeror or a director of the offeror.

9. An indication to the effect that any person who is in any doubt about the invitation or inducement should consult a person authorised under the Act.

10. An indication that, except insofar as the offer may be totally withdrawn and all persons released from any obligation incurred under it, the offer is open for acceptance by every recipient for the period of at least 21 days beginning with the day after the day on which the invitation or inducement in question was first communicated to recipients of the offer.

11. An indication of the date on which the invitation or inducement was first communicated to the recipients of the offer.

12. An indication that the acquisition of the shares or debentures to which the offer relates is not conditional upon the recipients approving, or consenting, to any payment or other benefit being made or given to any director or former director of the company in connection with, or as compensation or consideration for—

(a) his ceasing to be a director;

(b) his ceasing to hold any office held in conjunction with any directorship; or

(c) in the case of a former director, his ceasing to hold any office which he held in conjunction with his former directorship and which he continued to hold after ceasing to be a director.

13. An indication of the place where additional material listed in Part III may be inspected.

14. The audited accounts of the company in respect of the latest accounting reference period for which the period for laying and delivering accounts under the 2006 Act has passed or, if accounts in respect of a later accounting reference period have been delivered under the relevant legislation, as shown in those accounts and not the earlier accounts.

15. Advice to the directors of the company on the financial implications of the offer which is given by a competent person who is independent of and who has no substantial financial interest in the company or the offeror, being advice which gives the opinion of that person in relation to the offer.

16. An indication by the directors of the company, acting as a board, of the following matters—

(a) whether or not there has been any material change in the financial position or prospects of the company since the end of the latest accounting reference period in respect of which audited accounts have been delivered to the relevant registrar of companies under the relevant legislation;

(b) if there has been any such change, the particulars of it;

(c) any interests, in percentage terms, which any of them have in the shares in or debentures of the company . . . ;

(d) any interests, in percentage terms, which any of them have in the shares in or debentures of any offeror which is a body corporate . . .

17. An indication of any material interest which any director has in any contract entered into by the offeror and in any contract entered into by any member of any group of which the offeror is a member.

18. An indication as to whether or not each director intends to accept the offer in respect of his own beneficial holdings in the company.

19. In the case of an offeror which is a body corporate and the shares in or debentures of which are to be the consideration or any part of the consideration for the offer, an indication by the directors of the offeror that the information concerning the offeror and those shares or debentures contained in the document is correct.

20. If the offeror is making the offer on behalf of another person—

(a) an indication by the offeror as to whether or not he has taken any steps to ascertain whether that person will be in a position to implement the offer;

(b) if he has taken any such steps, an indication by him as to what those steps are; and

(c) the offeror's opinion as to whether that person will be in a position to implement the offer.

21. An indication that each of the following—

(a) each of the directors of the company;

(b) the offeror; and

(c) if the offeror is a body corporate, each of the directors of the offeror;

is responsible for the information required by Part I and this Part of this Schedule insofar as it relates to themselves or their respective bodies corporate and that, to the best of their knowledge and belief (having taken all reasonable care to ensure that such is the case) the information is in accordance with the facts and that no material fact has been omitted.

22. The particulars of—

(a) all shares in or debentures of the company; and

(b) all investments falling within paragraph 17, 19 or 21 of Schedule 1 so far as relating to shares in or debentures of the company;

which are held by or on behalf of the offeror or each offeror, if there is more than one, or if none are so held an appropriate negative statement.

23. An indication as to whether or not the offer is conditional upon acceptance in respect of a minimum number of shares or debentures being received and, if the offer is so conditional, what the minimum number is.

24. Where the offer is conditional upon acceptances, an indication of the date which is the latest date on which it can become unconditional.

25. If the offer is, or has become, unconditional an indication of the fact that it will remain open until further notice and that at least 14 days' notice will be given before it is closed.

26. An indication as to whether or not, if circumstances arise in which an offeror is able compulsorily to acquire shares of any dissenting minority under Chapter 3 of Part 28 of the Companies Act 2006 (c. 46), that offeror intends to so acquire those shares.

27. If shares or debentures are to be acquired for cash, an indication of the period within which the payment will be made.

28. (1) Subject to sub-paragraph (2), if the consideration or any part of the consideration for the shares or debentures to be acquired is shares in or debentures of an offeror—

(a) an indication of the nature and particulars of the offeror's business, its financial and trading prospects and its place of incorporation;

(b) the following information, in respect of any offeror which is a body corporate and in respect of the company, for the period of five years immediately preceding the date on which the invitation or inducement in question was first communicated to recipients of the offer—

(i) turnover,
(ii) profit on ordinary activities before and after tax,
(iii) extraordinary items,
(iv) profits and loss, and
(v) the rate per cent of any dividends paid, adjusted as appropriate to take account of relevant changes over the period and the total amount absorbed thereby.

(2) In the case of a body corporate—

(a) which was incorporated during the period of five years immediately preceding the date on which the invitation or inducement in question was first communicated to recipients of the offer; or

(b) which has, at any time during that period, been exempt from the provisions of Part 15 of the 2006 Act relating to the audit of accounts by virtue of section 477 or 480 of that Act . . . ;

the information described in sub-paragraph (1) with respect to that body corporate need be included only in relation to the period since its incorporation or since it last ceased to be exempt from those provisions of Part 15 of the 2006 Act.

29. Particulars of the first dividend in which any such shares or debentures will participate and of the rights attaching to them (including in the case of debentures, rights as to interest) and of any restrictions on their transfer.

30. An indication of the effect of the acceptance on the capital and income position of the holder of the shares in or debentures of the company.

31. Particulars of all material contracts (not being contracts which were entered into in the ordinary course of business) which were entered into by each of the company and the offeror during the period of two years immediately preceding the date on which the invitation or inducement in question was first communicated to recipients of the offer.

32. Particulars of the terms on which shares in or debentures of the company acquired in pursuance of the offer will be transferred and any restrictions on their transfer.

33. An indication as to whether or not it is proposed, in connection with the offer, that any payment or other benefit be made or given to any director or former director of the company in connection with, or as compensation or consideration for—

(a) his ceasing to be a director;

(b) his ceasing to hold any office held in conjunction with any directorship; or

(c) in the case of a former director, his ceasing to hold any office which he held in conjunction with his former directorship and which he continued to hold after ceasing to be a director;

and, if such payments or benefits are proposed, details of each one.

34. An indication as to whether or not there exists any agreement or arrangement between—

(a) the offeror or any person with whom the offeror has an agreement of the kind described in section 824 of the 2006 Act; and

(b) any director or shareholder of the company or any person who has been such a director or shareholder;

at any time during the period of twelve months immediately preceding the date on which the invitation or inducement in question was first communicated to recipients of the offer, being an agreement or arrangement which is connected with or dependent on the offer and, if there is any such agreement or arrangement, particulars of it.

35. An indication whether or not the offeror has reason to believe that there has been any material change in the financial position or prospects of the company since the end of the accounting reference period to which the accounts referred to in paragraph 14 relate, and if the offeror has reason to believe that there has been such a change, the particulars of it.

36. An indication as to whether or not there is any agreement or arrangement whereby any shares or debentures acquired by the offeror in pursuance of the offer will or may be transferred to any other person, together with the names of the parties to any such agreement or arrangement and particulars of all shares and debentures in the company held by such persons.

37. Particulars of any dealings—

(a) in the shares in or debentures of the company; and

(b) if the offeror is a body corporate, in the shares in or debentures of the offeror;

which took place during the period of twelve months immediately preceding the date on which the invitation or inducement in question was first communicated to recipients of the offer and which were entered into by every person who was a director of either the company or the offeror during that period; and, if there have been no such dealings, an indication to that effect.

38. In a case in which the offeror is a body corporate which is required to deliver accounts under the 2006 Act, particulars of the assets and liabilities as shown in its audited accounts in respect of the latest accounting reference period for which the period for laying and delivering accounts under the relevant legislation has passed or, if accounts in respect of a later accounting reference period have been delivered under the relevant legislation, as shown in those accounts and not the earlier accounts.

39. Where valuations of assets are given in connection with the offer, the basis on which the valuation was made and the names and addresses of the persons who valued them and particulars of any relevant qualifications.

40. If any profit forecast is given in connection with the offer, an indication of the assumptions on which the forecast is based.

PART III

Additional Material Available for Inspection

41. The memorandum and articles of association of the company.

42. If the offeror is a body corporate, the memorandum and articles of association of the offeror or, if there is no such memorandum and articles, any instrument constituting or defining the constitution of the offeror and, in either case, if the relevant document is not written in English, a certified translation in English.

43. In the case of a company that does not fall within paragraph 45—

(a) the audited accounts of the company in respect of the last two accounting reference periods for which the laying and delivering of accounts under the 2006 Act has passed; and

(b) if accounts have been delivered to the relevant registrar of companies, in respect of a later accounting reference period, a copy of those accounts.

44. In the case of an offeror which is required to deliver accounts to the registrar of companies and which does not fall within paragraph 45—

(a) the audited accounts of the offeror in respect of the last two accounting reference periods for which the laying and delivering of accounts under the 2006 Act has passed; and

(b) if accounts have been delivered to the relevant registrar of companies in respect of a later accounting reference period, a copy of those accounts.

45. In the case of a company or an offeror—

(a) which was incorporated during the period of three years immediately preceding the date on which the invitation or inducement in question was first communicated to recipients of the offer; or

(b) which has, at any time during that period, been exempt from the provisions of Part 15 of the 2006 Act relating to the audit of accounts by virtue of section 477 or 480 of that Act . . . ;

the information described in whichever is relevant of paragraph 43 or 44 with respect to that body corporate need be included only in relation to the period since its incorporation or since it last ceased to be exempt from those provisions of Part VII of the 1985 Act or Part VIII of the 1986 Order, as the case may be.

46. All existing contracts of service entered into for a period of more than one year between the company and any of its directors and, if the offeror is a body corporate, between the offeror and any of its directors.

47. Any report, letter, valuation or other document any part of which is exhibited or referred to in the information required to be made available by Part II and this Part of this Schedule.

48. If the offer document contains any statement purporting to have been made by an expert, that expert's written consent to the inclusion of that statement.

49. All material contracts (if any) of the company and of the offeror (not, in either case, being contracts which were entered into in the ordinary course of business) which were entered into during the period of two years immediately preceding the date on which the invitation or inducement in question was first communicated to recipients of the offer.

SCHEDULE 5

Articles 48 and 50A

STATEMENTS FOR CERTIFIED HIGH NET WORTH INDIVIDUALS AND SELF-CERTIFIED SOPHISTICATED INVESTORS

PART I

STATEMENT FOR CERTIFIED HIGH NET WORTH INDIVIDUALS

1. The statement to be signed for the purposes of article 48(2) (definition of high net worth individual) must be in the following form and contain the following content—

"Statement for Certified High Net Worth Individual

I declare that I am a certified high net worth individual for the purposes of the Financial Services and Markets Act 2000 (Financial Promotion) Order 2005.

I understand that this means:

(a) I can receive financial promotions that may not have been approved by a person authorised by the Financial Services Authority;

(b) the content of such financial promotions may not conform to rules issued by the Financial Services Authority;

(c) **by signing this statement I may lose significant rights;**

(d) I may have no right to complain to either of the following—

(i) the Financial Services Authority; or

(ii) the Financial Ombudsman Scheme;

(e) I may have no right to seek compensation from the Financial Services Compensation Scheme.

I am a certified high net worth individual because **at least one of the following applies**—

(a) I had, during the financial year immediately preceding the date below, an annual income to the value of £100,000 or more;

(b) I held, throughout the financial year immediately preceding the date below, net assets to the value of £250,000 or more. Net assets for these purposes do not include—

(i) the property which is my primary residence or any loan secured on that residence;

(ii) any rights of mine under a qualifying contract of insurance within the meaning of the Financial Services and Markets Act 2000 (Regulated Activities) Order 2001;

or

(iii) any benefits (in the form of pensions or otherwise) which are payable on the termination of my service or on my death or retirement and to which I am (or my dependants are), or may be, entitled.

I accept that I can lose my property and other assets from making investment decisions based on financial promotions.

I am aware that it is open to me to seek advice from someone who specialises in advising on investments.

Signature Date".

PART II

STATEMENT FOR SELF-CERTIFIED SOPHISTICATED INVESTORS

2. The statement to be signed for the purposes of article 50A(1) (definition of self-certified sophisticated investor) must be in the following form and contain the following content—

"Statement for Self-Certified Sophisticated Investor

I declare that I am a self-certified sophisticated investor for the purposes of the Financial Services and Markets Act (Financial Promotion) Order 2005.

I understand that this means:

(a) I can receive financial promotions that may not have been approved by a person authorised by the Financial Services Authority;

(b) the content of such financial promotions may not conform to rules issued by the Financial Services Authority;

(c) **by signing this statement I may lose significant rights;**

(d) I may have no right to complain to either of the following—

  (i) the Financial Services Authority; or

  (ii) the Financial Ombudsman Scheme;

(e) I may have no right to seek compensation from the Financial Services Compensation Scheme.

I am a self-certified sophisticated investor because **at least one of the following applies—**

(a) I am a member of a network or syndicate of business angels and have been so for at least the last six months prior to the date below;

(b) I have made more than one investment in an unlisted company in the two years prior to the date below;

(c) I am working, or have worked in the two years prior to the date below, in a professional capacity in the private equity sector, or in the provision of finance for small and medium enterprises;

(d) I am currently, or have been in the two years prior to the date below, a director of a company with an annual turnover of at least £1 million.

I accept that I can lose my property and other assets from making investment decisions based on financial promotions.

I am aware that it is open to me to seek advice from someone who specialises in advising on investments.

Signature Date".

Financial Services and Markets Act 2000 (Official Listing of Securities) Regulations 2001

S.I. 2001/2956

PART 1
GENERAL

1. Citation and commencement

These Regulations may be cited as the Financial Services and Markets Act 2000 (Official Listing of Securities) Regulations 2001 and come into force on the day on which section 74(1) comes into force.

2. Interpretation

(1) In these Regulations—

"the Act" means the Financial Services and Markets Act 2000;

"competent authority" is to be construed in accordance with section 72;

"the Financial Promotion Order" means the Financial Services and Markets Act 2000 (Financial Promotion) Order 2001;

"issuer" has the same meaning as is given, for the purposes of section 103(1), in regulation 4 below;

"non-listing prospectus" has the meaning given in section 87(2); and

"the Regulated Activities Order" means the Financial Services and Markets Act 2000 (Regulated Activities) Order 2001.

(2) Any reference in these Regulations to a section or Schedule is, unless otherwise stated or unless the context otherwise requires, a reference to that section of or Schedule to the Act.

PART 2
MISCELLANEOUS MATTERS PRESCRIBED FOR THE PURPOSES OF PART VI OF THE ACT

3. Bodies whose securities may not be listed

For the purposes of section 75(3) (which provides that no application for listing may be entertained in respect of securities issued by a body of a prescribed kind) there are prescribed the following kinds of body—

(a) where the securities are securities within the meaning of the Regulated Activities Order, a private company within the meaning of section 4(1) of the Companies Act 2006;

(b) an old public company within the meaning of section 1 of the Companies Consolidation (Consequential Provisions) Act 1985 or article 3 of the Companies Consolidation (Consequential Provisions) (Northern Ireland) Order 1986.

4. Meaning of "issuer"

(1) For the purposes of section 103(1), "issuer" has the meaning given in this regulation.

(2) In relation to certificates or other instruments falling within article 80 of the Regulated Activities Order (certificates representing certain securities), "issuer" means—

(a) . . .

(b) for all other purposes, the person who issued or is to issue the securities to which the certificates or instruments relate.

(3) In relation to any other securities, "issuer" means the person by whom the securities have been or are to be issued.

5. Meaning of "approved exchange"

For the purposes of paragraph 9 of Schedule 10, "approved exchange" means a recognised investment exchange approved by the Treasury for the purposes of the Public Offers of Securities Regulations 1995 (either generally or in relation to dealings in securities).

PART 3
PERSONS RESPONSIBLE FOR LISTING PARTICULARS, PROSPECTUSES AND NON-LISTING PROSPECTUSES

6. Responsibility for listing particulars

(1) Subject to the following provisions of this Part, for the purposes of Part VI of the Act the persons responsible for listing particulars (including supplementary listing particulars) are—

(a) the issuer of the securities to which the particulars relate;

(b) where the issuer is a body corporate, each person who is a director of that body at the time when the particulars are submitted to the competent authority;

(c) where the issuer is a body corporate, each person who has authorised himself to be named, and is named, in the particulars as a director or as having agreed to become a director of that body either immediately or at a future time;

(d) each person who accepts, and is stated in the particulars as accepting, responsibility for the particulars;

(e) each person not falling within any of the foregoing sub-paragraphs who has authorised the contents of the particulars.

(2) A person is not to be treated as responsible for any particulars by virtue of paragraph (1)(b) above if they are published without his knowledge or consent and on becoming aware of their publication he forthwith gives reasonable public notice that they were published without his knowledge or consent.

(3) When accepting responsibility for particulars under paragraph (1)(d) above or authorising their contents under paragraph (1)(e) above, a person may state that he does so only in relation to certain specified parts of the particulars, or only in certain specified respects, and in such a case he is responsible under paragraph (1)(d) or (e) above—

(a) only to the extent specified; and

(b) only if the material in question is included in (or substantially in) the form and context to which he has agreed.

(4) Nothing in this regulation is to be construed as making a person responsible for any particulars by reason of giving advice as to their contents in a professional capacity.

(5) Where by virtue of this regulation the issuer of any shares pays or is liable to pay compensation under section 90 for loss suffered in respect of shares for which a person has subscribed no account is to be taken of that liability or payment in determining any question as to the amount paid on subscription for those shares or as to the amount paid up or deemed to be paid up on them.

7. Securities issued in connection with takeovers and mergers

(1) This regulation applies where—

(a) listing particulars relate to securities which are to be issued in connection with—

(i) an offer by the issuer (or by a wholly-owned subsidiary of the issuer) for securities issued by another person ("A");

(ii) an agreement for the acquisition by the issuer (or by a wholly-owned subsidiary of the issuer) of securities issued by another person ("A"); or

(iii) any arrangement whereby the whole of the undertaking of another person ("A") is to become the undertaking of the issuer (or of a wholly-owned subsidiary of the issuer, or of a body corporate which will become such a subsidiary by virtue of the arrangement); and

(b) each of the specified persons is responsible by virtue of regulation 6(1)(d) above for any part ("the relevant part") of the particulars relating to A or to the securities or undertaking to which the offer, agreement or arrangement relates.

(2) In paragraph (1)(b) above the "specified persons" are—

(a) A; and

(b) where A is a body corporate—

(i) each person who is a director of A at the time when the particulars are submitted to the competent authority; and

(ii) each other person who has authorised himself to be named, and is named, in the particulars as a director of A.

(3) Where this regulation applies, no person is to be treated as responsible for the relevant part of the particulars under regulation 6(1)(a), (b) or (c) above but without prejudice to his being responsible under regulation 6(1)(d).

(4) In this regulation—

(a) "listing particulars" includes supplementary listing particulars; and

(b) "wholly-owned subsidiary" is to be construed in accordance with section 1159 of the Companies Act 2006 (and, in relation to an issuer which is not a body corporate, means a body corporate which would be a wholly-owned subsidiary of the issuer within the meaning of that section if the issuer were a body corporate).

8. Successor companies under legislation relating to electricity

(1) Where—

(a) the same document contains listing particulars relating to the securities of—

(i) two or more successor companies within the meaning of Part II of the Electricity Act 1989, or

(ii) two or more successor companies within the meaning of Part III of the Electricity (Northern Ireland) Order 1992; and

(b) the responsibility of any person for any information included in the document ("the relevant information") is stated in the document to be confined to its inclusion as part of the particulars relating to the securities of any one of those companies,

that person is not to be treated as responsible, by virtue of regulation 6 above, for the relevant information in so far as it is stated in the document to form part of the particulars relating to the securities of any other of those companies.

(2) "Listing particulars" includes supplementary listing particulars.

9. Specialist securities

(1) This regulation applies where listing particulars relate to securities of a kind specified by listing rules for the purposes of section 82(1)(c), other than securities which are to be issued in the circumstances mentioned in regulation 7(1)(a) above.

(2) No person is to be treated as responsible for the particulars under regulation 6(1)(a), (b) or (c) above but without prejudice to his being responsible under regulation 6(1)(d).

(3) "Listing particulars" includes supplementary listing particulars.

10–12. . . .

Directive 2004/109/EC of the European Parliament and of the Council of 15 December 2004

on the harmonisation of transparency requirements in relation to information about issuers whose securities are admitted to trading on a regulated market and amending Directive 2001/34/EC

THE EUROPEAN PARLIAMENT AND THE COUNCIL OF THE EUROPEAN UNION,

Having regard to the Treaty establishing the European Community, and in particular Articles 44 and 95 thereof,

Having regard to the proposal from the Commission,

Having regard to the opinion of the European Economic and Social Committee,

Having regard to the opinion of the European Central Bank,

Acting in accordance with the procedure laid down in Article 251 of the Treaty,

Whereas:

(1) Efficient, transparent and integrated securities markets contribute to a genuine single market in the Community and foster growth and job creation by better allocation of capital and by reducing costs. The disclosure of accurate, comprehensive and timely information about security issuers builds sustained investor confidence and allows an informed assessment of their business performance and assets. This enhances both investor protection and market efficiency.

(2) To that end, security issuers should ensure appropriate transparency for investors through a regular flow of information. To the same end, shareholders, or natural persons or legal entities holding voting rights or financial instruments that result in an entitlement to acquire existing shares with voting rights, should also inform issuers of the acquisition of or other changes in major holdings in companies so that the latter are in a position to keep the public informed.

(3) The Commission Communication of 11 May 1999, entitled 'Implementing the framework for financial markets: Action Plan', identifies a series of actions that are needed in order to complete the single marketfor financial services. The Lisbon European Council of March 2000 calls for the implementation of that Action Plan by 2005. The Action Plan stresses the need to draw up a Directive upgrading transparency requirements. That need was confirmed by the Barcelona European Council of March 2002.

(4) This Directive should be compatible with the tasks and duties conferred upon the European System of Central Banks (ESCB) and the Member States' central banks by the Treaty and the Statute of the European System of Central Banks and of the European Central Bank; particular attention in this regard needs to be given to the Member States' central banks whose shares are currently admitted to trading on a regulated market, in order to guarantee the pursuit of primary Community law objectives.

(5) Greater harmonisation of provisions of national law on periodic and ongoing information requirements for security issuers should lead to a high level of investor protection throughout the Community. However, this Directive does not affect existing Community legislation on units issued by collective investment undertakings other than the closed-end type, or on units acquired or disposed of in such undertakings.

(6) Supervision of an issuer of shares, or of debt securities the denomination per unit of which is less than EUR 1 000, for the purposes of this Directive, would be best effected by the Member State in which the issuer has its registered office. In that respect, it is vital to ensure consistency with Directive 2003/71/EC of the European Parliament and of the Council of 4 November 2003 on the prospectus to be published when securities are offered to the public or admitted to trading. Along the same lines, some flexibility should be introduced allowing third country issuers and Community companies issuing only securities other than those mentioned above a choice of home Member State.

(7) A high level of investor protection throughout the Community would enable barriers to the admission of securities to regulated markets situated or operating within a Member State to be

removed. Member States other than the home Member State should no longer be allowed to restrict admission of securities to their regulated markets by imposing more stringent requirements on periodic and ongoing information about issuers whose securities are admitted to trading on a regulated market.

(8) The removal of barriers on the basis of the home Member State principle under this Directive should not affect areas not covered by this Directive, such as rights of shareholders to intervene in the management of an issuer. Nor should it affect the home Member State's right to request the issuer to publish, in addition, parts of or all regulated information through newspapers.

(9) Regulation (EC) No 1606/2002 of the European Parliament and of the Council of 19 July 2002 on the application of international accounting standards has already paved the way for a convergence of financial reporting standards throughout the Community for issuers whose securities are admitted to trading on a regulated market and who are required to prepare consolidated accounts. Thus, a specific regime for security issuers beyond the general system for all companies, as laid down in the Company Law Directives, is already established. This Directive builds on this approach with regard to annual and interim financial reporting, including the principle of providing a true and fair view of an issuer's assets, liabilities, financial position and profit or loss. A condensed set of financial statements, as part of a half-yearly financial report, also represents a sufficient basis for giving such a true and fair view of the first six months of an issuer's financial year.

(10) An annual financial report should ensure information over the years once the issuer's securities have been admitted to a regulated market. Making it easier to compare annual financial reports is only of use to investors in securities markets if they can be sure that this information will be published within a certain time after the end of the financial year. As regards debt securities admitted to trading on a regulated market prior to 1 January 2005 and issued by issuers incorporated in a third country, the home Member State may under certain conditions allow issuers not to prepare annual financial reports in accordance with the standards required under this Directive.

(11) This Directive introduces more comprehensive half-yearly financial reports for issuers of shares admitted to trading on a regulated market. This should allow investors to make a more informed assessment of the issuer's situation.

(12) A home Member State may provide for exemptions from half-yearly reporting by issuers of debt securities in the case of:

— credit institutions acting as small-size issuers of debt securities, or

— issuers already existing on the date of the entry into force of this Directive who exclusively issue debt securities unconditionally and irrevocably guaranteed by the home Member State or by one of its regional or local authorities, or

— during a transitional period of ten years, only in respect of those debt securities admitted to trading on a regulated market prior to 1 January 2005 which may be purchased by professional investors only. If such an exemption is given by the home Member State, it may not be extended in respect of any debt securities admitted to a regulated market thereafter.

(13) The European Parliament and the Council welcome the Commission's commitment rapidly to consider enhancing the transparency of the remuneration policies, total remuneration paid, including any contingent or deferred compensation, and benefits in kind granted to each member of administrative, management or supervisory bodies under its Action Plan for 'Modernising Company Law and Enhancing Corporate Governance in the European Union' of 21 May 2003 and the Commission's intention to make a Recommendation on this topic in the near future.

(14) The home Member State should encourage issuers whose shares are admitted to trading on a regulated market and whose principal activities lie in the extractive industry to disclose payments to governments in their annual financial report. The home Member State should also encourage an increase in the transparency of such payments within the framework established at various international financial fora.

(15) This Directive will also make half-yearly reporting mandatory for issuers of only debt securities on regulated markets. Exemptions should only be provided for wholesale markets on the basis of a denomination per unit starting at EUR 50 000, as under Directive 2003/ 71/EC. Where debt securities are issued in another currency, exemptions should only be possible where the denomination per unit in such a currency is, at the date of the issue, at least equivalent to EUR 50 000.

(16) More timely and more reliable information about the share issuer's performance over the financial year also requires a higher frequency of interim information. A requirement should therefore be introduced to publish an interim management statement during the first six months and a second interim management statement during the second six months of a financial year. Share issuers who already publish quarterly financial reports should not be required to publish interim management statements.

(17) Appropriate liability rules, as laid down by each Member State under its national law or regulations, should be applicable to the issuer, its administrative, management or supervisory bodies, or persons responsible within the issuer. Member States should remain free to determine the extent of the liability.

(18) The public should be informed of changes to major holdings in issuers whose shares are traded on a regulated market situated or operating within the Community. This information should enable investors to acquire or dispose of shares in full knowledge of changes in the voting structure; it should also enhance effective control of share issuers and overall market transparency of important capital movements. Information about shares or financial instruments as determined by Article 13, lodged as collateral, should be provided in certain circumstances.

(19) Articles 9 and 10(c) should not apply to shares provided to or by the members of the ESCB in carrying out their functions as monetary authorities provided that the voting rights attached to such shares are not exercised; the reference to a 'short period' in Article 11 should be understood with reference to credit operations carried out in accordance with the Treaty and the European Central Bank (ECB) legal acts, in particular the ECB Guidelines on monetary policy instruments and procedures and TARGET, and to credit operations for the purpose of performing equivalent functions in accordance with national provisions.

(20) In order to avoid unnecessary burdens for certain market participants and to clarify who actually exercises influence over an issuer, there is no need to require notification of major holdings of shares, or other financial instruments as determined by Article 13 that result in an entitlement to acquire shares with regard to market makers or custodians, or of holdings of shares or such financial instruments acquired solely for clearing and settlement purposes, within limits and guarantees to be applied throughout the Community. The home Member State should be allowed to provide limited exemptions as regards holdings of shares in trading books of credit institutions and investment firms.

(21) In order to clarify who is actually a major holder of shares or other financial instruments in the same issuer throughout the Community, parent undertakings should not be required to aggregate their own holdings with those managed by undertakings for collective investment in transferable securities (UCITS) or investment firms, provided that such undertakings or firms exercise voting rights independently from their parent undertakings and fulfil certain further conditions.

(22) Ongoing information to holders of securities admitted to trading on a regulated market should continue to be based on the principle of equal treatment. Such equal treatment only relates to shareholders in the same position and does not therefore prejudice the issue of how many voting rights may be attached to a particular share. By the same token, holders of debt securities ranking pari passu should continue to benefit from equal treatment, even in the case of sovereign debt. Information to holders of shares and/or debt securities in general meetings should be facilitated. In particular, holders of shares and/or debt securities situated abroad should be more actively involved in that they should be able to mandate proxies to act on their behalf. For the same reasons, it should be decided in a general meeting of holders of shares and/or debt securities whether the use of modern information and communication technologies should become a reality.

In that case, issuers should put in place arrangements in order effectively to inform holders of their shares and/or debt securities, insofar as it is possible for them to identify those holders.

(23) Removal of barriers and effective enforcement of new Community information requirements also require adequate control by the competent authority of the home Member State. This Directive should at least provide for a minimum guarantee for the timely availability of such information. For this reason, at least one filing and storage system should exist in each Member State.

(24) Any obligation for an issuer to translate all ongoing and periodic information into all the relevant languages in all the Member States where its securities are admitted to trading does not foster integration of securities markets, but has deterrent effects on cross-border admission of securities to trading on regulated markets. Therefore, the issuer should in certain cases be entitled to provide information drawn up in a language that is customary in the sphere of international finance. Since a particular effort is needed to attract investors from other Member States and third countries, Member States should no longer prevent shareholders, persons exercising voting rights, or holders of financial instruments, from making the required notifications to the issuer in a language that is customary in the sphere of international finance.

(25) Access for investors to information about issuers should be more organised at a Community level in order to actively promote integration of European capital markets. Investors who are not situated in the issuer's home Member State should be put on an equal footing with investors situated in the issuer's home Member State, when seeking access to such information. This could be achieved if the home Member State ensures compliance with minimum quality standards for disseminating information throughout the Community, in a fast manner on a non-discriminatory basis and depending on the type of regulated information in question. In addition, information which has been disseminated should be available in the home Member State in a centralised way allowing a European network to be built up, acces- sible at affordable prices for retail investors, while not leading to unnecessary duplication of filing requirements for issuers. Issuers should benefit from free competition when choosing the media or operators for disseminating information under this Directive.

(26) In order to further simplify investor access to corporate information across Member States, it should be left to the national supervisory authorities to formulate guidelines for setting up electronic networks, in close consultation with the other parties concerned, in particular security issuers, investors, market participants, operators of regulated markets and financial information providers.

(27) So as to ensure the effective protection of investors and the proper operation of regulated markets, the rules relating to information to be published by issuers whose securities are admitted to trading on a regulated market should also apply to issuers which do not have a registered office in a Member State and which do not fall within the scope of Article 48 of the Treaty. It should also be ensured that any additional relevant information about Community issuers or third country issuers, disclosure of which is required in a third country but not in a Member State, is made available to the public in the Community.

(28) A single competent authority should be designated in each Member State to assume final responsibility for supervising compliance with the provisions adopted pursuant to this Directive, as well as for international cooperation. Such an authority should be of an administrative nature, and its independence from economic players should be ensured in order to avoid conflicts of interest. Member States may however designate another competent authority for examining that information referred to in this Directive is drawn up in accordance with the relevant reporting framework and taking appropriate measures in case of discovered infringements; such an authority need not be of an administrative nature.

(29) Increasing cross-border activities require improved cooperation between national competent authorities, including a comprehensive set of provisions for the exchange of information and for precautionary measures. The organisation of the regulatory and supervisory tasks in each Member State should not hinder efficient cooperation between the competent national authorities.

(30) At its meeting on 17 July 2000, the Council set up the Committee of Wise Men on the Regulation of European securities markets. In its final report, that Committee proposed the introduction of new legislative techniques based on a four-level approach, namely essential principles, technical implementing measures, cooperation amongst national securities regulators, and enforcement of Community law. This Directive should confine itself to broad 'framework' principles, while implementing measures to be adopted by the Commission with the assistance of the European Securities Committee established by Commission Decision 2001/528/EC should lay down the technical details.

(31) The Resolution adopted by the Stockholm European Council of March 2001 endorsed the final report of the Committee of Wise Men and the proposed four-level approach to make the regulatory process for Community securities legislation more efficient and transparent.

(32) According to that Resolution, implementing measures should be used more frequently, to ensure that technical provisions can be kept up to date with market and supervisory developments, and deadlines should be set for all stages of implementing rules.

(33) The Resolution of the European Parliament of 5 February 2002 on the implementation of financial services legislation also endorsed the Committee of Wise Men's report, on the basis of the solemn declaration made before the European Parliament the same day by the President of the Commission and the letter of 2 October 2001 addressed by the Internal Market Commissioner to the Chairman of the Parliament's Committee on Economic and Monetary Affairs with regard to safeguards for the European Parliament's role in this process.

(34) The European Parliament should be given a period of three months from the first transmission of draft implementing measures to allow it to examine them and to give its opinion. However, in urgent and duly justified cases, that period may be shortened. If, within that period, a Resolution is passed by the European Parliament, the Commission should re-examine the draft measures.

(35) Technical implementing measures for the rules laid down in this Directive may be necessary to take account of new developments on securities markets. The Commission should accordingly be empowered to adopt implementing measures, provided that they do not modify the essential elements of this Directive and provided that the Commission acts in accordance with the principles set out therein, after consulting the European Securities Committee.

(36) In exercising its implementing powers in accordance with this Directive, the Commission should respect the following principles:

— the need to ensure confidence in financial markets among investors by promoting high standards of transparency in financial markets;
— the need to provide investors with a wide range of competing investments and a level of disclosure and protection tailored to their circumstances;
— the need to ensure that independent regulatory authorities enforce the rules consistently, especially as regards the fight against economic crime;
— the need for high levels of transparency and consultation with all market participants and with the European Parliament and the Council;
— the need to encourage innovation in financial markets if they are to be dynamic and efficient;
— the need to ensure market integrity by close and reactive monitoring of financial innovation;
— the importance of reducing the cost of, and increasing access to, capital;
— the balance of costs and benefits to market participants on a long-term basis, including small and medium-sized businesses and small investors, in any implementing measures;
— the need to foster the international competitiveness of Community financial markets without prejudice to a much-needed extension of international cooperation;
— the need to achieve a level playing field for all market participants by establishing Community-wide regulations wherever appropriate;
— the need to respect differences in national markets where these do not unduly impinge on the coherence of the single market;

— the need to ensure coherence with other Community legislation in this area, as imbalances in information and a lack of transparency may jeopardise the operation of the markets and above all harm consumers and small investors.

(37) In order to ensure that the requirements set out in this Directive or the measures implementing this Directive are fulfilled, any infringement of those requirements or measures should be promptly detected and, if necessary, subject to penalties. To that end, measures and penalties should be sufficiently dissuasive, proportionate and consistently enforced. Member States should ensure that decisions taken by the competent national authorities are subject to the right of appeal to the courts.

(38) This Directive aims to upgrade the current transparency requirements for security issuers and investors acquiring or disposing of major holdings in issuers whose shares are admitted to trading on a regulated market. This Directive replaces some of the requirements set out in Directive 2001/34/EC of the European Parliament and of the Council of 28 May 2001 on the admission of securities to official stock exchange listing and on information to be published on those securities. In order to gather transparency requirements in a single act it is necessary to amend it accordingly. Such an amendment however should not affect the ability of Member States to impose additional requirements under Articles 42 to 63 of Directive 2001/34/EC, which remain valid.

(39) This Directive is in line with Directive 95/46/EC of the European Parliament and of the Council of 24 October 1995 on the protection of individuals with regard to the processing of personal data and on the free movement of such data.

(40) This Directive respects fundamental rights and observes the principles recognised in particular by the Charter of the Fundamental Rights of the European Union.

(41) Since the objectives of this Directive, namely to ensure investor confidence through equivalent transparency throughout the Community and thereby to complete the internal market, cannot be sufficiently achieved by the Member States on the basis of the existing Community legislation and can therefore be better achieved at Community level, the Community may adopt measures, in accordance with the principle of subsidiarity as set out in Article 5 of the Treaty. In accordance with the principle of proportionality, as set out in that Article, this Directive does not go beyond what is necessary in order to achieve these objectives.

(42) The measures necessary for implementing this Directive should be adopted in accordance with Council Decision 1999/468/EC of 28 June 1999 laying down the procedures for the exercise of implementing powers conferred on the Commission,

HAVE ADOPTED THIS DIRECTIVE:

CHAPTER I
GENERAL PROVISIONS

Article 1

Subject matter and scope

1. This Directive establishes requirements in relation to the disclosure of periodic and ongoing information about issuers whose securities are already admitted to trading on a regulated market situated or operating within a Member State.
2. This Directive shall not apply to units issued by collective investment undertakings other than the closed-end type, or to units acquired or disposed of in such collective investment undertakings.
3. Member States may decide not to apply the provisions mentioned in Article 16(3) and in paragraphs 2, 3 and 4 of Article 18 to securities which are admitted to trading on a regulated market issued by them or their regional or local authorities.
4. Member States may decide not to apply Article 17 to their national central banks in their capacity as issuers of shares admitted to trading on a regulated market if this admission took place before 20 January 2005.

Article 2

Definitions

1. For the purposes of this Directive the following definitions shall apply:
   (a) 'securities' means transferable securities as defined in Article 4(1), point 18, of Directive 2004/39/EC of the European Parliament and of the Council of 21 April 2004 on markets in financial instruments with the exception of money-market instruments, as defined in Article 4(1), point 19, of that Directive having a maturity of less than 12 months, for which national legislation may be applicable;
   (b) 'debt securities' means bonds or other forms of transferable securitised debts, with the exception of securities which are equivalent to shares in companies or which, if converted or if the rights conferred by them are exercised, give rise to a right to acquire shares or securities equivalent to shares;
   (c) 'regulated market' means a market as defined in Article 4(1), point 14, of Directive 2004/39/EC;
   (d) 'issuer' means a legal entity governed by private or public law, including a State, whose securities are admitted to trading on a regulated market, the issuer being, in the case of depository receipts representing securities, the issuer of the securities represented;
   (e) 'shareholder' means any natural person or legal entity governed by private or public law, who holds, directly or indirectly:
      (i) shares of the issuer in its own name and on its own account;
      (ii) shares of the issuer in its own name, but on behalf of another natural person or legal entity;
      (iii) depository receipts, in which case the holder of the depository receipt shall be considered as the shareholder of the underlying shares represented by the depository receipts;
   (f) 'controlled undertaking' means any undertaking
      (i) in which a natural person or legal entity has a majority of the voting rights; or
      (ii) of which a natural person or legal entity has the right to appoint or remove a majority of the members of the administrative, management or supervisory body and is at the same time a shareholder in, or member of, the undertaking in question; or
      (iii) of which a natural person or legal entity is a shareholder or member and alone controls a majority of the shareholders' or members' voting rights, respectively, pursuant to an agreement entered into with other shareholders or members of the undertaking in question; or
      (iv) over which a natural person or legal entity has the power to exercise, or actually exercises, dominant influence or control;
   (g) 'collective investment undertaking other than the closed-end type' means unit trusts and investment companies:
      (i) the object of which is the collective investment of capital provided by the public, and which operate on the principle of risk spreading; and
      (ii) the units of which are, at the request of the holder of such units, repurchased or redeemed, directly or indirectly, out of the assets of those undertakings;
   (h) 'units of a collective investment undertaking' means securities issued by a collective investment undertaking and representing rights of the participants in such an undertaking over its assets;
   (i) 'home Member State' means
      (i) in the case of an issuer of debt securities the denomination per unit of which is less than EUR 1 000 or an issuer of shares:
         — where the issuer is incorporated in the Union, the Member State in which it has its registered office;
         — where the issuer is incorporated in a third country, the Member State referred to in point (iii) of Article 2(1)(m) of Directive 2003/71/EC.

The definition of 'home' Member State shall be applicable to debt securities in a currency other than euro, provided that the value of such denomination per unit is, at the date of the issue, less than EUR 1 000, unless it is nearly equivalent to EUR 1 000;

(ii) for any issuer not covered by (i), the Member State chosen by the issuer from among the Member State in which the issuer has its registered office and those Member States which have admitted its securities to trading on a regulated market on their territory. The issuer may choose only one Member State as its home Member State. Its choice shall remain valid for at least three years unless its securities are no longer admitted to trading on any regulated market in the Community;

(j) 'host Member State' means a Member State in which securities are admitted to trading on a regulated market, if different from the home Member State;

(k) 'regulated information' means all information which the issuer, or any other person who has applied for the admission of securities to trading on a regulated market without the issuer's consent, is required to disclose under this Directive, under Article 6 of Directive 2003/6/EC of the European Parliament and of the Council of 28 January 2003 on insider dealing and market manipulation (market abuse), or under the laws, regulations or administrative provisions of a Member State adopted under Article 3(1) of this Directive;

(l) 'electronic means' are means of electronic equipment for the processing (including digital compression), storage and transmission of data, employing wires, radio, optical technologies, or any other electromagnetic means;

(m) 'management company' means a company as defined in Article 1a(2) of Council Directive 85/611/EEC of 20 December 1985 on the coordination of laws, regulations and administrative provisions relating to undertakings for collective investment in transferable securities (UCITS);

(n) 'market maker' means a person who holds himself out on the financial markets on a continuous basis as being willing to deal on own account by buying and selling financial instruments against his proprietary capital at prices defined by him;

(o) 'credit institution' means an undertaking as defined in Article 1(1)(a) of Directive 2000/12/EC of the European Parliament and of the Council of 20 March 2000 relating to the taking up and pursuit of the business of credit institutions;

(p) 'securities issued in a continuous or repeated manner' means debt securities of the same issuer on tap or at least two separate issues of securities of a similar type and/or class.

2. For the purposes of the definition of 'controlled undertaking' in paragraph 1(f)(ii), the holder's rights in relation to voting, appointment and removal shall include the rights of any other undertaking controlled by the shareholder and those of any natural person or legal entity acting, albeit in its own name, on behalf of the shareholder or of any other undertaking controlled by the shareholder.

3. In order to take account of technical developments on financial markets, to specify the requirements and to ensure the uniform application of paragraph 1, the Commission shall adopt, in accordance with Article 27(2a), (2b) and (2c), and subject to the conditions of Articles 27a and 27b, measures concerning the definitions set out in paragraph 1.

The Commission shall, in particular:

(a) establish, for the purposes of paragraph 1(i)(ii), the procedural arrangements in accordance with which an issuer may make the choice of the home Member State;

(b) adjust, where appropriate for the purposes of the choice of the home Member State referred to in paragraph 1(i)(ii), the three-year period in relation to the issuer's track record in the light of any new requirement under Community law concerning admission to trading on a regulated market; and

(c) establish, for the purposes of paragraph 1(l), an indicative list of means which are not to be considered as electronic means, thereby taking into account Annex V to Directive 98/34/EC of the European Parliament and of the Council of 22 June 1998 laying down a procedure for the provision of information in the field of technical standards and regulations and of rules on Information Society services in accordance with the regulatory procedure referred to in Article 27(2).

The measures referred to in points (a) and (b) of the second subparagraph shall be laid down by means of delegated acts in accordance with Article 27(2a), (2b) and (2c), and subject to the conditions of Articles 27a and 27b.

Article 3

Integration of securities markets

1. The home Member State may make an issuer subject to requirements more stringent than those laid down in this Directive.

   The home Member State may also make a holder of shares, or a natural person or legal entity referred to in Articles 10 or 13, subject to requirements more stringent than those laid down in this Directive.

2. A host Member State may not:
   (a) as regards the admission of securities to a regulated market in its territory, impose disclosure requirements more stringent than those laid down in this Directive or in Article 6 of Directive 2003/6/EC;
   (b) as regards the notification of information, make a holder of shares, or a natural person or legal entity referred to in Articles 10 or 13, subject to requirements more stringent than those laid down in this Directive.

CHAPTER II
PERIODIC INFORMATION

Article 4

Annual financial reports

1. The issuer shall make public its annual financial report at the latest four months after the end of each financial year and shall ensure that it remains publicly available for at least five years.

2. The annual financial report shall comprise:
   (a) the audited financial statements;
   (b) the management report; and
   (c) statements made by the persons responsible within the issuer, whose names and functions shall be clearly indicated, to the effect that, to the best of their knowledge, the financial statements prepared in accordance with the applicable set of accounting standards give a true and fair view of the assets, liabilities, financial position and profit or loss of the issuer and the undertakings included in the consolidation taken as a whole and that the management report includes a fair review of the development and performance of the business and the position of the issuer and the undertakings included in the consolidation taken as a whole, together with a description of the principal risks and uncertainties that they face.

3. Where the issuer is required to prepare consolidated accounts according to the Seventh Council Directive 83/349/ EEC of 13 June 1983 on consolidated accounts, the audited financial statements shall comprise such consolidated accounts drawn up in accordance with Regulation (EC) No 1606/2002 and the annual accounts of the parent company drawn up in accordance with the national law of the Member State in which the parent company is incorporated.

   Where the issuer is not required to prepare consolidated accounts, the audited financial statements shall comprise the accounts prepared in accordance with the national law of the Member State in which the company is incorporated.

4. The financial statements shall be audited in accordance with Articles 51 and 51a of the Fourth Council Directive 78/ 660/EEC of 25 July 1978 on the annual accounts of certain types of companies and, if the issuer is required to prepare consolidated accounts, in accordance with Article 37 of Directive 83/349/EEC.

The audit report, signed by the person or persons responsible for auditing the financial statements, shall be disclosed in full to the public together with the annual financial report.

5. The management report shall be drawn up in accordance with Article 46 of Directive 78/660/EEC and, if the issuer is required to prepare consolidated accounts, in accordance with Article 36 of Directive 83/349/EEC.

6. The Commission shall, in accordance with the procedure referred to in Article 27(2), adopt implementing measures in order to take account of technical developments in financial markets and to ensure the uniform application of paragraph 1. The Commission shall in particular specify the technical conditions under which a published annual financial report, including the audit report, is to remain available to the public.

Where appropriate, the Commission may also adapt the five-year period referred to in paragraph 1.

Article 5

Half-yearly financial reports

1. The issuer of shares or debt securities shall make public a half-yearly financial report covering the first six months of the financial year as soon as possible after the end of the relevant period, but at the latest two months thereafter. The issuer shall ensure that the half-yearly financial report remains available to the public for at least five years.

2. The half-yearly financial report shall comprise:

(a) the condensed set of financial statements;

(b) an interim management report; and

(c) statements made by the persons responsible within the issuer, whose names and functions shall be clearly indicated, to the effect that, to the best of their knowledge, the condensed set of financial statements which has been prepared in accordance with the applicable set of accounting standards gives a true and fair view of the assets, liabilities, financial position and profit or loss of the issuer, or the undertakings included in the consolidation as a whole as required under paragraph 3, and that the interim management report includes a fair review of the information required under paragraph 4.

3. Where the issuer is required to prepare consolidated accounts, the condensed set of financial statements shall be prepared in accordance with the international accounting standard applicable to the interim financial reporting adopted pursuant to the procedure provided for under Article 6 of Regulation (EC) No 1606/2002.

Where the issuer is not required to prepare consolidated accounts, the condensed set of financial statements shall at least contain a condensed balance sheet, a condensed profit and loss account and explanatory notes on these accounts. In preparing the condensed balance sheet and the condensed profit and loss account, the issuer shall follow the same principles for recognising and measuring as when preparing annual financial reports.

4. The interim management report shall include at least an indication of important events that have occurred during the first six months of the financial year, and their impact on the condensed set of financial statements, together with a description of the principal risks and uncertainties for the remaining six months of the financial year. For issuers of shares, the interim management report shall also include major related parties transactions.

5. If the half-yearly financial report has been audited, the audit report shall be reproduced in full. The same shall apply in the case of an auditors' review. If the half-yearly financial report has not been audited or reviewed by auditors, the issuer shall make a statement to that effect in its report.

6. The Commission shall adopt, in accordance with Article 27(2) or Article 27(2a), (2b) and (2c), in order to take account of technical developments on financial markets, measures to specify the requirements and ensure the uniform application of paragraphs 1 to 5 of this Article.

The Commission shall, in particular:

(a) specify the technical conditions under which a published half-yearly financial report, including the auditors' review, is to remain available to the public;

(b) clarify the nature of the auditors' review;

(c) specify the minimum content of the condensed balance sheet and profit and loss accounts and explanatory notes on these accounts, where they are not prepared in accordance with the international accounting standards adopted pursuant to the procedure provided for under Article 6 of Regulation (EC) No 1606/2002.

The measures referred to in point (a) shall be adopted in accordance with the regulatory procedure referred to in Article 27(2). The measures referred to in points (b) and (c) shall be laid down by means of delegated acts in accordance with Article 27(2a), (2b) and (2c), and subject to the conditions of Articles 27a and 27b.

Where appropriate, the Commission may also adapt the five-year period referred to in paragraph 1 by means of a delegated act in accordance with Article 27(2a), (2b) and (2c), and subject to the conditions of Articles 27a and 27b.

Article 6

Interim management statements

1. Without prejudice to Article 6 of Directive 2003/6/EC, an issuer whose shares are admitted to trading on a regulated market shall make public a statement by its management during the first six-month period of the financial year and another statement by its management during the second six-month period of the financial year. Such statement shall be made in a period between ten weeks after the beginning and six weeks before the end of the relevant six-month period. It shall contain information covering the period between the beginning of the relevant six-month period and the date of publication of the statement. Such a statement shall provide:
   - an explanation of material events and transactions that have taken place during the relevant period and their impact on the financial position of the issuer and its controlled undertakings, and
   - a general description of the financial position and performance of the issuer and its controlled undertakings during the relevant period.

2. Issuers which, under either national legislation or the rules of the regulated market or of their own initiative, publish quarterly financial reports in accordance with such legislation or rules shall not be required to make public statements by the management provided for in paragraph 1.

3. The Commission shall provide a report to the European Parliament and the Council by 20 January 2010 on the transparency of quarterly financial reporting and statements by the management of issuers to examine whether the information provided meets the objective of allowing investors to make an informed assessment of the financial position of the issuer. Such a report shall include an impact assessment on areas where the Commission considers proposing amendments to this Article.

Article 7

Responsibility and liability

Member States shall ensure that responsibility for the information to be drawn up and made public in accordance with Articles 4, 5, 6 and 16 lies at least with the issuer or its administrative, management or supervisory bodies and shall ensure that their laws, regulations and administrative provisions on liability apply to the issuers, the bodies referred to in this Article or the persons responsible within the issuers.

Article 8

Exemptions

1. Articles 4, 5 and 6 shall not apply to the following issuers:

   (a) a State, a regional or local authority of a State, a public international body of which at least one Member State is a member, the ECB, and Member States' national central banks whether or not they issue shares or other securities; and

   (b) an issuer exclusively of debt securities admitted to trading on a regulated market, the denomination per unit of which is at least EUR 100 000 or, in the case of debt securities denominated in a currency other than euro, the value of such denomination per unit is, at the date of the issue, equivalent to at least EUR 100 000.

2. The home Member State may choose not to apply Article 5 to credit institutions whose shares are not admitted to trading on a regulated market and which have, in a continuous or repeated manner, only issued debt securities provided that the total nominal amount of all such debt securities remains below EUR 100 000 000 and that they have not published a prospectus under Directive 2003/71/EC.

3. The home Member State may choose not to apply Article 5 to issuers already existing at the date of the entry into force of Directive 2003/71/EC which exclusively issue debt securities unconditionally and irrevocably guaranteed by the home Member State or by one of its regional or local authorities, on a regulated market.

4. By way of derogation from paragraph (1)(b), Articles 4, 5 and 6 shall not apply to issuers of exclusively debt securities the denomination per unit of which is at least EUR 50 000 or, in the case of debt securities denominated in a currency other than euro, the value of such denomination per unit is, at the date of the issue, equivalent to at least EUR 50 000, which have already been admitted to trading on a regulated market in the Union before 31 December 2010, for as long as such debt securities are outstanding.

CHAPTER III
ONGOING INFORMATION

SECTION I
INFORMATION ABOUT MAJOR HOLDINGS

Article 9

Notification of the acquisition or disposal of major holdings

1. The home Member State shall ensure that, where a shareholder acquires or disposes of shares of an issuer whose shares are admitted to trading on a regulated market and to which voting rights are attached, such shareholder notifies the issuer of the proportion of voting rights of the issuer held by the shareholder as a result of the acquisition or disposal where that proportion reaches, exceeds or falls below the thresholds of 5 %,10%,15 %,20%,25 %,30%,50 % and 75 %.

   The voting rights shall be calculated on the basis of all the shares to which voting rights are attached even if the exercise thereof is suspended. Moreover this information shall also be given in respect of all the shares which are in the same class and to which voting rights are attached.

2. The home Member States shall ensure that the shareholders notify the issuer of the proportion of voting rights, where that proportion reaches, exceeds or falls below the thresholds provided for in paragraph 1, as a result of events changing the breakdown of voting rights, and on the basis of the information disclosed pursuant to Article 15. Where the issuer is incorporated in a third country, the notification shall be made for equivalent events.

3. The home Member State need not apply:
   (a) the 30 % threshold, where it applies a threshold of one-third;
   (b) the 75 % threshold, where it applies a threshold of two-thirds.

4. This Article shall not apply to shares acquired for the sole purpose of clearing and settling within the usual short settlement cycle, or to custodians holding shares in their custodian capacity provided such custodians can only exercise the voting rights attached to such shares under instructions given in writing or by electronic means.

5. This Article shall not apply to the acquisition or disposal of a major holding reaching or crossing the 5 % threshold by a market maker acting in its capacity of a market maker, provided that:
   (a) it is authorised by its home Member State under Directive 2004/39/EC; and
   (b) it neither intervenes in the management of the issuer concerned nor exerts any influence on the issuer to buy such shares or back the share price.

6. Home Member States under Article 2(1)(i) may provide that voting rights held in the trading book, as defined in Article 2(6) of Council Directive 93/6/EEC of 15 March 1993 on the capital adequacy of investment firms and credit institutions, of a credit institution or investment firm shall not be counted for the purposes of this Article provided that:
   (a) the voting rights held in the trading book do not exceed 5 %, and
   (b) the credit institution or investment firm ensures that the voting rights attaching to shares held in the trading book are not exercised nor otherwise used to intervene in the management of the issuer.
7. The Commission shall adopt, by means of delegated acts in accordance with Article 27(2a), (2b) and (2c), and subject to the conditions of Articles 27a and 27b, measures in order to take account of technical developments on financial markets and to specify the requirements laid down in paragraphs 2, 4 and 5.
   The Commission shall specify, by means of delegated acts in accordance with Article 27(2a), (2b) and (2c), and subject to the conditions of Articles 27a and 27b, the maximum length of the 'short settlement cycle' referred to in paragraph 4 of this Article, as well as the appropriate control mechanisms by the competent authority of the home Member State.
   In addition, the Commission may draw up a list of the events referred to in paragraph 2 of this Article, in accordance with the regulatory procedure referred to in Article 27(2).

Article 10

Acquisition or disposal of major proportions of voting rights

The notification requirements defined in paragraphs 1 and 2 of Article 9 shall also apply to a natural person or legal entity to the extent it is entitled to acquire, to dispose of, or to exercise voting rights in any of the following cases or a combination of them:

(a) voting rights held by a third party with whom that person or entity has concluded an agreement, which obliges them to adopt, by concerted exercise of the voting rights they hold, a lasting common policy towards the management of the issuer in question;
(b) voting rights held by a third party under an agreement concluded with that person or entity providing for the temporary transfer for consideration of the voting rights in question;
(c) voting rights attaching to shares which are lodged as collateral with that person or entity, provided the person or entity controls the voting rights and declares its intention of exercising them;
(d) voting rights attaching to shares in which that person or entity has the life interest;
(e) voting rights which are held, or may be exercised within the meaning of points (a) to (d), by an undertaking controlled by that person or entity;
(f) voting rights attaching to shares deposited with that person or entity which the person or entity can exercise at its discretion in the absence of specific instructions from the shareholders;
(g) voting rights held by a third party in its own name on behalf of that person or entity;
(h) voting rights which that person or entity may exercise as a proxy where the person or entity can exercise the voting rights at its discretion in the absence of specific instructions from the shareholders.

Article 11

1. Articles 9 and 10(c) shall not apply to shares provided to or by the members of the ESCB in carrying out their functions as monetary authorities, including shares provided to or by members of the ESCB under a pledge or repurchase or similar agreement for liquidity granted for monetary policy purposes or within a payment system.
2. The exemption shall apply to the above transactions lasting for a short period and provided that the voting rights attaching to such shares are not exercised.

Article 12

Procedures on the notification and disclosure of major holdings

1. The notification required under Articles 9 and 10 shall include the following information:

(a) the resulting situation in terms of voting rights;
(b) the chain of controlled undertakings through which voting rights are effectively held, if applicable;
(c) the date on which the threshold was reached or crossed; and
(d) the identity of the shareholder, even if that shareholder is not entitled to exercise voting rights under the conditions laid down in Article 10, and of the natural person or legal entity entitled to exercise voting rights on behalf of that shareholder.

2. The notification to the issuer shall be effected as soon as possible, but not later than four trading days, the first of which shall be the day after the date on which the shareholder, or the natural person or legal entity referred to in Article 10,
(a) learns of the acquisition or disposal or of the possibility of exercising voting rights, or on which, having regard to the circumstances, should have learned of it, regardless of the date on which the acquisition, disposal or possibility of exercising voting rights takes effect; or
(b) is informed about the event mentioned in Article 9(2).

3. An undertaking shall be exempted from making the required notification in accordance with paragraph 1 if the notification is made by the parent undertaking or, where the parent undertaking is itself a controlled undertaking, by its own parent undertaking.

4. The parent undertaking of a management company shall not be required to aggregate its holdings under Articles 9 and 10 with the holdings managed by the management company under the conditions laid down in Directive 85/611/ EEC, provided such management company exercises its voting rights independently from the parent undertaking.
However, Articles 9 and 10 shall apply where the parent undertaking, or another controlled undertaking of the parent undertaking, has invested in holdings managed by such management company and the management company has no discretion to exercise the voting rights attached to such holdings and may only exercise such voting rights under direct or indirect instructions from the parent or another controlled undertaking of the parent undertaking.

5. The parent undertaking of an investment firm authorised under Directive 2004/39/EC shall not be required to aggregate its holdings under Articles 9 and 10 with the holdings which such investment firm manages on a client-by-client basis within the meaning of Article 4(1), point 9, of Directive 2004/39/EC, provided that:
— the investment firm is authorised to provide such portfolio management under point 4 of Section A of Annex I to Directive 2004/39/EC;
— it may only exercise the voting rights attached to such shares under instructions given in writing or by electronic means or it ensures that individual portfolio management services are conducted independently of any other services under conditions equivalent to those provided for under Directive 85/611/EEC by putting into place appropriate mechanisms; and
— the investment firm exercises its voting rights independently from the parent undertaking.
However, Articles 9 and 10 shall apply where the parent undertaking, or another controlled undertaking of the parent undertaking, has invested in holdings managed by such investment firm and the investment firm has no discretion to exercise the voting rights attached to such holdings and may only exercise such voting rights under direct or indirect instructions from the parent or another controlled undertaking of the parent undertaking.

6. Upon receipt of the notification under paragraph 1, but no later than three trading days thereafter, the issuer shall make public all the information contained in the notification.

7. A home Member State may exempt issuers from the requirement in paragraph 6 if the information contained in the notification is made public by its competent authority, under the conditions laid down in Article 21, upon receipt of the notification, but no later than three trading days thereafter.

8. In order to take account of technical developments on financial markets and to specify the requirements laid down in paragraphs 1, 2, 4, 5 and 6 of this Article, the Commission shall adopt, in accordance with Article 27(2a), (2b) and (2c), and subject to the conditions of Articles 27a and 27b, measures:
(a) . . .

(b) to determine a calendar of 'trading days' for all Member States;
(c) to establish in which cases the shareholder, or the natural person or legal entity referred to in Article 10, or both, shall effect the necessary notification to the issuer;
(d) to clarify the circumstances under which the shareholder, or the natural person or legal entity referred to in Article 10, should have learned of the acquisition or disposal;
(e) to clarify the conditions of independence to be complied with by management companies and their parent undertakings or by investment firms and their parent undertakings to benefit from the exemptions in paragraphs 4 and 5.

9. In order to ensure the uniform conditions of application of this Article and to take account of technical developments on financial markets, the European Supervisory Authority (European Securities and Markets Authority) (hereinafter 'ESMA'), established by Regulation (EU) No 1095/2010 of the European Parliament and of the Council may develop draft implementing technical standards to establish standard forms, templates and procedures to be used when notifying the required information to the issuer under paragraph 1 of this Article or when filing information under Article 19(3).
Power is conferred on the Commission to adopt the implementing technical standards referred to in the first subparagraph in accordance with Article 15 of Regulation (EU) No 1095/2010.

Article 13

1. The notification requirements laid down in Article 9 shall also apply to a natural person or legal entity who holds, directly or indirectly, financial instruments that result in an entitlement to acquire, on such holder's own initiative alone, under a formal agreement, shares to which voting rights are attached, already issued, of an issuer whose shares are admitted to trading on a regulated market.

2. The Commission shall adopt, by means of delegated acts in accordance with Article 27(2a), (2b) and (2c), and subject to the conditions of Articles 27a and 27b, measures in order to take account of technical developments on financial markets and to specify the requirements laid down in paragraph 1. It shall in particular determine:
(a) the types of financial instruments referred to in paragraph 1 and their aggregation;
(b) the nature of the formal agreement referred to in paragraph 1;
(c) the contents of the notification to be made . . . ;
(d) the notification period;
(e) to whom the notification is to be made.

3. In order to ensure uniform conditions of application of paragraph 1 of this Article and to take account of technical developments on financial markets, ESMA may develop draft implementing technical standards to establish standard forms, templates and procedures to be used when notifying the required information to the issuer under paragraph 1 of this Article or when filing information under Article 19(3).
Power is conferred on the Commission to adopt the implementing technical standards referred to in the first subparagraph in accordance with Article 15 of Regulation (EU) No 1095/2010.

Article 14

1. Where an issuer of shares admitted to trading on a regulated market acquires or disposes of its own shares, either itself or through a person acting in his own name but on the issuer's behalf, the home Member State shall ensure that the issuer makes public the proportion of its own shares as soon as possible, but not later than four trading days following such acquisition or disposal where that proportion reaches, exceeds or falls below the thresholdsof 5 % or 10 % of the voting rights. The proportion shall be calculated on the basis of the total number of shares to which voting rights are attached.

2. The Commission shall adopt, by means of delegated acts in accordance with Article 27(2a), (2b) and (2c), and subject to the conditions of Articles 27a and 27b, measures in order to take account of technical developments on financial markets and to specify the requirements laid down in paragraph 1.

Article 15

For the purpose of calculating the thresholds provided for in Article 9, the home Member State shall at least require the disclosure to the public by the issuer of the total number of voting rights and capital at the end of each calendar month during which an increase or decrease of such total number has occurred.

Article 16

Additional information

1. The issuer of shares admitted to trading on a regulated market shall make public without delay any change in the rights attaching to the various classes of shares, including changes in the rights attaching to derivative securities issued by the issuer itself and giving access to the shares of that issuer.
2. The issuer of securities, other than shares admitted to trading on a regulated market, shall make public without delay any changes in the rights of holders of securities other than shares, including changes in the terms and conditions of these securities which could indirectly affect those rights, resulting in particular from a change in loan terms or in interest rates.
3. The issuer of securities admitted to trading on a regulated market shall make public without delay of new loan issues and in particular of any guarantee or security in respect thereof. Without prejudice to Directive 2003/6/EC, this paragraph shall not apply to a public international body of which at least one Member State is member.

SECTION II
INFORMATION FOR HOLDERS OF SECURITIES ADMITTED TO TRADING ON A REGULATED MARKET

Article 17

Information requirements for issuers whose shares are admitted to trading on a regulated market

1. The issuer of shares admitted to trading on a regulated market shall ensure equal treatment for all holders of shares who are in the same position.
2. The issuer shall ensure that all the facilities and information necessary to enable holders of shares to exercise their rights are available in the home Member State and that the integrity of data is preserved. Shareholders shall not be prevented from exercising their rights by proxy, subject to the law of the country in which the issuer is incorporated. In particular, the issuer shall:
   (a) provide information on the place, time and agenda of meetings, the total number of shares and voting rights and the rights of holders to participate in meetings;
   (b) make available a proxy form, on paper or, where applicable, by electronic means, to each person entitled to vote at a shareholders' meeting, together with the notice concerning the meeting or, on request, after an announcement of the meeting;
   (c) designate as its agent a financial institution through which shareholders may exercise their financial rights; and
   (d) publish notices or distribute circulars concerning the allocation and payment of dividends and the issue of new shares, including information on any arrangements for allotment, subscription, cancellation or conversion.
3. For the purposes of conveying information to shareholders, the home Member State shall allow issuers the use of electronic means, provided such a decision is taken in a general meeting and meets at least the following conditions:
   (a) the use of electronic means shall in no way depend upon the location of the seat or residence of the shareholder or, in the cases referred to in Article 10(a) to (h), of the natural persons or legal entities;
   (b) identification arrangements shall be put in place so that the shareholders, or the natural persons or legal entities entitled to exercise or to direct the exercise of voting rights, are effectively informed;

(c) shareholders, or in the cases referred to in Article 10(a) to (e) the natural persons or legal entities entitled to acquire, dispose of or exercise voting rights, shall be contacted in writing to request their consent for the use of electronic means for conveying information and, if they do not object within a reasonable period of time, their consent shall be deemed to be given. They shall be able to request, at any time in the future, that information be conveyed in writing, and

(d) any apportionment of the costs entailed in the conveyance of such information by electronic means shall be determined by the issuer in compliance with the principle of equal treatment laid down in paragraph 1.

4. The Commission shall adopt, by means of delegated acts in accordance with Article 27(2a), (2b) and (2c), and subject to the conditions of Articles 27a and 27b, measures in order to take account of technical developments on financial markets, to take account of developments in information and communication technology and to specify the requirements laid down in paragraphs 1, 2 and 3. The Commission shall, in particular, specify the types of financial institution through which a shareholder may exercise the financial rights provided for in paragraph 2(c).

Article 18

Information requirements for issuers whose debt securities are admitted to trading on a regulated market

1. The issuer of debt securities admitted to trading on a regulated market shall ensure that all holders of debt securities ranking pari passu are given equal treatment in respect of all the rights attaching to those debt securities.

2. The issuer shall ensure that all the facilities and information necessary to enable debt securities holders to exercise their rights are publicly available in the home Member State and that the integrity of data is preserved. Debt securities holders shall not be prevented from exercising their rights by proxy, subject to the law of country in which the issuer is incorporated. In particular, the issuer shall:

(a) publish notices, or distribute circulars, concerning the place, time and agenda of meetings of debt securities holders, the payment of interest, the exercise of any conversion, exchange, subscription or cancellation rights, and repayment, as well as the right of those holders to participate therein;

(b) make available a proxy form on paper or, where applicable, by electronic means, to each person entitled to vote at a meeting of debt securities holders, together with the notice concerning the meeting or, on request, after an announcement of the meeting; and

(c) designate as its agent a financial institution through which debt securities holders may exercise their financial rights.

3. Where only holders of debt securities whose denomination per unit amounts to at least EUR 100 000 or, in the case of debt securities denominated in a currency other than euro whose denomination per unit is, at the date of the issue, equivalent to at least EUR 100 000, are to be invited to a meeting, the issuer may choose as venue any Member State, provided that all the facilities and information necessary to enable such holders to exercise their rights are made available in that Member State.

The choice referred to in the first subparagraph shall also apply with regard to holders of debt securities whose denomination per unit amounts to at least EUR 50 000 or, in the case of debt securities denominated in a currency other than euro, the value of such denomination per unit is, at the date of the issue, equivalent to at least EUR 50 000, which have already been admitted to trading on a regulated market in the Union before 31 December 2010, for as long as such debt securities are outstanding, provided that all the facilities and information necessary to enable such holders to exercise their rights are made available in the Member State chosen by the issuer.

4. For the purposes of conveying information to debt securities holders, the home Member State, or the Member State chosen by the issuer pursuant to paragraph 3, shall allow issuers the use of

electronic means, provided such a decision is taken in a general meeting and meets at least the following conditions:

(a) the use of electronic means shall in no way depend upon the location of the seat or residence of the debt security holder or of a proxy representing that holder;

(b) identification arrangements shall be put in place so that debt securities holders are effectively informed;

(c) debt securities holders shall be contacted in writing to request their consent for the use of electronic means for conveying information and if they do not object within a reasonable period of time, their consent shall be deemed to be given. They shall be able to request, at any time in the future, that information be conveyed in writing; and

(d) any apportionment of the costs entailed in the conveyance of information by electronic means shall be determined by the issuer in compliance with the principle of equal treatment laid down in paragraph 1.

5. The Commission shall adopt, by means of delegated acts in accordance with Article 27(2a), (2b) and (2c), and subject to the conditions of Articles 27a and 27b, measures in order to take account of technical developments on financial markets, to take account of developments in information and communication technology and to specify the requirements laid down in paragraphs 1 to 4. The Commission shall, in particular, specify the types of financial institution through which a debt security holder may exercise the financial rights provided for in paragraph 2(c).

CHAPTER IV
GENERAL OBLIGATIONS

Article 19

Home Member State control

1. Whenever the issuer, or any person having requested, without the issuer's consent, the admission of its securities to trading on a regulated market, discloses regulated information, it shall at the same time file that information with the competent authority of its home Member State. That competent authority may decide to publish such filed information on its Internet site.

Where an issuer proposes to amend its instrument of incorporation or statutes, it shall communicate the draft amendment to the competent authority of the home Member State and to the regulated market to which its securities have been admitted to trading. Such communication shall be effected without delay, but at the latest on the date of calling the general meeting which is to vote on, or be informed of, the amendment.

2. The home Member State may exempt an issuer from the requirement under paragraph 1 in respect of information disclosed in accordance with Article 6 of Directive 2003/6/EC or Article 12(6) of this Directive.

3. Information to be notified to the issuer in accordance with Articles 9, 10, 12 and 13 shall at the same time be filed with the competent authority of the home Member State.

4. The Commission shall adopt, by means of delegated acts in accordance with Article 27(2a), (2b) and (2c), and subject to the conditions of Articles 27a and 27b, measures in order to specify the requirements laid down in paragraphs 1, 2 and 3.

The Commission shall, in particular, specify the procedure in accordance with which an issuer, a holder of shares or other financial instruments, or a person or entity referred to in Article 10, is to file information with the competent authority of the home Member State under paragraph 1 or 3, respectively, in order to enable filing by electronic means in the home Member State.

Article 20

Languages

1. Where securities are admitted to trading on a regulated market only in the home Member State, regulated information shall be disclosed in a language accepted by the competent authority in the home Member State.

2. Where securities are admitted to trading on a regulated market both in the home Member State and in one or more host Member States, regulated information shall be disclosed:
   (a) in a language accepted by the competent authority in the home Member State; and
   (b) depending on the choice of the issuer, either in a language accepted by the competent authorities of those host Member States or in a language customary in the sphere of international finance.
3. Where securities are admitted to trading on a regulated market in one or more host Member States, but not in the home Member State, regulated information shall, depending on the choice of the issuer, be disclosed either in a language accepted by the competent authorities of those host Member States or in a language customary in the sphere of international finance.
   In addition, the home Member State may lay down in its law, regulations or administrative provisions that the regulated information shall, depending on the choice of the issuer, be disclosed either in a language accepted by its competent authority or in a language customary in the sphere of international finance.
4. Where securities are admitted to trading on a regulated market without the issuer's consent, the obligations under paragraphs 1, 2 and 3 shall be incumbent not upon the issuer, but upon the person who, without the issuer's consent, has requested such admission.
5. Member States shall allow shareholders and the natural person or legal entity referred to in Articles 9, 10 and 13 to notify information to an issuer under this Directive only in a language customary in the sphere of international finance. If the issuer receives such a notification, Member States may not require the issuer to provide a translation into a language accepted by the competent authorities.
6. By way of derogation from paragraphs 1 to 4, where securities whose denomination per unit amounts to at least EUR 100 000 or, in the case of debt securities denominated in a currency other than euro equivalent to at least EUR 100 000 at the date of the issue, are admitted to trading on a regulated market in one or more Member States, regulated information shall be disclosed to the public either in a language accepted by the competent authorities of the home and host Member States or in a language customary in the sphere of international finance, at the choice of the issuer or of the person who, without the issuer's consent, has requested such admission.
   The derogation referred to in the first subparagraph shall also apply to debt securities the denomination per unit of which is at least EUR 50 000 or, in the case of debt securities denominated in a currency other than euro, the value of such denomination per unit is, at the date of the issue, equivalent to at least EUR 50 000, which have already been admitted to trading on a regulated market in one or more Member States before 31 December 2010, for as long as such debt securities are outstanding.
7. If an action concerning the content of regulated information is brought before a court or tribunal in a Member State, responsibility for the payment of costs incurred in the translation of that information for the purposes of the proceedings shall be decided in accordance with the law of that Member State.

Article 21

Access to regulated information

1. The home Member State shall ensure that the issuer, or the person who has applied for admission to trading on a regulated market without the issuer's consent, discloses regulated information in a manner ensuring fast access to such information on a non-discriminatory basis and makes it available to the officially appointed mechanism referred to in paragraph 2. The issuer, or the person who has applied for admission to trading on a regulated market without the issuer's consent, may not charge investors any specific cost for providing the information. The home Member State shall require the issuer to use such media as may reasonably be relied upon for the effective dissemination of information to the public throughout the Community. The home Member State may not impose an obligation to use only media whose operators are established on its territory.

2. The home Member State shall ensure that there is at least one officially appointed mechanism for the central storage of regulated information. These mechanisms should comply with minimum quality standards of security, certainty as to the information source, time recording and easy access by end users and shall be aligned with the filing procedure under Article 19(1).
3. Where securities are admitted to trading on a regulated market in only one host Member State and not in the home Member State, the host Member State shall ensure disclosure of regulated information in accordance with the requirements referred to in paragraph 1.
4. The Commission shall adopt, by means of delegated acts in accordance with Article 27(2a), (2b) and (2c), and subject to the conditions of Articles 27a and 27b, measures to take account of technical developments on financial markets, to take account of developments in information and communication technology and to specify the requirements laid down in paragraphs 1, 2 and 3.
The Commission shall, in particular, specify:
(a) minimum standards for the dissemination of regulated information, as referred to in paragraph 1;
(b) minimum standards for the central storage mechanism as referred to in paragraph 2.
The Commission may also specify and update a list of media for the dissemination of information to the public.

Article 22

Guidelines

1. ESMA shall draw up guidelines, in accordance with Article 16 of Regulation (EU) No 1095/2010, with a view to further facilitating public access to information to be disclosed under Directive 2003/6/ EC, Directive 2003/71/EC and under this Directive.
The aim of those guidelines shall be the creation of:
(a) an electronic network to be set up at national level between national securities regulators, operators of regulated markets and national company registers covered by the First Council Directive 68/151/EEC of 9 March 1968 on coordination of safeguards which, for the protection of the interests of members and others, are required by Member States of companies within the meaning of the second paragraph of Article 48 of the Treaty, with a view to making such safeguards equivalent throughout the Community; and
(b) a single electronic network, or a platform of electronic networks across Member States.
2. The Commission shall review the results achieved under paragraph 1 by 31 December 2006 and may, in accordance with the procedure referred to in Article 27(2), adopt implementing measures to facilitate compliance with Articles 19 and 21.

Article 23

Third countries

1. Where the registered office of an issuer is situated in a third country, the competent authority of the home Member State may exempt that issuer from requirements under Articles 4 to 7, Article 12(6) and Articles 14 to 18, provided that the law of the third country in question lays down equivalent requirements or such an issuer complies with requirements of the law of a third country that the competent authority of the home Member State considers as equivalent.
The competent authority shall then inform ESMA of the exemption granted.
2. By way of derogation from paragraph 1, an issuer whose registered office is in a third country shall be exempted from preparing its financial statement in accordance with Article 4 or Article 5 prior to the financial year starting on or after 1 January 2007, provided such issuer prepares its financial statements in accordance with internationally accepted standards referred to in Article 9 of Regulation (EC) No 1606/ 2002.
3. The competent authority of the home Member State shall ensure that information disclosed in a third country which may be of importance for the public in the Community is disclosed in accordance with Articles 20 and 21, even if such information is not regulated information within the meaning of Article 2(1)(k).

4. In order to ensure the uniform conditions of application of paragraph 1, the Commission shall adopt, in accordance with the procedure referred to in Article 27(2), implementing measures:
   (i) setting up a mechanism ensuring the establishment of equivalence of information required under this Directive, including financial statements and information, required under the law, regulations or administrative provisions of a third country;
   (ii) stating that, by reason of its domestic law, regulations, administrative provisions, or of the practices or procedures based on the international standards set by international organisations, the third country where the issuer is registered ensures the equivalence of the information requirements provided for in this Directive.

   In the context of point (ii) of the first subparagraph, the Commission shall also adopt, by means of delegated acts in accordance with Article 27(2a), (2b) and (2c), and subject to the conditions of Articles 27a and 27b, measures concerning the assessment of standards relevant to the issuers of more than one country.

   The Commission shall, in accordance with the procedure referred to in Article 27(2), take the necessary decisions on the equivalence of accounting standards which are used by third-country issuers under the conditions set out in Article 30(3). If the Commission decides that the accounting standards of a third country are not equivalent, it may allow the issuers concerned to continue using such accounting standards during an appropriate transitional period.

   In the context of the third subparagraph, the Commission shall also adopt, by means of delegated acts in accordance with Article 27(2a), (2b) and (2c), and subject to the conditions of Articles 27a and 27b, measures aimed at establishing general equivalence criteria regarding accounting standards relevant to issuers of more than one country.
5. In order to specify the requirements laid down in paragraph 2, the Commission may adopt, by means of delegated acts in accordance with Article 27(2a), (2b) and (2c), and subject to the conditions of Articles 27a and 27b, measures defining the type of information disclosed in a third country that is of importance to the public in the Union.
6. Undertakings whose registered office is in a third country which would have required an authorisation in accordance with Article 5(1) of Directive 85/611/EEC or, with regard to portfolio management under point 4 of section A of Annex I to Directive 2004/39/EC if it had its registered office or, only in the case of an investment firm, its head office within the Community, shall also be exempted from aggregating holdings with the holdings of its parent undertaking under the requirements laid down in Article 12(4) and (5) provided that they comply with equivalent conditions of independence as management companies or investment firms.
7. In order to take account of technical developments in financial markets and to ensure the uniform application of paragraph 6, the Commission shall, in accordance with the procedure referred to in Article 27(2), adopt implementing measures stating that, by reason of its domestic law, regulations, or administrative provisions, a third country ensures the equivalence of the independence requirements provided for under this Directive and its implementing measures.

   The Commission shall also adopt, by means of delegated acts in accordance with Article 27(2a), (2b) and (2c), and subject to the conditions of Articles 27a and 27b, measures aimed at establishing general equivalence criteria for the purpose of the first subparagraph.
8. ESMA shall assist the Commission in carrying out its tasks under this Article in accordance with Article 33 of Regulation (EU) No 1095/2010.

CHAPTER V
COMPETENT AUTHORITIES

Article 24

Competent authorities and their powers

1. Each Member State shall designate the central authority referred to in Article 21(1) of Directive 2003/71/EC as the central competent administrative authority responsible for carrying out the

obligations provided for in this Directive and for ensuring that the provisions adopted pursuant to this Directive are applied. Member States shall inform the Commission and ESMA accordingly.

However, for the purpose of paragraph 4(h) Member States may designate a competent authority other than the central competent authority referred to in the first subparagraph.

2. Member States may allow their central competent authority to delegate tasks. Except for the tasks referred to in paragraph 4(h), any delegation of tasks relating to the obligations provided for in this Directive and in its implementing measures shall be reviewed five years after the entry into force of this Directive and shall end eight years after the entry into force of this Directive. Any delegation of tasks shall be made in a specific manner stating the tasks to be undertaken and the conditions under which they are to be carried out.

Those conditions shall include a clause requiring the entity in question to be organised in a manner such that conflicts of interest are avoided and information obtained from carrying out the delegated tasks is not used unfairly or to prevent competition. In any case, the final responsibility for supervising compliance with the provisions of this Directive and implementing measures adopted pursuant thereto shall lie with the competent authority designated in accordance with paragraph 1.

3. Member States shall inform the Commission, ESMA in accordance with Article 28(4) of Regulation (EU) No 1095/2010, and competent authorities of other Member States of any arrangements entered into with regard to the delegation of tasks, including the precise conditions for regulating the delegations.

4. Each competent authority shall have all the powers necessary for the performance of its functions. It shall at least be empowered to:

(a) require auditors, issuers, holders of shares or other financial instruments, or persons or entities referred to in Articles 10 or 13, and the persons that control them or are controlled by them, to provide information and documents;

(b) require the issuer to disclose the information required under point (a) to the public by the means and within the time limits the authority considers necessary. It may publish such information on its own initiative in the event that the issuer, or the persons that control it or are controlled by it, fail to do so and after having heard the issuer;

(c) require managers of the issuers and of the holders of shares or other financial instruments, or of persons or entities referred to in Articles 10 or 13, to notify the information required under this Directive, or under national law adopted in accordance with this Directive, and, if necessary, to provide further information and documents;

(d) suspend, or request the relevant regulated market to suspend, trading in securities for a maximum of ten days at a time if it has reasonable grounds for suspecting that the provisions of this Directive, or of national law adopted in accordance with this Directive, have been infringed by the issuer;

(e) prohibit trading on a regulated market if it finds that the provisions of this Directive, or of national law adopted in accordance with this Directive, have been infringed, or if it has reasonable grounds for suspecting that the provisions of this Directive have been infringed;

(f) monitor that the issuer discloses timely information with the objective of ensuring effective and equal access to the public in all Member States where the securities are traded and take appropriate action if that is not the case;

(g) make public the fact that an issuer, or a holder of shares or other financial instruments, or a person or entity referred to in Articles 10 or 13, is failing to comply with its obligations;

(h) examine that information referred to in this Directive is drawn up in accordance with the relevant reporting framework and take appropriate measures in case of discovered infringements; and

(i) carry out on-site inspections in its territory in accordance with national law, in order to verify compliance with the provisions of this Directive and its implementing measures. Where necessary under national law, the competent authority or authorities may use this power by applying to the relevant judicial authority and/or in cooperation with other authorities.

5. Paragraphs 1 to 4 shall be without prejudice to the possibility for a Member State to make separate legal and administrative arrangements for overseas European territories for whose external relations that Member State is responsible.
6. The disclosure to competent authorities by the auditors of any fact or decision related to the requests made by the competent authority under paragraph (4)(a) shall not constitute a breach of any restriction on disclosure of information imposed by contract or by any law, regulation or administrative provi- sion and shall not involve such auditors in liability of any kind.

Article 25

Professional secrecy and cooperation between Member States

1. The obligation of professional secrecy shall apply to all persons who work or who have worked for the competent authority and for entities to which competent authorities may have delegated certain tasks. Information covered by professional secrecy may not be disclosed to any other person or authority except by virtue of the laws, regulations or administrative provisions of a Member State.
2. Competent authorities of the Member States shall cooperate with each other, whenever necessary, for the purpose of carrying out their duties and making use of their powers, whether set out in this Directive or in national law adopted pursuant to this Directive. Competent authorities shall render assistance to competent authorities of other Member States.

2a. The competent authorities may refer to ESMA situations where a request for cooperation has been rejected or has not been acted upon within a reasonable time. Without prejudice to the Article 258 of the Treaty on the Functioning of the European Union (TFEU), ESMA may, in situations referred to in the first sentence, act in accordance with the powers conferred on it under Article 19 of Regulation (EU) No 1095/2010.

2b. The competent authorities shall cooperate with ESMA for the purposes of this Directive, in accordance with Regulation (EU) No 1095/2010.

2c. The competent authorities shall without delay provide ESMA with all information necessary to carry out its duties under this Directive and under Regulation (EU) No 1095/2010, in accordance with Article 35 of that Regulation.

3. Paragraph 1 shall not prevent the competent authorities from exchanging confidential information with, or from transmitting information to, other competent authorities, ESMA and the European Systemic Risk Board (ESRB) established by Regulation (EU) No 1092/2010 of the European Parliament and of the Council of 24 November 2010 on European Union macro-prudential oversight of the financial system and establishing a European Systemic Risk Board. Information thus exchanged shall be covered by the obligation of professional secrecy to which the persons employed or formerly employed by the competent authorities receiving the information are subject.
4. Member States and ESMA in accordance with Article 33 of Regulation (EU) No 1095/2010, may conclude cooperation agreements providing for the exchange of information with the competent authorities or bodies of third countries enabled by their respective legislation to carry out any tasks under this Directive in accordance with Article 24. Member States shall notify ESMA when they conclude cooperation agreements. Such an exchange of information is subject to guarantees of professional secrecy at least equivalent to those referred to in this Article. Such an exchange of information shall be intended for the performance of the supervisory task of the authorities or bodies mentioned. Where the information originates in another Member State, it shall not be disclosed without the express agreement of the competent authorities which disclosed it and, where appropriate, solely for the purposes for which those authorities gave their agreement.

Article 26

Precautionary measures

1. Where the competent authority of a host Member State finds that the issuer or the holder of shares or other financial instruments, or the person or entity referred to in Article 10, has committed

irregularities or infringed its obligations, it shall refer its findings to the competent authority of the home Member State.

2. If, despite the measures taken by the competent authority of the home Member State, or because such measures prove inadequate, the issuer or the security holder persists in infringing the relevant legal or regulatory provisions, the competent authority of the host Member State shall, afterinforming the competent authority of the home Member State, take, in accordance with Article 3(2), all the appropriate measures in order to protect investors. The Commission shall be informed of such measures at the earliest opportunity.

CHAPTER VI
DELEGATED ACTS AND IMPLEMENTING MEASURES

Article 27

Committee procedure

1. The Commission shall be assisted by the European Securities Committee, instituted by Article 1 of Decision 2001/528/ EC.
2. Where reference is made to this paragraph, Articles 5 and 7 of Decision 1999/468/EC shall apply, having regard to the provisions of Article 8 thereof, provided that the implementing measures adopted in accordance with that procedure do not modify the essential provisions of this Directive.
   The period laid down in Article 5(6) of Decision 1999/468/EC shall be set at three months.

2a. The power to adopt the delegated acts referred to in Article 2(3), Article 5(6), Article 9(7), Article 12(8), Article 13(2), Article 14(2), Article 17(4), Article 18(5), Article 19(4), Article 21(4), Article 23(4), Article 23(5) and Article 23(7) shall be conferred on the Commission for a period of 4 years from 4 January 2011. The Commission shall draw up a report in respect of delegated power at the latest 6 months before the end of the four-year period. The delegation of power shall be automatically extended for periods of an identical duration, unless the European Parliament or the Council revokes it in accordance with Article 27a.

2b. As soon as it adopts a delegated act, the Commission shall notify it simultaneously to the European Parliament and to the Council.

2c. The power to adopt delegated acts is conferred on the Commission subject to the conditions laid down in Articles 27a and 27b.

3. By 31 December 2010, and, thereafter, at least every three years, the Commission shall review the provisions concerning its implementing powers and present a report to the European Parliament and to the Council on the functioning of those powers. The report shall examine, in particular, the need for the Commission to propose amendments to this Directive in order to ensure the appropriate scope of the implementing powers conferred on the Commission. The conclusion as to whether or not amendment is necessary shall be accompanied by a detailed statement of reasons. If necessary, the report shall be accompanied by a legislative proposal to amend the provisions conferring implementing powers on the Commission.

Article 27a

Revocation of the delegation

1. The delegation of power referred to in Article 2(3), Article 5(6), Article 9(7), Article 12(8), Article 13(2), Article 14(2), Article 17(4), Article 18(5), Article 19(4) Article 21(4), Article 23(4), Article 23(5) and Article 23(7) may be revoked at any time by the European Parliament or by the Council.
2. The institution which has commenced an internal procedure for deciding whether to revoke a delegation of power shall endeavour to inform the other institution and the Commission within a reasonable time before the final decision is taken, indicating the delegated power which could be subject to revocation.

3. The decision of revocation shall put an end to the delegation of the power specified in that decision. It shall take effect immediately or at a later date specified therein. It shall not affect the validity of the delegated acts already in force. It shall be published in the *Official Journal of the European Union*.

Article 27b

Objections to delegated acts

1. The European Parliament or the Council may object to a delegated act within a period of 3 months from the date of notification. At the initiative of the European Parliament or the Council that period shall be extended by 3 months.
2. If, on the expiry of the period referred to in paragraph 1, neither the European Parliament nor the Council has objected to the delegated act, it shall be published in the *Official Journal of the European Union* and shall enter into force on the date stated therein.
   The delegated act may be published in the *Official Journal of the European Union* and enter into force before the expiry of that period if the European Parliament and the Council have both informed the Commission of their intention not to raise objections.
3. If either the European Parliament or the Council objects to a delegated act within the period referred to in paragraph 1, it shall not enter into force. In accordance with Article 296 TFEU, the institution which objects shall state the reasons for objecting to the delegated act.

Article 28

Penalties

1. Without prejudice to the right of Member States to impose criminal penalties, Member States shall ensure, in conformity with their national law, that at least the appropriate administrative measures may be taken or civil and/or administrative penalties imposed in respect of the persons responsible, where the provisions adopted in accordance with this Directive have not been complied with. Member States shall ensure that those measures are effective, proportionate and dissuasive.
2. Member States shall provide that the competent authority may disclose to the public every measure taken or penalty imposed for infringement of the provisions adopted in accordance with this Directive, save where such disclosure would seriously jeopardise the financial markets or cause disproportionate damage to the parties involved.

Article 29

Right of appeal

Member States shall ensure that decisions taken under laws, regulations, and administrative provisions adopted in accordance with this Directive are subject to the right of appeal to the courts.

CHAPTER VII
TRANSITIONAL AND FINAL PROVISIONS

Article 30

Transitional provisions

1. By way of derogation from Article 5(3) of this Directive, the home Member State may exempt from disclosing financial statements in accordance with Regulation (EC) No 1606/2002 issuers referred to in Article 9 of that Regulation for the financial year starting on or after 1 January 2006.
2. Notwithstanding Article 12(2), a shareholder shall notify the issuer at the latest two months after the date in Article 31(1) of the proportion of voting rights and capital it holds, in accordance with Articles 9, 10 and 13, with issuers at that date, unless it has already made a notification containing equivalent information before that date.

Notwithstanding Article 12(6), an issuer shall in turn disclose the information received in those notifications no later than three months after the date in Article 31(1).

3. Where an issuer is incorporated in a third country, the home Member State may exempt such issuer only in respect of those debt securities which have already been admitted to trading on a regulated market in the Community prior to 1 January 2005 from drawing up its financial statements in accordance with Article 4(3) and its management report in accordance with Article 4(5) as long as
   (a) the competent authority of the home Member State acknowledges that annual financial statements prepared by issuers from such a third country give a true and fair view of the issuer's assets and liabilities, financial position and results;
   (b) the third country where the issuer is incorporated has not made mandatory the application of international accounting standards referred to in Article 2 of Regulation (EC) No 1606/2002; and
   (c) the Commission has not taken any decision in accordance with Article 23(4)(ii) as to whether there is an equivalence between the abovementioned accounting standards and
      — the accounting standards laid down in the law, regulations or administrative provisions of the third country where the issuer is incorporated, or
      — the accounting standards of a third country such an issuer has elected to comply with.
4. The home Member State may exempt issuers only in respect of those debt securities which have already been admitted to trading on a regulated market in the Community prior to 1 January 2005 from disclosing half-yearly financial report in accordance with Article 5 for 10 years following 1 January 2005, provided that the home Member State had decided to allow such issuers to benefit from the provisions of Article 27 of Directive 2001/34/EC at the point of admission of those debt securities.

Article 31

Transposition

1. Member States shall take the necessary measures to comply with this Directive by 20 January 2007. They shall forthwith inform the Commission thereof.
   When Member States adopt these measures, they shall contain a reference to this Directive or shall be accompanied by such reference on the occasion of their official publication. The methods of making such reference shall be laid down by Member States.
2. Where Member States adopt measures pursuant to Articles 3(1), 8(2), 8(3), 9(6) or 30, they shall immediately communicate those measures to the Commission and to the other Member States.

Article 32

Amendments

With effect from the date specified in Article 31(1), Directive 2001/34/EC shall be amended as follows:

(1) In Article 1, points (g) and (h) shall be deleted;
(2) Article 4 shall be deleted;
(3) In Article 6, paragraph 2 shall be deleted;
(4) In Article 8, paragraph 2 shall be replaced by the following:
   '2. Member States may make the issuers of securities admitted to official listing subject to additional obligations, provided that those additional obligations apply generally for all issuers or for individual classes of issuers';
(5) Articles 65 to 97 shall be deleted;
(6) Articles 102 and 103 shall be deleted;
(7) In Article 107(3), the second subparagraph shall be deleted;
(8) In Article 108, paragraph 2 shall be amended as follows:
   (a) in point (a), the words 'periodic information to be published by the companies of which shares are admitted' shall be deleted;
   (b) point (b) shall be deleted;

(c) point (c)(iii) shall be deleted;

(d) point (d) shall be deleted.

References made to the repealed provisions shall be construed as being made to the provisions of this Directive.

Article 33

Review

The Commission shall by 30 June 2009 report on the operation of this Directive to the European Parliament and to the Council including the appropriateness of ending the exemption for existing debt securities after the 10-year period as provided for by Article 30(4) and its potential impact on the European financial markets.

Article 34

Entry into force

This Directive shall enter into force on the twentieth day following that of its publication in the Official Journal of the European Union.

Article 35

Addressees

This Directive is addressed to the Member States

Done at Strasbourg, 15 December 2004

Criminal Justice Act 1993

1996 c. 36

An Act . . . to amend and restate the law about insider dealing in securities . . .

[27th July 1993]

PART V
INSIDER DEALING

The offence of insider dealing

52. The offence

(1) An individual who has information as an insider is guilty of insider dealing if, in the circumstances mentioned in subsection (3), he deals in securities that are price-affected securities in relation to the information.

(2) An individual who has information as an insider is also guilty of insider dealing if—

(a) he encourages another person to deal in securities that are (whether or not that other knows it) price-affected securities in relation to the information, knowing or having reasonable cause to believe that the dealing would take place in the circumstances mentioned in subsection (3); or

(b) he discloses the information, otherwise than in the proper performance of the functions of his employment, office or profession, to another person.

(3) The circumstances referred to above are that the acquisition or disposal in question occurs on a regulated market, or that the person dealing relies on a professional intermediary or is himself acting as a professional intermediary.

(4) This section has effect subject to section 53.

53. Defences

(1) An individual is not guilty of insider dealing by virtue of dealing in securities if he shows—

(a) that he did not at the time expect the dealing to result in a profit attributable to the fact that the information in question was price-sensitive information in relation to the securities, or

(b) that at the time he believed on reasonable grounds that the information had been disclosed widely enough to ensure that none of those taking part in the dealing would be prejudiced by not having the information, or

(c) that he would have done what he did even if he had not had the information.

(2) An individual is not guilty of insider dealing by virtue of encouraging another person to deal in securities if he shows—

(a) that he did not at the time expect the dealing to result in a profit attributable to the fact that the information in question was price-sensitive information in relation to the securities, or

(b) that at the time he believed on reasonable grounds that the information had been or would be disclosed widely enough to ensure that none of those taking part in the dealing would be prejudiced by not having the information, or

(c) that he would have done what he did even if he had not had the information.

(3) An individual is not guilty of insider dealing by virtue of a disclosure of information if he shows—

(a) that he did not at the time expect any person, because of the disclosure, to deal in securities in the circumstances mentioned in subsection (3) of section 52; or

(b) that, although he had such an expectation at the time, he did not expect the dealing to result in a profit attributable to the fact that the information was price-sensitive information in relation to the securities.

(4) Schedule 1 (special defences) shall have effect.

(5) The Treasury may by order amend Schedule 1.

(6) In this section references to a profit include references to the avoidance of a loss.

Interpretation

54. Securities to which Part V applies

(1) This Part applies to any security which—

(a) falls within any paragraph of Schedule 2; and

(b) satisfies any conditions applying to it under an order made by the Treasury for the purposes of this subsection;

and in the provisions of this Part (other than that Schedule) any reference to a security is a reference to a security to which this Part applies.

(2) The Treasury may by order amend Schedule 2.

55. "Dealing" in securities

(1) For the purposes of this Part, a person deals in securities if—

(a) he acquires or disposes of the securities (whether as principal or agent); or

(b) he procures, directly or indirectly, an acquisition or disposal of the securities by any other person.

(2) For the purposes of this Part, "acquire", in relation to a security, includes—

(a) agreeing to acquire the security; and

(b) entering into a contract which creates the security.

(3) For the purposes of this Part, "dispose", in relation to a security, includes—

(a) agreeing to dispose of the security; and

(b) bringing to an end a contract which created the security.

(4) For the purposes of subsection (1), a person procures an acquisition or disposal of a security if the security is acquired or disposed of by a person who is—

(a) his agent,

(b) his nominee, or

(c) a person who is acting at his direction,

in relation to the acquisition or disposal.

(5) Subsection (4) is not exhaustive as to the circumstances in which one person may be regarded as procuring an acquisition or disposal of securities by another.

56. "Inside information", etc

(1) For the purposes of this section and section 57, "inside information" means information which—

(a) relates to particular securities or to a particular issuer of securities or to particular issuers of securities and not to securities generally or to issuers of securities generally;

(b) is specific or precise;

(c) has not been made public; and

(d) if it were made public would be likely to have a significant effect on the price of any securities.

(2) For the purposes of this Part, securities are "price-affected securities" in relation to inside information, and inside information is "price-sensitive information" in relation to securities, if and only if the information would, if made public, be likely to have a significant effect on the price of the securities.

(3) For the purposes of this section "price" includes value.

57. "Insiders"

(1) For the purposes of this Part, a person has information as an insider if and only if—

(a) it is, and he knows that it is, inside information, and

(b) he has it, and knows that he has it, from an inside source.

(2) For the purposes of subsection (1), a person has information from an inside source if and only if—

(a) he has it through—

(i) being a director, employee or shareholder of an issuer of securities; or

(ii) having access to the information by virtue of his employment, office or profession; or

(b) the direct or indirect source of his information is a person within paragraph (a).

58. Information "made public"

(1) For the purposes of section 56, "made public", in relation to information, shall be construed in accordance with the following provisions of this section; but those provisions are not exhaustive as to the meaning of that expression.

(2) Information is made public if—

(a) it is published in accordance with the rules of a regulated market for the purpose of informing investors and their professional advisers;

(b) it is contained in records which by virtue of any enactment are open to inspection by the public;

(c) it can be readily acquired by those likely to deal in any securities—

(i) to which the information relates, or

(ii) of an issuer to which the information relates; or

(d) it is derived from information which has been made public.

(3) Information may be treated as made public even though—

(a) it can be acquired only by persons exercising diligence or expertise;

(b) it is communicated to a section of the public and not to the public at large;

(c) it can be acquired only by observation;

(d) it is communicated only on payment of a fee; or

(e) it is published only outside the United Kingdom.

59. "Professional intermediary"

(1) For the purposes of this Part, a "professional intermediary" is a person—

(a) who carries on a business consisting of an activity mentioned in subsection (2) and who holds himself out to the public or any section of the public (including a section of the public constituted by persons such as himself) as willing to engage in any such business; or

(b) who is employed by a person falling within paragraph (a) to carry out any such activity.

(2) The activities referred to in subsection (1) are—

(a) acquiring or disposing of securities (whether as principal or agent); or

(b) acting as an intermediary between persons taking part in any dealing in securities.

(3) A person is not to be treated as carrying on a business consisting of an activity mentioned in subsection (2)—

(a) if the activity in question is merely incidental to some other activity not falling within subsection (2); or

(b) merely because he occasionally conducts one of those activities.

(4) For the purposes of section 52, a person dealing in securities relies on a professional intermediary if and only if a person who is acting as a professional intermediary carries out an activity mentioned in subsection (2) in relation to that dealing.

60. Other interpretation provisions

(1) For the purposes of this Part, "regulated market" means any market, however operated, which, by an order made by the Treasury, is identified (whether by name or by reference to criteria prescribed by the order) as a regulated market for the purposes of this Part.

(2) For the purposes of this Part an "issuer", in relation to any securities, means any company, public sector body or individual by which or by whom the securities have been or are to be issued.

(3) For the purposes of this Part—

(a) "company" means any body (whether or not incorporated and wherever incorporated or constituted) which is not a public sector body; and

(b) "public sector body" means—

(i) the government of the United Kingdom, of Northern Ireland or of any country or territory outside the United Kingdom;

(ii) a local authority in the United Kingdom or elsewhere;
(iii) any international organisation the members of which include the United Kingdom or another member State;
(iv) the Bank of England; or
(v) the central bank of any sovereign State.

(4) For the purposes of this Part, information shall be treated as relating to an issuer of securities which is a company not only where it is about the company but also where it may affect the company's business prospects.

Miscellaneous

61. Penalties and prosecution

(1) An individual guilty of insider dealing shall be liable—
(a) on summary conviction, to a fine not exceeding the statutory maximum or imprisonment for a term not exceeding six months or to both; or
(b) on conviction on indictment, to a fine or imprisonment for a term not exceeding seven years or to both.

(2) Proceedings for offences under this Part shall not be instituted in England and Wales except by or with the consent of—
(a) the Secretary of State; or
(b) the Director of Public Prosecutions.

(3) In relation to proceedings in Northern Ireland for offences under this Part, subsection (2) shall have effect as if the reference to the Director of Public Prosecutions were a reference to the Director of Public Prosecutions for Northern Ireland.

62. Territorial scope of offence of insider dealing

(1) An individual is not guilty of an offence falling within subsection (1) of section 52 unless—
(a) he was within the United Kingdom at the time when he is alleged to have done any act constituting or forming part of the alleged dealing;
(b) the regulated market on which the dealing is alleged to have occurred is one which, by an order made by the Treasury, is identified (whether by name or by reference to criteria prescribed by the order) as being, for the purposes of this Part, regulated in the United Kingdom; or
(c) the professional intermediary was within the United Kingdom at the time when he is alleged to have done anything by means of which the offence is alleged to have been committed.

(2) An individual is not guilty of an offence falling within subsection (2) of section 52 unless—
(a) he was within the United Kingdom at the time when he is alleged to have disclosed the information or encouraged the dealing; or
(b) the alleged recipient of the information or encouragement was within the United Kingdom at the time when he is alleged to have received the information or encouragement.

63. Limits on section 52

(1) Section 52 does not apply to anything done by an individual acting on behalf of a public sector body in pursuit of monetary policies or policies with respect to exchange rates or the management of public debt or foreign exchange reserves.

(2) No contract shall be void or unenforceable by reason only of section 52.

64. Orders

(1) Any power under this Part to make an order shall be exercisable by statutory instrument.

(2) No order shall be made under this Part unless a draft of it has been laid before and approved by a resolution of each House of Parliament.

(3) An order under this Part—
(a) may make different provision for different cases; and

(b) may contain such incidental, supplemental and transitional provisions as the Treasury consider expedient.

…

SCHEDULE 1

SPECIAL DEFENCES

Section 53(4)

Market makers

1.— (1) An individual is not guilty of insider dealing by virtue of dealing in securities or encouraging another person to deal if he shows that he acted in good faith in the course of—

(a) his business as a market maker, or

(b) his employment in the business of a market maker.

(2) A market maker is a person who—

(a) holds himself out at all normal times in compliance with the rules of a regulated market or an approved organisation as willing to acquire or dispose of securities; and

(b) is recognised as doing so under those rules.

(3) In this paragraph "approved organisation" means an international securities self-regulating organisation approved by the Treasury under any relevant order under section 22 of the Financial Services and Markets Act 2000.

Market information

2.— (1) An individual is not guilty of insider dealing by virtue of dealing in securities or encouraging another person to deal if he shows that—

(a) the information which he had as an insider was market information; and

(b) it was reasonable for an individual in his position to have acted as he did despite having that information as an insider at the time.

(2) In determining whether it is reasonable for an individual to do any act despite having market information at the time, there shall, in particular, be taken into account—

(a) the content of the information;

(b) the circumstances in which he first had the information and in what capacity; and

(c) the capacity in which he now acts.

3. An individual is not guilty of insider dealing by virtue of dealing in securities or encouraging another person to deal if he shows—

(a) that he acted—

(i) in connection with an acquisition or disposal which was under consideration or the subject of negotiation, or in the course of a series of such acquisitions or disposals; and

(ii) with a view to facilitating the accomplishment of the acquisition or disposal or the series of acquisitions or disposals; and

(b) that the information which he had as an insider was market information arising directly out of his involvement in the acquisition or disposal or series of acquisitions or disposals.

4. For the purposes of paragraphs 2 and 3 market information is information consisting of one or more of the following facts—

(a) that securities of a particular kind have been or are to be acquired or disposed of, or that their acquisition or disposal is under consideration or the subject of negotiation;

(b) that securities of a particular kind have not been or are not to be acquired or disposed of;

(c) the number of securities acquired or disposed of or to be acquired or disposed of or whose acquisition or disposal is under consideration or the subject of negotiation;

(d) the price (or range of prices) at which securities have been or are to be acquired or disposed of or the price (or range of prices) at which securities whose acquisition or disposal is under consideration or the subject of negotiation may be acquired or disposed of;

(e) the identity of the persons involved or likely to be involved in any capacity in an acquisition or disposal.

Price stabilisation

5.— (1) An individual is not guilty of insider dealing by virtue of dealing in securities or encouraging another person to deal if he shows that he acted in conformity with the price stabilisation rules or with the relevant provisions of Commission Regulation (EC) No. 2273/2003 of 22 December 2003 implementing Directive 2003/6/EC of the European Parliament and of the Council as regards exemptions for buy-back programmes and stabilisation of financial instruments.

(2) "Price stabilisation rules" means rules made under section 137Q of the Financial Services and Markets Act 2000.

SCHEDULE 2

SECURITIES

Section 54

Shares

1. Shares and stock in the share capital of a company ("shares").

Debt securities

2. Any instrument creating or acknowledging indebtedness which is issued by a company or public sector body, including, in particular, debentures, debenture stock, loan stock, bonds and certificates of deposit ("debt securities").

Warrants

3. Any right (whether conferred by warrant or otherwise) to subscribe for shares or debt securities ("warrants").

Depositary receipts

4.— (1) The rights under any depositary receipt.

(2) For the purposes of sub-paragraph (1) a "depositary receipt" means a certificate or other record (whether or not in the form of a document)—

(a) which is issued by or on behalf of a person who holds any relevant securities of a particular issuer; and

(b) which acknowledges that another person is entitled to rights in relation to the relevant securities or relevant securities of the same kind.

(3) In sub-paragraph (2) "relevant securities" means shares, debt securities and warrants.

Options

5. Any option to acquire or dispose of any security falling within any other paragraph of this Schedule.

Futures

6.— (1) Rights under a contract for the acquisition or disposal of relevant securities under which delivery is to be made at a future date and at a price agreed when the contract is made.

(2) In sub-paragraph (1)—

(a) the references to a future date and to a price agreed when the contract is made include references to a date and a price determined in accordance with terms of the contract; and

(b) "relevant securities" means any security falling within any other paragraph of this Schedule.

Contracts for differences

7.— (1) Rights under a contract which does not provide for the delivery of securities but whose purpose or pretended purpose is to secure a profit or avoid a loss by reference to fluctuations in—

(a) a share index or other similar factor connected with relevant securities;

(b) the price of particular relevant securities; or

(c) the interest rate offered on money placed on deposit.

(2) In sub-paragraph (1) "relevant securities" means any security falling within any other paragraph of this Schedule.

Financial Services Act 2012

2012 c. 21

An Act to amend the Bank of England Act 1998, the Financial Services and Markets Act 2000 and the Banking Act 2009; to make other provision about financial services and markets; to make provision about the exercise of certain statutory functions relating to building societies, friendly societies and other mutual societies; to amend section 785 of the Companies Act 2006; to make provision enabling the Director of Savings to provide services to other public bodies; and for connected purposes.

[19th December 2012]

PART 7
OFFENCES RELATING TO FINANCIAL SERVICES

89. Misleading statements

(1) Subsection (2) applies to a person ("P") who—

(a) makes a statement which P knows to be false or misleading in a material respect,

(b) makes a statement which is false or misleading in a material respect, being reckless as to whether it is, or

(c) dishonestly conceals any material facts whether in connection with a statement made by P or otherwise.

(2) P commits an offence if P makes the statement or conceals the facts with the intention of inducing, or is reckless as to whether making it or concealing them may induce, another person (whether or not the person to whom the statement is made)—

(a) to enter into or offer to enter into, or to refrain from entering or offering to enter into, a relevant agreement, or

(b) to exercise, or refrain from exercising, any rights conferred by a relevant investment.

(3) In proceedings for an offence under subsection (2) brought against a person to whom that subsection applies as a result of paragraph (a) of subsection (1), it is a defence for the person charged ("D") to show that the statement was made in conformity with—

(a) price stabilising rules,

(b) control of information rules, or

(c) the relevant provisions of Commission Regulation (EC) No 2273/2003 of 22 December 2003 implementing Directive 2003/6/EC of the European Parliament and of the Council as regards exemptions for buy-back programmes and stabilisation of financial instruments.

(4) Subsections (1) and (2) do not apply unless—

(a) the statement is made in or from, or the facts are concealed in or from, the United Kingdom or arrangements are made in or from the United Kingdom for the statement to be made or the facts to be concealed,

(b) the person on whom the inducement is intended to or may have effect is in the United Kingdom, or

(c) the agreement is or would be entered into or the rights are or would be exercised in the United Kingdom.

90. Misleading impressions

(1) A person ("P") who does any act or engages in any course of conduct which creates a false or misleading impression as to the market in or the price or value of any relevant investments commits an offence if—

(a) P intends to create the impression, and

(b) the case falls within subsection (2) or (3) (or both).

(2) The case falls within this subsection if P intends, by creating the impression, to induce another person to acquire, dispose of, subscribe for or underwrite the investments or to refrain from doing so or to exercise or refrain from exercising any rights conferred by the investments.

(3) The case falls within this subsection if—

(a) P knows that the impression is false or misleading or is reckless as to whether it is, and

(b) P intends by creating the impression to produce any of the results in subsection (4) or is aware that creating the impression is likely to produce any of the results in that subsection.

(4) Those results are—

(a) the making of a gain for P or another, or

(b) the causing of loss to another person or the exposing of another person to the risk of loss.

(5) References in subsection (4) to gain or loss are to be read in accordance with subsections (6) to (8).

(6) "Gain" and "loss"—

(a) extend only to gain or loss in money or other property of any kind;

(b) include such gain or loss whether temporary or permanent.

(7) "Gain" includes a gain by keeping what one has, as well as a gain by getting what one does not have.

(8) "Loss" includes a loss by not getting what one might get, as well as a loss by parting with what one has.

(9) In proceedings brought against any person ("D") for an offence under subsection (1) it is a defence for D to show—

(a) to the extent that the offence results from subsection (2), that D reasonably believed that D's conduct would not create an impression that was false or misleading as to the matters mentioned in subsection (1),

(b) that D acted or engaged in the conduct—

(i) for the purpose of stabilising the price of investments, and

(ii) in conformity with price stabilising rules,

(c) that D acted or engaged in the conduct in conformity with control of information rules, or

(d) that D acted or engaged in the conduct in conformity with the relevant provisions of Commission Regulation (EC) No 2273/2003 of 22 December 2003 implementing Directive 2003/6/EC of the European Parliament and of the Council as regards exemptions for buy-back programmes and stabilisation of financial instruments.

(10) This section does not apply unless—

(a) the act is done, or the course of conduct is engaged in, in the United Kingdom, or

(b) the false or misleading impression is created there.

91. Misleading statements etc in relation to benchmarks

(1) A person ("A") who makes to another person ("B") a false or misleading statement commits an offence if—

(a) A makes the statement in the course of arrangements for the setting of a relevant benchmark,

(b) A intends that the statement should be used by B for the purpose of the setting of a relevant benchmark, and

(c) A knows that the statement is false or misleading or is reckless as to whether it is.

(2) A person ("C") who does any act or engages in any course of conduct which creates a false or misleading impression as to the price or value of any investment or as to the interest rate appropriate to any transaction commits an offence if—

(a) C intends to create the impression,

(b) the impression may affect the setting of a relevant benchmark,

(c) C knows that the impression is false or misleading or is reckless as to whether it is, and

(d) C knows that the impression may affect the setting of a relevant benchmark.

(3) In proceedings for an offence under subsection (1), it is a defence for the person charged ("D") to show that the statement was made in conformity with—

(a) price stabilising rules,
(b) control of information rules, or
(c) the relevant provisions of Commission Regulation (EC) No 2273/2003 of 22 December 2003 implementing Directive 2003/6/EC of the European Parliament and of the Council as regards exemptions for buy-back programmes and stabilisation of financial instruments.

(4) In proceedings brought against any person ("D") for an offence under subsection (2) it is a defence for D to show—
(a) that D acted or engaged in the conduct—
(i) for the purpose of stabilising the price of investments, and
(ii) in conformity with price stabilising rules,
(b) that D acted or engaged in the conduct in conformity with control of information rules, or
(c) that D acted or engaged in the conduct in conformity with the relevant provisions of Commission Regulation (EC) No 2273/2003 of 22 December 2003 implementing Directive 2003/6/EC of the European Parliament and of the Council as regards exemptions for buy-back programmes and stabilisation of financial instruments.

(5) Subsection (1) does not apply unless the statement is made in or from the United Kingdom or to a person in the United Kingdom.

(6) Subsection (2) does not apply unless—
(a) the act is done, or the course of conduct is engaged in, in the United Kingdom, or
(b) the false or misleading impression is created there.

92. Penalties

(1) A person guilty of an offence under this Part is liable—
(a) on summary conviction, to imprisonment for a term not exceeding the applicable maximum term or a fine not exceeding the statutory maximum, or both;
(b) on conviction on indictment, to imprisonment for a term not exceeding 7 years or a fine, or both.

(2) For the purpose of subsection (1)(a) "the applicable maximum term" is—
(a) in England and Wales, 12 months (or 6 months, if the offence was committed before the commencement of section 154(1) of the Criminal Justice Act 2003);
(b) in Scotland, 12 months;
(c) in Northern Ireland, 6 months.

93. Interpretation of Part 7

(1) This section has effect for the interpretation of this Part.

(2) "Investment" includes any asset, right or interest.

(3) "Relevant agreement" means an agreement—
(a) the entering into or performance of which by either party constitutes an activity of a kind specified in an order made by the Treasury, and
(b) which relates to a relevant investment.

(4) "Relevant benchmark" means a benchmark of a kind specified in an order made by the Treasury.

(5) "Relevant investment" means an investment of a kind specified in an order made by the Treasury.

(6) Schedule 2 to FSMA 2000 (except paragraphs 25 and 26) applies for the purposes of subsections (3) and (5) with references to section 22 of that Act being read as references to each of those subsections.

(7) Nothing in Schedule 2 to FSMA 2000, as applied by subsection (6), limits the power conferred by subsection (3) or (5).

(8) "Price stabilising rules" and "control of information rules" have the same meaning as in FSMA 2000.

(9) In this section "benchmark" has the meaning given in section 22(6) of FSMA 2000.

94. Affirmative procedure for certain orders

(1) This section applies to the first order made under section 93.

(2) This section also applies to any subsequent order made under that section which contains a statement by the Treasury that the effect of the proposed order would include one or more of the following—

(a) that an activity which is not specified for the purposes of subsection (3)(a) of that section would become one so specified,

(b) that an investment which is not a relevant investment would become a relevant investment;

(c) that a benchmark which is not a relevant benchmark would become a relevant benchmark.

(3) A statutory instrument containing (alone or with other provisions) an order to which this section applies may not be made unless a draft of the instrument has been laid before Parliament and approved by a resolution of each House.

95. Consequential repeal

Section 397 of FSMA 2000 (which relates to misleading statements and practices and is superseded by the provisions of this Part) is repealed.

The City Code on Takeovers and Mergers (Introduction and General Principles)

INTRODUCTION

1 OVERVIEW

The Panel on Takeovers and Mergers (the "Panel") is an independent body, established in 1968, whose main functions are to issue and administer the City Code on Takeovers and Mergers (the "Code") and to supervise and regulate takeovers and other matters to which the Code applies in accordance with the rules set out in the Code. It has been designated as the supervisory authority to carry out certain regulatory functions in relation to takeovers pursuant to the Directive on Takeover Bids (2004/25/EC) (the "Directive"). Its statutory functions are set out in and under Chapter 1 of Part 28 of the Companies Act 2006 (as amended by The Companies Act 2006 (Amendment of Schedule 2) (No 2) Order 2009) (the "Act"). Rules are set out in the Code (including this Introduction, the General Principles, the Definitions and the Rules (and the related Notes and Appendices)) and the Rules of Procedure of the Hearings Committee. These rules may be changed from time to time, and rules may also be set out in other documents as specified by the Panel. Statutory rules also apply to the Isle of Man, Jersey and Guernsey: see sections 14, 15 and 16 respectively for more details. . . .

Further information relating to the Panel and the Code can be found on the Panel's website at www.thetakeoverpanel.org.uk. The Code is also available on the Panel's website.

2 THE CODE

Save for sections 2(c) and (d) (which each set out a rule), this section gives an overview of the nature and purpose of the Code.

(a) Nature and purpose of the Code

The Code is designed principally to ensure that shareholders in an offeree company are treated fairly and are not denied an opportunity to decide on the merits of a takeover and that shareholders in the offeree company of the same class are afforded equivalent treatment by an offeror. The Code also provides an orderly framework within which takeovers are conducted. In addition, it is designed to promote, in conjunction with other regulatory regimes, the integrity of the financial markets.

The Code is not concerned with the financial or commercial advantages or disadvantages of a takeover. These are matters for the company offeree and its shareholders. In addition, it is not the purpose of the Code either to facilitate or to impede takeovers. Nor is the Code concerned with those issues, such as competition policy, which are the responsibility of government and other bodies.

The Code has been developed since 1968 to reflect the collective opinion of those professionally involved in the field of takeovers as to appropriate business standards and as to how fairness to offeree company shareholders and an orderly framework for takeovers can be achieved. Following the implementation of the Directive by means of the Act, the rules set out in the Code have a statutory basis in relation to the United Kingdom and comply with the relevant requirements of the Directive. The rules set out in the Code also have a statutory basis in relation to the Isle of Man, Jersey and Guernsey: see sections 14, 15 and 16 respectively. . . .

(b) General Principles and Rules

The Code is based upon a number of General Principles, which are essentially statements of standards of commercial behaviour. These General Principles are the same as the general principles set out in Article 3 of the Directive. They apply to takeovers and other matters to which the Code applies. They are expressed in broad general terms and the Code does not define the precise extent of, or the limitations on, their application. They are applied in accordance with their spirit in order to achieve their underlying purpose.

In addition to the General Principles, the Code contains a series of rules. Although most of the rules are expressed in less general terms than the General Principles, they are not framed in technical language and, like the General Principles, are to be interpreted to achieve their underlying purpose. Therefore, their spirit must be observed as well as their letter.

(c) Derogations and Waivers

The Panel may derogate or grant a waiver to a person from the application of a rule (provided, in the case of a transaction and rule subject to the requirements of the Directive, that the General Principles are respected) either:

(i) in the circumstances set out in the rule; or

(ii) in other circumstances where the Panel considers that the particular rule would operate unduly harshly or in an unnecessarily restrictive or burdensome or otherwise inappropriate manner (in which case a reasoned decision will be given).

(d) Transitional provisions for offers which are not takeover bids under the Directive

In relation to any offer which is not a "takeover bid" within the meaning given in the Directive, anything done (or not done) with respect to a rule set out in the Code as in force before 6 April 2007 shall have effect from 6 April 2007 as done (or not done) with respect to that rule of the Code as in force from 6 April 2007 and any reference in the Code to a rule of the Code shall be construed as including a reference to that rule as in force before 6 April 2007.

These transitional provisions do not apply to the Channel Islands or the Isle of Man.

3 COMPANIES, TRANSACTIONS AND PERSONS SUBJECT TO THE CODE

This section (except for sections 3(d) and (e)) sets out the rules as to the companies, transactions and persons to which the Code applies.

(a) Companies

(i) UK, Channel Islands and Isle of Man registered and traded companies

The Code applies to all offers (not falling within paragraph (iii) below) for companies and Societas Europaea (and, where appropriate, statutory and chartered companies) which have their registered offices* in the United Kingdom, the Channel Islands or the Isle of Man if any of their securities are admitted to trading on a regulated market in the United Kingdom or on any stock exchange in the Channel Islands or the Isle of Man.

(ii) Other companies

The Code also applies to all offers (not falling within paragraph (i) above or paragraph (iii) below) for public and private companies† and Societas Europaea (and, where appropriate, statutory and chartered companies) which have their registered offices* in the United Kingdom, the Channel Islands or the Isle of Man and which are considered by the Panel to have their place of central management and control in the United Kingdom, the Channel Islands or the Isle of Man, but in relation to private companies only when:—

(A) any of their securities have been admitted to the Official List at any time during the 10 years prior to the relevant date; or

(B) dealings and/or prices at which persons were willing to deal in any of their securities have been published on a regular basis for a continuous period of at least six months in the 10 years prior to the relevant date, whether via a newspaper, electronic price quotation system or otherwise; or

---

* In the case of a UK unregistered company, the reference to "registered office" shall be read as a reference to the company's principal office in the UK.

† With respect to either a company having its registered office in the Isle of Man and which is incorporated there under the Companies Act 2006 (an Act of Tynwald), or a company having its registered office in Guernsey, the company will be treated as being subject to the Code only when any of the criteria in (A) to (D) of paragraph (ii) apply.

(C) any of their securities have been subject to a marketing arrangement as described in section 693(3)(b) of the Act at any time during the 10 years prior to the relevant date; or

(D) they were required to file a prospectus for the issue of securities with the registrar of companies or any other relevant authority in the United Kingdom, the Channel Islands or the Isle of Man or to have a prospectus approved by the UKLA at any time during the 10 years prior to the relevant date.

In each case, the relevant date is the date on which an announcement is made of a proposed or possible offer for the company or the date on which some other event occurs in relation to the company which has significance under the Code.

The Panel appreciates that the provisions of the Code may not be appropriate to all statutory and chartered companies referred to in paragraphs (i) and (ii) above or to all private companies falling within the categories listed in paragraph (ii) above and may accordingly apply the Code with a degree of flexibility in suitable cases.

(iii) Shared jurisdiction – UK and other EEA registered and traded companies

The Code also applies (to the extent described below) to offers for the following companies:

(A) a company which has its registered office* in the United Kingdom whose securities are admitted to trading on a regulated market in one or more member states of the European Economic Area but not on a regulated market in the United Kingdom;

(B) a company which has its registered office in another member state of the European Economic Area whose securities are admitted to trading only on a regulated market in the United Kingdom; and

(C) a company which has its registered office in another member state of the European Economic Area whose securities are admitted to trading on regulated markets in more than one member state of the European Economic Area including the United Kingdom, but not on a regulated market in the member state of the European Economic Area in which it has its registered office, if:

(I) the securities of the company were first admitted to trading only in the United Kingdom; or

(II) the securities of the company are simultaneously admitted to trading on more than one regulated market on or after 20 May 2006, if the company notifies the Panel and the relevant regulatory authorities on the first day of trading that it has chosen the Panel to regulate it; or

(III) the Panel is the supervisory authority pursuant to the second paragraph of Article 4(2)(c) of the Directive.

A company referred to in paragraphs (C)(II) or (III) must notify a Regulatory Information Service of the selection of the Panel to regulate it without delay.

The provisions of the Code which will apply to such offers shall be determined by the Panel on the basis set out in Article 4(2)(e) of the Directive. In summary, this means that:

- in cases falling within paragraph (A) above, the Code will apply in respect of matters relating to the information to be provided to the employees of the offeree company and matters relating to company law (in particular the percentage of voting rights which confers control and any derogation from the obligation to launch an offer, as well as the conditions under which the board of the offeree company may undertake any action which might result in the frustration of an offer) ("employee information and company law matters"); in relation to matters relating to the consideration offered (in particular the price) and matters relating to the offer procedure (in particular the information on the offeror's decision to make an offer, the contents of the offer document and the disclosure of the offer) ("consideration and procedural matters"), the rules of the supervisory authority of the member state determined in accordance with Article 4(2)(b) and (c) of the Directive as the relevant supervisory authority will apply; and
- in cases falling within paragraphs (B) or (C) above, the Code will apply in respect of consideration and procedural matters; in relation to employee information and company law

* In the case of a UK unregistered company, the reference to "registered office" shall be read as a reference to the company's principal office in the UK.

matters, the rules of the supervisory authority in the member state where the offeree company has its registered office will apply.

(iv) Open-ended investment companies

The Code does not apply to offers for open-ended investment companies as defined in Article 1(2) of the Directive.

(b) Transactions

In cases falling within paragraphs (a)(i) or (ii) above, the Code is concerned with regulating takeover bids and merger transactions of the relevant companies, however effected, including by means of statutory merger or scheme of arrangement (as defined in the Definitions Section). The Code is also concerned with regulating other transactions (including offers by a parent company for shares in its subsidiary, dual holding company transactions, new share issues, share capital reorganisations and offers to minority shareholders) which have as their objective or potential effect (directly or indirectly) obtaining or consolidating control of the relevant companies, as well as partial offers (including tender offers pursuant to Appendix 5) to shareholders for securities in the relevant companies. The Code also applies to unitisation proposals which are in competition with another transaction to which the Code applies.

In cases falling within paragraph (a)(iii) above, "offers" means only any public offer (other than by the company itself) made to the holders of the company's securities to acquire those securities (whether mandatory or voluntary) which follows or has as its objective the acquisition of control of the company concerned.

The Code applies to all the above transactions at whatever stage of their implementation, including possible transactions which have not yet been announced.

References in the Code to "takeovers" and "offers" include all transactions subject to the Code as referred to in this section.

The Code does not apply to offers for non-voting, non-equity capital unless they are offers required by Rule 15.

(c) Related matters

In addition to regulating the transactions referred to in section 3(b) above, the Code also contains rules for the regulation of things done in consequence of, or otherwise in relation to, takeovers and about cases where any such takeover is, or has been, contemplated or apprehended or an announcement is made denying that any such takeover is intended.

(d) Dual jurisdiction

Takeovers and other matters to which the Code applies may from time to time be subject to the dual jurisdiction of the Panel and an overseas takeover regulator, including offers for those companies within paragraph (a)(iii) above. In such cases, early consultation with the Panel is advised so that guidance can be given on how any conflicts between the relevant rules may be resolved and, where relevant, which provisions of the Code apply pursuant to Article 4(2)(e) of the Directive.

(e) Re-registration of a public company as a private company

A public company incorporated in the United Kingdom, the Channel Islands or the Isle of Man may decide to re-register as a private company as a result of which, pursuant to section 3(a) above, the Code may no longer apply to it. If the Code would no longer apply in such circumstances and the relevant company has more than one shareholder, early consultation with the Panel is advised before it re-registers as a private company so that guidance can be given by the Panel on the appropriate disclosure to be made to its shareholders about the implications of the loss of Code protection.

(f) Code responsibilities and obligations

The Code applies to a range of persons who participate in, or are connected with, or who in any way seek to influence, intervene in, or benefit from, takeovers or other matters to which the Code applies.

The Code also applies to all advisers to such persons, and all advisers in so far as they advise on takeovers or other matters to which the Code applies. Financial advisers to whom the Code applies have a particular responsibility to comply with the Code and to ensure, so far as they are reasonably able, that their client and its directors are aware of their responsibilities under the Code and will comply with them and that the Panel is consulted whenever appropriate.

The Code also applies to any directors, employees or representatives through whom any body corporate, partnership or other entity to which the Code applies acts. The Panel expects all bodies corporate, partnerships and other entities to which the Code applies to ensure that their relevant directors and employees receive appropriate and timely guidance in respect of the Code and will hold any such entity responsible for its directors' and employees' acts or omissions.

The Code imposes limitations on the manner in which directors can act in connection with takeovers, which may impinge on the duties that the directors of offeror and offeree companies might owe.

The Code applies in respect of the acts and omissions of any person in connection with a takeover or any other matter to which the Code applies, notwithstanding that the offeree company may since have ceased to be subject to the Code.

In this section 3(f), references to "directors" means, in relation to any body corporate, its directors and officers, in relation to any partnership, its partners, and, in relation to any other entity, those persons exercising equivalent functions on behalf of the entity concerned.

In cases of doubt, the Panel must be consulted as to the persons to whom the Code applies.

4 THE PANEL AND ITS COMMITTEES

Save for section 4(d) (which sets out a rule), this section gives an overview of the membership, functions, responsibilities and general activities of the Panel and certain of its Committees.

Details of various other Committees of the Panel are available on the Panel's website.

(a) The Panel

The Panel assumes overall responsibility for the policy, financing and administration of the Panel's functions and for the functioning and operation of the Code. The Panel operates through a number of Committees and is directly responsible for those matters which are not dealt with through one of its Committees.

The Panel comprises up to 35 members:

(i) the Chairman, who is appointed by the Panel;

(ii) up to three Deputy Chairmen, who are appointed by the Panel;

(iii) up to twenty other members, who are appointed by the Panel; and

(iv) individuals appointed by each of the following bodies:—

The Association for Financial Markets in Europe (with separate representation also for its Corporate Finance Committee and Securities Trading Committee)

The Association of British Insurers

The Association of Investment Companies

The Association of Private Client Investment Managers and Stockbrokers

The British Bankers' Association

The Confederation of British Industry

The Institute of Chartered Accountants in England and Wales

Investment Management Association

. . .

The National Association of Pension Funds.

The Chairman and the Deputy Chairmen are designated as members of the Hearings Committee. Each other Panel member appointed by the Panel under paragraphs (i) to (iii) above is designated upon appointment to act as a member of either the Panel's Code Committee or its Hearings Committee.

Up to twelve Panel members appointed by the Panel under paragraph (iii) above are designated as members of the Code Committee. The Panel may appoint designated alternates for such members of the Code Committee. One designated alternate may act as a member of the Panel (or the Code Committee) in a relevant member's place when he is unavailable.

Up to eight Panel members appointed by the Panel under paragraph (iii) above are designated as members of the Hearings Committee. The Panel may appoint designated alternates for such members of the Hearings Committee. One designated alternate may act as a member of the Panel (or the Hearings Committee) in a relevant member's place when he is unavailable.

The Panel members appointed by the bodies under paragraph (iv) above become members of the Panel's Hearings Committee without further designation by the Panel. Each of these bodies may appoint designated alternates for its appointees. One designated alternate may act as a member of the Panel (or the Hearings Committee) in the relevant member's place when he is unavailable. In performing their functions on the Hearings Committee, these members (and their alternates) act independently of the body which has appointed them (and not as that body's agent or delegate) and exercise their own judgment as to how to perform their functions and how to vote.

Details of the Panel and its Committees, and the names of members of the Panel and the designated alternates, are available on the Panel's website.

(b) The Code Committee

The Code Committee represents a spread of shareholder, corporate, practitioner and other interests within the Panel's regulated community. Up to twelve members of the Panel are designated by the Panel as members of the Code Committee. Its membership from time to time and Terms of Reference are available on the Panel's website.

The Code Committee carries out the rule-making functions of the Panel and is solely responsible for keeping the Code (other than those matters set out in sections 1, 2(a) and (b), 4(a),(b) and (c), 5, 7, 8, 13, 14, 15 and 16 of the Introduction, which are the responsibility of the Panel) under review and for proposing, consulting on, making and issuing amendments to those parts of the Code. The Code Committee's consultation procedures are set out in its Terms of Reference. Amendments to those matters set out in sections 1, 2(a) and (b), 4 (a),(b) and (c), 5, 7, 13, 14, 15 and 16 of the Introduction will usually be issued by the Panel. Amendments to those matters set out in section 8 of the Introduction will be agreed by the Takeover Appeal Board and will be issued by the Panel with immediate effect.

Matters leading to possible amendment to the Code might arise from a number of sources, including specific cases which the Panel has considered, market developments or particular concerns of those operating within the markets.

Once it has agreed that a particular matter is to be pursued, the Code Committee will prepare and publish a Public Consultation Paper ("PCP") seeking the views of interested parties on the proposals and setting out the background to, reasons for and (where available) full text of the proposed amendment. Consultation periods in relation to PCPs vary depending on the complexity of the subject, but will usually be between one and two months.

Following the end of the consultation period, the Code Committee will publish its conclusions on the proposed amendment, taking account of the responses to the PCP received, together with the final Code amendments in a Response Statement ("RS"). It is the Code Committee's policy to make copies of all non-confidential responses it receives to a PCP available on request.

In certain exceptional cases, the Code Committee might consider it necessary to amend the Code on an expedited basis, for example because a particular market development appears to the Code Committee to require that the proposed amendment be made more quickly than the usual public consultation process would permit. In such cases, the Code Committee will publish the amendment with immediate effect and without prior formal consultation, followed in due course by a PCP seeking views on the amendment, which might be later modified, or removed altogether, depending on the Code Committee's conclusions following the consultation process.

Where, in the opinion of the Code Committee, any proposed amendment to the Code either does not materially alter the effect of the provision in question or is a consequence of changes to relevant legislation or regulatory requirements, the Code Committee may publish the text of the amendment without any formal consultation process.

PCPs and RSs are available on the Panel's website.

(c) The Hearings Committee

The Hearings Committee of the Panel comprises the Chairman, up to three Deputy Chairmen, up to eight other members designated by the Panel and the individuals appointed by the bodies listed at paragraph (a)(iv) above. Its membership from time to time, Terms of Reference and Rules of Procedure are available on the Panel's website.

The principal function of the Hearings Committee is to review rulings of the Executive. The Hearings Committee also hears disciplinary proceedings instituted by the Executive when the Executive considers that there has been a breach of the Code (see section 11 below). The Hearings Committee may also be convened for hearings in certain other circumstances. The operations of the Hearings Committee are described in more detail in section 7 below.

The Hearings Committee is assisted in its proceedings by a secretary to the Hearings Committee, usually a partner in a law firm, acting as an officer of the Panel.

(d) Membership and representation restrictions

No person who is or has been a member (or an alternate of a member) of the Code Committee may simultaneously or subsequently be a member (or an alternate of a member) of the Hearings Committee or the Takeover Appeal Board.

When acting in relation to any proceedings before the Hearings Committee or the Takeover Appeal Board, the Panel shall do so only by an officer or member of staff (or a person acting as such).

5 THE EXECUTIVE

This section gives an overview of the functions, responsibilities and general activities of the Executive.

The day-to-day work of takeover supervision and regulation is carried out by the Executive. In carrying out these functions, the Executive operates independently of the Panel. This includes, either on its own initiative or at the instigation of third parties, the conduct of investigations, the monitoring of relevant dealings in connection with the Code and the giving of rulings on the interpretation, application or effect of the Code. The Executive is available both for consultation and also the giving of rulings on the interpretation, application or effect of the Code before, during and, where appropriate, after takeovers or other relevant transactions.

The Executive is staffed by a mixture of employees and secondees from law firms, accountancy firms, corporate brokers, investment banks and other organisations. It is headed by the Director General, usually an investment banker on secondment, who is an officer of the Panel. The Director General is assisted by Deputy Directors General, Assistant Directors General and Secretaries, each of whom is an officer of the Panel, and the various members of the Executive's permanent and seconded staff. In performing their functions, the secondees act independently of the body which has seconded them (and not as that body's agent or delegate). Further information about the membership of the Executive is available on the Panel's website.

6 INTERPRETING THE CODE

This section sets out the rules according to which the Executive issues guidance and rulings on the interpretation, application or effect of the Code.

The Executive gives guidance on the interpretation, application and effect of the Code. In addition, it gives rulings on points of interpretation, application or effect of the Code which are based on the particular facts of a case. References to "rulings" shall include any decision, direction, determination, order or other instruction made by or under rules.

(a) Interpreting the Code – guidance

The Executive may be approached for general guidance on the interpretation or effect of the Code and how it is usually applied in practice. It may also be approached for guidance in relation to a specific issue on a "no names" basis, where the person seeking the guidance does not disclose to the Executive the names of the companies concerned. In either case, the guidance given by the Executive is not binding, and parties or their advisers cannot rely on such guidance as a basis for taking any action without first obtaining a ruling of the Executive on a named basis.

In addition, the Executive may from time to time publish Practice Statements which provide informal guidance as to how the Executive usually interprets and applies particular provisions of the Code in certain circumstances. Practice Statements do not form part of the Code and, accordingly, are not binding and are not a substitute for consulting the Executive to establish how the Code applies in a particular case. Practice Statements are available on the Panel's website.

Panel Statements (see section 7(c) below), statements of the Takeover Appeal Board (see section 8(b) below) and publications of the Code Committee may also contain guidance on the interpretation, application or effect of the Code.

(b) Interpreting the Code – rulings of the Executive and the requirement for consultation

When a person or its advisers are in any doubt whatsoever as to whether a proposed course of conduct is in accordance with the General Principles or the rules, or whenever a waiver or derogation from the application of the provisions of the Code is sought, that person or its advisers must consult the Executive in advance. In this way, they can obtain a conditional ruling (on an ex parte basis) or an unconditional ruling as to the basis on which they can properly proceed and thus minimise the risk of taking action which might, in the event, be a breach of the Code. To take legal or other professional advice on the interpretation, application or effect of the Code is not an appropriate alternative to obtaining a ruling from the Executive.

In addition to giving rulings at the request of a party, the Executive may, on its own initiative, give rulings on the interpretation, application or effect of the Code where it considers it necessary or appropriate to do so.

The nature of the Executive's rulings will depend on whether or not the Executive is able to hear the views of other parties involved. If the Executive is not able to hear the views of other parties involved, it may give a conditional ruling (on an ex parte basis), which may be varied or set aside when any views of the other parties have been heard; if the Executive is able to hear the views of other parties involved, it may give an unconditional ruling. An unconditional ruling is binding on those who are made aware of it unless and until overturned by the Hearings Committee or the Takeover Appeal Board. In addition, such persons must comply with any conditional ruling given by the Executive for the purpose of preserving the status quo pending the unconditional ruling.

Rulings of the Executive, including any grant or refusal to grant a waiver or derogation from the application of any rules, may be referred to the Hearings Committee for review as set out in section 7 below.

7 HEARINGS COMMITTEE

This section gives an overview of the procedural rules which apply to the commencement of proceedings before the Hearings Committee and the procedures followed by the Hearings Committee in connection with hearings before it. The full Rules of Procedure of the Hearings Committee are available on the Panel's website.

(a) Hearings before the Hearings Committee

The Hearings Committee can be convened in the following circumstances:

(i) if a party to a takeover or any other person affected by a ruling of the Executive and with a sufficient interest in the matter, wishes to contest a ruling of the Executive, that party or person is entitled to request that the matter be reviewed by the Hearings Committee; or

(ii) the Executive may refer a matter for review by the Hearings Committee without itself giving a ruling where it considers that there is a particularly unusual, important or difficult point at issue; or

(iii) the Executive may institute disciplinary proceedings before the Hearings Committee when it considers that there has been a breach of the Code or of a ruling of the Executive or the Panel; or

(iv) in other circumstances where the Executive or the Hearings Committee considers it appropriate to do so.

The Hearings Committee can be convened at short notice, where appropriate.

(b) Time limits for applications for review by the Hearings Committee; applications with no reasonable prospect of success

Where a party to a takeover or any other person affected by a ruling of the Executive and with sufficient interest in the matter wishes a matter to be reviewed by the Hearings Committee, the Panel must be notified as soon as possible and, in any event (subject to the following paragraph), within such period as is reasonable in all the circumstances of the case (which shall not be longer than one month from the event giving rise to the application for review).

Where it considers necessary, the Executive may stipulate a reasonable time within which the Panel must be notified. Such time may, depending on the facts of the case, range from a few hours to the one month period referred to above. The Executive may also extend the usual one month period within which the Panel must be notified.

The Chairman (or, failing that, the chairman of the hearing as specified below) may, on behalf of the Hearings Committee, deal with applications for procedural directions, and may reject requests that the Hearings Committee be convened on any matter which he considers has no reasonable prospect of success, without convening the Hearings Committee and without holding a hearing.

(c) Conduct of hearings before the Hearings Committee

The quorum for Hearings Committee proceedings is five. The Chairman or, where he is unavailable, one of the Deputy Chairmen will usually preside as chairman of the proceedings in question ("chairman of the hearing"), although if the Chairman and all of the Deputy Chairmen are unavailable, another member of the Hearings Committee will be appointed by the Chairman (or, failing that, by the other members of the Hearings Committee) to act as chairman of the hearing.

The Hearings Committee usually conducts its hearings using the procedure set out in its Rules of Procedure, but it (or the chairman of the hearing) may vary such procedure in such manner as it (or he) considers appropriate for the fair and just conduct and determination of the case.

At hearings before the Hearings Committee, the case is usually presented in person by the parties, which include the Executive, or their advisers. Although not usual, parties may, if they so wish, be represented by legal advisers. Usually, the parties are required to set out their case briefly in writing beforehand. The parties are permitted to call such witnesses as they consider necessary, with the consent of the chairman of the hearing.

Proceedings before the Hearings Committee are usually in private, although the chairman of the hearing may, at his discretion, direct otherwise. Parties may request that the hearing be held in public. Any such request is considered and ruled upon by the chairman of the hearing (or, at the discretion of the chairman, by the Hearings Committee itself). In the event of a public hearing, the Hearings Committee or the chairman of the hearing may direct that the Hearings Committee should hear part or parts of the proceedings in private and may impose such other conditions relating to the non-disclosure of information relating to the proceedings as it or he considers necessary and appropriate.

In general, all parties are entitled to be present throughout the hearing and to see all papers submitted to the Hearings Committee. Occasionally, however, a party may wish to present evidence to the Hearings Committee which is of a confidential or commercially sensitive nature. In such exceptional cases, the Hearings Committee or the chairman of the hearing may, if satisfied that such course is justified, direct that the evidence in question be heard in the absence of some, or all, of the other parties involved.

The parties must at the earliest opportunity raise with the chairman of the hearing issues concerning possible conflicts of interest for members of the Hearings Committee and any other objections in relation to the proceedings. Any such issues will be resolved by a ruling of the chairman of the hearing.

Proceedings before the Hearings Committee are informal. There are no rules of evidence. A recording is taken for the Hearings Committee's own administrative purposes, but will not be retained once the proceedings are at an end. In addition, a transcript of the hearing is usually made. A party to the hearing may request a copy of the transcript, which may be provided subject to conditions, including conditions as to its confidentiality and use.

The Hearings Committee provides a copy of its ruling to the parties in writing as soon as practicable following the hearing. As part of the ruling, the Hearings Committee may give directions regarding the effects of the Executive's ruling (if any) and/or its ruling pending the outcome of an appeal (if any).

It is the usual policy of the Hearings Committee to publish its rulings by means of a Panel Statement issued as promptly as possible, having regard to all the circumstances of the case, after the ruling has been provided in writing to the parties. In certain circumstances, the Hearings Committee may issue a Panel Statement of its ruling (without providing supporting reasons) in advance of the publication of its full ruling. The chairman of the hearing may, upon application by any party, redact matters from any Panel Statement in order to protect confidential or commercially sensitive information.

If there is, or may be, an appeal to the Takeover Appeal Board against a ruling of the Hearings Committee (see section 8 below), the Hearings Committee (or the chairman of the hearing) may suspend publication of any Panel Statement, although an interim announcement may be made in these circumstances where appropriate. If there is an appeal, publication may, at the discretion of the chairman of the hearing, be suspended until after the decision of the Takeover Appeal Board or, in particular if the appeal is upheld, withheld altogether.

Panel Statements are available on the Panel's website.

Rulings of the Hearings Committee are binding on the parties to the proceedings and on those invited to participate in those proceedings, unless and until overturned by the Takeover Appeal Board.

(d) Procedural rulings

The chairman of the hearing may give such procedural rulings as he considers appropriate for the conduct and determination of the case. This includes, for the avoidance of doubt, the ability to extend or shorten any specified time limits.

(e) Right of appeal

Any party to the hearing before the Hearings Committee (or any person denied permission to be a party to the hearing before the Hearings Committee) may appeal to the Takeover Appeal Board against any ruling of the Hearings Committee or the chairman of the hearing (including in respect of procedural directions).

Notice of appeal, including a summary of the grounds of appeal and the remedy requested, must be given within such time as is stipulated by the Hearings Committee or the chairman of the hearing (or, at the discretion of the chairman, by the Hearings Committee itself) or, in the absence of such stipulation, within two business days of the receipt in writing of the ruling of the Hearings Committee or the chairman of the hearing in question.

8 TAKEOVER APPEAL BOARD

This section gives an overview of the Takeover Appeal Board (the "Board") and the procedures followed by the Board in connection with hearings before it. The full procedures of the Board are set out in its Rules, a copy of which is available on the Board's website at www.thetakeoverappealboard.org.uk.

(a) Status, purpose and membership of the Board

The Board is an independent body which hears appeals against rulings of the Hearings Committee. The Board's procedures are described in greater detail below.

The Chairman and Deputy Chairman of the Board will usually have held high judicial office, and are appointed by the Master of the Rolls. Other members, who will usually have relevant knowledge and experience of takeovers and the Code, are appointed by the Chairman (or, failing that, the Deputy Chairman) of the Board. The names of the members of the Board are available on the Board's website.

The Board is assisted in its proceedings by a secretary to the Board (who will not be the person who acted as secretary to the Hearings Committee in the same matter), usually a partner in a law firm.

(b) Conduct of hearings before the Board

The quorum for Board proceedings is three. However, the Board hearing an appeal will usually comprise at least five members. The Chairman or, where he is unavailable, the Deputy Chairman will usually preside as chairman of the proceedings in question ("chairman of the hearing"), although if they are unavailable, another member of the Board will be appointed by the Chairman (or, failing that, by the other members of the Board) to act as chairman of the hearing.

Proceedings before the Board are generally conducted in a similar way to those before the Hearings Committee as set out in section 7(c) above, using the procedure set out in the Board's Rules. In addition, the Board or the chairman of the hearing may give such directions as it or he considers appropriate for the conduct and determination of the case.

The chairman of the hearing may, on behalf of the Board, deal with appeals relating to procedural directions of the Hearings Committee, or appeals that he considers to have no reasonable prospect of success, without convening the Board and without holding an oral hearing.

The Board provides its decision to the parties in writing as soon as practicable. Decisions of the Board are usually published in a public statement, save for matters redacted in order to protect confidential or commercially sensitive information (redaction being allowed following a request by one of the parties to the hearing and at the discretion of the chairman of the hearing). Any public statement of the Board will be issued as promptly as possible, having regard to all the circumstances of the case, after the decision has been provided in writing to the parties. In certain circumstances, the Board may issue a public statement of its decision (without providing reasons at this stage) in advance of the publication of the full decision.

(c) Remedies

The Board may confirm, vary, set aside, annul or replace the contested ruling of the Hearings Committee. On reaching its decision, the Board remits the matter to the Hearings Committee with such directions (if any) as the Board (or the chairman of the hearing) considers appropriate for giving effect to its (or his) decision. The Hearings Committee will give effect to the Board's decision.

9 PROVIDING INFORMATION AND ASSISTANCE TO THE PANEL AND THE PANEL'S POWERS TO REQUIRE DOCUMENTS AND INFORMATION

This section sets out the rules according to which persons dealing with the Panel must provide information and assistance to the Panel.

(a) Dealings with and assisting the Panel

The Panel expects any person dealing with it to do so in an open and co-operative way. It also expects prompt co-operation and assistance from persons dealing with it and those to whom enquiries and other requests are directed. In dealing with the Panel, a person must disclose to the Panel any information known to them and relevant to the matter being considered by the Panel (and correct or update that information if it changes). A person dealing with the Panel or to whom enquiries or requests are directed must take all reasonable care not to provide incorrect, incomplete or misleading information to the Panel.

A person is entitled to resist providing information or documents on the grounds of legal professional privilege.

Where a matter has been determined by the Panel and a person becomes aware that information they supplied to the Panel was incorrect, incomplete or misleading, that person must promptly contact the Panel to correct the position. In addition, where a determination of the Panel has continuing effect (such as the grant of exempt status or a concert party ruling), the party or parties to that determination must promptly notify the Panel of any new information unless they reasonably consider that it would not be likely to have been relevant to that determination.

(b) Power to require documents and information

Section 947 of the Act gives the Panel certain powers to require documents and information. It provides that, where documents or information are reasonably required in connection with the exercise of its functions, the Panel may by notice in writing require any person:

(i) to produce any documents that are specified or described in the notice; or

(ii) to provide, in the form and manner specified in the notice, such information as may be specified or described in the notice,

within such reasonable period and at such place as is specified in the notice. It may also require any information or document so provided to be verified or authenticated in such manner as it may reasonably require. Where the Panel imposes a requirement under section 947 of the Act, the addressee must comply with that requirement. Failure to comply with any requirement is a breach of the Code.

A person is entitled to resist providing information or documents on the grounds of legal professional privilege.

10 ENFORCING THE CODE

Sections 10(a) to 10(c) set out certain rules pursuant to which the Panel enforces the Code. Section 10(e) sets out the "offer document rules" and the "response document rules" for the purposes of section 953 of the Act.

It is the practice of the Panel, in discharging its functions under the Code, to focus on the specific consequences of breaches of the Code with the aim of providing appropriate remedial or compensatory action in a timely manner. Furthermore, in respect of certain breaches of the Code, disciplinary action may be appropriate (see section 11 below). For the purposes of section 956(2) of the Act, no contravention of any requirement imposed by or under rules shall render any transaction void or unenforceable or affect the validity of any other thing.

(a) Requirement of promptness in dealings with the Executive

If a complaint is to be made that the Code has been breached, it must be made promptly, in default of which the Executive may, at its discretion, decide not to consider the complaint. Similarly, where a person who has made a complaint to the Executive fails to comply with a deadline set by the Executive, the Executive may decide to disregard the complaint in question.

(b) Compliance rulings

If the Panel is satisfied that:

(i) there is a reasonable likelihood that a person will contravene a requirement imposed by or under rules; or

(ii) a person has contravened a requirement imposed by or under rules,

the Panel may give any direction that appears to it to be necessary in order:

(A) to restrain a person from acting (or continuing to act) in breach of rules; or

(B) to restrain a person from doing (or continuing to do) a particular thing, pending determination of whether that or any other conduct of his is or would be a breach of rules; or

(C) otherwise to secure compliance with rules.

(c) Compensation rulings

Where a person has breached the requirements of any of Rules 6, 9, 11, 14, 15, 16.1 or 35.3 of the Code, the Panel may make a ruling requiring the person concerned to pay, within such period as is specified, to the holders, or former holders, of securities of the offeree company such amount as it thinks just and reasonable so as to ensure that such holders receive what they would have been entitled to receive if the relevant Rule had been complied with. In addition, the Panel may make a ruling requiring simple or compound interest to be paid at a rate and for a period (including in respect of any period prior to the date of the ruling and until payment) to be determined.

(d) Enforcement by the Courts

Under section 955 of the Act, the Panel may seek enforcement by the courts. If the court is satisfied that:

(i) there is a reasonable likelihood that a person will contravene a requirement imposed by or under rules; or

(ii) a person has contravened a requirement imposed by or under rules or a requirement imposed under section 947 of the Act,

the court may make any order it thinks fit to secure compliance with the requirement. Any failure to comply with a resulting court order may be a contempt of court.

(e) Bid documentation rules

For the purposes of section 953 of the Act, the "offer document rules" and the "response document rules" are those parts of Rules 24 and 25 respectively which are set out in Appendix 6 and, in each case, Rule 27 to the extent that it requires the inclusion of material changes to, or the updating of, the information in those parts of Rules 24 or 25, as the case may be, in relation to offer documents and offeree board circulars and the revised offer documents and subsequent offeree board circulars referred to in Rules 32.1 and 32.6 respectively.

11 DISCIPLINARY POWERS

This section sets out the disciplinary rules of the Panel in connection with breaches and alleged breaches of the Code.

(a) Disciplinary action

The Executive may itself deal with a disciplinary matter where the person who is to be subject to the disciplinary action agrees the facts and the action proposed by the Executive. In any other case, where it considers that there has been a breach of the Code, the Executive may commence disciplinary proceedings before the Hearings Committee. The person concerned is informed in writing of the alleged breach and of the matters which the Executive will present to the Hearings Committee. Disciplinary actions are conducted in accordance with the Rules of Procedure of the Hearings Committee, which are available on the Panel's website.

(b) Sanctions or other remedies for breach of the Code

If the Hearings Committee finds a breach of the Code or of a ruling of the Panel, it may:

(i) issue a private statement of censure; or

(ii) issue a public statement of censure; or

(iii) suspend or withdraw any exemption, approval or other special status which the Panel has granted to a person, or impose conditions on the continuing enjoyment of such exemption, approval or special status, in respect of all or part of the activities to which such exemption, approval or special status relates; or

(iv) report the offender's conduct to a United Kingdom or overseas regulatory authority or professional body (most notably the Financial Conduct Authority ("FCA")) so that that authority or body can consider whether to take disciplinary or enforcement action (for example, the FCA has power to take certain actions against an authorised person or an approved person who fails to observe proper standards of market conduct, including the power to fine); or

(v) publish a Panel Statement indicating that the offender is someone who, in the Hearings Committee's opinion, is not likely to comply with the Code. The Panel Statement will normally indicate that this sanction will remain effective for only a specified period. The rules of the FCA and certain professional bodies oblige their members, in certain circumstances, not to act for the person in question in a transaction subject to the Code, including a dealing in relevant securities requiring disclosure under Rule 8 (so called "cold-shouldering"). For example, the FCA's rules require a person authorised under the Financial Services and Markets Act 2000 ("FSMA") not to act, or continue to act, for any person in connection with a transaction to which the Code applies if the firm has reasonable grounds for believing that the person in question, or his principal, is not complying or is not likely to comply with the Code.

12 CO-OPERATION AND INFORMATION SHARING

This section summarises the relevant provisions of the Act and sets out the rules as to the basis on which the Panel will effect service of documents under Article 4(4) of the Directive and the professional secrecy obligations applying in relation to information held by the Panel in connection with the exercise of its functions which does not fall within section 948 of the Act.

Under section 950 of the Act, the Panel must, to the extent it has power to do so, take such steps as it considers appropriate to co-operate with:

(a) the FCA, the Prudential Regulation Authority and the Bank of England;

(b) other supervisory authorities designated for the purposes of the Directive; and

(c) regulators outside the United Kingdom having functions similar to the Panel, the FCA or the Prudential Regulation Authority, or similar to the regulatory functions of the Bank of England,

including by the sharing of information which the Panel is permitted to disclose (see below). It may also exercise its powers to require documents and information (see section 9(b) above) for this purpose.

Where any supervisory authority designated for the purposes of the Directive by another member state or any authority responsible for the supervision of capital markets in another member state requests the Panel to serve any legal document in pursuance of its obligation of co-operation under Article 4(4) of the Directive, the Panel shall serve that document by first class post to the address specified for service in the request, and shall inform the requesting authority accordingly. No other method of service will be adopted by the Panel, even where the request specifies another method of service. In cases where:

(a) no address for service is specified in the request; or
(b) the request specifies an address for service outside of the United Kingdom; or
(c) service of the document is validly refused by the party upon whom it is to be served; or
(d) the Panel has been unable to serve the document for any other reason,

the Panel shall return the document unserved to the requesting authority, along with a statement of the reasons for non-service.

Under section 948 of the Act, information received by the Panel in connection with the exercise of its statutory functions may not be disclosed without the consent of the individual (where it concerns a person's private affairs) or business to which it relates except as permitted by the Act. Schedule 2 of the Act (as amended by The Companies Act 2006 (Amendment of Schedule 2) (No 2) Order 2009) includes gateways to allow the Panel to pass information it receives to United Kingdom and overseas regulatory authorities and other persons in accordance with the conditions laid down in that Schedule. The circumstances in which this may occur include, but are not limited to, the circumstances falling within paragraph 11(b)(iv) above.

Information (in whatever form) relating to the private affairs of an individual or to any particular business not falling within section 948 of the Act which is created or held by the Panel in connection with the exercise of its functions, will not be disclosed by the Panel except as permitted in the circumstances set out in sections 948(2), (3) and (8) of the Act. A direct or indirect recipient of such information from the Panel may disclose it in the circumstances set out in sections 948(2), (3), (6) and (8) of the Act.

The Panel works closely with the FCA in relation to insider dealing and market abuse.

13 FEES AND CHARGES

The document charges set out in the Code shall be payable by the persons and in the circumstances set out in the Code.

Third parties shall pay such charges as the Panel may reasonably require for any goods (including copies of the Code) or services (including in relation to the granting, and maintenance, of exempt principal trader or exempt fund manager status as set out in the Definitions section of the Code) it provides. These charges are set out on the Panel's website.

14 ISLE OF MAN

Chapter 1 of Part 28 of the Act has been extended to the Isle of Man with certain modifications by The Companies Act 2006 (Extension of Takeover Panel Provisions) (Isle of Man) Order 2008 (as amended by The Companies Act 2006 (Extension of Takeover Provisions) (Isle of Man) Order 2009). The rules set out in the Code have statutory effect in the Isle of Man by virtue of the Orders.

15 JERSEY

The Panel has been appointed by the Companies (Appointment of Takeovers and Mergers Panel) (Jersey) Order 2009 made under Article 2 of the Companies (Takeovers and Mergers Panel) (Jersey) Law 2009 (the "Jersey Law"), to carry out certain regulatory functions in relation to takeovers and mergers under

Jersey law. The rules set out in the Code have statutory effect in Jersey by virtue of the Jersey Law and the Jersey Law contains provisions equivalent to the sections of the Act referred to in section 9(b), the second paragraph of section 10, section 10(d) and section 12 of the Introduction.

16 GUERNSEY

The Panel has been appointed under the Companies (Guernsey) Law, 2008 (the "Guernsey Law") to carry out certain regulatory functions in relation to takeovers and mergers under Guernsey law. The rules set out in the Code have statutory effect in Guernsey by virtue of the Guernsey Law and the Guernsey Law contains provisions equivalent to the sections of the Act referred to in section 9(b), the second paragraph of section 10, section 10(d) and section 12 of the Introduction.

GENERAL PRINCIPLES

1. All holders of the securities of an offeree company of the same class must be afforded equivalent treatment; moreover, if a person acquires control of a company, the other holders of securities must be protected.
2. The holders of the securities of an offeree company must have sufficient time and information to enable them to reach a properly informed decision on the bid; where it advises the holders of securities, the board of the offeree company must give its views on the effects of implementation of the bid on employment, conditions of employment and the locations of the company's places of business.
3. The board of an offeree company must act in the interests of the company as a whole and must not deny the holders of securities the opportunity to decide on the merits of the bid.
4. False markets must not be created in the securities of the offeree company, of the offeror company or of any other company concerned by the bid in such a way that the rise or fall of the prices of the securities becomes artificial and the normal functioning of the markets is distorted.
5. An offeror must announce a bid only after ensuring that he/she can fulfil in full any cash consideration, if such is offered, and after taking all reasonable measures to secure the implementation of any other type of consideration.
6. An offeree company must not be hindered in the conduct of its affairs for longer than is reasonable by a bid for its securities.

Directive 2004/25/EC of the European Parliament and of the Council of 21 April 2004 on takeover bids

(Text with EEA relevance)

THE EUROPEAN PARLIAMENT AND THE COUNCIL OF THE EUROPEAN UNION,
Having regard to the Treaty establishing the European Community, and in particular Article 44(1) thereof,
Having regard to the proposal from the Commission,
Having regard to the opinion of the European Economic and Social Committee,
Acting in accordance with the procedure laid down in Article 251 of the Treaty,
Whereas:

(1) In accordance with Article 44(2)(g) of the Treaty, it is necessary to coordinate certain safeguards which, for the protection of the interests of members and others, Member States require of companies governed by the law of a Member State the securities of which are admitted to trading on a regulated market in a Member State, with a view to making such safeguards equivalent throughout the Community.

(2) It is necessary to protect the interests of holders of the securities of companies governed by the law of a Member State when those companies are the subject of takeover bids or of changes of control and at least some of their securities are admitted to trading on a regulated market in a Member State.

(3) It is necessary to create Community-wide clarity and transparency in respect of legal issues to be settled in the event of takeover bids and to prevent patterns of corporate restructuring within the Community from being distorted by arbitrary differences in governance and management cultures.

(4) In view of the public-interest purposes served by the central banks of the Member States, it seems inconceivable that they should be the targets of takeover bids. Since, for historical reasons, the securities of some of those central banks are listed on regulated markets in Member States, it is necessary to exclude them explicitly from the scope of this Directive.

(5) Each Member State should designate an authority or authorities to supervise those aspects of bids that are governed by this Directive and to ensure that parties to takeover bids comply with the rules made pursuant to this Directive. All those authorities should cooperate with one another.

(6) In order to be effective, takeover regulation should be flexible and capable of dealing with new circumstances as they arise and should accordingly provide for the possibility of exceptions and derogations. However, in applying any rules or exceptions laid down or in granting any derogations, supervisory authorities should respect certain general principles.

(7) Self-regulatory bodies should be able to exercise supervision.

(8) In accordance with general principles of Community law, and in particular the right to a fair hearing, decisions of a supervisory authority should in appropriate circumstances be susceptible to review by an independent court or tribunal. However, Member States should be left to determine whether rights are to be made available which may be asserted in administrative or judicial proceedings, either in proceedings against a supervisory authority or in proceedings between parties to a bid.

(9) Member States should take the necessary steps to protect the holders of securities, in particular those with minority holdings, when control of their companies has been acquired. The Member States should ensure such protection by obliging the person who has acquired control of a company to make an offer to all the holders of that company's securities for all of their holdings at an equitable price in accordance with a common definition. Member States should be free to establish further instruments for the protection of the interests of the holders of securities, such as the obligation to make a partial bid where the offeror does not acquire control of the company or the obligation to announce a bid at the same time as control of the company is acquired.

(10) The obligation to make a bid to all the holders of securities should not apply to those controlling holdings already in existence on the date on which the national legislation transposing this Directive enters into force.

(11) The obligation to launch a bid should not apply in the case of the acquisition of securities which do not carry the right to vote at ordinary general meetings of shareholders. Member States should, however, be able to provide that the obligation to make a bid to all the holders of securities relates not only to securities carrying voting rights but also to securities which carry voting rights only in specific circumstances or which do not carry voting rights.

(12) To reduce the scope for insider dealing, an offeror should be required to announce his/her decision to launch a bid as soon as possible and to inform the supervisory authority of the bid.

(13) The holders of securities should be properly informed of the terms of a bid by means of an offer document. Appropriate information should also be given to the representatives of the company's employees or, failing that, to the employees directly.

(14) The time allowed for the acceptance of a bid should be regulated.

(15) To be able to perform their functions satisfactorily, supervisory authorities should at all times be able to require the parties to a bid to provide information concerning themselves and should cooperate and supply information in an efficient and effective manner, without delay, to other authorities supervising capital markets.

(16) In order to prevent operations which could frustrate a bid, the powers of the board of an offeree company to engage in operations of an exceptional nature should be limited, without unduly hindering the offeree company in carrying on its normal business activities.

(17) The board of an offeree company should be required to make public a document setting out its opinion of the bid and the reasons on which that opinion is based, including its views on the effects of implementation on all the company's interests, and specifically on employment.

(18) In order to reinforce the effectiveness of existing provisions concerning the freedom to deal in the securities of companies covered by this Directive and the freedom to exercise voting rights, it is essential that the defensive structures and mechanisms envisaged by such companies be transparent and that they be regularly presented in reports to general meetings of shareholders.

(19) Member States should take the necessary measures to afford any offeror the possibility of acquiring majority interests in other companies and of fully exercising control of them. To that end, restrictions on the transfer of securities, restrictions on voting rights, extraordinary appointment rights and multiple voting rights should be removed or suspended during the time allowed for the acceptance of a bid and when the general meeting of shareholders decides on defensive measures, on amendments to the articles of association or on the removal or appointment of board members at the first general meeting of shareholders following closure of the bid. Where the holders of securities have suffered losses as a result of the removal of rights, equitable compensation should be provided for in accordance with the technical arrangements laid down by Member States.

(20) All special rights held by Member States in companies should be viewed in the framework of the free movement of capital and the relevant provisions of the Treaty. Special rights held by Member States in companies which are provided for in private or public national law should be exempted from the 'breakthrough' rule if they are compatible with the Treaty.

(21) Taking into account existing differences in Member States' company law mechanisms and structures, Member States should be allowed not to require companies established within their territories to apply the provisions of this Directive limiting the powers of the board of an offeree company during the time allowed for the acceptance of a bid and those rendering ineffective barriers, provided for in the articles of association or in specific agreements. In that event Member States should at least allow companies established within their territories to make the choice, which must be reversible, to apply those provisions. Without prejudice to international agreements to which the European Community is a party, Member States should be allowed not to require companies which apply those provisions in accordance with the optional arrangements

to apply them when they become the subject of offers launched by companies which do not apply the same provisions, as a consequence of the use of those optional arrangements.

(22) Member States should lay down rules to cover the possibility of a bid's lapsing, the offeror's right to revise his/her bid, the possibility of competing bids for a company's securities, the disclosure of the result of a bid, the irrevocability of a bid and the conditions permitted.

(23) The disclosure of information to and the consultation of representatives of the employees of the offeror and the offeree company should be governed by the relevant national provisions, in particular those adopted pursuant to Council Directive 94/45/EC of 22 September 1994 on the establishment of a European Works Council or a procedure in Community-scale undertakings and Communityscale groups of undertakings for the purposes of informing and consulting employees, Council Directive 98/59/EC of 20 July 1998 on the approximation of the laws of the Member States relating to collective redundancies, Council Directive 2001/86/EC of 8 October 2001 supplementing the statute for a European Company with regard to the involvement of employees and Directive 2002/14/EC of the European Parliament and of the Council of 11 March 2002 establishing a general framework for informing and consulting employees in the European Community — Joint declaration of the European Parliament, the Council and the Commission on employee representation. The employees of the companies concerned, or their representatives, should nevertheless be given an opportunity to state their views on the foreseeable effects of the bid on employment. Without prejudice to the rules of Directive 2003/6/EC of the European Parliament and of the Council of 28 January 2003 on insider dealing and market manipulation (market abuse), Member States may always apply or introduce national provisions concerning the disclosure of information to and the consultation of representatives of the employees of the offeror before an offer is launched.

(24) Member States should take the necessary measures to enable an offeror who, following a takeover bid, has acquired a certain percentage of a company's capital carrying voting rights to require the holders of the remaining securities to sell him/her their securities. Likewise, where, following a takeover bid, an offeror has acquired a certain percentage of a company's capital carrying voting rights, the holders of the remaining securities should be able to require him/her to buy their securities. These squeeze-out and sell-out procedures should apply only under specific conditions linked to takeover bids. Member States may continue to apply national rules to squeeze-out and sellout procedures in other circumstances.

(25) Since the objectives of the action envisaged, namely to establish minimum guidelines for the conduct of takeover bids and ensure an adequate level of protection for holders of securities throughout the Community, cannot be sufficiently achieved by the Member States because of the need for transparency and legal certainty in the case of crossborder takeovers and acquisitions of control, and can therefore, by reason of the scale and effects of the action, be better achieved at Community level, the Community may adopt measures, in accordance with the principle of subsidiarity as set out in Article 5 of the Treaty. In accordance with the principle of proportionality as set out in that Article, this Directive does not go beyond what is necessary to achieve those objectives.

(26) The adoption of a Directive is the appropriate procedure for the establishment of a framework consisting of certain common principles and a limited number of general requirements which Member States are to implement through more detailed rules in accordance with their national systems and their cultural contexts.

(27) Member States should, however, provide for sanctions for any infringement of the national measures transposing this Directive.

(28) Technical guidance and implementing measures for the rules laid down in this Directive may from time to time be necessary, to take account of new developments on financial markets. For certain provisions, the Commission should accordingly be empowered to adopt implementing measures, provided that these do not modify the essential elements of this Directive and the Commission acts in accordance with the principles set out in this Directive, after consulting the European Securities Committee established by Commission Decision 2001/528/EC. The

measures necessary for the implementation of this Directive should be adopted in accordance with Council Decision 1999/468/EC of 28 June 1999 laying down the procedures for the exercise of implementing powers conferred on the Commission and with due regard to the declaration made by the Commission in the European Parliament on 5 February 2002 concerning the implementation of financial services legislation. For the other provisions, it is important to entrust a contact committee with the task of assisting Member States and the supervisory authorities in the implementation of this Directive and of advising the Commission, if necessary, on additions or amendments to this Directive. In so doing, the contact committee may make use of the information which Member States are to provide on the basis of this Directive concerning takeover bids that have taken place on their regulated markets.

(29) The Commission should facilitate movement towards the fair and balanced harmonisation of rules on takeovers in the European Union. To that end, the Commission should be able to submit proposals for the timely revision of this Directive,

HAVE ADOPTED THIS DIRECTIVE:

Article 1

Scope

1. This Directive lays down measures coordinating the laws, regulations, administrative provisions, codes of practice and other arrangements of the Member States, including arrangements established by organisations officially authorised to regulate the markets (hereinafter referred to as 'rules'), relating to takeover bids for the securities of companies governed by the laws of Member States, where all or some of those securities are admitted to trading on a regulated market within the meaning of Directive 93/22/EEC in one or more Member States (hereinafter referred to as a 'regulated market').
2. This Directive shall not apply to takeover bids for securities issued by companies, the object of which is the collective investment of capital provided by the public, which operate on the principle of risk-spreading and the units of which are, at the holders' request, repurchased or redeemed, directly or indirectly, out of the assets of those companies. Action taken by such companies to ensure that the stock exchange value of their units does not vary significantly from their net asset value shall be regarded as equivalent to such repurchase or redemption.
3. This Directive shall not apply to takeover bids for securities issued by the Member States' central banks.

Article 2

Definitions

1. For the purposes of this Directive:
   (a) 'takeover bid' or 'bid' shall mean a public offer (other than by the offeree company itself) made to the holders of the securities of a company to acquire all or some of those securities, whether mandatory or voluntary, which follows or has as its objective the acquisition of control of the offeree company in accordance with national law;
   (b) 'offeree company' shall mean a company, the securities of which are the subject of a bid;
   (c) 'offeror' shall mean any natural or legal person governed by public or private law making a bid;
   (d) 'persons acting in concert' shall mean natural or legal persons who cooperate with the offeror or the offeree company on the basis of an agreement, either express or tacit, either oral or written, aimed either at acquiring control of the offeree company or at frustrating the successful outcome of a bid;
   (e) 'securities' shall mean transferable securities carrying voting rights in a company;
   (f) 'parties to the bid' shall mean the offeror, the members of the offeror's board if the offeror is a company, the offeree company, holders of securities of the offeree company and the members of the board of the offeree company, and persons acting in concert with such parties;

(g) 'multiple-vote securities' shall mean securities included in a distinct and separate class and carrying more than one vote each.

2. For the purposes of paragraph 1(d), persons controlled by another person within the meaning of Article 87 of Directive 2001/34/EC shall be deemed to be persons acting in concert with that other person and with each other.

Article 3

General principles

1. For the purpose of implementing this Directive, Member States shall ensure that the following principles are complied with:
   (a) all holders of the securities of an offeree company of the same class must be afforded equivalent treatment; moreover, if a person acquires control of a company, the other holders of securities must be protected;
   (b) the holders of the securities of an offeree company must have sufficient time and information to enable them to reach a properly informed decision on the bid; where it advises the holders of securities, the board of the offeree company must give its views on the effects of implementation of the bid on employment, conditions of employment and the locations of the company's places of business;
   (c) the board of an offeree company must act in the interests of the company as a whole and must not deny the holders of securities the opportunity to decide on the merits of the bid;
   (d) false markets must not be created in the securities of the offeree company, of the offeror company or of any other company concerned by the bid in such a way that the rise or fall of the prices of the securities becomes artificial and the normal functioning of the markets is distorted;
   (e) an offeror must announce a bid only after ensuring that he/she can fulfil in full any cash consideration, if such is offered, and after taking all reasonable measures to secure the implementation of any other type of consideration;
   (f) an offeree company must not be hindered in the conduct of its affairs for longer than is reasonable by a bid for its securities.
2. With a view to ensuring compliance with the principles laid down in paragraph 1, Member States:
   (a) shall ensure that the minimum requirements set out in this Directive are observed;
   (b) may lay down additional conditions and provisions more stringent than those of this Directive for the regulation of bids.

Article 4

Supervisory authority and applicable law

1. Member States shall designate the authority or authorities competent to supervise bids for the purposes of the rules which they make or introduce pursuant to this Directive. The authorities thus designated shall be either public authorities, associations or private bodies recognised by national law or by public authorities expressly empowered for that purpose by national law. Member States shall inform the Commission of those designations, specifying any divisions of functions that may be made. They shall ensure that those authorities exercise their functions impartially and independently of all parties to a bid.
2. (a) The authority competent to supervise a bid shall be that of the Member State in which the offeree company has its registered office if that company's securities are admitted to trading on a regulated market in that Member State.
   (b) If the offeree company's securities are not admitted to trading on a regulated market in the Member State in which the company has its registered office, the authority competent to supervise the bid shall be that of the Member State on the regulated market of which the company's securities are admitted to trading.

If the offeree company's securities are admitted to trading on regulated markets in more than one Member State, the authority competent to supervise the bid shall be that of the Member State on the regulated market of which the securities were first admitted to trading.

(c) If the offeree company's securities were first admitted to trading on regulated markets in more than one Member State simultaneously, the offeree company shall determine which of the supervisory authorities of those Member States shall be the authority competent to supervise the bid by notifying those regulated markets and their supervisory authorities on the first day of trading.

If the offeree company's securities have already been admitted to trading on regulated markets in more than one Member State on the date laid down in Article 21(1) and were admitted simultaneously, the supervisory authorities of those Member States shall agree which one of them shall be the authority competent to supervise the bid within four weeks of the date laid down in Article 21(1). Otherwise, the offeree company shall determine which of those authorities shall be the competent authority on the first day of trading following that four-week period.

(d) Member States shall ensure that the decisions referred to in (c) are made public.

(e) In the cases referred to in (b) and (c), matters relating to the consideration offered in the case of a bid, in particular the price, and matters relating to the bid procedure, in particular the information on the offeror's decision to make a bid, the contents of the offer document and the disclosure of the bid, shall be dealt with in accordance with the rules of the Member State of the competent authority. In matters relating to the information to be provided to the employees of the offeree company and in matters relating to company law, in particular the percentage of voting rights which confers control and any derogation from the obligation to launch a bid, as well as the conditions under which the board of the offeree company may undertake any action which might result in the frustration of the bid, the applicable rules and the competent authority shall be those of the Member State in which the offeree company has its registered office.

3. Member States shall ensure that all persons employed or formerly employed by their supervisory authorities are bound by professional secrecy. No information covered by professional secrecy may be divulged to any person or authority except under provisions laid down by law.

4. The supervisory authorities of the Member States for the purposes of this Directive and other authorities supervising capital markets, in particular in accordance with Directive 93/22/EEC, Directive 2001/34/EC, Directive 2003/6/EC and Directive 2003/71/EC of the European Parliament and of the Council of 4 November 2003 on the prospectus to be published when securities are offered to the public or admitted to trading shall cooperate and supply each other with information wherever necessary for the application of the rules drawn up in accordance with this Directive and in particular in cases covered by paragraph 2(b), (c) and (e). Information thus exchanged shall be covered by the obligation of professional secrecy to which persons employed or formerly employed by the supervisory authorities receiving the information are subject. Cooperation shall include the ability to serve the legal documents necessary to enforce measures taken by the competent authorities in connection with bids, as well as such other assistance as may reasonably be requested by the supervisory authorities concerned for the purpose of investigating any actual or alleged breaches of the rules made or introduced pursuant to this Directive.

5. The supervisory authorities shall be vested with all the powers necessary for the purpose of carrying out their duties, including that of ensuring that the parties to a bid comply with the rules made or introduced pursuant to this Directive.

Provided that the general principles laid down in Article 3(1) are respected, Member States may provide in the rules that they make or introduce pursuant to this Directive for derogations from those rules:

(i) by including such derogations in their national rules, in order to take account of circumstances determined at national level and/or

(ii) by granting their supervisory authorities, where they are competent, powers to waive such national rules, to take account of the circumstances referred to in (i) or in other specific circumstances, in which case a reasoned decision must be required.

6. This Directive shall not affect the power of the Member States to designate judicial or other authorities responsible for dealing with disputes and for deciding on irregularities committed in the course of bids or the power of Member States to regulate whether and under which circumstances parties to a bid are entitled to bring administrative or judicial proceedings. In particular, this Directive shall not affect the power which courts may have in a Member State to decline to hear legal proceedings and to decide whether or not such proceedings affect the outcome of a bid. This Directive shall not affect the power of the Member States to determine the legal position concerning the liability of supervisory authorities or concerning litigation between the parties to a bid.

Article 5

Protection of minority shareholders, the mandatory bid and the equitable price

1. Where a natural or legal person, as a result of his/her own acquisition or the acquisition by persons acting in concert with him/her, holds securities of a company as referred to in Article 1(1) which, added to any existing holdings of those securities of his/hers and the holdings of those securities of persons acting in concert with him/her, directly or indirectly give him/her a specified percentage of voting rights in that company, giving him/her control of that company, Member States shall ensure that such a person is required to make a bid as a means of protecting the minority shareholders of that company. Such a bid shall be addressed at the earliest opportunity to all the holders of those securities for all their holdings at the equitable price as defined in paragraph 4.

2. Where control has been acquired following a voluntary bid made in accordance with this Directive to all the holders of securities for all their holdings, the obligation laid down in paragraph 1 to launch a bid shall no longer apply.

3. The percentage of voting rights which confers control for the purposes of paragraph 1 and the method of its calculation shall be determined by the rules of the Member State in which the company has its registered office.

4. The highest price paid for the same securities by the offeror, or by persons acting in concert with him/her, over a period, to be determined by Member States, of not less than six months and not more than 12 before the bid referred to in paragraph 1 shall be regarded as the equitable price. If, after the bid has been made public and before the offer closes for acceptance, the offeror or any person acting in concert with him/her purchases securities at a price higher than the offer price, the offeror shall increase his/her offer so that it is not less than the highest price paid for the securities so acquired.

   Provided that the general principles laid down in Article 3(1) are respected, Member States may authorise their supervisory authorities to adjust the price referred to in the first subparagraph in circumstances and in accordance with criteria that are clearly determined. To that end, they may draw up a list of circumstances in which the highest price may be adjusted either upwards or downwards, for example where the highest price was set by agreement between the purchaser and a seller, where the market prices of the securities in question have been manipulated, where market prices in general or certain market prices in particular have been affected by exceptional occurrences, or in order to enable a firm in difficulty to be rescued. They may also determine the criteria to be applied in such cases, for example the average market value over a particular period, the break-up value of the company or other objective valuation criteria generally used in financial analysis.

   Any decision by a supervisory authority to adjust the equitable price shall be substantiated and made public.

5. By way of consideration the offeror may offer securities, cash or a combination of both.

However, where the consideration offered by the offeror does not consist of liquid securities admitted to trading on a regulated market, it shall include a cash alternative.

In any event, the offeror shall offer a cash consideration at least as an alternative where he/she or persons acting in concert with him/her, over a period beginning at the same time as the period determined by the Member State in accordance with paragraph 4 and ending when the offer closes for acceptance, has purchased for cash securities carrying 5 % or more of the voting rights in the offeree company.

Member States may provide that a cash consideration must be offered, at least as an alternative, in all cases.

6. In addition to the protection provided for in paragraph 1, Member States may provide for further instruments intended to protect the interests of the holders of securities in so far as those instruments do not hinder the normal course of a bid.

Article 6

Information concerning bids

1. Member States shall ensure that a decision to make a bid is made public without delay and that the supervisory authority is informed of the bid. They may require that the supervisory authority must be informed before such a decision is made public. As soon as the bid has been made public, the boards of the offeree company and of the offeror shall inform the representatives of their respective employees or, where there are no such representatives, the employees themselves.

2. Member States shall ensure that an offeror is required to draw up and make public in good time an offer document containing the information necessary to enable the holders of the offeree company's securities to reach a properly informed decision on the bid. Before the offer document is made public, the offeror shall communicate it to the supervisory authority. When it is made public, the boards of the offeree company and of the offeror shall communicate it to the representatives of their respective employees or, where there are no such representatives, to the employees themselves.

Where the offer document referred to in the first subparagraph is subject to the prior approval of the supervisory authority and has been approved, it shall be recognised, subject to any translation required, in any other Member State on the market of which the offeree company's securities are admitted to trading, without its being necessary to obtain the approval of the supervisory authorities of that Member State. Those authorities may require the inclusion of additional information in the offer document only if such information is specific to the market of a Member State or Member States on which the offeree company's securities are admitted to trading and relates to the formalities to be complied with to accept the bid and to receive the consideration due at the close of the bid as well as to the tax arrangements to which the consideration offered to the holders of the securities will be subject.

3. The offer document referred to in paragraph 2 shall state at least:

(a) the terms of the bid;

(b) the identity of the offeror and, where the offeror is a company, the type, name and registered office of that company;

(c) the securities or, where appropriate, the class or classes of securities for which the bid is made;

(d) the consideration offered for each security or class of securities and, in the case of a mandatory bid, the method employed in determining it, with particulars of the way in which that consideration is to be paid;

(e) the compensation offered for the rights which might be removed as a result of the breakthrough rule laid down in Article 11(4), with particulars of the way in which that compensation is to be paid and the method employed in determining it;

(f) the maximum and minimum percentages or quantities of securities which the offeror undertakes to acquire;

(g) details of any existing holdings of the offeror, and of persons acting in concert with him/her, in the offeree company;
(h) all the conditions to which the bid is subject;
(i) the offeror's intentions with regard to the future business of the offeree company and, in so far as it is affected by the bid, the offeror company and with regard to the safeguarding of the jobs of their employees and management, including any material change in the conditions of employment, and in particular the offeror's strategic plans for the two companies and the likely repercussions on employment and the locations of the companies' places of business;
(j) the time allowed for acceptance of the bid;
(k) where the consideration offered by the offeror includes securities of any kind, information concerning those securities;
(l) information concerning the financing for the bid;
(m) the identity of persons acting in concert with the offeror or with the offeree company and, in the case of companies, their types, names, registered offices and relationships with the offeror and, where possible, with the offeree company;
(n) the national law which will govern contracts concluded between the offeror and the holders of the offeree company's securities as a result of the bid and the competent courts.

4. The Commission may adopt rules modifying the list in paragraph 3. Those measures, designed to amend non-essential elements of this Directive, shall be adopted in accordance with the regulatory procedure with scrutiny referred to in Article 18(2).
5. Member States shall ensure that the parties to a bid are required to provide the supervisory authorities of their Member State at any time on request with all the information in their possession concerning the bid that is necessary for the supervisory authority to discharge its functions.

Article 7

Time allowed for acceptance

1. Member States shall provide that the time allowed for the acceptance of a bid may not be less than two weeks nor more than 10 weeks from the date of publication of the offer document. Provided that the general principle laid down in Article 3(1)(f) is respected, Member States may provide that the period of 10 weeks may be extended on condition that the offeror gives at least two weeks' notice of his/her intention of closing the bid. L 142/18 EN Official Journal of the European Union 30.4.2004
2. Member States may provide for rules changing the period referred to in paragraph 1 in specific cases. A Member State may authorise a supervisory authority to grant a derogation from the period referred to in paragraph 1 in order to allow the offeree company to call a general meeting of shareholders to consider the bid.

Article 8

Disclosure

1. Member States shall ensure that a bid is made public in such a way as to ensure market transparency and integrity for the securities of the offeree company, of the offeror or of any other company affected by the bid, in particular in order to prevent the publication or dissemination of false or misleading information.
2. Member States shall provide for the disclosure of all information and documents required by Article 6 in such a manner as to ensure that they are both readily and promptly available to the holders of securities at least in those Member States on the regulated markets of which the offeree company's securities are admitted to trading and to the representatives of the employees of the offeree company and the offeror or, where there are no such representatives, to the employees themselves.

Article 9

Obligations of the board of the offeree company

1. Member States shall ensure that the rules laid down in paragraphs 2 to 5 are complied with.
2. During the period referred to in the second subparagraph, the board of the offeree company shall obtain the prior authorisation of the general meeting of shareholders given for this purpose before taking any action, other than seeking alternative bids, which may result in the frustration of the bid and in particular before issuing any shares which may result in a lasting impediment to the offeror's acquiring control of the offeree company.
   Such authorisation shall be mandatory at least from the time the board of the offeree company receives the information referred to in the first sentence of Article 6(1) concerning the bid and until the result of the bid is made public or the bid lapses. Member States may require that such authorisation be obtained at an earlier stage, for example as soon as the board of the offeree company becomes aware that the bid is imminent.
3. As regards decisions taken before the beginning of the period referred to in the second subparagraph of paragraph 2 and not yet partly or fully implemented, the general meeting of shareholders shall approve or confirm any decision which does not form part of the normal course of the company's business and the implementation of which may result in the frustration of the bid.
4. For the purpose of obtaining the prior authorisation, approval or confirmation of the holders of securities referred to in paragraphs 2 and 3, Member States may adopt rules allowing a general meeting of shareholders to be called at short notice, provided that the meeting does not take place within two weeks of notification's being given.
5. The board of the offeree company shall draw up and make public a document setting out its opinion of the bid and the reasons on which it is based, including its views on the effects of implementation of the bid on all the company's interests and specifically employment, and on the offeror's strategic plans for the offeree company and their likely repercussions on employment and the locations of the company's places of business as set out in the offer document in accordance with Article 6(3)(i). The board of the offeree company shall at the same time communicate that opinion to the representatives of its employees or, where there are no such representatives, to the employees themselves. Where the board of the offeree company receives in good time a separate opinion from the representatives of its employees on the effects of the bid on employment, that opinion shall be appended to the document.
6. For the purposes of paragraph 2, where a company has a two-tier board structure 'board' shall mean both the management board and the supervisory board.

Article 10

Information on companies as referred to in Article 1(1)

1. Member States shall ensure that companies as referred to in Article 1(1) publish detailed information on the following:
   (a) the structure of their capital, including securities which are not admitted to trading on a regulated market in a Member State, where appropriate with an indication of the different classes of shares and, for each class of shares, the rights and obligations attaching to it and the percentage of total share capital that it represents;
   (b) any restrictions on the transfer of securities, such as limitations on the holding of securities or the need to obtain the approval of the company or other holders of securities, without prejudice to Article 46 of Directive 2001/34/EC;
   (c) significant direct and indirect shareholdings (including indirect shareholdings through pyramid structures and crossshareholdings) within the meaning of Article 85 of Directive 2001/34/EC;
   (d) the holders of any securities with special control rights and a description of those rights;
   (e) the system of control of any employee share scheme where the control rights are not exercised directly by the employees;

(f) any restrictions on voting rights, such as limitations of the voting rights of holders of a given percentage or number of votes, deadlines for exercising voting rights, or systems whereby, with the company's cooperation, the financial rights attaching to securities are separated from the holding of securities;

(g) any agreements between shareholders which are known to the company and may result in restrictions on the transfer of securities and/or voting rights within the meaning of Directive 2001/34/EC;

(h) the rules governing the appointment and replacement of board members and the amendment of the articles of association;

(i) the powers of board members, and in particular the power to issue or buy back shares;

(j) any significant agreements to which the company is a party and which take effect, alter or terminate upon a change of control of the company following a takeover bid, and the effects thereof, except where their nature is such that their disclosure would be seriously prejudicial to the company; this exception shall not apply where the company is specifically obliged to disclose such information on the basis of other legal requirements;

(k) any agreements between the company and its board members or employees providing for compensation if they resign or are made redundant without valid reason or if their employment ceases because of a takeover bid.

2. The information referred to in paragraph 1 shall be published in the company's annual report as provided for in Article 46 of Directive 78/660/EEC and Article 36 of Directive 83/349/EEC.

3. Member States shall ensure, in the case of companies the securities of which are admitted to trading on a regulated market in a Member State, that the board presents an explanatory report to the annual general meeting of shareholders on the matters referred to in paragraph 1.

Article 11

Breakthrough

1. Without prejudice to other rights and obligations provided for in Community law for the companies referred to in Article 1(1), Member States shall ensure that the provisions laid down in paragraphs 2 to 7 apply when a bid has been made public.

2. Any restrictions on the transfer of securities provided for in the articles of association of the offeree company shall not apply vis-à-vis the offeror during the time allowed for acceptance of the bid laid down in Article 7(1).

Any restrictions on the transfer of securities provided for in contractual agreements between the offeree company and holders of its securities, or in contractual agreements between holders of the offeree company's securities entered into after the adoption of this Directive, shall not apply vis-à-vis the offeror during the time allowed for acceptance of the bid laid down in Article 7(1).

3. Restrictions on voting rights provided for in the articles of association of the offeree company shall not have effect at the general meeting of shareholders which decides on any defensive measures in accordance with Article 9.

Restrictions on voting rights provided for in contractual agreements between the offeree company and holders of its securities, or in contractual agreements between holders of the offeree company's securities entered into after the adoption of this Directive, shall not have effect at the general meeting of shareholders which decides on any defensive measures in accordance with Article 9. Multiple-vote securities shall carry only one vote each at the general meeting of shareholders which decides on any defensive measures in accordance with Article 9.

4. Where, following a bid, the offeror holds 75 % or more of the capital carrying voting rights, no restrictions on the transfer of securities or on voting rights referred to in paragraphs 2 and 3 nor any extraordinary rights of shareholders concerning the appointment or removal of board members provided for in the articles of association of the offeree company shall apply; multiple-vote securities shall carry only one vote each at the first general meeting of shareholders following closure of the bid, called by the offeror in order to amend the articles of association or to remove or appoint board members.

To that end, the offeror shall have the right to convene a general meeting of shareholders at short notice, provided that the meeting does not take place within two weeks of notification.

5. Where rights are removed on the basis of paragraphs 2, 3, or 4 and/or Article 12, equitable compensation shall be provided for any loss suffered by the holders of those rights. The terms for determining such compensation and the arrangements for its payment shall be set by Member States.

6. Paragraphs 3 and 4 shall not apply to securities where the restrictions on voting rights are compensated for by specific pecuniary advantages.

7. This Article shall not apply either where Member States hold securities in the offeree company which confer special rights on the Member States which are compatible with the Treaty, or to special rights provided for in national law which are compatible with the Treaty or to cooperatives.

Article 12

Optional arrangements

1. Member States may reserve the right not to require companies as referred to in Article 1(1) which have their registered offices within their territories to apply Article 9(2) and (3) and/or Article 11.

2. Where Member States make use of the option provided for in paragraph 1, they shall nevertheless grant companies which have their registered offices within their territories the option, which shall be reversible, of applying Article 9(2) and (3) and/or Article 11, without prejudice to Article 11(7).

   The decision of the company shall be taken by the general meeting of shareholders, in accordance with the law of the Member State in which the company has its registered office in accordance with the rules applicable to amendment of the articles of association. The decision shall be communicated to the supervisory authority of the Member State in which the company has its registered office and to all the supervisory authorities of Member States in which its securities are admitted to trading on regulated markets or where such admission has been requested.

3. Member States may, under the conditions determined by national law, exempt companies which apply Article 9(2) and (3) and/or Article 11 from applying Article 9(2) and (3) and/or Article 11 if they become the subject of an offer launched by a company which does not apply the same Articles as they do, or by a company controlled, directly or indirectly, by the latter, pursuant to Article 1 of Directive 83/349/EEC.

4. Member States shall ensure that the provisions applicable to the respective companies are disclosed without delay.

5. Any measure applied in accordance with paragraph 3 shall be subject to the authorisation of the general meeting of shareholders of the offeree company, which must be granted no earlier than 18 months before the bid was made public in accordance with Article 6(1).

Article 13

Other rules applicable to the conduct of bids

Member States shall also lay down rules which govern the conduct of bids, at least as regards the following:

(a) the lapsing of bids;
(b) the revision of bids;
(c) competing bids;
(d) the disclosure of the results of bids;
(e) the irrevocability of bids and the conditions permitted.

Article 14

Information for and consultation of employees' representatives

This Directive shall be without prejudice to the rules relating to information and to consultation of representatives of and, if Member States so provide, co-determination with the employees of the offeror and the offeree company governed by the relevant national provisions, and in particular those adopted pursuant to Directives 94/45/EC, 98/59/EC, 2001/86/EC and 2002/14/EC.

Article 15

The right of squeeze-out

1. Member States shall ensure that, following a bid made to all the holders of the offeree company's securities for all of their securities, paragraphs 2 to 5 apply.
2. Member States shall ensure that an offeror is able to require all the holders of the remaining securities to sell him/her those securities at a fair price. Member States shall introduce that right in one of the following situations:
   (a) where the offeror holds securities representing not less than 90 % of the capital carrying voting rights and 90 % of the voting rights in the offeree company,
   or
   (b) where, following acceptance of the bid, he/she has acquired or has firmly contracted to acquire securities representing not less than 90 % of the offeree company's capital carrying voting rights and 90 % of the voting rights comprised in the bid.

   In the case referred to in (a), Member States may set a higher threshold that may not, however, be higher than 95 % of the capital carrying voting rights and 95 % of the voting rights.
3. Member States shall ensure that rules are in force that make it possible to calculate when the threshold is reached.

   Where the offeree company has issued more than one class of securities, Member States may provide that the right of squeezeout can be exercised only in the class in which the threshold laid down in paragraph 2 has been reached.
4. If the offeror wishes to exercise the right of squeeze-out he/she shall do so within three months of the end of the time allowed for acceptance of the bid referred to in Article 7.
5. Member States shall ensure that a fair price is guaranteed. That price shall take the same form as the consideration offered in the bid or shall be in cash. Member States may provide that cash shall be offered at least as an alternative.

   Following a voluntary bid, in both of the cases referred to in paragraph 2(a) and (b), the consideration offered in the bid shall be presumed to be fair where, through acceptance of the bid, the offeror has acquired securities representing not less than 90 % of the capital carrying voting rights comprised in the bid.

   Following a mandatory bid, the consideration offered in the bid shall be presumed to be fair.

Article 16

The right of sell-out

1. Member States shall ensure that, following a bid made to all the holders of the offeree company's securities for all of their securities, paragraphs 2 and 3 apply.
2. Member States shall ensure that a holder of remaining securities is able to require the offeror to buy his/her securities from him/her at a fair price under the same circumstances as provided for in Article 15(2).
3. Article 15(3) to (5) shall apply mutatis mutandis.

Article 17

Sanctions

Member States shall determine the sanctions to be imposed for infringement of the national measures adopted pursuant to this Directive and shall take all necessary steps to ensure that they are put into effect. The sanctions thus provided for shall be effective, proportionate and dissuasive. Member States shall notify the Commission of those measures no later than the date laid down in Article 21(1) and of any subsequent change thereto at the earliest opportunity.

Article 18

Committee procedure

1. The Commission shall be assisted by the European Securities Committee established by Decision 2001/528/EC (hereinafter referred to as 'the Committee').
2. Where reference is made to this paragraph, Article 5a(1) to (4) and Article 7 of Decision 1999/468/EC shall apply, having regard to the provisions of Article 8 thereof.

Article 19

Contact committee

1. A contact committee shall be set up which has as its functions:
   (a) to facilitate, without prejudice to Articles 226 and 227 of the Treaty, the harmonised application of this Directive through regular meetings dealing with practical problems arising in connection with its application;
   (b) to advise the Commission, if necessary, on additions or amendments to this Directive.
2. It shall not be the function of the contact committee to appraise the merits of decisions taken by the supervisory authorities in individual cases.

Article 20

Revision

Five years after the date laid down in Article 21(1), the Commission shall examine this Directive in the light of the experience acquired in applying it and, if necessary, propose its revision. That examination shall include a survey of the control structures and barriers to takeover bids that are not covered by this Directive.

To that end, Member States shall provide the Commission annually with information on the takeover bids which have been launched against companies the securities of which are admitted to trading on their regulated markets. That information shall include the nationalities of the companies involved, the results of the offers and any other information relevant to the understanding of how takeover bids operate in practice.

Article 21

Transposition

1. Member States shall bring into force the laws, regulations and administrative provisions necessary to comply with this Directive no later than 20 May 2006. They shall forthwith inform the Commission thereof.

   When Member States adopt those provisions, they shall contain a reference to this Directive or shall be accompanied by such reference on the occasion of their official publication. The methods of making such reference shall be laid down by the Member States.
2. Member States shall communicate to the Commission the text of the main provisions of national law that they adopt in the fields covered by this Directive.

Article 22

Entry into force

This Directive shall enter into force on the 20th day after that of its publication in the *Official Journal of the European Union*.

Article 23

Addressees

This Directive is addressed to the Member States.

Done at Strasbourg, 21 April 2004.

Enterprise Act 2002

2002 c. 40

An Act to establish and provide for the functions of the Office of Fair Trading, the Competition Appeal Tribunal and the Competition Service; to make provision about mergers and market structures and conduct; to amend the constitution and functions of the Competition Commission; to create an offence for those entering into certain anti-competitive agreements; to provide for the disqualification of directors of companies engaging in certain anti-competitive practices; to make other provision about competition law; to amend the law relating to the protection of the collective interests of consumers; to make further provision about the disclosure of information obtained under competition and consumer legislation; to amend the Insolvency Act 1986 and make other provision about insolvency; and for connected purposes.

[7th November 2002]

PART 3
MERGERS

CHAPTER 1
DUTY TO MAKE REFERENCES

Duty to make references: completed mergers

22. Duty to make references in relation to completed mergers

(1) The OFT shall, subject to subsections (2) and (3), make a reference to the Commission if the OFT believes that it is or may be the case that—

(a) a relevant merger situation has been created; and

(b) the creation of that situation has resulted, or may be expected to result, in a substantial lessening of competition within any market or markets in the United Kingdom for goods or services.

(2) The OFT may decide not to make a reference under this section if it believes that—

(a) the market concerned is not, or the markets concerned are not, of sufficient importance to justify the making of a reference to the Commission; or

(b) any relevant customer benefits in relation to the creation of the relevant merger situation concerned outweigh the substantial lessening of competition concerned and any adverse effects of the substantial lessening of competition concerned.

(3) No reference shall be made under this section if—

(a) the making of the reference is prevented by section … 74(1) or 96(3) or paragraph 4 of Schedule 7;

(b) the OFT is considering whether to accept undertakings under section 73 instead of making such a reference;

(c) the relevant merger situation concerned is being, or has been, dealt with in connection with a reference made under section 33;

(d) a notice under section 42(2) is in force in relation to the matter or the matter to which such a notice relates has been finally determined under Chapter 2 otherwise than in circumstances in which a notice is then given to the OFT under section 56(1); …

(e) the European Commission is considering a request made, in relation to the matter concerned, by the United Kingdom (whether alone or with others) under article 22(1) of the EC Merger Regulation, is proceeding with the matter in pursuance of such a request or has dealt with the matter in pursuance of such a request; or

(f) subject to subsection (3A), a reasoned submission requesting referral to the European Commission has been submitted to the European Commission under article 4(5) of the EC Merger Regulation.

(3A) Subsection (3)(f) shall cease to apply if the OFT is informed that a Member State competent to examine the concentration under its national competition law has, within the time permitted by Article 4(5) of the EC Merger Regulation, expressed its disagreement as regards the request to refer the case to the European Commission; and this subsection shall be construed in accordance with that Regulation.

(4) A reference under this section shall, in particular, specify—

(a) the enactment under which it is made; and

(b) the date on which it is made.

(5) The references in this section to the creation of a relevant merger situation shall be construed in accordance with section 23, the reference in subsection (2) of this section to relevant customer benefits shall be construed in accordance with section 30 and the reference in subsection (3) of this section to a matter to which a notice under section 42(2) relates being finally determined under Chapter 2 shall be construed in accordance with section 43(4) and (5).

(6) In this Part "market in the United Kingdom" includes—

(a) so far as it operates in the United Kingdom or a part of the United Kingdom, any market which operates there and in another country or territory or in a part of another country or territory; and

(b) any market which operates only in a part of the United Kingdom;

and references to a market for goods or services include references to a market for goods and services.

(7) In this Part "the decision-making authority" means—

(a) in the case of a reference or possible reference under this section or section 33, the OFT or (as the case may be) the Commission; and

(b) in the case of a notice or possible notice under section 42(2) or 59(2) or a reference or possible reference under section 45 or 62, the OFT, the Commission or (as the case may be) the Secretary of State.

23. Relevant merger situations

(1) For the purposes of this Part, a relevant merger situation has been created if—

(a) two or more enterprises have ceased to be distinct enterprises at a time or in circumstances falling within section 24; and

(b) the value of the turnover in the United Kingdom of the enterprise being taken over exceeds £70 million.

(2) For the purposes of this Part, a relevant merger situation has also been created if—

(a) two or more enterprises have ceased to be distinct enterprises at a time or in circumstances falling within section 24; and

(b) as a result, one or both of the conditions mentioned in subsections (3) and (4) below prevails or prevails to a greater extent.

(3) The condition mentioned in this subsection is that, in relation to the supply of goods of any description, at least one-quarter of all the goods of that description which are supplied in the United Kingdom, or in a substantial part of the United Kingdom—

(a) are supplied by one and the same person or are supplied to one and the same person; or

(b) are supplied by the persons by whom the enterprises concerned are carried on, or are supplied to those persons.

(4) The condition mentioned in this subsection is that, in relation to the supply of services of any description, the supply of services of that description in the United Kingdom, or in a substantial part of the United Kingdom, is to the extent of at least one-quarter—

(a) supply by one and the same person, or supply for one and the same person; or

(b) supply by the persons by whom the enterprises concerned are carried on, or supply for those persons.

(5) For the purpose of deciding whether the proportion of one-quarter mentioned in subsection (3) or (4) is fulfilled with respect to goods or (as the case may be) services of any description, the decision-making authority shall apply such criterion (whether value, cost, price, quantity,

capacity, number of workers employed or some other criterion, of whatever nature), or such combination of criteria, as the decision-making authority considers appropriate.

(6) References in subsections (3) and (4) to the supply of goods or (as the case may be) services shall, in relation to goods or services of any description which are the subject of different forms of supply, be construed in whichever of the following ways the decision-making authority considers appropriate—

(a) as references to any of those forms of supply taken separately;

(b) as references to all those forms of supply taken together; or

(c) as references to any of those forms of supply taken in groups.

(7) For the purposes of subsection (6) the decision-making authority may treat goods or services as being the subject of different forms of supply whenever—

(a) the transactions concerned differ as to their nature, their parties, their terms or their surrounding circumstances; and

(b) the difference is one which, in the opinion of the decision-making authority, ought for the purposes of that subsection to be treated as a material difference.

(8) The criteria for deciding when goods or services can be treated, for the purposes of this section, as goods or services of a separate description shall be such as in any particular case the decision-making authority considers appropriate in the circumstances of that case.

(9) For the purposes of this Chapter, the question whether a relevant merger situation has been created shall be determined as at—

(a) in the case of a reference which is treated as having been made under section 22 by virtue of section 37(2), such time as the Commission may determine; and

(b) in any other case, immediately before the time when the reference has been, or is to be, made.

24. Time-limits and prior notice

(1) For the purposes of section 23 two or more enterprises have ceased to be distinct enterprises at a time or in circumstances falling within this section if—

(a) the two or more enterprises ceased to be distinct enterprises before the day on which the reference relating to them is to be made and did so not more than four months before that day; or

(b) notice of material facts about the arrangements or transactions under or in consequence of which the enterprises have ceased to be distinct enterprises has not been given in accordance with subsection (2).

(2) Notice of material facts is given in accordance with this subsection if—

(a) it is given to the OFT prior to the entering into of the arrangements or transactions concerned or the facts are made public prior to the entering into of those arrangements or transactions; or

(b) it is given to the OFT, or the facts are made public, more than four months before the day on which the reference is to be made.

(3) In this section—

"made public" means so publicised as to be generally known or readily ascertainable; and

"notice" includes notice which is not in writing.

25. Extension of time-limits

(1) The OFT and the persons carrying on the enterprises which have or may have ceased to be distinct enterprises may agree to extend by no more than 20 days the four month period mentioned in section 24(1)(a) or (2)(b).

(2) The OFT may by notice to the persons carrying on the enterprises which have or may have ceased to be distinct enterprises extend the four month period mentioned in section 24(1)(a) or (2)(b) if it considers that any of those persons has failed to provide, within the period stated in a notice under section 31 and in the manner authorised or required, information requested of him in that notice.

(3) An extension under subsection (2) shall be for the period beginning with the end of the period within which the information is to be provided and which is stated in the notice under section 31 and ending with—
(a) the provision of the information to the satisfaction of the OFT; or
(b) if earlier, the cancellation by the OFT of the extension.

(4) The OFT may by notice to the persons carrying on the enterprises which have or may have ceased to be distinct enterprises extend the four month period mentioned in section 24(1)(a) or (2)(b) if it is seeking undertakings from any of those persons under section 73.

(5) An extension under subsection (4) shall be for the period beginning with the receipt of the notice under that subsection and ending with the earliest of the following events—
(a) the giving of the undertakings concerned;
(b) the expiry of the period of 10 days beginning with the first day after the receipt by the OFT of a notice from the person who has been given a notice under subsection (4) and from whom the undertakings are being sought stating that he does not intend to give the undertakings; or
(c) the cancellation by the OFT of the extension.

(6) The OFT may by notice to the persons carrying on the enterprises which have or may have ceased to be distinct enterprises extend the four month period mentioned in section 24(1)(a) or (2)(b) if the European Commission is considering a request made, in relation to the matter concerned, by the United Kingdom (whether alone or with others) under article 22(1) of the EC Merger Regulation (but is not yet proceeding with the matter in pursuance of such a request).

(7) An extension under subsection (6) shall be for the period beginning with the receipt of the notice under that subsection and ending with the receipt of a notice under subsection (8).

(8) The OFT shall, in connection with any notice given by it under subsection (6), by notice inform the persons carrying on the enterprises which have or may have ceased to be distinct enterprises of the completion by the European Commission of its consideration of the request of the United Kingdom.

(9) Subject to subsections (10) and (11), where the four month period mentioned in section 24(1)(a) or (2)(b) is extended or further extended by virtue of this section in relation to a particular case, any reference to that period in section 24 or the preceding provisions of this section shall have effect in relation to that case as if it were a reference to a period equivalent to the aggregate of the period being extended and the period of the extension (whether or not those periods overlap in time).

(10) Subsection (11) applies where—
(a) the four month period mentioned in section 24(1)(a) or (2)(b) is further extended;
(b) the further extension and at least one previous extension is made under one or more of subsections (2), (4) and (6); and
(c) the same days or fractions of days are included in or comprise the further extension and are included in or comprise at least one such previous extension.

(11) In calculating the period of the further extension, any days or fractions of days of the kind mentioned in subsection (10)(c) shall be disregarded.

(12) No more than one extension is possible under subsection (1).

26. Enterprises ceasing to be distinct enterprises

(1) For the purposes of this Part any two enterprises cease to be distinct enterprises if they are brought under common ownership or common control (whether or not the business to which either of them formerly belonged continues to be carried on under the same or different ownership or control).

(2) Enterprises shall, in particular, be treated as being under common control if they are—
(a) enterprises of interconnected bodies corporate;
(b) enterprises carried on by two or more bodies corporate of which one and the same person or group of persons has control; or

(c) an enterprise carried on by a body corporate and an enterprise carried on by a person or group of persons having control of that body corporate.

(3) A person or group of persons able, directly or indirectly, to control or materially to influence the policy of a body corporate, or the policy of any person in carrying on an enterprise but without having a controlling interest in that body corporate or in that enterprise, may, for the purposes of subsections (1) and (2), be treated as having control of it.

(4) For the purposes of subsection (1), in so far as it relates to bringing two or more enterprises under common control, a person or group of persons may be treated as bringing an enterprise under his or their control if—

(a) being already able to control or materially to influence the policy of the person carrying on the enterprise, that person or group of persons acquires a controlling interest in the enterprise or, in the case of an enterprise carried on by a body corporate, acquires a controlling interest in that body corporate; or

(b) being already able materially to influence the policy of the person carrying on the enterprise, that person or group of persons becomes able to control that policy.

27. Time when enterprises cease to be distinct

(1) Subsection (2) applies in relation to any arrangements or transaction—

(a) not having immediate effect or having immediate effect only in part; but

(b) under or in consequence of which any two enterprises cease to be distinct enterprises.

(2) The time when the parties to any such arrangements or transaction become bound to such extent as will result, on effect being given to their obligations, in the enterprises ceasing to be distinct enterprises shall be taken to be the time at which the two enterprises cease to be distinct enterprises.

(3) In accordance with subsections (1) and (2) (but without prejudice to the generality of those subsections) for the purpose of determining the time at which any two enterprises cease to be distinct enterprises no account shall be taken of any option or other conditional right until the option is exercised or the condition is satisfied.

(4) Subsections (1) to (3) are subject to subsections (5) to (8) and section 29.

(5) The decision-making authority may, for the purposes of a reference, treat successive events to which this subsection applies as having occurred simultaneously on the date on which the latest of them occurred.

(6) Subsection (5) applies to successive events—

(a) which occur within a period of two years under or in consequence of the same arrangements or transaction, or successive arrangements or transactions between the same parties or interests; and

(b) by virtue of each of which, under or in consequence of the arrangements or the transaction or transactions concerned, any enterprises cease as between themselves to be distinct enterprises.

(7) The decision-making authority may, for the purposes of subsections (5) and (6), treat such arrangements or transactions as the decision-making authority considers appropriate as arrangements or transactions between the same interests.

(8) In deciding whether it is appropriate to treat arrangements or transactions as arrangements or transactions between the same interests the decision-making authority shall, in particular, have regard to the persons substantially concerned in the arrangements or transactions concerned.

28. Turnover test

(1) For the purposes of section 23 the value of the turnover in the United Kingdom of the enterprise being taken over shall be determined by taking the total value of the turnover in the United Kingdom of the enterprises which cease to be distinct enterprises and deducting—

(a) the turnover in the United Kingdom of any enterprise which continues to be carried on under the same ownership and control; or

(b) if no enterprise continues to be carried on under the same ownership and control, the turnover in the United Kingdom which, of all the turnovers concerned, is the turnover of the highest value.

(2) For the purposes of this Part (other than section 121(4)(c)(ii)) the turnover in the United Kingdom of an enterprise shall be determined in accordance with such provisions as may be specified in an order made by the Secretary of State.

(3) An order under subsection (2) may, in particular, make provision as to—

(a) the amounts which are, or which are not, to be treated as comprising an enterprise's turnover;

(b) the date or dates by reference to which an enterprise's turnover is to be determined;

(c) the connection with the United Kingdom by virtue of which an enterprise's turnover is turnover in the United Kingdom.

(4) An order under subsection (2) may, in particular, make provision enabling the decision-making authority to determine matters of a description specified in the order (including any of the matters mentioned in paragraphs (a) to (c) of subsection (3)).

(5) The OFT shall—

(a) keep under review the sum for the time being mentioned in section 23(1)(b); and

(b) from time to time advise the Secretary of State as to whether the sum is still appropriate.

(6) The Secretary of State may by order amend section 23(1)(b) so as to alter the sum for the time being mentioned there.

29. Obtaining control by stages

(1) Where an enterprise is brought under the control of a person or group of persons in the course of two or more transactions (in this section a "series of transactions") to which subsection (2) applies, those transactions may, if the decision-making authority considers it appropriate, be treated for the purposes of a reference as having occurred simultaneously on the date on which the latest of them occurred.

(2) This subsection applies to—

(a) any transaction which—

(i) enables that person or group of persons directly or indirectly to control or materially to influence the policy of any person carrying on the enterprise;

(ii) enables that person or group of persons to do so to a greater degree; or

(iii) is a step (whether direct or indirect) towards enabling that person or group of persons to do so; and

(b) any transaction by virtue of which that person or group of persons acquires a controlling interest in the enterprise or, where the enterprise is carried on by a body corporate, in that body corporate.

(3) Where a series of transactions includes a transaction falling within subsection (2)(b), any transaction occurring after the occurrence of that transaction is to be disregarded for the purposes of subsection (1).

(4) Where the period within which a series of transactions occurs exceeds two years, the transactions that may be treated as mentioned in subsection (1) are any of those transactions that occur within a period of two years.

(5) Sections 26(2) to (4) and 127(1), (2) and (4) to (6) shall apply for the purposes of this section to determine—

(a) whether an enterprise is brought under the control of a person or group of persons; and

(b) whether a transaction is one to which subsection (2) applies;

as they apply for the purposes of section 26 to determine whether enterprises are brought under common control.

(6) In determining for the purposes of this section the time at which any transaction occurs, no account shall be taken of any option or other conditional right until the option is exercised or the condition is satisfied.

30. Relevant customer benefits

(1) For the purposes of this Part a benefit is a relevant customer benefit if—

(a) it is a benefit to relevant customers in the form of—

(i) lower prices, higher quality or greater choice of goods or services in any market in the United Kingdom (whether or not the market or markets in which the substantial lessening of competition concerned has, or may have, occurred or (as the case may be) may occur); or

(ii) greater innovation in relation to such goods or services; and

(b) the decision-making authority believes—

(i) in the case of a reference or possible reference under section 22 or 45(2), as mentioned in subsection (2); and

(ii) in the case of a reference or possible reference under section 33 or 45(4), as mentioned in subsection (3).

(2) The belief, in the case of a reference or possible reference under section 22 or section 45(2), is that—

(a) the benefit has accrued as a result of the creation of the relevant merger situation concerned or may be expected to accrue within a reasonable period as a result of the creation of that situation; and

(b) the benefit was, or is, unlikely to accrue without the creation of that situation or a similar lessening of competition.

(3) The belief, in the case of a reference or possible reference under section 33 or 45(4), is that—

(a) the benefit may be expected to accrue within a reasonable period as a result of the creation of the relevant merger situation concerned; and

(b) the benefit is unlikely to accrue without the creation of that situation or a similar lessening of competition.

(4) In subsection (1) "relevant customers" means—

(a) customers of any person carrying on an enterprise which, in the creation of the relevant merger situation concerned, has ceased to be, or (as the case may be) will cease to be, a distinct enterprise;

(b) customers of such customers; and

(c) any other customers in a chain of customers beginning with the customers mentioned in paragraph (a);

and in this subsection "customers" includes future customers.

31. Information powers in relation to completed mergers

(1) The OFT may by notice to any of the persons carrying on the enterprises which have or may have ceased to be distinct enterprises request him to provide the OFT with such information as the OFT may require for the purpose of deciding whether to make a reference under section 22.

(2) The notice shall state—

(a) the information required;

(b) the period within which the information is to be provided; and

(c) the possible consequences of not providing the information within the stated period and in the authorised or required manner.

32. Supplementary provision for purposes of sections 25 and 31

(1) The Secretary of State may make regulations for the purposes of sections 25 and 31.

(2) The regulations may, in particular—

(a) provide for the manner in which any information requested by the OFT under section 31 is authorised or required to be provided, and the time at which such information is to be treated as provided (including the time at which it is to be treated as provided to the satisfaction of the OFT for the purposes of section 25(3));

(b) provide for the persons carrying on the enterprises which have or may have ceased to be distinct enterprises to be informed, in circumstances in which section 25(3) applies—

(i) of the fact that the OFT is satisfied as to the provision of the information requested by it or (as the case may be) of the OFT's decision to cancel the extension; and

(ii) of the time at which the OFT is to be treated as so satisfied or (as the case may be) of the time at which the cancellation is to be treated as having effect;

(c) provide for the persons carrying on the enterprises which have or may have ceased to be distinct enterprises to be informed, in circumstances in which section 25(5) applies—

(i) of the OFT's decision to cancel the extension; and

(ii) of the time at which the cancellation is to be treated as having effect;

(d) provide for the time at which any notice under section 25(4), (5)(b), (6) or (8) is to be treated as received;

(e) provide that a person is, or is not, to be treated, in such circumstances as may be specified in the regulations, as acting on behalf of a person carrying on an enterprise which has or may have ceased to be a distinct enterprise.

(3) A notice under section 25(2)—

(a) shall be given within 5 days of the end of the period within which the information is to be provided and which is stated in the notice under section 31; and

(b) shall inform the person to whom it is addressed of—

(i) the OFT's opinion as mentioned in section 25(2); and

(ii) the OFT's intention to extend the period for considering whether to make a reference.

(4) In determining for the purposes of section 25(1) or (5)(b) or subsection (3)(a) above any period which is expressed in the enactment concerned as a period of days or number of days no account shall be taken of—

(a) Saturday, Sunday, Good Friday and Christmas Day; and

(b) any day which is a bank holiday in England and Wales.

Duty to make references: anticipated mergers

33. Duty to make references in relation to anticipated mergers

(1) The OFT shall, subject to subsections (2) and (3), make a reference to the Commission if the OFT believes that it is or may be the case that—

(a) arrangements are in progress or in contemplation which, if carried into effect, will result in the creation of a relevant merger situation; and

(b) the creation of that situation may be expected to result in a substantial lessening of competition within any market or markets in the United Kingdom for goods or services.

(2) The OFT may decide not to make a reference under this section if it believes that—

(a) the market concerned is not, or the markets concerned are not, of sufficient importance to justify the making of a reference to the Commission;

(b) the arrangements concerned are not sufficiently far advanced, or are not sufficiently likely to proceed, to justify the making of a reference to the Commission; or

(c) any relevant customer benefits in relation to the creation of the relevant merger situation concerned outweigh the substantial lessening of competition concerned and any adverse effects of the substantial lessening of competition concerned.

(3) No reference shall be made under this section if—

(a) the making of the reference is prevented by section … 74(1) or 96(3) or paragraph 4 of Schedule 7;

(b) the OFT is considering whether to accept undertakings under section 73 instead of making such a reference;

(c) the arrangements concerned are being, or have been, dealt with in connection with a reference made under section 22;

(d) a notice under section 42(2) is in force in relation to the matter or the matter to which such a notice relates has been finally determined under Chapter 2 otherwise than in circumstances in which a notice is then given to the OFT under section 56(1); …

(e) the European Commission is considering a request made, in relation to the matter concerned, by the United Kingdom (whether alone or with others) under article 22(1) of the EC Merger Regulation, is proceeding with the matter in pursuance of such a request or has dealt with the matter in pursuance of such a request; or

(f) subject to subsection (3A), a reasoned submission requesting referral to the European Commission has been submitted to the European Commission under article 4(5) of the EC Merger Regulation.

(3A) Section 33(3)(f) shall cease to apply if the OFT is informed that a Member State competent to examine the concentration under its national competition law has, within the time permitted by Article 4(5) of the EC Merger Regulation, expressed its disagreement as regards the request to refer the case to the European Commission; and this subsection shall be construed in accordance with that Regulation.

(4) A reference under this section shall, in particular, specify—

(a) the enactment under which it is made; and

(b) the date on which it is made.

34. Supplementary provision in relation to anticipated mergers

(1) The Secretary of State may by order make such provision as he considers appropriate about the operation of sections 27 and 29 in relation to—

(a) references under this Part which relate to arrangements which are in progress or in contemplation; or

(b) notices under section 42(2), 59(2) or 67(2) which relate to such arrangements.

(2) An order under subsection (1) may, in particular—

(a) provide for sections 27(5) to (8) and 29 to apply with modifications in relation to such references or notices or in relation to particular descriptions of such references or notices;

(b) enable particular descriptions of events, arrangements or transactions which have already occurred—

(i) to be taken into account for the purposes of deciding whether to make such references or such references of a particular description or whether to give such notices or such notices of a particular description;

(ii) to be dealt with under such references or such references of a particular description or under such notices or such notices of a particular description.

Cases referred by European Commission under EC Merger Regulation

34A. Duty of OFT where case referred by the European Commission

(1) Subsection (2) applies if the European Commission has by a decision referred the whole or part of a case to the OFT under Article 4(4) or 9 of the EC Merger Regulation, or is deemed to have taken such a decision, unless an intervention notice is in force in relation to that case.

(2) Before the end of the preliminary assessment period, the OFT shall—

(a) decide whether to make a reference to the Commission under section 22 or 33; and

(b) inform the persons carrying on the enterprises concerned by notice of that decision and of the reasons for it.

(3) The OFT may, for the purposes of subsection (2), decide not to make a reference on the basis that it is considering whether to seek or accept undertakings under section 73 instead of making a reference; but a decision taken on that basis does not prevent the OFT from making a reference under section 22 or 33 in the event of no such undertakings being offered or accepted.

(4) In this section—

"the preliminary assessment period" means, subject to subsection (5), the period of 45 working days beginning with the day after the day on which the decision of the European Commission to refer the case is taken (or is deemed to have been taken); and

"working day" means any day which is not—

(a) a Saturday;

(b) a Sunday; or

(c) a day which is a European Commission holiday (as published in the Official Journal of the European Union before the beginning of the year in which it occurs).

(5) If the OFT has imposed a requirement under section 34B and it considers that the person on whom that requirement was imposed has failed to comply with it, the OFT may, by notice to the persons carrying on the enterprises concerned, extend the preliminary assessment period.

(6) The period of an extension under subsection (5) shall—

(a) begin with the end of the period within which the requirement under section 34B could be complied with; and

(b) end with the earlier of either compliance with the requirement to the satisfaction of the OFT or cancellation by the OFT of the extension.

(7) A notice under subsection (6) shall—

(a) be given within 5 working days of the end of the period mentioned in paragraph (a) of that subsection; and

(b) inform the person to whom it is addressed that the OFT is of the opinion mentioned in subsection (5) and that it intends to extend the preliminary assessment period.

34B. Power to request information in referred cases

(1) In a case mentioned in section 34A(1), the OFT may by notice to any of the persons carrying on the enterprises concerned request him to provide the OFT with such information as the OFT may require for the purpose of making a decision for the purposes of section 34A(2).

(2) The notice shall state—

(a) the information required;

(b) the period within which the information is to be provided;

(c) the manner (if any) in which the information is required to be provided; and

(d) the possible consequences—

(i) of not providing the information within the stated period; and

(ii) if a manner for its provision is stated in the notice, of not providing it in that manner.

Determination of references

35. Questions to be decided in relation to completed mergers

(1) Subject to subsections (6) and (7) and section 127(3), the Commission shall, on a reference under section 22, decide the following questions—

(a) whether a relevant merger situation has been created; and

(b) if so, whether the creation of that situation has resulted, or may be expected to result, in a substantial lessening of competition within any market or markets in the United Kingdom for goods or services.

(2) For the purposes of this Part there is an anti-competitive outcome if—

(a) a relevant merger situation has been created and the creation of that situation has resulted, or may be expected to result, in a substantial lessening of competition within any market or markets in the United Kingdom for goods or services; or

(b) arrangements are in progress or in contemplation which, if carried into effect, will result in the creation of a relevant merger situation and the creation of that situation may be expected to result in a substantial lessening of competition within any market or markets in the United Kingdom for goods or services.

(3) The Commission shall, if it has decided on a reference under section 22 that there is an anti-competitive outcome (within the meaning given by subsection (2)(a)), decide the following additional questions—

(a) whether action should be taken by it under section 41(2) for the purpose of remedying, mitigating or preventing the substantial lessening of competition concerned or any adverse effect which has resulted from, or may be expected to result from, the substantial lessening of competition;

(b) whether it should recommend the taking of action by others for the purpose of remedying, mitigating or preventing the substantial lessening of competition concerned or any adverse effect which has resulted from, or may be expected to result from, the substantial lessening of competition; and

(c) in either case, if action should be taken, what action should be taken and what is to be remedied, mitigated or prevented.

(4) In deciding the questions mentioned in subsection (3) the Commission shall, in particular, have regard to the need to achieve as comprehensive a solution as is reasonable and practicable to the substantial lessening of competition and any adverse effects resulting from it.

(5) In deciding the questions mentioned in subsection (3) the Commission may, in particular, have regard to the effect of any action on any relevant customer benefits in relation to the creation of the relevant merger situation concerned.

(6) In relation to the question whether a relevant merger situation has been created, a reference under section 22 may be framed so as to require the Commission to exclude from consideration—

(a) subsection (1) of section 23;

(b) subsection (2) of that section; or

(c) one of those subsections if the Commission finds that the other is satisfied.

(7) In relation to the question whether any such result as is mentioned in section 23(2)(b) has arisen, a reference under section 22 may be framed so as to require the Commission to confine its investigation to the supply of goods or services in a part of the United Kingdom specified in the reference.

36. Questions to be decided in relation to anticipated mergers

(1) Subject to subsections (5) and (6) and section 127(3), the Commission shall, on a reference under section 33, decide the following questions—

(a) whether arrangements are in progress or in contemplation which, if carried into effect, will result in the creation of a relevant merger situation; and

(b) if so, whether the creation of that situation may be expected to result in a substantial lessening of competition within any market or markets in the United Kingdom for goods or services.

(2) The Commission shall, if it has decided on a reference under section 33 that there is an anti-competitive outcome (within the meaning given by section 35(2)(b)), decide the following additional questions—

(a) whether action should be taken by it under section 41(2) for the purpose of remedying, mitigating or preventing the substantial lessening of competition concerned or any adverse effect which may be expected to result from the substantial lessening of competition;

(b) whether it should recommend the taking of action by others for the purpose of remedying, mitigating or preventing the substantial lessening of competition concerned or any adverse effect which may be expected to result from the substantial lessening of competition; and

(c) in either case, if action should be taken, what action should be taken and what is to be remedied, mitigated or prevented.

(3) In deciding the questions mentioned in subsection (2) the Commission shall, in particular, have regard to the need to achieve as comprehensive a solution as is reasonable and practicable to the substantial lessening of competition and any adverse effects resulting from it.

(4) In deciding the questions mentioned in subsection (2) the Commission may, in particular, have regard to the effect of any action on any relevant customer benefits in relation to the creation of the relevant merger situation concerned.

(5) In relation to the question whether a relevant merger situation will be created, a reference under section 33 may be framed so as to require the Commission to exclude from consideration—

(a) subsection (1) of section 23;

(b) subsection (2) of that section; or

(c) one of those subsections if the Commission finds that the other is satisfied.

(6) In relation to the question whether any such result as is mentioned in section 23(2)(b) will arise, a reference under section 33 may be framed so as to require the Commission to confine its

investigation to the supply of goods or services in a part of the United Kingdom specified in the reference.

37. Cancellation and variation of references under section 22 or 33

(1) The Commission shall cancel a reference under section 33 if it considers that the proposal to make arrangements of the kind mentioned in the reference has been abandoned.

(2) The Commission may, if it considers that doing so is justified by the facts (including events occurring on or after the making of the reference concerned), treat a reference made under section 22 or 33 as if it had been made under section 33 or (as the case may be) 22; and, in such cases, references in this Part to references under those sections shall, so far as may be necessary, be construed accordingly.

(3) Where, by virtue of subsection (2), the Commission treats a reference made under section 22 or 33 as if it had been made under section 33 or (as the case may be) 22, sections 77 to 81 shall, in particular, apply as if the reference had been made under section 33 or (as the case may be) 22 instead of under section 22 or 33.

(4) Subsection (5) applies in relation to any undertaking accepted under section 80, or any order made under section 81, which is in force immediately before the Commission, by virtue of subsection (2), treats a reference made under section 22 or 33 as if it had been made under section 33 or (as the case may be) 22.

(5) The undertaking or order shall, so far as applicable, continue in force as if—

(a) in the case of an undertaking or order which relates to a reference made under section 22, accepted or made in relation to a reference made under section 33; and

(b) in the case of an undertaking or order which relates to a reference made under section 33, accepted or made in relation to a reference made under section 22;

and the undertaking or order concerned may be varied, superseded, released or revoked accordingly.

(6) The OFT may at any time vary a reference under section 22 or 33.

(7) The OFT shall consult the Commission before varying any such reference.

(8) Subsection (7) shall not apply if the Commission has requested the variation concerned.

(9) No variation by the OFT under this section shall be capable of altering the period permitted by section 39 within which the report of the Commission under section 38 is to be prepared and published.

38. Investigations and reports on references under section 22 or 33

(1) The Commission shall prepare and publish a report on a reference under section 22 or 33 within the period permitted by section 39.

(2) The report shall, in particular, contain—

(a) the decisions of the Commission on the questions which it is required to answer by virtue of section 35 or (as the case may be) 36;

(b) its reasons for its decisions; and

(c) such information as the Commission considers appropriate for facilitating a proper understanding of those questions and of its reasons for its decisions.

(3) The Commission shall carry out such investigations as it considers appropriate for the purposes of preparing a report under this section.

(4) The Commission shall, at the same time as a report prepared under this section is published, give it to the OFT.

39. Time-limits for investigations and reports

(1) The Commission shall prepare and publish its report under section 38 within the period of 24 weeks beginning with the date of the reference concerned.

(2) …

(3) The Commission may extend, by no more than 8 weeks, the period within which a report under section 38 is to be prepared and published if it considers that there are special reasons why the report cannot be prepared and published within that period.

(4) The Commission may extend the period within which a report under section 38 is to be prepared and published if it considers that a relevant person has failed (whether with or without a reasonable excuse) to comply with any requirement of a notice under section 109.

(5) In subsection (4) "relevant person" means—

(a) any person carrying on any of the enterprises concerned;

(b) any person who (whether alone or as a member of a group) owns or has control of any such person; or

(c) any officer, employee or agent of any person mentioned in paragraph (a) or (b).

(6) For the purposes of subsection (5) a person or group of persons able, directly or indirectly, to control or materially to influence the policy of a body of persons corporate or unincorporate, but without having a controlling interest in that body of persons, may be treated as having control of it.

(7) An extension under subsection (3) or (4) shall come into force when published under section 107.

(8) An extension under subsection (4) shall continue in force until—

(a) the person concerned provides the information or documents to the satisfaction of the Commission or (as the case may be) appears as a witness in accordance with the requirements of the Commission; or

(b) the Commission publishes its decision to cancel the extension.

(9) References in this Part to the date of a reference shall be construed as references to the date specified in the reference as the date on which it is made.

(10) This section is subject to section 40.

40. Section 39: supplementary

(1), (2) …

(3) A period extended under subsection (3) of section 39 may also be extended under subsection (4) of that section and a period extended under subsection (4) of that section may also be extended under subsection (3) of that section.

(4) No more than one extension is possible under section 39(3).

(5) Where a period within which a report under section 38 is to be prepared and published is extended or further extended under section 39(3) or (4), the period as extended or (as the case may be) further extended shall, subject to subsections (6) and (7), be calculated by taking the period being extended and adding to it the period of the extension (whether or not those periods overlap in time).

(6) Subsection (7) applies where—

(a) the period within which the report under section 38 is to be prepared and published is further extended;

(b) the further extension and at least one previous extension is made under section 39(4); and

(c) the same days or fractions of days are included in or comprise the further extension and are included in or comprise at least one such previous extension.

(7) In calculating the period of the further extension, any days or fractions of days of the kind mentioned in subsection (6)(c) shall be disregarded.

(8) The Secretary of State may by order amend section 39 so as to alter any one or more of the following periods—

(a) the period of 24 weeks mentioned in subsection (1) of that section or any period for the time being mentioned in that subsection in substitution for that period;

(b) …

(c) the period of 8 weeks mentioned in subsection (3) of that section or any period for the time being mentioned in that subsection in substitution for that period.

(9) No alteration shall be made by virtue of subsection (8) which results in the period for the time being mentioned in subsection (1) … of section 39 exceeding 24 weeks or the period for the time being mentioned in subsection (3) of that section exceeding 8 weeks.

(10) An order under subsection (8) shall not affect any period of time within which the Commission is under a duty to prepare and publish its report under section 38 in relation to a reference under

section 22 or 33 if the Commission is already under that duty in relation to that reference when the order is made.

(11) Before making an order under subsection (8) the Secretary of State shall consult the Commission and such other persons as he considers appropriate.

(12) The Secretary of State may make regulations for the purposes of section 39(8).

(13) The regulations may, in particular—

(a) provide for the time at which information or documents are to be treated as provided (including the time at which they are to be treated as provided to the satisfaction of the Commission for the purposes of section 39(8));

(b) provide for the time at which a person is to be treated as appearing as a witness (including the time at which he is to be treated as appearing as a witness in accordance with the requirements of the Commission for the purposes of section 39(8));

(c) provide for the persons carrying on the enterprises which have or may have ceased to be, or may cease to be, distinct enterprises to be informed, in circumstances in which section 39(8) applies, of the fact that—

(i) the Commission is satisfied as to the provision of the information or documents required by it; or

(ii) the person concerned has appeared as a witness in accordance with the requirements of the Commission;

(d) provide for the persons carrying on the enterprises which have or may have ceased to be, or may cease to be, distinct enterprises to be informed, in circumstances in which section 39(8) applies, of the time at which the Commission is to be treated as satisfied as mentioned in paragraph (c)(i) above or the person concerned is to be treated as having appeared as mentioned in paragraph (c)(ii) above.

41. Duty to remedy effects of completed or anticipated mergers

(1) Subsection (2) applies where a report of the Commission has been prepared and published under section 38 within the period permitted by section 39 and contains the decision that there is an anti-competitive outcome.

(2) The Commission shall take such action under section 82 or 84 as it considers to be reasonable and practicable—

(a) to remedy, mitigate or prevent the substantial lessening of competition concerned; and

(b) to remedy, mitigate or prevent any adverse effects which have resulted from, or may be expected to result from, the substantial lessening of competition.

(3) The decision of the Commission under subsection (2) shall be consistent with its decisions as included in its report by virtue of section 35(3) or (as the case may be) 36(2) unless there has been a material change of circumstances since the preparation of the report or the Commission otherwise has a special reason for deciding differently.

(4) In making a decision under subsection (2), the Commission shall, in particular, have regard to the need to achieve as comprehensive a solution as is reasonable and practicable to the substantial lessening of competition and any adverse effects resulting from it.

(5) In making a decision under subsection (2), the Commission may, in particular, have regard to the effect of any action on any relevant customer benefits in relation to the creation of the relevant merger situation concerned.

…

127. Associated persons

(1) Associated persons, and any bodies corporate which they or any of them control, shall be treated as one person—

(a) for the purpose of deciding under section 26 whether any two enterprises have been brought under common ownership or common control;

(aa) for the purposes of section 58(2C); and

(b) for the purpose of determining what activities are carried on by way of business by any one person so far as that question arises in connection with paragraph 13(2) of Schedule 8.

(2) Subsection (1) shall not exclude from section 26 any case which would otherwise fall within that section.

(3) A reference under section 22, 33, 45 or 62 (whether or not made by virtue of this section) may be framed so as to exclude from consideration, either altogether or for a specified purpose or to a specified extent, any matter which, apart from this section, would not have been taken into account on that reference.

(4) For the purposes of this section—

(a) any individual and that individual's spouse, civil partner or partner and any relative, or spouse, civil partner or partner of a relative, of that individual or of that individual's spouse, civil partner or partner;

(b) any person in his capacity as trustee of a settlement and the settlor or grantor and any person associated with the settlor or grantor;

(c) persons carrying on business in partnership and the spouse, civil partner or partner and relatives of any of them; or

(d) two or more persons acting together to secure or exercise control of a body of persons corporate or unincorporate or to secure control of any enterprise or assets,

shall be regarded as associated with one another.

(5) The reference in subsection (1) to bodies corporate which associated persons control shall be construed in accordance with section 26(3) and (4).

(6) In this section "relative" means a brother, sister, uncle, aunt, nephew, niece, lineal ancestor or descendant (the stepchild of any person, or anyone adopted by a person, whether legally or otherwise, as his child being regarded as a relative or taken into account to trace a relationship in the same way as that person's child); and references to a spouse, civil partner or partner shall include a former spouse, civil partner or partner.

Council Regulation (EC) of 20 January 2004 on the control of concentrations between undertakings (the EC Merger Regulation)

No. 139/2004

THE COUNCIL OF THE EUROPEAN UNION,

Having regard to the Treaty establishing the European Community, and in particular Articles 83 and 308 thereof,

Having regard to the proposal from the Commission,

Having regard to the opinion of the European Parliament,

Having regard to the opinion of the European Economic and Social Committee,

Whereas:

(1) Council Regulation (EEC) No 4064/89 of 21 December 1989 on the control of concentrations between undertakings has been substantially amended. Since further amendments are to be made, it should be recast in the interest of clarity.

(2) For the achievement of the aims of the Treaty, Article 3(1)(g) gives the Community the objective of instituting a system ensuring that competition in the internal market is not distorted. Article 4(1) of the Treaty provides that the activities of the Member States and the Community are to be conducted in accordance with the principle of an open market economy with free competition. These principles are essential for the further development of the internal market.

(3) The completion of the internal market and of economic and monetary union, the enlargement of the European Union and the lowering of international barriers to trade and investment will continue to result in major corporate reorganisations, particularly in the form of concentrations.

(4) Such reorganisations are to be welcomed to the extent that they are in line with the requirements of dynamic competition and capable of increasing the competitiveness of European industry, improving the conditions of growth and raising the standard of living in the Community.

(5) However, it should be ensured that the process of reorganisation does not result in lasting damage to competition; Community law must therefore include provisions governing those concentrations which may significantly impede effective competition in the common market or in a substantial part of it.

(6) A specific legal instrument is therefore necessary to permit effective control of all concentrations in terms of their effect on the structure of competition in the Community and to be the only instrument applicable to such concentrations. Regulation (EEC) No 4064/89 has allowed a Community policy to develop in this field. In the light of experience, however, that Regulation should now be recast into legislation designed to meet the challenges of a more integrated market and the future enlargement of the European Union. In accordance with the principles of subsidiarity and of proportionality as set out in Article 5 of the Treaty, this Regulation does not go beyond what is necessary in order to achieve the objective of ensuring that competition in the common market is not distorted, in accordance with the principle of an open market economy with free competition.

(7) Articles 81 and 82, while applicable, according to the case-law of the Court of Justice, to certain concentrations, are not sufficient to control all operations which may prove to be incompatible with the system of undistorted competition envisaged in the Treaty. This Regulation should therefore be based not only on Article 83 but, principally, on Article 308 of the Treaty, under which the Community may give itself the additional powers of action necessary for the attainment of its objectives, and also powers of action with regard to concentrations on the markets for agricultural products listed in Annex I to the Treaty.

(8) The provisions to be adopted in this Regulation should apply to significant structural changes, the impact of which on the market goes beyond the national borders of any one Member State. Such concentrations should, as a general rule, be reviewed exclusively at Community level, in application of a 'one-stop shop' system and in compliance with the principle of subsidiarity. Concentrations not covered by this Regulation come, in principle, within the jurisdiction of the Member States.

(9) The scope of application of this Regulation should be defined according to the geographical area of activity of the undertakings concerned and be limited by quantitative thresholds in order to cover those concentrations which have a Community dimension. The Commission should report to the Council on the implementation of the applicable thresholds and criteria so that the Council, acting in accordance with Article 202 of the Treaty, is in a position to review them regularly, as well as the rules regarding pre-notification referral, in the light of the experience gained; this requires statistical data to be provided by the Member States to the Commission to enable it to prepare such reports and possible proposals for amendments. The Commission's reports and proposals should be based on relevant information regularly provided by the Member States.

(10) A concentration with a Community dimension should be deemed to exist where the aggregate turnover of the undertakings concerned exceeds given thresholds; that is the case irrespective of whether or not the undertakings effecting the concentration have their seat or their principal fields of activity in the Community, provided they have substantial operations there.

(11) The rules governing the referral of concentrations from the Commission to Member States and from Member States to the Commission should operate as an effective corrective mechanism in the light of the principle of subsidiarity; these rules protect the competition interests of the Member States in an adequate manner and take due account of legal certainty and the 'one-stop shop' principle.

(12) Concentrations may qualify for examination under a number of national merger control systems if they fall below the turnover thresholds referred to in this Regulation. Multiple notification of the same transaction increases legal uncertainty, effort and cost for undertakings and may lead to conflicting assessments. The system whereby concentrations may be referred to the Commission by the Member States concerned should therefore be further developed.

(13) The Commission should act in close and constant liaison with the competent authorities of the Member States from which it obtains comments and information.

(14) The Commission and the competent authorities of the Member States should together form a network of public authorities, applying their respective competences in close cooperation, using efficient arrangements for information- sharing and consultation, with a view to ensuring that a case is dealt with by the most appropriate authority, in the light of the principle of subsidiarity and with a view to ensuring that multiple notifications of a given concentration are avoided to the greatest extent possible. Referrals of concentrations from the Commission to Member States and from Member States to the Commission should be made in an efficient manner avoiding, to the greatest extent possible, situations where a concentration is subject to a referral both before and after its notification.

(15) The Commission should be able to refer to a Member State notified concentrations with a Community dimension which threaten significantly to affect competition in a market within that Member State presenting all the characteristics of a distinct market. Where the concentration affects competition on such a market, which does not constitute a substantial part of the common market, the Commission should be obliged, upon request, to refer the whole or part of the case to the Member State concerned. A Member State should be able to refer to the Commission a concentration which does not have a Community dimension but which affects trade between Member States and threatens to significantly affect competition within its territory. Other Member States which are also competent to review the concentration should be able to join the request. In such a situation, in order to ensure the efficiency and predictability of the system, national time limits should be suspended until a decision has been reached as to the referral of the

case. The Commission should have the power to examine and deal with a concentration on behalf of a requesting Member State or requesting Member States.

(16) The undertakings concerned should be granted the possibility of requesting referrals to or from the Commission before a concentration is notified so as to further improve the efficiency of the system for the control of concentrations within the Community. In such situations, the Commission and national competition authorities should decide within short, clearly defined time limits whether a referral to or from the Commission ought to be made, thereby ensuring the efficiency of the system. Upon request by the undertakings concerned, the Commission should be able to refer to a Member State a concentration with a Community dimension which may significantly affect competition in a market within that Member State presenting all the characteristics of a distinct market; the undertakings concerned should not, however, be required to demonstrate that the effects of the concentration would be detrimental to competition. A concentration should not be referred from the Commission to a Member State which has expressed its disagreement to such a referral. Before notification to national authorities, the undertakings concerned should also be able to request that a concentration without a Community dimension which is capable of being reviewed under the national competition laws of at least three Member States be referred to the Commission. Such requests for pre-notification referrals to the Commission would be particularly pertinent in situations where the concentration would affect competition beyond the territory of one Member State. Where a concentration capable of being reviewed under the competition laws of three or more Member States is referred to the Commission prior to any national notification, and no Member State competent to review the case expresses its disagreement, the Commission should acquire exclusive competence to review the concentration and such a concentration should be deemed to have a Community dimension. Such pre-notification referrals from Member States to the Commission should not, however, be made where at least one Member State competent to review the case has expressed its disagreement with such a referral.

(17) The Commission should be given exclusive competence to apply this Regulation, subject to review by the Court of Justice.

(18) The Member States should not be permitted to apply their national legislation on competition to concentrations with a Community dimension, unless this Regulation makes provision therefor. The relevant powers of national authorities should be limited to cases where, failing intervention by the Commission, effective competition is likely to be significantly impeded within the territory of a Member State and where the competition interests of that Member State cannot be sufficiently protected otherwise by this Regulation. The Member States concerned must act promptly in such cases; this Regulation cannot, because of the diversity of national law, fix a single time limit for the adoption of final decisions under national law.

(19) Furthermore, the exclusive application of this Regulation to concentrations with a Community dimension is without prejudice to Article 296 of the Treaty, and does not prevent the Member States from taking appropriate measures to protect legitimate interests other than those pursued by this Regulation, provided that such measures are compatible with the general principles and other provisions of Community law.

(20) It is expedient to define the concept of concentration in such a manner as to cover operations bringing about a lasting change in the control of the undertakings concerned and therefore in the structure of the market. It is therefore appropriate to include, within the scope of this Regulation, all joint ventures performing on a lasting basis all the functions of an autonomous economic entity. It is moreover appropriate to treat as a single concentration transactions that are closely connected in that they are linked by condition or take the form of a series of transactions in securities taking place within a reasonably short period of time.

(21) This Regulation should also apply where the undertakings concerned accept restrictions directly related to, and necessary for, the implementation of the concentration. Commission decisions declaring concentrations compatible with the common market in application of this Regulation should automatically cover such restrictions, without the Commission having to assess such

restrictions in individual cases. At the request of the undertakings concerned, however, the Commission should, in cases presenting novel or unresolved questions giving rise to genuine uncertainty, expressly assess whether or not any restriction is directly related to, and necessary for, the implementation of the concentration. A case presents a novel or unresolved question giving rise to genuine uncertainty if the question is not covered by the relevant Commission notice in force or a published Commission decision.

(22) The arrangements to be introduced for the control of concentrations should, without prejudice to Article 86(2) of the Treaty, respect the principle of non-discrimination between the public and the private sectors. In the public sector, calculation of the turnover of an undertaking concerned in a concentration needs, therefore, to take account of undertakings making up an economic unit with an independent power of decision, irrespective of the way in which their capital is held or of the rules of administrative supervision applicable to them.

(23) It is necessary to establish whether or not concentrations with a Community dimension are compatible with the common market in terms of the need to maintain and develop effective competition in the common market. In so doing, the Commission must place its appraisal within the general framework of the achievement of the fundamental objectives referred to in Article 2 of the Treaty establishing the European Community and Article 2 of the Treaty on European Union.

(24) In order to ensure a system of undistorted competition in the common market, in furtherance of a policy conducted in accordance with the principle of an open market economy with free competition, this Regulation must permit effective control of all concentrations from the point of view of their effect on competition in the Community. Accordingly, Regulation (EEC) No 4064/89 established the principle that a concentration with a Community dimension which creates or strengthens a dominant position as a result of which effective competition in the common market or in a substantial part of it would be significantly impeded should be declared incompatible with the common market.

(25) In view of the consequences that concentrations in oligopolistic market structures may have, it is all the more necessary to maintain effective competition in such markets. Many oligopolistic markets exhibit a healthy degree of competition. However, under certain circumstances, concentrations involving the elimination of important competitive constraints that the merging parties had exerted upon each other, as well as a reduction of competitive pressure on the remaining competitors, may, even in the absence of a likelihood of coordination between the members of the oligopoly, result in a significant impediment to effective competition. The Community courts have, however, not to date expressly interpreted Regulation (EEC) No 4064/89 as requiring concentrations giving rise to such non-coordinated effects to be declared incompatible with the common market. Therefore, in the interests of legal certainty, it should be made clear that this Regulation permits effective control of all such concentrations by providing that any concentration which would significantly impede effective competition, in the common market or in a substantial part of it, should be declared incompatible with the common market. The notion of 'significant impediment to effective competition' in Article 2(2) and (3) should be interpreted as extending, beyond the concept of dominance, only to the anti-competitive effects of a concentration resulting from the non-coordinated behaviour of undertakings which would not have a dominant position on the market concerned.

(26) A significant impediment to effective competition generally results from the creation or strengthening of a dominant position. With a view to preserving the guidance that may be drawn from past judgments of the European courts and Commission decisions pursuant to Regulation (EEC) No 4064/89, while at the same time maintaining consistency with the standards of competitive harm which have been applied by the Commission and the Community courts regarding the compatibility of a concentration with the common market, this Regulation should accordingly establish the principle that a concentration with a Community dimension which would significantly impede effective competition, in the common market or in a substantial part

thereof, in particular as a result of the creation or strengthening of a dominant position, is to be declared incompatible with the common market.

(27) In addition, the criteria of Article 81(1) and (3) of the Treaty should be applied to joint ventures performing, on a lasting basis, all the functions of autonomous economic entities, to the extent that their creation has as its consequence an appreciable restriction of competition between undertakings that remain independent.

(28) In order to clarify and explain the Commission's appraisal of concentrations under this Regulation, it is appropriate for the Commission to publish guidance which should provide a sound economic framework for the assessment of concentrations with a view to determining whether or not they may be declared compatible with the common market.

(29) In order to determine the impact of a concentration on competition in the common market, it is appropriate to take account of any substantiated and likely efficiencies put forward by the undertakings concerned. It is possible that the efficiencies brought about by the concentration counteract the effects on competition, and in particular the potential harm to consumers, that it might otherwise have and that, as a consequence, the concentration would not significantly impede effective competition, in the common market or in a substantial part of it, in particular as a result of the creation or strengthening of a dominant position. The Commission should publish guidance on the conditions under which it may take efficiencies into account in the assessment of a concentration.

(30) Where the undertakings concerned modify a notified concentration, in particular by offering commitments with a view to rendering the concentration compatible with the common market, the Commission should be able to declare the concentration, as modified, compatible with the common market. Such commitments should be proportionate to the competition problem and entirely eliminate it. It is also appropriate to accept commitments before the initiation of proceedings where the competition problem is readily identifiable and can easily be remedied. It should be expressly provided that the Commission may attach to its decision conditions and obligations in order to ensure that the undertakings concerned comply with their commitments in a timely and effective manner so as to render the concentration compatible with the common market. Transparency and effective consultation of Member States as well as of interested third parties should be ensured throughout the procedure.

(31) The Commission should have at its disposal appropriate instruments to ensure the enforcement of commitments and to deal with situations where they are not fulfilled. In cases of failure to fulfil a condition attached to the decision declaring a concentration compatible with the common market, the situation rendering the concentration compatible with the common market does not materialise and the concentration, as implemented, is therefore not authorised by the Commission. As a consequence, if the concentration is implemented, it should be treated in the same way as a non-notified concentration implemented without authorisation. Furthermore, where the Commission has already found that, in the absence of the condition, the concentration would be incompatible with the common market, it should have the power to directly order the dissolution of the concentration, so as to restore the situation prevailing prior to the implementation of the concentration. Where an obligation attached to a decision declaring the concentration compatible with the common market is not fulfilled, the Commission should be able to revoke its decision. Moreover, the Commission should be able to impose appropriate financial sanctions where conditions or obligations are not fulfilled.

(32) Concentrations which, by reason of the limited market share of the undertakings concerned, are not liable to impede effective competition may be presumed to be compatible with the common market. Without prejudice to Articles 81 and 82 of the Treaty, an indication to this effect exists, in particular, where the market share of the undertakings concerned does not exceed 25% either in the common market or in a substantial part of it.

(33) The Commission should have the task of taking all the decisions necessary to establish whether or not concentrations with a Community dimension are compatible with the common market, as

well as decisions designed to restore the situation prevailing prior to the implementation of a concentration which has been declared incompatible with the common market.

(34) To ensure effective control, undertakings should be obliged to give prior notification of concentrations with a Community dimension following the conclusion of the agreement, the announcement of the public bid or the acquisition of a controlling interest. Notification should also be possible where the undertakings concerned satisfy the Commission of their intention to enter into an agreement for a proposed concentration and demonstrate to the Commission that their plan for that proposed concentration is sufficiently concrete, for example on the basis of an agreement in principle, a memorandum of understanding, or a letter of intent signed by all undertakings concerned, or, in the case of a public bid, where they have publicly announced an intention to make such a bid, provided that the intended agreement or bid would result in a concentration with a Community dimension. The implementation of concentrations should be suspended until a final decision of the Commission has been taken. However, it should be possible to derogate from this suspension at the request of the undertakings concerned, where appropriate. In deciding whether or not to grant a derogation, the Commission should take account of all pertinent factors, such as the nature and gravity of damage to the undertakings concerned or to third parties, and the threat to competition posed by the concentration. In the interest of legal certainty, the validity of transactions must nevertheless be protected as much as necessary.

(35) A period within which the Commission must initiate proceedings in respect of a notified concentration and a period within which it must take a final decision on the compatibility or incompatibility with the common market of that concentration should be laid down. These periods should be extended whenever the undertakings concerned offer commitments with a view to rendering the concentration compatible with the common market, in order to allow for sufficient time for the analysis and market testing of such commitment offers and for the consultation of Member States as well as interested third parties. A limited extension of the period within which the Commission must take a final decision should also be possible in order to allow sufficient time for the investigation of the case and the verification of the facts and arguments submitted to the Commission.

(36) The Community respects the fundamental rights and observes the principles recognised in particular by the Charter of Fundamental Rights of the European Union. Accordingly, this Regulation should be interpreted and applied with respect to those rights and principles.

(37) The undertakings concerned must be afforded the right to be heard by the Commission when proceedings have been initiated; the members of the management and supervisory bodies and the recognised representatives of the employees of the undertakings concerned, and interested third parties, must also be given the opportunity to be heard.

(38) In order properly to appraise concentrations, the Commission should have the right to request all necessary information and to conduct all necessary inspections throughout the Community. To that end, and with a view to protecting competition effectively, the Commission's powers of investigation need to be expanded. The Commission should, in particular, have the right to interview any persons who may be in possession of useful information and to record the statements made.

(39) In the course of an inspection, officials authorised by the Commission should have the right to ask for any information relevant to the subject matter and purpose of the inspection; they should also have the right to affix seals during inspections, particularly in circumstances where there are reasonable grounds to suspect that a concentration has been implemented without being notified; that incorrect, incomplete or misleading information has been supplied to the Commission; or that the undertakings or persons concerned have failed to comply with a condition or obligation imposed by decision of the Commission. In any event, seals should only be used in exceptional circumstances, for the period of time strictly necessary for the inspection, normally not for more than 48 hours.

(40) Without prejudice to the case-law of the Court of Justice, it is also useful to set out the scope of the control that the national judicial authority may exercise when it authorises, as provided by national law and as a precautionary measure, assistance from law enforcement authorities in order to overcome possible opposition on the part of the undertaking against an inspection, including the affixing of seals, ordered by Commission decision. It results from the case-law that the national judicial authority may in particular ask of the Commission further information which it needs to carry out its control and in the absence of which it could refuse the authorisation. The case-law also confirms the competence of the national courts to control the application of national rules governing the implementation of coercive measures. The competent authorities of the Member States should cooperate actively in the exercise of the Commission's investigative powers.

(41) When complying with decisions of the Commission, the undertakings and persons concerned cannot be forced to admit that they have committed infringements, but they are in any event obliged to answer factual questions and to provide documents, even if this information may be used to establish against themselves or against others the existence of such infringements.

(42) For the sake of transparency, all decisions of the Commission which are not of a merely procedural nature should be widely publicised. While ensuring preservation of the rights of defence of the undertakings concerned, in particular the right of access to the file, it is essential that business secrets be protected. The confidentiality of information exchanged in the network and with the competent authorities of third countries should likewise be safeguarded.

(43) Compliance with this Regulation should be enforceable, as appropriate, by means of fines and periodic penalty payments. The Court of Justice should be given unlimited jurisdiction in that regard pursuant to Article 229 of the Treaty.

(44) The conditions in which concentrations, involving undertakings having their seat or their principal fields of activity in the Community, are carried out in third countries should be observed, and provision should be made for the possibility of the Council giving the Commission an appropriate mandate for negotiation with a view to obtaining non-discriminatory treatment for such undertakings.

(45) This Regulation in no way detracts from the collective rights of employees, as recognised in the undertakings concerned, notably with regard to any obligation to inform or consult their recognised representatives under Community and national law.

(46) The Commission should be able to lay down detailed rules concerning the implementation of this Regulation in accordance with the procedures for the exercise of implementing powers conferred on the Commission. For the adoption of such implementing provisions, the Commission should be assisted by an Advisory Committee composed of the representatives of the Member States as specified in Article 23,

HAS ADOPTED THIS REGULATION:

Article 1

Scope

1. Without prejudice to Article 4(5) and Article 22, this Regulation shall apply to all concentrations with a Community dimension as defined in this Article.

2. A concentration has a Community dimension where:
   (a) the combined aggregate worldwide turnover of all the undertakings concerned is more than EUR 5 000 million; and
   (b) the aggregate Community-wide turnover of each of at least two of the undertakings concerned is more than EUR 250 million,

   unless each of the undertakings concerned achieves more than two-thirds of its aggregate Community-wide turnover within one and the same Member State.

3. A concentration that does not meet the thresholds laid down in paragraph 2 has a Community dimension where:

(a) the combined aggregate worldwide turnover of all the undertakings concerned is more than EUR 2 500 million;
(b) in each of at least three Member States, the combined aggregate turnover of all the undertakings concerned is more than EUR 100 million;
(c) in each of at least three Member States included for the purpose of point (b), the aggregate turnover of each of at least two of the undertakings concerned is more than EUR 25 million; and
(d) the aggregate Community-wide turnover of each of at least two of the undertakings concerned is more than EUR 100 million,

unless each of the undertakings concerned achieves more than two-thirds of its aggregate Community-wide turnover within one and the same Member State.

4. On the basis of statistical data that may be regularly provided by the Member States, the Commission shall report to the Council on the operation of the thresholds and criteria set out in paragraphs 2 and 3 by 1 July 2009 and may present proposals pursuant to paragraph 5.
5. Following the report referred to in paragraph 4 and on a proposal from the Commission, the Council, acting by a qualified majority, may revise the thresholds and criteria mentioned in paragraph 3.

Article 2

Appraisal of concentrations

1. Concentrations within the scope of this Regulation shall be appraised in accordance with the objectives of this Regulation and the following provisions with a view to establishing whether or not they are compatible with the common market.
In making this appraisal, the Commission shall take into account:
(a) the need to maintain and develop effective competition within the common market in view of, among other things, the structure of all the markets concerned and the actual or potential competition from undertakings located either within or outwith the Community;
(b) the market position of the undertakings concerned and their economic and financial power, the alternatives available to suppliers and users, their access to supplies or markets, any legal or other barriers to entry, supply and demand trends for the relevant goods and services, the interests of the intermediate and ultimate consumers, and the development of technical and economic progress provided that it is to consumers' advantage and does not form an obstacle to competition.
2. A concentration which would not significantly impede effective competition in the common market or in a substantial part of it, in particular as a result of the creation or strengthening of a dominant position, shall be declared compatible with the common market.
3. A concentration which would significantly impede effective competition, in the common market or in a substantial part of it, in particular as a result of the creation or strengthening of a dominant position, shall be declared incompatible with the common market.
4. To the extent that the creation of a joint venture constituting a concentration pursuant to Article 3 has as its object or effect the coordination of the competitive behaviour of undertakings that remain independent, such coordination shall be appraised in accordance with the criteria of Article 81(1) and (3) of the Treaty, with a view to establishing whether or not the operation is compatible with the common market.
5. In making this appraisal, the Commission shall take into account in particular:
— whether two or more parent companies retain, to a significant extent, activities in the same market as the joint venture or in a market which is downstream or upstream from that of the joint venture or in a neighbouring market closely related to this market,
— whether the coordination which is the direct consequence of the creation of the joint venture affords the undertakings concerned the possibility of eliminating competition in respect of a substantial part of the products or services in question.

Article 3

Definition of concentration

1. A concentration shall be deemed to arise where a change of control on a lasting basis results from:
   (a) the merger of two or more previously independent undertakings or parts of undertakings, or
   (b) the acquisition, by one or more persons already controlling at least one undertaking, or by one or more undertakings, whether by purchase of securities or assets, by contract or by any other means, of direct or indirect control of the whole or parts of one or more other undertakings.
2. Control shall be constituted by rights, contracts or any other means which, either separately or in combination and having regard to the considerations of fact or law involved, confer the possibility of exercising decisive influence on an undertaking, in particular by:
   (a) ownership or the right to use all or part of the assets of an undertaking;
   (b) rights or contracts which confer decisive influence on the composition, voting or decisions of the organs of an undertaking.
3. Control is acquired by persons or undertakings which:
   (a) are holders of the rights or entitled to rights under the contracts concerned; or
   (b) while not being holders of such rights or entitled to rights under such contracts, have the power to exercise the rights deriving therefrom.
4. The creation of a joint venture performing on a lasting basis all the functions of an autonomous economic entity shall constitute a concentration within the meaning of paragraph 1(b).
5. A concentration shall not be deemed to arise where:
   (a) credit institutions or other financial institutions or insurance companies, the normal activities of which include transactions and dealing in securities for their own account or for the account of others, hold on a temporary basis securities which they have acquired in an undertaking with a view to reselling them, provided that they do not exercise voting rights in respect of those securities with a view to determining the competitive behaviour of that undertaking or provided that they exercise such voting rights only with a view to preparing the disposal of all or part of that undertaking or of its assets or the disposal of those securities and that any such disposal takes place within one year of the date of acquisition; that period may be extended by the Commission on request where such institutions or companies can show that the disposal was not reasonably possible within the period set;
   (b) control is acquired by an office-holder according to the law of a Member State relating to liquidation, winding up, insolvency, cessation of payments, compositions or analogous proceedings;
   (c) the operations referred to in paragraph 1(b) are carried out by the financial holding companies referred to in Article 5(3) of Fourth Council Directive 78/660/EEC of 25 July 1978 based on Article 54(3)(g) of the Treaty on the annual accounts of certain types of companies provided however that the voting rights in respect of the holding are exercised, in particular in relation to the appointment of members of the management and supervisory bodies of the undertakings in which they have holdings, only to maintain the full value of those investments and not to determine directly or indirectly the competitive conduct of those undertakings.

Article 4

Prior notification of concentrations and pre-notification referral at the request of the notifying parties

1. Concentrations with a Community dimension defined in this Regulation shall be notified to the Commission prior to their implementation and following the conclusion of the agreement, the announcement of the public bid, or the acquisition of a controlling interest.

   Notification may also be made where the undertakings concerned demonstrate to the Commission a good faith intention to conclude an agreement or, in the case of a public bid, where they have publicly announced an intention to make such a bid, provided that the intended agreement or bid would result in a concentration with a Community dimension.

For the purposes of this Regulation, the term 'notified concentration' shall also cover intended concentrations notified pursuant to the second subparagraph. For the purposes of paragraphs 4 and 5 of this Article, the term 'concentration' includes intended concentrations within the meaning of the second subparagraph.

2. A concentration which consists of a merger within the meaning of Article 3(1)(a) or in the acquisition of joint control within the meaning of Article 3(1)(b) shall be notified jointly by the parties to the merger or by those acquiring joint control as the case may be. In all other cases, the notification shall be effected by the person or undertaking acquiring control of the whole or parts of one or more undertakings.

3. Where the Commission finds that a notified concentration falls within the scope of this Regulation, it shall publish the fact of the notification, at the same time indicating the names of the undertakings concerned, their country of origin, the nature of the concentration and the economic sectors involved. The Commission shall take account of the legitimate interest of undertakings in the protection of their business secrets.

4. Prior to the notification of a concentration within the meaning of paragraph 1, the persons or undertakings referred to in paragraph 2 may inform the Commission, by means of a reasoned submission, that the concentration may significantly affect competition in a market within a Member State which presents all the characteristics of a distinct market and should therefore be examined, in whole or in part, by that Member State.

The Commission shall transmit this submission to all Member States without delay. The Member State referred to in the reasoned submission shall, within 15 working days of receiving the submission, express its agreement or disagreement as regards the request to refer the case. Where that Member State takes no such decision within this period, it shall be deemed to have agreed.

Unless that Member State disagrees, the Commission, where it considers that such a distinct market exists, and that competition in that market may be significantly affected by the concentration, may decide to refer the whole or part of the case to the competent authorities of that Member State with a view to the application of that State's national competition law.

The decision whether or not to refer the case in accordance with the third subparagraph shall be taken within 25 working days starting from the receipt of the reasoned submission by the Commission. The Commission shall inform the other Member States and the persons or undertakings concerned of its decision. If the Commission does not take a decision within this period, it shall be deemed to have adopted a decision to refer the case in accordance with the submission made by the persons or undertakings concerned.

If the Commission decides, or is deemed to have decided, pursuant to the third and fourth subparagraphs, to refer the whole of the case, no notification shall be made pursuant to paragraph 1 and national competition law shall apply. Article 9(6) to (9) shall apply mutatis mutandis.

5. With regard to a concentration as defined in Article 3 which does not have a Community dimension within the meaning of Article 1 and which is capable of being reviewed under the national competition laws of at least three Member States, the persons or undertakings referred to in paragraph 2 may, before any notification to the competent authorities, inform the Commission by means of a reasoned submission that the concentration should be examined by the Commission.

The Commission shall transmit this submission to all Member States without delay.

Any Member State competent to examine the concentration under its national competition law may, within 15 working days of receiving the reasoned submission, express its disagreement as regards the request to refer the case.

Where at least one such Member State has expressed its disagreement in accordance with the third subparagraph within the period of 15 working days, the case shall not be referred. The Commission shall, without delay, inform all Member States and the persons or undertakings concerned of any such expression of disagreement.

Where no Member State has expressed its disagreement in accordance with the third subparagraph within the period of 15 working days, the concentration shall be deemed to have a Community dimension and shall be notified to the Commission in accordance with paragraphs 1 and 2. In such situations, no Member State shall apply its national competition law to the concentration.

6. The Commission shall report to the Council on the operation of paragraphs 4 and 5 by 1 July 2009. Following this report and on a proposal from the Commission, the Council, acting by a qualified majority, may revise paragraphs 4 and 5.

Article 5

Calculation of turnover

1. Aggregate turnover within the meaning of this Regulation shall comprise the amounts derived by the undertakings concerned in the preceding financial year from the sale of products and the provision of services falling within the undertakings' ordinary activities after deduction of sales rebates and of value added tax and other taxes directly related to turnover. The aggregate turnover of an undertaking concerned shall not include the sale of products or the provision of services between any of the undertakings referred to in paragraph 4.

Turnover, in the Community or in a Member State, shall comprise products sold and services provided to undertakings or consumers, in the Community or in that Member State as the case may be.

2. By way of derogation from paragraph 1, where the concentration consists of the acquisition of parts, whether or not constituted as legal entities, of one or more undertakings, only the turnover relating to the parts which are the subject of the concentration shall be taken into account with regard to the seller or sellers.

However, two or more transactions within the meaning of the first subparagraph which take place within a two-year period between the same persons or undertakings shall be treated as one and the same concentration arising on the date of the last transaction.

3. In place of turnover the following shall be used:

(a) for credit institutions and other financial institutions, the sum of the following income items as defined in Council Directive 86/635/EEC, after deduction of value added tax and other taxes directly related to those items, where appropriate:

(i) interest income and similar income;

(ii) income from securities:

— income from shares and other variable yield securities,

— income from participating interests,

— income from shares in affiliated undertakings;

(iii) commissions receivable;

(iv) net profit on financial operations;

(v) other operating income.

The turnover of a credit or financial institution in the Community or in a Member State shall comprise the income items, as defined above, which are received by the branch or division of that institution established in the Community or in the Member State in question, as the case may be;

(b) for insurance undertakings, the value of gross premiums written which shall comprise all amounts received and receivable in respect of insurance contracts issued by or on behalf of the insurance undertakings, including also outgoing reinsurance premiums, and after deduction of taxes and parafiscal contributions or levies charged by reference to the amounts of individual premiums or the total volume of premiums; as regards Article 1(2)(b) and (3)(b), (c) and (d) and the final part of Article 1(2) and (3), gross premiums received from Community residents and from residents of one Member State respectively shall be taken into account.

4. Without prejudice to paragraph 2, the aggregate turnover of an undertaking concerned within the meaning of this Regulation shall be calculated by adding together the respective turnovers of the following:
   (a) the undertaking concerned;
   (b) those undertakings in which the undertaking concerned, directly or indirectly:
      (i) owns more than half the capital or business assets, or
      (ii) has the power to exercise more than half the voting rights, or
      (iii) has the power to appoint more than half the members of the supervisory board, the administrative board or bodies legally representing the undertakings, or
      (iv) has the right to manage the undertakings' affairs;
   (c) those undertakings which have in the undertaking concerned the rights or powers listed in (b);
   (d) those undertakings in which an undertaking as referred to in (c) has the rights or powers listed in (b);
   (e) those undertakings in which two or more undertakings as referred to in (a) to (d) jointly have the rights or powers listed in (b).
5. Where undertakings concerned by the concentration jointly have the rights or powers listed in paragraph 4(b), in calculating the aggregate turnover of the undertakings concerned for the purposes of this Regulation:
   (a) no account shall be taken of the turnover resulting from the sale of products or the provision of services between the joint undertaking and each of the undertakings concerned or any other undertaking connected with any one of them, as set out in paragraph 4(b) to (e);
   (b) account shall be taken of the turnover resulting from the sale of products and the provision of services between the joint undertaking and any third undertakings. This turnover shall be apportioned equally amongst the undertakings concerned.

Article 6

Examination of the notification and initiation of proceedings

1. The Commission shall examine the notification as soon as it is received.
   (a) Where it concludes that the concentration notified does not fall within the scope of this Regulation, it shall record that finding by means of a decision.
   (b) Where it finds that the concentration notified, although falling within the scope of this Regulation, does not raise serious doubts as to its compatibility with the common market, it shall decide not to oppose it and shall declare that it is compatible with the common market.

   A decision declaring a concentration compatible shall be deemed to cover restrictions directly related and necessary to the implementation of the concentration.
   (c) Without prejudice to paragraph 2, where the Commission finds that the concentration notified falls within the scope of this Regulation and raises serious doubts as to its compatibility with the common market, it shall decide to initiate proceedings. Without prejudice to Article 9, such proceedings shall be closed by means of a decision as provided for in Article 8(1) to (4), unless the undertakings concerned have demonstrated to the satisfaction of the Commission that they have abandoned the concentration.
2. Where the Commission finds that, following modification by the undertakings concerned, a notified concentration no longer raises serious doubts within the meaning of paragraph 1(c), it shall declare the concentration compatible with the common market pursuant to paragraph 1(b).

   The Commission may attach to its decision under paragraph 1(b) conditions and obligations intended to ensure that the undertakings concerned comply with the commitments they have entered into vis-à-vis the Commission with a view to rendering the concentration compatible with the common market.
3. The Commission may revoke the decision it took pursuant to paragraph 1(a) or (b) where:
   (a) the decision is based on incorrect information for which one of the undertakings is responsible or where it has been obtained by deceit,

or

(b) the undertakings concerned commit a breach of an obligation attached to the decision.

4. In the cases referred to in paragraph 3, the Commission may take a decision under paragraph 1, without being bound by the time limits referred to in Article 10(1).

5. The Commission shall notify its decision to the undertakings concerned and the competent authorities of the Member States without delay.

Article 7

Suspension of concentrations

1. A concentration with a Community dimension as defined in Article 1, or which is to be examined by the Commission pursuant to Article 4(5), shall not be implemented either before its notification or until it has been declared compatible with the common market pursuant to a decision under Articles 6(1)(b), 8(1) or 8(2), or on the basis of a presumption according to Article 10(6).

2. Paragraph 1 shall not prevent the implementation of a public bid or of a series of transactions in securities including those convertible into other securities admitted to trading on a market such as a stock exchange, by which control within the meaning of Article 3 is acquired from various sellers, provided that:

(a) the concentration is notified to the Commission pursuant to Article 4 without delay; and

(b) the acquirer does not exercise the voting rights attached to the securities in question or does so only to maintain the full value of its investments based on a derogation granted by the Commission under paragraph 3.

3. The Commission may, on request, grant a derogation from the obligations imposed in paragraphs 1 or 2. The request to grant a derogation must be reasoned. In deciding on the request, the Commission shall take into account inter alia the effects of the suspension on one or more undertakings concerned by the concentration or on a third party and the threat to competition posed by the concentration. Such a derogation may be made subject to conditions and obligations in order to ensure conditions of effective competition. A derogation may be applied for and granted at any time, be it before notification or after the transaction.

4. The validity of any transaction carried out in contravention of paragraph 1 shall be dependent on a decision pursuant to Article 6(1)(b) or Article 8(1), (2) or (3) or on a presumption pursuant to Article 10(6).

This Article shall, however, have no effect on the validity of transactions in securities including those convertible into other securities admitted to trading on a market such as a stock exchange, unless the buyer and seller knew or ought to have known that the transaction was carried out in contravention of paragraph 1.

Article 8

Powers of decision of the Commission

1. Where the Commission finds that a notified concentration fulfils the criterion laid down in Article 2(2) and, in the cases referred to in Article 2(4), the criteria laid down in Article 81(3) of the Treaty, it shall issue a decision declaring the concentration compatible with the common market.

A decision declaring a concentration compatible shall be deemed to cover restrictions directly related and necessary to the implementation of the concentration.

2. Where the Commission finds that, following modification by the undertakings concerned, a notified concentration fulfils the criterion laid down in Article 2(2) and, in the cases referred to in Article 2(4), the criteria laid down in Article 81(3) of the Treaty, it shall issue a decision declaring the concentration compatible with the common market.

The Commission may attach to its decision conditions and obligations intended to ensure that the undertakings concerned comply with the commitments they have entered into vis-à-vis the Commission with a view to rendering the concentration compatible with the common market.

A decision declaring a concentration compatible shall be deemed to cover restrictions directly related and necessary to the implementation of the concentration.

3. Where the Commission finds that a concentration fulfils the criterion defined in Article 2(3) or, in the cases referred to in Article 2(4), does not fulfil the criteria laid down in Article 81(3) of the Treaty, it shall issue a decision declaring that the concentration is incompatible with the common market.

4. Where the Commission finds that a concentration:

(a) has already been implemented and that concentration has been declared incompatible with the common market, or

(b) has been implemented in contravention of a condition attached to a decision taken under paragraph 2, which has found that, in the absence of the condition, the concentration would fulfil the criterion laid down in Article 2(3) or, in the cases referred to in Article 2(4), would not fulfil the criteria laid down in Article 81(3) of the Treaty,

the Commission may:

— require the undertakings concerned to dissolve the concentration, in particular through the dissolution of the merger or the disposal of all the shares or assets acquired, so as to restore the situation prevailing prior to the implementation of the concentration; in circumstances where restoration of the situation prevailing before the implementation of the concentration is not possible through dissolution of the concentration, the Commission may take any other measure appropriate to achieve such restoration as far as possible,

— order any other appropriate measure to ensure that the undertakings concerned dissolve the concentration or take other restorative measures as required in its decision.

In cases falling within point (a) of the first subparagraph, the measures referred to in that subparagraph may be imposed either in a decision pursuant to paragraph 3 or by separate decision.

5. The Commission may take interim measures appropriate to restore or maintain conditions of effective competition where a concentration:

(a) has been implemented in contravention of Article 7, and a decision as to the compatibility of the concentration with the common market has not yet been taken;

(b) has been implemented in contravention of a condition attached to a decision under Article 6(1)(b) or paragraph 2 of this Article;

(c) has already been implemented and is declared incompatible with the common market.

6. The Commission may revoke the decision it has taken pursuant to paragraphs 1 or 2 where:

(a) the declaration of compatibility is based on incorrect information for which one of the undertakings is responsible or where it has been obtained by deceit; or

(b) the undertakings concerned commit a breach of an obligation attached to the decision.

7. The Commission may take a decision pursuant to paragraphs 1 to 3 without being bound by the time limits referred to in Article 10(3), in cases where:

(a) it finds that a concentration has been implemented

(i) in contravention of a condition attached to a decision under Article 6(1)(b), or

(ii) in contravention of a condition attached to a decision taken under paragraph 2 and in accordance with Article 10(2), which has found that, in the absence of the condition, the concentration would raise serious doubts as to its compatibility with the common market; or

(b) a decision has been revoked pursuant to paragraph 6.

8. The Commission shall notify its decision to the undertakings concerned and the competent authorities of the Member States without delay.

Article 9

Referral to the competent authorities of the Member States

1. The Commission may, by means of a decision notified without delay to the undertakings concerned and the competent authorities of the other Member States, refer a notified concentration to the competent authorities of the Member State concerned in the following circumstances.
2. Within 15 working days of the date of receipt of the copy of the notification, a Member State, on its own initiative or upon the invitation of the Commission, may inform the Commission, which shall inform the undertakings concerned, that:
   (a) a concentration threatens to affect significantly competition in a market within that Member State, which presents all the characteristics of a distinct market, or
   (b) a concentration affects competition in a market within that Member State, which presents all the characteristics of a distinct market and which does not constitute a substantial part of the common market.
3. If the Commission considers that, having regard to the market for the products or services in question and the geographical reference market within the meaning of paragraph 7, there is such a distinct market and that such a threat exists, either:
   (a) it shall itself deal with the case in accordance with this Regulation; or
   (b) it shall refer the whole or part of the case to the competent authorities of the Member State concerned with a view to the application of that State's national competition law.

   If, however, the Commission considers that such a distinct market or threat does not exist, it shall adopt a decision to that effect which it shall address to the Member State concerned, and shall itself deal with the case in accordance with this Regulation.

   In cases where a Member State informs the Commission pursuant to paragraph 2(b) that a concentration affects competition in a distinct market within its territory that does not form a substantial part of the common market, the Commission shall refer the whole or part of the case relating to the distinct market concerned, if it considers that such a distinct market is affected.
4. A decision to refer or not to refer pursuant to paragraph 3 shall be taken:
   (a) as a general rule within the period provided for in Article 10(1), second subparagraph, where the Commission, pursuant to Article 6(1)(b), has not initiated proceedings; or
   (b) within 65 working days at most of the notification of the concentration concerned where the Commission has initiated proceedings under Article 6(1)(c), without taking the preparatory steps in order to adopt the necessary measures under Article 8(2), (3) or (4) to maintain or restore effective competition on the market concerned.
5. If within the 65 working days referred to in paragraph 4(b) the Commission, despite a reminder from the Member State concerned, has not taken a decision on referral in accordance with paragraph 3 nor has taken the preparatory steps referred to in paragraph 4(b), it shall be deemed to have taken a decision to refer the case to the Member State concerned in accordance with paragraph 3(b).
6. The competent authority of the Member State concerned shall decide upon the case without undue delay.

   Within 45 working days after the Commission's referral, the competent authority of the Member State concerned shall inform the undertakings concerned of the result of the preliminary competition assessment and what further action, if any, it proposes to take. The Member State concerned may exceptionally suspend this time limit where necessary information has not been provided to it by the undertakings concerned as provided for by its national competition law.

   Where a notification is requested under national law, the period of 45 working days shall begin on the working day following that of the receipt of a complete notification by the competent authority of that Member State.
7. The geographical reference market shall consist of the area in which the undertakings concerned are involved in the supply and demand of products or services, in which the conditions of competition are sufficiently homogeneous and which can be distinguished from neighbouring

areas because, in particular, conditions of competition are appreciably different in those areas. This assessment should take account in particular of the nature and characteristics of the products or services concerned, of the existence of entry barriers or of consumer preferences, of appreciable differences of the undertakings' market shares between the area concerned and neighbouring areas or of substantial price differences.

8. In applying the provisions of this Article, the Member State concerned may take only the measures strictly necessary to safeguard or restore effective competition on the market concerned.

9. In accordance with the relevant provisions of the Treaty, any Member State may appeal to the Court of Justice, and in particular request the application of Article 243 of the Treaty, for the purpose of applying its national competition law.

Article 10

Time limits for initiating proceedings and for decisions

1. Without prejudice to Article 6(4), the decisions referred to in Article 6(1) shall be taken within 25 working days at most. That period shall begin on the working day following that of the receipt of a notification or, if the information to be supplied with the notification is incomplete, on the working day following that of the receipt of the complete information.

   That period shall be increased to 35 working days where the Commission receives a request from a Member State in accordance with Article 9(2)or where, the undertakings concerned offer commitments pursuant to Article 6(2) with a view to rendering the concentration compatible with the common market.

2. Decisions pursuant to Article 8(1) or (2) concerning notified concentrations shall be taken as soon as it appears that the serious doubts referred to in Article 6(1)(c) have been removed, particularly as a result of modifications made by the undertakings concerned, and at the latest by the time limit laid down in paragraph 3.

3. Without prejudice to Article 8(7), decisions pursuant to Article 8(1) to (3) concerning notified concentrations shall be taken within not more than 90 working days of the date on which the proceedings are initiated. That period shall be increased to 105 working days where the undertakings concerned offer commitments pursuant to Article 8(2), second subparagraph, with a view to rendering the concentration compatible with the common market, unless these commitments have been offered less than 55 working days after the initiation of proceedings.

   The periods set by the first subparagraph shall likewise be extended if the notifying parties make a request to that effect not later than 15 working days after the initiation of proceedings pursuant to Article 6(1)(c). The notifying parties may make only one such request. Likewise, at any time following the initiation of proceedings, the periods set by the first subparagraph may be extended by the Commission with the agreement of the notifying parties. The total duration of any extension or extensions effected pursuant to this subparagraph shall not exceed 20 working days.

4. The periods set by paragraphs 1 and 3 shall exceptionally be suspended where, owing to circumstances for which one of the undertakings involved in the concentration is responsible, the Commission has had to request information by decision pursuant to Article 11 or to order an inspection by decision pursuant to Article 13.

   The first subparagraph shall also apply to the period referred to in Article 9(4)(b).

5. Where the Court of Justice gives a judgment which annuls the whole or part of a Commission decision which is subject to a time limit set by this Article, the concentration shall be reexamined by the Commission with a view to adopting a decision pursuant to Article 6(1).

   The concentration shall be re-examined in the light of current market conditions.

   The notifying parties shall submit a new notification or supplement the original notification, without delay, where the original notification becomes incomplete by reason of intervening changes in market conditions or in the information provided. Where there are no such changes, the parties shall certify this fact without delay.

The periods laid down in paragraph 1 shall start on the working day following that of the receipt of complete information in a new notification, a supplemented notification, or a certification within the meaning of the third subparagraph.

The second and third subparagraphs shall also apply in the cases referred to in Article 6(4) and Article 8(7).

6. Where the Commission has not taken a decision in accordance with Article 6(1)(b), (c), 8(1), (2) or (3) within the time limits set in paragraphs 1 and 3 respectively, the concentration shall be deemed to have been declared compatible with the common market, without prejudice to Article 9.

Article 11

Requests for information

1. In order to carry out the duties assigned to it by this Regulation, the Commission may, by simple request or by decision, require the persons referred to in Article 3(1)(b), as well as undertakings and associations of undertakings, to provide all necessary information.
2. When sending a simple request for information to a person, an undertaking or an association of undertakings, the Commission shall state the legal basis and the purpose of the request, specify what information is required and fix the time limit within which the information is to be provided, as well as the penalties provided for in Article 14 for supplying incorrect or misleading information.
3. Where the Commission requires a person, an undertaking or an association of undertakings to supply information by decision, it shall state the legal basis and the purpose of the request, specify what information is required and fix the time limit within which it is to be provided. It shall also indicate the penalties provided for in Article 14 and indicate or impose the penalties provided for in Article 15. It shall further indicate the right to have the decision reviewed by the Court of Justice.
4. The owners of the undertakings or their representatives and, in the case of legal persons, companies or firms, or associations having no legal personality, the persons authorised to represent them by law or by their constitution, shall supply the information requested on behalf of the undertaking concerned. Persons duly authorised to act may supply the information on behalf of their clients. The latter shall remain fully responsible if the information supplied is incomplete, incorrect or misleading.
5. The Commission shall without delay forward a copy of any decision taken pursuant to paragraph 3 to the competent authorities of the Member State in whose territory the residence of the person or the seat of the undertaking or association of undertakings is situated, and to the competent authority of the Member State whose territory is affected. At the specific request of the competent authority of a Member State, the Commission shall also forward to that authority copies of simple requests for information relating to a notified concentration.
6. At the request of the Commission, the governments and competent authorities of the Member States shall provide the Commission with all necessary information to carry out the duties assigned to it by this Regulation.
7. In order to carry out the duties assigned to it by this Regulation, the Commission may interview any natural or legal person who consents to be interviewed for the purpose of collecting information relating to the subject matter of an investigation. At the beginning of the interview, which may be conducted by telephone or other electronic means, the Commission shall state the legal basis and the purpose of the interview.

   Where an interview is not conducted on the premises of the Commission or by telephone or other electronic means, the Commission shall inform in advance the competent authority of the Member State in whose territory the interview takes place. If the competent authority of that Member State so requests, officials of that authority may assist the officials and other persons authorised by the Commission to conduct the interview.

Article 12

Inspections by the authorities of the Member States

1. At the request of the Commission, the competent authorities of the Member States shall undertake the inspections which the Commission considers to be necessary under Article 13(1), or which it has ordered by decision pursuant to Article 13(4). The officials of the competent authorities of the Member States who are responsible for conducting these inspections as well as those authorised or appointed by them shall exercise their powers in accordance with their national law.
2. If so requested by the Commission or by the competent authority of the Member State within whose territory the inspection is to be conducted, officials and other accompanying persons authorised by the Commission may assist the officials of the authority concerned.

Article 13

The Commission's powers of inspection

1. In order to carry out the duties assigned to it by this Regulation, the Commission may conduct all necessary inspections of undertakings and associations of undertakings.
2. The officials and other accompanying persons authorised by the Commission to conduct an inspection shall have the power:
   (a) to enter any premises, land and means of transport of undertakings and associations of undertakings;
   (b) to examine the books and other records related to the business, irrespective of the medium on which they are stored;
   (c) to take or obtain in any form copies of or extracts from such books or records;
   (d) to seal any business premises and books or records for the period and to the extent necessary for the inspection;
   (e) to ask any representative or member of staff of the undertaking or association of undertakings for explanations on facts or documents relating to the subject matter and purpose of the inspection and to record the answers.
3. Officials and other accompanying persons authorised by the Commission to conduct an inspection shall exercise their powers upon production of a written authorisation specifying the subject matter and purpose of the inspection and the penalties provided for in Article 14, in the production of the required books or other records related to the business which is incomplete or where answers to questions asked under paragraph 2 of this Article are incorrect or misleading. In good time before the inspection, the Commission shall give notice of the inspection to the competent authority of the Member State in whose territory the inspection is to be conducted.
4. Undertakings and associations of undertakings are required to submit to inspections ordered by decision of the Commission. The decision shall specify the subject matter and purpose of the inspection, appoint the date on which it is to begin and indicate the penalties provided for in Articles 14 and 15 and the right to have the decision reviewed by the Court of Justice. The Commission shall take such decisions after consulting the competent authority of the Member State in whose territory the inspection is to be conducted.
5. Officials of, and those authorised or appointed by, the competent authority of the Member State in whose territory the inspection is to be conducted shall, at the request of that authority or of the Commission, actively assist the officials and other accompanying persons authorised by the Commission. To this end, they shall enjoy the powers specified in paragraph 2.
6. Where the officials and other accompanying persons authorised by the Commission find that an undertaking opposes an inspection, including the sealing of business premises, books or records, ordered pursuant to this Article, the Member State concerned shall afford them the necessary assistance, requesting where appropriate the assistance of the police or of an equivalent enforcement authority, so as to enable them to conduct their inspection.
7. If the assistance provided for in paragraph 6 requires authorisation from a judicial authority according to national rules, such authorisation shall be applied for. Such authorisation may also be applied for as a precautionary measure.

8. Where authorisation as referred to in paragraph 7 is applied for, the national judicial authority shall ensure that the Commission decision is authentic and that the coercive measures envisaged are neither arbitrary nor excessive having regard to the subject matter of the inspection. In its control of proportionality of the coercive measures, the national judicial authority may ask the Commission, directly or through the competent authority of that Member State, for detailed explanations relating to the subject matter of the inspection. However, the national judicial authority may not call into question the necessity for the inspection nor demand that it be provided with the information in the Commission's file. The lawfulness of the Commission's decision shall be subject to review only by the Court of Justice.

Article 14

Fines

1. The Commission may by decision impose on the persons referred to in Article 3(1)b, undertakings or associations of undertakings, fines not exceeding 1% of the aggregate turnover of the undertaking or association of undertakings concerned within the meaning of Article 5 where, intentionally or negligently:
   (a) they supply incorrect or misleading information in a submission, certification, notification or supplement thereto, pursuant to Article 4, Article 10(5) or Article 22(3);
   (b) they supply incorrect or misleading information in response to a request made pursuant to Article 11(2);
   (c) in response to a request made by decision adopted pursuant to Article 11(3), they supply incorrect, incomplete or misleading information or do not supply information within the required time limit;
   (d) they produce the required books or other records related to the business in incomplete form during inspections under Article 13, or refuse to submit to an inspection ordered by decision taken pursuant to Article 13(4);
   (e) in response to a question asked in accordance with Article 13(2)(e),
      — they give an incorrect or misleading answer,
      — they fail to rectify within a time limit set by the Commission an incorrect, incomplete or misleading answer given by a member of staff, or
      — they fail or refuse to provide a complete answer on facts relating to the subject matter and purpose of an inspection ordered by a decision adopted pursuant to Article 13(4);
   (f) seals affixed by officials or other accompanying persons authorised by the Commission in accordance with Article 13(2)(d) have been broken.
2. The Commission may by decision impose fines not exceeding 10% of the aggregate turnover of the undertaking concerned within the meaning of Article 5 on the persons referred to in Article 3(1)b or the undertakings concerned where, either intentionally or negligently, they:
   (a) fail to notify a concentration in accordance with Articles 4 or 22(3) prior to its implementation, unless they are expressly authorised to do so by Article 7(2) or by a decision taken pursuant to Article 7(3);
   (b) implement a concentration in breach of Article 7;
   (c) implement a concentration declared incompatible with the common market by decision pursuant to Article 8(3) or do not comply with any measure ordered by decision pursuant to Article 8(4) or (5);
   (d) fail to comply with a condition or an obligation imposed by decision pursuant to Articles 6(1)(b), Article 7(3) or Article 8(2), second subparagraph.
3. In fixing the amount of the fine, regard shall be had to the nature, gravity and duration of the infringement.
4. Decisions taken pursuant to paragraphs 1, 2 and 3 shall not be of a criminal law nature.

Article 15

Periodic penalty payments

1. The Commission may by decision impose on the persons referred to in Article 3(1)b, undertakings or associations of undertakings, periodic penalty payments not exceeding 5% of the average daily aggregate turnover of the undertaking or association of undertakings concerned within the meaning of Article 5 for each working day of delay, calculated from the date set in the decision, in order to compel them:
   (a) to supply complete and correct information which it has requested by decision taken pursuant to Article 11(3);
   (b) to submit to an inspection which it has ordered by decision taken pursuant to Article 13(4);
   (c) to comply with an obligation imposed by decision pursuant to Article 6(1)(b), Article 7(3) or Article 8(2), second subparagraph; or;
   (d) to comply with any measures ordered by decision pursuant to Article 8(4) or (5).
2. Where the persons referred to in Article 3(1)(b), undertakings or associations of undertakings have satisfied the obligation which the periodic penalty payment was intended to enforce, the Commission may fix the definitive amount of the periodic penalty payments at a figure lower than that which would arise under the original decision.

Article 16

Review by the Court of Justice

The Court of Justice shall have unlimited jurisdiction within the meaning of Article 229 of the Treaty to review decisions whereby the Commission has fixed a fine or periodic penalty payments; it may cancel, reduce or increase the fine or periodic penalty payment imposed.

Article 17

Professional secrecy

1. Information acquired as a result of the application of this Regulation shall be used only for the purposes of the relevant request, investigation or hearing.
2. Without prejudice to Article 4(3), Articles 18 and 20, the Commission and the competent authorities of the Member States, their officials and other servants and other persons working under the supervision of these authorities as well as officials and civil servants of other authorities of the Member States shall not disclose information they have acquired through the application of this Regulation of the kind covered by the obligation of professional secrecy.
3. Paragraphs 1 and 2 shall not prevent publication of general information or of surveys which do not contain information relating to particular undertakings or associations of undertakings.

Article 18

Hearing of the parties and of third persons

1. Before taking any decision provided for in Article 6(3), Article 7(3), Article 8(2) to (6), and Articles 14 and 15, the Commission shall give the persons, undertakings and associations of undertakings concerned the opportunity, at every stage of the procedure up to the consultation of the Advisory Committee, of making known their views on the objections against them.
2. By way of derogation from paragraph 1, a decision pursuant to Articles 7(3) and 8(5) may be taken provisionally, without the persons, undertakings or associations of undertakings concerned being given the opportunity to make known their views beforehand, provided that the Commission gives them that opportunity as soon as possible after having taken its decision.
3. The Commission shall base its decision only on objections on which the parties have been able to submit their observations. The rights of the defence shall be fully respected in the proceedings. Access to the file shall be open at least to the parties directly involved, subject to the legitimate interest of undertakings in the protection of their business secrets.

4. In so far as the Commission or the competent authorities of the Member States deem it necessary, they may also hear other natural or legal persons. Natural or legal persons showing a sufficient interest and especially members of the administrative or management bodies of the undertakings concerned or the recognised representatives of their employees shall be entitled, upon application, to be heard.

Article 19

Liaison with the authorities of the Member States

1. The Commission shall transmit to the competent authorities of the Member States copies of notifications within three working days and, as soon as possible, copies of the most important documents lodged with or issued by the Commission pursuant to this Regulation. Such documents shall include commitments offered by the undertakings concerned vis-à-vis the Commission with a view to rendering the concentration compatible with the common market pursuant to Article 6(2) or Article 8(2), second subparagraph.
2. The Commission shall carry out the procedures set out in this Regulation in close and constant liaison with the competent authorities of the Member States, which may express their views upon those procedures. For the purposes of Article 9 it shall obtain information from the competent authority of the Member State as referred to in paragraph 2 of that Article and give it the opportunity to make known its views at every stage of the procedure up to the adoption of a decision pursuant to paragraph 3 of that Article; to that end it shall give it access to the file.
3. An Advisory Committee on concentrations shall be consulted before any decision is taken pursuant to Article 8(1) to (6), Articles 14 or 15 with the exception of provisional decisions taken in accordance with Article 18(2).
4. The Advisory Committee shall consist of representatives of the competent authorities of the Member States. Each Member State shall appoint one or two representatives; if unable to attend, they may be replaced by other representatives. At least one of the representatives of a Member State shall be competent in matters of restrictive practices and dominant positions.
5. Consultation shall take place at a joint meeting convened at the invitation of and chaired by the Commission. A summary of the case, together with an indication of the most important documents and a preliminary draft of the decision to be taken for each case considered, shall be sent with the invitation. The meeting shall take place not less than 10 working days after the invitation has been sent. The Commission may in exceptional cases shorten that period as appropriate in order to avoid serious harm to one or more of the undertakings concerned by a concentration.
6. The Advisory Committee shall deliver an opinion on the Commission's draft decision, if necessary by taking a vote. The Advisory Committee may deliver an opinion even if some members are absent and unrepresented. The opinion shall be delivered in writing and appended to the draft decision. The Commission shall take the utmost account of the opinion delivered by the Committee. It shall inform the Committee of the manner in which its opinion has been taken into account.
7. The Commission shall communicate the opinion of the Advisory Committee, together with the decision, to the addressees of the decision. It shall make the opinion public together with the decision, having regard to the legitimate interest of undertakings in the protection of their business secrets.

Article 20

Publication of decisions

1. The Commission shall publish the decisions which it takes pursuant to Article 8(1) to (6), Articles 14 and 15 with the exception of provisional decisions taken in accordance with Article 18(2) together with the opinion of the Advisory Committee in the Official Journal of the European Union.

2. The publication shall state the names of the parties and the main content of the decision; it shall have regard to the legitimate interest of undertakings in the protection of their business secrets.

Article 21

Application of the Regulation and jurisdiction

1. This Regulation alone shall apply to concentrations as defined in Article 3, and Council Regulations (EC) No 1/2003, (EEC) No 1017/68, (EEC) No 4056/86 and (EEC) No 3975/87 shall not apply, except in relation to joint ventures that do not have a Community dimension and which have as their object or effect the coordination of the competitive behaviour of undertakings that remain independent.
2. Subject to review by the Court of Justice, the Commission shall have sole jurisdiction to take the decisions provided for in this Regulation.
3. No Member State shall apply its national legislation on competition to any concentration that has a Community dimension.
   The first subparagraph shall be without prejudice to any Member State's power to carry out any enquiries necessary for the application of Articles 4(4), 9(2) or after referral, pursuant to Article 9(3), first subparagraph, indent (b), or Article 9(5), to take the measures strictly necessary for the application of Article 9(8).
4. Notwithstanding paragraphs 2 and 3, Member States may take appropriate measures to protect legitimate interests other than those taken into consideration by this Regulation and compatible with the general principles and other provisions of Community law.
   Public security, plurality of the media and prudential rules shall be regarded as legitimate interests within the meaning of the first subparagraph.
   Any other public interest must be communicated to the Commission by the Member State concerned and shall be recognised by the Commission after an assessment of its compatibility with the general principles and other provisions of Community law before the measures referred to above may be taken. The Commission shall inform the Member State concerned of its decision within 25 working days of that communication.

Article 22

Referral to the Commission

1. One or more Member States may request the Commission to examine any concentration as defined in Article 3 that does not have a Community dimension within the meaning of Article 1 but affects trade between Member States and threatens to significantly affect competition within the territory of the Member State or States making the request.
   Such a request shall be made at most within 15 working days of the date on which the concentration was notified, or if no notification is required, otherwise made known to the Member State concerned.
2. The Commission shall inform the competent authorities of the Member States and the undertakings concerned of any request received pursuant to paragraph 1 without delay.
   Any other Member State shall have the right to join the initial request within a period of 15 working days of being informed by the Commission of the initial request.
   All national time limits relating to the concentration shall be suspended until, in accordance with the procedure set out in this Article, it has been decided where the concentration shall be examined. As soon as a Member State has informed the Commission and the undertakings concerned that it does not wish to join the request, the suspension of its national time limits shall end.
3. The Commission may, at the latest 10 working days after the expiry of the period set in paragraph 2, decide to examine, the concentration where it considers that it affects trade between Member States and threatens to significantly affect competition within the territory of the Member State or States making the request. If the Commission does not take a decision within this period, it shall

be deemed to have adopted a decision to examine the concentration in accordance with the request.

The Commission shall inform all Member States and the undertakings concerned of its decision. It may request the submission of a notification pursuant to Article 4.

The Member State or States having made the request shall no longer apply their national legislation on competition to the concentration.

4. Article 2, Article 4(2) to (3), Articles 5, 6, and 8 to 21 shall apply where the Commission examines a concentration pursuant to paragraph 3. Article 7 shall apply to the extent that the concentration has not been implemented on the date on which the Commission informs the undertakings concerned that a request has been made.

Where a notification pursuant to Article 4 is not required, the period set in Article 10(1) within which proceedings may be initiated shall begin on the working day following that on which the Commission informs the undertakings concerned that it has decided to examine the concentration pursuant to paragraph 3.

5. The Commission may inform one or several Member States that it considers a concentration fulfils the criteria in paragraph 1. In such cases, the Commission may invite that Member State or those Member States to make a request pursuant to paragraph 1.

Article 23

Implementing provisions

1. The Commission shall have the power to lay down in accordance with the procedure referred to in paragraph 2:
   (a) implementing provisions concerning the form, content and other details of notifications and submissions pursuant to Article 4;
   (b) implementing provisions concerning time limits pursuant to Article 4(4), (5) Articles 7, 9, 10 and 22;
   (c) the procedure and time limits for the submission and implementation of commitments pursuant to Article 6(2) and Article 8(2);
   (d) implementing provisions concerning hearings pursuant to Article 18.
2. The Commission shall be assisted by an Advisory Committee, composed of representatives of the Member States.
   (a) Before publishing draft implementing provisions and before adopting such provisions, the Commission shall consult the Advisory Committee.
   (b) Consultation shall take place at a meeting convened at the invitation of and chaired by the Commission. A draft of the implementing provisions to be taken shall be sent with the invitation. The meeting shall take place not less than 10 working days after the invitation has been sent.
   (c) The Advisory Committee shall deliver an opinion on the draft implementing provisions, if necessary by taking a vote. The Commission shall take the utmost account of the opinion delivered by the Committee.

Article 24

Relations with third countries

1. The Member States shall inform the Commission of any general difficulties encountered by their undertakings with concentrations as defined in Article 3 in a third country.
2. Initially not more than one year after the entry into force of this Regulation and, thereafter periodically, the Commission shall draw up a report examining the treatment accorded to undertakings having their seat or their principal fields of activity in the Community, in the terms referred to in paragraphs 3 and 4, as regards concentrations in third countries. The Commission shall submit those reports to the Council, together with any recommendations.
3. Whenever it appears to the Commission, either on the basis of the reports referred to in paragraph 2 or on the basis of other information, that a third country does not grant undertakings having

their seat or their principal fields of activity in the Community, treatment comparable to that granted by the Community to undertakings from that country, the Commission may submit proposals to the Council for an appropriate mandate for negotiation with a view to obtaining comparable treatment for undertakings having their seat or their principal fields of activity in the Community.

4. Measures taken under this Article shall comply with the obligations of the Community or of the Member States, without prejudice to Article 307 of the Treaty, under international agreements, whether bilateral or multilateral.

Article 25

Repeal

1. Without prejudice to Article 26(2), Regulations (EEC) No 4064/89 and (EC) No 1310/97 shall be repealed with effect from 1 May 2004.
2. References to the repealed Regulations shall be construed as references to this Regulation and shall be read in accordance with the correlation table in the Annex.

Article 26

Entry into force and transitional provisions

1. This Regulation shall enter into force on the 20th day following that of its publication in the Official Journal of the European Union.
   It shall apply from 1 May 2004.
2. Regulation (EEC) No 4064/89 shall continue to apply to any concentration which was the subject of an agreement or announcement or where control was acquired within the meaning of Article 4(1) of that Regulation before the date of application of this Regulation, subject, in particular, to the provisions governing applicability set out in Article 25(2) and (3) of Regulation (EEC) No 4064/89 and Article 2 of Regulation (EEC) No 1310/97.
3. As regards concentrations to which this Regulation applies by virtue of accession, the date of accession shall be substituted for the date of application of this Regulation.
   This Regulation shall be binding in its entirety and directly applicable in all Member States.

ANNEX
CORRELATION TABLE

Regulation (EEC) No 4064/89	This Regulation
Article 1(1), (2) and (3)	Article 1(1), (2) and (3)
Article 1(4)	Article 1(4)
Article 1(5)	Article 1(5)
Article 2(1)	Article 2(1)
—	Article 2(2)
Article 2(2)	Article 2(3)
Article 2(3)	Article 2(4)
Article 2(4)	Article 2(5)
Article 3(1)	Article 3(1)
Article 3(2)	Article 3(4)
Article 3(3)	Article 3(2)
Article 3(4)	Article 3(3)
—	Article 3(4)
Article 3(5)	Article 3(5)

Article 4(1) first sentence	Article 4(1) first subparagraph
Article 4(1) second sentence	—
—	Article 4(1) second and third subparagraphs
Article 4(2) and (3)	Article 4(2) and (3)
—	Article 4(4) to (6)
Article 5(1) to (3)	Article 5(1) to (3)
Article 5(4), introductory words	Article 5(4), introductory words
Article 5(4) point (a)	Article 5(4) point (a)
Article 5(4) point (b), introductory words	Article 5(4) point (b), introductory words
Article 5(4) point (b), first indent	Article 5(4) point (b)(i)
Article 5(4) point (b), second indent	Article 5(4) point (b)(ii)
Article 5(4) point (b), third indent	Article 5(4) point (b)(iii)
Article 5(4) point (b), fourth indent	Article 5(4) point (b)(iv)
Article 5(4) points (c), (d) and (e)	Article 5(4) points (c), (d) and (e)
Article 5(5)	Article 5(5)
Article 6(1), introductory words	Article 6(1), introductory words
Article 6(1) points (a) and (b)	Article 6(1) points (a) and (b)
Article 6(1) point (c)	Article 6(1) point (c), first sentence
Article 6(2) to (5)	Article 6(2) to (5)
Article 7(1)	Article 7(1)
Article 7(3)	Article 7(2)
Article 7(4)	Article 7(3)
Article 7(5)	Article 7(4)
Article 8(1)	Article 6(1) point (c), second sentence
Article 8(2)	Article 8(1) and (2)
Article 8(3)	Article 8(3)
Article 8(4)	Article 8(4)
—	Article 8(5)
Article 8(5)	Article 8(6)
Article 8(6)	Article 8(7)
—	Article 8(8)
Article 9(1) to (9)	Article 9(1) to (9)
Article 9(10)	—
Article 10(1) and (2)	Article 10(1) and (2)
Article 10(3)	Article 10(3) first subparagraph, first sentence
—	Article 10(3) first subparagraph, second sentence
—	Article 10(3) second subparagraph
Article 10(4)	Article 10(4) first subparagraph
—	Article 10(4), second subparagraph

Article 10(5)	Article 10(5), first and fourth subparagraphs
—	Article 10(5), second, third and fifth sub-paragraphs
Article 10(6)	Article 10(6)
Article 11(1)	Article 11(1)
Article 11(2)	—
Article 11(3)	Article 11(2)
Article 11(4)	Article 11(4) first sentence
—	Article 11(4) second and third sentences
Article 11(5) first sentence	—
Article 11(5) second sentence	Article 11(3)
Article 11(6)	Article 11(5)
—	Article 11(6) and (7)
Article 12	Article 12
Article 13(1) first subparagraph	Article 13(1)
Article 13(1) second subparagraph, introductory words	Article 13(2) introductory words
Article 13(1) second subparagraph, point (a)	Article 13(2) point (b)
Article 13(1) second subparagraph, point (b)	Article 13(2) point (c)
Article 13(1) second subparagraph, point (c)	Article 13(2) point (e)
Article 13(1) second subparagraph, point (d)	Article 13(2) point (a)
—	Article 13(2) point (d)
Article 13(2)	Article 13(3)
Article 13(3)	Article 13(4) first and second sentences
Article 13(4)	Article 13(4) third sentence
Article 13(5)	Article 13(5), first sentence
—	Article 13(5), second sentence
Article 13(6) first sentence	Article 13(6)
Article 13(6) second sentence	—
—	Article 13(7) and (8)
Article 14(1) introductory words	Article 14(1) introductory words
Article 14(1) point (a)	Article 14(2) point (a)
Article 14(1) point (b)	Article 14(1) point (a)
Article 14(1) point (c)	Article 14(1) points (b) and (c)
Article 14(1) point (d)	Article 14(1) point (d)
—	Article 14(1) points (e) and (f)
Article 14(2) introductory words	Article 14(2) introductory words
Article 14(2) point (a)	Article 14(2) point (d)
Article 14(2) points (b) and (c)	Article 14(2) points (b) and (c)
Article 14(3)	Article 14(3)
Article 14(4)	Article 14(4)

Article 15(1) introductory words	Article 15(1) introductory words
Article 15(1) points (a) and (b)	Article 15(1) points (a) and (b)
Article 15(2) introductory words	Article 15(1) introductory words
Article 15(2) point (a)	Article 15(1) point (c)
Article 15(2) point (b)	Article 15(1) point (d)
Article 15(3)	Article 15(2)
Articles 16 to 20	Articles 16 to 20
Article 21(1)	Article 21(2)
Article 21(2)	Article 21(3)
Article 21(3)	Article 21(4)
Article 22(1)	Article 21(1)
Article 22(3)	—
—	Article 22(1) to (3)
Article 22(4)	Article 22(4)
Article 22(5)	—
—	Article 22(5)
Article 23	Article 23(1)
—	Article 23(2)
Article 24	Article 24
—	Article 25
Article 25(1)	Article 26(1), first subparagraph
—	Article 26(1), second subparagraph
Article 25(2)	Article 26(2)
Article 25(3)	Article 26(3)
—	Annex

Sale of Goods Act 1979

1979 c. 54

An Act to consolidate the law relating to the sale of goods

[6th December 1979]

PART I
CONTRACTS TO WHICH ACT APPLIES

1. Contracts to which Act applies

(1) This Act applies to contracts of sale of goods made on or after (but not to those made before) 1 January 1894.

(2) In relation to contracts made on certain dates, this Act applies subject to the modification of certain of its sections as mentioned in Schedule 1 below.

(3) Any such modification is indicated in the section concerned by a reference to Schedule 1 below.

(4) Accordingly, where a section does not contain such a reference, this Act applies in relation to the contract concerned without such modification of the section.

PART II
FORMATION OF THE CONTRACT

Contract of sale

2. Contract of sale

(1) A contract of sale of goods is a contract by which the seller transfers or agrees to transfer the property in goods to the buyer for a money consideration, called the price.

(2) There may be a contract of sale between one part owner and another.

(3) A contract of sale may be absolute or conditional.

(4) Where under a contract of sale the property in the goods is transferred from the seller to the buyer the contract is called a sale.

(5) Where under a contract of sale the transfer of the property in the goods is to take place at a future time or subject to some condition later to be fulfilled the contract is called an agreement to sell.

(6) An agreement to sell becomes a sale when the time elapses or the conditions are fulfilled subject to which the property in the goods is to be transferred.

3. Capacity to buy and sell

(1) Capacity to buy and sell is regulated by the general law concerning capacity to contract and to transfer and acquire property.

(2) Where necessaries are sold and delivered to a minor or to a person who by reason of ... or drunkenness is incompetent to contract, he must pay a reasonable price for them.

(3) In subsection (2) above "necessaries" means goods suitable to the condition in life of the minor or other person concerned and to his actual requirements at the time of the sale and delivery.

Formalities of contract

4. How contract of sale is made

(1) Subject to this and any other Act, a contract of sale may be made in writing (either with or without seal), or by word of mouth, or partly in writing and partly by word of mouth, or may be implied from the conduct of the parties.

(2) Nothing in this section affects the law relating to corporations.

Subject matter of contract

5. Existing or future goods

(1) The goods which form the subject of a contract of sale may be either existing goods, owned or possessed by the seller, or goods to be manufactured or acquired by him after the making of the contract of sale, in this Act called future goods.

(2) There may be a contract for the sale of goods the acquisition of which by the seller depends on a contingency which may or may not happen.

(3) Where by a contract of sale the seller purports to effect a present sale of future goods, the contract operates as an agreement to sell the goods.

6. Goods which have perished

Where there is a contract for the sale of specific goods, and the goods without the knowledge of the seller have perished at the time when the contract is made, the contract is void.

7. Goods perishing before sale but after agreement to sell

Where there is an agreement to sell specific goods and subsequently the goods, without any fault on the part of the seller or buyer, perish before the risk passes to the buyer, the agreement is avoided.

The price

8. Ascertainment of price

(1) The price in a contract of sale may be fixed by the contract, or may be left to be fixed in a manner agreed by the contract, or may be determined by the course of dealing between the parties.

(2) Where the price is not determined as mentioned in subsection (1) above the buyer must pay a reasonable price.

(3) What is a reasonable price is a question of fact dependent on the circumstances of each particular case.

9. Agreement to sell at valuation

(1) Where there is an agreement to sell goods on the terms that the price is to be fixed by the valuation of a third party, and he cannot or does not make the valuation, the agreement is avoided; but if the goods or any part of them have been delivered to and appropriated by the buyer he must pay a reasonable price for them.

(2) Where the third party is prevented from making the valuation by the fault of the seller or buyer, the party not at fault may maintain an action for damages against the party at fault.

Implied terms etc

10. Stipulations about time

(1) Unless a different intention appears from the terms of the contract, stipulations as to time of payment are not of the essence of a contract of sale.

(2) Whether any other stipulation as to time is or is not of the essence of the contract depends on the terms of the contract.

(3) In a contract of sale "month" prima facie means calendar month.

11. When condition to be treated as warranty

(1) This section does not apply to Scotland.

(2) Where a contract of sale is subject to a condition to be fulfilled by the seller, the buyer may waive the condition, or may elect to treat the breach of the condition as a breach of warranty and not as a ground for treating the contract as repudiated.

(3) Whether a stipulation in a contract of sale is a condition, the breach of which may give rise to a right to treat the contract as repudiated, or a warranty, the breach of which may give rise to a claim for damages but not to a right to reject the goods and treat the contract as repudiated,

depends in each case on the construction of the contract; and a stipulation may be a condition, though called a warranty in the contract.

(4) Subject to section 35A below where a contract of sale is not severable and the buyer has accepted the goods or part of them, the breach of a condition to be fulfilled by the seller can only be treated as a breach of warranty, and not as a ground for rejecting the goods and treating the contract as repudiated, unless there is an express or implied term of the contract to that effect.

(5) …

(6) Nothing in this section affects a condition or warranty whose fulfilment is excused by law by reason of impossibility or otherwise.

(7) Paragraph 2 of Schedule 1 below applies in relation to a contract made before 22 April 1967 or (in the application of this Act to Northern Ireland) 28 July 1967.

12. Implied terms about title, etc

(1) In a contract of sale, other than one to which subsection (3) below applies, there is an implied term on the part of the seller that in the case of a sale he has a right to sell the goods, and in the case of an agreement to sell he will have such a right at the time when the property is to pass.

(2) In a contract of sale, other than one to which subsection (3) below applies, there is also an implied term that—

(a) the goods are free, and will remain free until the time when the property is to pass, from any charge or encumbrance not disclosed or known to the buyer before the contract is made, and

(b) the buyer will enjoy quiet possession of the goods except so far as it may be disturbed by the owner or other person entitled to the benefit of any charge or encumbrance so disclosed or known.

(3) This subsection applies to a contract of sale in the case of which there appears from the contract or is to be inferred from its circumstances an intention that the seller should transfer only such title as he or a third person may have.

(4) In a contract to which subsection (3) above applies there is an implied term that all charges or encumbrances known to the seller and not known to the buyer have been disclosed to the buyer before the contract is made.

(5) In a contract to which subsection (3) above applies there is also an implied term that none of the following will disturb the buyer's quiet possession of the goods, namely—

(a) the seller;

(b) in a case where the parties to the contract intend that the seller should transfer only such title as a third person may have, that person;

(c) anyone claiming through or under the seller or that third person otherwise than under a charge or encumbrance disclosed or known to the buyer before the contract is made.

(5A) As regards England and Wales and Northern Ireland, the term implied by subsection (1) above is a condition and the terms implied by subsections (2), (4) and (5) above are warranties.

(6) Paragraph 3 of Schedule 1 below applies in relation to a contract made before 18 May 1973.

13. Sale by description

(1) Where there is a contract for the sale of goods by description, there is an implied term that the goods will correspond with the description.

(1A) As regards England and Wales and Northern Ireland, the term implied by subsection (l) above is a condition.

(2) If the sale is by sample as well as by description it is not sufficient that the bulk of the goods corresponds with the sample if the goods do not also correspond with the description.

(3) A sale of goods is not prevented from being a sale by description by reason only that, being exposed for sale or hire, they are selected by the buyer.

(4) Paragraph 4 of Schedule 1 below applies in relation to a contract made before 18 May 1973.

14. Implied terms about quality or fitness

(1) Except as provided by this section and section 15 below and subject to any other enactment, there is no implied term about the quality or fitness for any particular purpose of goods supplied under a contract of sale.

(2) Where the seller sells goods in the course of a business, there is an implied term that the goods supplied under the contract are of satisfactory quality.

(2A) For the purposes of this Act, goods are of satisfactory quality if they meet the standard that a reasonable person would regard as satisfactory, taking account of any description of the goods, the price (if relevant) and all the other relevant circumstances.

(2B) For the purposes of this Act, the quality of goods includes their state and condition and the following (among others) are in appropriate cases aspects of the quality of goods—

(a) fitness for all the purposes for which goods of the kind in question are commonly supplied,
(b) appearance and finish,
(c) freedom from minor defects,
(d) safety, and
(e) durability.

(2C) The term implied by subsection (2) above does not extend to any matter making the quality of goods unsatisfactory—

(a) which is specifically drawn to the buyer's attention before the contract is made,
(b) where the buyer examines the goods before the contract is made, which that examination ought to reveal, or
(c) in the case of a contract for sale by sample, which would have been apparent on a reasonable examination of the sample.

(2D) If the buyer deals as consumer or, in Scotland, if a contract of sale is a consumer contract, the relevant circumstances mentioned in subsection (2A) above include any public statements on the specific characteristics of the goods made about them by the seller, the producer or his representative, particularly in advertising or on labelling.

(2E) A public statement is not by virtue of subsection (2D) above a relevant circumstance for the purposes of subsection (2A) above in the case of a contract of sale, if the seller shows that—

(a) at the time the contract was made, he was not, and could not reasonably have been, aware of the statement,
(b) before the contract was made, the statement had been withdrawn in public or, to the extent that it contained anything which was incorrect or misleading, it had been corrected in public, or
(c) the decision to buy the goods could not have been influenced by the statement.

(2F) Subsections (2D) and (2E) above do not prevent any public statement from being a relevant circumstance for the purposes of subsection (2A) above (whether or not the buyer deals as consumer or, in Scotland, whether or not the contract of sale is a consumer contract) if the statement would have been such a circumstance apart from those subsections.

(3) Where the seller sells goods in the course of a business and the buyer, expressly or by implication, makes known—

(a) to the seller, or
(b) where the purchase price or part of it is payable by instalments and the goods were previously sold by a credit-broker to the seller, to that credit-broker,

any particular purpose for which the goods are being bought, there is an implied term that the goods supplied under the contract are reasonably fit for that purpose, whether or not that is a purpose for which such goods are commonly supplied, except where the circumstances show that the buyer does not rely, or that it is unreasonable for him to rely, on the skill or judgment of the seller or credit-broker.

(4) An implied term about quality or fitness for a particular purpose may be annexed to a contract of sale by usage.

(5) The preceding provisions of this section apply to a sale by a person who in the course of a business is acting as agent for another as they apply to a sale by a principal in the course of a business, except where that other is not selling in the course of a business and either the buyer knows that fact or reasonable steps are taken to bring it to the notice of the buyer before the contract is made.

(6) As regards England and Wales and Northern Ireland, the terms implied by subsections (2) and (3) above are conditions.

(7) Paragraph 5 of Schedule 1 below applies in relation to a contract made on or after 18 May 1973 and before the appointed day, and paragraph 6 in relation to one made before 18 May 1973.

(8) In subsection (7) above and paragraph 5 of Schedule 1 below references to the appointed day are to the day appointed for the purposes of those provisions by an order of the Secretary of State made by statutory instrument.

Sale by sample

15. Sale by sample

(1) A contract of sale is a contract for sale by sample where there is an express or implied term to that effect in the contract.

(2) In the case of a contract for sale by sample there is an implied term—

(a) that the bulk will correspond with the sample in quality;

(b) …

(c) that the goods will be free from any defect, making their quality unsatisfactory, which would not be apparent on reasonable examination of the sample.

(3) As regards England and Wales and Northern Ireland, the term implied by subsection (2) above is a condition.

(4) Paragraph 7 of Schedule 1 below applies in relation to a contract made before 18 May 1973.

Miscellaneous

15A. Modification of remedies for breach of condition in non-consumer cases

(1) Where in the case of a contract of sale—

(a) the buyer would, apart from this subsection, have the right to reject goods by reason of a breach on the part of the seller of a term implied by section 13, 14 or 15 above, but

(b) the breach is so slight that it would be unreasonable for him to reject them,

then, if the buyer does not deal as consumer, the breach is not to be treated as a breach of condition but may be treated as a breach of warranty.

(2) This section applies unless a contrary intention appears in, or is to be implied from, the contract.

(3) It is for the seller to show that a breach fell within subsection (1)(b) above.

(4) This section does not apply to Scotland.

15B. Remedies for breach of contract as respects Scotland

(1) Where in a contract of sale the seller is in breach of any term of the contract (express or implied), the buyer shall be entitled—

(a) to claim damages, and

(b) if the breach is material, to reject any goods delivered under the contract and treat it as repudiated.

(2) Where a contract of sale is a consumer contract, then, for the purposes of subsection (1)(b) above, breach by the seller of any term (express or implied)—

(a) as to the quality of the goods or their fitness for a purpose,

(b) if the goods are, or are to be, sold by description, that the goods will correspond with the description,

(c) if the goods are, or are to be, sold by reference to a sample, that the bulk will correspond with the sample in quality,

shall be deemed to be a material breach.

(3) This section applies to Scotland only.

PART III
EFFECTS OF THE CONTRACT

Transfer of property as between seller and buyer

16. Goods must be ascertained

Subject to section 20A below where there is a contract for the sale of unascertained goods no property in the goods is transferred to the buyer unless and until the goods are ascertained.

17. Property passes when intended to pass

(1) Where there is a contract for the sale of specific or ascertained goods the property in them is transferred to the buyer at such time as the parties to the contract intend it to be transferred.

(2) For the purpose of ascertaining the intention of the parties regard shall be had to the terms of the contract, the conduct of the parties and the circumstances of the case.

18. Rules for ascertaining intention

Unless a different intention appears, the following are rules for ascertaining the intention of the parties as to the time at which the property in the goods is to pass to the buyer.

Rule 1—

Where there is an unconditional contract for the sale of specific goods in a deliverable state the property in the goods passes to the buyer when the contract is made, and it is immaterial whether the time of payment or the time of delivery, or both, be postponed.

Rule 2—

Where there is a contract for the sale of specific goods and the seller is bound to do something to the goods for the purpose of putting them into a deliverable state, the property does not pass until the thing is done and the buyer has notice that it has been done.

Rule 3—

Where there is a contract for the sale of specific goods in a deliverable state but the seller is bound to weigh, measure, test, or do some other act or thing with reference to the goods for the purpose of ascertaining the price, the property does not pass until the act or thing is done and the buyer has notice that it has been done.

Rule 4—

When goods are delivered to the buyer on approval or on sale or return or other similar terms the property in the goods passes to the buyer:—

(a) when he signifies his approval or acceptance to the seller or does any other act adopting the transaction;

(b) if he does not signify his approval or acceptance to the seller but retains the goods without giving notice of rejection, then, if a time has been fixed for the return of the goods, on the expiration of that time, and, if no time has been fixed, on the expiration of a reasonable time.

Rule 5—

(1) Where there is a contract for the sale of unascertained or future goods by description, and goods of that description and in a deliverable state are unconditionally appropriated to the contract, either by the seller with the assent of the buyer or by the buyer with the assent of the seller, the property in the goods then passes to the buyer; and the assent may be express or implied, and may be given either before or after the appropriation is made.

(2) Where, in pursuance of the contract, the seller delivers the goods to the buyer or to a carrier or other bailee or custodier (whether named by the buyer or not) for the purpose of transmission to the buyer, and does not reserve the right of disposal, he is to be taken to have unconditionally appropriated the goods to the contract.

(3) Where there is a contract for the sale of a specified quantity of unascertained goods in a deliverable state forming part of a bulk which is identified either in the contract or by

subsequent agreement between the parties and the bulk is reduced to (or to less than) that quantity, then, if the buyer under that contract is the only buyer to whom goods are then due out of the bulk—

(a) the remaining goods are to be taken as appropriated to that contract at the time when the bulk is so reduced; and

(b) the property in those goods then passes to that buyer.

(4) Paragraph (3) above applies also (with the necessary modifications) where a bulk is reduced to (or to less than) the aggregate of the quantities due to a single buyer under separate contracts relating to that bulk and he is the only buyer to whom goods are then due out of that bulk.

19. Reservation of right of disposal

(1) Where there is a contract for the sale of specific goods or where goods are subsequently appropriated to the contract, the seller may, by the terms of the contract or appropriation, reserve the right of disposal of the goods until certain conditions are fulfilled; and in such a case, notwithstanding the delivery of the goods to the buyer, or to a carrier or other bailee or custodier for the purpose of transmission to the buyer, the property in the goods does not pass to the buyer until the conditions imposed by the seller are fulfilled.

(2) Where goods are shipped, and by the bill of lading the goods are deliverable to the order of the seller or his agent, the seller is prima facie to be taken to reserve the right of disposal.

(3) Where the seller of goods draws on the buyer for the price, and transmits the bill of exchange and bill of lading to the buyer together to secure acceptance or payment of the bill of exchange, the buyer is bound to return the bill of lading if he does not honour the bill of exchange, and if he wrongfully retains the bill of lading the property in the goods does not pass to him.

20. Passing of risk

(1) Unless otherwise agreed, the goods remain at the seller's risk until the property in them is transferred to the buyer, but when the property in them is transferred to the buyer the goods are at the buyer's risk whether delivery has been made or not.

(2) But where delivery has been delayed through the fault of either buyer or seller the goods are at the risk of the party at fault as regards any loss which might not have occurred but for such fault.

(3) Nothing in this section affects the duties or liabilities of either seller or buyer as a bailee or custodier of the goods of the other party.

(4) In a case where the buyer deals as consumer or, in Scotland, where there is a consumer contract in which the buyer is a consumer, subsections (1) to (3) above must be ignored and the goods remain at the seller's risk until they are delivered to the consumer.

20A. Undivided shares in goods forming part of a bulk

(1) This section applies to a contract for the sale of a specified quantity of unascertained goods if the following conditions are met—

(a) the goods or some of them form part of a bulk which is identified either in the contract or by subsequent agreement between the parties; and

(b) the buyer has paid the price for some or all of the goods which are the subject of the contract and which form part of the bulk.

(2) Where this section applies, then (unless the parties agree otherwise), as soon as the conditions specified in paragraphs (a) and (b) of subsection (1) above are met or at such later time as the parties may agree—

(a) property in an undivided share in the bulk is transferred to the buyer, and

(b) the buyer becomes an owner in common of the bulk.

(3) Subject to subsection (4) below, for the purposes of this section, the undivided share of a buyer in a bulk at any time shall be such share as the quantity of goods paid for and due to the buyer out of the bulk bears to the quantity of goods in the bulk at that time.

(4) Where the aggregate of the undivided shares of buyers in a bulk determined under subsection (3) above would at any time exceed the whole of the bulk at that time, the undivided share in the bulk

of each buyer shall be reduced proportionately so that the aggregate of the undivided shares is equal to the whole bulk.

(5) Where a buyer has paid the price for only some of the goods due to him out of a bulk, any delivery to the buyer out of the bulk shall, for the purposes of this section, be ascribed in the first place to the goods in respect of which payment has been made.

(6) For the purposes of this section payment of part of the price for any goods shall be treated as payment for a corresponding part of the goods.

20B. Deemed consent by co-owner to dealings in bulk goods

(1) A person who has become an owner in common of a bulk by virtue of section 20A above shall be deemed to have consented to—

(a) any delivery of goods out of the bulk to any other owner in common of the bulk, being goods which are due to him under his contract;

(b) any dealing with or removal, delivery or disposal of goods in the bulk by any other person who is an owner in common of the bulk in so far as the goods fall within that co-owner's undivided share in the bulk at the time of the dealing, removal, delivery or disposal.

(2) No cause of action shall accrue to anyone against a person by reason of that person having acted in accordance with paragraph (a) or (b) of subsection (1) above in reliance on any consent deemed to have been given under that subsection.

(3) Nothing in this section or section 20A above shall—

(a) impose an obligation on a buyer of goods out of a bulk to compensate any other buyer of goods out of that bulk for any shortfall in the goods received by that other buyer;

(b) affect any contractual arrangement between buyers of goods out of a bulk for adjustments between themselves; or

(c) affect the rights of any buyer under his contract.

Transfer of title

21. Sale by person not the owner

(1) Subject to this Act, where goods are sold by a person who is not their owner, and who does not sell them under the authority or with the consent of the owner, the buyer acquires no better title to the goods than the seller had, unless the owner of the goods is by his conduct precluded from denying the seller's authority to sell.

(2) Nothing in this Act affects—

(a) the provisions of the Factors Acts or any enactment enabling the apparent owner of goods to dispose of them as if he were their true owner;

(b) the validity of any contract of sale under any special common law or statutory power of sale or under the order of a court of competent jurisdiction.

22. Market overt

(1) …

(2) This section does not apply to Scotland.

(3) Paragraph 8 of Schedule 1 below applies in relation to a contract under which goods were sold before 1st January 1968 or (in the application of this Act to Northern Ireland) 29th August 1967.

23. Sale under voidable title

When the seller of goods has a voidable title to them, but his title has not been avoided at the time of the sale, the buyer acquires a good title to the goods, provided he buys them in good faith and without notice of the seller's defect of title.

24. Seller in possession after sale

Where a person having sold goods continues or is in possession of the goods, or of the documents of title to the goods, the delivery or transfer by that person, or by a mercantile agent acting for him, of the goods or documents of title under any sale, pledge, or other disposition thereof, to any person receiving the same in good faith and without notice of the previous sale, has the same effect as if the person making the delivery or transfer were expressly authorised by the owner of the goods to make the same.

25. Buyer in possession after sale

(1) Where a person having bought or agreed to buy goods obtains, with the consent of the seller, possession of the goods or the documents of title to the goods, the delivery or transfer by that person, or by a mercantile agent acting for him, of the goods or documents of title, under any sale, pledge, or other disposition thereof, to any person receiving the same in good faith and without notice of any lien or other right of the original seller in respect of the goods, has the same effect as if the person making the delivery or transfer were a mercantile agent in possession of the goods or documents of title with the consent of the owner.

(2) For the purposes of subsection (1) above—

(a) the buyer under a conditional sale agreement is to be taken not to be a person who has bought or agreed to buy goods, and

(b) "conditional sale agreement" means an agreement for the sale of goods which is a consumer credit agreement within the meaning of the Consumer Credit Act 1974 under which the purchase price or part of it is payable by instalments, and the property in the goods is to remain in the seller (notwithstanding that the buyer is to be in possession of the goods) until such conditions as to the payment of instalments or otherwise as may be specified in the agreement are fulfilled.

(3) Paragraph 9 of Schedule 1 below applies in relation to a contract under which a person buys or agrees to buy goods and which is made before the appointed day.

(4) In subsection (3) above and paragraph 9 of Schedule 1 below references to the appointed day are to the day appointed for the purposes of those provisions by an order of the Secretary of State made by statutory instrument.

26. Supplementary to sections 24 and 25

In sections 24 and 25 above "mercantile agent" means a mercantile agent having in the customary course of his business as such agent authority either—

(a) to sell goods, or

(b) to consign goods for the purpose of sale, or

(c) to buy goods, or

(d) to raise money on the security of goods.

PART IV
PERFORMANCE OF THE CONTRACT

27. Duties of seller and buyer

It is the duty of the seller to deliver the goods, and of the buyer to accept and pay for them, in accordance with the terms of the contract of sale.

28. Payment and delivery are concurrent conditions

Unless otherwise agreed, delivery of the goods and payment of the price are concurrent conditions, that is to say, the seller must be ready and willing to give possession of the goods to the buyer in exchange for the price and the buyer must be ready and willing to pay the price in exchange for possession of the goods.

29. Rules about delivery

(1) Whether it is for the buyer to take possession of the goods or for the seller to send them to the buyer is a question depending in each case on the contract, express or implied, between the parties.

(2) Apart from any such contract, express or implied, the place of delivery is the seller's place of business if he has one, and if not, his residence; except that, if the contract is for the sale of

specific goods, which to the knowledge of the parties when the contract is made are in some other place, then that place is the place of delivery.

(3) Where under the contract of sale the seller is bound to send the goods to the buyer, but no time for sending them is fixed, the seller is bound to send them within a reasonable time.

(4) Where the goods at the time of sale are in the possession of a third person, there is no delivery by seller to buyer unless and until the third person acknowledges to the buyer that he holds the goods on his behalf; but nothing in this section affects the operation of the issue or transfer of any document of title to goods.

(5) Demand or tender of delivery may be treated as ineffectual unless made at a reasonable hour; and what is a reasonable hour is a question of fact.

(6) Unless otherwise agreed, the expenses of and incidental to putting the goods into a deliverable state must be borne by the seller.

30. Delivery of wrong quantity

(1) Where the seller delivers to the buyer a quantity of goods less than he contracted to sell, the buyer may reject them, but if the buyer accepts the goods so delivered he must pay for them at the contract rate.

(2) Where the seller delivers to the buyer a quantity of goods larger than he contracted to sell, the buyer may accept the goods included in the contract and reject the rest, or he may reject the whole.

(2A) A buyer who does not deal as consumer may not—

(a) where the seller delivers a quantity of goods less than he contracted to sell, reject the goods under subsection (1) above, or

(b) where the seller delivers a quantity of goods larger than he contracted to sell, reject the whole under subsection (2) above,

if the shortfall or, as the case may be, excess is so slight that it would be unreasonable for him to do so.

(2B) It is for the seller to show that a shortfall or excess fell within subsection (2A) above.

(2C) Subsections (2A) and (2B) above do not apply to Scotland.

(2D) Where the seller delivers a quantity of goods—

(a) less than he contracted to sell, the buyer shall not be entitled to reject the goods under subsection (1) above,

(b) larger than he contracted to sell, the buyer shall not be entitled to reject the whole under subsection (2) above,

unless the shortfall or excess is material.

(2E) Subsection (2D) above applies to Scotland only.

(3) Where the seller delivers to the buyer a quantity of goods larger than he contracted to sell and the buyer accepts the whole of the goods so delivered he must pay for them at the contract rate.

(4) …

(5) This section is subject to any usage of trade, special agreement, or course of dealing between the parties.

31. Instalment deliveries

(1) Unless otherwise agreed, the buyer of goods is not bound to accept delivery of them by instalments.

(2) Where there is a contract for the sale of goods to be delivered by stated instalments, which are to be separately paid for, and the seller makes defective deliveries in respect of one or more instalments, or the buyer neglects or refuses to take delivery of or pay for one or more instalments, it is a question in each case depending on the terms of the contract and the circumstances of the case whether the breach of contract is a repudiation of the whole contract or whether it is a severable breach giving rise to a claim for compensation but not to a right to treat the whole contract as repudiated.

32. Delivery to carrier

(1) Where, in pursuance of a contract of sale, the seller is authorised or required to send the goods to the buyer, delivery of the goods to a carrier (whether named by the buyer or not) for the purpose of transmission to the buyer is prima facie deemed to be a delivery of the goods to the buyer.

(2) Unless otherwise authorised by the buyer, the seller must make such contract with the carrier on behalf of the buyer as may be reasonable having regard to the nature of the goods and the other circumstances of the case; and if the seller omits to do so, and the goods are lost or damaged in course of transit, the buyer may decline to treat the delivery to the carrier as a delivery to himself or may hold the seller responsible in damages.

(3) Unless otherwise agreed, where goods are sent by the seller to the buyer by a route involving sea transit, under circumstances in which it is usual to insure, the seller must give such notice to the buyer as may enable him to insure them during their sea transit; and if the seller fails to do so, the goods are at his risk during such sea transit.

(4) In a case where the buyer deals as consumer or, in Scotland, where there is a consumer contract in which the buyer is a consumer, subsections (1) to (3) above must be ignored, but if in pursuance of a contract of sale the seller is authorised or required to send the goods to the buyer, delivery of the goods to the carrier is not delivery of the goods to the buyer.

33. Risk where goods are delivered at distant place

Where the seller of goods agrees to deliver them at his own risk at a place other than that where they are when sold, the buyer must nevertheless (unless otherwise agreed) take any risk of deterioration in the goods necessarily incident to the course of transit.

34. Buyer's right of examining the goods

… Unless otherwise agreed, when the seller tenders delivery of goods to the buyer, he is bound on request to afford the buyer a reasonable opportunity of examining the goods for the purpose of ascertaining whether they are in conformity with the contract and, in the case of a contract for sale by sample, of comparing the bulk with the sample.

35. Acceptance

(1) The buyer is deemed to have accepted the goods subject to subsection (2) below—

(a) when he intimates to the seller that he has accepted them, or

(b) when the goods have been delivered to him and he does any act in relation to them which is inconsistent with the ownership of the seller.

(2) Where goods are delivered to the buyer, and he has not previously examined them, he is not deemed to have accepted them under subsection (1) above until he has had a reasonable opportunity of examining them for the purpose—

(a) of ascertaining whether they are in conformity with the contract, and

(b) in the case of a contract for sale by sample, of comparing the bulk with the sample.

(3) Where the buyer deals as consumer or (in Scotland) the contract of sale is a consumer contract, the buyer cannot lose his right to rely on subsection (2) above by agreement, waiver or otherwise.

(4) The buyer is also deemed to have accepted the goods when after the lapse of a reasonable time he retains the goods without intimating to the seller that he has rejected them.

(5) The questions that are material in determining for the purposes of subsection (4) above whether a reasonable time has elapsed include whether the buyer has had a reasonable opportunity of examining the goods for the purpose mentioned in subsection (2) above.

(6) The buyer is not by virtue of this section deemed to have accepted the goods merely because—

(a) he asks for, or agrees to, their repair by or under an arrangement with the seller, or

(b) the goods are delivered to another under a sub-sale or other disposition.

(7) Where the contract is for the sale of goods making one or more commercial units, a buyer accepting any goods included in a unit is deemed to have accepted all the goods making the unit; and in this subsection "commercial unit" means a unit division of which would materially impair the value of the goods or the character of the unit.

(8) Paragraph 10 of Schedule 1 below applies in relation to a contract made before 22 April 1967 or (in the application of this Act to Northern Ireland) 28 July 1967.

35A. Right of partial rejection

(1) If the buyer—

(a) has the right to reject the goods by reason of a breach on the part of the seller that affects some or all of them, but

(b) accepts some of the goods, including, where there are any goods unaffected by the breach, all such goods,

he does not by accepting them lose his right to reject the rest.

(2) In the case of a buyer having the right to reject an instalment of goods, subsection (1) above applies as if references to the goods were references to the goods comprised in the instalment.

(3) For the purposes of subsection (1) above, goods are affected by a breach if by reason of the breach they are not in conformity with the contract.

(4) This section applies unless a contrary intention appears in, or is to be implied from, the contract.

36. Buyer not bound to return rejected goods

Unless otherwise agreed, where goods are delivered to the buyer, and he refuses to accept them, having the right to do so, he is not bound to return them to the seller, but it is sufficient if he intimates to the seller that he refuses to accept them.

37. Buyer's liability for not taking delivery of goods

(1) When the seller is ready and willing to deliver the goods, and requests the buyer to take delivery, and the buyer does not within a reasonable time after such request take delivery of the goods, he is liable to the seller for any loss occasioned by his neglect or refusal to take delivery, and also for a reasonable charge for the care and custody of the goods.

(2) Nothing in this section affects the rights of the seller where the neglect or refusal of the buyer to take delivery amounts to a repudiation of the contract.

PART V
RIGHTS OF UNPAID SELLER AGAINST THE GOODS

Preliminary

38. Unpaid seller defined

(1) The seller of goods is an unpaid seller within the meaning of this Act—

(a) when the whole of the price has not been paid or tendered;

(b) when a bill of exchange or other negotiable instrument has been received as conditional payment, and the condition on which it was received has not been fulfilled by reason of the dishonour of the instrument or otherwise.

(2) In this Part of this Act "seller" includes any person who is in the position of a seller, as, for instance, an agent of the seller to whom the bill of lading has been indorsed, or a consignor or agent who has himself paid (or is directly responsible for) the price.

39. Unpaid seller's rights

(1) Subject to this and any other Act, notwithstanding that the property in the goods may have passed to the buyer, the unpaid seller of goods, as such, has by implication of law—

(a) a lien on the goods or right to retain them for the price while he is in possession of them;

(b) in case of the insolvency of the buyer, a right of stopping the goods in transit after he has parted with the possession of them;

(c) a right of re-sale as limited by this Act.

(2) Where the property in goods has not passed to the buyer, the unpaid seller has (in addition to his other remedies) a right of withholding delivery similar to and co-extensive with his rights of lien or retention and stoppage in transit where the property has passed to the buyer.

40. …

Unpaid seller's lien

41. Seller's lien

(1) Subject to this Act, the unpaid seller of goods who is in possession of them is entitled to retain possession of them until payment or tender of the price in the following cases:—

(a) where the goods have been sold without any stipulation as to credit;

(b) where the goods have been sold on credit but the term of credit has expired;

(c) where the buyer becomes insolvent.

(2) The seller may exercise his lien or right of retention notwithstanding that he is in possession of the goods as agent or bailee or custodier for the buyer.

42. Part delivery

Where an unpaid seller has made part delivery of the goods, he may exercise his lien or right of retention on the remainder, unless such part delivery has been made under such circumstances as to show an agreement to waive the lien or right of retention.

43. Termination of lien

(1) The unpaid seller of goods loses his lien or right of retention in respect of them—

(a) when he delivers the goods to a carrier or other bailee or custodier for the purpose of transmission to the buyer without reserving the right of disposal of the goods;

(b) when the buyer or his agent lawfully obtains possession of the goods;

(c) by waiver of the lien or right of retention.

(2) An unpaid seller of goods who has a lien or right of retention in respect of them does not lose his lien or right of retention by reason only that he has obtained judgment or decree for the price of the goods.

Stoppage in transit

44. Right of stoppage in transit

Subject to this Act, when the buyer of goods becomes insolvent the unpaid seller who has parted with the possession of the goods has the right of stopping them in transit, that is to say, he may resume possession of the goods as long as they are in course of transit, and may retain them until payment or tender of the price.

45. Duration of transit

(1) Goods are deemed to be in course of transit from the time when they are delivered to a carrier or other bailee or custodier for the purpose of transmission to the buyer, until the buyer or his agent in that behalf takes delivery of them from the carrier or other bailee or custodier.

(2) If the buyer or his agent in that behalf obtains delivery of the goods before their arrival at the appointed destination, the transit is at an end.

(3) If, after the arrival of the goods at the appointed destination, the carrier or other bailee or custodier acknowledges to the buyer or his agent that he holds the goods on his behalf and continues in possession of them as bailee or custodier for the buyer or his agent, the transit is at an end, and it is immaterial that a further destination for the goods may have been indicated by the buyer.

(4) If the goods are rejected by the buyer, and the carrier or other bailee or custodier continues in possession of them, the transit is not deemed to be at an end, even if the seller has refused to receive them back.

(5) When goods are delivered to a ship chartered by the buyer it is a question depending on the circumstances of the particular case whether they are in the possession of the master as a carrier or as agent to the buyer.

(6) Where the carrier or other bailee or custodier wrongfully refuses to deliver the goods to the buyer or his agent in that behalf, the transit is deemed to be at an end.

(7) Where part delivery of the goods has been made to the buyer or his agent in that behalf, the remainder of the goods may be stopped in transit, unless such part delivery has been made under such circumstances as to show an agreement to give up possession of the whole of the goods.

46. How stoppage in transit is effected

(1) The unpaid seller may exercise his right of stoppage in transit either by taking actual possession of the goods or by giving notice of his claim to the carrier or other bailee or custodier in whose possession the goods are.

(2) The notice may be given either to the person in actual possession of the goods or to his principal.

(3) If given to the principal, the notice is ineffective unless given at such time and under such circumstances that the principal, by the exercise of reasonable diligence, may communicate it to his servant or agent in time to prevent a delivery to the buyer.

(4) When notice of stoppage in transit is given by the seller to the carrier or other bailee or custodier in possession of the goods, he must re-deliver the goods to, or according to the directions of, the seller; and the expenses of the re-delivery must be borne by the seller.

Re-sale etc by buyer

47. Effect of sub-sale etc by buyer

(1) Subject to this Act, the unpaid seller's right of lien or retention or stoppage in transit is not affected by any sale or other disposition of the goods which the buyer may have made, unless the seller has assented to it.

(2) Where a document of title to goods has been lawfully transferred to any person as buyer or owner of the goods, and that person transfers the document to a person who takes it in good faith and for valuable consideration, then—

(a) if the last-mentioned transfer was by way of sale the unpaid seller's right of lien or retention or stoppage in transit is defeated; and

(b) if the last-mentioned transfer was made by way of pledge or other disposition for value, the unpaid seller's right of lien or retention or stoppage in transit can only be exercised subject to the rights of the transferee.

Rescission: and re-sale by seller

48. Rescission: and re-sale by seller

(1) Subject to this section, a contract of sale is not rescinded by the mere exercise by an unpaid seller of his right of lien or retention or stoppage in transit.

(2) Where an unpaid seller who has exercised his right of lien or retention or stoppage in transit re-sells the goods, the buyer acquires a good title to them as against the original buyer.

(3) Where the goods are of a perishable nature, or where the unpaid seller gives notice to the buyer of his intention to re-sell, and the buyer does not within a reasonable time pay or tender the price, the unpaid seller may re-sell the goods and recover from the original buyer damages for any loss occasioned by his breach of contract.

(4) Where the seller expressly reserves the right of re-sale in case the buyer should make default, and on the buyer making default re-sells the goods, the original contract of sale is rescinded but without prejudice to any claim the seller may have for damages.

PART 5A
ADDITIONAL RIGHTS OF BUYER IN CONSUMER CASES

48A. Introductory

(1) This section applies if—

(a) the buyer deals as consumer or, in Scotland, there is a consumer contract in which the buyer is a consumer, and

(b) the goods do not conform to the contract of sale at the time of delivery.

(2) If this section applies, the buyer has the right—

(a) under and in accordance with section 48B below, to require the seller to repair or replace the goods, or

(b) under and in accordance with section 48C below—

(i) to require the seller to reduce the purchase price of the goods to the buyer by an appropriate amount, or

(ii) to rescind the contract with regard to the goods in question.

(3) For the purposes of subsection (1)(b) above goods which do not conform to the contract of sale at any time within the period of six months starting with the date on which the goods were delivered to the buyer must be taken not to have so conformed at that date.

(4) Subsection (3) above does not apply if—

(a) it is established that the goods did so conform at that date;

(b) its application is incompatible with the nature of the goods or the nature of the lack of conformity.

48B. Repair or replacement of the goods

(1) If section 48A above applies, the buyer may require the seller—

(a) to repair the goods, or

(b) to replace the goods.

(2) If the buyer requires the seller to repair or replace the goods, the seller must—

(a) repair or, as the case may be, replace the goods within a reasonable time but without causing significant inconvenience to the buyer;

(b) bear any necessary costs incurred in doing so (including in particular the cost of any labour, materials or postage).

(3) The buyer must not require the seller to repair or, as the case may be, replace the goods if that remedy is—

(a) impossible, or

(b) disproportionate in comparison to the other of those remedies, or

(c) disproportionate in comparison to an appropriate reduction in the purchase price under paragraph (a), or rescission under paragraph (b), of section 48C(1) below.

(4) One remedy is disproportionate in comparison to the other if the one imposes costs on the seller which, in comparison to those imposed on him by the other, are unreasonable, taking into account—

(a) the value which the goods would have if they conformed to the contract of sale,

(b) the significance of the lack of conformity, and

(c) whether the other remedy could be effected without significant inconvenience to the buyer.

(5) Any question as to what is a reasonable time or significant inconvenience is to be determined by reference to—

(a) the nature of the goods, and

(b) the purpose for which the goods were acquired.

48C. Reduction of purchase price or rescission of contract

(1) If section 48A above applies, the buyer may—

(a) require the seller to reduce the purchase price of the goods in question to the buyer by an appropriate amount, or

(b) rescind the contract with regard to those goods,

if the condition in subsection (2) below is satisfied.

(2) The condition is that—

(a) by virtue of section 48B(3) above the buyer may require neither repair nor replacement of the goods; or

(b) the buyer has required the seller to repair or replace the goods, but the seller is in breach of the requirement of section 48B(2)(a) above to do so within a reasonable time and without significant inconvenience to the buyer.

(3) For the purposes of this Part, if the buyer rescinds the contract, any reimbursement to the buyer may be reduced to take account of the use he has had of the goods since they were delivered to him.

48D. Relation to other remedies etc

(1) If the buyer requires the seller to repair or replace the goods the buyer must not act under subsection (2) until he has given the seller a reasonable time in which to repair or replace (as the case may be) the goods.

(2) The buyer acts under this subsection if—

(a) in England and Wales or Northern Ireland he rejects the goods and terminates the contract for breach of condition;

(b) in Scotland he rejects any goods delivered under the contract and treats it as repudiated;

(c) he requires the goods to be replaced or repaired (as the case may be).

48E. Powers of the court

(1) In any proceedings in which a remedy is sought by virtue of this Part the court, in addition to any other power it has, may act under this section.

(2) On the application of the buyer the court may make an order requiring specific performance or, in Scotland, specific implement by the seller of any obligation imposed on him by virtue of section 48B above.

(3) Subsection (4) applies if—

(a) the buyer requires the seller to give effect to a remedy under section 48B or 48C above or has claims to rescind under section 48C, but

(b) the court decides that another remedy under section 48B or 48C is appropriate.

(4) The court may proceed—

(a) as if the buyer had required the seller to give effect to the other remedy, or if the other remedy is rescission under section 48C;

(b) as if the buyer had claimed to rescind the contract under that section.

(5) If the buyer has claimed to rescind the contract the court may order that any reimbursement to the buyer is reduced to take account of the use he has had of the goods since they were delivered to him.

(6) The court may make an order under this section unconditionally or on such terms and conditions as to damages, payment of the price and otherwise as it thinks just.

48F. Conformity with the contract

For the purposes of this Part, goods do not conform to a contract of sale if there is, in relation to the goods, a breach of an express term of the contract or a term implied by section 13, 14 or 15 above.

PART VI
ACTIONS FOR BREACH OF THE CONTRACT

Seller's remedies

49. Action for price

(1) Where, under a contract of sale, the property in the goods has passed to the buyer and he wrongfully neglects or refuses to pay for the goods according to the terms of the contract, the seller may maintain an action against him for the price of the goods.

(2) Where, under a contract of sale, the price is payable on a day certain irrespective of delivery and the buyer wrongfully neglects or refuses to pay such price, the seller may maintain an action for the price, although the property in the goods has not passed and the goods have not been appropriated to the contract.

(3) Nothing in this section prejudices the right of the seller in Scotland to recover interest on the price from the date of tender of the goods, or from the date on which the price was payable, as the case may be.

50. Damages for non-acceptance

(1) Where the buyer wrongfully neglects or refuses to accept and pay for the goods, the seller may maintain an action against him for damages for non-acceptance.

(2) The measure of damages is the estimated loss directly and naturally resulting, in the ordinary course of events, from the buyer's breach of contract.

(3) Where there is an available market for the goods in question the measure of damages is prima facie to be ascertained by the difference between the contract price and the market or current price at the time or times when the goods ought to have been accepted or (if no time was fixed for acceptance) at the time of the refusal to accept.

Buyer's remedies

51. Damages for non-delivery

(1) Where the seller wrongfully neglects or refuses to deliver the goods to the buyer, the buyer may maintain an action against the seller for damages for non-delivery.

(2) The measure of damages is the estimated loss directly and naturally resulting, in the ordinary course of events, from the seller's breach of contract.

(3) Where there is an available market for the goods in question the measure of damages is prima facie to be ascertained by the difference between the contract price and the market or current price of the goods at the time or times when they ought to have been delivered or (if no time was fixed) at the time of the refusal to deliver.

52. Specific performance

(1) In any action for breach of contract to deliver specific or ascertained goods the court may, if it thinks fit, on the plaintiff's application, by its judgment or decree direct that the contract shall be performed specifically, without giving the defendant the option of retaining the goods on payment of damages.

(2) The plaintiff's application may be made at any time before judgment or decree.

(3) The judgment or decree may be unconditional, or on such terms and conditions as to damages, payment of the price and otherwise as seem just to the court.

(4) The provisions of this section shall be deemed to be supplementary to, and not in derogation of, the right of specific implement in Scotland.

53. Remedy for breach of warranty

(1) Where there is a breach of warranty by the seller, or where the buyer elects (or is compelled) to treat any breach of a condition on the part of the seller as a breach of warranty, the buyer is not by reason only of such breach of warranty entitled to reject the goods; but he may—

(a) set up against the seller the breach of warranty in diminution or extinction of the price, or

(b) maintain an action against the seller for damages for the breach of warranty.

(2) The measure of damages for breach of warranty is the estimated loss directly and naturally resulting, in the ordinary course of events, from the breach of warranty.

(3) In the case of breach of warranty of quality such loss is prima facie the difference between the value of the goods at the time of delivery to the buyer and the value they would have had if they had fulfilled the warranty.

(4) The fact that the buyer has set up the breach of warranty in diminution or extinction of the price does not prevent him from maintaining an action for the same breach of warranty if he has suffered further damage.

(5) This section does not apply to Scotland.

53A. Measure of damages as respects Scotland

(1) The measure of damages for the seller's breach of contract is the estimated loss directly and naturally resulting, in the ordinary course of events, from the breach.

(2) Where the seller's breach consists of the delivery of goods which are not of the quality required by the contract and the buyer retains the goods, such loss as aforesaid is prima facie the difference between the value of the goods at the time of the delivery to the buyer and the value they would have had if they had fulfilled the contract.

(3) This section applies to Scotland only.

Interest, etc

54. Interest

Nothing in this Act affects the right of the buyer or the seller to recover interest or special damages in any case where by law interest or special damages may be recoverable, or to recover money paid where the consideration for the payment of it has failed.

PART VII
SUPPLEMENTARY

55. Exclusion of implied terms

(1) Where a right, duty or liability would arise under a contract of sale of goods by implication of law, it may (subject to the Unfair Contract Terms Act 1977) be negatived or varied by express agreement, or by the course of dealing between the parties, or by such usage as binds both parties to the contract.

(2) An express term does not negative a term implied by this Act unless inconsistent with it.

(3) Paragraph 11 of Schedule 1 below applies in relation to a contract made on or after 18 May 1973 and before 1 February 1978, and paragraph 12 in relation to one made before 18 May 1973.

56. Conflict of laws

Paragraph 13 of Schedule 1 below applies in relation to a contract made on or after 18 May 1973 and before 1 February 1978, so as to make provision about conflict of laws in relation to such a contract.

57. Auction sales

(1) Where goods are put up for sale by auction in lots, each lot is prima facie deemed to be the subject of a separate contract of sale.

(2) A sale by auction is complete when the auctioneer announces its completion by the fall of the hammer, or in other customary manner; and until the announcement is made any bidder may retract his bid.

(3) A sale by auction may be notified to be subject to a reserve or upset price, and a right to bid may also be reserved expressly by or on behalf of the seller.

(4) Where a sale by auction is not notified to be subject to a right to bid by or on behalf of the seller, it is not lawful for the seller to bid himself or to employ any person to bid at the sale, or for the auctioneer knowingly to take any bid from the seller or any such person.

(5) A sale contravening subsection (4) above may be treated as fraudulent by the buyer.

(6) Where, in respect of a sale by auction, a right to bid is expressly reserved (but not otherwise) the seller or any one person on his behalf may bid at the auction.

58. Payment into court in Scotland

In Scotland where a buyer has elected to accept goods which he might have rejected, and to treat a breach of contract as only giving rise to a claim for damages, he may, in an action by the seller for the price, be required, in the discretion of the court before which the action depends, to consign or pay into court the price of the goods, or part of the price, or to give other reasonable security for its due payment.

59. Reasonable time a question of fact

Where a reference is made in this Act to a reasonable time the question what is a reasonable time is a question of fact.

60. Rights etc enforceable by action

Where a right, duty or liability is declared by this Act, it may (unless otherwise provided by this Act) be enforced by action.

61. Interpretation

(1) In this Act, unless the context or subject matter otherwise requires—

"action" includes counterclaim and set-off, and in Scotland condescendence and claim and compensation;

"bulk" means a mass or collection of goods of the same kind which—

(a) is contained in a defined space or area; and

(b) is such that any goods in the bulk are interchangeable with any other goods therein of the same number or quantity;

"business" includes a profession and the activities of any government department (including a Northern Ireland department) or local or public authority;

"buyer" means a person who buys or agrees to buy goods;

"consumer contract" has the same meaning as in section 25(1) of the Unfair Contract Terms Act 1977; and for the purposes of this Act the onus of proving that a contract is not to be regarded as a consumer contract shall lie on the seller;

"contract of sale" includes an agreement to sell as well as a sale;

"credit-broker" means a person acting in the course of a business of credit brokerage carried on by him, that is a business of effecting introductions of individuals desiring to obtain credit—

(a) to persons carrying on any business so far as it relates to the provision of credit, or

(b) to other persons engaged in credit brokerage;

"defendant" includes in Scotland defender, respondent, and claimant in a multiple poinding;

"delivery" means voluntary transfer of possession from one person to another except that in relation to sections 20A and 20B above it includes such appropriation of goods to the contract as results in property in the goods being transferred to the buyer;

"document of title to goods" has the same meaning as it has in the Factors Acts;

"Factors Acts" means the Factors Act 1889, the Factors (Scotland) Act 1890, and any enactment amending or substituted for the same;

"fault" means wrongful act or default;

"future goods" means goods to be manufactured or acquired by the seller after the making of the contract of sale;

"goods" includes all personal chattels other than things in action and money, and in Scotland all corporeal moveables except money; and in particular "goods" includes emblements, industrial growing crops, and things attached to or forming part of the land which are agreed to be severed before sale or under the contract of sale and includes an undivided share in goods;

"plaintiff" includes pursuer, complainer, claimant in a multiplepoinding and defendant or defender counter-claiming;

"producer" means the manufacturer of goods, the importer of goods into the European Economic Area or any person purporting to be a producer by placing his name, trade mark or other distinctive sign on the goods;

"property" means the general property in goods, and not merely a special property;

…

"repair" means, in cases where there is a lack of conformity in goods for the purposes of section 48F of this Act, to bring the goods into conformity with the contract;

"sale" includes a bargain and sale as well as a sale and delivery;

"seller" means a person who sells or agrees to sell goods;

"specific goods" means goods identified and agreed on at the time a contract of sale is made and includes an undivided share, specified as a fraction or percentage, of goods identified and agreed on as aforesaid;

"warranty" (as regards England and Wales and Northern Ireland) means an agreement with reference to goods which are the subject of a contract of sale, but collateral to the main purpose of such contract, the breach of which gives rise to a claim for damages, but not to a right to reject the goods and treat the contract as repudiated.

(2) …

(3) A thing is deemed to be done in good faith within the meaning of this Act when it is in fact done honestly, whether it is done negligently or not.

(4) A person is deemed to be insolvent within the meaning of this Act if he has either ceased to pay his debts in the ordinary course of business or he cannot pay his debts as they become due, …

(5) Goods are in a deliverable state within the meaning of this Act when they are in such a state that the buyer would under the contract be bound to take delivery of them.

(5A) References in this Act to dealing as consumer are to be construed in accordance with Part I of the Unfair Contract Terms Act 1977; and, for the purposes of this Act, it is for a seller claiming that the buyer does not deal as consumer to show that he does not.

(6) As regards the definition of "business" in subsection (1) above, paragraph 14 of Schedule 1 below applies in relation to a contract made on or after 18 May 1973 and before 1 February 1978, and paragraph 15 in relation to one made before 18 May 1973.

62. Savings: rules of law etc

(1) The rules in bankruptcy relating to contracts of sale apply to those contracts, notwithstanding anything in this Act.

(2) The rules of the common law, including the law merchant, except in so far as they are inconsistent with the provisions of this Act, and in particular the rules relating to the law of principal and agent and the effect of fraud, misrepresentation, duress or coercion, mistake, or other invalidating cause, apply to contracts for the sale of goods.

(3) Nothing in this Act or the Sale of Goods Act 1893 affects the enactments relating to bills of sale, or any enactment relating to the sale of goods which is not expressly repealed or amended by this Act or that.

(4) The provisions of this Act about contracts of sale do not apply to a transaction in the form of a contract of sale which is intended to operate by way of mortgage, pledge, charge, or other security.

(5) Nothing in this Act prejudices or affects the landlord's right of hypothec . . . in Scotland.

63. Consequential amendments, repeals and savings

(1) Without prejudice to section 17 of the Interpretation Act 1978 (repeal and re-enactment), the enactments mentioned in Schedule 2 below have effect subject to the amendments there specified (being amendments consequential on this Act).

(2) The enactments mentioned in Schedule 3 below are repealed to the extent specified in column 3, but subject to the savings in Schedule 4 below.

(3) The savings in Schedule 4 below have effect.

64. Short title and commencement

(1) This Act may be cited as the Sale of Goods Act 1979.

(2) This Act comes into force on 1 January 1980.

SCHEDULE 1
MODIFICATION OF ACT FOR CERTAIN CONTRACTS

Section 1

Preliminary

1.— (1) This Schedule modifies this Act as it applies to contracts of sale of goods made on certain dates.

(2) In this Schedule references to sections are to those of this Act and references to contracts are to contracts of sale of goods.

(3) Nothing in this Schedule affects a contract made before 1 January 1894.

Section 11: condition treated as warranty

2. In relation to a contract made before 22 April 1967 or (in the application of this Act to Northern Ireland) 28 July 1967, in section 11(4) after "or part of them," insert "or where the contract is for specific goods, the property in which has passed to the buyer,".

Section 12: implied terms about title, etc

3. In relation to a contract made before 18 May 1973 substitute the following for section 12:—

12. Implied terms about title, etc

In a contract of sale, unless the circumstances of the contract are such as to show a different intention, there is—

(a) an implied condition on the part of the seller that in the case of a sale he has a right to sell the goods, and in the case of an agreement to sell he will have such a right at the time when the property is to pass;

(b) an implied warranty that the buyer will have and enjoy quiet possession of the goods;

(c) an implied warranty that the goods will be free from any charge or encumbrance in favour of any third party, not declared or known to the buyer before or at the time when the contract is made.

Section 13: sale by description

4. In relation to a contract made before 18 May 1973, omit section 13(3).

Section 14: quality or fitness (i)

5. In relation to a contract made on or after 18 May 1973 and before the appointed day, substitute the following for section 14:—

14. Implied terms about quality or fitness

(1) Except as provided by this section and section 15 below and subject to any other enactment, there is no implied condition or warranty about the quality or fitness for any particular purpose of goods supplied under a contract of sale.

(2) Where the seller sells goods in the course of a business, there is an implied condition that the goods supplied under the contract are of merchantable quality, except that there is no such condition—

(a) as regards defects, specifically drawn to the buyer's attention before the contract is made; or

(b) if the buyer examines the goods before the contract is made, as regards defects which that examination ought to reveal.

(3) Where the seller sells goods in the course of a business and the buyer, expressly or by implication, makes known to the seller any particular purpose for which the goods are being bought, there is an implied condition that the goods supplied under the contract are reasonably fit for that purpose, whether or not that is a purpose for which such goods are commonly supplied, except where the circumstances show that the buyer

does not rely, or that it is unreasonable for him to rely, on the seller's skill or judgment.

(4) An implied condition or warranty about quality or fitness for a particular purpose may be annexed to a contract of sale by usage.

(5) The preceding provisions of this section apply to a sale by a person who in the course of a business is acting as agent for another as they apply to a sale by a principal in the course of a business, except where that other is not selling in the course of a business and either the buyer knows that fact or reasonable steps are taken to bring it to the notice of the buyer before the contract is made.

(6) Goods of any kind are of merchantable quality within the meaning of subsection (2) above if they are as fit for the purpose or purposes for which goods of that kind are commonly bought as it is reasonable to expect having regard to any description applied to them, the price (if relevant) and all the other relevant circumstances.

(7) In the application of subsection (3) above to an agreement for the sale of goods under which the purchase price or part of it is payable by instalments any reference to the seller includes a reference to the person by whom any antecedent negotiations are conducted; and section 58(3) and (5) of the Hire-Purchase Act 1965, section 54(3) and (5) of the Hire-Purchase (Scotland) Act 1965 and section 65(3) and (5) of the Hire-Purchase Act (Northern Ireland) 1966 (meaning of antecedent negotiations and related expressions) apply in relation to this subsection as in relation to each of those Acts, but as if a reference to any such agreement were included in the references in subsection (3) of each of those sections to the agreements there mentioned.

Section 14: quality or fitness (ii)

6. In relation to a contract made before 18 May 1973 substitute the following for section 14:—

14. Implied terms about quality or fitness

(1) Subject to this and any other Act, there is no implied condition or warranty about the quality or fitness for any particular purpose of goods supplied under a contract of sale.

(2) Where the buyer, expressly or by implication, makes known to the seller the particular purpose for which the goods are required, so as to show that the buyer relies on the seller's skill or judgment, and the goods are of a description which it is in the course of the seller's business to supply (whether he is the manufacturer or not), there is an implied condition that the goods will be reasonably fit for such purpose, except that in the case of a contract for the sale of a specified article under its patent or other trade name there is no implied condition as to its fitness for any particular purpose.

(3) Where goods are bought by description from a seller who deals in goods of that description (whether he is the manufacturer or not), there is an implied condition that the goods will be of merchantable quality; but if the buyer has examined the goods, there is no implied condition as regards defects which such examination ought to have revealed.

(4) An implied condition or warranty about quality or fitness for a particular purpose may be annexed by the usage of trade.

(5) An express condition or warranty does not negative a condition or warranty implied by this Act unless inconsistent with it.

Section 15: sale by sample

7. In relation to a contract made before 18 May 1973, omit section 15(3).

Section 22: market overt

8. In relation to a contract under which goods were sold before 1 January 1968 or (in the application of this Act to Northern Ireland) 29 August 1967, add the following paragraph at the end of section 22(1):—

"Nothing in this subsection affects the law relating to the sale of horses."

Section 25: buyer in possession

9. In relation to a contract under which a person buys or agrees to buy goods and which is made before the appointed day, omit section 25(2).

Section 35: acceptance

10. In relation to a contract made before 22 April 1967 or (in the application of this Act to Northern Ireland) 28 July 1967, in section 35(1) omit "(except where section 34 above otherwise provides)".

Section 55: exclusion of implied terms (i)

11. In relation to a contract made on or after 18 May 1973 and before 1 February 1978 substitute the following for section 55:—

55. Exclusion of implied terms

(1) Where a right, duty or liability would arise under a contract of sale of goods by implication of law, it may be negatived or varied by express agreement, or by the course of dealing between the parties, or by such usage as binds both parties to the contract, but the preceding provision has effect subject to the following provisions of this section.

(2) An express condition or warranty does not negative a condition or warranty implied by this Act unless inconsistent with it.

(3) In the case of a contract of sale of goods, any term of that or any other contract exempting from all or any of the provisions of section 12 above is void.

(4) In the case of a contract of sale of goods, any term of that or any other contract exempting from all or any of the provisions of section 13, 14 or 15 above is void in the case of a consumer sale and is, in any other case, not enforceable to the extent that it is shown that it would not be fair or reasonable to allow reliance on the term.

(5) In determining for the purposes of subsection (4) above whether or not reliance on any such term would be fair or reasonable regard shall be had to all the circumstances of the case and in particular to the following matters—

(a) the strength of the bargaining positions of the seller and buyer relative to each other, taking into account, among other things, the availability of suitable alternative products and sources of supply;

(b) whether the buyer received an inducement to agree to the term or in accepting it had an opportunity of buying the goods or suitable alternatives without it from any source of supply;

(c) whether the buyer knew or ought reasonably to have known of the existence and extent of the term (having regard, among other things, to any custom of the trade and any previous course of dealing between the parties);

(d) where the term exempts from all or any of the provisions of section 13, 14 or 15 above if some condition is not complied with, whether it was reasonable at the time of the contract to expect that compliance with that condition would be practicable;

(e) whether the goods were manufactured, processed, or adapted to the special order of the buyer.

(6) Subsection (5) above does not prevent the court from holding, in accordance with any rule of law, that a term which purports to exclude or restrict any of the provisions of section 13, 14 or 15 above is not a term of the contract.

(7) In this section "consumer sale" means a sale of goods (other than a sale by auction or by competitive tender) by a seller in the course of a business where the goods—

(a) are of a type ordinarily bought for private use or consumption; and

(b) are sold to a person who does not buy or hold himself out as buying them in the course of a business.

(8) The onus of proving that a sale falls to be treated for the purposes of this section as not being a consumer sale lies on the party so contending.

(9) Any reference in this section to a term exempting from all or any of the provisions of any section of this Act is a reference to a term which purports to exclude or restrict, or has the effect of excluding or restricting, the operation of all or any of the provisions of that section, or the exercise of a right conferred by any provision of that section, or any liability of the seller for breach of a condition or warranty implied by any provision of that section.

(10) It is hereby declared that any reference in this section to a term of a contract includes a reference to a term which although not contained in a contract is incorporated in the contract by another term of the contract.

(11) Nothing in this section prevents the parties to a contract for the international sale of goods from negativing or varying any right, duty or liability which would otherwise arise by implication of law under sections 12 to 15 above.

(12) In subsection (11) above "contract for the international sale of goods" means a contract of sale of goods made by parties whose places of business (or, if they have none, habitual residences) are in the territories of different States (the Channel Islands and the Isle of Man being treated for this purpose as different States from the United Kingdom) and in the case of which one of the following conditions is satisfied:—

(a) the contract involves the sale of goods which are at the time of the conclusion of the contract in the course of carriage or will be carried from the territory of one State to the territory of another; or

(b) the acts constituting the offer and acceptance have been effected in the territories of different States; or

(c) delivery of the goods is to be made in the territory of a State other than that within whose territory the acts constituting the offer and the acceptance have been effected.

Section 55: exclusion of implied terms (ii)

12. In relation to a contract made before 18 May 1973 substitute the following for section 55:—

55. Exclusion of implied terms

Where a right, duty or liability would arise under a contract of sale by implication of law, it may be negatived or varied by express agreement, or by the course of dealing between the parties, or by such usage as binds both parties to the contract.

Section 56: conflict of laws

13.— (1) In relation to a contract on or after 18 May 1973 and before 1 February 1978 substitute for section 56 the section set out in sub-paragraph (3) below.

(2) In relation to a contract made otherwise than as mentioned in sub-paragraph (1) above, ignore section 56 and this paragraph.

(3) The section mentioned in sub-paragraph (1) above is as follows:—

56. Conflict of laws

(1) Where the proper law of a contract for the sale of goods would, apart from a term that it should be the law of some other country or a term to the like effect, be the law of any part of the United Kingdom, or where any such contract contains a term which purports to substitute, or has the effect of substituting, provisions of the law of some other country for all or any of the provisions of sections 12 to 15 and 55 above, those sections shall, notwithstanding that term but subject to subsection (2) below, apply to the contract.

(2) Nothing in subsection (1) above prevents the parties to a contract for the international sale of goods from negativing or varying any right, duty or liability which would otherwise arise by implication of law under sections 12 to 15 above.

(3) In subsection (2) above "contract for the international sale of goods" means a contract of sale of goods made by parties whose places of business (or, if they have none, habitual residences) are in the territories of different States (the Channel Islands and the Isle of Man being treated for this purpose as different States from the United Kingdom) and in the case of which one of the following conditions is satisfied:—

(a) the contract involves the sale of goods which are at the time of the conclusion of the contract in the course of carriage or will be carried from the territory of one State to the territory of another; or

(b) the acts constituting the offer and acceptance have been effected in the territories of different States; or

(c) delivery of the goods is to be made in the territory of a State other than that within whose territory the acts constituting the offer and the acceptance have been effected.

Section 61(1): definition of "business" (i)

14. In relation to a contract made on or after 18 May 1973 and before 1 February 1978, in the definition of "business" in section 61(1) for "or local or public authority" substitute "local authority or statutory undertaker".

Section 61(1): definition of "business" (ii)

15. In relation to a contract made before 18 May 1973 omit the definition of "business" in section 61(1).

SCHEDULE 2

CONSEQUENTIAL AMENDMENTS

Section 63

…

SCHEDULE 4

SAVINGS

Section 63

Preliminary

1. In this Schedule references to the 1893 Act are to the Sale of Goods Act 1893.

Orders

2. An order under section 14 (8) or 25 (4) above may make provision that it is to have effect only as provided by the order (being provision corresponding to that which could, apart from this Act, have been made by an order under section 192 (4) of the Consumer Credit Act 1974 bringing into operation an amendment or repeal making a change corresponding to that made by the order under section 14 (8) or 25 (4) above).

Offences

3. Where an offence was committed in relation to goods before 1st January 1969 or (in the application of this Act to Northern Ireland) 1st August 1969, the effect of a conviction in respect of the offence is not affected by the repeal by this Act of section 24 of the 1893 Act.

1893 Act, section 26

4. The repeal by this Act of provisions of the 1893 Act does not extend to the following provisions of that Act in so far as they are needed to give effect to or interpret section 26 of that Act, namely, the definitions of "goods" and "property" in section 62 (1), section 62 (2) and section 63 (which was repealed subject to savings by the Statute Law Revision Act 1908).

Things done before 1st January 1894

5. The repeal by this Act of section 60 of and the Schedule to the 1893 Act (which effected repeals and which were themselves repealed subject to savings by the Statute Law Revision Act 1908) does not affect those savings, and accordingly does not affect things done or acquired before 1st January 1894.

6. In so far as the 1893 Act applied (immediately before the operation of the repeals made by this Act) to contracts made before 1st January 1894 (when the 1893 Act came into operation), the 1893 Act shall continue so to apply notwithstanding this Act.

Unfair Contract Terms Act 1977

1977 c. 50

An Act to impose further limits on the extent to which under the law of England and Wales and Northern Ireland civil liability for breach of contract, or for negligence or other breach of duty, can be avoided by means of contract terms and otherwise, and under the law of Scotland civil liability can be avoided by means of contract terms

[26th October 1977]

PART I
AMENDMENT OF LAW FOR ENGLAND AND WALES AND NORTHERN IRELAND

Introductory

1. Scope of Part I

(1) For the purposes of this Part of this Act, "negligence" means the breach—

(a) of any obligation, arising from the express or implied terms of a contract, to take reasonable care or exercise reasonable skill in the performance of the contract;

(b) of any common law duty to take reasonable care or exercise reasonable skill (but not any stricter duty);

(c) of the common duty of care imposed by the Occupiers' Liability Act 1957 or the Occupiers' Liability Act (Northern Ireland) 1957.

(2) This Part of this Act is subject to Part III; and in relation to contracts, the operation of sections 2 to 4 and 7 is subject to the exceptions made by Schedule 1.

(3) In the case of both contract and tort, sections 2 to 7 apply (except where the contrary is stated in section 6(4)) only to business liability, that is liability for breach of obligations or duties arising—

(a) from things done or to be done by a person in the course of a business (whether his own business or another's); or

(b) from the occupation of premises used for business purposes of the occupier;

and references to liability are to be read accordingly but liability of an occupier of premises for breach of an obligation or duty towards a person obtaining access to the premises for recreational or educational purposes, being liability for loss or damage suffered by reason of the dangerous state of the premises, is not a business liability of the occupier unless granting that person such access for the purposes concerned falls within the business purposes of the occupier.

(4) In relation to any breach of duty or obligation, it is immaterial for any purpose of this Part of this Act whether the breach was inadvertent or intentional, or whether liability for it arises directly or vicariously.

Avoidance of liability for negligence, breach of contract, etc

2. Negligence liability

(1) A person cannot by reference to any contract term or to a notice given to persons generally or to particular persons exclude or restrict his liability for death or personal injury resulting from negligence.

(2) In the case of other loss or damage, a person cannot so exclude or restrict his liability for negligence except in so far as the term or notice satisfies the requirement of reasonableness.

(3) Where a contract term or notice purports to exclude or restrict liability for negligence a person's agreement to or awareness of it is not of itself to be taken as indicating his voluntary acceptance of any risk.

3. Liability arising in contract

(1) This section applies as between contracting parties where one of them deals as consumer or on the other's written standard terms of business.

(2) As against that party, the other cannot by reference to any contract term—

(a) when himself in breach of contract, exclude or restrict any liability of his in respect of the breach; or

(b) claim to be entitled—

(i) to render a contractual performance substantially different from that which was reasonably expected of him, or

(ii) in respect of the whole or any part of his contractual obligation, to render no performance at all,

except in so far as (in any of the cases mentioned above in this subsection) the contract term satisfies the requirement of reasonableness.

4. Unreasonable indemnity clauses

(1) A person dealing as consumer cannot by reference to any contract term be made to indemnify another person (whether a party to the contract or not) in respect of liability that may be incurred by the other for negligence or breach of contract, except in so far as the contract term satisfies the requirement of reasonableness.

(2) This section applies whether the liability in question—

(a) is directly that of the person to be indemnified or is incurred by him vicariously;

(b) is to the person dealing as consumer or to someone else.

Liability arising from sale or supply of goods

5. "Guarantee" of consumer goods

(1) In the case of goods of a type ordinarily supplied for private use or consumption, where loss or damage—

(a) arises from the goods proving defective while in consumer use; and

(b) results from the negligence of a person concerned in the manufacture or distribution of the goods,

liability for the loss or damage cannot be excluded or restricted by reference to any contract term or notice contained in or operating by reference to a guarantee of the goods.

(2) For these purposes—

(a) goods are to be regarded as "in consumer use" when a person is using them, or has them in his possession for use, otherwise than exclusively for the purposes of a business; and

(b) anything in writing is a guarantee if it contains or purports to contain some promise or assurance (however worded or presented) that defects will be made good by complete or partial replacement, or by repair, monetary compensation or otherwise.

(3) This section does not apply as between the parties to a contract under or in pursuance of which possession or ownership of the goods passed.

6. Sale and hire-purchase

(1) Liability for breach of the obligations arising from—

(a) section 12 of the Sale of Goods Act 1979 (seller's implied undertakings as to title, etc);

(b) section 8 of the Supply of Goods (Implied Terms) Act 1973 (the corresponding thing in relation to hire-purchase),

cannot be excluded or restricted by reference to any contract term.

(2) As against a person dealing as consumer, liability for breach of the obligations arising from—

(a) section 13, 14 or 15 of the 1979 Act (seller's implied undertakings as to conformity of goods with description or sample, or as to their quality or fitness for a particular purpose);

(b) section 9, 10 or 11 of the 1973 Act (the corresponding things in relation to hire-purchase),

cannot be excluded or restricted by reference to any contract term.

(3) As against a person dealing otherwise than as consumer, the liability specified in subsection (2) above can be excluded or restricted by reference to a contract term, but only in so far as the term satisfies the requirement of reasonableness.

(4) The liabilities referred to in this section are not only the business liabilities defined by section 1(3), but include those arising under any contract of sale of goods or hire-purchase agreement.

7. Miscellaneous contracts under which goods pass

(1) Where the possession or ownership of goods passes under or in pursuance of a contract not governed by the law of sale of goods or hire-purchase, subsections (2) to (4) below apply as regards the effect (if any) to be given to contract terms excluding or restricting liability for breach of obligation arising by implication of law from the nature of the contract.

(2) As against a person dealing as consumer, liability in respect of the goods' correspondence with description or sample, or their quality or fitness for any particular purpose, cannot be excluded or restricted by reference to any such term.

(3) As against a person dealing otherwise than as consumer, that liability can be excluded or restricted by reference to such a term, but only in so far as the term satisfies the requirement of reasonableness.

(3A) Liability for breach of the obligations arising under section 2 of the Supply of Goods and Services Act 1982 (implied terms about title etc in certain contracts for the transfer of the property in goods) cannot be excluded or restricted by references to any such term.

(4) Liability in respect of—

(a) the right to transfer ownership of the goods, or give possession; or

(b) the assurance of quiet possession to a person taking goods in pursuance of the contract,

cannot (in a case to which subsection (3A) above does not apply) be excluded or restricted by reference to any such term except in so far as the term satisfies the requirement of reasonableness.

(5) . . .

Other provisions about contracts

8. …

9. Effect of breach

(1) Where for reliance upon it a contract term has to satisfy the requirement of reasonableness, it may be found to do so and be given effect accordingly notwithstanding that the contract has been terminated either by breach or by a party electing to treat it as repudiated.

(2) Where on a breach the contract is nevertheless affirmed by a party entitled to treat it as repudiated, this does not of itself exclude the requirement of reasonableness in relation to any contract term.

10. Evasion by means of secondary contract

A person is not bound by any contract term prejudicing or taking away rights of his which arise under, or in connection with the performance of, another contract, so far as those rights extend to the enforcement of another's liability which this Part of this Act prevents that other from excluding or restricting.

Explanatory provisions

11. The "reasonableness" test

(1) In relation to a contract term, the requirement of reasonableness for the purposes of this Part of this Act, section 3 of the Misrepresentation Act 1967 and section 3 of the Misrepresentation Act (Northern Ireland) 1967 is that the term shall have been a fair and reasonable one to be included having regard to the circumstances which were, or ought reasonably to have been, known to or in the contemplation of the parties when the contract was made.

(2) In determining for the purposes of section 6 or 7 above whether a contract term satisfies the requirement of reasonableness, regard shall be had in particular to the matters specified in

Schedule 2 to this Act; but this subsection does not prevent the court or arbitrator from holding, in accordance with any rule of law, that a term which purports to exclude or restrict any relevant liability is not a term of the contract.

(3) In relation to a notice (not being a notice having contractual effect), the requirement of reasonableness under this Act is that it should be fair and reasonable to allow reliance on it, having regard to all the circumstances obtaining when the liability arose or (but for the notice) would have arisen.

(4) Where by reference to a contract term or notice a person seeks to restrict liability to a specified sum of money, and the question arises (under this or any other Act) whether the term or notice satisfies the requirement of reasonableness, regard shall be had in particular (but without prejudice to subsection (2) above in the case of contract terms) to—

- (a) the resources which he could expect to be available to him for the purpose of meeting the liability should it arise; and
- (b) how far it was open to him to cover himself by insurance.

(5) It is for those claiming that a contract term or notice satisfies the requirement of reasonableness to show that it does.

12. "Dealing as consumer"

(1) A party to a contract "deals as consumer" in relation to another party if—

- (a) he neither makes the contract in the course of a business nor holds himself out as doing so; and
- (b) the other party does make the contract in the course of a business; and
- (c) in the case of a contract governed by the law of sale of goods or hire-purchase, or by section 7 of this Act, the goods passing under or in pursuance of the contract are of a type ordinarily supplied for private use or consumption.

(1A) But if the first party mentioned in subsection (1) is an individual paragraph (c) of that subsection must be ignored.

(2) But the buyer is not in any circumstances to be regarded as dealing as consumer—

- (a) if he is an individual and the goods are second hand goods sold at public auction at which individuals have the opportunity of attending the sale in person;
- (b) if he is not an individual and the goods are sold by auction or by competitive tender.

(3) Subject to this, it is for those claiming that a party does not deal as consumer to show that he does not.

13. Varieties of exemption clause

(1) To the extent that this Part of this Act prevents the exclusion or restriction of any liability it also prevents—

- (a) making the liability or its enforcement subject to restrictive or onerous conditions;
- (b) excluding or restricting any right or remedy in respect of the liability, or subjecting a person to any prejudice in consequence of his pursuing any such right or remedy;
- (c) excluding or restricting rules of evidence or procedure;

and (to that extent) sections 2 and 5 to 7 also prevent excluding or restricting liability by reference to terms and notices which exclude or restrict the relevant obligation or duty.

(2) But an agreement in writing to submit present or future differences to arbitration is not to be treated under this Part of this Act as excluding or restricting any liability.

14. Interpretation of Part I

In this Part of this Act—

"business" includes a profession and the activities of any government department or local or public authority;

"goods" has the same meaning as in the Sale of Goods Act 1979:

"hire-purchase agreement" has the same meaning as in the Consumer Credit Act 1974;

"negligence" has the meaning given by section 1(1);

"notice" includes an announcement, whether or not in writing, and any other communication or pretended communication; and

"personal injury" includes any disease and any impairment of physical or mental condition.

PART II
AMENDMENT OF LAW FOR SCOTLAND

15. Scope of Part II

(1) This Part of this Act …, is subject to Part III of this Act and does not affect the validity of any discharge or indemnity given by a person in consideration of the receipt by him of compensation in settlement of any claim which he has.

(2) Subject to subsection (3) below, sections 16 to 18 of this Act apply to any contract only to the extent that the contract—

(a) relates to the transfer of the ownership or possession of goods from one person to another (with or without work having been done on them);

(b) constitutes a contract of service or apprenticeship;

(c) relates to services of whatever kind, including (without prejudice to the foregoing generality) carriage, deposit and pledge, care and custody, mandate, agency, loan and services relating to the use of land;

(d) relates to the liability of an occupier of land to persons entering upon or using that land;

(e) relates to a grant of any right or permission to enter upon or use land not amounting to an estate or interest in the land.

(3) Notwithstanding anything in subsection (2) above, section 16 to 18—

(a) do not apply to any contract to the extent that the contract—

(i) is a contract of insurance (including a contract to pay an annuity on human life);

(ii) relates to the formation, constitution or dissolution of any body corporate or unincorporated association or partnership;

(b) apply to—

a contract of marine salvage or towage;
a charter party of a ship or hovercraft;
a contract for the carriage of goods by ship or hovercraft; or,
a contract to which subsection (4) below relates,
only to the extent that—

(i) both parties deal or hold themselves out as dealing in the course of a business (and then only in so far as the contract purports to exclude or restrict liability for breach of duty in respect of death or personal injury); or

(ii) the contract is a consumer contract (and then only in favour of the consumer).

(4) This subsection relates to a contract in pursuance of which goods are carried by ship or hovercraft and which either—

(a) specifies ship or hovercraft as the means of carriage over part of the journey to be covered; or

(b) makes no provision as to the means of carriage and does not exclude ship or hovercraft as that means,

in so far as the contract operates for and in relation to the carriage of the goods by that means.

16. Liability for breach of duty

(1) Subject to subsection (1A) below, where a term of a contract , or a provision of a notice given to persons generally or to particular persons, purports to exclude or restrict liability for breach of duty arising in the course of any business or from the occupation of any premises used for business purposes of the occupier, that term or provision—

(a) shall be void in any case where such exclusion or restriction is in respect of death or personal injury;

(b) shall, in any other case, have no effect if it was not fair and reasonable to incorporate the term in the contract or, as the case may be, if it is not fair and reasonable to allow reliance on the provision.

(1A) Nothing in paragraph (b) of subsection (1) above shall be taken as implying that a provision of a notice has effect in circumstances where, apart from that paragraph, it would not have effect.

(2) Subsection (1)(a) above does not affect the validity of any discharge and indemnity given by a person, on or in connection with an award to him of compensation for pneumoconiosis attributable to employment in the coal industry, in respect of any further claim arising from his contracting that disease.

(3) Where under subsection (1) above a term of a contract or a provision of a notice is void or has no effect, the fact that a person agreed to, or was aware of, the term or provision shall not of itself be sufficient evidence that he knowingly and voluntarily assumed any risk.

17. Control of unreasonable exemptions in consumer or standard form contracts

(1) Any term of a contract which is a consumer contract or a standard form contract shall have no effect for the purpose of enabling a party to the contract—

(a) who is in breach of a contractual obligation, to exclude or restrict any liability of his to the consumer or customer in respect of the breach;

(b) in respect of a contractual obligation, to render no performance, or to render a performance substantially different from that which the consumer or customer reasonably expected from the contract;

if it was not fair and reasonable to incorporate the term in the contract.

(2) In this section "customer" means a party to a standard form contract who deals on the basis of written standard terms of business of the other party to the contract who himself deals in the course of a business.

18. Unreasonable indemnity clauses in consumer contracts

(1) Any term of a contract which is a consumer contract shall have no effect for the purpose of making the consumer indemnify another person (whether a party to the contract or not) in respect of liability which that other person may incur as a result of breach of duty or breach of contract, if it was not fair and reasonable to incorporate the term in the contract.

(2) In this section "liability" means liability arising in the course of any business or from the occupation of any premises used for business purposes of the occupier.

19. "Guarantee of consumer goods"

(1) This section applies to a guarantee—

(a) in relation to goods which are of a type ordinarily supplied for private use or consumption; and

(b) which is not a guarantee given by one party to the other party to a contract under or in pursuance of which the ownership or possession of the goods to which the guarantee relates is transferred.

(2) A term of a guarantee to which this section applies shall be void in so far as it purports to exclude or restrict liability for loss or damage (including death or personal injury)—

(a) arising from the goods proving defective while—

(i) in use otherwise than exclusively for the purposes of a business; or

(ii) in the possession of a person for such use; and

(b) resulting from the breach of duty of a person concerned in the manufacture or distribution of the goods.

(3) For the purposes of this section, any document is a guarantee if it contains or purports to contain some promise or assurance (however worded or presented) that defects will be made good by complete or partial replacement, or by repair, monetary compensation otherwise.

20. Obligations implied by law in sale and hire-purchase contracts

(1) Any term of a contract which purports to exclude or restrict liability for breach of the obligations arising from—

(a) section 12 of the Sale of Goods Act 1979 (seller's implied undertakings as to title etc.);

(b) section 8 of the Supply of Goods (Implied Terms) Act 1973 (implied terms as to title in hire-purchase agreements),

shall be void.

(2) Any term of a contract which purports to exclude or restrict liability for breach of the obligations arising from—

(a) section 13, 14 or 15 of the said Act of 1979 (seller's implied undertakings as to conformity of goods with description or sample, or as to their quality or fitness for a particular purpose);

(b) section 9, 10 or 11 of the said Act of 1973 (the corresponding provisions in relation to hire-purchase),

shall—

(i) in the case of a consumer contract, be void against the consumer;

(ii) in any other case, have no effect if it was not fair and reasonable to incorporate the term in the contract.

21. Obligations implied by law in other contracts for the supply of goods

(1) Any term of a contract to which this section applies purporting to exclude or restrict liability for breach of an obligation—

(a) such as is referred to in subsection (3)(a) below—

(i) in the case of a consumer contract, shall be void against the consumer, and

(ii) in any other case, shall have no effect if it was not fair and reasonable to incorporate the term in the contract;

(b) such as is referred to in subsection (3)(b) below, shall have no effect if it was not fair and reasonable to incorporate the term in the contract.

(2) This section applies to any contract to the extent that it relates to any such matter as is referred to in section 15(2)(a) of this Act, but does not apply to—

(a) a contract of sale of goods or a hire-purchase agreement; or

(b) a charter party of a ship or hovercraft unless it is a consumer contract (and then only in favour of the consumer).

(3) An obligation referred to in this subsection is an obligation incurred under a contract in the course of a business and arising by implication of law from the nature of the contract which relates—

(a) to the correspondence of goods with description or sample, or to the quality or fitness of goods for any particular purpose; or

(b) to any right to transfer ownership or possession of goods, or to the enjoyment of quiet possession of goods.

(4) . . .

22. Consequence of breach

For the avoidance of doubt, where any provision of this Part of this Act requires that the incorporation of a term in a contract must be fair and reasonable for that term to have effect—

(a) if that requirement is satisfied, the term may be given effect to notwithstanding that the contract has been terminated in consequence of breach of that contract;

(b) for the term to be given effect to, that requirement must be satisfied even where a party who is entitled to rescind the contract elects not to rescind it.

23. Evasion by means of secondary contract

Any term of any contract shall be void which purports to exclude or restrict, or has the effect of excluding or restricting—

(a) the exercise, by a party to any other contract, of any right or remedy which arises in respect of that other contract in consequence of breach of duty, or of obligation, liability for which could not by virtue of the provisions of this Part of this Act be excluded or restricted by a term of that other contract;

(b) the application of the provisions of this Part of this Act in respect of that or any other contract.

24. The "reasonableness" test

(1) In determining for the purposes of this Part of this Act whether it was fair and reasonable to incorporate a term in a contract, regard shall be had only to the circumstances which were, or ought reasonably to have been, known to or in the contemplation of the parties to the contract at the time the contract was made.

(2) In determining for the purposes of section 20 or 21 of this Act whether it was fair and reasonable to incorporate a term in a contract, regard shall be had in particular to the matters specified in Schedule 2 to this Act; but this subsection shall not prevent a court or arbiter from holding, in accordance with any rule of law, that a term which purports to exclude or restrict any relevant liability is not a term of the contract.

(2A) In determining for the purposes of this Part of this Act whether it is fair and reasonable to allow reliance on a provision of a notice (not being a notice having contractual effect), regard shall be had to all the circumstances obtaining when the liability arose of (but for the provision) would have arisen.

(3) Where a term in a contract or a provision of a notice purports to restrict liability to a specified sum of money, and the question arises for the purposes of this Part of this Act whether it was fair and reasonable to incorporate the term in the contract or whether it is fair and reasonable to allow reliance on the provision, then, without prejudice to subsection (2) above in the case of a term in a contract, regard shall be had in particular to—

(a) the resources which the party seeking to rely on that term or provision could expect to be available to him for the purpose of meeting the liability should it arise;

(b) how far it was open to that party to cover himself by insurance.

(4) The onus of proving that it was fair and reasonable to incorporate a term in a contract or that it is fair and reasonable to allow reliance on a provision of a notice shall lie on the party so contending.

25. Interpretation of Part II

(1) In this Part of this Act—

"breach of duty" means the breach—

(a) of any obligation, arising from the express or implied terms of a contract, to take reasonable care or exercise reasonable skill in the performance of the contract;

(b) of any common law duty to take reasonable care or exercise reasonable skill;

(c) of the duty of reasonable care imposed by section 2(1) of the Occupiers' Liability (Scotland) Act 1960;

"business" includes a profession and the activities of any government department or local or public authority;

"consumer" has the meaning assigned to that expression in the definition in this section of "consumer contract";

"consumer contract" means subject to subsections (1A) and (1B) below a contract … in which—

(a) one party to the contract deals, and the other party to the contract ("the consumer") does not deal or hold himself out as dealing, in the course of a business, and

(b) in the case of a contract such as is mentioned in section 15(2)(a) of this Act, the goods are of a type ordinarily supplied for private use or consumption;

and for the purposes of this Part of this Act the onus of proving that a contract is not to be regarded as a consumer contract shall lie on the party so contending;

"goods" has the same meaning as in the Sale of Goods Act 1979;

"hire-purchase agreement" has the same meaning as in section 189(1) of the Consumer Credit Act 1974;

"notice" includes an announcement, whether or not in writing, and any other communication or pretended communication;

"personal injury" includes any disease and any impairment of physical or mental condition.

(1A) Where the consumer is an individual, paragraph (b) in the definition of "consumer contract" in subsection (1) must be disregarded.

(1B) The expression of "consumer contract" does not include a contract in which—

(a) the buyer is an individual and the goods are second hand goods sold by public auction at which individuals have the opportunity of attending in person; or

(b) the buyer is not an individual and the goods are sold by auction or competitive tender.

(2) In relation to any breach of duty or obligation, it is immaterial for any purpose of this Part of this Act whether the act or omission giving rise to that breach was inadvertent or intentional, or whether liability for it arises directly or vicariously.

(3) In this Part of this Act, any reference to excluding or restricting any liability includes—

(a) making the liability or its enforcement subject to any restrictive or onerous conditions;

(b) excluding or restricting any right or remedy in respect of the liability, or subjecting a person to any prejudice in consequence of his pursuing any such right or remedy;

(c) excluding or restricting any rule of evidence or procedure;

(d) …

but does not include an agreement to submit any question to arbitration.

(4) …

(5) In sections 15 and 16 and 19 to 21 of this Act, any reference to excluding or restricting liability for breach of an obligation or duty shall include a reference to excluding or restricting the obligation or duty itself.

PART III
PROVISIONS APPLYING TO WHOLE OF UNITED KINGDOM

Miscellaneous

26. International supply contracts

(1) The limits imposed by this Act on the extent to which a person may exclude or restrict liability by reference to a contract term do not apply to liability arising under such a contract as is described in subsection (3) below.

(2) The terms of such a contract are not subject to any requirement of reasonableness under section 3 or 4: and nothing in Part II of this Act shall require the incorporation of the terms of such a contract to be fair and reasonable for them to have effect.

(3) Subject to subsection (4), that description of contract is one whose characteristics are the following—

(a) either it is a contract of sale of goods or it is one under or in pursuance of which the possession or ownership of goods passes; and

(b) it is made by parties whose places of business (or, if they have none, habitual residences) are in the territories of different States (the Channel Islands and the Isle of Man being treated for this purpose as different States from the United Kingdom).

(4) A contract falls within subsection (3) above only if either—

(a) the goods in question are, at the time of the conclusion of the contract, in the course of carriage, or will be carried, from the territory of one State to the territory of another; or

(b) the acts constituting the offer and acceptance have been done in the territories of different States; or

(c) the contract provides for the goods to be delivered to the territory of a State other than that within whose territory those acts were done.

27. Choice of law clauses

(1) Where the law applicable to a contract is the law of any part of the United Kingdom only by choice of the parties (and apart from that choice would be the law of some country outside the United Kingdom) sections 2 to 7 and 16 to 21 of this Act do not operate as part of the law applicable to the contract.

(2) This Act has effect notwithstanding any contract term which applies or purports to apply the law of some country outside the United Kingdom, where (either or both)—

(a) the term appears to the court, or arbitrator or arbiter to have been imposed wholly or mainly for the purpose of enabling the party imposing it to evade the operation of this Act; or

(b) in the making of the contract one of the parties dealt as consumer, and he was then habitually resident in the United Kingdom, and the essential steps necessary for the making of the contract were taken there, whether by him or by others on his behalf.

(3) In the application of subsection (2) above to Scotland, for paragraph (b) there shall be substituted—

"(b) the contract is a consumer contract as defined in Part II of this Act, and the consumer at the date when the contract was made was habitually resident in the United Kingdom, and the essential steps necessary for the making of the contract were taken there, whether by him or by others on his behalf.".

28. Temporary provision for sea carriage of passengers

(1) This section applies to a contract for carriage by sea of a passenger or of a passenger and his luggage where the provisions of the Athens Convention (with or without modification) do not have, in relation to the contract, the force of law in the United Kingdom.

(2) In a case where—

(a) the contract is not made in the United Kingdom, and

(b) neither the place of departure nor the place of destination under it is in the United Kingdom,

a person is not precluded by this Act from excluding or restricting liability for loss or damage, being loss or damage for which the provisions of the Convention would, if they had the force of law in relation to the contract, impose liability on him.

(3) In any other case, a person is not precluded by this Act from excluding or restricting liability for that loss or damage—

(a) in so far as the exclusion or restriction would have been effective in that case had the provisions of the Convention had the force of law in relation to the contract; or

(b) in such circumstances and to such extent as may be prescribed, by reference to a prescribed term of the contract.

(4) For the purposes of subsection (3) (*a*), the values which shall be taken to be the official values in the United Kingdom of the amounts (expressed in gold francs) by reference to which liability under the provisions of the Convention is limited shall be such amounts in sterling as the Secretary of State may from time to time by order made by statutory instrument specify.

(5) In this section,—

(a) the references to excluding or restricting liability include doing any of those things in relation to the liability which are mentioned in section 13 or section 25 (3) and (5); and

(b) "the Athens Convention" means the Athens Convention relating to the Carriage of Passengers and their Luggage by Sea, 1974; and

(c) "prescribed" means prescribed by the Secretary of State by regulations made by statutory instrument;

and a statutory instrument containing the regulations shall be subject to annulment in pursuance of a resolution of either House of Parliament.

29. Saving for other relevant legislation

(1) Nothing in this Act removes or restricts the effect of, or prevents reliance upon, any contractual provision which—

(a) is authorised or required by the express terms or necessary implication of an enactment; or

(b) being made with a view to compliance with an international agreement to which the United Kingdom is a party, does not operate more restrictively than is contemplated by the agreement.

(2) A contract term is to be taken—

(a) for the purposes of Part I of this Act, as satisfying the requirement of reasonableness; and

(b) for those of Part II, to have been fair and reasonable to incorporate,

if it is incorporated or approved by, or incorporated pursuant to a decision or ruling of, a competent authority acting in the exercise of any statutory jurisdiction or function and is not a term in a contract to which the competent authority is itself a party.

(3) In this section—

"competent authority" means any court, arbitrator or arbiter, government department or public authority;

"enactment" means any legislation (including subordinate legislation) of the United Kingdom or Northern Ireland and any instrument having effect by virtue of such legislation;

"statutory" means conferred by an enactment.

30. …

General

31. Commencement; amendments; repeals

(1) This Act comes into force on 1st February 1978.

(2) Nothing in this Act applies to contracts made before the date on which it comes into force; but subject to this, it applies to liability for any loss or damage which is suffered on or after that date.

(3) The enactments specified in Schedule 3 to this Act are amended as there shown.

(4) The enactments specified in Schedule 4 to this Act are repealed to the extent specified in column 3 of that Schedule.

32. Citation and extent

(1) This Act may be cited as the Unfair Contract Terms Act 1977.

(2) Part I of this Act extends to England and Wales and to Northern Ireland; but it does not extend to Scotland.

(3) Part II of this Act extends to Scotland only.

(4) This Part of this Act extends to the whole of the United Kingdom.

SCHEDULE 1

SCOPE OF SECTIONS 2 TO 4 AND 7

Section 1(2)

1. Sections 2 to 4 of this Act do not extend to—

(a) any contract of insurance (including a contract to pay an annuity on human life);

(b) any contract so far as it relates to the creation or transfer of an interest in land, or to the termination of such an interest, whether by extinction, merger, surrender, forfeiture or otherwise;

(c) any contract so far as it relates to the creation or transfer of a right or interest in any patent, trade mark, copyright or design right, registered design, technical or commercial information or other intellectual property, or relates to the termination of any such right or interest;

(d) any contract so far as it relates—

(i) to the formation or dissolution of a company (which means any body corporate or unincorporated association and includes a partnership), or

(ii) to its constitution or the rights or obligations of its corporators or members;

(e) any contract so far as it relates to the creation or transfer of securities or of any right or interest in securities.

2. Section 2(1) extends to—
(a) any contract of marine salvage or towage;
(b) any charterparty of a ship or hovercraft; and
(c) any contract for the carriage of goods by ship or hovercraft;
but subject to this sections 2 to 4 and 7 do not extend to any such contract except in favour of a person dealing as consumer.

3. Where goods are carried by ship or hovercraft in pursuance of a contract which either—
(a) specifies that as the means of carriage over part of the journey to be covered, or
(b) makes no provision as to the means of carriage and does not exclude that means,
then sections 2(2), 3 and 4 do not, except in favour of a person dealing as consumer, extend to the contract as it operates for and in relation to the carriage of the goods by that means.

4. Section 2(1) and (2) do not extend to a contract of employment, except in favour of the employee.

5. Section 2(1) does not affect the validity of any discharge and indemnity given by a person, on or in connection with an award to him of compensation for pneumoconiosis attributable to employment in the coal industry, in respect of any further claim arising from his contracting that disease.

SCHEDULE 2

"GUIDELINES" FOR APPLICATION OF REASONABLENESS TEST

Sections 11(2), 24(2)

The matters to which regard is to be had in particular for the purposes of sections 6(3), 7(3) and (4), 20 and 21 are any of the following which appear to be relevant—

(a) the strength of the bargaining positions of the parties relative to each other, taking into account (among other things) alternative means by which the customer's requirements could have been met;
(b) whether the customer received an inducement to agree to the term, or in accepting it had an opportunity of entering into a similar contract with other persons, but without having to accept a similar term;
(c) whether the customer knew or ought reasonably to have known of the existence and extent of the term (having regard, among other things, to any custom of the trade and any previous course of dealing between the parties);
(d) where the term excludes or restricts any relevant liability if some condition is not complied with, whether it was reasonable at the time of the contract to expect that compliance with that condition would be practicable;
(e) whether the goods were manufactured, processed or adapted to the special order of the customer.

SCHEDULE 3

AMENDMENT OF ENACTMENTS

Section 31(3)

…

SCHEDULE 4

REPEALS

Section 31(4)

…

Treaty on the Functioning of the European Union

(Articles 34, 36, 45, 49, 56, 101, 102)

PART THREE
UNION POLICIES AND INTERNAL ACTIONS

TITLE II
FREE MOVEMENT OF GOODS

CHAPTER 3
PROHIBITION OF QUANTITATIVE RESTRICTIONS BETWEEN MEMBER STATES

Article 34

Quantitative restrictions on imports and all measures having equivalent effect shall be prohibited between Member States.

Article 36

The provisions of Articles 34 and 35 shall not preclude prohibitions or restrictions on imports, exports or goods in transit justified on grounds of public morality, public policy or public security; the protection of health and life of humans, animals or plants; the protection of national treasures possessing artistic, historic or archaeological value; or the protection of industrial and commercial property. Such prohibitions or restrictions shall not, however, constitute a means of arbitrary discrimination or a disguised restriction on trade between Member States.

TITLE IV
FREE MOVEMENT OF PERSONS, SERVICES AND CAPITAL

CHAPTER 1
WORKERS

Article 45

1. Freedom of movement for workers shall be secured within the Union.
2. Such freedom of movement shall entail the abolition of any discrimination based on nationality between workers of the Member States as regards employment, remuneration and other conditions of work and employment.
3. It shall entail the right, subject to limitations justified on grounds of public policy, public security or public health:
   (a) to accept offers of employment actually made;
   (b) to move freely within the territory of Member States for this purpose;
   (c) to stay in a Member State for the purpose of employment in accordance with the provisions governing the employment of nationals of that State laid down by law, regulation or administrative action;
   (d) to remain in the territory of a Member State after having been employed in that State, subject to conditions which shall be embodied in implementing regulations to be drawn up by the Commission.
4. The provisions of this article shall not apply to employment in the public service.

CHAPTER 2
RIGHT OF ESTABLISHMENT

Article 49

Within the framework of the provisions set out below, restrictions on the freedom of establishment of nationals of a Member State in the territory of another Member State shall be prohibited. Such prohibition shall also apply to restrictions on the setting-up of agencies, branches or subsidiaries by nationals of any Member State established in the territory of any Member State.

Freedom of establishment shall include the right to take up and pursue activities as self-employed persons and to set up and manage undertakings, in particular companies or firms within the meaning of the second paragraph of Article 54, under the conditions laid down for its own nationals by the law of the country where such establishment is effected, subject to the provisions of the Chapter relating to capital.

CHAPTER 3
SERVICES

Article 56

Within the framework of the provisions set out below, restrictions on freedom to provide services within the Union shall be prohibited in respect of nationals of Member States who are established in a Member State other than that of the person for whom the services are intended.

The European Parliament and the Council, acting in accordance with the ordinary legislative procedure, may extend the provisions of the Chapter to nationals of a third country who provide services and who are established within the Union.

TITLE VII
COMMON RULES ON COMPETITION, TAXATION AND APPROXIMATION OF LAWS

CHAPTER 1
RULES ON COMPETITION

SECTION 1
RULES APPLYING TO UNDERTAKINGS

Article 101

1. The following shall be prohibited as incompatible with the internal market: all agreements between undertakings, decisions by associations of undertakings and concerted practices which may affect trade between Member States and which have as their object or effect the prevention, restriction or distortion of competition within the internal market, and in particular those which:
   (a) directly or indirectly fix purchase or selling prices or any other trading conditions;
   (b) limit or control production, markets, technical development, or investment;
   (c) share markets or sources of supply;
   (d) apply dissimilar conditions to equivalent transactions with other trading parties, thereby placing them at a competitive disadvantage;
   (e) make the conclusion of contracts subject to acceptance by the other parties of supplementary obligations which, by their nature or according to commercial usage, have no connection with the subject of such contracts.
2. Any agreements or decisions prohibited pursuant to this Article shall be automatically void.
3. The provisions of paragraph 1 may, however, be declared inapplicable in the case of:
   — any agreement or category of agreements between undertakings,
   — any decision or category of decisions by associations of undertakings,
   — any concerted practice or category of concerted practices,

which contributes to improving the production or distribution of goods or to promoting technical or economic progress, while allowing consumers a fair share of the resulting benefit, and which does not:

(a) impose on the undertakings concerned restrictions which are not indispensable to the attainment of these objectives;
(b) afford such undertakings the possibility of eliminating competition in respect of a substantial part of the products in question.

Article 102

Any abuse by one or more undertakings of a dominant position within the internal market or in a substantial part of it shall be prohibited as incompatible with the internal market in so far as it may affect trade between Member States.

Such abuse may, in particular, consist in:

(a) directly or indirectly imposing unfair purchase or selling prices or other unfair trading conditions;
(b) limiting production, markets or technical development to the prejudice of consumers;
(c) applying dissimilar conditions to equivalent transactions with other trading parties, thereby placing them at a competitive disadvantage;
(d) making the conclusion of contracts subject to acceptance by the other parties of supplementary obligations which, by their nature or according to commercial usage, have no connection with the subject of such contracts.

Commission Regulation (EU) on the application of Article 101(3) of the Treaty on the Functioning of the European Union to categories of vertical agreements and concerted practices

No. 330/2010

THE EUROPEAN COMMISSION,

Having regard to the Treaty on the Functioning of the European Union,

Having regard to Regulation No 19/65/EEC of the Council of 2 March 1965 on the application of Article 85(3) of the Treaty to certain categories of agreements and concerted practices, and in particular Article 1 thereof,

Having published a draft of this Regulation,

After consulting the Advisory Committee on Restrictive Practices and Dominant Positions,

Whereas:

(1) Regulation No 19/65/EEC empowers the Commission to apply Article 101(3) of the Treaty on the Functioning of the European Union by regulation to certain categories of vertical agreements and corresponding concerted practices falling within Article 101(1) of the Treaty.

(2) Commission Regulation (EC) No 2790/1999 of 22 December 1999 on the application of Article 81(3) of the Treaty to categories of vertical agreements and concerted practices defines a category of vertical agreements which the Commission regarded as normally satisfying the conditions laid down in Article 101(3) of the Treaty. In view of the overall positive experience with the application of that Regulation, which expires on 31 May 2010, and taking into account further experience acquired since its adoption, it is appropriate to adopt a new block exemption regulation.

(3) The category of agreements which can be regarded as normally satisfying the conditions laid down in Article 101(3) of the Treaty includes vertical agreements for the purchase or sale of goods or services where those agreements are concluded between non-competing undertakings, between certain competitors or by certain associations of retailers of goods. It also includes vertical agreements containing ancillary provisions on the assignment or use of intellectual property rights. The term 'vertical agreements' should include the corresponding concerted practices.

(4) For the application of Article 101(3) of the Treaty by regulation, it is not necessary to define those vertical agreements which are capable of falling within Article 101(1) of the Treaty. In the individual assessment of agreements under Article 101(1) of the Treaty, account has to be taken of several factors, and in particular the market structure on the supply and purchase side.

(5) The benefit of the block exemption established by this Regulation should be limited to vertical agreements for which it can be assumed with sufficient certainty that they satisfy the conditions of Article 101(3) of the Treaty.

(6) Certain types of vertical agreements can improve economic efficiency within a chain of production or distribution by facilitating better coordination between the participating undertakings. In particular, they can lead to a reduction in the transaction and distribution costs of the parties and to an optimisation of their sales and investment levels.

(7) The likelihood that such efficiency-enhancing effects will outweigh any anti-competitive effects due to restrictions contained in vertical agreements depends on the degree of market power of the parties to the agreement and, therefore, on the extent to which those undertakings face competition from other suppliers of goods or services regarded by their customers as interchangeable or substitutable for one another, by reason of the products' characteristics, their prices and their intended use.

(8) It can be presumed that, where the market share held by each of the undertakings party to the agreement on the relevant market does not exceed 30%, vertical agreements which do not contain certain types of severe restrictions of competition generally lead to an improvement in production or distribution and allow consumers a fair share of the resulting benefits.

(9) Above the market share threshold of 30%, there can be no presumption that vertical agreements falling within the scope of Article 101(1) of the Treaty will usually give rise to objective advantages of such a character and size as to compensate for the disadvantages which they create for competition. At the same time, there is no presumption that those vertical agreements are either caught by Article 101(1) of the Treaty or that they fail to satisfy the conditions of Article 101(3) of the Treaty.

(10) This Regulation should not exempt vertical agreements containing restrictions which are likely to restrict competition and harm consumers or which are not indispensable to the attainment of the efficiency-enhancing effects. In particular, vertical agreements containing certain types of severe restrictions of competition such as minimum and fixed resale-prices, as well as certain types of territorial protection, should be excluded from the benefit of the block exemption established by this Regulation irrespective of the market share of the undertakings concerned.

(11) In order to ensure access to or to prevent collusion on the relevant market, certain conditions should be attached to the block exemption. To this end, the exemption of non-compete obligations should be limited to obligations which do not exceed a defined duration. For the same reasons, any direct or indirect obligation causing the members of a selective distribution system not to sell the brands of particular competing suppliers should be excluded from the benefit of this Regulation.

(12) The market-share limitation, the non-exemption of certain vertical agreements and the conditions provided for in this Regulation normally ensure that the agreements to which the block exemption applies do not enable the participating undertakings to eliminate competition in respect of a substantial part of the products in question.

(13) The Commission may withdraw the benefit of this Regulation, pursuant to Article 29(1) of Council Regulation (EC) No 1/2003 of 16 December 2002 on the implementation of the rules on competition laid down in Articles 81 and 82 of the Treaty, where it finds in a particular case that an agreement to which the exemption provided for in this Regulation applies nevertheless has effects which are incompatible with Article 101(3) of the Treaty.

(14) The competition authority of a Member State may withdraw the benefit of this Regulation pursuant to Article 29(2) of Regulation (EC) No 1/2003 in respect of the territory of that Member State, or a part thereof where, in a particular case, an agreement to which the exemption provided for in this Regulation applies nevertheless has effects which are incompatible with Article 101(3) of the Treaty in the territory of that Member State, or in a part thereof, and where such territory has all the characteristics of a distinct geographic market.

(15) In determining whether the benefit of this Regulation should be withdrawn pursuant to Article 29 of Regulation (EC) No 1/2003, the anti-competitive effects that may derive from the existence of parallel networks of vertical agreements that have similar effects which significantly restrict access to a relevant market or competition therein are of particular importance. Such cumulative effects may for example arise in the case of selective distribution or non compete obligations.

(16) In order to strengthen supervision of parallel networks of vertical agreements which have similar anti-competitive effects and which cover more than 50% of a given market, the Commission may by regulation declare this Regulation inapplicable to vertical agreements containing specific restraints relating to the market concerned, thereby restoring the full application of Article 101 of the Treaty to such agreements,

HAS ADOPTED THIS REGULATION:

Article 1 Definitions

1. For the purposes of this Regulation, the following definitions shall apply:

(a) 'vertical agreement' means an agreement or concerted practice entered into between two or more undertakings each of which operates, for the purposes of the agreement or the concerted practice, at a different level of the production or distribution chain, and relating to the conditions under which the parties may purchase, sell or resell certain goods or services;

(b) 'vertical restraint' means a restriction of competition in a vertical agreement falling within the scope of Article 101(1) of the Treaty;

(c) 'competing undertaking' means an actual or potential competitor; 'actual competitor' means an undertaking that is active on the same relevant market; 'potential competitor' means an undertaking that, in the absence of the vertical agreement, would, on realistic grounds and not just as a mere theoretical possibility, in case of a small but permanent increase in relative prices be likely to undertake, within a short period of time, the necessary additional investments or other necessary switching costs to enter the relevant market;

(d) 'non-compete obligation' means any direct or indirect obligation causing the buyer not to manufacture, purchase, sell or resell goods or services which compete with the contract goods or services, or any direct or indirect obligation on the buyer to purchase from the supplier or from another undertaking designated by the supplier more than 80% of the buyer's total purchases of the contract goods or services and their substitutes on the relevant market, calculated on the basis of the value or, where such is standard industry practice, the volume of its purchases in the preceding calendar year;

(e) 'selective distribution system' means a distribution system where the supplier undertakes to sell the contract goods or services, either directly or indirectly, only to distributors selected on the basis of specified criteria and where these distributors undertake not to sell such goods or services to unauthorised distributors within the territory reserved by the supplier to operate that system;

(f) 'intellectual property rights' includes industrial property rights, know how, copyright and neighbouring rights;

(g) 'know-how' means a package of non-patented practical information, resulting from experience and testing by the supplier, which is secret, substantial and identified: in this context, 'secret' means that the know-how is not generally known or easily accessible; 'substantial' means that the know-how is significant and useful to the buyer for the use, sale or resale of the contract goods or services; 'identified' means that the know-how is described in a sufficiently comprehensive manner so as to make it possible to verify that it fulfils the criteria of secrecy and substantiality;

(h) 'buyer' includes an undertaking which, under an agreement falling within Article 101(1) of the Treaty, sells goods or services on behalf of another undertaking;

(i) 'customer of the buyer' means an undertaking not party to the agreement which purchases the contract goods or services from a buyer which is party to the agreement.

2. For the purposes of this Regulation, the terms 'undertaking', 'supplier' and 'buyer' shall include their respective connected undertakings.

'Connected undertakings' means:

(a) undertakings in which a party to the agreement, directly or indirectly:
   (i) has the power to exercise more than half the voting rights, or
   (ii) has the power to appoint more than half the members of the supervisory board, board of management or bodies legally representing the undertaking, or
   (iii) has the right to manage the undertaking's affairs;

(b) undertakings which directly or indirectly have, over a party to the agreement, the rights or powers listed in point (a);

(c) undertakings in which an undertaking referred to in point (b) has, directly or indirectly, the rights or powers listed in point (a);

(d)) undertakings in which a party to the agreement together with one or more of the undertakings referred to in points (a), (b) or (c), or in which two or more of the latter undertakings, jointly have the rights or powers listed in point (a);

(e) undertakings in which the rights or the powers listed in point (a) are jointly held by:

(i) parties to the agreement or their respective connected undertakings referred to in points (a) to (d), or

(ii) one or more of the parties to the agreement or one or more of their connected undertakings referred to in points (a) to (d) and one or more third parties.

Article 2 Exemption

1. Pursuant to Article 101(3) of the Treaty and subject to the provisions of this Regulation, it is hereby declared that Article 101(1) of the Treaty shall not apply to vertical agreements. This exemption shall apply to the extent that such agreements contain vertical restraints.

2. The exemption provided for in paragraph 1 shall apply to vertical agreements entered into between an association of undertakings and its members, or between such an association and its suppliers, only if all its members are retailers of goods and if no individual member of the association, together with its connected undertakings, has a total annual turnover exceeding EUR 50 million. Vertical agreements entered into by such associations shall be covered by this Regulation without prejudice to the application of Article 101 of the Treaty to horizontal agreements concluded between the members of the association or decisions adopted by the association.

3. The exemption provided for in paragraph 1 shall apply to vertical agreements containing provisions which relate to the assignment to the buyer or use by the buyer of intellectual property rights, provided that those provisions do not constitute the primary object of such agreements and are directly related to the use, sale or resale of goods or services by the buyer or its customers. The exemption applies on condition that, in relation to the contract goods or services, those provisions do not contain restrictions of competition having the same object as vertical restraints which are not exempted under this Regulation.

4. The exemption provided for in paragraph 1 shall not apply to vertical agreements entered into between competing undertakings. However, it shall apply where competing undertakings enter into a non-reciprocal vertical agreement and:

(a) the supplier is a manufacturer and a distributor of goods, while the buyer is a distributor and not a competing undertaking at the manufacturing level; or

(b) the supplier is a provider of services at several levels of trade, while the buyer provides its goods or services at the retail level and is not a competing undertaking at the level of trade where it purchases the contract services.

5. This Regulation shall not apply to vertical agreements the subject matter of which falls within the scope of any other block exemption regulation, unless otherwise provided for in such a regulation.

Article 3 Market share threshold

1. The exemption provided for in Article 2 shall apply on condition that the market share held by the supplier does not exceed 30% of the relevant market on which it sells the contract goods or services and the market share held by the buyer does not exceed 30% of the relevant market on which it purchases the contract goods or services.

2. For the purposes of paragraph 1, where in a multi party agreement an undertaking buys the contract goods or services from one undertaking party to the agreement and sells the contract goods or services to another undertaking party to the agreement, the market share of the first undertaking must respect the market share threshold provided for in that paragraph both as a buyer and a supplier in order for the exemption provided for in Article 2 to apply.

Article 4 Restrictions that remove the benefit of the block exemption — hardcore restrictions

The exemption provided for in Article 2 shall not apply to vertical agreements which, directly or indirectly, in isolation or in combination with other factors under the control of the parties, have as their object:

(a) the restriction of the buyer's ability to determine its sale price, without prejudice to the possibility of the supplier to impose a maximum sale price or recommend a sale price, provided that they do not amount to a fixed or minimum sale price as a result of pressure from, or incentives offered by, any of the parties;

(b) the restriction of the territory into which, or of the customers to whom, a buyer party to the agreement, without prejudice to a restriction on its place of establishment, may sell the contract goods or services, except:

(i) the restriction of active sales into the exclusive territory or to an exclusive customer group reserved to the supplier or allocated by the supplier to another buyer, where such a restriction does not limit sales by the customers of the buyer,

(ii) the restriction of sales to end users by a buyer operating at the wholesale level of trade,

(iii) the restriction of sales by the members of a selective distribution system to unauthorised distributors within the territory reserved by the supplier to operate that system, and

(iv) the restriction of the buyer's ability to sell components, supplied for the purposes of incorporation, to customers who would use them to manufacture the same type of goods as those produced by the supplier;

(c) the restriction of active or passive sales to end users by members of a selective distribution system operating at the retail level of trade, without prejudice to the possibility of prohibiting a member of the system from operating out of an unauthorised place of establishment;

(d) the restriction of cross-supplies between distributors within a selective distribution system, including between distributors operating at different level of trade;

(e) the restriction, agreed between a supplier of components and a buyer who incorporates those components, of the supplier's ability to sell the components as spare parts to end-users or to repairers or other service providers not entrusted by the buyer with the repair or servicing of its goods.

Article 5 Excluded restrictions

1. The exemption provided for in Article 2 shall not apply to the following obligations contained in vertical agreements:

(a) any direct or indirect non-compete obligation, the duration of which is indefinite or exceeds five years;

(b) any direct or indirect obligation causing the buyer, after termination of the agreement, not to manufacture, purchase, sell or resell goods or services;

(c) any direct or indirect obligation causing the members of a selective distribution system not to sell the brands of particular competing suppliers.

For the purposes of point (a) of the first subparagraph, a non- compete obligation which is tacitly renewable beyond a period of five years shall be deemed to have been concluded for an indefinite duration.

2. By way of derogation from paragraph 1(a), the time limi- tation of five years shall not apply where the contract goods or services are sold by the buyer from premises and land owned by the supplier or leased by the supplier from third parties not connected with the buyer, provided that the duration of the non-compete obligation does not exceed the period of occupancy of the premises and land by the buyer.

3. By way of derogation from paragraph 1(b), the exemption provided for in Article 2 shall apply to any direct or indirect obligation causing the buyer, after termination of the agreement, not to manufacture, purchase, sell or resell goods or services where the following conditions are fulfilled:

(a) the obligation relates to goods or services which compete with the contract goods or services;

(b) the obligation is limited to the premises and land from which the buyer has operated during the contract period;

(c) the obligation is indispensable to protect know-how transferred by the supplier to the buyer;

(d) the duration of the obligation is limited to a period of one year after termination of the agreement.

Paragraph 1(b) is without prejudice to the possibility of imposing a restriction which is unlimited in time on the use and disclosure of know-how which has not entered the public domain.

Article 6 Non-application of this Regulation

Pursuant to Article 1a of Regulation No 19/65/EEC, the Commission may by regulation declare that, where parallel networks of similar vertical restraints cover more than 50% of a relevant market, this Regulation shall not apply to vertical agreements containing specific restraints relating to that market.

Article 7 Application of the market share threshold

For the purposes of applying the market share thresholds provided for in Article 3 the following rules shall apply:

(a) the market share of the supplier shall be calculated on the basis of market sales value data and the market share of the buyer shall be calculated on the basis of market purchase value data. If market sales value or market purchase value data are not available, estimates based on other reliable market information, including market sales and purchase volumes, may be used to establish the market share of the undertaking concerned;

(b) the market shares shall be calculated on the basis of data relating to the preceding calendar year;

(c) the market share of the supplier shall include any goods or services supplied to vertically integrated distributors for the purposes of sale;

(d) if a market share is initially not more than 30% but subsequently rises above that level without exceeding 35%, the exemption provided for in Article 2 shall continue to apply for a period of two consecutive calendar years following the year in which the 30% market share threshold was first exceeded;

(e) if a market share is initially not more than 30% but subsequently rises above 35%, the exemption provided for in Article 2 shall continue to apply for one calendar year following the year in which the level of 3 5% was first exceeded;

(f) the benefit of points (d) and (e) may not be combined so as to exceed a period of two calendar years;

(g) the market share held by the undertakings referred to in point (e) of the second subparagraph of Article 1(2) shall be apportioned equally to each undertaking having the rights or the powers listed in point (a) of the second subparagraph of Article 1(2).

Article 8 Application of the turnover threshold

1. For the purpose of calculating total annual turnover within the meaning of Article 2(2), the turnover achieved during the previous financial year by the relevant party to the vertical agreement and the turnover achieved by its connected undertakings in respect of all goods and services, excluding all taxes and other duties, shall be added together. For this purpose, no account shall be taken of dealings between the party to the vertical agreement and its connected undertakings or between its connected undertakings.

2. The exemption provided for in Article 2 shall remain applicable where, for any period of two consecutive financial years, the total annual turnover threshold is exceeded by no more than 10%.

Article 9 Transitional period

The prohibition laid down in Article 101(1) of the Treaty shall not apply during the period from 1 June 2010 to 31 May 2011 in respect of agreements already in force on 31 May 2010 which do not satisfy the conditions for exemption provided for in this Regulation but which, on 31 May 2010, satisfied the conditions for exemption provided for in Regulation (EC) No 2790/1999.

Article 10 Period of validity

This Regulation shall enter into force on 1 June 2010.

It shall expire on 31 May 2022.

This Regulation shall be binding in its entirety and directly applicable in all Member States.

Council Regulation (EC) of 16 December 2002 on the implementation of the rules on competition laid down in Articles 81 and 82 of the Treaty

No. 1/2003

THE COUNCIL OF THE EUROPEAN UNION,

Having regard to the Treaty establishing the European Community, and in particular Article 83 thereof,

Having regard to the proposal from the Commission,

Having regard to the opinion of the European Parliament,

Having regard to the opinion of the European Economic and Social Committee,

Whereas:

(1) In order to establish a system which ensures that competition in the common market is not distorted, Articles 81 and 82 of the Treaty must be applied effectively and uniformly in the Community. Council Regulation No 17 of 6 February 1962, First Regulation implementing Articles 81 and 82 of the Treaty, has allowed a Community competition policy to develop that has helped to disseminate a competition culture within the Community. In the light of experience, however, that Regulation should now be replaced by legislation designed to meet the challenges of an integrated market and a future enlargement of the Community.

(2) In particular, there is a need to rethink the arrangements for applying the exception from the prohibition on agreements, which restrict competition, laid down in Article 81(3) of the Treaty. Under Article 83(2)(b) of the Treaty, account must be taken in this regard of the need to ensure effective supervision, on the one hand, and to simplify administration to the greatest possible extent, on the other.

(3) The centralised scheme set up by Regulation No 17 no longer secures a balance between those two objectives. It hampers application of the Community competition rules by the courts and competition authorities of the Member States, and the system of notification it involves prevents the Commission from concentrating its resources on curbing the most serious infringements. It also imposes considerable costs on undertakings.

(4) The present systemshould therefore be replaced by a directly applicable exception systemin which the competition authorities and courts of the Member States have the power to apply not only Article 81(1) and Article 82 of the Treaty, which have direct applicability by virtue of the case-law of the Court of Justice of the European Communities, but also Article 81(3) of the Treaty.

(5) In order to ensure an effective enforcement of the Community competition rules and at the same time the respect of fundamental rights of defence, this Regulation should regulate the burden of proof under Articles 81 and 82 of the Treaty. It should be for the party or the authority alleging an infringement of Article 81(1) and Article 82 of the Treaty to prove the existence thereof to the required legal standard. It should be for the undertaking or association of undertakings invoking the benefit of a defence against a finding of an infringement to demonstrate to the required legal standard that the conditions for applying such defence are satisfied. This Regulation affects neither national rules on the standard of proof nor obligations of competition authorities and courts of the Member States to ascertain the relevant facts of a case, provided that such rules and obligations are compatible with general principles of Community law.

(6) In order to ensure that the Community competition rules are applied effectively, the competition authorities of the Member States should be associated more closely with their application. To this end, they should be empowered to apply Community law.

(7) National courts have an essential part to play in applying the Community competition rules. When deciding disputes between private individuals, they protect the subjective rights under Community law, for example by awarding damages to the victims of infringements. The role of

the national courts here complements that of the competition authorities of the Member States. They should therefore be allowed to apply Articles 81 and 82 of the Treaty in full.

(8) In order to ensure the effective enforcement of the Community competition rules and the proper functioning of the cooperation mechanisms contained in this Regulation, it is necessary to oblige the competition authorities and courts of the Member States to also apply Articles 81 and 82 of the Treaty where they apply national competition law to agreements and practices which may affect trade between Member States. In order to create a level playing field for agreements, decisions by associations of undertakings and concerted practices within the internal market, it is also necessary to determine pursuant to Article 83(2)(e) of the Treaty the relationship between national laws and Community competition law. To that effect it is necessary to provide that the application of national competition laws to agreements, decisions or concerted practices within the meaning of Article 81(1) of the Treaty may not lead to the prohibition of such agreements, decisions and concerted practices if they are not also prohibited under Community competition law. The notions of agreements, decisions and concerted practices are autonomous concepts of Community competition law covering the coordination of behaviour of undertakings on the market as interpreted by the Community Courts. Member States should not under this Regulation be precluded from adopting and applying on their territory stricter national competition laws which prohibit or impose sanctions on unilateral conduct engaged in by undertakings. These stricter national laws may include provisions which prohibit or impose sanctions on abusive behaviour toward economically dependent undertakings. Furthermore, this Regulation does not apply to national laws which impose criminal sanctions on natural persons except to the extent that such sanctions are the means whereby competition rules applying to undertakings are enforced.

(9) Articles 81 and 82 of the Treaty have as their objective the protection of competition on the market. This Regulation, which is adopted for the implementation of these Treaty provisions, does not preclude Member States from implementing on their territory national legislation, which protects other legitimate interests provided that such legislation is compatible with general principles and other provisions of Community law. In so far as such national legislation pursues predominantly an objective different from that of protecting competition on the market, the competition authorities and courts of the Member States may apply such legislation on their territory. Accordingly, Member States may under this Regulation implement on their territory national legislation that prohibits or imposes sanctions on acts of unfair trading practice, be they unilateral or contractual. Such legislation pursues a specific objective, irrespective of the actual or presumed effects of such acts on competition on the market. This is particularly the case of legislation which prohibits undertakings from imposing on their trading partners, obtaining or attempting to obtain from them terms and conditions that are unjustified, disproportionate or without consideration.

(10) Regulations such as 19/65/EEC, (EEC) No 2821/71, (EEC) No 3976/87, (EEC) No 1534/91, or (EEC) No 479/92 empower the Commission to apply Article 81(3) of the Treaty by Regulation to certain categories of agreements, decisions by associations of undertakings and concerted practices. In the areas defined by such Regulations, the Commission has adopted and may continue to adopt so called 'block' exemption Regulations by which it declares Article 81(1) of the Treaty inapplicable to categories of agreements, decisions and concerted practices. Where agreements, decisions and concerted practices to which such Regulations apply nonetheless have effects that are incompatible with Article 81(3) of the Treaty, the Commission and the competition authorities of the Member States should have the power to withdraw in a particular case the benefit of the block exemption Regulation.

(11) For it to ensure that the provisions of the Treaty are applied, the Commission should be able to address decisions to undertakings or associations of undertakings for the purpose of bringing to an end infringements of Articles 81 and 82 of the Treaty. Provided there is a legitimate interest in doing so, the Commission should also be able to adopt decisions which find that an infringement has been committed in the past even if it does not impose a fine. This Regulation should also

make explicit provision for the Commission's power to adopt decisions ordering interim measures, which has been acknowledged by the Court of Justice.

(12) This Regulation should make explicit provision for the Commission's power to impose any remedy, whether behavioural or structural, which is necessary to bring the infringement effectively to an end, having regard to the principle of proportionality. Structural remedies should only be imposed either where there is no equally effective behavioural remedy or where any equally effective behavioural remedy would be more burdensome for the undertaking concerned than the structural remedy. Changes to the structure of an undertaking as it existed before the infringement was committed would only be proportionate where there is a substantial risk of a lasting or repeated infringement that derives from the very structure of the undertaking.

(13) Where, in the course of proceedings which might lead to an agreement or practice being prohibited, undertakings offer the Commission commitments such as to meet its concerns, the Commission should be able to adopt decisions which make those commitments binding on the undertakings concerned. Commitment decisions should find that there are no longer grounds for action by the Commission without concluding whether or not there has been or still is an infringement. Commitment decisions are without prejudice to the powers of competition authorities and courts of the Member States to make such a finding and decide upon the case. Commitment decisions are not appropriate in cases where the Commission intends to impose a fine.

(14) In exceptional cases where the public interest of the Community so requires, it may also be expedient for the Commission to adopt a decision of a declaratory nature finding that the prohibition in Article 81 or Article 82 of the Treaty does not apply, with a view to clarifying the law and ensuring its consistent application throughout the Community, in particular with regard to new types of agreements or practices that have not been settled in the existing case-law and administrative practice.

(15) The Commission and the competition authorities of the Member States should form together a network of public authorities applying the Community competition rules in close cooperation. For that purpose it is necessary to set up arrangements for information and consultation. Further modalities for the cooperation within the network will be laid down and revised by the Commission, in close cooperation with the Member States.

(16) Notwithstanding any national provision to the contrary, the exchange of information and the use of such information in evidence should be allowed between the members of the network even where the information is confidential. This information may be used for the application of Articles 81 and 82 of the Treaty as well as for the parallel application of national competition law, provided that the latter application relates to the same case and does not lead to a different outcome. When the information exchanged is used by the receiving authority to impose sanctions on undertakings, there should be no other limit to the use of the information than the obligation to use it for the purpose for which it was collected given the fact that the sanctions imposed on undertakings are of the same type in all systems. The rights of defence enjoyed by undertakings in the various systems can be considered as sufficiently equivalent. However, as regards natural persons, they may be subject to substantially different types of sanctions across the various systems. Where that is the case, it is necessary to ensure that information can only be used if it has been collected in a way which respects the same level of protection of the rights of defence of natural persons as provided for under the national rules of the receiving authority.

(17) If the competition rules are to be applied consistently and, at the same time, the network is to be managed in the best possible way, it is essential to retain the rule that the competition authorities of the Member States are automatically relieved of their competence if the Commission initiates its own proceedings. Where a competition authority of a Member State is already acting on a case and the Commission intends to initiate proceedings, it should endeavour to do so as soon as possible. Before initiating proceedings, the Commission should consult the national authority concerned.

(18) To ensure that cases are dealt with by the most appropriate authorities within the network, a general provision should be laid down allowing a competition authority to suspend or close a case on the ground that another authority is dealing with it or has already dealt with it, the objective being that each case should be handled by a single authority. This provision should not prevent the Commission from rejecting a complaint for lack of Community interest, as the case-law of the Court of Justice has acknowledged it may do, even if no other competition authority has indicated its intention of dealing with the case.

(19) The Advisory Committee on Restrictive Practices and Dominant Positions set up by Regulation No 17 has functioned in a very satisfactory manner. It will fit well into the new system of decentralised application. It is necessary, therefore, to build upon the rules laid down by Regulation No 17, while improving the effectiveness of the organisational arrangements. To this end, it would be expedient to allow opinions to be delivered by written procedure. The Advisory Committee should also be able to act as a forumfor discussing cases that are being handled by the competition authorities of the Member States, so as to help safeguard the consistent application of the Community competition rules.

(20) The Advisory Committee should be composed of representatives of the competition authorities of the Member States. For meetings in which general issues are being discussed, Member States should be able to appoint an additional representative. This is without prejudice to members of the Committee being assisted by other experts from the Member States.

(21) Consistency in the application of the competition rules also requires that arrangements be established for cooperation between the courts of the Member States and the Commission. This is relevant for all courts of the Member States that apply Articles 81 and 82 of the Treaty, whether applying these rules in lawsuits between private parties, acting as public enforcers or as review courts. In particular, national courts should be able to ask the Commission for information or for its opinion on points concerning the application of Community competition law. The Commission and the competition authorities of the Member States should also be able to submit written or oral observations to courts called upon to apply Article 81 or Article 82 of the Treaty. These observations should be submitted within the framework of national procedural rules and practices including those safeguarding the rights of the parties. Steps should therefore be taken to ensure that the Commission and the competition authorities of the Member States are kept sufficiently well informed of proceedings before national courts.

(22) In order to ensure compliance with the principles of legal certainty and the uniform application of the Community competition rules in a system of parallel powers, conflicting decisions must be avoided. It is therefore necessary to clarify, in accordance with the case-law of the Court of Justice, the effects of Commission decisions and proceedings on courts and competition authorities of the Member States. Commitment decisions adopted by the Commission do not affect the power of the courts and the competition authorities of the Member States to apply Articles 81 and 82 of the Treaty.

(23) The Commission should be empowered throughout the Community to require such information to be supplied as is necessary to detect any agreement, decision or concerted practice prohibited by Article 81 of the Treaty or any abuse of a dominant position prohibited by Article 82 of the Treaty. When complying with a decision of the Commission, undertakings cannot be forced to admit that they have committed an infringement, but they are in any event obliged to answer factual questions and to provide documents, even if this information may be used to establish against them or against another undertaking the existence of an infringement.

(24) The Commission should also be empowered to undertake such inspections as are necessary to detect any agreement, decision or concerted practice prohibited by Article 81 of the Treaty or any abuse of a dominant position prohibited by Article 82 of the Treaty. The competition authorities of the Member States should cooperate actively in the exercise of these powers.

(25) The detection of infringements of the competition rules is growing ever more difficult, and, in order to protect competition effectively, the Commission's powers of investigation need to be supplemented. The Commission should in particular be empowered to interview any persons who

may be in possession of useful information and to record the statements made. In the course of an inspection, officials authorised by the Commission should be empowered to affix seals for the period of time necessary for the inspection. Seals should normally not be affixed for more than 72 hours. Officials authorised by the Commission should also be empowered to ask for any information relevant to the subject matter and purpose of the inspection.

(26) Experience has shown that there are cases where business records are kept in the homes of directors or other people working for an undertaking. In order to safeguard the effectiveness of inspections, therefore, officials and other persons authorised by the Commission should be empowered to enter any premises where business records may be kept, including private homes. However, the exercise of this latter power should be subject to the authorisation of the judicial authority.

(27) Without prejudice to the case-law of the Court of Justice, it is useful to set out the scope of the control that the national judicial authority may carry out when it authorises, as foreseen by national law including as a precautionary measure, assistance from law enforcement authorities in order to overcome possible opposition on the part of the undertaking or the execution of the decision to carry out inspections in non-business premises. It results from the case-law that the national judicial authority may in particular ask the Commission for further information which it needs to carry out its control and in the absence of which it could refuse the authorisation. The case-law also confirms the competence of the national courts to control the application of national rules governing the implementation of coercive measures.

(28) In order to help the competition authorities of the Member States to apply Articles 81 and 82 of the Treaty effectively, it is expedient to enable themto assist one another by carrying out inspections and other fact-finding measures.

(29) Compliance with Articles 81 and 82 of the Treaty and the fulfilment of the obligations imposed on undertakings and associations of undertakings under this Regulation should be enforceable by means of fines and periodic penalty payments. To that end, appropriate levels of fine should also be laid down for infringements of the procedural rules.

(30) In order to ensure effective recovery of fines imposed on associations of undertakings for infringements that they have committed, it is necessary to lay down the conditions on which the Commission may require payment of the fine from the members of the association where the association is not solvent. In doing so, the Commission should have regard to the relative size of the undertakings belonging to the association and in particular to the situation of small and medium-sized enterprises. Payment of the fine by one or several members of an association is without prejudice to rules of national law that provide for recovery of the amount paid from other members of the association.

(31) The rules on periods of limitation for the imposition of fines and periodic penalty payments were laid down in Council Regulation (EEC) No 2988/74, which also concerns penalties in the field of transport. In a system of parallel powers, the acts, which may interrupt a limitation period, should include procedural steps taken independently by the competition authority of a Member State. To clarify the legal framework, Regulation (EEC) No 2988/74 should therefore be amended to prevent it applying to matters covered by this Regulation, and this Regulation should include provisions on periods of limitation.

(32) The undertakings concerned should be accorded the right to be heard by the Commission, third parties whose interests may be affected by a decision should be given the opportunity of submitting their observations beforehand, and the decisions taken should be widely publicised. While ensuring the rights of defence of the undertakings concerned, in particular, the right of access to the file, it is essential that business secrets be protected. The confidentiality of information exchanged in the network should likewise be safeguarded.

(33) Since all decisions taken by the Commission under this Regulation are subject to review by the Court of Justice in accordance with the Treaty, the Court of Justice should, in accordance with Article 229 thereof be given unlimited jurisdiction in respect of decisions by which the Commission imposes fines or periodic penalty payments.

(34) The principles laid down in Articles 81 and 82 of the Treaty, as they have been applied by Regulation No 17, have given a central role to the Community bodies. This central role should be retained, whilst associating the Member States more closely with the application of the Community competition rules. In accordance with the principles of subsidiarity and proportionality as set out in Article 5 of the Treaty, this Regulation does not go beyond what is necessary in order to achieve its objective, which is to allow the Community competition rules to be applied effectively.

(35) In order to attain a proper enforcement of Community competition law, Member States should designate and empower authorities to apply Articles 81 and 82 of the Treaty as public enforcers. They should be able to designate administrative as well as judicial authorities to carry out the various functions conferred upon competition authorities in this Regulation. This Regulation recognises the wide variation which exists in the public enforcement systems of Member States. The effects of Article 11(6) of this Regulation should apply to all competition authorities. As an exception to this general rule, where a prosecuting authority brings a case before a separate judicial authority, Article 11(6) should apply to the prosecuting authority subject to the conditions in Article 35(4) of this Regulation. Where these conditions are not fulfilled, the general rule should apply. In any case, Article 11(6) should not apply to courts insofar as they are acting as review courts.

(36) As the case-law has made it clear that the competition rules apply to transport, that sector should be made subject to the procedural provisions of this Regulation. Council Regulation No 141 of 26 November 1962 exempting transport from the application of Regulation No 17 should therefore be repealed and Regulations (EEC) No 1017/68, (EEC) No 4056/86 and (EEC) No 3975/87 should be amended in order to delete the specific procedural provisions they contain.

(37) This Regulation respects the fundamental rights and observes the principles recognised in particular by the Charter of Fundamental Rights of the European Union. Accordingly, this Regulation should be interpreted and applied with respect to those rights and principles.

(38) Legal certainty for undertakings operating under the Community competition rules contributes to the promotion of innovation and investment. Where cases give rise to genuine uncertainty because they present novel or unresolved questions for the application of these rules, individual undertakings may wish to seek informal guidance from the Commission. This Regulation is without prejudice to the ability of the Commission to issue such informal guidance,

HAS ADOPTED THIS REGULATION:

CHAPTER I
PRINCIPLES

Article 1

Application of Articles 81 and 82 of the Treaty

1. Agreements, decisions and concerted practices caught by Article 81(1) of the Treaty which do not satisfy the conditions of Article 81(3) of the Treaty shall be prohibited, no prior decision to that effect being required.
2. Agreements, decisions and concerted practices caught by Article 81(1) of the Treaty which satisfy the conditions of Article 81(3) of the Treaty shall not be prohibited, no prior decision to that effect being required.
3. The abuse of a dominant position referred to in Article 82 of the Treaty shall be prohibited, no prior decision to that effect being required.

Article 2

Burden of proof

In any national or Community proceedings for the application of Articles 81 and 82 of the Treaty, the burden of proving an infringement of Article 81(1) or of Article 82 of the Treaty shall rest on the party or the authority alleging the infringement. The undertaking or association of undertakings claiming the benefit of Article 81(3) of the Treaty shall bear the burden of proving that the conditions of that paragraph are fulfilled.

Article 3

Relationship between Articles 81 and 82 of the Treaty and national competition laws

1. Where the competition authorities of the Member States or national courts apply national competition law to agreements, decisions by associations of undertakings or concerted practices within the meaning of Article 81(1) of the Treaty which may affect trade between Member States within the meaning of that provision, they shall also apply Article 81 of the Treaty to such agreements, decisions or concerted practices. Where the competition authorities of the Member States or national courts apply national competition law to any abuse prohibited by Article 82 of the Treaty, they shall also apply Article 82 of the Treaty.
2. The application of national competition law may not lead to the prohibition of agreements, decisions by associations of undertakings or concerted practices which may affect trade between Member States but which do not restrict competition within the meaning of Article 81(1) of the Treaty, or which fulfil the conditions of Article 81(3) of the Treaty or which are covered by a Regulation for the application of Article 81(3) of the Treaty. Member States shall not under this Regulation be precluded from adopting and applying on their territory stricter national laws which prohibit or sanction unilateral conduct engaged in by undertakings.
3. Without prejudice to general principles and other provisions of Community law, paragraphs 1 and 2 do not apply when the competition authorities and the courts of the Member States apply national merger control laws nor do they preclude the application of provisions of national law that predominantly pursue an objective different fromthat pursued by Articles 81 and 82 of the Treaty.

CHAPTER II
POWERS

Article 4

Powers of the Commission

For the purpose of applying Articles 81 and 82 of the Treaty, the Commission shall have the powers provided for by this Regulation.

Article 5

Powers of the competition authorities of the Member States

The competition authorities of the Member States shall have the power to apply Articles 81 and 82 of the Treaty in individual cases. For this purpose, acting on their own initiative or on a complaint, they may take the following decisions:

— requiring that an infringement be brought to an end,
— ordering interimm easures,
— accepting commitments,
— imposing fines, periodic penalty payments or any other penalty provided for in their national law.

Where on the basis of the information in their possession the conditions for prohibition are not met they may likewise decide that there are no grounds for action on their part.

Article 6

Powers of the national courts

National courts shall have the power to apply Articles 81 and 82 of the Treaty.

CHAPTER III
COMMISSION DECISIONS

Article 7

Finding and termination of infringement

1. Where the Commission, acting on a complaint or on its own initiative, finds that there is an infringement of Article 81 or of Article 82 of the Treaty, it may by decision require the undertakings and associations of undertakings concerned to bring such infringement to an end. For this purpose, it may impose on them any behavioural or structural remedies which are proportionate to the infringement committed and necessary to bring the infringement effectively to an end. Structural remedies can only be imposed either where there is no equally effective behavioural remedy or where any equally effective behavioural remedy would be more burdensome for the undertaking concerned than the structural remedy. If the Commission has a legitimate interest in doing so, it may also find that an infringement has been committed in the past.
2. Those entitled to lodge a complaint for the purposes of paragraph 1 are natural or legal persons who can show a legitimate interest and Member States.

Article 8

Interim measures

1. In cases of urgency due to the risk of serious and irreparable damage to competition, the Commission, acting on its own initiative may by decision, on the basis of a prima facie finding of infringement, order interimm easures.
2. A decision under paragraph 1 shall apply for a specified period of time and may be renewed in so far this is necessary and appropriate.

Article 9

Commitments

1. Where the Commission intends to adopt a decision requiring that an infringement be brought to an end and the undertakings concerned offer commitments to meet the concerns expressed to them by the Commission in its preliminary assessment, the Commission may by decision make those commitments binding on the undertakings. Such a decision may be adopted for a specified period and shall conclude that there are no longer grounds for action by the Commission.
2. The Commission may, upon request or on its own initiative, reopen the proceedings:
   (a) where there has been a material change in any of the facts on which the decision was based;
   (b) where the undertakings concerned act contrary to their commitments; or
   (c) where the decision was based on incomplete, incorrect or misleading information provided by the parties.

Article 10

Finding of inapplicability

Where the Community public interest relating to the application of Articles 81 and 82 of the Treaty so requires, the Commission, acting on its own initiative, may by decision find that Article 81 of the Treaty is not applicable to an agreement, a decision by an association of undertakings or a concerted practice, either because the conditions of Article 81(1) of the Treaty are not fulfilled, or because the conditions of Article 81(3) of the Treaty are satisfied.

The Commission may likewise make such a finding with reference to Article 82 of the Treaty.

CHAPTER IV
COOPERATION

Article 11

Cooperation between the Commission and the competition authorities of the Member States

1. The Commission and the competition authorities of the Member States shall apply the Community competition rules in close cooperation.
2. The Commission shall transmit to the competition authorities of the Member States copies of the most important documents it has collected with a view to applying Articles 7, 8, 9, 10 and Article 29(1). At the request of the competition authority of a Member State, the Commission shall provide it with a copy of other existing documents necessary for the assessment of the case.
3. The competition authorities of the Member States shall, when acting under Article 81 or Article 82 of the Treaty, inform the Commission in writing before or without delay after commencing the first formal investigative measure. This information may also be made available to the competition authorities of the other Member States.
4. No later than 30 days before the adoption of a decision requiring that an infringement be brought to an end, accepting commitments or withdrawing the benefit of a block exemption Regulation, the competition authorities of the Member States shall inform the Commission. To that effect, they shall provide the Commission with a summary of the case, the envisaged decision or, in the absence thereof, any other document indicating the proposed course of action. This information may also be made available to the competition authorities of the other Member States. At the request of the Commission, the acting competition authority shall make available to the Commission other documents it holds which are necessary for the assessment of the case. The information supplied to the Commission may be made available to the competition authorities of the other Member States. National competition authorities may also exchange between themselves information necessary for the assessment of a case that they are dealing with under Article 81 or Article 82 of the Treaty.
5. The competition authorities of the Member States may consult the Commission on any case involving the application of Community law.
6. The initiation by the Commission of proceedings for the adoption of a decision under Chapter III shall relieve the competition authorities of the Member States of their competence to apply Articles 81 and 82 of the Treaty. If a competition authority of a Member State is already acting on a case, the Commission shall only initiate proceedings after consulting with that national competition authority.

Article 12

Exchange of information

1. For the purpose of applying Articles 81 and 82 of the Treaty the Commission and the competition authorities of the Member States shall have the power to provide one another with and use in evidence any matter of fact or of law, including confidential information.
2. Information exchanged shall only be used in evidence for the purpose of applying Article 81 or Article 82 of the Treaty and in respect of the subject-matter for which it was collected by the transmitting authority. However, where national competition law is applied in the same case and in parallel to Community competition law and does not lead to a different outcome, information exchanged under this Article may also be used for the application of national competition law.
3. Information exchanged pursuant to paragraph 1 can only be used in evidence to impose sanctions on natural persons where:
   — the law of the transmitting authority foresees sanctions of a similar kind in relation to an infringement of Article 81 or Article 82 of the Treaty or, in the absence thereof,
   — the information has been collected in a way which respects the same level of protection of the rights of defence of natural persons as provided for under the national rules of the

receiving authority. However, in this case, the information exchanged cannot be used by the receiving authority to impose custodial sanctions.

Article 13

Suspension or termination of proceedings

1. Where competition authorities of two or more Member States have received a complaint or are acting on their own initiative under Article 81 or Article 82 of the Treaty against the same agreement, decision of an association or practice, the fact that one authority is dealing with the case shall be sufficient grounds for the others to suspend the proceedings before them or to reject the complaint. The Commission may likewise reject a complaint on the ground that a competition authority of a Member State is dealing with the case.
2. Where a competition authority of a Member State or the Commission has received a complaint against an agreement, decision of an association or practice which has already been dealt with by another competition authority, it may reject it.

Article 14

Advisory Committee

1. The Commission shall consult an Advisory Committee on Restrictive Practices and Dominant Positions prior to the taking of any decision under Articles 7, 8, 9, 10, 23, Article 24(2) and Article 29(1).
2. For the discussion of individual cases, the Advisory Committee shall be composed of representatives of the competition authorities of the Member States. For meetings in which issues other than individual cases are being discussed, an additional Member State representative competent in competition matters may be appointed. Representatives may, if unable to attend, be replaced by other representatives.
3. The consultation may take place at a meeting convened and chaired by the Commission, held not earlier than 14 days after dispatch of the notice convening it, together with a summary of the case, an indication of the most important documents and a preliminary draft decision. In respect of decisions pursuant to Article 8, the meeting may be held seven days after the dispatch of the operative part of a draft decision. Where the Commission dispatches a notice convening the meeting which gives a shorter period of notice than those specified above, the meeting may take place on the proposed date in the absence of an objection by any Member State. The Advisory Committee shall deliver a written opinion on the Commission's preliminary draft decision. It may deliver an opinion even if some members are absent and are not represented. At the request of one or several members, the positions stated in the opinion shall be reasoned.
4. Consultation may also take place by written procedure. However, if any Member State so requests, the Commission shall convene a meeting. In case of written procedure, the Commission shall determine a time-limit of not less than 14 days within which the Member States are to put forward their observations for circulation to all other Member States. In case of decisions to be taken pursuant to Article 8, the time-limit of 14 days is replaced by seven days. Where the Commission determines a time-limit for the written procedure which is shorter than those specified above, the proposed time-limit shall be applicable in the absence of an objection by any Member State.
5. The Commission shall take the utmost account of the opinion delivered by the Advisory Committee. It shall inform the Committee of the manner in which its opinion has been taken into account.
6. Where the Advisory Committee delivers a written opinion, this opinion shall be appended to the draft decision. If the Advisory Committee recommends publication of the opinion, the Commission shall carry out such publication taking into account the legitimate interest of undertakings in the protection of their business secrets.
7. At the request of a competition authority of a Member State, the Commission shall include on the agenda of the Advisory Committee cases that are being dealt with by a competition authority of a

Member State under Article 81 or Article 82 of the Treaty. The Commission may also do so on its own initiative. In either case, the Commission shall inform the competition authority concerned. A request may in particular be made by a competition authority of a Member State in respect of a case where the Commission intends to initiate proceedings with the effect of Article 11(6).

The Advisory Committee shall not issue opinions on cases dealt with by competition authorities of the Member States. The Advisory Committee may also discuss general issues of Community competition law.

Article 15

Cooperation with national courts

1. In proceedings for the application of Article 81 or Article 82 of the Treaty, courts of the Member States may ask the Commission to transmit to them information in its possession or its opinion on questions concerning the application of the Community competition rules.
2. Member States shall forward to the Commission a copy of any written judgment of national courts deciding on the application of Article 81 or Article 82 of the Treaty. Such copy shall be forwarded without delay after the full written judgment is notified to the parties.
3. Competition authorities of the Member States, acting on their own initiative, may submit written observations to the national courts of their Member State on issues relating to the application of Article 81 or Article 82 of the Treaty. With the permission of the court in question, they may also submit oral observations to the national courts of their Member State. Where the coherent application of Article 81 or Article 82 of the Treaty so requires, the Commission, acting on its own initiative, may submit written observations to courts of the Member States. With the permission of the court in question, it may also make oral observations.

   For the purpose of the preparation of their observations only, the competition authorities of the Member States and the Commission may request the relevant court of the Member State to transmit or ensure the transmission to them of any documents necessary for the assessment of the case.
4. This Article is without prejudice to wider powers to make observations before courts conferred on competition authorities of the Member States under the law of their Member State.

Article 16

Uniform application of Community competition law

1. When national courts rule on agreements, decisions or practices under Article 81 or Article 82 of the Treaty which are already the subject of a Commission decision, they cannot take decisions running counter to the decision adopted by the Commission. They must also avoid giving decisions which would conflict with a decision contemplated by the Commission in proceedings it has initiated. To that effect, the national court may assess whether it is necessary to stay its proceedings. This obligation is without prejudice to the rights and obligations under Article 234 of the Treaty.
2. When competition authorities of the Member States rule on agreements, decisions or practices under Article 81 or Article 82 of the Treaty which are already the subject of a Commission decision, they cannot take decisions which would run counter to the decision adopted by the Commission.

CHAPTER V
POWERS OF INVESTIGATION

Article 17

Investigations into sectors of the economy and into types of agreements

1. Where the trend of trade between Member States, the rigidity of prices or other circumstances suggest that competition may be restricted or distorted within the common market, the Commission may conduct its inquiry into a particular sector of the economy or into a particular

type of agreements across various sectors. In the course of that inquiry, the Commission may request the undertakings or associations of undertakings concerned to supply the information necessary for giving effect to Articles 81 and 82 of the Treaty and may carry out any inspections necessary for that purpose.

The Commission may in particular request the undertakings or associations of undertakings concerned to communicate to it all agreements, decisions and concerted practices. The Commission may publish a report on the results of its inquiry into particular sectors of the economy or particular types of agreements across various sectors and invite comments from interested parties.

2. Articles 14, 18, 19, 20, 22, 23 and 24 shall apply mutatis mutandis.

Article 18

Requests for information

1. In order to carry out the duties assigned to it by this Regulation, the Commission may, by simple request or by decision, require undertakings and associations of undertakings to provide all necessary information.
2. When sending a simple request for information to an undertaking or association of undertakings, the Commission shall state the legal basis and the purpose of the request, specify what information is required and fix the time-limit within which the information is to be provided, and the penalties provided for in Article 23 for supplying incorrect or misleading information.
3. Where the Commission requires undertakings and associations of undertakings to supply information by decision, it shall state the legal basis and the purpose of the request, specify what information is required and fix the time-limit within which it is to be provided. It shall also indicate the penalties provided for in Article 23 and indicate or impose the penalties provided for in Article 24. It shall further indicate the right to have the decision reviewed by the Court of Justice.
4. The owners of the undertakings or their representatives and, in the case of legal persons, companies or firms, or associations having no legal personality, the persons authorised to represent them by law or by their constitution shall supply the information requested on behalf of the undertaking or the association of undertakings concerned. Lawyers duly authorised to act may supply the information on behalf of their clients. The latter shall remain fully responsible if the information supplied is incomplete, incorrect or misleading.
5. The Commission shall without delay forward a copy of the simple request or of the decision to the competition authority of the Member State in whose territory the seat of the undertaking or association of undertakings is situated and the competition authority of the Member State whose territory is affected.
6. At the request of the Commission the governments and competition authorities of the Member States shall provide the Commission with all necessary information to carry out the duties assigned to it by this Regulation.

Article 19

Power to take statements

1. In order to carry out the duties assigned to it by this Regulation, the Commission may interview any natural or legal person who consents to be interviewed for the purpose of collecting information relating to the subject-matter of an investigation.
2. Where an interview pursuant to paragraph 1 is conducted in the premises of an undertaking, the Commission shall inform the competition authority of the Member State in whose territory the interview takes place. If so requested by the competition authority of that Member State, its officials may assist the officials and other accompanying persons authorised by the Commission to conduct the interview.

Article 20

The Commission's powers of inspection

1. In order to carry out the duties assigned to it by this Regulation, the Commission may conduct all necessary inspections of undertakings and associations of undertakings.
2. The officials and other accompanying persons authorised by the Commission to conduct an inspection are empowered:
   (a) to enter any premises, land and means of transport of undertakings and associations of undertakings;
   (b) to examine the books and other records related to the business, irrespective of the medium on which they are stored;
   (c) to take or obtain in any formcopies of or extracts fromsuch books or records;
   (d) to seal any business premises and books or records for the period and to the extent necessary for the inspection;
   (e) to ask any representative or member of staff of the undertaking or association of undertakings for explanations on facts or documents relating to the subject-matter and purpose of the inspection and to record the answers.
3. The officials and other accompanying persons authorised by the Commission to conduct an inspection shall exercise their powers upon production of a written authorisation specifying the subject matter and purpose of the inspection and the penalties provided for in Article 23 in case the production of the required books or other records related to the business is incomplete or where the answers to questions asked under paragraph 2 of the present Article are incorrect or misleading. In good time before the inspection, the Commission shall give notice of the inspection to the competition authority of the Member State in whose territory it is to be conducted.
4. Undertakings and associations of undertakings are required to submit to inspections ordered by decision of the Commission. The decision shall specify the subject matter and purpose of the inspection, appoint the date on which it is to begin and indicate the penalties provided for in Articles 23 and 24 and the right to have the decision reviewed by the Court of Justice. The Commission shall take such decisions after consulting the competition authority of the Member State in whose territory the inspection is to be conducted.
5. Officials of as well as those authorised or appointed by the competition authority of the Member State in whose territory the inspection is to be conducted shall, at the request of that authority or of the Commission, actively assist the officials and other accompanying persons authorised by the Commission. To this end, they shall enjoy the powers specified in paragraph 2.
6. Where the officials and other accompanying persons authorised by the Commission find that an undertaking opposes an inspection ordered pursuant to this Article, the Member State concerned shall afford themthe necessary assistance, requesting where appropriate the assistance of the police or of an equivalent enforcement authority, so as to enable them to conduct their inspection.
7. If the assistance provided for in paragraph 6 requires authorisation froma judicial authority according to national rules, such authorisation shall be applied for. Such authorisation may also be applied for as a precautionary measure.
8. Where authorisation as referred to in paragraph 7 is applied for, the national judicial authority shall control that the Commission decision is authentic and that the coercive measures envisaged are neither arbitrary nor excessive having regard to the subject matter of the inspection. In its control of the proportionality of the coercive measures, the national judicial authority may ask the Commission, directly or through the Member State competition authority, for detailed explanations in particular on the grounds the Commission has for suspecting infringement of Articles 81 and 82 of the Treaty, as well as on the seriousness of the suspected infringement and on the nature of the involvement of the undertaking concerned. However, the national judicial authority may not call into question the necessity for the inspection nor demand that it be provided with the information in the Commission's file. The lawfulness of the Commission decision shall be subject to review only by the Court of Justice.

Article 21

Inspection of other premises

1. If a reasonable suspicion exists that books or other records related to the business and to the subject-matter of the inspection, which may be relevant to prove a serious violation of Article 81 or Article 82 of the Treaty, are being kept in any other premises, land and means of transport, including the homes of directors, managers and other members of staff of the undertakings and associations of undertakings concerned, the Commission can by decision order an inspection to be conducted in such other premises, land and means of transport.
2. The decision shall specify the subject matter and purpose of the inspection, appoint the date on which it is to begin and indicate the right to have the decision reviewed by the Court of Justice. It shall in particular state the reasons that have led the Commission to conclude that a suspicion in the sense of paragraph 1 exists. The Commission shall take such decisions after consulting the competition authority of the Member State in whose territory the inspection is to be conducted.
3. A decision adopted pursuant to paragraph 1 cannot be executed without prior authorisation from the national judicial authority of the Member State concerned. The national judicial authority shall control that the Commission decision is authentic and that the coercive measures envisaged are neither arbitrary nor excessive having regard in particular to the seriousness of the suspected infringement, to the importance of the evidence sought, to the involvement of the undertaking concerned and to the reasonable likelihood that business books and records relating to the subject matter of the inspection are kept in the premises for which the authorisation is requested. The national judicial authority may ask the Commission, directly or through the Member State competition authority, for detailed explanations on those elements which are necessary to allow its control of the proportionality of the coercive measures envisaged.

   However, the national judicial authority may not call into question the necessity for the inspection nor demand that it be provided with information in the Commission's file. The lawfulness of the Commission decision shall be subject to review only by the Court of Justice.
4. The officials and other accompanying persons authorised by the Commission to conduct an inspection ordered in accordance with paragraph 1 of this Article shall have the powers set out in Article 20(2)(a), (b) and (c). Article 20(5) and (6) shall apply mutatis mutandis.

Article 22

Investigations by competition authorities of Member States

1. The competition authority of a Member State may in its own territory carry out any inspection or other fact-finding measure under its national law on behalf and for the account of the competition authority of another Member State in order to establish whether there has been an infringement of Article 81 or Article 82 of the Treaty. Any exchange and use of the information collected shall be carried out in accordance with Article 12.
2. At the request of the Commission, the competition authorities of the Member States shall undertake the inspections which the Commission considers to be necessary under Article 20(1) or which it has ordered by decision pursuant to Article 20(4). The officials of the competition authorities of the Member States who are responsible for conducting these inspections as well as those authorised or appointed by themshall exercise their powers in accordance with their national law.

   If so requested by the Commission or by the competition authority of the Member State in whose territory the inspection is to be conducted, officials and other accompanying persons authorised by the Commission may assist the officials of the authority concerned.

CHAPTER VI
PENALTIES

Article 23

Fines

1. The Commission may by decision impose on undertakings and associations of undertakings fines not exceeding 1% of the total turnover in the preceding business year where, intentionally or negligently:
   (a) they supply incorrect or misleading information in response to a request made pursuant to Article 17 or Article 18(2);
   (b) in response to a request made by decision adopted pursuant to Article 17 or Article 18(3), they supply incorrect, incomplete or misleading information or do not supply information within the required time-limit;
   (c) they produce the required books or other records related to the business in incomplete form during inspections under Article 20 or refuse to submit to inspections ordered by a decision adopted pursuant to Article 20(4);
   (d) in response to a question asked in accordance with Article 20(2)(e),
   — they give an incorrect or misleading answer,
   — they fail to rectify within a time-limit set by the Commission an incorrect, incomplete or misleading answer given by a member of staff, or
   — they fail or refuse to provide a complete answer on facts relating to the subject-matter and purpose of an inspection ordered by a decision adopted pursuant to Article 20(4);
   (e) seals affixed in accordance with Article 20(2)(d) by officials or other accompanying persons authorised by the Commission have been broken.
2. The Commission may by decision impose fines on undertakings and associations of undertakings where, either intentionally or negligently:
   (a) they infringe Article 81 or Article 82 of the Treaty; or
   (b) they contravene a decision ordering interimm easures under Article 8; or
   (c) they fail to comply with a commitment made binding by a decision pursuant to Article 9.

   For each undertaking and association of undertakings participating in the infringement, the fine shall not exceed 10% of its total turnover in the preceding business year.

   Where the infringement of an association relates to the activities of its members, the fine shall not exceed 10% of the sum of the total turnover of each member active on the market affected by the infringement of the association.
3. In fixing the amount of the fine, regard shall be had both to the gravity and to the duration of the infringement.
4. When a fine is imposed on an association of undertakings taking account of the turnover of its members and the association is not solvent, the association is obliged to call for contributions from its members to cover the amount of the fine.

   Where such contributions have not been made to the association within a time-limit fixed by the Commission, the Commission may require payment of the fine directly by any of the undertakings whose representatives were members of the decision-making bodies concerned of the association.

   After the Commission has required payment under the second subparagraph, where necessary to ensure full payment of the fine, the Commission may require payment of the balance by any of the members of the association which were active on the market on which the infringement occurred.

   However, the Commission shall not require payment under the second or the third subparagraph from undertakings which show that they have not implemented the infringing decision of the association and either were not aware of its existence or have actively distanced themselves from it before the Commission started investigating the case.

The financial liability of each undertaking in respect of the payment of the fine shall not exceed 10% of its total turnover in the preceding business year.

5. Decisions taken pursuant to paragraphs 1 and 2 shall not be of a criminal law nature.

Article 24

Periodic penalty payments

1. The Commission may, by decision, impose on undertakings or associations of undertakings periodic penalty payments not exceeding 5% of the average daily turnover in the preceding business year per day and calculated from the date appointed by the decision, in order to compel them:
   (a) to put an end to an infringement of Article 81 or Article 82 of the Treaty, in accordance with a decision taken pursuant to Article 7;
   (b) to comply with a decision ordering interim measures taken pursuant to Article 8;
   (c) to comply with a commitment made binding by a decision pursuant to Article 9;
   (d) to supply complete and correct information which it has requested by decision taken pursuant to Article 17 or Article 18(3);
   (e) to submit to an inspection which it has ordered by decision taken pursuant to Article 20(4).
2. Where the undertakings or associations of undertakings have satisfied the obligation which the periodic penalty payment was intended to enforce, the Commission may fix the definitive amount of the periodic penalty payment at a figure lower than that which would arise under the original decision. Article 23(4) shall apply correspondingly.

CHAPTER VII
LIMITATION PERIODS

Article 25

Limitation periods for the imposition of penalties

1. The powers conferred on the Commission by Articles 23 and 24 shall be subject to the following limitation periods:
   (a) three years in the case of infringements of provisions concerning requests for information or the conduct of inspections;
   (b) five years in the case of all other infringements.
2. Time shall begin to run on the day on which the infringement is committed. However, in the case of continuing or repeated infringements, time shall begin to run on the day on which the infringement ceases.
3. Any action taken by the Commission or by the competition authority of a Member State for the purpose of the investigation or proceedings in respect of an infringement shall interrupt the limitation period for the imposition of fines or periodic penalty payments. The limitation period shall be interrupted with effect fromthe date on which the action is notified to at least one undertaking or association of undertakings which has participated in the infringement. Actions which interrupt the running of the period shall include in particular the following:
   (a) written requests for information by the Commission or by the competition authority of a Member State;
   (b) written authorisations to conduct inspections issued to its officials by the Commission or by the competition authority of a Member State;
   (c) the initiation of proceedings by the Commission or by the competition authority of a Member State;
   (d) notification of the statement of objections of the Commission or of the competition authority of a Member State.
4. The interruption of the limitation period shall apply for all the undertakings or associations of undertakings which have participated in the infringement.

5. Each interruption shall start time running afresh. However, the limitation period shall expire at the latest on the day on which a period equal to twice the limitation period has elapsed without the Commission having imposed a fine or a periodic penalty payment. That period shall be extended by the time during which limitation is suspended pursuant to paragraph 6.
6. The limitation period for the imposition of fines or periodic penalty payments shall be suspended for as long as the decision of the Commission is the subject of proceedings pending before the Court of Justice.

Article 26

Limitation period for the enforcement of penalties

1. The power of the Commission to enforce decisions taken pursuant to Articles 23 and 24 shall be subject to a limitation period of five years.
2. Time shall begin to run on the day on which the decision becomes final.
3. The limitation period for the enforcement of penalties shall be interrupted:
   (a) by notification of a decision varying the original amount of the fine or periodic penalty payment or refusing an application for variation;
   (b) by any action of the Commission or of a Member State, acting at the request of the Commission, designed to enforce payment of the fine or periodic penalty payment.
4. Each interruption shall start time running afresh.
5. The limitation period for the enforcement of penalties shall be suspended for so long as:
   (a) time to pay is allowed;
   (b) enforcement of payment is suspended pursuant to a decision of the Court of Justice.

CHAPTER VIII
HEARINGS AND PROFESSIONAL SECRECY

Article 27

Hearing of the parties, complainants and others

1. Before taking decisions as provided for in Articles 7, 8, 23 and Article 24(2), the Commission shall give the undertakings or associations of undertakings which are the subject of the proceedings conducted by the Commission the opportunity of being heard on the matters to which the Commission has taken objection. The Commission shall base its decisions only on objections on which the parties concerned have been able to comment. Complainants shall be associated closely with the proceedings.
2. The rights of defence of the parties concerned shall be fully respected in the proceedings. They shall be entitled to have access to the Commission's file, subject to the legitimate interest of undertakings in the protection of their business secrets. The right of access to the file shall not extend to confidential information and internal documents of the Commission or the competition authorities of the Member States. In particular, the right of access shall not extend to correspondence between the Commission and the competition authorities of the Member States, or between the latter, including documents drawn up pursuant to Articles 11 and 14. Nothing in this paragraph shall prevent the Commission from disclosing and using information necessary to prove an infringement.
3. If the Commission considers it necessary, it may also hear other natural or legal persons. Applications to be heard on the part of such persons shall, where they show a sufficient interest, be granted. The competition authorities of the Member States may also ask the Commission to hear other natural or legal persons.
4. Where the Commission intends to adopt a decision pursuant to Article 9 or Article 10, it shall publish a concise summary of the case and the main content of the commitments or of the proposed course of action. Interested third parties may submit their observations within a time limit which is fixed by the Commission in its publication and which may not be less than one

month. Publication shall have regard to the legitimate interest of undertakings in the protection of their business secrets.

Article 28

Professional secrecy

1. Without prejudice to Articles 12 and 15, information collected pursuant to Articles 17 to 22 shall be used only for the purpose for which it was acquired.
2. Without prejudice to the exchange and to the use of information foreseen in Articles 11, 12, 14, 15 and 27, the Commission and the competition authorities of the Member States, their officials, servants and other persons working under the supervision of these authorities as well as officials and civil servants of other authorities of the Member States shall not disclose information acquired or exchanged by them pursuant to this Regulation and of the kind covered by the obligation of professional secrecy. This obligation also applies to all representatives and experts of Member States attending meetings of the Advisory Committee pursuant to Article 14.

CHAPTER IX

EXEMPTION REGULATIONS

Article 29

Withdrawal in individual cases

1. Where the Commission, empowered by a Council Regulation, such as Regulations 19/65/EEC, (EEC) No 2821/71, (EEC) No 3976/87, (EEC) No 1534/91 or (EEC) No 479/92, to apply Article 81(3) of the Treaty by regulation, has declared Article 81(1) of the Treaty inapplicable to certain categories of agreements, decisions by associations of undertakings or concerted practices, it may, acting on its own initiative or on a complaint, withdraw the benefit of such an exemption Regulation when it finds that in any particular case an agreement, decision or concerted practice to which the exemption Regulation applies has certain effects which are incompatible with Article 81(3) of the Treaty.
2. Where, in any particular case, agreements, decisions by associations of undertakings or concerted practices to which a Commission Regulation referred to in paragraph 1 applies have effects which are incompatible with Article 81(3) of the Treaty in the territory of a Member State, or in a part thereof, which has all the characteristics of a distinct geographic market, the competition authority of that Member State may withdraw the benefit of the Regulation in question in respect of that territory.

CHAPTER X

GENERAL PROVISIONS

Article 30

Publication of decisions

1. The Commission shall publish the decisions, which it takes pursuant to Articles 7 to 10, 23 and 24.
2. The publication shall state the names of the parties and the main content of the decision, including any penalties imposed. It shall have regard to the legitimate interest of undertakings in the protection of their business secrets.

Article 31

Review by the Court of Justice

The Court of Justice shall have unlimited jurisdiction to review decisions whereby the Commission has fixed a fine or periodic penalty payment. It may cancel, reduce or increase the fine or periodic penalty payment imposed.

Article 32

...

Article 33

Implementing provisions

1. The Commission shall be authorised to take such measures as may be appropriate in order to apply this Regulation. The measures may concern, inter alia:
   (a) the form, content and other details of complaints lodged pursuant to Article 7 and the procedure for rejecting complaints;
   (b) the practical arrangements for the exchange of information and consultations provided for in Article 11;
   (c) the practical arrangements for the hearings provided for in Article 27.
2. Before the adoption of any measures pursuant to paragraph 1, the Commission shall publish a draft thereof and invite all interested parties to submit their comments within the time-limit it lays down, which may not be less than one month. Before publishing a draft measure and before adopting it, the Commission shall consult the Advisory Committee on Restrictive Practices and Dominant Positions.

CHAPTER XI
TRANSITIONAL, AMENDING AND FINAL PROVISIONS

Article 34

Transitional provisions

1. Applications made to the Commission under Article 2 of Regulation No 17, notifications made under Articles 4 and 5 of that Regulation and the corresponding applications and notifications made under Regulations (EEC) No 1017/68, (EEC) No 4056/86 and (EEC) No 3975/87 shall lapse as fromthe date of application of this Regulation.
2. Procedural steps taken under Regulation No 17 and Regulations (EEC) No 1017/68, (EEC) No 4056/86 and (EEC) No 3975/87 shall continue to have effect for the purposes of applying this Regulation.

Article 35

Designation of competition authorities of Member States

1. The Member States shall designate the competition authority or authorities responsible for the application of Articles 81 and 82 of the Treaty in such a way that the provisions of this regulation are effectively complied with. The measures necessary to empower those authorities to apply those Articles shall be taken before 1 May 2004. The authorities designated may include courts.
2. When enforcement of Community competition law is entrusted to national administrative and judicial authorities, the Member States may allocate different powers and functions to those different national authorities, whether administrative or judicial.
3. The effects of Article 11(6) apply to the authorities designated by the Member States including courts that exercise functions regarding the preparation and the adoption of the types of decisions foreseen in Article 5. The effects of Article 11(6) do not extend to courts insofar as they act as review courts in respect of the types of decisions foreseen in Article 5.
4. Notwithstanding paragraph 3, in the Member States where, for the adoption of certain types of decisions foreseen in Article 5, an authority brings an action before a judicial authority that is separate and different from the prosecuting authority and provided that the terms of this paragraph are complied with, the effects of Article 11(6) shall be limited to the authority prosecuting the case which shall withdraw its claim before the judicial authority when the Commission opens proceedings and this withdrawal shall bring the national proceedings effectively to an end.

Article 36

Amendment of Regulation (EEC) No 1017/68

Regulation (EEC) No 1017/68 is amended as follows:

1. Article 2 is repealed;
2. In Article 3(1), the words 'The prohibition laid down in Article 2' are replaced by the words 'The prohibition in Article 81(1) of the Treaty';
3. Article 4 is amended as follows:
   (a) In paragraph 1, the words 'The agreements, decisions and concerted practices referred to in Article 2' are replaced by the words 'Agreements, decisions and concerted practices pursuant to Article 81(1) of the Treaty';
   (b) Paragraph 2 is replaced by the following:
   '2. If the implementation of any agreement, decision or concerted practice covered by paragraph 1 has, in a given case, effects which are incompatible with the requirements of Article 81(3) of the Treaty, undertakings or associations of undertakings may be required to make such effects cease.'
4. Articles 5 to 29 are repealed with the exception of Article 13(3) which continues to apply to decisions adopted pursuant to Article 5 of Regulation (EEC) No 1017/68 prior to the date of application of this Regulation until the date of expiration of those decisions;
5. In Article 30, paragraphs 2, 3 and 4 are deleted.

Article 37

Amendment of Regulation (EEC) No 2988/74

In Regulation (EEC) No 2988/74, the following Article is inserted:

'Article 7a

Exclusion

This Regulation shall not apply to measures taken under Council Regulation (EC) No 1/2003 of 16 December 2002 on the implementation of the rules on competition laid down in Articles 81 and 82 of the Treaty.'

Article 38

Amendment of Regulation (EEC) No 4056/86

Regulation (EEC) No 4056/86 is amended as follows:

1. Article 7 is amended as follows:
   (a) Paragraph 1 is replaced by the following:
   '1. Breach of an obligation
   Where the persons concerned are in breach of an obligation which, pursuant to Article 5, attaches to the exemption provided for in Article 3, the Commission may, in order to put an end to such breach and under the conditions laid down in Council Regulation (EC) No 1/2003 of 16 December 2002 on the implementation of the rules on competition laid down in Articles 81 and 82 of the Treaty adopt a decision that either prohibits themfromcarrying out or requires themto performcertain specific acts, or withdraws the benefit of the block exemption which they enjoyed.'
   (b) Paragraph 2 is amended as follows:
   (i) In point (a), the words 'under the conditions laid down in Section II' are replaced by the words 'under the conditions laid down in Regulation (EC) No 1/2003';
   (ii) The second sentence of the second subparagraph of point (c)(i) is replaced by the following:
   'At the same time it shall decide, in accordance with Article 9 of Regulation (EC) No 1/2003, whether to accept commitments offered by the undertakings concerned with a view, inter alia, to obtaining access to the market for non-conference lines.'

2. Article 8 is amended as follows:
   (a) Paragraph 1 is deleted.
   (b) In paragraph 2 the words 'pursuant to Article 10' are replaced by the words 'pursuant to Regulation (EC) No 1/2003'.
   (c) Paragraph 3 is deleted;
3. Article 9 is amended as follows:
   (a) In paragraph 1, the words 'Advisory Committee referred to in Article 15' are replaced by the words 'Advisory Committee referred to in Article 14 of Regulation (EC) No 1/2003';
   (b) In paragraph 2, the words 'Advisory Committee as referred to in Article 15' are replaced by the words 'Advisory Committee referred to in Article 14 of Regulation (EC) No 1/2003';
4. Articles 10 to 25 are repealed with the exception of Article 13(3) which continues to apply to decisions adopted pursuant to Article 81(3) of the Treaty prior to the date of application of this Regulation until the date of expiration of those decisions;
5. In Article 26, the words 'the form, content and other details of complaints pursuant to Article 10, applications pursuant to Article 12 and the hearings provided for in Article 23(1) and (2)' are deleted.

Article 39

Amendment of Regulation (EEC) No 3975/87

Articles 3 to 19 of Regulation (EEC) No 3975/87 are repealed with the exception of Article 6(3) which continues to apply to decisions adopted pursuant to Article 81(3) of the Treaty prior to the date of application of this Regulation until the date of expiration of those decisions.

Article 40

Amendment of Regulations No 19/65/EEC, (EEC) No 2821/71 and (EEC) No 1534/91 Article 7 of Regulation No 19/65/EEC, Article 7 of Regulation (EEC) No 2821/71 and Article 7 of Regulation (EEC) No 1534/91 are repealed.

Article 41

Amendment of Regulation (EEC) No 3976/87

Regulation (EEC) No 3976/87 is amended as follows:

1. Article 6 is replaced by the following:

   'Article 6

   The Commission shall consult the Advisory Committee referred to in Article 14 of Council Regulation (EC) No 1/2003 of 16 December 2002 on the implementation of the rules on competition laid down in Articles 81 and 82 of the Treaty before publishing a draft Regulation and before adopting a Regulation.'
2. Article 7 is repealed.

Article 42

Amendment of Regulation (EEC) No 479/92

Regulation (EEC) No 479/92 is amended as follows:

1. Article 5 is replaced by the following:

   'Article 5

   Before publishing the draft Regulation and before adopting the Regulation, the Commission shall consult the Advisory Committee referred to in Article 14 of Council Regulation (EC) No 1/2003 of 16 December 2002 on the implementation of the rules on competition laid down in Articles 81 and 82 of the Treaty.'
2. Article 6 is repealed.

Article 43

Repeal of Regulations No 17 and No 141

1. Regulation No 17 is repealed with the exception of Article 8(3) which continues to apply to decisions adopted pursuant to Article 81(3) of the Treaty prior to the date of application of this Regulation until the date of expiration of those decisions.
2. Regulation No 141 is repealed.
3. References to the repealed Regulations shall be construed as references to this Regulation.

Article 44

Report on the application of the present Regulation

Five years from the date of application of this Regulation, the Commission shall report to the European Parliament and the Council on the functioning of this Regulation, in particular on the application of Article 11(6) and Article 17.

On the basis of this report, the Commission shall assess whether it is appropriate to propose to the Council a revision of this Regulation.

Article 45

Entry into force

This Regulation shall enter into force on the 20th day following that of its publication in the Official Journal of the European Communities.

It shall apply from1 May 2004.

This Regulation shall be binding in its entirety and directly applicable in all Member States.

Commission Notice

on agreements of minor importance which do not appreciably restrict competition under Article 81(1) of the Treaty establishing the European Community (*de minimis*)

(2001/C 368/07)

I

1. Article 81(1) prohibits agreements between undertakings which may affect trade between Member States and which have as their object or effect the prevention, restriction or distortion of competition within the common market. The Court of Justice of the European Communities has clarified that this provision is not applicable where the impact of the agreement on intra-Community trade or on competition is not appreciable.
2. In this notice the Commission quantifies, with the help of market share thresholds, what is not an appreciable restriction of competition under Article 81 of the EC Treaty. This negative definition of appreciability does not imply that agreements between undertakings which exceed the thresholds set out in this notice appreciably restrict competition. Such agreements may still have only a negligible effect on competition and may therefore not be prohibited by Article 81(1).
3. Agreements may in addition not fall under Article 81(1) because they are not capable of appreciably affecting trade between Member States. This notice does not deal with this issue. It does not quantify what does not constitute an appreciable effect on trade. It is however acknowledged that agreements between small and medium-sized undertakings, as defined in the Annex to Commission Recommendation 96/280/EC, are rarely capable of appreciably affecting trade between Member States. Small and medium-sized undertakings are currently defined in that recommendation as undertakings which have fewer than 250 employees and have either an annual turnover not exceeding EUR 40 million or an annual balance-sheet total not exceeding EUR 27 million.
4. In cases covered by this notice the Commission will not institute proceedings either upon application or on its own initiative. Where undertakings assume in good faith that an agreement is covered by this notice, the Commission will not impose fines. Although not binding on them, this notice also intends to give guidance to the courts and authorities of the Member States in their application of Article 81.
5. This notice also applies to decisions by associations of undertakings and to concerted practices.
6. This notice is without prejudice to any interpretation of Article 81 which may be given by the Court of Justice or the Court of First Instance of the European Communities.

II

7. The Commission holds the view that agreements between undertakings which affect trade between Member States do not appreciably restrict competition within the meaning of Article 81(1):
   (a) if the aggregate market share held by the parties to the agreement does not exceed 10% on any of the relevant markets affected by the agreement, where the agreement is made between undertakings which are actual or potential competitors on any of these markets (agreements between competitors); or
   (b) if the market share held by each of the parties to the agreement does not exceed 15% on any of the relevant markets affected by the agreement, where the agreement is made between

undertakings which are not actual or potential competitors on any of these markets (agreements between non-competitors).

In cases where it is difficult to classify the agreement as either an agreement between competitors or an agreement between non-competitors the 10% threshold is applicable.

8. Where in a relevant market competition is restricted by the cumulative effect of agreements for the sale of goods or services entered into by different suppliers or distributors (cumulative foreclosure effect of parallel networks of agreements having similar effects on the market), the market share thresholds under point 7 are reduced to 5%, both for agreements between competitors and for agreements between non-competitors. Individual suppliers or distributors with a market share not exceeding 5% are in general not considered to contribute significantly to a cumulative foreclosure effect (1). A cumulative foreclosure effect is unlikely to exist if less than 30% of the relevant market is covered by parallel (networks of) agreements having similar effects.

9. The Commission also holds the view that agreements are not restrictive of competition if the market shares do not exceed the thresholds of respectively 10%, 15% and 5% set out in point 7 and 8 during two successive calendar years by more than 2 percentage points.

10. In order to calculate the market share, it is necessary to determine the relevant market. This consists of the relevant product market and the relevant geographic market. When defining the relevant market, reference should be had to the notice on the definition of the relevant market for the purposes of Community competition law. The market shares are to be calculated on the basis of sales value data or, where appropriate, purchase value data. If value data are not available, estimates based on other reliable market information, including volume data, may be used.

11. Points 7, 8 and 9 do not apply to agreements containing any of the following hardcore restrictions:

(1) as regards agreements between competitors as defined in point 7, restrictions which, directly or indirectly, in isolation or in combination with other factors under the control of the parties, have as their object:

(a) the fixing of prices when selling the products to third parties;

(b) the limitation of output or sales;

(c) the allocation of markets or customers;

(2) as regards agreements between non-competitors as defined in point 7, restrictions which, directly or indirectly, in isolation or in combination with other factors under the control of the parties, have as their object:

(a) the restriction of the buyer's ability to determine its sale price, without prejudice to the possibility of the supplier imposing a maximum sale price or recommending a sale price, provided that they do not amount to a fixed or minimum sale price as a result of pressure from, or incentives offered by, any of the parties;

(b) the restriction of the territory into which, or of the customers to whom, the buyer may sell the contract goods or services, except the following restrictions which are not hardcore:

— the restriction of active sales into the exclusive territory or to an exclusive customer group reserved to the supplier or allocated by the supplier to another buyer, where such a restriction does not limit sales by the customers of the buyer,

— the restriction of sales to end users by a buyer operating at the wholesale level of trade,

— the restriction of sales to unauthorised distributors by the members of a selective distribution system, and

— the restriction of the buyer's ability to sell components, supplied for the purposes of incorporation, to customers who would use them to manufacture the same type of goods as those produced by the supplier;

(c) the restriction of active or passive sales to end users by members of a selective distribution system operating at the retail level of trade, without prejudice to the possibility of prohibiting a member of the system from operating out of an unauthorised place of establishment;

(d) the restriction of cross-supplies between distributors within a selective distribution system, including between distributors operating at different levels of trade;

(e) the restriction agreed between a supplier of components and a buyer who incorporates those components, which limits the supplier's ability to sell the components as spare parts to end users or to repairers or other service providers not entrusted by the buyer with the repair or servicing of its goods;

(3) as regards agreements between competitors as defined in point 7, where the competitors operate, for the purposes of the agreement, at a different level of the production or distribution chain, any of the hardcore restrictions listed in paragraph (1) and (2) above.

12.— (1) For the purposes of this notice, the terms "undertaking", "party to the agreement", "distributor", "supplier" and "buyer" shall include their respective connected undertakings.

(2) "Connected undertakings" are:

(a) undertakings in which a party to the agreement, directly or indirectly:

— has the power to exercise more than half the voting rights, or

— has the power to appoint more than half the members of the supervisory board, board of management or bodies legally representing the undertaking, or

— has the right to manage the undertaking's affairs;

(b) undertakings which directly or indirectly have, over a party to the agreement, the rights or powers listed in (a);

(c) undertakings in which an undertaking referred to in (b) has, directly or indirectly, the rights or powers listed in (a);

(d) undertakings in which a party to the agreement together with one or more of the undertakings referred to in (a), (b) or (c), or in which two or more of the latter undertakings, jointly have the rights or powers listed in (a);

(e) undertakings in which the rights or the powers listed in (a) are jointly held by:

— parties to the agreement or their respective connected undertakings referred to in (a) to (d), or

— one or more of the parties to the agreement or one or more of their connected undertakings referred to in (a) to (d) and one or more third parties.

(3) For the purposes of paragraph 2(e), the market share held by these jointly held undertakings shall be apportioned equally to each undertaking having the rights or the powers listed in paragraph 2(a).

Index